THE AMERICAN JOURNEY

A History of the United States

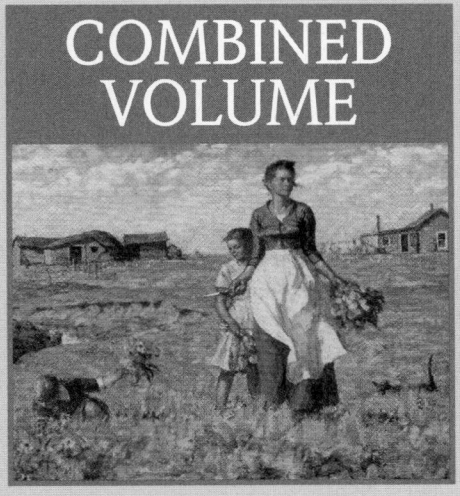

COMBINED VOLUME

THIRD EDITION

DAVID GOLDFIELD

CARL ABBOTT

VIRGINIA DEJOHN ANDERSON

JO ANN E. ARGERSINGER

PETER H. ARGERSINGER

WILLIAM L. BARNEY

ROBERT M. WEIR

PEARSON

Prentice Hall

Upper Saddle River, New Jersey 07458

Library of Congress Cataloging-in-Publication Data
The American journey : a history of the United States / David
  Goldfield . . . [et al.]. — 3rd ed.
    p. cm
  "Combined volume."
  Includes bibliographical references and index.
  ISBN 0-13-182553-4
  1.United States—History. I.Goldfield, David R.,
E178.1.A4925 2003
  973—dc21

2003040460

VP, Editorial Director: Charlyce Jones Owen
Senior Acquisitions Editor: Charles Cavaliere
Editor-in-Chief, Development: Rochelle Diogenes
Senior Development Editors: Roberta Meyer and Carolyn
    Viola-John
Editorial Assistant: Adrienne Paul
AVP, Director of Production and Manufacturing:
    Barbara Kittle
Project Manager: Lee Shenkman of Victory Productions, Inc.
Liaison Editor: Jean Lapidus
Prepress and Manufacturing Manager: Nick Sklitsis
Prepress and Manufacturing Buyer: Sherry Lewis
Creative Design Director: Leslie Osher

Art Director: Nancy Wells
Interior and Cover Designer: Kenny Beck
Cover Art: "The Prairie is my Garden,"
    Sodbusters/Homesteaders (1866-1900). Pugsly Union,
    South Dakota State University, Brooking. S.D.
Photo Researchers: Barbara Salz and Linda Sykes
Manager of Production Services: Guy Ruggiero
Map and Art Coordinator: Maria Piper
Copy Editor: Ruth Hein
Indexer: Northwind Editorial
Image Permission Coordinator: Craig A. Jones
Text Permissions: RGA Enterprises, Inc.

This book was set in 10.5/12 New Baskerville Roman by Victory Productions and was printed and bound by Von Hoffman Press, Inc. The cover was printed by Phoenix Color Corp.

Credits and acknowledgments for materials borrowed from other sources and reproduced with permission, in this textbook, appear on page C-1.

© 2004, 2001, 1998 by Pearson Education, Inc.
Upper Saddle River, New Jersey 07458

Printed in the United States of America
10 9 8 7 6 5 4 3 2 1

ISBN 0-13-182553-4
ISBN 0-13-184761-9 (Professional Copy)

PEARSON EDUCATION (UK) LIMITED, *London*
PRENTICE-HALL OF AUSTRALIA PTY. LIMITED, *Sydney*
PRENTICE-HALL CANADA INC., *Toronto*
PRENTICE-HALL HISPANOAMERICANA, S.A., *Mexico*
PRENTICE-HALL OF INDIA PRIVATE LIMITED, *New Delhi*
PRENTICE-HALL OF JAPAN, INC., *Tokyo*
PEARSON EDUCATION PTE. LTD., *Singapore*
EDITORA PRENTICE-HALL DO BRASIL, LTDA., *Rio de Janeiro*

FOR OUR STUDENTS,
WHO HELPED US WRITE THIS BOOK.

BRIEF CONTENTS

1 WORLDS APART   1

2 TRANSPLANTATION 1600–1685   35

3 THE CREATION OF NEW WORLDS   67

4 CONVERGENCE AND CONFLICT 1660s–1763   99

5 IMPERIAL BREAKDOWN 1763–1774   137

6 THE WAR FOR INDEPENDENCE 1774–1783   165

7 THE FIRST REPUBLIC 1776–1789   201

8 A NEW REPUBLIC AND THE RISE OF PARTIES 1789–1800   233

9 THE TRIUMPH AND COLLAPSE OF JEFFERSONIAN REPUBLICANISM 1800–1824   261

10 THE JACKSONIAN ERA 1824–1845   293

11 SLAVERY AND THE OLD SOUTH 1800–1860   323

12 THE MARKET REVOLUTION AND SOCIAL REFORM 1815–1850   351

13 THE WAY WEST   389

14 REFORMING ANTEBELLUM SOCIETY 1815–1850   417

15 BATTLE CRIES AND FREEDOM SONGS: THE CIVIL WAR 1861–1863   453

16 RECONSTRUCTION 1865–1877   497

17 A NEW SOUTH 1877–1900   529

18 INDUSTRY, IMMIGRANTS, AND CITIES 1870–1900   563

19 TRANSFORMING THE WEST 1865–1890   599

20 POLITICS AND GOVERNMENT 1877–1900   629

21 THE PROGRESSIVE ERA 1900–1917   659

22 CREATING AN EMPIRE 1865–1917   695

23 AMERICA AND THE GREAT WAR 1914–1920   723

24 TOWARD A MODERN AMERICA: THE 1920s   753

25 THE GREAT DEPRESSION AND THE NEW DEAL 1929–1939   783

26 WORLD WAR II 1939–1945   819

27 THE COLD WAR AT HOME AND ABROAD 1946–1952   855

28 THE CONFIDENT YEARS 1953–1964   885

29 SHAKEN TO THE ROOTS 1965–1980   919

30 THE REAGAN REVOLUTION AND A CHANGING WORLD 1981–1992   955

31 COMPLACENCY AND CRISIS 1993–2003   991

CONTENTS

American Views   xxi
From Then to Now   xxii
Maps   xxiii
Figures and Tables   xxvi
Overview Tables   xxviii
U.S. History Documents CD-ROM   xxix
Preface   xxxiii
About the Authors   xxxix
Student Tool Kit   xli

1

WORLDS APART

VOICES FROM THE AMERICAN JOURNEY:
   MOCTEZUMA   1
Native American Societies before 1492   2
   Paleo-Indians and the Archaic Period   3
   The Development of Agriculture   4
   Nonfarming Societies   5
   Mesoamerican Civilizations   5
   North American Cultures   7
   The Caribbean Islanders   9
West African Societies   9
   Geographical and Political Differences   11
   Family Structure and Religion   12
   European Merchants in West Africa and the
      Slave Trade   12
Western Europe on the Eve
   of Exploration   13
   The Consolidation of Political and Military
      Authority   13
Religious Conflict and the Protestant
      Reformation   13
Contact   16
   The Lure of Discovery   16
   Christopher Columbus and the Westward
      Route to Asia   17
   The Spanish Conquest and Colonization   19
   The Columbian Exchange   25
   Cultural Perceptions and Misperceptions   26
Competition for a Continent   27
   Early French Efforts in North America   27
   English Attempts in the New World   28
Conclusion   31
Review Questions   32
Key Terms   32
Recommended Reading   32
Additional Sources   32
Where to Learn More   33

2

TRANSPLANTATION 1600–1685

VOICES FROM THE AMERICAN JOURNEY:
   THOMAS DUDLEY   35
The French in North America   37
   The Quest for Furs and Converts   37
   The Development of New France   38
The Dutch Overseas Empire   39
   The Dutch East India Company   40
   The West India Company and
      New Netherland   40

English Settlement in the Chesapeake 42
The Ordeal of Early Virginia 42
The Importance of Tobacco 44
Maryland: A Refuge for Catholics 46
Life in the Chesapeake Colonies 47
The Founding of New England 48
The Pilgrims and Plymouth Colony 48
Massachusetts Bay Colony and
Its Offshoots 49
Families, Farms, and Communities
in Early New England 52
Competition in the Caribbean 55
Sugar and Slaves 55
A Biracial Society 57
The Proprietary Colonies 57
Early Carolina: Colonial Aristocracy
and Slave Labor 57
Pennsylvania: The Dream of Toleration
and Peace 60
New Netherland Becomes New York 62
Conclusion 62
Review Questions 63
Key Terms 63
Recommended Reading 63
Additional Sources 64
Where to Learn More 64

3

THE CREATION OF NEW WORLDS

VOICES FROM THE AMERICAN JOURNEY:
OLAUDAH EQUIANO 67
Indians and Europeans 68
Indian Workers in the Spanish
Borderlands 69
The Web of Trade 70
Displacing Native Americans in the
English Colonies 72
Bringing Christianity to Native Peoples 73
After the First Hundred Years: Conflict and
War 76
Africans and Europeans 80
Labor Needs and the Turn to Slavery 80
The Shock of Enslavement 81
African Slaves in the New World 82

African American Families and
Communities 88
Resistance and Rebellion 89
European Laborers in Early America 91
A Spectrum of Control 91
New European Immigrants 93
Conclusion 95
Review Questions 96
Key Terms 96
Recommended Reading 96
Additional Sources 96
Where to Learn More 97

4

CONVERGENCE AND CONFLICT 1660s–1763

VOICES FROM THE AMERICAN JOURNEY:
GEORGE WASHINGTON 99
Economic Development and Imperial Trade
in the British Colonies 101
The Regulation of Trade 101
The Colonial Export Trade and the Spirit of
Enterprise 103
The Import Trade and Ties of Credit 106
Becoming More Like England: The Growth of
Cities and Inequality 107
The Transformation of Culture 109
Goods and Houses 110
Shaping Minds and Manners 111
Colonial Religion and the Great Awakening 113
The Colonial Political World 116
The Dominion of New England and the Limits
of British Control 116
The Legacy of the Glorious Revolution 118
Diverging Politics in the Colonies and Great
Britain 119
Expanding Empires 121
British Colonists in the Backcountry 121
The Spanish in Texas and California 123
The French along the Mississippi and in
Louisiana 125
A Century of Warfare 125
Imperial Conflict and the Establishment of an
American Balance of Power, 1689–1738 126

King George's War Shifts the Balance,
1739–1754   127
The French and Indian War, 1754–1760:
A Decisive Victory   129
The Triumph of the British Empire, 1763   132
Conclusion   133
Review Questions   133
Key Terms   133
Recommended Reading   133
Additional Sources   134
Where to Learn More   134

5

IMPERIAL BREAKDOWN 1763–1774

VOICES FROM THE AMERICAN JOURNEY:
ELIZA FARMAR   137
Imperial Reorganization   139
British Problems   139
Dealing with the New Territories   141
Indian Affairs   142
Curbing the Assemblies   144
The Sugar and Stamp Acts   144
American Reactions   145
Constitutional Issues   145
Taxation and the Political Culture   146
Protesting the Taxes   147
The Aftermath of the Stamp
Act Crisis   149
A Strained Relationship   149
Regulator Movements   150
The Townshend Crisis   150
Townshend's Plan   150
American Boycott   151
The Boston Massacre   152
The "Quiet Period"   152
The Boston Tea Party   153
The Intolerable Acts   154
The Road to Revolution   154
American Response to the
Intolerable Acts   154
The First Continental Congress   155
The Continental Association   157
Political Divisions   157
Conclusion   160

Review Questions   161
Key Terms   161
Recommended Reading   161
Additional Sources   162
Where to Learn More   163

6

THE WAR FOR INDEPENDENCE 1774–1783

VOICES FROM THE AMERICAN JOURNEY:
JOHN LAURENS   165
The Outbreak of War and The Declaration
of Independence, 1774–1776   167
Mounting Tensions   167
The Loyalists' Dilemma   167
British Coercion and Conciliation   168
The Battles of Lexington and Concord   168
The Second Continental Congress,
1775–1776   170
Commander in Chief George
Washington   170
Early Fighting: Massachusetts, Virginia,
the Carolinas, and Canada   171
Independence   172
Republicanism   174
The Combatants   175
Professional Soldiers   175
Women in the Contending Armies   180
African American Participation
in the War   180
Native Americans and the War   181
The War in the North, 1776–1777   181
The British Army Hesitates: Battles in New York
and New Jersey   181
The Year of the Hangman: Victory at Saratoga
and Winter at Valley Forge   183
The War Widens, 1778–1781   184
The United States Gains an Ally   184
Fighting on the Frontier and at Sea   185
The Land War Moves South   186
American Counterattacks   188
The American Victory, 1782–1783   190
The Peace of Paris   190
The Components of Success   192

War and Society, 1775–1783 193
    The Women's War 193
    Effect of the War on African Americans 193
    The War's Impact on Native Americans 193
    Economic Disruption 193
    The Price of Victory 196
Conclusion 196
Review Questions 197
Key Terms 197
Recommended Reading 197
Additional Sources 198
Where to Learn More 199

7

THE FIRST REPUBLIC 1776–1789

VOICES FROM THE AMERICAN JOURNEY:
    WILLIAM SHEPARD 201
The New Order of Republicanism 203
    Defining the People 203
    The State Constitutions 207
    The Articles of Confederation 210
Problems at Home 210
    The Fiscal Crisis 211
    Economic Depression 212
    The Economic Policies of the States 214
    Congress and the West 216
Diplomatic Weaknesses 218
    Impasse with Britain 218
    Spain and the Mississippi River 219
Toward a New Union 221
    The Road to Philadelphia 221
    The Convention at Work 222
    Overview of the Constitution 224
    The Struggle over Ratification 225
Conclusion 228
Review Questions 229
Key Terms 229
Recommended Reading 230
Additional Sources 230
Where to Learn More 230

8

A NEW REPUBLIC AND THE RISE OF PARTIES 1789–1800

VOICES FROM THE AMERICAN JOURNEY:
    WILLIAM MACLAY 233
Washington's America 235
    The Uniformity of New England 235
    The Pluralism of the Mid-Atlantic Region 237
    The Slave South and Its Backcountry 239
    The Growing West 240
Forging a New Government 240
    "Mr. President" and the Bill of Rights 241
    Departments and Courts 241
    Revenue and Trade 242
    Hamilton and the Public Credit 242
    Reaction and Opposition 244
The Emergence of Parties 245
    The French Revolution 245
    Securing the Frontier 247
    The Whiskey Rebellion 247
    Treaties with Britain and Spain 250
    The First Partisan Election 251
The Last Federalist Administration 252
    The French Crisis and the XYZ Affair 252
    Crisis at Home 253
    The End of the Federalists 254
Conclusion 257
Review Questions 258
Key Terms 258
Recommended Reading 258
Additional Sources 259
Where to Learn More 259

9

THE TRIUMPH AND COLLAPSE OF JEFFERSONIAN REPUBLICANISM 1800–1824

VOICES FROM THE AMERICAN JOURNEY:
    ROSALIE CALVERT 261
Jefferson's Presidency 263
    Reform at Home 263

The Louisiana Purchase   266
Florida and Western Schemes   268
Embargo and a Crippled Presidency   269
Madison and the Coming of War   270
The Failure of Economic Sanctions   271
The Frontier and Indian Resistance   271
Decision for War   272
The War of 1812   273
Setbacks in Canada   273
Western Victories and British Offensives   276
The Treaty of Ghent and the Battle of New
Orleans   278
The Era of Good Feelings   280
Economic Nationalism   280
Judicial Nationalism   281
Toward a Continental Empire   282
The Breakdown of Unity   283
The Panic of 1819   283
The Missouri Compromise   284
The Election of 1824   287
Conclusion   288
Key Terms   289
Review Questions   289
Recommended Reading   289
Additional Sources   290
Where to Learn More   290

10

THE JACKSONIAN ERA 1824–1845

VOICES FROM THE AMERICAN JOURNEY:
BENJAMIN B. FRENCH   293
The Egalitarian Impulse   295
The Extension of White Male Democracy   295
The Popular Religious Revolt   297
The Rise of the Jacksonians   299
Jackson's Presidency   301
Jackson's Appeal   302
Indian Removal   303
The Nullification Crisis   305
The Bank War   308
Van Buren and Hard Times   309
The Panic of 1837   309
The Independent Treasury   311
Uproar over Slavery   312

The Rise of the Whig Party   312
The Party Taking Shape   313
Whig Persuasion   314
The Election of 1840   315
The Whigs in Power   316
Harrison and Tyler   316
The Texas Issue   317
The Election of 1844   318
Conclusion   318
Review Questions   319
Key Terms   319
Recommended Reading   319
Additional Sources   320
Where to Learn More   320

11

SLAVERY AND THE OLD SOUTH 1800–1860

VOICES FROM THE AMERICAN JOURNEY:
HANNAH CRAFTS   323
The Lower South   325
Cotton and Slaves   325
The Profits of Slavery   326
The Upper South   328
A Period of Economic Adjustment   329
The Decline of Slavery   331
Slave Life and Culture   332
Work Routines and Living Conditions   332
Families and Religion   334
Resistance   336
Free Society   337
The Slaveholding Minority   338
The White Majority   341
Free Black People   342
The Proslavery Argument   344
Conclusion   347
Review Questions   348
Key Terms   348
Recommended Reading   348
Additional Sources   348
Where to Learn More   349

12

THE MARKET REVOLUTION AND SOCIAL REFORM 1815–1850

VOICES FROM THE AMERICAN JOURNEY:
  ANGELINA GRIMKÉ   351
Industrial Change and Urbanization   353
  The Transportation Revolution   353
  Cities and Immigrants   357
  The Industrial Revolution   361
  Growing Inequality and New Classes   364
Reform and Moral Order   367
  The Benevolent Empire   368
  The Temperance Movement   369
  Women's Role in Reform   370
  Backlash against Benevolence   371
Institutions and Social Improvement   371
  School Reform   372
  Prisons, Workhouses, and Asylums   373
  Utopian Alternatives   375
Abolitionism and Women's Rights   378
  Rejecting Colonization   378
  Abolitionism   379
  The Women's Rights Movement   381
  Political Antislavery   382
Conclusion   383
Review Questions   385
Key Terms   385
Recommended Reading   385
Additional Sources   386
Where to Learn More   387

13

THE WAY WEST

VOICES FROM THE AMERICAN JOURNEY:
  GEORGE CATLIN   389
The Agricultural Frontier   391
  The Crowded East   391
  The Old Northwest   393
  The Old Southwest   395
The Frontier of the Plains Indians   397
  Tribal Lands   397
  The Fur Traders   399
  The Oregon Trail   400
The Mexican Borderlands   403
  The Peoples of the Southwest   403
  The Americanization of Texas   405
  The Push into California and the Southwest   406
Politics, Expansion, and War   408
  Manifest Destiny   408
  The Mexican War   410
Conclusion   413
Review Questions   414
Key Terms   414
Recommended Reading   414
Additional Sources   414
Where to Learn More   415

14

THE POLITICS OF SECTIONALISM 1846–1861

VOICES FROM THE AMERICAN JOURNEY:
  HARRIET BEECHER STOWE   417
Slavery in the Territories   419
  The Wilmot Proviso   419
  The Election of 1848   420
  The Gold Rush   421
  The Compromise of 1850   422
  Response to the Fugitive Slave Act   423
  Uncle Tom's Cabin   425
  The Election of 1852   426
Political Realignment   427
  Young America's Foreign Misadventures   427
  Stephen Douglas's Railroad Proposal   428
  The Kansas-Nebraska Act   428
  "Bleeding Kansas"   429
  Know-Nothings and Republicans: Religion and
    Politics   430
  The Election of 1856   432
  The Dred Scott Case   432
  The Lecompton Constitution   433
  The Lincoln-Douglas Debates   434
The Road to Disunion   435
  North-South Differences   436
  John Brown's Raid   438
  The Election of 1860   440

Secession Begins   442
Presidential Inaction   443
Peace Proposals   443
Lincoln's Views on Secession   444
Fort Sumter: The Tug Comes   444
Conclusion   448
Review Questions   450
Key Terms   450
Recommended Reading   450
Additional Sources   450
Where to Learn More   451

15

BATTLE CRIES AND FREEDOM SONGS: THE CIVIL WAR 1861–1865

VOICES FROM THE AMERICAN JOURNEY:
SULLIVAN BALLOU   453
Mobilization, North and South   455
War Fever   455
The North's Advantage in Resources   458
Leaders, Governments, and Strategies   459
The Early War, 1861–1862   461
First Bull Run   462
The War in the West   462
Reassessing the War: The Human Toll   463
The War in the East   465
Turning Points, 1862–1863   466
The Naval and the Diplomatic War   466
Antietam   467
Emancipation   468
From Fredericksburg to Gettysburg   471
Vicksburg, Chattanooga, and the West   474
The War Transforms the North   477
Wartime Legislation and Politics   477
The Northern Economy   479
Northern Women and the War   480
The Confederacy Disintegrates   481
Southern Politics   481
The Southern Economy   482
Southern Women and the War   483
The Union Prevails, 1864–1865   483
Grant's Plan to End the War   484
The Election of 1864 and Sherman's March   486
The Road to Appomattox and the Death of
Lincoln   490

Conclusion   492
Review Questions   493
Key Terms   493
Recommended Reading   494
Additional Sources   494
Where to Learn More   495

16

RECONSTRUCTION 1865–1877

VOICES FROM THE AMERICAN JOURNEY:
T. THOMAS FORTUNE   497
White Southerners and the Ghosts
of the Confederacy, 1865   499
More than Freedom: African American
Aspirations in 1865   500
Education   501
"Forty Acres and a Mule"   502
Migration to Cities   504
Faith and Freedom   505
Federal Reconstruction, 1865–1870   506
Presidential Reconstruction, 1865–1867   507
Congressional Reconstruction, 1867–1870
512
Southern Republican Governments   513
Counter-Reconstruction, 1870–1874   516
The Uses of Violence   516
The Failure of Northern Will   517
Liberal Republicans and the
Election of 1872   518
Redemption, 1874–1877   519
The Democrats' Violent Resurgence   519
The Weak Federal Response   519
The Election of 1876 and the Compromise
of 1877   520
The Memory of Reconstruction   520
The Failed Promise of Reconstruction   522
Sharecropping   523
Modest Gains and Future Victories   523
Conclusion   525
Review Questions   526
Key Terms   526
Recommended Reading   526
Additional Sources   526
Where to Learn More   527

17

A NEW SOUTH: ECONOMIC PROGRESS AND SOCIAL TRADITION 1877–1900

VOICES FROM THE AMERICAN JOURNEY:
  ANNA J. COOPER   529
The Newness of the New South   531
  An Industrial and Urban South   532
  The Limits of Industrial and Urban Growth   534
  Farms to Cities: Impact on Southern Society   537
The Southern Agrarian Revolt   538
  Cotton and Credit   539
  Southern Farmers Organize, 1877–1892   539
  Southern Populists   542
Women in the New South   543
  Church Work and Preserving Memories   543
  Women's Clubs   544
Settling the Race Issue   545
  The Fluidity of Southern Race Relations,
    1877–1890   545
  The White Backlash   546
  Lynch Law   546
  Segregation by Law   547
  Disfranchisement   548
  A National Consensus on Race   550
  Response of the Black Community   551
Conclusion   557
Review Questions   558
Key Terms   559
Recommended Reading   559
Additional Sources   559
Where to Learn More   560

18

INDUSTRY, IMMIGRANTS, AND CITIES 1870–1900

VOICES FROM THE AMERICAN JOURNEY:
  MARY ANTIN   563
New Industry   565
  Inventing Technology: The Electric Age   565
  The Corporation and Its Impact   567

The Changing Nature of Work   570
  Child Labor   571
  Working Women   571
  Responses to Poverty and Wealth   574
  Workers Organize   576
New Immigrants   579
  Old-World Backgrounds   579
  The Neighborhood   582
  The Job   583
  Nativism   584
  Roots of the Great Migration   586
New Cities   588
  Centers and Suburbs   589
  The New Middle Class   590
  A Consumer Society   591
  The Growth of Leisure Activities   592
Conclusion   594
Review Questions   594
Key Terms   594
Recommended Reading   595
Additional Sources   595
Where to Learn More   596

19

TRANSFORMING THE WEST 1865–1890

VOICES FROM THE AMERICAN JOURNEY:
  ANDREW J. RUSSELL   599
Subjugating Native Americans   601
  Tribes and Cultures   601
  Federal Indian Policy   603
  Warfare and Dispossession   603
  Life on the Reservation: Americanization   607
Exploiting the Mountains:
  The Mining Bonanza   610
  Rushes and Mining Camps   610
  Labor and Capital   613
Exploiting the Grass:
  The Cattle Kingdom   614
  Cattle Drives and Cow Towns   614
  Rise and Fall of Open-Range Ranching   615
  Cowhands and Capitalists   616

Exploiting the Earth: Homesteaders
   and Agricultural Expansion   617
   Settling the Land   617
   Home on the Range   621
   Farming the Land   622
Conclusion   624
Review Questions   625
Key Terms   625
Recommended Reading   625
Additional Sources   626
Where to Learn More   627

20

POLITICS AND GOVERNMENT 1877–1900

VOICES FROM THE AMERICAN JOURNEY:
   HORACE AND WILL TAFT   629
The Structure and Style of Politics   631
   Campaigns and Elections   631
   Partisan Politics   633
   Associational Politics   635
The Limits of Government   637
   The Weak Presidency   637
   The Inefficient Congress   637
   The Federal Bureaucracy and the Spoils System
      638
   Inconsistent State Government   638
Public Policies and National Elections   639
   Civil Service Reform   639
   The Political Life of the Tariff   640
   The Beginnings of Federal Regulation   641
   The Money Question   643
The Crisis of the 1890s   644
   Farmers Protest Inequities   644
   The People's Party   645
   The Challenge of the Depression   646
   The Battle of the Standards and the Election of
      1896   650
Conclusion   653
Review Questions   654
Key Terms   654
Recommended Reading   655

Additional Sources   656
Where to Learn More   656

21

THE PROGRESSIVE ERA 1900–1917

VOICES FROM THE AMERICAN JOURNEY:
   WASHINGTON POST   659
The Ferment of Reform   661
   The Context of Reform: Industrial and Urban
      Tensions   662
   Church and Campus   664
   Muckrakers   665
   The Gospel of Efficiency   665
   Labor's Demand for Rights   665
   Extending the Woman's Sphere   666
   Trans-Atlantic Influences   667
   Socialism   667
   Opponents of Reform   668
Reforming Society   668
   Settlement Houses and Urban Reform   668
   Protective Legislation for Women and Children
      670
   Reshaping Public Education   671
   Challenging Gender Restrictions   674
   Reforming Country Life   675
   Social Control and Moral Crusades   675
   For Whites Only?   677
Reforming Politics and Government   678
   Woman Suffrage   678
   Electoral Reform   679
   Municipal Reform   680
   Progressive State Government   680
Theodore Roosevelt and the Progressive
   Presidency   681
   TR and the Modern Presidency   681
   Roosevelt and Labor   682
   Managing Natural Resources   682
   Corporate Regulation   684
   Taft and the Insurgents   685
Woodrow Wilson and Progressive
   Reform   686
   The Election of 1912   686
   Implementing the New Freedom   687
   The Expansion of Reform   689

Conclusion   689
Review Questions   691
Key Terms   691
Recommended Reading   691
Additional Sources   692
Where to Learn More   693

22
CREATING AN EMPIRE 1865–1917

VOICES FROM THE AMERICAN JOURNEY:
   MAJOR-GENERAL LEONARD WOOD   695
The Roots of Imperialism   697
   Ideological Arguments   697
   Strategic Concerns   699
   Economic Designs   700
First Steps   700
   Seward and Blaine   701
   Hawaii   702
   Chile and Venezuela   704
The Spanish-American War   705
   The Cuban Revolution   705
   Growing Tensions   706
   War and Empire   706
   The Treaty of Paris   708
Imperial Ambitions: The United States and
   East Asia, 1899–1917   710
   The Filipino-American War   710
   China and the Open Door   712
   Rivalry with Japan and Russia   713
Imperial Power: The United States and
   Latin America, 1899–1917   713
   U.S. Rule in Puerto Rico   714
   Cuba as a U.S. Protectorate   714
   The Panama Canal   716
   The Roosevelt Corollary   717
   Dollar Diplomacy   717
   Wilsonian Interventions   718
Conclusion   719
Review Questions   720
Key Terms   720
Recommended Reading   720
Additional Sources   720
Where to Learn More   721

23
AMERICA AND THE GREAT WAR 1914–1920

VOICES FROM THE AMERICAN JOURNEY:
   RAY STANNARD BAKER   723
Waging Neutrality   725
   The Origins of Conflict   725
   American Attitudes   726
   The Economy of War   727
   The Diplomacy of Neutrality   727
   The Battle over Preparedness   729
   The Election of 1916   729
   Descent into War   730
Waging War in America   731
   Managing the War Economy   731
   Women and Minorities: New Opportunities,
      Old Inequities   733
   Financing the War   734
   Conquering Minds   735
   Suppressing Dissent   736
Waging War and Peace Abroad   737
   The War to End All Wars   737
   The Fourteen Points   740
   The Paris Peace Conference   741
Waging Peace at Home   742
   Battle over the League   744
   Economic Readjustment and
      Social Conflict   744
   The Red Scare   746
   The Election of 1920   747
Conclusion   748
Review Questions   749
Key Terms   749
Recommended Reading   749
Additional Sources   749
Where to Learn More   751

24

TOWARD A MODERN AMERICA THE 1920s

VOICES FROM THE AMERICAN JOURNEY:
UPTON SINCLAIR 753

The Economy That Roared 756
Boom Industries 756
Corporate Consolidation 757
Open Shops and Welfare Capitalism 757
Sick Industries 759

The Business of Government 760
Republican Ascendancy 760
Government Corruption 761
Coolidge Prosperity 761
The Fate of Reform 762

Cities and Suburbs 763
Expanding Cities 763
The Great Black Migration 763
Barrios 766
The Road to Suburbia 767

Mass Culture in the Jazz Age 767
Advertising the Consumer Society 768
Leisure and Entertainment 768
The New Morality 770
The Searching Twenties 770

Culture Wars 771
Nativism and Immigration Restriction 771
The Ku Klux Klan 772
Prohibition and Crime 773
Old-Time Religion and the Scopes Trial 774

A New Era in the World? 775
War Debts and Economic Expansion 775
Rejecting War 776
Managing the Hemisphere 778

Herbert Hoover and the Triumph
of the New Era 778
Conclusion 779
Review Questions 779
Key Terms 780
Recommended Reading 780
Additional Sources 780
Where to Learn More 781

25

THE GREAT DEPRESSION AND THE NEW DEAL 1929–1939

VOICES FROM THE AMERICAN JOURNEY: CARLOTTA
SILVAS MARTIN, EUNICE LANGDON, MERIDEL
LESEUR 783

Hard Times in Hooverville 786
Crash! 786
The Depression Spreads 788
"Women's Jobs" and "Men's Jobs" 789
Families in the Depression 789
"Last Hired, First Fired" 790
Protest 790

Herbert Hoover and the Depression 791
The Limits of Voluntarism 791
Repudiating Hoover: The Election of 1932 793

Launching the New Deal 794
Action Now! 794
Creating Jobs 795
Helping Some Farmers 796
The Flight of the Blue Eagle 796
Critics Right and Left 797

Consolidating the New Deal 800
Lifting Up and Weeding Out 800
Expanding Relief 802
The Roosevelt Coalition and the Election of
1936 803

The New Deal and American Life 804
Labor on the March 804
Women and the New Deal 804
Minorities and the New Deal 805
The New Deal: North, South, East,
and West 807
The New Deal and Public Activism 808

Ebbing of the New Deal 809
Challenging the Court 809
More Hard Times 809
Political Stalemate 809

Good Neighbors and Hostile Forces 810
Neutrality and Fascism 811
Edging Toward Involvement 814
Conclusion 814
Review Questions 815
Key Terms 815

Recommended Reading   815
Additional Sources   815
Where to Learn More   817

26

WORLD WAR II 1939–1945

VOICES FROM THE AMERICAN JOURNEY:
  ENRICO FERMI   819
The Dilemmas of Neutrality   821
  The Roots of War   821
  Hitler's War in Europe   822
  Trying to Keep Out   823
  Edging Toward Intervention   825
  The Brink of War   825
  December 7, 1941   827
Holding the Line   828
  Stopping Germany   828
  The Survival of Britain   830
  Retreat and Stabilization in the Pacific   830
Mobilizing for Victory   830
  Organizing the Economy   832
  The Enlistment of Science   833
  Men and Women in the Military   834
  The Home Front   836
  New Workers   837
  Clashing Cultures   838
  Internment of Japanese Americans   838
  The End of the New Deal   839
War and Peace   839
  Turning the Tide in Europe   840
  Operation OVERLORD   842
  Victory and Tragedy in Europe   844
  The Pacific War   846
  Searching for Peace   848
  How the Allies Won   849
Conclusion   851
Review Questions   852
Key Terms   852
Recommended Reading   852
Additional Sources   852
Where to Learn More   853

27

THE COLD WAR AT HOME AND ABROAD 1946–1952

VOICES FROM THE AMERICAN JOURNEY:
  BERNADETTE RISCHER WHEELER   855
Launching the Great Boom   856
  Reconversion Chaos   857
  Economic Policy   858
  The GI Bill   859
  Assembly-Line Neighborhoods   859
  Steps Toward Civil Rights   860
  Consumer Boom and Baby Boom   861
Truman, Republicans, and
  the Fair Deal   862
  Truman's Opposition   862
  Whistle-Stopping across America   864
  Truman's Fair Deal   864
Confronting the Soviet Union   865
  The End of the Grand Alliance   865
  The Truman Doctrine and the Marshall Plan
    867
  Soviet Reactions   867
  American Rearmament   868
Cold War and Hot War   868
  The Nuclear Shadow   869
  The Cold War in Asia   870
  NSC-68 and Aggressive Containment   872
  War in Korea, 1950–1953   872
  The Politics of War   874
The Second Red Scare   875
  The Communist Party and the
    Loyalty Program   876
  Naming Names to Congress   877
  Subversion Trials   878
  Senator McCarthy on Stage   879
  Understanding McCarthyism   880
Conclusion   880
Review Questions   881
Key Terms   882
Recommended Reading   882
Additional Sources   882
Where to Learn More   883

28
THE CONFIDENT YEARS 1953–1964

VOICES FROM THE AMERICAN JOURNEY:
MELBA PATTILLO BEALS   885
A Decade of Affluence   886
What's Good for General Motors   887
Reshaping Urban America   888
Comfort on Credit   889
The New 1950's Family   889
Inventing Teenagers   890
Turning to Religion   892
The Gospel of Prosperity   893
The Underside of Affluence   893
Facing Off with the Soviet Union   894
Why We Liked Ike   895
A Balance of Terror   895
Containment in Action   896
Global Standoff   898
John F. Kennedy and the Cold War   899
The Kennedy Mystique   899
Kennedy's Mistakes   900
Getting into Vietnam   901
Missile Crisis: A Line Drawn in the Waves   901
Science and Foreign Affairs   904
Righteousness Like a Mighty Stream:
The Struggle for Civil Rights   904
Getting to the Supreme Court   904
Deliberate Speed   905
Public Accommodations   906
The March on Washington, 1963   908
"Let Us Continue"   909
Dallas, 1963   909
War on Poverty   909
Civil Rights, 1964-1965   910
War, Peace, and the Landslide of 1964   911
Conclusion   914
Review Questions   915
Key Terms   915
Recommended Reading   916
Additional Sources   916
Where to Learn More   917

29
SHAKEN TO THE ROOTS 1965–1980

VOICES FROM THE AMERICAN JOURNEY:
BUZZ ALDRIN AND NEIL ARMSTRONG   919
The End of Consensus   920
Deeper into Vietnam   921
Voices of Dissent   923
New Left and Community Activism   926
The Feminist Critique   927
Youth Culture and Counterculture   928
Sounds of Change   928
Communes and Cults   929
Cities Under Stress   930
Diagnosing an Urban Crisis   930
Racial Rioting   931
Minority Separatism   931
Suburban Independence: The Outer City   934
The Year of the Gun, 1968   935
The Tet Offensive   935
LBJ's Exit   935
Red Spring   936
Violence and Politics: Kennedy, King,
and Chicago   937
Nixon and Watergate   937
Getting Out of Vietnam, 1969–1975   938
Nixon and the Wider World   939
Courting Middle America   940
Oil, OPEC, and Stagflation   940
Americans as Environmentalists   941
From Dirty Tricks to Watergate   942
The Ford Footnote   944
Jimmy Carter: Idealism and Frustration
in the White House   946
Carter, Energy, and the Economy   946
Closed Factories and Failed Farms   947
Building a Cooperative World   948
New Crises Abroad   948
Conclusion   950
Review Questions   951
Key Terms   951
Recommended Reading   952
Additional Sources   952
Where to Learn More   953

30

THE REAGAN REVOLUTION AND A CHANGING WORLD 1981–1992

VOICES FROM THE AMERICAN JOURNEY:
   CELIA NOUP   955
Reagan's Domestic Revolution   957
   Reagan's Majority   957
   The New Conservatism   961
   Reaganomics: Deficits and Deregulation   961
   Crisis for Organized Labor   962
   An Acquisitive Society   963
   Poverty amid Prosperity   964
   Consolidating the Revolution:
      George Bush   967
The Second (Short) Cold War   968
   Confronting the Soviet Union   968
   Risky Business: Foreign Policy Adventures   969
   Embracing *Perestroika*   971
   Crisis and Democracy in Eastern Europe   971
   The Persian Gulf War   974
Growth in the Sunbelt   976
   The Defense Economy   977
   New Americans   978
   Old Gateways and New   980
   The Graying of America   981
Values in Collision   981
   Women's Rights and Public Policy   981
   Coming Out   982
   Churches in Change   983
   Culture Wars   985
Conclusion   987
Review Questions   987
Key Terms   988
Recommended Reading   988
Additional Sources   988
Where to Learn More   989

31

COMPLACENCY AND CRISIS 1993–2003

VOICES FROM THE AMERICAN JOURNEY:
   JOHN MCNAMARA   991
The Politics of the Center   991
   The Election of 1992: A New Generation   993
   Policing the World   995
   Clinton's Neoliberalism   996
   Contract with America and the Election of
      1996   997
   The Dangers of Everyday Life   998
   Morality and Partisanship   999
A New Economy?   1000
   The Prosperous 1990s   1001
   The Service Economy   1001
   The High Tech Sector   1002
   An Instant Society   1003
   In the World Market   1006
Broadening Democracy   1007
   Americans in 2000   1007
   Women from the Grassroots to Congress   1008
   Minorities at the Ballot Box   1010
   Rights and Opportunities   1011
Edging into a New Century   1013
   The 2000 Election   1014
   Reaganomics Revisited   1015
   Downsized Diplomacy   1016
Paradoxes of Power   1017
   9-11-01   1018
   Security and Conflict   1019
   Iraq and Conflicts in the Middle East   1020
Conclusion   1021
Review Questions   1022
Key Terms   1022
Recommended Reading   1022
Additional Sources   1023
Where to Learn More   1023

APPENDIX   A-1
GLOSSARY   G-1
CREDITS   C-1
INDEX   I-1

AMERICAN VIEWS

CHAPTER

1 Cabeza de Vaca among the Indians (1530)   22

2 Miantonomo's Plea for Indian Unity (1642)   52

3 Mary Rowlandson Among the Indians   78

4 Boston Celebrates a New King (August 1727)   118

5 Social Status and the Enforcement of the Nonimportation Movement   158

6 A British Woman Observes an American Militia Exercise in 1775   176

7 A French Observer Describes a New Society   208

8 Little Turtle Defends the Miami Lands   248

9 Federalist Antiwar Resolutions   276

10 Memorial and Protest of the Cherokee Nation, 1836   306

11 A Letter from an Escaped Slave to His Former Master   338

12 Appeal of a Female Abolitionist   376

13 A Mexican View of the Texans in 1828   408

14 Lincoln on Slavery   446

15 A Soldier Promotes the Union Cause   473

16 Mississippi's 1865 Black Codes   508

17 Robert Smalls Argues Against Disfranchisement   552

18 Tenement Life   576

19 Zitkala-Sa's View of Americanization   608

20 A Populist Views American Government   648

21 Mother Jones and the Meaning of Child Labor in America   672

22 An Imperialist Views the World   702

23 Mobilizing America for Liberty   738

24 The Cult of Business   762

25 An Ohio Mayor on Unemployment and Relief   798

27 The Internment of Japanese Americans in 1942   840

27 Deciding on a Nuclear Arms Race   871

28 Two Presidents Assess the Implications of the Cold War   902

29 Grassroots Community Action   944

30 The Religious Imperative in Politics   984

31 Creating and Working in the New Economy   1004

FROM THEN TO NOW

CHAPTER

1 The Disappearance of Cod off
the Grand Banks 30

3 The Legacy of Slavery 94

6 The American Revolution and the
Teaching of American History 195

8 Hamilton's Legacy and the
National Debt 256

9 The Lewis and Clark Expedition in Their
World and Ours 286

11 The Economic Legacy of Slavery 346

12 Immigration: An Ambivalent Welcome 384

13 Manifest Destiny and American Foreign
Policy 412

14 Religion and Politics 448

15 Gettysburg 491

16 African American Voting Rights in the
South 524

17 The Confederate Battle Flag 556

19 The Legacy of Indian Americanization
622

20 Political Parties 654

21 The Environmental Movement 690

24 The Culture Wars 776

25 Social Security 812

26 Nuclear Weapons 850

28 Medical Research on Polio and AIDS 912

31 Loyalty in 2001 and 1917 1018

MAPS

CHAPTER 1

1-1 North American Culture Areas, c. 1500 6
1-2 West Africa and Europe in 1492 10
1-3 European Voyages of Discovery in the Atlantic in the Fifteenth and Sixteenth Centuries 18
1-4 Spanish, English, and French Settlements in North America in the Sixteenth Century 20

CHAPTER 2

2-1 New France, c. 1650 38
2-2 English and Dutch Mainland Colonies in North America, c. 1655 42
2-3 Principal European Possessions in the Caribbean in the Seventeenth Century 54
2-4 English North American Colonies, c. 1685 58

CHAPTER 3

3-1 A, B, & C Spanish and French Missions in North America 74
3-2 African Origins of North American Slaves, 1690–1807 82
3-3 Ethnic Distribution of Settler Population in British Mainland Colonies, c. 1755 95

CHAPTER 4

4-1 Anglo-American Transatlantic Commerce 104
4-2 Expanding Settlement, c. 1750 121
4-3 The French and Indian War, 1754–1763 128
4-4 European Empires in North America, 1750–1763 132

CHAPTER 5

5-1 Colonial Settlement and the Proclamation Line of 1763 141
5-2 The Quebec Act of 1774 155

CHAPTER 6

6-1 The Battles of Lexington and Concord 169
6-2 Early Fighting, 1775–1776 171
6-3 The War in the North, 1776–1777 182
6-4 The War on the Frontier, 1778–1779 187
6-5 The War in the South, 1778–1781 188
6-6 North America after the Peace of Paris, 1783 191

CHAPTER 7

7-1 Cession of Western Lands by the States 211
7-2 Disputed Territory in the West after the Treaty of Paris 220
7-3 The Ratification Vote on the Constitution 227

CHAPTER 8

8-1 Indian Land Cessions, 1784–1800 249
8-2 The Election of 1800 257

CHAPTER 9

9-1 The Louisiana Purchase and the Lewis and Clark Expedition 268
9-2 The War of 1812 274
9-3 The Missouri Compromise of 1820 and Territorial Treaties with Britain and Spain, 1818–1819 285
9-4 The Election of 1824 288

CHAPTER 10

10-1 Methods of Electing Presidential Electors, 1800 and 1824 296
10-2 The Election of 1828 301
10-3 Indian Removals 305
10-4 The Election of 1840 316

CHAPTER 11

11-1 The Spread of Slavery: New Slave States Entering the Union 326
11-2 Cotton and Other Crops in the South, 1860 330

CHAPTER 12

12-1 The Transportation Revolution, 354
12-2 A,& B The Growth of Cities 358, 359

CHAPTER 13

13-1 A,B,& C The Westward Shift of the
United States Population, 1790–1850 392
13-2 Western Overland Trails 401
13-3 Texas and Mexico after the Texas Revolt 406
13-4 The Mexican War 411

CHAPTER 14

14-1 The Compromise of 1850 424
14-2 The Kansas-Nebraska Act, 1854 429
14-3 Railroads in the United States, 1860 437
14-4 The Election of 1860 442
14-5 The Course of Secession 443

CHAPTER 15

15-1 From the First Bull Run to Antietam:
The War in the East, 1861–1862 462
15-2 The War in the West, 1861–1862 463
15-3 From Fredericksburg to Gettysburg: The War
in the East, December 1862–July 1863 472
15-4 The Battle of Gettysburg, July 1–3, 1863 474
15-5 Vicksburg and Chattanooga: The War in the
West, 1863 476
15-6 Grant and Lee in Virginia, 1864–1865 485
15-7 The Atlanta Campaign and Sherman's
March, 1864–1865 486

CHAPTER 16

16-1 Congressional Reconstruction, 1865–1877 512
16-2 The Election of 1876 522

CHAPTER 17

17-1 Railroads in the South,
1859 and 1899 534, 535

CHAPTER 18

18-1 Patterns of Immigration, 1820–1914 580
18-2 The Growth of America's Cities,
1880–1900 589

CHAPTER 19

19-1 Indian Land Cessions, 1860–1894 604
19-2 Economic Development of the West:
Railroads, Mining, and Cattle,
1860–1900 611
19-3 Population Density and Agricultural Land
Use in the Late Nineteenth Century 619

CHAPTER 20

20-1 The Two-Party Stalemate of the Late
Nineteenth Century 634
20-2 The Election of 1896 653

CHAPTER 21

21-1 Woman suffrage in the United States before
the ratification of the Nineteenth
Amendment 679
21-2 The growth of National Forests and National
Parks 683
21-3 The Election of 1912 688

CHAPTER 22

22-1 United States Expansion in the Pacific,
1867–1899 701
22-2 The Spanish-American War 707
22-3 The United States in the Caribbean 715

CHAPTER 23

23-1 The Election of 1916 730
23-2 The Western Front, 1918 740
23-3 Europe and the Middle East after the Treaty
of Versailles 743

CHAPTER 24
24-1 Population Shifts, 1920–1930 **765**
24-2 The Election of 1928 **784**

CHAPTER 25
25-1 The Election of 1932 **794**
25-2 The Dust Bowl **802**
25-3 The Tennessee Valley Authority **808**

CHAPTER 26
26-1 Axis Europe, 1941, on the Eve of Hitler's
Invasion of the Soviet Union **824**
26-2 A Global War **829**
26-3 World War II in the Pacific, from Pearl
Harbor to Midway **831**
26-4 States with Population Growth of 10 Percent
or More, 1940–1943 **833**
26-5 World War II in Europe, 1942–1945 **843**
26-6 World War II in the Pacific, 1942–1945 **847**

CHAPTER 27
27-1 The Election of 1948 **864**
27-2 Cold War in Europe **869**
27-3 The Landscape of Nuclear Weapons **872**
27-4 The Korean War **873**

CHAPTER 28
28-1 U.S. Intervention around the Caribbean
since 1954 **898**
28-2 The Election of 1960 **900**
28-3 SEATO and Other East Asian Countries with
Ties to the United States **903**

CHAPTER 29
29-1 The War in Vietnam **922**
29-2 The Election of 1968 **940**
29-3 The Election of 1976 **948**

CHAPTER 30
30-1 Election of 1980 **959**
30-2 Persian Gulf War **976**
30-3 Fast-Growing and Shrinking Metropolitan
Areas, 1900–2000 **977**

CHAPTER 31
31-1 Election of 1992 **995**
31-2 Women as Business Owners, 1992 **1010**
31-3 The Election of 2000 **1014**

FIGURES AND TABLES

FIGURES

1-1   Value of New World Treasure Imported into Spain, 1506–1655   **24**

2-1   European Populations of New France (Quebec) and English Colonies in 1650 and 1700   **40**

2-2   The Supply and Price of Chesapeake Tobacco, 1620–1700   **46**

3-1   Estimated Population of Selected Indian Peoples, 1600–1730   **70**

3-2   Destination of Slaves Imported from Africa to the Americas between 1451 and 1810   **81**

3-3   Estimated Population of Black and White Settlers in British Colonial Regions, 1650–1750   **84**

3-4   Ethnic Distribution of Non-Indian Inhabitants of British Mainland Colonies, c. 1770   **93**

4-1   Average Annual Value of Colonial Exports by Region, 1768–1772   **105**

4-2   Population Growth in British Mainland Colonies, 1700–1760   **122**

5-1   Value of American Exports to and Imports from England, 1763–1776   **152**

7-1   Growth of the Free Black Population between 1750 and 1800   **205**

7-2   American Exports to and Imports from Britain between 1783 and 1789   **213**

7-3   Land Ordinance of 1785   **217**

8-1   Ethnic Breakdown of the United States in 1790, by Region   **236**

10-1   Cotton Prices and the Value of Federal Land Sales in Five Southern States, 1825–1845   **310**

10-2   Voter Turnout in Presidential Elections, 1824–1840   **316**

11-1   U.S. Cotton Production, 1800–1860   **327**

11-2   The Changing Regional Pattern of Slavery in the South, 1800–1860   **331**

11-3   Slave, Free Black, and White Population in Southern States, 1850   **343**

12-1   Immigration to the United States, 1820–1860   **361**

12-2   Growth in Wealth Inequality, 1774–1860   **364**

12-3   Mob Violence and the Abolitionists   **381**

13-1   Overland Emigration to the West, 1840–1860   **401**

15-1   A Comparison of the Union and Confederate Control of Key Resources at the Outset of the Civil War   **458**

17-1   Per Capita Income in the South as a Percentage of the U.S. Average, 1860–1920   **536**

17-2   The Price of Cotton, 1869–1910   **539**

17-3   Disfranchisement and Educational Spending in the South, 1890–1910   **555**

18-1   Changes in the American Labor Force, 1870–1910   **567**

18-2   Immigration to the United States, 1870–1920   **581**

19-1 The Growth of Western Farming, 1860–1900 **620**

20-1 Voter Turnout in Presidential Elections, 1876–1924 **633**

20-2 Increase in Congressional Business, 1871–1901 **638**

21-1 Child Labor, 1870–1930 **670**

24-1 Registered Motor Vehicles, 1913–1929 **756**

24-2 Growing Income Inequality in the 1920s **759**

25-1 Distribution of Income in the United States, 1929–1946 **786**

25-2 Unemployment, 1925–1945 **788**

26-1 Making War: The United States Mobilizes, 1939–1945 **832**

27-1 The Suburbanizing Nation **860**

27-2 The Post-War Baby Boom: The U.S. Birthrate, 1930–1995 **861**

28-1 Households with Telephones, Televisions, and VCRs **890**

28-2 Working Women as a Percentage of All Women, 1950–1997 **891**

28-3 Defense Spending as a Percentage of Gross Domestic Product, 1950–1997 **896**

28-4 Poverty Rate, 1960–1997 **914**

29-1 The United States in Vietnam **923**

29-2 Year-to-Year Percentage Changes in the Consumer Price Index and Energy Prices **951**

30-1 Changes in Real Family Income, 1980–1990 **965**

30-2 Median Salary of Women and Men, 1960–1998 **966**

31-1 Women as a Percentage of High-Level Presidential Appointments, Lyndon Johnson to George W. Bush **1011**

31-2 Minorities and Women in Congress, 1869–1999 **1012**

TABLES

12-1 Impact of the Transportation Revolution on Traveling Time **353**

26-1 Military and Civilian Deaths in World War II **845**

30-1 Major Racial and Ethnic Minorities in the United States **979**

31-1 States with Highest Proportions of Minority Residents in 2000 **1008**

OVERVIEW TABLES

CHAPTER

1 The Columbian Exchange 25

2 English Colonies in the Seventeenth Century 59

3 Predominant Colonial Labor Systems, 1750 92

4 British Imperial Trade Regulations, 1651–1733 102

4 The Colonial Wars, 1689–1763 126

5 New Restraints and Burdens on Americans, 1759–1774 156

6 Important Battles of the Revolutionary War 178

7 The Articles of Confederation and the Constitution Compared 224

7 Federalists versus the Antifederalists 226

8 Federalist Party versus Republican Party 244

10 The Second Party System 313

11 Structure of Free Society in the South, c. 1860 340

12 Changes Promoting Growth in the Transformed Economy 360

12 Types of Antislavery Reform 380

13 Westward Expansion and the Growth of the Union, 1815–1850 396

14 South and North Compared in 1860 436

14 The Emerging Sectional Crisis 445

15 Major Battles of the Civil War, 1861–1865 489

16 Contrasting Views of Reconstruction: President and Congress 507

16 Constitutional Amendments and Federal Legislation of the Reconstruction Era 521

17 The March of Disfranchisement Across the South, 1889–1908 550

18 Workers Organize 578

19 Government Land Policy 618

20 Arguments in the Tariff Debates 641

21 Major Progressive Organizations and Groups 663

21 Major Laws and Constitutional Amendments of the Progressive Era 669

22 Rationales for Imperialism 699

22 U.S. Interventions in Latin America, 1891–1933 714

23 Major Government Wartime Agencies 731

24 Issues in the Culture Wars of the 1920s 772

25 Major Laws of the Hundred Days 795

26 The Decision to Use the Atomic Bomb 849

27 The Second Red Scare 876

28 Civil Rights in the South: The Struggle for Racial Equality 905

29 Why Were We in South Vietnam? 925

29 The Environmental Decades 942

30 Controlling Nuclear Weapons: Four Decades of Progress 972

30 Why Did the Cold War End? 975

31 Presidential Impeachment 1000

U.S. History Documents CD-ROM

Meeting of Three Cultures

Marco Polo Recounts His Travels Through Asia (1324)

Christopher Columbus, Letter to Ferdinand and Isabella of Spain (1494)

Alvar Núñez Cabeza de Vaca, "Indians of the Rio Grande" (1528–1536)

Jacques Cartier: First Contact with the Indians (1534)

Bartolomé de Las Casas, "Of the Island of Hispaniola" (1542)

Thomas Mun, from England's Treasure by Foreign Trade (1664)

Don Juan de Oñate, Plaus: A Settlement in New Mexico (1599)

The Founding of St. Augustine, 1565

The Columbian Exchange (1590)

Thomas Harriot, The Algonquian Peoples of the Atlantic Coast (1588)

Jose de Acosta, A Spanish Priest Speculates on the Origins of the Indians (1590)

Colonizing the New World

John White, The Lost Colony (1590)

Samuel de Champlain's Battle with the Iroquois, July 1609

An Act Concerning Servants and Slaves

Reasons for the Plantation in New England (1629)

John Winthrop, "A Model of Christian Charity" (1630)

The Taking of the Fort at Mystic: A Brief History of the Pequot War

The Trial of Anne Hutchinson (1638)

A Jesuit Priest Describes New Amsterdam (1642)

George Alsop, The Importance of Tobacco (1660)

The Examination and Confession of Ann Foster at Salem Village (1692)

Onandogas and Cayugas: Iroquois Chiefs Address the Governors of New York and Virginia (1684)

James Oglethorpe: The Stono Rebellion (1739)

Gottlieb Mittelberger, The Passage of Indentured Servants (1750)

Colonial America

Navigation Act of September13, 1660

Nathaniel Bacon's Challenge to William Berkeley and the Governor's Response (1676)

Early French Explorations of the Mississippi River (1673)

Edward Randolph Describes King Philip's War (1685)

Excerpt from Cotton Mather's "Memorable Providences, Relating to Witchcrafts and Possessions" (1689)

William Penn's Charter of Privileges (1701)

William Byrd II, Diary (1709)

Manners and Etiquette in the Eighteenth Century

"The Storm Arising in the West," George Washington Delivers a Warning to the French (1753)

The Closing of the Frontier (1763)

The Adventures of Daniel Boone (1769)

Alexander Falconbridge, The African Slave Trade (1788)

Olaudah Equiano, The Middle Passage (1788)

Prelude to Revolution

John Peter Zenger and the Responsibility of the Press (1734)

Declaration of the Injured Frontier Inhabitants [of Pennsylvania] (1764)

Benjamin Franklin, Testimony Against the Stamp Act (1766)

"Letters from a Farmer in Pennsylvania" (1767)

John Dickinson, from Letters from a Farmer in Pennsylvania (1768)

The Boston "Massacre" or Victims of Circumstance? (1770)

John Andrews to William Barrell, Letter Regarding the Boston Tea Party (1773)

Address of the Inhabitants of Anson County to Governor Martin (1774)

J. Hector St. John Crèvecoeur, "What Is an American?" (1782)

The American Revolution

Benjamin Franklin, "Observations Concerning the Increase of Mankind, Peopling of Countries, &c." (1751)

James Otis, The Rights of the British Colonies Asserted and Proved (1763)

The Crisis Comes to a Head: April 19, 1775

A Freelance Writer Urges His Readers to Use Common Sense (1776)

Abigail Adams and John Adams Letters; Abigail Adams Letter to Mercy Otis Warren

Petition of "A Grate Number of Blackes of the Province" to Governor Thomas Gage and the Members of the Massachusetts General Court (1774)

Joseph Warren, "Account of the Battle of Lexington" (1775)

Thomas Jefferson, "Original Rough Draught" of the Declaration of Independence (1776)

Rights of Women in an Independent Republic

The Rise of Partisan Warfare in the South (1778)

Forging a Constitution

Constitution of Pennsylvania (1776)

A Declaration of the Rights of the Inhabitants of the Commonwealth of Massachusetts (1780)

George Washington, The Newburgh Address (1783)

Henry Knox, Letter to George Washington (1786)

Marquis de Chastellux, Travels in North America (1786)

Shays's Rebellion: Letters of Generals William Shepard and Benjamin Lincoln to Governor James Bowdoin of Massachusetts (1787)

Divergent Reactions to Shays's Rebellion

The "Distracting Question" in Philadelphia (1787)

Patrick Henry Speaks Against Ratification of the Constitution (1788)

Benjamin Banneker, Letter to Thomas Jefferson (1791)

James Wilson, An Introductory Lecture To a Course of Law Lectures (1791)

Molly Wallace, Valedictory Oration (1792)

THE FEDERALIST ERA

James Madison Defends the Constitution (1788)

[William Maclay], "For the Independent Gazetteer" (1790)

Alexander Hamilton, Final Version of "An Opinion on the Constitutionality of an Act to Establish a Bank" (1791)

Questions Concerning the Constitutionality of the National Bank (1791)

Opposing Visions for the New Nation (1791)

An African American Calls for an End to Slavery (1791)

Backcountry Turmoil Puts the New Government to the Test (1794)

George Washington, Farewell Address (1796)

The Alien and Sedition Acts (1798)

Questions of Constitutionality and the Roots of Nullification (1798)

Reverend Peter Cartwright on Cane Ridge and the "New Lights" (1801)

Marbury v. Madison (1803)

JEFFERSON AND THE REPUBLIC

Memoirs of a Monticello Slave, as Dictated to Charles Campbell by Isaac" (1847)

Thomas Jefferson, "First Inaugural Address" (1801)

Margaret Bayard Smith Meets Thomas Jefferson (1801)

Constitutionality of the Louisiana Purchase (1803)

The United States Navy and the Bombardment of Tripoli (1803)

A Matter of Honor or Vengeance? (1804)

Fisher Ames, "The Republican. No. II" (1804)

Sacagawea Interprets for Lewis and Clark (1804)

An "Uncommon Genius" Advocates Indian Unity (1809)

Indian Hostilities (1812)

The British Attack Baltimore (1814)

Report and Resolutions of the Hartford Convention (1814)

Davy Crockett, Advice to Politicians (1833)

ECONOMIC AND SOCIAL CHANGE

The Western Country, "Extracts from Letters Published in Niles' Weekly Register" (1816)

The Cherokee Treaty of 1817

The Case for the Erie Canal

John Marshall Affirms the Power of the Federal Government

Thomas Jefferson Reacts to the "Missouri Question" (1820)

The Monroe Doctrine and a Reaction (1823)

Henry Clay, "Defense of the American System" (1832)

Imminent Dangers to the Free Institutions of the United States through Foreign Immigration (1835)

The Harbinger, Female Workers of Lowell (1836)

James F. Cooper, Notions of the Americans (1840)

Resolutions of the Boston Carpenters' Strike (1845)

The Trials of a Slave Girl

JACKSONIAN DEMOCRACY

Joseph Smith and the Beginnings of Mormonism (1823)

A "Corrupt Bargain" or Politics as Usual? (1824)

A Disaffected Mason Speaks Out Against the Order (1826)

The " Commoner" Takes Office (1828)

Andrew Jackson, First Annual Message to Congress (1829)

"Memorial of the Cherokee Nation" (1830)

Andrew Jackson, Veto of the Bank Bill (1832)

President Andrew Jackson's Proclamation Regarding Nullification (1832)

The Force Bill (1833)

Black Hawk, "Life of Black Hawk" (1833)

A French Traveler Reports on American Society (1835)

Female Industry Association, from the New York Herald (1845)

REFORMING THE NATION

Joshua and Sally Wilson Letters to George Wilson (1823)

Lyman Beecher, Six Sermons on Intemperance (1828)

"Early Habits of Industry," The Mother's Magazine (1834)

Charles Finney, "What a Revival of Religion Is" (1835)

Temperance and the Washingtonians (1836)

A Lowell Mill Girl Tells Her Story (1836)

"Petition of the Catholics of New York" (1840)

Ralph Waldo Emerson, "Self-Reliance" (1841)

Ja Norcom, Letter to Mary Matilda Norcom (1846)

Declaration of Sentiments and Resolutions, Woman's Rights Convention, Seneca Falls, New York (1848)

Horace Mann on Education and National Welfare

John Humphrey Noyes and Bible Communism (1845 and 1849)

Sojourner Truth, Address to the Woman's Rights Convention, Akron, Ohio (1851)

MANIFEST DESTINY

The Treaties of Velasco (May 14, 1836)

The Aroostook War (1839)

Across the Plains With Catherine Sager Pringle in 1844

John L. O'Sullivan, "The Great Nation of Futurity" (1845)

Thomas Corwin, Against the Mexican War (1847)

Chief Seattle, Oration (1854)

ANTEBELLUM SOUTH

State v. Boon (1801)

A Black Abolitionist Speaks Out (1829)

Nat Turner, Confession (1831)

An Abolitionist Defends the Amistad Mutineers (1839)

De Bow's Review, "The Stability of the Union," (1850)

Benjamin Drew, Narratives of Escaped Slaves (1855)

George Fitzhugh, "The Blessings of Slavery" (1857)

THE SECTIONAL CRISIS

William Lloyd Garrison, from The Liberator (1831)

Harriet Beecher Stowe, from Uncle Tom's Cabin

National Convention of Colored People, Report on Abolition (1847)

A Dying Statesman Speaks out Against the Compromise of 1850

Frederick Douglass, Independence Day Speech (1852)

Kansas Begins to Bleed (1856)

A White Southerner Speaks Out Against Slavery (1857)

Dred Scott v. Sanford (1857)

Abraham Lincoln, "A House Divided" (1858)

THE CIVIL WAR

Jefferson Davis, Address to the Provisional Congress of the Confederate States of America (1861)

The "Cornerstone Speech" (1861)

Mary Boykin Chesnut, A Confederate Lady's Diary (1861)

Why They Fought (1861)

A Confederate General Assesses First Bull Run (1861)

Charles Harvey Brewster, Three Letters from the Civil War Front (1862)

Clara Barton, Medical Life at the Battlefield (1862)

James Henry Gooding, Letter to President Lincoln (1863)

Abraham Lincoln, Gettysburg Address (1863)

John Dooley, Passages from a Journal (1863)

A Firsthand Account of the New York Draft Riots (1863)

Susie King Taylor, Reminiscences of an Army Laundress (1902)

General William Tecumseh Sherman on War (1864)

RECONSTRUCTION

"Address from the Colored Citizens of Norfolk, Virginia, to the People of the United States" (1865)

Carl Schurz, Report on the Condition of the South (1865)

Clinton B. Fisk, Plain Counsels for Freedmen (1865)

Mississippi Black Code (1865)

James C. Beecher, Report on Land Reform in the South Carolina Islands (1865, 1866)

The Memphis Riot (1866)

The Fourteenth Amendment (1868)

Albion W. Tourgee, Letter on Ku Klux Klan Activities (1870)

The Nation, "The State of the South" (1872)

Susan B. Anthony and the "New Departure" for Women (1873)

James T. Rapier, Testimony Before U.S. Senate Regarding the Agricultural Labor Force in the South (1880)

A Sharecrop Contract (1882)

NEW SOUTH, EXPANDING WEST

Edward Gould Buffum, Six Months in the Gold Mines (1850)

Lydia Allen Rudd, Diary of Westward Travel (1852)

Horace Greeley, An Overland Journey (1860)

Joseph G. McCoy, Historic Sketches of the Cattle Trade of the West and Southwest (1874)

Helen Hunt Jackson, from A Century of Dishonor (1881)

Congressional Report on Indian Affairs (1887)

Tragedy at Wounded Knee (1890)

Benjamin Harrison, Report on Wounded Knee Massacre and the Decrease in Indian Land Acreage (1891)

The Omaha Platform of the Populist Party (1892)

From Plessy v. Ferguson (1896)

W. E. B. Du Bois, from "Of Mr. Booker T. Washington and Others" (1903)

INDUSTRIALIZING AMERICA

Charles Loring Brace, "The Life of the Street Rats" (1872)

Progress and Poverty (1879)

The Gilded Age (1880)

Richard K. Fox, from Coney Island Frolics (1883)

Address by George Engel, Condemned Haymarket Anarchist (1886)

Edward Bellamy, from Looking Backward (1888)

The Assassination of President Garfield (1889)

Ida B. Wells-Barnett, from A Red Record (1895)

Booker T. Washington, Atlanta Exposition Address (1895)

United States Sanitary Commission, Sketch of Its Purposes (1864)

Lincoln Steffens, from The Shame of the Cities (1904)

Etiquette for the Upper Classes (1919)

Scientific Management (1919)

IMMIGRANT AND URBAN NATION

Memorial of the Chinese Six Companies to U. S. Grant, President of the United States (1876)

Plain Facts for Old and Young (1884)

Anglo-Saxon Culture Under Siege (1885)

How the Other Half Lives (1890)

The People's Party Platform (1892)

The Secret Oath of the American Protective Association (1893)

Adna Weber, The Growth of Cities in the Nineteenth Century (1899)

Lee Chew, Life of a Chinese Immigrant (1903)

Lincoln Steffens, from The Shame of the Cities (1904)

William T. Riordon, from Plunkitt of Tammany Hall (1905)

John Spargo, From The Bitter Cry of Children (1906)

Mary Antin, The Promised Land (1912)

AMERICA AROUND THE GLOBE

Josiah Strong, from Our Country (1885)

Henry Cabot Lodge, "The Business World vs. the Politicians" (1895)

Albert Beveridge, "The March of the Flag" (1898)

The Spanish-American War (1898)

William McKinley, "Decision on the Philippines" (1900)

The Boxer Rebellion (1900)

Theodore Roosevelt, Third Annual Message to Congress (1903)

Mark Twain, "Incident in the Philippines" (1924)

THE PROGRESSIVE ERA

Frederick Winslow Taylor, "A Piece-Rate System" (1896)

William Graham Sumner, What the Social Classes Owe to Each Other (1883)

Eugene V. Debs, "The Outlook for Socialism in the United States" (1900)

Platform Adopted by the National Negro Committee (1909)

James H. Patten, Chairman of the National Legislative Committee of the American Purity Federation, Testimony Before Congress (1910)

Jane Addams, Twenty Years at Hull House (1910)

Theodore Roosevelt, from The New Nationalism (1910)

Walker Percy, "Birmingham under the Commission Plan" (1911)

Helen M. Todd, "Getting Out the Vote" (1911)

Louis Brandeis, Other People's Money and How the Bankers Use It (1913)

Woodrow Wilson, from The New Freedom (1913)

Herbert Croly, Progressive Democracy (1914)

WORLD WAR ONE

The Great War
Boy Scouts of America from, "Boy Scouts Support the War
    Effort" (1917)
Letters from the Great Migration (1917)
American Troops in the Trenches (1918)
Eugene Kennedy, A "Doughboy" Describes the Fighting
    Front (1918)
Newton D. Baker, "The Treatment of German-Americans"
    (1918)
An Official Report
Woodrow Wilson, The Fourteen Points (1918)
Warren G. Harding, Campaign Speech at Boston (1920)
Edward Earle Purinton, "Big Ideas from Big Business" (1921)

THE 1920S AND MODERN AMERICA

J. Grimké, "Address of Welcome to the Men Who Have
    Returned from the Battlefront" (1919)
The Sahara of the Bozart (1920)
National Origins Quota Act, 1924
Advertisements (1925, 1927)
Family Planning 1926
Bartolomeo Vanzetti, Court Statement (1927)

DEPRESSION AND NEW DEAL

Herbert Hoover, Speech at New York City (1932)
FDR's First Inauguration Speech (1932)
Franklin Delano Roosevelt, Speech at San Francisco (1932)
Share the Wealth
The Victims of the Ku Klux Klan (1935)
Father Charles E. Coughlin, "A Third Party" (1936)
Mrs. Henry Weddington, Letter to President Roosevelt (1938)

WORLD WAR TWO

Albert Einstein, Letter to President Roosevelt (1939)
Charles Lindbergh, Radio Address (1941)
Franklin D. Roosevelt, The Four Freedoms (1941)
Franklin D. Roosevelt, Annual Message to Congress (1941)
A. Philip Randolph, "Why Should We March?" (1942)
Japanese Relocation Order, February 19, 1942
Sterling A. Brown, "Out of Their Mouths" (1942)

COLD WAR

George F. Kennan, "Long Telegram" (1946)
Kenneth MacFarland, "The Unfinished Work" (1946)
George Marshall, The Marshall Plan (1947)
Containment (1947)
Harry S Truman, The Truman Doctrine (1947)
Ronald Reagan, Testimony Before the House Un-American
    Activities Committee (1947)
Joseph R. McCarthy, from Speech Delivered to the
    Women's Club of Wheeling, West Virginia (1950)
National Security Council Memorandum Number 68 (1950)
Senator Joseph McCarthy's telegram to President Truman fol-
    lowing the 'Wheeling [W. Va.] Speech,' February 11, 1950

CONSENSUS AND CONFORMITY

The Kinsey Report (1948)
Brown v. *Board of Education* (1954)
Ladies Home Journal, "Young Mother" (1956)
Student Nonviolent Coordinating Committee, Statement of
    Purpose (1960)

THE CHANGING LIBERAL STATE

Dwight D. Eisenhower, Decision Not to Intervene at Dien
    Bien Phu (1954)
Charles Sherrod, Student Nonviolent Coordinating
    Committee Memorandum (1961)
John F. Kennedy, Cuban Missile Address (1962)
Students for a Democratic Society, The Port Huron
    Statement (1962)
John Lewis, Address at the March on Washington (1963)
The Civil Rights Act of 1964
The Tonkin Gulf Incident (1964)
Lyndon B. Johnson, Commencement Address at Howard
    University (1965)
Stokely Carmichael and Charles Hamilton, from *Black
    Power* (1967)
Donald Wheeldin, "The Situation in Watts Today" (1967)
Vietnamization (1969)

THE STRUGGLE FOR SOCIAL CHANGE

John F. Kennedy, Inaugural Address (1961)
The Feminist Mystique (1963)
Lyndon Johnson, The War on Poverty (1964)
National Organization for Women, Statement of Purpose
    (1966)
The Gay Liberation Front, Come Out (1970)
Swann v. *Charlotte-Mecklenburg Board of Education* (1971)
Roe v. *Wade* (1973)
Ione Malloy, Southie Won't Go (1975)
Jimmy Carter, The "Malaise" Speech (1979)

AMERICA AT THE MILLENNIUM

House Judiciary Committee, Conclusion on Impeachment
    Resolution (1974)
Ronald Reagan, First Inaugural Address (1981)
Ronald Reagan, Speech to the House of Commons (1982)
Ronald Reagan, Address to the National Association of
    Evangelicals (1983)
T. Boone Pickens, "My Case for Reagan" (1984)
Paul Craig Roberts, The Supply-Side Revolution (1984)
Bill Chappell, Speech to the American Security Council
    Foundation (1985)
Patricia Morrisroe, "The New Class" (1985)
George Bush, Address to the Nation Announcing Allied
    Military Action in the Persian Gulf (1991)

PREFACE

The path that led us to *The American Journey* began in the classroom with our students. Our goal is to make American history accessible to students. The key to that goal—the core of the book—is a strong clear narrative. American history is a compelling story and we seek to tell it in an engaging, forthright way. But we also provide students with an abundance of tools to help them absorb that story and put it in context. We introduce them to the concerns of the participants in America's history with primary source documents. The voices of contemporaries open each chapter, describing their own personal journeys toward fulfilling their dreams, hopes, and ambitions as part of the broader American journey. These voices provide a personal window on our nation's history, and the themes they express resonate throughout the narrative.

But if we wrote this book to appeal to our students, we also wrote it to engage their minds. We wanted to avoid academic trendiness, particularly the restricting categories that have divided the discipline of history over the last twenty years or so. We believe that the distinctions involved in the debates about multiculturalism and identity, between social and political history, between the history of the common people and the history of the elite, are unnecessarily confusing.

What we seek is integration—to combine political and social history, to fit the experience of particular groups into the broader perspective of the American past, to give voice to minor and major players alike because of their role in the story we have to tell.

APPROACH

In telling our story, we had some definite ideas about what we might include and emphasize that other texts do not—information we felt that the current and next generations of students will need to know about our past to function best in a new society.

CHRONOLOGICAL ORGANIZATION A strong chronological backbone supports the book. We have found that the jumping back and forth in time characteristic of some American history textbooks confuses students. They abhor dates but need to know the sequence of events in history. A chronological presentation is the best way to be sure they do.

GEOGRAPHICAL LITERACY We also want students to be geographically literate. We expect them not only to know what happened in American history, but where it happened as well. Physical locations and spatial relationships were often important in shaping historical events. The abundant maps in The American Journey—all numbered and called out in the text—are an integral part of our story.

REGIONAL BALANCE. *The American Journey* presents balanced coverage of all regions of the country. In keeping with this balance, the South and the West receive more coverage in this text than in comparable books.

POINT OF VIEW *The American Journey* presents a balanced overview of the American past. But "balanced" does not mean bland. We do not shy away from definite positions on controversial issues, such as the nature of early contacts between Native Americans and Europeans, why the political crisis of the 1850s ended in a bloody Civil War, and how Populism and its followers fit into the American political spectrum. If students and instructors disagree, that's great; discussion and dissent are important catalysts for understanding and learning.

RELIGION Nor do we shy away from some topics that play relatively minor roles in other texts, like religion. Historians are often uncomfortable writing about religion and tend to slight its influence. This text stresses the importance of religion in American society both as a source of strength and a reflection of some its more troubling aspects.

Historians mostly write for each other. That's too bad. We need to reach out and expand our audience. An American history text is a good place to start. Our students are not only our future historians, but more important, our future. Let their American journey begin.

FEATURES OF THE TEXT

The American Journey includes an array of features designed to make American history accessible to students. It provides more learning tools than any other U.S. history text.

- The **Student Tool Kit** that follows this preface helps students get the most out of the text and its features. It introduces students to key conventions of historical writing and it explains how to work with maps, graphs, tables, and other visuals.

- A new feature, **Voices from the American Journey**, opens each chapter. Consisting of letters, diary entries, and other first-hand accounts, these voices highlight the personal dimension of the American journey and show students the wealth and variety of experiences that make up this country's history. From Olaudah Equiano's narrative of his forced journey to Virginia as a slave, to the ultimate journey Sullivan Ballou made during the Civil War defending the Union, to Cambodian refugee Celia Noup's harrowing journey to California where she took her place as one of the thousands of new immigrants who are reshaping the face of our nation, "Voices from the American Journey" set the stage for the key themes that are explored in each chapter.

- The **American Views** box in each chapter contains a relevant primary source document. Taken from letters, diaries, newspapers, government papers, and other sources, these bring the people of the past and their concerns vividly alive. An introduction and prereading questions relate the documents to the text and direct students' attention to important issues. New "American Views" include the internment of Japanese Americans in Chapter 26 and working in the New Economy in Chapter 31.

- **America's Journey: From Then to Now**, found in more than half the chapters, relates important issues and events in each chapter to the issues and events of today, letting students see the relevance of history to their lives. Several are new to this edition. Examples include, "The Disappearance of Cod on the Grand Banks" (Chapter 1); "Medical Research on Polio and AIDS" (Chapter 28) and "Loyalty in 2001 and 1917" (Chapter 31).

- An **Outline** and **Key Topics** list give students a succinct overview of each chapter.

- **Overview Tables** in each chapter summarize complex issues.

- Chapter **Chronologies** help students build a framework of key events.

- **Third-level subheads**, new to the Third Edition, highlight key topics in the narrative and make them more accessible for study and review. In the sections on social history, for exam-

ple, these headings help highlight the roles of women and minorities in the American journey.

- **Key Terms** are highlighted within each chapter and defined in an end-of-book **Glossary**. The end of each chapter now includes a list of key terms and relevant page numbers.

- Chapter **Review Questions** help students review the material in each chapter and relate it to broader themes.

- A list of **Key Readings** and **Additional Sources** at the end of each chapter directs interested students to further information about the subject of the chapter.

- **Where To Learn More** sections describe important historical sites students can visit to gain a deeper understanding of the events discussed in the chapter. Websites for the historical sites as well as other websites relevant to the chapter topics are now included.

- Abundant maps, charts, and graphs help students understand important events and trends. The topographical detail in many of the maps helps students understand the influence of geography on history.

- Illustrations and photographs—tied to the text with detailed captions—provide a visual dimension to history. Approximately ninety new photos have been added to the Third Edition.

CHANGES TO THE THIRD EDITION

ORGANIZATION

- To make the text even more accessible to students—and to better match the teaching calendars of many institutions—the number of chapters in the Third Edition has been reduced from thirty-three to thirty-one.

- The chapters on urbanization and social change and reform movements in the antebellum period have been combined into a new chapter, "The Market Revolution and Social Reform" (Chapter 12). The chapter focuses on economic changes and industrialization as well as the connections between these forces and reform movements. Chapter 11, "Slavery and the Old South," now precedes this chapter.

- The Civil War is now treated in a single chapter (Chapter 15).
- The Eighties is now examined in an entirely re-vamped Chapter 30, "The Reagan Revolution and a Changing World."
- An all-new final chapter "Complacency and Crisis," examines America at the millennium and after September 11, 2001.

Taken together, these organizational changes make *The American Journey* an even more effective textbook for both students and instructors.

OTHER CHANGES

In the Third Edition of *The American Journey*, coverage of women, minorities, and Native Americans has been expanded. The active role of Native Americans in shaping the encounters with European settlers has been emphasized. Coverage of the institution of slavery and the Holocaust has also been expanded. Additional coverage of foreign policy during the 1980s and 1990s will help students understand the dilemmas our nation faces in the post-September 11th world. The following list highlights some of these additions:

- Chapter 1. Coverage of Native American and West African societies has been expanded significantly.
- Chapter 2. The Dutch mercantile empire, trade with West Africa, and the beginnings of the slave trade with the Portuguese and Dutch receive more discussion.
- Chapter 3. Coverage of Native Americans has been consolidated and expanded; their role as actors in the encounter with Europeans is emphasized. Increased coverage of the origins of slavery and its social and economic aspects.
- Chapter 6: Expanded coverage of Native Americans' role during the War for Independence.
- Chapter 20: Expanded coverage of women in politics, especially their partisan role and involvement in the temperance movement.
- Chapter 21. A section on trans-Atlantic influences during the Progressive era has been included. Coverage of the education of Native Americans, women in the election of 1912, and the antiprostitution campaign has been expanded.
- Chapter 25. A new section on foreign policy during the New Deal, which provides a background for understanding the U.S. role in World War II, has been added.

- Chapter 26. Discussion of the rise of anti-Semitism in Nazi Germany has been added and coverage of the Holocaust has been expanded. Coverage of the economic and social history of the war effort has been reorganized, and coverage of women and minorities in the war effort has been increased.
- Chapter 27. Includes fuller discussion of the Civil Rights movement.
- Chapter 28. Coverage of cultural history has been increased, a section on "Science and Foreign Affairs" has been added, and there is expanded discussion of Vietnam and LBJ.
- Chapter 29. Now examines the period from 1965—1980 in a single unit, examining feminism, suburban life, Vietnam, and de-industrialization.
- Chapter 30. Includes detailed discussion of the new conservatism and Reaganomics, in-depth treatment of social and cultural history of the period, coverage of women and poverty, and enhanced discussion of foreign policy.
- Chapter 31. Provides in-depth treatment of the New Economy, the Clinton presidency, the attacks of September 11, 2001, and America's role as the remaining superpower in a post-September 11th world.

SUPPLEMENTARY INSTRUCTIONAL MATERIALS

The American Journey comes with an extensive package of supplementary print and multimedia materials for both instructors and students.

PRINT SUPPLEMENTS

Instructor's Resource Manual

The *Instructor's Resource Manual* contains chapter outlines, chapter overviews, activities, discussion questions, readings, and information on audio-visual resources that are useful for lectures and assignments.

Test Item File

The *Test Item File* includes over 200 multiple-choice, true-false, essay, and map questions organized by chapter.

Prentice Hall Custom Test

This commercial-quality computerized test management program, available for Windows and Macintosh environments, allows instructors to select items from the Test Item File and design their own exams.

Transparency Pack

This set of transparencies provides instructors with full-color acetates of all the maps, charts, and graphs in the text for use in the classroom.

Practice Tests (Volumes I and II)

The two-volume *Practice Tests* provides students with a brief overview of each chapter; a list of chapter objectives; study exercises; and multiple-choice, short answer, and essay questions.

Retrieving the American Past: A Customized U.S. History Reader, 2003 Edition

This collection of documents is an on-demand history database written and developed by leading historians and educators. It offers eighty compelling modules on topics in American history, such as "Women on the Frontier," "The Salem Witchcraft Scare," "The Age of Industrial Violence," and "Native American Societies, 1870–1995." Approximately thirty-five pages in length, each module includes an introduction, several primary documents and secondary sources, follow-up questions, and recommendations for further reading. Instructor-originated material, including other readings and exercises, can be incorporated. Contact your local Prentice Hall representative for more information about this exciting custom-publishing option.

American Stories: Biographies in United States History

This two-volume collection of sixty-two biographies in United States history is free when packaged with *The American Journey*. Introductions, pre-reading questions, and suggested resources enrich this new supplement.

Prentice Hall and Penguin Bundle Program

Prentice Hall is pleased to provide adopters of *The American Journey* with an opportunity to receive significant discounts when copies of the text are bundled with Penguin titles in American history. Contact your local Prentice Hall representative for details.

Reading Critically about History

This brief guide provides students with helpful strategies for reading a history textbook. It is available free to students when packaged with *The American Journey*.

Understanding and Answering Essay Questions

This helpful guide provides analytical tools for understanding different types of essay questions and for preparing well-crafted essay answers. It is available free to students when packaged with *The American Journey*.

MULTIMEDIA SUPPLEMENTS

Companion Website

Available at http://www.prenhall.com/goldfield
The American Journey Companion Website™ offers students multiple choice, true-false, essay, identification, map labeling, and document questions based on material from the text, organized by the primary subtopics in each chapter. Additionally, the *Companion Website* provides numerous interactive maps tied to the text, source documents, and other interactive modules related to the content in each chapter. The Faculty Module contains materials for instructors, including the entire instructor's manual in PDF file, and downloadable presentations with maps, charts, graphs, summary tables, and illustrations.

U.S. History Documents CD-ROM

Bound in every new copy of *The American Journey*, and organized according to the main periods in American history, the U.S. History Documents CD-ROM contains over 300 primary sources in an easily-navigable PDF file. Each document is accompanied by essay questions that allow students to read important sources in U.S. history via the CD-ROM and respond online via a dedicated website.

Exploring America CD-ROM

The new *Exloring America CD-ROM* features thirty-one interactive learning activities that drill down to explore the impact of key episodes and developments in United States history, including such topics as industrialization, immigration, the women's suffrage movement, the Harlem Renaissance, the American Indian Movement, and globalization.

Evaluating Online Sources with Research Navigator, 2003 Edition

This brief guide focuses on developing critical thinking skills necessary to evaluate and use online sources. It provides a brief introduction to navigating the Internet with comprehensive references to History web sites. It also provides an access code and instruction on using Research Navigator, a powerful research tool that provides access to three exclusive databases of reliable source material: ContentSelect Academic Journal Database, *The New York Times* Search by Subject Archive, and Link Library.

Course Management Systems

For instructors interested in distance learning, Prentice Hall offers fully customizable, online courses with enhanced content, web links, online testing, and many other course-management features using the best available course management systems available, including WebCT, Blackboard, and CourseCompass. Contact your local Prentice Hall representative or visit our special Demonstration Central Website at http://www.prenhall.com/demo for more information.

ACKNOWLEDGMENTS

We would like to thank the reviewers whose thoughtful and often detailed comments helped shape this and the previous editions of *The American Journey*:

Joseph Adams, Saint Louis Community College
David Aldstadt, Houston Community College
William Allison, Weber State University
Janet Allured, McNeese State University
Tyler Anbinder, George Washington University
Michael Batinski, Southern Illinois University
Michael Bellesiles, Emory University
Eugene Berwanger, Colorado State University
Terry Bilhartz, Sam Houston State University
Fred Blue, Youngstown State University
Eric J. Bolsteri, University of Texas at Arlington
Charles Bolton, University of Arkansas at Little Rock
James Bradford, Texas A&M University
Michael Bradley, Motlow State Community College
Henry William Brands, Texas A&M University
Neal Brooks, Essex Community College
Richard Brown, University of Connecticut
Tom Bryan, Alvin Community College
Randolph Campbell, University of North Texas
Dale Carnagey, Blinn College
E. Wayne Carp, Pacific Lutheran University
JoAnn Carpenter, Florida Community College
David Castle, Ohio University, Eastern Campus
Andrew Cayton, Miami University
Bill Cecil-Fronsman, Washburn University
John Chalberg, Normandale Community College
Myles Clowers, San Diego City College
David Conrad, Southern Illinois University
William Corbett, Northeastern State University
Robert Cray, Montclair State College
Richard Crepeau, University of Central Florida
Samuel Crompton, Holyoke Community College
Gilbert Cruz, Glendale Community College
Light T. Cummins, Austin College
Paul K. Davis, University of Texas at San Antonio
Eugene Demody, Cerritos College
Joseph Devine, Stephen F. Austin State University
Donald Dewey, California State University
Leonard Dinnerstein, University of Arizona
Dean Dunlap, Rose State College
Marvin Dulaney, University of Texas at Arlington
Jonathan Earle, University of Kansas
Leflett Easley, Campbell University
Iris Engstrand, University of San Diego

Robin Fabel, Auburn University
Jay Fell, University of Colorado
Nancy Gabin, Purdue University
Scott Garrett, Paducah Community College
Marilyn Geiger, Washburn University
George Gerdow, Northeastern Illinois University
Gerald Ghelfi, Rancho Santiago College
Louis Gimelli, Eastern Michigan University
James Goode, Grand Valley State University
Gregory Goodwin, Bakersfield College
Ralph Goodwin, East Texas State University
Robert Greene, Morgan State University
Mark Grimsley, Ohio State University
Ira Gruber, U.S. Military Academy
Harland Hagler, University of North Texas
Steve Haley, Shelby State Community College
Gwendolyn Hall, Rutgers University
Timothy D. Hall, Central Michigan University
David Hamilton, University of Kentucky
Joe Hapak, Moraine Valley Community College
Ronald Hatzenbuchler, Idaho State University
David G. Hogan, Heidelberg College
Alfred Hunt, SUNY Purchase
John Ingham, University of Toronto
Priscilla Jackson-Evans, Longview Community College
Donald Jacobs, Northeastern University
Frederick Jaher, University of Illinois
John Johnson, University of Northern Iowa
Wilbur Johnson, Rock Valley College
Yvonne Johnson, Central Missouri State University
Yasuhide Kawashima, University of Texas at El Paso
Joseph E. King, Texas Tech University
Gene Kirkpatrick, Tyler Junior College
Lawrence Kohl, University of Alabama at Tuscaloosa
Michael Krenn, University of Miami
Michael Krutz, Southeastern Louisiana University
Robert LaPorte, North Texas University
Armand LaPotin, SUNY Oneonta
John LaSaine, University of Georgia
Bryan LeBeau, Creighton University
J. Edward Lee, Winthrop University
Mark Leff, University of Illinois, Urbana-Champaign
Richard Lowe, University of North Texas
Ed Lukes, Hillsborough Community College
Leo Lyman, Victor Valley College
Scott Martin, Bowling Green State University
Ronald McArthur, Atlantic Community College
Donald McCoy, University of Kansas
David McFadden, Fairfield University
Gerald MacFarland, University of Massachusetts
Thomas McLuen, Spokane Falls Community College
Peter C. Mancell, University of Kansas
Norman Markowitz, Rutgers University
Frank Marmolejo, Irvine Valley College
James Matray, New Mexico State University
Karen Miller, Oakland University
Otis Miller, Belleville Area College
Nancy Smith Midgette, Elon College

Worth Robert Miller, Southwest Missouri State University
Timothy Morgan, Christopher Newport University
Christopher Moss, University of Texas at Arlington
Harmon Mothershead, Northwest Missouri State University
Benjamin Newcomb, Texas Technological University
Elizabeth Nybakken, Mississippi State University
Colleen O'Connor, San Diego Mesa College
Chris Padgett, Weber State University
David Parker, Kennesaw State College
Peggy Pascoe, University of Utah
Christopher Phillips, Emporia State University
Thomas L. Powers, University of South Carolina, Sumter
Kay Pulley, Trinity Valley Community College
Norman Raiford, Greenville Technical College
John Rector, Western Oregon State University
Thomas C. Reeves, University of Wisconsin, Parkside
Gary Reichard, Florida Atlantic University
Joseph Reidy, Howard University
Ronald Reitvald, California State University, Fullerton
Howard Rock, Florida International University
Hal Rothman, University of Nevada, Las Vegas
Richard Sadler, Weber State University
Henry Sage, Northern Virginia Community College,
    Alexandria
Bufford Satcher, University of Arkansas at Pine Bluff
Sandra Schackel, Boise State University
Michael Schaller, University of Arizona
Dale Schmitt, East Tennessee State University
Ronald Schultz, University of Wyoming
Nancy Shoemaker, University of Connecticut
Rebecca Shoemaker, Indiana State University
Frank Siltman, U.S. Military Academy
David Sloan, University of Arkansas
J.B. Smallwood, University of North Texas
Sherry Smith, University of Texas at El Paso
Kenneth Stevens, Texas Christian University
William Stockton, Johnson County Community College
Mark Summers, University of Kentucky
William Tanner, Humbolt State University
Quintard Taylor, University of Oregon
Emily Teipe, Fullerton College
Frank Towers, Clarion University
Paula Trekel, Allegheny College
Stanley Underal, San Jose University
Andrew Wallace, Northern Arizona University
Harry Ward, University of Richmond
Ken Weatherbie, Del Mar College
Stephen Webre, Louisiana Tech University
Edward Weller, San Jacinto College, South
Michael Welsh, University of Northern Colorado
James Whittenberg, College of William and Mary
Brian Wills, Clinch Valley Community College
John Wiseman, Frostburg State University
James Woods, Georgia Southern University
Mark Wyman, Illinois State University
Neil York, Brigham Young University
William Young, Johnson County Community College
Nancy Zen, Central Oregon Community College

All of us are grateful to our families, friends, and colleagues for their support and encouragement. Jo Ann and Peter Argersinger would like in particular to thank Anna Champe, Linda Hatmaker, and John Willits; William Barney thanks Pamela Fesmire and Rosalie Radcliffe; Virginia Anderson thanks Fred Anderson, Kim Gruenwald, Ruth Helm, Eric Hinderaker, and Chidiebere Nwaubani; and David Goldfield thanks Frances Glenn and Jason Moscato. Jim Miller, Sylvia Mallory, and Sally Constable played key roles in the book's inception and initial development.

Finally, we would like to acknowledge the members of our Prentice Hall family. They are not only highly competent professionals but also pleasant people. We regard them with affection and appreciation. None of us would hesitate to work with this fine group again. We would especially like to thank our editorial team: Charles Cavaliere, senior acquisitions editor, Roberta Meyer, senior development editor, and Carolyn Viola-John for their creativity and skill in crafting the plan for the third edition, and for helping us to execute it. Charlyce Jones Owen, vice president and editorial director for the Humanities, who organized her team flawlessly; Heather Shelstad, executive marketing manager, and Beth Meija, marketing director, whose creative and informed marketing strategies demonstrated a unique insight into the textbook market; Kenny Beck and Nancy Wells, art directors, and Leslie Osher, creative design director; Jan Stephan and Jean Lapidus for keeping the production on schedule; Maria Piper, line art formatter; Barbara Salz and Linda Sykes for their photo research; Rochelle Diogenes, editor in chief for development, for ensuring that the book had the developmental resources it needed; Nick Sklitsis, manufacturing manager, Sherry Lewis, manufacturing buyer, and Yolanda deRooy, president of Prentice Hall's Humanities and Social Sciences division, who had the good sense to let her staff run with this book.

DG
CA
VDJA
JEA
PHA
WLB
RMW

ABOUT THE AUTHORS

David Goldfield received his Ph.D. in history from the University of Maryland. Since 1982 he has been Robert Lee Bailey Professor of History at the University of North Carolina in Charlotte. He is the author or editor of thirteen books on various aspects of southern and urban history. Two of his works—*Cotton Fields and Skyscrapers: Southern City and Region, 1607-1980* (1982) and *Black, White, and Southern: Race Relations and Southern Culture, 1940 to the Present* (1990)—received the Mayflower Award for non-fiction and were nominated for the Pulitzer Prize in history. His most recent book is *Still Fighting the Civil War: The American South and Southern History* (2002). When he is not writing history, Goldfield applies his historical craft to history museum exhibits, voting rights cases, and local planning and policy issues.

Carl Abbott is a professor of Urban Studies and planning at Portland State University. He taught previously in the history departments at the University of Denver and Old Dominion University, and held visiting appointments at Mesa College in Colorado and George Washington University. He holds degrees in history from Swarthmore College and the University of Chicago. He specializes in the history of cities and the American West and serves as co-editor of the *Pacific Historical Review.* His books include *The New Urban America: Growth and Politics in Sunbelt Cities* (1981, 1987), *The Metropolitan Frontier: Cities in the Modern American West* (1993), *Planning a New West: The Columbia River Gorge National Scenic Area* (1997), and *Political Terrain: Washington, D.C. from Tidewater Town to Global Metropolis* (1999). He is currently working on a comprehensive history of the role of urbanization and urban culture in the history of western North America.

Virginia DeJohn Anderson is Associate Professor of History at the University of Colorado at Boulder. She received her B.A. from the University of Connecticut. As the recipient of a Marshall Scholarship, she earned an M.A. degree at the University of East Anglia in Norwich, England. Returning to the United States, she received her A.M. and Ph.D. degrees from Harvard University. She is the author of *New England's Generation: The Great Migration and the Formation of Society and Culture in the Seventeenth Century* (1991) and several articles on colonial history, which have appeared in such journals as the *William and Mary Quarterly* and the *New England Quarterly.* She is currently finishing a book entitled *Creatures of Empire: People and Animals in Early America.*

Jo Ann E. Argersinger received her Ph.D. from George Washington University and is Professor of History at Southern Illinois University. A recipient of fellowships from the Rockefeller Foundation and the National Endowment for the Humanities, she is a historian of social, labor, and business policy. Her publications include *Toward a New Deal in Baltimore: People and Government in the Great Depression* (1988) and *Making the Amalgamated: Gender, Ethnicity, and Class in the Baltimore Clothing Industry* (1999).

Peter H. Argersinger received his Ph.D. from the University of Wisconsin and is Professor of History at Southern Illinois University. He has won several fellowships as well as the Binkley-Stephenson Award from the Organization of American Historians. Among his books on American political and rural history are *Populism and Politics* (1974), *Structure, Process, and Party* (1992), and *The Limits of Agrarian Radicalism* (1995). His current research focuses on the political crisis of the 1890s.

William L. Barney is Professor of History at the University of North Carolina at Chapel Hill. A native of Pennsylvania, he received his B.A. from Cornell University and his M.A. and Ph.D. from Columbia University. He has published extensively on nineteenth century U.S. history and has a particular interest in the Old South and the coming of the Civil War. Among his publications are *The Road to Secession* (1972), *The Secessionist Impulse* (1974), *Flawed Victory* (1975), *The Passage of the Republic* (1987), and *Battleground for the Union* (1989). He is currently finishing an edited collection of essays on nineteenth-century America and a book on the Civil War. Most recently, he has edited *A Companion to 19ᵗʰ-Century America* (2001) and finished *The Civil War and Reconstruction: A Student Companion* (2001).

Robert M. Weir is Distinguished Professor of History Emeritus at the University of South Carolina. He received his B.A. from Pennsylvania State University and his Ph.D. from Case Western Reserve University. He has taught at the University of Houston and, as a visiting professor, at the University of Southampton in the United Kingdom. His articles have won prizes from the Southeastern Society for the Study of the Eighteenth Century and the *William and Mary Quarterly.* Among his publications are *Colonial South Carolina: A History,* "The Last of American Freemen": Studies in the Political Culture of the Colonial and Revolutionary South, and, most recently, a chapter on the Carolinas in the new *Oxford History of the British Empire* (1998).

THE AMERICAN JOURNEY
THIRD EDITION

GET THE BOOK THAT **GETS YOUR STUDENTS.**

STUDENT TOOL KIT

When writing history, historians use maps, tables, graphs, and visuals to help their readers understand the past. What follows is an explanation of how to use the historian's tools that are contained in this book.

TEXT

Whether it is a biography of George Washington, an article on the Civil War, or a survey of American history such as this one, the text is the historian's basic tool for discussing the past. Historians write about the past using narration and analysis. Narration is the story line of history. It describes what happened in the past, who did it, and where and when it occurred. Narration is also used to describe how people in the past lived, how they passed their daily lives and even, when the historical evidence makes it possible for us to know, what they thought, felt, feared, or desired. Using analysis, historians explain why they think events in the past happened the way they did and offer an explanation for the story of history. In this book, narration and analysis are interwoven in each chapter.

STUDY AIDS

A number of features in this book are designed to aid in the study of history. Each chapter begins with Key Topics, a short list of the most important issues that will be covered in the chapter. The narrative is organized into three levels of subtopics, that carefully structure information (see example below). A Conclusion at the end of each chapter puts the subject of the chapter in the broader perspective of U.S. history. All of these study aids can be used to review important concepts.

HOLDING THE LINE

When Japan was considering war with the United States and Great Britain in 1940, Admiral Isoroku Yamamoto, the chief of Japan's Combined Fleet, weighed the chances for victory: "If I am told to fight

The Eastern Front and the Battle of Stalingrad.

The strategy recognized that the Eastern Front held the key to Allied hopes. In 1941, Germany had seized control of 45 percent of the Soviet population, 47 percent of its grain production, and more than 60

GET THE BEST PEDAGOGY:
Student Tool Kit

Wondering why your students need a Tool Kit to read and use this book? Because this Student Tool Kit allows you to rest assured that the book not only provides students with the best possible pedagogical features to enhance their learning, but that it also provides them with the insight they need to get the most out of them.

Immediately following the Preface, the Student Tool Kit offers students insight about how to use and follow the text so that they will get the most out of it. Indicative of the book's strong commitment to offering students the best pedagogy, the Tool Kit introduces them to the key conventions of historical writing, and offers clear explanations about how to read maps, graphs, primary source documents, photographs and tables, and much more. In this example, notice that the authors are explaining to students how to read maps, including visual annotations that draw their attention to the scale, the legend, and the caption. The authors also note the importance of paying attention to the topographical detail provided in the map, and provide instructions for how to access the interactive version of the map, *Map Exploration.*

Take a moment to look through the **Student Tool Kit,** and notice how it will help students use this text most effectively. Get Goldfield—and get your students the best pedagogy.

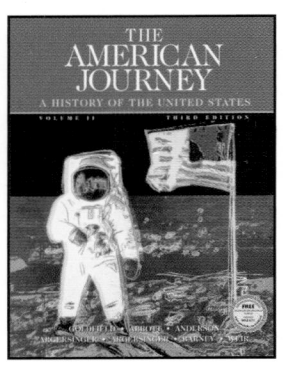

STUDENT TOOL KIT

When writing history, historians use maps, tables, graphs, and visuals to help their readers understand the past. What follows is an explanation of how to use the historian's tools that are contained in this book.

TEXT

Whether it is a biography of George Washington, an article on the Civil War, or a survey of American history such as this one, the text is the historian's basic tool for discussing the past. Historians write about the past using narration and analysis. Narration is the story line of history. It describes what happened in the past, who did it, and where and when it occurred. Narration is also used to describe how people in the past lived, how they passed their daily lives and even, when the historical evidence makes it possible for us to know, what they thought, felt, feared, or desired. Using analysis, historians explain why they think events in the past happened the way they did and offer an explanation for the story of history. In this book, narration and analysis are interwoven in each chapter.

STUDY AIDS

A number of features in this book are designed to aid in the study of history. Each chapter begins with Key Topics, a short list of the most important issues that will be covered in the chapter. The narrative is organized into three levels of subtopics, that carefully structure information (see example below). A Conclusion at the end of each chapter puts the subject of the chapter in the broader perspective of U.S. history. All of these study aids can be used to review important concepts.

HOLDING THE LINE

When Japan was considering war with the United States and Great Britain in 1940, Admiral Isoroku Yamamoto, the chief of Japan's Combined Fleet, weighed the chances of victory: "If I am told to fight regardless of the consequences, I shall run wild for the first six months or a year, but I have utterly no confidence for the second or third year." The admiral was right. Japan's armies quickly conquered most of Southeast Asia; its navy forced the United States on the defensive in the central Pacific. As it turned out, Japan's conquests reached their limit after six months, but, in early 1942, it was far from clear that such would be the case. At the same time, in Europe, Allied fortunes went from bad to worse. Again, no one knew that German and Italian gains would peak at midyear. Decisive turning points did not come until November 1942, a year after the United States had entered the war, and not until the middle of 1943 could the **Allies**–the United States, Britain, the Soviet Union, China, and other nations at war with Germany, Japan and Italy–begin with confidence to plan for victory.

STOPPING GERMANY

In December 1941, the United States plunged into a truly global war that was being fought on six distinct fronts (see Map 26–2). In North Africa, the British battled Italian and German armies that were trying to seize the Suez Canal, a critical transportation link to Asia. Along the 1,000 miles of the vast **Eastern Front**, Soviet armies held defensive positions against German

The Eastern Front and the Battle of Stalingrad.
The strategy recognized that the Eastern Front held the key to Allied hopes. In 1941, Germany had seized control of 45 percent of the Soviet population, 47 percent of its grain production, and more than 60 percent of its coal, steel, and aluminum industries. Hitler next sought to destroy the Soviet capacity to wage war. "Our aim," said the Führer Directive No. 41, "is to wipe out the entire defense potential remaining to the Soviets, and to cut them off. . . . from their most important centers of war industry." Hitler targeted southern Russia, an area rich in grain and oil. The thrust in 1942 was also designed to eliminate from the Middle East.

The scheme was easier to plan than to carry out in the fields of Russia. The offensive opened with stunning success. May's advance, however, stretched supply lines. Tanks ran out of fuel and spare parts. The horses that pulled German supply wagons died for lack of food.

The turning point of the war in Europe came at Stalingrad (present-day Volgograd), an industrial center on the western bank of the Volga River. After initially aiming at the city, German armies had turned south toward Russian oil fields, leaving a dangerous strongpoint on their flank that the German command decided to capture. In September and October, 1942, German, Italian, and Romanian soldiers fought their way house by house into the city. At night, the Soviets ferried their wounded across the Volga and brought in more ammunition. For both Hitler and Stalin, the

> Three levels of subtopics

MAPS

Maps are important historical tools. They show how geography has affected history and concisely summarize complex relationships and events. Knowing how to read and interpret a map is important to understanding history. Map 5-1 from Chapter 5 shows the British colonies on the eastern seaboard of North America in 1763, about twelve years before the American Revolution. It has three features to help you read it: a caption, a legend, and a scale. The caption explains the historical significance of the map. Here the caption tells us that in 1763 the British government sought to restrict colonial settlement west of the Appalachian Mountains to prevent conflict between colonists and Indians. Colonial frustration with this policy contributed to the outbreak of the American Revolution.

The legend and the scale appear in the lower right corner of the map. The legend provides a key to what the symbols on the map mean. The solid line stretching along the Appalachian Mountains from Maine to Georgia represents the Proclamation Line of 1763—the line meant to restrict colonial settlement. Cities are marked with a dot, capitals with a star, and forts by a black square. Spanish territory west of the Mississippi River is represented in yellow-brown; territory settled by Europeans is represented in green. The scale tells us that 7/8ths of an inch on the map represents 300 miles (about 480 kilometers) on the ground. With this information, estimates of the distance between points on the map are easily made.

The map also shows the topography of the region—its mountains, rivers, and lakes. This helps us understand how geography influenced history in this case. For example, the Appalachian Mountains divide the eastern seaboard from the rest of the continent. The mountains obstructed colonial migration to the west for a long time. By running the Proclamation Line along the Appalachians, the British hoped to use this natural barrier to separate Indians and colonists. Note how small the green areas are, that is, the areas of European settlement, relative to the immense size of North America. Note also how the map shows that the Europeans tended to settle near the coasts and along rivers and across plains.

MAP EXPLORATIONS

Many of the maps in each chapter are provided in a useful interactive version on the text's Companion Website. These maps are easily identified by a bar along the top that reads "Map Explorations." An interactive version of Colonial Settlements and the Proclamation Line of 1763 can be found at www.prenhall.com/goldfield/map5.1. The interactive version of this particular map provides an opportunity to pan over an enlarged version of the territory in question. Cities, forts, settlements, and terrain are shown in detail. By moving the cursor north, south, east, or west one can gain a bird's-eye view of the entire region.

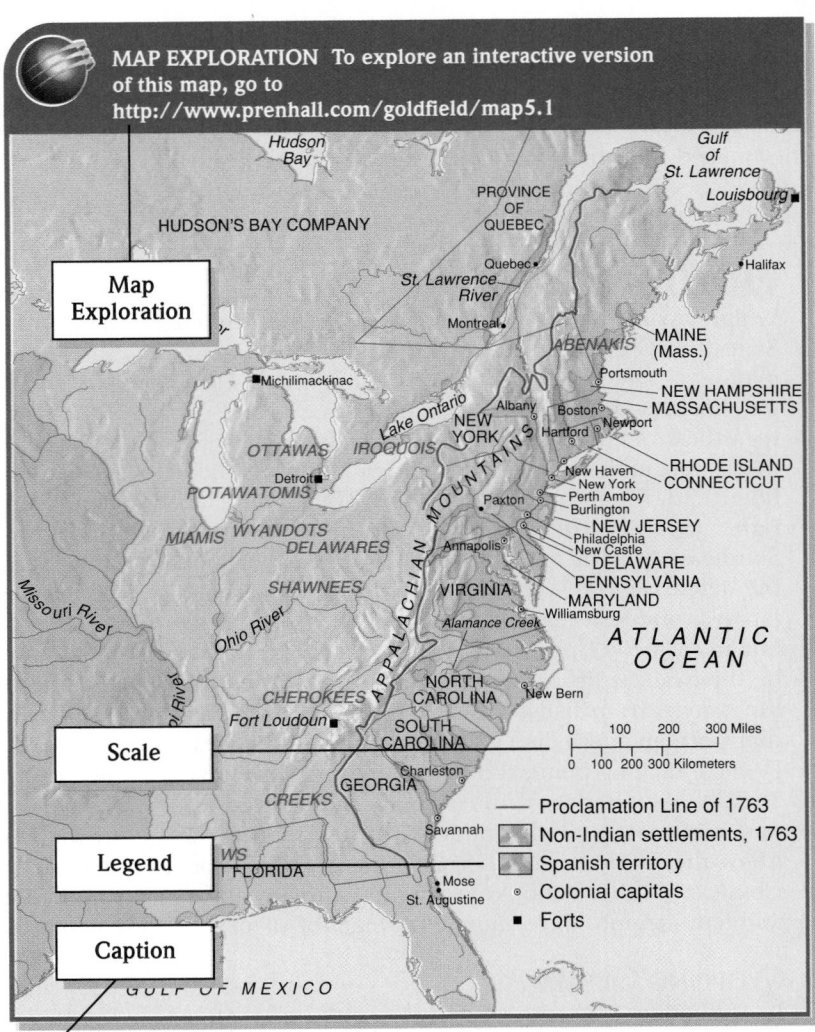

MAP EXPLORATION To explore an interactive version of this map, go to http://www.prenhall.com/goldfield/map5.1

MAP 5-1 Colonial Settlement and the Proclamation Line of 1763
This map depicts the regions claimed and settled by the major groups competing for territory in eastern North America. With the Proclamation Line of 1763, positioned along the crest of the Appalachian Mountains, the British government tried to stop the westward migration of settlers under its jurisdiction and thereby limit conflict with the Indians. The result, however, was frustration and anger on the part of land-hungry settlers.

GRAPHS

Historians use graphs to make comparisons and summarize trends. Comparisons can be between groups of people, regions of the country, products, time periods—whatever focuses the reader's attention on an important historical development. Various types of graphs are used in this book, including line graphs, pie charts, and bar graphs. The names denote the way the graphs are drawn to make comparisons. All graphs show the numbers of some significant factor—like people, goods, or prices—at a given time or how they fluctuated over a given period. Figure 18-2 is a line graph that shows the dramatic rise in immigration to the United States from eastern and southern Europe in the late nineteenth and early twentieth centuries. Figure 3-4, for example, is a pie chart—so called because it looks like a pie cut into slices. It shows the ethnic origins of the non-Indian population of the thirteen colonies at the start of the American Revolution. Figure 4-2 is a bar graph that compares the growth in population of the four major colonial regions.

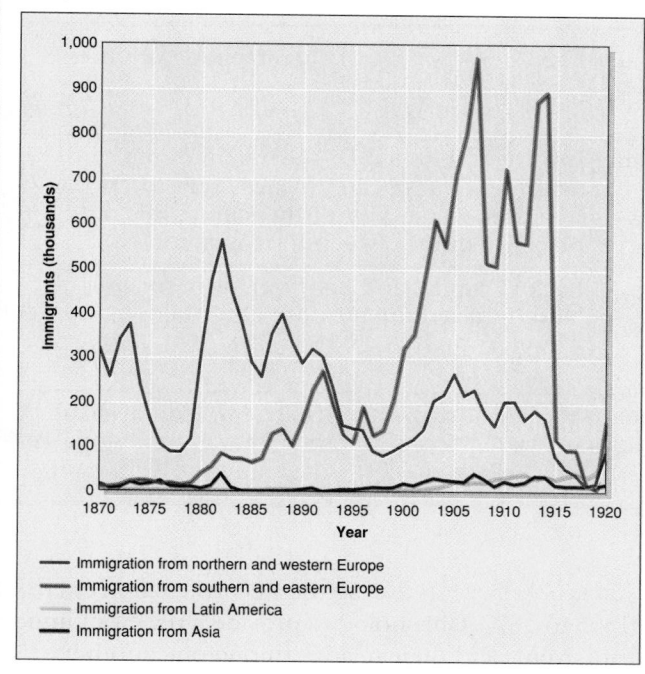

Immigration from northern and western Europe
Immigration from southern and eastern Europe
Immigration from Latin America
Immigration from Asia

FIGURE 18-2 Immigration to the United States, 1870–1915
The graph illustrates the dramatic change in immigration to the United States during the late nineteenth and early twentieth centuries. As immigration from northern and western Europe slackened, the numbers of newcomers from southern and eastern Europe swelled. Latin American and Asian immigration also increased during this period.

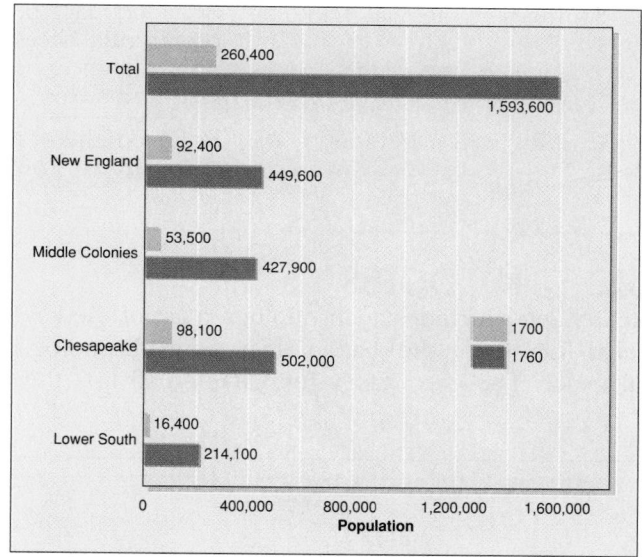

FIGURE 4-2   Population Growth in British Mainland Colonies, 1700–1760
Both natural increase and immigration contributed to a staggering rate of population growth in British North America. Some colonists predicted that Americans would soon outnumber Britain's inhabitants—a possibility that greatly concerned British officials.
Data Source: John J. McCusker and Russell R. Menard, *The Economy of British America, 1607–1789*, rev. ed. (1991). University of North Carolina Press.

FIGURE 3-4   Ethnic Distribution of Non-Indian Inhabitants of British Mainland Colonies, c. 1770
By the third quarter of the eighteenth century, the colonial population was astonishingly diverse. Only two out of three settlers claimed British ancestry (from England, Wales, Scotland, or northern Ireland), while one out of five was African in origin.
Data Source: Thomas L. Purvis, "The European Ancestry of the United States Population, 1790," *William and Mary Quarterly*, 3d series, 41 (1984), p. 98.

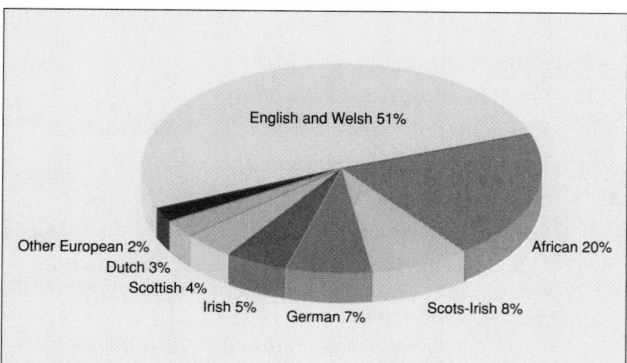

OVERVIEW TABLES

The Overview tables in this text are a special feature designed to highlight and summarize important topics within a chapter. The Overview table shown here, for example, summarizes the purpose and significance of the major laws and constitutional amendments passed during the Reconstruction era following the Civil War.

Overview

Constitutional Amendments and Federal Legislation of the Reconstruction Era

Amendment or Legislation	Purpose	Significance
Thirteenth Amendment (passed and ratified in 1865)	Prevented southern states from reestablishing slavery after the war	Final step toward full emancipation of slaves
Freedmen's Bureau Act (1865)	Oversight of resettlement, relief, education, and labor for former slaves	Involved the federal government directly in assisting the transition from slavery to freedom; worked fitfully to achieve this objective during its seven-year career
Southern Homestead Act (1866)	Provided black people preferential access to public lands in five southern states	Lack of capital and poor quality of federal land thwarted the purpose of the act
Civil Rights Act of 1866	Defined rights of national ~~citizenship~~	Marked an important change in federal–state relations, tilting balance of power to national

CHRONOLOGIES

Each chapter includes a Chronology, a list of the key events discussed in the chapter arranged in chronological order. The chronology for Chapter 16 lists the dates of key events during the Reconstruction era from 1865 to 1877. Chronologies provide a review of important events and their relationship to one another.

Chronology

1863	Lincoln proposes his Ten Percent Plan.
1864	Congress proposes the Wade-Davis Bill.
1865	Sherman issues Field Order No. 15.
	Freedmen's Bureau is established.
	Andrew Johnson succeeds to the presidency, unveils his Reconstruction plan.
	Massachusetts desegregates all public facilities.
	Black citizens in several southern cities organize Union Leagues.
	Former Confederate states begin to pass black codes.
1866	Congress passes Southern Homestead Act, Civil Rights Act of 1866.

Republican regimes topple in North Carolina and Georgia.

1871	Congress passes Ku Klux Klan Act.
1872	Freedmen's Bureau closes down.
	Liberal Republicans emerge as a separate party.
	Ulysses S. Grant is reelected.
1873	Severe depression begins.
	Colfax Massacre occurs.
	U.S. Supreme Court's decision in the Slaughterhouse cases weakens the intent of the Fourteenth Amendment.
	Texas falls to the Democrats in the fall elections.
1874	White Leaguers attempt a coup against the Re-

PRIMARY SOURCE DOCUMENTS

Historians find most of their information in written records, original documents that have survived from the past. These include government publications, letters, diaries, newspapers—whatever people wrote or printed, including many private documents never intended for publication. Each chapter in the book contains a feature called American Views—a selection from a primary source document. The example shown here is a letter from a Union soldier fighting during the Civil War. Each American Views feature begins with a brief introduction followed by several questions—for discussion or written response—on what the document reveals about key issues and events.

AMERICAN VIEWS

A Soldier Promotes the Union Cause

Introduction

Soldiers wrote their thoughts down in diaries, in letters to their families, and, as in the case of the infantryman here, D. Beardsley, from Tompkins County, New York, to newspapers. Morale faltered in both the civilian and military ranks on both sides during the Civil War as this excerpt indicates. At the same time, Beardsley is buoyed by the elevated sense of mission in Union ranks, brought about by Abraham Lincoln's Emancipation Proclamation, which took effect one month prior to this letter.

Questions

● How to balance civil liberties with the necessity of carrying on a war is a dilemma of all armed conflicts involving democratic societies. What does this soldier think about where the balance ought to occur?

● The writer refers to "desertion" in the ranks indicating a morale problem in the

In addition, each chapter begins with Voices from the American Journey, a brief firsthand account from an individual that powerfully recounts the personal journey he or she took in their lives. Each of these "voices" relates to the themes that follow in the chapter. The example here, from Chapter 18, is an excerpt from a letter written by Mary Antin, a Russian-Jewish immigrant who came to America at the turn of the last century.

We are forced to pick out our clothes from among all the others, with the steam blinding us; we choke, cough, entreat the women to give us time; they persist, "Quick! Quick!—or you'll miss the train!"—Oh, so we really won't be murdered! They are only making us ready for the continuing of our journey, cleaning us of all suspicions of dangerous sickness. Thank God! . . .

Oh, what solemn thoughts I had! How deeply I felt the greatness, the power of the scene! The immeasurable distance from horizon to horizon; . . . the absence of any object besides the one ship; . . . I was conscious only of sea and sky and something I did not understand. And as I listened to its solemn voice, I felt as if I had found a friend, and knew that I loved the ocean.

Mary Antin

Mary Antin, *The Promised Land* (Boston: Houghton Mifflin Company, 1912), chapter VIII.

UNITED STATES HISTORY DOCUMENT CD-ROM

Bound into every new copy of this textbook is a free U.S. History Document CD-ROM. This is a powerful resource for research and additional reading that contains more than 300 primary source documents central to U.S. History. Each document provides essay questions that are linked directly to a website where short-essay answers can be submitted online or printed out. A complete list of documents on the CD-Rom is found just before the Preface.

FROM THEN TO NOW

The feature called From Then to Now connects events and trends in the past to issues that confront Americans today, illustrating the value a historical perspective can contribute to our understanding of the world we live in. The example here, from Chapter 28, compares the fight against AIDS today with the search for a polio vaccine in the middle of the twentieth century.

FROM THEN TO NOW

Medical Research on Polio and AIDS

When Dr. Jonas Salk announced an effective vaccine for polio on April 12, 1955, the United States gained a new hero. In the confident mid-1950s, the polio vaccine seemed another proof of American ability to improve the world.

Poliomyelitis, or infantile paralysis, attacks the nervous system; it can paralyze the legs or kill by short-circuiting muscles in the throat and chest. Before 1900, infants had often encountered the polio virus in their first months and developed lifelong immunity. In the twentieth century, cleaner houses and streets delayed contact with polio until the preschool years or later, when the disease could be devastating. The virus sometimes struck adults; it cost Franklin Roosevelt the use of his legs when he was in his thirties, but most victims were children.

Fear of polio haunted American families after World War II. The disease killed fewer people than heart disease or cancer, but it seemed grossly unfair. Most Americans knew at least one child who hobbled through life on crutches and metal leg braces. Hospitals filled with new cases every summer—58,000 in 1952 alone. Many children clung to life inside iron lungs, metal cylinders that pumped air in and out of a hole in the throat.

Polio season peaked in July and August. Worried parents kept their children out of movie theaters and swimming pools, but the disease struck even the most careful families. One woman who grew up in the 1950s remembered: "Polio? That was the big fear when I was young. . . . I remember going to Dallas and seeing television for the first time. . . . Every day they would report 'another so many polio cases today.'"

Salk's announcement was welcome news. A generation later, President Ronald Reagan would list the polio vaccine with the steam engine and silicon chip as one of the great modern discoveries. By 2002, the number of new polio cases around the world had fallen to fewer than 1,000 in only ten countries—not including the United States.

However, medical research in the new century was vastly different than in the 1950s. Salk's work was financed largely by private contributions—many made by individuals and families to the March of Dimes. Fifty years later, the federal government is by far the largest supporter of medical research, spending to the

ANALYZING VISUALS

Like graphs and tables, visual images can provide as much insight into our nation's history as the written word. Within photographs and pieces of fine art lies emotional and historical meaning. Captions also provide valuable information, such as in the example below. When studying the image, consider questions such as: "Who are these people?"; "How were they feeling?"; "What event motivated this photograph or painting?"; and "What can be learned from the backdrop surrounding the focal point?" Such analysis allows for a fuller understanding of the people who lived the American journey.

Noted urban photographer Lewis Hine captures the cramped working conditions and child labor in this late nineteenth-century canning factory. Women and children provided a cheap and efficient work force for labor-intensive industries.

RECOMMENDED READINGS, ADDITIONAL SOURCES, AND WHERE TO LEARN MORE

At the end of each chapter are two lists of books—Recommended Readings and Additional Sources—that provide greater information about the topics discussed in the chapter. The section called Where to Learn More lists important historical sites and museums and related Websites that provide first-hand exposure to historical artifacts and settings.

GLOSSARY

Significant historical terms are called out in heavy type throughout the text and listed at the end of each chapter with appropriate page numbers. These are listed alphabetically and defined in a glossary at the end of the book.

Steele, Ian K. *Warpaths: Invasions of North America* (1994).

Washburn, Wilcomb E. *The Governor and the Rebel: A History of Bacon's Rebellion in Virginia* (1957).

White, Richard. *The Middle Ground: Indians, Empires, and Republics in the Great Lakes Region, 1650–1815* (1991).

Africans in America

Blackburn, Robin. *The Making of New World Slavery: From the Baroque to the Modern 1492–1800* (1997).

Breen, T. H., and Stephen Innes. *"Myne Owne Ground": Race and Freed   Virginia's   rn Shore,*

WHERE TO LEARN MORE

● **Ste. Marie among the Hurons, near Midland, Ontario, Canada.** This site contains a reconstructed Jesuit mission from the seventeenth century. There is a museum with information about seventeenth-century France as well as life among the Huron Indians. Further information may be found at www.saintemarieamongthehurons.on.ca.

● **Taos Pueblo, Taos, New Mexico.** Still a residence for Pueblo Indians, portions of this multistoried

→ *An unknown artist depicted the fateful first encounter between Moctezuma and Hernán Cortés on November 8, 1519. Forewarned of the Spaniards' arrival by a series of ominous portents, the Aztec ruler greeted Cortés with a mixture of majesty and apprehension. Less than a year later, Moctezuma was dead and by 1521 the Aztec empire had fallen to the Spanish.*

WORLDS APART

1

After a difficult journey of over two hundred miles, the exhausted man arrived at the royal palace in the grand city of Tenochtitlán. He had hurried all the way from the Gulf Coast with important news for the Aztec leader, Moctezuma.

Our lord and king, forgive my boldness. I am from Mictlancuauhtla. When I went to the shores of the great sea, there was a mountain range or small mountain floating in the midst of the water, and moving here and there without touching the shore. My lord, we have never seen the like of this, although we guard the coast and are always on watch.

[When Moctezuma sent some officials to check on the messenger's story, they confirmed his report.]

Our lord and king, it is true that strange people have come to the shores of the great sea. They were fishing from a small boat, some with rods and others with a net. They fished until late and then they went back to their two great towers and climbed up into them. . . . They have very light skin, much lighter than ours. They all have long beards, and their hair comes only to their ears.

Miguel Leon–Portilla, *The Broken Spears: The Aztec Account of the Conquest of Mexico* (Boston, 1962).

CHAPTER OUTLINE

Native American Societies before 1492
Paleo-Indians and the Archaic Period
The Development of Agriculture
Nonfarming Societies
Mesoamerican Civilizations
North American Cultures
The Caribbean Islanders

West African Societies
Geographical and Political Differences
Family Structure and Religion
European Merchants in West Africa and the Slave Trade

Western Europe on the Eve of Exploration
The Consolidation of Political and Military Authority
Religious Conflict and the Protestant Reformation

Contact
The Lure of Discovery
Christopher Columbus and the Westward Route to Asia
The Spanish Conquest and Colonization
The Columbian Exchange
Cultural Perceptions and Misperceptions

Competition for a Continent
Early French Efforts in North America
English Attempts in the New World

Conclusion

Moctezuma received news, like the messenger's initial report, filled with foreboding. Aztec religion placed great emphasis on omens and prophecies, which were thought to foreshadow coming events. Several unusual omens had recently occurred—blazing lights in the sky, one temple struck by lightning and another that spontaneously burst into flames, monstrous beings that appeared and then vanished. Now light-skinned strangers suddenly appeared offshore. Magicians regarded all these signs as unfavorable and warned that trouble lay ahead.

The messenger's journey to Tenochtitlán occurred in 1519. The "mountains" he saw were in fact the sails of European ships, and the strange men were Spanish soldiers under the command of Hernán Cortés. Like Columbus's voyage to the Caribbean in 1492, Cortés's arrival in Mexico is often considered a key episode in the European discovery of the "New World." But we might just as accurately view the messenger's entry into the Aztec capital as announcing the native Mexicans' discovery of a New World to the east, from which the strangers must

have come. Neither the Aztecs nor the Spaniards could have foreseen the far-reaching consequences of these twin discoveries. Before long, a variety of peoples—Native Americans, Africans, and Europeans—who had previously lived worlds apart would come together to create a world that was new to all of them.

This new world reflected the diverse experiences of the many peoples who built it. Improving economic conditions in the fifteenth and early sixteenth centuries propelled Europeans overseas to seek new opportunities for trade and settlement. Spain, Portugal, France, and England competed for political, economic, and religious domination within Europe, and their conflict carried over into the Americas. Native Americans drew upon their familiarity with the land and its resources, their patterns of political and religious authority, and their systems of trade and warfare to deal with the European newcomers. Africans did not come voluntarily to the Americas but were brought by the Europeans to work as slaves. They too would draw on their cultural heritage to cope with both a new land and a new, harsh condition of life.

KEY TOPICS

- Native American, West African, and European societies on the eve of contact
- The reasons for Europe's impulse to global exploration
- The Spanish, French, and English experiences in America in the sixteenth century
- Consequences of contact between the Old and New Worlds

NATIVE AMERICAN SOCIETIES BEFORE 1492

In 1492, the year Columbus landed on a tiny island in the Caribbean, perhaps 70 million people—nearly equal to the population of Europe at that time—lived on the continents of North and South America, most of them south of what is now the border between the United States and Mexico. They belonged to hundreds of groups, each with its own language or dialect, history, and way of life. In their own languages, many native groups called themselves "the original people" or "the true men." Europeans came to call them "Indians," following Columbus's mistaken first impression that he had arrived in the East Indies when his ships reached an island in the Bahamas.

From the start, the original inhabitants of the Americas were peoples in motion. The first migrants may have arrived over forty thousand years ago, traveling from central Siberia and slowly making their way to southern South America. These people, and subsequent migrants from Eurasia, probably traveled across a land bridge that emerged across what is now the Bering Strait. During the last Ice Age, much of the earth's water was frozen in huge glaciers. This process lowered ocean levels, exposing a 600-mile-wide land bridge between Asia and America. Recent research examining genetic and linguistic similarities between Asian and Native American populations suggests that there may have been later migrations as well. Asian seafarers may have crossed the Pacific to settle portions of western North and South America, while as recently as eight thousand years ago, a final

Chronology

c. 40,000–8,000 B.C.	Ancestors of Native Americans cross Bering land bridge.
c. 10,000–9000 B.C.	Paleo-Indians expand through the Americas.
c. 9000 B.C.	Extinction of large land mammals in North America.
c. 8000–1500 B.C.	Archaic Indian era.
c. 3000 B.C.	Beginnings of agriculture in Mesoamerica.
c. 1500 B.C.	Earliest mound-building culture begins.
c. 500 B.C.–A.D. 400	Adena-Hopewell mound-building culture.
c. A.D. 700–1600	Rise of West African empires.
c. 900	First mounds built at Cahokia. Ancestral Puebloan expansion.
c. 1000	Spread of Islam in West Africa.
c. 1000–1500	Last mound-building culture, the Mississippian.
c. 1290s	Ancestral Puebloan dispersal into smaller villages.
1400–1600	Renaissance in Europe.
1430s	Beginnings of Portuguese slave trade in West Africa.
1492	End of *reconquista* in Spain. Columbus's first voyage.
1494	Treaty of Tordesillas.
1497	John Cabot visits Nova Scotia and Newfoundland.
1497–1499	Vasco da Gama sails around Africa to reach India.
1517	Protestant Reformation begins in Germany.
1519–1521	Hernán Cortés conquers the Aztec empire.
1532–1533	Francisco Pizarro conquers the Inca empire.
1534–1542	Jacques Cartier explores eastern Canada for France.
1540–1542	Coronado explores southwestern North America.
1542–1543	Roberval's failed colony in Canada.
1558	Elizabeth I becomes queen of England.
1565	Spanish establish outpost at St. Augustine in Florida.
1560s–1580s	English renew attempts to conquer Ireland.
1587	Founding of "Lost Colony" of Roanoke.
1598	Spanish found colony at New Mexico.

migration may have brought Siberians to what is now Alaska and northern Canada.

PALEO-INDIANS AND THE ARCHAIC PERIOD

The earliest Americans, whom archaeologists call *Paleo-Indians*, traveled in small bands, tracking and killing mammoths, bison, and other large game. These animals were often easy prey, for they had never before encountered human hunters. Archaeologists working near present-day Clovis, New Mexico, have found numerous carefully crafted spear points—some of which may be over thirteen thousand years old—that testify to Paleo-Indians' expertise. Such efficient tools possibly contributed to overhunting, for by about 9000 B.C., mammoths, mastodons, and other large game had become extinct in the Americas. Climatic change also hastened the animals' disappearance. Around twelve thousand years ago, the world's climate began to grow warmer, turning grasslands

into deserts and reducing the animals' food supply. This meant that humans too had to find other food sources.

Between roughly 8000 B.C. and 1500 B.C. —what archaeologists call the Archaic period—Native Americans adapted to regional environments, learning to use local resources efficiently. Gradually, populations grew and people began living in larger communities. In these villages, men and women began to assume more specialized roles. Men did most of the hunting and fishing, activities that required travel. Women remained closer to home, gathering and preparing wild plant foods and caring for children. Each group made the tools it used, with men carving fishhooks and arrowheads and women making such items as bone needles and baskets.

Archaic Indians also collected local nonfood resources, such as minerals, rare shells, and bones, some of which were thought to have special spiritual significance. Native peoples traded these materials,

Women were the principal farmers in most Native American societies, growing corn, beans, and other crops that made up most of their food supply. This sixteenth-century French engraving shows Indian men preparing the soil for cultivation and Indian women sowing seeds in neat rows.

often over vast distances. At Indian Knoll, in western Kentucky, archaeologists have found copper from the Great Lakes area and shells from as far away as the Gulf of Mexico. Competition for control of lands where desirable materials could be found may have sparked conflict. Three bodies buried around 5000 B.C. in northwestern Alabama had stone arrowheads embedded in their backbones or ribcages, clear evidence of violent death.

Ideas as well as goods circulated among Archaic Indian peoples. Across the continent, human burials became more elaborate, suggesting that ideas about death and the afterlife passed between groups. Bodies might be wrapped in woven mats or cloths and the deceased's personal possessions placed in the grave. Certain valuable trade goods, such as exotic shell beads and animal figurines, accompanied some individuals to the grave, lending the deceased their spiritual power.

THE DEVELOPMENT OF AGRICULTURE

In the latter half of the Archaic period, some Native Americans made a momentous social and economic adaptation when they began farming. Agriculture in the Americas began around 3000 B.C., when the people of central Mexico started raising an ancient type of maize, or corn. Farming had already appeared independently in other parts of the world. People in the Middle East turned to agriculture around 9000 B.C.; a few thousand years later, farming appeared in South-

east Asia, China, and India. Archaeologists speculate that agriculture first developed in areas where population growth threatened to outrun the wild food supply. Women, with their knowledge of wild plants, probably discovered how to save seeds and cultivate them, becoming the world's first farmers.

At first, farming in the Americas supplemented a diet still largely dependent on hunting and gathering. But agriculture gradually became more widespread. In addition to maize, the main crop in both South and North America, farmers in Mexico, Central America, and the Peruvian Andes learned to cultivate peppers, beans, pumpkins, squash, avocados, sweet and white potatoes (native to the Peruvian highlands), and tomatoes. Mexican farmers also grew cotton. Maize and bean cultivation spread from Mexico in a wide arc to the north and east. Peoples in what is now the southwestern United States began farming between 1500 and 500 B.C., and by A.D. 200, farmers tilled the soil in present-day Georgia and Florida.

Wherever agriculture took hold, important social changes followed. Populations grew, because farming produced a more secure food supply than did hunting and gathering. Permanent villages appeared as farmers settled near their fields. In central Mexico, agriculture eventually sustained the populations of large cities. Trade in agricultural surpluses flowed through networks of exchange. In many Indian societies, women's status improved because of their role as the principal farmers. Specialized craft workers produced sophisticated pottery and baskets to store harvested grains. Even religious beliefs and practices reflected the centrality of farming. In describing the origins of their people, Pueblo Indians of the Southwest compared their emergence from the underworld to a maize plant sprouting from the earth.

The development of agriculture contributed to the diversity of Native American peoples. Even so, certain generalizations can be made about societies that developed within broad regions, or culture areas (see Map 1–1). Within each area, inhabitants shared basic patterns of subsistence and social organization, largely reflecting the natural environment to which they had adapted.

NONFARMING SOCIETIES

Throughout the North and West, Indians prospered without adopting agriculture. In the challenging environment of the Arctic and Subarctic, small nomadic bands moved seasonally to fish, follow game, and in the brief summers, gather wild berries. Far to the north, Eskimos and Aleuts hunted whales, seals, and other sea mammals. Farther inland, the Crees and other peoples followed migrating herds of caribou and moose. Northern peoples fashioned tools and weapons of bone and ivory, clothing and boats from animal skins, and houses of whalebones and hides or blocks of sod or snow. Many of their rituals and songs celebrated the hunt and the spiritual connection between humans and the animals on which they depended.

Along the Northwest Coast and Columbia River Plateau, abundant resources supported one of the most densely populated areas of North America. With rivers teeming with salmon and other fish, and forests full of game and edible plants, people prospered without resorting to farming. Among such groups as the Kwakiutls and Chinooks, extended families lived in large communal houses located in villages of up to several hundred residents. Local rulers displayed their prominence most conspicuously during potlatches, or ceremonies in which they gave away or destroyed food and other possessions. Artisans used the region's plentiful wood supply to make many items, including distinctive religious masks and memorial poles carved with images of supernatural beings.

Farther south, in present-day California, hunter-gatherers lived in smaller villages, several of which might be led by the same chief. These settlements usually adjoined oak groves, where Indians gathered acorns. Preparing the nuts was time-consuming, for they had to be ground into meal, leached with water to remove bitter acid, and then cooked. To protect their access to this important food, chiefs and villagers vigorously defended their territorial claims to the oak groves. Elsewhere, in the foothills of the Sierras, Indians periodically set fire to thick underbrush to hasten the growth of new shoots that would attract deer and other game.

Small nomadic bands in the Great Basin, where the climate was warm and dry, lived in caves and rock shelters, surviving on the region's limited resources. Shoshone hunters captured antelope in corrals and trapped small game, such as squirrels and rabbits. In what is now Utah and western Colorado, Utes hunted elk, bison, and mountain sheep and fished in mountain streams. Women gathered pinyon nuts, seeds, and wild berries. In hard times, people ate rattlesnakes, horned toads, and insects. They celebrated whenever food was plentiful and urged religious leaders to seek supernatural help when starvation loomed.

MESOAMERICAN CIVILIZATIONS

Mesoamerica, the birthplace of agriculture in North America, extends from central Mexico into Central America. A series of complex, literate, urban cultures emerged in this region beginning around 1200 B.C. Among the earliest was that of the Olmecs, who flourished on Mexico's Gulf Coast from about 1200 to 400 B.C. The Olmecs and other early Mesoamerican peoples built cities featuring large pyramids, developed religious practices that included human sacrifice, and devised calendars and writing systems. Two of the most prominent Mesoamerican civilizations to follow the Olmecs were that of the Mayans in the Yucatán and Guatemala and that of Teotihuacán in central Mexico.

The Mayans. Mayan civilization reached its greatest glory between about A.D. 150 and 900 in the southern Yucatán, creating Mesoamerica's most advanced writing and calendrical systems and developing a sophisticated mathematics that included the concept of zero. The Mayans of the southern Yucatán suffered a decline after 900, but there were still many thriving Mayan centers in the northern Yucatán when Europeans arrived in the Americas. The great city of Teotihuacán dominated central Mexico from the first century to the eighth century A.D. and influenced much of the rest of Mesoamerica through trade and conquest.

The Aztecs. Some two hundred years after the fall of Teotihuacán, the Toltecs, a warrior people, rose to prominence, dominating central Mexico from about 900 to 1100. In the wake of the Toltec collapse, the

MAP EXPLORATION To explore an interactive version of this map, go to
http://www.prenhall.com/goldfield/map1.1

Legend:
- Arctic
- Subarctic
- Northwest Coast
- Plateau
- Great Basin
- California
- Southwest
- Plains
- Eastern Woodlands (Northeast)
- Eastern Woodlands (Southeast)
- Mesoamerica
- Circum-Caribbean

MAP 1-1   North American Culture Areas, c. 1500
*Over the course of centuries, Indian peoples in North America developed distinctive cultures
suited to the environments in which they lived. Inhabitants of each culture area shared basic patterns of subsistence, craft work, and social organization. Most, but not all, Indian peoples combined farming with hunting and gathering.*

Aztecs, another warrior people, migrated from the north into the Valley of Mexico and built a great empire that soon controlled much of Mesoamerica. The magnificent Aztec capital, Tenochtitlán, was a city of great plazas, broad avenues, magnificent temples and palaces, ball courts, and busy marketplaces. Built on islands in the middle of Lake Texcoco, it was connected to the mainland by four broad causeways. In 1492, Tenochtitlán was home to some 200,000 people, making it one of the largest cities in the world at the time.

The great pyramid in Tenochtitlán's principal temple complex was the center of Aztec religious life. Here Aztec priests sacrificed human victims—by cutting open their chests and removing their still-beating hearts—to offer to the gods. Human sacrifice had been part of Mesoamerican religion since the time of the Olmecs. People believed that such ceremonies pleased the gods and prevented them from destroying the earth. The Aztecs, however, practiced sacrifice on a much larger scale than ever before. Hundreds, even thousands, of victims died in ceremonies that sometimes lasted for days.

Aztec culture expanded through continuous military conquest, driven by a quest for sacrificial victims and for wealth in the form of tribute payments of gold, food, and handcrafted goods. But as the empire grew, it became increasingly vulnerable to internal division. Neighboring peoples hated the Aztecs and submitted to them out of fear. With a powerful ally to lead them, they would readily turn on their overlords and bring the empire down.

NORTH AMERICAN CULTURES

North of Mexico, the introduction of a drought-resistant type of maize around 400 B.C. enabled a series of cultures sharing certain characteristics with Mesoamerica to develop. Beginning about 300 B.C., the Hohokams settled in southern Arizona, eventually building villages of several hundred people. Harvests of beans, corn, and squash (sometimes two a year), watered by a complex system of canals, fed Hohokam villagers. In large communities, inhabitants built ball courts similar to those found in Mexico. Artisans wove cotton cloth and made goods reflecting Mesoamerican artistic styles out of shell, turquoise, and clay. Extensive trade networks linked the Hohokams to people living as far away as California and Mexico. Their culture endured for over a thousand years but had disappeared by 1450.

Ancestral Puebloans.   Beginning about A.D. 1, Ancestral Puebloan peoples (sometimes called Anasazis) settled where the borders of present-day Colorado, Utah, Arizona, and New Mexico meet. They gradually adopted agriculture, first adding maize to a diet of wild foods and later beans and squash. Scarce rainfall, routed through dams and hillside terraces, watered the crops. Networks of roads carried people and goods between villages. Artisans crafted intricate baskets and distinctive black-on-white pottery for use and trade.

Ancestral Puebloans originally lived in villages built on mesas and canyon floors. These settlements

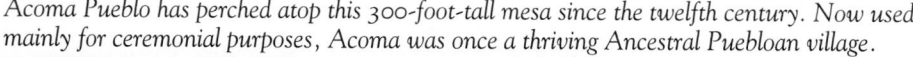

Acoma Pueblo has perched atop this 300-foot-tall mesa since the twelfth century. Now used mainly for ceremonial purposes, Acoma was once a thriving Ancestral Puebloan village.

included special rooms, or *kivas*, for religious ceremonies. The largest communal dwelling, Pueblo Bonito in New Mexico's Chaco Canyon, covered 3 acres and contained 650 to 800 rooms that housed about 1,200 people. Pueblo Bonito may have been the political and ceremonial center of Puebloan society from about A.D. 900 to 1100. After about 1200, villagers began carving multistoried stone houses into steep canyon walls. These spectacular dwellings were not easy places in which to live. They could be reached only by difficult climbs up steep cliffs and along narrow ledges, and water, food, and other goods had to be carried to them. Archaeologists now think that warfare and climate change worked together to force the Puebloans into these precarious homes. Around 1200, the climate of the Southwest grew colder, making it more difficult to grow enough to feed the large population. Food scarcity, in turn, may have set village against village and encouraged attacks by outsiders. Villagers probably resorted to cliff dwellings for defensive purposes as violence spread in the region. By 1300, survivors abandoned the cliff dwellings and dispersed into much smaller villages along the Rio Grande.

Their descendants include the Hopis and Zunis, as well as other Puebloan peoples in the desert Southwest. In 1492, many lived in large communal dwellings in permanent villages (*pueblo* is the Spanish word for "village"). Men did most of the farming—in contrast to the predominant pattern of women farmers elsewhere in Native America—and tilled irrigated fields of corn, beans, squash, and sunflowers. In their religious rituals, Pueblos directed prayers to the gods for enough rain for the all-important harvest.

Plains Indians.

The Great Plains of the continent's interior were much less densely settled than the desert Southwest. Scattered villages of Mandans, Pawnees, and other groups clung to tree-lined rivers. Women raised corn, squash, beans, and sunflowers and gathered wild plants for food and medicine. Men hunted bison, whose skin and bones were used for clothing, shelter, and tools. Plains Indians moved frequently, seeking more fertile land or better hunting. Wherever they went, they traded skins, food, and obsidian (a volcanic glass used for tools and weapons) with other native peoples.

Mound-building cultures.

The gradual spread of agriculture transformed native societies in the Eastern Woodlands, a vast territory extending from the Mississippi Valley to the Atlantic seaboard. Although the process began around 2500 B.C., farming was not firmly established until about A.D. 700. As agriculture

spread, several "mound-building" societies—named for the large earthworks their members constructed—developed in the Ohio and Mississippi Valleys. The oldest flourished in Louisiana between 1500 and 700 B.C. The members of the Adena-Hopewell culture, which appeared in the Ohio Valley between 500 B.C. and A.D. 400, lived in small villages spread over a wide area. They built hundreds of mounds, often in the shapes of humans, birds, and serpents. Most were grave sites, where people were buried with valuable goods. Many burial objects were made from materials obtained through long-distance trade, including Wyoming obsidian, Lake Superior copper, and Florida conch shells.

The last mound-building culture, the Mississippian, emerged between 1000 and 1500 in the Mississippi Valley. Mississippian farmers raised enough maize, squash, and beans to support sizable populations and major urban centers. One of the largest of these was **Cahokia**, located near present-day St. Louis. By 1250, Cahokia had perhaps thirty thousand residents, making it about the same size as medieval London and the largest American city north of Mexico. Its central feature was a 100-foot-high mound, the world's largest earthwork.

Cahokia dominated the Mississippi Valley, but numerous other towns, some with hundreds or thousands of residents, lay scattered across the Woodlands region, linked by extensive trade networks. In major towns, religious leaders conducted ceremonies in large temples built atop platform mounds. Powerful chiefs, thought to be related to the sun, ruled these communities. When a chief died, his wives and servants were killed in order to accompany him to the afterlife.

Mississippian culture began to decline in the thirteenth century. Food shortages (probably caused by a cooling climate) and warfare drove people from the great cities into the countryside. Yet elements of the culture survived among dispersed Woodlands Indians. Most people continued to subsist through maize and bean agriculture, living part of the year in villages where women tilled lands that men had cleared. Twice a year, after crops were planted and again after the harvest, villagers separated into family groups and dispersed into the forest. Men went off to hunt, while women and children foraged for wild plants. Although the large cities of the Mississippian era had disappeared, Woodlands Indians maintained long-distance trade links throughout the region, with such precious goods as copper, shell beads, and pearls passing among groups.

Woodlands villages generally contained 500 to 2000 people, led by chiefs who inherited their posi-

This artist's rendering, based on archaeological evidence, suggests the size and magnificence of the Mississippian city of Cahokia. By the thirteenth century, it was as populous as medieval London, and served as a center of trade for the vast interior of North America.

tions but ruled with the advice of groups of elders. In the North, Iroquois peoples took advantage of the demise of Cahokia to refocus trade and power in their own region, forming a confederation around 1450. The southern Woodlands region was more densely populated than the northern, largely because the warmer southern climate provided a longer growing season and more abundant wild foods. Patterns of settlement in the southern region, however, were more decentralized than in the north, with villages occasionally joining in loose regional confederacies.

THE CARIBBEAN ISLANDERS

The Caribbean islanders whom Columbus first encountered likewise descended from ancient cultures. Around 5000 B.C., mainland peoples began moving to the islands. Ancestors of the Tainos probably came from what is now Venezuela. The Guanahatabeys of western Cuba originated in Florida, and the Caribs of the easternmost islands moved from Brazil's Orinoco Valley. Surviving at first by hunting and gathering, island peoples began farming perhaps in the first century A.D. They raised manioc, sweet potatoes, maize, squash, beans, peppers, peanuts, and pineapple on clearings made in the tropical forests. Canoes carried trade goods throughout the Caribbean, as well as to Mesoamerica and coastal South America.

By 1492, as many as 4 million people may have inhabited the Caribbean islands. Powerful chiefs ruled over villages, conducted war and diplomacy, and controlled the distribution of food and other goods obtained as tribute from villagers. Island societies were divided into several ranks. An elite group aided the chief and supplied religious leaders. Below them were a large class of ordinary farmers and fishermen and a lower class of servants who worked for the elites. Elite islanders were easily recognized by their fine clothing, bright feather headdresses, and golden ear and nose ornaments—items that eventually attracted the attention of European visitors.

The histories of America's native peoples have largely been preserved in oral traditions and archaeological evidence, not written records, and for that reason may seem less distinct than the histories of Europeans and their descendants. But the New World, no less than the Old, had witnessed centuries of dynamic change. People adapted to many different environments, learning how to use local foods and resources not just to survive but to prosper. Empires rose and fell, and new ones took their place. Large cities flourished and disappeared. Periods of warfare occasionally disrupted the lives of thousands of individuals. At other times, military alliances sealed friendships, and networks of trade linked peoples across vast expanses of territory. Native Americans were thoroughly accustomed to dealing with new and challenging circumstances.

WEST AFRICAN SOCIETIES

In the three centuries after 1492, fully six out of seven people who crossed the Atlantic to the Americas were

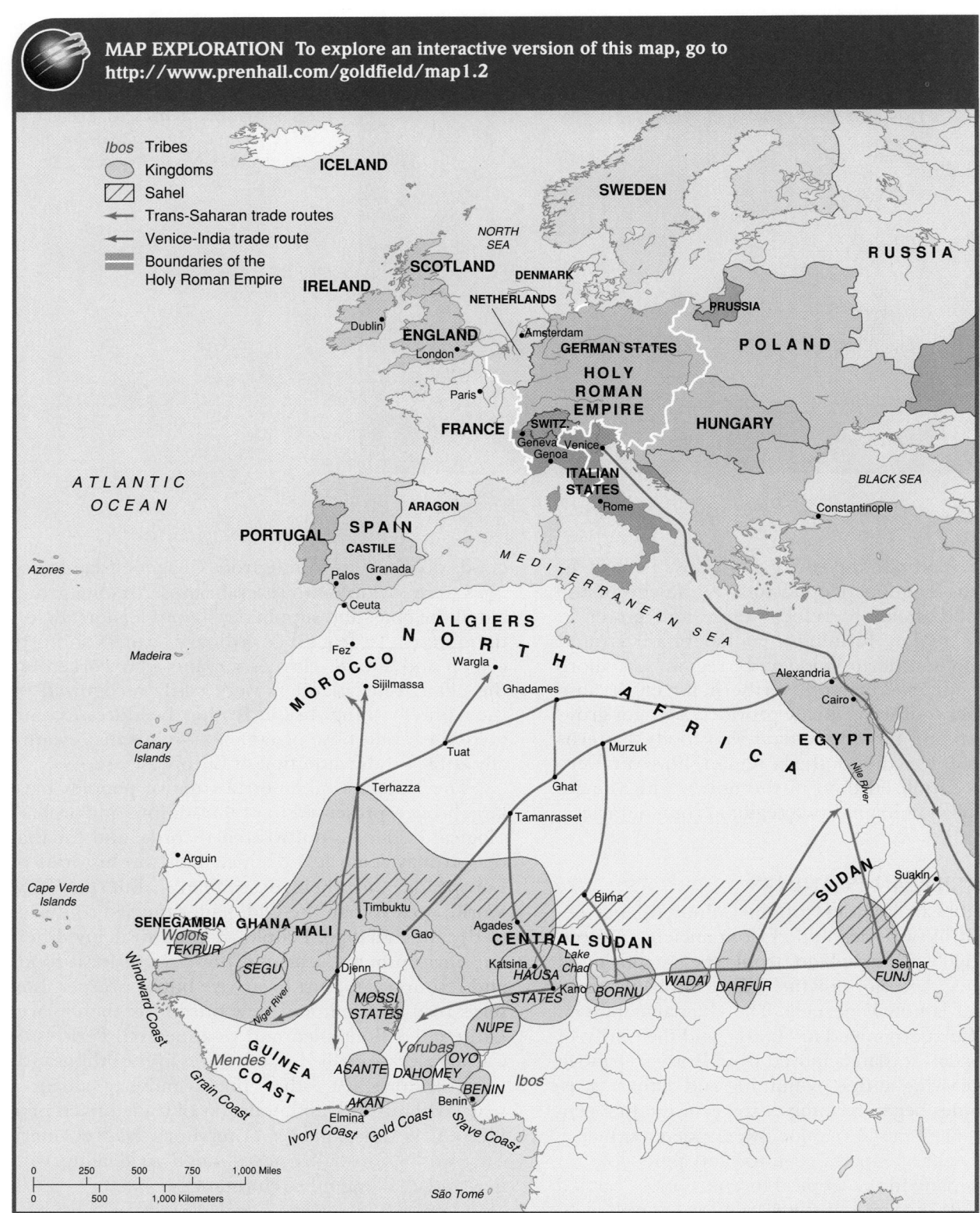

MAP EXPLORATION To explore an interactive version of this map, go to
http://www.prenhall.com/goldfield/map1.2

MAP 1-2 West Africa and Europe in 1492
Before Columbus's voyage, Europeans knew little about the world beyond the Mediterranean basin and the coast of West Africa. Muslim merchants from North Africa largely controlled European traders' access to African gold and other materials.

not Europeans but Africans. They came from the world's second largest continent and the one with the longest record of human habitation, where ancestors of modern humans (*homo sapiens*) appeared 130,000 or more years ago. Like the Americas, Africa had witnessed the rise of many ancient and diverse cultures (see Map 1-2). They ranged from the sophisticated Egyptian civilization that developed in the Nile Valley over 5000 years ago to the powerful twelfth-century chiefdoms of Zimbabwe to the West African empires that flourished in the time of Columbus and Cortés. The vast majority of Africans who came to the Americas after 1492 arrived as slaves, transported by Europeans eager to exploit their labor. Although they were involuntary immigrants, Africans could draw upon their ancient cultural heritages to help shape the New World in which they found themselves.

GEOGRAPHICAL AND POLITICAL DIFFERENCES

Most African immigrants to the Americas came from the continent's western regions. The West African city of Timbuktu was one of the continent's greatest cities in 1492. Located on the Niger River, the metropolis of perhaps seventy thousand people was the seat of the powerful Songhai empire, ruled by Sunni Ali with the support of a strong army and efficient bureaucrats. Timbuktu was a center of trade as well as government. A visitor in 1526 described its busy streets lined with "shops of artificers and merchants, and especially of such as weave linen and cotton cloth," and reported—with some exaggeration—that the inhabitants "are exceeding rich."

The Songhai empire was only the latest in a series of powerful states to develop in western Sudan, the vast plain lying south of the arid Sahara. One of the earliest, Ghana, rose to prominence in the eighth century and dominated West Africa for nearly three hundred years. Its successor, Mali, emerged around 1200 and lasted another three centuries. Songhai, the largest and wealthiest state, dominated the Sudan from around 1450 until it fell to a Moroccan invasion in 1591. Equivalently large empires did not appear in coastal West Africa, although the Asante, Dahomey, Oyo, and Bini kingdoms there grew to be quite powerful. Other coastal peoples, such as the Mendes and Igbos, were decentralized, living in autonomous villages where all adult males participated in making decisions.

Geographical as well as political differences marked the inland and coastal regions. In the vast grasslands of the Sudan, people raised cattle and cultivated millet and sorghum. In the 1500s, European visitors introduced varieties of Asian rice, which soon

Craftsmen from the West African kingdom of Benin were renowned for their remarkable bronze sculptures. This intricate bronze plaque depicts four African warriors in full military dress. The two tiny figures in the background may be Portuguese soldiers, who first arrived in Benin in the late fifteenth century.

became another important crop. On the coast—where rain falls nearly every day—people grew yams, bananas, and various kinds of beans and peas in forest clearings. They also kept sheep, goats, and poultry.

Artisans and merchants. West Africans were skilled artisans and particularly fine metalworkers. Smiths in Benin produced intricate bronze sculptures, and Asante craftsmen designed distinctive miniature gold weights. West African smiths also used their skills to forge weapons, attesting to the frequent warfare between West African states.

Complex trade networks linked inland and coastal states, and long-distance commercial connections tied West Africa to southern Europe and the Middle East. For centuries, mines in the area of present-day Guinea and Mali produced tons of gold each year. West African merchants exchanged gold with traders from North Africa for salt, a commodity so rare in West Africa that it was sometimes literally worth its weight in gold. In addition to gold, North African merchants bought pepper, leather, and ivory. The wealth generated by this trans-Saharan trade contributed to the rise of the Songhai and earlier empires.

Farming and gender roles. Most West Africans, however, were farmers, not merchants. A daily round of work, family duties, and worship defined their lives. West African men and women shared agricultural tasks. Men prepared fields for planting, while women cultivated the crops, harvested them, and dried grain for storage. Men also hunted and, in the grassland regions, herded cattle. Women in the coastal areas owned and cared for other livestock, including goats and sheep. West African women regularly traded goods, including the crops they grew, in local markets. In 1495, a Muslim African leader commented disapprovingly on the "free mixing of men and women in the markets and streets" in Timbuktu and other cities, but women merchants were essential to the vitality of local economies.

FAMILY STRUCTURE AND RELIGION

Family connections were exceedingly important to West Africans, helping to define each person's place in society. Children were especially cherished; one Yoruba proverb stated that "Without children you are naked." High rates of infant and child mortality made offspring all the more precious, for parents depended on their children for labor and for support in old age. In some regions, men who could afford to do so had more than one wife, thus increasing their chances of having surviving offspring. While ties between parents and children were of central importance, West Africans also emphasized their links with aunts, uncles, cousins, and grandparents. Groups of families formed clans that further extended an individual's kin ties. Most clans were patrilineal—tracing descent through the father's line—but some, for instance among the Akans and Igbos, were matrilineal. These links enmeshed West Africans in a web of family ties.

Religious beliefs magnified the powerful influence of family on African life. Africans believed that their ancestors acted as mediators between the worlds of the living and the dead. Families held elaborate funerals for deceased members to insure their passage into the realm of the spirits. Such rituals helped keep the memory of ancestors alive for younger generations.

West Africans worshiped a supreme being and several subordinate deities, believing that the gods often sent spirits to speak to people. Like Native Americans,

they performed ceremonies to insure the goodwill of the spiritual forces that suffused the natural world. West African medicine men and women used rituals to protect people from evil spirits and sorcerers. Religious ceremonies were held in sacred places—often near water—but not in buildings that Europeans recognized as churches. And like the Indians, West Africans preserved their faith through oral traditions.

Islam began to take root in West Africa around the eleventh century, probably introduced by Muslim traders from North Africa. By the fifteenth century, the cities of Timbuktu and Djenné had become centers of Islamic learning, attracting students from as far away as southern Europe. Some African rulers began keeping records in Arabic and enforcing Islamic law, but most West Africans probably retained traditional religious beliefs and practices.

EUROPEAN MERCHANTS IN WEST AFRICA AND THE SLAVE TRADE

Before the fifteenth century, Europeans knew little about Africa beyond its Mediterranean coast, which had been part of the Islamic world since the eighth century. Spain, much of which had been subject to Islamic rule before 1492, had stronger ties to North Africa than did most of Europe. But Christian merchants from other European lands had also traded for centuries with Muslims in the North African ports. When stories of West African gold reached the ears of European traders, they tried to move deeper into the continent. But they encountered powerful Muslim merchants intent on monopolizing the gold trade.

In the early fifteenth century, the kingdom of Portugal sought to circumvent this Muslim monopoly. Portuguese forces conquered Ceuta in Morocco and gained a foothold on the continent in 1415. Portuguese mariners gradually explored the West African coast, establishing trading posts along the way. Portuguese merchants exchanged horses, clothing, wine, lead, iron, and steel for African gold, grain, animal skins, cotton, pepper, and camels.

By the 1430s, the Portuguese had discovered perhaps the greatest source of wealth they could extract from Africa—slaves. People became slaves in various ways. Some Africans lost their freedom as punishment for crime, but the majority of slaves were captured in war. Slave raids into neighboring territories were a regular feature of African life. Slavery had long been a part of West African society. African law made land available to anyone willing to cultivate it—provided that no one else was using the same plot—and the possession of a large labor force to work the land became the principal means to wealth.

Slaves enriched their masters in a number of ways. Masters sold some slaves directly, tapping into a well-developed internal trade. Merchants from the Sahara frequently trekked to West Africa to exchange horses for slaves, and West Africans traded laborers among themselves. Most slaves worked at a variety of tasks for their owners. Many labored more or less independently as farmers, producing surplus crops for their masters. Some rulers acquired female slaves to serve as wives or concubines but also as workers. One Italian visitor to the small state of Warri reported in 1656 that its ruler had many slave wives who wove cloth for sale. Powerful Sudanese rulers employed large numbers of slaves as bureaucrats and soldiers, rewarding them for loyal service with good treatment and, occasionally, freedom.

Europeans who observed African slaves' relative freedom and variety of employment often concluded that slaves in Africa were "slaves in name only." Slavery in Africa was not necessarily a permanent status and did not automatically apply to the slaves' children. European purchasers of African slaves generally treated them much more harshly. Slavery for the unwilling African immigrants ensnared in it became even more oppressive as it developed in the Americas.

WESTERN EUROPE ON THE EVE OF EXPLORATION

When Columbus sailed from Spain in 1492, he left a continent recovering from the devastating warfare and disease of the fourteenth century and about to embark on the devastating religious conflicts of the sixteenth. Between 1337 and 1453, England and France had exhausted each other in a series of conflicts known as the Hundred Years' War. And between 1347 and 1351, an epidemic known as the Black Death (bubonic plague) wreaked havoc on a European population already suffering from persistent malnutrition. Perhaps a third of all Europeans died, with results that were felt for more than a century.

The plague left Europe with far fewer workers. To help the economy recover, the survivors learned to be more efficient and rely on technological improvements. Farmers selected the most fertile land to till, and artisans adopted labor-saving techniques to increase productivity. Metalworkers built larger furnaces with huge bellows driven by water power. Shipbuilders redesigned vessels with steering mechanisms that could be managed by smaller crews. Innovations in banking, accounting, and insurance also fostered economic recovery. Prosperity was distributed unevenly among social classes, however. In parts of England, France, Sweden, and the German states, peasants and workers protested rising rents and taxes that threatened to absorb most of their wages. Yet on the whole, Europe had a stronger, more productive economy in 1500 than ever before.

In much of western Europe, economic improvement encouraged an extraordinary cultural movement known as the Renaissance, a "rebirth" of interest in the classical civilizations of ancient Greece and Rome. The Renaissance originated in the city-states of Italy, where a prosperous and educated urban class promoted learning and artistic expression. Wealthy townspeople joined princes in becoming patrons of the arts, offering financial support to painters, sculptors, architects, writers, and musicians.

The daily lives of most Europeans, however, remained untouched by intellectual and artistic developments. Most Europeans were peasants, engaged in an annual round of agricultural labor. Within peasant families, men did most of the heavy field work, while women helped at planting and harvest time and cared for children, livestock, and the household. The economic recovery after the Black Death helped some families, but the lives of many remained hard. Crop failures and disease often brought great suffering to villages and towns.

European states were hierarchical, with their populations divided into fairly rigid classes. Monarchs stood at the top of society. Just below were the aristocrats, who, along with the royal family, dominated government and owned most of the land, receiving rents and labor services from peasants and rural artisans. Next, in descending order, came prosperous gentry families, independent landowners, and, at the bottom, landless peasants and laborers.

European society was also patriarchal, with men dominating political and economic life. Europe's rulers were, with few exceptions, men, and men controlled the Catholic Church. Inheritance was patrilineal, and only men could own property. According to an ideal not always upheld, Europeans thought that even the poorest man should be "as a king in his own house," ruling over his wife, children, and servants.

THE CONSOLIDATION OF POLITICAL AND MILITARY AUTHORITY

By the end of the fifteenth century, after more than a hundred years of incessant conflict, a measure of stability returned to the countries about to embark on overseas expansion. Ferdinand and Isabella of Spain, Louis XI of France, and Henry VII of England successfully asserted royal authority over their previously fragmented realms, creating strong state bureaucracies to control political rivals. They gave special trading privileges to merchants to gain their support, creating links that would later prove important in financing overseas expeditions. At the same time, Spain and Portugal negotiated an end to a long-running dispute about the succession to the throne of Castile, one of Spain's largest kingdoms.

The consolidation of military power went hand in hand with the strengthening of political authority. Portugal developed a strong navy to defend its seaborne merchants. Louis XI of France commanded a standing army, and Ferdinand of Spain created a palace guard to use against potential opponents. Before overseas expansion began, European monarchs exerted military force to extend their authority closer to home. Louis XI and his successors used warfare and intermarriage with ruling families of nearby provinces to expand French influence. In the early sixteenth century, England's Henry VIII sent soldiers to conquer Ireland. And the Spain of 1492 was forged from the successful conclusion of the *reconquista* ("reconquest") of territory from Muslim control.

Muslim invaders from North Africa first entered Spain in 711 and ruled much of the Iberian peninsula (which includes Spain and Portugal) for centuries. Beginning in the mid-eleventh century, Christian armies embarked on a long effort to reclaim the region. By 1450, only the southern tip of Spain remained under Muslim control. After the marriage of Ferdinand of Aragon and Isabella of Castile in 1469 united Spain's two principal kingdoms, their combined forces completed the *reconquista*. Granada, the last Muslim stronghold, fell in 1492, shortly before Columbus set out on his first voyage.

RELIGIOUS CONFLICT AND THE PROTESTANT REFORMATION

Even as these rulers sought to unify their realms, religious conflicts began to tear Europe apart. For more than a thousand years, Catholic Christianity had united western Europeans in one faith. All Christians believed that God sent his only son, Jesus Christ, to suffer crucifixion, die, and rise from the dead in order to redeem humans from sin and give them eternal life. The Catholic Church built on this faith included an elaborate hierarchy of clergy, ranging upward from parish priests to bishops, archbishops, and cardinals, culminating in Christ's representative on earth, the pope. It also supported monastic orders whose members often lived and prayed apart from society.

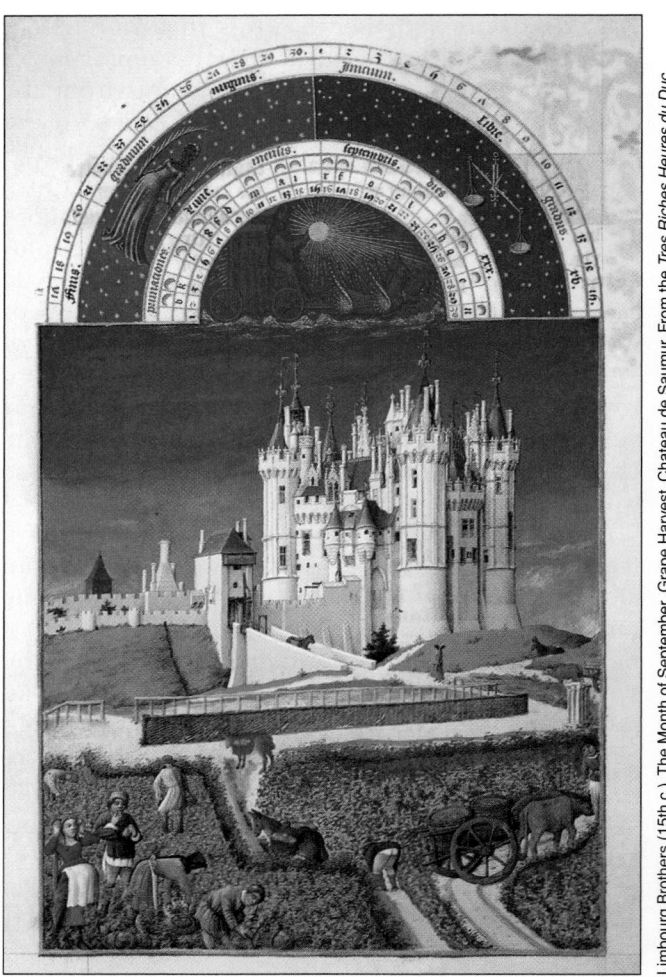

This illustration from a fifteenth-century French manuscript shows the sharp social divisions of late medieval Europe. In the forefront, a peasant family gathers in the grape harvest. The enormous fortified castle in the background was the home of an aristocratic family whose wealth derived in good part from the labor of peasants.

By the sixteenth century, the Catholic Church had accumulated enormous wealth and power. The pope wielded influence not only as a spiritual leader but also as the political ruler of parts of Italy. The church owned considerable property throughout Europe. Many Christians, especially in northern Europe, began to criticize the worldliness of the popes and the church itself for corruption, abuse of power, and betrayal of the legacy of Christ.

In 1517, a German monk, Martin Luther, invited open debate on a set of propositions critical of church practices and doctrines. Luther believed that the church had become too insistent on the performance of good works, such as charitable donations or other actions intended to please God. He called for a return to what he understood to be the purer practices and beliefs of the early church, emphasizing that salvation came not by good deeds but only by faith in God. With the help of the newly invented printing press, his ideas spread widely, inspiring a challenge to the Catholic Church that became known as the **Reformation**.

When the Catholic church refused to compromise, Luther and other critics withdrew to form their own religious organizations. Luther emphasized the direct, personal relationship of God to the individual believer. He urged people to take responsibility for their own spiritual growth by reading the Bible, which he translated for the first time into German. What started as a religious movement, however, quickly acquired an important political dimension.

Sixteenth-century Germany was a fragmented region of small kingdoms and principalities jealous of their independence. They were officially part of the Holy Roman Empire, but only loosely so, and many German princes resisted efforts by the Catholic empire to assert its authority. Realizing that religious protest reinforced their claims to independence, many princes supported Luther for both spiritual and secular reasons. When the Holy Roman Empire under Charles V (who was also king of Spain) tried to silence them, the reformist princes protested. From that point on, these princes—and all Europeans who supported religious reform—became known as **Protestants**.

The Protestant movement took a more radical turn under the influence of the French reformer John Calvin, who emphasized the doctrine of **predestination**. Calvin maintained that an all-powerful and all-knowing God chose at the moment of creation which humans would be saved and which would be damned. Each person's fate is thus foreordained, or predestined, by God, although we cannot know our fate during our lifetimes. Good Calvinists struggled to behave as God's chosen, continually searching their souls for evidence of divine grace.

Calvin founded a religious community consistent with his principles at Geneva, a Swiss city-state near the French border. Men who claimed to be "saints," or God's chosen people, led the city's government. They drove out nonbelievers, subjected all citizens to a rigid discipline, and made Geneva the center of Protestant reform in Europe. But neither Lutherans nor Calvinists could contain the powerful Protestant impulse. In succeeding years, other groups formed, split, and split again, increasing Europe's religious fragmentation.

From Germany and Geneva the Protestant Reformation spread to France, the Netherlands, Eng-

This 1568 woodcut of a European printshop shows workers setting type in the background, while the men in front print pages for a book. The invention of the printing press revolutionized European society, making information accessible to anyone who could read. During the Reformation, both Protestants and Catholics used the press to spread their views and attack their opponents.

land, and Hungary. The new religious ideas particularly interested literate city-dwellers, such as merchants and skilled artisans, who were attracted to Protestant writings as well as the sermons of Protestant preachers. Peasants adopted the new ideas more slowly, although German peasants, claiming Luther as inspiration, staged an unsuccessful revolt against their masters in 1524. Luther disavowed them, however, and supported the German princes in their brutal suppression of the revolt.

The Reformation addressed spiritual needs that the Catholic Church had left unfulfilled, but it also fractured the religious unity of western Europe and spawned a century of warfare unprecedented in its bloody destructiveness. Protestants fought Catholics in France and the German states. Popes initiated a "Counter-Reformation" to strengthen the Catholic Church—in part by internal reform and in part by persecuting its opponents and reimposing religious conformity. Europe thus fragmented into warring camps just at the moment when Europeans were coming to terms with their discovery of America and seeking ways to exploit its wealth.

CONTACT

Religious fervor, political ambition, and the desire for wealth propelled European nations into overseas expansion as well as conflict at home. Portugal, Spain, France, and England competed to establish footholds on other continents in an intense scramble for riches and dominance. The success of these early endeavors was a reflection of Europe's prosperity and a series of technological breakthroughs that enabled its mariners to navigate beyond familiar waters.

By 1600, Spain had emerged as the apparent winner among the European competitors for New World dominance. Its astonishingly wealthy empire included vast territories in Central and South America. The conquerors of this empire attributed their success to their military superiority and God's approval of their imperial ambitions. In reality, it was the result

Advances in ship design, including the development of the caravel pictured in this fifteenth-century woodcut, made transoceanic voyages possible. The arrangement of sails allowed the caravel to catch the trade winds and move more quickly across the high seas.

of a complex set of interactions with native peoples as well as an unanticipated demographic catastrophe.

THE LURE OF DISCOVERY

The potential rewards of overseas exploration captured the imaginations of a small but powerful segment of European society. Most people, busy making a living, cared little about distant lands. But certain princes and merchants anticipated spiritual and material benefits from voyages of discovery. The spiritual advantages included making new Christian converts and blocking Islam's expansion—a Christian goal that dated back to the eleventh-century Crusades against the Muslims in the Middle East and continued with the *reconquista*. On the material side, the voyages would contribute to Europe's prosperity by increasing trade.

Merchants especially sought access to Asian spices like pepper, cinnamon, ginger, and nutmeg that added interest to an otherwise monotonous diet and helped preserve certain foods. Wealthy Europeans paid handsomely for small quantities of spices, making it worthwhile to transport them great distances. But the overland spice trade—and the trade in other luxury goods such as silk and furs—spanned thousands of miles, involved many middlemen, and was controlled at key points by Muslim merchants. One critical center was Constantinople, the bastion of Christianity in the eastern Mediterranean. When it fell to the Ottomans—the Muslim rulers of Turkey—in 1453, Europeans feared that caravan routes to Asia would be disrupted. This encouraged merchants to turn westward and seek alternate routes.

The reorientation of European trade benefited western Italian cities such as Genoa as well as Portugal and Spain, whose ports gave access to the Mediterranean and the Atlantic Ocean. Mariners ventured farther into ocean waters, seeking direct access to the African gold trade and, eventually, a sea route around Africa to Asia. Had it not been for a set of technological developments that reduced the risks of ocean sailing, such lengthy voyages into unexplored areas would have been impossible.

Advances in navigation and shipbuilding. Ocean voyages required sturdier ships than those that plied the Mediterranean. Because oceangoing mariners traveled beyond sight of coastal features, they also needed reliable navigational tools. In the early fifteenth century, Prince Henry of Portugal, excited by the idea of overseas discovery, sponsored the efforts of shipbuilders, mapmakers, and other workers to solve these practical problems.

By 1500, enterprising artisans had made several important advances. Iberian shipbuilders perfected the caravel, a ship whose narrow shape and steering rudder suited it for ocean travel. Ship designers combined square sails (good for speed) with triangular lateen sails, which increased maneuverability. Two Arab inventions—the magnetic compass and the astrolabe (which allowed mariners to determine their position in relation to a star's known location in the sky)—gained popularity among European navigators. As sailors acquired practical experience on the high seas, mapmakers recorded their observations of landfalls, wind patterns, and ocean currents.

After Portugal's conquest of the Moroccan city of Ceuta in 1415, its mariners slowly worked their way along Africa's western coast, establishing trading posts where they exchanged European goods for gold, ivory, and slaves (see Map 1–3). Bartolomeu Días reached the southern tip of Africa in 1488. Eleven years later, Vasco da Gama brought a Portuguese fleet around Africa to India, opening a sea route to Asia. These initiatives gave Portugal a virtual monopoly on Far Eastern trade for some time.

The Atlantic islands and the slave trade.
The new trade routes gave strategic importance to the islands that lie in the Atlantic off the west coast of Africa and Europe. Spain and Portugal vied for control of the Canary Islands, located 800 miles southwest of the Iberian peninsula. Spain eventually prevailed in 1496 by defeating the islands' inhabitants. Portugal acquired Madeira and the Cape Verde Islands, along with a set of tiny islands off Africa's Guinea Coast.

Sugar, like Asian spices, commanded high prices in Europe, so the conquerors of the Atlantic islands began to cultivate sugar cane on them, on large plantations worked by slave labor. In the Canaries, the Spanish first enslaved the native inhabitants. When disease and exhaustion reduced their numbers, the Spanish brought in African slaves, often purchased from Portuguese traders. On uninhabited islands, the Europeans imported African slaves from the start. São Tomé and the other small islands off the Guinea Coast eventually became important way stations in the transatlantic slave trade.

These island societies, in which a small European master class dominated a much larger population of native peoples or imported African slaves, were to provide a model for Spain's and Portugal's later exploitation of their American colonies. In 1494, two years after his first voyage to the New World, Christopher Columbus wrote to Ferdinand and Isabella of Spain to suggest that Caribbean islanders could be sold as slaves in order to cover the costs of exploration. He found the inhabitants to be "a people very savage and suitable for the purpose, and well made and of very good intelligence." They "will be better than any other slaves," he went on, "and their inhumanity they will immediately lose when they are out of their own land."

CHRISTOPHER COLUMBUS AND THE WESTWARD ROUTE TO ASIA

Columbus's proposal revealed him to be very much a man of his time. Born in Genoa in 1451, he later lived in Portugal and Spain and as a young man visited Africa's Guinea Coast and Madeira. He was thus thoroughly familiar with slavery and regarded the enslavement of Caribbean islanders as an extension of established practice.

Columbus was also not the first European to believe that he could reach Asia by sailing westward. The idea developed logically during the fifteenth century as mariners gained knowledge and experience from their exploits in the Atlantic and around Africa. Columbus himself may have gained valuable experience on a voyage to Iceland. He also read widely in geographical treatises and paid close attention to the stories and rumors that circulated among mariners.

Most Europeans knew that the world was round, but most also scoffed at the idea of a westward voyage to Asia, believing that it would take so long that no ship could carry enough supplies. Columbus's confidence that he could make the voyage grew from a mathematical error. He mistakenly calculated the earth's circumference as 18,000 (rather than 24,000) miles and so concluded that Asia lay just 3,500 miles west of the Canary Islands. Columbus first sought financial support from the king of Portugal, whose advisers disputed his calculations and warned him that he would starve at sea before reaching Asia. Undaunted, he turned to Portugal's rival, Spain.

Columbus tried to convince Ferdinand and Isabella that his plan suited Spain's national goals. If he succeeded, Spain could grow rich from Asian trade, send Christian missionaries to Asia (a goal in keeping with the religious ideals of the *reconquista*), and perhaps enlist the Great Khan of China as an ally in the long struggle with Islam. If he failed, the "enterprise of the Indies" would cost little. The Spanish monarchs nonetheless kept Columbus waiting nearly seven years—until 1492, when the last Muslim stronghold at Granada fell to Spanish forces—before they gave him their support.

After thirty-three days at sea, Columbus and his men reached the Bahamas, probably landing on what is now called Watling Island. They spent four

MAP 1-3   European Voyages of Discovery in the Atlantic in the Fifteenth and Sixteenth Centuries
During the fifteenth and sixteenth centuries, Europeans embarked on voyages of discovery that carried them to both Asia and the Americas. Portugal dominated the ocean trade with Asia for most of this period. In the New World, reports of Spain's acquisition of vast wealth soon led France and England to attempt to establish their own territorial claims.

A decidedly European view of Columbus's landing on Guanahani appears in this late sixteenth-century print. Columbus and his men, armed with guns and swords, are resplendent in European attire, while nearly naked Indians offer them gifts. To the left, Spaniards erect a cross to claim the land for Christianity. In the upper right, frightened natives flee into the woods.

months exploring the Caribbean and visiting several islands, including Hispaniola (now the site of Haiti and the Dominican Republic) and Cuba. Although puzzled not to find the fabled cities of China or Japan, Columbus believed that he had reached Asia. Three more voyages, between 1493 and 1504, however, failed to yield clear evidence of an Asian landfall or samples of Asian riches. Columbus reported that the islands he encountered contained "great mines of gold and other metals" and spices in abundance, yet all he brought back to Isabella and Ferdinand were strange plants and animals, some gold ornaments, and several kidnapped Taino Indians.

Obsessed with the wealth he had promised himself and others, Columbus and his men turned violent, sacking the villages of Tainos and Caribs and demanding tribute in gold. But Caribbean gold reserves, found mainly on Hispaniola, Puerto Rico, and Cuba, were not extensive. The Spanish forced native gangs to pan rivers for the precious nuggets. Dissatisfied with the meager results, Columbus sought other sources of wealth. His plan to enslave islanders was a desperate attempt to show that the Indies could yield a profit. It earned him a sharp rebuke from Queen Isabella, who, at least initially, opposed enslaving people she considered to be new Spanish subjects. This royal fastidiousness was short-lived, however. Within thirty years of Columbus's first voyage, Spanish exploitation of native labor had brought the native populations of many Caribbean islands close to extinction.

Columbus died in Spain in 1506, still convinced he had found Asia. What he had done was to set in motion a process that would transform both sides of the Atlantic. It would eventually bring wealth to many Europeans and immense suffering to Native Americans and Africans.

THE SPANISH CONQUEST AND COLONIZATION

Of all European nations, Spain was best suited to take advantage of Columbus's discovery. Its experience with the *reconquista* gave it both a religious justification for conquest (bringing Christianity to nonbelievers) and an army of seasoned soldiers—*conquistadores*—eager to seek their fortunes in America now that the last Muslims had been expelled from Spain. In addition, during the *reconquista* and the conquest of the Canary Islands, Spain's rulers had developed efficient techniques for controlling newly conquered lands that could be applied to New World colonies.

The Spanish first consolidated their control of the Caribbean, establishing outposts on Cuba, Puerto Rico, and Jamaica (see Map 1–4). The *conquistadores*

First published in 1535, this woodcut shows Taino Indians panning for gold. Columbus and his men, desperate for riches to bring back to Spain but unaware that gold reserves on most Caribbean islands were quite small, compelled the Indians to search for the precious metal. After only a few decades of forced labor and harsh treatment, the native populations of the islands had all but disappeared.

MAP 1-4   **Spanish, English, and French Settlements in North America in the Sixteenth Century**
By the end of the sixteenth century, only Spain had established permanent settlements in North America. French outposts in Canada and at Fort Caroline, as well as the English settlement at Roanoke, failed to thrive. European rivalries for North America, however, would intensify after 1600.

were more interested in finding gold and slaves than in creating permanent settlements. Leaving a trail of destruction, they attacked native villages and killed or captured the inhabitants. By 1524, the Tainos had all but died out; the Caribs survived on more isolated islands until the eighteenth century. Spanish soldiers then ventured to the mainland. Juan Ponce de León led an expedition to Florida in 1513. In that same

year, Vasco Núñez de Balboa arrived in Central America, crossing the isthmus of Panama to the Pacific Ocean.

The end of the Aztec Empire.   In 1519, Hernán Cortés and six hundred soldiers—the light-skinned strangers who inspired the Indian messenger to rush to Moctezuma—landed on the coast of Mexico. Their subsequent actions more than fulfilled the Aztec king's belief that the Spaniards' arrival was an evil omen. "I and my companions," Cortés announced, "suffer from a disease of the heart which can be cured only with gold." By 1521, Cortés and his men had conquered the powerful Aztec empire. The Spanish soldiers also discovered riches beyond their wildest dreams. They "picked up the gold and fingered it like monkeys," reported one Aztec witness. They were "transported by joy, as if their hearts were illumined and made new."

The swift, decisive Spanish victory depended on several factors. In part, the Spanish enjoyed certain technological advantages. Their guns and horses often enabled them to overwhelm larger groups of Aztec foot soldiers armed with spears and wooden swords edged with obsidian. But technology alone cannot account for the conquest of a vastly more numerous enemy, capable of absorbing far higher losses in combat.

Cortés benefited from two other factors. First, he exploited divisions within the Aztec empire. The Spanish acquired indispensable allies among subject Indians who resented Aztec domination, tribute demands, and seizure of captives for religious sacrifice. Cortés led only six hundred Spanish soldiers but eventually gained 200,000 Indian allies eager to throw off Aztec rule.

A second and more important factor was disease. One of Cortés's men was infected with smallpox, which soon devastated the native population. European diseases had been unknown in the Americas, and Indians lacked resistance to them. Historians estimate that nearly 40 percent of the inhabitants of central Mexico died of smallpox within a year. Other diseases followed, including typhus, measles, and influenza. By 1600, the population of Mexico may have declined from over 15 million to less than a million people.

In this illustration from a Spanish monk's history of the Aztecs, Moctezuma observes a comet plummeting toward the earth, an omen that he believed presaged disaster for his people. The appearance of the comet coincided with the first reports of white-skinned strangers arriving on the coast of Mexico.

AMERICAN VIEWS

Cabeza de Vaca among the Indians (1530)

Álvar Núñez Cabeza de Vaca came to the New World in 1527 in search of riches, not suffering. But the Spanish expedition of which he was a member met disaster shortly after it arrived in Florida on a mission to conquer the region north of the Gulf of Mexico. Of an original group of three hundred soldiers, only Cabeza de Vaca and three other men (including one African slave) survived. They did so by walking thousands of miles overland from the Gulf Coast to northern Mexico, an eight-year-long ordeal that tested the men's wits and physical endurance. Instead of entering Indian villages as proud conquistadors, Cabeza de Vaca and his companions encountered native peoples from a position of weakness. In order to survive, they had to adapt to the ways of the peoples across whose land they passed. After Cabeza de Vaca made it back to Mexico City, he described his experiences in an official report to the King of Spain. This remarkable document offers vivid descriptions of the territory extending from northern Florida to northern Mexico and the many peoples who inhabited it. It is equally interesting, as this extract suggests, for what it reveals about Cabeza de Vaca himself and the changes he made in the interest of survival.

- While living among the Capoques, what sort of work did Cabeza de Vaca have to do, and why?
- Why did Cabeza de Vaca decide to become a merchant? What advantages did this way of life offer him?
- Why did the Indians welcome Cabeza de Vaca into their communities, even though he was a stranger?

Aztec society and culture collapsed in the face of appalling mortality. "The illness was so dreadful," one survivor recalled, "that no one could walk or move. The sick were so utterly helpless that they could only lie on their beds like corpses, unable to move their limbs or even their heads. . . . If they did move their bodies, they screamed with pain." The epidemic ravaged families, wiped out whole villages, and destroyed traditional political authority. Early in their bid to gain control of the Aztec empire, the Spanish seized Moctezuma, and eventually put him to death. They did not have to kill his successor, however, for he died of disease less than three months after gaining the throne.

The fall of the Inca Empire. In 1532, Francisco Pizarro and 180 men, following rumors of even greater riches than those of Mexico, discovered the Inca empire high in the Peruvian Andes. It was the largest empire in the Americas, stretching more than two thousand miles from what is now Ecuador to Chile. An excellent network of roads and bridges linked this extensive territory to the imperial capital of Cuzco. Economically prosperous from trade and agricultural production based on complex irrigation systems, the empire was also prone to political division. The Spaniards arrived at a moment of weakness for the empire. A few years before, the Inca ruler had died, probably from smallpox, and civil war had broken out between two of his sons. The victor, Atahualpa, was on his way from the empire's northern provinces to claim his throne in Cuzco when Pizarro intercepted him. Pizarro took Atahualpa hostage and despite receiving a colossal ransom—a roomful of gold and silver—had him killed. The Spaniards then captured Cuzco, eventually extended control over the whole empire, and established a new capital at Lima.

I had to stay with the Capoques more than a year. Because of the hard work they put me to, and their harsh treatment, I resolved to flee to the people of Charruco in the forests of the main.... My life had become unbearable. In addition to much other work, I had to grub roots in the water or from underground in the canebrakes. My fingers got so raw that if a straw touched them they would bleed. The broken canes often slashed my flesh; I had to work amidst them without benefit of clothes.

So I set to contriving how I might transfer to the forest-dwellers, who looked more propitious. My solution was to turn to trade.

[Escaping to Charruco about February 1530,] I did my best to devise ways of making my traffic profitable so I could get food and good treatment. The various Indians would beg me to go from one quarter to another for things they needed; their incessant hostilities made it impossible for them to travel cross-country or make many exchanges.

But as a neutral merchant I went into the interior as far as I pleased.... My principal wares were cones and other pieces of sea-snail, conchs used for cutting, sea-beads, and a fruit like a bean [from mesquite trees] which the Indians value very highly, using it for a medicine and for a ritual beverage in their dances and festivities. This is the sort of thing I carried inland. By barter I got and brought back to the coast skins, red ochre which they rub on their faces, hard canes for arrows, flint for arrowheads, with sinews and cement to attach them, and tassels of deer hair which they dye red.

This occupation suited me; I could travel where I wished, was not obliged to work, and was not a slave. Wherever I went, the Indians treated me honorably and gave me food, because they liked my commodities. They were glad to see me when I came and delighted to be brought what they wanted. I became well known; those who did not know me personally knew me by reputation and sought my acquaintance. This served my main purpose, which all the while was to determine an eventual road out.

Source: Cyclone Covey, ed., *Cabeza de Vaca's Adventures in the Unknown Interior of America*, pp. 66–67. Reprinted by permission of Scribner, a Division of Simon & Schuster. © 1961 by Macmillan Publishing Company.

By 1550, Spain's New World empire extended from the Caribbean through Mexico to Peru. It was administered from Spain by the Council of the Indies, which enacted laws for the empire and supervised an elaborate bureaucracy charged with their enforcement. The council aimed to project royal authority into every village in New Spain in order to maintain political control and extract as much wealth as possible from the land and its people.

For more than a century, Spanish ships crossed the Atlantic carrying seemingly limitless amounts of silver, gold, and jewels from the colonies. To extract this wealth, the colonial rulers subjected the native inhabitants of New Spain to compulsory tribute payments and forced labor. Tens of thousands of Indians toiled in silver mines in Peru and Bolivia and on sugar plantations in the Caribbean. When necessary, Spaniards imported African slaves to supplement a native labor force ravaged by disease and exhaustion.

Spanish incursions to the north. The desire for gold eventually lured Spaniards farther into North America. In 1528, an expedition to Florida ended in disaster when the Spanish intruders provoked an attack by Apalachee Indians. Most of the Spanish survivors eventually perished, but Álvar Núñez Cabeza de Vaca and three other men (including an African slave) escaped from their captors and managed to reach Mexico after a grueling eight-year journey. In a published account of his ordeal, Cabeza de Vaca insisted that the interior of North America contained a fabulously wealthy empire (see "American Views: Cabeza de Vaca among the Indians").

This report inspired other Spaniards to seek the treasures that had eluded its author. In 1539, Hernán de Soto—who tried unsuccessfully to get Cabeza de Vaca to serve as a guide—led an expedition from Florida to the Mississippi River. Along the way, the Spaniards harassed the native peoples, demanding provisions, burning villages, and capturing women to be servants and concubines. De Soto, who reportedly enjoyed "the sport of hunting Indians on horseback," ordered natives who resisted him to be mutilated, thrown to dogs, or burned alive. He and his men also exposed the Indians to deadly European diseases. Although weakened by native resistance, the expedition kept up its rampage for three years, turning toward Mexico only after de Soto died in 1542. In these same years, Francisco Vásquez de Coronado led three hundred troops on an equally destructive expedition through present-day Arizona, New Mexico, and Colorado on a futile search for the mythical Seven Cities of Cíbola, rumored to contain hoards of gold and precious stones.

The failure to find gold and silver halted the Spanish attempt to extend their empire to the north. By the end of the sixteenth century, they maintained just two precarious footholds north of Mexico. One was at St. Augustine, on Florida's Atlantic coast. Founded in 1565, this fortified outpost served as a naval base to defend Spanish treasure fleets from raids by English and French privateers. The other settlement was located far to the west in what is now New Mexico. Juan de Oñate, on a futile search for silver mines, claimed the region for Spain in 1598. He and his men proceeded to antagonize the area's inhabitants. In one surprise attack, the Spaniards destroyed the ancient town of Acoma, killing or enslaving most of the residents. Having earned the enmity of the Pueblo people—astonishing even his own superiors with his brutality—Oñate barely managed to keep his tiny colony together.

Almost from the start of the conquest, the bloody tactics of men such as Oñate aroused protest back in Spain. The Indians' most eloquent advocate was Bartolomé de Las Casas, a Dominican priest shamed by his own role (as a layman) in the conquest of Hispaniola. In 1516, the Spanish king appointed him to the newly created office of Protector of the Indians, but his efforts had little effect. To publicize the horrors he saw, Las Casas wrote *In Defense of the Indians,* including graphic descriptions of native sufferings. Instead of eliciting Spanish reforms, however, his work inspired Protestant Europeans to create the "Black Legend," an exaggerated story according to which a fanatical Catholic Spain sought to spread its control at any cost.

The seeds of economic decline.

Meanwhile, the vast riches of Central and South America glutted Spain's treasury. Between 1500 and 1650, an estimated 181 tons of gold and 16,000 tons of silver were shipped from the New World to Spain, making it the richest and most powerful state in Europe (see Figure 1–1). But this influx of American treasure had unforeseen consequences that would soon undermine Spanish predominance.

In 1492, the Spanish crown, determined to impose religious conformity after the *reconquista,* expelled from Spain all Jews who refused to become Christians. The refugees included many leading merchants who had contributed significantly to Spain's economy. The remaining Christian merchants, now awash in American riches, saw no reason

FIGURE 1-1   Value of New World Treasure Imported into Spain, 1506–1655
During the sixteenth and early seventeenth centuries, Spain was the only European power to reap great wealth from North America. The influx of New World treasure, however, slowed the development of Spain's economy in the long run. [Note: A ducat was a gold coin.]

Data Source: J.H. Elliott, *Imperial Spain, 1469–1716* (1964), p. 175.

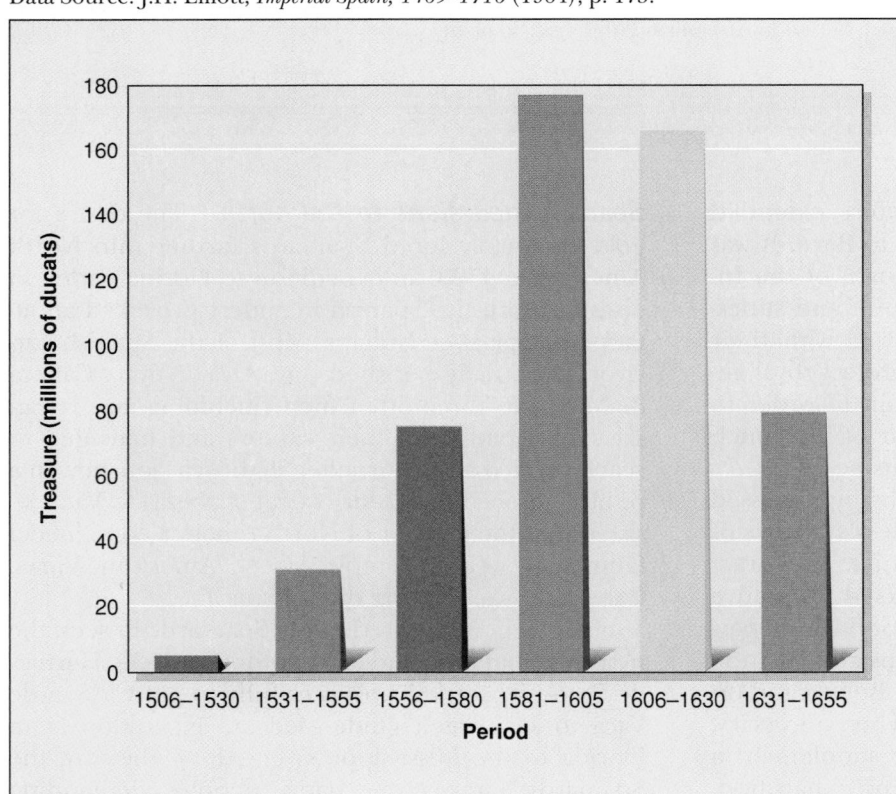

Overview

The Columbian Exchange

	From Old World to New World	From New World to Old World
Diseases	Smallpox, measles, plague, typhus, influenza, yellow fever, diphtheria, scarlet fever	Syphilis
Animals	Horses, cattle, pigs, sheep, goats, donkeys, mules, black rats, honeybees, cockroaches	Turkeys
Plants	Wheat, sugar, barley, coffee, rice, dandelion and other weeds	Maize, beans, peanut, potato, sweet potato, manioc, squash, papaya, guava, tomato, avocado, pineapple, chili pepper, cocoa

to invest in new trade or productive enterprises that might have sustained the economy once the flow of New World treasure diminished. As a result, Spain's economy eventually stagnated.

Compounding the problem, the flood of American gold and silver inflated prices throughout Europe, hurting both workers, whose wages failed to rise as fast, and aristocrats, who were dependent on fixed rents from their estates. Most damaging of all, Spain's monarchs wasted their American wealth fighting expensive wars against their European enemies that ultimately only weakened the nation. By 1600, some disillusioned Spaniards were arguing that the conquest had brought more problems than benefits to their country.

THE COLUMBIAN EXCHANGE

Spain's long-term economic decline was just one of many consequences of the conquest of the New World. The arrival of Europeans in America set in motion a whole series of changes. In the long run, the biological consequences of contact—what one historian has called the **Columbian Exchange**—proved to be the most momentous (see the Overview table, "The Columbian Exchange").

The most catastrophic result of the exchange was the exposure of Native Americans to Old World diseases. Europeans and Africans, long exposed to these diseases, had developed some immunity to them. Native Americans, lacking such contact, had not. The Black Death of 1347–1351, Europe's worst epidemic, killed perhaps a third of its population. Epidemics of smallpox, measles, typhus, and influenza struck Native Americans with far greater force, killing half, and sometimes as much as 90 percent, of the people in communities exposed to them. The only American disease to infect the Old World was syphilis, a serious but

far less catastrophic malady, which appeared in Spain just after Columbus returned from his first voyage.

Another important aspect of the Columbian exchange was the introduction of Old World livestock to the New World, which began when Columbus brought horses, sheep, cattle, pigs, and goats with him on his second voyage in 1493. Native Americans had few domesticated animals (mainly dogs, and, in the Peruvian Andes, llamas and alpacas). The large European beasts created problems as well as opportunities for native peoples. With few natural predators to limit their numbers, livestock populations boomed in the New World, competing with native mammals for grazing. At least at first, the Indians' unfamiliarity with the use of horses in warfare often gave mounted European soldiers a decisive military advantage. But some native groups adopted these animals for their own purposes. Yaquis, Pueblos, and other peoples in the Southwest began to raise cattle and sheep. By the eighteenth century, Plains Indians had reoriented their culture around the use of horses, which had become essential for travel, hunting buffalo, and carrying burdens. Horses also became a primary object for trading and raiding among Plains peoples.

European ships carried unintentional passengers as well. The black rat, a carrier of disease, arrived on the first voyages. So did insects, including honeybees, previously unknown in the New World. Ships also brought weeds such as thistles and dandelions, whose seeds were often embedded in hay for animal fodder.

Europeans brought a variety of seeds and plants in order to grow familiar foods. Columbus's men planted wheat, chickpeas, melons, onions, and fruit trees on Caribbean islands. Although they optimistically reported that crops "sprouted in three days and were ready to eat by the twenty-fifth day," they—and later colonists—often found that European plants

Smallpox wreaked havoc among Native Americans who lacked biological resistance to European diseases. This drawing by Aztec illustrators shows Aztec victims of a smallpox epidemic that struck Tenochtitlán in 1520. Historians estimate that up to 40 percent of the population of central Mexico died within a year. This catastrophic decline weakened the Aztecs' ability to resist the Spanish conquest of their land.

did not always grow quite so easily. As a result, Europeans learned to cultivate native foods, such as corn, tomatoes, squash, beans, and potatoes, as well as non-food plants such as tobacco and cotton. They carried many of these plants back to Europe, enriching Old World diets with new foods. By the late seventeenth century, potatoes had become the mainstay of the Irish diet. Throughout Europe, new foods contributed to a sharp rise in population—thus, in time, swelling the numbers of Europeans eager to leave their overcrowded communities for the New World.

CULTURAL PERCEPTIONS AND MISPERCEPTIONS

For thousands of years, Indian and European societies developed in isolation from one another. When members of these societies met for the first time, confusion inevitably resulted. Even simple transactions produced unexpected results. When Columbus showed swords to Caribbean islanders, for example, "they took them by the edge and through ignorance cut themselves" because they had never touched metal weapons. The first Indians whom Cortés allowed aboard a Spanish ship fainted at the sound of a large cannon being fired. French explorers were similarly taken by surprise when they choked while smoking

Iroquois tobacco, which they thought tasted like "powdered pepper." These were relatively minor mishaps and were soon overshadowed by more substantial interactions which seemed to exaggerate the differences between Indians and Europeans.

Religion was extremely important to both Native Americans and Europeans, but differences in forms and practices encouraged misunderstandings. Most Indians believed that the universe contained friendly and hostile spiritual forces in human and other-than-human forms (such as plants, animals, and stars). People interacted with the spirit world through ceremonies that often involved exchanging gifts and performing certain rituals. North of Mexico, Indians passed on religious beliefs through oral traditions, not in writing. To Europeans accustomed to worshiping one God in an organized church and preserving their beliefs in a written Bible, Indian traditions were incomprehensible. When Columbus noted that the Tainos on the Caribbean island of Guanahani had no churches, he concluded that "I do not detect in them any religion." Some Europeans, including Cortés, went further, assuming that Indians worshiped the Devil. Indians, in turn, often found Christianity confusing and at first rejected European pressure to convert. As some Iroquois explained to colonists, "We do not know that God, we have never seen him, we know not who he is."

Different understandings of the roles of men and women provided another source of confusion. Europeans assumed that men were naturally superior to women and should dominate them and rule society. They disapproved of the less rigid gender divisions among Native American peoples. Wampanoags and Powhatans sometimes accepted female leaders, for instance, and Huron women helped to select male chiefs. Many Indian societies, including the Pueblos, Hurons, and Iroquois, were matrilineal, tracing descent through the mother's family instead of the father's, as Europeans did. In matrilineal societies, married couples lived with the wife's family, children inherited property from their mother's brother, and rulers succeeded to their positions through their mother's family line. Europeans, accustomed to societies in which men did most agricultural work, also objected to Indian women's dominant role in farming and assumed that men's hunting was more for recreation than subsistence. They often concluded that Indian women lived "a most slavish life." Indians, in turn, sometimes thought that European men failed to make good use of their wives. In Massachusetts, some native men ridiculed colonists "for spoiling good working creatures" by not making their women work in the fields.

These were some of the many cultural differences that separated Indian and European societies. In order for natives and newcomers to get along peaceably with each other, each side would have to adapt to the new circumstances under which both groups now lived. At first, such harmony seemed possible. Columbus initially reported that the Taino Indians "became so much our friends that it was a marvel." But it soon became clear that Europeans intended to dominate the lands they discovered. Only three days after he arrived in America, Columbus announced his intention "not to pass by any island of which I did not take possession" and soon speculated on the possibility of enslaving Indians. Such claims to dominance sparked vigorous resistance from native peoples everywhere who strove to maintain their autonomy in a changed world.

COMPETITION FOR A CONTINENT

Spain's New World bonanza attracted the attention of other European states eager to share in the wealth. Portugal soon acquired its own profitable piece of South America. In 1494, the pope resolved the conflicting claims of Portugal and Spain with the **Treaty of Tordesillas**. The treaty drew a north–south line approximately 1,100 miles west of the Cape Verde Islands. Spain received all lands west of the line, while Portugal held sway to the east. This limited Portugal's New World empire to Brazil, where settlers followed the precedent of the Atlantic island colonies and established sugar plantations worked by slave labor. But the treaty also protected Portugal's claims in Africa and Asia, which lay east of the line.

France and England, of course, rejected the papal grant of the Western Hemisphere to Spain and Portugal. Their initial challenges to Spanish dominance in the New World, however, proved quite feeble. Domestic troubles—largely sparked by the Protestant Reformation—distracted the two countries from the pursuit of empire. By the close of the sixteenth century, both France and England insisted on their rights to New World lands, but neither had created a permanent settlement to support its claim.

EARLY FRENCH EFFORTS IN NORTH AMERICA

France was a relative latecomer to New World exploration. In 1494, French troops invaded Italy, beginning a long and ultimately unsuccessful war with the Holy Roman Empire. Preoccupied with European affairs, France's rulers paid little attention to America. But when news of Cortés's exploits in Mexico arrived in the 1520s, King Francis I wanted his own New World empire to enrich France and block further Spanish expansion.

In 1524, Francis sponsored a voyage by Giovanni da Verrazano, an Italian navigator, who mapped the North American coast from present-day South Carolina to Maine. During the 1530s and 1540s, the French mariner Jacques Cartier made three voyages in search of rich mines to rival those of Mexico and Peru. He explored the St. Lawrence River up to what is now Montreal, hoping to discover a water route through the continent to Asia (what came to be called the Northwest Passage). His second voyage, in 1535, nearly ended in disaster. Unaware of the harshness of Canadian winters, he and his crew almost froze to death and suffered from scurvy, a disease caused by a lack of vitamin C. Many men died, and the rest survived only because the Iroquois showed them how to make a vitamin-rich concoction of boiled white cedar needles and bark.

On his third voyage, in 1541, Cartier was to serve under the command of a nobleman, Jean-François de la Rocque, Sieur de Roberval, who was commissioned by the king to establish a permanent settlement in Canada. Troubles in recruiting colonists delayed Roberval, who—when he finally set sail in 1542—ended up taking convicts as his settlers. Cartier sailed ahead, gathered samples of what he thought were gold and diamonds, and returned to France without Roberval's permission.

This first attempt to found a permanent French colony failed miserably. Roberval's expedition was poorly organized, and his cruel treatment of the convicts provoked several uprisings. The Iroquois, suspicious of repeated French intrusions on their lands, saw no reason to help them. A year after they arrived in Canada, Roberval and the surviving colonists were back in France. Their return coincided with news that the gold brought back by Cartier was iron pyrite ("fool's gold") and the diamonds were worthless quartz crystals.

Disappointed with their Canadian expeditions, the French made a few brief forays to the south, establishing outposts in what is now South Carolina in 1562 and Florida in 1564. They soon abandoned the Carolina colony (though not before the starving settlers resorted to cannibalism), and Spanish forces captured the Florida fort. Then, back in France, a prolonged civil war broke out between Catholics and Protestants. Renewed interest in colonization would have to await the return of peace at home.

ENGLISH ATTEMPTS IN THE NEW WORLD

The English were quicker than the French to stake a claim to the New World but no more successful at colonization. In 1497, King Henry VII sent John Cabot, an Italian mariner, to explore eastern Canada on England's behalf. But neither Henry nor any of his wealthy subjects would invest the funds necessary to follow up on Cabot's discoveries. For nearly half a century, English contact with America was limited to the seasonal voyages of fishermen who lived each summer in Newfoundland, fished offshore, and returned in autumn with ships full of cod.

The lapse in English activity in the New World stemmed from religious troubles at home. Between 1534 and 1558, England changed its official religion several times. King Henry VIII, who had once defended the Catholic Church against its critics, took up the Protestant cause when the pope refused to annul his marriage to Catherine of Aragon. In 1534, Henry declared himself the head of a separate Church of England and seized the Catholic Church's English property. Because many English people sympathized with the Protestant cause, there was relatively little opposition to Henry's actions. But in 1553, Mary—daughter of the spurned Catherine of Aragon—became queen and tried to bring England back to Catholicism. She had nearly three hundred Protestants burned at the stake for their beliefs (earning her the nickname "Bloody Mary"), and many others went into exile in Europe.

After Mary's brief but destructive reign, which ended with her death in 1558, her half-sister Elizabeth, a committed Protestant, became queen. Elizabeth ruled for forty-five years (1558–1603), restoring Protestantism as the state religion, bringing stability to the nation, and renewing England's interest in the New World. She and her subjects saw colonization not only as a way to gain wealth and political advantage but also as a Protestant crusade against Catholic domination.

The Colonization of Ireland.
England's first target for colonization, however, was not America but Ireland. Located less than 60 miles west of England and populated by Catholics, Ireland threatened to be-

come a base from which Spain or another Catholic power might invade England. Henry VIII had tried, with limited success, to bring the island under English control in the 1530s and 1540s. Elizabeth renewed the attempt in the 1560s with a series of brutal expeditions that destroyed Irish villages and slaughtered the inhabitants. Several veterans of these campaigns later took part in New World colonization and drew on their Irish experience for guidance.

Two aspects of that experience were particularly important. First, the English transferred their assumptions about Irish "savages" to Native Americans. Englishmen in America frequently observed similarities between Indians and the Irish. "When they [the Indians] have their apparel on they look like Irish," noted one Englishman. "The natives of New England," he added, "are accustomed to build their houses much like the wild Irish." Because the English held the "wild Irish" in contempt, these observations encouraged them to scorn the Indians. When Indians resisted their attempts at conquest, the English recalled the Irish example, claiming that native "savagery" required brutal suppression.

Second, the Irish experience influenced English ideas about colonial settlement. English conquerors set up "plantations" surrounded by palisades on seized Irish lands. These plantations were meant to be civilized outposts in a savage land. Their aristocratic owners imported Protestant tenants from England and Scotland to farm the land. Native Irish people, considered too wild to join proper Christian communities, were excluded. English colonists in America followed this precedent when they established plantations that separated English and native peoples.

Expeditions to the New World.
Sir Humphrey Gilbert, a notoriously cruel veteran of the Irish campaigns, became fascinated with the idea of New World colonization. He composed a treatise to convince Queen Elizabeth to support such an endeavor. The queen, who counted Gilbert among her favorite courtiers, authorized several exploratory voyages, including Martin Frobisher's three trips in 1576–1578 in search of the Northwest Passage to Asia. Frobisher failed to find the elusive passage and sent back shiploads of glittering ore that proved to be fool's gold. Elizabeth had better luck in allowing privateers, such as John Hawkins and Francis Drake, to raid Spanish ships and New World ports for gold and silver. The plunder taken during these raids enriched both the sailors and their investors—one of whom was the queen herself.

Meanwhile, Gilbert continued to promote New World settlement, arguing that it would increase

England's trade and provide a place for the nation's unemployed people. Like many of his contemporaries, Gilbert believed that England's "surplus" population threatened social order. The population was indeed growing, and economic changes often made it difficult for people to support themselves. Many landlords, for instance, had been converting farmland into sheep pastures. They profited from the wool trade, but their decision threw tenant families off the land. Gilbert suggested offering free land in America to English families willing to emigrate.

In 1578, Gilbert received permission to set up a colony along the North American coast. It took him five years to organize an expedition to Newfoundland, which he claimed for England. After sailing southward seeking a more favorable site for a colony, Gilbert headed home, only to be lost at sea during an Atlantic storm. The impetus for English colonization did not die with him, however, for his half-brother, Sir Walter Raleigh (another veteran of the Irish wars), immediately took up the cause.

Algonquian Indian village of Pomeiooc, North Carolina: Watercolor, c. 1585 by John White.

John White's picture of the village of Pomeiooc offers a rare glimpse of a sixteenth-century Eastern Woodlands Indian community. The village is surrounded by a palisade with two entrances; evidence suggests that White exaggerated the spacing of the poles in order to depict the houses inside. Eighteen dwellings constructed of poles and mats are clustered around the village circumference; inside some of them raised sleeping platforms can be seen. Many of the villagers are clustered around a central fire, while others are working or conversing.

The Roanoke Colony.

In 1584, Raleigh sent an expedition to find a suitable location for a colony. Learning that the Carolina coast seemed promising, Raleigh sent men in 1585 to build a settlement on Roanoke Island. Most colonists were soldiers fresh from Ireland who refused to grow their own food, insisting that the Roanoke Indians should feed them. When the local chief, Wingina, organized native resistance, they killed him. Eventually, the colonists, disappointed not to have found gold or precious stones and exhausted by a harsh winter, returned to England in 1586.

Two members of these early expeditions, however, left a more positive legacy. Thomas Hariot studied the Roanoke and Croatoan Indians and identified plants and animals in the area, hoping that some might prove to be profitable commodities. John White drew maps and painted a series of watercolors depicting the natives and the coastal landscape. When Raleigh tried once more, in 1587, to found a colony, he chose White to be its leader.

This attempt also failed. The ship captain dumped the settlers—who, for the first time, included women and children—on Roanoke Island so that he could pursue Spanish treasure ships. White waited until his granddaughter, Virginia Dare (the first English child born in America), was safely born and then sailed to England for supplies. But the outbreak of war with Spain delayed his return for three years. Spain had gathered an immense fleet to invade England, and all English ships were needed for defense. Although England defeated the Armada in

FROM THEN TO NOW

The Disappearance of Cod off the Grand Banks

Not long after John Cabot returned from his voyage to America in 1497, rumors began to swirl in port towns and European capitals alike. The Italian mariner who had sailed on behalf of England, it was said, had discovered astonishingly rich fishing grounds. One envious diplomat reported to the duke of Milan that Cabot and his men had caught enormous numbers of cod simply by dropping weighted baskets into the sea. As it happened, Basque fishermen sailing from ports in northern Spain and southwestern France already knew about these fishing grounds. But Cabot's discovery spread the news and soon fishermen from all over western Europe scrambled to capture some of the bounty for themselves. By the 1550s, over a hundred ships a year traveled from French ports alone to fish in the waters of the Grand Banks off the coasts of Newfoundland and Labrador.

In 1994, on the eve of the five-hundredth anniversary of Cabot's historic voyage, Brian Tobin, a Canadian fisheries minister, reported that cod had become so scarce in the Grand Banks that fishing was no longer commercially viable. He announced that a moratorium on At-lantic cod fishing, first declared in 1992, would have to be extended. This measure was the latest in a series of efforts to address the decline in the cod population. In 1977, Canada's government had prohibited foreign fishing vessels from working within 200 miles of the Canadian coast. Nine years later, foreign boats fishing just beyond the 200-mile limit were no longer allowed to visit the city of St. John's in Newfoundland for repairs and supplies. Although these measures were designed mainly to protect Canadian fisheries from competition rather than to address issues of conservation, they clearly recognized that a valuable resource was in grave danger.

How had such abundant codfish stocks declined so dramatically? Ecological and historical factors combined to produce this result. Cod prefer to swim near the ocean floor in shallow waters, and migrate to even shallower places rich in plankton and krill—such as the Grand Banks—when they are ready to spawn. These locations are particularly vulnerable to climatic change, and that in turn affects the cod. Ten years after Canada de-

---

1588, White could not obtain a relief ship for Roanoke until 1590.

White found the colony deserted. Digging through the ruins of the village, he found "my books torn from the covers, the frames of some of my pictures and Maps rotten and spoiled with rain." He also saw the word CROATOAN carved on a post and assumed that the colonists had moved to nearby Croatoan Island. But bad weather prevented him from searching there. For years, English and Spanish mariners reported seeing white people along the coast of Chesapeake Bay. But no Roanoke colonists were ever found. They may have moved to the mainland and intermarried with local Indians. One historian has speculated that they survived until 1607 when Powhatan Indians, angered by the appearance of more English settlers, killed them. The actual fate of the "Lost Colony" at Roanoke will probably never be known.

At this point, Raleigh gave up on North America and turned his attention to his Irish plantations. But England's interest in colonization did not wane. In 1584, Richard Hakluyt had aroused enthusiasm for America by writing the *Discourse on the Western Planting* for the queen and her advisers. He argued that England would prosper from the expansion of trade and the sale of New World commodities. Once the Indians were civilized, Hakluyt added, they would eagerly purchase English goods. Equally important, England could plant "sincere religion" (that is, Protestant Christianity) in the New World and prevent the power of "the Spanish king from flowing over all the face . . . of America."

clared the moratorium on fishing, cod populations on the Grand Banks have yet to rebound. Some scientists speculate that the depletion of the Earth's ozone layer may be allowing ultraviolet rays to penetrate shallower ocean waters, killing off young cod at a high rate.

Centuries of fishing have also taken their toll. Cabot's voyage sparked tremendous interest in the Grand Banks fisheries. By the middle of the sixteenth century, 60 percent of all the fish eaten in Europe was cod, and most of it came from the Grand Banks region. English and French fishing enterprises found particularly lucrative markets in Mediterranean countries, whose primarily Catholic populations had to abstain from eating meat on Fridays and during the six weeks of Lent because of religious restrictions. By the eighteenth century, New England colonists, plying the waters off their own coast as well as near the Grand Banks, had initiated a thriving trade with the West Indies, where planters purchased relatively cheap salted cod to feed their slaves. After the Revolution, victorious Americans insisted that Great Britain recognize their "right to take fish of every kind on the Grand Bank." This provision became part of the 1783 Treaty of Paris, testify-ing to the continued significance of the fishing industry.

Economic competition also encouraged technological developments. By the early nineteenth century, most fishermen had switched from using handlines—single baited hooks fastened to a weight and dropped in the water—to longlines, consisting of ropes anywhere from half a mile to four or more miles long, with baited hooks attached every three feet or so. Gill nets, positioned just above the ocean floor to catch "ground feeders" like cod, eventually made enormous catches possible. These changes, combined with the transition from sailing vessels to boats using first steam power and then diesel fuel, spelled doom for the once-plentiful supplies of cod on the Grand Banks.

Experts differ on whether cod populations can recover. In addition to the possible effects of climatic change, cod continue to be threatened by overfishing. In February of 2002, Canadian officials investigated reports of foreign boats ignoring the moratorium on cod and infringing on the 200-mile limit. The long-term legacy of John Cabot's voyage may well be the disappearance of the resource that drew him and so many early European adventurers to North America in the first place.

Hakluyt's arguments fired the imaginations of many people, and the defeat of the Spanish Armada only emboldened England to challenge Spain's New World dominance. The experience of Roanoke should have tempered that enthusiasm, illustrating the problems as well as benefits of colonization. The colony's fate underscored the need for adequate funding, the unsuitability of soldiers as colonists, and the need to maintain good relations with the Indians. But the English were slow to learn these lessons; when they resumed colonization efforts in 1607, they repeated Roanoke's mistakes, with disastrous results for the people involved. As it was, the sixteenth century ended with no permanent English settlement in the New World.

CONCLUSION

Dramatic changes occurred in North America during the century after Moctezuma's messenger spotted the Spanish ships. Europeans, eager for wealth and power, set out to claim a continent that just a hundred years earlier they had not dreamed existed. African slaves were brought to the Caribbean, Mexico, and Brazil, and forced to labor under extremely harsh conditions for white masters in unfamiliar lands. The Aztec and Incan empires collapsed in the wake of the Spanish conquest. In the Caribbean and parts of Mexico and Peru, untold numbers of native peoples succumbed to European diseases they had never before encountered.

And yet conditions in 1600 bore clearer witness to the past than to the future. Despite all that had happened, North America was still Indian country. Only Spain had established North American colonies, and even its soldiers struggled to expand north of Mexico. Spain's outposts in Florida and New Mexico staked claims to territory that it did not really control. Except in Mexico and the Caribbean, Europeans had merely touched the continent's shores—often only briefly. In 1600, despite the virulent epidemics, native peoples (even in Mexico) still greatly outnumbered European and African immigrants. The next century, however, brought many powerful challenges both to native control and to the Spanish monopoly of settlement.

REVIEW QUESTIONS

1. How did the Aztecs who first glimpsed Spanish ships off the coast of Mexico describe to Moctezuma what they had seen? What details most captured their attention?

2. Compare men's and women's roles in Native American, West African, and European societies. What were the similarities and differences? How did differences between European and Native American gender roles lead to misunderstandings?

3. Many of the first European colonizers in North America were military veterans. What impact did this have on their relations with Indian peoples?

4. Why did Spain so quickly become the dominant colonial power in North America? What advantages did it enjoy over France and England?

5. What role did religion play in early European efforts at overseas colonization? Did religious factors always encourage colonization, or did they occasionally interfere with European expansion?

KEY TERMS

Aztecs (p. 7)

Cahokia (p. 8)

Columbian Exchange (p. 25)

Predestination (p. 15)

Protestants (p. 15)

Reconquista (p. 14)

Reformation (p. 15)

Tordesillas, Treaty of (p. 27)

RECOMMENDED READING

Covey, Cyclone, ed. *Cabeza de Vaca's Adventures in the Unknown Interior of America* (1998). A remarkable account of the Spanish explorer's harrowing eight-year-long journey from Florida to Mexico.

Hassig, Ross. *Mexico and the Spanish Conquest* (1994). A brief account of Cortés's expedition, focusing on the military aspects of the Spanish conquest.

Josephy, Alvin M., Jr. *America in 1492: The World of the Indian Peoples before the Arrival of Columbus* (1991). A collection of essays describing the wide variety of Indian cultures in North America prior to contact with Europeans.

Leon-Portillo, Miguel. *The Broken Spears: The Aztec Account of the Conquest of Mexico* (1962). Reprints of translated Indian chronicles, providing a moving account of the Aztec experience of the Spanish conquest.

Phillips, William D., Jr., and Carla Rahn Phillips. *The Worlds of Christopher Columbus* (1992). A judicious biography of Columbus that places him firmly in the context of fifteenth-century European culture.

Thornton, John. *Africa and Africans in the Making of the Atlantic World, 1400–1680*, 2nd ed. (1998). A thorough examination of the causes and consequences of the movement of Africans throughout the Atlantic world and the rise of the slave trade.

ADDITIONAL SOURCES

Native American Cultures

Bragdon, Kathleen J. *Native People of Southern New England, 1500–1650* (1996).

Clendinnen, Inga. *Aztecs: An Interpretation* (1991).

Fagan, Brian M. *Ancient North America: The Archaeology of a Continent*, 3rd ed. (2000).

Fiedel, Stuart J. *Prehistory of the Americas*, 2nd ed. (1992).

Jennings, Francis. *The Founders of America: How Indians Discovered the Land, Pioneered in It, and Created Great Classical Civilizations . . .* (1993).

Milner, George. *The Cahokia Chiefdom: The Archaeology of a Mississippian Society* (1998).

Rouse, Irving. *The Tainos: Rise and Decline of the People Who Greeted Columbus* (1992).

West African Society

Bohannan, Paul, and Curtin, Philip. *Africa and Africans*, 3rd ed. (1988).

Fage, J. D. *A History of West Africa: An Introductory Survey*, 4th ed. (1969).

Olaniyan, Richard, ed. *African History and Culture* (1982).

Reader, John. *Africa: A Biography of the Continent* (1998).

Europe in the Age of Discovery

Bainton, Roland H. *Here I Stand: A Life of Martin Luther* (1955).

Braudel, Fernand. *The Mediterranean and the Mediterranean World in the Age of Philip II*, 2nd ed. (1966; English trans., 1972).

Canny, Nicholas. *Making Ireland British, 1580–1650* (2000).

Cantor, Norman F. *In the Wake of the Plague: The Black Death and the World It Made* (2001).

Cipolla, Carlo M. *Guns, Sails, and Empire: Technological Innovation and the Early Phases of European Expansion, 1400–1700* (1965).

Elliott, J. H. *Imperial Spain, 1469–1716* (1964).

Lewis, Bernard. *Cultures in Conflict: Christians, Muslims, and Jews in the Age of Discovery* (1995).

Morison, Samuel Eliot. *The European Discovery of America: The Northern Voyages*, A.D. *500–1600* (1971).

Morison, Samuel Eliot. *The European Discovery of America: The Southern Voyages*, A.D. *1492–1616* (1974).

Scammell, G. V. *The First Imperial Age: European Overseas Expansion, c. 1400–1715* (1989).

Conquest and Colonization

Andrews, Kenneth R. *Trade, Plunder, and Settlement: Maritime Enterprise and the Genesis of the British Empire, 1480–1630* (1984).

Crosby, Alfred W., Jr. *Ecological Imperialism: The Biological Expansion of Europe, 900–1900* (1986).

De Las Casas, Bartolomé. *Short Account of the Destruction of the Indies* (several editions).

Eccles, W. J. *France in America*, rev. ed. (1990).

Elliott, J. H. *The Old World and the New, 1492–1650* (1970).

Hudson, Charles. *Knights of Spain, Warriors of the Sun: Hernando de Soto and the South's Ancient Chiefdoms* (1997).

Kupperman, Karen Ordahl. *Roanoke: The Abandoned Colony* (1984).

Meinig, D. W. *The Shaping of America*, Vol. 1: *Atlantic America, 1492–1800* (1986).

Seed, Patricia. *Ceremonies of Possession in Europe's Conquest of the New World 1492–1640* (1995).

Todorov, Tzvetan. *The Conquest of America* (1984).

Weber, David J. *The Spanish Frontier in North America* (1992).

Where to Learn More

- **Cahokia Mounds State Historic Site, Collinsville, Illinois.** This site, occupied from A.D. 600-1500, was the largest Mississippian community in eastern North America. It now includes numerous exhibits, and archaeological excavations continue in the vicinity. The website, www.siue.edu/CAHOKIAMOUNDS, contains information and photos of archaeological excavations, as well as a link to a virtual tour.

- **Mashantucket Pequot Museum, Mashantucket, Connecticut.** This tribally owned and operated complex offers a view of eastern Woodlands Indian life, focusing on the Pequots of eastern Connecticut. Exhibits include dioramas, films, interactive programs, and a reconstructed sixteenth-century Pequot village. The homepage for the Mashantucket Pequot Museum and Research Center is www.mashantucket.com.

- **Mesa Verde National Park, Colorado.** Occupied by Ancestral Puebloan peoples as early as A.D. 550, the area contains a variety of sites, from early pithouses to spectacular cliff dwellings. The official National Park webpage for Mesa Verde is www.nps.gov/meve. Information on individual houses and sites within the park, plus travel and lodging information can be found at www.mesa.verde.national-park.com.

- **St. Augustine, Florida.** Founded in 1565, St. Augustine is the site of the first permanent Spanish settlement in North America. Today the restored community resembles a Spanish colonial town, with narrow, winding streets and seventeenth- and eighteenth-century buildings. The site also contains the restored Castillo de San Marcos, now a national park. The official website for Historic St. Augustine, www.oldcity.com/his2.html, provides considerable information about the origins and development of the Spanish settlement.

 Please refer to the document CD-ROM for primary sources related to this chapter.

→ *The unknown artist who painted this portrait of Elizabeth Freake and her daughter Mary*
(c.1671) captured the quiet elegance of prosperous second-generation New Englanders. The
wife of a successful merchant, Mrs. Freake wears a pearl necklace and a skirt edged with gold
embroidery. Her collar, and her baby's bonnet and sleeves, are edged with fine Dutch lace.

Oil on canvas, 42 1/2 x 36 3/4 in. (108 x 93.4 cm). Worcester Art Museum. Worcester, Massachusetts.

TRANSPLANTATION
1600–1685

2

Boston in New England

March 28, 1631

To the Right Honorable my very good lady, the Lady Bridget, Countess of Lincoln,

Madam:

I have . . . thought fit to commit to memory our present condition and what hath befallen us since our arrival here . . . . [I] must do [so] rudely, having yet no table nor other room to write in than by the fireside upon my knee in this sharp winter. . . .

[In] April 1630 we set sail from old England with four good ships. And in May following, eight more followed, two having gone before in February and March and two more following in June and August, besides another set out by a private merchant. These seventeen ships arrived all safe in New England for the increase of the plantation here this year 1630, but made a long, a troublesome and costly voyage, being all windbound long in England and hindered with contrary winds after they set sail, and so scattered with mists and tempests that few of them arrived together. . . .

[Once we disembarked in mid-June, after more than nine weeks at sea] we began to consult of the place of our sitting down, for Salem, where we landed, pleased us not. And to that purpose some were sent to the Bay to search

CHAPTER OUTLINE

The French in North America
The Quest for Furs and Converts
The Development of New France

The Dutch Overseas Empire
The Dutch East India Company
The West India Company and New Netherland

English Settlement in the Chesapeake
The Ordeal of Early Virginia
The Importance of Tobacco
Maryland: A Refuge for Catholics
Life in the Chesapeake Colonies

The Founding of New England
The Pilgrims and Plymouth Colony
Massachusetts Bay Colony and Its Offshoots
Families, Farms, and Communities in Early New England

Competition in the Caribbean
Sugar and Slaves
A Biracial Society

The Proprietary Colonies
Early Carolina: Colonial Aristocracy and Slave Labor
Pennsylvania: The Dream of Toleration and Peace
New Netherland Becomes New York

Conclusion

up the rivers for a convenient place. . . . [We] found a place . . . three leagues up Charles river, and thereupon unshipped our goods into other vessels and with much cost and labor brought them in July to Charlestowne, but there receiving advertisements by some of the late arrived ships from London and Amsterdam of some French preparations against us . . . we were forced to change counsel and for our present shelter to plant dispersedly. . . . This dispersion troubled some of us, but help it we could not. . . . The best counsel we could find out was to build a fort to retire to, in some convenient place, if an enemy pressed thereunto, after we should have fortified ourselves against the injuries of wet and cold.

Everett Emerson, ed., *Letters from New England: The Massachusetts Bay Colony, 1629–1638* (Amherst, 1976).

Thomas Dudley, the man who wrote this letter, was 54 years old when he decided to move with his family to New England. He had reached an age when most men avoided making such major changes in their lives. Married for 27 years, Thomas and his wife Dorothy had six children ranging in age from 9 to 25 years old. Dudley had prospered in England by working as a steward for local aristocrats, including the Countess of Lincoln to whom he addressed his letter. A man of talent and education, he had been chosen to serve as deputy governor of the new colony of Massachusetts. Eager as he was to see the colony succeed, Dudley worried that it might not survive its first months.

The Countess of Lincoln, reading this letter in the warmth of her grand home, could not help but sense the contrast between her comfortable situation and the hardships Dudley endured. Neither could she miss the deputy governor's preoccupation with the French, who had established a colony in Canada. Remote as they were from England and Europe, the English colonists worried more about Old World enemies than about hostile reactions from the Indians whose lands they now occupied.

Rumors of a French attack sparked concern that Massachusetts would make an easy target if all settlers clustered in a single community. So Dudley and his companions planted "dispersedly" in seven towns around Boston Harbor and agreed to seek shelter in the hastily-constructed fort should French ships appear over the horizon.

The Dudleys ended up in Newtown (now Cambridge) and not only survived but prospered. Thomas Dudley went on to serve four terms as governor and accumulate a large estate to bequeath to his seven surviving children. He died in July 1653 at the age of 76, an unusually long life span for the seventeenth century. But Dudley could not have predicted such a happy outcome in the first difficult months following his voyage to America. His journey took place at a time of increased rivalry among European nations for New World territory. England's greatest adversaries were France and the Netherlands. Each nation scrambled to claim pieces of the North American mainland and islands in the Caribbean, hoping to match Spain's earlier success. As Thomas Dudley's letter suggests, this international race for overseas possessions was never far from colonists' minds.

KEY TOPICS

- Development of New France
- The Dutch Empire and New Netherland
- Diversity of English colonies in the seventeenth century
- Growth of staple crop economies in the southern and Caribbean colonies
- Role of religion in the founding of colonies
- Creation of biracial slave societies in the West Indies and Carolina

Chronology

1603–1625	James I reigns as king of England.
1607	Founding of English colonies at Jamestown and Sagadahoc.
1608	Establishment of French colony at Quebec.
1619	First Africans arrive in Jamestown.
	Virginia's House of Burgesses meets for the first time.
1620	Founding of Plymouth Colony in New England.
	Mayflower Compact signed.
1620s	Tobacco boom in Virginia.
1624	Dutch found colony of New Netherland.
1625	Virginia becomes a royal colony.
	Fort Amsterdam founded.
1625–1649	Charles I reigns as king of England.
1627	English colony at Barbados founded.
1630	Massachusetts Bay Colony founded.
1630–1642	Great Migration to New England.
1634	Lord Baltimore (Cecilius Calvert) founds proprietary colony of Maryland.
1635–1636	Roger Williams banished from Massachusetts, founds Providence, Rhode Island.
1637	Anne Hutchinson banished from Massachusetts.
	Pequot War.
1638	New Haven colony founded.
1640s	Sugar cultivation and slavery established in West Indies.
1642–1660	English Civil War and Interregnum.
1649	Maryland's Act for Religious Toleration.
1660	Charles II restored to English throne; reigns until 1685.
1663	Founding of Carolina colony.
1664	New Netherland conquered by the English, becomes New York.
	New Jersey established.
1673	French explorers reach the Mississippi River.
1681	Founding of Pennsylvania.

THE FRENCH IN NORTH AMERICA

In the mid-sixteenth century, religious warfare between Catholics and Protestants at home had interrupted France's efforts to establish a foothold in North America. So long as this conflict divided the nation, the only French subjects who maintained regular contact with the New World were fishermen making seasonal voyages to the bountiful waters of the Grand Banks off the coast of Newfoundland. But in the early seventeenth century, once King Henry IV restored civil order in France, the situation changed dramatically. With the creation of permanent settlements first along the St. Lawrence River and later in the continent's interior, France staked its claim to an expansive and profitable New World empire.

THE QUEST FOR FURS AND CONVERTS

French fishermen who set up frames on the Newfoundland shore to dry their catch frequently encountered Indians interested in trading beaver pelts for European goods. There was a ready market for these furs in Europe, where broad-brimmed beaver hats had become highly fashionable. Thus furs joined fish as a source of wealth, and a reason for French explorers and entrepreneurs to establish the colony of New France.

In 1608, Samuel de Champlain led an expedition more than 130 miles up the St. Lawrence River to found a permanent settlement at Quebec. This village was eventually joined by two others—Trois-Rivières (founded 1634) and Montreal (1642)—located farther up the river (see Map 2–1). For several decades, the colony was managed by the Company of New France, a private corporation working on its own behalf as well as in France's imperial interests. At first New France grew slowly; by the 1660s, there were only 3,200 colonists clustered in and around the three main villages.

The fur trade supporting the colony's development functioned as a partnership between Indians and Europeans. Indians performed most of the work–trapping beavers, preparing skins, carrying pelts from the interior to trading posts along the St. Lawrence–in return for axes, knives, metal pots, and glass beads. At first, some colonists anticipated that economic ties between the two peoples would be supplemented by marital ones, as French traders

MAP 2-1 New France, c. 1650
By 1650, New France contained a number of thinly populated settlements along the St. Lawrence River Valley and the eastern shore of Lake Huron. Most colonists lived in Quebec and Montreal; other sites served mainly as fur-trading posts and Jesuit missions to the Huron Indians.

took Indian wives. Intermarriage, however, was never widespread, occurring mainly among *coureurs de bois* ("woods runners"), independent fur traders who ventured into the forests to live and trade among native peoples. Much to the consternation of colonial officials, these traders often seemed to abandon their French ways for Indian ones.

Indian peoples such as the Montagnais and Hurons welcomed the French not only as trading partners, but also as military allies, making sure that the newcomers understood that the two roles had to be linked. As a result, the fur trade entangled the French in rivalries among Indian groups that long predated European contact. Champlain's alliance with the Hurons and other St. Lawrence Valley Indians drew the French into conflict with their Iroquois enemies, forcing colonial authorities for more than a century thereafter to engage in delicate diplomatic maneuvers to ensure New France's security.

For some French colonists, saving Indian souls was even more important than profiting from furs. Beginning in the 1630s, Jesuit missionaries—members of a Catholic religious order founded during the Counter-Reformation—tried to convince Indians to come to the French settlements to hear

Christian preaching and learn European ways. When that tactic failed, Jesuits traveled to native villages and learned native languages, bringing Christianity directly to Indian populations.

At times, this strategy aroused Indian suspicions. Jesuits who baptized dying victims of epidemics raised fears that the priests themselves might have caused the outbreak of disease. By the 1650s, however, the Jesuits claimed to have produced thousands of genuine converts, some of whom formed separate native Christian communities. They also publicized extraordinary examples of Indian piety, particularly the story of Kateri Tekakwitha. An orphaned Mohawk girl who joined the Christian Indian village of Kahnawake, Tekakwitha sparked a religious revival among other female converts and went on to become the first Native American candidate for sainthood.

THE DEVELOPMENT OF NEW FRANCE

After 1663, New France underwent several important changes. Keen on asserting his royal authority, King Louis XIV disbanded the Company of New France and assumed direct control of the colony, entrusting one of his key ministers, Jean-Baptiste Colbert, with its administration. Political reorganization followed. New France was henceforth ruled by two royal appointees: a governor charged with military and diplomatic affairs, and an *intendant* who oversaw colonial finances and the judicial system. The French government also vastly improved Canada's military defenses, investing money in the construction of forts and sending several companies of professional soldiers. This was a greater investment in defense than English kings would provide for their colonies until the middle of the eighteenth century.

The king and Colbert launched a massive campaign to increase French migration to the colony. Colbert arranged to send over 700 women—called *filles du roi*, or king's daughters—to provide wives in a colony where there were six men of marriageable age for every unmarried French woman. Many male immigrants were *engagés*, or **indentured servants** who agreed to work for three years in return for food, lodging, a small salary, and a return passage to France.

Despite these efforts, only about 250 French immigrants arrived each year. Several factors contributed to this reluctance to emigrate, not least of which was Canada's reputation as a distant and inhospitable place. "Canada has always been regarded as a country at the end of the world," admitted one official. Rumors

Because Indians expected their trading partners also to be military allies, Europeans were often drawn into native conflicts. This illustration, from Samuel de Champlain's 1613 description of the founding of New France, shows him joining his Huron allies in an attack on the Iroquois.

about frigid winters and surprise Indian attacks dissuaded many potential colonists. In addition, the government required settlers to be Catholic (although Protestants often resided in Canada temporarily), reducing the pool from which colonists could be recruited. In the end, nearly three out of four immigrants who went to Canada returned home.

By 1700, the population had increased to about 15,000 (less than 7 percent of the English population in the mainland colonies that year; see Figure 2-1), mostly clustered in the three major towns along the St. Lawrence. This growth testified to a remarkable level of natural increase. Because land for farms was readily available, couples faced few obstacles in supporting themselves. Since *engagés* could not marry until their labor contracts had expired, men tended to wed around the age of 28. Intense competition for marriageable women drove the average age for brides before 1660 down to as young as 16. It was not unknown for some women to bear ten or even fifteen children. As late as 1666, only one out of three French settlers were women, and very few women failed to find husbands. Some who remained single chose to do so, preferring a religious vocation with the Ursulines or one of the other orders of nuns, devoting their energies to teaching or administering care to the sick and indigent.

Many families established farms along the St. Lawrence river, producing wheat and other provisions mostly for local consumption. Often the land was technically owned by a gentleman, or *seigneur*, who received a rent payment. *Seigneurs* claimed other privileges, including rights to fishing and timber, and collected other fines and taxes. Though powerful, these gentlemen never enjoyed anything comparable to the status of aristocrats with vast estates back in France.

French officials sought to restrict settlement to the St. Lawrence Valley, fearing that further expansion would render the empire impossible to defend. The impetus to move inland however, could not be restrained. By the 1670s, French traders and missionaries had reached the Mississippi river. In 1681–82, Robert, Sieur de La Salle, followed the Mississippi to the Gulf of Mexico, claiming the entire valley (which he named Louisiana in honor of the king) for France. When officials tried to restrict the direct trade between Indians and the *coureurs de bois,* many of these Frenchmen simply drifted off to settle in what eventually became known as the *pays des Illinois* along the Mississippi. This expansion of French influence alarmed the English, who had founded colonies along the Atlantic seaboard and feared a growing French presence in the west.

Prosperous and expansive, if not completely manageable from Paris, Canada provided France with a secure foothold on the North American mainland. Its successful establishment contributed to an escalating European competition for land and trade in the New World. It would not be long before new rivals entered onto the scene.

THE DUTCH OVERSEAS EMPIRE

Small but densely populated, the Dutch Republic joined the scramble for empire in the early seventeenth century. The Northern Provinces, sometimes known as Holland, had declared their independence from Spain (whose kings ruled the region as leaders of the Holy Roman Empire) in 1581, although sporadic fighting continued for another half-century. The new republic, dominated by Protestants, was intent on challenging Catholic Spain's power for religious as well as

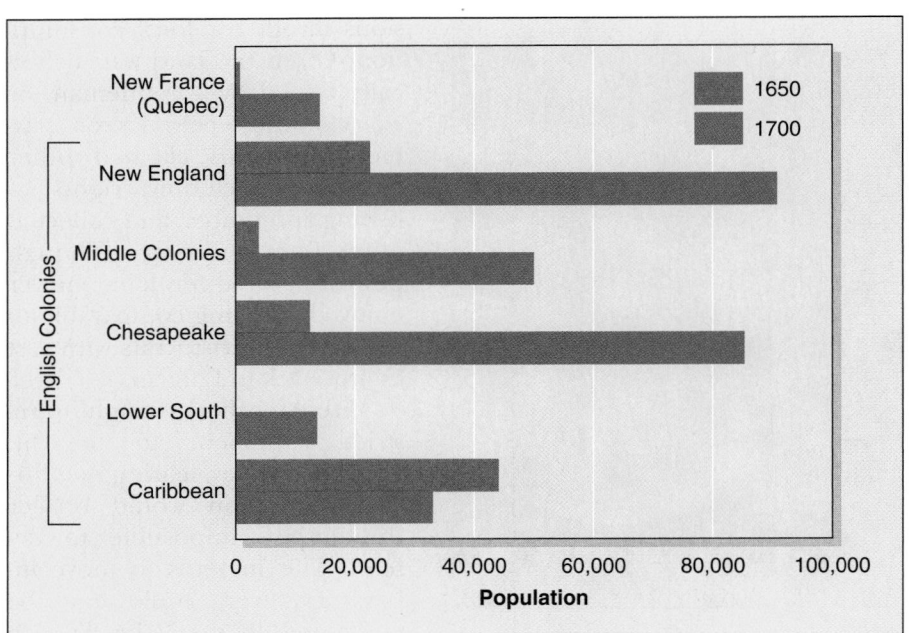

FIGURE 2-1 **European Populations of New France (Quebec) and English Colonies in 1650 and 1700**
Although New France's population grew rapidly between 1650 and 1700, it remained only a tiny fraction of the population of England's North American colonies. By 1700, English colonists on the mainland outnumbered New France's inhabitants by a factor of about 16 to 1.

Data Source: From John J. McCusker and Russell R. Menard, *The Economy of British America, 1607–1789* (1985). The University of North Carolina Press.

political reasons in the New World as well as the Old. More than any other factor, however, the desire for profit drove the Dutch quest for colonies.

THE DUTCH EAST INDIA COMPANY

By 1600, the Dutch had become the leading economic power in Europe. Skilled craftsmen specialized in the production of fine textiles, jewelry, glass, and colored tiles, making the Republic the dominant manufacturing center on the Continent. Amsterdam emerged as a key financial capital, particularly after the Bank of Amsterdam was founded in 1609. The centerpiece of Dutch prosperity, however, was commerce, which expanded dramatically in the first decades of the seventeenth century.

The Dutch Republic served as a major center of world trade. Bulk goods such as grain, salt, lumber, and fish arrived from the Baltic countries. Merchants established an equally lucrative trade in luxury items, including sugar, dyestuffs, wine, and other Mediterranean products. By 1590, the Dutch had supplanted the English as primary traders with Russia for timber and furs. Before long, thousands of Dutch ships plied the world's oceans and the Republic's earnings from foreign trade may have surpassed those of the rest of Europe combined. This commercial vitality provided the context for overseas expansion.

The instrument of colonial dominance was the Dutch East India Company, founded in 1602. Eager to reap profits from spices and other exotic goods,

the Company challenged what had until then been a virtual Portuguese monopoly of Asian trade. Its first success was the capture of the Spice Islands (now Indonesia and East Timor), followed by the takeover of Batavia (Jakarta), Ceylon (Sri Lanka), and Sumatra. The Company established trading posts on the Gold Coast of West Africa, where it competed with the Portuguese in the slave trade, and at the Cape of Good Hope on Africa's southern tip. Its far-flung commercial net eventually encompassed parts of India and Formosa (Taiwan). These possessions sealed Dutch trading predominance for decades to come.

THE WEST INDIA COMPANY AND NEW NETHERLAND

The Dutch next set their sights on the Americas, creating the West India Company in 1621. After taking control of West African slave-trading posts and temporarily occupying part of Brazil, the West India Company moved into the Caribbean (acquiring four islands by the 1640s) and North America. Its claim to the Connecticut, Hudson, and Delaware valleys stemmed from the 1609 voyage of Henry Hudson, an Englishman sailing for the Dutch, who discovered the river that bears his name.

The first permanent Dutch settlers on mainland North America arrived in 1624 to set up a fur-trading post at Fort Orange (now Albany). Two years later, Peter Minuit and a company of Protestant refugees established New Amsterdam on Manhattan Island, which Minuit had purchased from the Indians. The

Cornelius de Zeeuw depicted a prosperous Dutch merchant family in this sixteenth-century painting. The arrangement of figures indicates the hierarchies of gender and age that prevailed in Dutch society, while the family members' serious expressions suggest their strict Calvinist beliefs.

Hudson River corridor between these two settlements became the heart of the New Netherland colony. Like New France, its economic focus was the fur trade. Dutch merchants forged ties with the Iroquois, who brought furs to exchange for European tools and weapons.

In the 1630s, to help supply colonial traders, the West India Company offered large landed estates (called patroonships) to wealthy Dutchmen who would be responsible for populating them with tenant farmers. The plan never really worked, in part because most would-be patroons disliked company-imposed limits on their rights, and in part because few Dutch people wanted to emigrate only to live as peasants. At its peak, New Netherland's colonists only numbered about ten thousand.

What they lacked in numbers the colonists made up for in divisiveness. New Netherland became a magnet for religious refugees from Europe, as well as a destination for Africans acquired through the slave trade. (In 1638, about 100 Africans—free and slave—lived in New Amsterdam, constituting nearly a third of that city's population.) Ethnic differences hindered a sense of community. In 1643, a French Jesuit visitor reported hearing at least eighteen languages spoken on the streets of New Amsterdam. Among the colony's Dutch, German, French, English, Swedish, Portuguese, and African settlers were Calvinists, Lutherans, Quakers, Catholics, Jews, and Muslims.

The West India Company, more interested in making money than keeping order, dispatched several inept but aggressive governors who made an unstable situation worse by provoking conflict with Indians. Although colonists generally maintained good relations with their Iroquois trading partners on the upper Hudson River, they had far less friendly dealings with Algonquian peoples around New Amsterdam. In one particularly gruesome incident in 1645, Governor Willem Kieft ordered a massacre at an encampment of Indian refugees who

This engraving depicts New Amsterdam in 1643 as a bustling port. The figures of African laborers in the background attest to the importance of slavery in the Dutch colonial city, where perhaps a quarter of the residents had been born in Africa.

had refused to pay tribute. A horrified Dutch witness described Indian children being "thrown into the river, and when the fathers and mothers endeavored to save them, the soldiers would not let them come on land, but made both parents and children drown." He saw victims "with their hands, some with their legs cut off, and some holding their entrails in their arms." Ten years later, Governor Peter Stuyvesant antagonized Susquehannock Indians along the Delaware River by seizing a small Swedish colony where the Susquehannocks had traded.

Such actions provoked retaliatory raids by the Indians, further weakening the colony. Though profitable, the fur trade did not generate the riches to be found in other parts of the Dutch empire. By the 1650s and 1660s, New Netherland increasingly looked like a poor investment to company officials back in Europe.

ENGLISH SETTLEMENT IN THE CHESAPEAKE

Following the Roanoke colony's disappearance after 1587 (see Chapter 1), twenty years passed before the English again attempted to settle in America. When they did, in 1607, it was in the lower Chesapeake Bay region. The new settlement, Jamestown, at first seemed likely to share Roanoke's dismal fate. But it endured, eventually developing into the prosperous colony of Virginia. The reason for Virginia's success was an American plant—tobacco—that commanded good prices from European consumers. Tobacco also underlay the economy of a neighboring colony, Maryland, founded by English settlers on the northern and eastern shores of Chesapeake Bay, and had a profound influence on the development of Chesapeake society.

THE ORDEAL OF EARLY VIRGINIA

In 1606, several English merchants, convinced that they could succeed where others had failed, petitioned King James I for a charter incorporating two companies to attempt New World settlement. One, the London, or Virginia, Company, included merchants from the city of London; the other, the Plymouth Company, included merchants from England's western ports. James I issued a charter granting the companies two tracts of land along the mid-Atlantic coast but refrained from investing any money himself in such a risky enterprise. These **joint-stock compa-**

nies sold shares to investors (who expected a profit in return) to raise money for colonization.

The Jamestown colony. Three small ships carried 104 settlers, all men, to the mouth of Chesapeake Bay in May 1607 (see Map 2–2). On a peninsula about fifty miles up a river they named the James in honor of their king, the colonists built a fortified settlement they called Jamestown. Hoping to earn quick profits for Virginia Company investors, they immediately began hunting for gold and exploring the James in search of the Northwest Passage to Asia. But Jamestown was no Mexico. All they found was disappointment and suffering. The swampy region was a perfect breeding area for malarial mosquitoes and parasites carrying other diseases. Spending all their time in search of riches, the settlers neglected to plant crops, and their food sup-

MAP 2-2 English and Dutch Mainland Colonies in North America, c. 1655
Early English colonies clustered in two areas of the Atlantic seaboard—New England and the Chesapeake Bay. Between them lay Dutch New Netherland, with settlements stretching up the Hudson River. The Dutch also acquired territory at the mouth of the Delaware River in 1655 when they seized a short-lived Swedish colony located there.

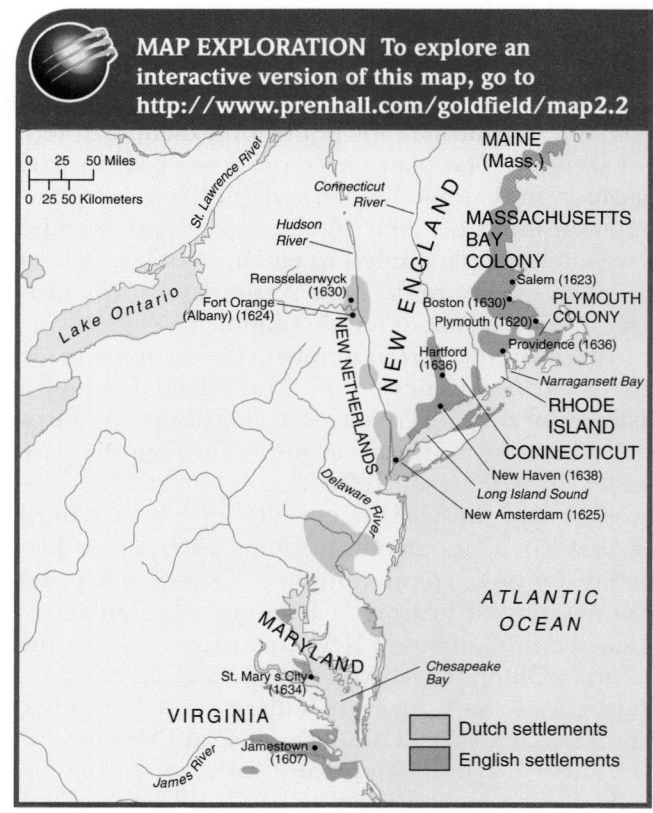

MAP EXPLORATION To explore an interactive version of this map, go to http://www.prenhall.com/goldfield/map2.2

plies dwindled. By January 1608, only thirty-eight colonists were still alive.

After the disastrous first year, the colony's governing council turned to Captain John Smith for leadership. Just 28 years old, Smith was a seasoned adventurer who had fought against Spain in the Netherlands and the Ottoman Turks in Hungary. He imposed military discipline on Jamestown, organizing settlers into work gangs and decreeing that "he that will not worke shall not eate." His high-handed methods revived the colony but antagonized certain settlers who believed that their social status exempted them from manual labor and who bristled at taking orders from a man of lower social rank. When a gunpowder explosion wounded Smith in 1609 and forced him to return to England, his enemies had him replaced as leader.

Once again, the colony nearly disintegrated. Shiploads of new settlers arrived, only to starve or die of disease. Of the five hundred people in Jamestown in the autumn of 1609, just sixty remained alive by the spring of 1610—some of whom survived only by eating their dead companions. Facing financial ruin, company officials back in England tried to conceal the state of the colony. They reorganized the company twice and sent more settlers, including glassmakers, winegrowers, and silkmakers, in a desperate effort to find a marketable colonial product. They experimented with harsh military discipline, instructing governors to enforce a legal code—the *Lawes Divine, Morall and Martiall*—that prescribed the death penalty for offenses as trivial as swearing or killing a chicken. When it became clear that such severity discouraged immigration, the company tried more positive inducements.

The first settlers had been expected to work together in return for food and other necessities; only Company stockholders were to share in the colony's profits. But surviving settlers wanted land, so governors began assigning small plots to those who finished their terms of service to the company. In 1616, the company instituted the **headright system**, giving 50 acres to anyone who paid his own way to Virginia and an additional 50 for each person (or "head") he brought with him.

In 1619, three other important developments occurred. That year, the company began transporting women to become wives for planters and induce them to stay in the colony. It was also the year in which the first Africans arrived in Virginia. In addition, the company created the first legislative body in English America, the **House of Burgesses**, setting a precedent for the establishment of self-government in other English colonies. Landowners elected representatives to the House of Burgesses, which, subject to the approval of the company, made laws for Virginia. In 1621 the *Lawes Divine, Morall and Martiall* gave way to a code based on English common law.

Despite these changes, the settlers were still unable to earn the company a profit, and life in the colony barely improved. To make things worse, the headright system expanded English settlement beyond Jamestown. This strained the already tense relations between the English and the Indians onto whose lands they had intruded.

The Powhatan Confederacy and the colonists.

When the English arrived in 1607, they planted their settlement in the heart of territory ruled by the Indian leader Powhatan, who was then at the peak of his power. Chief of a confederacy of about thirty tribes with some fourteen thousand people, including 3,200 warriors, Powhatan had little to fear at first from the struggling English outpost. After an initial skirmish with English soldiers, he sent gifts of food, assuming that by accepting the gifts, the colonists acknowledged their dependence on him. Further action against the settlers seemed unnecessary, because they seemed fully capable of destroying themselves.

This conclusion was premature. Armed colonists began seizing corn from Indian villages whenever the natives refused to supply it voluntarily. During one raid in 1609, John Smith held a pistol to the chest of Opechancanough, Powhatan's younger brother, until the Indians ransomed him with corn. Protesting that the English came "to invade my people and possesse my Country," Powhatan besieged Jamestown and tried to starve the colony to extinction. The colony was saved by the arrival of reinforcements from England, but war with the Indians continued until 1614.

The marriage of the colonist John Rolfe to Pocahontas, Powhatan's daughter, helped seal the peace in 1614. Pocahontas had briefly been held captive by the English during the war and had been instructed in English manners and religion by Rolfe. Sent to negotiate with Powhatan in the spring of 1614, Rolfe asked the chief for his daughter's hand. Powhatan gave his consent, and Pocahontas—baptized in the Church of England and renamed Rebecca—became Rolfe's wife.

Powhatan died in 1618, and Opechancanough succeeded him as chief. Still harboring intense resentment against the English, the new chief made plans for retaliation. Pocahontas had died on a trip to England in 1617, severing the tie between her family and the English. With new settlers arriving each year and the ranks of his warriors depleted by

This illustration shows John Smith seizing the scalplock of Opechancanough, Chief Powhatan's brother, during an English raid on an Indian village. Smith released his prisoner only after Indians ransomed him with corn. Thirteen years later, Opechancanough led a surprise attack against the colonists.

the ravages of European diseases, Opechancanough could not wait long to act. Early in the morning on March 22, 1622, hundreds of Indian men traveled to the scattered English settlements, as if they meant to visit or trade. Instead, they attacked the unsuspecting colonists, killing 347 by the end of the day—more than one-fourth of the English population.

Opechancanough assumed that the survivors would recognize his authority and confine themselves to trading posts in Jamestown. Instead, they plotted revenge. Believing that "now we have just cause to destroy them by all meanes possible," English forces struck at native villages, killing the inhabitants and burning cornfields. At peace talks held in April 1623, the English served poisoned wine to their enemies, killing two hundred more. During the ensuing nine years of war, the English treated the In-dians with a ferocity that recalled their earlier subjugation of the Irish.

Although Opechancanough's attack failed to restrain the colonists, it destroyed the Virginia Company. Economic activity ceased as settlers retreated to fortified garrisons. The company went bankrupt, and a royal commission investigating the 1622 attack was shocked to discover that nearly ten times more colonists had died from starvation and disease than at the hands of Indians. King James had little choice but to dissolve the company in 1624, and Virginia became a royal colony the following year. The settlers continued to enjoy a measure of self-government through the House of Burgesses, but now the king chose the colony's governor and council, and royal advisers monitored its affairs.

THE IMPORTANCE OF TOBACCO

Ironically, the demise of the Virginia Company helped the colony succeed. In their search for a marketable product, settlers had begun growing tobacco after 1610. Europeans had acquired a taste for tobacco in the late sixteenth century when the Spanish brought samples from the West Indies and Florida. Initially expensive, it became popular among wealthy consumers. The high price appealed to Virginians, but they found that native Virginia leaf was of poor quality. John Rolfe began experimenting with seeds from Trinidad, which did much better. The first cargo of Virginia-grown tobacco arrived in England in 1617 and sold at a highly profitable 3 shillings per pound.

Settlers immediately planted tobacco everywhere—even in the streets of Jamestown. Company officials, unwilling to base the colony's economy on a single crop, tried to restrict annual production to 100 pounds per person. Colonists, busy "rooting in the ground about Tobacco like Swine" as one observer reported, ignored these restrictions. But it was only after company rule ended that tobacco planting really surged.

Between 1627 and 1669, annual tobacco exports climbed from 250,000 pounds to more than 15 million pounds. As the supply grew, the price per pound plunged from 13 pence in 1624 to a mere penny in the late 1660s, where it remained for the next half century. What had once been a luxury product thus became affordable for Europeans of average means. Now thoroughly dependent on tobacco for their livelihood, the only way colonists could compensate for falling prices was to grow even more, pushing exports to England to more than 20 million pounds per year by the late 1670s (see Figure 2-2).

Virginia-grown tobacco found a ready market among European consumers such as this contemplative smoker. As tobacco prices declined during the seventeenth century due to increased production, even people of modest means could take up the habit of smoking.

Tobacco shaped nearly every aspect of Virginia society, from patterns of settlement to the recruitment of colonists. Planters scrambled to claim lands near navigable rivers so that ships could easily reach their plantations and carry their crops to market. As a result, the colonists dispersed into plantations located along waterways—wherever, one governor wrote, "a choice veine of rich ground invited them, and further from neighbours the better." Colonists competed to produce the biggest and best crop and get it to market the fastest, hoping to enjoy even a small price advantage over everyone else.

The key to success was to control a large labor force. Tobacco kept workers busy nine months of the year. Planters sowed seeds in the early spring, transplanted seedlings a few weeks later, and spent the summer pinching off the tops of the plants (to produce larger leaves) and removing worms. After the harvest, the leaves were "cured"—dried in ventilated sheds—and packed in large barrels. During the winter, planters cleared and fenced more land and made barrels for next year's crop. Working on his own, one planter could tend two thousand plants, which yielded about 500 pounds of cured tobacco. Early on, when the price was high, this supplied a comfortable income. But as the price plummeted, planters could keep up only by producing more tobacco, and to do that they needed help.

The planters turned to England, importing thousands of indentured servants, or contract workers, who agreed to a fixed term of labor, usually four to seven years, in exchange for free passage to Virginia. The master provided food, shelter, clothing, and, at the end of the term of service, "freedom dues" paid in corn and clothing. Between 1625 and 1640, an estimated one thousand or more indentured servants arrived each year. Some were orphans; others were condemned criminals given a choice between execution and transportation to Virginia. The vast majority, however, came from the ranks of England's unemployed, who emigrated in hopes of "bettering their condition in a Growing Country."

Most found such hopes quickly dashed. Servants died in alarming numbers from disease, and those who survived faced years of backbreaking labor. Masters squeezed as much work out of them as possible with long hours and harsh discipline. Some servants died from mistreatment. Richard Price beat his servant, Endymion Inleherne, for "being a common runaway and one that did use to feign himself sick," so severely that the young man died. A jury refused to charge Price with murder, reasoning that Inleherne deserved punishment and Price had not intended to kill him. Few masters matched Price's cruelty, but because the courts (administered by masters) favored masters' authority over servants' rights, those who did generally escaped prosecution.

New obstacles faced servants who managed to survive their terms of indenture. For every ex-servant who became a landholder, dozens died in poverty. To prevent freed servants from becoming economic rivals, established planters avoided selling them good land, particularly after tobacco prices hit bottom in the 1660s. Many ex-servants found land only in places less suitable for tobacco cultivation and more vulnerable to Indian attack. Forced to choose between eking a "poor living with hard labor out of the ground in a terrible Wilderness" or giving up all hope for ownership and either becoming ten-

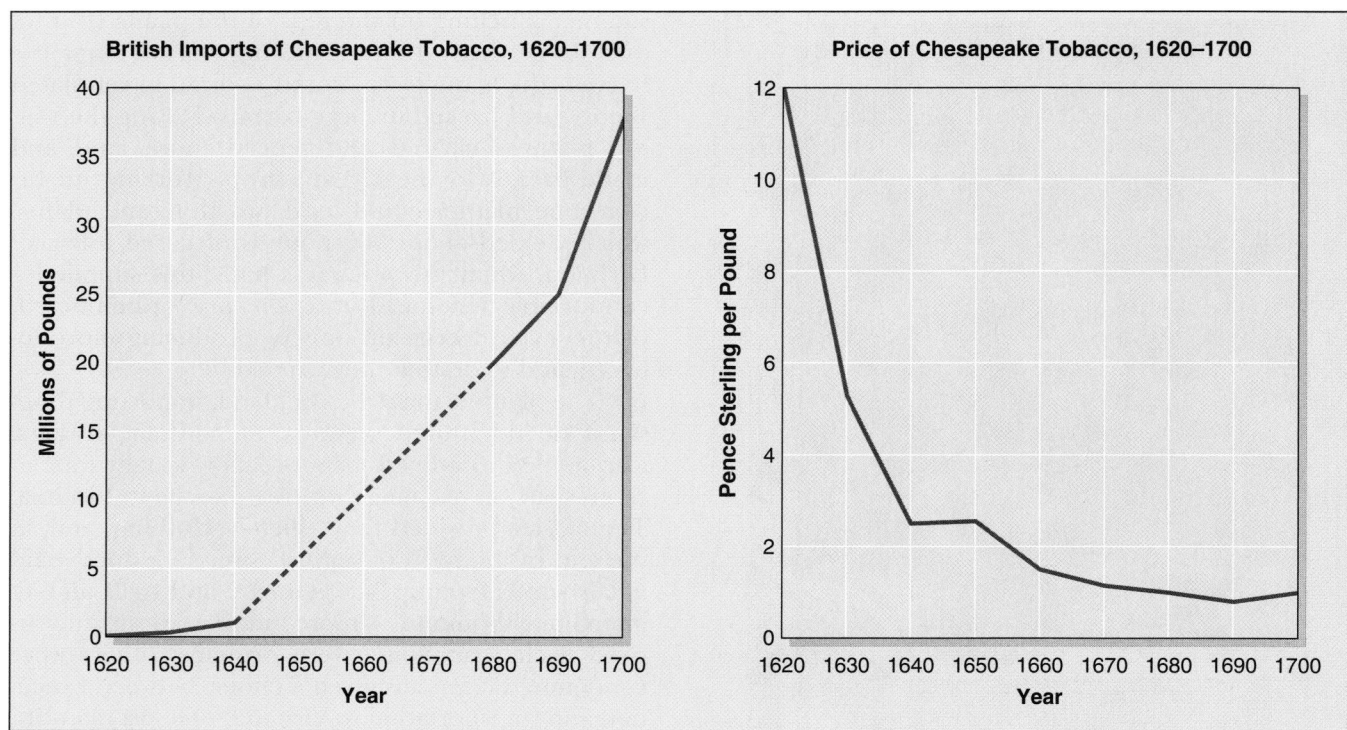

FIGURE 2-2 The Supply and Price of Chesapeake Tobacco, 1620–1700
*Tobacco cultivation dominated the economy of the Chesapeake region throughout the
seventeenth century. As planters brought more and more land under cultivation, the amount of
tobacco exported to Britain shot up and the price plummeted. (As the dashed line indicates, no
data on tobacco imports are available for the years 1640–1680.)*

Data Source: From Russell R. Menard, "The Tobacco Industry in the Chesapeake Colonies,
1617–1730: An Interpretation," *Research in Economic History, 5* (1980), app. Jai Press, Inc.

ants or laborers, ex-servants were a discontented
group. In 1675, their discontent would flare into rebellion (discussed in Chapter 3).

MARYLAND: A REFUGE FOR CATHOLICS

The success of tobacco in Virginia encouraged further English colonization in the Chesapeake Bay region. In 1632, King Charles I granted 10 million acres
of land north of the bay to the nobleman George
Calvert, Lord Baltimore. Unlike Virginia, which was
founded by a joint-stock company, Maryland was a
proprietary colony—the sole possession of Calvert
and his heirs. They owned all the land, which they
could divide up as they pleased, and had the right to
set up the colony's government.

Calvert, who was Catholic, intended Maryland to
be a refuge for others of his faith. When Queen Elizabeth's accession made England a Protestant nation,
Catholics became a disadvantaged minority. They
paid double taxes and could not worship in public,
hold political office, or send their children to univer-

sities. In Maryland, Calvert wanted Catholic colonists
to enjoy economic and political power. He intended
to divide the land into manors—large private estates
like those of medieval England—and distribute them
to wealthy Catholic friends. These manor lords
would live on rents collected from tenant farmers,
hold the most important governmental offices, and
run their own law courts.

Calvert died before settlement began, and it was
the sad fate of his son, Cecilius, to see his father's plans
unravel. The majority of colonists, who began arriving
in 1634, were Protestants who despised Catholics. Refusing to live as tenants on Catholic estates, they
claimed land of their own—a process that accelerated
after 1640, when Maryland adopted a headright system like Virginia's as a way to recruit settlers.

Maryland's problems intensified when civil war
broke out in England in 1642. For years, political
and religious disputes had divided the nation.
Charles I, who became king in 1625, clashed with
Puritans who called for further reform of the
Church of England. He also antagonized many gov-

ernment leaders by dissolving Parliament in 1629 and ruling on his own for eleven years. Needing funds to suppress a rebellion in Scotland in 1640, however, Charles was forced to recall Parliament. Its leaders, sympathetic to the Puritan cause, quickly turned against him. Both king and Parliament recruited armies and went to war in 1642. Parliamentary forces triumphed, and in 1649, they executed Charles. For the next decade, England was governed as a protectorate, not a monarchy. Oliver Cromwell, a Puritan general, ruled until his death in 1658. His son, Richard, proved an inept successor, however, and in 1660 a group of army officers invited Charles's exiled son to accept the throne.

During the 1640s and 1650s, Maryland Protestants took advantage of the upheaval in England to contest the Calverts' control of the colony. To pacify them, Cecilius Calvert established a legislature, assuming that Protestants would dominate the elective lower house while he could appoint Catholics to the upper house. In 1649, Calvert also approved the **Act for Religious Toleration**, the first law in America to call for freedom of worship for all Christians, but even this brought no peace. The Protestant majority, supported during the 1650s by Cromwell and Parliament, continued to resist Catholic political influence, at one point passing a law that prohibited Catholics from voting.

Instead of the peaceful Catholic refuge Calvert intended, Maryland soon resembled neighboring Virginia. Its settlers raised tobacco and imported as many indentured servants as possible. Because Maryland initially provided freed servants with 50 acres of land, more became landholders than in Virginia. As in Virginia, however, economic opportunity diminished after 1660 when the price of tobacco dropped. Maryland's settlers enjoyed more peaceful relations with the Indians than Virginians had, but they fought intensely among themselves. Throughout the seventeenth century, Protestants kept up their opposition to the proprietor's control of land and political power and resisted all attempts by Catholics to govern the colony that was supposed to have been theirs.

LIFE IN THE CHESAPEAKE COLONIES

Few people could have predicted how much life in the Chesapeake colonies would differ from England. Many of those differences stemmed from the region's distinctive population. Because of their labor needs, masters preferred to recruit young men in their teens and twenties as indentured servants, importing three or four times as many of them as women. As a result,

the populations of Virginia and Maryland were overwhelmingly young and male. Even as late as 1700, Virginia had three English men for every two women.

As a consequence of this gender imbalance, many male ex-servants found that marriage was as remote a possibility as landownership. Very few chose Indian wives: John Rolfe's union with Pocahontas was one of only three English-Indian marriages in seventeenth-century Virginia. One planter suggested that, in contrast to Englishmen's experience, the Chesapeake was a "paradise for women" because their scarcity made them the object of men's competition. While few unmarried women failed to find husbands, and widows usually remarried soon after their spouses' deaths, their lives were hardly easy.

Malaria and other diseases inflicted hardship on nearly everyone. Few colonists lived past 50, and women's susceptibility to disease during pregnancy meant that many of them barely made it to 40. Such high mortality, combined with late marriages (because servants could not wed until their terms were up), limited the size of families and thus slowed population growth from natural increase. As many as one out of four children died in their first year, and more than half failed to reach the age of 20.

Under such conditions, the only way the populations of the Chesapeake colonies could grow during most of the seventeenth century was through continued heavy importation of servants. The number of English settlers rose from about 8,000 in 1640 to 24,000 in 1660. Still mostly young and mostly male, the immigrants helped the region's distinctive demographic patterns persist until the end of the century.

These conditions hindered colonists from reproducing customary patterns of family life. The frequency of early death produced unusual households, containing various combinations of stepparents and children from different marriages living under the same roof. There were so many orphans in Maryland that the colony created special courts to protect whatever property they might have inherited. Many women would be widows at some point in their lives, which gave them temporary control over the family property. Husbands often arranged for their widows to manage their estates, until such time as the eldest son reached age 21. Few women ever received land outright, and if widows remarried, their new spouses usually took control of the estates left by their first husbands. As in England itself, the Chesapeake colonies accorded women little formal authority within society.

The precariousness of life encouraged settlers to invest every penny of profit in land and labor, postponing investment in goods that would bring a more comfortable existence. Early houses were often no larger than 16 by 20 feet, with one or two rooms. Poor settlers slept on the floor on straw mattresses and had few other furnishings—often not even a chair or bench to sit on. Rich planters owned more goods, but often of poor quality. In 1655, for instance, William Brocas, a prominent colonial official, owned several curtains "very thin and much worn," seven chairs "most of them unusefull," and seven guns "most unfixt." Nearly everyone subsisted on a rude diet of pork and corn. Servants and poor colonists had no choice but to accept crude living conditions. Their more fortunate neighbors tolerated discomfort in order to invest in family estates where their descendants might live in greater luxury.

Rough as these conditions were, they far surpassed the circumstances of most native peoples in the Chesapeake. The English population may have been growing slowly, but it still overwhelmed the Indian population which increasingly suffered high mortality from European diseases. Opechancanough led the Powhatans on another raid against the colonists in 1644, killing nearly 500 of them, but this had a far less devastating effect than his attack of 1622 because the colonists now outnumbered the Indians. By 1685, there were more than ten colonists for every Indian living in eastern Virginia. By that point, many Native Americans in the Chesapeake had retreated to their own towns, keeping their distance from the colonists in hopes of preserving control over dwindling lands and maintaining a measure of independence from English domination.

THE FOUNDING OF NEW ENGLAND

The first English attempt to settle the northeastern coast of North America, what would soon be called New England, was a miserable failure. In 1607, the same year that the Virginia Company founded Jamestown, the Plymouth Company sent two ships with 120 Englishmen (and one Indian captive from an earlier raid) to found a colony at the mouth of the Sagadahoc River in present-day Maine. The colonists alienated the Abenaki Indians who lived there (and who consequently refused to trade with the belligerent newcomers), suffered through a harsh winter, and abandoned their settlement the next summer. But explorers and fishermen continued to visit the area, and it was not long before the English renewed their efforts to settle New England.

Six colonies appeared in the region between 1620 and 1640, settled by thousands of people troubled by religious, political, and economic upheavals in England. Even before the colonists established permanent settlements, New England's native population felt the effects of European contact. Between 1616 and 1618, a terrible epidemic swept through coastal New England, killing up to 90 percent of the Indians living there. The devastated survivors were struggling to cope with the consequences of this disaster just as colonists began to arrive.

THE PILGRIMS AND PLYMOUTH COLONY

Plymouth Colony, the first of the New England settlements, was founded in 1620. Its origins lay in religious disputes that had plagued England since the late sixteenth century. Most of Queen Elizabeth's subjects approved of her efforts to keep England a Protestant nation, but some reformers believed that she had not rid the Church of England of all Catholic practices. The enemies of these reformers, ridiculing them for wanting to purify the Church of England (or **Anglican** Church) of all corruption, called them Puritans.

Following the doctrine of predestination taught by John Calvin and other Protestant reformers, English Puritans believed in an all-powerful God who, at the moment of Creation, determined which humans would be saved and which would be damned. They held that salvation came through faith alone, not good works, and urged believers to seek a direct, personal relationship with God. The centerpiece of their spiritual life was conversion: the transforming experience that occurred when individuals felt the stirrings of grace in their souls and began to hope that they were among the saved. Those who experienced conversion were considered saints and acquired new strength to live godly lives.

Puritans believed that certain Anglican practices interfered with conversion and the believer's relationship with God. They rejected the Book of Common Prayer, which regulated Anglican worship, insisting that ministers should pray from the heart and preach from the Bible. They objected when Anglican clergy wore rich vestments that set them apart from ordinary Christians. And they objected to any church organization above the level of individual congregations, seeing no need for bishops and archbishops. But what they hated most about the Anglican Church was that anyone could be a member. Puritans believed that everyone should attend church services, but they wanted church membership, which conferred the right to partake in the Lord's Supper, or communion, to be limited to saints who had experienced conversion.

Puritans thus insisted on further reform. Elizabeth and the rulers who followed her—who as monarchs were the "supreme heads" of the Church of England—disagreed and tried to silence them. James I viewed the Puritans' demands as a challenge to his authority and threatened to "harry them out of the land." Some Puritans, known as **separatists**, were convinced that the Church of England would never change and left it to form their own congregations. One such group, mainly artisans and middling farmers from the village of Scrooby, in Nottinghamshire, became the core of Plymouth Colony.

The Scrooby separatists, seeking refuge from persecution, left England in 1607–1608 for Holland, where they stayed for more than a decade. Although they could worship in peace there, many struggled to make a living and feared that their children were being tempted by the worldly pleasures of Dutch city life. Some Scrooby separatists contemplated moving to America and contacted the Plymouth Company, which was eager to make another colonization attempt after the Sagadahoc failure. Called **Pilgrims** because they thought of themselves as spiritual wanderers, they were joined by other separatists and by nonseparatist "strangers" hired to help get the colony started. In all, 102 men, women, and children set sail on the *Mayflower* in September 1620.

After a long and miserable voyage, they landed near Massachusetts Bay. Because this was about 200 miles north of the land their charter permitted them to settle, some of the "strangers" claimed that they were no longer legally bound to obey the expedition's separatist leaders. To prevent the colony from disintegrating into factions before their ship had even landed, the leaders drafted the Mayflower Compact, a document that bound all signers to abide by the decisions of the majority.

The Pilgrims settled at Plymouth, the site of a Wampanoag village recently depopulated by disease. William Bradford, a Pilgrim leader and Plymouth's governor for many years, described finding abandoned cornfields, a clearing "where lately a house had been," Indian graves, and baskets of corn buried underground. Although it helped feed them for a while, this corn was not enough to prevent the Pilgrims from suffering their first winter through a terrible "starving time" that left nearly half of them dead.

When two natives, Squanto and Samoset, emerged from the woods the next spring and began speaking English, the surviving Pilgrims marveled at them as "special instruments sent of God." Samoset had learned English from traders, and Squanto had learned it in England, where he lived for a time after being kidnapped by a sea captain. Upon his return to New England, Squanto found that he was the sole survivor of the Patuxets, who had succumbed to disease while he had been away. The two native men approached the Pilgrims on behalf of Massasoit, the Wampanoag leader. Although suspicious of the newcomers, the Wampanoags thought the Pilgrims might be useful allies against Wampanoag enemies, such as the Narragansetts, who had escaped the recent epidemics.

In 1621, the Wampanoags and the Pilgrims signed a treaty of alliance, although each side (working through translators) understood its terms differently. The Pilgrims assumed that Massasoit had submitted to the superior authority of King James, whereas Massasoit assumed that he and the English king were equal partners. Until his death in 1622, Squanto offered advice to each side, hoping to achieve honor and influence as a mediator.

Economic ties strengthened the alliance. The Indians taught the English how to plant corn and traded corn with them for manufactured goods. The Pilgrims also exchanged corn with other Indians to the north for furs, which they shipped back to England to help pay off their debts to English investors. In the autumn of 1621, Indians and Pilgrims gathered for a feast celebrating the settlers' first harvest—an event Americans still commemorate as the first Thanksgiving.

Plymouth remained small, poor, and weak, never exceeding about seven thousand settlers. Although its families achieved a modest prosperity, the colony as a whole never produced more than small shipments of furs, fish, and timber to sell in England. It took the Pilgrims more than twenty years to repay their English creditors. After 1630, the first New England colony was overshadowed by a new and more powerful neighbor, Massachusetts Bay.

MASSACHUSETTS BAY COLONY AND ITS OFFSHOOTS

Not long after his arrival in New England, Thomas Dudley became a member of a Puritan church. Dudley, like the other Puritans who founded Massachusetts, shared many beliefs with the Pilgrims of Plymouth Colony—with one important exception. They insisted that the Anglican Church could be reformed and so were not separatists. When they went to New England, it was to create godly churches to serve as models for English reform. And England, they believed, was in more desperate need of reformation than ever.

Charles I, who became king in 1625, opposed Puritans more forcefully than his father had and supported changes in Anglican worship that recalled Catholic practices. England at the time also suffered from economic troubles—including crop failures and a depression in the wool industry—that many Puritans saw as signs of God's displeasure with their country, encouraging them to move to the New World.

In 1629, a group of Puritan merchants and gentlemen received a royal charter for a joint-stock enterprise, the Massachusetts Bay Company, to set up a colony north of Plymouth. Its founding members included Thomas Dudley and John Winthrop, a prosperous lawyer chosen to lead the new colony. In the spring of 1630, a fleet of eleven ships carried the Winthrops, Dudleys, and about a thousand other men, women and children across the Atlantic.

Before Winthrop's ship landed, he preached a lay sermon, called "A Model of Christian Charity," to his fellow passengers, describing his vision of the society they were about to create. The governor reminded them of their goal "to do more service to the Lord." They should "love one another with a pure heart" and place the good of all above private ambitions. Winthrop argued that the Lord had made them his chosen people and that as a result, "we shall be as a city upon a hill, the eyes of all people are upon us." If they failed to live up to God's expectations, he would punish them, and the spectacle of their failure would allow their enemies "to speak evil of the ways of God." With this mingled encouragement and threat ringing in their ears, the emigrants set about establishing their colony. Within a few months of their landing, they founded Boston and six adjoining towns.

Stability, conformity, and intolerance.
Winthrop described the settlers' mission in New England as a **covenant**, or contract, with God, binding them to meet their religious obligations in return for God's favor. The settlers also created covenants to define their duties to one another. When they founded towns, colonists signed covenants agreeing to live together in peace. The settlers of Dedham, for example, agreed to "walk in a peaceable conversation," seeking "the good of each other." Worshipers in each town's church likewise wrote covenants binding themselves to live in harmony.

The desire for peace and purity could breed intolerance. Settlers scrutinized their neighbors for signs of unacceptable behavior. Standards for church membership were strict; only those who could prove they were saints by describing their conversion expe-

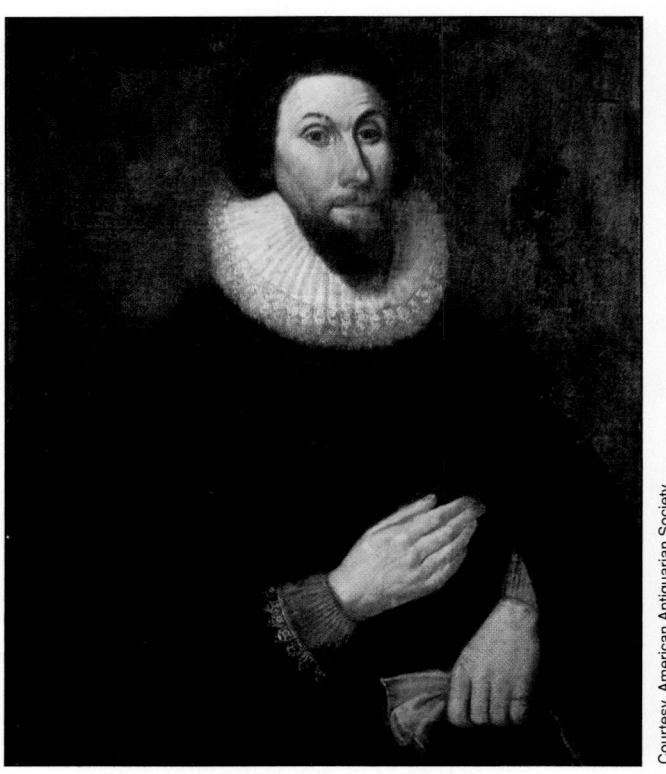

John Winthrop (1588–1649) served as the Massachusetts Bay Colony's governor for most of its first two decades. Throughout his life, Winthrop—like many fellow Puritans—struggled to live a godly life in a corrupt world.

riences were admitted. But the insistence on covenants and conformity also created a remarkably stable society, far more peaceable than Virginia's.

That stability was enhanced by the development of representative government. Colony leaders in effect translated the charter of the Massachusetts Bay Company into a plan of government, a process completed by 1634. The General Court, which initially included only the shareholders of the joint-stock company, was transformed into a two-house legislature. Freemen—adult males who held property and were church members—had the right to elect representatives to the lower house, as well as eighteen members (called "assistants") to the upper house. They also chose a governor and a deputy governor.

The Connecticut Valley and the Pequot War.
At least thirteen thousand settlers came to New England and established dozens of towns between 1630 and 1642, when the outbreak of the English Civil War halted emigration. The progress of settlement was generally untroubled in coastal Massachusetts, but when colonists moved into the Connecticut River Valley, ten-

sions with Indians grew rapidly. These erupted in 1637 in the brief, tragic conflict called the **Pequot War**.

English settlers from Massachusetts first arrived in the Connecticut Valley in the mid-1630s. The migration accelerated in 1636 when the Reverend Thomas Hooker led part of his congregation from Cambridge, Massachusetts, to what became Hartford. The new arrivals found themselves in a dangerous situation. For several years, the Pequot Indians had used their partnership with Dutch traders in the region to monopolize the trade in European goods and exert dominance over their native neighbors. This political and economic strategy was endangered in 1633 when the Dutch built an outpost near the site of Hartford and invited the Pequots' rivals—including the Narragansetts and Mohegans—to trade. The Pequots, suffering terribly from a recent smallpox epidemic, resented losing their special trading rights and approached Massachusetts Bay as an ally against the Dutch. But when English settlers poured into Connecticut and demanded Pequot submission to English authority as the price of an alliance, the Pequots turned against them too in a struggle to retain control over the land and trade of eastern Connecticut.

The English settlers allied with the Pequots' enemies, the Narragansetts and Mohegans. Together they overwhelmed the Pequots in an astonishingly bloody war. In May 1637, English forces surrounded a Pequot village inhabited mainly by women and children, located on the Mystic River. They set it ablaze and shot anyone who tried to escape. Between three hundred and seven hundred Pequots died, a toll that shocked the settlers' Indian allies, who protested that English-style warfare was "too furious, and slays too many men" (see "American Views: Miantonomo's Plea for Indian Unity").

The English, for their part, thanked God for giving them "so speedy a victory over so proud and insulting an enemy." After the surviving Pequots had fled or been sold into slavery, many more settlers moved to Connecticut, which soon declared itself a separate colony. In 1639, the settlers adopted the Fundamental Orders, creating a government similar to that of Massachusetts, and the English government granted them a royal charter in 1662.

Roger Williams and the founding of Rhode Island.
Massachusetts spun off other colonies as its population expanded in the 1630s and dissenters ran afoul of its intolerant government. Puritan leaders tried to suppress unorthodox religious opinions whenever they emerged, for fear that God would interpret their failure to do so as a breach of their covenant with Him. Some dissenting colonists, however, refused to conform. Roger Williams, who founded Rhode Island, was one such irrepressible dissenter. Williams was a separatist minister who declared that because Massachusetts churches had not rejected the Church of England, they shared its corruption. He opposed government interference in religious affairs—such as laws requiring settlers to attend worship services—and argued for the separation of church and state. Williams even attacked the Massachusetts charter, insisting that the king had no right to grant Indian lands to English settlers.

Despite his fiery opinions, Williams was an immensely likable man; even Governor Winthrop remained on friendly terms with him and tried to persuade him to change his views. When Williams refused to be silenced, the General Court sentenced him to banishment, intending to ship him back to England. But in the winter of 1635, Williams slipped away and followed Winthrop's advice to "steer my course to Narragansett Bay." There he and a few followers found refuge among the Narragansett Indians, from whom he purchased land for the village of Providence, founded in 1636. More towns soon sprang up nearby when a new religious crisis, provoked by a woman named Anne Hutchinson, sent additional refugees to Rhode Island from Massachusetts.

Anne Hutchinson's challenge to the Bay Colony.
Anne Hutchinson arrived in Boston from England with her husband and seven children in 1634. Welcomed by the town's women for her talents as a midwife, she also began to hold religious meetings in her house. During these meetings, she denounced several ministers, who had taught worshipers that there were certain spiritual exercises they could perform that might prepare them for sainthood. Hutchinson insisted that there was nothing humans could do to encourage God to make them saints. She implied that any minister who taught otherwise could not be a saint himself, in which case he had no authority over the true saints in his church.

Many people, including prominent Boston merchants, flocked to Hutchinson's meetings. But her critics believed her to be a dangerous antinomian (someone who claimed to be free from obedience to moral law), because she seemed to maintain that saints were accountable only to God and not to any worldly authority. Her opponents also objected to her teaching of mixed groups of men and women. Governor Winthrop complained that such behavior was neither "comely in the sight of God nor fitting for your sex." This comment suggests that Hutchinson's breach of normal gender roles, which placed

AMERICAN VIEWS

Miantonomo's Plea for Indian Unity (1642)

Until European colonization began to force a change in outlook, the native inhabitants of North America never thought of themselves as one people, any more than Europe's residents considered themselves "Europeans." Miantonomo, a Narragansett living in Rhode Island, was one of the first native leaders to call for a unified response to English intrusion. With the gruesome lessons of the Pequot War fresh in his mind, he urged the Montauks of Long Island to put aside their differences with the Narragansetts and join them in opposing the settlers. His appeal, recorded by Lion Gardiner, an English officer during the Pequot War, was uttered in vain. Captured by the English and tried and convicted of the murder of an Indian, Miantonomo was turned over to a Mohegan rival for execution.

- How did Miantonomo describe Indian life before the arrival of the English?
- What changes occurred as a result of their settlement?

Brothers, we must be as one as the English are, or we shall all be destroyed. You know our fathers had plenty of deer and skins and our plains were full of game and turkeys, and our coves and rivers were full of fish.

But, brothers, since these Englishmen have seized our country, they have cut down the

Source: Steven Mintz, ed., *Native American Voices: A History and Anthology* (1995), pp. 84–85. Reprinted with permission of Brandywine Press.

grass with scythes, and the trees with axes. Their cows and horses eat up the grass, and their hogs spoil our bed of clams; and finally we shall all starve to death; therefore, stand not in your own light, I ask you, but resolve to act like men. All the sachems both to the east and the west have joined with us, and we are resolved to fall upon them at a day appointed, and therefore I come secretly to you, [be]cause you can persuade your Indians to do what you will.

---

women subordinate to men, upset him as much as her religious views did. Colony magistrates arrested her and tried her for sedition—that is, for advocating the overthrow of the government.

During her trial, Hutchinson mounted a lively defense. When asked to explain her views, she reminded her opponents of their objections to her teaching and asked them, "Why do you call me to teach the court?" In the end, however, the court found her guilty and banished her from the colony. With many of her followers, she moved to Rhode Island, where Roger Williams had proclaimed a policy of religious toleration. Other followers returned to England or moved north to what became in 1679 the separate colony of New Hampshire.

At the height of the Hutchinson controversy, a group of zealous Puritan emigrants led by the Reverend John Davenport arrived in Boston. Appalled

by the religious turmoil, they departed for the coast of Long Island Sound, where they founded New Haven in 1638. Davenport's efforts to impose perfect Puritan conformity in his colony made Massachusetts seem easygoing in comparison. But New Haven failed to thrive, and in 1662, the poor, intolerant, and isolated colony was absorbed into Connecticut.

FAMILIES, FARMS, AND COMMUNITIES IN EARLY NEW ENGLAND

"This plantation and that of Virginia went not forth upon the same reasons," declared one of Massachusetts's founders. Virginians came "for profit," whereas New Englanders emigrated to bear witness to their Puritan faith. They too hoped for economic prosperity but believed that it would come only if God blessed their efforts to create a godly society. Most New Eng-

Most New Englanders came in family groups, bringing many children with them. The lace and ribbons on the clothing of the Mason children, depicted in this 1670 portrait, suggest that they came from a well-to-do family. Like many seventeenth-century portraits, this one is rich in symbolism. The cane in David Mason's hand indicates his status as the male heir, while the rose held by his sister Abigail was a symbol of childhood innocence.

land settlers arrived in the brief span between the founding of Massachusetts in 1630 and 1642, when the outbreak of the English Civil War convinced many Puritans to stay at home and fight on Parliament's behalf against the king. Unlike the unmarried young men who moved in great numbers to Virginia, most New Englanders settled with their families. This had important implications for the development of New England society.

Even though emigration from England slowed to a trickle after 1642, New England's population continued to grow. By 1660, the number of colonists exceeded 33,000. This demographic expansion stemmed from the initial emigration of families. With a more balanced sex ratio (about three men to two women) than there was in the early Chesapeake, marriage and childbearing were more common. Emigrant families that already had children produced more of them, and newly married couples soon added to the population. Families frequently had seven or eight children, compared to the two or three offspring common to Chesapeake families.

Settling in a region with a healthier climate, New Englanders were also largely spared early deaths from malaria and other diseases that ravaged Chesapeake settlers and devastated Indian populations.

Most children survived to reach adulthood and form families of their own. Many New Englanders enjoyed unusually long lives (for the seventeenth century), reaching their seventies and even eighties. Unlike most Chesapeake children, young New Englanders got to know their grandparents.

Long-lived parents exercised considerable control over their children's lives. This was especially true for sons, who could not marry until their fathers provided them with sufficient land to support a family. Because fathers depended on their sons for labor, they often postponed granting them the means to economic independence until they were 26 or 27. Daughters, too, contributed their labor to the household economy, but generally married between the ages of 21 and 23. They also depended on the willingness of their fathers to supply them with a dowry (usually livestock and household goods) to bring to their new homes.

Women in early New England. In New England, as in other colonies and England itself, women were assumed to be legally and economically dependent on the men in their families. Since fewer New England marriages were shortened by the early death of a spouse, fewer New England women experienced widowhood, the one time in their lives when they might enjoy legal independence and exercise control over property. During the seventeenth century, widows occasionally exercised more extensive property rights than the law dictated. By law, they had "dower rights" to possess one-third the value of the husband's personal estate and to use one-third of the land for the remainder of their lives. Many husbands, however, gave their widows control over greater amounts of property, perhaps to recognize their important contributions to building the family estate.

Women's economic contributions were indeed central to the family's success. In addition to raising the children, women performed essential domestic tasks, including cooking, sewing, gardening, and cleaning. Many also engaged in household production and traded the fruits of their labor with other families. They cared for poultry and sold eggs, made butter and cheese, brewed beer, and spun yarn. Wives of shopkeepers and craftsmen occasionally managed their husbands' businesses when the men had to travel or became ill.

Community and economic life. New Englanders' lives were shaped not only by their families, but by their towns. Unlike Chesapeake colonists, who tended to disperse into separate plantations, New Englanders clustered into more populous communities that eventually contained between fifty and a

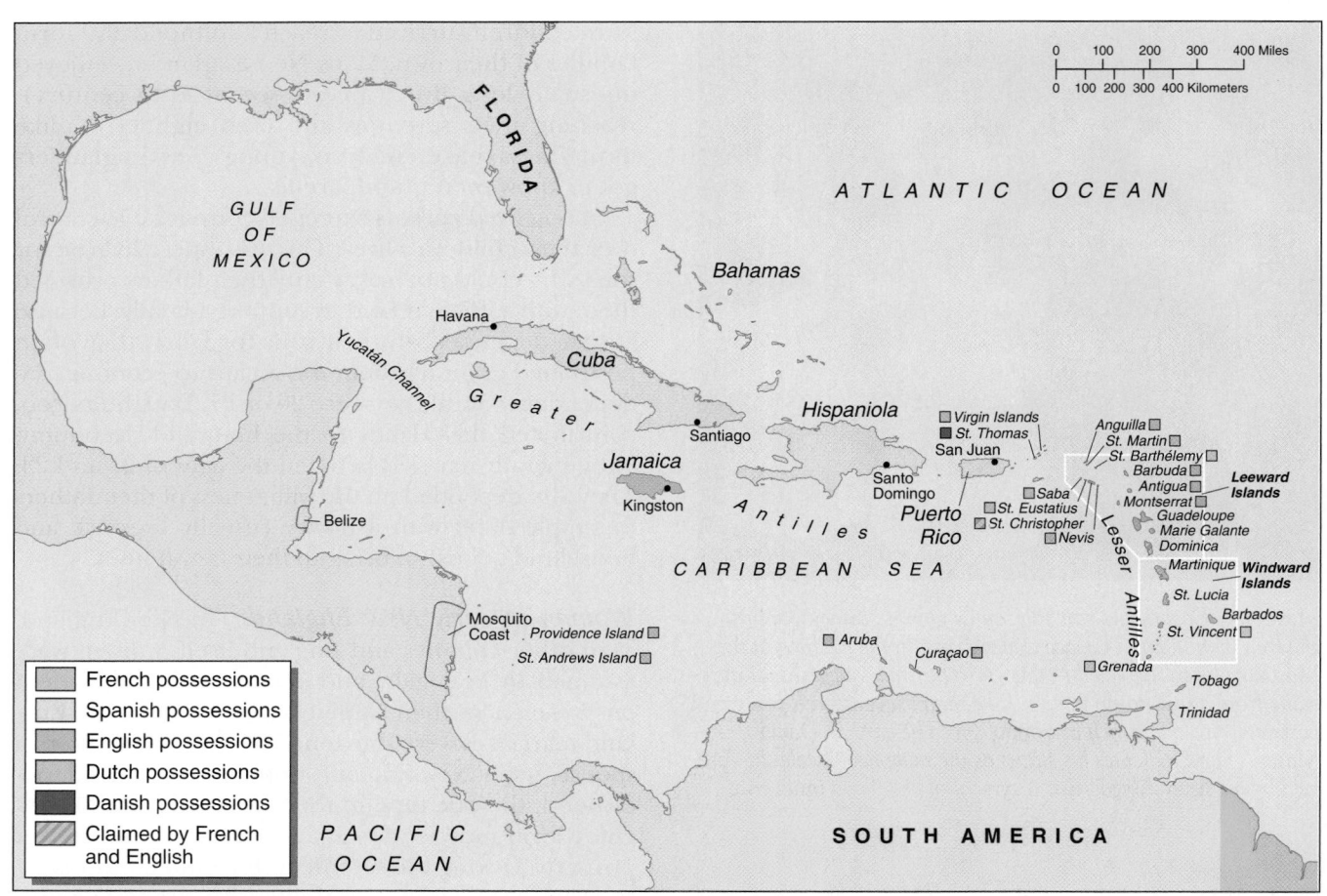

MAP 2-3   Principal European Possessions in the Caribbean in the Seventeenth Century
Europeans scrambled for control of Caribbean islands, where they raised sugar cane with slave labor. On many islands, Africans soon formed the majority of the population. In some cases, colonists from one European country settled on lands claimed by a rival power. For instance, English settlers established bases in Belize and on the Mosquito Coast, both of which were claimed by Spain.

hundred or so families. The Massachusetts government strongly encouraged town formation by granting tracts of land to groups of families who promised to settle together. Once they received a grant, the families in a group divided it among themselves, allotting each family a farm of sufficient size to support its members. Social distinctions were maintained: people who had higher standing in England received larger farms than those of lower status. Land that the original families could not yet use was held "in common" to be distributed to their children as they grew up. Once they found a town they liked, families tended to stay in place. Grown children, inheriting parental estates and finding spouses nearby, often settled in the same community as their parents.

At the center of each town stood the meetinghouse, used both for religious and secular purposes. Every Sunday, townspeople gathered there to listen to the minister preach God's word. The importance Puritans placed on worship with fellow Christians helped promote community feeling. At other times, the meetinghouse served as a town hall, where men assembled to discuss matters ranging from local taxes to making sure everyone's fences were mended. Massachusetts law required towns with at least fifty families to support a school (so children could learn to read the Bible) and men often wrangled at town meetings over the choice of a schoolmaster and what salary to pay him. Townsmen tried to reach decisions by consensus, although that was not always possible. To oversee day-to-day local affairs, they chose five to seven trusted neighbors to serve as selectmen. Each town could also elect two men to represent it in the colony legislature. Many towns neglected to do so, either because their citizens could not afford to pay the representative's expenses or because they lacked sufficient interest in outside political affairs.

Economic life likewise centered on the family and the town. New England's stony soil and short growing season offered few ways to get rich, but most people achieved a modest prosperity mainly by farming. They grew corn and other foods and raised livestock to feed their families, selling or trading what they could not use. Their goal was to achieve what they called competency—the possession of enough property to ensure the family's economic independence. Without the income generated by a staple crop like tobacco, New England farmers lacked adequate resources to hire large numbers of indentured servants and so relied on family members. Even children as young as five or six contributed their labor to the household economy, perhaps by caring for younger siblings or fetching water and wood.

No family could produce all that it needed, so New Englanders regularly traded goods and services with their neighbors. A skilled carpenter might erect a house—usually larger and sturdier than the ramshackle dwellings of Chesapeake settlers—in return for barrels of salted beef. Men with several sons sent them to help neighbors whose children were too young to work. Midwives delivered babies in return for cheese or eggs. Women nursed sick neighbors, whom they might one day call on for similar help. These sorts of transactions allowed most New Englanders to enjoy a fairly comfortable life, one that many Virginians might have envied.

Lacking a single staple crop like tobacco, New England prospered by exploiting a variety of resources, developing a diversified economy that was less vulnerable to depression than Virginia's. Farmers sent livestock and meat to merchants to be marketed abroad. Fishermen caught thousands of pounds of cod, haddock, and other fish to be sold in Europe. Some of the region's timber found its way abroad, but most of it ended up in shipyards. New Englanders became such skilled shipbuilders and seafaring merchants that by the 1670s, London merchants were complaining about competition from them. England itself had little use for the dried fish, livestock, salted meat, and wood products that New England vessels carried, but enterprising merchants found exactly the market they needed in the West Indies.

COMPETITION IN THE CARIBBEAN

The Spanish claimed all Caribbean islands by right of Columbus's discovery, but during the seventeenth century, French, Dutch, and English adventurers boldly defied them. Spain retained the largest and most lucrative islands—Cuba, Hispaniola, Puerto Rico, Trinidad—but others were seized, one by one, by rival European powers. The French eventually obtained Guadaloupe, Martinique, St. Lucia, St. Vincent, and smaller outposts in the Leeward and Windward Islands. Aruba, Curaçao, St. Martin, Saba, and St. Eustatius became Dutch possessions. Even the Danes took control of St. Thomas in the Virgin Islands. England's share of the West Indies included Antigua, Barbados, Montserrat, Nevis, and St. Christopher; in 1655, the English wrested Jamaica from Spain (see Map 2–3). Although a few English efforts, including an attempt to found a Puritan colony on Providence Island off Nicaragua's coast, failed, the West Indies soon became the jewel of England's empire in the Americas.

Europeans competed for these islands at first in the hope that they would yield precious metals and also provide bases for privateering expeditions. It eventually became clear that the islands would produce treasure of another sort—sugar, which was in great demand in Europe. In order to reap the enormous profits that sugar could bring, Caribbean planters of all nationalities imported enormous numbers of African people to work as slaves under the harshest conditions to be found in the New World.

SUGAR AND SLAVES

The Spanish and Portuguese first experimented with sugar production on Atlantic islands such as São Tomé and the Canaries in the fifteenth century, importing their workers from Africa. Europeans prized sugar as a sweetener, preservative, decoration—even a medicine—and paid high prices for it. Columbus accordingly brought sugar canes to the New World on his second voyage, in 1493. Soon after the Spanish began growing sugar on Santo Domingo, they began importing African slaves as workers because Indian slaves were dying in great numbers. The Spanish brought sugar to the South American mainland as well, as did the Portuguese, who turned Brazil into one of the world's major producers. And everywhere that sugar flourished, first Indian slaves and then enslaved African workers could be found. It seemed as if Europeans could not imagine growing sugar any other way. For the Portuguese and Dutch, who dominated the African slave trade, sugar and slaves provided twin sources of profit. In the early seventeenth century, Portugal alone shipped 10,000 to 20,000 Africans to the New World every year.

The English in the Caribbean eventually made the same decisions, after a false start. Like the early Virginians, the first English colonists who came to

In this seventeenth-century drawing, African slaves are shown toiling in a Brazilian sugar mill. Similar scenes prevailed on Barbados and other Caribbean colonies dominated by sugar production.

the West Indies in the 1620s and 1630s raised tobacco and imported indentured servants to work their fields. By that time, however, tobacco prices were dropping. Moreover, the disease environment of the West Indies proved even harsher than that of the Chesapeake and settlers died in great numbers. That thousands came anyway testified more to their hopes for prosperity than their actual chances of success. Until the 1660s the islands actually attracted more emigrants than the mainland colonies did.

By the 1640s, a Barbados planter boasted of "a great change on this island of late from the worse to the better, praised be God." That change was a shift from tobacco to sugar cane. Dutch merchants helped finance this transition. The Dutch, who had briefly taken control of Brazil, were being driven out by the Portuguese, and looked to the English islands as a new market for the Dutch slave trade. They taught the English how to grow sugar, supplied them with slaves, and dominated the marketing of the English crop. Before long, many English sugar planters grew astonishingly wealthy. In 1646, a 500-acre plantation on Barbados sold for £16,000—more than the whole island had been worth just a few years before. On average, the estate of a Caribbean sugar planter was worth four times as much as a prosperous Chesapeake plantation.

Sugar rapidly transformed the West Indies. Planters deforested whole islands to raise sugar cane. They stopped planting food crops and raising livestock—thereby creating a demand for lumber and provisions that boosted New England's economy. In 1647, John Winthrop noted that Barbadians "had rather buy food at very dear rates than produce it by labor, so infinite is the profit of sugar works."

For some years after the transition to sugar, English planters continued to import white indentured servants, including some kidnapped English and Irish youths, and supplemented the labor force with African slaves. They eventually grew dissatisfied with this labor force. Due to the islands' unhealthy environment and extremely harsh working conditions, servants died in great numbers. England could barely meet the demand for workers, and English workers, if they survived, often proved rebellious. Given the example of prosperous Spanish and Portuguese plantations using slave labor, and the willingness of the Dutch to supply them with slaves, the English too switched to African laborers whom they considered better suited to agricultural work in a tropical climate. The planters' choice has been called an "unthinking decision," but it had an enormous impact on English colonial life, first in the islands and then on the mainland, where slavery would develop later in the seventeenth century (see Chapter 3).

A BIRACIAL SOCIETY

As happened on virtually all Caribbean islands, the English West Indies developed a biracial plantation society—the first in the English colonial world. By 1700, more than 250,000 slaves had been brought to the English islands, and they soon constituted a majority of the population. In Barbados, black slaves increased from 50 percent to more than 70 percent of the population between 1660 and 1700. Slaves lived in wretched conditions, underfed, poorly dressed, and housed in rough huts. They labored six days a week from sunrise to sunset—except at harvest time, when they toiled seven days a week in round-the-clock shifts. Masters considered them property, often branding them like livestock and hunting them with bloodhounds when they ran away.

Laws, sometimes called **slave codes**, declared slavery to be a lifelong condition that passed from slave parents to their children. Slaves had no legal rights and were under the complete control of their masters. Only rarely would masters who killed slaves face prosecution, and those who did and were found guilty were subject only to fines. Slaves, in contrast, faced appalling punishments even for minor offenses. They could be whipped, branded, or maimed for stealing food or harboring a runaway compatriot. Serious crimes such as murder or arson brought execution without trial. Slaves who rebelled were burned to death.

Astonishingly, slaves managed to preserve some elements of normal life even under these brutal conditions. When masters began to import African women as well as men—hoping to create a self-reproducing labor force—slaves formed families and preserved at least some African traditions. They gave their children African names (although masters often gave them English names as well). They celebrated with African music and worked to the rhythm of familiar songs. And they drew on their West African heritage to perform elaborate funeral rituals, often burying their dead with food and other goods to accompany them on the journey to what they believed to be a much happier afterlife.

Some planters, profiting handsomely from their slaves' toil, lived better than many English gentlemen. They indulged in large houses, fine furnishings, and expensive clothing. Even so, many hated the hot, humid West Indian climate and feared the constant threat of disease. After making their fortunes, planters often fled to England, leaving their estates under the care of hired overseers.

But sugar made relatively few white colonists wealthy. Its production required a heavy investment in land, slaves, mills, and equipment. As great planters took vast amounts of land for themselves, freed servants and small farmers struggled to survive. After 1650, many of these poor men, looking for other places to live, headed for the mainland. They were joined by planters looking for a place to expand their operations once most of the good land on the islands had been brought under cultivation.

THE PROPRIETARY COLONIES

The initial burst of English colonization ended in 1640 when England tottered on the brink of civil war. With the accession of Charles II to the throne in 1660, however, interest in North America revived. Charles II needed to reward the supporters who had remained loyal to him during his long exile in France. One of the easiest ways for him to do so was with huge grants of American land. During his reign (1660–1685), four new colonies—Carolina, Pennsylvania, New Jersey, and New York—resulted from such grants (see Map 2-4). All were proprietary colonies, essentially the private property of the people to whom they had been given. Two of them—Carolina and Pennsylvania—like the earlier proprietary colony of Maryland, provided their owners the chance to test idealistic social visions. The origins of New York and New Jersey as English colonies, by contrast, lay not in proprietary visions of social harmony but in the stern reality of military conquest (see the Overview table, "English Colonies in the Seventeenth Century").

EARLY CAROLINA: COLONIAL ARISTOCRACY AND SLAVE LABOR

In 1663, Charles II granted a group of supporters an enormous tract of land stretching from southern Virginia to northern Florida. The proprietors, who included several Barbados planters, called their colony Carolina, after *Carolus*, the Latin form of the king's name. They envisioned it growing from the few English outposts already in the region, established by settlers from New England and the West Indies, into a prosperous, orderly society.

One of the proprietors, Anthony Ashley Cooper, working closely with his secretary, John Locke, devised the **Fundamental Constitutions of Carolina**, a plan to ensure the colony's stability by balancing property ownership and political rights. It called for the creation of a colonial aristocracy, who would own two-fifths of the land and wield extensive political power. Below them, a large class of freeholders would own small farms and elect representatives to

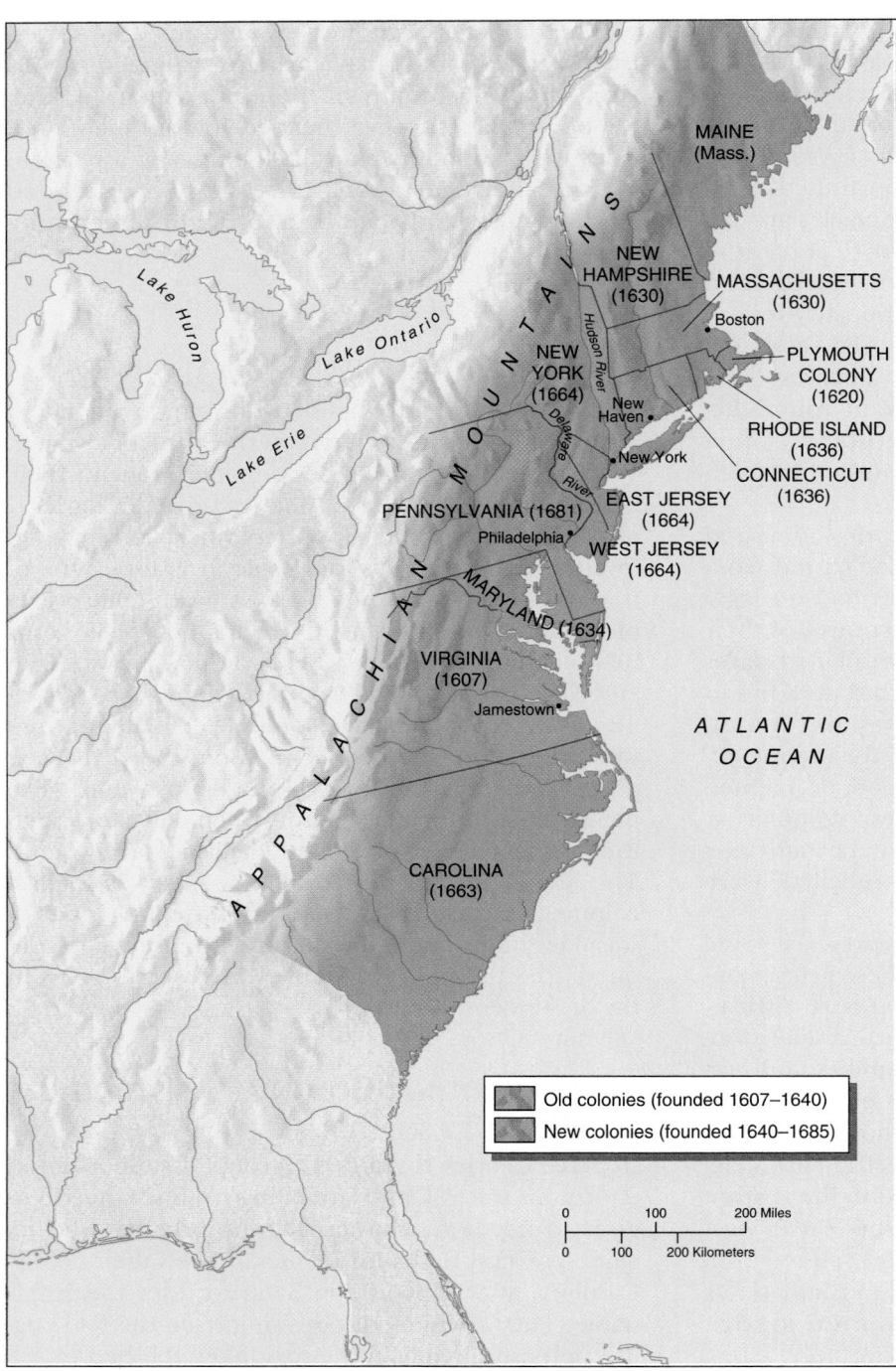

MAP 2-4   English North American Colonies, c. 1685
After the restoration of Charles II in 1660, several large proprietary colonies joined earlier English settlements in New England and the Chesapeake. By 1685, a growing number of English settlers solidified England's claim to the Atlantic coast from Maine (then part of Massachusetts Bay Colony) to the southern edge of Carolina.

an assembly. At the bottom of the social order would be slaves.

This plan never went into effect. People moved in from Virginia and the West Indies and settled where they pleased. They even voted in the assembly to reject the Fundamental Constitutions. They antagonized the Indians in the region, who numbered perhaps fifteen thousand when settlers first arrived. When English traders first appeared, eager to buy deerskins, many Indians had welcomed them. But they grew hostile when traders began selling guns to some tribes in exchange for captives from rival tribes. The captives were later sold as slaves to the West Indies. Native resentments deepened as settlers moved onto their lands. The result was a deadly cycle of violence.

The colonists at first raised livestock to be sold to the West Indies. But the introduction of rice in Carolina in the 1690s transformed the settlers' economy, making it, as one planter noted, "as much their staple Commodity, as Sugar is to Barbados and Jamaica, or Tobacco to Virginia and Maryland." The English had never grown rice, but West Africans had raised it since the 1500s. Rice cultivation in Carolina coincided with an increase in the number of African slaves there, who probably introduced the crop. Ironically, the profits earned from rice persuaded Carolina planters to invest even more heavily in slave labor.

Carolina society soon resembled the sugar islands from which many of its founders had come. By 1708, there were more black slaves than white settlers in the colony, and two decades after that, black people outnumbered white people by two to one. Rice farming required a substantial investment in land, labor, and equipment, including dikes and dams for flooding fields. Those who could afford such an investment set themselves up as planters in Carolina's coastal rice district, acquiring large es-

Overview

English Colonies in the Seventeenth Century

Colony	Date of Founding	Established Religion	Economy	Government
Virginia	1607	Anglican	Tobacco	Royal (after 1625)
Plymouth	1620	Puritan	Mixed farming	Corporate
St. Christopher	1624	Anglican	Sugar	Royal
Barbados	1627	Anglican	Sugar	Royal
Nevis	1628	Anglican	Sugar	Royal
Massachusetts (including present-day Maine)	1630	Puritan	Mixed farming, fishing, shipbuilding	Corporate
New Hampshire	1630 (first settlement, annexed to Mass. 1643–1679; royal colony after 1679)	Puritan	Mixed farming	Corporate (royal after 1679)
Antigua	1632	Anglican	Sugar	Royal
Montserrat	1632	Anglican	Sugar	Royal
Maryland	1634	None (Anglican after 1692)	Tobacco	Proprietary
Rhode Island	1636	None	Mixed farming	Corporate
Connecticut	1636	Puritan	Mixed farming	Corporate
New Haven	1638	Puritan	Mixed farming	Corporate
Jamaica	1655 (captured from Spanish)	Anglican	Sugar	Royal
Carolina	1663	Anglican	Rice	Proprietary
New York	1664 (captured from Dutch)	None	Mixed farming, furs	Proprietary (royal after 1685)
New Jersey	1664	None	Mixed farming	Proprietary
Pennsylvania	1681	None	Wheat, mixed farming	Proprietary

tates and forcing poorer settlers to move elsewhere.

Some of these dislocated settlers went to the northern part of Carolina, where the land and climate were unsuited to rice. There they raised tobacco and livestock, and produced pitch, tar, and timber products from the region's pine forests. So different were the two regions that the colony formally split into two provinces—North and South Carolina—in 1729.

South Carolina rice planters became some of the wealthiest colonists on the mainland. But their luxurious style of life came at a price. As Carolina began to look "more like a negro country than like a country settled by white people," planters dreaded the prospect of slave rebellion. To avert this nightmare, they enacted slave codes as harsh as those of the sugar islands.

Although John Locke went on to become one of England's most important philosophers, the visionary

Thomas Coram's oil painting (c. 1770) shows the main residence and slave quarters on the Mulberry Plantation near Charleston, South Carolina. The distinctive steep-roofed design of the slave cabins on the left probably reflects African building styles. Slave quarters may not have been located quite as close to the main house as this picture suggests.

plan he and Cooper had devised for Carolina disintegrated on contact with American conditions. Carolina would not be a harmonious colony that balanced wealth and power; it evolved instead into a racially divided society founded on the oppression of a black majority and permeated by fear.

PENNSYLVANIA: THE DREAM OF TOLERATION AND PEACE

Even as early Carolina diverged from the plans of its founders, another Englishman dreamed of creating a colonial utopia. William Penn put his plans into action in 1681, when Charles II granted him a huge tract of land north of Maryland as payment for a royal debt owed to Penn's father. Penn intended his colony to be a model of justice and peace, as well as a refuge for members of the Society of Friends, or **Quakers**, a persecuted religious sect to which Penn himself belonged.

The Society of Friends was one of many radical religious groups that emerged in England during the civil war. Like the separatists, Quakers abandoned the Church of England as hopelessly corrupt. But they went even further in their beliefs. Rejecting predestination, they maintained that every soul had a spark of grace and that salvation was possible for all who heeded that "Inner Light." They rejected trained clergy and elaborate church rituals as unnecessary to salvation. Instead of formal religious services, Quakers held meetings at which silence reigned until someone, inspired by the Inner Light, rose to speak.

Quaker beliefs had disturbing social and political implications. Although they did not advocate complete equality of the sexes, Quakers granted women spiritual equality with men, allowing them to preach, hold separate prayer meetings, and exercise authority over "women's matters." Arguing that social distinctions were not the work of God, Quakers refused to defer to their betters. People of lower social rank were expected to remove their hats in the presence of superiors, but Quakers would not do so. And instead of the formal *you*,

Quakers addressed superiors with the informal *thee* and *thou*. Because their faith required them to renounce the use of force, Quakers also refused to perform military service, which their enemies considered tantamount to treason.

When English authorities began harassing Quakers, William Penn, who was himself jailed briefly, conceived his plan for a New World refuge. He aimed to launch a "holy experiment," a harmonious society governed by brotherly love. Knowing that Quakers were unwelcome in the existing colonies—Massachusetts had hanged four of them—Penn looked elsewhere. His aristocratic background gave him advantages that other Quakers, who were mainly of humble origins, lacked. Using his father's connection with the king, he acquired the land that became Pennsylvania ("Penn's Woods") and recruited settlers from among Europe's oppressed peoples and persecuted religious sects. By 1700, eighteen thousand emigrants had left England, Wales, Scotland, Ireland, and various German provinces for the new colony.

Many came in families and settled in an area occupied by the Delaware Indians, whose numbers, though still substantial, had recently been reduced by disease and warfare. The "holy experiment" required colonists to live "as Neighbours and friends" with the Indians as well as with one another. Penn aimed to accomplish this by paying Indians for land and regulating trade. As long as Penn controlled his colony, relations between the settlers and the Indians were generally peaceful—so much so that refugee Indians from nearby colonies moved into Pennsylvania. Relations between Penn and the settlers, however, were less cordial.

In the **Frame of Government**, his constitution for Pennsylvania, Penn remained true to his Quaker principles with a provision allowing for religious freedom. But true to his aristocratic origins, he designed a legislature with limited powers and reserved considerable authority for himself. When Penn returned to England after a brief stay in the colony (1682–1684), the settlers immediately began squabbling among themselves. The governor and council, both appointed by Penn, fought with elected members of the assembly. Penn's opponents—many of whom were fellow Quakers—objected to his proprietary privileges, including his control of foreign trade and his collection of fees from landholders. Settlers on the lower Delaware River, which the crown had added to Penn's colony to give its port city, Philadelphia, access to the sea, gained autonomy for themselves with their own legislature, in effect creating an unofficial colony that later became Delaware.

No colonial proprietor was more idealistic than William Penn, shown here in a portrait made in about 1698 by Francis Place. Penn wanted Pennsylvania to be a place of peace, prosperity, and religious toleration—especially for his fellow Quakers. The colony eventually became an economic success but failed to achieve the social harmony that Penn had wanted.

A disappointed Penn lamented that the settlers had become "so brutish." He spent his fortune on his beloved colony, only to die in debt with his hopes for a harmonious society dashed. Settlers continued to fight among themselves, and with Penn's heirs, after his death. A flood of increasingly aggressive immigrants undermined peaceful relations with the Indians, forcing many natives to abandon their homelands and move west.

By 1720, Pennsylvania's ethnically and religiously diverse colonists numbered more than thirty thousand. The colony had some of the richest farmland along the Atlantic coast and was widely known as the "best poor man's country in the world." Growing wheat and other crops, the settlers lived mostly on scattered farms rather than in towns. From the busy port of Philadelphia, ships carried much of the harvest to markets in the West Indies and southern Europe. Penn's "holy experiment" in social harmony may have failed, but, as a thriving colony, Pennsylvania succeeded handsomely.

NEW NETHERLAND BECOMES NEW YORK

The proprietary colonies of New York and New Jersey were carved out of the Dutch colony of New Netherland. Competition between the English and the Dutch had intensified in the mid-seventeenth century as the two peoples struggled for trade supremacy on the high seas. Their antagonism generated two Anglo-Dutch wars, first in 1652–1654, and again in 1665–1667. In the New World, tensions were heightened by the presence of numerous English colonists on Long Island, which the Dutch claimed for themselves. The governors of New Netherland at first welcomed the *Yankees* (a Dutch word for "land pirates") in the expectation that crops raised on their prosperous farms would enrich Dutch trade. At the same time, Dutch leaders worried about the English settlers' loyalty.

In 1664, Charles II brought matters to a head by claiming that since the site of New Netherland lay within the bounds of the original charter of Virginia, the land belonged to England. He granted the territory to his brother James, Duke of York, who sent ships to Long Island to back up England's claim. Their arrival provoked a rebellion by the island's English colonists, leading the Dutch governor, Peter Stuyvesant—who commanded just 150 soldiers—to surrender without firing a shot.

The Duke of York became proprietor of this new English possession, which was renamed New York. James immediately created another colony, New Jersey, when he granted some of the land to a group of his supporters. New Jersey's proprietors struggled to control the diverse people already living there and fighting among themselves. At one point the colony split in two parts, East and West Jersey, which reunited to become a single royal colony in 1702 when the frustrated proprietors surrendered their rights to the king.

New York, which James retained for himself, was the most valuable part of the former Dutch colony. It included the port of New York City (the former New Amsterdam) and the Hudson Valley with its fur trade. James, who succeeded his brother to the English throne in 1685, encouraged Dutch colonists to remain on rather generous terms and promoted immigration from England to strengthen the colony and gain income from land sales. By 1700, the settlers numbered twenty thousand.

For nearly twenty years after its takeover by the English, New York lacked something all other English colonies had—a representative assembly. The Dutch had never created one, and James saw no reason to change that policy, despite the friction it created with his colonists. Particularly after neighboring New Jersey and Pennsylvania created their own assemblies, however, New Yorkers pressed their proprietor to follow suit. Only in 1683, when it became clear that New York might lose population to Pennsylvania, did James relent and create the assembly that brought New York into line with other English colonies.

CONCLUSION

During the seventeenth century, France, the Netherlands, and England competed for land and trade in North America, with France and England gaining colonies on the mainland and all three joining Spain in the Caribbean. New France's small and scattered settlements clung to the St. Lawrence River Valley. The profits from the fur trade encouraged the French to maintain friendly relations with their Indian allies and ensured that French kings would monitor the colony's affairs and invest in its defense. English colonization, by contrast, was a more haphazard process. English kings granted charters—sometimes to joint-stock companies (Virginia, Plymouth, Massachusetts), sometimes to proprietors (Maryland, Carolina, New York, New Jersey, Pennsylvania)—and let the colonies develop more or less on their own. England had no equivalent in the seventeenth century of the imperial bureaucracies Spain and France created to manage their New World holdings.

The result was a highly diverse set of English colonies stretching from the Maine coast to the Caribbean. Settlers adjusted to different environments, developed different economies and labor systems, and worshiped in different churches. In South Carolina, New York, Pennsylvania, the West Indies, the majority of settlers were not even of English origin. What held these colonies together—besides their establishment under English charters and their enmity toward the Spanish and French—was an overlay of common English institutions of government. By the mid-1680s, all the colonies had legislatures that provided for self-government and laws and judicial institutions based on English models.

The planting of French, Dutch, and English colonies not only ended Spain's monopoly of settlement in North America but also challenged the Indians' hold on the continent. Forced to deal with a rising tide of settlers and often to choose sides between European antagonists, native peoples had to adapt to rapidly changing circumstances. Transplanted Europeans adapted too, not only in their dealings with native peoples but also in finding and controlling the supply of laborers they needed to make their colonies prosper. For English colonists this meant the widespread adoption of slavery, an institution that did not exist in England itself. For millions of Africans, the result was forced migration to the New World.

REVIEW QUESTIONS

1. According to Thomas Dudley's letter to the Countess of Lincoln, why did the first Massachusetts colonists worry about their safety? What preparations did they think were necessary to insure the survival of their colony?

2. Comparing French, Dutch, and English colonies, which ones attracted the most settlers, and which the fewest? In what colonies were women scarce? What impact did these differences in emigration have on the various colonies' development?

3. Which English settlements were proprietary colonies? Did they share any common characteristics? What plans did the various proprietors have for their colonies, and to what extent were those plans put into effect?

4. When Virginia's settlers first arrived, they encountered a numerous and powerful confederation of Powhatan Indians. New England's colonists, in contrast, began settlement after epidemics had drastically reduced the local native population. In what ways did the presence or absence of substantial Indian populations affect each region's early history?

5. In both Massachusetts and Pennsylvania, religion figured prominently as a motive for settlement. What were the religious beliefs of the settlers in each colony, and how did those beliefs help shape each colony's development?

6. Three colonial regions—the Chesapeake, the West Indies, and Carolina—developed economies dependent on staple crops. What were those crops? In what ways did staple crop agriculture shape society in each region?

KEY TERMS

Act for Religious Toleration (p. 46)

Anglican (p. 48)

Coureur de bois (p. 37)

Covenant (p. 49)

Frame of Government (p. 61)

Fundamental Constitutions of Carolina (p. 57)

Headright system (p. 42)

House of Burgesses (p. 42)

Indentured servants (p. 38)

Joint-stock company (p. 41)

Pequot War (p. 50)

Pilgrims (p. 48)

Proprietary colony (p. 46)

Puritans (p. 46)

Quakers (p. 60)

Separatists (p. 48)

Slave codes (p. 57)

RECOMMENDED READING

Anderson, Virginia DeJohn. *New England's Generation: The Great Migration and the Formation of Society and Culture in the Seventeenth Century* (1991). Examines the experiences of nearly seven hundred emigrants to New England and explores the ways in which the composition of the settler population shaped New England society.

Dunn, Richard S. *Sugar and Slaves: The Rise of the Planter Class in the English West Indies, 1624–1713* (1972). The authoritative account of British settlement in the West Indies and the development of the slave labor system.

Greer, Allan. *The People of New France* (1997). A brief and readable overview of the origins and development of New France.

Morgan, Edmund S. *American Slavery, American Freedom: The Ordeal of Colonial Virginia* (1975). A vividly written account of the founding of Virginia and the development of an unfree labor system that remains the best study of an early American colony.

Wood, Peter H. *Black Majority: Negroes in Colonial South Carolina from 1670 through the Stono Rebellion* (1974). A study of the founding of South Carolina that emphasizes the contributions of the black slaves who eventually comprised a majority of the colony's settlers.

ADDITIONAL SOURCES

New France
Choquette, Leslie. *Frenchmen into Peasants: Modernity and Tradition in the Peopling of French Canada* (1997).

Eccles, W. J. *Essays on New France* (1987).

Moogk, Peter. *La Nouvelle France: The Making of French Canada—A Cultural History* (2000).

New Netherland
Israel, Jonathan. *The Dutch Republic: Its Rise, Greatness, and Fall, 1477–1806* (1995).

Price, J. L. *The Dutch Republic in the Seventeenth Century* (1998).

Rink, Oliver. *Holland on the Hudson: An Economic and Social History of Dutch New York* (1986).

Chesapeake Society
Carr, Lois Green, Russell R. Menard, and Lorena S. Walsh. *Robert Cole's World: Agriculture and Society in Early Maryland* (1991).

Horn, James. *Adapting to a New World: English Society in the Seventeenth-Century Chesapeake* (1994).

Rutman, Darrett, and Anita Rutman. *A Place in Time: Middlesex County, Virginia, 1650–1750* (1984).

New England
Cave, Alfred. *The Pequot War* (1996).

Hall, David D. *Worlds of Wonder, Days of Judgment: Popular Religious Belief in Early New England* (1989).

Main, Gloria. *Peoples of a Spacious Land: Families and Cultures in Colonial New England* (2001).

Morgan, Edmund S. *Puritan Dilemma: The Story of John Winthrop* (1958).

Ulrich, Laurel Thatcher. *Good Wives: Image and Reality in the Lives of Women in Northern New England, 1650–1750* (1982).

The West Indies
Beckles, Hilary. *White Servitude and Black Slavery in Barbados, 1627–1715* (1989).

Bridenbaugh, Carl and Roberta Bridenbaugh. *No Peace Beyond the Line: The English in the Caribbean, 1624–1690* (1972).

Mintz, Sidney. *Sweetness and Power: The Place of Sugar in Modern History* (1985).

The Proprietary Colonies
Dunn, Richard S., and Mary Maples Dunn, eds. *The World of William Penn* (1986).

Goodfriend, Joyce D. *Before the Melting Pot: Society and Culture in Colonial New York City, 1664–1730* (1992).

Illick, Joseph. *Colonial Pennsylvania: A History* (1976).

Levy, Barry. *Quakers and the American Family: British Settlement in the Delaware Valley* (1988).

Ritchie, Robert. *The Duke's Province: A Study of New York Politics and Society, 1664–1691* (1977).

Weir, Robert. *Colonial South Carolina: A History* (1983).

WHERE TO LEARN MORE

- Jamestown Settlement, near Williamsburg, Virginia. Site includes replicas of first English passenger ships to Virginia, a reconstructed Powhatan Village, the recreated James Fort, and galleries with Indian and English artifacts. Visitors can also see archaeological excavations of site of the actual James Fort, as well as sample artifacts recovered from the area.

  For updated information about archaeological excavations at Jamestown, see www.apva.org. At http:jeffersonvillage.virginia.edu, you can take a virtual tour of the Jamestown settlement.

- St. Mary's City, Maryland. Visitors to this site of the first permanent settlement under the Calvert family may tour the area and view exhibits and living history programs that describe life in early Maryland. The website www.somd.com contains information about the historic site of St. Mary's City and has links to a virtual tour of the area.

- Plimoth Plantation, Plymouth, Massachusetts. A living history museum, Plimoth Plantation recreates colony life in the year 1627. There are reproductions of the English village and a Wampanoag settlement. Visitors may also see a replica of the Mayflower. For a virtual tour, go to pilgrims.net/plimothplantation/vtour. Information on Pilgrims and early years of the colony can be found at pilgrims.net/plymouth/history.

- Pennsbury Manor, Morrisville, Pennsylvania. A reconstruction of William Penn's seventeenth-century plantation, this site includes furnished buildings and restored gardens. There are also guided tours and demonstrations of colonial crafts. Both www.bucksnet.com/pennsbury and www.pennsburymanor.org provide information about William Penn, the historic site, and various activities at the manor.

 Please refer to the document CD-ROM for primary sources related to this chapter.

→ As the top portion of this eighteenth-century French engraving suggests, the horrors of slavery began as soon as Africans were torn from their families and marched to ships anchored off the coast. The bottom part of the picture shows how tightly slaves were packed below the decks of these vessels, evidence that merchants' thirst for profit overrode concerns for the slaves' health or welfare.

THE CREATION OF NEW WORLDS

3

One day [in 1756], when all our people were gone out to their work as usual, and only I and my sister were left to mind the house, two men and a woman got over our walls, and in a moment seized us both; and without giving us time to cry out, or to make any resistance, they stopped our mouths and ran off with us into the nearest wood. Here they tied our hands, and continued to carry us as far as they could. . . . Thus I continued to travel, both by land and by water, through different countries and various nations, till at the end of six or seven months after I had been kidnapped, I arrived at the sea coast. . . .

The first object that saluted my eyes when I arrived on the coast was the sea, and a slave ship, which was then riding at anchor, and waiting for its cargo. These filled me with astonishment, that was soon converted into terror, which I am yet at a loss to describe. . . . I was immediately handled and tossed up to see if I was sound, by some of the crew; and I was now persuaded that I had got into a world of bad spirits, and that they were going to kill me. Their complexions too, differing so much from ours, their long hair, and the language they spoke, which was very different from any I had ever heard, united to confirm me in this belief. . . . I asked . . . if we were not to be eaten by those white men with horrible looks, red faces, and long hair. . . .

In a little time after, amongst the poor chained men, I found some of my own nation. . . . They gave me to

CHAPTER OUTLINE

Indians and Europeans
Indian Workers in the Spanish Borderlands
The Web of Trade
Displacing Native Americans in the English Colonies
Bringing Christianity to Native Peoples
After the First Hundred Years: Conflict and War

Africans and Europeans
Labor Needs and the Turn to Slavery
The Shock of Enslavement
African Slaves in the New World
African American Families and Communities
Resistance and Rebellion

European Laborers in Early America
A Spectrum of Control
New European Immigrants

Conclusion

> understand we were to be carried to these white people's country to work for them. . . . [Many weeks later] we were landed up a river a good way from the sea, about Virginia county, where we saw few of our native Africans, and not one soul who could talk to me.

Olaudah Equiano, *The Interesting Narrative of the Life of Olaudah Equiano, or Gustavus Vassa, The African.*

Olaudah Equiano, born in 1745 in the African kingdom of Benin, was only a boy when his terrifying journey to America began. The son of an Igbo chief, he was caught in the web of an expanding transatlantic slave trade that reached from the African interior to nearly every port town in the Americas and the Caribbean. From modest beginnings in the sixteenth century, the slave trade had expanded dramatically, transforming all societies it touched. Equiano's Virginia scarcely resembled that of John Smith. Tobacco still reigned supreme, but by the mid-eighteenth century, more black workers than white ones bent their backs to the hoe. Slavery had spread from England's Caribbean colonies to dominate the Chesapeake settlements as well.

At the same time, in Virginia and elsewhere in North America, Indian peoples faced new challenges as they endeavored to maintain their independence despite a flood of immigrants from Europe and Africa. Depending on the circumstances, Indians employed different tactics—adaptation, coexistence, diplomacy, resistance—to assert their claims to land and their right to participate in the events and deliberations that affected their lives as much as those of colonists. The America to which Olaudah Equiano had been forcibly transported remained a place where Indian voices had to be heeded.

Equiano's journey did not end in Virginia. Over the next quarter-century, he visited nearly every part of England's empire and beyond—traveling to other mainland colonies, the West Indies, England, Turkey, Portugal, and Spain. He worked as the servant of a naval officer, a barber, a laborer, an overseer, saving money until he could purchase his own freedom. Such an extraordinary career testified to Equiano's versatility, resilience, and determination. It also bore witness to the emergence of an international market for laborers, which—like slavery and Indian relations—shaped the development of North America. Thousands of people from England, Scotland, Ireland, and Germany attempted to take advantage of that market and seek their fortunes in America, increasing the white population and expanding onto new lands. The interactions of Indians, Africans, and Europeans created not one but many New Worlds.

KEY TOPICS

- Patterns of contact between Native Americans and Spanish, French, and English colonists
- The development of slavery and other labor systems in early America
- The formation of African American communities
- Causes and consequences of European immigration to America

INDIANS AND EUROPEANS

Although, by 1750, European colonists and African slaves together outnumbered Indians north of the Rio Grande, Native Americans continued to dominate much of the continent. The colonists remained clustered along the coasts and had yet to make significant movement into the interior. Some native peoples had scarcely seen any colonists. Indians living along the northern Pacific coast, for instance, met their first white men—Russian fur traders—only in the 1740s. By this time, the Pueblos of the Southwest, the Hurons of Canada, and the Algonquians of the Atlantic seaboard had more than a century's experience dealing with Europeans and their American-born descendants.

The character of the relationship between Indians and Europeans depended on more than relative population size and the length of time they had been in contact. It was also shaped by the intentions of the newcomers—whether they came to extract resources, to trade, to settle, or to gain converts—and

Chronology

1440s	Portuguese enter slave trade in West Africa.
c. 1450	Iroquois form Great League of Peace and Power.
1610–1614	First war between English settlers and Powhatan Indians.
1619	First Africans arrive in Virginia.
1622–1632	Second war between English settlers and Powhatan Indians.
1637	Pequot War in New England.
1640s	Slave labor begins to dominate in the West Indies.
	First phase of the Beaver Wars.
1651	First "praying town" established at Natick, Massachusetts.
1661	Maryland law defines slavery as lifelong, inheritable status.
1670	Virginia law defines status of slaves.
1675–1676	King Philip's War in New England.
1676	Bacon's Rebellion in Virginia.
1680	Pueblo Revolt in New Mexico.
1680s	Second phase of Beaver Wars begins.
1690s	Shift from white indentured servants to black slaves as principal labor force in the Chesapeake.
1701	Iroquois adopt policy of neutrality toward French and English.
1711–1713	Tuscarora War in Carolina.
1713	Beginnings of substantial Scottish, Scots-Irish, and German immigration to colonies.
1715–1716	Yamasee War in Carolina.
1720s	Black population begins to increase naturally in English mainland colonies.
1732	Georgia established.
1739	Stono Rebellion in South Carolina.
1741	Slave conspiracy discovered in New York City.
1750	Slavery legalized in Georgia.
1760–1775	Peak of European and African immigration to English colonies.

the responses of particular Native American groups intent on preserving their cultures. The result was a variety of regionally distinctive New World communities. Many of the strategies Native Americans developed as they adapted to new conditions and tried to counter the intrusions of settlers would persist into the twentieth century.

INDIAN WORKERS IN THE SPANISH BORDERLANDS

More than any other European colonists, the Spanish sought direct control over Indians who labored in their mines or in their fields. Their ability to marshal Indian workers for Spanish gain depended on two factors: the existence of sizable Indian communities and Spanish military force. In North America outside of Mexico itself, these conditions could be found in New Mexico, and to a lesser extent in Florida. Native villages provided plenty of workers as well as existing structures of government that the Spanish could convert to their own uses. At the same time, Spanish soldiers insured that the Indians obeyed orders even though they greatly outnumbered the colonists.

One of the Spaniards' most important methods of labor control was the *encomienda*. Encomiendas, granted to influential Spaniards in New Mexico, gave these colonists the right to collect tribute from the native peoples living on a specific piece of land. That tribute usually took the form of corn, blankets, and animal hides, which the Spanish could either use themselves or sell. It was not supposed to include forced labor, but often it did.

The *repartimiento* was another Spanish technique for exploiting Native American labor. This was a mandatory draft of Indian labor for public projects, such as building forts, bridges, and roads. Laws stated that native workers should be paid and limited the length of their service, but the Spanish often ignored these provisions and sometimes compelled Indians to work on private estates.

Spaniards also acquired laborers by ransoming captives that Indian groups seized from one another. This practice was called *rescate*, and it obliged rescued Indians to work for those who had paid their ransom. These "freed" Native Americans usually became servants in Spanish households, often for years. Some colonial families welcomed them as

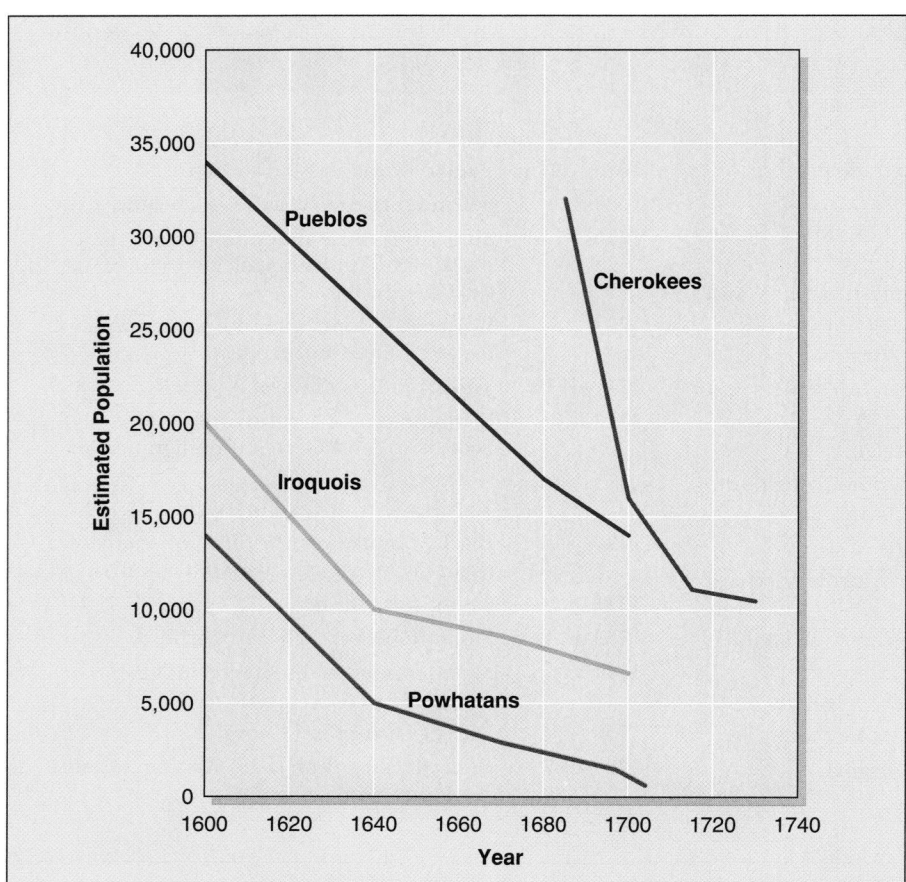

FIGURE 3-1   Estimated Populations of Selected Indian Peoples, 1600–1730
Indian populations shrank dramatically due to diseases brought by Europeans from the Old World. By about 1750, native peoples had become a minority of the inhabitants of America north of the Rio Grande.
Data Sources: Daniel Richter, *The Ordeal of the Longhouse* (1992); Helen Rountree, *Pocahontas's People* (1990); David Weber, *The Spanish Frontier in North America* (1992); Peter Wood, et al., eds., *Powhatan's Mantle* (1989).

foster members, but others mistreated them and even sold them into slavery.

Together these Spanish strategies for controlling Indian labor aroused considerable resentment on the part of native peoples. Spanish demands for labor and tribute remained constant, even when Indian populations declined from disease or crops failed in bad weather. Workers who resisted were severely punished by their masters or by soldiers. Resentments simmered beneath a surface of cooperation until late in the seventeenth century, when longstanding native anger burst forth in rebellion.

THE WEB OF TRADE

Not all economic exchanges between Indians and Europeans were as directly coercive as the *encomiendas* imposed by the Spanish. In many other instances,

Indians used trade relations to exert considerable influence over Europeans. They made colonists understand that Native Americans thought of trade not simply as an economic activity but rather as one aspect of a broader alliance between peoples. If Europeans wished to trade with Indians, they would have to prove their friendship by offering gifts such as wampum (shell beads used as a kind of currency) and military aid as well as manufactured goods. The names that native peoples bestowed on their European neighbors and allies often indicated the kinds of goods they provided. The Narragansetts in New England, for instance, called the English "coat-men" or "knife-men."

The French were among the most successful in adapting to the Native American understanding of trade, for they knew that good relations were essential to keeping New France's fur trade operating smoothly. The fur trade benefited Indians too. "The Beaver does everything perfectly well," noted one native leader; "it makes kettles, hatchets, swords, knives, bread; and, in short, it makes everything." Initially, Indians used European goods as raw materials to be reshaped as they saw fit. Thus copper kettles might be cut into pieces and hammered into ornaments instead of used for cooking. As such goods became more readily available, Indians replaced traditional objects with them: metal kettles for ceramic pots, wool blankets for skins and furs, metal knives for stone ones, glass beads for carved shells.

The benefits of trade were immediate and obvious, but most of the problems were slower to appear. The one exception was the problem of disease, which followed almost immediately from Indians' contacts with European traders (see Figure 3–1). The Huron population declined by half in just six years between 1634 and 1640. Indians trading with the Dutch in New Netherland in the 1650s insisted that they had once been "ten times as numerous as

This eighteenth-century engraving illustrates, in idealized form, the way Indian peoples traded furs for European goods. The barrel may have contained kettles or other metalware packed in sawdust, while the bale to the left probably held cloth.

Courtesy of the Library of Congress

they now are," but "their population had been melted down" by smallpox.

Although Indian hunters enjoyed considerable autonomy in their work, French merchants began to use economic pressure to exert greater control over them. By supplying Indians with trade goods in advance, merchants obligated them to bring in furs as payment. One year's hunting, in short, paid the previous year's debts. If hunters tried to avoid payment, merchants refused to give them any more of the trade goods they needed. Extending credit in this way allowed the French to control native workers without having to subjugate them.

The French could control the Indians through credit because native peoples had grown increasingly dependent on European manufactures. In many communities, Indians had abandoned native crafts and instead relied on imported goods. As a result, they had no alternative but to increase their hunting in order to have enough furs to trade for what they needed. "The Cloaths we wear, we cannot make ourselves," a Carolina Cherokee observed in 1753. "We cannot make our Guns. . . . Every necessary Thing in Life we must have from the white People." One consequence of this predicament was overhunting; as early as the 1640s, beaver could no longer be found in much of New England, New York, and Pennsylvania.

Trade with Europeans eventually encouraged violence and warfare. Indians had certainly fought one another before European colonization. But these wars were generally limited in scope and destructiveness. In much of eastern North America, "mourning wars" predominated. Warriors conducted raids mainly to seize captives rather than to kill large numbers of their enemies. The captives would either be ritually killed to avenge the deaths of individuals lost in earlier conflicts or adopted into the captors' group to replace the dead. After Europeans arrived, Indians adapted the mourning war tradition to deal with new circumstances. Warriors raided their enemies to replace family members lost to disease and fought to avenge losses resulting from the increasingly fierce competition for a diminishing supply of fur-bearing animals. The proliferation of firearms made the conflicts deadlier, and more casualties led to further mourning wars.

The **Beaver Wars,** a long struggle between the Hurons and the Iroquois that began in the 1640s, illustrated the ferocity of such contests. The Hurons were trading partners and allies with the French, and the Iroquois had forged ties with Dutch merchants in the Hudson River Valley. The Iroquois belonged to a league composed of five separate nations: the Mohawks, Oneidas, Onondagas, Cayugas, and Senecas. The **Great League of Peace and Power** had formed c. 1450, initially as a religious organization designed to eliminate mourning wars among the five nations and strengthen them in their conflicts with Indians outside the league.

To satisfy the European demand for furs, the Hurons and Iroquois both hunted beaver at an unsustainable rate. By the 1630s, they had killed nearly all the beavers on their own lands and began to look elsewhere for furs. The Hurons started to raise more corn, intending to trade the surplus for furs with Indians living north of the Great Lakes, where beavers were still abundant. The Iroquois, however, began to raid Huron trading parties and then to attack Huron villages.

The Iroquois triumphed in this struggle largely because the Dutch supplied them with guns while the French were reluctant to arm the Hurons. In the end, the Hurons were destroyed. Thousands were killed or captured, and many others fled westward. A French traveler reported seeing no Hurons in "districts which, not ten years ago, I reckoned to contain eight or ten thousand men. . . . A little farther on, were but the shells of cabins abandoned to the fury of the enemy—those who had dwelt in them having fled into the forest."

The cycle of warfare did not end with the Hurons' destruction. To maintain control over the fur supply, the victorious Iroquois went on to challenge Indian nations near the Great Lakes and in the Ohio Valley. Although trade brought improvements to native life, cemented alliances with Europeans, and strengthened the economic and diplomatic positions of such successful participants as the Iroquois, over the long run its disadvantages—especially Indians' eventual dependence on Europeans and the escalation of violence—threatened to overshadow its benefits.

DISPLACING NATIVE AMERICANS IN THE ENGLISH COLONIES

In New France and New Netherland, where the fur trade took precedence over farming, Indians always outnumbered Europeans. This numerical superiority and their key role as suppliers of furs to the Europeans allowed native peoples to negotiate with settlers from a position of strength and to retain control of much of their land. The situation was much different in the English colonies, whose settlers came to farm and thus competed directly with Indians for land. It did not help matters that, as Indian populations declined as the result of onslaughts of European diseases, colonial populations burgeoned through immigration and natural increase. As early as 1650,

colonists outnumbered Native Americans in coastal Massachusetts and eastern Virginia.

English settlers at first assumed that there was enough land for everyone. Colonists thrilled at the sight of what they considered vast unoccupied territory. "The Indians are not able to make use of the one fourth part of the Land," declared one New England settler. Another insisted that the natives "do but run over the grass, as do also the foxes and wild beasts" and that therefore the "spacious and void" land was free for the taking.

Land use and property rights. But the settlers misunderstood how Indians used their territory. Eastern Algonquian peoples moved frequently to take advantage of the land's diversity. They cleared areas for villages and planting fields, which native women farmed until the soil grew less fertile. Then they moved to a new location, allowing the former village site to return to forest. In ten to twenty years, they or their descendants might return to that site to clear and farm it again. Indians often built villages near the seacoast or rivers so that they could fish and use reeds and grasses for weaving. In the winter, village communities broke up into small bands to hunt in the forest for deer and other animals.

Thus what the colonists considered "vacant" lands were in fact either being used for nonfarming activities or recovering from human occupation in order to be farmed in years to come. Settlers who built towns on abandoned native village sites deprived the Indians of these future planting fields. Indians tolerated such intrusions for a while, but competition from the rapidly increasing settlers threatened their survival.

Disputes between Europeans and Indians frequently arose from misunderstandings about the definition of land ownership and property rights. Indian villages claimed sovereignty over a certain territory, which their members collectively used for farming, fishing, hunting, and gathering. No Indian claimed individual ownership of a specific tract of land. Europeans, of course, did, and for them ownership conferred on an individual the exclusive right to use or sell a piece of land.

These differences created problems whenever Indians transferred land to settlers. The settlers assumed that they had obtained complete rights to the land, whereas the Indians assumed that they had given the settlers not the land itself but only the right to use it. The Indians soon learned what the English meant by a land sale, however, because it was the English understanding that prevailed, enforced in the settlers' courts under the settlers' laws.

Many of the settlers' agricultural practices also strained relations with the Indians. Cutting down forests destroyed Indian hunting lands. When colonists dammed rivers, they disturbed Indian fishing. When they surrounded their fields with log fences and stone walls, they made trespassers of natives who crossed them. Colonial laws prohibited Indians from burning parts of the forest—something they had regularly done to destroy underbrush and make the woods suitable for hunting and travel—because settlers feared that fires might spread to their property. Yet the colonists felt free to let their cattle and pigs loose to graze in the woods and meadows, where they could wander into unfenced Indian cornfields and damage the crops.

Colonial land acquisition.

As their numbers grew, the colonists displaced Indian inhabitants, acquiring their lands in various ways. Some colonial leaders, such as Roger Williams in Rhode Island and William Penn of Pennsylvania, insisted on buying land. But even purchasers who tried to be fair encountered difficulties. Because Indians owned land collectively, only their leaders had the authority to negotiate sales. Settlers, however, sometimes bought land from individual Indians, who had no right to sell it. Because land transfers were usually arranged through interpreters and recorded in English, Indians were not always fully informed of the terms of sale. And even Indians who willingly sold land to begin with grew resentful as colonists approached them for more. Finally, native peoples could be forced to sell land to settle debts they had run up with English creditors.

Settlers occasionally obtained land by fraud. In 1734, for instance, James Logan of Pennsylvania produced what he insisted was a copy of a deed from 1686 by which the Delaware Indians had supposedly transferred a large tract of land to William Penn. Although Logan did not have the original deed and there was no reference to it in the colony's land records, the Delawares eventually had to give up the territory. By the eighteenth century, some colonists moved farther inland, simply settled on Indian lands without any legal pretense at all, and appealed to colonial governments for help when the Indians objected. Land speculators amplified this kind of unrest on the edges of settlement as they sought to acquire land as cheaply as possible and sell it for as much as they could.

Finally, colonists often seized Indian lands in the aftermath of war, as befell, among many others, the Pequots in 1637 in Connecticut and, in Carolina, the Tuscaroras in 1713 and the Yamasees in 1715. In each case, settlers moved onto land left vacant as native peoples were killed, captured, and dispersed by colonial forces. Sometimes colonial leaders contrived for some Indian groups to help them displace others. During the Pequot War, Narragansetts aided Connecticut settlers' efforts to oust the Pequots. Carolina colonists enlisted the help of the Yamasees against the Tuscaroras and then turned to the Cherokees to help them against the Yamasees.

Some Indians who survived warfare and disease staved off the worst effects of English encroachments by regrouping to form new native communities just beyond the edges of colonial settlements. The Catawba Nation in the Carolina Piedmont employed this strategy to preserve their independence and, as a nineteenth-century visitor observed, "be Indians still." Although English colonists continued to covet Catawba lands, the Carolina government realized the advantages of having friendly native allies in a volatile frontier region and tried to discourage settlers' incursions.

Such small victories helped to sustain Indian autonomy in various parts of the English colonies. But the general trend was hardly encouraging. The colonists' insatiable hunger for land generated relentless pressure on native peoples, who were viewed more as impediments to English expansion than as trading partners or potential neighbors. Once the pattern of mutual suspicion and territorial competition had been established, it would be difficult to alter.

BRINGING CHRISTIANITY TO NATIVE PEOPLES

In addition to trade and settlement, religion played a powerful role in shaping relations between Native Americans and Europeans in colonial North America. The three major New World empires of Spain, France, and England competed for Indians' souls as well as their lands and riches.

Catholic missionaries in Spanish colonies.

Franciscan priests were the driving force behind Spain's efforts to control its colonies of New Mexico and Florida (see Map 3–1). Spain valued both regions for strategic reasons. Its bases in Florida helped protect Spanish ships bearing treasure from the mines of Mexico and Peru and discouraged the southward spread of English settlement. New Mexico similarly served as a buffer between the silver mines of northern Mexico and roaming Plains Indians. Neither colony attracted many settlers, however, because neither offered much opportunity for wealth. When Franciscan missionaries proposed to move in, Spanish officials, who were eager to back up their claims

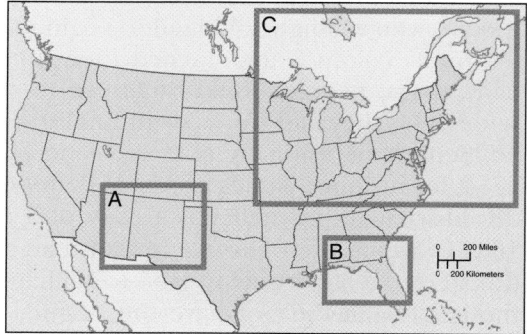

MAP 3-1   Spanish and French Missions in Seventeenth-Century North America
*Spanish Franciscans in New Mexico (A) and Florida (B) and French Jesuits in New France
(C) devoted considerable effort to converting native peoples to Catholic Christianity.*

with a more visible Spanish presence, agreed and even provided financial support.

Franciscans settled near native villages in New Mexico and Florida in order to convert their inhabitants to Christianity. The priests wore their finest vestments and displayed religious paintings and statues, trying to impress the Indians with European goods and Catholic ceremonies. They gave away bells, knives, cloth, and food. According to one Franciscan in New Mexico, these gifts functioned as bait,

bringing Indians to the missions "like fish to the fish hook." The natives believed that accepting these gifts obliged them to listen to the priests' Christian message and help the Franciscans build houses and churches.

After brief religious instruction, the missionaries convinced many Indians to accept baptism into the Catholic Church and with it, the promise of salvation and a heavenly afterlife. Although many of these conversions were doubtless genuine, they also had practical motivations. They often followed epidemics that devastated native villages but spared the Spanish, leading many Indians to wonder if the Christian God might indeed be more powerful than their own gods. In New Mexico, the Spanish offered Pueblo converts protection against Apache raids and access to Franciscan storehouses in times of famine. Ironically, the corn in the storehouses often came from the Indians' own fields, collected by the Spanish as tribute.

The Franciscans insisted that converts abandon their former ways of life and adopt Spanish food, clothing, gender relations, and work routines along with Catholicism. Their efforts met with mixed success. Many Indians, particularly in the densely settled communities of New Mexico, preferred to supplement native beliefs and practices with the new teachings. They added Jesus, Mary, and the Catholic saints to the list of Indian supernatural beings and considered missionaries as counterparts of, rather than replacements for, native religious leaders. Because missionaries reacted to this spiritual mixture with horror, inflicting severe punishments that sometimes led to victims' deaths, native peoples often practiced their own rituals in secret. Some groups, such as the Zuni and Hopi peoples, responded to the missionaries' intolerance by rejecting Christianity altogether. By the mid-seventeenth century, Spanish missionaries claimed to have made thousands of converts, many of whom were mestizos—people of mixed Spanish and Indian ancestry—occupying a difficult position between two cultures. Christianity had been securely planted in the Spanish borderlands, but not quite as deeply as the missionaries assumed.

French Jesuits in Canada.
To a certain extent, French Jesuits in Canada followed a similar strategy, moving to native villages and seeking to awe Indians with European technology and Catholic rituals. Priests exhibited the "magical" powers of clocks and magnets before Indian audiences and impressed native peoples by predicting eclipses. Missionaries demonstrated their ability to read and write, which fascinated Indian peoples who had no experience with written language. "All this serves to gain their affections, and to render them more docile when we introduce the admirable and incomprehensible mysteries of our Faith," explained one priest, who assumed that suitably impressed Indians would then "accept without reply what we say to them."

When Indians failed to relinquish their religious beliefs quite so easily, French missionaries resorted to economic pressure. They convinced merchants to sell guns only to converted Indians and to offer them other trade goods at a discount. Such tactics doubtless brought some success but, as in New Mexico, the crises engendered by epidemics more often than not sparked an upsurge in conversions. Converts in New France also preferred to meld Catholic teachings with native beliefs. Missionaries hardly condoned this response; one Jesuit complained that Indians "cannot suffer any opposition to their ceremonies." Vastly outnumbered by the Indians and intent on achieving their ultimate goal of winning souls for the Christian God, Jesuits resigned themselves at least in the short run to a gradual approach. "One must be careful before condemning a thousand things among their customs," warned one priest, because to do so would "greatly offend minds brought up and nourished in another world." Although the Jesuits were just as convinced of their own cultural superiority as any other Europeans, they reduced the potential for confrontation with the Indians by accepting small changes in converts at first in hopes of a wholesale transformation to follow.

Missionaries in English colonies.
The Protestant English were less successful at attracting Native

This Jesuit missionary, wearing his distinctive Catholic vestments, is baptizing an Indian in New France. French Jesuits proved to be more tolerant than most European missionaries in allowing Indian converts to retain at least some of their own customs.

This ball-headed war club, carved of maple wood, is thought to have been owned by King Philip, who led a confederation of Wampanoags and other New England Indians in a war against the colonists in 1675–1676. It is inlaid on both sides with pieces of white and purple wampum, which supposedly represented the number of English and Indian enemies killed.

American converts. Puritans frowned on the rituals and religious objects that drew Indians to Catholicism, but Protestant practices, including lengthy sermons and an emphasis on Bible study, held little allure for Indians accustomed to a more ritualistic spiritual life. Even so, Protestant missionaries achieved some success, principally in New England. Beginning in the 1650s and 1660s, Puritan ministers such as John Eliot and Thomas Mayhew, Jr. attracted converts. Eliot helped to establish several "praying towns," where Indians received instruction in Protestant Christianity and English ways. By 1674, about 2,300 Indians resided in these towns.

Elsewhere in the English colonies, missionaries enjoyed little success. Anglican missionaries in the southern colonies did not even begin conversion work until the eighteenth century and then often directed their efforts toward settlers who seemed to need religious instruction more urgently than the Indians. In the 1730s and 1740s, German Moravians, a Protestant group that stressed personal piety, managed to convert some Indians in western Pennsylvania. Although individual ministers showed genuine interest in conversion, and Anglican officials in England devoted some resources to missionary activities by the eighteenth century, the Protestant English never matched the efforts of Spanish or French Catholics. Rapidly growing English colonial populations were more interested in acquiring Indian lands than in converting Indian peoples.

AFTER THE FIRST HUNDRED YEARS: CONFLICT AND WAR

After nearly a century of European settlement, violence between colonists and Indians erupted in all three North American empires. Each deadly encounter—**King Philip's War** in New England, **Bacon's Rebellion** in Virginia, the **Pueblo Revolt** in New Mexico, and the resumption of the Beaver Wars in New France—reflected distinctive features of English, Spanish, and French patterns of colonization.

King Philip's War. The growing frustration of the Wampanoags, who had befriended the Pilgrims more than a half-century earlier, with the land-hungry settlers whose towns now surrounded them sparked King's Philip's War, which broke out in 1675. Massasoit's younger son, Metacom—called King Philip by the English—led the Wampanoags and struggled to preserve their independence against the incursions of the colonists, who now numbered more than fifty thousand. He had little reason to trust the colonists. His older brother had died mysteriously while being questioned by colonial officials about rumors of an Indian conspiracy. Philip himself had been accused of plotting against the settlers and then forced to sign a treaty submitting to English authority.

In the spring of 1675, a colonial court found three Wampanoags guilty of murdering a Christian Indian who had warned the English of Wampanoag preparations for war. Despite Philip's protest that the evidence against the men was tainted, the court sentenced them to be hanged. This act convinced the Wampanoags that they had to strike back against the English before it was too late. Only "a small part of the dominion of my ancestors remains," declared Philip. "I am determined not to live until I have no country." The final blow occurred in June 1675, when colonists killed an Indian they found looting an abandoned house and then ignored the Indians' outrage at the murder.

Native warriors attacked outlying villages in Plymouth Colony, moved into the Connecticut River Valley, and then turned eastward again to strike towns within 20 miles of Boston. As the Narragansetts and other groups joined the uprising, Philip successfully eluded the combined forces of Massachusetts, Connecticut, and Plymouth for months (see "American Views: Mary Rowlandson

Among the Indians" on page 78). By the summer of 1676, however, the Indians were exhausted, weakened by disease and food shortages. Philip moved into western New England, where his men clashed with the powerful Mohawks, long-standing enemies of the Wampanoags and allies of English fur traders in New York. Philip died in an ambush in August 1676, and the war ended soon after.

At least a thousand colonists and perhaps three thousand Indians died in King Philip's War. One out of every sixteen male colonists of military age was killed, making this the deadliest conflict in American history in terms of the proportion of casualties to total population. The Indians succeeded in forcing back the line of settlement—it would be forty years before colonists again occupied land they had first claimed before the war—but lost what remained of their independence in New England. The victorious English sold many native survivors, including Philip's wife and young son, into slavery in the West Indies. Others they employed in marginal jobs or confined in one of the few remaining praying towns. Philip's head, impaled on a stake, was left for decades just outside Plymouth as a grisly warning of the price to be paid for resisting colonial expansion.

Bacon's Rebellion.

As King Philip's War raged in New England, a bloody conflict erupted in Virginia that had a similarly devastating effect on that colony's native population. Frustrated by shrinking economic opportunities in eastern Virginia, where established planters controlled all the good land, many settlers, including new arrivals and recently freed indentured servants, moved to Virginia's western frontier. There they came into conflict with the region's resident Indians. In the summer of 1675, a group of frontier settlers attacked the Susquehannocks in order to seize their lands. The Indians struck back, prompting Nathaniel Bacon, a young, wealthy planter who had only recently arrived in Virginia, to lead the settlers in a violent campaign against all Indians, even those at peace with the colonial government. Governor William Berkeley ordered Bacon and his men to stop their attacks. They defied him and marched on Jamestown, turning a war between settlers and Indians into a rebellion of settlers against the colonial authorities.

The rebels believed that Berkeley and the colonial government represented the interests of established tobacco planters who wanted to keep men like themselves from emerging as potential competitors. Desperate because of the low price of tobacco, they demanded lower taxes and easier access to land—meaning, in effect, the right to take land from the In-

dians. Berkeley offered to build forts along the frontier to protect the settlers from the Indians, but the rebels were not interested in protection. What they wanted was help in exterminating the Indians. They captured and burned the colonial capital at Jamestown, forcing Berkeley to flee. Free to direct their aggression against Indians once more, they burned Indian villages and massacred the inhabitants. Trying to appease the rebels, the House of Burgesses passed measures allowing them to seize lands belonging to Indians who had left their villages without permission—even though many had fled to escape the rebels. The assembly also legalized the enslavement of Indians.

By the time troops arrived from England to put down the rebellion, Bacon had died of a fever and most of his men had drifted home. Berkeley arrested and hanged twenty-three rebels, but the real victims of the rebellion were Virginia's Indians. The remnants of the once-powerful Powhatans lost their remaining lands and either moved west or lived in poverty on the edges of English settlement. In the wake of the rebellion, hatred of Indians became a permanent feature of frontier life in Virginia, and government officials appeared more eager to spend money "for extirpating all Indians" than for maintaining peaceful relations.

The Pueblo Revolt.

In 1680, the Pueblo Revolt against the Spanish in New Mexico had a very different outcome than did the rebellion in Virginia or the war in New England. Nearly 20,000 Pueblo Indians had grown increasingly restless under the harsh rule of only 2,500 Spaniards. Incessant Spanish demands for tribute under the *encomienda* system fed native discontent. A prolonged drought that began in the 1660s only increased their distress. Corn harvests dwindled, and many people starved. The Apaches, who had once traded with the Pueblos for corn, now raided their storehouses instead, and Spanish soldiers could not stop them.

The spark that ignited the revolt, however, was an act of religious persecution. Spanish officials unwisely chose this troubled time to stamp out all remaining traces of Pueblo religion. In 1675, the governor arrested forty-seven native religious leaders on charges of sorcery. The court ordered most of them to be publicly whipped and released but sentenced four of them to death.

Led by Popé, one of the freed leaders, the outraged Pueblos organized for revenge. A growing network of rebels emerged as Spanish soldiers marched into Pueblo villages and destroyed kivas, the chambers that Indians used for religious ceremonies. Working from the village of Taos in northern New

AMERICAN VIEWS

Mary Rowlandson Among the Indians

In February 1676, in the midst of King Philip's War, Indian warriors attacked the town of Lancaster, Massachusetts. They killed many inhabitants and took 23 colonists captive, including Mary Rowlandson and three of her children. Rowlandson spent the next three months traveling with various groups of Nipmucs, Narragansetts, and Wampanoags. She suffered physically and emotionally, watching her youngest daughter die in her arms and worrying about her other two children, from whom she was frequently separated. During her captivity, Rowlandson survived by accepting her fate and adapting to the Indians' way of life. Finally, with an English victory imminent, Rowlandson was ransomed and rejoined her husband (who had been away at the time of the attack) and family. In 1682, she published an account of her captivity in which she explored the meaning of her experience. Rowlandson's narrative proved so popular that three editions were printed in the first year.

- How did Rowlandson describe the Indians? How did she characterize her encounter with King Philip?
- In what ways did Rowlandson accommodate herself to the Indians' way of life? How did she employ her skills to fit in? Did her gender make a difference in her experience of captivity?
- How did Rowlandson's Puritan faith shape her narrative?

We travelled on till night; and in the morning, we must go over the River to Philip's crew. When I was in the Cannoo, I could not but be amazed at the numerous crew of Pagans that were on the Bank on the

---

Mexico, by the summer of 1680, Popé commanded an enormous force of rebels drawn from twenty Pueblo villages. On August 10, they attacked the Spanish settlements. Popé urged them to "break up and burn the images of the holy Christ, the Virgin Mary and the other saints, the crosses, and everything pertaining to Christianity" and ordered Indian converts to "plunge into the rivers and wash themselves" to remove the taint of baptism. Within a few weeks, the rebels had destroyed or damaged every Spanish building and killed more than four hundred Spaniards, including twenty-one of the colony's thirty-three missionaries. By October, all Spaniards had fled New Mexico.

They did not return for thirteen years. By then, internal rivalries had split the victorious Pueblo coalition, and Popé had been overthrown as leader. Few Pueblo villages offered much resistance to the new Spanish intrusion. Even so, the Spanish now understood the folly of pushing the Indians too far. Fearful of inciting another rebellion, officials reduced demands for tribute, and ended the *encomienda* system. The Franciscans eased their attacks on Pueblo religion. New Spanish governors, backed by military force, were responsible for keeping peace as best they could in a place where Indians still outnumbered Europeans.

The Iroquois adopt neutrality. The Iroquois experience in the last phase of the Beaver Wars threatened to parallel that of the Indians of New England and Virginia rather than that of the Pueblos in New Mexico. What began as a struggle between the Iroquois and western native peoples for control of the fur trade blossomed into a larger conflict as it was absorbed into the imperial rivalry between England and other side. When I came ashore, they gathered all about me, I sitting alone in the midst: I observed they asked one another questions, and laughed, and rejoyced over their Gains and Victories. Then my heart began to fail: and I fell a weeping which was the first time to my remembrance, that I wept before them. Although I had met with so much Affliction, and my heart was many times ready to break, yet could I not shed one tear in their sight: but rather had been all this while in a maze, and like one astonished: but now I may say as, Psal. 137.1 *By the rivers of Babylon, there we sat down: yea, we wept when we remembered Zion.* There one of them asked me, why I wept, I could hardly tell what to say: yet I answered, they would kill me: No, said he, none will hurt you. Then came one of them and gave me two spoon-fulls of Meal to comfort me. . . . Then I went to see King Philip, he bade me come in and sit down, and asked me whether I would smoke (a usual Complement now adayes amongst Saints and Sinners) but this no way suited me. For though I had formerly used Tobacco, yet I had left it ever since I was first taken, *It seems to be a bait, the devil lays to make men loose their precious time.* . . .

During my abode in this place, Philip spake to me to make a shirt for his boy, which I did, for which he gave me a shilling: I offered the money to my master, but he bade me keep it: and with it I bought a piece of Horse flesh. Afterwards he asked me to make a Cap for his boy, for which he invited me to Dinner. I went, and he gave me a Pancake, about as big as two fingers; it was made of parched wheat, beaten, and fryed in Bears grease, but I thought I never tasted pleasanter meat in my life. There was a Squaw who spake to me to make a shirt for her *Sannup* [husband], for which she gave me a piece of Bear. Another asked me to knit a pair of Stockins, for which she gave me a quart of Pease. . . . Hearing that my son was come to this place, I went to see him, and found him lying flat upon the ground: I asked him how he could sleep so? He answered me, *That he was not asleep, but at Prayer;* and lay so, that they might not observe what he was doing. I pray God he may remember these things now he is returned in safety.

Source: Neal Salisbury, ed., *The Sovereignty and Goodness of God, Together with the Faithfulness of His Promises Displayed. . . .* (Boston, 1997), pp. 82–83.

France. Although the Iroquois suffered devastating losses similar to those inflicted on the Indians in the English colonies, they did not similarly suffer a loss of independence. The key to Iroquois survival in the war's aftermath was the adoption of a position of neutrality between the European powers.

Looking for new trading partners to replace the Hurons, the French turned in the 1680s to the Ottawas, Wyandots, and other Indian peoples living near the Great Lakes. But the Iroquois had begun to raid these same peoples for furs and captives, much as they had attacked the Hurons in the first phase of the Beaver Wars in the 1640s. They exchanged the furs for European goods with English traders, who had replaced the Dutch as their partners after the conquest of New Netherland. Many of the captives were adopted into Iroquois families, replacing victims of warfare and disease. When the French

moved into the Great Lakes territory, the Iroquois objected to their attempt to "have all the Bevers" for themselves.

The French attacked the Iroquois to prevent them and their English allies from extending their influence in the west. In June 1687, a combined force of French and Christian Indian soldiers invaded the lands of the Senecas, the westernmost of the five nations of the Iroquois League. The Iroquois retaliated by besieging a French garrison at Niagara, where nearly two hundred soldiers starved to death, and killing hundreds of colonists in attacks on French villages along the St. Lawrence River.

The French participated much more directly and suffered greater losses in this renewal of the Beaver Wars than they had in the fighting of the 1640s. In 1689, France and England went to war in Europe, and the struggle between them and their

Indian allies for control of the fur trade in North America became part of a larger imperial contest between the two countries. The European powers made peace in 1697, but calm did not immediately return to the Great Lakes region.

The conflict was even more devastating for the Iroquois. The English, still solidifying their control over their new colony of New York, provided minimal military assistance, and the Iroquois suffered heavy casualties. Perhaps a quarter of their population died from disease and warfare by 1689. The devastation encouraged Iroquois diplomats to find a way to extricate themselves from future English–French conflicts. The result, in 1701, was a pair of treaties, negotiated separately with Albany and Montreal, that recognized Iroquois neutrality and, at least for several decades, prevented either the English or the French from dominating the western lands.

Each of these conflicts grew from a distinctive pattern of contact between different groups of colonists and native peoples. English settlers fought with Wampanoags, Powhatans, and Susquehannocks for control of land, and the losers were the outnumbered Indians. Spanish colonists clashed with Pueblos over religion, and the more numerous natives won a temporary victory and accommodation in the long run with the Spanish Catholic minority. French soldiers battled with the Iroquois over control of the fur trade until both sides agreed to an uneasy truce. In each case, nearly a century of contact culminated in a struggle that revealed the fragility of Indian autonomy as European populations continued to grow and to seek domination.

AFRICANS AND EUROPEANS

The movement of Africans to the Americas was one of the largest forced migrations in world history. By the time New World slavery finally ended, with its abolition in Brazil in 1888, over twelve million Africans had arrived on American shores. From a relatively small stream in the sixteenth century, African migration ac-

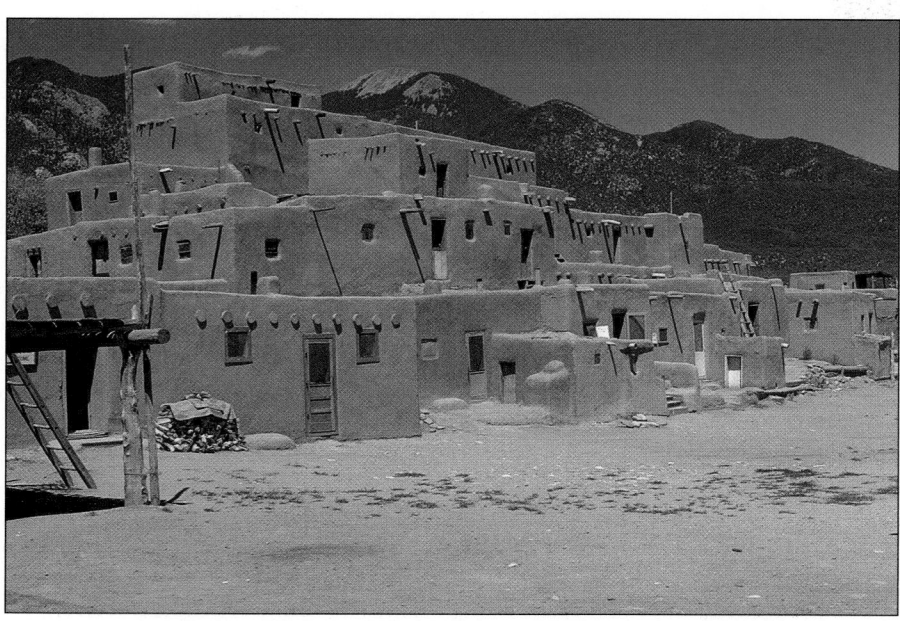

One of the many pueblos scattered along the Rio Grande valley, Taos served as Popé's headquarters at the start of the Pueblo Revolt in August 1680. Within a few weeks, the Indians drove the Spanish from New Mexico and destroyed most of their settlements. The Spanish did not return until 1693.

celerated to a great flood by the 1700s. Over 350,000 Africans crossed the Atlantic before 1600. More than five times as many, nearly 1.8 million Africans, arrived in the Americas in the seventeenth century. In the eighteenth century, another 6.1 million African migrants reached American destinations.

Virtually all Africans arrived as slaves, making the history of African experience in the Americas inseparable from the history of slavery and the slave trade. As one eighteenth-century English observer noted, Africans became "the strength and sinews of this western world," performing much of the labor of colonization. The vast majority of African slaves ended up in Brazil, the West Indies, or New Spain. Only 1 out of 20 Africans came to the British mainland colonies, but this still amounted to well over 300,000 individuals (see Figure 3–2). Their presence transformed English colonial societies everywhere, but particularly in the South. At the same time, Africans were themselves transformed. Out of their diverse African ethnic backgrounds and the experience of slavery itself they gradually forged new identities as African American peoples.

LABOR NEEDS AND THE TURN TO SLAVERY

Europeans in the New World were thrilled to find that land was abundant and quite cheap by European standards. They were perplexed, however, by

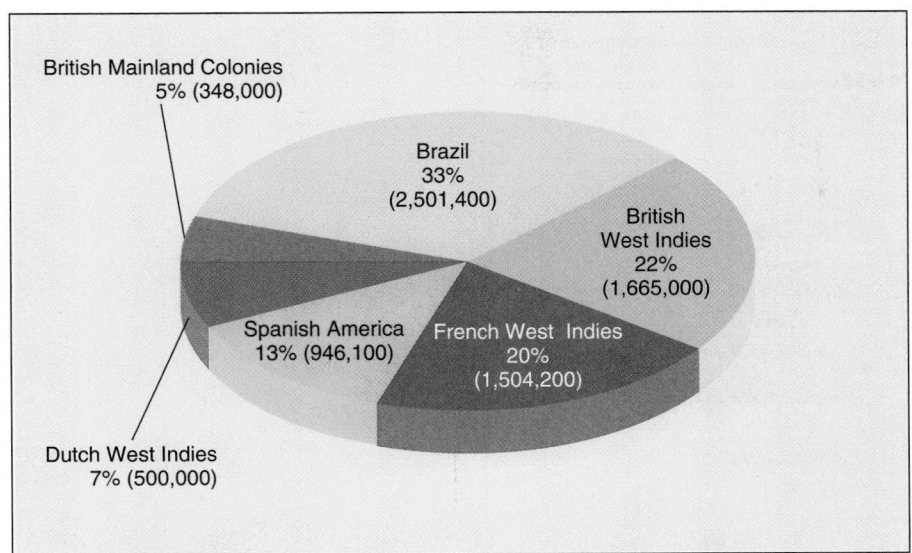

FIGURE 3-2 Destination of Slaves Imported from Africa to the Americas between 1451 and 1810
Approximately 7.5 million Africans were brought as slaves to the Americas before 1810. The vast majority went to the Caribbean, Mexico, and South America, where they toiled in mines and on sugar plantations.
Data Source: Philip Curtin, *The Atlantic Slave Trade: A Census* (1969), p. 268.

the unexpectedly high cost of labor. In Europe, the reverse had been true. There land was expensive but labor cheap, because competition for jobs among large numbers of workers pushed wages down. Colonial workers commanded high wages because there were so few of them compared to the supply of land waiting to be developed. Making matters worse, few settlers wanted to work for others when they could get farms of their own. The scarcity and high cost of labor created a major problem for colonial employers, leading some to turn to enslaved Africans as a solution.

The development of slavery in the colonies was not inevitable. Europeans had owned slaves (both white and black) long before the beginning of American colonization, but slaves formed a small—and shrinking—minority of European laborers. By the fifteenth century, slavery had all but disappeared in northern Europe except as punishment for serious crimes. English laws in particular protected the personal freedom of the king's subjects.

Slavery persisted longer in southern Europe and the Middle East. In both regions, religion influenced the choice of who was enslaved. Because neither Christians nor Muslims would hold as slaves members of their own faiths, Arab traders turned to sub-Saharan Africa to find slaves who did not belong to either religion. Eventually the Arabic word for slave—*'abd*—became a synonym for "black man." By

the fifteenth century, a durable link between slave status and black skin had been forged in European minds.

Europeans in the New World, however, first attempted to force Indians into slavery as a way of addressing the labor shortage. Columbus's enslavement of Caribbean islanders marked only the beginning. Spaniards held Indian slaves in all their New World colonies, as did the Portuguese in Brazil. French Canadians enslaved Pawnee Indians captured in wars in the North American interior. English colonists condemned Indian enemies they captured in wartime to slavery as punishment for their opposition to English rule. And in early Carolina, English traders saw an opportunity to profit by enslaving Indians without any judicial niceties. They encouraged Indians "to make War amongst themselves to get Slaves" whom the traders could buy and then resell to West Indian and local planters.

Native American slaves, however, could not fill the colonists' labor needs. Everywhere disease and harsh working conditions reduced their numbers. English colonists also discovered practical reasons not to enslave Indians. When traders incited Indian wars to gain slaves, bloodshed often spread to English settlements. Moreover, enslaved Indian men refused to perform agricultural labor, which they considered women's work. Because they knew the land so well, Indians could easily escape and make their way back to their own people. As a result, although the Indian slave trade persisted in the English colonies through the eighteenth century (and there were still Indian slaves in the nineteenth century), by 1700 it had given way to a much larger traffic in Africans. Virtually all European colonizers had, by that point, made the same decision to rely principally on African laborers.

THE SHOCK OF ENSLAVEMENT

European traders did not themselves enslave Africans. Instead, they relied on other Africans to capture slaves for them, tapping into a preexisting African slave trade and helping to expand it beyond previous bounds. With the permission of local rulers, Europeans built forts and trading posts (called factories) on the West African coast and bought slaves from African traders (see Map 3–2). African rulers occasionally enslaved and sold their own people as punishment for crimes, but most slaves were seized by one group from another. Attracted by European cloth, iron, liquor, guns, and other goods, West Africans fought increasingly among themselves to secure captives and began kidnapping individuals from the interior.

People of all social ranks ended up on the slave ships. Some had been slaves in Africa; others had been village leaders or, like Olaudah Equiano, members of chiefs' families and the educated elite. In 1730, for example, Mandingo tribesmen captured Job ben Solomon, an accomplished Arabic scholar of the Fula tribe of Senegal, and sold him to English traders. In the end, slavery reduced all Africans, regardless of their social origins, to the same degraded status.

Once captured, slaves marched in chains to the coast, to be confined in cages called *barracoons* until there were enough to fill a ship. Captains examined them to insure their fitness and branded them like cattle with a hot iron. The slaves then boarded canoes to be ferried to the ships. Desperation overwhelmed some of them, who, according to an English captain, jumped "out of the canoos. . . . and kept under water till they were drowned, to avoid being taken up and saved." Slaves brought aboard ships waiting to leave for America sometimes mutinied. These rebellions, fought against great odds, rarely succeeded.

Slaves who could not escape while still in Africa suffered through a horrendous six- to eight-week-long ocean voyage known as the **Middle Passage**. Captains wedged men below decks into spaces about 6 feet long, 16 inches wide, and 30 inches high. Women and children were packed even more tightly. Except for brief excursions on deck for forced exercise, slaves remained below decks, where the air grew foul from the vomit, blood, and excrement in which the terrified victims lay. "The shrieks of the women, and the groans of the dying," recalled Olaudah Equiano, "rendered it a scene of horror almost in-

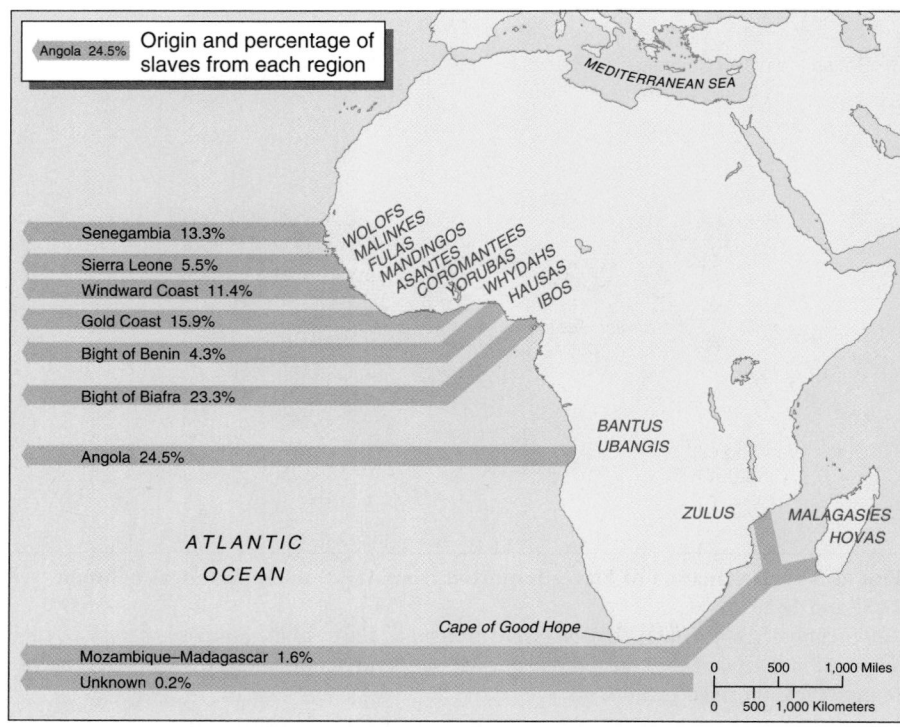

MAP 3-2   African Origins of North American Slaves, 1690–1807
Nearly all slaves in English North America were West Africans. Most had been captured or purchased by African slave traders, who then sold them to European merchants.

conceivable." Some slaves went insane. Others tried to commit suicide by jumping overboard or starving themselves. Captains force-fed those who refused to eat, prying their mouths open and pouring food in through a funnel. On many voyages, between 5 and 20 percent of the slaves perished from disease, but captains had usually packed the ships tightly enough to make a profit from selling the rest.

Those who survived the dreadful voyage endured the fear and humiliation of sale. Sometimes buyers rushed aboard ship in a scramble to choose slaves. Planters generally preferred males and often sought slaves from particular African ethnic groups, in the belief that some Africans would work harder than others. Ship captains also sold slaves at public auctions, where purchasers poked them, looking for signs of disease. Many terrified Africans, like Equiano, thought they were going to be eaten.

AFRICAN SLAVES IN THE NEW WORLD

The Spanish and Portuguese first brought Africans to the Americas, using them to replace or supplement the dwindling numbers of Indian slaves toiling in silver mines and on sugar plantations. The Dutch, who scrambled for a share of the lucrative slave trade, quickly followed suit. English colonists, less familiar with slavery, adopted it more slowly. West Indian planters were the first Englishmen to do so on a large scale in the 1640s, buying thousands of slaves from Portuguese and Dutch traders to work on sugar plantations. In most other English colonies, however, different economic conditions either postponed or prevented slavery's widespread adoption.

Slavery in the southern colonies.

Black slaves first arrived in Virginia in 1619, but they did not form a significant portion of the colony's population until the end of that century (see Figure 3–3). For decades, tobacco planters saw no reason to switch from white indentured servants to slaves. Servants (because they worked for masters only for a period of years rather than for life) cost less than slaves, were more readily available, and were familiar. For most of the seventeenth century, by contrast, slaves were expensive, difficult to obtain, and exotic. By the 1680s, however, planters in the Chesapeake colonies of Virginia and Maryland began to shift from servants to slaves.

Two related developments caused this change. First, white indentured servants became harder to find. Fewer English men and women chose to emigrate as servants after 1660 because an improving economy in England provided jobs for them at home. At the same time, Virginia's white population tripled between 1650 and 1700, rapidly increasing the number of planters now competing for a shrinking supply of laborers. Planters also faced competition from newer colonies. Pennsylvania and New Jersey, with generous land policies, attracted immigrant laborers away from the longer-settled Chesapeake colonies.

Second, even as white servants grew scarcer, African slaves became more available, largely because of changes in the slave trade. Before the 1660s, Dutch and Portuguese merchants who dominated the trade mainly supplied their own colonies and the profitable West Indian market. But beginning in 1674, England's Royal African Company began shipping slaves to English buyers in the Caribbean and on the mainland. The supply of slaves surged after 1698, when the Royal African Company lost its special trading rights and many English merchants and New Englanders entered the fiercely competitive trade.

Chesapeake planters eventually found reasons besides availability to prefer slaves to servants. Although more expensive than servants, slaves were a better long-term investment. Because slave status passed from slave mothers to their children, buying both men and women gave planters a self-reproducing labor force. Runaway black slaves were more easily recaptured than were escaped servants, who blended into the white population. And unlike indentured servants, slaves were slaves for life. They would never compete as planters with their former masters or, like Nathaniel Bacon's followers, pose a threat to order if they failed to prosper.

Chesapeake planters had already come to see white servants as possessions, people whose labor could be bought and sold like any other commodity. This attitude doubtless eased the transition in the 1680s and 1690s to the much harsher system of slavery. In Carolina, of course, the introduction of slavery was not gradual at all. Slaves arrived there right from the start, brought in the 1670s by colony founders accustomed to slavery in Barbados. By 1720, slavery was firmly embedded in all the southern colonies except sparsely settled North Carolina. In that year, one-third of Virginia's settler population, and nearly three-quarters of South Carolina's, were black.

Slavery grew rapidly in the southern colonies because it answered the labor needs of planters engaged in the commercial production of tobacco and rice. The demand for slaves became so powerful that it

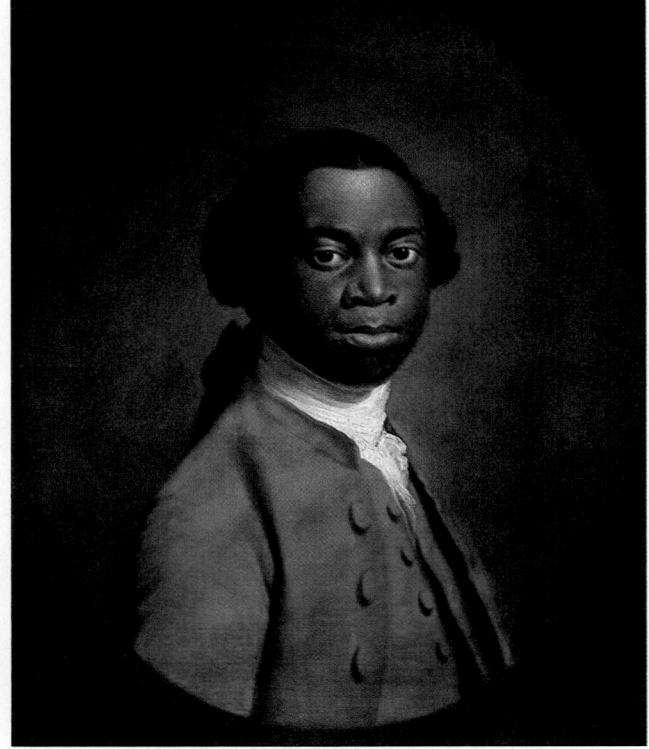

The freed slave Olaudah Equiano appears in this 1780 portrait by an unknown artist. After purchasing his freedom, Equiano wrote a vivid account of his capture in Africa and his life in slavery. One of the first such accounts to be published (in 1789), this narrative testified to slavery's injustice and Equiano's own fortitude and talents.

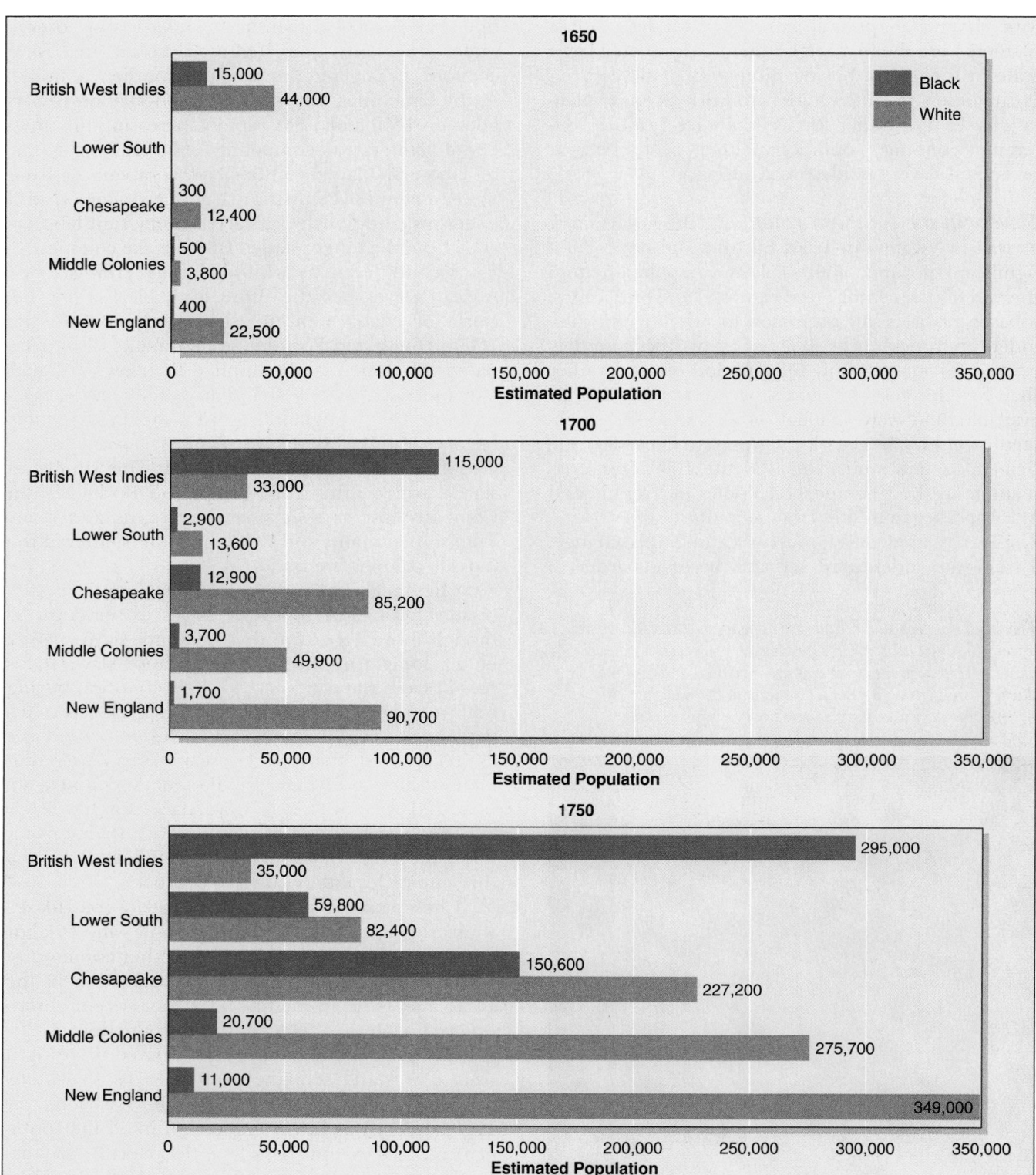

FIGURE 3-3   **Estimated Population of Black and White Settlers in British Colonial Regions, 1650–1750**
Settler populations increased rapidly in all colonial regions, but the racial composition varied. By 1750, black people overwhelmingly predominated in the West Indies and were quite numerous in the southern colonies; north of Maryland, however, their numbers remained small.

Data Source: John J. McCusker and Russell Menard, *The Economy of British America, 1607–1789* (1985).

Although this watercolor of a slave ship bound for Brazil dates from the nineteenth century, it depicts a scene common on slavers in the 1700s. The artist's attention to detail suggests both the misery of the slaves' surroundings and the dignity of the individuals forced to live under such conditions.

destroyed James Oglethorpe's plan to keep them out of the new colony of Georgia, founded in 1732. Oglethorpe intended Georgia to be a refuge for English debtors, who normally were jailed until they could repay their creditors. His idea was to send debtors to Georgia to produce such exotic goods as silk and wine, benefiting both themselves and the English economy. Only rice turned a profit in Georgia, however, and

colonists insisted that they needed slaves to keep up with South Carolina's planters. By 1750, Georgia's founders reluctantly legalized slavery; by 1770, slaves made up nearly half of the colony's population.

Slavery in the northern colonies.   Far fewer slaves lived north of the Chesapeake, although they were present in every British colony. They were too

This 1769 broadside advertised the arrival of a cargo of West African slaves in Charleston, South Carolina. By that date, slaves made up over two-thirds of the colony's settlers. Note that nearly equal numbers of men and women have been imported. This practice would eventually contribute to the formation of slave families and communities.

expensive for most northern farmers—who mainly produced food for their families, not staple crops for an international market—to use profitably. This was not true, however, for farmers with larger properties in parts of Long Island, the Hudson Valley, Rhode Island, northern New Jersey, and southeast Pennsylvania, where commercial wheat farming and livestock raising prevailed. Especially in the eighteenth century, these landowners acquired significant numbers of slaves. By the 1760s, for instance, one-fifth of the farmers in Chester County, Pennsylvania, owned slaves. Some rural slaves also worked in local indus-

tries, such as tanneries and iron foundries, often alongside white servants and hired laborers.

Northern slaves could often be found in cities, especially busy ports such as Newport, Rhode Island, where newly arrived Africans landed. At the start of the eighteenth century, one out of six Philadelphia residents was a slave; by 1740, slaves made up 15 percent of the city's workingmen. In mid-eighteenth-century New York City, slaves comprised between 12 and 14 percent of the population. Urban slaves worked at a variety of occupations, including seafaring and maritime trades such as rope and sail making. Many were domestic servants in the homes of rich merchants, gentlemen, and professionals. Substantial numbers found employment as artisans, to such an extent that white workers occasionally protested that they were being left behind. In 1737, for instance, New York City's white coopers complained about "the pernicious custom of breeding slaves to trades whereby the honest and industrious tradesmen [are] reduced to poverty for want of employ."

Changing race relations in the colonies.   Race relations in the mainland colonies were less rigid in the seventeenth century than they would later become. Before 1700, slaves did not form a majority of the population in any colony, a situation that may have made them seem less threatening to white people. Most seventeenth-century Chesapeake planters did not own slaves. Those who did often held only a few slaves along with white servants. In these households, white and black people lived and worked in close contact. Black slaves and white servants ran away together and cooperated during Bacon's Rebellion. In some areas, free black people—often slaves who had bought their own freedom—prospered in an atmosphere of racial tolerance that would be unthinkable by the eighteenth century.

The career of an ambitious black Virginian named Anthony Johnson, for example, resembled that of many white settlers—a remarkable achievement, given that he arrived in the colony in 1621 as a slave known only as "Antonio a Negro." Johnson's master allowed him to marry and start a family while he was still a slave and may even have allowed Anthony to earn the money to purchase his and his family's liberty. Once free, the Johnsons settled near their former master in eastern Virginia. By 1651, Johnson owned a 250-acre plantation, and his sons eventually acquired even larger estates. Like white settlers, Johnson occasionally took his neighbors to court and even successfully sued them. He and his sons also owned slaves. When his plantation burned to the ground in 1653, local authorities granted

Johnson relief from taxes in recognition of his family's "hard labor and known services" in supporting themselves.

Anthony Johnson belonged to the first or what one historian has called the "charter" generation of American slaves, and his experience reveals how much slavery changed over time. This generation of slaves mainly came from African port towns, where Europeans and Africans had mingled for generations, or by way of the West Indies or New Netherland. Familiar with European ways, often fluent in European languages, they acquired skills and knowledge that enabled them to bargain with their masters in ways their descendants would not be able to replicate. They came in small groups, cultivated their masters as patrons, negotiated for property of their own, and often gained their freedom. They enjoyed such advantages because they came to colonies where slavery had not yet become firmly embedded, where the meaning of bondage was still being worked out.

As this nineteenth-century engraving indicates, slaves were often subjected to humiliating physical inspections so that potential buyers could be convinced of their good health and strength.

Repressive laws and slave codes.

But Johnson's descendants, and the generations of slaves and free black people who came after them, encountered much harsher conditions. Once slavery became the dominant labor system in the Chesapeake, tobacco planters no longer welcomed free black people, fearing that they might encourage slaves to escape. In 1691, Virginia's legislature prohibited individual masters from freeing their slaves. Eight years later, lawmakers passed another measure requiring newly freed black people to leave the colony altogether. Black people like the Johnsons, who were already free, suffered under an increasing burden of legal discrimination. Laws prohibited them from employing white servants, holding office, bearing arms, and voting. Free black people paid extra taxes and suffered more severe punishments than white people did for the same crimes. Interracial marriages, never common, were prohibited as "shameful Matches."

Bad as the situation of free black people had grown, the condition of slaves was far worse. Slave codes, laws governing slavery, essentially reduced an entire class of human beings to property. In Virginia, from the middle of the seventeenth century on, a series of new laws added to slaves' oppression. A 1662 measure defined slavery as a lifelong and inherited status that passed from slave mothers to their children—even children with white fathers. Masters who might have felt uneasy about holding fellow Christians as slaves were relieved in 1667 when another law stated that baptism would not release slaves from bondage. Two years later, the House of Burgesses gave masters the power of life and death over their slaves, decreeing that masters would not be charged with felony if their slaves died during punishment. These and other measures were gathered into a comprehensive slave code in Virginia in 1705. Additional restrictions prohibited slaves from testifying in court against white colonists, required them to carry passes whenever they left their masters' estates, and forbade them to gather in groups of more than four people.

Slave codes appeared virtually everywhere, North and South, but were particularly harsh in the southern colonies. White colonists in the Tidewater Chesapeake and South Carolina feared the consequences of a growing black population. One South Carolina planter predicted in 1720 that slaves would soon rise up against their masters because black people were "too numerous in proportion to the White Men there."

The changing composition of the slave labor force also created tensions. Unlike the charter generation, slaves who arrived in the eighteenth century usually came from the African interior and had had less contact with European customs and language. Worried planters commented on the strange appearance and behavior of these people, with whom they could barely communicate. Their uneasiness, of course, scarcely compared to the Africans' harrowing experience of being torn away from the only world they knew and thrust into the harsh and unfamiliar condition of slavery.

AFRICAN AMERICAN FAMILIES AND COMMUNITIES

The harshness of slaves' condition could be relieved somewhat by the formation of close ties with others who shared their circumstances. For those ties to be created, however, several developments had to occur. Slaves had to become sufficiently numerous in specific localities so that black people could have regular contact with one another. Ethnic and language barriers carried over from Africa had to erode so that slaves could communicate with one another. And for family ties to be formed, there had to be adequate numbers of slave women as well as men. Because these conditions were slow to develop, occurring at different rates in different colonies, the formation of African American families and communities was delayed until well into the eighteenth century.

The situation was perhaps most difficult for slaves in the northern colonies. Many slaves there lived alone or in pairs with their master's family, with few opportunities to associate with fellow slaves. Only in cities and on substantial commercial farms were slaves numerous enough to create their own communities. The formation of families, however, was slowed by a relative scarcity of women. When slave families did appear, husbands and wives often lived in different households as the property of different masters.

The rise of the creole slave population. Slaves were far more numerous in the southern colonies, and it is there that African American families and communities emerged with greater success. This fact was especially true in South Carolina and parts of the Tidewater Chesapeake, where in certain localities slaves formed a majority of the population. Even more significant, these regions witnessed the rise of a creole, or American-born, slave population by about the 1750s. This development distinguished slavery in the mainland British colonies from that in the West Indies, where disease and overwork killed so many slaves that the black population grew only because of the constant importation of Africans.

The rise of a creole slave population in the Chesapeake and in Carolina set off a chain of related events that fostered family and community life. Creoles lived longer than African immigrants, and creole women usually bore twice as many children as African-born mothers. This circumstance allowed the slave population to grow by natural increase and more closely resemble a normal population of men and women, children and elders. Greater equality between the numbers of men and women helped in the creation of families. At the same time, creole slaves grew up without personal memories of Africa, and thus African ethnic differences receded in importance. Most creoles knew some English and spoke dialects, such as Gullah in parts of South Carolina, that mixed English and African words and speech patterns, so that they were able to communicate with other slaves and form African American communities.

Work and family life. Most of a slave's life was structured by work. The vast majority of southern slaves were field hands. On tobacco plantations, they toiled in gangs supervised by overseers. In Carolina, rice planters allowed their workers more flexibility, assigning them tasks in the morning and permitting them free time after they finished. On large plantations, masters selected some slave men to be trained as shoemakers, weavers, or tailors and chose others as drivers or leaders of work gangs. With the exception of nurses and cooks, few slave women avoided the drudgery of field labor. If they had families, the end of the day's work in the fields only marked the start of domestic duties back in the slave quarters. But no matter how onerous, work did not absorb every minute of the slaves' lives, and in the intervals around their assigned duties many slaves nurtured ties of family and community. Combining aspects of their African heritage and American experience, they created a new identity for themselves.

By the late eighteenth century, more than half of Chesapeake and Carolina slaves lived in family groups. These were fragile units, subject to the whims of masters who did not recognize slave marriages as legal, who broke up families by sale, and who could take slave women as sexual partners at will. Many slave husbands and wives resided on different plantations, although on larger Carolina estates two-parent slave households grew increasingly common. Over time, dense kinship networks formed, linking slaves across greater distances. To a certain extent, kinship structures reflected West African influences. Slaves placed great emphasis on kin connections, even using familiar terms such as "aunt" and "uncle" to address friends. Some slave husbands, like West African men, took more than one wife. In naming their children, slaves mingled old and new practices, sometimes giving them the African names of distant kin and sometimes using English names.

Community life and religion. Community life forged ties between slave families and single slaves on the plantations and offered further opportunities to preserve elements of African heritage. Traces of African religious practices endured in America. Magical charms and amulets have been found buried in slave quarters, indicating that certain spiritual ceremonies may have been conducted out of sight of white masters. Slave conjurors told fortunes, concocted herbal potions, and placed curses on their clients' enemies. Reflecting their West African background, slaves placed great emphasis on funerals, in the belief that relatives remained members of kin communities even after death. Funerals were sometimes divided into two distinct ceremonies. First, the deceased received a somber burial, often with beads or other ceremonial objects placed in the grave; some weeks later, slaves played music and danced at livelier funeral rites.

Christianity offered little competition to African religious practices during most of the colonial period. Few masters showed much interest in converting their slaves. Evangelical ministers, who began to preach to slave audiences around the middle of the eighteenth century, did gain some converts, but the widespread adoption of Christianity by slaves did not occur until after the Revolution.

African influences shaped aspects of slaves' recreational activity and material life. Slave musicians used African-style instruments, including drums and banjos, to accompany traditional songs and dances. In parts of South Carolina, slaves enjoyed *papaw*, an African game with dice. Storytellers entertained audiences with folk tales that may have had African roots. Where slaves were allowed to build their own houses, they often incorporated African elements into the designs—for instance, by using mud walls and roofs thatched with palmetto leaves. Their gardens frequently contained African foods such as millet, yams, peppers, and sesame seeds along with European and Native American crops.

Family and community ties gave a sense of belonging and dignity to people whose masters treated them as outcasts. Working and living together, slaves preserved at least some elements of African culture despite the harrowing conditions of their forced migration. Out of their African past and their American experience, they created new identities as African Americans as they coped with the oppressiveness of slavery.

RESISTANCE AND REBELLION

Even as family ties made a life in bondage more tolerable, they made it more difficult for slaves to attempt escape or contemplate rebellion. Slaves who resisted their oppression ran the risk of endangering families and friends as well as themselves. But the powerful desire for freedom and the spirit of resistance were not easily suppressed, and slaves found numerous ways to defy the dehumanization that slavery entailed.

Running away from a master was a desperate act, but thousands of slaves did just that. Few runaways shared the mistaken impression of some new arrivals in eighteenth-century Virginia who thought they could "find the Way back to their own Country." But deciding where else to go posed a problem. Escape out of the South did not bring freedom because slavery was legal in every colony. After 1733, some runaways went to Florida, where Spanish officials promised them freedom. Others tried to survive on their own in the woods or join the Indians—a choice that carried the risk of capture or death. South Carolina planters paid Indians to catch escaped slaves, largely to sow seeds of distrust between the two peoples and prevent them from joining forces against white colonists. For slaves with families, running away carried the high emotional cost of separation from loved ones as well as physical danger. Perilous as it was, escape proved irresistible to some slaves, especially young males. In a few isolated areas on the South Carolina frontier, runaways formed "maroon" settlements, always on the lookout for the white soldiers sent to attack them.

Many slaves chose less perilous ways to resist their bondage. Landon Carter, one of Virginia's wealthiest tobacco planters, once complained that his slaves "seem to be quite dead hearted and either cannot or will not work." He did not seem to realize that he had become the target of forms of resistance more subtle, but every bit as real, as running away. Slaves worked slowly, broke tools, and pretended to be ill in order to conserve strength and exert some control over their working lives. When provoked, they also took more direct action, damaging crops, stealing goods, and setting fire to their masters' barns, houses, and fields. Slaves with knowledge of poisonous plants occasionally tried to kill their white owners, although the penalty for being caught was to be burned to death.

The most serious, as well as the rarest, form of resistance was organized rebellion. South Carolinians and coastal Virginians, who lived in regions where

This eighteenth-century painting from South Carolina records the preservation of certain African traditions in American slave communities. The dance may be Yoruba in origin, while the stringed instrument and drum were probably modeled on African instruments.

Abby Aldrich Rockefeller Folk Art Center, Williamsburg, VA.

black people outnumbered white people, had a particular dread of slave revolt. But because rebellions required complete secrecy, careful planning, and access to weapons, they were extremely hard to organize. No slave rebellion succeeded in the British colonies. Rumors usually leaked out before any action had been taken, prompting severe reprisals against the alleged conspirators. In Charleston, South Carolina, rumors of a planned uprising in 1740 led to the torture and execution of fifty black suspects. The following year, thirty-five alleged rebels (including four white people) were executed in New York City.

Two slave revolts did occur in the colonial period, however, and instilled lasting fear in the white colonists. In 1712 in New York City, where black people made up perhaps 20 percent of the population, about twenty slaves set a building on fire and killed nine white men who came to put it out. The revolt was quickly suppressed. The court tried forty-three rebels and sentenced twenty-four to death. Their punishments revealed the extent of white terror: thirteen were hanged, three burned at the stake, one starved to death, and one broken on the wheel. Six committed suicide before execution.

The **Stono Rebellion**, colonial America's largest slave uprising, occurred in South Carolina in 1739. It began when about twenty slaves—including several recently arrived Angolans—broke into a store and armed themselves with stolen guns. As the rebels marched southward along the Stono River, their ranks grew to perhaps a hundred. Heading for freedom in Spanish Florida, they attacked white settlements along the way. White troops (with Indian help) defeated the rebels within a week, but tensions remained high for months. The death toll, in the end, was about two dozen white people and perhaps twice as many black rebels. Planters boasted that they "did not torture one Negroe, but only put them to an easy death," although one settler claimed that white soldiers "Cutt off their heads and set them up at every Mile Post they came to."

In the wake of the Stono Rebellion, South Carolina's assembly passed a law requiring stricter supervision of slave activities. Other measures encouraged more white immigration to offset the colony's black majority. But the colony continued to rely on the labor system that generated so much fear and brutality. In South Carolina, as in the rest of the southern colonies, planters considered slavery indispensable to their economic survival and would not willingly give it up. Their slaves, in turn, obeyed when necessary, resisted when possible, and kept alive the hope that freedom would one day be theirs.

EUROPEAN LABORERS IN EARLY AMERICA

Slavery was one of several responses to the scarcity of labor in the New World. It took hold mainly in areas where the profits from growing export crops such as sugar, rice, and tobacco offset the high purchase price of slaves and where a warm climate permitted year-round work. Elsewhere European masters and employers found various ways to acquire and manage European laborers. Indentured servitude, forced labor, tenancy, and the extension of credit, all aimed at limiting the freedom of some people in order to make them work for others.

A SPECTRUM OF CONTROL

In the English colonies, slavery was merely the most oppressive extreme in a spectrum of practices designed to exert control over workers and relieve the problems caused by the easy availability of land and the high cost of labor. Most colonial laborers were, in some measure, unfree (see the Overview table, "Predominant Colonial Labor Systems, 1750").

One-half to two-thirds of all white immigrants to the English colonies arrived as indentured servants, bound by contract to serve masters for a period of years. Tens of thousands of people accepted temporary servitude in return for passage across the Atlantic and the chance for a more prosperous future in America. But indentured servants, though less costly than slaves, carried too high a price for farmers who raised crops mainly for subsistence rather than for sale. Thus, although servants could be found in every colony, they were most common in the Chesapeake and, to a lesser extent, in Pennsylvania, where they produced export crops valuable enough to enable their masters to feed, clothe, and shelter them—and still make a profit.

Slaves replaced white indentured servants in Chesapeake tobacco fields during the eighteenth century. Masters continued to import servants for a while to fill skilled jobs but in time trained the more plentiful slaves to fill those positions. Thus, by the middle of the eighteenth century, white servitude, although it still existed in the Chesapeake region as well as in Pennsylvania and New York, was in decline as a dominant labor system.

Eighteenth-century Chesapeake planters also availed themselves of another unfree labor source: transported English convicts. Lawmakers in England saw transportation as a way of getting rid of large numbers of criminals who might otherwise be executed. Between 1718 and 1775, nearly fifty thousand convicts were sent to the colonies, 80 percent of whom ended up in the Chesapeake. Most were young, lower-class males forced by economic hardship to turn to lives of crime. Although some colonists objected to England's policy of sending its undesirables to America, labor-hungry planters eagerly bought them for seven-year terms at relatively low prices and exploited them ruthlessly. A few convicts eventually prospered in America, but most faced lives as miserable as those they had known in England.

An arrangement similar to indentured servitude—the **redemptioner** system—brought many families, especially from German provinces, to the colonies in the eighteenth century. Instead of negotiating contracts for service before leaving Europe, as indentured servants did, redemptioners promised to redeem, or pay, the costs of passage on arrival in America. They often paid part of the fare themselves before sailing. If they could not raise the rest of it soon after landing, the ship captain who brought them sold them into servitude. The length of their service depended on how much they still owed. Most Germans went to Pennsylvania, where they hoped to find friends or relatives willing to help them pay off their debt quickly

Purchasing slaves, servants, or convicts did not make sense for everyone. Colonists who owned undeveloped land faced many tasks—cutting trees, clearing fields, building fences and barns—that brought no immediate profit. Rather than buy expensive laborers to accomplish these ends, landowners rented undeveloped tracts to families without property. Both tenants and landlords benefited from this arrangement. Tenants enjoyed greater independence than servants and could save toward the purchase of their own farms. The landlord secured the labor necessary to transform his property into a working farm, thus increasing the land's value. He also received an annual rent payment, usually a portion of the tenant's crop, and eventually profited from selling the land, often to the tenant family who had rented it. Tenancy worked best in Pennsylvania, New Jersey, and the Hudson and Connecticut River Valleys, where farmers raised wheat and other grains for the market.

Overview

Predominant Colonial Labor Systems, 1750

	Colony	Labor System
New England	Massachusetts	Family farms
	Connecticut	Family farms
	New Hampshire	Family farms
	Rhode Island	Family farms
Middle Colonies	New York	Family farms, tenancy
	Pennsylvania and Delaware	Indentured servitude, tenancy, family farms
	New Jersey	Family farms, tenancy
South	Maryland	Slavery
	Virginia	Slavery
	North Carolina	Family farms, slavery
	South Carolina	Slavery

Merchants eager to develop New England's fisheries devised other means to fill their labor needs. Because it was fairly easy to get a farm, few New Englanders cared to take on the difficult and risky job of fishing. Moreover, few could afford the necessary equipment, including boats, sails, provisions, and salt (used for preserving fish). Merchants learned to recruit fishermen by advancing credit to coastal villagers so that they could outfit their own boats. To pay off the debt, the fishermen were legally bound to bring their catch to the merchant, who then sold it to Europe and the West Indies. Many fishermen ran up such large debts that they were obliged to continue supplying fish to their creditors, whether they wanted to or not. Toward the end of the seventeenth century, as the rising population of coastal villages lowered the cost of labor, merchants abandoned the credit system and paid wages to fishermen instead.

In the northern colonies, the same conditions that made men reluctant to become fishermen deterred them from becoming farm laborers, except perhaps for high wages. Paying high wages, however, or the high purchase cost of servants or slaves was difficult, if not impossible, for New Englanders with farms that produced no export crops and could not be worked during cold winter months. So northern farmers turned to the cheapest and most dependable workers they could find—their children.

Children as young as 5 or 6 years old began with simple tasks and moved on to more complex work as they grew older. By the time they were in their late teens, girls knew how to run households, and boys knew how to farm. Instead of contracts or outright coercion, fathers used their ownership of property to prolong the time their sons worked for them. Young men could not marry until they could set up their own households and relied on their fathers to provide them with land to do so. Fathers often waited until their sons were in their mid-twenties, compelling them until then to invest their labor in the paternal estate.

Thus New England's labor shortage produced strong ties of dependency between generations. Fathers kept their sons working for them as long as possible; sons accepted this arrangement because they had no other way to become independent farmers. They would eventually employ their own children in the same way. As New England's population increased in the eighteenth century, and vacant land grew scarcer, the price of labor came down. Some fathers could then afford to hire occasional helpers and loosen their hold on their sons, allowing them to marry earlier.

Property owners in all the English colonies found different ways to control the laborers they so desperately needed. But where property owners saw problems—high wages (often twice what workers in England received) and abundant land (which deterred colonists from working for others when they could have their own farms)—others saw opportunities. For tens of thousands of Europeans, the chance to own or rent a farm or to find steady employment made North America an irresistible magnet, promising a prosperity that was beyond their reach at home.

NEW EUROPEAN IMMIGRANTS

European immigrants flooded into America in the seventeenth and eighteenth centuries (see Figure 3–4). Nearly 250,000 Scots-Irish people—descendants of Protestant Scots who had settled in northern Ireland in the sixteenth and seventeenth centuries—came to the colonies after 1718, when their landlords raised rents to intolerable levels. Tens of thousands of immigrants arrived from Scotland during the same period, some seeking economic improvement and some sent as punishment for rebellions against the king in 1715 and 1745. Thousands of Irish Catholics arrived as servants, redemptioners, and convicts. By 1773, the tremendous outflow of Britons to America sparked debate in England over whether emigration should be prohibited lest the British Isles themselves be left empty.

Continental Europe contributed another stream of emigrants. Perhaps 100,000 German Protestants left the Rhine Valley, where war, economic hardship, and religious persecution had brought misery. French Protestants (known as Huguenots) began emigrating after 1685, when their faith was made illegal in France, and continued to arrive for decades. Swiss Protestants likewise fled religious persecution. Even a few Poles, Greeks, Italians, and Jews reached the colonies in the eighteenth century.

Many emigrants responded to pamphlets and newspaper articles that exaggerated the bright prospects of life in America. Others studied more realistic accounts from friends and relatives who had already emigrated. One Scot who had moved to North Carolina warned his countrymen that at first "poor people will meet with many Difficulties" but they should "take courage and Come to this Country [for] it will be of Benefitt" to their families. Landowners eager for workers sent agents to port towns to recruit new arrivals to become tenants, often on generous terms. One happy immigrant wrote to his wife, who remained behind in England, that he had signed a lease for a farm in New York that exempted him from paying rent for the first 5 years and charged him only 7 pence an acre after that.

Streams of emigrants flowed to places where land was cheap and labor most in demand (see Map 3–3). Few went to New England, where descendants of the first settlers already occupied the best land. They also avoided areas where slavery predominated—the Chesapeake Tidewater and lowland South Carolina—in favor of the foothills of the Appalachian Mountains, from western Pennsylvania to the Carolinas. There, one emigrant declared, a "poor man that will incline to work may have the value of his labour."

This observation, though partly true, did not tell the whole story. Any person who came as a servant, redemptioner, or tenant learned that his master or landlord received much of "the value of his labour."

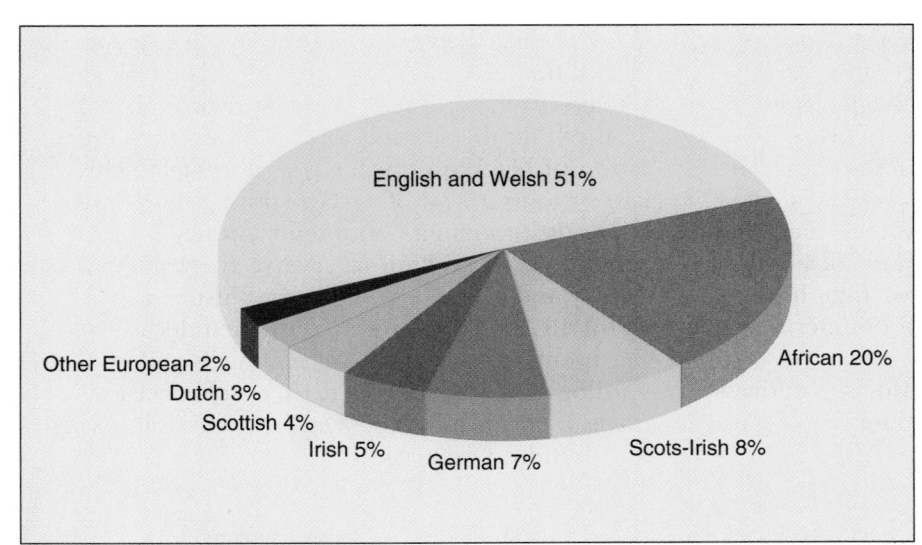

English and Welsh 51%
African 20%
Scots-Irish 8%
German 7%
Irish 5%
Scottish 4%
Dutch 3%
Other European 2%

FIGURE 3-4 Ethnic Distribution of Non-Indian Inhabitants of British Mainland Colonies, c. 1770
By the third quarter of the eighteenth century, the colonial population was astonishingly diverse. Only two out of three settlers claimed British ancestry (from England, Wales, Scotland, or northern Ireland), while one out of five was African in origin.

Data Source: Thomas L. Purvis, "The European Ancestry of the United States Population, 1790," *William and Mary Quarterly*, 3d series, 41 (1984), p. 98.

FROM THEN TO NOW

The Legacy of Slavery

As the twenty-first century begins, Americans continue to grapple with the social, economic, and political consequences of the nation's past involvement in the enslavement of Africans. Slavery's roots extend deeply into American history, reaching back before nationhood itself. White colonists, facing a New World labor shortage in the seventeenth century, chose to fill their need for workers by purchasing slaves from Africa. Seeking to produce as much tobacco, rice, or sugar as they could for as little cost as possible, they left a painful legacy that has shaped America's history for centuries.

By the early eighteenth century, slavery was a fixture in every colony, and white colonists had come to associate slave status with black skin. The Revolution, with its rhetoric of freedom, challenged slavery but did not end it. It took another, far bloodier, war in the following century to accomplish that end. But the constitutional amendments outlawing slavery and guaranteeing black people's civil rights that passed after the Civil War—important milestones though they were—still could not eradicate the racism that had become deeply ingrained in American life.

Even today, well over a century after the Civil War ended, problems persist. Many black Americans have joined the middle class, but many others continue to suffer from discrimination and poverty. Black Americans' average incomes lag behind those of white people, fewer black people attend college, more of them live in impoverished neighborhoods in decaying urban centers. Black victims occasionally become targets of hate crimes merely because of the color of their skin. To a considerable extent, these economic and social dislocations, and the racial attitudes that help to shape them, can be traced to the lingering effects of slavery.

Recent public and private efforts to address the condition of African Americans have sought to highlight that longstanding connection. In 1997, for instance, President Bill Clinton appointed a commission to study the persistent problem of race in America. That he chose an historian, John Hope Franklin, to head the group suggested that Clinton recognized the link between America's past involvement with slavery and the nation's current racial divisions. But when some of his supporters subsequently urged Clinton to issue a formal apology for slavery, he refused to take what would have been a highly controversial step.

The reluctance of political leaders to take on such a sensitive issue may explain the recent search for private remedies. Among the most prominent of these efforts was a federal lawsuit filed in March 2002 against the Aetna Insurance Company, the FleetBoston Financial Corporation, and the CSX Corporation. A group of black plaintiffs charged that these companies profited from slavery in the past, and ought to make restitution. In the 1850s the Aetna Insurance Company, for example, made money insuring the lives of slaves. Deandria Farmer-Paellmann, the lead plaintiff in the lawsuit and a descendant of slaves, discovered the connection as she researched the slave reparations issue for a law-school class. These companies, she suggested, "should be held responsible, and later on down the road there will be more companies."

Whether these suits will be any more successful than the push for a presidential apology remains to be seen. How reparations, if granted, would be used to ameliorate the condition of black Americans is also unclear. This lawsuit joins a host of earlier strategies, including constitutional amendments and civil rights legislation, in seeking to reverse the legacy of slavery and to make equality and justice a reality for all Americans. Even in the first decade of the twenty-first century, the nation is still contending with the consequences of decisions made by some of the earliest colonists almost four hundred years ago.

CONCLUSION

Eighteenth-century America offered a strikingly diverse mosaic of peoples and communities. Along the St. Lawrence River lay Kahnawake, a village of Mohawks and Abenakis who had adopted Catholicism and French ways under Jesuit instruction. In Andover, Massachusetts, New Englanders tilled fields that their Puritan grandparents had cleared. German immigrants seeking spiritual perfection populated the isolated Pennsylvania settlement of Ephrata. The hundred or so slaves on Robert Carter's Virginia plantation at Nomini Hall gathered on Sunday evenings to nurture ties of community with songs and dances, while the master cultivated his very different sense of community with the neighboring planters whom he invited to the great house to sip fine wine. In North Carolina, Swiss settlers rebuilt the coastal town of New Bern, destroyed during the Tuscarora War, while 100 miles farther west, Scottish emigrants cleared land for farms near present-day Fayetteville. Catawba Indians formed new villages in the South Carolina foothills to distance themselves from white settlers. In Mose, Florida, near St. Augustine, runaway slaves farmed and gathered shellfish under the protection of Spanish soldiers. Far to the west, the Spanish, mestizo, and Pueblo residents of Santa Fe warily reestablished ties broken during the Pueblo Revolt.

In these and many other communities, peoples from three continents adapted to one another and to American conditions. Indians struggled with the consequences of disease, trade, religious conversion, settlement, and warfare resulting from European immigration. Some native peoples managed to preserve their autonomy, others did not. Millions of African slaves suffered under the most repressive labor regime but fought its grip whenever possible. Slave communities testified to African Americans' assertion of their humanity in the face of a system that sought to deny it. English settlers became landowners in unprecedented numbers and adopted new ways to control laborers, reinventing slavery, unknown in England for centuries. For many European immigrants, the colonies offered the chance for economic improvement. Impoverished servants, transported convicts, and slaves, however, found America to be no land of opportunity

As the eighteenth century wore on, the North American colonies attracted more attention from their home countries. Spain, France, and England all recognized the colonies' growing economic power and strove to harness it to block the expansion of their rivals. Everywhere the effort to strengthen imperial ties created ambivalence among colonists.

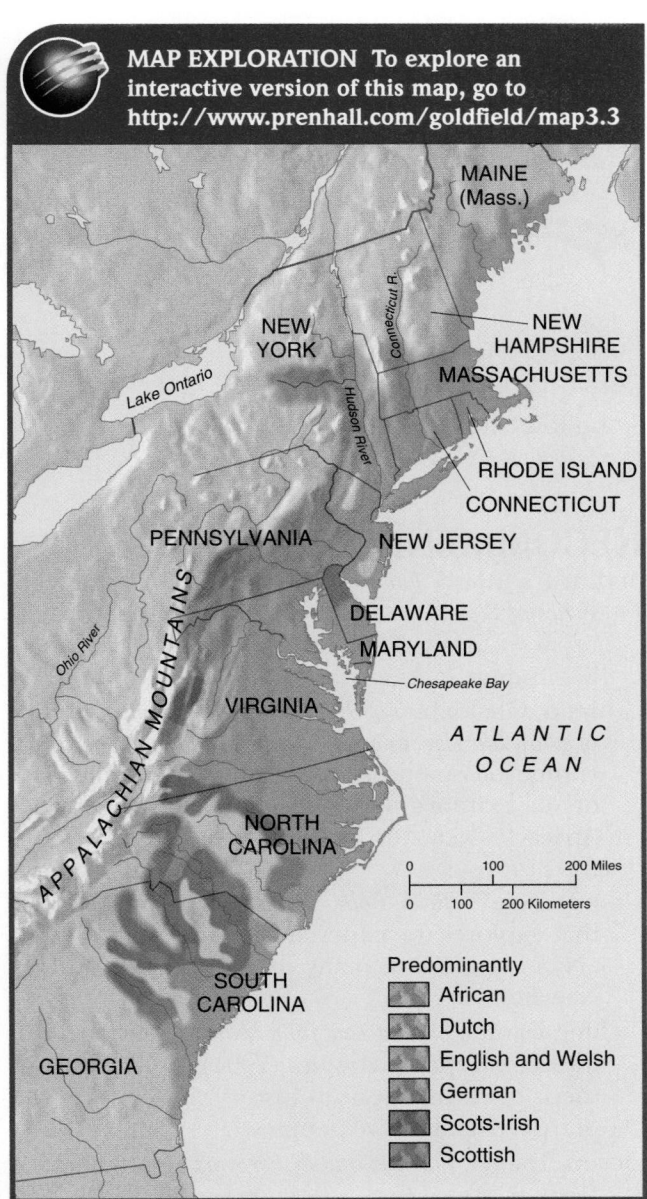

MAP 3-3   Ethnic Distribution of Settler Population in British Mainland Colonies, c. 1755
Settlers of different ethnic backgrounds tended to concentrate in certain areas. Only New Englanders were predominantly English, while Africans dominated in the Chesapeake Tidewater and South Carolina. German, Scottish, and Scots-Irish immigrants often settled in the backcountry.

Not all emigrants realized their dreams of becoming independent landowners. The scarcity of labor in the colonies led as easily to the exploitation of white workers as of slaves and Indians. Even so, for many people facing bleak prospects in Europe, the chance that emigration might bring prosperity was too tempting to ignore.

Because the English settlers were by far the most numerous, their responses were the most pronounced. As they saw more clearly the differences between themselves and England itself, some colonists began to defend their distinctive habits, while others tried more insistently than ever to imitate English ways. The tension between new and old had, of course, characterized colonial development from the start. What made the eighteenth century distinctive were the many ways in which those tensions worked themselves out.

REVIEW QUESTIONS

1. The first phase of Olaudah Equiano's journey into slavery took him from Africa's interior to the coast. What part of this journey most frightened him? Why?

2. English colonists experienced more frequent, and more violent, conflicts with Indians than the settlers of New France did. Why was this so? What factors affected Indian–European relations in the two colonial regions?

3. Why were Catholic missionaries more successful than Protestants in converting Indians to Christianity in early America?

4. When did Chesapeake planters switch from servants to slaves? What factors contributed to their decision to make this change?

5. By about 1750, more slaves in the mainland British colonies were creoles (American-born) than African-born. What effects did this have on the formation of African American communities in America?

6. Different labor systems predominated in various regions of British America. How did the economy of each region help determine its labor system?

7. Tens of thousands of European immigrants came to America in the eighteenth century, but they tended to settle only in certain colonial regions. What destinations did they favor and why?

KEY TERMS

Bacon's Rebellion (p. 76)

Beaver Wars (p. 71)

Encomienda (p. 69)

Great League of Peace and Power (p. 71)

King Philip's War (p. 76)

Middle Passage (p. 82)

Pueblo Revolt (p. 76)

Redemptioner (p. 91)

Repartimiento (p. 69)

Rescate (p. 69)

Stono Rebellion (p. 90)

RECOMMENDED READING

Berlin, Ira. *Many Thousands Gone: The First Two Centuries of Slavery in North America* (1998). A magisterial synthesis of the evolution of slavery from its beginnings in America through the Revolution.

Equiano, Olaudah. *The Interesting Narrative of the Life of Olaudah Equiano, or Gustavus Vassa, the African* (numerous editions). A vivid and moving story of an extraordinary individual's passage from Africa to New World slavery and, ultimately, to freedom.

Moore, Brian. *Black Robe* (1985). A powerful novel that explores the experiences of a Jesuit missionary among the Indians in seventeenth-century New France.

Richter, Daniel. *Facing East from Indian Country: A Native History of Early America* (2001). A brilliant synthesis of early American history viewed from the perspective of native peoples.

Vickers, Daniel. *Farmers and Fishermen: Two Centuries of Work in Essex County, Massachusetts, 1630–1830* (1994). A beautifully written and sophisticated analysis that explores the way in which settlers adapted their English experiences to deal with the shortages of labor and capital in New England.

ADDITIONAL SOURCES

Indians and Europeans

Axtell, James. *The Indians' New South: Cultural Change in the Colonial Southeast* (1997).

Calloway, Colin. *New Worlds for All: Indians, Europeans, and the Remaking of Early America* (1997).

Cronon, William. *Changes in the Land: Indians, Colonists, and the Ecology of New England* (1983).

Delage, Denys. *Bitter Feast: Amerindians and Europeans in Northeastern North America, 1600–64* (English ed., 1993).

Drake, James. *King Philip's War: Civil War in New England, 1675–1676* (2000).

Gutierrez, Ramon. *When Jesus Came, the Corn Mothers Went Away: Marriage, Sexuality, and Power in New Mexico, 1500–1846* (1991).

Hinderaker, Eric. *Elusive Empires: Constructing Colonialism in the Ohio Valley, 1673–1800* (1997).

Knaut, Andrew L. *The Pueblo Revolt of 1680: Conquest and Resistance in Seventeenth-Century New Mexico* (1995).

Merrell, James H. *Into the American Woods: Negotiators on the Pennsylvania Frontier* (1999).

Rountree, Helen. *Pocahontas's People: The Powhatan Indians of Virginia through Four Centuries* (1990).

Steele, Ian K. *Warpaths: Invasions of North America* (1994).

Washburn, Wilcomb E. *The Governor and the Rebel: A History of Bacon's Rebellion in Virginia* (1957).

White, Richard. *The Middle Ground: Indians, Empires, and Republics in the Great Lakes Region, 1650–1815* (1991).

Africans in America

Blackburn, Robin. *The Making of New World Slavery: From the Baroque to the Modern 1492–1800* (1997).

Breen, T. H., and Stephen Innes. *"Myne Owne Ground": Race and Freedom on Virginia's Eastern Shore, 1640–1676* (1980).

Curtin, Philip. *The Atlantic Slave Trade: A Census* (1969).

Davis, David Brion. *The Problem of Slavery in Western Culture* (1966).

Jordan, Winthrop. *White over Black: American Attitudes toward the Negro, 1550–1812* (1968).

Littlefield, Daniel. *Rice and Slaves: Ethnicity and the Slave Trade in Colonial South Carolina* (1981).

Morgan, Philip. *Slave Counterpoint: Black Culture in the Eighteenth-Century Chesapeake & Lowcountry* (1998).

Morris, Thomas. *Southern Slavery and the Law 1619–1860* (1996).

Mullin, Michael. *Africa in America: Slave Acculturation and Resistance in the American South and the British Caribbean 1736–1831* (1994).

Piersen, William. *Black Yankees: The Development of an Afro-American Subculture in Eighteenth-Century New England* (1988).

Wood, Betty. *The Origins of American Slavery: Freedom and Bondage in the English Colonies* (1997).

Labor Systems and European Immigration

Bailyn, Bernard. *The Peopling of British North America: An Introduction* (1986).

Bailyn, Bernard. *Voyagers to the West: A Passage in the Peopling of America on the Eve of the Revolution* (1986).

Baseler, Marilyn. *"Asylum for Mankind": America 1607–1800* (1998).

DeWolfe, Barbara, ed. *Discoveries of America: Personal Accounts of British Emigrants to America in the Revolutionary Era* (1997).

Ekirch, A. Roger. *Bound for America: The Transportation of British Convicts to the Colonies, 1718–1775* (1987).

Griffin, Patrick. *The People With No Name: Ireland's Ulster Scots, America's Scots Irish, and the Creation of a British Atlantic World, 1689–1764* (2001).

Innes, Stephen, ed. *Work and Labor in Early America* (1988).

Roeber, A. G. *Palatines, Liberty, and Property: German Lutherans in Colonial British America* (1993).

Salinger, Sharon V. *"To Serve Well and Faithfully": Labor and Indentured Servants in Pennsylvania, 1682–1800* (1987).

Wokeck, Marianne. *Trade in Strangers: The Beginnings of Mass Migration to North America* (1999).

WHERE TO LEARN MORE

- **Ste. Marie among the Hurons, near Midland, Ontario, Canada.** This site contains a reconstructed Jesuit mission from the seventeenth century. There is a museum with information about seventeenth-century France as well as life among the Huron Indians. Further information may be found at www.saintemarieamongthehurons.on.ca.

- **Taos Pueblo, Taos, New Mexico.** Still a residence for Pueblo Indians, portions of this multistoried pueblo date from the fifteenth century. This was the site from which Popé directed the beginnings of the Pueblo Revolt in 1680. Pictures and other information are available at www.cr.nps.gov/worldheritage/taos.htm.

- **Ephrata Cloister, Ephrata, Pennsylvania.** Founded by German immigrants in the eighteenth century, the Ephrata community attracted religious pietists. The site now contains a museum, buildings that reflect medieval German architectural styles, and a collection of decorative art objects. The website www.cob-net.org/cloister.htm includes a biography of Ephrata's founder, Johann Conrad Beissel.

- **Carter's Grove Slave Quarter, near Williamsburg, Virginia.** Site includes reconstructed eighteenth-century slave quarters on original site where slave cabins once stood. Costumed African American interpreters show visitors around and tell stories about actual slaves who lived on the plantation. Information about the house and plantation can be found at www.williamsburg.com/plant/carter.html. Pictures of the plantation may also be seen at www.wise.virginia.edu.

 Please refer to the document CD-ROM for primary sources related to this chapter.

→ *This painting hung over the fireplace in the home of eighteenth-century Massachusetts merchant Moses Marcy. The ledger book and the trading ship symbolize the central figure's commercial career. The fine wineglass in his hand, the elegant punch bowl on the table, and the gracious home in the background represent the prosperity that trade could bring.*

Old Sturbridge Village Photo by Henry E. Peach. 20.19.1

CONVERGENCE AND CONFLICT
1660s–1763

4

Virginia 26th April 1763

Mr. Lawrence

Be pleased to send me a genteel sute of Cloaths made of superfine broad Cloth handsomely chosen; I shou|l|d have Inclosed |for| you my measure but in a general way they are so badly taken here that I am convinced it wou|l|d be of very little service; I wou|l|d have you therefore take measure of a Gentleman who wears well made Cloaths of the following size—to wit—Six feet high & proportionably made; if any thing rather Slender than thick for a Person of that highth with pretty long arms & thighs— You will take care to make the Breeches longer than those you sent me last, & I wou|l|d have you keep the measure of the Cloaths you now make by you and if any alteration is required, in my next |letter| it shall be pointed out. Mr Cary will pay your Bill—& I am Sir Yr Very H|um|ble Serv|an|t . . .

George Washington

W.W. Abbot and Dorothy Twohig, eds., *The Papers Of George Washington*, Colonial Series, vol. 7 (Charlottesville, 1990).

CHAPTER OUTLINE

Economic Development and Imperial Trade in the British Colonies
The Regulation of Trade
The Colonial Export Trade and the Spirit of Enterprise
The Import Trade and Ties of Credit
Becoming More Like England: The Growth of Cities and Inequality

The Transformation of Culture
Goods and Houses
Shaping Minds and Manners
Colonial Religion and the Great Awakening

The Colonial Political World
The Dominion of New England and the Limits of British Control
The Legacy of the Glorious Revolution
Diverging Politics in the Colonies and Great Britain

Expanding Empires
British Colonists in the Backcountry
The Spanish in Texas and California
The French along the Mississippi and in Louisiana

A Century of Warfare
Imperial Conflict and the Establishment of an American Balance of Power, 1689–1738
King George's War Shifts the Balance, 1739–1754
The French and Indian War, 1754–1760: A Decisive Victory
The Triumph of the British Empire, 1763

Conclusion

George Washington, along with a few dozen other privileged Virginians, had traveled to Williamsburg for a visit that mixed politics, business, and pleasure. Like Washington, these men had come to the capital to represent their respective counties in the House of Burgesses. When not engaged in government business, they attended to private affairs. They arranged to ship tobacco from their plantations to England, to pay outstanding debts, or to seek credit until the harvest was in. Washington was surely not the only one to take the opportunity to write to his London tailor and order the fashionable clothing that advertised his status as a gentleman. He and his fellow burgesses donned their best coats and breeches to attend evening dinner parties and theater performances that enlivened days otherwise devoted to debating politics and rendering accounts.

April 1763 marked the fourth time Washington had gone to Williamsburg to take his seat in the legislature. Each journey carried him further away from a youth spent as a surveyor and soldier toward his future as a respected planter and public servant. Just 31 years old in 1763, he had recently married Martha Custis, a wealthy widow, and inherited his older brother's plantation at Mount Vernon. He had served his king in battle during the Seven Years' War; now he was eager to exchange his military uniform for the "genteel" broadcloth suits appropriate to his new station. Washington already owned vastly more land than most English gentlemen. With land and wealth to support his ambitions, he wanted to live, look, and behave like an English country gentleman, not merely like a Virginia planter.

But Washington could not be sure what an English gentleman wore. While some of his fellow Virginia planters, like William Byrd, had been sent to England to obtain education and social graces to smooth over the rough edges of their provincial origins, Washington had never been to England and trusted neither his own judgment nor Williamsburg tailors to know how a proper English gentleman should dress. So, while he instructed Mr. Lawrence about measurements and fabric quality, Washington said nothing about the color or style of his new suit. He had to trust his tailor to make him clothing as suitable for the drawing rooms of London as for the parlors of Williamsburg.

Throughout British America, colonists who had achieved wealth and power tried, like Washington, to imitate the habits and manners of the English gentry. Their aspirations testified to important developments in the eighteenth century. Prosperity and the demand of a growing population for English products tied the colonies ever more tightly into a trade network centered on the imperial metropolis, London. The flow of goods and information between England and America fueled the desires of Washington and other successful colonists for acceptance as transatlantic members of the English elite. No longer a collection of rough outposts clinging to the Atlantic seaboard, British America was growing in size and sophistication.

These developments in Britain's American colonies brought them to the attention of European statesmen, who increasingly factored North America into their economic, political, diplomatic, and military calculations. Parliament devised legislation that would channel tobacco and other colonial goods into England and away from its European competitors. Spain and France viewed the economic growth and geographic expansion of British North America as a threat to their own colonial possessions, and they responded aggressively by augmenting their territorial claims. With expansion came conflict, and with conflict, war: a series of four imperial wars, which themselves became powerful engines of change in the New World.

KEY TOPICS

- Development of closer connections between Britain and the colonies
- Rising aspirations of the colonial elite
- Eighteenth-century religious life
- Political developments in England and the colonies
- Renewed competition among Britain, France, and Spain in North America
- Impact of imperial warfare in North America

Chronology

1651–1733	Parliament passes series of Navigation Acts to regulate imperial trade.
1660	Charles II becomes king of England.
1662	Halfway Covenant adopted by Massachusetts clergy.
1685	James II becomes king of England.
1686–1689	Dominion of New England.
1688	Glorious Revolution in England; James II loses the throne.
1689	William and Mary become English monarchs; Leisler's Rebellion begins in New York.
1689–1697	King William's War in America.
1691–1692	Witchcraft trials in Salem, Massachusetts.
1698	First French settlements near mouth of Mississippi River.
1701	Iroquois adopt policy of neutrality toward France and Britain.
1702–1713	Queen Anne's War in America.
1718	Establishment of San Antonio, Texas; New Orleans founded.
1734–1735	Jonathan Edwards leads religious revival in Northampton, Massachusetts.
1739	Great Awakening begins in Middle Colonies with George Whitefield's arrival.
1744–1748	King George's War in America.
1754–1763	Seven Years' War in America.
1760s	Spanish begin establishing missions in California.

ECONOMIC DEVELOPMENT AND IMPERIAL TRADE IN THE BRITISH COLONIES

The greatest assets that Great Britain could call on in its competition with other European nations were a dynamic economy and a sophisticated financial system that put commerce at the service of the state. In the century after 1690, England became the most advanced economic power in Europe. England's leaders came to see colonies as indispensable to the nation's economic welfare. Colonies supplied raw materials unavailable in the mother country, and colonists and Indians provided a healthy market for English manufactured goods.

As the eighteenth century progressed, colonial economies grew in tandem with England's. Parliament knitted the colonies into an empire with commercial legislation, while British merchants traded with and extended credit to growing numbers of colonial merchants and planters. Over time, these developments made colonial societies resemble England more closely than ever before and integrated the economies of the colonies with that of the metropolis in a vast transatlantic system.

THE REGULATION OF TRADE

England, Holland, and France competed vigorously in transatlantic trade. To capture a greater share of commerce, England pursued a policy of national self-sufficiency in which its American colonies played a key role (see the Overview table, "British Imperial Trade Regulations, 1651–1733"). Between 1651 and 1733, Parliament passed laws that regulated trade to insure that more wealth flowed into England's treasury than out of it. This governmental intervention in the economy for the purpose of increasing national wealth—called **mercantilism**—aimed to draw the colonies into a mutually beneficial relationship with England.

Parliament enacted four types of mercantilist regulations. The first aimed at ending Dutch dominance in England's overseas trade. Beginning with the Navigation Act of 1651, all trade in the empire had to be conducted in English or colonial ships, with crews of which at least half were Englishmen or colonists. The act stimulated rapid growth in both England's merchant marine and New England's shipping industry. Shipbuilding and earnings from what was called the carrying trade soon became the most profitable sector of New England's economy.

The second type of legislation channeled most colonial trade through England, giving it control over raw materials it would otherwise have to buy from rival nations. Certain colonial goods, called **enumerated products**, could be shipped only to England or to another English colony. These goods initially included tobacco, sugar, indigo, and cotton; other products, such as rice, were added later.

Overview

British Imperial Trade Regulations, 1651–1733

Name of Act	Key Features
Navigation Act of 1651	Aimed to eliminate Dutch competition in overseas trade
	Required most goods to be carried in English or colonial ships
	Required crews to be at least half English
Navigation Act of 1660	Required all colonial trade to be carried in English ships
	Required master and three-quarters of crew to be English
	Created list of enumerated goods, such as tobacco and sugar, that could be shipped only to England or another English colony
Staple Act of 1663	Required products from Europe, Asia, and Africa to be landed in England before being shipped to the colonies
Plantation Duty Act of 1673	Attempted to reduce smuggling
	Required captains of colonial ships to post bond that they would deliver enumerated goods to England or pay the "plantation duty" that would be owed in England
Navigation Act of 1696	Plugged loopholes in earlier laws
	Created vice-admiralty courts in colonies to enforce trade regulations
Woolens Act of 1699	Forbade export of woolen cloth made in the colonies, to prevent competition with English producers
Hat Act of 1732	Prohibited export of colonial-made hats
Molasses Act of 1733	Placed high tax on French West Indian and other foreign molasses imported into colonies to encourage importation of British West Indian molasses

These laws also required European goods to pass through England before they could be shipped to the colonies. When these goods entered English ports, they were taxed, making them more expensive and encouraging colonists to buy English-made items.

The third and fourth sorts of regulation further enhanced the advantage of English manufacturers who produced for the colonial market. Parliament subsidized certain goods, including linen, gunpowder, and silks, to allow manufacturers to undersell European competitors in the colonies. Other laws protected English manufacturers from colonial competition by prohibiting colonists from manufacturing wool, felt hats, and iron on a large scale.

England's commercial goals were largely achieved. The Dutch eventually lost their preeminence in the Atlantic trade. Colonial trade helped the English economy to grow and contributed to London's emergence as western Europe's largest city. Although some tobacco and rice planters complained about restraints on their freedom to seek markets on their own, the colonies as a whole prospered. Between 1650 and 1770, the colonial economy expanded twice as fast as England's did. Colonists enjoyed protected markets for their staple crops and low prices on English imports. Because colonial merchants operated on equal terms with English traders, they could take full advantage of commercial opportunities within the empire.

Occasionally, merchants evaded these laws by smuggling. Customs officials, sent over from England beginning in the 1670s, were hard-pressed to stop them. Although they derived much of their income from fines collected from smugglers, officials generally found it easier to accept bribes and look

Scenes like this were common in the dockyards at Deptford and other parts of eighteenth-century London. Boxes and barrels of English goods were loaded aboard sailing ships that returned months later with sugar, tobacco, rice, and other products from every part of England's worldwide empire.

the other way when a suspicious ship arrived in port with, say, an illicit cargo of French West Indian sugar. Most colonial trade, however, followed the proper routes. By not pushing for perfect compliance, British officials did not put too much pressure on a system that in fact worked remarkably well.

THE COLONIAL EXPORT TRADE AND THE SPIRIT OF ENTERPRISE

By the mid-eighteenth century, the Atlantic had become a busy thoroughfare of international commerce (see Map 4–1). Between 1700 and 1770, the number of British merchant ships nearly tripled,

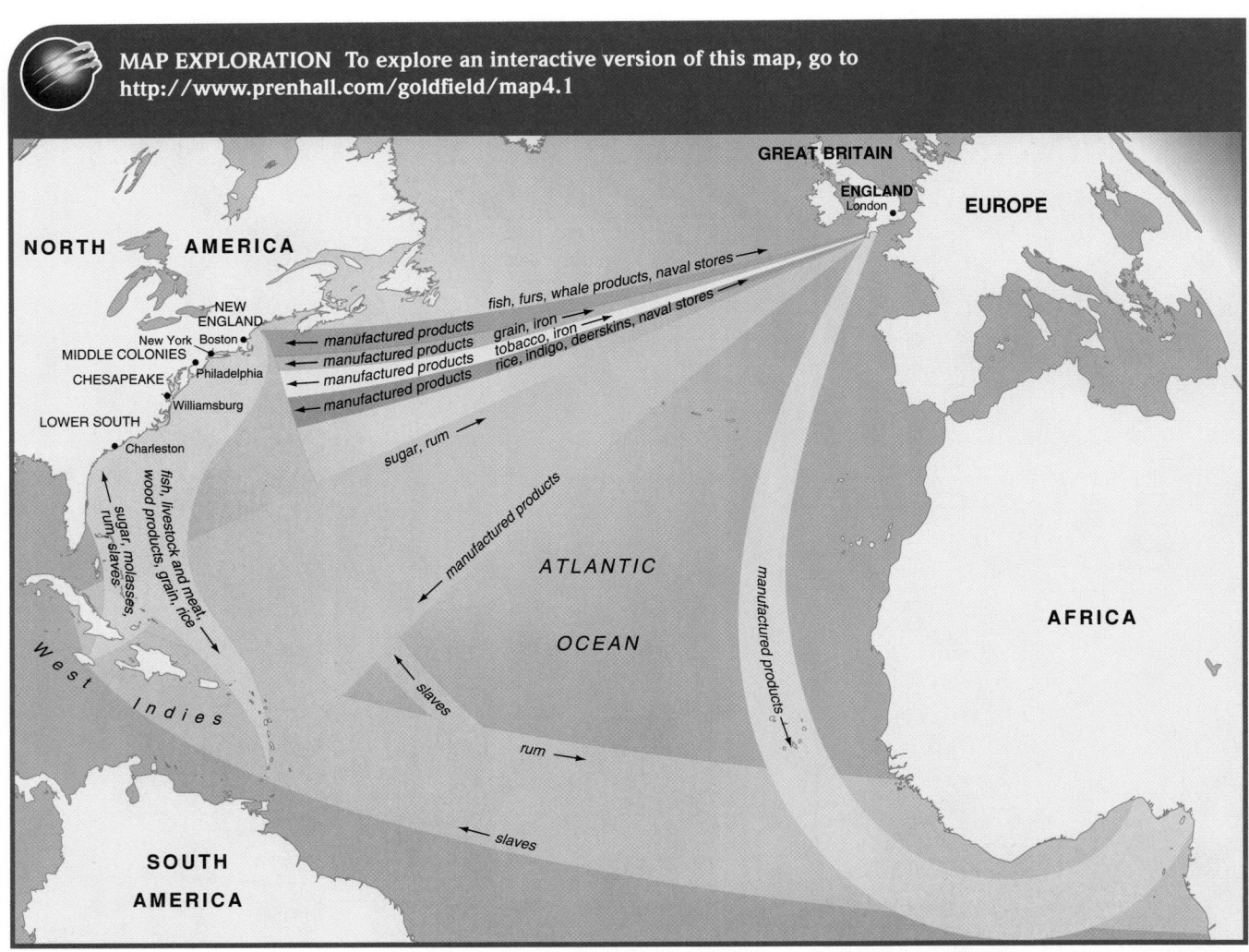

MAP EXPLORATION To explore an interactive version of this map, go to http://www.prenhall.com/goldfield/map4.1

MAP 4-1 Anglo-American Transatlantic Commerce
By the eighteenth century, Great Britain and its colonies were enmeshed in a complex web of trade. Britain exchanged manufactured goods for colonial raw materials, while Africa provided the enslaved laborers who produced the most valuable colonial crops.

from 3,300 to 9,400. They, along with colonial vessels, carried goods and people from Great Britain, continental Europe, and West Africa to the British colonies and returned tons of raw materials to the Old World. At the heart of Anglo-American trade lay the highly profitable commerce in staple crops, most of which were produced by slave labor.

West Indian sugar far surpassed all other colonial products in importance (see Figure 4–1). By the late 1760s, the value of sugar and sugar by-product exports reached almost £4 million per year—nearly 50 percent more than the total value of exports from all the other British American colonies combined. Prominent West Indian planters joined with the English merchants who marketed their sugar to lobby Parliament for favorable treatment. Because

these planters and merchants—known as the sugar interest—wielded so much economic power, politicians listened. It was at their insistence that Parliament in 1733 passed the Molasses Act, which taxed sugar products from foreign sources, especially the French West Indies. Parliament also removed sugar from the list of enumerated items in 1739, allowing merchants to ship it directly from the islands to southern Europe.

Tobacco from the Chesapeake colonies was the second most valuable staple crop. Exports worth about £750,000 arrived each year in England during the late 1760s. Nearly 90 percent of the crop was later reexported to continental Europe. Persistent low prices, however, led many tobacco planters to sow some of their land with wheat after about 1750. This

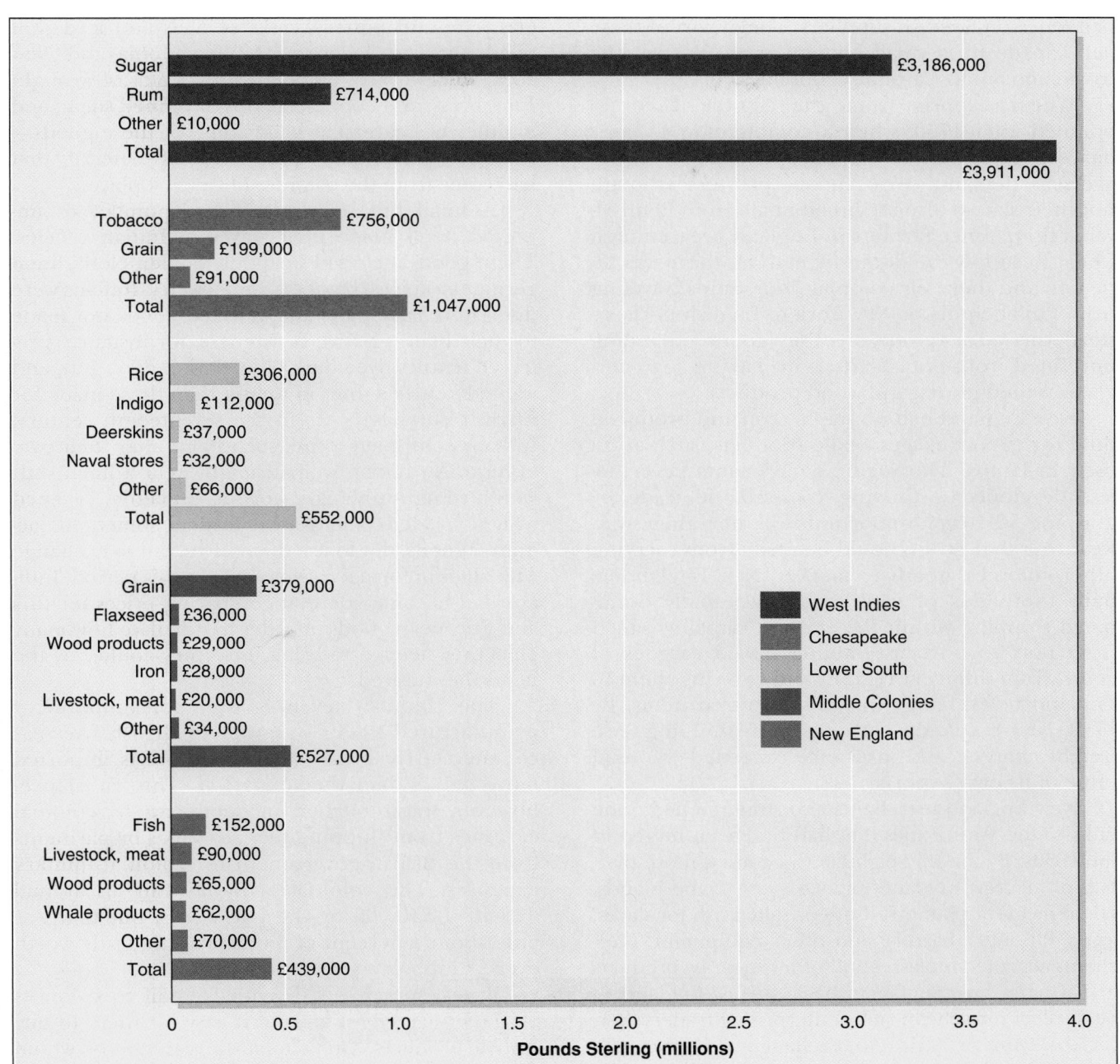

FIGURE 4-1   Average Annual Value of Colonial Exports by Region, 1768–1772
Staple crops—especially sugar—produced by slave labor were the most valuable items exported from Britain's North American colonies.

Data Source: John J. McCusker and Russell R. Menard, *The Economy of British America, 1607–1789*, rev. ed. (1991). University of North Carolina Press.

change lessened their dependence on tobacco and allowed them to take advantage of the high demand for flour in southern Europe and the West Indies.

Exports of rice and indigo (a plant that produced an expensive blue dye used in textile manufacture), helped make South Carolina planters some of the richest mainland colonists. Most of the rice went to England and the West Indies, although, after 1731, Parliament permitted direct shipments to southern Europe. Parliament encouraged indigo production by granting subsidies to growers and placing stiff taxes on foreign indigo. It also subsidized colonial production of naval stores—such as tar, pitch, and turpentine—to reduce England's dependence on Swedish suppliers. The export of these items made up a small but important part of the North and South Carolina economies.

Wheat exports from the Middle Colonies boomed after 1750, when a combination of poor harvests and warfare in Europe created strong overseas demand. West Indian planters (though not their slaves) also ate bread made from Pennsylvania flour. Since farmers in England grew enough wheat to supply the domestic market, there was little demand there for colonial flour. Ships traveling from Philadelphia or New York to English ports instead carried a variety of other goods, including unrefined iron, potash (used in making soap and glass), salted meats, and wood products.

New England had no staple crop and produced little for export except whale products, such as oil used in lamps. The region's merchants nevertheless developed a thriving transatlantic trade by grasping whatever opportunities came their way. Realizing that profits could be made from carrying other colonies' goods to market, New Englanders built thousands of vessels and eventually dominated shipping within the empire. Captains sailed from port to port, assembling mixed cargoes of goods from different regions and carrying them to England to exchange for manufactured items. By 1770, New England's earnings from shipping fees, freight charges, and insurance exceeded the total value of its own exports.

New England merchants also strengthened trade links to the West Indies that had first been forged in the 1650s. By the mid-eighteenth century, more than half of all New England exports went to the islands: salted meat for planters' dinners, salted fish for slaves, wood for sugar barrels, and other equipment. Merchants accepted molasses and other sugar by-products in payment, bringing them back to New England to be distilled into cheap rum. Enterprising traders then carried rum to Africa to exchange for slaves. Although English merchants dominated the African slave trade, New Englanders also profited. Less than 10 percent of New England's population were slaves, but because New Englanders trafficked in human cargo and provisioned the West Indies, their commercial economy depended on the institution of slavery.

THE IMPORT TRADE AND TIES OF CREDIT

By the late 1760s, over £4 million worth of English manufactured goods flowed into the colonies. This import trade satisfied a demand for items that could not be produced—at least not cheaply—in North America. Bales of English cloth and leather, crates of

glassware and pottery, casks of nails and lead shot piled onto the wharves of Philadelphia and New York. Dockworkers emptied ships' holds of wrought iron, brass, and copper, barrels of refined sugar, and bundles of beaverskin hats. Some of these goods—ironware, sugar, hats—were made of materials that had come from the colonies in the first place.

A small but not insignificant number of imported items made their way into Indian villages. These goods included weapons, woolen cloth, linen garments, knives, hatchets, and jewelry. Indians were discerning customers and rejected goods not made to their liking. Native consumers, for instance, preferred textiles dyed dark blue, dark red, or gray, and wanted kettles lighter in weight than those made for English purchasers. As in the seventeenth century, Indians continued to use such items after their own fashion. An Indian woman might wear a linen shift with an English blanket worn as a mantle, fastened with a beaded belt. Native leaders sometimes acquired goods, not to use themselves, but to exchange with allies in formal ceremonies. By this period, Indians had become adept at comparing prices for furs and European goods in order to calculate how many pelts they needed to bring in so they could buy the items they desired.

The colonists' even heavier consumption of manufactured goods was vital to British overseas commerce. In terms of value, colonists imported more goods than they exported. This imbalance, however, was remedied in good part by colonial earnings from shipping fees as well as by payments from the British government for colonial military expenses. The colonial economy ran an annual deficit of £40,000 by the late 1760s, but that was only about 1 percent of a transatlantic trade worth over £4 million a year.

British merchants extended credit to colonists on generous terms, making it easy for them to buy British products. Great tobacco planters, of whom Washington was typical, virtually lived on the easy credit that British merchants provided. These merchants marketed the planters' tobacco and supplied them with English goods, charging the costs of purchase and transportation against the profits they expected the next year's crop to bring.

Easy credit let planters indulge themselves, and many ordered English goods without stopping to worry about how they would pay for them. Gradually they sank into debt. A Virginian noted that in the 1740s, no planter would have dared run up a debt of £1,000 but that by the 1760s, "Ten times that sum is . . . spoke of with Indifference." When trade was brisk and tobacco prices high, neither the planters nor their

During the eighteenth century, quantities of imported English manufactures began to appear in many colonial houses. This elegant mahogany clothespress, made in England in the 1740s, may have graced the Boston home of Charles Apthorp, once called "the greatest and most noble merchant" in America.

British creditors worried. But when tobacco prices dropped or an international crisis made overseas trading risky, creditors called in the debts owed to them. At such times, colonial debtors realized how much they (like Indians involved in European trade) depended on goods and credit supplied by distant merchants.

BECOMING MORE LIKE ENGLAND: THE GROWTH OF CITIES AND INEQUALITY

As colonial commerce grew, so did colonial cities—the connecting points in the economic network tying the colonies to London. Boston, New York, Philadelphia, and Charleston were as large as many British provincial towns. By 1770, Philadelphia's population had reached 30,000, New York's 25,000, Boston's 16,000, and Charleston's 12,000. A fifth city, Baltimore, was rapidly developing at the best

harbor on Chesapeake Bay. Only about 5 percent of all mainland colonists lived in cities, but the influence of urban centers far outweighed their size.

European visitors marveled at America's bustling cities and remarked on their resemblance to England's. One Englishman declared in 1759 that Philadelphia "must certainly be the object of every one's wonder and admiration." Less than 80 years old, it already boasted three thousand houses, impressive public buildings, "handsomely built" streets, two libraries, eight or ten churches, and a college (chartered as the College of Philadelphia in 1755, now the University of Pennsylvania). This same visitor judged Boston to be a "most flourishing" place with "much the air of some of our best country towns in England."

All colonial cities (like England's major ones) were seaports, and Europeans took note of the appearance and activity of their dockyards. Oceangoing ships sailed "right up to the town" of Philadelphia on the Delaware River, according to one observer. Boston had "a very fine wharf, at least half a mile long, undertaken at the expense of a number of private gentlemen" to facilitate shipping. New York, then as now, had one of the world's finest harbors, from which it conducted "a more extensive commerce than any town in the English North American provinces."

Indeed, in their bustle and cosmopolitan atmosphere, colonial cities resembled English provincial cities more than they did the farming villages of the American countryside. Cities provided all sorts of amenities, including inns, taverns, coffeehouses, theaters, and social clubs. Their populations were much more diverse in ethnic origin and religion. Dr. Alexander Hamilton, a Scottish immigrant, recalled dining at a Philadelphia tavern with "Scots, English, Dutch, Germans, and Irish" and "Roman Catholicks, Church [of England] men, Presbyterians, Quakers, Newlightmen, Methodists, Seventh day men, Moravians, Anabaptists, and one Jew." In addition, the African American population in the northern colonies tended to live in cities. By 1750, slaves made up 20 percent of New York City's population, about 10 percent of Philadelphia's, and nearly 9 percent of Boston's.

Artisans in colonial cities. Colonial cities had higher proportions of artisans than did rural villages. Perhaps two out of three adult white males living in cities worked at a craft. Many of them—shipbuilders, ropemakers, sailmakers—labored at trades directly related to overseas commerce. Others produced pottery, furniture, paper, glassware, iron tools, and various household items. Colonial products tended to be somewhat cruder and cheaper than British-made goods. Yet talented colonists such as the Boston silversmith Paul Revere and the Philadelphia furniture maker John Folwell fashioned goods that would have been prized possessions in any English gentleman's home.

Colonial manufacturing took place not in factories but in workshops often attached to artisans' houses. Artisans managed a workforce consisting of their wives and children, along with journeymen or apprentices. Usually teenage boys, apprentices contracted to work for a master for 4 to 7 years in order to learn the "mysteries" of his craft. Like indentured servants, they received no wages but worked for food, clothing, shelter, and a small payment at the end of their service. Once an apprentice finished his training, he became a journeyman, working for a master but now earning wages and saving until he could afford to set up his own shop. Like farmers, colonial artisans valued household independence and aimed to limit the time during which they worked for others.

Many artisans flourished in colonial cities. Adino Paddock, for example, moved from the countryside to Boston in 1736 to learn how to make the light carriages known as chaises. By 1758, he had his own shop, and as his business prospered, Bostonians elected him to important local offices. As a gesture of public spirit, Paddock arranged for the transplanting of elm trees on Boston Common, to beautify the city where he had made his fortune, which by 1775 amounted to more than £3,000.

Paddock's rise was more spectacular than that of most craftsmen, since prosperity for urban artisans was by no means guaranteed. In Philadelphia, artisans typically accumulated property worth £50 to £200, enough for a modest subsistence. Workers at less skilled crafts often earned only a bare living, and ordinary laborers faced seasonal unemployment. The irregular delivery of raw materials idled even the most industrious artisans. Silversmiths, tailors, and furniture makers, relying on overseas suppliers of metal, cloth, and exotic woods, suffered when supply ships sank or wars hindered ocean traffic. Makers of luxury goods also feared downturns in the economy, for such trends discouraged nervous customers from purchasing their wares.

Cities like Philadelphia, New York, and Charleston provided an important setting for some women to support themselves with craft work. Mary Wallace and Clementia Ferguson, for instance, stitched fashionable hats and dresses for New York customers. Nonetheless, even in cities, women's options were limited. Most employed women were widows striving to maintain a family business until sons grew old enough to take over. This was true for printers such as Elizabeth Timothy, who ran the *South Carolina Gazette* after her husband's death in 1739, and Anne Catherine Green, who managed the *Maryland Gazette* for nine years. Other widows toiled at less prestigious—and less remunerative—jobs as nurses, laundresses, and boardinghouse keepers.

The growing gap between rich and poor.
Wherever colonists engaged heavily in commerce—in cities or on plantations—the gap between rich and poor widened during the eighteenth century. In 1687, the richest 10 percent of Boston residents owned 46 percent of the taxable property in the town; by 1771, the top tenth held 63 percent of taxable wealth. Similar changes occurred in Philadelphia. In South Carolina and the Chesapeake, many planters added to the already substantial estates they had inher-

This view of the Philadelphia waterfront dates from 1720. It shows how the city had developed into one of British America's principal ports just forty years after its founding.

Peter Cooper "The Southeast Prospect of the City of Philadelphia," ca. 1720. The

John Singleton Copley's portrait of the silversmith Paul Revere, painted about 1769, depicts one of Boston's most prominent artisans. As colonists grew wealthier, some commissioned portraits for their homes to serve as emblems of their rising social aspirations. Even so, Copley despaired that America would ever provide a suitable market for his artistic talents and he eventually moved to England.

ited. This elite group controlled vast amounts of land and of slaves. It became increasingly difficult for newcomers to enter their ranks. At the same time, the colonies' growing reliance on slave labor—especially in the South—created a sizeable class of impoverished people denied the chance to better their condition. By 1770, slaves, for whom America was anything but a land of opportunity, constituted one out of five British colonists.

To address the growing problem of poverty among white colonists, cities built workhouses, and towns collected funds for poor relief in greater amounts than ever before. Many poor people were aged or ill, without families to help them. Able-bodied workers forced to accept public relief usually owed their misfortune to temporary downturns in the economy, more often than not the result of wartime dislocations. Such was the case in

1757, for example, when Boston's leaders complained about rising poor relief expenses. England was then at war with France, and the British commander in chief had halted Boston's overseas trade, a military expedient that hurt the city's economy.

Even in the worst of times, no more than one out of ten white colonists (mainly city dwellers) depended on public assistance. For free black people who were unemployed and denied public relief, conditions were far worse. A Pennsylvania law went so far as to allow them to be enslaved. This was a threat no impoverished white colonist faced. And, bad as it was, the problem of poverty among white colonists had not reached anything like the levels seen in England. As much as one-third of England's population regularly received relief, and the numbers swelled during hard times. Eighteenth-century white colonists, on average, enjoyed a higher standard of living than most English or other Europeans. So long as land was available—even if one had to move to the edges of settlement to get it—colonists could at least eke out a bare subsistence, and many did much better.

No one would have mistaken Philadelphia for London or Virginia planters for British lords. Even so, colonial society resembled Great Britain more than ever before. The growth of cities mirrored British urban development. The widening gap between rich and poor convinced many colonists that their society had at last matured from its crude beginnings. Eighteenth-century Britons on both sides of the Atlantic believed that societies ought to be organized hierarchically, that God intended for people to be arranged in ranks from rich to poor. The more America resembled Britain, many colonists assumed, the more stable and prosperous it would be.

THE TRANSFORMATION OF CULTURE

Despite the convergence of English and colonial society, many influential settlers worried that America remained culturally inferior to Great Britain. Just as Washington trusted a London tailor to make him a fashionable suit—assuming that Virginia tailors could not do the job—other colonial gentlemen tended to see American architecture, fashion, manners, and intellectual life as at best poor imitations of superior British models. During the eighteenth century, newly prosperous colonists strove to overcome this provincial sense of inferiority. They built grand houses and filled them with imported goods, cultivated what they took to be the manners of the British gentry, and followed English and European intellectual developments. Some colonial gentlemen even reshaped their religious beliefs to reflect European notions that God played only an indirect role in human affairs.

These elite aspirations, however, were not shared by most settlers. The majority of colonists, although they might purchase a few imported goods, had little interest in copying the manners of the English elite, and very few of them altered their spiritual beliefs to fit European patterns. Indeed, familiar religious practices flourished in eighteenth-century America, and when a tremendous revival swept through the colonies beginning in the 1730s, religion occupied center stage in American life.

As second- and third-generation Chesapeake planters achieved greater prosperity, they often remodeled their homes to make larger and more imposing structures. This watercolor depicts Green Spring Mansion as it looked in 1770, significantly modified from the smaller brick dwelling where Governor William Berkeley lived a century earlier.

GOODS AND HOUSES

Eighteenth-century Americans imported more manufactured products from England with every passing year. This practice did not simply reflect the growth of the colonial population, for the rate at which Americans bought British goods exceeded the rate of population increase. Colonists owned more goods, often of better quality, than their parents and grandparents had possessed.

In the less secure economic climate of the seventeenth century, colonists had limited their purchases of goods, investing instead in land to pass on to their children. But by the eighteenth century, prosperous colonists felt secure enough to buy goods to make their lives more comfortable. Chairs replaced benches, and carpets covered wooden floors. Colonists hung mirrors and perhaps a portrait or two on their walls. At mealtimes, the table might be covered with a damask cloth and set with individual porcelain plates instead of a common wooden dish. Wealthier colonists ate with forks and knives, not just spoons.

Benjamin Franklin described such changes in his own household. Accustomed to eating his breakfast of bread and milk with a pewter spoon from an earthenware bowl, he found it one morning "in a China Bowl with a Spoon of Silver" that had cost "the enormous Sum of three and twenty Shillings." His wife, Deborah, justified the purchase by declaring "that she thought her Husband deserved a Silver Spoon & China Bowl as well as any of his Neighbors." Deborah Franklin knew that silver and china, although they served the same

function as pewter and earthenware, signified her family's prosperity and good taste. Many colonists likewise acquired such goods to advertise their refined style of life.

By the 1760s, nearly every item that George Washington ordered from his London agent could have been purchased in Philadelphia. But Washington wanted the latest English styles and even worried that his agent might take advantage of him by sending goods that were no longer in fashion in England. He once complained that "instead of getting things good and fashionable . . . we often have Articles sent Us that cou[l]d only have been us[e]d by our Forefathers in the days of yore." Washington's desires were hardly unique. One visitor to Maryland, astonished at the speed with which colonists adopted English styles, declared that he was "almost inclined to believe that a new fashion is adopted earlier by the polished and affluent American than by many opulent persons" in London. Colonial shopkeepers regularly assured the "ladies and gentlemen" among their customers that their wares reflected the latest English styles.

Prosperous colonists built grand houses where they lived in greater comfort than ever before. In the seventeenth century, Virginia's governor lived in the finest house in the colony—a four-room dwelling. His eighteenth-century counterpart, however, resided in Williamsburg in the Governor's Palace, an elegant two-storied mansion designed after British architectural styles. By the 1730s, numerous southern planters had built "great houses" with expensive paneling and marble fireplaces. Others transformed older houses into more stylish residences. Washington extensively remodeled Mount Vernon, adding a second story and extra wings on each side to create a home fit for a gentleman. In the northern colonies, merchants built the most impressive houses, often following architectural pattern books imported from England.

These houses were not only larger but also different in design from the homes of less affluent colonists. Most settlers lived in one- or two-room dwellings and thus cooked, ate, and slept in the same chamber. Under such conditions, privacy was virtually unknown. But the owners of great houses could devote rooms to specialized uses. Cooking and other domestic work took place in back or in separate outbuildings. Private bedrooms were located upstairs, allowing first-floor rooms to be used for public activities. The most distinctive feature of these grand homes was the parlor, an elaborately decorated room used for receiving guests and entertaining them with music, dancing, and card games. Parlor doors often opened onto lawns and formal gardens where guests could stroll and engage in polite conversation.

Prosperous colonists did not build such homes merely to advertise their wealth. They wanted to create the proper setting for a refined way of life, emulating the English gentry in their country estates and London townhouses. But they knew that the true measure of their gentility lay not just in where they lived and what they owned but in how they behaved.

SHAPING MINDS AND MANNERS

Colonists knew that the manners of English gentlefolk set them apart from ordinary people. Many Americans therefore imported "courtesy books," which contained the rules of polite behavior. In previous centuries, such books had prepared princes for life at court and for their future duties as kings. Eighteenth-century versions advised would-be gentlemen on how to show regard for social rank, practice personal cleanliness, and respect other people's feelings.

The young George Washington studied such books carefully. At the age of 13, he copied 110 rules from *Youth's Behaviour, or Decency in Conversation among Men,* including such advice as "In the Presence of Others Sing not to yourself with a humming Noise, nor Drum with your Fingers or Feet" and "In Company of those of Higher Quality than yourself Speak not till you are ask'd a Ques-

tion then Stand upright put of[f] your Hat and Answer in few words." Many colonists subscribed to English journals such as *The Tatler* and *The Spectator* that printed articles describing good manners.

Women, too, cultivated genteel manners. In Charleston, South Carolina, and other colonial cities, dozens of girls' boarding schools advertised instruction in "the different branches of Polite Education." Female pupils received only the rudiments of intellectual training in reading, writing, and arithmetic, for it was assumed that women had little need of such accomplishments. Only rarely did young women receive a more rigorous education, for few parents thought it appropriate to their gender. The private schools' curriculum instead focused on French, music, dancing, and fancy needlework. These were skills that advertised girls' genteel status and prepared them for married lives as mistresses of great houses, mothers of future gentlemen and ladies, and hostesses of grand entertainments.

Such entertainments proliferated in the eighteenth century. Invitations to balls, musical performances, and fancy dinners circulated among well-bred neighbors. Women who could afford to do so invited their neighbors to tea parties, where they could display good manners and fine silver and china at the same time. Robert Carter, one of Virginia's wealthiest gentlemen, once hosted an "elegant" dinner that lasted for nearly eight hours. Between half past four and seven o'clock, Carter's guests enjoyed a sumptuous meal. Then they turned to dancing and card playing, and only at midnight did they begin to return to their homes. Such occasions excluded ordinary settlers and reinforced elite colonists' sense of themselves as a separate—and better—class of people.

Some people expressed their gentility through more intellectual pursuits, taking advantage of the relatively high literacy rates among white colonists. In New England, where settlers placed great emphasis on Bible study, about 70 percent of men and 45 percent of women could read and write. Only a third of men in the southern colonies, and even fewer women, could read and write, but even these literacy rates were higher than among England's general population. Eighteenth-century colonists enjoyed greater access to printed material than ever before. In 1704, the *Boston News-Letter* became the first continuously published newspaper in British America. By the 1760s nearly every colony had a regularly published newspaper, printers were publishing almanacs,

Robert Feke (1707–1752), Portrait of Benjamin Franklin (1706–1790), c. 1746, Oil on canvas, 127 x 102 cm. Courtesy of the Harvard University Portrait Collection. Bequest of Dr. John Collins Warren, 1856

Painted at about the time Franklin retired from his printing business, this portrait depicts the one-time craftsman as an aspiring gentleman. Wearing a wig and a shirt with ruffled cuffs, Franklin would no longer work with his hands but would pursue his scientific experiments and other studies.

and booksellers opened shops in several cities. Prominent colonists, intent on developing America's intellectual life, began to participate in a transatlantic world of ideas.

These colonists, however, were consumers of British and European ideas rather than producers of an American intellectual tradition. They imported thousands of books, subscribed to British journals, and established libraries in cities such as Philadelphia, Charleston, and New York where borrowing privileges could be purchased for a modest fee. Libraries and private collections contained sermons and other religious writings, classical Greek and Roman texts, political and philosophical works by prominent European thinkers, and mainly British examples of poetry, drama, essays, and novels. Colonists with literary aspirations emulated their favorite writers. Students at Harvard in Cambridge (founded in 1636) modeled their college newspaper on an English periodical, *The Spectator.* In Virginia, William Byrd II, whose father got his

start as an Indian trader and tobacco farmer, advertised his own genteel pretensions by composing verse in the style of contemporary English poets. The young Thomas Jefferson copied out passages from the English novel *Tristram Shandy.* Benjamin Franklin honed his writing skills by rewriting essays from *The Spectator* and comparing his versions to the originals.

Educated colonists were especially interested in the new ideas that characterized what has been called the **Age of Enlightenment**. The European thinkers of the Enlightenment drew inspiration from recent advances in science—such as the English scientist Isaac Newton's explanation of the laws of gravity—that suggested that the universe operated according to natural laws that human reason could discover. They also drew on the work of the English philosopher John Locke, who maintained that God did not dictate human knowledge but rather gave us the power to acquire knowledge through experience and understanding. The hallmark of Enlightenment thought was a belief in the power of human reason to improve the human condition.

This optimistic worldview marked a profound intellectual shift. Enlightenment thinkers rejected earlier ideas about God's unknowable will and continued intervention in human and natural events. They instead assigned God a less active role as the creator of the universe, who had set the world running according to predictable laws, and then let nature—and human beings—shape events. Such ideas inspired a growing international community of scholars to try to discover the laws of nature and to work toward human progress.

Colonial intellectuals sought membership in this scholarly community. A few of them—the Reverend Cotton Mather of Massachusetts, William Byrd, Benjamin Franklin—gained election to the Royal Society of London, the most prestigious learned society in England. Most of their scholarly contributions were unimpressive. Byrd, for instance, sent the Royal Society a rather superficial manuscript titled "An Account of a Negro Boy That Is Dappled in Several Places of His Body with White Spots."

Benjamin Franklin, by contrast, achieved genuine intellectual prominence. Even as a youth, Franklin hungered after learning and demonstrated a particular gift for science. His experiments with a kite proved that lightning was electricity (a natural force whose properties were poorly understood at the time) and gained him an international reputation. He also found practical uses for his scientific knowledge. Franklin invented the lightning rod (which prevented fires in wooden buildings by channeling the electrical charge of a lightning bolt into the ground), bifocal spectacles, the iron "Franklin stove" (in which wood burned more efficiently than in fireplaces), and the glass harmonica, an instrument that made him famous among European musicians and composers.

If Franklin's career embodied the Enlightenment ideal of the rational exploration of nature's laws, it also revealed the limited impact of Enlightenment thought in colonial America. Only a few prosperous and educated colonists could afford such intellectual pursuits. Franklin came from humble origins—his father was a maker of candles and soap—but his success as a printer eventually allowed him to retire from business at the age of 42. Only then did he purchase the equipment for his electrical discoveries and begin his scientific work, devoting the "leisure during the rest of my life for philosophical studies and amusements." Franklin's equipment—and leisure—were as much badges of gentlemanly status as George Washington's London-made suit.

Most colonists remained ignorant of scientific advances and Enlightenment ideas. Unlike aspiring gentlemen and ladies, they had little leisure to devote to literature and polite conversation. When they found time to read, they picked up not a courtesy book or *The Spectator* but the Bible, which was the best-selling book of the colonial era. Religion principally shaped the way in which they viewed the world and explained human and natural events.

COLONIAL RELIGION AND THE GREAT AWAKENING

Church steeples dominated the skylines of colonial cities. By the 1750s, Boston and New York each had eighteen churches, and Philadelphia boasted twenty. Churches and meetinghouses likewise dominated country towns, though more sparsely in the scattered settlements of the South than in the northern colonies. Often the largest and finest buildings in town, they bore witness to the diverse and thriving condition of religion in America.

In all New England colonies except Rhode Island, the Puritan (or Congregationalist) faith was the established religion. The many Congregational churches in the region, headed by ministers trained at Harvard College and Yale (founded in 1701), served the majority of its colonists and re-

ceived financial support from their taxes. Though proud of the Puritan tradition that had inspired New England's origins, ministers and believers nonetheless had to adapt to changing social and religious conditions.

The principal adaptation consisted of a move away from strict requirements for church membership. In order to keep their churches pure, New England's founders had required prospective members to give convincing evidence that they had experienced a spiritual conversion. Once admitted, members could receive communion and have their children baptized. By the 1660s, however, fewer colonists sought admission under such strict standards, which left them and their unbaptized children outside the church. To address this problem, the clergy in 1662 adopted the **Halfway Covenant**, which allowed adults who had been baptized (because their parents were church members), but who had not themselves experienced conversion, to have their own children baptized. The Halfway Covenant slowly gained acceptance in subsequent decades. By the 1680s, some ministers made church admission even easier, requiring members only to demonstrate knowledge of the Christian faith and to live godly lives.

The Congregational Church also had to accept a measure of religious toleration in New England. In 1691, Massachusetts received a royal charter granting "liberty of Conscience" to all Protestants, bringing the colony into line with England's religious policy. Anglicans and Baptists eventually won exemptions from paying taxes to support the Congregational Church. At the same time, some Congregationalist preachers began emphasizing personal piety and good works in their sermons, ideas usually associated with Anglicanism. These changes indicated a shift away from the Puritan exclusiveness of New England's early years.

In the South, the established Church of England consolidated its authority in the early eighteenth century but never succeeded in exerting effective control over spiritual life. The bishop of London began appointing agents to oversee church matters, and the Society for the Propagation of the Gospel in Foreign Parts, founded in 1701, attempted to provide ministers for colonial parishes. Even so, these parishes often lacked trained clergy, and those who did emigrate encountered unexpected obstacles.

Many a parson in England could easily ride from one side of his parish to the other in an hour, but Anglican clergymen in the southern colonies served parishes that were vast and sparsely settled.

One South Carolina parish contained 10,400 square miles—and only seven hundred white residents. Ministers also found that influential planters, who had grown used to running parishes when preachers were unavailable, resisted their efforts to take control of churches. Aware that the planters' taxes paid their salaries, many ministers found it easiest simply to preach and behave in ways that offered the least offense. Frontier regions often lacked Anglican churches and clergymen altogether. In such places, dissenting religious groups, such as Presbyterians, Quakers, and Baptists, gained followers among people neglected by the Anglican establishment.

No established church dominated in the Middle Colonies of New York, New Jersey, and Pennsylvania. The region's ethnically diverse population and William Penn's policy of religious toleration guaranteed that a multitude of groups would compete for followers. One observer, accustomed to an established church, characterized these conditions as a "soul-destroying whirlpool." Yet religion flourished in the Middle Colonies. By the middle of the eighteenth century, the region had more congregations per capita than even New England.

Groups such as the Quakers and the Mennonites, who did not believe in having specially trained ministers, easily formed new congregations in response to local demand. Lutheran and German Reformed churches, however, required European-educated clergy, who were always scarce. Pious laymen held worship services in their homes even as they sent urgent letters overseas begging for ordained ministers. When more Lutheran and Reformed clergy arrived in the 1740s and 1750s, they sometimes discovered, as Anglican preachers did in the South, that laymen balked at relinquishing control of the churches. Lutheran and Reformed ministers also learned that their professional training alone could not command respect; their congregations demanded that they be powerful preachers. Because so many other religious alternatives were available, these ministers had to compete for their parishioners' allegiance.

Bewildering spiritual diversity, relentless religious competition, and a comparatively weak Anglican Church, all distinguished the colonies from England. Yet in one important way, religious developments during the middle third of the eighteenth century drew the colonies closer to England. A great transatlantic religious revival, originating in Scotland and England, first touched the Middle Colonies in the 1730s. In 1740–1745, it struck the northern colonies with the force of a hurricane, and in the 1760s, the

John Wollaston "George Whitefield" ca.1770. By courtesy of the National Portrait Gallery, London.

George Whitefield (who, contemporaries noted, was cross-eyed) enjoyed a remarkable career as a powerful preacher on both sides of the Atlantic. This portrait shows him preaching indoors to a rapt audience. During his tour of the colonies, Whitefield reportedly had a similar effect on crowds of thousands who gathered outdoors to hear his sermons.

last phase of the revival spread through the South. America had never seen anything like this immense revival, which came to be called the **Great Awakening**.

By 1730, Presbyterians in Pennsylvania had split into factions over such issues as the disciplining of church members and the requirement that licensed ministers have university degrees. One group, led by an immigrant Scottish evangelist, William Tennent, Sr., and his four sons, denounced their opponents as men more interested in regulations than conversion. In the 1730s, Tennent set up the Log College in Neshaminy, Pennsylvania, to train his sons and other young men to be evangelical ministers. What began as a dispute among clergymen eventually blossomed into a broader challenge to religious authority. That challenge gained momentum in late 1739, when one of the most charismatic evangelists of the century, George Whitefield, arrived in the colonies from England.

Whitefield, an Anglican priest, had experienced an uncommonly intense religious conversion while he was still a university student. Already famous in Britain as a preacher of great emotional fervor, he embarked on a tour of the colonies in the winter of 1739–1740. As soon as Whitefield landed in Delaware, his admirers whipped up local enthusiasm, insuring that he would preach to huge crowds in Pennsylvania and New Jersey. Whitefield's powerful preaching on the experience of conversion lent support to the Presbyterian faction led by the Tennents and sparked local revivals. Whitefield then moved on to New England, where some communities had already experienced small, local awakenings. In 1734–1735, for instance, the Congregationalist minister Jonathan Edwards had led a revival in Northampton, Massachusetts, urging his parishioners to recognize their sinfulness and describing hell in such a terrifying way that many despaired of their salvation.

Whitefield's tour through the colonies knitted these scattered local revivals into the Great Awakening. Crowds gathered in city squares and open fields to listen to his sermons. Whitefield exhorted his audiences to examine their souls for evidence of the "indwelling of Christ" that would indicate that they were saved. He criticized most ministers for emphasizing good works and "head-knowledge" instead of the emotional side of religion.

Whitefield's open-air sermons scarcely resembled the colonists' accustomed form of worship. Settlers normally gathered with family and neighbors in church for formal, structured services. They sat in pews assigned on the basis of social status, with wealthier members in front and poorer folk in the back. Such worship services reinforced standards of order and community hierarchy. But Whitefield's sermons were highly dramatic performances. He preached for hours in a booming voice, accompanying his words with spirited gestures and even occasionally dissolving in tears. Thousands of strangers, jostling in crowds that often outnumbered the populations of several villages put together, wept along with him. When the sermon ended, his listeners dispersed, many never to see each other again.

In the wake of Whitefield's visits, Benjamin Franklin noted, "it seem'd as if all the World were growing Religious." Revivals and mass conversions often followed his appearances, to the happy astonishment of local clergy. But their approval evaporated when more extreme revivalists appeared. Gilbert Tennent, William's son, followed Whitefield to Boston and derided the town's ministers as unconverted "dead Drones." James Davenport—a preacher so erratic that many thought him mad—claimed that God gave him the knowledge of other ministers' spir-

itual state and routinely denounced by name those he "knew" to be damned. Once, in the midst of a sermon urging his audience to rid itself of worldly finery, Davenport set an example by tearing off his velvet breeches and throwing them into a bonfire. Officials who valued civic order soon tried to silence such extremists by passing laws that prohibited them from preaching in a town without the local minister's permission.

Disputes between individuals converted in the revivals—called **New Lights**—and those who were not (Old Lights) split churches. New Lights insisted, as the separatist founders of Plymouth once had, that they could not remain in churches with sinful members and unconverted ministers and so left to form new churches. "Formerly the People could bear with each other in Charity when they differ'd in Opinion," lamented one colonist, "but they now break Fellowship and Communion with one another on that Account."

The Awakening came late to the southern colonies, but it was there, in the 1760s, that it produced perhaps its greatest controversy. Many southern converts became Baptists, combining their religious criticism of the Anglicans with a condemnation of the wealthy planters' way of life. Plainly dressed Baptists criticized the rich clothes, drinking, gambling, and pride of Virginia's gentry. Planters, in turn, viewed Baptists as dangerous people who could not "meet a man upon the road, but they must ram a text of Scripture down his throat." Most of all, they hated the Baptists for their willingness to preach to slaves. More than once, irate gentlemen burst in on Baptist services and beat the preacher senseless.

Although the revivals themselves gradually waned, the Great Awakening had a lasting impact on colonial society. It forged new links between Great Britain and the colonies. Evangelical ministers on both sides of the Atlantic exchanged correspondence. Periodicals such as *The Christian History*—over which Whitefield exercised considerable control—informed British and American subscribers of advances in true religion throughout the empire.

In the colonies, the Awakening brought numerous changes. It led to the founding of new colleges to serve members of different religious denominations. Middle Colony evangelicals founded the College of New Jersey (now Princeton University) in 1746. In the 1760s, New England Baptists established the College of Rhode Island (now Brown University). An evangelical wing of the Dutch Reformed Church founded Queens College (now Rutgers University) in 1766. These colleges drew their exclusively male students from all colonies, not just the local area.

The revivals also brought newcomers into Christian congregations. Chesapeake slaves responded to the evangelists' message and—often contrary to the intent of white preachers—drew lessons from sermons about the equality of humankind. A few black preachers circulated among slave quarters, spreading the message of salvation and freedom. The impact of revivalism on Indians was less dramatic, but still significant. Evangelicals enjoyed their greatest success in small Native American communities, whose inhabitants were attracted to a less formal style of preaching, particularly in New England. Native converts often urged fellow Indians to heed the Christian message of self-discipline, not to emulate English colonists, but to revitalize villages beset by alcoholism and other problems linked to European domination. Samson Occom, a Mohegan convert and the best-known native preacher, worked as a missionary among the Montauks on Long Island. His experience of poor pay and white prejudice, however, discouraged other converts from following his example.

The Awakening did not greatly increase women's church membership, since women already constituted majorities in many congregations. But by emphasizing the emotional power of Christianity, revivals accorded greater legitimacy to what were thought to be women's more sensitive temperaments. And some women, such as Bathsheba Kingsley, were inspired by the power of their conversions to become traveling preachers. More often, female evangelicals stayed within the bounds of social convention and limited their activities to conducting prayer meetings for other women.

Everywhere, the New Light challenge to established ministers and churches undermined habits of deference to authority. Revivalists urged colonists to think for themselves in choosing which church to join and which minister to follow, not just to conform to what the rest of the community did. As their churches fractured, colonists—particularly New Englanders—faced more choices than ever before in their religious lives.

The exercise of religious choice also influenced political behavior. Voters noticed whether candidates for office were New or Old Lights and cast their ballots for men on their own side. Tactics first used to mobilize religious groups—such as organizing committees and writing petitions and letters—proved useful for political activities as well. Though hardly the intent of Whitefield or other revivalists, the Awakening thus fostered greater political awareness and participation among colonists.

THE COLONIAL POLITICAL WORLD

The political legacy of the Great Awakening—particularly the emphasis on individual choice and resistance to authority—corresponded to developments in the colonial political world. For most of the seventeenth century, ties within the empire developed from trade rather than governance. But as America grew in wealth and population, king and Parliament sought to manage colonial affairs more directly than before.

In the late seventeenth century, upheavals on both sides of the Atlantic seemed to confirm for both colonists and Englishmen a common interest in protecting the rights and liberties they derived from their shared heritage. The English overthrew King James II, and the people of New England successfully resisted the king's attempt to impose autocratic government in the colonies. But even as colonists and Englishmen asserted their common political culture at the dawn of the eighteenth century, differences in their political practices and ideas began to emerge.

THE DOMINION OF NEW ENGLAND AND THE LIMITS OF BRITISH CONTROL

Before 1650, England made little attempt to exert centralized control in North America. Each colony more or less governed itself, and most political activity occurred at the town or county level. Local officials kept the peace, resolved disputes, hired schoolmasters, arranged for the construction of roads and bridges, and collected taxes. Busy with the routines of daily life, most colonists devoted little time, and even less interest, to politics.

When Charles II became king in 1660, he initially showed little interest in the colonies except as sources of land and government offices with which he could reward his supporters. The grandest prizes, of course, were the great proprietorships, such as Pennsylvania and Carolina, but the creation of a rudimentary imperial bureaucracy also yielded rewards for the king to distribute. With the passage of mercantilist regulations governing colonial trade, for example, Parliament required customs officers to administer the imperial trading system and thus created a certain number of jobs.

Charles's brother James, the Duke of York, envisioned a more tightly controlled empire. He encouraged Charles to appoint military officers with strong ties of loyalty to him, as royal governors in

America. In 1675, James convinced Charles to create the Lords of Trade, a committee of the Privy Council (the group of nobles who served as royal advisers), to oversee colonial affairs.

When James became king in 1685, the whole character of the empire abruptly changed. Seeking to transform it into something much grander and more susceptible to England's control, James set out to reorganize it along the lines of Spain's empire, combining the colonies into three or four large provinces. He appointed powerful governors to carry out policies that he himself would formulate.

James began in the north, creating the **Dominion of New England** out of eight previously separate colonies stretching from Maine (then part of Massachusetts) to New Jersey. He chose Sir Edmund Andros, a former army officer, to govern the vast region with an appointive council but no elective assembly. Andros moved to Boston and initially gained some support from merchants excluded from politics by Massachusetts's insistence that only church members could vote. But he eventually antagonized them and other New Englanders by rigidly enforcing the Navigation Acts, limiting towns to just one annual meeting, remodeling the law courts, challenging property titles, and levying taxes without the colonists' consent. He even compelled Boston Puritans to share a meetinghouse with Anglicans.

Events in England ultimately sealed the fate of the Dominion. For years, English Protestants had worried about James's absolutist governing style and his conversion to Catholicism. Their fears increased in 1688, when the queen bore a son to carry on a Catholic line of succession. Parliament's leaders invited James's Protestant daughter, Mary, and her husband, William of Orange, the Stadtholder of the Netherlands, to take over the throne. In November 1688, William landed in England and gained the support of most of the English army. In December, James fled to France, ending a bloodless coup known as the **Glorious Revolution**.

Bostonians overthrew Andros the following April, even before they knew for sure that William was king, and later they had him shipped back to England. Massachusetts colonists hoped that their original charter of 1629 would be reinstated, but a new one was issued in 1691. It made several important changes. Massachusetts now included within its borders what had formerly been Plymouth Colony as well as Maine. Its colonists no longer elected their governor, who would instead be appointed by the monarch. Voters no longer had to be church members, and religious toleration was extended to all Protestants.

The new charter ended exclusive Puritan control in Massachusetts but also restored political stability. During the three years between Andros's overthrow and the arrival of a royal governor in 1692, the colony lacked a legally established government. In this atmosphere of uncertainty, an outbreak of accusations of witchcraft in Salem grew to unprecedented proportions. Colonists, like most Europeans of the time, believed in the existence of witches—humans who acted as Satan's agents and used supernatural powers to hurt their enemies. Over the years, New Englanders had executed a dozen or so accused witches, usually older women. But in the winter of 1691–1692, when several young girls of Salem experienced fits and other strange behavior, hundreds of settlers were accused of witchcraft, and nineteen were hanged. Salem's crisis occurred against a backdrop of local economic change, but it gathered momentum because the Dominion crisis had generated uncertainty about political and legal authority. Special courts had to be created to deal with the witchcraft outbreak. The judges' unusual methods, including the acceptance of "spectral evidence," or accusers' uncorroborated testimony that they had seen apparitions, later aroused considerable criticism.

The impact of the Glorious Revolution in other colonies likewise reflected local conditions. In New York, after Andros's deputy left, Jacob Leisler, a rich merchant and militia captain, gained power and ruled in a dictatorial fashion, persecuting men against whom he held personal grievances. Too slow in relinquishing command to the newly arrived royal governor in 1691, Leisler was arrested for treason and executed. In Maryland, Protestants used the occasion of William and Mary's accession to the throne to lobby for the end of the Catholic proprietorship. They were partly successful. The Calvert family lost its governing powers but retained rights to vast quantities of land. The Anglican Church became the established faith, and Catholics were barred from public office.

The colonists rejected James, not English authority in general. Their motives (especially in New England) largely reflected powerful anti-Catholic sentiment. William's firm Protestantism reassured them, and most colonists assumed that

AMERICAN VIEWS

Boston Celebrates a New King (August 1727)

The first colonial newspaper, the *Boston News-Letter*, appeared in that city in 1704. By the 1720s, Bostonians could choose from three newspapers, and New York and Philadelphia each had one. Published weekly, these papers mainly reported on English and European affairs and often reprinted essays by prominent English political writers. Their pages carried little local news, on the assumption that colonists could learn of this by word of mouth. But when truly extraordinary events occurred, such as the accession of a new British monarch, colonial newspapers reported on the local response. The following extract describes Bostonians' reaction to news that George II had become Britain's new king.

- How did Bostonians commemorate the new king's accession?
- What does this reveal about their attitudes toward George II and British government in general?
- Who was invited to the "splendid Entertainment," and what does this reveal about the structure of Boston society?

On Wednesday Morning by order of His Honour William Dummer, Esq., our Lieut. Governour & Commander in chief[,] three Regiments of the Militia and five Troops of horse were under arms in the great street before the State-house, making a very fine appearance. The number of Spectators exceeded the Men in Arms, covering the houses on every side. As soon as the Herauld had said his Amen to God Save the King, the loud and joyful Huzza's of so great a multitude rent the skies, the Regiments made a tripple discharge, the Castle Forts & Ships fir'd their cannon; and a splendid Entertainment follow'd for the Lieut. Governour and his Majesty's Council, Officers, Justices, and the Rev[eren]d Ministers present; with suitable provisions for the Regiments and Troops. The bells rung all the day, and in the Evening the

Rejoycing was continued with Fireworks and Bonfires, and the whole Town illuminated in an extraordinary manner, the Windows of each story of the Houses in the principal streets having three or four rows of candles in them. The streets were fill'd all the Evening with the Gentry of both Sexes, who appear'd with much decency and gravity, and with gayety and chearfulness. At nine of the clock a welcome rain, after a time of much heat and drought, put an end to the Ceremony. . . . We pray God, by whom Kings reign, that the royal smiles of His Majesty King George the Second, and the happy influences of his wise and just Government, may ever be falling on all his Majesty's Dominions, and on this loyal and dutiful Province in particular.

Source: *New England Weekly Journal* (August 21, 1727).

life would return to normal. But the Glorious Revolution in England and the demise of the Dominion had long-lasting effects that shaped political life in England and America for years to come.

THE LEGACY OF THE GLORIOUS REVOLUTION

In England, the Glorious Revolution signaled a return to political stability after years of upheaval. English people celebrated the preservation of their rights from the threat of a tyrannical king. In 1689, Parliament passed the Bill of Rights, which justified James's ouster and bound future monarchs to abide by the rule of law. They could not suspend parliamentary laws, collect taxes, or engage in foreign wars without Parliament's consent, or maintain a standing army in peacetime. Parliamentary elections and meetings would follow a regular schedule, without royal interference. In sum, Parliament claimed to be the crown's equal partner in governing England.

Colonists, too, celebrated the vindication of their rights as Englishmen. They believed that their successful resistance to Andros confirmed that their membership in the empire was founded on voluntary allegiance and not on forced submission to the mother country. Observing the similarity between Parliament and the colonial assemblies, they concluded that their own legislatures had a critical role in governance and in the protection of their rights and liberties. On both sides of the Atlantic, representative government had triumphed.

In fact, Parliament claimed full authority over the colonies and did not recognize their assemblies as its equal. For more than a half-century, however, it did not vigorously assert that authority. At the same time, William and his immediate successors lacked James's compulsion to control the colonies. William did make a few changes to imperial administration. In 1696, he replaced the Lords of Trade with a new committee, the Board of Trade. This advisory body gathered information from the colonies and recommended policy changes but itself had no executive role. William also approved the Navigation Act of 1696, which closed loopholes in earlier laws and created vice-admiralty courts in the colonies similar to those of England. Admiralty judges settled maritime disputes and smuggling cases without using juries.

During the early eighteenth century, Parliament and royal ministers confined their attention to matters of trade and military defense and otherwise left the colonies on their own. This mild imperial rule, later called the era of "salutary neglect," allowed the colonies to grow in wealth, population, and self-government. It also encouraged colonial self-confidence, leading colonists to assume equality with the English as members of the empire.

DIVERGING POLITICS IN THE COLONIES AND GREAT BRITAIN

English people on both sides of the Atlantic believed that politics ought to reflect social organization. They often compared the state to a family. Just as fathers naturally headed families, adult men led societies. In particular, adult male property holders, who enjoyed economic independence, claimed the right to vote and hold office. Women (who generally could not own property), propertyless men, and slaves had no political role because they, like children, were subordinate to the authority of others. Their dependence on husbands, fathers, masters, or employers—who could influence their political decisions—rendered them incapable of exercising freedom of choice.

States, like families, worked best when all members fulfilled their responsibilities. Rulers ought to govern with the same fairness and benevolence that fathers presumably exercised within their families. When George II became king in 1727, he reassured Parliament of his "constant care" to "secure to All My subjects, the full Enjoyment of their religious and civil Rights." In return for protection, the people owed their rulers the same obedience that children accorded their parents. The House of Commons responded to George II's assurance of goodwill with its own promise of "Duty, Zeal and Affection to Your Majesty's Person and Government." Such phrases often disguised actual struggles between rulers and people but nevertheless expressed firmly held ideals.

Eighteenth-century people also believed that government should reflect society's hierarchical organization. In England, this idea was embodied in the institutions of monarchy and Parliament. The crown, of course, represented the interests of the royal family. Parliament represented society's two main divisions: the aristocracy in the House of Lords and the common people in the House of Commons. Americans shared the view that government should mirror social hierarchies but found it much more difficult to put the idea into practice.

American society grew closer to the British model during the eighteenth century but was never identical to it. Thus its political structure would never fully mirror that of England. One obvious difference was that America lacked an aristocracy. In England, the members of this tiny privileged minority were easily recognizable by their great wealth, prestigious family lines, leisured lives, and official titles of nobility. British America had elites but no titled aristocracy. Elite colonists were often just two or three generations removed from humble beginnings. Hence the acute anxiety that inspired George Washington and other colonial gentlemen to seek refinement, to gain the automatic recognition that England's more secure elites enjoyed.

In both England and America, land ownership was the prerequisite for political participation, on the grounds that it freed people from dependence on others and gave them a stake in society. In England, this requirement sharply limited participation. By the mid-eighteenth century, only one-tenth of all English heads of households owned all the country's land, and thus only a correspondingly tiny proportion of men could vote. Landholding in America, however, was much more widespread. By late in life, a large majority of white male farmers owned the land they tilled. The expansion of landholding swelled the ranks of voters. In most colonies, 50 to 75 percent of white men were eligible to vote, although not all exercised this right at election time.

Distinctive social conditions in England and America also gave rise to different notions of political representation. Electoral districts for Parliament came in a confusing mixture of shapes, reflecting their status in past centuries. Once-important towns sent representatives on the basis of their former prominence. Dunwich even retained its right to elect a parliamentary representative long after the city itself had washed into the North Sea. At the same time, rapidly growing cities, such as Manchester, lacked any representative at all. Some English radicals protested this inequity during the eighteenth century. Most of their countrymen, however, accepted the idea of **virtual representation**, which held that representatives served the interests of the nation as a whole, not just the locality from which they came. They assumed that since the colonists held interests in common with English people at home, they were virtually represented in Parliament, just like Manchester's residents.

Since the founding of their colonies, however, Americans had experienced **actual representation** and believed that elected representatives should be directly responsive to local interests. They were accustomed to sending written instructions to their legislators, informing them how to vote on important issues. Colonial representatives, unlike members of Parliament, resided in their districts. The Americans' experience with actual representation made them extremely skeptical of Parliament's claims to virtual representation. For the first half of the eighteenth century, however, Parliament did not press this claim, and the tensions between the two ideas remained latent.

The most direct political confrontations between England and the colonies instead focused on the role of colonial governors. In every colony except Connecticut and Rhode Island (where voters chose the executive), either the king or proprietors appointed the governors. Their interests thus lay with their English patrons and not the colonies. More important, governors exercised greater powers over the colonial assemblies than the king (after the Glorious Revolution) did over Parliament. Governors could veto laws enacted by the assemblies and initiate legislation in consultation with councilors, whom they appointed. They could delay legislative sessions and dissolve the assemblies at will. Governors could also nominate and dismiss colonial judges as they wished.

In practice, several conditions hampered governors' efforts to exercise their legal authority. Many arrived with detailed instructions on how to govern, a condition that limited their ability to negotiate with colonists over sensitive issues. Governors controlled few offices or other prizes with which to buy the allegiance of their opponents. They struggled to dominate assemblies that grew in size as the colonial population expanded. And in several colonies, including Massachusetts and New York, governors relied on the assemblies to appropriate the money for their salaries—a financial dependence that restrained even the most autocratic executive.

In response to the perceived, if not always realized, threat of powerful governors, colonial assemblies asserted themselves as never before. They sent agents (including such prominent figures as Benjamin Franklin) to England to lobby on behalf of colonial interests. Local factions fought for election to the increasingly important legislature, leading to some of the most contentious politics in the British Empire. Governors often stood on the sidelines, either frustrated with their inability to govern or, at times, enlisted on the side of one faction or another.

Decades of struggles with governors led colonists to exalt the assemblies' role as the guarantors of their liberties. In 1738, one Pennsylvanian went so far as to declare that the "necessity of reducing the form of this government to the British mode" by strengthening the executive was a "wicked" design. Most colonists, however, accepted the loose and sometimes contradictory political ties of empire. They assumed that their connections to Britain were voluntary, based on common identity and rights. So long as Parliament treated the Americans as partners in empire and refrained from ruling by coercion, colonists could celebrate British government as "the most perfect combination of human powers in society . . . for the preservation of liberty and the production of happiness."

By the middle of the eighteenth century, the blessings of British government extended to more colonists than ever before. The population of

British America grew rapidly and spread out over vast amounts of land. The expansion of British settlement, in turn, alarmed other European powers with American colonies. Both Spain and France launched new settlements as the competition for the continent entered a new and volatile phase.

EXPANDING EMPIRES

During the first half of the eighteenth century, England, Spain, and France all enlarged their North American holdings according to patterns established during the previous century. England's empire expanded in tandem with the unrelenting growth of its colonial population. Spain and France still relied on missionaries, soldiers, and traders to stake their claims to American territory. In the eighteenth century, as in the seventeenth, English settlement displaced native peoples. Newly established Spanish and French colonies, however, contained small numbers of Europeans amid much larger populations of Indians. Over time, these empires came into closer contact with one another, intensifying the competition for land, trade, resources, and Indian allies (see Map 4–2).

BRITISH COLONISTS IN THE BACKCOUNTRY

Population growth in British North America during the eighteenth century was truly astonishing. The non-Indian population in the mainland

MAP 4-2   Expanding Settlement, c. 1750
Imperial rivalries drove Spain, France, and England to expand their North American empires in the mid-eighteenth century. Once again, this sparked conflict with native peoples as well as with European competitors.

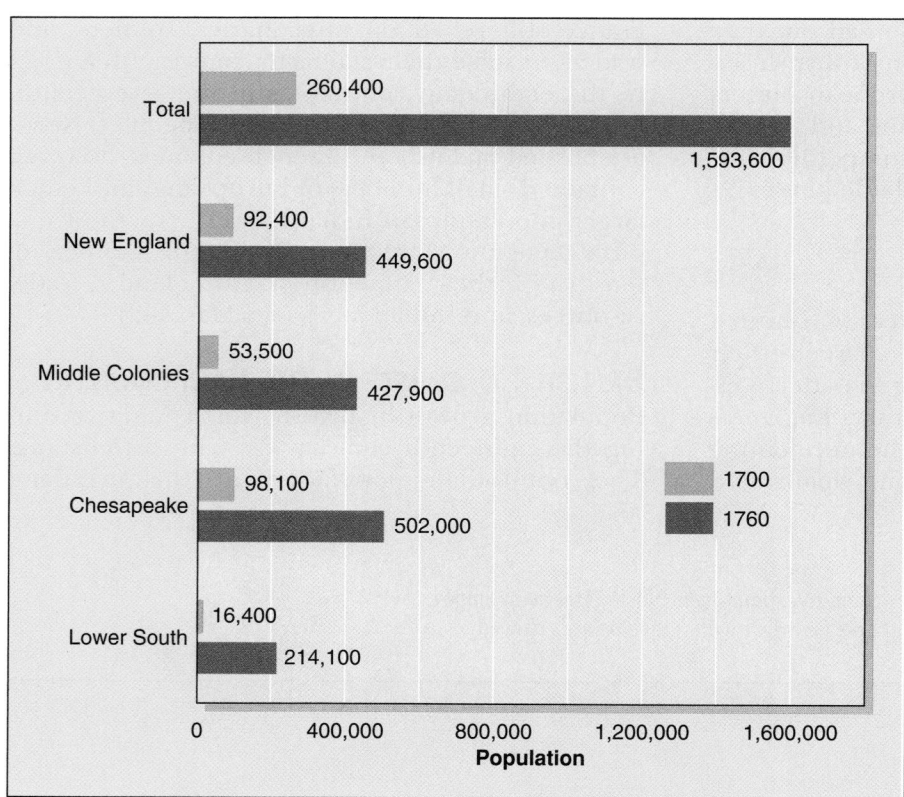

FIGURE 4-2 Population Growth in British Mainland Colonies, 1700–1760
Both natural increase and immigration contributed to a staggering rate of population growth in British North America. Some colonists predicted that Americans would soon outnumber Britain's inhabitants—a possibility that greatly concerned British officials.
Data Source: John J. McCusker and Russell R. Menard, *The Economy of British America, 1607–1789*, rev. ed. (1991). University of North Carolina Press.

colonies numbered about 260,000 in 1700; by 1760, it had increased to over 1.5 million (see Figure 4–2). In 1750, Benjamin Franklin predicted that if the colonial population continued to grow at this rate, within two hundred years "the greatest Number of Englishmen will be on this Side" of the Atlantic Ocean.

Much of this growth stemmed from natural increase. Many white families, particularly in the northern colonies, had between five and ten children, most of whom survived to produce more offspring. The descendants of a single couple could, after three or four generations, people small towns. When 80-year-old Judith Coffin, the matriarch of an unusually large Massachusetts family, died in 1705, she had a total of 177 children and grandchildren. By the mid-eighteenth century, even the slave population, first in the Chesapeake and later in the Lower South, began to reproduce itself, although more slowly than the white population.

Immigration also boosted the population, making some regions grow faster than others. Thou-

sands of Scots-Irish and German settlers, in addition to thousands of African slaves, helped the population of the Lower South increase at nearly twice the rate of New England, which attracted few immigrants (and therefore remained the most thoroughly English of all colonial regions). Pennsylvania absorbed a continuous stream of immigrants. By 1770, it had 240,000 settlers, ten times the number it had in 1710. Indeed, extensive German immigration worried Pennsylvania leaders. Like Benjamin Franklin, they feared that the newcomers would "never adopt our Language or Customs" and would soon "be so numerous as to Germanize us."

Most of the coast from Maine to Georgia was settled by 1760, forcing new immigrants to move inland. Descendants of earlier settlers often joined them, seeking farms that could no longer be had in the more crowded towns of their birth. New Englanders pushed up the Connecticut River Valley and into the hills of western Massachusetts. Settlement in New York followed the Hudson, Mohawk, and Schoharie Rivers deep into the interior. But the most dramatic expansion occurred in the foothills and valleys of the Appalachian Mountains from Pennsylvania to Georgia, a region known as the backcountry.

Between 1730 and 1770, nearly a quarter of a million German, Scots-Irish, and English colonists entered the backcountry. For the most part, they raised crops and livestock for subsistence on small, isolated farms. Community life developed slowly, in part because many backcountry settlers moved frequently. In addition, a surplus of men among the first settlers delayed the formation of families.

Contemporary observers derided the crudeness of frontier life. William Byrd scornfully described one backcountry house as a "castle containing of one dirty room with a dragging door to it that will neither open or shut." Charles Woodmason, an English-born Anglican missionary, was appalled by the sight of western Carolina settlers

This log house, built in Pennsylvania in the early eighteenth century, suggests the sort of dwellings that dotted the backcountry. Most such houses would have been smaller than this two-story example. Scandinavian colonists, who settled on the lower Delaware River in the early seventeenth century, introduced log construction to America.

who "Live in Logg Cabbins like Hogs." Most of them, he reported, were "very loose, dissolute, Idle People—Without either Religion or Goodness." Genteel observers offered what they considered the most damaging insult by referring to such settlers as "white Indians."

These comments reflect emerging tensions between backcountry settlements and older seacoast communities. George Washington, William Byrd, and other coastal planters acquired vast tracts of western land with the intent of selling it to these "crude" settlers. During the 1740s and 1750s, scores of Virginia planters, northern merchants, and London investors formed companies whose purpose was to profit from this kind of land speculation. Their interests collided with those of many backcountry settlers, including squatters who occupied the land without acquiring legal title in the hope that their labor in clearing farms would establish their property rights.

Backcountry settlers often complained that rich eastern planters, who dominated the colonial legislatures, ignored western demands for adequate representation. Many argued that the crudeness of frontier life was only temporary. Perhaps the best measure of their desire to resemble eastern planters was the spread of slaveholding among prosperous backcountry farmers. In one western Virginia county in 1750, only one-fifth of the household heads owned slaves. Just nineteen years later, more than half of them did.

Tensions grew throughout the backcountry as English settlers encroached on Indian lands. Colonists who moved to Pennsylvania's fertile Susquehanna Valley displaced Delawares, Shawnees, and other native peoples who had sought refuge there from earlier white migrations. In South Carolina, the Catawbas moved to ever more remote sites to keep their distance from white settlers. Indians moving to avoid friction with whites, however, frequently encroached on lands claimed by other tribes—particularly those of the Iroquois Confederacy—leading to conflict among native peoples.

Even where British settlers had not yet appeared, English and Scottish traders could often be found, aggressively pursuing trade with the Indians. Spanish and French observers feared this commercial expansion even more than they did the movement of settlers. Knowing that the Indians viewed trade as a counterpart to military alliance, they worried that the English, with cheaper and better trade goods, would lure away their native allies. In response, the Spanish and French expanded their own territorial claims and tried to strengthen relations with Indian peoples.

THE SPANISH IN TEXAS AND CALIFORNIA

Spain worried that its existing North American colonies would be overwhelmed by its enemies. Florida had become the target of English raiders from South Carolina, who attacked Spanish missions with the help of local Indians. Years of religious persecution and forced labor encouraged Florida's Indians to oppose the Spanish, but the natives also wanted English trade goods, such as guns, which Spanish traders were officially prohibited from selling. Spain maintained a precarious hold on coastal bases at St. Augustine, San Marcos de Apalachee, and Pensacola. By the mid-eighteenth century, however, control of Florida's interior effectively passed to Indian bands allied with English (and in the west, French) traders.

In 1700, New Mexico still suffered from the effects of the Pueblo Revolt. Spanish farmers and ranchers slowly moved back up the Rio Grande Valley. Franciscans returned to build fewer missions than before. Fearful of sparking another revolt, the priests eased their labor demands and avoided outright religious persecution, allowing the Pueblos to retain many of their customs and religious practices. New Mexican officials worried about news brought by Apache hunters that Frenchmen had been seen on the plains. French traders did not reach Santa Fe until 1739, but persistent rumors of

This panel of an eighteenth-century painting by an unknown Mexican artist is representative of a genre of portraits illustrating the categories Spanish colonists developed to designate the offspring of various kinds of mixed marriage. This one, labeled Español, con India, Mestizo, *depicts a Spanish father, an Indian mother, and their mestizo child. The scarcity of European women made mixed marriage common in Spanish colonies. Such unions were exceedingly rare in the English colonies, where cultural preferences and the relative abundance of European women discouraged intermarriage.*

their approach fueled Spanish fears that New Mexico would fall into French hands.

To create a buffer zone around their existing colonies, the Spanish moved into Texas and California. Franciscan priests led the way into east Texas, establishing several missions between 1690 and 1720. San Antonio was founded in 1718 as a way station between the Rio Grande and east Texas missions; its fortified chapel, San Antonio de Valero, later became famous as the Alamo. The Spanish advance into Texas, however, met with resistance from the French (who also had outposts on the Gulf Coast) and from the Caddos and other Indians armed with French guns. Efforts to fill east Texas with settlers from Spain, Cuba, and the Canary Islands, all failed when Spanish officials could not guarantee their safety. With only 1,800 settlers there as late as 1742, Spain exerted a weak hold on Texas.

Sixteenth-century Spaniards had considered building outposts in California to supply ships traveling between Mexico and the Philippines but were deterred by the region's remoteness. Spanish interest revived in the 1760s, when it seemed that Russia, which had built fur-trading posts in Alaska, might occupy California. Largely through the efforts of two men—José de Gálvez, a royal official, and Junípero Serra, a Franciscan priest—the Spanish constructed a string of forts and missions from San Diego north to San Francisco between 1769 and 1776.

They initially encountered little opposition from California's Indians, who lived in small, scattered villages and lacked experience with organized warfare. With no European rivals nearby to compete with them, the Spanish erected an extensive mission system designed to convert and educate Indians and set them to work. Thousands of native laborers farmed irrigated fields and tended horses, sheep, and cattle. They did so under extremely harsh conditions.

According to one observer, Indians who became Christians and settled at the missions endured a fate "worse than that of slaves." The Spanish worked them hard and maintained them in overcrowded, unsanitary dwellings. Native women suffered from sexual exploitation by Spanish soldiers. Epidemics of European diseases swept through the Indian population, reducing it from 300,000 in 1769 to about 200,000 fifty years later. Signs of native resistance met with quick and cruel punishment—including whipping, burning, and execution—so that the Indians would not (as one official later wrote) "come to know their power" over the vastly outnumbered Spanish. (As late as 1790, California had only 990 Spanish residents.) Despite the gruesome consequences, Indians staged several revolts during the eighteenth century, but Spanish soldiers usually suppressed them quickly.

Spain's empire grew, even as it weakened, during the eighteenth century. Its scattered holdings north of the Rio Grande functioned as colonies of another colony—Mexico—shielding it from foreign incursion. The scarcity of Spanish settlers, especially women, encouraged racial intermixture in the borderlands and insured that racial distinctions would never be drawn as sharply there as in the English colonies. From the beginning, Spain's vision of empire had rested not on extensive settlement but on expansive territorial claims backed up by soldiers and missionaries who subjugated native peoples in order to control their labor for Spanish profit. After 1700, however, the limitations of this coercive approach to empire, which had served Spain well for nearly two centuries, became apparent. As their experiences in Florida and Texas vividly demonstrated, the Spanish simply could not compete with the vigorous commercial empires of France and England.

THE FRENCH ALONG THE MISSISSIPPI AND IN LOUISIANA

French expansion followed major waterways of the St. Lawrence River, the Great Lakes, and the Mississippi into the heart of North America. Explorers reached the Mississippi Valley in the 1670s. Within twenty years, French outposts appeared along the Gulf Coast. New Orleans, the capital and main port of French Louisiana, was founded in 1718. Soon forts, trading posts, and villages sprang up in the continent's interior and formed a chain of way stations between Canada and the Gulf of Mexico, with military garrisons strategically located on lakes and rivers. Concerned about defending scattered settlements, French officials forbade colonists to move into the interior. But colonists went anyway, building six villages along the Mississippi in a place they called the pays des Illinois.

The first Illinois settlers were independent fur traders (*coureurs de bois,* or "woods runners") unwilling to return to Canada after the French government tried to prohibit their direct trade with Indians. Many found Christian Indian wives and began farming the rich lands along the river. Several hundred emigrants from Canada eventually joined them. The settlers, using the labor of their families and of black and Indian slaves, produced profitable surpluses of wheat, corn, and livestock to feed the growing population of New Orleans and the lower Mississippi Valley.

French Louisiana contained a remarkably diverse population of Indian peoples, French soldiers and settlers, and German immigrants, as well as African slaves who, by the 1730s, outnumbered European colonists. Settlers and slaves raised some tobacco and indigo as cash crops, but Louisiana's economy depended mainly on food crops, herding, fishing, and the deerskin trade. Discouraged by the lack of profits, French officials and merchants neglected Louisiana, and even Catholic missionaries failed to establish a strong presence. Significant European emigration to Louisiana essentially ceased after the 1720s.

But the French approach to empire in Louisiana as in Canada had always depended more on

Indian alliances than on settlement. Louisiana's principal allies were the Choctaws, whom one military official called "the bulwark of the colony." The Choctaws and other native allies offered trade and military assistance in return for guns, trade goods, French help in fighting English raiders seeking Indian slaves, and occasional French mediation of Indian disputes.

French expansion along the Mississippi Valley drove a wedge between Florida and Spain's other mainland colonies; it also blocked the westward movement of English settlers. But France's enlarged empire was only as strong as the Indian alliances on which it rested. Preserving good relations was expensive, however, requiring the constant exchange of diplomatic gifts and trade goods. When France ordered Louisiana officials to limit expenses and reduce Indian gifts in 1745, the officials objected that the Choctaws "would ask for nothing better than to have such pretexts in order to resort to the English."

The fear of losing Indian favor preoccupied officials in 1745 because at that moment France's empire in America consisted of two disconnected pieces: New France, centered in the St. Lawrence Valley and the Great Lakes basin, and Louisiana, stretching from New Orleans to the pays des Illinois. Between them lay a thousand miles of wilderness, through which only one thoroughfare passed—the Ohio River. For decades, communication between the two parts of France's North American empire posed no problem because Indians in the Ohio Valley allowed the French free passage through their lands. If that policy ended, however, France's New World empire would be dangerously divided.

A CENTURY OF WARFARE

The expansion of empires in North America reflected the policies of European states locked in a relentless competition for power and wealth. From the time of the Glorious Revolution, English foreign policy aimed at limiting the expansion of French influence. This, in turn, resulted in a series of four wars. As the eighteenth century wore on, the conflicts between the two countries increasingly involved their American colonies as well as Spain and its colonies. The outcome of each of the wars in America depended no less on the participation of colonists and Indians than on the policies and strategies of the European powers. The conclusion of the final conflict signaled a dramatic

Overview

The Colonial Wars, 1689–1763

Name in the Colonies	European Name and Dates	Dates in America	Results for Britain
King William's War	War of the League of Augsburg, 1688–1697	1689–1697	Reestablished balance of power between England and France
Queen Anne's War	War of Spanish Succession, 1702–1714	1702–1713	Britain acquired Nova Scotia
King George's War	War of Austrian Succession, 1739–1748	1744–1748	Britain returned Louisbourg to France British settlers began moving westward Weakening of Iroquois neutrality
French and Indian War	Seven Years' War, 1756–1763	1754–1763	Britain acquired Canada and all French territory east of Mississippi Britain gained Florida from Spain

shift in North American history (see the Overview table, "The Colonial Wars, 1689–1763").

IMPERIAL CONFLICT AND THE ESTABLISHMENT OF AN AMERICAN BALANCE OF POWER, 1689–1738

When he became king of England in 1688, the Dutch Protestant William of Orange was already fighting the War of the League of Augsburg against France's Catholic king, Louis XIV. Almost immediately, William brought England into the conflict. The war lasted until 1697 and ended, as most European wars of this period did, in a negotiated peace that reestablished the balance of power. Little territory changed hands, either in this war or in the War of the Spanish Succession (1702–1713), which followed it

In America, these two imperial wars—known to British colonists as **King William's War** and **Queen Anne's War**, after the monarchs on the throne at the time—ended with equal indecisiveness. New France's Indian allies attacked New England's north-

ern frontier with devastating success, destroying the Massachusetts town of Deerfield in 1704. New Englanders struck back at the exposed settlements of Acadia, which ultimately entered the British Empire as Nova Scotia, and tried unsuccessfully to seize Quebec. Neither war caused more than marginal changes for the colonies in North America. Both had profound effects, however, on the English state and the Iroquois League.

All European states of the eighteenth century financed their wars by borrowing. But the English were the first to realize that wartime debts did not necessarily have to be repaid during the following peace. The government instead created a funded debt. Having borrowed heavily from large joint-stock corporations, the government agreed to use tax revenues to pay interest on those loans, but it did not agree to pay off the loans themselves. The corporations agreed because the interest payments amounted to a steady form of income that over the long run could amount to more than the original loans. In this way, England became the first European country to harness its national economy efficiently to military ends.

As the debt grew larger, more and more taxes were necessary to pay interest on it. Taxes also rose to pay for a powerful navy and a standing army. When the treasury created a larger and more efficient bureaucracy to collect taxes, many Englishmen grew nervous. Their anxiety emerged as a strain of thought known as **Country**, or **"Real Whig," ideology**. Country ideology stressed the threats that a standing army and a powerful state posed to personal liberty. It also emphasized the dangers of taxation to property rights and the need for property holders to retain their right to consent to taxation. Real Whig politicians publicized their fears but could not stop the growth of the state. In every successive war, the claims of national interest and patriotism—and the prospect of profit for parties rich enough to lend money to the government—overrode the objections of those who feared the expansion of state power.

In America, the first two imperial wars transformed the role of the Iroquois League. After the English took over New Netherland in 1664, the Five Nations cultivated trading connections with them and later allied with England during King William's War. But the English offered little help when the French and their Indian allies attacked the Iroquois during that conflict. By 1700, the Iroquois League had suffered such horrendous losses—perhaps a quarter of the population had died from causes related to the war—that its leaders sought an alternative to direct alliance with the British.

With the so-called **Grand Settlement of 1701**, the Iroquois adopted a policy of neutrality with regard to the French and British Empires. Their goal was to refrain from alliances with either European power—which were likely to fight each other again—and instead maneuver between them. The Iroquois's strategic location between New France and the English colonies allowed them to serve as a geographical and diplomatic buffer between the two. Neutral Iroquois diplomats could play the English against the French, gaining favors from one side in return for promises not to ally with the other. This neutralist policy insured that for nearly fifty years neither England nor France could gain ascendancy in North America.

Iroquois neutrality offered benefits to the Europeans as well as the Indians. The English, for instance, began to negotiate with them for land. The

This cartoon, the first to appear in a colonial American newspaper, was printed in the Pennsylvania Gazette *in the spring of 1754. It refers to the plan for a colonial union that was put forward at the Albany Congress. The image alludes to the folk belief that a severed snake could revive if its parts were rejoined before sundown.*

Iroquois claimed sovereignty over much of the country west of the Middle and Chesapeake colonies. To smooth relations with the English, the Iroquois sold them land formerly occupied by Delawares and Susquehannocks. This transaction simultaneously helped to satisfy the colonists' land hunger and to enrich the Iroquois League.

Meanwhile a neutral Iroquois League claiming control over the Ohio Valley and blocking English access across the Appalachian Mountains helped the French protect the strategic corridor of the Ohio and Mississippi Valleys that linked Canada and Louisiana. If the English ever established a permanent presence in the Ohio Valley, however, the Iroquois would cease to be of use to the French. The Iroquois remained reasonably effective at keeping the British out of the Valley until the late 1740s. The next European war, however, altered these circumstances, increasing French anxiety about their empire and compelling British strategists to incorporate their colonies into war plans more fully than ever before.

KING GEORGE'S WAR SHIFTS THE BALANCE, 1739–1754

The third confrontation between Britain and France in Europe, the War of the Austrian Succession—**King George's War** to the British colonists—began as a small war between Britain and Spain in 1739. Its immediate cause was British attempts to poach on trade

MAP EXPLORATION To explore an interactive version of this map, go to http://www.prenhall.com/goldfield/map4.3

British territory

French territory

Disputed between Britain and France

■ British forts

■ French forts

✳ British victories

✳ French victories

MAP 4-3   The French and Indian War, 1754–1763
Most of the battles of the French and Indian War occurred in the frontier regions of northern and western New York and the Ohio Valley. The influx of settlers into these areas created tensions that eventually developed into war.

to Spain's Caribbean colonies. But in 1744, France joined in the war against Britain. An Anglo-French conflict once again erupted in North America.

New Englanders saw yet another chance to attack Canada. This time, their target was the great fortress of Louisbourg on Cape Breton Island, a naval base that dominated the Gulf of St. Lawrence. An expedition from Massachusetts and Connecticut, supported by a squadron of Royal Navy warships, captured Louisbourg in 1745. This success cut Canada off from French reinforcement and resupply. English forces should now have been able to conquer New France.

Instead, politically influential merchants in Albany, New York, chose to continue their profitable trade with the enemy over Lake Champlain, enabling Canada to hold out until the end of the war.

When the peace treaty was signed in 1748, Britain, which had fared badly in the European fighting, returned Louisbourg to France. This diplomatic adjustment, routine by European standards, shocked New Englanders. At the same time, New York's illegal trade with the enemy appalled British administrators. They began thinking of ways to prevent such independent behavior in any future war.

King George's War furnished an equal share of shocks for New France, which had suffered more than in any previous conflict. Even before the war's end, aggressive English traders from Pennsylvania began moving west to buy furs from Indians who had once traded with the French. The movements of these traders, along with the appearance of Virginians in the Ohio Valley after 1748, gravely concerned the French.

In 1749, the governor general of New France set out to assert direct control over the region by building a set of forts from Lake Erie to the Forks of the Ohio (where the Monongahela and Allegheny Rivers meet to form the Ohio River). This decision signaled the end of France's commitment to Iroquois neutrality. Instead of enjoying their old position as neutral mediators, the chiefs of the Iroquois League now found themselves trapped between empires edging closer to confrontation in the Ohio Valley.

The Iroquois, in fact, had never exerted direct power in the Ohio Country. Their control instead depended on their ability to dominate the peoples who actually lived there—western Senecas, as well as the Delawares and Shawnees, both in theory Iroquois dependents. The appearance of English traders in the valley offering goods on better terms than the French or the Iroquois had ever provided undermined Iroquois dominance.

The Ohio Valley Indians increasingly ignored Iroquois claims of control and pursued their own independent course. One spur to their disaffection from the Iroquois was the 1744 **Treaty of Lancaster**, by which Iroquois chiefs had sold the rights to trade at the Forks of the Ohio to a group of Virginia land speculators. The Virginians assumed that these trading rights included the right to acquire land for eventual sale to settlers. The Ohio Valley Indians found this situation intolerable, as did the French. When, in 1754, the government of Virginia sent out a small body of soldiers under Lieutenant Colonel George Washington to protect Virginia's claims to the Forks of the Ohio, the French struck decisively to stop them.

THE FRENCH AND INDIAN WAR, 1754–1760: A DECISIVE VICTORY

In April 1754, French soldiers overwhelmed a group of Virginians who had been building a small fort at the Forks of the Ohio. They then erected a much larger fort of their own, Fort Duquesne, on the spot. The French intended to follow up by similarly ousting Washington's weak, untrained troops, who had encamped further up the Monongahela River. However, at the end of May, Washington's men killed or captured all but one of the members of a small French reconnaissance party. The French decided to teach the Virginians a lesson. On July 3, they attacked Washington at his encampment, Fort Necessity. The following day, with a quarter of his troops killed or wounded, Washington surrendered.

Even before news of these engagements reached Britain, imperial officials worried that the Iroquois might ally with the French. Britain ordered New York's governor to convene an intercolonial meeting in Albany—known as the Albany Congress—to discuss matters with the Iroquois. Several prominent colonists, including Governor William Shirley of Massachusetts and Benjamin Franklin, took advantage of the occasion to put forward the **Albany Plan of Union**, which called for an intercolonial union to coordinate colonial defense, levy taxes, and regulate Indian affairs. But the colonies, too suspicious of one another to see their common interests, rejected the Albany Plan. Meanwhile, events in the west took a turn for the worse.

The French expulsion of the Virginians left the Indians of the region, Delawares and Shawnees, with no choice but to ally with the French in what came to be called the French and Indian War (see Map 4–3). Soon French and Indian attacks fell like hammer blows on backcountry settlements from

This, the earliest known portrait of George Washington, was painted by Charles Willson Peale in 1772. It depicts him in his military uniform from the French and Indian War. Military service helped to strengthen Washington's ties with the British Empire.

Washington/Custis/Lee Collection, Washington and Lee University, Lexington, VA.

Pennsylvania to the Carolinas. The Iroquois tried to remain neutral, but their neutrality no longer mattered. Europeans were at last contending directly for control of the Ohio Country.

The **French and Indian War** blazed in America for two years before it erupted as a fourth Anglo-French war in Europe in 1756. Known in Europe as the Seven Years' War (1756–1763), it involved fighting in the Caribbean, Africa, India, and the Philippine Islands as well as in Europe and North America. It was unlike any other eighteenth-century conflict, not only in its immense scope and expense but also in its decisive outcome.

The war had two phases in North America—one from 1754 to 1758 and the other from 1758 through 1760—that corresponded to shifts in European involvement. During the first phase, the French enjoyed a string of successes as they followed what had been a proven strategy in previous conflicts—guerrilla war. Relying on Indian allies acting with Canadian soldiers, the French raided

English frontier settlements, killing and capturing hundreds of civilians and forcing tens of thousands more to flee. Then they attacked fortified outposts whenever the opportunity appeared. This style of warfare allowed the Canadians' Indian allies—who came from all over the Northeast and the upper Midwest—to act independently in choosing targets and tactics.

The first full campaign of the war, in 1755, saw not only the British colonial frontiers collapsing in terror but also a notable defeat inflicted on the troops Britain had dispatched to attack Fort Duquesne. The British commander in chief, Major General Edward Braddock, with immense self-confidence and no real knowledge of the countryside or his enemy, marched to within 10 miles of Fort Duquesne, only to have his 1,450-man force surrounded and destroyed by Indians and Canadian militiamen. Braddock's defeat set the tone for virtually every military engagement of the next three years and opened a period of demoralization and internal conflict in the British colonies.

Britain responded to Braddock's defeat by sending a new commander in chief with more trained British soldiers. The new commander, Lord Loudoun, tried to set colonial military affairs on a professional footing. He insisted on managing every aspect of the war effort, not only directing the campaigns but also dictating the amount of support, in men and money, that each colony would provide. The colonists, who had plenty of experience with war, had never experienced anything like Loudoun's high-handed style and grew increasingly stubborn in response to it. Colonial soldiers, who had volunteered to serve under their own officers, objected to Loudoun's command. By the end of 1757, a year of disastrous military campaigns, colonial assemblies were also refusing to cooperate.

Britain's aim had been to "rationalize" the war by making it conform to European professional military standards. This approach required soldiers to advance in formation in the face of massed musket fire without breaking rank. It needed iron discipline, which was enforced—as in the British army—by savage punishments, including hundreds of lashes at the whipping post. Few colonial volunteers met professional standards, and few colonists thought them necessary, especially when British soldiers suffered defeat after defeat at the hands of French and Indian guerrillas. British officers assumed that colonial soldiers were simply lazy cowards. But colonial volunteers, appalled to see men lashed "till the blood came out at the knee" of their breeches, saw British officers as brutal task-masters.

They resisted all efforts to impose such discipline on their own units, even to the point of desertion and mutiny.

Despite the astonishing success of their guerrilla tactics, the French, too, began moving toward a more European style of warfare. In the process, they destroyed their strategic and tactical advantages. In 1756, the Marquis de Montcalm, a strong proponent of European professional standards of military conduct, assumed command of French forces. In his first battle, the successful siege of Fort Oswego, New York, Montcalm was horrified by the behavior of his Indian allies, which included killing wounded prisoners, taking personal captives, and collecting scalps as trophies. He came to regard the Indians—so essential to the defense of New France—as mere savages.

Following his next victory, the capture of Fort William Henry, New York, Montcalm conformed to European practice by allowing the defeated garrison to go home in return for the promise not to fight again. Montcalm's Indian allies, a thousand or more strong, were not to take prisoners, trophies, or plunder. The tragic result came to be known as the Massacre of Fort William Henry. Feeling betrayed by their French allies, the Indians took captives and trophies anyway, killing as many as 185 defenders and capturing about 300 people. This action not only outraged the New England colonies (most of the victims were New Englanders) but also alienated the Indians on whom the defense of Canada depended. Ironically, Montcalm's efforts to limit the war's violence—to impose European standards of conduct—prepared the way for the British army and its colonial auxiliaries to win an unlimited victory.

For at the same time that the Europeanization of the war was weakening the French, the British moderated their policies and reached accommodation with the colonists. A remarkable politician came to power in London as England's chief war minister. William Pitt, who as secretary of state directed the British war effort from late 1757 through 1761, realized that friction between the colonists and the commander in chief arose from the colonists' sense that they were bearing all the financial burdens of the war without having any say in how the war was fought. Pitt's ingenious solutions were to promise reimbursements to the colonies in proportion to their contribution to the war effort, to deemphasize the power of the commander in chief, and to replace the arrogant Loudoun with a less objectionable officer.

Pitt's money and measures restored colonial morale. He sent thousands of British soldiers to America to fight alongside colonial troops. As the Anglo-American forces grew stronger, they operated more successfully, seizing Louisbourg again in 1758. Once more, Canada experienced crippling shortages of supplies, weapons, and trade goods. But this time, unlike the situation in 1745, the Anglo-Americans were united and able to take advantage of the situation. British emissaries persuaded the Delawares and Shawnees to abandon their French alliance, and late in 1758, an Anglo-American force again marched on Fort Duquesne. In command of its lead battalion was Colonel George Washington. The French defenders, abandoned by their native allies and confronted by overwhelming force, blew up the fort and retreated to the Great Lakes.

From this point on, the Anglo-Americans suffered no setbacks, and the French won no victories.

The war became a contest in which the larger, better-supplied army would triumph. Montcalm, forced back to Quebec, decided to risk everything in a European-style, open-field battle against a British force led by General James Wolfe. At the Battle of Quebec (September 13, 1759), Montcalm lost the gamble—and his life (as did the victorious General Wolfe).

But the French had not yet lost the war. If they could revive their Indian alliances, with weapons and trade goods sent from France, the French still had a chance to recover. What finally decided the outcome of the war in America was not the Battle of Quebec but two other developments: the Battle of Quiberon Bay in France (November 20, 1759) and the Iroquois' decision to join the Anglo-American side in 1760. The sea battle cost the French navy its ability to operate on the Atlantic, preventing it from carrying the reinforcements and

In his most famous painting, American artist Benjamin West depicted the death of the British general James Wolfe at the Battle of Quebec. He portrays Wolfe as a glorious martyr to the cause of British victory. In the left foreground, West added the figure of an Indian, a "noble savage" who contemplates the meaning of Wolfe's selfless sacrifice of his life.

MAP 4-4 European Empires in North America, 1750–1763
Great Britain's victory in the French and Indian War transformed the map of North America. France lost its mainland colonies, England claimed all lands east of the Mississippi, and Spain gained nominal control over the Trans-Mississippi West.

supplies Canada needed to survive. Montcalm's successor could not rebuild the Indian alliances he so desperately needed. At the same time, the Iroquois decision to enter the war on the side of the Anglo-Americans tipped the balance irrevocably against the French. The last ragged, hungry defenders of Canada, surrounded at Montreal by a vastly superior Anglo-American-Iroquoian force, surrendered on September 8, 1760.

THE TRIUMPH OF THE BRITISH EMPIRE, 1763

The war pitting Britain against France and Spain (which had entered the fighting as a French ally in 1762), concluded with an uninterrupted series of British victories. In the Caribbean, where every valuable sugar island the French owned came under British control, the culminating event was the surrender of Havana on August 13, 1762. Even more spectacular was Britain's capture of the Philippine capital of Manila on October 5—a victory that literally carried British power around the world.

These conquests created the unshakable conviction that British arms were invincible. An immense surge of British patriotism spread throughout the American colonies. When news of the conquest of Havana reached Massachusetts, bells rang, cannons fired salutes, and bonfires blazed. General John Winslow of Plymouth, a portly man, rejoiced by becoming "so intoxicated as to jump on the table, and break a great number of bowls."

Hostilities ended formally on February 10, 1763, with the conclusion of the **Treaty of Paris**. France regained its West Indian sugar islands—its most valuable colonial possessions—but lost the rest of its North American empire. France ceded to Britain all its claims to lands east of the Mississippi River (except the city of New Orleans) and compensated Spain for the losses it had sustained as an ally by handing over all claims to the Trans-Mississippi West and the port of New Orleans (see Map 4-4). Britain returned Cuba and the Philippines to

Spain and in compensation received Florida. Now Great Britain owned everything east of the Mississippi, from the Gulf of Mexico to Hudson's Bay. With France and Spain both humbled and on the verge of financial collapse, Britain seemed preeminent in Europe and ready to dominate in the New World. Never before had Americans felt more pride in being British, members of the greatest empire on earth.

CONCLUSION

The George Washington who ordered a suit from England in 1763 longed to be part of the elite of the great British Empire. If he feared any threat to his position in that elite, it was not Parliament and the king but the uncomfortably large debts he owed to his London agents for the goods he wanted or perhaps the unruly Baptists who challenged the superiority of the great planters. But those worries, though real, were merely small, nagging doubts, shared by most of his fellow planters.

What was more real to Washington was the great victory that the British empire had just gained over France, a victory that he had helped to achieve. With the French eliminated as an imperial power in North America, Washington could look forward to increasing his fortune by speculating in the western lands he knew so well. For Washington, as for virtually all other colonial leaders, 1763 was a moment of great promise and patriotic devotion to the British Empire. It was a time to rejoice in the fundamental British identity and liberty and rights that seemed to ensure that life in the colonies would be better and more prosperous than ever.

REVIEW QUESTIONS

1. Why did George Washington prefer to order a suit from London rather than trust a Virginia tailor to make him one? How does his decision reflect elite colonists' attitudes about American society and culture in the eighteenth century?

2. In what ways did economic ties between Britain and the colonies grow closer in the century after 1660?

3. What was the Great Awakening, and what impact did it have? How did it affect different groups in colonial society?

4. In what ways were colonial and British political ideas and practices similar? In what ways were they different?

5. Why did England, Spain, and France renew their competition for North America in the eighteenth century?

6. What role did warfare play in North America in the eighteenth century? What role did the Iroquois play?

KEY TERMS

Actual representation (p. 120)

Age of Enlightenment (p. 112)

Albany Plan of Union (p. 129)

Country, or "Real Whig" ideology (p. 127)

Dominion of New England (p. 117)

Enumerated products (p. 102)

French and Indian War (p. 129)

Glorious Revolution (p. 117)

Grand Settlement of 1701 (p. 127)

Great Awakening (p. 114)

Halfway Covenant (p. 113)

King George's War (p. 127)

King William's War (p. 126)

Mercantilism (p. 102)

New Lights (p. 115)

Queen Anne's War (p. 126)

Treaty of Lancaster (p. 129)

Treaty of Paris (p. 132)

Virtual representation (p. 120)

RECOMMENDED READING

Anderson, Fred. *Crucible of War: The Seven Years' War and the Fate of Empire in British North America, 1754–1766* (2000). A vivid narrative of the last great imperial war.

Bushman, Richard L. *The Refinement of America: Persons, Houses, Cities* (1992). A sophisticated exploration of the quest for gentility in early America.

Franklin, Benjamin. *Autobiography* (numerous editions). The classic account of Franklin's rise from poor beginnings to prominence in colonial Philadelphia.

McCusker, John J., and Russell R. Menard. *The Economy of British America, 1607–1789,* rev. ed. (1991). The most comprehensive study of the economies of each colonial region.

Stout, Harry S. *The Divine Dramatist: George Whitefield and the Rise of Modern Evangelicalism* (1991). A clear and thorough account of Whitefield's career and the religious context in which it occurred.

ADDITIONAL SOURCES

Colonial Economic Development

Marshall, Peter, and Glyn, Williams, eds. *The British Atlantic Empire before the American Revolution* (1980).

Steele, Ian K. *The English Atlantic, 1675–1740: An Exploration of Communication and Community* (1986).

Walton, Gary M., and James F. Shepherd. *The Economic Rise of Early America* (1979).

Waterhouse, Richard. *A New World Gentry: The Making of a Merchant and Planter Class in South Carolina, 1670–1770* (1989).

Religion, Society, and Culture in Early America

Bonomi, Patricia. *Under the Cope of Heaven: Religion, Society, and Politics in Colonial America* (1986).

Boyer, Paul, and Stephen Nissenbaum. *Salem Possessed: The Social Origins of Witchcraft* (1974).

Breen, Timothy H. *Tobacco Culture: The Mentality of the Great Tidewater Planters on the Eve of Revolution* (1985).

Brown, Richard D. *Knowledge Is Power: The Diffusion of Information in Early America, 1700–1865* (1991).

Bushman, Richard L. *From Puritan to Yankee: Character and the Social Order in Connecticut, 1690–1765* (1967).

Butler, Jon. *Becoming America: The Revolution before 1776* (2000).

Dayton, Cornelia Hughes. *Women Before the Bar: Gender, Law, & Society in Connecticut, 1639–1789* (1995).

Demos, John. *Entertaining Satan: Witchcraft and the Culture of Early New England* (1982).

Hall, Gwendolyn Midlo. *Africans in Colonial Louisiana: The Development of Afro-Creole Culture in the Eighteenth Century* (1992).

Isaac, Rhys. *The Transformation of Virginia, 1740–1790* (1982).

Karlsen, Carol. *The Devil in the Shape of a Woman: Witchcraft in Colonial New England* (1987).

May, Henry. *The Enlightenment in America* (1976).

Colonial and Imperial Politics

Bailyn, Bernard. *The Origins of American Politics* (1968).

Bliss, Robert. *Revolution and Empire: English Politics and the American Colonies in the Seventeenth Century* (1990).

Brewer, John. *The Sinews of Power: War, Money, and the English State, 1688–1783* (1989).

Bushman, Richard. *King and People in Provincial Massachusetts* (1985).

Johnson, Richard. *Adjustment to Empire: The New England Colonies, 1675–1715* (1981).

Jones, J. R. *Country and Court: England, 1658–1714* (1978).

Lovejoy, David S. *The Glorious Revolution in America, 1660–1692* (1972).

Morgan, Edmund S. *Inventing the People: The Rise of Popular Sovereignty in England and America* (1988).

Nash, Gary B. *The Urban Crucible: The Northern Seaports and the Origins of the American Revolution,* abr. ed. (1986).

Shannon, Timothy. *Indians and Colonists at the Crossroads of Empire: The Albany Congress of 1754* (1999).

Speck, W. A. *Stability and Strife: England, 1714–1760* (1977).

The Expansion of Empires

Chipman, Donald E. *Spanish Texas, 1519–1821* (1992).

Hinderaker, Eric. *Elusive Empires: Constructing Colonialism in the Ohio Valley 1673–1800* (1997).

Mancall, Peter. *Valley of Opportunity: Economic Culture along the Upper Susquehanna, 1700–1800* (1991).

Richter, Daniel. *Ordeal of the Longhouse: The Peoples of the Iroquois League in the Era of European Colonization* (1992).

Usner, Daniel H., Jr. *Indians, Settlers, and Slaves in a Frontier Exchange Economy: The Lower Mississippi Valley before 1783* (1992).

Weber, David J. *The Spanish Frontier in North America* (1992).

Imperial Warfare

Black, Jeremy. *Britain as a Military Power, 1688–1815* (1999).

Jennings, Francis. *Empire of Fortune: Crowns, Colonies, and Tribes in the Seven Years' War in America* (1988).

Selesky, Harold. *War and Society in Colonial Connecticut* (1990).

Steele, Ian K. *Betrayals: Fort William Henry and the "Massacre"* (1990).

Titus, James. *The Old Dominion at War: Society, Politics, and Warfare in Late Colonial Virginia* (1991).

WHERE TO LEARN MORE

● **Mission Parkway, San Antonio, Texas.** Three Spanish missions (Mission Nuestra Señora de la Purisma Concepción, Mission San Francisco de la Espada, Mission San Juan Capistrano) founded in the early eighteenth century are located along this road. Their architecture indicates that they were intended to be fortifications as well as churches. The website http://hotx.com/missions/ has links to each mission, offering pictures, descriptions, and historical background.

● **Ste. Genevieve Historic District, Ste. Genevieve, Missouri.** This restored site of an early eighteenth-century French settlement in the pays des Illinois contains many historic buildings open for tours. A general description of the site is at the website http://rosecity.net/rhr/stegenevieve.html. Descriptions and pictures of historic houses can be found at http://www.ste-genevieve.com/histsite.htm.

● **Colonial Williamsburg, Williamsburg, Virginia.** A reconstruction of the capital of eighteenth-century Virginia, this site covers 173 acres and contains many restored and rebuilt structures, including houses, churches, the House of Burgesses, and the Governor's Palace. Many educational and cultural programs are available. Historical interpreters, dressed in period costume, provide information about eighteenth-century Chesapeake life. The website www.colonialwilliamsburg.com/history/index.cfm has a variety of links that include biographical information on eighteenth-century residents of Williamsburg, aspects of colonial life, and material culture. The link to "Electronic Field Trips" has information on how to arrange for an interactive television program and special Internet activities.

● **Mount Vernon, Virginia.** Site of George Washington's much refurbished home. There is also a reconstructed gristmill and barn, as well as various outbuildings. Exhibits include information on Washington's agricultural experiments. The website www.mountvernon.org offers virtual tours of the house and grounds, as well as information on "George Washington, Pioneer Farmer."

● **Johnson Hall, Johnstown, New York.** Eighteenth-century home of William Johnson, who served as Superintendent of Indian Affairs and directed much of Britain's diplomacy with the Iroquois. Biographical information and pictures can be found at the website www.johnstown.com/city/johnson.html.

● **Berkeley and Westover Plantations, Charles City, Virginia.** These two eighteenth-century James River plantations suggest the elegance of elite planters' lives. The house and grounds at Berkeley are open to the public, the grounds only at Westover, the home of William Byrd. Pictures, descriptions of the sites, and background on their owners can be found at www.jamesriverplantations.org, which has links to each plantation.

 Please refer to the document CD-ROM for primary sources related to this chapter.

→ *Having apparently originated in a May Day-like celebration of the repeal of the Stamp Act in the spring of 1766, liberty poles were particularly characteristic of New York City, where citizens of all social classes supported their erection (as in the picture). However, British soldiers repeatedly destroyed them, thereby prompting serious rioting. Elsewhere, liberty trees served similar symbolic functions. John C. McRae of New York published this print in 1875.*

IMPERIAL BREAKDOWN
1763–1774

5

Philadelphia, January 1774

My Dear Jack,

Your Uncle wrote the 27 Dec. by Capt. Ayres who brought the Tea. His ship came within four miles of this City on Sunday the 26th where she was stopped, not being suffered to come any farther…. The inhabitants sent a Supply of fresh provisions & a Pilot on board [who put them on course for England]. I believe they were glad they came off so well, for at Boston they threw it all into the River, and it would have gone near to have shared the same fate here, but the Capt. had more prudence than to endeavour to force a landing by which means he prevented a great deal of Mischief & Confusion, for they were all determined to oppose it. They think now that the India Company will get the Act which imposes a duty of 3d per pound repealed and then send more over.

Kensington, September 19, 1774

Dear Jack,

The Congress [The First Continental Congress] are now Setting here & have been a fortnight but nothing Transpires. All is kept a profound Secret. There was a [false] report the other day of the Town of Boston being Bombarded by the Men of War lying off the Town…which Occasioned a general consternation along the Continent,

CHAPTER OUTLINE

Imperial Reorganization
British Problems
Dealing with the New Territories
Indian Affairs
Curbing the Assemblies
The Sugar and Stamp Acts

American Reactions
Constitutional Issues
Taxation and the Political Culture
Protesting the Taxes

The Aftermath of the Stamp Act Crisis
A Strained Relationship
Regulator Movements

The Townshend Crisis
Townshend's Plan
American Boycott
The Boston Massacre
The "Quiet Period"
The Boston Tea Party
The Intolerable Acts

The Road to Revolution
American Response to the Intolerable Acts
The First Continental Congress
The Continental Association
Political Divisions

Conclusion

and in some parts of the Country they Armed and Marched to the Number of 15,000 & more were getting ready.... In Short the Provinces are determined one and all to stand by each other. What the Consequences will be we don't know. To be sure thy |they|may send Men of War and destroy the Towns on the sea shore but its Impossible to take the Country, and the damage they do in destroying the Towns will fall on the English in the end.

Kensington Nov 1, 1774

My Dear Jack,

Our Congress are broke up and are come to a great Spirited Resolves . . . together with a petition to his Majestie. . . . It is to be published and they have bound themselves to abide by those resolves . . . and if Necessitated to repel force with force. All Importation ceases after the first of December next.

April 28, 1775

Dear Jackey,

The Provinces are all Arming themselves, and the men are almost all for inlisting as fast as they take them so am afraid we shall have Troublesome times. I heartily wish the Authors of all this Mischief may be brought to Justice.

Kensington June 28, 1775

My Dear Jack,

All the Provinces |are| arming and Training in the same Manner, for they are all determined to die or be Free. It is not the low Idle Fellows that fight only for pay but Men of great property are Common Soldiers who say they are fighting for themselves and Posterity. . . . . The People are getting in Manufactures of different sorts, particularly Salt Peter and Gunpowder. The Smiths are almost all turnd Gunsmiths and cannot work fast enough. God knows how it will end but I fear it will be very bad on both sides, and if your drivalish minestry and parliament dont make some concessions and Repeal the Acts, England will lose America for as I said before they are determined to be free.

Eliza Farmar

Pennsylvania Magazine of History and Biography, vol. 40 (1916): 199-207.

Eliza Farmar and her family had recently moved to Kensington, a suburb of Philadelphia, when she wrote these letters, and her ties to relatives in England remained strong. Jack, the recipient of these letters, was her nephew and a clerk in the London office of the East India Company, whose shipment of tea precipitated the Boston Tea Party. Although she hoped that he might come to America, she minced no words in emphasizing the determination of Americans to resist British measures that appeared to infringe upon their freedoms. These letters accordingly chronicle a psychological counterpart to her move to Kensington. She began both journeys as an English subject; she ended them as an American citizen. Her initial reports of political developments, though sympathetic to the colonial point of view, were fairly objective, but by the eve of the Revolution she had disowned the British government by referring to "your ministry and parliament" as "drivalish," a slip of the pen that covered ineffective and devilish.

Like most colonists, she started out proud to be a British subject and part of Britain's increasingly powerful empire. Americans had fought the king's enemies as well as their own in a series of imperial wars and had gloried in British successes. But over the course of the eighteenth century, they had also developed a sense of their identity as Americans. Largely governing themselves through their own legislatures, they believed that they enjoyed all the rights of British subjects anywhere.

But in the wake of the French and Indian War, British authorities found themselves with a burdensome debt and vastly increased territory to administer. In response, they attempted to change the way they governed the colonies and, for the first time, imposed direct taxes on the colonists. Most Americans saw these measures as violations of their rights and opposed them, although they disagreed over how far to carry their resistance.

KEY TOPICS

- British problems and policies in North America after the French and Indian War
- Native Americans' conflicts with the colonists
- The American reaction to British attempts to tax the colonies
- Social tensions and the Regulator movements in the Carolinas
- Intercolonial union and resistance to British measures

IMPERIAL REORGANIZATION

At the close of the French and Indian War, British officials adopted a new and ultimately disastrous course in dealing with America. Lacking experience and led by the young and somewhat naive new monarch, George III, they panicked at the magnitude of the problems confronting them. Trying to fix a relationship between England and the colonies that most Americans would have said was not broken, they took measures that worked mostly to the disadvantage of the colonies. As one contemporary critic observed, "A great Empire and little minds go ill together."

BRITISH PROBLEMS

Britain's empire in 1763 was, in fact, immense, and the problems its rulers faced were correspondingly large. Its territories in North America stretched from Hudson's Bay in the north to the Caribbean Sea in the south and from the Atlantic Ocean west to the Mississippi River. Britain also had possessions in the Mediterranean region, Africa, and India. It still faced threats, if diminished ones, from its traditional European enemies. French territory on the North American mainland had been reduced to two tiny islands in the Gulf of St. Lawrence. But France would be eager for revenge, and French inhabitants in the recently acquired territories might prove disloyal to their new rulers in any future war between the two countries.

Spain was less powerful militarily than France but a more significant presence on the North American mainland. In the territorial settlement at the end of the French and Indian War, it surrendered East and West Florida to Britain but got back its possessions in Cuba and the Philippines that the British had captured. Spain acquired Louisiana from its French ally as compensation for the loss of the Floridas. Shocked by their inability to defend Cuba and the Philippines, Spanish officials stepped up the pace of reforms that they had begun making earlier in the century. Following the efficient French model of colonial government, they appointed *intendants*—generally Spaniards rather than colonials—to insure better tax collection. Spain also expelled the Jesuit order from its dominions, because Jesuit priests were too independent of royal control to suit Spanish officials. And Spain strengthened its military forces in much of the empire, including Mexico, which then encompassed Texas, New Mexico, and California as well as present-day Mexico.

Spain began to establish settlements in California in 1769 (see Chapter 4), but these were too weak and too far from the British colonies on the eastern seaboard to worry officials in London. British authorities were similarly little concerned about Louisiana, though it was closer and more populated. As for Florida, under British control after 1763, the Spanish authorities evacuated it completely, taking with them not only the free black population of Mose (a settlement of former slaves who had escaped from Georgia and South Carolina) but even the bones of one of the late royal governors.

Protecting and controlling the old and new territories in North America as inexpensively as possible presented British officials with difficult questions. How should they administer the new territories? How should they deal with Indians likely to resist further encroachments on their lands? And perhaps most vexing, how could they rein in the seemingly out-of-control colonists in the old territories?

Permitting most of the new areas to have their own assemblies appeared inadvisable but unavoidable if these areas were to attract settlers. Believing that the increasing power of the legislatures had long since "unhinged" the government of the older colonies, British authorities hoped to avoid similar unruliness in the new territories. In fact, they had long wanted to roll back the power of the old colonial assemblies. But Britain had needed the cooperation of these assemblies during the years of war with France. Now, with France vanquished, imperial officials felt that they could crack down on the local governments. Some British statesmen, however, recognized that this new approach was risky. With France gone from the continent, Americans would be less dependent on Britain for protection and therefore more inclined to resist unpopular restrictions.

Resentment against American conduct during the war also colored British thinking. Some of the colonies had failed to enlist their quota of recruits, and for this the British blamed the local assemblies. Worse yet, some Americans continued to smuggle goods to and from the enemy in the French West Indies during the war. Illicit trade was so common in New England that it cost Britain more to operate the customs service in America than it collected in duties.

England emerged from the war with what was then an immense national debt of approximately £146 million, nearly double the amount at the beginning of the conflict. Interest payments alone

Chronology

1759–1761	Cherokee War takes place.		**1766**	Stamp Act repealed; Declaratory Act passed.
1760	George III becomes king.			New York Assembly refuses to comply with the Quartering Act.
1761–1762	Writs of Assistance case in Massachusetts.		**1767**	Townshend duties imposed.
1763	Peace of Paris ends French and Indian War.			Regulator movements begin in North and South Carolina.
	Spanish accelerate imperial reforms.		**1770**	Boston Massacre takes place.
	British troops remain in America.			Tea duty retained, other Townshend duties repealed.
	Proclamation Line of 1763 limits western expansion of colonial settlement.		**1771**	North Carolina Regulator movement defeated.
	Pontiac's Rebellion begins.		**1772**	*Gaspee* burned.
	Paxton Boys murder peaceful Indians.			Committees of Correspondence formed.
	Virginia Court decides Parson's Cause.		**1773**	Boston Tea Party takes place.
1764	Sugar Act passed.		**1774**	Coercive Acts passed.
	Currency Act passed.			Quebec Act passed.
1765	Quartering Act passed.			First Continental Congress meets and agrees to boycott British imports.
	Stamp Act passed.			
	Stamp Act Congress meets in New York.			

accounted for half the government's annual expenditures after the war. Alarmed by the unprecedented debt, many Britons concluded that Americans should bear more of the financial burden of running the empire. The colonists certainly appeared prosperous to British soldiers who had served in America. But compared to the English, who paid on average perhaps a third of their income in taxes, many Americans normally rendered no more than 5 percent. An economic recession—triggered by the reduction in spending that followed the war—put further pressure on British officials to reduce taxes in England.

DEALING WITH THE NEW TERRITORIES

In 1763, the British government took several important steps to deal with the new territories, protect the old colonies, and maintain peace with the Indians. One was to keep a substantial body of troops—10,000 were initially planned—stationed in America even in peacetime. Another, announced in the royal **Proclamation of 1763**, was to establish civilian governments in East and West Florida (Canada remained under military rule). A third, in the same proclamation, was to temporarily forbid white settlement west of the Appalachian Mountains. The purpose of the **Proclamation Line** restricting white settlement was presumably twofold: to keep white settlers and Indians apart, preventing fighting between them, and to hold the colonists closer to the coast where they would be easier to control (see Map 5–1). Permanent arrangements for the Mississippi Valley could come later, after British officials had time to ponder matters.

Neither the Proclamation Line nor the stationing of troops in America was particularly wise. The

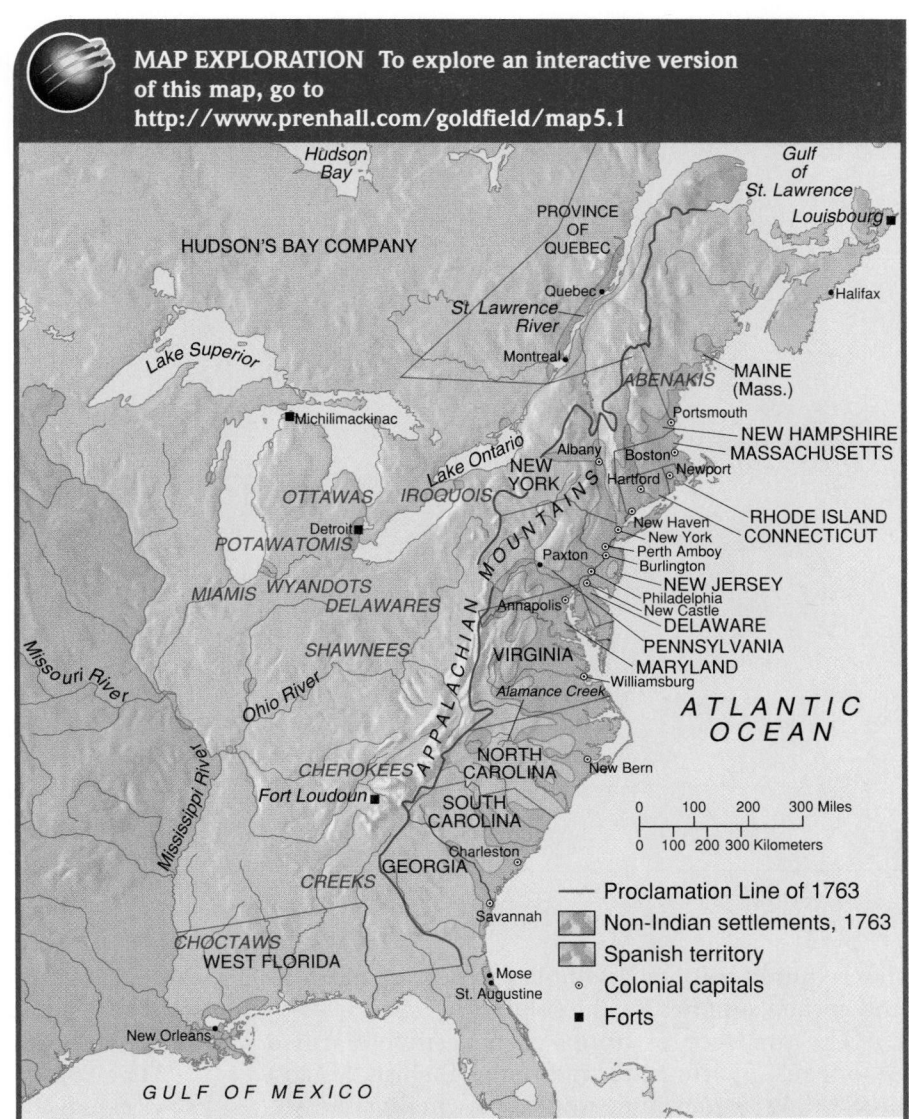

MAP EXPLORATION To explore an interactive version of this map, go to http://www.prenhall.com/goldfield/map5.1

MAP 5-1   Colonial Settlement and the Proclamation Line of 1763
This map depicts the regions claimed and settled by the major groups competing for territory in eastern North America. With the Proclamation Line of 1763, positioned along the crest of the Appalachian Mountains, the British government tried to stop the westward migration of settlers under its jurisdiction and thereby limit conflict with the Indians. The result, however, was frustration and anger on the part of land-hungry settlers.

Proclamation Line provoked resentment because it threatened to deprive settlers and speculators in the rapidly developing colonies of the land they coveted. Some who had moved into the Ohio area were forcefully removed. Other Americans merely ignored the restriction. Moreover, someone had to pay for the troops, forcing the British government to take additional measures that further provoked American resentment. These measures included the imposition of direct taxes and the passage of **Quartering Acts**

IN THE BLUE RIDGE.

This clearing and cabin in the Blue Ridge Mountains of the southern Appalachian chain typifies the hope and homes of many small farmers who resented the British Proclamation Line of 1763, which barred white settlement west of the eastern continental divide.

that required colonial assemblies to provide barracks and certain supplies for the soldiers.

The presence of troops in peacetime alarmed Americans. Sharing the traditional English distrust of standing armies, they wondered whether the soldiers were there to coerce rather than protect them. And the military presence may, in fact, have made imperial authorities less cautious in dealing with the colonies. Given their wariness, Americans would doubtless have objected to the troops and to the taxes necessary to support them even if the troops had done an exemplary job of protecting the frontiers. But conflicts with Indians cast doubt on their ability to do even that.

INDIAN AFFAIRS

If Britain confronted complex problems in North America, Native Americans would have said those problems were nothing compared to their own troubles in dealing with the British. Colonial settlers and their livestock were displacing Indians from their ancient lands. Free-flowing rum and rampant cheating among traders were making the fur and deer-

skin trades increasingly violent. Each of the colonies tried to regulate its Indian traders, but lack of coordination made most of these efforts ineffective.

The British victory over the French and the westward expansion of British territory undermined the Indians' traditional strategies and alignments. British officials no longer found Native American neutrality or military help as important as they once had. Increasingly superfluous as allies and unable to play the European powers off against each other, Native Americans lost much of their former ability to protect themselves by any means short of military resistance. The British took advantage of this increasing vulnerability: Traders exploited the Indians, and settlers encroached on their lands.

Two major Indian wars—one breaking out in the late 1750s, during the closing years of the French and Indian War, and the other erupting in its aftermath in the early 1760s—tested British policy toward Native Americans. The first conflict, the **Cherokee War**, took place in the southern Appalachian highlands. Though increasingly alarmed at the abuses and encroachments of their white neighbors, the Cherokees had long remained allies of the British. But in 1759,

The legend on this scrimshaw powder horn, "New Map of Carolina and Likewise a plan of Ye Cherokee Nation Conqurd by the arme Commandt by Lieutt Col Jas Grant," and the date, 1762, suggest that the soldier who engraved it was, like his commander, British and that he finished his elaborate depiction of the campaign shortly after the Cherokee War.

Cherokee warriors (who were returning home from a campaign with the British against the French and their Indian allies in western Pennsylvania) may have stolen horses belonging to Virginia colonists. The colonists attacked the Cherokees, killing some of them. The Cherokees retaliated with attacks on western settlements in all of the southern colonies. In 1760, they captured Fort Loudoun in eastern Tennessee, stuffing the commander's mouth full of dirt and telling him, "Dog, since you are so hungry for land, eat your fill." Three expeditions, manned by British as well as colonial troops, eventually forced the Cherokees to agree, in a 1761 treaty, to surrender land in the Carolinas and Virginia to the colonists.

The second major conflict, **Pontiac's Rebellion**, broke out in 1763 among Indians in the Great Lakes and Ohio Valley regions formerly claimed by France. Many Native American groups feared that the British planned to exterminate them and take their lands now that the French could no longer help them. They also resented the increased stinginess of British traders and officials, who were no longer forced to compete commercially with the French to secure Indian allegiance. These concerns helped to inspire a united effort to resist the British and revitalize Indian cultures. Neolin, also known as the Delaware Prophet, urged Native Americans to reject European goods and ways. Pontiac, an Ottawa chief, joined other chiefs in leading at least eight major groups of Native Americans in attacking British forces and American settlers from the Great Lakes to Virginia in 1763.

Pontiac's Rebellion raged until 1766. During intermittent negotiations, Pontiac insisted that British possession of the old French forts in western Pennsylvania and Ohio did not give Great Britain title to the area. The French, he maintained, had been there merely as tenants of the Indians, not owners of the land. But the British eventually forced the Indians to give up portions of their territory in return for compensation and guarantees that traditional hunting grounds in the Ohio Valley would remain theirs.

At one point during the war, a British commander used germ warfare against the Indians, sending them blankets that smallpox victims had used. Settlers in Paxton township (near modern Harrisburg, Pennsylvania) were equally unrestrained. Angered by the Pennsylvania Assembly's lack of aggressive action against the Indians, the settlers lashed out at convenient targets, massacring their peaceful neighbors, the Conestogas. Facing arrest and trial for this outrage, the so-called Paxton Boys marched toward Philadelphia, threatening the Pennsylvania Assembly. Benjamin Franklin convinced them to disperse. Despite the government's efforts, the Paxton Boys were never effectively prosecuted for their acts.

Pontiac's Rebellion and the Cherokee War were costly for both sides, claiming the lives of hundreds of Indians and white settlers. Hoping to prevent such outbreaks, British officials began experimenting with centralized control of Indian affairs during the 1760s. Following the recommendations of the

Albany Congress in 1754 (see Chapter 4), they had already created two districts, northern and southern, for the administration of Indian affairs, each with its own superintendent. The Proclamation of 1763, and the line it established restricting further white settlement, gave these officials increased responsibility for protecting the Indians against the encroachments of settlers. But land-hungry Americans objected to efforts to keep them off Indian lands, and white traders resented restrictions on their activities. Centralized control of the fur and deerskin trades also proved to be expensive for the British government. British authorities therefore permitted several adjustments in the Indian boundary line and in 1768 returned supervision of the Indian traders to the individual colonies. But such tacit recognition of local autonomy conflicted with imperial authorities' plans to restrict the powers of the colonial assemblies.

CURBING THE ASSEMBLIES

As early as the 1750s, in an episode known as the **Parson's Cause**, British authorities took advantage of opportunities to curb the American legislatures. Anglican ministers in Virginia drew tax-supported salaries computed in pounds of tobacco. As a result, when a drought in the mid-1750s caused a sharp rise in tobacco prices, they expected a windfall. The Virginia House of Burgesses, however, restricted their payment to two pennies a pound, below the market value of the tobacco that backed their salaries. Lobbying by the clergy convinced the king to disallow the Two Penny Act, and some Virginia clergymen sued for the unpaid portion of their salaries.

In the most famous of these cases, the Virginia government was defended by Patrick Henry, a previously obscure young lawyer who looked like "a Presbyterian clergyman, used to haranguing the people." Henry gained instant notoriety when he declared that a king who vetoed beneficial acts became a tyrant and thereby forfeited "all right to his subjects' obedience." Given Henry's eloquence, and its own sense of fair play, the jury found in favor of the suing minister but awarded him only one penny in damages. This pittance reflected the hostility many Virginians of all denominations felt toward the pretensions of the Anglican clergy.

Meanwhile, still in response to the Two Penny Act, the crown further dismayed Virginians by instructing the colony's governor not to sign any new law that modified existing laws unless it contained a suspending clause making it inoperative until the king approved it. This restriction severely hampered the assembly's ability to respond to emergencies such as the drought. As one Virginian observed, it "put us under the despotic Power of a French or Turkish Government; for what is the real Difference between a French Edict and an English Instruction if they are both equally absolute?" The legislators of the colony, Virginians maintained, had the "Right to enact ANY Law they shall think necessary for their INTERNAL Government."

British authorities also sought to restrict the power of colonial legislatures to issue legal tender currency, paper notes that could be used to settle debts. These notes frequently depreciated to only a fraction of their face value in British money. Not surprisingly, British merchants who had to accept them felt cheated and complained. Parliament had responded in 1751 by forbidding further issues of legal tender paper money in New England. In the **Currency Act** of 1764, Parliament extended this restriction to the rest of the colonies, prohibiting all of them from printing their own legal tender paper money. Because the new restrictions came when most colonies were in an economic recession, Americans considered this step an especially burdensome attempt to curtail the assemblies' powers. To deprive them of their paper money was, in the words of one American, "downright Robbery." Worse, however, was yet to come.

THE SUGAR AND STAMP ACTS

In 1764, the British Parliament, under Prime Minister George Grenville, passed the American Revenue Act, commonly known as the **Sugar Act**. The main purpose of this act, as stated in its preamble, was "for improving the revenue of this kingdom." To generate funds, the Sugar Act and its accompanying legislation combined new and revised duties on colonial imports with strict provisions for collecting these impositions. The act lowered the duty on molasses from the French West Indies from 6 pence a gallon to 3 pence a gallon. Smugglers had long evaded the earlier duty with bribes to customs officials. By lowering the duty and improving its collection, Grenville hoped to capture for the crown what customs officials had been siphoning off for themselves without excessively increasing the shippers' cost of business.

The Sugar Act legislation also lengthened the list of enumerated products—goods that could be sent only to England or within the empire—and required that ships carry elaborate new documents certifying the legality of their cargoes. The purpose of the new paperwork was to prevent illegal trade with other countries. A ship's captain, however, could have his entire cargo seized if any of the complicated documents were out of order.

To enforce these cumbersome regulations, the British government continued to use the Royal Navy to seize smugglers' ships, a practice authorized by the Revenue Act of 1762 during the French and Indian War. It also ordered colonial customs collectors to discharge their duties personally. Previously, the collectors had often lived in England, leaving the work of collection in the colonies to poorly paid deputies, who were susceptible to bribes. Finally, Parliament gave responsibility for trying violations of the laws to a new vice-admiralty court in Halifax, Nova Scotia. Vice-admiralty courts had jurisdiction over maritime affairs. Unlike other courts, they normally operated without a jury and were therefore more likely to enforce trade restrictions. For this reason, and because of the remote location of the Halifax court—getting to it would be a hardship—Americans immediately opposed this provision of the Sugar Act. In response, Parliament created three more-conveniently located vice-admiralty courts in Boston, Philadelphia, and Charleston, a decision that was not exactly what the colonists had had in mind.

In the spring of 1765, Parliament enacted another tax on Americans, the **Stamp Act**. This legislation required all valid legal documents, as well as newspapers, playing cards, and various other papers, to bear a government-issued stamp, for which there was a charge. The Sugar Act, though intended to raise revenue, appeared to fall within Britain's accepted authority to regulate commerce; the Stamp Act, by contrast, was the first internal tax (as opposed to an external trade duty) that Parliament had imposed on the colonies. Grenville, a lawyer, realized that it raised a constitutional issue: Did Parliament have the right to impose direct taxes on Americans when Americans had no elected representatives in Parliament? Following the principle of virtual representation—that members of Parliament served the interests of the nation as a whole, not just the locality from which they came—Grenville maintained that it did. Americans, he would find, vigorously disagreed, and so did some members of Parliament. One, Colonel Isaac Barré, who had served in the colonies, opposed the Stamp Act and referred to Americans as "Sons of Liberty"—a label Americans would soon adopt for themselves.

AMERICAN REACTIONS

The measures Britain took to solve its financial and administrative problems first puzzled, then shocked, and eventually outraged Americans. The colonists

had emerged from the French and Indian War believing that they had done their fair share and more toward making Great Britain ruler of the greatest empire the world had yet seen. They expected to be rewarded for their efforts and treated with the respect that they assumed they deserved. They were certain that as British Americans they shared in the glory and enjoyed all the rights of Englishmen in England. The new restrictions and taxes accordingly hit them like a slap in the face, made worse by a postwar economic recession in many of the colonies.

CONSTITUTIONAL ISSUES

To Americans, it was self-evident that the British measures were unfair. It was difficult to contend, however, that the British authorities had no right

The last issue of the Pennsylvania Journal *on the day before the Stamp Act was to go into effect. Note the caricature of a stamp in the lower right corner. William Bradford, who printed this paper, was one of the organizers of the Sons of Liberty in Philadelphia.*

to impose them. The king and Parliament were considered the sovereign, or highest, authority in the empire. Then as now, the **British Constitution** was not a single written document. It consisted, rather, of the accumulated body of English law and custom, including acts of Parliament. How, then, could the colonists claim that an act of Parliament was unconstitutional?

Constitutional conflict surfaced early in Massachusetts over the issue of **writs of assistance**. These general search warrants, which gave customs officials in America the power to inspect virtually any building suspected of holding smuggled goods, had to be formally renewed at the accession of a new monarch. When George III became king in 1760, Massachusetts merchants—perhaps out of a fondness for smuggling as well as for liberty—sought to block the reissuance of the writs. Their attorney, James Otis, Jr., arguing before the Massachusetts superior court, called the writs "instruments of slavery." Parliament, he maintained, lacked the authority to empower colonial courts to issue them. Otis lost, but "then and there," a future president of the United States, John Adams, would later write, "the child independence was born."

TAXATION AND THE POLITICAL CULTURE

The constitutional issue that most strained the bond between the colonies and the empire was taxation. British measures on other issues annoyed and disturbed Americans, and their cumulative effect helped to alienate the colonists from England. But it was outrage over taxation—the most fundamental issue— that would be the midwife of American independence. Because Parliament had customarily refrained from taxing them, Americans assumed that it could not, and because their own assemblies had taxed them, they believed that those legislatures were in fact their parliaments.

Most Americans, including many who would later side with the British, believed that to deprive them of the right to be taxed only by their own elected representatives was to deny them one of the most basic rights of Englishmen. If taxes were imposed "without our having a legal Representation where they are laid," one American asked, "are we not reduced from the Character of free Subjects to the miserable State of tributary Slaves?"

British subjects everywhere believed that Parliament's exclusive authority to impose taxes on its constituents made Britain the freest country in the world. British officials, who believed in parliamentary sovereignty, counted the colonists among those constituents. Americans, who understood that their

interests might conflict with those of England, thought otherwise. Given the selfishness of human nature, they believed that to have governing officials who could do unto them without doing the same to themselves was to risk disaster.

American views on taxation and the role of government reflected the influence of country ideology. As mentioned in Chapter 4, this opposition political philosophy emerged in England in the late seventeenth and early eighteenth centuries partly in response to the development of Britain's powerful standing army and navy. It viewed these forces, and the financial measures needed to support them, as threats to personal liberty. Country ideology proceeded from two basic assumptions: that human beings are selfish and that they need governments to protect them from one another. But country ideology also held that government power, no matter how necessary or to whom entrusted, is inherently aggressive and expansive. According to the English political philosopher John Locke, rulers have the authority to enforce law "only for the public good." When government exceeds this proper function, the people have the right to change it. Only in the last resort does this right justify revolution; the preferable alternative is a system with less-disruptive ways of protecting the freedom of the people.

Country ideology stressed that in the English system of government, it was the duty of Parliament, in particular the House of Commons (which represented the people as a whole), to check the executive power of the crown. The House of Commons's control of taxation enabled it to curb tyrannical rulers. When the crown did its job properly, the Commons appropriated the necessary funds; when rulers infringed on the liberty of the people, the Commons restrained them by withholding taxes.

Such important responsibilities required the people's representatives to be men of sufficient property and judgment to make independent decisions. A representative should be "virtuous" (meaning public-spirited), and he should avoid political partisanship, because divisions within the House of Commons could undermine its ability to resist or curb the executive. A representative of the appropriate social status who exhibited the proper behavior deserved the deference of his constituents. They should assume, in other words, that he was more qualified to understand and manage public affairs than they were, and they should accordingly follow his lead. But if he did not measure up, the people should be able to vote him out.

Country ideology appealed to Americans for a number of reasons. In part, colonists were drawn to it as they were to other English ideas and trends. The works of Alexander Pope, the most widely read English poet of the eighteenth century and a proponent of a version of country ideology, appeared in many colonial libraries. So also did the works of two readable and prolific country ideology publicists, John Trenchard and Thomas Gordon, who collaborated in writing *Cato's Letters* (1720–1724) and the *Independent Whig* (1721). More important, country ideology's suspicion of those in power suited American politics on the local level, where rivalries and factionalism fostered distrust between those with and without power. And it emboldened the many Americans who feared they had no voice in the decisions of the government in London on matters of vital importance to them. Finally, with its insistence on the important political role of the propertied elite, country ideology appealed to America's local gentry. It suggested that it was their duty, as elected political officials, to safeguard the freedom of their constituents.

These ideas have had an enduring influence on American politics, surfacing even today in the suspicion of Washington and "big government." During the eighteenth century, they predisposed Americans to value local control and to expect the worst from remote governments. In so doing, they helped inspire the American Revolution. Many Americans were ready to attribute any new imperial regulations or taxes to a conspiracy of corrupt British officials to tyrannize them.

PROTESTING THE TAXES

Given this ideological background, the initial American response to the Sugar Act was surprisingly mild. This was because the new taxes it imposed took the form of duties on trade and thus appeared consistent with the earlier Navigation Acts. The actual reaction varied from colony to colony in ways that reflected regional self-interest. The speaker of the legislature in one southern colony commented that it was "much divided" over the effects of the act and would probably not petition against it. In New England, by contrast, the Sugar Act threatened to cut into the profits of the lucrative smuggling trade with the French West Indies. As a result, people there and in other northern colonies were quicker to recognize the act's implications. The legislative body that imposed it—Parliament—and whose constituents in England stood to gain from it was not accountable to the people on whom it was imposed, the colonists. As one alarmed colonist noted, if his fellow Americans

submitted to any tax imposed by Parliament, they were dumb and docile donkeys; "more Sacks, more Sacks," or burdens, were coming.

The size of the burden was less important than the principle involved. To Americans steeped in country ideology, direct taxation by London threatened to undercut the elected representatives' power of the purse and thereby remove the traditional first line of defense against a tyrannical executive. Thus all the assemblies eventually passed resolutions flatly maintaining that any parliamentary tax on America, including the Sugar Act, was unconstitutional. Colonists in New York, their assembly stated, claimed to be exempt from taxation by anyone but their own representatives not "as a Privilege" but "as their Right." By the end of 1764, New York merchants had joined the artisans and merchants of Boston in a **nonimportation movement**, an organized boycott of British manufactured goods. The goal was to cut into the profits of British employers, inducing them and the workers laid off as a result to bring pressure on the government to back down.

Unlike the Sugar Act, the Stamp Act had an equal impact throughout the colonies, and the response to it was swift and vociferous. Newspapers and pamphlets were filled with denunciations of the supposedly unconstitutional measure, and in taverns everywhere outraged patrons roundly condemned it. "The minds of the freeholders," wrote one observer, "were inflamed . . . by many a hearty damn of the Stamp Act over bottles, bowls and glasses." Parliament, Americans were convinced, did not represent them. Its members did not share their economic interests and would not pay the taxes that they imposed on Americans. Parliament therefore could not legitimately tax Americans.

The colonial legislatures were also quick to condemn the new measure. Virginia's lower house was the first to act, approving Patrick Henry's strong resolutions against the Stamp Act. These were then reprinted in newspapers throughout the colonies, and other legislatures passed similar formal objections.

Popular protest also expressed widespread outrage at the Stamp Act. Crowds had long gathered in the colonies for public purposes, such as closing houses of prostitution or rolling back exorbitant price increases. With a postwar economic slump in some of the colonies, many people now turned to direct action. The **Sons of Liberty**, a collection of loosely organized protest groups, put pressure on stamp distributors and British authorities. In August 1765, a Boston crowd led by Ebenezer MacIntosh, a volunteer fireman with engine company number nine and a shoemaker, demolished property belonging to a revenue agent, and another mob sacked Lieutenant Governor Thomas Hutchinson's house. About a month later, other rioters roamed the streets of New York, smashing windows and telling the governor, "[Y]ou'll die a Martyr to your own villany . . . and every man, that assists you, shall be, surely, put to Death." The Sons of Liberty organized similar demonstrations in other cities but kept most of them more peaceful with tighter discipline.

Members of the Sons of Liberty included people from all ranks of society. The leaders, however, came mostly from the middle and upper classes. Often pushed by more radical common people, some of the elite doubtless joined in the hope of protecting their own positions and interests. Indeed, in Charleston, slaves paraded through the streets crying, "Liberty!" much to the dismay of their masters and the rest of the city's white population.

Movement leaders were also concerned that violence could discredit the American cause. Even the fiery Samuel Adams, one of the leading organizers of the protest in Boston, would later claim, "I am no friend to Riots." Still, he added, "when the People are oppressed," they will be "discontented, and they are not to be blamed."

Partly as a result of the growing unrest, leaders throughout the colonies determined to meet and agree on a unified response to Britain. As Christopher Gadsden of South Carolina, an ardent advocate of American rights and opponent of taxation, observed at the time, "There ought to be no New England men, no New Yorker, etc. known on the Continent, but all of us Americans." Nine colonies eventually sent delegates, including Gadsden, to the **Stamp Act Congress**, which met in New York City in October 1765. A humorist in the Carolina legislature, who had opposed sending anyone, observed that the gathering would produce a most unpalatable combination: New England would throw in fish and onions; the middle provinces, flaxseed and flour; Virginia and Maryland, tobacco; North Carolina, pitch, turpentine, and tar; South Carolina, indigo and rice—and Georgia would sprinkle the whole with sawdust. "Such an absurd jumble will you make if you attempt to form [a] union among such discordant materials as the thirteen British provinces," he concluded. A quick-witted member of the assembly shot back that he would not choose his colleague for a cook, but that the congress would prepare a dish fit for any king.

It did indeed. The congress adopted the **Declaration of Rights and Grievances**, which denied Parliament's right to tax the colonies, and petitioned both king and Parliament to repeal the Stamp and Sugar acts. Parliament, unwilling to acknowledge this challenge to its authority, refused to receive the colonial petitions.

As protests spread, the stamp distributors got the message and resigned "for the welfare of the people." In some areas, Americans went about their business as usual without using stamped paper. In other places, they avoided activities that required taxed items. They also stepped up the boycott of British goods that had begun in response to the Sugar Act. British merchants, hurt by this economic pressure, petitioned Parliament for repeal of the Stamp Act, and a new ministry obliged them by rescinding it in March 1766. Modifications in the provisions of the Sugar Act came later in the year.

Samuel Adams, the leader of the Boston radicals, as he appeared to John Singleton Copley in the early 1770s. In this famous picture, thought to have been commissioned by another revolutionary leader, John Hancock, Adams points to legal documents guaranteeing American rights.

A satirical British engraving from 1766 showing English politicians burying the Stamp Act, "born 1765 died 1766." The warehouses in the background symbolize the revival of trade with America.

THE AFTERMATH OF THE STAMP ACT CRISIS

During the Stamp Act crisis, Benjamin Franklin appeared before Parliament to present American objections to the Stamp and Sugar acts. Some members apparently concluded from his remarks that the colonists would accept port duties but would oppose direct taxes. They were wrong. At this point, Americans were in no mood to accept any tax imposed by Parliament.

Americans in turn misunderstood the **Declaratory Act** that accompanied the repeal of the Stamp Act. Intended to make Parliament's retreat more acceptable to its members, this act stated that Parliament had the right to "legislate for the colonies in all cases whatsoever." Did *legislate* mean *tax*? Not necessarily, for taxes were traditionally deemed to be a voluntary gift to the king from the people acting through their own representatives. (This is why money bills, as distinct from other acts, had to originate in the House of Commons.) Americans therefore tended to consider the Declaratory Act a mere face-saving gesture. Unfortunately, it was more than that. As one colonist later observed, it created a "platform for the Invincible Reasoning from the

Mouths of four and twenty pounders [cannons]."

A STRAINED RELATIONSHIP

Most members of Parliament continued to believe that they represented everyone in the empire and that they could therefore tax people in the colonies as well as in England. Americans believed just as strongly that "in taxing ourselves and making Laws for our own internal government . . . we can by no means allow our Provincial legislatures to be subordinate to any legislative power on earth."

Relations were never quite the same between England and America after the Stamp Act crisis. Each side became ever more suspicious of the other. Americans were convinced that they had forced British authorities to back down and that, if need be, they could do it again. Or so they told themselves every March 18, the anniversary of the repeal of the Stamp Act. This date became an occasion for celebration, giving Americans a national holiday before they had a nation.

An exchange between British merchants and their American correspondents in the wake of the Stamp Act's repeal illustrates how far apart Englishmen and Americans had become. The British merchants lectured the Americans, enjoining them "to express filial duty and gratitude to your parent country." To which one Virginia planter tartly replied, "We rarely see anything from your side of the water free from the authoritative style of a master to a schoolboy." This, he observed, was more than "a little ridiculous."

Events likewise testified to continuing tensions between the two sides. When British authorities required Massachusetts to compensate those who had suffered damage in the Stamp Act rioting, the legislature complied but pardoned the rioters. In 1767, an irritated Parliament then passed an act suspending the New York legislature because it had not complied with the Quartering Act of 1765. This law required colonial assemblies to provide facilities and certain supplies for royal troops. The New York legislature finally obeyed before the suspending act went into effect, and it remained in business. But such incidents boded ill for the hopes of some colonists that a British government that had repealed the Stamp Act would prove cooperative in other ways.

REGULATOR MOVEMENTS

In 1766, a committee of the South Carolina legislature appointed to consider "the State of the Province" recommended that it establish courts in the rapidly growing backcountry and petition Parliament for repeal of the Currency Act. These suggestions were prompted by mounting unrest in the southern backcountry. Vigilante groups calling themselves **Regulators** had emerged in North Carolina in response to official corruption and in South Carolina in response to lawlessness. High taxes and high court costs in North Carolina oppressed the colony's western farmers. Because the Currency Act reduced the amount of money in circulation, it compounded their problems, leaving them "crouched beneath their sufferings" and unable to pay their debts and taxes. In South Carolina, the devastation and disruptions of the Cherokee War left a legacy of violence. Outlaws roamed the backcountry, stealing livestock and raiding isolated houses. In both colonies, because representation in the assemblies failed to reflect the rapidly growing backcountry populations, legislatures were slow to respond to their needs. As a result, the Regulators did by extralegal action what they could not do through legal channels. In North Carolina, they closed courts and intimidated tax officials. In South Carolina, they pursued outlaws and whipped people suspected of harboring them.

These activities brought the Regulators into conflict with the local elites of both North and South Carolina. British officials, however, only made matters worse. Instead of encouraging the assemblies to increase western representation, the crown did exactly the opposite. As part of its effort to limit the power of colonial legislatures, it forbade them from increasing their size. Americans termed this instruction "perhaps [as] peculiar as any that have been given on the continent." As for the shortage of currency, Lord Hillsborough, the secretary of state for the colonies, callously informed North Carolinians that "no Consideration of a possible local inconvenience" would prompt Britain to modify the "sound Principles" of the Currency Act. And instead of approving legislation in South Carolina that would have established courts in the backcountry, British officials disallowed it because it specified that judges would hold their positions contingent on good behavior rather than at the pleasure of the crown.

Thanks to such help from London as well as to their own mistakes, a crisis confronted local authorities by 1767. In South Carolina, the assembly belatedly reapportioned itself, giving the backcountry some representation, and permitted the crown to dictate the terms of judicial appointments. These and other concessions to western residents narrowly averted bloodshed. But in North Carolina, fighting broke out in 1771. Governor William Tryon led the local militia against the Regulators who had gathered near Alamance Creek. There, he ordered the Regulators to disperse or his men would fire. "Fire and be damned," someone replied, and gunfire erupted, killing 29 men and wounding more than 150 on both sides. During the next several weeks, seven Regulators were hanged and six thousand pardoned.

The confrontation in North Carolina was the most serious of its kind, but similar social tensions were apparent in other colonies. To deal with them, colonial leaders had to understand local conditions and be able to act on their knowledge. But British attempts to reform colonial governments threatened to hamstring them.

THE TOWNSHEND CRISIS

British authorities had not given up the idea of taxing the colonies with the repeal of the Stamp Act in 1766. Little over a year later, Parliament passed a new collection of taxes, the Townshend duties. Another crisis ensued, lasting until an American boycott of British goods forced repeal of most of the new duties. The relatively quiet period that followed ended when Britain made a serious attempt to enforce compliance with the one Townshend duty still on the books, the duty on tea.

TOWNSHEND'S PLAN

Charles Townshend became the leading figure in Britain's government in 1767. A former member of the Board of Trade, he thought he understood the colonies, and he knew that many members of Parliament still wanted to tax Americans. The legislation that bears his name, the **Townshend Duty Act**,

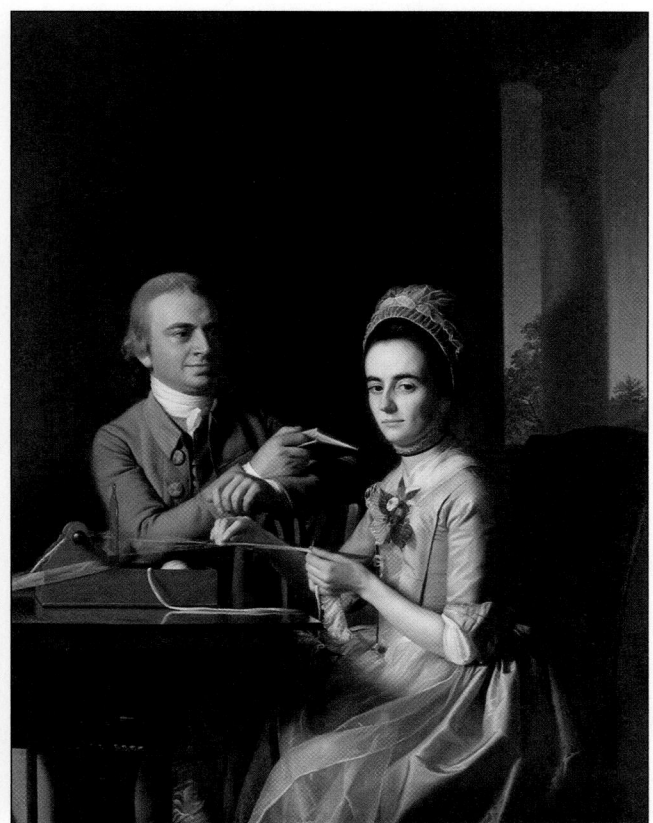

Mr. and Mrs. Thomas Mifflin of Philadelphia. A prominent merchant and radical opponent of British policy toward the colonies, Mifflin and his wife were visiting Boston in 1773, when John Singleton Copley painted them. Working at a small loom, Sarah Morris Mifflin weaves a decorative fringe. She no doubt did the same during the nonimportation movement against the Townshend duties, thereby helping to make importation of such goods from England unnecessary.

was intended to help pay the cost of government in America. It imposed new duties, or external taxes, which Townshend believed the colonists were willing to accept, but no direct, or internal, taxes like the Stamp Tax. The duties covered a number of items the colonists regularly imported—tea, paper, paint, lead, and glass. To make sure that the duties were collected, British authorities added a new board of customs commissioners for America and located its headquarters in Boston, the presumed home of many smugglers.

Coming on top of the threatened suspension of the New York legislature, the Townshend Duty Act seemed to foreshadow greater British interference in colonial affairs. And the new customs officials were, in fact, far more diligent than their predecessors. One of them, taking advantage of technicalities in the law, entrapped Henry Laurens, a prominent merchant in South Carolina. Other officials harassed the wealthy Boston merchant John Hancock, perhaps because he was openly contemptuous of them. Seizing his appropriately named vessel *Liberty,* they accused him of smuggling. Hancock may indeed have violated the acts of trade at times, but in this case the accusations were apparently false. The incident sparked a riot in Boston during which a crowd on the waterfront roughed up members of the customs service. British authorities responded in 1768 by sending troops to Boston. The soldiers would remain there amid mounting hostility for the next year and a half.

AMERICAN BOYCOTT

The Townshend duties, like the stamp tax, provoked resistance throughout the colonies. Rejecting the argument that duties were somehow different from taxes, John Dickinson, a wealthy lawyer who wrote under the pen name A Farmer in Pennsylvania, asserted that a tax was a tax, whatever its form. The purpose of the taxes—to help pay the costs of government in the colonies, including the salaries of governors and judges—also seemed dangerous. Americans believed it was the role of their own assemblies to raise revenues for these costs. By bypassing the assemblies, the Townshend Act threatened to undermine their authority.

There was no equivalent to the Stamp Act Congress in response to the Townshend Act, because British officials (acting through the colonial governors) barred the assemblies from sending delegates to such a meeting. Even so, Americans gradually organized an effective nonimportation movement. When, for example, the governor of Virginia dissolved the House of Burgesses for resolutions opposing British measures, the members met on their own in the Raleigh Tavern at Williamsburg and adopted a nonimportation agreement. Once again, vigilant laborers and artisans threatened violators of the general boycott with physical violence, but few disturbances occurred. Many Americans signed subscription lists binding themselves, with the other signers, to buy only goods made in the colonies and nothing made in Great Britain. Handbills, like one urging "the Sons and Daughters of LIBERTY" to shun a particular Boston merchant, brought pressure to bear on uncooperative importers. To avoid imported English textiles, American women spun more thread and wove more cloth at home. Wearing homespun became a moral virtue, a sign of self-reliance, personal

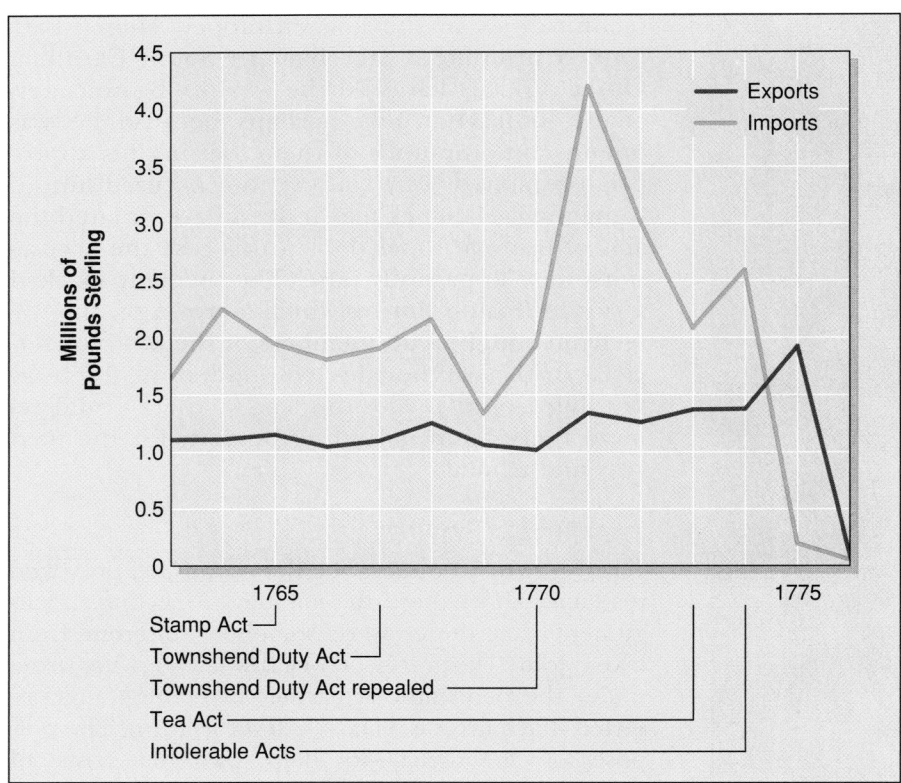

FIGURE 5-1   Value of American Exports to and Imports from England, 1763–1776
This figure depicts the value of American exports to and imports from England. The decrease of imports in 1765–1766 and the even sharper drop in 1769 illustrate the effect of American boycotts in response to the Stamp Act and Townshend duties.

Data Source: U.S. Bureau of the Census, *Historical Statistics of the United States, Colonial Times to 1970, Bicentennial Edition, Part 1* (1975).

independence, and the rejection of "corrupting" English luxuries (see "American Views: Social Status and the Enforcement of the Nonimportation Movement" page 158).

The nonimportation movement forged a sense of common purpose among all who participated in it—men and women, southern planters and northern artisans alike—giving them the sense of belonging to a larger community of fellow Americans. Although it was at this point more an imagined community than a political community, it was real enough and large enough to reduce imports from Britain by 40 percent after only one year.

Because Britain had increased its exports to Europe since the Stamp Act crisis, it took longer than before for the nonimportation movement to produce a reaction in London (see Figure 5–1). Still, the troubles in America contributed to the king's decision to appoint a new prime minister, Lord North. Thinking—and even looking—remarkably alike, George III and North complemented each other. At

the king's insistence, North would remain prime minister until 1782. In 1770, he was prepared to concede that the Townshend duties had been counterproductive because they interfered with British trade. But when Parliament repealed most of them, it left the duty on tea. This symbolic equivalent of the Declaratory Act served to assert Parliament's continuing right to tax the colonies.

THE BOSTON MASSACRE

Ironically, on the same day that North proposed that Parliament rescind most of the Townshend duties—March 5, 1770—British troops fired on American civilians in Boston. This incident, which came to be known to Americans everywhere as the **Boston Massacre**, resulted from months of increasing friction between townspeople and the British troops stationed in the city. The townspeople complained that the soldiers insulted them, leered at women, and competed for scarce jobs. Samuel Adams recounted these real and imagined misdeeds in a column called "A Journal of the Times" that he circulated to other American cities. The hostility was so great, complained a British officer, that "twenty" soldiers could be "knocked down in the Streets" and nothing be heard of it, but if a soldier merely kicked a resident, "the Town is immediately in an Alarm."

The Boston Massacre occurred when angry and frightened British soldiers fired on a crowd that was pelting them with sticks and stones. Five men died, including Crispus Attucks—subsequently described as "that half Indian, half negro and altogether rowdy"— who has since become the most celebrated casualty of the incident. To preserve order, the troops withdrew from the city. Later two prominent local lawyers successfully defended the soldiers accused of murder.

THE "QUIET PERIOD"

In the so-called Quiet Period that followed, no general grievance united all Americans. But in almost

The Boston Massacre, March 5, 1770, in an engraving by Paul Revere. Copied from an earlier print, Revere's widely circulated version shows—somewhat inaccurately—well-organized soldiers firing on helpless civilians; the names of the dead, including Crispus Attucks, appear below.

every colony, issues continued to simmer. In Massachusetts and South Carolina, for example, the royal governors temporarily moved the meeting places of the legislatures to small towns miles away from the capital, "for the sole Purpose," as the Declaration of Independence would later charge, "of fatiguing them into compliance" with British measures.

Local circumstances produced a more spectacular confrontation in Rhode Island. The crew of a British revenue schooner, the *Gaspee,* had been patrolling Narragansett Bay, seizing smugglers and, it was said, stealing livestock and cutting down farmers' fruit trees for firewood. When the *Gaspee* ran aground while chasing some American ships, Rhode Islanders got even. Led by John Brown, a local merchant, they boarded the vessel, shot its captain in the buttocks, and putting him and his crew ashore, burned the ship. The British government appointed a commission of inquiry with instructions to arrest the culprits and send them to England for trial. Despite its offer of a reward for information about the incident, the commission learned nothing. The British attempt to stamp out

smuggling in the colonies was so heavy-handed that it offended the innocent more than it frightened the guilty.

Such incidents, and in particular the British threat to send Americans to England for trial, led American leaders to resolve to keep one another informed about British actions. Twelve colonies established **committees of correspondence** for this purpose. Leaders in Boston established similar committees in Massachusetts. There would soon be plenty for these organizations to do, for Boston was about to become the scene of a showdown between imperial authority and colonial resistance.

THE BOSTON TEA PARTY

During the Quiet Period, Americans drank smuggled (and therefore untaxed) Dutch tea. Partly as a result, the British East India Company, which had the exclusive right to distribute tea in the British Empire, nearly went bankrupt. Lord North tried to rescue it with the **Tea Act of 1773.** The act permitted the company to ship tea from its warehouses in Britain without paying the duty normally collected there. Because its tea would therefore be cheaper, British authorities assumed that Americans would buy it and simultaneously pay the old Townshend duty. The company selected a few merchants to act as its exclusive agents in the colonies. These merchants stood to reap substantial profits from their position.

This plan angered Americans. Some may have been jealous at being excluded from the tea trade. Most, however, were outraged at the attempt to trick them into paying the tax on tea. Thousands decided not to touch the stuff. Newspapers discussed its dangers to the body as well as to the body politic and offered recipes for substitutes. "To their great honor," according to the newspapers, many women rejected the tea and put pressure on others to do likewise, while schoolboys collected and burned tea leaves.

Thomas Hutchinson, who had been lieutenant governor of Massachusetts during the Stamp Act riots, was now the colony's royal governor. Two of his sons were among those chosen to be the East India Company's agents. In most other cities, threats from the Sons of Liberty convinced the captains of the tea ships to return to England without landing their cargo. Hutchinson, however, was determined to have the tea unloaded in Boston, and he barred the tea ships there from leaving. As a result, violence once again erupted in the city.

When the Sons of Liberty realized that they could not force the ships to leave, they decided on dramatic

LIBERTY.TREE

The BOSTONIAN'S Paying the EXCISE-MAN, or TARRING & FEATHERING

"The Bostonian's Paying the Excise-Man or Tarring & Feathering." This print, published in London in 1774, satirizes American resistance to British tax measures. Four men representing a broad range of social classes pour tea down the throat of a tax collector while the Boston Tea Party takes place in the background.

action. On December 16, 1773, Samuel Adams reportedly told a large gathering at Old South Meeting House that it "could do nothing more to preserve the liberties of America." This remark was apparently a prearranged signal for what came to be known as the **Boston Tea Party**. War whoops immediately answered him from the street outside, and a well-organized band of men disguised as Indians raced aboard the *Dartmouth* and two other tea ships, broke open 342 chests of tea, and heaved the contents into the harbor. In a similar action in 1774, residents of Annapolis, Maryland, forced some merchants to burn their own ship when it arrived with dutied tea.

THE INTOLERABLE ACTS

The destruction of property in the Boston Tea Party shocked many Americans. Surprised and angry, British officials reacted even more strongly. Parlia-

ment passed a series of repressive measures known as the **Coercive Acts**. The first of these, effective June 1, 1774, was the Boston Port Act, which closed the port of Boston to all incoming and outgoing traffic until the East India Company and the crown received payment for the destroyed tea and lost duties. The Administration of Justice Act, which followed, declared that an official who, while performing his duties, killed a colonist could be tried in England (where he would almost certainly receive sympathetic treatment) rather than in Massachusetts. The third measure, the Massachusetts Government Act, drastically modified that colony's charter of 1691. Under the old document, the legislature had elected members to the governor's council; henceforth, the crown would appoint them. And appointed, rather than elected, sheriffs would now name juries. In addition, the Massachusetts Government Act limited the number of town meetings that could be held without the governor's prior approval. In another measure, the British government made its commander in chief in America, General Thomas Gage, the governor of Massachusetts and, in the Quartering Act of 1774, declared that the troops under his command could be lodged in virtually any uninhabited building.

On the same day that Parliament enacted these measures, it also passed the **Quebec Act**. This statute enlarged the boundaries of Quebec south to the Ohio River and stipulated that it be governed by an appointed governor and council but no elected assembly (see Map 5–2). The act also provided for the trial of civil cases without a jury and gave the Catholic Church the same privileges that it had enjoyed under the French. The colonists linked the Quebec Act with the Coercive Acts and labeled them the **Intolerable Acts**.

THE ROAD TO REVOLUTION

Americans throughout the colonies considered the Intolerable Acts so threatening that they organized another gathering, the **First Continental Congress**, to respond to them. Congress renewed the nonimportation movement and took measures to enforce it strictly. These measures widened the gap between those who supported British authorities and those who opposed them.

AMERICAN RESPONSE TO THE INTOLERABLE ACTS

Americans found the territorial, administrative, and religious provisions of the Quebec Act deeply disturbing. As one royal governor observed, "The securing of lands for the rising Generation is a matter of great importance to a poor and provident Man with a large family." The Quebec Act, however, gave Canada jurisdiction over lands in the area north of the Ohio River claimed by Connecticut, Pennsylvania, and Virginia. This deprived settlers of their hoped-for homesteads and land speculators of their hoped-for profits, angering both. The administrative provisions of the act—appointed government, no assemblies, no jury for civil cases—also suggested to Americans what Britain might have in store for them.

Americans had similar fears about the religious provisions of the Quebec Act. During the 1760s, some Anglican clergymen had sought to have a bishop appointed for America. But most Americans, including Anglicans, opposed this proposal. They were convinced that the creation of such an office would strengthen the Anglican Church at the expense of other denominations, weaken local control of religious affairs, and require the payment of additional taxes. Many Americans believed that British authorities had scrapped the idea. The Quebec Act's concessions to Canadian Catholics, however, seemed to resurrect it in more ominous form. As one Virginian had observed, the hierarchical organization of the Anglican Church was "a Relick of the Papal Incroachments" on English law. The Quebec Act accordingly "gave a General Alarm to all Protestants," whose ministers throughout the continent warned their congregations that they might be "bound by Popish chains."

American reaction to the religious provisions of the Quebec Act may have been exaggerated, but some features of the Coercive Acts were cause for real concern. The Boston Port Act arbitrarily punished innocent and guilty Bostonians alike. The Administration of Justice Act—which some with vivid imaginations dubbed the Murder Act—seemed to declare an open season on colonists, allowing crown officials to kill them without fear of punishment. The Massachusetts Government Act raised the more realistic fear that no colonial charter was safe. A Parliament that had stripped the Massachusetts legislature of an important power might equally decide to abolish the lower houses of all the colonies.

Nightmarish scenarios filled the colonial newspapers. One clergyman observed that the terms of the Coercive Acts were such that if someone were to "make water" on the door of the royal customs house, an entire colonial city "might be laid in Ashes." He undoubtedly knew that he exaggerated, but his words embodied real fear and anger, and many other Americans shared his feelings. Trying to

MAP EXPLORATION   To explore an interactive version of this map, go to http://www.prenhall.com/goldfield/map5.2

☐ British Colonies, Possessions, and claims   ☐ Spanish Possessions
☐ Quebec   — Quebec boundary, 1774, as later defined
— Quebec boundary, 1763

Hudson Bay

HUDSON'S BAY COMPANY

Lake Superior   QUEBEC 1774   Lake Ontario   St. Lawrence River   ATLANTIC OCEAN

Mississippi River   Lake Michigan   Lake Huron   Lake Erie

Ohio River   THE THIRTEEN COLONIES

LOUISIANA

WEST FLORIDA   EAST FLORIDA

0   300 Miles
0   300 Kilometers

MAP 5-2   The Quebec Act of 1774
The Quebec Act enlarged the boundaries of the Canadian province southward to the Ohio River and westward to the Mississippi, thereby depriving several colonies of claims to the area granted to them by their original charters.

make an example of Boston, British authorities had taken steps that united Americans as nothing had ever done before (see the Overview table, "New Restraints and Burdens on Americans, 1759–1774").

THE FIRST CONTINENTAL CONGRESS

Massachusetts wanted to respond to the Intolerable Acts with an immediate renewal of the nonimportation movement. Leaders in other colonies wanted to organize a more coordinated response and called for another meeting like the Stamp Act Congress. The colonies accordingly agreed to send delegates to a

Overview

New Restraints and Burdens on Americans, 1759–1774

	Limits on Legislative Action	Curbs on Territorial Expansion	Burdens on Colonial Trade	Imposition of New Taxes
1759	Royal instructions restrict the ability of the Virginia assembly to pass timely legislation.			
1762			Writs of assistance issued. Revenue Act authorizes Navy to help enforce customs regulation.	
1763		Proclamation Line keeps white settlement east of the Appalachians.	Peacetime use of the navy and new customs officials to enforce Navigation Acts.	
1764	Currency Act limits the colonial legislatures' ability to issue paper money.		Vice-admiralty courts strengthened for Sugar Act.	Sugar Act imposes taxes for revenue (modified 1766).
1765				Quartering Act requires assemblies to provide facilities for royal troops. Stamp Act imposes internal taxes on various items (repealed 1766).
Declaratory Act proclaims Parliament's right to legislate for colonies in all cases whatsoever.				
1767	Royal instructions limit the size of colonial assemblies.		Vice-admiralty courts strengthened for Townshend duties. American Customs Service established in Boston.	Townshend duties imposed on some imported goods in order to pay colonial officials. (All but tax on tea repealed, 1770.)
1773				Tea Act reduces duty and prompts Boston Tea Party.
1774 (Intolerable Acts)	Massachusetts Government Act limits town meetings, changes legislature, and violates Massachusetts charter.	Quebec Act enlarges Quebec at expense of colonies with claims in the Ohio River Valley.	Boston Port Act closes harbor until East India Company's tea is paid for.	Quartering Act of 1774 declares that troops could be lodged in virtually any uninhabited building in Boston.

meeting in Philadelphia that came to be called the First Continental Congress. Because royal governors attempted to prevent the meeting by barring the legislatures from naming delegates, the colonies called extralegal public meetings for the purpose. In the end, all the colonies except Georgia were represented.

The First Continental Congress met at Carpenter's Hall in Philadelphia from September 5 to October 26, 1774, with fifty-five delegates present at one time or another. All were leading figures in their home colonies, but only a few knew members from elsewhere. Each colony had one vote, irrespective of the size of its delegation. Some of the more conservative participants favored a compromise with Britain. The speaker of the Pennsylvania Assembly, Joseph Galloway, introduced a measure reminiscent of the Albany Plan of Union. It called for creation of an American "grand council" that would have veto power over parliamentary legislation dealing with America. His plan failed in the Congress by one vote. Instead, those who favored stronger measures—such as Samuel Adams and his cousin John, Patrick Henry, and Christopher Gadsden—prevailed. They persuaded most of their colleagues to endorse the **Suffolk Resolves**, which had been passed at a meeting held in Suffolk County (the site of Boston). These strongly worded resolves denounced the Coercive Acts as unconstitutional, advised the people to arm, and called for general economic sanctions against Britain. Learning of them, one British official told an American, "If these Resolves of your people are to be depended on, they have declared War against us."

THE CONTINENTAL ASSOCIATION

The Congress created the **Continental Association** to organize and enforce sanctions against the British. As a first step, the Association pledged Americans to cut off imports from Britain after December 1, 1774. If the dispute with Britain was not resolved by September 1775, the Association called for barring most exports to Britain and the West Indies. Voters in every district throughout the colonies were to choose committeemen to enforce the terms of the Association. All who violated them were to be considered "enemies of American liberty." Their names were to be published, and associators (people agreeing to the Association) would "break off all dealings" with them.

Congress also issued a declaration of rights and grievances summarizing its position. This declaration condemned most of the steps taken by British authorities since 1763, but "cheerfully" consented to trade regulations for the good of the whole empire. In addition, the Congress sent addresses to the people of America, to the inhabitants of Great Britain, and to the king. The address to the king asked him to use his "royal authority and interposition" to protect his loyal subjects in America. The words were significant, for protection and allegiance were considered the reciprocal duties of a sovereign and his people. After agreeing to convene again on May 10, 1775, if its grievances had not been redressed by then, the First Continental Congress adjourned.

The proceedings of the First Continental Congress revealed division as well as agreement among its delegates. All the delegates believed that the Coercive Acts were unconstitutional, but they differed on methods to resist them. Only a minority was prepared to take up arms against Britain. Most representatives tried to protect the interests of their own colonies. Those from Virginia and Maryland, for example, insisted that the embargo on exports not begin until planters had finished shipping the current tobacco crop. Even more alarming, some South Carolina delegates, in an early example of the sectional stubbornness that would culminate nearly a century later in the United States Civil War, threatened to walk out of the meeting unless the nonexportation agreement omitted rice, most of which went to northern Europe by way of Britain. To placate the Carolinians, northerners agreed to the exemption. Gadsden, the most radical of the South Carolina delegates, was disgusted with his self-serving South Carolina colleagues. Their actions, he felt, betrayed the spirit of united purpose Patrick Henry had spoken of so stirringly earlier in the Congress: "The distinctions between Virginians, Pennsylvanians, New Yorkers and New Englanders are no more. I am not a Virginian, but an American."

POLITICAL DIVISIONS

In the wake of the First Continental Congress, Americans were forced to take sides for and against the Continental Association. At this point, not even such well-known radicals as Samuel Adams and Gadsden were advocating independence. Throughout the pre-Revolutionary period, most colonists hoped and expected that imperial authorities would change their policy toward America. English history, Americans believed, was full of instances in which the resolute opposition of a free people forced oppressive ministries and tyrannical kings to back down. They were confident that it could happen again.

AMERICAN VIEWS

Social Status and the Enforcement of the Nonimportation Movement

Many Americans enthusiastically supported the nonimportation movement called in response to the Townshend Duty Act crisis of the late 1760s. A few, however, openly opposed it. Among these was the aristocratic William Henry Drayton of South Carolina, who objected to the composition of the committee that had been chosen to enforce the nonimportation agreement in his region. The committee included artisans and shopkeepers, men who Drayton claimed, should have no role in public affairs. Their education prepared them only "to cut up a beast in the market to the best advantage, to cobble an old shoe in the neatest manner, or to build a necessary house [outhouse]," not to make public policy. As the following document makes clear, deference had its limits, and the committeemen emphatically disagreed with him. Drayton was later to reverse himself and actively support the Continental Association's ban on importing British goods in 1775. "The people" wanted it, he would later explain, and "it was our duty, to satisfy our constituents; as we were only servants of the public [at large]."

- Who makes policy in the United States today?
- What qualifications do you think they should have?
- How do your answers to these questions differ from Drayton's? From the "Mechanicks's"?
- How would you explain Drayton's later switch?

The Mechanicks of the General Committee to William Henry Drayton

The gracious Giver of all good things, has been pleased to bestow a certain principle on mankind, which properly may be called common sense: But, though every man hath a natural right to a determined portion of this ineffable ray of the Divinity, yet, to the misfortune of society, many persons fall short of this most necessary gift of God; the want of which cannot be compensated by all the learning of the schools.

The Mechanicks pretend to nothing more, than having a claim from nature, to their share in this inestimable favour, in common with Emperors and Kings, and, were it safe to carry the comparison still higher, they would say with William-Henry Drayton himself; who, in his great condescention, has been pleased to allow us a place amongst human beings: But whether it might have happened from an ill construc-

What Americans were divided over was the extent of Parliament's authority over them and the degree to which they could legitimately challenge its power. As British officials failed, with the passing of time, to accommodate American views of their rights, Americans began in increasing numbers to challenge London's control over them. The experience of James Wilson, a Pennsylvania lawyer, illustrates this shift. In *Considerations on the Nature and Extent of the Legislative Authority of the British Parliament* tion of his sensory, or his upper works being damaged by some rough treatment of the person who conducted his birth, we know not; however so it is, that, to us, he seems highly defective in this point, whatever exalted notions he may entertain of his own abilities.

By attending to the dictates of common sense, the Mechanicks have been able to distinguish between RIGHT and WRONG; in doing which indeed no great merit is claimed, because every man's own feelings will direct him thereto, unless he obstinately, or from a pertinacious opinion of his own superior knowledge, shuts his eyes, and stoickally submits to all the illegal encroachments that may be made on his property, by an ill-designing and badly-informed ministry.

Mr. Drayton may value himself as much as he pleases, on his having had a liberal education bestowed on him, tho' the good fruits thereof have not hitherto been conspicuous either in his public or private life: He ought however to know, that this is not so absolutely necessary to these, who move in the low sphere of mechanical employments. But still, though he pretends to view them with so contemptuous and oblique an eye, these men hope, that they are in some degree useful to society, without presuming to make any comparisons between themselves and him, except with regard to love for their country; for he has amply shewn, that an attachment of this sort is not one of his ruling passions. Nor does he appear in the least to have regarded the peace and good order of that community of which he is a member; otherwise he would not wilfully, and without any cause, have knocked his head against ninety-nine out of every hundred of the people, not only in this province, but of all North-America,

not one of whom bore him any malice, nor yet do, though they may entertain what opinions they please, with respect to his want of patriotism, from his having proved a Felo de se [murderer of himself] in this point.

After an avowal of principles, incompatible with the essential rights of freemen under the English constitution, surely, no parish in this province, will ever think it prudent, to trust their interests in such hands, for the time to come? Besides, who can say he ever shewed any capacity for business, when he was honoured with a seat in the House of Assembly? . . .

Mr. Drayton may be assured, that so far from being ashamed of our trades, we are in the highest degree thankful to our friends, who put us in the way of being instructed in them; and that we bless God for giving us strength and judgment to pursue them, in order to maintain our families, with a decency suitable to their stations in life. Every man is not so lucky as to have a fortune ready provided to his hand, either by his own or his wife's parents, as has been his lot; nor ought it to be so with all men; and Providence accordingly hath wisely ordained otherwise, by appointing the greatest part of mankind, to provide for their support by manual labour; and we will be bold to say, that such are the most useful people in a community. . . .

We are, Yours, &c.
MECHANICKS of the COMMITTEE.
October 3d, 1769.

Source: *South Carolina Gazette*, October 5, 1769; reprinted in *The Letters of Freeman, etc.: Essays on the Nonimportation Movement in South Carolina* by William Henry Drayton, ed. Robert M. Weir (1977), University of South Carolina Press, pp. 111–114.

(published in 1774), Wilson wrote that he set out to find a reasonable dividing line between those areas in which Parliament had legitimate authority over the colonies and those in which it did not. But the more he thought, the more he became convinced

"that such a line does not exist" and that there can be "no medium between acknowledging and denying that power in all cases." Wilson therefore concluded that Parliament had no authority at all over the colonies, that the colonies' only legal governing bodies were their own assemblies, and that their only link to the British Empire was through the king, to whom colonists owed allegiance. British authorities and their American supporters strongly disagreed, insisting that Parliament had complete authority over the colonies.

During 1774 and early 1775, as the British–American confrontation grew more heated, lively debates raged in newspapers and pamphlets, and the colonists became increasingly polarized. In the last months before the outbreak of the American Revolution, the advocates of colonial rights began to call themselves **Whigs** and condemned their opponents as **Tories**. These traditional English party labels dated from the late seventeenth century, when the Tories had supported the accession of the Catholic King James II; the Whigs had opposed it. By calling themselves Whigs and their opponents Tories (loyalist was a more accurate label), the advocates of colonial rights cast themselves as champions of liberty and their enemies as defenders of religious intolerance and royal absolutism.

CONCLUSION

All Americans, Whigs and loyalists alike, had considered themselves good British subjects. But Americans were a more diverse and more democratic people than the English. A considerably larger percentage of them could participate in government, and for all practical purposes, they had been governing themselves for a long time.

British officials recognized the different character of American society and feared it might lead Americans to reject British control. But the steps they took to prevent this outcome had the opposite effect.

From Britain's perspective, the measures it took in the wake of the French and Indian War were a reasonable response to its administrative and financial problems in the colonies. Taken one by one from the colonists' perspective, however, they were a rain of blows that finally impelled them to rebel.

No wonder that Americans, whose political ideology had already made them wary of governmental power, believed that they were the victims of a conspiracy in London to deprive them of their liberty. That Parliament should be a party to this presumed conspiracy particularly shocked and offended them. Because it was the representative body in the government, Americans had long considered it their "friend," though they were certain that it was not composed of their representatives.

Yet Americans probably should not have been surprised at Parliament's role. After the Glorious Revolution, virtually the only institutional limitation on Parliament was Parliament itself. That the most powerful part of the British government should concern itself with the empire after 1763 seemed only natural in Britain; that its American counterparts should defend their own rights seemed only reasonable in America. The American assemblies, after all, had modeled themselves on Parliament. Indeed, both Parliament and the colonial assemblies were doing what similar bodies throughout Europe were also doing at roughly the same time—asserting their powers and defending their liberties against encroachments from above and below.

The attempts to protect their accustomed autonomy first brought the colonial assemblies into conflict with Parliament. Asserting their rights led the individual colonies to greater cooperatation among themselves. This development, in turn, led to increasingly widespread resistance, then to rebellion, and finally to revolution. Moving imperceptibly from one stage to the next, Americans grew conscious of their common interests and their differences from the English. They became aware, as Benjamin Franklin would later write, of the need to break "through the bounds, in which a dependent people had been accustomed to think, and act" so that they might "properly comprehend the character they had assumed."

That working men and members of the elite dressed as Indians had joined in the dangerous act of defiance known as the Boston Tea Party also foreshadowed coming developments. No one now knows for certain why they adopted that particular disguise, but Indians were a traditional symbol of the new world. And those who were making a new political world were risking much—even, it would shortly turn out, life itself.

REVIEW QUESTIONS

1. What do Eliza Farmer's letters tell us about the crisis over dutied tea in 1773 and 1774? What does she think has caused the crisis and who was at fault? What makes her increasingly sympathetic to the colonial position? How widespread is the American claim of rights in her estimation? What makes her think the colonists have any chance of success in resisting British impositions?

2. How did the British victory and French withdrawal from North America after the French and Indian War affect the relations between Native Americans and white settlers? Between British authorities and Americans?

3. What was the relationship between the French and Indian War and changes in British policy toward America? What problems were British officials trying to solve in 1763? What difficulties confronted Americans in 1763? How did the expectations of American and British authorities differ in 1763? Why were the new policies offensive to Americans?

4. How was stationing British troops in America related to British taxation of the colonists? Why did the colonists consider taxation by Parliament an especially serious threat to their freedom as well as to their pocketbooks?

5. How did Americans oppose the new measures? Who participated in the various forms of resistance? How effective were the different kinds of resistance? What were the effects of American resistance to British measures on their own sense of identity as Americans? What were the effects on their own internal politics?

6. What led to the meeting of the First Continental Congress? What steps did the Congress take? What did it expect to achieve? What were the differences between Whigs and Tories?

KEY TERMS

Boston Massacre (p. 152)

Boston Tea Party (p. 154)

British Constitution (p. 146)

Cherokee War (p. 142)

Coercive Acts (p. 154)

Committees of correspondence (p. 153)

Continental Association (p. 157)

Currency Act (p. 144)

Declaration of Rights and Grievances (p. 148)

Declaratory Act (p. 149)

First Continental Congress (p. 154)

Intolerable Acts (p. 154)

Nonimportation movement (p. 147)

Parson's Cause (p. 144)

Pontiac's Rebellion (p. 143)

Proclamation Line (p. 141)

Proclamation of 1763 (p. 141)

Quartering Acts (p. 141)

Quebec Act (p. 154)

Regulators (p. 150)

Sons of Liberty (p. 147)

Stamp Act (p. 145)

Stamp Act Congress (p. 148)

Sugar Act (p. 144)

Suffolk Resolves (p. 157)

Tea Act of 1773 (p. 153)

Tories (p. 160)

Townshend Duty Act (p. 150)

Whigs (p. 160)

Writs of assistance (p. 146)

RECOMMENDED READING

Bailyn, Bernard. *The Ideological Origins of the American Revolution,* 2nd ed. (1992). A clear and illuminating account of how the colonists' ideas about politics prepared them to resist British measures.

Countryman, Edward. *The American Revolution* (1985). A brief, readable general history of the Revolutionary period that focuses on the involvement of the common people.

Morison, Samuel Eliot, ed. *Sources and Documents Illustrating the American Revolution, 1764–1788, and the Formation of the Federal Constitution* (1965). The most readily available and conveniently used collection of documents (mostly official) from the era of the American Revolution.

Raphael, Ray. *A People's History of the American Revolution: How Common People Shaped the Fight for Independence* (2001). A readable, popular synthesis of much recent scholarship.

ADDITIONAL SOURCES

Imperial Reorganization

Alden, John R. *John Stuart and the Southern Colonial Frontier: A Study of Indian Relations, War, Trade, and Land Problems in the Southern Wilderness, 1754–1775* (1944, 1966).

Anderson, Fred. *Crucible of War: The Seven Years' War and the Fate of Empire in British North America, 1754–1766* (2000).

Barrow, Thomas C. *Trade and Empire: The British Customs Service in Colonial America, 1660–1775* (1967).

Bonwick, Colin. *The American Revolution* (1991).

Brooke, John. *King George III* (1972).

Cashin, Edward J. *William Bartram and the American Revolution on the Southern Frontier* (2000).

Dowd, Gregory. *A Spirited Resistance: The North American Indian Struggle for Unity, 1745–1815* (1992).

Hatley, Tom. *The Dividing Paths: Cherokees and South Carolinians through the Era of Revolution* (1993).

Langford, Paul. *A Polite and Commercial People: England, 1727–1783* (1989).

Peckham, Howard H. *Pontiac and the Indian Uprising* (1947).

Richter, Daniel. *Facing East from Indian Country: A Native History of Early America* (2001).

Shy, John. *Toward Lexington: The Role of the British Army in the Coming of the American Revolution* (1965).

Snapp, J. Russell. *John Stuart and the Struggle for Empire on the Southern Frontier* (1996).

Sosin, Jack M. *Whitehall and the Wilderness: The Middle West in British Colonial Policy, 1760–1775* (1961).

Weber, David J. *The Spanish Frontier in North America* (1992).

White, Richard. *The Middle Ground: Indians, Empires, and Republics in the Great Lakes Region, 1650–1815* (1991).

American Reactions

Breen, Timothy H. "Ideology and Nationalism on the Eve of the American Revolution: Revisions Once More in Need of Revising," *Journal of American History* (1998), 13-39.

Brown, Richard D. *Revolutionary Politics in Massachusetts: The Boston Committee of Correspondence and the Towns, 1772–1774* (1970).

Brown, Richard M. *The South Carolina Regulators* (1963).

Calhoon, Robert M. *Dominion and Liberty: Ideology in the Anglo-American World, 1660–1801* (1994).

Colbourn, H. Trevor. *The Lamp of Experience: Whig History and the Intellectual Origins of the American Revolution* (1965).

Countryman, Edward. *A People in Revolution: The American Revolution and Political Society in New York, 1760–1790* (1981).

Egnal, Marc. *A Mighty Empire: The Origins of the American Revolution* (1988).

Ekirch, Robert A. *"Poor Carolina": Politics and Society in Colonial North Carolina, 1729–1776* (1981).

Greene, Jack P. *Negotiated Authorities: Essays in Colonial Political and Constitutional History* (1994).

Greene, Jack P., *Understanding the American Revolution: Issues and Actors* (1995).

Hoerder, Dirk. *Crowd Action in Revolutionary Massachusetts, 1765–1780* (1977).

Jensen, Merrill. *The Founding of a Nation: A History of the American Revolution, 1763–1776* (1968).

Klein, Rachel N. *Unification of a Slave State: The Rise of the Planter Class in the South Carolina Backcountry, 1760–1808* (1990).

Knollenberg, Bernhard. *Origin of the American Revolution, 1759–1766* (1960).

Krawczynski, Keith. *William Henry Drayton: South Carolina Revolutionary Patriot* (2001).

Kurtz, Stephen G. and James H. Hutson, eds., *Essays on the American Revolution* (1973).

Labaree, Benjamin W. *The Boston Tea Party* (1964).

Maier, Pauline. *From Resistance to Revolution: Colonial Radicals and the Development of American Opposition to Britain, 1765–1776* (1972).

Maier, Pauline., *The Old Revolutionaries: Political Lives in the Age of Samuel Adams* (1980).

Morgan, Edmund S. *The Birth of the Republic, 1763–1789, 3rd ed.* (1992).

Morgan, Edmund S., and Helen M. Morgan, *The Stamp Act Crisis: Prologue to Revolution* (1963, 1995).

Nash, Gary B. *The Urban Crucible: The Northern Seaports and the Origins of the American Revolution* (1986).

Pole, J. R., and Jack P. Greene, eds., *A Companion to the American Revolution* (2000).

Reid, John P. *Constitutional History of the American Revolution: The Power to Tax* (1987).

Ryerson, Richard A. *"The Revolution Is Now Begun": The Radical Committees of Philadelphia, 1765–1776* (1978).

Thomas, Peter D. G. *The Townshend Duties Crisis: The Second Phase of the American Revolution, 1767–1773* (1987).

Ubbelohde, Carl. *The Vice-Admiralty Courts and the American Revolution* (1960).

Whittenburg, James P. "Planters, Merchants, and Lawyers: Social Change and the Origins of the North Carolina Regulation," *William and Mary Quarterly*, 34 (1977), 214–238.

Zobel, Hiller B. *The Boston Massacre* (1970).

The Road to Revolution

Ammerman, David. *In the Common Cause: American Response to the Coercive Acts of 1774* (1974).

Brown, Wallace. *The Good Americans: The Loyalists in the American Revolution* (1969).

Calhoon, Robert M. *The Loyalists in Revolutionary America, 1760–1781* (1973).

Clark, J. C. D. *The Language of Liberty, 1660–1832: Political Discourse and Social Dynamics in the Anglo-American World* (1994).

Doll, Peter. *Revolution, Religion, and National Identity: Imperial Nationalism in British North America, 1745–1795* (2000).

Holton, Woody. *Forced Founders: Indians, Debtors, Slaves, and the Making of the American Revolution in Virginia* (1999).

McCullough, David. *John Adams* (2001).

Nelson, William H. *The American Tory* (1961).

Rakove, Jack N. *The Beginnings of National Politics: An Interpretive History of the Continental Congress* (1979).

Young, Alfred F. *The Shoemaker and the Tea Party: Memory and the American Revolution* (1999).

WHERE TO LEARN MORE

- **Charleston, South Carolina.** Many buildings date from the eighteenth century. Officials stored tea in one of them—the Exchange—to prevent a local version of the Boston Tea Party. The website for Historic Charleston, http://www.cr.nps.gov/nr/travel/charleston, provides a map, a list of buildings, and information about them.

- **Philadelphia, Pennsylvania.** Numerous buildings and sites date from the eighteenth century. Independence National Historical Park, between Second and Sixth streets on Walnut and Chestnut streets, contains Carpenter's Hall, where the First Continental Congress met, and the Pennsylvania State House (now known as Independence Hall), where the Declaration of Independence was adopted. Philadelphia's Historic Mile, http://www.ushistory.org/tour/index.html, provides a virtual tour of the great landmarks of the city, including Independence Hall.

- **Boston, Massachusetts.** Many important buildings and sites in this area date from the seventeenth and eighteenth centuries. They include Faneuil Hall (Dock Square), where many public meetings took place prior to the Revolution, and the Old State House (Washington and State streets), which overlooks the site of the Boston Massacre. The Freedom Trail, http://www.thefreedomtrail.org/virtual_tour.html, provides a well illustrated virtual tour of the historic sites.

- **Fort Michilimackinac National Historic Landmark, Mackinaw City, Michigan.** Near the south end of the Mackinac Bridge, the present structure is a modern restoration of the fort as it was when Pontiac's Rebellion took a heavy toll of its garrison. The Mackinac State Historic Parks website, http://www.mackinacparks.com/michilimackinac/html, provides a brief description and photographs of the reconstructed colonial village and fort.

Please refer to the document CD-ROM for primary sources related to this chapter.

�{ *George Washington's Tent. Plunkett Fleeson, a well-known Philadelphia upholsterer, made a set of three tents for Washington in 1776. One was for sleeping, one for dining, and one for baggage. This one, which measures 18 by 28 feet, could have served multiple purposes.*

Smithsonian Museum.

THE WAR FOR INDEPENDENCE
1774–1783

6

Headquarters, Valley Forge

January 14, 1778

I barely hinted to you my dearest Father my desire to augment the Continental Forces from an untried Source . . . . I would solicit you to cede me a number of your able bodied men Slaves, instead of leaving me a fortune. I would bring about a twofold good, first I would advance those who are unjustly deprived of the Rights of Mankind to a State which would be a proper Gradation between abject Slavery and perfect Liberty and besides I would reinforce

CHAPTER OUTLINE

The Outbreak of War and The Declaration of Independence, 1774–1776

Mounting Tensions
The Loyalists' Dilemma
British Coercion and Conciliation
The Battles of Lexington and Concord
The Second Continental Congress, 1775–1776
Commander in Chief George Washington
Early Fighting: Massachusetts, Virginia, the Carolinas, and Canada
Independence
Republicanism

GET THE BEST DRAMA:
Voices from the American Journey

Personal letters and diary entries fascinate us because they are real and intimate, and history is humanized through them. What better way than to let students feel the drama of the American story than with authentic, first-hand accounts of the events that shaped our nation's history?

New to the Third Edition, *Voices from the American Journey* features spotlight an authentic letter or diary entry at the beginning of each chapter, offering students dramatic "voices" from their past. Chosen to reflect the growing importance in understanding social history, these features trace America's personal, compelling trials and triumphs over time. Such voices allow us to touch the lives of the people about whom history is written.

In this example on page 165, John Laurens—a 23 year-old born in South Carolina but educated abroad and an aide to General Washington—is writing to his father to make an earnest plea on behalf of the cause of the American Revolution. His father, who is a wealthy slaveholder in South Carolina and president of the Continental Congress, is resistant to the notion that he enlist some of his slaves to fight on behalf of American freedom, thus pursuing a bit of freedom for themselves. More can be learned about John Laurens and the outcome of this debate on pages 166-167. *Other examples may be found on pages 67, 351, 454, 563, 659 and 920.*

Take a moment to look at this edition's *Voices from the American Journey* features, and see how they highlight the personal, highly dramatic dimension of the American journey. Notice that they set the stage for the key themes that are explored in each chapter, and how they infuse character and excitement into our nation's past. Get Goldfield—and get your students the best drama.

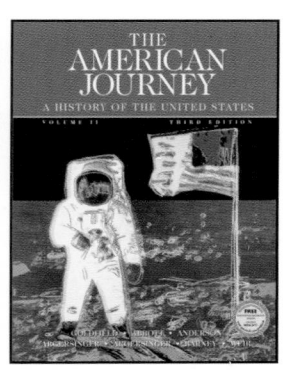

GET THE BOOK THAT GETS YOUR STUDENTS.

The authors of THE AMERICAN JOURNEY, THIRD EDITION **take educating students very seriously.** Every aspect of this new edition is geared towards providing the most important scholarship, as well as the best tools to ensure your students have a positive experience with our textbook, regardless of their individual learning style.

In addition, Prentice Hall believes in providing you with the most flexibility and your students with the most value for their investment. Therefore, we are offering THE AMERICAN JOURNEY, THIRD EDITION in a variety of options to serve your teaching needs, plus a selection of value packages designed to satisfy your students' budget concerns. In every way, THE AMERICAN JOURNEY is the book that gets your students.

GET THE BEST TEXT

- **The Best Pedagogy: Student Tool Kit** *(refer to tab 1 in this text)*
- **The Best Drama:** *Voices from the American Journey (refer to tab 2 in this text)*
- **The Best Maps:** *Map Explorations (refer to tab 3 in this text)*
- **The Best Presentation: Overviews and 3-Level Heads** *(refer to tab 4 in this text)*
- **The Best Relevance:** *From Then To Now (refer to tab 5 in this text)*
- **The Best Documents:** *American Views (refer to tab 6 in this text)*

GET THE BEST OPTIONS

THE AMERICAN JOURNEY: A HISTORY OF THE UNITED STATES, THIRD EDITION is available in the following formats, all of which include the FREE, exclusive **U.S. History Documents CD-ROM** from Prentice Hall:

- *Combined Edition—includes Chapters 1-31:* 0-13-182553-4
- *Volume 1—includes Chapters 1-15:* 0-13-182552-6
- *Volume 2—includes Chapters 16-31:* 0-13-182550-X

THE AMERICAN JOURNEY is also available in a convenient Brief Edition.

GET THE BEST PACKAGES

Take advantage of these SPECIAL VALUE PACKAGES available with new copies of THE AMERICAN JOURNEY, THIRD EDITION by Goldfield, et al. Get your students these great savings when your bookstore uses the corresponding package ISBNs below:

- **Combined Edition:**
   —*with FREE Study Guide/Practice Test:* 0-13-130271-X
   —*with FREE* **Common Sense** *by Thomas Paine AND* **The Jungle** *by Upton Sinclair:* 0-13-130272-8

- **Volume I:**
   —*with FREE Study Guide/Practice Test:* 0-13-130273-6
   —*with FREE* **Common Sense** *by Thomas Paine:* 0-13-130274-4

- **Volume II:**
   —*with FREE Study Guide/Practice Test:* 0-13-130275-2
   —*with FREE* **The Jungle** *by Upton Sinclair:* 0-13-130276-0

Additional FREE Value Packages are available. For details, please contact your local Prentice Hall sales representative.

PRENTICE HALL HISTORY
Connecting the past with the future
www.prenhall.com/history

THE WAR FOR INDEPENDENCE
1774–1783

6

> Headquarters, Valley Forge
>
> January 14, 1778
>
> I barely hinted to you my dearest Father my desire to augment the Continental Forces from an untried Source . . . . I would solicit you to cede me a number of your able bodied men Slaves, instead of leaving me a fortune. I would bring about a twofold good, first I would advance those who are unjustly deprived of the Rights of Mankind to a State which would be a proper Gradation between abject Slavery and perfect Liberty and besides I would reinforce the Defenders of Liberty with a number of gallant Soldiers . . . . If I could obtain authority for the purpose I would have a Corps of such men trained, uniformly clad, equip'd and ready in every respect to act at the opening of the next Campaign.
>
> Headquarters, Valley Forge
>
> February 2, 1778
>
> My dear Father,
>
> The more I reflect upon the difficulties and delays which are likely to attend the completing our Continental Regiments, the more anxiously is my mind bent upon the Scheme which I lately communicated to you . . . . I was aware of having that monster popular Prejudice open-mouthed against me . . . [and] of being obliged to combat the arguments and perhaps the intrigues of interested

CHAPTER OUTLINE

The Outbreak of War and The Declaration of Independence, 1774–1776
Mounting Tensions
The Loyalists' Dilemma
British Coercion and Conciliation
The Battles of Lexington and Concord
The Second Continental Congress, 1775–1776
Commander in Chief George Washington
Early Fighting: Massachusetts, Virginia, the Carolinas, and Canada
Independence
Republicanism

The Combatants
Professional Soldiers
Women in the Contending Armies
African American Participation in the War
Native Americans and the War

The War in the North, 1776–1777
The British Army Hesitates: Battles in New York and New Jersey
The Year of the Hangman: Victory at Saratoga and Winter at Valley Forge

The War Widens, 1778–1781
The United States Gains an Ally
Fighting on the Frontier and at Sea
The Land War Moves South
American Counterattacks

The American Victory, 1782–1783
The Peace of Paris
The Components of Success

The War and Society, 1775–1783
The Women's War
Effect of the War on African Americans
The War's Impact on Native Americans
Economic Disruption/The Price of Victory

Conclusion

persons. But zeal for the public Service and an ardent desire to assert the rights of humanity determined me to engage in this arduous business. . . .

You seem to think my dear Father, that men reconciled by long habit to the miseries of their Condition would prefer their ignominious bonds to the untasted Sweets of Liberty, especially when offer'd upon the terms which I propose. I confess indeed the minds of this unhappy species must be debased by a Servitude from which they can hope for no Relief but Death and that every motive to action but Fear must be also nearly extinguished in them. But do you think they are so perfectly moulded to their State as to be insensible that a better exists? Will the galling comparison between themselves and their masters leave them unenlightened in this respect? Can their Self-Love be so totally annihilated as not frequently to induce ardent wishes for a change? . . . I am tempted to believe that this trampled people have so much human left in them, as to be capable of aspiring to the rights of men by noble exertions, if some friend to mankind would point the Road, and give them prospect of Success.

I have long deplored the wretched State of these men and considered in their history, the bloody wars excited in Africa to furnish America with Slaves. The Groans of despairing multitudes toiling for the Luxuries of Merciless Tyrants. I have had the pleasure of conversing with you sometimes upon the means of restoring them to their rights. When can it be better done than when their enfranchisement may be made conducive to the Public Good.

John Laurens

Henry Laurens Papers, vol 12, pp. 305, 390-392.

John Laurens wrote these letters to his father, Henry, at one of the low points of the American Revolution, when victory seemed most remote. The letters reveal much, not only about the course of the war but also about the aspirations and limitations of the Revolutionary generation. Henry, a wealthy slaveholder from South Carolina, was president of the Continental Congress; his son John was an aide to General Washington while the Continental Army occupied winter quarters at Valley Forge.

John, then 23 years old, had been born in South Carolina but educated for the most part in Geneva and London, where he had been exposed to some of the most progressive currents of the Enlightenment. Among these were compassion for the oppressed and the conviction that slavery should be abolished. As the controversy between Britain and its colonies grew from a family quarrel into a war for independence, John became increasingly impatient to enlist in a cause that appealed deeply to him. The American version of republicanism combined a New Whig distrust of central authority with a belief in a government rooted in the public spirit of a virtuous citizenry. Clinging fervently to this ideology, Americans at first expected to defeat the British Army with a zealous citizens' militia. But as the war intensified, they learned that they could prevail only by developing an equally professional fighting force of their own. With vital French assistance, the new American army eventually overcame the enemy, but the Continental Army was often critically short of soldiers. During the summer of 1776, for example, Britain had 30,000 troops in New York City; at Valley Forge in 1777-1778, Washington had 8,200 men fit for duty.

Aware of this discrepancy in manpower, Laurens saw an opportunity to solve two problems at once when he returned to America in 1777. Enlisting slaves in the Army would provide blacks with a stepping stone to freedom and American forces with desperately needed troops. His father, however, was a conditional emancipationist—though he detested slavery—and conditions were never quite right for him. John, however, tried and failed repeatedly to convince legislatures in the deep south to enroll black troops in exchange for their freedom.

John's journey from South Carolina to Europe and back in his idealistic quest for social justice ended on the banks of the Combahee River in South Carolina, where he died in one of the last skirmishes of the war. "Where liberty is," he once wrote, "there is my country." Americans won their independence, but eight long years of warfare strained and in some ways profoundly altered the fabric of American society, though not as much as Laurens had wished.

KEY TOPICS

- Mounting tensions with Britain
- Declaring independence
- The contending forces
- The major campaigns of the Revolution
- The alliance with France
- The peace settlement
- The social effects of the war

THE OUTBREAK OF WAR AND THE DECLARATION OF INDEPENDENCE, 1774–1776

After the Boston Tea Party, both the British and the Americans knew that they were approaching a crisis. A British officer in Massachusetts commented in late 1774 that "it is thought by every body here" that British forces would soon have "to take the field." "The people in general are very enraged," he explained, and some would "defend what they call their Liberties," to the death. Many Americans also expected a military confrontation but continued to hope that the king would not "reason with us only by the roar of his Cannon."

MOUNTING TENSIONS

In May 1774, General Thomas Gage, the commander in chief of the British army in America, replaced Thomas Hutchinson as governor of Massachusetts. After Gage dissolved the Massachusetts legislature, the General Court, it defied him by assembling anyway. Calling itself the Provincial Congress, the legislature in October 1774 appointed an emergency executive body, the **Committee of Safety**, headed by John Hancock, which began stockpiling weapons and organizing militia volunteers. Some localities had already provided for the formation of special companies of **Minute Men**, who were to be ready at "a minute's warning in Case of an alarm."

Enforcing the Continental Association's boycott of British goods, local committees sometimes assaulted suspected loyalists and destroyed their property. The increasingly polarized atmosphere, combined with the drift toward military confrontation, drove a growing wedge between American loyalists and the patriot anti-British American Whigs.

THE LOYALISTS' DILEMMA

Loyalists and Whigs began to part company in earnest during the fall and winter of 1774–1775 as the threat of war mounted. Much like other Americans, loyalists came from all walks of life and all social classes. Most were farmers, though officeholders and professionals were more numerous among them than in the population at large. Many recent immigrants to the colonies, as well as some locally unpopular minorities (Scots in the South, Anglicans in New England), also remained loyal because they felt that the crown offered them some protection against more established Americans. Most loyalists believed, in short, that they had something to lose—including their honor—if America broke with Britain. During the War for Independence, about 19,000 American men would join British provincial units and fight to restore royal authority. (This compares with the perhaps 200,000 who served in some military capacity on the rebel side.) Including those who did not actually fight, the loyalists numbered close to half a million men and women— some 20 percent of the colonies' free population. Of

Chronology

1775	April 19: Battles of Lexington and Concord.
	May 10: Second Continental Congress meets.
	June 17: Battle of Bunker Hill.
	December 31: American attack on Quebec.
1776	January 9: Thomas Paine's *Common Sense*.
	July 4: Declaration of Independence.
	September 15: British take New York City.
	December 26: Battle of Trenton.
1777	January 3: Battle of Princeton.
	September 11: Battle of Brandywine Creek.
	October 17: American victory at Saratoga.
	Runaway inflation begins.
	Continental Army winters at Valley Forge.
1778	February 6: France and the United States sign an alliance.
	June 17: Congress refuses to negotiate with British peace commissioners.
	July 4: George Rogers Clark captures British post in the Mississippi Valley.
	December 29: British capture Savannah.
1779	June 21: Spain declares war on Britain.
	Americans devastate the Iroquois country.
	September 23: John Paul Jones captures the British ship *Serapis*.
1780	May 12: Fall of Charleston, South Carolina.
	October 7: Americans win Battle of Kings Mountain.
	Nathanael Greene takes command in the South.
1781	January 17: Americans defeat British at Battle of Cowpens.
	March 15: Battle of Guilford Court House.
	October 19: Cornwallis surrenders at Yorktown.
1783	March 15: Washington quells the Newburgh "Conspiracy."
	September 3: Peace of Paris signed.
	November 21: British begin evacuating New York.

these, up to 100,000 would leave with the British forces at the end of the war.

BRITISH COERCION AND CONCILIATION

Britain held parliamentary elections in the fall of 1774, but if Americans hoped that the outcome would change the government's policy toward them, they were disappointed. Few British voters paid much attention to colonial affairs or to opposition criticism of Prime Minister Lord North's handling of them. As one member of Parliament later noted, a robbery near London "would make more conversation than all the disturbances of America." North's supporters won easily. Angry and alarmed at the colonists' challenge to Parliament's sovereignty, they took a hard line. Under North's direction, in February 1774, Parliament resolved that Massachusetts was in rebellion and prohibited the New England colonies from trading outside the British Empire or sending their ships to the North Atlantic fishing grounds. Similar restrictions on most of the other colonies soon followed.

Meanwhile, in a gesture of appeasement, Parliament endorsed Lord North's **Conciliatory Proposition** that pledged not to tax the colonies if they would voluntarily contribute to the defense of the empire. British authorities, however, would decide what was a sufficient contribution. Parliament, as a result, would remain sovereign and the colonial legislatures strictly subordinate to it.

Had the Conciliatory Proposition specified a maximum colonial contribution and had it been offered ten years earlier, the colonists might have found it acceptable. Now it was too late. North's government, in any case, had already sent orders to General Gage to take decisive action against the Massachusetts rebels. These orders triggered the first clash between British and American forces.

THE BATTLES OF LEXINGTON AND CONCORD

Gage received his orders on April 14, 1775. On the night of April 18, he assembled seven hundred men on the Boston Common and marched them toward the little towns of Lexington and Concord, some 20 miles away (see Map 6-1). Their mission was to arrest rebel leaders Samuel Adams and John Hancock (then staying in Lexington) and to destroy the military supplies the Committee of Safety had assembled at Concord. Patriots in Boston got wind of the troop movements and sent out riders—one of them the silversmith Paul Revere—to warn their fellows. Adams and Hancock escaped.

When the British soldiers reached Lexington at dawn, they found about seventy armed militiamen drawn up in formation on the village green. Their

MAP 6-1   The Battles of Lexington and Concord
This map shows the area around Boston, Massachusetts, where in April 1775 British and American forces fought the first military engagements of the Revolution.

precise intentions are not clear. Outnumbered ten to one, they probably did not plan to begin a fight. More likely, they were there in a show of defiance, to demonstrate that Americans would not run at the sight of a superior British force.

Months of mounting tension exploded on the Lexington green. A British major ordered the militia to disperse. They were starting to obey when a shot cracked through the dawn stillness. No one now knows who fired. The British responded with a volley

that killed or wounded eighteen Americans.

The British troops pressed on to Concord and burned what few supplies the Americans had not been able to hide. When their rear guard came under patriot fire at Concord's North Bridge, the British panicked. As they retreated to Boston, patriot Minute Men and other militia harried them from both sides of the road. By the time the column reached safety, 273 British soldiers were dead, wounded, or missing. The four thousand Americans who had shot at them along the way suffered nearly a hundred dead, wounded, and missing.

News of the fighting at the **Battles of Lexington and Concord** spread quickly. Patriots in Providence, Rhode Island, knew of it by evening of the Wednesday on which it occurred. Rumors of the fighting had already reached New York by the time an express rider confirmed the stories at noon the following Sunday. The Philadelphia newspaper *Pennsylvania Packet* carried the story the next Monday. Williamsburg's *Virginia Gazette* printed an account on May 4, only two weeks after the event. South Carolinians knew by May 9, and Georgians probably soon after. The speed with which distant colonies heard

This dramatic engraving of the first battle of the American Revolution at Lexington, Massachusetts, on April 19, 1775, is not the photographic work of an eyewitness to events but a close approximation to it. Ralph Earl, a painter, and Amos Doolittle, an engraver, walked over the battlefields at Lexington and Concord a few days after the engagement, interviewed spectators and participants, and collaborated in producing four large engravings that depicted the events with considerable accuracy. This scene from the first plate shows British troops firing on the American militia at Lexington.

This fine portrait of George Washington appears in multiple versions depicting the victorious general against different backgrounds, including the battles of Princeton and Yorktown. The painter, Charles Willson Peale, served under Washington at Princeton, and the French commander at Yorktown, the Count de Rochambeau, took an appropriate version home with him in 1783.

about the outbreak of fighting suggests both the importance Americans attached to it and the extraordinary efforts patriots made to spread word of it. Everywhere, news of Lexington and Concord spurred Whigs into action.

The shots fired that April morning would, in the words of the nineteenth-century Concord philosopher and poet Ralph Waldo Emerson, be "heard round the world." They signaled the start of the American Revolution. And that revolution helped inspire the French Revolution in 1789 and other revolutions in Europe and Latin America.

THE SECOND CONTINENTAL CONGRESS, 1775–1776

By the time the **Second Continental Congress** convened in Philadelphia on May 10, 1775, it had a war on its hands. After Gage's troops had limped back into Boston from Lexington and Concord, patriot militia surrounded the city and laid siege to it. On the first day the Congress met, militia forces from Vermont under Ethan Allen and from Massachusetts under Benedict Arnold overwhelmed the British garrison at Fort Ticonderoga at the southern end of Lake Champlain. Rebel forces elsewhere seized arms and ammunition from royal storehouses.

Assuming leadership of the rebellion, the Congress in the succeeding months became, in effect, a national government. It called for the patchwork of local forces to be organized into the **Continental Army**, authorized the formation of a navy, established a post office, and authorized the printing of paper continental dollars to meet its expenses. Denying Parliament's claim to govern the colonies but not yet ready to declare themselves independent, the delegates sought to preserve their ties to Britain by expressing loyalty to the crown. In the **Olive Branch Petition**, addressed to George III on July 5, they asked the king to protect his American subjects from the military actions ordered by Parliament. The following day, Congress approved the **Declaration of the Causes and Necessity of Taking Up Arms**, asserting the resolve of American patriots "to die freemen, rather than to live slaves." And at the end of the month, it formally rejected North's Conciliatory Proposition.

COMMANDER IN CHIEF GEORGE WASHINGTON

To take command of the patriot forces around Boston—the newly named Continental Army—Congress turned to George Washington. John Adams, a Whig leader from Massachusetts, first nominated Washington. Selecting the Virginian, Adams realized, would help transform a local quarrel in New England into a continental conflict involving all of British North America. Adams and his fellow delegates also expected Washington's leadership to help attract recruits from Virginia, which was then the most populous colony. Despite (or perhaps because of) his experience in the French and Indian War, Washington claimed to feel inadequate to the task, but by attending the Congress in military uniform, he seemed to be volunteering for it.

He was the ideal person for the job. Some of his contemporaries had quicker minds and broader educations; Washington, however, was blessed with good judgment, a profound understanding of both the uses and the limitations of power, and a quiet air of authority. In short, he had the gift of command. He soon also realized that the fate of the patriot cause depended on the survival of the army. Early in the war, he almost suffered catastrophic military defeat at least twice, but he learned from his mistakes and thereafter did not risk lives unnecessarily. The troops in turn revered him. In a crisis, wrote a man who served under him, "his likeness was worth more . . . than the British would have given for his person"—presumably a great deal.

EARLY FIGHTING: MASSACHUSETTS, VIRGINIA, THE CAROLINAS, AND CANADA

General Gage, finding himself besieged in Boston after the fighting at Lexington and Concord, decided to seize and fortify territory south of Boston, where his cannons could command the harbor. But the Americans seized high ground first, entrenching themselves on Breeds Hill north of town. On June 17, 1775, Gage sent 2,200 well-trained soldiers to drive the 1,700 patriot men and boys from their new position. The British succeeded, but at great cost. In three assaults, they suffered more than a thousand casualties. The Americans, who retreated when they ran short of gunpowder, lost just under four hundred dead or wounded. One glum British officer observed afterward that another such victory "would have ruined us." Misnamed for another hill nearby, this encounter has gone down in history as the Battle of Bunker Hill (see Map 6-2).

Washington, who arrived in Boston after the battle, took command of the American forces there in early July. Months of standoff followed, with neither side able to dislodge the other. During the winter of 1775–1776, however, the Americans dragged some sixty cannons—the largest weighing as much as a ton—300 miles through snow and over mountains from Fort Ticonderoga to Boston. In March 1776, Washington mounted the newly arrived guns to overlook Boston harbor, putting the British in an indefensible position. The British then evacuated Boston—which really had no strategic value for them—and moved

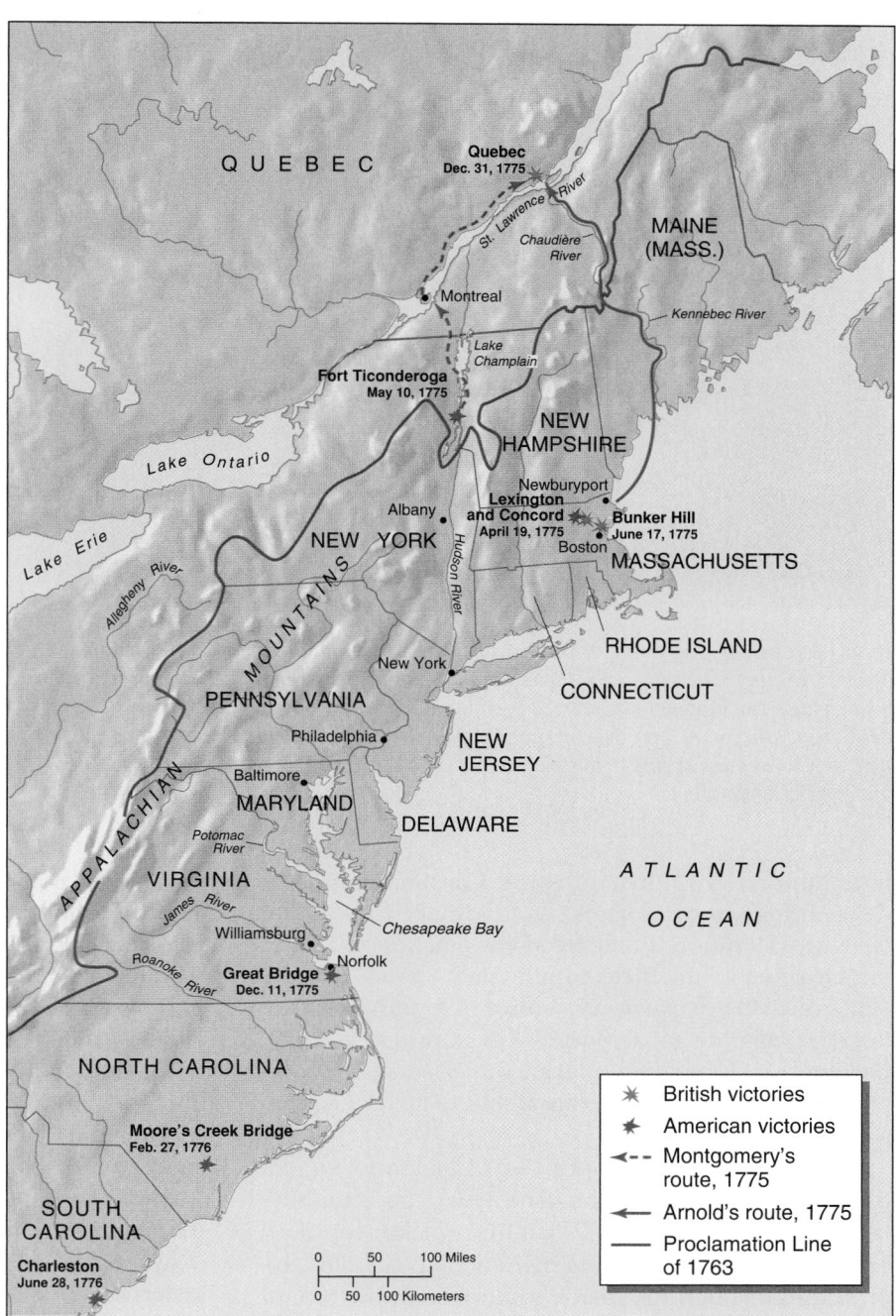

MAP 6-2   Early Fighting, 1775–1776
As this map clearly reveals, even the earliest fighting occurred in widely scattered areas, thereby complicating Britain's efforts to subdue the Americans.

their troops to Halifax, Nova Scotia. New England was for the moment secure for the patriots.

Fighting in the South also went well for the patriots. Virginia's last royal governor, Lord Dunmore, fled the capital, Williamsburg, and set up a base in nearby Norfolk. Promising freedom to slaves who joined him, he succeeded in raising a small force of black and white loyalists. On December 9, 1775, he sent these men, with some British marines, to attack a much larger force of

In this painting of The Battle of Bunker Hill, the artist John Trumbull highlighted the death of Major General Joseph Warren of the Massachusetts militia. Like Trumbull, historians have traditionally emphasized prominent historical figures. More recently, however, they have focused on the common people, such as the militiamen, black and white, who appear at the margins of this picture but who composed the majority of the American forces fighting that day.

nine hundred Virginia and North Carolina patriots at Great Bridge, near Norfolk. As it advanced up a long causeway, Dunmore's little band was slaughtered. Their march, one British officer commented, was an "extravagant Folly." On February 27, a force of loyalist Scots suffered a similar defeat at Moore's Creek Bridge in North Carolina. In June 1776, patriot forces successfully repulsed a large British expedition sent to attack Charleston, South Carolina.

In contrast, an attempt to win Canada to the patriot side met with disaster. Two American armies attacked Canada in late 1775. One quickly captured Montreal. The other, under Benedict Arnold, approached through the Maine wilderness in the face of great hardships. The two forces linked up outside heavily fortified Quebec. On December 31, their hasty attack failed, and most of the Americans who participated in it were captured. The Siege of Quebec dragged on into the spring, when a British fleet relieved the city and fresh troops forced the Americans back to Lake Champlain. Canada remained a British province.

INDEPENDENCE

The stunning American successes in New England and the South in late 1775 and early 1776 bolstered the patriots' confidence as attempts to promote an

Anglo-American reconciliation failed.

In August 1775, King George III rejected the Congress's Olive Branch Petition. Instead, he issued a proclamation declaring the colonies in rebellion and denying them his protection. In December, Parliament barred all exports from the American colonies. These aggressive actions, especially the king's, persuaded many colonists to abandon their loyalty to the crown. More and more, Whigs began to think seriously of declaring full independence from Britain.

At this critical moment, a ne'er-do-well Englishman, recently arrived on American soil, gave the cause of independence a powerful boost. Thomas Paine was by trade a corsetmaker—and twice a fired tax collector. He was also a man of radical ideas—which he expressed forcefully in the everyday English of ordinary people—and he became a powerful polemicist for the American cause. Benjamin Franklin, in London as a lobbyist for the colonies, recognized Paine's talent and gave him letters of introduction when he sailed for America in 1774. In his pamphlet *Common Sense,* published in Philadelphia in January 1776, Paine denounced King George and made the case for independence. He ridiculed the absurdity of "supposing a continent to be perpetually governed by an island." America, he maintained, would be better off on every count if it were independent. The king, Paine said bluntly, was "the Royal Brute" whose tyranny should be thrown off. This assertion, which not long before would have shocked even Whigs, seemed self-evident now in light of the king's rejection of the Olive Branch Petition. Simple common sense, Paine concluded, dictated that " 'TIS TIME TO PART."

Common Sense, which promptly sold more than 100,000 copies throughout the colonies, helped predispose Americans toward independence. Tactical considerations also led patriot leaders toward a formal separation from Great Britain. Such a move would make it easier for America to gain desperately needed aid from foreign countries, especially from England's ancient enemy, France. Declaring independence would also give the local political elites leading the re-

Thomas Jefferson, author of the Declaration of Independence and future president of the United States. Mather Brown, an American artist living in England, painted this picture of Jefferson for John Adams while the two men were in London on diplomatic missions in 1786. A companion portrait of Adams that Jefferson ordered for himself also survives. Brown's sensitive portrait of a thoughtful Jefferson is the earliest known likeness of him.

sistance to British rule a solid legal basis for their newly claimed authority. Accordingly, most of the American states (as the rebellious colonies now called themselves) either instructed or permitted their delegates in the Congress to vote for independence.

On June 7, 1776, Virginian Richard Henry Lee introduced in the Congress a resolution stating that the united colonies "are, and of right ought to be, free and independent States." Postponing a vote on the issue, the Congress appointed a committee to draw up a declaration of independence. The committee turned to a young Virginian named Thomas Jefferson to compose the first draft. "You can write ten times better than I," John Adams supposedly told Jefferson. On June 28, after making revisions in Jefferson's proposed text, the committee presented the document to Congress. In the debate that followed, the South Carolina, Pennsylvania, and New York delegations initially opposed independence. As it became clear that

the majority favored it, the Pennsylvania and South Carolina delegations switched sides, and the New York delegation decided to abstain. A few delegates—including the notable patriot leaders John Dickinson and Robert Morris of Pennsylvania—clung to the hope of maintaining loyal ties to the crown. But when the Congress voted on the resolution for independence on July 2, 1776, all voting delegations approved it. After further tinkering with the wording, the Congress officially adopted the **Declaration of Independence** on July 4, 1776.

Congress intended the declaration to be a justification for America's secession from the British Empire. Jefferson later maintained that he did not write any more than what everyone was thinking. The political theory that lies behind the declaration is known as the **contract theory of government**. Developed by the late-seventeenth-century English philosopher John Locke and others, the contract theory maintains that legitimate government rests on an agreement between the people and their rulers. The people are bound to obey their rulers only so long as the rulers offer them protection. Jefferson's prose, however, transformed what might have been a bland, legalistic rehash of the contract theory into one of history's great statements of human rights.

The Declaration of Independence consists of a magnificently stated opening assumption, two premises, and a powerful conclusion. The opening assumption is that all men are created equal, that they therefore have equal rights, and that they can neither give up these rights nor allow them to be taken away. The first premise—that people establish governments to protect their fundamental rights to life, liberty, and property—is a restatement of contract theory. (With a wonderful flourish reflecting the Enlightenment's optimism about human potential, Jefferson changed "property" to "the pursuit of happiness.") The second premise is a long list of charges meant to prove that George III had failed to defend his American subjects' rights. This indictment, the heart of the declaration, justified the Americans' rejection of their hitherto legitimate ruler. Then followed the dramatic conclusion: that Americans could rightfully overthrow King George's rule and replace it with something more satisfactory to them.

Historians have spilled oceans of ink debating Jefferson's use of the expression "all men." Almost certainly he was thinking in the abstract and meant "humanity in general." In practice, of course, many people were excluded from full participation in eighteenth-century American society. Women had no formal political rights and limited legal rights.

This British engraving published in 1783 depicts one of the many public readings of the Declaration of Independence that occurred throughout the United States during the weeks following its adoption by the Second Continental Congress on July 4, 1776.

Propertyless white and free black men had similarly restricted rights, and slaves enjoyed no rights at all. (Although himself a slaveowner, Jefferson was deeply troubled by American slavery. He had wanted to include a denunciation of the slave trade among the charges against George III in the Declaration of Independence, but the Congress took it out, believing that to blame the king for this inhumane business would appear hypocritical.) But if the words "all men are created equal" had limited practical meaning in 1776, they have ever since confronted Americans with a moral challenge to make good on them.

REPUBLICANISM

Americans reacted to news of the Declaration of Independence with mixed emotions. There was rejoicing as orators read the declaration to great crowds. Soldiers fired noisy salutes, and candles lit up the windows of public buildings at night. But even many who favored independence worried about how Americans would govern themselves. Most Whigs, animated by the political ideology known as **republicanism**, thought a republican government was best suited to American society.

John Adams once complained that republicanism was too shadowy a concept to define, and indeed it was a complex, changing body of ideas, values, and assumptions. Closely related to country (New Whig) ideology, republicanism was derived from the political ideas of classical antiquity, Renaissance Europe, and early modern England. It held that self-government—either directly by the citizens of a country or indirectly by their elected representatives—provided a more reliable foundation for the good society and individual freedom than did rule by kings. Thus drawing on contract theory, as in the Declaration of Independence, republicanism called for government by consent of the governed. Drawing on country ideology, it was suspicious of excessively centralized government and insistent on the need for a virtuous, public-spirited citizenry. The benefits of monarchy depended on the variable abilities of monarchs; the character of republican government depended on the virtue of the people. Republicanism therefore helped to give the American Revolution a moral dimension.

But other than a state that was not ruled by a hereditary king, what was a republic? And what were the chances that one would survive? Every educated person knew, of course, that ancient Rome and Athens had been republics. Classical political theory, beginning with the ancient Greek thinkers Plato and Aristotle, had insisted that republics could endure only as long as their citizens remained virtuous and self-sacrificing. Once individual citizens, greedy for wealth and power, began fighting among themselves, a republic would certainly collapse. A failed republic would give way to the despotism of one-man rule or to oligarchy—rule by a narrow clique of rich men—or, worst of all, to the "mob rule" of ignorant and violent common people. Europe's three surviving republics in the eighteenth century—the Netherlands, Switzerland, and Venice—seemed to bear out this dismal picture: All were rather corrupt and uninspiring societies, and none of them was at all democratic.

But Americans had at hand a more recent example of a republic than ancient Athens or Rome, one more closely linked to their own history than the republics of eighteenth-century Europe. During the

English Civil War of the mid-seventeenth century, English Puritans had for a time replaced the monarchy with a republican "Commonwealth," dedicated to advancing the "common weal," or common good. Most eighteenth-century Americans thought of the Puritan Commonwealth as a misguided product of fanaticism that had ended in a military dictatorship. However, some New Englanders, spiritual descendants of the Puritans, considered the Commonwealth to have been a noble experiment. To them, the American Revolution offered another chance to establish a republic of the godly.

"When the mere Politician weighs the Danger or Safety of his Country," warned one clergyman, "he computes them in Proportion to its Fortresses, Arms, Money, Provisions, Numbers of Fighting Men, and its Enemies." But, the clergyman continued, the "Christian Patriot" calculates them "by its Numbers of Sinful or praying People, and its Degrees of Holiness or Vice." Such language recalled the Great Awakening; it reached beyond the upper classes who had been directing resistance to the British and mobilized ordinary people for what their ministers repeatedly assured them was a just war against sin and despotism. Out of this fusion of republican theory (with which only the educated were familiar) and the religious heritage that all Americans understood, a common belief developed that Americans must have "resolution enough to forgo Self gratification" and be willing to stake their all "upon the prospect of Securing freedom and happiness to future Generations."

THE COMBATANTS

At the outset of the American Revolution, republican fervor produced a spontaneous eruption of patriotism that to skeptical foreign observers looked like religious fanaticism. The experience of Lancaster, Pennsylvania, where more men responded to a call for volunteers than were then needed, leaving disappointed men behind, was shared elsewhere. But this enthusiastic flocking to the colors eventually waned, and in any case, its results were often unsatisfactory.

Republican theory mistrusted professional armies as the instruments of tyrants. A free people, republicans insisted, relied for defense on their own patriotism. When individual or community rights were in danger, free men should grab their muskets from over the fireplace, assemble as the local militia, take care of the problem, and go home (see "American Views: A British Woman Observes an American Militia Exercise in 1775"). But militiamen, as one American general observed, had trouble coping with "the shocking scenes of war" because they were not "steeled by habit or fortified by military pride." In real battles, they often proved unreliable. Americans therefore faced a hard choice: Develop a professional army or lose the war. In the end, they did what they had to do. While state militias continued to offer support, it was the disciplined forces of the Continental Army that won the crucial battles. To be sure, when the war was over, Americans tried to forget about their professional troops; in American mythology, it was the "embattled farmers"—Minute Men at Lexington and Concord, swamp fighters in the South—who had won independence. But long before the struggle was over, toughened Continental soldiers knew better.

PROFESSIONAL SOLDIERS

Drawing on their colonial experience and on republican theory, the new state governments first tried to meet their military needs by relying on the militia and by creating new units based on short-term enlistments. Officers, particularly in the North, were often elected, and their positions depended on personal popularity. As a result, their orders sometimes sounded more like requests than commands, and rules were lax. Discipline became a major problem in both the militia and the new state units, and often volunteers had barely received basic training before their term of duty ended and they returned home.

Washington tightened things up in the new Continental Army. Eventually, he prevailed on Congress to adopt stricter regulations and to require enlistments for three years or the duration of the war. Although he used militia effectively, his consistent aim was to turn the Continental Army into a disciplined force that could defeat the British in the large engagements of massed troops characteristic of eighteenth-century European warfare. Guerrilla fighters shooting from behind trees like "savages" had their place in the American war effort, but they could never win a decisive, formal battle. And only such a "civilized" victory would impress the other European powers and establish the legitimacy of the United States.

Many soldiers of fortune, as well as a few idealists, offered their services to American representatives in Europe. So many came to the United States that both Washington and Congress soon regarded most of them as nuisances. But several proved especially valuable in helping Washington forge a professional army. France's 19-year-old Marquis de Lafayette was one of the youngest, wealthiest, and most idealistic. Two Poles, Tadeusz Kosciuszko, an

AMERICAN VIEWS

A British Woman Observes an American Militia Exercise in 1775

The following description of North Carolinians preparing for war in 1775 comes from the travel journal of Janet Schaw, a Scotswoman visiting her brother Robert in America. Robert Schaw, although he was appointed a colonel in the North Carolina militia, disapproved of the American cause and eventually refused to take the oath of allegiance to the new state government. His wife, by contrast, according to Janet Schaw, was "so rooted an American, that she detests every thing that is European." Early in June 1775 Janet Schaw saw the militia train outside of Wilmington under their commander, Robert Howe, who later became a major general in the Continental Army. She returned to Scotland in late 1775.

- What does this passage suggest about Janet Schaw's own views of the American cause?
- How accurately do you think it reflects the effectiveness of milita forces?
- What does it suggest about the relationship between patriots and loyalists?

We came down in the morning in time for the review, which the heat made as terrible to the spectators as to the soldiers, or what you please to call them. They had certainly fainted under it, had not the constant draughts of grog supported them. Their exercise was that of bush-fighting, but it appeared so confused and so perfectly different from any thing I ever saw, I cannot say whether they performed it well or not; but this I know that they were heated with rum till capable of committing the most shocking outrages. We stood in the balcony of Doctor Cobham's [a future loyalist] house and they were reviewed on a field mostly covered with what are called here scrubby oaks which are only a little better than brushwood. They at last however assembled on the plain field, and I must really laugh while I recollect their figures: 2000 men in their shirts and trousers, preceded by a very ill beat-drum and a fiddler, who was also in his shirt with a long sword and a cue at his hair, who played with all his might. They made indeed a most unmartial appearance. But the worst figure there can shoot from behind a bush and kill even a General Wolfe.

Before the review was over, I hear a cry of tar and feather. I was ready to faint at the idea of this dreadful operation. I would have gladly quitted the balcony, but was so much afraid the Victim was one of my friends, that I was not able to move; and he indeed proved to be one, tho' in a humble station. For it was Mr. Neilson's [a loyalist] poor English groom. You can hardly conceive what I felt when I saw him dragged forward, poor devil, frighted out of his wits. However at the request of some of the officers, who had been Neilson's friends, his punishment was changed into that of mounting on a table and begging pardon for having smiled at the regt. He was then drummed and fiddled out of the town, with a strict prohibition of ever being seen in it again.

Source: [Janet Schaw], *Journal of a Lady of Quality; Being the Narrative of a Journey from Scotland to the West Indies, North Carolina, and Portugal, in the Years 1774 to 1776*, ed. Evangeline Walker Andrews in Collaboration with Charles McLean Andrews (1923). Yale University Press.

engineer, and Kazimierz Pulaski, a cavalry commander who would be mortally wounded at the Battle of Savannah in 1779, also rendered good service. Johann Kalb, a bogus baron from Germany, became a general and died heroically at Camden, South Carolina, in 1780. Most useful of all, probably, was Baron von Steuben. His title, too, was new, but he had experience in the Prussian army, continental Europe's best. He also knew how to get along with American soldiers by explaining the reasons for his orders. He became the Continental Army's drillmaster, and thanks partly to him, Washington's troops increasingly came to resemble their disciplined European counterparts.

The enemy British troopers—and the nearly thirty thousand German mercenaries (Americans called them "Hessians") whom the British government also employed—offered Americans the clearest model of a professional army. British regulars were not (as Americans, then and later, assumed) the "dregs of society." Most enlisted men did come from the lower classes and from economically depressed areas, but many also had skills. British officers usually came from wealthy families or had simply purchased their commissions. Only in rare cases did a man rise from the enlisted ranks to commissioned officer status.

Most British troops carried the "Brown Bess" musket. With bayonet attached, it was almost 6 feet long and weighed over 16 pounds. It fired a lead ball slightly more than 1/2 inch in diameter, which might hit its target at up to 100 yards. Skilled troops could get off more than two rounds per minute under combat conditions. In battle, soldiers usually stood close together in lines three deep. They were expected to withstand bombardment without flinching, fire on command in volleys, charge with the bayonet, and use their heavy musket stock (the wooden end) to crush the skulls of any wounded enemy they strode over.

Military life was tough. On the march, seasoned troops carrying 60-pound packs normally covered about 15 miles a day but could go 30 miles in a "forced" march. In most weather conditions, they wore heavy woolen uniforms dyed bright red for visibility on smoke-filled battlefields (hence their nickname "Redcoats"). In their barracks, British soldiers doubled up in a bed slightly over 4 feet wide; in the field, they were often wet, crawling with lice, and hungry. Under the best conditions, they ate mainly beef or salt pork and bread. They were frequently undernourished, however, and many more died of disease than of injury in battle. Medical care was, by modern standards, primitive. Treatments for illness included bleeding and purging (induced vomiting and diarrhea). Serious arm or leg wounds usually meant amputation, without antiseptics or anesthetics. But unless a man was extraordinarily lucky, a body wound or amputation usually proved fatal. If loss of blood or infection did not kill him immediately, tetanus probably would do so later.

Severe discipline held soldiers in line. Striking an officer or deserting could bring death; lesser offenses usually incurred a beating. Several hundred lashes, "well laid on" with the notorious cat-o'-nine-tails (a whip with multiple cords, each ending in a nasty little knot or a metal ball), were not uncommon.

Soldiers amused themselves with gambling (despite regulations against it) and drinking. As one foreign officer serving with the British lamented, America was a terrible country where one drank "to get warm, or to get cool, or . . . because you get no letters." Perhaps two-thirds of the Redcoats were illiterate, and all suffered from loneliness and boredom. Camaraderie and a legendary loyalty to their regiments sustained them.

After the winter of 1777–1778, conditions in the Continental Army came to resemble those of the British army. Like British regulars, American recruits tended to be low on the social scale. They included young men without land, indentured servants, some criminals and vagrants—in short, men who lacked better prospects. The chances for talented enlisted men to win an officer's commission were greater in the Continental Army than in the British army. As a German prisoner of war observed, American troops tended to be taller than their British counterparts. And despite their ragged uniforms, they carried themselves like soldiers. Indeed, Continental soldiers frequently had little more than "their ragged shirt flaps to cover their nakedness," and more than once their bare marching feet left bloody tracks in the snow.

Both British and American authorities had trouble supplying their troops. Both sides suffered from bureaucratic inefficiencies, but the fundamental problems of each were different. The British had plenty of hard-coin money with a stable value, which many American merchants and farmers were happy to take in payment for supplies. But the British had to rely mostly on supplies shipped to them from the British Isles. The Continental Army, by contrast, had to pay for supplies in paper money, both Continental dollars and state-issued currency, whose value sank steadily as the war progressed. After 1780, the burden of provisioning the Continental Army fell on the states, which did little better than Congress had done. Unable to obtain sufficient supplies, the army

Overview

Important Battles of the Revolutionary War

	Battle	Date	Outcome
Early Fighting	Lexington and Concord, Massachusetts	April 19, 1775	Contested
	Fort Ticonderoga, New York	May 10, 1775	American victory
	Breeds Hill ("Bunker Hill"), Boston, Massachusetts	June 17, 1775	Contested
	Great Bridge, Virginia	Dec. 9, 1775	American victory
	Quebec, Canada	Dec. 31, 1775	British repulse American assault
	Moore's Creek Bridge, North Carolina	Feb. 27, 1776	American victory
The War in the North	Brooklyn Heights, New York	Aug. 27, 1776	British victory
	White Plains, New York	Oct. 28, 1776	British victory
	Trenton, New Jersey	Dec. 26, 1776	American victory
	Princeton, New Jersey	Jan. 3, 1777	American victory
	Brandywine Creek, Pennsylvania	Sept. 11, 1777	British victory (opened way for British to take Philadelphia)
	Saratoga, New York	Sept. 19 and Oct. 17, 1777	American victory (helped persuade France to form an alliance with United States)
	Monmouth Court House, N. J.	June 28, 1778	Contested
The War on the Frontier	Wyoming Valley, Pennsylvania	June and July 1778	British victory
	Kaskaskia and Cahokia, Illinois; Vincennes, Indiana	July 4, 1778– Feb. 23, 1779	American victories strengthen claims to Mississippi Valley
	Cherry Valley, New York	Nov. 11, 1778	British victory
The War in the South	Savannah, Georgia	Dec. 29, 1778	British victory (took control of Georgia)
	Kettle Creek, Georgia	Feb. 14, 1779	American victory
	Savannah, Georgia	Sept. 3– Oct. 28, 1779	British victory (opened way for British to take Charleston)
	Charleston, South Carolina	Feb. 11– May 12, 1780	British victory
	Camden, South Carolina	Aug. 16, 1780	British victory
	Kings Mountain, South Carolina	Oct. 7, 1780	American victory
	Cowpens, South Carolina	Jan. 17, 1781	American victory
	Guilford Court House, North Carolina	March 15, 1781	Contested
	Yorktown, Virginia	Aug. 30– Oct. 19, 1781	American victory (persuaded Britain to end the war)

Ye Foil'd, Ye Baffled Brittons This Behold   To fave their Country and Promote its Weal
Nor longer urge your Pardons,Threats or Gold; Difdaining Bribes to wound a righteous Caufe
See in each virtuous face Patr'otic Zeal   While ANDRE falls a victim to the Laws.

This print, Ye Foil'd, Ye Baffled Brittons, shows the capture of Major John André, the British agent who acted as the go-between for British authorities and the American General Benedict Arnold, who planned to turn over the American fortress at West Point to them. The three militiamen who captured André, who was later hanged as a spy, reportedly refused a bribe for his release. The strange facial expressions of all the participants were probably the artist's crude attempt to indicate surprise.

sometimes provoked resentment by threatening to seize them by force. This, in turn, increased the public's republican distrust of its own professional army.

Feeling themselves outcasts from an uncaring society, the professional soldiers of the Continental Army developed a community of their own. The soldiers were "as strict a band of brotherhood as Masons," one later wrote, and their spirit kept them together in the face of misery. They groused, to be sure—sometimes alarmingly. In May 1780, Connecticut troops at Washington's camp in Morristown, New Jersey, staged a brief mutiny. A more serious mutiny erupted on January 1, 1781, when armed units from Pennsylvania stationed in New Jersey marched to Philadelphia demanding their arrears in pay. The Pennsylvania Executive Council met part of the soldiers' demands, but some of the men left the service. Washington ordered subsequent mutinies by New Jersey and Pennsylvania troops suppressed by force.

Occasionally, American officers let their disgruntlement get out of hand. The most notorious such case was that of Benedict Arnold, a general who compiled a distinguished record during the first three years of the war but then came to feel himself shabbily treated by Congress and his superiors. Seeking better rewards for his abilities, he offered to surrender the strategic fort at West Point (which he commanded) to the enemy. Before he could act, however, his plot was discovered, and he fled to the British, serving with them until the end of the war. Among Americans, his name became a synonym for traitor.

What was perhaps the most serious expression of army discontent—one that threatened the future of republican institutions and civilian government in the United Sates—occurred in March 1783, after the fighting was over. At the time, Washington's troops were stationed near Newburgh, New York, waiting to disband and for the Congress to decide how to settle up with them. During the war, the Congress had promised officers a pension of half-pay for life (the custom in Great Britain), but now many veterans demanded instead full pay for six years. When the Congress failed to grant real assurances that any pay would be forthcoming, hotheaded young officers called a meeting that could have led to an armed uprising and military coup. General Washington, who had scrupulously deferred to civilian authority throughout the war, asked permission to address the gathering and, in a dramatic speech, subtly warned the men of all that they might lose by insubordination. A military coup would "open the flood Gates of Civil discord" and "deluge" the nation in blood; loyalty now, he said, would be "one more distinguished proof" of their patriotism. With the fate of the Revolution and the honor of the army hanging in the balance, the movement collapsed. Officers and politicians behind the "conspiracy" were probably only bluffing, using the threat of a discontented army to frighten the states into granting the Congress the power (which it then lacked) to levy taxes so that it would have the funds to pay the army. If so, they may not have realized the potential harm they threatened. In any case, the Continental Army thereafter disbanded without further serious incidents.

WOMEN IN THE CONTENDING ARMIES

Women accompanied many units on both sides, as was common in eighteenth-century warfare. A few were prostitutes. Some were officers' wives or mistresses, but most were the married or common-law consorts of ordinary soldiers. These "camp followers" cooked and washed for the troops, occasionally helped load artillery, and provided most of the nursing care. A certain number in a company were subject to military orders and were authorized to draw rations and pay.

The role of these women found its way into American folklore in the legend of Molly Pitcher (perhaps Mary Ludwig Hays, the wife of a Continental artillery sergeant), who heroically carried water to gunners to cool them and their overheated guns at the Battle of Monmouth Court House in 1778. Numberless, nameless other women accompanying the troops also found themselves under fire. A British officer fighting in New York, for example, reported discovering three American bodies, one a woman with cartridges in her hands. A few women even managed to serve in the Continental Army's ranks. One was discharged only when she was hospitalized for illness and her sex was discovered.

AFRICAN AMERICAN PARTICIPATION IN THE WAR

Early in the war, some royal officials sought to recruit black slaves into the loyalist forces with a promise of freedom. Such was the case with Lord Dunmore, for example, whose black and white troops met disaster at Great Bridge in some of the earliest fighting of the war. Unfortunately for the British, these offers proved counterproductive, frightening and enraging potentially loyalist slaveowners and driving them to the Whig side. Thus it was not until June 30, 1779, that the British commander in chief, Sir Henry Clinton, promised to allow slaves who fled from rebel owners to join the royal troops to "follow . . . any Occupation" they wished. Hedged as this promise of freedom was, news of it spread quickly among the slave communities, and late in the war, enough black people flocked to the British army in South Carolina and Georgia to make feeding and housing them a serious problem.

The British shared the racial prejudices of many Americans, however, and, despite their efforts to recruit African Americans, were reluctant to arm them. Instead, the British put most of the ex-slaves to work as agricultural or construction workers (many of the free and enslaved blacks accompanying American troops were similarly employed). A few relatively

John Laurens, who hoped to raise black troops in South Carolina as a prelude to the general abolition of slavery, was the only member of George Washington's staff to be killed in battle. This commemorative portrait by Charles Willson Peale bears the Latin inscription "sweet and proper it is to die for one's country."

well equipped black British dragoons (mounted troops), however, saw some combat in South Carolina, much to the horror of local Whigs. Some of these troops later formed the nucleus of the postwar First and Second British West India Regiments.

Approximately five thousand African Americans fought against the British and for American independence, hundreds of them in the Continental Army. Many were freemen from Massachusetts and Rhode Island. Several free black men served among the defenders at Bunker Hill, and at least one distinguished himself sufficiently for his commander to commend him as "an experienced officer as well as an excellent soldier."

But farther south, as we have seen, John Laurens, a young Carolina patriot, repeatedly but vainly tried to convince the South Carolina assembly to raise and arm black troops. (On the contrary, the legislature eventually voted to give slaves confiscated from loyalists to white volunteers as a reward for their service in the state regiments.) It is therefore scarcely surprising that, as one Whig put it, many black people were "a little Toryfied," especially in the South.

NATIVE AMERICANS AND THE WAR

At first, most of the approximately 200,000 Native Americans east of the Mississippi River would probably have preferred to remain neutral. Like some Oneidas who were explicit on the subject, other Indian peoples generally hoped to stay out of the white man's conflict. Knowing that Indian allies would cost money and might be unpredictable, the British and Americans initially took them at their word. But Indians' skills and manpower were valuable, and by 1776 both sides sought their assistance. Forced to choose, many Native Americans favored the British, hoping thereby to safeguard their lands. "Remember," one Cherokee chief once told Virginians, the crucial "difference is about our land." Their prewar experience made them believe that British officials would protect them against white settlers whereas an American victory would sweep away all restraints on these incursions. The British were also in a better position to provide trade goods and arms. Accordingly, many Indian peoples, including the Cherokees, Creeks, Choctaws, and Chickasaws in the South, decided that it was in their interest to back the British. Cherokee warriors therefore raided the southern frontier starting in 1776. Virginians, North and South Carolinians, and ultimately Tennesseans countered with expeditions that repeatedly devastated Cherokee towns. But when older chiefs sought peace, Dragging Canoe (Tsi'yugunsi'ny) and the more militant younger men established new communities on the Chickamauga River in northern Georgia and continued to fight.

Pushed and pulled by the British and the Americans, other Indian groups also split. Among these were the members of the powerful Iroquois Confederation in upstate New York. Under the leadership of Thayendanegea—known to whites as Joseph Brant—the Mohawks and some of the other Iroquois nations supported the British, while most of the Oneidas and Tuscaroras joined the Americans. Thus some Iroquois attacked the northern frontiers of New York and Pennsylvania in 1777 and 1778; another Iroquois guided the American expedition that retaliated in 1779. Brother, sometimes quite literally, killed brother.

In other cases, though, the war promoted greater unity among Native Americans. Despite factionalism, the Shawnees, Delawares, Miamis, Wyandots, and others in the Ohio Valley eventually forged an alliance to preserve their control of the area with British support. And a few Native American nations even aided the Americans with relative unanimity. Most of these were small groups, like the Catawbas of South Carolina, who lived in the midst of white settlements.

In sum, the British had more Indian allies, but they seldom made unrestricted use of them. Because Native Americans pursued their own purposes, British control of them was frequently tenuous, and the result could sometimes be counterproductive. In one such incident an Indian attack in the Hudson River Valley resulted in the mistaken scalping of Jane McCrae, the fiancee of a British officer. Whig propagandists exploited this tragedy to the fullest. Neither side, however, had a monopoly on atrocities; both the Americans and the British committed more than their share.

THE WAR IN THE NORTH, 1776–1777

The Revolutionary War can be divided into three phases. In the first, from the outbreak of fighting in 1775 to 1778, most of the important battles took place in New England, New York, New Jersey, and Pennsylvania. During these years, the Americans faced the British alone. But in 1778, France entered the war on the American side, opening the second phase of the war. Fighting in the second phase would rage from 1778 to 1781 mainly in the South, at sea, and on the western frontier. The third phase of the war, from late 1781 to 1783, saw little actual fighting. With American victory assured, attention shifted to the diplomatic maneuvering leading up to the Peace of Paris (1783), which ended the war and recognized American independence.

THE BRITISH ARMY HESITATES: BATTLES IN NEW YORK AND NEW JERSEY

During the first phase of the war, the British concentrated on subduing New England, the hotbed of what they saw as "rebellious principles." Replacing General Gage, the government appointed Sir William Howe as commander in chief of British forces and his brother, Richard Howe, as admiral of the naval forces in North American waters. New York City had been the headquarters of the British army during the late colonial period, and the Howes decided to make it their base of operations. To counter this move, Washington moved his forces to New York

MAP 6-3 The War in the North, 1776–1777
Most of the fighting between the British and Americans during the first part of the war occurred in the North, partly because British authorities assumed that the New England colonies were the most rebellious.

in the spring of 1776. In August 1776, the Howes landed troops on Long Island and, in the Battle of Brooklyn Heights, quickly drove the American forces deployed there from Brooklyn Heights and back to Manhattan Island (see Map 6-3).

Following instructions to negotiate peace as well as wage war, Richard Howe then met with three envoys from Congress on Staten Island on September 11, 1776. The British commanders were prepared to offer fairly generous terms but could not grant independence. The Americans would accept nothing less. So, despite a fine meal of cold meat and wine, the meeting produced no substantive negotiations.

In the ensuing weeks, British forces overwhelmed Washington's forces, driving them out of Manhattan and then, moving north, clearing them from the area around the city at the Battle of White Plains. But the Howes were hesitant to deal a crushing blow, and the Americans were able to retreat across New Jersey into Pennsylvania. The American cause seemed lost, however; the Congress fled from Philadelphia to Baltimore, and the Continental Army almost melted away. The enlistments for most of his troops expired on January 1, and Washington realized that without a success, he would soon have no army left.

On Christmas night, he led his forces back across the icy Delaware from Pennsylvania and, in the Battle of Trenton, launched an unorthodox surprise attack on a garrison of Hessian mercenaries at Trenton, New Jersey, on the morning of December 26. Still in the midst of their Christmas celebrations, the Hessians quickly surrendered. A week later, in the Battle of Princeton, Washington overwhelmed a British force at Princeton, New Jersey. Thereafter, Washington withdrew to winter quarters in Morristown, New Jersey, and the Howes made no further effort to pursue him. Both sides suspended operations until the spring.

"These are the times that try men's souls." So wrote Tom Paine—briefly a volunteer in the Continental Army—of these difficult months. "The summer soldier and the sunshine patriot will, in this crisis, shrink from the service of his country; but he that stands it NOW, deserves the love and thanks of man and woman."

The victories at Trenton and Princeton boosted morale and saved the American cause. But why did the Howes not annihilate the Continental Army while they had the chance? Perhaps, as a favorite Whig ditty had it, it was because Sir William Howe was "snug" abed with his mistress in New York. More significantly, the Howe brothers themselves were not entirely in favor of the war. Seeking to restore peace as well as end the rebellion, they wanted to regain loyal subjects, not alienate them. But if they had inflicted a crushing defeat on the Americans, they would have risked making them permanent enemies of British rule. In short, the British had sound political reasons for not beating the Americans too thoroughly. By the time it later became apparent that this cautious strategy was not working and the Howe brothers had been replaced with more aggressive commanders, the British had lost their best chance to win the war.

THE YEAR OF THE HANGMAN: VICTORY AT SARATOGA AND WINTER AT VALLEY FORGE

Contemporaries called 1777 the Year of the Hangman because the triple sevens suggested a row of gallows. Living up to its ominous name, it was indeed a crucial year for the American cause.

The British began the year by mounting a major effort to end the rebellion. Their strategy was to send a force south from Canada down the Hudson River to link up with the Howes in New York City, separate New England from the rest of the states, and then crush the rebellion in that most recalcitrant region. Unfortunately, there was no effort to coordinate strategy between the forces advancing from Canada and the forces under the command of the Howes in New York. Thus in the end, poorly planned, poorly executed, and unsupported from the South, the campaign ended in disaster for the British.

Some five thousand Redcoats and three thousand German mercenaries assembled in Canada during the winter of 1776–1777. Ravaged by disease, the troops were unable to bury their dead until the frozen ground thawed in the spring. (To amuse himself, the officer in charge of the morgue arranged the dead around a room in lifelike poses, a morbid joke that did nothing to calm the nerves of survivors.) Under the command of the jaunty, high-living, and popular "Gentleman Johnny" Burgoyne, the army finally set off in June with 1,500 horses hauling its heavy artillery and ponderous supply train. A second, smaller column, supported by an Indian force under Thayendanegea (Joseph Brant) set out to the west to capture an American fort near Oriskany, New York, and then join up with Burgoyne's main force.

Crossing Lake Champlain, Burgoyne's army made a splendid spectacle. Indians in lightly bobbing canoes led the way, followed by row after row of boats filled with uniformed regulars resplendent in the bright sunshine. On July 5, Burgoyne's army recaptured Fort Ticonderoga, but success eluded him after that.

Trouble began as the troops started moving overland through the woods at the southern end of the lake. Forced to clear away huge trees in its path felled by American axmen, the army crawled along at only 2 or 3 miles a day. Early in August, the column under Colonel Barry St. Leger that had been sent west from the Montreal area failed to capture the American fort near Oriskany and turned back to Canada. Burgoyne's Indian allies under Joseph Brant likewise went home. Promised reinforcements never arrived. Ten days later, a Whig militia force wiped out a force of eight hundred men that

Burgoyne had sent into Vermont to round up badly needed horses.

By October 1777, Burgoyne's army was down to less than six thousand men and facing disaster. A force of nearly three thousand Continentals and nine thousand militia, commanded by General Horatio Gates, had now assembled to confront the British. The Americans exerted relentless pressure on the harassed and dispirited invaders. Unable to break through the American lines, Burgoyne surrendered to Gates following the Battle of Saratoga on October 17, 1777.

Burgoyne's defeat was a stunning reversal for the British. It also gave the American cause a significant boost in the eyes of foreign observers. It would prove an important factor in convincing the French, in particular, eager for a way to strike back at their old enemy, the British, to recognize America as an ally and join the fighting on the American side.

While Burgoyne was making his way to disaster, General William Howe, rather than moving north to support him, was making plans to destroy Washington's army and capture Philadelphia. In July 1777, Howe's troops sailed from New York to Chesapeake Bay and from there marched on Philadelphia from the south. They met Washington's army on the banks of Brandywine Creek, near the Pennsylvania–Delaware border. An American teenager who fought for the first time that day recalled that some men stiffened their courage by drinking a concoction of liquor and gunpowder. The young man himself could not stomach it, but it may have worked for some of his companions. They put up a good fight before giving way with a loss of 1,200 killed or captured (twice as many as the British).

Howe occupied Philadelphia, and his men settled down in comfortable winter quarters. The Congress fled to York, Pennsylvania, and the Continental Army established its own winter camp outside Philadelphia, at Valley Forge. Here Washington was joined by his wife, Martha, in a small stone farmhouse, surrounded by the log huts that his men built for themselves.

The Continental Army's miserable winter at **Valley Forge** has become legendary in American history. Suffering from cold, disease, and starvation, as many as 2,500 soldiers died. Meanwhile, some congressmen and a few unhappy officers intrigued unsuccessfully to replace Washington with Gates as commander in chief. Yet despite the suffering of the troops, the Continental Army managed, over the course of the winter, to transform itself into a disciplined professional army. Under the watchful eye of General von Steuben, the soldiers drilled endlessly.

Just before the encampment broke up in the spring, they put on an impressive demonstration of their new skills, including a precisely timed wave of massed musket volleys. Pleased observers felt that Washington at last had an army capable of meeting the British on equal terms. With the coming of spring, American prospects improved dramatically.

THE WAR WIDENS, 1778–1781

Since late 1776, Benjamin Franklin and a team of American diplomats had been in Paris negotiating French support for the patriot cause. In the winter of 1777–1778, aware that a Franco-American alliance was close, Parliament belatedly tried to end the rebellion by giving the Americans everything they wanted except independence itself. A peace commission sailed to America with authorization to grant the former colonies full autonomy, including the exclusive right to tax themselves, in return for a resumption of allegiance to the crown. But France and the United States concluded an alliance on February 6, 1778, and news of it reached America before the British commission arrived. Seeing independence within reach, Congress refused to negotiate.

Foreign intervention would transform the American Revolution into a virtual world war, engaging British forces in heavy fighting not only in North America but also in the West Indies and India. In the end, had it not been for French assistance, the American side probably would not have won the clear-cut victory it did.

THE UNITED STATES GAINS AN ALLY

If the American victory at Saratoga had persuaded the French that the United States had a viable future, Washington's defeat at Brandywine Creek suggested it was a fragile one. Hoping to get even with their old enemy, Britain, the French had already been secretly supplying some aid to the United States. They now became convinced that they needed to act quickly lest further reverses force the Americans to agree to a reconciliation with Britain. The agreements they signed with the United States included both a commercial treaty and a military alliance. Both sides promised to fight together until Britain recognized the independence of the United States, and France pledged not to seek the return of lands in North America.

French entry into the war was the first step in the consolidation of a formidable alliance of European powers eager to see Britain humbled and to gain trading rights in the former British colonies. In turn, France persuaded Spain to declare war on Britain in June 1779. Unlike France, Spain never recognized the independence of the United States and would give it only minimal financial aid. Spain did, however, contribute important logistical support. Much of the salt used to preserve American soldiers' provisions came from Spanish possessions. American agents also purchased other supplies in Spanish New Orleans, and American privateers used New Orleans as a base. More important, the Spanish fleet augmented the naval power of the countries arrayed against Great Britain.

Meanwhile, Catherine the Great of Russia suggested that European powers form a League of Armed Neutrality to protect their trade with the United States and other warring countries against British interference. Denmark and Sweden soon joined; Austria, the Netherlands, Portugal, Prussia, and Sicily eventually followed. Britain, however, quickly went to war with Holland, ostensibly over another issue (to avoid war with the League), but really to cut off Dutch trade with the United States.

Great Britain thus found itself nearly completely isolated and even, briefly, threatened with invasion. In the spring of 1779, a joint Franco-Spanish fleet tried to ferry thousands of French troops across the English Channel but abandoned the effort after weeks at sea. These threats did not frighten the British leaders into suing for peace. On the contrary, they inspired a wave of patriotism that swelled enlistments in the armed forces. But facing challenges on a worldwide scale, British officials were forced to make several important changes in policy and strategy.

Accordingly, early in the spring of 1778, the British replaced the Howes with a tough new commander, Sir Henry Clinton, instructing him to detach some of his troops to attack the French West Indies. To replace them, Clinton sought closer cooperation with Britain's Indian and loyalist allies. Knowing that he now faced a serious French threat, Clinton also began consolidating his forces. He evacuated Philadelphia and pulled his troops slowly back across New Jersey to New York.

On June 28, 1778, Washington caught up with the British and engaged them at the Battle of Monmouth Court House. The day was hot and the battle hard-fought. For a while, it looked as if the now well-trained Americans might win, but a mix-up in orders cost Washington the victory. This inconclusive battle proved to be the last major engagement in the North for the rest of the war. Clinton withdrew to New York, and Continental troops occupied the hills along the Hudson Valley north of the city. The war shifted to other fronts.

FIGHTING ON THE FRONTIER AND AT SEA

Native Americans called Kentucky "a dark and bloody ground," a designation that took on added meaning when Indians began raiding the territory in 1777 on British instructions. The nerve center for coordinating these attacks was the British post of Detroit, and the Americans accordingly made plans to capture it. Two expeditions from Pittsburgh in 1778 failed completely. A third, under Virginian George Rogers Clark, although it never reached Detroit, was more successful (see Map 6-4). In July 1778 Clark's force of 175 frontiersmen captured three key British settlements in the Mississippi Valley: Kaskaskia, Cahokia, and Vincennes. These successes may have strengthened American claims to the West at the end of the war.

Blood also ran on the Pennsylvania and upstate New York frontiers. In the summer of 1778, a British force of one hundred loyalists and five hundred Indians struck settlers in north-central Pennsylvania's Wyoming Valley. After the Americans' Forty Fort surrendered on July 4, raiders killed the wounded and fleeing defenders. A similar mix of attackers in November 1778 burned farmsteads and slaughtered civilians at Cherry Valley, New York. Both raids became the stuff of legends and stimulated equally savage reprisals against the Indians. Congress authorized an expedition against the Iroquois, and in the late summer of 1779, more than four thousand Continental soldiers and state militia swept through the Finger Lakes region of New York, destroying forty-one Indian villages and the crops that supported them. Among the Seneca, not enough food remained to keep even "a child one day from perishing with hunger." As a result, some five thousand Iroquois sought refuge with the British at Fort Niagara.

Anglo-American clashes at sea had begun in 1775, shortly after the Battles of Lexington and Concord, and would continue until the end of the war as Americans struggled to break the British navy's blockade. Great Britain was the preeminent sea power of the age, and the United States never came close to matching it, in either the number or the size of its ships. But Congress did its best to challenge the British at sea. In 1775, it authorized the construction of thirteen frigates—medium-sized, relatively fast ships, mounting thirty-two guns—as well as the purchase of several merchant vessels for conversion to warships. By contrast, the Royal Navy in 1779 had

"Paul Jones Shooting a Sailor." Color engraving from the Olds Collection #366, no negative number. Collection of The New York Historical Society.

This engraving, published in London in 1779, shows an apocryphal incident during the battle in which John Paul Jones's ship Bon Homme Richard *defeated the British* Serapis. *During the fighting, Jones supposedly shot an American sailor who attempted to lower the ship's flag as a sign of surrender; actually Jones only knocked him down with a pistol. Legend (and the artist) may have confused this incident with another earlier one—while Jones was still a Scotsman (note the bonnet)—in which Jones did kill a mutineer.*

more than a hundred large and heavily armed "ships of the line." The Americans therefore engaged in what was essentially a guerrilla war at sea. Their naval flag, appropriately, pictured a rattlesnake and bore the motto, "Don't Tread on Me."

The country's first naval hero, Scottish-born John Paul Jones, was primarily a hit-and-run raider. Originally named only John Paul, he had gone to sea at age 12. He took the name Jones as an alias after he killed a fellow sailor during a mutiny. In the colonies by chance when the war broke out, this adventurer offered his services to the Congress. As commander of the new frigate *Ranger,* it was Jones who brought news of the American victory at Saratoga to France in early 1777. After delivering the news—an announcement that helped Franklin clinch the alliance

with France—Jones raided the British coast, inspiring local panic.

Franklin helped secure Jones an old French merchant ship, which he outfitted for war and renamed the *Bon Homme Richard* in honor of Franklin's famous *Poor Richard's Almanac.* After capturing seventeen enemy vessels, he encountered the formidable *H.M.S. Serapis* in the North Sea on September 23, 1779. Completely outgunned, Jones brought his ship close enough to make his small-arms fire more effective. Asked by the British if he were surrendering, Jones gave the legendary reply, "I have not yet begun to fight." Lashing the two ships together, Jones and his men battled the crew of the *Serapis* for more than four hours, much of it by moonlight. Finally, the *Serapis* surrendered. Jones's crew took possession of the British vessel and left the crippled *Bon Homme Richard* to sink.

The Congress and the individual states supplemented America's naval forces by commissioning individual sea captains to outfit their merchant vessels with guns and act as privateers. In effect legalized pirates, these privateers preyed on British shipping. They sold the goods they seized and divided the proceeds among their crews according to rank. The crews of captured vessels became prisoners of war. Successful privateering could bring wealth but required stealth and speed. One particularly fast vessel cruised off New York towing a buoy to make itself look like a lumbering merchantman under full sail. Once within range of a potential prize, the crew cut away the buoy and took the cannons out from under wraps. Such tactics paid off. Some two thousand American privateers captured more than six hundred British ships and forced the British Navy to spread itself thin doing convoy duty.

THE LAND WAR MOVES SOUTH

During the first three years of the war, the British had made little effort to mobilize what they believed to be considerable loyalist strength in the South. In 1778, however, facing a threat from France and with their forces in the North concentrated and inactive, they gave Southern loyalists a key role in a new strategy for subduing the rebellion. After first sending Redcoats sweeping through a large area, they would leave behind a Tory militia to reestablish loyalty to the crown and suppress local Whigs. The British hoped by this strategy to recapture everything from Georgia to Virginia; they would deal with New England later.

The British southern strategy began to unfold in November 1778, when General Clinton dispatched 3,500 troops to take control of Georgia (see Map 6-5). Meeting only light resistance, they quickly seized

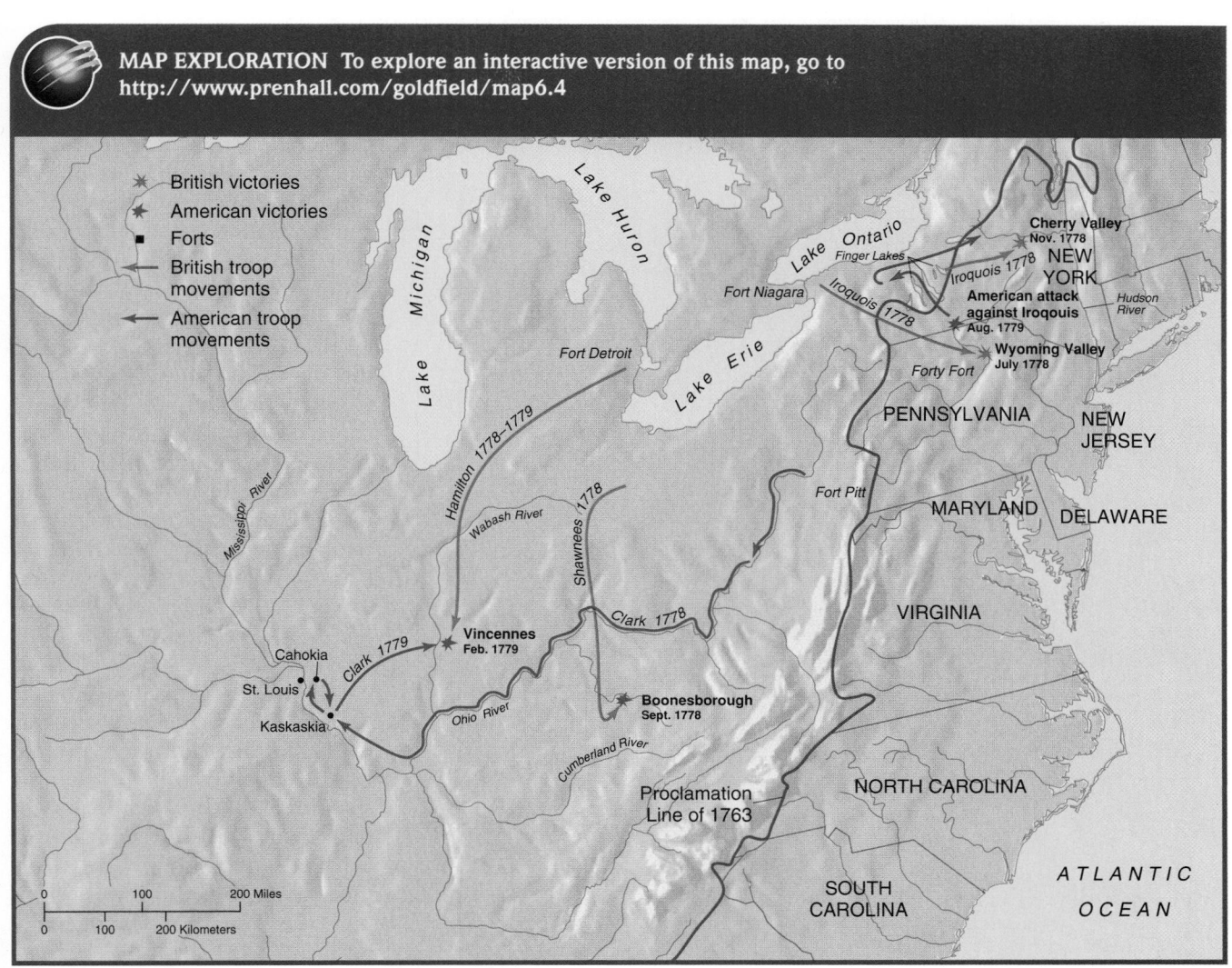

MAP EXPLORATION To explore an interactive version of this map, go to http://www.prenhall.com/goldfield/map6.4

MAP 6-4   **The War on the Frontier, 1778–1779**
Significant battles in the Mississippi Valley and the frontiers of the seaboard states added to the ferocity of the fighting and strengthened some American claims to western lands.

Savannah and Augusta. Indeed, enough inhabitants seemed happy to have the British back for the old colonial government to be restored under civilian control. After their initial success, however, the British suffered some serious setbacks. The Spanish entered the war and seized British outposts on the Mississippi and Mobile rivers. And in February 1779, at the Battle of Kettle Creek, South Carolina's Whig militia decimated a loyalist militia contingent that was trying to fight its way from the North Carolina back-country to Georgia to join up with British troops.

But the Americans could not beat the British army. In late September and early October 1779, a combined force of 5,500 American and French troops, supported by French warships, laid siege to Savannah. Moving too slowly to encircle the city, they allowed British reinforcements to get through.

Then, impatient to get their ships away from the hurricane-prone coast, the French forced the Americans to launch a premature assault on the city on October 9. The assault failed, and the French sailed off.

The way was now open for the British to attack Charleston, the military key to the Lower South. In December 1779, Clinton sailed through storm-battered seas from New York to the Carolina coast with about nine thousand troops. In the Battle of Charleston, he encircled the city, trapping the patriot forces inside. On May 12, 1780, more than five thousand Continentals and militia laid down their arms—the worst American defeat of the war and the largest single loss of United States troops to a foreign army until the surrender of American forces in the Philippines to Japan in 1942. Not everyone—even in Charleston—gave up. One woman there attacked a loyalist quartered in her house with an ax.

MAP 6-5 The War in the South, 1778–1781
During the latter part of the war, most of the major engagements occurred in the South. British forces won most of the early ones but could not control the immense territory involved and eventually surrendered at Yorktown.

Redcoats striking into the Carolina backcountry. At the South Carolina–North Carolina border, British troops under Colonel Banastre Tarleton overwhelmed a detachment of 350 Virginia Continentals trying to retreat homeward after coming too late to Charleston's aid. When the Continentals offered to surrender, Tarleton slaughtered most of them. So complete did the British success seem that Clinton tried to force the American troops whom he had taken prisoner to resume their duties as British subjects and join the loyalist militia. Thinking that matters were now well in hand, Clinton sailed back to New York, leaving the southern troops under the command of Lord Cornwallis.

Clinton's confidence that the South had returned securely to the loyalist camp was premature. Atrocities like Tarleton's slaughter of the Virginians inflamed anti-British feelings. And Clinton's decision to force former rebels into the loyalist militia backfired, infuriating real loyalists—who saw their enemies getting off lightly—as well as Whigs. Atrocities and reprisals mounted on both sides as Whigs continued to defy British authority. "Tarleton's Quarter" and "a Georgia parole" (a bullet in the back) became Whig euphemisms for "take no prisoners."

AMERICAN COUNTERATTACKS

In the summer of 1780, Congress dispatched a substantial Continental force to the South under General Horatio Gates, the hero of Saratoga. Local patriots flocked to join him. But Gates was reckless. Pushing through North Carolina, his men tried to subsist on green corn. Weakened by diarrhea, they blundered into Cornwallis's British army near Camden, South

But the British were now poised to sweep all the South before them. Most local Whigs, thinking the Revolution over, at first offered little resistance to

Carolina, on August 16, and suffered a complete rout. More than one thousand Americans were killed or wounded and many captured. Gates—transformed from the hero of Saratoga into the goat of Camden— fled to Hillsborough, North Carolina.

American morale revived on October 7, 1780, when "over mountain men" (militia) from Virginia, western North and South Carolina, and what is today eastern Tennessee inflicted a defeat on the British at Kings Mountain, South Carolina. And in December 1780, Nathanael Greene replaced the discredited Gates, bringing competent leadership to the Continentals in the South.

The daring and resourceful Greene realized that he would need an unorthodox strategy to defeat Cornwallis's larger army of seasoned professional troops. He divided his forces, keeping roughly half with him in northeastern South Carolina and sending the other half westward under General Daniel Morgan. Cornwallis ordered Tarleton to pursue Morgan's troops, who retreated northward until they reached an open area in South Carolina called Hannah's Cowpens. There Morgan rallied his men, reportedly inspiring them with the sight of his scarred back; he had been flogged by order of a British court martial during the French and Indian War. At the Battle of Cowpens on January 17, 1781, Morgan cleverly posted his least reliable troops, the militia, in the front line, telling them to run after firing two volleys. When Tarleton attacked, the militia fired and withdrew. Thinking that the American ranks had broken, the Redcoats charged—straight into devastating fire from Morgan's Continentals. Tarleton escaped, but his reputation for invincibility had been destroyed.

Cornwallis now badly needed a battlefield victory. Burning his army's excess baggage, he set off in hot pursuit of Greene and Morgan, who had rejoined forces. The Continentals had the advantage of knowing the country, which was laced with rain-swollen rivers. Greene's officers often arranged to have boats waiting at the deeper crossings. Finally, on February 13, 1781, Greene's tired men crossed the Dan River into Virginia, and Cornwallis gave up the chase, marching his equally exhausted Redcoats southward. To his surprise, Cornwallis now found himself pursued—though cautiously, to be sure—by Greene. On March 15, the opposing forces met at Guilford Court House (near present-day Greensboro, North Carolina) in one of the war's bloodiest battles. At one point, with the two sides tangled in hand-to-hand combat, the Americans drove the British back. To blunt the onslaught, Cornwallis fired cannon directly into the melee, mowing down friend and foe alike. Thanks

to such tactics, the British still held the field at the end of the day. But, as one Englishman observed, "another such victory would destroy the British Army." Cornwallis had to retreat to the coastal town of Wilmington, North Carolina, to rest and regroup. Abandoning his most seriously wounded men, he carried the rest back in wagons, their broken bones poking through their wounds as they bounced along rutted roads.

By the late summer of 1781, British fortunes were waning in the Lower South. The Redcoats held only the larger towns and the immediately surrounding countryside. With their superior staying power, they won most major engagements, but these victories brought them no lasting gain. As General Greene observed of the Americans, "We fight, get beat, and rise and fight again." When the enemy pressed him too hard, Greene retreated out of reach, advancing again as the British withdrew.

Patriot guerrilla forces, led by such colorful figures as "Gamecock" Thomas Sumter, and "Swamp Fox" Francis Marion, disrupted British communications between their Charleston headquarters and outlying garrisons. The loyalist militias that the British had hoped would pacify the countryside proved unequal to the task. Whig militiamen had often driven out any loyalists before a British sweep. And those who did welcome the British found themselves the targets of Whig retaliation once the Redcoats had left. Thus, although Greene never defeated the Redcoats outright, his campaign was a strategic success. The British could not hold what they had taken; the Americans had time on their side.

Disappointed and frustrated, Cornwallis decided to conquer Virginia to cut off Greene's line of supply and to destroy Whig resolve. British forces, including units commanded by turncoat Benedict Arnold, had already been raiding the state. Cornwallis marched north to join them, reaching Yorktown, Virginia, during the summer of 1781.

The final military showdown of the war was at hand. By now, five thousand French soldiers were in America ready to fight alongside the Continentals, and a large French fleet in the West Indies had orders to support an attack on the British in North America. Faking preparations for an assault on British-occupied New York, the Continentals (commanded by Washington) and the French headed for the Chesapeake. Cornwallis and his six thousand Redcoats soon found themselves besieged behind their fortifications at Yorktown by 8,800 Americans and 7,800 French. A French naval victory gave the allies temporary command of the waters around Yorktown. Cornwallis had nowhere to go, and Clinton—still in New York—could not reinforce him quickly enough. On October 19, 1781, the British army surrendered. The defeated men filed between rows of American and French troops to lay down their arms while a British band mournfully played a tune reputedly called "The World Turned Upside Down." When he learned the news in London, the British prime minister, Lord North, took it like "a ball in his breast." "It is all over," he groaned.

THE AMERICAN VICTORY, 1782–1783

The British surrender at Yorktown marked the end of major fighting in North America, though skirmishes continued for another year. In April 1782, the Royal Navy defeated the French fleet in the Caribbean, strengthening the British bargaining position. George III had insisted on continuing the war for so long because he feared that conceding American independence would threaten British rule in Canada and the West Indies. But the majority in Parliament now felt that enough men and money had been wasted trying to keep the Americans within the empire. In March 1782, the king accepted Lord North's resignation and appointed Lord Rockingham as prime minister, with a mandate to make peace.

THE PEACE OF PARIS

The peace negotiations, which took place in Paris, were lengthy. The Americans demanded independence, handsome territorial concessions—Franklin, the senior American negotiator, asked for all of Canada—and access to the rich British-controlled fishing grounds in the North Atlantic. The new British prime minister, Lord Shelburne (Rockingham had died in 1782), was inclined to be conciliatory. By making concessions, he hoped to help British merchants recover their lost colonial trade. The French had achieved their objective—to weaken the British—and now wanted out of an increasingly costly worldwide war. Spain had not won its most important goal, the recovery of British-held Gibraltar, and thus gave the Americans no support at all.

The American negotiators, Franklin, John Adams, and John Jay, masterfully threaded their way among these conflicting interests. With good reason, they feared that the French and Spanish would strike a bargain with the British at the expense of the United States—one that might, for example, confine the new country to a narrow coastal strip or allow Britain to retain areas such as New York City and Charleston, which its troops still occupied. As a result, the Americans disregarded Congress's instructions to avoid making peace unilaterally. Instead, they secretly worked out their own arrangements with the British that would meet Shelburne's objective of restoring Anglo-American commercial ties. On November 30, 1782, the negotiators signed a preliminary Anglo-American treaty of peace. Its terms were embodied in the final **Peace of Paris**, signed by all the belligerents on September 3, 1783.

The Peace of Paris gave the United States nearly everything it sought except Canada (which

The surrender of Lord Cornwallis at Yorktown on October 19, 1781, led to the British decision to withdraw from the war. Cornwallis, who claimed to be ill, absented himself from the ceremony and is not in the picture. Washington, who is astride the horse under the American flag, designated General Benjamin Lincoln (on the white horse in the center) as the one to accept the submission of a subordinate British officer. John Trumbull, who painted The Battle of Bunker Hill and some three hundred other scenes from the Revolutionary War, finished this painting while he was in London about fifteen years after the events depicted. A large copy of the work now hangs in the rotunda of the United States Capitol in Washington, D.C.

Surrender of Lord Cornwallis at Yorktown, by John Trumbull (American, 1756–1843).Oil on canvas, 20 7/8 x 30 5/8 in.

MAP EXPLORATION To explore an interactive version of this map, go to
http://www.prenhall.com/goldfield/map6.6

MAP 6-6   **North America after the Peace of Paris, 1783**
*The results of the American Revolution redrew the map of North America, confining Britain to
Canada and giving the United States most of the area east of the Mississippi River, though Spain
controlled its mouth for most of the next twenty years.*

was never really a serious issue). Great Britain acknowledged that the United States was "free, sovereign and independent." The northern boundary of
the new nation extended west from the St. Croix
River (which separated Maine from Nova Scotia)
past the Great Lakes to what were thought to be the
headwaters of the Mississippi River (see Map 6-6).
The Mississippi itself—down to just north of New Orleans—formed the western border. Spain acquired
the provinces of East and West Florida from Britain.
This territory included a substantial chunk of present-day Louisiana, Mississippi, Alabama, and Geor-

gia. The treaty did not, however, provide the United
States with access to the Gulf of Mexico, a situation
that would be a source of diplomatic friction for
years.

Several provisions of the treaty addressed impor-
tant economic issues. Adams, on behalf of his fellow
New Englanders, insisted on a provision granting
American fishermen access to the waters off eastern
Canada. The treaty also required that British forces,
on quitting American soil, were to leave behind all
American-owned property, including slaves. Another
provision declared existing debts between citizens of

Benjamin West's painting of the American commissioners who negotiated the Peace of Paris includes, from left to right, John Jay, John Adams, Benjamin Franklin, and Franklin's grandson, who served as the commissioners' secretary. A fourth American commissioner who arrived only at the end of the negotiations, Henry Laurens, stands in the background. The British commissioners, who would have occupied the blank space on the right, did not sit for their portraits. Chagrin at the outcome of the war probably contributed to their absence, but an apocryphal story attributed it to the reluctance of Richard Oswald, who was blind in one eye, to have his portrait painted.

Britain and the United States still valid, giving British merchants hope of collecting on their American accounts. Congress was to "recommend" that the states restore rights and property taken from loyalists during the war. Nothing was said about the slave trade, which Jay had hoped to ban.

THE COMPONENTS OF SUCCESS

The War for Independence was over. In December 1783, the last British transports put to sea with troops evacuated from New York. Despite the provisions of the peace treaty and the objections of southern planters, about three thousand African Americans went with them. General Guy Carleton, who had replaced Clinton as commander in chief after Yorktown, agreed to keep a list of these people, but he refused to renege on British promises of freedom for slaves who fled rebel owners. (Carleton's list survived and has recently been published.)

Washington's Continental Army had already disbanded in the summer of 1783 (but not, as we have seen, before a dispute over pay came close to provoking a military coup). On December 4, the American commander said an emotional farewell to his officers at New York City's Fraunces Tavern, and on December 23, at Annapolis, Maryland, he resigned his commission to the Congress. Like the legendary citizen-soldier Cincinnatus, who after defending the

ancient Roman Republic gave up his power and went back to plowing his land, Washington went home to Mount Vernon. By now he had won the respect of friend and foe alike. "You are," one British aristocrat would write to him, "the only human being for whom I ever felt an awful reverence." Only a natural genius, other Britons said, could have accomplished what he did. How else could one explain the victory of ragtag provincials over the world's greatest military and naval power?

Washington's leadership was just one of the reasons why the Americans won the Revolutionary War. French assistance played a crucial role. Some historians contend that without the massive infusion of French men and money in 1781, the Revolution would have failed. The British also contributed heavily to their own downfall. Their fatal mistakes included bureaucratic inefficiency, hesitant command, and, worst of all, overconfidence. British authorities consistently underestimated the enormous difficulty of waging war 3,000 miles from home in an era of slow and uncertain communications. The people they sought to conquer were sparsely distributed over an area that stretched more than 1,500 miles from Maine to Georgia. There was no natural center whose capture would severely cripple the rest of the country. British forces occupied, at one time or another, most of the important seaports and state capitals—Boston, New York, Philadelphia,

Charleston, and Savannah—but patriot forces driven from these centers could simply regroup in another location. Finally, Great Britain had tried to solve a political problem by military means. An occupying army is far more likely to alienate people than to secure their goodwill.

Yet it took 175,000 to 200,000 soldiers—Continentals and militia troops—to prevent Great Britain from recovering the colonies. Of these, some seven thousand died in battle. Perhaps ten thousand more succumbed to disease while on active duty, another 8,500 died while prisoners of war, and nearly 1,500 were reported missing in action. More than eight thousand were wounded and survived. Those who served in the Continental Army, probably more than half of all who fought, served the longest and saw the most action. Their casualty rate—30 to 40 percent—may have been the highest of any war in which the United States has been engaged. In proportion to the population, these losses would be the equivalent of more than two million people in the United States today.

WAR AND SOCIETY, 1775–1783

Regular combatants were not the only ones to suffer during the struggle for independence. Eight years of warfare also produced profound dislocations throughout American society. Military service wrenched families apart, sporadic raids by each side brought the war home to vast numbers of people, and everyone endured economic disruptions. As a forge of nationhood, the Revolution tested all Americans, whatever their standing as citizens.

THE WOMEN'S WAR

Everywhere women had to see their husbands, sons, brothers, and fiancés go off to fight and die. Like Mary Silliman in Connecticut, they waited, trying to stay calm until they knew "what tidings God" had for them. At first, with spirits still running high, Mary's letters to her husband, Selleck, reveal an affectionate lightheartedness. "These cold nights make me shudder for you," she wrote, adding "Oh, King George, what hardships does thy tyranny put thy late subjects to!" Selleck responded with similarly suggestive banter. Later, the couple's letters grew less playful. Then her husband was captured. The daily round of domestic duties helped to keep her going, but his extended absence increased her burdens and enlarged her responsibilities.

Such circumstances elevated women's domestic status. Couples began referring to "our"—not "my" or "your"—property. Wives frequently grew more knowledgeable about a family's financial condition than long-absent husbands. "What shall I do my Dearest? I wish I had Your Advice," wrote Selleck Silliman to his wife after he had been released from captivity.

Women also assumed new public roles during the conflict. Some nursed the wounded. More wove cloth for uniforms. The Ladies' Association of Philadelphia was established in 1780 to demonstrate women's patriotism and raise money to buy shirts for the army. Though women might not be able to march "to glory by the same path as the Men," wrote the association's founder, "we should at least equal and sometimes surpass them in our love for the public good." Similar associations formed in other states.

Despite their increasing private responsibilities and new public activities, it did not occur to most women to encroach very far on traditional male prerogatives. When John Adams's wife, Abigail, urged him and the Second Continental Congress to "Remember the Ladies," she was not expecting equal political rights. What she wanted, rather, was some legal protections for women and recognition of their value and need for autonomy in the domestic sphere. "Remember," she cautioned, "all Men would be Tyrants if they could." Why not, then, make it impossible for "the vicious and lawless" to abuse women with impunity? "I will never consent to have our sex considered in an inferior point of light," she wrote.

Republican ideology, responding to the changing status of women, assigned them a role that was at once exalted and subordinate. It was their job to nurture wise, virtuous, and public-spirited men. It was this view of women that would prevail in the post-Revolutionary era.

EFFECT OF THE WAR ON AFRICAN AMERICANS

In the northern states, where slavery was already economically marginal and where black men were welcome as volunteers in the Continental Army, the Revolutionary War helped to bring an end to slavery, although it remained legal there for some time (see Chapter 7). In the South, however, slavery was integral to the economy, and white planters viewed it as crucial to their postwar recovery. Thus, although British efforts to recruit black soldiers brought freedom to thousands and temporarily undermined slavery in the South, the war ultimately strengthened the institution, especially in

American soldiers at Yorktown in 1781 as drawn by a young officer in the French army, Jean-Baptiste-Antoine de Verger. The African American on the left is an infantryman of the First Rhode Island Regiment; the next, a musketeer; the third, with the fringed jacket, a rifleman. The man on the right is a Continental artilleryman, holding a lighted match used to fire cannons.

the negotiations in Paris. The Iroquois told a British commander that if the English really "had basely betrayed them by pretending to give up their Country to the Americans without their Consent, or Consulting them, it was an Act of Cruelty and injustice that Christians only were capable of doing." With the Americans now claiming their country by conquest, the Revolutionary War was for most Native Americans a disaster that opened the floodgates to a torrent of white settlers. During 1779 and 1780 alone, approximately 20,000 settlers streamed into Kentucky. Five years later, there were reportedly 2,200 squatter families in parts of Ohio where the United States government forbade settlement.

the Carolinas and Georgia. Of the African Americans who left with the British at the end of the war, many, both slave and free, went to the West Indies. Others settled in Canada, and some eventually went back to Africa, where Britain established the colony of Sierra Leone for them.

THE WAR'S IMPACT ON NATIVE AMERICANS

Survivors among the approximately thirteen thousand Native Americans who fought for the British did not have the option of leaving with them at the end of the war. How many died during the war is not known, but certainly many did. Not only the Iroquois but other groups lost much. The Americans repeatedly invaded the Cherokees' homeland in the southern Appalachian Mountains. "There was no withstanding them," recalled a Cherokee chief of the many frontiersmen who assaulted his people. "They dyed their hands in the blood of many of our Women and children, burnt seventeen towns, destroyed all our provisions," and spread famine across the land. Americans also attacked the Shawnees of Ohio. In one notorious incident, militiamen even massacred peaceful Christian Indians at Gnadenhutten, Ohio.

With the peace treaty of 1783, Britain surrendered its territory east of the Mississippi, shocking and infuriating the Native Americans living there. They had not surrendered, and none of them had been at

ECONOMIC DISRUPTION

The British and American armies both needed enormous quantities of supplies. This heavy demand disrupted the normal distribution of goods and drove up real prices seven- or eightfold. The widespread use of depreciating paper money by the American side amplified this rise in prices and triggered severe inflation.

When the British did not simply seize what they needed, they paid for it in hard currency—gold and silver. American commanders, by contrast, had to rely on paper money because the Congress and the states had almost no hard currency at their disposal. The Continental dollar, however, steadily declined in value, and by March 1780, the Congress was forced to admit officially that it was worthless. (The popular expression, "not worth a Continental" suggests that the public had long since reached this conclusion.) Thus, not surprisingly, American farmers and merchants, whatever their political opinions, sometimes sold food to the British while their own forces went hungry.

Necessity, not folly, drove Congress and the states to rely on the printing press. Rather than alienate citizens by immediately raising taxes to pay for the war, the states printed paper money supposedly redeemable through future tax revenues. Because the quantity of this paper money rose faster than the supply of goods and services, prices skyrocketed, and the value of the money plunged. By April 1779, as

FROM THEN TO NOW

The American Revolution and the Teaching of American History

In October 1994, TV viewers saw politically conservative talk show host Rush Limbaugh hold up a history book and begin ripping out pages. "Here's Paul Revere. He's gone," he exclaimed, and out went a page. "Here's George Washington. . . . He's gone. . . ." More pages bit the dust. "This is what we're doing to American history with this stupid new book, folks." The volume that prompted his outburst was the National History Standards—"the standards from hell" according to conservative critics. In response to such outbursts, Gary Nash, a leading author of the standards and an expert in early American history, repeatedly went on television to defend them, appearing in one twenty-four hour period on ABC, NBC, and PBS.

The furor arose out of a bipartisan attempt to improve education in the nation's schools. In 1989, President George H. W. Bush and the nation's governors announced that it was time "to establish clear national performance goals, goals that will make us internationally competitive . . . in the twenty-first century." The plan called for knowledgeable professionals to establish voluntary guidelines governing what schools should expect students to know about several core subjects, including history. The development of the history standards, which involved thousands of historians and history teachers, took more than two and a half years.

The heated reaction to the standards caught many by surprise, but it probably should not have. History, Nash has pointed out, is "unceasingly controversial because it provides so much of the substance for the way a society defines itself." This is certainly true of the history of the American Revolution—the focus of much of the ire of the standard's critics—because it is from the Revolution that the founding propositions of the nation emerged.

The authors of the standards wanted students to learn the results of recent research that has given voice to African Americans, Native Americans, women, and ordinary people and documented their active role in history. But critics complained that including this material would unduly diminish coverage of prominent figures like Revere and Washington. They also worried that calling attention, say, to African American life under slavery or to such incidents as the Paxton Boys' assault on their Indian neighbors would darken the narrative of American history.

How should one tell the story of the United States? A state legislature once resolved that school textbooks should emphasize "the history of hearts and souls inspired by wonderful American principles and traditions." Those who wrote the National History Standards believed that the "governing narrative" should be "the struggle to fulfill the American ideals of liberty, equal justice, and equality" as "various groups [sought] to elbow their way under the canopy of the nation's founding promises."

Compromise eventually quieted the controversy. After the Senate rejected the history standards, blue-ribbon panels of experts reviewed them, recommended some changes, and predicted that the revised version would make an important contribution toward "developing a responsible and productive citizenry." And indeed, teachers and school administrators throughout the country now regularly consult the revised standards to help them design an appropriate history curriculum.

But such controversies—or "memory wars"— have long been, and doubtless will remain, a recurring part of American history as competing segments of society seek to sanction their aspirations and achievement with differing versions of the common past.

Washington commented, "a wagon load of money will scarcely purchase a wagon load of provisions." Savvy people tried to spend money before its value could drop further, whereas those who had salable commodities such as grain tended to hoard them in the hope that the price would go even higher. Prices also climbed much faster than wages, leaving many working people impoverished. As always happens in times of severe inflation, people resorted to bartering and demanded price-fixing laws. But often there was nothing to barter, and price controls never worked for long.

The rampant inflation was demoralizing and divisive. Lucky speculators and unscrupulous profiteers grew rich, while ordinary and patriotic people suffered. These conditions sparked more than thirty protest demonstrations. In October 1779, frustrated Philadelphia militiamen marched on the house of a local Whig leader, demanding better enforcement of price controls. The confrontation left six people dead but otherwise achieved little. Freebooters—rovers in search of plunder—sailed Long Island Sound in boats with such names as *Retrieve My Losses,* ostensibly to harry the British but all too often to trade with them. As usual, war and its deprivations brought out both the best and the worst in human nature.

Nevertheless, the successful outcome of the war and the stable peace that followed suggest that most Americans somehow managed to cope. But during the last years of the conflict, their economic and psychological reserves ran low. The total real wealth of private individuals declined by an average of 0.5 percent annually from 1774 to 1805, even with the returning prosperity of the 1790s. Such statistics suggest the true economic cost of the War for Independence. And the atrocities committed on both sides provide nearly as accurate an indicator of the conflict's psychological cost.

THE PRICE OF VICTORY

Most American and British commanders tried to keep hostilities "civilized"—if such a characterization can ever be applied to a war—but discipline sometimes broke down among regular troops. Controlling militias or civilians acting on their own was even more difficult, demonstrating once again that civil wars and guerrilla struggles often rank among the worst of human conflicts. Residents of contested areas near British-occupied cities, such as New York and Charleston, lived in almost constant danger. Their plight emerges starkly from an incident in New Jersey in 1779, when a roving Tory band

knocked on the door of a Whig militiaman. Entering his house, they announced that he was a dead man. Drinking his liquor and terrorizing his wife, they argued about how to execute him until one of the intruders abruptly resolved the dispute by shooting him. Whigs could be equally brutal. Late in the war, British sympathizers in the Lower South compiled a list of more than three hundred loyalists who had been massacred by Whigs—some, the survivors claimed, while they slept.

Although the British were probably the worse offenders, both sides burned, plundered, and murdered. One can see the results in a returning refugee's description of the area around Beaufort, South Carolina, in the early 1780s: "All was desolation. . . . Robberies and murders are often committed on the public roads. The people that remain have been peeled, pillaged, and plundered. Poverty, want, and hardship appear in almost every countenance . . . , and the morals of the people are almost entirely extirpated."

CONCLUSION

Despite the devastation and divisiveness of the war, many people in Europe and the United States were convinced that it represented something momentous. *The Annual Register,* an influential British magazine reflecting respectable opinion, commented accurately in 1783 that the American Revolution "has already overturned those favourite systems of policy and commerce, both in the old and in the new world, which the wisdom of the ages, and the power of the greatest nations, had in vain endeavored to render permanent; and it seems to have laid the seeds of still greater revolutions in the history and mutual relations of mankind."

Americans, indeed, had fired a shot heard round the world. Thanks in part to its heavy investment in the American Revolution, France suffered a grave financial crisis in the late 1780s. This, in turn, ushered in the political crisis that culminated in the French Revolution of 1789. The American Revolution helped to inspire among French people (including soldiers returning from service in America) an intense yearning for an end to arbitrary government and undeserved social inequalities. Liberty also proved infectious to thousands of German troops who had come to America as mercenaries but elected to stay as free citizens after the war was over. Once prosperous but distant provinces of a far-flung empire, the North American states had become an independent confederation, a grand experiment in republicanism whose fate mattered to enlightened men and women throughout the Western world. In his written farewell to the rank and file of his troops at the end of October 1783, Washington maintained that "the enlarged prospects of happiness, opened by the confirmation of our independence and sovereignty, almost exceed the power of description."

He urged those who had fought with him to maintain their "strong attachments to the union" and "prove themselves not less virtuous and useful as citizens, than they have been persevering and victorious as soldiers." The work of securing the promise of the American Revolution, Washington knew, would now shift from the battlefield to the political arena.

REVIEW QUESTIONS

1. Who were the loyalists, and how many of them were there? What attempts did the British and Americans make in 1775 to avert war? Why did these steps fail?

2. What actions did the Second Continental Congress take in 1775 and 1776? Why did it choose George Washington as the commander of its army? Why was he a good choice?

3. Why did Congress declare independence in July 1776? How did Americans justify their claim to independence?

4. What was republicanism, and why was the enthusiasm that it inspired insufficient to win the war?

5. What were the chief characteristics of the British and American armies?

6. Why were most of the early battles fought in the northern states? Why did the British not crush the Americans immediately? Why did France decide to enter the war as an ally of the United States? What effect did French entry into the war have on British strategy?

7. Why did the initial British victories in the South not win the war for them? Why did the United States ultimately win? What did it obtain by winning?

8. What were the effects of the war on American society? What impact did it have on the status of women? On the lives of African Americans? What did John Laurens intend for African Americans? Why did he think ex-slaves would make good soldiers? Why did his plan fail? How did the war affect Native Americans? What was the price of victory—for the victors and for the vanquished? What were the immediate results of the American victory?

KEY TERMS

Battles of Lexington and Concord (p. 168–169)

Committee of Safety (p. 167)

Conciliatory Proposition (p. 168)

Continental Army (p. 170)

Contract theory of government (p. 173)

Declaration of Independence (p. 173)

Declaration of the Causes and Necessity of Taking Up Arms (p. 170)

Minute Men (p. 167)

Olive Branch Petition (p. 170)

Peace of Paris (p. 190)

Republicanism (p. 174)

Second Continental Congress (p. 170)

Valley Forge (p. 184)

RECOMMENDED READING

Buel, Joy D., and Richard Buel, Jr. *The Way of Duty: A Woman and Her Family in Revolutionary America* (1984). A readable and unusually full biography of Mary Fish of Connecticut, who lived from 1736 to 1818. Her experiences during the Revolutionary War while her husband, Selleck Silliman, was a prisoner of the British have become the subject of a good movie, "Mary Silliman's War" (1993).

Conway, Stephen. *The War of American Independence, 1775–1783* (1995). A short, accessible account that emphasizes the degree to which the American Revolution was the first modern war.

Dann, John C. ed. *The Revolution Remembered: Eyewitness Accounts of the War for Independence* (1980). A collection of seventy-nine narratives by veterans seeking pensions for their Revolutionary War service; sometimes poignant and frequently illuminating.

Gross, Robert A. *The Minutemen and Their World* (1976). An example of "history from the bottom up" that provides a close look at the Minute Men of Concord from the late colonial period through the Revolution.

Maier, Pauline. *American Scripture: Making the Declaration of Independence* (1997). A readable account of the adoption of the Declaration of Independence and its later reputation.

Shy, John. *A People Numerous and Armed: Reflections on the Military Struggle for American Independence* (1990). A collection of essays on various aspects of the American Revolution by a perceptive military historian; full of interesting ideas.

Weigley, Russell F. *The Partisan War: The South Carolina Campaign of 1780–1782* (1970). A short, stimulating account of the American recovery of the Lower South that takes "the perspective of our recent insights into unconventional war" and communist successes in Vietnam.

ADDITIONAL SOURCES
The Outbreak of War and the Declaration of Independence

Adams, Willi Paul et al, "Interpreting the Declaration of Independence by Translation: A Round Table," *Journal of American History* (1999), pp. 1280–1458.

Calhoon, Robert M. *The Loyalists in Revolutionary America, 1760–1781* (1973).

Ellis, Joseph. *American Sphinx: The Character of Thomas Jefferson* (1996).

Fischer, David H. *Paul Revere's Ride* (1994).

Flexner, James T. *Washington: The Indispensable Man* (1984).

Foner, Eric. *Tom Paine and Revolutionary America* (1976).

Hamowy, Ronald. "Jefferson and the Scottish Enlightenment: A Critique of Garry Wills's Inventing America," *William and Mary Quarterly* (1979), pp. 503–523.

Higginbotham, Don. *The War of American Independence: Military Attitudes, Policies, and Practice, 1763–1789* (1971).

Middlekauff, Robert. *The Glorious Cause: The American Revolution, 1763–1789* (1982).

The Combatants

Billias, George A. ed. *George Washington's Generals* (1964).

Billias, George A. ed. *George Washington's Opponents: British Generals and Admirals in the American Revolution* (1969).

Frey, Sylvia R. *The British Soldier in America: A Social History of Military Life in the Revolutionary Period* (1981).

Gardiner, Robert. *Navies and the American Revolution, 1775–1783* (1996).

Mayer, Holly A. *Belonging to the Army: Camp Followers and Community during the American Revolution* (1996).

Neimeyer, Charles P. *America Goes to War: A Social History of the Continental Army* (1996).

Royster, Charles. *A Revolutionary People at War: The Continental Army and American Character, 1775–1783* (1979).

Wright, Robert K. *The Continental Army* (1984).

The War in the North

Gruber, Ira D. *The Howe Brothers and the American Revolution* (1972).

Kennett, Lee B. *The French Forces in America, 1780–1783* (1977).

Kwasny, Mark V. *Washington's Partisan War, 1775–1783* (1996).

Martin, James Kirby. *Benedict Arnold, Revolutionary Hero: An American Warrior Reconsidered* (1997).

Rosswurm, Steven. *Arms, Country, and Class: The Philadelphia Militia and "Lower Sort" during the American Revolution, 1775–1783* (1987).

Stinchcombe, William C. *The American Revolution and the French Alliance* (1969).

The War Widens

Frey, Sylvia R. *Water from the Rock: Black Resistance in a Revolutionary Age* (1991).

Graymont, Barbara. *The Iroquois in the American Revolution* (1972).

Hoffman, Ronald, Thad W. Tate, and Peter J. Albert, eds. *An Uncivil War: The Southern Backcountry during the American Revolution* (1985).

Mintz, Max. *Seeds of Empire: The American Revolutionary Conquest of the Iroquois* (1999).

O'Donnell, James H. *Southern Indians in the American Revolution* (1973).

Smith, Paul H. *Loyalists and Redcoats: A Study in British Revolutionary Policy* (1964).

Thayer, Theodore. *Nathanael Greene: Strategist of the American Revolution* (1960).

Wickwire, Franklin, and Mary Wickwire. *Cornwallis: The American Adventure* (1970).

The American Victory

Dull, Jonathan R. *A Diplomatic History of the American Revolution* (1985).

Mackesy, Piers. *The War for America, 1775–1783* (1964).

Martin, James K., and Mark E. Lender. *A Respectable Army: The Military Origins of the Republic, 1763–1789* (1982).

Morris, Richard B. *The Peacemakers: The Great Powers and American Independence* (1965).

Peckham, Howard H. *The Toll of Independence: Engagements and Battle Casualties of the American Revolution* (1974).

The War and Society

Brown, Wallace. *The Good Americans: The Loyalists in the American Revolution* (1969).

Buel, Richard Jr. *Dear Liberty: Connecticut's Mobilization for the Revolutionary War* (1980).

Calloway, Colin G. *The American Revolution in Indian Country: Crisis and Diversity in Native American Communities* (1995).

Hodges, Graham Russell, ed. *The Black Loyalist Directory: African Americans in Exile after the American Revolution* (1996).

Hoffman, Ronald, and Peter J. Albert, eds. *The Transforming Hand of Revolution: Reconsidering the American Revolution as a Social Movement* (1995).

Hoffman, Ronald, and Peter J. Albert. *Women in the Age of the American Revolution* (1989).

Kerber, Linda. *Women of the Republic: Intellect and Ideology in Revolutionary America* (1980).

Leiby, Adrian C. *The Revolutionary War in the Hackensack Valley: The Jersey Dutch and the Neutral Ground, 1775–1783* (1962).

Massey, Gregory. *John Laurens and the American Revolution* (2000).

Norton, Mary Beth. *Liberty's Daughters: The Revolutionary Experience of American Women, 1750–1800* (1980).

Ward, Harry M. *The War for Independence and the Transformation of American Society* (1999).

Young, Alfred F., ed. *The American Revolution: Explorations in the History of American Radicalism* (1976).

WHERE TO LEARN MORE

- **Gnadenhutten Monument and Schoenbrunn Village near New Philadelphia, Ohio.** Reconstructed buildings mark the Moravian Indian settlement whose inhabitants were massacred in 1782. The website for the museum and park, http://www.geocities.com/tusc_hat/gnaden.html, gives a brief history of the village and Revolutionary War massacre.

- **Independence National Historical Park, Philadelphia, Pennsylvania.** Independence Hall, where Congress adopted the Declaration of Independence, is the most historic building in Philadelphia. The informative website can be accessed through Links to the Past: National Park Service Cultural Resources' comprehensive listing of historic sites in the National Park system, http://www.cr.nps.gov.

- **Kings Mountain National Military Park and Cowpens National Battlefield, South Carolina.** Situated approximately 20 miles apart, these were the sites of two battles in October 1780 and January 1781 that turned the tide of the war in the South. Both have museums and exhibits. The official site is accessible through Links to the Past: National Park Service Cultural Resources, http://www.cr.nps.gov. But see also Battles of the American Revolutionary War, http://www.ilt.columbia.edu/k12/history/aha/battles.html, for a brief description of the battles and their contexts.

- **Minute Man National Historical Park, Lexington and Concord, Massachusetts.** There are visitors' centers at both Lexington and Concord with explanatory displays. Visitors may also follow the self-guided Battle Road Automobile Tour. The official website is accessible through Links to the Past: National Park Service Cultural Resources, http://www.cr.nps.gov.

- **Saratoga National Historical Park, New York.** The park preserves and commemorates the American victory that led to French entry into the war. There is a museum with artifacts from the battlefield. Both the explanatory displays and the topography of the area make this an especially illuminating site. The official website is accessible through Links to the Past: National Park Service Cultural Resources, http://www.cr.nps.gov.

- **Valley Forge National Historical Park, Valley Forge, Pennsylvania.** Reconstructed huts convey a sense of life in the Continental Army camp at Valley Forge during the hard winter of 1777–1778. The official website is accessible through Links to the Past: National Park Service Cultural Resources, http://www.cr.nps.gov.

- **Yorktown Battlefield, Colonial National Historical Park, Yorktown, Virginia.** The park commemorates the great American victory here. Innovative exhibits enable visitors to follow the course of the war from a multicultural perspective. The official website is accessible through Links to the Past: National Park Service Cultural Resources, http://www.cr.nps.gov.

 Please refer to the document CD-ROM for primary sources related to this chapter.

→ *The federal ship Hamilton was the center of attention in the grand procession staged by supporters of the Constitution in New York City in 1788.*

THE FIRST REPUBLIC
1776–1789

7

Springfield Jan. 26, 1787

Sir,

The unhappy time is come in which we have been obliged to shed blood. Shays, who was at the head of about twelve hundred men, marched yesterday afternoon about four o'Clock, towards the public buildings in battle array. He marched his men in an open column by plattoons. I sent several times [through aides] to him to know what he was after, or what he wanted. His reply was, he wanted barracks, and barracks he would have and stores. The answer returned was he must purchase them dear, if he had them. He still proceeded on his march until he approached within two hundred and fifty yards of the arsenal. He then made a halt. I immediately sent Major Lyman, one of my aides, and Capt Buffington to inform him not to march his troops any nearer to Arsenal on his peril, as I was stationed here by order of your Excellency and the Secretary at War, for the defence of the public property, in case he did I should surely fire on him and his men. [After rebuffing Lyman and Buffington,] Shays immediately put his troops in motion, and marched on rapidly near one hundred yards. I then ordered Major Stephens, who commanded the Artillery, to fire upon them. He accordingly did. The two first shott he endeavored to overshoot them, in hopes they would have taken warning without firing among them, but it had no effect on them. Major Stevens

CHAPTER OUTLINE

The New Order of Republicanism
Defining the People
The State Constitutions
The Articles of Confederation

Problems at Home
The Fiscal Crisis
Economic Depression
The Economic Policies of the States
Congress and the West

Diplomatic Weaknesses
Impasse with Britain
Spain and the Mississippi River

Toward a New Union
The Road to Philadelphia
The Convention at Work
Overview of the Constitution
The Struggle over Ratification

Conclusion

then directed his shott thro' the center of his column. The fourth or fifth shot put their whole column into the utmost confusion. Shays made an attempt to display [spread out] the column, but in vain. We had one howitz which was loaded with grape shot, which when fired, gave them great uneasiness. Had I been disposed to destroy them, I might have charged upon their rear and flanks with my Infantry and the two field pieces, and could have killed the greater part of his whole army within twenty five minutes. There was not a single musket fired on either side. I found three men dead on the spot, and one wounded, who is since dead. …

I am, Sir, with great respect, <u>Your</u> Excellency's most

Obedient hble Servt
W. Shepard

General Shepard to Governor Bowdoin, Jan. 26, 1787, in *American Historical Review*, Vol. 2: July 1897, p. 694.

William Shepard, the commander of the Hampshire County militia, informed Massachusets Governor James Bowdoin that the armed insurgents led by Daniel Shays had been routed the previous day in their attempt to seize the federal arsenal at Springfield. Shays was a hitherto obscure Revolutionary war captain. Born in 1747 in eastern Massachusetts, he had escaped rural poverty by acquiring his own farm before the outbreak of the Revolution. He enlisted in 1775 and served the patriot cause for five years before returning to his farm in Pelham, a village of small-scale farmers with a tradition of resisting outside authorities. Like many of his fellow farmers in western Massachusetts, Shays faced hard times in the 1780s. A combination of falling farm prices, a shortage of money, heavy taxes, and mounting debts produced an economic crisis that threatened more and more farmers with imprisonment for debt and, worse yet, the loss of their farms, the basis of their independence. Faced with an unresponsive state legislature controlled by eastern merchants and creditors, angry farmers reacted much as they had during the revolutionary agitation against the British a decade earlier: they organized, protested, and shut down the county courts. By 1786 Shays had emerged as one of their key leaders, and the ragtag army of farmers that he marched against the Springfield arsenal now aimed at nothing less than the overthrow of the state government.

State leaders and eastern merchants were horrified by this armed challenge to their authority. In quickly mobilizing forces to suppress the rebellion, they acted on their belief that the Revolution had been fought to forge a society founded on the rule of law and contract, in which the established order would be upheld. Liberty for them was equated with the right of the individual to pursue wealth and amass property. By contrast, the struggling farmers and artisans supportive of the cause of the rebels defined the liberty won in the Revolution more strongly in terms of the right of communities to defend their interests against the threat of moneyed and aristocratic elites.

Driven out of Massachusetts when his army quickly collapsed in 1787, Shays once again became an obscure figure. Few noticed when he died impoverished in upstate New York in 1825. Still, the movement that bears his name, more than any other domestic disturbance in the 1780s, dramatized the fragile nature and conflicting values of America's first republic under the Articles of Confederation. Providing for little more than a loose union of the states, the Articles were ratified in 1781. The years that followed were a period of trial and error marked by a running debate over the meaning of liberty and the extent of power to be entrusted to a national government. Americans favoring a stronger, more centralized government repeatedly cited Shays's Rebellion as an example of the impending chaos that would destroy the republic unless fundamental changes were made. Those changes came with the writing and ratification of the Constitution of the United States in 1788.

KEY TOPICS

- Republicanism and the political philosophy of the new state constitutions
- Internal problems in the United States under the Articles of Confederation
- Efforts of Britain and Spain to exploit the weaknesses of the United States after the Revolution
- The movement for a stronger national government
- The drafting and ratification of the United States Constitution

THE NEW ORDER OF REPUBLICANISM

As royal authority collapsed during the Revolution, various provincial congresses and committees assumed power in each of the former colonies. The Continental Congress, seeking to build support for the war effort, was concerned that these new institutions should have a firm legal and popular foundation. In May 1776, the Congress called on the colonies to form new state governments "under the authority of the people."

This call reflected the political philosophy of republicanism that animated the Revolution (see Chapter 6). To Americans, republicanism meant, first and foremost, that legitimate political authority derives from the people. It is they who are sovereign, not the king or the aristocracy. The people should elect the officials who govern them, and those officials should represent the interests of the people who elected them. Another key aspect of republicanism was the revolutionary idea that the people could define and limit governmental power through written constitutions.

Thus for many Americans, the Congress's call reflected the root purpose of the Revolution—to banish aristocratic tyranny and reconstruct government in the states on republican principles. But if those principles included the idea that legitimate government flowed from the people, it was not always clear just who was included in "the people."

DEFINING THE PEOPLE

When news of the peace treaty with Britain reached New Bern, North Carolina, in June 1783, the citizens held a grand celebration. As reported by Francisco de Miranda, a visiting Spanish officer, "There was a barbecue [a roast pig] and a barrel of rum, from which the leading officials and citizens of the region promiscuously drank with the meanest and lowest kind of people, holding hands and drinking from the same cup. It is impossible to imagine, without seeing it, a more purely democratic gathering."

For Miranda, this boisterous mingling of all citizens as seeming equals confirmed the central tenet of republicanism, the belief that the people were sovereign. But republicanism also taught that political rights should be limited to those who owned private property, because the independent will required for informed political judgment required economic self-sufficiency. This, in effect, restricted political participation to propertied white men. Virtually everyone else—propertyless white men, servants legally bound to others, women, slaves and most free black people—were denied political rights. As for Native Americans, they were outside the U.S. body politic and exercised political rights within their own nations.

Because the ownership of property was relatively widespread among white men, some 60 to 85 percent of adult white men could participate in politics—a far higher proportion than elsewhere in the world of the eighteenth century. The greatest concentration of the remaining 25 percent or so shut out of the political process were unskilled laborers and mariners living in port cities. The city's working poor still included indentured servants, bound by contract to give personal service for a fixed time. The walking poor—vagrants and transients—might be jailed by local authorities, confined to workhouses, or hired out in public auctions for fixed terms of labor. Those who incurred debts they were unable to pay faced imprisonment.

Women and the Revolution. The Revolution did little to change the traditional patriarchal assumption that politics and public life should be the exclusive domain of men. Women, according to republican beliefs, were part of the dependent class and belonged under the control of propertied men—their husbands and fathers. Under common law (the custom-

Chronology

1776 States begin writing the first constitutions.	States begin to issue more paper money.
1777 Articles of Confederation proposed.	Treaty of Fort McIntosh.
1781 Articles ratified.	**1786** Shays's Rebellion breaks out.
1783 Americans celebrate independence and the peace treaty with Britain.	Jay-Gardoqui Treaty defeated.
	Annapolis Convention.
1784 Onset of the postwar depression.	**1787** Constitutional Convention at Philadelphia.
Spain closes the Mississippi.	Northwest Ordinance.
Separatist plots in the West.	**1788** Constitution ratified and goes into effect.
Treaty of Fort Stanwix.	Publication of *The Federalist.*
1785 Land Ordinance of 1785.	

ary, largely unwritten, law that Americans had inherited from Britain), women surrendered their property rights at marriage unless they made special arrangements to the contrary. Legally and economically, husbands had complete control over their wives. As a result, argued Theophilus Parsons of Massachusetts in 1778, women were, as a matter of course, "so situated as to have no wills of their own."

To be sure, some women saw in the political and social enthusiasm of the Revolution an opportunity to protest the most oppressive features of their subordination. "I won't have it thought that because we are

the weaker sex as to bodily strength we are capable of nothing more than domestic concerns," wrote Eliza Wilkinson of South Carolina. Men, she lamented, "won't even allow us liberty of thought and that is all I want." Such protests, however, had little enduring effect. Most women were socialized to accept that their proper place was in the home with their families.

Gender-specific language—including such terms as "men," "Freemen," "white male inhabitants," and "free white men"—explicitly barred women from voting in almost all state constitutions of the 1770s. Only the New Jersey constitution of 1776 defined **suffrage**—the right to vote—in gender-free terms, extending it to all adults "worth fifty pounds." As a result, until 1807, when the state legislature changed the constitution, propertied women, including widows and single women, enjoyed the right to vote in New Jersey.

The Revolution otherwise did bring women a few limited gains. They benefited from slightly less restrictive divorce laws and gained somewhat greater access to educational and business opportunities, changes that reflected the relative autonomy of many women during the war when their men were off fighting. The perception of women's moral status also rose. As the Philadelphia physician Benjamin Rush argued in his *Thoughts upon Female Education* (1787), educated

With the exception of New Jersey, where women meeting the property qualifications were eligible to vote, the state constitutions of the Revolutionary era prohibited women from voting.

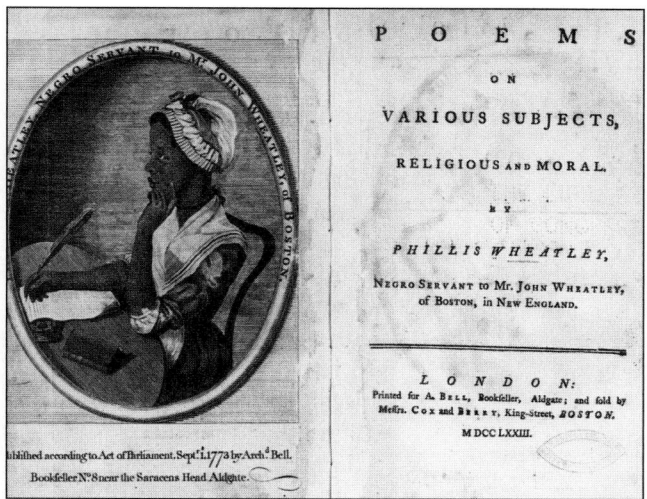

Phillis Wheatley was an acclaimed African American poet. Kidnapped into slavery as a child in Africa, she was a domestic slave to the Wheatley family of Boston when her first poems were published in 1773.

and morally informed women were needed to instruct "their sons in the principles of liberty and government." Often called republican motherhood, this more positive view of women's influence entrusted mothers with the responsibility of passing on republican virtues from one generation to the next.

The Revolution and African Americans in the South.

The Revolution had a more immediate impact on the lives of many African Americans, triggering the growth of free black communities and the development of an African American culture. Changes begun by the Revolution were the main factor in the tremendous increase of free blacks from a few thousand at midcentury to more than 100,000 by 1800 (see Figure 7–1). One key to this increase was a shift in the religious and intellectual climate. Revolutionary principles of liberty and equality and evangelical notions of human fellowship convinced many whites for the first time to challenge black slavery. In 1784, Virginia Methodists condemned slavery as "contrary to the Golden Law of God on which hang all the Laws and Prophets, and the unalienable Rights of Mankind, as well as every Principle of Revolution." As many whites grew more hostile to slavery, blacks began to seize opportunities for freedom that emerged from the disruptions of the war and the needs of both sides for military manpower.

Upwards of fifty thousand slaves, or one in ten of those in bondage, gained their freedom as a result of the war. One route was through military service, which generally carried a promise of freedom. When the British began raising black troops, the Americans followed suit. All the states except Georgia and South Carolina recruited black regiments. Some five thousand blacks served in the Continental armies, and they, like their counterparts in British units, were mostly slaves. Most slaves who gained freedom during the war, however, were those who fled their owners and made their way to the port cities of the North.

By making slave property generally less secure, the Revolution encouraged many masters to free their slaves. Once freed, blacks tried to break all the bonds of their former servitude. "Negro Soloman," his former owner griped, "now free, prefers to mould bricks rather than serve me." A Delaware mistress felt rejected when a slave she had freed spurned her offer of employment with a friend and found her own job. "I cannot help think," she noted sourly, that "it is too generally the case with all those of colour to be ungrateful." As the number of free blacks increased, those still enslaved grew bolder in their efforts to gain freedom. "Henny," warned a Maryland slaveowner in 1783, "will try to pass for a free woman as several have lately been set free in this neighbourhood."

Northern blacks and the Revolution.

If the control mechanisms of slavery experienced some strain in the South during the Revolution, in the North, where slaves were only a small percentage of the population, they crumbled. Most northern states ended slavery between 1777 and 1784. New York

FIGURE 7-1   Growth of the Free Black Population between 1750 and 1800
Gradual emancipation in the North, the freeing of many slaves by their owners in the South, and the opportunities for freedom offered by the Revolution, all contributed to an explosive growth in the free population of African Americans in the second half of the eighteenth century.

Source: *A Century of Population Growth in the United States, 1790–1900* (1909). p. 80. Data for 1750 estimated.

The Mother Bethel Church in Philadelphia, dedicated in 1794, was home to the first independent black congregation in America and the founding establishment of the African Methodist Episcopal denomination. Churches were central to the community life of black Northerners and provided leadership in the struggle for racial justice.

followed in 1799 and New Jersey in 1804. Nonetheless, although a majority of northern whites now agreed that slavery was incompatible with the Revolution's commitment to **natural rights** (the inherent human rights to life and liberty) and human freedom, they refused to sanction a sudden emancipation. The laws ending slavery in most of the northern states called for only the children of slaves to be freed, and only when they reached adulthood.

Northern blacks had to struggle to overcome white prejudice. Although black males were allowed to vote if they met the property qualifications, most were poor and held little property. Facing discrimination in jobs and housing, barred from juries, and denied a fair share of funds for schools, urban blacks had to rely on their own resources. With the help of the small class of property holders among them, they began establishing their own churches and self-help associations.

The Revolution's Impact on Native Americans.

Most Indian peoples had stayed neutral during the war or fought for the British (see Chapter 6). Just as the Americans sought to shake off British control, so the Indians, especially the western tribes and most of the Iroquois Confederation, sought to free themselves from American dominance. The British defeat was thus a double blow, depriving the Indians of a valuable ally and exposing them to the wrath of the victorious patriots. Late in the war a British officer observed of the pro-British southern Indians, "The minds of these people appear as much agitated as those of the unhappy Loyalists, they have very seriously proposed to abandon their country and accompany us [in an evacuation], having made all the world their enemies by their attachment to us."

The state governments, as well as the Confederation Congress, now treated Indian lands after the Revolution as a prize of war to be distributed to white settlers. Territorial demands on the Indians escalated, and even the few tribes that had furnished troops for the American side struggled to maintain control over most of their homelands. As they did so, it was clear that white Americans did not consider Native Americans to be part of their republican society. With the exception of Massachusetts, the states denied voting and legal rights to the Indians within their borders.

Still, it must be stressed that most Native Americans did not want or expect equal rights within the new American republic. They viewed themselves as belonging to their own nations, composed of distinct villages and settlements, with a common culture and interests. What they wanted were political rights and control over land within their nations. Above all, they were fiercely independent. As George Rogers Clark wrote in 1783 of the Indians he had fought during the Revolution, "They have no notion of being dependent on Either the brittish or americans, But would make war on both if Equally Insulted."

In seeking to defend their independence against the growing pressure of white Americans on their lands, Native Americans forged new confederacies in the 1780s that temporarily united them against a common enemy. They were encouraged in these efforts by the imperial powers of England and Spain, both of whom sought to curb the westward expansion of the United States. Thus, the immediate impact of the Revolution on Native Americans was a mixed one. On the one hand, the Revolution had created a new expansionist power in the United States that was intent on settling lands already occupied by Indians. On the other hand, American victory in the Revolution had broken the British monopoly of power in the region west of the Appalachian Mountains. Before the United States could consolidate its claim over the region, new imperial rivalries sprang up that allowed Native Americans to stake out a political middle ground between the competing powers. Throughout the 1780s, Native Americans continued to act as independent political agents in playing off outside powers against each other.

THE STATE CONSTITUTIONS

"Oppose everything that leans to aristocracy, of power in the hands of the rich and chief men exercised to the oppression of the poor." So the voters of Mecklenburg County, North Carolina, instructed their delegates to the state's constitutional convention in 1776. These instructions reflect a basic premise embodied in the new state constitutions of the Revolutionary period: Power had to be checked to insure individual liberty and safeguard against tyranny.

Ten new state constitutions were in place by the end of 1777. In Connecticut and Rhode Island, the new constitutions simply amended the existing colonial charters, which already provided for extensive self-rule, by dropping all references to royal authority. Massachusetts, the only state to hold elections for a special constitutional convention, ratified its constitution in 1780.

All these constitutions were written documents, a striking departure from the English practice of treating a constitution as a collection of customary rights and practices that had evolved over time. In the American view, a constitution was a formal expression of the people's sovereignty, a codification of the powers of government and the rights of citizenship that functioned as a fundamental law to which all public authority was held accountable.

Because Americans had come to associate tyranny with the privileges of royal governors, all the new state constitutions cut back sharply on executive power. Annual elections were now the norm for governors, who were also made subject to impeachment—charges of misconduct, resolved at a public trial—and limited in the number of terms they could serve. Most important, for it struck at what patriots felt was the main source of executive domination and corruption, governors lost control over patronage, the power to appoint executive and judicial officials.

As the new constitutions curbed the power of governors, they increased that of the legislatures, making them the focal point of government. Colonial assemblies had been in the forefront of popular opposition to British authority, and the state legislatures that succeeded them were now seen as the most trustworthy defenders of individual liberty. The new constitutions expanded the power of the legislatures to appoint officials and to oversee military and financial matters. To make the legislatures more expressive of the popular will, the new constitutions included provisions that lowered property requirements for voting and officeholding, mandated annual elections, increased the number of seats in the legislatures, and made representation more proportional to the geographical distribution of population. Upper houses were made independent of the executive office and opened to popular election, as opposed to the colonial practice of having their members appointed by the governor.

Americans knew that legislatures, too, could act tyrannically, as they believed Britain's Parliament had done. So in a final check on arbitrary power, each state constitution eventually included some form of a **bill of rights** that set explicit limits on the power of government to interfere in the lives of citizens. The Virginia Declaration of Rights, written by the planter George Mason and adopted in June 1776, set the precedent for this notable republican feature. By 1784, the constitutions of all thirteen states had provisions guaranteeing religious liberty, freedom of the press, and a citizen's right to such fair legal practices as trial by jury.

Toward religious pluralism. The new constitutions weakened but did not always sever the traditional tie between church and state for the support of religion. Many Americans held, as the Massachusetts Constitution of 1780 put it, that "the happiness of a people, and the good order and preservation of civil government, essentially depend upon piety, religion, and morality." Reflecting this belief, many states, notably in New England, levied taxes for the support of religion. The states of New England also continued to maintain Congregationalism as the established, or state-supported, religion, while allowing dissenting Baptists and Methodists to use funds from the compulsory religious taxes to support their ministers. The "common people," explained the Baptist leader Isaac Backus, insisted that they had "as good a right to judge and act for themselves in matter of religion as civil rulers or the learned clergy."

The mid-Atlantic states lacked the religious uniformity of New England. The region supported several prominent denominations—Quaker, Episcopalian, Presbyterian, Dutch Reformed, and Lutheran—and none was able to dominate the others. This pluralism checked legislative efforts to impose

AMERICAN VIEWS

A French Observer Describes a New Society

In 1782, J. Hector St. John Crèvecoeur, a Frenchman who had lived and traveled in British North America, published his impressions of America. The following selection from his *Letters from an American Farmer* captures the striking optimism and sense of newness that he found. More so than any other literary work, the *Letters* stamped the new American republic, especially in the minds of Europeans, as the home of the world's freest and most equal people.

- What is Crèvecoeur's image of America? Do you believe it was overly optimistic?
- Why does Crèvecoeur put such emphasis on the absence of titles and great disparities of wealth?
- Just what was so new about America to Crèvecoeur?
- Why did Crèvecoeur ignore African slaves in his definition of the American? What happened to Native Americans in his account of the making of the American?

I wish I could be acquainted with the feelings and thoughts which must agitate the heart and present themselves to the mind of an enlightened Englishman when he first lands on this continent. . . . He is arrived on a new continent; a modern society offers itself to his contemplation, different from what he had hitherto seen. It is not composed, as in Europe, of great lords who possess everything and of a herd of people who have nothing. Here are no aristocratical families, no courts, no kings, no bishops, no ecclesiastical dominion, no invisible power giving to a few a very visible one, no great manufactures employing thousands, no great refinements of luxury. The rich and the poor are not so far removed

---

religious taxes or designate any denomination as the established church. In the South, where many Anglican (or Episcopalian) clergymen had been Tories, the Anglican Church lost its former established status. Thomas Jefferson, in Virginia's religious freedom law of 1786, went so far as to assert that "our civil rights have no dependence on our religious opinions any more than on opinions in physics or geometry."

Radical and conservative visions of republicanism.

Although in general the executive lost power and the legislature gained power under the new state constitutions, the actual structure of each state government reflected the outcome of political struggles between those holding a radical vision of republicanism and those holding a conservative vision. The democratically inclined radicals wanted to open government to all male citizens. The conservatives, fearing "mob rule," wanted to limit government to an educated elite of substantial property holders. Although they agreed that government had to be derived from the people, most conservatives, like Jeremy Belknap of New Hampshire, thought that the people had to be "taught . . . that they are not able to govern themselves."

In South Carolina, where conservative planters gained the upper hand, the constitution mandated property qualifications that barred 90 percent of the state's white males from holding elective public office. By contrast, Pennsylvania had the most democratic and controversial constitution. Many of Pennsylvania's conservatives had discredited themselves during the Revolution by remaining neutral or loyal to the crown. The Scots-Irish farmers and Philadelfrom each other as they are in Europe. Some few towns excepted, we are all tillers of the earth, from Nova Scotia to West Florida. We are a people of cultivators scattered over an immense territory, communicating with each other by means of good roads and navigable rivers, united by the silken bands of mild government, all respecting the laws without dreading their power, because they are equitable. We are all animated with the spirit of an industry which is unfettered and unrestrained, because each person works for himself . . . . A pleasing uniformity of decent competence appears throughout our habitations. The meanest of our log-houses is a dry and comfortable habitation. Lawyer and merchant are the fairest titles our towns afford; that of a farmer is the only appellation of the rural inhabitants of our country. It must take some time ere he can reconcile himself to our dictionary, which is but short in words of dignity and names of honour . . . . We have no princes for whom we toil, starve, and bleed; we are the most perfect society now existing in the world. Here man is free as he ought to be, nor is this pleasing equality so transitory as many others are. Many ages will not see the shores of our great lakes replenished with inland nations, nor the unknown bounds of North America entirely peopled. . . .

The next wish of this traveller will be to know whence came all these people. They are a mixture of English, Scotch, Irish, French, Dutch, Germans, and Swedes. From this promiscuous breed, that race now called Americans have arisen. . . .

What, then, is the American, this new man? He is either an European or the descendant of an European; hence that strange mixture of blood, which you will find in no other country . . . . He is an American, who, leaving behind him all his ancient prejudices and manners, receives new ones from the new mode of life he has embraced, the new government he obeys, and the new rank he holds. He becomes an American by being received in the broad lap of our Alma Mater. Here individuals of all nations are melted into a new race of men, whose labours and posterity will one day cause great changes in the world.

Source: J. Hector St. John Crèvecoeur, *Letters from an American Farmer and Sketches of Eighteenth-Century America*, ed. Albert E. Stone (1986), pp. 66–70.

---

phia artisans who stepped into the resulting political vacuum held an egalitarian view of republicanism. The constitution they pushed through in 1776 gave the vote to all free males who paid taxes, regardless of wealth, and eliminated property qualifications for officeholding. In addition, the constitution concentrated power in a unicameral (single-house) legislature, eliminating both the office of governor and the more elite upper legislative house. To prevent the formation of an entrenched class of officeholders, the constitution's framers also required legislators to stand for election annually and barred them from serving more than four years out of seven.

The constitutions of the other states, although not as bold in their democratic reforms as Pennsylvania's, typically enhanced the political influence of ordinary citizens more than the constitution of South Carolina did. Unlike the colonial assemblies, the new bicameral (two-house) legislatures included substantially more artisans and small farmers and were not controlled by men of wealth. The proportion of legislators who came from a common background—those with property valued under £200—more than tripled to 62 percent in the North and more than doubled in the South from the 1770s to the 1780s.

This growing political equality was accompanied by demands that those in government be more responsive to the people. Summing up the prevailing view among Americans about the proper basis for government, William Hooper of North Carolina wrote in 1776, "Rulers must be conceived as the creatures of the people, made for their use, accountable to them, and subject to removal as soon as they act inconsistent with the purposes for which they were formed."

THE ARTICLES OF CONFEDERATION

Once the Continental Congress decided on independence in 1776, it needed to create a legal basis for a permanent union of the states. John Dickinson of Pennsylvania, a reluctant supporter of independence, presented a draft plan for such a union as early as the summer of 1776. Dickinson favored a strong central government to prevent the collapse of the social order that he feared might follow the overthrow of imperial rule. The Congress, however, fundamentally altered Dickinson's original plan to recognize the sovereign power of the individual states. According to the key provision of the **Articles of Confederation** that the Congress finally submitted to the states more than a year later, in November 1777, "Each State retains its sovereignty, freedom and independence, and every power, jurisdiction and right, which is not by this confederation expressly delegated to the United States, in Congress assembled." The effect was to create a loose confederation of autonomous states.

The powers the Articles of Confederation delegated to the central government were extremely limited, in effect little more than those already exercised by the Continental Congress. There were no provisions for a national judiciary or a separate executive branch of government. The Articles made Congress the sole instrument of national authority but restricted it with a series of constitutional safeguards that virtually eliminated any possibility that it could ever threaten the interests of the states. Each state had only one vote in Congress, making each politically equal regardless of its size or population. State legislatures were to choose their congressional delegations in annual elections, and delegates could serve only three years out of six. Delegates were expected to follow the instructions of their state legislatures and could be recalled at any time. Important measures, such as those dealing with finances or war and peace, required approval from a majority of nine state delegations voting in the Congress. Amendments to the Articles of Confederation, including the levying of national taxes, required the unanimous consent of the states.

The Congress had authority primarily in the areas of foreign policy and national defense. It could declare war, make peace, conduct foreign affairs, negotiate with Native Americans, and settle disputes between the states. It had no authority, however, to raise troops or impose taxes on its own; it could only ask the states to supply troops and money and hope that they would comply.

The central principle behind the Articles was the fear of oppressive, centralized power encroaching on the freedoms for which the Revolution was fought. In the end, as Edward Rutledge, a delegate from South Carolina to the Continental Congress, put it, the new Confederation Congress was vested "with no more Power than is absolutely necessary." "It is freedom, Gentlemen, it is freedom, & not a choice of the forms of servitude for which we contend," resolved the residents of West Springfield, Massachusetts, in instructions to their congressional representatives in 1778.

Most states quickly ratified the Articles of Confederation, but Maryland stubbornly held out until March 1781. Because they needed the approval of all thirteen states, it was not until then that the Articles officially took effect. Surprisingly, given the prevailing deep suspicion of central power, what caused the delay was the demand of some states to give Congress a power not included in the Articles submitted for ratification in 1777.

The issue here concerned the unsettled lands in the West between the Appalachian Mountains and the Mississippi River (see Map 7–1). Some states claimed these lands by virtue of their colonial charter rights, and led by Virginia and Massachusetts, they insisted on maintaining control over these territories. The so-called landless states—those with no claim to the West—insisted that it be set aside as a national domain, a reserve of public land controlled by Congress for the benefit of all the states. Land speculators who had purchased huge blocs of land from the Indians before the Revolution sided with the landless states. Many of them leading politicians, they expected that the Congress would be more likely to honor their land titles than would the individual states.

The British threat to the Chesapeake area in early 1781 finally broke the impasse that had delayed final approval of the Articles. Though retaining control of Kentucky, Virginia gave up its claim in the west to a vast area extending north of the Ohio River. In turn, Maryland, the last holdout among the landless states and now desperate for military aid from the Congress, agreed to ratify the Articles. After more than three years of debate and the airing of jealousies among the states, the final cementing of the original Union was decidedly anticlimactic.

PROBLEMS AT HOME

Neither prosperity nor political stability accompanied the return of peace in 1783. The national government struggled to avoid bankruptcy, and in 1784, an economic depression struck the country. As fiscal problems deepened over the next few years, creditor and debtor groups clashed angrily in state legislatures. When legislatures passed measures that provided relief to debtors at the expense of creditors, the

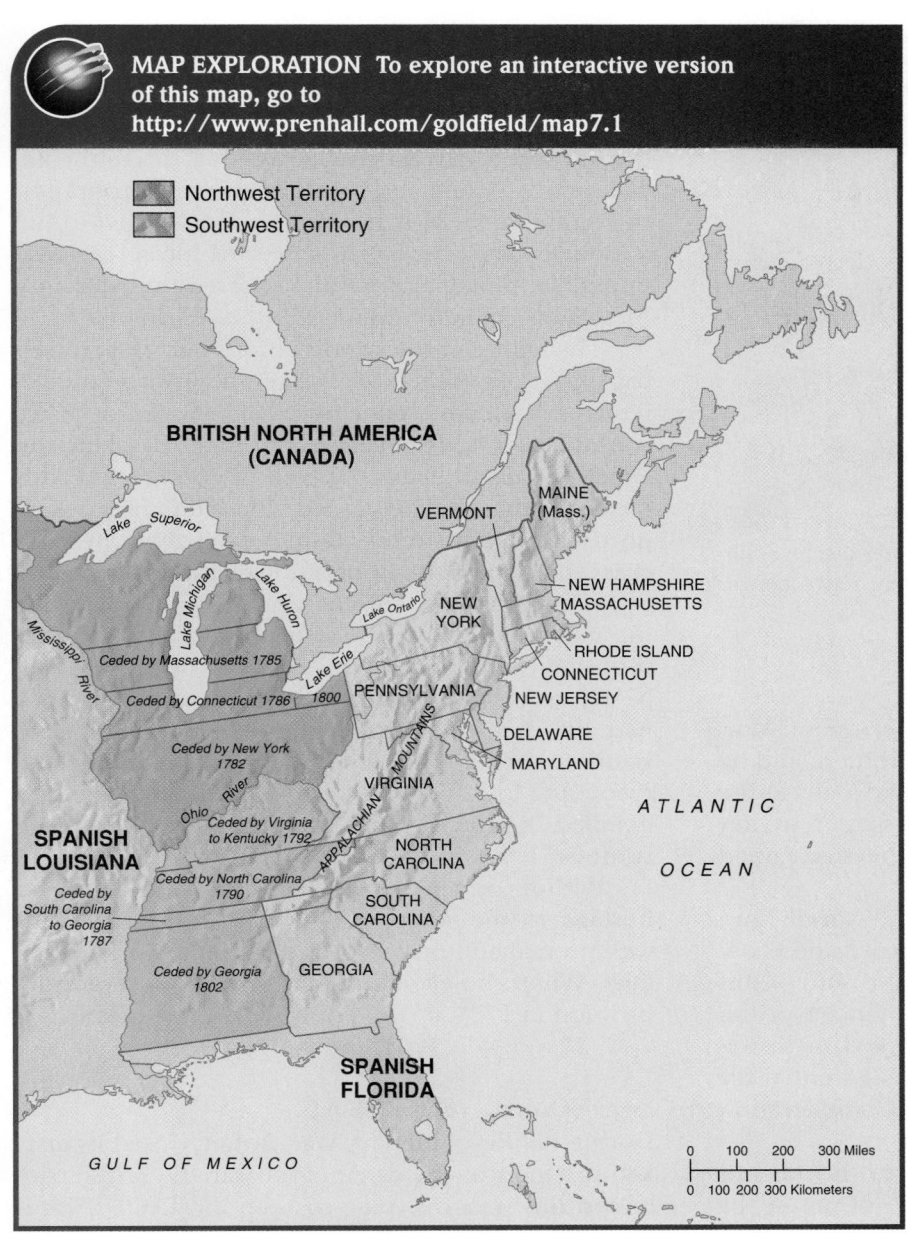

MAP EXPLORATION To explore an interactive version of this map, go to http://www.prenhall.com/goldfield/map7.1

Northwest Territory
Southwest Territory

BRITISH NORTH AMERICA
(CANADA)

Lake Superior
Lake Michigan
Lake Huron
Lake Ontario
Lake Erie
Mississippi River

VERMONT
MAINE (Mass.)
NEW HAMPSHIRE
MASSACHUSETTS
NEW YORK
RHODE ISLAND
CONNECTICUT
NEW JERSEY
PENNSYLVANIA
DELAWARE
MARYLAND

Ceded by Massachusetts 1785
Ceded by Connecticut 1786 | 1800
Ceded by New York 1782
Ohio River
Ceded by Virginia to Kentucky 1792
VIRGINIA
APPALACHIAN MOUNTAINS

SPANISH LOUISIANA

Ceded by South Carolina to Georgia 1787
Ceded by North Carolina 1790
NORTH CAROLINA
SOUTH CAROLINA

Ceded by Georgia 1802
GEORGIA

SPANISH FLORIDA

GULF OF MEXICO

ATLANTIC OCEAN

0   100   200   300 Miles
0 100 200 300 Kilometers

MAP 7-1   Cession of Western Lands by the States
Eight states had claims to lands in the West after the Revolution, and their willingness to cede them to the national government was an essential step in the creation of a public domain administered by Congress.

The Fiscal Crisis.

The Continental Congress and the states had incurred heavy debts to finance the Revolutionary War. Unable to impose and collect sufficient taxes to cover the debts and without reserves of gold or silver, they had little choice but to borrow funds and issue certificates or bonds pledging repayment. The Congress had the largest responsibility for meeting the war's costs, and to do so, it printed close to $250 million in paper notes backed only by its good faith. By the end of the war in 1781, these Continental dollars were nearly worthless, and the national debt—primarily certificates issued by the Continental Loan Office—stood at $11 million. As Congress issued new securities to settle claims by soldiers and civilians, this sum rose to $28 million within just a few years.

The Congress never did put its tottering finances on a sound footing, and its fiscal problems ultimately discredited the Articles of Confederation in the eyes of the **nationalists,** a loose bloc of congressmen, army officers, and public creditors who wanted to strengthen the Confederation at the expense of the states. The nationalists first began to organize in the dark days of 1780 and 1781, when inflation was rampant, the army was going unpaid, the Congress had ceased paying interest on the public debt, and the war effort itself seemed in danger of collapsing. Galvanized by this crisis, the nationalists rallied behind Robert Morris, a Philadelphia merchant appointed as superintendent of finance for the Confederation government.

Morris sought to enhance national authority through a bold program of financial and political reform. He began by securing a charter from Congress in 1781 for the Bank of North America, the nation's first commercial bank. Located in Philadelphia and partly owned by private investors, the bank had close

creditors decried what they saw as the interference of ignorant majorities with the rights of private property. Raising the cry of "legislative despotism," the abuse of power by tyrannical lawmakers, the creditors joined their voices to those who early on had wanted the power of the states curbed by a stronger central government. The only solid accomplishment of the Confederation Congress during this troubled period was to formulate an orderly and democratic plan for the settlement of the West under national controls.

Issued in 1777, this Georgia four-dollar banknote was an example of the type of paper money used to finance the Revolutionary War.

connections to the Confederation government. Morris wanted it to serve as a national institution, and he used it to hold government funds, make loans to the government, and issue bank notes—paper money that could be used to settle debts and pay taxes owed to the United States.

Morris was able to resume some specie payments, and he temporarily brought order and economy to the nation's finances. As a result of his reforms, he came to be called the Financier of the Revolution. Nonetheless, he was blocked in his efforts to gain the taxing power that was essential for restoring the shattered credit of the Confederation government.

Morris's larger objective, central to the aims of the nationalists, was to create a "bond of union" by having the Congress assume payment of the entire national debt. Settling this debt would lead the propertied classes—the people who had financed the war and held the debt—to identify their economic self-interest with the effective exercise of power by the national government.

But to achieve this political goal, Morris had to gain for the Congress what it had always lacked: the power to tax. In 1781, he proposed a national impost, or tariff, of 5 percent on imported goods. Because this was a national tax, it required an amendment to the Articles of Confederation and the consent of all thirteen states. Twelve of the states quickly ratified the impost amendment, but Rhode Island—critically dependent on its own import duties to finance its war debt—rejected it, sending it

down to defeat. When a revised impost plan was considered two years later, New York blocked its passage.

These failures doomed Morris's financial reforms. He left office in 1784, and in the same year, the Bank of North America severed its ties to the national government and became a private corporation in Pennsylvania. Morris remained committed to the nationalist cause and would see his ideas resurface under the financial programs of Treasury Secretary Alexander Hamilton in the 1790s (see Chapter 8).

The failure of the impost tax was one of many setbacks that put the nationalists temporarily on the defensive. With the conclusion of peace in 1783, confidence in state government returned, taking the edge off calls to invest the central government with greater authority. The states continued to balk at supplying the money requisitioned from them by Congress and denied the Congress even limited authority to regulate foreign commerce. Most ominously for the nationalist cause, the states began to assume responsibility for part of the national debt. By 1786, New Jersey, Pennsylvania, Maryland, and New York had absorbed one-third of the debt by issuing state bonds to their citizens in exchange for national securities. As Morris had warned in 1781, such a policy entailed "a principle of disunion . . . which must be ruinous."

Without the power to tax, the Congress was a hostage to the sovereignty of the individual states with no real authority over the nation's economic affairs. When the economy plunged into a severe depression in 1784, it could only look on helplessly.

ECONOMIC DEPRESSION

During the Revolutionary War, Britain closed its markets to American goods. After the war, the British continued this policy, hoping to keep the United States weak and dependent. In the summer of 1783, they excluded Americans from the lucrative trade with the British West Indies. Before the Revolution, this trade in foodstuffs and timber with the sugar islands had been the primary means by which the colonists had built up the credits they needed to offset their imports from Britain.

Meanwhile, British merchants were happy to satisfy America's pent-up demand for consumer goods after the war. A flood of cheap British imports inundated the American market, and coastal merchants made them available to inland traders and shopkeepers by extending easy credit terms. In turn, these local businessmen sold the goods to farmers and artisans in the interior. Ultimately, however, the British merchants required payment in hard currency, gold and silver coins. Without access to its former export markets, America's only source of hard currency was foreign loans obtained by Congress and what money the French army had spent during the war. This was soon exhausted as America's trade deficit with Britain—the excess of imports over exports—ballooned in the early 1780s to £5 million (see Figure 7–2).

The result was an immense bubble of credit that finally burst in 1784, triggering a depression that would linger for the balance of the decade. As merchants began to press debtors for immediate payment, prices collapsed (they fell more than 25 percent between 1784 and 1786), and debtors were unable to pay. The best most could hope for was to avoid bankruptcy.

Small farmers everywhere had trouble paying their taxes. In 1786, James Swan of Massachusetts wrote of farmers in his state: "There is no family that does not want some money for some purposes, and the little which the farmer carries home from market, must be applied to other uses, besides paying off the [tax] collector's bills." Rural shopkeepers often could not move goods unless they agreed to barter them for farm produce. Abigail Dwight, who ran a small store in western Massachusetts, reported in 1785 that "most of these People sell on credit for To-Morrow at large—for very little Cash stirring this way—to be pay'd for in old Horses—cows—some Boards—cabbages—turnips—Potatoes etc."

In the cities, wages fell 25 percent between 1785 and 1789, and workers began to organize. They called for tariffs to protect them from cheap British imports and for legislative measures to promote American manufacturers. In the countryside, farmers faced a wave of lawsuits for the collection of debts and the dread possibility of losing their land. "To be tenants to landlords, we know not who," protested the farmers of Conway, Massachusetts, "and pay rent for lands, purchased with our money, and converted from howling wilderness, into fruitful fields, by the sweat of our brows, seems. . . truly shocking."

With insufficient money in circulation to raise prices and reverse the downturn, the depression fed on itself. Congress was powerless to raise cash and was unable to pay off its old debts, including what it owed to the Revolutionary soldiers. Many state governments made things worse by imposing heavy taxes payable in the paper money they had issued during the Revolution. The result was to further reduce the amount of money in circulation, thus increasing deflationary pressures and forcing prices still lower.

Britain's trade policies caused particular suffering among New England merchants. No longer protected under the old Navigation Acts as British vessels, American ships were now barred from most ports in the British Empire. Incoming cargoes from the West Indies to New England fell off sharply, and the market for whale oil and fish, two of New England's major exports, dried up. The economy of the mid-Atlantic region held up somewhat better, but even there the loss of the provisioning trade to the British West Indies in grains, livestock, and dairy products cut into the income of merchants and farmers and forced layoffs among artisans who serviced the shipping trade.

In the southern states, British policies compounded the problem of recovering from the physical

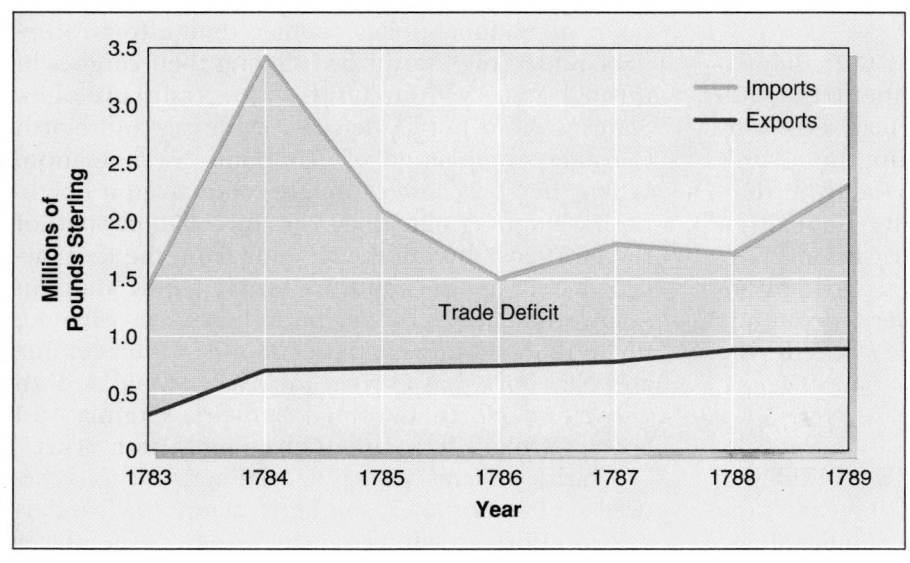

FIGURE 7-2   American Exports to and Imports from Britain between 1783 and 1789

During the 1780s, the United States imported far more from Britain than it exported there. The resulting huge trade deficit drained the country of gold and silver and was a major factor in the credit crisis that triggered an economic depression in the middle of the decade.

Source: *U.S. Bureau of the Census, Historical Statistics of the United States: Colonial Times to 1970, Part 2.* (1975) p. 1176.

damage and labor disruptions inflicted by the war. Some 10 percent of the region's slaves had fled during the war, and production levels on plantations fell in the 1780s. Chesapeake planters needed a full decade to restore the prewar output of tobacco, and a collapse in tobacco prices in 1785 left most of them in the same chronic state of indebtedness that had plagued them on the eve of the Revolution.

Farther south, in the Carolina lowcountry, the plantation economy was crippled throughout the 1780s. War damage had been extensive, and planters piled up debts to purchase additional slaves and repair their plantations and dikes. In spite of these investments, rice production was slow to recover. Burdened by new British duties on American rice, planters saw their rice exports fall by 50 percent. Small farmers in the pine barrens of North Carolina likewise had to adjust to the loss of their formerly protected British market for naval stores—tar, pitch, and turpentine.

By the late 1780s, the worst of the depression was over and an upturn was under way in the mid-Atlantic states. Food exports to continental Europe were on the rise, and American merchants were developing new trading ties with India and China. Commercial treaties with the Dutch, Swedes, and Prussians also opened up markets that had been closed to the colonists. Nonetheless, a full recovery had to await the 1790s.

The depression of the 1780s was the culmination of a decade of painful adjustment that followed the wrenching of the American economy from its traditional moorings within the British trading empire. A stagnant economy and burdensome debt combined with a growing population (there were 50 percent more Americans in 1787 than there had been in 1775) to reduce living standards. With more losers than winners, economic conflict dominated the politics of the states during the Confederation period.

THE ECONOMIC POLICIES OF THE STATES

The depression had political repercussions in all the states. Britain was an obvious target of popular anger,

Depicted here in a folding fan, the Empress of China *was the first American ship to undertake an extensive trading voyage to China. Sailing out of New York in February 1784,* the Empress of China *returned on May 11, 1785, and netted a profit of $37,000 for the investors who had financed the voyage. Building trading contracts to new markets in Asia and Europe helped the United States break its economic dependence on England.*

and merchants poorly positioned to adjust to the postwar dislocations of trade led a campaign to slap retaliatory duties on British ships and special taxes on the goods they carried. Likewise artisans and workers, especially in the North, pushed for tariff barriers against cheap British goods as a way to encourage domestic manufacturing and protect their jobs and wages. Most northern states imposed anti-British measures, but these varied from state to state, limiting their impact and producing squabbles when goods imported in one state were shipped to another.

State legislatures in the North responded to the protests of artisans by passing tariffs, but the lack of a uniform, national policy doomed their efforts. Shippers evaded high tariffs by bringing their cargoes in through states with no tariffs or less restrictive ones. States without ports, such as New Jersey and North Carolina, complained of economic discrimination. When they purchased foreign goods from a neighboring shipping state, they were forced to pay part of the tariff cost, but all the revenue from the tariff accrued only to the importing state. James Madison neatly summarized the plight of these states when he noted that "New Jersey, placed between Philadelphia and New York, was likened to a cask tapped at both ends; And North Carolina, between Virginia and South Carolina, to a patient bleeding at both Arms."

Tariff policies also fed sectional tensions between northern and southern states that undermined efforts to confer on the Congress the power to regulate commerce. The agrarian states of the South, which had little in the way of manufacturing to protect, had interests that differed from those of the states of the North. With the exception of Virginia, they favored free trade policies that encouraged British imports. Southern planters were also happy to take advantage of the low rates charged by British ships for transporting their crops to Europe; by doing so, they put pressure on northern shippers to reduce their rates.

The most bitter divisions exposed by the depression of the 1780s, however, were not between states but between debtors and creditors within states. As the value of debt securities the states had issued to raise money dropped during the Revolutionary War, speculators bought them up for a fraction of their face value and then put pressure on the states to raise taxes and repay the debts in full in hard currency. Wealthy landowners and merchants likewise supported higher taxes and the rapid repayment of debts in hard currency. Arrayed against these creditor groups by the mid-1780s was a broad coalition of debtors composed of middling farmers, small shop-

This clash between Shays's rebels and government troops at the Springfield arsenal marked the violent climax of the agrarian protests of the 1780s.

keepers, artisans, laborers, and people who had overextended themselves speculating in western land. The debtors wanted the states to issue paper money that they could use instead of hard money—gold and silver—to pay their debts. The paper money would have an inflationary effect, raising wages and the prices of farm commodities and reducing the value of debts contracted in hard currency. The townspeople of Atkinson, New Hampshire, expressing the feelings of many hard-pressed rural areas, put the issue this way: "For want of a suitable medium of trade the Citizens of this State are altogether unable to pay their public taxes, or private debts, or even to support the train of needless and expensive lawsuits, which alone would be an insupportable burden."

This was the economic context in which **Shays's Rebellion** exploded in the fall of 1786. Farm foreclosures and imprisonments for failure to pay debts had skyrocketed in western Massachusetts. Facing a collapse in farm prices and an impoverishing burden of debt, farmers petitioned the state legislators for economic relief. They complained of heavy taxes and the shortage of money and demanded legislation that would temporarily prohibit creditors from seizing farms and processing suits for debt. When the creditor and seaboard interests in the legislature refused to pass any relief measures, some two thousand farmers took up arms against the state government in Shays's Rebellion.

Outside of western Massachusetts, discontented debtors generally stopped short of armed resistance. Whereas the Shaysite rebels had felt betrayed by a state government that had rejected their demands, debtor interests elsewhere were often successful in changing the monetary policy of their states. In 1785 and 1786, seven states enacted laws for new paper money issues. In most cases, the result was a qualified success. Controls on the supply of the new money kept it from depreciating rapidly, so that its inflationary effect was mild. It was used chiefly to provide loans to farmers so that they could meet their tax or mortgage payments. Combined with laws that prevented or delayed creditors from seizing property from debtors to satisfy debts, the currency issues helped keep a lid on popular discontent.

The most notorious exception to this pattern of fiscal responsibility was in Rhode Island, already nicknamed "Rogue's Island" for the sharp trading practices of its merchants. A rural party that gained control of the Rhode Island legislature in 1786 pushed through a currency law that flooded the state with paper money that could be used to pay all debts. Creditors who balked at accepting the new money at face value were subject to heavy penalties. Shocked, they went into hiding or left the state entirely, and merchants denounced the law as outright fraud.

The actions of the debtor party in Rhode Island alarmed conservatives everywhere, confirming their fears that legislative bodies dominated by common farmers and artisans rather than, as before the Revolution, by men of wealth and social distinction, were dangerous. One South Carolina conservative declared that he could see nothing but an "open and outrageous . . . violation of every principle of justice" in paper money and debt relief laws. Conservatives, creditors, and nationalists alike now spoke of a democratic tyranny that would have to be checked if the republic were to survive and protect its property holders.

CONGRESS AND THE WEST

The Peace of Paris and the surrender of charter claims by the states gave the Congress control of a magnificent expanse of land between the Appalachian Mountains and the Mississippi River. This was the first American West. In what would prove the most enduring accomplishment of the Confederation government, the Congress set forth a series of effective provisions for its settlement, governance, and eventual absorption into the Union.

The Congress took several steps to establish its jurisdiction in the West. Asserting for the national government the right to formulate Indian policy, the Congress negotiated a series of treaties with the Indians beginning in 1784 for the abandonment of their land claims in the West. By threatening to use military force, congressional commissioners in 1784 coerced the Iroquois Confederation of New York to cede half of its territory to the United States in the Treaty of Fort Stanwix. Similar tactics in 1785 resulted in the Treaty of Fort McIntosh in which the Wyandots, Chippewas, Delawares, and Ottawas ceded much of their land in Ohio. Against the opposition of states intent on grabbing Indian lands for themselves, Congress resolved in 1787 that its treaties were binding on all the states. And anxious for revenue, Congress insisted on payment from squatters who had filtered into the West before provisions had been made for land sales.

The most pressing political challenge was to secure the loyalty of the West to the new and fragile Union. To satisfy the demands of settlers for self-government, the Congress resolved as early as 1779 that new states would be carved out of the western domain with all the rights of the original states. An early plan for organizing the territories, the Ordinance of 1784, was largely the work of Thomas Jefferson. In it, he proposed to create ten districts, or territories, each of which could apply for admission as a state when its population equaled that of the free inhabitants in the least populous of the existing states. Jefferson also proposed that settlers be permitted to choose their own officials, and he called for the prohibition of slavery in the West after 1800. Shorn of its no-slavery features, the ordinance passed Congress but was never put into practice.

As settlers and speculators began pouring into the West in 1784, however, the Congress was forced to move quickly to formulate a policy for conveying its public land into private hands. If it could not regulate land sales and pass on clear titles, Congress would, in effect, have surrendered its claim to govern. One way or another, settlers were going to get their land, but a pell-mell process of private acquisitions in widely scattered settlements threatened to touch off costly Indian wars, deprive the national government of vitally needed revenue, and encourage separatist movements. The members of Congress had to act on national land policy, warned a western Pennsylvanian, or else "lose the only opportunity they ever will have of extending their power and influence over this new region."

The Congress responded with the **Land Ordinance of 1785**. The crucial feature of this seminal legislation was its stipulation that public lands be surveyed in a rectangular grid pattern before being offered for sale (see Figure 7-3). By requiring that land first be plotted into townships of thirty-six uniform sections of 640 acres each, the ordinance adopted the New England system of land settlement, an approach that promoted compact settlements and produced undisputed land titles. In sharp contrast was the typical southern pattern, whereby settlers picked out a piece of land in a large tract ahead of a precise survey and then fought each other in the courts to secure legal title. In an effort to avoid endless litigation, Congress opted for a policy geared to order and regularity.

Congress also attempted to attract a certain type of settler to the West by offering the plots of 640 acres at the then hefty sum of no less than $640, or $1 per acre, payable in hard currency or its equivalent. The goal here was to keep out the shiftless poor and reserve the West for enterprising and presumably law-abiding farm families who could afford the entry cost. Concerned about westerners' reputation for lawlessness and afraid that the primitive living conditions might cause them to lapse into savagery, Congress also set aside the income from the sale of the sixteenth section in each township for the sup-

GRAPHIC EXPLORATION To explore an interactive version of this graph, go to http://www.prenhall.com/goldfield/fig7.3

FIGURE 7-3   Land Ordinance of 1785
The precise uniformity of the surveying system initiated in the Land Ordinance of 1785 created a rectangular grid pattern that was the model for all future land surveyed in the public domain.

port of public schools. Support for education, as a congressional report of 1783 put it, would help provide for "security against the increase of feeble, disorderly and dispersed settlements in those remote and extended territories [and] against the depravity of manners which they have a tendency to produce."

Before any land sales occurred under the Ordinance of 1785, impatient settlers continued to push north of the Ohio River and claim homesteads as squatters. They clashed both with local Indian tribes and with the troops sent by the Congress to evict them. Impatient itself with the slow process of surveying, the Congress sold off 1.5 million acres to a group of New England speculators organized as the Ohio Company. The speculators bought the land with greatly depreciated loan-office certificates that had been issued to Revolutionary War veterans, and their cost per acre averaged less than 10 cents in hard money. They now pressed their allies in Congress to establish a governmental structure for the West that would protect their investment by bringing the unruly elements in the West under control.

Both the Congress and speculators wanted political stability and economic development in the West and a degree of supervision for settlers commonly viewed in the East as "but little less savage than the Indians." What was needed, wrote James Monroe of Virginia, were temporary controls—made acceptable by the promise of eventual statehood—that "in effect" would place the western territories under "a colonial government similar to that which prevail'd in these States previous to the revolution." The **Northwest Ordinance of 1787,** the most significant legislative act of the Confederation Congress, filled this need, creating a political structure for the territories and a phased process for achieving statehood that neatly blended public and private interests.

According to the ordinance, controls on a new territory were to be strictest in the early stage of settlement, when Congress would appoint a territorial government consisting of a governor, a secretary, and three judges. When a territory reached a population of five thousand adult males, those with 50 acres of land or more could elect a legislature. The actions of the legislature, however, were subject to an absolute veto by the governor. Once a territory had a population of sixty thousand, the settlers could draft a constitution and apply for statehood "on an equal footing with the original states in all respects whatsoever."

Unlike Jefferson's Ordinance of 1784, which called for ten states, the Northwest Ordinance of 1787 stipulated that only three to five states were to be formed out of the Northwest. This change was because the admission of new states would weaken the control over Congress that the original thirteen states wanted to maintain for themselves as long as possible. Although less democratic in many respects than Jefferson's plan in mandating a period of outside control by Congress, the 1787 ordinance did provide greater protection for property rights as well as a bill of rights guaranteeing individual freedoms. Most significant, it prohibited slavery.

Southern congressmen agreed to the slavery ban, in part because they feared that planters in the new states would compete with them in the production of slave-produced staples such as tobacco. More importantly, however, they expected slavery to be permitted in the region south of the Ohio River that was still under the administrative authority of Virginia, North Carolina, and Georgia in the 1780s. Indeed, slavery was allowed in this region when the **Southwest Ordinance of 1790** brought it under national control, a decision that would have grave consequences in the future sectionalization of the United States.

Although the Northwest Ordinance applied only to the national domain north of the Ohio River, it provided the organizational blueprint by which all future territory was brought into the Union. It went into effect immediately and set the original Union on a course of dynamic expansion through the addition of new states.

DIPLOMATIC WEAKNESSES

In the international arena of the 1780s, the United States was a weak and often ridiculed nation. Under the Articles of Confederation, the Congress had the authority to negotiate foreign treaties but no economic or military power to enforce their terms. Unable to regulate commerce or set tariffs, Congress had no leverage with which to pry open the restricted trading empires of France, Spain, and most important, Britain.

France and the United States, allies during the Revolutionary War, remained on friendly terms after it. The United States even had a favorable trade balance with France, selling more there than it bought. Britain, however, treated its former colonies with contempt, and Spain was also openly antagonistic to the new nation. Both Britain and Spain sought to block American expansion into the trans-Appalachian West. And a dispute with Spain over the West produced the most serious diplomatic crisis of the period, one that spilled over into domestic politics, increasing sectional tensions between northern and southern states and leading many to question the country's chances of survival. As this crisis unfolded, the British remained poised to exploit any additional signs of American weakness.

IMPASSE WITH BRITAIN

The Confederation Congress was unable to resolve any of the major issues that poisoned Anglo-American relations in the 1780s. Key among those issues were provisions in the peace treaty of 1783 that concerned prewar American debts to the British and the treatment of Loyalists by the patriots. Britain used what it claimed to be America's failure to satisfy those provisions to justify its own violations of the treaty. The result was a diplomatic deadlock that hurt American interests in the West and in foreign trade.

Article 4 of the peace treaty called for the payment of all prewar debts at their "full value in sterling money"—that is, in gold or silver coin. Among the most numerous of those with outstanding debts to British creditors were tobacco planters in the Chesapeake region of Virginia and Maryland. During the Revolution, the British army had carried off and freed many of the region's slaves without compensating the planters. Still angry, the planters were in no mood to repay their debts. Working out a scheme with their respective legislatures, they agreed only to pay the face value of their debts to their state treasuries in state or Continental paper money. Since this money was practically worthless, the planters in effect repudiated their debts.

During the Revolution, all the states had passed anti-Loyalist legislation, and many state governments had seized Loyalists' lands and goods, selling them to raise revenue for the war effort. Upwards of 100,000 Loyalists fled to Canada and England, and their property losses ran into millions of dollars. Articles 5 and 6 of the peace treaty pledged the Congress to "recommend" to the states that they stop persecuting Loyalists and restore confiscated Loyalist property. But wartime animosities remained high, ebbing only gradually as the 1780s wore on. Despite the pleadings of John Jay, the secretary for foreign affairs in the Confederation government, the states were slow to rescind their punitive legislation or allow the recovery of confiscated property.

Combined with the matter of the unpaid debts, the continued failure of the states to make restitution to the Loyalists gave the British a convenient pretext to hold on to the forts in the West that they had promised to relinquish in the Treaty of Paris. Their refusal to abandon the forts, which extended from Lake Champlain in upstate New York westward along the Great Lakes, was part of an overall strategy to keep the United States weak, divided, and small. The continued British presence in the region effectively shut Americans out of the fur trade with the Indians. It also insulted the sovereignty of the United States and threatened the security of its northern frontier. In 1784, exasperated New Yorkers warned the Congress that unless the British were forced to leave, New York would "be compelled to consider herself as left to pursue her own Councils, destitute of the Protection of the United States." Elsewhere, the British, spurred on by Canadian officials, encouraged secessionist movements in the Northwest and sought out Indian allies to fight for a possible buffer state south of the Great Lakes that would keep Americans hemmed in along the Atlantic seaboard.

Throughout the 1780s, the British also explored the possibility of entering into an economic alliance with Vermont. Created in 1777 out of land claimed by both New York and New Hampshire, Vermont proclaimed itself an independent republic, free from the control of the British Parliament and the American Congress. Ethan Allen and his brothers Ira

and Levi held the power in Vermont politics, and their ambitious schemes for profiting from the sale of such raw materials as lumber and naval stores depended on a favorable treaty with Britain. The Allen brothers initiated a series of negotiations with the British in the 1780s in which they offered a treaty of friendship in exchange for recognition of Vermont's independence and trading privileges within the British Empire. The British were tempted but held back for fear of unduly antagonizing the United States. (Most Vermonters were strongly pro-American in their loyalties, and in 1791, after settlement of the disputed land claims, Vermont joined the Union as the fourteenth state.)

Although concerned by British provocations in the West and fears that the British would convert Vermont into a client state, American officials viewed Britain's retaliatory trade policies as the gravest threat to American security and prosperity. John Adams, the American minister to London, sought in vain to counter Britain's anti-American economic policies. "I may reason till I die to no purpose," Adams reported to Jay in June 1785, and he complained that he was treated as a complete "cypher."

Adams soon concluded that the British would never lift their trading and shipping restrictions until forced to do so by a uniform American system of discriminatory duties on British goods. The problem was that a uniform policy was impossible to achieve under the Articles of Confederation. Retaliatory navigation acts by individual states did little good because they left the British free to play one state off another. Adams could denounce Parliament as a "parcel of sots" for restricting American trade, but only with a strong, centralized government could Americans fashion a navigation system that would command Britain's respect.

SPAIN AND THE MISSISSIPPI RIVER

At the close of the Revolutionary War, Spain reimposed barriers on American commerce within its empire. Anxious to maintain as large a buffer zone as possible between its Louisiana and Florida possessions and the restless Americans, Spain also refused to recognize the southern and western boundaries of the United States as specified in the treaty with Britain in 1783, holding out instead for a more northerly border (see Map 7–2). And of greatest consequence, it denied the claim of the United States to free navigation of the entire length of the Mississippi River.

The Mississippi question was explosive because on its resolution hinged American settlement and control of the entire western region south of the

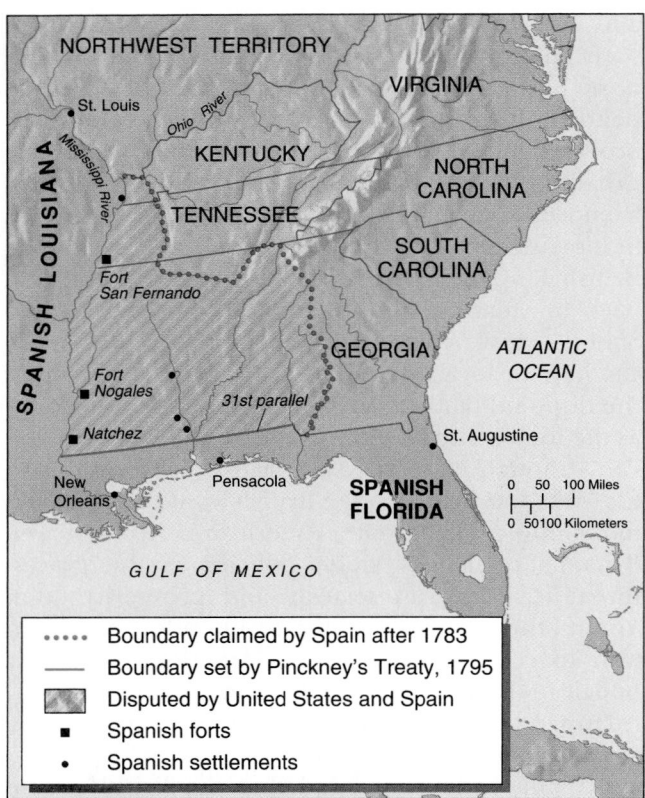

MAP 7-2   Disputed Territory in the West after the Treaty of Paris

Throughout the 1780s, Spain asserted title to a large area in the West south of the Ohio River.

Ohio River. Southerners were rapidly moving into this area, and the slave South expected to gain new support for an alliance against the commercial North as new slave states were created south of the Ohio. Free navigation of the Mississippi was essential to the realization of these expectations. Only with access to the Mississippi and the commercial right of deposit at New Orleans—that is, the right to transfer cargoes to oceangoing vessels—could the region's farmers, then mostly in what would become Tennessee and Kentucky, profitably reach national and international markets.

In the wake of the Revolution, the settlers of Kentucky, which was still part of Virginia, and Tennessee, which was still part of North Carolina, flirted with the idea of secession. According to a 1785 report, settlers in Kentucky felt that they did "not at present enjoy a greater portion of liberty [under Virginia] than an American colony might have done a few years ago had she been allowed a Representation in the British Parliament." Impatient to secure both political independence and the economic benefits that would come with access to the Mississippi, the

separatists were not particular about whom they dealt with. They became entangled in a web of diplomatic intrigue that included the Spanish, the Indians, and American authorities east of the mountains.

Spain sought to trade on the divided loyalties of American speculators and frontier settlers to its advantage, employing some of them as spies and informers. Led by General James Wilkinson in Kentucky, these agents encouraged separatist plots and talk of a western confederation under Spanish protection. Spain likewise sought to exploit divisions among Indian groups. In a bewildering variety of treaties negotiated by the Congress, individual Southern states, and land speculators, white Americans laid claim to much of the ancestral land of the major Indian nations in the Southeast—the Cherokee, Chickasaw, Choctaw, and Creek. Fraud was rampant, and many Native Americans believed, with good reason, that they had never been consulted in the dispossession of their land. The Spanish responded by recruiting disaffected Indians into an alliance system of their own. Their staunchest allies came from a faction of the Creeks led by Alexander McGillivray, the son of a trader father and a half-French, half-Creek mother. Supplied with arms from the Spanish, these Creeks succeeded in forcing white settlers off their tribal land in Georgia.

Spain stepped up pressure on the West in the summer of 1784, when it closed the Mississippi River within Spanish territory to American trade. Hoping now to benefit from American weakness, Spain also opened negotiations for a long-term settlement with the United States. The Spanish negotiator, Don Diego de Gardoqui, offered a deal that cleverly played the interests of the North against those of the South and West. In exchange for an American agreement to surrender claims to navigate the Mississippi for thirty years, Gardoqui proposed to grant the United States significant trading concessions in the Spanish Empire that would open new markets and new sources of hard money to the financially pressed merchants of the northeastern states. John Jay, his American negotiating partner, reluctantly accepted the offer.

When Jay released the terms of the proposed treaty with Spain in 1786, Congress erupted in angry debate. Southerners, who had taken the lead in the settlement of the West, accused Jay of selling out their interests. The treaty threatened the agrarian alliance they hoped to forge with the West, increasing the odds that the West would break from the East and go its own way. Vowing that they would not surrender the West, southern congressmen united to

This portrait, sketched in about 1790 by John Trumbull, is the only known likeness of Alexander McGillivray, a Creek leader who effectively played off Spanish and American interests in the Southeast to gain a measure of independence for the Creeks in the 1780s.

TOWARD A NEW UNION

In June 1786, a worried John Jay wrote to General George Washington that he was "uneasy and apprehensive; more so than during the war. Then we had a fixed object. . . . The case is now altered; we are going and doing wrong, and therefore I look forward to evils and calamities, but without being able to guess at the instrument, nature, or measure of them." Other nationalists fully shared Jay's forebodings. Everywhere they saw unsolved problems and portents of disaster: unpaid debts, social unrest, squabbling states, sectional hostilities, the uncertain status of the West, blocked channels of trade, foreign intrigues, and a paralyzing lack of centralized authority and purpose. They feared that the republic's very survival was now at stake.

In September 1786, delegates from several states met at the **Annapolis Convention,** in Annapolis, Maryland, seeking to devise a uniform system of commercial regulation for the country. While there, a group of nationalist leaders called on all the states to send delegates to a convention at Philadelphia "to devise such further provisions as shall appear to them necessary to render the constitution of the Federal Government adequate to the exigencies of the Union." The leaders who met at the **Constitutional Convention** in Philadelphia forged an entirely new framework of governance, the **Constitution of the United States,** that called for a federal republic with a powerful and effective national government. In 1788, after a close struggle in state ratifying conventions, the Constitution was adopted.

THE ROAD TO PHILADELPHIA

The road to Philadelphia began at Mount Vernon, George Washington's estate in Virginia. Commissioners from Maryland and Virginia met there in March 1785 to resolve jurisdictional and navigational disputes over the Potomac River and Chesapeake Bay, waters shared by the two states. Washington had a personal stake in hosting the conference, for he was president of the Potomac Company, a newly formed group of investors hoping to build a series of canals linking the Potomac River with the Shenandoah and Ohio Valleys. The meeting went so well that the participants invited representatives from Delaware and Pennsylvania to join them at a conference in Annapolis the following year to formulate policies for interstate commerce on the waterways that linked the Chesapeake region and the Ohio Valley. James Madison then broadened the scope of the Annapolis Conference to include representatives from all thirteen states for a general discussion of how best to promote and regulate interstate trade.

defeat the treaty. Nine states' votes were required for ratification under the Articles, and Jay's treaty could gain only seven—all in the North.

The regional antagonisms exposed by the Jay-Gardoqui talks heightened the alarm over the future of the republic provoked by Shays's Rebellion earlier in 1786. The Union had never appeared more fragile or the Congress under the Articles of Confederation so powerless to resolve its differences. Southerners openly calculated the value of remaining in a Union seemingly dominated by the commercial North, and Westerners warned that unless they were upheld on the Mississippi issue, they would consider themselves "relieved from all Federal Obligations and fully at Liberty to exact alliances & Connections wherever they find them." As the sense of crisis deepened in 1786, the nationalists grew in influence and numbers. Led by Alexander Hamilton of New York and James Madison of Virginia, they now argued that only a radical political change could preserve the republic and fulfill the promise of its greatness.

Only nine states decided to send delegates to the Annapolis Convention, and only those from five states had actually arrived when the nationalists, at the prompting of Madison and Hamilton, abruptly adjourned the meeting. They then called on the states and the Congress to approve a full-scale constitutional convention for Philadelphia in May 1787.

The timing of the call for the Philadelphia Convention could not have been better. During the fall and winter of 1786, the agrarian protests unleashed by Shays's Rebellion in Massachusetts spilled over into other states. Coupled with talk of a dismemberment of the Union in the wake of the Jay-Gardoqui negotiations, the agrarian unrest strengthened the case of the nationalists for more centralized authority.

All the states except Rhode Island, which wanted to retain exclusive control over its own trade, sent delegates to Philadelphia. The fifty-five men who attended the convention represented an extraordinary array of talent and experience. Chiefly lawyers by training or profession, most of them had served in the Confederation Congress, and more than one-third had fought in the Revolution. Extremely well educated by the standards of the day, the delegates were members of the intellectual as well as the political and economic elite. As a group, they were far wealthier than the average American. Most had investments in land and the public securities of the United States. At least nineteen owned slaves. Their greatest asset as a working body was their common commitment to a nationalist solution to the crisis of confidence they saw gripping the republic. Most of the strong supporters of the Articles of Confederation refused to attend, perhaps because, as Patrick Henry of Virginia remarked, they "smelt a rat."

THE CONVENTION AT WORK

When it agreed to the Philadelphia Convention, Congress authorized only a revision of the Articles of Confederation. Almost from the start, however, the delegates set about replacing the Articles altogether. Their first action was to elect George Washington unanimously as the convention's presiding officer, gaining credibility for their deliberations from his prestige. The most ardent nationalists then immediately seized the initiative by presenting the **Virginia Plan**. Drafted by James Madison, this plan replaced the Confederation Congress with a truly national government, organized like most state governments, with a bicameral legislature, an executive, and a judiciary.

Two features of the Virginia Plan stood out. First, it granted the national Congress power to legislate "in all cases in which the separate states are incompetent" and to nullify any state laws that in its judgment were contrary to the "articles of Union." Second, it made representation in both houses of the Congress proportional to population. This meant that the most populous states would have more votes in Congress than the less populous states, giving them effective control of the government. In short, Madison sought to all but eliminate the independent authority of the states while also forcing the smaller states to defer to the more populous ones in national affairs.

Delegates from the small states countered with the **New Jersey Plan**, introduced on June 15 by William Paterson. This plan kept intact the basic structure of the Confederation Congress—one state, one vote—but otherwise amended the Articles by giving the national government the explicit power to tax and to regulate domestic and foreign commerce. In addition, it gave acts of Congress precedence over state legislation, making them "the supreme law of the respective states."

The Great Compromise. The New Jersey Plan was quickly voted down, and the convention remained deadlocked for another month over how to apportion state representation in the national government. The issue was finally resolved on July 16 with the so-called **Great Compromise**. Based on a proposal by Roger Sherman of Connecticut, the compromise split the differences between the small and large states. Small states were given equal footing with large states in the Senate, or upper house, where each would have two votes. In the lower house, the House of Representatives, the number of seats was made proportional to population, giving larger states the advantage. The Great Compromise also settled a sectional dispute over representation between the free (or about to be free) states and slave states. The southern states wanted slaves counted for apportioning representation in the House but excluded from direct tax assessments. The northern states wanted slaves counted for tax assessments but excluded for apportioning representation. To settle the issue, the Great Compromise settled on an expedient, if morally troubling, formula: Free residents were to be counted precisely; to that count would be added three-fifths "of all other persons," excluding Indians not taxed. Thus the slave states gained additional political representation while the states in the North received assurances that the owners of nonvoting slaves would have to bear part of the cost of any direct taxes levied by the new government.

Washington presides over the Constitutional Convention.

The Great Compromise ended the first phase of the convention, which had focused on the general framework of a stronger national government. In its next phase, the convention debated the specific powers to be delegated to the new government. It was at this point that the sectional cleavage between North and South over slavery and other issues came most prominently to the fore. As Madison had warned in late June, "the great division of interests" in the United States would arise from the effect of states "having or not having slaves."

Regulation of commerce and the issue of slavery.

The sectional clash first erupted over the power of Congress to regulate commerce. At issue was whether Congress could regulate trade and set tariffs by a simple majority vote. Southerners worried that a northern majority would pass navigation acts favoring northern shippers and drive up the cost of sending southern commodities to Europe. To counter this threat, delegates from the Lower South demanded that a two-thirds majority be required to enact trade legislation. Suddenly, the central plank

in the nationalists' program—the unified power to force trading concessions from Britain—was endangered. A frustrated Madison urged his fellow southerners to remember that "as we are laying the foundation of a great empire, we ought to take a permanent view of the subject."

In the end, Madison had his way; the delegates agreed that enacting trade legislation would require only a simple majority. In return, however, southerners exacted concessions on the slavery issue. When planters from South Carolina and Georgia made it clear that they would agree to join a new Union only if they could continue to import slaves, the convention abandoned a proposal to ban the foreign slave trade. Instead, following the lead of Roger Sherman of Connecticut, who argued that emancipation sentiment would eventually lead to abolition of slavery anyway, antislavery New Englanders reached a compromise with the delegates from the Lower South: Congress would be barred from acting against the slave trade for twenty years. In addition, bowing to the fears of planters that Congress could use its taxing power to undermine slavery, the convention denied Congress the right to tax exports from any state. And to alleviate southern concerns that slaves might escape to freedom in the North, the new Constitution included an explicit provision calling on any state to return "persons held to Service or Labour" in another.

After settling the slavery question in late August, the convention had one last significant hurdle to clear: the question of the national executive. For months the delegates had gone around in circles debating how presidents should be elected, how long they should serve, and what their powers should be. But in early September, eager to wrap matters up and close to exhaustion after working through a long, hot summer, they moved quickly to resolve these issues.

The office of the chief executive.

In large part because of their confidence in General Washington, whom nearly everyone expected to be the first president, the delegates fashioned a chief executive office with broad discretionary powers. The prerogatives of the president included the rank of commander in chief of the armed forces, the authority to conduct foreign affairs and negotiate treaties, the right to appoint diplomatic and judicial officers, and the power to veto congressional legislation. The president's term of office was set at four years, with no limits on how often an individual could be reelected.

Determining how to elect the president proved a thorny problem. The delegates envisioned a forceful, energetic, and independent executive, insulated from the whims of an uninformed public and the intrigues of the legislature. As a result, they rejected both popular election and election by Congress. The solution they hit upon was the convoluted system of an "electoral college." Each state was left free to determine how it would choose presidential electors equal to the number of its representatives and senators. These electors would then cast votes to select a president. If no candidate received a majority of the electoral votes, the election would be turned over to the House of Representatives, where each state would have one vote.

After a style committee polished the wording in the final draft of the Constitution, thirty-nine of the forty-two delegates still in attendance signed the document on September 17. The Preamble, which originally began with a list of the states, was reworded at the last minute to begin simply: "We the people of the United States, in order to form a more perfect Union . . ." This subtle change had significant implications. By identifying the people, and not a collection of states, as the source of authority, it emphasized the national vision of the framers and their desire to create a government quite different from a confederation of states.

OVERVIEW OF THE CONSTITUTION

Although not as strong as the most committed nationalists would have liked, the central government outlined in the Constitution was to have far more powers than those entrusted to Congress under the Articles of Confederation (see the Overview table, "The Articles of Confederation and the Constitution Compared.") The Constitution's provision for a strong, single-person executive had no precedent in the Articles. Nor did the provision for a Supreme Court. The Constitution vested this court, as well as the lower courts that Congress was empowered to establish, with the judicial power of the United States. In addition, the Constitution specifically delegated to Congress the powers to tax, borrow and coin money, regulate commerce, and raise armed forces that the Confederation government had lacked.

Most of the economic powers of Congress came at the expense of the states, which were prohibited from passing tariffs, issuing money, or—in an obvi-

Overview

The Articles of Confederation and the Constitution Compared

	Articles	Constitution
Sovereign power of the central government	No power to tax or raise armies	Power granted on taxes and armed forces
Source of power	Individual states	Shared through federalism between states and the national government
Representation in Congress	Equal representation of states in a unicameral Congress	A bicameral legislature with equal representation of the states in the Senate and proportional representation in the House
Amendment process	Unanimous consent of the states	Consent of three-fourths of the states
Executive	None provided for	Office of the president
National judiciary	None provided for	The Supreme Court

ous reference to the debtor relief legislation of the 1780s—enacting any law that infringed on the contractual rights of creditors to collect money from debtors. Further curbing the sovereignty of the states was a clause stipulating that the Constitution and all national legislation and treaties were to be "the supreme law of the land." This clause has subsequently been interpreted as giving the central government the power to declare state laws unconstitutional

A no-nonsense realism, as well as a nationalist outlook, infused the Constitution. Its underlying political philosophy was that, in Madison's wonderful phrase, "ambition must be made to counter ambition." Madison and the other members of the national elite who met at Philadelphia were convinced that self-interest, not disinterested virtue, motivated political behavior. As proof, they cited what to them was the sorry record of the state governments in protecting property rights and promoting social order. In their view, these governments were failures because they had been captured by unrestrained majorities corrupted by the selfishness of competing interest groups. Accepting interest group politics as inevitable and seeking to prevent a tyrannical majority from forming at the national level, the architects of the Constitution designed a central government in which competing blocs of power counterbalanced one another.

The Constitution placed both internal and external restraints on the powers granted to the central government. The functional division of the government into executive, legislative, and judicial branches, each with ways to keep the others from exercising excessive power, created an internal system of checks and balances. For example, the Senate's authority to approve or reject presidential appointments and to ratify or reject treaties was a curb on the powers of the executive. The president commanded the armed forces, but only Congress could declare war. The president could veto congressional legislation, but Congress could override that veto with a two-thirds vote. To pass in the first place, legislation had to be approved by both the House of Representatives, which, with its membership proportional to population, represented the interests of the people at large, and the Senate, which represented the interests of the states. And as an ultimate check against executive abuse of power, Congress could indict, convict, and remove from office a president who tried to set himself above the law.

Although the Constitution did not explicitly grant it, the Supreme Court soon claimed the right to invalidate acts of Congress and the president that it found to be unconstitutional. This power of **judicial review** provided another check against legislative and executive authority. To guard against an arbitrary federal judiciary, the Constitution empowered Congress to determine the size of the Supreme Court and to indict and remove federal judges appointed by the president.

The external restraints on the central government were to be found in the nature of its relationship to the state governments. This relationship was based on **federalism**, the division of power between local and central authorities. By listing specific powers for Congress, the Constitution implied that all other powers were to be retained by the states. Thus, while strengthening the national government, the Constitution did not obliterate the sovereign rights of the states, leaving them free to curb the potential power of the national government in the ambiguous areas between national and state sovereignty.

This ambiguity in the federalism of the Constitution was both its greatest strength and its greatest weakness. It allowed both nationalists and advocates of states' rights to support the Constitution. But the issue of slavery, left unresolved in the gray area between state and national sovereignty, would continue to fester, sparking sectional conflict over the extent of national sovereignty that would plunge the republic into civil war three-quarters of a century later.

THE STRUGGLE OVER RATIFICATION

The realism the Philadelphia delegates displayed in the drafting of the Constitution extended to the procedure they devised for implementing it. Knowing full well that they had exceeded their instructions by proposing an entirely new government, not an amended version of the Articles, and aware that the Articles' requirement of unanimous consent by the state legislatures to any amendment would result in certain defeat, they boldly bypassed both Congress and the state legislatures.

The last article of the Constitution stipulated that it would go into effect when it had been ratified by at least nine of the states acting through specially elected popular conventions. Influenced by the nationalist sentiments of many of its members, one-third of whom had attended the Philadelphia Convention, and perhaps weary of its own impotence, the Congress accepted this drastic and not clearly legal procedure, submitting the Constitution to the states in late September 1787.

The delegates in Philadelphia had excluded the public from their proceedings. The publication of the text of the Constitution lifted this veil of secrecy and touched off a great political debate. Although those who favored the Constitution could most accurately have been defined as nationalists, they referred to themselves as **Federalists**, a term that helped deflect charges that they favored an excessive centralization of political authority. By default, the opponents of the Constitution were known as **Antifederalists**, a negative-sounding label that obscured their support of the state-centered sovereignty that most Americans associated with federalism. Initially outmaneuvered in this way, the Antifederalists never did mount an effective campaign to counter the Federalists' output of pamphlets, speeches, and newspaper editorials (see the Overview table, "Federalists versus the Antifederalists").

The Antifederalists did attract some men of wealth and social standing. Three of them—Elbridge Gerry of Massachusetts and George Mason and Edmund Randolph of Virginia—had been delegates at Philadelphia but refused to sign the Constitution. They feared that the new national government would swallow up the state governments.

Most Antifederalists, however, were backcountry farmers, men with mud on their boots who lived far from centers of communication and market outlets for their produce. They distrusted the social and commercial elite, and many Antifederalists saw in the Constitution a sinister plot by this elite "to lord it over the rest of their fellow citizens, to trample the poorer part of the people under their feet that they may be rendered their servants and slaves." The Antifederalists clung to the belief that only a small republic, one composed of relatively homogeneous social interests, could secure the voluntary attachment of the people necessary for a free government. They argued that a large republic, such as the one framed by the Constitution, would inevitably become tyrannical because it was too distant and removed from the interests of common citizen-farmers.

However much the Antifederalists attacked the Constitution as a danger to the individual liberties

Overview

Federalists versus the Antifederalists

	Federalists	Antifederalists
Position on the Constitution	Favored the Constitution	Opposed the Constitution
Position on the Articles of Confederation	Felt the Articles had to be abandoned	Felt the Articles needed only to be amended
Position on the power of the states	Sought to curb the power of the states with a new central government	Felt the power of the states should be paramount
Position on the need for a bill of rights	Initially saw no need for a bill of rights in the Constitution	Saw the absence of a bill of rights in the proposed Constitution as a threat to individual liberties
Position on the optimum size of the republic	Believed a large republic could best safeguard personal freedoms	Believed only a small republic formed on common interests could protect individual rights
Source of support	Commercial farmers, merchants, shippers, artisans, holders of the national debt	State-centered politicians, most backcountry farmers

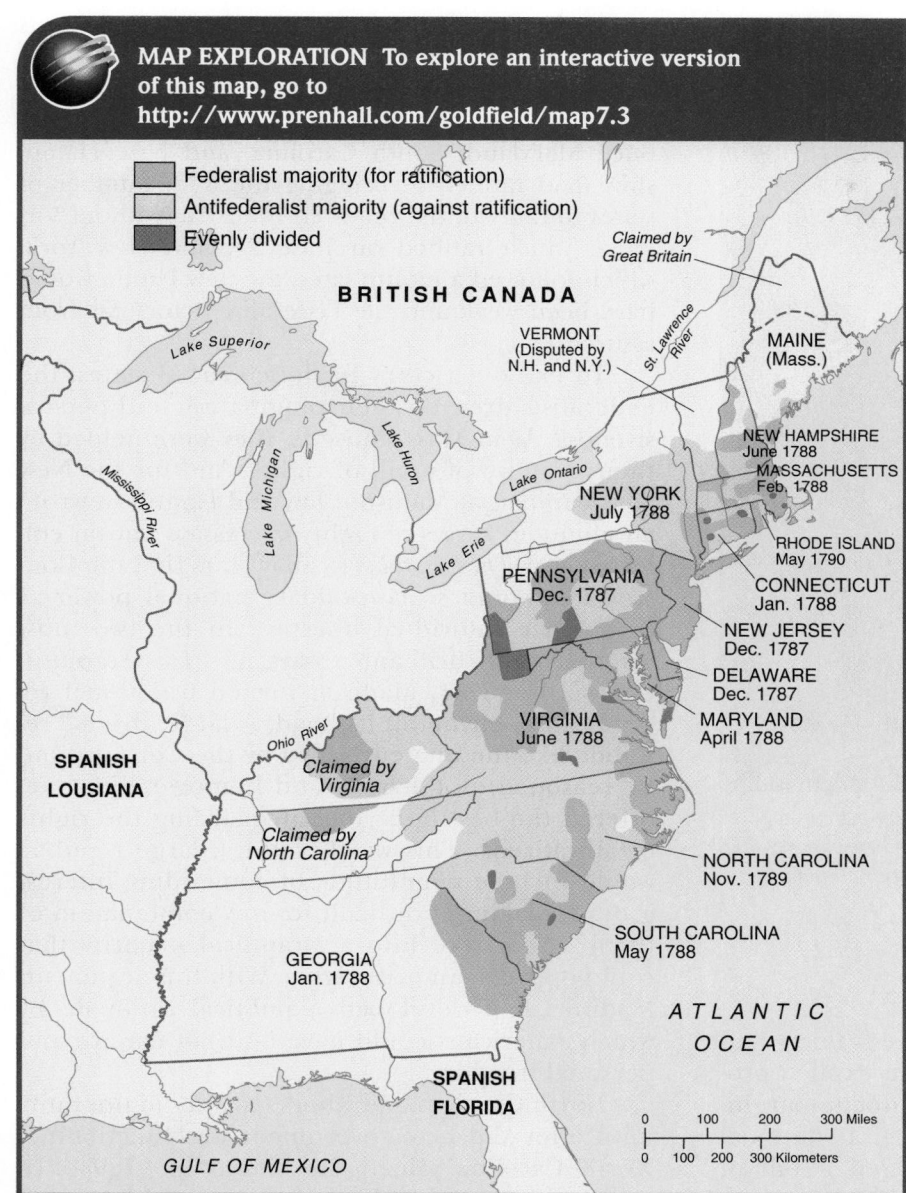

MAP EXPLORATION To explore an interactive version of this map, go to http://www.prenhall.com/goldfield/map7.3

- Federalist majority (for ratification)
- Antifederalist majority (against ratification)
- Evenly divided

BRITISH CANADA

Claimed by Great Britain

Lake Superior

Lake Michigan

Lake Huron

Lake Ontario

Lake Erie

Mississippi River

VERMONT (Disputed by N.H. and N.Y.)

St. Lawrence River

MAINE (Mass.)

NEW HAMPSHIRE June 1788

MASSACHUSETTS Feb. 1788

NEW YORK July 1788

RHODE ISLAND May 1790

PENNSYLVANIA Dec. 1787

CONNECTICUT Jan. 1788

NEW JERSEY Dec. 1787

DELAWARE Dec. 1787

Ohio River

MARYLAND April 1788

SPANISH LOUSIANA

VIRGINIA June 1788

Claimed by Virginia

Claimed by North Carolina

NORTH CAROLINA Nov. 1789

SOUTH CAROLINA May 1788

GEORGIA Jan. 1788

ATLANTIC OCEAN

SPANISH FLORIDA

GULF OF MEXICO

0 100 200 300 Miles
0 100 200 300 Kilometers

MAP 7-3   The Ratification Vote on the Constitution
Aside from some frontier districts exposed to possible foreign attack, the strongest support for the Constitution came from coastal and interior areas tied into a developing commercial economy.

cities and commercial farming areas along the coast.

With talent, intellect, and political savvy on their side, the Federalists skillfully built on the momentum for change that had developed out of the crisis atmosphere of 1786. They successfully portrayed the Constitution as the best opportunity to erect a governing structure capable of preserving and extending the gains of the Revolution.

Conservatives shaken by Shays's Rebellion lined up behind the Constitution. So, too, did groups—creditors, merchants, manufacturers, urban artisans, commercial farmers—whose interests would be promoted by economic development. The enhanced powers of the national government held out the promise of protecting the home market from British imports, enlarging foreign markets for American exports, promoting a stable and uniform currency, and raising revenues to pay off the Revolutionary War debt.

In the early stages, the Federalists scored a string of easy victories (see Map 7–3). Delaware ratified the Constitution on December 7, 1787, and within a month, so, too, had Pennsylvania, New Jersey, Georgia, and Connecticut. Except for Pennsylvania, these were small, sparsely populated states that stood to benefit economically or militarily from a stronger central government. The Constitution carried in the larger state of Pennsylvania because of the Federalists' strength in the commercial center of Philadelphia.

The Federalists faced their toughest challenge in the large states that had generally been more successful in going it alone during the 1780s. One of the most telling arguments of the Antifederalists in these and other states was the absence of a

and local independence that they believed the Revolution had been fought to safeguard, they were no political match for the Federalists. They lacked the social connections, access to newspapers, and self-confidence of the more cosmopolitan and better-educated Federalists. In addition, the Federalists could more easily mobilize their supporters, who were concentrated in the port

Although physically frail, James Madison, shown here in a portrait made in about l815, was a formidable thinker whose essays in The Federalist *endure as a lasting contribution to political theory.*

bill of rights in the Constitution. The framers had felt it unnecessary to include such an explicit protection of individual rights in a document intended to specify the powers of a national government and had barely discussed a bill of rights in Philadelphia. Realizing the importance of the issue, and citing Article 5 of the Constitution, which provided for an amendment process, the Federalists promised to recommend amending the Constitution with a bill of rights once it was ratified. By doing so, they split the ranks of the Antifederalists in Massachusetts. After the Federalists gained the support of two venerable heroes of the Revolution, John Hancock and Sam Adams, the Massachusetts convention approved the Constitution by a close vote in February 1788. To win over Hancock, the Federalists had played on his vanity, suggesting that they would back him for a top national post. Adams was convinced to back the Federalists by demonstrations of Boston artisans in favor of national tariff protection.

The major hurdles remaining for the Federalists were Virginia, the most populous state, and the strategically located New York. Technically, the Constitution could have gone into effect without them once Maryland, South Carolina, and New Hampshire had ratified it, bringing the total number of states to ratify to the required nine. But without Virginia, which ratified on June 25, and New York, which followed a month later, the new Union would have been weak and the Federalist victory far from assured.

To eke out victory in these crucial states, the Federalists drew on their pragmatism and persuasiveness. As in Massachusetts, they were helped by their promise of a bill of rights. And for the New York campaign, Madison, Jay, and Hamilton wrote an eloquent series of eighty-five essays known collectively as *The Federalist* to allay fears that the Constitution would so consolidate national power as to menace individual liberties. In the two most original and brilliant essays in *The Federalist*, essays 10 and 51, Madison turned traditional republican doctrine on its head. A large, diverse republic like the one envisaged by the Constitution, he reasoned, not a small and homogeneous one, offered the best hope for safeguarding the rights of all citizens. This was because a large republic would include a multitude of contending interest groups, making it difficult for any combination of them to coalesce into a tyrannical majority that could oppress minority rights. With this argument, Madison had developed a political rationale by which Americans could have both an empire and personal freedom.

North Carolina and Rhode Island did not ratify until after the new government was functioning. North Carolina joined the Union in 1789 once Congress submitted the amendments that constituted the Bill of Rights. The obstinate Rhode Islanders stayed out until 1790, when Congress forced them in with a threat of commercial reprisal.

CONCLUSION

In freeing themselves from British rule, Americans embarked on an unprecedented wave of constitution-making that sought to put into practice abstract principles of republicanism that held that political power should derive from the people. Between 1776 and 1780, Americans developed a unique system of constitutionalism. They proclaimed the supremacy of constitutions over ordinary legislation; detailed the powers of government in a written document; provided protection for individual freedoms in bills of rights; and fashioned a process for framing governments through the election of delegates to a special constitutional convention and the popular ratification of the work of that convention. In all of these areas, Americans were pioneers in demonstrating to the rest of the world how common citizens could create their own governments.

The curbs on centralized power that characterized the state constitutions also applied to what amounted to the first national constitution, the Articles of Confederation. Indeed, the inability of the Confederation Congress to exercise effective power in the areas of taxation and foreign trade was a crippling flaw that thoroughly discredited the Articles in the eyes of the nationalist-minded leaders who had emerged during the Revolution. These leaders overthrew the Articles at the Constitutional Convention in 1787 and en-

gineered a peaceful revolution in securing the ratification of the Constitution. Their victory in creating a new central government with real national powers was built on the foundation of constitutional concepts and mechanisms that Americans had laid down in their state constitutions. The new Contitution did rest on the consent of the governed, and it endured because it could be amended to reflect shifts in popular will and to widen the circle of Americans granted the rights of political citizenship.

Accepting as a given that self-interest drove political action, the framers of the Constitution designed the new national government to turn ambition against itself. They created rival centers of power that forced selfish factions to compete in a constant struggle to form a workable majority. That struggle occurred both within the national government and between that government and the states in the American system of federalism. The Constitution thus set the stage for an entirely new kind of national politics.

REVIEW QUESTIONS

1. How would you assess the decisions made by Shepard and Shays that resulted in the clash at the Springfield arsenal? Can you imagine any way in which the crisis could have been resolved short of violence?

2. How would you define republicanism? Do you believe that Americans today still believe in the basic tenets of republicanism?

3. What was so unprecedented about the new state constitutions, and what principles of government did they embody?

4. What were the problems of the economy in the 1780s, and why did clashes between debtors and creditors become so divisive? Do you think that an economic recovery could have been achieved under the Articles of Confederation?

5. Do you feel that the diplomatic weaknesses of the United States under the Articles were as serious as its internal problems? What were the sources of those weaknesses, and what threat did they pose for national unity?

6. What sorts of men drafted the Constitution in 1787, and how representative were they of all Americans? What explains the differences between the Federalists and Antifederalists? Do you think they shared the same vision of what they wanted America to become? How widespread was the popular backing for the Constitution, and what accounts for its ratification?

KEY TERMS

Annapolis Convention (p. 221)

Antifederalists (p. 226)

Articles of Confederation (p. 210)

Bill of rights (p. 207)

Constitutional Convention (p. 221)

Constitution of the United States (p. 221)

Federalism (p. 225)

Federalists (p. 226)

Great Compromise (p. 222)

Judicial review (p. 225)

Land Ordinance of 1785 (p. 216)

Nationalists (p. 211)

Natural rights (p. 205)

New Jersey Plan (p. 222)

Northwest Ordinance of 1787 (p. 218)

Shays's Rebellion (p. 215)

Southwest Ordinance of 1790 (p. 218)

Suffrage (p. 204)

Virginia Plan (p. 222)

RECOMMENDED READINGS

Beeman, Richard, Stephen Botein, and Edward C. Carter, III, eds., *Beyond Confederation: Origins of the Constitution and American National Identity* (1987). These twelve essays offer a fine overview of the competing ideologies and issues that shaped the history of the 1780s and pushed the republic toward a new frameweork of government in the Constitution.

Crèvecoeur, J. Hector St. John. *Letters from an American Farmer and Sketches of Eighteenth-Century America, ed. Albert E. Stone* (1986). This modern reprint of Crèvecoeur's work provides an accessible account of Americans and their living conditions in the late eighteenth century.

Jensen, Merrill. *The New Nation: A History of the United States during the Confederation, 1781–1787* (1948). This work makes the strongest case for the Articles as a tentative success that was overturned in a conservative reaction that exaggerated threats to social order.

Morris, Richard B. *The Forging of the Union, 1781–1789* (1987). The best-balanced synthesis of the 1780s, this book documents the creative statesmanship of the leaders of the Constitutional Convention.

Wood, Gordon. *The Creation of the American Republic, 1776–1787* (1969). This masterful study is indispensable for understanding the transformation in American republicanism between the winning of independence and the ratification of the Constitution.

ADDITIONAL SOURCES

The New Order of Republicanism

Block, Ruth H. *Visionary Republic: Millennial Themes in American Thought, 1756–1800* (1985).

Frey, Sylvia R. *Water from the Rock: Black Resistance in a Revolutionary Age* (1991).

Kerber, Linda. *Women of the Republic* (1980).

Pole, J. R. *Political Representation in England and the Origins of the American Republic* (1966).

Wood, Gordon. *The Radicalism of the American Revolution* (1992).

Problems at Home

Davis, Joseph L. *Sectionalism in American Politics, 1774–1787* (1977).

Hoffman, Ronald L. and Peter Albert, eds., *Sovereign States in an Age of Uncertainty* (1981).

Main, Jackson Turner. *Political Parties before the Constitution* (1973).

Onuf, Peter S. *The Origins of the Federal Republic* (1983).

Richards, Leonard L. *Shays's Rebellion: The American Revolution's Final Battle* (2002)

Diplomatic Weaknesses

Hoxie, Frederick E. Ronald Hoffman, and Peter J. Albert, eds. *Native Americans and the Early Republic* (1999).

Ritcheson, Charles T. *Aftermath of Revolution: British Policy toward the United States, 1783–1795* (1969).

Van Alstyne Richard W. *The Rising American Empire* (1980).

Toward a New Nation

Beard, Charles. *An Economic Interpretation of the Constitution* (1913).

Brown, Roger H. *Redeeming the Republic: Federalists, Taxation, and the Origins of the Constitution* (1993).

Cornell, Saul. *The Other Founders: Anti-Federalism and the Dissenting Tradition in America, 1788-1828* (1999).

Duncan, Christopher M. *The Anti-Federalists and Early American Political Thought* (1995).

Gillespie, Michael Allen, and Michael Lienesch, eds. *Ratifying the Constitution* (1989).

McDonald, Forrest. *Novus Ordo Seclorum: The Intellectual Origins of the Constitution* (1985).

Morris, Richard B. *Witness at the Creation* (1985).

WHERE TO LEARN MORE

- **South Street Seaport Museum, New York City, New York.** Maritime commerce was the lifeblood of the postrevolutionary economy. The artifacts and the exhibits here offer a fine introduction to the seafaring world of the port city that became the nation's first capital in the new federal Union. See www.southstseaport.org for more on the impact of trade on the development of New York and information on preservation projects underway in the city.

- **Independence National Historical Park, Philadelphia, Pennsylvania.** Walks and guided tours through this historic district enable one to grasp much of the physical setting in which the delegates to the Constitutional Convention met. The website www.nps.gov/inde/home.htm includes a virtual tour of many of the collections at the park, a portrait gallery of leading figures in the Revolution, and a look at the archaeological projects underway in the park

- **Northern Indiana Center for History, South Bend, Indiana.** The permanent exhibition on the St. Joseph River valley of northern Indiana and southern Michigan explains the material world of this region and how it changed as first Europeans and then Americans mingled and clashed with the Native American population. At www.centerforhistory.org/ one can learn more about the center and the variety of programs that it offers.

 Please refer to the document CD-ROM for primary sources related to this chapter.

DEC 26.
1776

THE DEFENDER OF THE MOTHERS,
WILL BE
THE PROTECTOR OF THE DAUGHTERS.

→ *This engraving shows respectful crowds greeting Washington as he passes through Trenton on the way to New York City for his inauguration as president.*

A NEW REPUBLIC AND THE RISE OF PARTIES
1789–1800

8

April 30, 1789
New York City

This is the great important day. Goddess of Etiquette assist me while I describe it. . . . The President was conducted out of the middle window into the Gallery [of Federal Hall] and the Oath administered by the Chancellor [Robert R. Livingston, Chancellor of New York]. Notice that the Business was done, was communicated to the Croud by Proclamation. . . . who gave three Cheers. . . . As the Company returned into the Senate Chamber, the president took the Chair, and the Senate and representatives their Seats. He rose & all arose also and [he] addressed them [in his inaugural address]. This great Man was agitated and embarrassed more than ever he was by the levelled Cannon or pointed Musket. He trembled and several times could scarce make out to read, tho it must be supposed he had often read it before. He put part of the fingers of his left hand, into the side, of what I think the Taylors call the fall, of his Breetches. Changing the paper into his left hand, after some time, he then did the same with some of the fingers of his right hand. When he came to the Words *all the World*, he made a flourish with his right hand, which left rather an ungainly impression . . . . He was dressed in deep brown, with Metal buttons,

CHAPTER OUTLINE

Washington's America
The Uniformity of New England
The Pluralism of the Mid-Atlantic Region
The Slave South and Its Backcountry
The Growing West

Forging a New Government
"Mr. President" and the Bill of Rights
Departments and Courts
Revenue and Trade
Hamilton and the Public Credit
Reaction and Opposition

The Emergence of Parties
The French Revolution
Securing the Frontier
The Whiskey Rebellion
Treaties with Britain and Spain
The First Partisan Election

The Last Federalist Administration
The French Crisis and the XYZ Affair
Crisis at Home
The End of the Federalists

Conclusion

233

with an Eagle on them, White Stockings a Bag and Sword—from the Hall there was a grand Procession to St. Pauls Church where prayers were said by the Bishop. The Procession was well conducted and without accident, as far as I have heard. The Militias were all under Arms. [They] lined the Street near the Church, made a good figure and behaved well. The Senate returned to their Chamber after Service, formed & took up the Address . . . . In the Evening there were grand fire Works . . . . and after this the People went to bed.

[William Maclay]

Kenneth R. Bowling and Helen E. Veit, eds., *The Diary of William Maclay and Other Notes on Senate Debates*, March 4, 1789 – March 3, 1791 (Baltimore: The Johns Hopkins University Press, 1988), pp. 11–13.

Senator William Maclay of Pennsylvania wrote this account in his personal journal of the inauguration of George Washington as the first president of the United States at Federal Hall in New York City on April 30, 1789. Born in Pennsylvania in 1737 of Scotch-Irish parents, Maclay had amassed sizeable wealth as a surveyor and lawyer by the eve of the Revolution. He held a number of popularly elected offices in the 1780s before his selection by the Pennsylvania legislature in September 1788 as one of the state's first two U.S. senators. A Presbyterian with a strong sense of rectitude that often made him overly critical of others, he quickly broke with the Washington administration over its fiscal and diplomatic policies. Before his death in 1804, he switched his political allegiance to an opposition party led by Thomas Jefferson.

Washington's shakiness at his inaugural that so obviously pained Maclay reflected the shaky start of the country's new government. Two states, North Carolina and Rhode Island, had not yet ratified the Constitution and were still outside the federal Union. The newly elected members of Congress felt no urgency to assume their duties. They had been scheduled to meet in New York on March 4, 1789, to count the ballots of the electoral college and officially confirm Washington's election, but only one-quarter of them had arrived by then. A month would go by before the minimum needed to count the ballots could be mustered. Washington, his dignity ruffled by this show of congressional disinterest, dallied at Mount Vernon until formally notified of his election.

He had every reason to dread taking on the burden of the presidency. As head of the new national government, he would put at risk the legendary status he had achieved during the Revolution. Most Americans intensely feared centralized authority, which is why the framers deliberately left the word *national* out of the Constitution. Washington somehow had to establish loyalty to a new government whose main virtue in the eyes of many was the very vagueness of its defined powers.

The Constitution had created the framework for a national government, but pressing problems demanded the fleshing out of that framework. The government urgently needed revenue to begin paying off the immense debt incurred during the Revolution. It also had to address unstable conditions in the West. Remote from the seat of power and wooed by the British north of the Ohio River and by the Spanish in the lower Mississippi Valley, western settlers wavered in their loyalties. Ultimately, the key to solving these and other problems was to establish the new republic's legitimacy. Washington and his supporters had to inspire popular backing for the government's right to exercise authority.

The realities of governing would soon shatter the nonpartisan ideal that had prevailed when the Constitution was ratified. By the end of Washington's first term, two political parties had begun to form. The Federalist party (the name came from that used by the original backers of the Constitution), which included Washington and his successor, John Adams, favored a strong central government. The opposition party, the Jeffersonian Republicans, took shape as a result of differences over financial policy and the American response to the French Revolution. Led by Thomas Jefferson, the Republicans were distrustful of excessive central power.

The Federalists, who governed through 1800, succeeded in showing a doubting world ruled by kings and queens that the American experiment in republican government could work. But as inheritors of a political tradition that equated parties with factions—temporary coalitions of selfish private interests—the Federalists doubted the loyalty of the Republicans. When the Federalists under President Adams attempted to suppress the Republicans, the stage was set for the critical election of 1800. Jefferson's victory in that election ended both Federalist rule and the republic's first major internal crisis.

KEY TOPICS

- Regional diversity of the United States in 1789
- Laying the foundations of American government during Washington's first term
- Hamilton's financial policies
- The emergence of parties during Washington's second term
- The Adams administration and the election of 1800

WASHINGTON'S AMERICA

Who were the Americans whom Washington was called on to lead when he became president? There is no easy answer. In 1789, as now, Americans identified and grouped themselves according to many factors, including race, sex, class, ethnicity, religion, and degree of personal freedom. Geographical factors, including climate and access to markets, further divided them into regions and sections. The resulting hodgepodge sorely tested the assumption—and it was never more than an assumption in 1789—that a single national government could govern Americans as a whole (see Figure 8–1).

THE UNIFORMITY OF NEW ENGLAND

The national census of 1790 counted nearly 4 million Americans, one in four of whom lived in New England. Although often viewed as the most typically "American" part of the young nation, New England in fact was rather atypical. It alone of the nation's formative regions had largely shut itself off from outsiders. Puritan notions of religious liberty that prevailed in the region extended only to those who subscribed to the Calvinist orthodoxy of the dominant Congregationalist church. Geography conspired with this religious exclusiveness to limit population diversity. New England's poor soils and long, cold winters made it an impractical place to cultivate cash crops like the tobacco and rice of the South. As a result, New England farmers had little need of imported white indentured servants or black slaves. Family members, helped by neighbors and the occasional hired hand, provided the labor on New England farms.

Puritan values and a harsh environment thus combined to make New England the most religiously and ethnically uniform region in the United States. Most of the people living there were descended from English immigrants who had arrived in the seventeenth century. Small pockets of Quakers, Baptists, and Catholics had gained the legal right of worship by the 1720s, but Congregationalism remained the official, state-supported religion in Connecticut and Massachusetts. Blacks and Indians together barely constituted 3 percent of New England's population. The few remaining Indians lived on reservations of inferior land, which they usually left only to find work as servants or day laborers.

New Englanders found slavery incompatible with the natural rights philosophy that had emerged during the Revolution and gradually began to abolish it in the 1780s. Slavery had, in any case, always been marginal in New England's economy. Owning slaves as domestic servants or artisans had been a status symbol for wealthy urban whites in Boston, Portsmouth, and Newport. As a result, about 20 percent of New England's small African American population lived in cities, in contrast to the white population, 90 percent of which lived in the countryside. Freed slaves and their descendants tended to remain in the cities, where jobs were easier for them to find than in rural areas.

Women outnumbered men in parts of New England in 1789. This pattern—not found in other parts of the country—was the result of the pressure of an expanding population and the practice of dividing family farms among male heirs. As farms in the older, more densely settled parts of New England were divided into ever smaller lots, many young men migrated west in search of cheap, arable land. They first pushed into the hilly regions of northern New England and then, by the 1790s, through the Mohawk River Valley into New York. Thus by 1789, women formed a slight majority in Connecticut, Massachusetts, and Rhode Island.

Despite their superior numbers, women in New England, as elsewhere, remained subordinate to men. Even so, the general testing of traditional authority that accompanied the Revolution led some New England women to question male power. The Massachusetts poet Judith Sargeant Murray, for example, published essays asserting that women were the intellectual equals of men. Murray was the first woman to argue publicly in favor of equal educational opportunities for young women, and she boldly asserted that women should learn how to become economically independent.

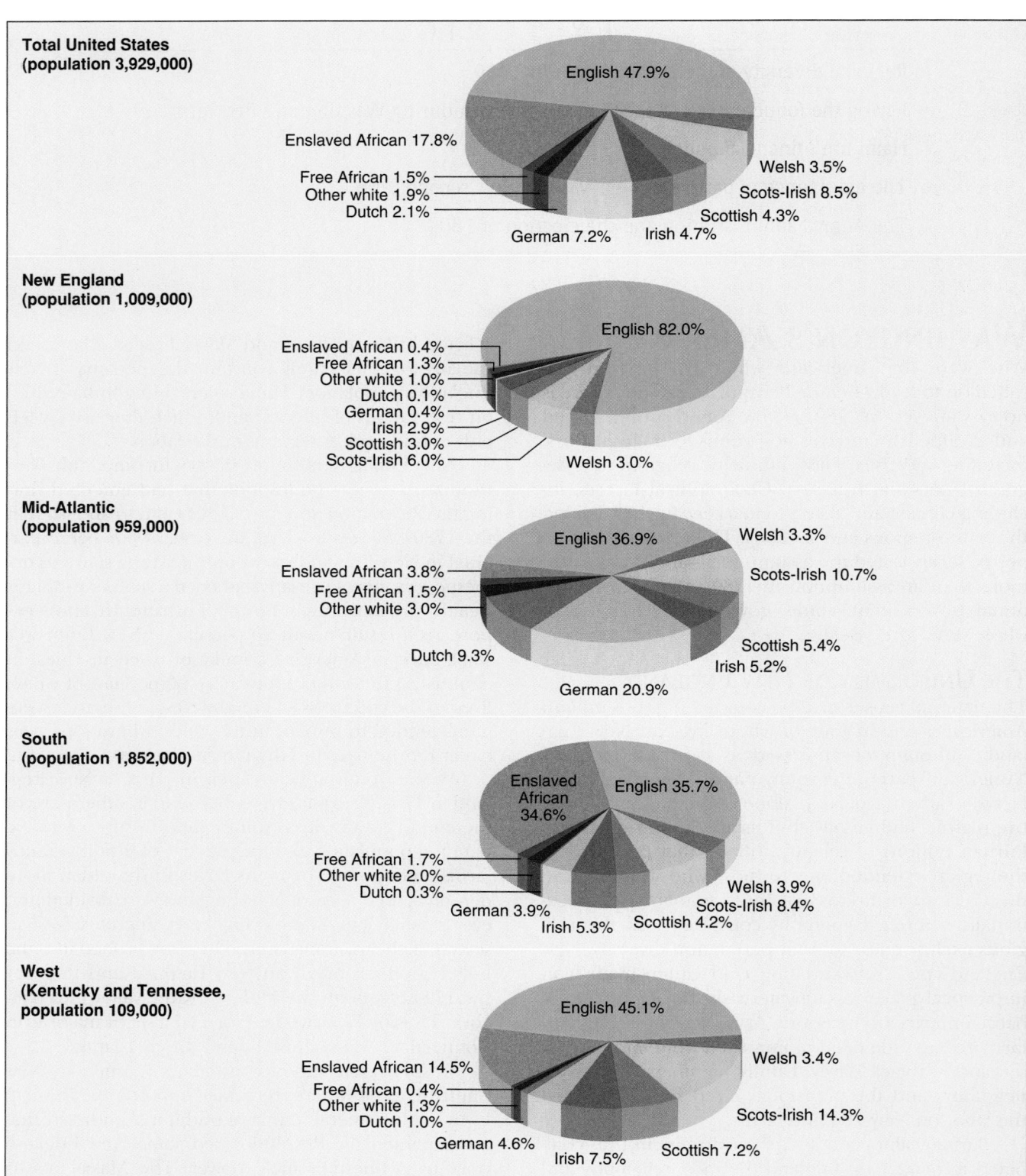

FIGURE 8-1 **Ethnic Breakdown of the United States in 1790, by Region.**
Unique racial and ethnic patterns shaped each of the nation's four major regions in 1790.
New England was most atypical in its lack of racial or ethnic diversity.

Source: "The Statistics of the Population of the United States," comp. Francis A. Walker (1872), pp. 3–7; Thomas L. Purvis, "The European Ancestry of the United States Population, 1790," *William and Mary Quarterly*, 41 (1984), p. 98.

This painting of a young woman reading—General Schumacker's Daughter, by Jacob Maentel—reflects women's increasing access to education in the early years of the nation. Nearly four hundred female academies and seminaries were established between 1790 and 1830.

Republican ideology, emphasizing the need of women to be intellectually prepared to raise virtuous, public-spirited children, also led reformers in New England to seek equal access for women to education. In 1789, Massachusetts became the first state to allocate funds specifically for girls' elementary education. And beginning in the 1780s, wealthy residents of eastern cities set up private academies for women that would later provide the foundation for women's higher education. Liberalized divorce laws in New England also allowed a woman to seek legal separation from an abusive or unfaithful spouse.

In other respects, political and social life in New England remained rooted in the Puritan past. Age, property, and reputation determined one's standing in a culture that valued a clearly defined social order. The moral code that governed town life promoted curbs on individual behavior for the benefit of the community as a whole. With their notions of collective liberty, New Englanders subscribed to a version of republicanism that favored strong government, setting themselves apart from most other Americans, who embraced a more individualistic idea of liberty and a republicanism suspicious of government power. New Englanders perceived government as a divine institution with a moral responsibility to intervene in people's lives. Acting through town meetings, they taxed themselves for public services at rates two to four times higher than in the rest of the country. Their courts were also far more likely than those elsewhere to punish individuals for crimes against public order (like failing to observe the Sabbath properly) and sexual misconduct.

THE PLURALISM OF THE MID-ATLANTIC REGION

The states of the mid-Atlantic region—New York, New Jersey, and Pennsylvania—were the most ethnically and religiously diverse in the nation. People of English descent constituted somewhat less than 40 percent of the population. Other major ethnic groups included the Dutch and Scots-Irish in New York and Germans and Scots-Irish in New Jersey and Pennsylvania. With ethnic diversity came religious diversity. Transplanted New Englanders, who brought their Congregationalism and Yankee twang with them when they settled Long Island and northern New Jersey, made up about 40 percent of New York's ethnic English population. Among others of English descent, Anglicans predominated in New York, and Quakers in New Jersey and Pennsylvania. The Dutch, concentrated in the lower Hudson Valley, had their own Dutch Reformed Church, and most Germans were either Lutherans or **pietists** such as Mennonites and Moravians, who stressed personal piety over theological doctrine. The Presbyterian Scots-Irish settled heavily in the backcountry.

This mosaiclike pattern of ethnic and religious groupings was no accident. In contrast to Puritan New England, the Middle Colonies had offered freedom of worship to attract settlers. In addition, economic opportunities for newcomers were much greater than in New England. The soil was better, the climate was milder, and market outlets for agricultural products were more abundant. These conditions made the mid-Atlantic region the nation's first breadbasket. It produced surpluses of wheat, flour, and corn that were shipped out of New York and Philadelphia, the two largest cities in North America by 1790. Commercial agriculture fed urban growth and created a greater demand for labor in both rural and urban areas than in New England. The influx of

Chronology

1789 Inauguration of Washington.	Suppression of the Whiskey Rebellion in western Pennsylvania.
Congress establishes the first federal departments.	**1795** Jay's Treaty with Britain ratified.
French Revolution begins.	Treaty of Greenville with Ohio Indians.
1790 Hamilton submits the first of his financial reports to Congress.	**1796** Pinckney's Treaty with Spain ratified.
1791 Bill of Rights ratified.	Washington's Farewell Address.
Congress charters the Bank of the United States.	John Adams elected president.
1792 St. Clair's defeat along the Wabash.	**1797** Beginning of the Quasi-War with France.
Reelection of Washington.	**1798** XYZ Affair.
1793 France goes to war against Britain, Spain, and Holland.	Alien and Sedition Acts.
Genêt Mission.	Provisional army and direct tax.
Washington issues Proclamation of Neutrality.	Virginia and Kentucky Resolutions.
1794 Ohio is opened with the victory of General Anthony Wayne at the Battle of Fallen Timbers.	**1799** Fries's Rebellion in Pennsylvania.
	1800 Franco-American Accord.
	Thomas Jefferson elected president.

Germans and Scots-Irish into the region in the eighteenth century occurred in response to this demand.

The demand for labor had also been met by importing African slaves. Blacks, both free and enslaved, made up 5 percent of the mid-Atlantic population in 1790, and as in New England, they were more likely than whites to live in the maritime cities. New York had more slaveholders in 1790 than any other American city except Charleston, South Carolina. About 40 percent of white families in the city's nearby rural outposts of Queens, Brooklyn, and Staten Island owned slaves, a rate as high as in Maryland and South Carolina.

Despite its considerable strength in the port cities and adjacent rural areas, slavery was never an economically vital institution in most of the mid-Atlantic region. The region's major cash crop, wheat, required seasonal labor, which did not warrant tying up capital in slaves. Commercial agriculture did not rest on a slave base, nor did it produce a politically powerful class of planters. As a result, slavery in the mid-Atlantic region gave way to the demands for emancipation inspired by the natural rights philosophy of the Revolution.

Pennsylvania in 1780, New York in 1799, and New Jersey in 1804, each passed laws of gradual emancipation. These laws did not free adult slaves but provided that children born of a slave mother were to be freed at ages ranging between 18 and 28. Soon after the laws were passed, however, adult slaves began hastening their own freedom. They ran away,

set fires, and pressured their owners to accept cash payments in return for a short, fixed term of labor service. But even as they gained their freedom, African Americans had to confront enduring white racism. The comments of one white New Yorker suggest what they were up against. "We may sincerely advocate the freedom of black men," he wrote, "and yet assert their moral and physical inferiority."

The diversity of the mid-Atlantic region created a complex political environment. Competing cultural and economic interests prevented the kind of broad consensus on the meaning of republicanism that had emerged in New England. Some mid-Atlantic groups favored a strong central government to foster economic development and maintain traditional authority. Others wanted to keep government weak so as to foster a republican equality that would promote individual freedom.

Those who supported strong government included mercantile and financial leaders in the cities and commercial farmers in the countryside. These people tended to be Anglicans, Quakers, and Congregationalists of English descent. Those opposing them and favoring a more egalitarian republicanism tended to come from the middle and lower classes. They included subsistence farmers in the backcountry and artisans and day laborers in the cities. Most were Scots-Irish Presbyterians, but those in opposition also included Dutch Calvinists and German Lutherans. Fiercely independent and proud of their liberties, they resented the claims of the wealthy to political authority. They resisted government aid to business as a form of political corruption that unfairly enriched those who were already economically powerful.

THE SLAVE SOUTH AND ITS BACKCOUNTRY

In the South—the region from Maryland and Delaware to Georgia—climate and soil conditions favored the production of cash staples for world markets. Cultivating these crops required backbreaking labor that white immigrants preferred to avoid. As Thomas Jefferson put it, "In a warm climate no man will work for himself, who can make another labor for him." Southern planters relied on the coerced labor of African slaves, whose numbers made the South the most populous region in the country.

Just under 40 percent of all Southerners were slaves, but their concentration varied within the region. They were a majority in the Chesapeake Tidewater region, where slave ownership was widely distributed among white tobacco planters, including small and middling growers as well as the few great plantation owners. Farther south, in the tidal swamps of the South Carolina and Georgia lowcountry, where draining and clearing the land required huge inputs of labor, blacks outnumbered whites five to one. Slave ownership there was more concentrated than in the Tidewater. Large planters, the richest men in the country, worked hundreds of slaves in the production of rice, indigo, and sea-island cotton. Because yellow fever and malaria plagued the Carolina lowcountry, whites avoided the area, and the death rate among slaves was very high.

Slaves were less numerous in the Piedmont, or foothill, region of the South that lies between the coastal plain and the Appalachian highlands. Although sons of Tidewater planters had expanded tobacco production with slave labor into the Piedmont of Virginia and South Carolina, this was predominantly an area of nonslaveholding farmers. They relied on family labor to raise livestock, corn, and wheat. In the southern mountains, sloping to the southwest from the Blue Ridge in Virginia, the general absence of marketable crops diminished the demand for slave labor.

The free black population in the South had grown rapidly during the 1780s. Thousands of slaves fled behind British lines to win their freedom, and patriots freed others as a reward for enlisting in their forces. The Revolutionary values of liberty and equality also led many slave owners to question the morality of slavery. Legislatures in the Upper South passed laws making it financially easier than before for masters to manumit (free) their slaves. In Virginia alone, ten thousand slaves were manumitted in the 1780s. Slavery remained the foundation of the southern economy, however, and whites feared competition from freed blacks. As a result,

A frontier log cabin, such as this, was a squalid, rough-hewn structure that could be built in a day with the help of neighbors.

no southern state embarked on a general program of emancipation, and slavery in the region survived the turbulence of the Revolutionary era.

Economic conditions in the South, where the raw poverty of the backcountry offset the great wealth of the lowcountry, stamped the region's politics and culture. Tidewater planters were predominantly Anglican and of English descent. Piedmont farmers were more likely to be Scots-Irish Presbyterians and Baptists. More evangelical in their religion, and with simpler habits and tastes, the backcountry Baptists denounced the lowcountry planters for their luxury and arrogance. The planters retaliated by trying unsuccessfully to suppress the backcountry evangelicals.

The planters were indeed proud, domineering, and given to ostentatious displays of their wealth. An English traveler observed that Virginia planters "are haughty and jealous of their liberties, impatient of restraint, and can scarcely bear the thought of being controlled by any superior power." Planters understood liberty to mean the power of white males, unchecked by any outside authority, to rule over others. The only acknowledged check on this power was the planter's sense of duty, his obligation to adhere to an idealized code of conduct befitting a gentleman and a man of honor.

Backcountry farmers also jealously guarded their liberties. "They are," noted a late-eighteenth-century traveler, "extremely tenacious of the rights and liberties of republicanism. They consider themselves on an equal footing with the best educated people of the country, and upon the principles of equality they intrude themselves into every company." Backcountry farmers shared with the planters a disdain for government and restraints on the individual. But they opposed the planters' belief in a social hierarchy based on wealth and birth that left both poor whites and black slaves in a subordinate position.

THE GROWING WEST

Between the Appalachian Mountains and the Mississippi River stretched the most rapidly growing region of the new nation, the West. Land-hungry settlers poured across the mountains once the British recognized the American claim to the region in the Treaty of Paris. During the 1780s, the white population of the West exploded from less than 10,000 to 200,000. The region's Native American population was, by contrast, about 150,000.

Indians strongly resisted white claims on their lands. A confederation of tribes in the Ohio Valley, led by the Miamis and supplied with firearms by the British in exchange for furs, kept whites out of the Old Northwest territory, the area north of the Ohio River. South of the Ohio, white settlements were largely limited to Kentucky and Tennessee. In what is today Alabama and Mississippi, the Creeks and their allies blocked American expansion.

Most white migrants in Kentucky and Tennessee were the young, rural poor from the seaboard slave states. The West offered them the opportunity to claim their own farms and gain economic independence, free from the dominance of planters and the economic competition of slave labor. But planters also saw the West as a land of opportunity. The planters of Tidewater Virginia were especially likely to speculate in vast tracts of western land. And many planters' sons migrated to the West with a share of the family's slaves to become planters in their own right. This process laid the foundation for the extension of slavery into new regions. As early as 1790, slaves made up more than 10 percent of the population of Tennessee and Kentucky.

Life in the western settlements was harsh and often cruel. Mortality was high, especially among infants. Travelers from the East described settlers living in crudely built log cabins with squalid, filthy interiors infested with fleas and lice. Easterners also found an appallingly casual acceptance of violence in the West. Men commonly settled disputes in knife-slashing, eye-gouging brawls.

Isolation and uncertainty haunted frontier life. The Appalachians posed a formidable barrier to social and economic intercourse with the East. Few settlers had the labor resources, which chiefly meant slaves, to produce an agricultural surplus for shipment to market down the Ohio and Mississippi Rivers. Most farmers lived at a semisubsistence level. Many of them, mostly Scots-Irish, did not own the land they cultivated. These squatters, as they were called, occupied the land hoping someday to obtain clear title to it.

In Kentucky, squatters, aligned with a small class of middling landowners, spearheaded the movement for political separation from Virginia that gained statehood for the territory in 1792. (In similar fashion, white settlers in Vermont established their independence from New York and New Hampshire and gained statehood in 1791.) The settlers wanted to break the control that Tidewater planters had gained over most of the land and lucrative government offices in Kentucky. In their minds, planters, officeholders, land speculators, and gentlemen of leisure were all part of an aristocracy tied to the distant government in Richmond and intent on robbing them of their liberty. As one proponent of statehood proudly announced, "I never was a frend to larned men for I see it is those sort of fokes who always no how to butter thare own bred and care not for others."

Despite the movement in Kentucky for statehood, the ultimate political allegiance of the West was uncertain in 1790. Westerners wanted the freedom to control their own affairs and outlets for their crops. Apparently, they were willing to strike a deal with any outside power offering to meet these needs. The British, contrary to the terms of the Treaty of Paris, had not abandoned their military posts in the Old Northwest. Using their military position and close ties with the Indians as leverage, the British encouraged separatist movements north of the Ohio River.

Spain posed a more serious threat. It rejected the American claim to the 31st parallel as the southern boundary of the United States and asserted that most of the area south of the Ohio and east of the Mississippi was Spanish territory. Most important, Spain controlled New Orleans and hence the main outlet on the Mississippi River for western produce. Washington had warned in 1784 that the political loyalties of the West wavered "on a pivot," and the future of the region loomed as a major test for his administration.

FORGING A NEW GOVERNMENT

The Congress that assembled in New York (a temporary capital) from 1789 to 1791 faced a challenge scarcely less daunting than that of the Constitutional Convention of 1787. It had to give form and substance to the framework of the new national government outlined in the Constitution. Executive departments had to be established, a federal judiciary organized, sources of revenue found, terms of international trade and foreign policy worked out, and a commitment to add a bill of rights to the Constitution honored.

Staunch supporters of the new government had easily carried the first national elections in 1788 and enjoyed large majorities in both houses of Congress. These people brought superb administrative talents to the task of governing. Many, however, were clumsy politicians and unsympathetic to the egalitarian sensibilities of the electorate. By 1792, they faced growing political opposition.

"MR. PRESIDENT" AND THE BILL OF RIGHTS

The first problem for Washington and Congress was to decide just how the chief executive of the new republic should be addressed. Vice President John Adams of Massachusetts and his like-minded colleagues in the Senate wanted a title with dignity, something that imparted proper respect both for the office and for national political authority. They preferred "His Highness." In a debate that tied up Congress for a month, the more democratically inclined members of the House argued that such a title smacked of a longing for monarchical rule. Adams and the others grudgingly agreed to accept "Mr. President."

Whatever his title, Washington was intent on surrounding the presidency with an aura of respectability. Dismayed by the hordes of visitors and officeseekers who immediately invaded his rented mansion in New York, he set down strict rules for his interactions with the public. He met with visitors twice a week for an hour and bowed with republican deference to the people but refused to shake hands. He traveled outside New York in a luxurious coach pulled by six horses, and at all times he carried himself with stern reserve. After a dinner with the president, one senator remarked that "as usual the company was as grave as at a funeral."

While Washington was laying down guidelines for presidential etiquette, Congress got down to business. James Madison, now a representative from Virginia, early emerged as the most forceful leader in the House. He pushed for speedy action on the bill of rights, which the Federalists had promised to add to the Constitution during the ratification debate. To allay the fears of Antifederalists that the Constitution granted too much power to the national government, the Federalists had promised to consider amendments that protected both individual rights and liberties and the rights of states. But Madison, concerned not to have the new government immediately hobbled by concessions to states, astutely kept the focus of the amendments on personal liberties. He submitted nineteen amendments, and

Congress soon settled on twelve. Ten of these amendments, known collectively as the **Bill of Rights**, were ratified by the states and became part of the Constitution as of December 15, 1791.

The Bill of Rights has been one of the most enduring legacies of the first Congress. Most of the first eight amendments are concerned with individual rights. They guarantee religious freedom, freedom of expression, and the safeguarding of individuals and their property against arbitrary legal proceedings. Only three amendments speak of state interests. Citing the necessity of a "well regulated Militia" for "the security of a free State," the Second Amendment guarantees "the right of the people to keep and bear Arms." This assured the states that they could rely on their militias for protection against federal tyranny. The Ninth and Tenth Amendments stipulate that the powers not granted to the national government in the Constitution are retained by the people and the states.

The Bill of Rights broadened the government's base of popular support. Once Congress submitted the amendments to the states for ratification, North Carolina (1789) and Rhode Island (1790) overcame their lingering objections and joined the Union. The Bill of Rights also assured Americans that the central government would not try to impose on them a uniform national culture.

DEPARTMENTS AND COURTS

In the summer of 1789, Congress authorized the first executive departments: the State Department for foreign affairs, the Treasury for finances, and the War Department for the nation's defense. These departments already existed under the Articles of Confederation, and the only debate about them concerned the extent of presidential control over the officials who would head them. The Constitution gave the president the right to nominate public officials but required the consent of the Senate to confirm their appointments. The Constitution was silent, however, on whether or not the president could dismiss an official without the Senate's consent. Congress decided that the president could do so, setting an important precedent that bolstered presidential power. Department heads would now be closely bound to the president. As a group, they would evolve into the cabinet, the president's chief advisory body.

Greater controversy attended the creation of the federal judiciary. The Constitution called for "one Supreme Court" but left it up to Congress to authorize lower federal courts. The framers were deliberately vague about the federal judiciary because Antifederalists and proponents of states' rights did not want national courts enforcing a uniform judicial system. National courts, they argued, would be far removed from the people and would act as engines of oppression.

The **Judiciary Act of 1789** represented an artful compromise that balanced the concerns of the Antifederalists and states' rights advocates with the concerns of nationalists who strongly opposed leaving matters of national law up to state courts. It created a hierarchical national judiciary based on thirteen federal district courts, one for each state. Appeals from these courts were to be heard in one of three circuit courts, and the Supreme Court was to have the final say in contested cases. In a major concession to the Antifederalists, however, the act limited jurisdiction in federal courts to legal issues stemming from the Constitution and the laws and treaties of the national government. The distinctive legal systems and customs of the states remained intact. State courts would continue to hear and rule on the vast majority of civil and criminal cases.

REVENUE AND TRADE

The government's most pressing need was for revenue. Aware that Congress under the Articles of Confederation had been crippled by its inability to secure a reliable source of income, Madison acted to put the finances of the new federal government on a firm footing. Nearly everyone agreed that the government's chief source of income should be a tariff on imported goods and tonnage duties (fees based on cargo capacity) on ships entering American ports. The United States imported most of its manufactured goods, as well as many raw materials, and foreign-owned ships accounted for nearly half of entering tonnage.

The **Tariff Act of 1789** was designed primarily to raise revenue, not to protect American manufacturers by keeping out foreign goods with high duties. It did, however, seek to protect a few industries thought vital to the economic health of the nation. Thus it levied a duty of 5 percent on most imported goods but imposed tariffs as high as 50 percent on a limited number of items such as steel, salt, cloth, and tobacco. The debate on the Tariff Act provoked some sectional sparring. In general, manufacturers, who were concentrated in the North, wanted high tariffs for protection against foreign competition. In contrast, farmers and southern planters wanted low tariffs to keep down the cost of the manufactured goods they purchased.

Madison originally hoped to use tonnage duties not only to raise revenue but also to strike at foreign nations that had not signed a commercial treaty with the United States. He had in mind specifically Great Britain. Since the Revolution, Britain had kept its trading empire closed to American merchants while at the same time exploiting the United States as a market for its manufactured goods. In contrast, France, America's ally during the Revolution, had a commercial treaty with the United States that recognized the American position on equal trading relations and the rights of neutral shippers during war.

Madison wanted to punish the British with a duty of 60 cents per ton on British ships entering American ports, twice the proposed duty on French ships. He hoped to dislodge the British from their dominant position in American markets and to open up overseas trade for American and French shippers.

Madison's duties were, in effect, a declaration of economic warfare against Britain, but they failed to pass Congress, defeated by an unlikely coalition of sectional interests. Southerners voted against them because they feared their result would be to give New England merchants a monopoly on the carrying trade and raise the cost of shipping tobacco to Europe. But northern merchants, presumably the beneficiaries of the duties, also opposed them. They were leery of disrupting their profitable trade with Britain, especially with the economic slump of the 1780s abating. The **Tonnage Act of 1789**, as finally passed, treated all foreign ships equally. Foreign-owned and foreign-built ships were to pay a duty of 50 cents a ton; foreign-owned but American-built ships were to pay a duty of 30 cents a ton. The duty for American ships was only 6 cents a ton.

HAMILTON AND THE PUBLIC CREDIT

The Treasury was the largest and most important new department. To its head, Alexander Hamilton of New York, fell the task of bringing order to the nation's ramshackle finances. The basic problem was the huge debt left over from the Revolution. With interest going unpaid, the debt was growing, and by 1789, it had reached $52 million. Most of this—about $40 million—was held by Americans in the form of securities and certificates issued during the Revolution. Foreigners, mostly French and Dutch, held another $12 million. In addition, state governments had debts totaling close to $25 million. Until the government set up and honored a regular schedule for paying interest, the nation's public credit would be worthless. Unable to borrow, the government would collapse.

More than any other individual, Hamilton imparted energy and purpose to the Washington administration. He was ambitious, egotistical, and overbearing. When he spoke of the people, he usually did so with a sneer. But he also had a brilliant financial mind and a sweeping vision of national greatness. He was convinced that the economic self-interests of the wealthy and well-born offered the only sound foundation for the success of the new government.

This painting of about 1797 captures the bustle of commercial activity in New York at the end of the eighteenth century. The large building to the left is the Tontine Coffee House, the site of insurance offices and the Stock Exchange.

Born illegitimate in the West Indies in 1755 and orphaned at the age of 13, Hamilton craved power and social connections. Friends impressed with his potential sent him as a teenager to New York City for an education at Kings College (now Columbia University). An eager patriot, he served as Washington's personal aide during the Revolution. Washington's backing enabled him to marry into a wealthy New York family. He now had an entry into the world of the social and economic elite, and he parlayed it into a flourishing legal practice and a rising political career. With no ancestral loyalties to any individual state, he brought an unabashed nationalism to Washington's cabinet. And with a conviction, born of his own rise, that wealth and power were synonymous, he made no apologies for trying to link the interests of the government with those of the wealthy.

At the request of Congress, Hamilton prepared a series of reports on the nation's finances and economic condition. In the first, issued in January 1790, Hamilton proposed a bold plan to address the Revolutionary War debt. The federal government, he maintained, should fund the national debt at full face value. To do this, he proposed exchanging the old debt, including accrued interest, for new government bonds bearing interest at about 4 percent. In addition, Hamilton maintained that the federal government should assume the remaining war debt of the state governments. The intent of this plan was to give the nation's creditors an economic stake in the

stability of the new nation and to subordinate state financial interests to those of the central government.

In his second report, issued in December 1790, Hamilton called for an excise tax (a tax on the production, sale, or consumption of a commodity) on distilled whiskey produced within the United States. The purpose of the tax was to raise additional revenue for interest payments on the national debt. It would also establish the government's authority to levy internal taxes on its citizens.

The third report, which followed quickly after the second, recommended the chartering of a national bank, the Bank of the United States. Hamilton patterned his proposed bank after the Bank of England and intended it to meet a variety of needs. Jointly owned by the federal government and private investors, it would serve as the fiscal (financial) and depository agent of the government and make loans to businesses. Through a provision that permitted up to three-fourths of the value of bank stock to be purchased with government bonds, the bank would create a market for public securities and hence raise their value. Most important, the bank would provide the nation with a stable currency. At the time, the country had only three private banks, and specie—hard currency in the form of gold and silver coins—was scarce. The government needed a reliable source of money, as did the economy as a whole. Hamilton proposed to allow the Bank of the United States to issue money in the form of paper banknotes that would be backed by a small reserve of specie and the security of government bonds. His goal was both to strengthen the economy and to consolidate the power of the national government.

Hamilton's final report, issued in December 1791, recommended government actions to promote industry. Looking, as always, to the British model of economic development, he argued that the United States would never become a great power until it diversified its largely agrarian economy. As long as the nation imported most of its manufactured goods, Hamilton warned, it would be no more than a second-rate power. Moreover, American manufacturers, saddled with both high labor costs and primitive technology, would

OVERVIEW

Federalist Party versus Republican Party

Federalists	Republicans
Favored strong central government	Wanted to limit the role of the national government
Supported Hamilton's economic program	Opposed Hamilton's economic program
Opposed the French Revolution	Generally supported the French Revolution
Supported Jay's Treaty and closer ties to Britain	Opposed Jay's Treaty and favored closer ties to France
In response to the threat of war with France, proposed and passed the Direct Tax of 1798, the Alien and Sedition Acts, and legislation to enlarge the size of the army	Opposed the Alien and Sedition Acts and the enlarged army as threats to individual liberties
Drew strongest support from New England; lost support in the mid-Atlantic region after 1798	Drew strongest support from the South and West

remain at a severe competitive disadvantage unless they received government assistance. Hamilton advocated aid in the form of protective tariffs (high tariffs meant to make imported goods more expensive than domestic goods) for such industries as iron, steel, and shoemaking—which had already begun to establish themselves—and direct subsidies to assist with start-up costs for other industries. Hamilton believed that such "patronage," as he called it, would ultimately foster interregional economic dependence. An industrializing Northeast, for example, would depend on the South and West for foodstuffs for its workers and raw materials for its factories. In turn, farmers and planters would buy manufactured goods from the Northeast. Thus, in Hamilton's vision, manufacturing, like a national currency, would be a great national unifier.

REACTION AND OPPOSITION

The breadth and boldness of Hamilton's program invited opposition. For many people, it reflected a vision of the nation that challenged their deeply held beliefs about the purpose and meaning of the American Revolution. Opposition began to emerge with the first report on the public credit and quickly solidified along economic, ideological, and sectional lines.

About half the members of Congress owned some of the nation's debt, and nearly all of them agreed with Hamilton that it should be paid off. Some opponents, however, were concerned that Hamilton's plan was unfair. Hard times had forced most of the original holders of the debt—by and large, ordinary citizens—to sell their certificates to speculators at a fraction of their face value. Should the government, asked Madison, reward speculators with a windfall profit when the debt was paid back in full and forget about the true patriots who had sustained the Revolution in its darkest hours?

Others objected, on republican grounds, that Hamilton had no intention of actually eliminating the government's debt. He envisioned instead a permanent debt, with the government making regular interest payments as they came due. The debt, in the form of government securities, would serve as a vital prop for the support of moneyed groups. One congressman saw this as a violation of "that great principle which alone was the cause of the war with Great Britain . . . that taxation and representation should go hand in hand." Future generations, he argued, would be unfairly taxed for a debt incurred by the present generation.

Opposition to Hamilton's proposal to have the federal government assume state debts reflected sectional differences. With the exception of South Carolina, the southern states had already paid back a good share of their war debts. Thus Hamilton's plan stood to benefit the northern states disproportionately. Because Hamilton had linked the funding of the national debt with the assumption of state debts, southern opposition to assumption threatened funding as well. Tensions mounted as the deadlock continued into the summer of 1790. Frustrated over southern intransigence, New Englanders muttered about seceding. Southerners responded in kind. A Virginia senator charged that disunion would be a small price to pay to escape "the rule of a fixed insolent northern majority."

Tempers cooled when a compromise was reached in July. Southerners agreed to accept funding in its original form because, as Hamilton correctly noted, it would be impractical, if not impossible, to distinguish between the original and current holders of the national debt. Assumption passed after Hamilton cut a deal with Virginians James Madison and Thomas Jefferson. In exchange for southern support of assumption, Hamilton agreed to line up northern votes for locating the nation's permanent capital on the banks of the Potomac River, where it would be surrounded by the slave states of Maryland and Virginia. The package was sweetened by extra grants of federal money to states with small debts.

Hamilton's alliance with Madison and Jefferson proved short-lived, dissolving when Madison led the congressional opposition to Hamilton's proposed bank. Madison and most other Southerners viewed the bank as evidence of a willingness to sacrifice the interests of the agrarian South in favor of the financial and industrial interests of the North. They feared that the bank, with its power to dispense economic favors, would re-create in the United States the kind of government corruption and privilege they associated with Great Britain. They argued that the Constitution did not explicitly authorize Congress to charter a bank or any other corporation.

The bank bill passed Congress on a vote that divided along sectional lines. Madison's objections, however, left Washington concerned that the bank might not be constitutional. He sought the cabinet's opinion, provoking the first great debate over how the Constitution should be interpreted. Thomas Jefferson, the secretary of state, sided with Madison and for the first time openly clashed with Hamilton. Taking a strict constructionist position, he argued that all powers the Constitution had not expressly delegated to the national government were reserved to the states under the Tenth Amendment. Hamilton, in a brilliant rejoinder, argued that Article 1, Section 8, of the Constitution, which declares that Congress has the right to "to make all laws which shall be necessary and proper" to exercise its powers and those of the federal government, gives Congress implicit authority beyond its explicitly enumerated powers. With this broad constructionist position, he won Washington to his side.

With Washington's signature on the bill, Hamilton's bank was chartered for twenty years. Congress also passed a hefty 25 percent excise tax on distilled liquor. Little, however, of Hamilton's plan to promote manufacturing survived the scrutiny of the agrarian opposition. Tariff duties were raised moderately in 1792, but no funds were forthcoming to accelerate industrial development.

THE EMERGENCE OF PARTIES

By the end of Washington's first term, Americans were dividing into two camps. On one side stood those who still called themselves **Federalists**. These were the supporters of Hamilton's program—speculators, creditors, merchants, manufacturers, and commercial farmers. They were the Americans most fully integrated into the market economy and in control of it. Concentrated in the North, they included New England Congregationalists and mid-Atlantic Episcopalians (former Anglicans), members of the more socially prestigious churches. In both economic and cultural terms, the Federalists were drawn from the more privileged segments of society.

Jefferson and Madison shrewdly gave the name **Republican** to the party that formed in opposition to the Federalists, thus identifying it with individual liberties and the heritage of the Revolution. The Republicans accused Hamilton and the Federalists of attempting to impose a British system of economic privilege and social exploitation. The initial core of the party consisted of southern planters and backcountry Scots-Irish farmers. These were Americans outside the market economy or skeptical of its benefits. They feared that the commercial groups favored by Hamilton would corrupt politics in their pursuit of power and foster commerce and manufacturing at the expense of agriculture. The Republicans were committed to an agrarian America in which power remained in the hands of farmers and planters.

In 1792, parties were still in a formative stage. The political divisions that had appeared first in Congress and then spread to Washington's cabinet did not yet extend very deeply into the electorate. Washington remained aloof from the political infighting and was still seen as a great unifier. Unopposed, he was reelected in 1792. However, a series of crises in his second term deepened and broadened the incipient party divisions. By 1796, rival parties were contesting the presidency and vying for the support of an increasingly politically organized electorate.

THE FRENCH REVOLUTION

The French Revolution began in 1789, and in its early phase, most Americans applauded it. France had been an ally of the United States during the Revolutionary War and now seemed to be following the example of its American friends in shaking off monarchical rule. By 1792, however, the French Revolution had turned violent and radical. Its supporters confiscated the property of aristocrats and the church, slaughtered suspected enemies, and executed the king, Louis XVI. In early 1793, republican France was at war against Britain and the European powers.

The excesses of the French Revolution and the European war that erupted in its wake touched off a bitter debate in America. Federalists drew back in horror from France's new regime. They insisted that the terror unleashed by the French was far removed from the reasoned republicanism of the American Revolution. As the *Federalist Gazette* of the United States argued: "The American Revolution, it ought to be repeated, was not accomplished as the French has been, by massacres, assassinations, or proscriptions." For the Republicans, the French remained the standard-bearers of the cause of liberty for common people everywhere. Jefferson admitted that the French Revolution was tarnished by the loss of innocent lives, "but rather than it should have failed, I would have seen half the earth desolated." He was convinced that "the liberty of the whole earth was depending on the issue in the contest."

Franco-American relations.   When the new French ambassador, Edmond Genêt arrived in the United States in April 1793—just as the debate in America over the French Revolution was heating up—Franco-American relations reached a turning point. The two countries were still bound to one another by the Franco-American Alliance of 1778. The alliance required the United States to assist France in the defense of its West Indian colonies and to open American ports to French privateers if France were attacked. Genêt, it soon became clear, hoped to embroil the United States in the French war against the British. He commissioned American privateers to attack British shipping and tried to enlist an army of frontiersmen to attack Spanish possessions in Louisiana and Florida.

Genêt's actions, as well as the enthusiastic receptions that greeted him as he traveled from Charleston to Philadelphia (chosen in 1790 as the temporary national capital), forced Washington to call a special cabinet meeting. The president feared that Genêt would stampede Americans into the European war, with disastrous results for the nation's finances. The bulk of America's foreign trade was with the British, and tariff duties on British imports were the main source of revenue to pay for Hamilton's assumption and funding programs. Hamilton urged Washington to declare American neutrality in the European war, maintaining that the president could commit the nation to neutrality on his own authority when Congress, as was then the case, was not in session. Hamilton also wanted to suspend the military and commercial

treaties of 1778 with France and refuse diplomatic recognition of Genêt. Jefferson, although he too wanted to avoid war, opposed Hamilton on these issues. Disputing Washington's power to act on his own, Jefferson maintained that the warmaking powers of Congress reserved for it alone the right to issue a declaration of neutrality.

Washington steered a middle course. He granted Genêt a formal (but cold) reception and took no action to suspend the Franco-American treaties. But he accepted Hamilton's argument on his authority to declare neutrality and issued a proclamation on April 22, 1793, stating that the United States would be "friendly and impartial toward the belligerent powers."

Despite this proclamation, Genêt continued to meddle. He finally exceeded Washington's patience in the summer of 1793, when he grandly announced that he would take his case directly to the American people and force a cowardly administration to stand up for French rights. Washington was on the verge of forcing Genêt's recall to France in August when news arrived that a new and more radical French government had decided to bring Genêt back as a political prisoner. The president graciously permitted Genêt to remain in America as a private citizen. Had he returned to France, he would have faced almost certain execution.

The growth of Democratic-Republican societies. Genêt quickly faded from public view, but American politics became more open and aggressive in the wake of his visit. Pro-French enthusiasm lived on in a host of grass-roots political organizations known as the Democratic-Republican societies. Nearly forty of these societies formed in 1793 and 1794. As their name suggests, these societies reflected a belief that democracy and republicanism were one and the same. This was a new concept in American politics. Democracy had traditionally been equated with anarchy and mob rule. The members of the new societies argued to the contrary that only democracy—meaning popular participation in politics and direct appeals by politicians to the people—could maintain the revolutionary spirit of 1776 because the people were the only true guardians of that spirit. As a letter writer to the *Newark Gazette* put it: "It must be the mechanics and farmers, or the poorer class of people (as they are generally called), that must support the freedom which they and their fathers purchased with their blood—the nobility will never do it—they will be always striving to get the reins of government into their own hands, and then they can ride the people at pleasure."

The Democratic-Republican societies attacked the Washington administration for failing to assist France, and they expressed the popular feeling that Hamilton's program favored the rich over the poor.

member of Gen. Anthony Wayne's staff.

This painting by an officer on General Wayne's staff shows Little Turtle, a Miami chief, speaking through an interpreter to General Wayne (with one hand behind his back) during the negotiations that led to the Treaty of Greenville.

For the first time, Washington himself was personally assailed in the press.

The core members of the societies were urban artisans whose egalitarian views shocked the Federalists, who expected deference, not criticism and political activism, from the people. In their view, the Democratic-Republicans were rabble-rousers trying to dictate policy to the nation's natural leaders. The Federalists harshly condemned the emergence of organized political dissent from below, but in so doing they only enhanced the popular appeal of the growing Republican opposition.

SECURING THE FRONTIER

Control of the West remained an elusive goal throughout Washington's first term. Indian resistance in the Northwest Territory initially prevented whites from pushing north of the Ohio River. The powerful Miami Confederacy, led by Little Turtle, routed two ill-trained American armies in 1790 and 1791. The 1791 encounter, which took place on the banks of the Wabash River in western Ohio, was the worst defeat an American army ever suffered in frontier fighting. More than nine hundred soldiers were killed or wounded, and the commander, General Arthur St. Clair, was lucky to survive. The southern frontier was quieter, but the Spanish continued to use the Creeks and Cherokees as a buffer against American penetration south of the Tennessee River.

By 1793, many western settlers felt abandoned by the national government. They believed that the government had broken a promise to protect them against Indians and foreigners. Much of the popularity of the Democratic-Republican societies in the West fed off these frustrations. Westerners saw the French, who were at war with Britain and Spain, as allies against the foreign threat on the frontier, and they forwarded resolutions to Congress embracing the French cause. These resolutions also demanded free and open navigation on the Mississippi River. This, in the minds of Westerners, was their natural right. Without it, they would be forever impoverished. "If the interest of Eastern America requires that we should be kept in poverty," argued the Mingo Creek society of western Pennsylvania, "it is unreasonable from such poverty to exact contributions. The first, if we cannot emerge from, we must learn to bear, but the latter, we never can be taught to submit to."

Submission to national authority, however, was precisely what the Federalists wanted from both the Indians and the western settlers. St. Clair's humiliating defeat in 1791 prompted a reorganization of the War Department. By the summer of 1794, Washington's administration felt prepared to move against the Indians. This time, it sent into the Ohio region not the usual ragtag crew of militia and unemployed city dwellers but a force built around veterans from the professional army. The commander, General Anthony Wayne, was a savvy, battle-hardened war hero.

Wayne's victory on August 4, 1794, at the Battle of Fallen Timbers, near present-day Toledo, broke the back of Indian military resistance in Ohio. In the resulting **Treaty of Greenville**, signed in August 1795, twelve tribes ceded most of the present state of Ohio to the U.S. government in return for an annual payment of $9,500. The Ohio country was now open to white settlement (see Map 8–1 and American Views).

THE WHISKEY REBELLION

Within a few months of Wayne's victory at Fallen Timbers, another American army was on the move. The target this time were the so-called whiskey rebels of

AMERICAN VIEWS

Little Turtle Defends the Miami Lands

The climax of what had become a thirty-year war between Native Americans and white settlers for control of the Ohio country came in 1794 with the American victory at the Battle of Fallen Timbers. The most innovative and successful of the Indian leaders who had emerged in the conflict was the Miami war chief Mishiki-nakwa, or Little Turtle as he was known by whites. The following is from one of Little Turtle's speeches during the peace negotiations with the victorious Americans at Greenville, Ohio, in July, 1795.

- How would you characterize Little Turtle's stance during the negotiations and his attitude toward Wayne?
- On what basis did Little Turtle justify the land claims of the Miamis in the Ohio country? How would this differ from the way in which whites staked their claim to the land?
- How did Little Turtle explain his leadership of the Miamis and how did this differ from white notions of leadership?
- What might account for the divisions among the Indians that were cited by Little Turtle?

"General Wayne: I hope you will pay attention to what I now say to you. I wish to inform you where your younger brothers, the Miamies, live, and, also, the Pottawatamies of St. Joseph's, together with the Wabash Indians. You have pointed out to us the boundary line between the Indians and the United States, but I now take the liberty to inform you, that the line cuts off from the Indians a large portion of country, which has been enjoyed by my forefathers time immemorial, without molestation or dispute. The print of my ancestors' houses are every where to be seen in this portion . . . . It is well known by all my brothers present, that my forefathers kindled the first fire at Detroit; from thence, he extended his lines to the head waters of Scioto; from thence, down the Ohio, to the mouth of the Wabash, and from thence to Chicago, on Lake Michigan . . . . I have now informed you of the boundaries of the Miami nation, where the Great Spirit placed my forefathers a long time ago, and charged him not to sell or part with his lands, but to preserve them for his posterity. This charge has been handed down to me . . . . I was much surprised to find that my other brothers differed so much from me on this subject: for their conduct would lead one to suppose, that the Great Spirit, and their forefathers, had not given them the same charge that was give[n] to me, but, on the contrary, had directed them to sell their lands to any white man who wore a hat, as soon as he should ask it of them. Now, elder brother, your younger brothers, the Miamies, have pointed out to you their country, and also to our brothers present. When I hear your remarks and proposals on this subject [of Miami lands], I will be ready to give you an answer; I came with an expectation of hearing you say good things, but I have not heard what I have expected."

Source: "Documents, Legislative and Executive, of the Congress of the United States, From the First Session of the First to the Third Session of the Thirteenth Congress, Inclusive: commencing March 3, 1789, and ending March 3, 1815. Vol. IV" (Washington: Gales and Seaton, 1832), pp. 570–571.

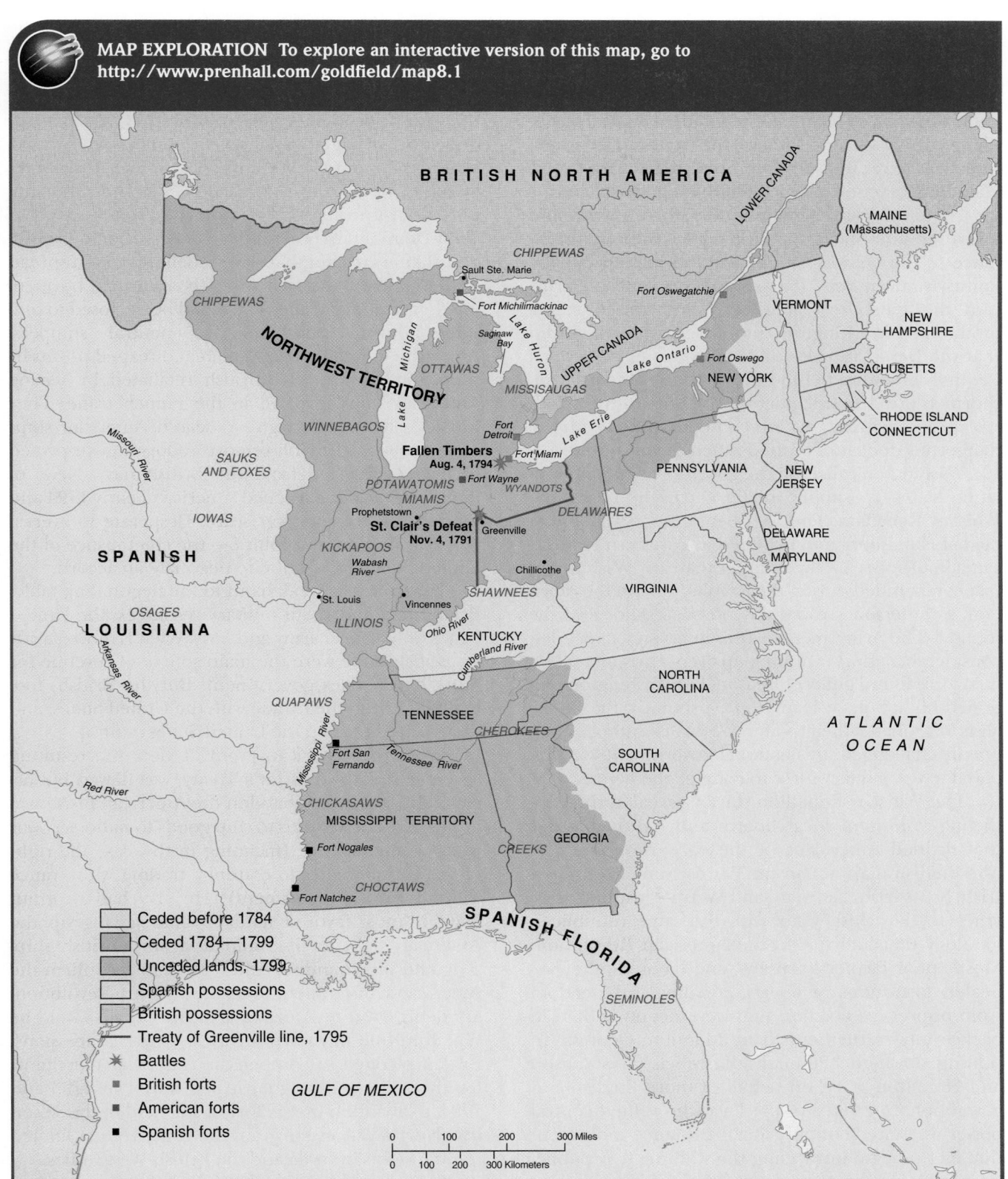

MAP 8-1　Indian Land Cessions, 1784–1800
The persistent pressure of white settlers and the military forces of the new national government forced Native Americans to cede huge tracts of their western lands.

western Pennsylvania, who were openly resisting Hamilton's excise tax on whiskey. This tax had always been unpopular among western farmers. The high cost of transport across the mountains made it unprofitable for them to sell their grain in the east. But by distilling corn or rye into whiskey, they reduced it enough in bulk to lower transportation costs and earn a profit. Hamilton's excise tax wiped out these profits.

Hamilton was determined to enforce the tax and assert the supremacy of national laws. Although resistance to the tax was widespread, he singled out the Pennsylvania rebels. It was easier to send an army into the Pittsburgh area than into the Carolina mountains. Washington, moreover, was convinced that the Democratic-Republican societies of western Pennsylvania were behind the defiance of federal authority there. He welcomed the opportunity to chastise these organizations, which he identified with the dangerous doctrines of the French Revolution.

Washington called on the governors of the mid-Atlantic states to supply militia forces to crush the **Whiskey Rebellion**. The 13,000-man army that assembled at Harrisburg and marched into western Pennsylvania in October 1794 was larger than any Washington had commanded during the Revolution. But the rebellion, as Jefferson sardonically noted, "could never be found." The army met no resistance and expended considerable effort rounding up twenty prisoners. Two men were found guilty of treason, but Washington pardoned both. Still, at Hamilton's insistence, the Federalists had made their point: When its authority was openly challenged, this national government was prepared to use military force to compel obedience.

The Whiskey Rebellion starkly revealed the conflicting visions of local liberty and national order that divided Americans of the early republic. The non-English majority on the Pennsylvania frontier—Irish, Scots-Irish, German, and Welsh—justified resistance to the whiskey tax with the same republican ideology that had fueled the American Revolution. Mostly poor farmers, artisans, and laborers, they appealed to notions of liberty, equality, and freedom from oppressive taxation that were deeply rooted in backcountry settlements from Maine to Georgia. In putting down the Pennsylvania rebels, Washington and Hamilton acted on behalf of more English and cosmopolitan groups in the East who valued central power as a check on any local resistance movement that might begin unraveling the still fragile republic.

TREATIES WITH BRITAIN AND SPAIN

Much of the unrest in the West stemmed from the menacing presence of the British and Spanish on the nation's borders. Washington's government had the resources to suppress Indians and frontier dissidents but lacked sufficient armed might to push Spain and especially Britain out of the West.

The British, embroiled in what they saw as a life-or-death struggle against revolutionary France, clamped a naval blockade on France and its colonies in the Caribbean in the fall of 1793. They also supported an uprising of slaves on the French island of Saint-Domingue (present-day Haiti), enraging southern planters fearful that slave rebellions might spread to the United States. The French countered by opening their colonial trade, which had been closed to outsiders during peacetime, to neutral shippers. American merchants stepped in and reaped profits by supplying France. The British retaliated by seizing American ships involved in the French trade. They further claimed the right to search American ships and impress, or forcibly remove, sailors they suspected of having deserted from the British navy. News of these provocations reached America in early 1794 and touched off a major war scare. Desperate to avert a war, Washington sent John Jay, the chief justice of the United States, to London to negotiate an accord.

Jay brought a weak hand to the negotiating table. Britain had enormous military resources, the United States only a small army and navy. What is more, tariffs on British trade were the main source of revenue for the United States government. But the British, too, benefited from their trade with the United States, and they wanted to keep the United States neutral.

From the American point of view, the resulting agreement, known as **Jay's Treaty**, was flawed but acceptable. Jay had to abandon the American insistence on the right of neutrals to ship goods to nations at war without interference (meaning in this case the right of the United States to continue trading with France without British harassment). He also had to grant Britain "most favored nation" status, giving up the American right to discriminate against British shipping and merchandise. And he had to reconfirm the American commitment to assure that pre-Revolutionary debts owed by Americans to the British would be repaid in full. In return for these major concessions, Britain pledged to compensate American merchants for the ships and cargoes it had seized in 1793 and 1794, to abandon the six forts it still held in the American Northwest, and to grant the United States limited trading rights in India and the British West Indies.

Signed in November 1794, Jay's Treaty caused an uproar in the United States when its terms became known in March 1795. Southerners saw in it another sellout of their interests. It required them to pay their prewar debts to British merchants but was silent about the slaves Britain had carried off during the Revolution. And the concessions Britain did make seemed to favor the North, especially New England merchants and shippers. Republicans, joined now by urban artisans, were infuriated that Jay had stripped them of their chief weapon—economic retaliation—for breaking free of British commercial dominance. The Senate ratified the treaty in June 1795, but only because Washington backed it.

Jay's Treaty, combined with a string of French victories in Europe in 1795, convinced Spain to adopt a more conciliatory attitude toward the United States. With France apparently gaining the upper hand in the war, Spain was anxious to shift its allegiance from Britain to France. But it saw the Jay treaty as the beginning of an Anglo-American alliance and decided to reach an agreement with the United States before it changed sides, lest the United States and Britain combine forces to challenge Spain's American possessions. In the **Treaty of San Lorenzo** (also known as Pinckney's Treaty) of 1795, Spain accepted the American position on the 31st parallel as the northern boundary of Spanish Florida and granted American farmers the right of free transit through the port of New Orleans.

THE FIRST PARTISAN ELECTION

Partisanship—open identification with one of the two parties—steadily rose in the 1790s, fueled in large measure by a new print culture. The first opposition newspaper, the *National Gazette,* appeared in 1791, and the number of newspapers more than doubled within the decade. Circulated and discussed in taverns and coffeehouses, newspapers helped draw ordinary Americans into the political process. Ongoing involvement in the raucous, celebratory political culture that Americans fashioned also politicized them. Through festivals on July 4 honoring the nation's independence, street parades and demonstrations favoring or opposing such events as the French Revolution or Jay's Treaty, and an endless stream of toasts, speeches, banquets, and broadsides, various groups publicly proclaimed and acted out their version of what it meant to be an American. No single version held sway. National self-identity varied by class, race, sex, and region, but as newspaper reports of local activities were copied and disseminated across the country, Americans could feel that they were joined in a collective effort to define what the nation meant to them. As a national identity was being forged and contested, lines of partisanship were marked and deepened. Depending upon the group staging the celebration, Republican or Federalist doctrines were on display. Each of the parties

competed with the other to lay claim to the Revolutionary heritage of freedom and independence.

Women also participated in this public arena of political activism. Although denied formal political rights, they wrote and attended plays with explicit political messages, joined in patriotic rituals, and organized their own demonstrations. To show their support for the French Revolution, women in Menetomy, Massachusetts, wore liberty caps and cockades, the symbols of the French cause. Two widows in Charleston, South Carolina—one American, the other French—went further in July 1793, when they staged a clever form of street theater in front of a large crowd. As reported by a Charleston newspaper, "after having repudiated their husbands on account of their ill-treatment, [they] conceived the design of living together in the strictest union and friendship in order to give a pledge of their fidelity [and] requested that their striped gowns should be penned together, that their children should be looked upon as one family, while their mothers showed them an equal affection." Here was a double-edged message. Just as a union of the French and the Americans could dispense with the need for Britain, so, it appeared, two women could enjoy domestic bliss without the need for husbands. Shocked by such pro-French sympathies and declarations of women's independence, the Federalists moved quickly to find a safe outlet for women's political activism. They invited women to join Federalist-sponsored events that denounced the French Revolution as a threat to all civilized order. By the late 1790s, both parties were seeking to broaden their popular appeal by including women in their partisan rallies.

As partisanship spread, no symbol of traditional authority, Washington included, was safe from challenge. Washington complained bitterly to friends that his political opponents had maligned him "in such exaggerated and indecent terms as could scarcely be applied to a . . . notorious defaulter, or a even a common pickpocket." He announced his decision to retire from public life in his Farewell Address of September 1796. Devoting most of this address to a denunciation of partisanship, he invoked the republican ideal of disinterested, independent statesmanship as the only sure and virtuous guide for the nation. He warned against any permanent foreign alliances and cautioned that the Union itself would be endangered if parties continued to be characterized "by geographical discriminations—*Northern* and *Southern*, *Atlantic* and *Western*—whence designing men may endeavor to excite a belief that there is a real difference of local interests and views."

Confirming Washington's fears, the election of 1796 was the first openly partisan election in American history. John Adams was the Federalist candidate and

Thomas Jefferson the Republican candidate. Each was selected by a party caucus, a meeting of party leaders. As a result of disunity in the Federalist ranks, the election produced the anomaly of a Federalist president (Adams) and a Republican vice president (Jefferson). Written with no thought of organized partisan competition for the presidency, the Constitution simply stated that the presidential candidate with the second highest number of electoral votes would become vice president. In this case, that candidate was Jefferson, and the result was a new administration badly divided from the start.

Despite the election's confused outcome, the sectional pattern in the voting was unmistakable. Only the solid support of regional elites in New England and the mid-Atlantic states enabled the Federalists to retain the presidency. Adams received all the northern electoral votes, with the exception of Pennsylvania's. Jefferson was the overwhelming favorite in the South.

THE LAST FEDERALIST ADMINISTRATION

The Adams administration got off to a rocky start from which it never recovered. The vice president was the leader of the opposition party; key members of the cabinet, which Adams had inherited from Washington, owed their primary loyalty to Hamilton; and the French, who saw Adams as a dupe of the British, instigated a major crisis that left the threat of war hanging over the entire Adams presidency. Adams had been a lawyer before the Revolution; he was a veteran of both Continental Congresses, had been a diplomat in Europe for a decade, and had served as Washington's vice president for eight years. But despite this extraordinarily rich background in public affairs, he was politically naive. Scrupulously honest but quick to take offense, he lacked the politician's touch for inspiring personal loyalty and crafting compromises based on a realistic recognition of mutual self-interest. But putting the interests of the country before those of his party, he almost single-handedly prevented a nearly certain war with France and a possible civil war at home. The price he paid was a badly split Federalist

With the horrors of the French Revolution forming a backdrop, this cartoon depicts France as a five-headed monster demanding a bribe from the three Americans sent by Adams. The Federalists hoped that such anti-French sentiments would lead to an open war.

party that refused to unite behind him when he sought reelection in 1800.

THE FRENCH CRISIS AND THE XYZ AFFAIR

An aggressive coalition known as the Directory gained control of revolutionary France in 1795 and denounced the Jay treaty as evidence of an Anglo-American alliance against France. When Jefferson and the pro-French Republicans lost the election of 1796, the Directory turned openly hostile. In short order, the French annulled the commercial treaty of 1778 with the United States, ordered the seizure of American ships carrying goods to the British, and declared that any American sailors found on British ships, including those forcibly pressed into service, would be summarily executed. By the time Adams had been in office barely three months, the French had already confiscated more than three hundred American ships.

In the fall of 1797, Adams sent three commissioners to Paris in an effort to avoid war. The French treated the three with contempt. Having just conquered the Netherlands and detached Spain from its British alliance, France was in no mood to compromise. Through three intermediaries—identified by Adams only as X, Y, and Z when he informed Congress of the negotiations—the French foreign minister demanded a large bribe to initiate talks and an American loan of $12 million.

In April 1798, the Senate published a full account of the insulting behavior of the French in what came to be called the **XYZ Affair**. The public was indignant, and war fever swept the country. The Federalists, who had always warned against the French, enjoyed greater popularity than they ever had or ever would again. Congress acted to upgrade the navy, which had languished since the Revolutionary War. Funds were provided to build and arm forty new ships. Responsibility for naval affairs, formerly divided between the Treasury and War Departments, was consolidated in a new Department of the Navy. By the fall of 1798, American ships were waging an undeclared war against the French in Caribbean waters, a conflict that came to be known as the **Quasi-War**.

The Federalists in Congress, dismissing Republican objections, also voted to create a vastly expanded army. They tripled the size of the regular army to ten thousand men and authorized a special provisional army of fifty thousand. Congress put the provisional army under Washington's command, but he declined to come out of retirement except for a national emergency. In the meantime, he insisted that Hamilton be appointed second in command and given charge of the provisional army's field operations. To pay for both the expanded army and the naval rearmament, the Federalists pushed through the Direct Tax of 1798, a levy on the value of land, slaves, and dwellings.

CRISIS AT HOME

The thought of Hamilton in charge of a huge army convinced many Republicans that their worst nightmares were about to materialize. One congressman shuddered that "the monarchy-loving Hamilton is now so fixed, as to be able, with one-step, to fill the place of our present commander in chief." Adams shared such fears. He was furious that Hamilton had been forced on him as commander of the provisional army. Years later, he wrote that "the British faction was determined to have a war with France, and Alexander Hamilton at the head of the army and then Pres. of U.S. Peace with France was therefore treason against their fundamental maxims and reasons of State." As the Republicans immediately sensed and Adams came to realize, Hamilton's supporters, known as the High Federalists, saw the war scare with France as an opportunity to stamp out dissent, cement an alliance with the British, and strengthen and consolidate the powers of the national government.

Congressional Pugilists, caricature 1798. Neg. #33995. Collection of The New-York Historical Society

This contemporary cartoon shows Republican Matthew Lyon, in the center with the fire tongs, fighting against Roger Griswold, a Connecticut Federalist. This brawl in Congress on February 15, 1798, revealed the depth of the feeling that now divided the Republicans and Federalists.

The Federalists passed four laws in the summer of 1798, known collectively as the **Alien and Sedition Acts** that confirmed the Republicans' fears. Three of these acts were aimed at immigrants, especially French and Irish refugees who voted for the Republicans. The acts convinced hundreds of immigrants to flee the country to avoid possible arrest. The Alien Enemies Act empowered the president to deport foreigners who came from countries at war with the United States. The more sweeping Alien Friends Act authorized the president to expel any alien resident he suspected of subversive activities. The Naturalization Act extended the residency requirement for American citizenship (and hence the right to vote) from five to fourteen years.

The most dangerous of the four acts in the minds of Republicans was the Sedition Act, a measure that made it a federal crime to engage in any combination or conspiracy against the government or to utter or print anything "false, scandalous and malicious" against the government. Federalist judges were blatantly partisan in their enforcement of the Sedition Act. Twenty-five individuals, mostly Republican editors, were indicted under the act, and ten were convicted. The most celebrated case involved Matthew Lyon, a Republican congressman from Vermont. Indicted for publishing a letter criticizing President Adams, he was reelected to Congress in December 1798 while still in jail.

Facing a Congress and a Supreme Court dominated by the Federalists, Jefferson and Madison turned to the safely Republican legislatures of Kentucky and Virginia for a forum from which to attack the constitutionality of the Alien and Sedition Acts. Taking care to keep their authorship secret, they each drafted a set of resolutions—Jefferson for the Kentucky legislature and Madison for the Virginia legislature—that challenged the entire centralizing program of the Federalists. In doing so, they produced the first significant articulation of the southern stand on **states' rights**.

The resolutions—adopted in the fall of 1798—proposed a compact theory of the Constitution. They asserted that the states had delegated specific powers to the national government for their common benefit. It followed that the states reserved the right to rule whether the national government had unconstitutionally assumed a power not granted to it. If a state decided that the national government had exceeded its powers, it could "interpose" its authority to shield its citizens from a tyrannical law. In a second set of resolutions, the Kentucky legislature introduced the doctrine of **nullification**, the right of a state to render null and void a national law it deemed unconstitutional.

Jefferson and Madison hoped that these resolutions would rally voters to the Republican party as the defender of threatened American liberties. Yet not a single additional state seconded them. In the end, what aroused popular rage against the Federalists was not legislation directed against aliens and subversives but the high cost of Federalist taxes.

The Direct Tax of 1798 fell on all owners of land, dwellings, or slaves and provoked widespread resentment. Enforcing it required an army of bureaucrats—more than five hundred for the state of Pennsylvania alone. In February 1799, in the heavily German southeastern counties of Pennsylvania, a group of men led by an auctioneer named John Fries released tax evaders from prison in Bethlehem. President Adams responded to Fries's Rebellion with a show of force, but the fiercest resistance the soldiers he sent to Pennsylvania encountered was from irate farm wives, who doused them with hot water. Fries and two other men were arrested, convicted of treason, and sentenced to be executed. (Adams later pardoned them.) But the Federalists had now lost much of their support in Pennsylvania.

THE END OF THE FEDERALISTS

The events in Pennsylvania reflected an air of menace that gripped the country as the campaign of 1800 approached. The army was chasing private citizens whose only crime in the eyes of many was that they were honoring their Revolutionary heritage by resisting hateful taxes. Federal soldiers also roughed up Republican voters at polling places. No wonder Adams later wrote that

Short and pudgy, Adams had little of Hamilton's physical presence as a natural leader. But he had a first-rate mind and the political courage to place the nation's needs above those of his Federalist party when he peacefully ended the Quasi-War with France.

"the army was as unpopular as if it had been a ferocious wild beast let loose upon the nation to devour it." Southern Republicans talked in private of the possible need to resist Federalist tyranny by force and, failing in that, to secede from the Union. Hamilton and the High Federalists saw in the Kentucky and Virginia resolutions "a regular conspiracy to overturn the government." Reports that Virginia intended to strengthen its militia heightened their anxieties, and they proposed to meet force with force. Speaking of Virginia, Hamilton said that "the government must not merely defend itself, it must attack and arraign its enemies."

No one did more to defuse this charged atmosphere than President Adams. The Federalists depended for their popular support on the expectation of a war with France, which as late as 1798 had swept them to victory in the congressional elections. Still, Adams refrained from asking for a declaration of war. The United States had been successful in the Quasi-War against France. By early 1799, French ships had been forced out of the Caribbean and American coastal waters. And in Europe, the tide of war had turned against the French. As a result, Adams believed that the French would now be more open to conciliation. Of greater importance, Adams recognized that war with France could trigger a civil war at home. Hamilton and the High Federalists, he realized, would use war as an excuse to crush the Republican opposition in Virginia. Fearful of Hamilton's intentions and unwilling to run the risk of militarizing the government and saddling it with a huge war debt, Adams broke with his party and decided to reopen negotiations with France in February 1799.

The **Franco-American Accord of 1800** that resulted from Adams's initiative released the United States from its 1778 alliance with France. It also obligated the United States to surrender all claims against the French for damages done to American shipping during the Quasi-War. The negotiations in Paris dragged on through the election of 1800, but for the Hamiltonian Federalists, the political damage had already been done. The prospect of peace with France deprived them of their trump card in the election. The Republicans could no longer be branded as the traitorous friends of an enemy state. The enlarged army, with no foe to fight, became a political embarrassment, and the Federalists dismantled it. Although rumors of possible violence continued to circulate, the Republicans grew increasingly confident that they could peacefully gain control of the government.

The Federalists nonetheless ran a very competitive race in 1800. Adams's peace policy bolstered his popularity. And because American merchants had profited from supplying both sides in the European war, the country was enjoying a period of prosperity that benefited the president and his party. The Federalists put on a show of unity when they nominated Adams and Charles C. Pinckney of South Carolina as their presidential candidates at their party caucus. But the wounds opened by Adams's decision to broker a peace with France continued to fester. Hamilton and his friends felt that Adams had betrayed them, and Hamilton wrote a scathing attack on the president in a letter that fell into the hands of Aaron Burr, a crafty politician from New York whom the Republicans had teamed up with Jefferson for the presidential election. Burr published the letter, airing the Federalists' squabblings in public.

The Federalists, hampered by party disunity, could not counter the Republicans' aggressive orga-

REPUBLICANS

Turn out, turn out and save your Country from ruin !

From an *Emperor*—from a *King*—from the iron grasp of a *British Tory Faction*—an unprincipled banditti of British speculators. The hireling tools and emissaries of his majesty king George the 3d have thronged our city and diffused the poison of principles among us.

DOWN WITH THE TORIES, DOWN WITH THE BRITISH FACTION,

Before they have it in their power to enslave you, and reduce your families to distress by heavy taxation. Republicans want no Tribute-liars—they want no ship Ocean-liars—they want no Rufus King's for Lords —they want no Varick to lord it over them—they want no Jones for senator, who fought with the British against the Americans in time of the war.—But they want in their places such men as

Jefferson & Clinton,

who fought their Country's Battles in the year '76

By associating their Federalist opponents with the hated Tories of the American Revolution, the Republicans appealed to the voters as the true defenders of American liberation.

nizational tactics. They found it distasteful to appeal to common people. One party member lamented that the Republicans sent spokesmen "to every class of men, and even to every individual man, that can be gained. Every threshing floor, every husting, every party at work on a house-frame or raising a building, the very funerals are infected with bawlers or whisperers against government."

Wherever they organized, the Republicans attacked the Federalists as monarchists plotting to undo the gains of the Revolution. The Federalists responded with emotional appeals that depicted Jefferson as a godless revolutionary whose election would usher in a reign of terror. "The effect," intoned the Reverend William Linn, "would be to destroy religion, introduce immorality, and loosen all bonds of society."

Attacks like Linn's reflected the fears of Calvinist preachers that a tide of disbelief was about to submerge Christianity in the United States. Church attendance had declined in the 1790s, particularly among men, and perhaps no more than one in twenty Americans was a member of any church. **Deism**, an Enlightenment religious philosophy popular among the leaders of the Revolutionary era, was making inroads among common citizens as well. Deists viewed God as a kind of master clockmaker who created the laws by which the universe runs but otherwise leaves it alone. They rejected revelation for reason, maintaining that the workings of nature alone reveal God's design. In 1794, the famed pamphleteer Thomas Paine, in *The Age of Reason,* denounced churches as "human

FROM THEN TO NOW

Hamilton's Legacy and the National Debt

The debate over the national debt that figured so prominently in the rise of party politics in the 1790s has continued to echo throughout American history. The tripling of the debt in the 1980s, combined with a recession that hit during the presidency of George Bush, sharpened these debates and made the debt a major issue in the election of 1992.

Well into the twentieth century, a Jeffersonian bias against a large public debt dominated the fiscal policy of the federal government. Until 1930, government revenues usually exceeded expenditures, and the surplus was used to reduce the debt. Even so, except for a brief time in the mid-1830s during Andrew Jackson's presidency, the debt was never actually extinguished. This was because economic depressions periodically reduced government income, and wars periodically forced huge increases in expenditures, keeping the government perpetually in debt.

By 1860, the national debt was smaller than it had been when Alexander Hamilton took office as the first secretary of the treasury. To pay for the unprecedented expenses of the Civil War, however, the government borrowed funds, and by 1866, the debt had skyrocketed. The government then committed itself to lowering the debt, and, by the 1890s, when a depression ended twenty-eight consecutive years of budget surplus, it had declined by two-thirds. World War I began a similar cycle—a runup of the debt followed by a gradual reduction—until the onset of the Great Depression of the 1930s began a dramatic change in government policy toward the debt.

Under President Franklin Roosevelt's New Deal, the federal government responded to the length and severity of the depression with new relief programs that drove up outlays while revenues plunged. In what was highly unusual for peacetime, budget deficits piled up, and the national debt rose. It was the cost of World War II, however, that sent the debt soaring. By 1946 it stood at $271 billion, more than the entire economic output of the country. This time, after the war, the creation of surpluses to reduce the debt did not top the government agenda. On the contrary, the onset of the Cold War began an extended period of massive defense spending. At the same time, the government built on the New Deal with new spending on domestic welfare.

Many economists argue that the government's deficit spending since World War II has kept the economy healthy and helped to avert a new depression. In any case the size of the debt relative to the economy as a whole has declined since World War II—even after the runup of the 1980s—because the economy has grown faster than the debt.

Why, then, were the debt and federal deficits such potent political issues in 1992? One reason was surely that the country was just then emerging from a recession. All aspects of the economy were under intense scrutiny, as voters fearful for their jobs struggled with their own debt loads. Renewed economic growth and budgetary restraint allayed those fears by the late 1990s, when the budget was in surplus and the government was paying down some of the national debt. In the presidency of George W. Bush, however, another economic recession and the costs associated with the war on terrorism quickly converted projections of federal budgetary surpluses for the first decade of the twenty-first century into warnings of a new series of deficits. Whether this will revive concerns about the national debt that Jeffersonians first voiced in the 1790s remains to be seen.

---

inventions set up to terrify and enslave mankind, and monopolize power and profit."

These developments convinced Calvinist ministers, nearly all of them Federalists, that the atheism of the French Revolution was infecting American republicanism. They lashed out at the Republicans, the friends of the French Revolution, as perverters of religious and social order. Jefferson, a deist known for his free thinking in religion, bore the brunt of their attack in 1800.

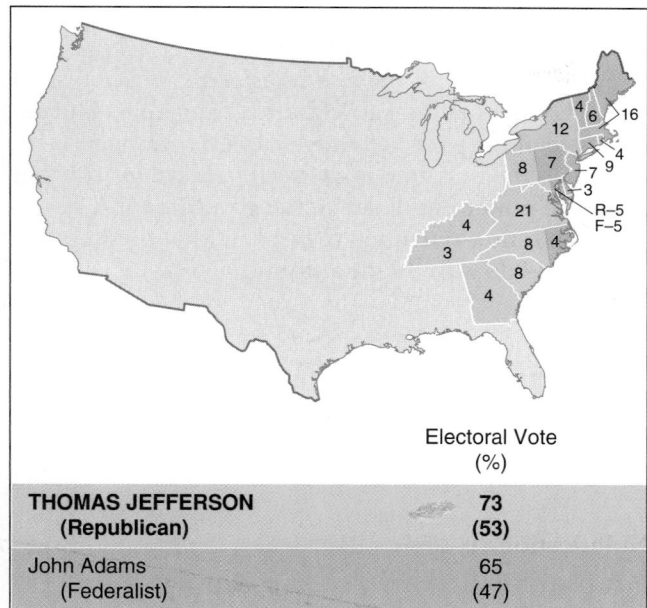

Electoral Vote
(%)

THOMAS JEFFERSON (Republican)	73 (53)
John Adams (Federalist)	65 (47)

MAP 8-2   The Election of 1800
The sharp erosion of Federalist strength in New York and Pennsylvania after 1798 swung the election of 1800 to the Republicans.

The Republicans won the election by mobilizing voters through strong party organizations. Voter turnout in 1800 was twice what it had been in the early 1790s, and most of the new voters were Republicans. The Direct Tax of 1798 cost the Federalists the support of commercial farmers in the mid-Atlantic states. Artisans in port cities had already switched to the Republicans in protest over Jay's Treaty, which they feared left them exposed to a flood of cheap British imports. Adams carried New England and had a smattering of support elsewhere. With New York added to their solid base in the South and the backcountry, the Jeffersonians gained an electoral majority (see Map 8–2).

Party unity among Republican electors was so strong that Jefferson and Burr each received seventy-three electoral votes. Consequently the election was thrown into the House of Representatives, which, until the newly elected Congress was seated, was still dominated by Federalists. Hoping to deny Jefferson the presidency, the Federalists in the House backed Burr. They believed that he was untainted by the Revolutionary virus that made Jefferson seem so dangerous, even though Hamilton, who faced Burr as a political rival in New York, sought to convince them otherwise. The result was a deadlock that persisted into the early months of 1801. Pennsylvania and Virginia mobilized their state militias, a clear message that the Republicans were prepared to use force against what Jefferson termed any "legislative usurpation" of the people's will as expressed in the election.

On February 16, 1801, the Federalists yielded. Informed through intermediaries that Jefferson would not dismantle Hamilton's fiscal system, enough Federalists cast blank ballots to give Jefferson the majority he needed for election. The Twelfth Amendment to the Constitution, ratified in 1804, prevented a similar impasse from arising again by requiring electors to cast separate ballots for president and vice president.

CONCLUSION

In 1789, the American republic was little more than an experiment in self-government. The Federalists provided a firm foundation for that experiment. Hamilton's financial program, neutrality in the wars of the French Revolution, and the diplomatic settlement with Britain in Jay's Treaty bequeathed the young nation a decade of peace and prosperity.

Federalist policies, however, provoked strong opposition rooted in conflicting economic interests and contrasting regional views over the meaning of liberty and government in the new republic. Federalist leadership initially depended on a coalition of regional elites in New England, the mid-Atlantic region, and the slave districts of the South. Each of these elites favored the establishment of effective national power, though often for different reasons. Merchants in Congregationalist New England were concerned mainly with reviving their British trading connections and reversing what they saw as the social and moral decline of the 1780s. Quaker and Episcopal businessmen and commercial farmers in the mid-Atlantic states wanted a central government to promote economic development at home and expand markets aboard. Southern slaveholders, hoping to expand into the West, needed a national government strong enough to secure the trans-Appalachian region.

The Federalist coalition split during Washington's second term when southern planters joined urban artisans and backcountry Scots-Irish farmers in opposing Jay's Treaty and the commercially oriented program of the Federalists. During John Adams' administration, Quaker and German farmers in the mid-Atlantic states defected from the Federalists over the tax legislation of 1798, and three of the four regions of the country lined up behind the Republicans. The new Republican majority was united by their belief that the actions of the New England Federalists—the expansion of the army, the imposition of new taxes, and the passage of the Alien and Sedition Acts—threatened individual liberty and regional autonomy. Non-English groups and farmers south of New England turned to the Republicans as the upholders of these threatened freedoms.

The openly partisan politics of the 1790s surprised the country's founders, who equated parties with the evils of factionalism. They had not foreseen that parties would forge a necessary link between the rulers and the ruled and create a mechanism by which group values and regional interests could be given a political voice. Party formation climaxed in the election of 1800, when the Republicans ended the Federalists' rule. The Republicans won by embracing the popular demand for a more egalitarian social and political order.

To the credit of the Federalists, they relinquished control of the national government peacefully. The importance of this precedent can scarcely be exaggerated. It marked the first time in modern political history that a party in power handed over the government to its opposition. It now remained to be seen what the Republicans would do with their newfound power.

REVIEW QUESTIONS

1. What role did the "people" play in Washington's inauguration in 1789? What was the purpose of the grand procession and why were the militia present?

2. What was distinctive about the four regions of the United States in 1790? What were the common values and goals that brought white Americans together?

3. What were the major problems confronting the Washington administration, and how effectively were they resolved?

4. Who were the Federalists and the Republicans, and how did they differ over the meaning of liberty and the power of the national government? What were the major steps in the formation of two distinct parties in the early United States?

5. Why did regional differences tend to pit the North against the South by the late 1790s?

6. How did the XYZ Affair lead to a political crisis in the United States? Why did the Federalists believe that they would benefit from a war against France?

7. Jefferson called his election in 1800 the "revolution of 1800." What do you think he meant? Would you agree with him?

KEY TERMS

Alien and Sedition Acts (p. 253)

Bill of Rights (p. 241)

Deism (p. 255)

Federalists (p. 245)

Franco-American Accord of 1800 (p. 255)

Jay's Treaty (p. 250)

Judiciary Act of 1789 (p. 242)

Nullification (p. 254)

Pietists (p. 237)

Quasi-War (p. 253)

Republican (Jeffersonian) (p. 245)

States' rights (p. 254)

Tariff Act of 1789 (p. 242)

Tonnage Act of 1789 (p. 242)

Treaty of Greenville (p. 247)

Treaty of San Lorenzo (p. 251)

Whiskey Rebellion (p. 250)

XYZ Affair (p. 252)

RECOMMENDED READING

Elkins, Stanley, and Eric McKitrick. *The Age of Federalism* (1993). A magisterial work of narrative history that includes brilliant sketches of the major political actors in the 1790s.

Flexner, James T. *George Washington and the New Nation, 1783–1793* (1969) and *George Washington: Anguish and Farewell, 1793–1799* (1972). These two volumes stand out for their readable and informative account of Washington's political career after the Revolution.

Freeman, Joanne B. *Affairs of Honor: National Politics in the New Republic* (2001). By showing how politicians in the early republic based their behavior on codes of male honor, this study offers a fresh way of understanding the often bitter political divisions of the 1790s.

Hofstadter, Richard. *The Idea of a Party System, 1780–1840* (1969). This book combines political and intellectual history in a graceful account of how Americans gradually came to accept political parties as a legitimate expression of the popular will.

Lipset, Seymour. *The First New Nation: The United States in Historical and Comparative Perspective* (1963). This work draws on insights from political sociology to show what was unique and enduring in America's pioneering role as a new nation with a written constitution.

Miller, John C. *The Federalist Era, 1789–1801* (1960). This older work is still of great value for its relatively brief and well-balanced overview of the Washington and Adams administrations.

Waldstreicher, David. *In the Midst of Perpetual Fetes: The Making of American Nationalism, 1776–1820* (1997). An imaginatively conceived work that reveals how Americans in the early republic created their own sense of nationalism through popular festivals, street parades, and other forms of political celebration at the local level.

ADDITIONAL SOURCES

Washington's America

Horseman, Reginald. *The Frontier in the Formative Years, 1783–1815* (1970).

McColley, Robert. *Slavery and Jeffersonian Virginia* (1964).

Nash, Gary B. *Forging Freedom: The Formation of Philadelphia's Black Community, 1720–1840* (1988).

Newman, Simon P. *Parades and the Politics of the American Street* (1997).

Smith, Billy G. The *"Lower Sort": Philadelphia's Laboring People, 1750–1800* (1990).

Ulrich, Laurel Thatcher. *A Midwife's Tale: The Life of Martha Ballard, Based on Her Diary, 1785–1812* (1990).

Wallace, Anthony F. C. *The Death and Rebirth of the Seneca* (1970).

Wood, Betty. *Women's Work, Men's Work: The Informal Slave Economies of Lowcountry Georgia* (1995).

Forging a New Government

Cunliffe, Marcus. *George Washington: Man and Monument* (1958).

Ketcham, Ralph. *Presidents above Party: The First American Presidency, 1789–1829* (1984).

Kohn, Richard H. *Eagle and Sword: The Federalists and the Creation of the Military Establishment in America, 1783–1802* (1975).

Phelps, Glenn A. *George Washington and American Constitutionalism* (1993).

Stourzh, Gerald. *Alexander Hamilton and the Idea of Republican Government* (1970).

Ellis, Joseph J. *Founding Brothers: The Revolutionary Generation* (2000)

The Emergence of Parties

Appleby, Joyce. *Capitalism and a New Social Order: The Republican Vision of the 1790s* (1984).

Buel. Richard Jr., *Securing the Revolution: Ideology in American Politics, 1789–1815* (1972).

Branson, Susan. *Those Fiery Frenchified Dames: Women and Political Culture in Early National Philadelphia* (2001)

Cunningham, Noble E. Jr., *The Jeffersonian Republicans: The Formation of Party Organization, 1789–1801* (1957).

De Conde, Alexander. *Entangling Alliance: Politics and Diplomacy under George Washington* (1958).

Slaughter, Thomas P. *The Whiskey Rebellion: Frontier Epilogue to the American Revolution* (1986).

Young, Alfred F. *The Democratic Republicans of New York: The Origins, 1763–1797* (1967).

The Last Federalist Administration

Dauer, Manning *The Adams Federalists* (1953).

Kurtz, Stephen G. *The Presidency of John Adams: The Collapse of Federalism, 1795–1800* (1957).

Sharp, Roger. *American Politics in the Early Republic: The New Nation in Crisis* (1993).

Sisson, Daniel. *The American Revolution of 1800* (1974).

Smith, James M. *Freedom's Fetters: The Alien and Sedition Laws and American Civil Liberties*, rev. ed. (1966).

Stinchcombe, William. *The XYZ Affair* (1980).

WHERE TO LEARN MORE

- **Cincinnati Historical Society, Cincinnati, Ohio.** Collections include written and visual materials on the history of the Old Northwest Territory. Visit its website www.cincymuseum.org/ for information on its programs and the accessibility of its printed and audiovisual collections.

- **Federal Hall National Memorial, New York, New York.** This museum and historic site holds artifacts relating to President Washington's inauguration. Its website www.nps.gov/feha/ includes a printable travel guide to various sites in Manhattan administered by the National Parks Service.

- **Hamilton Grange National Memorial, New York, New York.** The home of Alexander Hamilton contains materials on his life. A brief history of the home and Hamilton's life can be found at its website www.nps/gov/hagr/.

- **Adams National Historic Site, Quincy, Massachusetts.** This site preserves buildings and manuscripts associated with four generations of the Adams family. See its website www.nps.gov/adam/ for information on guided tours and the various homes that are part of the site.

 Please refer to the document CD-ROM for primary sources related to this chapter.

➜ *The low point in what many Americans viewed as A Second War of Independence—the War of 1812—came when British troops seized and burned Washington, D.C., on August 24, 1814.*

THE TRIUMPH AND COLLAPSE OF JEFFERSONIAN REPUBLICANISM
1800–1824

Riversdale, 30 August 1814

My dear Sister,

Since I started this letter [on Aug. 9] we have been in a state of continual alarm, and now I have time to write only two or three lines to ask you to tell Papa that we are alive, in good health, and I hope safe from danger. I am sure that you have heard the news of the battle of Bladensburg where the English defeated the American troops with Madison 'not at their head, but at their rear.'

From there they went to Washington where they burned the Capitol, the President's House, all the public offices, etc. During the battle I saw several cannonballs with my own eyes, and I will write all the details to your husband. At the moment the English ships are at Alexandria which is also in their possession.

I don't know how all this will end, but I fear very badly for us. It is probable that it will also bring about a dissolution of the union of the states, and in that case, farewell to the public debt. You know I have predicted this outcome for a long time. Wouldn't it be wise to send your husband here without delay, in order to plan with me the best course to pursue for Papa's interests as well as yours?

This letter will go, I think, by a Dutch ship. If I have time with the confusion we are in, I will write again in a

CHAPTER OUTLINE

Jefferson's Presidency
Reform at Home
The Louisiana Purchase
Florida and Western Schemes
Embargo and a Crippled Presidency

Madison and the Coming of War
The Failure of Economic Sanctions
The Frontier and Indian Resistance
Decision for War

The War of 1812
Setbacks in Canada
Western Victories and British Offensives
The Treaty of Ghent and the Battle of New Orleans

The Era of Good Feelings
Economic Nationalism
Judicial Nationalism
Toward a Continental Empire

The Breakdown of Unity
The Panic of 1819
The Missouri Compromise
The Election of 1824

Conclusion

few days, perhaps by the same vessel. At present my house is full of people every day and at night my bedroom is full of rifles, pistols, sabers, etc. Many thanks to your husband for the information in his letter of 27 April, and tell him that I invested all his money in the May loan [of the U.S. Treasury]. Please give many greetings to my dear Father and to Charles [her brother]. Embrace your children for me and believe me,

Your affectionate sister,
Rosalie E. Calvert

Margaret Law Callcott, ed., *Mistress of Riversdale: The Plantation Letters of Rosalie Stier Calvert, 1795–1821* (Baltimore: The Johns Hopkins University Press, 1991), pp. 271–272.

Rosalie Calvert, from her plantation home in nearby Bladensburg, Maryland, wrote to her sister in Europe with news of the British attack on Washington, D.C. in August 1814, the low point of the American cause in the War of 1812. The youngest of three children in a wealthy Belgian family that had fled the advancing armies of revolutionary France, Rosalie was sixteen when her family arrived in Philadelphia in the summer of 1794. Her father, Henri J. Stier, had planned in advance for his family's departure and brought with him a sizeable fortune in gold, U.S. currency, and paintings. The family lived off the income from Henri's investments in U.S. securities and, unsurprisingly, was strongly Federalist in its political leanings. After resettling in Annapolis, most of the Stiers returned to Europe in 1803 when political conditions had stabilized. Left behind was Rosalie, entrusted with the management of the family's financial holdings. In 1799, Rosalie had married George Calvert, a descendent of the proprietors of the Maryland colony and a kinsman of the Washingtons.

The Calverts lived at Riversdale, a home built by her father, and shared in the responsibilities of managing three plantations worked by slave labor. Rosalie's wealth and elite social standing deepened her political conservatism. Moreover, the coming to power of the Jeffersonian Republicans in 1801 triggered bitter memories of the revolutionary turmoil she had experienced as a young woman in Belgium. In her eyes, Jefferson and his followers were demagogues who catered to the poor and threatened to infect America with the political radicalism of the French Revolution. She blamed the coming of the War of 1812 on ignorant, ill-conceived Republican policies and feared that the war would unleash massive unrest within the United States. Particularly alarming was the news that a mob in Baltimore had brutally beaten twelve prominent Federalists for their antiwar stand. Thus the sense of "continual alarm" that runs through her letter in August 1814, at a time when the war had spilled over into her home.

Her fears were overblown. The United States did weather the War of 1812 and the Calverts were spared any property damage at their Riversdale estate. Rosalie, however, survived the war by only six years. Her great wealth could not shield her from the duties of a wife, most notably frequent childbearing. The strain of having nine children and suffering one miscarriage in twenty-one years of marriage is likely to have contributed to her death at the age of 43 from congestive heart failure.

Despite her denunciations of the Republicans, Jefferson and his Republican successors, James Madison and James Monroe, succeeded in promoting the growth and independence of the United States in the first quarter of the nineteenth century. Expansionist policies to the south and west more than doubled the size of the republic and fueled the westward spread of slavery. The war against Britain from 1812 to 1815, if less than a military triumph, nonetheless freed Americans to look inward for economic development.

At the height of Republican success during the Era of Good Feelings just after the War of 1812, the Federalist party collapsed. Without an organized opposition to enforce party discipline among themselves, the Republicans soon followed the Federalists into political oblivion. The nation's expansion produced two crises—a financial panic and a battle over slavery in Missouri—that shattered the façade of republican unity. By the mid-1820s, a new party system was emerging.

KEY TOPICS

- The domination of the Republicans and the collapse of the Federalist party
- The territorial expansion of the United States to the west and the south
- The growth of nationalism and of sectional rivalry
- The first national crisis over slavery
- The collapse of the Republican party

JEFFERSON'S PRESIDENCY

Thomas Jefferson believed that a true revolution had occurred in 1800, a peaceful overthrow of the Federalist party and its hated principles of government consolidation and military force. In his eyes, the defeat of the monarchical Federalists reconfirmed the true political legacy of the Revolution by restoring the republican majority to its rightful control of the government.

Unlike the Hamiltonian Federalists, whose commercial vision of America accepted social and economic inequalities as inevitable, the Jeffersonians wanted a predominantly agrarian republic based on widespread economic equality for white yeomen families. Without such equality, Jefferson was convinced, the privileged few would threaten the people's liberties. Contemporary political thought held that all societies went through stages of economic development that ended in the consolidation of power and suppression of liberties by a wealthy minority. Jefferson hoped to break that cycle through territorial expansion that would add enough land to maintain self-reliant farmers as the guardians of republican freedoms.

Jefferson's first administration was a solid success. A unified Republican party reduced the size and scope of the federal government, allowed the Alien and Sedition Acts to lapse, and celebrated the Louisiana Purchase. An enfeebled Federalist party weakly opposed Jefferson's reelection in 1804. His second term, however, was a bitter disappointment, marked by the massive unpopularity of Jefferson's embargo on American foreign trade. The embargo, designed to compel warring Britain and France to recognize American rights as a neutral shipper, failed at home and abroad. As a result, Jefferson left his successor, James Madison, a divided party, a revived Federalism, and an unresolved crisis in foreign affairs.

REFORM AT HOME

Jefferson set the style and tone of his administration from the beginning. He was the first president to be inaugurated in Washington, D.C., and his inauguration was as unpretentious as the raw and primitive capital city itself. Then little more than a scraggly collection of huts, a few boardinghouses, and unfinished public buildings, Washington lacked, one senator ruefully noted, "only houses, wine cellars, learned men, amiable women, and other trifles to make our city perfect." Jefferson walked from his lodgings to the Capitol building to be sworn in. His dress was neat but shorn of such gentlemanly refinements as a wig. He emphasized in his inaugural address the overwhelming commitment of Americans to the "republican form" of government and affirmed his own support of civil liberties as an American principle.

Believing that the Federalists had promoted aristocratic pretensions and courtly intrigue through such practices as weekly levees (formal receptions) for presidential guests, Jefferson replaced the levees with small, men-only dinners, where he aired his political views. This effort to achieve republican purity in governance, one that denied women any political role, created a void in the capital's social life that was filled by the wives of cabinet members and women drawn from the social elite. It was their dinner parties and receptions that enabled politically minded women and men to come together, lobby on behalf of friends and relatives, and build the networks that influenced how political offices and favors were distributed. These occasions provided a setting in which politicking could occur in a capital where the formal institutions of power—the executive, legislative, and judicial branches of government—were cut off from each other, not only by the distance between their physical locations, but also by the constitutional doctrine of separation of powers. Influential Washington hostesses soon wielded a good deal of informal political power as they helped make possible a national political culture.

The cornerstone of Republican domestic policy was retrenchment, a return to the frugal, simple federal

Chronology

1801 Thomas Jefferson is inaugurated, the first Republican president. John Marshall becomes chief justice.

1802 Congress repeals the Judiciary Act of 1801.

1803 *Marbury v. Madison* sets the precedent of judicial review by the Supreme Court.

Louisiana Purchase.

Lewis and Clark expedition begins.

1804 Vice President Aaron Burr kills Alexander Hamilton in a duel.

Judges John Pickering and Samuel Chase impeached by Republicans.

Jefferson is reelected.

1806 Britain and France issue orders restricting neutral shipping.

Betrayal of the Burr conspiracy.

1807 Chesapeake affair.

Congress passes the Embargo Act.

Congress prohibits the African slave trade.

1808 James Madison elected president.

1809 Repeal of the Embargo Act.

Passage of the Nonintercourse Act.

1810 Macon's Bill No. 2 reopens trade with Britain and France.

United States annexes part of West Florida.

Georgia state law invalidated by the Supreme Court in *Fletcher v. Peck*.

1811 Battle of Tippecanoe and defeat of the Indian confederation.

Charter of the Bank of the United States expires.

1812 Congress declares war on Britain.

American loss of Detroit.

Madison reelected.

1813 Perry's victory at Battle of Put-in-Bay.

Battle of the Thames and death of Tecumseh.

1814 Jackson crushes the Creeks at the Battle of Horseshoe Bend.

British burn Washington, D.C., and attack Baltimore.

Macdonough's naval victory on Lake Champlain turns back a British invasion.

Hartford Convention meets.

Treaty of Ghent signed.

1815 Jackson routs British at the Battle of New Orleans.

1816 Congress charters the Second Bank of the United States and passes a protective tariff.

James Monroe elected president.

1817 Rush–Bagot Treaty demilitarizes the Great Lakes.

1818 Anglo–American Accords on trade and boundaries.

Jackson's border campaign in Spanish East Florida.

1819 Trans-Continental Treaty between United States and Spain.

Beginning of the Missouri controversy.

Financial panic sends economy into a depression.

Dartmouth College v. Woodward upholds the charter rights of corporations.

McCulloch v. Maryland upholds constitutionality of the Bank of the United States.

1820 Missouri Compromise on slavery in the Louisiana Purchase.

Monroe reelected.

1823 Monroe Doctrine proclaims western hemisphere closed to further European colonization.

1825 John Quincy Adams elected president by the House of Representatives

establishment the Jeffersonians believed to be the original intent of the Constitution. Determined to root out what they viewed as the corruption and patronage of a government bloated by the power-grasping Federalists, the Republicans began with fiscal policy. Jefferson's secretary of the treasury was Albert Gallatin, a native of Switzerland who emerged in the 1790s as the best financial mind in the Republican party. He convinced Jefferson that the Bank of the United States was essential for financial stability and blocked efforts to dismantle it. Unlike Hamilton, however, Gallatin thought that a large public debt was a curse, a drag on productive capital, and an unfair burden on future generations. He succeeded in reducing the national debt from $83 million in 1800 to $57 million by 1809.

Gallatin's conservative fiscal policies shrank both the spending and taxes of the national government. The Republicans eliminated all internal taxes, including the despised tax on whiskey. Slashes in the military budget kept government expenditures below the level of 1800. The army was cut back to three thousand men, and the navy was nearly eliminated. Jefferson's

Jane Braddick Petticolas (1791-1852) "View of the West Front of Monticello and Garden" 1825, watercolor on paper, 13 5/8 x 18 1/18 inches. Edward Owen/Monticello/Thomas Jefferson Foundation, Inc.

The classical design and bucolic setting of Monticello, Jefferson's home outside Charlottesville, Virginia, visually expressed both his aristocratic tastes and his vision of a harmonious agrarian republic.

defense strategy called for gunboats and coastal fortifications. If the country were invaded, he would rely on the militia—citizen soldiers commanded by professional officers, to be trained at the newly established (1802) military academy at West Point. The cuts in military spending, combined with soaring revenues from customs collections, left Gallatin with a surplus in the budget that he could devote to debt repayment.

Jeffersonian reform targeted the political character, as well as the size, of the national government. Of the six hundred officeholders appointed by Washington and Adams, Jefferson estimated that only six were Republicans. He moved to break the Federalist stranglehold on federal offices and appoint officials with sound Republican principles. Arch-Federalists, those Jefferson deemed guilty of misusing their offices for openly political reasons, were immediately replaced, and Republicans filled other posts opened up by attrition. By the time Jefferson left the presidency in 1809, Republicans held nearly all the appointive offices.

Jefferson moved most aggressively against the Federalists in the judiciary. Just days before they relinquished power, the Federalists passed the Judiciary Act of 1801. This act created sixteen new circuit courts; added nearly two hundred federal marshals, attorneys, and clerks; and reduced the size of the Supreme Court from six justices to five by stipulating that the next vacancy was not to be filled. The Jeffersonians were enraged. The Federalists already monopolized all federal judgeships, and this last-minute legislation both enlarged the judiciary and packed it with more Federalists appointed by Adams, the outgoing president. To add insult to injury, the Federalists had even tried to insure that Jefferson would be unable to appoint a Republican to the Supreme Court when the next opening occurred.

The Republicans fought back. Now dominant in Congress, they quickly repealed the Judiciary Act of 1801, replacing it with a measure that eliminated the new judgeships and restored the size of the Supreme Court to six members, each with responsibility for one

Dolley Madison, the engaging young wife of James Madison, Jefferson's secretary of state, served as the unofficial social hostess in the White House during the administration of Jefferson, a widower.

of the circuit courts. Frustrated Federalists now turned to John Marshall, a staunch Federalist appointed chief justice of the United States by President Adams in 1801, hoping that he would rule that Congress had acted unconstitutionally in removing the recently appointed federal judges. Marshall moved carefully to avoid an open confrontation. He was aware that the Republicans contended that Congress and the president had at least a coequal right with the Supreme Court to decide constitutional questions.

The issue came to a head in the case of **Marbury v. Madison** (1803), which centered on Secretary of State James Madison's refusal to deliver a commission to William Marbury, one of Adams's "midnight appointments" as a justice of the peace for the District of Columbia. Marshall held that although Marbury had a legal right to his commission, the Court had no jurisdiction in the case. The Court ruled that the section of the Judiciary Act of 1789 granting it the power to order the delivery of Marbury's commission was unconstitutional because it conferred on

the Court a power not specified in Article 3 of the Constitution on cases of original jurisdiction. Stating that it was "emphatically the province and duty of the judicial department to say what the law is," Marshall created the precedent of judicial review, the power of the Supreme Court to rule on the constitutionality of federal law. Although not invoked again until the Dred Scott decision of 1857, this doctrine was of pivotal importance for the future of the Court. Marshall had brilliantly turned a threatening situation into a success for the judiciary.

Marshall's assertion of the Court's power deepened Republican suspicions of judicial tyranny. Demanding popular election for all judges, radical Republicans rejected the entire notion of an appointed judiciary. Jefferson did not want to go that far, but he felt strongly that judges should be accountable to the popular will.

At the urging of the radicals, congressional Republicans brought formal charges against two notorious Federalist judges. One of them, John Pickering, a district judge from New Hampshire and a mentally unstable alcoholic, was convicted and removed from office. The other was bigger game: Justice Samuel Chase of the Supreme Court, the most obnoxious Federalist still in a position of national power. For all his blatant partisanship, however, Chase was clearly sane, and he escaped conviction in the Senate in early 1805, when the Republicans failed to show that he was guilty of "high crimes and misdemeanors," the constitutionally defined grounds for removal from office. His acquittal ended the Republican offensive against the judiciary.

THE LOUISIANA PURCHASE

In foreign affairs, fortune smiled on Jefferson during his first term. The European war that had almost sucked in the United States in the 1790s subsided. Britain and France agreed on a truce in 1802. Meanwhile, Jefferson, despite his distaste for a strong navy, ordered a show of force in the Mediterranean to punish the Barbary pirates who were preying on American shipping and taking American sailors hostage.

For years, the North African states of Morocco, Algeria, Tunis, and Tripoli had demanded cash tribute from foreigners trading in the Mediterranean. Jefferson stopped the payments in 1801, and when attacks on American shipping resumed, he retaliated by sending warships and marines to the Mediterranean. The tribute system continued until 1815, but thanks to the success of U.S. forces in Tripoli, Jefferson got much better terms.

The Anglo-French peace was a mixed blessing for the United States. Although it removed any im-

William Clark sketched a Columbia River salmon on this page of his journal.

mediate threat of war, the return of peace also allowed Spain and France to reclaim their colonial trade in the Western Hemisphere. American shippers were thus deprived of the windfall profits they had earned while dominating that trade during the European war. Of greater long-range concern, the new military ruler of France, Napoleon Bonaparte, was now free to develop his plans for reviving the French empire in America. In a secret treaty with Spain in 1800, Napoleon reacquired for France the Louisiana Territory, a vast, vaguely defined area stretching between the Mississippi River and the Rocky Mountains.

Sketchy, unconfirmed reports of the treaty reached Jefferson in the spring of 1801, and he was immediately alarmed. He had long believed that Spain, proud but militarily impotent, would be powerless to stem the spread of the expanding American population into its territories in western North America. Indeed, Spanish military officials in Louisiana had repeatedly called in vain for mili-

tary reinforcements to block the Americans, this "new and vigorous people . . . advancing and multiplying in the silence of peace." France, by contrast, was a formidable opponent. French control of the Mississippi Valley, combined with the British presence in Canada, threatened to hem in the United States and deprive Jefferson's farmers of their empire for liberty.

Jefferson was prepared to reverse the traditional foreign policy of his party in order to eliminate this threat. He opened exploratory talks with the British on an Anglo-American alliance to drive the French out of Louisiana. Looking toward the possibility of war, he also strengthened American forces in the Mississippi Valley and secured congressional approval for the Lewis and Clark expedition through upper Louisiana. Although best known for its scientific discoveries, this expedition was designed initially as a military mission. Jefferson applied diplomatic and military pressure to induce Napoleon to sell New Orleans and a small slice of coastal territory to its east to the United States. This was his main objective: to possess New Orleans and control the mouth of the Mississippi River, outlet to world markets. To his surprise, Napoleon suddenly decided in early 1803 to sell all of the immense Louisiana Territory to the Americans (see Map 9–1).

Napoleon's failure to reconquer Saint-Domingue (modern-day Haiti) was instrumental in his about-face on plans for a revived French empire in America. He had envisioned this rich sugar island as the jewel of his new empire and intended to use the Louisiana Territory as a granary to supply the island. During the upheavals of the French Revolution, the slaves on the island, led by Touissant L'Ouverture, rebelled in a bloody and successful bid for independence. Napoleon sent a large army to reassert French control, but it succumbed to the islanders' fierce resistance.

Without firm French control of Saint-Domingue, Louisiana was of little use to Napoleon. And when the U.S. Congress passed resolutions threatening an American attack on New Orleans, he realized that he was likely to have to fight to keep it. With a renewed war against Britain looming, he had better use for his troops in Europe and wanted to keep Americans neutral. For $15 million (including about $4 million in French debts owed to American citizens), he offered to part with the whole of Louisiana. The cost to the United States was about 3.5 cents per acre.

Jefferson, the strict constructionist, now turned pragmatist. Despite the lack of any specific authorization in the Constitution for the acquisition of foreign territory or the incorporation as American citizens of the fifty thousand French and Spanish descendants then living in Louisiana, he accepted

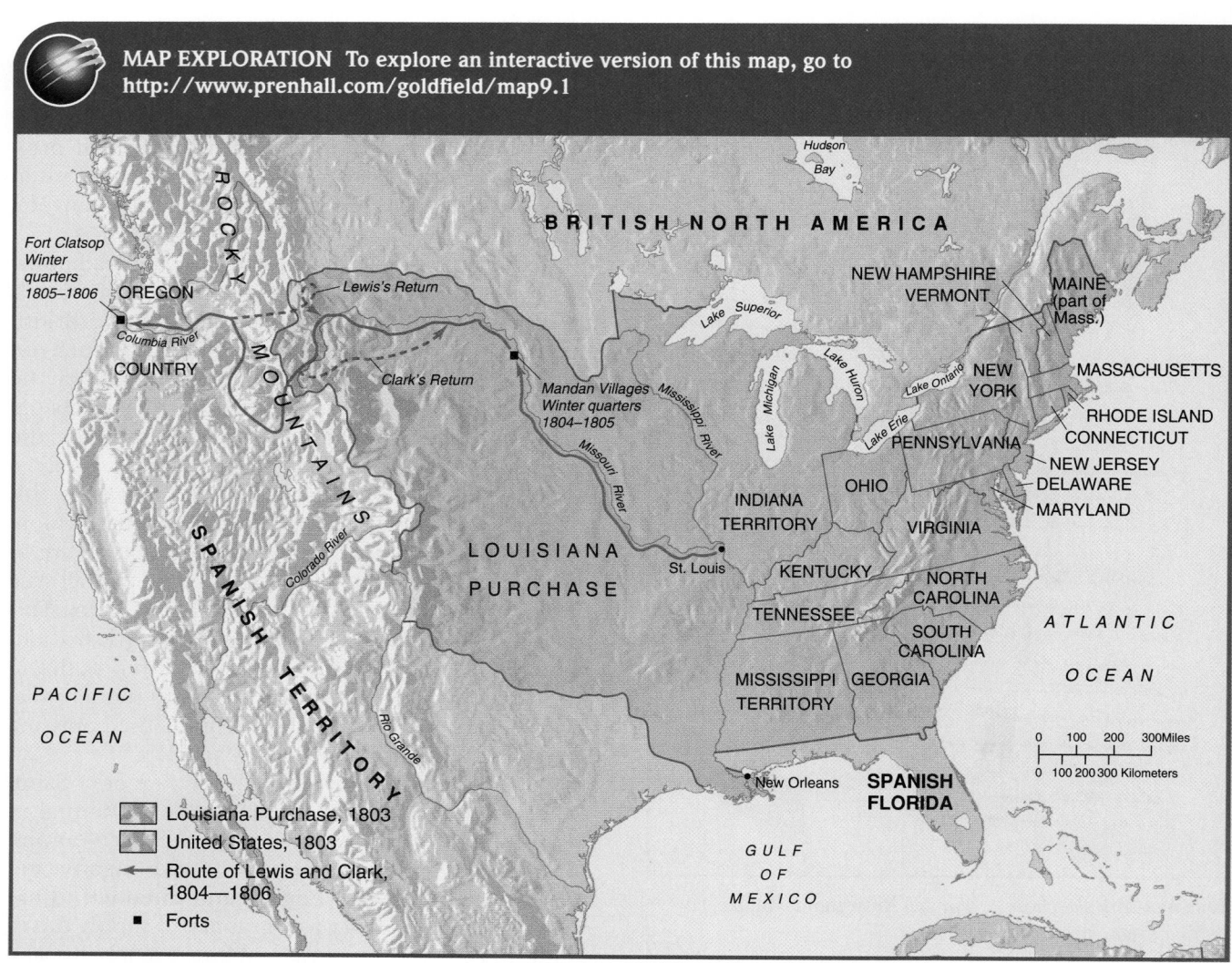

MAP EXPLORATION To explore an interactive version of this map, go to http://www.prenhall.com/goldfield/map9.1

MAP 9-1 **The Louisiana Purchase and the Lewis and Clark Expedition**
The vast expanse of the Louisiana Purchase was virtually unknown territory to Americans before the Lewis and Clark expedition gathered a mass of scientific information about it.

Napoleon's deal. The Louisiana Purchase doubled the size of the United States and offered seemingly endless space to be settled by yeoman farmers.

Jefferson was willing, as the Federalists had been when they were in power, to stretch the Constitution to support his definition of the national good. Conversely, it was now the Federalists, fearful of a further decline in their political power, who relied on a narrow reading of the Constitution in a futile attempt to block the Louisiana acquisition.

FLORIDA AND WESTERN SCHEMES

The magnificent prize of Louisiana did not satisfy Republican territorial ambitions. Still to be gained were river outlets on the Gulf Coast essential for the development of plantation agriculture in Alabama

and Mississippi. As Secretary of State Madison later bluntly explained, "The free navigation of these rivers was inseparable from the very existence of the United States." The boundaries of the Louisiana Purchase were so vague that Jefferson felt justified in claiming Spanish-held Texas and the Gulf Coast eastward from New Orleans to Mobile Bay, including the Spanish province of West Florida. Against stiff Spanish opposition, he pushed ahead with his plans to acquire West Florida. This provoked the first challenge to his leadership of the party.

Once it was clear that Spain did not want to sell West Florida to the United States, Jefferson accepted Napoleon's offer to act as a middleman in the acquisition. Napoleon's price was $2 million. He soon lost interest in the project, however, and Jefferson lost prestige in 1806, when he pushed an

The caption on this 1807 illustration of a deserted pier in Portland, Maine—"And the grass literally grew upon the wharves."—reflects the hardship Jefferson's embargo caused as it choked off the American export trade.

"And the grass literally grew upon the wharves."

appropriations bill through Congress to pay for Napoleon's services. Former Republican stalwarts in Congress denounced the bill as bribe money and staged a party revolt against the president's devious tactics.

Jefferson's failed bid for West Florida emboldened Westerners to demand that Americans seize the territory by force. In 1805 and 1806, Aaron Burr, Jefferson's first vice president, apparently became entangled in an attempt at just such a land grab.

Republicans had been suspicious of Burr since his dalliance with the Federalists in their bid to make him, rather than Jefferson, president in 1800. He further alienated the party when he involved himself with the efforts of a minority of die-hard Federalists known as the Essex Junto. The members of this group feared that incorporation of the vast Louisiana Purchase into the United States would leave New England powerless in national affairs. Picking up on states' rights themes first used by Jefferson in the Kentucky Resolutions, they concocted a plan for a northern confederacy. New York was central to their scheme. Rebuffed by Hamilton, they turned to Burr and backed him in the New York gubernatorial race of 1804. Burr lost, largely because Hamilton denounced him. The enmity between the two men reached a tragic climax in July 1804, when Burr killed Hamilton in a duel at Weehawken, New Jersey. Facing murder charges in New Jersey and New York, Burr fled to the West and lined up followers for a separatist plot.

The Burr conspiracy remains mysterious. Burr was undoubtedly eager to pry land loose from the Spanish and Indians, and he may have been thinking of carving out a separate western confederacy in the lower Mississippi Valley. Whatever he had in mind, he blundered in relying on General James Wilkinson as a co-conspirator. Wilkinson, the military governor of the Louisiana Territory and also a double agent for Spain, betrayed Burr. He was tried for treason in 1807, and Jefferson made extraordinary efforts to secure his conviction. He was saved by the insistence of Chief Justice Marshall that the Constitution defined treason only as the waging of war against the United States or the rendering of aid to its enemies. The law also required the direct testimony of two witnesses to an "overt act" of treason for conviction. Lacking such witnesses, the government failed to prove its case, and Burr was acquitted.

EMBARGO AND A CRIPPLED PRESIDENCY

Concern about a possible war against Britain in 1807 soon quieted the uproar over Burr's trial. After Britain and France had resumed their war in 1803, the United States became enmeshed in the same quarrels over neutral rights, blockades, ship seizures, and impressments of American sailors that had almost dragged the country into war in the 1790s. Britain proclaimed a blockade of the European continent, which was controlled by Napoleon, and confiscated the cargoes of ships attempting to run the blockade. Napoleon retaliated with seizures of ships that adhered to the blockade by submitting to British searches and accepting the British-imposed licensing system for trading with Europe. Caught in the middle, but eager to supply both sides, was the American merchant marine, the world's largest carrier of neutral goods.

American merchants and shippers had taken full advantage of the opportunities opened by the European war. During the flush years from 1793 to 1807, American ship tonnage tripled, and the value of exports soared fivefold. Despite French and British restrictions, American merchants traded with anyone they pleased. They dominated commerce, not only between Britain and the United States, but also between the European continent and the French and Spanish colonies in the West Indies. Profits were so great that merchants made money even when only one-third of their ships evaded the blockades.

In June 1807, however, a confrontation known as the ***Chesapeake* Incident** nearly triggered an Anglo-American war. A British ship, the *Leopard,* ordered a U.S. frigate, the *Chesapeake,* to submit to a search in coastal waters off Norfolk. When the commander of the *Chesapeake* refused, the *Leopard* opened fire. Three Americans were killed, eighteen were wounded, and four others (one of whom was subsequently hanged) were impressed as alleged deserters from the Royal Navy. Although Federalists worried that "our rogue of a President will glory in a war with England," Jefferson resisted the popular outcry for revenge. Instead, he barred American ports to British warships and called both for monetary compensation and for an end to impressment.

Britain offered in response only a belated apology and a promise of reparations. Still, Jefferson desperately wanted to avoid conflict. The country was woefully unprepared for war, and he passionately believed that international law should resolve international disputes. In a resort to the Republican idealism that had animated the Revolution, Jefferson called for a trade embargo as a substitute for war. The **Embargo Act of 1807**, an expression of Jefferson's policy of "peaceable coercion," prohibited American ships from clearing port to any nation until Britain and France repealed their trading restrictions on neutral shippers.

The premise of the embargo was that Europe was so dependent on American foods and raw materials that it would do America's bidding if faced with a cutoff. This premise was not so much wrong as unrealistic. The embargo did hurt Europe, but the people who first felt the pain were British textile workers and slaves in the colonies, hardly those who wielded the levers of power. Meanwhile, politically influential landlords and manufacturers benefited from short-term shortages by jacking up prices.

The American export trade and its profits dried up with Jefferson's self-imposed blockade. Except for manufacturers, who now had the American market to themselves, nearly all economic groups suffered under the embargo. Especially hard hit were New England shippers and merchants, and they accused the Republicans of near-criminal irresponsibility for forcing a depression on the country. Jefferson responded to these criticisms and to widespread violations of the embargo with a series of enforcement acts. These acts put real teeth into the embargo and consolidated executive powers far beyond what the Federalists themselves had been able to achieve while in power.

As the embargo tightened and the 1808 presidential election approached, the Federalist party revived. The Federalist presidential candidate, Charles C. Pinckney—running against Secretary of State James Madison, Jefferson's handpicked successor—polled three times as many votes as he had in 1804. Madison won only because he carried the South and the West, the Republican heartland.

Before Madison took office, the Republicans abandoned Jefferson's embargo. Britain and France had remained defiant, and at home the embargo had become an intolerable political burden. The embargo ended on March 3, 1809, and was immediately replaced by the Nonintercourse Act, a measure that prohibited American trade only with Britain and France. At the president's discretion, trade could be reopened with either nation once it lifted its restrictions on American shipping.

MADISON AND THE COMING OF WAR

Frail-looking and short, Madison struck most contemporaries as an indecisive and weaker version of Jefferson. He never did succeed in escaping from his predecessor's shadow. Nor did he succeed, as president, in keeping America at peace. Yet in intellectual toughness and resourcefulness he was at least Jefferson's equal. He failed because of an inherited foreign policy that was partly of his own making as Jefferson's secretary of state. The Republicans' idealistic stand on neutral rights was ultimately untenable unless backed up by military and political force. Madison concluded as much when he decided on war against Britain in the spring of 1812.

A war against America's old enemy also promised to restore unity to a Republican party increasingly divided over Madison's peaceful diplomacy. What was at stake for Madison was not just the defense of America's economic independence but also the legacy of republicanism itself, now under attack by monarchists in Britain and their presumed American friends in the resurgent Federalist party. Thus did Madison and his fellow Republicans push for a war they were eager but unprepared to fight.

THE FAILURE OF ECONOMIC SANCTIONS

Early in his administration, Madison convinced himself that the impasse in Anglo–American relations was about to be broken. Britain benefited from the Nonintercourse Act at the expense of France. Unlike the embargo, which had kept American vessels at home, nonintercourse permitted ship clearances. Once at sea, American ships were kept away from France and steered to England by the strong British navy. Perhaps in recognition of this unintended consequence of the new American policy, the British began to relax their restrictions on neutral shipping, known as the Orders in Council, in favor of U.S. commerce. At the same time, the British minister in Washington, David Erskine, reached an agreement with Madison that called for completely rescinding the Orders in Council as they applied to the United States. In return, Madison pledged to terminate nonintercourse against Britain while maintaining it against France.

Madison set June 10, 1809, as the date for the resumption of Anglo–American trade. Unfortunately, Erskine had exceeded his instructions, and the Madison–Erskine agreement was disavowed as soon as news of it reached London. Although Madison reimposed sanctions on Britain in August, he was left looking the fool.

With Madison floundering, Congress stepped in with its own policy in 1810. Macon's Bill No. 2, named after congressman Nathaniel Macon, threw open American trade to everyone but stipulated that if either France or England lifted its restrictions, the president would resume trading sanctions against the other. A concession to mercantile interests in New England and the mid-Atlantic states, Macon's bill also bought Madison time before he had to decide between war or submission to the British Orders in Council. Thanks to Napoleon's duplicity, however, that time was short.

Napoleon made an offer in August 1810 that Madison felt he had to accept. The French emperor promised to withdraw his decrees against American shipping on the condition that if Britain did not follow suit, Madison would force the British to respect American rights. Madison took the bait. He was under no illusion as to Napoleon's honesty, but he was desperate to apply pressure on the British to match the apparent French concessions. To Madison's chagrin, Napoleon's offer was an utter fraud. French seizures of American ships continued. By the time his duplicity became clear, Napoleon had already succeeded in worsening Anglo–American tensions. In November 1810, Madison reimposed nonintercourse against Britain, putting the two nations on a collision course.

THE FRONTIER AND INDIAN RESISTANCE

Mounting frustrations in the South and West also pushed Madison toward a war against Britain. Nearly one million Americans lived west of the Appalachian Mountains in 1810, a tripling of the western population in just a decade. Cheap, fertile land and markets for crops down the Ohio and Mississippi River systems drew farm families from the East. Farm prices, including those for the southern staples of cotton and tobacco, plunged when Jefferson's embargo shut off exports, and they stayed low after the embargo was lifted. Blame for the persistent agricultural depression focused on the British and their stranglehold on overseas trade after 1808. As a glut of American goods piled up in English ports, prices remained depressed.

Western settlers also accused the British of inciting Indian resistance. After the *Chesapeake* incident, the British did seek alliances with Indians in the Old Northwest, reviving the strategy of using them as a buffer against any American move on Canada. However, it was the unceasing demand of Americans for ever more Indian land, not any British incitements, that triggered the **pan-Indian resistance movement** that so frightened western settlers on the eve of the War of 1812.

In the Treaty of Greenville (1795) (see Chapter 8), the American government had promised that any future acquisitions of Indian land would have to be approved by all native peoples in the region. Nonetheless, government agents continued to play one group against another and divide groups from within by lavishing money and goods on the more accommodationist Christianized Indians. By such means, William Henry Harrison, the governor of the Indiana Territory, procured most of southern Indiana in the Treaty of Vincennes of 1804. Two extraordinary leaders, the Shawnee chief Tecumseh and his brother, the Prophet Tenkswatawa, channeled Indian outrage over this treaty into a movement to unify tribes throughout the West for a stand against the white invaders.

The Prophet Tenkswatawa was the spiritual leader of the pan-Indian movement that sought to revitalize native culture and block the spread of white settlement in the Old Northwest.

The message of pan-Indianism was unwavering: White encroachments had to be stopped and tribal and clan divisions submerged in a return to native rituals and belief systems. As preached by Tecumseh and the Prophet, Indian land could be saved and self-respect regained only through tribal cooperation and a spiritual rebirth. Tenkswatawa had undergone such a rebirth when he saved himself from alcoholism, and much of the passion he brought to preaching reflected his own sense of redemption. With the assistance of Tecumseh, Tenkswatawa established the Prophet's Town in 1808. At the confluence of the Wabash and Tippecanoe Rivers in north-central Indiana, this encampment became headquarters of an intertribal confederation. As he tried to explain to the worried Governor Harrison, his goals were peaceful. He admonished his followers, "[Do] not take up the tomahawk, should it be offered by the British, or by the long knives: do not meddle with any thing that does not belong to you, but mind your own business, and cultivate the ground, that your women and your children have enough to live on."

That ground, of course, was the very reason the Indians could not live in peace and dignity. White settlers wanted it and would do anything to get it. In November 1811, Harrison marched an army to Prophet's Town and provoked the Battle of Tippecanoe. The Indian encampment was on land claimed by the U.S. government in the Treaty of Fort Wayne (1809). Tecumseh was absent, off on a recruiting mission among the southern tribes, and without his restraining influence, impetuous young braves attacked Harrison's army. Losses were heavy on both sides, but Harrison regrouped his forces, drove the surviving Indians away, and burned the abandoned town. Harrison's victory came at a high cost: Tecumseh now joined forces with the British, leaving the frontier more unsettled than ever.

While Harrison's aggressiveness was converting fears of a British–Indian alliance into a self-fulfilling prophecy, expansionist-minded southerners struck at Britain through Spain, now its ally against Napoleon. With the covert support of President Madison, American adventurers staged a bloodless revolt in Spanish West Florida between Louisiana and the Pearl River. They raised the American flag and declared their independence. This "republic" was quickly recognized by the U.S. government and annexed as part of Louisiana in 1811. Spanish possession of the rest of Florida still galled southern planters anxious to remove the territory as a sanctuary for fugitive slaves.

Hatred of Native Americans, expansionist pressures, the lingering agricultural depression, and impatience with the administration's policy of economic coercion, all pointed in the same direction—a war against Britain coupled with an American takeover of British Canada and Spanish Florida. This was the rallying cry of the **War Hawks**, the forty or so prowar congressmen swept into office in 1810. Generally younger men from the South and West, the War Hawks were led by Henry Clay of Kentucky. Along with other outspoken nationalists, such as John C. Calhoun of South Carolina, Clay played a key role in building congressional support for Madison's growing aggressiveness on the British issue.

DECISION FOR WAR

In July 1811, Madison issued a Proclamation calling Congress into an early session on November 4. By the time of the announcement, Madison had probably accepted the inevitability of war against Britain. Deceived by Napoleon and dismissed by the British as the head of a second-rate power, Madison had run out of diplomatic options and was losing control of his party.

When Congress met, Madison tried to lay the groundwork for war. Although he did not rule out a peaceful settlement, he called for military preparations and stressed his "deep sense of the crisis." In

January 1812, the authorized size of the army was increased from 10,000 to 35,000 men. Still, fewer than 7,000 men were actually under arms throughout the spring, and Congress refused to enlarge the navy. The Republican-controlled Congress also balked at raising taxes to pay for a war that seemed ever more likely. In opposing Madison, many Republicans cited their party's traditional view of high taxes and a strong military as the tools of despots.

Madison secretly asked Congress on April 1 for a sixty-day embargo, a move designed to give American merchant ships time to return safely to their home ports. On June 1, he sent a war message to Congress in which he laid out the stark alternative of submission or resistance to British control of American commerce. Madison was now convinced that British commercial restrictions were not just a defensive measure aimed at France but an aggressive attempt to reduce the United States to the permanent status of colonial dependent.

For Madison and most other Republicans, the impending conflict was a second war for independence. Free and open access to world markets was certainly at stake, but so was national pride. The arrogant British policy of impressment was a humiliating affront to American honor and headed the list of grievances in Madison's war message.

A divided Congress declared war on Britain. The vote in the House on June 4 was seventy-nine in favor and forty-nine opposed; on June 17, the Senate concurred, nineteen to thirteen. The vote split along regional, economic, and party lines. Support for the war was strongest in regions whose economies had been damaged the most by the British blockades and control of Atlantic commerce. Thus the South and the West, trapped in an agricultural depression and anxious to eliminate foreign threats at their frontiers, favored war. Conversely, mercantile New England—a region that had, ironically, prospered as a result of British interference with ocean commerce—opposed the war.

The votes that carried the war declaration came from northern Republicans, who saw the impending struggle as a defense of America's experiment in self-government. Nine-tenths of the congressional Republicans voted for war, but not a single Federalist did so. For the Federalists, the real enemy was France, which had actually seized more American ships than had the British. From their strongholds in coastal New England, the Federalists condemned the war as a French-inspired plot and predicted that it would end in financial ruin.

The Federalists' anger increased when they learned that the British had been prepared to yield on one of the most prominent issues in the coming of war. On June 23, the British government revoked for one year its Orders in Council against the United States. A poor harvest and the ongoing economic pressure exerted by Madison had finally caused hard times in England and produced a policy reversal intended to placate the Americans. This concession, however, did not address impressment or monetary compensation, and news of it did not reach America until August. For Madison, it was too little too late, and he remained committed to war.

THE WAR OF 1812

The Republicans led the nation into a war it was unprepared to fight (see Map 9–2). Still, the apparent vulnerability of Canada to invasion made it possible to envision an American victory. Canada was thinly populated, poorly defended, and exposed to a potentially huge American army of militiamen. Yet bungled American invasions verged on tragicomedy, and British-Canadian forces and their Indian allies stymied American advances. For much of the war, Britain was preoccupied with Napoleon in Europe. When free to concentrate on the American sideshow in 1814, the British failed to secure naval control of the Great Lakes, their minimal strategic objective, and their counterinvasions of the United States bogged down. By the fall of 1814, both sides were eager for an end to the military stalemate.

Internal dissent endangered the Union as much as did British troops. The war exacerbated Federalist disenchantment with southern dominance of national affairs. Nearly all Federalists believed that pro-French fanatics and slaveholding agrarians in the Republican party had consistently sacrificed the commercial interests of New England. A minority of Federalists were convinced that New England could never regain its rightful place in shaping national policy and was prepared to lead a secession movement. Although blocked by party moderates at the Hartford Convention in 1814, the secessionists tarred Federalism with the brush of treason. Consequently, the Republicans, the party that brought the country to the brink of a military disaster, emerged from the war more powerful than ever.

SETBACKS IN CANADA

The outbreak of the **War of 1812** unleashed deep emotions that often divided along religious lines. From their strongholds in the Congregationalist churches in New England, the Federalists preached

MAP 9-2   The War of 1812
Most of the battles of the War of 1812 were fought along the Canadian–American border, where American armies repeatedly tried to invade Canada. Despite the effectiveness of the British naval blockade, the American navy was successful in denying the British strategic control of the Great Lakes. Andrew Jackson's smashing victory at the Battle of New Orleans convinced Americans that they had won the war.

that all true Christians opposed a war "against the nation from which we are descended, and which for many generations has been the bulwark of the religion we profess." Such antiwar sentiments, however, outraged the Baptists and Methodists, the largest and most popularly rooted denominations. They believed, as resolved by the Georgia Baptist Association in 1813, that the British government was "corrupt, arbitrary, and despotic" and that the war was "just, necessary, and indispensable."

Fiercely loyal to Madison, who had championed religious freedom in Virginia, these Methodists and Baptists harbored old grudges against the established churches of both Britain and New England for suppressing their religious rights. Especially for the Baptists, the war became something of a crusade to secure civil and religious liberties against their traditional enemies. For Spencer Houghton Cone, a lieutenant in a company of sharpshooters and a future president of the National Baptist Convention, service in the war seemed "as much the duty of the Christian as the honor of the soldier."

Madison hoped to channel this Christian, anti-British patriotism into the conquest of Canada. Two out of three Canadians were native-born Americans who, it was assumed, would welcome the United States Army with open arms. Only five thousand British troops were initially stationed in Canada, and Canadian militia were outnumbered nine to one by their American counterparts. No wonder Madison and his advisers felt that Canada was ripe for the taking— "a mere matter of marching," as Jefferson put it.

Canada was also the only area where the United States could strike directly against British forces. Although officially a war to defend America's neutrality on the high seas, the War of 1812 was largely a land war. The United States simply did not have enough ships to do more than harass the powerful British navy. Against sixteen ships in the U.S. Navy, only seven of which were top-of-the-line frigates (warships), the British could deploy more than two hundred vessels.

By seizing Canada, Madison also hoped to weaken Britain's navy and undercut its navigation system. Madison had been convinced that withholding American foodstuffs and provisions from the British West Indies would quickly force the British to yield to American economic pressure. But the British turned to Canada as an alternative source of supplies. Madison hoped to close off that source. And if, as Madison expected, Napoleon denied the British access to the naval stores of the Baltic region in Europe, an American monopoly on Canadian lumber would cripple British naval power. Facing such a threat, the British would have to end the war on American terms.

Madison's strategic vision was clear, but its execution was pathetic. Three offensives against Canada in 1812 were embarrassing failures. In the first, in July, General William Hull crossed into Canada from Detroit and invited Canadians to join the American cause. He found few takers. Meanwhile, Fort Michilimackinac fell, and Tecumseh's warriors cut Hull's communications. Hull hurried back to Detroit, only to surrender his army on August 16 to the smaller British-Indian force.

The loss of Detroit, preceded a day earlier by the abandonment of Fort Dearborn (present-day Chicago) and the massacre of its inhabitants, exposed western settlements to the full fury of frontier warfare. Americans in the Indiana Territory fled outlying areas for the safety of forts in the interior. The acting territorial governor scarcely exaggerated when he proclaimed, "Our former frontiers are now wilds and our inner Settlements have become frontiers." By the end of the year, the British controlled half of the Old Northwest.

Farther east, the Americans botched two offensives in 1812. In October, an American thrust across the Niagara River was defeated when a New York state militia refused to cross the river to join the regular army troops on the Canadian side. This left the isolated forces under General Stephen Van Rensselaer easy prey for the British at the Battle of Queenston Heights. Then the long-delayed third offensive, north from Lake Champlain, turned into a bloodless fiasco. It was aimed at Montreal, the center of British

POLICE.

WHEREAS authentic intelligence has been received that the Government of the United States of America did, on the 18th instant, declare War against the United Kingdom of Great Britain and Ireland and its dependencies, Notice is hereby given, that all Subjects or Citizens of the said United States, and all persons claiming American Citizenship, are ordered to quit the City of Quebec, on or before TWELVE o'clock at Noon, on WEDNESDAY next, and the District of Quebec on or before 12 o'clock at noon on FRIDAY next, on pain of arrest.   ROSS CUTHBERT, C. Q. S. & Inspector of Police.

The Constables of the City of Quebec are ordered to assemble in the Police Office at 10 o'clock to-morrow morning, to receive instructions.

Quebec, 29th June, 1812.

Fearful of an American invasion, Canadian authorities ordered American residents expelled at the beginning of the War of 1812.

operations in Canada. General Henry Dearborn, the leader of the expedition, turned back in late November when he discovered, as Van Rensselaer had, that his militias would not leave their states.

Republican expectations of victory in Canada had been wishful thinking. Most Canadians fought against, not with, the Americans. Reliance on state militias proved disastrous. Poorly trained and equipped, the militias, when they did show up for battle, could not match the discipline of British soldiers or the fighting skills of their Native American allies. Nor was American generalship on a par with that of the British. Primitive land communications made the movement and coordination of troops a nightmare. New England, the obvious base for operations against the strategically critical St. Lawrence River Valley—the entry point for all British supplies and reinforcements—withheld many of its state

AMERICAN VIEWS

Federalist Antiwar Resolutions

As the policies of the Madison administration in the spring of 1812 increasingly pointed toward war against Great Britain, New England Federalists mounted protest meetings in an effort to preserve peace. Passed at a meeting in Providence, Rhode Island, on April 7, 1812, the following resolutions make the Federalist case for the disastrous consequences of a war against Britain and reveal the depths of the party divisions over foreign policy.

- On what grounds did the Federalists accuse the Republicans of an anti-British bias?
- What did the Federalists argue would be the results of a war against Britain?
- How could the Federalists now depict France, America's ally during the Revolutionary War, as a greater threat to American freedoms than Britain?

Voted and Resolved unanimously,

That, in our opinion, the peace, prosperity and happiness of these United States, are in great jeopardy; inasmuch as, we have the strongest reasons to believe, the general government have determined to make war on Great-Britain . . . .

We are further confirmed in our apprehensions . . . by the evident partiality [the Republicans] have for a long time manifested towards one of the belligerents; and their deep-rooted enmity towards the other. The decrees of both nations equally violate our neutral rights; but France by her Berlin Decree, was the first aggressor; and still persists in capturing and burning our vessels on the high seas; and in robbing, imprisoning, and insulting our citizens; yet all these atrocities have been either palliated, or excused; while every effort has been made to excite the prejudices and animosities of our people against Great Britain. British vessels are excluded from our harbors; and our citizens are forbidden to import goods of the growth and manufacture of Britain and her dependen-

---

forces from national service. Consequently, the invasions were piecemeal ineffective forays launched from western areas where anti-British and anti-Indian sentiment ran high.

All the Republicans had to show for the first year of the war were morale-boosting but otherwise insignificant naval victories. In individual combat between ships, the small American navy acquitted itself superbly. Early in the war, American privateers harassed British merchant vessels, but the easy pickings were soon gone. British squadron ships redeployed to protect shipping, and other warships kept up a blockade that stifled American commerce.

Military setbacks and antiwar feelings in much of the Northeast hurt the Republicans in the election of 1812. Madison won only narrowly. Federalists and other disaffected Northerners rallied behind DeWitt Clinton, an antiadministration Republican from New York. The now familiar regional pattern in voting repeated itself. Madison swept the electoral vote of the South and West. He ran poorly in the Northeast and won only because his party held on to Pennsylvania.

WESTERN VICTORIES AND BRITISH OFFENSIVES

American forces fared better in 1813. Motivation remained high because, as Major Isaac Roach of an artillery regiment noted, many Americans believed that "it had become a jest and byword in England that this country could not be kicked into war." In September, the navy won a major engagement on Lake Erie that opened up a supply line in the western theater. Comcies; at the same time that French privateers are suffered to refit in American ports; and French goods are received, and protected, by our government . . . . All this, too, is done, when our trade to France, is of little value; and that to England, and her dependence is, of more importance to the United States, than with all the world besides.

Resolved, That . . . believing as we most sincerely do, that a war with England, at this time, is neither necessary, nor expedient, we deem it a duty which we owe to our families, and to our country, to use our utmost efforts to avert so great a calamity; and . . . we are of opinion that this expression ought to be given in the approaching elections. If we choose Democratic [Republican] State Rulers, we choose war; if we choose Federal State Rulers, we choose peace . . . .

But should we, forgetful of our duties, elect democratic rulers, and thereby let loose this wild spirit of war, what calamities, and horrors must spread themselves over those devoted States! All the taxes proposed must fall upon us; our foreign and coasting commerce be cut off; our fisheries be destroyed; our agriculture neglected . . . . The destruction of our navigation would interrupt, and we fear, ruin our numerous, and flourishing manufactories; for, when the enemies['] ships cover our coasts, we can

neither obtain the necessary materials, nor export the manufactured goods.

But these evils are only the beginning of sorrows. When war arrives, what will give protections to our harbours and maritime towns? [The enemy] will . . . make a war of frequent, and sudden descent on our long, and defenceless sea-coast. Ships manned, and now moored on the other side of the Atlantic Ocean, can, in forty days, be riding on the waters of our bay and river. What could then save our sea-port towns, together with all the vessels in our harbours from conflagration, pillage, and military exaction?

Dreadful are these consequences of war: but more dreadful will await us. A war with England will bring us into alliance with France. This alliance would make the last page of our history as a nation. All the horrors of war might be endured; but who can endure to become a Slave?—If we are allied to that putrid pestilence of tyranny; our laws, freedom, independence, national name and glory, are blotted out from the memory of man—If Bonaparte sends to this country, ships, and French soldiers, and French generals, we shall soon be like Holland, and Italy, and Switzerland, and every other country where this scourge of nations has been permitted to set his foot.

---

modore Oliver Hazard Perry attacked the British fleet in the **Battle of Put-in-Bay**, on the southwestern shore of the lake, and forced the surrender of all six British ships. The victory signaled General William Henry Harrison to launch an offensive in the West.

With the loss of Lake Erie, the British were forced to abandon Detroit. Harrison caught up with the British garrison and their Indian allies on the banks of the Thames River in southern Ontario. Demonstrating bold leadership and relying on battle-tested western militias, Harrison won a decisive victory. Tecumseh, the most visionary of the Indian warriors, was killed, and the backbone of the Indian resistance was broken. The Old Northwest was again safe for American settlement.

The Battle of the Thames ended British plans for an Indian buffer state. But by 1814, Britain had big-

ger goals in mind. A coalition of European powers forced Napoleon to abdicate in April 1814, thus freeing Britain to focus on the American war. It now seemed poised to break the military stalemate with a clear-cut victory.

British strategy in 1814 called for two major offensives—an invasion south from Montreal down Lake Champlain in upstate New York and an attack on Louisiana aimed at seizing New Orleans with a task force out of Jamaica. Meanwhile, diversionary raids along the mid-Atlantic coast were to pin down American forces and undermine morale. The overall objective was nothing less than a reversal of America's post-1783 expansion. If the invasions succeeded, the British would have been in a strong position to force a southward adjustment of the Canadian–American boundary and to claim the Louisiana Purchase territory.

The British attacks could hardly have come at a worse time for the Madison administration. The Treasury was nearly bankrupt. Against the wishes of Treasury Secretary Gallatin, Congress had refused to preserve the Bank of the United States when its charter expired in 1811. Lacking both a centralized means of directing wartime finances and any significant increase in taxes, the Treasury was forced to rely on makeshift loans. These loans were poorly subscribed, largely because the cash-rich New England banks refused to buy them. Inflation also became a problem when state banks, no longer restrained by the controls of a national bank, overissued paper money in the form of bank notes.

As the country's finances tottered toward collapse, political dissent in New England was reaching a climax. In 1814, the British extended their blockade of American commerce northward to include New England. Federalist merchants and shippers, who had earlier profited from their illegal trade with the British, now felt the economic pinch of the war. Cries for resistance against "Mr. Madison's war" culminated in a call issued by the Massachusetts legislature for a convention to consider "a radical reform of the national compact." The convention was scheduled for December in Hartford, Connecticut.

The darkest hour came in August 1814. A British amphibious force occupied and torched Washington, D.C., in retaliation for an American raid on York (now Toronto), the capital of Upper Canada. The defense of Washington was slipshod at best, and a local inhabitant can be excused for scribbling on a wall: "The capital and the Union lost by cowardice." Still, the British actions stiffened American resistance, and the failure of a follow-up attack on Baltimore deprived the British of any strategic gain. Baltimore's defenses held, stirring Francis Scott Key, a young lawyer who viewed the bombardment from a British prisoner-of-war ship, to write "The Star-Spangled Banner." Fittingly in this strange war, the future national anthem was set to the tune of a British drinking song.

The Chesapeake campaign was designed to divert American attention from the major offensive General George Prevost was leading down the shores of Lake Champlain. Prevost commanded the largest and best-equipped army the British had yet assembled. His opponent was Commodore Thomas Macdonough, one of several young, talented regional commanders Madison appointed late in the war. On September 11, at the **Battle of Plattsburgh**, Macdonough smashed a British fleet on Lake Champlain.

Having counted on that fleet to protect his supply lines, Prevost retreated to Canada.

The tide had turned. When news of the setbacks at Baltimore, and especially at Plattsburgh, reached England, the foreign office scaled back the demands it had been making on American negotiators at peace talks in the city of Ghent, in present-day Belgium. The British were ready for peace, but one of their trump cards had yet to be played—the southern offensive against New Orleans. The outcome of that campaign could still upset whatever was decided at Ghent.

THE TREATY OF GHENT AND THE BATTLE OF NEW ORLEANS

By the fall of 1814, the British were eager to get on with redrawing the map of post-Napoleonic Europe, restoring profitable relations with America, and reducing their huge war debt. The British negotiators at Ghent agreed to a peace treaty on terms the Americans were delighted to accept. The **Treaty of Ghent**, signed on Christmas Eve, 1814, simply restored relations to their status at the start of the war. No territory changed hands, and nothing was said about impressment or the rights of neutrals.

The ink had barely dried on the Treaty of Ghent when the British government sent reinforcements to General Edward Pakenham, the commander of the Louisiana invasionary force. By this action, the British indicated that they were not irrevocably committed to the peace settlement, which, though signed, could not be formally ratified until weeks had passed while it was sent across the Atlantic. The British had always held that the Louisiana Purchase was fraudulent (they insisted that Louisiana was never Napoleon's to sell), and they were prepared to install a new government in Louisiana if Pakenham succeeded. Far from being an anticlimax to a war that was already over, the showdown between British and American forces at the Battle of New Orleans in January 1815 had immense strategic significance for the United States.

The hero of New Orleans, in song and legend, was Andrew Jackson. A planter-politician from Tennessee, Jackson rose to prominence during the war as a ferocious Indian fighter. The Creeks of Alabama and Georgia, much like the Shawnees farther north, had undergone a religious revival that culminated in a military effort to drive American settlers out of their tribal homelands. As a general in the Tennessee militia, Jackson crushed Indian resistance in the Old Southwest at the Battle of Horseshoe Bend

The seizure and burning of Washington, D.C., by British troops on August 24, 1814, marked the republic's most humiliating defeat in the War of 1812.

in March 1814. He then forced the vanquished Creeks to cede two-thirds of their territory to the United States.

After his Indian conquests, Jackson was promoted to general in the regular army and given command of the defense of the Gulf Coast. In November 1814, he seized Pensacola in Spanish Florida to deny the British its use as a supply depot and then hurried to defend New Orleans. The overconfident British frontally attacked Jackson's lines on January 8, 1815. The result was a massacre. Artillery fire laid down by French-speaking cannoneers from New Orleans accounted for most of the carnage. More than two thousand British soldiers were killed or wounded. American casualties totaled twenty-one.

Strategically, Jackson's smashing victory at New Orleans ended any possibility of a British sphere of influence in Louisiana. Politically, it was a deathblow to Federalism. At the Hartford Convention in December, party moderates had forestalled talk of secession with a series of proposed constitutional amendments designed to limit southern power in national affairs. At the top of their list was a demand for eliminating the three-fifths clause by which slaves were counted for purposes of congressional representation. They also wanted to require a two-thirds majority in Congress for the admission of new states, declarations of war, and the imposition of embargoes. These demands became public as Americans were rejoicing over the Treaty of Ghent and Jack-

Creek war leader Red Eagle surrenders to Andrew Jackson after the Battle of Horseshoe Bend in 1814.

son's routing of the British. Set against the revived nationalism that marked the end of the war, the Federalists now seemed to be parochial sulkers who put regional interests above the national good. Worse yet, they struck many Americans as quasi-traitors who had been prepared to desert the country in the face of the enemy. As a significant political force, Federalism was dead.

THE ERA OF GOOD FEELINGS

In 1817, on the occasion of a presidential visit by James Monroe, a Boston newspaper proclaimed the **Era of Good Feelings**, an expression that nicely captured the spirit of political harmony and sectional unity that washed over the republic in the immediate postwar years. National pride surged with the humbling of the British at New Orleans, the demise of the Federalists lessened political tensions, and the economy boomed. The Republicans had been vindicated, and for a short time they enjoyed de facto status as the only governing party.

At the end of Madison's presidency, and in the first administration of his successor, James Monroe of Virginia, the Republicans embarked on a program of economic nationalism that would have pleased Alexander Hamilton. In foreign policy, they moved aggressively to stake out American leadership in the Western Hemi-

sphere. A series of decisions handed down by the Supreme Court also reinforced the postwar nationalism. In 1819, however, an economic depression and a bitter controversy over slavery shattered the harmony. The nationalist tide set in motion by the end of the war had run its course, and the Republicans divided on sectional and economic issues.

ECONOMIC NATIONALISM

The War of 1812 had taught the Republicans to appreciate old Federalist doctrines on centralized national power. In his annual message of December 1815, Madison outlined a program of economic nationalism that was pushed through Congress by Henry Clay and John C. Calhoun, the most prominent of the new generation of young, nationalist-minded Republicans.

The first order of business was to create a new national bank. Reliance on state banks for wartime financing had proved a major mistake. The banks lacked sufficient capital reserves or, as occurred in New England, held them back. Demand for credit was met by a flood of state bank notes that fell in value because there was insufficient gold and silver to back them. Many banks suspended specie payments for their notes, and inflation was a persistent problem. After the British burned Washington, the Treasury was temporarily bankrupt, and throughout the war it could borrow only at high interest rates. Fiscal stability required the monetary coordination and restraint that only a new Bank of the United States could provide.

Introduced by Calhoun, the bank bill passed Congress in 1816. Modeled after Hamilton's original bank and also headquartered in Philadelphia, the **Second Bank of the United States** was capitalized at $35 million, making it by far the nation's largest bank. Its size and official status as the depository and dispenser of the government's funds gave the bank tremendous economic power. It also enjoyed the exclusive privilege of being able to establish branches in any state.

After moving to repair the fiscal damage of the war, the Republicans then acted to protect what the war had fostered. Embargoes followed by three years of war forced American businessmen to manufacture goods they previously had imported. This was especially the case with iron and textile goods long supplied by the British. In 1815 and again in 1816, the British inundated the American market with cheap imports to strangle American industry in its infancy. Responding to this challenge to the nation's economic independence, the Republicans passed the Tariff of 1816, the first protective tariff in American history. The act levied duties of 20 to 25 percent on imported goods that could be produced in the United States.

Responding to pressure from the War Department and western states, Congress earmarked revenue from the tariff and $1.5 million from the Bank of the United States (a cash payment in return for its charter) for transportation projects. The lack of a road system in the trans-Appalachian region had severely hampered troop movements during the war. Also, as settlers after the war moved onto lands seized from the pro-British Indians, western congressmen demanded improved outlets to eastern markets.

In early 1817, an internal improvements bill passed Congress. Despite the soaring rhetoric of John C. Calhoun, the bill's sponsor, seeking to "bind the republic together with a perfect system of roads and canals," President Madison remained unmoved. Though in agreement with the bill's objectives, he was convinced that the Constitution did not permit federal financing of primarily local projects. He vetoed the bill just before he left office.

Congressional passage of Calhoun's internal improvements bill marked the pinnacle of the Republicans' economic nationalism. Frightened by the sectional disunity of the war years, a new generation of Republicans jettisoned many of the ideological trappings of Jefferson's original agrarian party. Their program was a call for economic, and therefore political, unity. Such unity was to be achieved through a generous program of national subsidies consisting of tariffs for manufacturers in the Northeast and transportation funds for planters and farmers in the South and West. The new national bank would provide a uniform currency and credit facilities for the internal exchange of raw materials and manufactured goods.

Support for this program was strongest in the mid-Atlantic and western states, the regions that stood to gain the most economically. Opposition centered in the Southeast, notably among die-hard proponents of states' rights in the old tobacco belt of Virginia and North Carolina and in New England, a region not only well served already by banks and a road network but also anxious not to be politically overshadowed by the rising West. This opposition took on an increasingly hard edge in the South as the Supreme Court outlined an ever more nationalist interpretation of the Constitution.

JUDICIAL NATIONALISM

Under Chief Justice John Marshall, the Supreme Court had long supported the nationalist perspective Republicans began to champion after the war. A Virginia Federalist whose nationalism was forged during his service in the Revolutionary War, Marshall dominated the Court throughout his tenure (1801–1835) by his forceful personality and the logical power of his nationalist convictions. Two principles defined Marshall's jurisprudence: the primacy of the Supreme

This 1830 painting shows Chief Justice John Marshall in the full robes of his office. Marshall's leadership molded the Supreme Court into an effective instrument of the national government.

Court in all matters of constitutional interpretation and the sanctity of contractual property rights. In *Fletcher v. Peck*, (1810), for example, the Court ruled that a Georgia law voiding a land grant made by an earlier legislature—on the grounds that it had involved massive fraud—violated the constitutional provision barring any state from "impairing the obligation of contracts." Marshall held that despite the fraud, the original land grant constituted an unbreakable legal contract.

Out of the political limelight since the Burr trial in 1807, the Court was thrust back into it by two controversial decisions in 1819. The first involved Dartmouth College and the attempt by the New Hampshire legislature to amend its charter in the direction of greater public control over this private institution. In *Dartmouth College v. Woodward*, the Court ruled that Dartmouth's original royal charter of 1769 was a contract protected by the Constitution. Hence the state of New Hampshire could not alter that charter without the prior consent of the college. By so sanctifying charters or acts of incorporation as contracts, the Court prohibited states from interfering with the rights and privileges they had bestowed on private corporations.

The second important decision in 1819, *McCulloch v. Maryland*, rested on a positive assertion of national power over the states. The case involved the Bank of the United States. Many state bankers were jealous of the privileges of the national bank, and this resentment was shared by legislators who viewed the bank's branches as an infringement on the states' economic sovereignty. In 1818, the Maryland legislature placed a heavy tax on the branch of the Bank of the United States established in Baltimore (and on all other banks in the state established without legislative authority). James McCulloch, the cashier of the Baltimore branch, refused to pay the tax. This set up a test case that involved two fundamental legal issues: Was the bank itself constitutional? And could a state tax federal property within its borders?

A unanimous Court, in language similar to but even more sweeping than that used by Alexander Hamilton in the 1790s, upheld the constitutional authority of Congress to charter a national bank and thereby regulate the nation's currency and finances. As long as the end was legitimate "within the scope of the Constitution," Congress had full power to use any means not expressly forbidden by the Constitution to achieve that end. As for Maryland's claim of a constitutional right to tax a federal agency, Marshall stressed that "the power to tax involves the

power to destroy." Surely, he reasoned, when the people of the United States ratified the Constitution, they did not intend the federal government to be controlled by the states or rendered powerless by state action. Here was the boldest statement to date of the loose or "implied powers" interpretation of the Constitution and a ringing rebuke to the compact theory of the Union outlined by Southerners in the Virginia and Kentucky Resolutions and picked up by disgruntled Federalists in New England.

TOWARD A CONTINENTAL EMPIRE

Marshall's legal nationalism paralleled the diplomatic nationalism of John Quincy Adams, secretary of state from 1817 to 1825. A former Federalist and the son of the second president, Adams broke with the party over its refusal to support an expansionist policy and held several diplomatic posts under the Madison administration. Adams made few friends as a negotiator. A British statesman once described him as "doggedly and systematically repulsive." Still, he was an effective diplomat. Convinced in his Puritan soul that God and nature had ordained that America stretch from the Atlantic to the Pacific as a beacon of liberty to the world, Adams used whatever tactics were necessary to realize that vision.

Adams shrewdly exploited Britain's desire for friendly and profitable relations after the War of 1812. The British wanted access to American cotton and foodstuffs in exchange for manufactured goods and investment capital. The United States wanted more trading opportunities in the British Empire and a free hand to deal with Spain's disintegrating empire in the Americas.

The **Rush–Bagot Agreement** of 1817 signaled the new pattern of Anglo–American cooperation. The agreement strictly limited naval armaments on the Great Lakes, thus effectively demilitarizing the border with Canada. The **Anglo–American Accords** of the following year resolved several issues left hanging after the war. Of great importance to New England, the British once again recognized American fishing rights off Labrador and Newfoundland. The boundary of the Louisiana Territory abutting Canada was set at the 49th parallel, and both nations agreed to the joint occupation of Oregon, the territory in the Pacific Northwest that lay west of the Rocky Mountains.

Having secured the northern flank of the United States, Adams was now free to deal with the South and West. Adams wanted all of Florida and an undisputed American window on the Pacific. The adversary here was Spain. Much weaker than it had been in the eighteenth century and struggling to suppress independence movements in its South American possessions, Spain resorted to delaying tactics in trying to hold off the tenacious Adams. Negotiations remained deadlocked until Andrew Jackson gave Adams the leverage he needed.

In March 1818, Jackson led his troops across the border into Spanish Florida. He destroyed encampments of the Seminole Indians, seized two Spanish forts, and executed two British subjects on the grounds that they were dealing arms to the Seminoles for raids on the Alabama–Georgia frontier. Despite later protestations to the contrary, Jackson had probably exceeded his orders. He might well have been censured by the Monroe administration had not Adams supported him, telling Spain that Jackson was defending American interests and warning that he might be unleashed again.

Spain yielded to the American threat in the **Trans-Continental Treaty of 1819.** The United States annexed East Florida, and Spain recognized the prior American seizures of West Florida in 1810 and 1813. Adams secured an American hold on the Pacific Coast by drawing a boundary between the Louisiana Purchase and the Spanish Southwest that ran stepwise up the Sabine, Red, and Arkansas Rivers to the Continental Divide and then due west along the 42nd parallel to the Pacific (see Map 9-3). Spain renounced any claim to the Pacific Northwest; the United States in turn renounced its shaky claim to Texas under the Louisiana Purchase and assumed $5 million in Spanish debts to American citizens.

Adams's success in the Spanish negotiations turned on the British refusal to threaten war or assist Spain in the wake of Jackson's highhanded actions in Florida. Spanish possessions and the lives of two British subjects were worth little when weighed against the economic advantages of retaining close trading ties with the United States. Moreover, Britain, like the United States, had a vested interest in developing trade with newly independent Latin American countries now free of Spain's former imperial monopoly. Recognizing this common interest, George Canning, the British foreign minister, proposed in August 1823 that the United States and Britain issue a joint declaration opposing any European attempt to recolonize South America or to assist Spain in regaining its colonies.

President Monroe rejected the British overture, but only at the insistence of Adams. Canning's offer had a string attached to it: a mutual pledge by the British and Americans not to annex former Spanish territory. But Adams was confident that within a gen-

eration, the United States would acquire California, Texas, and perhaps Cuba as well. He wanted to maintain the maximum freedom of action for future U.S. policy and avoid any impression that America was beholden to Britain. Thus originated the most famous diplomatic statement in early American history, the **Monroe Doctrine**.

In his annual message to Congress in December 1823, Monroe declared that the Americas "are henceforth not to be considered as subjects for future colonization by any European power." In turn, Monroe pledged that the United States would not interfere in the internal affairs of European states. With its continental empire rapidly taking shape and new Latin American republics to be courted, the United States was more than willing to proclaim a special position for itself as the guardian of New World liberties.

THE BREAKDOWN OF UNITY

For all the intensity with which he pursued his continental vision, John Quincy Adams worried in early 1819 that "the greatest danger of this union was in the overgrown extent of its territory, combining with the slavery question." His words were prophetic. A sectional crisis flared in 1819 over slavery and its expansion when the territory of Missouri sought admission to the Union as a slave state. Simultaneously, a financial panic ended postwar prosperity and crystallized regional discontent over banking and tariff policies. Party unity cracked under these pressures, and each region backed its own presidential candidate in the wide-open election of 1824.

THE PANIC OF 1819

From 1815 to 1818, Americans enjoyed a wave of postwar prosperity. European markets were starved for American goods after a generation of war and trade restrictions, and farmers and planters met that demand by expanding production and bringing new land into cultivation. The availability of public land in the West on easy terms of credit sparked a speculative frenzy, and land sales soared. State banks and, worse yet, the Bank of the United States fed the speculation by making loans in the form of bank notes far in excess of their hard-currency reserves. Before the bubble burst, cotton prices doubled to 30 cents a pound, real-estate values became wildly inflated, and the money Westerners owed the federal government for the purchase of public lands rose to $21 million, an amount greater than the value of all western farm goods.

European markets for American cotton and food supplies returned to normal by late 1818. In January 1819, cotton prices sank in England, and the Panic of 1819 was on. Cotton was the most valuable American export, and expected returns from the staple were the basis for an intricate credit network anchored in Britain. The fall in cotton prices triggered a credit contraction that soon engulfed the overextended American economy. Commodity prices fell across the board, and real-estate values collapsed, especially in and around western cities.

A sudden shift in policy by the Bank of the United States virtually guaranteed that the economic downturn would settle into a depression. The Bank stopped all loans, called in all debts, and refused to honor drafts drawn on its branches in the South and West. Hardest hit by these policies were farmers and businessmen in the West, a region that had piled up debt in the expectation that the income generated by postwar prosperity would return a tidy profit. Bankruptcies mushroomed as creditors forced the liquidation of farms and real estate. For westerners, the Bank of the United States now became "the Monster," a ruthless institution controlled by eastern aristocrats, who callously destroyed the hopes of farmers.

Southern resentment over the hard times brought on by low cotton prices focused on the tariff. Planters charged that the Tariff of 1816 unfairly raised their costs and amounted to an unconstitutional tax levied for the sole benefit of northern manufacturers. Unreconstructed Jeffersonians, now known as the Old Republicans, spearheaded a sharp reaction against the South's flirtation with nationalist policies in the postwar period. Taking their cue from John Taylor, a Virginia planter and agrarian philosopher, they demanded a return to strict states' rights doctrines. If Northerners, they asked, could stretch the Constitution to incorporate a bank or impose a protective tariff, what could prevent them from emancipating the slaves?

THE MISSOURI COMPROMISE

Until 1819, slavery had not been a major divisive issue in American politics. The Northwest Ordinance of 1787, which banned slavery in federal territories north of the Ohio River, and the Southwest Ordinance of 1790, which permitted slavery south of the Ohio, represented a compromise that had allowed slavery in areas where climate and soil conditions favored slave-based agriculture. What was unforeseen in the 1780s, however, was the explosive demand for slave-produced cotton generated by the

English textile industry in the early nineteenth century. At the republic's founding in 1787, slavery was identified with the declining tobacco economy of the South Atlantic states, and many Americans felt, perhaps wishfully, that the institution would gradually wither away.

Despite the prohibition of the African slave trade in 1807 (under the sectional compromise of 1787 this was the first year in which Congress could exercise this power), all hopes for the natural death of slavery were gone by 1819. Kentucky, Tennessee, Louisiana, Mississippi, and Alabama had all been added to the Union as slave states since 1787. Florida had just been annexed and surely would be another slave state. A thriving cotton market was underwriting slavery's expansion across the South, and even Missouri, a portion of the Louisiana Purchase that Northerners initially assumed would be inhospitable to slavery, had fallen under the political control of slaveholders.

The Missouri issue increased long-simmering northern resentment over the spread of slavery and the southern dominance of national affairs under the Virginia presidents. In February 1819, James Tallmadge, a Republican congressman from New York, introduced an amendment in the House mandating a ban on future slave imports and a program of gradual emancipation as preconditions for the admission of Missouri as a state. Missourians, as well as Southerners in general, rejected the Tallmadge Amendment. The states, they argued, had absolute sovereignty in the drafting of their constitutions, and any attempt by Congress to set conditions for statehood was unconstitutional. Nonetheless, a solid phalanx of northern congressmen supported the amendment.

Without a two-party system in which each of the parties had to compromise to protect its intersectional interests, voting followed sectional lines. The northern-controlled House passed the amendment, but it was repeatedly blocked in the Senate, which was evenly divided between free and slave states. The debates were heated, and Southerners spoke openly of secession if Missouri were denied admission as a slave state.

The stalemate over Missouri persisted into the next session of Congress. Finally, Speaker of the House Henry Clay engineered a compromise in March 1820. Congress put no restrictions on slavery in Missouri, and the admission of Missouri as a slave state was balanced by the admission of Maine (formerly part of Massachusetts) as a free state. In return for their concession on Missouri, northern

MAP EXPLORATION To explore an interactive version of this map, go to http://www.prenhall.com/goldfield/map9.3

Rush-Bagot Treaty of 1817 and Anglo-American Accords of 1818

Trans-Continental Treaty of 1819

Missouri Compromise, 1820

Territory closed to slavery by Missouri Compromise

Slave states and territories

Free states and territories

MAP 9-3   The Missouri Compromise of 1820 and Territorial Treaties with Britain and Spain, 1818–1819

Treaties with Britain and Spain in 1818 and 1819 clarified and expanded the nation's boundaries. Britain accepted the 49th parallel as the boundary between Canada and the United States in the Trans-Mississippi West to the Oregon Country; Spain ceded Florida to the United States and agreed to a boundary stretching to the Pacific between the Louisiana Purchase territory and Spanish possessions in the Southwest. Sectional disputes over slavery led to the drawing of the Missouri Compromise line of 1820 that prohibited slavery in the Louisiana Territory north of 36°30'.

congressmen demanded a prohibition on slavery in the remainder of the Louisiana Purchase north of the 36° 30' parallel, the southern boundary of Missouri (see Map 9–3). With the **Missouri Compromise**, the Louisiana Purchase was closed to slavery in the future, except for the Arkansas Territory and what would become the Indian Territory of Oklahoma. The compromise almost unraveled when Missouri submitted a constitution the following November that required the state legislature to bar the entry of free black people. This mandate violated the guarantee in the U.S. Constitution that "the citizens of each State shall be entitled to all privileges and immunities of citizens in the several

FROM THEN TO NOW

The Lewis and Clark Expedition in Their World and Ours

In its day the Lewis and Clark expedition was as daring a venture as space exploration is today. The expedition, which began in 1803, ended in 1806, and lasted 863 days, brought Americans their first knowledge of the vast territory they had secured in the Louisiana Purchase. Traveling more than seven thousand miles by foot, boat, and horseback from St. Louis to the Pacific Coast and back, the explorers compiled a detailed record of their experiences and observations. In these journals they have bequeathed to us a vivid picture of the natural environment of the trans-Mississippi West before white settlement.

The West described by Lewis and Clark was a land of change, diversity, and abundance. The Missouri River that their party of forty-five followed to the north and west up to central Montana was wild and unpredictable. Its currents were ceaselessly eroding its banks, forming and displacing sandbars, and cutting new channels as they deposited soil eroded from the Rocky Mountains onto its immense floodplain. Today, a series of dams has tamed the river, controlling floods, generating electricity, and diverting water for irrigation. But the dams have had unforeseen consequences. The fertile sediments the Missouri once deposited on its floodplain, replenishing the soil in the farm states of the midwest, now flow into the Gulf of Mexico. As Midwesterners learned in the summer of 1993, the levees and retaining walls that confine the river can sometimes result in floods far more disastrous than ever occurred under natural conditions.

Lewis and Clark passed through regions of incredible biological diversity and abundance. They catalogued 122 animals and 178 plants that were new to American science. Traveling through present-day South Dakota in September,

States." Missouri's restrictionist policy obviously denied African American citizens this constitutional right to move from one state to any other state. Southerners were quick to point out, however, that free states as well as slave states already restricted the rights of free black people to vote or to serve in the militia.

The nearly universal acceptance by white Americans of second-class citizenship for free black Americans permitted Clay to dodge the issue. Missouri's constitution was accepted with the proviso that it "shall never be construed" to discriminate against citizens in other states. In short, with meaningless words that begged the issue of Missouri's defiance of the federal Constitution, the Missouri Compromise was salvaged. With this sacrifice of the claims of free black citizens for equal treatment, the Union survived its first great sectional crisis over slavery.

The Missouri crisis made white southerners aware that they were now a political minority within the Union. More rapid population growth in the North had reduced southern representation in the House to just over 40 percent. Of greater concern was the crystallization in Congress of a northern majority arraigned against the expansion of slavery. Southern threats of secession died out in the aftermath of the Missouri Compromise, but it was an open question whether the sectional settlement really solved the intertwined issues of slavery and expansion or merely sidestepped them for a day of final reckoning.

1804, Lewis observed "Vast herds of Buffaloe deer elk and Antelopes . . . feeding in every direction as far as the eye of the observer could reach." Upon seeing the salmon in the Columbia River in 1805, Clark wrote that their numbers were "almost inconceivable."

Before the end of the nineteenth century, the great herds of grazing animals in the West and the carnivores that stalked them had nearly been wiped out by government-sponsored extermination programs. The industrialization of the Pacific Northwest in the twentieth century reduced the natural habitat essential for the spawning and rearing of salmon, and their numbers fell sharply. Even more striking, most of the vast prairie landscape that Lewis and Clark crossed from the Mississippi Valley to the Rocky Mountains has disappeared, replaced by uniform fields of row-to-row crops. The prairie grasslands were once the largest ecosystem in North America, a patchwork of native grasses and herbs that supported a wide diversity of habitats.

Lewis and Clark were hardly romantic sentimentalists. Their West was dangerous and threatening, and their supplies included the latest in scientific equipment. They fully shared American notions of progress, and they carefully noted locations that were favorably situated for settlement. Still, the West they saw often left them with a sense of awe. For Lewis, the White Cliffs of the Missouri River in Montana were a spectacle "of visionary enchantment." He described the Great Falls of the Missouri as "the grandest sight I ever beheld."

The journals of Lewis and Clark provide a baseline from which to gauge how much the West has changed, putting Americans in a better position to preserve what is left and even restore some of what has been lost.

In commemoration of their epic expedition, President George W. Bush designated 2003 through 2006 as the Lewis and Clark Bicentennial. Beginning at Monticello in January 2003, a series of bicentennial events will highlight key dates and stages in the expedition and allow the public to gain a sense of how their journey unfolded. For information on these events, access the website listed in Web Resources.

THE ELECTION OF 1824

The election of 1820 made Monroe, like both his Republican predecessors, a two-term president. Monroe was the uncontested choice of his party, and the Federalists were too weak to run a candidate. Although Monroe won all but one of the electoral votes, Republican unity was more apparent than real. Voters had no choice in 1820, and without two-party competition, no outlets existed for expressing popular dissatisfaction with the Republicans. Instead, the Republicans split into factions as they began jockeying almost immediately for the election of 1824 (see Map 9–4).

The politics of personality dominated Monroe's second administration. Monroe had no obvious successor, and five candidates competed to replace him. All of them were nominal Republicans, and three were members of his cabinet. Secretary of War John C. Calhoun soon dropped out. He preferred to accept a nomination as vice president, confident that his turn would come in 1828. The other candidates—Secretary of the Treasury William Crawford from Georgia, Secretary of State John Quincy Adams from Massachusetts, Henry Clay from Kentucky, and Andrew Jackson from Tennessee—each had a strong regional following. As the Republican party fragmented, sectional loyalties were replacing partisan allegiances.

The early favorite was Crawford. He was the "official" party nominee in the sense that he had received the support of the congressional caucus, but most Republicans had boycotted the caucus, by now a

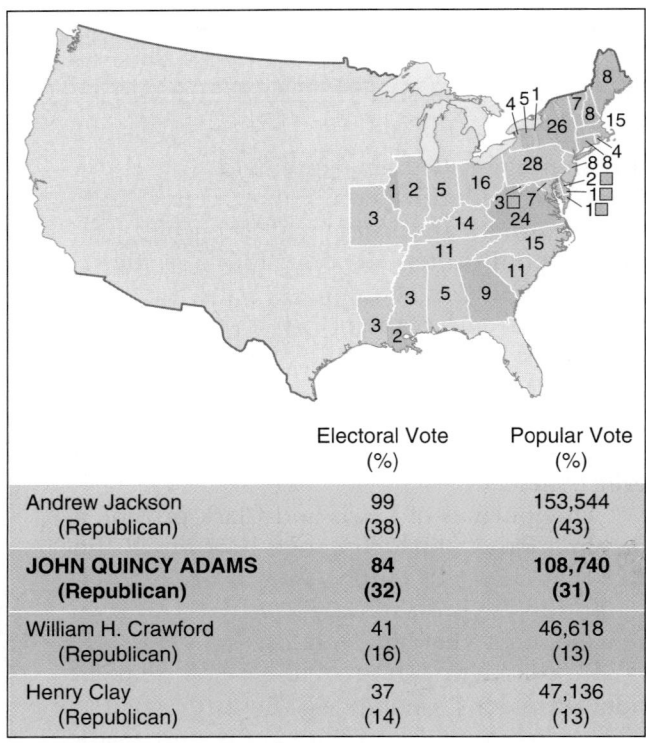

	Electoral Vote (%)	Popular Vote (%)
Andrew Jackson (Republican)	99 (38)	153,544 (43)
JOHN QUINCY ADAMS (Republican)	**84 (32)**	**108,740 (31)**
William H. Crawford (Republican)	41 (16)	46,618 (13)
Henry Clay (Republican)	37 (14)	47,136 (13)

MAP 9-4   The Election of 1824
The regional appeal of each of the four presidential candidates in the election of 1824 prevented any candidate from receiving a majority of the electoral vote. Consequently, and as set forth in the Constitution, the House of Representatives now had to choose the president from the three leading candidates. Its choice was John Quincy Adams.

useless relic of past party unity. Clay, Jackson, and Adams were nominated by their state legislatures. None of the candidates ran on a platform, but Crawford was identified with states' rights and Clay and Adams with centralized government. Clay in particular was associated with the national bank, protective tariffs, and federally funded internal improvements, a package of federal subsidies he called the **American System**. Jackson took no stand on any of the issues.

Jackson's noncommittal stance turned out to be a great asset. It helped him to project the image of a military hero, fresh from the people, who was unsullied by any connection with Washington politicians, whom the public associated with hard times and sectional controversies. He was the highest vote-getter (43 percent of the popular vote), but none of the four candidates had a majority in the electoral college.

As in 1800, the election was thrown into the House of Representatives. Each state had one vote,

and the choice was from among the top three in the electoral college. Clay, who had received the fewest electoral votes, was eliminated. Crawford had suffered a debilitating stroke and was no longer a viable candidate. Thus it came down to Adams or Jackson. Anxious to undercut Jackson, his chief rival in the West, Clay used his influence as speaker of the House to line up support for Adams, a fellow advocate of a strong centralized government.

Adams won the election, and he immediately named Clay as his secretary of state, the office traditionally viewed as a stepping-stone to the presidency. Jackson and his followers were outraged. They smelled a "corrupt bargain" in which Clay had bargained away the presidency to the highest bidder. Vowing revenge, they began building a new party that would usher in a more democratic era of mass-based politics.

CONCLUSION

In 1800, the Republicans were an untested party whose coming to power frightened many Federalists into predicting the end of the Union and constitutional government. The Federalists were correct in sensing that their days of power had passed, but they underestimated the ideological flexibility the Republicans would reveal once in office and the imaginative ways in which Jefferson and his successors would wield executive power to expand the size of the original Union. Far from being anarchists and demagogues, the Republicans were shrewd empire builders astute enough to add to their base of political support in the South and West. They also paved the way for the nation to evolve as a democratic republic rather than the more aristocratic republic preferred by the Federalists.

Most Federalists never did learn the art of popular electioneering, and they were too elitist to have any desire to do so. Although foreign-policy issues arising out of Jefferson's and Madison's attempts to assert American neutral rights during the Anglo-French war kept the Federalists alive and even briefly revived the party, the British posed the greatest test to Republican leadership. The Republicans chose war rather than surrendering their claims of American rights. Jackson's victory at the Battle of New Orleans ended the war in an American burst of glory, and the Federalists were swept aside by the postwar surge of nationalism.

By the mid-1820s, the Republicans were about to join the Federalists as political dinosaurs. The Republican era ended when the party became a victim of its own success. With no Federalist threat to enforce party discipline, the Republicans lost their organizational strength. Embracing economic nationalism after the war made the party's original focus on states' rights all but meaningless. Ideologically and organizationally adrift, the party split into regional coalitions in the wake of the Missouri controversy and the panic of 1819. But before it dissolved, the party left as its most enduring legacy the foundations of a continental empire.

REVIEW QUESTIONS

1. What changes did the Republicans bring to the federal government? How did their policies differ from those of their Federalist predecessors?

2. Why were the Republicans so intent on expanding the boundaries of the United States, and why did the Federalists oppose an expansionist program?

3. What factors accounted for the Federalists' inability to regain national power after they lost the election of 1800?

4. What external and internal factors drew the United States into war against Britain? Could this war have been avoided?

5. What accounted for the difficulties of the United States in waging the War of 1812, and why was the war widely viewed as a great American victory? How did the war lead to an increasing pattern of diplomatic cooperation between the United States and Britain?

6. Why was Rosalie Calvert so critical of the Republican Party and U.S. entry into the War of 1812? To what extent would New England Federalists have shared her views?

7. What explains the upsurge of nationalism that underlay the Era of Good Feelings? Why were the Republicans unable to maintain their party unity after 1819?

KEY TERMS

American System (p. 288)

Anglo-American Accords (p. 282)

Chesapeake Incident (p. 270)

Dartmouth College v. Woodward (p. 282)

Embargo Act of 1807 (p. 270)

Era of Good Feelings (p. 280)

Fletcher v. Peck (p. 282)

Ghent, Treaty of (p. 278)

Marbury v. Madison (p. 266)

Missouri Compromise (p. 285)

Monroe Doctrine (p. 283)

New Orleans, Battle of (p. 271)

Pan-Indian resistance movement (p. 271)

Plattsburgh, Battle of (p. 278)

Put-in-Bay, Battle of (p. 277)

Rush-Bagot Agreement (p. 282)

Second Bank of the United States (p. 280)

Trans-Continental Treaty of 1819 (p. 283)

War Hawks (p. 272)

War of 1812 (p. 273)

RECOMMENDED READING

Allgor, Catherine. *Parlor Politics: In Which the Ladies of Washington Help Build a City and a Government* (1999). A witty and engagingly written work that describes how women exercised political power in the early republic.

Hickey, Donald R. *The War of 1812: A Forgotten Conflict* (1989). Breaks no new ground, but presents a complete and very readable account of all aspects of the war.

McCoy, Drew R. *The Elusive Republic: Political Economy in Jeffersonian America* (1980). A gracefully written study that examines how attitudes on economic development influenced Jeffersonian notions of republicanism and were central to the Republicans' stand on free trade.

Onuf, Peter S., ed. *Jeffersonian Legacies* (1993). A collection of essays that presents the latest thinking on the extraordinary range of Jefferson's activities.

Smelser, Marshall. *The Democratic Republic, 1801–1815* (1968). Gives a sound overview of the Jefferson and Madison administrations. Smelser portrays Jefferson as a political moderate adept at wielding power and offers a spirited defense of Madison's record as a war president.

Vidal, Gore. *Burr* (1973). A superbly entertaining novel that satirically brings to life the leading personalities of Jefferson's America.

Weeks, William Earl. *John Quincy Adams and American Global Empire* (1992). Presents Adams as a cynical, tough-minded negotiator utterly driven by his vision of an American continental empire. Though questioning his tactics, Weeks confirms Adams's reputation as America's greatest secretary of state.

ADDITIONAL SOURCES

Jefferson's Presidency

Ambrose, Stephen. *Undaunted Courage: Meriwether Lewis, Thomas Jefferson, and the Opening of the American West* (1996).

Banning, Lance. *The Jeffersonian Persuasion: Evolution of a Party Ideology* (1978).

Ben-Atar, Doron S. *The Origins of Jeffersonian Commercial Policy and Diplomacy* (1993).

Cunningham, Jr. Noble E. *The Jeffersonian Republicans in Power: Party Operations, 1801–1809* (1963).

De Conde, Alexander. *This Affair of Louisiana* (1976).

Kennon, Donald R. ed., *A Republic for the Ages: The United States Capitol and the Political Culture of the Early Republic* (1999)

Fischer, David Hackett. *The Revolution of American Conservation: The Federalist Party in the Era of Jeffersonian Democracy* (1965).

McDonald, Forrest. *The Presidency of Thomas Jefferson* (1976).

Young, James Sterling. *The Washington Community, 1800–1828* (1966).

Madison and the Coming of War

Brown, Roger H. *The Republic in Peril* (1964).

Dowd, Gregory Evans. *A Spirited Resistance: The North American Indian Struggle for Unity, 1745–1815* (1992).

Edmunds, R. David. *The Shawnee Prophet* (1983) and Tecumseh and the Quest for Indian Leadership (1984).

Owsley, Jr. Frank Lawrence. and Smith Gene H. *Filibusters and Expansionists: Jeffersonian Manifest Destiny* (1997).

Perkins, Bradford. *Prologue to War: England and the United States, 1805–1812* (1961).

Rutland, Robert A. *Madison's Alternatives: The Jeffersonian Republicans and the Coming of War* (1975).

The War of 1812

Banner, James M. *To the Hartford Convention: The Federalists and the Origins of Party Politics in the Early Republic, 1789–1815* (1967).

Edmunds, R. David. *Tecumseh and the Quest for Indian Leadership* (1984).

Gribbin, William. *The Churches Militant: The War of 1812 and American Religion* (1973).

Horsman, Reginald. *The War of 1812* (1969).

Stagg, J. C. A. *Mr. Madison's War: Politics, Diplomacy, and Warfare in the Early Republic, 1783–1830* (1983).

Watts, Steven. *The Republic Reborn: War and the Making of Liberal America* (1987).

The Era of Good Feelings

Bemis, Samuel Flagg. *John Quincy Adams and the Foundations of American Foreign Policy* (1949).

Cunningham, Noble E. Jr. *The Presidency of James Monroe* (1996).

Livermore, Shaw. *The Twilight of Federalism: The Disintegration of the Federalist Party, 1815–1830* (1962).

May, Ernest R. *The Making of the Monroe Doctrine* (1975).

White, G. Edward. *The Marshall Court and Cultural Change, 1815–1835* (1991).

The Breakdown of Unity

Moore, Glover. *The Missouri Compromise, 1819–1821* (1953).

Rothbard, Murray N. *The Panic of 1819: Reactions and Policies* (1962).

WHERE TO LEARN MORE

- **Fort McHenry National Monument, Baltimore, Maryland.** This historic site preserves the fort that was the focal point of the British attack on Baltimore and contains a museum with materials on the battle and the writing of "The Star-Spangled Banner." For the military history of the fort and the archeological work at the site, see www.nps.gov/fomc/archeology/overview.html.

- **Tippecanoe Battlefield Museum, Battle Ground, Indiana.** This museum includes artifacts from the Indian and white settlement of Indiana and visual materials on the Battle of Tippecanoe of 1811. The museum's website at www.tcha.mus.in.us/battlefield.htm   includes an account of the battle and its aftermath.

- **Monticello, Charlottesville, Virginia.** The architecturally unique home of Thomas Jefferson and the headquarters for his plantation serves as a museum that provides insights into Jefferson's varied interests. Information on educational programs and upcoming events at Monticello, as well as the new Jefferson Library in Charlottesville, can be found at www.monticello.org/.

- **Montpelier, Montpelier Station, Virginia.** The museum here was the home of James Madison, and it includes material on his life as a politician and planter. Its website at www.montpelier.org/ provides information on tours and programs and a look at the archeological findings at Montpelier.

- **Perry's Victory and International Peace Memorial, Put-in-Bay, Ohio.** At the site of Perry's decisive victory on Lake Erie in 1813 now stands a museum that depicts the role of the Old Northwest in the War of 1812. For a printable travel guide and information on the new visitor center, see www.nps.gov/pevi/.

- **Lewis and Clark Expedition.** This site provides a wealth of information and resources including photo essays, interactive maps, web resources, a list of planned events, the journals of the expedition, and a bibliography of recent works. http://www.time.com/time/2002/lewis_clark

 Please refer to the document CD-ROM for primary sources related to this chapter.

→ *This early nineteenth-century painting of a polling place in Philadelphia illustrates the growing
involvement of common Americans in politics. As suffrage broadened and more Americans
came out to vote, elections became more heated and emotional.*

John L. Krimmel, Painting, (1786-1821), Oil on Canvas, H. 16 3/8" x W. 25 5/8". (AN: 59.131) Courtesy, Winterthur Museum,
"Election Day in Philadelphia" (1815) - DETAIL.

THE JACKSONIAN ERA
1824–1845

10

Newport, New Hampshire
September, 1828

Wherever a person may chance to be in company, he will hear nothing but politicks discussed. In the ballroom, or at the dinner table, in the Stagecoach & in the tavern; even the social chitchat of the tea table must yield up to the everlasting subject.

How many friendships are broken up! With what rancor the political war is carried on between the editorial corps! To what meanness[,] vulgarity & abuse is that champion of liberty, in proper hands, the press prostituted! With what lies and scandal does the columns of almost every political paper abound! I blush for my country when I see such things, & I often tremble with apprehension that our Constitution will not long withstand the current which threatens to overwhelm it. Our government is so based that an honest difference between American citizens must always exist. But the rancorous excitement which now threatens our civil liberties and a dissolution of this Union does not emanate from an honest difference of opinion, but from a determination of an unholy league to trample down an Administration, be it ever so pure, & be its acts ever so just. It must not be. There is a kind Providence that overlooks the destinies of this Nation and will not suffer it to be overthrown by a party of aspiring office seekers & political demagogues.

Benjamn B. French

Donald B. Cole and John J. McDonough, eds., *Witness to the Young Republic: A Yankee's Journal, 1828–1870* (Hanover, N.H.: University Press of New England, 1989), pp. 15–16.

CHAPTER OUTLINE

The Egalitarian Impulse
The Extension of White Male Democracy
The Popular Religious Revolt
The Rise of the Jacksonians

Jackson's Presidency
Jackson's Appeal
Indian Removal
The Nullification Crisis
The Bank War

Van Buren and Hard Times
The Panic of 1837
The Independent Treasury
Uproar over Slavery

The Rise of the Whig Party
The Party Taking Shape
Whig Persuasion
The Election of 1840

The Whigs in Power
Harrison and Tyler
The Texas Issue
The Election of 1844

Conclusion

Benjamin Brown French, a young editor and county clerk in Newport, New Hampshire, penned these words in his journal in September 1828. Like most other Americans, he was amazed—indeed, shocked—by the intense, seemingly all-pervasive partisanship stirred up in the presidential election of 1828 between Andrew Jackson and John Quincy Adams. Whether measured by the vulgar personal attacks launched by a partisan press, the amount of whiskey and beef consumed at political barbecues, or the huge increase in voter turnout, this election marked the entrance of ordinary Americans onto the political stage.

The sense of shock soon wore off for French. The son of a wealthy Federalist lawyer with whom he was always at odds, French broke with his father when, at the age of twenty-five, he married without his permission. With no income, job, or family support, he now began to make a business out of law, politics, and journalism. In so doing he was part of the first generation of professional politicians, young men who compensated for their lack of social connections and family wealth by turning to politics as a means of earning an income and building a career. The partisanship that French found so disturbing in 1828 quickly became the basis of his livelihood. After rejecting his father's politics by joining the Democrats in 1831, he spent most of his subsequent years as a political officeholder in Washington, holding a variety of appointive jobs. His own fortunes initially depended on the political success of his Democratic party. Then, after breaking with the Democrats in the 1850s over the slavery issue, he succeeded in finding government employment in Republican administrations until his death in 1870.

What had made possible French's career was an ongoing democratization of American politics that gathered momentum in the early decades of the nineteenth century. The number and potential power of the voters expanded, and professional politicians realized that party success now depended on reaching and organizing this enlarged electorate. Men like French, working for the party, could help them do this. The "Jacksonian Democrats," named for their leader, Andrew Jackson, were the first party to learn this fundamental lesson. Trumpeting Andrew Jackson as the friend of the common man and the foe of aristocratic privilege, they won a landslide victory in 1828 and held national power through the 1830s. The Jacksonians promised to protect farmers and workers from the monied elite, whom they portrayed as the enemies of equality and the corruptors of public morality.

By the mid-1830s, the Whig party had formed in opposition to the Jacksonians. The Whigs offered an ordered vision of American progress and liberty, anchored in the use of governmental power to expand economic opportunities and promote morality. By embracing electoral techniques of popular appeal first used by the Democrats, the Whigs captured the presidency in 1840. Their triumph heralded a new party system, one based on massive voter turnouts and two-party competition in every state.

The luckless Whigs failed to capitalize on their victory in 1840. Their newly elected president, William Henry Harrison, died shortly after entering office, and Vice President John Tyler, his successor, blocked the Whigs' economic program. Spurned by the Whigs as a traitor, Tyler then reopened the explosive question of slavery and territorial expansion by pushing to annex the independent republic of Texas, where slavery was legal.

The Democrats regained power in 1844 by skillfully exploiting the Texas issue, but they set an ominous precedent. Debates over the expansion of slavery became embedded in the political system, and the greatest strength of the mass-based parties—their ability to tap and unleash popular emotions—now became their greatest weakness. The slavery issue began to take on a life of its own beyond the control of party leaders. The seeds of the Civil War were being sown.

KEY TOPICS

- The rise of new political parties: Jacksonian Democrats and Whigs
- The disfranchisement of free black people and women
- Birth of the Whig party
- The Second Great Awakening
- The Bank War
- The growing conflict over slavery

THE EGALITARIAN IMPULSE

Political democracy, defined as the majority rule of white males, was far from complete in early nineteenth-century America. Acting on the belief that only property owners with a stake in society should have a voice in governing it, the landed and commercial elites of the Revolutionary era erected legal barriers against the full expression of majority sentiments. These barriers—property requirements for voting and officeholding, the prevalence of appointed over elected offices, and the overrepresentation of older and wealthier regions in state legislatures—came under increasing attack after 1800 and were all but eliminated by the 1820s.

As politics opened to mass participation, a democratization movement in American religion also gathered momentum. Popular styles of religious leadership and worship emerged in a broad reaction to the formalism and elitism of the dominant Protestant churches. The same egalitarian impulse drove these twin democratic revolutions, and both movements represented an empowerment of the common man. Popular movements now spoke his language and appealed to his quest for republican equality. (Women would have to wait longer.) John Quincy Adams and his followers never understood the more democratic America of the 1820s. As a result, they were easily routed in the election of 1828 by those who did—the **Jacksonian Democrats**.

THE EXTENSION OF WHITE MALE DEMOCRACY

In 1789, Congress set the pay of representatives and senators at $6 a day plus travel expenses. By 1816, inflation had so eroded this salary that many government clerks earned more than members of Congress. Thus Congress thought itself prudent and justified when it voted itself a hefty raise to $1,500 a year. The public thought otherwise. In a resolution typical of the popular response, the citizens of Saratoga, New York, accused Congress of "wanton extravagance" and "a daring and profligate trespass against . . . the *morals* of the *Republic.*" The outcry stunned the politicians, who found themselves deluged with protests decrying their greed.

So sharp was the reaction against the Salary Act of 1816 that 70 percent of the members of Congress were turned out of office at the next election. Congress quickly repealed the salary increase, but not before John C. Calhoun spoke for many in Congress when he plaintively asked, "Are we bound in all cases to do what is popular?" The answer was apparently yes. As Richard M. Johnson

of Kentucky noted, "The presumption is, that the people are always right."

The people had spoken in 1816, and the politicians got the message. The uproar over the Salary Act marked a turning point in the transition from the deferential politics of the Federalist-Republican period to the egalitarianism of the coming Jacksonian era. Since the War of 1812, demands for a greater popular voice in government had noticeably quickened the pace of democratization. The public would no longer passively accept decisions handed down by local elites or established national figures.

Individual states, not the federal government, defined who could vote. Six states—Indiana, Mississippi, Illinois, Alabama, Missouri, and Maine—entered the Union between 1816 and 1821, and none of them required voters to own property. Meanwhile, proponents for suffrage liberalization won major victories in the older eastern states. Constitutional conventions in Connecticut in 1818 and Massachusetts and New York in 1821 eliminated property requirements for voting. By the end of the 1820s, universal white male suffrage was the norm everywhere except Rhode Island, Virginia, and Louisiana.

Extending the suffrage and democratic reform.

Broadening the suffrage was part of a general democratization of political structures and procedures in the state governments. Representation in most state legislatures was made more equal by giving more seats to newer, rapidly growing regions in the backcountry. States removed or reduced property qualifications for officeholding. The selection of local officials and, in many cases, judges, was taken out of the hands of governors and executive councils and given to the voters in popular elections. With the end of oral or "stand-up" voting, the act of casting a ballot became more private and freer from the intimidation of influential neighbors. Written ballots were the norm by the 1820s. Most significant for national politics, voters acquired the power to choose presidential electors. In 1800, only two states had provided for a statewide popular vote in presidential elections. By 1824, most did so, and by 1832 only South Carolina still clung to the practice of having the state legislature choose the electors (see Map 10–1).

Several currents swelled the movement for democratic reform. Limiting voting rights to those who owned landed property seemed increasingly elitist when economic changes were producing new classes—workers, clerks, and small tradesmen—whose livelihoods were not tied directly to the land. At the same time, the middling and lower ranks of society demanded the ballot and access to offices to protect

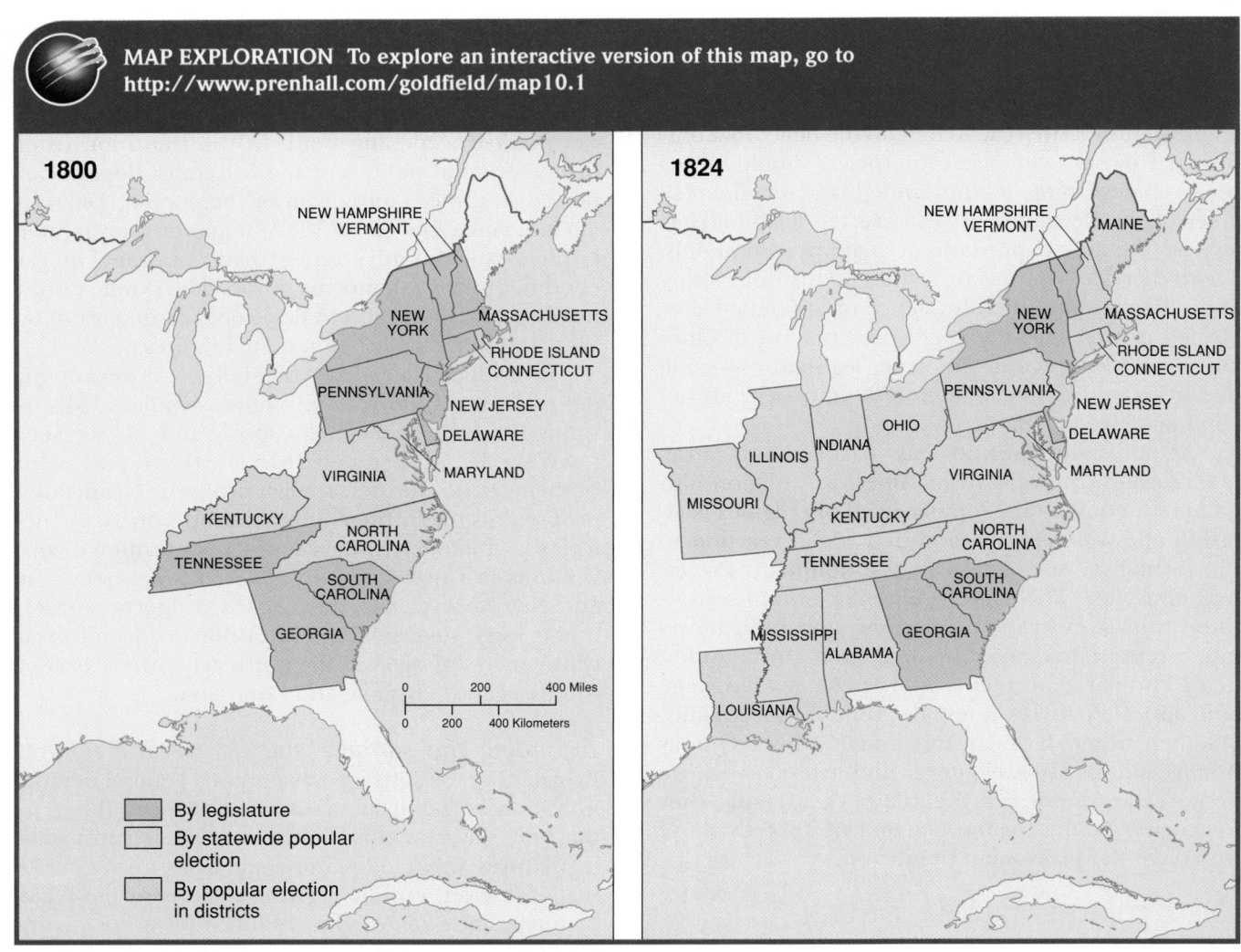

MAP EXPLORATION To explore an interactive version of this map, go to
http://www.prenhall.com/goldfield/map10.1

MAP 10-1 Methods of Electing Presidential Electors, 1800 and 1824
The Constitution permits each state legislature to choose the method of electing presidential electors for its state. In 1800 the legislatures in most states appointed the electors. By 1824 most states had adopted more democratic systems in which electors pledged to specific presidential candidates were selected by popular vote in statewide elections.

Data Source: U.S. Bureau of the Census, *Historical Statistics of the United States, Colonial Times to 1957 (1960)*, p. 681.

themselves from the commercial and manufacturing interests, who benefited most from economic change. Propertyless laborers in Richmond argued in an 1829 petition that "virtue [and] intelligence are not among the products of the soil. Attachment to property, often a sordid sentiment, is not to be confounded with the sacred flame of patriotism."

Of greatest importance, however, was the incessant demand that all white men be treated equally. Seth Luther, an advocate for workers' rights, insisted that "we wish nothing, but those equal rights, which were designed for us all." The logical extension of the ideology of the American Revolution, with its leveling attacks against kings and aristocrats, this demand for

equality made republicanism by the 1820s synonymous with simple majority rule. If any white male was the equal of any other, regardless of wealth or property holdings, then only the will of the majority could be the measure of a republican government.

The disfranchisement of free blacks and women.

As political opportunities expanded for white males, they shrank for women and free black people. In the state constitutions of the Revolutionary era, free black males who met the minimum property requirements usually had the same voting rights as white males. New Jersey's constitution of 1776 was exceptional in also granting the suffrage to single women

Chronology

1826	Disappearance of William Morgan.
1827	Emergence of the Anti-Masons, the first third party.
1828	Andrew Jackson elected president.
	John C. Calhoun writes *The South Carolina Exposition and Protest*.
1830	Congress passes the Indian Removal Act.
1831	William Lloyd Garrison starts publication of *The Liberator*.
	Nat Turner leads a slave uprising in Virginia.
1832	Jackson vetoes bill for rechartering the Second Bank of the United States; Bank War begins.
	South Carolina nullifies the Tariffs of 1828 and 1832.
	Jackson reelected.
1833	Congress passes the Force Act and the Compromise Tariff.
	American Anti-Slavery Society established.

1834	Whig party begins to organize.
1836	Texas War of Independence and establishment of the Republic of Texas.
	Congress passes first gag rule on abolitionist petitions.
	Van Buren elected president.
1837	Panic of 1837 sets off a depression.
1840	Independent Treasury Act passes.
	William Henry Harrison elected as first Whig president.
1841	John Tyler succeeds to presidency on death of Harrison.
1842	United States and Britain sign the Webster-Ashburton Treaty.
1844	James K. Polk elected president.
	Gag rule repealed.
1845	Texas admitted to the Union.

and widows who owned property. By the early 1800s, race and gender began to replace wealth and status as the basis for defining the limits of political participation. Thus, when New Jersey's new constitution in 1807 broadened suffrage by requiring only a simple taxpaying qualification to vote, it specifically denied the ballot to women and free black men. In state after state, the same constitutional conventions that embraced universal suffrage for white men deprived black men of the vote or burdened them with special property qualifications. Moreover, none of the ten states that entered the Union from 1821 to 1861 allowed black suffrage. African Americans protested in vain. "Foreigners and aliens to the government and laws," complained black New Yorkers in 1837, "strangers to our institutions, are permitted to flock to this land and in a few years are endowed with all the privileges of citizens; but we native born Americans . . . are most of us shut out." By the 1850s, black males could vote only in certain New England states.

The linkage of democracy with white manhood was not accidental. Advocates of greater democratization explicitly argued that only white males had the intelligence and love of liberty to be entrusted with political rights. Women, they said, were too weak and emotional, black people too lazy and lascivious. In denouncing distinctions drawn on property as artificial and demeaning, the white egalitarians simultaneously erected new distinctions based on race

and sex that were supposedly natural and hence immutable. Thus personal liberties were now to be guarded, not by propertied gentlemen but by all white men, whose equality ultimately rested on assumptions of their shared natural superiority over women and nonwhite people.

THE POPULAR RELIGIOUS REVOLT

In religion as well as politics, ordinary Americans demanded a greater voice in the early nineteenth century. Insurgent religious movements rejected the formalism and traditional Calvinism of the Congregational and Presbyterian churches, the dominant Protestant denominations in Washington's America. In a blaze of fervor known as the **Second Great Awakening** (recalling the Great Awakening of colonial America), evangelical sects led by the Methodists and Baptists radically transformed the religious landscape between 1800 and 1840. A more popularly rooted Christianity moved outward and downward as it spread across frontier areas and converted marginalized and common folk. By 1850, one in three Americans was a regular churchgoer, a dramatic increase since 1800.

The Baptists and Methodists, both spinning off numerous splinter groups, grew spectacularly and were the largest religious denominations by the 1820s. The key to their success was their ability to give

"Camp Meeting," color lithograph by Kennedy and Lucas after painting by A. Rider, c. 1835, negative number 26275. © collection of the New York Historical Society, NYC.

The Second Great Awakening originated on the frontier. Preachers were adept at arousing emotional fervor, and women in particular responded to the evangelical message of spiritual equality open to all who would accept Christ into their lives.

religious expression to the same popular impulse behind democratic reform. Especially in the backcountry of the South and West, where the first revivals occurred, itinerant preachers reshaped religion to fit the needs and values of ordinary Americans.

Evangelical Christianity emphasized personal, heartfelt experience that would produce a spiritual rebirth. Preaching became a form of theater in which scenes of damnation and salvation were acted out by both preacher and audience. The emotional force unleashed at the mass revivals known as camp meetings astounded observers. "The scene that then presented itself to my mind was indescribable," recalled James Finley of the camp meeting at Cane Ridge, Kentucky, in 1801. "At one time I saw at least five hundred swept down in a moment, as if a battery of a thousand guns had been opened upon them, and then immediately followed shrieks and shouts that rent the very heavens."

The evangelical religion of the traveling preachers was democratic in its populist rejection of traditional religious canons and its encouragement of

organizational forms that gave a voice to popular culture. Salvation was no longer simply bestowed by an implacable God as taught by the Calvinist doctrine of individual predestination (see Chapter 1). Ordinary people could now actively choose salvation, and this possibility was exhilarating. "Why, then, I can be saved!" exclaimed Jesse Lee upon hearing a Methodist preacher in Massachusetts. "I have been taught that only a part of the race could be saved, but if this man's singing be true, all may be saved." Evangelical churches bound the faithful into tightly knit communities that expressed and enforced local values and standards of conduct. Their hymns borrowed melodies from popular music and were accompanied by fiddles and other folk instruments.

Evangelicalism was a religion of the common people, and it appealed especially to women and African Americans. The revivals converted about twice as many women as men. Excluded from most areas of public life, women found strength and comfort in the evangelical message of Christian love and equality. As the wife of a Connecticut minister explained, church membership offered them a welcome release from "being treated like beasts of burden [and] drudges of domineering masters." In the first flush of evangelical excitement, female itinerant preachers spread the gospel up and down the East Coast. By thus defying social convention, these women offered a model of independent action. Other women organized their own institutions within denominations still formally controlled by men. Women activists founded and largely directed hundreds of church-affiliated charitable societies and missionary associations.

Evangelicalism also empowered black Americans. African American Christianity experienced its first sustained growth in the generation after the Revolutionary War. As a result of their uncompromising commitment to convert slaves, the Baptists and Methodists led the way. They welcomed slaves at their revivals, encouraged black preachers, and above all else, advocated secular and spiritual equality. Many of the early Baptist and Methodist preachers directly challenged slavery. In converting to Methodism, one slave stated that "from the sermon I heard, I felt that God had made all men free and equal, and that I ought not to be a slave." Perceiving in it the promise of liberty and deliverance, the slaves received the evangelical gospel in loud, joyous, and highly emotional revivals. They made it part of their own culture, fusing Christianity with folk beliefs from their African heritage.

But for all its liberating appeal to women and African Americans, evangelicalism was eventually limited by race and gender in much the same way as the democratic reform movement. Denied positions of authority in white-dominated churches and resentful of white opposition to integrated worship, free black northerners founded their own independent churches.

As increasing numbers of planters embraced evangelicalism after the 1820s, southern evangelicals first muted their attacks on slavery and then developed a full-blown religious defense of it based on the biblical sanctioning of human bondage. They similarly cited the Old Testament patriarchs to defend the unquestioned authority of fathers over their households, the masters of slaves, women, and children. Many popular religious sects in the North also used a particular reading of the Bible to exalt the independence of white males at the expense of the dependence of everyone else.

In religion as well as politics, white men retained the power in Jacksonian America. Still, the Second Great Awakening removed a major intellectual barrier to political democracy. Traditional Protestant theology—whether Calvinist, Anglican, or Lutheran—viewed the mass of humanity as sinners predestined to damnation and hence was loath to accept the idea that those same sinners, by majority vote, should make crucial political decisions. In rejecting this theology, ordinary Americans made a fundamental intellectual breakthrough. "Salvation open to all" powerfully reinforced the legitimacy of "one man, one vote."

THE RISE OF THE JACKSONIANS

The Jacksonian Democrats were the first party to mold and organize the democratizing impulse in popular culture. At the core of the Jacksonian appeal was the same rejection of established authority that was the hallmark of the secular and religious populists. Much like the revivalists and the democratic reformers, the Jacksonians also fashioned techniques of communication that tapped into the hopes and fears of ordinary Americans. In so doing, they built the first mass-based party in American history.

In Andrew Jackson the new **Democratic Party** that formed between 1824 and 1828 had the perfect candidate for the increasingly democratic temperament of the 1820s. Born of Scots-Irish ancestry on the Carolina frontier in 1767, Jackson was a self-made product of the southern backcountry. Lacking any formal education, family connections, or inherited wealth to ease his way, he relied on his own wits and raw courage to carve out a career as a frontier lawyer and planter in Tennessee. He won fame as the military savior of the republic with his victory at the Battle of New Orleans. Conqueror of the British, the Spanish, and the Indians, all of whom had blocked frontier expansion, he achieved incredible popularity in his native South. His strengths and prejudices were those most valued by the restless, mobile Americans to whom he became a folk hero.

As a presidential candidate, Jackson's image was that of the antielitist champion of the people. "Take for your President a man from your own body, untainted by the corruption of a court and uninitiated in Cabinet secrets," urged a New Jersey Jackson convention in 1824. Jackson lost the election of 1824, but his defeat turned out to be a blessing in disguise. The wheeling and dealing in Congress that gave the presidency to John Quincy Adams enveloped that administration in a cloud of suspicion from the start. It also enhanced Jackson's appeal as the honest tribune of the people whose rightful claim to the presidency had been spurned by intriguing politicians in Washington. His supporters now claimed that the people, as well as Jackson, had been swindled by the "corrupt bargain" between Adams and Clay (see page 287). Moreover, the ill-fated Adams presidency virtually destroyed itself. Though the same age as Jackson, Adams seemed

To the opponents of the Jacksonians, elections had become a degrading spectacle in which conniving Democratic politicians, such as the one shown below handing a voting ticket to the stereotypical Irishman in the light coat, were corrupting the republic's political culture.

frozen in an eighteenth-century past, in which aloof gentlemanly statesmen disdainfully refused to turn to the people for support. Uncomfortable with the give-and-take of politics or the very idea of building a coalition to support himself, Adams was out of touch with the political realities of the 1820s.

Just how out of touch was revealed when Adams delivered his first annual message to Congress in 1825. He presented a bold vision of an activist federal government promoting economic growth, social advancement, and scientific progress. Such a vision might have received a fair hearing in 1815, when postwar nationalism was in full stride. In 1825, it amounted to political suicide. Postwar nationalism had dissolved into sectional bickering and burning resentments against banks, tariffs, and the political establishment, which were blamed for the hard times after the Panic of 1819. The Jacksonians charged that an administration born in corruption now wanted to waste the people's money by promoting more corruption and greed. And when Adams urged Americans not "to proclaim to the world that we are palsied by the will of our constituents," the Jacksonians attacked him as an arrogant aristocrat contemptuous of the common man.

Little of Adams's program passed Congress, and his nationalist vision drove his opponents into the

Jackson camp. Southern planters jumped onto the Jackson bandwagon out of fear that Adams might use federal power against slavery; more Westerners joined because Adams revived their suspicions of the East. The most important addition came from New York, where Martin Van Buren had built the **Albany Regency**, a tightly disciplined state political machine.

Van Buren was a new breed of politician, a professional who made a business out of politics. The son of a tavern keeper, he quickly grasped, as a young lawyer, how politics could open up career opportunities. The discipline and regularity of strict party organization gave him and others from the middling ranks a winning edge in competition against their social betters. In battling against the system of family-centered wealth and prestige on which politics had previously been based, Van Buren redefined parties as something good in and of themselves. Indeed, he and his followers argued that parties were indispensable instruments for the successful expression of the popular will against the dominance of elites.

State leaders such as Van Buren organized the first national campaign that relied extensively on new techniques of mass mobilization. In rallying support for Jackson against Adams in 1828, these state leaders put together chains of party-subsidized newspapers and coordinated a frantic schedule of meetings and rallies. Grassroots Jackson committees reached out to the voters by knocking on their doors, pressing party literature into their hands, dispensing mass-produced medals and buttons with a likeness of Jackson, and lavishly entertaining all who would give them a hearing. Politics became a folk spectacle as torchlight parades awakened sleepy towns and political barbecues doled out whiskey and food to farmers from the surrounding countryside.

The election of 1828 centered on personalities, not issues. This in itself was a victory for Jackson's campaign managers, who proved far more skillful in the new presidential game of image making than did their Adams counterparts, now known as the National Republicans. Although both sides tried to depict the other's candidate as morally unfit, the

Jackson men were more in tune with a public sentiment that identified Adams's call for a strong government with special privileges for the favored few. Thus for many voters, Adams personified a discredited elite and Jackson the voice of the people.

Jackson carried every state south and west of Pennsylvania in 1828 and polled 56 percent of the popular vote (see Map 10–2). Voter turnout shot up to 55 percent from the apathetic 25 percent of 1824. Adams ran well only in New England and in commercialized areas producing goods for outside markets. Aside from the South, where he was virtually untouchable, Jackson's appeal was strongest among ordinary Americans who valued their local independence and felt threatened by outside centers of power beyond their control. He rolled up heavy majorities from Scots-Irish farmers in the Baptist-Methodist evangelical belt of the backcountry and from unskilled workers with an Irish Catholic background. To these voters, Jackson was a double hero, for he had defeated their hated British enemy and promised to do the same to the Yankee capitalists of the Northeast and all the elitist politicians. Democracy, they were convinced, had at last come to presidential politics.

JACKSON'S PRESIDENCY

Once in office, Jackson proved to be the most forceful and energetic president since Jefferson. Like a military chieftain tolerating no interference from his subordinates, Jackson dominated his presidency with the sheer force of his personality. At one time or another, his administration angered southern planters, frightened eastern bankers and commercial interests, and outraged New England reformers. Nonetheless, Jackson remained popular because he portrayed himself as the embodiment of the people's will.

The Jacksonians had no particular program in 1828, and Jackson shrewdly had avoided taking a stand on divisive issues. Apart from removing Indians to areas west of the Mississippi River, Jackson's first term was notable primarily for its political infighting. Two political struggles that came to a head in 1832–1833—the **Bank War** and the **nullification crisis**—

This 1845 painting captures the heroic, forceful side of Andrew Jackson that made him so appealing to many voters.

MAP 10-2   The Election of 1828
Andrew Jackson won a decisive victory in 1828 by sweeping the South and West and making major inroads in the Northeast.

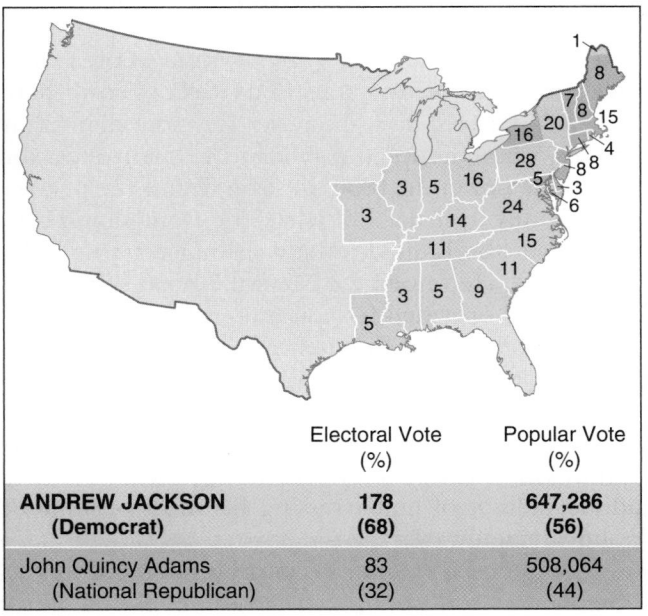

	Electoral Vote (%)	Popular Vote (%)
ANDREW JACKSON (Democrat)	**178** **(68)**	**647,286** **(56)**
John Quincy Adams (National Republican)	83 (32)	508,064 (44)

stamped the Jacksonians with a lasting party identity. By destroying the Second Bank of the United States and rejecting the attempt of South Carolina to nullify (or annul) a national tariff, Jackson firmly established the Democrats as the enemy of special privilege, the friend of the common man, and the defender of the Union. Consequently, even when Jackson stepped down in 1837, the Democrats were so identified with the interests of the people that they were able to elect Martin Van Buren, who had none of Jackson's personal magnetism or broad appeal.

JACKSON'S APPEAL

Jackson's inauguration struck many conservatives as ushering in a vulgar new order in national affairs. A vast crowd poured into Washington to applaud the people's hero. They cheered loudly when Jackson took his oath of office and then rushed to the White House for a postinauguration reception. Any semblance of order broke down as they pressed in on waiters trying to serve them refreshments. Bowls of liquor-laced punch went flying, and glass and china crashed to the floor as a seeming mob surged through the White House. "But it was the People's day," reported one conservative onlooker, "and the People's President and the People would rule. God grant that one day or other, the People do not put down all rule and rulers."

Ordinary Americans identified with Jackson as with no earlier president, and he convinced them that he was using his office as the instrument of their will. Although led by wealthy planters and entrepreneurs who were hardly average Americans, the Jacksonians skillfully depicted themselves as the champions of the common man against the aristocratic interests, who had enriched themselves through special privileges granted by the government. Jackson proclaimed his task as one of restoring the federal government to the ideal of Jeffersonian republicanism, in which farmers and artisans could pursue their individual liberty free of any government intervention that favored the rich and powerful.

Jackson began his assault on special privilege by proclaiming a reform of the appointment process for federal officeholders. Accusing his predecessors, especially Adams, of having created a social elite of self-serving bureaucrats, he vowed to make government service more responsive to the popular will. He insisted that federal jobs required no special expertise or training and proposed to rotate honest, hardworking citizens in and out of the civil service.

Jackson's reform of the federal bureaucracy had more style than substance. He removed only about one-fifth of the officeholders he inherited, and most of his appointees came from the same relatively high-status groups as the Adams people. But by providing a democratic rationale for government ser-

THE GREAT CHEESE LEVEE.

The first president to be openly embraced by the people as one of their own, Jackson received many gifts while president. One of the gifts was a 1,400-pound cheese, which he offered to well-wishers at a public reception.

vice, he opened the way for future presidents to move more aggressively against incumbents. Thus emerged the **spoils system**, in which the victorious party gave government jobs to its supporters and removed the appointees of the defeated party. This parceling out of jobs was a powerful technique for building party strength, because it tied party loyalty to the reward of a federal appointment.

When Jackson railed against economic privilege, he most often had in mind Henry Clay's American System (see Chapter 9). Clay's program called for a protective tariff, a national bank, and federal subsidies for internal improvements; his goal was to bind Americans together in an integrated national market. To the Democrats, Clay's system represented government favoritism at its worst, a set of costly benefits at the public's expense for special-interest groups, who corrupted politicians in their quest for economic power. In 1830, Jackson found the perfect opportunity to strike a blow for the Democratic conception of the limited federal role in economic development. He vetoed the Maysville Road Bill, which would have provided federal money for a road to be built entirely within Kentucky. The bill was unconstitutional, he claimed, because it benefited only the citizens of Kentucky and not the American people as a whole. Moreover, since the Maysville project was within Clay's congressional district, Jackson had the added delight of embarrassing his most prominent political enemy.

On the issue of internal improvements, as well as bureaucratic reform, the Democrats placed party needs ahead of ideology. Jackson's Maysville veto did not rule out congressional appropriations for projects deemed beneficial to the general public. This pragmatic loophole gave Democrats all the room they needed to pass more internal-improvement projects during Jackson's presidency than during all of the previous administrations together. Having built a mass party, the Democrats soon discovered that they had to funnel federal funds to their constituents back home.

Any support Jackson might have lost among market-minded entrepreneurs and farmers in the West by his Maysville veto was more than made up by the popularity of his Indian removal policy. Jackson's strongest base of support was in the West and South, and by driving Native Americans from these regions, he more than lived up to his billing as the friend of the common (white) man.

INDIAN REMOVAL

Some 125,000 Indians lived east of the Mississippi when Jackson became president. The largest concen-

Sequoyah, a Cherokee scholar, developed a written table of syllables for the Cherokee language that enabled his people to publish a tribal newspaper in both Cherokee and English.

SE-QUO-YAH

tration was in the South, where five Indian nations—the Cherokees, Creeks, Choctaws, Chickasaws, and Seminoles—controlled millions of acres of land in what soon would become the great cotton frontiers of southwestern Georgia and central Alabama and Mississippi. That, of course, was the problem: Native Americans held land that white farmers coveted for their own economic gain.

Pressure from the states to remove the Indians had been building since the end of the War of 1812. It was most intense in Georgia. In early 1825, Georgia authorities finalized a fraudulent treaty that ceded most of the Creek Indians' land to the state. When Adams tried to obtain fairer terms for the Creeks in a new treaty, he was brazenly denounced in Georgia, which based its case for grabbing Indian territory on the inviolability of states' rights. Georgia dared Adams to do something about it; not willing to risk an armed confrontation between federal and state authorities, Adams backed down.

In 1828, Georgia moved against the Cherokees, the best-organized and most advanced (by white standards) of the Indian nations. By now a prosperous society of small farmers with their own newspaper and schools for their children, the Cherokees wanted to avoid the fate of their Creek neighbors. In 1827, they adopted a constitution declaring themselves an independent nation with complete sovereignty over their land. The Georgia legislature reacted by placing the Cherokees directly under state law, annulling Cherokee laws and even the right of the Cherokees to make laws, and legally defining the Cherokees as tenants on land belonging to the state of Georgia. By also prohibiting Indian testimony in cases against white people, the legislature stripped the Cherokees of any legal rights. They were now easy prey for white settlers, who scrambled onto Cherokee land after gold was discovered in northern Georgia in 1829. Alabama and Mississippi followed Georgia's lead in denying Indians legal rights.

Thus the stage was set for what Jackson always considered the most important measure of the early days of his administration, the **Indian Removal Act**. Jackson had no qualms about allowing state officials to override federal protection of Native Americans. He had long considered the federal policy of negotiating with the Indians as sovereign entities a farce. But it was awkward politically for the president to declare that he had no intention of enforcing treaty obligations of the U.S. government. The way out of this dilemma was to remove Native Americans from the center of the dispute. In his first annual message, Jackson sided with state authorities in the South and advised the Indians "to emigrate beyond the Mississippi or submit to the laws of those States." This advice enabled Jackson to pose as the friend of the Indians, the

For the Cherokees, the Trail of Tears stretched 1,200 miles from the homeland in the East to what became the Indian Territory in Oklahoma.

wise father who would lead them out of harm's way and save them from rapacious white people.

Congress acted on Jackson's recommendation in the Indian Removal Act of 1830. The act appropriated $500,000 for the negotiation of new treaties under which the southern Indians would surrender their territory and be removed to land in the trans-Mississippi area (primarily present-day Oklahoma). Although force was not authorized and Jackson stressed that removal should be voluntary, no federal protection was provided for Indians harassed into leaving by land-hungry settlers. Ultimately, Jackson did deploy the U.S. Army, but only to round up and push out Indians who refused to comply with the new removal treaties.

And so most of the Indians left the eastern United States—the Choctaws in 1830, the Creeks and Chickasaws in 1832, and the Cherokees in 1838 (see Map 10–3). The government was ill-prepared to supervise the removal. The private groups who won the federal contracts for transporting and provisioning the Indians were those who had entered the low-est bids; they were a shady lot, interested only in a quick profit. Thousands of Indians, perhaps as many as one-fourth of those who started the trek, died on the way to Oklahoma, the victims of cold, hunger, disease, and the general callousness of the white people they met along the way. "It is impossible to conceive the frightful sufferings that attend these forced migrations," noted a Frenchman who observed the Choctaw removal. It was indeed, as recalled in the collective memory of the Cherokees, a **Trail of Tears**.

Tribes that resisted removal were attacked by white armies. Federal troops joined local militias in 1832 in suppressing the Sauk and Fox Indians of Illinois and Wisconsin in what was called **Black Hawk's War**. More a frantic attempt by the Indians to reach safety on the west bank of the Mississippi than an actual war, this affair ended in the slaughter of five hundred Indian men, women, and children by white troops and their Sioux allies. The Seminoles held out in the swamps of Florida for seven years between 1835 and 1842 in what became the longest Indian war in American history. Their resistance continued even after their leader, Osceola, was captured while negotiating under a flag of truce.

Jackson forged ahead with his removal policy despite the opposition of eastern reformers and Protestant missionaries. Aligned with conservatives concerned by Jackson's cavalier disregard of federal treaty obligations, they came within three votes of defeating the removal bill in the House of Representatives. Jackson ignored their protests (see "American Views: Memorial and Protest of the Cherokee Nation, 1836" page 306) as well as the legal rulings of the Supreme Court. In *Cherokee Nation v. Georgia* (1831) and *Worcester v. Georgia* (1832), the Court ruled that Georgia had violated the U.S. Constitution in extending its jurisdiction over the Cherokees. Chief Justice John Marshall defined Indian tribes as "dependent domestic nations" subject only to the authority of the federal government. Marshall may have won the legal argument, but he was powerless to enforce his decisions without Jackson's cooperation. Aware that southerners and westerners were on his side, Jackson ignored the Supreme Court rulings and pushed Indian removal to its tragic conclusion.

MAP 10-3   Indian Removals

The fixed policy of the Jackson administration and pressure from the states forced Native Americans in the 1830s to migrate from their eastern homelands to a special Indian reserve west of the Mississippi River

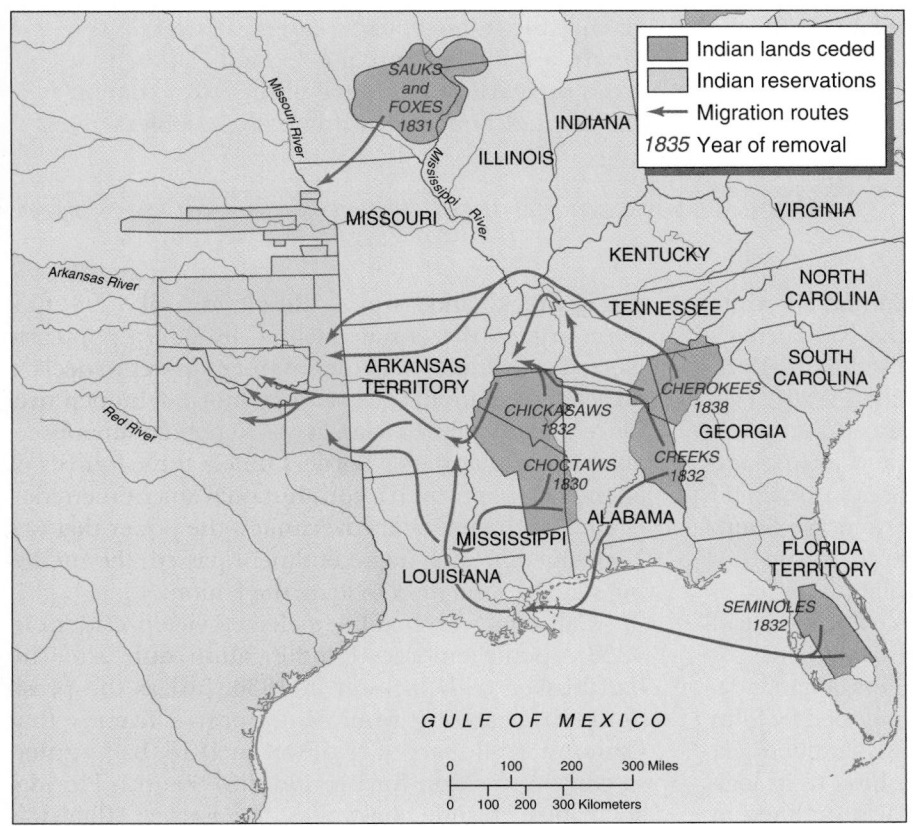

THE NULLIFICATION CRISIS

Jackson's stand on Indian removal confirmed the impression of many of his followers that when state and national power conflicted, he could be trusted to side with the states. But when states' rights forces in South Carolina, known as the nullifiers, directly challenged Jackson in the early 1830s over tariff policy—the most sensitive issue involving the power of the national government—they precipitated the nullification crisis, the most serious sectional crisis since the Missouri debates of 1819–1820. And Jackson, for all his talk of states' rights when it came to Indian policy, revealed himself to be an ardent nationalist on the issue of majority rule in the Union. He won the showdown with South Carolina and established the nationalist credentials of his Democratic party. In reaction to his strong stand, however, the solid front of Democratic power in the South began to crack.

After the first protective tariff in 1816, rates increased further in 1824 and then jumped to 50 percent in 1828 in what was denounced as the "Tariff of Abominations." Southerners were especially angry over the last tariff, because it had been contrived by northern Democrats to win additional northern support for Jackson in his presidential campaign. The outcry was loudest in South Carolina, an old cotton state losing population to the West in the 1820s as cotton prices remained low after the Panic of 1819. What fueled antitariff sentiment was not just the economic argument that high tariffs worsened the agricultural depression in the state by raising the cost of manufactured goods purchased by farmers and planters and lowering the foreign demand for agricultural exports. Protective tariffs were also denounced as an unconstitutional extension of national power over the states; many southern planters feared that they were only a prelude to forced emancipation of the slaves.

South Carolina was the only state where African Americans made up the majority of the population. Slaves were heavily concentrated in the marshes and tidal flats south of Charleston, the lowcountry district of huge rice

AMERICAN VIEWS

Memorial and Protest of the Cherokee Nation, 1836

Of the major tribes in the Southeast, the Cherokees fought longest and hardest against the Jacksonian policy of Indian removal. Led by their principal chief, John Ross, the son of a Scot and a mixed-blood Cherokee woman, they submitted the following protest to Congress against the fraudulent 1835 Treaty of New Echota forced on them by the state of Georgia. Although clearly opposed by an overwhelming majority of the Cherokees, this treaty provided the legal basis for the forced removal of the Cherokee people from Georgia to the Indian Territory.

- On what legal grounds did the Cherokees base their protest? What pledges had been made to them by the U.S. government?

- What did the Cherokees mean when they said they had been "taught to think and feel as the American citizen"? If the Cherokees had become "civilized" by white standards, why did most whites still insist on their removal?

- Why would President Jackson have allowed white intruders to remain on land reserved by treaties for the Cherokees?

- Do you feel that the Cherokees were justified in believing that they had been betrayed by the American government?

The undersigned representatives of the Cherokee nation, east of the river Mississippi, impelled by duty, would respectfully submit . . . the following statement of facts: It will be seen, from the numerous treaties between the Cherokee nation and the United States, that from the earliest existence of this government, the United States, in Congress assembled, re-

---

plantations. Here black people outnumbered white people ten to one in the summer months. Nat Turner's Rebellion, a bloody slave uprising in Virginia in 1831, and earlier aborted rebellions in the 1820s (see Chapter 11) left fearful planters convinced that growing antislavery agitation in the North and in England was feeding slave unrest. The disturbances so far would be "nothing to what we shall see," warned the South Carolina planter James Hamilton, Jr., "if we do not stand manfully at the Safety Valve of Nullification."

Led by the lowcountry planters, the antitariff forces in South Carolina controlled state politics by 1832. They called themselves the nullifiers, a name derived from the constitutional theory developed by John C. Calhoun in an anonymous tract of 1828 titled *The South Carolina Exposition and Protest*. Pushing to its logical extreme the states' rights doctrine first outlined in the Kentucky and Virginia Resolutions of 1798, Calhoun argued that a state, acting through a popularly elected convention, had the sovereign power to declare an act of the national government null and inoperative. Once a state nullified a law, it was to remain unenforceable within that state's borders unless three-fourths of all the states approved a constitutional amendment delegating to the national government the power that was challenged. If such an amendment passed, the nullifying state had the right to leave the Union.

Calhoun, who had been elected vice president in 1828, openly embraced nullification only after he had broken with Jackson in 1830. Just as the president was learning from Van Buren's friends that Calhoun, while secretary of war in 1818, had wanted to censure Jackson for his raid into Spanish Florida, a curious episode known as the Eaton Affair was ceived the Cherokees and their nation into favor and protection; and that the chiefs and warriors, for themselves and all parts of the Cherokee nation, acknowledged themselves and the said Cherokee nation to be under the protection of the United States of America, and of no other sovereign whatsoever: they also stipulated, that the said Cherokee nation will not hold any treaty with any foreign power, individual State, or with individuals of any State: that for, and in consideration of, valuable concessions made by the Cherokee nation, the United States solemnly guaranteed to said nation all their lands not ceded, and pledged the faith of the government, that "all white people who have intruded, or may hereafter intrude, on the lands reserved for the Cherokees, shall be removed by the United States, and proceeded against, according to the provisions of the act, passed 30th March, 1802," entitled "An act to regulate trade and intercourse with the Indian tribes, and to preserve peace on the frontiers." It would be useless to recapitulate the numerous provisions for the security and protection of the rights of the Cherokees, to be found in the various treaties between their nation and the United States. The Cherokees were happy and prosperous under a scrupulous observance of treaty stipulations by the government of the United States, and from the fostering hand extended over them, they made rapid advances in civilization, morals, and in the arts and sciences. Little did they anticipate, that when taught to think and feel as the American citizen, and to have with him a common interest, they were to be despoiled by their guardian, to become strangers and wanderers in the land of their fathers, forced to return to the savage life, and to seek a new home in the wilds of the far west, and that without their consent. An instrument purporting to be a treaty with the Cherokee people, has recently been made public by the President of the United States, that will have such an operation, if carried into effect. This instrument, the delegation aver before the civilized world, and in the presence of Almighty God, is fraudulent, false upon its face, made by unauthorized individuals, without the sanction, and against the wishes, of the great body of the Cherokee people. Upwards of fifteen thousand of those people have protested against it, solemnly declaring they will never acquiesce.

Source: U.S. Congress, *Executive Documents* (1836)

reaching a climax. When the wives of Jackson's cabinet members, led by Floride Calhoun, pointedly snubbed Peggy Eaton, the wife of Jackson's secretary of war, on the grounds that she was a "loose woman" who had driven her first husband to suicide, Jackson was convinced that Calhoun was plotting to discredit his administration.

The political consequences of the Eaton affair included not only Calhoun's fall from Jackson's favor but also the resignation of the entire cabinet. Much of the rancor stemmed from the belief of elite Washington women that Peggy Eaton had violated the rules of women's political behavior. Rather than exerting influence indirectly by using social gatherings to lobby on behalf of male friends, as Washington women had done since the 1790s, she seemingly sought power in her own right by appealing directly to Jackson for his support. Moreover, as the daughter of a tavernkeeper, she was overstepping her bounds by claiming political influence that Washington society felt belonged only to women of the social elite.

In addition to losing out at the national level, Calhoun also faced the danger of losing control of his political base in South Carolina. Unless he publicly identified himself with nullification, his leadership of the state would be threatened. With Calhoun's approval, a South Carolina convention in November 1832 nullified the tariffs of 1828 and 1832 (a compromise tariff that did not reduce rates to a low enough level to satisfy the nullifiers). The convention decreed that customs duties were not to be collected in South Carolina after February 1, 1833.

Calhoun always insisted that nullification was not secession. He further defended his doctrine as a constitutional means of protecting minority rights within a Union dominated by a tyrannical national majority. Jackson rejected such reasoning as the talk of a scheming disunionist. He considered nullification a dangerous and nonsensical perversion of the Constitution, and he vowed to crush any attempt to block the enforcement of federal laws. He told a congressman from South Carolina that "if a single drop of blood shall be shed there in opposition to the laws of the United States, I will hang the first man I can lay my hand on engaged in such treasonable conduct, upon the first tree I can reach."

In January 1833, Jackson, in the Force Bill, asked for and received from Congress full authorization to put down nullification by military force. Simultaneously, he worked to defuse nullification by supporting a new tariff that would cut duties by half within two years. Because Jackson's opponents in Congress did not want him to get political credit for brokering a compromise, they pushed through their own tariff measure. The Compromise Tariff of 1833 lowered duties to 20 percent but extended the reductions over a ten-year period. Up against this combination of the carrot and the stick, the nullifiers backed down.

Jackson reacted swiftly and decisively when challenged by the nullifiers. His stand established the principle of national supremacy grounded in the will of the majority. Despite his victory, however, states'-rights doctrines remained popular both in the South and among many northern Democrats. South Carolina had been isolated in its stand on nullification, but many southerners, and especially slaveholders, agreed that the powers of the national government had to be strictly limited. Their quarrel with the nullifiers was one of tactics, not of objectives. Moreover, by dramatically affirming his right to use force against a state in defense of the Union, Jackson drove many planters out of the Democratic party. In the shock waves set off by the nullification crisis, a new anti-Jackson coalition began to form in the South.

THE BANK WAR

What amounted to a war against the Bank of the United States became the centerpiece of Jackson's presidency and a defining event for the Democratic party. The Bank War erupted in 1832, when Jackson was presented with draft legislation for the early rechartering of the national bank. His thunderous veto kept banking and currency issues in the forefront of national politics for the remainder of the decade.

Like most Westerners, Jackson distrusted banks. Because gold and silver coins were scarce and the national government did not issue or regulate paper currency, money consisted primarily of notes issued as loans by private and state banks. These bank notes fluctuated in value in accordance with the reputation and creditworthiness of the issuing banks. In the credit-starved West, banks were particularly unreliable. Many were "wildcat" operations that made a quick profit by issuing notes without the gold or silver reserves to redeem them and then skipping town when they were on the verge of being found out. Even when issued by honest bankers, notes often could not be redeemed at face value because of market conditions. All of this struck many Americans, and especially farmers and workers, as inherently dishonest. They wanted to be paid in "real" money, gold or silver coin, and they viewed bankers as parasites who did nothing but fatten their own pockets by manipulating paper money.

The largest and most powerful bank was the Bank of the United States, and citizens who were wiped out or forced to retrench drastically by the Panic of 1819 never forgave the Bank for saving itself at the expense of its debtors. Still, under the astute leadership of a new president, Nicholas Biddle of Philadelphia, the Bank performed well in the 1820s. Prosperous times had returned, and the Bank underwrote the economic expansion with its healthy credit reserves and stable banknotes. By 1832, the Bank was as popular as it ever would be.

Beginning with his first annual message, Jackson had been making noise about not rechartering the Bank, at least in its present form. Searching for an issue to use against Jackson in the presidential campaign of 1832, Clay then forced Jackson's hand. Clay convinced Biddle to apply to Congress for a new charter, even though the current charter would not expire until 1836. Confident of congressional approval, Clay reasoned that he had Jackson trapped. If Jackson went along with the new charter, Clay could take credit for the measure. If he vetoed it, Clay could attack Jackson as the enemy of a sound banking system.

Clay's clever strategy backfired. Jackson turned on him and the Bank with a vengeance. As he told his heir apparent, "The bank, Mr. Van Buren, is trying to kill me, but *I will kill it!*" Jackson and his advisers realized that the Bank was vulnerable as a symbol of privileged monopoly, a monstrous institution that deprived common Americans of their right to compete equally for economic advantage. Moreover, many of these advisers were also state bankers and local developers, who backed Jackson precisely because they wanted to be free of federal restraints on their business activities. On July 10, 1832, Jackson vetoed the rechartering bill for the Bank in a message that appealed both to state bankers and to foes of all banks. He took a ringing "stand against all new grants of monopolies and exclusive privileges,

This Democratic cartoon portrays Jackson as the champion of the people attacking the Bank of the United States, a many-headed monster whose tentacles of corruption spread throughout the states.

"pet banks," state banks controlled by loyal Democrats.

Jackson won the Bank War, but he left the impression that the Democrats had played fast and loose with the nation's credit system. The economy overheated in his second term. High commodity prices and abundant credit, both at home and abroad, propelled a buying frenzy of western lands. Prices soared, and inevitably the speculative bubble had to burst. When it did, the Democrats would be open to the charge of having squandered the people's money by shifting deposits to reckless state bankers who were part of a corrupt new alliance between the government and private economic interests. Jackson was out of office when the Panic of 1837 hit; Van Buren, his successor, paid the political price for Jackson's economic policies.

against any prostitution of our Government to the advancement of the few at the expense of the many."

The business community and eastern elites lashed out at Jackson's veto as the demagogic ravings of an economic fool. For Biddle, the veto message had "all the fury of a chained panther, biting the bars of his cage." In rejecting Jackson's claims that the Bank had fostered speculative and corrupt financial practices, the pro-Bank forces had the better of the economic argument. But Jackson won the political battle, and he went to the people in the election of 1832 as their champion against the banking aristocracy. Although his support was no stronger than it had been in 1828, he easily defeated Clay, the candidate of the short-lived National Republican party that had also backed Adams in 1828.

Having blocked the rechartering of the Bank when Congress failed to override his veto, Jackson then set out to destroy it, claiming his reelection in 1832 as a mandate to do so. In Roger B. Taney he finally found a secretary of the treasury (his first two choices refused) who agreed to sign the order removing federal deposits from the Bank in 1833. Drained of its lifeblood, the deposits, the Bank was reduced by 1836 to seeking a charter as a private corporation in the state of Pennsylvania. In the meantime, the government's monies were deposited in

VAN BUREN AND HARD TIMES

Like John Adams and James Madison, Martin Van Buren followed a forceful president who commanded a strong popular following. Fairly or not, he would come out, as they did, second best compared to his predecessor. Where Jackson forged ahead regardless of consequences, Van Buren tended to hang back, carefully calculating all the political angles. This trait served him poorly as president.

Facing a sharp economic downturn, Van Buren appeared indecisive and unwilling to advance a bold program. When the rise of a radical **abolitionist movement** in the North revived sectional tensions over slavery, he awkwardly straddled the divisive issue. Van Buren's difficult position was made worse by his cautious political style. In the end, he undermined himself by failing to offer a compelling vision of his presidency.

THE PANIC OF 1837

Van Buren was barely settled into the White House when the nation was rocked by a financial panic. For over a decade, the economy had benefited from a favorable business cycle. Easy credit and the availability of territories opened up by Jackson's Indian removal policy generated a stampede to buy land in the West. Government land sales ballooned from under 4 million acres in 1833 to 20 million acres by 1836. As in 1817 and 1818, Americans piled up debt on the assumption that the good times would never end. A banking crisis in 1837 painfully reintroduced economic reality.

Even as it expanded, the American economy had remained vulnerable to disruptions in the supply of foreign capital and the sale of agricultural exports that underpinned prosperity. The key foreign nation was Britain, a major source of credit and demand for exports. In late 1836, the Bank of England tightened its credit policies. Concerned with the large outflow of specie to the United States, it raised interest rates and reduced the credit lines of British merchants heavily involved in the American trade. Consequently, the British demand for cotton fell and with it the price of cotton (see Figure 10–1). Because cotton, as the leading export, was the main security for most loans issued by American banks and mercantile firms, its drop in value set off a chain reaction of contracting credit and falling prices. When panic-stricken investors rushed to the banks to redeem their notes in specie, the hard-pressed banks suspended specie payments.

The shock waves hit New Orleans in March 1837 and spread to the major New York banks by May. What began as a bank panic soon dragged down the entire economy. Bankruptcies multiplied, investment capital dried up, and business stagnated. State governments, which had borrowed lavishly in the heady optimism of the boom years to finance canals and other internal improvements, slashed their budgets and halted all construction projects. Nine states in the South and West defaulted (stopped making payments) on their bonds. Workers in the shoe, textile, mining, and construction indus-

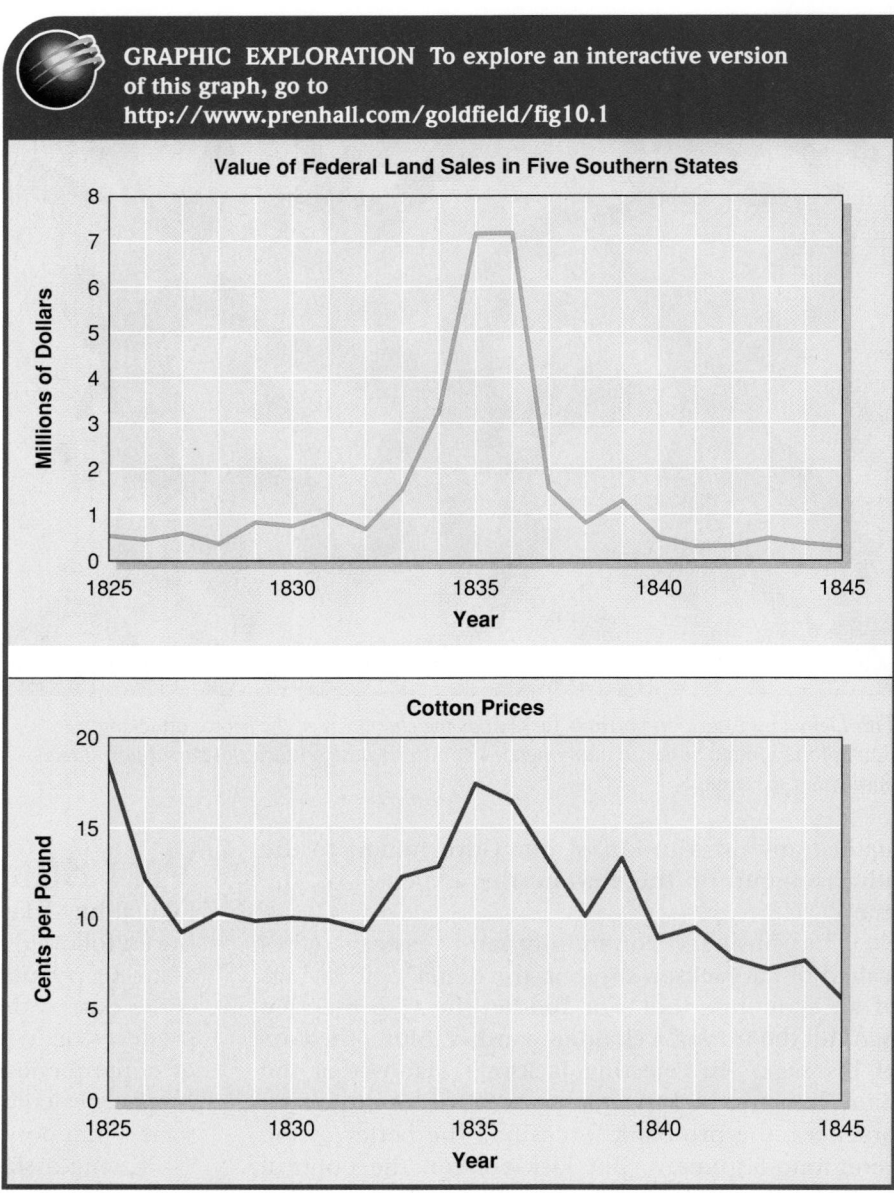

GRAPHIC EXPLORATION To explore an interactive version of this graph, go to http://www.prenhall.com/goldfield/fig10.1

FIGURE 10-1 Cotton Prices and the Value of Federal Land Sales in Five Southern States, 1825–1845
Because the U.S. economy was heavily dependent on cotton exports as a source of credit, the collapse of cotton prices—and a corresponding plunge in the sale of federal land after a speculative runup in the newer cotton regions of the South—triggered a financial panic in the late 1830s.
Data Source: Douglas C. North, *The Economic Growth of the United States, 1790–1860* (1966), tab. A-X, p. 257.

tries suddenly found themselves without jobs. As unemployment mounted and workers mobilized mass protest meetings in eastern cities, conservatives feared the worst. "Workmen thrown out of employ by the hundred daily," nervously noted a wealthy merchant in New York City in May 1837. He half expected that "we shall have a revolution here."

After a brief recovery in 1838, another round of credit contraction drove the economy into a depression that did not bottom out until 1843. In the manufacturing and commercial centers of the Northeast, unemployment reached an unheard-of 20 percent. The persistence of depressed agricultural prices meant that farmers and planters who had incurred debts in the 1830s faced the constant threat of losing their land or their slaves. Many fled west to avoid their creditors.

THE INDEPENDENT TREASURY

Although the Democrats bore no direct responsibility for the economic downturn, they could not avoid being blamed for it. Their political opponents, now coalescing as the **Whig party**, pointed to Jackson's destruction of the Bank of the United States, an act that, they claimed, had undermined business confidence. In their view, Jackson had then compounded his error by trying to force a hard-money policy on the state banks that had received federal deposits. The "pet banks" were required to replace small-denomination bank notes with coins or hard money. This measure, it was hoped, would protect the farmers and workers from being paid in depreciated bank notes.

Jackson had taken his boldest step against paper money when he issued the **Specie Circular** of 1836, which stipulated that large tracts of public land could be bought only with specie. Aimed at breaking the speculative spiral in land purchases, the Specie Circular is likely to have contributed to the Panic of 1837 by requiring the transfer of specie to the West for land transactions just when eastern banks were strapped for specie reserves to meet demands on their own bank notes. Bankers and speculators denounced Jackson for unwarranted government interference with the natural workings of the economy and blundering into a monetary disaster.

Conservative charges of Democratic irresponsibility were overblown, but the Democrats were caught on the horns of a dilemma. By dramatically politicizing the banking issue and removing federal monies from the national bank, the Democrats had in effect assumed the burden of protecting the people from the paper aristocrats in the banking and business commu-

Broken families and demoralized workers were among the litany of evils blamed on the Panic of 1837.

nity. Once they shifted treasury receipts to selected state banks, they had to try to regulate these banks. Otherwise they would be accused of creating a series of little "monsters" and feeding the paper speculation they so decried. But any regulatory policy contradicted the Democratic commitment to limiting governmental power. A restrictive policy, especially one aimed at replacing bank notes with specie, was bound to upset business interests and drive them out of the Democratic party. Worse yet, even the "pet banks" joined in the general suspension of specie payments when the Panic of 1837 hit. Thus the banks favored by the Democrats proved themselves unworthy of the people's trust.

The only way out of the dilemma was to make a clean break between the government and banking. Van Buren reestablished the Democrats' tarnished image as the party of limited government when he came out for the **Independent Treasury System**. Under this plan, the government would dispense with banks entirely. The Treasury would conduct its business only in gold and silver coin and would store its specie in regional vaults or subtreasuries. First proposed in 1837, the Independent Treasury System finally passed Congress in 1840 on the heels of a second wave of bank failures.

The Independent Treasury System made more political than economic sense. It restored the ideological purity of the Democrats as the friends of honest money, but it prolonged the depression. Specie locked up in government vaults was unavailable for loans in the private banking system that could have expanded the credit needed to revive the economy. The end result was to reduce the money supply and further depress prices.

UPROAR OVER SLAVERY

In 1831, William Lloyd Garrison of Boston inaugurated a radical new phase in northern attacks on slavery with the publication of his abolitionist paper *The Liberator*. The abolitionists embraced the doctrine of immediatism, an immediate moral commitment to begin the work of emancipation. Inspired by the wave of religious revivals sweeping the North in the late 1820s, they seized on slavery as the greatest sin of all. With the righteous wrath of evangelical ministers, they called on all Americans to recognize their Christian duty to end a system of human bondage that deprived the enslaved of their God-given right to be free moral beings. (For more on the abolitionists, see Chapter 11.)

The abolitionists touched off a political uproar when they launched a propaganda offensive in 1835. Taking advantage of technological improvements in the printing industry, they produced over a million pieces of antislavery literature, much of which was sent to the South through the U.S. mails. Alarmed white Southerners vilified the abolitionists as fanatics intent on enticing the slaves to revolt. Abolitionist tracts were burned, and, with the open approval of Jackson, southern postmasters violated federal law by censoring the mails to keep out antislavery materials.

Unable to receive an open hearing in the South, the abolitionists now focused on Congress. Beginning in 1836 and continuing through Van Buren's presidency, hundreds of thousands of antislavery petitions, some of them with thousands of signatures, flooded into Congress. Most of them called for the abolition of slavery in the District of Columbia. Southern congressmen responded by demanding that free speech be repressed in the name of southern white security. The enemy, they were convinced, was fanaticism, and nearly all agreed with Francis Pickens of South Carolina that they must "meet it and strangle it in its infancy." The strangling took the form of the **gag rule**, a procedural device whereby antislavery petitions were automatically tabled with no discussion.

The gag rule first passed in 1836 and was renewed in a series of raucous debates through 1844. Only the votes of some three-fourths of the northern Democrats enabled the southern minority to have its way. With Van Buren's reluctant support, the gag rule became a Democratic party measure, and it identified the Democrats as a prosouthern party in the minds of many Northerners. Ironically, while Van Buren was attacked in the North as a lackey of the slave interests, he was damned in the South, if only because he was a nonslaveholder from the North, as being unsafe on the slavery issue. In short, tensions over slavery and the economy seemingly doomed Van Buren to be cast as a vacillating president fully trusted by neither section.

THE RISE OF THE WHIG PARTY

The early opponents of the Democrats were known as the National Republicans, a label that captured the nationalist vision of former Jeffersonian Republicans who adhered to the economic program of Henry Clay and John Quincy Adams. The Bank War and Jackson's reaction to nullification shook loose pro-Bank Democrats and many southern states' righters from the original Jacksonian coalition, and these groups joined the opposition to Jackson. By 1834, the anti-Jacksonians started to call themselves Whigs, a name associated with the eighteenth-century American and

British opponents of monarchical tyranny. The name stuck because of the party's constant depiction of Jackson as King Andrew, an executive tyrant who ran roughshod over congressional prerogatives and constitutional liberties.

By 1840, the Whigs had mastered the techniques of political organization and mobilization pioneered by the Democrats in the late 1820s. They ran William Henry Harrison, their own version of a military hero, and swept to victory. The **second party system** of intense national competition between Whigs and Democrats was now in place (see the Overview table, "The Second Party System"). It would dominate politics until the rise of the antislavery Republican party in the 1850s.

THE PARTY TAKING SHAPE

The Whig party was born in the congressional reaction to Jackson's Bank veto and his subsequent attacks on the national bank. Led by the unlikely trio of Henry Clay and Daniel Webster, nationalists from the West and New England, and John C. Calhoun, a states' righter from the South, the congressional opposition accused Jackson of demagogic appeals to the poor against the rich. What upset them, apart from the specific content of Jackson's policies, was how he enforced his will. Jackson wielded his executive power like a bludgeon. Whereas all earlier presidents together had used the veto only ten times, Jackson did so a dozen times. He openly defied the Supreme Court and Congress, be it on Indian or banking policy, and unlike any of his predecessors, he took each case directly to the people. It seemed to his opponents that Jackson was threatening to undermine the constitutional system of checks and bal-

ances and bypass the established leadership of public-spirited gentlemen who had hitherto ruled on behalf of the people.

Local and state coalitions of the Whigs sent an anti-Jackson majority to the House of Representatives in 1835. The most powerful of these coalitions was in New York, where a third party, the **Anti-Masons**, joined the Whigs. The party had originated in western New York in the late 1820s as a grassroots response to the sudden disappearance and presumed murder of William Morgan, an itinerant artisan who threatened to expose the secrets of the Order of Freemasons. An all-male order steeped in ritual and ceremony, the Masons united urban and small-town elites into a tightly knit brotherhood through personal contacts and mutual aid. When efforts to investigate Morgan's disappearance ran into a legal dead end, rumors spread that the Masons constituted a vast conspiracy that conferred special privileges and legal protection on its exclusive members. To combat this "monster," farmers and townspeople flocked to the new Anti-Masonic party. They sought, in the words of an 1831 Anti-Masonic address, "equal rights and equal privileges among the freemen of the country."

Western New York, an area of religious fervor and rapid economic change after the opening of the Erie Canal in 1825, provided fertile ground for the growth of the new party. With close ties to rural landlords and town creditors, the Masons were vulnerable to the charge of economic favoritism. In addition, evangelicals accused the Masons of desecrating the Christian faith with their secret rituals. The Anti-Masons were thus the first party to combine demands for equal opportunity with calls for the moral reform of a sinful society.

Overview

The Second Party System

	Democrats	Whigs
Ideology	Favor limited role of federal government in economic affairs and in matters of individual conscience; support territorial expansion	Favor government support for economic development and controls over individual morality; opposed to expansion
Voter support	Mainly subsistence farmers, unskilled workers, and Catholic immigrants	Mainly manufacturers, commercial farmers, skilled workers, and northern evangelicals
Regional strength	South and West	New England and Upper Midwest

Although it spread into New England and the neighboring mid-Atlantic states, the Anti-Mason party was unable to sustain itself. Its presidential candidate in 1832, William Wirt of Maryland, won only Vermont. Recognizing that the opponents of the Anti-Masons were usually the entrenched local interests of the Democratic party, shrewd politicians, led by Thurlow Weed and William Seward of New York, took up the movement and absorbed most of it into the anti-Jackson coalition. They thus broadened the Whigs' mass base and added an egalitarian message to their appeal.

By 1836, the Whigs were strong enough to mount a serious challenge for the presidency. However, they still lacked an effective national organization that could unite their regional coalitions behind one candidate. They ran three candidates—Daniel Webster of Massachusetts, William Henry Harrison of Ohio, and Hugh Lawson White of Tennessee—and some Whigs hoped that the regional popularity of these candidates would siphon off enough votes from Van Buren to throw the election into the House of Representatives. The strategy, if such it can be called, failed. Van Buren won an electoral majority by holding on to the populous mid-Atlantic states and improving on Jackson's showing in New England. Still, the Whigs were encouraged by the results. Compared to Jackson, Van Buren did poorly in what had been the overwhelmingly Democratic South. He lost Tennessee and Georgia and barely carried the popular vote elsewhere. The South was now open to further Whig inroads.

WHIG PERSUASION

The Whigs, like the Democrats, based their mass appeal on the claim that they could best defend the republican liberties of the people. Whereas the Democrats attributed the threat to those liberties to privileged monopolies of government-granted power, the Whigs found it in the expansive powers of the presidency as wielded by Jackson and in the party organization that put Jackson and Van Buren into office. In 1836, the Whigs called for the election of "a president of the nation, not a president of party." Underlying this call was the persistent Whig belief that parties undermined individual liberties and the public good by fostering and rewarding the selfish interests of the party faithful. Although the Whigs dropped much of this ideology when they themselves matured as a party, they never lost their fear of the presidency as an office of unchecked, demagogic power. They always insisted that Congress should be the locus of power in the federal system.

If the Whigs were more reluctant than the Democrats to accept political change in the form of mass-based parties, they were quicker to embrace economic change in the form of banks and manufacturing corporations. Most Whigs viewed governmental power as a positive force to promote economic development. They favored encouraging the spread of banking and paper money, chartering corporations, passing protective tariffs to support American manufacturers, and opening up new markets for farmers through government-subsidized transportation projects. Such policies, they held, would widen economic opportunities for more and more Americans and provide positive incentives for material self-improvement.

The Whigs' economic program appealed mostly to Americans who were benefiting from economic change or expecting to do so. They drew heavily from commercial and planting interests in the South. They were also the party of bankers, manufacturers, small-town entrepreneurs, farmers prospering from the market outlets of canals and railroads, and skilled workers who valued a high tariff as protection from the competition of goods produced by cheap foreign labor. These Whig groups also tended to be native-born Protestants of New England or Yankee ancestry, particularly those caught up in the religious revivals of the 1820s and 1830s. The strongest Whig constituencies comprised an arc of Yankee settlements stretching from rural New England through central New York and around the southern shores of the Great Lakes.

Whether as economic promoters or evangelical reformers, Whigs believed in promoting social progress and harmony through an interventionist government. The Whigs favored such social reforms as prohibiting the consumption of alcohol; preserving the sanctity of the Protestant Sabbath through bans on business activities on Sundays; caring for orphans, the physically handicapped, and the mentally ill in state-run asylums and hospitals; and teaching virtuous behavior and basic knowledge through a centralized system of public education. Whig ideology blended economic, social, and spiritual reform into a unified message of uplift. An activist government would provide the economic opportunities and moral guidance for a harmonious, progressive society of freely competing individuals whose behavior would be shaped by the evangelical norms of thrift, sobriety, and self-discipline.

Much of the Whigs' reform impulse was directed against non-English and Catholic immigrants, those Americans whom the Whigs believed most needed to be taught the virtues of self-control and disciplined work habits. Not coincidentally, these groups—the Scots-Irish in the backcountry, the Reformed Dutch,

This cotton banner used by the Whigs in the campaign of 1840 celebrated their ticket as the friends of common Americans who had been raised in a log cabin.

and Irish and German Catholics—were the most loyal Democrats. They resented the aggressive moralism of the Whigs and the legislative attempts to interfere with their drinking habits and Sunday amusements. These Democrats were typically subsistence farmers on the periphery of market change and unskilled workers forced by industrial change to abandon their hopes of ever opening their own shops. They equated an activist government with special privileges for the economically and culturally powerful and identified with the Democrats' demand for keeping the government out of the economy and individual religious practices.

THE ELECTION OF 1840

One of the signs of the Whigs' maturing as a party was their decision in 1840 to place victory above principle. Because of the lingering economic depression, Democratic rule had been discredited for many voters. Aside from the Independent Treasury Act and legislation establishing a ten-hour workday for federal employees, the Van Buren administration had no program to combat the Whig charge of helplessness in the face of economic adversity. Henry Clay, who promised that his American System would revive the economy with government aid, appeared the most

likely Whig candidate for president against Van Buren in 1840. Yet the power brokers in the party dumped Clay, who represented the ideological heart of the party, for their version of a popular military hero, William Henry Harrison of Ohio.

Harrison had run surprisingly well as one of the Whigs' regional candidates in 1836 and had revealed a common touch with the voters that the Whigs generally lacked. Unlike Clay, he was untainted by any association with the Bank of the United States, the Masonic Order, or slaveholding. As the victor at the Battle of Tippecanoe and a military hero in the War of 1812, he enabled Whig image makers to cast him, like Jackson, as the honest, patriotic soldier worthy of the people's trust. In a decision that came back to haunt them, the Whigs geographically balanced their ticket by selecting John Tyler, a planter from Virginia, as Harrison's running mate. Tyler was an advocate of states' rights and a former Democrat who had broken with Jackson over the Force Bill.

The Democrats inadvertently gave the Whig campaign a tremendous boost. A Democratic editor wisecracked that "Old Granny" Harrison (he was 67) was such a simpleton that he would like nothing better than to retire to a log cabin with a government pension and a barrel of hard cider. Pouncing on this sneer, the Whigs created a Harrison who never was—a yeoman farmer of humble origins and homespun tastes, whose rise to prominence was a democratic model of success for other Americans to follow. Thus Harrison, who was descended from the Virginia slaveholding aristocracy, became a symbol of the common man, and the Whigs were finally able to shed their aristocratic image. Indeed, they pinned the label of the dandified and elitist aristocrat on Van Buren. "Martin Van Ruin," as effectively portrayed by the Whigs, squandered public revenue on effete luxuries and was concerned only with the spoils of office.

The Whigs beat the Democrats at their own game of mass politics in 1840. They reversed the roles and symbolism of the Jackson–Adams election of 1828 and seized the high ground as the party of the people. In a further adaptation of earlier Democratic initiatives, the Whigs put together a frolicking campaign of slogans, parades, and pageantry. Politics became a carnival in which voters were shamelessly wooed with food, drink, and music in huge rallies complete with live animals and gigantic buckskin balls that were triumphantly rolled from one rally to another. Clay muttered with some disgust that he regretted the need "of appealing to the feelings and passions of our Countrymen, rather than to their reasons and their judgments." Nonetheless, such hoopla was now essential for electoral victory.

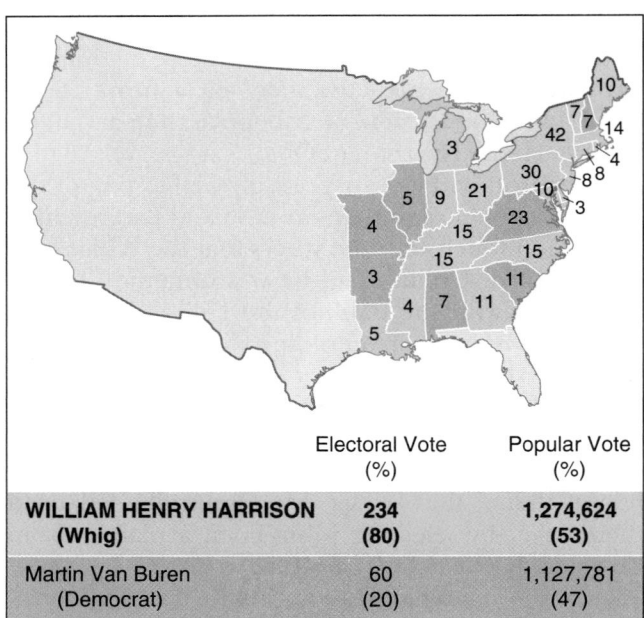

MAP 10-4 The Election of 1840
Building upon their strength in the commercializing North, the Whigs attracted enough rural voters in the South and West to win the election of 1840.

	Electoral Vote (%)	Popular Vote (%)
WILLIAM HENRY HARRISON (Whig)	**234 (80)**	**1,274,624 (53)**
Martin Van Buren (Democrat)	60 (20)	1,127,781 (47)

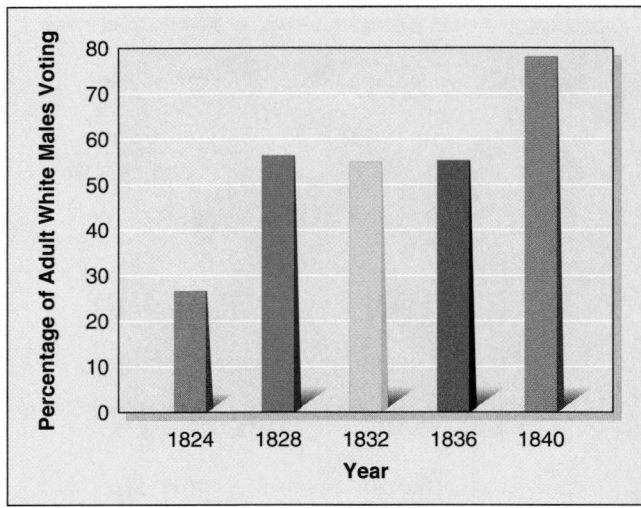

FIGURE 10-2 Voter Turnout in Presidential Elections, 1824–1840
The creation of mass-based political parties dramatically increased voter turnout in presidential elections. Voting surged in 1828 with the emergence of the Jacksonian Democratic Party and again in 1840 when the Whig Party learned to appeal to the mass electorate.

Data Source: Richard P. McCormick, "New Perspectives on Jacksonian Politics" in *The Nature of Jacksonian America*, ed. Douglas T. Miller (1972), p. 103.

The Whigs gained control of both Congress and the presidency in 1840. Harrison won 53 percent of the popular vote, and for the first time the Whigs carried the South (see Map 10–4). With the arrival of politics as mass spectacle, the turnout surged to an unprecedented 78 percent of eligible voters, a whopping increase over the average of 55 percent in the three preceding presidential elections (see Figure 10–2). The Whigs claimed most of the new voters and were now fully competitive with the Democrats in all parts of the nation. As the new majority party, they finally had the opportunity, or so they thought, to implement their economic program.

THE WHIGS IN POWER

Although the Whigs had been noncommittal on their plans during the campaign of 1840, it was common knowledge that Clay would move quickly on Whig economic policies by marshaling his forces in Congress and trying to dominate a pliant Harrison. But Harrison died from pneumonia in April 1841, barely a month after his inauguration, ruining Clay's plans. Tyler, Harrison's successor, was a particularly rigid states'-rights ideologue, who betrayed party expectations by blocking key pieces of Clay's program. The Whigs reacted by reading Tyler out of the party.

In 1843, Tyler latched on to the annexation of the slaveholding Republic of Texas as an issue that might get him back into the good graces of the Democratic party and establish his own successful record as president. At the end of his administration, Tyler did succeed in securing the annexation of Texas, but his main accomplishment was to shift the focus of national politics from economic issues to sectional ones of territorial expansion. Running on an expansionist platform, the Democrats regained the presidency in 1844.

HARRISON AND TYLER

Perhaps the Democrats had been right that Harrison was too old for the demands of the presidency. He fumed that "I am bothered almost to death with visitors. I have not time to attend to my person, not even to change my shirt, much less to attend to the public business." Still, for all his grumblings, he was the type of president the Whigs wanted. He had pledged to follow the dictates of party leaders in Congress and defer to the judgment of his cabinet. Bowing to Clay's demands, he agreed to call Congress into special session to act on Whig party measures. Thus his death was a real blow to Whig hopes of establishing the credibility of their party as an effective agent for positive change.

Just how serious that blow was soon became apparent when Tyler became president, the first vice president to succeed on the death of a president. Tyler was cut from quite different cloth from Harrison. This stiff, unbending planter subscribed to a states'-rights agrarian philosophy that put him at odds with the urban and commercial elements of the Whig party even in his home state of Virginia. Clay's economic nationalism struck him as a program of rank corruption that surrendered the constitutional rights of the South to power-hungry politicians and manufacturers in the North. Clay refused to cultivate Tyler's prickly pride with soothing gestures, and he forged ahead with the party agenda—the repeal of the Independent Treasury System and its replacement by a new national bank, a protective tariff, and the distribution of the proceeds of the government's public land sales to the states as funds for internal improvements.

A Democratic observer predicted in mid-May 1841 that "the Whigs will be very much disappointed by the course which the President will feel himself constitutionally bound to pursue." Tyler used the negative power of presidential vetoes to stymie the Whig program. He twice vetoed bills to reestablish a national bank. The second veto led to the resignation of the cabinet he had inherited from Harrison, save for Secretary of State Daniel Webster, who was in the midst of negotiations with the British. Enraged congressional Whigs then expelled Tyler from the party.

A now desperate Clay sought to salvage what was left of his American System. He lined up southern votes for the distribution of federal funds to the states by agreeing to a ceiling of 20 percent on tariff rates. Westerners were won over by Clay's support for the Preemption Act of 1841, a measure that allowed squatters to purchase up to 160 acres of public land at the minimum government price of $1.25 per acre. This act was popular in the West because squatters no longer had to match the bids of speculators at government land sales.

Clay's legislative wizardry got him nowhere. When the Whigs passed a higher tariff in 1842 with a provision for distribution, Tyler vetoed it and forced them to settle for a protective tariff with no distribution. In the end, Clay had no national bank, no funds for internal improvements, and only a slightly higher tariff. Although Clay's leadership of the Whigs was strengthened, Tyler had deprived that leadership of meaning by denying the Whigs the legislative fruits of their victory in 1840.

THE TEXAS ISSUE

Constrained by his states'-rights view to a largely negative role in domestic policy, Tyler was a much more forceful president in foreign policy, an area in which the Constitution gives the chief executive considerable latitude. In 1842, Tyler's secretary of state, Daniel Webster, wrapped up his negotiations with the British over a long-standing boundary dispute. The **Webster–Ashburton Treaty** of that year established the boundary between British Canada and Maine and parts of the Upper Midwest. An agreement was also reached to cooperate in suppressing the African slave trade. Webster now resigned from the cabinet to join his fellow Whigs, allowing Tyler to follow a pro-southern policy of expansion that he hoped would gain him the Democratic nomination for the presidency in 1844. His goal was the annexation of Texas.

Texas had been a slaveholding republic since 1836, when rebellious Americans, joined by some tejanos (Texans of Mexican descent), declared their independence from Mexico. Jackson extended diplomatic recognition before leaving office, but he refused the new nation's request to be annexed to the United States out of fear of provoking a war with Mexico, which did not recognize Texan independence. But he was also aware that the addition of Texas, a potentially huge area for the expansion of plantation slavery, would inflame sectional tensions and endanger Van Buren's chances in the upcoming presidential election. In private, however, he urged Texans to seize harbors on the Pacific Coast from Mexican control and thus make annexation more attractive to the commercial interests of the Northeast.

For the sake of sectional harmony, party leaders sidestepped the Texas issue after 1836. Spurned by the Whigs and anxious to return to the Democrats, Tyler renewed the issue in 1843 to curry favor among southern and western Democrats. He replaced Webster as secretary of state with a proannexationist Virginian, Abel P. Upshur, and secretly opened negotiations with the Texans. After Upshur's death in an accidental explosion on the battleship *Princeton,* John C. Calhoun, his successor, completed the negotiations and dramatically politicized the slavery issue. In the spring of 1844, Calhoun and Tyler submitted to the Senate a secretly drawn up treaty annexing Texas to the United States. Calhoun also made public his correspondence with Richard Pakenham, the British minister in Washington. In his letter, Calhoun accused the British of seeking to force emancipation on Texas in return for economic aid and a British-brokered Mexican recognition of Texan independence. These British efforts, warned Calhoun, were just the opening wedge in a master plan to block American expansion and destroy slavery in the South. After pointedly defending slavery as a benign institution, Calhoun concluded that the security and preservation of the Union demanded the annexation of Texas.

The Pakenham letter hit the Senate like a bombshell, convincing antislavery Northerners that the annexation of Texas was a slaveholders' conspiracy to extend slavery and swell the political power of the South. In June 1844, the Senate rejected Calhoun's treaty of annexation by a two-to-one margin. All but one Whig senator voted against it. Still, the issue was hardly dead. Thanks to Tyler and Calhoun, Texas dominated the election of 1844.

THE ELECTION OF 1844

The Whig and Democratic National Conventions met in the spring of 1844 in the midst of the uproar over Texas. Both Clay, who had the Whig nomination locked up, and Van Buren, who was the strong favorite for the Democratic one, came out against immediate annexation. Clay's stand was consistent with Whig fears that territorial expansion would disrupt the party's plans for ordered economic development. But Van Buren's anti-Texas stand cost him his party's nomination. In a carefully devised strategy, western and southern Democrats united to deny him the necessary two-thirds vote of convention delegates. A deadlocked convention turned to James K. Polk of Tennessee, a confirmed expansionist who had the blessing of Jackson, the party's patriarch.

To counter the charge that they were a prosouthern party, the Democrats ran in 1844 on a platform that linked Oregon to Texas as territorial objectives. Oregon had first attracted public attention during the Tyler presidency. Glowing reports from Protestant missionaries of the boundless fertility of Oregon's Willamette Valley triggered a migration to the new promised land on the shores of the Pacific by midwestern farm families still reeling from the Panic of 1837. At the same time, the report of a naval expedition sent to explore the Pacific aroused the interest of New England merchants in using Oregon as a jumping-off point for expanded trade with China.

Some six thousand Americans were in Oregon by the mid-1840s, and demands mounted, especially from northern Democrats, that the United States abandon its 1818 agreement of joint occupation with the British and lay exclusive claim to Oregon as far north as the 54°40' parallel, the border with Russian-owned Alaska. These were bold, even reckless, demands, because the actual area of American settlement in Oregon was south of the Columbia River, itself well south of even the 49th parallel. Nonetheless, the Polk Democrats seemed to endorse them when they asserted an American claim "to the whole of the Territory of Oregon."

Polk's expansionist program united the Democrats and enabled them to campaign with much more enthusiasm than in 1840. Acquiring Texas and Oregon not only held out the economic hope of cheap, abundant land to debt-burdened farmers in the North and planters in the South but also played on the anti-British sentiments of many voters. In contrast, the Whig campaign was out of focus. Clay sensed that his opposition to the immediate annexation of Texas was hurting him in the South, and he started to hedge by saying that he would accept Texas if the conditions were right. This wavering, however, failed to stem the defection of proslavery southern Whigs to the Democrats and cut into his support among antislavery Whigs in the North. Clay lost to Polk by less than 2 percent of the popular vote.

Tyler claimed Polk's victory as a mandate for the immediate annexation of Texas. He knew that it would still be impossible to gain the two-thirds majority in the Senate necessary for the approval of a treaty. Thus he resorted to the constitutionally unprecedented expedient of a joint resolution in Congress inviting Texas to join the Union. By the narrow margin of twenty-seven to twenty-five, the Senate concurred with the House in favor of annexation. Tyler signed the joint resolution on March 1, 1845.

Although Tyler had failed to secure the Democratic nomination in 1844, he had gained Texas. He also had the satisfaction of getting revenge against the Whigs, the party that had disowned him. Texas, more than any other issue, defeated Clay and the Whigs in 1844.

CONCLUSION

The Jacksonian era ushered in a revolution in American political life. Responding to a surge of democratization that was in full swing by the 1820s, politicians learned how to appeal to a mass electorate and to build disciplined parties that channeled popular desires into distinctive party positions. In the two decades after 1824, voter participation in national elections tripled, and Democrats and Whigs competed on nearly equal terms in every region.

Although the origins of a national political culture can be traced back to the Federalists and Jeffersonian Republicans, politics did not fully enter the mainstream of American life until the rise of the second party system of Democrats and Whigs. The election of 1824 revived interest in presidential politics, and Jackson's forceful style of leadership highlighted the presidency as the focal point of American politics. Professional politicians soon mastered the art of tailoring issues and images to reach the widest popular audience. Voters in favor of government aid for economic development and a social order based on Protestant moral controls turned to the Whigs' program of economic and moral activism. Conversely, those who saw an activist government as a threat to their economic and cultural equality turned to the Democrats.

The national issues around which the Democrats and Whigs organized and battled down to 1844 were primarily economic. As long as this was the case, party competition tended to diffuse sectional tensions and strengthen a national political culture. Slavery, in the form of the Texas question, replaced the economy as the decisive issue in the election of 1844. With this shift, party appeals began to focus on the place of slavery in American society, creating an escalating politics of sectionalism. Within a decade, the slavery issue would rip apart the second party system.

REVIEW QUESTIONS

1. Explain the democratic movements of the early nineteenth century. What role did race and gender play in these movements?

2. What distinguished Jackson's presidency from those of his predecessors? How did he redefine the role of the president?

3. How was the Bank War central to the development of the Democratic and Whig parties? Why did the political debates of the 1830s focus on financial issues?

4. In terms of ideology and voter appeal, how did the Democrats and Whigs differ? How did each party represent a distinctive response to economic and social change?

5. How would you describe the changes in American politics between 1824 and 1840? What accounted for these changes?

6. How did the annexation of Texas emerge as a political issue in the early 1840s? Why were the Democrats more in favor of territorial expansion than the Whigs?

7. What do you think accounted for the sense of shock, even outrage, with which Benjamin Brown French reacted to the partisanship of the election of 1828?

KEY TERMS

Abolitionist movement (p. 309)

Albany Regency (p. 300)

Anti-Masons (p. 313)

Bank War (p. 301)

Black Hawk's War (p. 304)

Democratic Party (p. 299)

Gag rule (p. 312)

Independent Treasury System (p. 312)

Indian Removal Act (p. 303)

Jacksonian Democrats (p. 295)

Nullification crisis (p. 301)

Second Great Awakening (p. 297)

Second party system (p. 313)

Specie Circular (p. 311)

Spoils system (p. 302)

Trail of Tears (p. 304)

Webster-Ashburton Treaty (p. 317)

Whig party (p. 311)

RECOMMENDED READING

Altschuler, Glenn C., and Stuart M. Blumin. *Rude Republic: Americans and their Politics in the Nineteenth Century* (2000). A recent work that argues that historians have exaggerated the extent of popular involvement in the party politics of the nineteenth century.

Cole, Donald B. *The Presidency of Andrew Jackson* (1993). A revisionist look at Jackson's presidency that argues that he was an uncertain leader who failed in his efforts to resist the spread of the market revolution that was transforming America.

Feller, Daniel. *The Jacksonian Promise: America, 1815–1840* (1995). An up-to-date survey that emphasizes the optimism and innovation of the Jacksonian era.

Meyers, Marvin. *The Jacksonian Persuasion* (1960). A gracefully written work that explores the beliefs of the Jacksonians and concludes that their agrarian values made them fearful of economic change.

Pessen, Edward. *Jacksonian America* (1985). A revisionist work that argues that Democrats and Whigs, for all their talk of democratic change, were driven primarily by the goal of acquiring office as an end in itself.

Remini, Robert V. *The Life of Andrew Jackson* (1988). A lively account of Jackson's career, written by his most noted biographer.

Schlesinger, Arthur Jr. *The Age of Jackson* (1945). Remains the enduring statement of the democratic impulse behind the Jackson movement.

Sellers, Charles. *The Market Revolution: Jacksonian America, 1815–1846* (1991). A boldly conceived work that places responses to market change at the center of the era's political development.

de Tocqueville, Alexis. *Democracy in America,* ed. Phillips Bradley, 2 vols. (1945). An often quoted classic, still popular for its firsthand depiction of Jacksonian society and institutions.

Varon, Elizabeth R. *We Mean To Be Counted: White Women and Politics in Antebellum Virginia* (1998). A recent work that reveals the surprising extent to which elite white women in Virginia engaged in partisan politics.

Watson, Harry. *Liberty and Power: The Politics of Jacksonian America* (1990). A very readable and concise synthesis of Jacksonian politics.

ADDITIONAL SOURCES

The Egalitarian Impulse

Butler, Jon. *Awash in a Sea of Faith: Christianizing the American People* (1990).

Hargreaves, Mary W. M. *The Presidency of John Quincy Adams* (1985).

Hatch, Nathan O. *The Democratization of American Christianity* (1989).

Peterson, Merrill D., ed. *Democracy, Liberty, and Property: The State Constitutional Conventions of the 1820s* (1966).

Williamson, Chilton. *American Suffrage from Property to Democracy, 1760–1860* (1960).

Jackson's Presidency

Debo, Angie. *And Still the Waters Run: The Betrayal of the Five Civilized Tribes* (1940; reprint, 1972).

Ellis, Richard E. *The Union at Risk: Jacksonian Democracy, States' Rights, and the Nullification Crisis* (1987).

Freehling, William W. *Prelude to Civil War: The Nullification Controversy in South Carolina, 1816–1836* (1966).

Remini, Robert V. *Andrew Jackson and the Bank War* (1967).

Rogin, Michael Paul. *Fathers and Children: Andrew Jackson and the Subjugation of the American Indian* (1975).

Ward, John William. *Andrew Jackson: Symbol for an Age* (1955).

Van Buren and Hard Times

McFaul, John M. *The Politics of Jacksonian Finance* (1972).

McGrane, Reginald Charles. *The Panic of 1837* (1924).

Sharp, Roger. *The Jacksonians versus the Banks: Politics in the States after the Panic of 1837* (1970).

Temin, Peter. *The Jacksonian Economy* (1969).

Wilson, Major L. *The Presidency of Martin Van Buren* (1984).

The Rise of the Whig Party

Ashworth, John. *"Agrarians" and "Aristocrats": Party Political Ideology in the United States, 1837–1846* (1983).

Howe, Daniel Walker. *The Political Culture of the American Whigs* (1979).

Kohl, Lawrence Frederick. *The Politics of Individualism: Parties and the American Character in the Jacksonian Era* (1989).

McCormick, Richard P. *The Second American Party System* (1966).

Peterson, Merrill. *The Great Triumvirate: Webster, Clay, and Calhoun* (1987).

The Whigs in Power

Brock, William R. *Parties and Political Conscience* (1979).

Holt, Michael F. *The Rise and Fall of the American Whig Party* (1999).

Merk, Frederick. *Slavery and the Annexation of Texas* (1972).

Peterson, Norma Louis. *The Presidencies of William Henry Harrison and John Tyler* (1990).

Remini, Robert V. *Henry Clay: Statesman for the Union* (1991).

WHERE TO LEARN MORE

● Rice Museum, Georgetown, South Carolina. Rice planters were the leaders of the nullification movement, and the interpretive materials here on the history of rice cultivation help one understand how slave labor was employed to produce their great wealth. Maps to the museum and news of special events can be found at www.ricemuseum.com/.

- The Hermitage, Hermitage, Tennessee. This site, the plantation home of Andrew Jackson, includes a museum with artifacts of Jackson's life. Its website www.thehermitage.com/ lists events and programs and examines the archeological projects undertaken at the Hermitage.

- Martin Van Buren National Historic Site, Kinderhook, New York. The site preserves Lindenwald, Van Buren's home after he left the presidency, and includes a library with materials on Van Buren and his political era. Its recently expanded website www.nps.gov/mava/home.htm discusses the history of Lindenwald and includes a virtual tour of its art collection.

 Please refer to the document CD-ROM for primary sources related to this chapter.

→ *The spectacle of the slave market was commonplace in the cities of the antebellum South. The above scene is of a slave auction in Richmond, Virginia.*

SLAVERY AND THE OLD SOUTH
1800–1860

11

Had Mrs Wheeler condemned me to the severest corporal punishment, or exposed me to be sold in the public slave market in Wilmington[N.C.]I should probably have resigned myself with apparent composure to her cruel behests. But when she sought to force me into a compulsory union with a man whom I could only hate and despise it seemed that rebellion would be a virtue, that duty to myself and my God actually required it, and that whatever accidents or misfortunes might attend my flight nothing could be worse than what threatened my stay.

Marriage like many other blessings I considered to be especially designed for the free, and something that all the victims of slavery should avoid as tending essentially to perpetuate that system. Hence to all overtures of that kind from whatever quarter they might come I had invariably turned a deaf ear. I had spurned domestic ties not because my heart was hard, but because it was my unalterable resolution never to entail slavery on any human being. And now when I had voluntarily renounced the society of those I might have learned to love should I be compelled to accept one, whose person, and speech, and manner could not fail to be ever regarded by me with loathing and disgust. Then to be driven in to the fields beneath the eye and lash of the brutal overseer, and those miserable huts, with their promiscuous crowds of dirty, obscene and degraded objects, for my home I could not, I would not bear it.

Hannah Crafts

Henry Louis Gates, Jr., ed., *The Bondwoman's Narrative* (New York: Warner Books, 2002), pp. 206–207.

CHAPTER OUTLINE

The Lower South
Cotton and Slaves
The Profits of Slavery

The Upper South
A Period of Economic Adjustment
The Decline of Slavery

Slave Life and Culture
Work Routines and Living Conditions
Families and Religion
Resistance

Free Society
The Slaveholding Minority
The White Majority
Free Black People

The Proslavery Argument

Conclusion

Hannah Crafts was the name adopted by an African American woman after escaping from slavery in the late 1850s. This passage is from *The Bondwoman's Narrative,* a recently discovered manuscript that stands as the only known novel written by a female black slave. Although the precise identity of Crafts remains uncertain, the evidence strongly suggests that she was a house slave of John Hill Wheeler of North Carolina who fled north in the spring of 1857, married a Methodist clergyman, and merged into the black middle class of southern New Jersey. As a fugitive slave in the North, Crafts risked recapture at any time prior to the outbreak of the Civil War. Her decision not to publish her autobiographical slave narrative might well have been based on the fear that the intimate details she included on the Wheeler family would reveal her whereabouts to an owner intent on reclaiming her. Among the other details in the novel are the searingly candid observations on the brutalized living conditions that field slaves were forced to endure.

Knowing from firsthand experience that masters frequently violated the sanctity of slave marriages and, under the law, could keep any resulting children as slaves, she believed that all slaves should remain celibate: "plain, practical common sense must teach every observer that any situation involving such responsibilities as marriage can only be filled with profit, and honor, and advantage by the free." Triggering her decision to flee was Mrs. Wheeler's demand that she "marry" the field hand Bill—that is, submit to being raped by a man she despised and to living in the squalor of the huts in the slave quarter.

The system of slavery that Crafts described with revulsion increasingly defined the South as a distinctive region in the antebellum United States. Indeed, only the widespread presence of slaves makes it possible to speak of the South as a single region despite its geographical and cultural diversity. It was black slavery that created a bond among white Southerners and cast them in a common mold.

Not only did slavery make the South distinctive, it was also the source of the region's immense agricultural wealth, the foundation on which planters built their fortunes, the basis for white upward mobility, and the means by which white people controlled a large black minority. Slavery also frightened white Southerners with a vision of what might happen to them should they not protect their own personal liberties, including, paradoxically, the liberty to enslave African Americans. Southern white men were thus quick to take offense at any challenge to their honor or independence. A code of honor for planters demanded an apology or vindication in a duel for any insult, whether real or perceived. Precisely because slavery was so deeply embedded in southern life and customs, white leadership reacted to mounting attacks on slavery after 1830 with an ever more defiant defense of the institution. That defense, in turn, reinforced a growing sense of sectionalism among white Southerners, the belief that their values divided them from their fellow citizens in the Union.

Economically and intellectually, the Old South developed in stages. The South of 1860 was geographically much larger and more diverse than it had been in 1800, but it was also more uniformly committed to a single cash crop, cotton. Demand for cotton had exploded as the industrial revolution made the mass production of textiles possible. New England mill owners were now as dependent on slavery as southern planters were. Cotton became king, as contemporaries put it, and it provided the economic basis for southern sectionalism. During the reign of King Cotton, however, regional differences emerged between the Lower South, where the linkage between cotton and slavery was strong, and the Upper South, where slavery was relatively less important and the economy was more diversified.

KEY TOPICS

- How the increasing demand for cotton made slavery highly profitable in the Lower South

- The decline of slavery after 1800 in the increasingly diversified economy of the Upper South

- Slave culture and slave resistance

- The divisions of free white society

- The southern defense of slavery in response to increasing attacks from northern abolitionists

Chronology

1790s	Large-scale conversions of slaves to Christianity begin.
1793	Eli Whitney patents the cotton gin.
1800	Gabriel Prosser leads a rebellion in Richmond, Virginia.
1808	Congress prohibits the African slave trade.
1811	Slaves rebel in Louisiana.
1816–1819	First cotton boom in the South.
1822	Denmark Vesey's Conspiracy fails in Charleston, South Carolina.
1831	Nat Turner leads a rebellion in Southampton County, Virginia.
1831–1832	Virginia legislature debates and rejects gradual emancipation.
1832	Thomas R. Dew publishes the first full-scale defense of slavery.
1837–1845	Slavery issue divides Presbyterians, Methodists, and Baptists into separate sectional churches.
1845	Florida and Texas, the last two slave states, are admitted to the Union.
1850s	Cotton production doubles.
1857	Hinton R. Helper publishes *The Impending Crisis of the South*.

THE LOWER SOUTH

South and west of South Carolina in 1800 stretched some of the best cotton land in the world. A long growing season, adequate rainfall, navigable rivers, and untapped fertility gave the Lower South—consisting, in 1850, of South Carolina, Georgia, Florida, Alabama, Mississippi, Louisiana, and Texas—incomparable natural advantages for growing cotton. Ambitious white Southerners exploited these advantages by extending slavery after 1800 to the newer cotton lands that opened up in the Lower South (see Map 11–1). Cotton production and slavery thus went hand in hand.

COTTON AND SLAVES

Before 1800, slavery was associated with the cash crops of tobacco, rice, and Sea Island (or long-staple) cotton. Tobacco, the mainstay of the colonial Chesapeake economy, severely depleted the soil. Its production had stagnated after the Revolutionary War, when it lost its formerly protected markets in Britain.

Rice and long-staple cotton—named for its long, silky fibers—were profitable but geographically limited to the humid sea islands and tidal flats off the coast of South Carolina and Georgia. Like sugar cane, introduced into Louisiana in the 1790s, they required a huge capital investment in special machinery, dikes, and labor.

Upland, or short-staple, cotton faced none of these constraints, once the cotton gin removed the technical barrier to its commercial production. It could be planted far inland, and small farmers could grow it profitably because it required no additional costs for machinery or drainage systems.

As a result, after the 1790s, the production of short-staple cotton boomed. Moreover, like the South's other cash crops, upland cotton was well suited for slave labor because it required fairly continuous tending throughout most of the year. Once the harvest was in—a time when northern agricultural workers were laid off—the slaves cleared land, cut wood, and made repairs. The long work year maximized the return on capital invested in slave labor.

Despite the care required, the cultivation of cotton left plenty of time for slaves to grow food. The major grain in the southern diet was corn, which nicely complemented the labor cycle of cotton. Corn needed little attention while cotton was being harvested and could be planted earlier or later than cotton during the long growing season. Surplus corn could be fed to hogs and converted into pork. Because almost all cotton farms and plantations also raised corn and hogs, the South virtually fed itself.

The linkage of cotton and slaves was at the heart of the plantation system that spread westward after the War of 1812. From its original base in South Carolina and Georgia, the cotton kingdom moved into the Old Southwest and then into Texas and Arkansas. As wasteful agricultural practices exhausted new lands, planters moved to the next cotton frontier farther west. Cotton output exploded from 73,000 bales (each bale weighed close to 500 pounds) in 1800 to more than 2 million bales by midcentury, thanks to the fertility of virgin land and technological changes, such as improved seed varieties and steam-powered cotton gins (see Figure 11-1). Slave labor accounted for more than 90 percent of cotton production.

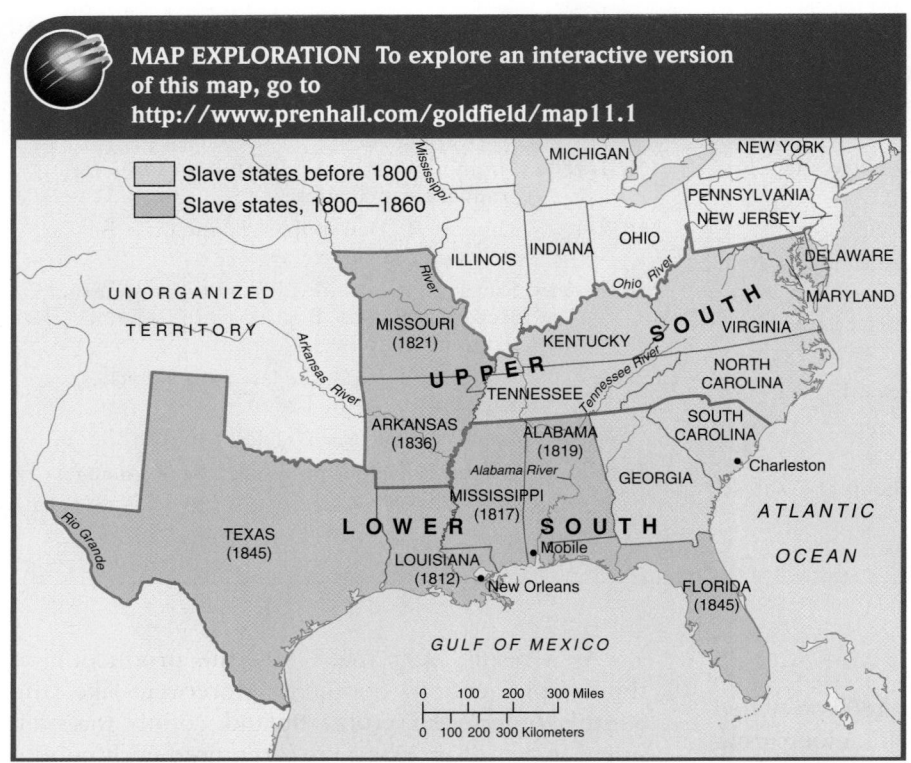

MAP EXPLORATION To explore an interactive version of this map, go to http://www.prenhall.com/goldfield/map11.1

MAP 11-1 The Spread of Slavery: New Slave States Entering the Union, 1800-1850. *Seven slave states entered the Union after 1800 as cotton production shifted westward.*

Plantations, large productive units specializing in a cash crop and employing at least twenty slaves, were the leading economic institution in the Lower South. Planters were the most prestigious social group, and, though less than 5 percent of white families were in the planter class, they controlled more than 40 percent of the slaves, cotton output, and total agricultural wealth. Most had inherited or married into their wealth, but they could stay at the top of the South's class structure only by continuing to profit from slave labor.

Plantations were generally more efficient producers of cotton than were small farms. Planters had the best land because only they commanded the labor resources to exploit the wet bottomlands, drain the swamps, or clear the raw jungle in the Mississippi Delta. They were also more likely than farmers to belong to agricultural reform societies that made them aware of superior varieties of seed and the most progressive techniques of cultivation. Most important, the ownership of twenty or more slaves enabled planters to use gangs to do both routine and specialized agricultural work. This **gang system**, a cruder version of the division of labor that was being introduced in northern factories, permitted a regimented pace of work that would have been impossible to impose on free

agricultural workers. Teams of field hands, made up of women as well as men, had to work at a steady pace or else feel the lash. They were supervised by white overseers and black drivers, slaves selected for their management skills and agricultural knowledge.

By 1850, the plantations of the Lower South were larger and more specialized than was the case elsewhere in the South, and the wealth of their owners was more ostentatiously displayed. More clusters of slave cabins, overseers' quarters, and cotton gins dotted the countryside. The few towns were little more than a haphazard collection of plain wooden houses scattered around a tavern, country store, and blacksmith's shop. "During two days' sail on the Alabama River from Mobile to Montgomery," noted a traveler in 1860, "I did not see so many houses standing together in any one spot as could be dignified with the appellation of village."

The plantation districts of the Lower South stifled the growth of towns and the economic enterprise they fostered. Planters, as well as ordinary farmers, strove to be self-sufficient. The most significant economic exchange—exporting cotton—took place in international markets and was handled by specialized commission merchants in Charleston, Mobile, and New Orleans. The Lower South had amassed great wealth, but most outsiders saw no signs of progress there.

THE PROFITS OF SLAVERY

Slavery was profitable on an individual basis. Most modern studies indicate that the average rate of return on capital invested in a slave was about 10 percent a year, a rate that at least equaled what was available in alternative investments in the South or the North. Not surprisingly, the newer regions of the cotton kingdom in the Lower South, with the most productive land and the greatest commitment to plantation agriculture, consistently led the nation in per capita income.

The profitability of slavery ultimately rested on the enormous demand for cotton outside the South. This demand grew at about 5 percent a year during

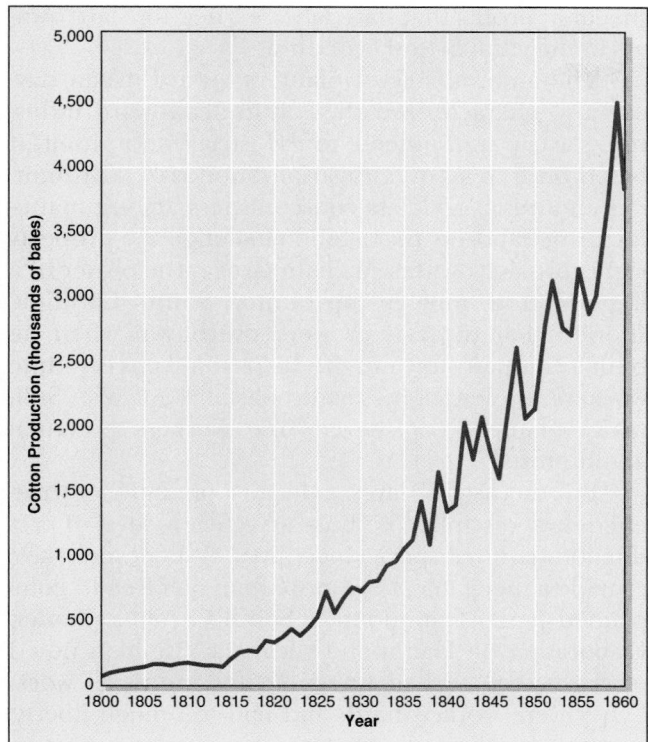

FIGURE 11-1   U.S. Cotton Production, 1800–1860
Cotton production spiraled upward after 1800, and the South became the world's leading supplier.

Data Source: U.S. Bureau of the Census, *Historical Statistics of the United States* (1960).

the first half of the nineteenth century. Although cotton prices fluctuated like those of any other commodity in an unregulated market, demand was so strong that prices held steady at around 10 cents a pound in the 1850s, even as southern production of cotton doubled. Textile mills in Britain were always the largest market, but demand in continental Europe and the United States grew even faster after 1840.

Southern law defined slaves as chattel, the personal property of their owners, and their market value increased along with the profitability of slavery. Prices for a male field hand rose from $250 in 1815 to $900 by 1860. Prices at any given time varied according to the age, sex, and skills of the slave, as well as overall market conditions, but the steady appreciation of prices for slaves meant that slave owners could sell their human chattel and realize a profit over and above what they had already earned from the slaves' labor. This was especially the case with slave mothers; the children they bore increased the capital assets of their owners. Slave women of childbearing age were therefore valued nearly as much as male field hands.

The domestic slave trade brought buyers and sellers of slaves together. Slaves flowed from the older areas of the Upper South to the newer plantation districts in the Lower South. Indeed, when Congress ended the African slave trade in 1807 and it became difficult to smuggle in significant numbers of African slaves, planters in the Deep South had to depend on the internal trade for the bulk of their labor supply. This trade was extensive: more than 800,000 slaves were moved between regions in the South from 1790 to 1860, and professional slave traders transported at least 60 percent of them. Drawing on lines of credit from banks, the traders paid cash for slaves, most of whom they bought from plantations in the Upper South. By selling these slaves in regional markets where demand had driven up the price, they turned a tidy profit.

The sheer size of the internal slave trade indicates just how profit-driven slave owners were. Few of them hesitated to break up slave families for sale when market conditions were right. About half of all slave sales separated family members. Slave children born in the Upper South after 1820 stood a one-in-three chance of being sold during their lifetime. Most of the profits from slave labor and sales went into buying more land and slaves. As long as slaves employed in growing cash staples returned 10 percent a year, slave owners had little economic incentive to shift their capital resources into manufacturing or urban development. The predictable result was that industrialization and urbanization fell far behind the levels in the free states, creating what outsiders came to decry as southern "backwardness." The South had one-third of the nation's population in 1860 but produced by value only 10 percent of the nation's manufacturing output. Fewer than one in ten Southerners lived in a city, compared to more than one in three northeasterners and one in seven midwesterners.

Nowhere was the indifference of planters to economic diversification more evident than in the Lower South, which had the smallest urban population and the fewest factories. Planters here were not opposed to economic innovations that promised greater profits, but they feared social changes that might undermine the stability of slavery. Urbanization and industrialization both entailed such risks.

Most planters suspected that the urban environment weakened slavery. An editorial in the *New Orleans Crescent* charged that slaves in the city were "demoralized to a deplorable extent, all owing to the indiscriminate license and indulgence extended them by masters, mistresses, and guardians, and to the practice of forging passes, which has now be-

Collection of The New-York Historical Society, negative number 47843

African American field hands return from a South Carolina cotton field in the 1860s. The economy of the prewar South was based on the production of cotton by a large enslaved labor force.

come a regular business in New Orleans." For a white person, a "demoralized" slave was one who behaved as if free. Urban slaves, though scarcely free, enjoyed a degree of personal and economic independence that blurred the line between freedom and servitude.

Urban slavery. Urban slaves were artisans, semiskilled laborers, and domestics, and, unlike their rural counterparts, they usually lived apart from their owners. They had much more freedom than field hands to move around, interact with white people and other black people, and experiment with various social roles. Many of them, especially if they had a marketable skill, such as carpentry or tailoring, could hire out their labor and retain some wages for themselves after reimbursing their owners. In short, the direct authority of the slave owner was less clear-cut in the town than in the country.

Urban slavery declined from 1820 to 1860 as slaves decreased from 22 percent to 10 percent of the urban population. This decline reflected both doubts about the stability of slavery in an urban setting and

the large profits that slave labor earned for slave owners in the rural cotton economy.

The ambivalence of planters toward urban slavery also characterized their attitudes toward industrial slavery and, indeed, to industrialization itself. If based on free labor, industrialization risked promoting an antislavery class consciousness among manufacturing laborers that would challenge the property rights of slave owners. William Gregg, the owner of a large cotton mill in upcountry South Carolina, showed that these fears were overblown when he built a company town in the 1840s that kept his white workers under tight, paternalistic controls. Still, many planters considered free workers potential abolitionists.

But the use of slaves as factory operatives threatened slave discipline because an efficient level of production required special incentives. "Whenever a slave is made a mechanic, he is more than half freed," complained James Hammond, a South Carolina planter. Elaborating on Hammond's fears, a Virginian noted of slaves that he had hired out for industrial work, "They were worked hard, and had too much liberty, and were acquiring bad habits. They earned money by overwork, and spent it for whisky, and got a habit of roaming about and *taking care of themselves*; because, when they were not at work in the furnace, nobody looked out for them."

The anxieties of planters over industrialization and their refusal to shift capital from plantation agriculture to finance it insured that manufacturing played only a minor economic role in the Lower South. Planters supported industrialization only as an adjunct, not an alternative, to the plantation economy. Thus planters did invest in railroads and factories, but their holdings remained concentrated in land and slaves. They augmented their income by renting slaves to manufacturers and railroad contractors but were quick to recall these slaves to work on the plantations when they were needed.

No more than 5 percent of the slaves in the Lower South ever worked in manufacturing, and most of these were in rural enterprises serving local markets too small to interest northern manufacturers. Ever concerned to preserve slavery, planters would not risk slave discipline or the profits of cotton agriculture by embracing the unpredictable changes that industrialization was sure to bring.

THE UPPER SOUTH

Climate and geography distinguished the Upper South from the Lower South. The eight slave states

The internal slave trade was the primary means by which the slaves of the Upper South were brought into the plantation markets of the Old Southwest. This illustration shows professional slave traders driving a chained group of slaves, known as a coffle, to perspective buyers in the Lower South.

of the Upper South lay north of the best growing zones for cotton. The northernmost of these states —Delaware, Maryland, Kentucky, and Missouri— bordered on free states and were known as the Border South. The four states south of them —Virginia, North Carolina, Tennessee, and Arkansas—constituted a middle zone. Slavery was entrenched in all these states, but it was less dominant than in the cotton South.

The key difference, from which others followed, was the suitability of the Lower South for growing cotton with gangs of slave laborers. Except for prime cotton districts in middle Tennessee, eastern Arkansas, and parts of North Carolina, the Upper South lacked the fertile soil and long growing season necessary for the commercial production of cotton, rice, or sugar (see Map 11–2). Consequently, the demand for slaves was less than it was in the Lower South. Two-thirds of white southerners lived in the Upper South in 1860, but they held only 45 percent of all slaves. Percentages of slave ownership and of slaves in the overall population were roughly half those in the cotton South. While the Lower South was undergoing a cotton boom after the War of 1812, the Upper South was mired in a long economic slump, from which it did not emerge until the 1850s. The improved economy of the Upper South in the late antebellum period increasingly relied on free labor, a development that

many cotton planters feared would diminish southern unity in defense of slavery.

A PERIOD OF ECONOMIC ADJUSTMENT

To inhabitants and visitors alike, vast stretches of the Upper South presented a dreary spectacle of exhausted fields and depopulation in the 1820s and 1830s. The soil was most depleted where tobacco had been cultivated extensively. Even where the land was still fertile, farmers could not compete against the agricultural commodities that the fresher lands of the Old Southwest produced. Land values fell as farmers dumped their property and headed west. "Emigration is here raging with all the strength of fanaticism," wrote a Virginian in 1837, "and nothing else can be talked of but selling estates, at a great sacrifice, and '*packing off*' for the '*far west.*'"

Agricultural reform emerged in the 1830s as one proposed solution to this economic crisis. Its leading advocate was Edmund Ruffin, a Virginia planter who tirelessly promoted the use of marl (shell deposits) to neutralize the overly acidic and worn-out soils of the Upper South. He also called for deeper plowing, systematic rotation of crops, and upgrading the breeding stock for animal husbandry.

Ruffin's efforts, and those of the agricultural societies and fairs spawned by the reform movement, met with some success, especially in the 1840s, when

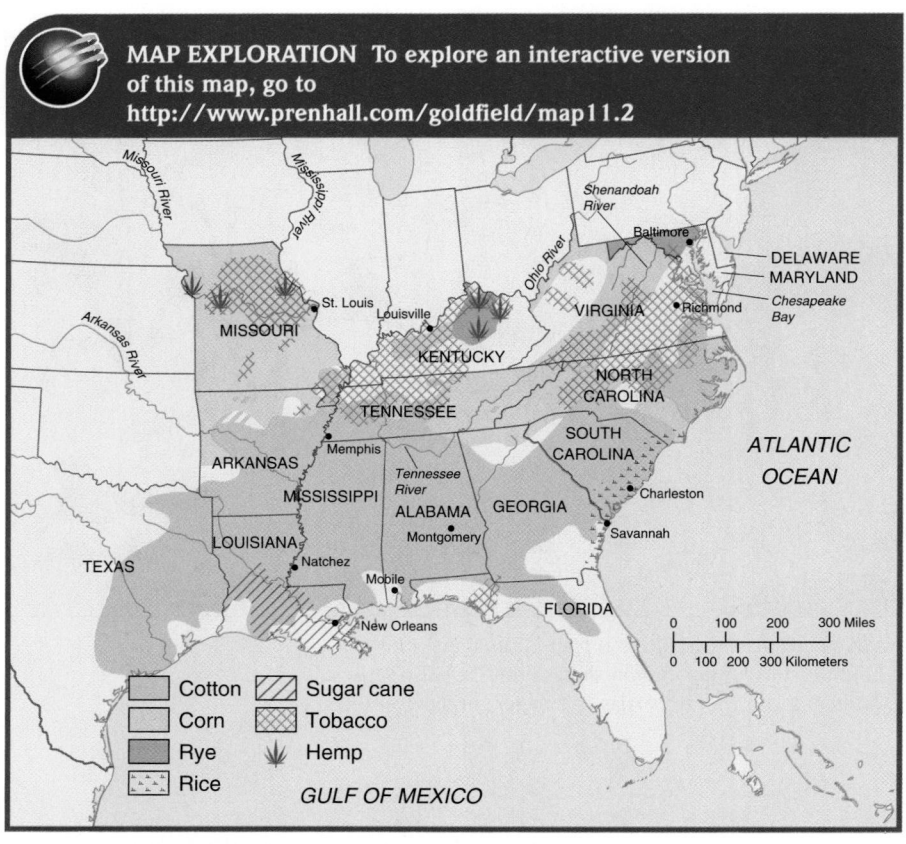

MAP EXPLORATION To explore an interactive version of this map, go to http://www.prenhall.com/goldfield/map11.2

MAP 11-2 Cotton and Other Crops in the South, 1860
Most of the Upper South was outside the cotton belt where the demand for slave labor was greatest.

Shenandoah Valley and northern sections of Virginia grew wheat, and in the former tobacco districts of the Virginia and North Carolina Tidewater, wheat, corn, and garden vegetables became major cash crops.

Expanding urban markets and a network of internal improvements facilitated this transition to general farming. Both these developments were outgrowths of the movement for industrial diversification launched in the 1820s in response to the heavy outflow of population from the Upper South.

Growing urbanization. Although not far advanced by northern standards, urbanization and industrialization in the Upper South were considerably greater than in the Lower South. The region had twice the percentage of urban residents of the cotton South, and it contained the leading manufacturing cities in the slave states—St. Louis, Baltimore, and Louisville. By 1860, the Upper South accounted for three-fourths of the South's manufacturing capital and output and nearly all of its heavy industry. Canals and railroads linked cities and countryside in a denser transportation grid than in the Lower South.

With an economy more balanced among agriculture, manufacturing, and trade than a generation earlier, the Upper South at midcentury was gradually becoming less tied to plantation agriculture and slave labor. The rural majority increasingly prospered by growing foodstuffs for city-dwellers and factory workers. The labor market for railroad construction and manufacturing work was strong enough to attract northern immigrants and help reduce the loss of the native-born population that had migrated to other states.

The economic adjustment in the Upper South converted the labor surplus of the 1820s into a labor scarcity by the 1850s. "It is a fact," noted Edmund Ruffin in 1859, "that labor is greatly deficient in all Virginia, and especially in the rich western counties, which, for want of labor, scarcely yet yield in the proportion of one tenth of their capacity." Ruffin's commitment to agricultural reform was exceeded only by

the prices of all cash staples fell. Still, only a minority of farmers ever embraced reform. These were generally the well-educated planters who read the agricultural press and could afford to change their farming practices. The landscape of Ruffin's beloved Virginia Tidewater still provoked travelers to remark, as one did in the early 1850s, "I've heard 'em say out West that old Virginny was the mother of statesmen—reckon she must be about done, eh? This 'ere's about the barrenest look for a mother ever I see."

Although soil exhaustion and wasteful farming persisted, agriculture in the Upper South had revived by the 1850s. A rebound in the tobacco market accounted for part of this revival, but the growing profitability of general farming was responsible for most of it.

Particularly in the Border South, the trend was toward agricultural diversification. Farmers and planters lessened their dependence on slave labor or on a single cash crop and practiced a thrifty, efficient agriculture geared to producing grain and livestock for urban markets. Western Maryland and the his devotion to slavery. Like many planters in the cotton states, he feared that free labor was about to replace scarce and expensive slave labor in Virginia and much of the Upper South.

THE DECLINE OF SLAVERY

Slave owners tended to exaggerate all threats to slavery, and Ruffin was no exception. But slavery was clearly growing weaker in the Upper South by the 1850s (see Figure 11-2). The decline was most evident along the northern tier of the Upper South, where the proportion of slaves to the overall population fell steadily after 1830. By 1860, slaves in the Border South had dropped to 2 percent of the population in Delaware, 13 percent in Maryland, 19 percent in Kentucky, and 10 percent in Missouri. In Virginia, from 1830 to 1860, slaves fell from 39 to 31 percent of the population.

Elsewhere in the Upper South, slavery was more or less holding its own by the 1850s. Tobacco and cotton planters in North Carolina and Tennessee continued to rely heavily on slave labor, but most small farmers were indifferent, if not opposed, to the institution. Only in Arkansas, whose alluvial lands along the Mississippi River offered a new frontier for plantation agriculture, was slavery growing rapidly. Slaves, however, still made up only 25 percent of the population of Arkansas in 1860 and were confined mainly to the southeastern corner of the state. Geographically dominated by the Ozark Highlands, Arkansas was best suited to general farming.

The region's role as a slave exporter to the Lower South hastened the decline of slavery in the Upper South. In every decade after 1820, the internal slave trade drained off about 10 percent of the slaves in the Upper South—virtually the entire natural increase. Slave traders initially made most of their purchases in Virginia and Maryland, but by the 1850s, they were also active in the Carolinas, Kentucky, and Missouri. New Orleans, Memphis, and Natchez, Mississippi, were the major western distribution points for the slaves, who were sent west both by sea and by land.

Selling slaves to the Lower South reinforced the Upper South's economic stake in slavery at a time when the institution was otherwise barely profitable there. The sale of surplus slaves was a windfall for planters whose slaves had become an economic burden. This same windfall gave planters the capital to embark on agricultural reform and shift out of tobacco production. Investment capital in the Upper South was not flowing into slave property but into economic diversification that expanded urban manufacturing. Both of these structural changes increas-

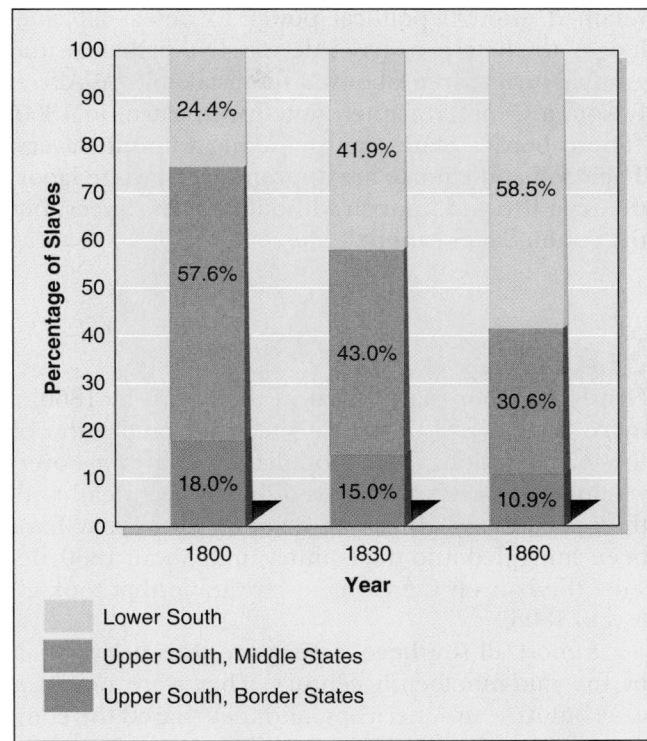

FIGURE 11-2 The Changing Regional Pattern of Slavery in the South, 1800–1860
As the nineteenth century progressed, slavery increasingly became identified with the cotton-growing Lower South.

ingly put slavery at a competitive disadvantage against free labor.

The wheat, small grains, and fodder crops that replaced tobacco in much of the Upper South did not require the nearly continuous attention of a work force. Unlike tobacco, wheat needed intensive labor only at planting and during the short harvest. Thus, as planters abandoned tobacco, they kept fewer slaves and relied on seasonal and cheap agricultural workers to meet peak labor demand.

The cheapness and flexibility of free labor made it better suited than slave labor for general farming. Urban manufacturers likewise wanted workers who could be hired and fired at a moment's notice. Despite the successful use of slaves in tobacco manufacturing and at the large Tredegar Iron Works in Richmond, immigrant workers displaced slaves in most of the factories in the Border South. By 1860, slaves made up just 1 percent of the population in St. Louis and Baltimore, the South's major industrial cities.

Slavery was in economic retreat across the Upper South after 1830. There were still plantation districts with large concentrations of slaves, and slave owners retained enough political power to defeat all challenges to their property interests. Nevertheless, the gradual turn to free labor was unmistakable. As Alfred Iveson, a Georgia planter, noted with alarm in 1860, "Those border States can get along without slavery. Their soil and climate are appropriate to white labor; they can live and flourish without African slavery; but the cotton States cannot."

SLAVE LIFE AND CULTURE

Nearly 4 million slaves lived in the South by 1860, a more than fivefold increase since the ratification of the Constitution. This population gain was overwhelmingly due to an excess of births over deaths, although as many as fifty thousand Africans may have been smuggled into the country until about 1860, despite the ban on the African slave trade that took effect in 1808.

Almost all southern slaves were thus native-born by the mid-nineteenth century. They were not Africans but African Americans, and they shared the common fate of bondage. By resisting an enslavement they could not prevent, they shaped a culture of their own that eased their pain and raised their hopes of someday being free. They managed to retain their dignity despite the humiliations to which they were subjected. In their family life and religious beliefs, slaves found the strength to sustain themselves under nearly intolerable circumstances.

WORK ROUTINES AND LIVING CONDITIONS

Being treated as a piece of property to be worked for profit and bought and sold when financially advantageous to one's owners—this was the legal and economic reality that all slaves confronted. Each southern state had its own **slave codes**, laws defining the status of slaves and the rights of masters; the codes gave slave owners near-absolute power over their human property.

"The right of personal liberty in the slave is utterly inconsistent with the idea of slavery," wrote Thomas R. R. Cobb of Georgia in a legal treatise on slavery. The slave codes, accordingly, severely restricted the lives of slaves. Slaves could not own property, make contracts, possess guns or alcohol, legally marry (except in Louisiana), leave plantations without the owner's written permission, or testify against their masters or any other white person in a court of law. Many states also prohibited teaching a slave to read or write. The law assumed that the economic self-interest of masters in their slave property gave slaves adequate legal protection against injuries inflicted by others. The murder

of a slave by a master was illegal, but in practice, the law and community standards looked the other way if a disobedient slave was killed while being disciplined.

The slave codes penalized any challenge to a master's authority or any infraction of plantation rules. Whippings were the most common authorized punishment: twenty lashes on the bare back for leaving a plantation without a pass, one hundred lashes for writing a pass for another slave, and so on. Striking a master, committing arson, or conspiring to rebel were punishable by death.

The owner, as expressed in the Alabama Slave Code of 1852, had "the right to the time, labor and services of the slave." This, of course, was the whole purpose of owning a slave. Most masters recognized that it made good business sense to feed, clothe, and house their slaves well enough to insure productive labor and to encourage a family life that would enable the slave population to reproduce itself. Thus planters' self-interest probably improved the living standards for slaves in the first half of the nineteenth century, and the slave population grew at a rate only slightly below that of white Southerners.

However, planters rarely provided more than the bare necessities. The slaves lived mainly on rations of

Five generations are represented in this photograph of an African American family on a South Carolina plantation. The photograph was taken in 1862, soon after the family gained its freedom during the Civil War.

cornmeal and salt pork, supplemented with vegetables they grew on the small garden plots that many planters permitted and with occasional catches of game and fish. This diet provided ample calories but often insufficient vitamins and nutrients to protect slaves (as well as the many poor whites who ate the same diet) against such diseases as beriberi and pellagra. Intestinal disorders were chronic, and dysentery and cholera were common. About 20 percent of the slaves on a typical plantation were sick at any given time. Infant mortality was twice as high among slaves as among white southerners in 1850; so was mortality among slave children up to age 14. According to one study, the life expectancy for slaves at birth was 21 to 22 years—roughly half the white life expectancy.

Planters furnished slaves with two sets of coarse clothing, one for summer and one for winter. Their housing, typically a 15-by-15-foot one-room cabin for five or six occupants, provided little more than basic shelter against the elements. "They were built of logs," a traveler noted of slave cabins in South Carolina, "with no windows—no opening at all, except the doorway, with a chimney of sticks and mud; with no trees about them, no porches, or shades, of any kind. Except for the chimney . . . I should have conjectured that it had been built for a powder-house, or perhaps an ice-house—never for an animal to sleep in."

Small and unadorned, slave cabins emphasized, not only the planters' desire to minimize housing costs, but also their determination to treat slaves as a regimented, collective population. Large planters placed these cabins in a row—an arrangement that projected precision and undifferentiated order. Slaves expressed their own individuality by furnishing their cabins with handmade beds and benches and by pushing for the right to put in gardens.

The diet and housing of most slaves may have been no worse than that of the poorest whites in both the North and the South, but their workload was undoubtedly heavier. Just over half of the slave population at midcentury was concentrated on plantation units with twenty or more slaves, and most of these slaves worked as field hands in gang labor. Overseers freely admitted that they relied on whippings to make slaves work in these gangs.

Most plantation slaves toiled at hard physical labor from sunup to sundown. The work was more intense and sustained than that of white farmers or white factory hands. The fear of the whip on a bare back set the pace. At daybreak, recalled Solomon Northrup of his enslavement on a Louisiana plantation, "the fears and labors of another day begin; and until its close there is no such thing as rest. [The

Especially on large plantations, slave nursemaids cared for the young children in the white planter's family.

slave] fears he will be caught lagging through the day; he fears to approach the gin-house with his basket-load of cotton at night; he fears, when he lies down, that he will oversleep himself in the morning."

Some 15 to 20 percent of plantation slaves were house servants or skilled artisans who had lighter and less regimented workloads than field hands. Some planters used the prospect of transfer to these relatively privileged positions as an incentive to field hands to work harder. Extra rations, time off on weekends, passes to visit a spouse on a nearby plantation, and the right to have a garden plot were among the other incentives planters used to keep labor productivity high. However, what a planter viewed as privileges, benevolently bestowed, slaves quickly came to see as customary rights. Despite the power of the whip, if planters failed to respect these "rights," slave morale would decline, and the work routine would be interrupted.

Nearly three-fourths of the slaves worked on plantations and medium-sized farms. Most of the remainder—those in units with fewer than ten slaves—worked on small farms in close contact with the master's family. Their workloads were more varied and sometimes less taxing than those of plantation hands, but these slaves were also more directly exposed to the whims of their owners and were less likely to live in complete family units. Slave couples in small holdings were more likely to live on separate farms. The owners of only a few slaves were also more vulnerable than were planters to market downturns that could force them to sell slaves and further divide families.

Of all slaves, 10 percent were not attached to the land, laboring instead at jobs that most white workers shunned. Every southern industry—but most particularly extractive industries such as mining and lumbering—relied heavily on slaves. The Tredegar Iron Company in Richmond, the largest iron foundry in the South, used slaves as its main workforce after 1847, partly to curb strikes by its white workers. Racial tensions often flared in southern industry, and when the races worked together, skilled white laborers typically insisted on being placed in supervisory positions.

Digging coal as miners or shoveling it as stokers for boilers on steamboats, laying down iron for the railroads or shaping hot slabs of it in a foundry, industrial slaves worked at least as hard as field hands. Compared to plantation slaves, however, they had more independence off the job and greater opportunities to earn money of their own. Because many of them had to house and feed themselves, they could also enjoy more time free from direct white scrutiny. By undertaking extra factory work, known as "overwork," industrial slaves could earn $50 or more a month, money they could use to buy goods for their families or, in rare cases, to purchase their freedom.

FAMILIES AND RELIGION

The core institution of slave life was the family. Except in Louisiana, southern law did not recognize slave marriages, but masters permitted, even encouraged, marital unions in order to raise the morale of their labor force and increase its value by having it produce marketable children. Slaves embraced their families as a source of loving warmth and strength in a system that treated them as commodities.

Despite all the obstacles arrayed against them, many slave marriages produced enduring commitments and a supportive moral code for family members. Most slave unions remained intact until the death or, frequently, the sale of one spouse. Close to one-third of slave marriages were broken up by sales or forced removals. A slave bitterly recalled that "the separation of slaves in this way is little thought of. A few masters regard their union as sacred, but where one does, a hundred care nothing about it."

Both parents were present in about two-thirds of slave families—the same ratio as in contemporary peasant families in western Europe. Although the father's role as protector of and provider for his wife and children had no standing under slavery, most slave fathers struggled to help feed their families by hunting and fishing, and they risked beating and death to defend their wives from sexual abuse by the overseer or master. Besides their field labors, slave mothers had all the burdens of pregnancy, child care, laundry, and cooking. After escaping from slavery, Sojourner Truth told how she placed her babies in a basket hanging from a tree while she worked in the field and had older children care for them.

No anguish under slavery was more heartrending than that of a mother whose child was sold away from her. "Oh, my heart was too full!" recalled Charity Bowery on being told that her boy Richard was sold. "[My mistress] had sent me away on an errand, because she didn't want to be troubled with our cries. I hadn't any chance to see my poor boy. I shall never see my poor boy. I shall never see him again in this world. My heart felt as if it was under a great load."

Charity Bowery's experience was hardly unique. Slave parents had to suppress the rage they felt at their powerlessness to protect their children from the cruelties of slavery. Slave accounts are full of stories of children running in vain to their parents to save them from a whipping. Most parents could only teach their children the skills of survival in a world in which white people had a legal monopoly on violence. The most valuable of these skills was the art of hiding one's true feelings from white people and telling them what they wanted to hear. As a perceptive traveler noted: "When therefore a white man approaches [the slaves] with inquiries concerning their condition, they are at once put upon their guard, and either make indefinite and vague replies, or directly contradict their real sentiments."

Extensive kinship ties provided a support network for the vulnerable slave family. Thickest on the older and larger plantations, these networks included both blood relatives and other significant people. Children were taught to address elders as "Aunt" and "Uncle" and fellow slaves as "sister" and "brother." Parents thus helped prepare their children for the day when the family might be divided. If separated from a parent, a child could turn to relatives or the larger slave community for care and assistance.

Slaves followed West African customs by prohibiting marriage between cousins and by often naming their children after departed grandparents. They also drew on an African heritage kept alive through folk-

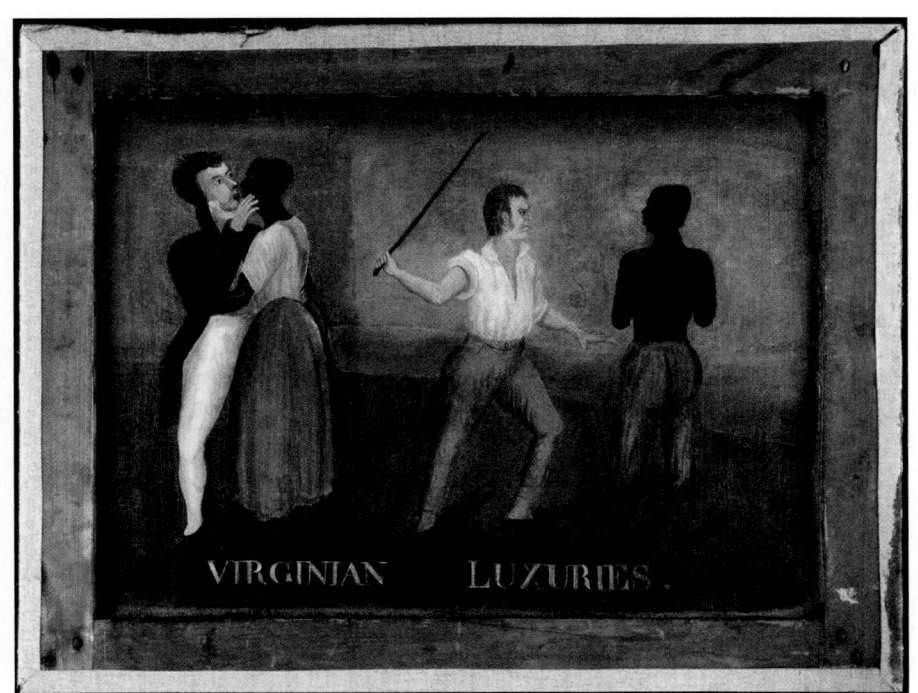

Satirically entitled "Virginian Luxuries," this antislavery painting sought to expose how the unchecked power of slaveowners resulted in the physical beating and sexual abuse of their slaves.

Promised Land of love and justice. By blending biblical imagery into their spirituals, the slaves expressed their yearning for freedom: "Didn't my Lord deliver Daniel/Then why not every man?"

The initial exposure of slaves to Christianity usually came from evangelical revivalists, and slaves always favored the Baptists and Methodists over other denominations. The evangelical message of universal spiritual equality confirmed the slaves' sense of personal worth. Less formal in both their doctrines and organization than the Presbyterians and Episcopalians, the evangelical sects allowed the slaves more leeway to choose their own preachers and engage in their physical call-and-response pattern of worship. Perhaps because they baptized by total immersion, which evoked the purifying power of water so common in African religions, the Baptists gained the most slave converts.

lore and oral histories to create a religion that fit their needs. The ancestors of nineteenth-century slaves brought no common religion with them when they were taken to the New World. However, beliefs common to a variety of African religions survived. Once slaves began to embrace Christianity in the late eighteenth century, they blended these beliefs into an African Christianity.

In keeping with African traditions, the religion of the slaves fused the natural and spiritual worlds, accepted the power of ghosts over the living, and relied on an expressive form of worship in which the participants shouted and swayed in rhythm with the beat of drums and other instruments. Associated with reverence for ancestors, dance was sacred in Africa. Spirituals, the religious songs of the slaves, were sung in a dance known in America as the ring shout. Moving counterclockwise and stamping their feet to establish a beat, slaves blended dance and song in a religious ceremony that helped them to endure oppression and sustain their self-confidence.

By most estimates, no more than 20 percent of slaves ever converted to Christianity. Those who did found in Christianity a message of deliverance rooted in the liberation of Moses's people from bondage in Egypt. The Jesus of the New Testament spoke to them as a compassionate God who had shared their burden of suffering, so that all peoples could hope to find the

Most planters were pragmatic about encouraging Christianity among their slaves. Like every other aspect of the slaves' lives, they favored it only if they could control it. Thus, while many planters allowed black preachers at religious services on their plantations, they usually insisted that white observers be present. Worried that abolitionist propaganda might attract the slaves to Christianity as a religion of secular liberation, some planters in the late antebellum period tried to convert their slaves to their own version of Christianity. They invited white ministers to their plantations to preach a gospel of passivity and obedience, centered on Paul's call for servants to "obey in all things your Masters."

Although most slaves viewed the religion of their owners as hypocritical and the sermons of white ministers as propaganda, they feigned acceptance of the religious wishes of their masters. They attended the special slave chapels some masters built and sat in segregated galleries in white churches on Sunday mornings. But in the evening, out of sight of the master or overseer, they held their own services in the woods and listened to their own preachers. As much as they could, the slaves hid their religious life from white people. Many slaves experienced religion as a spiritual rebirth that gave them the inner strength to endure their bondage. As one recalled, "I was born a slave and lived through some hard times. If it had not been for my God, I don't know what I would have done."

RESISTANCE

Open resistance to slavery was futile. The persistently disobedient slave would be sold "down river" to a harsher master or, in extreme cases, killed. The fate of Richard, Charity Bowery's son who was sold away from her, typified that of the openly defiant slave. He resisted the efforts of his new owner in Alabama to break his will. When the owner threatened to shoot him if he did not consent to being whipped, Richard replied, "Shoot away, I won't come to be flogged." The master shot and killed him.

Although the odds of succeeding were infinitesimal, slaves as desperate as Richard did plot rebellions. Four major uprisings occurred in the nineteenth century. The first, **Gabriel Prosser's Rebellion** in 1800, involved about fifty armed slaves around Richmond, though perhaps as many as one thousand slaves knew about Prosser's plans. The failure to seize a key road to Richmond and a warning to white authorities by a slave informer doomed the rebellion before it got under way. State authorities executed Prosser and twenty-five of his followers.

A decade later, in what seems to have been a spontaneous bid for freedom, several hundred slaves in the river parishes (counties) above New Orleans marched on the city. Poorly armed, they were no match for the U.S. Army troops and militiamen who stopped them. More than sixty slaves died, and the heads of the leading rebels were posted on poles along the Mississippi River to warn others of the fate that awaited rebellious slaves.

The most carefully planned slave revolt, **Denmark Vesey's Conspiracy**, like Prosser's, failed before it got started. Vesey, a literate carpenter and lay preacher in Charleston who had purchased his freedom with the money he had won in a lottery, planned the revolt in the summer of 1822. Vesey drew on biblical passages, antislavery sentiments in Congress he had gleaned from newspaper reports on the Missouri Compromise debates, and the successful revolt of slaves in Haiti to inspire his followers. He tried to steel the courage of his coconspirators by telling them that his chief lieutenant, Gullah Jack, a conjurer, or voodoo doctor, would cast spells on their enemies. He assigned teams of rebels specific targets, such as the municipal guardhouse and arsenal. Once Charleston was secured, the rebels apparently planned to flee to Haiti. The plot collapsed when two domestic servants betrayed it. White authorities responded swiftly and savagely. They hanged thirty-five conspirators, including Vesey,

After eluding his white pursuers for two months, Nat Turner, the leader of the South's most famous slave revolt, was captured on October 30, 1831.

and banished thirty-seven others. After destroying the African Methodist Episcopal Church where Vesey had preached and the conspirators had met, they tried to seal off the city from subversive outsiders by passing the Negro Seamen's Act, which mandated the imprisonment of black sailors while their ships were berthed in Charleston.

One slave revolt, **Nat Turner's Rebellion**, in Southampton County, Virginia, did erupt before it could be suppressed. Turner was a literate field hand driven by prophetic visions of black vengeance against white oppressors. Like Vesey, he was well versed in the Bible. Convinced by what he called "signs in heaven" that he should "arise and prepare myself and slay my enemies with their own weapons," he led a small band of followers on a murderous rampage in late August 1831. The first white man to be killed was Joseph Travis, Turner's owner, known for his lenient treatment of slaves. In the next two days, sixty other white people were also killed. An enraged posse, aided by slaves, captured or killed most of Turner's party. Turner hid for two months before being apprehended. He and more than thirty other slaves were executed, and panicky white people killed more than a hundred other slaves.

Slaves well understood that the odds against a successful rebellion were insurmountable. They could see who had all the guns. White people were also more numerous. In contrast to the large black majorities in the slave societies of the West Indies

After fleeing from slavery in Maryland in 1849, Harriet "Moses" Tubman, standing on the left, risked reenslavement by returning to the South on several occasions to assist other slaves in escaping. She is photographed here with some of those she helped free.

and Brazil—majorities made possible only by the continuous, heavy importation of Africans—slaves made up only one-third of the population of the antebellum American South. They lacked the numbers to overwhelm the white population and could not escape to mountain hideaways or large tracts of jungle. Surveillance by mounted white patrols—part of the police apparatus of slavery—limited organized rebellion by slaves to small, local affairs that were quickly suppressed.

Nor could many slaves escape to freedom. Few runaways made it to Canada or to a free state. White people could stop black people and demand to see papers documenting their freedom or right to travel without a master. The **Underground Railroad**, a secret network of stations and safe houses organized by Quakers and other black and white antislavery activists, provided some assistance. However, fellow slaves or free black people, especially in the cities of the Border South, provided the only help most runaways could count on. Out of more than 3 million slaves in the 1850s, only about a thousand a year permanently escaped. (See "American Views: A Letter from an Escaped Slave to His Former Master.")

The few who made it to the North did so by running at night and hiding during the day. The most ingenious resorted to clever stratagems. Henry "Box" Brown arranged to have himself shipped in a box from Richmond to Philadelphia. Ellen Craft, a light-skinned slave who could pass as white, disguised herself as a male slaveholder accompanied by his dark-skinned servant (her husband, William). What could have

been a fatal flaw in their plan as they traveled from Savannah to Philadelphia—their inability to write and hence sign their names or document their assumed identities—was overcome by having Ellen pose as a sickly, rheumatic master whose right hand had to be kept bandaged.

Running away was common, but most runaways fled no farther than to nearby swamps and woods. Most voluntarily returned or were tracked down by bloodhounds within a week. Aside from protesting a special grievance or trying to avoid punishment, these slaves usually wanted to visit a spouse or loved one. Occasionally, runaways could bargain for lenient treatment in return for faithful service in the future. Most were severely punished. Such temporary flights from the master's control siphoned off some of the anger that might otherwise have erupted in violent, self-destructive attacks on slave owners. All planters had heard about the field hand who took an ax to an overseer, the cook who poisoned her master's family, or the house servant who killed a sleeping master or mistress.

Slaves resisted complete domination by their masters in less overt ways. They mocked white people in folktales like those about Brer Rabbit, for example, in which weak but wily animals cunningly outsmart their stronger enemies. Slave owners routinely complained of slaves malingering at work, abusing farm animals, losing tools, stealing food, and committing arson. These subversive acts of protest never challenged the system of slavery itself, but they did help slaves to maintain a sense of dignity and self-respect.

FREE SOCIETY

The abolitionists and the antislavery Republican Party of the 1850s portrayed the social order of the slave South as little more than haughty planters lording it over shiftless poor white people. The reality was considerably more complex. Planters, who set the social tone for the South as a whole, did act superior, but they were a tiny minority and had to contend with an ambitious middle class of small slaveholders and a majority of nonslaveholding farmers. Some landless white people on the margin of rural society

AMERICAN VIEWS

A Letter from an Escaped Slave to His Former Master

In 1859, Jackson Whitney was one of six thousand fugitive slaves living in Canada, a sanctuary of freedom beyond the reach of the Fugitive Slave Act of 1850. Like most fugitives, he was male, and he had been forced to leave his family behind in Kentucky. His letter, as well as other direct testimony by African Americans about their experiences and feelings while enslaved, gives us information about slavery that only the slaves could provide.

- How would you characterize the tone of Whitney's letter? How did he express his joy at being a free man?
- How did Whitney feel that Riley, his former owner, had betrayed him?
- What did Whitney mean by the phrase "a slave talking to 'massa' "? How did he indicate that he had been hiding his true feelings as a slave?
- How did Whitney contrast his religious beliefs and those of Riley? How did he expect Riley to be punished?
- What pained Whitney about his freedom in Canada, and what did he ask of Riley?

March 18, 1859
Mr. Wm. Riley, Springfield, Ky. —Sir:

I take this opportunity to dictate a few lines to you, supposing you might be curious to know my whereabouts. I am happy to inform you that I am in Canada, in good health, and have been here several days. Perhaps, by this time, you have concluded that robbing a woman of her husband, and children of their father does not pay, at least in your case; and I thought, while lying in jail by your direction, that if you had no remorse or conscience that would make you feel for a poor, broken-hearted man, and his worse-than-murdered wife and child, . . . and could

---

fit the stereotype of "poor whites," but they were easily outnumbered by self-reliant farmers who worked their own land. Southern cities, though small by northern standards, provided jobs for a growing class of free workers who increasingly clashed with planters over the use of slave labor.

These same cities, notably in the Upper South, were also home to the nation's largest concentration of free black people. Their freedom, though restricted, contradicted the racial justification of slavery. They competed with white workers for jobs, and by the 1850s pressure was mounting on them to leave the South or be enslaved. The free society in the South was surely more diverse than its antislavery critics charged, but overriding racism bonded most white people together to defend the prerogatives of white supremacy.

THE SLAVEHOLDING MINORITY

The white-columned plantation estate approached from a stately avenue of shade trees and framed by luxuriant gardens remains the most popular image of the slave South. In fact, such manorial estates were utterly unrepresentative of the lifestyle of the typical slaveholder. Only the wealthiest planters could live in such splendor, and they constituted less than 1 percent of southern white families in 1860. Yet displayed not by any entreaty or permission be induced to do as you promised you would, which was to let me go with my family for $800—but contended for $1,000, when you had promised to take the same you gave for me (which was $660.) at the time you bought me, and let me go with my dear wife and children! but instead would render me miserable, and lie to me, and to your neighbors . . . and when you was at Louisville trying to sell me! then I thought it was time for me to make my feet feel for Canada, and let your conscience feel in your pocket. —Now you cannot say but that I did all that was honorable and right while I was with you, although I was a slave. I pretended all the time that I thought you, or some one else had a better right to me than I had to myself, which you know is rather hard thinking.

—You know, too, that you proved a traitor to me in the time of need, and when in the most bitter distress that the human soul is capable of experiencing; and could you have carried out your purposes there would have been no relief. But I rejoice to say that an unseen, kind spirit appeared for the oppressed, and bade me take up my bed and walk—the result of which is that I am victorious and you are defeated. I am comfortably situated in Canada, working for George Harris [another fugitive slave from Kentucky who had bought a farm in Canada] . . . .

There is only one thing to prevent me being entirely happy here, and that is the want of my dear wife and children, and you to see us enjoying ourselves together here. I wish you could realize the contrast between Freedom and slavery; but it is not likely that we shall ever meet again on this earth.

But if you want to go to the next world and meet a God of love, mercy, and justice, in peace; who says, "Inasmuch as you did it to the least of them my little ones, you did it unto me"—making the professions that you do, pretending to be a follower of Christ, and tormenting me and my little ones as you have done—[you] had better repair the breaches you have made among us in this world, by sending my wife and children to me; thus preparing to meet your God in peace; for, if God don't punish you for inflicting such distress on the poorest of His poor, then there is no use of having any God, or talking about one . . . .

I hope you will consider candidly, and see if the case does not justify every word I have said, and ten times as much. You must not consider that it is a slave talking to 'massa' now, but one as free as yourself.

I subscribe myself one of the abused of America, but one of the justified and honored of Canada.

Jackson Whitney

Source: John W. Blassingame, ed., *Slave Testimony: Two Centuries of Letters, Speeches, Interviews, and Autobiographies* (Louisiana State University Press, 1977).

---

in their homes and grounds, their wealth and status were so imposing that they created an idealized image of grace and grandeur that has obscured the cruder realities of the slave regime.

Only in the rice districts of the South Carolina lowcountry and in the rich sugar parishes and cotton counties of the Mississippi Delta were large planters more than a small minority of the slaveholding class, let alone the general white population. Families of the planter class—those who held a minimum of twenty slaves—constituted only around 3 percent of all southern families in 1860. Fewer than one out of five planter families—less than 1 percent of all families—owned more than fifty slaves. Far from conspicuously exhibiting their wealth, most planters lived in drab log cabins. "The planter's home is generally a rude ungainly structure, made of logs, rough hewn from the forest; rail fences and rickety gates guard its enclosures," complained a speaker to the Alabama horticultural society in 1851. "We murder our soil with wasteful culture because there is plenty of fresh land West—and we live in tents and huts when we might live in rural palaces." Most planters wanted to acquire wealth, not display it. They were restlessly eager to move on and abandon their homes when the allure of profits from a new cotton frontier

Overview

Structure of Free Society in the South, c. 1860

Group	Size	Characteristics
Large planters	Less than 1 percent of white families	Owned fifty or more slaves and plantations in excess of one thousand acres; the wealthiest class in America
Planters	About 3 percent of white families	Owned twenty to forty-nine slaves and plantations in excess of one hundred acres; controlled bulk of southern wealth and provided most of the political leaders
Small slaveholders	About 20 percent of white families	Owned fewer than twenty slaves and most often fewer than five; primarily farmers, though some were part of a small middle class in towns and cities
Nonslaveholding whites	About 75 percent of white families	Mostly yeomen farmers who owned their own land and stressed production for family use; one in five owned neither slaves nor land and squatted on least desirable land where they planted some corn and grazed some livestock; in cities they worked as artisans or, more typically, day laborers
Free blacks	About 3 percent of all free families	Concentrated in the Upper South; hemmed in by legal and social restrictions; mostly tenants or farm laborers; about one-third lived in cities and generally were limited to lowest-paying jobs

promised to relieve them of the debts they had incurred to purchase their slaves.

Most planters expected their wives to help supervise the slaves and run the plantation. Besides raising her own children, the plantation mistress managed the household staff, oversaw the cooking and cleaning, gardened, dispensed medicine and clothing to the slaves, and often assisted in their religious instruction. When guests or relatives came for an extended visit, the wife had to make all the special arrangements that this occasion entailed. When the master was called off on a business or political trip, she kept the plantation accounts. In many respects, she worked harder than her husband.

Planters' wives often complained in their journals and letters of their isolation from other white women and the physical and mental toil of managing slaves. Still, they enjoyed a wealth and status unknown to most southern women and only rarely questioned the institution of slavery. Their deepest anger stemmed from their humiliation by husbands who kept slave mistresses or sexually abused slave women. Bound by their duties as wives not to express this anger publicly, and unwilling to renounce the in-

stitution that both victimized and benefited them, white women tended to vent their frustrations on black women whose alleged promiscuity they blamed for the sexual transgressions of white males. "Sometimes white mistresses will surmise that there is an intimacy between a slave woman & the master," recalled a former slave, "and perhaps she will make a great fuss & have her whipped, & perhaps there will be no peace until she is sold."

Despite the tensions and sexual jealousies that it aroused, the ownership of slaves was the surest means of social and economic advancement for most white families. Most slave owners, however, never attained planter status. Nine in ten slave owners in 1860 owned fewer than twenty slaves, and fully half of them had fewer than five. Many white people also rented a few slaves on a seasonal basis.

Generally younger than the planters, small slaveholders were a diverse lot. About 10 percent were women, and another 20 percent or so were merchants, businessmen, artisans, and urban professionals. Most were farmers trying to acquire enough land and slaves to enter the ranks of planters. To keep costs down, they often began by purchasing children, the cheapest slaves available, or a young slave family, so that they could add to their slaveholdings as the slave mother bore more children.

Other slaveholding farmers had inherited their slaves and were trying to regain their fathers' planter status. Partible inheritance—the equal division of property among children—was the norm in the nineteenth-century South. Except among the richest planter families, this division reduced the sons to modest slaveholders who had to struggle to build their own plantations.

Small slaveholders had scant economic security. A deadly outbreak of disease among their slaves or a single bad crop could destroy their credit and force them to sell their slaves to clear their debts. Owners of fewer than ten slaves stood a fifty-fifty chance

James Cameron (1817-1882), "Colonel and Mrs. James A. Whiteside, son Charles and servants." Oil on canvas; c. 1858-1859. Hunter Museum of Art, Chattanooga, Tennessee, Gift of Mr. and Mrs. Thomas Whiteside.

Colonel James A. Whiteside and his family were among the small elite of white Southerners who enjoyed the wealth and ease of life on a large plantation. Reflecting the ideal of patriarchy, this portrait, c. 1858, projects the colonel as a figure of power and authority.

within a decade of dropping out of the slaveholding class. Nor could small holders hope to compete directly with the planters. In any given area suitable for plantations, they were gradually pushed out as planters bought up land to raise livestock or more crops. In general, only slave owners who had established themselves in business or the professions had the capital reserves to rise into the planter elite.

Especially in the Lower South, owning slaves was a necessary precondition for upward mobility, but it was hardly a sufficient one. Slaveholders who failed to advance had nonetheless acquired a badge of social respectability. As a Baptist opponent of slavery put it, "Without slaves a man's children stand but poor chance to marry in reputation." Aside from conferring status, owning a few slaves could relieve a white household of much hard domestic labor. "I wish to God every head of a family in the United States had one [slave] to take the drudgery and menial service off his family," proclaimed Andrew Johnson of Tennessee in the U.S. Senate. (Johnson replaced Abraham Lincoln as president in 1865.)

THE WHITE MAJORITY

Three-fourths of southern white families owned no slaves in 1860. Although most numerous in the Upper South, nonslaveholders predominated wherever the soil and climate were not suitable for plantation agriculture. Most were yeoman farmers who worked their own land with family labor.

These farmers were quick to move when times were bad and their land was used up, but once settled in an area, they formed intensely localized societies in which fathers and husbands held sway over their families. The community extended 5 to 10 miles around the nearest country store or county courthouse. Networks of kin and friends provided labor services when needed, fellowship in evangelical churches, and staple goods that an individual farm could not produce. Social travel and international markets, so central to the lives of planters, had little relevance in the farmers' community-centered existence. The yeomanry aimed to be self-sufficient and limited market involvement to the sale of livestock and an occasional cotton crop that could bring in needed cash.

Yeoman farmers jealously guarded their independence, and in their tight little worlds of face-to-face relationships, they demanded that planters treat them as social equals. Ever fearful of being reduced to dependence, they avoided debt and sought to limit government authority. Rather than risk financial ruin by buying slaves on credit to grow cotton, they grew food crops and depended on their sons and, when needed, their wives and daughters to work the fields. Far longer than most northern farmers, and in part because poor transportation raised the cost of manufactured goods, they continued to make their own clothes, shoes, soap, and other consumer items.

Nonslaveholding farmers from the mountains and planters on the bottomlands rarely mixed, and their societies developed in isolation from each other. In areas where there were both small farms and scattered plantations, the interests of the yeomen and the planters were often complementary. Planters provided local markets for the surplus grain and livestock of nonslaveholders and, for a small fee, access to grist mills and gins for grinding corn and cleaning cotton. They lent small sums to poorer neighbors in emergencies or to pay taxes. The yeomen staffed the slave patrols and became overseers on the plantations. Both groups sought to protect property rights from outside interference and to maintain a system of racial control in which white liberties rested on black degradation.

When yeomen and planters did clash, it was usually over economic issues. Large slaveholders needing better credit and marketing facilities gravitated toward the Whig Party, which called for banks and internal improvements. Nonslaveholding farmers, especially in the Lower South, tended to be Democrats who opposed banks and state-funded economic projects. They considered bankers grasping outsiders who wanted to rob them of their economic independence, and they suspected that state involvement in the economy led only to higher taxes and increased the public debt. These partisan battles, however, rarely involved a debate about the merits of slavery. As long as planters deferred to the egalitarian sensibilities of the yeomen by courting them at election time and promising to safeguard their liberties, the planters were able to maintain broad support for slavery across class lines.

Around 15 percent of rural white families owned neither land nor slaves. These were the so-called "poor whites," stigmatized by both abolitionists and planters as lazy and shiftless. The abolitionists considered them a kind of underclass who proved that slavery so degraded the dignity of labor that it led people to shun work and lapse into wretched poverty. To the planters, they were a constant nuisance and a threat to slave discipline. Planters habitually complained that poor whites demoralized their slaves by showing that a person could survive without steady labor. Planters also accused them of trading guns and alcohol with slaves for stolen plantation property. Despite the efforts of slaveowners to crack down on this illicit trade, poor whites and slaves continued to swap goods and socially intermingle on the fringes of the plantations.

Some landless white people did live down to their negative stereotype. Still, the "poor white trash" label with which they were stigmatized is misleading. Most were resourceful and enterprising enough to supply themselves with all the material comforts they wanted. Back in the swamps and pine barrens shunned by planters and yeomen alike, they squatted on a few acres of land, put up crude cabins for shelter, planted some corn, and grazed livestock in the surrounding woods. Aided by the mild southern climate, they had all the corn and pork they could eat. Not having to do steady work for survival, they hunted, fished, and took orders from no one. Although poor by most standards, they were also defiantly self-reliant.

Nonslaveholders were a growing majority in southern cities, especially among the working classes. These urban workers shared no agricultural interests or ties with the planters. Nor were most of them, especially in the unskilled ranks, southern-born. Northerners and immigrants dominated the urban work force.

Free workers, especially Irish and German immigrants, increasingly replaced slaves in urban labor markets. These white workers bitterly resented competition from black slaves, and their demands to exclude slaves from the urban workplace reinforced planters' belief that cities bred abolitionism. When urban laborers protested against slave competition in the 1850s, planters singled them out as the nonslaveholders most likely to attack slavery.

FREE BLACK PEOPLE

A few southern black people—6 percent of the total in 1860—were "free persons of color" and constituted 3 percent of the free population in the South (see Figure 11–2). These free black people occupied a precarious and vulnerable position between degraded enslavement and meaningful freedom. White intimidation and special legal provisions known as **black codes** (found throughout the North as well) denied them nearly all the rights of citizenship. Because of the legal presumption in the South that all black people were slaves, they had to carry freedom papers, official certificates of their freedom. They were shut out of the political process and could not testify against white people in court. Many occupations, especially those involved in the communication of ideas, such as the printing trades, were closed to them.

Every slave state forbade the entry of free black people, and every municipality had its own rules and regulations that forced them to live as an inferior caste. In Charleston, for example, a free black person could not smoke a cigar or carry a cane in public. Any sign of upward mobility or intimation of equal standing was ruthlessly suppressed. White people had the right of way, and a free black person who bumped into a white person on the street was likely to be flogged.

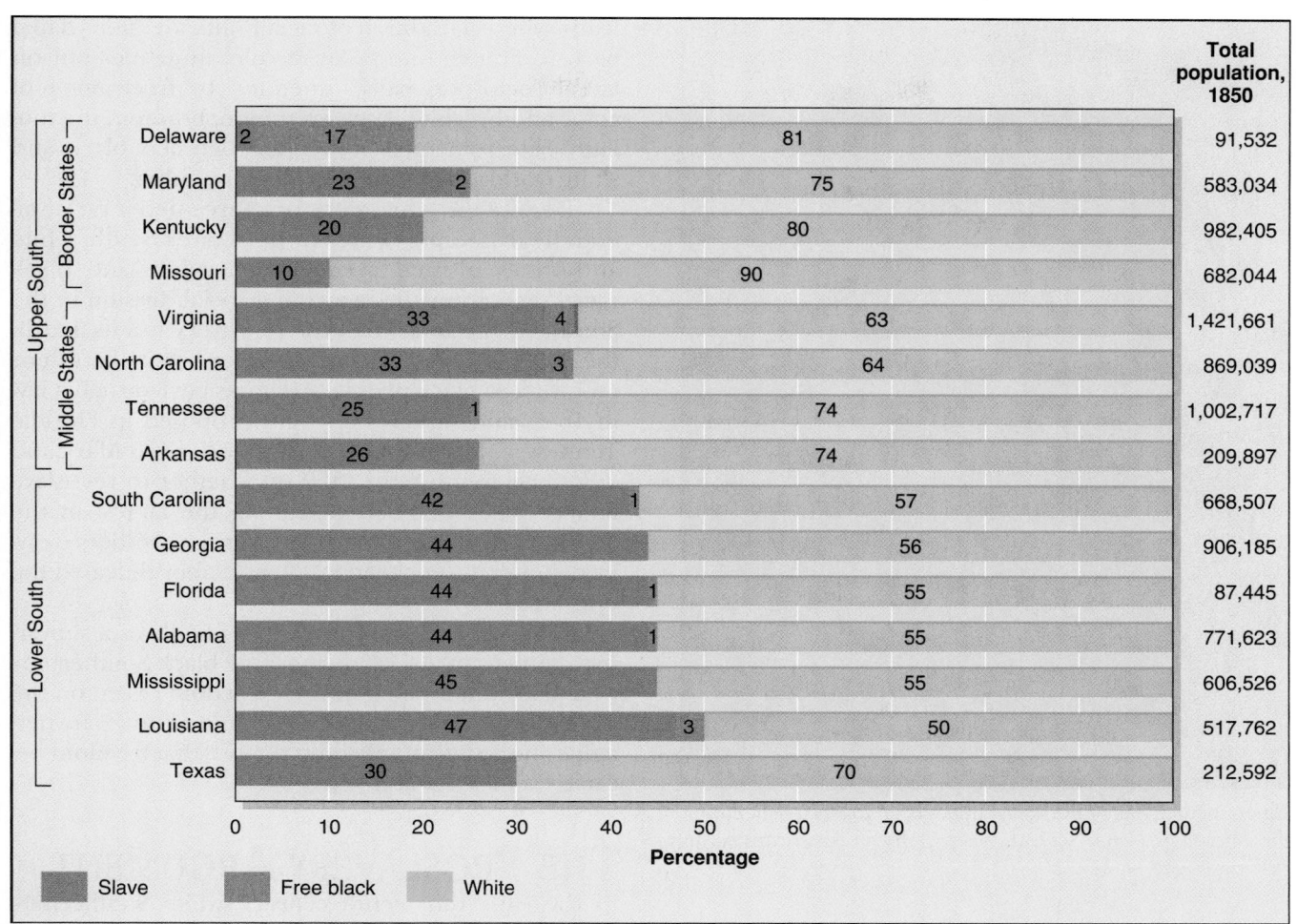

FIGURE 11-3 Slave, Free Black, and White Population in Southern States, 1850
Except for Texas, slaves by 1850 comprised over 40 percent of the population in every state of the Lower South. The small population of free black people was concentrated in the Upper South.

More than four-fifths of the southern free black population lived in the Upper South. Most were the offspring of slaves freed by private manumissions between 1780 and 1800, when slavery temporarily loosened in the Chesapeake region in the wake of the Revolutionary War. Manumissions dropped sharply after 1810, the result of heightened white anxieties over slave security after Prosser's Rebellion and the rising demand for slaves in the Lower South. From 1810 to 1860, only 13 percent of black people in the Upper South were free.

As in the North, legal barriers and white prejudice generally confined free black people to the poorest-paying and most menial work. In rural areas, a handful became independent farmers, but most worked as farm laborers or tenants. The best economic opportunities were in the cities, where some found factory jobs and positions in the skilled trades. Because the South had a general shortage of skilled labor, free black artisans—carpenters, barbers, shoemakers, tai-lors, and plasterers—could earn a respectable income. Indeed, the percentage of black people in the skilled trades was generally higher in the South than in the North. Talented artisans, such as Thomas Day, widely recognized as the finest cabinetmaker in North Carolina, could command a premium in wages from white employers.

One-third of free black people in the Upper South lived in cities, a much higher proportion than among white people. Cities offered black people, not only jobs, but also enough social space to found their own churches and mutual-aid associations. Especially after 1840, urban African American churches proliferated to become the center of black community life. Church Sunday schools and day schools provided black people practically their only access to education, which they persisted in pursuing despite white opposition. A "good education," declared a black schoolmaster in Baltimore, "is the *sine qua non* as regards the elevation of our people.

The Granger Collection, New York.

Barbering was one of the skilled trades open to black men during the antebellum years. Several wealthy African Americans began their careers as barbers.

Less than 2 percent of the black people in the Lower South were free in 1860. Given the greater profitability of slavery there, manumissions were rare. Most of the Lower South's free black population descended from black emigrants who fled the revolutionary unrest in Haiti in the 1790s. These refugees were artisans, shopkeepers, and farmers who settled primarily in Charleston and New Orleans. Able to secure a solid economic footing, they left their descendants wealthier than any other free black people in the United States. Free black people in the Lower South were more likely than those in the Upper South to have a marketable skill, and two-thirds of them lived in cities.

A light skin also enhanced the social standing of free black people among color-conscious whites in the Lower South. Nearly 70 percent of free black people in 1860 were mulattoes, and from their ranks came nearly all of the very small number of black planters. Mulattoes could count on greater white patronage, and they monopolized the best jobs available to free black people. A mulatto elite emerged in Charleston, Mobile, and New Orleans that carefully distanced itself from most black people, slave or free. In New Or-

leans, where a tradition of racially mixed unions dated back to French and Spanish rule, mulattoes put on lavish "octoroon balls," attended by freewomen of color and by white men. Even here, however, the mulatto elite remained suspended between black and white worlds, never fully accepted by either.

Despite the emergence of a three-tiered racial hierarchy in the port cities of the Lower South, white authorities insisted on making a white and black racial dichotomy the overriding social division in the South. As the racial defense of slavery intensified in the 1850s, more calls were made for laws to banish or enslave free black people. Arkansas passed such a law in 1859, and similar bills were proposed in Florida, Tennessee, Mississippi, and Missouri. Even Maryland held a referendum in 1859 on whether to reenslave its free black population, among the largest in the South. Only the opposition of nonslaveholders heavily dependent on cheap free black labor defeated the referendum.

Despised and feared by white people as a subversive element in a slave society, free black Southerners were daily reminded that their freedom rested on the whims of the white majority. As white attitudes turned uglier in the late antebellum period, that freedom became ever less secure.

THE PROSLAVERY ARGUMENT

In the early nineteenth century, white Southerners made no particular effort to defend slavery because the institution was not under heavy outside attack. If pressed, most white people would have called slavery a necessary evil, an unfortunate legacy from earlier generations that was needed to maintain racial peace.

The 1830s marked a turning point. After the twin shocks of Nat Turner's Rebellion and the onset of the abolitionist crusade (for more on this crusade, see Chapter 12), white mobs emerged to stifle any open criticism of slavery in the Lower South. White Southerners also began to develop a defense of slavery. By the 1850s, politicians, intellectuals, and evangelical ministers were arguing that it was a positive good, an institution ordained by God as the foundation of southern prosperity, white democracy, and Christian instruction for heathen Africans. Slavery, they insisted, was a mild, paternalistic, and even caring institution.

This defense obviously portrayed slavery as the defenders imagined it, not as it was. However comforting it may have been to individual slaveholders, the argument failed to convince abolitionists or southern dissenters who condemned slavery on moral and economic grounds.

Evangelical Protestantism dominated southern religious expression by the 1830s, and its ministers took the lead in combating abolitionist charges that slavery was a moral and religious abomination. Except for a radical minority of antislavery evangelicals in the Upper South, a group largely silenced or driven out by the conservative reaction following Nat Turner's uprising, the southern churches had always supported slavery. This support grew more pronounced and articulate once the abolitionists stepped up their attacks on slavery in the mid-1830s.

Southern evangelicals accepted the Bible as God's literal word, and through selective reading they found abundant evidence in it to proclaim slavery fully in accord with His moral dictates. They pointed out, for example, that the patriarchs of Israel owned slaves. Slavery was practiced throughout the Roman world at the time of Christ, they noted, and the apostles urged obedience to all secular laws, including those governing slavery.

Southern evangelicals also turned to the Bible to support their argument that patriarchal authority—the unquestioned power of the father—was the basis of all Christian communities. Part of that authority extended over slaves, and slavery thus became a matter of family governance, a domestic institution in which Christian masters of slaves, unlike capitalist masters of free "wage slaves" in the North, accepted responsibility for caring for their workers in sickness and old age. Far from being a moral curse, slavery was part of God's plan to Christianize an inferior race and teach its people how to produce raw materials that benefited the world's masses.

The growing commitment of southern evangelicals to slavery as a positive good clashed with the antislavery position and the generally more liberal theology of northern evangelicals. In 1837, the Presbyterians split along sectional lines in part because of differences over slavery. In 1844, and as a direct result of the slavery issue, the Methodist Episcopal Church, the nation's largest, divided into northern and southern churches. The Baptists did the same a year later. These religious schisms foreshadowed the sectionalized political divisions of the 1850s; they also severed

As this 1841 cartoon reflects, a staple of proslavery propaganda was to contrast the allegedly contented and healthy lot of slaves with that of starving factory workers exploited by the system of wage labor.

one of the main emotional bonds between whites in the North and the South.

The religious defense of slavery was central to the slaveholding ethic of paternalism that developed after 1830. By the 1850s, planters commonly described slaves as members of an extended family who were treated better than free workers in the North. This language often reflected the psychological need of planters to feel appreciated, even loved, as caring parents by their slave dependents. Some evangelical masters tried to act as moral stewards to their slaves and to curb the worst features of their bondage. Led by Charles Colcock Jones, a minister and planter in the Georgia lowcountry, they founded religious missions to the slaves and sought reforms, such as legal measures, that would prevent the separation of slave families. Such slaveholders, however, were a minority, and efforts to reform slavery failed largely because masters would accept no limits on their power to control and work their slaves as they saw fit.

The crusade to sanctify slavery won few converts outside the South. Most northern churches did not endorse abolitionism but did have moral qualms about slavery. In a particularly stinging rebuke to southern church leaders in the 1850s, black abolitionists succeeded in having slaveholders barred from international religious conventions.

More common than the biblical defense of slavery was the racial argument that black people were unfit for freedom among white people. Drawing in part on

FROM THEN TO NOW

The Economic Legacy of Slavery

The South today enjoys one of the highest rates of economic growth in the nation and plays host to business conglomerates, bank mergers, and Olympic games. Yet as late as the 1930s, the South was so impoverished that it was labeled the nation's number-one economic problem. The key to this remarkable transformation was the way in which the South finally overcame the economic legacy of slavery.

Because slavery persisted in the South and was abolished in the North, the Northern and Southern economies developed separately before the Civil War. The key difference was the markedly lower level of Southern investment in manufacturing and transportation compared to the levels in the North. Slaveowners had invested two-thirds of their wealth in slaves and were reluctant to promote changes that would diversify their economy along northern lines through the introduction of manufacturing based on low-wage labor. On the contrary, they had every incentive to keep wages high to protect the value of their investment in human labor.

The end of slavery reversed the basic dynamic shaping the southern economy. Planters now had to derive their wealth primarily from their land, not their slaves. As a result, they encouraged low-wage policies that transformed many former slaves and poor white farmers into impoverished tenant farmers and sharecroppers. When cotton prices began a steady decline in the 1870s, Southern investors turned to manufacturing in an effort to generate economic growth, but the abundance of cheap agricultural labor kept industrial wage rates well below the national level. Consequently, the South attracted little in the way of outside labor. And with investment opportunities more attractive elsewhere, it attracted little capital for modernizing its factories. Education in the South likewise remained behind, because the white southern elite was leery of reforms that would increase workers' skills and encourage them to leave the region in search of better wages. Thus, although southern industry grew, it remained labor-intensive and failed to keep pace with the region's rising population. By the 1930s, when the Great Depression hit, the South was mired in poverty and backwardness.

Sweeping new federal policies initiated in the wake of the Depression began fundamentally to change the Southern economy, raising wages and bringing them more in line with the national average. Farm subsidies encouraged planters to take land out of production, forcing poor tenants and sharecroppers to leave the land and migrate out of the region. Abundant, well-paying jobs in Northern factories during World War II accelerated the outflow of the South's low-skill workers. Meanwhile, federal money poured into the South for new defense plants and war-related projects.

By the 1950s, the formerly insulated, low-wage southern economy had turned the corner. Southern politicians dropped the region's corporate taxes to the lowest in the nation and became adept at attracting new sources of capital and large federal subsidies. After initially opposing the black-led civil rights revolution of the 1950s and 1960s, most of the white business elite backed the formal end of racial segregation in an attempt to improve the South's image. Today, well over a century after slavery had placed it on a separate path of economic development, the Southern economy has lost nearly all traces of its distinctiveness and can boast of being in the forefront of national economic trends.

the scientific wisdom of the day, the racial defense alleged that black people were naturally lazy and inherently inferior to white people. If freed, so went the argument, they would turn to crime and sexually assault white women. Only the controls of slavery enabled the races to coexist in the South. Slavery as necessary racial control was a central theme in Thomas R. Dew's *Review of the Debates in the Virginia Legislature of 1831 and 1832*, the first major justification of slavery by a Southerner. Dew, a Tidewater planter, was responding to a proposal for gradual emancipation that had been introduced into the Virginia legislature. Although the plan was defeated (largely because the eastern plantation counties were overrepresented in the legislature), upper-class conservatives such as Dew were alarmed by the potentially dangerous class division it had revealed between slaveholders and nonslaveholders. He tried to unite white people on the issue of race.

The racial argument resonated powerfully among white people because nearly all of them, including those otherwise opposed to slavery, dreaded emancipation. The attitude of a Tennessee farmer, as recorded by a northern traveler in the 1850s, was typical: "He said he'd always wished there hadn't been any niggers here . . . , but he wouldn't like to have them free." Unable to conceive of living in a society with many free black people, most white people could see no middle ground between slavery and the presumed social chaos of emancipation.

The existence of *black* slavery also had egalitarian implications for the nonslaveholding majority of whites. Slavery supposedly spared white Southerners from the menial, degrading labor that white northerners had to perform. Moreover, because slaves lacked political rights, champions of slavery argued that black bondage buttressed the political liberties of all white males by removing from politics the leveling demands of the poor and propertyless for a redistribution of wealth.

Despite its apparent success in forging white solidarity, the racial argument could be turned on its head and used to weaken slavery. Most white Northerners were about as racist as their southern counterparts, but they were increasingly willing to end slavery on the grounds that the stronger white race should help black people improve themselves as free persons. In short, nothing in the internal logic of racist doctrines required enslaving black people. That same logic also encouraged some white Southerners to challenge the economic prerogatives of slaveholders. Why, for example, should any white people, as members of the master race, be forced into economic competition against skilled slave artisans? Why should not all nonagricultural jobs be legally reserved for white people? Doctrines of black inferiority could not

prevent white unity from cracking when the economic interests of nonslaveholders clashed with those of planters.

CONCLUSION

Slavery and a biracial social order defined the South as a distinctive region. The spread of plantation agriculture across the Lower South after 1830 deepened the involvement of white Southerners in cotton and slavery. At the same time, an abolitionist movement in the North attacked slavery on moral grounds and demanded that it be abolished. As southern interests became more enmeshed in an institution that outsiders condemned, religious and intellectual leaders portrayed slavery as a Christian institution and a positive good necessary for white democracy and harmonious race relations. Proslavery ideologues stridently insisted that the South was separate from and superior to the rest of the nation.

The proslavery argument depicted a nearly ideal society blessed by class and racial harmony. In reality, social conditions in the slave South were contradictory and conflict-ridden. Slaves were not content in their bondage. They dreamed of freedom and sustained that dream through their own forms of Christianity and the support of family and kin. Relations between masters and their slaves were antagonistic, not affectionate, and wherever the system of control slackened, slaves resisted their owners.

Nor did all white southerners, who confronted increasing economic inequality after 1830, accept racial slavery as in their best interests. It divided as well as united them. The publication in 1857 of Hinton Rowan Helper's *The Impending Crisis of the South,* a scathing indictment by a white North Carolinian of slavery's harmful effect on economic opportunities for average white people, vividly showed that not all were convinced by the proslavery argument.

During the 1850s, the size of the slaveholding class fell from 31 percent of Southern white families to 25 percent. Slaveowners were a shrinking minority, and slavery was in decline throughout the Upper South. In the Border South, free labor was replacing slavery as the dominant means of organizing economic production. In these states, slavery was a vulnerable institution. Planters were not fooled by the public rhetoric of white unity. They knew that slavery was increasingly confined to the Lower South and that elsewhere in the South white support for it was gradually eroding. Planters feared the double-edged challenge to their privileged positions of outside interference with slavery and internal white disloyalty. By the 1850s, many of them were concluding that the only way to resolve their dilemma was to make the South a separate nation.

REVIEW QUESTIONS

1. What factors accounted for the tremendous expansion of cotton production in the South? How was this expansion linked to slavery and westward movement?

2. What differentiated the Upper South from the Lower South? What role did slavery play in each region after 1815?

3. How would you characterize the life of a plantation slave? What insights does Hannah Crafts's opening account provide into the special vulnerability of slave women? Why were religion and family such key features of the world that slaves built for themselves? What evidence is there of resistance and rebellion among the slaves?

4. How did most nonslaveholding white Southerners live? What values did they prize most highly? Why did most nonslaveholders accept slavery or at least not attack it directly?

5. What was the position of free black Southerners in southern society? How were their freedoms restricted?

6. How did white Southerners attempt to defend slavery and reconcile it with Christianity?

KEY TERMS

Black codes (p. 342)

Denmark Vesey's Conspiracy (p. 336)

Gabriel Prosser's Rebellion (p. 336)

Gang system (p. 326)

Nat Turner's Rebellion (p. 336)

Slave codes (p. 332)

Underground Railroad (p. 337)

RECOMMENDED READING

Bowman, Shearer. *Masters and Lords: Mid-19th Century U.S. Planters and Prussian Junkers* (1993). A fascinating study in comparative history that portrays southern planters as agrarian capitalists.

Freehling, William W. *The Road to Disunion: Secessionists at Bay, 1776-1854* (1990). A fine introduction to the social diversity of the Old South, especially strong in exploring the tensions over slavery between the Upper South and the Lower South.

Gates, Henry Louis, Jr., ed. *The Bondwoman's Narrative* (2002). A superb introduction by the editor helps the reader appreciate just how unique is this autobiographical novel by a self-educated house slave.

Genovese, Eugene D. *Roll, Jordan, Roll: The World the Slaveholders Made* (1974). A richly textured study of slavery that is an excellent source for the interaction between masters and slaves. Genovese argues that paternalistic relations of dependent rights and obligations characterized slavery.

Johnson, Walter. *Soul by Soul: Life Inside the Antebellum Slave Market* (1999). An innovative study that takes the reader inside the daily life of the slave market and lays bare its multiple meanings for slave, slave trader, and slaveholder.

Morris, Cristopher. *Becoming Southern: The Evolution of a Way of Life, Warren County and Vicksburg, Mississippi, 1770–1860* (1995). A well-crafted study that reveals how central slavery was to the evolving self-consciousness of rural white southerners.

Oakes, James. *The Ruling Race* (1982). A relatively short but provocative history of the slave-owning class that stresses the restless, acquisitive nature of the small slave owners, the most typical holders of slaves.

Stampp, Kenneth M. *The Peculiar Institution* (1956). A work that has aged well and is still the best one-volume history of southern slavery; it leaves no doubt that slavery was both brutal and profitable.

Wyatt-Brown, Bertram. *Southern Honor: Ethics and Behavior in the Old South* (1982). Valuable for its insights into the culture of the planter class and the notions of honor that structured social relations among all white people.

ADDITIONAL SOURCES
The Lower South

Fogel, Robert W., and Stanley Engerman. *Time on the Cross: The Economics of American Negro Slavery* (1974).

Ford, Lacy K., Jr. *Origins of Southern Radicalism: The South Carolina Upcountry, 1800–1860* (1988).

Lockley, Timothy J. *Lines in the Sand: Race and Class in Lowcountry Georgia, 1750-1860* (2001).

McCurry, Stephanie. *Masters of Small Worlds* (1995).

Thornton, J. Mills, III. *Politics and Power in a Slave Society* (1978).

Vlach, John Michael. *The Planter's Prospect: Privilege and Slaves in Plantation Paintings* (2002).

Wright, Gavin. *The Political Economy of the Cotton South* (1978).

The Upper South

Allmendinger, David F. *Ruffin: Family and Reform in the Old South* (1990).

Bailey, Fred Arthur. *Class and Tennessee's Confederate Generation* (1987).

Crofts, David W. *Old Southampton: Politics and Society in a Virginia County, 1834–1869* (1992).

Fields, Barbara J. *Slavery and Freedom on the Middle Ground: Maryland during the Nineteenth Century* (1985).

McKenzie, Robert Tracey. *One South or Many? Plantation Belt and Upcounty in Civil War Era Tennessee* (1994).

Tadman, Michael. *Speculators and Slaves: Masters, Traders, and Slaves in the Old South* (1989).

Slave Life and Culture

Blassingame, John W. *The Slave Community: Plantation Life in the Antebellum South* (1972).

Dew, Charles B. *Bond of Iron: Master and Slave at Buffalo Forge* (1994).

Gutman, Herbert G. *The Black Family in Slavery and Freedom, 1750–1925* (1974).

Kolchin, Peter. *Unfree Labor: American Slavery and Russian Serfdom* (1987).

McDonald, Roderick A. *The Economy and Material Culture of Slaves* (1993).

Starobin, Robert. *Industrial Slavery in the Old South* (1970).

Wade, Richard C. *Slavery in the Cities* (1964).

Free Society

Berlin, Ira. *Slaves without Masters: The Free Negro in the Antebellum South* (1974).

Bolton, Charles C. *Poor Whites of the Antebellum South* (1994).

Bynum, Victoria E. *Unruly Women: The Politics of Social and Sexual Control in the Old South* (1992).

Cecil-Fronsman, Bill. *Common Whites: Class and Culture in Antebellum North Carolina* (1992).

Fox-Genovese, Elizabeth. *Within the Plantation Household: Black and White Women of the Old South* (1988).

Harris, J. William. *Plain Folk and Gentry in a Slave Society* (1985).

Owsley, Frank. *Plain Folk in the South* (1949).

The Proslavery Argument

Bailey, David L. *Shadow on the Church: Southwestern Evangelical Religion and the Issue of Slavery, 1783–1860* (1985).

Fredrickson, George M. *The Black Image in the White Mind* (1971).

Genovese, Eugene D. *The Slaveholders' Dilemma: Freedom and Progress in Southern Conservative Thought, 1820-1860* (1992).

Jenkins, W. S. *Pro-Slavery Thought in the Old South* (1935).

Mathews, Donald G. *Religion in the Old South* (1977).

McKivigan, John R., and Mitchell Snay, eds. *Religion and the Antebellum Debate over Slavery* (1998).

Snay, Mitchell. *Gospel of Disunion: Religion and Separatism in the Antebellum South* (1993).

WHERE TO LEARN MORE

- **The Anacostia Museum Center for African American History.** This museum of the Smithsonian Institution explores American history and cultures from an African American perspective. Go to www.si.edu/anacostia/ for information on its exhibits and a calendar of events.

- **Appalachian Museum of Berea College, Berea, Kentucky.** This museum is an excellent source for understanding the lifestyles and material culture of the nonslaveholding farmers in the Appalachian highlands. For an overview of its exhibits, see www.museum.appstate.edu/exhibits/exhibits.shtml.

- **Cottonlandia Museum, Greenwood, Mississippi.** The library and museum depict the history of cotton in the Mississippi Delta. Special collections include some Native American artifacts. Information on its displays can be found at www.gcvg.com/CL.html.

- **Jarrell Plantation, Juliette, Georgia.** This state historic site consists of a fifteen-building farm complex that conveys a good sense of the physical dimensions of a nineteenth-century Georgia plantation. For a visual tour of the plantation, go to www.mylink.net/~jarrell/.

- **Meadow Farm Museum, Richmond, Virginia.** The archives and museum are especially strong on southern farm life in the mid-nineteenth century. A description of the museum is at www.co.henrico.va.us/rec/kmfarm.html.

 Please refer to the document CD-ROM for primary sources related to this chapter.

✦ *Whether at home or on the road, the contributions of women were indispensable to the success of ante-*
bellum reform movements.

THE MARKET REVOLUTION AND SOCIAL REFORM
12
1815–1850

East Boylston, Mass. 10th mo. 2d, 1837

Dear Friend: . . .

The investigation of the rights of the slave has led me to a better understanding of my own. I have found the Anti-Slavery cause to be the high school of morals in our land — the school in which *human rights* are more fully investigated, and better understood and taught, than in any other. Here a great fundamental principle is uplifted and illuminated, and from this central light, rays innumerable stream all around. Human beings have *rights*, because they are *moral* beings: the rights of *all* men grow out of their moral nature; and as all men have the same moral nature, they have essentially the same rights. These rights may be wrested from the slave, but they cannot be alienated: his title to himself is as perfect *now*, as is that of Lyman Beecher [a prominent minister]: it is stamped on his moral being, and is, like it, imperishable. Now if rights are founded on the nature of our moral being, then the *mere circumstance of sex* does not give to man higher rights and responsibilities, than to woman. To suppose that it does, would be to deny the self-evident truth, that the "physical constitution is the mere instrument of the moral nature." To suppose that it does, would be to break up utterly the relations, of the two natures, and to reverse their functions, exalting the animal nature into a monarch, and humbling the moral into a slave; making the former a pro-

CHAPTER OUTLINE

Industrial Change and Urbanization

The Transportation Revolution
Cities and Immigrants
The Industrial Revolution
Growing Inequality and New Classes

Reform and Moral Order

The Benevolent Empire
The Temperance Movement
Women's Role in Reform
Backlash against Benevolence

Institutions and Social Improvement

School Reform
Prisons, Workhouses, and Asylums
Utopian Alternatives

Abolitionism and Women's Rights

Rejecting Colonization
Abolitionism
The Women's Rights Movement
Political Antislavery

Conclusion

prietor, and the latter its property. When human beings are regarded as *moral* beings, *sex*, instead of being enthroned upon the summit, . . . sinks into insignificance and nothingness. My doctrine then is, that whatever it is morally right for man to do, it is morally right for woman to do. Our duties originate, not from difference of sex, but from the diversity of our relations in life, the various gifts and talents committed to our care, and the different eras in which we live.

Angelina Emily Grimké

Aileen S. Kraditor, ed., *Up From the Pedestal: Selected Writings in the History of American Feminism* (New York: Quadrangle, 1968), pp. 62–63.

Angelina Grimké wrote the above as part of a public letter to Catherine Beecher, a pioneer in women's education and the daughter of the evangelical preacher Lyman Beecher mentioned in the letter. In 1837, on an abolitionist lecture tour in New England with her sister Sarah, Angelina had become the first American woman to defy the social taboo against women speaking in public to a mixed audience of men and women. Catherine Beecher was among the many critics of the Grimké sisters, and Angelina publicly responded to her attacks.

Born in 1805 to a wealthy slaveholding family in Charleston, Angelina was the daughter of a prominent jurist. Despite all the social and economic benefits that membership in the planter class conferred upon her, she passionately rejected slavery when she became a young adult. As was also true for her sister, this rejection was part of a religious conversion to Quakerism. Angelina left her home in Charleston in 1829 and joined Sarah in Philadelphia. The sisters joined the abolitionist movement in 1835, and within two years had become the crusade's most celebrated (and notorious) platform lecturers. As Angelina made clear in her letter to Beecher, her commitment to women's rights flowed out of her exposure to abolitionism.

Soon after her marriage in 1838 to the abolitionist Theodore Weld, Angelina compiled much of the first-hand documentation on slavery that contributed to the popular success of Weld's *American Slavery As It Is*, an antislavery tract that appeared in 1839. For reasons that still remain mysterious, her marriage also coincided with her withdrawal from public life for a dozen years. Although she resumed her reform activities in the 1850s and worked for the emancipation of the slaves during the Civil War, she only rarely spoke in public. Before her death in 1879, Angelina learned that her brother Henry, who had become the family patriarch after the death of her father in 1819, had fathered three slave children, whom he retained as slaves. Her worst fears of the corrupting influence of slavery had been confirmed.

Although Angelina, in her commitment to radical reform, was hardly typical of antebellum American women, let alone women of the planter class, her journey from a privileged life in Charleston to one of social activism in the North speaks to the radicalizing potential of the reform impulse that swept over the nation after the War of 1812.

This reform impulse was strongest in the North, where traditional social and economic relations were undergoing wrenching changes as a market revolution accelerated the spread of cities, factories, and commercialized farms. Cities grew at the fastest relative rate in American history. Urbanization also brought new production patterns and increasingly separated one's home from one's place of work. New middle and working classes evolved in response to such changes, which were the most pronounced in the Northeast. The North was also the area where the emotional fires of evangelical revivals burned the hottest.

The religious message of the Second Great Awakening that began in the early 1800s provided a framework for responding to the changes that accompanied the market revolution. New within mainstream Protestantism was the belief that anyone who sought salvation could attain it, not just those whom God had predestined to be saved. Evangelicalism taught that in both the spiritual and secular realms, individuals were accountable for their own actions. Through Christian activism, individuals could strive toward moral perfectibility. Social evils, and the sinful consequences of economic and social changes, could be cleansed if only good Christians would help others find the path of righteousness.

The first wave of reform after the War of 1812 focused on individual behavior, targeting drinking, gambling, sexual misconduct, and Sabbath-breaking. By the 1830s, a second phase of reform turned to institutional solutions for crime, poverty, and social delinquency, largely untouched by voluntary moral suasion. The third phase of the reform cycle rejected the social beliefs and practices that prescribed fixed and subordinate positions to certain Americans based on race and also on sex. This radical phase culminated in the abolitionist and women's right's movement.

KEY TOPICS

- The increasing industrialization of the U.S. economy between 1815 and 1850

- The growth of cities and the emergence of both a new middle-class society and a lower class of working poor

- New wealth and the increasing inequalities among the rich, the middle class, and the working classes

- The rise of the reform movement after the War of 1812

- The growth of abolitionist agitation and sentiment in the North

- Women's crucial role in the reform movements and the rise of an organized women's rights movement

INDUSTRIAL CHANGE AND URBANIZATION

In 1820, four in five of the free labor force worked in agriculture, and manufacturing played a minor role in overall economic activity. Over the next three decades, however, the United States joined England as a world leader in industrialization. By 1850, manufacturing accounted for one-third of total commodity output, and nonfarm employment had more than doubled to 45 percent of the labor force.

The most direct cause of this rapid and sustained surge in manufacturing was the increasing consumption within the United States of the goods the country was producing. The **transportation revolution** dramatically reduced transportation costs and shipping times, opened up new markets for farmers and manufacturers alike, and provided an ongoing incentive for expanding production (see Table 12–1). As agricultural and manufactured goods were exchanged more efficiently, a growing home market continually stimulated the development of American manufacturing.

THE TRANSPORTATION REVOLUTION

Aside from some 4,000 miles of toll roads in the Northeast, the nation had nothing approaching a system of transportation in 1815. The cost of moving goods by land transportation was prohibitively high. It cost just as much to haul heavy goods by horse-drawn wagons 30 miles into the interior as to ship them 3,000 miles across the Atlantic Ocean. Water transportation was much

cheaper, but it was limited to the coast or navigable rivers. Thus, only farmers located near a city or a river could grow surplus crops for sale in an outside market. Western farm surpluses followed the southerly flow of the Ohio and Mississippi river systems to market outlets in New Orleans.

Steamboats and canals. Steamboats provided the first transportation breakthrough. In 1807, Robert Fulton demonstrated their commercial practicality when he sent the *Clermont* 150 miles up the Hudson River from New York City to Albany. By the 1820s, steamboats had reduced the cost and the time of upriver shipments by 90 percent. As steamboats spread to western waters, more and more farmers could now reap the economic benefits of exporting corn, pork, and other regional foodstuffs.

Western trade did not start to flow eastward until the completion of the Erie Canal in 1825, the first and most successful of the artificial waterways designed to link eastern seaboard cities with western markets (see Map 12–1). Funded by the

TABLE 12.1			
Impact of the Transportation Revolution on Traveling Time			
Route	**1800**	**1830**	**1860**
New York to Philadelphia	2 days	1 day	Less than 1 day
New York to Charleston	More than 1 week	5 days	2 days
New York to Chicago	6 weeks	3 weeks	2 days
New York to New Orleans	4 weeks	2 weeks	6 days

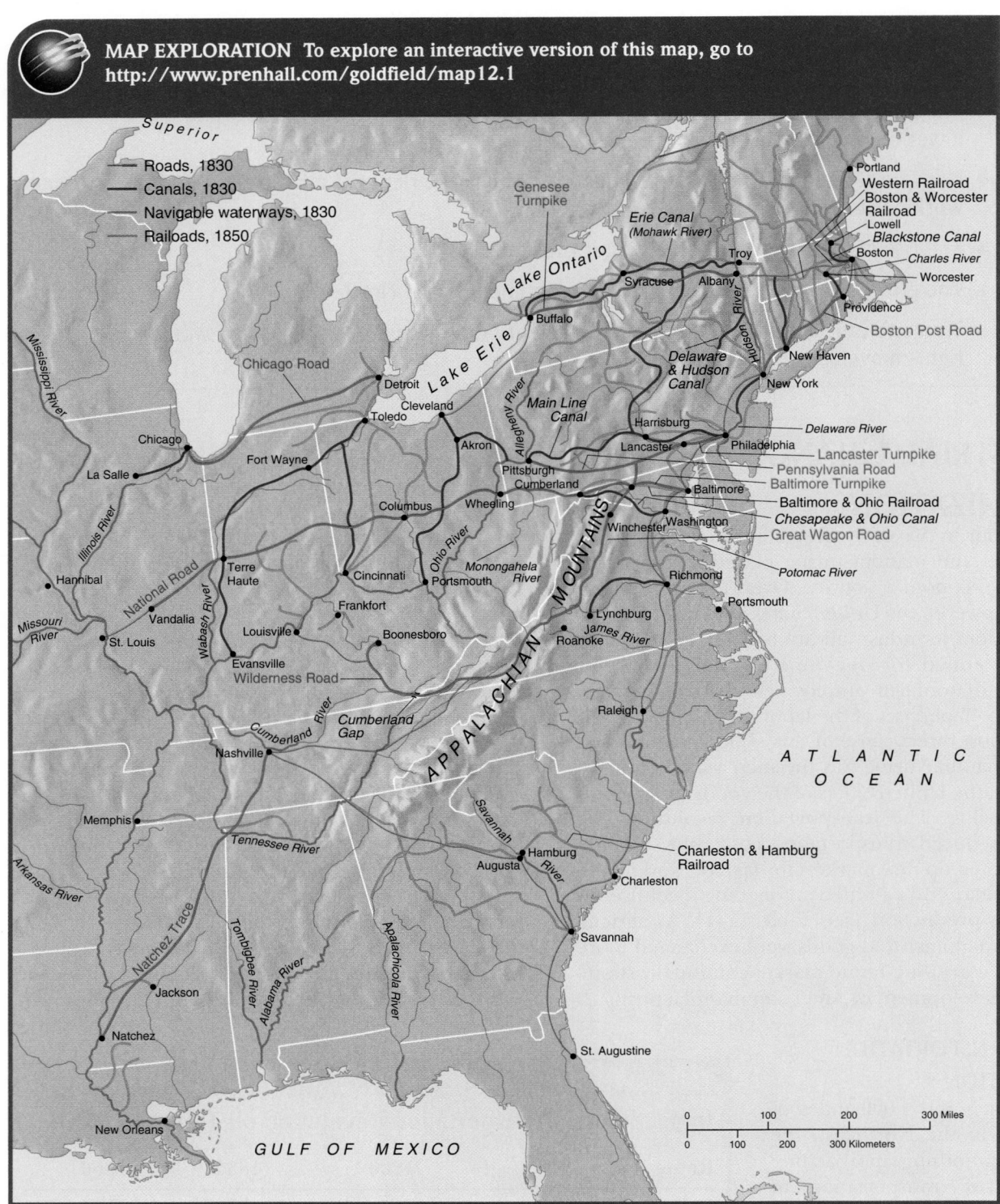

MAP EXPLORATION To explore an interactive version of this map, go to
http://www.prenhall.com/goldfield/map12.1

MAP 12-1 The Transportation Revolution

By 1830, a network of roads, canals, and navigable rivers was spurring economic growth in the first phase of the Transportation Revolution. By 1850, railroads, the key development in the second phase of the Transportation Revolution, were opening up additional areas to commercial activity.

THE AMERICAN JOURNEY
THIRD EDITION

GET THE BOOK THAT **GETS YOUR STUDENTS.**

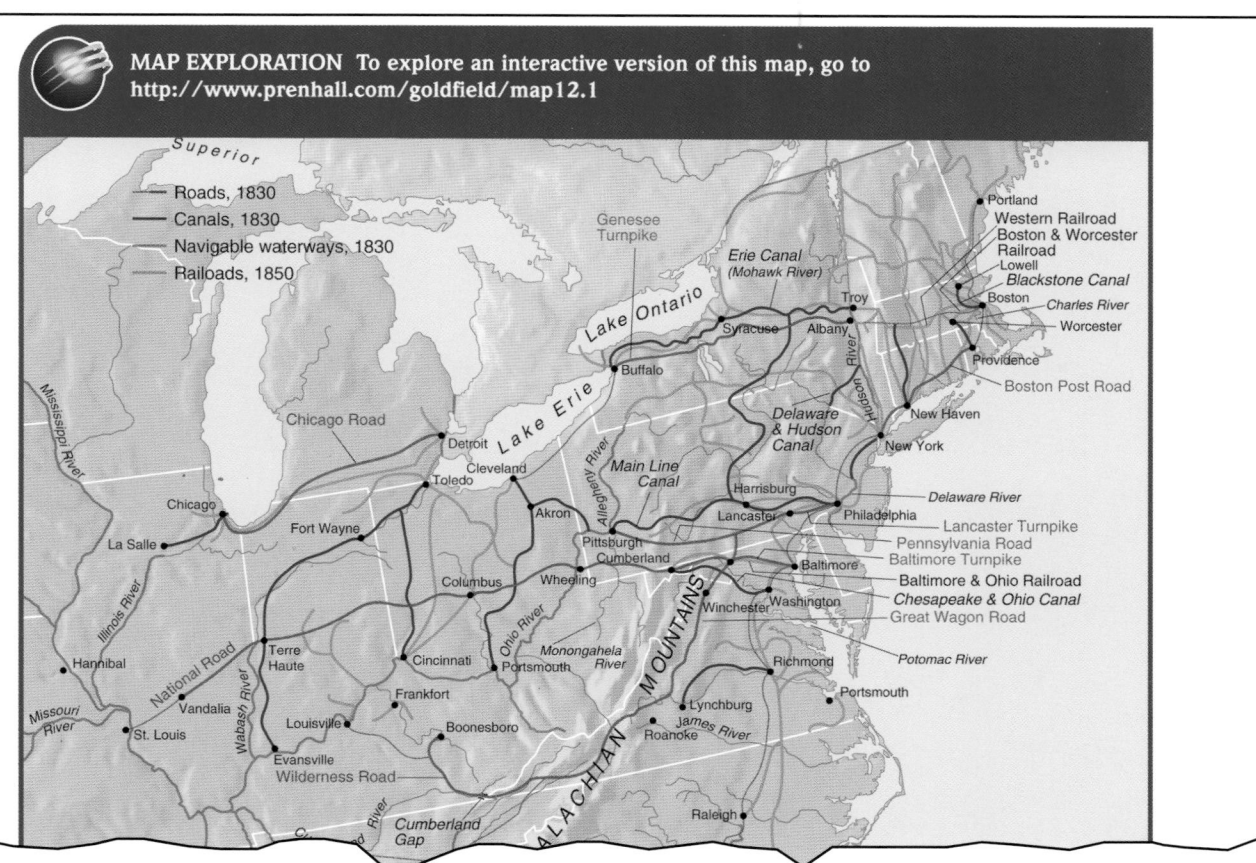

MAP EXPLORATION To explore an interactive version of this map, go to
http://www.prenhall.com/goldfield/map12.1

GET THE BEST MAPS:
Map Explorations

Understanding the American journey means developing geographical literacy to clarify not only what happened and where it happened, but most importantly the significance of the relationship between the two. What better way to impart this crucial piece of history to students than with detailed maps and interactive maps?

The abundant maps in **THE AMERICAN JOURNEY, THIRD EDITION**—all called out in the text—tell a visually stimulating, highly integral part of the American story. Detailed maps with insightful captions appear throughout this book to show students the importance of the physical locations and spatial relationships that were often important in shaping American history. What's more, interactive versions, or *Map Explorations* are featured on its state-of-the-art Companion Website™ at *www.prenhall.com/goldfield*.

Map Explorations allow students to interact with these maps in creative ways, with drag and drop exercises, labeling, panning to view a larger picture, or with animations. Critical thought questions accompany the *Map Exploration* on the website to enhance students' complete understanding. In this example on page 354, students explore a large detailed map of The Transportation Revolution that depicts how the early network of roads and rivers was contributing to economic growth in the 1830's, thus spurring commercial activity throughout this region. When students visit the *Map Exploration* on the Companion Website™, they will experience an interactive version of this map. *Other examples may be found on pages 128, 249, 268, 463, 611, 707, and 922.*

Take a moment to look at **THE AMERICAN JOURNEY**'s maps and *Map Explorations*. Notice how they will help your students understand the significant role geography played as American history took shape. Get Goldfield—and get your students the best maps.

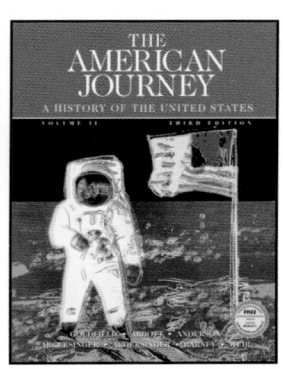

GET THE BOOK THAT GETS YOUR STUDENTS.

The authors of THE AMERICAN JOURNEY, THIRD EDITION **take educating students very seriously.** Every aspect of this new edition is geared towards providing the most important scholarship, as well as the best tools to ensure your students have a positive experience with our textbook, regardless of their individual learning style.

In addition, Prentice Hall believes in providing you with the most flexibility and your students with the most value for their investment. Therefore, we are offering THE AMERICAN JOURNEY, THIRD EDITION in a variety of options to serve your teaching needs, plus a selection of value packages designed to satisfy your students' budget concerns. In every way, THE AMERICAN JOURNEY is the book that gets your students.

GET THE BEST TEXT

- **The Best Pedagogy: Student Tool Kit** *(refer to tab 1 in this text)*
- **The Best Drama:** *Voices from the American Journey (refer to tab 2 in this text)*
- **The Best Maps:** *Map Explorations (refer to tab 3 in this text)*
- **The Best Presentation: Overviews and 3-Level Heads** *(refer to tab 4 in this text)*
- **The Best Relevance:** *From Then To Now (refer to tab 5 in this text)*
- **The Best Documents:** *American Views (refer to tab 6 in this text)*

GET THE BEST OPTIONS

THE AMERICAN JOURNEY: A HISTORY OF THE UNITED STATES, THIRD EDITION is available in the following formats, all of which include the FREE, exclusive **U.S. History Documents CD-ROM** from Prentice Hall:

- *Combined Edition—includes Chapters 1-31:* 0-13-182553-4
- *Volume 1—includes Chapters 1-15:* 0-13-182552-6
- *Volume 2—includes Chapters 16-31:* 0-13-182550-X

THE AMERICAN JOURNEY is also available in a convenient Brief Edition.

GET THE BEST PACKAGES

Take advantage of these SPECIAL VALUE PACKAGES available with new copies of THE AMERICAN JOURNEY, THIRD EDITION by Goldfield, et al. Get your students these great savings when your bookstore uses the corresponding package ISBNs below:

- **Combined Edition:**
  —*with FREE Study Guide/Practice Test:* 0-13-130271-X
  —*with FREE Common Sense by Thomas Paine AND The Jungle by Upton Sinclair:* 0-13-130272-8

- **Volume I:**
  —*with FREE Study Guide/Practice Test:* 0-13-130273-6
  —*with FREE Common Sense by Thomas Paine:* 0-13-130274-4

- **Volume II:**
  —*with FREE Study Guide/Practice Test:* 0-13-130275-2
  —*with FREE The Jungle by Upton Sinclair:* 0-13-130276-0

Additional FREE Value Packages are available. For details, please contact your local Prentice Hall sales representative.

PRENTICE HALL HISTORY
Connecting the past with the future
www.prenhall.com/history

Chronology

1790	Samuel Slater opens the first permanent cotton mill in Rhode Island.
1793	Eli Whitney patents the first cotton gin.
1807	Robert Fulton's steamboat, the *Clermont*, makes its pioneering voyage up the Hudson River.
1814	The Boston Associates opens its Waltham mill, the first textile factory to mechanize all phases of production.
1817	Construction on the Erie Canal begins.
	American Colonization Society is founded.
1819–1823	Economic depression.
1824	In *Gibbons v. Ogden*, the Supreme Court strikes down a state monopoly over steamboat navigation.
1825	Erie Canal is completed.
1826	American Temperance Society launches its crusade.
1828	The Baltimore and the Ohio, the most important of the early railroads, is chartered.
1829	David Walker publishes *Appeal to the Colored Citizens of the World.*
1830	Joseph Smith founds the Church of Jesus Christ of Latter-day Saints.
1830–1831	Evangelical revivals are held in northern cities.
1831	William Lloyd Garrison begins publishing *The Liberator.*
1833	Slaves in the British Empire are emancipated.
	American Anti-Slavery Society is organized.

1834	New York Female Reform Society is founded.
	Female workers at the Lowell Mills stage their first strike.
1836	Congress passes gag rule.
1837	Horace Mann begins campaign for school reform in Massachusetts.
	Antiabolitionist mob kills Elijah P. Lovejoy.
	In *Charles River Bridge v. Warren Bridge*, the Supreme Court encourages economic competition by ruling that presumed rights of monopolistic privileges could not be used to block new economic enterprises.
1839–1843	Economic depression.
1840	Abolitionists split into Garrisonian and anti-Garrisonian societies.
	Political abolitionists launch the Liberty party.
1841	Brook Farm is established.
	Dorothea Dix begins her work to improve conditions for the mentally ill.
1842	Massachusetts Supreme Court in *Commonwealth v. Hunt* strengthens the legal right of workers to organize trade unions.
1845	Potato famine in Ireland sets off a mass migration of Irish to the United States.
1846–1848	Mormons migrate to the West.
1847	John Humphrey Noyes establishes the Oneida Community.
1848	Seneca Falls Convention outlines a program for women's rights.

New York legislature, the Erie Canal stretched 364 miles from Albany to Buffalo, a small port on Lake Erie. Begun at a time when the United States had barely 100 miles of canals, its construction by Irish immigrants was the greatest engineering feat of its era. An immediate success, the Erie reduced the cost of sending freight from Buffalo to New York City by more than 90 percent, and by the 1840s, it was pulling in more western trade than was being sent to New Orleans on the Mississippi River.

Anxious to match the Erie's success, other states launched plans for competing canals to the West. More than 3,000 miles of canal were in place by 1840, but no other canal could overcome the tremendous advantage of the Erie's head start in fixing trading patterns along its route. Before the Panic of 1837 abruptly ended the canal boom by drying up financing, three broad networks of canals had been built. One set linked seaboard cities on the Atlantic with their agricultural hinterlands, another connected the Mid-Atlantic states with the Ohio River Valley, and a third funneled western grain to ports on the Great Lakes.

Railroads. Railroads were the last and ultimately the most important link in the transportation improvements that spurred economic development in Jacksonian America. Moving at 15 to 20 miles per hour—four times as fast as a canal boat and twice the speed of a stagecoach—the railroads of the 1830s struck Americans as a radically new technology that overturned traditional notions of time and space. "I

Canal boats below a lock at the Junction of the Erie with the Northern (Champlain) Canals. Aquatint by John Hill.

cannot describe the strange sensation produced on seeing the train of cars come up. And when I started in them . . . it seemed like a dream," exclaimed Christopher Columbus Baldwin of Massachusetts when he saw his first railroad car in 1835.

In 1825, the same year the Erie Canal was completed, the world's first general-purpose railroad, the Stockton and Darlington, opened in England. The construction of the first American railroads began in the late 1820s, and they all pushed outward from seaboard cities eager to connect to the western market. One of the first, the Baltimore and Ohio, was to cross the Appalachians and connect Baltimore with Wheeling, Virginia, on the Ohio River. The Boston and Worcester linked New England and the eastern terminus of the Erie at Albany. By 1840, U.S. rail mileage had drawn even with that of the canals and was twice as extensive as the total for all of Europe. The rails now became the most dynamic booster of interregional trade. Whereas the canal network stopped expanding after 1840, the railroads tripled their mileage in the 1840s. Revenues from freight traffic exceeded those from passenger travel for the first time in 1849. By then, trunk lines built westward from Atlantic Coast cities had reached the Great Lakes and the Ohio Valley and were about to enter the Mississippi Valley.

The rail network in place by mid-century was already altering the North-South sectional balance. The bulk of western trade no longer went downriver to New Orleans but was shipped to the East. Moving in the opposite direction to the West were northern-born settlers, manufactured goods, and cultural values that increas-ingly unified the free states east of the Mississippi into a common economic and cultural unit. As their distinctions blurred, the Northeast and the Old Northwest were becoming just the North. Significantly, no direct rail connection linked the North and the South.

Government and the transportation revolution.

Both national and state government played an active role in promoting the transportation revolution. Given high construction costs and the uncertainty of future profits, private investors were leery of risking their scarce capital in long-term transportation projects. State legislatures stepped in and furnished some 70 percent of the funding for canals and about half of all railroad capital. By the 1830s, the states were also making it easier for private businesses, and especially those in transportation, to receive the legal privileges of incorporation. Paramount among these privileges was the protection of limited liability—that is, the limiting of an investor's liability to one's direct financial stake in the company—and the power of eminent domain—the legal right to purchase whatever land was needed for rights-of-way. The federal government provided engineers for railroad surveys, lowered tariff duties on iron used in rail construction, and granted subsidies to the railroads in the form of public land. Most important, however, were two decisions of the Supreme Court that helped open up the economy to competition. In *Gibbons v. Ogden* (1824), the Court overturned a New York law that had given Aaron Ogden a monopoly on steamboat service between New York and New Jersey. Thomas Gibbons, Ogden's competitor, had a federal license for the coastal trade. The right to compete under the national license, the Court ruled, took legal precedence over Ogden's monopoly. The decision affirmed the supremacy of the national government to regulate interstate commerce.

A new Court, presided over by Roger B. Taney, who became chief justice when John Marshall died in 1835, struck a bolder blow against monopoly in the landmark case of *Charles River Bridge v. Warren Bridge* in 1837. Taney ruled in favor of the Warren Bridge Company by deciding that the older Charles River Bridge Company had not received a monopoly from Massachusetts to collect tolls across the Charles River. Any uncertainties in the charter rights of corpo-

New York City's busy harbor was the entry to the largest metropolitan center that emerged in the nineteenth-century U.S.

rations, reasoned Taney, should be resolved in favor of the broader community interests that would be served by free and open competition.

CITIES AND IMMIGRANTS

Barely one in twenty Americans in the 1790s lived in an urban area (defined by the federal census as a place with a population of 2,500 or more) and Philadelphia, with a population just over 40,000, was the nation's largest city. By 1850, more than one in seven Americans was a city-dweller, and the nation had ten cities whose population exceeded fifty thousand (see Map 12–2). The transportation revolution triggered this surge in urban growth. The cities that prospered and grew were those with access to the expanding network of cheap transport on steamboats, canals, and railroads. This network opened up the rural interior for the purchase of farm commodities by city merchants and the sale of finished goods by urban importers and manufacturers. A huge influx of immigrants after the mid-1840s and simultaneous advances in steam engines provided the cheap labor and sources of power that increasingly made cities focal points of manufacturing production.

The port cities. America's largest cities in the early nineteenth century were its Atlantic ports: New York, Philadelphia, Baltimore, and Boston. As late as the 1820s, these four cities held more than half the total urban population and packed together merchants, artisans, and laborers near the waterfronts that were their economic lifeblood. All these cities grew as a result of transportation improvements, but only New York experienced phenomenal growth. By 1810, New

York had become the largest American city, and its population exceeded 800,000 by the 1850s. One-third of the nation's exports and more than three-fifths of its imports passed through New York between 1820 and 1860. No wonder poet Walt Whitman trumpeted this metropolis as "the great place of the Western Continent, the heart, the brain, the focus, the main spring, the pinnacle, the extremity, the no more beyond of the new world."

New York's harbor gave oceangoing ships direct, protected access to Manhattan Island, and from there, the Hudson River provided a navigable highway flowing 150 miles north to Albany, deep in the state's agricultural interior. No other port was so ideally situated for trade. And no other had the advantage of access to the Erie Canal. New York City benefited, not only from the increased volume of western foodstuffs sent east across the Erie and then down the Hudson River for export to Europe, but also from the swelling flow of finished goods shipped out of New York for sale in the West to farmers increasingly specializing in the production of cash crops. New Yorkers plowed the profits of this commerce into local real estate—which soared in value fifty-fold between 1823 and 1836— and into financial institutions such as the New York Stock Exchange, founded in 1817. The city's banks brought together the capital that made New York the country's chief financial center.

As they grew, the Atlantic ports pioneered new forms of city transportation. Omnibuses—horse-drawn coaches carrying up to twenty passengers—and steam ferries were in common use by the 1820s. The first commuter railroad, the Boston and Worcester,

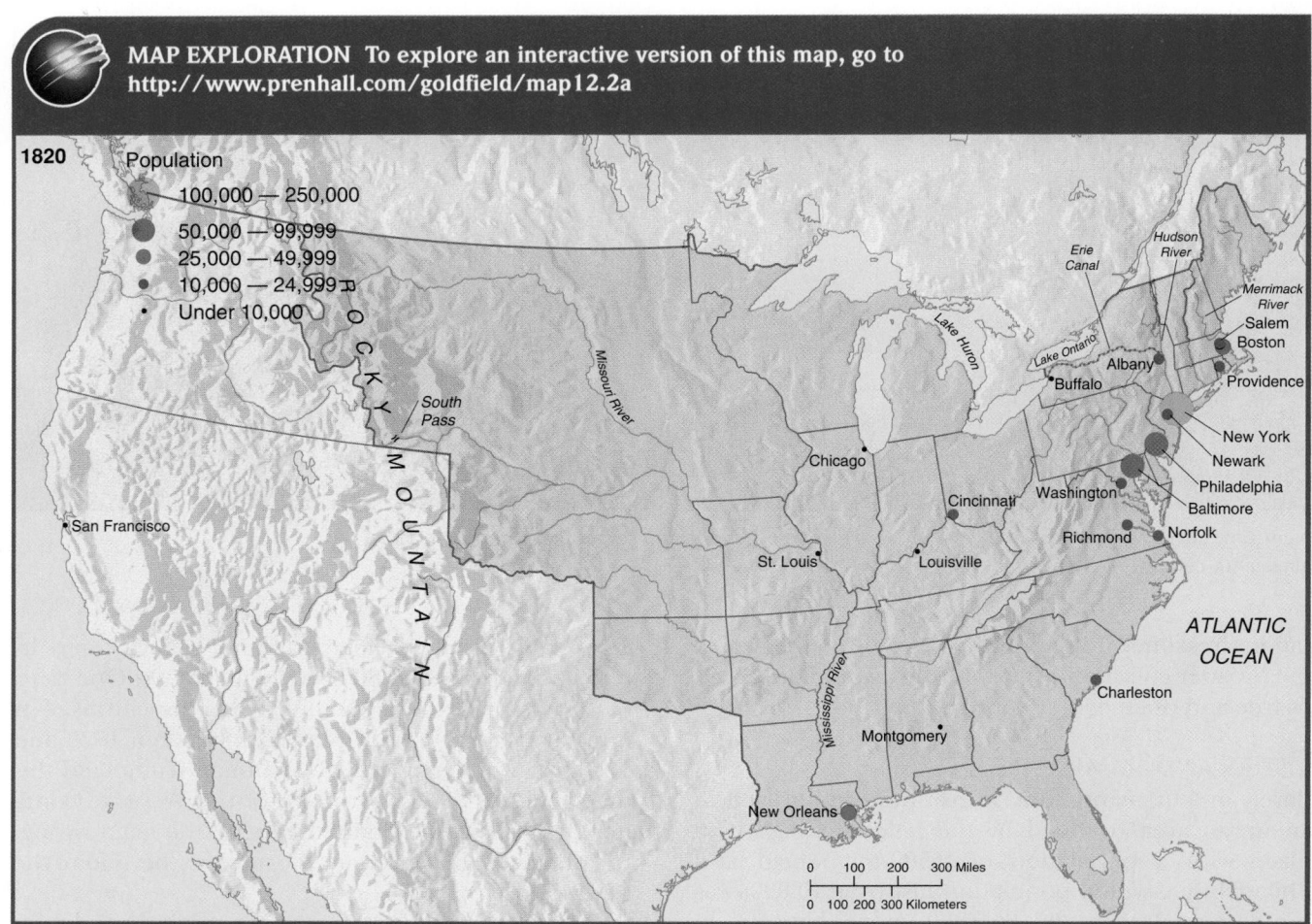

MAP EXPLORATION To explore an interactive version of this map, go to
http://www.prenhall.com/goldfield/map12.2a

MAP 12-2 **The Growth of Cities, 1820-1860**
In 1820, most cities were clustered along the Atlantic seaboard. By 1860, new transportation outlets—canals and railroads—had fostered the rapid growth of cities in the interior, especially at trading locations with access to navigable rivers or to the Great Lakes. Much of this growth occurred in the 1850s.
Data Source: *Statistical Abstract of the United States.*

began service in 1838. At mid-century, horse-drawn street railway lines moved at speeds of about 6 miles an hour, overcoming some of the limitations of the "walking cities" of the early nineteenth century.

Accompanying this growth were the first slums, the most notorious of which was the Five Points district of New York City. In 1842, the English novelist Charles Dickens described this area of tenement houses, brothels, and saloons as "these narrow ways, diverging to the right and left, and reeking everywhere with dirt and filth." Small, flimsy wooden structures, often crammed into a back alley, housed the working poor in cramped, fetid conditions. Backyard privies, supplemented by chamber pots, were the standard means of disposing of human wastes. These outhouses overflowed in heavy rain and often contaminated private wells, the source of

drinking water. Garbage and animal wastes simply accumulated on streets, scavenged by roving packs of hogs.

Inland cities. Largely because of their newness, the cities in the interior escaped the worst of these slum conditions. It was here, away from the seaboard, that the rate of urban growth was the highest. Among the fastest-growing cities was Rochester, New York, a village that the opening of the Erie Canal transformed into a major flour-milling center. Pittsburgh, at the head of the Ohio River, was the first western city to develop a manufacturing sector to complement its exchange function. With access to the extensive coalfields of western Pennsylvania, Pittsburgh had a cheap fuel that provided the high heat needed to manufacture

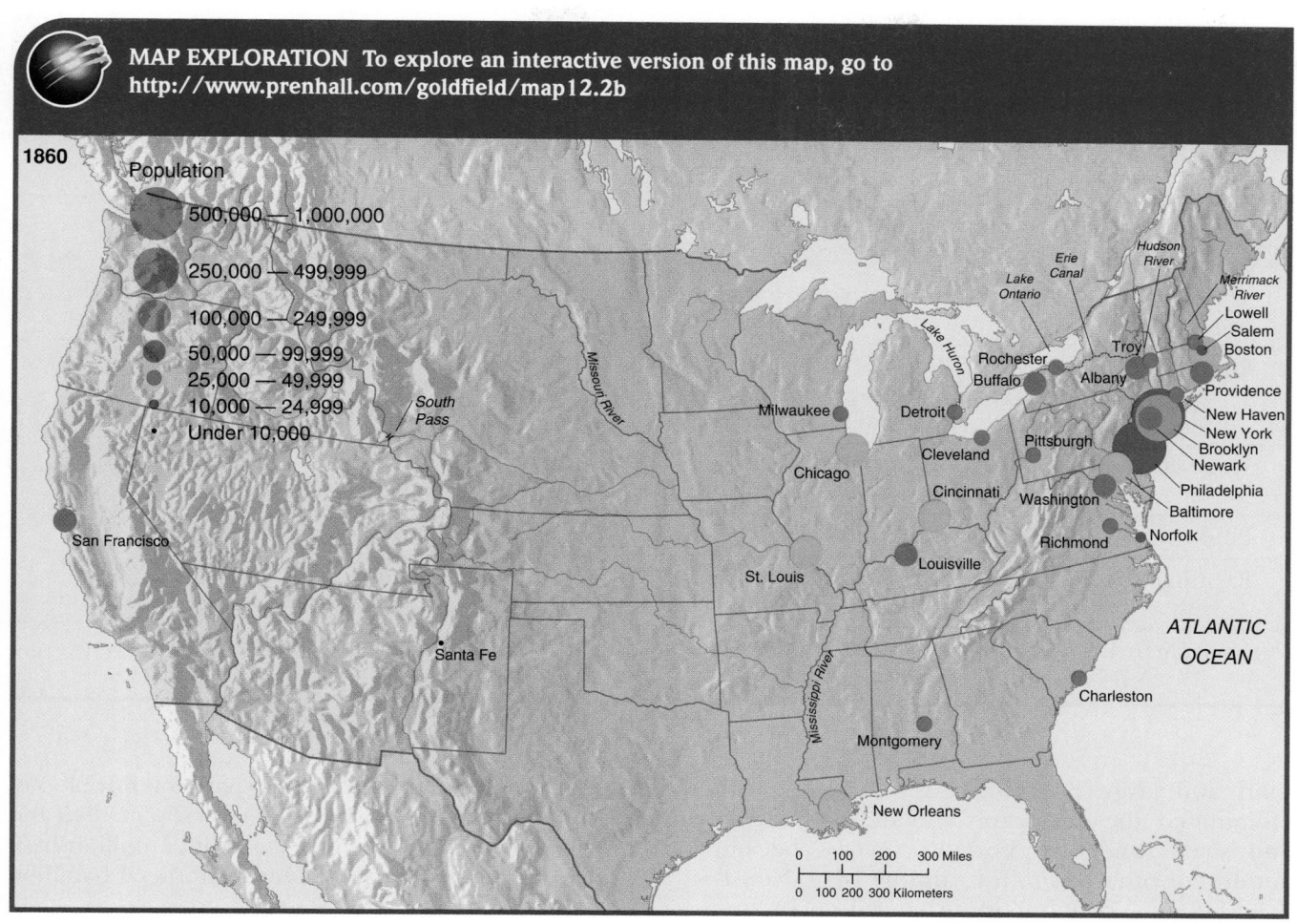

MAP EXPLORATION To explore an interactive version of this map, go to http://www.prenhall.com/goldfield/map12.2b

iron and glass. It emerged as America's best-known and most polluted manufacturing city. Cincinnati, downstream on the Ohio, soon became famous for its hogs. "Porkopolis," as it was called, was the West's first meatpacking center. St. Louis, just below the merger of the Missouri and the Mississippi Rivers, prospered by servicing American trade with the trans-Mississippi West.

By the 1840s, the Great Lake ports of Cleveland, Detroit, Milwaukee, and Chicago were the dynamic centers of western urbanization. Their combined population increased twenty-five-fold between 1830 and 1850. The Great Lakes served as an extension of the Erie Canal, and cities on the lakes where incoming and outgoing goods had to be unloaded for transshipment benefited enormously. They attracted settlers and soon evolved into regional economic centers serving the surrounding agricultural communities. They also aggressively promoted themselves into major rail hubs and thus reaped the

economic advantages of being at the juncture of both water and rail transport.

New industrial cities. The only other cities growing as fast as the Great Lakes ports were the new industrial towns. The densest cluster of these was in rural New England along the fall line of rivers, where the rapidly falling water provided cheap power to drive the industrial machinery of factories and machine shops. Each town was tied to a transportation network that brought in raw cotton for the textile mills from the mercantile centers of Boston and Providence and shipped out the finished goods.

Lowell, Massachusetts, was America's first large-scale planned manufacturing city. Founded in 1822 by Boston businessmen, Lowell was built around the falls of the Merrimack River. Within a decade, rural fields had been transformed into a city of eighteen thousand people. Multistoried brick factories surrounded by detached housing for the supervisory

Overview

Changes Promoting Growth in the Transformed Economy

Sector	1815	1850
Travel and transportation	By foot and horse-drawn wagon	Cheaper and faster with canals, steamboats, and railroads opening up new markets
Population	Overwhelmingly native-born, rural, and concentrated east of the Appalachian Mountains	Four times larger as a result of natural increase and surge of immigration after 1840; settlement of West and growth of cities
Wage labor	Native-born, primarily women and children in manufacturing	Expanding as rural poor and immigrants enter the manufacturing work force
Power	Water-driven mills	Steam-driven engines
Farming	Subsistence-oriented; surplus sold in localized markets	Commercialized agriculture spreading in response to improvements in transportation
Manufacturing	Small-scale production in household units and artisan shops	Large-scale production in eastern cities and factories

staff and large boardinghouses for the workers dominated the landscape and defined the city's industrial functions. Lowell's success became a model for others to follow, and by 1840, New England led the North in both urbanization and industrialization.

Immigration. Swelling the size of nearly all the cities was a surge of immigrants after the 1830s. From 1840 to 1860 the number of immigrants, 4.2 million, increased tenfold over the number that had come in the two preceding decades. At midcentury, most of the population in New York was foreign-born, and in all the port cities of the Northeast, immigrants dominated the manufacturing work force. Most of these immigrants were Irish and German (see Figure 12–1).

In the 1840s, economic and political upheavals in Europe spurred mass migration, mostly to the United States. Catholic peasants of Ireland, dominated by their Protestant English land-lords, eked out a subsistence as tenants on tiny plots of land. A potato blight wiped out the crop in 1845 and 1846, and in the next five years about 1 million Irish died of malnutrition and disease. Another 1.5 million fled, many to the United States.

Lowell was the nation's leading textile center and the second-largest city in Massachusetts by 1850. The building with the cupola and the structure with dormers and chimneys were part of the mill complex. The two detached buildings were boardinghouses for the young women who worked in the mills.

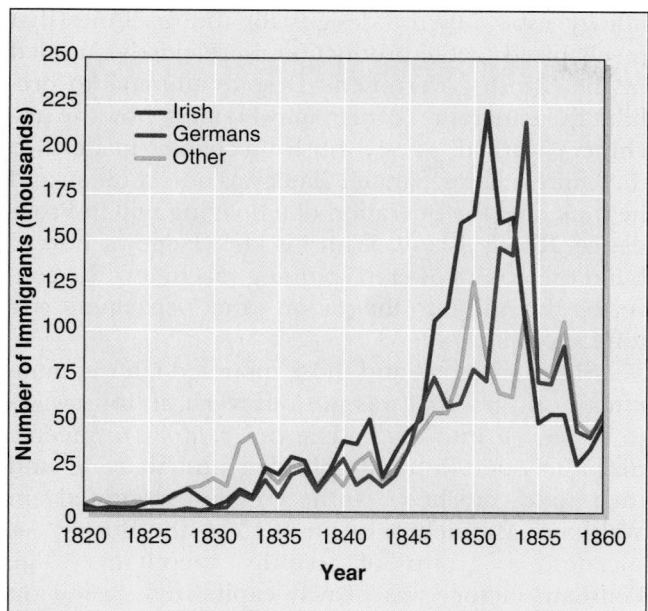

FIGURE 12-1   Immigration to the United States, 1820-1860
The potato famine in Ireland and economic and political unrest on the Continent led to a surge in immigration in the 1840s. The pace slackened in the mid-1850s, when economic conditions in Europe improved.

Data Source: U.S. Bureau of the Census, *Historical Statistics of the United States, Colonial Times to 1957* (1960), p. 57.

The Irish had no money to buy land or move west unless they joined construction gangs for canals and railroads. Without marketable skills, they had to take the worst and lowest-paying jobs: ragpickers, porters, day laborers, and unskilled factory hands. Wives and daughters became laundresses and maids for the urban middle class. Packed into dark cellars, unventilated attics, and rank tenements, the Irish suffered from very high mortality rates. Still, cash wages and access to food made the American city enviable, compared to the prospect of starvation in Ireland. Urging her parents to join her, Margaret McCarthy, an Irish domestic servant, wrote in 1850 that New York was a place "where no man or woman ever Hungered or ever will and where you will not be Seen Naked . . . where you would never want or be at a loss for a good Breakfast and Dinner."

German immigrants were second in number only to the Irish by the 1850s. They came to America to escape poor harvests and political turmoil. Far more Germans than Irish had owned property as farmers, artisans, and shopkeepers and had the capital to purchase land in the West and the skills to join the ranks of small businessmen in the cities. They were also more likely than the Irish to have entered the country through Baltimore or New Orleans, southern ports engaged in the tobacco and cotton trade with continental Europe. From there they fanned out into the Mississippi and Ohio Valleys. More so than the Irish, German immigrants settled in rural areas, but they also gravitated to cities, and by the 1850s they were close to a majority in some of the large cities of the Midwest and Northeast. With their diversified skills, they found ample economic opportunities in the fast-growing cities of the West and a setting in which to build neighborhoods of German-speaking shops, churches, schools, and benevolent societies. These tightly knit communities published their own newspapers and met most of the immigrant's cultural and economic needs.

About four in five of all the immigrants arriving after 1840 settled in the New England and mid-Atlantic states. Their sheer numbers transformed the size and ethnic composition of the working class, especially in the cities of the Northeast. And their cheap labor provided the final ingredient in the expansion of industrialization that began after the War of 1812.

THE INDUSTRIAL REVOLUTION

The Northeast led America's industrial revolution. In 1815, this region had the largest cities, the most developed capital markets, the readiest access to the technological skills of artisans, and the greatest supply of available labor. The first large-scale factories, the textile mills, were erected in New England in the 1820s. For the next thirty years, the United States had the most rapidly developing industrial economy in the world.

The household and the small workshop were the sites of manufacturing in Jefferson's America. Wider markets for household manufactures began to develop in the late eighteenth century with the coming of the **putting-out system**. Local merchants furnished ("put out") raw materials to rural households and paid at a piece rate for the labor that converted those raw materials into manufactured products. The supplying merchant then marketed and sold these goods.

In the cities and larger towns, most manufacturing was done by artisans, skilled craftsmen who were also known as mechanics. Working in their own shops and with their own tools, they produced small batches of finished goods. Artisans and their families fed, clothed, and housed the urban population and constituted close to half the population in the seaport cities. Each artisan had a specific skill that set him above common laborers. These skills came from hands-on experience and craft traditions that were handed down from one generation to the next.

The "mysteries of the craft" were taught by master craftsmen to the journeymen and apprentices who lived with them and worked in their shops. Journeymen had learned the skills of their craft but lacked the

John Neagle (American, 1796–1865), "Pat Lyon at the Forge," 1826–27. Oil on canvas, 93 3/4 x 68 in. (238.1 x 172.7 cm). Henry H. and Zoe Oliver Sherman Fund, 1975.806. Courtesy, Museum of Fine Arts, Boston. Reporduced with permission. (c)2000 Museum of Fine Arts.

As revealed in this portrait of the blacksmith Pat Lyon, the self-image of the artisans was closely related to the pride and dignity they derived from their craft work.

capital to open their own shops. Before establishing their own businesses, they saved their earnings and honed their skills while working for a wage under a master. Apprentices were adolescent boys legally sent by their fathers to live with and obey a master craftsman in return for being taught a trade. By the terms of the contract, known as an indenture, the master also provided for the apprentice's schooling and moral upbringing. An apprentice could reasonably expect to be promoted to journeyman in his late teens and begin advancement toward his competency, a secure income from an independent trade that would enable him to support a family.

The factory system of production that would undercut both household and artisanal manufacturing after 1815 had several advantages. First, the factories could produce goods far more quickly and cheaply per worker than could artisans or rural households. Factories subdivided the specialized skills of the artisan into a series of semiskilled tasks, a process foreshadowed by the putting-out system. Second, factories put workers under systematic controls. And in the final stage of industrialization, they boosted workers' productivity through the use of power-driven machinery.

Britain pioneered the technological advances that drove early industrialization. The secrets of this technology, especially the designs for the machines that mechanized textile production, were closely guarded by the British government. Despite attempts to prohibit the emigration of artisans who knew how the machinery worked, some British mechanics made it to the United States. Samuel Slater was one of them, and he took over the operation of a fledging mill in Providence, Rhode Island. With his knowledge of how to build the water-powered spinning machinery, he converted the mill into the nation's first permanent cotton factory in 1790.

Slater's factory, and those modeled after it, manufactured yarn that was put out to rural housewives to be woven into cloth. The first factory to mechanize the operations of spinning and weaving and turn out finished cloth was incorporated in Waltham, Massachusetts, in 1813 by the Boston Associates, a group of wealthy merchants. The Waltham factory was heavily capitalized, relied on the latest technology, and recruited its work force from rural farm families.

The first real spurt of factory building came with the closing off of British imports during the Embargo and the War of 1812. Hundreds of new cotton and woolen mills were established from 1808 to 1815. But the great test of American manufacturing came after 1815, when peace with Britain brought a flood of cheap British manufactured goods. If factories were to continue to grow, American manufacturers had to reach more consumers in their home market and overcome the British advantage of lower labor costs.

Sources of labor.   Industrial labor was more expensive in America than in England, where the high cost of land forced the rural poor into the cities to find work. By contrast, land was cheap and plentiful in the United States, and Americans preferred the independence of farm work to the dependence of factory labor. Consequently, the first mill workers were predominately children. For example, the mills that advertised in the *Massachusetts Spy* in the 1820s called for families "of five or six children each." The owners set up the father on a plot of company-owned land, provided piecework for the mother, and put the children to work in the mills.

Although this so-called **Rhode Island system** of family employment sufficed for small mills, it was inadequate for the larger, more mechanized factories that were built in New England after the War of 1812. These mill owners recruited single, adolescent daughters of farmers from across New England as their laborers in the **Waltham system**. Jemima Sanborn, one of these young farm daughters, explained that she had left home for the mills because of "the hard times to get a living off the farm for so large a family." Although

Shown here working at power looms under the supervision of a male overseer, young single women constituted the bulk of the labor force in the first textile factories of New England.

factory wages were low (a little over a dollar per week, after deductions for room and board), they were more than these young women could earn doing piecework in the home or as domestics. The wages also brought a liberating degree of financial independence. "When they felt the jingle of silver in their pockets," recalled Harriet Hanson Robinson of her fellow workers at Lowell in the 1830s, "there for the first time, their heads became erect and they walked as if on air."

To overcome parental fears that their daughters might be exposed to the same morally corrupting conditions associated with mill work in Britain, New England manufacturers set up paternalistic moral controls. Single female workers had to live in boardinghouses owned by the company. Curfews were imposed, visitors were screened, and church attendance was mandatory. Still, the mill women had to work six days a week from dawn to dusk for low wages. They tended clattering, fast-moving machinery in a work environment kept humid to minimize the snapping of threads in the machines. There were limits to what these women would endure, and in 1834 and 1836 the female hands at Lowell "turned out" to protest wage reductions in demonstrations that were the largest strikes in American history up to that time.

After the economic downturn of the late 1830s, conditions in the mills grew worse. By the mid-1840s, however, the Irish, desperate for work, sent their children into the mills at an earlier age than Yankee families had. These workers did not leave after two or three years of building up a small dowry for marriage, as many New Englanders did. By the early 1850s, more than half the textile operatives were Irish women.

In the mid-Atlantic region, where the farm population was more prosperous than in New England and

fewer young women were available for factory work, immigrants were an important source of manufacturing workers as early as the 1820s. They played an especially crucial role in urban manufacturing. The port cities lacked usable water power, but by drawing on a growing pool of cheap, immigrant labor, manufacturers could expand production while driving down the cost. Particularly in finished consumer goods, such as the clothing and leather industries, where low-paid workers could stitch cloth or sole a shoe, urban manufacturing became labor-intensive, depending more heavily on workers than on investment in machines and other capital.

Except in New England textile factories and the smaller factories and shops in the seaboard cities, native-born males were the largest group of early manufacturing workers. They came from poor rural families that lacked enough land to pass on to male heirs. As late as 1840, women, including those working at home, made up about half of the manufacturing work force and one-quarter of the factory hands. Regardless of their sex, few of these workers brought any specific skills to their jobs, and hence they had little bargaining power. Economic necessity forced them to accept low wages and harsh working conditions. The sheer increase in their numbers, as opposed to any productivity gains from technological innovations, accounted by 1850 for two-thirds of the gains in manufacturing output.

Technological gains. After 1815, American manufacturers began to close the technological gap with Britain. They did so by drawing on the versatile, practical skills of American mechanics. The Dominy family of Easthampton, Long Island, for example, worked with wood and iron, built grist mills, and made clocks and watches. Mechanics experimented with new designs, improved old ones, and patented inventions that found industrial applications outside their own crafts.

The most famous early American invention was the cotton gin. Eli Whitney, a Massachusetts Yankee who, as a teenager, had turned out knives and blades at a forge on his father's farm, built the first prototype of the gin in 1793 while working as a tutor on a Georgia plantation. By cheaply and quickly removing the seeds from cotton fibers, the cotton gin spurred the cultivation of cotton across the South.

Whitney also pushed the idea of basing production on interchangeable parts. After receiving a federal contract to manufacture muskets, he designed new milling machines and turret lathes that transformed the technology of machine tool production. The federal arsenal at Harpers Ferry, Virginia, developed machine tools that could manufacture standardized, interchangeable parts. The new techniques were first applied in 1815 to the manufacture of wooden clocks and by the 1840s to sewing machines, farm machinery, and watch parts. The **American system of manufacturing**—low-cost, standardized mass production, built around interchangeable parts stamped out by machines—was America's unique contribution to the industrial revolution.

As the pace of technological innovation accelerated after 1840, so did the growth of manufacturing. Indeed, the 1840s registered the highest rate of expansion in the manufacturing sector of the economy in the nineteenth century. The adoption of the stationary steam engine in urban manufacturing fueled much of this expansion. High-pressure steam engines enabled power-driven industry to locate in the port cities of the Northeast. Steam power and more mechanized manufacturing also benefited the booming cities in the Great Lakes corridor of the Old Northwest. With limited access to water power, early manufacturing in the West was confined to the processing of farm goods. By turning to steam power and new machine tools, western manufacturers after 1840 enlarged their region's industrial base and created a new industry, the mass production of agricultural implements. The West was the center of the farm-machinery industry, and the region produced 20 percent of the nation's manufacturing output by the 1850s.

A greater control over natural resources, as well as new technologies, drove industrial growth. To provide their mills with a steady, reliable source of water—one that would not be affected by the whims of nature—the Boston Associates constructed a series of dams and canals that extended to the headwaters of the Merrimack River in northern New Hampshire. Inevitably, the ecology of the region under control changed. The level of the lakes was altered, the flow of rivers interrupted, the upward migration of spawning fish blocked, and the foraging terrain of wild game flooded. Farmers protested when their fields and pastures were submerged, but lawyers for the Boston Associates successful argued that water, like any other natural resource, should be treated as a commodity that could contribute to economic progress. Increasingly, the law treated nature as an economic resource to be engineered and bought and sold.

GROWING INEQUALITY AND NEW CLASSES

In the first half of the nineteenth century, the economy grew three times faster than in the eighteenth century, and per capita income doubled. Living standards for most Americans improved. Houses, for those who could afford them, became larger and better furnished and heated. There was a price to be paid, however, for the benefits of economic growth. Half of the adult white males were propertyless at mid-century. Wealth had become more concentrated, and extremes of wealth and poverty eroded the Jeffersonian ideal of a republic of independent proprietors who valued liberty because they were economically free.

The gap between the rich and the poor widened considerably in the early phases of industrialization (see Figure 12–2). In 1800, the richest 10 percent of Americans owned 40 to 50 percent of the national wealth. By the 1850s, that share was about 70 percent. The most glaring discrepancies in wealth appeared in the large cities. In all cities by the 1840s, the top 10 percent of the population owned 80 percent of urban wealth. Most of the urban rich had been born wealthy, the offspring of old-money families who had married and invested wisely. They belonged to exclusive clubs, attended lavish balls and dinners, and were waited on

FIGURE 12-2 Growth in Wealth Inequality, 1774–1860
The two benchmark years for the gathering of data on the nationwide distribution of wealth are 1774 and 1860. Specialized studies on regions and subregions indicate that wealth inequality increased most sharply from the 1820s to 1850, the period that coincides with early industrialization.

Data Source: Jeffrey G. Williamson and Peter H. Lindert, *American Inequality: A Macroeconomic History* (1980), p. 38.

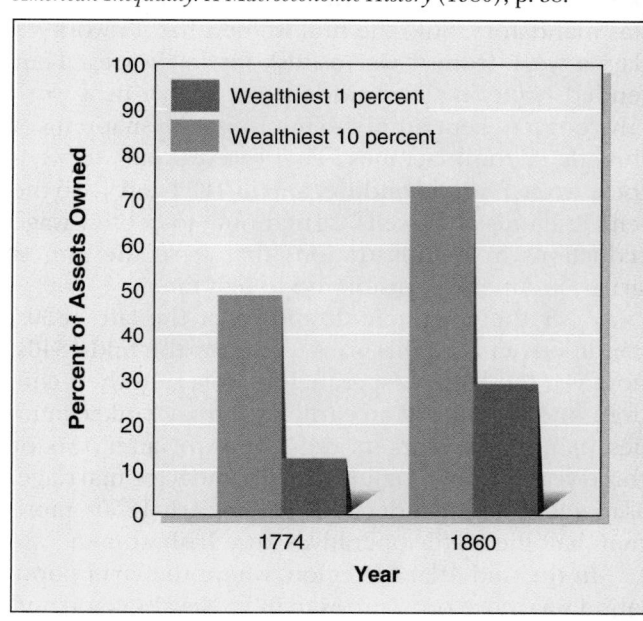

by a retinue of servants in their mansions, and generally recoiled from what they considered the "mob government" ushered in by the Jacksonian Democrats. As one of the urban elite noted, it was a society "characterized by a spirit of exclusiveness and persecution unknown in any other country. Its gradations not being regulated according to rank and titles, selfishness and conceit are its principal elements; and its arbitrary distinctions the more offensive, as they principally refer to fortune."

The new middle class.

The faster pace of economic growth that enabled the urban rich to increase their wealth also created opportunities for a rapidly expanding new middle class. This class grew as new employment opportunities opened up in non-manual work. Most of these jobs were in northern cities and bustling market towns, where the need was greatest for office and store clerks, managerial personnel, sales agents, and independent retailers. The result by mid-century was a new middle class superimposed on the older one of independent farmers, artisans, shopkeepers, and professionals.

This scene, entitled "The Tea Room," by Henry Sargent in his 1821 painting, depicts how the wealthy elite in Boston used their social gatherings to set themselves apart as an elegantly cultured class.

The Tea Party, about 1824 Henry Sargent, American, 1770-1845 Oil on canvas 163.51 x 133.03 cm (64 3/8 x 52 3/8 in.) Museum of Fine Art, Boston Gift of Mrs. Horatio A. Lamb in memory of Mr. and Mrs. Winthrop Sargent 19.12 (c) 2003 Museum of Fine Art

The apparent separation of work and home constituted the first step in the forging of a distinctive identity for the new middle class. As the market revolution advanced, the workplace increasingly became a specialized location of production or selling. Middle-class fathers now left for work in the morning, while mothers governed households that were primarily residential units and places of material comfort, where growing quantities of consumer goods—pianos, carpets, draperies, mirrors, oil lamps, and ornate furniture—were on display. Having servants—domestic service being the single largest field of employment in the cities—became a status symbol. Shunned as degrading by most native-born white women, these low-paying jobs were filled by African-American and young immigrant (especially Irish) women. Work had not left the middle-class home; instead, it was disguised as the "domestic duties" of middle-class wives who supervised the servants.

Besides turning to etiquette books for advice on proper manners in public and in the home, the middle class also tried to shape its behavior by the tenets of evangelical religion. Revivals swept northern cities in the late 1820s. Charles G. Finney led the most dramatic and successful ones in the cities along the Erie Canal in upstate New York. Finney preached that salvation was available to those who willed it. He also stressed that both economic and moral success depended on the virtues of sobriety, self-restraint, and hard work. Aggressiveness and ambition at work were not necessarily sinful so long as businessmen reformed their own moral lives and helped others do the same. This message was immensely reassuring to employers and entrepreneurs, for it confirmed and sanctified their own pursuit of economic self-interest. It also provided them with a religious inspiration for attempting to exert moral control over their communities and employees. **Temperance**—the prohibition of alcoholic beverages—was the greatest of the evangelically inspired reforms, and abstinence from alcohol became the most telling evidence of middle-class respectability.

Women and the cult of domesticity.

In a reversal of traditional Calvinist doctrine, the evangelical ministers

This pen-and-watercolor drawing of a middle-class family in 1832 illustrates how the home, as it lost its productive functions, became idealized as a center of domestic refinement and material comfort.

of the northern middle class enshrined women as the moral superiors of men. Though considered weak and passive, women were also held to be uniquely pure and pious. Women, who easily outnumbered men at Sunday services and weeknight prayer meetings, were now responsible for converting their homes into loving, prayerful centers of domesticity, and the primary task of motherhood became the Christian nurturing of souls entrusted to a mother's care. "There is a ministry that is older and deeper and more potent than ours," wrote a liberal Presbyterian clergyman; "it is the ministry that presides over the crib and impresses the first gospel influence on the infant soul."

This sanctified notion of motherhood reflected and reinforced shifting patterns of family life. Families became smaller as the birthrate fell by 25 percent in the first half of the nineteenth century. The decline was greatest in the urban middle class after 1820. Children were no longer an economic asset as they had been on a family farm. Middle-class couples consciously limited the size of their families, and women stopped having children at an earlier age. As a result, parents were able to devote more care and financial resources to child rearing. Middle-class children lived

at home longer than children had in the past and received more schooling than working-class children.

Beginning in the 1820s, ministers and female writers elevated the family role of middle-class women into a **cult of domesticity**. This idealized conception of womanhood insisted that the biological differences of God's natural order determined separate social roles for men and women. Characterized as strong, aggressive, and ambitious, men naturally belonged to the competitive world of business and politics. Women's providential task was to preserve religion and morality in the home and family. Held to be innately weak, nurturing, and selfless, only they possessed the moral purity necessary for rearing virtuous children and preserving the home as a refuge from the outside world.

The working classes. The economic changes that produced a new middle class also fundamentally transformed the working class. In the preindustrial United States, the working class was predominately native-born and of artisan origins. By mid-century, most urban workers were immigrants or the children of immigrants and had never been artisans in a skilled craft.

Job skills, sex, race, and ethnicity, all divided workers after 1840. Master craftsmen were the most highly skilled and best-paid members of the labor force. As industrialization proceeded, the unity of the old artisan class splintered. Ambitious master craftsmen with access to capital ignored craft traditions to rise into the ranks of small businessmen and manufacturers. They expanded output and drove down the cost of production by contracting out work at piece wages and hiring the cheapest workers they could find. The result was to transform the apprentice system into a system of exploited child labor.

By the 1830s, most journeymen were becoming a class of permanent wage earners with little prospect of opening their own shops. They denounced the new industrial relations as a "system of mental and physical slavery." To protect their liberties from what they considered a new aristocracy of manufacturers, they organized workingmen's parties in the 1830s, centered in the eastern cities. At the top of these parties' list of reforms were free public education, the abolition of imprisonment for debt, and a ten-hour workday. But the depression of 1839-1843 forced mechanics to concentrate on their economic survival, and the Democrats siphoned off many of their political leaders.

Early trade unions. Journeymen also turned to trade union activity in the 1820s and 1830s to gain better wages, shorter hours, and enhanced job security. Benefiting from a strong demand for their skills, workers in the building trades organized the first unions. They were soon followed by shoemakers, printers, and weavers, workers in trades where pressure on urban journeymen was the most intense. Locals from various trades formed the National Trades Union, the first national union, in 1834. The new labor movement launched more than 150 strikes in the mid-1830s.

Although the Panic of 1837 decimated union membership, the early labor movement did achieve two notable victories. First, by the late 1830s, it had forced employers to accept the ten-hour day as the standard for most skilled workers. Second, in a landmark decision handed down in 1842, the Massachusetts Supreme Court ruled in *Commonwealth* v. *Hunt* that a trade union was not necessarily subject to laws against criminal conspiracies and that a strike could be used to force employers to hire only union members.

The unions were the defenders of artisanal rights and virtues, and they ignored workers whose jobs had never had craft status. As massive immigration merged with industrialization after 1840, this basic division between workers widened. On one side was the male, Protestant, and native-born class of skilled artisans. On the other side was the working-class majority of factory laborers and the unskilled. These workers were predominately immigrants and women who worked for a wage as domestic or factory hands. On average, they earned less than $500 a year, about half what skilled workers earned. Their financial survival rested on a family economy in which all members contributed whatever they could earn.

Increasingly fearing these workers as a threat to their job security and Protestant values, in the 1840s, American-born artisans joined **nativist** organizations that sought to curb mass immigration from Europe and limit the political rights of Catholic immigrants. Whereas the immigrants viewed temperance as business-class meddling in their lives, the nativist workers tended to embrace the evangelical, middle-class ideology of temperance and self-help. One of the few issues that brought these groups together was the nearly universal demand of white workers that black workers be confined to the most menial jobs.

Gender also divided workers. Working-class men shared the dominant ideology of female dependence. They measured their own status as husbands by their ability to keep their wives and daughters from having to work. Beginning in the 1830s, male workers argued that their wages would be higher if women were barred from the labor force. A report of the National Trades Union in 1836 insisted that a woman's "efforts to sustain herself and her family are actually the same as tying a stone around the neck of her natural protector, Man, and destroying him with the weight she has brought to his assistance."

With these views, male workers helped lock wage-earning women into the lowest-paying and most exploited jobs. "If we do not come forth in our defence, what will become of us?" asked Sarah Monroe of New York City in the midst of a strike by seamstresses in 1831. Women tried to organize as workers, but the male labor movement refused to lend much support. The men tried to channel the discontent of women workers into "proper female behavior" and generally restricted their assistance to pushing for legislation that would limit the hours worked by women and children—a stand that enhanced their male image as protectors of the family.

REFORM AND MORAL ORDER

The rapidity and extent of the social and economic changes that accompanied the market revolution were disorienting, even frightening, to many Americans. This was particularly the case with religious leaders and wealthy businessmen in the East. They saw signs of moral wickedness and disorder all around them in the more fluid, materialistic society that was emerging. In their eyes, licentiousness was rampant in the cities and the evils of drink were causing workers to forsake God and their families. Alarmed by what they perceived as a breakdown in moral authority, they sought to impose moral discipline on Americans.

These eastern elites, with the indispensable support of their wives and daughters, created a network of voluntary church-affiliated reform organizations known collectively as the **benevolent empire**. Revivals in the 1820s and 1830s then broadened the base of reform to include the newly evangelicalized middle class in northern cities and towns. From this class emerged the temperance crusade, the largest reform movement in the pre-Civil War United States.

THE BENEVOLENT EMPIRE

For the Reverend Lyman Beecher, the United States in 1814 presented "a scene of destitution and wretchedness." From his Presbyterian pulpit in Litchfield, Connecticut, and then in Boston, he became the leader of a clerical drive to restore morality to America.

The United States these ministers valued was one of respectable churchgoers whose behavior conformed to Puritan and Federalist standards of freedom as defined and ordered by an educated clergy. Evangelical businessmen in the seaboard cities backed the call to restore moral order. Worried by the increasing number of urban poor, wealthy merchants contributed vital financial support for a network of reform associations, which grew to include the American Board of Commissioners for Foreign Missions (1810), the American Bible Society (1816), the American Sunday School Union (1824), the American Tract Society (1825), and the American Home Missionary Society (1826).

The reform societies built on the Second Great Awakening's techniques of organization and communication. The Protestant reformers sent out speakers on regular schedules along prescribed routes. They developed organizations that maintained a constant pressure for reform. National and local boards of directors supervised the work of salaried managers, who inspired volunteers to combat sin among the unconverted. When steam presses and stereotype plates halved the cost of printing and dramatically increased its speed, the American Bible Society was the first organization to exploit this revolution in the print media. Between 1790 and 1830, the number of religious newspapers grew from

fourteen to more than six hundred. By then, religious presses were churning out more than 1 million Bibles and 6 million tracts a year.

A host of local societies targeted individual vices. Their purpose, as summed up by a Massachusetts group, the Andover South Parish Society for the Reformation of Morals, was "to discountenance [discourage] immorality, particularly Sabbath-breaking, intemperance, and profanity, and to promote industry, order, piety, and good morals." These goals linked social and moral discipline, appealing both to churchgoers concerned about godlessness and profit-oriented businessmen eager to curb their workers' unruly behavior.

With volunteers drawn largely from the teenage daughters of evangelical businessmen, Sunday interdenominational schools combined elementary education with the teaching of the Bible and Protestant principles. The American Sunday School Union coordinated local efforts and published books and periodicals. By 1832, nearly 10 percent of all American children aged 5 to 14 were attending one of eight thousand Sunday schools.

The boldest expression of the drive to enhance Protestant Christian power was the **Sabbatarian movement**. In 1828, evangelicals led by Lyman Beecher formed the General Union for Promoting the Observance of the Christian Sabbath. Their immediate goal was the repeal of a law passed by Congress in 1810, directing post offices to deliver mail on Sunday. This law symbolized to Protestant reformers the moral degeneracy into which the republic had fallen. Their broader mission was to enforce local statutes that shut down business and leisure activities on Sundays. The Sabbatarians considered such statutes no less "necessary to the welfare of the state" than "laws against murder and polygamy."

In 1829, insisting on the separation of church and state, the Democratic Congress upheld the postal law of 1810, a crippling setback to the Sabbatarian crusade. The Sabbatarians had outraged canal operators, hotel keepers, tavern owners and other businesses threatened with the loss of their Sunday trade. Businessmen, workingmen, Southern evangelicals, and religious conservatives, all felt that the Sabbath purists had gone too far in a movement now seen as a threat to civil liberties and the rights of private property.

The General Union disbanded in 1832, but it left an important legacy for future reform movements. On the one hand, it developed techniques that converted the reform impulse into direct political action. In raising funds, training speakers, holding rallies, disseminating literature, lobbying for local Sunday regulations, and coordinating a petition to Congress, the

Sabbatarians created an organizational model for other reformers to follow in mobilizing public opinion and influencing politicians. On the other hand, the failure of the Sabbatarians revealed that a new approach was needed that encouraged individuals to reform themselves without coercive controls. It soon emerged in the temperance movement.

THE TEMPERANCE MOVEMENT

Temperance—the drive against the consumption of alcohol—had the greatest impact on the most people of any reform movement. Its success rested on what Lyman Beecher called "a new moral power." Dismayed by the popular resistance to the coercive moralism of the first wave of Protestant reform, evangelicals concluded that reform had to rest on persuasion, and it had to begin with the voluntary decision of individuals to free themselves from sin. For these evangelicals, the self-control to renounce alcohol became the key to creating a harmonious Christian society of self-regulating citizens.

In 1826, evangelicals founded the **American Temperance Society** and took control of the movement. Their goal was to bring about a radical change in American attitudes toward alcohol and its role in social life. By 1830, American consumption of alcohol reached an all-time high of 7.1 gallons of pure alcohol per year for every American aged 14 and over (about three times present-day levels). "Liquor at that time," recalled a carpenter, "was used as commonly as the food we ate." Taverns easily outnumbered churches as centers of community sociability. Alcohol was used to pay both common laborers and itinerant preachers on the early Methodist circuit. Masters and journeymen shared a drink as a customary way of taking a break from work, and no wedding, funeral, or meeting of friends was complete without alcohol.

For the temperance crusade to succeed, the reformers had to finance a massive propaganda campaign and link it to an organization that could mobilize and energize thousands of people. They built such a mass movement by merging temperance into the network of churches and lay volunteers that the benevolent empire had developed and by adopting the techniques of revivals to win new converts.

Evangelical reformers denounced intemperance as the greatest sin of the land. In the words of the Reverend Herman Humphrey, it deprived "its victims of the means of grace . . . . If there is any evil which hardens the heart faster, . . . or quickens hatred [of] God and man into a more rapid and frightful maturity, I know not what it is." Alcohol represented all that was wrong in America—crime, poverty, insanity, broken families, boisterous politicking, Sabbath-breaking.

This temperance poster depicts the evangelical virtues of faith, hope, and charity in battle against the evil temptations of drinking.

This message was thundered from the pulpit and the public lectern. Thanks to the generous financial subsidies of such wealthy benefactors as Stephen Van Rensselaer and Edward Delavan of New York, it was also broadcast in millions of tracts printed on the latest high-speed presses. As in the revivals, temperance rallies combined emotionally charged sermons with large, tearful prayer meetings to evoke guilt among sinners, who would then seek release by taking the pledge of abstinence.

Within a decade, the American Temperance Society had more than five thousand local chapters and statewide affiliates, most of them in the Northeast. A million members had pledged abstinence by 1833. Women constituted one third to over half of the members in local temperance societies. Lacking legal protections against abusive husbands who drank away the family resources, women had a compelling reason to join the crusade. As the moral protectors of the family, they pressured their husbands to take the teetotaler's pledge and stick by it, raised sons to shun alcohol, and banished liquor from their homes. By the 1840s, temperance and middle-class domesticity had become synonymous.

The first wave of temperance converts came from the upper and middle classes. Businessmen welcomed temperance as a model of self-discipline in their efforts to regiment factory work. Young, upwardly mobile professionals and petty entrepreneurs learned in temperance how to be thrifty, self-controlled, and more respectable and creditworthy. Many of them presumably agreed with *The Temperance Recorder* that "the enterprise of this country is so great, and competition so eager in every branch of business . . ., that profit can only result from . . . *temperance*."

Temperance made its first significant inroads among the working classes during the economic depression of 1839–1843. Joining together in what they called Washington Temperance Societies, small businessmen and artisans, many of them reformed drunkards, carried temperance into working-class districts. The Washingtonians gained a considerable following by insisting that workers could survive the depression only if they stopped drinking and adopted the temperance ethic of frugality and self-help. Their wives organized auxiliary societies and pledged to enforce sobriety and economic restraint at home.

In a telling measure of the temperance movement's success, per capita consumption of alcohol had fallen to less than two gallons by 1845. In 1851, Maine passed the first statewide prohibition law. Other northern states followed suit, but antitemperance coalitions soon overturned most of these laws outside New England. Nonetheless, alcohol consumption remained at the low level set in the 1840s.

WOMEN'S ROLE IN REFORM

The first phase of women's reform activities represented an extension of the domestic ideal promoted in the Cult of Domesticity. Assumptions about their unique moral qualities permitted, and even encouraged, women to assume the role of "social mother" by organizing on behalf of the orphaned and the widowed. Founded in 1797, the Society for the Relief of Poor Widows with Small Children in New York typified these early approaches to reform. The women in the society came from socially prominent families. Motivated by religious charity and social duty, they visited poor women and children, dispensed funds, and set up work programs. However, they limited their benevolence to the "deserving poor"—socially weak but morally strong people who had suffered personal misfortune—and screened out all who were thought to be unworthy.

The revivalist call in the 1820s for moral action inspired middle-class women to join voluntary female groups. They founded maternal associations, where they prayed and fasted for the moral strength to save the souls of their children. Other associations sponsored revivals, visited the poor, established Sunday Schools, and distributed Bibles and religious tracts. These reformers widened the public role of women, but their efforts also reinforced cultural stereotypes of women as nurturing helpmates who deferred to males as the wielders of economic and political power.

A second phase in the reform efforts by women developed in the 1830s. Unlike their benevolent counterparts, the reformers now began to challenge male prerogatives and move beyond moral suasion.

The temperance crusade brought women out of their homes and into the streets to pray in front of taverns filled with drunken men.

The crusade against prostitution exemplified the new militancy. Women seized leadership of the movement in 1834 with the founding of the New York Female Moral Reform Society. In the pages of their journal, *Advocate for Moral Reform*, members identified male greed and licentiousness as the causes for the fallen state of women. Identified, too, were the male patrons of the city's brothels. The society blamed businessmen for the low wages that forced some women to resort to prostitution and denounced lustful men for engaging in "a regular crusade against [our] sex."

In 1839, this attack on the sexual double standard became a national movement with the establishment of the **American Female Moral Reform Society**. With 555 affiliates throughout the evangelical heartland of the North, female activists mounted a lobbying campaign that, unlike earlier efforts, bypassed prominent men and reached out to a mass audience for signatures. By the 1840s, such unprecedented political involvement enabled women to secure the first state laws criminalizing seduction and adultery.

Other women's groups developed a more radical critique of American society and its male leadership. The Boston Seamen's Aid Society, founded in 1833 by

Sarah Josepha Hale, a widow with five children, soon rejected the benevolent tradition of distinguishing between the "respectable" and the "unworthy" poor. Hale discovered that her efforts to guide poor women toward self-sufficiency flew in the face of the low wages and substandard housing that trapped her clients in poverty. She concluded in 1838 that "it is hardly possible for the hopeless poor to avoid being vicious." Hale attacked male employers for exploiting the poor. "Combinations of selfish men are formed to beat down the price of female labor," she wrote in her 1836 annual report, "and then they call the diminished rate the market price."

BACKLASH AGAINST BENEVOLENCE

Some of the benevolent empire's harshest critics came out of the populist revivals of the early 1800s. They considered the Protestant reformers' program a conspiracy of orthodox Calvinists from old-line denominations to impose social and moral control on behalf of a religious and economic elite. The goal of the "orthodox party," warned the Universalist *Christian Intelligencer*, was the power of "governing the nation"; the societies they formed "are but so many strings . . ., the ultimate design of which is to draw them into power."

These criticisms revealed a profound mistrust of the emerging market society. In contrast to the evangelical reformers, drawn from the well-educated business and middle classes who were benefiting from economic change, most evangelical members of the grass-roots sects and followers of the itinerant preachers were unschooled, poor, and hurt by market fluctuations that they could not control. Often they were farmers forced by debt to move west or artisans and tradesmen displaced by new forms of factory production and new commercial outlets. Socially uprooted and economically stranded, they found a sense of community in their local churches and resisted control by wealthier, better-educated outsiders. Above all, they clung to beliefs that shored up the threatened authority of the father over his household.

With the elevation of women to the status of moral guardians of the family and agents of benevolent reform outside the household, middle-class evangelicalism in the Northeast was becoming feminized. This new social role for women was especially threatening—indeed, galling—for men who were the causalities of the more competitive economy. Raised on farms where the father had been the unquestioned lawgiver and provider, these men attacked feminized evangelicalism for undermining their paternal authority. They found in Scripture an affirmation of patriarchal power for any man, no matter how poor or economically dependent.

The **Church of Jesus Christ of Latter-day Saints** (also known as the **Mormon Church**) represented the most enduring religious backlash of economically struggling men against the aggressive efforts of reforming middle-class evangelicals. Joseph Smith, who established the church in upstate New York in 1830, came from a New England farm family uprooted and impoverished by market speculations gone sour. He and his followers were alienated, not only from the new market economy but also from what they saw as the religious and social anarchy around them.

Based on Smith's divine revelations as set forth in *The Book of Mormon* (1830), their new faith offered converts to Mormonism both a sanctuary as a biblical people and a release from social and religious uncertainties. They believed that the mainstream evangelical churches had corrupted Christ's original gospel. "This generation abounds in ignorance, superstition, selfishness, and priestcraft," charged the Mormon John Whitmer; "for this generation is truly led by . . . hireling priests whose God is the substance of the world's goods."

Mormonism provided a defense of communal beliefs centered on male authority that was reassuring to rural families seeking refuge from individualism and economic dislocation. It assigned complete spiritual and secular authority to men. Unlike female-dominated evangelicalism, men led their families into Mormonism. Only through subordination and obedience to their husbands could women hope to gain salvation.

To be a Mormon was to join a large extended family that was part of a shared enterprise. Men bonded their labor in a communal economy to benefit all the faithful. A law of tithing, instituted in 1841, required Mormons to give 10 percent of their property to the church upon conversion and 10 percent of their annual income thereafter. Driven by a strong sense of social obligation, the Mormons forged the most successful alternative vision in antebellum America to the individualistic Protestant republic of the benevolent reformers. (For the Mormons' role in the westward movement, see Chapter 13.)

INSTITUTIONS AND SOCIAL IMPROVEMENT

Although evangelical Protestantism was its mainspring, antebellum reform also had its roots in the European Enlightenment. Like the evangelicals inspired by religious optimism, reformers drawing on Enlightenment doctrines of progress had unbounded faith in social improvement. They saw in America an unlimited potential to fashion a model republic of virtuous, intelligent citizens.

Studies published in the 1820s that documented increasing urban poverty, crime, and teenage delinquency created a sense of urgency for many reformers. Guided by the Enlightenment belief that environmental conditions shaped human character, reformers created a new system of public schooling in the North. They also prodded state legislatures to fund penitentiaries for criminals, asylums for the mentally ill, reformatories for the delinquent, and almshouses for the poor.

As reformers were implementing new institutions for shaping individual character after 1820, a host of utopian communities sprang up. These communities also tapped into an impulse for human betterment. They typically rejected either private property or families based on monogamous marriage and offered a communitarian life designed to help a person reach perfection. Most of these communities were short-lived because the new forms of social and economic organization they promoted were far too radical for all but a handful of Americans.

SCHOOL REFORM

"An ignorant people always has been and always will be a degraded and oppressed people—they are always at the mercy of the corrupt and designing," cautioned Philadelphia school officials in their annual report for 1836 where they warned, "if we fail by Education to awake—guide—confirm the moral energies of our people, we are lost!" Secular revivalists as much as they were institutional innovators, the school reformers embarked on a crusade to save America from ignorance and vice.

Before the 1820s, schooling in America was an informal, haphazard affair that nonetheless met the basic needs for reading, writing, and arithmetic skills of an overwhelmingly rural population. Private tutors and academies for the wealthy, a few charitable schools for the urban poor, and rural one-room schoolhouses open for a few months a year constituted formal education at the primary level.

The first political demands for free tax-supported schools originated with the **Workingmen's movement** in eastern cities in the 1820s. Decrying what the Philadelphia Working Men's Committee in 1830 described as "a monopoly of talent, which consigns the multitude to comparative ignorance, and secures the balance of knowledge on the side of the rich and the rulers," workers called for free public education. In pushing for what they called "equal republican education," they were also seeking to guarantee that all citizens, no matter how poor, could achieve meaningful liberty and equality.

Their proposals, however, met stiff resistance from wealthier property holders, who refused to be taxed to pay for the education of working-class children.

The breakthrough in public education came in New England, where the disruptive forces of industrialization and urbanization were felt the earliest. Increased economic inequality, growing numbers of impoverished Irish Catholic immigrants, and the emergence of a mass democracy based on nearly universal white male suffrage convinced reformers of the need for state-supported schools.

In 1837, the Massachusetts legislature established the nation's first state board of education. The head of the board for the next twelve years was Horace Mann, a former Whig politician and temperance advocate who now tirelessly championed educational reform. Mann demanded that the state government assume centralized control over Massachusetts schools. All schools should have the same standards of compulsory attendance, strict discipline, common textbooks, professionally trained teachers, and graded, competitive classes of age-segregated students.

Once this system was in place, Mann promised, the schools would become "the great equalizer of the conditions of men—the balance-wheel of the social machinery." Poverty would no longer threaten social disruption because the ignorant would have the knowledge to acquire property and wealth. Education, Mann stated, "does better than disarm the poor of their hostility against the rich; it prevents being poor." Trained in self-control and punctuality, youths would be able to take advantage of economic opportunities and become intelligent voters concerned with the rights of property.

Democrats in the Massachusetts legislature denounced Mann's program as "a system of centralization and of monopoly of power in a few hands, contrary in every respect, to the true spirit of our democratical institutions." The laboring poor, who depended for economic survival on the wages their children could earn, resisted compulsory-attendance laws and a longer school year. Farmers fought to maintain local control over schooling and to block the higher taxes needed for a more comprehensive and professionalized system. The Catholic Church protested the thinly veiled attempts of the reformers to indoctrinate all students in the moral strictures of middle-class Protestantism. Catholics began, at great expense, to build their own parochial schools.

Mann and his allies nonetheless prevailed in most of the industrializing states. The educational reformers received strong support from the professional and

16   ECLECTIC FIRST READER.

LESSON XI.

Boys at Play.

Can you fly a kite? See how the boy flies his kite. He holds the string fast, and the wind blows it up.

Now it is high in the air, and looks like a bird. When the wind blows hard, you must hold fast, or your kite will get away.

Boys love to run and play.

But they must not be rude. Good boys do not play in a rude way, but take care not to hurt any one.

Moral Lessons such as this one for boys at play filled the pages of the McGuffey's readers.

business constituencies of the Whig party. Manufacturers hoped that the schools would turn out a more obedient and punctual labor force, and the more skilled and prosperous workers saw in public education a key to upward mobility for their children.

Most important for its political success, school reform appealed to the growing northern middle class. Opposing both the "vicious passions" of the poor and the "idle luxury" of the rich, schools would instill the moral and economic discipline that the middle class deemed essential for a progressive and ordered society. Teaching morality and national pride was central to the educational curriculum, and from the popular McGuffey Readers used as a classroom text, students learned such lessons as "God gives a great deal of money to some persons, in order that they may assist those [who] are poor."

Out of the northern middle class also came the young female teachers who increasingly staffed elementary schools. Presumed by their nature to be more nurturing than men, women now had an entry into teaching, the first profession open to them. Be-

sides, women could also be paid far less than men; school boards assumed that they would accept low wages while waiting to be married.

Just over 50 percent of the white children between 5 and 19 years of age in the United States were enrolled in school in 1850—the highest percentage in the world at the time. Working-class parents were quicker to pull their children out of school at an early age than higher-income middle-class parents. Planters continued to rely on private tutors or academies for their children, and southern farmers saw little need for public education. The slave states, especially in the Lower South, lagged behind the rest of the nation in public education.

PRISONS, WORKHOUSES, AND ASYLUMS

Up to this time, Americans had depended on voluntary efforts to cope with crime, poverty, and social deviance. Convinced that these efforts were now inadequate, reformers turned to public authorities to establish a host of new institutions—penitentiaries, workhouses, mental hospitals, orphanages, and reformatories—to deal with social problems.

All these public institutions reflected a new attitude toward conditions that had been regarded as inevitable and irreversible. For example, eighteenth-century Americans never thought of rehabilitating criminals. Prisons were simple structures whose only purpose was to hold criminals before they were fined, whipped, mutilated, or executed in a public ritual that drew large crowds of festive onlookers. But the institutional reformers of the Jacksonian era believed that criminals, as well as the poor and other deviants, could be morally redeemed.

The reformers held that people's environments shaped their character for good or evil. The Boston Children's Friend Society was devoted to the young, "whose plastic natures may be molded into images of perfect beauty, or . . . perfect repulsiveness." Samuel Gridley Howe, a prison reformer, proclaimed: "Thousands of convicts are made so in consequence of a faulty organization of society . . . . They are thrown upon society as a sacred charge; and that society is false to its trust, if it neglects any means for their reformation." In the properly ordered environment of new institutions, discipline and moral character would be instilled in criminals and other deviants who lacked the self-control to resist the corrupting vices and temptations that pervaded society.

Reformers had particularly high expectations for the penitentiary systems pioneered in Pennsylvania and New York in the 1820s. As two French observers noted in the early 1830s, "The penitentiary system . . . to them seems the remedy for all the evils of society." Unlike earlier prisons, the penitentiaries were huge, imposing structures that isolated the prisoners from each other and the outside world. Inmates in the New York system pioneered in the 1820s worked together in gangs during the day, but under the Pennsylvania plan, each prisoner was held in solitary confinement.

No longer were criminals to be brutally punished or thrown together under inhumane conditions that perpetuated a cycle of moral depravity. Now, cut off from all corrupting influences, forced to learn that hard work teaches moral discipline, and uplifted by religious literature, criminals would be guided toward becoming law-abiding, productive citizens.

Workhouses.

The same philosophy of reform provided the rationale for asylums to house the poor and the insane. The number of transient poor and the size of urban slums increased as commercial capitalism uprooted farmers from the land and undercut the security of craft trades. Believing that the poor, much like criminals, had only themselves to blame, public officials and their evangelical allies prescribed a therapeutic regimen of discipline and physical labor to cure the poor of their moral defects. The structured setting for that regiment was the workhouse.

The custodians of the workhouses banished drinking, gambling, and idleness. Under the workhouse rules in New York, officers could "rightly exercise . . . a measure of moral force upon the will of these persons, to induce them to do that which their own uncultivated understanding might oppose." Officers were to administer their duties "with strictness —severity." Their prime responsibility was to supervise the inmates in a tightly scheduled daily routine built around manual labor. Once purged of their laziness and filled with self-esteem as the result of work discipline, the poor would be released to become useful members of society.

Asylums for the Mentally Ill.

Public insane asylums offered a similar order for the mentally ill. Reformers believed that too many choices in a highly mobile, materialistic, and competitive society drove some people insane. Following the lead of New York and Massachusetts in the 1830s, twenty-eight states had established mental hospitals by 1860. These facilities set rigid rules and work assignments to teach patients how to order their lives.

In the early 1840s Dorothea Dix, a Massachusetts schoolteacher, discovered that the insane in her home state were dumped into jails and almshouses, where they suffered filthy, inhumane treatment. She found the insane "confined . . . in cages, closets, cellars,

In the concern etched in her face, this photograph captures the compassion that Dorothea Dix brought to her crusade for mental health reform.

stalls, pens! Chained, naked, beaten with rods, and lashed into obedience." Horrified, Dix lobbied state legislatures across the nation for the next twenty years to improve treatment for the mentally ill.

While the reformers did provide social deviants with cleaner and safer living conditions, their penitentiaries and asylums succeeded more in classifying and segregating their inmates than in reforming them. Submission to routine turned out not to be the best builder of character. Witnessing the rigorous control of every movement of the isolated prisoners at the Eastern State Penitentiary in Philadelphia, the English novelist Charles Dickens declared "this slow and daily tampering with the mysteries of the brain to be immeasurably worse than any torture of the body."

Penitentiaries, reformatories, and workhouses failed to eliminate or noticeably check poverty, crime, and vice. Refusing to question their basic premise that repressive institutions could promote individual responsibility, reformers abandoned their environmental explanations for deviance. By mid-century, they were defining deviants and dependents as permanent misfits with ingrained character defects. The asylums remained; but, stripped of their earlier optimism, they became little more than holding pens for the outcasts of society.

UTOPIAN ALTERNATIVES

Unlike the reformers, who aimed to improve the existing order by guiding individuals to greater self-discipline, the utopians sought perfection by withdrawing from society and its confining institutions. A radically new social order, not an improved old one, was their goal.

Though following different religious and secular philosophies of communitarian living, all the utopians wanted to fashion a more rational and personally satisfying alternative to the competitive materialism of antebellum America. Nearly all the communities sought to transform the organization and rewards of work, thus challenging the prevailing dogmas about private property.

The most successful utopian communities were religious sects whose reordering of both sexual and economic relations departed most sharply from middle-class norms. The **Shakers**, at their height in the 1830s, attracted some six thousand followers. Named for the convulsive dancing that was part of their religious ceremonies, the Shakers traced their origins to the teachings of Ann Lee ("Mother Lee"). An illiterate factory laborer in mid-eighteenth-century England, Lee had a revelation in 1770 that the Second Coming of Christ was to be fulfilled in her own womanly form, the embodiment of the female side of God. Fired by another vision in 1774, Lee led eight of her followers to America, where, after her death in 1784, her disciples established the first Shaker community in New Lebanon, New York.

Organized around doctrines of celibacy and **communism**, Shaker communities held all property in common. The sexes worked and lived apart from each other. Dancing during religious worship brought men and women together and provided an emotional release from enforced sexual denial. As an early Shaker leader explained, "There is no labor which so fully absorbs all the faculties of soul and body, as real spiritual devotion and energetic exercise in sacred worship." In worldly as well as spiritual terms, women enjoyed an equality in Shaker life that the outside world denied them. For this reason, twice as many women as men joined the Shakers.

The Shakers gradually dwindled. Their rule of celibacy meant, of course, that they could propagate themselves only be recruiting new members, and few new converts joined the movement after 1850. Viewed as eccentric outsiders by contemporaries, the Shakers today are best remembered for the beautiful simplicity of the furniture and other household objects they made in their workshops.

John Humphrey Noyes, a graduate of Dartmouth who studied for the ministry at Yale, founded another utopian community that offered women a liberating alternative to the burdens of monogamous marriage and constant child rearing. Noyes preached that marriage, the selfish "exclusive possession of one woman to one man," was the main barrier to perfection. He proposed instead "complex marriage," the mutual love for each other of all those who had been saved. His goal was a religious society in which cooperative arrangements between men and women regulated child care and the distribution of property.

After he had been drummed out of the ministry for his radical teachings, Noyes established the **Oneida Community** in upstate New York in 1847. He attracted over two hundred followers with his perfectionist vision of plural marriage, community nurseries, group discipline, and common ownership of property. Charged with adultery, Noyes fled to Canada in 1879, but the Oneida Community, reorganized in 1881 as a joint-stock company in the United States and committed thereafter to conventional sexual mores, survived into the twentieth century.

Secular utopians aspired to perfect social relations through the rational design of planned communities. Bitter critics of the social evils of industrialization, they tried to construct models for a social order free from poverty, unemployment, and inequality. They envisioned cooperative communities that balanced agricultural and industrial pursuits in a mixed economy that recycled earnings to the laborers who actually produced the wealth.

Despite their high expectations, nearly all the planned communities ran into financial difficulties and soon collapsed. The pattern was set by the first of the controversial socialist experiments, **New Harmony** in Indiana, the brainchild of the wealthy Scottish industrialist and philanthropist Robert Owen. A proponent of utopian **socialism**, Owen promised to create a new order where "the degrading and pernicious practices in which we are now well trained, of buying cheap and selling dear, will be rendered unnecessary" and "union and co-operation will supersede individual interest." But within two years of its founding in 1825, New Harmony fell victim to inadequate financing and internal bickering.

The economic misery of the depression of the 1840s revived interest in utopian ventures and helped popularize the ideas of Charles Fourier, a French utopian who proposed to restore dignity to labor and end poverty by dividing society into phalanxes, cooperative units of workers who lived communally. Scores of **Fourierist communities** were set up, but few survived into the 1850s.

About the only secular cooperative that gained lasting fame was **Brook Farm** in West Roxbury, Massa-

AMERICAN VIEWS

Appeal of a Female Abolitionist

Lydia Maria Child's Appeal, published in Boston in 1833, was a landmark in abolitionist literature for both the thoroughness of its attack on slavery and its refutation of racist ideology and discrimination. This condemnation of racial prejudice was the most radical feature of abolitionist ideology. It directly challenged the deeply held beliefs and assumptions of nearly all white Americans, in the North as well as the South. Racism and slavery, as Child shows in this excerpt from her Appeal, fed off one another in the national curse of slavery.

- How does Child argue that northern white people must bear some of the responsibility for perpetuating slavery?
- What arguments does Child make against racial discrimination in northern society?
- What did Child mean when she wrote that "the Americans are peculiarly responsible for the example they give"? Do you agree with her?
- How does Child deal with the charge that the abolitionists threatened the preservation of the Union?

While we bestow our earnest disapprobation on the system of slavery, let us not flatter ourselves that we are in reality any better than our brethren of the South. Thanks to our soil and climate, and the early exhortions of the Quakers, the form of slavery does not exist among us; but the very spirit of the hateful and mischievous thing is here in all its strength. . . . Our prejudice against colored people is even more inveterate than it is at the South. The planter is often attached to his negroes, and lavishes caresses and kind words upon them, as he would on a favorite hound: but our cold-hearted, ignoble prejudice admits of no exception—no intermission.

The Southerners have long continued habit, apparent interest and dreaded danger, to palliate the wrong they do; but we stand without excuse. . . . If the free States wished to cherish the system of slavery forever, they could not take a more direct course than they now do. Those who are kind and liberal on all other subjects, unite with the selfish and the proud in their unrelenting efforts to keep the colored

---

chusetts (today part of Boston). Established in 1841, Brook Farm was a showcase for the transcendentalist philosophy of Ralph Waldo Emerson. A former Unitarian minister in Boston, Emerson taught that intuition and emotion could grasp a truer ("transcendent") reality than could the senses alone. The Boston intellectuals drawn to Brook Farm in the 1840s saw it as a refuge from the pressures and coarseness of commercial society, a place where they could realize the Emersonian ideal of spontaneous creativity. Although disbanded after six years as an economic failure, Brook Farm inspired intellectuals such as Nathaniel Hawthorne, who briefly lived there. In turn, his writings and those of other writers influenced by **transcendentalism** flowed into the great renaissance of American literature in the mid-nineteenth century, an outpouring of work that grappled with Emersonian themes of individualism and the reshaping of the American character.

In an 1837 address at Harvard titled "The American Scholar," Emerson had called for a distinctly national literature devoted to the democratic possibilities of American life. "The literature of the poor, the feelings of the child, the philosophy of the street, population in the lowest state of degradation; and the influence they unconsciously exert over children early infuses into their innocent minds the same strong feelings of contempt. . . .

The state of public feeling not only makes it difficult for the Africans to obtain information, but it prevents them from making profitable use of what knowledge they have. A colored man, however intelligent, is not allowed to pursue any business more lucrative than that of a barber, a shoe-black, or waiter. These, and all other employments, are truly respectable, whenever the duties connected with them are faithfully performed; but it is unjust that a man should, on account of his complexion, be prevented from performing more elevated uses in society. Every citizen ought to have a fair chance to try his fortune in any line of business, which he thinks he has ability to transact. Why should not colored men be employed in the manufactories of various kinds? If their ignorance is an objection, let them be enlightened, as speedily as possible. If their moral character is not sufficiently pure, remove the pressure of public scorn, and thus supply them with motives for being respectable. All this can be done. It merely requires an earnest wish to overcome a prejudice, which . . . is in fact opposed to the spirit of our religion, and contrary to the instinctive good feelings of our nature. . . . When the majority heartily desire a change, it is effected, be the difficulties what they may. The Americans are peculiarly responsible for the example they give; for in no other country does the unchecked voice of the people constitute the whole of government. . . .

The strongest and best reason that can be given for our supineness on the subject of slavery, is the fear of dissolving the Union. The Constitution of the United States demands our highest reverence. . . . But we must not forget that the Constitution provides for any change that may be required for the general good. The great machine is constructed with a safety valve, by which any rapidly increasing evil may be expelled whenever the people desire it.

If the Southern politicians are determined to make a Siamese question of this also—if they insist that the Union shall not exist without slavery—it can only be said that they join two things, which have no affinity with each other, and which cannot permanently exist together. —They chain the living and vigorous to the diseased and dying; and the former will assuredly perish in the infected neighborhood.

The universal introduction of free labor is the surest way to consolidate the Union, and enable us to live together in harmony and peace. If a history is ever written entitled "The Decay and Dissolution of the North American Republic," its author will distinctly trace our downfall to the existence of slavery among us.

Source: Lydia Maria Child, *An Appeal in Favor of That Class of Americans Called Africans* (originally published 1833), ed. Carolyn L. Karcher (University of Massachusetts Press, 1996).

the meaning of household life, are the topics of the time," he proclaimed. Writers soon responded to Emerson's call.

Walt Whitman, whose *Leaves of Grass* (1855) foreshadowed modern poetry in its use of free verse, shared Emerson's faith in the possibilities of individual fulfillment, and his poems celebrated the democratic variety of the American people. Henry David Thoreau, Emerson's friend and neighbor, embodied the transcendentalist fascination with nature and self-discovery by living in relative isolation for sixteen months at Walden Pond, near Concord, Massachu-

setts. His *Walden, or Life in the Woods* (1854) became an American classic. "I went to the woods," he wrote, "because I wished to . . . confront only the essential facts of life, and see if I could not learn what it had to teach, and not, when I came to die, discover that I had not lived."

Nathaniel Hawthorne and Herman Melville, the greatest novelists of the American renaissance, focused on the existence of evil and the human need for community. In *The Scarlet Letter* (1850) and *The House of the Seven Gables* (1851), Hawthorne probed themes of egoism and pride to reveal the underside of the human soul. Melville's *Moby Dick* (1851) depicted the consequences of a competitive individualism unchecked by a social conscience. In his relentless pursuit of the great white whale, Captain Ahab destroys himself and his crew.

Much of the appeal of the utopian communities flowed from the same concern about the splintering and selfishness of antebellum society that animated Hawthorne and Melville. The works of these novelists have endured, but the utopian experiments quickly collapsed. Promising economic security and social harmony to buttress a threatened sense of community, the utopians failed to lure all but a few Americans from the acquisitiveness and competitive demands of the larger society.

ABOLITIONISM AND WOMEN'S RIGHTS

Abolitionism emerged from the same religious impulse that energized reform throughout the North. Like other reformers, the abolitionists came predominately from evangelical, middle-class families, particularly those of New England stock. What distinguished the abolitionists was their insistence that slavery was *the* great national sin, mocking American ideals of liberty and Christian morality.

Under the early leadership of William Lloyd Garrison, the abolitionists uncompromisingly attacked not only slaveholders but also all others whose moral apathy helped support slavery. After provoking a storm of protest in both the North and South, the abolitionist movement split in 1840. Crucial in this division was Garrison's support of women's rights. Most abolitionists broke with him and founded their own antislavery organization. Female abolitionists took the lead in organizing a separate women's rights movement.

REJECTING COLONIZATION

In the early nineteenth century, when slavery was expanding westward, almost all white Americans regardless of class or region were convinced that emancipation would lead either to a race war or the debasement of their superior status through racial interbreeding. This paralyzing fear of general emancipation, rooted in pervasive racism, long shielded slavery from sustained attack.

In 1817, antislavery reformers from the North and the South, founded the **American Colonization Society**. Slaveholding politicians from the Upper South—notably Henry Clay, James Madison, and President James Monroe—were the leading organizers of the society. Gradual emancipation accompanied by the removal of black people from America to Africa was the only solution that white reformers could imagine for ridding the nation of slavery and avoiding a racial bloodbath. Their goal was to make America all free *and* all white.

The American Colonization Society had no real chance of success. No form of emancipation, no matter how gradual, could appeal to slaveowners who could profit from the demand for their slaves in the Lower South. Moreover, the society could never afford to purchase the freedom of any significant number of slaves. Almost all the African Americans it transported to Liberia, the West African colony it helped found, were already free. At the height of its popularity in the 1820s, the society sent only fourteen hundred colonists to Africa. During that same decade, the American slave population increased by more than 450,000.

Free African Americans bitterly attacked the colonizers' central assumption that free black people were unfit to live as free citizens in America. Typical of the colonizers' racist thinking was the claim by Henry Clay in 1827 that the "free coloured" were the "most vicious" of all Americans. "Contaminated themselves, they extend their vices to all around them, to the slaves and to the whites." The annual report of the American Colonization Society in 1824 approvingly quoted a New England minister who said of the free African Americans: "You cannot raise him from the abyss of his degradation. You may call him free . . . but you cannot bleach him into the enjoyment of freedom."

Most free African Americans were native-born, and they considered themselves Americans with every right to enjoy the blessings of republican liberty. As a black petition in 1817 stated, banishment from America "would not only be cruel, but in direct violation of the principles, which have been the boast of this republic."

Organizing through their own churches in northern cities, free African Americans founded some fifty abolitionist societies, offered refuge to fugitive slaves, and launched the first African-American newspaper in 1827, *Freedom's Journal.* David Walker, a free black man who had moved from North Carolina to Massachusetts, published his ***Appeal to the Colored Citizens of the World*** in 1829. In a searing indictment of white greed and hypocrisy, he rejected colonization and insisted that "America is more our country, than it is the whites'—we have enriched it with our *blood and tears.*" He warned white America that "wo, wo, will be to you if we have to obtain our freedom by fighting."

As if in response to this call for revolutionary resistance by the enslaved, Nat Turner's Rebellion exploded in the summer of 1831 (see Chapter 11). Both alarmed and inspired by the increased tempo of black militancy, a small group of antislavery white people abandoned all illusions about colonization and embarked on a radically new approach for eradicating slavery.

ABOLITIONISM

William Lloyd Garrison, a Massachusetts printer and the leading figure in early abolitionism, became coeditor of an antislavery newspaper in Baltimore in 1829. Before the year was out, Garrison was arrested and convicted of criminal libel for his editorials against a Massachusetts merchant engaged in the domestic slave trade (the foreign or African slave trade had been prohibited in 1807), and he spent seven weeks in jail before a wealthy New York City philanthropist paid his $100 fine. Recognizing that his lack of freedom in jail paled against that of the slave, Garrison emerged with an unquenchable hatred of slavery. Returning to Boston, he launched his own antislavery newspaper, *The Liberator*, in 1831. A year later, he was instrumental in founding the New England Anti-Slavery Society.

As militant as the free African Americans who comprised the bulk of the early subscribers to *The Liberator*, Garrison thundered, "If we would not see our land deluged in blood, we must instantly burst asunder the shackles of the slaves." He committed abolitionism to the twin goals of immediatism—an immediate moral commitment to end slavery—and racial equality. Only by striving toward these goals, he insisted, could white America ever hope to end slavery without massive violence.

The demand of the abolitionists for the legal equality of black people was as unsettling to public opinion as their call for immediate, uncompensated emancipation. Discriminatory laws, aptly characterized by the abolitionist Lydia Maria Child as "this legalized contempt of color," restricted the political and civil liberties of free African Americans in every state. Denied the vote outside New England, segregated in all public facilities, prohibited from moving into several western states, and excluded from most jobs save menial labor, free black people everywhere were walled off as an inferior caste, unfit for equality.

The illustration on the masthead of this 1831 issue of The Liberator *condemns the relegation of slaves to the legal status of chattel, mere livestock to be bought and sold, no different from cattle or horses. Revulsion at the treatment of human beings as property was central to the abolitionist indictment of slavery.*

Garrison, harsh and uncompromising in denouncing slavery and advocating black rights, instilled the antislavery movement with moral urgency. But without the organizational and financial resources of a national society, the message of the early Garrisonians rarely extended beyond free black communities in the North. The success of British abolitionists in 1833, when gradual, compensated emancipation was enacted for Britain's West Indian colonies, inspired white and black abolitionists to gather at Philadelphia in December 1833 and form the **American Anti-Slavery Society**.

Arthur and Lewis Tappan, two wealthy merchants who dominated the abolitionist movement in New York City, provided financial backing for the Anti-Slavery Society. The young evangelical minister Theodore Dwight Weld, fusing abolitionism with the moral passion of religious revivalism, brought the antislavery message of the eastern radicals to the West in 1834 with the revivals he preached at Lane Theological Seminary in Cincinnati. The "Lane rebels," students gathered by Weld, fanned out as itinerant agents to seek converts for abolitionism throughout the Yankee districts of the rural North. Weld's *American Slavery as It Is: Testimony of a Thousand Witnesses*, a massively documented indictment of slavery, became a bestseller in 1839.

Revivalist exhortations were just one of the techniques the abolitionists exploited to mobilize public opinion against slavery. They spread their message through rallies, paid lecturers, children's games and toys, and the printed word. Drawing on the experience of reformers in Bible and tract societies, the

Overview

Types of Antislavery Reform

Type	Definition	Example
Gradualist	Accepts notions of black inferiority and attempts to end slavery gradually by purchasing the freedom of slaves and colonizing them in Africa	American Colonization Society
Immediatist	Calls for immediate steps to end slavery and denounces slavery and racial prejudice as moral sins	Abolitionists
Political Antislavery	Recognizes slavery in states where it exists but insists on keeping slavery out of the territories	Free-Soilers

abolitionists harnessed steam power to the cause of moral suasion. They distributed millions of antislavery tracts, and by the late 1830s, abolitionist sayings appeared on posters, emblems, song sheets, and even candy wrappers.

Women were essential in all of these activities. From the very beginning of the movement, they established their own antislavery societies as auxiliaries to the national organizations run and dominated by men. As Christian wives and mothers, they identified with the plight of the black family under slavery. Initially, their gender-segregated role was limited to raising funds, circulating petitions, and visiting homes to gain converts. Often operating out of local churches, women were grass-roots organizers of a massive petition campaign that the abolitionists launched in the mid-1830s. Women signed more than half of the antislavery memorials sent to Congress. "There would be but a few abolition petitions if the ladies . . . would let us alone," complained a Mississippi congressman.

The abolitionists focused their energies on mass propaganda because they saw their role as social agitators who had to break through white apathy and change public opinion. By 1840 they had succeeded in enlisting nearly 200,000 Northerners in two thousand local affiliates of the American Anti-Slavery Society. Most whites, however, remained unmoved, and some violently opposed the abolitionists.

Antiabolitionist mobs in the North went on a rampage in the mid-1830s (see figure 12–3). They disrupted antislavery meetings, beat and stoned speakers, destroyed printing presses, burned the homes of the wealthy benefactors of the movement, and vandalized free black neighborhoods in a wave of terror that drove many black people from several

northern cities. Although Garrison and Weld, the most frequent targets of mob violence, escaped with their lives, Elijah P. Lovejoy, an abolitionist editor in Illinois, was killed by a mob in 1837. Local elites, especially those with profitable ties to the slave economy of the South, often incited the mobs, whose fury expressed the anxieties of semi-skilled and common laborers that they might lose their jobs if freed slaves move north.

In the South, the hostility to abolitionism took the form of burning and censoring antislavery literature, offering rewards for the capture of leading abolitionists to stand trial for allegedly inciting slave revolts, and tightening up slave codes and the surveillance of free black people. Meanwhile, Democrats in Congress yielded to slaveholding interests in 1836 by passing a gag rule that automatically tabled antislavery petitions with no debate, infringing Americans' constitutional right to petition their representatives for the redress of grievances.

The hostility and violence abolitionism provoked convinced Garrison and some of his followers that American institutions and values were fundamentally flawed. In 1838, Garrison helped found the New England Non-Resistant Society, dedicated to the belief that a complete moral regeneration, based on renouncing force in all human relationships, was necessary if America were ever to live up to its Christian and republican ideals. The Garrisonian nonresistants rejected all coercive authority, whether expressed in human bondage, clerical support of slavery, male dominance in the patriarchal family, the racial oppression of back people, or the police power of government. The logic of their stand as Christian **anarchists** drove them to denounce all formal political activities and even the legitimacy of the Union, based as it was on a pact with slaveholders.

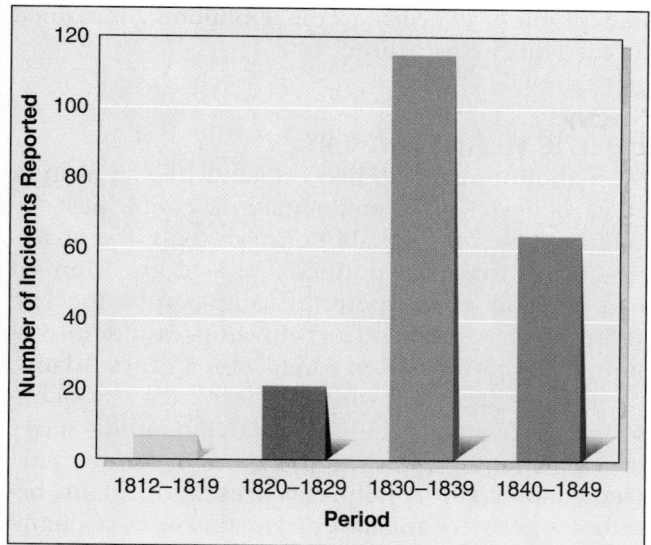

FIGURE 12-3   Mob Violence and the Abolitionists
Civil disturbances resulting in attacks on individuals or property increased sharply in the 1830s. The abolitionist campaign to flood the country with antislavery literature triggered much of this surge. Nearly half of the mob activity in the 1830s was directed against the abolitionists.

Data Source: Leonard L. Richards, *"Gentlemen of Property and Standing": Anti-Abolitionist Mobs in Jacksonian America* (1970).

Garrison's opponents within the abolitionist movement accused him of alienating the public by identifying the antislavery cause with radical attacks on traditional authority. His support for the growing demand of antislavery women to be treated as equals in the movement brought the factional bickering to a head and split the American Anti-Slavery Society. In turn, the opposition of most male abolitionists to the public activities of their female counterparts provoked a militant faction of these women into founding their own movement to achieve equality in American society.

THE WOMEN'S RIGHTS MOVEMENT

Feminism grew out of abolitionism because of the parallels many women drew between the exploited lives of the slaves and their own subordinate status in northern society. Considered biologically inferior to men, women were denied the vote, deprived of property or control of any wages after marriage, and barred from most occupations and advanced education. "In striving to cut [the slave's] irons off, we found most surely that we were manacled *ourselves*," argued Abby Kelley, a Quaker abolitionist.

In 1837, Angelina and Sarah Grimké, the South Carolina born abolitionists, attracted large crowds of men and women to their antislavery lectures in New England. By publicly lecturing to a "promiscuous" (mixed) audience of men and women, they defied restrictions on women's proper role and enraged the Congregational clergy of Massachusetts. Harshly criticized for their unwomanly behavior, the Grimkés publicly responded with an indictment of the male patriarchy and the shocking assertion that "men and women are *created equal*! They are both moral and accountable beings and whatever is right for man to do is right for woman."

Now more sensitive than ever to the injustice of their assigned role as men's submissive followers, antislavery women demanded an equal voice in the abolitionist movement. Despite strong opposition from many of his fellow male abolitionists, Garrison helped Abby Kelley win a seat on the business committee of the American Anti-Slavery Society at its convention in 1840. The anti-Garrisonians walked out of the convention and formed a separate organization, the American and Foreign Anti-Slavery Society.

What was rapidly becoming known as the "woman question" also disrupted the 1840 World Anti-Slavery Convention in London. The refusal of the convention to seat the American female delegates was the final indignity that transformed the discontent of women into a self-conscious movement for women's equality. Two of the excluded delegates, Lucretia Mott and Elizabeth Cady Stanton, vowed to build an organization to "speak out for *oppressed* women."

Their work went slowly. Early feminists were dependent on the abolitionists for most of their followers, and they were unable to do more than hold local meetings and sponsor occasional speaking tours. Many women sympathetic to the feminist movement hung back lest they be shunned in their communities. A minister's wife in Portsmouth, New Hampshire, spoke for many of these women when she wrote to a feminist friend, "There are but few here who think of women as anything more than slave or plaything, and they think I am different from most women."

In 1848, Stanton and Mott were finally able to call the first national convention ever devoted to women's rights at Seneca Falls, in upstate New York. The **Seneca Falls Convention** issued the **Declaration of Sentiments**, a call for full female equality. Modeled directly on the Declaration of Independence, it identified male patriarchy as the source of women's oppression and demanded the vote for women as a sacred and inalienable right of republican citizenship. This call for suffrage raised the prospect of women's self-determination as independent citizens.

Mobs of angry men often broke up meetings organized by women to vote. Shown here is a male escort offering protection to Lucretia Mott and another suffragette at one such meeting.

The Seneca Falls agenda defined the goals of the women's movement for the rest of the century. The call for the vote met the stiffest opposition, and male legislators refused to budge. The feminists' few successes before the Civil War came in economic rights. By 1860, fourteen states had granted women greater control over their property and wages—most significantly, under New York's Married Women's Property Act of 1860. Largely the result of the intense lobbying of Susan B. Anthony, the act established women's legal right to their own wage income and to sue fathers and husbands who tried to deprive them of their wages.

Despite such successes, the feminist movement did not attract broad support. Most women found in the doctrine of separate spheres a reassuring feminine identity that they could express either at home or in benevolent and reform societies. Within the reform movement as a whole, women's rights were al-

ways of minor concern, as the abolitionists remained focused on emancipation.

POLITICAL ANTISLAVERY

Most abolitionists who had broken with Garrison in 1840 believed that emancipation could best be achieved by moving abolitionism into the mainstream of American politics. Political abolitionism had its roots in the petition campaign of the late 1830s. Congressional efforts to suppress the discussion of slavery backfired when John Quincy Adams, the former president who had become a Massachusetts congressman, resorted to an unending series of parliamentary ploys to get around the gag rule (see chapter 10). A failure as president, Adams became a hero to antislavery Northerners, a champion of the constitutional right to petition Congress for redress of grievances. White Northerners who had shown no interest in abolitionism as a moral crusade for black people now began to take a stand against slavery when the issue involved the civil liberties of whites and the dominant political power of the South. By the hundreds of thousands, they signed abolitionist petitions in 1837 and 1838 to protest the gag rule and the admission of Texas as a slave state.

In 1840, anti-Garrisonian abolitionists tried to turn this new antislavery constituency into an independent political party. They formed the **Liberty Party** and ran James G. Birney, a former slaveholder converted by Weld to abolitionism, as their candidate for the presidency. He failed to draw even 1 percent of the total popular vote, but antislavery districts dominated by evangelical New Englanders elected several antislavery congressmen.

The Liberty Party opposed any expansion of slavery in the territories, condemned racial discrimination in the North as well as slavery in the South, and won the support of most black abolitionists. "To it," recalled Samuel Ward of New York, "I devoted my political activities; with it I lived my political life." In 1843, a national African-American convention in Buffalo endorsed the Liberty party.

This political activism was part of a concerted effort by African Americans to assert leadership in an antislavery movement that rarely treated them as equals. Frederick Douglass was their most dynamic spokesman. After escaping from slavery in 1838, Douglass became a spellbinding lecturer for abolitionism and in 1845 published his classic autobiography, *Narrative of the Life of Frederick Douglass, an American Slave.* Increasingly dissatisfied with Garrison's Christian pacifism and his stand against political action, Douglass broke with Garrison in 1847 and founded a black abolitionist newspaper, *The North Star*. The break became irreparable in 1851 when Douglass publicly denied the Garrisonian position that the Constitution was a proslavery document. If properly interpreted, Douglass insisted, "the Constitution is a *glorious liberty document*," and he called for a political war against slavery.

That war had started in the 1840s with the Liberty Party. Although the party elected only one of its candidates to Congress (Gerrit Smith of New York), it kept slavery in the limelight of national politics. Led by Joshua R. Giddings, a small but vocal bloc of antislavery politicians began to popularize the frightening concept of "the Slave Power"—a vast conspiracy of planters and their northern lackeys that had seized control of the federal government and was plotting to spread slavery and subvert any free institutions that opposed it. As proof, they cited the gag rule shutting off debate on slavery and the campaign of the Tyler administration to annex slaveholding Texas. The Michigan Liberty party in 1843 claimed that slavery was "not only a monstrous legalized system of wickedness . . . but an overwhelming political monopoly . . . which has thus tyrannically subverted the constitutional liberties of more than 12,000,000 of nominal American freemen." The Liberty Party blamed the depression of 1839–1843 on the "withering and impoverishing effect of slavery on the free States." Planters, it was charged, had reneged on their debts to northern creditors and manipulated federal policies on banking and tariffs to the advantage of the South.

The specter of the Slave Power made white liberties, and not black bondage, central to northern concerns about slavery. This shift redefined the evil of slavery to appeal to the self-interests of white Northerners who had rejected the moral appeals of the Garrisonians. White people who had earlier been apathetic now began to view slavery as a threat to their rights of free speech and self-improvement through free labor untainted by the degrading competition of slave labor.

Birney again headed the Liberty Party ticket in 1844, but he ran only marginally stronger than in 1840. Nonetheless, the image of the Slave Power predisposed many Northerners to see the expansionist program of the incoming Polk administration as part of a southern plot to secure more territory for slaveholders at the expense of northern farmers. Northern fears that free labor would be shut out of the new territories won in the Mexican War provided the rallying cry for the Free-Soil Party of 1848 that foreshadowed the more powerful Republican Party of the late 1850s.

After escaping to freedom in 1838, Frederick Douglass became a commanding figure in the abolitionist movement. His speeches denouncing slavery were fiery and eloquent.

Frederick Douglass (1817?-1895). Oil on canvas, c. 1844, attr. to E. Hammond. The Granger Collection.

CONCLUSION

With surprising speed after 1815, transportation improvements, technological innovations, and expanding markets drove the economy on a path toward industrialization. Wealth inequality increased, old classes were reshaped, and new ones formed. These changes were most evident in the Northeast, where capital, labor, and growing urban markets spurred the acceleration of manufacturing. The reform impulse that both reflected and shaped these changes was also strongest in the Northeast.

The new evangelical Protestantism promised that human perfectibility was possible if individuals strove to free themselves from sin. Influenced by this promise, the northern middle class embraced reform causes that sought to improve human character. Temperance, the most widely accepted of these causes, changed American drinking habits and established sobriety as the cultural standard for respectable male behavior. Middle-class reform also emphasized institutional solutions for what were now defined as the social problems of ignorance, crime, and poverty.

FROM THEN TO NOW

Immigration: An Ambivalent Welcome

Americans have long extended an ambivalent welcome to newcomers. In the mid-nineteenth century, employment posters often read "Irish Need Not Apply," and today stepped-up border patrols seek to keep out Mexican and other Latin American immigrants. Yet America is a nation settled and built by immigrants whose founding ideals promise equality and opportunity to all. And for much of its history it has offered asylum for the world's oppressed.

In the early years of the republic, Federalists worried that immigrants from Europe might be contaminated by the radical ideas of the French revolution and sought to make it harder for them to become naturalized citizens. The nation's first naturalization law in the 1790s also barred black immigrants from citizenship. The first sustained attack against newcomers, however, emerged as a result of the surge in immigration during the 1840s and 1850s. It was directed by established immigrant groups—the descendants of settlers from Britain and northwestern Europe—at unfamiliar newcomers, particularly the Irish.

Nativist arguments of that time have found an echo in all subsequent immigration debates. The Irish, it was claimed, would take jobs away from American workers and lower their wages. Taxpayers would have to foot the bill for the strains the newcomers imposed on schools, hospitals, and other civic services. The ignorant immigrants would corrupt the political process. Nativists especially feared religious contamination, claiming that the Catholicism of the Irish was alien to the Protestant values held to be indispensable to the preservation of American liberties. So many Irish arrived so quickly that many nativists were convinced of a Papal plot to undermine American freedom. "The bloody hand of the Pope," one wrote, "has stretched itself forth to our destruction."

Eventually the Irish and Germans merged into the economic and political fabric of American life. But in the late nineteenth century a massive new immigrant surge dominated by people from Southern and Eastern Europe seeking economic opportunity and fleeing religious oppression transformed American society and renewed nativist fears. This time, race replaced religion as the basis for drawing invidious comparisons between established residents and the newcomers. Pseudo-scientific theories relegated Jews, Slavs, and Mediterranean peoples, together with Africans, to an inferior status below people of Northern European and especially Anglo-Saxon descent. The newcomers, it was claimed, were unfit for democratic government and would endanger American civilization. Strict anti-immigrant legislation in the 1920s sharply curtailed immigration from outside the Western Hemisphere, banning Asians entirely and setting quotas based on national origin for others.

Recent concerns about immigration result from the unforeseen consequences of a 1965 reform in immigration law that abolished quotas. Since then, immigration has risen sharply, and the national origin of the immigrants has diverged from previous patterns. By the 1980s, Europeans constituted but 10 percent of the newcomers. The bulk of the remainder came from Asia (40 percent) and Mexico, Central America, and the Caribbean. Once again, anti-immigrant voices worry that alien newcomers are threatening the cohesiveness of the nation's institutions and values. But, once again as well, a more inclusive vision of American identity and ideals seems likely to prevail as the newcomers establish themselves. As Abraham Lincoln expressed it, "There was no exclusively American race entitled to claim liberty by heredity. What held the nation together was an idea of equality that every newcomer could claim and defend by free choice."

The most radical of the reform movements focused on women's equality and the elimination of slavery. The women's rights movement emerged out of women's involvement in reform, especially in abolitionism. Feminism and abolitionism triggered a backlash from the more conservative majority. This backlash prevented women from gaining legal and political equality, the major demand of the feminists, and convinced most abolitionists that they had to switch from moral agitation to political persuasion. The political abolitionists soon found that the most effective approach in widening the antislavery appeal was their charge that a Slave Power conspiracy threatened the freedoms of white Northerners.

REVIEW QUESTIONS

1. Why were improvements in transportation so essential to the growth of the economy after 1815? What were the nature and scope of these improvements?

2. What is an industrial revolution? How can we explain the surge in manufacturing in the United States from 1815 to 1850?

3. What was the religious impulse behind the first wave of reform? What innovations in reaching a mass audience did the benevolent reformers pioneer?

4. What drew women into reform? Why did many of them feel a special affinity for abolitionism?

5. Why was abolitionism the most radical reform of all?

6. Why do you think so few Southern women of the plantation class followed Angelina Grimké on her journey from social privilege to social activism?

KEY TERMS

American Anti-Slavery Society (p. 379)
American Colonization Society (p. 378)
American Female Reform Society (p. 370)
American system of manufacturing (p. 364)
American Temperance Society (p. 369)
Anarchists (p. 380)
Appeal to the Colored Citizens of the World (p. 378)
Benevolent empire (p. 368)
Brook Farm (p. 375)
Charles River Bridge v. Warren Bridge (p. 356)
Church of Jesus Christ of Latter-day Saints (Mormon Church) (p. 371)
Communism (p. 375)
Cult of domesticity (p. 366)

Declaration of Sentiments (p. 381)
Fourierist communities (p. 375)
Gibbons v. Ogden (p. 356)
Liberty Party (p. 382)
Mormon Church (p. 371)
Nativist (p. 367)
New Harmony (p. 375)
Oneida Community (p. 375)
Putting-out system (p. 361)
Rhode Island system (p. 362)
Sabbatarian movement (p. 368)
Seneca Falls Convention (p. 381)
Shakers (p. 375)
Socialism (p. 375)
Temperance (p. 365)
Transcendentalism (p. 376)
Transportation revolution (p. 353)
Waltham system (p. 362)
Workingmen's movement (p. 372)

RECOMMENDED READING

Abzug, Robert H. *Cosmos Crumbling: American Reform and the Religious Imagination* (1994). Provides a fresh look at antebellum reform by using the lives of individual reformers to show how Protestant Christianity inspired a rethinking of American values in a period of rapid economic change.

Boydston, Jeanne. *Home and Work: Housework, Wages, and the Ideology of Labor in the Early Republic* (1990). Shows how issues of gender shaped the emergence of a market for labor and influenced the very notion of work itself.

Cochran, Thomas C. *Frontiers of Change: Early Industrialization in America* (1981). Argues for the importance of cultural factors in the rise and scope of manufacturing in the United States before 1850.

Davis, David Brion, ed. *Antebellum American Culture* (1979). This superb collection of source materials covers all facets of the commitment to reform and institutional change.

Larkin, Jack. *The Reshaping of Everyday Life, 1790–1840* (1988). A very readable depiction of how social and economic changes were reflected in the rhythms and customs of daily life in the first half of the nineteenth century.

Licht, Walter. *Industrializing America: The Nineteenth Century* (1995). This smoothly written survey interprets industrialization as both a product and a promoter of economic and social change.

Mintz, Steven. *Moralists and Modernizers: America's Pre-Civil War Reformers* (1995). A recent survey that demonstrates how both the fears and possibilities of change influenced the impulse of reform.

Stewart, James Brewer. *Holy Warriors: The Abolitionists and American Society* (1978). Provides the best brief overview of abolitionism and what distinguished it from the mainstream of the reform tradition.

ADDITIONAL SOURCES

Industrial Change and Urbanization

Anbinder, Tyler. *Five Points* (2001).

Blumin, Stuart M. *The Emergence of the Middle Class: Social Experience in the American City, 1760–1900* (1989).

Bushman, Richard L. *The Refinement of America: Persons, Houses, Cities* (1992).

Dublin, Thomas. *Women at Work: The Transformation of Work and Community in Lowell, Massachusetts, 1826–1860* (1979).

Fishlow, Albert. *American Railroads and the Transformation of the Ante-Bellum Economy* (1965).

Handlin, Oscar. *Boston's Immigrants: A Study of Acculturation*, rev. ed. (1959).

Horowitz, Morton J. *The Transformation of American Law, 1790–1860* (1977).

Johnson, Paul E. *A Shopkeeper's Millennium: Society and Revivals in Rochester, New York, 1815–1837* (1978).

Laurie, Bruce. *Artisans into Workers: Labor in Nineteenth-Century America* (1989).

Pessen, Edward. *Riches, Class, and Power before the Civil War* (1973).

Roediger, David. *The Wages of Whiteness: Race and the Making of the American Working Class* (1991).

Ryan, Mary. *Cradle of the Middle Class: The Family in Oneida County, New York, 1790–1865* (1981).

Shaw, Ronald E. *Canals for a Nation: The Canal Era in the United States, 1790–1860* (1990).

Stansel, Christine. *City of Women: Sex and Class in New York, 1789–1860* (1986).

Steinberg, Theodore. *Nature Incorporated: Industrialization and the Waters of New England* (1991).

Wade, Richard C. *The Urban Frontier* (1964).

Wilentz, Sean. *Chants Democratic: New York City and the Rise of the American Working Class, 1790–1865* (1984).

Reform and Moral Order

Cott, Nancy F. *The Bonds of Womanhood: "Woman's Sphere" in New England, 1780–1835* (1977).

Cross, Whitney R. *The Burned-Over District: The Social and Intellectual History of Enthusiastic Religion in Western New York, 1800–1850* (1950).

Epstein, Barbara Leslie. *The Politics of Domesticity: Women, Evangelicalism, and Temperance in Nineteenth-Century America* (1981).

Foster, Charles I. *An Errand of Mercy: The Evangelical United Front* (1960).

Ginzberg, Lori D. *Women and the Work of Benevolence: Morality, Politics, and Class in the 19th-Century United States* (1990).

Hanley, Mark Y. *Beyond a Christian Commonwealth: The Protestant Quarrel with the American Republic, 1830–1860* (1994).

Smith-Rosenberg, Carroll. *Religion and the Rise of the American City* (1971).

Rorabaugh, W. J. *The Alcoholic Republic* (1979).

Walters, Ronald A. *American Reformers, 1815–1860* (1978).

Winn, Kenneth H. *Exiles in a Land of Liberty: Mormons in America, 1830–1846* (1989).

Wosh, Peter J. *Spreading the Word: The Bible Business in Nineteenth-Century America* (1994).

Institutions and Social Improvement

Capper, Charles, and Conrad Edick Wright, eds. *Transient and Permanent: The Transcendentalist Movement and its Contexts* (1999).

Grob, Gerald N. *Mental Institutions in America: Social Policy to 1875* (1973).

Guarneri, Carl J. *The Utopian Alternative: Fourierism in Nineteenth-Century America* (1991).

Hirsh, Adam Jay. *The Rise of the Penitentiary* (1992).

Kaestle, Carl F. *Pillars of the Republic: Common Schools and American Society, 1780–1860* (1983).

Katz, Michael B. *In the Shadow of the Poorhouse: A Social History of Welfare in America* (1986).

Rothman, David. *The Discovery of the Asylum: Social Order and Disorder in the New Republic* (1971).

Stein, Stephen J. *The Shaker Experience in America* (1992).

Abolitionism and Women's Rights

Basch, Norma. *In the Eyes of the Law: Women, Marriage, and Property in Nineteenth-Century New York* (1982).

Du Bois, Ellen. *Feminism and Suffrage: The Emergence of an Independent Women's Movement, 1848–1869* (1978).

Hewitt, Nancy A. *Women's Activism and Social Change: Rochester, New York, 1822–1872* (1984).

Isenberg, Nancy. *Sex and Citizenship in Antebellum America* (1998).

Jeffrey, Julie Roy. *The Great Silent Army of Abolitionism: Ordinary Women in the Antislavery Movement* (1998).

Litwack, Leon F. *North of Slavery: The Negro in the Free States, 1790–1860* (1961).

Lumpkin, Katharine Du Pre. *The Emancipation of Angelina Grimké* (1974).

McKivigan, John R. *The War against Proslavery Religion: Abolitionism and the Northern Churches, 1830–1865* (1984).

Newman, Richard S. *The Transformation of American Abolitionism: Fighting Slavery in the Early Republic* (2002).

Rael, Patrick. *Black Identity and Black Protest in the Antebellum North* (2002).

Richards, Leonard L. *The Slave Power: The Free North and Southern Domination, 1780–1860* (2000).

Ripley, C. Peter, et al., eds. *Witness for Freedom: African-American Voices on Race, Slavery, and Emancipation* (1993).

Staudenraus, Philip J. *The African Colonization Movement, 1816–1865* (1961).

WHERE TO LEARN MORE

- **Baltimore Center for Urban Archaeology, Baltimore, Maryland.** Operated by Baltimore City Life Museum, the center has a large collection of artifacts depicting urban life in the eighteenth and nineteenth centuries and a working archaeological library.

- **Hanford Mills Museum, East Meredith, New York.** This museum preserves and interprets water-powered machinery and explains the role played by local mills in the community life of the nineteenth century. For a map and links to events, workshops, and education programs, visit www.hanfordmills.org/.

- Slater Hill Historic Site, Pawtucket, Rhode Island. The Sylvanus Brown House of 1758, the Slaren Mill of 1793, and the Wilkinson Mill of 1810 are on the site. An extensive library and holdings provide insight into the social and economic world of the early industrial revolution. Information on hours, collections, and exhibits can be found at www.artcom.com/museums/vs/sz/02862-06.htm.

- **Erie Canal Museum, Syracuse, New York.** The museum houses extensive collections on the building and maintenance of the Erie Canal, and its photo holdings visually record much of the history of the canal. In addition to information on exhibits, tours, and school programs, its website, www.eriecanalmuseum.org/, includes pictures of a replica of an Erie Canal line boat.

- **Historic New Harmony, New Harmony, Indiana.** The tours and museum holdings at this preserved site offer a glimpse into the communal living that Robert Owen tried to promote in his utopian plan. For a brief history of New Harmony and links to special events and programs at the site, go to www.newharmony.org/.

- **Oberlin College Library, Oberlin, Ohio.** Oberlin was a hotbed of reform agitation, and the tracts, broadsides, photographs, and other memorabilia here are especially rich on the activities of white evangelicals and black abolitionists. For an introduction to the library and its holdings, visit www.oberlin.edu/library/.

- **Shaker Museum at South Union, Kentucky.** The exhibits, artifacts, and archives are a superb source for understanding the history and material culture of the Shakers and other radical sects. Its website, www.shakermuseum.com/, includes a brief history of the Shakers, photographs of restored buildings, and an overview of the museum's holdings.

- **Women's Rights Historical Park, Seneca Falls, New York.** The park provides an interpretive overview of the first women's rights convention and includes among its historical sites the restored home of Elizabeth Cady Stanton. Go to www.nps.gov/wori/wrnhp.htm for links to the museum's summer calendar of events and information on programs.

 Please refer to the document CD-ROM for primary sources related to this chapter.

→ As depicted in this painting by George Catlin, Native Americans were still the dominant power on the Great Plains when this Comanche war party met up with a scouting expedition of the U.S. Army in the 1830s. Within a decade, a wave of white settlement challenged the power in a series of clashes for control of the Trans-Mississippi West.

THE WAY WEST 13

"On an occasion when I had interrogated a Sioux chief, on the upper Missouri, about their Government — their punishments and tortures of prisoners, for which I had freely condemned them for the cruelty of the practice, he took occasion, when I had got through, to ask *me* some questions relative to modes in the *civilized world*, which, with his comments upon them, were nearly as follows: and struck me, as I think they must every one, with great force.

He . . . told me he had often heard that white people hung their criminals by the neck, and choked them to death like dogs, and those their own people; to which I answered, "yes." He then told me he had learned that they shut each other up in prisons, where they keep them a great part of their lives *because they can't pay money*! I replied in the affirmative to this, which occasioned great surprise and excessive laughter, even among the women. . . . He said . . . that he had been along the Frontier, and a good deal amongst the white people, and he had seen them whip their little children — a thing that is very cruel — he had heard also, from several white *medicine-men*, that the Great Spirit of the white people was the child of a white woman, and that he was at the last put to death by the white people! This seemed to be a thing that he had not been able to comprehend, and he concluded by saying, 'the Indians' Great Spirit got no mother — the Indians no kill him, he never die." He put me a chapter of other questions as to the

CHAPTER OUTLINE

The Agricultural Frontier
The Crowded East
The Old Northwest
The Old Southwest

The Frontier of the Plains Indians
Tribal Lands
The Fur Traders
The Oregon Trail

The Mexican Borderlands
The Peoples of the Southwest
The Americanization of Texas
The Push into California and the Southwest

Politics, Expansion, and War
Manifest Destiny
The Mexican War

Conclusion

trespasses of the white people on their lands—their continual corruption of the morals of their women—and digging open the Indians' graves to get their bones, &c. To all of which I was compelled to reply in the affirmative, and quite glad to close my note-book, and quietly to escape from the throng that had collected around me, and saying (though to myself and silently), that these and an hundred other vices belong to the civilized world, and are practiced upon (but certainly, in no instance, reciprocated by) the "cruel and relentless savage."

George Catlin

Virgil J. Vogel, ed., *A Documentary History of the American Indian* (New York: Harper and Row, 1972), pp. 138–139.

George Catlin, one of the great illustrators of the West of the American Indians, recorded these words in the 1830s when he traveled over the trans-Mississippi West painting and sketching, in his words, "the looks and customs of the vanishing races of native man in America." Unlike most whites of his generation, he approached Indian cultures with respect, and he was astute enough to realize that native peoples had a valid critique of the culture and values of white America. Born in 1796 in the Wyoming Valley of northeastern Pennsylvania, an area wracked by Indian raids during the Revolutionary War, including one in which his mother was held captive, he was raised among memories of Indians and their warfare. After attending law school in Litchfield, Connecticut, and briefly practicing law, he turned to painting and portraiture as a career in the 1820s. He was so taken with the physical grace and dignity of a group of Indians visiting Philadelphia in 1824 that he committed his life's work to a visual recording of Indian history and customs.

From his first contact with the tribes along the upper Missouri River in the early 1830s, Catlin sensed that he was witness to a way of life that was about to vanish. He worked at a feverish pace to create a pictorial record of what he saw in a collection of art he called "Catlin's Indian Gallery." The proceeds from exhibiting his work in Europe enabled him to live quite comfortably in the 1840s, but falling prey to a vice of the "civilized" world that the Sioux chief failed to mention, he suffered a severe setback in 1852 when a financial speculation went sour. He had to pledge his art collection as security to obtain a large loan, and he never did succeed in redeeming the loan. A failure as an entrepreneur, he nonetheless succeeded brilliantly as an artist in depicting the Native American peoples of the trans-Mississippi West just at the moment they were about to be engulfed by a surging tide of white settlement.

Some 300,00 Americans traveled the Oregon Trail in the 1840s and 1850s in a trek that eventually made the United States a nation that spanned the continent. These overlanders, as they came to be known, were part of a restless tide of white migration that eventually saw more than fifty thousand Americans a year migrate west of the Appalachians after the War of 1812.

After moving into the area between the Appalachian Mountains and the Mississippi River—the American West of the early nineteenth century—migrants headed beyond the Mississippi River in the 1840s. The edge of settlement pushed into the Louisiana Purchase territory and across a huge area of plains, desert, mountains, and ocean coast that had seen few American settlers before 1840.

The broad expanse of the trans-Mississippi region (stretching from the Mississippi Valley to the Pacific Coast) had become the new American West by midcentury. The West became a meeting ground of people from diverse cultures as Anglo-Americans came into contact and conflict with the Indians of the Plains and the Mexicans of the Southwest. Convinced of the superiority of their political and cultural values, Anglo-Americans asserted a God-given right to spread across the continent and impose their notions of liberty and democracy on peoples whose land they coveted. In the process, they defeated and subjugated those who stood in their way.

Manifest Destiny was the label for this presumed providential right, and it provided a justification for the aggressively expansionist Democratic administration of James K. Polk that came to power in 1845. The most dramatic result of these policies was the Mexican War of 1846–1848, which made California and the present-day Southwest part of the American continental empire.

KEY TOPICS

- Western migration spurred by economic and demographic pressures in the East after the War of 1812

- The development of free commercial agriculture tied to eastern markets and increased industrialization and urbanization of the Old Northwest

- The development of a plantation economy based on cotton and slavery in the Old Southwest

- Manifest Destiny and westward expansion, relegating Native Americans and Mexican-Americans to subjugated status

- U.S. annexation of Texas and the wresting of the Southwest and California from Mexico

THE AGRICULTURAL FRONTIER

The U.S. population ballooned from 5.3 million in 1800 to more than 23 million by 1850. The population grew about 33 percent per decade, and four-fifths of this extraordinary gain was from natural increase—the surplus of births over deaths. As the population expanded, it shifted westward. Fewer than one in ten Americans lived west of the Appalachians in 1800; by 1850, about half did (see Map 13–1).

The tremendous amount of land available for settlement accounted for both phenomena. Through purchase and conquest, the land area of the United States more than tripled in the first half of the nineteenth century. Here was space where Americans could raise the large families of a rural society in which, on average, six to eight children survived to adolescence. Millions of fertile acres lured eastern families ever westward to the next agricultural frontier.

Declining soil fertility and rising population pressure in the rural East propelled these migrations. A common desire for greater economic opportunity, however, resulted in two distinct western societies by the 1840s. North of the Ohio River, in the Old Northwest, free labor and family farms defined the social order. South of the Ohio was the Old Southwest, a society dominated by slave labor and the plantation.

THE CROWDED EAST

Looking back at his rural youth, Omar H. Morse recalled, "My Parents were in very limited circumstances financially yet blessed with a large family of children which is a poor man's capital though capital of this kind is not considered very available in case of financial Depression." Born in 1824 in the upstate New York village of Hastings, Morse was typical of the hard-pressed eastern youth who moved west after the War of 1812. With no prospect of inheriting land from his father and tired of taking orders as a farmhand for temporary wages, he moved in the 1840s to Wisconsin, where he found what he thought was "the most beautiful spot of country on God's green Earth." Even after this fresh start, bad luck and too many debts prevented Morse from ever achieving landed independence. He lost three farms and eventually settled in Minnesota, where he worked at odd jobs and built houses. Heading west did not guarantee economic success, but it was the best option open to land-starved easterners who dreamed of leaving a productive farm to their children.

By the early nineteenth century, land was scarce in the East, especially in New England. After generations of population growth and subdivisions of landholdings to male heirs, most New England communities no longer had enough arable land to satisfy all the young men who wanted their own farms. Even such recently opened areas as Vermont felt the pressure of rural overpopulation.

Land was more productive and expensive farther south, in the mid-Atlantic states. Based on the major export crop of wheat, agriculture was more commercialized than in New England, and economic inequality was thus higher. Successful farmers became wealthy by specializing in wheat and hiring the rural poor to work their fields. One-third to one-half of the young men in the commercialized agricultural districts of New Jersey and Pennsylvania were landless by the end of the eighteenth century. These men and their families, many of whom were recently arrived Scots-Irish and German immigrants, led the western migration from Pennsylvania.

The pressure to move west was greatest in the slave states along the eastern seaboard. Although population

MAP EXPLORATION To explore an interactive version of this map, go to
http://www.prenhall.com/goldfield/map13.1

MAP 13-1 **The Westward Shift of the United States Population, 1790–1850**
With a speed that was unimaginable in 1790, the United States quickly became a continental nation that stretched from the Atlantic to the Pacific by 1850. Particularly dramatic was the population growth in what became the Midwest.

density here was just two-thirds of that in New England, ordinary white farmers faced even more limited prospects of economic advancement. Landholdings were more concentrated and the soil more exhausted than in the Northeast. Repeated plantings of tobacco in Virginia and Maryland and of cotton farther south had depleted the soil throughout much of the region. In the Chesapeake states, established planters with extensive capital and labor resources shifted to wheat production or bought out their nonslaveholding neighbors. Tenants who wanted their own land and small farmers tired of competing against slave labor were forced west across the mountains. They were joined by the sons of planters. Despite marriages arranged to keep land within the wealthy families, there was no longer enough good land left to carve out plantations for all the younger sons.

By the early 1800s, the young and the poor in the rural East faced limited opportunities for social mobility and economic independence. They had every incentive to head west, where fertile land was abundant, accessible, and at $2 to $3 per acre, far cheaper than in the East. Land was the basis of wealth and social standing, and its ownership separated the independent from the dependent, the rooted from the rootless. According to the principles of Jeffersonian democracy, the independent farmer was the backbone of the republic, the virtuous citizen who made republican government possible. "Those who labor in the earth," Jefferson wrote in 1785, "are the chosen people of God . . . whose breasts He has made his peculiar deposit for substantial and genuine virtue."

The western settler, observed a traveler on the Missouri frontier in the 1820s, wanted "to be a freeholder, to have plenty of rich land, and to be able to settle his children around him." Government policy under the Jeffersonian Republicans and Jacksonian Democrats attempted to make it easier to reach these goals. Central to the land policy of the federal government after 1800 was the conviction that political liberties rested on the broadest possible base of land ownership. Thus public policy and private aspirations merged in the belief that access to land was the key to preserving American freedom.

When Jefferson took office in 1801, the minimum price for public land was $2 per acre, and a block of 320 acres had to be purchased at one time. By the 1830s, the price was down to $1.25 per acre, and the minimum purchase was only 80 acres. Congress also protected squatters, who had settled on public land before it was surveyed, from being outbid by speculators at land sales. The Preemption Act of 1841 guaranteed the right to purchase up to 160 acres at the minimum price of $1.25 when the public auction was held.

THE OLD NORTHWEST

The number of Americans who settled in the heartland of the Old Northwest—Ohio, Indiana, and Illinois—rose tenfold from 1810 to 1840. Ohio had already entered the Union in 1803; Indiana joined in 1816, Illinois in 1818. The end of the War of 1812 and the abandonment by the British of their former Indian allies opened up the region to a flood of migrants.

Travelers passing through the Ohio Valley just after the war were astonished by the number of Americans

Chronology

1803–1806	Lewis and Clark travel up the Missouri River in search of a water route to the Pacific.	1837	Smallpox epidemic hits the Plains Indians.
1816	Settlers surge into the trans-Appalachian region.	1842	First large parties of migrants set out on the Oregon Trail.
1821	Mexico gains its independence from Spain.	1845	United States annexes Texas.
	Santa Fe Trail opens.		Democrats embrace Manifest Destiny.
	Stephen F. Austin establishes the first American colony in Texas.	1846	Mexican War breaks out.
			United States and Britain reach an agreement in Oregon.
1824	Rocky Mountain Fur Company begins the rendezvous system.	1847	Mormons begin settlement of Utah.
1830	Congress creates the Indian Territory.	1848	Oregon Territory is organized.
1834	Protestant missions are established in Oregon.		Treaty of Guadalupe Hidalgo ends the Mexican War.
	Santa Anna seizes power in Mexico.	1851	Fort Laramie Treaty with the Plains Indians is signed.
1836	Texas wins its independence from Mexico.		

trekking west. Wagonloads of migrants bounced along turnpikes to disembark on the Ohio River at Pittsburgh and Wheeling, where they bought flatboats to carry them down the Ohio to the interior river valleys. Moving north across the Ohio were families from the hill country of Virginia and Kentucky. These two streams of migrants, one predominantly northern and the other southern, met in the lower Midwest and viewed each other as strangers. Lucy Maynard, a New Englander living in south-central Illinois, noted that her neighbors were "principally from Indiana and Kentucky, some from Virginia, all friendly but very different from our people in their manners and language and every other way."

A mosaic of settlements.

The Old Northwest was less a melting pot in which regional cultures merged than a mosaic of settlements in which the different values and folkways of regional cultures from throughout the East took root and expanded. Belts of migration generally ran along a line from east to west as settlers sought out soil types and ecological conditions similar to those they had left behind. Thus the same North–South cultural differences that existed along the Atlantic seaboard in 1800 were to be found half a century later in the Mississippi Valley.

A transplanted Yankee culture from New England and upstate New York spread over the upper Midwest—northern Ohio, Indiana, and Illinois, as well as Michigan and Wisconsin. These westerners were Whiggish in their politics, tended to be antislavery, and valued a communal sense of responsibility that regulated moral behavior and promoted self-improvement. The highland southerners who settled the lower Midwest—southern Ohio, Indiana, and Illinois, as well as Kentucky—were Democrats: They fiercely distrusted any centralized authority, political or moral, and considered Yankees intolerant do-gooders. Holding the balance of cultural and political power were the migrants from Pennsylvania and New Jersey, who were accustomed to ethnic diversity and the politics of competing economic groups. They settled principally in central Ohio, Indiana, and Illinois. By emphasizing economic growth and downplaying the cultural politics that pitted Yankees against Southerners, they built a consensus around community development.

Much as they had done in the East, the early settlers practiced a diversified agriculture to feed and shelter their families. The first task was to clear the land and sow a crop of corn, a hardy grain that required little care. Wild game and livestock left to forage in the woods supplemented the corn-based diet.

It took about ten years of backbreaking labor to create an 80-acre farm in heavily wooded sections. Because the Northwest Ordinance of 1787 had barred slavery north of the Ohio, settlers had to do the work themselves or hire farmhands. The work of women was essential for the success of the farm and the production of any salable surplus. Wives and daughters helped to tend the field crops, milked cows and churned butter, and they produced the homespun cloth that, along with their dairy goods, found a market in the first country stores on the frontier. Charlotte Webb Jacobs, from the Sugar Creek community on the Illinois prairie, proudly recalled, "I made everything that we wore; I even made my towels and table cloths, sheets and everything in the clothing line."

Because outside labor was scarce and expensive, communities pooled their efforts for such tasks as raising a cabin. Groups of settlers also acted as a cooperative unit at public land auctions. Local associations known as **claims clubs** enforced the extralegal right of squatters to enter noncompetitive bids on land they had settled and improved. Members of the clubs physically intimidated speculators who refused to step aside until local settlers had acquired the land they wanted.

The high cost of hauling goods to outside markets kept the early frontier economy barely above self-sufficiency. Any surplus was sold to newcomers moving into the area or bartered with local storekeepers for such essentials as salt, sugar, and metalwares. This initial economy, however, soon gave way to a more commercially oriented agriculture when steamboats, canals, and railroads opened up vast new markets (see Chapter 12). Western lands were at least twice as fertile as those in the East, and farmers could now profit from their bountiful yields.

The first large market was in the South, down the corridor of the Ohio and Mississippi Rivers, and its major staples were corn and hogs. By the 1830s, the Erie Canal and its feeder waterways in the upper Midwest began to reorient much of the western farm trade to the Northeast. Wheat, because of its ready marketability for milling into flour, became the major cash crop for the northern market.

Wheat production skyrocketed when settlers overcame their initial reluctance to farming in a treeless terrain and moved into the prairies of Indiana and Illinois in the 1840s. New plows—a cast-iron one patented by Jethro Wood in 1819 and a steel version developed by John Deere in 1837—helped break the thick prairie sod. The plows were followed in the 1840s by horse-drawn mechanical harvesters designed and manufactured by Cyrus McCormick. Traditional harvesting methods that relied on a worker using a scythe with a cradle frame were slow and relatively expensive. An experienced worker could cut no more than two acres a day. The same worker with the new machinery could harvest twelve acres a day, and the per-acre cost of labor fell dramatically. Once railroads provided direct access to eastern markets, the Midwest became the nation's breadbasket.

Although southern cotton was the raw material that fueled New England textile factories in the first stages of industrialization, the commercialization of agriculture in the West also contributed to the growth of eastern manufacturing. The productivity of western farms supplied eastern manufacturers with inexpensive raw materials for processing into finished goods. By flooding national markets with corn and wheat, western produce not only supplied eastern workers with cheap food but also forced noncompetitive eastern farmers either to move west or to work in factories in eastern cities. In turn, the West itself became an ever-growing market for eastern factory goods. For example, nearly half of the nation's iron production in the 1830s was fashioned into farm implements.

In the 1820s, the Old Northwest was just emerging from semisubsistence and depended on the southern trade. Thirty years later it had become part of a larger Midwest whose economy was increasingly integrated with that of the Northeast. Settlers continued to pour into the region, and three additional states—Michigan (1837), Iowa (1846), and Wisconsin (1848)—joined the Union.

The combination of favorable farm prices and steadily decreasing transportation costs generated a rise in disposable income that was spent on outside goods or invested in internal development. A network of canals and railroads was laid down, and manufacturing cities grew from towns favorably situated by water or rail transport. There was still room for subsistence farming, but the West north of the Ohio was now economically specialized and socially diverse.

THE OLD SOUTHWEST

"The *Alabama Feaver* rages here with great violence and has carried off vast numbers of our Citizens," wrote a North Carolina planter in 1817 about the westward migration from his state. "I am apprehensive, if it continues to spread as it has done, it will almost depopulate the country."

The planter, James Graham, had reason to be concerned. About as many people migrated from the old slave states in the East to the Old Southwest as those states gained by natural increase in the 1820s and 1830s. By 1850, more than 600,000 white settlers from Maryland, Virginia, and the Carolinas lived in slave states to the south and west, and many of them had brought their slaves with them. Indeed, from 1790 to 1860, more than 800,000 slaves were moved from the South Atlantic region into the Old Southwest.

Soaring cotton prices after the War of 1812 and the smashing of Indian confederations during the war, which opened new lands to white settlement, propelled the first surge of migration into the Old Southwest (see Map 13–1). Before cotton prices plunged in the Panic of 1819, planters flooded into western Tennessee and the Black Belt, a crescent-shaped band of rich, black loamy soil arcing westward from Georgia through central Alabama and Mississippi. Migration surged anew in the 1830s when cotton prices were again high and the Chickasaws and Choctaws had been forced out of the incredibly fertile Delta country between the Yazoo and Mississippi Rivers (see Chapter 10). The 1840s brought Texas fever to replace the Alabama fever of the 1810s, and a steady movement to the Southwest rounded out the contours of the cotton South. In less than thirty years, six new slave states—Mississippi (1817), Alabama (1819), Missouri (1821), Arkansas (1836), Florida (1845), and Texas (1845)—joined the Union (see the Overview table, "Westward Expansion and the Growth of the Union, 1815–1850").

Cyrus McCormick pioneered the development of horse-drawn mechanical reapers. Shown here demonstrating his reaper to potential customers, McCormick helped revolutionize American agriculture with labor-saving machinery that made possible far larger harvests of grain crops.

The southwestern frontier attracted both slave-holding planters and small independent farmers. The planters, though a minority, had the capital or the credit to acquire the best lands and the slave labor to make those lands productive. In abandoning the light, sandy, and overworked soils of eastern plantations for the far richer alluvial and prairie soils of the Old Southwest, these slaveholders were responding both to the need for fresh land and to the extraordinary demand for short-staple cotton. As one North Carolina planter put it, Alabama would be a "garden of plenty" compared to the "old-fields and empty corn-houses" of his native state.

Short-staple cotton could be grown anywhere with a minimum of 210 consecutive frost-free days. The crop, however, was of minor commercial importance before the 1790s, when Eli Whitney's gin eliminated the problem of removing the sticky, green seeds from cotton fiber, an essential step in preparing it to be spun and woven into cloth. Meanwhile, the mechanization of the British textile industry had created a seemingly unquenchable demand for raw cotton. No place in the world was better positioned to meet that demand than the American South. Most important, a slave labor force was available to work the land. Led by the booming output of the new plantations in the Old Southwest, the South increased its share of world cotton production from 9 percent in 1800 to 68 percent in 1850.

Thanks to cotton and slavery, aggressive, hard-driving planters loomed large in the Old Southwest. But small independent yeoman farmers, most with no slaves, were far more typical on the southern frontier. Usually settling in the valleys, on the ridges, and in the hill country, they often soon sold out to neighboring planters and headed west again. Like the yeoman farmer Gideon Linecum, they relished "the pleasure of frequent change of country."

The yeomanry moved onto the frontier in two waves. The first consisted of stockmen-hunters, a restless, transient group that spread from the pine barrens in the Carolina backcountry to the coastal plain of eastern Texas. These pioneers prized unfettered independence and measured their wealth in the livestock left to roam and fatten on the sweet grasses of uncleared forests. They were quick to move on when farmers, the second wave, started to clear the land for crops.

Like the stock herders, the yeoman farmers valued self-sufficiency and the leisure to hunt and fish. In pursuit of these goals, they practiced a diversified agriculture aimed at feeding their families. Corn and pork were the mainstays of their diet, and both could readily be produced as long as there was room for the open-range herding of swine and for patches of corn and small grains. The more ambitious farmers, usually those who owned one or two slaves, grew some cotton, but most preferred to avoid the economic risks of cotton production. The yeoman's chief source of labor was his immediate family, and to expand that labor force to produce cotton meant going into debt to purchase slaves. That debt could easily cost the yeoman his farm if the price of cotton fell.

Measured by per capita income, and as a direct result of the profits from slave-produced cotton on virgin soils, the Old Southwest was a wealthier society than the Old Northwest in 1850. In the short term, the settlement of the Old Southwest was also more significant for national economic development. Cot-

Overview

Westward Expansion and the Growth of the Union, 1815–1850

New Free States	New Slave States	Territories (1850)
Indiana, 1816	Mississippi, 1817	Minnesota
Illinois, 1818	Alabama, 1819	Oregon
Maine, 1820	Missouri, 1821	New Mexico
Michigan, 1837	Arkansas, 1836	Utah
Iowa, 1846	Florida, 1845	
Wisconsin, 1848	Texas, 1845	

ton accounted for more than half the value of all American exports after the mid-1830s. More than any other commodity, cotton paid for American imports and underpinned national credit. But southern prosperity was not accompanied by the same economic development and social change as in the Old Northwest. Compared to the slave West in 1860, the free-labor West was twice as urbanized, and far more of its workforce was engaged in nonagricultural pursuits.

The Southwest Ordinance, enacted by Congress in 1790, opened all territories south of the Ohio River to slavery. Slaves, land, and cotton were the keys to wealth on the southern frontier, and agricultural profits were continually plowed back into more land and slaves to produce more cotton. In contrast, prosperous farmers in the Old Northwest had no slaves to work additional acres. Hence they were much more likely to invest their earnings in promotional schemes designed to attract settlers whose presence would raise land values and increase business for local merchants and entrepreneurs. As early as the 1840s, rural communities in the Old Northwest were supporting bustling towns that offered jobs in trade and manufacturing on a scale far surpassing anything in the slave West. By the 1850s, the Midwest was almost as urbanized as the Northeast had been in 1830, and nearly half its labor force no longer worked on farms.

The Old Southwest remained overwhelmingly agricultural. Once the land was settled, the children of the first generation of slaveholders and yeomen moved west to the next frontier rather than compete for the good land that was left. Relatively few newcomers took their place. By the 1850s, Kentucky, Tennessee, Alabama, and Mississippi—the core states of the Old Southwest—were all losing more migrants than they were gaining.

THE FRONTIER OF THE PLAINS INDIANS

Few white Americans had ventured west of the Mississippi by 1840. What scanty knowledge there was of this huge inland expanse was the result of government-sponsored expeditions. Reports of explorations of the southern plains by Zebulon Pike in 1806 and Stephen Long in 1819 dismissed the area as the Great American Desert—an arid, treeless landscape with little agricultural potential, fit only for the Indians being removed from the East. The vast plains and plateaus climbing westward to the foothills of the Rocky Mountains in a seemingly endless ocean of grass were unfamiliar and intimidating to farmers accustomed to the wooded, well-watered, humid East.

Moreover, Americans had no legal claim to much of the trans-Mississippi West—or merely the paper title of the Louisiana Purchase, to which none of the native inhabitants had acquiesced. Beyond Texas and the boundary line drawn by the Trans-Continental Treaty of 1819 lay the northern possessions of Mexico. Horse-mounted Indian tribes dominated by the Sioux were a formidable power on the central Plains northward to the Canadian boundary.

Before the 1840s, Americans lacked the interest, numbers, and concerted military power to control this Far West, held by other peoples. Only fur trappers and traders, who worked with and not against the powerful Sioux, had pushed across the Great Plains and into the Rockies. The 1840s brought a sudden change, a large migration westward that radically altered the ecology of the Great Plains. Farm families trapped in an agricultural depression and enticed by Oregon's bounty turned the trails blazed by the fur traders into ruts on the **Oregon Trail**, the route that led to the first large settlement of Americans on the Pacific Coast.

TRIBAL LANDS

At least 350,000 Native Americans lived in the plains and mountains of the trans-Mississippi West in 1840. They were loosely organized into tribal groups, each with its own territory and way of life. Most of them inhabited the Great Plains region that lay north and west of the Indian Territory reserved for eastern tribes in the present state of Oklahoma. The point where the prairies of the Midwest gave way to the higher, drier plains marked a rough division between predominantly agricultural tribes to the east and nomadic, hunting tribes to the west. The Kansas, Osages, and Omahas in what is now Kansas and Iowa and the Arikaras, Mandans, and Hidatsas along the upper Missouri River grew corn, beans, and squash and lived in semipermanent villages, much as woodland Indians had in the East. On the open plains were hunting and raiding peoples, such as the western Sioux, Crows, Cheyennes, and Arapahos.

In the 1830s, the U.S. government set aside a broad stretch of country between the Platte River to the north and the Red River to the south (most of what is now Oklahoma and eastern Kansas) exclusively for Indians. This Indian Territory was reserved for tribes resettled from the East under the Indian Removal Act of 1830 and for village-living groups native to the area. Many government officials envisioned this territory as a permanent sanctuary that would separate Indians from white people and allow them to live in peace on allotments of land granted to individual tribes as compensation for the territory they had ceded to the federal government in earlier treaties. However, even as Congress was debating the idea of a permanent Indian reserve, the pressure on native peoples in the Mississippi Valley both from raiding parties of Plains Indians and the incessant demands of white farmers and speculators for land was rendering a stable Indian–white boundary untenable.

On the eve of Indian removal in the East, the Sauks, Foxes, Potawatomis, and other Indian peoples inhabited Iowa. The defeat of the Sauks and Foxes in what white Americans called Black Hawk's War of 1832 opened Iowa to white settlement and forced tribes to cede land. In 1838, Congress created the Territory of Iowa, which encompassed all the land between the Mississippi and Missouri Rivers north of the state of Missouri. The remaining Indians were now on the verge of being pushed completely out of the region. Throughout the upper Mississippi Valley in the 1830s, other groups suffered a similar fate, and the number of displaced Indians swelled.

The first to be displaced were farming peoples whose villages straddled the woodlands to the east and the open plains to the west. These border tribes were caught in a vise between the loss of their land to advancing white people and the seizure of their horses and agricultural provisions by Indian raiders from the plains. The Pawnees were among the hardest hit.

By the 1830s, the Pawnees were primarily an agricultural people who embarked on seasonal hunts for game in the Platte River Valley. In 1833, they signed a treaty with the U.S. government in which they agreed to withdraw from south of the Platte in return for subsidies and military protection from the hostile Indians on the plains. Once they moved north of the Platte, the Pawnees were attacked by Sioux who seized control of the prime hunting grounds. Sioux raiders seeking provisions and horses also harassed Pawnee agricultural villages. When the Pawnees in desperation filtered back south of the Platte, in violation of the treaty of 1833, they encountered constant harassment from white settlers. In vain the Pawnee leaders cited the provisions of the same treaty that promised them protection from the Sioux. Forced back north of the Platte by the U.S. government, the Pawnees were eventually driven out of their Nebraska homeland by the Sioux.

The Sioux were the dominant power on the northern and central Great Plains, more than able to hold their own against white Americans in the first half of the nineteenth century. The Tetons, Yanktons, and Yanktonais constituted the main divisions of the western Sioux. In the eighteenth century, these western Sioux had separated from their woodland kin (known as the Santee Sioux), left their homeland along the headwaters of the Mississippi River, and pushed onto the Minnesota prairies. Armed with guns they had acquired from the French, the western Sioux dominated the prairies east of the Missouri River by 1800.

The Sioux learned to use the horse from the Plains Indians. Introduced to the New World by the Spanish, horses had revolutionized the lives of native peoples on the Great Plains. As they acquired more horses through trading and raids, the Plains Indians evolved a distinctly new and nomadic culture. Horses made buffalo hunting vastly more productive, they made it easier to transport bulky possessions, and they made possible an aggressive, highly mobile form of warfare. The Sioux were the most successful of all the tribes in melding two facets of white culture, the gun and the horse, into an Indian culture of warrior-hunters.

Although the Sioux frequently fought other tribes, casualties from these encounters were light. The Sioux and other Plains Indians fought, not to kill the greatest number of the enemy, but rather to dominate hunting grounds and to win individual honor by "counting coup" (touching a live foe). When an Army officer in 1819 urged the Sioux to make peace with the Chippewas, Little Crow, a Santee Sioux, explained why war was preferable: "Why, then, should we give up such an extensive country to save the life of a man or two annually?"

When the United States acquired title to the Great Plains in the Louisiana Purchase of 1803, the western Sioux economy was based on two seasonally restricted systems of hunting. In summer, the Sioux hunted buffalo on horse on the plains. In winter, they

Shown here is a Lakota shirt, c. 1850, that was specially woven for those Sioux warriors who had distinguished themselves in battle. The blue and yellow dyes symbolize sky and earth, and the strands of human hair represent the acts of bravery performed in defense of the Lakota people.

trapped beaver. In great spring trading fairs, the western Sioux exchanged their buffalo robes and beaver pelts for goods acquired by the Santee Sioux from European traders.

As the supply of beaver dwindled and the demand for buffalo hides from American and European traders increased in the early 1800s, the Sioux extended their buffalo hunts. In a loose alliance with the Cheyennes and Arapahos, Sioux war parties pushed aside or subjugated weaker tribes to the south and west of the Missouri River basin. The Sioux gained access to new sources for buffalo and raided the village tribes for horses and provisions. Reduced to a dependent status, these tribes were forced to rely on the Sioux for meat and trading goods.

Epidemic diseases brought to the plains by white traders helped Sioux expansion. Because they lived in small wandering bands, the Sioux were less susceptible to these epidemics than the more sedentary village peoples. The Sioux were also one of the first tribes to be vaccinated against smallpox by doctors sent up the Missouri River by the Bureau of Indian Affairs in the early 1830s. Smallpox reached the plains in the 1780s, and a major epidemic in 1837 probably halved the region's Indian population. Particularly hard hit were tribes attempting to resist the Sioux advance. Sioux losses were relatively light and, unlike the other tribes, their population grew.

Some 25,000 strong by 1850, the western Sioux had increased in power and numbers since they first encountered American officials during the Lewis and Clark Expedition in 1804 and 1805. Even then,

Jefferson had cautioned Lewis to cultivate good relations with the Sioux "because of their immense power." "These are the vilest miscreants of the savage race," Lewis and Clark wrote of the Sioux, "and must ever remain the pirates of the Missouri, until such measures are pursued by our government as will make them feel a dependence on its will for their supply of merchandise."

Words were one thing, gaining power over the Sioux another. Americans could vilify the Sioux, but they could not force them into dependence in the first half of the nineteenth century. The Sioux continued to extend their influence, and they were shrewd enough to align themselves with the Americans whenever their interests dictated conciliation.

THE FUR TRADERS

"Curiosity, a love of wild adventure, and perhaps also a hope of profit—for times are hard, and my best coat has a sort of sheepish hang-dog hesitation to encounter fashionable folk—combined to make me look upon the project with an eye of favour." As best he could recollect, these were the motives that induced Warren A. Ferris, a New York civil engineer, to join the American Fur Company in 1829 at the age of 19 and go west as a fur trapper and mountain man. When Ferris joined up, the American fur trade in the trans-Mississippi West—and the spirit of adventure it stirred—was at its height. During their golden age in the 1820s and 1830s, the trappers blazed the trails that far greater numbers of white settlers would follow in the 1840s.

The western fur trade originated in the rivalry between British and American companies for profitable furs, especially beaver pelts. Until the early 1820s, the Hudson's Bay Company, a well-capitalized British concern, dominated the trans-Mississippi fur trade. A breakthrough for American interests came in 1824 when two St. Louis businessmen, William Henry Ashley and Andrew Henry of the Rocky Mountain Fur Company, developed the rendezvous system, which eliminated the need for permanent and costly posts deep in Indian territory. In keeping with Indian traditions of periodic intertribal meetings, the rendezvous system brought together trappers, Indians, and traders in a

The annual rendezvous in Wyoming of fur trappers and traders was a multinational affair in which Anglo Americans, French Canadians, Mexican Americans, and Native Americans gathered to trade, drink, and swap stories.

The Denver Public Library, Western History Department

grand annual fair at a designated site in the high mountain country of Wyoming. White trappers and Indians exchanged the animal skins they had gathered in the seasonal hunt for the guns, traps, tobacco, whiskey, textiles, and other trading goods that agents of the fur companies in St. Louis brought to the fair.

The mountain men signed up for two- or three-year stints with the fur companies. Except for the annual fairs, they lived isolated, hard lives in the wilderness. Their closest relations were with Indians, and about 40 percent of the trappers married Indian women, unions that often linked them economically and diplomatically to their bride's tribe.

Living conditions in the wilderness were primitive, even brutal. Mortality rates among trappers ran as high as 80 percent a year. Death often came suddenly from an accidental gunshot wound, an encounter with a grizzly, or an arrow from an Indian whose hunting grounds a trapper had transgressed. Survival required techniques that a "civilized" American would find repellent. Many a trapper avoided death from dehydration by sucking blood from the sliced vein of a horse or drinking the watery contents from the stomach of a buffalo carcass. "Peg-Leg" Smith became a legend for amputating his own leg after a bullet shattered it.

For all its dangers, the life of a trapper appealed to unattached young men like Warren Ferris. They were fleeing the confinements, as well as the comforts, of white civilization and were as free as they could be. When on a hunt with the Indians, they were part of a spectacle unknown to other white Americans, one that was already passing into history. "Fancy to yourself," Ferris asked readers of his published journals, "three thousand horses of every variety of size and colour, with trappings almost as varied as their appearance . . . ridden by a thousand souls . . . their persons fantastically ornamented. . . . Listen to the rattle of numberless lodgepoles [trailed] by packhorses. . . . Yonder see a hundred horsemen pursuing a herd of antelopes." He was describing the color, bustle, and motion at the start of a hunt with the Salish Indians of Montana in the 1830s, played out on "a beautiful level prairie, with dark blue snow-capped mountains in the distance for the locale."

Such spectacles were increasingly rare after 1840, the year of the last mountain men's rendezvous on the Green River in Wyoming. The most exploitative phase of the fur trade in the 1830s had ravaged the fur-bearing animals and accelerated the spread of smallpox among the tribes. Whiskey, the most profitable item among the white man's trading goods, had corrupted countless Indians and undermined the vitality of tribal cultures.

The mountain men were about to pass into legend, but before they did, they explored every trail and path from the front (or eastern) range of the Rockies to the Pacific. They had gone where no white people had gone before. The main trading corridor of the fur trade—up the lower Missouri to the North Platte and across the plains to the South Pass, a wide plateau crossing the Continental Divide, and into the Wyoming basin—became the main overland route to the West that migrating farm families followed in the 1840s. The mountain men had removed the mystery of western geography, and in so doing they hastened the end of the frontier conditions that had made their unique way of life possible.

THE OREGON TRAIL

The ruts are still there. One can follow them to the horizon in the Platte River Valley of Nebraska and the dry tablelands of Wyoming, Idaho, and Nevada. They were put there by the wheels of wagons hauled by oxen on a jolting 2,000-mile journey across plains, mountains, and deserts from Missouri to Oregon, Utah, and California (see Map 13–2). Some 150,000 Americans made this overland trek in the heyday of the Oregon Trail in the 1840s and early 1850s (see Figure 13–1). Most of them walked alongside their wagons. They covered up to fifteen miles a day on a trip that lasted close to six months.

This 1845 painting depicts a trapper taking an Indian bride. It was a solemn ceremony in which the calumet, or peace pipe, was smoked and the trapper acquired his bride with goods such as guns and blankets.

Alfred Jacob Miller (American, 1810-1874), The Trapper's Bride, oil on canvas, Museum purchase. Joslyn Art Museum, Omaha, Nebraska

Map 13-2　Western Overland Trails
The great overland trails to the West began at the Missouri River. The Oregon Trail crossed South Pass in Wyoming and then branched off to Oregon, California, or Utah. The Santa Fe Trail carried American goods and traders to the Mexican Southwest.

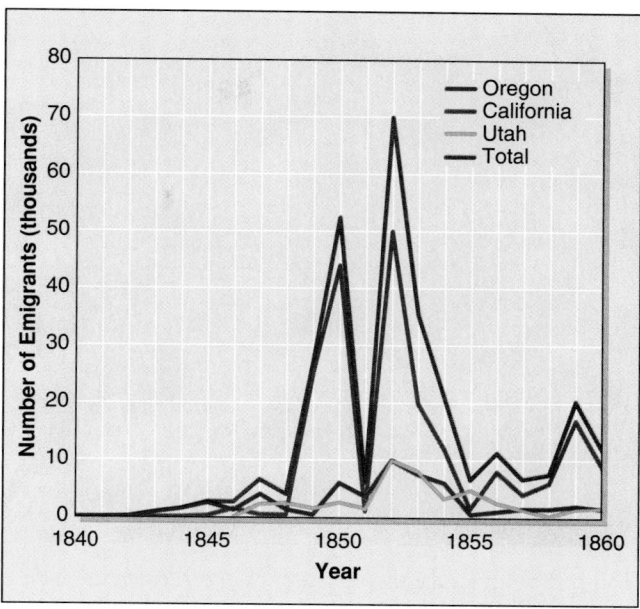

Figure 13-1　Overland Emigration to the West, 1840–1860
Immigration to the trans-Mississippi West steadily increased in the 1840s as farm families moved to Oregon or Utah. After the discovery of gold in California in 1849, California attracted the bulk of the emigrants, many of whom were single men hopeful of striking it rich.

Data Source: John D. Unruh, Jr., *The Plains Across: The Overland Emigrants and the Trans-Mississippi West, 1840–60* (1982), pp. 84–85.

Before the 1830s, few Americans had heard of Oregon, and practically none lived there. Under an agreement reached in 1818, the Oregon Country was still jointly administered by the United States and Great Britain. Furs—whether beaver pelts or the skins of the Pacific sea otter—had attracted a few American trappers and merchants, but the British-controlled Hudson's Bay Company dominated the region. Protestant missionaries established the first permanent white settlements in the 1830s. Under the leadership of Jason Lee, they set up their missions in the fertile Willamette Valley, south of the Columbia River. Reports of Oregon's fertility that the missionaries sent east sparked the first popular interest in the region, especially among Midwestern farmers stuck in the agricultural depression that followed the Panic of 1837.

While the missionaries were publicizing Oregon and attracting future settlers, they were failing in their efforts to convert the Indians of the region to Christianity. Unlike the trappers, the missionaries sought to change the entire structure of Indian life and beliefs. But with their numbers already thinned by the diseases brought in by the trappers, Oregon tribes such as the

Cayuses refused to abandon their traditional culture based on hunting and fishing to become laborers for white farmers. During a measles epidemic in 1847, the Cayuses killed two of the most prominent missionaries, Marcus and Narcissa Whitman. In retaliation, white Americans, who now numbered more than five thousand, virtually exterminated the Cayuses.

The first large party of overlanders on the Oregon Trail left Independence, Missouri, for the Willamette Valley in 1842. Independence and St. Joseph in Missouri and, by the 1850s, Council Bluffs in Iowa were the jumping-off points for the Oregon Trail. Each town competed to capture the lucrative trade of outfitting the migrants. There was more than enough trade to go around. Merchants profited from supplying, usually at inflated prices, wagons, mules, oxen, guns, ammunition, and staples like flour, bacon, and sugar.

Most overlanders were young farm families from the Midwest, who had moved at least once before in their restless search for the perfect farm that would keep them out of debt. Indeed, Medorum Crawford said of one family that made the journey to Oregon with him in 1842 and then quickly left for California, "They had practically lived in the wagon for more than twenty years, only remaining in one locality long

This sketch reveals the sheer physical exertion demanded of the emigrants as they pushed across the Plains on the Oregon Trial.

enough to make a crop, which they had done in every State and Territory in the Mississippi Valley."

Usually the male head of a household made the decision to move. Women often regretted giving up ties with kin and friends, which provided security and assistance in their isolated, rural lives. They were well aware of the dangers of childbirth on a long, hard journey. Besides their usual work of minding the children and cooking and cleaning, they would now have to help drive wagons and tend livestock. Still, many women were also optimistic about the journey. "Ho— for California—at last we are on the way," exclaimed Helen Carpenter in 1857, "and with good luck may

In trunks such as this, women transported their fine pieces of china to the West on the Oregon Trial.

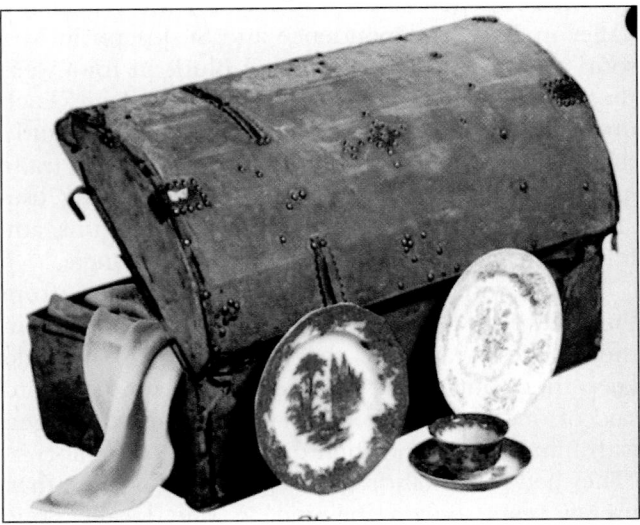

some day reach the 'promised land.'" A study of 159 women's trail diaries indicates that about one-third of the women strongly favored the move. Margaret Frink, for example, recalled that she "never had occasion to regret the prolonged hardships of the toilsome journey." By adapting to the new conditions of trail life— pitching tents, yoking oxen, cooking over open fires, and gathering buffalo chips (dried dung used for fuel)—women learned skills that would help them start a new life in the West.

The journey was long and dangerous. In the 1840s, some five thousand of the ninety thousand men, women, and children who set out on the Oregon Trail died along the way. But although the overlanders were terrified of encountering Indians—who, they assumed, would be hostile—few died from Indian attacks. As long as the wagon trains were just passing through their lands, the Plains Indians left the white people alone. At first they watched with bemused curiosity, and then, as the white migrants kept coming, they traded game for clothing and ammunition. Indians killed only 115 migrants in the 1840s, and trigger-happy white migrants provoked most clashes. Disease, especially cholera, was the great killer. Second to disease were accidents, especially drownings that resulted when drivers tried to force overloaded wagons across swollen rivers.

Cooperation between families was the key to a successful overland crossing. The men in a party often drew up a formal, written constitution at the start of a trip spelling out the assignments and work responsibilities of each wagon. Before the trail was well marked, former mountain men hired on as captains to lead wagon trains. Timing was crucial. A wagon train had to leave late enough in the spring to get good grass in Nebraska for the oxen and mules. Too early a departure, and the wagon train risked getting bogged down in spring mud; too late a departure, and it risked being trapped in the snows of the Pacific coastal ranges.

Before "Oregon fever" had run its course, the flow of white settlers across the continent radically changed the economy and ecology of the Great Plains. Pressure mounted on plants and animals, reducing the land's ability to support all the tribes accustomed to living off it. Intertribal warfare intensified as the supply of buffalo and other game dwindled. Far from being separated from white people by a permanent line of division, the Plains Indians now stood astride the main path of white migration to the Pacific.

In response, officials in the Bureau of Indian Affairs organized a great gathering of the tribes in 1851. At this conference they pushed through the Fort Laramie Treaty, the first U.S. government attempt to draw boundaries within which to contain the Plains Indians. In exchange for accepting limitations on their movement and for the loss of game, the tribes were to receive annual compensation of $50,000 a year for fifty years (later reduced by the U.S. Senate to ten years).

Most of the Indians at the Fort Laramie conference were the Sioux and their allies. The Sioux viewed the treaty as confirming their dominant power on the Great Plains. When American negotiators tried to restrict Sioux hunting to north of the Platte, the Sioux demanded and received treaty rights to lands south of the Platte as well. "These lands once belonged to the Kiowas and the Crows," argued a western Sioux, "but we whipped those nations out of them, and in this we did what the white men do when they want the lands of the Indians." This was an argument white Americans could understand, and they conceded the point.

The Fort Laramie Treaty represented a standoff between the Sioux and the U.S. government, the two great powers on the Plains. If neither yielded its claims to the region, war between them would be inevitable.

THE MEXICAN BORDERLANDS

By the mid-1840s, parties of emigrant Americans were beginning to branch off the main Oregon Trail on their way to Utah and California. These areas were then part of the northern borderlands of Mexico. Mostly a semiarid and thinly populated land of high plateaus, dry basins, and desert bisected north to south by mountain ranges, the borderlands had been part of the Spanish empire in North America. Mexico inherited this territory when it won independence from Spain in 1821. The borderlands covered roughly 1 million square miles; today, they comprise the American Southwest from Texas to California. Mexico's hold on this region was always weak. It lost Texas in 1837, and, in the next decade, the American penetration of Utah and California set the stage for the American seizure of most of the rest in the Mexican War.

THE PEOPLES OF THE SOUTHWEST

Diverse peoples lived in the Southwest. Imperial Spain had divided them into four main groupings: Indians, full-blooded Native Americans who retained their own languages and customs; mestizos, those of racially mixed ancestry, usually Spanish and Indian;

criollos, American-born whites of Spanish ancestry; and Spaniards.

By far the smallest group were the Spaniards. Compared to the English, few Spaniards emigrated to the New World, and most who did were men. Consequently, Spanish males married or lived with native women, creating a large class of mestizos. Despite their small numbers, the Spanish, along with the criollos, monopolized economic and political power. This wealthy elite controlled the labor of the *mestizos* in the predominantly ranching economy of the borderlands.

The largest single group in the borderlands were the Indians, about half the population in the 1820s. Most had not come under direct Spanish or Mexican control. Those who had were part of the mission system. This instrument of Spanish imperial policy forced Indians to live in a fixed area, to convert to Catholicism, and to work as agricultural laborers.

Spanish missions, most of them established by the Franciscan order, aimed both to Christianize and "civilize" the Indians, making them loyal imperial subjects. Mission Indians were forced to abandon their native economies and culture and settle in agricultural communities under the tight supervision of the friars (see Chapter 1). Spanish soldiers and royal officials, who lived in military garrisons known as presidios, accompanied the friars.

The largest concentration of Indians—some 300,000 when the Spanish friars arrived in the 1760s—was in California. Most of these—the Paiutes, Chumashes, Pomos, Shastas, and a host of smaller tribes—occupied their own distinct ecological zones

This painting by Alfred James Miller depicts the busy interior of Fort Laramie in 1837.

where they gathered and processed what the rivers, forests, and grasslands provided. Fish and game were abundant, and wild plants and nuts, especially acorns, provided grain and flour. The Paiutes in the Owens Valley perfected an intricate system for irrigating wild grasses, but only the Yumans along the Colorado River in southeastern California practiced full-scale agriculture. The Spanish marveled at their lush fields of wheat, maize, beans, tobacco, and melons. The Yumans also had an elaborate religion based on an oral tradition of dream songs. (Dream songs remain a distinctive feature of Native American culture.)

The paintings by George Catlin are among the best visual sources for understanding the material culture of the Plains Indians. This painting, c. 1834, shows how central was the buffalo in the life of the Comanches, the most powerful tribe on the Southern Plains.

The major farming Indians east of California were the Pueblo peoples of Arizona and New Mexico. Named after the adobe or stone community dwellings in which they lived atop mesas or on terraces carved into cliffs, the Pueblo Indians were a peaceful people closely bound to small, tightly knit communities. (*Pueblo* is Spanish for "village.") Indeed, some of their dwellings, such as those of the Hopis in Arizona or the Acomas in New Mexico, have been continuously occupied for more than 500 years. Corn and beans were the staples of their irrigation-based agriculture. Formally a part of the Spanish mission system, they had incorporated the Catholic God and Catholic rituals into their own polytheistic religion, which stressed the harmony of all living things with the forces of nature. They continued to worship in their underground sanctuaries known as *kivas*.

Once the Pueblos made their peace with the Spaniards after their great revolt in 1680 (see Chapter 3), their major enemies were the nomadic tribes that lived by hunting and raiding. These tribes outnumbered the Pueblos four to one and controlled most of the Southwest until the 1850s. The horse, which many of the tribes acquired during Spain's temporary retreat from the region during the late seventeenth century in the wake of the Pueblo Revolt, was the basis of their way of life. As the horse frontier spread, the peoples of the southern Plains gained enormous mobility and the means of ranging far and wide for the economic resources that sustained their transformation into societies of mounted warriors.

West of the pueblos around Taos was the land of the Navajos, who herded sheep, raised some crops, and raided other tribes from their mountain fastness. Spilling over onto Navajo lands, the Southern Utes ranged up and down the canyon lands of Utah. The Gila Apaches were the dominant tribe south of Albuquerque and westward into Arizona. To the east in the Pecos River Valley roamed bands of Mescalero and Jicarillo Apaches. On the broad plains rolling northward from the Texas panhandle and southward into northern Mexico were war parties of Comanches and Kiowas.

The Comanches, a branch of the mountain Shoshonis who moved to the plains when horses became available, were the most feared of the nomadic peoples. Utterly fearless, confident, and masterful horsemen, they gained a reputation of mythic proportions for their prowess as mounted warriors. For food and clothing, they relied on the immense buffalo herds of the southern plains. For guns, horses, and other trading goods, they lived off their predatory raids. When the Santa Fe Trail opened in the early 1820s, their shrewdness as traders gave them a new source of firearms that strengthened their raiding prowess.

The three focal points of white settlement in the northern borderlands of Mexico—Texas, New Mexico, and Alta California (as distinguished from Lower, or Baja, California)—were never linked by an effective network of communications or transportation. Navigable rivers were few, and travel was limited to tortuous journeys along Indian and Spanish trails that barely indented the dry and largely barren landscape. Each of these settlements was an isolated offshoot of Hispanic culture with a semiautonomous economy based on ranching and a mostly illegal trade with French, British, and American merchants that brought in a trickle of needed goods.

Neither Spain, which tried to seal off its northern outposts from economic contact with foreigners, nor Mexico, which opened up the borderlands to outsiders, had integrated this vast region into a unified economic or political whole. Indeed, Mexico's most pressing problem in the 1820s was protecting its northern states from the Comanches. To serve as a buffer against the Comanches, the Mexican government in 1821 invited Americans into Texas, opening the way to the eventual American takeover of the territory.

THE AMERICANIZATION OF TEXAS

The Mexicans faced the same problems governing Texas that the Spanish had. Mexico City was about a thousand miles from San Antonio, the center of Hispanic settlement in Texas, and communications were slow and cumbersome. The ranching elite of *Tejanos* (Spanish-speaking Mexicans born in Texas) had closer economic ties to American Louisiana than they did to Coahuila, the Mexican state to which Texas was formally attached. These large ranchers had long been smuggling horses and cattle into Louisiana in exchange for manufactured items and tobacco. Markets for farm crops were limited, and the ranchers and a scattered class of tenant farmers produced little surplus food. This low agricultural productivity, combined with the low birthrate among mission Indians, outbreaks of disease, and the generally hostile frontier environment, sharply restricted population growth. Only some five thousand Mexicans lived in Texas in the 1820s.

Sparsely populated and economically struggling, Mexican Texas shared a border with the United States along the Sabine River in Louisiana and the Red River in the Arkansas Territory (see Map 13-2). The threat that the nearby Americans posed to Mexico's security was obvious to Mexican officials. As one of them early noted with alarm: "If we do not take the present opportunity to people Texas, day by day the strength of the United States will grow until it will annex Texas, Coahuila, Saltillo, and Nuevo León like the Goths, Visigoths, and the other tribes that assailed the Roman Empire." However, attempts to promote immigration into Texas from other parts of Mexico failed. Reasoning that the Americans were going to come in any event and anxious to build up the population of Texas against Indian attacks, the Mexican government encouraged Americans to settle in Texas by offering huge grants of land in return for promises to accept Mexican citizenship, convert to Catholicism, and obey the authorities in Mexico City.

The first American *empresario*—the recipient of a large grant in return for a promise to bring in settlers—was Stephen F. Austin. He had inherited a huge Spanish grant from his father, Moses Austin, a Missourian who had had business dealings with the Spanish since 1797. After having the grant confirmed by the new Mexican government in 1821, Stephen Austin founded the first American colony in Texas. The Austin grant encompassed 18,000 square miles. Other grants were smaller but still lavish. The *empresarios* stood to grow wealthy by leasing out land, selling parcels to settlers, and organizing the rest into large-scale farms that produced cotton with slave labor in the bottomlands of the Sabine, Colorado, and Brazos Rivers. For the Americans who followed in their wake, Texas was a dream come true—the chance to acquire good land that was so cheap that it was almost free. As early as 1830, eastern and south-central Texas was becoming an extension of the plantation economy of the Gulf coastal plain. More than 25,000 white settlers, with around a thousand slaves, had poured into the region (see "American Views: A Mexican View of the Texans in 1828").

More Americans moved into Texas with slaves than the Mexicans had anticipated. Many settlers simply ignored Mexican laws, especially the Emancipation Proclamation of 1829 that forbade slavery in the Republic of Mexico. In 1830, the Mexican government attempted to assert its authority. It levied the first taxes on the Americans, prohibited the further importation of slaves, and closed the international border to additional immigration. Still, another ten thousand Americans spilled across the border in the early 1830s, and they continued to bring in slaves.

Unlike the *empresarios,* many of whom became Catholic and married into elite *Tejano* families, these newcomers lived apart from Mexicans and rejected Mexican citizenship. Cultural tensions escalated. Believing that they belonged to a superior race of liberty-loving white Anglo-Saxons, most of these new arrivals sneered at the Mexicans as a mongrelized race of black people, Indians, and Spaniards and resented having to submit to their rule. They considered Catholicism a despotic, superstitious religion and ignored legal requirements that they convert to it.

A clash became inevitable in 1835 when General Santa Anna, elected president of Mexico in 1833, overturned the liberal Mexican constitution of 1824. He established himself as a dictator in 1834, and his centralist rule ended any hope of the Americans *empresarios* and their *Tejano* allies that Texas might become an autonomous state within a federated Mexico. Skirmishing between Mexican troops and rebellious Texans began in the fall of 1835.

At first, the Anglo–*Tejano* leadership did not renounce all ties with Mexico. When these leaders drafted a constitution in November 1835, they sought to overthrow Santa Anna, restore the constitution of 1824, and win separate statehood for Texas within a liberal Mexican republic. Santa Anna, however, refused to compromise. When he raised a large army to crush the uprising, he radicalized the rebellion and pushed its leaders to declare complete independence on March 2, 1836. Four days later, a Mexican army of 4,000 annihilated the 187 defenders of the **Alamo,** an abandoned mission in San Antonio. A few weeks later at Goliad, another 300 Texans were killed after they had agreed to surrender (see Map 13–3).

"Remember the Alamo!" and "Remember Goliad!" were powerful rallying cries for the beleaguered Texans. Volunteers from the American South rushed to the aid of the main Texan army, commanded by Sam Houston. A product of the Tennessee frontier and a close friend of Andrew Jackson's, Houston did Jackson proud by catching the overconfident Santa Anna off guard in eastern Texas. Houston's victory in April 1836 at the Battle of San Jacinto established the independence of Texas. Captured while trying to flee, Santa Anna signed a treaty in May 1836, recognizing Texas as an independent republic with a boundary on the south and west at the Rio Grande. However, the Nueces River to the north of the Rio Grande had been the administrative border of Texas under Mexican rule. The Mexican Congress rejected the treaty, and the boundary remained in dispute.

Soon forgotten during the ensuing eight years of Texas independence was the support that many

MAP 13-3 **Texas and Mexico after the Texas Revolt**
The Battle of San Jacinto was the decisive American victory that gained the independence of Texas, but the border dispute between Texas and Mexico would not be resolved until the Mexican War a decade later.

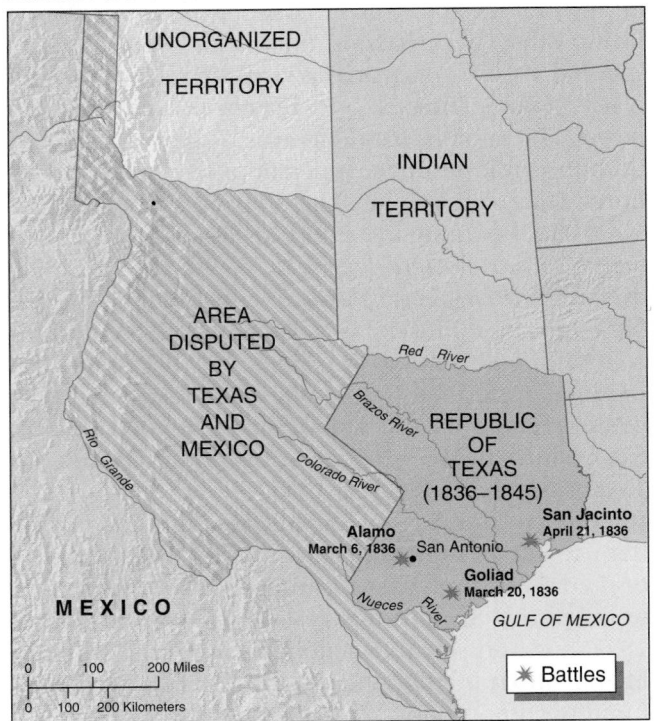

Tejanos had given to the successful revolt against Mexican rule. In part because Mexico refused to recognize the Texas Republic, Anglos feared Tejanos as a subversive element. Pressure mounted on them to leave, especially after Santa Anna launched a major counterattack in 1842, capturing San Antonio. Those who stayed lost much of their land and economic power as Anglos used their knowledge of American legal codes or just plain chicanery to reduce the *Tejanos* to second-class citizens.

More difficult to subordinate were the Comanches. While president of Texas, Houston tried to fix a permanent boundary between the Comanches and white settlers, but Texas pride and ongoing white encroachments on Indian land undercut his efforts. By the early 1840s, Texans and Comanches were in a state of nearly permanent war. Only the force of the federal army after the Civil War ended the Comanches' long reign as the effective rulers of the high, dry plains of northern and western Texas.

THE PUSH INTO CALIFORNIA AND THE SOUTHWEST

Mexican rule in California was always weak. The Sonoran desert and the resistance of the Yuman Indians in southeastern California cut off Mexico from any direct land contact with Alta California. Only irregular communications were maintained over a long sea route. For *Californios,* Californians of Spanish descent, Mexico was literally *la otra banda,* "the other shore." In trying to strengthen its hold on this remote and thinly populated region, the Mexican government relied on a program of economic development. As in Texas, however, Mexican policy had unintended consequences.

The centerpiece of the Mexican program was the secularization of the missions. This policy opened up the landholdings of the Catholic Church to private ownership and released the mission Indians from paternalistic bondage. Small allotments of land were set aside for the Indians, but most returned to their homelands. Those who remained became a source of cheap labor for the *rancheros* who carved up the mission lands into huge cattle ranches. Thus by the 1830s, California had entered what is called the *rancho* era. The main beneficiaries of this process, however, were not Mexican authorities but the American traders who responded to the economic opportunities presented by the privatization of the California economy.

New England merchants had been trading in California since the 1780s. What first attracted them were the seal fisheries off the California coast, a source of otter pelts highly prized in the China trade. After the seals had been all but exterminated by the 1820s, Yankee merchants shipped out hides and tallow, a trade fed by the immense cattle resources of the *rancheros,* to

New England for processing into shoes and candles. Ships from New England and New York sailed around Cape Horn to California ports, where they unloaded trading goods. Servicing this trade in California was a resident colony of American agents, some three hundred strong by the mid-1840s.

Whereas Yankees dominated the American colonies in coastal California, it was mostly midwestern farm families who filtered into the inner valleys of California from the Oregon Trail in the 1830s and 1840s. About one in ten of the overland parties took a cutoff on the Trail near Fort Hall on the Snake River that led them across the deserts of northern Nevada to a passage across the Sierra Nevada near Lake Tahoe. At the end of the journey, they dropped down into the fertile Sacramento River Valley. Nearly a thousand Americans had arrived by 1846.

California belonged to Mexico in name only by the early 1840s. The program of economic development had strengthened California's ties to the outside world at the expense of Mexico. American merchants and California *rancheros* ran the economy, and both groups had joined separatist movements against Mexican rule. Unlike the *Californios*, who were ambivalent about their future political allegiance, the Americans wanted to be part of the United States and assumed that California would shortly be annexed. With the outbreak of the Mexican War in 1846, their wish became reality.

Except for Utah, the American push into the interior of the Mexican Southwest followed the California pattern of trade preceding settlement. When Mexico liberalized the formerly restrictive trading policies of Spain, American merchants opened up the nine-hundred-mile-long **Santa Fe Trail** from Independence, Missouri, to Santa Fe, New Mexico. Starved for mercantile goods, the New Mexicans were a small but highly profitable market. They paid for their American imports with gold, silver, and furs.

Brent's Old Fort, an impregnable adobe structure built on the Arkansas River at the point where the Santa Fe Trail turned to the southwest and Taos, was the fulcrum for the growing economic influence of Americans over New Mexican affairs. Completed in 1832, the fort enabled the Brent brothers from Missouri to control a flourishing and almost monopolistic trade with Indians, trappers, caravans on the Santa Fe Trail, and the large landowners and merchants of New Mexico. This trade pulled New Mexico into the cultural and economic orbit of the United States and undermined what little sovereign power Mexico held in the region.

Although only a few hundred Americans were permanent residents of New Mexico in the 1840s, they had married into the Spanish-speaking landholding elite and were themselves beginning to receive large grants of land. Ties of blood and common economic interests linked this small group of American businessmen with an influential faction of the local elite. American merchants and New Mexican landlords were further united by their growing disdain for the instability of Mexican rule, Santa Anna's dictatorship, and sporadic attempts by Mexico to levy heavy taxes on the Santa Fe trade. Another bond was their concern over the aggressive efforts of the Texans to seize eastern New Mexico. After thwarting an 1841 Texan attempt to occupy Santa Fe, the leaders of New Mexico increasingly looked to the United States to protect their local autonomy. They quickly decided to cooperate with the American army of invasion when the Mexican War got under way. Over the opposition of the clergy and ranchers still loyal to Mexico, this group was instrumental in the American takeover of New Mexico.

At the extreme northern and inner reaches of the Mexican borderlands lay Utah. Dominated by an intermountain depression called the Great Basin, Utah was a starkly beautiful but dry region of alkaline flats, broken tablelands, cottonwood canyons, and mountain ranges. It was home to the Bannocks, Utes, Navajos, Hopis, and small bands of other Indians. Aside from trading ties with the Utes, Spain and Mexico had largely ignored this remote region. Its isolation and lack of white settlers, however, were precisely what made Utah so appealing to the leaders of the Mormons, the Church of Jesus Christ of Latter-day Saints. For the Mormons in the 1840s, Utah became the promised land in which to build a new Zion.

Founded by Joseph Smith in upstate New York in the 1820s, Mormonism grew rapidly within a communitarian framework that stressed hard work and economic cooperation under the leadership of patriarchal leaders. The economic success of close-knit Mormon communities, combined with the righteous zeal of their members, aroused the fears and hostility of non-Mormons. Harassed out of New York, Ohio, and Missouri, the Mormons thought they had found a permanent home by the late 1830s in Nauvoo, Illinois. But the murder of Joseph Smith and his brother by a mob in 1844 convinced the beleaguered Mormons that they had to leave the settled East for a refuge of their own in the West. In 1846 a group of Mormons migrated to the Great Basin in Utah. Under the leadership of Brigham Young, they established a new community in 1847 at the Great Salt Lake on the western slopes of the Wasatch Mountains. Ten thousand Mormons joined them.

The Mormons thrived in the arid desert. Their intense communitarianism was ideally suited to dispensing land and organizing an irrigation system that coordinated water rights with the amount of land under production. To their dismay, however, they learned in 1848 that they had not left the United

AMERICAN VIEWS

A Mexican View of the Texans in 1828

By the late 1820s, Mexico was reassessing its policy of encouraging American immigration to Texas. Concerned over the large numbers and uncertain loyalties of the American settlers, the government appointed a commission in 1827 ostensibly to survey the boundary between Louisiana and the province of Texas. The real purpose of the commission was to recommend policy changes that would strengthen Mexico's hold on Texas. The following excerpt is from a journal kept by José María Sánchez, the draftsman of the boundary commission.

- Why was the Mexican government so ineffective in maintaining control over Texas?
- What was the appeal of Texas for Americans? How did most of them enter Texas and take up land?
- Why did Sánchez have such a low opinion of the Americans in the Austin colony? What did he think of Stephen Austin?
- Why did the Mexicans fear that they would lose Texas?

The Americans from the north have taken possession of practically all the eastern part of Texas, in most cases without the permission of the authorities. They immigrate constantly, finding no one to prevent them, and take possession of the *sitio* [location] that best suits them without either asking leave or going through any formal-ity other than that of building their homes. Thus the majority of inhabitants in the Department are North Americans, the Mexican population being reduced to only Bejar, Nacogdoches, and La Bahía del Espíritu Santo, wretched settlements that between them do not number three thousand inhabitants, and the new village of

States after all. The Union acquired Utah, along with the rest of the northern borderlands of Mexico, as a result of the Mexican War. (For more on the Mormons, see Chapter 12.)

POLITICS, EXPANSION, AND WAR

The Democrats viewed their victory in the election of 1844 (see Chapter 10) as a popular mandate for expansion. They had campaigned on a platform that boldly demanded both Texas and the "reoccupation" of Oregon up to 54°40'.

James K. Polk, the new Democratic president, fully shared the expansionist vision of his party. The greatest prize in his eyes was California. Although silent in public on California for fear of further antagonizing the Mexicans, who had never accepted the loss of Texas, Polk made the acquisition of California the cor-nerstone of his foreign policy. When he was stymied in his efforts to purchase California and New Mexico, he tried to force concessions from the Mexican government by ordering American troops to the mouth of the Rio Grande, far within the territory claimed by Mexico. When the virtually inevitable clash of arms occurred in late April 1846, war broke out between the United States and Mexico.

Victory resulted in the **Mexican Cession of 1848**, which added a half-million square miles to the United States. Polk's administration also finalized the acquisition of Texas and reached a compromise with the British on the Oregon Territory that recognized American sovereignty in the Pacific Northwest up to the 49th parallel. The United States was now a nation that spanned a continent.

MANIFEST DESTINY

With a phrase that soon entered the nation's vocabulary, John L. O'Sullivan, editor and Democratic politi-

Guadalupe Victoria that has scarcely more than seventy settlers. The government of the state, with its seat at Saltillo, that should watch over the preservation of its most precious and interesting department, taking measures to prevent its being stolen by foreign hands, is the one that knows the least not only about actual conditions, but even about its territory. . . . Repeated and urgent appeals have been made to the Supreme Government of the Federation regarding the imminent danger in which this interesting Department is of becoming the prize of the ambitious North Americans, but never has it taken any measures that may be called conclusive. . . .

[Sánchez goes on to describe the village of Austin and the American colony founded by Stephen Austin.]

Its population is nearly two hundred persons, of which only ten are Mexicans, for the balance are all Americans from the North with an occasional European. Two wretched little stores supply the inhabitants of the colony: one sells only whiskey, rum, sugar, and coffee; the other, rice, flour, lard, and cheap cloth. . . . The Americans from the North, at least the great part of those I have seen, eat only salted meat, bread made by themselves out of corn meal, coffee, and home-made cheese. To these the greater part of those who live in the village add strong liquor, for they are in general, in my opinion, lazy people of vicious character. Some of them cultivate their small farms by planting corn; but this task they usually entrust to their negro slaves, whom they treat with considerable harshness. Beyond the village in an immense stretch of land formed by rolling hills are scattered the families brought by Stephen Austin, which today number more than two thousand persons. The diplomatic policy of this empresario, evident in all his actions, has, as one may say, lulled the authorities into a sense of security, while he works diligently for his own ends. In my judgment, the spark that will start the conflagration that will deprive us of Texas, will start from this colony. All because the government does not take vigorous measures to prevent it. Perhaps it does not realize the value of what it is about to lose.

cian, proclaimed in 1845 America's "manifest destiny to overspread and to possess the whole of the continent which Providence has given us for the development of the great experiment of Liberty and federated self-government entrusted to us." Central to Manifest Destiny was the assumption that white Americans were a special people. Part of that sense of specialness was religiously inspired and dated back to the Puritans' belief that God had appointed them to establish a New Israel cleansed of the corruption of the Old World. Evangelical revivals in the early nineteenth century then added an aggressive sense of urgency to America's presumed mission to spread the benefits of Protestantism and Christian civilization. Protestant missionaries, as in Oregon, were often in the vanguard of American expansion.

What distinguished the special American mission as enunciated by Manifest Destiny was its explicitly racial component. Between 1815 and 1850, the term Anglo-Saxon, originally loosely applied to English-speaking peoples, acquired racial overtones, in keeping with the then current interest of European and American scientists in defining, classifying, and ranking human races (with themselves, of course, at the top). Caucasian Anglo-Saxon Americans, as the descendants of ancient Germanic tribes that purportedly brought the seeds of free institutions to England, were now said to be the foremost race in the world. This superior racial pedigree they claimed for themselves gave white Americans the natural right to expand westward, a chosen people carrying the blessings of democracy and progress. Only they, it was argued, had the energy, industriousness, and innate love of liberty to establish a successful free government.

Advocates of Manifest Destiny insisted that American expansion would be irresistible and peaceful. They were not warmongers calling for conquest. Still, the doctrine was undeniably a self-serving justification for what other peoples would see as territorial aggrandizement. Certainly, that was true of the Mexican-Ameri-

In this late-1872 evocation of the spirit of Manifest Destiny, Indians retreat westward as white settlers, guided by a diaphanously-clad America, spread the benefits of American civilization.

cans and Native Americans who lost land and cultural independence as they were brought under American control. Manifest Destiny and popular stereotypes lumped Indians and Mexicans together as inferior peoples. An emigrant guide of 1845 spoke of the Mexican Californians as "scarcely a visible grade in the scale of intelligence, above the barbarous tribes by whom they are surrounded." For Waddy Thompson, an American minister to Mexico in the early 1840s, the Mexicans in general were "lazy, ignorant, and, of course, vicious and dishonest." This alleged Mexican inferiority was attributed to racial intermixture with the Indians, who, it was said, were hopelessly unfit for civilization.

Manifest Destiny was closely associated with the Democratic party. For Democrats, expansionism would counterbalance the debilitating effects of industrialization and urbanization. As good Jeffersonians, they stressed the need for more land to realize the ideal of a democratic republic rooted in the virtues and rough equality of independent farmers. For their working-class Irish constituency, the Democrats touted the broad expanses of the West as the surest means to escape the misery of wage slavery. It was no coincidence that O'Sullivan was a Democrat or that he feared that the spread of factories would produce an impoverished class of workers in America as it had in England.

As a manifesto for expansion, Manifest Destiny captured the popular imagination when the country was still mired in a depression after the Panic of 1837. The way out of the depression, according to many Democrats, was to revive the export trade to soak up the agricultural surplus. Thomas Hart Benton, a De-

mocratic senator from Missouri, was the leading spokesman for the vast potential of an American trade with India and China—a trade to be secured by American possession of the harbors on the Pacific Coast.

THE MEXICAN WAR

Once in office, Polk proved far more conciliatory with the British than with the Mexicans. Despite a stridently anti-British tone in his annual message to Congress in December 1845, Polk was willing to compromise on Oregon because he dreaded the possibility of a two-front war against both the Mexicans and the British. Mexico had severed diplomatic ties with the United States over the annexation of Texas (see Chapter 10), and a war could break out at any time.

In the spring of 1846, after Polk had abrogated the agreement on the joint occupation of Oregon, the British offered a compromise that they had earlier rejected. They agreed to a boundary at the 49th parallel if they were allowed to retain Vancouver Island in Puget Sound. Polk sent the offer to the Senate, which quickly approved it in June 1846. British–American trade continued to flourish, Mexico lost a potential ally, and, most important, Polk could now concentrate on the Mexican War that had erupted a month earlier.

Unlike Oregon, where he backed off from extravagant territorial claims, Polk refused to budge on the American claim (inherited from the Texans, when the United States annexed Texas in 1845) that the Rio Grande was the border between Texas and Mexico. The Mexicans insisted that the Nueces River, a hundred miles to the north of the Rio Grande, was the border, as it had been when Texas was part of Mexico. An immense territory was at stake, for the headwaters of the Rio Grande were in northern New Mexico, and a boundary on the Rio Grande would more than double the size of Texas.

Citing rumors of a Mexican invasion, Polk sent 3,500 troops under General Zachary Taylor to the Nueces River in the summer of 1845. Polk also stepped up his efforts to acquire California. He instructed Thomas Larkin, the American consul in Monterey, California, to inform the *Californios* and Americans that the United States would support them if they revolted against Mexican rule. Polk also secretly ordered the U.S. Pacific naval squadron to seize

MAP EXPLORATION To explore an interactive version of this map, go to
http://www.prenhall.com/goldfield/map13.4

MAP 13-4   The Mexican War
Victories under General Zachary Taylor in northern Mexico secured the Rio Grande as the boundary between Texas and Mexico. Colonel Stephen Kearny's expedition won control of New Mexico, and reinforcements from Kearny assured the success of American troops landed by the Pacific Squadron in gaining Alta California for the United States. The success of General Winfield Scott's amphibious invasion at Vera Cruz and his occupation of Mexico City brought the war to an end.

California ports if war broke out with Mexico. Polk's final effort at peaceful expansion was the Slidell mission in November 1845. He sent John L. Slidell to Mexico City to offer $30 million to purchase California and New Mexico and to secure the Rio Grande boundary.

When Polk learned that the Mexican government had refused to receive Slidell, he set out to draw Mexico into a war that would result in the American acquisition of California. In early 1846, he ordered General Taylor to advance to the Rio Grande, deep in the dis-

puted border region. Taylor blockaded the mouth of the Rio Grande (an aggressive act even if the river had been an international boundary) and built a fort on the northern bank across from the Mexican town of Matamoros. The Mexicans attacked and were repulsed on April 24.

Even before the news reached Washington, Polk had decided on war, on the grounds that the Mexican government had unjustifiably refused to sell territory to the United States and had fallen behind on debt payments owed to American citizens.

FROM THEN TO NOW

Manifest Destiny and American Foreign Policy

From the birth of the nation in 1776 to the U.S. war on terrorism in the wake of the attacks on September 11, 2001, a sense of mission has often imbued American foreign policy. Manifest Destiny was one expression of that sense of mission.

Thomas Paine, in *Common Sense*, declared that America had the "power to begin the world over again." The shining force of the American republic's free government, Paine believed, would redeem those suffering under despotic monarchies. According to the lofty rhetoric of Manifest Destiny, America would fulfill this divinely ordained mission by absorbing all the people of North America—at least those deemed capable of self-government—into the republic.

Manifest Destiny helped inspire the American surge to the Pacific and justify the Mexican War. But the war also provoked a contrary fear: Was the United States guilty of an imperial conquest that threatened liberty rather than promoting it? When expansionists pushed for the acquisition of all of Mexico, opponents objected. Mexicans, they claimed, were unfit to join Anglo-Saxon Americans in assuming the responsibilities of self-rule. At the same time, to subject Mexico to colonial rule would deny it the democratic liberty that Manifest Destiny promised. Consequently, the All Mexico movement soon collapsed.

After cresting in the 1840s, Manifest Destiny lost its appeal. Expansionists in the late nineteenth century invoked Manifest Destiny to justify America's acquisition of an overseas empire following the Spanish-American War, but the new empire did not really fit that model. The advocates of Manifest Destiny had envisioned neighboring peoples in North America voluntarily joining the Republic. According to critics, the new empire, on the contrary, rested on the once-despised imperialist doctrines of Old World Europe. For former President Grover Cleveland, the annexation of the Hawaiian Islands in 1898 was "a perversion of our national mission," a signal that the nation was prepared to "abandon old landmarks and . . . follow the lights of monarchical hazards."

Cleveland and the other anti-imperialists lost the turn-of-the-century debate over whether the nation should acquire dependent possessions abroad. Still, by insisting, with Thomas Paine, that America's true mission must be to serve as the "model republic" for others to follow, they established the theme that characterized at least the public face of American diplomacy in the twentieth century. President Woodrow Wilson, for example, justified American intervention in World Was I as a moral crusade to save democracy in Europe, and he sought in vain to bring the United States into a new international body—the League of Nations—designed to curb aggressive nations and prevent future wars. Wilsonian idealism infused the foreign policy of President Franklin D. Roosevelt during World War II and inspired the formation of the United Nations. Throughout the Cold War, America identified itself as the protector of democratic freedoms from the threat of international communism. In the post–Cold War world, Presidents George Bush and Bill Clinton cited the need to uphold human rights as grounds for U.S. military intervention abroad. President George W. Bush has gone further by claiming that the United States has the right to use preemptive force against any "evil power" deemed a threat to world peace and the future security of the United States.

Critics have charged that the mantle of human rights cloaks the pursuit of less noble U.S. interests in other nations. Whether or not this critique is valid, it is clear that as the twenty-first century dawns, any interventionist foreign policy must present itself in the idealistic terms of a special American mission if it is to have public support.

Informed of the clash between Mexican and American troops in early May (it took ten days for the news to reach Washington), he sent a redrafted war message to Congress on May 9 asserting that Mexico "has invaded our territory, and shed American blood on American soil." Congress declared war on May 13, 1846.

The war was a stunning military success for the United States (see Map 13–4). The Mexicans fought bravely, but they lacked the leadership, modern artillery, and naval capacity to check the American advances. By the end of 1846, Polk had gained his objectives in the Mexican borderlands. An army sent west under Colonel Stephen W. Kearny occupied New Mexico. The conquest was relatively bloodless, because most of the local elite cooperated with the American authorities. Sporadic resistance was largely confined to poorer Mexicans and the Pueblo Indians, who feared that their land would be confiscated. The largest uprising, one that was ruthlessly suppressed, was the **Taos Revolt** in January 1847, led by Jesús Trujillo and Tomasito, a Pueblo chieftain. A sympathetic observer described the rebels as "those who defend to the last their country and their homes."

Kearny's army then moved to Tucson and eventually linked up in southern California with pro-American rebels and U.S. forces sent ashore by the Pacific squadron. As in New Mexico, the stiffest resistance came from ordinary Mexicans and the Spanish-speaking Indians.

Despite the loss of its northern provinces, Mexico refused to concede defeat. After Taylor had established a secure defensive line in northeastern Mexico with a victory at Monterrey in September 1846 and repulsed a Mexican counterattack at Buena Vista in February 1847, Polk directed General Winfield Scott to invade central Mexico. Following an amphibious assault on Vera Cruz in March 1847, Scott captured Mexico City in September.

After a frustrating delay while Mexico reorganized its government, peace talks finally got under way and concluded in the Treaty of Guadalupe Hidalgo, signed on February 2, 1848. Mexico surrendered its claim to Texas north of the Rio Grande and ceded Alta California and New Mexico (including present-day Arizona, Utah, and Nevada). The United States paid $15 million, assumed over $3 million in claims of American citizens against Mexico, and agreed to grant U.S. citizenship to Mexicans resident in its new territories.

Polk had gained his strategic goals, but the cost was thirteen thousand American lives (most from diseases such as measles and dysentery), fifty thousand Mexican lives, and the poisoning of Mexican–American relations for generations. The war also, as will be seen in Chapter 14, heightened sectional tensions over slavery and weakened the political structure that was vital to preserving the Union.

CONCLUSION

Americans were an expansionist people. Though not necessarily proof of Manifest Destiny, their surge across the continent between 1815 and 1850 was fully in keeping with their restless desire for independence on a plot of land. Population pressure on overworked farms in the East impelled much of this westward migration, but, by the 1840s, expansion had seemingly acquired a momentum all its own, one that increasingly rejected the claims of other peoples to the land.

Far from being a process of peaceful, evolutionary, and democratic change, as was once thought, expansion involved the spread of slavery, violent confrontations, and the uprooting and displacement of native peoples. By 1850, the earlier notion of reserving the trans-Mississippi West as a permanent Indian country had been abandoned. The Sioux and Comanches were still feared by white settlers, but their final subjugation was not far off. The derogatory stereotypes of Mexican-Americans that were a staple of both popular thought and expansionist ideology showed clearly that American control after the Mexican War would relegate Spanish-speaking people to second-class status.

However misleading and false much of it was, the rhetoric of Manifest Destiny did highlight a central truth. A broad, popular base existed for expanding across the continent. As the Mexican War made clear, the United States was now unquestionably the dominant power in North America. The only serious threat to its dominance in the near future would come from inside, not outside, its continental domain.

REVIEW QUESTIONS

1. What accounted for the westward movement of Americans? How did the presence or absence of slavery affect developmental patterns in the new settlements?

2. How was the West of the Plains Indians transformed after 1830 as peoples migrated both within the region and into it from various directions? Why were the Sioux so powerful? How did they interact with other Native Americans and the U.S. government?

3. Who lived in the Mexican borderlands of the Southwest? Why was it so difficult for Mexican authorities to maintain effective control of the region? What role did trade play in the American penetration of the Southwest?

4. What did Americans mean by Manifest Destiny? Why was territorial expansion so identified with the Democratic party?

5. Who was responsible for the outbreak of the Mexican War? Were Mexicans the victims of American aggression?

6. How valid was the Sioux chief's indictment of the pretensions of white civilization as related to George Catlin?

KEY TERMS

Alamo (p. 406)

Californios (p. 406)

Claims clubs (p. 394)

Empresarios (p. 405)

Manifest Destiny (p. 390)

Mexican Cession of 1848 (p. 408)

Oregon Trail (p. 397)

Santa Fe Trail (p. 407)

Taos Revolt (p. 413)

Tejanos (p. 405)

RECOMMENDED READING

Billington, Ray Allen. *The Far Western Frontier, 1830–1860* (1956). Still a useful survey and an excellent example of an older approach to the West from the perspective of white people entering the region with their values of freedom and individualism.

Brandon, Richard. *The Last Americans: The Indian in American Culture* (1974). A beautifully written, panoramic account that looks at Indian cultures and their interactions with the spread of white settlement.

Limerick, Patricia Nelson. *The Legacy of Conquest: The Unbroken Past of the American West* (1987). A forcefully argued work that overturns many stereotypes and places the federal government and cultural antagonisms at the center of western history.

Meinig, D. W. *The Shaping of America*, Vol. 2: *Continental America, 1800–1867* (1993). A comprehensive work that offers a distinctive interpretation of continental expansion from the perspective of historical geography.

Merk, Frederick. *Manifest Destiny and Mission in American History* (1963). Valuable not only for its revisionist look at the appeal of Manifest Destiny in the 1840s but also for its insights into how a sense of mission influenced American foreign policy in the future.

Milner, Clyde A. II, Carol A. O'Connor, and Martha A. Sandweiss, eds. *The Oxford History of the American West* (1994). A comprehensive collection of essays that summarize much of the best work in the modern rethinking of the history of the American West.

Stephanson, Anders. *Manifest Destiny: American Expansionism and the Empire of Right* (1995). A tightly argued study that traces Manifest Destiny back to its roots in Puritan ideology and shows how, in revised form, it continued to influence American foreign policy well into the twentieth century.

White, Richard. *"Its Your Misfortune and None of My Own": A History of the American West* (1991). An outstanding work that draws on cultural and environmental approaches to show how complex and often unequal relationships among a host of peoples shaped the history of the West.

ADDITIONAL SOURCES

The Agricultural Frontier

Cashin, Joan E. *A Family Venture: Men and Women on the Southern Frontier* (1991).

Faragher, John Mack. *Sugar Creek: Life on the Illinois Prairie* (1986).

Gates, Paul W. *The Farmer's Age: Agriculture, 1815–1860* (1962).

Moore, John Hebron. *The Emergence of the Cotton Kingdom in the Old Southwest: Mississippi, 1770–1860* (1987).

Hudson, John C. *Making the Corn Belt: A Geographical History of Middle-Western Agriculture* (1994).

Rohrbough, Malcolm J. *The Trans-Appalachian Frontier: People, Societies, and Institutions, 1775–1850* (1978).

The Frontier of the Plains Indians

Clark, Malcolm Jr. *Eden Seekers: The Settlement of Oregon, 1810–1862* (1981).

De Voto, Bernard. *Across the Wide Missouri* (1947).

Goetzmann, William H. *Exploration and Empire: The Explorer and Scientist in the Winning of the American West* (1966).

Jeffrey, Julie R. *Frontier Women: The Trans-Mississippi West, 1840–1880* (1979).

Moore, John H., ed. *The Political Economy of the North American Indians* (1993).

Unruh, John. *The Plains Across: The Overland Emigrations and the Trans-Mississippi West, 1840–1860* (1979).

Elliott West, *The Way to the West: Essays on the Central Plains* (1995).

White, Richard. *The Roots of Dependency: Subsistence, Environment, and Social Change Among the Choctaws, Pawnees, and Navajos* (1983).

The Mexican Borderlands

Acuña, Rudolfo. *Occupied America: A History of Chicanos* (1988).

Gonzales, Manuel G. *Mexicanos: A History of Mexicans in the United States* (1999).

Lack, Paul D. *The Texas Revolutionary Experience: A Political and Social History, 1835–1836* (1992).

Lamar, Howard R. *The Far Southwest, 1846–1912* (1966).

Lecompte, Janet. *Pueblo, Hardscabble, Greenhorn: The Upper Arkansas, 1832–1856* (1978).

Phillips, George Harwood. *Indians and Intruders in Central California, 1769–1849* (1993).

Roberts, Randy, and James L. Olsen, *A Line in the Sand: The Alamo in Blood and Memory* (2001).

Tijerina, Andres. *Tejanos and Texas under the Mexican Flag, 1821–1836* (1994).

Weber, David J. *The Mexican Frontier, 1821–1846: The American Southwest under Mexico* (1982).

Politics, Expansion, and War

Griswold del Castillo, Richard. *The Treaty of Guadalupe Hidalgo: A Legacy of Conflict* (1990).

Eisenhower, John S. D. *So Far from God: The U.S. War with Mexico* (1989).

Hietala, Thomas R. *Manifest Design: American Aggrandizement in Late Jacksonian America* (1985).

Horsman, Reginald. *Race and Manifest Destiny: The Origins of American Racial Anglo-Saxonism* (1981).

Johannsen, Robert W. *To the Halls of Montezuma: The Mexican War in the American Imagination* (1985).

Sellers, Charles G. *James K. Polk: Continentalist, 1843–1846* (1966).

WHERE TO LEARN MORE

- **Indian Pueblo Cultural Center, Albuquerque, New Mexico.** This center provides an excellent orientation to the culture, crafts, and community life of the Pueblo and Southwestern Indians. It also includes much material on archaeological findings. **Visit** www.indianpueblo.org/ **for a calendar of events and an introduction to the history of the** nineteen pueblos.

- **Museum Association of American Frontier and Fur Trade, Chadron, Nebraska.** The library in the museum holds archives, maps, and some photographs dealing with the western fur trade. **In addition to an event calendar, its website** www.stepintohistory.com/states/NE/Fur_Trade.htm **provides links to other museums and preservation sites.**

- **Indian Museum of North America, Crazy Horse, South Dakota.** This is one of the best sources for learning of the culture of the Teton Sioux and other American and Canadian tribes on the Great Plains. Holdings include outstanding examples of Indian art and artifacts. **For information on exhibits, educational and cultural programs, and special collections of Native American art, go to** www.crazyhorse.org/museum.shtml.

- **Living History Farms, Des Moines, Iowa.** This site includes several working farms, operated as they were at different points in the nineteenth century, as well as a mid-twentieth-century farm. A vintage town with a general store, church, and other buildings has also been re-created. **Its website** www.lhf.org/ **lists events and provides a look at four farm sites.**

- **Scotts Bluff National Monument, Gering, Nebraska.** Scotts Bluff was a prominent landmark on the Oregon Trail, and the museum exhibits here have interpretive material on the trail and the western phase of expansion. Go to www.nps.gov/scbl/ to print a park travel guide and to access a website devoted to the frontier photographer and artist William Henry Jackson.

- **Conner Prairie, Noblesville, Indiana.** The museum and historic area re-create a sense of life on the Indiana frontier during the period of the Old Northwest. www.connerprairie.org .

- **Fort Union National Monument, Watrous, New Mexico.** Fort Union was a nineteenth-century military post, and the holdings and exhibits in the museum relate to frontier military life and the Santa Fe Trail. **For a printable travel guide and a history of the park that includes bibliographical aides, go to** www.nps.gov/foun/.

 Please refer to the document CD-ROM for primary sources related to this chapter.

➜ *Vivid illustrations accompanied the numerous editions of* Uncle Tom's Cabin *depicting the brutal realities of slavery and the unmerited suffering of the slave. These images sharpened the tragedy of Harriet Beecher Stowe's story. Here, Tom dies following a savage beating.*

THE POLITICS OF SECTIONALISM

1846–1861

14

December 16, 1852

My Dear Madam,

So you want to know what sort of woman I am! Well, if this is any object, you shall have statistics free of charge. To begin, then, I am a little bit of a woman,—somewhat more than forty, about as thin and dry as a pinch of snuff— never very much to look at in my best days and looking like a used up article now.

I was married when I was twenty-five years old to a man rich in Greek and Hebrew and Latin and Arabic, and alas, rich in nothing else . . . . But then I was abundantly furnished with wealth of another sort. I had two little curly headed twin daughters to begin with and my stock in this line has gradually increased, till I have been the mother of seven children, the most beautiful and the most loved of whom lies buried near my Cincinnati residence. It was at his dying bed and at his grave that I learned what a poor slave mother may feel when her child is torn away from her. In those depths of sorrow which seemed to me immeasurable, it was my only prayer to God that such anguish might not be suffered in vain. There were circumstances about his death of such peculiar bitterness, of what seemed almost cruel suffering that I felt that I could never be consoled for it unless this crushing of my own heart might enable me to work out some great good to others.

CHAPTER OUTLINE

Slavery in the Territories

The Wilmot Proviso
The Election of 1848
The Gold Rush
The Compromise of 1850
Response to the Fugitive Slave Act
Uncle Tom's Cabin
The Election of 1852

Political Realignment

*Young America's Foreign
    Misadventures*
Stephen Douglas's Railroad Proposal
The Kansas-Nebraska Act
"Bleeding Kansas"
*Know-Nothings and Republicans:
    Religion and Politics*
The Election of 1856
The Dred Scott Case
The Lecompton Constitution
The Lincoln–Douglas Debates

The Road to Disunion

North–South Differences
John Brown's Raid
The Election of 1860
Secession Begins
Presidential Inaction
Peace Proposals
Lincoln's Views on Secession
Fort Sumter: The Tug Comes

Conclusion

I allude to this here because I have often felt that much that is in that book had its root in the awful scenes and bitter sorrow of that summer. It has left now, I trust, no trace on my mind except a deep compassion for the sorrowful, especially for mothers who are separated from their children . . . .

This horror, this nightmare abomination! Can it be in my country! It lies like lead on my heart, it shadows my life with sorrow; the more so that I feel, as for my own brothers, for the South, and am pained by every horror I am obliged to write, as one who is forced by some awful oath to disclose in court some family disgrace. . . . .

Yours affectionately,

H. B. Stowe

Harriet Beecher Stowe to Eliza Cabot Follen, December 16, 1852; from Jeanne Boydston, Mary Kelley, Anne Margolis, *The Limits of Sisterhood* (Chapel Hill: University of North Carolina Press, 1988), 178–180.

Harriet Beecher Stowe, while writing to poet and fellow abolitionist, Eliza Cabot Follen, in the year that *Uncle Tom's Cabin* became an international best-seller, revealed how being a wife and a mother influenced her perception of slavery and inspired her writing. The deep piety and self-effacement expressed in the letter, as well as her transparent grief over the loss of her son, typified mid-nineteenth-century correspondence between women. Her beloved son had died of cholera in 1849; that wrenching event, coupled with the passage of the Fugitive Slave Act a year later, galvanized Stowe to pour her grief and indignation into a novel about plantation slavery.

Slavery was yet an abstract concept to most white Northerners at the time. Stowe personalized it in a way that made them see it as an institution that not just oppressed black people but destroyed families and debased well-meaning Christian masters as well. The deep piety expressed in the letter permeated the book and changed people's moral perceptions about slavery.

Stowe had grown up in a family of evangelical Protestant ministers and abolitionists. Her father, Lyman Beecher, was a prominent evangelical reformer. He had moved his large family from New England to Cincinnati in 1832 to assume the presidency of Lane Theological Seminary, where he used his office to promote the abolition of slavery. All six of his sons became ministers. Two of his three daughters, Catharine and Harriet, became accomplished writers. In Beecher's view, evangelical Christianity erased the line between public and private. Personal and societal salvation were closely con-

nected, a principle that is apparent in Harriet's letter. Stowe went on to write ten novels, became a popular children's-book author and wrote extensively on family and travel matters. She died in 1896, in Hartford, Connecticut, at the age of 85.

As slavery took on a personal and tragic meaning for Stowe, so it would move from being just another political issue to a moral crusade. Stowe's personal journey transformed into a political passion; with the millions who read her book, the political became personal. Yet, the anguish she expressed in her writing and the outrage it generated among her readers was hardly prefigured when a relatively obscure Congressman from Pennsylvania stepped forward in 1846 with a modest proposal that not only placed slavery front and center as a national political issue, a position that only strengthened over the next fifteen years, but would shake the Union to its very core.

Slavery was not, of course, a new political issue: the debate over the Missouri Compromise, the nullification controversy, and the battles in Congress over abolitionist mailings and petitions had roiled the political waters for nearly a generation prior to 1846. But after 1846, the clashes between northern and southern congressmen over issues relating to slavery became more frequent and more difficult to resolve. In the coming years, several developments—including white Southerners' growing consciousness of themselves as a minority, the mixture of political issues with religious questions, and the rise of the Republican party—would aggravate sectional antagonism. But the flash point that first brought it to the fore was the issue of slavery in the territories acquired from Mexico.

418

KEY TOPICS

- The controversy over slavery in the territories and the attempt to resolve it
- The causes and consequences of political realignment in the 1850s
- Why Lincoln was elected in 1860
- The secession crisis and why the political system could not fix it

SLAVERY IN THE TERRITORIES

Whatever its boundaries over the years, the West symbolized the hopes and dreams of white Americans. It was the region of fresh starts, of possibilities. To exclude slavery from the western territories was to exclude white Southerners from pursuing their vision of the American dream. Exclusion meant, an Alabamian declared, "that a free citizen of Massachusetts was a better man and entitled to more privileges than a free citizen of Alabama." Northern politicians disagreed. They argued that exclusion preserved equality—the equality of all white men and women to live and work without competition from slave labor or rule by despotic slaveholders. The issue of slavery in the territories became an issue of freedom for both sides.

From the late 1840s until 1861, northern and southern leaders attempted to fashion a solution to the problem of slavery in the territories. Four proposals dominated the debate:

- Outright exclusion
- Extension of the Missouri Compromise line to the Pacific
- Popular sovereignty—allowing the residents of a territory to decide the issue
- Protection of the property of slaveholders (meaning their right to own slaves) even if few lived in the territory

The first major debate on these proposals occurred during the early days of the Mexican War and culminated with the Compromise of 1850.

THE WILMOT PROVISO

In August 1846, David Wilmot, a Pennsylvania Democrat, offered an amendment to an appropriations bill for the Mexican War. The language of the **Wilmot Proviso** stipulated that "as an express and fundamental condition to the acquisition of any territory from the Republic of Mexico . . . neither slavery nor involuntary servitude shall ever exist in any part of said territory." This language deliberately reflected Thomas Jefferson's Northwest Ordinance of 1787, which prohibited slavery in the Old Northwest. The proviso did not apply to Texas, which had become a state before the war began.

Wilmot explained that he wanted only to preserve the territories for "the sons of toil, of my own race and own color." By thus linking the exclusion of slavery in the territories to freedom for white people, he hoped to generate support across the North, regardless of party, and even in some areas of the Upper South.

Linking freedom for white people to the exclusion of slaves infuriated Southerners. It implied that the mere proximity of slavery was degrading and that white Southerners were therefore a degraded people, unfit to join other Americans in the territories. Georgia's Whig senator, Robert Toombs, issued a warning that reflected the feelings of many Southerners: "I do not hesitate to avow before this House and the Country, and in the presence of the living God, that if, by your legislation, you seek to drive us from the territories of California and New Mexico, purchased by the common blood and treasure of the whole people . . . , thereby attempting to fix a national degradation upon half the states of this Confederacy, I am for disunion."

Northern congressmen replied in kind. An Ohio Congressman declared, "We [the North] will establish a cordon of free states that shall surround you; and then we will light up the fires of liberty on every side until they melt your present chains and render all your people free." Now a majority in the House of Representatives (because the population of the northern states was greater than that of the southern states), northern lawmakers passed more than fifty versions of the proviso between 1846 and 1850. In the Senate, however, where each state had equal representation, the proviso was consistently rejected and never became law.

The proviso debate sowed distrust and suspicion between Northerners and Southerners. Congress had divided along sectional lines before, but seldom

Chronology

1846 Wilmot Proviso is submitted to Congress but is defeated.

1848 Gold is discovered in California.

Whig party candidate Zachary Taylor defeats Democrat Lewis Cass and Free-Soiler Martin Van Buren for the presidency.

1850 California applies for statehood.

President Taylor dies; Vice President Millard Fillmore succeeds him.

Compromise of 1850 is passed.

1851 Harriet Beecher Stowe publishes *Uncle Tom's Cabin.*

1852 Democrat Franklin Pierce is elected president in a landslide over Whig candidate Winfield Scott.

Whig party disintegrates.

1853 National Black Convention called in Rochester, New York, to demand repeal of the Fugitive Slave Act.

1854 Ostend Manifesto is issued.

Kansas-Nebraska Act repeals the Missouri Compromise.

Know-Nothing and Republican parties are formed.

1855 Civil war erupts in "Bleeding Kansas."

William Walker attempts a takeover of Nicaragua.

1856 "Sack of Lawrence" occurs in Kansas; John Brown makes a retaliatory raid at Pottawatomie Creek.

Democratic congressman Preston Brooks of South Carolina canes Massachusetts senator Charles Sumner in the U.S. Senate.

Democrat James Buchanan is elected president over Republican John C. Frémont and American (Know-Nothing) candidate Millard Fillmore.

1857 Supreme Court issues *Dred Scott* decision.

Kansas territorial legislature passes the proslavery Lecompton Constitution.

Panic of 1857 begins.

1858 Senatorial candidates Abraham Lincoln and Stephen A. Douglas hold series of debates in Illinois.

1859 John Brown's Raid fails at Harpers Ferry, Virginia.

1860 Constitutional Union party forms.

Democratic party divides into northern and southern factions.

Republican candidate Abraham Lincoln is elected president over southern Democratic candidate John C. Breckinridge, northern Democratic candidate Stephen A. Douglas, and Constitutional Unionist candidate John Bell.

South Carolina secedes from the Union.

1861 The rest of the Lower South secedes from the Union.

Crittenden Plan and Tyler's Washington peace conference fail.

Jefferson Davis assumes presidency of the Confederate States of America.

Lincoln is inaugurated.

Fort Sumter is bombarded; Civil War begins.

Several Upper South states secede.

---

had divisions become so personal. The leaders of both the Democratic and Whig parties, disturbed that the issue of slavery in the territories could so monopolize Congress and poison sectional relations, sought to defuse the issue as the presidential election of 1848 approached.

THE ELECTION OF 1848

Both Democrats and Whigs wanted to avoid identification with either side of the Wilmot Proviso controversy, and they selected their presidential candidates accordingly. The Democrats nominated Michigan senator Lewis Cass, a veteran party stalwart, whose public career stretched back to the War of 1812. Cass understood the destructive potential of the slavery issue. In 1847, he suggested that territorial residents, not Congress, should decide slavery's fate. This solution,

popular sovereignty, had a do-it-yourself charm: Keep the politicians out of it, and let the people decide. Cass was deliberately ambiguous, however, on when the people should decide. The timing was important. If residents could decide only when applying for statehood, slavery would be legal up to that point. The ambiguity aroused more fears than it allayed.

The Whigs were silent on the slavery issue. Reverting to their winning 1840 formula of nominating a war hero, they selected General Zachary Taylor of Mexican War fame. If the Whigs were looking for someone with no political record, they found him in the squat and craggy-faced Taylor. Taylor belonged to no party and had never voted. He was also inarticulate to the point of unintended humor. In one address, he intoned: "We are at peace with all of the world, and seek to maintain . . . amity with the rest of mankind." If one had to guess his views, his background provided some clues. He lived in Louisiana in the Lower South, he owned a hundred-slave plantation, and his now-deceased daughter had been married to Jefferson Davis, Mississippi's staunch proslavery senator.

Taylor's background disturbed many antislavery northern Whigs. These Conscience Whigs along with remnants of the old Liberty party and a scattering of northern Democrats bolted their parties and formed the Free-Soil party. The name reflected the party's vow to keep the territories free. Its slogan—"Free soil, free speech, free labor, free men"—was a catalog of white liberties that the South had allegedly violated over the previous decade.

The Free-Soilers' appeal centered on their opposition to slave labor in the territories. Free labor, they believed, could not compete with bonded labor. Slavery condemned the white worker to unemployment, poverty, and eventually a condition little better than slavery itself. The party nominated former president Martin Van Buren. The old New Yorker, who had remained active in state politics, had little hope of winning. But he could wield some influence if he were to prevent one of the major party candidates from winning a majority of electoral votes, thereby throwing the election into the House of Representatives.

Chalking up one out of seven northern votes, Van Buren ran strongly enough in eleven of the fifteen northern states to deny the winning candidate in those states a majority of the votes cast. But he could not overcome Taylor's strength in the South. Taylor was elected, giving the nation its first president from the Lower South.

THE GOLD RUSH

Events in distant California would leave Taylor little time to savor his victory. By the time he took office in March 1849, a gold rush was under way in that territory recently acquired from Mexico. John Sutter, a Swiss immigrant, contracted with James Marshall in late 1847 to build a sawmill on his property at the junction of the American and Sacramento Rivers in central California. In January 1848, Marshall was nearly finished with his project when something caught his eye: "I reached my hand down and picked it up; it made my heart thump, for I was certain it was gold. The piece was about half the size and shape of a pea. Then I saw another." Few believed the story at first, but Sam Brannan, a San Francisco merchant, witnessed Marshall's finds and literally ran shouting through the streets of the sparsely settled town about the new discovery. Brannan would become the wealthiest man in California, provisioning miners and staking claims.

Through 1849 and 1850, more than 100,000 hopefuls flooded into California. Anarchy and geology combined to form a volatile mixture in appropriately named settlements such as Hangtown, Gouge Eye, and Whiskeytown. One unfortunate miner wrote back east to his family in 1850: "I take this opportunity of writing these few lines to you hoping to find you in good health. Me and Charley is sentenced to be hung at five o/clock for robbery. Give my best to Frank and Sam." Though the overland or overseas treks took months, and travelers battled disease, weather, and each other, the lure of gold—easy to get at with just simple tools—was a powerful motivator.

Huge fortunes accrued, not only from the gold, but from supplying the miners. Young Levi Strauss experimented with trousers made out of canvas that miners particularly favored; two brothers, Henry Wells and William Fargo offered banking, transportation, and mail services for the newcomers. The rush also attracted migrants from around the world. California soon became a polyglot empire of Chinese, Chileans, Mexicans, Irish, Germans, and Turks. Blacks, mostly slaves brought by southern masters, also roamed the gold fields.

By 1853 gold mining operations had undergone structural and technological changes that made many miners superfluous. The new hydraulic extraction techniques also severely damaged the pristine rivers of central California.

Almost overnight, San Francisco was transformed from a modest port to a cosmopolitan metropolis. In 1847, a typical lot in the town cost $16; by 1849, that same lot sold for $45,000. During these two years, the town burned to the ground no less than six times,

Taking a break from digging and panning for gold, a group of Forty-Niners pose for the camera. Notice the African-American miner on the far left.

and six times the residents rebuilt on an ever grander scale. By the mid-1850s, a half-billion dollars in gold money had passed through the city, and a good bit of it stayed. The city by then boasted a fine theater, an opera house, and more newspapers than any other city in the world save London. The image of California, and of the West in general, as wild or golden, dates from this era. But the romance of California and the wealth it generated loomed more troubling back east as the territory filled up with people in 1849. For the western dream would soon become ensnared in the conflict over slavery.

THE COMPROMISE OF 1850

When the territory's new residents began asking for statehood and drafted a state constitution, the document contained no provision for slavery. The constitution reflected antiblack rather than antislavery sentiment. Keeping California white shielded residents against social and economic interaction with black people. In the context of territorial politics, "free" became a synonym for "whites only."

If Congress accepted the residents' request for statehood, California would enter the Union as a free state. The Union at the time consisted of fifteen free states and fifteen slave states. The admission of California would tip the balance and give free states a majority in the Senate. California, with its rapidly growing population, would also add to the sixty-one-vote majority the North enjoyed in the House of Representatives. New Mexico (which then included most of present-day New Mexico, Arizona, small parts of Nevada, and Colorado) appeared poised to follow suit and enter the Union as the seventeenth free state. Southerners saw their political power slipping away. Northern leaders saw an opportunity to stop the extension of slavery and reduce southern influence in the federal government.

When Congress confronted the issue of California statehood in December 1849, partisans on both sides began marshaling forces for what promised to be a long and bitter struggle. Because nine Free-Soil candidates had won seats in the House of Representatives, neither Whigs nor Democrats held a majority there. South Carolina senator John C. Calhoun understood that only a politically unified South could protect its interests. He urged southern congressmen to ignore party ties and unite behind a plan he proposed to gain federal protection for slavery in the territories. Most southern Whigs ignored Calhoun and waited to hear from President Taylor before abandoning him and their party.

No one, at first, knew where Taylor stood. Although a political novice, the president was not stupid. Recognizing his lack of political experience, he selected Whig senator William H. Seward of New York as his adviser. Seward, a committed antislavery man, was one of the most hated politicians in the South; Taylor, a slaveholder from Louisiana, was distrusted by many northern members of his party. This odd match provided the first insight into the president's thinking on California.

He supported, it turned out, a version of popular sovereignty and favored allowing California and the other territories acquired from Mexico to decide the slavery issue for themselves. Under normal circumstances, the residents of a new territory organized a territorial government under the direction of Congress. When the territory's population approached thirty thousand or so, residents could draft a constitution and petition Congress for statehood. California already easily exceeded the population threshold. Taylor proposed bypassing the territorial stage—and congressional involvement in it—and having California and New Mexico admitted as states directly. (Before his inauguration in March 1849, he had already privately encouraged people in both territories to write state constitutions and to request admission.) The result would be to bring both into the Union as free states.

Although Seward no doubt encouraged him in it, Taylor's position was his own. The president was a nationalist and a strong believer in Manifest Destiny. He did not oppose slavery, but he abhorred the slavery issue because it threatened his vision of a continental empire. He was thus willing to forgo the extension of slavery into the territories. Southerners were certain to object strongly. But the president had a chilling message for them: "Whatever dangers may threaten [the Union] I shall stand by it and maintain it in its integrity."

Southerners resisted Taylor's plan, and Congress deadlocked on the territorial issue. Henry Clay then stepped forward with his last great compromise. To break the impasse, Clay urged that Congress should take four steps:

- Admit California as a free state, as its residents clearly preferred.
- Allow the residents of the New Mexico and Utah territories to decide the slavery issue for themselves too.
- End the slave trade in the District of Columbia.
- Pass a new fugitive slave law to enforce the constitutional provision stating that a person "held to Service or Labor in one state . . . escaping into another . . . shall be delivered upon Claim of the party to whom such Service or Labor may be due."

Clay's proposal provoked a historic Senate debate that began in February 1850, featuring America's three most prominent statesmen—Clay, Calhoun, and Daniel Webster—together for the last time. The emaciated Calhoun, who would be dead in two months, had to be carried into the Senate chamber. Too weak to read his remarks, he passed them to Virginia senator James M. Mason. Calhoun argued that the compromise did not resolve the slavery issue to the South's satisfaction, and he proposed to give Southerners in Congress the right to veto legislation in Congress as a way to safeguard their minority rights. Webster stood up to support the compromise, at deep political peril to himself. His Massachusetts constituents detested the fugitive-slave provision, which gave southern slaveholders the right to "invade" northern states to reclaim escaped slaves. Webster declared that he came to the debate "not as a Massachusetts man, nor as a Northern man, but as an American." He would swallow the fugitive slave law to save the Union.

After tumultuous deliberation that lasted into the summer of 1850, the Senate rejected the compromise. Calhoun had died at the end of March 1850, even before the debate ended. The 73-year-old Clay, exhausted, left Washington to recover his health. He would die less than two years later. Webster, estranged from fellow northern Whigs, left the Senate and went to his grave a few months after Clay.

President Taylor, who had vowed to veto any compromise, died unexpectedly of a stomach ailment after overindulging in cherries and milk in the hot sun at a July 4 celebration in Washington. Vice President Millard Fillmore, a pro-Clay New Yorker, assumed the presidency after Taylor's death. Compared with Taylor, who had stormed around the White House daring Southerners to attempt secession, Fillmore was a backroom man, quiet, at home with the cigar-and-brandy crowd, and effective with the deal. Fillmore let it be known that he favored Clay's package and would sign it if passed.

Although the Senate had rejected the compromise, Illinois senator Stephen A. Douglas kept it alive. A small man with a large head that gave him a mushroomlike appearance, Douglas epitomized the promise of American life for men of his generation. A native Vermonter, he migrated first to New York, then to Illinois as a teenager; read law; and developed a voracious appetite for politics. By the age of 28, he had already served as state legislator, chairman of the state Democratic party, and judge of the state supreme court. He envisioned an urban, industrial West linked to the East by a vast railroad network eventually extending to the Pacific. Above all, Douglas professed an unbending nationalism. To him, according to a biographer, "the Union was sacred, the symbol of all human progress." After his election to Congress in 1842, the Little Giant, as his constituents affectionately called him, developed a reputation as an astute parliamentarian and a tenacious debater.

Like Webster, Douglas feared for the Union if the compromise failed. Realizing that it would never pass as a package, he proposed to break it up into its components and hold a separate vote on each. With a handful of senators voting for all parts, and with different sectional blocs supporting one provision or another, Douglas engineered a majority for the compromise, and Fillmore signed it.

The Compromise of 1850 (see Map 14–1) was not a compromise in the sense of opposing sides consenting to certain terms desired by the other. The North gained California but would have done so in any case. Southern leaders looked to the West and saw no slave territories awaiting statehood. Their future in the Union appeared to be one of numerical and economic decline, and the survival of their institutions seemed doubtful. They gained the **Fugitive Slave Act**, which reinforced their right to seize and return to bondage slaves who had fled to free territory, but it was slight consolation. One Lower South senator termed it "useless." Because most slaves who escaped to the North did so from neighboring slave states, the law affected mainly the states of the Upper South. Few slave owners from the Lower South would bear the expense and uncertainty of chasing an escaped slave into free territory. And the North's hostile reception to the law made Southerners doubt their commitment to the compromise.

RESPONSE TO THE FUGITIVE SLAVE ACT

The Fugitive Slave Act was ready-made for abolitionist propaganda mills and heartrending stories. A few months after Congress passed it, a Kentucky slaveholder visited Madison, Indiana, and snatched a black man from his wife and children, claiming that the man had escaped nineteen years earlier. Black people living in northern communities feared capture, and some escaped across the Canadian border. Several northern cities and states vowed resistance, but except for a few publicized cases, northern authorities typically cooperated with southern slave owners to help them retrieve their runaway property. The effect of the act on public opinion, however, was to polarize North and South even further.

The strongest reaction to the act was in the black communities of the urban North. Previously, black abolitionists in the North had focused on freeing slaves in the South. The Fugitive Slave Act brought the danger of slavery much closer to home. No black per-

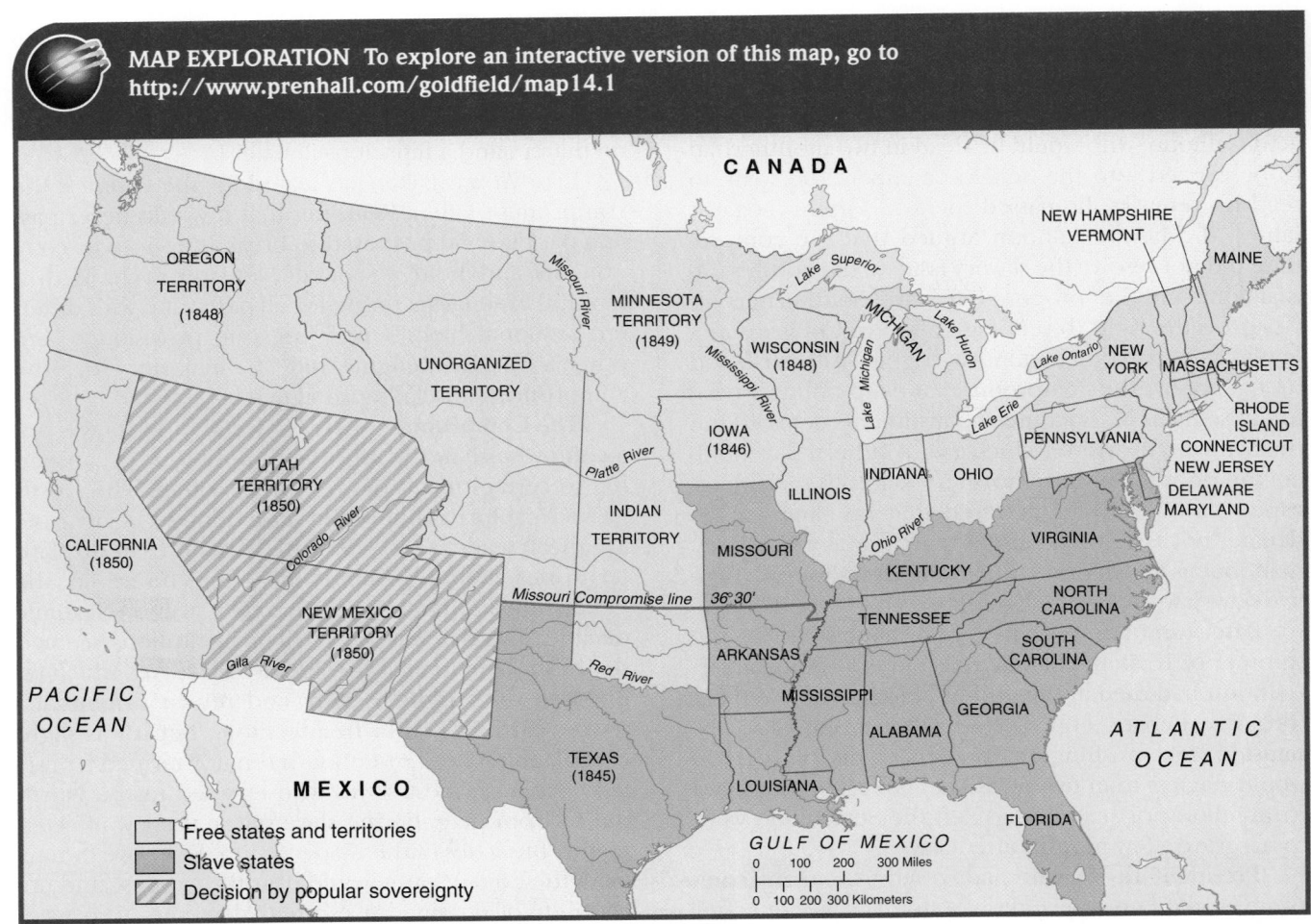

MAP EXPLORATION To explore an interactive version of this map, go to
http://www.prenhall.com/goldfield/map14.1

MAP 14-1   The Compromise of 1850
*Given the unlikely prospect that any of the western territories would opt for slavery,
the compromise sealed the South's minority status in the Union.*

son was safe under the new law. Mistaken identity, the support of federal courts for slaveholders' claims, and the presence of informants made reenslavement a real possibility. The lives that 400,000 black northerners had constructed, often with great difficulty, appeared suddenly uncertain.

Black Northerners formed associations to protect each other and repel—violently, if necessary—any attempt to capture and reenslave them. Boston's black leaders created the League of Freedom. Black Chicagoans organized the Liberty Association, with teams assigned to "patrol the city, spying for possible slave-hunters." Similar associations appeared in Cleveland and Cincinnati. Frederick Douglass, an escaped slave himself, explained the need for such organizations: "We must be prepared . . . to see the streets . . . running with blood . . . should this law be put into operation." Some black people left the United States. In October 1850, two hundred left Pittsburgh for On-

tario, Canada, vowing that "they would die before being taken back into slavery." As many as twenty thousand African Americans may have found their way across the border during the 1850s in response to fears over capture and reenslavement. Another solution was proposed by Martin Delany, a prominent black abolitionist. He argued for the establishment of a black homeland at several potential sites in Central or South America or on the west coast of Africa. "Go we must," he wrote in 1852. "To remain here in North America and be crushed to the earth in vassalage and degradation, we never will."

During the early 1850s, black Northerners gathered in conventions to demand the repeal of the Fugitive Slave Act. Frederick Douglass convened the National Black Convention in Rochester, New York, in July 1853, at which he established a national council of black leaders to address issues of political and civil rights. Although the council was short-lived, it re-

CAUTION!!

COLORED PEOPLE

OF BOSTON, ONE & ALL,

You are hereby respectfully CAUTIONED and advised, to avoid conversing with the

Watchmen and Police Officers of Boston,

For since the recent ORDER OF THE MAYOR & ALDERMEN, they are empowered to act as

KIDNAPPERS

AND

Slave Catchers,

And they have already been actually employed in KIDNAPPING, CATCHING, AND KEEPING SLAVES. Therefore, if you value your LIBERTY, and the *Welfare of the Fugitives* among you, *Shun* them in every possible manner, as so many *HOUNDS* on the track of the most unfortunate of your race.

Keep a Sharp Look Out for KIDNAPPERS, and have TOP EYE open.

APRIL 24, 1851.

The Fugitive Slave Act threatened the freedom of escaped slaves living in the North, and even of free black Northerners. This notice, typical of warnings posted in northern cities, urged Boston's African American population to take precautions.

flected a growing militancy. Less than a year later, for example, a black New York City woman schoolteacher defied that city's public transit segregation ordinance and succeeded in pressing state legislators to strike down the law.

On several occasions, black Northerners fought to defend their rights. In September 1851, Edward Gorsuch, a Maryland slaveholder, went to Christiana, Pennsylvania, where two of his escaped slaves were living. A fugitive slave named William Parker had organized the town's black community to defend against such an incident. Gorsuch located the two fugitives in a house occupied by Parker and a dozen other armed black men. Another fifty black people and some white people arrived and surrounded Gorsuch, his son, two other relatives, two neighbors, and a federal marshal. Gunfire erupted, wounding both Gorsuch and his son. As the elder Gorsuch lay on the ground, a group of black women "rushed from the

house with corn cutters and scythe blades [and] hacked the bleeding and lifeless body."

How much of this militancy filtered down to slaves in the South is difficult to say. Slaveholders noted an increase in black resistance during the early 1850s. A white Virginian noted in 1852 that "it is useless to disguise the fact, its truth is undeniable, that a greater degree of insubordination has been manifested by the negro population within the last few months, than at any previous period in our history as a state." Southerners often concocted tales of slave plots and unrest during times of national distress. But even if the Virginia writer exaggerated, his concern reflected genuine southern anxiety.

UNCLE TOM'S CABIN

Sectional controversy over the Fugitive Slave Act was relatively modest compared to the firestorm abolitionist writer Harriet Beecher Stowe ignited with the publication of a novel about southern slavery. *Uncle Tom's Cabin*, which first appeared in serial form in 1851, moved many northern white people from the sidelines of the sectional conflict to more active participation.

At the beginning of *Uncle Tom's Cabin*, a Kentucky slave owner is reluctantly forced by financial ruin to sell some of his slaves. Among them are the son of two mulatto slaves, George and Eliza Harris, and an older slave, Tom. Eliza escapes across the ice-choked Ohio River, clutching her son to her breast as slave catchers and their bloodhounds pursue them. Tom submits to sale to a New Orleans master. When that master dies, Tom is sold to Simon Legree, who owns a plantation on the Red River in Louisiana. Legree is vicious and sadistic—the only major slaveholding character in the book whom Stowe portrays in this manner. Tom, a devout Christian, remains loyal and obedient until Legree asks him to whip another slave. When Tom refuses, Legree beats him to death. Legree, incidentally, is from Vermont.

Stowe offered, not abstractions, but characters who seemed real. She aimed to evoke strong emotions in the reader. The broken family, the denial of freedom, and the Christian martyr were emotional themes. The presence of mulattoes in the book testified to widespread interracial and extramarital sex, which Northerners, then in the midst of a religious revival, viewed as an abhorrent sin destructive to family life. And the depiction of southern masters struggling unsuccessfully with their consciences focused public attention on how slavery subverted Christianity.

Uncle Tom's Cabin created a sensation in the United States and abroad. The book sold 10,000 copies in its first week and 300,000 within a year. By the time of the Civil War, it had sold an unprecedented 3 million copies in the United States and tens of thousands more in Europe. Stowe's book gave slavery a face; it changed people's moral perceptions about the institution in an era of deep Protestant piety; it was a Sermon on the Mount for a generation of Northerners seeking witness for their Christianity and a crusade on behalf of their faith. It transformed abolitionism, bringing a movement—whose extreme rhetoric many Northerners had previously viewed with disapproval—to the edge of respectability.

For Southerners, *Uncle Tom's Cabin* was a damnable lie, a political tract disguised as literature. One Southerner denounced the book as a "criminal prostitution of the high functions of the imagination to the pernicious intrigues of sectional animosity." Some Southerners retaliated with crude plays and books of their own. In these versions of slavery, no slave families were broken up, no slaves were killed, and all masters were models of Christian behavior. Few Northerners, however, read these southern responses. The writers penned them more to convince fellow Southerners that slavery was necessary and good than to change opinions in the North.

An advertisement for Uncle Tom's Cabin. *The book became a worldwide best-seller illuminating the tragedy of slavery in its corruption of family, human dignity, and Christianity.*

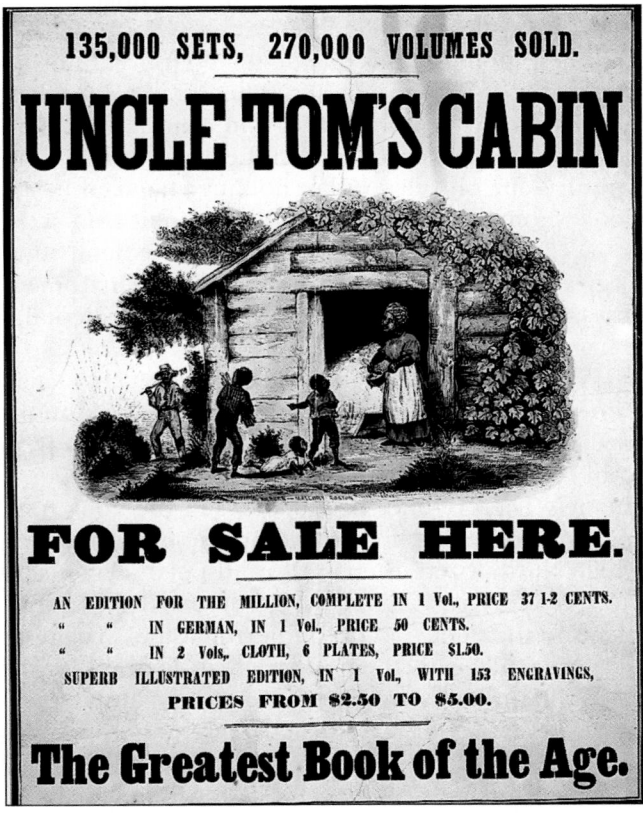

Black Northerners embraced *Uncle Tom's Cabin.* Frederick Douglass's National Black Convention resolved that the book was "a work plainly marked by the finger of God" on behalf of black people. Some black people hoped that the book's popularity would highlight the hypocrisy of white Northerners who were quick to perceive evil in the South but were often blind to discrimination against African Americans in the North. Despite reactions to Stowe's book, however, black Northerners continued to face voting restrictions, segregation, and official harassment.

THE ELECTION OF 1852

While the nation read and reacted to *Uncle Tom's Cabin,* a presidential election campaign took place. The Compromise of 1850 had divided the Whigs deeply. Northern Whigs perceived it as a capitulation to southern slaveholding interests and refused to support the renomination of President Millard Fillmore. Many southern Whigs, angered by the suspicions and insults of their erstwhile northern colleagues, abandoned the party. Although the Whigs nominated Mexican War hero and Virginian Winfield Scott for president, few southern Whigs viewed the nonslaveholding general as a friend of their region.

The Democratic Party entered the campaign more united. Despite reservations, both northern and southern wings of the party announced their support for the Compromise of 1850. Southern Democrats viewed the party's nominee, Franklin Pierce of New Hampshire, as safe on the slavery issue despite his New England heritage. Pierce satisfied Northerners as a nationalist devoted to the idea of Manifest Destiny. He belonged to Young America, a mostly Democratic group that advocated extending American influence into Central and South America and the Caribbean with an aggressive foreign policy. His service in the Mexican War and his good looks and charm won over doubters from both sections.

Given the disarray of the Whigs and the relative unity of the Democrats, the election results were predictable. Pierce won overwhelmingly with 254 electoral votes to Scott's 42. But Pierce's landslide victory could not obscure the deep fissures in the American party system. The Whigs, although they would continue to run local candidates through the rest of the 1850s, were finished as a national party. And the Democrats, despite their electoral success, emerged frayed from the election. In the Lower South, conflicts within the party between supporters and opponents of the Compromise of 1850 had overshadowed the contests between Democrats and Whigs. Southern Democrats had wielded great influence at the party's nominating convention and dominated party policy, clouding its prospects in the North. During the election, much of the party's support in the North had come from the first-time votes of mainly Catholic immigrants. But the growing political influence of Catholics alarmed evangelical Protestants of both parties, thus adding religious bigotry to the divisive issues undermining the structure of the national parties.

As Franklin Pierce took office in March 1853, it seemed that the only thing holding Democrats together was the thirst for political patronage. The low voter turnout in the 1852 election—Whig participation declined by 10 percent and Democratic participation by 17 percent, mostly in the Lower South—reflected public apathy and disgust at the prevailing party system. As the slavery issue confronted the nation with the most serious challenge it had faced since its inception, American voters were losing faith in their parties' ability to govern and in each other.

POLITICAL REALIGNMENT

Franklin Pierce, only forty-eight when he took office, was one of the youngest presidents in American history. He hoped to duck the slavery issue by focusing on Young America's dreams of empire. During the 1840s, the nationalist appeal of Manifest Destiny had helped elect Democrat James K. Polk to the presidency and had bolstered support for the Mexican War. Americans were still susceptible to nationalist fervor. For all their sectional, religious, ethnic, and racial differences, they shared a common language and political institutions. New technologies like the railroad and the telegraph were working to bind them together physically as well. The country was optimistic, and its possibilities for advancement seemed limitless. As Florida senator Stephen R. Mallory claimed, "It is no more possible for this country to pause in its career, than for the free and untrammeled eagle to cease to soar." But President Pierce's attempts to forge national sentiment around an aggressive foreign policy failed. And his administration's inept handling of a new territorial controversy in Kansas forced him to confront the slavery debate.

As Missouri senator Thomas Hart Benton, a Democrat, had realized during the debates over the Wilmot Proviso in 1848, no matter what policies a president pursued, Congress and the American people would interpret them in the light of their impact, real or potential, on slavery. The issue, said Benton, was like the plague of frogs that God had inflicted on the Egyptians to convince them to release the Hebrews from bondage. "You could not look upon the table but there were frogs, you could not sit down at the banquet but there were frogs, you could not go to the bridal couch and lift the sheets but there were frogs!" So it was with "this black question, forever on the table, on the nuptial couch, everywhere!"

Franklin Pierce lacked the skilled leadership the times demanded. Troubled by alcoholism, worried about his chronically ill wife, and grief-stricken over the death of three young sons, including one in a train wreck, Pierce presided weakly over the nation and increasingly deferred to proslavery interests in his policies.

YOUNG AMERICA'S FOREIGN MISADVENTURES

Pierce's first missteps occurred in pursuit of Young America's foreign ambitions. The administration turned a greedy eye toward Spanish-ruled Cuba, just ninety miles off the coast of Florida. Spanish authorities were harassing American merchants exporting sugar from Cuba and the American naval vessels protecting the merchants' ships. Southerners supported an aggressive Cuba policy, seeing the island as a possible new slave state. And nationalists saw great virtue in replacing what they perceived as a despotic colonial regime with a democratic government under the guidance of the United States.

In October 1854, three American diplomats met in Ostend, Belgium, to discuss Cuba. It is not clear whether Pierce approved or even knew of their meeting, but the diplomats believed that they had the administration's blessing. One of them, the American minister to Spain, Pierre Soulé of Louisiana, was especially eager for the United States to acquire Cuba. The group composed a document on Cuba called the Ostend Manifesto that claimed that the island belonged "naturally to the great family of states of which the Union is the Providential Nursery." The implication was that Spain's control of Cuba was unnatural. The United States would offer to buy Cuba from Spain, but if Spain would not sell, the authors warned, "by every law, human and Divine, we shall be justified in wresting it from Spain."

The Ostend Manifesto caused an uproar and embarrassed the Pierce administration when it became public. In the polite world of nineteenth-century diplomacy, it was a significant breach of etiquette. Other nations quickly denounced it as a "buccaneering document" and a "highwayman's plea." It provoked a similar reaction in the United States, raising suspicions in the North that the South was willing to provoke a war with Spain to expand the number of slaveholding states.

Meanwhile, the Pierce administration's aggressive foreign policy encouraged private citizens to pursue Young America's goals in Latin America. Such was the case of self-styled "General" William Walker and his private army, "the immortals." Newspaper reporters loved the diminutive Walker, whose exploits provided excellent copy. The popular press called him "the grey-eyed man of destiny." Walker moved from Tennessee to California, and in 1853, after gathering arms and men, he invaded Mexican-owned Baja California and proclaimed a republic. Before he could establish a permanent government and legalize slavery, the Mexican authorities tossed him out. Undaunted, Walker and his followers plunged into the civil war that had erupted in Nicaragua in May 1855. He gained control of the country by the end of the year, proclaimed himself president, and invited southern slaveholders to take up residence. The Pierce administration immediately recognized Walker's government; the people of Nicaragua did not. Backed by other Central American countries, they fought to oust the little general. Congressional pressure forced the Pierce administration to cool its support for Walker, and his financial resources dried up. His foes overthrew him in 1857, and he fled Nicaragua on an American naval vessel. After two more abortive attempts at conquest in Central America, he was executed by a Honduran firing squad in 1860.

These and other setbacks frustrated Pierce's hope that foreign adventures would mute the angry debate over slavery. Instead, the proslavery overtones of the Cuban fiasco and Walker's open courting of southern support sharpened sectional conflict. As Pierce was fumbling in foreign policy, Senator Stephen A. Douglas of Illinois was developing a national project that also promised to draw the country together—the construction of a transcontinental railroad and the settling of the land it traversed. The result was worse conflict and the first outbreak of sustained sectional violence.

STEPHEN DOUGLAS'S RAILROAD PROPOSAL

Douglas, like many Westerners, wanted a transcontinental railroad. He himself had a personal stake in railroad building in that he owned some Chicago real estate and speculated in western lands. Railroads and the people and business they carried drove up property values. But beyond personal gain, Douglas, the supreme nationalist, understood that a transcontinental railroad would tie the nation together. Not only would it physically link East and West, it would also help spread American democracy. In short, a transcontinental railroad made good economic and political sense.

Douglas had in mind a transcontinental route extending westward from Chicago through the Nebraska Territory. Unfortunately for his plans, Indians already occupied this region, many of them on land the U.S. government had set aside as Indian

Territory and barred to white settlement. "How," Douglas complained, "are we to develop, cherish, and protect our immense interests and possessions on the Pacific with a vast wilderness 1,500 miles in breadth, filled with hostile savages, and cutting off all direct communication?" Removing the "Indian barrier" and establishing white government were "first steps," in the senator's view, toward a "tide of emigration and civilization."

Once again, and not for the last time, the federal government responded by reneging on earlier promises and forcing Indians to move. In 1853, President Pierce sent agents to convince the Indians in the northern part of the Indian Territory to cede land for the railroad.

With the Indian "obstacle" removed, Douglas sought congressional approval to establish a government for the Nebraska Territory. But southern senators defeated his proposal. They objected to it not only because it called for a northern rather than southern route for the transcontinental railroad but also because the new territory lay above the Missouri Compromise line and would enter the Union as yet another free state. Bowing to southern pressure, Douglas rewrote his bill and resubmitted it in January 1854. He predicted that the new bill would "raise a hell of a storm." He was right.

THE KANSAS-NEBRASKA ACT

Douglas's Kansas-Nebraska Bill split the Nebraska Territory into two territories, Kansas and Nebraska, with the implicit understanding that Kansas would become a slave state and Nebraska a free state. Consistent with Douglas's belief in popular sovereignty, it left the actual decision on slavery to the residents of the territories. But because it allowed Southerners to bring slaves into an area formerly closed to slavery, it repealed the Missouri Compromise (see Map 14–2).

Northerners of all parties were outraged. The Missouri Compromise had endured for thirty-four years as a basis for sectional accord on slavery. Now it was threatened, northern leaders charged, by the South's unquenchable desire to spread slavery and expand its political power. In defense of the bill, Douglas claimed that it was unlikely that a majority in either territory would vote for slavery. But a group of northern leaders of Douglas's own Democratic party countered vehemently that repealing the Missouri Compromise was more than a political maneuver. Using language indicative of the way religious and conspiratorial imagery had infected political debate, transforming it into a contest of good against evil, of liberty against oppression, they said it was "a gross violation of a sacred pledge," "a criminal betrayal of precious rights," and "part and parcel of

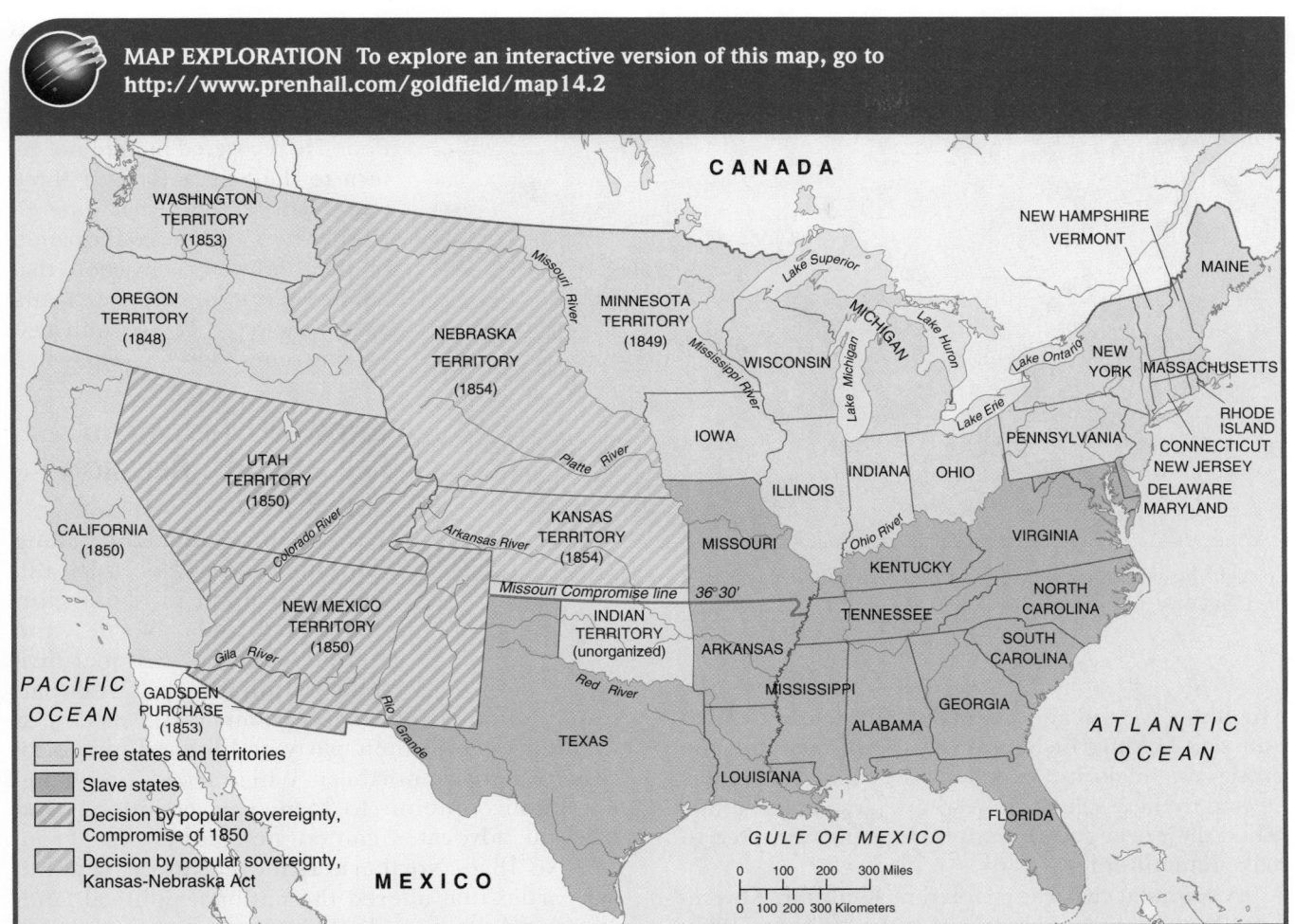

MAP EXPLORATION To explore an interactive version of this map, go to http://www.prenhall.com/goldfield/map14.2

MAP 14-2 **The Kansas Nebraska Act, 1854.**
The Kansas-Nebraska Act of 1854, which divided the Nebraska Territory in two and repealed the Missouri Compromise, reopened the incendiary issue of slavery in the territories.

an atrocious plot" to make a free territory a "dreary region of despotism, inhabited by masters and slaves." President Pierce, however, backed the bill, assuring the support of enough northern Democrats to secure it a narrow victory. The **Kansas-Nebraska Act** was law.

In August 1854, shortly after Congress adjourned, Douglas left Washington for his home in Chicago, to rest and mend political fences. He did not enjoy a pleasant journey home. "I could travel," he later recalled, ". . . by the light of my own effigy on every tree we passed." Arriving in Chicago, he addressed a large hostile crowd outside his hotel balcony. As he departed, he lost his temper and blurted, "It is now Sunday morning. I'll go to church; you can go to hell."

"BLEEDING KANSAS"

Because of its fertile soil, favorable climate, and location adjacent to the slave state of Missouri, Kansas was the most likely of the new territories to support slav-

ery. As a result, both Southerners and antislavery Northerners began an intensive drive to recruit settlers and establish a majority there. Speaking for the antislavery forces, William H. Seward said in the Senate, "We will engage in competition for the virgin soil of Kansas, and God give this victory to the side which is strong in numbers as it is in right." South Carolina editor Robert Barnwell Rhett accepted the challenge, urging fellow Southerners to "send men to Kansas, ready to cast in their lot with the proslavery part there and able to meet Abolitionism on its own issue, and with its own weapons."

As proslavery residents of Missouri poured into Kansas, antislavery organizations funded and armed their own migrants. In March 1855, proslavery forces, relying on the ineligible votes of Missouri residents, fraudulently elected a territorial legislature. This legislature promptly passed a series of harsh measures, including a law mandating the death penalty for aiding

Armed Missourians cross the border into Kansas to vote illegally for a proslavery government in 1855.

a fugitive slave and another making it a felony to question slaveholding in Kansas. For good measure, the proslavery majority expelled the few free-staters elected to the assembly. In response, free-staters established their own government in Topeka and vowed to make Kansas white.

A sporadic civil war erupted in Kansas in November 1855 and reached a climax in the spring of 1856. Journalists dubbed the conflict **"Bleeding Kansas."** On May 21, a group of proslavery officials attacked the free-state stronghold of Lawrence, subjecting it to a heavy artillery barrage. No one was killed, but the town suffered substantial damage. Eastern newspapers, exaggerating the incident, called it "the sack of Lawrence." Three days later, antislavery agitator John Brown, originally from Connecticut, went with several sympathizers to Pottawatomie Creek south of Lawrence in search of proslavery settlers. Armed with razor-sharp broadswords, they split the skulls and hacked the bodies of five men.

Kansans were not the only Americans bleeding over slavery. Five days before the **"sack of Lawrence,"** Massachusetts senator Charles Sumner delivered a long-winded diatribe, "The Crime Against Kansas," full of personal insults against several Southerners, especially elderly South Carolina senator Andrew P. Butler. Two days after Sumner's outburst, and a day after the story of the sack of Lawrence appeared in the newspapers, Butler's cousin, South Carolina congressman Preston Brooks, entered a mostly vacant Senate chamber, where Sumner sat working on a speech. Seeking to defend his

cousin's honor, Brooks raised his walking cane and beat Sumner over the head. Bloody and unconscious, the senator slumped to the floor. He recovered but did not return to the Senate for over three years. His empty chair offered Northerners' mute confirmation of their growing conviction that Southerners were despotic. Southerners showered Brooks with new walking canes.

KNOW-NOTHINGS AND REPUBLICANS: RELIGION AND POLITICS

The Sumner incident, along with the Kansas-Nebraska Bill and the civil war in Kansas, further polarized North and South, widening sectional divisions within the political parties. Some northern Democrats distanced themselves from their party and looked for political alternatives; northern Whigs seized on changing public opinion to form new coalitions; and free-soil advocates gained new adherents. From 1854 to 1856, Northerners moved into new political parties that altered the national political landscape and sharpened sectional conflict.

Although the slavery issue was mainly responsible for party realignment in the North, other factors played a role as well. Nearly 3.5 million immigrants entered the United States between 1848 and 1860, the greatest influx in American history in proportion to the total population. Some of these newcomers, especially the Germans, were escaping failed democratic revolutions in Europe. They were predominantly middle-class Protestants who, along with fewer German Catholics and Jews, settled mostly in the cities, where they established shops and other businesses. More than 1 million of the immigrants, however, were poor Irish Roman Catholics, fleeing their homeland to avoid starvation.

The Irish immigrants made their homes in northern cities, at the time in the midst of Protestant revivals and reform. They also competed for jobs with native-born Protestant workers. Because the Irish would work for lower wages, the job competition bred animosity and sometimes violence. Culturally, the Irish held different views on keeping the Sabbath, and they preferred to send their children to separate sectarian schools. But it was their Roman Catholic religion that most concerned some urban Protestants. These Protestants associated Catholicism with despotism and immorality, the same evils they attributed to Southerners. For their part, the Irish made it clear that they had little use for Protestant reform, especially temperance and abolitionism. The clash of cultures would soon further disturb a political environment increasingly in flux over the slavery issue.

Democrats wooed the Irish newcomers. The champions of individual rights against intrusive government and meddling reformers, they supported the strict separation of church and state. Evangelical Protestants, especially those who were not Democrats, took a different view. They believed that the assertion of individual rights led to chaos and had to be countered by evangelically led reform. And that reform must be legislated. As a Boston minister wrote during the debate on the Wilmot Proviso, "The great problem for the Christian world now to accomplish is to effect a closer union between religion and politics . . . . We must make men to do good and be good."

Evangelicals supported government action on a wide variety of issues, from drinking to slavery to economic policy. To the reformers, every political issue had moral overtones. Those who disagreed with them were not merely political opponents but obstacles to the creation of a righteous society. These views, though, blurred the lines not only between church and state but also between the expiation of sin and the elimination of the sinner.

New parties emerged from this cauldron of religious, ethnic, and sectional strife. Anti-immigrant, anti-Catholic sentiment gave rise to the **Know-Nothing Party**, which began as a secret organization in July 1854. Its name derived from the reply that members gave when asked about the party: "I know nothing." Although strongest in the North, Know-Nothing chapters blossomed in several southern cities that had experienced some immigration since 1848, among them Richmond, Louisville, New Orleans, and Savannah. The party's members in both North and South were mostly former Whigs. In addition to their biases against Catholics and foreigners, the Know-Nothings shared a fear that the slavery issue could destroy the Union. But because attempts to solve the issue seemed only to increase sectional tensions, the Know-Nothings hoped to ignore it.

Know-Nothing candidates fared surprisingly well in local and congressional elections during the fall of 1854, carrying 63 percent of the statewide vote in Massachusetts and making strong showings in New York and Pennsylvania. In office, Know-Nothings achieved some notable reforms. In Massachusetts, where they pursued an agenda similar to that of the Whigs in earlier years, they secured administrative reforms and supported public health and public education programs.

The Know-Nothings' anti-Catholicism, however, overshadowed their reform agenda. In several states and cities, they passed legislation barring Catholics from public office and unsuccessfully sought to increase the time required for an immigrant to become a citizen from one year to twenty-one years. The Know-Nothings also fostered anti-Catholic violence such as a bloody election day riot that erupted in Louisville, Kentucky, in 1855.

Ethnic and religious bigotry were weak links to hold together a national party. Southern and northern Know-Nothings soon fell to quarreling among themselves over slavery, despite their vow to avoid it, and the party split. Many northern Know-Nothings soon found a congenial home in the new **Republican Party**.

The Republican Party formed in the summer of 1854 from a coalition of antislavery Conscience Whigs and Democrats disgusted with the Pierce administration's Kansas policy. Like the Know-Nothings, the Republicans advocated strong state and federal governments to promote economic and social reforms. But the new party did not espouse the Know-Nothings' anti-Catholic and anti-immigrant positions. The overriding bond among Republicans was their opposition to the extension of slavery in the territories.

Reflecting its opposition to slavery, the Republican party was an antisouthern sectional party. The overwhelming majority of its members were Northerners. Northern Whig merchants and entrepreneurs who joined the party were impatient with southern obstruction in Congress of federal programs for economic development, such as a transcontinental railroad, harbor and river improvements, and high tariffs to protect American industries (located mostly in the North) from foreign competition. In a bid to keep slavery out of the territories, the Republicans favored limiting homesteads in the West to 160 acres. Not incidentally, populating the territories with northern whites would ensure a western base for the new party.

Heightened sectional animosity laced with religious and ethnic prejudice fueled the emergence of new parties and the weakening of old political affiliations in the early 1850s. Accompanying the political realignment were diverging views on the proper role of government. As the nation prepared for the presidential election of 1856, the Democrats had become a party top-heavy with Southerners; the Know-Nothings splintered along sectional lines; some Whigs remained active under the old party name, mainly on the state and local levels in North and South; and the Republican party was becoming an important political force in the North and, to Southerners, the embodiment of evil.

THE ELECTION OF 1856

The presidential election of 1856 proved one of the strangest in American history. The Know-Nothings and the Republicans faced a national electorate for the first time. The Democrats were deeply divided over the Kansas issue. Rejecting both Pierce and Douglas, they turned instead to a longtime insider, James Buchanan. This Pennsylvanian's major asset was that he had been absent from the country the previous three years as ambassador to Great Britain and was thus untainted by the Kansas controversy. The members of the increasingly powerful southern wing of the party supported him because he had cooperated with them during his more than thirty years in Congress. Northerners accepted him primarily because of his clean slate on Kansas and because he hailed from a state crucial to a Democratic victory.

The Republicans passed over their most likely candidate, the New York senator and former Whig William H. Seward. Instead, they followed a tried-and-true Whig precedent and nominated a military hero, John C. Frémont, a handsome, dark-haired soldier of medium height and medium intelligence. His wife, Jessie Benton, the daughter of Missouri senator Thomas Hart Benton, was his greatest asset. In effect, she ran the campaign and wisely encouraged her husband to remain silent.

The Know-Nothings split into the "South Americans" and the "North Americans." The South Americans nominated Millard Fillmore, although he was not a Know-Nothing. The North Americans eventually and reluctantly embraced Frémont, despite the widespread but mistaken belief that he was a Roman Catholic.

Openly reviling what they called the "Black Republican party," Southerners threatened disunion if Frémont won. Virginia governor Henry A. Wise declared that Frémont's election "would be an open, overt proclamation of public war." Georgia's fire-eating Senator Robert Toombs concurred, warning that "the election of Frémont would be the end of the Union, and ought to be."

Buchanan claimed to be the only national candidate on the ballot. Writing to a colleague before the election, he stated, "I consider that all incidental questions are comparatively of little importance . . . when compared with the grand and appalling issue of Union or Disunion." Voters agreed, for Buchanan bested Frémont in the North and Fillmore in the South to win the presidency.

The overall result pleased Southerners, but the details left them uncomfortable. Buchanan won by carrying every southern state and the Lower North—Pennsylvania, New Jersey, Illinois, Indiana, and California. But Frémont, a political novice running on his party's first national ticket, carried eleven free states, and the rest he lost by scant margins to Buchanan. It was a remarkable showing for a two-year-old party. In the South and border states, Fillmore managed more than 40 percent of the vote and carried Maryland, despite bearing the standard of a fragmented party.

Buchanan, who brought more than a generation of political experience to the presidency, would need every bit and more. He had scarcely settled into office when two major crises confronted him: a Supreme Court decision that challenged the right of Congress to regulate slavery in the territories and renewed conflict over Kansas.

THE DRED SCOTT CASE

Dred Scott was a slave owned by an army surgeon based in Missouri. In the 1830s and early 1840s, he had traveled with his master to the state of Illinois and the Wisconsin Territory before returning to Missouri. In 1846, Scott sued his master's widow for freedom on the grounds that the laws of Illinois and the Wisconsin Territory barred slavery. After a series of appeals, the case reached the Supreme Court. Chief Justice Roger Taney of Maryland, joined by five other justices of the nine-member Supreme Court (five of whom came from slave states), dismissed Scott's suit two days after Buchanan's inauguration in March 1857. There is evidence that Buchanan had urged the Court to issue a sweeping ruling on slavery in the territories that would set the question to rest once and for all. Although Buchanan apparently did not suggest which way he wanted the Court to rule, such contact between the executive and the judicial branches of government concerning a pending case was inappropriate. In any case, Taney's opinion, far from settling the sectional debate over slavery, deepened it.

Taney's opinion contained two bombshells. First, using dubious logic and failing to take into account the status of African Americans in several northern states, he argued that black people were not citizens of the United States. Because Scott was not a citizen, he could not sue. In reaching this conclusion, Taney noted that the framers of the Constitution had never intended citizenship for slaves. The framers, according to Taney, respected a long-standing view that slaves were "beings of an inferior order . . . so far inferior that they had no rights which the white man was bound to respect."

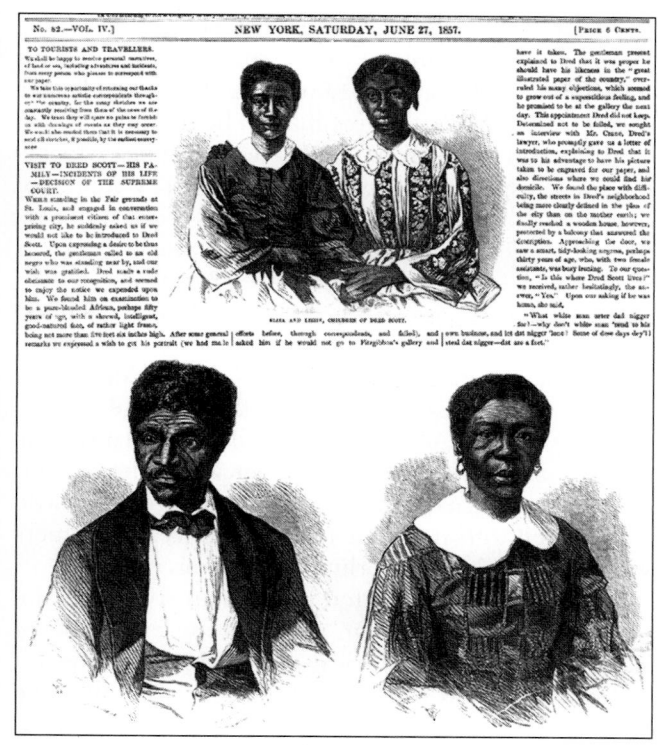

Dred Scott and his wife Harriet are portrayed here with their children as an average middle-class family, an image that fueled Northern opposition to the Supreme Court's 1857 decision that denied both Scott's freedom and his citizenship.

Second, Taney held that even if Scott had standing in court, his residence in the Wisconsin Territory did not make him a free man. This was because the Missouri Compromise, which was still in effect in the 1840s, was, in Taney's view, unconstitutional. (The Wisconsin Territory lay above the compromise line.) The compromise, the Chief Justice explained, deprived citizens of their property (slaves) without the due process of law granted by the Fifth Amendment to the U.S. Constitution. In effect, Taney ruled that Congress could not bar slavery from the territories.

Black Americans reacted bitterly to the **Dred Scott Decision**. Throughout the struggle of black abolitionists to free their compatriots in the South, they had appealed to the basic American ideals of freedom, liberty, and self-determination. Now Taney was saying that these ideals did not apply to black people. Throughout the urban North, African Americans held meetings to denounce the decision. One gathering in Philadelphia in April 1857 resolved "that the only duty the colored man owes to a constitution under which he is declared to be an inferior and degraded being . . . is to denounce and repudiate it." A statewide black convention in Ohio objected in even stronger language: "If the Dred Scott dictum be the true . . . law of the land, then are the founders of the American Republic convicted by their descendants of base hypocrisy, and colored men absolved from all allegiance to a government which withdraws all protection." The gap between American ideals and the application of those ideals to black Americans had never been wider or more apparent.

The decision also shocked Republicans. The right of Congress to ban slavery from the territories, which Taney had apparently voided, was one of the party's central tenets. Republicans responded by ignoring the implications of the decision for the territories while promising to abide by it so far as it affected Dred Scott himself. Once in office, Republicans vowed, they would seek a reversal. This position allowed them to attack the decision without appearing to defy the law.

The Dred Scott decision boosted Republican fortunes in the North even as it seemed to undercut the party. Fears of a southern Slave Power conspiracy, which some had dismissed as fanciful and politically motivated, now seemed justified. If Congress could not ban slavery from the territories, Republicans asked, how secure was the right of states to ban slavery within their borders? A small group of slaveholders, they charged, was holding nonslaveholding white people hostage to the institution of slavery.

THE LECOMPTON CONSTITUTION

Establishing a legitimate government in Kansas was the second major issue to bedevil the Buchanan administration. The president made a good start, sending his friend and fellow Pennsylvanian Robert Walker (then a resident of Mississippi) to Kansas as territorial governor to oversee the election of a constitutional convention in June 1857. Walker, though sickly, was a man of integrity.

The violence had subsided in Kansas, and prospects had grown for a peaceful settlement. But free-staters, fearing that the slavery forces planned to stuff the ballot box with fraudulent votes, announced a boycott of the June election. As a result, proslavery forces dominated the constitutional convention, which was held in Lecompton. And Walker, although a slaveholder, let it be known that he thought Kansas would never be a slave state. He thus put himself at odds with proslavery residents from the outset.

Walker convinced the free-staters to vote in October to elect a new territorial legislature. The returns gave the proslavery forces a narrow victory, but Walker discovered irregularities. In McGee, Kansas, twenty voters somehow had cast twelve hundred votes for proslavery candidates. And in Oxford, a community of a mere six houses, 1,601 names appeared on the voting rolls, all in the same handwriting and all copied from the Cincinnati city directory. Walker threw out these returns, and the free-staters took control of the territorial legislature for the first time.

Undeterred, the proslavery forces drafted a proslavery constitution at the constitutional convention in Lecompton. Buchanan, who had promised Southerners a proslavery government in Kansas, dismissed Walker before he could rule on the Lecompton Constitution, then ignored the recommendation of Walker's successor that he reject it. He submitted the **Lecompton Constitution** to the Senate for approval even though it clearly sidestepped the popular sovereignty requirement of the Kansas-Nebraska Act.

As with the Kansas-Nebraska Act, many Northerners were outraged by the Lecompton Constitution. The proslavery Kansans behind the constitution had a record of fraud, and Buchanan's own appointee had advised him against it. Northern Democrats facing reelection refused to support a president of their own party and, though the constitution passed in the Senate, Democratic opposition killed it in the House. Among Lecompton's opponents was Stephen A. Douglas, who justified his vote with an impassioned defense of popular sovereignty, which the president and proslavery Kansans had openly defied.

Douglas knew that the Dred Scott decision and Buchanan's support of the Lecompton Constitution would help the Republicans and hurt him and his fellow northern Democrats in the 1858 congressional elections. The **Panic of 1857**, a severe economic recession that lingered into 1858, also worked to the advantage of the Republicans. The Democratic administration did nothing as unemployment rose, starvation stalked the streets of northern cities, and homeless women and children begged for food and shelter. Republicans claimed that government intervention—specifically, Republican-sponsored legislation to raise certain tariffs, give western land to homesteaders, and fund transportation projects—could have prevented the panic. The Democrats' inaction, they said, reflected the southern Slave Power's insensitivity to northern workers.

Southerners disagreed. The panic had scarcely touched them. Cotton prices were high, and few southern banks failed. Cotton seemed indeed to be king. The financial crisis in the North reinforced the southern belief that northern society was corrupt and greedy. The Republicans' proposed legislative remedies, in their view, would enrich the North and beggar the South.

Such were the issues confronting Douglas as he returned home to Illinois in the summer of 1858 to begin his reelection campaign.

THE LINCOLN–DOUGLAS DEBATES

Douglas faced a forceful opponent. The Republicans had nominated Abraham Lincoln, a 49-year-old lawyer and former Whig congressman. The Kentucky-born Lincoln had risen from modest circumstances to become a prosperous lawyer in the Illinois state capital of Springfield. His marriage to wealthy and well-connected Mary Todd helped both his law practice and his pocketbook. After one term in Congress from 1847 to 1849, he returned to his law practice but maintained his interest in politics. Strongly opposed to the extension of slavery into the territories, he considered joining the Republican Party after the passage of the Kansas-Nebraska Act. Lincoln had developed a reputation as an excellent stump speaker with a homespun sense of humor, a quick wit, and a self-deprecating style that fit well with the small-town residents and farmers who composed the majority of the Illinois electorate.

But substance counted more than style with Illinois voters. Most of them opposed the extension of slavery into the territories, although generally not out of concern for the slaves. Illinois residents, like most Northerners, wanted to keep the territories free for white people. Few voters would support dissolving the Union over the slavery issue. Douglas, who knew his constituents well, branded Lincoln a dangerous radical for warning, in a biblical paraphrase, that the United States, like "a house divided against itself," could not "endure permanently half slave and half free."

Lincoln could not allow the charge of radicalism to go unanswered. Little known beyond the Springfield area, he also had to find a way to gain greater exposure. So, in July 1858, he challenged Douglas to a series of debates across the state. Douglas was reluctant to provide exposure for his lesser-known opponent, but he could not reject Lincoln's offer outright, lest voters think he was dodging his challenger. He agreed to debates in seven of the state's nine congressional districts.

The **Lincoln–Douglas debates** were defining events in American politics. Farmers rode into such market towns as Ottawa, Galesburg, Alton, and Freeport, bringing their families and picnic baskets. They settled in their wagons or on the ground under trees to hear the two great debaters confront each other on the most troubling issue of the day. What a sight it must have been, the stubby-legged, animated, barrel-chested Little Giant engaging the gangly, deliberate former rail-splitter, Abe Lincoln.

The debates put the differences between Lincoln and Douglas, Republicans and Democrats, and North and South into sharp focus. At Freeport, Lincoln asked Douglas to reconcile popular sovereignty, which

Abraham Lincoln making a point at Coles County (Illinois) Fairgrounds, 1858. His U.S. Senate opponent, Stephen A. Douglas, sitting at Lincoln's right, waits his turn. The Lincoln-Douglas debates captivated Illinois voters who turned out in great numbers to witness the rhetorical fireworks.

Douglas had long championed, with the *Dred Scott* decision, which seemed to outlaw it by prohibiting a territorial legislature from excluding slavery before statehood. Douglas replied with what became known as the Freeport Doctrine. Slavery, he argued, could exist in a territory only if residents passed a law to protect it. Without such a law, no slaveholders would move in, and the territory would be free. Thus, if residents did nothing, there could be no slavery in the territory.

For Douglas, slavery was not a moral issue. What mattered was what white people wanted. If they wanted slavery, fine; if they did not, fine also. Lincoln and many Republicans had a very different view. For them, slavery was a moral issue. As such, it was independent of what the residents of a territory wanted. In the final Lincoln-Douglas debate, Lincoln turned to his rival and explained:

> The real issue in this controversy . . . is the sentiment on the part of one class that looks upon the institution of slavery *as a wrong*, and of another class that does not look upon it as a wrong . . . . The Republican party . . . look upon it as being a moral, social and political wrong . . . and one of the methods of treating it as a wrong is to make provision that it shall grow no

larger . . . . That is the real issue . . . . It is the eternal struggle between these two principles—right and wrong—throughout the world.

Abolitionists and evangelicals had been saying much the same thing. But Lincoln was calm and nonaccusatory, his measured words more like a conversation than a sermon. And people listened.

Lincoln tempered his moralism with practical politics. He took care to distance himself from abolitionists, asserting that he abided by the Constitution and did not seek to interfere where slavery existed. Privately, however, he prayed for its demise. Nor did he agree, publicly at least, with abolitionist calls for racial equality. Several times during the debates he noted "a physical difference between the white and black races" that would "forever forbid the two races living together on terms of social and political equality." At the Springfield debate, he echoed the wishes of most white Illinoisans when he declared, "What I would most desire would be the separation of the white and black races." Indeed, he had once advocated sending freed slaves to Africa. Slavery was immoral, but inequality was not. The Republican party was antislavery, but it did not advocate racial equality.

Illinois voters retained a narrow Democratic majority in the state legislature, which reelected Douglas to the U.S. Senate. (State legislatures elected senators until 1913, when the Seventeenth Amendment provided for direct election by the people.) But Douglas alienated southern Democrats with his strong defense of popular sovereignty and lost whatever hope he had of becoming the standard-bearer of a united Democratic party in 1860. Lincoln lost the senatorial contest but won national respect and recognition.

Despite Lincoln's defeat in Illinois, the Republicans made a strong showing in the 1858 congressional elections across the North. The increased Republican presence and the sharpening sectional divisions among Democrats portended a bitter debate over slavery in the new Congress. Americans were viewing issues and each other more than ever before in sectional terms. Northern and Southern took on meanings that expressed a great deal more than geography.

THE ROAD TO DISUNION

The unsatisfying Compromise of 1850, the various misadventures in the Caribbean and Central America, "Bleeding Kansas" and "Bleeding Sumner," and the

Dred Scott case convinced many Northerners that Southerners were conspiring with the federal government to restrict their political and economic liberties. Southerners interpreted the response to these same events as evidence of a northern conspiracy to gain increased power in the federal government and reduce the South's political and economic influence. There were no conspiracies, but with so little goodwill on either side, hostility predominated. Slavery, above all, accounted for the growing divide.

When abolitionist John Brown, who had avenged the "sack of Lawrence" in 1856, led a raid against a federal arsenal at Harpers Ferry, Virginia, in 1859 in the vain hope of sparking a slave revolt, he brought the frustrations of both sides of the sectional conflict to a head. The presidential election campaign of 1860 began before the uproar over the raid had subsided. In the course of that contest, one of the last nationally unifying institutions, the Democratic party, broke apart. The election of Abraham Lincoln, an avowedly sectional candidate, triggered a crisis that defied peaceful resolution.

Although the crisis spiraled into a civil war, this outcome did not signal the triumph of sectionalism over nationalism. Ironically, in defending their stands, both sides appealed to time-honored nationalist and democratic sentiments. Southern secessionists believed they were the true keepers of the ideals that had inspired the American Revolution. They were merely re-creating a more perfect Union. It was not they, but the Republicans, who had sundered the old Union by subverting the Constitution's guarantee of liberty. Lincoln similarly appealed to nationalist themes, telling Northerners that the United States was "the last best hope on earth."

Northerners and Southerners both appealed to nationalism and democracy but applied different meanings to those concepts. These differences underscored how far apart the sections had grown. When Southerners and Northerners looked at each other, they no longer saw fellow Americans; they saw enemies.

NORTH–SOUTH DIFFERENCES

Behind the ideological divide that separated North and South lay real and growing social and economic differences (see the Overview table, "South and North Compared in 1860"). As the North became increasingly urban and industrial, the South remained primarily rural and agricultural. The urban population of the free states increased from 10 to 26 percent between 1820 and 1860. In the South, in the same period, it increased only from 5 to 10 percent. Likewise the proportion of the northern work force in agriculture declined from 68 percent to 40 percent between 1800 and 1860, whereas in the South it increased from 82 percent to 84 percent. Northern farmers made up for the decline in farm workers by relying on machinery instead. In 1860, the free states had twice the value of farm machinery per worker as the slave states had.

Overview

South and North Compared in 1860

	South	North
Population	Biracial; 35 percent African American	Overwhelmingly white; less than 2 percent African American
Economy	Growing though relatively undiversified; 84 percent of work force in agriculture	Developing through industrialization and urbanization; 40 percent of workforce in agriculture
Labor	Heavily dependent on slave labor, especially in Lower South	Free wage labor
Factories	15 percent of national total	85 percent of national total; concentrated in the Northeast
Railroads	Approximately ten thousand miles of track; primarily shorter lines, with fewer links to trunk lines	Approximately twenty thousand miles of track; more effectively linked in trunk lines connecting east and west
Literacy	17 percent illiteracy rate for free population	6 percent illiteracy rate

The demand for farm machinery in the North reflected growing demand for manufactured products in general. The need of city-dwellers for ready-to-wear shoes and clothing, household iron products, processed foods, homes, workplaces, and public amenities boosted industrial production in the North. In contrast, in the South, the slower rate of urbanization, the lower proportion of immigrants, and the region's labor-intensive agriculture kept industrial development modest. The proportion of manufacturing capital invested in the South declined from 31 to 16 percent between 1810 and 1860. In 1810, per capita investment in industrial enterprises was 2.5 times greater in the North than in the South; in 1860, it was 3.5 times greater.

The rate of urban and industrial growth in the North was greater than anywhere else in the world in the early nineteenth century. As a result, the South inevitably suffers by comparison. Even when compared to the West, however, the South was falling behind. The South and West had about the same levels of manufacturing investment and urban population in the 1850s, but the rate of growth was even greater in the West than in the North. What is more, a vast railroad network linked the West to the Northeast rather than the South (see Map 14–3).

MAP 14-3   Railroads in the United States, 1860
A vast network of railroads honeycombed the North and West by 1860. While the South made considerable progress in railroad construction during the 1850s, its lines had many different gauges, and it lacked suitable connections to the West.

More subtle distinctions between North and South became evident as well by midcentury. Southerners tended to be more violent than Northerners. The slave states had a higher homicide rate than the free states, and more Southerners carried weapons. Southern values stressed courtesy, honor, and courage. Southerners were more inclined to military service than Northerners. They had proportionately more cadets enrolled in the United States Military Academy at West Point; more than 60 percent of the volunteer soldiers for the Mexican War hailed from the South; and, excluding West Point and the Naval Academy at Annapolis, seven of the nation's eight military colleges were located in the South.

The South had a high illiteracy rate, nearly three times greater than the North—eight times greater if black Southerners are included. The "ideology of literacy," as one historian called it, was not as widespread in the South as in the North. Northerners, for example, supported far more public schools and libraries than Southerners. In the South, education was barred by law to slaves and limited for most white people. Many white leaders viewed education more as a privilege for the well-to-do than a right for every citizen. A South Carolinian wrote in the 1850s that "it is better that a part should be fully and highly educated and the rest utterly ignorant."

Evangelical Protestantism attracted increasing numbers in both North and South, but its character differed in the two regions. The Methodist Church divided along sectional lines over slavery in 1844, and the Baptists split the following year. The Presbyterians splintered in 1837 over mainly doctrinal issues, but the rupture became complete in 1861. In the North, evangelical Protestants viewed social reform as a prerequisite for the Second Coming of Christ. As a result, they were in the forefront of most reform movements. Southern evangelicals generally defended slavery.

Slavery accounted for many of the differences between the North and the South. Investment in land and slaves limited investment in manufacturing. The availability of a large slave labor force reduced the need for farm machinery and limited the demand for manufactured products. Slaves were relatively immobile. They did not migrate to cities in massive numbers as did northern farmers. Nor could they quickly fill the labor demands of an expanding urban economy. Agriculture usually took precedence.

Slavery also divided northern from southern churches. And it accounted for the contrast between the inward, otherworldly emphasis of southern theology and the reformist theology of northern evangelicals. Southerners associated black slavery with white freedom; Northerners associated it with white degradation.

· Slavery contributed to the South's martial tradition and its lukewarm attitude toward public education. Fully 95 percent of the nation's black population lived in the South in 1860, and 90 percent of these were slaves. As a result, the South was often a region on edge. Fearful of revolt, especially in the 1850s, when rumors of slave discontent ran rampant, white people felt compelled to maintain patrols and militias in constant readiness. The South was also determined to keep slaves as ignorant as possible. Educated slaves would be susceptible to abolitionist propaganda and more inclined to revolt.

The South's defense of slavery and the North's attack on it fostered an array of stereotypes that exaggerated the real differences between the sections. Like all stereotypes, these reduced individuals to dehumanized categories. They encouraged the people of each section to view those of the other less as fellow Americans than as aliens in their midst.

Southerners saw Northerners as crass and materialistic but themselves as generous and compassionate. Northerners saw Southerners as brutal and backward, themselves as progressive and temperate. Southerners perceived themselves as honorable and chaste and saw Northerners as corrupt and loose living. Northerners saw Southerners as perverse and lazy, themselves as righteous and hardworking. The South, according to Southerners, was the land of moonlight and magnolias (an image actually originated in the North), while the North was the region of muggings and mudslinging. Northerners saw Southerners as lords of the lash and themselves as angels of mercy.

Ironically, although slavery increasingly defined the character of the South in the 1850s, a growing majority of white Southerners did not own slaves. Slavery nonetheless implicated nonslaveholders in ways that assured their support for it. By satisfying the demand for labor on large plantations, it relieved many rural white Southerners from serving as farmhands and enabled them to work their own land. Slaveholders also recruited nonslaveholders to suppress slave violence or rebellion. It was nonslaveholders, for example, who often manned patrols and militia companies. Some nonslaveholders hoped to purchase slaves someday. Many dreamed of migrating westward to the next cotton frontier where they might find greater opportunity to own land and slaves. This dream not only bound white Southerners together on slavery but also prompted their strong support for southern access to the western territories. Finally, regardless of a white man's social or economic status, he shared an important feature with the largest slaveholder: As long as racial slavery existed, the color of his skin made him a member of a privileged class that could never be enslaved.

While white Southerners were more united on slavery than on other issues, their defense of slavery presented them with a major dilemma. It left them vulnerable to moral condemnation because, in the end, slavery was morally indefensible. By the 1850s, most western nations had condemned and abolished the institution. And because Northerners controlled the flow of information through the popular newspapers and the national network of communications, credit, and commerce, Southerners were likely to find themselves increasingly isolated. A minority in their own country and a lonely voice for a despised institution that was for them a significant source of wealth, Southerners were understandably jittery.

JOHN BROWN'S RAID

Shortly after he completed his mayhem at Pottawatomie Creek, John Brown left Kansas and approached several New England abolitionists for funds to continue his private war in the territory. By 1857, Brown had become a rustic celebrity in New England. He had dined at Ralph Waldo Emerson's home, had tea with Henry David Thoreau, and discussed theology with the abolitionist minister Theodore Dwight

Weld. Brown's frontier dress, rigid posture, reticent manner, and piercing eyes gave him the appearance of a biblical prophet. After several failed businesses, more than twenty lawsuits for nonpayment of debts, and a brush with horse rustling, he had at last found his life's calling: He had become a moderately successful fund-raiser for his own violent frontier exploits.

But when Brown returned to Kansas in late 1857, he discovered that peace had settled over that troubled territory. Residents now cared more about making money than about making war. Leaving Kansas for the last time, he went east with a new plan. He proposed to attack and capture the federal arsenal at Harpers Ferry, Virginia, a small town near the Maryland border. The assault, Brown imagined, would spark a slave uprising in the area, eventually spreading to the rest of the state. With funds from his New England friends, he equipped a few dozen men and hired an English army officer to train them.

When Brown outlined his scheme to Frederick Douglass, the noted black abolitionist warned him against it. But his white New England friends were less cautious, and a group of six prominent abolitionists (the "Secret Six") gave Brown additional funds for his project.

Brown and his "army" moved to a Maryland farmhouse in the summer of 1859 to train and complete planning for the raid. On the night of October 16, 1859, he and twenty-two followers captured the federal arsenal at Harpers Ferry and waited for the slaves to rally to his banner. Meanwhile, the townspeople alerted outside authorities. The Virginia militia and a detachment of United States Marines under the command of Colonel Robert E. Lee arrived and put a quick end to **John Brown's Raid**. They wounded Brown and killed or captured most of his force.

Brown had launched the operation without provisions and at a site from which escape was impossible. Although the primary goal of the attack had been to inspire a slave insurrection, no one had bothered to inform the local slaves. And despite the secret nature of the expedition, Brown had left behind a mountain of documents at the Maryland farmhouse. He had tried to conquer the state of Virginia with twenty-two men and an ill-conceived plan. Was he crazy? As the *Boston Post* editorialized after the raid, "John Brown may be a lunatic, [but if so] then one-fourth of the people of Massachusetts are madmen."

Although the *Post* may have exaggerated, the editorial reflected an article of faith among many abolitionists that, given the signal, slaves would immediately throw off their chains, slaughter their masters, and join a rebellion. But even those slaves in the area who knew of the raid understood the odds against Brown

JOHN BROWN AT HARPER'S FERRY.

John Brown's ill-planned raid at Harpers Ferry, Virginia, nears its desperate end as the trapped abolitionist and his supporters fall to a contingent of U.S. Marines led by Colonel Robert E. Lee, October 18, 1859.

and had the good sense not to join him. As Abraham Lincoln observed, "It was not a slave insurrection. It was an attempt by white men to get up a revolt among slaves, in which the slaves refused to participate."

The raid, though foolish and unsuccessful, played on Southerners' worst fears of slave rebellion, adding a new dimension: Here was an attack engineered not from within the South but from the North. Some southern white people may have dismissed the ability or even the desire of slaves to mount revolts on their own, but they less easily dismissed the potential impact of outside white agitators.

The state of Virginia tried Brown on the charge of treason to the state. Brown, recovering from his wounds, attended most of the trial on a stretcher. The trial was swift but fair. The jury sentenced Brown to hang. Throughout his brief imprisonment and trial, Brown maintained a quiet dignity that impressed even his jailers. The governor of Virginia spoke admiringly of him as "a man of clear head, of courage, fortitude, and simple ingenuousness." Speaking to the court after his sentencing, Brown suggested that he was God's agent in a holy war: "I believe that to have interfered as I have done . . . in behalf of [God's] despised poor, is no wrong, but right. Now, if it is deemed necessary that I should forfeit my life for the furtherance of the ends of justice, and mingle my blood further with the blood of my children and with the blood of millions in this slave country whose rights are disregarded by wicked, cruel, and unjust enactments, I say, let it be done."

Some Northerners compared Brown's execution with the death of a religious martyr. The abolitionist William Lloyd Garrison asked readers of *The Liberator* to "let the day of [Brown's] execution . . . be the occasion of such a public moral demonstration against the bloody and merciless slave system as the land has never witnessed." When the state of Virginia hanged Brown, church bells tolled across the North. Thoreau compared Brown with Jesus and called the abolitionist "an angel of light." Emerson observed that Brown would "make the gallows glorious like the cross." Writing to Margaretta Mason, wife of the Virginia senator James M. Mason, abolitionist Lydia Maria Child asserted that "in this enlightened age, all despotisms ought to come to an end by the agency of moral and rational means. But if they resist such agencies, it is in the order of Providence that they must come to an end by violence." Most Northerners, however, including many Republicans, had condemned the raid. Still, the dignity of Brown's death touched many. Condemning the deed, they nevertheless embraced the cause.

The outpouring of northern grief over Brown's death convinced white Southerners that the threat to their security was not over. The discovery of Brown's correspondence at his Maryland farmhouse further fueled southern rancor, and Southerners increasingly ceased to believe northern disclaimers about the raid. Senator Mason asserted in Congress that "John Brown's invasion was condemned [in the North] only because it failed." Several members of the Secret Six had ties to the Republican party, and Southerners targeted them for special censure. Mississippi senator Jefferson Davis remarked that the Republican party "was organized on the basis of making war" against the South.

John Brown's Raid significantly changed southern public opinion. However much they defended slavery, most Southerners were for the Union. The northern reaction to John Brown's trial and death, however, troubled them. The *Richmond Whig*, a newspaper that had reflected moderate Upper South opinion for decades, observed in early 1860 that "recent events have wrought almost a complete revolution in the sentiments, the thoughts, the hopes, of the oldest and steadiest conservatives in all the southern states. . . . There are thousands upon . . . thousands of men in our midst who, a month ago, scoffed at the idea of a dissolution of the Union as a madman's dream, but who now hold the opinion that its days are numbered, its glory perished."

It was one thing to condemn slavery in the territories but another to attack it violently where it was long established. Southerners now saw in the Republican party the embodiment of John Brown's ideals and actions. So, in their view, the election of a Republican president would be a death sentence for the South.

The impact of this shifting sentiment was immediately apparent in Congress when it reconvened three days after Virginia hanged Brown. Debate quickly turned tense and ugly. South Carolina Senator James H. Hammond captured the mood well, when he remarked of his colleagues on the Senate floor that "the only persons who do not have a revolver and a knife are those who have two revolvers." The southern and northern wings of the Democratic party were now almost totally estranged. Southern Democrats seemed concerned only to promote an extreme proslavery agenda rather than to initiate real legislation.

THE ELECTION OF 1860

An atmosphere of mutual sectional distrust and animosity characterized the campaign for the presidential election of 1860. In April, the Democratic party, the sole surviving national political organization, held its convention in Charleston, South Carolina. The location was not conducive to sectional reconciliation. The city had been a hotbed of nullification sentiment during the 1830s, and talk of disunion had surfaced periodically ever since, especially in the influential *Charleston Mercury*, edited by Robert Barnwell Rhett. At the convention, Charlestonians packed the galleries and cheered for their favorite extremists.

Northern Democrats arrived in Charleston united behind Stephen A. Douglas. Although they constituted a majority of the delegates, they could not muster the two-thirds majority vote necessary to nominate their candidate. Other issues, however, were decided on a simple majority vote, permitting northern Democrats to defeat a platform proposal for a federal slave code in the territories.

Southern extremists who favored secession hoped to disrupt the convention and divide the party. They reasoned that the Republicans would then win the presidency, providing the South with the justification to secede. The platform vote gave them the opportunity they were seeking. Accompanied by spectators' cheers, delegates from five Lower South states—South Carolina, Florida, Mississippi, Louisiana, and Texas—walked out. The Arkansas and Georgia delegations joined them the following day.

Still without a nominee, the Democrats agreed to reconvene in Baltimore in June. This time, the Upper South delegations marched out when Douglas Democrats, in a commanding majority, refused to seat the Lower South delegations that had walked out in Charleston. The remaining delegates nominated

Douglas for president. The bolters, who included almost all southern delegates plus a few Northerners loyal to President Buchanan, met in another hall and nominated John C. Breckinridge of Kentucky.

The disintegration of the national Democratic party alarmed those Southerners who understood that it would insure the election of a Republican president in November. The *Memphis Appeal* warned that "the odium of the Black-Republican party has been that it is *Sectional.*" Should Southerners now allow a group of "restless and reckless or misguided men to destroy the national Democratic party?" the *Appeal* asked. Its emphatic answer was, "No!"

The *Appeal* reflected the sentiment of many former Whigs, mainly from the Upper South, who would not support Breckinridge and could not support Douglas. Together with Whig allies in the North who had not defected to the Republican party, they met in Baltimore in May 1860 to form the **Constitutional Union Party** and nominated John Bell of Tennessee for president.

Sensing victory, the Republicans convened in Chicago. If they could hold the states won by Frémont in 1856, add Minnesota (a new Republican-leaning state), and win Pennsylvania and one of three other Lower North states—Illinois, Indiana, or New Jersey—their candidate would win. These calculations dictated a platform and a candidate who could appeal to the four Lower North swing states, where antislavery sentiment was not so strong.

The issue of slavery in the territories had dominated the Republicans' 1856 platform. Now they embraced other issues as well, presenting themselves as the party of sound economy, business, and industry. Delegates enthusiastically cheered a tariff plank calling for the protection of American industry.

In selecting an appropriate presidential nominee, the Republicans faced a dilemma. Senator William H. Seward came to Chicago as the leading Republican candidate. But his immoderate condemnation of Southerners and slavery made moderate northern voters wary of him, and these were precisely the voters the party needed for victory.

Reservations about Seward benefited Abraham Lincoln. A year after his losing 1858 Senate campaign, he had embarked on a speaking tour of the East at the invitation of influential newspaper editor Horace Greeley. Lincoln's lieutenants at the convention stressed their candidate's moderation and morality, distancing him from both the abolitionists and Seward. Moreover, Chicago was Lincoln's home turf, and he had many friends working for him at the convention. When Seward faltered, Lincoln rose and won the Republican nomination.

True to their Whig heritage, the Republicans staged a colorful campaign, featuring drill teams as well as organized groups of young men called the **Wide Awakes**, outfitted in flowing black oilcloth capes. Douglas supporters countered by enrolling teams of "Little Giants." Breckinridge and Bell followed suit, and soon large groups of young men were marching all over the country in support of one candidate or another. The theme was political, but the atmosphere was an odd mix of military parade and religious revival.

The presidential campaign of 1860 actually comprised two campaigns. In the South, the contest was between Breckinridge and Bell; in the North, it was Lincoln against Douglas. Breckinridge and Bell had scattered support in the North, as did Douglas in the South, but in the main this was a sectional election. Lincoln did not even appear on the ballot in most southern states.

Lincoln's strategy was to say practically nothing. He spent the entire campaign in Springfield, Illinois. When he did speak, it was to a reporter or friends, but not in a public forum. He discounted southern threats of disunion if he were to become president. Other Republicans dismissed southern talk of secession as well. Republican leaders thought the South too fragmented to unite behind a move as drastic as disunion. "The South," Greeley wrote dismissively, "could no more unite upon a scheme of secession than a company of lunatics could conspire to break out of bedlam."

Douglas campaigned hard, trying to convince the electorate that the Union hung in the balance. Breckinridge, like Lincoln in the North, sought to assure voters that he was not the disunion candidate. And Bell ran a low-key campaign, venturing out of Tennessee infrequently. He reiterated his support of the Constitution and the Union but said little else.

In those days, states held gubernatorial elections on different days, even in different months, from the national presidential election. When, in mid-October, Republicans had swept the statehouses in two crucial states—Pennsylvania and Indiana—Douglas made an extraordinary decision, but one consistent with his ardent nationalism. He abandoned his campaign and headed south at great personal peril to urge Southerners to remain in the Union now that Lincoln's election was inevitable.

Lincoln became the nation's sixteenth president, with 40 percent of the popular vote (see Map 14–4). Bell won the three Upper South states of Virginia, Kentucky, and Tennessee. Douglas, though second

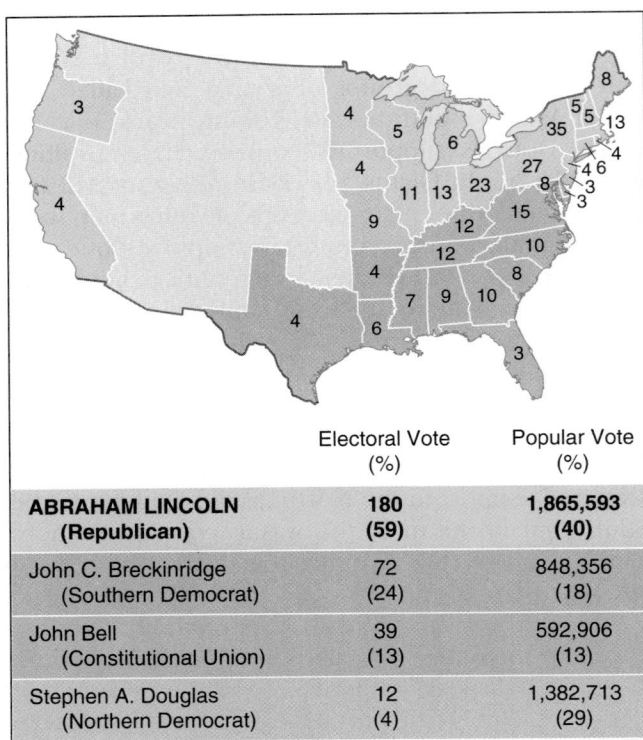

	Electoral Vote (%)	Popular Vote (%)
ABRAHAM LINCOLN (Republican)	**180** **(59)**	**1,865,593** **(40)**
John C. Breckinridge (Southern Democrat)	72 (24)	848,356 (18)
John Bell (Constitutional Union)	39 (13)	592,906 (13)
Stephen A. Douglas (Northern Democrat)	12 (4)	1,382,713 (29)

MAP 14-4 The Election of 1860
The election returns from 1860 vividly illustrate the geography of sectionalism.

after Lincoln in the popular balloting, won the undivided electoral vote of only one state, Missouri.

Lincoln took most northern states by significant margins and won all the region's electoral votes except three in New Jersey. This gave him a substantial majority of 180 electoral votes. Breckinridge won eleven southern states but received a majority of the popular vote cast in just four. In the South as a whole, his opponents, Bell and Douglas, together reaped 55 percent of the popular vote, confirming Republicans' skepticism about southern determination to secede.

The urban vote in the 1860 election is intriguing. Lincoln fared worst in the larger cities of the North, and urban voters drubbed Breckinridge in the South. City-dwellers tended to vote for the centrist candidates, Douglas and Bell. The close commercial ties of North and South, the tendency of immigrants in northern cities to vote Democratic, and the concern of affluent urban residents that disunion could bring economic uncertainty motivated their votes. The owners of large plantations in the South similarly had a strong economic interest in preserving the Union and tended to vote for the southern centrist, Bell. But the United States was still a nation mostly of farms and small towns,

and rural communities returned strong majorities for Lincoln in the North and Breckinridge in the South.

SECESSION BEGINS

The events following Lincoln's election demonstrated how wildly mistaken were those who dismissed southern threats of secession. Four days after Lincoln's victory, the South Carolina legislature called on the state's citizens to elect delegates to a convention to consider secession. Meeting on December 20, the delegates voted unanimously to leave the Union. By February 1, six other states—Mississippi, Florida, Alabama, Georgia, Louisiana, and Texas—had all held similar conventions and decided to leave the Union (see Map 14–5). Representatives from the seven seceding states met to form a separate country, the **Confederate States of America**. On February 18, Jefferson Davis was sworn in as its president.

Curiously, for a people trumpeting the virtues of democratic government, no seceding state submitted its secession ordinance for popular referendum. Further, though subsequent generations of white southerners would dwell on states' rights as the precipitating cause of secession, leaders of the new Confederate nation emphasized slavery as the state right most valued. A month after the formation of the Confederacy, Alexander H. Stephens of Georgia, vice president of the new government, praised the just-framed Confederate Constitution in the following words:

> [T]he new Constitution has put at rest forever all the agitating questions relating to our peculiar institution—African slavery as it exists amongst us—the proper status of the negro in our form of civilization. This was the immediate cause of the late rupture and present revolution . . . . Our new Government'[s] . . . foundations are laid, its cornerstone rests, upon the great truth that the negro is not equal to the white man; that slavery, subordination to the superior race, is his natural and normal condition. [Applause.] This, our new Government, is the first, in the history of the world, based upon this great physical, philosophical, and moral truth.

The swiftness of secession in the Lower South obscured divisions in most states over the issue. Secessionists barely secured a majority in the Georgia and Louisiana conventions. In Mississippi, Florida, and Alabama, the secessionist majority was more comfortable, but pro-Union candidates polled a significant minority of votes. With Lincoln headed for the White House, the greatest support for secession came from large land-

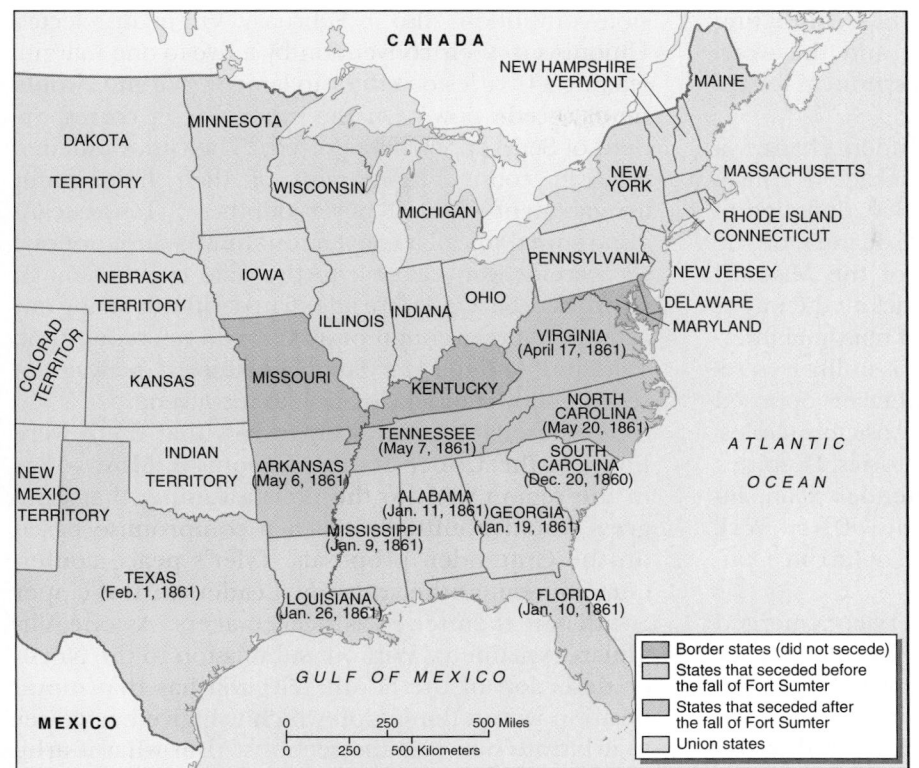

MAP 14-5   The Course of Secession
Before the firing on Fort Sumter in April 1861, the Confederacy consisted primarily of states in the Lower South. After Sumter, and after President Lincoln called upon them for troops, the Upper South states of Virginia, North Carolina, Tennessee, and Arkansas seceded.

owners in counties in which slaves comprised a majority of the population. Support for secession was weakest among small, nonslaveholding farmers.

Secessionists mounted an effective propaganda campaign, deftly using the press to convince voters to elect their delegates to the state conventions. Framing the issue as a personal challenge to every southern citizen, they argued that it would be cowardly to remain in the Union, a submission to despotism and enslavement. Southerners, they maintained, were the true heirs to the spirit of 1776. Lincoln and the Republicans were like King George III and the British—they meant to deny Southerners the right to life, liberty, and the pursuit of happiness.

Unionists, in response, could only offer voters a wait-and-see strategy. By remaining in the Union, they argued, Southerners could extract concessions from the Republicans that would protect their institutions.

PRESIDENTIAL INACTION

Because Lincoln would not take office until March 4, 1861, it was the Buchanan administration that had to cope with the secession crisis during the critical months of December and January. The president's failure to work out a solution with Congress as secession fever swept the Lower South further undermined Unionist forces in the seceding states.

When Buchanan lost the support of northern Democrats over the Lecompton Constitution, he turned to the South for support and filled his cabinet with Southerners. Now, facing the secession crisis, he proposed holding a constitutional convention to amend the Constitution in ways that would satisfy the South's demands on slavery. This outright surrender to southern demands, however, had no chance of passing in Congress.

Thereafter, Buchanan's administration quickly fell apart. As the Lower South states left the Union, their representatives and senators left Washington, and with them went Buchanan's closest advisers and key cabinet officials. Commenting on the emotionally charged atmosphere in the Senate as prominent Southerners gave their farewells and departed, one observer wrote, "There was everywhere a feeling of suspense, as if, visibly, the pillars of the temple were being withdrawn and the great Government structure was tottering."

Buchanan, a lame duck, bereft of friends and advisers, did little more than condemn secession. He was reluctant to take action that would limit the options of the incoming administration or, worse, tip the balance in the Upper South toward secession. He hoped that waiting might bring an isolated Lower South to its senses and give efforts to mediate the sectional rift a chance to succeed.

PEACE PROPOSALS

Previous sectional conflicts, dating from the Missouri Compromise of 1820, had brought forth the ingenuity and good will of political leaders to effect a compromise and draw the Union back from the brink of disintegration. Both ingenuity and good will were scarce commodities in the gray secession winter of 1860–1861. Yet, a few men believed that the opportunity, though slim, for compromise still existed. The difficulty was that the two conflicting sides had little trust of each other and the word "compromise" was viewed as more a synonym for capitulation than salvation.

Kentucky senator John J. Crittenden chaired a Senate committee that proposed a package of constitutional amendments in December 1860, designed to solve the sectional crisis. The central feature of the Crittenden Plan was the extension of the Missouri Compromise line through the territories all the way to the state of California. The plan was of marginal interest to the South, however, because it was unlikely to result in any new slave states. And Republicans opposed it because it contradicted one of their basic principles, the exclusion of slavery from the territories. Despite a flood of letters supporting the Crittenden Plan, including a petition from 38,000 citizens of New York City, Republicans successfully bottled it up in Congress and prevented action on it.

Meanwhile, ex-president John Tyler emerged from retirement to lead an effort by the border states—the Upper South and the Lower North—to forge a peace. Delegates from these states responded to Tyler's invitation and met in February 1861 at the Willard Hotel in Washington. But the plan the conference produced differed little from Crittenden's, and it, too, got nowhere in Congress.

LINCOLN'S VIEWS ON SECESSION

President-elect Lincoln monitored the secession of the Lower South states and the attempts to reach a compromise from his home in Springfield. Although he said nothing publicly, he made it known that he did not favor compromises like those proposed by Crittenden and Tyler. As he put it to a friend, "We have just carried an election on principles fairly stated to the people. Now we are told in advance, the government shall be broken up, unless we surrender to those we have beaten, before we take the offices. . . . If we surrender, it is the end of us, and of the government."

Lincoln counted on Unionist sentiment to keep the Upper South from seceding. Like Buchanan, he felt that the longer the Lower South states remained isolated, the more likely they would be to return to the fold. For a while, events seemed to bear him out. In North Carolina, the *Wilmington Herald* responded to South Carolina's secession by asking readers, "Will you suffer yourself to be spit upon in this way? Are you submissionists to the dictation of South Carolina . . . are you to be called cowards because you do not follow the crazy lead of that crazy state?"

One by one, Upper South states registered their support for the Union. North Carolinians went to the polls in February and turned down the call for a secession convention. Also in February, Virginians elected Unionists to their convention by a five-to-one margin, leading a Charleston editor to lament, "Virginia would never secede now." On the other side, a correspondent of Senator Seward rejoiced, "The Gulf Confederacy can count Virginia out of their little family arrangement—she will never join them." Tennesseans also refused to call a convention. In Missouri, not one secessionist won election to the state convention. In Kentucky, the legislature adjourned without taking any action on a convention or a statewide referendum on secession. And the Maryland legislature, already out of session, showed no inclination to reconvene.

A closer look, however, reveals that there were limits to the Upper South's Unionism. Most voters in the region went to the polls assuming that Congress would eventually reach a compromise based on the Crittenden proposals, Tyler's peace conference, or some other remedy. Leaders in the Upper South saw themselves as peacemakers. As one Virginian explained, "Without submission to the North or desertion of the South, Virginia has that moral position within the Union which will give her power to arbitrate between the sections." But what if arbitration failed? Or what if the Lower South states precipitated a crisis that forced the Upper South to choose sides? It was unlikely that the Upper South would abide the use of federal force against its southern neighbors.

Lincoln believed that the slavery issue had to come to a crisis before the nation could solve it. Although he said in public that he would never interfere with slavery in the slave states, the deep moral revulsion he felt toward the institution left him more ambivalent in private. As he confided to a colleague in 1860, "The tug has to come, and better now, than any time hereafter" (see "American Views: Lincoln on Slavery").

FORT SUMTER: THE TUG COMES

In his inaugural address on March 4, 1861, Abraham Lincoln denounced secession and vowed to uphold federal law but tempered his firmness with a conciliatory conclusion. Addressing Southerners specifically, he assured them, "We are not enemies but friends. . . . Though passion may have strained, it must not break our bonds of affection. The mystic chords of memory, stretching from every battlefield, and patriot grave, to every living heart and hearthstone, all over this broad land, will yet swell the chorus of the Union, when again touched, as surely they will be, by the better angels of our nature."

Southerners wanted concessions, not conciliation, however. The new president said nothing about slavery in the territories, nothing about constitutional

Overview

The Emerging Sectional Crisis

Event	Year	Effect
Wilmot Proviso	1846	Congressman David Wilmot's proposal to ban slavery from territories acquired from Mexico touched off a bitter sectional dispute in Congress.
Compromise of 1850	1850	Law admitted California as a free state, granted the population of Utah and New Mexico Territories the right to decide on slavery, and established a new and stronger Fugitive Slave Act, all of which "solved" the territorial issue raised by the Wilmot Proviso but satisfied neither North nor South and planted the seeds of future conflict.
Election of 1852	1852	Results confirmed demise of the Whig party, initiating a period of political realignment.
Kansas-Nebraska Act	1854	Law created the Kansas and Nebraska Territories and repealed the Missouri Compromise of 1820 by leaving the question of slavery to the territories' residents. Its passage enraged many Northerners, prompting some to form the new Republican party.
"Bleeding Kansas"	1855–1856	Sometimes violent conflict between pro- and antislavery forces in Kansas further polarized the sectional debate.
Election of 1856	1856	Presidency was won by Democrat James Buchanan of Pennsylvania, but a surprisingly strong showing by the recently formed Republican party in the North set the stage for the 1860 election.
Dred Scott Case	1857	The Supreme Court ruling that slaves were not citizens and that Congress had no authority to ban slavery from the territories boosted Republican prospects in the North.
Lecompton	1857	Proslavery document, framed by a fraudulently elected Constitution convention in Kansas and supported by President Buchanan, further convinced Northerners that the South was subverting their rights.
John Brown's Raid	1859	Unsuccessful attempt to free the South's slaves, this attack on a federal arsenal in Harpers Ferry, Virginia, increased sectional tension.
Election of 1860	1860	Republican Abraham Lincoln won a four-way race for the presidency. The last major national party, the Democrats, disintegrated. Lower South states seceded.
Fort Sumter	1861	Confederate forces attacked the fort in April 1861, Lincoln called for troops, and several Upper South states seceded. The Civil War was underway.

amendments proposed by Crittenden and Tyler, and nothing about the release of federal property in the South to the Confederacy. Even some Northerners hoping for an olive branch were disappointed. As one Ohio editor wrote, Lincoln's policies would "stain the soil and color the waters of the entire continent." But Lincoln was hoping for time—time to get the Lower South states quarreling with one another, time to allow Union sentiment to build in the Upper South,

and time to convince Northerners that the Union needed preserving. He did not get that time.

One day after Lincoln's inauguration, Major Robert Anderson (like Lincoln, a native Kentuckian), the commander of **Fort Sumter** in Charleston harbor, informed the administration that he had only four to six weeks' worth of provisions left. Sumter was one of three southern forts still under federal control. Confederate batteries had ringed the fort, and Anderson

AMERICAN VIEWS

Lincoln on Slavery

In the weeks after the 1860 election, northern and southern leaders sought out President-elect Abraham Lincoln for his views on slavery. Yet, Lincoln had spoken often on the institution in the years immediately preceding the election. His speech two years earlier, excerpted here, offered an unequivocal statement of Lincoln's moral and philosophical opposition to slavery. Implied in that speech was the fact that the contradiction between American ideals and slavery could not be brokered, compromised, or ignored.

- How do Lincoln's actions from his election in November 1860 to the firing on Fort Sumter in April 1861 reflect the principles enunciated in his Springfield address?

- The two letters, one to fellow Illinois Republican Lyman Trumbull and the other to Virginia Democrat John A. Gilmer, indicate Lincoln's firm opposition to the extension of slavery into the territories. Are they consistent with the views expressed in Springfield two years earlier?

- Despite the difference in tone, do you think the letters both say essentially the same thing?

Speech of Hon. Abraham Lincoln
Springfield, Illinois, June 17, 1858
We are now far into the fifth year since policy was initiated with the avowed object and confident promise of putting an end to slavery agitation. Under the operation of that policy, that agitation has not only not ceased, but has constantly augmented. In my opinion, it will not cease until a crisis shall have been reached and passed. "A house divided against itself can-

---

estimated that only a force of at least twenty thousand troops could run the gauntlet and provision and defend the fort. Anderson assumed that Lincoln would understand the hopeless arithmetic and order him to evacuate Fort Sumter. The commanding general of the army, Winfield Scott, advised the president accordingly, as did many members of his cabinet. Lincoln stalled.

News of Anderson's plight changed the mood in the North. The Slave Power, some said, was holding him and his men hostage. Frustration grew over Lincoln's silence and inaction. The Confederacy's bold resolve seemed to contrast sharply with the federal government's confusion and inertia. "The bird of our country," cracked New York diarist George Templeton Strong, "is a debilitated chicken, disguised in eagle feathers . . . . We are a weak, divided, disgraced people unable to maintain our institutional existence."

By the end of March, nearly a month after Anderson had informed Lincoln of the situation at Fort Sumter, the president finally moved. By this time, northern public opinion and Lincoln's cabinet (with Secretary of State Seward a notable exception) favored an effort to provision Major Anderson.

Seward made a last, desperate attempt to avert armed conflict by drawing on the reservoir of common American nationalism. He suggested that Lincoln trump up charges of Spanish and French aggression in the Caribbean and convene Congress to declare war. Seward hoped that his absurd plan would draw seceding states back into the Union to make common cause against Spain and France. Lincoln politely rejected the advice and ordered an expedition to provision Fort Sumter.

The president still hoped to avoid a confrontation. He did not send the troops that Anderson had not stand." I believe this government cannot endure permanently half slave and half free. I do not expect the Union to be dissolved; I do not expect the house to fall; but I do expect it will cease to be divided. It will become all one thing, or the other . . . . So I say in relation to the principle that all men are created equal, let it be as nearly reached as we can. If we cannot give freedom to every creature, let us do nothing that will impose slavery upon any other creature . . . . I leave you, hoping that the lamp of liberty will burn in your bosoms until there shall no longer be a doubt that all men are created free and equal.

> Springfield, Ills. Dec. 10, 1860
> Hon. L. Trumbull
> My dear Sir: Let there be no compromise on the question of extending slavery. If there be, all our labor is lost, and ere long, must be done again. The dangerous ground—that into which some of our friends have a hankering to run—is Pop[ular] Sov[ereignty]. Have none of it. Stand firm. The tug has to come, & better now, than any time hereafter. Yours as ever,
> A. Lincoln

> Springfield, Ill. Dec. 15, 1860
> Hon. John A. Gilmer:
> My dear Sir: . . . I have no thought of recommending the abolition of slavery in the District of Columbia, nor the slave trade among the slave states . . . and if I were to make such recommendation, it is quite clear Congress would not follow it. As to the use of patronage in the slave states, where there are few or no Republicans, I do not expect to inquire for the politics of the appointee, or whether he does or not own slaves . . . . In one word, I never have been, am not now, and probably never shall be, in a mood of harassing the people, either North or South. On the territorial question, I am inflexible . . . . On that, there is a difference between you and us; and it is the only substantial difference. You think slavery is right and ought to be extended; we think it is wrong and ought to be restricted. For this, neither has any just occasion to be angry with the other.
> Your obt. Servt.
> A. Lincoln

Source: John G. Nicolay and John Hay, eds., *Works of Abraham Lincoln, vol. 6* (New York, Century Co.,1905).

requested. Instead he ordered unarmed boats to proceed to the fort, deliver the provisions, and leave. Only if the Confederates fired on them were they to force their way into the fort with the help of armed reinforcements. Lincoln notified South Carolina authorities that he intended to do nothing more than "feed the hungry."

At Charleston, Confederate general P.G.T. Beauregard had standing orders to turn back any relief expedition. But President Davis wanted to take Sumter before the provisions arrived to avoid fighting Anderson and the reinforcements at the same time. He also realized that the outbreak of fighting could compel the Upper South to join the Confederacy. But his impatience to force the issue placed the Confederacy in the position of firing, unprovoked, on the American flag and at a man who had become a national hero.

On April 10, Davis ordered Beauregard to demand the immediate evacuation of Fort Sumter. Anderson refused but wondered what the hurry was, considering that his provisions would run out in a few days. The remark gave Beauregard pause and prompted additional negotiations. Anderson did not yield, and before dawn on April 12, 1861, the first Confederate shell whistled down on the fort. After more than a day of shelling, during which more than five thousand artillery rounds struck Fort Sumter, Anderson surrendered. Remarkably, neither side suffered any casualties, a deceptive beginning to an exceptionally bloody war.

When the verdict of Fort Sumter reached President Lincoln, he called on the southern states still in the Union to send troops to put down the rebellion. Refusing to make war on South Carolina, the Upper South states of Virginia, North Carolina, Tennessee,

FROM THEN TO NOW

Religion and Politics

When evangelical Protestantism first emerged in the late eighteenth century, its adherents advocated the separation of church and state. By the 1850s, however, the social landscape of America had changed. A wave of immigrants, many of them Roman Catholic, threatened Protestant dominance. Growing cities and rapid technological and economic change strained the traditional moral and social order. Alarmed by these changes, evangelicals entered the political arena. Their convictions, as we saw in Chapter 12, helped drive the antebellum reform movement.

The give and take of politics, however, posed a challenge to the evangelical belief in an absolute truth grounded in the Bible. Eventually the two great evangelical crusades of the 1850s—anti-Catholicism and abolitionism—were subsumed within the Republican Party. And after the Civil War, the Republican Party gradually lost its radical fervor.

By the twentieth century, the evangelical movement had begun to turn away from politics and revert to its traditional focus on saving souls. In 1950, Jerry Falwell, an emerging evangelical leader, declared himself "a soul-winner and a separatist," meaning he wanted little involvement with society at large, much less with politics. But then came the upheavals of the 1960s and 1970s that challenged traditional morality and authority, including the Supreme Court's decision in *Roe v. Wade* to legalize abortion. In addition, the Internal Revenue Service began questioning the tax-exempt status of various religious groups. Once again, a changing social landscape compelled evangelicals to enter the political arena, this time to defend themselves against what they perceived to be an encroaching government. Organizations emerged to mobilize evangelical voters, including Jerry Falwell's Moral Majority in the late 1970s and Pat Robertson's Christian Coalition in 1989.

In the 1850s the Northeast was the center of evangelical politics. Now evangelical political organizations speak with a mostly Southern accent. In the 1850s opposition to slavery was the focus

and Arkansas seceded, and the Confederacy expanded to eleven states.

CONCLUSION

When David Wilmot submitted his amendment to ban slavery from the territories gained from Mexico, he could not have foreseen that the debate he unleashed would end in civil war just fifteen years later. Northerners and Southerners had lived together in one nation for nearly eighty years. During that time, they had reached accommodations on slavery at the Constitutional Convention of 1787, in the Compromises of 1820 and 1850, and on numerous lesser occasions. But they could not reach agreement during the 1850s. By that time, the slavery issue had become weighted with so much moral and political freight that it defied easy resolution. Throughout the Western world, attitudes toward slavery were changing. Northern evan-

gelical Protestants in the 1840s and 1850s branded slavery a sin and slaveholders sinners. The overwhelming popularity of *Uncle Tom's Cabin* both tapped and fed this sentiment.

Political conflict over slavery coalesced around northern efforts to curtail southern expansion and power and southern attempts to maintain their power and influence in the federal government by planting the institution in the western territories. This conflict eventually helped undo the Compromise of 1850 and turned Stephen A. Douglas's railroad bill into a battle royal over Kansas. Unable to resolve sectional differences over slavery, the Whigs disintegrated, and the Democrats divided into northern and southern factions. The Republican party formed from the political debris. Ethnic and religious conflicts further disturbed the political landscape and contributed to party realignment.

Northerners and Southerners eventually interpreted any incident or piece of legislation as an attempt of evangelical politics. Now it is opposition to abortion and other social issues that have risen to prominence with the end of the Cold War and the nation's growing prosperity. Evangelical activists have once again found a home in the Republican Party. The Democrats, they believe, are too permissive and too committed to abortion rights, just as nineteenth century Democrats had been committed to the defense of slavery.

And again, as in the 1850s, evangelical involvement has heated political discourse with the language of righteousness. In 1992, Randall Terry, founder of Operation Rescue, a militant antiabortion organization, wrote in his newsletter that "to vote for Bill Clinton is to sin against God." In a similar if more flowery declaration, a New England evangelical journal proclaimed the 1856 presidential contest a choice between "the bloodstained ticket of the Democratic party, responsible for the murder of your brothers and mine on the plains of Kansas," and a Republican ticket designated by "the God of peace and purity as the one that shall smile upon you."

Most Americans today, as in the 1850s, recoil from the overt intrusion of religion into politics, and groups like the Christian Coalition have had only limited success in electing their favored candidates. Despite these disappointments, they have been as wary of compromise as their nineteenth-century predecessors. As one evangelical leader explained in 1999: "I would rather go to bed with a clear conscience after losing."

But if evangelical political organizations cannot gain control of Congress and the presidency, it is unlikely that their social agenda—which, in addition to antiabortion legislation, includes prayer in school, the posting of the Ten Commandments in public places, and laws restricting the rights of homosexuals—will be enacted. Today, some evangelical strategists call for a "popular front" approach, allying themselves with candidates not openly associated with the evangelical agenda. Abolitionists in the 1850s faced the same quandary between ideological purity and political pragmatism. Their support of Abraham Lincoln in 1860 reflected a bow toward pragmatism, a course that ultimately proved successful for their cause, but not without a bloody civil war.

by one side to gain moral and political advantage at the other's expense. Northerners viewed the Dred Scott decision, the Lecompton Constitution, and the southern reaction to John Brown's Raid as evidence of a Slave Power conspiracy to deny white Northerners their constitutional rights. Southerners interpreted northern reaction to these same events as evidence of a conspiracy to rob them of security and equality within the Union.

By 1861, the national political parties that had muted sectional animosities were gone, and so were national church organizations and fraternal associations. The ideals that had inspired the American Revolution remained in place, especially the importance of securing individual liberty against encroachment by government. But with each side interpreting them differently, these ideals served more to divide than to unite. Southerners viewed the North in general and the Republican party in particular as threats to their individual liberties. Lincoln's victory, they believed, robbed the national government of its traditional role as "a disinterested and dispassionate umpire." Northerners believed that the South was conspiring to rob them of their individual rights as well and that only a redeemed federal government stood between their freedom and the despotism of the Slave Power. Both sides claimed for themselves the role of guardian of the Revolutionary tradition. Lincoln's election left Northerners feeling vindicated and Southerners feeling vulnerable.

Ironically, as Americans in both sections talked of freedom and self-determination, the black men and women in their midst had little of either. Lincoln went to war to preserve the Union; Davis, to defend a new nation. Slavery was the spark that ignited the conflict, but white America seemed more comfortable embracing abstract ideals than real people. Northerners and Southerners would confront this irony during the bloodiest war in American history—but they would not resolve it.

REVIEW QUESTIONS

1. How do you account for the great success of Harriet Beecher Stowe's *Uncle Tom's Cabin?*

2. If you were a Democratic representative from your state to the U.S. Congress in 1854, what would your position be on the Kansas-Nebraska Bill? What if you were a Whig?

3. Discuss the role of evangelical religion in sharpening the sectional conflict between North and South.

4. Between the time he was elected president in November and his inauguration in March, what options did Abraham Lincoln have for resolving the sectional crisis?

5. Northerners and Southerners appealed to the same American ideals in support of their respective positions. Could they both have been correct?

KEY TERMS

"Bleeding Kansas" (p. 430)

Compromise of 1850 (p. 423)

Confederate States of America (p. 442)

Constitutional Union Party (p. 441)

Dred Scott Decision (p. 433)

Fort Sumter (p. 445)

Fugitive Slave Act (p. 423)

John Brown's Raid (p. 439)

Kansas-Nebraska Act (p. 429)

Know-Nothing Party (p. 431)

Lecompton Constitution (p. 434)

Lincoln-Douglas debates (p. 434)

Panic of 1857 (p. 434)

Popular Sovereignty (p. 420)

Republican Party (p. 431)

"Sack of Lawrence" (p. 430)

Wide Awakes (p. 441)

Wilmot Proviso (p. 419)

RECOMMENDED READING

Freehling, William W. *The Road to Disunion, Vol. 1: Secessionists at Bay, 1776–1854* (1990). A detailed and lively treatment of events and personalities in the years leading up to passage of the Kansas-Nebraska Act.

Potter, David M. *The Impending Crisis, 1848–1861* (1976). Remains the most comprehensive analysis of the coming of the war; a balanced account that is especially strong on political events.

Stowe, Harriet Beecher. *Uncle Tom's Cabin* (1852; reprint edition 1982, with notes by Kathryn Kish Sklar). Reading this book is essential for understanding why and how it generated so much controversy and intensified sectional antagonisms in the early 1850s.

ADDITIONAL SOURCES

Slavery in the Territories

Berwanger, Eugene H. *The Frontier against Slavery: Western Anti-Negro Prejudice and the Slavery Extension Controversy* (1967).

Hamilton, Holman. *Prologue to Conflict: The Crisis and Compromise of 1850* (1966).

Hedrick, Joan D. *Harriet Beecher Stowe: A Life* (1993).

Johnson, Susan Lee. *Roaring Camp: The Social World of the California Gold Rush* (2000).

May, Robert E. *The Southern Dream of a Caribbean Empire, 1854–1861* (1973).

Morrison, Michael E. *Slavery and the American West: The Eclipse of Manifest Destiny and the Coming of the Civil War* (1997).

Peterson, Merrill. *The Great Triumvirate: Webster, Clay, and Calhoun* (1987).

Quarles, Benjamin. *Black Abolitionists* (1969).

Rohrbough, Malcolm J. *Days of Gold: The California Gold Rush and the American Nation* (1997).

Political Realignment

Anbinder, Tyler. *Nativism and Slavery: The Northern Know-Nothings and the Politics of the 1850s* (1992).

Carwardine, Richard J. *Evangelicals and Politics in Antebellum America* (1993).

Cooper, William J., Jr. *The South and the Politics of Slavery, 1828–1856* (1978).

Fehrenbacher, Don E. *Slavery, Law, and Politics: The Dred Scott Case in Historical Perspective* (1981).

Foner, Eric. *Free Soil, Free Labor, Free Men: The Ideology of the Republican Party before the Civil War* (1970).

Gienapp, William. *Origins of the Republican Party, 1852–1856* (1987).

Holt, Michael F. *The Political Crisis of the 1850s* (1978).

Howe, Daniel Walker. "The Evangelical Movement and Political Culture in the North during the Second Party System," *Journal of American History*, 77 (March 1991): 1216–1239.

Johannsen, Robert W. *The Frontier, the Union, and Stephen A. Douglas* (1989).

Johannsen, Robert W. ed. *The Lincoln–Douglas Debates of 1858* (1965).

Long, Kathryn Teresa. *The Revival of 1857–58: Interpreting an American Religious Awakening* (1998).

SenGupta, Ganja. *For God and Mammon: Evangelicals and Entrepreneurs, Masters and Slaves in Territorial Kansas, 1854–1860* (1996).

Rawley, James A. *Race and Politics: "Bleeding Kansas" and the Coming of the Civil War* (1969).

von Frank, Albert J. *The Trials of Anthony Burns: Freedom and Slavery in Emerson's Boston* (1998).

Wolff, Gerald W. *The Kansas-Nebraska Bill: Party, Section, and the Coming of the Civil War* (1977).

The Road to Disunion

Banks, Russell. *Cloudsplitter* (1997).

Barney, William L. *The Road to Secession: A New Perspective on the Old South* (1972).

Craven, Avery. *The Growth of Southern Nationalism, 1848–1861* (1953).

Crofts, Daniel W. *Reluctant Confederates: Upper South Unionists in the Secession Crisis* (1989).

Current, Richard N. *Lincoln and the First Shot* (1963).

Dew, Charles B. *Apostles of Disunion: Southern Secession Commissioners and the Causes of the Civil War* (2001).

Johnson, Michael P., and James L. Roark, eds. *No Chariot Let Down: Charleston's Free People of Color on the Eve of the Civil War* (1984).

McCardell, John. *The Idea of a Southern Nation: Southern Nationalists and Southern Nationalism, 1830–1860* (1979).

McPherson, James M. "Antebellum Southern Exceptionalism: A New Look at an Old Question," *Civil War History*, 29 (September 1983): 230–244.

Snay, Michael. *Gospel of Disunion: Religion and Separatism in the Antebellum South* (1993).

Stampp, Kenneth M. *America in 1857: A Nation on the Brink* (1990).

Walther, Eric H. *The Fire-Eaters* (1992).

WHERE TO LEARN MORE

- The Underground Railroad Freedom Center, Cincinnati, Ohio. The Center provides information on the Northern response to the Fugitive Slave Act. **www.undergroundrailroad.org**.

- Adair Cabin and John Brown Museum, John Brown Memorial Park, Osawatomie, Kansas. Maintained by the Kansas Historical Society, the cabin (which once belonged to John Brown's sister) and the museum are located on the site of the Battle of Osawatomie, one of the critical events of "Bleeding Kansas." **www.kshs.org/places/adair.htm**.

- Constitution Hall, Lecompton, Kansas. This site, also run by the Kansas State Historical Society, is where proslavery delegates framed the controversial Lecompton Constitution that increased sectional discord. **www.kshs.org/places/constit.htm**.

- Harpers Ferry National Historical Park, West Virginia. Exhibits interpret John Brown's Raid and re-create some of the atmosphere and structures of the 1850s village and the federal arsenal. **www.nps.gov/hafe**.

- "A House Divided," mounted by the Chicago Historical Society, Chicago. This exhibit depicts the major events of the sectional crisis during the 1850s, the election of 1860, and the coming of the Civil War. It continued until 2001. **www.chicagohs.org**.

- Fort Sumter National Monument, Charleston, South Carolina. This historic site interprets the bombardment of the fort and the events that immediately preceded the Civil War. **www.nps.gov/fosu**.

 Please refer to the document CD-ROM for primary sources related to this chapter.

➔ *Awaiting combat, 1861: Union Soldiers from New York relax at camp awaiting orders to move to the front. The young men show great confidence and determination for their coming engagements, though one fellow to the left of the tent, perhaps a teenager far from home, seems to long for something as he stares beyond the camera. At this early stage of the war, a combination of romance and apprehension enveloped these hopeful recruits. Note also the young African American with a broom sitting apart from the soldiers.*

BATTLE CRIES AND FREEDOM SONGS
THE CIVIL WAR 1861–1865

15

July 14, 1861
Camp Clark, Washington, DC

My very dear Sarah:

The indications are very strong that we shall move in a few days—perhaps tomorrow. And lest I should not be able to write you again I feel impelled to write a few lines that may fall under your eye when I am no more. Our movement may be one of a few days' duration and be full of pleasure. And it may be one of severe conflict and death to me. "Not my will but thine o God be done." If it is necessary that I should fall on the battle-field for my Country I am ready. I have no misgivings about, or lack of confidence in the cause in which I am engaged, and my courage does not halt or falter. I know how American Civilization now leans upon the triumph of the government and how great a debt we owe to those who went before us through the blood and suffering of the Revolution. And I am willing—perfectly willing—to lay down all my joys in this life, to help maintain this government, and to pay that debt. But my dear wife, when I know that with my own joys I lay down nearly all of yours, and replace them in this life with cares and sorrows, when after having eaten for long years the bitter fruit of orphanage myself, I must offer it as the only sustenance to my dear little children, is it weak or dishonorable that while the banner of my purpose floats calmly and

CHAPTER OUTLINE

Mobilization, North and South
War Fever
The North's Advantage in Resources
Leaders, Governments, and Strategies

The Early War, 1861–1862
First Bull Run
The War in the West
Reassessing the War: The Human Toll
The War in the East

Turning Points, 1862–1863
The Naval War and the Diplomatic War
Antietam
Emancipation
From Fredericksburg to Gettysburg
Vicksburg, Chattanooga, and the West

The War Transforms the North
Wartime Legislation and Politics
The Northern Economy
Northern Women and the War

The Confederacy Disintegrates
Southern Politics
The Southern Economy
Southern Women and the War

The Union Prevails, 1864–1865
Grant's Plan to End the War
The Election of 1864 and Sherman's March
The Road to Appomattox and the Death of Lincoln

Conclusion

proudly in the breeze, underneath, my unbounded love for you my darling wife and children should struggle in fierce though useless contest with my love of country? . . .

Sarah, my love for you is deathless, it seems to bind me with mighty cables that nothing but omnipotence can break; and yet my love of Country comes over me like a strong wind and bears me irresistibly with all those chains to the battle-field.

The memories of the blissful moments I have enjoyed with you come crowding over me, and I feel most deeply grateful to God and you, that I have enjoyed them for so long. And how hard it is for me to give them up and burn to ashes the hopes and future years, when, God willing, we might still have lived and loved together, and see our boys grown up to honorable manhood around us. . . . If I do not [return], my dear Sarah, never forget how much I loved you, nor that when my last breath escapes me on the battle-field, it will whisper your name.

Forgive my many faults, and the many pains I have caused you. How thoughtless, how foolish I have sometimes been! . . .

But, O Sarah, if the dead can come back to this earth and flit unseen around those they love, I shall be with you, in the gladdest days and the darkest nights . . . always, always, and if there be a soft breeze upon your cheek, it shall be my breath[;] as the cool air fans your throbbing temple, it shall be my spirit passing by. Sarah do not mourn me dead; think I am gone and wait for thee, for we shall meet again . . .

Sullivan

Sullivan Ballou to Sarah Ballou, July 14, 1861. Geoffrey C. Ward, et al., *The Civil War: An Illustrated History* (New York: Alfred A. Knopf, 1990), 82–83.

Sullivan Ballou's letter to his wife on the eve of the First Battle of Bull Run typified the sentiments of the civilian armies raised by both North and South: a clear purpose of the importance of their mission, a sense of foreboding, an appeal and acknowledgment of the guiding hand of God, and, most of all, words of love for family. Such romantic expressions were common in mid-nineteenth-century American correspondence between husband and wife, lover and loved.

Yet, the Civil War lent an urgency to such expressions. Most of the soldiers had no combat experience and, aside from some perfunctory training, knew little about military life before going into battle. Just a few months earlier, Major Sullivan Ballou of the Second Regiment, Rhode Island Volunteers, was a thirty-two-year-old attorney, having risen to the bar from a childhood of poverty. He lived a quiet life in Providence with his wife, Sarah, and their two young sons, Edgar and Willie. But the events of the 1850s stoked Ballou's interest in politics and he became a dedicated Republican and devoted supporter of Abraham Lincoln. When the war came, he did not hesitate in his responsibility to the union and what it stood for. He volunteered and was sent to Washington, D.C., to await further orders. He wrote this letter from his camp. A few days later, those orders arrived and Ballou and his company marched to Manassas, Virginia, where they engaged Confederate troops on July 21 at the First Battle of Bull Run. Sullivan Ballou was killed during the battle.

Sullivan Ballou took the ultimate journey for his beliefs and his love. The Civil War preserved the Union, abolished slavery, and killed at least 620,000 soldiers—more than in all other wars the country fought, from the Revolution to the Korean conflict, combined. To come to terms with it is to try to reconcile its great accomplishments with its awful consequences. In the spring of the war, that time of sanguine expectation in April 1861, all things seemed possible on both sides as flags waved, bands played, and politicians orated. But war is a hard thing, and Union and freedom came at a dear price. We are still paying off its legacy.

When the war began, only a small minority of Northerners linked the preservation of the Union with the abolition of slavery. By 1863, Union and freedom had become inseparable Federal objectives. The Confederacy fought for independence and the preservation of slavery. The Confederate objectives dictated a defensive military strategy; the Union objectives dictated an offensive strategy. But during the war's early years, both sides faced similar problems—raising an army, financing the war effort, mobilizing the civilian population, and marshaling resources. The Confederates confronted the added burden of starting a government from scratch with relatively fewer resources than the Federals.

At the end of the war's first year, the Confederacy's strong military position east of the Appalachians belied its numerical and economic inferiority. Confederate advances resulted as much from the bungling of Union commanders as from the gallant efforts of the South's own forces. By the end of 1862, Union officers had begun to expose Southern military shortcomings, and Federal officials had expanded the North's war aims to include the abolition of slavery. Within a year, the trans-Mississippi portion of the Confederacy capitulated as dissent and despair mounted on the home front. A slim victory at Gettysburg, Sherman's destructive and demoralizing march through Georgia, and the relentless assaults of new Union commander Ulysses S. Grant overwhelmed Confederate resistance and civilian hope. The North, too, suffered social and political disruption, but the marvelous elixir of battlefield victory did wonders to allay these ills.

Black Southerners seized the initiative in the war against slavery, especially in the months after the Emancipation Proclamation, eventually joining Union forces in combat against their former masters. Soon, another war to secure the fruits of freedom would begin.

KEY TOPICS

- The comparative economic and human resources of the North and South

- Confederate and Union military strategies

- Steps leading to the Emancipation Proclamation

- The impact of the war on Northern political, economic, and social life

- How military reversals affected Confederate political and economic life and civilian morale

- The meaning of the Civil War for the nation and its citizens

MOBILIZATION, NORTH AND SOUTH

Neither side was prepared for a major war. The Confederacy lacked a national army. Each Southern state had a militia, but, by the 1850s, these companies had become more social clubs than fighting units. Aside from private boats and some captured Federal vessels, the Confederacy also lacked a navy. The Union had a regular army of only sixteen thousand men, most of whom were stationed west of the Mississippi River. Their major concern had been to intervene between white settlers and Indians.

Each government augmented these meager military reserves with thousands of new recruits and developed a bureaucracy to mount a war effort. At the same time, the administrations of Presidents Lincoln and Davis secured the loyalty of their civilian populations and devised military strategies for a war of indeterminate duration. How North and South went about these tasks reflected both the different objectives of the two sides and the distinctive personalities of their leaders, Abraham Lincoln and Jefferson Davis.

WAR FEVER

The day after Major Robert Anderson surrendered Fort Sumter, President Lincoln moved to enlarge his small, scattered army by mobilizing state militias for ninety days. Four states—Virginia, Arkansas, North Carolina, and Tennessee—refused the call and seceded from the Union. About one-third of the officer corps in the regular army, including some of the

Chronology

1861 April	Confederates fire on Fort Sumter; Civil War Begins.
July	First Battle of Bull Run.
1862 February	Forts Henry and Donelson fall to Union Forces.
March	Peninsula Campaign Begins.
	Battle of Glorieta Pass, New Mexico.
April	Battle of Shiloh.
	New Orleans falls to Federal Forces.
May	Union captures Corinth, Mississippi.
July	Seven Days' Battles end.
	Congress passes the Confiscation Act
August	Second Battle of Bull Run.
September	Battle of Antietam.
December	Battle of Fredericksburg.
1863 January	Emancipation Proclamation takes effect.
May	Battle of Chancellorsville; Stonewall Jackson is mortally wounded.
July	Battle of Gettysburg.
	Vicksburg falls to Union Forces.

	New York Draft Riot occurs
	Black Troops of the 54th Massachusetts Volunteer Infantry Regiment Assault Fort Wagner outside Charleston.
September	Battle of Chickamauga.
November	Battle of Chattanooga.
1864 May	Battle of the Wilderness.
June	Battle of Cold Harbor.
September	Sherman captures Atlanta.
November	President Lincoln is reelected.
	Sherman begins his march to the sea.
1865 January	Congress passes Thirteenth Amendment to the Constitution, outlawing slavery (ratified December 1865).
February	Charleston surrenders.
March	Confederate Congress authorizes enlistment of black soldiers.
April	Federal troops enter Richmond.
	Lee surrenders to Grant at Appomattox Court House.
	Lincoln is assassinated.

highest-ranking officers, resigned their commissions to join the Confederacy. Still, Lincoln seemed likely to meet his target of 75,000 troops.

Lincoln's modest ninety-day call-up reflected the general belief, North and South, that the war would end quickly. The *New York Times* predicted that the "local commotion" in the South would be put down "in thirty days." Some Southerners believed that the Yankees would quit after the first battle. "Just throw three or four shells among those blue-bellied Yankees," a North Carolinian blustered, "and they'll scatter like sheep." Not everyone thought the war would be brief. William T. Sherman, who had recently headed a Louisiana military academy and would become one of the Union's few great commanders, wrote in April 1861, "I think it is to be a long war—very long—much longer than any politician thinks."

Northerners closed ranks behind the president after the Confederacy's attack on Fort Sumter. Leading Democrat Stephen A. Douglas called on the Republican Lincoln to offer his and his party's support. "There can be no neutrals in this war," Douglas said, "only patriots—or traitors." Residents of New York

City, where sympathy for the South had probably been greater than anywhere else in the North, now sponsored huge public demonstrations in support of the war effort. One New Yorker exclaimed, "It seems as if we never were alive till now; never had a country till now." The city council appropriated $1 million to raise and equip Union regiments. Vigilance committees intimidated pro-Southern newspapers. And American flags flew everywhere. The *New York Daily Tribune*, an abolitionist paper, made the objective of this patriotic fervor clear: "We mean to conquer [the Southern people]—not merely to defeat, but to conquer, to SUBJUGATE them—and we shall do this the most mercifully, the more speedily we do it. But when the rebellious traitors are overwhelmed in the field, and scattered like leaves before an angry wind, it must not be to return to peaceful and contented homes. They must find poverty at their firesides, and see privation in the anxious eyes of mothers and rags of children."

Southerners were equally eager to support their new nation. A *London Times* correspondent traveling in the South witnessed large crowds with "flushed

Departure of the 7th Regiment, N.Y.S.M., April 19, 1861, April 19, 1861 George Hayward, American (born England) about 1800–1872 (?). Graphite pencil, transparent and opaque watercolor on paper Karolik cat. no 961, fig 194 Sheet: 36.7 x 51.3 cm (14

A rousing send-off for the Union's 7th Regiment in 1861 reflects the optimism and enthusiasm of citizens at the beginning of the war.

faces, wild eyes, screaming mouths." They punctuated stirring renditions of "Dixie" with the high-pitched piercing sounds that would later be known as the "rebel yell." Enlistment rallies, wild send-offs at train stations, and auctions and balls to raise money for the troops were staged throughout the Confederacy during the war's early months. As in the North, war fever fired hatred of the enemy. A Louisiana plantation overseer wrote:

My prayer Sincerely to God is that Every Black Republican in the Hole combined whorl Either man women o chile that is opposed to negro slavery . . . shal be trubled with pestilences & calamitys of all kinds & drag out the Balance of there existence in misry & degradation with Scarsely food & rayment enughf to keep sole & body to geather and O God I pray the to Direct a bullet or a bayonet to pirce the art of every northern Soldier that invades southern Soil.

As war fever gripped North and South, volunteers on both sides rushed to join, quickly filling the quotas of both armies. Most soldiers were motivated by patriotism, a desire to defend their homes and loved ones, and a craving for glory and adventure. A recruitment poster in one Massachusetts town promised "travel and promotion" as well as good pay. Some men succumbed to the pressure of companions and sweethearts. A young Alabamian received a package from his fiancée with a skirt, a petticoat, and a note demanding "wear these or volunteer!" The initial enthusiasm, however, wore off quickly. After four months of war, a young Confederate soldier admitted, "I have seen quite enough of a soldier's life to satisfy me that it is not what it is cracked up to be."

The South in particular faced a contradiction between its ideology and the demands of full-scale war. Southerners were loyal to their localities, counties, and states. Southern leaders had been fighting for decades to defend states' rights against national authority. Now these same leaders had to forge the states of the Confederacy into a nation. By early spring 1862, the Confederate government was compelled to order the first general draft in U.S. history. It required three years' service for men between eighteen and thirty-five (a range later expanded from seventeen to fifty). In 1864, the Confederate Congress added a compulsory reenlistment provision. At that point, the only way a recruit could get out of the army was to die or desert.

The Confederate draft law allowed several occupational exemptions. Among them was an infamous provision that allowed one white man on any plantation with more than twenty slaves to be excused from service. The reason for the exemption was to assure the security and continued productivity of large plantations, not to protect the privileged, but it led some Southerners to conclude that the struggle had become "a rich man's war but a poor man's fight."

The initial flush of enthusiasm faded in the North as well. Responding to a federal call for additional troops, some Northern states initiated a draft during the summer of 1862. In March 1863, Congress passed the Enrollment Act, a draft law that, like the Confederate draft, allowed for occupational exemptions. A provision that allowed a draftee to hire a substitute aroused resentment among working-class Northerners. Anger at the draft—as well as poor working conditions—sparked several riots during 1863. But the North was less dependent on conscription than was the South. Only 8 percent of Union forces were drafted, compared to 20 percent for the Confederacy.

The complaints of many rank-and-file soldiers may give the impression that only people of lesser or modest means fought, but in fact the armies of both sides included men from all walks of life, from common laborers to clerks to bankers. An undetermined number of women, typically disguised as men, also served in both armies. Perhaps as many as three hundred women joined the Union ranks, and about half that number enlisted in the Confederate army. They joined for the same reasons as men: adventure, patriotism, and glory

THE NORTH'S ADVANTAGE IN RESOURCES

The resources of the North—including its population, industrial and agricultural capacity, and transportation network—greatly exceeded those of the South (see

Figure 15-1). The 2.1 million men who fought for the Union represented roughly half the men of military age in the North. The 900,000 men who fought for the Confederacy, by contrast, represented fully 90 percent of its eligible population. Irish and German immigrants continued to flow into the North during the war, although at a slower rate than before 1861, and thousands of them enlisted, often as substitutes for native-born Northerners. Nearly 200,000 African Americans, most of them ex-slaves from the South, took up arms for the Union. Not until the last month of the war did the Confederacy consider arming slaves.

The Confederacy compensated somewhat for its numerical disadvantage by requiring long tours of duty, which meant that its forces tended to be more experienced than those of the Union. But the Union's greater numbers left the South vulnerable to a war of attrition. As one Confederate veteran explained to a Union veteran several years after the war, "When one of your men got killed, a dozen took his place. When one of our boys died, it was just another good man gone."

At the beginning of the war, the North controlled 90 percent of the nation's industrial capacity. It had seventeen times more cotton and woolen cloth than the South, thirty times more boots and shoes, and thirty-two times more firearms. The North had dozens of facilities for producing the tools to make war materiel; the South had no such factories and only one munitions plant, the Tredegar Iron Works in Richmond. Northern farms, more mechanized than their Southern counterparts, produced record harvests of meat, grains, and vegetables. Southern farms were also productive, but the South lacked the North's capacity to transport and distribute food efficiently. The railroad system in the North was more than twice the size of the South's.

FIGURE 15-1   A Comparison of the Union and Confederate Control of Key Resources at the Outset of the Civil War

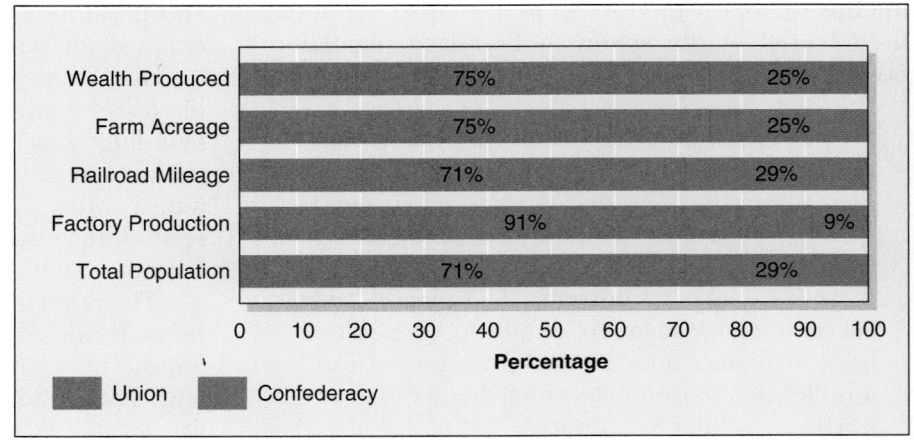

Thanks to the North's abundance of resources, no soldier in any previous army had ever been outfitted as well as the blue-uniformed Union trooper. The official color of the Confederate uniform was gray, although a dusty brown shade was more common. Most Southern soldiers, however, did not wear distinguishable uniforms, especially toward the end of the war. They also often lacked proper shoes or any footwear at all. In winter and on certain road surfaces, this shortage was a severe handicap. When the Confederate general Robert E. Lee invaded Maryland in 1862, he left behind several thousand barefoot soldiers because they could not march on gravel roads. Still, the South never lost a battle because of insufficient supplies or inadequate weaponry. New foundries opened, and manufacturing enterprises in Augusta, Georgia; Selma, Alabama; and elsewhere joined the Tredegar Iron Works in keeping the Confederate armies equipped with the weapons and other supplies they needed to keep fighting.

Unstable finances proved more of a handicap to the Confederacy than its relatively low industrial capacity. The Confederate economy—and its treasury—depended heavily on cotton exports. But a Union naval blockade and the ability of textile manufacturers in Europe to find new sources of supply restricted this crucial source of revenue. The imposition of taxes would have improved the Confederacy's finances, but Southerners resisted taxation. The government sold interest-bearing bonds to raise money, but as Confederate fortunes declined, so did bond sales. With few other options, the Confederacy financed more than 60 percent of the $1.5 billion it spent on the war with printing-press money. Inflation spiraled out of control, demoralizing civilians.

The Union had more abundant financial resources than the Confederacy, and the Federal government was more successful than the Confederate government at developing innovative ways to meet the great cost of the war. Its first recourse was to borrow money by selling long-term interest-bearing bonds and shorter-term interest-bearing treasury notes. Together these bonds accounted for 66 percent of the $4 billion that the Union raised to wage the war. Like the Confederacy, the Federal government issued paper money—bills derisively known as "greenbacks"—that was not backed by gold or silver. But the Federal government also offset its expenses with the country's first income tax, which citizens could pay in greenbacks—a move that bolstered the value and credibility of the paper currency. These financial measures eliminated the need for wage and price controls and rationing and warded off ruinous inflation in the North.

LEADERS, GOVERNMENTS, AND STRATEGIES

Leadership ability, like resources, played an important role in the war. It was up to the leaders of the two sides to determine and administer civilian and military policy, to define the war objectives of each side, and to inspire a willingness to sacrifice in both citizens and soldiers.

Confederate president Jefferson Davis had to build a government from scratch during a war. Abraham Lincoln at least had the benefit of an established governmental structure, a standing army, healthy financial resources, and established diplomatic relations with the nations of Europe.

Davis and Lincoln were both born in Kentucky within a year and 100 miles of each other. Davis, like Lincoln, was born into modest circumstances. He attended the military academy at West Point, where he was a mediocre student. He abandoned his military career after seven years of service and married the sixteen-year-old daughter of General Zachary Taylor. Davis and his bride moved to a plantation in Mississippi, where she soon died of yellow fever. Immersing himself in books and cotton farming, Davis had emerged as a gentleman planter by the 1840s and married Varina Howell in 1845. He returned to military service during the Mexican war, fought well, and used his success to become a senator from Mississippi in 1847. He served as secretary of war under President Franklin Pierce and returned to the Senate in 1857.

Although Davis's career qualified him for the prodigious task of running the Confederacy, aspects of his character compromised his effectiveness. He had a sharp intellect but related awkwardly to people and was not "one of the boys." Colleagues found him aloof. He was inclined to equate compromise with weakness and interpreted any opposition as a personal attack. His wife commented, "[I]f anyone disagrees with Mr. Davis he resents it and ascribes the difference to the perversity of his opponent." Davis was also fatalistic. According to his wife, when he heard that the Confederate Congress had selected him as president, he spoke of it "as a man might speak of a sentence of death."

Southerners viewed themselves as the genuine heirs of the American Revolution and the true defenders of the United States Constitution. If the South were to establish itself as a separate country, however, Southerners had to renounce their American identity and develop one of their own. But on what distinctive aspects of Southern life could the Confederacy build such an identity? Slavery was distinctively Southern, but most white Southerners, even if they believed that slavery served their interests, did not own slaves.

Southerners had forcefully advanced the ideology of states' rights, but, with its emphasis on the primacy of state sovereignty over central authority, states' rights, too, was a weak foundation on which to build a national consciousness.

Although Southerners fought for a variety of reasons, protecting their homes and families remained paramount. When these were threatened or destroyed, where would loyalty lie? Did Davis, or anyone else for that matter, possess the skill to hold together a new nation that was more like the nation it had renounced than anything that could replace it?

Northerners, like Southerners, needed a convincing reason to endure the prolonged sacrifice of the Civil War. For them, the struggle was a distant one, fought mostly on Southern soil, far from their homes. Lincoln and other Northern leaders secured support by convincing their compatriots of the importance of preserving the Union. Lincoln eloquently articulated this view, framing the war as more than a military conquest. In a message to Congress on July 4, 1861, he explained that the struggle to preserve the Union was "not altogether for today; it is for a vast future." The president viewed the conflict in global terms, its results affecting the hopes for democratic government around the world. He concluded that the war "embraces more than the fate of these United States. It presents to the whole family of man, the question, whether a constitutional republic . . . can or cannot maintain its territorial integrity, against its own domestic foes."

Lincoln handled disagreement better than Davis did. He defused tense situations with folksy humor, and his simple eloquence captured the imagination of ordinary people, even if it did not persuade his political enemies. Lincoln viewed himself as a man of the people. He was not aloof, like Davis. Friends and critics alike agreed that Lincoln made himself available to them. Lincoln generated the type of affection among rank-and-file soldiers that eluded Davis. The President's occasional visit to the front generated both amusement and gratitude from the troops, owing to his ungainly appearance on a horse, and his easy way of conversing with the men. They serenaded "Old Abe," as they called him affectionately with the popular tune, "We Are Coming Father Abraham." There is no record of Confederate tunesmiths composing similar ditties for their leaders. But even if Jefferson Davis had been as effective and beloved a leader as Lincoln, it is unlikely that he could have overcome the odds against him. The key to Southern independence lay less with the Confederacy's president than with its forces on the battlefield.

Lincoln's fight for the border states.

The secession of Virginia, Arkansas, North Carolina, and Tennessee left four border slave states—Maryland, Delaware, Kentucky, and Missouri—hanging in the balance. Were Maryland and Delaware to secede, the federal capital at Washington, D.C., would be surrounded by Confederate territory. The loss of Kentucky and Missouri would threaten the borders of Iowa, Illinois, Indiana, and Ohio and remove the Deep South from the threat of imminent invasion. Kentucky's manpower, livestock, and waterways were as important to hold for the Union as they were to gain for the Confederacy. The state also had special symbolic significance, as the birthplace of the rival presidents, Lincoln and Davis. Lincoln viewed Kentucky as the key to retaining the three other border states: "I think to lose Kentucky is nearly to lose the whole game. Kentucky gone, we cannot hold Missouri, nor, as I think, Maryland. . . . We would as well consent to separation at once, including the surrender of this capital."

Lincoln adopted a "soft" strategy to secure the border states, stressing the restoration of the Union as the sole objective of Federal military operations and assuring border residents that his government would not interfere with slavery. Union commanders barred fugitive slaves from their camps during the first year of the war, promising "to keep the war a lily-white crusade," as one officer put it. But, early reports from the four states were troubling. The four governors displayed polite indifference or overt hostility to the Federal government.

Maryland's strategic location north of Washington, D.C., rendered its loyalty to the Union vital. Although a majority of its citizens opposed secession, a mob attack on Union troops passing through Baltimore in April 1861 indicated strong pro-Southern sentiment. Lincoln dispatched Federal troops to monitor the fall elections in the state, placed its legislature under military surveillance, and arrested officials who opposed the Union cause, including the mayor of Baltimore. This show of force guaranteed the pro-Union candidate for governor an overwhelming victory and saved Maryland for the Union. Delaware, although nominally a slave state, remained staunchly for the Union.

Missourians settled their indecision by combat. The fighting culminated with a Union victory in March 1862 at the Battle of Pea Ridge, Arkansas. Pro-Confederate Missourians refused to concede defeat and waged an unsuccessful guerrilla war over the next two years.

Kentucky never seceded but attempted to remain neutral at the outset of the war. The legislature was pro-Union, the governor pro-Southern. Both sides ac-

Artist Winslow Homer's depiction of the place soldiers spent most of their time—camp. A soldier's life was boredom occasionally interspersed with fierce and deadly combat.

tively recruited soldiers in the state. In September 1861, when Confederate forces invaded Kentucky and Union forces moved to expel them, the state became one of the war's battlegrounds.

Although Virginia went with the Confederacy, some counties in the western part of the state opposed the state's secession and, as early as the summer of 1861, took steps to establish a pro-Union state. In June 1863, West Virginia became the nation's thirty-fifth state.

Strategies and tactics. To a great extent, the political objectives of each side determined its military strategy. Southerners wanted independence and protection of their institutions; Northerners fought to preserve the Union. The North's goal required conquest. Federal forces had to invade the South, destroy its armies, and rout its government. The Confederacy, for its part, did not need to conquer the North. Fighting a defensive battle in its own territory, the South had only to hang on until growing Northern opposition to the war or some decisive Northern military mistake convinced the Union to stop fighting.

But the South's strategy had two weaknesses. First, it demanded more patience than the South had shown in impulsively attacking Fort Sumter. Second, the South might not have sufficient resources to draw

out the war long enough to swing Northern public opinion behind peace. The question was: What would break first, Northern support for the war or Southern ability to wage it?

THE EARLY WAR, 1861–1862

The North's offensive strategy dictated the course of the war for the first two years. In the West, the federal army's objectives were to hold Missouri, Kentucky, and Tennessee for the Union, to control the Mississippi River, and eventually to detach the area west of the Appalachians from the rest of the Confederacy. In the East, Union forces sought to capture Richmond, the Confederate capital. The U.S. Navy imposed a blockade along the Confederate coast and pushed into inland waterways to capture Southern ports.

The Confederates defended strategic locations throughout their territory or abandoned them when prudence required. Occasionally, taking advantage of surprise or terrain, Southern forces ventured out to engage Union armies. Between engagements, each side sniped at, bushwhacked, and trapped the other.

By the end of 1862, the result remained in the balance. Although Union forces attained some success in the West, Southern armies there remained intact. In the East, where resourceful Confederate leaders several times stopped superior Union forces, Southerners clearly had the best of it.

FIRST BULL RUN

By July 1861, when the border states appeared more secure for the Union, President Lincoln shifted his attention southward and ordered Union general Irvin McDowell to move Federal forces into Virginia to take Richmond (see Map 15-1). Confronting McDowell twenty miles southwest of Washington at Manassas, an important junction in the railway that supplied the Confederate capital, was a Confederate army under General P.G.T. Beauregard. Their armies clashed on July 21 at the First Battle of Bull Run (known to the Confederacy as the first battle of Manassas). Union troops seemed at first on the verge of winning. But Beauregard's forces, along with General Joseph E. Johnston's reinforcements, repulsed the assault, scattering not only the Union army, but also hundreds of picnickers who had come out from Washington to watch the fight. At the height of the battle, General Barnard Bee of South Carolina called out to Colonel Thomas J. Jackson for assistance. Jackson, a Virginia college professor turned officer, either did not hear Bee or chose to ignore him. In exasperation, Bee shouted, "There stands Jackson—like a damned stone wall!" The rebuke became, in the curious alchemy of battlefield gossip, a shorthand for courage and steadfastness. Jackson's men henceforth called him "Stonewall."

Bull Run dispelled some illusions and reinforced others. It boosted Southerners' confidence and seemed to confirm their boast that one Confederate could whip ten Yankees, even though the opposing armies were of relatively equal strength when the fighting began. The Union rout planted the suspicion in Northern minds that perhaps the Confederates were invincible and destroyed the widespread belief in the North that the war would be over quickly.

THE WAR IN THE WEST

While federal forces retreated in Virginia, they advanced in the west. Two Confederate forts on the Tennessee–Kentucky border, Fort Henry on the Tennessee river and Fort Donelson on the Cumberland River, guarded the strategic waterways that linked Tennessee and Kentucky to the Mississippi valley. The forts also defended Nashville, the Tennessee state capital (see Map 15-2). In February 1862, Union general Ulysses S. Grant coordinated a land and river campaign against the forts, with Flag Officer Andrew H. Foote who commanded a force of ironclad Union gunboats.

Grant, recently promoted to brigadier general, had resigned from the military in the 1850s after a mediocre career marked by bouts of excessive drink-

MAP 15-1   From First Bull Run to Antietam: The War in the East, 1861-1862
The early stages of the war demonstrated the strategies of both Confederate and Union forces. Federal troops stormed into Virginia hoping to capture Richmond and bring a quick end to the war. Through a combination of poor generalship and Confederate tenacity, they failed. Confederate troops hoped to defend their territory, prolong the war, and eventually win their independence as Northern patience evaporated. They proved successful initially, but, with the abandonment of the defensive strategy and the invasion of Maryland in the fall of 1862, the Confederates suffered a political and morale setback at Antietam.

ing. Before rejoining the army, he had worked in his family's struggling leather business in Illinois. A plain-looking man, with dark-brown hair and a beard streaked with gray, he often looked as if he had slept in his uniform. Behind the rumpled appearance lay a flexible military mind that would eventually grasp how the Civil War must be won.

Grant appreciated the strategic importance of river systems in the conquest of the western Confederacy. His combined river and land campaign caught the Southerners unprepared and outflanked. By February 16, both forts had fallen. The Union victory drove a wedge into Southern territory and closed the Confederacy's quickest path to the west from Virginia and the Carolinas. The Confederacy's only safe link across the Appalachians was now through Georgia. The Confederacy never recovered the strategic advantage in the West after the loss of Forts Henry and Donelson.

Grant next moved his main army south to Pittsburgh Landing on the Tennessee River, to prepare for an assault on the key Mississippi River port and rail center of Vicksburg. After blunting a surprise Confederate attack at Shiloh Church near Pittsburgh Landing, Grant pushed the Southerners back to Corinth, Mississippi.

Federal forces complemented their victories at Shiloh and Corinth with another important success in the western Confederacy. Admiral David G. Farragut, who remained a Unionist even though born in Tennessee, blasted the Confederate river defenses protecting New Orleans and sailed a federal fleet into the city in April 1862. The result was to open 200 miles of the Mississippi River, the nation's most vital commercial waterway, to Union traffic. With the fall of Memphis to union forces in June, Vicksburg remained the only major river town still in Confederate hands. The western losses exposed a major problem with the Confederates' defensive strategy: their military reserves were stretched too thin to defend their vast territory.

REASSESSING THE WAR: THE HUMAN TOLL

The fierce fighting at Shiloh wrought unprecedented carnage. More American soldiers were lost at Shiloh than in all of the nation's wars combined up to that

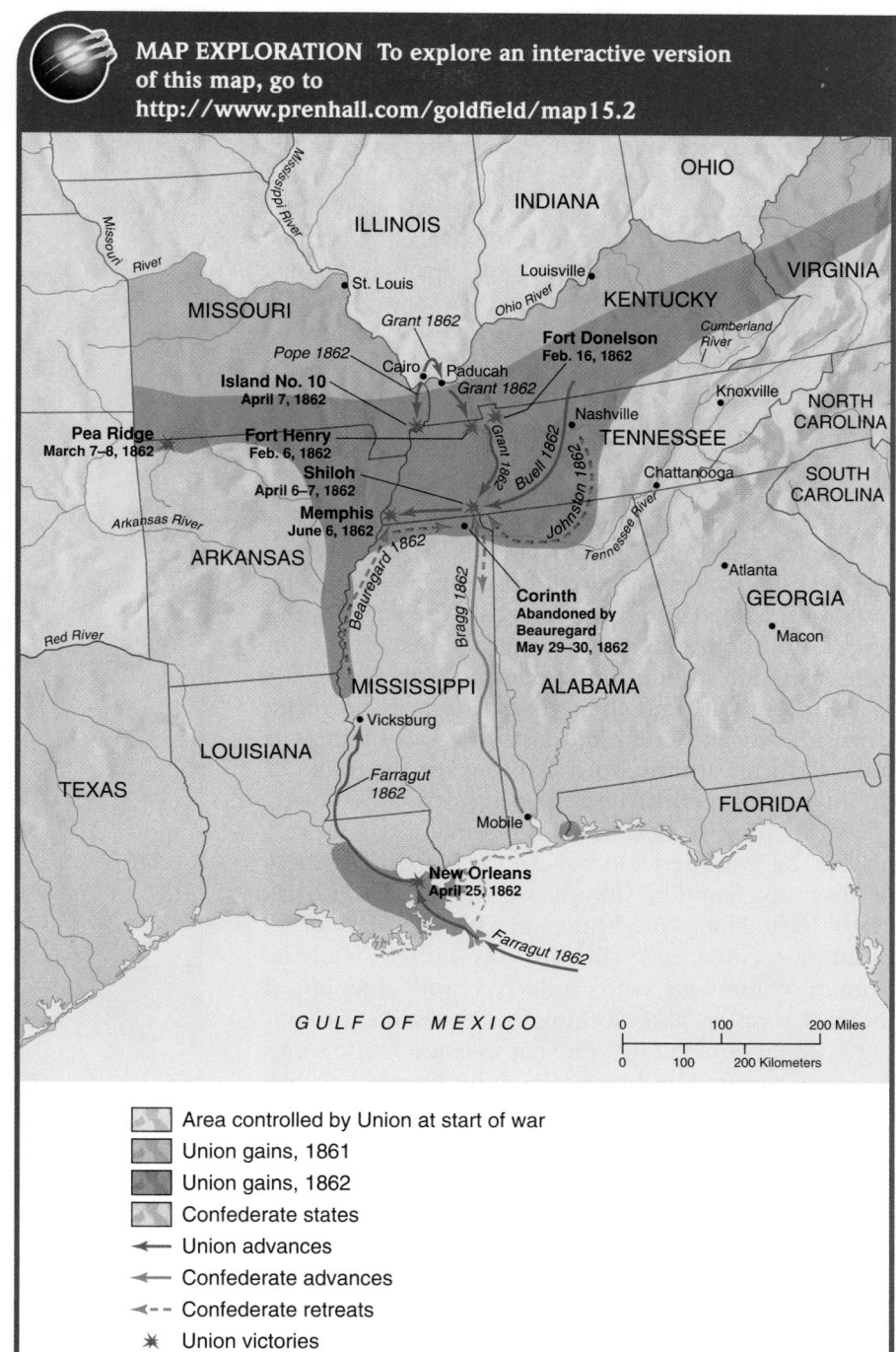

MAP EXPLORATION To explore an interactive version of this map, go to http://www.prenhall.com/goldfield/map15.2

MAP 15-2   **The War in the West, 1861-1862**
Because of the early Union emphasis on capturing Richmond, the war in the West seemed less important to Northerners. But, from a strategic standpoint, the victories at Forts Henry and Donelson, which drove a wedge into southern territory and closed the Confederacy's quickest path to the West from Virginia and the Carolinas, and the capture of New Orleans and its Mississippi River port were crucial and set the stage for greater Federal success in the West in 1863.

time. Each side suffered more than ten thousand casualties. By the time the smoke had cleared, the soldiers' view of the war had undergone a major transformation. The initial enthusiasm and bravado were replaced by the sober realization that death or capture was a likely outcome and that heroism, courage, and piety did not guarantee survival. "Too shocking, too horrible," a Confederate survivor of Shiloh wrote. "God grant that I may never be the partaker in such scenes again . . . when released from this I shall ever be an advocate of peace." A Union soldier wrote of "the dead and dying lying in masses, some with arms, legs, and even their jaws shot off, bleeding to death, and no one to wait upon them to dress their wounds."

Landing in a hospital scarcely improved a wounded or ill soldier's chances of survival. Kate Cumming, a nurse at a Confederate hospital in Corinth, wrote of soldiers brought from the battle "mutilated in every imaginable way." The wounded lay packed together on the floor, and Cumming negotiated the rooms with great difficulty to avoid stepping on the dead and dying. Piercing the air were the screams of men undergoing amputations, often with little or no anesthetic. Some pleaded with physicians to kill them and end their misery. Others bore the pain stoically and entrusted last words and letters to nurses, dying with the word "Mother" or the name of their wife or sweetheart on their lips.

Women on both sides played a major role in caring for the wounded and sick. In the North, members of the U.S. Sanitary Commission attempted to upgrade hospital and medical care. This voluntary organization, formed in April 1861, was staffed mainly by women volunteers who collected and distributed medical supplies and clothing and advised on cleaning hospitals and camps. The commission made some headway during the first year of the war, but in the months after Shiloh and with the resumption of fighting in the east, the extent of casualties often overwhelmed the dedicated volunteers. And the bloodiest fighting lay ahead.

Even if a soldier escaped death on the battlefield and survived a hospital stay, he still faced the possibility of death from disease. Roughly twice as many men died from disease as on the battlefield during the Civil War. Heaps of garbage, contaminated food and water, and swarming mosquitoes, flies, and lice created unhealthy camp conditions. Typhoid, commonly and appropriately known as "camp fever," claimed the most lives.

Many soldiers turned to religion for consolation in response to the growing carnage. The frequency of camp prayer meetings and revivals increased after Shiloh. Many a recruit carried books with such titles as *Satan's Bait* and *A Mother's Parting Words to her Soldier Boy* in his knapsack. Soldiers often gathered with their

Several hundred women, disguised as men, made their contribution to the war effort by enlisting. Frances Clalin served with Federal forces in Missouri. Many were found out after suffering wounds or illness.

comrades to sing hymns before retiring for the night. Stories circulated of a Bible that stopped a bullet whistling toward a soldier's heart. But veterans knew that a deck of cards did just as well, and they understood that neither Bibles nor cards offered protection against artillery.

Some soldiers, responding to constant danger and fear, talked or yelled loudly. The Confederate rebel yell probably served to relieve some of the tension of battle as well as to frighten the enemy. Others shook so much that they fell down, unable to control their limbs. A few soldiers could not wake up in the morning without being doused with cold water; "they wanted to stay out, they couldn't bear to remember all this mess waiting with first light."

The harsh conditions of camp life often strained relations between officers and enlisted men. Soldiers also suffered from boredom. Battles rarely lasted more than a day or two. While in camp between engagements, a recruit faced seemingly incessant drilling (loading and firing a rifle required nine separate steps) and heavy chores such as chopping wood and hauling water. Typically, he spent what little time remained resting, writing, reading, and eating. To relieve their anxieties, soldiers talked about home and loved ones, upcoming or recent battles, and food. Soldiers also fought the boredom and harsh physical conditions of camp life by singing, playing cards, and competing in sports like footracing and makeshift forms of football and baseball.

Women camp followers cooked, did laundry, and provided sexual services for a price. The two capitals, Washington and Richmond, had notorious vice districts. A Confederate recruit lamented that "almost half of the women in the vicinity of the army, married and unmarried, are lost to all virtue." Both armies experienced soaring rates of venereal disease.

By 1862, the war's carnage and brutality had dispelled any lingering notions of war as a chivalrous enterprise. At a battle in Virginia that year, Stonewall Jackson reprimanded a Confederate general who had ordered his men not to shoot at a Union officer riding before his own men, rallying them on. "This is no ordinary war," Jackson said, "and the brave and gallant Federal officers are the very kind that must be killed. Shoot the brave officers and the cowards will run away and take the men with them." The reluctance of some commanders to pursue retreating armies or to initiate campaigns resulted in part from their recognition of how awful the war really was.

THE WAR IN THE EAST

With Grant and Farragut squeezing the Confederacy in the West, Lincoln ordered a new offensive against Richmond in the East that he believed would end the war. Following the defeat at Bull Run, he had shaken up the Union high command and appointed General George B. McClellan to lead what was now called the Army of the Potomac.

A West Point graduate, McClellan had served with distinction in the Mexican war. Called back into active duty at the outbreak of the war, he assumed command of the Army of the Potomac, which was no more than a collection of raw recruits and disgruntled veterans. McClellan succeeded in transforming it into a disciplined fighting force. He was well liked by his soldiers, who referred to him affectionately as "Little Mac." Mc-

Clellan returned their affection, perhaps too much. A superb organizer, he would prove overly cautious on the field of battle.

In March 1862, at the outset of the Peninsula Campaign, McClellan moved his 112,000-man army out of Washington and maneuvered his forces by boat down the Potomac River and Chesapeake Bay to the peninsula between the York and James Rivers southeast of the Confederate capital. Union forces took Yorktown, Williamsburg, and Norfolk. Confederate general Joseph E. Johnston, withdrew his forces up the peninsula toward Richmond, preparing for what most felt would be the decisive battle of the war. McClellan, moving ponderously up the peninsula, clashed with Johnston's army inconclusively at Seven Pines in late May 1862. Johnston was badly wounded in the clash, and president Davis replaced him with General Robert E. Lee, who renamed the forces under his command the Army of Northern Virginia.

Lee was from a prominent Virginia family long accustomed to power and command. His father, "Light-Horse Harry" Lee, had been a Revolutionary

A career army officer who resigned his commission to serve his state and new country, Confederate General Robert E. Lee's quiet courage and sense of duty inspired his men.

War hero. Lee attended West Point, served with distinction in the Mexican War, and commanded the federal force that captured John Brown at Harpers Ferry in 1859. In 1831, he married Mary Custis, the daughter of George Washington's adopted son. Their gracious home in Arlington, Virginia, had a commanding view of the Potomac and Washington, D.C. Before the war, it had seemed as if Lee would live out his days as a soldier-farmer, much like his wife's grandfather.

In 1860, the army posted Lee to Texas, where he watched the secession drama unfold. He opposed secession but was unwilling to take up arms against his native Virginia. Refusing an offer from Winfield Scott to take command of Federal forces, he resigned from the U.S. Army and went with Virginia after it left the Union.

Lee's reserved and aristocratic bearing masked a gambler's disposition. One fellow officer noted, "his name might be Audacity. He will take more chances, and take them quicker than any other general in this country." Under his daring leadership, the Confederacy's defensive strategy underwent an important shift.

Lee seized the initiative on June 25, 1862, attacking McClellan's right flank. Although inconclusive, the attack pushed the nervous McClellan into a defensive position. For a week, the armies sparred in a series of fierce engagements known collectively as the Seven Days' Battles. More than thirty thousand men were killed or wounded on both sides, the deadliest week of the war so far. Although McClellan prevailed in these contests, the carnage so shocked him that he withdrew to Harrison's Landing on the James River. An exasperated Lincoln replaced McClellan with John Pope. Although Lee had saved Richmond, his troops had suffered frightfully. He had lost one-fourth of his eighty thousand–man army, but he remained convinced of the wisdom of his offensive-defensive strategy.

Lee went to work to vindicate these tactics. A series of inconclusive skirmishes brought Union and Confederate armies together once more, near Manassas Junction. The Second Battle of Bull Run was as much a disaster for the Union as the first had been. Lee's generalship completely befuddled Pope and again saved Richmond. Lee and the Army of Northern Virginia were developing a reputation for invincibility.

TURNING POINTS, 1862–1863

The impressive Confederate victories in the East masked the delicate condition of Southern fortunes.

The longer the Confederacy held off Union offensives, the greater the likelihood of securing the South's independence. But the longer the war continued, the higher the probability that the Confederacy's shortcomings in men, finances, and materiel would erode its ability to keep fighting. Lee's offensive-defensive strategy seemed to be working, but it raised the possibility that the Confederacy could exhaust its men and resources before it sealed its independence.

The waning summer months of 1862 brought other concerns to the Davis administration in Richmond. The Union navy was choking the South's commercial link with Europe. Davis looked to the nations of Europe for diplomatic recognition as well as for trade.

But the most important arena of the war remained the battlefield. Having stymied the Union war machine, Lee contemplated a bold move—a thrust into Northern territory to bring the conflict to the North and stoke Northerners' rising hostility to the war. It was a bold plan that might end the war and secure Southern independence—or hasten an otherwise inevitable Union victory.

President Lincoln also harbored a bold plan. Gradually during the spring and summer of 1862, the president had concluded that emancipation of the Confederacy's slaves was essential for preserving the Union. Emancipation would provide Federal forces with both moral and strategic advantages over their foes. But Lincoln was reluctant to take this step before the Union's fortunes on the battlefield improved. Without a significant victory, emancipation would appear to be an act of desperation. As the fall of 1862 approached, both Union and Confederate governments prepared for the most significant conflicts of the war to date.

THE NAVAL AND THE DIPLOMATIC WAR

The Union's naval strategy was to blockade the Southern coast and capture its key seaports and river towns. The intention was to prevent arms, clothing, and food from reaching the Confederacy and keep cotton and tobacco from leaving. Destroying the South's ability to carry on trade would also prevent the Confederacy from raising money to purchase the goods it needed to wage war. This vital trade brought the Confederacy into contact with European nations, a connection they hoped to reinforce on the diplomatic front as well.

The naval war. Neither side had much of a navy at the outset of the war. With more than three thousand miles of Confederate coastline to cover, the Union blockade was weak at first. As time passed and the number of ships in the Union navy grew, the blockade tightened. The skyrocketing prices of Southern staples on world markets by 1862 attested to the effectiveness of the Union strategy.

Understandably, the Confederate naval strategy was to break the blockade and defend the South's vital rivers and seaports. The Confederacy built several warships to serve as blockade runners and as privateers to attack Union merchants ships, and, briefly, they disrupted Federal operations before Union vessels regained the advantage. Historians disagree about the effectiveness of the Union naval blockade, but with limited resources and capital, the Confederacy was heavily dependent on the flow of trade. Any restriction in that flow hurt the Southern cause.

The diplomatic front.

Southerners, remembering the crucial role that timely French assistance had played in the American Revolution, thought that the recognition of their independence by overseas governments would legitimize their cause in the eyes of the world.

Great Britain had several reasons to support the Confederate cause. After two wars and a succession of diplomatic wrangles, it had no great love of the United States. If the country divided, it would pose less of a threat to British economic and territorial ambitions. Some British textile magnates also supported the Confederacy because they feared a drastic reduction in the supply of Southern cotton.

British foreign policy, however, had been anti-slavery for a quarter century, and the slavery issue turned many Britons against the South. The Union cause had support in high ruling circles, especially from Queen Victoria, as well as from middle-class and working-class Britons. One working-class leader declared the Confederate cause "odious and . . . blasphemous" and hoped for a reunited America that would become "the hope of freedom, and a refuge for the oppressed of every race and of every clime."

Emperor Napoleon III of France, who had imperial designs on Mexico, favored the Confederacy. A restored Union, he thought, would pose a greater threat to his ambitions than a divided one. But Napoleon feared antagonizing the powerful British and would not intervene unilaterally in the Confederate cause.

He did, however, take advantage of the Civil War, by invading Mexico in June 1863 and installing Austrian archduke Maximilian as emperor. In November, however, Union forces occupied the border town of Brownsville, Texas, an unmistakable signal to the French not to expand their adventure. Following the Civil War, the United States government prevailed upon France to withdraw from Mexico. Patriot insurgents, led by Benito Juárez, who would become president of Mexico, captured and killed Maximilian, restoring Mexican rule and removing the last vestige of a foreign threat on United States borders.

The Russians were probably the staunchest supporters of the Union abroad. The odd friendship between the Western world's most autocratic country and its most democratic one resulted primarily from political expediency. The Russian tsar, Alexander II, saw the United States as a counterweight to British power. There was also some sympathy for the North's opposition to slavery in Russia, where the tsar had abolished serfdom (a form of slavery) in 1861.

Southerners were convinced that their cotton was so important to the world economy that they could use it as a diplomatic bargaining chip. "You dare not to make war on cotton. . . . cotton is king." So declared South Carolina senator James H. Hammond in a warning to the North in 1858. But King Cotton was no more successful at coercing the British—who had large cotton reserves and an alternate source of supply in Egypt—into granting recognition to the Confederacy than it was at stopping the North from going to war against the South.

The Davis administration did chalk up some minor diplomatic victories early in the war. Great Britain declared itself neutral and allowed British merchants to sell arms and supplies to both Confederate and Union forces. This policy especially benefited the Confederacy, with its limited arsenal. France followed with a similar concession.

In the end, the Confederacy's hopes for diplomatic recognition depended on its ability to show that it could secure its independence on the battlefield. After Lee's victories in Virginia in the spring of 1862 and his subsequent decision to invade the North, British intervention in the war grew more likely. The British government had more or less decided that if Lee emerged victorious from his planned invasion, it would press for mediation. William Gladstone, England's future prime minister, believed that Lee would achieve his goal. He concluded that "we may anticipate with certainty the success of the Southern states so far as regards their separation from the North."

ANTIETAM

The alarming arithmetic of the offensive-defensive strategy convinced Lee that the South could not sustain a prolonged conflict. He knew that his army must keep the pressure on Union forces and, if possible, destroy them quickly. Union success in the Mississippi valley threatened to cut the Confederacy in two and deprive it of the resources of a vast chunk of territory. Within a year, the Confederacy might cease to exist west of the Appalachians. He desperately needed a dramatic victory.

In September 1862, Lee crossed the Potomac into Maryland as his band played "Maryland, My Maryland" for the unimpressed residents. He was on his way to cut off the Pennsylvania Railroad at Harrisburg. Lee established camp at Frederick, scattering his army at various sites, convinced that McClellan and the Army of the Potomac would not attack him.

At this point, luck intervened for the North. At an abandoned Confederate encampment, a Union corporal found three wrapped cigars on the ground, evidently tossed out by a careless Confederate officer. To the corporal's amazement, the wrapping was a copy of Lee's orders for the disposition of his army. But even with this information, "Little Mac" moved so cautiously that Lee had time to gather his and Jackson's regiments and retreat to defensive positions at Sharpsburg, Maryland, along Antietam creek. There Lee's army of 39,000 men came to blows with McClellan's army of 75,000.

The Battle of Antietam saw the bloodiest single day of fighting in American history. About 2,100 Union soldiers and 2,700 Confederates died on the battlefield, and another 18,500, equally divided, were wounded. McClellan squandered his numerical superiority with uncoordinated and timid Union attacks. Although the armies had fought to a tactical draw, the battle was a strategic defeat for the Confederacy. In the battle's aftermath, Lee's troops limped back across the Potomac into Virginia and McClellan did not pursue.

Antietam marked a major turning point in the war. It kept Lee from directly threatening Northern industry and financial institutions. It prompted Britain and France to abandon plans to grant recognition to the Confederacy. And it provided Lincoln with the victory he needed to announce the abolition of slavery.

EMANCIPATION

President Lincoln despised slavery, but he had always maintained that preserving the Union was his primary war goal. "If I could save the Union without freeing any slave I would do it," he wrote to the newspaper editor Horace Greeley in August 1862, "and if I could save it by freeing all the slaves I would do it; and if I could save it by freeing some and leaving others alone, I would also do that." An astute politician, Lincoln realized that he had to stress union and equivocate on slavery to keep the Northern public united in support of the war. But from the war's out-set, the possibility of emancipation as a war objective was considered in the Republican Congress, within the Union army, and among citizens throughout the Northern states. Northern soldiers, as they moved South, saw slaves building trenches, earthworks, bridges, and roads for the Confederate army as well as working Southern farms. As a result, pressure grew within the Union army to declare emancipation as a way of depriving the South and the Confederate army of its labor force.

Lincoln said in his inaugural address that he had "no purpose, directly or indirectly, to interfere with the institution of slavery in the states where it exists." By March 1862, however, his moral repugnance toward slavery, and the military arguments for abolition, led him to propose a resolution, which Congress adopted, supporting the compensated emancipation of slaves. The measure died, however, when Congress failed to appropriate funds for it and slaveholders in the border states expressed no interest in the plan.

Pressure from Northern civilians, Union soldiers, and Congress for some form of emancipation mounted in the spring of 1862. In response, the Republican Congress prohibited slavery in the territories and abolished slavery in the District of Columbia. The act emancipating the district's slaves called for compensating slave owners and colonizing the freed slaves in black republics, such as Haiti and Liberia. Then, in July 1862, Congress passed the **Confiscation Act,** which ordered the seizure of land from disloyal Southerners and the emancipation of their slaves.

Although support for emancipation had grown both in the army and among civilians, Lincoln still faced political considerations that dictated against it. Emancipation was still not favored by a majority in the North, especially not in the border states. The thousands of Irish Catholic immigrants who entered the Union army and who had competed with black workers for jobs in Northern cities during the 1850s were especially opposed to emancipation, fearing a loss of economic security. They also resented the abolitionists' Protestant moralizing. The Roman Catholic Archbishop John Hughes of New York declared that "We Catholics, and a vast majority of our brave troops in the field, have not the slightest idea of carrying on a war that costs so much blood and treasure just to gratify a clique of abolitionists in the North." But other considerations favored emancipation. Freeing the slaves would appeal to the strong antislavery sentiment in Britain and gain support for the Union cause abroad. And it would weaken the Confederacy's ability to wage war by removing a crucial source of labor.

The Emancipation Proclamation.

By mid-1862, the president had resolved to act on his moral convictions and proclaim emancipation. Taking the advice of Secretary of State Seward, however, he decided to wait for a battlefield victory so that the measure would not appear an act of desperation. Antietam gave the president his opening, narrow though it was, and on September 22, 1862, he announced his intention to issue the **Emancipation Proclamation,** to take effect January 1, 1863, in all states still in rebellion. The proclamation exempted slaves in the border states loyal to the Union and in areas under Federal occupation.

Southerners reacted to the Emancipation Proclamation with outrage. Some viewed it as an invitation to race war and conjured up fears of freed slaves slaying white women and children while their men were at the battlefront. Jefferson Davis, taking a positive view, thought that the proclamation would invigorate the Southern war effort. Some observers abroad were skeptical. One London newspaper, noting that emancipation did not apply to all slaves, stated, "the principle is not that a human being cannot justly own another, but that he cannot own him unless he is loyal to the United States."

Northerners generally approved of the emancipation proclamation. Although abolitionists comprised a minority of the Northern population, most civilians and soldiers accepted emancipation for its military advantages. A private in the Army of the Potomac who had previously expressed serious reservations about emancipation wrote home his support for "putting away any institution if by so doing it will help put down the rebellion."

The Emancipation Proclamation represented far more than its qualified words and phrases expressed. "A mighty act," Massachusetts governor John Andrew called it. Lincoln had freed the slaves. He and the Union war effort were now tied to the cause of freedom. What began as a war to save the Union had became a holy war of deliverance. Freedom and Union entwined in the public consciousness of the North. As Lincoln noted in his December 1862 message to Congress, "[I]n giving freedom to the slave, we assure freedom to the free." Emancipation also unified the Republican party and strengthened the president's hand in conducting the war.

"Stealing" freedom.

As word of the Emancipation Proclamation raced through the slave grapevine, slaves rejoiced that their long-awaited day of jubilee had arrived. But the proclamation only continued a process that had begun when the first Union armies invaded the South. In the months before freedom came, many slaves had run away to Union camps, dug Union trenches, and scouted for Federal troops.

Southern masters fought to deter their slaves by severely punishing the families of black men who fled to the Union lines. They used the courts and slave catchers to reclaim runaways. Some Confederate masters protected their investments by removing slaves to Texas or to areas far from federal forces. And a few slave owners whipped, sold, and even killed their slaves to prevent them from joining the Union troops.

But in the end, slaveholders could not stem the tide of slaves fleeing toward the Union lines and freedom. The 1862 Confiscation Act included slaves with other Confederate property as the "contraband" of war and subject to confiscation, a term Union general Benjamin Butler had applied to escaped slaves as early as May 1861. As they helped the Union cause, contrabands also sought to help fellow slaves "steal" their freedom. When Union forces occupied part of the Georgia coast in April 1862, for example, March Haynes, a slave who had worked as a river pilot in Savannah, began smuggling slaves to the Union lines. Federal general Quincy Adams Gilmore provided a swift boat for Haynes's missions. In return, Haynes supplied Gilmore with "exact and valuable information" on the strength and location of Confederate defenses.

The former slaves who arrived at Federal camps after emancipation often encountered poor conditions but relished their freedom nonetheless. A Northern missionary in occupied Louisiana wrote in 1863 that he was surrounded by "negroes in uniform, negroes in rags, negroes in frame houses, negroes living in tents, negroes living in rail pens covered with brush, and negroes living under brush piles without any rails, negroes living on the bare ground with the sky for their covering; all hopeful . . . every one pleading to be taught, willing to do anything for learning."

The Emancipation Proclamation accelerated the slaves' flight from bondage. Personally fighting to secure their freedom and liberating those still enslaved became the objective of many, for after 1863, ex-slaves served in increasing numbers in the Union army.

Black troops in the Union Army.

More than 80 percent of the roughly 180,000 black soldiers and 20,000 black sailors who fought for the Union were slaves and free black men from the South. For the typical black Southerner who joined the army, the passage from bondage to freedom came quickly. Making his escape from his master, he perhaps "stole" his family as well. He typically experienced his first days of freedom behind Union lines, where he may have

Even before the Emancipation Proclamation, slaves throughout the South "stole" their freedom. After the Proclamation, the trickle of black slaves abandoning their masters became a flood as they sought freedom behind Union lines.

learned to read and write. Finally, he put on the Federal uniform, experiencing, as one black Southern volunteer commented, "the biggest thing that ever happened in my life."

As early as August 1862, five thousand African Americans had enrolled in the Union army in the occupied Sea Islands off South Carolina despite a widely publicized Confederate directive promising to shoot black prisoners of war. This threat was later withdrawn when Union officers declared that they would do the same with Confederate prisoners. The Confederacy, however, held fast to its refusal to parole, or send back, captured black soldiers, a policy that led to the end of prisoner exchanges in early 1863 and contributed to horrible conditions in overcrowded prisoner-of-war camps on both sides.

Initially, the enlistment of black soldiers in South Carolina encountered opposition in the North. By early 1863, however, public opinion was changing. One reason was that white Northerners realized that the enlistment of African Americans relieved them in comparable numbers from military service. President Lincoln strongly advocated enlisting former slaves. In March 1863, he wrote, with exaggerated enthusiasm, "[T]he bare sight of 50,000 armed and drilled black soldiers on the banks of the Mississippi would end the rebellion at once." On the contrary, the appearance of black Union troops infuriated the Confederates. After a battle at Milliken's Bend, Louisiana, in 1863, for example, observers found dead Confederate and black Union soldiers entangled in each other's arms and impaled on one another's bayonets.

COME AND JOIN US BROTHERS.
PUBLISHED BY THE SUPERVISORY COMMITTEE FOR RECRUITING COLORED REGIMENTS
1210 CHESTNUT ST. PHILADELPHIA.

Once orders were issued allowing the recruitment of black troops, posters like this one appeared throughout the North. The illustrations stressed the dignity and manhood of military service but also showed segregated soldiers and white officers.

But for black volunteers, the promise of freedom and redemption outweighed the dangers of combat. Black abolitionists campaigned tirelessly for the enlistment of free black men and fugitive slaves in the Union army. Frederick Douglass, whose son Lewis distinguished himself in the all-black 54th Massachusetts Volunteer Infantry Regiment, explained in early 1863, "Once let the black man get upon his person the brass letters, 'U.S.,' let him get an eagle on his buttons and a musket on his shoulder and bullets in his pockets, and there is no power on earth which can deny that he has earned the right to citizenship in the United States." Other black abolitionists took up the refrain. Sojourner Truth, a former slave who saw many of her thirteen children sold into slavery, canvassed Northern cities to rally public opinion for the deployment of black troops.

Although black soldiers were eager to engage the enemy and fought as ably as their white comrades, they received lower pay and performed the most menial duties in camp. Abolitionists and black leaders in the North pressured President Lincoln for more equitable treatment of African American recruits. When Frederick Douglass complained to Lincoln about the lower pay that black troops received, the president defended the practice, noting that "their enlistment was a serious offense to popular prejudice" and the fact "that they were not to receive the same pay as white soldiers seemed a necessary concession to smooth the way to their employment at all as soldiers."

Despite discrimination, black soldiers fought valiantly at Port Hudson, Louisiana; near Charleston; and, late in the war, at the siege of Petersburg, Virginia. After hearing of African American troops fighting Confederate forces nearby, one young white Mississippian wrote in her diary, "it is said the Negro regiments fought there like mad demons." The most celebrated black encounter with Confederate troops occurred in July 1863, during a futile assault by the 54th Massachusetts Regiment on Fort Wagner outside Charleston The Northern press, previously lukewarm toward black troops, heaped praise on the effort. "Through the cannon smoke of that dark night," intoned a writer in the *Atlantic Monthly*, "the manhood of the colored race shines before many eyes that would not see."

If only President Lincoln could find such gallantry among his generals! George McClellan had failed to follow his advantage at Antietam in September 1862, allowing Lee's army to escape to Virginia and remain a formidable fighting force. And despite Union successes in the West, the Confederate forces massed there remained largely intact.

FROM FREDERICKSBURG TO GETTYSBURG

In late 1862, after Antietam, the president replaced McClellan with General Ambrose E. Burnside. The new chief of the Army of the Potomac, an imposing physical presence, sported bushy whiskers on his cheeks that came to be known as "sideburns," a transposition of the two parts of his name. Despite his commanding stature, Burnside was shy and insecure. Claiming incompetence, he had twice refused the command. His judgment proved better than Lincoln's.

Fredericksburg. Moving swiftly against Lee's dispersed army in northern Virginia, Burnside reached the Rappahannock river opposite Fredericksburg in November 1862 (see Map 15-3). But the pontoon bridges to ford his 120,000 soldiers across the river arrived three weeks late, giving Lee an opportunity to gather his 78,000 men. On December 13, the Union forces launched a poorly coordinated and foolish frontal assault that the Confederates repelled, inflicting heavy federal casualties. Burnside, having performed to his own expectations, was relieved of his command, and Major General Joseph Hooker was installed in his place.

MAP 15-3 From Fredericksburg to Gettysburg: The War in the East, December 1862-July 1863
By all logic, the increasingly outgunned and outfinanced Confederacy should have been showing signs of faltering by 1863. But bungling by Union generals at Fredericksburg and Chancellorsville sustained Southern fortunes and encouraged Robert E. Lee to attempt another Northern invasion.

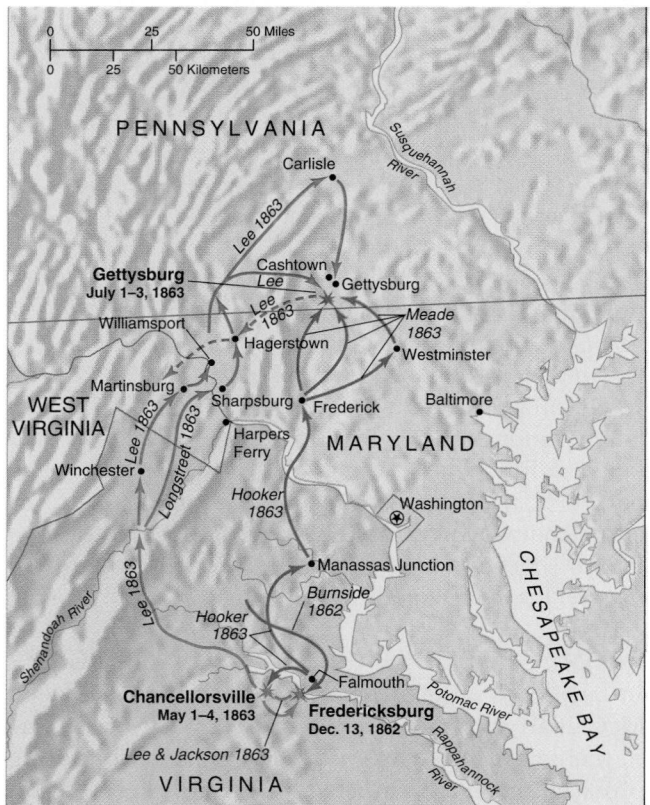

Chancellorsville.
The hard-drinking Hooker lacked Burnside's humility but not his incompetence. Resuming the offensive in the spring of 1863, Hooker hoped to outflank Lee. But the Confederate commander surprised Hooker by sending Stonewall Jackson to outflank the Union right. Between May 1 and May 4, Lee's army delivered a series of crushing attacks on Hooker's forces at Chancellorsville. Outnumbered two to one, Lee had pulled off another stunning victory—but at a high cost. Lee lost some thirteen thousand men, fewer than Hooker's seventeen thousand, but more than the Confederacy could afford.

Lee also lost Stonewall Jackson at Chancellorsville. Nervous Confederate sentries mistakenly shot and wounded him as he returned from a reconnoitering mission, and he died a few days later. Known for his lightning strikes at the enemy and his brilliant understanding of the tactics of modern warfare, Jackson had helped Lee win some of the Confederacy's most stunning victories in 1862. Lee recognized the tragedy of Jackson's loss for himself and his country. "Any victory," the Confederate commander wrote, "would be dear at such a price. I know not how to replace him."

Still, Lee appeared invincible. Chancellorsville thrust Lincoln into another bout of despair. "My God!" he exclaimed in agony, "What will the country say! What will the country say!" Meanwhile, Lee, to take advantage of the Confederacy's momentum and the Union's gloom, planned another bold move. On June 3, 1863, the 75,000-man Army of Northern Virginia broke camp and headed North once again (see "American Views: A Soldier Promotes the Union Cause").

Gettysburg.
President Lincoln sent the Union Army of the Potomac after Lee. But General Hooker dallied, requested more troops, and allowed the Confederates to march from Maryland into Pennsylvania. An infuriated Lincoln replaced Hooker with George Gordon Meade.

Lee and Meade were personal friends—they had served together during the Mexican war—and the change in command worried the Confederate general. He had counted on the bungling Hooker as his opponent. "General Meade," he commented prophetically, "will commit no blunder in my front."

Lee's Army of Northern Virginia occupied a wide swath of Pennsylvania territory from Chambersburg to Wrightsville along the Susquehanna River, across from the state capital at Harrisburg. When Lee learned of Meade's movements, he ordered his troops to consolidate in a defensive position at Cashtown, 45 miles from Harrisburg. That the greatest battle of the war erupted at nearby Gettysburg was pure chance. A

AMERICAN VIEWS

A Soldier Promotes the Union Cause

Soldiers wrote their thoughts down in diaries, in letters to their families, and, as in the case of the infantryman here, D. Beardsley, from Tompkins County, New York, to newspapers. Morale faltered in both the civilian and military ranks on both sides during the Civil War as this excerpt indicates. At the same time, Beardsley is buoyed by the elevated sense of mission in Union ranks, brought about by Abraham Lincoln's Emancipation Proclamation, which took effect one month prior to this letter.

- How to balance civil liberties with the necessity of carrying on a war is a dilemma of all armed conflicts involving democratic societies. What does this soldier think about where the balance ought to occur?

- The writer refers to "desertion" in the ranks indicating a morale problem in the Union armies. Why was this the case in February 1863?

- What impact does this soldier hope the Emancipation Proclamation will have on the war effort in the North?

I having the honor of being a volunteer from old Tompkins County, and also fighting under the same banner and for the same principles that Washington did—still holding to my priviledges [sic] as a citizen of the United States, I think it will not be out of place for me to speak a few words through your columns, to the good people of my native county. . . .

If our Government would have no rebellion, she must pluck the tares of rebellion from the heart of the nation; and if we would have this rebellion crushed, we must cease to have traitors in power. Let that class in the Northern States, who would kiss the red hand of treason for a momentary peace, remember that the hand will be no less red by the kiss, or the blow no less sure by the pause; and I would humbly beg the people of the North, in the name of a soldier for the Union, that they will, in this dark and trying hour of our country's history, give us

their undivided support, first, by stripping all power from the traitors at home, and then by their repentant prayers for our success in battles. . . . A few have deserted, and may God have mercy upon them. Let them go, their *blood* is altogether too poor to enrich the soil of worn out Virginia. We want the blood of patriots to make it bring forth the fruits of freedom. . . . We hope that in future the people and the army will become more pure, and work with a nobler purpose of heart. The first step toward this reformation has already been taken. We begin to see that all men have rights, whether white or black, and we hope that when the smoke of battle shall have cleared away, that the bright sun of peace will shine upon a truly free people.

Source: D. Beardsley, "Co. K, 137th Reg't, N.Y. Vols" that appeared in the *Ithaca Journal*, March 3, 1863; dated February 16, 1863 and written from Acquia Landing, Virginia.

Confederate brigade left Cashtown to confiscate much-needed shoes in Gettysburg. Meeting federal cavalry resistance near the town, the brigade withdrew. On July 1, 1863, a larger Confederate force advanced toward Gettysburg to disperse the cavalry and seize the shoes. What the Confederates did not realize

was that the entire Army of the Potomac was coming up behind the cavalry (see map 15-4).

During the first day of battle, July 1, the Confederates appeared to gain the upper hand, forcing Union forces back from the town to a new position on Cemetery Hill. On the second day, the entire Union army

MAP 15-4   The Battle of Gettysburg, July 1-3, 1863
In a war that lasted four years, it is difficult to point to the decisive battle. But clearly, the outcome during those hot July days at Gettysburg set the tone for the rest of the war. The result was unclear until the final day of battle, and, even then, it might have gone either way. Winning by a whisker was enough to propel Union armies to a string of victories over the next year and to throw Confederate forces back on their defenses among an increasingly despairing population. Gettysburg marked the last major Southern invasion of the North.

was in place, but the Confederates seized the initiative and took several key locations along Cemetery Ridge before federal forces pushed them back to the previous day's positions. Although the opposing sides had suffered heavy casualties, both armies were intact; and, if anything, Lee had the advantage. On July 3, the third

day of the battle, Lee made a fateful error. Believing that the center of Meade's line was weak, he ordered an all-out assault against it. The night before, Meade had remarked to his colleague, Brigadier General John Gibbon, "if Lee attacks tomorrow, it will be in your front. He has made attacks on both our flanks and failed and if he concludes to try it again, it will be on our center." Thus Meade was prepared for Lee's assault.

The next morning, a bright, hot summer day, the Confederates launched an assault on Culp's Hill, only to fall back by noon. The key battle of the day occurred at three in the afternoon at Cemetery Ridge, preceded by a fierce artillery duel. When the Union guns suddenly went silent, the Confederates, thinking they had knocked them out, began a charge led by General George Pickett. As the Confederate infantry marched out with battle colors flying, the Union artillery opened up again and tore apart the charging Southerners. Some managed to reach their objective, a low stone wall at the crest of the hill, but the federals who held the wall outnumbered them and pushed them back. The Confederates retreated down the gentle slope strewn with their fallen comrades, the hopes of a Southern victory dashed. Half of Pickett's thirteen–thousand–man division lay dead or wounded.

After the battle, Lee explained his disastrous frontal assault: "I believed my men were invincible." After Pickett's charge, Lee rode among his troops and urged them to brace for a final Union assault. The attack never came. Meade allowed Lee to withdraw into Maryland and cross the Potomac to Virginia.

Gettysburg was the bloodiest battle of the war. The Union suffered 23,000 casualties; the Confederacy, 28,000. The battle's outcome boosted morale in the North and drained Lee's army of men and materiel. Yet Lincoln blasted Meade for failing to follow up on his victory. "I do not believe you appreciate the magnitude of the misfortune involved in Lee's escape," he wrote to his general. "He was within your easy grasp, and to have closed upon him would, in connection with our other late successes, have ended the war. As it is, the war will be prolonged indefinitely. . . . Your golden opportunity is gone, and I am distressed immeasurably because of it." Convinced by his aides that Meade would resign when he read the letter, Lincoln never sent it.

VICKSBURG, CHATTANOOGA, AND THE WEST

As Union forces thwarted Confederate dreams in Pennsylvania, Federal troops bore down on strategic Rebel strongholds in the Western theater of the war. Union military success in the West would seriously compromise the South's ability to move goods and men across rail lines and over waterways, and leave its

These Union and Confederate dead at Gettysburg represent the cost of the war, the price of freedom. President Lincoln transformed the battleground from a killing field to a noble symbol of sacrifice for American ideals. Gettysburg continues to occupy a special place in our nation's history and in the memory of its citizens.

forces vulnerable to the ultimate Western prize, the Confederate bread basket, Georgia.

Vicksburg.

When Lincoln mentioned "our other late successes" in his letter to Meade, he was referring to another crucial Union victory. On July 4, one day after Pickett's charge at Gettysburg, the city of Vicksburg, the last major Confederate stronghold on the Mississippi, surrendered to Ulysses S. Grant.

Grant had demonstrated an ability to use his forces creatively, swiftly, and with a minimum loss of life in his campaigns in the western Confederacy, but Vicksburg presented him with several strategic obstacles (see Map 15-5). In 1862, the formidable defenses on the city's western edge, which towered over the Mississippi, had thwarted a Union naval assault, and the labyrinth of swamps, creeks, and woods, protecting the city from the north, had foiled General Sherman. The only feasible approaches appeared to be from the south and east.

By March 1863, Grant, had devised a brilliant plan to take Vicksburg that called for rapid maneuvering and expert coordination. Grant had his twenty thousand Union troops ferried across the Mississippi from the Louisiana side at a point south of Vicksburg. Then he marched them quickly into the interior of

Mississippi. They moved northeastward, captured the Mississippi state capital at Jackson, and turned west toward Vicksburg. On May 22, 1863, Grant settled down in front of the city, less than 600 yards from Confederate positions. Grant's tight siege and the Union navy's bombardment from the river cut the city off completely. As food stores dwindled, residents were forced to eat mules and rats to survive. Their situation hopeless, General John Pemberton and his thirty-thousand-man garrison surrendered on July 4.

Chattanooga.

As Grant was besieging Vicksburg in June 1863, Union general William S. Rosecrans, commanding the Army of the Cumberland, advanced on Confederate general Braxton Bragg, whose Army of Tennessee held Chattanooga, a "doorway" on the railroad that linked Richmond to the lower South. The capture of the city would complete the uncoupling of the West from the eastern Confederacy.

Bragg lacked confidence in his men and consistently overestimated the force and cunning of his enemy. At Rosecrans's approach, he abandoned Chattanooga and took up positions at nearby Chickamauga Creek. When the two armies clashed at Chickamauga on September 19, Bragg pushed Rosecrans back to Chattanooga. Bragg seized the railroad leading into Chattanooga and bottled up Rosecrans there, much as Grant had confined Pemberton at Vicksburg. Both sides had suffered heavily. Suddenly, the Union's careful strategy for the conquest of the western Confederacy seemed in jeopardy.

The Confederate position on the heights overlooking Chattanooga appeared impregnable. But the Confederate camp was plagued by dissension, with some officers openly questioning Bragg's ability. President Davis considered replacing him but had no one else available with Bragg's experience. Instead, Davis ordered General James Longstreet (along with one-third of Bragg's army) on a futile expedition against Union forces at Knoxville, Tennessee. Converging on Chattanooga with reinforcements, Union generals Grant, Sherman, and Hooker took advantage of the

MAP 15-5   Vicksburg and Chattanooga: The War in the West, 1863
Devising a brilliant strategy, Union General Ulysses S. Grant took the last major Mississippi River stronghold from Confederate hands on July 4, 1863, dealing a significant economic and morale blow to Southern forces. Coupled with the defeat at Gettysburg a day earlier, the fall of Vicksburg portended a bitter finale to hopes for Southern independence. Grant completed his domination of the West by joining forces with several Union generals to capture Chattanooga and push Confederate forces into Georgia, setting the stage for the capture of that key southern state by the Federals in 1864.

divided Confederate army to break the siege and force Bragg's army to retreat into Georgia. The Union now dominated most of the West and faced an open road to the East.

The war in the Trans-Mississippi West.

The Confederacy's reverses at Vicksburg and Chattanooga mirrored its misfortunes farther west of the Mississippi River. Although a relatively minor theater of war, the territory west of the Mississippi provided supplies and strategic advantages for the Confederate West. Success in the Trans-Mississippi West could occupy Federal troops and relieve pressure from other parts of the Confederacy while allowing food and munitions to reach desperate Southern armies.

Native American tribes in the Trans-Mississippi West, such as the Navajos, Dakotas, and Lakotas, spent a good deal of the Civil War battling Federal troops for territory and resources, quite apart from the sectional conflict. Three regiments of Cherokee Indians, however, led by Colonel (later Brigadier General) Stand Watie, fought for the South at the Battle of Pea Ridge in 1862. The Union won the battle and, with it, control of Missouri and northern Arkansas. Most battles between pro-Union and pro-Confederate Native American forces occurred in the Indian Territory (now Oklahoma).

Texas was critical to Confederate fortunes, both as a source of supply for the East and as a base for the conquest of the Far West. President Davis envisaged a continental Confederacy that included California, with its gold fields and Pacific ports. The ports would give the Confederacy access to Asian trade and, Davis reasoned, weaken the Federal naval blockade.

Texas, however, was far from secure. It suffered from internal dissent and violence on its borders. Not all Texans supported secession. As early as 1862, areas of northern Texas, a Unionist stronghold before the war, rebelled against Confederate authorities and were brutally suppressed. Germans in the Fredericksburg-San Antonio area openly defied the Confederacy from 1862 until the war's end. And the Mexican population in southern Texas supported the Union. On the state's western border, Comanches raided homesteaders at will until late 1864. In the east and along the southern frontier in the lower Rio Grande Valley, Union gunboats and troops disrupted Confederate supply lines. For a time, Texas maintained commercial contact with the rest of the Confederacy through Matamoros Mexico. The Mexican connection was vexing to the Lincoln administration, given the presence of the French and their puppet government from 1863 on. But by 1864, with the Union in control of the

Mississippi, and Federal troops along the Mexican border, Texas had lost its strategic importance.

The Confederacy's transcontinental aspirations died early in the war. In March 1862, a Confederate army seeking to conquer the Southwest was defeated by Union forces at the Battle of Glorieta Pass in New Mexico. The Southwest, from New Mexico to California, would remain firmly in Union hands.

WAR TRANSFORMS THE NORTH

Union successes in 1863 had a profound impact on both sides. For the North, hopes of victory and reunion increased. The federal government expanded its bureaucracy to wage war efficiently, and a Republican-dominated Congress passed legislation that broadened federal power and furthered the war effort. The Lincoln administration faced opposition on these measures and on its conduct of the war from within Congress, from the Democratic party, and from state leaders. But it successfully weathered dissent, thanks to the president's political skill, the desire of the Republicans to remain in power, and the Union's improving military fortunes. Boosted by federal economic legislation and wartime demand, the Northern economy boomed. Women entered the work force in growing numbers. But labor unrest and class and racial tensions suggested that prosperity had a price.

WARTIME LEGISLATION AND POLITICS

Before the Civil War, the federal government rarely affected citizens' lives directly. But raising troops, protecting territory, and mobilizing the economy for war required a strong and active central government. With the departure of the South from the Union, Republicans dominated all branches of the federal administration. This left them in a position to test the constitutional limits of federal authority.

Suppressing dissent.

President Lincoln began almost immediately to use executive authority to suppress opposition to the war effort in the North. In one of his most controversial actions, he issued a temporary suspension of the writ of habeas corpus, the constitutional requirement that protects a defendant against illegal imprisonment. Suspending it allowed authorities to arrest suspected Confederate agents and hold them indefinitely, a procedure sanctioned by the Constitution "when in cases of rebellion or invasion the public safety may require it." Explaining his extraordinary actions in a July 4, 1861, message to Congress, Lincoln stated, "it became necessary for me to choose whether I should let the government fall into ruin, or whether . . . availing myself of the broader powers conferred by the Constitution in case of insurrection, I would make an effort to save it." The suspension became permanent in September 1862 and was used primarily in the border states to detain those suspected of trading with the enemy, defrauding the War Department, and evading the draft.

Executive sanctions fell particularly hard on the Democratic party. "Disloyalty" was difficult to define in the midst of war. Though many Democrats opposed secession and supported the Union, they challenged the president on the conduct of the war, on emancipation, and on Lincoln's coolness toward peace initiatives. A few had ties with Confederate agents. Republicans called these dissenters "**Copperheads**," after the poisonous snake.

Despite the suspension of habeas corpus, Lincoln compiled a fairly good record for upholding basic American civil liberties. Although the authorities shut down a handful of newspapers temporarily, the administration made no attempt to control the news or subvert the electoral process. Two major elections were held during the war. In the first, the off-year election in 1862, Republicans retained control of Congress but lost several seats to Democrats. In the presidential election of 1864, Lincoln won reelection in a hard-fought contest.

While fellow Republicans sometimes chastised the president for violating civil liberties, mismanaging military command assignments, or moving too slowly on emancipation, they rarely threatened to disrupt the party. But there was dissent in the Republican party, and it had an effect on national policy. **Radical Republicans** hounded Lincoln from early in his administration, establishing the Joint Committee on the Conduct of the War to examine and monitor military policy. Some of them accused Democratic generals, including McClellan, of deliberately subverting the war effort with their poor performance. They also pressed Lincoln for quicker action on emancipation, though they supported the president on most crucial matters.

Boosting the economy. Lincoln likewise supported his party on an array of initiatives in Congress. Republicans used the federal government to enhance individual opportunities, especially in the West. The **Homestead Act**, passed in May 1862, granted 160 acres free to any settler in the territories who agreed to improve the land (by cultivating it and erecting a house) within five years of the grant. The act was also a boon for railroad companies.

Other legislation to boost the nation's economy and the fortunes of individual manufacturers and farmers included the **Land Grant College Act** of 1862, a protective tariff that same year, and the National Banking Act of 1863. The Land Grant Act awarded the proceeds from the sale of public lands to the states for the establishment of colleges offering instruction in "agriculture and mechanical arts." (President Buchanan had vetoed an earlier version of this act.) The tariff legislation protected Northern industry from foreign competition while raising revenue for the Union. The National Banking Act of 1863 replaced the bank notes of individual states, which were often backed by flimsy reserves and subject to wild fluctuations in value, with a uniform national currency.

Changes in the disposition of federal lands, the protective tariff, and the establishment of a national banking system presaged the active role the federal government would henceforth play in shaping the nation's economy. These measures helped sustain the Union war effort and enjoyed widespread support. The expansion of government into other areas, however, aroused opposition in some quarters, none more than the draft laws.

Conscription and the Draft Riots. Congress passed the first national conscription law in 1863. Almost immediately, evasion, obstruction, and weak enforcement threatened to undermine it. As military authorities began arresting draft dodgers and deserters, secret societies formed to harbor draftees and instruct them on evasion.

Conflicts between citizens and federal officials over the draft sometimes erupted in violence. The worst draft riot occurred in New York City in July 1863. Opposition to what many perceived as the Republican's war ran deep in New York, and support for the Democratic party was strong. The city's merchants were hurting from their lost trade in Southern cotton, and its Irish workers feared competition for jobs from freed slaves migrating to the North.

The **New York Draft Riot** began when a mostly Irish mob, protesting conscription, burned the federal marshal's headquarters. Racial and class antagonisms quickly joined antidraft anger as the mob went on a rampage through the city's streets, fighting police, plundering houses of the wealthy, and crying, "Down with the rich!" The rioters hanged two black New Yorkers who wandered into their path and burned the Colored Orphan Asylum. City authorities and the police stood by, unable or unwilling to stem the riot, which claimed more than one hundred lives. It was finally quelled by army units fresh from Gettysburg, along with militia and naval units. The draft resumed a month later.

The lynching of a black New Yorker during the Draft Riot in July 1863. The violence against black people during the riot reflected decades of racial tensions, especially between Irish immigrants and black residents, over jobs and housing.

THE NORTHERN ECONOMY

"The North," one historian has said, "was fighting the South with one hand and getting rich with the other behind its back." After an initial downturn during the uncertain months preceding the war, the Northern economy picked up quickly. High tariffs and massive federal spending soon made up for the loss of southern markets and the closing of the Mississippi river. Profits skyrocketed for some businesses. The earnings of the Erie Railroad, for example, jumped from $5 million in 1860 to $10 million in 1863. New industries boomed, and new inventions increased manufacturing efficiency, as in the sewing machine industry, which was first commercialized in the 1850s. Technological advances there greatly increased the output of the North's garment factories. Production of petroleum, a lubricant, increased from 84,000 gallons to 128 million gallons during the war.

Despite the loss of manpower to the demands of industry and the military, the productivity of Northern agriculture grew during the war. As machines replaced men on the farm, the manufacturers of farm machinery became wealthy. Crop failures in Europe dramatically increased the demand for American grain. "Old King Cotton's dead and buried; brave young Corn is king," went a popular Northern refrain of the day.

Trade unions and strikebreakers. Working people should have benefited from wartime prosperity.

With men off to war and immigration down, labor was in short supply. Although wages increased, prices rose more. Declining real wages led to exploitation, especially of women in garment factories. The trade union movement, which suffered a serious setback in the depression of 1857, revived. Local unions of shoemakers, carpenters, and miners emerged in 1862 across the North, and so did a few national organizations. By 1865, more than 200,000 northern workers belonged to labor unions.

Employers struck back at union organizing by hiring strikebreakers, usually African Americans. Labor conflicts between striking white workers and black strikebreakers sparked riots in New York City and Cincinnati. The racial antagonism accounted in part for workers' opposition to Lincoln's Emancipation Proclamation and for the continued strength of the Democratic party in Northern cities.

Profiteers and corruption. The promise of enormous profits bred greed and corruption as well as exploitation. Illicit trade between North and South was inevitable when cotton could be bought at 20 cents a pound in New Orleans and sold for $1.90 a pound in Boston. Profiteers not only defied the government to trade with the enemy but also sometimes swindled the government outright. Some merchants reaped high profits supplying the army with shoddy (a word coined during the war denoting poor quality shoes) goods at inflated prices. A writer for *Harper's Weekly* complained that "soldiers, on the first day's march or in the earliest storm, found their clothes . . . scattering to the wind in rags."

Some Northerners viewed the spending spree uneasily. They were disturbed to see older men flaunting their wealth while young men were dying on the battlefield. "The lavish profusion in which the old Southern cotton aristocracy used to indulge," wrote an indignant reporter for the *New York World*, "is completely eclipsed by the dash, parade, and magnificence of the new Northern shoddy aristocracy. . . . [T]he individual who makes the most money—no matter how—and spends the most money—no matter for what—is considered the greatest man."

Comments like these hinted at the deep social and ethical problems that were emerging in Northern society and would become more pronounced in the decades after the Civil War. For the time being, the benefits of economic development for the Union cause outweighed its negative consequences. The thriving Northern economy fed, clothed, and armed the Union's soldiers and kept most civilians employed and well fed. Prosperity and the demands of a wartime economy also provided Northern women with unprecedented opportunities.

NORTHERN WOMEN AND THE WAR

More than 100,000 Northern women took jobs in factories, sewing rooms, and arsenals during the civil war. Stepping in for their absent husbands, fathers, and sons, they often performed tasks previously reserved for men but at lower pay. The expanding bureaucracy in Washington also offered opportunities for many women. The United States Treasury alone employed 447 women in the war years. And unlike private industry, the Federal government paid women and men equally for the same work.

Women also had the opportunity to serve the war effort directly in another profession previously dominated by men—nursing. Physicians and officers, however, although they tolerated women nurses as nurturing morale boosters, thought little of their ability to provide medical care. Women sometimes challenged this condescending view, braving dismissal to confront the medical-military establishment head-on. Clara Barton, among the most notable nurses of the war, treated soldiers on the battlefield at great peril to her safety and to the consternation of officers. One of them remarked to her, "Miss Barton, this is a rough and unseemly position for you, a woman, to occupy." She shot back, "Is it not as rough and unseemly for these pain-racked men?" The officer temporarily suspended Barton for her candor. A British journalist, impressed by Barton and the thousands of women like her, commented that no conflict in history was so much "a woman's war" as the Civil War.

If the war created opportunities for many women, it also left tens of thousands widowed and devastated. In a society that assumed that men supported women, the death of a husband could be a financial and psychological disaster. Many women were left to survive on meager pensions with few skills they could use to support themselves.

The new economic opportunities the war created for women left Northern society more open to a broader view of women's roles. One indication of this change was the admission of women to eight previously all-male state universities after the war. Like the class and racial tensions that surfaced in Northern cities, the shifting role of women during the Civil War hinted at the promises and problems of postwar life. The changing scale and nature of the American economy, the expanded role of government, and the shift in class, racial, and gender relations are all trends that signaled what historians call the "modernization" of American society. Many of these trends began before the war, but the war highlighted and accelerated them.

Nurse Ann Bell tends a fallen Union soldier. Although medical practices were primitive and many young men died from poorly treated wounds or disease, the U.S. Sanitary Commission attempted to improve care in Union hospitals during the war. The war helped open nursing as a respectable occupation for women.

THE CONFEDERACY DISINTEGRATES

Even under the best of conditions, the newly formed political and economic institutions of the Confederacy would have had difficulty maintaining control over the country's class and racial tensions. But as battlefield losses mounted, the Confederacy disintegrated.

Victory is a marvelous glue. Defeat dissolves the bonds that hold a small society, such as the Confederacy, together and exposes the large and small divisions within it. After 1863, defeat infected Confederate politics, ruined the Southern economy, and eventually invaded the hearts and minds of the Southern people. What is remarkable is that such losses did not demoralize the Confederacy sooner. In fact, desertion rates did not exceed those of the Union forces, and Lee's Army of Northern Virginia included about as many men in the spring of 1865 as it had in the spring of 1863. True, civilians battled the policies of the Richmond government, but they protested less the sacrifices that war engendered than the unequal sharing of these burdens, including taxation, the military draft, food shortages, and inflation. Disillusionment against the Confederate government did not erode support for Lee and his army. The South pinned its waning hopes on its defensive military strategy. If it could prolong the conflict a little longer, perhaps a war-weary North would replace Lincoln and the Republicans in the 1864 elections with a Democratic president and Congress inclined to make peace.

SOUTHERN POLITICS

Dissent plagued Southern politics before the end of the war's first year. Residents of western Virginia mounted a secession movement of their own, declaring themselves for the union and forming the new state of West Virginia. Several counties in northern Alabama, in German-speaking districts in Texas, and throughout the mountains of Tennessee and North Carolina contemplated similar action.

As the war turned against the Confederacy, Southerners increasingly turned against each other. Some joined the peace societies that emerged as early as 1861 in Arkansas and soon after in most other Southern states. North Carolinians opposed to the war formed the Order of the Heroes of America, whose members not only demonstrated for peace but took control of the Piedmont and mountain sections of the state as well. Other Southerners preferred quieter dissent. They refused to join the army, pay taxes, or obey laws prohibiting trade with the enemy.

States' rights, a major principle of the seceding states, proved an obstacle to the Davis administration's efforts to exert central authority. The governors of Georgia and North Carolina gave the Richmond government particular difficulty, hoarding munitions, soldiers, supplies, food, and money. Even cooperative governors refused to allow state agents to collect taxes for the Confederacy.

Unlike Abraham Lincoln, Jefferson Davis could not appeal to party loyalty to control dissent because the Confederacy had no parties. Davis's frigid personality, his insistence on attending to minute details, and his inability to accept even constructive criticism gracefully, also set him apart from Lincoln and worsened political tensions within the Confederacy.

Several parts of the South began clamoring for peace during the fateful summer of 1863. In a tour of his state that year, North Carolina political leader Jonathan Worth heard calls for the overthrow of the Davis administration and a separate peace with the North. "Every man [I] met," he concluded "was for reconstruction on the basis of the old [U.S.] constitution." By November 1864, the Confederacy suffered as much from internal disaffection as from the attacks of Union armies. Confederate authorities could not suppress civilian unrest in Virginia, North Carolina, and Tennessee, and Union spies operated openly in Mobile, Wilmington, and Richmond.

Davis and other Confederate leaders might have averted some of these political problems had they succeeded in building a strong sense of Confederate nationalism among soldiers and civilians. They tried several strategies to do so. For example, Davis tried to identify the Confederacy's fight for independence with the American Revolution of 1776. But egalitarian revolutionary ideals quickly lost their appeal in the face of poverty, starvation, and defeat. Davis also tried to cast the Confederacy as a bastion of freedom standing up to Lincoln's despotic abuse of executive authority, but he, too, eventually invoked authority similar to Lincoln's. Confederate religious leaders sought to distinguish their new nation from the North by referring to Southerners as God's "chosen people." But when Confederate military fortunes declined, religious leaders drew back from such visions of collective favor and stressed the need for individual salvation.

In a devout society convinced it was fighting a holy war, some Southerners sought some moral failing to account for their mounting losses. Some identified slavery as the culprit. A Confederate leader in South Carolina asked in 1864, "Are we not fighting against the moral sense of the world? Can we hope to succeed in such a struggle?" in a similar vein, a Louisiana woman admitted that "always I felt that moral guilt of it [slavery], felt how impossible it must be for an owner of slaves to win his way into heaven."

THE SOUTHERN ECONOMY

Defeat came to the South, according to one historian, "not because the government failed to mobilize the South's resources" but "because there was virtually nothing left to mobilize." By 1863, the Confederacy was having a difficult time feeding itself. Destruction of farms by both sides and growing Union control of waterways and rail lines restricted the distribution of food. Speculators held certain commodities off the market to drive up prices, making shortages of food, cloth, and medicines worse. Bread riots erupted in Mobile, Atlanta, and Richmond. In Mobile, a group of women marched under banners reading "Bread or Blood" and "Bread and Peace." Armed with hatchets, they looted stores for food and clothing. In a show of grim humor, people in Southern cities held "starvation parties" at which they served only water. "Deaths from starvation have absolutely occurred," a Confederate official in the state informed President Davis in 1864.

Southern soldiers had marched off to war in neat uniforms with shiny buttons, many leaving behind self-sustaining families. But in August 1863, diarist Mary Chesnut, wife of a Confederate official in Richmond, watched ten thousand men marching near Richmond and commented, "Such rags and tags as we saw now. Most garments and arms were . . . taken from the enemy." The soldiers' families were threadbare as well. The prohibitive cost of new clothing prompted a group of women in northern Georgia to raid a textile mill for calico cloth in 1863. During the winter of 1863–1864, women lined their clothes with rags and newspapers to keep warm. In the devastated areas near battle sites, civilians survived by selling fragments of dead soldiers' clothing stripped off their bodies and by collecting spent bullets and selling them for scrap.

The predations of both Union and Confederate soldiers further threatened civilians in the South. The women and children left alone on farms and plantations were vulnerable to stragglers and deserters from both armies who sometimes robbed, burned houses, raped, and murdered. Southerners also feared that slaves on isolated plantations would rise up against their masters. Most slaves, however, were more intent on escape than revenge. There was no point in murdering the master or his family when freedom was just out the door and down the road to the Union lines. Escaped slaves had children, husbands, wives, and other relatives to find and spirit away to Union camps. The business of freedom was too time-consuming to waste on white people. Leave it to God to mete out punishment for the evil of bondage.

Wartime food shortages, skyrocketing inflation, and rumors of hoarding and price-gouging drove women in several Southern cities to protest violently. Demonstrations like the 1863 food riot shown here reflected a larger rending of Southern society as Confederate losses and casualties mounted on the battlefield. Some Southern women placed survival and providing for their families ahead of boosting morale and silently supporting a war effort that had taken their men away. Their defection hurt the Confederate cause.

Some slaves felt genuine affection for the families they served and stayed on with them even after the war. Some protected white Southerners from Union soldiers and hid valuables for them. But women forced to manage plantations alone could never be sure where their slaves stood. Mary Chesnut wrote in her diary about her mother's butler, "He looks over my head—he scents freedom in the air." As slaves stopped working and abandoned plantations, the women left to run them had to work the fields themselves.

As Confederate casualties mounted, more and more Southern women and children, like their Northern counterparts, faced the pain of grief. Funeral processions became commonplace in the cities and black the color of fashion. With little food, worthless money, and a husband or father gone forever, the future looked bleak.

SOUTHERN WOMEN AND THE WAR

In the early days of the Civil War, Southern white women continued to live their lives according to antebellum conventions. Magazine articles urged them to preserve themselves as models of purity for men debased by the violence of war. The Southern woman, by her moral example, "makes the Confederate soldier a gentleman of honor, courage, virtue and truth, instead of a cut-throat and vagabond," opined one magazine. She would buttress the nation's morale through the wavering fortunes of war. On her shoulders rested "the destinies of the Southern Confederacy," the *Natchez Weekly Courier* declared.

Women flooded newspapers and periodicals with patriotic verses and songs. A major theme of these works, illustrated by the following example from the *Richmond Record* in September 1863, was the need to suppress grief and fear for the good of the men at the front:

> The maid who binds her warrior's sash
> And smiling, all her pain dissembles,
> The mother who conceals her grief
> [had] shed as sacred blood as e'er
> Was poured upon the plain of battle.

A Virginia woman confided to her diary, "We must learn the lesson which so many have to endure—to struggle against our feelings."

By the time of the Civil War, such emotional concealment had become second nature to planters' wives. They had long had to endure their anguish over their husbands' nocturnal visits to the slave quarters. They were used to the condescension of men who assumed them to be intellectually inferior. And they accepted in bitter, self-sacrificing silence the contradiction between the myth of the pampered leisure they were presumed to enjoy and the hard demands their lives actually entailed. But some Southern women chafed at their supporting role and, as Confederate manpower and materiel needs became acute, took on new productive responsibilities. Initially, they did so within the domestic context: Women formed clubs to sew flags and uniforms. To raise money for the war effort, they held benefits and auctions and collected jewelry and other valuables.

Soon, however, the needs of the Confederacy drew women outside the home to fill positions vacated by men. They managed plantations. They worked in the fields alongside slaves, and, if they had worked there before, they worked harder. They worked in factories to make uniforms and munitions. They worked in government offices as clerks and secretaries. They taught school. A few, like Belle Boyd and Rose O'Neal Greenhow, spied for the Confederacy. And many, like their Northern counterparts, served as nurses. Eventually, battlefield reverses and economic collapse undermined all these roles, leaving women and men alike struggling simply to survive.

As the war dragged on and the Southern economy and the social order deteriorated, even the patriots suffered from resentment and doubt. By 1864, many women were helping their deserting husbands or relatives elude Confederate authorities. In Randolph County, North Carolina, for example, two women torched a barn belonging to a state official in charge of rounding up deserters. Incidents like these convinced authorities that women were mainly responsible for desertion in the last years of the war. A North Carolina official explained that "desertion takes place because desertion is encouraged. . . . and though the ladies may not be willing to concede the fact, they are nevertheless responsible . . . for the desertion in the army and the dissipation in the country."

By 1864, many Southern white women had tired of the war. What had begun as a sacred cause had disintegrated into a nightmare of fear and deprivation. Uprooted from their homes, some women wandered through the war-ravaged South, exposed to violence, disease, and hunger and seeking shelter where they could find it. Those women fortunate enough to remain in their homes turned to work, others to protest, and many to religion. Some devoutly religious women concluded that it was God, not the Yankees, who had brought destruction on the South for its failure to live up to its responsibilities to women and children. Others blamed their men. After a series of reverses in the Confederate West, one woman confided to her diary that "If our soldiers continue to behave so disgracefully, we *women* had better take the field and send them home to raise chickens." Women greeted defeated troops retreating from Vicksburg with shouts of "We are disappointed in you!" However, despite hardship and privation, support for the Confederacy persisted among some women accompanied by a fierce hatred of the enemy. One woman displayed the bones of a Federal soldier in her yard and another hoped for a "Yankee skull" to use as a jewelry box.

THE UNION PREVAILS, 1864–1865

Despite the union's dominant military position after Vicksburg and Gettysburg and the Confederacy's mounting home-front problems, three obstacles to

White family "refugeeing." In advance of Union armies, tens of thousands of Southern families fled to safer locales, a bitter exodus that fulfilled the Federals' vow to bring the war to the South's civilian population.

Union victory remained. Federal troops under General William T. Sherman controlled Chattanooga and the gateway to Georgia, but the Confederate Army of Tennessee, commanded by Joseph E. Johnston, was still intact, blocking Sherman's path to Atlanta. Robert E. Lee's formidable Army of Northern Virginia still protected Richmond. And the Confederacy still controlled the rich Shenandoah Valley, which fed Lee's armies and supplied his cavalry with horses. In March 1864, President Lincoln brought General Ulysses S. Grant to Washington and appointed him commander of all Union armies. Grant set about devising a strategy to overcome these obstacles.

GRANT'S PLAN TO END THE WAR

Grant brought two innovations to the final campaign. First, he coordinated the Union war effort. Before, the Union's armies in Virginia and the West had operated independently, giving Confederate leaders the opportunity to direct troops and supplies to whichever arena most needed them. Now Grant proposed to deprive them of that option. The Union's armies in Virginia and the Lower South would attack at the same time, keeping steady pressure on all fronts. Second, Grant changed the tempo of the war. Before, long periods of rest had intervened between battles. Grant, with the advantage of superior numbers, proposed nonstop warfare. He wanted to "hammer continuously against the armed force of the enemy and his resources, until by mere attrition, if in no other way, there should be nothing left to him but an equal submission with the

loyal section of our common country to the constitution and laws of the land."

Although Grant's strategy ultimately worked, several problems and miscalculations undermined its effectiveness. With Sherman advancing in Georgia, Grant's major focus was Lee's army in Virginia. But Grant underestimated Lee. The Confederate general thwarted him for almost a year and inflicted horrendous casualties on his army. Confederate forces under Jubal Early drove off Union forces from the Shenandoah Valley in June 1864, depriving Grant of troops and allowing the Confederates to maintain their supply lines. And the incompetence of General Benjamin Butler, charged with advancing up the James River to Richmond in May 1864 to relieve Lee's pressure on Grant, further eroded Grant's plan. Finally, Grant contended with disaffection in his officer corps. Many of his officers felt enduring loyalty to General George McClellan, whom Lincoln had dismissed in 1862, and considered Grant a mediocrity who had triumphed in the West only because his opposition there had been third-rate.

Lee's only hope was to make Grant's campaign so costly and time-consuming that the Northern general would abandon it before the Southerners ran out of supplies and troops. But despite problems and setbacks, Grant kept relentless pressure on Lee. Tied down in Virginia, the Confederate general was unable to send troops to help slow Sherman's advance in Georgia.

From the Wilderness to Cold Harbor. Grant and General George Meade began their campaign against Lee in May 1864, crossing the Rapidan River near Fredericksburg, Virginia, and marching toward an area known as the Wilderness (see Map 15-6). Lee attacked the Army of the Potomac, which outnumbered his 118,000 to 60,000, in the thickets of the Wilderness on May 5 and 6 before it could reach open ground. The densely wooded terrain reduced the Union army's advantage in numbers and artillery. Much of the fighting involved fierce hand-to-hand combat. Exchanges of gunfire at close range set the dry underbrush ablaze. Wounded soldiers, trapped in the fires, begged their comrades to shoot them before they burned to death. The toll was frightful—eighteen

MAP EXPLORATION To explore an interactive version of this map, go to http://www.prenhall.com/goldfield/map15.6

Area controlled by Union
Area controlled by Confederacy
Union advances
Confederate advances
Confederate retreats
Fortifications
Union victories
Confederate victories

MAP 15-6   Grant and Lee in Virginia, 1864-1865
The engagements in Virginia from May 1864 to April 1865 between the two great generals for the Union and the Confederacy proved decisive in ending the Civil War. Although General Lee fared well enough in the Wilderness, Spotsylvania, and Cold Harbor campaigns, the sheer might and relentlessness of Grant and his army wore down the Confederate forces. When Petersburg fell after a prolonged siege on April 2, 1865, Richmond, Appomattox, and dreams of Southern independence soon fell as well.

thousand casualties on the Union side, ten thousand for the Confederates. Union commanders would have pulled back and rested after such an encounter. But Grant, relentless in the pursuit of the enemy, startled Lee's army by pushing on. "Surprise and disappointment were the prevailing emotions," one Southerner wrote, "when we discovered after the contest in the Wilderness that General Grant was not going to retire." Lee's offensive in the Battle of the Wilderness

was his last. From then on, his army was on the defensive against Grant's relentless pursuit.

Marching and fighting, his casualties always higher than Lee's, Grant continued South. Attacking the entrenched Confederate army at Spotsylvania, his army suffered another eighteen thousand casualties to the Confederates' eleven thousand. Undeterred, Grant moved on toward Cold Harbor, where Lee's troops again awaited him in entrenched positions. Flinging his army against withering Confederate fire on June 3, he lost seven thousand men in eight minutes.

In less than a month of fighting, the Army of the Potomac had lost 55,000 men. The slaughter undermined Grant's support in Northern public opinion and led peace advocates to renew their quest for a cease-fire. With antiwar sentiment growing in the North as the presidential elections approached in November, Lee's defensive strategy seemed to be working.

At this point, Grant decided to change his tactics. Abandoning his march on Richmond from the north, he shifted his army south of the James River to approach the Confederate capital from the rear. Wasting no time, he crossed his army over the James and, on June 17, 1864, surprised the Confederates with an attack on Petersburg, a critical rail junction 23 miles south of Richmond. It was a brilliant maneuver, but the hesitant actions of Union corps commanders gave Lee time to reinforce the town's defenders. Both armies dug in for a lengthy siege.

Atlanta. While Grant engaged Lee in Virginia, Union forces under William T. Sherman in Georgia engaged in a deadly dance with the Army of Tennessee under the command of Joseph E. Johnston as they began the Atlanta Campaign, a scheme to take Atlanta, Georgia (see Map 15-7). Johnston had replaced the incompetent Braxton Bragg after the Confederate

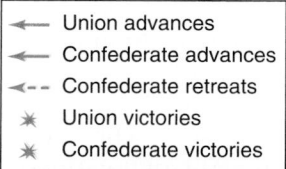

- ← Union advances
- ← Confederate advances
- ◄-- Confederate retreats
- ✳ Union victories
- ✳ Confederate victories

MAP 15-7   The Atlanta Campaign and Sherman's March, 1864-1865
General William T. Sherman, a brilliant tactician who generally refused to be goaded into a frontal assault, "danced" with Confederate general Joseph E. Johnston until an impatient Jefferson Davis replaced Johnston with Hood, and soon Atlanta was in Federal hands. The fall of Atlanta opened the way to the rest of Georgia, a key supply state for the Confederacy. With orders not to harm the civilian population. Sherman's men took their wrath out on property as they made their way through Georgia and South Carolina.

debacle at Chattanooga in late 1863. He shared Lee's belief that the Confederacy's best hope lay in a defensive strategy. Hoping to lure Sherman into a frontal assault, Johnston settled his forces early in May at Dalton, an important railroad junction in Georgia 25 miles south of Chattanooga and seventy-five miles north of Atlanta. The wily Union general declined to attack and instead made a wide swing around the Confederates, prompting Johnston to abandon Dalton, rush south, and dig in again at Resaca to prevent Sherman from cutting the railroad. Again Sherman swung around without an assault, and again Johnston rushed south to cut him off, this time at Cassville.

This waltz continued for two months, until Johnston had retreated to a strong defensive position on Kennesaw Mountain, barely twenty miles north of Atlanta. At this point, early in July, Sherman decided to attack, with predictably disastrous consequences. The Union suffered three thousand casualties, the Confederates only six hundred. Sherman would not make such a mistake again. He resumed his maneuvering and by mid-July had forced Johnston into defensive positions on Peachtree Creek just north of Atlanta.

President Davis feared that Johnston would let Sherman take Atlanta without a fight and dance with the Union general until the sea stopped them both. Davis dismissed Johnston and installed John Bell Hood of Texas in his place. This was a grave error. Hood, in the opinion of those who fought for him, had a "lion's heart" but a "wooden head."

In late July, Hood began a series of attacks on Sherman, beginning at Peachtree Creek on July 20, and was thrown back each time with heavy losses. Sherman launched a series of flanking maneuvers around the city in late August that left Hood in danger of being surrounded. The Confederate general had no choice but to abandon Atlanta and save his army. On the night of September 1, Hood evacuated the city, burning everything of military value.

The loss of Atlanta was a severe blow to the Confederacy. Several of the South's major railroads converged at the city, and its industries helped arm and clothe the South's armies. Atlanta's fall also left Georgia's rich farmland at the mercy of Sherman's army.

Most significant, the fall of Atlanta revived the morale of the war-weary North and helped assure Lincoln's reelection in November. The last hope of the Confederacy—that a peace candidate would replace Lincoln and end the war—had faded. As the disconsolate editor of the *Richmond Examiner* explained, the "disaster at Atlanta [came] in the very nick of time" to "save the party of Lincoln from irretrievable ruin. . . . [I]t will obscure the prospect of peace, late so bright. It will also diffuse gloom over the South."

THE ELECTION OF 1864 AND SHERMAN'S MARCH

Before Sherman's victory at Atlanta, Northern dismay over Grant's enormous losses and his failure to take Richmond raised the prospect of a Democratic election victory. Nominating George B. McClellan, the former commander of the Union's armies, as their presidential candidate, the Democrats appealed to the voters as the party of peace. They also appealed to

Union General Ulysses S. Grant had the pews from a local church moved to a grove of trees where he and his officers planned the following day's assault on Confederate troops at Cold Harbor, Virginia. Grant appears at the left of the photograph, leaning over a bench and studying a map.

the antiemancipation sentiment that was strong in some parts of the North.

The fall of Atlanta and the Union's suddenly improved military fortunes undermined Democratic prospects. Another Union victory three weeks before the elections gave Lincoln a further boost and diminished McClellan's chances. Since September, Union forces, under General Philip H. Sheridan, had been on the offensive in the Shenandoah Valley. In lightning cavalry raids on farms and supply depots, they destroyed valuable Confederate food reserves. And, in a decisive battle on October 19, they overwhelmed the valley's Confederate defenders. Lee had now been deprived of a vital source of supply.

The Republican victory.   In the voting on November 8, Lincoln captured 55 percent of the popular vote, losing only New Jersey, Delaware, and Kentucky. Republicans likewise swept the congressional elections, retaining control of both the Senate and the House of Representatives.

The Republican victory reinforced the Union commitment to emancipation. A proposed constitutional amendment outlawing slavery everywhere in the United States, not just those areas still in rebellion, passed Congress and was ratified as the **Thirteenth Amendment** to the U.S. Constitution in 1865. All earlier amendments related to government powers and functions; this was the first to outlaw a domestic institution previously protected by the Constitution and state law.

Sherman's March to the Sea.

After Sherman took Atlanta, he proposed to break Confederate resistance once and for all by marching his army to the sea and destroying everything in its path. Sherman's March got under way on November 15. His force of sixty thousand men encountering little resistance, entered Savannah on December 22, 1864, and presented the city to Lincoln as a Christmas present. Just a few weeks earlier, Union forces in Tennessee had routed Hood's army at the Battle of Franklin and then crushed it entirely at the Battle of Nashville. Hood's defeat removed any threat to Sherman's rear.

Sherman's March reached a triumphant conclusion in February 1865 when black Federal troops of the 55th Massachusetts Regiment marched into battered Charleston, South Carolina. The illustration captures both the destructiveness of the total war General Sherman waged on Georgia and South Carolina and the hope among former slaves for a new birth of freedom.

Sherman resumed his march in February 1865, heading for South Carolina, the heart of the Confederacy and the state where the Civil War had begun. "The truth is," Sherman wrote a friend, "the whole army is burning with an insatiable desire to wreak vengeance on South Carolina." South Carolinians sent taunting messages promising stiff resistance, but these served only further to provoke Sherman's troops. They pushed aside the small force that assembled to oppose them, wreaked greater destruction in South Carolina than they had in Georgia, and burned the state capitol at Columbia. Sherman sent the colonel of a black regiment to receive the surrender of Charleston and ordered black troops to be the first to take possession of the city. The soldiers marched in singing "John Brown's Body" to the cheers of the city's black population.

Sherman ended his march in Goldsboro, North Carolina, in March 1865 after repelling a surprise Confederate attack at Bentonville led by the restored Joseph E. Johnston and the remnants of the Army of Tennessee. Behind the Union army lay a barren swath 425 miles long from Savannah to Goldsboro.

Arming the Confederacy's slaves.

In a move reflecting their desperation in March 1865, Confederate leaders revived a proposal that they had previously rejected to arm and free slaves. Slaves had served involuntarily in the Confederate army, and a number of free black Louisianans had volunteered for service in Southern ranks early in the war. But this proposal represented a major policy shift. President Davis hoped it would gain the Confederacy not only a military benefit but also diplomatic recognition from countries that had balked because of slavery.

The issue divided Confederate leaders. Confederate general Howell Cobb argued that "if slaves will make good soldiers, our whole theory of slavery is wrong." Others thought that it was preferable to abandon slavery than to lose independence. A Confederate congressman from Georgia wrote to a friend in October 1864 that if the South lost the war, slavery was over anyway, and "we and our children will be slaves, while our freed Negroes will lord it over us." But if the Confederacy enlisted slaves, it could "win our independence, and have liberty and homes for ourselves and our children."

Not surprisingly, slaves themselves greeted the proposal with little enthusiasm. They might have found service in the Confederate army an acceptable alternative to bondage earlier in the war, but not now, with Union victory imminent. Mary Chesnut recalled in March 1865 that early in the war, when her husband "spoke to his Negroes about it, his head men were keen to go in the army, to be free and get a bounty after the war. Now they say coolly that they don't want freedom if they have to fight for it. That means they are pretty sure of having it anyway."

Overview

Major Battles of the Civil War, 1861–1865

Battle or Campaign	Date	Outcome and Consequences
First Bull Run	July 21, 1861	Confederate victory, destroyed the widespread belief in the North that the war would end quickly, fueled Confederate sense of superiority
Forts Henry and Donelson	Feb. 6–16, 1862	Union victory, gave the North control of strategic river systems in the western Confederacy and closed an important link between the eastern and western Confederacy
Shiloh Church	Apr. 6–7, 1862	Union victory, high casualties transformed attitudes about the war on both sides
Seven Days' Battles	June 25–July 1, 1862	Standoff, halted Union General McClellan's advance on Richmond in the Peninsula Campaign
Second Bull Run	Aug. 29–30, 1862	Confederate victory, reinforced Confederate general Robert E. Lee's reputation for invincibility
Antietam	Sept. 17, 1862	Standoff, halted Lee's advance into the North, eliminated Confederacy's chance for diplomatic recognition, encouraged Lincoln to issue the Emancipation Proclamation
Fredericksburg	Dec. 13, 1862	Confederate victory, revived morale of Lee's army
Chancellorsville	May 2–6, 1863	Confederate victory, Confederate General Stonewall Jackson killed, encouraged Lee to again invade North
Gettysburg	July 1–3, 1863	Union victory, halted Confederate advance in the North, major psychological blow to Confederacy
Vicksburg	Nov. 1862–July 1863	Union victory; closed the key Confederate port on the Mississippi, also dealt a severe blow to Confederate cause
Chattanooga	Aug.–Nov. 1863	Union victory, solidified Union dominance in the West
Wilderness and Cold Harbor	May and June 1864	Both Confederate victories inflicted huge losses on Grant's army; turned public opinion against Grant but failed to force him to withdraw
Atlanta	May–September 1864	Union victory; Confederacy lost key rail depot and industrial center
Sherman's March	November 1864–March 1865	Nearly unopposed, Sherman's army cut a path of destruction through Georgia and South Carolina, breaking Southern morale
Battles of Franklin and Nashville	November and December 1864	Union victories in Tennessee; effectively destroyed Army of Tennessee
Siege of Petersburg	June 1864–April 1865	Long stalemate ended in Union victory; led to fall of Richmond and surrender of Lee's army at Appomattox Court House

On March 13, 1865, a reluctant Confederate Congress passed a bill to enlist black soldiers, but without a provision offering them freedom. President Davis and the war office bypassed the equivocal congressional legislation ten days later, issuing a general order that promised immediate freedom to slaves who enlisted. The war ended before the order could have any effect. The irony was that in the summer of 1864, a majority of Northerners probably would have accepted reunion without emancipation had the Confederacy abandoned its fight.

THE ROAD TO APPOMATTOX AND THE DEATH OF LINCOLN

With Sherman's triumph in Georgia and the Carolinas and Sheridan's rout of the Confederates in the Shenandoah Valley, Lee's army remained the last obstacle to Union victory. On April 1, Sheridan's cavalry seized a vital railway junction on Lee's right flank, forcing Lee to abandon Petersburg and the defense of Richmond. He tried a daring run westward toward Lynchburg, hoping to secure much-needed supplies and to join Johnston's Army of Tennessee in North Carolina to continue the fight.

President Davis fled Richmond with his cabinet and headed toward North Carolina. Richard Gill Forrester, a seventeen-year-old black youth, awoke to find the evacuation underway. He reached under his bed and pulled out an American flag. Maneuvering through the chaotic streets, young Forrester reached the state capitol building, climbed to the top, and affixed the banner to the flagpole. Union troops occupied the Confederate capital on April 3, and, two days later, President Lincoln walked through its streets to

This photograph of Abraham Lincoln was taken four days before John Wilkes Booth assassinated him in Ford's Theatre.

the cheers of his army and an emotional reception from thousands of black people. "I know I am free," shouted one black spectator, "for I have seen Father Abraham and felt him."

The surrender at Appomattox. Grant's army of 60,000 outran Lee's diminishing force of 35,000 and cut off his escape at Appomattox Court House, Virginia, on April 7. Convinced that further resistance was futile, the Confederate commander met Grant on April 9, 1865, in the McLean house at Appomattox to sign the documents of surrender. The Union general offered generous terms, allowing Lee's men to go home unmolested and to take with them horses or mules "to put in a crop." Grant reported feeling "sad and depressed" at "the downfall of a foe who had fought so long and valiantly, and had suffered so much for a cause, though that cause was, I believe, one of the worst for which a people ever fought." Lee rode through the thinned ranks of his troops, who crowded around him in silent tribute, brushing the general's boots and the withers of his horse with their hats.

Though some Southerners entertained fleetingly the idea of launching a guerilla campaign against Union forces, most were sick of the war. One Confederate leader, traveling through the stricken South in April 1865, reported that soldiers and civilians alike considered any continuation of the conflict, "madness." Joseph E. Johnston surrendered to Sherman near Durham, North Carolina, on April 26. On May 10, Union cavalry captured President Davis in southern Georgia. On May 26, Texas general Kirby Smith surrendered his trans-Mississippi army, and the Civil War came to an end.

The death of Lincoln. Washington greeted the Confederate surrender at Appomattox with predictable and raucous rejoicing—torchlight parades, cannon salutes, and crowds spontaneously bellowing "The Star-Spangled Banner." On April 11, President Lincoln addressed a large crowd from the White House balcony and spoke briefly of his plans to reconstruct the South with the help of persons loyal to the Union, including recently freed slaves. At least one listener found the speech disappointing. A sometime actor and full-time Confederate patriot, John Wilkes Booth, muttered to a friend in the throng, "That means nigger citizenship. Now, by God, I'll put him through. That is the last speech he will ever make."

On the evening of April 14, Good Friday, the president went to Ford's Theatre in Washington to view a comedy, *Our American Cousin*. During the per-

FROM THEN TO NOW

Gettysburg

Each year more than 1.8 million visitors track across Pennsylvania's rolling hills to retrace the steps of the competing armies as they fought the Battle of Gettysburg in July 1863. The fascination has become big business at the Gettysburg National Military Park, where tourists spend more than $40 million annually on items ranging from Pickett's Charge T-shirts to faked battlefield relics. For a nation not ordinarily fixated on the past, the devotion to this battle—to which a majority of Americans have no ancestral connections—is extraordinary. What accounts for it?

The Civil War was a defining event in American history, and the Battle of Gettysburg was the defining moment of the Civil War, a guidepost on the American journey. The battle has thus become a metaphor for the national ideals the war brought into focus, symbolizing them in an enduring form for subsequent generations of Americans and serving as a reminder of the work still to be done to translate those ideals into reality for all. The battle also emerged as a symbol of national reconciliation after the fratricidal conflict of the war.

For generations of white Southerners after the Civil War, Gettysburg was the place where the young men of a doomed cause displayed incomparable courage against long odds. "For every southern boy fourteen years old," William Faulkner wrote, "not once but whenever he wants it, there is the instant when it's still not yet two o'clock"—the hour before Pickett's Charge—"on that July afternoon in 1863."

But today most Americans, North and South, see Gettysburg not as a missed opportunity, but, thanks to President Lincoln's famous address dedicating the battlefield cemetery, as a place that gives meaning to the sacrifices of both sides. Consecrating the battlefield to a renewal of the nation's founding ideals, Lincoln asked his listeners to "highly resolve that these dead shall not have died in vain that this nation, under God, shall have a new birth of freedom and that government of the people, by the people, for the people, shall not perish from the earth." In the years after the war, veterans from both sides came to the battlefield seeking reconciliation, posing together for pictures and shaking hands. Tourists strike similar poses today.

African Americans, however, have not by and large shared the national fascination with Gettysburg and make up less than 3 percent of the visitors to the battlefield. "When you're black," the African American historian Allan B. Ballard explained, "the great battlefield holds mixed messages." Although the National Park Service, which oversees the site, has put up an exhibit on the role of African American troops in the Civil War, black visitors remain ambivalent about the place. Aware of the long and continuing struggle they would face to secure true equality in American society after the Civil War, they see irony in Lincoln's call for "a new birth of freedom." Yet, if, as Ballard notes, "we are still fighting our civil wars," at Gettysburg at least, it is possible for Americans today to see and learn how their freedoms were paid for in blood and to reflect, in Lincoln's words, on the "unfinished work which they who fought here have thus far so nobly advanced."

---

formance, Booth shot the president, wounding him mortally, then jumped from Lincoln's box to the stage shouting *"sic semper tyrannis"* ("Thus ever to tyrants") and fled the theater. Union troops tracked him down to a barn in northern Virginia and killed him. Investigators arrested eight accomplices, who had conspired with Booth to murder other high officials in addition to Lincoln. Four of the accomplices were hanged. Besides the president, however, the only other official attacked was Secretary of State Seward, who received serious but not fatal knife wounds.

Southerners reacted to Lincoln's assassination with surprisingly mixed emotions. Many saw in the death of the man they had regarded as their bitterest enemy for four years some slight hope of relief for the South's otherwise bleak prospects. But General Johnston and others like him understood Lincoln's influence with the radical elements in the Republican party who were pressing for harsh terms against the South. The president's death, Johnston wrote, was "the greatest possible calamity to the South."

CONCLUSION

Just before the war, William Sherman had warned a friend from Virginia, "You people of the South don't know what you are doing. This country will be drenched in blood. . . . [W]ar is a terrible thing." He was right. More than 365,000 Union soldiers died during the war, 110,000 in battle, and more than 256,000 Confederate soldiers, 94,000 of them in battle. Total casualties on both sides, including wounded, were more than 1 million.

Southern armies suffered disproportionately higher casualties than did Northern armies. One in four Confederate soldiers died or endured debilitating wounds, compared to one in ten Federal soldiers. During the first year after the war, Mississippi allocated one-fifth of its budget to artificial limbs. Compounding the suffering of the individuals behind these gruesome statistics was the incalculable suffering—in terms of grief, fatherless children, women who never married, families never made whole—of the people close to them.

The war devastated the South. The region lost one-fourth of its white male population between the ages of 20 and 40. It also lost two-fifths of its livestock and half its farm machinery. Union armies destroyed many of the South's railroads and shattered its industry. Between 1860 and 1870, the wealth of the South declined by 60 percent, and its share of the nation's total wealth dropped from more than 30 percent to 12 percent. The wealth of the North, in contrast, increased by half in the same period.

The Union victory solved the constitutional question about the right of secession and sealed the fate of slavery. The issue that dominated the prewar sectional debate had vanished. Now when politicians intoned in Independence Day orations or campaign speeches about the ideals of democracy and freedom, the glaring reality of human bondage would no longer mock their rhetoric.

For black Southerners, emancipation was the war's most significant achievement. Journalists sponsored by the federal government who recorded the testimony of ex-slaves in the 1930s during the Great Depression, seventy years after emancipation, found their memory of the jubilee as fresh as yesterday. Lincoln entered African-American folklore as a larger-than-life figure. At age 91, Fanny Burdock of Valdosta, Georgia, told a recorder a common tale of seeing Lincoln "coming all dusty and on foot" past her Georgia home.

> We run right to the fence and had the oak bucket and the dipper. When he draw up to us, he so tall, black eyes so sad. Didn't say not one word, just looked hard at all us, every one us crying. We give him nice cool water from the dipper. Then he nodded and set off and we just stood there till he get to being dust then nothing. After, didn't our owner or nobody credit it, but me and all my kin, we knowed. I still got the dipper to prove it.

The Civil War stimulated other changes that grew more significant over time. It did not make the Union an industrial nation, but it taught the effectiveness of centralized management, new financial techniques, and the coordination of production, marketing, and distribution. Entrepreneurs would apply these lessons to create the expanding corporations of the postwar American economy.

Likewise, the war did not revolutionize gender relations in American society; but, by opening new opportunities to women in fields such as nursing and teaching, it helped lay the foundation for the woman's suffrage movement of the 1870s and 1880s.

For many Americans, especially black and white Southerners, the war was the most important event in their lives. It had a devastating impact on the families and friends of those who died. But it was not responsible for every postwar change in American society, and it left many features of American life intact. The experience of pulling together in a massive war effort, for example, did not soften class antagonisms. European socialist and father of communism Karl Marx hailed Lincoln as a son of the working class and predicted that "as the American War of independence initiated a new era of ascendancy for the middle class, so the American anti-slavery war will do for the working classes." But capitalism, not labor, triumphed during the war. And it was industrialists and entrepreneurs, not working people, who most benefited from the war's bonanza. Lincoln brutally suppressed strikes at defense plants and threw labor leaders into military prisons.

The war to end slavery changed some American racial attitudes, especially in the North. When Lincoln broadened the war's objectives to include the abolition of slavery, he connected the success of the Union to freedom for the slave. At the outset of the Civil War, only a small minority of Northerners considered themselves abolitionists. After the Emancipation Proclamation, every Northern soldier became a liberator. By the end of the war, perhaps a majority of Northerners supported granting freedmen the right to vote and to equal protection under the law, even if they believed (as many did) that black people were inferior to white people. The courage of black troops and the efforts of African American leaders to link the causes of reunion and freedom were influential in bringing about this shift.

Most white Southerners did not experience a similar enlightenment. Some were relieved by the end of slavery, but most greeted it with fear, anger, and regret. For them, the freed slaves would be living reminders of the South's defeat and the end of a way of life grounded in white supremacy.

If the Civil War resolved the sectional dispute of the 1850s by ending slavery and denying the right of the Southern states to secede, it created two new equally troubling problems: how to reunite South and North and how to deal with the legacy of slavery. At his last cabinet meeting on April 14, Lincoln gave little indication of how he intended to proceed on these problems. He seemed inclined to be conciliatory, cautioning against reprisals on Confederate leaders and noting the courage of General Lee and his officers. The president said nothing about the rights of freedmen, although earlier statements indicated that he favored suffrage, but not social equality, for African Americans.

America's greatest crisis had closed. In its wake, former slaves tested their new freedom, and the nation groped for reconciliation. The struggle to preserve the Union and abolish slavery had renewed and vindicated the nation's ideals. It was time to savor the hard-fought victories before plunging into the uncertainties of Reconstruction.

In November 1863, President Lincoln was asked to say a few words at the dedication of the federal cemetery at Gettysburg. There, surrounded by a somber scene of fresh graves, Lincoln bound the cause of the Union to that of the country's founders: "Fourscore and seven years ago our fathers brought forth upon this continent a new nation, conceived in liberty and dedicated to the proposition that all men are created equal. Now we are engaged in a great civil war, testing whether that nation, or any nation so conceived and so dedicated can long endure." A Union victory, Lincoln hoped, would not only honor the past but also call forth a new nation, cleansed of its sins, to serve as an inspiration, to oppressed peoples around the world. He called on the nation to resolve "that the nation shall, under God, have a new birth of freedom; and that government of the people, by the people, for the people, shall not perish from the earth." Not only did the two-minute Gettysburg Address capture what Union supporters were fighting for, but it also connected their sacrifices to the noble causes of freedom and democratic government. That would be both the hope and the challenge of the peace that followed a hard war.

REVIEW QUESTIONS

1. How did the Union and the Confederacy compare in terms of resources, leadership, and military strategies in the period 1861–1863? What impact did these factors have on the course of the war?

2. What was the significance of the battles of Antietam and Gettysburg? In what ways were they turning points in the Civil War?

3. What effects did the Emancipation Proclamation have on both the Union and Confederate causes?

4. Compare and contrast the roles played by women, in the North and in the South, during the Civil War, and explain how their actions and activities aided or hindered the war effort of their respective nations.

5. Given the enormity of the losses in lives and property, it is not surprising that some historians have attributed major changes in American society to the Civil War. But other historians claim that the Civil War's impact has been exaggerated. Analyze and assess what the Civil War did or did not accomplish.

6. Sullivan Ballou made the ultimate sacrifice for his cause. Why did he fight?

KEY TERMS*

Confiscation Act (p. 468)

Copperheads (p. 478)

Emancipation Proclamation (p. 469)

Homestead Act (p. 478)

Land Grant College Act (p. 478)

New York Draft Riot (p. 478)

Radical Republicans (p. 478)

Thirteenth Amendment (p. 487)

* See the Overview table, on p. 489 for important battles of the Civil War.

RECOMMENDED READING

Crane, Stephen. *The Red Badge of Courage* (Originally published 1895; reprinted various dates). The Civil War did not inspire great American novels. But this is a notable exception that depicts, not only the horrors of combat, but also its impact on the soldiers who fought.

McPherson, James M. *Battle Cry of Freedom: the Civil War Era* (1982). This book is probably the best account of the war in print. The author draws a number of interesting conclusions on several controversial topics from military strategy to the home front.

ADDITIONAL SOURCES

Mobilization, North and South

Cooper, William J. *Jefferson Davis: American* (2000).

Current, Richard N. *Lincoln's Loyalists: Union Soldiers from the Confederacy* (1992).

Davis, William C. *"A Government of Our Own": the Making of the Confederacy* (1994).

Donald, David. *Lincoln* (1995).

Faust, Drew Gilpin. *The Creation of Confederate Nationalism: Ideology and Identity in the Civil War* (1988).

Marszalek, John P. *Sherman: A Soldier's Passion for Order* (1993).

Rable, George C. *The Confederate Republic: A Revolution Against Politics* (1994).

Royster, Charles. *The Destructive War: William Tecumseh Sherman, Stonewall Jackson, and the Americans* (1991).

Thomas, Emory M. *Robert E. Lee: A Biography* (1995).

The Early War, 1861–1862

Cooling, Benjamin Franklin. *Forts Henry and Donelson: The Key to the Confederate Heartland* (1988).

Daniel, Larry J. *Shiloh: The Battle That Changed the Civil War* (1997).

Fellman, Michael. *Inside War: The Guerrilla Conflict in Missouri during the Civil War* (1989).

Linderman, Gerald F. *Embattled Courage: The Experience of Combat in the American Civil War* (1989).

McPherson, James M. *What They Fought For, 1861–1865* (1994).

Robertson, James I. *Stonewall Jackson: the Man, the Soldier, the Legend* (1997).

Sears, Stephen W. *George B. McClellan: the Young Napoleon* (1988).

Turning Points, 1862–1863

Berlin, Ira, et al., eds. *Freedom: A Documentary History of Emancipation, 1861–1867*, Ser. 1, Vol. 1: *The Destruction of Slavery* (1985).

Cox, LaWanda. *Lincoln and Black Freedom: A Study in Presidential Leadership* (1981).

Foner, Eric. *Nothing but Freedom: Emancipation and its Legacy* (1983).

Josephy Jr., Alvin M. *The Civil War in the American West* (1993).

McFeely, William S. *Grant: A Biography* (1981).

Quarles, Benjamin. *The Negro in the Civil War* (1953).

Reardon, Carol. *Pickett's Charge in History and Memory* (1997).

Sears, Stephen W. *Landscape Turned Red: The Battle of Antietam* (1983).

Smith, David Paul. *Frontier Defense in the Civil War: Texas' Rangers and Rebels* (1992).

Wills, Garry. *Lincoln at Gettysburg: The Words That Remade America* (1992).

War Transforms the North

Baker, Kevin. *Paradise Alley: A Novel* (2002)

Neely, Mark E. Jr., *The Fate of Liberty: Abraham Lincoln and Civil Liberties* (1991).

Pryor, Elizabeth B. *Clara Barton: Professional Angel* (1987).

Richardson, Heather Cox. *The Greatest Nation of the Earth: Republican Economic Policies During the Civil War* (1997).

The Confederacy Disintegrates

Ash, Stephen V. *When the Yankees Came: Conflict and Chaos in the Occupied South, 1861–1865* (1995).

Campbell, Edward D. C. Jr., and Kym S. Rice, eds. *A Woman's War: Southern Women, Civil War, and the Confederate Legacy* (1996).

Clinton, Catherine, and Nina Silber, eds. *Divided Houses: Gender and the Civil War* (1992).

Durden, Robert F. *The Gray and the Black: The Confederate Debate on Emancipation* (1972).

Faust, Drew Gilpin. *Mothers of Invention: Women of the Slaveholding South in the American Civil War* (1996).

Grimsely, Mark. *The Hard Hand of War: Union Policy Toward Southern Civilians, 1861–1865* (1995).

Whites, Leeann. *The Civil War as a Crisis in Gender: Augusta, Georgia, 1860-1890* (1995).

Woodward, C. Vann, ed. *Mary Chesnut's Civil War* (1981).

The Union Prevails

Beringer, Richard E., Herman Hattaway, Archer Jones, and William N. Still, Jr. *Why the South Lost the Civil War* (1986).

Glatthaar, Joseph T. *The March to the Sea and Beyond* (1985).

Thomas, Emory. *The Confederate Nation, 1861–1865* (1979).

WHERE TO LEARN MORE

- **Museum of the Confederacy, Richmond, Virginia.** This museum has rotating exhibits on various aspects of the Confederate effort during the Civil War, both on the home front and on the battlefield. The Confederate White House, which is open to the public, is next door to the museum. [www.moc.org].

- **Gettysburg National Military Park, Gettysburg, Pennsylvania.** An excellent and balanced interpretation awaits the visitor at this national park. [www.nps.gov/gett/].

- **Antietam National Battlefield, Sharpsburg, Maryland.** Also an excellent and balanced interpretation at this battlefield site. [www.nps.gov/anti/].

- **Ford's Theatre National Historical Site, Washington, DC.** The place where John Wilkes Booth assassinated President Abraham Lincoln not only depicts those events, including artifacts from the assassination, but also presents period plays. [www.nps.gov/foth/index2.htm].

- **Appomattox Court House, Appomattox, Virginia.** What historian Bruce Catton termed "a stillness at Appomattox" can be felt at the McLean house in this south-central Virginia town. The house is much as it was when Confederate General Robert E. Lee surrendered his forces to Union General Ulysses S. Grant on April 9, 1865. An almost reverential solitude covers the house and the well-maintained grounds today. [www.nps.gov/apco/].

 Please refer to the document CD-ROM for primary sources related to this chapter.

THE "ABRAHAM LINCOLN SCHOOL" FOR FREEDMEN, NEW ORLEANS, LOUISIANA.—[PHOTOGRAPHED BY LILIENTHAL, NEW ORLEANS.]

➜ Barred from literacy during the slavery era, freedmen devoured learning after the Civil War. Their classrooms ranged from one-room cabins to more grandiose structures such as this, the Abraham Lincoln School for Freedmen in New Orleans.

RECONSTRUCTION 16
1865–1877

Marianna, Florida 1866

The white academy opened about the same time the church opened the school for the Negro children. As the colored children had to pass the academy to reach the church it was easy for the white children to annoy them with taunts and jeers. The war passed from words to stones which the white children began to hurl at the colored. Several colored children were hurt and, as they had not resented the rock-throwing in kind because they were timid about going that far, the white children became more aggressive and abusive.

One morning the colored children armed themselves with stones and determined to fight their way past the academy to their school. [They] approached the academy in formation whereas in the past they had been going in pairs or small groups. When they reached hailing distance, a half dozen white boys rushed out and hurled their missiles. Instead of scampering away, the colored children not only stood their ground and hurled their missiles but maintained a solemn silence. The white children, seeing there was no backing down as they expected, came rushing out of the academy and charged the colored children.

During some fifteen minutes it was a real tug of war. In the close fighting the colored children got the advantage gradually and began to shove the white children back. As they pressed the advantage the white children broke away

CHAPTER OUTLINE

White Southerners and the Ghosts of the Confederacy, 1865

More than Freedom: African American Aspirations in 1865
Education
"Forty Acres and a Mule"
Migration to Cities
Faith and Freedom

Federal Reconstruction, 1865–1870
Presidential Reconstruction, 1865–1867
Congressional Reconstruction, 1867–1870
Southern Republican Governments

Counter-Reconstruction, 1870–1874
The Uses of Violence
The Failure of Northern Will
Liberal Republicans and the Election of 1872

Redemption, 1874–1877
The Democrats' Violent Resurgence
The Weak Federal Response
The Election of 1876 and the Compromise of 1877
The Memory of Reconstruction

The Failed Promise of Reconstruction
Sharecropping
Modest Gains and Future Victories

Conclusion

and ran for the academy. The colored fighters did not follow them but made it hot for the laggards until they also took to their heels. There were many bruises on both sides, but it taught the white youngsters to leave the colored ones alone thereafter.

T. Thomas Fortune, *Norfolk Journal and Guide*

T. Thomas Fortune, "Norfolk Journal and Guide," August 20, 1927, reprinted in Dorothy Sterling, ed., *The Trouble They Seen: Black People Tell the Story of Reconstruction* (Garden City, NY: Doubleday & Co., 1976): 22–24.

T. Thomas Fortune, a New York newspaper editor, recalled this battle between black and white schoolchildren sixty years earlier, at the beginning of the Reconstruction era. In the scheme of things, it did not amount to much. However, for ten-year-old Thomas, born a slave in Marianna, the incident encapsulated well the dilemma of Reconstruction. In the journey from slavery to freedom, education emerged as an important element of full citizenship for African Americans. The eagerness with which black children (and adults) flooded schools—often spaces converted in churches and staffed initially by white missionaries from the North—was matched by the hostility of the white community who resented any advance by the former bondsmen and any pretense of equality that education implied.

Reconstruction was not merely a series of white aggressions against African American aspirations, followed by black retreats. The former slaves did not shy away from asserting their rights, any more than they had waited patiently for the Emancipation Proclamation to induce them to leave their plantations. The violence and disorder that punctuated Southern society after the Civil War was due in part to the refusal of blacks to relinquish their dreams of equal citizenship, including the right to a decent education.

Young Thomas did not back down, though by 1878 he understood that the promise that characterized his schoolboy days could not be realized in the South. The journey from slavery to freedom, he felt, would always be incomplete in the South. Together with his young bride, Carrie Smiley of Jacksonville, Florida, Thomas left for New York City, where he obtained a job as a printer for the *New York Sun*. Shaped by his early years in Florida, and the difficulties involved in obtaining a decent education, Fortune used the pages of the *Sun* to promote equality of education for all races and for integrated public schools in New York State. He died there in 1928. New York's gain was the South's loss, a process repeated many times over in the decades after the Civil War as talented young black men and women left the region of their birth and their ancestors. It was a double tragedy for the South: losing people who could have rebuilt a shattered region, and missing the opportunity to create a society based on racial equality.

The position of African Americans in American society was one of the two great issues of the Reconstruction era. Americans of both sections disagreed about how much freedom to grant the former slaves, almost all of whom lived in the South. The other great issue was how and under what terms to readmit the former Confederate states. The Constitution was silent on the subject. As with the issue of black equality, opinions in both sections varied widely.

The formation of a national consensus on freedom and reunification began with the demands and hopes of three broad groups. One was the Republican party, which controlled the federal government and determined its policies. Most Republicans were unwilling to accept the seceding states back in the Union without an expression of loyalty and a commitment to protecting the rights of freedmen. A second group, the more than 4 million former slaves, demanded voting rights, access to education, and the opportunity to seek economic self-sufficiency. Few black Northerners yet enjoyed all these benefits, and few white Southerners could conceive of former slaves possessing them. The third group, white Southerners, hoped to restore their shattered lives, fortunes, and dignity. In their vision of a renewed South, black people remained subservient and the federal government stopped interfering in southern affairs.

Between 1865 and 1867, under President Andrew Johnson's Reconstruction plan, white Southerners pretty much had their way with the former slaves and with their own state governments. Congressional action between 1867 and 1870 attempted to balance black rights and home rule, with mixed results. After 1870, white Southerners gradually regained control of their states and localities, often through violence and intimidation, denying black Southerners their political gains while Republicans in Washington lost interest in policing their former enemies.

By the time the last federal troops left the South in 1877, white Southerners had prevailed. The Confederate states had returned to the Union with all of their rights and many of their leaders restored. And the freed slaves remained in mostly subservient positions with few of the rights and privileges enjoyed by other Americans.

KEY TOPICS

- African American aspirations and southern white expectations

- Federal government plans to bring the South back into the Union and secure freedom for former slaves

- Southern Republican efforts to keep the allegiance of black voters and win white support

- Why and how Reconstruction ended

WHITE SOUTHERNERS AND THE GHOSTS OF THE CONFEDERACY, 1865

Confederate soldiers—generals and troops alike—returned to devastated homes they could scarcely recognize. General Braxton Bragg returned to his "once prosperous" Alabama home to find "all, all was lost, except my debts." Bragg and his wife found temporary shelter in a slave cabin. Yeomen farmers, the backbone of the Confederacy, found uprooted fences, farm animals dead or gone, and buildings destroyed. With no income or savings to soften their plight, they and their families wandered about in a living nightmare, seeking shelter where they could. They lived in morbid fear of vengeful former slaves or the hated Yankee soldiers wreaking more damage. "The demoralization is complete," a Georgia girl noted.

Their cause lost and their society reviled, white Southerners lived through the summer and fall of 1865 surrounded by ghosts—the ghosts of lost loved ones, joyful times, bountiful harvests, self-assurance, and slavery. Defeat shook the basic tenets of their religious beliefs. A North Carolinian cried, "Oh, our God! What sins we must have been guilty of that we should be so humiliated by Thee now!" Some praised God for delivering the South from the sin of slavery. A Virginia woman expressed thanks that "we white people are no longer permitted to go on in such wickedness, heaping up more and more wrath of God upon our devoted heads."

But many other white Southerners refused to accept their defeat as a divine judgment. How could they, as a devout people, believe that God had abandoned them? Instead, they insisted, God had spared the South for a greater purpose. They came to view the war as the **Lost Cause** and interpreted it, not as a lesson in humility, but as an episode in the South's journey to salvation. Robert E. Lee became the patron saint of this cause, his poignant nobility a contrast to the crassness of the Yankee warlords. White Southerners would not allow the memory of the bloody struggle to die, transforming it into a symbol of courage against great odds and piety against sin. Eventually, they believed, redemption would come.

The Southern white view of the Civil War (and of Reconstruction) was not a deliberate attempt to falsify history, but rather a need to justify and rationalize the devastation and loss of life that accompanied the Confederate defeat. This view, in which the war became the Lost Cause, and Reconstruction became the Redemption, also served to forge a community among white Southerners at a time of great unrest. A common religion solidified that bond and sanctified it. The Lost Cause also enabled white Southerners to move on with their lives and concentrate on rebuilding their shattered region. The Lost Cause was less a backward-looking perspective than it was a historical rationalization that enabled believers to hope for a better future. The regrettable feature of elevating the Civil War to a noble, holy enterprise was that it implied a stainless Old South, a civilization worth fighting and dying for. This new history required the return of the freedmen, if not to the status of slaves, then at least to their lowly place in society. This new history also ignored the savagery of the war by romanticizing the conflict.

The Lost Cause would not merely exist as a memory, but also as a three-dimensional depiction of Southern history across the landscape, in rituals and celebrations, and as the educational foundation for future generations. The statues of the common Confederate soldier erected typically on the most important site in a town, the courthouse square; the commemorations of Confederate Memorial Day, the birthdays of prominent Confederate leaders, and the reunions of veterans, all marked with flourishing oratory, brass bands, parades, and related spectacles; and the textbooks insuring that the white history of the South was implanted into young minds and the legacy carried down through the generations—all of these insured

Chronology

1863	Lincoln proposes his Ten Percent Plan.
1864	Congress proposes the Wade-Davis Bill.
1865	Sherman issues Field Order No. 15.
	Freedmen's Bureau is established.
	Andrew Johnson succeeds to the presidency, unveils his Reconstruction plan.
	Massachusetts desegregates all public facilities.
	Black citizens in several southern cities organize Union Leagues.
	Former Confederate states begin to pass black codes.
1866	Congress passes Southern Homestead Act, Civil Rights Act of 1866.
	Ku Klux Klan is founded.
	Fourteenth Amendment to the Constitution is passed (ratified in 1868).
	President Johnson goes on a speaking tour.
1867	Congress passes Military Reconstruction Acts, Tenure of Office Act.
1868	President Johnson is impeached and tried in the Senate for defying the Tenure of Office Act.
	Republican Ulysses S. Grant is elected president.
1869	Fifteenth Amendment passed (ratified 1870).
1870	Congress passes Enforcement Act.
	Republican regimes topple in North Carolina and Georgia.
1871	Congress passes Ku Klux Klan Act.
1872	Freedmen's Bureau closes down.
	Liberal Republicans emerge as a separate party.
	Ulysses S. Grant is reelected.
1873	Severe depression begins.
	Colfax Massacre occurs.
	U.S. Supreme Court's decision in the Slaughterhouse cases weakens the intent of the Fourteenth Amendment.
	Texas falls to the Democrats in the fall elections.
1874	White Leaguers attempt a coup against the Republican government of New Orleans.
	Democrats win off-year elections across the South amid widespread fraud and violence.
1875	Congress passes Civil Rights Act of 1875.
1876	Supreme Court's decision in *United States v. Cruikshank* nullifies Enforcement Act of 1870.
	Outcome of the presidential election between Republican Rutherford B. Hayes and Democrat Samuel J. Tilden is contested.
1877	Compromise of 1877 makes Hayes president and ends Reconstruction.

that the Lost Cause would not only be an interpretation of the past, but also the basic reality of the present and the foundation for the future.

Fifteen years after the war, Mark Twain traveled the length of the East Coast. After visiting a gentlemen's club in Boston, he recalled that the conversation had covered a variety of topics, none of which included the Civil War. Northerners had relegated that conflict to history books and moved on. Such was not the case in the South. There, defeat and destruction demanded rationalization and remembrance. Thus Twain reported that, unlike in the North, gentlemen's talk in Atlanta inevitably wandered to the war and to heroism and sacrifice. "In the South," Twain wrote, "the war is what A.D. is elsewhere: they date from it." Such people would not accept the changes implied by defeat. They would fight to preserve as much of their past as the victors allowed. For the past was both their present and their future.

Most white Southerners approached the great issues of freedom and reunification with unyielding views. They saw African Americans as adversaries whose attempts at self-improvement were a direct challenge to white people's beliefs in their own racial superiority. White Southerners saw outside assistance to black Southerners as another invasion. The Yankees may have destroyed their families, their farms, and their fortunes, but they would not destroy the racial order. The war may have ended slavery, but white Southerners were determined to preserve strict racial boundaries.

MORE THAN FREEDOM: AFRICAN AMERICAN ASPIRATIONS IN 1865

Black Southerners also had a particular perspective on the Civil War and Reconstruction, the former as a great victory for freedom and the latter as a time of great possibility. But their view did not matter; it

This engraving shows Southerners decorating the graves of rebel soldiers at Hollywood Memorial Cemetery in Virginia, in 1867. Northerners and Southerners alike honored their war dead. But in the South, the practice of commemorating fallen soldiers became an important element in maintaining the myth of the Lost Cause that colored white Southerners' view of the war.

was invisible or, worse, distorted, in books, monuments, and official accounts. If, as British writer George Orwell later argued, "who controls the present controls the past, and who controls the past controls the future," then the vanishing black perspective is not surprising. The ferocity with which white Southerners attempted to take back their governments and their social structure was not only about nostalgia; it was about power and the legitimacy that power conferred.

And, of course, the black perspective was decidedly different from that of whites. As early as 1863, black Southerners carved out a very different interpretation of the Civil War which, to them, was a war of liberation, not a Lost Cause. At an emancipation parade in Norfolk that year, black women took joy in stomping on Confederate flags and burning an effigy of Jefferson Davis. Less raucous displays followed the war, especially on July 4, which, until well into the 1880s, was primarily a black holiday. And how it must have incensed white Southerners to see their former slaves celebrate their defeat and humiliation.

Yet, the response of Southern whites to black aspirations still stunned African Americans who believed, naively perhaps, that what they sought—education, land, access to employment, and equality in law and politics—were so basic to American citizenship that no one would or could deny them these modest objectives. The former slaves did not initially even dream of social equality; far less did they plot the kind of vengeful murder and mayhem white people feared. They did harbor two potentially contradictory aspirations. The first was to be left alone, free of white supervision. Responding to the key question of the time, "What shall we do with the Negro?" the former slave and abolitionist Frederick Douglass responded, "Do nothing . . . . Give him a chance to stand on his own legs! Let him alone!" But former slaves also wanted land, voting and civil rights, and education. To secure these, they needed the intervention and support of the white power structure.

In 1865, African Americans had reason to hope that their dreams of full citizenship might be realized. They enjoyed a reservoir of support for their aspirations among some Republican leaders. The views of James A. Garfield, Union veteran, U.S. congressman, and future president, were typical of these Republicans. Commenting on the ratification of the Thirteenth Amendment, Garfield asked, "What is freedom? Is it the bare privilege of not being chained? . . . If this is all, then freedom is a bitter mockery, a cruel delusion."

The first step Congress took beyond emancipation was to establish the Bureau of Refugees, Freedmen, and Abandoned Lands in March 1865. Congress envisioned the **Freedmen's Bureau**, as it came to be called, as a multipurpose agency to provide social, educational, and economic services, advice, and protection to former slaves and destitute white Southerners. The Bureau marked the federal government's first foray into social welfare legislation. Congress also authorized the bureau to rent confiscated and abandoned farmland to freedmen in forty-acre plots, with an option to buy. This auspicious beginning belied the great disappointments that lay ahead.

EDUCATION

The greatest success of the Freedmen's Bureau was in education. The bureau coordinated more than fifty northern philanthropic and religious groups, which, in turn, established three thousand freedmen's schools in the South, serving 150,000 men, women, and children.

Initially, single young women from the Northeast comprised much of the teaching force. One of them, 26-year-old Martha Schofield, came to Aiken, South Carolina, from rural Pennsylvania in 1865. Like many of her colleagues, she had joined the abolitionist movement as a teenager and decided to make teaching her life's work. Her strong Quaker beliefs reflected the importance of Protestant Christianity in motivating the young missionaries. When her sponsoring agency, the Pennsylvania Freedmen's Relief Association, folded in 1871, her school closed. Undaunted, she opened another school on her own, and, despite chronic financial problems and the hostility of Aiken's white citizens, she and the school

The Freedmen's Bureau, Northern churches, and missionary societies established more than three thousand schools, attended by some 150,000 men, women, and children in the years after the Civil War. At first, mostly young white women from the Northeast staffed these schools.

endured. (Since 1953, her school has been part of the Aiken public-school system.)

By the time Schofield opened her own school in 1871, black teachers outnumbered white teachers in the "colored" schools. The financial troubles of northern missionary societies and declining interest in the freedmen's condition among white Northerners opened opportunities for black teachers. Support for them came from black churches, especially the African Methodist Episcopal (AME) Church.

The former slaves crowded into basements, shacks, and churches to attend school. "The children . . . hurry to school as soon as their work is over," wrote a teacher in Norfolk, Virginia, in 1867. "The plowmen hurry from the field at night to get their hour of study. Old men and women strain their dim sight with the book two and a half feet distant from the eye, to catch the shape of the letter. I call this heaven-inspired interest."

At the end of the Civil War, only about 10 percent of black Southerners were literate, compared with more than 70 percent of white Southerners. Within a decade, black literacy had risen above 30 percent. Joseph Wilson, a former slave, attributed the rise to "this longing of ours for freedom of the mind as well as the body."

Some black Southerners went on to one of the thirteen colleges established by the American Missionary Association and black and white churches. Between 1860 and 1880 more than one thousand black Southerners earned college degrees at institutions still serving students today, such as Howard University in Washington, D.C.; Fisk University in Nashville; Hampton Institute (now University); Tuskegee Institute; and Biddle Institute (now Johnson C. Smith University) in Charlotte.

Pursuing freedom of the mind involved challenges beyond those of learning to read and write. Many white Southerners condemned efforts at "Negro improvement." They viewed the time spent on education as wasted, forcing the former slaves to catch their lessons in bits and pieces between work, often by candlelight or on Sundays. White Southerners also harassed white female teachers, questioning their morals and threatening people who rented rooms to them. The *Atlanta Constitution,* in a vicious caricature, suggested that Harriet Beecher Stowe planned to establish a freedmen's school near Atlanta "for the benefit of mulatto children that have been born in the South since its invasion by Yankee school-marms."

After the Freedmen's Bureau folded in 1872 and many of the northern societies that supported freedmen's education collapsed or cut back their involvement, education for black Southerners became more haphazard.

"FORTY ACRES AND A MULE"

Although education was important to the freed slaves in their quest for civic equality, land ownership offered them the promise of economic independence. For generations, black people had worked southern farms and had received nothing for their labor. An overwhelmingly agricultural people, freedmen looked to farm ownership as a key element in their transition from slavery to freedom. "Gib us our own land and we take care of ourselves," a Charleston freedman asserted to a Northern visitor in 1865. "But without land, de ole massas can hire or starve us, as dey please."

Even before the war's end, rumors circulated through black communities in the South that the government would provide each black family with forty acres and a mule. These rumors were fueled by General William T. Sherman's **Field Order No. 15** in January 1865, which set aside a vast swath of abandoned land along the South Atlantic coast from the Charleston area to northern Florida for grants of up to forty acres. The Freedmen's Bureau likewise raised expectations when it was initially authorized to rent forty-acre plots of confiscated or abandoned land to freedmen.

By June 1865, about forty thousand former slaves had settled on "Sherman land" along the southeastern coast. In 1866, Congress passed the **Southern Homestead Act**, giving black people preferential access to public lands in five southern states. Two years later, the Republican government of South Carolina initiated a land-redistribution program financed by the sale of state bonds. The state used proceeds from the bond sales to purchase farmland, which it then resold to freedmen, who paid for it with state-funded long-term low-interest loans. By the late 1870s, more than fourteen thousand African American families had taken advantage of this program.

The highest concentration of black land ownership was in the Upper South and in areas of the Lower South with better economic conditions and less white hostility toward black people. By 1890, one out of three black farmers in the Upper South owned his land, compared to one out of five for the South as a whole. In Virginia, 43 percent of black farmers owned the land they farmed.

Land ownership did not insure financial success. Most black-owned farms were small and on marginal land. The value of these farms in 1880 was roughly half that of white-owned farms. Black farmers also had trouble obtaining credit to purchase or expand their holdings. A lifetime of field work left some freedmen without the managerial skills to operate a farm. The hostility of white neighbors and their refusal to lend tools or animals, share work, sell land, or offer advice also played a role in thwarting black aspirations. Black farmers often had the most success when groups of families settled together, as in the farm community of Promise Land in upcountry South Carolina.

Milk sampling at Hampton Institute. Hampton, which opened in Virginia in 1868, was one of the first of several schools established with the help of Northern philanthropic and missionary societies to allow freedmen to pursue a college education. Hampton stressed agricultural and vocational training. The military uniforms were typical for male students, black and white, at agricultural and mechanical schools.

The vast majority of former slaves, however, especially those in the Lower South, never fulfilled their dreams of land ownership. Rumors to the contrary, the federal government never intended to implement a land-redistribution program in the South. General Sherman viewed his field order as a temporary measure to support freedmen for the remainder of the war. President Andrew Johnson nullified the order in September 1865, returning confiscated land to its former owners. Even Republican supporters of black land ownership questioned the constitutionality of seizing privately owned real estate. Most land-redistribution programs that did emerge after the war, including government-sponsored programs, required black farmers to have capital. But in the impoverished postwar economy of the South, it was difficult for them to acquire it.

Republican party rhetoric of the 1850s extolled the virtues and dignity of free labor over the degradation of slave labor. Free labor usually meant working for a wage or under some other contractual arrangement. But unlike slaves, according to the then prevailing view, free laborers could enjoy the fruits of their work and might someday become owners or entrepreneurs themselves. It was self-help, not government assistance, that guaranteed individual success. After the war, many white Northerners envisioned former slaves assuming the status of free laborers, not necessarily of independent landowners.

For most officials of the Freedmen's Bureau, who shared these views, reviving the southern economy was a higher priority than helping former slaves acquire farms. They wanted both to get the crop in the field and start the South on the road to a free labor system. They thus encouraged freedmen to work for their former masters under contract and to postpone their quest for land. Bureau and military officials lectured former slaves on the virtues of staying home and working "faithfully" in the fields.

At first, agents of the Freedmen's Bureau supervised labor contracts between former slaves and masters. But after 1867, bureau surveillance declined. Agents assumed that both black laborers and white landowners had become accustomed to the mutual obligations of contracts. The bureau, however, underestimated the power of white landowners to coerce favorable terms or to ignore those they did not like. Contracts implied a mutuality that most planters could not accept in their relations with former slaves. As the northern journalist Whitelaw Reid noted in 1865, planters "have no sort of conception of free labor. They do not comprehend any law for controlling laborers, save the law of force."

The former slaves had their own views of their proper place in the labor hierarchy. If they could not own land in the short term, they would strive for the best labor arrangement in the meantime. As early as 1862, slaves behind Union lines abandoned the gang system of labor, which they associated with slavery and dependence. In contracts with planters (usually their former masters) after the war, freedmen in most of the South insisted on working the land independently with their families. By contrast, freedmen in the rice districts along the South Atlantic coast retained their task system of labor, which allowed them flexibility and a degree of independence.

Throughout the South in 1865 and 1866, landlords complained of a chronic labor shortage, although few freedmen had left the region. The alleged shortage was the result of former slaves' refusal to work under conditions that resembled slavery. The withdrawal of black women from field work also contributed to the impression of a labor shortage. By staying home to care for their families, black women avoided the economic and sexual exploitation of the slavery era. They also sought to place themselves on an equal social footing with white plantation women, who likewise worked in the home and not in the fields.

MIGRATION TO CITIES

While some black Southerners asserted their rights as workers on southern farms, others affirmed their freedom by moving to towns and cities. Even before the war, the city had offered slaves and free black people a measure of freedom unknown in the rural South. After the war, African Americans moved to cities to find families, seek work, escape the tedium and supervision of farm life, or simply to test their right to move about.

For these same reasons, white people disapproved of black migration to the city. It reduced the labor pool for farms. It also gave black people more opportunities to associate with white people of similar social status, to compete for jobs, and to establish schools, churches, and social organizations, fueling their hopes for racial equality. White people felt confident that they could fix the freedmen's place in southern society on the farm; the city was another matter.

Between 1860 and 1870, the African American population in every major southern city rose significantly. In Atlanta, for example, black people accounted for one in five residents in 1860 and nearly one in two by 1870. Some freedmen came to cities initially to reunite with their families. Every city newspaper after the war carried advertisements from former slaves seeking their mates and children. In 1865, the Nashville *Colored Tennessean* carried this poignant plea: "During the year 1849, Thomas Sample carried away from this city, as his slaves, our daughter, Polly, and son. . . . We will give $100 each for them to any person who will assist them . . . to get to Nashville, or get word to us of their whereabouts."

Once in the city, freedmen had to find a home and a job. They usually settled for the cheapest accommodations in low-lying areas or on the outskirts of town, where building codes did not apply. Rather than developing one large ghetto, as happened in many northern cities, black Southerners lived in several concentrations in and around cities. Sometimes armed with a letter of reference from their former masters, black people went door to door to seek employment. Many found work serving white families—as guards, laundresses, maids—for very low wages. Both skilled and unskilled laborers found work rebuilding war-torn cities such as Atlanta. Frederick Ayer, a Freedmen's Bureau agent in Atlanta, reported to a colleague in 1866 that "many of the whites are making most vigorous efforts to retrieve their broken fortunes and . . . rebuild their dwellings and shops. . . . This furnished employment to a large number of colored people as Masons, Carpenters, Teamsters, and Common Workmen."

Most rural black Southerners, however, arrived in cities untrained in the kinds of skills sought in an urban work force and so worked as unskilled laborers.

In both Atlanta and Nashville, black people comprised more than 75 percent of the unskilled workforce in 1870. Their wages were at or below subsistence level. A black laborer in Richmond admitted to a journalist in 1870 that he had difficulty making ends meet on $1.50 a day. "It's right hard," he reported. "I have to pay $15 a month rent, and only two little rooms." His family survived because his wife took in laundry, while her mother watched the children. Considering the laborer's struggle, the journalist wondered, "Were not your people better off in slavery?" The man replied, "Oh, no sir! We're a heap better off now . . . . We're men now, but when our masters had us we was only change in their pockets."

The black church was the center of African American life in the postwar urban South. Most black churches formed after the Civil War, but some, such as the first African Baptist Church in Richmond, shown here in an 1874 engraving, traced their origins to before 1861.

FAITH AND FREEDOM

Religious faith framed and inspired the efforts of African Americans to test their freedom on the farm and in the city. White Southerners used religion to transform the Lost Cause from a shattering defeat to a premonition of a greater destiny. Black Southerners, in contrast, saw emancipation in biblical terms as the beginning of an exodus from bondage to the Promised Land.

Some black churches in the postwar South originated in the slavery era, but most split from white-dominated congregations after the war. White churchgoers deplored the expressive style of black worship, and black churchgoers were uncomfortable in congregations that treated them as inferiors. A separate church also reduced white surveillance.

The First African Baptist Church in Richmond, founded before the war, originated in a white Baptist congregation. An 1846 agreement allowed black worshipers to hold separate services, but only with a white minister officiating. In 1866, the white pastor resigned, noting that black worshipers "would naturally and justly prefer a minister of their own color." The white church transferred the deed to the black congregation that year, and the Reverend James Henry Holmes, a former slave, became their first black pastor. The church flourished under Holmes, paid off its debt, and by the 1870s boasted the largest black congregation in the United States.

The church became a primary focus of African American life. It gave black people the opportunity to hone skills in self-government and administration that white-dominated society denied them. Within the supportive confines of the congregation, they could assume leadership positions, render important decisions, deal with financial matters, and engage in politics. The church also operated as an educational institution. Local governments, especially in rural areas, rarely constructed public schools for black people; churches often served that function. The desire to read the Bible inspired thousands of former slaves to attend the church school.

The church also spawned other organizations that served the black community over the next century. Burial societies, Masonic lodges, temperance groups, trade unions, and drama clubs originated in churches. By the 1870s, African Americans in Memphis had more than two hundred such organizations. They often came together to celebrate such holidays as Independence Day on July 4 and the anniversary of the Emancipation Proclamation on January 1. These commemorations antagonized white people and further divided the black and white communities.

African Americans took great pride in their churches, which became visible measures of their progress. In Charleston, the first building erected after the war was a black church. The First Colored Baptist Church in Nashville became a landmark for its imposing brick and stone façade. Black people donated a greater proportion of their earnings to their churches than did white people.

The church and the congregation were a cohesive force in black communities. They supported families under stress from discrimination and poverty. Husbands and wives joined church-affiliated societies together. Their children joined organizations such as the Young Rising Sons and Daughters of the New Testament. The church enforced family and religious values, punishing violaters guilty of such infractions as adultery. Black churchwomen—both working class and middle class—were especially prominent in the family-oriented organizations.

Most black churches looked inward to strengthen their members against the harsh realities of postwar southern society. Few ministers dared to engage in or even support protest activities. Some, especially those in the Colored Methodist Episcopal Church, counseled congregants to abide by the rules of second-class citizenship and to trust in God's will to right the wrongs of racism.

Northern-based denominations, however, notably the AME Church, were more aggressive advocates of black rights. AME ministers stressed the responsibility of individual black people to realize God's will of racial equality.

Henry McNeal Turner, probably the most influential AME minister of his day, helped expand the denomination into the South from its small primarily northern base at the end of the Civil War. The white Southern Methodist church granted the nineteen-year-old Turner a license to preach in 1853. He served as an itinerant minister for both black and white congregations during the next five years. In 1858, he joined the AME Church and moved north to lead a congregation in Baltimore. After serving as a U.S. Army chaplain, Turner moved to Georgia and evangelized former slaves who thronged to an activist church with black roots. Within five years, the AME Church had grown to 500,000 members, 80 percent of whom lived in the South. Turner entered Georgia politics in the late 1860s and held several state elective offices. His church elevated him to bishop in 1880.

Turner's career and the efforts of former slaves in the classroom, on the farm, in cities, and in the churches reflect the enthusiasm and expectations with which black Southerners greeted freedom. But the majority of white Southerners were unwilling to see those expectations fulfilled. For this reason, African Americans could not secure the fruits of their emancipation without the support and protection of the federal government. The issue of freedom was therefore inextricably linked to the other great issue of the era—the rejoining of the Confederacy to the Union, as expressed in federal Reconstruction policy.

FEDERAL RECONSTRUCTION, 1865–1870

When the Civil War ended in 1865, no acceptable blueprint existed for reconstituting the Union. President Lincoln believed that, at heart, a majority of white Southerners were Unionists and that they could and should undertake the task of reconstruction. He favored a conciliatory policy toward the South in order, as he put it in one of his last letters, "to restore the Union, so as to make it . . . a Union of hearts and hands as well as of States." He counted on the loyalists to be fair with respect to the rights of the former slaves.

The president had outlined his policy as early as 1863, when he proposed to readmit a seceding state if 10 percent of its prewar voters took an oath of loyalty to the Union and it prohibited slavery in a new state constitution. But this Ten Percent Plan did not require states to grant equal civil and political rights to former slaves, and many Republicans in Congress thought it was not stringent enough. In 1864, a group of them responded with the Wade-Davis Bill, which required a majority of a state's prewar voters to pledge their loyalty to the Union and demanded guarantees of black equality before the law. The bill was passed at the end of a congressional session, but Lincoln kept it from becoming law by refusing to sign it (an action known as a "pocket veto").

Lincoln, of course, died before he could implement a Reconstruction plan. His views on reconstructing the Union during the war did not necessarily prefigure how his views would unfold after the war. Above all, Lincoln was flexible on the issue, prepared to tailor his proposals to suit the situation. As noted of his proposed Proclamation of Amnesty, promulgated in 1863 as a way to ease the rebellious states back into the Union, "[A]s bad promises are better broken than kept, I shall treat this as a bad promise, and break it, whenever I shall be convinced that keeping it is adverse to the public interest." Given this flexibility, and given his commitment in the Gettysburg Address to promote "a new birth of freedom," it is likely that had white Southerners resisted black civil rights, Lincoln would have responded with harsher terms. But his successor, Andrew Johnson, lacked both his flexibility and his appreciation for the importance of black freedom.

The controversy over these plans introduced during the war reflected two obstacles to Reconstruction that would continue to plague the ruling Republicans after the war. First, neither the Constitution nor legal precedent offered any guidance on whether the president or Congress should take the lead on Reconstruction policy. Second, there was no agreement on what that policy should be. Proposals requiring various preconditions for readmitting a state—loyalty oaths, new constitutions with certain specific provisions, guarantees of freedmen's rights—all provoked vigorous debate.

President Andrew Johnson, some conservative Republicans, and most Democrats believed that because the Constitution made no mention of secession, the southern states had been in rebellion but had never left the Union, and that therefore there was no need for a formal process to readmit them. Moderate and radical Republicans disagreed, arguing that the defeated states had forfeited their rights. Moderates and radicals parted company, however, on the conditions necessary for readmission to the Union. The radicals wanted to treat the former Confederate states as territories—or "conquered provinces"—subject to congressional legis-

lation. Moderates wanted to grant the seceding states more autonomy and limit federal intervention in their affairs while they satisfied the conditions of readmission. No group held a majority in Congress, and legislators sometimes changed their positions (see the Overview table, "Contrasting Views of Reconstruction").

PRESIDENTIAL RECONSTRUCTION, 1865–1867

When the Civil War ended in April 1865, Congress was not in session and would not reconvene until December. Thus, the responsibility for developing a Reconstruction policy initially fell on Andrew Johnson, who succeeded to the presidency upon Lincoln's assassination. Johnson seemed well suited to the difficult task. The new president's personal and political background was promising to his Republican colleagues. Johnson was born in humble circumstances in North Carolina in 1808. He learned the tailoring trade and struck out for Tennessee as a teenager to open a tailor shop in the eastern Tennessee town of Greenville. Gaining his education informally, he

Overview

Contrasting Views of Reconstruction: President and Congress

Politician or Group	Policy on Former Slaves	Policy on Readmission of Former Confederate States
President Johnson	Opposed to black suffrage	Maintained that rebellious states were already readmitted
	Silent on protection of black civil rights	Granted pardons and restoration of property to all who swore allegiance to the United States
	Opposed to land redistribution	
Radical Republicans	Favored black suffrage	Favored treating rebellious states as territories and establishing military districts*
	Favored protection of black civil rights	Favored limiting franchise to black people and loyal white people
	Favored land redistribution	
Moderate Republicans	Favored black suffrage	Favored some restrictions on white suffrage*
	Favored protection of civil rights	Favored requiring states to meet various requirements before being readmitted*
	Opposed land redistribution	Split on military rule

*True of most but not all members of the group.

AMERICAN VIEWS

Mississippi's 1865 Black Codes

White Southerners, especially landowners and business owners, feared emancipation would produce a labor crisis; freedmen, they expected, would either refuse to work or strike hard bargains with their former masters. White Southerners also recoiled from the prospect of having to treat their former slaves as full social equals. Thus, beginning in late 1865, several southern states, including Mississippi, enacted laws designed to control black labor, mobility, and social status. Northerners responded to the codes as a provocation, a bold move to deny the result of the war and its consequences.

- How did the black codes fit into President Andrew Johnson's Reconstruction program?
- Some Northerners charged that the black codes were a backdoor attempt at reestablishing slavery. Do you agree?
- If southern states enacted black codes to stabilize labor relations, how did the provisions below effect that objective?

From An Act to Confer Civil Rights on Freedmen, and for other Purposes

Section 1. All freedmen, free negroes and mulattoes may sue and be sued, implead and be impleaded, in all the courts of law and equity of this State, and may acquire personal property, and choose in action, by descent or purchase, and may dispose of the same in the same manner and to the same extent that white persons may: Provided, That the provisions of this section shall not be so construed as to allow any freedman, free negro or mulatto to rent or lease any lands or tenements except in incorporated cities or towns, in which places the corporate authorities shall control the same.

---

prospered modestly, purchased a few slaves, and began to pursue politics. He was elected alderman, mayor, state legislator, congressman, governor, and then, in 1856, U.S. senator. Johnson was the only southern senator to remain in the U.S. Senate after secession. This defiant Unionism won him acclaim in the North and credibility among Republican leaders, who welcomed him into their party. During the war, as military governor of Tennessee, he solidified his Republican credentials by advocating the abolition of slavery in Tennessee and severe punishment of Confederate leaders. His views landed him on the Republican ticket as the candidate for vice president in 1864. Indiana Republican congressman George W. Julian, who advocated harsh terms for the South and broad rights for black people, viewed Johnson's accession to the presidency in 1865 as "a godsend."

Most Northerners and many Republicans approved Johnson's Reconstruction plan when he un-

veiled it in May 1865. Johnson extended pardons and restored property rights, except in slaves, to Southerners who swore an oath of allegiance to the Union and the Constitution. Southerners who had held prominent positions in the Confederacy, however, and those with more than $20,000 in taxable property had to petition the president directly for a pardon, a reflection of Johnson's disdain for wealthy whites. The plan had nothing to say about the voting rights and civil rights of former slaves.

Northern Democrats applauded the plan's silence on these issues and its promise of a quick restoration of the southern states to the Union. They expected the southern states to favor their party and expand its political power. Republicans, although some of them would have preferred the plan to have provided for black suffrage, approved of the restoration of property rights to white Southerners. This position was consistent with their view of former slaves as

Section 7. Every civil officer shall, and every person may, arrest and carry back to his or her legal employer any freedman, free negro, or mulatto who shall have quit the service of his or her employer before the expiration of his or her term of service without good cause; and said officer and person shall be entitled to receive for arresting and carrying back every deserting employee aforesaid the sum of five dollars, and ten cents per mile from the place of arrest to the place of delivery; and the same shall be paid by the employer, and held as a set off for so much against the wages of said deserting employee: Provided, that said arrested party, after being so returned, may appeal to the justice of the peace or member of the board of police of the county, who, on notice to the alleged employer, shall try summarily whether said appellant is legally employed by the alleged employer, and has good cause to quit said employer. Either party shall have the right of appeal to the county court, pending which the alleged deserter shall be remanded to the alleged employer or otherwise disposed of, as shall be right and just; and the decision of the county court shall be final.

From An Act to Amend the Vagrant Laws of the State
Section 2. All freedmen, free negroes and mulattoes in this State, over the age of eighteen years, found on the second Monday in January, 1866, or thereafter, with no lawful employment or business, or found unlawful assembling themselves together, either in the day or night time, and all white persons assembling themselves with freedmen, Free negroes or mulattoes, or usually associating with freedmen, free negroes or mulattoes, on terms of equality, or living in adultery or fornication with a freed woman, freed negro or mulatto, shall be deemed vagrants, and on conviction thereof shall be fined in a sum not exceeding, in the case of a freedman, free negro or mulatto, fifty dollars, and a white man two hundred dollars, and imprisonment at the discretion of the court, the free negro not exceeding ten days, and the white man not exceeding six months.

Source: "Laws in Relation to Freedmen," 39 Congress, 2 Session, Senate Executive Document 6, Freedmen's Affairs, 182–86.

laborers, not property owners. Republicans also hoped that Johnson's conciliatory terms might attract some white Southerners to the Republican party.

White Southerners, however, were not so favorably impressed with Johnson's plan, and their response turned northern public opinion against the president. On the two great issues of freedom and reunion, white Southerners quickly demonstrated their eagerness to reverse the results of the Civil War. Although most states accepted President Johnson's modest requirements, several objected to one or more of them. Mississippi and Texas refused to ratify the Thirteenth Amendment, which abolished slavery. Alabama accepted only parts of the amendment. South Carolina declined to nullify its secession ordinance. No southern state authorized black voting. When Johnson ordered special congressional elections in the South in the fall of 1865, the all-white electorate returned many prominent Confederate leaders to office.

In late 1865, the newly elected southern state legislatures revised their antebellum slave codes. The updated **black codes** allowed local officials to arrest black people who could not document employment and residence or who were "disorderly" and sentence them to forced labor on farms or road crews. The codes also restricted black people to certain occupations, barred them from jury duty, and forbade them to possess firearms. Apprenticeship laws permitted judges to take black children from parents who could not, in the judges' view, adequately support them. Given the widespread poverty in the South in 1865, the law could apply to almost any freed black family. Northerners looking for contrition in the South found no sign of it. Worse, President Johnson did not seem perturbed about this turn of events.

The Republican-dominated Congress reconvened in December 1865 in a belligerent mood. A few radical Republicans pushed for swift retribution. George

W. Julian thundered that he would "indict, convict and hang Jefferson Davis in the name of God; as for Robert E. Lee, unmolested in Virginia, hang him too." His colleague, Benjamin F. Wade, suggested that "if the negroes by insurrection would contrive to slay one-half of the White Southerners, the remaining half would then hold them in respect and treat them with justice." Few in Congress took these statements seriously. Nonetheless, a consensus formed among radical Republicans, who comprised nearly half of the party's strength in Congress, that to gain readmission, a state would have to extend suffrage to black citizens, protect freedmen's civil rights, and have its white citizens officially acknowledge these rights. Some radicals also supported the redistribution of land to former slaves, but few pressed for social equality. They envisioned a new South of modest farms, some owned by former slaves, and a Republican party built on an alliance between black people and white loyalists.

Thaddeus Stevens of Pennsylvania led the radical forces in the House of Representatives, while the abolitionist veteran Charles Sumner of Massachusetts rallied radicals in the Senate. Stevens had established himself as a partisan for black political rights in the North as early as the 1840s. As a congressman during the Civil War, he pushed Lincoln to free and arm the slaves and later to extend them the right to vote. Stevens dreamed of a South populated by white and black yeoman farmers. With no large plantations and few landless farmers, the South would become an ideal republic, a boon to the rest of the nation, instead of a burden. Few shared his vision, and when he died in 1868, a reporter noted that "no man was oftener outvoted." Yet he remained the conscience of the House, a standard of idealism in an age of growing cynicism. His epitaph read in part, "The principle which I advocated through a long life, Equality of Man before his Creator."

Sumner was among the foremost abolitionist politicians before the Civil War. His combative nature won him few friends, even within his own party. As fierce as Stevens in the promotion of black civil and political rights after the war, he also believed that the Reconstruction era offered a "golden moment" to remake the South into an egalitarian region. Sumner died in 1874 as his dream was fading. The last piece of Reconstruction legislation, the Civil Rights Act of 1875, became a posthumous tribute to his uncommon ability to overcome the racial prejudices of the day with a vision of a colorblind society.

But the radicals could not unite behind a program, and it fell to their moderate colleagues to take the first step toward a congressional Reconstruction plan. The moderates shared the radicals' desire to protect the former slaves' civil and voting rights. But they would not support land redistribution schemes or punitive measures against prominent Confederates. The moderates' first measure, passed in early 1866, extended the life of the Freedmen's Bureau and provided it with authority to punish state officials who failed to extend to black citizens the civil rights enjoyed by white citizens. But President Johnson vetoed the legislation.

Undeterred, Congress passed the Civil Rights Act of 1866 in direct response to the black codes. The act specified the civil rights to which all U.S. citizens were entitled. In creating a category of national citizenship with rights that superseded state laws restricting them, the act changed federal–state relations (and in the process overturned the Dred Scott decision). President Johnson vetoed the act, but it became law when Congress mustered a two-thirds majority to override his veto—the first time in American history that Congress passed major legislation over a president's veto.

Andrew Johnson's position reflected both his view of government and his racial attitudes. The Republican president remained a Democrat in spirit. Republicans had expanded federal power during the Civil War. Johnson, however, like most Democrats, favored more of a balance between federal and state power. He also shared with many of his white southern neighbors a belief in black inferiority and a view that white plantation owners had conspired to limit the economic and political power of white yeomen like himself. Johnson supported abolition assuming that, once free, black people would emigrate to Africa. Given the president's views and his inflexible temperament, a clash between him and Congress became inevitable.

To keep freedmen's rights safe from presidential vetoes, state legislatures, and federal courts, the Republican-dominated Congress moved to incorporate some of the provisions of the 1866 Civil Rights Act into the Constitution. The **Fourteenth Amendment**, which Congress passed in June 1866, addressed the issues of civil and voting rights. It guaranteed every citizen equality before the law. The two key sections of the amendment prohibited states from violating the civil rights of their citizens, thus outlawing the black codes, and gave states the choice of enfranchising black people or losing representation in Congress. Some radical Republicans expressed disappointment that the amendment, in a reflection of northern ambivalence, failed to give the vote to black people outright.

The amendment also disappointed advocates of woman suffrage, for the first time using the word *male* in the Constitution to define who could vote. Wendell Phillips, a prominent abolitionist, counseled them, "One question at a time. This hour belongs to the Negro." Susan B. Anthony, who had campaigned for the abolition of slavery before the war and helped

"Selling a Freeman to Pay his Fine at Monticello, Florida." This 1867 engraving shows how the black codes of the early Reconstruction era reduced former slaves to virtually their pre-Civil War status. Scenes such as this convinced Northerners that the white South was unrepentant and prompted congressional Republicans to devise their own Reconstruction plans.

mount a petition drive that collected 400,000 signatures for the Thirteenth Amendment, formed the American Equal Rights Association in 1866 with her colleagues to push for woman suffrage at the state level.

The Fourteenth Amendment had little immediate impact on the South. Although enforcement of black codes diminished, white violence against black people increased. In the 1870s, several decisions by the U.S. Supreme Court would weaken the amendment's provisions. Eventually, however, it would play a major role in securing the civil rights of African Americans.

President Johnson encouraged Southern white intransigence by openly denouncing the Fourteenth Amendment. In August 1866, at the start of the con-

gressional election campaign, he undertook an unprecedented tour of key northern states to sell his message of sectional reconciliation to the public. Although listeners appreciated Johnson's desire for peace, they questioned his claims of southern white loyalty to the Union. The president's diatribes against the Republican Congress won him followers in those northern states with a reservoir of opposition to black suffrage. But the tone and manner of his campaign offended many as undignified. In the November elections, the Democrats suffered embarrassing defeats in the North as Republicans managed better than two-thirds majorities in both the House and Senate, sufficient to override presidential vetoes. Radical Republicans, joined by moderate colleagues buoyed by the election results and revolted by the president's and the South's intransigence, seized the initiative when Congress reconvened.

CONGRESSIONAL RECONSTRUCTION, 1867–1870

The radicals' first salvo in their attempt to take control over Reconstruction occurred with the passage over President Johnson's veto of the Military Reconstruction Acts. The measures, passed in March 1867, inaugurated a period known as **Congressional Reconstruction** or Radical Reconstruction. Congress divided the ex-Confederate states (except for Tennessee, the only southern state that had ratified the Fourteenth Amendment and been readmitted to the Union) into five military districts, each headed by a general (see Map 16–1). The commanders' first order of business was to conduct voter-registration campaigns to enroll black people and bar white people who had held office before the Civil War and who had supported the Confederacy. The eligible voters would then elect delegates to a state convention to write a new constitution that guaranteed universal manhood suffrage. Once a majority of eligible voters ratified the new constitution and the Fourteenth Amendment, their state would be eligible for readmission to the Union.

MAP 16-1   Congressional Reconstruction, 1865–1877
When Congress wrested control of Reconstruction policy from President Andrew Johnson, it divided the South into the five military districts depicted here. The commanding generals for each district held the authority both to hold elections and to decide who could vote.

Legend:
- Boundaries of the five military districts
- Former Confederate states
- 1868 Date of readmission to Union
- (1874) Date of reestablishment of conservative Democratic party control

The Reconstruction Acts fulfilled the radicals' three major objectives. First, they secured the freedmen's right to vote. Second, they made it likely that southern states would be run by Republican regimes that would enforce the new constitutions, protect former slaves' rights, and maintain the Republican majority in Congress. Finally, the acts set standards for readmission that required the South to accept the consequences of defeat: the preeminence of the federal government and the end of involuntary servitude.

To limit presidential interference with their policies, Republicans passed the Tenure of Office Act, prohibiting the president from removing certain officeholders without the Senate's consent. Johnson, angered at what he believed was an unconstitutional attack on presidential authority, deliberately violated the act by firing Secretary of War Edwin M. Stanton, a leading radical, in February 1868. The House responded to this defiance by approving articles of impeachment against a president for the first time in American history. After a trial, the Senate voted 35 to 19 to convict the president, one vote short of the two-thirds necessary to remove him from office. The seven Republicans who voted against their party did so, not out of respect for the president, but because they feared that a conviction would damage the office of the presidency and violate the constitutional separation of powers. The outcome weakened the radicals and eased the way for a moderate Republican, Ulysses S. Grant, to gain the party's nomination for president in 1868.

The Republicans viewed the 1868 presidential election as a referendum on Congressional Reconstruction. They supported black suffrage in the South but equivocated on allowing African Americans to vote in the North. Black Northerners could vote in only eight of the twenty-two northern states, and, between 1865 and 1869, white Northerners had rejected equal suffrage referendums in eight of eleven states. Republicans "waved the bloody shirt," reminding voters of Democratic disloyalty, the sacrifices of war, and the peace only Republicans could redeem. Democrats denounced Congressional Reconstruction as federal tyranny and, in openly racist appeals, warned white voters that a Republican victory would mean black rule. Grant won the election, but his margin of victory was uncomfortably narrow. Reflecting growing ambivalence in the North over issues of race and federal authority, New York's Horatio Seymour, the Democratic presidential nominee, probably carried a majority of the nation's white vote. Black voters' overwhelming support for Grant probably provided him his margin of victory.

Casting a ballot. Black voters in Richmond vote on a state constitutional convention in 1867. A key objective of Congressional Reconstruction was to secure the voting rights of freedmen.

The Republicans retained a strong majority in both houses of Congress and managed to pass another major piece of Reconstruction legislation, the **Fifteenth Amendment**, in February 1869. In response to growing concerns about voter fraud and violence against freedmen, the amendment guaranteed the right of American men to vote, regardless of race. Although the amendment provided a loophole allowing states to impose restrictions on the right to vote based on literacy or property qualifications, it was nonetheless a milestone. It made the right to vote perhaps the most distinguishing characteristic of American citizenship.

The Fifteenth Amendment allowed states to keep the franchise a male prerogative, angering many in the woman-suffrage movement more than had the Fourteenth Amendment. The resulting controversy severed the ties between the movement and Republican politics. Susan B. Anthony broke with her abolitionist colleagues and opposed the amendment. A fellow abolitionist and woman suffragist, Elizabeth Cady Stanton, charged that the amendment created an "aristocracy of sex." In an appeal brimming with ethnic and racial animosity, Stanton warned that "if you do not wish the lower orders of Chinese, African, Germans and Irish, with their low ideas of womanhood to make

laws for you and your daughters . . . awake to the danger . . . and demand that woman, too, shall be represented in the government!" Such language created a major rift in the nascent women's movement. Women who supported the amendment formed the New England Woman Suffrage Association, challenging Anthony's American Equal Rights Association.

SOUTHERN REPUBLICAN GOVERNMENTS, 1867–1870

Away from Washington, the first order of business for the former Confederacy was to draft state constitutions. The documents embodied progressive principles new to the South. They mandated the election of numerous local and state offices. Self-perpetuating local elites could no longer appoint themselves or cronies to powerful positions. The constitutions committed southern states, many for the first time, to public education. Lawmakers enacted a variety of reforms, including social welfare, penal reform, legislative reapportionment, and universal manhood suffrage.

The Republican regimes that gained control in southern states promoted vigorous state government and the protection of civil and voting rights. Three diverse Republican constituencies supported these governments. One consisted of white natives, most of them yeomen farmers. Residing mainly in the upland regions of the South and long ignored by lowland planters and merchants in state government, some had supported the Union during the war. The conflict had left many of them devastated. They struggled to keep their land and hoped for an easing of credit and for debt-stay laws to help them escape foreclosure. They wanted public schools for their children and good roads to get their crops to market. Some urban merchants and large planters also called themselves Republicans. Many were Whigs before the war, and a few had been Unionists. They were attracted to the party's emphasis on economic development, especially railroad construction, and would become prominent in Republican leadership after 1867, forming a majority of party elected officials.

Collectively, opponents called these native white Southerners **scalawags**, a derogatory term for an idle or mischievous person derived from Scalloway, the name of a district on Scotland's Shetland Islands known for its scraggly livestock. The term was first applied in western New York before the Civil War to an idle person, and then to a mischievous one. Although their opponents may have perceived them as a unified group, scalawags held a variety of views. Planters and merchants opposed easy debt and credit arrangements and the use of their taxes to support programs other than railroads or port improvements. Yeomen farmers desperately needed the debt and credit legislation to retain their land. And even though they supported public schools and road building—which would require increased state revenues—they opposed higher taxes.

Northern transplants, or **carpetbaggers**, as many Southern whites called them, constituted a second group of southern Republicans. The term also had antebellum origins, referring to a suspicious stranger. Cartoonists depicted carpetbaggers as shoddily dressed and poorly groomed, their worldly possessions in a ratty cloth satchel, slinking into a town and swindling the locals before departing with their ill-gotten gains. The reality was far different from the caricature. Thousands of Northerners came south during and after the war. Many were Union soldiers who simply enjoyed the climate and perhaps married a local woman. Most were drawn by economic opportunity. Land was cheap and the price of cotton high. Although most carpetbaggers had supported the Republican party before they moved south, few became politically active until the cotton economy nosedived in 1866. Financial concerns were not all that motivated carpetbaggers to enter politics; some hoped to aid the freedmen.

Carpetbaggers never comprised more than 2 percent of any state's population. Most white Southerners viewed them as an alien presence, instruments of a hated occupying force. They provoked resentment because they seemed to prosper while most Southerners struggled in poverty. And they further estranged themselves from their neighbors by supporting and participating in the Republican state governments that most white people despised. In Alabama, local editors organized a boycott of northern-owned shops. "STARVE THEM OUT!" they wrote. "Don't put your foot in the doors of their shops, offices, and stores. Purchase from true men and patronize those of known Southern sympathies." Because many of them tended to support extending political and civil rights to black Southerners, carpetbaggers were also often at odds with their fellow white Republicans, the scalawags.

African Americans constituted the Republican party's largest southern constituency. In three states—South Carolina, Mississippi, and Louisiana—they also constituted the majority of eligible voters. They viewed the franchise as the key to civic equality and economic opportunity and demanded an active role in party and government affairs.

Black people began to take part in southern politics even before the end of the Civil War, especially in cities occupied by Union forces. In February 1865, black people in Norfolk, Virginia, gathered to demand a say in the new government that Union supporters were forming in that portion of the state. In April, they created the Colored Monitor Union club, modeled after regular Republican party organizations in north-

ern cities, called **Union Leagues**. They demanded "the right of universal suffrage" for "all loyal men, without distinction of color." Black people in other southern cities held similar meetings, seeking inclusion in the democratic process in order to protect their freedom. As a member of the Alexandria, Virginia, black Union League argued in August 1865, "The only salvation for us . . . is in the possession of the ballot. Give us this, and we will protect ourselves."

White Southerners viewed these developments with alarm but could not at first counter them. Despite white threats, black Southerners thronged to Union League meetings in 1867, even forging interracial alliances in states such as North Carolina and Alabama. Focusing on political education and recruitment, the leagues successfully mobilized black voters. In 1867, more than 90 percent of eligible black voters across the South turned out for elections. Black women, even though they could not vote, also played a role. During the 1868 presidential campaign, for example, black maids and cooks in the South wore but-

As white paramilitary organizations in the South attacked African American civil and political rights, South Carolina Congressman Robert B. Elliott rose in the House of Representatives in January 1874 to present a ringing endorsement of Charles Sumner's Civil Rights Bill. The illustration also depicts southern black aspirations for and justification of the basic rights of citizenship, the results of which Elliott embodied.

tons touting the candidacy of the Republican presidential nominee, Ulysses S. Grant.

Black Southerners were not content just to vote; they also demanded political office. White Republican leaders in the South often took the black vote for granted. But on several occasions after 1867, black people threatened to run independent candidates, support rival Democrats, or simply stay home unless they were represented among Republican nominees. These demands brought them some success. The number of southern black congressmen in the U.S. House of Representatives increased from two in 1869 to seven in 1873, and more than six hundred African Americans, most of them former slaves from plantation counties, were elected to southern state legislatures between 1867 and 1877.

White fears that black officeholders would enact vengeful legislation proved unfounded. African Americans generally did not promote race-specific legislation. Rather, they supported measures such as debt relief and state funding for education that benefited all poor and working-class people. Like all politicians, however, black officials in southern cities sought to enact measures beneficial to their constituents. In Atlanta, for example, black officeholders had a sidewalk laid in front of a prominent black church and diverted a road scheduled to cut through a black neighborhood. In Richmond, black people secured an ordinance forbidding the robbing of black graves to supply medical schools with corpses. And they succeeded in having a black police commissioner appointed in Jacksonville, Florida. Gains like these underscored the advantages of suffrage for the African American community.

During the first few years of Congressional Reconstruction, Republican governments walked a tightrope, attempting to lure moderate Democrats and unaffiliated white voters into the party without slighting the black vote. They used the lure of patronage power and the attractive salaries that accompanied public office. In 1868, for example, Louisiana's Republican governor, Henry C. Warmoth, appointed white conservatives to state and local offices, which he divided equally between ex-Confederate veterans and black people, and repealed a constitutional provision disfranchising former Confederate officials.

Republicans also gained support by expanding the role of state government to a degree unprecedented in the South. Southern Republican administrations appealed to hard-pressed upland white constituents by prohibiting foreclosure and passing stay laws that allowed farm owners additional time to repay debts. They undertook building programs that benefited both black and white citizens, erecting hospitals, schools, and orphanages. Stepping further into social policy than most northern states at the time, Republican governments in the South expanded women's property rights, enacted legislation against child abuse, and required child support from fathers of mulatto children. In South Carolina, the Republican government provided medical care for the poor; in Alabama, it provided free legal aid for needy defendants.

Despite these impressive policies, southern Republicans were unable to hold their diverse constituency together. Although the party had some success among white yeoman farmers, the liberal use of patronage to attract white conservatives failed to gain it many new adherents. At the same time, it alienated the party's core supporters, who resented seeing their former enemies rewarded with lucrative offices.

The high costs of their activist policies further undermined the Republicans by forcing them to raise state taxes. In Mississippi—where the Republican governor built a public-school system for both black and white students, founded a black university, reorganized the state judiciary, built new courthouses and two state hospitals, and pushed through legislation giving black people equal access to public facilities—the state debt soared to $1.5 million between 1869 and 1873. This was in an era in which state budgets rarely exceeded $1 million.

Unprecedented expenditures and the liberal use of patronage sometimes resulted in waste and corruption. Officials charged with selecting railroad routes, appointing lesser officials, and erecting public buildings were well positioned to benefit from their power. Their high salaries offended many in an otherwise impoverished region. Problems like these were not limited to the South. They were pervasive throughout the country in the 1860s and 1870s. The perception of dishonesty was nonetheless damaging to governments struggling to build legitimacy among a skeptical white electorate.

The excesses of some state governments, high taxes, contests over patronage, and conflicts over the relative roles of white and black party members opened rifts in Republican ranks. Patronage triggered intraparty warfare. Every office secured by a Democrat created a disappointed Republican. Class tensions erupted in the party as economic development policies, favored by former Whigs, sometimes superseded relief and social service legislation supported by small farmers. The failure of Alabama Republicans to deliver on promises of debt relief and land redistribution eroded the significant support the party had enjoyed among upcountry white voters. There were differences among black voters too. In the Lower South, divisions that had developed in the prewar era between urban, lighter-skinned free black people and darker, rural slaves persisted into the Reconstruction era. In many southern states, black clergy, because of their independence from white support and their important spiritual and educational role, became leaders. But most preached salvation in the next world rather than equality in this one, conceding more to white people than their rank-and-file constituents.

COUNTER-RECONSTRUCTION, 1870–1874

Republicans might have survived battles over patronage, differences over policy, and the resentment provoked by extravagant expenditures and high taxes. But they could not overcome racism and the violence it generated. Racism killed Republican rule in the South because it deepened divisions within the party, encouraged white violence, and eroded support in the North. Southern Democrats discovered that they could use race baiting and racial violence to create solidarity among white people that overrode their economic and class differences. Unity translated into election victories.

Northerners responded to the persistent violence in the South, not with outrage, but with a growing sense of tedium. They came to accept the arguments of white Southerners that it was folly to allow black people to vote and hold office. Racism became respectable. Noted intellectuals and journalists espoused "scientific" theories that claimed to demonstrate the natural superiority of white people over black people. These theories influenced the Liberal Republicans, followers of a new political movement that splintered the Republican Party, further weakening its will to pursue Reconstruction policy.

By 1874, Americans were concerned with an array of domestic problems that overshadowed Reconstruction. A serious economic depression left them more preoccupied with survival than racial justice. Corruption convinced many that politics was part of the nation's problems, not a solution to them. With the rest of the nation thus distracted and weary, white Southerners reclaimed control of the South.

THE USES OF VIOLENCE

Racial violence preceded Republican rule. As African Americans moved about, attempted to vote, haggled over labor contracts, and carried arms as part of occupying Union forces, they tested the patience of white Southerners. In a racial world turned upside down from the white perspective, any black assertion of equality seemed threatening.

Cities, where black and white people competed for jobs and where black political influence was most visible, became flashpoints for interracial violence. In

May 1866, the collision of two wagons in Memphis, one driven by a white carter, the other by a black carter, touched off three days of white attacks on black people and black neighborhoods. Forty-six black people and two white people died in the fray, and five black women were raped. The white mob destroyed black churches, schools, and homes.

White paramilitary groups flourished in the South during the Reconstruction era and were responsible for much of the violence directed against African Americans. Probably the best known of these groups was the **Ku Klux Klan**. Founded in Tennessee by six Confederate veterans in 1866, the Klan was initially a social club. Prominent ex-Confederates such as General John B. Gordon and General Nathan Bedford Forrest, allegedly the first Grand Wizard of the Klan, saw the political potential of the new organization. Within a year, the Klan had spread throughout the South. In 1867, when black people entered politics in large numbers, the Klan unleashed a wave of terror against them. Klan night riders in ghostlike disguises intimidated black communities. The Klan directed much of its violence toward subverting the electoral process. One historian has estimated that roughly 10 percent of all black delegates to the 1867 state constitutional conventions in the South became victims of political violence during the next decade.

Not all Klan attacks had political objectives. Klansmen struck against anyone, black or white, who, they believed, had violated racial boundaries. A Georgia Klansman murdered a freedman because he could read and write. Klansmen in Florence, South Carolina, killed a black man who rented a plantation "because such a thing ought not to be." And in 1868, Klansmen murdered three southern white Republican Georgia state legislators. Membership in the Klan crossed class lines. Race became an issue on which white people, regardless of differing economic interests, could agree.

By 1868, white paramilitary organizations permeated the South. Violence was particularly severe in election years in Louisiana, which had a large and active black electorate. Before the presidential election of 1868, for example, white Louisianans killed at least seven hundred Republicans, including the black leader William R. Meadows, who was dragged from his home and shot and beheaded in front of his family. As the election neared, white mobs roamed New Orleans, attacking black people and breaking up Republican rallies. The violence cut the Republican vote in the state by 50 percent from the previous spring.

The most serious example of political violence in Louisiana, if not in the entire South, occurred in Colfax in 1873, when a white Democratic mob attempted to wrest control of local government from Republicans. For three weeks, black defenders held the town against the white onslaught. When the white mob finally broke through, they massacred the remaining black defenders, including those who had surrendered and laid down their weapons.

Racial violence and the combative reaction it provoked both among black people and Republican administrations energized white voters. Democrats regained power in North Carolina, for example, after the state's Republican governor enraged white voters by calling out the militia to counter white violence during the election of 1870. That same year, the Republican regime in Georgia fell as well.

Some Republican governments countered the violence successfully for a time. Republican Governor Edmund J. Davis of Texas, for example, organized a special force of two hundred state policemen to round up Klan night riders. Between 1870 and 1872, Davis's force arrested six thousand and broke the Klan in Texas. Arkansas Governor Powell Clayton launched an equally successful campaign against the Klan in 1869. But other governors hesitated to enforce laws directed at the Klan, fearing that to do so would further alienate white people.

The federal government responded with a variety of legislation. One example was the Fifteenth Amendment, ratified in 1869, which guaranteed the right to vote. Another was the Enforcement Act of 1870, which

The Klan directed violence at African Americans primarily for political activity. Here, a black man, John Campbell, vainly begs for mercy in Moore County, North Carolina, in August 1871.

authorized the federal government to appoint supervisors in states that failed to protect voting rights. When violence and intimidation persisted, Congress followed with a second, more sweeping measure, the Ku Klux Klan Act of 1871. This law permitted federal authorities, with military assistance, if necessary, to arrest and prosecute members of groups that denied a citizen's civil rights if state authorities failed to do so. The Klan Act was not successful in curbing racial violence, as the Colfax Massacre in 1873 made vividly clear. But with it, Congress, by claiming the right to override state authority to bring individuals to justice, established a new precedent in federal–state relations.

THE FAILURE OF NORTHERN WILL

The success of political violence after 1871 reflected less the inadequacy of congressional legislation than the failure of will on the part of northern Republicans to follow through on commitments to southern Republican administrations. The erosion of northern support for Congressional Reconstruction began as early as the presidential election of 1868. The Republican candidate Ulysses S. Grant's campaign theme that year was "Let Us Have Peace," a reference to the political turmoil in the South.

The commitment to voting rights for black Southerners, widespread among Republicans in 1865 and affirmed in the Fifteenth Amendment, faded as well. American politics in the 1870s seemed increasingly corrupt and irresponsible. Scandal abounded. The Democratic boss William M. Tweed and his associates transformed Tammany Hall, a Democratic Club, into a full-fledged political machine that robbed New York City of an astounding $100 million. Federal officials allowed private individuals to manipulate the stock market for spectacular gains. Several members of Congress and President Grant's vice president exchanged government favors for railroad stock. And the president's secretary of war was caught selling contracts to firms supplying goods to Indians.

A growing number of Americans attributed the debacle to the expansion of the right to vote. Voting was a privilege to be earned, they maintained, not a basic right of citizenship. And black people, according to some Republicans, had not earned that right.

The racist assumption behind this view found growing support among intellectuals. Racism gained an aura of scientific respectability in the late nineteenth century. Science was held in high esteem at the time, helping assure public acceptance of the putatively scientific views of the racial theorists. According to those views, some peoples are inherently inferior to others, a natural state of affairs that no government interference can change.

According to white racial theorists, it was folly to grant suffrage to African Americans, because an inferior race (black) could not hold power over a superior race (white). Black people, because of their race, could not understand the basic principles of democracy. Thus, Missouri's Republican senator Carl Schurz looked on with equanimity as white terror toppled Republican regimes in the South in 1872. He urged his colleagues to let affairs run their course and admit that southern black voters and officeholders "were ignorant and inexperienced; that the public business was an unknown world to them, and that in spite of the best intentions they were easily misled." Allowing an unfit people to vote resulted in a "more disastrous process than rebellion," intoned *The Nation*, a leading Republican journal, in 1872. The perpetual turmoil in the South, the extravagances of some Republican southern administrations, and their persistent inability to attract sufficient numbers of white voters all reinforced the view that these governments were unnatural.

Black people were not the only targets of racial theory. Immigrants were also said to derive from inferior races. Their growing numbers coincided with the flourishing of corrupt political machines in northern cities, fueling Republican reservations about an unrestricted franchise. Like black people, immigrants were held to be incapable of understanding the American electoral process. As one Republican leader observed, "What is bad among ignorant foreigners in New York will not be good among ignorant natives in South Carolina."

Concerns about the quality of the electorate reflected the rising stakes of public office in post–Civil War America. The urban industrial economy boomed in the five years after the war. Engineers flung railroads across the continent. Steam propelled factories to unprecedented levels of productivity and ships to new speed records. Discoveries of rich natural resources such as oil and iron presaged a new age of industrial might. Republicans promoted and benefited from the boom, and it influenced their priorities. Railroad, mining, and lumber lobbyists crowded Washington and state capitals begging for financial and land subsidies and favorable legislation. In an era before conflict-of-interest laws, leading Republicans sat on the boards of railroads, land development companies, and industrial corporations. While the federal government denied land to the freedman, it doled out millions of acres to corporations. Issues of fiscal responsibility, tariffs, and hard money replaced freedom and reunion, moving the Republican party, as *The Nation* explained in 1874, "out of the region of the Civil War."

Not all Republicans approved the party's promotion of economic development. Some questioned the prudence of government intervention in the "natural" operation of the economy. The emerging scandals of the Grant administration led to calls for reform. Republican governments, North and South, were condemned for their lavish spending and high taxes.

The reform movement attracted an assortment of groups concerned about the size, activism, and expense of government. Business leaders decried the ability of wealthy lobbyists to influence economic decisions. An influential group of intellectuals and opinion makers lamented the inability of politicians to understand "natural" laws. Some reformers expressed alarm at the federal government's increasing intervention in the affairs of the states since the Civil War. And some Republicans joined the reform movement out of fear that Democrats would capitalize on the turmoil in the South and the political scandals in the North to reap huge electoral victories in 1872.

LIBERAL REPUBLICANS AND THE ELECTION OF 1872

Liberal Republicans, as those reformers called themselves, put forward an array of suggestions to improve government and save the Republican party. They advocated civil service reform to reduce reliance on patronage and the abuses that accompanied office seeking. To limit government and reduce artificial economic stimuli, the reformers called for tariff reduction and an end to federal land grants to railroads. For the South, they recommended a general amnesty for white people and a return to "local self-government" by men of "property and enterprise."

When the Liberals failed to convince other Republicans to adopt their program, they broke with the party. Taking advantage of this split, the Democrats forged an alliance with the Liberals. Together, they nominated journalist Horace Greeley to challenge Ulysses S. Grant for the presidency in the election of 1872. Grant won resoundingly, helped by high turnout among black voters in the South. He carried all southern states except Georgia, Tennessee, and Texas. Elsewhere, Republicans again used the tactic of waving the bloody shirt to good effect. It was the Republicans, they declared, who had saved the Union, the Democrats who had almost destroyed it. Greeley had been a staunch Republican during the Civil War and had spent most of his career attacking Democrats. Republicans used his own words against him. Many Democratic voters stayed home.

The election suggested that the excesses of the Grant administration had not yet exceeded public tolerance and that the Republican experiment in the South retained some public support. But Greeley had helped the Republicans by running an inept campaign. Within a year, an economic depression, continued violence in the South, and the persistent corruption of the Grant administration would turn public opinion against the Republicans. With this shift, support for Reconstruction and black rights would also fade.

REDEMPTION, 1874–1877

For southern Democrats, the Republican victory in 1872 underscored the importance of turning out larger numbers of white voters and restricting the black vote. They accomplished these goals over the next four years with a surge in political violence. Southern Democrats operated in the secure knowledge that federal authorities would not intervene against them. Preoccupied with corruption and economic crisis and increasingly indifferent, if not hostile, to African American aspirations, most Americans looked the other way. The elections of 1876—on the local, state, and national levels—affirmed the triumph of white Southerners. Reconstruction did not end; it was overthrown.

In a religious metaphor that matched their view of the Civil War as a lost crusade, southern Democrats called their victory "Redemption" and depicted themselves as **Redeemers**, holy warriors who had saved the South from the hell of black Republican rule. Generations of American boys and girls would learn this interpretation of the Reconstruction era, and it would affect race relations for nearly a century.

THE DEMOCRATS' VIOLENT RESURGENCE

The violence between 1874 and 1876 differed in several respects from earlier attempts to restore white government by force. Attackers operated more openly and more closely identified themselves with the Democratic party. Mounted, gray-clad ex-Confederate soldiers flanked Democratic candidates at campaign rallies and "visited" black neighborhoods afterward to discourage black people from voting. With black people intimidated and white people already prepared to vote, election days were typically quiet.

Democrats swept to victory across the South in the 1874 elections. "A perfect reign of terror" redeemed Alabama for the Democrats. The successful appeal to white supremacy inspired a massive white turnout to unseat Republicans in Virginia, Florida (legislature only), and Arkansas. Texas had fallen to the Democrats in 1873. Only South Carolina, Missis-

sippi, and Louisiana—states with large black populations—survived the debacle. But the relentless tide of terror would soon overwhelm them as well.

In Louisiana, a group of elite Democrats in New Orleans organized a military organization, known as the White League, in 1874 to challenge the state's Republican government. In September 1874, more than eight thousand White Leaguers staged a coup to overthrow the Republican government of New Orleans. The city's police, commanded by the former Confederate general James Longstreet, and the intervention of nearby federal troops saved the government and prevented a wholesale slaughter. But the incident only inspired White Leaguers to redouble their efforts.

Few Reconstruction politicians endured greater trials than one Louisiana Republican, Marshall Harvey Twitchell. Born in Vermont, he led black troops during the Civil War and settled in Louisiana after the war. He married the daughter of a prominent plantation owner and launched a successful business career. But with the advent of Congressional Reconstruction, Twitchell entered politics and built a powerful Republican organization in Red River Parish. The hospitable reception he had until then enjoyed in his adopted state quickly evaporated. During the 1874 election campaign, White Leaguers murdered his brother and two brothers-in-law. Two years later, White Leaguers shot him six times in an assassination attempt. Although he lost both arms, he survived. He left Louisiana in 1877, never to return.

THE WEAK FEDERAL RESPONSE

Unrest such as events in Louisiana also plagued Mississippi and South Carolina. When South Carolina Governor Daniel H. Chamberlain could no longer contain the violence in his state in 1876, he asked the president for help. Grant acknowledged the gravity of Chamberlain's situation but would offer him only the lame hope that South Carolinians would exercise "better judgment and cooperation" and assist the governor in bringing offenders to justice "without aid from the federal Government."

Congress responded to the violence with the Civil Rights Act of 1875. Introduced by Charles Sumner, the bill went through several variations. Congress finally passed a watered-down version after Sumner's death. The act prohibited discrimination against black people in public accommodations such as theaters, parks, and trains and guaranteed freedmen's rights to serve on juries. It had no provision for voting rights, which Congress presumed the Fifteenth Amendment protected. The only way to enforce the law was for individuals to bring grievances related to it before federal courts in the South.

As this Thomas Nast cartoon makes clear, the paramilitary violence against black Southerners in the early 1870s threatened, not only the voting rights of freedmen, but their dreams of education, prosperity, and family life as well. In this context, the slogan, "The Union As It Was" is highly ironic.

When black people tested the law by trying to make free use of public accommodations, they were almost always turned away. Some filed suit, with disappointing results. A Texas judge fined a Galveston theater $500 for refusing to allow black people to sit wherever they wanted, but most judges either interpreted the law narrowly or declared it unconstitutional. In 1883, the U.S. Supreme Court agreed and overturned the act, declaring that only the states, not Congress, could redress "a private wrong, or a crime of the individual."

THE ELECTION OF 1876 AND THE COMPROMISE OF 1877

Reconstruction officially ended with the presidential election of 1876 in which the Democrat Samuel J. Tilden ran against the Republican Rutherford B. Hayes. Republicans again waved the bloody shirt, touting their role in preserving the Union during the Civil War, but they ignored Reconstruction. The Democrats hoped that their resurgent strength in the South and a respectable showing in the North would bring them the White House. The scandals of the Grant administration, northern weariness with southern Republican governments, and the persisting economic depression worked in the Democrats' favor.

When the ballots were counted, it appeared that Tilden, a conservative New Yorker respectable enough for northern voters and Democratic enough for white southerners, had won. But despite a majority in the popular vote, disputed returns in three southern states left him with only 184 of the 185 electoral votes needed to win (see Map 16–2). The three states—Florida, South Carolina, and Louisiana—were the last in the South still to have Republican administrations.

Both camps maneuvered intensively in the months following the election to claim the disputed votes. Congress appointed a fifteen-member commission to settle the issue. Because the Republicans controlled Congress, they held a one-vote majority on the commission.

Southern Democrats wanted Tilden to win, but they wanted control of their states more. They were willing to deal. As one South Carolina newspaper editorialized in February 1877, "It matters little to us who rules in Washington, if South Carolina is allowed to have [Democratic governor Wade] Hampton and Home Rule." Hayes intended to remove federal support from the remaining southern Republican governments anyway. It thus cost him nothing to promise to do so in exchange for the contested electoral votes. Republicans also made vague promises to invest in the southern economy and support a southern transcontinental railroad, but these were secondary. What the South wanted most was to be left alone, and that is what it got. The so-called Compromise of 1877 installed Hayes in the White House and gave Democrats control of all state governments in the South. Congress never carried through on the economic promises, and southern Democrats never pressed it to.

Southern Democrats emerged the major winners from the **Compromise of 1877.** President Hayes and his successors into the next century left the South alone. In practical terms, the Compromise signaled the revocation of civil rights and voting rights for black Southerners. The Fourteenth and Fifteenth Amendments would be dead letters in the South until well into the twentieth century. On the two great issues confronting the nation at the end of the Civil War, reunion and freedom, the white South had won. It reentered the Union largely on its own terms with the freedom to pursue a racial agenda consistent with its political, economic, and social interests.

THE MEMORY OF RECONSTRUCTION

Southern Democrats used the memory of Reconstruction to help maintain themselves in power. It would join the Lost Cause, as part of the glorious

Overview

Constitutional Amendments and Federal Legislation of the Reconstruction Era

Amendment or Legislation	Purpose	Significance
Thirteenth Amendment (passed and ratified in 1865)	Prevented southern states from reestablishing slavery after the war	Final step toward full emancipation of slaves
Freedmen's Bureau Act (1865)	Oversight of resettlement, relief, education, and labor for former slaves	Involved the federal government directly in assisting the transition from slavery to freedom; worked fitfully to achieve this objective during its seven-year career
Southern Homestead Act (1866)	Provided black people preferential access to public lands in five southern states	Lack of capital and poor quality of federal land thwarted the purpose of the act
Civil Rights Act of 1866	Defined rights of national citizenship	Marked an important change in federal–state relations, tilting balance of power to national government
Fourteenth Amendment (passed 1866; ratified 1868)	Prohibited states from violating the rights of their citizens	Strengthened the Civil Rights Act of 1866 and guaranteed all citizens equality before the law
Military Reconstruction Acts (1867)	Set new rules for the readmission of ex-Confederate states into the Union and secured black voting rights	Initiated Congressional Reconstruction
Tenure of Office Act (1867)	Required congressional approval for the removal of any official whose appointment had required Senate confirmation	A congressional challenge to the president's right to dismiss Cabinet members that led to President Andrew Johnson's impeachment trial
Fifteenth Amendment (passed 1869; ratified 1870)	Guaranteed the right of all American male citizens to vote regardless of race	The basis for black voting rights
Civil Rights Act of 1875	Prohibited racial discrimination in jury selection, public transportation, and public accommodations	Rarely enforced; Supreme Court declared it unconstitutional in 1883

fight to preserve the civilization of the Old South. As white Southerners elevated Civil War heroes into saints, and battles into holy struggles, Reconstruction became the Redemption. If the South was crucified at Appomattox, it was resurrected at every courthouse square and political office throughout the once-defeated land. For white Southerners—white Democrats in particular—had rescued the South from a purgatory of black rule and federal oppression. Whenever southern Democrats felt

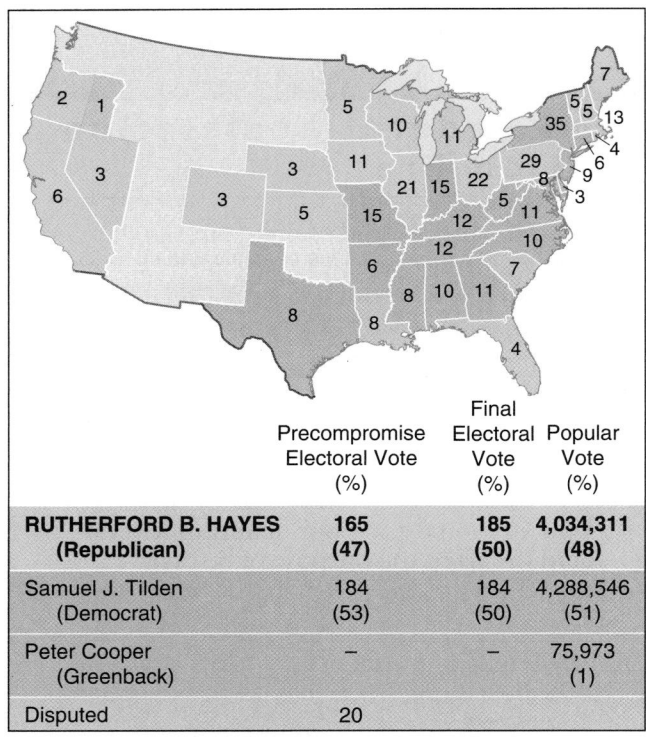

	Precompromise Electoral Vote (%)	Final Electoral Vote (%)	Popular Vote (%)
RUTHERFORD B. HAYES (Republican)	**165 (47)**	**185 (50)**	**4,034,311 (48)**
Samuel J. Tilden (Democrat)	184 (53)	184 (50)	4,288,546 (51)
Peter Cooper (Greenback)	–	–	75,973 (1)
Disputed	20		

MAP 16-2   The Election of 1876
The Democrat Samuel J. Tilden won a majority of the popular vote but eventually fell short of an electoral vote majority when the contested electoral votes of Florida, Louisiana, and South Carolina went to his Republican opponent, Rutherford B. Hayes. The map also indicates the Republicans' failure to build a base in the South after more than a decade of Reconstruction.

threatened over the next century, they reminded their white constituents of the sacrifices and heroism of war, the "horrors of Reconstruction," the menace of black rule, and the cruelty of Yankee occupiers. The southern view of Reconstruction permeated textbooks, films, and standard accounts of the period. By the early 1900s, professional historians at the nation's finest institutions concurred in this view, ignoring contrary evidence and rendering the story of African Americans invisible. By that time, therefore, most Americans believed that the policies of Reconstruction had been misguided and had brought great suffering to the white South. The widespread acceptance of this view allowed the South to maintain its system of racial segregation and exclusion without interference from the federal government.

Not all memories of Reconstruction conformed to this thesis. In 1913, John R. Lynch, a former black Republican congressman from Mississippi, published *The Facts of Reconstruction* to "present the other side." He hoped that his book would "bring to public notice those things that were commend-

able and meritorious, to prevent the publication of which seems to have been the primary purpose of nearly all who have thus far written upon that important subject." But most Americans ignored his book. Two decades later, a more forceful defense, W.E.B. Du Bois's *Black Reconstruction* (1935), met a similar fate. An angry Du Bois attacked the prevailing view of Reconstruction as "one of the most stupendous efforts the world ever saw to discredit human beings, an effort involving universities, history, science, social life and religion."

The national historical consensus grew out of a growing national reconciliation concerning the war, a mutual agreement that both sides had fought courageously and that it was time to move on. Immediately after the Civil War, a number of prominent white Southerners urged their neighbors to work on rebuilding the South rather than hating the Yankees. But general reconciliation remained on hold until the end of Reconstruction, when white Southerners reclaimed both their governments and their dominance over African Americans. Once that recovery occurred, the bonds grew quickly as joint battlefield commemorations stressed mutual bravery and shared sacrifice. Lost in all the good will was the tacit agreement among both Southern and Northern whites that the South was now free to work out its own resolution to race relations.

There is much to be said in favor of sectional reconciliation as opposed to persistent animosity. There are enough examples in the world today of antagonists in the same country never forgetting or never forgiving their bloody histories. Ideally, Americans could have had *both* healing and justice, but instead, they settled for the former. Frederick Douglass, prescient as ever, worried about the peace that followed the Civil War and what it would mean for race relations: "If war among the whites brought peace and liberty to the blacks, what will peace among the whites bring?" But white Americans seemed intent on shaking hands and getting on with their lives. As novelist William Dean Howells quipped, "What the American public always wants is a tragedy with a happy ending."

THE FAILED PROMISE OF RECONSTRUCTION

The price of this happy ending was the faltering dream that freedmen held at the outset of Reconstruction—a dream of economic independence, political equality, and dignity in the eyes of the law and their white neighbors. As Republican governments and black voters succumbed to the southern white reign of terror in the early 1870s, the *Atlanta Constitution* chided black people for being so presumptuous as to want to participate in the democratic process. Politics, the Constitution intoned, "was not intended . . . for the blacks, but for the whites. . . . This government is still a white man's government, and will remain forever such. The superior intelligence of the white race . . . will for all time secure political ascendancy." The *Constitution* excused the freedman for his delusion, blaming the "infamous carpetbagger and the radical [Republican] party."

If the demise of Reconstruction elicited a sigh of relief from most white Americans, black Southerners greeted it with frustration. Their dreams of land ownership faded as a new labor system relegated them to a lowly position in southern agriculture. Redemption reversed their economic and political gains and deprived them of most of the civil rights they had enjoyed under Congressional Reconstruction. Although they continued to vote into the 1890s, they had by 1877 lost most of the voting strength and political offices they held. Rather than becoming part of southern society, they were increasingly set apart from it, valued only for their labor.

Still, the former slaves were better off in 1877 than in 1865. They were free, however limited their freedom. Some owned land; some held jobs in cities. They raised their families in relative peace and experienced the spiritual joys of a full religious life. They socialized freely with relatives and friends, and they moved about. The Reconstruction amendments to the Constitution guaranteed an array of civil and political rights and, though Southern states would evade and federal courts would eviscerate, eventually these guarantees would form the basis of the civil rights revolution after World War II. But that outcome was long, too long, in the future. By 1877, the "golden moment"—an unprecedented opportunity for the nation to live up to its ideals by extending equal rights to all its citizens, black and white alike—had passed.

SHARECROPPING

When they lost political power, black Southerners also lost economic independence. As the Freedmen's Bureau retreated from supervising farm labor contracts and opportunities for black people to possess their own land dried up, the bargaining power of black farm laborers decreased, and the power of white landlords increased. The faltering southern economy contributed to the loss of labor autonomy

as well. Cash wages were at first high enough and rental agreements between tenant farmers and landlords at first fair enough for black farmers to be able to buy their own tools and perhaps a few extra acres. But the dramatic decline of cotton prices soon after the war reduced cash surpluses in an already cash-poor region. Unable now to purchase their own animals or tools and lacking cash to buy food and other necessities at local stores, freedmen were forced to barter their crops for credit.

The upshot was that by the late 1870s, most former slaves in the rural South had been drawn into a subservient position in a new labor system called **sharecropping**. The premise of this system was relatively simple: The landlord furnished the sharecroppers with a house, a plot of land to work, seed, some farm animals, and farm implements and advanced them credit at a store the landlord typically owned. In exchange, the sharecroppers promised the landlord a share of their crop, usually one-half. The croppers kept the proceeds from the sale of the other half to pay off their debts at the store and save or spend as they and their families saw fit. In theory, a sharecropper could save enough to secure economic independence.

But white landlords perceived black independence as both contradictory and subversive. With landlords holding the accounts at the store, black sharecroppers found that the proceeds from their share of the crop never left them very far ahead. In exchange for extending credit to sharecroppers, store owners felt justified in requiring collateral, but sharecroppers had no assets other than the cotton they grew. So southern states passed crop lien laws, which gave the store owner the right to the following year's crop in exchange for the current year's credit. If the following year's harvest could not pay off the debt, the sharecropper sank deeper into dependence. Some found themselves in perpetual debt and worked as virtual slaves. They could not simply abandon their debts and go to another farm, because the new landlord would check their references. Those found to have jumped their debts could end up on a prison chain gang. Not all white landlords cheated their tenants, but given the sharecroppers' innocence regarding accounting methods and crop pricing, the temptation to do so was great. Thus weak cotton prices conspired with white chicanery to keep black people economically dependent.

MODEST GAINS AND FUTURE VICTORIES

Black Southerners experienced some advances in the decade after the Civil War, but these owed little

FROM THEN TO NOW

African American Voting Rights in the South

Right from the end of the Civil War, white Southerners resisted African American voting rights. Black people, with equal determination, used the franchise to assert their equal right to participate in the political process. Black voting rights proved so contentious that Congress sought to secure them with the Fourteenth and Fifteenth Amendments to the U.S. Constitution. But U.S. Supreme Court decisions in *United States v. Cruikshank* (1876) and in the Civil Rights Cases (1883) undermined federal authority to protect the rights of freedmen, including voting rights. A combination of violence, intimidation, and legislation effectively disfranchised black Southerners by the early twentieth century.

During the 1960s, a period some historians have referred to as the Second Reconstruction, Congress passed legislation designed to override state prohibitions and earlier court decisions limiting African American voting rights. The key measure, the 1965 Voting Rights Act, not only guaranteed black Southerners (and later, other minorities) the right to register and vote but also protected them from procedural subterfuges, many of which dated from the first Reconstruction era, that would dilute their votes. These protections proved necessary because of the extreme racial polarization of Southern elections: White people rarely voted for black candidates.

To insure African American candidates an opportunity to win elections, the federal government after 1965 insisted that states and localities establish procedures to increase the likelihood of such a result. As part of this process, the federal government also monitored state redistricting for Congressional elections, which occurs every decade in response to population shifts recorded in the national census.

By the early 1990s, states were being directed to draw districts with majority-black voting populations to insure African American representation in the U.S. Congress and in state legislatures.

The federal government cited the South's history of racial discrimination and racially polarized voting to justify these districts. But white Southerners challenged such claims, as they had more than a century earlier, and their challenges proved successful in federal court.

In 1993, the U.S. Supreme Court issued a decision in a North Carolina redistricting case, *Shaw v. Reno*, that struck down a majority-black Congressional district in that state. Subsequent decisions in other southern districts produced similar rulings. The general principle followed by the Court has been that if race is a key justification for drawing these districts, then they violate the Fourteenth Amendment, which, according to the Court majority, demands color-blind electoral procedures. But, as the late Supreme Court Justice William Brennan noted, "to read the Fourteenth Amendment to state an abstract principle of color-blindness is itself to be blind to history." The framers of the Reconstruction Amendments had the protection of the rights of the freedmen (including and especially voting rights) in mind when they wrote those measures. One voting rights expert has charged that the Court rulings have ushered in a "Second Redemption."

But it is also true that beginning in 1998 and continuing through the 2002 elections, black Congressional incumbents in Georgia and North Carolina, running in redrawn districts in which black voters were in the minority (and less than 40 percent, at that) won reelection. These results may indicate that racially polarized voting may be diminishing in the South, although they may also reflect the power of incumbency and the weak campaigns of the challengers. In any case, the issue of African American voting rights in the South and the degree to which the federal government may or may not intercede to protect those rights remains as much at issue as it was more than a century ago.

to Reconstruction. Black families functioned as economic and psychological buffers against unemployment and prejudice. Black churches played crucial roles in their communities. Self-help and labor organizations offered mutual friendship and financial assistance. All of these institutions existed in the slavery era, although on a smaller scale. And some of them, such as black labor groups, schools, and social welfare associations, endured because comparable white institutions excluded black people.

Black people also scored some modest economic successes during the Reconstruction era, mainly from their own pluck. In the Lower South, black per capita income increased 46 percent between 1857 and 1879, compared with a 35 percent decline in white per capita income. Sharecropping, oppressive as it was, represented an advance over forced and gang labor. Collectively, black people owned more than $68 million worth of property in 1870, a 240 percent increase over 1860, but the average worth of each was only $408. Those who had been free before the war sometimes fared worse after it, especially property-owning free black people in the Lower South. Black city dwellers, especially in the Upper South, fared somewhat better. The overwhelming majority of black people, however, were landless agricultural laborers eking out a meager income that merchants and landlords often snatched to cover debts.

The Fourteenth and Fifteenth Amendments to the Constitution are among the few bright spots in Reconstruction's otherwise dismal legacy. The Fourteenth Amendment guaranteed former slaves equality before the law; the Fifteenth Amendment protected their right to vote. Both amendments elevated the federal government over the states by protecting freedmen from state attempts to deny them their rights. But the benefits of these two landmark amendments did not accrue to African Americans until well into the twentieth century. White Southerners effectively nullified the Reconstruction amendments, and the U.S. Supreme Court virtually interpreted them, and other Reconstruction legislation, out of existence.

In the *Slaughterhouse* **cases** (1873), the Supreme Court contradicted the intent of the Fourteenth Amendment by decreeing that most citizenship rights remained under state, not federal, control. In *United States v. Cruikshank* (1876), the Court overturned the convictions of some of those responsible for the Colfax Massacre, ruling that the Enforcement Act applied only to violations of black rights by states, not individuals. Within the next two decades, the Supreme Court would uphold the legality of racial segregation

and black disfranchisement, in effect declaring that the Fourteenth and Fifteenth Amendments did not apply to African Americans. The Civil War had killed secession forever, but states' rights enjoyed a remarkable revival.

As the historian John Hope Franklin accurately concluded, Reconstruction "had no significant or permanent effect on the status of the black in American life. . . . [Black people] made no meaningful steps toward economic independence or even stability."

CONCLUSION

Formerly enslaved black Southerners had entered freedom with many hopes, among the most prominent of which was to be let alone. White Southerners, after four bloody years of unwanted attention from the federal government, also longed to be left alone. But they did not include their ex-slaves as equals in their vision of solitude. Northerners, too, began to seek escape from the issues and consequences of the war, eventually abandoning their commitment to secure civil and voting rights for black Southerners.

White Southerners robbed black Southerners of their gains and sought to reduce them again to servitude and dependence, if not to slavery. But in the processs, the majority of white Southerners lost as well. Yeoman farmers missed an opportunity to break cleanly from the Old South and establish a more equitable society. Instead, they allowed the old elites to regain power and gradually ignore their needs. They preserved the social benefit of a white skin at the cost of almost everything else. Many lost their farms and sank into tenancy, leasing land from others. Fewer had a voice in state legislatures or the U.S. Congress. A new South, rid of slavery and sectional antagonism, had indeed emerged, redeemed, regenerated, and disenthralled. But the old South lingered on in the new like Spanish moss on live oaks.

As federal troops left the South to be redeployed restraining striking workers in the North and suppressing Native Americans on the Great Plains, an era of possibility for American society ended, and a new era began. "The southern question is dead," a Charleston newspaper proclaimed in 1877. "The question of labor and capital, work and wages" had moved to the forefront. The chance to redeem the sacrifice of a bloody civil war with a society that fulfilled the promise of the Declaration of Independence and the Constitution for all citizens slipped away. It would take a new generation of African Americans a long century later to revive it.

REVIEW QUESTIONS

1. Given the devastation in the South after the Civil War and the loss of property, lives, and hope among many white Southerners, do you think they should they have supported black aspirations for civil rights, land, and suffrage? How differently would things have turned out if they had?

2. Some historians have placed a great deal of the blame for Reconstruction's failures on the backs of southern Republicans. Is this fair? Explain your response.

3. Black people did achieve some notable gains during Reconstruction, despite its overall failure. What were those gains?

4. In T. Thomas Fortune's recollection of a boyhood incident, why was it important for him and his friends to fight back?

KEY TERMS

Black codes (p. 509)

Carpetbaggers (p. 514)

Compromise of 1877 (p. 520)

Congressional Reconstruction (p. 512)

Field Order No. 15 (p. 503)

Fifteenth Amendment (p. 513)

Fourteenth Amendment (p. 510)

Freedmen's Bureau (p. 501)

Ku Klux Klan (p. 516)

Lost Cause (p. 499)

Redeemers (p. 519)

Scalawags (p. 513)

Sharecropping (p. 523)

Slaughterhouse cases (p. 525)

Southern Homestead Act (p. 503)

Union Leagues (p. 514)

United States v. Cruikshank (p. 525)

RECOMMENDED READING

Du Bois, W. E. B. *Black Reconstruction in America, 1860–1880* (1935). An early and long-ignored study by the foremost black scholar of his time that refuted the contemporary historical wisdom that Reconstruction was a horror visited on the South by an overbearing federal government and ignorant, willful black people.

Foner, Eric. *Reconstruction: America's Unfinished Revolution, 1863–1877* (1988). The standard work on Reconstruction, notable for its emphasis on the experience and aspirations of black Southerners.

Foster, Gaines M. *Ghosts of the Confederacy: Defeat, the Lost Cause, and the Emergence of the New South, 1865 to 1913* (1987). A fine picture of how the memory of the Civil War affected white Southerners and their views on Reconstruction policy.

Litwack, Leon. *Been in the Storm So Long: The Aftermath of Slavery* (1979). An eloquent account of the early days of freedom from the freedmen's perspective, up to 1867.

Tourgée, Albion W. *A Fool's Errand* (1879). A novel written by an Ohioan who migrated to North Carolina in 1865 to take advantage of economic opportunities in the state and eventually became involved in politics, with his frustrations with Reconstruction and his keen analysis of racism as important themes.

ADDITIONAL SOURCES

White Southerners and the Ghosts of the Confederacy

Blight, David W. *Race and Reunion: The Civil War in American Memory* (2001).

Edwards, Laura F. *Gendered Strife and Confusion: The Political Culture of Reconstruction* (1997).

Goldfield, David, *Still Fighting the Civil War: The American South and Southern History* (2002).

Black Aspirations beyond Freedom

Berlin, Ira, et al. *Freedom: A Documentary History of Emancipation, 1861–1867. The Wartime Genesis of Free Labor: The Lower South* (1990).

Cimbala, Paul A., and Randall M. Miller, eds. *The Freedmen's Bureau and Reconstruction: A Reconsideration* (1999).

Fitzgerald, Michael W. *The Union League Movement in the Deep South: Politics and Agricultural Change during Reconstruction* (1989).

Gutman, Herbert G. *The Black Family in Slavery and Freedom, 1750–1925* (1976).

Jaynes, Gerald. *Branches Without Roots: The Genesis of the Black Working Class in the American South, 1862–1882* (1986).

Jones, Jacqueline. *Labor of Love, Labor of Sorrow: Black Women, Work, and the Family from Slavery to the Present* (1985).

Kolchin, Peter. *First Freedom: The Responses of Alabama's Blacks to Emancipation and Reconstruction* (1972).

Rabinowitz, Howard N. *Race Relations in the Urban South, 1865–1890* (1978).

Rabinowitz, Howard N., ed. *Southern Black Leaders of the Reconstruction Era* (1982).

Thornbrough, Emma Lou. ed. *Black Reconstructionists* (1972).

Williamson, Joel. *After Slavery: The Negro in South Carolina During Reconstruction, 1861–1877* (1965).

Federal Reconstruction, 1865–1870

Abbott, Richard. *The Republican Party and the South, 1855–1877* (1986).

Belz, Herman. *A New Birth of Freedom: The Republican Party and Freedmen's Rights, 1861–1866* (1976).

Benedict, Michael Les. *A Compromise of Principle: Congressional Republicans and Reconstruction, 1863–1869* (1974).

Harris, William C. *With Charity for All: Lincoln and the Restoration of the Union* (1997).

McFeely, William S. *Grant: A Biography* (1981).

Moneyhon, Carl H. *Republicanism in Reconstruction Texas* (1980).

Perman, Michael. *Reunion without Compromise: The South and Reconstruction, 1865–1868* (1973).

Rose, Willie Lee. *Rehearsal for Reconstruction: The Port Royal Experiment* (1964).

Summers, Mark W. *Railroads, Reconstruction, and the Gospel of Prosperity: Aid Under the Radical Republicans, 1865–1877* (1984).

Trefousse, Hans. *The Radical Republicans: Lincoln's Vanguard for Racial Justice* (1969).

Counter-Reconstruction, 1870–1874

Current, Richard N. *Those Terrible Carpetbaggers: A Reinterpretation* (1988).

Duncan, Russell. *Entrepreneur for Equality: Governor Rufus Bullock, Commerce, and Race in Post-Civil War Georgia* (1994).

Hyde, Samuel C., Jr. *Pistols and Politics: The Dilemma of Democracy in Louisiana's Florida Parishes, 1810–1899* (1996).

Perman, Michael. *The Road to Redemption: Southern Politics, 1869–1879* (1984).

Rable, George C. *But There Was No Peace: The Role of Violence in the Politics of Reconstruction* (1984).

Trelease, Allen W. *White Terror: The Ku Klux Klan Conspiracy and Southern Reconstruction* (1971).

Redemption, 1874–1877

Campbell, Randolph B. *Grass-Roots Reconstruction in Texas, 1865–1880* (1997).

Woodward, C. Vann. *Reunion and Reaction: The Compromise of 1877 and the End of Reconstruction* (1951).

The Failure of Reconstruction

Angell, Stephen Ward. *Bishop Henry McNeal Turner and African-American Religion in the South* (1992).

Franklin, John Hope. *Reconstruction after the Civil War* (1961).

Ransom, Roger L., and Richard Sutch. *One Kind of Freedom: The Economic Consequences of Emancipation* (1977).

Richardson, Heather Cox. *The Death of Reconstruction: Race, Labor, and Politics in the Post-Civil War North, 1865–1901* (2001).

Stampp, Kenneth M. *The Era of Reconstruction, 1865–1877* (1965).

WHERE TO LEARN MORE

- Penn Center Historic District, St. Helena Island, South Carolina. The Penn School was a sea-island experiment in the education of free black people established by northern missionaries Laura Towne and Ellen Murray in 1862 that they operated until their deaths in the early 1900s. The Penn School became Penn Community Services in 1948, serving as an educational institution, health clinic, and a social service agency. **www.penncenter.com**.

- Hampton University Museum, Hampton, Virginia. Hampton University was founded by the Freedmen's Bureau in 1868 to provide "practical" training in the agricultural and mechanical fields for former slaves. In addition to a history of the institution, the museum includes one of the oldest collections of African art in the United States. **www.hamptonu.edu/museum**.

- Beauvoir, Biloxi, Mississippi. The exhibits at Beauvoir, the home of Jefferson Davis, evoke the importance of the Lost Cause for the white survivors of the Confederacy. Especially interesting is the Jefferson Davis Soldiers Home on the premises and the Confederate Veterans Cemetery. Davis spent his retirement in Beauvoir. **www.beauvoir.org**.

- Levi Jordan Plantation, Brazoria County, Texas. This site provides an excellent depiction and interpretation of the lives of sharecroppers and tenants during and immediately after the Reconstruction era. The site is especially valuable for demonstrating the transition from slavery to sharecropping. **www.webarchaeology.com**.

 Please refer to the document CD-ROM for primary sources related to this chapter.

→ *The economic advance of African Americans in the South during the decades after the Civil War against great odds provided one of the more inspiring success stories of the era. But it was precisely this success, as depicted here at Dr. McDougald's Drug Store in Georgia, in 1900, that infuriated whites who believed that the African American's place in the South resided in menial and subservient occupations.*

A NEW SOUTH: ECONOMIC PROGRESS AND SOCIAL TRADITION 1877–1900

17

The colored woman of to-day occupies . . . a unique position in this country . . . . She is confronted by both a woman question and a race problem . . . . While the women of the white race can with calm assurance enter upon the work they feel by nature appointed to do [including reform efforts both inside and outside the home], while their men give loyal support and appreciative countenance to [these] efforts, recognizing in most avenues of usefulness the propriety and the need of woman's distinctive co-operation, the colored woman too often finds herself hampered and shamed by a less liberal sentiment . . . on the part of those for whose opinion she cares most . . . .

You do not find the colored woman selling her birthright for a mess of pottage . . . . It is largely our women in the South to-day who keep the black men solid in the Republican party. The black woman can never forget—however lukewarm the party may to-day appear—that it was a Republican president who struck the manacles from her own wrists and gave the possibilities of manhood to her helpless little ones; and to her mind a Democratic Negro is a traitor and a time-server.

To be a woman in a . . . [new] age carries with it a privilege and an opportunity never implied before. But to be a woman of the Negro race in America, and to be able to grasp the deep significance of the possibilities of the crisis,

CHAPTER OUTLINE

The Newness of the New South
An Industrial and Urban South
The Limits of Industrial and Urban Growth
Farms to Cities: Impact on Southern
    Society

The Southern Agrarian Revolt
Cotton and Credit
Southern Farmers Organize,
    1877–1892
Southern Populists

Women in the New South
Church Work and Preserving Memories
Women's Clubs

Settling the Race Issue
The Fluidity of Southern Race
    Relations, 1877–1890
The White Backlash
Lynch Law
Segregation by Law
Disfranchisement
A National Consensus on Race
Response of the Black Community

Conclusion

is to have a heritage, it seems to me, unique in the ages. In the first place, the race is young and full of the elasticity and hopefulness of youth. All its achievements are before it . . . . Everything to this race is new and strange and inspiring. There is a quickening of its pulses and a glowing of its self-consciousness. Aha, I can rival that! I can aspire to that! I can honor my name and vindicate my race! Something like this, it strikes me, is the enthusiasm which stirs the genius of young Africa in America; and the memory of past oppression and the fact of present attempted repression only serve to gather momentum for its irrepressible power . . . . What a responsibility then to have the sole management of the primal lights and shadows! Such is the colored woman's office. She must stamp weal or woe on the coming history of this people. May she see her opportunity and vindicate her high prerogative.

Anna J. Cooper,
A Voice from the South, 1892

Anna Julia Cooper, *A Voice from the South* (Xenia, OH: The Aldine Printing House, 1892): 134–135, 138–140, 142–145. The book may be accessed from the Internet: http://docsouth.unc.edu/church/cooper/cooper.html

Anna J. Cooper undertook an incredible journey that took her from slavery at her birth in Raleigh, North Carolina, in 1858 to a doctoral degree at the Sorbonne in Paris, France, and to a prominent career as an educator. Throughout her life she remained a firm believer in the role women, especially black women, should play in striking down both white supremacy and male domination. In 1892, Cooper published *A Voice from the South*, excerpted here. The book appeared at a time when the first African American generation raised in freedom generated a relatively prosperous, educated middle-class intent on challenging the limits of race in the New South. The assertiveness of this generation alarmed their white counterparts who launched a campaign of violence and repression, mainly directed at black men.

Despite these tensions and threats, Cooper's tone reflects the optimism of the New South and an enthusiasm for the expanding public role of women.

At the same time, her critical assessment of black men is scarcely concealed. She implies that black men have held black women back, unlike their white counterparts, though Cooper overestimated white women's freedom of choice outside the home. Cooper also suggests that black men share at least some of the blame for the white assault on their political rights. Her solution for racial advancement and, presumably, for white hostility to black aspirations is to increase the public profile of black women. But, however "new" the New South may have been, traditional views of Southern whites on race and gender rendered that solution untenable.

By the early 1900s, Cooper lived in Washington, D.C. and had immersed herself in the woman-suffrage movement as well as promoting female education. She would live to see the dawn of a new racial and gender era in the South and in America, but that journey would take many years and many lives. Cooper died at the age of 106 in 1964.

KEY TOPICS

- Continuity and change between the Old South and the New South
- The origins and nature of southern Populism
- Women's roles in the New South
- How and why segregation and disfranchisement changed race relations in the South

THE NEWNESS OF THE NEW SOUTH

Southerners of both races and genders shared Anna J. Cooper's optimism in the decades after Reconstruction. Despite the destruction of war and the turmoil of Reconstruction, Southerners worked to rebuild their stricken region as both a testimony to their ability to rise from the ashes, and as a way to secure a measure of economic independence from their former Civil War enemies. Southerners did what other Americans were doing between 1877 and 1900 — they built railroads, erected factories, and moved to towns and cities, only on a smaller scale and with more modest results. The factories did not dramatically alter the South's rural economy, and the towns and cities did not make it an urban region. The changes, nonetheless, brought political and social turmoil, emboldening black people, like Cooper, to assert their rights, encouraging women to work outside the home and pursue public careers, and frightening some white men.

By 1900, southern white leaders, urban and rural, had used the banner of white supremacy to stifle dissent. They removed African Americans from political life and constricted their social and economic role. The New South was thus like a cake with fancy new layers piled high on a very old crust. The appearance was American, but the taste was southern. The New South, however, is not solely a southern story. The racial solutions that emerged from the South by 1900 established a legacy only partially dissolved by the civil rights movement of the 1960s. If, as the black leader W.E.B. Du Bois predicted in 1903, the major American problem of the twentieth century would be "the problem of the color line," that line was drawn most emphatically down South.

The New South's "newness" was to be found primarily in its economy, not in its social relations, though the two were connected and complementary. After Reconstruction, new industries absorbed tens of thousands of first-time industrial workers from impoverished rural areas. Southern cities grew faster than those in any other region of the country. A burst of railroad construction linked these cities to one another and to the rest of the country, giving them increased commercial prominence. Growing in size and taking on new functions, cities extended their influence into the countryside with newspapers, consumer products, and new values. But this urban influence had important limits. It did not bring electricity, telephones, public health services, or public schools to the rural South. It did not greatly broaden the rural economy with new jobs. And it left the countryside without the daily contact with the outside world that fostered a broader perspective.

The Democratic party dominated southern politics after 1877, significantly changing the South's political system. Through various deceits, Democrats purged most black people and some white people from the electoral process and suppressed challenges to their leadership. The result was the emergence by 1900 of the **Solid South**, a period of white Democratic party rule that lasted into the 1950s.

Although most southern women remained at home or on the farm, piecing together families shattered by war, some enjoyed new options after 1877. Middle-class women in the cities, both white and black, became increasingly active in civic work and reform. They organized clubs, preserved and promoted the memories of war, lobbied for various causes, and

The pride of accomplishment is evident in this photograph of the Georgia State College class of 1900. By this time, a number of black institutions of higher education in the South were turning out ambitious and talented graduates who faced an increasingly grim future in their native region.

assumed regional leadership on a number of important issues. Tens of thousands of young white women from impoverished rural areas found work in textile mills, in city factories, or as servants. These new options posed a challenge to prevailing views about the role of women but ultimately did not change them.

The status of black Southerners changed significantly between 1877 and 1900. The members of the first generation born after Emancipation sought more than just freedom as they came of age. They also expected dignity and self-respect and the right to work, to vote, to go to school, and to travel freely. White Southerners responded with the equivalent of a second Civil War—and they won. By 1900, black Southerners found themselves more isolated from white Southerners and with less political power than at any time since 1865. Despite these setbacks, they succeeded, especially in the cities, in building a rich community life and spawning a vibrant middle class.

AN INDUSTRIAL AND URBAN SOUTH

Since the 1850s, public speakers calling for economic reform in the South had been rousing audiences with the tale of the burial of a southern compatriot. The man's headstone, his clothes, the coffin, and the gravediggers' tools, all came from the North. Only the corpse and the earth of his grave were southern. The speakers urged their listeners to found industries, build railroads, and grow great cities, so that the South could make its own goods and no one in the future would have to suffer the indignity of journeying to the next world accompanied by Yankee artifacts.

It is unclear whether such admonitions worked. Certainly, Southerners manufactured very little in 1877, less than 10 percent of the national total. By 1900, however, they boasted a growing iron and steel industry, textile mills that rivaled those of New England, a world-dominant tobacco industry, and a timber-processing industry that helped make the South a leading furniture-manufacturing center. A variety of regional enterprises also rose to prominence, among them the maker of what would become the world's favorite soft drink, Coca-Cola.

Steel mills and textiles.   Birmingham, barely a scratch in the forest in 1870, exemplified one aspect of what was new about the New South. Within a decade, its iron and steel mills belched the smoke of progress across the northern Alabama hills. By 1889, Birmingham had surpassed the older southern iron center of Chattanooga, Tennessee, and was preparing to challenge Pittsburgh, the nation's preeminent steelmaking city.

Chronology

1872 Texas and Pacific Railway connects Dallas to eastern markets.

1880 First southern local of the Women's Christian Temperance Union is formed in Atlanta.

1881 Booker T. Washington establishes Tuskegee Institute.

1882 Agricultural Wheel is formed in Arkansas.

1883 Laura Haygood founds the home mission movement in Atlanta.

1884 James B. Duke automates his cigarette factory.

1886 Dr. John Pemberton creates Coca-Cola.

Southern railroads conform to national track gauge standards.

1887 Charles W. Macune expands the Southern Farmer's Alliance from its Texas base to the rest of the South.

1888 The Southern Farmers' Alliance initiates a successful boycott of jute manufacturers.

1890 Mississippi becomes the first state to restrict black suffrage with literacy tests.

1892 The Populist party forms.

1894 United Daughters of the Confederacy is founded.

Populist and Republican fusion candidates win control of North Carolina.

1895 Booker T. Washington delivers his "Atlanta Compromise" address.

1896 Populists endorse the Democratic presidential candidate and fade as a national force.

In *Plessy v. Ferguson*, the Supreme Court permits segregation by law.

1898 North Carolina Mutual Life Insurance is founded.

Democrats regain control of North Carolina.

1903 W.E.B. Du Bois publishes *The Souls of Black Folk*.

1905 James B. Duke forms the Southern Power Company.

Thomas Dixon publishes *The Clansman*.

1906 Bloody race riots break out in Atlanta.

1907 Pittsburgh-based U.S. Steel takes over Birmingham's largest steel producer.

The southern textile industry also experienced significant growth during the 1880s. Although the South had manufactured cotton products since the early decades of the nineteenth century, chronic shortages of labor and capital kept the industry small. In the 1870s, however, several factors drew local investors into textile enterprises. The population of the rural South was rising, but farm income was low, ensuring a steady supply of cheap labor. Cotton was plentiful and cheap. Mixing profit and southern patriotism, entrepreneurs promoted a strong textile industry as a way to make the South less dependent on northern manufactured products and capital. The entrepreneurs located their mills mostly in rural areas, not in cities. The center of the industry was in the Carolina Piedmont, a region with good railroads, plentiful labor, and cheap energy. By 1900, the South had surpassed New England to become the nation's foremost textile-manufacturing center.

Tobacco and Coca-Cola.

The South's tobacco industry, like its textile industry, predated the Civil War. Virginia was the dominant producer, and its main product was chewing tobacco. The discovery of bright-leaf tobacco, a strain suitable for smoking in the form of cigarettes, changed Americans' tobacco habits. In 1884, James B. Duke installed the first cigarette-making machine in his Durham, North Carolina, plant. By 1900, Duke's American Tobacco Company controlled 80 percent of all tobacco manufacturing in the United States.

Although not as important as textiles or tobacco in 1900, a soft drink developed by an Atlanta pharmacist, Dr. John Pemberton, eventually became the most renowned southern product in the world. Pemberton developed the drink—a mixture of oils, caffeine, coca leaves, and cola nuts—in his backyard in an effort to find a good-tasting cure for headaches. He called his concoction Coca-Cola. It was not an overnight success, and Pemberton, short of cash, sold the rights to it to another Atlantan, Asa Candler, in 1889. Candler tinkered with the formula to improve the taste and marketed the product heavily. By the mid-1890s, Coca-Cola enjoyed a national market. Southerners were such heavy consumers that the Georgia Baptist Association felt compelled to warn its members "the more you drink, the more you want to drink. We fear great harm will grow out of this sooner or later, to our young people in particular." The Baptists may have been on to something, as Coca Cola's original formula did, in fact, include chemically active coca leaves.

Railroads and growth.

Southern railroad construction boomed in the 1880s, outpacing the rest of the nation. Overall, southern track mileage doubled between 1880 and 1890, with the greatest increases in Texas and Georgia (see Map 17–1). By 1890, nine out of ten Southerners lived in a county with a railroad running through it. In 1886, the southern railroads agreed to conform to a national standard for track width, firmly linking the region into a national transportation network and insuring quick and direct access for southern products to the booming markets of the Northeast.

The railroads connected many formerly isolated small southern farmers to national and international agricultural markets. At the same time, it gave them access to a whole new range of products, from fertilizers to fashions. Drawn into commercial agriculture, the farmers were now subject to market fluctuations, their fortunes rising and falling with the market prices for their crops. To an extent unknown before the Civil War, the market now determined what farmers planted, how much credit they could expect, and on what terms.

The railroad also opened new areas of the South to settlement and economic development. In 1892, according to one guidebook, Florida was "in the main inaccessible to the ordinary tourist, and unopened to the average settler." But railroad construction boomed in the state in the 1890s, and by 1912, there were tourist hotels as far south as Key West. Railroads also penetrated the Appalachian Mountains, expanding markets for farmers but also opening the area to outside timber and coal-mining interests.

The railroad increased the prominence of interior cities at the expense of older cities along the southern Atlantic and Gulf Coasts. Antebellum ports such as New Orleans, Charleston, and Savannah declined as commerce rode the rails more than the water. Cities such as Dallas, Atlanta, Nashville, and Charlotte, astride great railroad trunk lines, emerged to lead southern urban growth. No fewer than five major rail lines converged on Atlanta by the 1870s. As early as 1866, that city had become "the radiating point for Northern and Western trade coming Southward, and . . . the gate through which passes Southern trade and travel going northward." When the Texas and Pacific Railway linked Dallas to eastern markets in 1872, it was a small town of three thousand people. Eight years later, its population had grown to more than ten thousand, and within thirty years it had become the South's twelfth-largest city. By 1920, New Orleans and Norfolk were the only coastal ports still among the ten most populous southern cities.

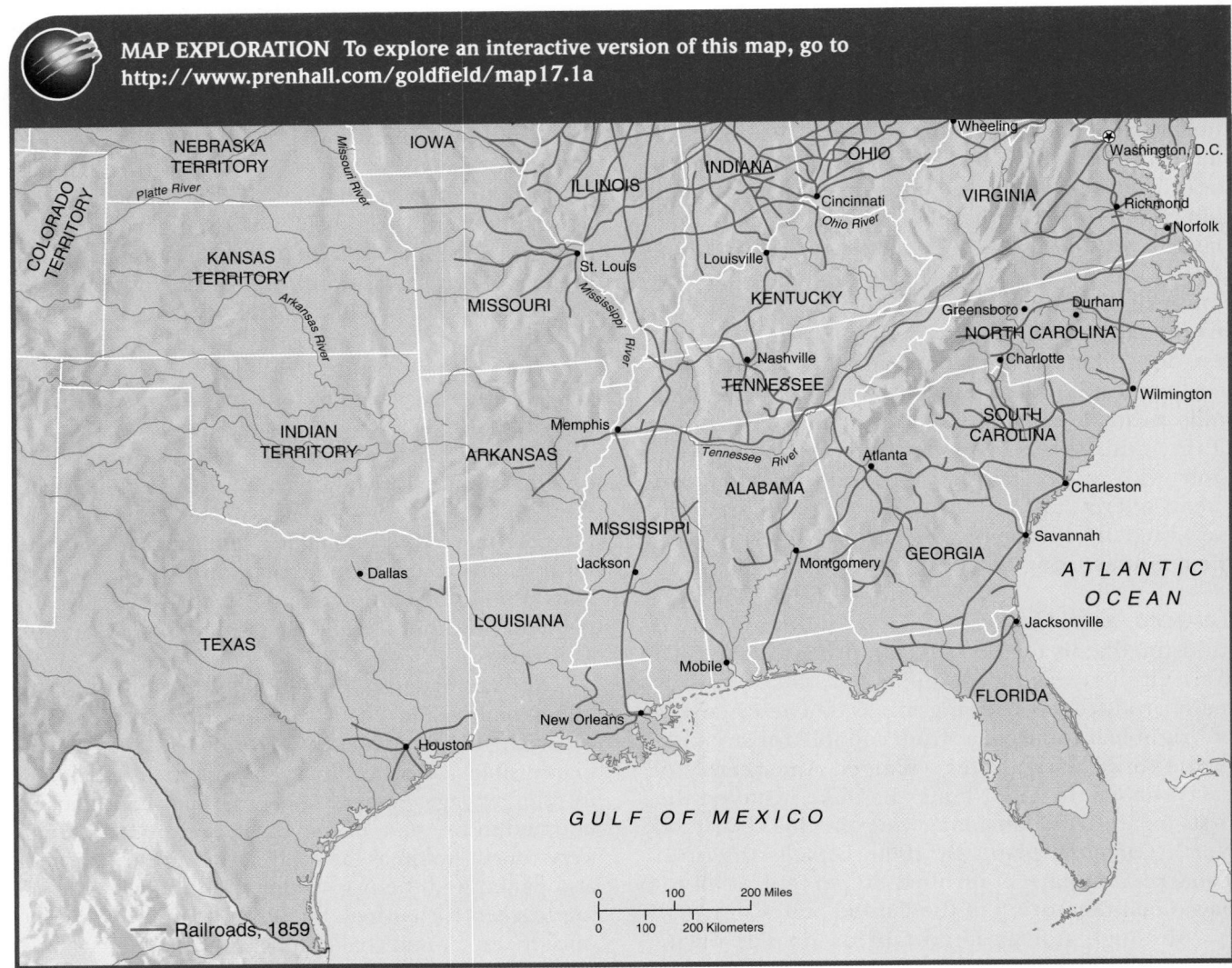

MAP EXPLORATION To explore an interactive version of this map, go to
http://www.prenhall.com/goldfield/map17.1a

MAP 17-1   Railroads in the South, 1859 and 1899
*A postwar railroad construction boom promoted commercial agriculture and industry in the
South. Unlike the railroads of the prewar South, uniform gauges and connections to major trunk
lines in the North linked Southerners to the rest of the nation. Northern interests, however,
owned the major southern railroads in 1899, and most of the products flowing northward were
raw materials to be processed by northern industry or shipped elsewhere by northern merchants.*

Railroads also spurred the growth of smaller
towns that marketed and processed farm products for
the surrounding countryside. A town on a rail line
that invested in a cotton press and a cottonseed-oil
mill would become a marketing hub for the surrounding countryside within a day's wagon ride away. Local
merchants would stock the latest fashions from New
York, canned foods, and current issues of popular
magazines such as the *Atlantic* or *Harper's*. The number of towns with fewer than five thousand people
doubled between 1870 and 1880 and had doubled
again by 1900. During the 1880s, southern urban

growth was twice the national average. By 1900, one
out of six Southerners lived in an urban place.

THE LIMITS OF INDUSTRIAL AND URBAN GROWTH

Rapid as it was, urban and industrial growth in the
South barely kept pace with that of the booming
North (see Chapter 18). Between 1860 and 1900, the
South's share of the nation's manufacturing increased
only marginally from 10.3 percent to 10.5 percent,
and its share of the nation's capital declined slightly

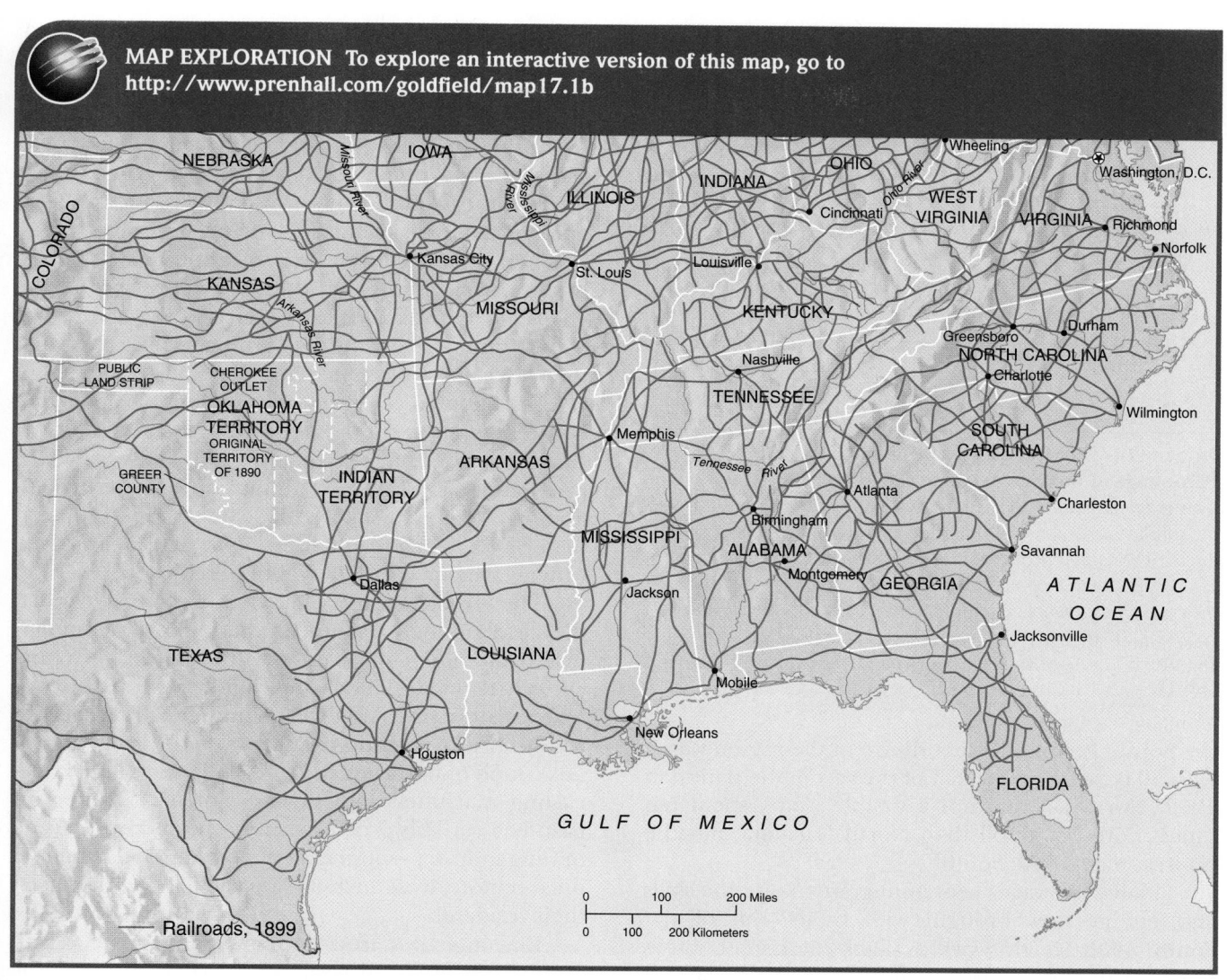

MAP EXPLORATION To explore an interactive version of this map, go to
http://www.prenhall.com/goldfield/map17.1b

Railroads, 1899

from 11.5 percent to 11 percent. About the same percentage of people worked in manufacturing in the southern states east of the Mississippi in 1900 as in 1850. Between 1860 and 1880, the per capita income of the South declined from 72 percent of the national average to 51 percent, and by 1920 it had recovered to only 62 percent (see Figure 17–1).

A weak agricultural economy and a high rural birthrate depressed wages in the South. Southern industrial workers earned roughly half the national average manufacturing wage during the late nineteenth century. Business leaders promoted the advantages of this cheap labor to northern investors. In 1904, a Memphis businessman boasted that his city "can save the northern manufacturer . . . who employs 400 hands, $50,000 a year on his labor bill."

Effects of low wages.
Despite their attractiveness to industrialists, low wages undermined the southern economy in several ways. Poorly paid workers did not buy much, keeping consumer demand low and limiting the market for southern manufactured goods. They also could not provide the southern states with much tax revenue, restricting the states' ability to fund services like public education. Low wages meant that mostly low-skilled, labor-intensive industries flourished in the South. Well-educated workers would have been overqualified for work in such industries. They would either go north, where factories needed skilled labor to produce high-quality goods and run complicated machinery, or agitate for higher wages and better working conditions in the South. Birmingham, Alabama, for example, probably spent more on public education than any other southern city, but the skilled workers in its steel mills tended to leave as soon as they could for higher-wage opportunities in northern cities like Pittsburgh and Cleveland. As a result, investment in education lagged in

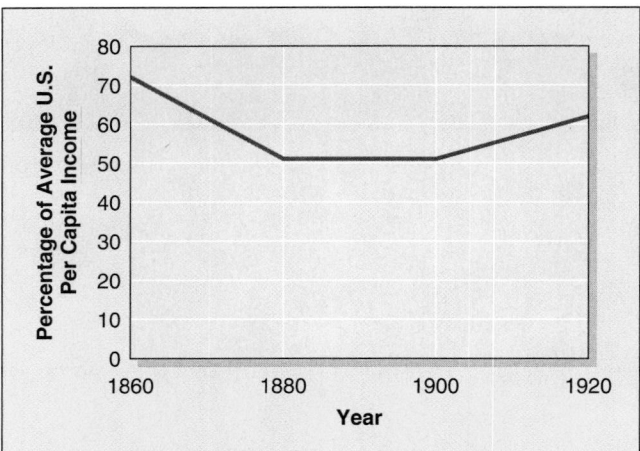

FIGURE 17-1 **Per Capita Income in the South as a Percentage of the U.S. Average, 1860-1920**
This graph illustrates the devastating effect of the Civil War on the southern economy. Southerners began a slow recovery during the 1880s that accelerated after 1900. But even as late as 1920, per capita income in the South was still lower relative to the country as a whole than it had been before the Civil War.
Data Source: Richard A. Easterlin, "Regional Economic Trends, 1840-1950," in *American Economic History*, ed. Seymour E. Harris (1961).

the South. Per-pupil expenditure in the region was at least 50 percent below that of the rest of the nation in 1900. North Dakota, not a wealthy state, spent ten times more per pupil than North Carolina, not the poorest state in the South.

Finally, low wages kept immigrants—and the skills and energy they brought with them—out of the South. With steady work available at higher wages north of the Mason-Dixon line, only a scattering of Italian farm laborers, Chinese railroad workers, and Jewish peddlers ventured below it. Between 1860 and 1900—during one of the greatest waves of immigration the United States has yet experienced—the foreign-born population of the South actually declined from about 10 percent to less than 2 percent.

Limited capital.

Why did the South not do better? Why did it not benefit more from the rapid expansion of the national economy in the last three decades of the nineteenth century? The simple answer is that, despite its growing links to the national economy, the South remained a region apart.

The Civil War had wiped out the South's capital resources, leaving it in effect an economic colony of the North. Northern goods flowed into the South, but northern capital, technology, and people did not. Northern-based national banks emerged in the wake of the Civil War to fund northern economic expansion. The South, in contrast, had few banks, and those

lacked sufficient capital reserves to fuel an equivalent expansion there. In 1880, Massachusetts alone had five times as much bank capital as the entire South.

Investment in the South seemed riskier and less promising than investment in the vibrant northern economy. As a result, northern banks imposed higher interest rates and shorter terms on loans to Southerners than on loans to their northern customers. Some northern capital came south nonetheless. When southern rail lines failed during a depression in the 1870s, northern financiers purchased the companies at bargain prices. By the 1890s, northern firms owned the five major rail lines serving the South.

With limited access to other sources of capital, the South's textile industry depended on thousands of small investors in towns and cities. These investors avoided risk and shunned innovation. Most textile operations remained small-scale. The average southern firm in 1900 was capitalized at $11,000, compared with an average of $21,000 elsewhere.

The lumber industry, the South's largest, typified the shortcomings of southern economic development in the late nineteenth century. It required little capital, relied on unskilled labor, and processed its raw materials on site. After clear-cutting—felling all the trees—in one region, sawmills moved quickly to the next stand of timber, leaving behind a bare landscape, rusting machinery, and a work force no better off than before. This process—later repeated by the coal-mining industry—inflicted environmental damage on once remote areas such as Appalachia, and displaced their residents.

Birmingham's iron and steel industry also suffered from financial weakness. Part of the fault lay with mill owners, who relied on cheap black labor rather than investing in expensive technology. Another problem was the limited market for steel in the mostly agricultural South. Southern farmers compounded this problem by relying on people and mules instead of farm machinery. Pittsburgh-based U.S. Steel took over Birmingham's largest steel producer in 1907. Thereafter, pricing policies favoring Pittsburgh plants limited Birmingham's growth. Pittsburgh also won the competition for technology and skilled labor.

The tobacco industry, however, avoided the problems that plagued other southern enterprises. James B. Duke's American Tobacco Company was so immensely profitable that he became, in effect, his own bank. With more than enough capital to install the latest technology in his plants, Duke bought out his competitors. He then diversified into electric power generation, investing in an enterprise that became the Southern Power Company in 1905 (and later the

Duke Power Company). He also endowed what became Duke University.

Southern industry fit into a narrow niche of late-nineteenth-century American industrialization. With an unskilled and uneducated work force, poor access to capital and technology, and a weak consumer base, the South processed raw agricultural products and produced cheap textiles, cheap lumber products, and cheap cigarettes. "Made in the South" became synonymous with bottom-of-the-line goods. In the North, industrialization usually occurred in an urban context and promoted rapid urban growth. This was not the case in the South. Most textile mills were typically located in the countryside, often in mill villages, where employers could easily recruit families and keep them isolated from the distractions and employment alternatives of the cities. The timber industry similarly remained a rural-based enterprise. Tobacco manufacturing helped Durham and Winston, North Carolina, grow, but they remained small compared to northern industrial cities. Duke moved his corporate headquarters to New York to be near that city's financial, advertising, and communications services.

FARMS TO CITIES: IMPACT ON SOUTHERN SOCIETY

If industrialization in the South was limited compared to the North, it nonetheless had an enormous impact on southern society. In the southern Piedmont, for example, textile mills erupted from the red clay and transformed a portion of the farm population into an industrial work force. Failed farmers moved to textile villages to earn a living. Entire families secured employment and often a house in exchange for their labor. Widows and single young men also moved to the mills, usually the only option outside farm work in the South. Nearly one-third of the textile mill labor force by 1900 consisted of children under the age of fourteen, and women. They worked twelve hours a day, six days a week, although some firms allowed a half-day off on Saturday. They had worked long hours on the farm, too, but now they became the target of concern of middle-class urban reformers, who viewed factory work as destructive of individual and family life.

Southern urban growth, which also paled in comparison with that of the North, had a similarly disproportionate impact on southern society. One observer noted the changes in a North Carolina town between 1880 and 1900. The town in 1880 presented a sorry aspect: rutted roads, a shanty for a school, a few forlorn churches, and perhaps three prominent families. Twenty years later, another railroad, bustling commerce, and textile mills had produced a new scene: paved streets, two public schools—one for black children, one for white children—and a cosmopolitan frame of mind among its residents. "The men have a wider range of activities and the women have more clothes." Discussions changed from local gossip to

By the 1890s, textile mills were a common sight in towns throughout the South. The mills provided employment for impoverished rural families, especially women and children.

"the prices of certain stocks in New York." The town now had electric lights, paved streets, and a direct train to New York. In another twenty years, the observer predicted, it will be "very like hundreds of towns in the Middle West."

In 1880, southern towns often did not differ much from the countryside in appearance, economy, religion, and outlook. Over the next twenty years, the gap between town and country widened. By 1900, a town in the New South would boast a business district and more elegant residences than before. It would have a relatively prosperous economy and more frequent contact with other parts of the country. Its influence would extend into the countryside. Mail, the telegraph, the railroad, and the newspaper brought city life to the attention of farm families. In turn, farm families visited nearby towns and cities more often. A South Carolina writer related in 1900 that "[c]ountry people who . . . went to town annually or semiannually, can now go quickly, safely, pleasantly, and cheaply several times a day." Many never returned to the farm. "Cheap coal, cheap lights, convenient water supply offer inducements; society and amusements draw the young; the chance to speculate, to make a sudden rise in fortunes, to get in the swim attracts others."

The urban South drew the region's talented and ambitious young people. White men, like William Henry Belk, moved to cities to open shops or take jobs as bank clerks, bookkeepers, merchants, and salesmen. White women worked as retail clerks, telephone operators, and office personnel. Black women filled the growing demand for laundresses and domestic servants. And black men also found prospects better in towns than on the farm, despite a narrow and uncertain range of occupations available to them.

The excitement that drew some Southerners to their new cities repelled others. To them, urbanization and the emphasis on wealth, new technology, and display represented a second Yankee conquest. The cities, they feared, threatened to infect the South with northern values, undermining southern grace, charm, faith, and family. Ministers warned against traffic with the urban devil, whose temptations could overcome even the most devout individual. Evangelist Sam Jones, a reformed alcoholic, chose Atlanta for his largest revivals in the 1890s, challenging its residents to keep the Sabbath holy, reject alcohol, and obey the Golden Rule.

Country people held ambivalent views of the city. Farm children looked forward to the Saturday excursion to town, when they would gaze in shop windows, watch people rushing about, wonder at the workings of electricity, and drink a "Co'Cola" at the drugstore. Their parents shared some of this excitement but experienced apprehension as well. They were disturbed by the easy blurring of class and racial distinctions in town and offended by the scorn with which town folk sometimes treated them.

White Southerners in town and country, who not long ago had lived similar lives, grew distant. Evelyn Scott recalled how rural folk looked to her when they visited her town, Clarksville, Tennessee, at the turn of the century:

> These beings [farmers and their families] I regarded as from another planet. . . . The little girls whose petticoats were never of a length with their frocks; the little boys whose misfit "store pants" were cut of material . . . uncongenial . . . to the human form; the misses in muslin dresses of [a] diluted [pink] color; . . . already-weary mothers wearing hats on which reposed entire flimsy gardens and orchards, or else pathetically alighted, stuffed birds! [They engaged] in bouts of window-shopping in which stoical hearts and vacant imaginations were replenished.

Once the backbone of the South, small landholding white farmers and their families like those Scott thought so alien had fallen on hard times. The market that lured them into commercial agriculture threatened to take away their independence. They faced the loss of their land and livelihood. Their way of life no longer served as the standard for the South. New South spokesmen promoted cities and industries and ordered farmers to get on board the train of progress before it left the station without them.

THE SOUTHERN AGRARIAN REVOLT

Even more than before the Civil War, cotton dominated southern agriculture between 1877 and 1900. And the economics of cotton brought despair to cotton farmers. Those who grew two other traditional southern cash crops—rice and tobacco—fared better. Rice and tobacco production increased, and Louisiana and Arkansas overtook South Carolina in rice production. Steady demand, however, allowed rice and tobacco growers to maintain a decent standard of living. Cotton was another matter. The size of the cotton crop continued to set annual records after 1877. Fertilizers revived supposedly exhausted soils in North and South Carolina, turning them white with cotton. The railroad opened new areas for cultivation in Mississippi and eastern Texas. But the price of cotton fell while the price of fertilizers, agricultural tools, food, and most other necessities went up (see Figure 17–2). As a

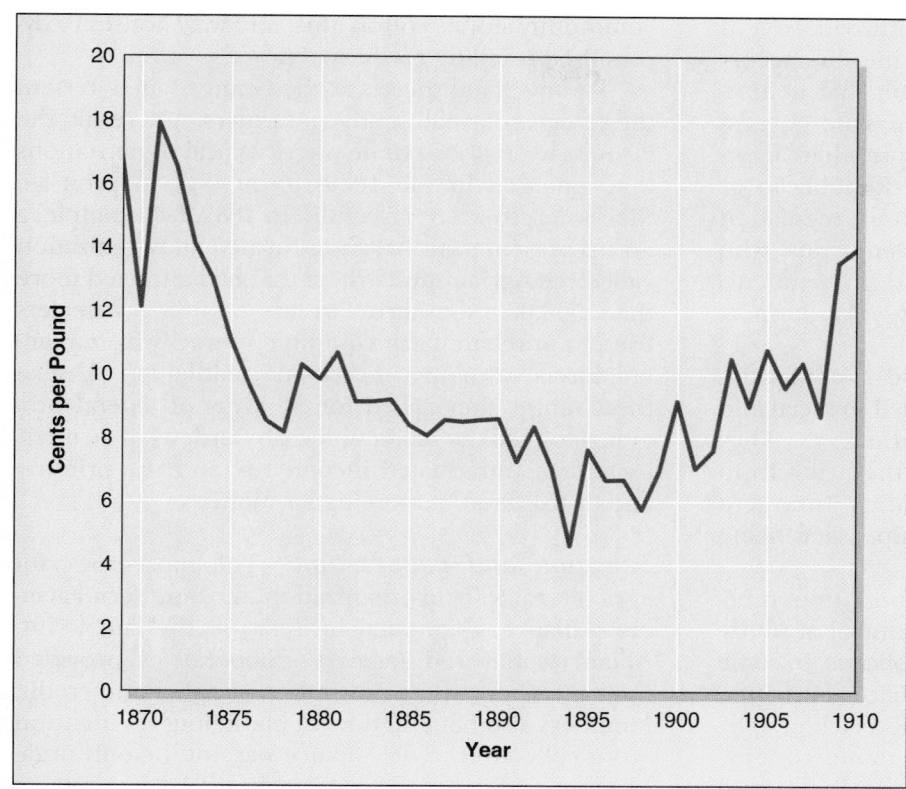

FIGURE 17-2   The Price of Cotton, 1869-1910
The steadily declining price of cotton after the Civil War—from 18 cents a pound to 5 cents a pound by the early 1890s—reflected extreme overproduction. Behind the numbers lay an impoverished rural South.

Data Source: U.S. Department of Commerce, *Historical Statistics of the United States: Colonial Times to 1957.*

result, the more cotton the farmers grew, the less money they made.

Before the Civil War, the South fed itself. After the war, with railroads providing direct access to major cotton-marketing centers, farmers cultivated more land in cotton and less in food crops. The South became an importer of food. As a common lament went in 1893, "Five-cent cotton, forty-cent meat, how in the world can a poor man eat?"

COTTON AND CREDIT

The solution to this agrarian dilemma seemed simple: Grow less cotton. But that course was not possible for several reasons. In a cash-poor economy, credit ruled. Cotton was the only commodity instantly convertible into cash and hence the only commodity accepted for credit. Food crops generated less income per acre than cotton, even in the worst years. Local merchants, themselves bound in a web of credit to merchants in larger cities, accepted cotton as collateral. As cotton prices plummeted, the merchants required their customers to grow more cotton to make up the differ-

ence. "No cotton, no credit" became a standard refrain throughout the South after 1877.

For small landowning farmers, credit proved addictive. Trapped in debt by low cotton prices and high interest rates, they lost their land in record numbers. Both black farmers and white farmers were affected. But white farmers were more likely than black farmers to own their farms, and the effect on them was more dramatic. Less than one-third of white farmers in the South were tenants or sharecroppers just after the Civil War. By the 1890s, nearly half were.

Some areas did diversify. Good rail connections in Georgia, for example, made peach farming profitable for some farmers. Railroads likewise helped cattle ranching spread in Texas. But few crops or animals had the geographical range of cotton. Soil type, rainfall, animal parasites, and frost made alternatives unfeasible for many farmers. Cotton required no machinery or irrigation system. James Barrett, a farmer outside Augusta, Georgia, said of his experiment with diversification in 1900: "I have diversified, and I have not made any money by diversification. . . . I grow green peas and everything I know of. I have raised horses, cows, and hogs, and I have diversified it for the last three years and have not been able to make a dollar."

SOUTHERN FARMERS ORGANIZE, 1877–1892

As their circumstances deteriorated, southern farmers fought back. They engaged in barter when they could. They supplemented their income with occasional jobs off the farm and by selling eggs or vegetables. They lobbied for debt-stay laws and formed farmer organizations. They had lived a communal life of church, family, and kin. Now they would widen the circle of their community to include other farmers sharing their plight. These were not naive country folk—most owned their own land and participated in the market economy. They just wanted to make the market fairer, to lower interest rates and ease credit, to regulate railroad freight rates, and to keep the prices of necessities in check.

But these goals required legislation that neither the federal government nor southern state governments were inclined to support. No presidential administration between 1877 and 1900, Republican or Democrat, favored debt relief or extensive regulation of business. And the Redeemer Democrats who gained control of the southern state governments after Reconstruction represented large landowners and merchants, not poor farmers.

To strengthen their authority and suppress dissent, the Redeemer Democrats appealed to racial and regional solidarity among white Southerners. They portrayed themselves as having saved the South from the rule of black people and Republicans. Insurgent farmers who challenged this leadership risked being branded as disloyal.

The Democrats nonetheless faced opposition beginning soon after they had wrested control of southern state governments from the Republicans. In some states, like North Carolina, the Republicans retained support in mountain areas and among black people. In addition, disaffected white farmers mounted independent political campaigns against the Redeemers in several states in the late 1870s and early 1880s, to demand currency reform and the easing of credit. But the Democrats, in firm control of the election machinery throughout the South, turned back these challenges. Although Independents at one point succeeded in gaining control of the Virginia legislature, their few other victories were confined to the local level. Hard-pressed farmers began to organize on a broader scale.

Southern farmers joined their colleagues nationwide to address common grievances related to pricing, credit, and tax policies. Though some of the southern farmers' problems resulted from conditions particular to the South, agricultural distress became widespread in the decades after 1870. By 1875, nearly 250,000 southern landowners had joined the National Grange of the Patrons of Husbandry or, more popularly, simply the **Grange** (see Chapter 20). The leaders of the Grange, however, were large landowners. Their interests were not the same as the small farmers who made up the organization's rank and file. The Grange leadership in the South, for example, while nominally concerned about issues of concern to small farmers, such as exploitative merchants and excessive railroad freight rates, favored policies—like fence laws to pen animals and protect crops and controls on farm labor—that hurt small farmers. The rank-and-file members, by contrast, pushed a more radical agenda, including establishing

community stores, cotton gins, and warehouses to bypass the prevailing credit system.

Despite a few successes, the Grange failed to stem the reverses of small southern farmers. As a result, the farmers were drawn to new agricultural organizations that emerged in the 1880s, promising to promote their interests more forcefully. In 1882, for example, a group of farmers in Arkansas formed an organization called the **Agricultural Wheel** that had attracted more than 500,000 southern farmers by 1887. Wheelers tried to purchase farm equipment directly from manufacturers, avoiding merchant middlemen. Unlike the Grange, they called for an array of federal programs to ease the credit and cash burdens of farmers, including a graduated income tax and the printing and distribution of more paper money.

Salvation and cooperation. The most powerful agricultural reform organization, the **Southern Farmers' Alliance**, originated in Texas in the late 1870s. Alliance-sponsored farmers' cooperatives provided their members with discounts on supplies and credit. Members also benefited from marketing their cotton crops collectively. The Alliance was not the only organization to form cooperatives, but it was unique in the messianic zeal with which it promoted them. Although it endorsed some candidates for office, the Alliance was not a political party and did not challenge Democratic domination of the South.

The Alliance was still very much a Texas organization in 1887 when Charles W. Macune, a Wisconsin native, became its driving force. Macune sent a corps of speakers to create a network of southern cooperatives. Within two years, the Alliance had spread throughout the South and into the North and West. By 1890, it claimed more than a million members. With the exception of a few large landowners and some tenant farmers, almost all were small farmers who owned their own land. The success of the Alliance reflected both the desperate struggle of these small farmers to keep their land and the failure of other organizations to help them.

The Alliance operated like a religious denomination. Its leaders preached a message of salvation through cooperation to as many as twenty thousand people at huge revival-like rallies. Qualifications for membership included a belief in the divinity of Jesus and the literal truth of the Bible. Alliance speakers, many of them rural ministers, often held meetings in churches. In their talks, they combined biblical nostrums with economic policy and stressed the importance of doing good as much as good farming. They urged members to visit "the homes where lacerated hearts are bleeding, to assuage the suffering of a

The faces of this white sharecropper family in North Carolina reflect the harshness of farm life in the late nineteenth- and early twentieth-century South, a period when thousands of Southerners, white and black alike, slipped from land ownership to sharecropping.

brother or a sister, bury the dead, care for the widows and educate the orphans." The Alliance lobbied state legislatures to fund rural public schools. To increase the sense of community, the Alliance sponsored picnics, baseball games, and concerts.

The Alliance became for many small farmers a surrogate government and church in a region where public officials and many mainline Protestant ministers ignored their needs. It imposed strict morality on its members, prohibiting drinking, gambling, and sexual misconduct. Alliance leaders criticized many Baptist, Methodist, and Presbyterian ministers for straying from the traditional emphasis on individual salvation and for defending a status quo that benefited large planters and towns. Cyrus Thompson, the North Carolina Alliance president and a prominent Methodist, declared in 1889 that "the church today stands where it has always stood, on the side of human slavery."

Some Alliance members left their churches for new religious groups. The Holiness movement, which began in the North before the Civil War, revived among Texas farmers in the mid-1880s. Holiness disciples advocated simple dress, avoided coffee and pork, and swore off all worldly amusements. The members of the Church of God, which formed in the mountains of Tennessee and North Carolina in 1886, similarly sought to cleanse themselves of secular evils. The new churches promoted a vision of an egalitarian

South. They accepted women on an equal basis, and occasionally black people as well. As many as a third of Holiness preachers were women.

Women also found an active role as officers and speakers in the Alliance. As a Texas woman declared, "The Alliance has come to redeem woman from her enslaved condition. She is admitted into the organization as the equal of her brother, and the ostracism which has impeded her intellectual progress in the past is not met with."

Unlike some of the new religious movements, however, the Alliance did not accept black members. Black farmers formed the first **Colored Farmers' Alliance** in Texas in 1886. The Colored Alliance had fewer landowners and more tenants and sharecroppers in its ranks than the white organization. It concerned itself with issues relevant to this constituency, such as higher wages for cotton pickers. In 1891, the Colored Alliance attempted a region-wide strike over farm wages but was unable to enforce it in the worsening southern economy.

The white Alliance had better results with a protest over price fixing. To protect cotton shipped to market, farmers wrapped it in a burlaplike material called jute. In 1888, jute manufacturers combined to raise the price from 7 cents to as much as 14 cents a yard. The Alliance initiated a jute boycott throughout the South, telling farmers to use cotton bagging as an alternative. The protest worked, forcing the chastened jute manufacturers to offer farmers their product at a mere 5 cents per yard.

Storing cotton. This success encouraged Macune to pursue a more ambitious project. Low cotton prices and a lack of cash kept farmers poor. To address these problems, Macune proposed his **subtreasury plan.** Alliance members were to store their crops in a subtreasury (a warehouse), keeping their cotton off the market until the price rose. In the meantime, the government would loan the farmers up to 80 percent of the value of the stored crops at a low interest rate of 2 percent per year. This arrangement would free farmers from merchants' high interest rates and crop liens.

Macune urged Alliance members to endorse political candidates who supported the subtreasury scheme. Many Democratic candidates for state legislatures throughout the South did endorse it and were elected, with Alliance backing, in 1890. Once in office, however, they failed to deliver.

The failure of the subtreasury plan combined with a steep drop in cotton prices after 1890 undermined the Alliance. Its cooperatives collapsed as crop liens cut down small landowners as though with scythes. A Georgia Allianceman wrote in 1891 that "Hundreds of farmers will be turned adrift, and thousands of acres of our best land allowed to grow up in weeds through lack of necessary capital to work them." Alliance membership declined by two-thirds in Georgia that year. Desperate Alliance leaders merged their organization with a new national political party in 1892, the People's or **Populist Party**. Populists appropriated the Alliance program and challenged Democrats in the South and Republicans in the West. The merger reflected desperation more than calculation.

SOUTHERN POPULISTS

Northern farmers, like their southern counterparts, faced growing financial pressure in the 1880s that by the early 1890s had led them too to join the Alliance. Just as southern farmers had turned to the Democratic Party to redress their grievances, northern farmers turned to the dominant party in the northern farming states—the Republican Party—to redress theirs. Like the Democrats, the Republicans failed to respond. Beginning in Kansas in 1890, disillusioned farmers formed the People's Party, soon called the Populist Party. The Populists held their first national nominating convention in Omaha in July 1892.

The Populists supported a wide range of reforms, many adopted from the Alliance, including the direct election of United States senators by popular vote rather than by state legislatures, an income tax, woman suffrage, government ownership of railroads, and various proposals to ease credit. As we will see in Chapter 20, the Populists stirred up national politics between 1892 and 1896. In the South, they challenged the Democratic Party, sometimes courting Republicans, including black voters.

Southern populists were ambivalent about African Americans. On the one hand, black people constituted a potential voting bloc the Populists could ill afford to ignore. On the other hand, appealing to black voters would expose Populists to demagogic attacks from Democrats for undermining white supremacy, frightening away potential white backers. Populists who wanted to extend the hand of fellowship to black people risked withering fire from Democrats. The *Baton Rouge Daily Advocate*, for example, informed its readers in 1892 that the Populist Party was "the most dangerous and insidious foe of white supremacy." Many southern Populists, including former members of the Alliance, supported segregation and never made the gesture of racial reconciliation.

Despite the risks, in at least two southern states, Texas and Georgia, Populists openly appealed for black votes. In Texas, the black Populist John B. Rayner, the "silver-tongued orator of the colored race," spoke to racially mixed audiences around the state. The Texas Populist platform called for "equal justice and protection under the law to all citizens without reference to race, color or nationality." In Georgia, the Populist leader Tom Watson supported a biracial party organization and counseled white people to accept black people as partners in their common crusade. "You are kept apart," Watson told black and white Georgians, "that you may be separately fleeced of your earnings. You are made to hate each other because upon that hatred is rested the keystone of the arch of financial despotism which enslaves you both."

Despite Rayner's and Watson's efforts, most black people remained loyal to the Republican Party for its role in abolishing slavery and for the few patronage crumbs the party still threw their way. Black people also suspected Populists' motives. The party appealed mainly to small, landowning farmers, not, as most black Southerners were, unpropertied tenants and sharecroppers. And even the Texas Populists, while appealing for black support, opposed black office-holding and jury service.

Unwilling or unable to mobilize black voters and unsuccessful in dislodging white voters from the Democratic party, the Populists finished a distant third in the 1892 presidential election. In the South, their only significant inroads were in the state legislatures of Texas, Alabama, and Georgia. Even in these states, widespread voter fraud among Democrats undermined Populist strength.

Despite a deepening economic depression, the Populists had only a few additional successes in the South after 1892. Their major victory was in North Carolina in 1894. Republicans had remained a political force in the state's mountain counties and among black people in its eastern part. Adopting a fusion strategy, the Populists ran candidates on a combined ticket with Republicans. The fusion candidates captured the governorship and state legislature. Once in office, they overhauled the state electoral machinery, eased voter registration procedures, and established nonpartisan electoral panels to monitor elections. Reflecting Populist influence, they also imposed limits on interest rates, increased expenditures for education, and raised taxes on railroads.

Higher cotton prices and returning prosperity in the late 1890s, however, undermined Populist support in North Carolina, as in the rest of the South. In 1896, the Populists assisted in their own nationwide demise by merging with the Democrats for the presidential election of 1896. In 1898, Democrats surged back into office in North Carolina on the strength of a virulent white supremacy campaign and promptly undid the work of the fusionists.

WOMEN IN THE NEW SOUTH

Just as farm women found their voices in the Alliance movement of the 1880s, a growing group of middle-class white and black urban women entered the public realm and engaged in policy issues. In the late-nineteenth-century North, women became increasingly active in reform movements, including woman suffrage, labor legislation, social welfare, and city planning. Building on their antebellum activist traditions, northern women, sometimes joining with men, sought to improve the status of women.

Because antebellum reform movements included abolitionism, they had made little headway in the South. As a result, southern women had a meager reform tradition to build on. The war also left them ambivalent about independence. With husbands, fathers, and brothers dead or incapacitated, many women had to care for themselves and their families in the face of defeat and deprivation. Some determined never again to depend on men. Others, responding to the stress of running a farm or business, would have preferred less independence.

The response of southern white men to the war also complicated women's efforts to improve their status. Southern men had been shaken by defeat. They had lost the war and placed their families in peril. Many responded with alcoholism and violence. To regain their self-esteem, they recast the war as a noble crusade rather than a defeat. And they imagined southern white women as paragons of virtue and purity who required men to defend them. Demands for even small changes in traditional gender roles would threaten this image. Southern women understood this and never mounted an extensive reform campaign like their sisters in the North. Some middle-class women were openly hostile to reform, and others adopted conservative causes more inclined to reinforce the role of men in southern society than to challenge it.

Despite such limitations, middle-class southern women found opportunities to broaden their social role and enter the public sphere in the two decades after 1880. They found these opportunities primarily in the cities, where servants, stores, and schools freed them of many of the productive functions—such as making clothing, cooking, and child care—that burdened their sisters in the country and kept them tied to the home.

CHURCH WORK AND PRESERVING MEMORIES

Southern women waded warily into the public arena, using channels men granted them as natural extensions of the home, such as church work. The movement to found home mission societies, for example, was led by single white women in the Methodist church. Home missions promoted industrial education among the poor and helped working-class women become self-sufficient. The home mission movement reflected an increased interest in missionary work among white southern evangelical churches. Laura Haygood, an Atlantan who had served as a missionary in China, founded a home mission in Atlanta when she returned in 1883. Lily Hammond, another Atlantan, extended the mission concept when she opened settlement houses in black and white neighborhoods in Atlanta in the 1890s. Settlement houses, pioneered in New York in the 1880s, promoted middle-class values in poor neighborhoods and provided them with a permanent source of services. In the North, they were privately sponsored. In the South, they were supported by the Methodist church and known as Wesley Houses, after John Wesley, the founder of Methodism.

Religion also prompted southern white women to join the **Women's Christian Temperance Union (WCTU)**. The first southern local formed in Lucy Haygood's church in Atlanta in 1880. Temperance reform, unlike other church-inspired activities, involved women directly in public policy. Women framed temperance and the prohibition of alcohol as a family issue—alcohol ruined families, victimizing innocent women and children. WCTU members visited schools to educate children about the evils of alcohol, addressed prisoners, and blanketed men's meetings with literature. As a result, they became familiar with the South's abysmal school system and its archaic criminal justice system. They thus began advocating education and prison reform as well as legislation against alcohol.

By the 1890s, many WCTU members realized that they could not achieve their goals unless women had the vote. Rebecca Latimer Felton, an Atlanta suffragist and WCTU member, reflected the frustration of her generation of southern women in an address to working women in 1892:

But some will say—you women might be quiet—you can't vote, you can't do anything! Exactly so—we have kept quiet for nearly a hundred years hoping to see relief come to the women of this country—and it hasn't come. How long must our children be slain? If a mad dog should come into my yard, and attempt to bite my child or myself—would you think me out of my place, if I killed him with a dull meat axe? . . . [You] would call that woman a brave woman . . . and yet are we to sit by while drink ruins our homes?

Despite the WCTU's roots in southern churches, the activism of its members alarmed some southern men. WCTU rhetoric implied a veiled attack on men. Felton, for example, often referred to men who drank as "beasts." And WCTU members had many other issues besides prohibition on their agenda. When the WCTU held its national convention in Atlanta in 1890, local Baptist and Methodist ministers launched a bitter attack against the organization, claiming that it drew women into activities contrary to the Scriptures and that its endorsement of woman suffrage subverted traditional family values.

Few women, however, had such radical objectives in mind. Rebecca Felton's own career highlighted the essentially conservative nature of the reform movement among middle-class women in the New South. Born in 1835 to a wealthy planter family, she attended college and married Dr. William H. Felton, a physician and minister twelve years her senior. During the Civil War and its aftermath, the Feltons eked out a modest living teaching school and working a small farm. Four of their five children died. Seeing southern families worse off than her own, Felton threw herself into a variety of reform activities, ranging from woman suffrage to campaigns against drinking, smoking, and Coca-Cola. She fought for child-care facilities and sex education, as well as compulsory school attendance, and she pushed for the admission of women to the University of Georgia. But she strongly supported textile operators over textile workers and defended white supremacy. She had no qualms about the lynching of black men—executing them without trial—"a thousand times a week if necessary" to preserve the purity of white women. In 1922, she became the first woman member of the U.S. Senate. By any definition, Felton was a reformer, but like most middle-class southern women, she had no interest in challenging the class and racial inequities of the New South.

The dedication of southern women to commemorating the memory of the Confederate cause also suggested the conservative nature of middle-class women's reform in the New South. Ladies' Memorial Associations formed after the war to insure the proper burial of Confederate soldiers and suitable markings for their graves. The associations joined with men to erect monuments to Confederate leaders and, by the 1880s, to the common soldier. These activities reinforced white solidarity and constructed a common heritage for all white Southerners regardless of class or location. By the 1890s, women planned monuments in prominent civic spaces in the urban South. Their efforts sparked interest in city planning and city beautification. A new organization, the United Daughters of the Confederacy (UDC), appeared in 1894 to preserve southern history and honor its heroes. Although men formed similar associations, women remained the most active protectors of regional memory. Work for the Lost Cause reflected traditional roles, but it also offered a way for women to hone leadership and organizational skills, preparing them for less traditional public activities in the 1890s. Gertrude Thomas, for example, one of the South's leading suffragists, played an important role in the Georgia UDC.

WOMEN'S CLUBS

A broader spectrum of southern middle-class women joined women's clubs than joined church-sponsored organizations or memorial associations. Most clubs began in the 1880s as literary or self-improvement societies that had little interest in reform. By 1890, most towns and cities boasted at least several women's clubs and perhaps a federated club organization. But, also by that time, some clubs and their members had begun to discuss political issues such as child labor reform, educational improvement, and prison reform. The Arkansas Federation of Women's Clubs launched a boycott of goods produced by "exploited" labor in 1903. The Lone Star (Texas) Federation scrutinized public hospitals, almshouses, and orphanages at the turn of the century. Its president asserted, "The Lone Star Federation stands for the highest and truest type of womanhood—that which lends her voice as well as her hand." Southern women's club members sought out their sisters in the North. As Georgia's federated club president, Mrs. A.O. Granger, wrote in 1906, "Women of intellectual keenness in the South could not be left out of the awakening of the women of the whole country to a realization of the responsibility which they properly had in the condition of their fellow-women and of the children."

This pursuit of solidarity with women in the North did not extend to the members of black women's

The Confederate battle flag on this parade float reflects its emerging status as an icon of the Lost Cause in the late nineteenth century.

clubs in the South. The activities of black women's clubs paralleled those of white women's clubs. Only rarely, however—as at some meetings of the Young Women's Christian Association (YWCA) or occasional meetings in support of prohibition—did black and white club members interact.

Some white clubwomen expressed sympathy for black women privately, but publicly they maintained white solidarity. Most were unwilling to sacrifice their own reform agenda to the cause of racial reconciliation. Women suffragists in the South, for example, did not make common cause with black people. On the contrary, some used racial solidarity as a weapon to promote white women's right to vote, arguing that the combined vote of white men and women would further white interests.

The primary interest of most southern white women's clubs was the plight of young white working-class and farm women. This interest reflected the growing number of such women in the work force. Single and adrift in the city, many worked for low wages, and some slipped into prostitution. The clubs sought to help them make the transition from rural to urban life or to improve their lives on the farm. To this end, they focused on child labor reform and on upgrading public education.

SETTLING THE RACE ISSUE

The assertiveness of a new generation of African Americans, especially those in urban areas, in the 1880s and 1890s provided the impetus and opportunity for white leaders to secure white solidarity. To counter black aspirations, white leaders enlisted the support of young white Southerners, convincing them that the struggle for white supremacy would place them beside the larger-than-life heroes of the Civil War generation. African Americans resisted the resulting efforts to deprive them of their remaining freedoms. Though some left the South, many more built new lives and communities within the restricted framework white Southerners allowed them.

THE FLUIDITY OF SOUTHERN RACE RELATIONS, 1877–1890

Race relations remained remarkably fluid in the South between the end of Reconstruction and the early 1890s. Despite the departure of federal troops and the end of Republican rule, many black people continued to vote and hold office. Some Democrats even courted the black electorate. Though segregation ruled .in churches, schools, and in some organizations and public places after the Civil War, black people and white people continued to mingle, do business with each other, and often maintain cordial relations.

In 1885, T. McCants Stewart, a black journalist from New York, traveled to his native South Carolina, expecting a rough reception once his train headed south from Washington, D.C. To his surprise, the conductor allowed him to remain in his seat while white riders sat on baggage or stood. He provoked little reaction among white passengers when he entered the dining car. Some of them struck up a conversation with him. Stewart, who admitted he had begun his journey with "a chip on my shoulder . . . [daring] any man to knock it off," now observed that "the whites of the South are really less afraid to [have] contact with colored people than the whites of the North." In Columbia, South Carolina, Stewart found that he could move about with no restrictions. "I can ride in first-class cars. . . . I can go into saloons and get refreshments even as in New York. I can stop in and drink a glass of soda and be more politely waited upon than in some parts of New England."

Other black people corroborated Stewart's experiences. John Gray Lucas, a native of Pine Bluff, Arkansas, attended law school in Boston. There, in an 1887 newspaper interview, Lucas noted that three of Pine Bluff's eight city councilmen and half the police force were black and that black people encountered no segregation or discrimination in public careers.

Given the racial climate in Pine Bluff, Lucas wondered "why more colored young men from the North did not make Arkansas their home. It is an inviting field for them, and a grand opportunity to make something of themselves." Lucas followed his own advice and returned to Pine Bluff, where he embarked on a successful legal career in the 1890s.

During the 1880s, black people joined interracial labor unions and continued to be active in the Republican party. They engaged in business with white people. In the countryside, African Americans and white people hunted and fished together, worked side by side at sawmills, and traded with each other. Cities were segregated more by class than by race, and people of both races sometimes lived in the same neighborhoods. To be sure, black people faced discrimination in employment and voting and random retaliation for perceived violations of racial barriers. But those barriers were by no means fixed.

THE WHITE BACKLASH

The black generation that came of age in this environment demanded full participation in American society. As the young black editor of Nashville's *Fisk Herald* proclaimed in 1889, "We are not the Negro from whom the chains of slavery fell a quarter of a century ago.... We are now qualified, and being the equal of whites, should be treated as such." Charles Price, an educator from North Carolina, admonished colleagues in 1890, "If we do not possess the manhood and patriotism to stand up in the defense of . . . constitutional rights and protest long, loud and unitedly against their continual infringements, we are unworthy of heritage as American citizens and deserve to have fastened on us the wrongs of which many are disposed to complain."

For many in the generation of white Southerners who came of age in the same period, this assertiveness rankled. These young white people, raised on the myth of the Lost Cause, were continually reminded of the heroism and sacrifice of their fathers during the Civil War. Confronted with what was, for many, worse conditions than their families had enjoyed before the war, they resented the changed status of black people. For them, black people replaced the Yankees as the enemy; they saw it as their mis-

sion to preserve white purity and dominance. Echoing these sentiments, David Schenck, a Greensboro, North Carolina, businessman, wrote in 1890 that "the breach between the races widens as the young free negroes grow up and intrude themselves on white society and nothing prevents the white people of the South from annihilating the negro race but the military power of the United States Government." Using the Darwinian language popular among educated white people at the time, Schenck concluded, "I pity the Negro, but the struggle is for the survival of the fittest race."

The South's deteriorating rural economy and the volatile politics of the late 1880s and early 1890s exacerbated the growing tensions between assertive black people and threatened white people. So too did the growth of industry and cities in the South. In the cities, black and white people came in close contact, competing for jobs and jostling each other for seats on streetcars and trains. Racist rhetoric and violence against black people accelerated in the 1890s.

LYNCH LAW

In 1892, three prominent black men—Tom Moss, Calvin McDowell, and William Stewart—opened a grocery on the south side of Memphis, an area with a large African American population. The People's Grocery prospered, while a white-owned store across the street struggled. The proprietor of the white-owned store, W. H. Barrett, was incensed. He secured an indictment against Moss, McDowell, and Stewart for maintaining a public nuisance. Outraged black

Lynching became a public spectacle, a ritual designed to reinforce white supremacy. Note the matter-of-fact satisfaction of the spectators to this gruesome murder of a black man.

community leaders called a protest meeting at the grocery during which two people made threats against Barrett. Barrett learned of the threats, notified the police, and warned the gathering at the People's Grocery that white people planned to attack and destroy the store. Nine sheriff's deputies, all white, approached the store to arrest the men who had threatened Barrett. Fearing Barrett's threatened white assault, the people in the grocery fired on the deputies, unaware who they were, and wounded three. When the deputies identified themselves, thirty black people surrendered, including Moss, McDowell, and Stewart, and were imprisoned. Four days later, deputies removed the three owners from jail, took them to a deserted area, and shot them dead.

The men at the People's Grocery had violated two of the unspoken rules that white Southerners imposed on black Southerners to maintain racial barriers: They had prospered, and they had forcefully challenged white authority. During 1892, a year of political agitation and economic depression, 235 lynchings occurred in the South. White mobs lynched nearly two thousand black Southerners between 1882 and 1903. During the 1890s, **lynchings** occurred at the rate of 150 a year. Most lynchers were working-class whites with rural roots, who were struggling in the depressed economy of the 1890s and enraged at the fluidity of urban race relations. The men who murdered Moss, McDowell, and Stewart, for example, had recently moved to Memphis from the countryside, where they had been unable to make a living farming.

The silence or tepid disapproval of white leaders condoned this orgy of violence. The substitution of lynch law for a court of law seemed a cheap price to pay for white solidarity at a time when political and economic pressures threatened entrenched white leaders. In 1893, Atlanta's Methodist bishop, Atticus G. Haygood, typically a spokesman for racial moderation, objected to the torture some white lynchers inflicted on their victims but added, "Unless assaults by Negroes on white women and little girls come to an end, there will most probably be still further displays of vengeance that will shock the world."

Haygood's comments reflect the most common justification for lynching—the presumed threat posed by black men to the sexual virtue of white women. Sexual "crimes" could include remarks, glances, and gestures. Yet only 25 percent of the lynchings that took place in the thirty years after 1890 had some alleged sexual connection. Certainly, the men of the People's Grocery had committed no sex crime. Lynchers did not carry out their grisly crimes to end a rape epidemic; they killed to keep black men in their place and to restore their own sense of manhood and honor.

Ida B. Wells, who owned a black newspaper in Memphis, used her columns to publicize the People's Grocery lynchings. The great casualty of the lynchings, she noted, was her faith that education, wealth, and upright living guaranteed black people the equality and justice they had long sought. The reverse was true. The more black people succeeded, the greater was their threat to white people. She investigated other lynchings, countering the claim that they were the result of assaults on white women. When she suggested that, on the contrary, perhaps some white women were attracted to black men, she enraged the white citizens of Memphis, who destroyed her press and office. Exiled to Chicago, Wells devoted herself to the struggle for racial justice.

SEGREGATION BY LAW

Southern white lawmakers sought to cement white solidarity and ensure black subservience in the 1890s by instituting **segregation** by law and the **disfranchisement** of black voters. Racial segregation restricting black Americans to separate and rarely equal public facilities had prevailed nationwide before the Civil War. After 1870, the custom spread rapidly in southern cities. In Rich-

Ida B. Wells, an outspoken critic of lynching, fled to Chicago following the People's Grocery lynchings in Memphis in 1892 and became a national civil-rights leader.

mond by the early 1870s, segregation laws required black people registering to vote to enter through separate doors and registrars to count their ballots separately. The city's prison and hospitals were segregated. So too were its horse-drawn railways, its schools, and most of its restaurants, hotels, and theaters.

During the same period, many northern cities and states, often in response to protests by African Americans, were ending segregation. Massachusetts, for example, had passed the nation's first public accommodations law in May 1865, desegregating all public facilities. Cities such as New York, Cleveland, and Cincinnati desegregated their streetcars. Chicago, Cleveland, Milwaukee, and the entire state of Michigan desegregated their public school systems. Roughly 95 percent of the nation's black population, however, lived in the South. Integration in the North, consequently, required white people to give up very little to black people. And as African American aspirations increased in the South during the 1890s as their political power waned, they became more vulnerable to segregation by law at the state level. At the same time, migration to cities, industrial development, and technologies such as railroads and elevators increased the opportunities for racial contact and muddled the rules of racial interaction.

Much of the new legislation focused on railroads, a symbol of modernity and mobility in the New South. Local laws and customs could not control racial interaction on interstate railroads. White passengers objected to black passengers' implied assertion of economic and social equality when they sat with them in dining cars and first-class compartments. Black Southerners, by contrast, viewed equal access to railroad facilities as a sign of respectability and acceptance. When southern state legislatures required railroads to provide segregated facilities, black people protested.

The railroad segregation laws required the railroads to provide "separate but equal" accommodations for black passengers. Railroads balked at the expense involved in doing so and provided black passengers with distinctly inferior facilities. Many lines refused to sell first-class tickets to black people and treated them roughly if they sat in first-class seats or tried to eat in the dining car. In 1890, Homer Plessy, a black Louisianan, refused to leave the first-class car of a railroad traveling through the state. Arrested, he filed suit, arguing that his payment of the first-class fare entitled him to sit in the same first-class accommodations as white passengers. He claimed that under his right of citizenship guaranteed by the Fourteenth Amendment, neither the state of Louisiana nor the railroad could discriminate against him on the basis of color. The Constitution, he claimed, was colorblind.

The U.S. Supreme Court ruled on the case, *Plessy v. Ferguson*, in 1896. In a seven-to-one decision, the Court held that Louisiana's railroad segregation law did not violate the Constitution as long as the railroads or the state provided equal accommodations for black passengers. The decision left unclear what "equal" meant. In the Court's view, "Legislation is powerless to eradicate racial instincts," meaning that segregation of the races was natural and transcended constitutional considerations. The only justice to vote against the decision was John Marshall Harlan, a Kentuckian and former slave owner. In a stinging dissent, he predicted that the decision would result in an all-out assault on black rights. "The destinies of the two races . . . are indissolubly linked together," Harlan declared, "and the interests of both require that the common government of all shall not permit the seeds of race hate to be planted under the sanction of law."

Harlan's was a prophetic dissent. Both northern and southern states enacted new segregation laws in the wake of *Plessy v. Ferguson*. In practice, the separate facilities for black people these laws required, if provided at all, were rarely equal. A sense of futility, time, expense, and physical danger dissuaded black people from challenging the statutes. Protests in the press, appeals to white leaders, and occasional boycotts failed to stem the rising tide. By 1900, segregation by law extended to public conveyances, theaters, hotels, restaurants, parks, and schools.

The segregation statutes came to be known collectively as **Jim Crow laws**, after the blackface stage persona of Thomas Rice, a white northern minstrel-show performer in the 1820s. Reflecting white stereotypes of African Americans, Rice caricatured Crow as a foolish, elderly, lame slave who spoke in an exaggerated dialect.

Economic segregation followed social segregation. Before the Civil War, black men had dominated crafts such as carpentry and masonry. By the 1890s, white men were replacing them in these trades and excluding them from new trades such as plumbing and electrical work. Trade unions, composed primarily of craft workers, began systematically to exclude African Americans. Although the steel and tobacco industries hired black workers, most other manufacturers turned them away. Confined increasingly to low or unskilled positions in railroad construction, the timber industry, and agriculture, black people underwent deskilling—a decline in workforce expertise—after 1890. With lower incomes from unskilled labor, they faced reduced opportunities for better housing and education.

DISFRANCHISEMENT

With economic and social segregation came political isolation. The authority of post-Reconstruction Redeemer governments had rested on their ability to

"JIM CROW" CARS

For Virginia Afro-Americans, as Well as Those of Kentucky, Tennessee and Several Other Southern States.

An Attempt to Extend the Provisions of the Outrageous Law to Street Cars.

The Constitutionality of the Law to be Attacked in the Courts by an Electric Street Car Company and Prominent Virginia Afro-Americans.

Richmond, Va.—Since Sunday week, July 1, the "Jim Crow" car law passed by the Virginia legislature last January, and signed by Gov. Tyler in spite of the remonstrance of nearly every influential colored man in Virginia, has been in force. It requires every railroad and, some attorneys say, every street car company in the state to provide separate cars for the exclusive use of colored people. Negroes are not allowed to ride on the cars intended for the use of the whites, and vice versa; but any Negro forcing himself upon a car for whites, and refusing to leave when requested to do so, may be forcibly ejected

Segregation by law accelerated after the 1896 Plessy v. Ferguson decision, but public conveyances often failed to abide by the "equal" portion of the separate-but-equal ruling. African Americans in the South fought racial separation and exclusion vigorously, as this excerpt from a black newspaper in Cleveland attests. July 14, 1900.

limit and control the black vote. Following the political instability of the late 1880s and the 1890s, however, white leaders determined to disfranchise black people altogether, thereby reinforcing white solidarity and eliminating the need to consider black interests. Obstacles loomed—the Fifteenth Amendment, which guaranteed freedmen the right to vote, and a Republican-dominated Congress—but with a national consensus emerging in support of white supremacy, they proved easy to circumvent.

Rural and urban white elites engineered the disfranchisement campaigns. Support for disfranchisement was especially strong among large landowners in the South's plantation districts, where heavy concentrations of black people threatened their political domination. Urban leaders, especially after the turmoil of the 1890s, looked on disfranchisement as a way to stabilize politics and make elections more predictable.

The movement to reduce or eliminate the black vote in the South began in the 1880s and continued through the early 1900s (see the Overview table, "The March of Disfranchisement across the South, 1889–1908"). Democrats enacted a variety of measures to attain their objectives without violating the letter of the Fifteenth Amendment. They complicated the registration and voting processes. States enacted **poll taxes**, requiring citizens to pay to vote. They adopted the secret ballot, which confused and intimidated illiterate black voters accustomed to using ballots with colors to identify parties. States set literacy and educational qualifications for voting or required prospective registrants to "interpret" a section of the state constitution. To avoid disfranchising poor, illiterate white voters with these measures, states enacted **grandfather clauses**, granting the vote automatically to anyone whose grandfather could have voted prior to 1867 (the year Congressional Reconstruction began). The grandfathers of most black men in the 1890s had been slaves, ineligible to vote.

Tennessee was the first state to pass disfranchising legislation. In 1889, it required the secret ballot and a poll tax in four cities—Nashville, Memphis, Chattanooga, and Knoxville—where African Americans often held a balance of power. A year later, Mississippi amended its constitution to require voters to pass a literacy test and to prove that they "understood" the state constitution. The laws granted the registrar wide latitude in interpreting the accuracy of the registrant's understanding. When a journalist asked an Alabama lawmaker if Jesus Christ could pass his state's "understanding" test, the legislator replied, "That would depend entirely on which way he was going to vote."

Lawmakers sold white citizens on franchise restrictions with the promise that they would apply only to black voters and would scarcely affect white voters.

Overview

The March of Disfranchisement across the South, 1889–1908

Year	State	Strategies
1889	Florida	Poll tax
1889	Tennessee	Poll tax
1890	Mississippi	Poll tax, literacy test, understanding clause
1891	Arkansas	Poll tax
1893, 1901	Alabama	Poll tax, literacy test, grandfather clause
1894, 1895	South Carolina	Poll tax, literacy test, understanding clause
1894, 1902	Virginia	Poll tax, literacy test, understanding clause
1897, 1898	Louisiana	Poll tax, literacy test, grandfather clause
1899, 1900	North Carolina	Poll tax, literacy test, grandfather clause
1902	Texas	Poll tax
1908	Georgia	Poll tax, literacy test, understanding clause, grandfather clause

This promise proved untrue. Alarmed by the Populist uprising, Democratic leaders used disfranchisement to gut dissenting parties. During the 1880s, minority parties in the South consistently polled an average of 40 percent of the statewide vote; by the mid-1890s, that figure had diminished to 30 percent, despite the Populist insurgency. Turnout dropped even more dramatically. In Mississippi, for example, voter turnout in gubernatorial races during the 1880s averaged 51 percent; during the 1890s, it was 21 percent. Black turnout in Mississippi, which averaged 39 percent in the 1880s, plummeted to near zero in the 1890s. Overall turnout, which averaged 64 percent during the 1880s, fell to only 30 percent by 1910.

Black people protested disfranchisement vigorously. When 160 South Carolina delegates gathered to amend the state constitution in 1895, the six black delegates among them mounted a passionate but futile defense of their right to vote. Black delegate W. J. Whipper noted the irony of white people clamoring for supremacy when they already held the vast majority of the state's elected offices. He also pointed out that African Americans voted responsibly where they had a majority and frequently elected white candidates. Robert Smalls, the state's leading black politician, urged delegates not to turn their backs on the state's black population (see "American Views: Robert Smalls Argues against Disfranchisement"). Such pleas fell on deaf ears.

A NATIONAL CONSENSUS ON RACE

How could the South get away with it? How could Southerners openly segregate, disfranchise, and lynch African Americans without a national outcry? Apparently, the majority of Americans in the 1890s subscribed to the notion that black people were inferior to white people and deserved to be treated as second-class citizens. Contemporary depictions of black people show scarcely human stereotypes: black men with bulbous lips and bulging eyes, fat black women wearing turbans and smiling vacuously, and black children contentedly eating watermelon or romping with jungle animals. These images appeared on cereal boxes, in advertisements, in children's books, in newspaper cartoons, and as lawn ornaments. Popular theater of the day featured white men in blackface cavorting in ridiculous fashion and singing songs such as "All Coons Look Alike to Me" and "I Wish My Color Would Fade." Among the widely read books of the era was *The Clansman,* a glorification of the rise of the Ku Klux Klan by Thomas Dixon, a North Carolinian living in New York City and an ardent white supremacist. D.W. Griffith transformed *The Clansman* into an immensely popular motion picture epic under the title *Birth of a Nation.*

Intellectual and political opinion in the North bolstered southern policy. So-called scientific racism purported to establish white superiority and black inferiority on biological grounds. Northern-born pro-

THE AMERICAN JOURNEY
THIRD EDITION

GET THE BOOK THAT **GETS YOUR STUDENTS.**

Overview

The March of Disfranchisement across the South, 1889–1908

Year	State	Strategies
1889	Florida	Poll tax
1889	Tennessee	Poll tax
1890	Mississippi	Poll tax, literacy test, understanding clause
1891	Arkansas	Poll tax
1893, 1901	Alabama	Poll tax, literacy test, grandfather clause
1894, 1895	South Carolina	Poll tax, literacy test, understanding clause
1894, 1902	Virginia	Poll tax, literacy test, understanding clause
1897, 1898	Louisiana	Poll tax, literacy test, grandfather clause
1899, 1900	North Carolina	Poll tax, literacy test, grandfather clause
1902	Texas	Poll tax
1908	Georgia	Poll tax, literacy test, understanding clause, grandfather clause

GET THE BEST PRESENTATION: Overviews and 3-Level Heads

American history can be an intricate story and THE AMERICAN JOURNEY, THIRD EDITION tells it in an engaging, forthright manner. How better to present otherwise complex text material than to organize it with a visually and intellectually stimulating presentation that students find interesting, balanced, and structured to fit their learning needs?

■ **Overview Boxes.** These tables are placed liberally throughout the text to highlight and visually summarize important topics within a chapter, making otherwise complex issues easier to digest. Overviews are consistently students' favorite learning tools in the text.

In this example on page 550 regarding Disfranchisement, the authors help students clarify the measures some Southern states implemented to limit the right to vote to a select audience in order to maintain political control.

■ **3-Level Heads.** On page 552 you will notice that in the Third Edition, the already highly accessible narrative of the text is made even easier for students to read by breaking each chapter into 3 levels of heads. See *"An urban middle class."*

Other examples can be found on pages 59, 178, 226, 489, 521, 699, 731, and 849.

Take a moment to look through the Overviews and 3-Level Heads in **THE AMERICAN JOURNEY**, and notice how these features make the text easy to follow and enjoyable to read. Get Goldfield—and get your students the best presentation.

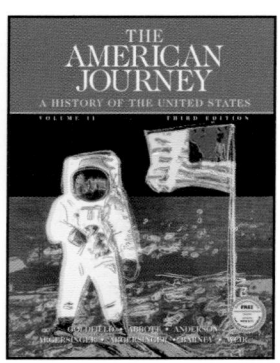

GET THE BOOK THAT GETS YOUR STUDENTS.

The authors of THE AMERICAN JOURNEY, THIRD EDITION **take educating students very seriously.** Every aspect of this new edition is geared towards providing the most important scholarship, as well as the best tools to ensure your students have a positive experience with our textbook, regardless of their individual learning style.

In addition, Prentice Hall believes in providing you with the most flexibility and your students with the most value for their investment. Therefore, we are offering THE AMERICAN JOURNEY, THIRD EDITION in a variety of options to serve your teaching needs, plus a selection of value packages designed to satisfy your students' budget concerns. In every way, THE AMERICAN JOURNEY is the book that gets your students.

GET THE BEST TEXT

- **The Best Pedagogy: Student Tool Kit** (refer to tab 1 in this text)
- **The Best Drama:** *Voices from the American Journey* (refer to tab 2 in this text)
- **The Best Maps:** *Map Explorations* (refer to tab 3 in this text)
- **The Best Presentation: Overviews and 3-Level Heads** (refer to tab 4 in this text)
- **The Best Relevance:** *From Then To Now* (refer to tab 5 in this text)
- **The Best Documents:** *American Views* (refer to tab 6 in this text)

GET THE BEST OPTIONS

THE AMERICAN JOURNEY: A HISTORY OF THE UNITED STATES, THIRD EDITION is available in the following formats, all of which include the FREE, exclusive **U.S. History Documents CD-ROM** from Prentice Hall:

- *Combined Edition—includes Chapters 1-31: 0-13-182553-4*
- *Volume 1—includes Chapters 1-15: 0-13-182552-6*
- *Volume 2—includes Chapters 16-31: 0-13-182550-X*

THE AMERICAN JOURNEY is also available in a convenient Brief Edition.

GET THE BEST PACKAGES

Take advantage of these SPECIAL VALUE PACKAGES available with new copies of THE AMERICAN JOURNEY, THIRD EDITION by Goldfield, et al. Get your students these great savings when your bookstore uses the corresponding package ISBNs below:

- **Combined Edition:**
  —*with FREE Study Guide/Practice Test: 0-13-130271-X*
  —*with FREE Common Sense by Thomas Paine AND The Jungle by Upton Sinclair: 0-13-130272-8*

- **Volume I:**
  —*with FREE Study Guide/Practice Test: 0-13-130273-6*
  —*with FREE Common Sense by Thomas Paine: 0-13-130274-4*

- **Volume II:**
  —*with FREE Study Guide/Practice Test: 0-13-130275-2*
  —*with FREE The Jungle by Upton Sinclair: 0-13-130276-0*

Additional FREE Value Packages are available. For details, please contact your local Prentice Hall sales representative.

PRENTICE HALL HISTORY
Connecting the past with the future
www.prenhall.com/history

PULLMAN Compartment Cars
CINCINNATI, INDIANAPOLIS, CHICAGO.

THROUGH TRAINS
CINCINNATI, DAYTON, TOLEDO, DETROIT.

INTERIOR OF DINING CARS ON THE CINCINNATI, HAMILTON & DAYTON R.R.

Racial stereotypes permeated American popular culture by the turn of the twentieth century. Images like this advertisement for Pullman railroad cars, which depicts a deferential black porter attending to white passengers, reinforced racist beliefs that black people belonged in servile roles. Immersed in such images, white people assumed they depicted the natural order of things.

fessional historians reinterpreted the Civil War and Reconstruction in the white South's favor. Historian William A. Dunning, the generation's leading authority on Reconstruction, wrote in 1901 that the North's "views as to the political capacity of the blacks had been irrational." Respected journals openly supported disfranchisement and segregation. The progressive journal *Outlook* hailed disfranchisement because it made it "impossible in the future for ignorant, shiftless, and corrupt negroes to misrepresent their race in political action." Harvard's Charles Francis Adams, Jr., chided colleagues who disregarded the "fundamental, scientific facts" that, he claimed, demonstrated black inferiority. The *New York Times*, summarizing this national consensus in 1903, noted that "practically the whole country" supported the "southern solution" to the race issue, because "there was no other possible settlement."

These views permeated Congress, which made no effort to block the institutionalization of white supremacy in the South after 1890, and the courts, which upheld discriminatory legislation. As a delegate at the Alabama disfranchisement convention of 1901 noted, "The race problem is no longer confined to the States of the South, [and] we have the sympathy instead of the hostility of the North."

By the mid-1890s, Republicans were so entrenched in the North and West that they did not need southern votes to win presidential elections or to control Congress. Besides, business-oriented Republicans found common ground with conservative southern Democrats on fiscal policy and foreign affairs. Their attention, diverted by economic problems and labor unrest, no longer rested on the South. The emerging consensus on the meaning of the Civil War and Reconstruction, part of the national reconciliation discussed in the previous chapter, also worked against a federal response to the elimination of black rights in the South.

As the white consensus on race emerged, the status of African Americans slipped in the North as well as the South. Although no northern states threatened to deny black citizens the right to vote, they did increase segregation. The booming industries of the North generally did not hire black workers. Antidiscrimination laws on the books since the Civil War went unenforced. In 1904, 1906, and 1908, race riots erupted in Springfield, Ohio; Greensburg, Indiana; and Springfield, Illinois; matching similar disturbances in Wilmington, North Carolina, and Atlanta, Georgia.

RESPONSE OF THE BLACK COMMUNITY

American democracy had, it seemed, hung out a "whites only" sign. How could African Americans respond to the growing political, social, and economic restrictions on their lives? Given white America's hostility, protest proved ineffective, even dangerous. African Americans organized more than a dozen boycotts of streetcar systems in the urban South between 1896 and 1908 in an effort to desegregate them, but not one succeeded. The Afro-American Council, formed in 1890 to protest the deteriorating conditions of black life, accomplished little and disbanded in 1908. W.E.B. Du Bois organized an annual Conference on Negro Problems at Atlanta University beginning in 1896, but it produced no effective plan of action.

A few black people chose to leave the South. In 1879, Benjamin "Pap" Singleton, a Nashville real estate agent, led several thousand black migrants to Kansas. Henry McNeal Turner of Georgia, an African

AMERICAN VIEWS

Robert Smalls Argues against Disfranchisement

Born in Beaufort, South Carolina, in 1839, Robert Smalls served as a slave pilot in Charleston Harbor. In 1862, he emancipated himself, with his family and friends, when he delivered a Confederate steamer, *The Planter*, to a Union fleet blockading the harbor. He entered politics in 1864 as a delegate from his state to the Republican National Convention. He helped write South Carolina's Reconstruction constitution, which, among its provisions, guaranteed the right of former slaves to vote and hold office. Smalls won election to the state house of representatives in 1869, the state senate in 1871, and the U.S. House of Representatives in 1875. With opportunities for African Americans to hold public office declining following Reconstruction, Smalls secured appointment as collector of the Port of Beaufort, a federal post he occupied until his death in 1915. In the speech excerpted here—delivered to the South Carolina Constitutional Convention of 1895—he bitterly assails the state's plan to disfranchise black voters.

- From the white perspective, what is Smalls's most telling argument against the disfranchisement and the planned strategies to implement it?
- How does Smalls depict the black citizens of South Carolina?
- Why were white political leaders unmoved by Smalls's plea?

Mr. President, this convention has been called for no other purpose than the disfranchisement of the negro . . . .

The negroes are paying taxes in the south on $263,000,000 worth of property. In South Carolina, according to the census, the negroes pay tax on $12,500,000 worth of property. That was in 1890. You voted down without discussion . . . a proposition for a simple property and education qualification [for

---

Methodist Episcopal (AME) bishop, promoted migration to Liberia, but only a few hundred made the trip in the late 1870s, Turner not included, and most of those returned disappointed. Most black people who moved in the 1890s stayed within the South, settling in places like Mississippi, Louisiana, and Texas, where they could find work with timber companies or farming new lands that had opened to cotton and rice cultivation.

An urban middle class.   More commonly, black people withdrew to develop their own rich community life within the restricted confines white society permitted them. Particularly in the cities of the South, they could live relatively free of white surveillance and even white contact. In 1890, fully 70 per-

cent of black city dwellers lived in the South; and between 1860 and 1900, the proportion of black people in the cities of the South rose from one in six to more than one in three. The institutions, businesses, and families that black people began painstakingly building during Reconstruction continued to grow, and in some cases flourish, after 1877.

By the 1880s, a new black middle class had emerged in the South. Urban-based, professional, business-oriented, and serving a primarily black clientele, its members fashioned an interconnected web of churches, fraternal and self-help organizations, families, and businesses. Black Baptists, AME, and AME Zion churches led reform efforts in the black community, seeking to eliminate drinking, prostitution, and other vices in black neighborhoods.

voting]. What do you want? . . . In behalf of the 600,000 negroes in the State and the 132,000 negro voters all that I demand is that a fair and honest election law be passed. We care not what the qualifications imposed are, all that we ask is that they be fair and honest, and honorable, and with these provisos we will stand or fall by it. You have 102,000 white men over 21 years of age, 13,000 of these cannot read nor write. You dare not disfranchise them, and you know that the man who proposes it will never be elected to another office in the State of South Carolina . . . . Fifty-eight thousand negroes cannot read nor write. This leaves a majority of 14,000 white men who can read and write over the same class of negroes in this State. We are willing to accept a scheme that provides that no man who cannot read nor write can vote, if you dare pass it. How can you expect an ordinary man to "understand and explain" any section of the Constitution, to correspond to the interpretation put upon it by the manager of election, when by a very recent decision of the supreme court, composed of the most learned men in State, two of them put one construction upon a section, and the other justice put an entirely different construction upon it. To embody

such a provision in the election law would be to mean that every white man would interpret it aright and every negro would interpret it wrong . . . . Some morning you may wake up to find that the bone and sinew of your country is gone. The negro is needed in the cotton fields and in the low country rice fields, and if you impose too hard conditions upon the negro in this State there will be nothing else for him to do but to leave. What then will you do about your phosphate works? No one but a negro can work them; the mines that pay the interest on your State debt. I tell you the negro is the bone and sinew of your country and you cannot do without him. I do not believe you want to get rid of the negro, else why did you impose a high tax on immigration agents who might come here to get him to leave?

Now, Mr. President we should not talk one thing and mean another. We should not deceive ourselves. Let us make a Constitution that is fair, honest and just. Let us make a Constitution for all the people, one we will be proud of and our children will receive with delight.

———————————

Source: *The Columbia State*, October 27, 1895.

African American fraternal and self-help groups, led by middle-class black people, functioned as surrogate welfare organizations for the poor. Some groups, such as the Colored Masons and the Colored Odd Fellows, paralleled white organizations. Black membership rates usually exceeded those in the white community. More than 50 percent of Nashville's black men, for example, belonged to various fraternal associations in the city. Fraternal orders also served as the seedbed for such business ventures as the North Carolina Mutual Life Insurance Company, founded in Durham in 1898. Within two decades, North Carolina Mutual became the largest black-owned business in the nation and helped transform Durham into the "capital of the black middle class." Durham's thriving black business district included several black-owned insurance firms, banks, and a textile mill. Most southern cities boasted active black business districts by the 1890s.

Nashville's J.C. Napier typified the activism of the African American urban middle class in the New South era. He belonged to two of the city's prominent black churches, was active in Republican politics, played an important role in several temperance and fraternal societies, served as president of the local black YMCA chapter, and, as an attorney, helped his fellow African Americans with numerous legal matters. Before disfranchisement in the 1890s, Napier used his leverage to secure the appointment of black teachers for black schools and of black applicants to the police force and fire department.

The offices of the North Carolina Mutual Life Insurance Company, around 1900. Founded by John Merrick, C.C. Spaulding, and Dr. A.M. Moore (all of whom appear in this picture), this Durham-based insurance company became one of the most successful black enterprises in the country.

The African American middle class worked especially hard to improve black education (see Figure 17–3). Declining black political power encouraged white leaders to reduce funding for black public education. Black students in cities had only makeshift facilities; those in the countryside had almost no facilities. By the early 1900s, the student–teacher ratio in Nashville's segregated school system was thirty-three to one for white schools but seventy-one to one for black schools. To improve these conditions, black middle-class leaders solicited educational funds from northern philanthropic organizations.

Black women's roles. Black women played an increasingly active and prominent role in African-American communities after 1877, especially in cities. The experience of Ida B. Wells illustrates this trend. When she moved to Memphis from Mississippi in 1884, she entered an environment that, despite her race and gender, offered her opportunities for intellectual growth and a professional career. In December 1886, for example, she attended a lecture at an interracial Knights of Labor meeting (see Chapter 18). Earlier that year, she witnessed a religious revival conducted by the nation's leading evangelist, Dwight Moody. The following year, Wells began her journal-

ism career and soon purchased a one-third interest in a local black newspaper.

Black women's clubs evolved to address the new era in race relations. Most African American women in southern cities worked as domestics or laundresses. Black women's clubs supported day-care facilities for working mothers and settlement houses in poor black neighborhoods modeled after those in northern cities. Atlanta's Neighborhood Union, founded by Lugenia Burns Hope in 1908, provided playgrounds and a health center and secured a grant from a New York foundation to improve black education in the city. Black women's clubs also established homes for single black working women to protect them from sexual exploitation, and they worked for woman suffrage "to reckon with men who place no value on her [black woman's] virtue," as Nannie H. Burroughs of the National Association of Colored Women argued at the turn of the century.

After disfranchisement, middle-class black women assumed an even more pivotal role in the black community. They often used their relations with prominent white women and organizations such as the WCTU and the Young Womens Christian Association (YWCA) to press for public commitments to improve the health and education of African Americans. Absent political pressure from black men, as well as the danger of African American males asserting themselves in the tense racial climate after 1890, black women became critical spokespersons for their race.

The extension of black club work into rural areas of the South, where the majority of the African-American population lived, to educate families about hygiene, nutrition, and child care, anticipated similar efforts among white women after 1900. But unlike their white counterparts, these middle-class black women worked with limited resources in a context of simmering racial hostility and political and economic impotence. In response, they nurtured a self-help strategy to improve the conditions of the people they sought to help. One of the most prominent African American leaders of the late nineteenth and early twentieth centuries, Booker T. Washington, adopted a similar approach to racial uplift.

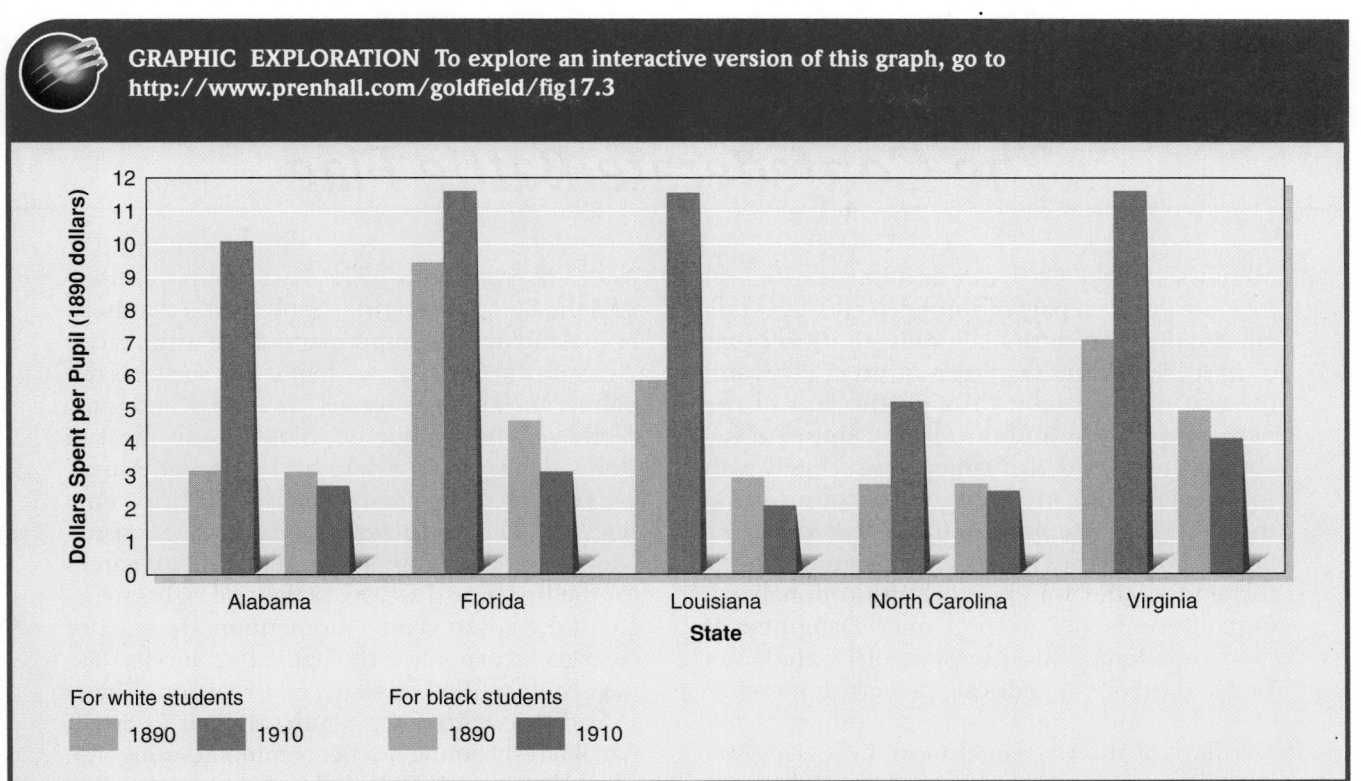

GRAPHIC EXPLORATION To explore an interactive version of this graph, go to
http://www.prenhall.com/goldfield/fig17.3

FIGURE 17-3   **Disfranchisement and Educational Spending in the South, 1890-1910**
By barring black people from the political process, franchise restrictions limited their access to government services. Educational expenditures—which increased for white people but decreased for black people following disfranchisement—provide one measure of the result.

Data Source: Robert A. Margo, "Disfranchisement, School Finance, and the Economics of Segregated Schools in the United States South, 1890-1910," Ph.D. diss., Harvard University, 1982.

Booker T. Washington's accommodation.

Born a slave in Virginia in 1856, Washington and his family worked in the salt and coal mines of West Virginia after the Civil War. Ambitious and flushed with the postwar enthusiasm for advancement that gripped freedmen, he enrolled in Hampton Normal and Agricultural Institute, the premier black educational institution in the South at that time. Washington worked his way through Hampton, graduated, taught for a time, and then, in 1881, founded the Tuskegee Institute for black students in rural Alabama. Washington thought that his students would be best served if they learned a trade and workplace discipline. By learning industrial skills, he maintained, black people could secure self-respect and economic independence. As a result, Tuskegee emphasized vocational training over the liberal arts.

Washington argued that African Americans should accommodate themselves to segregation and disfranchisement until they could prove their economic worth to American society. In exchange for this accommodation, however, white people should help provide black people with the education and job training they would need to gain their independence. Washington articulated this position, known as the **Atlanta Compromise**, in a speech at the Atlanta Cotton States and International Exposition in 1895. Despite his conciliatory public stance, Washington secretly helped to finance legal challenges to segregation and disfranchisement. The social and economic realities of the South, meanwhile, frustrated his educational mission. Increasingly, black people were shut out of the kinds of jobs for which Washington hoped to train them. Facing a depressed rural economy and growing racial violence, they had little prospect of advancement.

W.E.B. Du Bois attacks the Atlanta Compromise.

Another prominent African American leader, W.E.B. Du Bois, challenged Washington's acceptance of black social inequality. Born in Massachusetts in 1868, Du Bois was the first African American to earn a doctorate at Harvard. Du Bois promoted self-help, education, and black pride. A gifted teacher and writer, he taught at Atlanta University and wrote eighteen books

FROM THEN TO NOW

The Confederate Battle Flag

Memories of the Civil War and Reconstruction formed a crucial part of southern civic and religious culture from the late nineteenth century onward. Southerners perceived themselves and the rest of the nation through the lens of the heroic Lost Cause and the alleged abuses of Reconstruction, and the symbols associated with those events took on the status of icons. During the 1890s, the memory industry that white political and religious leaders had promoted since the end of the war became institutionalized. Organizations such as the United Daughters of the Confederacy and the Sons of Confederate Veterans strove to educate a new generation of white Southerners on the meanings of the sacrifices of the war generation, bolstering the imposition of white supremacy through racial segregation and disfranchisement.

The Confederate battle flag emerged from this process as an icon of the Lost Cause and a symbol of white supremacy. Alabama, for example, redesigned its state flag in the 1890s to resemble more closely the battle flag. Its red St.

Andrews cross on a white background symbolized the blood spilled in defense of the Southern homeland and the supremacy of the white race.

Still, the Confederate battle flag itself was displayed mostly at veterans' reunions and only rarely at other public occasions—until the late 1940s, that is, when civil rights for African Americans emerged as a national issue for the first time since the Reconstruction era. In 1948, Mississippians waved the flag at Ole Miss football games for the first time. In 1956, as the civil rights struggle in the South gained momentum, the state of Georgia incorporated the battle flag into its state flag. And, in 1962, as sit-ins and Freedom Riders spread throughout the South, officials in South Carolina—claiming to be commemorating the Civil War centennial—hoisted the battle flag above the State House in Columbia.

Long after the centennial celebration concluded, the battle flag continued to fly in Columbia. This official display became a focus of heated controversy. Proponents argued that the battle flag represents heritage, not hate. Opponents de-

---

on various aspects of black life in America. In *The Souls of Black Folk*, published in 1903, he described the strengths of black culture and attacked Washington's Atlanta Compromise. Du Bois was a cofounder, in 1910, of the **National Association for the Advancement of Colored People (NAACP)**, an interracial organization dedicated to restoring African American political and social rights.

Despite their differences, which reflected their divergent backgrounds, Washington and Du Bois agreed on many issues. Both had reservations about allowing illiterate black people to vote, and both believed that black success in the South required some white assistance. As Du Bois wrote in *The Souls of Black Folk*, "Any movement for the elevation of the Southern Negro needs the cooperation, the sympathy, and the support of the best white people in

order to succeed." But it became apparent to Du Bois that "the best white people" did not care to elevate black Southerners. In 1906, after a bloody race riot in Atlanta, Du Bois left the South, a decision millions of black Southerners would make over the next two decades.

A curtain had descended between black and white, North and South, on the issue of race. Northerners did not care to look behind that curtain to acknowledge the injustice of southern treatment of black people. As long as it provided the raw materials for the North's new urban industrial economy and maintained the peace, the South could count on the rest of the country not to interfere in its solution to race relations. Indeed, to the extent that most white Americans concerned themselves with race, they agreed with the southern solution.

nounced it as a symbol of white supremacy. In the mid-1990s, South Carolina's Republican Governor David Beasley, seeking to defuse the issue, proposed removing the flag from atop the Capitol and installing it at a nearby history museum. The resulting firestorm of protest from some of the Governor's white constituents forced him to reverse himself, however, and contributed to his defeat in his bid for reelection.

The flag controversy erupted again in 1999, when South Carolina's state Democratic Party chairman urged voters to return a Democratic legislature that would, once and for all, remove the flag from the State Capitol. The angry response from both Republicans and some Democrats forced the new Democratic governor to quickly distance himself from the proposal. Then, in July 1999, the National Association for the Advancement of Colored People (NAACP) announced a national boycott of South Carolina, beginning in January 2000. Facing the loss of convention and tourist revenues, business groups pleaded with lawmakers to lower the flag, which they did in July 2000. But the flag's new home, near a monument on the Capitol grounds, is even more visible to the public, prompting the continuation of the NAACP boycott.

In 2001, Mississippians voted overwhelmingly to keep their state flag which includes the battle flag. That same year, an interracial group of Georgia legislators agreed to remove the battle flag from the state banner; the new design includes the Confederate emblem, but only as part of a ribbon that includes all of the flags that have flown over Georgia through its history. Legislators did not submit the new design to a referendum, though in 2003, Georgia's recently-elected Republican Governor Sonny Perdue reversed that decision.

When people in other parts of the country sometimes remark that white Southerners are still fighting the Civil War, it is controversies like the one over the battle flag that they have in mind. But the controversy is less about the past than it is about the way we use history to shape our understanding of the society we live in and our vision of its future. At issue is not just history, but whose history. In that sense the flag controversy, as much as it picks at wounds more than a century old, can at least generate positive dialogue. Even so, in the interests of reconciliation, it may be time for Southerners to follow Robert E. Lee's final order to his men and "Furl the flag, boys."

CONCLUSION

In many respects, the South was more like the rest of the nation in 1900 than at any other time since 1860. Southern cities hummed with activity and industries from textiles to steel dotted the southern interior. Young men and women migrated to southern cities to pursue opportunities unavailable to their parents. Advances in the production and marketing of cigarettes and soft drinks would soon make southern entrepreneurs and their products household names. Southerners ordered fashions from Sears, Roebuck catalogs and enjoyed electric lights, electric trolleys, and indoor plumbing as much as other urban Americans.

Americans idealized the South—not the urban industrial South, but a mythical South of rural grace and hospitality. National magazines and publishers rushed to print stories about this land of moonlight and magnolias, offering it as a counterpoint to the crowded, immigrant-infested, factory-fouled, money-grubbing North. It was this fantasy South that white people in both the North and the South imagined as they came to a common view on race and reconciled their differences. Northern journalists offered admiring portraits of such southern heroes as Robert E. Lee, of whom one declared in 1906, "[T]he nation has a hero to place beside her greatest." The Republican-dominated Congress agreed to care for the graves of the Confederate dead and ordered the return to the South of captured Confederate flags.

White Southerners cultivated national reconciliation but remained fiercely dedicated to preserving the peculiarities of their region: a one-party political

Booker T. Washington (left) and W.E.B. Du Bois (right). The differences between these two prominent black leaders reflected in part the differences between the North and the South in the late nineteenth and early twentieth centuries. The northern-born Du Bois challenged segregation and pinned his hopes for improving the condition of African Americans on a talented elite. The southern-born Washington counseled acquiescence to segregation, maintaining that black people could ultimately gain the acceptance of white society through self-improvement and hard work.

system, disfranchisement, and segregation by law. The region's urban and industrial growth, impressive from the vantage of 1865, paled before that of the North. The South remained a colonial economy characterized more by deep rural poverty than urban prosperity.

How one viewed the New South depended on one's vantage point. White Northerners accepted at face value the picture Southerners painted for them of a chastened and prosperous, yet still attractive, region. Middle-class white people in the urban South enjoyed the benefits of a national economy and a secure social position. Middle-class white women enjoyed increased influence in the public realm, but not to the extent of their northern sisters. And the institutionalization of white supremacy gave even poor white farmers and factory workers a place in the social hierarchy a rung or two above the bottom.

For black people, the New South proved a crueler ruse than Reconstruction. No one now stepped forward to support their cause and stem the erosion of their economic independence, political freedom, and civil rights. Yet they did not give up the American dream, nor did they give up the South for the most part. They built communities and worked as best they could to challenge restrictions on their freedom.

The New South was thus both American and southern. It shared with the rest of the country a period of rapid urban and industrial growth. But the legacy of war and slavery still lay heavily on the South, manifesting itself in rural poverty, segregation, and black disfranchisement. The burdens of this legacy would limit the attainments of both black and white Southerners for another half-century, until Americans finally rejected racial inequality as an affront to their national ideals.

REVIEW QUESTIONS

1. In what ways did the growing activism of white middle-class women, the increasing assertiveness of young urban black people, and the persistence of the agricultural depression affect the politics of the South in the late 1880s and early 1890s?

2. We associate segregation and disfranchisement with reactionary political and social views. Yet many white people who promoted both seriously believed them to be reforms. How could white people hold such a view?

3. What strategies did black Southerners employ in response to the narrowing of economic and political opportunities in the New South?

4. What accounted for Anna J. Cooper's optimism for African American women in the South at a time when southern whites began an extensive legal and physical assault on black civil rights?

KEY TERMS

Agricultural Wheel (p. 540)

Atlanta Compromise (p. 555)

Colored Farmer's Alliance (p. 541)

Disenfranchisement (p. 547)

Grandfather clause (p. 549)

Grange (p. 540)

Jim Crow laws (p. 548)

Lynching (p. 547)

National Association for the Advancement of Colored People (NAACP) (p. 556)

Plessy v. Ferguson (p. 548)

Poll taxes (p. 549)

Populist party (p. 542)

Segregation (p. 547)

Solid South (p. 531)

Southern Farmers' Alliance (p. 540)

Subtreasuray Plan (p. 541)

Women's Christian Temperance Union (WCTU) (p. 543)

RECOMMENDED READING

Ayers, Edward L. *The Promise of the New South: Life After Reconstruction* (1992). Illuminates how the people of the late-nineteenth-century South accommodated the conflict between the economic and cultural legacies of the slave South and the currents of modernity, such as industrialization and the creation of a national state.

Gaston, Paul M. *The New South Creed: A Study in Southern Mythmaking* (1970). Provides an important assessment of how New South booster rhetoric matched up against the economic reality; especially good at examining how New South spokesmen turned images of the Old South and other southern traditions to the ends of urban and industrial development.

Rabinowitz, Howard N. *Race Relations in the Urban South, 1865–1890* (1978). A fine survey of how African Americans built communities in the urban South despite the worsening racial situation after Reconstruction.

Williamson, Joel. *The Crucible of Race: Black–White Relations in the American South since Emancipation* (1984). An innovative work that details the racial attitudes of white Southerners and reveals how elites particularly used race to further political and social objectives.

Woodward, C. Vann. *Origins of the New South, 1877–1913* (1951). A classic interpretation of the New South era that stresses the discontinuities between Old South and New.

ADDITIONAL SOURCES

The Newness of the New South

Billings, Dwight B. Jr. *Planters and the Making of a "New South"* (1979).

Burton, Orville Vernon. *In My Father's House Are Many Mansions: Family and Community in Edgefield County, South Carolina* (1985).

Carlton, David L. *Mill and Town in South Carolina, 1880–1920* (1980).

Clark, Thomas D. *Pills, Petticoats, and Plows: The Southern Country Store* (1944).

Davis, Harold E. *Henry Grady's New South: Atlanta, a Brave and Beautiful City* (1990).

Doyle, Don H. *New Men, New Cities, New South: Atlanta, Nashville, Charleston, Mobile, 1860–1910* (1990).

Durden, Robert F. *The Dukes of Durham, 1865–1929* (1975).

Eller, Ronald D. *Miners, Millhands, and Mountaineers: Industrialization of the Appalachian South, 1880–1920* (1982).

Hall, Jacqueline Dowd, et al. *Like a Family: The Making of a Southern Cotton Mill World* (1987).

Hearden, Patrick J. *Independence and Empire: The New South's Cotton Mill Campaign, 1865–1901* (1982).

Horwitz, Tony, *Confederates in the Attic: Dispatches from the Unfinished Civil War* (1998).

Lewis, W. David, *Sloss Furnaces and the Rise of the Birmingham District: An Industrial Epic* (1994).

Russell, James M. *Atlanta, 1847–1890: City Building in the Old South and the New* (1988).

Tilley, Nannie M. *The R. J. Reynolds Tobacco Company* (1985).

Wright, Gavin, *Old South, New South: Revolutions in the Southern Economy since the Civil War* (1986).

The Southern Agrarian Revolt

Barnes, Donna. *Farmers in Rebellion: The Rise and Fall of the Southern Farmers' Alliance and People's Party in Texas* (1987).

Barr, Alwyn. *Reconstruction to Reform: Texas Politics, 1876–1906* (1971).

Daniel, Pete. *Breaking the Land: The Transformation of Cotton, Tobacco and Rice Cultures since 1880* (1985).

Fite, Gilbert. *Cotton Fields No More: Southern Agriculture, 1865–1890* (1984).

Goodwyn, Lawrence. *Democratic Promise: The Populist Moment in America* (1976).

Hahn, Steven. *The Roots of Southern Populism: The Transformation of the Georgia Upcountry, 1850–1890* (1983).

McMath, Robert Jr. *The Populist Vanguard: A History of the Southern Farmers' Alliance* (1975).

Minnix, Kathleen. *Laughter in the Amen Corner: The Life of Evangelist Sam Jones* (1993).

Newby, I. A. *Plain Folk in the New South: Social Change and Cultural Persistence, 1880–1915* (1989).

Ownby, Ted. *Subduing Satan: Religion, Recreation, and Manhood in the Rural South, 1865–1920* (1990).

Ransom, Roger, and Richard Sutch. *One Kind of Freedom: The Economic Consequences of Emancipation* (1977).

Wallenstein, Peter. *From Slave South to New South: Public Policy in Nineteenth-Century Georgia* (1987).

Webb, Samuel L. *Two-Party Politics in the One-Party South: Alabama's Hill Country, 1874–1920* (1997).

Wiener, Jonathan. *Social Origins of the New South: Alabama, 1860–1885* (1978).

Woodman, Harold D. *King Cotton and His Retainers: Financing and Marketing the Cotton Crop of the South, 1800–1925* (1968).

Woodward, C. Vann. *Tom Watson: Agrarian Rebel* (1938).

Women in the New South

Bernhard, Virginia, et al., eds. *Southern Women: Histories and Identities* (1992).

Enstam, Elizabeth York. *Women and the Creation of Urban Life: Dallas, Texas, 1843–1920* (1998).

Friedman, Jean E. *The Enclosed Garden: Women and Community in the Evangelical South, 1830–1900* (1985).

Gilmore, Glenda Elizabeth. *Gender and Jim Crow: Women and Politics of White Supremacy in North Carolina, 1896–1920* (1996).

Green, Elna C. *Southern Strategies: Southern Women and the Woman Suffrage Question* (1997).

Higginbotham, Evelyn Brooks. *Righteous Discontent: The Women's Movement in the Black Baptist Church, 1880–1920* (1993).

Hunter, Tera W. *To 'Joy My Freedom: Southern Black Women's Lives and Labors after the Civil War* (1997).

Lumpkin, Katharine DuPre. *The Making of a Southerner* (1947).

McArthur, Judith N. *Creating the New Woman: The Rise of Southern Women's Progressive Culture in Texas, 1893–1918* (1998).

McDowell, John P. *The Social Gospel in the South: The Woman's Home Mission Movement in the Methodist Episcopal Church, South, 1886–1939* (1982).

Scott, Anne Firor. *The Southern Lady: From Pedestal to Politics, 1830–1930* (1970).

Sims, Anastatia, *The Power of Femininity in the New South: Women's Organizations and Politics in North Carolina, 1880–1930* (1997).

Terrell, Mary Church, *A Colored Woman in a White World* (1980).

Thomas, Mary Martha. *The New Woman in Alabama: Social Reforms and Suffrage, 1890–1920* (1992).

Turner, Elizabeth Hayes. *Women, Culture, and Community: Religion and Reform in Galveston, 1880–1920* (1997).

Wheeler, Marjorie Spruill. *New Women of the New South: The Leaders of the Woman Suffrage Movement in the Southern States* (1993).

Settling the Race Issue

Ayers, Edward L. *Vengeance and Justice: Crime and Punishment in the Nineteenth-Century American South* (1984).

Beatty, Bess. *A Revolution Gone Backwards: The Black Response to National Politics, 1876–1896* (1987).

Brundage, W. Fitzhugh. *Lynching in the New South: Georgia and Virginia, 1880–1930* (1993).

Cell, John W. *The Highest Stage of White Supremacy: The Origins of Segregation in South Africa and the American South* (1982).

Clayton, Bruce. *The Savage Ideal: Intolerance and Intellectual Leadership in the South, 1890–1914* (1972).

Dailey, Jane. *Before Jim Crow: The Politics of Race in Postemancipation Virginia* (2000).

Greenwood, Janette Thomas. *Bittersweet Legacy: The Black and White "Better Classes" in Charlotte, 1850–1910* (1994).

Hale, Grace Elizabeth. *Making Whiteness: The Culture of Segregation in the South, 1890–1940* (1998).

Harlan, Louis R. *Booker T. Washington: The Making of a Black Leader, 1856–1901* (1972).

Kantrowitz, Stephen. *Ben Tillman and the Reconstruction of White Supremacy* (2000).

Kenzer, Robert C. *Enterprising Southerners: Black Economic Success in North Carolina, 1865–1915* (1997).

Kousser, J. Morgan, *The Shaping of Southern Politics: Suffrage Restriction and the Establishment of the One-Party South, 1880–1910* (1974).

Letwin, Daniel. *The Challenge of Interracial Unionism: Alabama Coal Miners, 1878–1921* (1998).

Litwack, Leon F. *Trouble in Mind: Black Southerners in the Age of Jim Crow* (1998).

Lofgren, Charles A. *The Plessy Case: A Legal-Historical Interpretation* (1987).

Meier, August. *Negro Thought in America, 1880–1915: Racial Ideologies in the Age of Booker T. Washington* (1963).

Prather, H. Leon. *We Have Taken a City: The Wilmington Racial Massacre and Coup of 1898* (1989).

Silber, Nina. *The Romance of Reunion: Northerners and the South* (1993).

Tolnay, Stewart E. and E. M. Beck. *A Festival of Violence: An Analysis of Southern Lynchings, 1882–1930* (1995).

Weare, Walter B. *Black Business in the New South: A Social History of the North Carolina Mutual Life Insurance Company* (1973).

Woodward, C. Vann. *The Strange Career of Jim Crow* (1955).

WHERE TO LEARN MORE

- **Levine Museum of the New South, Charlotte, North Carolina.** The museum has exhibits on various New South themes and a permanent exhibit on the history of Charlotte and the Carolina Piedmont. www.museumofthenewsouth.org.

- **Atlanta History Center, Atlanta, Georgia.** The major exhibit, "Metropolitan Frontiers, 1835–2000," includes a strong segment on the New

South era, including the development of separate black and white economies in Atlanta. The Herndon home, also on the grounds of the center, has an exhibit on black upper-class life in Atlanta from 1880 to 1930. www.atlhist.org/exhibitions/html/metropolitan_frontiers.htm.

- **Sloss Furnaces National Historical Landmark, Birmingham, Alabama.** The site recalls the time when Birmingham challenged Pittsburgh as the nation's primary steel-producing center. www.slossfurnaces.com.

 Please refer to the document CD-ROM for primary sources related to this chapter.

➜ Photographer Lewis Hine's portrait of a young Jewish woman arriving from Russia at Ellis Island 1905. Like hundreds of thousands of other immigrants who passed through the portals of New York harbor, this young woman's expression carries the hope, fear, and remembrance that touched her fellow wanderers as they embarked on their new life in America.

INDUSTRY, IMMIGRANTS, AND CITIES

1870–1900

18

CHAPTER OUTLINE

New Industry
Inventing Technology: The Electric Age
The Corporation and Its Impact
The Changing Nature of Work
Child Labor
Working Women
Responses to Poverty and Wealth
Workers Organize

New Immigrants
Old-World Backgrounds
The Neighborhood
The Job
Nativism
Roots of the Great Migration

New Cities
Centers and Suburbs
The New Middle Class
A Consumer Society
The Growth of Leisure Activities

Conclusion

We were homeless, houseless, and friendless in a strange place. We had hardly money enough to last us through the voyage for which we had hoped and waited for three long years. We had suffered much that the reunion we longed for might come about; we had prepared ourselves to suffer more in order to bring it about, and had parted with those we loved, with places that were dear to us in spite of what we passed through in them, never again to see them, as we were convinced—all for the same dear end. With strong hopes and high spirits that hid the sad parting, we had started on our long journey. And now we were checked so unexpectedly but surely . . . When my mother had recovered enough to speak, she began to argue with the *gendarme*, telling him our story and begging him to be kind. The children were frightened and all but I cried. I was only wondering what would happen . . . .

Here we had been taken to a lonely place; . . . our things were taken away, our friends separated from us; a man came to inspect us, as if to ascertain our full value; strange-looking people driving us about like dumb animals, helpless and unresisting; children we could not see crying in a way that suggested terrible things; ourselves driven into a little room where a great kettle was boiling on a little stove; our clothes taken off, our bodies rubbed with a slippery substance that might be any bad thing; a shower of warm water let down on us without warning . . . .

We are forced to pick out our clothes from among all the others, with the steam blinding us; we choke, cough, entreat the women to give us time; they persist, "Quick! Quick!—or you'll miss the train!"—Oh, so we really won't be murdered! They are only making us ready for the continuing of our journey, cleaning us of all suspicions of dangerous sickness. Thank God! . . .

Oh, what solemn thoughts I had! How deeply I felt the greatness, the power of the scene! The immeasurable distance from horizon to horizon; . . . the absence of any object besides the one ship; . . . I was conscious only of sea and sky and something I did not understand. And as I listened to its solemn voice, I felt as if I had found a friend, and knew that I loved the ocean.

Mary Antin

Mary Antin, *The Promised Land* (Boston: Houghton Mifflin Company, 1912), chapter VIII.

Mary Antin, a thirteen-year old Jewish girl from Russia, describes her family's perilous journey from the persecution of Jews in tsarist Russia to the ship that sailed from Hamburg, Germany, that would take her to Boston in far-away America. In 1894, Mary and her mother and sisters set out from their village to join her father in Boston.

Millions of European immigrants made similar journeys across the Atlantic (as did Chinese and Japanese immigrants, across the Pacific), a trip fraught with danger, unpredictable detours, occasional heartbreak, the sundering of family ties, and the fear of the unknown. So powerful was the promise of American life for the migrants that they willingly risked these obstacles to come to the United States. Mary wrote this extended letter to her uncle, who remained behind, during the first few months after her arrival in Boston. The letter was both a way of conveying the details of her family's exodus and of maintaining contact with a world and a family she had left behind.

Mary recalls the fear and frustration of being removed from the train at the Russian-German border by Russian police because of improper documents. Once her mother had settled the issue with the help of a local Jewish family, they reboarded the train to Berlin. Outside that city, they were once again removed from the train and, though they did not immediately understand what was happening, German authorities had arranged for a thorough cleansing and health inspection, since a cholera epidemic was raging in Russia. As the excerpt ends, you can sense Mary's exultation of joy and freedom as the ship leaves Hamburg for the open ocean and the place that lay beyond the horizon.

For Mary, America did indeed prove to be *The Promised Land*, as she titled her emigration memoir, published in 1912. At the age of fifteen, she published her first poem in the *Boston Herald* and, after attending Barnard College in New York City, she wrote on immigrant issues, lectured widely, and worked for Theodore Roosevelt's Progressive Party. She fought against immigration restriction legislation and promoted public education as the main channel of upward mobility for immigrants. Though some have viewed her work as a bit too optimistic and perhaps naïve, her own life is a strong testament of how a teenage girl moved from a medieval life in tsarist Russia to a career as a respected writer in the United States.

Mary and her family were part of a major demographic and economic transformation in the United States between 1870 and 1900. Rapid industrial development changed the nature of the work force and the workplace. Large factories staffed by semiskilled laborers displaced the skilled artisans and small shops that had dominated American industry before 1870. Industrial development also accelerated urbanization. Between the Civil War and 1900, the proportion of the nation's population living in cities—swelled by migrants from the countryside and immigrants from Europe and Asia—increased from 20 to 40 percent, a rate of growth twice that of the population as a whole. During the 1880s alone, more than 5 million immigrants came to the United States, twice as many as in any previous decade.

The changes in American life were exhilarating for some, tragic for others. New opportunities opened as old opportunities disappeared. Vast new wealth was created, but poverty increased. New technologies eased life for some but left others untouched. It would be the great dilemma of early-twentieth-century America to reconcile these contradictions and satisfy the American quest for a decent life for all within the new urban industrial order.

Few locations encapsulated this dilemma better than Philadelphia during the Centennial Exposition of 1876, marking the nation's hundredth birthday. More than 8 million people would visit the site over the following six months. There they witnessed the ingenuity of the world's newest industrial power. Thomas Edison explained his new automatic telegraph, and Alexander Graham Bell demonstrated his telephone to the wonder of on-lookers. A giant Corliss steam engine loomed over the entrance to Machinery Hall, dwarfing the other exhibits and providing them with power. "Yes," a visitor concluded, "it is in these things of iron and steel that the national genius most freely speaks."

For many Americans, however, the fanfare of the exposition rang hollow. The country was in the midst of a depression that had begun in 1873 and would not bottom out until 1877. Tens of thousands were out of work, and countless others had lost their savings in bank failures and sour investments. With the typical daily wage a dollar, most Philadelphians could

not afford the exposition's 50-cent admission price. They celebrated instead at "Centennial City," a rag-tag collection of cheap bars, seedy hotels, small restaurants, and circus sideshows hurriedly constructed of wood and tin along a muddy mile-long strip across the street from the exposition's sturdy halls and manicured lawns.

This small area of Philadelphia reflected the promise and failure of late-nineteenth century America, a period often called the **Gilded Age**. The term is taken from the title of a novel by Mark Twain that satirizes the materialistic excesses of his day. It serves as a shorthand description of the shallow worship of wealth—and the veneer of respectability and prosperity covering deep economic and social divisions—that characterized the period.

KEY TOPICS

- The technological and organizational innovations behind the emergence of large industrial corporations

- Changes in the American workforce in the urban-industrial economy and the reaction of organized labor

- The impact of the new immigration and the start of African-American migration to the cities of the North

- The changing physical and social structure of the industrial city

- New patterns of residence and recreation in the consumer society

NEW INDUSTRY

Between 1870 and 1900, the United States transformed itself from an agricultural nation—a nation of farmers, merchants, and artisans—into the world's foremost industrial power, producing more than one-third of the world's manufactured goods. By the early twentieth century, factory workers made up one-fourth of the work force, and agricultural workers had dropped from a half to less than a third (see Figure 18–1). A factory with a few dozen employees would have been judged fair-sized in 1870. By the early twentieth century, many industries employed thousands of workers in a single plant. Some industries—petroleum, steel, and meatpacking, for example—had been unknown before the Civil War.

Although the size of the industrial workforce increased dramatically, the number of firms in a given industry shrank. Mergers, changes in corporate management and the organization of the workforce, and a compliant government left a few companies in con-

trol of vast segments of the American economy. Workers, reformers, and eventually government challenged this concentration of economic power.

INVENTING TECHNOLOGY: THE ELECTRIC AGE

Technology played a major role in transforming factory work and increasing the scale of production. Steam engines, like the giant Corliss engine at the Centennial Exposition and, later, electricity, freed manufacturers from dependence on water power. Factories no longer had to be located by rivers. They could be built anywhere accessible to the transportation system and a concentration of labor. Technology also enabled managers to substitute machines for workers, skewing the balance of power in the workplace toward employers. And it transformed city life, making available a host of new conveniences. By the early twentieth century, electric lights, appliances, ready-made clothing, and store-bought food eased middle-class life. Electric trolleys whisked

Chronology

1869 The Knights of Labor is founded in Philadelphia.

1870 John D. Rockefeller forms the Standard Oil Company.

Congress passes the Naturalization Act barring Asians from citizenship.

1876 The Centennial Exposition opens in Philadelphia.

1877 The Great Uprising railroad strike, the first nationwide work stoppage in the United States, provokes violent clashes between workers and federal troops.

1879 Thomas Edison unveils the electric light bulb.

1880 Founding of the League of American Wheelmen in 1880 helps establish bicycling as one of urban America's favorite recreational activities.

1881 Assassination of Russian Tsar Alexander II begins a series of pogroms that triggers a wave of Russian Jewish immigration to the United States.

1882 Congress passes the Chinese Exclusion Act.

First country club in the United States founded in Brookline, Massachusetts.

1883 National League merges with the American Association and opens baseball to working-class fans.

1886 The Neighborhood Guild, the nation's first settlement house, opens in New York City.

Riot in Chicago's Haymarket Square breaks the Knights of Labor.

American Federation of Labor is formed.

1887 Anti-Catholic American Protective Association is formed.

1888 Wanamaker's department store introduces a "bargain room," and competitors follow suit.

1889 Jane Addams opens Hull House, the nation's most celebrated settlement house, in Chicago.

1890 Jacob A. Riis publishes *How the Other Half Lives*.

1891 African-American Chicago physician Daniel Hale Williams establishes Provident Hospital, the nation's first interracially staffed hospital.

1892 General Electric opens the first corporate research and development division in the United States.

Strike at Andrew Carnegie's Homestead steelworks fails.

1894 Pullman Sleeping Car Company strike fails.

Immigration Restriction League is formed.

1895 American-born Chinese in California form the Native Sons of the Golden State to counter nativism.

1897 George C. Tilyou opens Steeplechase Park on Coney Island in Brooklyn, New York.

1898 Congress passes the Erdman Act to provide for voluntary mediation of railroad labor disputes.

---

clerks, salespeople, bureaucrats, and bankers to new urban and suburban subdivisions. Electric streetlights lit up city streets at night. Amusement parks drew crowds with mechanical attractions scarcely imaginable a generation earlier. Movies entertained the masses. As the historian and novelist Henry Adams put it at the turn of the century, "In the essentials of life . . . the boy of 1854 stood nearer [to] the year one than to the year 1900."

For much of the nineteenth century, the United States was dependent on the industrial nations of Europe for technological innovation. American engineers often went to England and Germany for education and training, and the textile industry, railroads, and the early steel industry benefited from German and English inventions.

In the late nineteenth century, the United States changed from a technological borrower to a technological innovator. By 1910, a million patents had been issued in the United States, 900,000 of them after 1870. Nothing represented this shift better than

Thomas A. Edison's development of a practical electric lightbulb and electric generating system. Edison's invention transformed electricity into a new and versatile form of industrial energy. It also reflected a change in the relationship between science and technology. Until the late nineteenth century, advances in scientific theory usually followed technological innovation, rather than the other way around. Techniques for making steel, for example, developed before scientific theories emerged to explain how they worked. Textile machinery and railroad technology developed similarly. In contrast, a theoretical understanding of electricity preceded its practical use as a source of energy. Scientists had been experimenting with electricity for half a century before Edison unveiled his lightbulb in 1879. Edison's research laboratory at Menlo Park, New Jersey, also established a model for corporate-sponsored research and development that would rapidly increase the pace of technological innovation.

Edison was a problem student, who had only three months of formal schooling. But he spent much

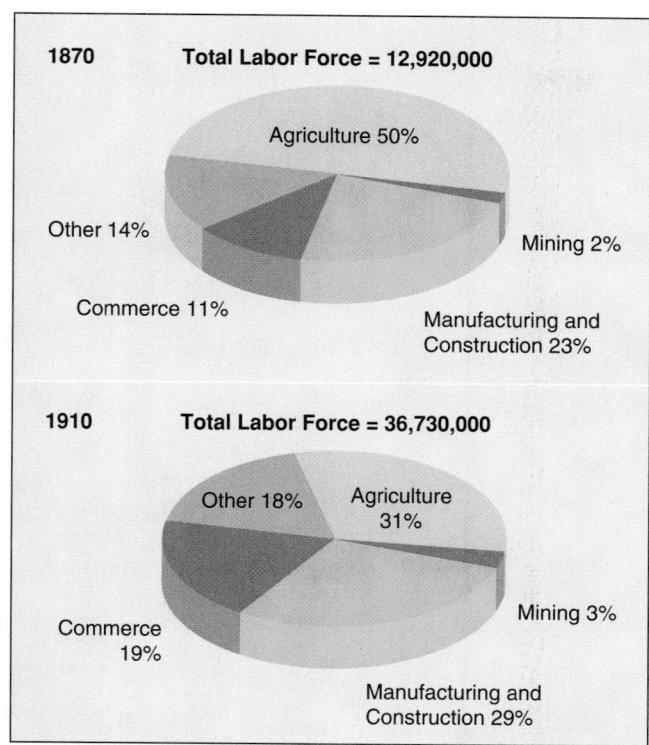

1870   **Total Labor Force = 12,920,000**

Agriculture 50%

Other 14%

Mining 2%

Commerce 11%

Manufacturing and
Construction 23%

1910   **Total Labor Force = 36,730,000**

Other 18%   Agriculture 31%

Commerce 19%

Mining 3%

Manufacturing and
Construction 29%

FIGURE 18-1   Changes in the American Labor Force, 1870-1910

The transformation of the American economy in the late nineteenth century changed the nature and type of work. By 1910, the United States was an urban, industrial nation with a matching workforce that toiled in factories and for commercial establishments (including railroads) and, less frequently, on farms.

of his childhood at home reading and experimenting with chemistry. In 1863, at the age of 16, he began working as a telegraph operator, devoting his spare time to inventing. Over the next 14 years, he produced several practical devices, including a system for carrying multiple messages on the same telegraph wire and an improved automatic stock ticker. With the money he earned from the stock ticker, he built a factory in Newark. In 1876, he gave up the factory, established his research laboratory at Menlo Park, and turned his attention to the electric light.

Scientists had already discovered that passing an electric current through a filament in a vacuum produced light. They had not yet found a filament, however, that could last for more than a few minutes. Edison tried a variety of materials, from grass to hair from a colleague's beard, before succeeding with charred thread. In 1879, he produced a bulb that burned for an astounding 45 hours. Then he devised a circuit that provided an even flow of current through the filament. After thrilling a crowd with the spectacle of five hundred lights ablaze on New Year's Eve in 1879, Edison went on to build a power station

in New York City to serve businesses and homes by 1882. The electric age had begun.

Edison's initial success touched off a wave of research and development in Germany, Austria, Great Britain, France, and the United States. Whoever could light the world cheaply and efficiently held the key to an enormous fortune. Ultimately, the prize fell, not to Edison, but to Elihu Thomson, a high school chemistry teacher in Philadelphia. Thomson, like Edison, enjoyed dabbling in electricity. Leaving teaching to devote himself to research full time, Thomson founded his own company and in 1883 moved to Connecticut, where he experimented with transformers and electric trolley equipment. Thomson purchased Edison's General Electric Company in 1892 and established the country's first corporate research and development division. His scientists produced what was then the most efficient lightbulb design, and by 1914, General Electric was producing 85 percent of the world's lightbulbs.

Following this precedent, other American companies established research and development laboratories. Standard Oil, U.S. Rubber, the chemical giant Du Pont, and the photographic company Kodak, all became world leaders in their respective industries because of innovations their laboratories developed.

The process of invention that emerged in the United States gave the country a commanding technological lead. But the modernization of industry that made the United States the world's foremost industrial nation after 1900 reflected organizational as well as technological innovation. As industries sought efficient ways to apply technology and expand their markets within and beyond national borders, their workforces expanded, and their need for capital mounted. Coping with these changes required significant changes in corporate management.

THE CORPORATION AND ITS IMPACT

The modern corporation provided the structural framework for the transformation of the American economy. A corporation is an association of individuals with legal rights and liabilities separate from those of its members. This form of business organization had existed since colonial times but became a significant factor in the American economy with the growth of railroad companies in the 1850s. A key feature of a corporation is the separation of ownership from management. A corporation can raise capital by selling stock—ownership shares—to people with no direct role in running it. The shareholders benefit from dividends drawn on profits and, if the corporation thrives, from the rising value of its stock.

The corporation had two major advantages over other forms of business organization that made it

Electricity conquered space and the night. The yellow glow of incandescent bulbs, the whiz of trolleys, and the rumble of elevated railways energize The Bowery, an emerging entertainment district in lower Manhattan at the end of the nineteenth century.

attractive to investors. First—unlike a partnership, which can dissolve when a partner dies—a corporation can outlive its founders. This durability permits long-term planning. Second, a corporation's officials and shareholders are not personally liable for its debts. If it goes bankrupt, they stand to lose only what they have invested in it.

As large corporations emerged in major American industries, they had a ripple effect on the economy. To build plants, merge with or acquire other companies, develop new technology, and hire workers, large corporations needed huge supplies of capital. They turned to the banks to help meet those needs, and the banks grew in response. The corporations stimulated technological change as they looked for ways to speed production, improve products, and lower costs. As they grew, they generated jobs.

Large industrial corporations also changed the nature of work. Into the late nineteenth century, well-paid skilled artisans, typically native-born, dominated the industrial workplace. Operating alone or in groups, they controlled the pace of their work, their output, and even the hiring and firing of coworkers. By the early twentieth century, control of the workplace was shifting to managers, and semiskilled and unskilled workers were replacing skilled artisans. These new workers, often foreign-born, performed repetitive tasks for low wages.

Because corporations usually located factories in cities, they stimulated urban growth. Large industrial districts sprawled along urban rivers and near urban rail lines. There were exceptions. Southern textile manufacturers tended to locate plants in villages and small towns and on the outskirts of larger cities. A few northern entrepreneurs also constructed industrial communities outside major cities to save on land costs and insure control over labor. George Pullman, for example, built his railway car manufacturing plant outside Chicago in 1880. Nonetheless, by 1900, fully 90 percent of all manufacturing occurred in cities.

Two organizational strategies—**vertical integration** and **horizontal integration**—helped successful corporations reduce competition and dominate their industries. Vertical integration involved the consolidation of all functions related to a particular industry, from the extraction and transport of raw materials to manufacturing and finished-product distribution and sales. Vertical integration reduced a company's dependence on outside suppliers, cutting costs and delays. Geographical dispersal went hand in hand with vertical integration. Different functions—a factory and its source of raw materials, for example—were likely to be in different places, a development made possible by such advances in communication as the telephone. The multiplication of functions also prompted the growth of corporate bureaucracy.

The development of the meatpacking industry provides a good example of vertical integration. Meat is perishable and cannot be transported long distances without refrigeration. To reach eastern markets, cattlemen had to ship live animals in cattle cars from western ranges to major rail centers like Chicago. Since only 40 percent of a steer is edible, shippers were paying freight charges for a lot of commercially useless weight. In addition, some animals died in transit, and many lost weight.

Gustavus Swift, a Boston native who moved to Chicago in 1875, realized that refrigerated railway cars would make it possible to ship butchered meat, eliminating the need to transport live cattle. He invented a refrigerated car but could not sell it to the major railroads because they feared losing their substantial investment in cattle cars and pens. Swift had the cars built himself and convinced a Canadian railroad with only a small stake in cattle shipping to haul them to eastern markets. He established packing houses in Omaha and Kansas City, near the largest cattle markets; built refrigerated warehouses at key distribution points; and hired a sales force to convince eastern butchers of the quality of his product. He now controlled the production, transportation, and distribution of his product, the essence of vertical integration. By 1881, he was shipping $200,000 worth of beef a week. Competitors soon followed his example.

Horizontal integration involved the merger of competitors in the same industry. John D. Rockefeller's Standard Oil Company pioneered horizontal integration in the 1880s.

Born in western New York State, the son of a traveling patent-medicine salesman, Rockefeller moved to Ohio at the age of 14 in 1853. Serving as family head during his father's frequent absences, Rockefeller developed a capacity for leadership, a thirst for hard work, and a devotion to the Baptist Church. He began invest-

A family takes a spin in their Model T Ford with the boys up front. The Ford Motor Company built affordable machines for the expanding middle-class, changing patterns of recreation and expanding work commutes and tourism.

ing in Cleveland oil refineries by his mid-twenties and formed Standard Oil in 1870. Using a variety of tactics—including threats, deceit, and price wars—Rockefeller rapidly acquired most of his competitors. Supported by such investment bankers as J.P. Morgan, Standard Oil controlled 90 percent of the nation's oil refining by 1890. Acquiring oil fields and pipelines as well as refineries, it achieved both vertical and horizontal integration. Rockefeller's dominant position allowed him to impose order and predictability on the industry, insuring a continuous flow of profits. He closed inefficient refineries, opened new ones, and kept his operations up to date with the latest technologies.

Almost as soon as oil gained widespread prominence, the electric light bulb appeared to dim the prospects of oil as the world's universal illuminant. But the invention of the internal combustion engine and the growth of automobile and truck manufacturing after 1900 suddenly made an inconsequential by-product of the refining process—gasoline—an indispensable fuel. By that time, the refining and production of oil had spread to Texas and Oklahoma, with the discovery of oil at Spindletop Hill, near Beaumont, Texas. The Texas oil fields dwarfed the Pennsylvania basin and soon surpassed their eastern rivals in output, spawning towns from the Gulf Coast to the Permian Basin in West Texas, and new companies such as the Texas Oil Company (Texaco) and Gulf Oil, breaking Rockefeller's near-monopoly. The petroleum industry represented one of the earliest shifts of industrial wealth from the Northeast and Midwest to the South and Southwest.

Other entrepreneurs achieved similar dominance in other industries and amassed similarly enormous

The industrial revolution in the United States generated enormous sums of wealth and, prior to the federal income tax in 1913, magnates such as railroad tycoon William K. Vanderbilt, whose Louis XVI dining room is pictured here, could keep it all. The opulent room was part of Vanderbilt's summer retreat in Newport, Rhode Island. The rest of the year he resided in an $11 million mansion on the corner of Fifty-First Street and Fifth Avenue in New York City.

fortunes. James B. Duke, who automated cigarette manufacturing, gained control of most of the tobacco industry. Andrew Carnegie consolidated much of the U.S. steel industry within his Carnegie Steel Company (later U.S. Steel). By 1900, Carnegie's company was producing one-quarter of the country's steel.

The concentration of American industry in the hands of a few powerful corporations alarmed many Americans. Giant corporations threatened to restrict opportunities for small entrepreneurs like the shopkeepers, farmers, and artisans who abounded at midcentury. In the words of one historian, the corporations "seemed to signal the end of an open, promising America and the beginning of a closed, unhappier society." Impersonal and governed by profit, the modern corporation challenged the ideal of the self-made man and the belief that success and advancement would reward hard work. These concerns eventually prompted the federal and state govern-

ments to respond with antitrust and other regulatory laws (see Chapters 20 and 21).

Tabloid newspapers reinforced distrust of the corporations with exposés of the sharp business practices of corporate barons such as Rockefeller and Carnegie and accounts of the sumptuous lifestyles of the corporate elite. Public concern notwithstanding, however, the giant corporations helped increase the efficiency of the American economy, raise the national standard of living, and transform the United States into a major world power. Corporate expansion generated jobs that attracted rural migrants and immigrants by the millions from Europe and Asia to American cities.

THE CHANGING NATURE OF WORK

From the perspective of the workers, immigrant and native-born alike, the growth of giant corporations was a mixed blessing. The corporations provided abundant jobs, but they firmly controlled working conditions. A Pennsylvania coal miner spoke for many of his fellows in the 1890s when he remarked, "The working people of this country . . . find monopolies as strong as government itself. They find capital as rigid as absolute monarchy. They find their so-called independence a myth."

As late as the 1880s, shops of skilled artisans were responsible for most manufacturing in the United States. Since the mid-century, however, industrialists had been introducing ways to simplify manufacturing processes so they could hire low-skilled workers. This deskilling process accelerated in the 1890s in response to new technologies, new workers, and workplace reorganization. By 1906, according to a U.S. Department of Labor report, industrial labor had been reduced to minute, low-skilled operations, making skilled artisans obsolete.

Mechanization and technological innovation did not reduce employment, although they did eliminate some jobs, most of them skilled. On the contrary, the birth of whole new industries—steel, automobiles, electrical equipment, cigarettes, food canning, and machine tools—created a huge demand for workers. Innovations in existing industries, like railroads, similarly spurred job growth. The number of people working for U.S. railroads increased from eighty thousand to more than 1 million between 1860 and 1910.

Ironically, it was a shortage of skilled workers as much as other factors that encouraged industrialists to mechanize. Unskilled workers cost less than did the scarce artisans. And with massive waves of immigrants arriving from Europe and Asia between 1880 and 1920 (joined after 1910 by migrants from the American South), the supply of unskilled workers seemed limitless.

Low salaries and long hours. The new workers, however, shared little of the wealth generated by industrial expansion and enjoyed few of the gadgets and products generated by the new manufacturing. The Eastern European immigrants who comprised three-quarters of U.S. Steel's work force during the first decade of the twentieth century received less than $12.50 a week, significantly less than the $15.00 a week a federal government survey in 1910 calculated that an urban family needed to subsist.

Nor did large corporations put profits into improved working conditions. In 1881, on-the-job accidents maimed or killed thirty thousand railroad workers. Safety equipment existed that could have prevented many of these injuries, but the railroads refused to purchase it. At a U.S. Steel plant in Pittsburgh, injuries or death claimed one out of every four workers between 1907 and 1910. In Chicago's meat plants, injuries were commonplace. Workers grew careless from fatigue and long-term exposure to the extreme temperatures of the workplace. Meat cutters working rapidly with sharp knives often sliced fingers off their numb hands. Upton Sinclair wrote in his novel *The Jungle* (1906), a chronicle of the killing floors of meatpacking plants in Chicago, "It was to be counted as a wonder that there were not more men slaughtered than cattle."

Factory workers typically worked ten hours a day, six days a week in the 1880s. Steel workers put in twelve hours a day. Because the mills operated around the clock, once every two weeks, when the workers changed shifts, one group took a "long turn" and stayed on the job for twenty-four hours.

Long hours affected family life. By Sunday, most factory workers were too tired to do more than sit around home. During the week, they had time only to eat and sleep. As one machinist testified before a U.S. Senate investigative committee in 1883:

> They were pretty well played out when they come home, and the first thing they think of is having something to eat and sitting down, and resting, and then of striking a bed. Of course when a man is dragged out in that way he is naturally cranky, and he makes all around him cranky . . . and staring starvation in the face makes him feel sad, and the head of the house being sad, of course the whole family are the same, so the house looks like a dull prison.

Workers lived as close to the factory as possible, to reduce the time and expense of getting to work. The environment around many factories, however, was almost as unwholesome as the conditions inside. A visitor to Pittsburgh in 1884 noticed "a drab twilight" hanging over the areas around the steel mills, where "gas-lights, which are left burning at mid-day, shine out of the murkiness with a dull, reddish glare." Industrial wastes fouled streams and rivers around many plants. The factories along the Cuyahoga River in Cleveland turned that waterway into an open sewer by the turn of the century.

Big factories were not characteristic of all industries after 1900. In some, like the "needle," or garment, trade, operations remained small scale. But salaries and working conditions in these industries were, if anything, worse than in the big factories. The garment industry was dominated by small manufacturers who assembled clothing for retailers from cloth provided by textile manufacturers. The manufacturers squeezed workers into small, cramped, poorly ventilated **sweatshops**. These might be in attics or lofts or even in the workers' own dwellings. Workers pieced together garments on the manufacturer's sewing machines. A government investigator in Chicago in the 1890s described one sweatshop in a three-room tenement where the workers—a family of eight—both lived and worked: "The father, mother, two daughters, and a cousin work together making trousers at seventy-five cents a dozen pairs . . . . They work seven days a week . . . . Their destitution is very great."

CHILD LABOR

Child labor was common in the garment trade and other industries. Shocked reformers in the 1890s told of the devastating effect of factory labor on children's lives, citing cases like that of a 7-year-old girl whose legs were paralyzed and deformed because she toiled "day after day with little legs crossed, pulling out bastings from garments."

Industries that employed many children were often dangerous, even for adults. In the gritty coal mines of Pennsylvania, breaker boys, youths who stood on ladders to pluck waste matter from coal tumbling down long chutes, breathed harmful coal dust all day. Girls under sixteen made up half the work force in the silk mills of Scranton and Wilkes-Barre, Pennsylvania. Girls with missing fingers from mill accidents were a common sight in those towns.

By 1900, Pennsylvania and a few other states had passed legislation regulating child labor, but enforcement of these laws was lax. Parents desperate for income often lied about their children's age, and authorities were often sympathetic toward mill or mine owners, who paid taxes and provided other civic benefits.

WORKING WOMEN

Women accompanied children into the work force outside the home in increasing numbers after 1870.

Noted urban photographer Lewis Hine captures the cramped working conditions and child labor in this late nineteenth-century canning factory. Women and children provided a cheap and efficient work force for labor-intensive industries.

The comparatively low wages of unskilled male workers often required women family members to work as well. The head of the Massachusetts Bureau of Labor Statistics observed in 1882, "A family of workers can always live well, but the man with a family of small children to support, unless his wife works also, has a small chance of living properly." Between 1870 and 1920, the number of women and children in the workforce more than doubled.

Like child labor, the growing numbers of women in the workforce alarmed middle-class reformers. They worried about the impact on family life and on the women themselves. Working-class men were also concerned. The trend toward deskilling favored women. Employers, claiming that women worked only for supplemental money, paid them less than men. A U.S. Department of Labor commissioner asserted that women worked only for "dress or pleasure." In one St. Louis factory in 1896, women received $4 a week for work for which men were paid $16 a week. Women chafed under this wage system but had no recourse

other than to quit. An Iowa shoe saleswoman complained in 1886, "I don't get the salary the men clerks do, although this day I am 600 sales ahead! Call this justice? But I have to grin and bear it, because I am so unfortunate as to be a woman."

Most women worked out of economic necessity. In 1900, fully 85 percent of wage-earning women were unmarried and under the age of 25. They supported siblings and contributed to their parents' income. A typical female factory worker earned $6 a week in 1900. On this wage, a married woman might help pull her family up to subsistence level. For a single woman on her own, however, it allowed little more, in writer O. Henry's words, "than marshmallows and tea." Her lodging rarely consisted of more than one room.

Yet, even with their limited wages, working women found ways to enjoy their leisure time. They went to dances, visited amusement parks such as Brooklyn's Coney Island (formerly a mostly male preserve), and crowded into theaters. They met young men at these venues under relatively safe conditions as proprietors insured order to attract and keep female customers, who would, in turn, draw the young men. Though these cheap amusements sometimes scandalized middle-class reformers, working women viewed them as both an escape from the restrictions of work and a declaration of independence from their families.

Over time, more work options opened to women, but low wages and poor working conditions persisted. Women entered the needle trades after widespread introduction of the sewing machine in the 1870s. Factories gradually replaced sweatshops in the garment industry after 1900, but working conditions improved little.

The downtown department store became a significant female place in the late nineteenth century, as shopping increasingly held a feminine connotation. These emporiums also provided employment opportunities for working-class young women. Store managers staffed the sales floor with workers who would be both deferential and knowledgeable for the customer. The salesgirls enjoyed some latitude in their positions, which factory girls could not approach. Management felt some compulsion toward fair treatment of the sales staff, fearing their employees might turn their anger toward the customer. Managers provided salesgirls with lunchrooms, gymnasiums, libraries, and infirmaries. Despite the long hours and low pay, the lure of working in a glittering showplace and wielding at least a little autonomy, rendered this job the most coveted for working-class young women.

On the factory floor, young women had less room for negotiation, as the customer was far removed from the manufacturing process, but they banded together, sometimes in labor unions after 1900 to demand and receive concessions from management. Working women, no less than working men, refused to be inanimate recipients of bosses' decrees and working conditions. The factory, though less so than the department store, was a space for negotiation between worker and management. And, if a young woman could obtain some basic skills, other opportunities loomed as well.

The introduction of the typewriter transformed clerical office work, dominated by men until the 1870s, into a female preserve. Women were alleged to have the greater dexterity and tolerance for repetition that the new technology required. But they earned only half the salary of the men they replaced. Middle-class parents saw office work as clean and honorable, compared with factory or sales work. Consequently, clerical positions drew growing numbers of native-born women into the urban work force after 1890. A top-paid office worker in the 1890s earned as much as $900 a year. Teaching, another acceptable occupation for middle-class women, typically paid only $500 a year.

By the turn of the century, women were gaining increased access to higher education. Coeducational colleges were rare, but by 1900 there were many women-only institutions. By 1910, women comprised 40 percent of all American college students, compared

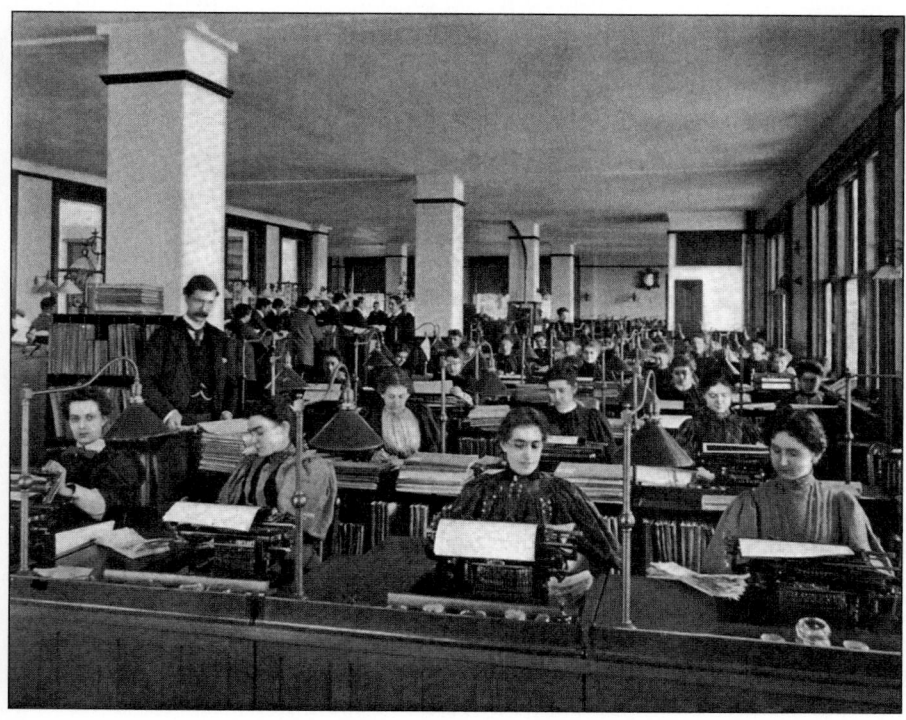

Before the typewriter was invented, male workers dominated office staffs. However, employers believed that women exhibited greater dexterity with the new machines and, besides, they could pay them less. Notice the male supervisor.

to 20 percent in 1870. Despite these gains, many professions—including those of physician and attorney—remained closed to women. Men still accounted for more than 95 percent of all doctors in 1900. Women also were rarely permitted to pursue doctoral degrees.

Most women college graduates found employment in such "nurturing" professions as nursing, teaching, and library work. Between 1900 and 1910, the number of trained women nurses increased sevenfold. In response to the growing problems of urban society, a relatively new occupation, social work, opened to women. There were one thousand women social workers in 1890 and nearly thirty thousand by 1920. Reflecting new theories on the nurturing role of women, school boards after 1900 turned exclusively to female teachers for the elementary grades.

Despite these gains, women's work remained segregated. More than 90 percent of all wage-earning women in 1900 worked at occupations in which women comprised the great majority of workers. Some reforms meant to improve working conditions for women reinforced this state of affairs. Protective legislation restricted women to "clean" occupations and limited their ability to compete with men in other jobs. As an economist explained in 1901, "The wage bargaining power of men is weakened by the competition of women and children, hence a law restricting the hours of women and children may also be looked upon as a law to protect men in their bargaining power."

Women also confronted negative stereotypes. Most Americans in 1900 believed a woman's proper role was to care for home and family. The single working woman faced doubts about her virtue. The system of "treating" on dates reinforced stories about loose salesgirls, flirtatious secretaries, and easy factory workers. Newspapers and magazines published exposés of working girls descending into prostitution. These images encouraged sexual harassment at work, which was rarely punished.

Working women faced a difficult dilemma. To justify their desire for education and training, they had to argue that these would enhance their roles as wives and mothers. To gain improved wages and working conditions, they increasingly supported protective legislation that restricted their opportunities in the workplace.

RESPONSES TO POVERTY AND WEALTH

Concerns about working women merged with larger anxieties about the growing numbers of impoverished workers in the nation's cities during the 1890s and the widening gap between rich and poor. While industrial magnates flaunted their fabulous wealth, working men and women led hard lives on meager salaries and in crowded dwellings. In his exposé of poverty in New York, *How the Other Half Lives* (1890), the Danish-born urban reformer Jacob Riis wrote that "the half that is on top cares little for the struggles, and less for the fate of those who are underneath so long as it is able to hold them there and keep its own seat."

The urban poor included workers as well as the unemployed, aged, widowed, and disabled. The industrial economy strained working-class family life. Workplace accidents and deaths left many families with only one parent. Infant mortality among the working poor was nearly twice the citywide norm in 1900. Epidemic diseases, especially typhoid, an illness spread by impure water, devastated crowded working-class districts. Poverty compounded itself in various ways. For example, the poor paid twice as much for coal to heat their homes as better-off people, because they could afford to buy it only in small quantities.

Inadequate housing was the most visible badge of poverty. Crammed into four- to six-story buildings on tiny lots, **tenement** apartments in urban slums were notorious for their lack of ventilation and light. According to Jacob Riis, a typical apartment in New York's Mulberry Bend neighborhood consisted of a parlor—a combined living room and kitchen—and "two pitch-dark coops called bedrooms." The furniture included three beds, "if the old boxes and heaps of foul straw can be called by that name," which gave off an appalling smell. In 90-degree July heat, temperatures inside soared to 115 degrees.

Authorities did nothing to enforce laws prohibiting overcrowding for fear of leaving people homeless. The population density of New York's tenement district in 1894 was 986.4 people per acre, the highest in the world at the time. (Today, the densest areas of American cities rarely exceed 400 people per acre, and only Calcutta, India, and Lagos, Nigeria, approach the crowding of turn-of-the-century New York; today Manhattan has 84 residents per acre.)

One early attempt to deal with these conditions was the **settlement house**. The settlement house movement, which originated in England, sought to moderate the effects of poverty through neighborhood reconstruction. New York's Neighborhood Guild, established in 1886, was the first settlement house in the country; Chicago's **Hull House**, founded in 1889 by Jane Addams, a young Rockford (Illinois) College graduate, became the most famous. Addams had visited settlement houses in England and thought the idea would work well in American cities.

The settlement house typically did not dispense charity. Rather, it provided the working poor with facilities and education to help them improve their environment and, eventually, to escape it. By 1900, there

The new industrial age created great wealth and abject poverty, and the city became the stage upon which these hard economic lessons played out. Here, a "modest" Fifth Avenue mansion in turn-of-the-century New York City; further downtown, Jacob Riis found this tenement courtyard.

were more than one hundred settlement houses throughout the country.

Hull House, a rambling old residence in a working-class immigrant neighborhood, quickly became a neighborhood institution. On Saturday evenings, Italian immigrants and their families came to settle legal disputes. Hull House also catered to native-born Americans, who formed the Young Citizens' Club to discuss municipal issues. Addams renovated an adjacent saloon and transformed it into a gym. She began a day nursery as well. When workers at a nearby knitting factory went on strike, Addams arbitrated the conflict.

The poor seldom lived near large urban parks and could not afford to join athletic clubs. Settlement-house gyms, like the one Addams built for Hull House, provided them with much-needed recreational space. So too did the athletic fields and playgrounds built adjacent to public schools after 1900.

The Gospel of Wealth.

Late-nineteenth-century political ideology discouraged more comprehensive efforts to remedy urban poverty until the Progressive Era (discussed in Chapter 21). According to the **Gospel of Wealth**, a theory popular among industrialists, intellectuals, and some politicians, any intervention on behalf of the poor was of doubtful benefit. Hard work and perseverance, in this view, led to wealth. Poverty, by implication, resulted from the flawed character of the poor. Steel tycoon Andrew Carnegie sought to soften this doctrine by stressing the responsibility of the affluent to set an example for the working class and to return some of their wealth to the communities in which they lived. Carnegie, accordingly, endowed libraries, cultural institutions, and schools throughout the country. Beneficial as they might be, however, these philanthropic efforts scarcely addressed the causes of poverty, and few industrialists followed Carnegie's example.

A flawed attempt to apply Charles Darwin's theory of biological evolution to human society emerged as a more common justification than the Gospel of Wealth for the growing gap between rich and poor. According to the theory of **Social Darwinism**, the human race evolves only through competition. The fit survive, the weak perish, and humanity moves forward. Wealth reflects fitness; poverty, weakness. For

AMERICAN VIEWS

Tenement Life

In 1890, the Danish immigrant Jacob A. Riis published *How the Other Half Lives*, an exposé of living conditions among immigrants in New York City's Lower East Side neighborhood. The book, complete with vivid photographs, caused a sensation. At a time when newspapers and magazines competed for readers with lurid tales of urban life, Riis's detailed and gruesome depictions shocked readers and provided an impetus for housing reform in New York and, eventually, across the urban nation. Riis's scientific tone, devoid of sensationalism, rendered the scenes that more dramatic. For a nation that valued family life and the sanctity of childhood, Riis's accounts of how the environment, inside and outside the tenement, destroyed young lives provided moving testimony that for some, and perhaps many immigrants, the "promise" had been taken out of the Promised Land.

- What is Jacob Riis's attitude toward the tenement dwellers?
- Considering the destitute character of the family Riis describes, what sort of assistance do you think they receive?
- Why do you suppose the authorities were reluctant to enforce sanitary, capacity, and building regulations in these neighborhoods?

Look into any of these houses, everywhere the same piles of rags, of malodorous bones and musty paper all of which the sanitary police flatter themselves they have banished . . . . Here is a "parlor" and two pitch-dark coops called bedrooms. Truly, the bed is all there is room for. The family teakettle is on the stove, doing duty for the time being as a wash-boiler. By night it will have returned to its proper use again, a practical illustration of how poverty . . .

---

governments or private agencies to interfere with this natural process is futile. Thus, Columbia University president Nicholas Murray Butler, claiming that "nature's cure for most social and political diseases is better than man's," warned against charity for the poor in 1900. Standard Oil's John D. Rockefeller concurred, asserting that the survival of the fittest is "the working out of a law of nature and a law of God."

Social Darwinism provided some industrialists with an excuse to do nothing to relieve the causes of poverty. Workers, caught between harsh theory and harsher reality, began to take matters into their own hands.

WORKERS ORGANIZE

The growing power of industrial corporations and the declining power of workers generated social tensions reminiscent of the sectional crisis that triggered the Civil War. Wild swings in the business cycle—the fluc-tuation between periods of growth and contraction in the economy—aggravated these tensions. Two pro-longed depressions, one beginning in 1873 and the other in 1893, threw as many as 2 million laborers out of work. Skilled workers, their security undermined by deskilling, were hit particularly hard. Their hopes of becoming managers or starting their own businesses disappearing, they saw the nation "drifting," as a car-penter put it in 1870, "to that condition of society where a few were rich, and the many very poor."

Beginning after the depression of 1873 and con-tinuing through World War I, workers fought their loss of independence to industrial capital by organiz-ing and striking (see the Overview table, "Workers Or-ganize"). The first episode in this conflict was the railroad strike of 1877, sometimes referred to as the **Great Uprising**. The four largest railroads, in the midst of a depression and in the wake of a series of pay makes both ends meet. One, two, three beds are there, if the old boxes and heaps of foul straw can be called by that name; a broken stove with crazy pipe from which the smoke leaks at every joint, a table of rough boards propped up on boxes, piles of rubbish in the corner. The closeness and smell are appalling . . . .

Well do I recollect the visit of a health inspector to one of these tenements on a July day when the thermometer outside was climbing high in the nineties; but inside, in that awful room, with half a dozen persons washing, cooking, and sorting rags, lay the dying baby alongside the stove, where the doctor's thermometer ran up to 115 degrees! Perishing for the want of a breath of fresh air in this city of untold charities! . . .

A message came one day last spring summoning me to a Mott Street tenement in which lay a child dying from some unknown disease. With the "charity doctor" I found the patient on the top floor, stretched upon two chairs in a dreadfully stifling room. She was gasping in the agony of peritonitis [abdominal infection] that had already written its death-sentence on her wan and pinched face. The whole family,

father, mother, and four ragged children, sat around looking on with the stony resignation of helpless despair that had long since given up the fight against fate as useless. A glance around the wretched room left no doubt as to the cause of the children's condition. "Improper nourishment," said the doctor, which translated to suit the place, meant starvation. The father's hands were crippled from lead poisoning. He had not been able to work for a year. A contagious disease of the eyes, too long neglected, had made the mother and one of the boys nearly blind. The children cried with hunger . . . . For months the family had subsisted on two dollars a week from the priest, and a few loaves and a piece of corned beef which the sisters sent them on Saturday. The doctor gave direction for the treatment of the child, knowing that it was possible only to alleviate its sufferings until death should end them, and left some money for food for the rest. An hour later, when I returned, I found them feeding the dying child with ginger ale, bought for two cents a bottle at the pedlar's cart down the street. A pitying neighbor had proposed it as the one thing she could think of as likely to make the child forget its misery.

---

cuts over the previous four years, agreed to slash wages yet again. When Baltimore & Ohio Railroad workers struck in July to protest the cut, President Rutherford B. Hayes dispatched federal troops to protect the line's property. The use of federal troops infuriated railroad workers throughout the East and Midwest, and they stopped work as well. Violence erupted in Pittsburgh when the state militia opened fire on strikers and their families, killing twenty-five, including a woman and three children. As news of the violence spread, so did the strike, as far as Galveston, Texas, and San Francisco. Over the next two weeks, police and federal troops continued to clash with strikers. By the time this first nationwide work stoppage in American history ended, more than one hundred had been killed. The wage cuts remained.

Despite its ultimate failure, the Great Uprising was notable for the way workers cooperated with one another across ethnic and, in some cases, racial lines. The experience proved important in the next major upheaval, nine years later.

The **Knights of Labor**, a union of craft workers founded in Philadelphia in 1869, grew dramatically after the Great Uprising under the leadership of Terence V. Powderly. Reflecting the views of many skilled workers, the Knights saw "an inevitable . . . conflict between the wage system of labor and [the] republican system of government." Remarkably inclusive for its time, the Knights welcomed black workers and women to its ranks. Victories in several small railroad strikes in 1884 and 1885 boosted its membership to nearly one million workers by 1886.

In that year, the Knights led a movement for an eight-hour workday. Ignoring the advice of the national leadership to avoid strikes, local chapters staged more than 1,500 strikes involving more than 340,000

Overview

Workers Organize

Organization	History	Strategies
Knights of Labor	Founded in 1869; open to all workers; declined after 1886	Disapproved of strikes; supported a broad array of labor reforms, including cooperatives; favored political involvement
American Federation of Labor	Founded in 1886; open to craft workers only and organized by craft; hostile to blacks and women; became the major U.S. labor organization after 1880s	Opposed political involvement; supported a limited number of labor reforms; approved of strikes

workers. Workers also organized boycotts against manufacturers and ran candidates for local elections. Social reformer Henry George made a strong, though losing, effort in the New York City mayoral race, and labor candidates won several local offices in Chicago.

Employers fought back. They convinced the courts to order strikers back to work and used local authorities to arrest strikers for trespassing or obstructing traffic. In early May 1886, police killed four unarmed workers during a skirmish with strikers in Chicago. Rioting broke out when a bomb exploded at a meeting in Haymarket Square to protest the slayings. The bomb killed seven policemen and four strikers and left one hundred people wounded. Eight strike leaders were tried for the deaths, and despite a lack of evidence linking them to the bomb, four were executed.

The Haymarket Square incident, and a series of disastrous walkouts that followed it, weakened the Knights of Labor. By 1890, it had shrunk to less than 100,000 members. Thereafter, the **American Federation of Labor** (AFL), formed in 1886, became the major organizing body for skilled workers.

The AFL was much less ambitious, and less inclusive, than the Knights of Labor. Led by a British immigrant, Samuel Gompers, it emphasized **collective bargaining**—negotiations between management and union representatives—to secure workplace concessions. The AFL also discouraged political activism. With this business unionism, the AFL proved more effective than the Knights of Labor at meeting the needs of skilled workers, but it left out the growing numbers of unskilled workers, black workers, and women workers, to whom the Knights had given a glimmer of hope.

Rather than including all workers in one large union, the AFL organized skilled workers by craft. It

then focused on a few basic workplace issues important to each craft. Workers at a given factory might be represented by five or more craft unions instead of one umbrella organization. This organizing technique assured that rank-and-file members in a union shared similar objectives. The result was greater cohesion and discipline. In 1889 and 1890, more than 60 percent of AFL-sponsored strikes were successful, a remarkable record in an era when most strikes failed. A series of work stoppages in the building trades between 1888 and 1891, for example, won an eight-hour day and a national agreement with builders.

Responding to this success, employers determined to break the power of craft unions just as they had destroyed the Knights. In 1892, Andrew Carnegie dealt the steelworkers' union a major setback in the Homestead strike. Carnegie's manager, Henry Clay Frick, announced to workers at Carnegie's Homestead plant in Pennsylvania that he would negotiate only with workers individually and not renew the union's collective bargaining contract. Expecting a strike, Frick locked the union workers out of the plant and hired three hundred armed guards to protect the nonunion ("scab") workers he planned to hire in their place. Union workers, with the help of their families and unskilled workers, seized control of Homestead's roads and utilities. In a bloody confrontation, they drove back Frick's forces. Nine strikers and seven guards died. But Pennsylvania's governor called out the state militia to open the plant and protect the nonunion workers. After four months, the union capitulated. With this defeat, skilled steelworkers lost their power on the shop floor. Eventually, mechanization cost them their jobs.

In 1894, workers suffered another setback in the Pullman strike, against George Pullman's Palace Sleeping Car Company. The strike began when the

During the Great Uprising of 1877, federal troops clashed with striking workers. Here, the Maryland militia fires at strikers in Baltimore, killing twelve. As Reconstruction ended, government attention shifted from the South to quelling labor unrest.

no more than 7 percent of the American work force was organized by 1900.

By that time, a dramatic change in the industrial work force was afoot. As the large factories installed labor- and time-saving machinery, unskilled foreign-born labor flooded onto the shop floor. For many reasons, not least of which were the adjustments required for life in a new country, labor radicalism was not a high priority for many of the newcomers. Immigrants not only transformed the workplace, but also transformed the cities where they settled and the nation many eventually adopted. In the process, they changed themselves.

company cut wages for workers at its plant in the "model" suburb it built outside Chicago, without a corresponding cut in the rent it charged workers for their company-owned housing. When Pullman rejected their demands, the workers appealed for support to the American Railway Union (ARU), led by Eugene V. Debs. The membership of the ARU, an independent union not affiliated with the AFL, had swelled to more than 150,000 workers after it won a strike earlier in 1894 against the Great Northern Railroad. On behalf of the Pullman strikers, Debs ordered a boycott of any trains with Pullman cars. The result was to disrupt train travel in several parts of the country. The railroads claimed to be innocent victims of a local dispute, and with growing public support, they fired workers who refused to handle trains with Pullman cars. Debs called for all ARU members to walk off the job, crippling rail travel nationwide. When Debs refused to honor a federal court injunction against the strike, President Cleveland, at the railroads' request, ordered federal troops to enforce it. Debs was arrested, and the strike and the union were broken.

These setbacks, and the depression that began in 1893, left workers and their unions facing an uncertain future. But growing public opposition to the use of troops, the high-handed tactics of industrialists, and the rising concerns of Americans about the power of big business sustained the unions. Workers would call more than 22,000 strikes over the next decade, the majority of them union-sponsored. Still,

NEW IMMIGRANTS

The late nineteenth century was a period of unprecedented worldwide population movements. The United States was not the only New World destination for the migrants of this period. Many also found their way to Brazil, Argentina, and Canada.

The scale of overseas migration to the United States after 1870, however, dwarfed all that preceded it. Between 1870 and 1910, the country received more than 20 million immigrants. Before the Civil War, most immigrants came from northern Europe. Most of the new immigrants, by contrast, came from southern and eastern Europe. Swelling their ranks were migrants from Mexico and Asia, as well as internal migrants moving from the countryside to American cities (see Map 18–1 and Figure 18–2).

OLD-WORLD BACKGROUNDS

The people of southern and eastern Europe had long been accustomed to migrating within Europe on a seasonal basis to find work to support their families. In the final quarter of the nineteenth century, however, several factors drove migrants beyond the borders of Europe and into the Western Hemisphere.

A growing rural population combined with unequal land distribution to create economic distress in late-nineteenth-century Europe. With land ownership concentrated in increasingly fewer hands, more and more people found themselves working ever smaller plots as laborers rather than owners. In Poland, laborers accounted for 80 percent of the

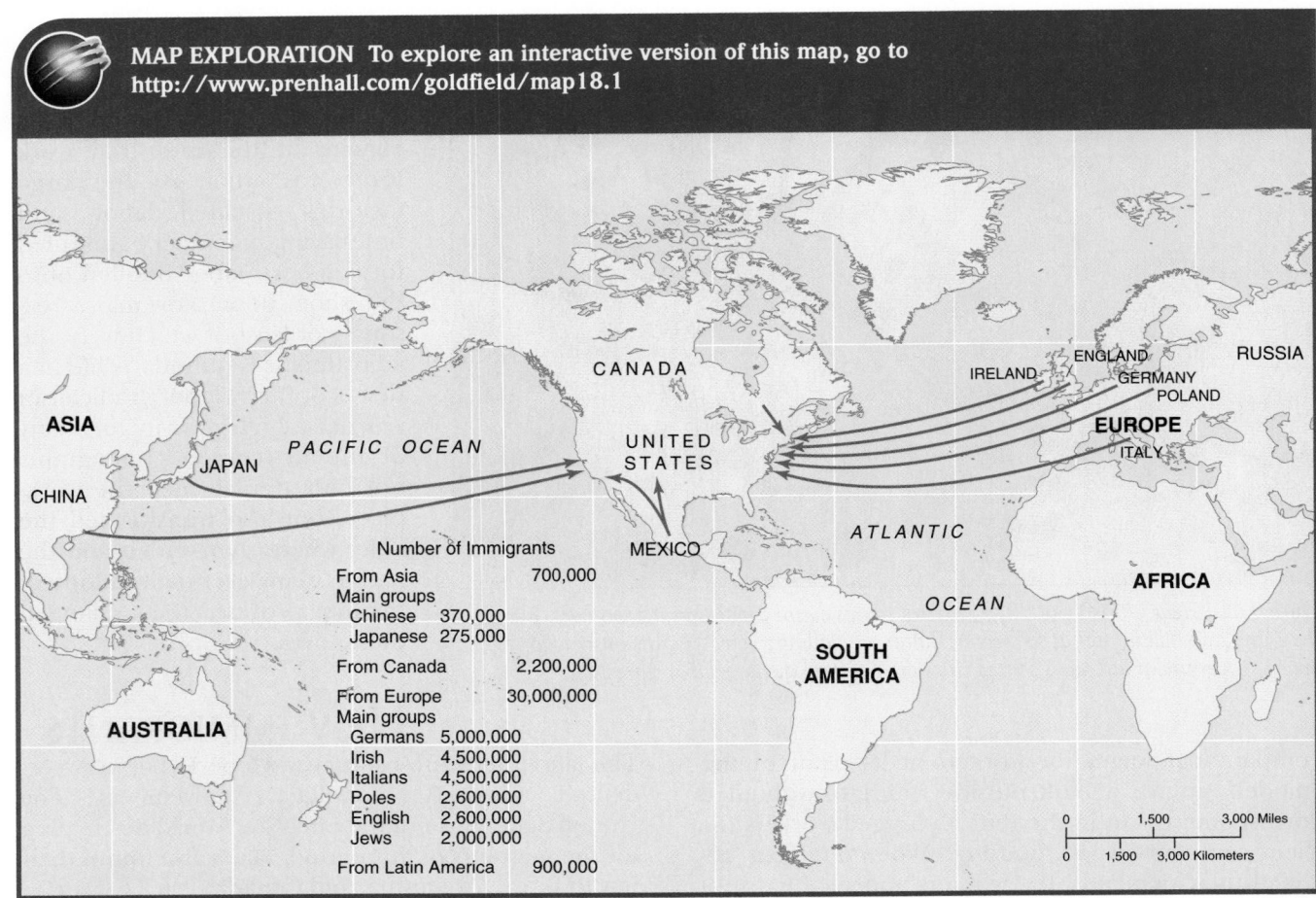

MAP EXPLORATION To explore an interactive version of this map, go to
http://www.prenhall.com/goldfield/map18.1

Number of Immigrants

From Asia	700,000
Main groups	
Chinese	370,000
Japanese	275,000
From Canada	2,200,000
From Europe	30,000,000
Main groups	
Germans	5,000,000
Irish	4,500,000
Italians	4,500,000
Poles	2,600,000
English	2,600,000
Jews	2,000,000
From Latin America	900,000

MAP 18-1   **Patterns of Immigration, 1820-1914**
*The migration to the United States was part of a worldwide transfer of population that acceler-
ated with the Industrial Revolution and the accompanying improvement in transportation.*

agricultural population in the 1860s. Similar conditions prevailed in the Mezzogiorno region of southern Italy, home of three out of four Italian
emigrants to America. Declining farm commodity
prices and the deterioration of the road system in
southern Italy contributed to a general agricultural
depression. Absentee landlords abused workers and
neglected the land.

For Russian Jews, religious persecution compounded economic hardship. In tsarist Russia, Jews
could not own real estate and were barred from
work in farming, teaching, the civil service, and the
law. Confined to designated cities, they struggled to
support themselves. After the assassination of Tsar
Alexander II in 1881, which some leaders falsely
blamed on Jews, the government sanctioned a series
of violent attacks on Jewish settlements; these attacks were known as **pogroms**. At the same time, the
government forced Jews into fewer towns, deepening their poverty and making them easier targets for
violence.

Economic hardship and religious persecution
were not, of course, new to Europe. What made the
late nineteenth century different was that new transportation technologies permitted people to leave.
Railroad construction boomed in Europe during the
1870s and 1880s as Germany and Great Britain
sought markets for their iron and steel. Steamship
companies in several European countries built giant
vessels to transport passengers quickly and safely
across the Atlantic. The companies sent agents into
Russia, Poland, Italy, and the Austro-Hungarian Empire to solicit business.

Sometime during the 1880s, an agent from the
Hamburg-American Line (HAPAG), a German
steamship company, visited a village in the Russian
Ukraine where the great-grandparents of one of this
book's authors lived. Shortly after his visit, they
boarded a train to Austrian-occupied Poland and
Hamburg. There, they boarded a HAPAG steamer
emblazoned with a large banner proclaiming
"Willkommen" ("Welcome"). Like Mary Antin, whose

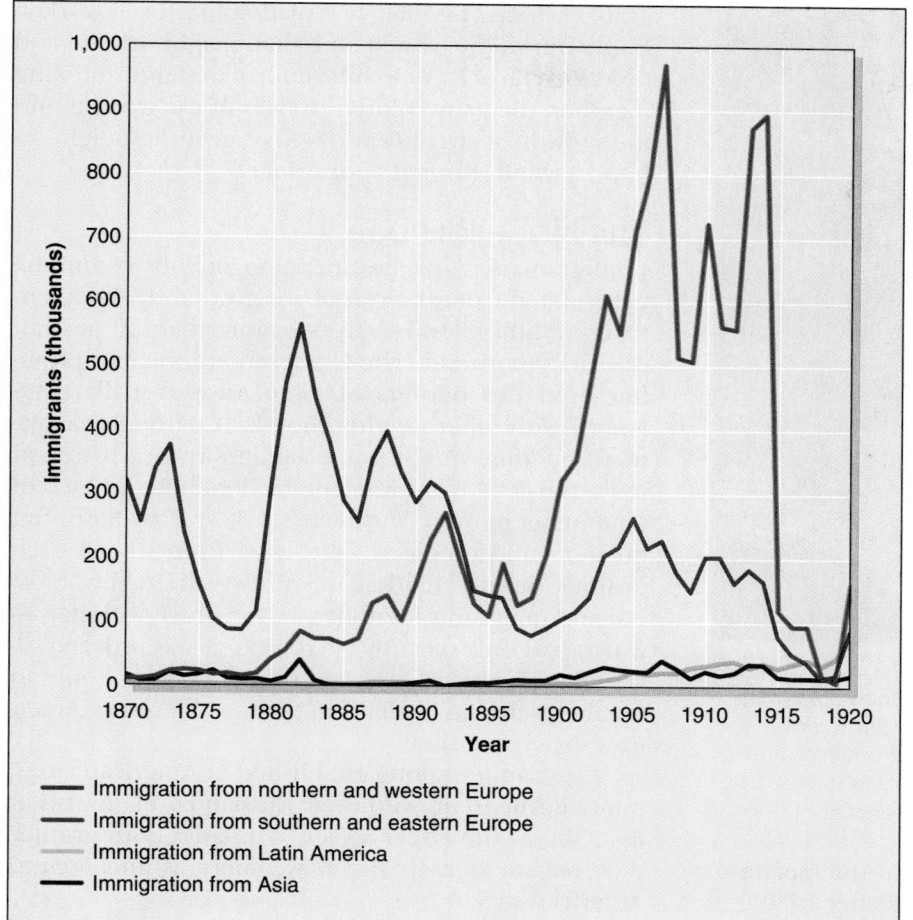

FIGURE 18-2 Immigration to the United States, 1870–1915
The graph illustrates the dramatic change in immigration to the United States during the late nineteenth and early twentieth centuries. As immigration from northern and western Europe slackened, the numbers of newcomers from southern and eastern Europe swelled. Latin American and Asian immigration also increased during this period.

recollection begins this chapter, just boarding that ship, they felt that they were entering the United States. Millions of others like them sailed on ocean liners from Germany, Italy, and Great Britain over the next thirty years.

Chinese and Japanese immigrants also came to the United States in appreciable numbers for the first time during the late nineteenth century. Most Chinese immigrants came from Canton in South China, a region of great rural poverty. They worked on railroads and in mines throughout the West and as farm laborers in California. Many eventually settled in cities such as San Francisco, where they established residential enclaves referred to as Chinatowns. The Chinese population in the United States peaked at about 125,000 in 1882.

Japanese began immigrating to the United States beginning in the late 1880s, driven by a land shortage even more acute than that in Europe. The first wave came by way of Hawaii, to work on farms in California, taking the place of Chinese workers, who had moved to the cities. By 1900, there were some fifty thousand

Japanese immigrants in the United States, nearly all on the West Coast.

Wherever they came from, most migrants saw the ocean as a two-way highway. They intended to stay only a year or two, long enough to earn money to buy land or, more likely, to enter a business back home and improve life for themselves and their families. Roughly half of all immigrants to the United States between 1880 and World War I returned to their country of origin. Some made several round trips. Jews, unwelcome in the lands they left, were the exception. No more than 10 percent of Jewish immigrants returned to Europe, and very few Jews from Russia, who accounted for almost 80 percent of Jewish immigrants after 1880, went back home.

Most newcomers were young men. (Jews, again, were the exception: Reflecting their intention to stay in their new home, they tended to migrate in families.) Immigrants easily found work in the nation's booming cities. The quickest way to make money was in the large urban factories, with their voracious

Southern Pacific

Chinese workers hewed out western forests to build the great railroads of the late nineteenth century. Here, Chinese immigrants work in the Sierras to construct the Central Pacific Railroad. Such workers suffered harsh living and working conditions; some among those who survived found their way to cities such as San Francisco and Seattle to create new and better lives.

demands for unskilled labor. Except for the Japanese, few immigrants came to work on farms after 1880.

By 1900, women began to equal men among all immigrant groups as young men who decided to stay, sent for their families. In a few cases, entire villages migrated, drawn by the good fortune of one or two compatriots, a process called **chain migration**. The success of Francesco Barone, a Buffalo tavern owner, convinced eight thousand residents of his former village in Sicily to migrate to that city, many arriving on tickets Barone purchased.

Immigrants tended to live in neighborhoods among people from the same homeland. Their native culture helped shape their response to their new home. For Italians from the Mezzogiorno, for example, the family was the basic institution for obtaining work and securing assistance in times of stress, death, or sickness. Family ties were so strong that voluntary associations in the towns of the Mezzogiorno were rare. In the United States, immigrants from southern Italy, almost alone among European and Asian migrants, rarely formed neighborhood or ethnic associations.

The desire of the new immigrants to retain their cultural traditions led contemporary observers to doubt their ability to assimilate into American society. Even sympathetic observers, such as social workers, marveled at the utterly foreign character of immi-

grant districts. In 1900, a Philadelphia social worker, Emily Dinwiddie, visited an Italian neighborhood and described "black-eyed children, rolling and tumbling together, the gaily colored dresses of the women and the crowds of street vendors, that give the neighborhood a wholly foreign appearance."

THE NEIGHBORHOOD

Immigrants did not live in homogeneous communities isolated from the rest of society. Rarely did a particular ethnic group comprise more than 50 percent of a neighborhood. The Chinese were the exception, but even the borders of Chinatowns usually overlapped with other neighborhoods. A particular apartment building might house families from Abruzzi in Italy, and Jews from Kiev might dominate a block of tenements in New York City's Lower East Side, but greater concentrations were rare. Even to call such districts "Jewish" or "Italian" distorts the reality. Most Italian immigrants identified not so much with Italy—which had only recently been unified—as with the village of their birth. Only with time did they come to see themselves as "Italian" in the way the rest of American society saw them.

German Jews, long established in American cities, wanted little to do with their Russian coreligionists at first. Yet, as the larger society conflated both groups, they began to help the newcomers assimilate into American society.

In smaller cities and in the urban South, where foreign-born populations were smaller, ethnic groups were more geographically dispersed, though occasionally they might inhabit the same neighborhood. In turn-of-the-century Memphis, for example, Irish, Italian, and Jewish immigrants lived cheek by jowl in a single immigrant district (called the Pinch), sharing schools and recreational space even as they led their singular institutional, religious, and family lives.

Immigrants maintained their cultural traditions through the establishment of religious and communal institutions. Charitable organizations were frequently connected to religious institutions. The church or synagogue became the focal point for immigrant neighborhood life. Much more than a place of worship, it was a school for transmitting Old World values and language to American-born children. The church or synagogue also functioned as a recreational facility and a gathering place for community leaders. In Jewish communities, associations called *landsmanshaften* arranged for burials, jobs, housing, and support for the sick, poor, and elderly.

Because religious institutions were so central to their lives, immigrant communities insisted on maintaining control over them. Polish parishioners wanted

Mulberry Street, New York, 1905. The vibrant, predominantly Russian Jewish Lower East Side of New York at first reflected more the culture of the homeland than of the United States. Language, dress, ways of doing business, keeping house, and worshiping, all followed Old World patterns. Gradually, thanks especially to the influence of school-age children, a blend of Russian Jewish and United States traditions emerged.

Polish priests, and Russian Jewish communities wanted Russian rabbis. The nationality of parish priests became such a heated topic for some Catholic national groups that they threatened to secede from the church, a movement the hierarchy squelched.

Religious institutions played a less formal role among Chinese and Japanese neighborhoods. For them, the family functioned as the source of religious activity and communal organization. Chinatowns were organized in clans of people with the same surname. An umbrella organization called the Chinese Consolidated Benevolent Association emerged; it functioned like the Jewish *landsmanshaften*. Perhaps most important, the association shipped the bones of deceased members back to China for burial in ancestral cemeteries. A similar association, the Japanese Association of America, governed the Japanese community in the United States. This organization was sponsored by the Japanese government, which was sensitive to mistreatment of its citizens abroad and anxious that immigrants set a good example. The Japanese Association, unlike other ethnic organizations, actively encouraged assimilation and stressed the importance of Western dress and learning English.

Ethnic newspapers, theaters, and schools supplemented associational life for immigrants. These institutions reinforced Old-World culture while informing immigrants about American ways. Thus, the *Jewish Daily Forward*, first published in New York in 1897, re-

minded readers of the importance of keeping the Sabbath while admonishing them to adopt American customs.

THE JOB

If the neighborhood provided a familiar and supportive environment for the immigrant, work offered the ultimate reward for coming to America. All immigrants perceived the job as the way to independence and as a way out, either back to the Old World or into the larger American society.

Immigrants typically received their first job with the help of a countryman. Italian, Chinese, Japanese, and Mexican newcomers worked with contractors who placed them in jobs. These middlemen often provided housing, loans, and other services for recent arrivals. They exacted a fee, sometimes extortionate, for their services. In an era before employment agencies, however, they efficiently matched immigrants with jobs. Other immigrant groups, such as Poles and Russian Jews, often secured work through their ethnic associations or village or family connections. Poles in the meatpacking industries in Chicago, for example, recommended relatives to their bosses. Family members sometimes exchanged jobs with one another.

The type of work available to immigrants depended on their skills, the local economy, and local discrimination. Mexican migrants to southern California, for example, concentrated in railroad construction. Mostly unskilled, they replaced Chinese laborers when the federal government excluded Chinese immigration after 1882. Mexicans built the interurban rail lines of Los Angeles in 1900 and established communities at their construction camps. Los Angeles businessmen barred Mexicans from other occupations. Similarly, Chinese immigrants were confined to work in laundries and restaurants within the boundaries of Los Angeles's Chinatown. There were no commercial laundries in China.

The Japanese who came to Los Angeles around 1900 were forced into sectors of the economy native-born white people had either shunned or failed to exploit. The Japanese turned this discrimination to their benefit when they transformed the cultivation of market garden crops into a major agricultural enterprise. By 1904, Japanese farmers owned more than fifty thousand acres in California. George Shima, who came to California from Japan in 1889 with a little capital, made himself the "Potato King" of the Sacramento Delta. By 1913, Shima owned 28,000 acres of farmland.

Other ethnic groups in other parts of the country had to conform to similar constraints. Greeks in Chicago, for example, restricted to food services, established restaurants, fruit distributorships, and ice-cream factories throughout the city.

Stereotypes also channeled immigrants' work options, sometimes benefiting one group at the expense of another. Jewish textile entrepreneurs, for example, sometimes hired only Italians because they thought them less prone to unionization than Jewish workers. Other Jewish bosses hired only Jewish workers, hoping that ethnic loyalty would overcome the lure of the unions. Pittsburgh steelmakers preferred Polish workers to the black workers who began arriving in northern cities in appreciable numbers after 1900. This decision began the decades-long tradition of handing down steel mill jobs through the generations in Polish families.

Jews, alone among European ethnic groups, found work almost exclusively with one another. Among the factors contributing to this pattern may have been the discrimination Jews faced in eastern Europe, the existence of an established Jewish community when they arrived, and their domination of the needle trades. Jews comprised three-quarters of the more than half-million workers in New York City's garment industry in 1910. Jews were also heavily concentrated in the retail trade.

Like their native-born counterparts, few married immigrant women worked outside the home, but unlike the native-born, many Italian and Jewish women did piecework for the garment industry in their apartments. Unmarried Polish women often worked in factories or as domestic servants. Japanese women, married and single, worked with their families on farms. Until revolution in China in 1911 began to erode traditional gender roles, married Chinese immigrant women typically remained at home.

The paramount goal for many immigrants was to work for themselves, rather than for someone else. Some immigrants, like George Shima, parlayed their skills and a small stake into successful businesses. Most new arrivals, however, had few skills, and no resources beyond their wits, with which to realize their dreams. Major banks at the time were unlikely to extend even a small business loan to a budding ethnic entrepreneur. Family members and small ethnic-based community banks provided the initial stake for most immigrant businesses. Many of these banks failed, but a few survived and prospered. For example, the Bank of Italy, established by Amadeo Pietro Giannini in San Francisco in 1904, eventually grew into the Bank of America, one of the nation's largest financial institutions today.

Immigrants could not fully control their own destinies in the United States, any more than native-born Americans could. The vagaries of daily life, including death, disease, and bad luck, thwarted many immigrants' dreams. Hard work did not always insure success. Add to these the difficulty of cultural adjustment to an unfamiliar environment, and the newcomer's confident hopes could fade quickly. Almost all immigrants, however, faced an obstacle that by its nature white native-born Americans did not. They faced it on the job, in the city at large, and even in their neighborhoods: the antiforeign prejudice of American nativism.

NATIVISM

Despite the openness of American borders in the nineteenth century, and contrary to the nation's reputation as a refuge from foreign persecution and poverty, immigrants have not always received a warm reception. Ben Franklin groused about the "foreignness" of German immigrants during the colonial era. From the 1830s to 1860, nativist sentiment, directed mainly at Irish Catholic immigrants, expressed itself in occasional violence and job discrimination. Anti-immigrant sentiment gave rise to an important political party, the Know-Nothings, in the 1850s.

When immigration revived after the Civil War, so did antiforeign sentiment. But late-nineteenth-century **nativism** differed in two ways from its antebellum predecessor. First, the target was no longer Irish Catholics, but the even more numerous Catholics and Jews of southern and eastern Europe, people whose languages and usually darker complexions set them apart from the native-born majority. Second, late-nineteenth-century nativism had a pseudoscientific underpinning. As we saw in Chapter 16, the so-called "scientific" racism of the period maintained that some people are inherently inferior to others. There was, in this view, a natural hierarchy of race. At the top, with the exception of the Irish, were northern Europeans, especially those of Anglo-Saxon descent. Following below them were French, Slavs, Poles, Italians, Jews, Asians, and Africans. Social Darwinism, which justified the class hierarchy, reinforced scientific racism.

When the "inferior" races arrived in the United States in significant numbers after 1880, nativists sounded the alarm. A prominent Columbia University professor wrote in 1887 that Hungarians and Italians were "of such a character as to endanger our civilization." Nine years later, the director of the U.S. census warned that eastern and southern Europeans were "beaten men from beaten races. They have none of the ideas and aptitudes which fit men to take up readily and easily the problem of self-care and self-government." The result of unfettered migration would be "race suicide."

The popular press translated these scientific pronouncements into blunter language. In the mid-1870s, a Chicago newspaper described recently arrived Bohemian immigrants (from the present-day Czech Republic) as "depraved beasts, harpies, decayed physically and spiritually, mentally and morally, thievish and licentious." A decade later, with eastern Europeans still pouring into Chicago, another newspaper suggested: "Let us whip these slavic wolves back to the European dens from which they issue, or in some way exterminate them." The *New York Times*, demurring from such an extreme, suggested instead some form of restriction. Referring to Russian Jewish and Italian immigrants, the *Times* concluded that Americans "pretty well agreed" that these foreigners were "of a kind which we are better without." The rhetoric of the scientific press was scarcely less extreme. *Scientific American* magazine warned immigrants to "assimilate" quickly or "share the fate of the native Indians" and face "a quiet but sure extermination."

Such sentiments generated proposals to restrict foreign immigration. The treatment of the Chinese provided a precedent. Chinese immigrants had long worked for low wages, under harsh conditions, in mining and railroad construction in the West. Their different culture and their willingness to accept low wages provoked resentment among native- and European-born workers. Violence against Chinese laborers increased during the 1860s and 1870s. In 1870, the Republican-dominated Congress passed the Naturalization Act, which limited citizenship to "white persons and persons of African descent." The act was specifically intended to prevent Chinese from becoming citizens—a ban not lifted until 1943—but it affected other Asian groups also. The Chinese Exclusion Act of 1882, passed following another decade of anti-Chinese pressure, made the Chinese the only ethnic group in the world that could not emigrate freely to the United States. Even this drastic measure did not satisfy one Knights of Labor official, who in 1885 viewed the conflict between Chinese and native-born labor in the perspective of the 1850s sectional crisis (with a modern Darwinian twist): "This is the old irrepressible conflict between slave and white labor. God grant there may be survival of the fittest." Anti-Asian violence raced through mining communities in the West for the next two years.

Labor competition also contributed to the rise of another anti-immigrant organization. A group of skilled workers and small businessmen formed the American Protective Association (APA) in 1887 and claimed half a million members a year later. The APA sought to limit Catholic civil rights in the United States to protect the jobs of Protestant workingmen.

The Immigration Restriction League (IRL), formed in 1894 in the midst of a depression, took a more modest and indirect approach. The IRL proposed to require prospective immigrants to pass a literacy test that they presumed most southern and eastern Europeans would fail. Cynically reaching out to native-born workers, the IRL vowed that its legislation would protect "the wages of our workingmen against the fatal competition of low-price labor."

The IRL ultimately failed to have its literacy requirement enacted. The return of prosperity and the growing preference of industrialists for immigrant labor put an end to calls for formal restrictions on immigration for the time being. Less than thirty years later, however, Congress would enact major restrictive legislation aimed at southern and eastern European immigrants. In the meantime, IRL propaganda encouraged northern universities to establish quotas limiting the admission of new immigrants, especially Jews.

Immigrants and their communal associations fought attempts to restrict immigration. The Japanese government even hinted at violent retaliation if Congress ever enacted restrictive legislation similar to that imposed on the Chinese. But most immigrants believed that the more "American" they became, the less prejudice they would encounter.

Accordingly, leaders of immigrant groups stressed the importance of assimilation.

In 1895, a group of American-born Chinese in California formed a communal association called the Native Sons of the Golden State (a deliberate response to a nativist organization that called itself the Native Sons of the Golden West). Stressing the need to assimilate, the association's constitution declared, "It is imperative that no members shall have sectional, clannish, Tong [a secret fraternal organization] or party prejudices against each other. . . . Whoever violates this provision shall be expelled." A guidebook written at the same time for immigrant Jews recommended that they "hold fast," calling that attitude "most necessary in America. Forget your past, your customs, and your ideals . . . . A bit of advice to you: do not take a moment's rest. Run, do, work, and keep your own good in mind." Although it is doubtful whether most Jewish immigrants followed this advice whole, it nonetheless reflects the way the pressure to conform modified the cultures of all immigrant groups.

Assimilation connotes the loss of one culture in favor of another. The immigrant experience of the late nineteenth and early twentieth centuries might better be described as a process of adjustment between old ways and new. It was a dynamic process that resulted in entirely new cultural forms. It rarely followed a straight line toward or from the culture of origin. The Japanese, for example, had not gone to Los Angeles to become truck farmers, but circumstances led them to that occupation, and they used their cultural heritage of hard work, strong family ties, and sober living to make a restricted livelihood successful. Sometimes economics and the availability of alternatives resulted in modifications of traditions that nonetheless maintained their spirit. In the old country, Portuguese held *festas* every Sunday honoring a patron saint. In New England towns, they confined the tradition to their churches, instead of parading through the streets. And instead of baking bread themselves, Portuguese immigrant women were happy to buy all the bread they needed from local bakers.

In a few cases, the New World offered greater opportunities to follow cultural traditions than the Old. Young women who migrated from Italy's Abruzzi region to Rochester, New York, found that it was easier to retain their Old World moral code in late-nineteenth-century Rochester, where young men outnumbered them significantly. At the same time, the enhanced economic prospects in Rochester enabled them to marry earlier than they would have in their hometown. It also allowed these young women to work outside the home, something women rarely did in Abruzzi. Financial security allowed them to construct the nuclear household that was the cultural ideal in the old country. In a similar way, Sicilians who migrated to lower Manhattan discovered that ready access to work and relatively high geographical mobility permitted them to live near and among their extended families much more easily than they could in Sicily.

Despite the antagonism of native-born white people toward recent immigrants, the greatest racial divide in America remained that between black and white. Newcomers quickly caught on to this distinction and sought to assert their "whiteness" as a common bond with other European immigrant groups and a badge of acceptance into the larger society. Nativists, however, often lumped immigrants into the "black" category. The word "guinea," for example, which originally referred to African slaves, emerged as a derogatory epithet for Italians and, occasionally, Greeks, Jews, and Puerto Ricans. When the Louisiana legislature debated disfranchisement in 1898, a lawmaker explained that "according to the spirit of our meaning when we speak of 'white man's government,' Italians are as black as the blackest negro in existence." For immigrants, therefore, becoming "white" —distancing themselves from African American culture and people—was often part of the process of adjusting to American life, especially as increasing numbers of black Southerners began moving to northern cities.

ROOTS OF THE GREAT MIGRATION

Nearly 90 percent of African Americans still lived in the South in 1900, most in rural areas. Between 1880 and 1900, however, black families began to move into the great industrial cities of the Northeast and Midwest. They were drawn by the same economic promise that attracted overseas migrants and were pushed by growing persecution in the South. They were also responding to the appeals of black Northerners. As a leading black newspaper, the *Chicago Defender* argued in the early 1900s, "To die from the bite of frost is far more glorious than at the hands of a mob. I beg you, my brother, to leave the benighted land." Job opportunities probably outweighed all other factors in motivating what became known as the **Great Migration**. Letters to the *Defender* spoke much less of the troubled life in the South than of the promise of a new, more productive life in the North.

In most northern cities in 1900, black people typically worked as common laborers or domestic servants. They competed with immigrants for jobs, and in most cases they lost. Immigrants even claimed jobs that black workers once dominated, such as barbering

An African American religious meeting, New York City, early 1900s. Black migrants from the South found vibrant communities in northern cities typically centered around black churches and their activities. Like immigrants from Asia and Europe, who sought to transplant the culture of their homelands within the urban United States, black migrants reestablished southern religious and communal traditions in their new homes.

and service work in hotels, restaurants, and transportation. Fannie Barrier Williams, a turn-of-the-century black activist in Chicago, complained that between 1895 and 1905, "the colored people of Chicago have lost . . . nearly every occupation of which they once had almost a monopoly."

Black women had particularly few options in the northern urban labor force outside of domestic service, although they earned higher wages than they had for similar work in southern cities. The retail and clerical jobs that attracted young working-class white women remained closed to black women. Employers rejected them for any job involving direct contact with the public. As one historian concluded, advertisers and corporate executives demanded "a pleasing physical appearance (or voice)—one that conformed to a native-born white American standard of female beauty [and served] as an important consideration in hiring office receptionists, secretaries, department store clerks, and telephone operators." Addie W. Hunter, who qualified for a civil-service clerical position in Boston, could not find work to match her

training. She concluded in 1916, "For the way things stand at present, it is useless to have the requirements. Color . . . will always be in the way."

The lack of options black migrants confronted in the search for employment matched similar frustrations in their quest for a place to live. Even more than foreign immigrants, they were restricted to segregated urban ghettos. Small black ghettos existed in antebellum northern cities. In 1860, four out of every five black residents of Detroit lived in a clearly defined district, for example. After the Civil War, black ghettos emerged in southern and border cities. In Washington, D.C., black residents comprised nearly 80 percent of the population in a twenty-block area in the southwest quadrant of the city. In the 1890s, black people dominated an area east of downtown Atlanta known as Sweet Auburn, after the avenue that cut through the neighborhood. As black migration to northern cities accelerated after 1900, the pattern of residential isolation became more pronounced. The black districts in northern cities were more diverse than those in southern cities. Migration brought rural Southerners, urban Southerners, and West Indians together with the black Northerners already living there. People of all social classes lived in these districts.

The difficulties that black families faced to make ends meet paralleled in some ways those of immigrant working-class families. Restricted job options, however, limited the income of black families, even with black married women five times more likely to work than married white women. In black families, moreover, working teenage children were less likely to stay home and contribute their paychecks to the family income.

Popular culture reinforced the marginalization of African Americans. Vaudeville and minstrel shows, popular urban entertainment around 1900, featured songs belittling black people and black characters with names like Useless Peabody and Moses Abraham Highbrow. Immigrants frequented these shows and absorbed the culture of racism from them. The new medium of film perpetuated the negative stereotypes.

In the North as in the South, African Americans sought to counter the hostility of the larger society by building their own community institutions. An emerging middle-class leadership—including Robert Abbott, publisher of the *Chicago Defender*—sought to develop black businesses. Despite these efforts, chronic lack of capital kept black businesses mostly small and confined to the ghetto. Immigrant groups often pooled extended family capital resources or tapped ethnic banks. With few such resources at their disposal, black businesses failed at a high rate. Most black people worked outside the ghetto for white employers. Economic marginalization often attracted unsavory businesses—dance halls, brothels, and bars—to black neighborhoods. One recently arrived migrant from the South complained that in his Cleveland neighborhood, his family was surrounded by loafers, "gamblers [and] pocket pickers; I can not raise my children here like they should be. This is one of the worst places in principle you ever looked on in your life."

Other black institutions proved more lasting than black businesses. In Chicago in 1891, black physician Daniel Hale Williams established Provident Hospital, the nation's first interracially staffed hospital, with the financial help of wealthy white Chicagoans. Although it failed as an interracial experiment, the hospital thrived, providing an important training ground for black physicians and nurses.

The organization of black branches of the Young Men's and Young Women's Christian Association provided living accommodations, social facilities, and employment information for black young people. Many black migrants to northern cities—perhaps a majority—were single, and the Y provided them guidance and a "home." White people funded many black Y projects but did not accept black members in their chapters. By 1910, black settlement houses modeled after white versions appeared in several cities.

NEW CITIES

Despite the hardships associated with urban life, the American city continued to act, in the words of the contemporary novelist Theodore Dreiser, as a "giant magnet." Immigration from abroad and migration from American farms to the cities resulted in an urban explosion during the late nineteenth century (see Map 18–2). In 1850, six cities had a population exceeding 100,000; by 1900, thirty-eight did. In 1850, only 5 percent of the nation's population lived in cities of more than 100,000 inhabitants; by 1900, the figure was 19 percent. The nation's population tripled between 1860 and 1920, but the urban population increased ninefold. Of the 1,700 cities listed in the 1900 census, less than 2 percent even existed in 1800.

In Europe, a few principal cities, such as Paris and Berlin, absorbed most of the urban growth during this period. In the United States, by contrast, growth was more evenly distributed among many cities. In 1820, about 18 percent of the urban population of the United States lived in New York, the nation's largest city; by 1890, its share had fallen to 7 percent. Put another way, many U.S. cities experienced the pains of rapid growth and industrialization in the late nineteenth century.

Despite the relative evenness of growth, a distinctive urban system had emerged by 1900, with New York and Chicago anchoring an urban-industrial core extending in a crescent from New England to the cities bordering the Great Lakes. This region included nine of the nation's ten largest cities in 1920. Such Western cities as Denver, San Francisco, and Los Angeles emerged as dominant urban places in their respective regions but did not challenge the urban core for supremacy. Southern cities, limited in growth by low consumer demand, low wages, and weak capital formation, were drawn into the orbit of the urban core. Atlanta, an offspring of the railroad, prospered as the region's major way station for funneling wealth into the urban North. Dallas emerged as Atlanta's counterpart in the western South (see Chapter 17).

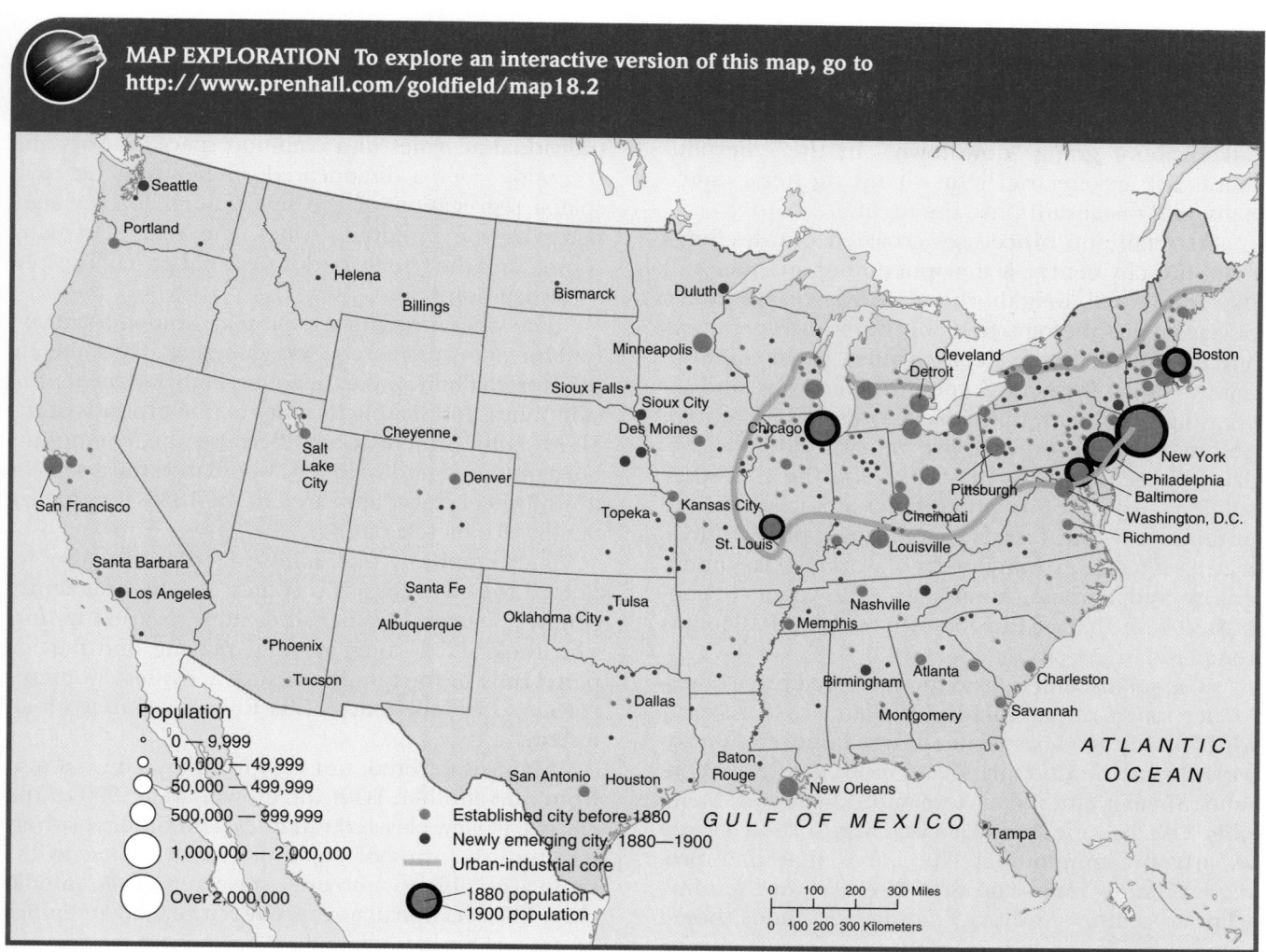

MAP EXPLORATION To explore an interactive version of this map, go to
http://www.prenhall.com/goldfield/map18.2

MAP 18-2   **The Growth of American Cities, 1880-1900**
Several significant trends stand out on this map. First is the development of an urban-industrial core, stretching from New England to the Midwest, where the largest cities were located. And second is the emergence of relatively new cities in the South and West, reflecting the national dimensions of innovations in industry and transportation.

Urban growth highlighted the growing divisions in American society. The crush of people and the emergence of new technologies expanded the city outward and upward as urban dwellers sorted themselves by social class and ethnic group. While the new infrastructure of water and sewer systems, bridges, and trolley tracks kept steel mills busy, it also fragmented the urban population by allowing settlements well beyond existing urban boundaries. The way people satisfied their needs for food, clothing, and shelter stimulated the industrial economy while distinguishing one class from another. Although urban institutions emerged to counter these divisive trends, they could not overcome them completely.

CENTERS AND SUBURBS

The centers of the country's great cities changed in scale and function in this era, achieving a prominence they would eventually lose in the twentieth century. Downtowns expanded up and out as tall buildings arose—monuments to business and finance—creating towering urban skylines. Residential neighborhoods were pushed out, leaving the center dominated by corporate headquarters and retail and entertainment districts.

Corporate heads administered their empires from downtown, even if their factories were located on the urban periphery or in other towns and cities. Banks and insurance companies clustered in such financial centers as Atlanta's Five Points district, to service the corporations. Department stores and shops clustered in retail districts in strategic locations along electric trolley lines. It was to these areas that urban residents usually referred when they talked about going "downtown." In the entertainment district, electric lights lit up theaters, dance halls, and restaurants into the night.

As retail and office uses crowded out dwellings from the city center, a new phenomenon emerged: the residential neighborhood. Advances in transportation technology, first the horse-drawn railway and, by the 1890s, the electric trolley, eased commuting for office workers. Some in the growing and increasingly affluent middle class left the crowded, polluted city altogether to live in new residential suburbs. These people did not abandon the city—they still looked to it for its jobs, schools, libraries, and entertainment—but they rejected it as a place to live, leaving it to the growing ranks of working-class immigrants and African Americans. This pattern contrasted with that of Europe, where the middle class remained in the city.

The suburb emerged as the preferred place of residence for the urban middle class after 1870. As early as 1873, Chicago boasted nearly one hundred suburbs with a combined population of more than fifty thousand. Smaller cities like Cleveland, Richmond, Memphis, Omaha, and San Francisco also sprouted large suburban communities. The ideals that had promoted modest suburban growth earlier in the nineteenth century—privacy, aesthetics, and home ownership—became increasingly important to the growing numbers of middle-class families after 1880.

Consider the Russells of Short Hills, New Jersey. Short Hills lay 18 miles by railroad from New York City. William Russell; his wife, Ella Gibson Russell; and their six children moved there from Brooklyn in the late 1880s, seeking a "pleasant, cultured people whose society we could enjoy" and a cure for Russell's rheumatism. Russell owned and managed a small metal brokerage in New York and enjoyed gardening, reading, and socializing with his new neighbors. Ella Russell cared for their six children with the help of a servant and also found time for several clubs and charities.

The design of the Russells's home reflected the principles Catharine Beecher and Harriet Beecher Stowe outlined in their suburban home bible, *American Woman's Home* (1869). The kitchen, according to Beecher and Stowe, should be organized for expedience and hygiene. The home's utilities should be confined to a central core, freeing wall areas for other functions. The new technology of central heating made it unnecessary to divide a house into many small rooms, each with its own fireplace or stove. Taking advantage of this change, Beecher and Stowe recommended that a home's ground floor have fewer but larger rooms, to encourage the family to pursue their individual activities in a common space. Parlors and reception rooms disappeared, along with the rigid spatial segregation of the sexes. Such former standards as the children's wing, the male "smoking room," and the female parlor were not part of the new suburban home.

The once prevailing view that women were too frail for vigorous exercise was changing. Thus, the entire Russell family was to be found enjoying the tennis, swimming, and skating facilities on the grounds of the Short Hills Athletic Club. Because the community bordered on undeveloped woodland traversed by trails, "wheel clubs" appeared in the 1880s to organize families for bicycle outings.

The emphasis on family togetherness also reflected the changing role of men in late-nineteenth-century society. Beecher and Stowe praised fathers who took active roles in child rearing and participated fully in the family's leisure activities. Women's roles also broadened, as Ella Russell's club work attested.

Suburbs differed, not only from the city, but also from one another. With the growth after 1890 of the electric trolley, elevated rail lines, and other relatively inexpensive forms of commuter travel, suburbs became accessible to a broader spectrum of the middle class. The social structure, architecture, and amenities of suburbs varied, depending on the rail service and distance from the city. The commuter railroad remained popular among people like the Russells who could afford the time and expense of commuting to and from the city center—a distance of fifteen miles or more. The trolley and elevated railroads generated modest middle-class urban neighborhoods and suburbs, with densities decreasing and income increasing toward the ends of the lines. But for the working class—even skilled artisans—suburban living remained out of reach.

The suburb underscored the growing fragmentation of life in and around American cities in the late nineteenth century. Residence, consumer habits, and leisure activities reflected growing social and class divisions. Yet, at the same time, the growing materialism of American society promised a common ground for its disparate ethnic, racial, and social groups.

THE NEW MIDDLE CLASS

From the colonial era, America's urban middle class had included professionals—physicians, lawyers, ministers, educators, editors—as well as merchants, shopkeepers, and skilled artisans (until they dropped from the middle class in the late nineteenth century). In the late nineteenth century, industrial technology and urban growth expanded the urban middle class to include salespeople, factory supervisors, managers, civil servants, technicians, and a broad range of "white-collar" office workers such as insurance agents, bank tellers, and legal assistants. This newer middle class set national trends in residential patterns, consumption, and leisure.

The more affluent members of the new middle class, like the Russells, repaired to new subdivisions within and outside the city limits. Simple row houses sheltered the growing numbers of clerks and civil servants who remained in the city. These dwellings contrasted sharply with the crowded one- or two-room apartments that confined the working class. Rents for these apartments ran as much as $3 a week, at a time when few workers made more than $9 or $10.

A CONSUMER SOCIETY

The new middle class transformed America into a consumer society. In earlier times, land had been a symbol of prestige. Now it was things. And the new industries obliged with a dazzling array of goods and technologies to make life easier and allow more time for family and leisure.

By 1910, the new middle class lived in all-electric homes, with indoor plumbing and appliances unavailable twenty years earlier. A typical kitchen might include an electric coffeepot, a hot plate, a chafing dish, and a toaster. These items eased food preparation. The modern city dweller worked by the clock, not by the sun. Eating patterns changed: cold packaged cereals replaced hot meats at breakfast; fast lunches of Campbell's soup—"a meal in itself"— or canned stews weaned Americans from the heavy lunch. Jell-O appeared in the 1890s, touted as America's "most quick and easy" dessert. In Nashville at the same time, Joel Cheek ground and blended coffee beans in his store for customers' convenience. He convinced the city's Maxwell House Hotel to serve his new concoction, and in 1907, when President Theodore Roosevelt visited the hotel and drained his cup, he turned to Cheek and declared that the coffee was "good to the very last drop." A slogan and Maxwell House coffee were born.

Advertising played an important role in the consumer society. Advertisers told Americans what they wanted; they created demand and developed loyalty for brand-name products. In early-twentieth-century New York, a six-story-high Heinz electric sign was a sensation, especially the forty-foot-long pickle at its top.

The middle class liked anything that saved time: trolleys, trains, electric razors, vacuum cleaners. The telephone replaced the letter for everyday communication; it was quicker and less formal. By 1900, some 1.4 million phones were in service, and many middle-class homes had one. The new technology introduced new terms that reflected the pace of urban life: "I'll give you a buzz" or "Give me a ring."

The middle class liked its news in an easy-to-read form. Urban tabloids multiplied after 1880, led by Joseph Pulitzer's *New York World* and William Randolph Hearst's *New York Journal*. The newspapers organized the news into topical sections, used bold headlines and graphics to catch the eye, ran human interest stories to capture the imagination, inaugurated sports pages to attract male readers, and offered advice columns for women. And they opened their pages to a wide range of attractive advertising, much of it directed to women, who did about 90 percent of the shopping in American cities by 1900.

As the visual crowded out the printed in advertising, newspapers, and magazines, these materials became more accessible to a wider urban audience. Although mainly middle class in orientation, the tabloid press drew urban society together with new features such as the comic strip, which first appeared in the 1890s, and heart-rending personal sagas drawn from real life. Immigrants, who might have had difficulty reading small-type newspapers, received their initiation into the mainstream of American society through the tabloids.

In a similar manner, the department store, essentially a middle-class retail establishment, became one of the city's most democratic forums and the focus of the urban downtown after 1890. Originating in the 1850s and 1860s, with the construction of retail palaces such as Boston's Jordan Marsh, Philadelphia's Wanamaker & Brown, New York's Lord & Taylor, and Chicago's Marshall Field, the department store came to epitomize the bounty of the new industrial capitalism. At the time of the Philadelphia Exposition in 1876, only thirty or so department stores existed; by 1920, there were thousands. They exuded limitless abundance with their extensive inventories, items for every budget, sumptuous surroundings, and efficient, trained personnel.

At first, most department-store customers were middle-class married women. Not expected to work and with disposable income and flexible schedules, these women had the means and time to wander department store aisles. The stores catered to their tastes—and the current emphasis on home and domesticity—with such items as prefabricated household furnishings, ready-made clothing, toys, and stationery.

Industry churned out uniform, high-quality products in abundance, and middle-class salaries absorbed them. Department stores maintained consumers' interest with advertising campaigns arranged around holidays such as Easter and Christmas, the seasons, and the school calendar. Each event required new clothing and accessories, and the ready-made clothing industry changed fashions accordingly.

Soon the spectacle and merchandise of the department store attracted shoppers from all social strata, not just the middle class. "The principal cause of the stores' success," one shopper explained in 1892, "is the fact that their founders have understood the necessity of offering a new democracy whose needs and habits" are satisfied "in the cheapest possible way," providing "a taste for elegance and comfort unknown to previous generations." Though many less affluent women came merely to "window-shop" (a new expression inspired by the large plate-glass display windows retailers installed in their stores to attract customers), some came to buy. After 1890, department stores increasingly hired young immigrant women, to cater to their growing foreign-born clientele.

The department store was the turn-of-the-century shopping mall and provided another inexpensive amusement for young working-class people, especially immigrants. Mary Antin recalled how she and her teenage friends and sister would spend their Saturday nights in 1898 patrolling "a dazzlingly beautiful palace called a 'department store.'" It was there that Mary and her sister "exchanged our hateful homemade European costumes . . . for real American machine-made garments, and issued forth glorified in each other's eyes."

By 1900, department stores had added sporting goods and hardware sections and were attracting customers from a wide social spectrum. When Wanamaker's introduced a "bargain room" in 1888, other retail stores—including Filene's famous "Automatic Bargain Basement" in Boston—followed suit.

THE GROWTH OF LEISURE ACTIVITIES

The expanding floor space devoted to sporting goods reflected the growth of leisure in urban society. And like other aspects of that society, leisure and recreation both separated and cut across social classes. The leisure activities of the wealthy increasingly removed them from the rest of urban society. For them, the good life required such prerequisites as a mansion on Fifth Avenue, carriages and horses for transportation, a pony for the younger children, a sad-

dle horse for the older ones, and a yacht. As such sports as football became important extracurricular activites at Harvard, Yale, and other elite universities, intercollegiate games became popular occasions for the upper class to congregate and, not incidentally, to discuss business. For exercise and recreation, the elite gathered at the athletic clubs and country clubs that emerged as open spaces disappeared in the city. High fees and strict membership criteria kept these clubs exclusive. The first country club in the United States was founded in Brookline, Massachusetts, a Boston suburb, in 1882. Country clubs built golf courses for men and tennis courts primarily for women. The clubs offered a suburban retreat, away from the diverse middle- and working-class populations, where the elite could play in privacy.

Middle-class urban residents could not afford country clubs, but they rode electric trolleys to the end of the line to enjoy suburban parks and bicycle and skating clubs. Reflecting the emphasis on family togetherness in late-nineteenth-century America, both men and women participated in these sports. Bicycling in particular became immensely popular. New bikes cost at least $50, putting them beyond the reach of the working class.

If college football was the rage among the elite, baseball was the leading middle-class spectator sport. Organized baseball originated among the urban elite before the Civil War. The middle class took over the sport after the war. Baseball epitomized the nation's transition from a rural to an urban industrial society. Reflecting rural tradition, it was played on an expanse of green, usually on the outskirts of the city. It was leisurely; unlike other games, it had no time limit. Reflecting industrial society, however, it had clearly defined rules and was organized into leagues. Professional leagues were profit-making enterprises, and, like other enterprises, they frequently merged. Initially, most professional baseball games were played on weekday afternoons, making it hard for working-class spectators to attend. After merging with the American Association (AA) in 1883, the National League adopted some of the AA's innovations to attract more fans, including beer sales, cheap admission, and, despite the objections of Protestant churches, Sunday games.

The tavern, or saloon, was the workingman's club. Typically an all-male preserve, the saloon provided drink, cheap food, and a place for workingmen to read a newspaper, socialize, and learn about job opportunities. Advances in refrigeration in the 1870s allowed large breweries such as Anheuser-Busch and Pabst to distribute their product nationwide. Alcoholism was a severe problem in cities, especially, though not exclusively, among working-class men,

Amusement for the masses. Better transportation, more leisure time, and disposable income fueled escapes such as Luna Park in Coney Island, Brooklyn, a place where people could come together and have fun in a relatively controlled environment.

fueling the prohibition movement of the late nineteenth century.

Amusement parks, with their mechanical wonders, were another hallmark of the industrial city. Declining trolley fares made these parks accessible to the working class around 1900. Unlike taverns, they provided a place for working-class men and women to meet and date.

The most renowned of these parks was Brooklyn's Coney Island. In 1897, George C. Tilyou opened Steeplechase Park on Coney Island. He brought an invention by George Washington Ferris—a giant rotating vertical wheel, equipped with swinging carriages—to the park from Chicago, and the Ferris Wheel quickly became a Coney Island signature. Together with such attractions as mechanical horses and 250,000 of Thomas Edison's light bulbs, Steeplechase dazzled patrons with its technological wonders. It was quickly followed by Luna Park and Dreamland, and the Coney Island attractions became collectively

known as "the poor man's paradise." Immigrant entrepreneurs, seeing a good thing, flocked to Coney Island to set up sideshows, pool halls, taverns, and restaurants. One German immigrant opened a small café serving sausages that he named "frankfurters" after his native Frankfurt. Locals called them "Coney Island hots" or "hot dogs" because they resembled the dachshund, a German-bred dog.

After 1900, the wonders of Coney Island began to lure people from all segments of an increasingly diverse city. Sightseers came from around the world. Notables such as Herman Melville, Mark Twain, and even Sigmund Freud (what did he think of Dreamland?) rubbed shoulders with factory workers, domestics, and department store clerks. In much the same manner, baseball was becoming a national pastime as games attracted a disparate crowd of people with little in common but their devotion to the home team.

Increasing materialism had revealed great fissures in American urban society by 1900. Yet places like deparment stores, baseball parks, and amusement parks provided democratic spaces for some interaction. Newspapers and schools also offered diverse groups the vicarious opportunity to share similar experiences.

CONCLUSION

The new industrial order, the changing nature of work, the massive migrations of populations from the countryside and abroad, and the rise of great cities changed the American landscape in the late nineteenth century. By 1900, the factory worker and the department store clerk were more representative of the new America than the farmer and small shopkeeper. Industry and technology had created thousands of new jobs, but they also eliminated the autonomy many workers had enjoyed and limited their opportunities to advance.

Immigrants thronged to the United States to realize their dreams of economic and religious freedom. They found both to varying degrees but also discovered a darker side to the promise of American life. The great cities thrilled newcomers with their possibilities and their abundance of goods and activities. But the cities also bore witness to the growing divisions in American society. As the new century dawned, the prospects for urban industrial America seemed limitless, yet the stark contrasts that had appeared so vividly inside and outside the Centennial Exposition persisted and deepened.

Still, it would be wrong to depict the nation in 1900 as merely a larger and more divided version of itself in 1876. Although sharp ethnic, racial, and class differences persisted, the nation seemed better poised to address them in 1900 than it had a quarter-century earlier. Labor unions, ethnic organizations, government legislation, and new urban institutions promised ways to remedy the worst abuses of the new urban, industrial economy.

REVIEW QUESTIONS

1. Were there ways to achieve the benefits of industrialization without its social costs, or did the nation's political and economic systems make that impossible?

2. How did working-class women respond to the new economy? How did their participation and responses differ from that of working-class men?

3. When historians speak of immigrant groups adjusting rather than assimilating to American society, what do they mean?

4. The growing fragmentation of urban life reflected deep divisions in modern urban industrial society. At the same time, there were forces that tended to overcome these divisions. What were these forces, and were they sufficient to bridge the divisions?

5. How did Old World conditions influence Mary Antin's adjustment to American life? Would individuals from other immigrant groups express similar sentiments, or is Mary's reaction specific to her Jewish background?

KEY TERMS

American Federation of Labor (p. 578)

Chain migration (p. 582)

Collective bargaining (p. 578)

Gilded Age (p. 565)

Gospel of Wealth (p. 575)

Great Migration (p. 586)

Great Uprising (p. 576)

Horizontal integration (p. 569)

Hull House (p. 574)

Knights of Labor (p. 577)

Nativism (p. 584)

Pogroms (p. 580)

Settlement house (p. 574)

Social Darwinism (p. 575)

Sweatshops (p. 571)

Tenements (p. 574)

Vertical integration (p. 569)

RECOMMENDED READING

Blumin, Stuart M. *The Emergence of the Middle Class: Social Experience in the American City, 1760–1900* (1989). Analyzes the key factors in the emergence of the urban middle class, especially in the late nineteenth century, and the impact of that class on urban society and culture.

Bodnar, John. *The Transplanted: A History of Immigrants in Urban America* (1985). An excellent starting point for learning about the diverse immigrant experience in the United States that is also sensitive to conditions in the countries of origin.

Daniels, Roger. *Coming to America: A History of Immigration and Ethnicity in American Life* (1990). Preferred by some to Bodnar's survey. The book's great virtue is its coverage of all immigrant groups; the discussion of Asian immigrants is especially good.

Dreiser, Theodore. *Sister Carrie* (1900). One of the best novels to capture life in late-nineteenth-century Chicago and New York. Few detail so clearly the moral and economic dilemmas newcomers faced in the fast-evolving American urban environment.

Higham, John. *Strangers in the Land: Patterns of American Nativism, 1860–1925* (1965). Despite its age, serves as an excellent overview of and introduction to the subject of nativism; especially good in setting the context of nativism in American society and politics

ADDITIONAL SOURCES
New Industry

Bazerman, Charles. *The Languages of Edison's Light* (1999).

Bellamy, Edward. *Looking Backward* (1888).

Benson, Susan Porter. *Counter Cultures: Saleswomen, Managers, and Customers in American Department Stores, 1890–1940* (1986).

Boris, Eileen. *Home to Work: Motherhood and the Politics of Industrial Homework in the United States* (1994).

Buder, Stanley. *Pullman: An Experiment in Industrial Order and Community Planning, 1880–1930* (1967).

Carlson, W. Bernard. *Innovation as a Social Process: Elihu Thomson and the Rise of General Electric, 1870–1900* (1991).

Davies, Marjorie. *Woman's Place Is at the Typewriter, 1870–1930* (1982).

Davis, Allan F. *Spearheads for Reform: The Social Settlements and the Progressive Movement, 1890–1914* (1967).

Dye, Nancy Schrom. *As Equals and as Sisters: Feminism, the Labor Movement, and the Women's Trade Union League of New York* (1981).

Enstad, Nan. *Ladies of Labor, Girls of Adventure: Working Women, Popular Culture, and Labor Politics at the Turn of the Twentieth Century* (1999).

Gilfoyle, Timothy J. *City of Eros: New York City, Prostitution, and the Commercialization of Sex, 1790–1920* (1992).

Gutman, Herbert. *Work, Culture, and Society in Industrializing America* (1976).

Katzman, David M. *Seven Days a Week: Women and Domestic Service in Industrializing America* (1978).

Kaufman, Stuart. *Samuel Gompers and the Origins of the American Federation of Labor, 1848–1896* (1973).

Kessler-Harris, Alice. *Out to Work: A History of Wage-Earning Women in the United States* (1982).

Lane, James B. *Jacob A. Riis and the American City* (1974).

Montgomery, David. *The Fall of the House of Labor: The Workplace, the State, and American Labor Activism, 1865–1925* (1987).

Sinclair, Upton. *The Jungle* (1906).

Stromquist, Shelton. *A Generation of Boomers: The Pattern of Railroad Labor Conflict in Nineteenth-Century America* (1987).

Tentler, Leslie Woodcock. *Wage-Earning Women: Industrial Work and Family Life, 1900–1930* (1979).

Tygiel, Jules. *Workingmen in San Francisco, 1880–1901* (1992).

Voss, Kim. *The Making of American Exceptionalism: The Knights of Labor and Class Formation in the Nineteenth Century* (1994).

New Immigrants

Blanck, Dag. *Becoming Swedish-American: The Construction of an Ethnic Identity in the Augustana Synod, 1860–1917* (1997).

Cahan, Abraham. *The Rise of David Levinsky* (1917).

Camarillo, Albert. *Chicanos in a Changing Society: From Mexican Pueblos to American Barrios in Santa Barbara and Southern California, 1848–1930* (1979).

Chen, Yong. *Chinese San Francisco, 1850-1943: A Trans-Pacific Community* (2000).

Clark, Dennis. *The Irish in Philadelphia: Ten Generations of Urban Experience* (1973).

Daniels, Roger. *Not Like Us: Immigrants and Minorities in America, 1890–1924* (1997).

Diner, Hasia. *Erin's Daughters in America* (1983).

Gabaccia, Donna. *From Sicily to Elizabeth Street: Housing and Social Change among Italian Immigrants, 1880–1930* (1984).

Gabaccia, Donna. *From the Other Side: Women, Gender, and Immigrant Life in the U.S., 1820–1990* (1994).

Glenn, Evelyn Nakano. *Issei, Nisei, War Bride: Three Generations of Japanese American Women in Domestic Service* (1986).

Harzig, Christiane, ed. *Peasant Maids—City Women: From the European Countryside to Urban America* (1997).

Howe, Irving. *World of Our Fathers* (1976).

Ignatiev, Noel. *How the Irish Became White* (1995).

Jacobson, Matthew Frye. *Whiteness of a Different Color: European Immigrants and the Alchemy of Race* (1998).

Kessner, Thomas. *The Golden Door: Italian and Jewish Immigrant Mobility in New York City, 1880–1915* (1977).

Kraut, Alan M. *The Huddled Masses: The Immigrant in American Society, 1880–1921* (1982).

Kusmer, Kenneth. *A Ghetto Takes Shape: Black Cleveland, 1870–1930* (1976).

Lerda, Valeria Gennaro, ed. *From "Melting Pot" to Multiculturalism: The Evolution of Ethnic Relations in the United States and Canada* (1990).

Mauk, David C. *The Colony that Rose from the Sea: Norwegian Maritime Migration and Community in Brooklyn, 1850–1910* (1997).

Modell, John. *The Economics and Politics of Racial Accommodation: The Japanese of Los Angeles, 1900–1942* (1977).

Roediger, David R. *The Wages of Whiteness: Race and the Making of the American Working Class* (rev. ed. 1999).

Smith, Betty. *A Tree Grows in Brooklyn* (1943).

Stewart, Kenneth L., and Arnoldo De Leon. *Not Room Enough: Mexicans, Anglos, and Socio-Economic Change in Texas, 1850–1900* (1993).

Vecoli, Rudolph J., and Suzanne M. Sinke, eds. *A Century of European Migrations, 1830–1930* (1991).

Wong, K. Scott, and Sucheng Chan, eds. *Claiming America: Constructing Chinese American Identities during the Exclusion Era* (1998).

New Cities

Barth, Gunther. *Instant Cities: Urbanization and the Rise of San Francisco and Denver* (1975).

Barth, Gunther. *City People: The Rise of Modern City Culture in Nineteenth-Century America* (1982).

Beckert, Sven. *The Monied Metropolis: New York City and the Consolidation of the American Bourgeoisie, 1850–1896* (2001).

Bluestone, Daniel. *Constructing Chicago* (1991).

Burrows, Edwin G., and Mike Wallace. *Gotham: A History of New York City to 1898* (1998).

Couvares, Francis G. *The Remaking of Pittsburgh: Class and Culture in an Industrializing City, 1877–1919* (1984).

Deutsch, Sarah. *Women and the City: Gender, Space, and Power in Boston, 1870–1940* (2000).

Ebner, Michael H. *Creating Chicago's North Shore: A Suburban History* (1988).

Fishman, Robert. *Bourgeois Utopias: The Rise and Fall of Suburbia* (1987).

Foy, Jessica, and Thomas J. Schlereth, eds. *American Home Life, 1880–1930: A Social History of Spaces and Services* (1991).

Hood, Clifton. *722 Miles: The Building of the Subways and How They Transformed New York* (1993).

Jackson, Kenneth T. *Crabgrass Frontier: The Suburbanization of the United States* (1985).

Kasson, John F. *Amusing the Millions: Coney Island at the Turn of the Century* (1978).

Miller, Donald L. *City of the Century: The Epic of Chicago and the Making of America* (1996).

Mohl, Raymond A. *A New City: Urban America in the Industrial Age, 1860–1920* (1985).

Peiss, Kathy. *Cheap Amusements: Working Women and Leisure in Turn-of-the-Century New York* (1986).

Platt, Harold L. *The Electric City: Energy and the Growth of the Chicago Area, 1880–1930* (1991).

Rosenzweig, Roy. *Eight Hours for What We Will: Workers and Leisure in an Industrial City, 1870–1920* (1983).

Sklar, Kathryn Kish. *Catharine Beecher: A Study of Domesticity* (1973).

Warner, Sam Bass Jr. *Streetcar Suburbs: The Process of Growth in Boston, 1870–1900* (1962).

Wright, Gwendolyn. *Moralism and the Model Home: Domestic Architecture and Cultural Conflict in Chicago, 1873–1913* (1980).

WHERE TO LEARN MORE

- **Edison National Historic Site, West Orange, New Jersey.** The site contains the Edison archives, including photographs, sound recordings, and industrial and scientific machinery. Its twenty historic structures dating from the 1880–1887 period include Edison's home and laboratory. www.nps.gov/edis.

- **Japanese American National Museum, Los Angeles, California.** Housed in a converted Buddhist temple, this museum includes artifacts and photographs of early Japanese immigration and settlement. The core exhibit is "Issei Pioneers: Japanese Immigration to Hawaii and the Mainland from 1885 to 1924." www.janm.org.

- **Pasa al Norte.** This museum, located in El Paso, Texas, serves as the Mexico-United States International Immigration History Center. Its exhibits focus on the importance of El Paso ("the Southwest Ellis Island") as a port-of-entry between the United States and Mexico from the late sixteenth century to the present. utminers.utep.edu/panihm/default.htm.

- **Missouri Historical Society, St. Louis, Missouri.** The Society displays a long-term exhibition accompanied by public programs called, "St. Louis in the Gilded Age," which focuses on the changes generated by industrialization and urban development in St. Louis from 1865 to 1900. www.mohistory.org.

- **Senator John Heinz Pittsburgh Regional History Center, Pittsburgh, Pennsylvania.** Through its long-term exhibition, "Points in Time: Building a Life in Western Pennsylvania, 1750–Today," the Center explores the growth of the Pittsburgh metropolitan area, especially its expansion during the great industrial boom at the turn of the twentieth century. www.pghhistory.org.

- **Angel Island State Park, San Francisco Bay.** Angel Island served as a detention center from 1910 to 1940 for Asian immigrants who were kept there for days, months, and, in some cases, years, while immigration officials attempted to ferret out illegal entries. Exhibits depict the era through pictures and artifacts. www. angelisland.org.

- **Strawbery Banke, Portsmouth, New Hampshire.** This museum includes an exhibit and audiovisual presentations on the adjustment of one immigrant family to American life: "Becoming Americans: The Shapiro Story, 1898–1929," presents the story of an immigrant Jewish family in the context of immigration to the small, coastal city of Portsmouth at the turn of the twentieth century. www.strawberybanke.org.

- **Statue of Liberty National Monument and Ellis Island, New York, New York.** More than 12 million immigrants were processed at Ellis Island between 1892 and 1954. The exhibits provide a fine overview of American immigration history during this period. There is an ongoing oral history program as well. www.nps.gov/stli.

 Please refer to the document CD-ROM for primary sources related to this chapter.

➜ *This idealized 1875 engraving presents a harmonious image of western expansion and railroad construction that belies a more complex and distruptive reality, particularly for Native Americans.*

"Railroad building on the Great Plains, colored engraving, 1875" (Granger Collection 4E239.36).

TRANSFORMING THE WEST 19
1865–1890

After a pleasant ride of about six miles we attained a very high elevation, and, passing through a gorge of the mountains, we entered a level, circular valley, about three miles in diameter, surrounded on every side by mountains. The track is on the eastern side of the plain, and at the point of junction extends in nearly a southwest and northeast direction. Two lengths of rails are left for today's work. . . . At a quarter to nine A.M. the whistle of the C.P. [Central Pacific Railroad] is heard, and soon arrives, bringing a number of passengers. . . . Two additional trains arrive from the East. At a quarter to eleven the Chinese workmen commenced leveling the bed of the road with picks and shovels, preparatory to placing the ties. . . . At a quarter past eleven the Governor's train arrived. The engine was gayly decorated with little flags and ribbons, the red, white, and blue. At 12 M. the rails were laid, and the iron spikes driven. The last tie that was laid is 8 feet long, 8 inches wide, and 6 inches thick. It is of California laurel, finely polished, and is ornamented with a silver escutcheon bearing the following inscription: "The last tie laid on the Pacific Railroad, May 10th, 1869." . . .

The point of contact is 1,085 4/5 miles from Omaha, leaving 690 miles for the C.P. portion of the work. The engine Jupiter, of the C.P., and engine 119, of the U.P.R.R. [Union Pacific Railroad] moved up within thirty feet of each other. . . . Three cheers were given for the Government

CHAPTER OUTLINE

Subjugating Native Americans
Tribes and Cultures
Federal Indian Policy
Warfare and Dispossession
Life on the Reservation:
   Americanization

Exploiting the Mountains: The Mining Bonanza
Rushes and Mining Camps
Labor and Capital

Exploiting the Grass: The Cattle Kingdom
Cattle Drives and Cow Towns
Rise and Fall of Open-Range Ranching
Cowhands and Capitalists

Exploiting the Earth: Homesteaders and Agricultural Expansion
Settling the Land
Home on the Range
Farming the Land

Conclusion

of the United States, for the railroad, for the President, for the Star Spangled Banner, for the laborers, and for those who furnished the means respectively. The four spikes—two gold and two silver—were furnished by Montana, Idaho, California, and Nevada. They were about seven inches long, and a little larger than the iron spike. Dr. Harkness, of Sacramento, on presenting to Governor Stanford a spike of pure gold, delivered a short and appropriate speech. The Hon. F.A. Tuttle, of Nevada, presented Dr. Durant with a spike of silver, saying: 'To the iron of the East, and the gold of the West, Nevada adds her link of silver to span the continent and wed the oceans.' . . . The two locomotives then moved up until they touched each other, . . . and at one P.M., under an almost cloudless sky, and in the presence of about one thousand one hundred people, the completion of the greatest railroad on earth was announced.

Andrew J. Russell, "The Completion of the Pacific Railroad," *Frank Leslie's Illustrated Newspaper,* June 5, 1869.

Andrew J. Russell's short journey on the morning of May 10, 1869, from Ogden to Promontory Summit, Utah, enabled him to document what he called "the completion of the greatest work of the age, by which this vast continent is spanned, from ocean to ocean, by the iron path of travel and commerce." But Russell had already been on the road two years, living in his darkroom-wagon or in railroad construction camps, working as the official Union Pacific photographer. The transcontinental railroad itself was still longer in the making, having been authorized in 1862, but it symbolized the classic American journey, a people and a nation moving westward.

The construction of the transcontinental railroad also set a precedent for western development. The two railroads that met in a desolate sagebrush basin were huge corporate enterprises, not individual efforts, and corporations would dominate western growth as much as they did eastern industrialization. The crowd of onlookers had good reason to give three cheers for the federal government, for it played a crucial role in railroad construction, as in virtually all aspects of western development. Congress had authorized the Union Pacific and Central Pacific to build the railroad link, given them the right-of-way for their tracks, and provided huge land grants and financial subsidies.

The railroads' dependence on capital investment, engineering knowledge, technological innovations, and labor skills also typified western development. Their labor forces both reflected and reinforced the region's racial and ethnic diversity. European immigrants, Mexicans, Paiute Indians, both male and female, and especially Chinese, recruited in California and Asia, chiseled the tunnels through the mountains, built the bridges over the gulches, and laid the ties and rails across the plains. But Russell had the Chinese workers step back so as not to appear in the famous photographs he took at Promontory, an indication of the racism that marred so many western achievements.

This photograph, taken by A.J. Russell, records the celebration at the joining of the Central Pacific and Union Pacific railroads on May 10, 1869, at Promontory Summit, Utah. Railroads transformed the American West, linking the region to outside markets, spurring rapid settlement, and threatening Indian survival.

Laying track as quickly as possible to collect the subsidies awarded by the mile, the railroad corporations adopted callous and reckless construction tactics, resulting in waste, deaths (perhaps as many as a thousand Chinese), and environmental destruction—all consequences that would similarly characterize other forms of economic development in the West. And as with most American undertakings in the West, the construction provoked conflict with the Cheyenne, Sioux, and other tribes. As one railroad official declared, "we've got to clean the damn Indians out or give up building the Union Pacific Railroad."

The most important feature of the railroad, however, was that traffic moved in both directions. The transcontinental and subsequent railroads helped move soldiers, miners, cattle raisers, farmers, merchants, and other settlers into the West, but they also enabled the West to send precious metals, livestock, lumber, and wheat to the growing markets in the East. Thus the railroad both integrated the West into the rest of the nation and made it a crucial part of the larger economic revolution that transformed America after the Civil War.

KEY TOPICS

- The subjugation of Native Americans in the West, their confinement to reservations, and the attempted destruction of their culture

- The integration of the West into the national economy through the construction of transcontinental railroads

- The flood of migrants to the West in the late nineteenth century seeking work as railroad workers, miners, cowboys, and farmers

- The transformation of mining, ranching, and farming in the West from individual pursuits to corporate enterprises

SUBJUGATING NATIVE AMERICANS

The initial obstacle to exploiting the West was the people already living there, who used its resources in their own way and held different concepts of progress and civilization. For despite Easterners' image of the West as an unsettled wilderness, Native Americans had long inhabited it and had developed a variety of economies and cultures. As whites pressed westward, they attempted to subjugate the Indians, displace them from their lands, and strip them of their culture. Conquest gradually forced Indians onto desolate reservations, but efforts to destroy their beliefs and transform their way of life were less successful.

TRIBES AND CULTURES

Throughout the West, Indians had adapted to their environment, developing subsistence economies ranging from simple gathering to complex systems of irrigated agriculture. Each activity encouraged their sensitivity to the natural world, and each had social and political implications.

In the Northwest, abundant food from rich waters and dense forests gave rise to complex and stable Indian societies. During summer fishing runs, the Tillamooks, Chinooks, and other tribes caught salmon that, after being dried in smokehouses, sustained them throughout the year. During the mild winters, they developed artistic handicrafts, elaborate social institutions, and a satisfying religious life.

At the opposite environmental extreme, the Cahuillas of the southern California desert survived only through their ability to extract food and medicines from desert plants. In the dry and barren Great Basin of Utah and Nevada, Shoshones and Paiutes ate grasshoppers and other insects to supplement their diet of rabbits, mice, and other small animals. Such harsh environments restricted the size, strength, and organizational complexity of societies. Needing to spend most of their time searching for food, these Indians lived in small family groups in flimsy huts rather than established villages.

In the Southwest, the Pueblos dwelled in permanent towns of adobe buildings and practiced intensive agriculture. Because tribal welfare depended on maintaining complex irrigation systems, the Zunis, Hopis, and other Pueblos emphasized community solidarity rather than individual ambition. Town living encouraged social stability and the development of

Chronology

1858 Gold is discovered in Colorado and Nevada.

1860 Gold is discovered in Idaho.

1862 Homestead Act is passed.

Gold is discovered in Montana.

1864 Militia slaughters Cheyennes at Sand Creek, Colorado.

1867 Cattle drives make Abilene the first cow town.

1868 Fort Laramie Treaty is signed.

1869 First transcontinental railroad is completed.

1874 Gold is discovered in the Black Hills.

Turkey Red wheat is introduced to Kansas.

Barbed wire is patented.

1876 Indians devastate U.S. troops in the Battle of the Little Bighorn.

1879 "Exodusters" migrate to Kansas.

1885 Chinese massacred at Rock Springs, Wyoming.

1887 Dawes Act is passed.

1890 Government troops kill two hundred Sioux at Wounded Knee, South Dakota.

1892 Mining violence breaks out at Coeur d'Alene, Idaho.

1893 Western Federation of Miners is organized.

---

complex effective governments, elaborate religious ceremonies, and creative arts. Navajos, Apaches, and other nomadic tribes in the region relied on sheep-herding and hunting.

The most numerous Indian groups lived on the Great Plains. The largest of these tribes included the Lakotas or Sioux, who ranged from western Minnesota through the Dakotas; the Cheyennes and Arapahos, who controlled much of the central plains between the Platte and Arkansas Rivers; and the Comanches, predominant on the southern plains. Two animals dominated the lives of these peoples: the horse, which enabled them to move freely over the plains and to use the energy stored in its valuable grasses, and the buffalo, which provided meat, hides, bones and horns for tools, and a focus for spiritual life.

The importance of the horse, which had gradually spread northward after having been introduced to America by the Spanish in the sixteenth century, indicates that Indian lives constantly adapted to changing conditions, including the appearance of Europeans and then Americans. Trade with whites, often mediated by other tribes, brought Indians new tools, weapons, and other useful products as well as new opportunities and challenges, but their societies were resilient, thanks especially to procedures, rituals, and beliefs devised over generations to assure tribal identity and stability.

Clashing values. Despite their diversity, all tribes emphasized community welfare over individual interest. Their economies were based on subsistence rather than profit. They tried to live in harmony with nature to ward off sickness, injury, death, or misfortune. And they were intensely religious, absorbed

with the need to establish proper relations with supernatural forces that linked human beings with all other living things. The connections among these basic values appeared in the frequent religious rituals regulating hunting. The Sioux, for example, performed ceremonies in which they accorded respect to the buffalo's soul, sought its forgiveness for having to kill it, and promised not to be wasteful, so that the animals would not depart and bring starvation on the tribe. These connections also shaped Indians' attitude toward land, which they regarded—like air and water—as part of nature to be held and used communally, not as an individual's personal property from which others could be excluded.

White and Indian cultural values were incompatible. Disdaining Native Americans and their religion, white people condemned them as "savages" to be converted or exterminated. Rejecting the concept of communal property, most settlers demanded land for the exclusive use of ambitious individuals. Ignoring the need for natural harmony, they followed their own culture's goal of extracting wealth from the land for a market economy.

No one expressed these cultural differences better than the great Sioux leader Sitting Bull. Referring to the forces of the spirit world, he declared:

It is through this mysterious power that we too have our being and we therefore yield to our neighbors, even our animal neighbors, the same right as ourselves, to inhabit this land. Yet, hear me, people. We have now to deal with another race. . . . Possession is a disease with them. These people have made many rules that the rich may break but the poor may not. . . . They claim this mother of ours, the earth, for their own and fence their neighbors away; they deface her with their buildings. . . . That nation is like a spring freshet that overruns its banks and destroys all who are in its path. We cannot dwell side by side.

FEDERAL INDIAN POLICY

The government had in the 1830s adopted the policy of separating whites and Indians (see Chapter 13). Eastern tribes were moved west of Missouri and resettled on land then scorned as "the Great American Desert," unsuitable for white habitation and development. This division presumed a permanent frontier with perpetual Indian ownership of western America. It collapsed in the 1840s, when the United States acquired Texas, California, and Oregon, and migrants crossed Indian lands to reach the West Coast. Mormons developed a trail through Indian country in 1847 and settled on Indian lands; gold and silver discoveries beginning in 1848 prompted miners to invade Indian lands. Rather than curbing white entry into Indian country, the government built forts along the overland trails and ordered the army to punish Indians who threatened travelers.

White migration devastated the Indians, already competing among themselves for the limited resources of the Plains. Migrants' livestock destroyed crucial timber and pastures along streams in the semiarid region; trails disrupted buffalo grazing patterns and eliminated buffalo from tribal hunting ranges. The Pawnees in particular suffered from the violation of their hunting grounds. One observer reported that "their trail could be followed by the dead bodies of those who starved to death." The Plains Indians also suffered from diseases the white migrants introduced. Smallpox, cholera, measles, whooping cough, and scarlet fever, for which Indians had no natural immunity, swept through the tribes. Cholera killed more than half of the Comanches and Kiowas, and most other tribes lost up to 40 percent of their population from the new diseases. Emigrants along the Platte River routes came across "villages of the dead."

By the early 1850s, white settlers sought to occupy Indian territory. Recognizing that the Great American Desert could support agriculture, they pressed on the eastern edge of the plains and demanded the removal of the Indians. Simultaneously, railroad companies developed plans to lay tracks across the plains. To promote white settlement, the federal government decided to relocate the tribes to separate and specific reserves. In exchange for accepting such restrictions, the government would provide the tribes with annual payments of livestock, clothing, and other materials. To implement this policy, the government negotiated

treaties, extinguishing Indian rights to millions of acres (see Map 19–1), and ordered the army to keep Indians on their assigned reservations.

These actions alarmed Native Americans. One Cherokee complained of a government official "with a pocket full of money and his mouth full of lies. Some chiefs he will bribe, some he will flatter and some he will make drunk; and the result . . . will be called a treaty." And the treaties the army enforced were not always what the Indians, however reluctantly, had accepted. White negotiators sometimes omitted from the formal documents provisions that Indians had insisted upon, and at times Congress sharply reduced the annual payments or the size of reservations promised in treaties. The commissioner of Indian affairs aptly described the Indians' lot: "By alternate persuasion and force these tribes have been removed, step by step, from mountain to valley, and from river to plain, until they have been pushed halfway across the continent. They can go no further; on the ground they now occupy the crisis must be met, and their future determined."

WARFARE AND DISPOSSESSION

Most smaller tribes accepted the government's conditions, but larger tribes resisted. From the 1850s to the 1880s, warfare engulfed the advancing frontier. Indians sometimes initiated conflict, especially in the form of small raids, but invading Americans bore ultimate responsibility for these wars. Even the men who led the white military assault conceded as much. General Philip Sheridan, for example, declared of the Indians: "We took away their country and their means of support, broke up their mode of living, their habits of life, introduced disease and decay among them, and it was for this and against this that they made war. Could anyone expect less?"

One notorious example of white aggression occurred in 1864, at Sand Creek, Colorado. Gold discoveries had attracted a flood of white miners and settlers onto land only recently guaranteed to the Cheyennes and Arapahos. Rather than enforcing the Indians' treaty rights, however, the government compelled the tribes to relinquish their lands, except for a small tract designated as the Sand Creek reservation. But white settlers wanted to eliminate the Indian presence altogether. John Chivington, a Methodist minister who had organized Denver's first Sunday school, led a militia force to the Sand Creek camp of a band of Cheyennes under Black Kettle, an advocate of peace and accommodation. An American flag flew over the camp. Under Chivington's orders to "kill and scalp all, big and little," the militia attacked Black Kettle's sleeping camp without warning. With howitzers and rifles,

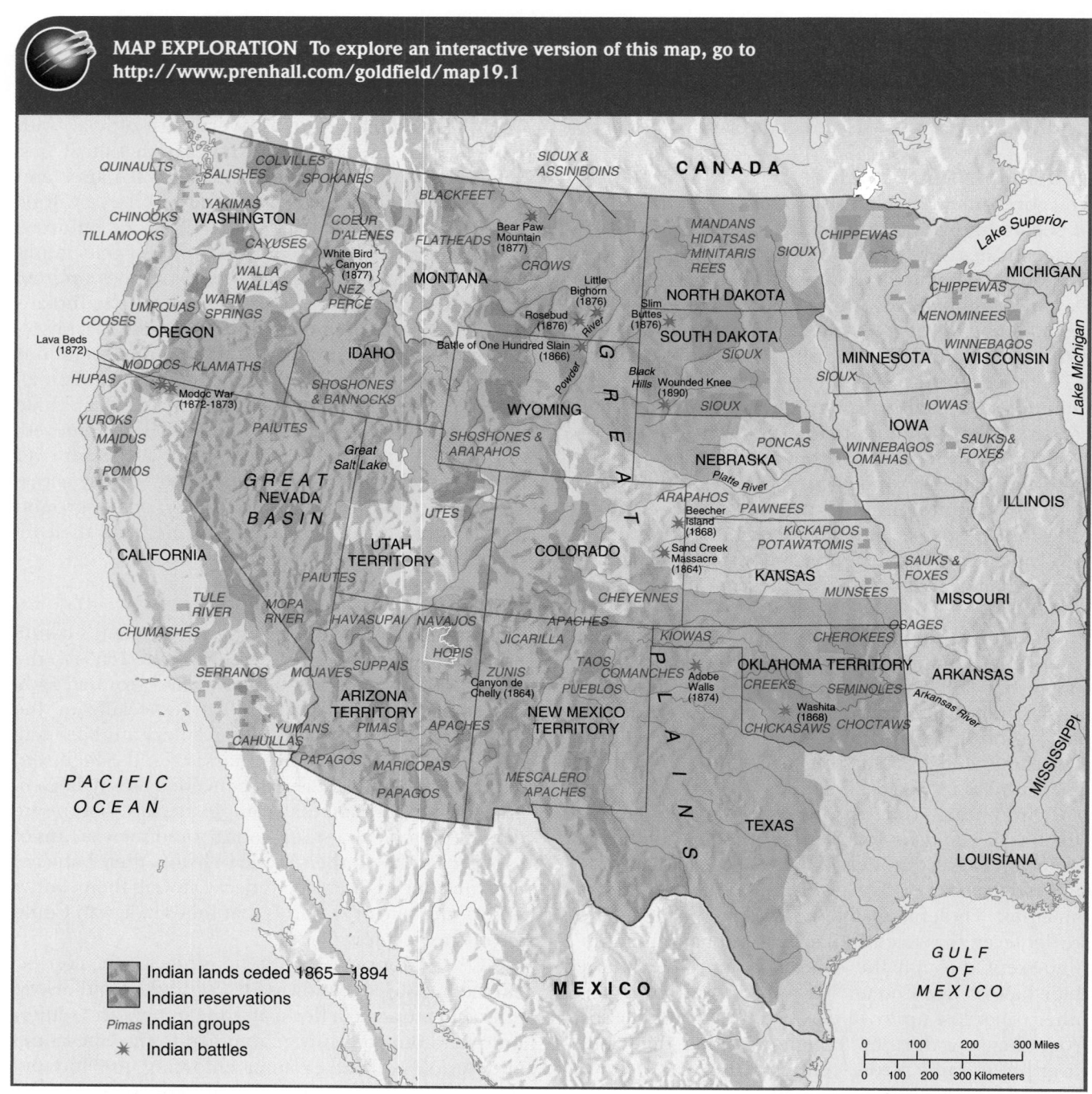

MAP EXPLORATION To explore an interactive version of this map, go to http://www.prenhall.com/goldfield/map19.1

MAP 19-1 Indian Land Cessions, 1860–1894
As white people pushed into the West to exploit its resources, Indians were steadily forced to cede their lands. By 1900 they held only scattered parcels, often in areas considered worthless by white people. Restricted to these reservations, tribes endured official efforts to suppress Indian customs and values.

the soldiers fired into the camp and then assaulted any survivors with swords and knives. One white trader later described the helpless Indians: "They were scalped, their brains knocked out; the [white] men used their knives, ripped open women, clubbed little children, knocked them in the head with their guns, beat their brains out, mutilated their bodies in every sense of the word."

The **Sand Creek Massacre** appalled many Easterners. The Cheyennes, protested the commissioner of Indian affairs, were "butchered in cold blood by troops in the service of the United States." A congressional investigating committee denounced Chivington for "a foul and dastardly massacre which would have disgraced the veriest savage among those who were the victims of his cruelty." Westerners, however, justified the brutality as a means to secure their own opportunities. One western newspaper demanded, "Kill all the Indians that can be killed. Complete extermination is our motto."

While assaults on smaller tribes usually "succeeded," other tribes were more formidable. None was more powerful than the Sioux, whose military skills had been honed in conflicts with other tribes. An army offensive against the Sioux in 1866 failed completely. Entire units deserted in fear and frustration; others were crushed by the Sioux. On the Bozeman Trail, in what the Lakotas called the Battle of One Hundred Slain, the Sioux wiped out an army detachment led by a captain who had boasted that he would destroy the Sioux nation. General William T. Sherman, who had marched through Georgia against Confederates, knew that the odds were different in the West. Fifty Plains In-

dians, he declared, could "checkmate" three thousand soldiers. General Philip Sheridan calculated that the army suffered proportionately greater losses fighting Indians than either the Union or the Confederacy had suffered in the Civil War.

With the army unable to defeat the Sioux and their allies, and with many Easterners shocked by both the military's indiscriminate aggression and the expense of the fighting, the government sued for peace. Describing white actions as "uniformly unjust," a federal peace commission in 1868 negotiated the **second Treaty of Fort Laramie**, in which the United States abandoned the Bozeman Trail and other routes and military posts on Sioux territory—one of the few times Indians forced the whites to retreat. The United States also guaranteed the Sioux permanent ownership of the western half of South Dakota and the right to inhabit and hunt in the Powder River country in Wyoming and Montana, an area to be henceforth closed to all white people.

This engraving, showing passengers shooting buffalo from a train crossing the plains, suggests the often casual approach Americans took toward the Western environment. The destruction of the buffalo herds, for both profit and "sport," also destroyed the basis of the Plains Indians' economy and culture.

THE FAR WEST.—SHOOTING BUFFALO ON THE LINE OF THE KANSAS-PACIFIC RAILROAD.

There is no photograph of Crazy Horse, but Amos Bad Heart Bull drew this pictograph of his murder at Fort Robinson, Nebraska, September 7, 1877. Bayoneted in the back, the great Sioux warrior told his followers: "It is no use to depend on me. I am going to die."

For several years, peace prevailed on the northern plains, but in 1872, the Northern Pacific Railroad began to build westward on a route that would violate Sioux territory. Rather than stopping the railroad, the government sent an army to protect the surveyors. Sherman drew up plans for the war that he expected the construction to provoke. He regarded railroad expansion as the most important factor in defeating the Indians, for it would allow troops to travel as far in a day as they could march in weeks. Other technological developments, from the telegraph to rapid-fire weapons, also undercut the skills of the Indian warrior.

The destruction of the buffalo also threatened Native Americans. From 1872 to 1874, white hunters killed 4 million buffalo. Railroad survey and construction parties disrupted grazing areas, and hunters working for the railroads killed hordes of buffalo, both to feed construction crews and to prevent the animals from obstructing rail traffic. Hide hunters slaughtered even more of the beasts for their skins, leaving the bodies to rot. Reporters found vast areas covered with "decaying, putrid, stinking remains." Federal officials encouraged the buffalo's extermination because it would destroy the Indians' basis for survival.

The climactic provocation of the Sioux began in 1874, when Colonel George A. Custer led an invasion to survey the Black Hills for a military post and to confirm the presence of gold. Thousands of white miners then illegally poured onto Sioux land. Ignoring Sioux demands that the government enforce the Fort Laramie treaty, the army insisted that the Indians leave their Powder River hunting grounds. When the Sioux refused, the army attacked. The Oglala Sioux, under Crazy Horse, repulsed one prong of this offensive at the Battle of the Rosebud in June 1876 and then joined a larger body of Sioux under Sitting Bull and their Cheyenne and Arapaho allies to overwhelm a second American column, under Custer, at the **Battle of the Little Bighorn**.

But the Indians could not follow up their dramatic victory. They had to divide their forces to find fresh grass for their horses and to hunt for their own food. Without such limitations, the U.S. Army relentlessly pursued the separate bands to exhaustion. "We have been running up and down in this country, but they follow us from one place to another," lamented Sitting Bull. He led his followers to Canada, but the other bands capitulated in the winter of 1876–1877. In the end, the conquest of the northern plains came, not through any decisive victory, but through attrition and the inability of the traditional Indian economy to support resistance to the technologically and numerically superior white forces.

The defeat of the Sioux nearly completed the Indian Wars. Smaller tribes, among them the Kiowas, Modocs, and Utes, had been overrun earlier. In the Northwest, the Nez Percé resisted in 1877 when the government reneged on its agreement to protect their land. Outwitting and outfighting the larger forces of the U.S. Army over a 1,500-mile retreat toward Canada, the exhausted Nez Percé surrendered after being promised a return to their own land. But the government refused to honor that pledge, too, and imprisoned the tribe in Oklahoma, where more than a third perished within a few years.

In the Southwest, the Navajos and the Comanches were subdued, as the Sioux had been, by persistent pursuit that prevented them from obtaining food. The last to abandon resistance were the Apaches, under Geronimo. In 1886, he and thirty-six followers, facing five thousand U.S. troops, finally surrendered. Geronimo and other Apaches were sent to a military prison in Florida; the tribes were herded onto reservations. The Oglala chief Red Cloud concluded of the white invasion: "They made us many promises, more than I can remember, but they never kept but one. They promised to take our land, and they took it."

LIFE ON THE RESERVATION: AMERICANIZATION

Conquering the tribes and taking their land were only the initial objectives of government policy. The next goal was to require Indians to adopt white ways, instilled by education and religion and enforced when necessary by the military. This goal did not involve assimilation but merely "Americanization," an expression of cultural conquest.

The government received aid from many Christian denominations, which had long proposed nonviolent methods of controlling Indians. Beginning in the 1860s, they gained influence in reaction to the military's brutality. Religious groups helped to staff the reservations as agents, missionaries, or civilian employees. Protestant philanthropists supervised Indian affairs and controlled several private organizations that worked to shape Indian policy, including the Indian Rights Association and the Women's National Indian Association. Reformers wanted to change Indian religious and family life, train Indian children in Protestant beliefs, and force Indians to accept private ownership and market capitalism.

Confined to reservations, Indians were a captive audience for white reformers. Furthermore, with their very survival dependent on government rations and annual payments stipulated by treaties, Indians were "compelled by sheer necessity," as one federal official said, to accept government orders "or starve." One Paiute woman wailed, "Our poor children are crying to us for food, and we are powerless to help the little ones." Government agents of the Bureau of Indian Affairs used their power to undermine tribal authority and destroy traditional Indian government, prohibiting tribal councils from meeting and imprisoning tribal leaders.

White activists sought to destroy Indian religion because it was "pagan" and because it helped Indians resist assimilation. Protestant religious groups persuaded the Bureau of Indian Affairs to frame a criminal code prohibiting and penalizing tribal religious practices. Established in 1884, the code remained in effect until 1933. It was first invoked to ban the Sun Dance, the chief expression of Plains Indian religion. To enforce the ban, the government withheld rations and disrupted the religious ceremonies that

Dressed in their school uniforms, Indian children sit under the U.S. flag. Government and missionary schools sought to promote "Americanization" and to suppress native cultures. Such education, said one member of Congress, "is the solution of the vexed Indian problem."

AMERICAN VIEWS

Zitkala-Sa's View of Americanization

Zitkala-Sa, or Red Bird, was an eight-year-old Sioux girl when she was taken from her South Dakota reservation in 1884 and placed in a midwestern missionary school, where she encountered what she called the "iron routine" of the "civilizing machine." Here she recalls her first day at the school.

- What lessons were the missionaries trying to teach Zitkala-Sa by their actions?
- What lessons did Zitkala-Sa learn?

Soon we were being drawn rapidly away by the white man's horses. When I saw the lonely figure of my mother vanish in the distance, a sense of regret settled heavily upon me. . . . I no longer felt free to be myself, or to voice my own feelings. The tears trickled down my cheeks, and I buried my face in the folds of my blanket. Now the first step, parting me from my mother, was taken, and all my belated tears availed nothing. . . . Trembling with fear and distrust of the palefaces . . . I was as frightened and bewildered as the captured young of a wild creature. . . .

[At the missionary school,] the constant clash of harsh noises, with an undercurrent of many voices murmuring an unknown tongue, made a bedlam within which I was securely tied.

And though my spirit tore itself in struggling for its lost freedom, all was useless. . . .

We were placed in a line of girls who were marching into the dining room. . . . A small bell was tapped, and each of the pupils drew a chair from under the table. Supposing this act meant they were to be seated, I pulled out mine and at once slipped into it from one side. But when I turned my head, I saw that I was the only one seated, and all the rest at our table remained standing. Just as I began to rise, looking shyly around to see how chairs were to be used, a second bell was sounded. All were seated at last, and I had to crawl back into my chair again. I heard a man's voice at one end of the hall, and I looked around to see him. But all others hung their heads over their plates. As I glanced at the

---

transmitted traditional values. In 1890, to suppress the Ghost Dance religion, the army even used artillery, firing exploding shells, and killed at least two hundred Sioux men, women, and children at Wounded Knee, South Dakota, in what became known as the **Wounded Knee Massacre**.

Missionaries attempted to convert Indians to Christianity but often found them reluctant to accept the creed of their conquerors. As one Crow Indian explained,

We found there were too many kinds of religion among white men for us to understand, and that scarcely any two white men agreed which was the right one to learn. This bothered us a good deal until we saw that the white man did not take his religion any more seriously than he did his laws,

and that he kept both of them just . . . to use when they might do him good in his dealings with strangers. These were not our ways. We kept the laws we made and lived our religion.

The government and religious groups also used education to eliminate Indian values and traditions. They isolated Indian children from tribal influences at off-reservation boarding schools. Troops often seized Indian children for these schools, where they were confined until after adolescence. The schoolchildren were forced to speak English, attend Christian services, and profess white American values (see "American Views: Zitkala-Sa's View of Americanization").

Finally, the government and the religious reformers imposed the economic practices and values of long chain of tables, I caught the eyes of a pale-face woman upon me. Immediately I dropped my eyes, wondering why I was so keenly watched by the strange woman. The man ceased his mutterings, and then a third bell was tapped. Every one picked up his knife and fork and began eating. I began crying instead, for by this time I was afraid to venture anything more.

But this eating by formula was not the hardest trial in that first day. Late in the morning, my friend Judewin gave me a terrible warning. Judewin knew a few words of English; and she had overheard the paleface woman talk about cutting our long, heavy hair. Our mothers had taught us that only unskilled warriors who were captured had their hair shingled by the enemy. Among our people, short hair was worn by mourners, and shingled hair by cowards!

. . . I remember being dragged out, though I resisted by kicking and scratching wildly. In spite of myself, I was carried downstairs and tied fast in a chair. I cried aloud, shaking my head all the while until I felt the cold blades of the scissors against my neck, and heard them gnaw off one of my thick braids. Then I lost my spirit. . . . My long hair was shingled like a coward's. In my anguish I moaned for my mother, but no one came to comfort me. Not a soul reasoned quietly with me, as my own mother used to do; for now I was only one of many little animals driven by a herder. . . .

I blamed the hard-working, well-meaning, ignorant [missionary] woman who was inculcating in our hearts her superstitious ideas. Though I was sullen in all my little troubles, as soon as I felt better I was . . . again actively testing the chains which tightly bound my individuality like a mummy for burial. . . .

Many specimens of civilized peoples visited the Indian school. The city folks with canes and eyeglasses, the countrymen with sunburnt cheeks and clumsy feet, forgot their relative social ranks in an ignorant curiosity. Both sorts of these Christian palefaces were alike astounded at seeing the children of savage warriors so docile and industrious. . . .

In this fashion many [whites] have passed idly through the Indian schools during the last decade, afterward to boast of their charity to the North American Indian. But few there are who have paused to question whether real life or long-lasting death lies beneath this semblance of civilization.

Source: Zitkala-Sa, "The School Days of an Indian Girl" (1900). Reprinted in *American Indian Stories* (Glorieta, NM: Rio Grande Press, 1976).

white society on Indians. Government agents taught Indian men how to farm and distributed agricultural implements; Indian women were taught household tasks. These tactics reduced the status of Indian women, whose traditional responsibility for agriculture had guaranteed them respect and authority. Nor could men farm successfully on reservation lands, which whites had already rejected as unproductive. Kiowa chief Little Mountain suggested that if the president wanted Indians to raise corn, he should send them land fit for corn production. Whites, however, believed that the real obstacle to economic prosperity for the Indians was their rejection of private property. The Indians' communal values, the reformers argued, inhibited the pursuit of personal success that lay at the heart of capitalism. As one Bureau of Indian Affairs official declared, Indians must be taught to be more "mercenary and ambitious to obtain riches." To force such values on Indians, Congress in 1887 passed the **Dawes Act**, which divided tribal lands among individual Indians. Western settlers who had no interest in the Indians supported the law because it provided that reservation lands not allocated to individual Indians should be sold to white settlers. Under this "reform," the amount of land held by Indians declined by more than half by 1900.

White acquisition and exploitation of Indian land seemed to be the only constant in the nation's treatment of Native Americans. Assimilation itself failed because most Indians clung to their own values and rejected as selfish, dishonorable, and obsessively materialistic those favored by whites. As Big Bear, a chief of the Otoe-Missouria, defiantly declared, "You cannot make white men of us. That is one thing you can't do." But if it was not yet clear what place Native Americans would have in America, it was at least clear by 1900 that they would no longer stand in the way of western development.

EXPLOITING THE MOUNTAINS: THE MINING BONANZA

Migrants to the American West exploited the region's natural resources in pursuit of wealth and success. Some were rewarded; others met tragedy and failure. In either case, the challenges they confronted and the ventures they initiated gave rise to romantic images: the West as a land of adventure, opportunity, and freedom; pioneers as self-reliant individuals. Promoters, artists, and novelists developed these images into a heroic legend that movies, television, and politicians perpetuated. All too often, however, reality differed from legend. Opportunites were frequently short-lived and rarely available to all; individualism often gave way to group, corporate, or government action; nature and technology mocked self-reliance. The appeal of the cherished images made the reality harder to bear.

In the later nineteenth century, the West experienced several stages of economic development, but all of them transformed the environment, produced economic and social conflict, and integrated the region into the modern national economy. The first stage of development centered on mining, which attracted swarms of eager prospectors into the mountains and deserts in search of gold and silver. They founded vital communities, stimulated the railroad construction that brought further development, and contributed to the disorderly heritage of the frontier (see Map 19–2). But few gained the wealth they had expected.

RUSHES AND MINING CAMPS

The first important gold rush in the Rocky Mountains came in Colorado in 1859. More than 100,000 prospectors crowded into Denver and the nearby mining camps. Simultaneously, the discovery of the famous Comstock Lode in Nevada produced an eastward rush of miners from California. Some seventeen thousand claims were made around Virginia City, Nevada, the main mining camp. Strikes in the northern Rockies followed in the 1860s. Boise City and Lewiston in Idaho and Helena in Montana became major mining centers, and other camps prospered briefly before fading into ghost towns. The last of the frontier gold rushes came in 1874 on the Sioux reservation in the Black Hills of South Dakota, where the roaring mining camp of Deadwood flourished. Later, other minerals shaped frontier development: silver in Nevada, silver and lead in Colorado and Idaho, silver and copper in Arizona and Montana.

Mining camps were often isolated by both distance and terrain. They frequently consisted of only flimsy shanties, saloons, crude stores, dance halls, and brothels, all hastily built by entrepreneurs. Such towns reflected the speculative, exploitive, and transitory character of mining itself. And yet they did contribute to permanent settlement by encouraging agriculture, industry, and transportation in the surrounding areas.

The camps had an unusual social and economic structure. Their population was overwhelmingly male. In 1860, for example, about 2,300 men and only 30 women lived in the Nevada mining camps of Virginia City and Gold Hill. Women found far fewer economic opportunities than men did on the mining frontier. Some did become prospectors themselves; in Montana, women, "skirts hiked up," were reported working claims. But most stayed within conventional domestic spaces. Several opened lodging houses or hotels. Those with less capital worked as seamstresses and cooks and took in washing. The few married women often earned more than their husbands by boarding other miners willing to pay for the trappings of family life. When one found that miners would pay ten dollars for a biscuit made by a woman, she confessed: "In my dreams that night I saw crowds of bearded miners striking gold from the earth with every blow of the pick, each one seeming to leave a share for me."

Prostitution. But the largest source of paid employment for women was prostitution, a flourishing consequence of the gender imbalance. A few women prospered. Mary Josephine Welch, an entrepreneurial Irish immigrant, settled in Helena in 1867 and established the Red Light Saloon, the first of many saloons, dance halls, and brothels that she owned and operated. Most women who engaged in such activities, however, were far less successful. Many women became prostitutes because their other economic options were limited. As one Denver prostitute later noted, "I went into the sporting life for business reasons and no other. It was a way for a woman in those days to make money and I made it." And most prostitutes who entered brothels already suffered from economic hardship or a broken family. Some Chinese women were virtually sold into prostitution. One California newspaper in the 1870s described a scene resembling antebellum slave auctions, with Chinese women "stripped and paraded onto a platform where prospective buyers could inspect and bid." But prostitution usually only worsened their distress. By the 1890s, as men gained control of the vice trade from the madams, violence, suicide, alcoholism, disease,

MAP EXPLORATION To explore an interactive version of this map, go to
http://www.prenhall.com/goldfield/map19.2

MAP 19-2 Economic Development of the West: Railroads, Mining, and Cattle, 1860–1900
The spread of the railroad network across the West promoted economic development by providing access to outside markets for its resources. The discovery of precious metals often attracted the railroads, but stockraisers had to open cattle trails to reach the railheads.

drug addiction, and poverty overcame most prostitutes. Public authorities showed little concern for the abuse and even murder of prostitutes, although they used "sporting women" to raise revenue by fining or taxing them. Condemning such moral indifference, middle-class Protestant women in Denver and other cities established "rescue homes" to protect or rehabilitate prostitutes and dance-hall girls from male vice and violence. But their attempts to impose piety and purity had little success; male community leaders valued social order less than they did economic opportunity.

Saloon society.   The gender imbalance in mining camps also made saloons prevalent among local businesses. An 1879 business census of Leadville, Colorado, reported 10 dry-goods stores, 4 banks, and 4 churches, but 120 saloons, 19 beer halls, and 118 gambling houses. Saloons were social centers in towns where most miners lived in crowded and dirty tents and rooming houses. As Mark Twain wrote in *Roughing It* (1872), his account of Virginia City, "The cheapest and easiest way to become an influential man and be looked up to by the community at large, was to stand behind a bar, wear a cluster-diamond pin, and sell whiskey."

The male-dominated saloon society of mining camps generated social conflict. One observer of the Montana camps reported that men, "unburdened by families, drink whenever they feel like it, whenever they have money to pay for it, and whenever there is nothing else to do.... Bad manners follow, profanity becomes a matter of course.... Excitability and nervousness brought on by rum help these tendencies along, and then to correct this state of things the pistol comes into play." Disputes over mining claims could become violent, adding to the disorder. The California mining town of Bodie experienced twenty-nine killings between 1877 and 1883, a homicide rate higher than that of any U.S. city a century later. But such killings occurred only within a small group of males—young, single, surly, and armed—who were known as the Badmen of Bodie. Daily life for most people was safe.

Social violence.   Indeed, personal and criminal violence, which remains popularly associated with the West, was less pervasive than collective violence. This, too, affected mining camps and was aggravated by their ethnic and racial diversity. Irish, Germans, English, Chinese, Australians, Italians, Slavs, and Mexicans, among others, rushed into the mining regions. In many camps, half the population was foreign-born and another fourth consisted of first-generation Americans. Virginia City was such a mixed community that Germans, Mexicans, Chinese, French, Cornish, and Welsh each had their own churches, bands, and other social organizations and celebrated their own national holidays.

The uninhibited saloon society of Western mining and cattle towns, depicted here in an 1870s Montana engraving, gave rise to Eastern notions of the Wild West but was generally short-lived.

The European immigrants who sometimes encountered nativist hostility in the East experienced less animosity in the West, but nonwhite minorities often suffered. In particular, white people frequently drove Mexicans and Chinese from their claims or refused to let them work in higher-paid occupations in the mining camps. The Chinese had originally migrated to the California gold fields and thereafter spread to the new mining areas of the Rockies and the Great Basin, where they worked in mining when possible, operated laundries and restaurants, and held menial jobs like hauling water and chopping wood. In 1870, more than a quarter of Idaho's population and nearly 10 percent of Montana's was Chinese. Where they were numerous, the Chinese built their own communities and maintained their customs.

But racism and fear of economic competition sparked hostility and violence against the Chinese almost everywhere. In Colorado, town leaders boasted of having driven all Chinese out of Leadville by 1879, and white citizens destroyed Denver's Chinatown in 1880. The worst anti-Chinese violence occurred in Rock Springs, Wyoming, in 1885 when white miners killed twenty-eight unresisting Chinese miners and drove away all seven hundred residents from the local Chinatown. Although the members of the mob were well known, the grand jury, speaking for the

Chinese miners in Idaho operate the destructive water cannons used in hydraulic mining. Technological changes made most miners wage workers for companies.

Idaho State Historical Society

quartz, or lode, mining, sometimes called hard-rock mining. Time, money, and technology were required to sink a shaft into the earth, timber underground chambers and tunnels, install pumps to remove underground water and hoists to lower men and lift out rock, and build stamp mills and smelters to treat the ore.

Such complex, expensive, and permanent operations necessarily came under corporate control. Often financed with eastern or British capital, the new corporations integrated the mining industry into the larger economy. Hard rock mining produced more complex ores than could be treated in remote mining towns, but, with the new railroad network, they were shipped to smelting plants as far away as Kansas City and St. Louis and then to refineries in eastern cities. Western ores thus became part of national and international business. The mining industry's increasing development of lower-grade deposits led to greater capital investment and larger operations employing more workers and machinery.

white majority, found no cause for legal action: "Though we have examined a large number of witnesses, no one has been able to testify to a single criminal act committed by any known white person." Such community sanction for violence against racial minorities made mob attacks one of the worst features of the mining camps.

LABOR AND CAPITAL

New technology had dramatic consequences for both miners and the mining industry. Initially, mining was an individual enterprise in which miners used simple tools, such as picks and shovels, wash pans, and rockers, to work shallow surface deposits known as placers. Placer mining attracted prospectors with relatively little capital or expertise, but surface deposits were quickly exhausted. More complex and expensive operations were needed to reach the precious metal buried in the earth.

Hydraulic mining, for example, required massive capital investment to build reservoirs, ditches, and troughs to power high-pressure water cannons that would pulverize hillsides and uncover the mineral deposits. California's North Bloomfield Gravel Mining Company owned hundreds of miles of ditches and used more than a million gallons of water a day to feed its huge water nozzles. Still more formidable was

Effects of corporate mining. Quartz mining thus helped usher the mining frontier into a more stable period. But the new corporate mining had disturbing effects. Its impact on the environment was horrendous. Hydraulic mining washed away hillsides, depositing debris in canyons and valleys to a depth of 100 feet or more, clogging rivers and causing floods, and burying thousands of acres of farmland. Such damage provoked an outcry and eventually led to government regulation. Fewer Westerners worried about sterile slag heaps or toxic fumes that belched from smelters and killed the vegetation for miles. They were the signs of progress. One Montana corporate leader even praised the arsenic fumes that permeated Butte for giving women "beautiful complexions."

Corporate mining also hurt miners, transforming them into wage workers with restricted opportunities. "It is useless to say that here all have an equal chance," conceded a Colorado newspaper in 1891. Miners' status declined as new machinery, such as power drills, reduced the need for skilled laborers and enabled employers to hire cheaper workers from eastern and southern Europe. Mining corporations, moreover, did little to protect miners' health or safety. Miners died in cave-ins, explosions, and fires or from the great heat and poisonous gases in underground mines. Others contracted silicosis, lead poisoning, or other diseases or were crippled or killed by machines. Miners called power hoists "man killers" because they frequently crushed and dismembered workers. Investigating the new machinery in 1889, the Montana inspector of mines concluded that "death lurks even in the things which are designed as benefits."

Unions and union busting. To protect themselves, miners organized unions. These functioned as benevolent societies, using members' dues to pay benefits to injured miners or their survivors. Several unions established hospitals. Union halls offered an alternative to the saloons by serving as social and educational centers. The Miners' Union Library in Virginia City was the largest library in Nevada. Unions also promoted miners' interests on the job by striking against wage cuts and campaigning for mine safety. They convinced states to pass mine safety laws and, beginning in the 1880s, to appoint mine inspectors. The chief role of these state officials was, in the words of a Colorado inspector, to decide "How far should an industry be permitted to advance its material welfare at the expense of human life?" The industry itself, however, often provided the answer to that question, for mining companies frequently controlled state power and used it to crush unions. Thus, in 1892, in the Coeur d' Alene district of Idaho, mining companies locked out strikers and imported a private army, which battled miners in a bloody gunfight. Management next persuaded the governor and the president to send in the state militia and the U.S. Army. State officials then suppressed the strike and the union by confining all union members and their sympathizers in stockades.

Strikes, union busting, and violence continued for years. When mining companies in Utah, Colorado, and Montana pursued the same aggressive tactics of lockouts and wage cuts, the local miners' unions in the West united for strength and self-protection. In 1893, they formed one of the nation's largest and most militant unions, the Western Federation of Miners.

Violence and conflict were attributable not to frontier lawlessness but to the industrialization of the mines. Both management's tactics—blacklisting union members, locking out strikers, obtaining court injunctions against unions, and using soldiers against workers—and labor's response mirrored conditions in the industrial East. In sum, western mining, reflecting the industrialization of the national economy, had been transformed from a small-scale prospecting enterprise characterized by individual initiative and simple tools into a large-scale corporate business characterized by impersonal management, outside capital, advanced technology, and wage labor.

EXPLOITING THE GRASS: THE CATTLE KINGDOM

The development of the range-cattle industry opened a second stage of exploitation of the late-nineteenth-century West. It reflected the needs of an emerging eastern urban society, the economic possibilities of the grasslands of the Great Plains, the technology of the expanding railroad network, and the requirements of corporations and capital. It also brought "cow towns" and urban development to the West. The fabled cowboy, though essential to the story, was only a bit player.

CATTLE DRIVES AND COW TOWNS

The cattle industry originated in southern Texas, where the Spanish had introduced cattle in the eighteenth century. Developed by Mexican ranchers, "Texas longhorns" proved well adapted to the plains grasslands. By the 1860s, they numbered about 5 million head. Texans attempted to market these cattle as early as the 1850s, driving some herds on dusty journeys through New Mexico and Arizona to California and others to Missouri and Illinois. These latter drives disturbed local residents, angered farmers who feared that Texas cattle diseases might infect their own livestock, and prompted quarantine laws against the herds.

Following the Civil War, however, industrial expansion in the East and Midwest enlarged the urban market for food and increased the potential value of Texas steers. The extension of the railroad network into the West, moreover, opened the possibility of tapping that market without antagonizing farmers en route. The key was to establish a shipping point on the railroads west of the settled farming regions, a step first taken in 1867 by Joseph McCoy, an Illinois cattle shipper. McCoy selected Abilene, Kansas—in his words "a very small, dead place, consisting of about one dozen log huts." But Abilene was also the western railhead of the Kansas Pacific Railroad and was ringed by lush grasslands for cattle. McCoy bought 250 acres for a stockyard and imported lumber for stock pens, loading facilities, stables, and a hotel for cowhands. Texans opened the **Chisholm Trail** through Indian Territory to drive their cattle northward to Abilene. Within three years, a million and a half cattle reached Abilene, divided into herds of several thousand, each directed by a dozen cowhands on a "long drive" taking two to three months.

Cow town life. The cattle trade attracted other entrepreneurs who created a bustling town. Bankers prospered enough to convince one reporter in 1873 that "banks are as fat a thing as gold mines." Grocers, tailors, bootmakers, laundresses, barbers, druggists, blacksmiths, lawyers, and hotelkeepers provided consumer goods and services. Entertainments mushroomed: saloons, gambling rooms, dance halls, billiard parlors, and brothels. As both railroads and settlement advanced westward, a series of other cow towns—Ellsworth, Wichita, Dodge City, Cheyenne—attracted the long drives, cattle herds, and urban development.

As with the mining camps, the cow towns' reputation for violence was exaggerated. They adopted gun-control laws, prohibiting the carrying of handguns within city limits, and established police forces to maintain order. The primary duties of law officers were arresting drunks, fixing sidewalks, and collecting fines. The cow towns regulated, rather than prohibited, prostitution and gambling, for merchants viewed these vices as necessary to attract the cattle trade. Thus, the towns taxed prostitutes and gamblers and charged high fees for liquor licenses. By collecting such "sin taxes," Wichita was able to forgo general business taxes, thereby increasing its appeal to prospective settlers.

Not all cow towns became cities like Wichita, which by 1888 boasted of "Fine Educational Institutions, Magnificent Business Blocks, Elegant Residences, and Extensive Manufacturers"; most, like Abilene, dwindled into small towns serving farm populations. But cow towns, again like mining camps, contributed to the growth of an urban frontier. Railroads often determined the location and growth of western cities, providing access to markets for local products, transporting supplies and machinery for residents, and attracting capital for commercial and industrial development. When railroads reached El Paso, Texas, for example, it became a shipping point for cattle but then built its own packing houses and opened smelters to process Arizona ores. Its Mexican workers clustered in barrios and developed their own religious and social organizations—just as San Francisco's Chinese did in Chinatown or European immigrants did in eastern cities. This urbanization demonstrated how western developments paralleled those in older regions. The West, in fact, had become the most urban region in the nation by 1890, with two-thirds of its population living in communities of at least 2,500 people.

RISE AND FALL OF OPEN-RANGE RANCHING

The significance of the long drive to the cow towns faded as cattle raising expanded beyond Texas. Indian removal and extension of the railroads opened land for ranching in Kansas, Nebraska, Wyoming, Colorado, Montana, and the Dakotas. Cattle reaching Kansas were increasingly sold to stock these northern ranges rather than for shipment to the packing houses. Ranches soon spread across the Great Plains and into the Great Basin, the Southwest, and even eastern Oregon and Washington. This expansion was helped by the initially low investment that ranching required. Calves were cheap, and grass was mostly free. Ranchers did not buy, but merely used, the grazing lands of the open range, which was public land. It sufficed to acquire title to the site for a ranch house and a water source, because controlling access to water in semiarid lands gave effective control of the surrounding public domain "the same as though I owned it," as one rancher explained. Ranchers thus needed to invest only in horses, primitive corrals, and bunkhouses. Their labor costs were minimal: They paid cowboys in the spring to round up new calves for branding and in the fall to herd steers to market.

By the early 1880s, the high profits from this enterprise and an expanding market for beef attracted speculative capital and reshaped the industry. Eastern and European capital flooded the West, with British investors particularly prominent. Some investors went into partnership with existing ranchers, providing capital in exchange for expertise and management. Wisconsin investors formed the Three Rivers Land and Cattle Company of New Mexico, for example, by buying into a ranch owned and operated by Susan Barber, whom they then employed as general manager. Barber was unusual in the male-dominated industry (a newspaper praised her for making cowboys "respect the customs of civilization"), but the managerial skills she demonstrated were necessary for success. On a larger scale, British and American corporations acquired, expanded, and managed huge ranches. In 1883, the Swan Land and Cattle Company controlled a tract in Wyoming 130 miles long and 40 to 100 miles wide, with more than 100,000 head of cattle.

Effects of corporate control. Large companies soon dominated the industry, just as they had gained control of mining. They also worked together to enhance their power, especially by restricting access to the range and by intimidating small competitors. Some large companies illegally enclosed the open range, building fences to exclude newcomers and minimize labor costs by reducing the number of cowboys needed to control the cattle. One Wyoming

Employees of the Prairie Cattle Company at the ranch headquarters in Dry Cimarron, New Mexico, in 1888. The company, a British corporation, held eight thousand square miles of land.

newspaper complained: "some morning we will wake up to find that a corporation has run a wire fence about the boundary lines of Wyoming, and all within the same have been notified to move." And a Coloradan wondered, "Will the government protect us if we poor unite and cut down their fences and let our stock have some of Uncle Sam's feed as well as them?"

The corporate cattle boom overstocked the range and threatened the industry itself. Overgrazing replaced nutritious grasses with sagebrush, Russian thistle, and other plants that livestock found unpalatable. Droughts in the mid-1880s further withered vegetation and enfeebled the animals. Millions of cattle starved or froze to death in terrible blizzards in 1886 and 1887. These ecological and financial disasters destroyed the open-range cattle industry. The surviving ranchers reduced their operations, restricted the size of their herds, and tried to insure adequate winter feed by growing hay. To further reduce their dependence on natural vegetation, they introduced drought-resistant sorghum and new grasses; to reduce their dependence on rainfall, they drilled wells and installed windmills to pump water.

COWHANDS AND CAPITALISTS

One constant in the cattle industry was the cowboy, but his conditions and opportunities changed sharply over time and corresponded little to the romantic image of a dashing individual free of social constraints. Cowboys' work was hard, dirty, seasonal, te-

dious, sometimes dangerous, and poorly paid. Many early cowboys were white Southerners unwilling or unable to return home after the Civil War. Black cowhands made up perhaps 25 percent of the trail-herd outfits. Many others, especially in Texas and the Southwest, were Mexicans. Indeed, Mexicans developed most of the tools, techniques, and trappings that characterized the cattle industry: from boots, chaps, and the "western" saddle to roundups and roping. Black and Mexican cowboys were often relegated to the more lowly jobs, such as wrangler—a "dust-eater" who herded horses for others to use—but most served as ordinary hands on ranch or trail. Except in the few all-black outfits, they were rarely ranch or trail bosses. Texas cowboys dominated the early years of ranching and trailing, but as the industry expanded northward, more cowboys came from rural Kansas, Nebraska, and neighboring states.

Initially, in the frontier-ranching phase dominated by the long drive, cowboys were seasonal employees who worked closely with owners. Often the sons or neighbors of ranchers, they frequently expected to become independent stock raisers themselves. They typically enjoyed the rights to "maverick" cattle, or put their own brand on unmarked animals they encountered, and to "run a brand," or to own their own cattle while working for a ranch. These informal rights provided opportunities to acquire property and move up the social ladder.

As ranching changed with the appearance of large, corporate enterprises, so did the work and work relationships of cowhands. The power and status of employer and employees diverged, and the cowboys' traditional rights disappeared. Employers redefined mavericking as rustling and prohibited cowhands from running a brand of their own. One cowboy complained that these restrictions deprived a cowhand of his one way "to get on in the world." But that was the purpose: Cowboys were to be workers, not potential ranchers and competitors. To increase labor efficiency, some companies prohibited their cowboys from drinking, gambling, and carrying guns.

Unions and strikes. Cowboys sometimes responded to these structural transformations the same way skilled workers in the industrial East did—by forming unions and striking. The first strike occurred in Texas in 1883, when the Panhandle Stock Association, representing large operators, prohibited ranch hands from owning their own cattle and imposed a standard wage. More than three hundred cowboys struck seven large ranches for higher wages—$50 rather than $30 per month—and the right to brand mavericks for themselves and to run small herds on the public domain. Ranchers evicted the cowboys, hired scabs, and brought in the Texas Rangers to drive the strikers from the region.

Other strikes also failed because corporate ranches and their stock associations had the power, and cowhands faced long odds in their efforts to organize. They were isolated across vast spaces and had little leverage in the industry. Members of the Northern New Mexico Cowboys Union, formed in 1886, recognized their weakness. After asking employers for "what we are worth after many years' experience," they conceded, "We are dependent on you."

The transformation of the western cattle industry and its integration into a national economy dominated by corporations thus made the cherished image of cowboy independence and rugged individualism more myth than reality. One visitor to America in the late 1880s commented: "Out in the fabled West, the life of the 'free' cowboy is as much that of a slave as is the life of his Eastern brother, the Massachusetts mill-hand. And the slave-owner is in both cases the same—the capitalist."

EXPLOITING THE EARTH: HOMESTEADERS AND AGRICULTURAL EXPANSION

Even more than ranching and mining, agricultural growth boosted the western economy and bound it tightly to national and world markets. In this process, the government played a significant role, as did the railroads, science and technology, eastern and foreign capital, and the dreams and hard work of millions of rural settlers. The development of farming produced remarkable economic growth, but it left the dreams of many unfulfilled.

SETTLING THE LAND

Federal land grants to railroads had helped open the West to outside influences, and mining and cattle interests had also exploited public lands. To stimulate agricultural settlement, Congress passed the most famous land law, the **Homestead Act** of 1862 (see the Overview table, "Government Land Policy"). The measure of-

fered 160 acres of free land to anyone who would live on the plot and farm it for five years. The act promised opportunity and independence to ambitious farmers. The governor of Nebraska exclaimed, "What a blessing this wise and humane legislation will bring to many a poor but honest and industrious family."

Limits of the Homestead Act. Despite the apparently liberal land policy, however, prospective settlers found less land open to public entry than they expected. Federal land laws did not apply in much of California and the Southwest, where Spain and Mexico had previously transferred land to private owners, or in all of Texas. Elsewhere, the government had given away 181 million acres to railroads, transferred millions more to the states to sell for educational and other purposes (the Morrill Act provided the foundation for state agricultural colleges), and set aside millions of acres of former Indian land for sale rather than for homesteading. Moreover, other laws provided for easy transfer of public lands to cattle companies, to other corporations exploiting natural resources, and to land speculators.

Thus, settlers in Kansas, Nebraska, Minnesota, and the Dakotas in the late 1860s and early 1870s often found most of the best land unavailable for homesteading and much of the rest remote from transportation facilities and markets. As much as 40 percent of the land in Kansas, for example, was closed to homesteading, which prompted the editor of the *Kansas Farmer* to complain that "the settlement of the state is retarded by land monopolists, corporate and individual." Although 375,000 farms were claimed by 1890 through the Homestead Act—a success by any measure—most settlers had to purchase their land.

The Homestead Act also reflected traditional eastern conceptions of the family farm, which were inappropriate in the West. A farm of 160 acres would have suited conditions in eastern Kansas or Nebraska, but farther west, larger-scale farming was necessary. And the law ignored the need for capital—for machinery, buildings, livestock, and fencing—that was required for successful farming on the Great Plains.

Promoting settlement. Thus other forces assumed responsibility for promoting settlement. Newspaper editors trumpeted the prospects of their region. Land companies, eager to sell their speculative holdings, sent agents through the Midwest and Europe to encourage migration. Steamship companies, hoping to sell transatlantic tickets, advertised the opportunities in the American West across Europe. Religious and

OVERVIEW

Government Land Policy

Legislation	Result
Railroad land grants (1850–1871)	Granted 181 million acres to railroads to encourage construction and development
Homestead Act (1862)	Gave 80 million acres to settlers to encourage settlement
Morrill Act (1862)	Granted 11 million acres to states to sell to fund public agricultural colleges
Other grants	Granted 129 million acres to states to sell for other educational and related purposes
Dawes Act (1887)	Allotted some reservation lands to individual Indians to promote private property and weaken tribal values among Indians and offered remaining reservation lands for sale to whites (by 1906, some 75 million acres had been acquired by whites)
Various laws	Permitted direct sales of 100 million acres by the Land Office

ethnic groups encouraged immigration. The Scandinavian Immigration Society generated both publicity and settlers for Minnesota; the Hebrew Emigrant Aid Society established Jewish agricultural colonies in Kansas and North Dakota. On a larger scale, the Mormons organized the Perpetual Emigrating Fund Company, which helped more than 100,000 European immigrants settle in Utah and Idaho. Their agricultural communities, relying on communal cooperation under church supervision, succeeded where individual efforts often failed in developing this region.

Most important, railroad advertising and promotional campaigns attracted people to the West. In 1882 alone, the Northern Pacific distributed more than 630,000 pieces of promotional literature in English, Swedish, Dutch, Danish, and Norwegian. "The glowing accounts of the golden west sent out by the R.R. companies," one pioneer later recalled, had convinced her that "they were doing a noble work to let poor people know there was such a grand haven they could reach." Only later did she realize the railroads' selfish motive. Not only would they profit from selling their huge land reserves to settlers, but a successful agricultural economy would produce crops to be shipped east and a demand for manufactured goods to be shipped west on their lines. The railroads therefore advanced credit to prospective farmers, provided transportation assistance, and extended technical and agricultural advice.

Prospective settlers crowd the U.S. Land Office in Garden City, Kansas, in 1885. The rush of people into the West from throughout the world contributed to the diversity of the region's population.

Thus encouraged, migrants poured into the West, occupying and farming more acres between 1870 and 1900 than Americans had in the previous 250 years (see Figure 19–1). Farmers settled in every region (see Map 19–3). Many went to California, Oregon, and Washington, where American development had begun much earlier. Some journeyed into the arid Great Basin and Rocky Mountains or the Southwest, where they often acquired land at the expense of the long-established Mexican population. Most, however, streamed into the Great Plains states, from the Dakotas to Texas. Much of Oklahoma was settled in virtually a single day in 1889, when the government opened up lands previously reserved for Indians.

So many Americans migrated west that many states east of the plains actually lost population during the 1870s. White migrants predominated in the mass migration, but African Americans initiated one of its most dramatic episodes, a millenarian folk movement they called the Exodus. Seeking to escape the misery and repression of the post-Reconstruction South, these poor "Exodusters" established several dozen black communities in 1879 in Kansas and Nebraska on the agricultural frontier. The Exodusters, said one observer, "regarded Kansas as a modern Canaan." But many of the new settlers came from Europe, sometimes in a chain migration of entire villages, bringing with them not only their own attitudes toward the land but also special crops, skills, settlement patterns, and agricultural practices. Peasants from Norway, Sweden, and Denmark flocked to Minnesota. Germans, Russians, and Irish put down roots across Texas, Kansas, Nebraska, and the Dakotas. French, Germans, and Italians developed vineyards, orchards, and nurseries in California, where laborers from Japan and Mexico arrived to work in fields and canneries. By 1890, the foreign-born population of North Dakota exceeded 40 percent, and nonnatives made up much of the population in California and

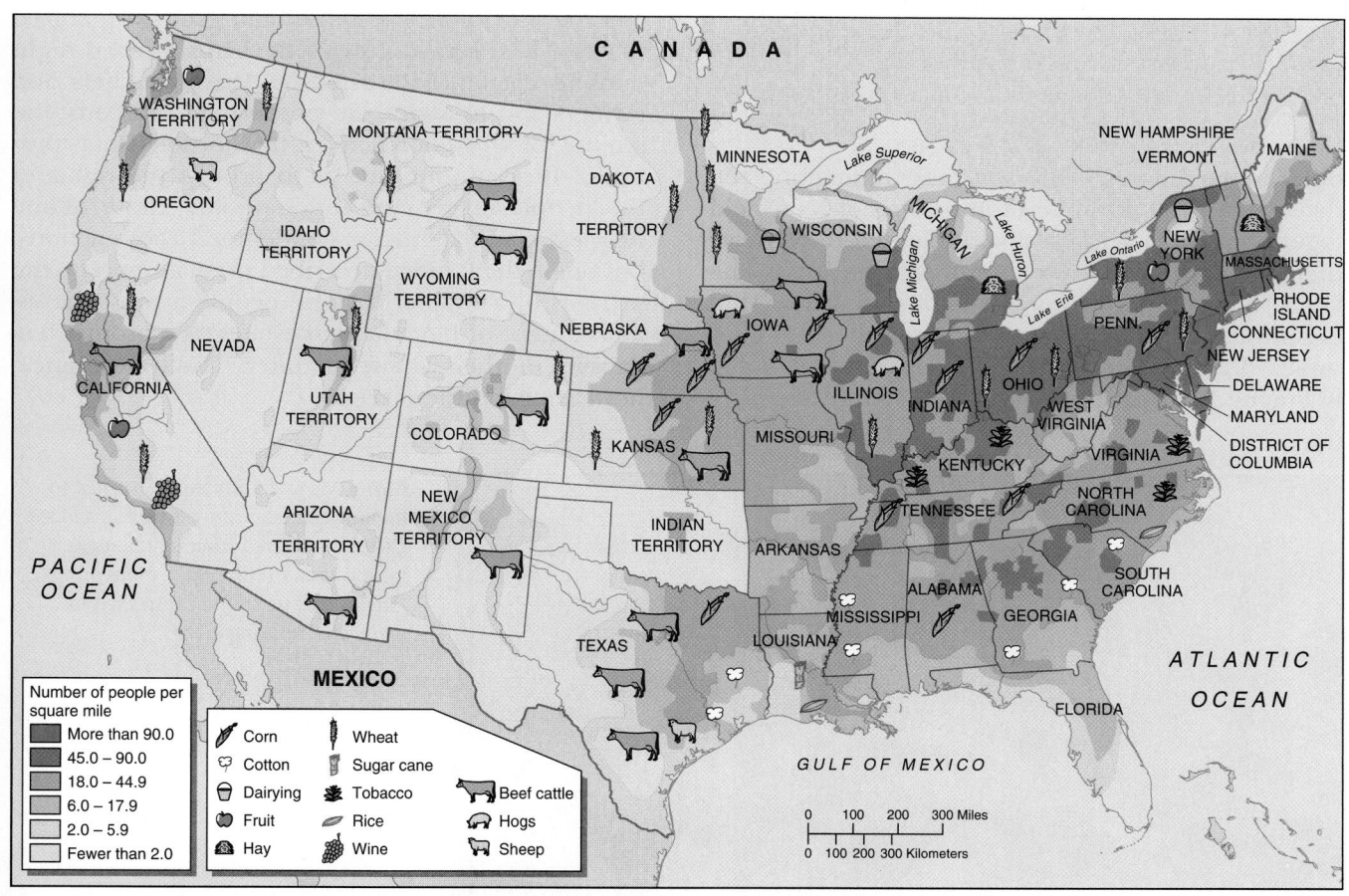

MAP 19-3   Population Density and Agricultural Land Use in the Late Nineteenth Century
Economic integration of the West promoted regional agricultural specialization. Stockraising and grain production dominated the more sparsely settled West, while the South grew the labor-intensive crops of cotton, tobacco, and sugar cane, and other areas concentrated on dairy products, fruit, and other crops for nearby urban markets.

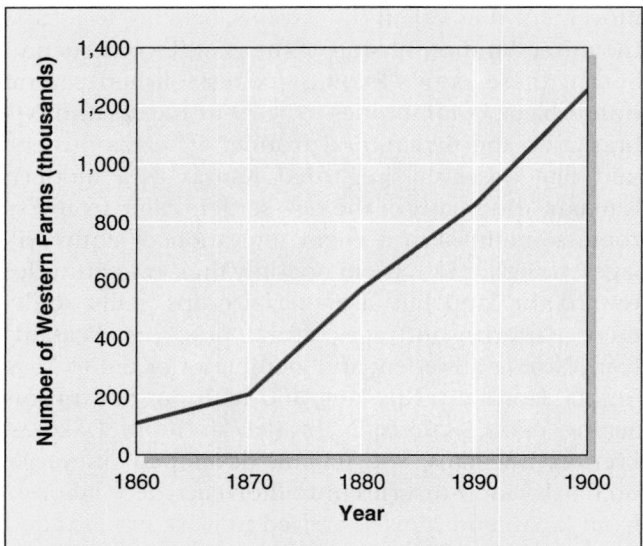

FIGURE 19-1   The Growth of Western Farming, 1860–1900
Indian removal, railroad expansion, and liberal land policies drew farm families into the West from much of Europe as well as the East. Technological innovations like barbed wire and farm machinery soon enabled them to build farms, but economic, social, and environmental challenges remained.

Data Source: Historical Statistics of the United States (1975).

other western states. Generally, these immigrants settled together in separate ethnic communities, held together by their church, and attempted to preserve their language and customs rather than be assimilated. Some Swedish congregations in rural Minnesota feared that prayers in English would go unheard, and as late as 1926, the only non-Bohemian in Prague, Nebraska, was the railroad depot agent.

Hispanic losses.   Migrants moved into the West in search of opportunity, which they sometimes seized at the expense of others already there. In the Southwest, Hispanics had long lived in village communities largely outside a commercial economy, farming small tracts of irrigated land and herding sheep on communal pastures. But as more Anglos, or white Americans, arrived as cattle raisers, railroad and mining developers, land speculators, and commercial farmers, their political and economic influence undermined traditional Hispanic society. Congress restricted the original Hispanic land grants to only the villagers' home lots and irrigated fields, throwing open most of their common lands to newcomers. Hispanic title was confirmed to only 2 million of the 37.5 million acres at stake. Anglo ranchers and settlers manipulated the federal land system to control these lands. The notorious Santa Fe Ring, a group of lawyers and land speculators, seized millions of acres through fraud and legal chicanery.

Spanish Americans resisted these losses, in court or through violence. One militant group, organized as *Las Gorras Blancas* (the White Caps), staged night raids to cut fences erected by Anglo ranchers and farmers and to attack the property of railroads, the symbol of the encroaching new order. "Our purpose," they announced, "is to protect the rights of the people in general and especially those of the helpless classes." Anglos condemned these actions, but one federal judge described them as merely "the protests of a simple, pastoral people against the establishment of large landed estates, or baronial feudalism, in their native country." Such resistance, however, had little success.

Division of Cultural Resources, Wyoming Department of Commerce.

Many Mexican Americans turned to mining as the Southwest was developed. But they suffered from a dual wage system that discriminated in favor of Anglos and were often restricted to segregated housing areas.

As their landholdings shrank, Hispanic villagers could not maintain their pastoral economy. Few turned to homesteading, for that would have required dispersed settlement and abandoning the village and its church, school, and other cultural institutions. Thus many Hispanics became seasonal wage laborers in the Anglo-dominated economy, sometimes working as stoop labor in the commercial sugar-beet fields that emerged in the 1890s, sometimes working on the railroads or in the mines. Women also participated in this new labor market. Previously crucial to the subsistence village economy, they now sought wage labor as cooks and domestic servants in railroad towns and mining camps. Such seasonal labor enabled Hispanics to maintain their villages and provided sufficient income to adopt some Anglo technology, such as cookstoves and sewing machines. But if Hispanics retained some cultural autonomy, they had little influence over the larger processes of settlement and development that restricted their opportunities and bound them to the western and national economy.

HOME ON THE RANGE

In settling the West, farm families encountered many difficulties, especially on the Great Plains, where they had to adapt to a radically new environment. The scarcity of trees on the plains meant that there was little wood for housing, fuel, and fencing. Until they had reaped several harvests and could afford to import lumber, pioneer families lived in houses made of sod. Though inexpensive and sturdy, sod houses were also dark and dirty. Snakes, mice, and insects often crawled out of the walls and roofs. Describing how a snake would "fall down on the bed," one child noted, "Mother would grab the hoe and there was something doing and after the fight was over Mr. Bull Snake was dragged outside." Small wonder that one Nebraska homesteader recalled that her first sight of a sod house "sickened me."

Women's work.   For fuel, settlers often had to rely on buffalo or cattle "chips"—dried dung—which repelled some newcomers. One farmer reported in 1879 that

> it was comical to see how gingerly our wives handled these chips at first. They commenced by picking them up between two sticks, or with a poker. Soon they used a rag, and then a corner of their apron. Finally, growing hardened, a wash after handling them was sufficient. And now? Now it is out of the bread, into the chips and back again—and not even a dust of the hands!

A farm family poses in front of its sod house. Successful farming on the Great Plains required all members of the family to work hard and adapt to new conditions, but as one newspaper reported, many settlers always felt like "strangers in a strange land."

The scarcity of water also complicated women's domestic labor. They often transported water over long distances, pulling barrels on "water sleds" or carrying pails on neck yokes. They melted snow on the stove for wash water and used the same water over again for different chores. Where possible, they also helped to dig wells by hand.

Some women farmed the land themselves. Single women could claim land under the Homestead Act, and, in some areas, women claimants made up 18 percent of the total and succeeded more frequently than men in gaining final title. At times, married women operated the family farm by themselves while their husbands worked elsewhere to earn the money needed for seeds, equipment, and building supplies. In the 1870s, one Dakota woman recounted the demands women faced:

> I had lived on a homestead long enough to learn some fundamental things: that while a woman had more independence here than in any other part of the world, she was expected to contribute as much as a man—not in the same way, it is true, but to the same degree; that people who fought the frontier had to be prepared to meet any emergency; that the person who wasn't willing to try anything once wasn't equipped to be a settler.

Isolation and community.   Isolation and loneliness troubled many early settlers on the plains. Women

FROM THEN TO NOW

The Legacy of Indian Americanization

The assumptions, objectives, and failures of the Americanization policies of the nineteenth century continue to affect American Indians more than a century later. Although periodically modified (see Chapter 25), these policies long persisted, as did their consequences. In the 1970s official investigations reported that the continuing attempts of the Bureau of Indian Affairs to use education to force Indians into an Anglo-American mold "have been marked by near total failure, haunted by prejudice and ignorance."

Similarly, the economic problems on reservations in the nineteenth century foreshadowed conditions a century later. Today, Indians rank at the bottom of almost all measures of economic well-being. Lack of economic opportunity leaves isolated reservations with unemployment rates averaging 40 percent. Off the reservation, discrimination, limited skills, and inadequate capital further restrict Indians' job prospects.

Indians also continue to suffer from poor health standards. They have the highest rates of infant mortality, pneumonia, hepatitis, tuberculosis, and suicide in the nation and a life expectancy twenty-five years less than the national average.

Indian culture, however, did not succumb to the pressure to Americanize. In the words of a Shoshone writer, "Indian history didn't end in the 1800s. Indian cultures . . . evolve, grow, and continually try to renew themselves."

In recent decades, Indian peoples have begun to reclaim their past and assert control over their future. Dramatic protests—most notably a confrontation in 1973 between Indian activists and the FBI at Wounded Knee, the site of the notorious 1890 massacre—have called attention to Indian grievances. But Indians have

especially suffered because they frequently had less contact with other people than farm men, who conducted their families' business in town and participated in such public activities as political meetings. One farm woman complained that "being cut off from everybody is almost too much for me." Luna Kellie recalled that from her Nebraska farm "there were no houses in sight and it seemed like the end of the world." The worst agony for many was the silence, unbroken by the sound of neighbors, the rush of water over rocks, or even—in the absence of trees—songbirds or rustling leaves. To break the silence, to provide some music and color, many homesteading families kept canaries among their few belongings.

Over time, conditions improved. "It does beet all how fast this country is getting up," wrote one South Dakota woman in 1886. "I'm looking round and see two new houses been put up since yesterday." As population increased, women in particular worked to bind isolated households into communities by organizing social activities and institutions. They held fairs, dances, and picnics and established churches, schools, and libraries, thereby gaining both companionship and a sense of purpose. Rural families also created agricultural cooperatives and other economic organizations that encouraged community action. External institutions also developed to serve the rural population. Few were more important than Rural Free Delivery, which eventually brought letters, newspapers, magazines, and advertisements to farm families' doorsteps, or mail-order houses, which made available to farm people such helpful goods as stoves, sewing machines, and shoes. After acquiring her first Montgomery Ward catalog in 1885, one Wyoming woman declared it "impossible to exaggerate the importance of . . . this book of wonder." Such changes helped incorporate Westerners into the larger society.

FARMING THE LAND

Pioneer settlers had to make daunting adjustments to develop the agricultural potential of their new land. Advances in science, technology, and industry made such adjustments possible. The changes would not only reshape the agricultural economy but also bring also moved effectively to regain control of the institutions that define their cultural identity. They have established community schools and tribal community colleges that provide a bilingual, bicultural education, seeking to preserve traditions while opening new opportunities. They have built tribal museums and visitor centers in order to shape the presentation of their histories and cultures. By the late 1990s there were more than 200 such institutions, from the Seneca-Iroquois museum in upstate New York to the Makah Tribal Museum on the Olympic peninsula.

Indians have also secured legal recognition of their right to their cultural patrimony. The Native American Graves Protection and Repatriation Act of 1990 gives Indian communities the right to reclaim, or "repatriate," material artifacts and skeletal remains from museums and historical societies. The Native American Religious Freedom Act of 1978 affirmed their right to practice their traditional religions and have access to sacred sites. Indian dance—once suppressed by white authorities—has revived, and the powwow has become a national Indian institution and symbol of Indian identity.

With the help of historians and lawyers, Indians are also winning enforcement of long-ignored treaty provisions guaranteeing them land ownership and water, hunting, and fishing rights. Court decisions have recognized the right of tribes to permit gambling on their reservations, and some tribes have built profitable casinos, attracting economic development that creates new job opportunities for their people and permits them to stay on their land.

Indians still confront hostility and condescension reminiscent of attitudes a century ago. A white museum official, for example—seeking to prevent the repatriation of Pawnee artifacts—claimed recently that Indians do not have a real religion. But Indians have proved resilient in preserving their cultural heritage and keeping it vibrant for future generations.

---

their own great challenges to traditional rural values and expectations.

Growing crops. Fencing was an immediate problem, for crops needed to be shielded from livestock. But without timber, farmers could not build wooden fences. Barbed wire, developed in the mid-1870s, solved the problem. By 1900, farmers were importing nearly 300 million pounds of barbed wire each year from eastern and midwestern factories.

The aridity of most of the West also posed difficulties. In California, Colorado, and a few other areas, settlers used streams fed by mountain snowpacks to irrigate land. Elsewhere, enterprising farmers developed variants of the "dry farming" practices that the Mormons had introduced in Utah, attempting to maximize the limited rainfall. Some farmers erected windmills to pump underground water. The scarce rainfall also discouraged the cultivation of many of the crops that supported traditional general agriculture and encouraged farmers to specialize in a single cash crop for market. Gradually, many plains farmers turned from corn to wheat, especially the drought-resistant Turkey Red variety of hard winter wheat that German Mennonites had introduced into Kansas from Russia. Government agencies and agricultural colleges contributed to the success of such adaptations, and private engineers and inventors also fostered agricultural development. Related technological advancements included grain elevators that would store grain for shipment and load it into rail cars mechanically and mills that used corrugated, chilled-iron rollers rather than millstones to process the new varieties of wheat.

Mechanization and technological innovations also made possible the large-scale farming practiced in semiarid regions. Farmers required special plows to break the tough sod, new harrows to prepare the soil for cultivation, grain drills to plant the crop, and harvesting and threshing machines to bring it in. Thanks to more and better machines, agricultural efficiency and productivity shot up. By the 1890s, machinery permitted the farmer to produce eighteen times more wheat than hand methods had. Nearly a thousand corporations were manufacturing agricultural machinery to meet the demands of farmers, who purchased implements in steadily mounting quantities.

Growing tensions. These developments reflected both the expansion of agriculture and its increasing dependence on the larger society. Western commercial farmers needed the high demand of eastern and midwestern cities and the expanding world market. The rail network provided essential transportation for their crops; the nation's industrial sector produced necessary agricultural machinery. Banks and loan companies extended the credit and capital that allowed farmers to take advantage of mechanization and other new advances; and many other businesses graded, stored, processed, and sold their crops. In short, because of its market orientation, mechanization, and specialization, western agriculture relied on other people or impersonal forces as it was incorporated into the national and international economy.

When conditions were favorable—good weather, good crops, and good prices—western farmers prospered. Too often, however, they faced adversity. The early years of settlement were unusually wet, but, even then, periodic droughts brought crop failures. Other natural hazards also disrupted production. Especially alarming were plagues of grasshoppers, forming what one woman called a "cloud so dense that the sun was obscured and the earth was in darkness." Grasshoppers ate crops, clothing, and bedding; they attacked sod houses and chewed woodwork and furniture. "In a few hours," one newspaper reported, "many fields that had hung thick with long ears of golden maize were stripped of their value and left only a forest of bare yellow stalks that in their nakedness mocked the tiller of the soil." Private relief organizations distributed food, clothing, and seed to farm families suffering from droughts and grasshoppers in the 1870s, and state governments and Congress appropriated public funds to combat destitution on the agricultural frontier.

In the late 1880s, drought coincided with a slump in crop prices. The large European market that had encouraged agricultural expansion in the 1870s and early 1880s contracted after 1885, when several nations erected trade barriers to U.S. commodities. More important, America's production competed with that from Argentina, Canada, Australia, and Russia, and a world surplus of grain drove prices steadily downward. The average price of wheat dropped from $1.19 a bushel in 1881 to only $0.49 in 1894; prices for other farm commodities also declined.

Squeezed between high costs for credit, transportation, and manufactured goods and falling agri-cultural prices, western farmers faced disaster. They responded by lashing back at their points of contact with the new system. They especially condemned the railroads, believing that the companies exploited farmers' dependence by charging excessive and discriminatory freight rates. Luna Kellie complained of the railroads, "The minute you crossed the Missouri River your fate both soul and body was in their hands. What you should eat and drink, what you should wear, everything was in their hands and they robbed us of all we produced except enough to keep body and soul together and many many times not that."

Farmers censured the grain elevators in the local buying centers. Often owned by eastern corporations, including the railroads themselves, elevators allegedly exploited their local monopoly to cheat farmers by fixing low prices or misrepresenting the quality of wheat. A Minnesota state investigation found systematic fraud by elevators, which collectively cost farmers a massive sum.

Farmers also denounced the bankers and mortgage lenders who had provided the credit for them to acquire land, equipment, and machinery. Much of the money had come from eastern investors, seeking the higher interest rates in the West. With failing crops and falling prices, however, the debt burden proved calamitous for many farmers. Beginning in 1889, many western farms were foreclosed.

Stunned and bitter, western farmers concluded that their problems arose because they had been incorporated into the new system, an integrated economy directed by forces beyond their control. And it was a system that did not work well. "There is," one of them charged, "something radically wrong in our industrial system. There is a screw loose."

CONCLUSION

In a few decades, millions of people had migrated westward in search of new opportunities. With determination, ingenuity, and hard work they had settled vast areas, made farms and ranches, built villages and cities, brought forth mineral wealth, and imposed their values on the land. These were remarkable achievements, though tempered by a shameful treatment of Indians and an often destructive exploitation of natural resources. But if most Westerners took pride in their accomplishments, and a few enjoyed wealth and power, many also grew discontented with the new conditions they encountered as the "Wild" West receded.

The farmers' complaints indicted the major processes by which the West was developed and exploited in the late nineteenth century. Railroad expansion, population movements, eastern investment, corporate control, technological innovations, and government policies had incorporated the region fully into the larger society. Indians experienced this incorporation most thoroughly and most tragically, losing their lands, their traditions, and often their lives; the survivors were dependent on the decisions and actions of interlopers determined to impose "Americanization," the name itself implying the imposition of national patterns.

Cowboys and miners also learned that the frontier merely marked the cutting edge of eastern industrial society. Both were wage workers, often for corporations controlled by eastern capital, and if industrial technology directly affected miners more than cowhands, neither could escape integration into the national economy by managerial decisions, transportation links, and market forces. Most settlers in the West were farmers, but they too learned that their distinctive environment did not insulate them from assimilation into larger productive, financial, and marketing structures.

Western developments, in short, reflected and interacted with those of eastern industrial society. The processes of incorporation drained away Westerners' hopes along with their products, and many of the discontented would demand a serious reorganization of relationships and power. Led by angry farmers, they turned their attention to politics and government, where they encountered new obstacles and opportunities.

REVIEW QUESTIONS

1. Why was the completion of the first transcontinental railroad, described by Andrew J. Russell, celebrated from Boston to San Francisco? How did western railroads shape the settlement and development of the West and affect the East as well?

2. What factors were most influential in the subjugation of American Indians?

3. What were the major goals of federal Indian policy, and how did they change?

4. How did technological developments affect Indians, miners, and farmers in the West?

5. How did the federal government help transform the West?

KEY TERMS

Chisholm Trail (p. 614)

Dawes Act (p. 609)

Homestead Act (p. 617)

Little Bighorn, Battle of the (p. 606)

Sand Creek Massacre (p. 604)

Second Treaty of Fort Laramie (p. 605)

Wounded Knee Massacre (p. 608)

RECOMMENDED READING

Dykstra, Robert R. *The Cattle Towns* (1968). A classic analysis of town building and social conflict in Kansas cattle towns, both fascinating and fun to read.

Fite, Gilbert C. *The Farmers' Frontier, 1865–1900* (1966). A comprehensive account of agricultural settlement in all areas of the West.

Lingenfelter, Richard E. *The Hardrock Miners: A History of the Mining Labor Movement in the American West, 1863–1893* (1974). An important analysis of the relationship between the labor movement and the industrialization of the western mines.

Paul, Rodman W. *The Far West and the Great Plains in Transition* (1988). A valuable survey of regional development that devotes particular attention to mining.

Riley, Glenda. *The Female Frontier: A Comparative View of Women on the Prairie and the Plains* (1988). A useful guide to women's experiences in the West.

Utley, Robert M. *The Indian Frontier of the American West, 1846–1890* (1984). A balanced survey of United States–Indian relations in the late nineteenth century.

Weeks, Philip. *Farewell, My Nation: The American Indian and the United States, 1820–1890,* 2nd ed. (2001). Modern discussions of Indian policy that provide insights into the perspectives of the Indians.

White, Richard. *"It's Your Misfortune and None of My Own": A New History of the American West* (1991). An important and original analysis of the development of the West that highlights environmental, ethnic, labor, and social history.

Wyman, Mark. *Hard Rock Epic: Western Miners and the Industrial Revolution, 1860–1910* (1979). Miners experiencing the dual frontiers of the West and the industrial revolution.

ADDITIONAL SOURCES

General Studies

Armitage, Susan, and Elizabeth Jameson, eds. *The Women's West* (1987).

Butler, Anne M. *Daughters of Joy, Sisters of Misery: Prostitutes in the American West* (1985).

Cronon, William. *Nature's Metropolis: Chicago and the Great West* (1991).

Hine, Robert V. *Community on the American Frontier: Separate but Not Alone* (1980).

Jameson, Elizabeth, and Susan Armitage, eds. *Writing the Range: Race, Class, and Culture in the Women's West* (1997).

Jeffrey, Julie Roy. *Frontier Women* (1998).

Limerick, Patricia Nelson. *The Legacy of Conquest* (1987).

Milner, Clyde A., Carol A. O'Connor, and Martha A. Sandweiss, eds. *The Oxford History of the American West* (1994).

Pascoe, Peggy, *Relations of Rescue: The Search for Female Moral Authority in the American West* (1990).

Riley, Glenda. *A Place to Grow: Women in the American West* (1992).

Robbins, William G. *Colony and Empire: The Capitalist Transformation of the American West* (1994).

West, Elliott. *The Way to the West* (1995).

Worster, Donald. *Rivers of Empire: Water, Aridity, and the Growth of the American West* (1985).

Native Americans

Adams, David W. *Education for Extinction: American Indians and the Boarding School Experience* (1995).

Fritz, Henry. *The Movement for Indian Assimilation, 1860–1890* (1963).

Gibson, Arrell Morgan. *The American Indian, Prehistory to the Present* (1980).

Hoxie, Frederick E. *A Final Promise: The Campaign to Assimilate the Indians, 1880–1920* (1984).

Hutton, Paul. *Phil Sheridan and His Army* (1985).

Iverson, Peter. *The Navajos* (1990).

Josephy, Alvin M. Jr. *The Nez Percé Indians and the Opening of the Northwest* (1965).

Mardock, Robert. *The Reformers and the Indian* (1971).

McDonnell, Janet. *The Dispossession of the American Indian* (1991).

Utley, Robert M. *The Lance and the Shield: The Life and Times of Sitting Bull* (1993).

Washburn, Wilcomb E. *The Indian in America* (1975).

West, Elliott. *The Contested Plains: Indians, Goldseekers, and the Rush to Colorado* (1998).

Wishart, David. *An Unspeakable Sadness: The Dispossession of the Nebraska Indians* (1994).

Wooster, Robert. *The Military and United States Indian Policy, 1865–1903* (1988).

The Mining Bonanza

Emmons, David. *The Butte Irish: Class and Ethnicity in an American Mining Town* (1989).

James, Ronald, and Elizabeth Raymond, eds. *Comstock Women: The Making of a Mining Community* (1998).

Marks, Paula M. *Precious Dust: The American Gold Rush Era* (1994).

Paul, Rodman W. *Mining Frontiers of the Far West, 1848–1880* (1963).

Peterson, Richard H. *The Bonanza Kings: The Social Origins and Business Behavior of Western Mining Entrepreneurs* (1977).

Petrik, Paula. *No Step Backward: Women and Family on the Rocky Mountain Mining Frontier, Helena, Montana* (1987).

Rohrbough, Malcolm. *Aspen: The History of a Silver-Mining Town* (1986).

Smith, Duane A. *Mining America: The Industry and the Environment* (1987).

Smith, Duane A. *Rocky Mountain Mining Camps: The Urban Frontier* (1967).

Spence, Clark. *British Investments and the American Mining Frontier* (1958).

West, Elliott. *The Saloon on the Rocky Mountain Mining Frontier* (1979).

Zhu, Liping. *A Chinaman's Chance: The Chinese on the Rocky Mountain Mining Frontier* (1997).

The Cattle Kingdom

Atherton, Lewis. *The Cattle Kings* (1961).

Carlson, Paul. *The Cowboy Way* (2000)

Dale, Edward. *The Range Cattle Industry* (1969).

Dary, David. *Cowboy Culture* (1981).

Durham, Philip, and Everett L. Jones. *The Negro Cowboys* (1965).

Gressley, Gene M. *Bankers and Cattlemen* (1966).

Haywood, C. Robert. *Victorian West: Class and Culture in Kansas Cattle Towns* (1991).

Lopez, David E. "Cowboy Strikes and Unions," *Labor History* 18 (Summer 1977): 325–340.

Miner, H. Craig. *Wichita: The Early Years, 1865–1880* (1982).

Skaggs, Jimmy M. *The Cattle Trailing Industry* (1973).

Walker, Don D. *Clio's Cowboys* (1981).

The Expansion of Agriculture

Bogue, Allan G. *Money at Interest: The Farm Mortgage on the Middle Border* (1955).

Isern, Thomas. *Bull Threshers and Bindlestiffs: Harvesting and Threshing on the North American Plains* (1990).

Miner, H. Craig. *West of Wichita: Settling the High Plains of Kansas, 1865–1890* (1986).

Nelsen, Jane Taylor, ed. *Prairie Populist: The Memoirs of Luna Kellie* (1992).

Painter, Nell. *Exodusters: Black Migration to Kansas after Reconstruction* (1976).

Pisani, Donald J. *From the Family Farm to Agribusiness: The Irrigation Crusade in California and the West* (1984).

Pisani, Donald J. *To Reclaim a Divided West: Water, Law, and Public Policy* (1992).

Shannon, Fred A. *The Farmer's Last Frontier: Agriculture, 1860–1897* (1945).

Ethnic and Cultural Frontiers

Camarillo, Albert. *Chicanos in a Changing Society* (1979).

Chan, Sucheng. *This Bittersweet Soil: The Chinese in California Agriculture* (1986).

Deutsch, Sarah. *No Separate Refuge: Culture, Class, and Gender on an Anglo-Hispanic Frontier in the American Southwest* (1987).

Garcia, Mario T. *Desert Immigrants: The Mexicans of El Paso, 1880–1920* (1981).

Gjerde, Jon. *From Peasants to Farmers: The Migration from Balestrand, Norway, to the Upper Midwest* (1985).

Luebke, Frederick C. *Ethnicity on the Great Plains* (1980).

McQuillan, D. Aidan. *Prevailing over Time: Ethnic Adjustment on the Kansas Prairies, 1875–1925* (1990).

Takaki, Ronald. *Strangers from a Different Shore: A History of Asian Americans* (1989).

WHERE TO LEARN MORE

- **Bodie State Historic Park, Bodie, California.** The largest authentic ghost town in the West, Bodie was an important mining center from the 1860s to the 1880s. About 170 buildings remain, including a museum with mining equipment and artifacts of everyday life. www.bodie.net/.

- **Little Bighorn Battlefield National Monument, Crow Agency, Montana.** The site of Custer's crushing defeat includes a monument to the Seventh Cavalry atop Last Stand Hill. A new authorized Indian Memorial will include sacred texts, artifacts, and pictographs of the Plains Indians. www.nps.gov/libi/home.htm.

- **American Historical Society of Germans from Russia Museum, Lincoln, Nebraska.** This unique museum, consisting of a complex of re-stored homes, exhibitions, and archives, preserves the history and culture of Germans who emigrated to Russia and then to the American Great Plains, where they contributed importantly to the development of a multicultural society and an agricultural economy.

- **National Museum of the American Indian, New York, New York.** Part of the Smithsonian Institution, this museum has a collection of artifacts illustrative of more than ten thousand years of the Native American culture. www.nmai.si.edu/index.asp.

- **National Cowboy Hall of Fame, Oklahoma City, Oklahoma.** This large institution contains an outstanding collection of Western art, displays of cowboy and Indian artifacts, and both kitschy exhibitions of the mythic, Hollywood West and serious galleries depicting the often hard realities of the cattle industry. Its many public programs also successfully combine fun with learning. www.cowboyhalloffame.org/index2.html.

- **Golden Spike National Historic Site, near Promontory, Utah.** The completion of the transcontinental railroad here in 1869 is reenacted from May to October, using reproductions of the original locomotives. Visitors can drive the route of the railroad, now a National Backway Byway through abandoned mining and railroad towns, from Promontory to Nevada. Virtual tour, history, and tourist links on www.nps./gov/gosp.

- **Fort Laramie, National Historic Site, near Guernsey, Wyoming.** A fur-trading post, stop on the Oregon Trail, site of treaty negotiations with the Plains Indians, and staging area for military campaigns, Fort Laramie is now a living history museum with many original buildings. For a virtual tour of the fort and information about visiting see www.nps.gov/fola/.

 Please refer to the document CD-ROM for primary sources related to this chapter.

→ An engraving of New Yorkers celebrating their party's national convention at Madison Square Garden in 1888 conveys the popular enthusiasm and mass participation that characterized American politics in the late nineteenth century.

POLITICS AND GOVERNMENT 20
1877–1900

Cincinnati, Ohio
September 28, 1884

Dear Fanny,

Will has been appointed chief supervisor and so has to take means to prevent fraud at the election. He must appoint assistants for each ward.

Horace
October 12, 1884

Dear Father,

Will has no time for anything but the election and his duties as chief supervisor. . . . I am afraid the election will be a stormy one & violence will not surprise me. I am one of a citizens' committee of the 18th ward and we propose to be on hand from 6 in the morning till the votes are counted at night.

Horace
October 22, 1884

Dear Mother,

We had an exciting time election day. The Democrats tried to introduce their Southern methods into northern elections and succeeded in one or two wards, but in general the U.S. Deputy Marshals managed to keep the scoundrels

CHAPTER OUTLINE

The Structure and Style of Politics
Campaigns and Elections
Partisan Politics
Associational Politics

The Limits of Government
The Weak Presidency
The Inefficient Congress
The Federal Bureaucracy and the Spoils System
Inconsistent State Government

Public Policies and National Elections
Civil Service Reform
The Political Life of the Tariff
The Beginnings of Federal Regulation
The Money Question

The Crisis of the 1890s
Farmers Protest Inequities
The People's Party
The Challenge of the Depression
The Battle of the Standards and the Election of 1896

Conclusion

quiet. The negroes in many precincts voted at the risk of their lives. I saw a man shot & killed about fifteen feet from me at our polling place. . . . He drew a pistol on a Deputy Marshal but the Deputy was too quick for him.

Horace
October 22, 1884

Dear Father,

In the 5th, 8th, and 19th Wards the marshals were utterly useless and were soon overpowered. The police did nothing except to set on [incite] the crowd. . . . The negroes were driven away from the polls, beaten and wounded and exposed to as much abuse as they could have been south of Mason's and Dixon's line. No colored votes were polled in those precincts after twelve o'clock.

Will

William H. Taft Papers, Manuscript Division, Library of Congress.

Horace and Will Taft wrote regularly to their parents and sister Fanny to keep them informed of the 1884 congressional election in their hometown of Cincinnati. Alphonso, Louise, and Fanny Taft, all staunch Republicans, were desperate for such political news. Alphonso's high standing in his party had led to important political appointments, first to President Ulysses S. Grant's cabinet and then as American minister to Austria. Now in Vienna, they eagerly awaited news of their party's success.

As the Taft brothers reported, voters in the city had a complicated and difficult journey to the polls, and some did not reach their destination. The lead-up to the election had electrified the city, as rabid partisans had staged competing torchlight parades, with thousands of uniformed marchers organized into companies, brigades, and divisions; orators had stirred the huge crowds for hours with patriotic, religious, and cultural bombast. And amid such excitement, the election itself did produce the violence Horace had expected. The Republican brothers condemned the Democrats for intimidating African Americans and others likely to vote Republican, "importing" Democratic voters from other states and "colonizing" them in Cincinnati, and using the local police force as a partisan organization to frighten or arrest Republicans attempting to reach the ballot box.

But there was a Democratic version of events as well. The U.S. marshals so praised by Horace had been appointed by Republican federal officials under Will's supervision. And many of those marshals were merely thugs, paid and armed by the Lincoln Club, a local Republican campaign organization, and often interested simply in improving Republican election prospects. As Will conceded, they first "drove from the city the night before election" hundreds of Democrats they alleged might commit election fraud. On election day itself they sought to incite violence in the city's Irish wards to keep other Democratic voters from the polls, and they made mass arrests of others trying to vote, often claiming that they were Kentucky Democrats who had crossed the Ohio River to "colonize" Cincinnati's election. Several times deputies fired point-blank into Democratic crowds around the polls. As Will admitted to his father about those deputies, "it is attended with risk to furnish revolvers to men who are close to or belong to the criminal class."

"The Democrats are so mad at not being able to perpetrate these frauds," Will concluded with unwitting irony, "that they are trying to get even by crying fraud at us."

Not all American elections in the late nineteenth century were as riotous as this Cincinnati contest. (And both Democrats and Republicans were eventually convicted of illegal voting and election fraud, while Alphonso Taft congratulated his two sons for the "risk and labor" they had undertaken in the election.) But in many ways it suggested much about

American politics at the time. From the military-style campaign to the rough act of voting itself, elections were a masculine business—although women were intensely interested. Marked by pageantry and hoopla, campaigns attracted mass participation but often avoided substantive policy issues. The two major political parties shaped campaigns and controlled elections, which were usually tumultuous if not always violent. Partisan divisions overlapped with ethnic, racial, and other social divisions, and the question of suffrage was a contested one. Partisanship often determined both the membership and the activities of government agencies, even those nominally charged with the maintenance of public order. The lack of a common national election day, which allowed Kentuckians to vote in Cincinnati's October election without missing their own, reflected localism—the belief that local concerns took precedence over national concerns. One newspaper even denied the legitimacy of federal involvement in the city's elections, declaring that federal deputies "can all be kicked and cuffed about like ordinary citizens, and will be compelled to take their chances with common people on election day."

These features of late-nineteenth century politics would eventually be transformed in significant ways. But while they endured, they shaped not only campaigns and elections but the form and role of government as well. As for William Howard Taft, he moved up the political ladder, eventually becoming President of the United States. His success, he explained, stemmed from his father's reputation, his own loyalty to his party, and keeping his "plate the right side up when offices were falling."

KEY TOPICS

- The exuberant partisan politics and the close balance between parties in the late nineteenth century

- The inability of a weak federal government to address problems of America's industrializing economy

- The pressure for civil service reform

- The tariff issue

- Monetary policy and the call for free silver

- Agricultural protest and the emergence of the Populist party

- The end of political stalemate after the election of 1896

THE STRUCTURE AND STYLE OF POLITICS

Politics in the late nineteenth century was an absorbing activity. Campaigns and elections expressed social values as they determined who held the reins of government. Political parties dominated political life. They organized campaigns, controlled balloting, and held the unswerving loyalty of most of the electorate. While the major parties worked to maintain a sense of unity and tradition among their followers, third parties sought to activate those the major parties left unserved. Other Americans looked outside the electoral arena to fulfill their political goals.

CAMPAIGNS AND ELECTIONS

Political campaigns and elections generated remarkable public participation and enthusiasm. They constituted a major form of entertainment at a time when recreational opportunities were limited. Campaign pageantry absorbed communities large and small. In cities and towns across the nation, thousands of men in elaborate uniforms marched in massive torchlight parades to demonstrate partisan enthusiasm. The small town of Emporia, Kansas, once witnessed a campaign rally of twenty thousand people, several times its population. A parade of wagons stretched 5 miles, reported the proud local newspaper. "When the head of the procession was under the equator the tail was

Chronology

1867 Patrons of Husbandry (the Grange) is founded.

1869 Massachusetts establishes the first state regulatory commission.

1873 Silver is demonetized in the "Crime of '73."

1874 Woman's Christian Temperance Union is organized.

1875 U.S. Supreme Court, in *Minor v. Happersett*, upholds denial of suffrage to women.

1876 Greenback Party runs presidential candidate.

1877 Rutherford B. Hayes becomes president after disputed election.

Farmers' Alliance is founded.

Supreme Court, in *Munn v. Illinois*, upholds state regulatory authority over private property.

1878 Bland-Allison Act obliges the government to buy silver.

1880 James A. Garfield is elected president.

1881 Garfield is assassinated; Chester A. Arthur becomes president.

1883 Pendleton Civil Service Act is passed.

1884 Grover Cleveland is elected president.

1886 Supreme Court, in *Wabash v. Illinois*, rules that only the federal government, not the states, can regulate interstate commerce.

1887 Interstate Commerce Act is passed.

1888 Benjamin Harrison is elected president.

1890 Sherman Antitrust Act is passed.

McKinley Tariff Act is passed.

Sherman Silver Purchase Act is passed.

National American Woman Suffrage Association is organized.

Wyoming enters the Union as the first state with woman suffrage.

1892 People's Party is organized.

Cleveland is elected to his second term as president.

1893 Depression begins.

Sherman Silver Purchase Act is repealed.

1894 Coxey's Army marches to Washington.

Pullman strike ends in violence.

1895 Supreme Court, in *Pollock v. Farmers' Loan and Trust Company*, invalidates the federal income tax.

Supreme Court, in *United States v. E.C. Knight Company*, limits the Sherman Antitrust law to commerce, excluding industrial monopolies.

1896 William Jennings Bryan is nominated for president by Democrats and Populists.

William McKinley is elected president.

1900 Currency Act puts U.S. currency on the gold standard.

coming around the north pole." Political picnics and camp meetings served a comparable function in rural areas. Attending party meetings and conventions, listening to lengthy speeches appealing to group loyalties and local pride, gathering at the polls to watch the voting and the counting, celebrating victory and drowning the disappointment of defeat—all these provided social enjoyment and defined popular politics.

The excitement of political contests prompted the wife of Chief Justice Morrison Waite to write longingly on election day, 1876, "I should want to vote all day." But women—though they often identified with and endorsed a political party—could not vote at all in national elections. Justice Waite himself had just a year earlier written the unanimous opinion of the Supreme Court (in *Minor v. Happersett*) that the Constitution did not confer suffrage on women. Men generally believed that weakness and sentimentality disqualified women from the fierce conflicts of the public realm.

Virtually all men participated in politics. In many states, even immigrants not yet citizens were eligible to vote and flocked to the polls. African Americans voted regularly in the North and irregularly in the South before being disfranchised at the end of the century. Overall, turnout was remarkably high, averaging nearly 80 percent of eligible voters in presidential elections between 1876 and 1900, a figure far greater than ever achieved thereafter (see Figure 20-1).

Political parties mobilized this huge electorate. They kept detailed records of voters, transported them to the polls, saw that they were registered where necessary, and sometimes even paid their poll taxes or naturalization fees to make them eligible. With legal regulations and public machinery for elections negligible, parties dominated the campaigns and elections. Many states did not have meaningful registration laws, making it difficult to determine voter eligibility. Until the 1890s, most states had no laws to ensure secrecy in voting, and balloting often took place in open rooms or on sidewalks. Election clerks and judges were not public officials but partisans chosen by the political parties.

Nor did public authorities issue official ballots. Instead voters used party tickets, strips of paper printed by the parties. These had only the names of the candidates of the party issuing them and often varied in size and color. The voter's use of a ballot thus revealed his party allegiance. Tickets were distributed by paid party workers known as peddlers or hawkers, who stationed themselves near the polls, each trying to force his ticket on prospective voters. These contending hawkers contributed greatly to election day chaos. Fighting and intimidation were so commonplace at the polls that one state supreme court ruled in 1887 that they were "acceptable" features of elections.

As the court recognized, the open and partisan aspects of the electoral process did not necessarily lead to election fraud, however much they shaped the nature of political participation. In these circumstances, campaigns and elections provided opportunities for men to demonstrate publicly their commitment to their party and its values, thereby reinforcing their partisan loyalties.

Nonvoting women, too, often exhibited their partisanship in this exciting political environment. Women wrote partisan literature and gave campaign speeches; Anna Dickinson, one of the period's most popular orators, was hired by the Republican National Committee to campaign in the East and Midwest. Sometimes partisan women acted together with men; other times they worked through separate women's organizations. J. Ellen Foster established the Woman's National Republican Association in 1888 and built it into an organizing machine for the Republican Party with numerous state and local clubs. In these partisan groups women discussed and circulated party literature and devised plans to influence elections. Their partisanship was so deeply embedded that they remained loyal Republicans even when their party repudiated woman suffrage. "What discourages me about women," noted suffragist Susan B. Anthony, was that they care more for "[their] political party . . . than for [their] own political rights."

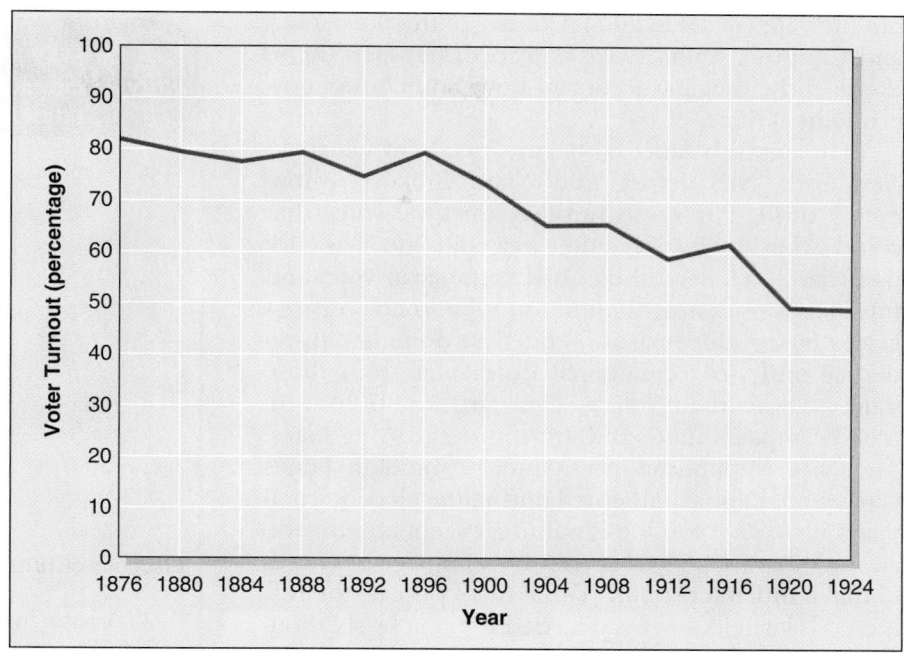

FIGURE 20-1   Voter Turnout in Presidential Elections, 1876–1924
The exciting partisan politics of the late nineteenth century produced very high voter turnouts, but as party competition declined and states enacted more restrictive voting regulations, popular participation in elections fell in the twentieth century.

PARTISAN POLITICS

A remarkably close balance prevailed between the two major parties in the elections of this era. Democrats and Republicans had virtually the same level of electoral support, one reason they worked so hard to get

The campaign pageantry of a Republican parade in Canton, Ohio, in 1896 illustrates the central role played by political parties in entertaining, organizing, and mobilizing voters. Over a century later, parties have lost many of their functions and much of their popular support.

out the vote (see Map 20-1). Control of the presidency and Congress shifted back and forth between them. Rarely did either party control both branches of government at once.

The party balance also gave great influence to New York, New Jersey, Ohio, and Indiana, whose evenly divided voters controlled electoral votes that could swing an election either way. Said one New York politician, "We need the entire Republican vote, and this means work and attention in every school district in the State." Both parties tended to nominate presidential and vice presidential candidates from those states to woo their voters. The parties also concentrated campaign funds and strategy on the swing states. Thus the Republican presidential candidate James Garfield of Ohio commented during the election campaign in 1880: "Nothing is wanting except an immediate and liberal supply of money for campaign expenses to make Indiana certain. With a victory there, the rest is easy." Garfield narrowly carried Indiana by six thousand votes and the nation by nine thousand, out of 9.2 million cast. His victory was not the outcome of a contest over great issues but of carefully organized, tightly balanced parties mobilizing their supporters.

Party loyalty. Interrelated regional, ethnic, religious, and local factors determined the party affiliations of most Americans. Economic issues, although important to the politics of the era, generally did not decide party ties. Farmers, for example, despite often shared economic concerns, affiliated with both major parties. Like religious belief and ethnic identity, partisan loyalty was largely a cultural trait passed from parents to children—a situation that helps to explain the electoral stability of most communities.

Republicans were strongest in the North and Midwest, where they benefited from their party's role as the defender of the Union in the Civil War. "Republicanism in [Iowa] is not a logical conviction," reported one journalist in 1884; "it is a baleful fanaticism. . . . The war is still in progress in this region. . . . The women are worse than the men; they are intolerant, ferocious, implacable." But not all Northerners voted for the Grand Old Party, or GOP. The Republican Party appealed primarily to old-stock Americans and other Protestants, including those of German and Scandinavian descent. African Americans, loyal to the party that had emancipated and enfranchised the slaves of the South, also supported the GOP where they could vote. Democrats were strongest in the South, where they stood as the defender of the traditions of the region's white population. But Democrats also drew support in the urban Northeast, especially from Catholics and recent immigrants.

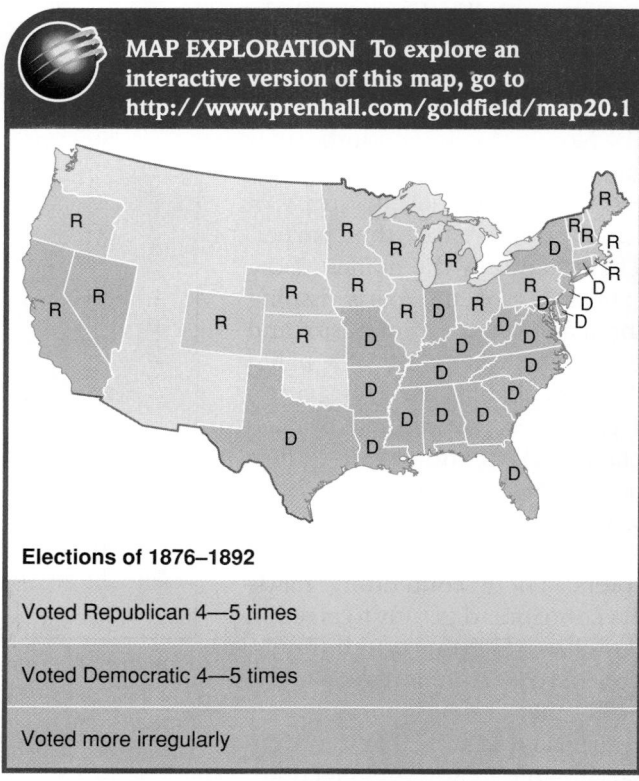

MAP 20-1   The Two-Party Stalemate of the Late Nineteenth Century
Strong parties, staunch loyalties, and an evenly divided electorate made for exciting politics but often stalemated government in the late nineteenth century. Most states voted consistently for one of the major parties, leaving the few swing states like New York and Indiana the scenes of fierce partisan battles.

Party identities. Each major party thus consisted of a complex coalition of groups with differing traditions and interests. One observer of the Democratic Party in California described it as "a sort of Democratic happy family, like we see in the prairie-dog villages, where owls, rattlesnakes, prairie dogs, and lizards all live in the same hole." This internal diversity often provoked conflict and threatened party stability. To hold its coalition together, each party identified itself with a theme that appealed broadly to all its constituents, while suggesting that it was menaced by the members and objectives of the opposing party.

Republicans identified their party with nationalism and national unity and attacked the Democrats as an "alliance between the embittered South and the slums of the Northern cities." They combined a "bloody shirt" appeal to the memories of the Civil War with campaigns for immigration restriction and cultural uniformity. Seeing a threat to American society in efforts by Catholic immigrants to preserve their ethnic and cultural traditions, for example, Republican legislatures in several states in the 1880s and 1890s enacted laws regulating parochial schools, the use of foreign languages, and alcohol consumption.

Democrats portrayed themselves as the party of limited government and "personal liberties," a theme that appealed both to the racism of white Southerners and the resentment immigrants felt about the nativist meddling the Republicans favored. The Democrats' commitment to personal liberties had limits. They supported the disfranchisement of African Americans, the exclusion of Chinese immigrants, and the dispossession of American Indians. Nevertheless, their emphasis on traditional individualism and localism proved popular.

The partisan politics of both major parties culminated in party machines, especially at the local level. Led by powerful bosses, such as the Democrat Richard Croker of New York and the Republican George Cox of Cincinnati, these machines controlled not only city politics but also municipal government. Party activists used well-organized ward clubs to mobilize working-class voters, who were rewarded by municipal jobs and baskets of food or coal doled out by the machine. Such assistance was often necessary, given the lack of public welfare systems, but to buy votes the machine also sold favors. Public contracts and franchises were peddled to businesses whose high bids covered kickbacks to the machine.

Third parties.   The partisan politics of the era left room for several third parties, organized around specific issues or groups. The **Prohibition Party** persistently championed the abolition of alcohol but also supported electoral reforms such as woman suffrage, economic reforms such as railroad regulation and income taxes, and social reforms including improved race relations. It won as many as a quarter of a million votes, drawn mostly from Republicans, and its strong showing in New York may have cost the GOP the presidential election in 1884.

Some farmers and workers, fed up with the major parties, formed larger but shorter-lived third parties. These parties charged that Republicans and Democrats had failed to respond to economic problems caused by industrialization or, worse still, had deliberately promoted powerful business interests at the expense of ordinary Americans. The **Greenback Party** of the 1870s denounced "the infamous financial legislation which takes all from the many to enrich the few." Its policies of labor reform and currency inflation (to stimulate and democratize the economy) attracted supporters from Maine to Texas. Other significant third parties included the Anti-Monopoly party, the Union Labor party, and, most important, the People's or **Populist Party** of the 1890s. Although third parties often won temporary success at the local or regional level, they never permanently displaced the major parties or undermined traditional voter allegiances.

ASSOCIATIONAL POLITICS

Associations of like-minded citizens, operating outside the electoral arena, played an increasingly important role in late-nineteenth-century politics. These organizations worked to achieve public policies beneficial to their members. Farmers organized many such groups, most notably the Patrons of Husbandry, known familiarly as the Grange (see Chapter 17). Established in 1867, with both women and men eligible for membership, the Grange had 22,000 local lodges and nearly a million members by 1875. Its campaign for public regulation of the rates charged by railroads and grain elevators helped convince midwestern states to pass the so-called **Granger laws**. The Grange also sought reforms in the nation's financial system. Although it inspired the formation of small independent farmers' parties in the Midwest and on the Pacific coast, the Grange itself remained nonpartisan.

The Grange rejected partisanship but not politics. This sympathetic cartoon shows a Granger trying to warn Americans blindly absorbed in partisan politics of the dangers of onrushing industrialization.

To the Grangers' dismay, industrialists also formed pressure groups. Organizations such as the American Iron and Steel Association and the American Protective Tariff League lobbied Congress for high tariff laws and made campaign contributions to friendly politicians of both parties. A small group of conservative reformers known derisively as **Mugwumps** (the term derives from the Algonquian word for "chief") objected to both tariffs and the government regulations farmers favored as interfering with "natural" economic laws. They devoted most of their efforts, however, to campaigning for honest and efficient government through civil-service reform. They organized the National Civil Service Reform League to publicize their plans, lobby Congress and state legislatures, and endorse sympathetic candidates. Other pressure groups focused on cultural politics. The rabidly anti-Catholic American Protective Association, for example, agitated for laws restricting immigration, taxing church property, and inspecting Catholic religious institutions.

Women as activists.

Women were also active in associational politics. Susan B. Anthony and others formed groups to lobby Congress and state legislatures for constitutional amendments extending the right to vote to women. The leading organizations merged in 1890 as the **National American Woman Suffrage Association**. Despite the opposition of male politicians of both major parties, suffragists had succeeded by the mid-1890s in gaining full woman suffrage in four western states—Wyoming, Colorado, Idaho, and Utah—and partial suffrage (the right to vote in school elections) in several other states, east and west.

Other women influenced public issues through social service organizations. Although the belief that women belonged in the domestic sphere limited their involvement in electoral politics, it furnished a basis for political action focused on welfare and moral reform. With petition campaigns, demonstrations, and lobbying, women's social service organizations sought to remedy poverty and disease, improve education and recreation, and provide day nurseries for the children of workingwomen. The Illinois Woman's Alliance—

A meeting in 1880 of the National Woman Suffrage Association protested the exclusion of women from electoral politics. Susan B. Anthony noted with regret that "to all men woman suffrage is only a side issue."

organized in 1888 by suffragists, women assemblies of the Knights of Labor, and middle-class women's clubs—investigated the conditions of women and children in workshops and factories, campaigned successfully for protective labor legislation and compulsory school-attendance laws, and obtained greater representation of women on the Chicago school board. The Woman's Municipal League, organized in New York City in 1894, described itself as a "political club" for women concerned with "education, sanitation, public health, and police and fire protection."

Women also combined domesticity and politics in the temperance movement. Alcoholism, widespread in American society, was regarded as a major cause of crime, wife abuse, and broken homes. The temperance movement thus invoked women's presumed moral superiority to address a real problem that fell within their accepted sphere. The Woman's Christian Temperance Union (WCTU) gained a massive membership by campaigning for restrictive liquor laws. It helped secure prohibition or local-option laws in a dozen states and was particularly successful in persuading legislatures to require temperance education in the public schools.

Under the leadership of Frances Willard, the WCTU built on traditional women's concerns to develop an important critique of American society. Reversing the conventional view, Willard argued that alcohol abuse was a result, not a cause, of poverty and social disorder. Under the slogan of "Home Protection," the WCTU inserted domestic issues into the political sphere with a campaign for social and economic reforms far beyond temperance. It particularly sought to strengthen and enforce laws against rape. Willard bitterly noted that twenty states fixed the age of consent at ten and that "in Massachusetts and Vermont it is a greater crime to steal a cow" than to rape a woman. The WCTU also pushed for improved health conditions, reached out to the Knights of Labor to support workplace reforms, and lobbied for federal aid to education, particularly as a means to provide schooling for black children in the South. It eventually supported woman suffrage as well, on the grounds that women needed the vote to fulfill their duty to protect home, family, and morality. The organization further expanded its political activities in 1887 by making Ada Bittenbender, a Nebraska attorney, its Superintendent on Legislation, and she established an effective office in Washington, testifying before Congress, drafting model legislation, and otherwise developing lobbying techniques that other special interest groups have subsequently followed.

THE LIMITS OF GOVERNMENT

Despite the popular enthusiasm for partisan politics and the persistent pressure of associational politics, government in the late nineteenth century was neither active nor productive by present standards. The receding government activism of the Civil War and Reconstruction years coincided with a resurgent belief in localism and **laissez-faire** policies. In addition, a Congress and presidency divided between the two major parties, a small and inefficient bureaucracy, and judicial restraints joined powerful private interests to limit the size and objectives of the federal government.

THE WEAK PRESIDENCY

The presidency was a weak and restricted institution. The impeachment of President Johnson at the outset of Reconstruction had undermined the office. President Grant clearly subordinated it to the legislative branch by deferring to Congress on appointments and legislation. Other factors contributed as well. The men who filled the office between 1877 and 1897— Republicans Rutherford B. Hayes (1877–1881), James A. Garfield (1881), and Chester A. Arthur (1881–1885); Democrat Grover Cleveland (1885–1889 and 1893–1897); and Republican Benjamin Harrison (1889–1893)—were all honest and generally capable. Each had built a solid political record at the state or federal level. But they were all conservatives, with a narrow view of the presidency, and proposed few initiatives. The most aggressive of them, Cleveland, used

his energy in a singularly negative fashion, vetoing two-thirds of all the bills Congress passed, more than all his predecessors combined. Cleveland once vetoed a relief measure for drought-stricken Texas farmers with the statement that "though the people support the Government, the Government should not support the people." This attitude limited government action.

The presidents of this era viewed their duties as chiefly administrative. They made little effort to reach out to the public or to exert legislative leadership. In 1885, Woodrow Wilson, at the time a professor of history and government, described "the business of the president" as "not much above routine" and concluded that the office might "not inconveniently" be made purely administrative, its occupant a sort of tenured civil servant. (Wilson, who helped transform the presidency into a powerful office in the twentieth century, took a very different view when he became president himself in 1913.) Benjamin Harrison devoted as many as six hours a day to dealing with office seekers, and Garfield lamented, "My day is frittered away by the personal seeking of people, when it ought to be given to the great problems which concern the whole country."

The presidency was also hampered by its limited control over bureaus and departments, which responded more directly to Congress, and by its small staff. Indeed, the president's staff consisted of no more than a half-dozen secretaries, clerks, and telegraphers. As Cleveland complained, "If the President has any great policy in mind or on hand he has no one to help him work it out."

THE INEFFICIENT CONGRESS

Congress was the foremost branch of the national government. It exercised authority over the federal budget, oversaw the cabinet, debated public issues, and controlled legislation. Its members were often state and national party leaders, who were strong-willed and, as one senator conceded, "tolerated no intrusion from the President or from anybody else."

But Congress was scarcely efficient. Its chambers were noisy and chaotic, and members rarely devoted their attention to the business at hand. Instead, they played cards, read newspapers, or sent a page to get fruit or tobacco from the vendors who lined the hallways of the capitol. The repeated shifts in party control of Congress also impeded effective action. So, too, did the loss of experienced legislators to rapid turnover. In some Congresses, a majority of members were first-termers.

Procedural rules, based on precedents from a simpler time and manipulated by determined partisans, hindered congressional action. Some rules restricted the introduction of legislation; others prevented its passage. The most notorious rule required that a quorum be not only present but voting. When the House was narrowly divided along party lines, the minority could block all business simply by refusing to answer when the roll was called.

But as a nationalizing economy required more national legislation, business before Congress grew relentlessly (see Figure 20-2). The expanding scale of congressional work prompted a gradual reform of procedures and the centralization of power in the Speaker of the House and the leading committees. These changes did not, however, create a coherent program for government action.

THE FEDERAL BUREAUCRACY AND THE SPOILS SYSTEM

Reflecting presidential weakness and congressional inefficiency, the federal bureaucracy remained small and limited in the late nineteenth century. There were little more than fifty thousand government employees in 1871, and three-fourths of them were local postmasters scattered across the nation. Only six thousand, from President Grant to janitors, worked in Washington. The number of federal employees doubled to 100,000 in 1881 and grew again to 157,000 in 1891 and to 239,000 in 1901. It was still the postal service, however, that absorbed most of this increase.

FIGURE 20-2 Increase in Congressional Business, 1871–1901
Industrialization, urbanization, and western expansion brought increased demands for government action, but the party stalemate, laissez-faire attitudes, and inefficient public institutions often blocked effective responses.

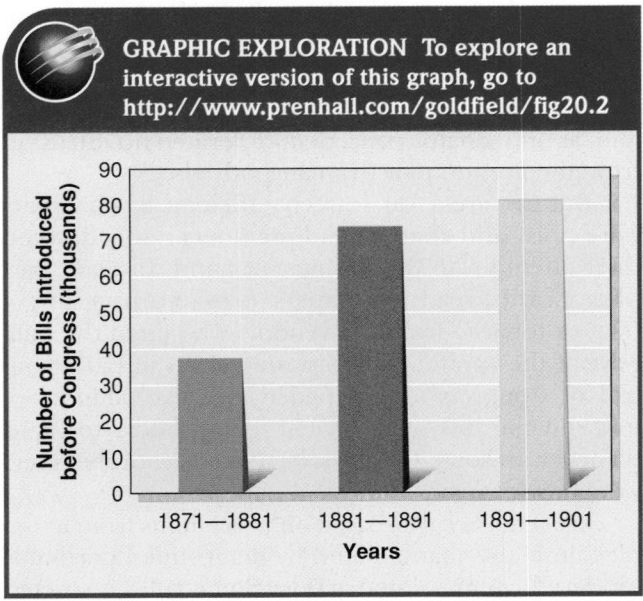

GRAPHIC EXPLORATION To explore an interactive version of this graph, go to http://www.prenhall.com/goldfield/fig20.2

The system for selecting and supervising federal officials had developed gradually in the first half of the century. Known as the spoils system, its basic principle was that victorious politicians awarded government jobs to party workers, with little regard for qualifications, and ousted the previous employees. Appointees then typically promised part of their salary and time to the political interests of their patron or party. The spoils system played a crucial role in all aspects of politics. It enabled party leaders to strengthen their organizations, reward loyal party service, and attract the political workers needed to mobilize the electorate. Supporters described it as a democratic system that offered opportunities to many citizens and prevented the emergence of an entrenched bureaucracy.

Critics, however, charged that the system was riddled with corruption, abuse, and inefficiency. Rapid turnover bred instability; political favoritism bred incompetence. One secretary of the navy, appointed at the behest of Indiana's Republican machine, was said to have exclaimed during his first official inspection of a ship: "Why, the thing's hollow!" Certainly the spoils system was ineffective for filling positions that required special clerical skills, such as typing, or scientific expertise like that required by the Weather Bureau (established in 1870) or the U.S. Geological Survey (established in 1879). Even worse, the spoils system also absorbed the president and Congress in unproductive conflicts over patronage.

INCONSISTENT STATE GOVERNMENT

State governments were more active than the federal government. Considered closer and more responsible to the people, they had long exercised police power and regulatory authority. They collected taxes for education and public works, and they promoted private enterprise and public health. Still, they did little by today's standards. Few people thought it appropriate for government at any level to offer direct help to particular social groups. Some state governments contracted in the 1870s and 1880s following the wartime activism of the 1860s. Newly elected Democratic governors hewed to their party's narrow view of government, and new state constitutions restricted the scope of public authority. California's constitution of 1879, for example, limited the state government's authority so sharply that one wit even proposed abolishing the legislature, "and any person who shall be guilty of suggesting that a Legislature be held, shall be punished as a felon without the benefit of clergy."

But state governments gradually expanded their role in response to the stresses produced by industrialization. Following the lead of Massachusetts in 1869, a majority of states had by the turn of the century created commissions to investigate and regulate industry. Public intervention in other areas of the industrial economy soon followed. One observer noted in 1887 that state governments enacted many laws and established numerous state agencies in "utter disregard of the laissez-faire principle." In Minnesota, for example, the state helped farmers by establishing a dairy commission, prohibiting the manufacture or sale of margarine, creating a bureau of animal industry, and employing state veterinarians. In the lumber industry, state officials oversaw every log "from the woods to the saw-mill." State inspectors examined Minnesota's steam boilers, oil production, and sanitary conditions. Other laws regulated railroads, telegraphs, and dangerous occupations, prohibited racial discrimination in inns, and otherwise protected the public welfare.

Not all such agencies and laws were effective, nor were all state governments as diligent as Minnesota's. Southern states, especially, lagged, and one Midwesterner complained that his legislature merely "meets in ignorance, sits in corruption, and dissolves in disgrace every two years." Still, the widening scope of state action represented a growing acceptance of public responsibility for social welfare and economic life and laid the foundation for more effective steps in the early twentieth century.

PUBLIC POLICIES AND NATIONAL ELECTIONS

Several great issues dominated the national political arena in the late nineteenth century, including civil service reform, tariffs, and business and financial regulation. Civil-service reform attracted relatively little popular interest, but Americans argued passionately about even the smallest details of tariff, regulatory, and financial legislation. Rarely, however, did these issues clearly and consistently separate the major political parties. Instead, they divided each party into factions along regional, interest, and economic lines. As a consequence, these leading issues often played only a small role in determining elections and were seldom resolved by government action.

CIVIL SERVICE REFORM

Reform of the spoils system emerged as a prominent issue during the Hayes administration. Such reformers as the Mugwumps wanted a professional civil service, based on merit and divorced from politics. They wanted officeholders to be selected on the basis of competitive written examinations and protected from removal on political grounds. They expected such a

system to promote efficiency, economy, and honesty in government. But they also expected it to increase their own influence and minimize that of "mere politicians." As one Baltimore Mugwump said, civil-service reform would replace ignorant and corrupt officeholders with "gentlemen . . . who need nothing and want nothing from government except the satisfaction of using their talents," or at least with "sober, industrious . . . middle-class persons who have taken over . . . the proper standards of conduct."

Not all Americans agreed with such haughty views. The *New York Sun* denounced "the proposition that men shall be appointed to office as the result of examinations in book learning and that they shall remain in office during life. . . . We don't want an aristocracy of office-holders in this country." And a Midwestern newspaper declared, "A free land develops free men. They will accept no dictation from men who claim superior virtue or superior wisdom."

President Hayes favored civil-service reform but did not fully renounce the spoils system. He rewarded

In this 1881 cartoon, the evil spirit of partisanship threatens a government clerk hesitating to kick back an assessed portion of his salary to the party in power. Civil service reformers wanted to eliminate political factors in staffing the federal bureaucracy.

those who had helped to elect him, permitted party leaders to name or veto candidates for the cabinet, and insisted that his own appointees contribute funds to Republican election campaigns. But he rejected the claims of some machine leaders and office seekers and proposed reforms, which Congress promptly blocked. He struck a blow for change, however, when he fired Chester A. Arthur from his post as New York customs-house collector after an investigation pronounced Arthur's patronage system "unsound in principle, dangerous in practice, . . . and calculated to encourage and perpetuate the official ignorance, inefficiency, and corruption. . . ."

The weakness of the civil-service reformers was dramatically underscored in 1880 when the Republicans, to improve their chances of carrying the crucial state of New York, nominated Arthur for vice president on a ticket headed by James Garfield of Ohio. They won, and Garfield immediately found himself enmeshed in the demands of the unreformed spoils system. He once complained to his wife, "I had hardly arrived before the door-bell began to ring and the old stream of office-seekers began to pour in. They had scented my coming and were lying in wait for me like vultures for a wounded bison. All day long it has been a steeple chase, I fleeing and they pursuing." Within a few months of his inauguration in 1881, Garfield was assassinated by a disappointed and crazed office seeker, and Arthur became president.

Public dismay over this tragedy finally spurred changes in the spoils system. Arthur himself urged Congress to act, and in 1883, it passed the **Pendleton Civil Service Act**. This measure prohibited federal employees from soliciting or receiving political contributions from government workers and created the Civil Service Commission to administer competitive examinations to applicants for government jobs. The act gave the commission jurisdiction over only about 10 percent of federal positions but contained a provision that allowed presidents to extend its authority. And subsequent presidents did so, if sometimes only to prevent their own appointees from being turned out by a succeeding administration. A professional civil service free from partisan politics gradually emerged, strengthening the executive branch's ability to handle its increasing administrative responsibilities.

The new emphasis on merit and skill rather than party ties opened new opportunities to women. Federal clerks were nearly exclusively male as late as 1862, but by the early 1890s, women held a third of the clerical positions in the executive departments in Washington. These workers constituted the nation's first substantial female clerical labor force. Their work in public life challenged the conventional belief that a woman's ability and personality limited her to the domestic sphere. To succeed, clerks had to be assertive and competent, to acquire managerial skills, and to think of their careers as permanent, not temporary. Julia Henderson described her work as an examiner of accounts in the Interior Department in 1893 as "brain work of a character that requires a knowledge not only of the rulings of this Department, but also those of the Treasury, Second Auditor, Second Comptroller, and Revised Statutes; demanding the closest and most critical attention, together with a great deal of legal and business knowledge."

THE POLITICAL LIFE OF THE TARIFF

Americans debated heatedly over tariff legislation throughout the late nineteenth century. This complex issue linked basic economic questions to partisan, ideological, and regional concerns. Tariffs on imported goods provided revenue for the federal government and protected American industry from European competition. They thus promoted industrial growth but often allowed favored industries to garner high profits. By the 1880s, tariffs covered four thousand items and generated more revenue than the government needed to carry on its limited operations.

Reflecting its commitment to industry, the Republican Party vigorously championed protective tariffs. Party leaders also claimed that American labor benefited from tariff protection. "Reduce the tariff, and labor is the first to suffer," declared William McKinley of Ohio. Most Democrats, by contrast, favored tariff reduction, a position that reflected their party's relatively laissez-faire outlook. They argued that lower tariffs would encourage foreign trade and, by reducing the treasury surplus, minimize the temptation for the government to pursue activist policies. They pointed out the discriminatory effects of high tariffs, which benefited some interests, such as certain manufacturers, but hurt others, such as some farmers, while raising the cost of living for all (see the Overview table, "Arguments in the Tariff Debates").

The differences between the parties, however, were often more rhetorical than substantial. They disagreed only about how high tariffs should be and what interests they should protect. Regardless of party position, congressmen of both parties voted for tariffs that would benefit their districts. California Democrats called for protective duties on wool and raisins, products produced in California; Massachusetts Republicans, to aid their state's shoe manufacturers, supported tariffs on shoes but opposed tariffs on leather. A Democratic senator from Indiana, elected on a campaign pledge to reduce tariffs, summed up the prevailing rule succinctly: "I am a

Overview

Arguments in the Tariff Debates

Area Affected	High-Tariff Advocates	Low-Tariff Advocates
Industry	Tariffs promote industrial growth.	Tariffs inflate corporate profits.
Employment	Tariffs stimulate job growth.	Tariffs restrict competition.
Wages and prices	Tariffs permit higher wages.	Tariffs increase consumer prices.
Government	Tariffs provide government revenue.	Tariffs violate the principle of laissez-faire and produce revenues that tempt the government to activism.
Trade	Tariffs protect the domestic market.	Tariffs restrict foreign trade.

protectionist for every interest which I am sent here by my constituents to protect."

In the 1884 campaign, the Republican presidential candidate, James G. Blaine, maintained that prosperity and high employment depended on high duties. The Democrats' platform endorsed a lowered tariff, but their candidate, New York governor Grover Cleveland, generally ignored the issue. Unable to address this and other important issues, both parties resorted to scandalmongering. The Democrats exploited Blaine's image as a beneficiary of the spoils system, which convinced the Mugwumps to bolt to Cleveland. Blaine's nomination, resolved the Massachusetts Mugwumps, was "an insult to the conscience of the country." Republicans responded by exposing Cleveland as the father of an illegitimate child. One observer called the election "a more bitter, personal, and disgusting campaign than we have ever seen."

Cleveland continued to avoid the tariff issue for three years after his election, until the growing treasury surplus and rising popular pressure for tariff reduction prompted him to act. He devoted his entire 1887 annual message to attacking the "vicious, inequitable, and illogical" tariff, apparently making it the dominant issue of his 1888 reelection campaign. Once again, however, the distinctive political attribute of the period—intense and organized campaigning between closely balanced parties—forced both Democrats and Republicans to blur their positions. Cleveland proposed a Democratic platform that ignored his recent message and did not even use the word tariff. When the party convention adopted a tariff-reduction plank, Cleveland complained bitterly and named high-tariff advocates to manage his campaign. "What a predicament the party is placed in," lamented one

Texas Democrat, with tariff reform "for its battle cry and with a known protectionist . . . as our chairman." Cleveland won a slightly larger share of popular votes than his Republican opponent, Benjamin Harrison of Indiana, but Harrison carried the electoral college, indicating the decisive importance of strategic campaigning, local issues, and large campaign funds rather than great national issues.

The triumphant Republicans raised tariffs to unprecedented levels with the McKinley Tariff Act of 1890. McKinley praised the law as "protective in every paragraph and American on every page," but it provoked a popular backlash that helped return the Democrats to power. Still, the Democrats made little effort to push tariff reform. The *Atlanta Constitution* mused about such tariff politics in a bit of doggerel:

> It's funny 'bout this tariff—how they've lost it
>   or forgot;
> They were rushing it to Congress once; their
>   collars were so hot
> They could hardly wait to fix it 'till we har-
>   vested a crop;
> Was it such a burnin' question that they had
>   to let it drop?

THE BEGINNINGS OF FEDERAL REGULATION

While business leaders pressed for protective tariffs and other public policies that promoted their interests, they otherwise used their great political influence to insure governmental laissez-faire. Popular pressure nonetheless compelled Congress to take the first steps toward the regulation of business with the passage of the **Interstate Commerce Act** in 1887 and the **Sherman Antitrust Act** in 1890.

The rapid growth of great industrial corporations and their disruptive effects on traditional practices and values profoundly alarmed the public (see Chapter 18). Farmers condemned the power of corporations over transportation facilities and their monopolization of industries affecting agriculture, from those that manufactured farm machinery to those that ran flour mills. Small business owners suffered from the destructive competition of corporations, workers were exploited by their control of the labor market, and consumers felt victimized by high prices. The result was a growing demand to rein in the corporations.

Popular concern focused first on the nation's railroads, the preeminent symbol of big business. Both farm groups and business shippers complained of discriminatory rates levied by railroads. Consumers condemned the railroads' use of pooling arrangements to suppress competition and raise rates. The resulting pressure was responsible for the Granger laws enacted in several midwestern states in the 1870s to regulate railroad freight and storage rates.

At first, the Supreme Court upheld this legislation, ruling, in *Munn v. Illinois* (1877), that state governments had the right to regulate private property when it was "devoted to a public use." But in 1886, the Court ruled in *Wabash, St. Louis, and Pacific Railway Company v. Illinois* that only the federal government could regulate interstate commerce. This decision effectively ended state regulation of railroads but simultaneously increased pressure for congressional action. "Upon no public question are the people so nearly unanimous as upon the proposition that Congress should undertake in some way the regulation of interstate business," concluded a Senate committee. With the support of both major parties, Congress in 1887 passed the Interstate Commerce Act.

The act prohibited rebates, discriminatory rates, and pooling and established the **Interstate Commerce Commission (ICC)** to investigate and prosecute violations. The ICC was the first federal regulatory agency. But its powers were too limited to be effective. Senator Nelson Aldrich of Rhode Island, a leading spokesman for business interests, described

PUCK.

THE BOSSES OF THE SENATE.

"The Bosses of the Senate," a political cartoon of 1889, depicts the popular belief that huge corporate trusts controlled the government and corrupted public policy. This conviction helped fuel the demand for antitrust legislation but may not have been allayed by the weaknesses of the Sherman Act.

the law as an "empty menace to great interests, made to answer the clamor of the ignorant." Presidents did little to enforce it, and railroads continued their objectionable practices. They frustrated the commission by refusing to provide required information and endlessly appealing its orders to a conservative judiciary. In its first fifteen years, only one court case was decided in favor of the ICC. Not surprisingly, then, popular dissatisfaction with the railroads continued into the twentieth century. Californian Frank Norris, in his novel *The Octopus* (1901), likened them to "a gigantic parasite fattening upon the lifeblood of an entire commonwealth."

Many people saw railroad abuses as indicative of the dangers of corporate power in general and demanded a broader federal response. As with railroad regulation, the first antitrust laws—laws intended to break up or regulate corporate monopolies—were passed by states. Exposés of the monopolistic practices of such corporations as Standard Oil forced both major parties to endorse national antitrust legislation during the campaign of 1888. In 1890, Congress enacted the Sherman Antitrust Act with only a single vote in opposition. But this near unanimity concealed real differences over the desirability and purpose of the law. Although it emphatically prohibited any combination in restraint of trade (any attempt to restrict competition), it was otherwise vaguely written and hence weak in its ability to prevent abuses. The courts further weakened the act, and presidents of both parties made little effort to enforce it. Essentially still unfettered, large corporations remained an ominous threat in the eyes of many Americans.

THE MONEY QUESTION

Persistent wrangling over questions of currency and coinage made monetary policy the most divisive political issue in the late nineteenth century. President Garfield suggested the complexities of this subject when he wryly declared that a member of Congress had been committed to an asylum after "he devoted himself almost exclusively to the study of the currency, became fully entangled with the theories of the subject, and became insane." Despite the sometimes arcane and difficult nature of the money question, millions of Americans adopted positions on it and defended them with religious ferocity.

Creditors, especially bankers, as well as conservative economists and many business leaders favored limiting the money supply. They called this a **sound money** policy and insisted that it would insure economic stability, maintain property values, and retain investor confidence. Farmers and other debtors complained that this deflationary monetary policy would exacerbate the trend toward depressed prices in the American economy. They feared that it would depress already low crop prices, drive debtors further into debt, and restrict economic opportunities. They favored expanding the money supply to match the country's growing population and economy. They expected this inflationary policy to raise prices, stimulate the economy, reduce debt burdens, and increase opportunities.

The conservative leadership of both major parties supported the sound money policy, but their rank-and-file membership, especially in the West and the South, included many inflationists. As a result, the parties avoided confronting each other on the money issue.

The conflict between advocates of sound money and inflation centered on the use of paper money—"greenbacks"—and silver coinage. The greenback controversy had its roots in the Civil War. To meet its expenses during the war, the federal government issued $450 million in greenbacks—paper money backed only by the credit of the United States, not by gold or silver, the traditional basis of currency. After the war, creditors demanded that these greenbacks be withdrawn from circulation. Debtors and other Americans caught up in a postwar depression favored retaining the greenbacks and even expanding their use.

In 1875, sound money advocates in Congress enacted a deflationary law that withdrew some greenbacks from circulation and required that the remainder be convertible into gold after 1878. This action forced the money issue into electoral politics. Outraged inflationists organized the Greenback Party. They charged that the major parties had "failed to take the side of the people" and instead supported the "great moneyed institutions." The Greenbackers polled more than a million votes in 1878 and elected fourteen members of Congress, nearly gaining the balance of power in the House. As the depression faded, however, so did interest in the greenback issue, and the party soon withered.

The silver issue. Inflationists then turned their attention to the silver issue, which would prove more enduring and disruptive. Historically, the United States had been on a bimetallic standard; that is, it used both gold and silver as the basis of its currency. But after the 1840s, the market price of silver rose above the currency value assigned to it by the government. Silver miners and owners began to sell the metal for commercial use rather than to the government for coinage, and little silver money circulated. In 1873, Congress passed a law "demonetizing" silver, making gold the only standard for American currency. Gold-standard supporters hoped that the law would promote international trade by aligning U.S. financial policy with that of Great Britain, which insisted on gold-based currency. But they also wanted to prevent new silver discoveries in the American West from expanding the money supply.

Indeed, silver production soon boomed, flooding the commercial market and dropping the value of the metal. Dismayed miners wanted the Treasury Department to purchase their surplus silver on the old terms and demanded a return to the bimetallic system. More important, the rural debtor groups seeking currency inflation joined in this demand, seeing the return to silver coinage as a means to reverse the long deflationary trend in the economy. Many passionately denounced the "Crime of '73" as a conspiracy of eastern bankers and foreign interests to control the money system to the detriment of ordinary Americans.

Again, both major parties equivocated. Eastern conservatives of both parties denounced silver; Southerners and Westerners demanded **free silver**, meaning unlimited silver coinage. One New York Democrat complained that western and southern members of his party were "mad as wild Texas steers on this silver dollar business. As we pass each other in the streets they seem to sneer, and hiss through their teeth the words 'gold bug,' and look as if they would like to spit upon [us]."

By 1878, a bipartisan coalition succeeded in passing the Bland-Allison Act. This compromise measure required the government to buy and coin at least $2 million of silver a month. However, the government never exceeded the minimum, and the law had little inflationary effect. Republican President Arthur and Democratic President Cleveland recommended repealing the Bland-Allison Act, but the parties avoided the silver issue in their national platforms, fearing its divisive effect.

As hard times hit rural regions in the late 1880s, inflationists secured passage of the Sherman Silver Purchase Act of 1890. The Treasury now had to buy a larger volume of silver and pay for it with treasury notes redeemable in either gold or silver. But this, too, produced little inflation, because the government did not coin the silver it purchased, redeemed the notes only with gold, and, as western silver production increased further, had to spend less and less to buy the stipulated amount of silver. Debtors of both parties remained convinced that the government favored the "classes rather than the masses." Gold standard advocates (again, of both parties) were even less happy with the law and planned to repeal it at their first opportunity. The division between them was deep and bitter.

THE CRISIS OF THE 1890S

In the 1890s, social, economic, and political pressures created a crisis for both the political system and the government. A third-party political challenge generated by agricultural discontent disrupted traditional party politics. A devastating depression spawned social misery and labor violence. Changing public attitudes led to new demands on the government and a realignment of parties and voters. These developments, in turn, set the stage for important political, economic, and social changes in the new century.

FARMERS PROTEST INEQUITIES

The agricultural depression that engulfed the Great Plains and the South in the late 1880s brought misery and despair to millions of rural Americans. Falling crop prices and rising debt overwhelmed many people already exhausted from overwork and alarmed by the new corporate order. "At the age of 52 years, after a long life of toil, economy, and self-denial, I find myself and family virtual paupers," lamented one Kansan. His family's farm, rather than being "a house of refuge for our declining years, by a few turns of the monopolistic crank has been rendered valueless." To a large extent, the farmers' plight stemmed from conditions beyond control, including bad weather and an international overproduction of farm products. Seeking relief, however, the farmers naturally focused on the inequities of railroad discrimination, tariff favoritism, a restrictive financial system, and apparently indifferent political parties.

Credit inequities. Angry farmers particularly singled out the systems of money and credit that worked so completely against agricultural interests. Government rules for national banks directed credit into the urbanized North and East at the expense of the rural South and West and prohibited loans on farm property and real estate. As a result, farmers had to turn to other sources of credit and pay higher interest rates. In the West, farmers borrowed from mortgage companies to buy land and machinery.

Declining crop prices made it difficult for them to pay their debts and often required them to borrow more and at higher rates. In hard times, mortgage foreclosures crushed the hopes of many farmers. In the South, the credit shortage interacted with the practices of cotton marketing and retail trade to create the sharecropping system, which trapped more and more farmers, black and white, in a vicious pattern of exploitation. The government's policies of monetary deflation worsened the debt burden for all farmers.

Freight rates and tariffs. Farmers protested other features of the nation's economic system as well. Railroad freight rates were two or three times higher in the West and South than in the North and East. The near-monopolistic control of grain elevators and cotton brokerages in rural areas left farmers feeling exploited. Protective tariffs on agricultural machinery and other manufactured goods further raised their costs. The failure of political parties and the government to devise effective regulatory and antitrust measures or to correct the inequities in the currency, credit, and tariff laws capped the farmers' anger. By the 1890s, many were convinced that the nation's economic and political institutions were aligned against them.

Farmers organize. In response, farmers turned to the **Farmers' Alliance**, the era's greatest popular movement of protest and reform. Originating in Texas, the Southern Farmers' Alliance spread throughout the South and across the Great Plains to the Pacific coast. African American farmers organized the Colored Farmers' Alliance. The Northwestern Farmers' Alliance spread westward and northward from Illinois to Nebraska and Minnesota. In combination, these groups constituted a massive grassroots movement committed to economic and ultimately to political reform.

The Farmers' Alliance restricted its membership to men and women of the "producing class" and urged them to stand "against the encroachments of monopolies and in opposition to the growing corruption of wealth and power." At first, the Alliance attempted to establish farmers' cooperatives to market crops and purchase supplies. Although some co-ops worked well, most soon failed because of the opposition of established merchants and other business interests. Railroads suppressed Alliance grain elevators by refusing to handle their wheat. In Leflore County, Mississippi, when members of the Colored Farmers' Alliance shifted their trade to an Alliance store, local merchants provoked a conflict in which state troops killed twenty-five black farmers, including the local leaders of the Colored Alliance.

The Alliance also developed ingenious proposals to remedy rural credit and currency problems. In the South, the Alliance pushed the subtreasury system, which called on the government to warehouse farmers' cotton and advance them credit based on its value (see Chapter 17). In the West, the Alliance proposed a system of federal loans to farmers, using land as security. This land-loan scheme, like the subtreasury system, was a political expression of greenbackism; it would have expanded the money supply while providing immediate relief to distressed farmers. These proposals were immensely popular among farmers, but the major parties and Congress rejected them. The Alliance also took up earlier calls for free silver, government control of railroads, and banking reform, again to no avail. Denouncing the indifference of the major political parties and the institutions of government, William A. Peffer, the influential editor of the Alliance newspaper the *Kansas Farmer*, declared that the "time has come for action. The people will not consent to wait longer. . . . The future is full of retribution for delinquents."

THE PEOPLE'S PARTY

In the West, discontented agrarians organized independent third parties to achieve reforms the major parties had ignored. State-level third parties appeared in the elections of 1890 under many names. All eventually adopted the labels "People's" or "Populist," which were first used by a Kansas party that formed in June 1890. The founders of the Kansas People's Party included members of the Farmers' Alliance, the Knights of Labor, the Grange, and the old Greenback party. The new party's campaign, marked by grim determination and fierce rhetoric, set the model for Populist politics and introduced many of the movement's leaders. These people, women as well as men, were earnest organizers and powerful orators. One was *Kansas Farmer* editor Peffer. Others included "Sockless Jerry" Simpson, Annie Diggs, and Mary E. Lease.

When hostile business and political leaders attacked the Populist plans as socialistic, Lease retorted, "You may call me an anarchist, a socialist, or a communist. I care not, but I hold to the theory that if one man has not enough to eat three times a day and another has $25,000,000, that last man has something that belongs to the first." Lease spoke as clearly against the colonial status experienced by the South and West: "The great common people of this country are slaves, and monopoly is the master. The West and South are bound and prostrate before the manufacturing East."

The Populist parties proved remarkably successful. They gained control of the legislatures of Kansas and Nebraska and won congressional elections in Kansas, Nebraska, and Minnesota. Their victories came at the expense of the Republicans, who had traditionally controlled politics in these states, and contributed to a massive defeat of the GOP in the 1890 midterm elections after the passage of the McKinley Tariff and the Sherman Silver Purchase Act.

Established interests ridiculed the Populists unmercifully. This hostile cartoon depicts the People's Party as an odd assortment of radical dissidents committed to a "Platform of Lunacy."

A PARTY OF PATCHES.
Grand Balloon Ascension—Cincinnati, May 20th, 1891.

Thereafter, Populists gained further victories throughout the West. In the mountain states, where their support came more from miners than from farmers, they won governorships in Colorado and Montana. On the Pacific coast, angry farmers found allies among urban workers in Seattle, Tacoma, Portland, and San Francisco, where organized labor had campaigned for reform since the 1880s. The Populists elected a governor in Washington, congressmen in California, and legislators in all three states. Even in the Southwest, where territorial status limited political activity, Populist parties emerged. In Oklahoma, the party drew support from homesteaders and tenant farmers; in Arizona, from miners and railroad workers; in New Mexico, from small stockraisers and poor Hispanics threatened by corporate ranches and land companies.

In the South, the Alliance did not initially form third parties but instead attempted to seize control of the dominant Democratic Party by forcing its candidates to pledge support to the Alliance platform. The rural southern electorate then swept these "Alliance Democrats" into office, electing four governors, several dozen members of Congress, and a majority of legislators in eight states.

With their new political power, farmers enacted reform legislation in many western states. New laws regulated banks and railroads and protected poor debtors by capping interest rates and restricting mortgage foreclosures. Others protected unions and mandated improved workplace conditions. Still others made the political system more democratic. Populists were instrumental, for example, in winning woman suffrage in Colorado and Idaho, although the united opposition of Democrats and Republicans blocked their efforts to win it in other states. In the South, the Democratic Party frustrated reform, and most Alliance Democrats repudiated their Alliance pledges and remained loyal to their party and its traditional opposition to governmental activism.

National action. Populists soon realized that successful reform would require national action. They met in Omaha, Nebraska, on July 4, 1892, to organize a national party and nominated former Greenbacker James B. Weaver for president. The party platform, known as the **Omaha Platform**, rejected the laissez-faire policies of the old parties: "We believe that the powers of government—in other words, of the people, should be expanded . . . to the end that oppression, injustice, and poverty shall eventually cease in the land." It demanded government ownership of the railroads and the telegraph and telephone systems, a national currency issued by the government rather than by private banks, the subtreasury system, free

and unlimited silver coinage, a graduated income tax, and the redistribution to settlers of land held by railroads and speculative corporations. Accompanying resolutions endorsed the popular election of senators, the secret ballot, and other electoral reforms to make government more democratic and responsive to popular wishes. When the platform was adopted, "cheers and yells," one reporter wrote, "rose like a tornado from four thousand throats and raged without cessation for 34 minutes, during which women shrieked and wept, men embraced and kissed their neighbors . . . in the ecstasy of their delirium."

The Populists left Omaha to begin an energetic campaign. Weaver toured the western states and with Mary Lease invaded the Democratic stronghold of the South where some Populists, such as Tom Watson of Georgia, tried to mobilize black voters. Southern Democrats, however, used violence and fraud to intimidate Populist voters and cheat Populist candidates out of office. Some local Populist leaders were murdered, and Weaver was driven from the South. One Democrat confessed that Alabama's Populist gubernatorial candidate "carried the state, but was swindled out of his victory . . . with unblushing trickery and corruption." Southern Democrats also appealed effectively to white supremacy, undermining the Populist effort to build a biracial reform coalition.

Elsewhere, too, Populists met disappointment. Midwestern farmers unfamiliar with Alliance ideas and organization ignored Populist appeals and stood by their traditional political allegiances. So did most eastern working-class voters, who learned little of the Populist program beyond its demand for inflation, which they feared would worsen their own conditions.

The Populists lost the election but showed impressive support for a new organization. They garnered more than a million votes (one out of every twelve cast), carried several western states, and won hundreds of state offices throughout the West and in pockets of the South, such as Texas and North Carolina. Populist leaders began immediately working to expand their support, to the alarm of both southern Democrats and northern Republicans.

THE CHALLENGE OF THE DEPRESSION

The emergence of a significant third-party movement was but one of many developments that combined by the mid-1890s to produce a national political crisis. A harsh and lengthy depression began in 1893, cruelly worsening conditions not only for farmers but for most other Americans as well. Labor unrest and violence engulfed the nation, reflecting workers' distress but frightening more comfortable Americans. The persistent failure of the major parties to respond to serious problems contributed mightily to growing popular discontent. Together these developments constituted an important challenge to America's new industrial society and its government.

Although the Populists had not triumphed in 1892, the election nonetheless reflected the nation's spreading dissatisfaction. Voters decisively rejected President Harrison and the incumbent Republicans in Congress; turning again to the other major party, they placed the Democrats in control of Congress and Grover Cleveland back in the White House. But the conservative Cleveland was almost oblivious to the mounting demand for reform. He delivered an inaugural address championing the doctrine of laissez-faire and rejecting government action to solve social or economic problems.

Cleveland's resolve was immediately tested when the economy collapsed in the spring of 1893. Railroad overexpansion, a weak banking system, tight credit, and plunging agricultural prices all contributed to the disaster. So too did a depression in Europe, which reduced American export markets and prompted British investors to sell their American investments for gold. Within a few months, hundreds of banks closed, and thousands of businesses, including the nation's major railroads, went bankrupt. By winter, 20 percent of the labor force was unemployed, and the jobless scavenged for food in a country that had no public unemployment or welfare programs. "Never within memory," said one New York minister, "have so many people literally starved to death as in the past few months."

Churches, local charity societies, and labor unions tried to provide relief but were overwhelmed. Most state governments offered little relief beyond encouraging private charity to the homeless. In Kansas, however, the Populist governor insisted that traditional laissez-faire policies were inadequate: "It is the duty of government to protect the weak, because the strong are able to protect themselves." (See "American Views: A Populist Views American Government.") Cleveland disagreed and showed little sympathy for the struggling. The functions of the government, he said in 1893, "do not include the support of the people."

Appeals for federal action.

If Cleveland and Congress had no idea how the federal government might respond to the depression, some thoughtful Americans did. Jacob Coxey, a Populist businessman from Ohio, proposed a government public-works program for the unemployed to be financed with paper money. This plan would improve the nation's infrastructure, create jobs for the unemployed, and provide an inflationary stimulus to counteract the depression's deflationary effects. In short, Coxey was advocating positive government action to combat the depression. Elements of his plan would be adopted for mitigating economic downturns in the twentieth century; in 1894, it was too untraditional for Congress to consider.

Coxey organized a march of the unemployed to Washington as "a petition with boots on" to support his ideas. **Coxey's Army** of the unemployed, as the excited press dubbed it, marched through the industrial towns of Ohio and Pennsylvania and into Maryland, attracting attention and support. Other armies formed in eastern cities from Boston to Baltimore and set out for the capital. Some of the largest armies organized in the western cities of Denver, San Francisco, and Seattle. Three hundred men in an army from Oakland elected as their commander Anna Smith, who promised to "land my men on the steps of the Capitol at Washington." "I'm not afraid of anything," Smith explained. "I have a woman's heart and a woman's sympathy, and these lead me to do what I have done for these men, even though it may not be just what a woman is expected to do."

Lewis Fry, the organizer of the Los Angeles army, declared: "If the government has a right to make us die in time of war, we have the right to demand of her the right to live in time of peace." Fry's five hundred marchers captured a train to cross the desert regions of the Southwest and were feted and fed by townspeople from Tucson to El Paso. When the Southern Pacific uncoupled the train's locomotive and left the marchers stranded without food or water in West Texas for five days, the governor of Texas threatened to hold the railroad responsible for murder "by torture and starvation." Texas citizens quickly raised funds to speed the army on to St. Louis. From there it marched to Washington on foot.

The sympathy and assistance with which Americans greeted these industrial armies reflected more than anxiety over the depression and unemployment. As one economist noted, what distinguished the Populists and Coxeyites from earlier reformers was their appeal for federal action. Their substantial public support suggested a deep dissatisfaction with the failure of the government to respond to social and economic needs.

Nonetheless, the government acted to suppress Coxey. When he reached Washington with six hundred marchers, police and soldiers arrested him and his aides, beat sympathetic bystanders in a crowd of twenty thousand, and herded the marchers into detention camps. Unlike lobbyists for business and finance, Coxey was not permitted to reach Congress to

AMERICAN VIEWS

A Populist Views American Government

An educator, merchant, and former editor, Lorenzo D. Lewelling became one of the most articulate champions of the Populist party and its principles. Elected governor of Kansas in 1892, he headed what was heralded as "The First People's Party Government on Earth." On January 9, 1893, Lewelling delivered his inaugural address, in which he declared, "I appeal to the people of this great commonwealth to array themselves on the side of humanity and justice." The following passages from that speech sketch out both Lewelling's views of the 1890s and his "dream of the future."

- How does Lewelling's rhetoric reflect the deep divisions of the 1890s?
- What is Lewelling's view of the proper role of government?
- For what does Lewelling criticize the government of the 1890s?
- What does Lewelling mean by his statement that "the rich have no right to the property of the poor"?

The survival of the fittest is the government of brutes and reptiles, and such philosophy must give place to a government which recognizes human brotherhood. It is the province of government to protect the weak, but the government today is resolved into a struggle of the masses with the classes for supremacy and bread, until business, home, and personal integity are trembling in the face of possible want in the family. Feed a tiger regularly and you tame and make him harmless, but hunger makes tigers of men. If it be true that the poor have no right to the property of the rich let it also be declared that the rich have no right to the property of the poor.

It is the mission of Kansas to protect and advance the moral and material interests of all its citizens. It is its especial duty at the present time to protect the producer from the ravages of combined wealth. National legislation has for twenty years fostered and protected the interests of the few, while it has left the South and West to supply the products with which to feed and clothe the world, and thus to become the servants of wealth.

The demand for free coinage has been refused. The national banks have been permitted to withdraw their circulation, and thus the interests of the East and West have been diverged until the passage of the McKinley bill culminated in their diversement. The purchasing power of the dollar has become so great [that] corn, wheat, beef, pork, and cotton have

deliver his statement urging the government to assist "the poor and oppressed."

Protecting big business. The depression also provoked labor turmoil. In 1894, there were some 1,400 industrial strikes, involving nearly 700,000 workers, the largest number of strikers in any year in the nineteenth century. Cleveland had no response except to call for law and order. One result was the government's violent suppression of the Pullman strike (see Chapter 18).

In a series of decisions in 1895, the Supreme Court strengthened the bonds between business and government. First, it upheld the use of a court-ordered injunction to break the Pullman strike. As a result, injunctions became a major weapon for courts and corporations against labor unions, until Congress finally limited their use in 1932. Next, in *United States v. E.C. Knight Company*, the Court gutted the Sherman Antitrust Act by ruling that manufacturing, as opposed to commerce, was beyond the reach of federal regulation. The Court thus allowed the American scarcely commanded a price equal to the cost of production.

The instincts of patriotism have naturally rebelled against these unwarranted encroachments of the power of money. Sectional hatred has also been kept alive by the old powers, the better to enable them to control the products and make the producer contribute to the millionaire; and thus, while the producer labors in the field, the shop, and the factory, the millionaire usurps his earnings and rides in gilded carriages with liveried servants. . . .

The problem of today is how to make the State subservient to the individual, rather than to become his master. Government is a voluntary union for the common good. It guarantees to the individual life, liberty, and the pursuit of happiness. The government then must make it possible for the citizen to enjoy liberty and pursue happiness. If the government fails of these things, it fails in its mission. . . . If old men go to the poor-house and young men go to prison, something is wrong with the economic system of the government.

What is the State to him who toils, if labor is denied him and his children cry for bread? What is the State to the farmer who wearily drags himself from dawn till dark to meet the stern necessities of the mortgage on the farm? What is the State to him if it sanctions usury and other legal forms by which his home is destroyed and his innocent ones become a prey to the fiends who lurk in the shadow of civilization? What is the State to the business man,

early grown gray, broken in health and spirit by successive failures; anxiety like a boding owl his constant companion by day and the disturber of his dreams by night? How is life to be sustained, how is liberty to be enjoyed, how is happiness to be pursued under such adverse conditions as the State permits if it does not sanction? Is the State powerless against these conditions?

This is the generation which has come to the rescue. Those in distress who cry out from the darkness shall not be heard in vain. Conscience is in the saddle. We have leaped the bloody chasm and entered a contest for the protection of home, humanity, and the dignity of labor.

The grandeur of civilization shall be emphasized by the dawn of a new era in which the people shall reign, and if found necessary they will "expand the powers of government to solve the enigmas of the times." The people are greater than the law or the statutes, and when a nation sets its heart on doing a great and good thing it can find a legal way to do it.

I have a dream of the future. I have the evolution of an abiding faith in human government, and in the beautiful vision of a coming time I behold the abolition of poverty. A time is foreshadowed when the withered hand of want shall not be outstretched for charity; when liberty, equality, and justice shall have permanent abiding places in the republic.

Source: *People's Party Paper* (Atlanta), January 20, 1893.

Sugar Refining Company, a trust controlling 90 percent of the nation's sugar, to retain its great power. Finally, the Court invalidated an income tax that agrarian Democrats and Populists had maneuvered through Congress. The conservative Court rejected the reform as an "assault upon capital." A dissenting judge noted that the decision gave vested interests "a power and influence" dangerous to the majority of Americans.

Not until 1913, and then only with an amendment to the Constitution, would it be possible to adopt an

equitable system of taxation. Surveying these developments, farmers and workers increasingly concluded that the government protected powerful interests while ignoring the plight of ordinary Americans.

Certainly the callous treatment shown workers contrasted sharply with Cleveland's concern for bankers as he managed the government's monetary policy in the depression. Cleveland blamed the economic collapse on the Sherman Silver Purchase Act, which he regarded as detrimental to business confidence and a threat to the nation's gold reserve. He

Jacob Coxey's "Army" of the unemployed marches to Washington, D.C., in 1894. Many such "industrial armies" were organized during the depressed 1890s, revealing dissatisfaction with traditional politics and limited government.

persuaded Congress in 1893 to repeal the law, enraging southern and western members of his own party. These Silver Democrats condemned Cleveland for betraying the public good to "the corporate interests."

Cleveland's policy failed to end the depression. By 1894, the Treasury began borrowing money from Wall Street to bolster the gold reserve. These transactions benefited a syndicate of bankers headed by J.P. Morgan. It seemed to critics that an indifferent Cleveland was helping rich bankers profit from the nation's economic agony. "A set of vampires headed by a financial trust has control of our destiny," cried one rural newspaper.

THE BATTLE OF THE STANDARDS AND THE ELECTION OF 1896

The government's unpopular actions, coupled with the unrelenting depression, alienated workers and farmers from the Cleveland administration and the Democratic party. In the off-year elections of 1894, the Democrats suffered the greatest loss of congressional seats in American history. Populists increased their

vote by 42 percent, making especially significant gains in the South, but the real beneficiaries of the popular hatred of Cleveland and his policies were the Republicans. Denouncing Cleveland's "utter imbecility," they gained solid control of Congress as well as state governments across the North and West. All three parties began to plan for the presidential election of 1896.

As hard times persisted, the silver issue came to overshadow all others. Some Populist leaders, hoping to broaden the party's appeal, had already begun to emphasize silver rather than the more radical but divisive planks of the Omaha Platform. Weaver declared the silver issue "the line upon which the battle should be fought. It is the line of least resistance and we should hurl our forces against it at every point." Many southern and western Democrats, who had traditionally favored silver inflation, also decided to stress the issue, both to undercut the Populists and to distance themselves and their party from the despised Cleveland. ("I hate the very ground that man walks on," said one Alabama Democrat.) In 1895, leading Democrats began using the silver issue to reorganize their party and displace Cleveland and his conservative supporters. They held rallies and conventions across the South and West, distributed silver literature, and argued that free silver would finally end the depression.

McKinley and the Republicans.

The dissension among Democrats pleased Republicans. William McKinley, governor of Ohio and author of the McKinley Tariff Act of 1890, emerged as the leader of a crowd of hopeful Republican presidential candidates. His candidacy benefited particularly from the financial backing and political management of Mark Hanna, a wealthy Ohio industrialist. Hanna thought McKinley's passion for high tariffs as the key to revived prosperity would appeal to workers as well as to industry and business. As governor, McKinley had reached out to workers by supporting prolabor legislation and by avoiding the anti-Catholic positions that alienated immigrants from the Republicans. Nonetheless, he shared Hanna's conviction that government should actively promote business interests; he was not Hanna's puppet, as opponents sometimes claimed.

Republicans nominated McKinley on the first ballot at their 1896 convention. Their platform called for high tariffs but also endorsed the gold standard, placating eastern delegates but prompting several western Silver Republicans to withdraw from the party.

Bryan and the Silverites.

The Democratic convention met shortly thereafter. Embattled supporters of the gold standard soon learned that the silver crusade had made them a minority in the party. With a fervor that conservatives likened to "scenes of the French Revolution," the Silver Democrats revolutionized their party. They adopted a platform repudiating Cleveland and his policies and endorsing free silver, the income tax, and tighter regulation of trusts and railroads. A magnificent speech supporting this platform by William Jennings Bryan helped convince the delegates to nominate him for president. Bryan was only 36 years old but he had already served in Congress, edited an important newspaper, and gained renown for his oratorical skills and popular sympathies.

Holding their convention last, the Populists now faced a terrible dilemma. The Democratic nomination of Bryan on a silver platform undercut their hopes of attracting into their own ranks disappointed reformers from the major parties. Bryan, moreover, had already worked closely with Nebraska Populists, who now urged the party to endorse him rather than split the silver vote and insure the victory of McKinley and the gold standard. Other Populists

William Jennings Bryan in 1896. A powerful orator of great human sympathies, Bryan was adored by his followers as "the majestic man who was hurling defiance in the teeth of the money power." Nominated three times for the presidency by the Democrats, he was never elected.

argued that fusing—joining with the Democrats—would cost the Populists their separate identity and subordinate their larger political principles to the issue of free silver. After anguished discussion, the Populists nominated Bryan for president but named a separate vice presidential candidate, Tom Watson of Georgia, in an effort to maintain their identity. They hoped the Democrats would reciprocate by replacing their nominee with Watson, but the Democrats ignored the overture. The Populists' strength was in the South and West, regions that Bryan would control anyway. They could offer him little help in the battle for the Midwest and East, what Bryan called "the enemy's country."

Money and oratory.

The campaign was intense and dramatic, with each side demonizing the other. Terrified by the thought of Bryan's election, eastern financial and business interests contributed millions of dollars to Hanna's campaign for McKinley. Standard Oil alone provided $250,000, about the same amount as the Democrats' total national expenses. Hanna used these funds to organize an unprecedented kind of campaign. Shifting the emphasis from parades to information, Republicans issued 250 million campaign documents in a dozen languages, warning of economic disaster should Bryan be elected and the bimetallic standard be restored, but promising that McKinley's election would finally end the depression. Republicans were aided by a national press so completely sympathetic that many newspapers not only shaped their editorials but distorted their news stories to Bryan's disadvantage.

Lacking the Republicans' superior resources, the Democrats relied on Bryan's superb speaking ability and youthful energy. Bryan was the first presidential candidate to campaign systematically for election, speaking hundreds of times to millions of voters. By contrast, McKinley stayed home in Canton, Ohio, where he conducted a "front porch" campaign. Explaining his refusal to campaign outside Canton, McKinley said, "I might just as well put up a trapeze . . . and compete with some professional athlete as go out speaking against Bryan." But Hanna brought groups of Republicans from all over the country to visit McKinley every day, and McKinley reiterated his simple promise of prosperity.

In the depression, that appeal proved enough. As the Democratic candidate, Bryan was, ironically, burdened with the legacy of the hated Cleveland administration. The intense campaign brought a record voter turnout. McKinley won decisively by capturing the East and Midwest as well as Oregon and California (see Map 20-2). Bryan carried the traditionally Democratic South and the mountain and plains states, where Populists and silverites dominated. He failed to gain support in either the Granger states of the Midwest or the cities of the East. His silver campaign had little appeal to industrial workers. Hanna realized that Bryan was making a mistake in subordinating other popular grievances to silver: "He's talking silver all the time, and that's where we've got him."

Bryan immediately wrote a personal account of the campaign, which he optimistically titled *The First Battle*. But Bryan and the Democrats would not win subsequent battles, at least not on the issues of the 1890s. The elections of 1894 and 1896 ended the close balance between the major parties. Cleveland's failures, coupled with an economic recovery in the wake of the election of 1896, gained the Republicans a reputation as the party of prosperity and industrial

This Republican campaign poster of 1896 depicts William McKinley standing on sound money and promising a revival of prosperity. The depression of the 1890s shifted the electorate into the Republican column.

progress, firmly establishing them in power for years to come. By contrast, the Democratic party receded into an ineffectual sectional minority dominated by southern conservatives, despite Bryan's liberal views.

The People's party simply dissolved. Demoralized by fusion with the Democrats, who had earlier violently repressed them, many southern Populists dropped out of politics. The Democrats' disfranchisement laws, directed at discontented poor white Southerners as well as poor black Southerners, further undermined the Populists in the South. In the West, the silver tide of 1896 carried many Populists into office, but with their party collapsing, they had no hope of reelection. By 1898, the Populist party had virtually disappeared. Its reform

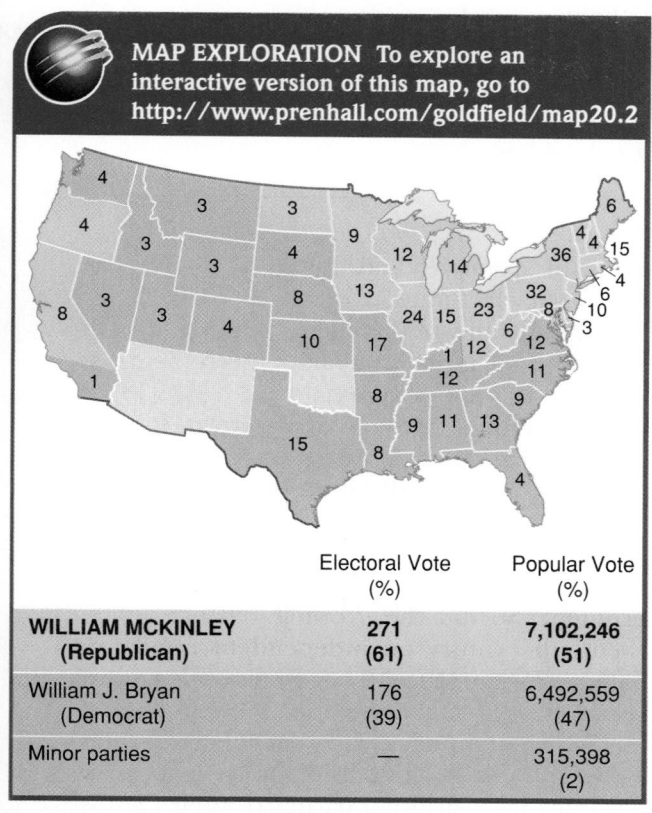

MAP EXPLORATION To explore an interactive version of this map, go to http://www.prenhall.com/goldfield/map20.2

	Electoral Vote (%)	Popular Vote (%)
WILLIAM MCKINLEY **(Republican)**	**271** **(61)**	**7,102,246** **(51)**
William J. Bryan (Democrat)	176 (39)	6,492,559 (47)
Minor parties	—	315,398 (2)

MAP 20-2   The Election of 1896
William Jennings Bryan carried most of the rural South and West, but his free silver campaign had little appeal to more urban and industrial regions, which swung strongly to Republican candidate William McKinley.

legacy, however, proved more enduring. The issues it raised would continue to shape state and national politics.

McKinley plunged into his presidency. Unlike his predecessors, he had a definite, if limited, program, consisting of tariff protection, sound money, and overseas expansion. He worked actively to see it through Congress and to shape public opinion, thereby helping establish the model of the modern presidency. He had promised prosperity, and it returned, although not because of the record high tariff his party enacted in 1897 or the Currency Act of 1900, which firmly established the gold standard. Prosperity returned, instead, because of reviving markets and a monetary inflation that resulted from the discovery of vast new deposits of gold in Alaska, Australia, and South Africa. The silverites had recognized that an expanding industrial economy required an expanding money supply. Ironically, the new inflation was greater than the inflation that

would have resulted from free silver. With the return of prosperity and the decline of social tensions, McKinley easily won reelection in 1900, defeating Bryan a second time.

CONCLUSION

In late-nineteenth-century America, politics and government often seemed at cross purposes. Political contests were exciting events, absorbing public attention, attracting high voter turnout, and often raising issues of symbolic or substantive importance. Closely balanced political parties commanded the zealous support of their constituents and wielded power and influence. The institutions of government, by contrast, were limited in size, scope, and responsibility. A weakened presidency and an inefficient Congress, hampered by a restrictive judiciary, were often unable to resolve the very issues that were so dramatically raised in the political arena. The persistent disputes over tariff and monetary policy illustrate this impasse. But the issue that most reflected it was civil-service reform. The patronage system provided the lifeblood of politics but also disrupted government business.

The localism, laissez-faire, and other traditional principles that shaped both politics and government were becoming increasingly inappropriate for America's industrializing society. New challenges were emerging that state and local governments could not effectively solve on their own. The national nature of the railroad network, for example, finally brought the federal government into the regulatory arena, however imperfectly, with the Interstate Commerce Act of 1887. Both the depression of the 1890s and the popular discontent articulated most clearly by the Populist rejection of laissez-faire underscored the need for change and discredited the limited government of the Cleveland administration.

By the end of the decade, the political system had changed. The Republicans had emerged as the dominant party, ending the two-party stalemate of previous decades. Campaign hoopla in local communities had given way to information-based campaigns directed by and through national organizations. A new, activist presidency was emerging. And the disruptive currency issue faded with the hard times that had brought it forth. Still greater changes were on the horizon. The depression and its terrible social and economic consequences undermined traditional ideas about the responsibilities of government and increased public support for activist policies. The stage was set for the Progressive Era.

FROM THEN TO NOW

Political Parties

Few things in contemporary American politics present a sharper contrast to the nineteenth century than the role of political parties. In the late nineteenth century, parties dominated politics. They commanded the allegiance of Americans, controlled the selection of candidates, mobilized voters, shaped voting behavior, provided ballots, and ran elections. They also shaped public policies and, through patronage, staffed government positions. At the beginning of the twenty-first century, parties do virtually none of these things.

This transformation began at the end of the nineteenth century. Extreme partisanship prompted states to assert control over elections. The corruption attributed to party machines led gradually to such changes as nonpartisan municipal elections and increased public control over parties. Restrictions on campaign expenditures reduced the party hoopla that had made politics so exciting and voter turnout so high. The connection between parties and voters declined further as new voters unfamiliar

with the passions and loyalties of the past joined the electorate.

The inability of the major parties to deal effectively with important national problems, so evident in the depression of the 1890s, prompted Americans to find other ways to influence public policy. Associational groups that had acted outside the partisan arena evolved into effective special-interest lobbying groups. Civil-service reform, beginning with the Pendleton Act, steadily reduced party influence in government. So did the growing reliance in the twentieth century on independent regulatory commissions, rather than partisan legislative committees, to make and implement policies.

In recent decades, party decline has accelerated. The introduction and spread of primary elections have stripped parties of their control over nominations. Individual candidates have come increasingly to rely more on personal organizations than on the party apparatus to manage campaigns. Candidates often appeal for

REVIEW QUESTIONS

1. In their letters to their parents, the Taft brothers simply condemned the personal morality and behavior of their Democratic opponents in Cincinnati's election, but there were social and institutional factors that shaped the disorderly nature of elections in the late nineteenth century. What were those factors and how did they operate in American politics?

2. What social and institutional factors determined the role of government? How and why did the role of government change during this period?

3. What factors determined the party affiliation of

American voters? Why did so many third parties develop during this era?

4. How might the planks of the Omaha Platform have helped solve farmers' troubles?

5. What factors shaped the conduct and outcome of the election of 1896? How did that contest differ from earlier elections?

KEY TERMS

Coxey's Army (p. 647)

Farmers' Alliance (p. 644)

Free silver (p. 643)

votes as individuals rather than as party members and communicate directly to voters through the mass media, relying less on the old door-to-door personal campaign requiring party workers. Television, in particular, with its focus on dramatic and personal sound bites, is better at promoting individual candidates than it is at presenting such abstract entities as parties.

Campaign finance reform laws have reduced party control over the funding of campaigns. So too has the rise of political action committees (PACs) as an important source of support for candidates. PACs represent particular interests, not a collection of interests, as parties do. Candidates dependent on specific interests find it harder to make broader partisan appeals.

Polls show fewer and fewer Americans identifying with a particular party and indicate that partisanship has greatly declined as a factor in voting decisions. Americans increasingly regard parties as neither meaningful nor even useful, let alone essential to democratic government. Nearly half of the electorate favors making all elections nonpartisan or even abolishing parties. More and more people believe that interest groups better represent their political needs than parties. At the same time, fewer and fewer Americans bother to vote. Those who do are much more likely than before to split their ticket, voting for candidates of different parties for different offices. This often results in divided government—with the presidency controlled by one party and Congress by the other. The resulting stalemate increases public cynicism about parties.

Of course, parties endure and retain some importance. Election laws favor the two established parties and obstruct independent candidacies. Public funds subsidize party activities, and party coffers harvest unregulated "soft money" campaign contributions. Congress and state legislatures continue to rely on party divisions to organize their leadership and committee structures, and party discipline still influences the way legislators vote. But while such institutional factors guarantee the continued presence of a two-party system, the parties themselves no longer enjoy the influence they had in the nineteenth century.

Granger laws (p. 635)

Greenback Party (p. 635)

Interstate Commerce Act (p. 641)

Interstate Commerce Commission (ICC) (p. 642)

Laissez-faire (p. 637)

Mugwumps (p. 636)

National American Woman Suffrage Association (p. 636)

Omaha Platform (p. 646)

Pendleton Civil Service Act (p. 640)

Populist Party (p. 635)

Prohibition Party (p. 635)

Sherman Antitrust Act (p. 641)

Sound money (p. 643)

RECOMMENDED READING

Cherny, Robert W. *American Politics in the Gilded Age* (1997). An excellent brief analysis, emphasizing the importance of parties in both elections and public policy.

Keller, Morton. *Affairs of State: Public Life in Late Nineteenth Century America* (1977). A detailed and fascinating account of the changing dimensions of government and politics.

McMath, Robert C. Jr. *American Populism: A Social History, 1877–1898* (1993). The best modern history of Populism; balanced and readable.

Summers, Mark. *The Gilded Age* (1997). A useful survey that effectively captures the complexities of the era.

Williams, R. Hal. *Years of Decision: American Politics in the 1890s* (1978). A valuable synthesis of the scholarship on the political currents of the 1890s.

ADDITIONAL SOURCES

The Structure and Style of Politics

Argersinger, Peter H. *Structure, Process, and Party* (1992).

Baker, Paula. "The Domestication of Politics: Women and American Political Society, 1780–1920," *American Historical Review* 89 (1984): 620–647.

Bordin, Ruth. *Frances Willard: A Biography* (1986).

Bordin, Ruth. *Woman and Temperance* (1981).

Edwards, Rebecca. *Angels in the Machinery: Gender in American Party Politics* (1997).

Goldberg, Michael. *An Army of Women: Gender and Politics in Gilded Age Kansas* (1997).

Gustafson, Melanie Susan. *Women and the Republican Party* (2001).

Kleppner, Paul. *The Third Electoral System, 1853–1892* (1979).

McCormick, Richard L. *The Party Period and Public Policy* (1986).

McGerr, Michael. *The Decline of Popular Politics: The American North, 1865–1928* (1988).

Schneirov, Richard. *Labor and Urban Politics* (1998).

Shafer, Byron, and Anthony Badger. *Contesting Democracy* (2001).

Silbey, Joel. *The American Political Nation, 1838–1893* (1991).

The Limits of Government

Aron, Cindy. *Ladies and Gentlemen of the Civil Service: Middle-Class Workers in Victorian America* (1987).

Brock, William R. *Investigation and Responsibility: Public Responsibility in the United States, 1865–1900* (1984).

Campbell, Ballard C. *Representative Democracy: Public Policy and Midwestern Legislatures in the Late Nineteenth Century* (1980).

Garraty, John A. *The New Commonwealth, 1877–1890* (1968).

Hoogenboom, Ari. *Rutherford B. Hayes: Warrior and President* (1996).

Skowronek, Stephen. *Building a New American State: The Expansion of National Administrative Capacities* (1982).

Thompson, Margaret S. *The "Spider Web": Congress and Lobbying* (1985).

White, Leonard D. *The Republican Era* (1958).

Public Policies and National Elections

Hoogenboom, Ari. *Outlawing the Spoils: A History of the Civil Service Movement, 1865–1883* (1961).

Marcus, Robert D. *Grand Old Party: Political Structure in the Gilded Age, 1880–1896* (1971).

Morgan, H. Wayne. *From Hayes to McKinley* (1969).

Reitano, Joanne. *The Tariff Question in the Gilded Age: The Great Debate of 1888* (1995).

Ritter, Gretchen. *Goldbugs and Greenbacks: The Antimonopoly Tradition and the Politics of Finance* (1997).

Socolofsky, Homer E. and Allan B. Spetter. *The Presidency of Benjamin Harrison* (1987).

Sproat, John. *The Best Men: Liberal Reformers in the Gilded Age* (1968).

Summers, Mark. *Rum, Romanism, and Rebellion: The Making of a President, 1884* (2000).

The Crisis of the 1890s

Argersinger, Peter H. *Populism and Politics: W. A. Peffer and the People's Party* (1974).

Clanton, Gene. *Populism: The Humane Preference* (1991).

Glad, Paul. *McKinley, Bryan, and the People* (1964).

Goodwyn, Lawrence. *The Populist Moment* (1978).

Jensen, Richard. *The Winning of the Midwest: Social and Political Conflict, 1888–1896* (1971).

Kousser, J. Morgan. *The Shaping of Southern Politics* (1974).

Larson, Robert W. *Populism in the Mountain West* (1986).

McSeveney, Samuel. *The Politics of Depression* (1972).

Miller, Worth Robert. *Oklahoma Populism* (1987).

Ostler, Jeffrey. *Prairie Populism* (1993).

Ross, William G. *A Muted Fury: Populists, Progressives, and Labor Unions Confront the Courts* (1994).

Schneirov, Richard, Shelton Stromquist, and Nick Salvatore. *The Pullman Strike and the Crisis of the 1890s* (1999).

Schwantes, Carlos A. *Coxey's Army: An American Odyssey* (1985).

Shaw, Barton. *The Wool-Hat Boys: Georgia's Populist Party* (1984).

Welch, Richard. *The Presidencies of Grover Cleveland* (1988).

WHERE TO LEARN MORE

- **Rest Cottage, Evanston, Illinois.** Frances Willard's home, from which she directed the Woman's Christian Temperance Union, is carefully preserved as a museum. The Willard Memorial Library contains more memorabilia and papers of Willard and the WCTU. www.wctu.org/house.html.

- **President Benjamin Harrison's Home, Indianapolis, Indiana.** President Harrison's brick Italianate mansion, completed in 1875, has been completely restored with the family's furniture and keepsakes. The former third-floor ballroom serves as a museum with exhibits of many artifacts of the Harrisons' public and private lives. www.presidentbenjaminharrison.org/.

- **Fairview, Lincoln, Nebraska.** A National Historic Landmark, Fairview was the home of William Jennings Bryan, who described it as "the Monticello of the West." Faithfully restored to depict the Bryan family's life in the early 1900s, it includes a museum and interpretive center. www.bryanlgh.org/aboutus/fairviewhistory.htm.

- **Susan B. Anthony House National Historic Landmark, Rochester, New York.** This modest house was the home of the prominent suffragist and contains Anthony's original furnishings and personal photographs. www.susanbanthonyhouse.org/main.html.

- **Rutherford B. Hayes Presidential Center, Fremont, Ohio.** This complex contains President Hayes's home, office, and extensive grounds together with an excellent library and museum holding valuable collections of manuscripts, artifacts, and photographs illustrating his personal interests and political career. www.rbhayes.org/.

- **James A. Garfield Home, Mentor, Ohio.** Operated by the Western Reserve Historical Society as a museum, Garfield's home is the site of his successful 1880 front-porch campaign for president. www.nps.gov/jaga/index.htm.

 Please refer to the document CD-ROM for primary sources related to this chapter.

→ *The great woman suffrage parade leaves Capitol Hill and heads for the White House, March 3, 1913.*
Dramatic tactics and careful organizing like those that marked this parade helped secure reform in the
Progressive Era.

"The head of a suffrage parade at Washington, D.C." oil over a photograph, 1913 (Granger Collection 4E1028.04).

THE PROGRESSIVE ERA 21
1900–1917

Five thousand women, marching in the woman suffrage pageant yesterday, practically fought their way foot by foot up Pennsylvania avenue, through a surging mass of humanity that completely defied the Washington police, swamped the marchers, and broke their procession into little companies. The women, trudging stoutly along under great difficulties, were able to complete their march only when troops of cavalry from Fort Myer were rushed into Washington to take charge of Pennsylvania avenue. No inauguration has ever produced such scenes, which in many instances amounted to little less than riots. . . .

The parade in itself, in spite of the delays, was a great success. . . . As a spectacle the pageant was entrancing. Beautiful women, posing in classic robes, passed in a bewildering array, presenting an irresistible appeal to the artistic, and completely captivating the hundred thousand spectators who struggled for a view along the entire route.

Miss Margaret Foley, bearing aloft a large "Votes for Women" flag, and Mrs. G. Farquhar, carrying an American flag, led the procession. . . . After the float reading, "We Demand an Amendment to the United States Constitution Enfranchising the Women of This Country," came a body of ushers clad in light blue capes. . . . Two large floats . . . represented the countries in which women are working for equal rights, followed by a large body of

CHAPTER OUTLINE

The Ferment of Reform
The Context of Reform: Industrial and Urban Tensions
Church and Campus
Muckrakers
The Gospel of Efficiency
Labor's Demand for Rights
Extending the Woman's Sphere
Trans-Atlantic Influences
Socialism
Opponents of Reform

Reforming Society
Settlement Houses and Urban Reform
Protective Legislation for Women and Children
Reshaping Public Education
Challenging Gender Restrictions
Reforming Country Life
Social Control and Moral Crusades
For Whites Only?

Reforming Politics and Government
Woman Suffrage
Electoral Reform
Municipal Reform
Progressive State Government

Theodore Roosevelt and the Progressive Presidency
TR and the Modern Presidency
Roosevelt and Labor
Managing Natural Resources
Corporate Regulation
Taft and the Insurgents

Woodrow Wilson and Progressive Reform
The Election of 1912
Implementing the New Freedom
The Expansion of Reform

Conclusion

women on foot dressed in street clothes, who bore the banners and pennants of scores of suffrage associations throughout the world. . . . The Homemakers . . . were dressed in long purple robes over their street clothes. Following them came a float, "In Patriotic Service," . . . and Miss Lillian Wald, the walking leader of a large body of women who followed the float, dressed as trained nurses, with gray caps and coats.

Miss Margaret Gage and Maurice Cohen, wearing college gowns with mortar boards, represented "Education," which was followed by nearly 1,000 women of the college section. . . . A group of young girls in blue capes represented the wage-earners, followed by "A Labor Story," which depicted the crowded condition of tenements, with women and children bendng over sewing machines, dirty and disheveled, in squalid quarters.... [Then followed] the women in the government section, all wearing light blue capes, . . . the business women, dressed in similar manner. . . . the teachers, . . . the social workers, . . . the white and pink costumed delegation of "writers," . . . club women and women clergy.

The greatest ovation was given to "General" Rosalie Jones, who led her little band of hikers from New York over rough roads and through snow and rain to march for the "cause." . . .

But there were hostile elements in the crowd through which the women marched. . . . Passing through two walls of antagonistic humanity, the marchers for the most part kept their temper. They suffered insult and closed their ears to jibes and jeers. Few faltered, although several of the older women were forced to drop out from time to time.

The pageant moved up Pennsylvania avenue with great difficulty and surrounded with some danger. Crowds surged into the streets, completely overwhelming the police and stopping the pageant's progress. Mounted police charged into the crowds, but failed at times to drive them back, even with the free use of clubs. In more than an hour the pageant had moved only ten blocks.

Miss Inez Milholland, a New York society girl, mounted on her white horse and dressed as a herald, finally rode up beside a mounted policeman, and helped charge the crowd. Miss Milholland gesticulated and shouted at the crowd and rode her horse into it with good effect. . . .

When the surging multitude was driven back in one place it flowed back into the street at another. The pageant slowly moved along, sometimes not more than a dozen feet at a time. . . .

As a result of the unruly spirit of the biggest crowd that ever witnessed a parade on Pennsylvania avenue, or of the inactivity of the police, who seemed powerless to protect the marching suffragists, the Emergency Hospital last night was filled to overflowing. . . . While an automobile and ambulance and horse-drawn vehicle ran back and forth, with all the surgeons in the institution taking turns at riding on it, people who had fainted or been overcome by exhaustion, or crushed and trampled, were brought to the hospital."

Washington Post, March 4, 1913.

Inez Milholland's charge and the jumbled news accounts from the *Washington Post* reporters all convey the intensity of the dramatic woman suffrage parade on March 3, 1913. But the women's difficult journey down Pennsylvania Avenue that day, suggestive of the much longer journey to achieve woman suffrage itself, illustrated critical features of life in the **Progressive Era**.

Important movements challenged traditional relationships and attitudes—here involving women's role in American life—and often met strong resistance. "Progressives" seeking reforms organized their supporters across lines of class, education, occupation, geography, gender, and, at times, race and ethnicity—as the variety of groups in the suffrage parade demonstrated. Rather than rely on traditional partisan politics, reformers adopted new political techniques, including lobbying and demonstrating, as nonpartisan pressure groups. Reform work begun at the local and state levels—where the suffrage movement had already met some success—inexorably moved to the national level as the federal government expanded its authority and became the focus of political interest. Finally, this suffrage demonstration revealed the exceptional diversity of the progressive movement, for the women marched, in part, against Woodrow Wilson, who had campaigned for the presidency as a progressive.

However, woman suffrage did not define progressivism. Indeed, in a sense, there was no "progressive movement," for progressivism had no unifying organization, central leadership, or consensus on objectives. Instead, it represented the coalescing of different and sometimes even contradictory movements that sought changes in the nation's social, economic, and political life. But reformers did share certain convictions. They believed that industrialization and urbanization had produced serious social disorders, from city slums to corporate abuses. They believed that new ideas and methods were required to correct these problems. In particular, they rejected the ideology of individualism in favor of broader concepts of social responsibility, and they sought to achieve social order through organization and efficiency. Finally, most progressives believed that government itself, as the organized agent of public responsibility, should address social and economic problems.

Other Americans resisted the progressives' plans. The interaction among the reformers and the conflict with their opponents made the two decades before World War I a period of remarkable ferment and excitement. The progressives' achievements, and their failures, profoundly shaped America.

KEY TOPICS

- The nature of progressivism
- Women and progressivism
- Antidemocratic aspects of progressivism
- Strengthening of the executive under Roosevelt
- Climax of progressivism under Woodrow Wilson

THE FERMENT OF REFORM

The diversity of progressivism reflected the diverse impulses of reform. Reformers responded to the tensions of industrialization and urbanization by formulating programs according to their own interests and priorities. Clergy and professors provided new ideas to guide remedial action. Journalists exposed corporate excesses and government corruption and stirred public demand for reform. Business leaders sought to curtail disorder through efficiency and regulation, while industrial workers struggled to improve the horrible conditions in which they worked and lived. Women organized to protect their families and homes from new threats and even to push beyond such domestic issues. Nearly every movement for change encountered fierce opposition. But in raising new issues and proposing new ideas, progressives helped America grapple with the problems of industrial society. (See the Overview table, "Major Progressive Organizations and Groups.")

Chronology

1893–1898	Depression grips the nation.
1898	South Dakota adopts initiative and referendum.
	National Consumers' League is organized.
1900	Robert La Follette is elected governor of Wisconsin.
1901	United States Steel Corporation is formed, the world's largest business at the time.
	President William McKinley is assassinated; Theodore Roosevelt becomes president.
	Socialist Party of America is organized.
	Galveston, Texas, initiates the city commission plan.
1902	Antitrust suit is filed against Northern Securities Company.
	Mississippi enacts the first direct primary law.
	National Reclamation Act is passed.
	Roosevelt intervenes in coal strike.
1903	Women's Trade Union League is organized.
1904	National Child Labor Committee is formed.
	Roosevelt is elected president.
1905	Industrial Workers of the World is organized.
1906	Hepburn Act strengthens the Interstate Commerce Commission.

	Meat Inspection Act extends government regulation.
	Pure Food and Drug Act is passed.
1908	*Muller v. Oregon* upholds maximum workday for women.
	William Howard Taft is elected president.
1910	National Association for the Advancement of Colored People is organized.
	Ballinger-Pinchot controversy erupts.
1912	Children's Bureau is established.
	Progressive Party organizes and nominates Roosevelt.
	Woodrow Wilson is elected president.
1913	Sixteenth and Seventeenth Amendments are ratified.
	Underwood-Simmons Tariff Act establishes an income tax.
	Federal Reserve Act creates the Federal Reserve System.
1914	Federal Trade Commission is established.
	Harrison Act criminalizes narcotics.
1915	National Birth Control League is formed.
1916	Keating-Owen Act prohibits child labor.
1917	Congress enacts literacy test for immigrants.
1920	Nineteenth Amendment is ratified.

THE CONTEXT OF REFORM: INDUSTRIAL AND URBAN TENSIONS

The origins of progressivism lay in the crises of the new urban-industrial order that emerged in the late nineteenth century. The severe depression and consequent mass suffering of the 1890s, the labor violence and industrial armies, the political challenges of Populism and an obviously ineffective government shattered the complacency many middle-class Americans had felt about their nation and made them aware of social and economic inequities that rural and working-class families had long recognized. Many Americans began to question the validity of social Darwinism and the laissez-faire policies that had justified unregulated industrial growth. They began to reconsider the responsibilities of government and, indeed, of themselves for social order and betterment.

By 1900, a returning prosperity had eased the threat of major social violence, but the underlying problems intensified. Big business, which had disrupted traditional economic relationships in the late nineteenth century, suddenly became bigger in a series of mergers between 1897 and 1903, resulting in huge new business combinations. The formation in 1901 of the United States Steel Corporation, the world's largest firm, symbolized this development. Such giant corporations threatened to squeeze opportunities for small firms and workers, dominate markets, and raise social tensions. They also inspired calls for public control.

Industrial growth affected factory workers most directly. Working conditions were difficult and often dangerous. Most workers still toiled nine to ten hours a day; steelworkers and textile employees usually worked twelve-hour shifts. Wages were minimal; an economist in 1905 calculated that 60 percent of all adult male breadwinners made less than a living wage. Family survival, then, often required women and children to work, often in the lowest-paid, most exploited positions. Southern cotton mills employed

Overview

Major Progressive Organizations and Groups

Group	Activity
Social Gospel movement	Urged churches and individuals to apply Christian ethics to social and economic problems
Muckrakers	Exposed business abuses, public corruption, and social evils through investigative journalism
Settlement House movement	Attempted through social work and public advocacy to improve living and working conditions in urban immigrant communities
National Consumers' League (1898)	Monitored businesses to insure decent working conditions and safe consumer products
Women's Trade Union League (1903)	United workingwomen and their middle-class "allies" to promote unionization and social reform
National Child Labor Committee (1904)	Campaigned against child labor
Country Life movement	Attempted to modernize rural social and economic conditions according to urban-industrial standards
National American Woman Suffrage Association	Led the movement to give women the right to vote
Municipal reformers	Sought to change the activities and structure of urban government to promote efficiency and control
Conservationists	Favored efficient management and regulation of natural resources rather than uncontrolled development or preservation

children as young as seven; coal mines paid twelve-year-old slate pickers thirty-nine cents for a ten-hour day. Poor ventilation, dangerous fumes, open machinery, and an absence of safety programs threatened not only workers' health but their lives as well. Such conditions were gruesomely illustrated in 1911, when a fire killed 146 workers, most of them young women, trapped inside the factory of the Triangle Shirtwaist Company in New York because management had locked the exits. The fire chief found "skeletons bending over sewing machines." The United States had the highest rate of industrial accidents in the world. Half a million workers were injured and thirty thousand killed at work each year. These terrible conditions cried out for reform.

Other Americans saw additional social problems in the continuing flood of immigrants who were transforming America's cities. From 1900 to 1917, more than 14 million immigrants entered the United States, and most became urban dwellers. By 1910, immigrants and their children comprised more than 70 percent of the population of New York, Chicago, Buf-

falo, Milwaukee, and other cities. Most of the arrivals were so-called new immigrants from southern and eastern Europe, rather than the British, Irish, Germans, and Scandinavians who had arrived earlier. More than 3 million Italians disembarked; another 2.5 million came from the diverse nationalities of the Russian empire. Several hundred thousand Japanese also arrived, primarily in California, as did increasing numbers of Mexicans. Crowding into urban slums, immigrants overwhelmed municipal sanitation, education, and fire protection services. One Russian described his new life as "all filth and sadness."

Many native-born Americans associated the immigrants with rampant urban crime and disease and with city bosses and government corruption. Ethnic prejudices abounded. Woodrow Wilson, then president of Princeton University, declared in 1902, "The immigrant newcomers of recent years are men of the lowest class from the South of Italy, and men of the meaner sort out of Hungary and Poland, men out of the ranks where there was neither skill nor energy, nor any initiative or quick intelligence." Americans

Overcome with grief, families of the victims of the Triangle Shirtwaist fire later received from the factory owners $75.00 for each life lost. Still mourning, family members asked, "Justice, what justice?"

of the Old Stock often considered the predominantly Catholic and Jewish newcomers a threat to social stability and cultural identity and so demanded programs to reform either the urban environment or the immigrants themselves.

CHURCH AND CAMPUS

Many groups, drawing from different traditions and inspirations, responded to such economic and social issues. Reform-minded Protestant ministers were especially influential, creating the **Social Gospel movement**, which sought to introduce religious ethics into industrial relations and appealed to churches to meet their social responsibilities. Washington Gladden, a Congregational minister in Columbus, Ohio, was one of the earliest Social Gospelers. Shocked in 1884 by a bloody strike crushed by wealthy members of his own congregation, Gladden began a ministry to working-class neighborhoods that most churches ignored. He endorsed unions and workers' rights and proposed replacing a cruelly competitive wage system with profit sharing.

A more profound exponent of the Social Gospel was Walter Rauschenbusch, a Baptist minister who had served impoverished immigrants in New York's slums. In his book *Christianity and the Social Crisis* (1907), he argued that Christians should support social reform to alleviate poverty, slums, and labor exploitation. He attacked low wages for transforming workers "into lean, sallow, hopeless, stupid, and vicious young people, simply to enable some group of stockholders to earn 10 percent." Such ideas were popularized by Charles Sheldon, a Kansas minister, whose book *In His Steps* sold 23 million copies and called on Americans to act in their

daily lives as they believed Jesus Christ would in the same circumstances.

The Social Gospel was part of an emerging liberal movement in American religion. Scholars associated with this movement discredited the literal accuracy of the Bible and emphasized instead its general moral and ethical lessons. These modernists also abandoned theological dogmatism for a greater tolerance of other faiths and became more interested in social problems. To some extent, liberal Protestantism had its Jewish and Catholic counterparts. Reform Judaism renounced certain ancient religious practices and favored adapting to American life; liberal Catholics urged their church to modernize its theological and social positions, especially by showing sympathy for labor unions. But most Jewish immigrants followed Old World habits, and liberal Catholicism was checked in 1907 when Pope Pius X condemned modernism for questioning the church's authority.

Thus the Social Gospel movement flowered among certain Protestant denominations, especially Episcopalians, Congregationalists, and Methodists. It climaxed in 1908 in the formation of the Federal Council of Churches of Christ in America. The council, representing thirty-three religious groups, adopted a program that endorsed welfare and regulatory legislation to achieve social justice. By linking reform with religion (as "applied Christianity," in the words of Washington Gladden), the Social Gospel movement gave progressivism a powerful moral drive that affected much of American life.

The Social Gospel movement provided an ethical justification for government intervention to improve the social order. Scholars in the social sciences also gradually helped turn public attitudes in favor of reform by challenging the laissez-faire views of social Darwinists and traditional academics. In *Applied Sociology* (1906), Lester Ward called for social progress through rational planning and government intervention rather than through unrestrained and unpredictable competition. Economists rejected laissez-faire principles in favor of state action to accomplish social evolution. Industrialization, declared economist Richard T. Ely, "has brought to the front a vast number of social problems whose solution is impossible without the united efforts of church, state, and science."

MUCKRAKERS

Journalists also spread reform ideas by developing a new form of investigative reporting known as **muckraking**. Technological innovations that sharply reduced production costs had recently made possible the mass circulation of magazines, and editors competed to attract an expanding urban readership. Samuel S. McClure was the first to introduce promotional gimmicks and serialized popular fiction in *McClure's Magazine*; he then sent his reporters to uncover political and corporate corruption. Sensational exposés sold magazines, and soon *Cosmopolitan, Everybody's,* and other journals began publishing investigations of business abuses, dangerous working conditions, and the miseries of slum life.

Muckraking articles aroused indignant public demands for reform. Lincoln Steffens detailed the corrupt links between "respectable" businessmen and crooked urban politicians in a series of articles called "The Shame of the Cities." Ida Tarbell revealed John D. Rockefeller's sordid construction of Standard Oil. Muckraking novels also appeared. *The Octopus* (1901), by Frank Norris, dramatized the Southern Pacific Railroad's stranglehold on California's farmers, and *The Jungle* (1906), by Upton Sinclair, exposed nauseating conditions in Chicago's meatpacking industry.

THE GOSPEL OF EFFICIENCY

Many progressive leaders believed that efficiency and expertise could control or resolve the disorder of industrial society. President Theodore Roosevelt (1901–1909)—who called muckrakers irresponsible radicals—spoke for more moderate reformers by praising the "gospel of efficiency." Like many other progressives, he admired corporations' success in applying management techniques to guide economic growth. Drawing from science and technology as well as from the model of the corporation, many progres-

sives attempted to manage or direct change efficiently. They used scientific methods to collect extensive data and relied on experts for analysis and recommendations. "Scientific management," a concept often used interchangeably with "sound business management," seemed the key to eliminating waste and inefficiency in government, society, and industry. Rural reformers thought that "scientific agriculture" could bring prosperity to the impoverished southern countryside; urban reformers believed that improvements in medical science and the professionalization of physicians through uniform state licensing standards could eradicate the cities' wretched health problems.

Business leaders especially advocated efficiency, order, and organization. Industrialists were drawn to the ideas of Frederick Taylor, a proponent of scientific management, for cutting factory labor costs. Taylor proposed to increase worker efficiency through imposed work routines, speedups, and mechanization. Workers, Taylor insisted, should "do what they are told promptly and without asking questions. . . . It is absolutely necessary for every man in our organization to become one of a train of gear wheels." By assigning workers simple and repetitive tasks on machines, Taylorization made their skills expendable and enabled managers to control the production, pace of work, and hiring and firing of personnel. Stripped of their influence and poorly paid, factory workers shared little of the wealth generated by industrial expansion and scientific management. When labor complained, one business leader declared that unions failed "to appreciate the progressivism of the age."

Sophisticated managers of big business combinations saw some forms of government intervention as another way to promote order and efficiency. In particular, they favored regulations that could bring about safer and more stable conditions in society and the economy. Government regulations, they reasoned, could reassure potential consumers, open markets, mandate working conditions that smaller competitors could not provide, and impose systematic procedures that competitive pressures would otherwise undercut.

LABOR'S DEMAND FOR RIGHTS

Industrial workers with different objectives also hastened the ferment of reform. Workers resisted the new rules of efficiency experts and called for improved wages and working conditions and reduced work hours. They and their middle-class sympathizers sought to achieve some of these goals through state intervention, demanding laws to compensate workers injured on the job, curb child labor, and regulate the employment of women. Sometimes they succeeded. After the Triangle Shirtwaist fire, for example, urban politicians with working-class constituencies created the New York State Factory Commission and enacted dozens of laws dealing with fire hazards, machine safety, and wages and hours for women.

Workers also organized unions to improve their lot. The American Federation of Labor (AFL) claimed 4 million members by 1920. But it recruited mainly skilled workers, particularly native-born white males. New unions organized the factories and sweatshops where most immigrants and women worked. Despite strong employer resistance, the International Ladies Garment Workers Union (1900) and the Amalgamated Clothing Workers (1914) organized the garment trades, developed programs for social and economic reforms, and led their members—mostly young Jewish and Italian women—in spectacular strikes. The "Uprising of the 20,000," a 1909 strike in New York City, included months of massive rallies, determined picketing, and police repression. One observer marveled at the women strikers' "emotional endurance, fearlessness, and entire willingness to face danger and suffering."

A still more radical union tried to organize miners, lumberjacks, and Mexican and Japanese farm workers in the West, black dockworkers in the South, and immigrant factory hands in New England. Founded in 1905, the Industrial Workers of the World (IWW), whose members were known as **"Wobblies,"** used sit-down strikes, sit-ins, and mass rallies, tactics adopted by other industrial unions in the 1930s and the civil rights movement in the 1960s. "Respectable people" considered the Wobblies violent revolutionaries, but most of the violence was committed against them. Private employers and public officials used every method, legal and illegal, to destroy the Wobblies, but broader labor unrest nonetheless stimulated the reform impulse.

EXTENDING THE WOMAN'S SPHERE

Women reformers and their organizations played a key role in progressivism. Women responded not merely to the human suffering caused by industrialization and urbanization but also to related changes in their own status and role. By the early twentieth century, more women than before were working outside the home—in the factories, mills, and sweatshops of the industrial economy and as clerks in stores and offices. In 1910, more than one-fourth of all workers were women, increasing numbers of them married. Their importance in the workforce and participation in unions and strikes challenged assumptions that woman's "natural" role was to be a submissive housewife. Shrinking family size, labor-saving household

equipment, and changing social expectations enabled middle-class women to find more time and opportunities to pursue activities outside the home. Better educated than previous generations, they also acquired interests, information, skills, and confidence relevant to a larger public setting.

The women's clubs that had begun multiplying in the late nineteenth century became seedbeds of progressive ideas in the early twentieth century. Often founded for cultural purposes, women's clubs soon adopted programs for social reform and gave their members a route to public influence. In 1914, an officer of the General Federation of Women's Clubs proudly declared that every cause for social reform had "received a helpful hand from the clubwomen." Generally, however, the clubs focused on public issues affecting women, home, and family.

Women also joined or created other organizations that pushed beyond the limits of traditional domesticity. "Woman's place is in the home," observed one progressive, but "no longer is the home encompassed by four walls." By threatening healthy and happy homes, urban problems required that women become "social housekeepers" in the community. The National Congress of Mothers, organized in 1897, worried about crime and disease and championed kindergartens, foster-home programs, juvenile courts, and compulsory school attendance.

Still more aggressive were the National Consumers' League, formed in 1898, and the Women's Trade Union League (WTUL; 1903), both of which organized women across class lines to promote social change. Led by the crusading Florence Kelley, the National Consumers' League tried to protect both women wage earners and middle-class housewives by monitoring stores and factories to insure decent working conditions and safe products. The WTUL united working women and their self-styled middle-class "allies" to unionize women workers and eliminate sweatshop conditions. Its greatest success came in the 1909 garment workers' strike when the allies—dubbed by one worker the "mink brigade"—assisted strikers with relief funds, bail money, food supplies, and a public-relations campaign. This cooperation, declared one WTUL official, demonstrated the "sisterhood of women."

Although most progressive women stressed women's special duties and responsibilities as social housekeepers, others began to demand women's equal rights. In 1914, for example, critics of New York's policy of dismissing women teachers who married formed a group called the Feminist Alliance and demanded "the removal of all social, political, economic and other discriminations which are based upon sex, and the award of all rights and duties in all fields on the basis of individual capacity alone." With these new organizations and ideas, women gave important impetus and direction to the reform sentiments of the early twentieth century.

TRANSATLANTIC INFLUENCES

A major source of America's progressive impulse lay outside its borders. European nations were already grappling with many of the same problems that stemmed from industrialization and urbanization, and they provided guidance, examples, and possible solutions. As one American observer said in 1915: What "the men and women who call themselves progressive . . . propose to do is to bring the United States abreast of Germany and other European countries in the matter of remedial legislation." Progressive reformers soon learned that

Striking garment workers and their supporters in the 1909 "Uprising" in New York City. Working women and their allies contributed to the growing pressure for improved working conditions.

the particular political, economic, and social structures of America required modifying, adapting, or even abandoning these imported ideas, but their influence was obvious.

University study in Europe taught Americans the limits of their traditional laissez-faire attitudes and the possibilities of state action. Trained in Germany, the economist Richard T. Ely returned to academic positions in America, teaching that government "is the agency through which we must work." International influences were particularly strong in the Social Gospel movement, symbolized by William T. Stead, a British social evangelist, whose idea of a "Civic Church" (a partnership of churches and reformers) captured great attention in the United States. Stead himself went to Chicago to promote "a broad and clear social programme," and his book, *If Christ Came to Chicago*, helped inspire Sheldon's *In His Steps*.

Muckrakers not only exposed American problems but looked for foreign solutions. *McClure's* sent Ray Stannard Baker to Europe in 1900 "to see why Germany is making such progress"; *Everybody's* sent Charles E. Russell around the world in 1905 to describe the social advances in Europe and New Zealand, which he called "this practical Utopia of the South Seas"; a third muckraking magazine reported extensively on what it termed "foreign experiment stations abroad."

Institutional connections also linked progressives with European reformers. The American Association for Labor Legislation, for example, was founded in

1905 as an offshoot of the International Association for Labor Legislation, founded in 1900 by French, Belgian, and German social economists. And the transatlantic movement of reform ideas and organizations flowed both ways: The National Consumers' League also began as a European import but eventually inspired affiliates of its own in France, Germany, and Switzerland.

By 1912, American consumer activists, trade unionists, factory inspectors, and feminists participated in regular international conferences on labor legislation, child welfare, social insurance, and housing reform and returned home with new ideas and strategies. State governments organized commissions to analyze European policies and agencies for lessons that might be applicable in the United States.

SOCIALISM

The growing influence of socialist ideas also promoted the spirit of progressivism. Socialists never attracted a large following, even among workers (see Chapter 18), but their criticism of the industrial economy gained increasing attention in the early twentieth century. American socialists condemned social and economic inequities, criticized limited government, and demanded public ownership of railroads, utilities, and communications. They also campaigned for tax reforms, better housing, factory inspections, and recreational facilities for all. Such muckrakers as Lincoln Steffens and Upton Sinclair were committed socialists, as were some Social Gospel ministers and labor leaders, but the most prominent socialist was Eugene Debs. In 1901, Debs helped organize the Socialist Party of America. In the next decade, the party won many local elections, especially in Wisconsin and New York, where it drew support from German and Russian immigrants, and in Oklahoma, among poor tenant farmers. Socialism was also promoted by newspapers and magazines, including the *Appeal to Reason* in Girard, Kansas, which had a circulation of 500,000 by 1906. "Socialism is coming," the *Appeal* proclaimed. "It's coming like a prairie fire and nothing can stop it."

Most progressives considered socialist ideas too drastic. Nevertheless, socialists contributed importantly to the reform ferment, not only by providing support for reform initiatives but often also by prompting progressives to push for some changes to undercut increasingly attractive radical alternatives.

OPPONENTS OF REFORM

Not all Americans supported progressive reforms, and many people regarded as progressives on some issues opposed change in other areas. Social Gospeler Rauschenbusch, for instance, opposed expanding women's rights. More typically, opponents of reform held consistently traditional attitudes, like the conservatives who saw in feminism the orthodox bogies of "non-motherhood, free love, easy divorce, economic independence for all women, and other demoralizing and destructive theories."

Social Gospelers themselves faced opposition. Reacting to the rise of religious liberalism, Protestant traditionalists emphasized what they termed fundamental beliefs. Particularly strong among evangelical denominations with rural roots, these **fundamentalists** stressed personal salvation rather than social reform. "To attempt reform in the black depths of the great city," said one, "would be as useless as trying to purify the ocean by pouring into it a few gallons of spring water." Indeed, the urban and industrial crises that inspired Social Gospelers to preach reform drove many evangelical leaders to endorse social and political conservatism. The most famous evangelist, the crude but spellbinding Billy Sunday, scorned all reforms but prohibition and denounced labor unions, women's rights, and business regulation as violating traditional values. Declaring that the Christian mission was only to save individual souls, he condemned the Social Gospel as "godless social service nonsense" and attacked its advocates as "infidels and atheists."

Business interests, angered by exposés of corporate abuse and corruption, attacked muckrakers. To capture public opinion, business groups such as the American Bankers' Association accused muckrakers of promoting socialism. Such major corporations as Standard Oil cre-

ated public-relations bureaus to improve their image and to identify business, not its critics, with the public interest. "The voice of the public," one press agent proclaimed, was "spoken through the Chamber of Commerce." Advertising boycotts discouraged magazines from running critical stories, and credit restrictions forced some muckraking journals to suspend publication. By 1910, the heyday of muckraking was over.

Labor unions likewise encountered resistance. Led by the National Association of Manufacturers, business groups denounced unions as corrupt and radical, hired thugs to disrupt them, organized strike-breaking agencies, and used blacklists to eliminate union activists. The antiunion campaign peaked in Ludlow, Colorado, in 1914. John D. Rockefeller's Colorado Fuel and Iron Company used armed guards and the state militia to shoot and burn striking workers and their families. The courts aided employers by issuing injunctions against strikes and prohibited unions from using boycotts, one of their most effective weapons.

Progressives campaigning for government intervention and regulation also met stiff resistance. Many Americans objected to what they considered unwarranted interference in private economic matters. Their political representatives were called the "Old Guard," implying their opposition to political and economic change. The courts often supported these attitudes. In *Lochner v. New York* (1905), the Supreme Court overturned a maximum-hours law on the grounds that it deprived employers and employees of their "freedom of contract." Progressives constantly had to struggle against such opponents, and progressive achievements were limited by the persistence and influence of their adversaries.

REFORMING SOCIETY

With their varied motives and objectives, progressives worked to transform society by improving living conditions, educational opportunities, family life, and social and industrial relations. (See the Overview table, "Major Laws and Constitutional Amendments of the Progressive Era.") They sought what they called social justice, but their plans for social reform sometimes also smacked of social control—coercive efforts to impose uniform standards on a diverse population. Organized women dominated the movement to reform society, but they were supported, depending on the goal, by Social Gospel ministers, social scientists, urban immigrants, labor unions, and even some conservatives eager to regulate personal behavior.

SETTLEMENT HOUSES AND URBAN REFORM

The spearheads for social reform were settlement houses, community centers in urban immigrant

Overview

Major Laws and Constitutional Amendments of the Progressive Era

Legislation	Effect
New York Tenement House Law (1901)	Established a model housing code for safety and sanitation
Newlands Act (1902)	Provided for federal irrigation projects
Hepburn Act (1906)	Strengthened authority of the Interstate Commerce Commission
Pure Food and Drug Act (1906)	Regulated the production and sale of food and drug products
Meat Inspection Act (1906)	Authorized federal inspection of meat products
Sixteenth Amendment (1913)	Authorized a federal income tax
Seventeenth Amendment (1913)	Mandated the direct popular election of senators
Underwood-Simmons Tariff Act (1913)	Lowered tariff rates and levied the first regular federal income tax
Federal Reserve Act (1913)	Established the Federal Reserve System to supervise banking and provide a national currency
Federal Trade Commission Act (1914)	Established the FTC to oversee business activities
Harrison Act (1914)	Regulated the distribution and use of narcotics
Smith-Lever Act (1914)	Institutionalized the county agent system
Keating-Owen Act (1916)	Indirectly prohibited child labor
Eighteenth Amendment (1919)	Instituted prohibition
Nineteenth Amendment (1920)	Established woman suffrage

neighborhoods. Reformers created four hundred settlement houses, largely modeled after Hull House in Chicago, founded in 1889 by Jane Addams, after she had visited Toynbee Hall in London, the first settlement house. Settlement houses often reflected the ideals of the Social Gospel. "A simple acceptance of Christ's message and methods," wrote Addams, "is what a settlement should stand for." Yet most were secular institutions, avoiding religion to gain the trust of Catholic and Jewish immigrants.

Most settlements were led and staffed primarily by middle-class young women, seeking to alleviate poverty and do useful, professional work when most careers were closed to them. Settlement work did not immediately violate prescribed gender roles because it initially focused on the "woman's sphere"—family, education, domestic skills, and cultural "uplift." Thus settlement workers organized kindergartens and nurseries; taught classes in English, cooking, and personal hygiene; held musical performances and poetry readings; and sponsored recreation.

However, settlement workers soon saw that the root problem for immigrants was widespread poverty that required more than changes in individual behavior. Unlike earlier reformers, they regarded many of the evils of poverty as products of the social environment rather than of moral weakness. Slum dwellers, Addams sadly noted, suffered from "poisonous sewage, contaminated water, infant mortality, adulterated food, smoke-laden air, juvenile crime, and unwholesome crowding." Thus, settlement workers campaigned for stricter building codes to improve slums, better urban sanitation systems to enhance public health, public parks to revive the urban environment, and laws to protect women and children.

Their crusade for housing reform demonstrated the impact that social reformers often had on urban life. His work at the University Settlement in New York City convinced Lawrence Veiller that "the improvement of the homes of the people was the starting point for everything." Organizing pressure groups to promote tenement house reform, Veiller relied on settle-

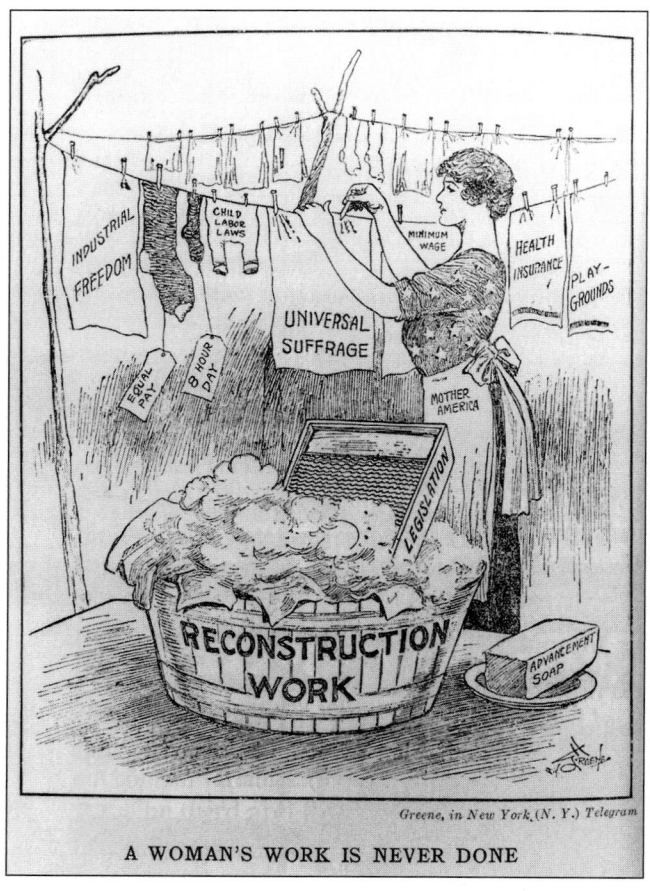

A WOMAN'S WORK IS NEVER DONE

Women's activism was critically important in reconstructing American life during the Progressive Era. Busily engaged in social housekeeping, Mother America uses corrective legislation to clean the dirty laundry of industrialization and injustice.

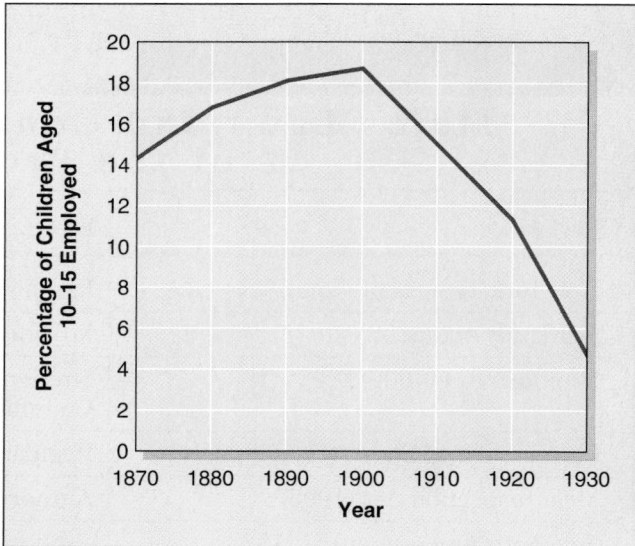

FIGURE 21-1   Child labor, 1870–1930.
Nearly 2 million children worked in factories and fields in 1900, twice the number as in 1870. Progressives' efforts to curtail child labor through laws for compulsory education and a minimum working age encountered resistance, and change came slowly.
Data Source: U.S. Bureau of the Census.

ment workers to help investigate housing conditions, prepare public exhibits depicting rampant disease in congested slums, and agitate for improvements. Based on their findings, Veiller drafted a new housing code limiting the size of tenements and requiring toilet facilities, ventilation, and fire protection. In 1901, the New York Tenement House Law became a model for other cities. To promote uniform building codes throughout the nation, the tireless Veiller founded the National Housing Association in 1910.

PROTECTIVE LEGISLATION FOR WOMEN AND CHILDREN

While settlement workers initially undertook private efforts to improve society, many reformers eventually concluded that only government power could achieve social justice. They demanded that state and federal governments protect the weak or disadvantaged. As Veiller insisted, it was "unquestionably the duty of the state" to enforce justice in the face of "greed on the part of those who desire to secure for themselves an undue profit."

The maiming and killing of children in industrial accidents made it "inevitable," Addams said, "that efforts to secure a child labor law should be our first venture into the field of state legislation." The National Child Labor Committee, organized in 1904, led the campaign to curtail child labor (see Figure 21-1). Reformers documented the problem with extensive investigations and also benefited from the public outrage stirred by socialist John Spargo's muckraking book *The Bitter Cry of the Children* (1906). In 1900, most states had no minimum working age; by 1914, every state but one had such a law. Effective regulation, however, required national action, for many state laws were weak or poorly enforced (see "American Views: Mother Jones and the Meaning of Child Labor in America").

Stiff resistance came from manufacturers who used child labor, conservatives who opposed government action as an intrusion into family life, and some poor parents who needed their children's income. But finally, Congress in 1912 established the Children's Bureau to investigate the welfare of children. Julia Lathrop, from Hull House, directed the Bureau, the first government agency headed and staffed almost entirely by women. In 1916, the Keating-Owen Act prohibited the interstate shipment of goods manufactured by children. But the law was weaker than

The famous photographer Lewis Hine used his camera to document child labor. The eight-year-old girl on the right in this 1911 photograph of women and children working in an Alabama canning factory had been shucking oysters for three years.

that of many states and did not cover most child workers. Even so, the Supreme Court declared the measure unconstitutional.

Social reformers also lobbied for laws regulating the wages, hours, and working conditions of women and succeeded in having states from New York to Oregon pass maximum-hours legislation. After the Supreme Court upheld such laws in *Muller v. Oregon* (1908), thirty-nine states enacted new or stronger laws on women's maximum hours between 1909 and 1917. Fewer states established minimum wages for women. In 1912, Massachusetts created a commission to recommend such wages, and within a year, eight midwestern and western states authorized wage commissions to set binding rates. But few other states followed these examples.

Protective legislation for women posed a troubling issue for reformers. In California, for example, middle-class clubwomen favored protective legislation on grounds of women's presumed weakness. They wanted to preserve "California's potential motherhood." More radical progressives, as in the socialist-led Women's Trade Union League of Los Angeles, supported legislation to help secure economic independence and equality in the labor market for women, increase the economic strength of the working class, and serve as a precedent for laws improving conditions for all workers.

Progressive Era lawmakers adopted the first viewpoint. They limited protective legislation to measures reflecting the belief that women needed paternalist protection, even by excluding them from

certain occupations. Laws establishing a minimum wage for women, moreover, usually set a wage level below that reported by the wage commissions as subsistence rates. Protective legislation thus assured women, not economic independence, but continued dependence on husbands or fathers. In practice, then, the laws reinforced women's subordinate place in the labor force.

Social-justice reformers forged the beginnings of the welfare state in further legislation. Prompted by both humanitarian and paternalistic urgings, many states began in 1910 to provide "mothers' pensions" to indigent widows with dependent children. Twenty-one states, led by Wisconsin in 1911, enacted workers' compensation programs, ending the custom of holding workers themselves liable for injuries on the job.

Compared to social insurance programs in western Europe, however, these were feeble responses to the social consequences of industrialization. Attempts by various reform groups to follow up workers' compensation laws with health insurance and old-age pension programs went nowhere. Business groups and other conservative interests curbed the movement toward state responsibility for social welfare. Few more advances would come until the New Deal (1930s) and the Great Society (1960s), both heirs of progressivism in their commitment to governmental activism.

RESHAPING PUBLIC EDUCATION

Concerns about child labor overlapped with increasing attention to public schools. The rapid influx of

AMERICAN VIEWS

Mother Jones and the Meaning of Child Labor in America

Born in Ireland in 1830, the legendary Mother Jones (Mary Harris Jones) became one of America's greatest social activists, organizing workers, participating in strikes, and protesting social and industrial conditions from the 1870s through the 1920s. Here she recounts one of her efforts to end child labor, one of the most persistent reform goals of the Progressive Era. Using the techniques of exposure and publicity characteristic of the period and adroitly employing patriotic symbols and references, Jones skillfully raised troubling questions about the concepts of social and economic opportunity that many Americans associated with national development and identity.

- How did Mother Jones direct public attention to child labor?
- How did she invoke the treasured American concept of opportunity to gain support for her goal?
- What did she argue was the relationship between child labor and the privileged status of other Americans?
- How successful was her crusade against child labor?

In the spring of 1903 I went to Kensington, Pennsylvania, where 75,000 textile workers were on strike. Of this number at least 10,000 were little children. The workers were striking for more pay and shorter hours. Every day little children came into Union Headquarters, some with their hands off, some with the thumb missing, some with their fingers off at the knuckle. They were stooped little things, round shouldered and skinny. Many of them were not over ten years of age. . . .

We assembled a number of boys and girls one morning in Independence Park and from there we arranged to parade with banners to the court house where we would hold a meeting.

A great crowd gathered in the public square in front of the city hall. I put the little boys with their fingers off and hands crushed and maimed on a platform. I held up their mutilated hands and showed them to the crowd and made the statement that Philadelphia's

immigrants, as well as the demands of the new corporate workplace, generated interest in education not only as a means of advancement but also as a tool for assimilation and the training of future workers. Middle-class women supported public-school reforms. In 1900, for example, women's clubs in North Carolina launched a program to improve school buildings, increase teachers' salaries, and broaden the curriculum. Claiming efficiency and expertise,

school administrators also pushed for changes, both to upgrade their own profession and to expand their public influence. And some intellectuals predicted that schools themselves could promote social progress and reform. The philosopher John Dewey sketched his plans for such progressive education in *The School and Society* (1899).

The modern urban public school system emerged between 1880 and 1920. Compulsory school attend-mansions were built on the broken bones, the quivering hearts, and drooping heads of these children. . . .

I called upon the millionaire manufacturers to cease their moral murders, and I cried to the officials in the open windows opposite, "Some day the workers will take possession of your city hall, and when we do, no child will be sacrificed on the altar of profit."

The reporters quoted my statement that Philadelphia mansions were built on the broken bones and quivering hearts of children. The Philadelphia papers and the New York papers got into a squabble with each other over the question. The universities discussed it. Preachers began talking. That was what I wanted. Public attention on the subject of child labor.

The matter quieted down for a while and I concluded the people needed stirring up again. . . . I decided to go with the children to see President Roosevelt to ask him to have Congress pass a law prohibiting the exploitation of childhood. I thought that President Roosevelt might see these mill children and compare them with his own little ones who were spending the summer at the seashore at Oyster Bay. . . .

Everywhere we had meetings, showing up with living children, the horrors of child labor. . . . [In New Jersey] I called on the mayor of Princeton and asked for permission to speak opposite the campus of the University. I said I wanted to speak on higher education. The mayor gave me permission. A great crowd gathered, professors and students and the people;

and I told them that the rich robbed these little children of any education of the lowest order that they might send their sons and daughters to places of higher education. . . . And I showed those professors children in our army who could scarcely read or write because they were working ten hours a day in the silk mills of Pennsylvania. . . .

[In New York] I told an immense crowd of the horrors of child labor in the mills around the anthracite region and . . . I showed them Gussie Rangnew, a little girl from whom all the childhood had gone. Her face was like an old woman's. Gussie packed stockings in a factory, eleven hours a day for a few cents a day. . . . "Fifty years ago there was a cry against slavery and men gave up their lives to stop the selling of black children on the block. Today the white child is sold for two dollars a week to the manufacturers."

. . . We marched down to Oyster Bay but the president refused to see us and he would not answer my letters. But our march had done its work. We had drawn the attention of the nation to the crime of child labor. And while the strike of the textile workers in Kensington was lost and the children driven back to work, not long afterward the Pennsylvania legislature passed a child labor law that sent thousands of children home from the mills, and kept thousands of others from entering the factory until they were fourteen years of age.

Source: *The Autobiography of Mother Jones*, 3rd ed. (Chicago: Kerr Publishing Company, 1977).

ance laws, kindergartens, age-graded elementary schools, professional training for teachers, vocational education, parent-teacher associations, and school nurses all became standard elements in American education. School reformers believed these measures to be both educationally sound and important for countering slum environments. As Jacob Riis contended, the kindergartner would "rediscover . . . the natural feelings that the tenement had smothered." Others supported the kindergarten as "the earliest opportunity to catch the little Russian, the little Italian, the little German, Pole, Syrian, and the rest and begin to make good American citizens of them." Further socialization came through vocational courses intended to instill discipline in poor students and prepare them to become productive adults.

Public education in the South lagged behind the North. An educational awakening, supported by northern philanthropy and southern reformers, brought improvements after 1900. Per capita expenditures for education doubled, school terms were extended, and high schools spread across the region. But the South frittered away its limited resources on a segregated educational system that shortchanged both races. Black Southerners particularly suffered, for the new programs increased the disparity in funding for white and black schools. South Carolina spent twelve times as much per white pupil as per black pupil. Booker T. Washington complained in 1906 that the educational reforms meant "almost nothing so far as the Negro schools are concerned." As a northern critic observed, "To devise a school system which shall save the whites and not the blacks is a task of such delicacy that a few surviving reactionaries are willing to let both perish together."

Racism also underlay important changes in schooling of American Indians. The earlier belief that education would promote equality and facilitate assimilation increasingly gave way to a conviction that Indians were inferior and fit, at best, merely for manual labor. One speaker told the National Education Association in 1901 that those concerned with Indian education "can learn many things from the dealings of our southern friends with the plantation Negro." The plantation system, he maintained, was a "much more successful school for the training of a barbarous race than is the reservation." Such educators now rejected the notion of a common school education for Indian children in favor of manual training which would enable Indians to fill menial jobs and whites to "turn their attention to more intellectual employments." Educators also renounced the practice of integrating Indian children into previously all-white classrooms, a policy begun in 1891. The superintendent of the Chilocco, Oklahoma, school believed that the new commitment to practical vocational education "solved the Indian problem," but critics noted that limiting Indian children to a rudimentary and segregated education merely doomed them to the margins of American society.

CHALLENGING GENDER RESTRICTIONS

Most progressives held fairly conservative, moralistic views about sexuality and gender roles. Margaret Sanger, however, radically challenged conventional ideas of the social role of women. Despite great opposition, she initiated the modern birth control movement. A public-health nurse and an IWW organizer, she soon made the struggle for reproductive rights her personal crusade. Her mother had died at the age of 49 after eighteen pregnancies, and Sanger saw in New York's immigrant neighborhoods the plight

of poor women worn out from repeated pregnancies or injured or dead from self-induced knitting-needle abortions. Despite federal and state laws against contraceptives, Sanger began promoting birth control as a way to avert such tragedies. In 1914, Sanger published a magazine, *Woman Rebel*, in which she argued that "a woman's body belongs to herself alone. It does not belong to the United States of America or any other government on the face of the earth." Prohibiting contraceptives meant "enforced motherhood," Sanger declared. "Women cannot be on an equal footing with men until they have full and complete control over their reproductive function."

Sanger's crusade attracted support from many women's and labor groups, but it also infuriated those who regarded birth control as a threat to the family and morality. Indicted for distributing information about contraception, Sanger fled to Europe. Other women took up the cause, forming the Na-

Margaret Sanger, who coined the phrase "birth control," campaigned to make contraceptive information and devices available. Through her writings, speeches, and publicized arrests and trials, Sanger helped build an important movement.

tional Birth Control League in 1915 to campaign for the repeal of laws restricting access to contraceptive information and devices. They had little immediate success, but their cause would triumph in later generations.

REFORMING COUNTRY LIFE

Although most progressives focused on the city, others sought to reform rural life, both to modernize its social and economic conditions and to integrate it more fully into the larger society. They worked to improve rural health and sanitation, to replace inefficient one-room schools with modern consolidated ones under professional control, and to extend new roads and communication services into the countryside. To further these goals, President Theodore Roosevelt created the Country Life Commission in 1908. The country lifers had a broad program for social and economic change, involving expanded government functions, activist government agencies staffed by experts, and the professionalization of rural social services.

Agricultural scientists, government officials, and many business interests also sought to promote efficient, scientific, and commercial agriculture. A key innovation was the county-agent system: the U.S. Department of Agriculture and business groups placed an agent in each county to teach farmers new techniques and to encourage changes in the rural social values that had spawned the Populist radicalism that most progressives decried. Farmers, it was hoped, would acquire materialistic values and learn "economy, order, . . . patriotism, and a score of other wholesome lessons," as one progressive put it in 1910. The Smith-Lever Act (1914) provided federal subsidies for county agents throughout the country. Its purpose, claimed Woodrow Wilson, was to produce "an efficient and contented population" in rural America.

Few farmers, however, welcomed these efforts. As one Illinois county agent said in 1915, "Farmers, as a whole, resent exceedingly those forces which are at work with missionary intent trying to uplift them." School consolidation meant the loss of community control of education; good roads would raise taxes and chiefly benefit urban business interests. Besides, most farmers believed that their problems stemmed, not from rural life, but from industrial society and its nefarious trusts, banks, and middlemen. Rural Americans did not want their lives revolutionized.

Even so, rural people were drawn into the larger urban-industrial society during the Progressive Era. Government agencies, agricultural colleges, and rail-

roads and banks steadily tied farmers to urban markets. Telephones and rural free delivery of mail lessened countryside isolation but quickened the spread of city values. Improved roads and the coming of the automobile eliminated many rural villages and linked farm families directly with towns and cities. Consolidated schools wiped out the social center of rural neighborhoods and carried children out of their communities, many never to return.

SOCIAL CONTROL AND MORAL CRUSADES

The tendency toward social control evident in the movements to pass protective legislation and transform country life also marked other less attractive progressive efforts. These efforts, moreover, often meshed with the restrictive attitudes that conservative Americans held about race, religion, immigration, and morality. The result was widespread attempts to restrict certain groups and control behavior.

Controlling immigrants.   Many Americans wanted to limit immigration for racist reasons. Nativist agitation in California prompted the federal government to secure restrictions on Japanese immigration in 1907. Californians, including local progressives, also hoped to curtail the migration of Mexicans. A Stanford University researcher condemned Mexicans as an "undesirable class" compared to "the more progressive races," and in 1916 the Los Angeles County supervisors urged the federal government to deport Mexican immigrants.

Nationally, public debate focused on restricting the flow of new immigrants from southern and eastern Europe. Some labor leaders believed that immigration held down wages and impeded unionization; many sociologists thought it created serious social problems; other Americans disliked the newcomers on religious, cultural, or ethnic grounds. Many backed their prejudice with a distorted interpretation of Darwinism, labeling the Slavic and Mediterranean peoples "inferior races." As early as 1894, nativists had organized the Immigration Restriction League, which lobbied for a literacy test for admission, sure that it would "bear most heavily upon the Italians, Russians, Poles, Hungarians, Greeks, and Asiatics, and very lightly or not at all upon English-speaking immigrants or Germans, Scandinavians, and French." Congress enacted a literacy law in 1917.

Other nativists demanded the "Americanization" of immigrants already in the country. The Daughters of the American Revolution sought to inculcate loyalty, patriotism, and conservative values. Settlement workers and Social Gospelers promoted a gentler kind of Americanization by helping immigrants adapt to their new life with classes in English and home mission campaigns, but they too attempted to transfer their own values to the newcomers. The most prominent advocate of Americanization was a stereotypical progressive, Frances Kellor. She studied social work at the University of Chicago, worked in New York settlement houses, wrote a muckraking exposé of employment agencies that exploited women, and became director of the New York Bureau of Immigration. In 1915, she helped organize the National Americanization Committee and increasingly emphasized destroying immigrants' old-country ties and imposing an American culture.

Prohibition. Closely linked to progressives' worries about immigrants was their campaign for **prohibition**. This movement engaged many of the progressives' basic impulses. Social workers saw liquor as a cause of crime, poverty, and family violence; employers blamed it for causing industrial accidents and inefficiency; Social Gospel ministers condemned the "spirit born of hell" because it impaired moral judgment and behavior. But also important was native-born Americans' fear of new immigrants—"the dangerous classes, who are readily dominated by the saloon." Many immigrants, in fact, viewed liquor and the neighborhood saloon as vital parts of daily life, and so prohibition became a focus of nativist hostilities, cultural conflict, and Americanization pressures. In the South, racism also figured prominently. Alexander McKelway, the southern secretary for the National Child Labor Committee, endorsed prohibition as a way to maintain social order and white supremacy. McKelway himself drank, but he helped organize the North Carolina Anti-Saloon League to deny alcohol to African Americans, whom he considered naturally "criminal and degenerate."

Protestant fundamentalists also stoutly supported prohibition, working through the Anti-Saloon League, founded in 1893. Their nativism and antiurban bias surfaced in demands for prohibition to prevent the nation's cities from lapsing into "raging mania, disorder, and anarchy." With most urban Catholics and Jews opposing prohibition—the Central Conference of American Rabbis denounced it as "born of fanaticism"—the Anti-Saloon League justified imposing its reform on city populations against their will: "Our nation can only be saved by turning the pure stream of country sentiment . . . to flush out the cesspools of cities and so save civilization from pollution."

With these varied motivations, prohibitionists campaigned for local and state laws against the manufacture and sale of alcohol. Beginning in 1907, they proved increasingly successful, especially in the South, Midwest, and Far West. By 1917, twenty-six states had prohibition laws. Congress then approved the Eighteenth Amendment, which made prohibition the law of the land by 1920.

Less controversial was the drive to control narcotics, then readily available. Patent medicines commonly contained opium, heroin, and cocaine (popularly used for hay fever), and physicians known as "dope doctors" openly dispensed drugs to paying customers. Inaccurate assumptions that addiction was spreading in "the fallen and lower classes"—and particularly among black people and immigrants—prompted calls for restrictive legislation. In 1914, Congress passed the Harrison Act, prohibiting the distribution and use of narcotics for other than medicinal purposes.

Suppressing prostitution. Reformers also sought to suppress the "social evil" of prostitution. Like crowded slums, sweatshops, and child labor, the "vice districts" where prostitution flourished were seen as part of the exploitation and disorder in the industrial cities. Women's low wages as factory workers and domestic servants explained some of the problem, as pointed out by a *McClure's* muckraking article entitled "The Daughters of the Poor." But nativism spurred public concern, as when New York officials insisted that most prostitutes and brothel owners, some of whom "have been seducers of defenseless women all their lives," were foreign-born.

The response to prostitution was typical of progressivism: investigation and exposure, a reliance upon experts—boards of health, medical groups, clergy— for recommendations, and enactment of new laws. The New York City Committee of Fifteen, organized in 1900, investigated prostitution in response to complaints of clergymen and concerns about links among vice districts, urban political machines, and corrupt business interests. Its report dismissed as ineffective the European attempts to regulate prostitution. The progressive solution emerged in state and municipal action abolishing the "red light" districts previously tolerated and in a federal law, the Mann Act of 1910, prohibiting the interstate transport of women "for immoral purposes."

California provided other examples of progressives' interest in social control and moral reform. The state assembly, described by the *San Francisco Chronicle* as "a legislature of progressive cranks," prohibited gambling, cardplaying, and prizefighting. Los Angeles—influenced by the aptly named Morals Efficiency League—banned premarital sex and introduced artistic censorship. One critic in 1913 complained that the reformers' "frenzy of virtue" made "Puritanism . . . the inflexible doctrine of Los Angeles."

FOR WHITES ONLY?

Racism permeated the Progressive Era. In the South, progressivism was built on black disfranchisement and segregation. Like most white Southerners, progressives believed that racial control was necessary for social order and that it enabled reformers to address other social problems. Such reformers also invoked racism to gain popular support for their objectives. In Georgia, for instance, child labor reformers warned that while white children worked in the Piedmont textile mills, black children were going to school: Child labor laws and compulsory school attendance laws were necessary to maintain white supremacy.

The Flanner House, a black settlement house in Indianapolis, provided the black community with many essential services, including health care. In addition to this baby clinic, pictured in 1918, it established a tuberculosis clinic at a time when the city's public hospitals refused to treat black citizens afflicted with the disease.

Governors Hoke Smith of Georgia and James Vardaman, "the White Chief," of Mississippi typified the link between racism and reform in the South. These men supported progressive reforms, but they also viciously attacked black rights. Their racist demagogy incited antiblack violence throughout the South. Antiblack race riots, like that produced in Atlanta by Smith's election in 1906, and lynching—defended on the floor of the U.S. Senate by a southern progressive—were part of the system of racial control that made the era a terrible time for African Americans.

Even in the North, where relatively few black people lived, race relations deteriorated. Civil rights laws went unenforced, black customers were excluded from restaurants and hotels, and schools were segregated. A reporter in Pennsylvania found "this disposition to discriminate against Negroes has greatly increased within the past decade." Antiblack race riots exploded in New York in 1900 and in Springfield, Illinois—Abraham Lincoln's hometown—in 1908.

Black activism But although most white progressives promoted or accepted racial discrimination and most black Southerners had to adapt to it, black progressive activism was growing. Even in the South, some African Americans struggled to improve conditions. In Atlanta, for example, black women created

progressive organizations and established settlement houses, kindergartens, and day care centers. With public parks reserved for white people, the Gate City Day Nursery Association built and supervised a playground on the campus of Atlanta Baptist College. The women of the Neighborhood Union, organized in 1908, even challenged the discriminatory policies of Atlanta's board of education, demanding equal facilities and appropriations for the city's black schools. They had only limited success, but their efforts demonstrated a persisting commitment to reforming society.

In the North, African Americans more openly criticized discrimination and rejected Booker T. Washington's philosophy of accommodation. Ida Wells-Barnett, the crusading journalist who had fled the South for Chicago, became nationally prominent for her militant protests. She fought fiercely against racial injustices, especially school segregation, agitated for woman suffrage, and organized kindergartens and settlement houses for Chicago's black migrants.

Still more important was W.E.B. Du Bois, who campaigned tirelessly against all forms of racial discrimination. In 1905, Du Bois and other black activists met in Niagara Falls, Canada, to make plans to promote political and economic equality. In 1910, this **Niagara Movement** joined with a small group of white reformers, including Jane Addams, to organize the National Association for the Advancement of Colored People. The NAACP sought to overthrow segregation and establish equal justice and educational opportunities. As its director of publicity and research, Du Bois launched the influential magazine *The Crisis* to shape public opinion. "Agitate," he counseled, "protest, reveal the truth, and refuse to be silenced." By 1918, the NAACP had 44,000 members in 165 branches. Two generations later, it would successfully challenge the racial discrimination that most early-twentieth-century white progressives either supported or tolerated.

REFORMING POLITICS AND GOVERNMENT

Progressives of all kinds clamored for the reform of politics and government. But their political activism was motivated by different concerns, and they sometimes pursued competing objectives. Many wanted to change procedures and institutions to promote greater democracy and responsibility. Others hoped to improve the efficiency of government, to eliminate corruption, or to increase their own influence. All justified their objectives as necessary to adapt the political system to the nation's new needs.

WOMAN SUFFRAGE

One of the most important achievements of the era was woman suffrage. The movement had begun in the mid-nineteenth century, but suffragists had been frustrated by the prevailing belief that women's "proper sphere" was the home and the family. Males dominated the public sphere, including voting. Woman suffrage, particularly when championed as a step toward women's equality, seemed to challenge the natural order of society, and it generated much opposition, not only among men but among tradition-minded women as well. "Housewives," announced the Women's Anti-Suffrage Association of Massachusetts, "you do not need a ballot to clean out your sink spout. A handful of potash and some boiling water is quicker."

In the early twentieth century, suffragists began to outflank this opposition. Under a new generation of leaders, such as Carrie Chapman Catt, they adopted activist tactics, including parades, mass meetings, and "suffrage tours" by automobile. They also organized by political districts and attracted working-women and labor unions. By 1917, the National American Woman Suffrage Association had over 2 million members.

Combining traditional appeals to patriotism and women's moral purity with new activist tactics, including parades like this in New York City, woman suffragists eventually achieved the greatest democratic reform of the Progressive Era.

But some suffrage leaders shifted arguments to gain more support. They argued for woman suffrage within—not against—traditional ideas about women's role. Rather than insisting on the "justice" of woman suffrage or emphasizing equal rights, they spoke of the special moral and maternal instincts women could bring to politics if allowed to vote. The suffrage movement now appeared less a radical, disruptive force than a vehicle for extending traditional female benevolence and service to society. Many suffragists, particularly among working-class groups, remained committed to the larger possibilities they saw in suffrage, but the new image of the movement increased public support by appealing to conventional views of women. Noted one Nebraska undergraduate, women students no longer feared "antagonizing the men or losing invitations to parties by being suffragists."

Gradually, the suffrage movement began to prevail (see Map 21-1). In 1910, Washington became the first state since the mid-1890s to approve woman suffrage, followed by California in 1911 and Arizona, Kansas, and Oregon in 1912. Suffragists also mounted national action, such as the dramatic inaugural parade in

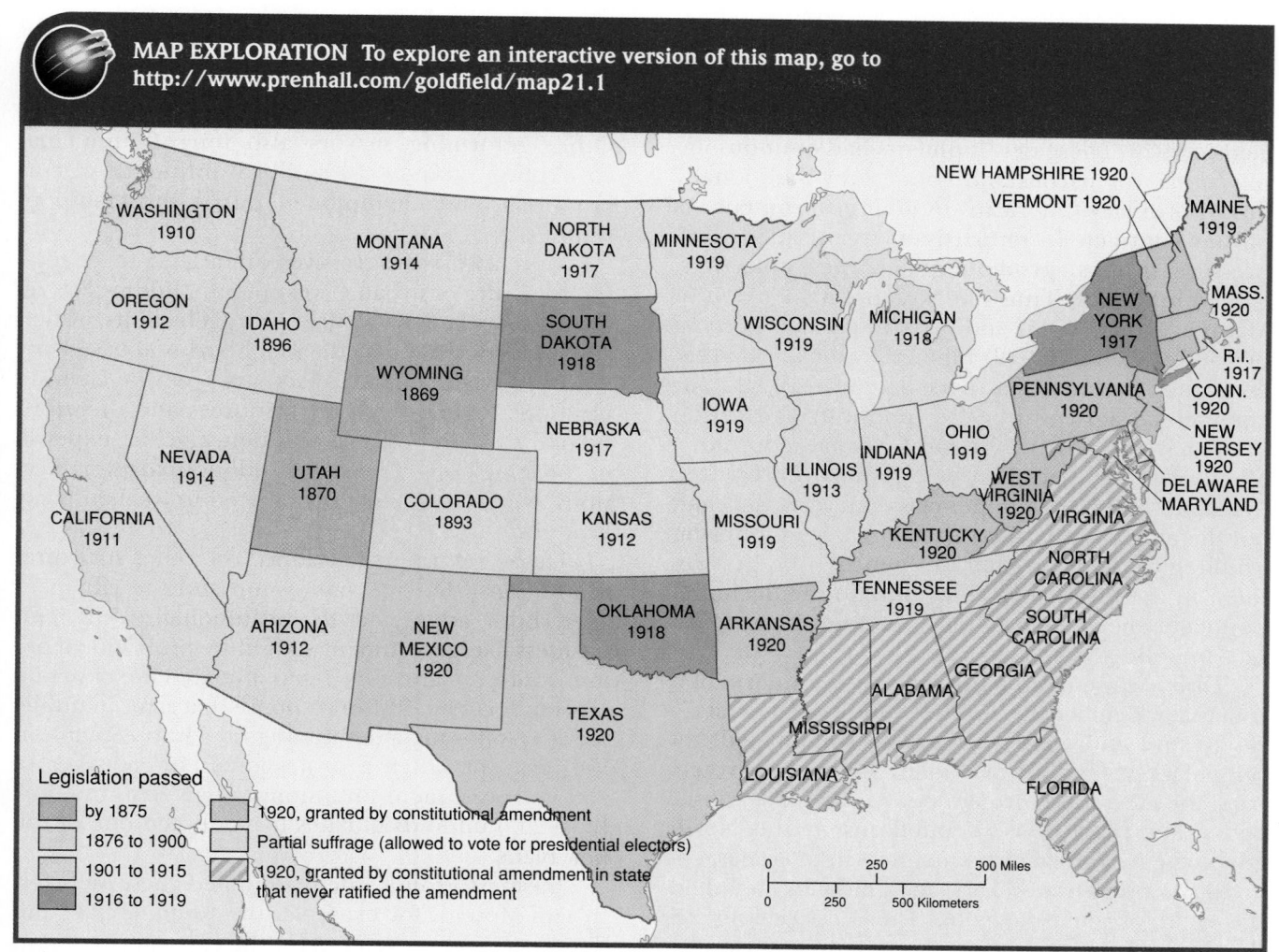

MAP EXPLORATION To explore an interactive version of this map, go to
http://www.prenhall.com/goldfield/map21.1

Legislation passed

- by 1875
- 1876 to 1900
- 1901 to 1915
- 1916 to 1919
- 1920, granted by constitutional amendment
- Partial suffrage (allowed to vote for presidential electors)
- 1920, granted by constitutional amendment in state that never ratified the amendment

MAP 21-1   Woman suffrage in the United States before the ratification of the Nineteenth Amendment.

Beginning with Wyoming in 1869, woman suffrage slowly gained acceptance in the West, but women in the South and much of the East got the ballot only when the Nineteenth Amendment was ratified in 1920.

March 1913 described at the beginning of this chapter. The violence surrounding that event outraged public opinion, revived interest in a federal constitutional amendment to grant women the vote, and prompted women to send petitions and organize pilgrimages to Washington from across the country. By 1919, thirty-nine states had established full or partial woman suffrage, and Congress finally approved an amendment. Ratified by the states in 1920, the **Nineteenth Amendment** marked a critical advance in political democracy.

ELECTORAL REFORM

Other electoral reforms changed the election process and the meaning of political participation. The so-called **Australian ballot** adopted by most states during the 1890s provided for secret voting, freeing voters from intimidation and making vote buying and other corruption more difficult. It also replaced the individual party tickets with an official ballot listing all candidates and distributed by public officials. The Australian ballot led to quiet, orderly elections. One Cincinnati editor, recalling the "howling mobs" and chaos at the polls in previous elections, declared, "The political bummer and thug has been relegated to the background . . . while good citizenship . . . has come to the front."

Government responsibility for the ballot soon led to public regulation of other parts of the electoral process previously controlled by parties. Beginning with Mississippi in 1902, nearly every state provided for direct primaries to remove nominations from the boss-ridden caucus and convention system. Many states also reformed campaign practices.

These reforms weakened the influence of political parties. Their decreasing ability to mobilize voters was reflected in a steady decline in voter participation, from 79 percent in 1896 to 49 percent in 1920. These developments had ominous implications, for parties and voting had traditionally linked ordinary Americans to their government. As parties contracted, nonpartisan organizations and pressure groups, promoting narrower objectives, gained influence. Thus the National Association of Manufacturers (1895) and the United States Chamber of Commerce (1912) lobbied for business interests; the National Farmers Union (1902), for commercial agriculture; the American Federation of Teachers (1916), for professional educators. Many·of these special-interest groups represented the same middle- or upper-class interests that had led the attack on parties. Their organized lobbying would give them greater influence over government in the future and contribute to the declining popular belief in the value of voting or participation in politics.

Disfranchisement more obviously undermined American democracy. In the South, Democrats—progressive and conservative alike—eliminated not only black voters but also many poor white voters from the electorate through poll taxes, literacy tests, and other restrictions. Republicans in the North adopted educational or literacy tests in ten states, enacted strict registration laws, and gradually abolished the right of aliens to vote. These restrictions reflected both the progressives' anti-immigrant prejudices and their obsessions with social control and with purifying politics and "improving" the electorate. Such electoral reforms reduced the political power of ethnic and working-class Americans, often stripping them of their political rights and means of influence.

MUNICIPAL REFORM

Antiparty attitudes also affected progressives' efforts to reform municipal government, which they regarded as inefficient and corrupt, at least partly because of the power of urban political machines. Muckrakers had exposed crooked alliances between city bosses and business leaders that resulted in wasteful or inadequate municipal services. In some cities, urban reformers attempted to break these alliances and improve conditions for those suffering most from municipal misrule. For example, in Toledo, Ohio, Samuel "Golden Rule" Jones won enough working-class votes to be elected mayor four times despite the hostility of both major parties. Serving from 1897 to 1904, Jones opened public playgrounds and kindergartens, es-

tablished the eight-hour day for city workers, and improved public services. Influenced by the Social Gospel, he also provided free lodging for the homeless and gave his own salary to the poor. Other reforming mayors also fought municipal corruption, limited the political influence of corporations, and championed public ownership of utilities.

More elitist progressives attempted to change the structure of urban government. Middle-class reformers worked to replace ward elections, which could be controlled by the neighborhood-based city machine, with at-large elections. To win citywide elections required greater resources and therefore helped swell middle-class influence at the expense of working-class wards. So did nonpartisan elections, which reformers introduced to weaken party loyalties.

Urban reformers developed two other structural innovations: the city commission and the city manager. Both attempted to institutionalize efficient, business-like government staffed by professional administrators. Galveston, Texas, initiated the city-commission form in 1901 in response to a crisis in public services following a devastating tidal wave. Staunton, Virginia, appointed a professional city manager to run its government on a nonpartisan basis in 1908. By 1920, hundreds of cities had adopted one of the new plans.

Business groups often promoted these reforms. In Des Moines, for example, the Commercial Club dominated the movement for the city commission in 1906, and its president declared that "the professional politician must be ousted and in his place capable businessmen chosen to conduct the affairs of the city." Again, then, reform in municipal government often shifted political power from ethnic and working-class voters, represented however imperfectly by partisan elections, to smaller groups with greater resources.

PROGRESSIVE STATE GOVERNMENT

Progressives also reshaped state government. Some tried to democratize the legislative process, regarding the legislature—the most important branch of state government in the nineteenth century—as ineffective and even corrupt, dominated by party bosses and corporate influences. The Missouri legislature reportedly "enacted such laws as the corporations paid for, and such others as were necessary to fool the people." Populists had first raised such charges in the 1890s and proposed novel solutions: the **initiative** and the **referendum**. The initiative enabled reformers themselves to propose legislation directly to the electorate, bypassing an unresponsive legislature; the referendum permitted voters to approve or reject legislative measures. South Dakota Populists established the first system of "direct legislation" in 1898, and progressives adopted these innovations in twenty other states between 1902 and 1915.

Conservative opponents and procedural difficulties, however, often blocked these reforms. And the reforms could be turned against progressives themselves. In the state of Washington in 1914, an initiative to establish an eight-hour workday was defeated by an electorate alarmed by conservative propaganda, and organized labor had to fight seven referendum measures, such as an antipicketing law, that conservative legislators had promoted. The head of the state federation of labor concluded that the people could be "fooled and confused" when they voted directly on legislation.

Other innovations also expanded the popular role in state government. The **Seventeenth Amendment**, ratified in 1913, provided for the election of U.S. senators directly by popular vote instead of by state legislatures. Beginning with Oregon in 1908, ten states adopted the **recall**, enabling voters to remove unsatisfactory public officials from office.

As state legislatures and party machines were curbed, dynamic governors such as Robert La Follette in Wisconsin, Charles Evans Hughes in New York, and Hiram Johnson in California pushed progressive programs into law. Elected governor in 1900, "Fighting Bob" La Follette turned Wisconsin into "the laboratory of democracy." "His words bite like coals of fire," wrote one observer. "He never wearies and he will not allow his audience to weary." Overcoming fierce opposition from "stalwart" Republicans, La Follette established direct primaries, railroad regulation, the first state income tax, workers' compensation, and other important measures before being elected to the U.S. Senate in 1906.

La Follette also stressed efficiency and expertise. The Legislative Reference Bureau that he created was staffed by university professors to advise on public policy. He used regulatory commissions to oversee railroads, banks, and other interests. Most states followed suit, and expert commissions became an important feature of state government, gradually gaining authority at the expense of local officials. An observer in Virginia noted in 1912 that the emphasis on efficiency and expertise caused the government to "delegate all new functions, and some old ones, to state departments or commissions instead of to county officers."

"Experts" were presumed to be disinterested and therefore committed to the general welfare. In practice, however, regulators were subject to pressures from competing interest groups, and some commissions became captives of the very industries they were supposed to control. This irony was matched by the contradiction between the expansion of democracy through the initiative and referendum and the increasing reliance on nonelected professional experts to set and implement public policy. Such inconsistencies emphasize the complex mixture of ideas, objectives, and groups that were reshaping politics and government.

THEODORE ROOSEVELT AND THE PROGRESSIVE PRESIDENCY

When a crazed anarchist assassinated William McKinley in 1901, Theodore Roosevelt entered the White House, and the progressive movement gained its most prominent leader. The son of a wealthy New York family, Roosevelt had been a New York legislator, U.S. civil service commissioner, and assistant secretary of the navy. After his exploits in the Spanish–American War, he was elected governor of New York in 1898 and vice president in 1900. His public life was matched by an active private life, in which he both wrote works of history and obsessively pursued what he called the "strenuous life": boxing, wrestling, hunting, rowing, even ranching and chasing rustlers in Dakota Territory. His own son observed that Roosevelt "always wanted to be the bride at every wedding and the corpse at every funeral."

Roosevelt's frenetic activity, aggressive personality, and penchant for self-promotion worried some Americans. Mark Twain fretted that "Mr. Roosevelt is the Tom Sawyer of the political world of the twentieth century; always showing off; always hunting for a chance to show off; in his frenzied imagination the Great Republic is a vast Barnum circus with him for a clown and the whole world for audience." But Roosevelt's flamboyance and ambitions made him the most popular politician of the time and enabled him to dramatize the issues of progressivism and to become the first modern president.

TR AND THE MODERN PRESIDENCY

Roosevelt rejected the limited role of Gilded Age presidents. He believed that the president could do anything to meet national needs that the Constitution did not specifically prohibit. "Under this interpretation of executive power," he later recalled, "I did and caused to be done many things not previously done. . . . I did not usurp power, but I did greatly broaden the use of executive power." Indeed, the expansion of government power and its consolidation in the executive branch were among his most significant accomplishments.

Rather than deferring to Congress, Roosevelt exerted legislative leadership. He spelled out his policy goals in more than four hundred messages to Congress, sent drafts of bills to Capitol Hill, and intervened to win passage of "his" measures. Some members of Congress resented such "executive arrogance" and "dictatorship." Roosevelt generally avoided direct challenges to the conservative Old Guard Republicans who controlled Congress, but his activities helped shift the balance of power within the national government.

Roosevelt also reorganized the executive branch. He believed in efficiency and expertise, which he attempted to institutionalize in special commissions and administrative procedures. To promote rational policymaking and public management, he staffed the expanding federal bureaucracy with able professionals. Here, too, he provoked opposition. The president, complained one Republican, was "trying to concentrate all power in Washington . . . and to govern the people by commissions and bureaus."

Finally, Roosevelt encouraged the development of a personal presidency by exploiting the public's interest in their exuberant young president. He established the first White House press room and skillfully handled the mass media. His endless and well-reported activities, from playing with his children in the White House to wrestling, hiking, and horseback-riding with various notables, made him a celebrity, "TR" or "Teddy." The publicity not only kept TR in the spotlight but also enabled him to mold public opinion.

ROOSEVELT AND LABOR

One sign of TR's vigorous new approach to the presidency was his handling of a coal strike in 1902. Members of the United Mine Workers Union walked off their jobs, demanding higher wages, an eight-hour day, and recognition of their union. The mine owners closed the mines and waited for the union to collapse. But led by John Mitchell, the strikers held their ranks. The prospect of a freezing winter frightened consumers. Management's stubborn arrogance contrasted with the workers' orderly conduct and willingness to negotiate and hardened public opinion against the owners. TR's legal advisers told him that the government had no constitutional authority to intervene.

As public pressure mounted, however, Roosevelt invited both the owners and the union leaders to the White House and declared that the national interest made government action necessary. Mitchell agreed to negotiate with the owners or to accept an arbitration commission appointed by the president. The owners, however, refused even to speak to the miners and demanded that Roosevelt use the army to break the union, as Cleveland had done in the Pullman strike in 1894.

Roosevelt was not a champion of labor, and he had favored shooting the Pullman strikers. But as president, he believed his role was to mediate social conflict for the public good. Furious with the owners' "arrogant stupidity" and "insulting" attitude toward the presidency, Roosevelt announced that he would use the army to seize and operate the mines, not to crush the union. Questioned about the constitutionality of such an action, Roosevelt bellowed, "To hell with the Constitution when the people want coal." Reluctantly, the owners accepted the arbitration commission they had previously rejected. The commission gave the miners a 10 percent wage increase and a nine-hour day, but not union recognition, and permitted the owners to raise coal prices by 10 percent. Roosevelt described his intervention as simply giving both labor and management a "square deal." It also set important precedents for an active government role in labor disputes and a strong president acting as a steward of the public.

MANAGING NATURAL RESOURCES

Federal land policy had helped create farms and develop transportation, but it had also ceded to speculators and business interests much of the nation's forests, mineral deposits, waterpower sites, and grazing lands. Reckless exploitation of these resources alarmed a new generation that believed the public welfare required the **conservation** of natural resources through efficient and scientific management. Conservationists achieved early victories in the Forest Reserve Act (1891) and the Forest Management Act (1897), which authorized the federal government to withdraw timberlands from development and to regulate grazing, lumbering, and hydroelectric sites in the forests (see Map 21-2).

Roosevelt built on these beginnings and his friendship with Gifford Pinchot to make conservation a major focus of his presidency. Pinchot had been trained in French and German scientific forestry practices. Appointed in 1898 to head the new Division of Forestry (renamed the Forest Service in 1905), he brought rational management and regulation to resource development. With his advice, TR used presidential authority to triple the size of the forest reserves to 150 million acres, set aside another 80 million acres valuable for minerals and petroleum, and establish dozens of wildlife refuges. In 1908, Roosevelt held a White House conference of state and federal officials that led to the creation of the National Conservation Commis-

MAP EXPLORATION To explore an interactive version of this map, go to
http://www.prenhall.com/goldfield/map21.2

MAP 21-2 **The growth of National Forests and National Parks.**
*Rapid exploitation of the West prompted demands to preserve its spectacular scenery and protect
its remaining forests. In 1872 Yellowstone became the first National Park, and the National
Forest system began in the 1890s. Conservation became increasingly important during the
Progressive Era but often provoked western hostility.*

sion, forty-one state conservation commissions,
and widespread public support for the conservation movement.

Not everyone, of course, agreed with TR's con-
servationist policies. Some favored **preservation**,
hoping to set aside land as permanent wilderness,
whereas Roosevelt favored a scientific and efficient
rather than uncontrolled use of resources. Pinchot
declared, "Wilderness is waste." Preservationists won
some victories, saving a stand of California's giant
redwoods and helping create the National Park Service in 1916, but more Americans favored the utili-
tarian emphasis of early conservationists.

Other interests opposed conservation completely. While some of the larger timber and mineral
companies supported conservation as a way to
guarantee long-run profits, smaller western entrepreneurs often cared only about quick returns.
Many Westerners, moreover, resented having Easterners make key decisions about western growth
and saw conservation as a perpetuation of this colonial subservience. Many ranchers refused to pay federal grazing fees. Colorado arsonists set forest fires
to protest the creation of forest reserves.

But Westerners were happy to take federal money
for expensive irrigation projects that private capital

Theodore Roosevelt and John Muir on a 1903 camping trip in Yosemite, which was set aside as a national park largely through Muir's activism. Roosevelt was less interested in such preservation and eventually supported flooding a spectacular valley in the park in order to provide a water supply for San Francisco.

would not undertake. They favored the 1902 National Reclamation Act, which established what became the **Bureau of Reclamation**. Its engineers were to construct dams, reservoirs, and irrigation canals, and the government was to sell the irrigated lands in tracts no larger than 160 acres. The act helped shape the modern West. With massive dams and networks of irrigation canals, it reclaimed fertile valleys from the desert. Unfortunately, the bureau did not enforce the 160-acre limitation and thus helped create powerful corporate farms in the West.

CORPORATE REGULATION

Nothing symbolized Roosevelt's active presidency better than his popular reputation as a "trust buster." TR took office at a time of public anxiety about corporate power, but he did not share that anxiety. On the contrary, he regarded the formation of large business combinations to be the result of a natural and beneficial process. But he understood the political implications of the public's concern. Although business leaders and Old Guard conservatives opposed

any government intervention in the large trusts, Roosevelt knew better. "You have no conception of the revolt that would be caused if I did nothing," he said privately. To satisfy popular clamor, ensure social stability, and still retain the economic advantages of big modern corporations, TR proposed to "develop an orderly system, and such a system can only come through the gradually exercised right of efficient government control." Rather than invoking "the foolish antitrust law," he favored government regulation to prevent corporate abuses and defend the public interest. "Misconduct," not size, was the issue. Roosevelt preferred to use government agencies to work with corporations to avoid lawsuits. But he did sue some "bad trusts."

In 1902, the Roosevelt administration filed its most famous antitrust suit, against the Northern Securities Company, a holding company organized by J.P. Morgan to control the railroad network of the Northwest. For TR, this suit was an assertion of government power that reassured a worried public and made corporate responsibility more likely. In 1904, the Supreme Court ordered the dissolution of the Northern Securities Company. Ultimately, Roosevelt brought forty-four antitrust suits against business combinations, but, except for a few like Standard Oil, he avoided the giant firms. Many of the cases had inconclusive outcomes, but Roosevelt was more interested in establishing a regulatory role for government than in breaking up big businesses.

Elected president in his own right in 1904 over the colorless and conservative Democratic candidate, Judge Alton B. Parker, Roosevelt responded to the growing popular demand for reform by pushing further toward a regulatory government. He proposed legislation "to work out methods of controlling the big corporations without paralyzing the energies of the business community." In 1906, Congress passed the Hepburn Act, the Pure Food and Drug Act, and the Meat Inspection Act. All three were compromises between reformers seeking serious government control of the industries and political defenders and lobbyists of the industries themselves.

The Hepburn Act authorized the Interstate Commerce Commission to set maximum railroad rates and extended its jurisdiction. It was a weaker law than many progressives had wanted, but it marked the first time the federal government gained the power to set rules in a private enterprise. The two other laws aimed at consumer protection in food and drugs. In part, this legislation reflected public demand, but many business leaders also supported government regulation, convinced that it would expand their markets by certifying the quality of their

Roosevelt enjoyed this cartoon illustrating his distinction between good trusts, restrained by government regulations for public welfare, and bad trusts. On those he put his foot down.

had extended government powers dangerously, but in fact his accomplishments had been relatively modest because of his need to compromise in Congress. As La Follette noted, Roosevelt's "cannonading filled the air with noise and smoke, which confused and obscured the line of action, but, when the battle cloud drifted by and the quiet was restored, it was always a matter of surprise that so little had really been accomplished."

TAFT AND THE INSURGENTS

TR handpicked his successor as president: a loyal lieutenant, William Howard Taft. A member of a prominent Ohio political family, Taft had been a federal judge, governor-general of the Philippines, and secretary of war. Later he would serve as chief justice of the United States. But if Roosevelt thought that Taft would be a successful president, continuing his policies and holding the Republican party together, he was wrong. Taft's election in 1908, over Democrat William Jennings Bryan in his third presidential campaign, led to a Republican political disaster.

Taft did preside over important progressive achievements. His administration pursued a more active and successful antitrust program than Roosevelt's. He supported the Mann-Elkins Act (1910), which extended the ICC's jurisdiction to telephone and telegraph companies. Taft set aside more public forest lands and oil reserves than Roosevelt had. He also supported a constitutional amendment authorizing an income tax, which went into effect in 1913 under the **Sixteenth Amendment**. One of the most important accomplishments of the Progressive Era, the income tax would provide the means for the government to expand its activities and responsibilities.

Nevertheless, Taft soon alienated progressives and floundered into a political morass. His problems were twofold. First, the Republicans were divided. Midwestern reform Republicans, led by La Follette, clashed with more conservative Republicans led by Senator

products and drive their smaller competitors out of business. The laws thus did extend government supervision and regulation over business to protect the public health and safety, but they also served some corporate purposes.

Despite the compromises and weaknesses in the three laws, TR contended that they marked "a noteworthy advance in the policy of securing federal supervision and control over corporations." In 1907 and 1908, he pushed for an eight-hour workday, stock market regulation, and inheritance and income taxes. Republican conservatives in Congress blocked such reforms, and tensions increased between the progressive and conservative wings of the party. Old Guard Republicans thought Roosevelt

Nelson Aldrich of Rhode Island. Second, Taft was politically inept. He was unable to mediate between these two groups, and the party split apart.

Reformers wanted to restrict the power of the speaker of the House, "Uncle Joe" Cannon, a reactionary who blocked reform. After seeming to promise support, Taft backed down when conservatives threatened to defeat important legislation. The insurgents in Congress eventually restricted the speaker's powers, but they never forgave what they saw as Taft's betrayal. The tariff also alienated progressives from Taft. He had campaigned in 1908 for a lower tariff to curb inflation, and midwestern Republicans favored tariff reduction to trim the power of big business. But when they introduced tariff reform legislation, the president failed to support them, and Aldrich's Senate committee added 847 amendments, many of which raised tariff rates. Taft justified his inaction as avoiding presidential interference with congressional business, but this excuse clashed with TR's example and the reformers' expectations. Progressives concluded that Taft had sided with the Old Guard against real change.

That perception solidified when Taft stumbled into a controversy over conservation. Gifford Pinchot had become embroiled in a complex struggle with Richard Ballinger, Taft's secretary of the interior. Ballinger, who was closely tied to western mining and lumbering interests, favored private development of public lands. When Pinchot challenged Ballinger's role in a questionable sale of public coal lands in Alaska to a J.P. Morgan syndicate, Taft upheld Ballinger and fired Pinchot. Progressives concluded that Taft had repudiated Roosevelt's conservation policies.

Progressives determined to replace Taft, whom they now saw as an obstacle to reform. In 1911, the National Progressive League organized to champion La Follette for the Republican nomination in 1912. Roosevelt rejected an appeal for support, convinced that a challenge to the incumbent president was both doomed and divisive. Besides, his own position was closer to Taft's than to what he called "the La Follette type of fool radicalism." But Taft's political blunders increasingly angered Roosevelt. Condemning Taft as "disloyal to our past friendship," TR began to campaign for the Republican nomination himself. In thirteen state primaries, he won 278 delegates, to only 46 for Taft. But most states did not then have primaries; that situation allowed Taft to dominate the Republican convention and win renomination. Roosevelt's forces formed a third party—the Progressive party—and nominated the former president. The Republican split almost guaranteed victory for the Democratic nominee, Woodrow Wilson.

WOODROW WILSON AND PROGRESSIVE REFORM

The pressures for reform called forth many new leaders. The one who would preside over progressivism's culmination, and ultimately its collapse, was Woodrow Wilson. Elected president in 1912 and 1916, he mediated among differing progressive views to achieve a strong reform program, enlarge the power of the executive branch, and make the White House the center of national politics.

THE ELECTION OF 1912

Despite the prominence of Roosevelt and La Follette, progressivism was not simply a Republican phenomenon. In Congress, Southern Democrats more consistently supported reform measures than Republicans did, and the Democratic leader William Jennings Bryan surpassed Roosevelt as a persistent advocate of significant reform. As the Republicans quarreled during Taft's administration, Democrats pushed progressive remedies and achieved major victories in the state and congressional elections of 1910. To improve the party's chances in 1912, Bryan announced that he would step aside. The Democratic spotlight shifted to the governor of New Jersey, Woodrow Wilson.

Born in Virginia as the son and grandson of Presbyterian ministers, Wilson combined public eloquence with a cold personality; he balanced a self-righteousness that led to stubborn inflexibility with an intense ambition that permitted the most expedient compromises. Wilson first entered public life as a conservative, steeped in the limited government traditions of the South. As president of Princeton University, beginning in 1902, he became a prominent representative of middle-class respectability and conservative causes. In 1910, New Jersey's Democratic bosses selected him for governor to head off the progressives, but, once in office, Wilson championed popular reforms and immediately began to campaign as a progressive for the party's 1912 presidential nomination.

Wilson's progressivism differed from that of Roosevelt in 1912. TR emphasized a strong government to promote economic and social order. He defended big business as inevitable and healthy provided that government control ensured that it would benefit the entire nation. Roosevelt called this program the **New Nationalism**, reflecting his belief in a powerful state

A portrait of Woodrow Wilson by Edward Charles Tarbell. A strong president, Wilson led Congress to enact sweeping and significant legislation.

scope of the federal government, which he hoped to minimize. (This position, shot back the alarmed Roosevelt, meant the repeal of "every law for the promotion of social and industrial justice.")

Roosevelt's stance on social legislation attracted many women into political action. As Jane Addams observed, "their long concern for the human wreckage of industry has come to be considered politics." The Progressive party also endorsed woman suffrage, accepted women as convention delegates, and pledged to assure women equal representation on party committees. The *New York Times* exaggerated in claiming that the 1912 campaign had become "feminized," but certainly women activists welcomed the opportunity of participating "in party affairs before the vote is won" and thereby "answering forcibly many of the objections to the vote" for women.

Despite his personal popularity, however, TR was unable to add progressive Democrats to the Republicans who followed him into the Progressive party, dooming him to defeat. Other reform voters embraced the Socialist candidate, Eugene V. Debs, who captured 900,000 votes—6 percent of the total. Taft played little role in the campaign. "I might as well give up as far as being a candidate," he lamented. "There are so many people in the country who don't like me."

and a national interest. He also supported demands for social welfare, including workers' compensation and the abolition of child labor.

Wilson was horrified by Roosevelt's vision. His **New Freedom** program rejected what he called TR's "regulated monopoly." Wilson wanted "regulated competition," with the goverment's role limited to breaking up monopolies through antitrust action and preventing artificial barriers like tariffs from blocking free enterprise. Wilson opposed social welfare legislation as "paternalistic," reaching beyond the proper

Wilson won an easy electoral college victory, though he received only 42 percent of the popular vote and fewer popular votes than Bryan had won in any of his three campaigns (see Map 21-3). Roosevelt came in second, Taft third. The Democrats also gained control of Congress, giving Wilson the opportunity to enact his New Freedom program.

IMPLEMENTING THE NEW FREEDOM

As president, Wilson built on Roosevelt's precedent to strengthen executive authority. He summoned

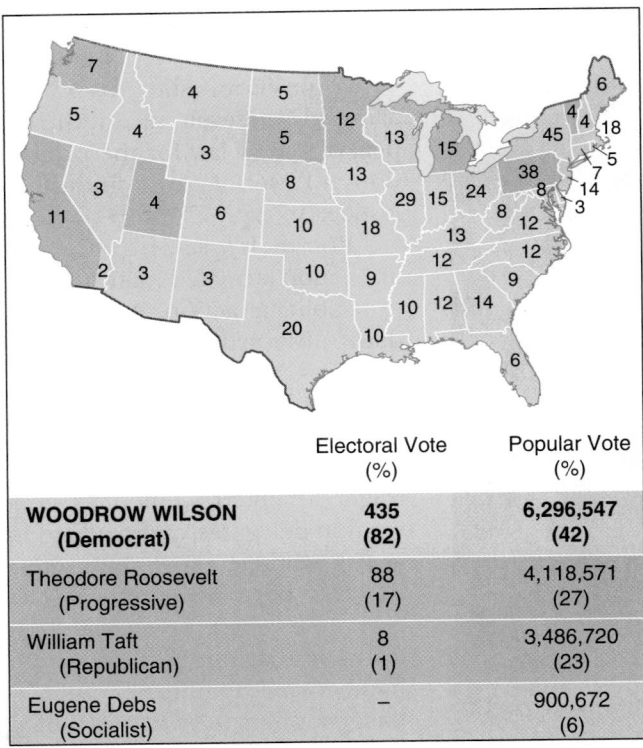

	Electoral Vote (%)	Popular Vote (%)
WOODROW WILSON (Democrat)	**435** **(82)**	**6,296,547** **(42)**
Theodore Roosevelt (Progressive)	88 (17)	4,118,571 (27)
William Taft (Republican)	8 (1)	3,486,720 (23)
Eugene Debs (Socialist)	–	900,672 (6)

MAP 21-3 **The Election of 1912.**
The split within the Republican party enabled Woodrow Wilson to carry most states and become president even though he won only a minority of the popular vote.

Congress into special session in 1913 and delivered his message in person, the first president to do so since John Adams. Wilson proposed a full legislative program and worked forcefully to secure its approval. He held regular conferences with Democratic leaders and had a private telephone line installed between the Capitol and the White House to keep tabs on congressional actions. When necessary, he appealed to the public for support or doled out patronage and compromised with conservatives. With such methods and a solid Democratic majority, Wilson gained approval of important laws.

Wilson turned first to the traditional Democratic goal of reducing the high protective tariff, the symbol of special privileges for industry. "The object of the tariff duties," he announced, "must be effective competition." He forced through the **Underwood-Simmons Tariff Act** of 1913, the first substantial reduction in duties since before the Civil War. The act also levied the first income tax under the recently ratified Sixteenth Amendment. Conservatives condemned the "revolutionary" tax, but it was designed simply to compensate for lower tariff rates. The top tax rate paid by the wealthiest was a mere 7 percent.

Wilson next reformed the nation's banking and currency system, which was inadequate for a modernizing economy. A panic in 1907 and a subsequent congressional investigation had dramatized the need for a more flexible and decentralized financial system. Wilson skillfully maneuvered a compromise measure through Congress, balancing the demands of agrarian progressives for government control with the bankers' desires for private control. The **Federal Reserve Act** of 1913 created twelve regional Federal Reserve banks that, although privately controlled, were to be supervised by the Federal Reserve Board, appointed by the president. The law also provided for a flexible national currency and improved access to credit. Serious problems remained, but the new system promoted the progressive goals of order and efficiency and fulfilled Wilson's New Freedom principle of introducing limited government regulation while preserving private business control.

Wilson's third objective was new legislation to break up monopolies. To this end, he initially supported the Clayton antitrust bill, which prohibited unfair trade practices and sharply restricted holding companies. But when business leaders and other progressives strenuously objected, Wilson reversed himself. Opting for continuous federal regulation rather than for the dissolution of trusts, Wilson endorsed the creation of the **Federal Trade Commission (FTC)** to oversee business activity and prevent illegal restrictions on competition.

The Federal Trade Commission Act of 1914 dismayed many of Wilson's early supporters because it embraced the New Nationalism's emphasis on positive regulation. Roosevelt's 1912 platform had proposed a federal trade commission; Wilson now accepted what he had earlier denounced as a partnership between trusts and the government that the trusts would dominate. Indeed, Wilson's conservative appointments to the FTC insured that the agency would not seriously interfere with business, and by the 1920s, the FTC had become virtually a junior partner of the business community.

The fate of the Clayton antitrust bill after Wilson withdrew his support reflected his new attitude toward big business. Congressional conservatives gutted the bill with crippling amendments before permitting it to become law in 1914. As one senator complained, "When the Clayton bill was first written, it was a raging lion with a mouth full of teeth. It has degenerated to a tabby cat with soft gums, a plaintive mew, and an anemic appearance. It is a sort of legislative apology to the trusts, delivered hat in hand, and accompanied by assurances that no discourtesy is intended."

Wilson now announced that no further reforms were necessary—astonishing many progressives whose objectives had been completely ignored. Wilson refused to support woman suffrage and helped kill legislation abolishing child labor and expanding credits to farmers. Race relations provided a flagrant instance of Wilson's indifference to issues of social justice. Raised in the South, he believed in segregation and backed the southern Democrats in his cabinet when they introduced formal segregation within the government itself. Government offices, shops, restrooms, and restaurants were all segregated; employees who complained were fired. Federal officials in the South discharged black employees wholesale. One Georgia official promised that there would be no more government jobs for African Americans: "A Negro's place is in the cornfield."

THE EXPANSION OF REFORM

Wilson had won in 1912 only because the Republicans had split. By 1916, Roosevelt had returned to the GOP, and Wilson realized that he had to attract some of TR's former followers. Wilson therefore abandoned his opposition to social and economic reforms aiding specific groups and promoted measures he had previously condemned as paternalistic and unconstitutional. But he had also grown in the White House and now recognized that some problems could be resolved only by positive federal action. "Old political formulas," he said, "do not fit the present."

To assist farmers, Wilson in 1916 convinced Congress to pass the Federal Farm Loan Act. This law, which Wilson himself had rejected twice earlier, provided farmers with federally financed, long-term agricultural credits. The Warehouse Act of 1916 improved short-term agricultural credit. The Highway Act of 1916 provided funds to construct and improve rural roads through the adoption of the "dollar-matching" principle by which the federal government would expand its power over state activities in the twentieth century.

Wilson and the Democratic Congress also reached out to labor. Wilson signed the Keating-Owen Act prohibiting the interstate shipment of products made by child labor. In 1902, Wilson had denounced Roosevelt's intervention in the coal strike, but in 1916 he broke a labor-management impasse and averted a railroad strike by helping pass the Adamson Act establishing an eight-hour day for railway workers. Wilson also pushed the Kern-McGillicuddy Act, which achieved the progressive goal of a workers' compensation system for federal employees. Together, these laws marked an important advance toward government regulation of the labor market.

Wilson also promoted activist government when he nominated Louis Brandeis to the Supreme Court. Known as the "people's lawyer," Brandeis had successfully defended protective labor legislation before the conservative judiciary. The nomination outraged conservatives, including William Howard Taft and the American Bar Association. Brandeis was the first Jew nominated to the court, and anti-Semitism motivated some of his opponents. Wilson overcame a vicious campaign against Brandeis and secured his confirmation.

By these actions, Wilson brought progressivism to a culmination of sorts and consolidated reformers behind him for a second term. Less than a decade earlier, Wilson the private citizen had assailed government regulation and social legislation; by 1916, he had guided an unprecedented expansion of federal power. His own transformation symbolized the development of progressivism itself.

CONCLUSION

In the early twentieth century, progressive reformers responded to the tensions of industrial and urban development by moving to change society and government. Rejecting an earlier emphasis on individualism and laissez-faire, they organized to promote social change and an interventionist state. Programs and laws to protect women, children, and injured workers testified to their compassion; the creation of new agencies and political techniques indicated their interest in order and efficiency; campaigns to end corruption, whether perceived in urban political machines, corporate influence, drunkenness, or "inferior" immigrants, illustrated their self-assured vision of the public good.

Progressivism had its ironies and paradoxes. It called for democratic reforms—and did achieve woman suffrage, direct legislation, and popular election of senators—but helped disfranchise black Southerners and northern immigrants. It advocated social justice but often enforced social control. It demanded responsive government but helped create bureaucracies largely removed from popular control. It endorsed the regulation of business in the public interest but forged regulatory laws and commissions that tended to aid business. Some of these seeming contradictions reflected the persistence of traditional attitudes and the necessity to accommodate conservative opponents; others revealed the progressives' own limitations in vision, concern, or nerve.

FROM THEN TO NOW

The Environmental Movement

Many of the issues that concern environmentalists today were first raised by the conservationists and preservationists of the Progressive Era. Conservationists favored the planned and regulated management of America's natural resources for the public benefit. Led by Theodore Roosevelt, they dominated the new agencies like the Forest Service that were responsible for federal lands. In contrast, preservationists—like John Muir, who founded the Sierra Club in 1892—sought to protect wilderness from any development whatsoever. Opposing both were those who championed the uncontrolled development of public lands.

Preservationists' reasons for protecting wilderness were primarily aesthetic—to preserve natural splendors intact for future generations. By the second half of the twentieth century, however, the disturbing consequences of technological change, rapid economic development, and spiraling population growth began to raise the stakes. Air pollution from smokestack industries and automobile exhaust damaged natural vegetation and caused respiratory diseases; water pollution from sewage and chemical waste spread disease; and oil spills fouled beaches and devastated marine habitats.

Public concern over these problems gave birth to the environmental movement, which drew on the legacy of both the conservation and preservation movements but had wider interests and broader support than either. Responding to the environmental movement's quickly growing strength, Congress in the 1970s passed laws to protect endangered species, reduce pollution, limit the use of pesticides, and control hazardous waste. The Environmental Protection Agency, created in 1970, subsequently became the largest federal regulatory agency.

Again, however, as during the Progressive Era, efforts to protect the environment encountered opposition from proponents of unrestricted development, especially in the West. In the Sagebrush Rebellion in the late 1970s and 1980s, some Westerners condemned "outside" federal regulation and tried to seize control of public lands for private exploitation. One oil company dismissed catastrophic oil spills as merely "Mother Earth letting some oil come out."

Four Republican presidents from the West—Californians Richard Nixon and Ronald Reagan and Texans George Bush and George W. Bush, all closely tied to oil and real estate interests—sought in varying degrees to curtail environmental policies, agencies, and budgets and to promote development. This repudiation of Theodore Roosevelt's conservationism reflected the shift of the party's base to the sunbelt. As one Nixon adviser said, when a pipeline across the Alaskan wilderness was approved, "Conservation is not in the Republican ethic."

Ronald Reagan in particular was convinced that environmental protection fundamentally conflicted with economic growth. The business executives and corporate lawyers he appointed to key federal positions rescinded or weakened environmental regulations.

Congress, the courts, and the public, however, resisted efforts to weaken environmental policy. "Green" groups proliferated, demanding greater attention to environmental issues; some, like Greenpeace, undertook direct action to protect the environment, and even Western communities organized to oppose strip mining, nuclear power plants, and toxic waste dumping.

Despite fluctuations, public opinion and mainstream politics now appear to favor greater environmental protection. Debate is sure to continue over the cost and effectiveness of specific policies. But as ever more challenging ecological problems arise—such as ozone depletion and global warming—Americans are increasingly inclined to stand with Theodore Roosevelt and John Muir in looking to the federal government for effective action to meet them.

THE AMERICAN JOURNEY
THIRD EDITION

GET THE BOOK THAT **GETS YOUR STUDENTS.**

FROM THEN TO NOW

The Environmental Movement

Many of the issues that concern environmentalists today were first raised by the conservationists and preservationists of the Progressive Era. Conservationists favored the planned and regulated management of America's natural resources for the public benefit. Led by Theodore Roosevelt, they dominated the new agencies like the Forest Service that were responsible for federal lands. In contrast, preservationists—like John Muir, who founded the Sierra Club in 1892—sought to protect wilderness from any development whatsoever. Opposing both were those who championed the uncontrolled development of public lands.

Preservationists' reasons for protecting wilderness were primarily aesthetic—to preserve natural splendors intact for future generations. By the second half of the twentieth century, how

the Sagebrush Rebellion in the late 1970s and 1980s, some Westerners condemned "outside" federal regulation and tried to seize control of public lands for private exploitation. One oil company dismissed catastrophic oil spills as merely "Mother Earth letting some oil come out."

Four Republican presidents from the West—Californians Richard Nixon and Ronald Reagan and Texans George Bush and George W. Bush, all closely tied to oil and real estate interests—sought in varying degrees to curtail environmental policies, agencies, and budgets and to promote development. This repudiation of Theodore Roosevelt's conservationism reflected the shift of the party's base to the sunbelt. As one Nixon adviser said, when a pipeline across the Alaskan wilderness was approved, "Conservation

GET THE BEST RELEVANCE:
From Then to Now

History comes with us into the present in many ways. It marks our journey through time, with names and dates of the people whose triumphs and trials are forerunners to those happening today.

What better way to capture and hold your students' attention than with relevant accounts of how their history has had a profound impact on their own lives today?

From Then to Now features throughout this text will help your students connect events and trends of the past to issues that they and their fellow Americans confront. These insightful features enable students to gain an historical perspective that contributes to their understanding of the world in which they live today. In this example on page 690 the authors take a look at The Environmental Movement and how many of the issues we face today were raised during the Progressive Era of the late 1800's-early 1900's. *Other examples may be found on pages 94, 286, 412, 812, 850, and 912.*

Take a moment to look at the *From Then to Now* features in every chapter of this book, and notice how they will impart upon your students the profound impact that history holds in the cumulative store of the human experience that it represents. Get Goldfield—and get your students the best relevance.

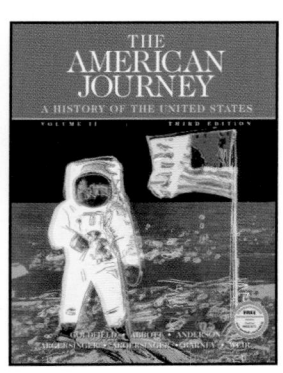

But both the successes and the failures of progressivism revealed that the nature of politics and government had changed significantly. Americans had come to accept that government action could resolve social and economic problems, and the role and power of government expanded accordingly. The emergence of an activist presidency, capable of developing programs, mobilizing public opinion, directing Congress, and taking forceful action, epitomized this key development.

These important features would be crucial when the nation fought World War I, which brought new challenges and dangers to the United States. The Great War would expose many of the limitations of progressivism and the naiveté of the progressives' optimism.

REVIEW QUESTIONS

1. How and why did the presidency change during the Progressive Era?

2. How did the progressive concern for efficiency affect social reform efforts, public education, government administration, and rural life?

3. How and why did the relationship between business and government change during this time?

4. Why did social reform and social control often intermingle in the Progressive Era? Can such objectives be separate?

5. What factors, old and new, stimulated the reform movements of progressivism?

6. How did the role of women change during the Progressive Era? How did that affect progressivism itself?

7. Why did the demand for woman suffrage provoke such determined support and such bitter opposition, as illustrated by the reporters' accounts of the 1913 parade and riot in Washington, D.C.?

KEY TERMS

Australian ballot (p. 679)
Bureau of Reclamation (p. 684)
Conservation (p. 682)
Federal Reserve Act (p. 688)
Federal Trade Commission (p. 688)
Fundamentalists (p. 668)
Initiative (p. 680)
Muckraking (p. 665)
New Freedom (p. 687)
New Nationalism (p. 686)
Niagrara Movement (p. 677)
Nineteenth Amendment (p. 679)

Preservation (p. 683)
Progressive Era (p. 661)
Prohibition (p. 676)
Recall (p. 681)
Referendum (p. 680)
Seventeenth Amendment (p. 681)
Sixteenth Amendment (p. 685)
Social Gospel Movement (p. 664)
Underwood-Simmons Tariff Act (p. 688)
Wobblies (p. 666)

RECOMMENDED READING

Addams, Jane. *Twenty Years at Hull House* (1910). Jane Addams's own classic story of settlement work.

Clements, Kendrick A. *The Presidency of Woodrow Wilson* (1992). An excellent book that provides important new information on both Wilson and the presidency.

Deverell, William, and Tom Sitton. *California Progressivism Revisited* (1994). A valuable collection of essays that examines the complex motivations underlying progressivism in California.

Diner, Steven J. *A Very Different Age: Americans of the Progressive Era* (1998). An engaging survey of the era, stressing social history.

Gould, Lewis L. *The Presidency of Theodore Roosevelt* (1991). A balanced and comprehensive account of TR's presidency.

Link, Arthur S., and Richard L. McCormick. *Progressivism* (1983). A superb brief analysis of the complexities and scholarly interpretations of progressivism.

Sinclair, Upton. *The Jungle* (1906). The most famous muckraking novel.

Wiebe, Robert. *The Search for Order, 1877–1920.* (1967). A masterful essay that emphasizes the organizational thrust of middle-class progressives.

ADDITIONAL SOURCES

The Ferment of Reform

Blair, Karen. *The Clubwoman as Feminist: True Womanhood Redefined, 1868–1914* (1980).

Chambers, John W. *The Tyranny of Change* (2nd ed., 1992).

Chesler, Ellen. *Woman of Valor: The Life of Margaret Sanger* (1992).

Cott, Nancy. *The Grounding of Modern Feminism* (1987).

Curtis, Susan. *A Consuming Faith: The Social Gospel and Modern American Culture* (1991).

Danbom, David B. *"The World of Hope": Progressives and the Struggle for an Ethical Public Life* (1987).

Dubofsky, Melvyn. *We Shall Be All: A History of the Industrial Workers of the World* (1969).

Marsden, George. *Fundamentalism and American Culture* (1980).

May, Henry. *Protestant Churches and Industrial America* (1949).

Peiss, Kathy. *Cheap Amusements: Working Women and Leisure in Turn-of-the-Century New York* (1986).

Rodgers, Daniel. *Atlantic Crossings: Social Politics in a Progressive Age* (1998**).**

Salvatore, Nick. *Eugene V. Debs: Citizen and Socialist* (1982).

Scott, Anne Firor. *Natural Allies: Women's Associations in American History* (1991).

Shore, Elliott. *Talkin' Socialism: J. A. Wayland and the Role of the Press in American Radicalism* (1988).

Wheeler, Margaret Spruill. *New Women of the New South* (1993).

Reforming Society

Boyer, Paul. *Urban Masses and Moral Order in America* (1978).

Carson, Mina. *Settlement Folk: Social Thought and the American Settlement Movement* (1990).

Crocker, Ruth H. *Social Work and Social Order* (1992).

Danbom, David. *The Resisted Revolution: Urban America and the Industrialization of Agriculture* (1979).

Davis, Allen F. *American Heroine: The Life and Legend of Jane Addams* (1973).

Davis, Allen F. *Spearheads of Reform: The Social Settlements and the Progressive Movement* (1968).

Dorsett, Lyle. *Billy Sunday and the Redemption of Urban America* (1991).

Dye, Nancy S. *As Equals and as Sisters: Feminism, the Labor Movement, and the Women's Trade Union League of New York* (1980).

Frankel, Noralee, and Nancy S. Dye. *Gender, Class, Race, and Reform in the Progressive Era* (1991).

Gorn, Elliott. *Mother Jones: The Most Dangerous Woman in America* (2001).

Hamm, Richard. *Shaping the Eighteenth Amendment* (1995).

Harlan, Louis. *Booker T. Washington: The Wizard of Tuskegee* (1983).

Higham, John. *Strangers in the Land: Patterns of American Nativism* (1963).

Ladd-Taylor, Molly. *Mother-Work: Women, Child Welfare, and the State, 1890-1930* (1994).

Lindenmeyer, Kriste. *A Right to Childhood: The U.S. Children's Bureau and Child Welfare* (1997).

Link, William A. *The Paradox of Southern Progressivism* (1992).

Lubove, Roy. *The Progressives and the Slums* (1962).

Muncy, Robyn. *Creating a Female Dominion in American Reform, 1890–1935* (1991).

Nelson, Daniel. *Frederick W. Taylor and the Rise of Scientific Management* (1980).

Payne, Elizabeth Anne. *Reform, Labor, and Feminism: Margaret Dreier Robins and the Women's Trade Union League* (1988).

Timberlake, James. *Prohibition and the Progressive Movement* (1963).

Reforming Politics and Government

Baker, Jean H. ed. *Votes for Women* (2002).

Buenker, John D. *Urban Liberalism and Progressive Reform* (1973).

DuBois, Ellen Carol. *Harriot Stanton Blatch and the Winning of Woman Suffrage* (1997).

Graham, Sara Hunter. *Woman Suffrage and the New Democracy* (1996).

Grantham, Dewey. *Southern Progressivism* (1983).

Gustafson, Melanie S. *Women and the Republican Party* (2001).

Holmes, William F. *The White Chief: James Kimble Vardaman* (1970).

Kirby, Jack Temple. *Darkness at the Dawning: Race and Reform in the Progressive South* (1972).

Kousser, J. Morgan. *The Shaping of Southern Politics* (1974).

McCormick, Richard L. *From Realignment to Reform: Political Change in New York State, 1893–1910* (1983).

McGerr, Michael E. *The Decline of Popular Politics* (1986).

Pegram, Thomas. *Partisans and Progressives* (1992).

Reynolds, John F. *Testing Democracy: Electoral Behavior and Progressive Reform in New Jersey* (1988).

Schiesl, Martin. *The Politics of Efficiency: Municipal Administration and Reform in America* (1977).

Thelen, David P. *The New Citizenship: Origins of Progressivism in Wisconsin* (1972).

Thelen, David P. *Robert M. La Follette and the Insurgent Spirit* (1976).

Unger, Nancy. *Fighting Bob La Follette: The Righteous Reformer* (2000).

Wesser, Robert F. *Charles Evans Hughes: Politics and Reform in New York State* (1967).

Wright, James E. *The Progressive Yankees: Republican Reformers in New Hampshire* (1987).

Theodore Roosevelt and the Progressive Presidency

Blum, John M. *The Republican Roosevelt* (1954).

Brands, H.W. *T.R.: The Last Romantic* (1997).

Burton, David. *The Learned Presidency: Theodore Roosevelt, William Howard Taft, Woodrow Wilson* (1988).

Coletta, Paolo. *The Presidency of William Howard Taft* (1973).

Harbaugh, William H. *Power and Responsibility: The Life and Times of Theodore Roosevelt* (1961).

Hays, Samuel P. *Conservation and the Gospel of Efficiency: The Progressive Conservation Movement* (1962).

Keller, Morton. *Regulating a New Economy* (1990).

Kolko, Gabriel. *The Triumph of Conservatism* (1963).

Morris, Edmund. *Theodore Rex* (2002).

Mowry, George E. *The Era of Theodore Roosevelt, 1900–1912* (1958).

Sanders, Elizabeth. *Roots of Reform: Farmers, Workers, and the American State* (1999).

Sklar, Martin. *The Corporate Reconstruction of American Capitalism* (1988).

Worster, Donald. *Rivers of Empire: Water, Aridity, and the Growth of the American West* (1985).

Woodrow Wilson and Progressive Reform

Blum, John M. *Woodrow Wilson and the Politics of Morality* (1956).

Clements, Kendrick A. *Woodrow Wilson* (1987).

Cooper, John Milton, Jr. *The Warrior and the Priest: Woodrow Wilson and Theodore Roosevelt* (1983).

Gould, Lewis L. *Reform and Regulation: American Politics, From Roosevelt to Wilson* (1996).

Hecksher, August. *Woodrow Wilson* (1991).

Link, Arthur. *Woodrow Wilson and the Progressive Era* (1954).

Livingston, James. *Origins of the Federal Reserve System* (1986).

Sarasohn, David. *The Party of Reform: Democrats in the Progressive Era* (1989).

Thompson, John A. *Woodrow Wilson* (2002).

Urofsky, Melvin. *Louis D. Brandeis and the Progressive Tradition* (1981).

WHERE TO LEARN MORE

- **John Muir National Historic Site, Martinez, California.** The architecture and furnishings of this seventeen-room house reflect the interests of John Muir, the writer and naturalist who founded the Sierra Club and led the preservationists in the Progressive Era. www.nps. gov/jomu/.

- **National Museum of American History, Smithsonian Institution, Washington, D.C.** A permanent exhibition, "Parlor to Politics: Women and Reform, 1890–1925," uses design, artifacts, and recent scholarship to vividly illustrate the changing role of women in the Progressive Era. It effectively emphasizes their work in settlement houses and their growing politicization and demonstrates the importance of the work of black women's organizations.

- **Hull House, Chicago, Illinois.** This pioneering settlement house is now a museum on the campus of the University of Illinois, Chicago. www.uic.edu/jaddams/hull/hull_house.html.

- **Lowell National Historic Park, Lowell, Massachusetts.** "The Working People," a permanent exhibition, uses artifacts and photographs to chart the activities of immigrant workers at different times in the past, particularly during the Progressive Era. www.nps.gov/lowe/.

- **Lower East Side Tenement Museum, New York City, New York.** A six-story tenement building containing twenty-two apartments, this museum vividly illustrates the congested and unhealthy living conditions of urban immigrants from the 1870s to the early twentieth century. See www.tenement.org/ for a virtual tour.

- **Sagamore Hill, Oyster Bay, New York.** Theodore Roosevelt's home is now a National Historic Site and open to the public. www.nps.gov/sahi/.

- **William Howard Taft National Historic Site, Cincinnati, Ohio.** Taft was born in this house, the only national Taft memorial. An informative tour focuses on Taft's public and private life.

- **Staunton, Virginia.** The birthplace and childhood home of Woodrow Wilson, restored with period furnishings, reveals many of the influences that shaped Wilson's career.

 Please refer to the document CD-ROM for primary sources related to this chapter.

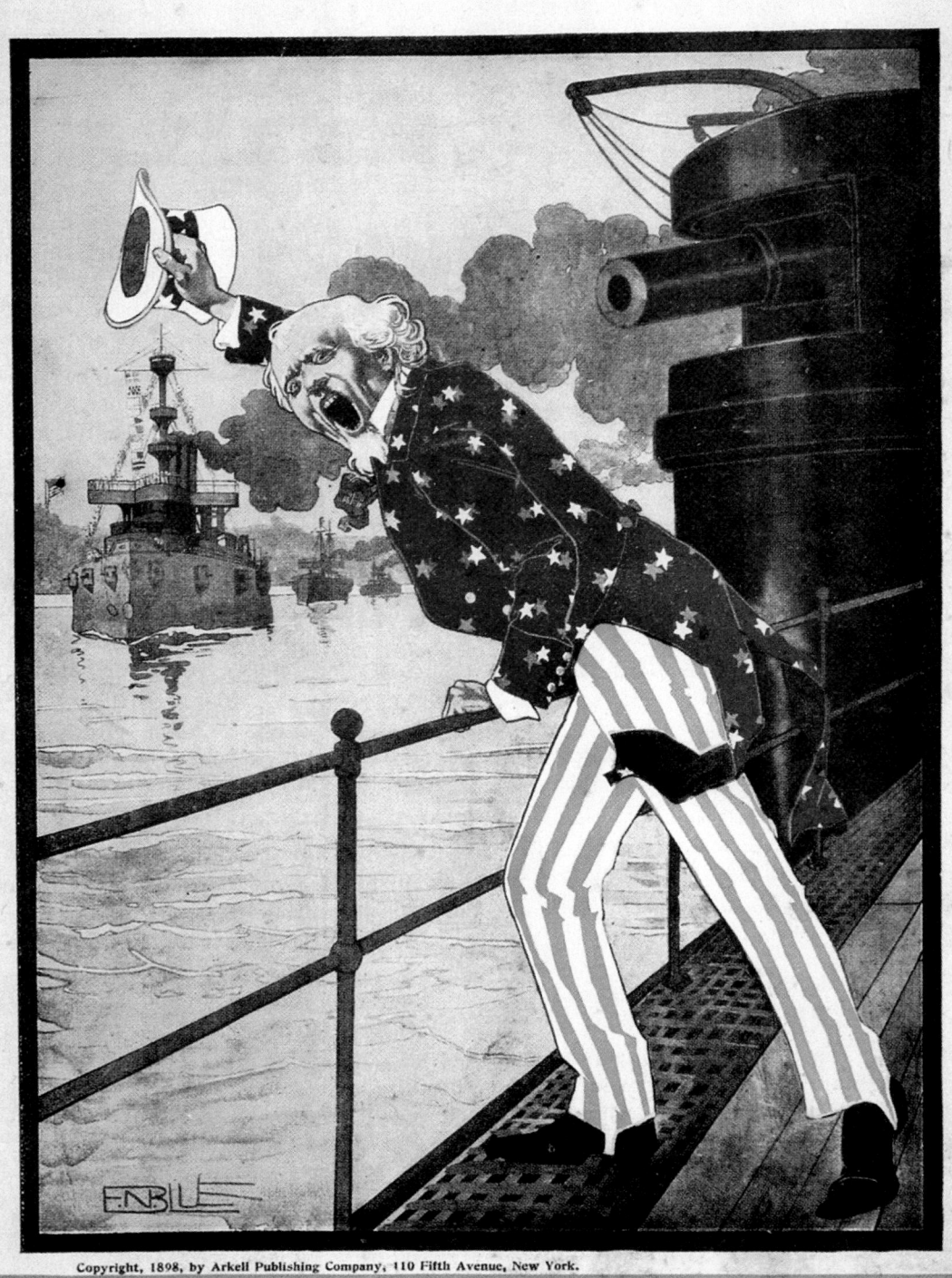

➔ *A jubilant Uncle Sam celebrates victory in the Spanish-American War and anticipates the building of an American Empire.*

CREATING AN EMPIRE 22
1865–1917

Havana, Cuba

October 1901

When the Spanish-American war was declared the United States took a step forward, and assumed a position as protector of the interests of Cuba. It became responsible for the welfare of the people, politically, mentally, and morally. The mere fact of freeing the island from Spanish rule has not ended the care which this country should give. . . . The effect will be to uplift the people, gaining their permanent friendship and support and greatly increasing our own commerce. At present there are two million people requiring clothing and food, for but a small proportion of the necessaries of life are raised on the island. It is folly to grow food crops when sugar and tobacco produce such rich revenues in comparison. The United States should supply the Cubans with their breadstuffs, even wine, fruit, and vegetables, and should clothe the people. . . . The money received for their crops will be turned over in a great measure in buying supplies from the United States. . . .

Naturally the manufacturers of the United States should have precedence in furnishing machinery, locomotives, cars, and rails, materials for buildings and bridges, and the wide diversity of other supplies required, as well as fuel for their furnaces. With the present financial and commercial uncertainty at an end the people of the island will . . . come into the American market as customers for products of many kinds.

CHAPTER OUTLINE

The Roots of Imperialism
Ideological Arguments
Strategic Concerns
Economic Designs

First Steps
Seward and Blaine
Hawaii
Chile and Venezuela

The Spanish-American War
The Cuban Revolution
Growing Tensions
War and Empire
The Treaty of Paris

Imperial Ambitions: The United States and East Asia, 1899–1917
The Filipino-American War
China and the Open Door
Rivalry with Japan and Russia

Imperial Power: The United States and Latin America, 1899–1917
U.S. Rule in Puerto Rico
Cuba as a U.S. Protectorate
The Panama Canal
The Roosevelt Corollary
Dollar Diplomacy
Wilsonian Interventions

Conclusion

The meeting of the Constitutional Convention on November 5th will be an event in Cuban history of the greatest importance, and much will depend upon the action and outcome of this convention as to our future control of the island. . . . I considered it unwise to interfere, and I have made it a settled policy to permit the Cubans to manage every part of their constitution-making. This has been due to my desire to prevent any possible charge of crimination being brought against the United States in the direction of their constitutional affairs. . . .

There is no distrust of the United States on the part of the Cubans, and I know of no widespread antipathy to this country, its people, or its institutions. There are, of course, a handful of malcontents, as there must be in every country. . . .

I could not well conceive how the Cubans could be otherwise than grateful to the United States for its efforts in their behalf. The reconstruction of the island has proceeded rapidly from the first, and I think the transformation is without any superior in the history of modern times. The devastation of the long war had left the island in an unparalleled condition when the United States interfered, and in the brief time since the occupation of the island by American troops the island has been completely rehabilitated—agriculturally, commercially, financially, educationally, and governmentally. This improvement has been so rapid and so apparent that no Cuban could mistake it. To doubt in the face of these facts that their liberators were not still their faithful friends would be impossible.

Major–General Leonard Wood, "The Future of Cuba," *The Independent* 54 (January 23, 1902): 193–194; and Wood, "The Cuban Convention," *The Independent* 52 (November 1, 1900): 265–266.

General Leonard Wood's reports on Cuba, then under his control as military governor, captured the complex mixture of attitudes and motives that underlay the journey of the United States from a developing nation to a world power. Plans for economic expansion, a belief in national mission, a sense of responsibility to help others, scarcely hidden religious impulses and racist convictions—all combined in an uneasy mixture of self-interest and idealism. Such a variety of motives, to say nothing of the positive spin that Wood could impart to them, helped garner support for the new policies that the nation's leaders adopted, including extending American control over Cuba.

Wood himself had taken a symbolic journey in American expansionism. His earlier career had been on the American southwestern frontier, with the troops chasing the Apache under Geronimo, but in 1898 he and Theodore Roosevelt formed the Rough Riders cavalry to participate in the Spanish-American War in Cuba. As Wood wrote on the transport ships headed for that Spanish colony: "this is the first great expedition our country has sent overseas and marks the commencement of a new era in our relations with the world." Upon Spain's surrender, Cuba came under United States military occupation, and Wood was appointed military governor of the island.

Wood's support for the war was reflected as well in his activities as a colonial administrator. Convinced of the superiority of American institutions, he favored their expansion. The United States had a responsibility, he believed, to uplift those less able. But expansion would promote American interests as well. Thus, Wood brought improved sanitation, schools, and transportation to Cuba, but he instituted these reforms through an authoritarian government and regarded Cubans as backward and incapable of self-government. And at the same time, he expected that American business interests would "naturally" be the beneficiaries of his reorganization of Cuban life. Thus Wood combined changes that satisfied paternalistic or humanitarian instincts with attempts to incorporate Cuba into America's new commercial empire, fulfilling the traditional colonial role of providing raw materials and serving as a market for American products and capital.

The tension between what one friend called the "righteous" and the "selfish" aspects of expanding American influence lay beneath the surface in Wood's reports. His claim that he was not interfering with Cuba's constitutional convention was disingenuous, for he had already undertaken to limit those who could participate as voters or delegates and was even then devising means to restrict its autonomy. And in his repeated insistence that the Cubans were "grateful" for the intervention of "their faithful friends," the Americans, Wood obviously protested too much: Cubans, as well as Filipinos, Puerto Ricans, and others, rarely perceived American motives or American actions as positively as did Wood and other proponents of American expansion. Military victory in the Spanish-American War had provided the United States with an extensive empire, status as a world power, and opportunities and problems that would long shape American foreign policy.

KEY TOPICS

- Why the United States became an imperial power in the 1890s
- The Spanish-American War and the colonial empire the United States gained as a result
- U.S. involvement in Asia, and the tensions with Japan that resulted
- U.S. predominance in the Caribbean and Latin America

THE ROOTS OF IMPERIALISM

The United States had a long-established tradition of expansion across the continent. Through purchase, negotiation, or conquest, the vast Louisiana Territory, Florida, Texas, New Mexico, California, and Oregon had become U.S. territory. Indeed, by the 1890s, Republican Senator Henry Cabot Lodge of Massachusetts boasted that Americans had "a record of conquest, colonization, and territorial expansion unequalled by any people in the nineteenth century." Lodge now urged the country to build an overseas empire, emulating the European model of **imperialism** based on the acquisition and exploitation of colonial possessions. Other Americans favored a less formal empire, in which United States interests and influence would be assured through extensive trade and investments rather than through military occupation. Still others advocated a cultural expansionism in which the nation exported its ideals and institutions. All such expansionists could draw from many sources to support their plans. Some cited political, religious, and racial ideas; some were concerned with national security and power; others pointed to economic trends at home and abroad (see the Overview table, "Rationales for Imperialism").

IDEOLOGICAL ARGUMENTS

Scholars, authors, politicians, and religious leaders provided interlocking ideological arguments for the new imperialism. Some intellectuals, for example, invoked social Darwinism, maintaining that the United States should engage in a competitive struggle for wealth and power with other nations. "The survival of the fittest," declared one writer, was "the law of nations as well as a law of nature." As European nations expanded into Asia and Africa in the 1880s and 1890s, seeking colonies, markets, and raw materials, these advocates argued that the United States had to adopt similar policies to insure national success.

Related to social Darwinism was a pervasive belief in racial inequality and, particularly, in the superiority of people of English, or Anglo-Saxon, descent. To many Americans, the industrial progress, military strength, and political development of England and the United States were proof of an Anglo-Saxon superiority that carried with it a responsibility to extend the blessings of their rule to less able people. John Fiske, a philosopher and historian, popularized these ideas in his oft-repeated lecture "Manifest Destiny." "The work which the English race began when it colonized North America," Fiske declaimed, "is destined to go on until every land on the earth's surface that is not already the seat of an old civilization shall become English in its language, in its religion, in its political habits and traditions, and to a predominant extent in the blood of its people." As a popular expression put it, colonialism was the "white man's burden," carrying with it a duty to aid and uplift other peoples. Such attitudes led some expansionists to favor imposing American ideas and practices on other cultures, regardless

Chronology

1861–1869	Seward serves as secretary of state.
1867	U.S. purchases Alaska from Russia.
1870	Annexation of the Dominican Republic is rejected.
1881	Naval Advisory Board is created.
1887	United States gains naval rights to Pearl Harbor.
1889	First Pan-American Conference is held.
1890	Alfred Thayer Mahan publishes *The Influence of Sea Power upon History*.
1893	Harrison signs but Cleveland rejects a treaty for the annexation of Hawaii.
1893–1897	Depression increases interest in economic expansion abroad.
1894–1895	Sino-Japanese War is fought.
1895	U.S. intervenes in Great Britain–Venezuelan boundary dispute.
	Cuban insurrection against Spain begins.
1896	William McKinley is elected president on an imperialist platform.
1898	Spanish-American War is fought.
	Hawaii is annexed.
	Anti-Imperialist League is organized.
	Treaty of Paris is signed.
1899–1902	Filipino-American War is fought.
1899	Open Door note is issued.
1901	Theodore Roosevelt becomes president.
1903	Platt Amendment restricts Cuban autonomy.
	Panama "revolution" is abetted by the United States.
1904	United States acquires the Panama Canal Zone.
	Roosevelt Corollary is announced.
1904–1905	Russo-Japanese War is fought.
1905	Treaty of Portsmouth ends the Russo-Japanese War through U.S. mediation.
1906–1909	United States occupies Cuba.
1907–1908	Gentlemen's Agreement restricts Japanese immigration.
1909	United States intervenes in Nicaragua.
1912–1933	United States occupies Nicaragua.
1914	Panama Canal opens.
1914–1917	United States intervenes in Mexico.
1915–1934	United States occupies Haiti.
1916–1924	United States occupies the Dominican Republic.
1917	Puerto Ricans are granted U.S. citizenship.
1917–1922	United States occupies Cuba.

of those cultures' own values and customs. The political scientist John W. Burgess, for example, concluded that Anglo-Saxons "must have a colonial policy" and "righteously assume sovereignty" over "incompetent" or "barbaric races" in other lands.

Reflecting such aggressiveness, as well as Darwinian anxieties, some Americans endorsed expansion as consistent with their ideals of masculinity. Forceful expansion would be a manly course, relying upon and building strength and honor among American males. Men who would not shirk the challenges of empire would thereby improve their ability to compete in the international arena. "Pride of race, courage, manliness," predicted one enthusiast, would be both the causes and the consequences of assertive foreign policies.

American missionaries also promoted expansionist sentiment. Hoping to evangelize the world, American religious groups increased the number of Protestant foreign missions sixfold from 1870 to 1900. Women in particular organized foreign missionary societies and served in the missions. Missionaries publi-

cized their activities throughout the United States, generating interest in foreign developments and support for what one writer called the "imperialism of righteousness." Abroad they pursued a religious transformation that often resembled a cultural conversion, for they promoted trade, developed business interests, and encouraged westernization through technology and education as well as religion. Sometimes, as in the Hawaiian Islands, American missionaries even promoted annexation by the United States.

Indeed, the American religious press endlessly repeated the themes of national destiny, racial superiority, and religious zeal. The Reverend J.H. Barrows in early 1898 lectured on the "Christian conquest of Asia," suggesting that American Christianity and commerce would cross the Pacific to fulfill "the manifest destiny of the Christian Republic." Missionaries also contributed to the imperial impulse by describing their work, as Barrows did, in terms of the "conquest" of "enemy" territory. Thus, while missionaries were motivated by what they considered to be idealism and often brought real benefits to other lands, especially in education and health, religious sentiments reinforced the ideology of American expansion.

STRATEGIC CONCERNS

Other expansionists were motivated by strategic concerns, shaped by what they saw as the forces of history and geography. America's location in the Western Hemisphere, its coastlines on two oceans, and the ambitions and activities of other nations, particularly Germany and Britain, convinced some Americans that the United States had to develop new policies to protect and promote its national security and interests. Alfred Thayer Mahan, a naval officer and president of the Naval War College, emphasized the importance of a strong navy for national greatness in his book *The Influence of Sea Power Upon History*. To complement that navy, Mahan proposed that the United States build a canal across the isthmus of Panama to link its coasts, acquire naval bases in the Caribbean and the Pacific to protect the canal, and annex Hawaii and other Pacific islands to promote trade and service the fleet. The United States must "cast aside the policy of isolation which befitted her infancy," Mahan declared, and "begin to look outward."

An American missionary and her Chinese converts study the Bible in Manchuria in 1903 under a U. S. flag. American missionaries wanted to spread the Gospel abroad but inevitably spread American influence as well.

Mahanism found a receptive audience. President Benjamin Harrison declared in 1891 that "as to naval stations and points of influence, we must look forward to a departure from the too conservative opinions which have been held heretofore." Still more vocal advocates of Mahan's program were a group of nationalistic Republicans, predominantly from the Northeast.

Overview

Rationales for Imperialism

Category	Beliefs
Racism and social Darwinism	Convictions that "Anglo-Saxons" were racially superior and should dominate other peoples, either to ensure national success, establish international stability, or benefit the "inferior" races by imposing American ideas and institutions on them
Righteousness	The conviction that Christianity, and a supporting American culture, should be aggressively spread among the benighted peoples of other lands
Mahanism	The conviction, following the ideas advanced by Alfred Thayer Mahan, that U.S. security required a strong navy and economic and territorial expansion
Economics	A variety of arguments holding that American prosperity depended on acquiring access to foreign markets, raw materials, and investment opportunities

They included such politicians as Henry Cabot Lodge and Theodore Roosevelt, such journalists as Whitelaw Reid of the *New York Tribune* and Albert Shaw of the *Review of Reviews*, and such diplomats and lawyers as John Hay and Elihu Root.

Conscious of European colonialism, these men favored imperial expansion, as Shaw wrote, "for the sake of our destiny, our dignity, our influence, and our usefulness." Theodore Roosevelt promoted Mahan's ideas when he became assistant secretary of the navy in 1897, but he was even more militaristic. Praising "the most valuable of all qualities, the soldierly virtues," Roosevelt declared in 1897: "No triumph of peace is quite so great as the supreme triumphs of war." One British observer concluded on the eve of the Spanish-American War that Mahan's influence had transformed the American spirit, serving "as oil to the flame of 'colonial expansion' everywhere leaping into life" (see "American Views: An Imperialist Views the World").

Even so, Mahan was not solely responsible for the large navy policy popular among imperialists. Its origins went back to 1881, when Congress established the Naval Advisory Board, which successfully lobbied for larger naval appropriations. An extensive program to replace the navy's obsolete wooden ships with modern cruisers and battleships was well under way by 1890, when the first volume of Mahan's book appeared. The United States soon possessed the formidable navy the expansionists wanted. This larger navy, in turn, demanded strategic bases and coaling stations. One writer indicated the circular nature of this development by noting in 1893 that Manifest Destiny now meant "the acquisition of such territory, far and near," that would secure "to our navy facilities desirable for the operations of a great naval power."

ECONOMIC DESIGNS

One reason for the widespread support for a larger navy was its use to expand and protect America's international trade. Nearly all Americans favored economic expansion through foreign trade. Such a policy promised national prosperity: larger markets for manufacturers and farmers, greater profits for merchants and bankers, more jobs for workers. Far fewer favored the acquisition of colonies that was characteristic of European imperialism. Commercial, as opposed to colonial, goals were the primary objective. As one diplomat declared in 1890, the nation was more interested in the "annexation of trade" than in the annexation of territory.

The United States had long aggressively fostered American trade, especially in Latin America and East Asia. As early as 1844, the United States had negotiated a trade treaty with China, and ten years later a squadron under Commodore Matthew Perry had forced the Japanese to open their ports to American products. In the late nineteenth century, the dramatic expansion of the economy caused many Americans to favor more government action to open foreign markets to American exports. Alabama Senator John Morgan had the cotton and textiles produced in the New South in mind when he warned in 1882: "Our home market is not equal to the demands of our producing and manufacturing classes and to the capital which is seeking employment. . . . We must either enlarge the field of our traffic, or stop the business of manufacturing just where it is." More ominous, a naval officer trying to open Korea to U.S. products declared in 1878, "At least one-third of our mechanical and agricultural products are now in excess of our wants, and we must *export* these products or *deport* the people who are creating them."

Exports, particularly of manufactured goods, which grew ninefold between 1865 and 1900, did increase greatly in the late nineteenth century. Still, periodic depressions fed these fears of overproduction. The massive unemployment and social unrest that accompanied these economic crises also provided social and political arguments for economic relief through foreign trade.

In the depression of the 1890s, with the secretary of state seeing "symptoms of revolution" in the Pullman strike and Coxey's Army of unemployed workers (see Chapter 20), this interest in foreign trade became obsessive. More systematic government efforts to promote trade seemed necessary, a conclusion strengthened by new threats to existing American markets. In that tumultuous decade, European nations raised tariff barriers against American products, and Japan and the European imperial powers began to restrict commercial opportunities in the areas of China that they controlled. Many American leaders decided that the United States had to adopt decisive new policies or face economic catastrophe.

FIRST STEPS

Despite the growing ideological, strategic, and economic arguments for imperialism, the government only fitfully interested itself in foreign affairs before the mid-1890s. It did not pursue a policy of isolationism from international affairs, for the nation maintained normal diplomatic and trade ties and at times vigorously intervened in Latin America and East Asia. But in general the government deferred to the initiative of private interests, reacted haphazardly to outside events, and did little to create a professional foreign service.

SEWARD AND BLAINE

Despite this generally passive and ineffective approach, two secretaries of state, William H. Seward, secretary under Presidents Abraham Lincoln and Andrew Johnson (1861–1869), and James G. Blaine, secretary under Presidents James Garfield and Benjamin Harrison (1881, 1889–1892), laid the foundation for a larger and more aggressive American role in world affairs. Seward possessed an elaborate imperial vision, based on his understanding of commercial opportunities, strategic necessities, and national destiny. In his concerns for opening East Asia to American commerce and establishing American hegemony over the Caribbean, he anticipated the subsequent course of American expansion. His hopes of annexing Canada and Greenland went unfulfilled, but he did purchase Alaska from Russia in 1867, approve the navy's occupation of the Midway Islands in the Pacific, push American trade on a re-

luctant Japan, and repeatedly try to acquire Caribbean naval bases (see Map 22-1). But his policy of expansion, as one observer noted, "went somewhat too far and too fast for the public," and many of his plans fizzled. Congressional opposition frustrated his efforts to obtain Haiti and the Dominican Republic and to purchase the Danish West Indies; Colombia blocked his attempt to gain construction rights for a canal across the isthmus of Panama.

The Grant administration (1869–1877) haphazardly pursued some of Seward's goals but met resistance. When Grant attempted to take over the Dominican Republic in 1870, for example, the Senate defeated the annexation treaty. Opponents of overseas expansion complained of its cost, worried about the "alien races" it would incorporate into the nation, and, above all, condemned it as contrary to basic American principles. Such anticolonial sentiments would weaken, however, in the next generation.

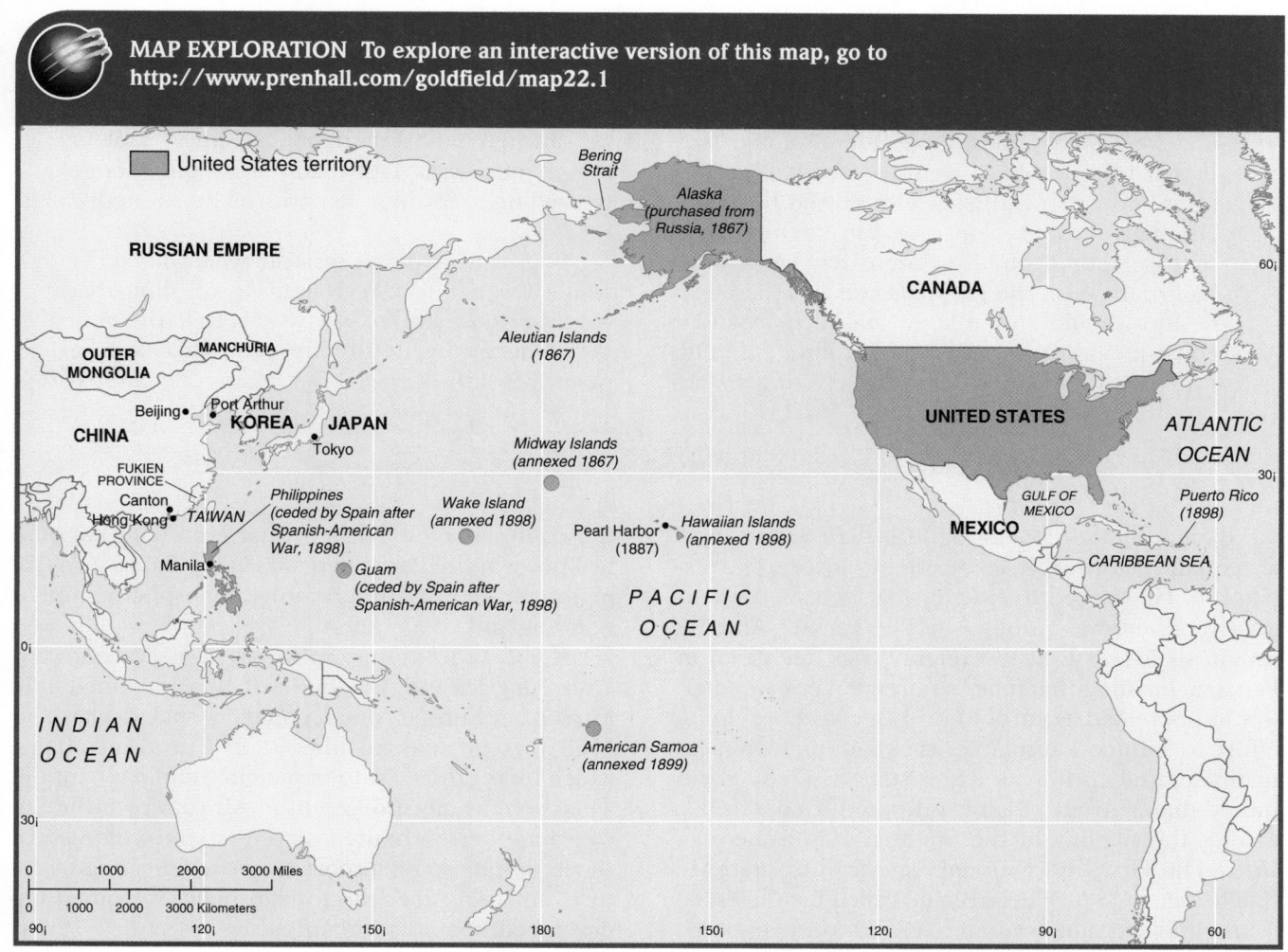

MAP EXPLORATION To explore an interactive version of this map, go to
http://www.prenhall.com/goldfield/map22.1

MAP 22-1   **United States Expansion in the Pacific, 1867-1899**
Pursuing visions of a commercial empire in the Pacific, the United States steadily expanded its territorial possessions as well as its influence there in the late nineteenth century.

AMERICAN VIEWS

An Imperialist Views the World

Theodore Roosevelt, Henry Cabot Lodge, Alfred Thayer Mahan, and other influential imperialists frequently corresponded with one another, expressing their views forcefully if not always in depth. The following excerpts are from Roosevelt's private correspondence in 1897, while he was assistant secretary of the Navy and before the Spanish-American War began.

- In what ways does Roosevelt reflect the influence of Mahan?
- What is Roosevelt's view of war?
- How does Roosevelt view European nations?
- How does he view the independence of other nations in the Western Hemisphere?

I suppose that I need not tell you that as regards Hawaii I take your views absolutely, as indeed I do on foreign policy generally. If I had my way we would annex those islands tomorrow. If that is impossible I would establish a protectorate over them. I believe we should build the Nicaraguan canal at once, and in the meantime that we should build a dozen new battleships, half of them on the Pacific Coast; and these battleships should have a large coal capacity and a consequent increased radius of action. . . . I think President Cleveland's action [in rejecting the an-

nexation of Hawaii] was a colossal crime, and we should be guilty of aiding him after the fact if we do not reverse what he did. I earnestly hope we can make the President [McKinley] look at things our way. Last Saturday night Lodge pressed his views upon him with all his strength.

I agree with all you say as to what will be the result if we fail to take Hawaii. It will show that we either have lost, or else wholly lack, the masterful instinct which alone can make a race great. I feel so deeply about it I hardly dare ex-

---

Blaine, though less thoughtful than Seward, was an equally vigorous, if inconsistent, advocate of expansion. He worked to extend what he called America's "commercial empire" in the Pacific. And he sought to insure U.S. sovereignty over any canal in Panama, insisting that it be "a purely American waterway to be treated as part of our own coastline." In an effort to induce Latin American nations to import manufactured products from the United States rather than Europe, Blaine proposed a conference among the nations of the Western Hemisphere in 1881. The First International American Conference finally met in 1889. There Blaine called for the establishment of a customs union to reduce trade barriers. He expected this union to strengthen U.S. control of hemispheric markets. The Latin American nations, however, wary of economic subordination to the colossus of the north, rejected Blaine's plan. Instead,

the conference established what eventually came to be known as the **Pan American Union**. Based in Washington, it helped to promote hemispheric understanding and cooperation.

If U.S. officials were increasingly assertive toward Latin America and Asia, however, they remained little involved in Europe (one secretary of state declared in 1885 that he had no interest in European affairs, which he regarded "with impatience and contempt"). They were wholly indifferent to Africa, which the European powers were then carving up into colonies. In short, despite some important precedents for the future, much of American foreign policy remained undeveloped, sporadic, and impulsive.

HAWAII

Blaine regarded Hawaii as "indispensably" part of "the American system." As early as 1842, the United States press myself in full. The terrible part is to see that it is the men of education who take the lead in trying to make us prove traitors to our race.

I fully realize the importance of the Pacific coast. . . . But there are big problems in the West Indies also. Until we definitely turn Spain out of those islands (and if I had my way that would be done tomorrow), we will always be menaced by trouble there. We should acquire the Danish Islands [in the West Indies], and by turning Spain out should serve notice that no strong European power, and especially not Germany, should be allowed to gain a foothold by supplanting some weak European power. I do not fear England; Canada is a hostage for her good behavior.

I wish we had a perfectly consistent foreign policy, and that this policy was that every European power should be driven out of America, and every foot of American soil, including the nearest islands in both the Pacific and the Atlantic, should be in the hands of independent American states, and so far as possible in the possession of the United States or under its protection.

To speak with a frankness which our timid friends would call brutal, I would regard a war

with Spain from two standpoints: first, the advisability on the grounds both of humanity and self-interest of interfering on behalf of the Cubans, and of taking one more step toward the complete freeing of America from European dominion; second, the benefit done our people by giving them something to think of which isn't material gain, and especially the benefit done our military forces by trying both the Navy and the Army in actual practice. I should be very sorry not to see us make the experiment of trying to land, and therefore feed and clothe, an expeditionary force [on Cuba], if only for the sake of learning from our own blunders. I should hope that the force would have some fighting to do. It would be a great lesson, and we would profit much by it.

I wish there was a chance that the [U.S. battleship] Maine was going to be used against some foreign power; by preference Germany—but I am not particular, and I'd take even Spain if nothing better offered.

Source: Reprinted by permission of the publisher from *The Letters of Theodore Roosevelt* Volume I 1868–1898, selected and edited by Elting E. Morison, Cambridge: Harvard University Press.

---

had announced its opposition to European control of Hawaii, a key way station in the China trade, where New England missionaries and whalers were active. Although the islands remained under native monarchs, American influence grew, particularly as other Americans arrived to establish sugar plantations and eventually dominate the economy.

Treaties in 1875 and 1887 integrated the islands into the American economy and gave the United States control over Pearl Harbor on the island of Oahu. In 1887, the United States rejected a proposal from Britain and France for a joint guarantee of Hawaii's independence and endorsed a new Hawaiian constitution that gave political power to wealthy white residents. The obvious next step was U.S. annexation, which Blaine endorsed in 1891.

A combination of factors soon impelled American planters to bid for annexation. The McKinley Tariff

Act of 1890 effectively closed the U.S. market to Hawaiian sugar producers, facing them with economic ruin. At the same time, Queen Liliuokalani moved to restore native control of Hawaiian affairs. To insure market access and protect their political authority, the American planters decided to seek annexation to the United States. In 1893, they overthrew the queen. John Stevens, the American minister, ordered U.S. Marines to help the rebels. He then declared an American protectorate over the new Hawaiian government and wired Washington: "The Hawaiian pear is now fully ripe, and this is the golden hour for the United States to pluck it." A delegation from the new provisional government, containing no native Hawaiians, went to Washington to draft a treaty for annexation. President Harrison signed the pact but could not get Senate approval before the new Cleveland administration took office.

Grover Cleveland immediately called for an investigation of the whole affair. Soon convinced that "the undoubted sentiment of the people is for the Queen, against the provisional Government, and against annexation," Cleveland apologized to the queen for the "flagrant wrong" done her by the "reprehensible conduct of the American minister and the unauthorized presence on land of a military force of the United States." But the American-dominated provisional government refused to step down, and Cleveland's rejection of annexation set off a noisy debate in the United States.

Many Republicans strongly supported annexation, which they regarded as merely part of a larger plan of expansion. One eastern Republican manufacturer called for the annexation of Hawaii as the first step toward making the Pacific "an American ocean, dominated by American commercial enterprise for all time." On the West Coast, where California business interests had close ties with the islands, the commercial and strategic value of Hawaii seemed obvious. The *San Francisco Examiner* declared, "Hoist the Stars and Stripes. It is a case of manifest destiny." Reflecting racial imperialism, others argued that annexation would both fittingly reward the enterprising white residents of Hawaii and provide an opportunity to civilize native Hawaiians.

Democrats generally opposed annexation. They doubted, as Missouri Senator George Vest declared, whether the United States should desert its traditional principles and "venture upon the great colonial system of the European powers." Most Democrats believed, as one argued, that "the mission of our nation is to build up and make a greater country out of what we have, instead of annexing islands."

The Hawaiian episode of 1893 thus foreshadowed the arguments over imperialism at the end of the century and emphasized the policy differences between Democrats and the increasingly expansionist Republicans.

CHILE AND VENEZUELA

American reactions to developments in other countries in the 1890s also reflected an increasingly assertive national policy and excitable public opinion. In 1891, American sailors on shore leave in Chile became involved in a drunken brawl that left two of them dead, seventeen injured, and dozens in jail. The incident heightened the already tense relations between the United States and Chile. After supporting the unpopular (and losing) side in a recent Chilean revolution, President Harrison had warned the new leaders that "sometime it may be necessary to instruct them." Now, encouraged by a combative navy, he threatened military retaliation against Chile,

COASTING.
The old horse was too slow for Uncle Sam.

As other imperial powers look on, the United States abandons its traditional principles to rush headlong into world affairs. Uncle Sam would not always find it a smooth ride.

provoking an outburst of bellicose nationalism in the United States. Harrison relented only when Chile apologized and paid an indemnity.

A few years later, the United States again threatened war over a minor issue but against a more formidable opponent. Though opposed to annexing Hawaii, President Cleveland adopted an increasingly aggressive policy in Latin America. In 1895, he intervened in a boundary dispute between Great Britain and Venezuela over British Guiana. Cleveland was motivated not only by the long-standing U.S. goal of challenging Britain for Latin American markets but also by ever more expansive notions of the **Monroe Doctrine** and the authority of the United States. He also seized on this foreign policy issue to divert public attention from a severe economic depression. Secretary of State Richard Olney sent Britain a blunt note (a "twenty-inch gun," Cleveland called it) demanding arbitration of the disputed territory and stoutly asserting American supremacy in the Western Hemisphere. Cleveland urged Congress to establish a commission to determine the boundary and enforce its decision by war if necessary. The astonished British ambassador reported an "extraordinary state of excitement into which the Congress of the United States and the whole country were thrown by the warlike Message . . . a condition of mind which can only be described as hysterical." As war fever swept the United States, Britain agreed to arbitration, recognizing the limited nature of the issue that so convulsed Anglo-American relations.

The United States' assertion of hemispheric dominance angered Latin Americans, and their fears deepened when it decided arbitration terms with Britain without consulting Venezuela, which protested before bowing to American pressure. The United States had intervened less to protect Venezuela from the British bully than to advance its own hegemony. The further significance of the Venezuelan crisis, as Captain Mahan noted, lay in its "awakening of our countrymen to the fact that we must come out of our isolation . . . and take our share in the turmoil of the world."

But if these bold steps in Hawaii, Chile, and Venezuela indicated an increasing role for the United States in world affairs, the nation had yet to adopt a consistent policy for expanding its influence. That would happen in the next few years.

THE SPANISH-AMERICAN WAR

The forces pushing the United States toward imperialism and international power came to a head in the Spanish-American War. The war had its origins in Cuba's quest for independence from the oppressive colonial control of Spain. The struggle activated Americans' long-standing interest in the island. Many sympathized with the Cuban rebels' yearning for freedom, others worried that disorder in Cuba threatened their own economic and political interests, and some thought that United States intervention would increase its influence in the Caribbean and along key Pacific routes to Asian markets. But few foresaw that the war that finally erupted in 1898 would dramatically change America's relationships with the rest of the world and give it a colonial empire.

THE CUBAN REVOLUTION

In the nineteenth century, Cubans rebelled repeatedly against Spanish rule. One rebellion, the Ten Years' War from 1868 to 1878, had been brutally suppressed, but not before drawing American interest and sympathy. Cuba was the last major European colony in Latin America, with an economic potential that attracted American business interests and a strategic significance for any Central American canal. In the 1880s, Spanish control became increasingly harsh, even while American investors expanded their economic influence in Cuba. Cuban discontent erupted again in 1895, when the Cuban patriot José Martí launched another revolt.

The rebellion was a classic guerrilla war, in which the rebels controlled the countryside and the Spanish army, the towns and cities. American economic interests were seriously affected, for both Cubans and Spaniards destroyed American property and disrupted American trade. The Cleveland administration, motivated as much by a desire to protect American property and establish a safe environment for further investments as by a concern for Cuban rights, urged Spain to adopt reforms. But the brutality with which Spain attempted to suppress the revolt promoted American sympathy for the Cuban insurgents. Determined to cut the rebels off from their peasant supporters, the Spanish herded most civilians into "reconcentration camps," where tens of thousands died of starvation and disease.

Americans' sympathy was further aroused by the sensationalist **yellow press**. To attract readers and boost advertising revenues, the popular press of the day adopted bold headlines, fevered editorials, and real or exaggerated stories of violence, sex, and corruption. A circulation war between William Randolph Hearst's *New York Journal* and Joseph Pulitzer's *New York World* helped stimulate interest in Cuban war. "Blood on the roadsides, blood on the fields, blood on the doorsteps, blood, blood, blood! The old, the young, the weak, the crippled—all are butchered without mercy," the *World* feverishly reported of Cuba. "Is there no nation wise enough, brave enough to aid this blood-smitten land?" Failure to intervene to protect the innocent from Spanish lust and cruelty, insisted the yellow journalists, would be dishonorable and cowardly.

The nation's religious press, partly because it reflected the prejudice many Protestants held against Catholic Spain, also advocated American intervention. One religious newspaper endorsed an American war against Spain as God's instrument for attacking "that system of iniquity, the papacy." Another promised that if war came, "every Methodist preacher will be a recruiting officer" for the American military. The *Catholic Herald* of New York sarcastically referred to the "bloodthirsty preachers" of the Protestant churches, but such preachers undeniably influenced American opinion against Spain.

As the Cuban rebellion dragged on, more and more Americans advocated intervention to stop the carnage, protect U.S. investments, or uphold various principles. Expansionists, such as Roosevelt and Lodge, clamored for intervention, but so did their opponents. Populists, for example, sympathized with a people seeking independence from colonial rule and petitioned Congress to support the crusade for Cuban freedom; conservative Democrats hoped that the excitement of intervention and war "might do much towards directing the minds of the people from imaginary ills, the relief of which is erroneously supposed to be reached by 'Free Silver.'" In the election of 1896, both major parties endorsed Cuban independence. The Democratic platform expressed "sympathy to the people of Cuba in their heroic struggle for liberty." The Republican platform not only wished Cubans success in "their determined contest for liberty" but urged intervention on the grounds that Spain was "unable to protect the property or lives of resident American citizens."

GROWING TENSIONS

In his 1897 inaugural address, President William McKinley outlined an expansionist program ranging from further enlargement of the navy to the annexation of Hawaii and the construction of a Central American canal in Nicaragua, but his administration soon focused on Cuba. McKinley's principal complaint was that chronic disorder in Cuba disrupted America's investments and agitated public opinion. Personally opposed to military intervention, McKinley first used diplomacy to press Spain to adopt reforms that would settle the rebellion. Following his instructions, the U.S. minister to Spain warned the Spanish government that if it did not quickly establish peace, the United States would take whatever steps it "should deem necessary to procure this result." In late 1897, Spain modified its brutal military tactics and offered limited autonomy to Cuba. But Cubans insisted on complete independence, a demand that Spain refused to grant.

Relations between the United States and Spain deteriorated. In early 1898, the *New York Journal* published a private letter from the Spanish minister to the United States that mocked McKinley as "weak and a bidder for the admiration of the crowd." (The *Journal* called the letter "the worst insult to the United States in its history.") McKinley found more troubling the letter's intimation that Spain was not negotiating in good faith. Only days later, on February 15, 1898, the U.S. battleship *Maine* blew up in Havana harbor, killing 260 men. The Spanish were not responsible for the tragedy, which a modern naval inquiry has attributed to an internal accident. But many Americans agreed with Theodore Roosevelt, the assistant secretary of the navy, who called it "an act of dirty treachery on the part of the Spaniards" and told McKinley that only war was "compatible with our national honor." Others demanded war, in the words of an Illinois politician, "if we would uphold our manhood." Cried another: "American manhood" required "avenging innocent blood." Thus understandings of appropriate male conduct also influenced decisions as to how the nation should act.

Popular anger was inflamed, but the sinking of the *Maine* by itself did not bring war, though it did restrict McKinley's options and pressure him to be more assertive toward Spain. One newspaper expressed its hope to see "any signs, however faint, of manhood in the White House." Other pressures soon began to build on the president. Increasingly, business interests favored war as less disruptive than a volatile peace that threatened their investments. Senator Lodge reported a consensus "that this situation must end. We cannot go on indefinitely with this strain, this suspense, and this uncertainty, this tottering upon the verge of war. It is killing to business." Further, McKinley feared that a moderate policy would endanger congressional candidates. Again Senator Lodge, although hesitant to suggest "war for political reasons," nevertheless advised McKinley, "If the war in Cuba drags on through the summer with nothing done, we shall go down in the greatest [election] defeat ever known."

At the end of March 1898 (when the French ambassador in Washington reported that "a sort of bellicose fury has seized the American nation"), McKinley sent Spain an ultimatum. He demanded an armistice in Cuba, an end to the reconcentration policy, and the acceptance of American arbitration, which implied Cuban independence. Desperately, Spain made concessions, abolishing reconcentration and declaring a unilateral armistice. But McKinley had already begun war preparations, withdrawing American diplomats from Cuba and Spain, ordering the navy to prepare for war, and drafting a war message for Congress. He submitted that message on April 11, asking for authority to use force against Spain "in the name of humanity, in the name of civilization, in behalf of endangered American interests." Congress declared war on Spain on April 25, 1898.

A few national leaders welcomed the war as a step toward imperialism, but there was little popular support for such a policy. Most interventionists were not imperialists, and Congress added the **Teller Amendment** to the war resolution, disclaiming any intention of annexing Cuba and promising that Cubans would govern themselves. Congress also refused to approve either a canal bill or the annexation of Hawaii. Nevertheless, the Spanish-American War did turn the nation toward imperialism.

WAR AND EMPIRE

The decisive engagement of the war took place not in Cuba but in another Spanish colony, the Philippines, and it involved the favored tool of the expansionists, the new navy (see Map 22-2). In 1897, McKinley had approved plans for an attack on the Philippines in the event of war with Spain. Once war was declared, Commodore George Dewey led the U.S. Asiatic squadron into Manila Bay and destroyed the much weaker Spanish fleet on May 1, 1898. This dramatic victory galvanized expansionist sentiment in the United States. The navy had long coveted Manila Bay as a strategic harbor, but other Americans, casting an eye on commercial opportunities in China, saw a greater significance in the victory. With Dewey's triumph, ex-

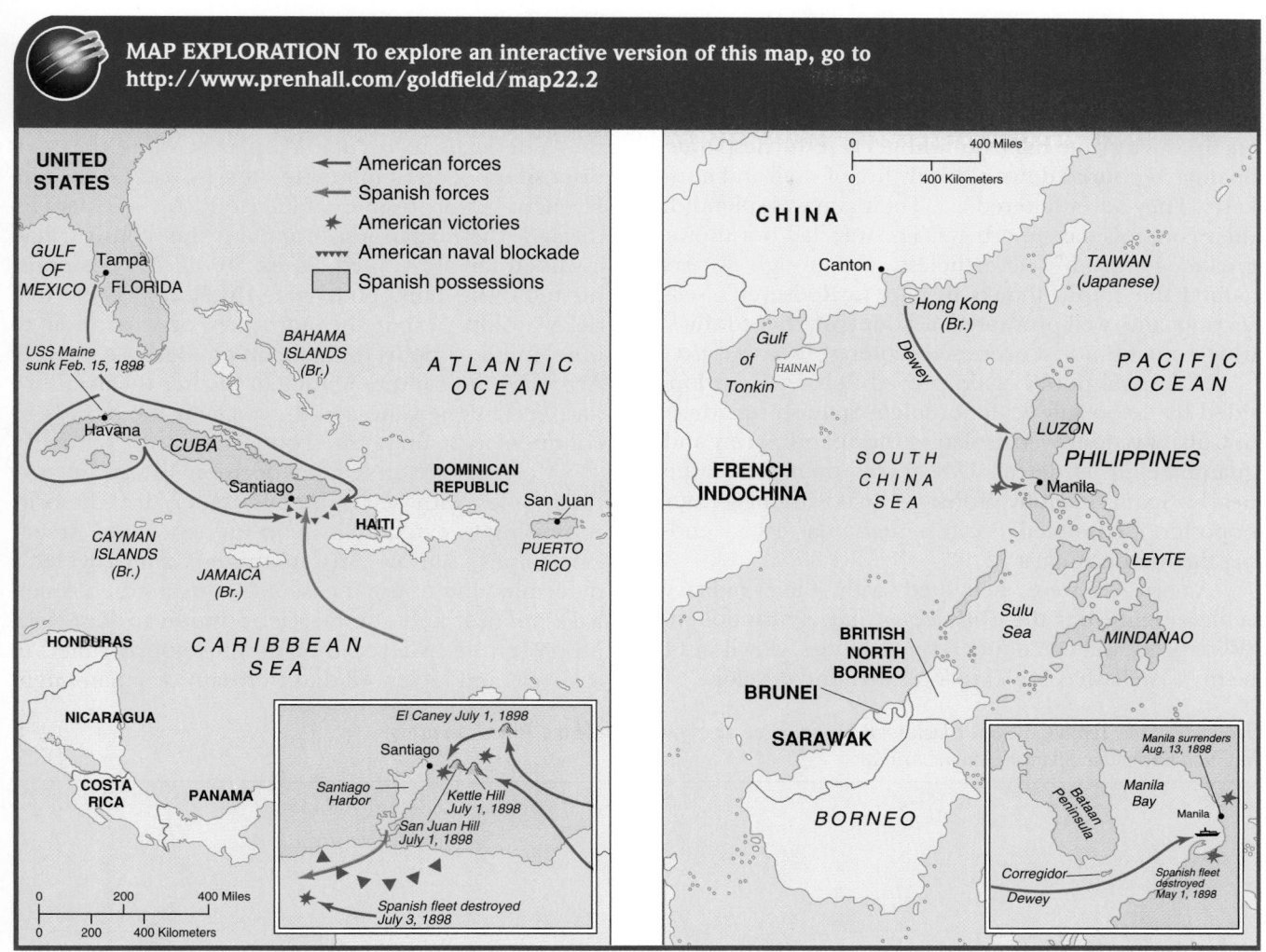

MAP EXPLORATION To explore an interactive version of this map, go to
http://www.prenhall.com/goldfield/map22.2

MAP 22-2 The Spanish-American War
*The United States gained quick victories in both theaters of the Spanish-American War.
Its naval power proved decisive, with Commodore Dewey destroying one enemy fleet in the
Philippines and a second U.S. naval force cutting off the Spanish in Cuba.*

ulted one expansionist, "We are taking our proper rank among the nations of the world. We are after markets, the greatest markets now existing in the world." To expand this foothold in Asia, McKinley ordered troops to the Philippines, postponing the military expedition to Cuba itself.

Dewey's victory also precipitated the annexation of Hawaii, which had seemed hopeless only weeks before. Annexationists now pointed to the islands' strategic importance as stepping stones to Manila. "To maintain our flag in the Philippines, we must raise our flag in Hawaii," the *New York Sun* contended. McKinley himself privately declared, "We need Hawaii just as much and a good deal more than we did California. It is Manifest Destiny." In July, Congress approved annexation, a decision welcomed by Hawaii's white minority. Natives solemnly protested this step taken "without reference to the consent of the people

of the Hawaiian Islands." Filipinos would soon face the same American imperial impulse.

Military victory also came swiftly in Cuba, once the U.S. Army finally landed in late June. Victory depended largely on Spanish ineptitude, for the American army was poorly led, trained, and supplied. Troops had to fight with antiquated weapons and wear wool uniforms in the sweltering tropics. They were issued rotting and poisoned food by a corrupt and inefficient War Department. More than five thousand Americans died of diseases and accidents brought on by such mismanagement; only 379 were killed in battle. State militias supplemented the small regular army, as did volunteer units, such as the famous Rough Riders, a cavalry unit of cowboys and eastern dandies assembled by Leonard Wood and Theodore Roosevelt.

While the Rough Riders captured public attention, other units were more effective. The 10th Negro

Cavalry, for example, played the crucial role in capturing San Juan Hill, a battle popularly associated with the Rough Riders. One war correspondent wrote of the black soldiers' charge: "They followed their leaders up the terrible hill from whose crest the desperate Spaniards poured down a deadly fire of shell and musketry. They never faltered. . . . Their aim was splendid, their coolness was superb. . . . The war had not shown greater heroism." Nevertheless, the Rough Riders gained the credit, thanks in part to Roosevelt's self-serving and well-promoted account of the conflict, which one humorist proposed retitling *Alone in Cuba.*

U.S. naval power again proved decisive. In a lopsided battle on July 3, the obsolete Spanish squadron in Cuba was destroyed, isolating the Spanish army and guaranteeing its defeat. U.S. forces then seized the nearby Spanish colony of Puerto Rico without serious opposition. Humbled, Spain signed an armistice ending the war on August 12.

Americans were delighted with their military achievements, but the *Philadelphia Inquirer* cautioned, "With peace will come new responsibilities, which must be met. We have colonies to look after and develop."

THE TREATY OF PARIS

The armistice required Spain to accept Cuban independence, cede Puerto Rico and Guam (a Pacific island between Hawaii and the Philippines), and allow the Americans to occupy Manila, pending the final disposition of the Philippines at a formal peace conference. The acquisition of Puerto Rico and Guam indicated the expansionist nature the conflict had assumed for the United States. So did the postponement of the Philippine issue. McKinley knew that delay would permit the advocates of expansion to build public support for annexation. Because the U.S. Army did not capture Manila until after the armistice had been signed, he could not claim the islands by conquest, as Spain pointed out.

McKinley defended his decision to acquire the Philippines with self-righteous imperialist rhetoric, promising to extend Christian influence and American values. But he was motivated primarily by a determination to use the islands to strengthen America's political and commercial position in East Asia. Moreover, he believed the Filipinos poorly suited to self-rule, and he feared that Germany or Japan might

Troopers of the Tenth Cavalry. Black soldiers composed nearly a fourth of the American army in Cuba during the Spanish-American War.

seize the Philippines if the United States did not. Meeting in Paris in December, American and Spanish negotiators settled the final terms for peace. Spain agreed—despite Filipino demands for independence—to cede the Philippines to the United States.

The decision to acquire the Philippines sparked a dramatic debate over the ratification of the Treaty of Paris. Imperialists invoked the familiar arguments of economic expansion, national destiny, and strategic necessity, while asserting that Americans had religious and racial responsibilities to advance civilization by uplifting backward peoples. The *United States Investor* spoke for business leaders, for example, in demanding the Philippines as "a base of operations in the East" to protect American interests in China; other economic expansionists argued that the Philippines themselves had valuable resources and were a market for American goods or warned that "our commercial rivals in the Orient" would grab the islands if the United States did not. The *Presbyterian Banner* spoke for what it termed a nearly unanimous religious press in affirming "the desirability of America's retaining the Philippines as a duty in the interest of human freedom and Christian progress." The United States, it concluded, was "morally compelled to become an Asiatic power." Conveniently ignoring that most Filipinos were Catholic, the *Baptist Union* insisted, "The conquest by force of arms must be followed up by conquest for Christ." And some imperialists argued that conquering and holding the Philippines as colonies would create among Americans the "physical manhood" and "character of force" presumably necessary in the international Darwinian struggle.

Opponents of the treaty raised profound questions about national goals and ideals. They included such prominent figures as the civil-service reformer Carl Schurz, the steel baron Andrew Carnegie, the social reformer Jane Addams, the labor leader Samuel Gompers, and the author Mark Twain. Their organizational base was the Anti-Imperialist League, which campaigned against the treaty, distributing pamphlets, petitioning Congress, and holding rallies. League members' criticisms reflected a conviction that imperialism was a repudiation of America's moral and political traditions embodied in the Declaration of Independence. The acquisition of overseas colonies, they argued, conflicted with the nation's commitment to liberty and its claim to moral superiority. They regarded as loathesome and hypocritical the transformation of a war to free Cuba into a campaign for imperial conquest and subjugation.

William Jennings Bryan ridiculed the imperialists' arguments of national destiny: "When the desire to steal becomes uncontrollable in an individual he is declared to be a kleptomaniac and is sent to an asylum;

By portraying only liberation and uplift, a nationalistic cartoonist omits the more negative features of America's quest for empire.

when the desire to grab land becomes uncontrollable in a nation we are told that the 'currents of destiny are flowing through the hearts of men.'" Some African Americans derided the rhetoric of Anglo-Saxon superiority that underlay imperialism, and even organized the Black Man's Burden Association to promote Philippine independence.

But other arguments were less high-minded. Many anti-imperialists objected to expansion on the racist grounds that Filipinos were inferior and unassimilable. Gompers feared that cheap Asian labor would undercut the wages and living standards of American workers. The *San Francisco Call*, representing California-Hawaiian sugar interests, also wanted no competition from the Philippines.

The debate over the treaty became bitter. Furious at the opponents of empire, Roosevelt called them "little better than traitors." Carl Schurz responded that McKinley himself had earlier termed territorial annexation through conquest "a criminal act of aggression"; the President's seizure of the Philippines, Puerto Rico, and Hawaii, said Schurz, had perverted a legitimate concern for Cuba into "a war of selfish ambition and conquest."

Finally, on February 6, 1899, the Senate narrowly ratified the treaty. All but two Republicans supported the pact; most Democrats opposed it, although several voted for the treaty after Bryan suggested that approval was necessary to end the war and detach the Philippines from Spain. Thereafter, he hoped, a congressional resolution would give the Filipinos their independence. But by a single vote, the Republicans defeated a Democratic proposal for Philippine independence once a stable government had been established; the United States would keep the islands.

Bryan attempted to make the election of 1900 a referendum on "the paramount issue" of imperialism, promising to free the Philippines if the Democrats won. But other issues determined the outcome. Some of the most ardent anti-imperialists were conservatives who remained loyal to McKinley because they could not tolerate Bryan's economic policies. Republicans also benefited from the prosperity the country experienced under McKinley after the hard 1890s, and they played on the nationalist emotions evoked by the war, especially by nominating the "hero of San Juan Hill," Theodore Roosevelt, for vice president. "If you choose to vote for America, if you choose to vote for the flag for which we fought," Roosevelt said, "then you will vote to sustain the administration of President McKinley." Bryan lost again, as he had in 1896, and under Republican leadership, the United States became an imperial nation.

Roosevelt's well-advertised exploits in the Spanish-American War propelled his political career. After being elected governor of New York in 1898, he received the Republican nomination for vice president in 1900 and often seemed to overshadow President McKinley.

IMPERIAL AMBITIONS: THE UNITED STATES AND EAST ASIA, 1899–1917

In 1899, as the United States occupied its new empire, Assistant Secretary of State John Bassett Moore observed that the nation had become "a world power. . . . Where formerly we had only commercial interests, we now have territorial and political interests as well." American policies to promote those expanded interests focused first on East Asia and Latin America, where the Spanish-American War had provided the United States with both opportunities and challenges. In Asia, the first issue concerned the fate of the Philippines, but looming beyond it were American ambitions in China, where other imperial nations had their own goals.

THE FILIPINO-AMERICAN WAR

Filipino nationalists, like Cuban insurgents, were already fighting Spain for their independence before the sudden American intervention. The Filipino leader, Emilio Aguinaldo, welcomed Dewey's naval victory as the sign of a *de facto* alliance with the United States; he then issued a declaration of independence and proclaimed the Philippine Republic. His own troops captured most of Luzon, the Philippines' major island, before the U.S. Army arrived. But the Filipinos' optimism declined as American officials acted in an increasingly imperious manner toward them, first refusing to meet with the "savages," then insisting that Filipino forces withdraw from Manila or face "forcible action," and finally dismissing the claims of Aguinaldo and "his so-called government." When the Treaty of Paris provided for U.S. ownership rather than independence, Filipinos felt betrayed. Mounting tensions erupted in a battle between American and Filipino troops outside Manila on February 4, 1899, sparking a long and brutal war.

Ultimately, the United States used nearly four times as many soldiers to suppress the Filipinos as it had to defeat Spain in Cuba and, in a tragic irony, employed many of the same brutal methods for which it had condemned Spain. Recognizing that "the Filipino masses are loyal to Aguinaldo and the government which he heads," U.S. military leaders adopted ever harsher measures, often directed at civilians, who were crowded into concentration camps in which perhaps 200,000 died. Americans often made little effort to distinguish between soldiers and noncombatants, viewing all Filipinos with racial antagonism. After reporting one massacre of a thousand men, women, and children, an American soldier declared, "I am in my glory when I can sight my gun on some dark skin and pull the trigger."

Before the military imposed censorship on war news, reporters confirmed U.S. atrocities; one wrote that "American troops have been relentless, have killed to exterminate men, women, and children, prisoners and captives, active insurgents and suspected people, from lads of 10 and up." A California newspaper defended such actions with remarkable candor: "There has been too much hypocrisy about this Philippine business. . . . Let us all be frank. WE DO NOT WANT THE FILIPINOS. WE DO WANT THE PHILIPPINES. All of our troubles in this annexation matter have been caused by the presence in the Philippine Islands of the Filipinos. . . . The more of them killed the better. It seems harsh. But they must yield before the superior race."

The overt racism of the war repelled African Americans. John Mitchell, a Virginia editor, condemned all the talk of "white man's burden" as deceptive rhetoric for brutal acts that could not be "defended either in moral or international law." Mitchell argued that white Southerners needed missionary work more than freedom-loving Filipinos.

"With the government acquiescing in the oppression and butchery of a dark race in this country and the enslaving and slaughtering of a dark race in the Philippines," he concluded, "we think it time to call all missionaries home and have them work on our own people."

Other Americans also denounced the war. The Anti-Imperialist League revived, citing the war as proof of the corrosive influence of imperialism on the nation's morals and principles. Women figured prominently in mass meetings and lobbying efforts to have the troops returned, their moral stature further undercutting the rationale for colonial wars. Professors addressed antiwar rallies on college campuses. "Alas, what a fall," one University of Michigan professor told his audience. "Within the circuit of a single year to have declined from the moral leadership of mankind into the common brigandage of the robber nations of the world." By 1902, the realities of imperial policy—including American casualties—disillusioned most of those who had clamored to save Cuba.

The Filipino-American War was documented extensively by photographers. "First position near Manila" shows soldiers of the Twentieth Kansas Infantry Regiment deployed early in what would become a lengthy and brutal war.

By that time, however, the American military had largely suppressed the rebellion, and the United States had established a colonial government headed by an American governor general appointed by the president. Filipino involvement in the government was limited on educational and religious grounds. Compared to the Americans' brutal war policies, U.S. colonial rule was relatively benign, though paternalistic. William Howard Taft, the first governor general, launched a program that brought the islands new schools and roads, a public-health system, and an economy tied closely to both the United States and a small Filipino elite. Independence would take nearly half a century.

CHINA AND THE OPEN DOOR

America's determined involvement in the Philippines reflected its preoccupation with China. By the mid-1890s, other powers threatened prospects for American commercial expansion in China. Japan, after defeating China in 1895, annexed Taiwan and secured economic privileges in the mainland province of Fukien (Fujian); the major European powers then competed aggressively to claim other areas of China as their own **spheres of influence**. In Manchuria, Russia won control of Port Arthur (Lüshun) and the right to construct a railway. Germany secured a ninety-nine-year lease on another Chinese port and mining and railroad privileges on the Shandong Peninsula. The British wrung special concessions in Kowloon, opposite Hong Kong, and in other Chinese provinces, as well as a port facing the Russians in Manchuria. France gained a lease on ports and exclusive commercial privileges in southern China.

These developments alarmed the American business community, which was confident that, given an equal opportunity, the United States would prevail in international trade because of its efficient production and marketing systems. But the creation of exclusive spheres of influence would limit the opportunity to compete. In early 1898, business leaders organized the Committee on American Interests in China to lobby Washington to promote American trade in the shrinking Chinese market. The committee persuaded the nation's chambers of commerce to petition the McKinley administration to act. This campaign influenced McKinley's interest in acquiring the Philippines, but the Philippines, in the words of Mark Hanna, were only a "foothold"; China was the real target. The State Department soon reported that, given overproduction for the home market, "the United States has important interests at stake in the partition of commercial facilities in regions which are likely to offer developing markets for its goods. Nowhere is

A FAIR FIELD AND NO FAVOR.
UNCLE SAM: "I'm out for commerce, not conquest."

The United States usually preferred the "annexation of trade" to the annexation of territory. The Open Door policy promised to advance American commercial expansion, but Uncle Sam had to restrain other imperialists with colonial objectives.

this consideration of more interest than in its relation to the Chinese Empire."

In 1899, the government moved to advance those interests. Without consulting the Chinese, Secretary of State John Hay asked the imperial powers to maintain an **Open Door** for the commercial and financial activities of all nations within their Chinese spheres of influence. Privately, Hay had already approved a plan to seize a Chinese port for the United States, if necessary to join in the partition of China, but equal opportunity for trade and investment would serve American interests far better. It would avoid the expense of military occupation, avert further domestic criticism of U.S. imperialism, and guarantee a wider sphere for American business.

The other nations replied evasively, except for Russia, which rejected the Open Door concept. In 1900, an antiforeign Chinese nationalist movement known as the Boxers laid seige to the diplomatic quarters in Beijing. The defeat of the Boxer Rebellion by a multinational military force, to which the United States contributed troops, again raised the prospect of a division of China among colonial powers. Hay sent a second Open Door note, reaffirming "the principle of equal and impartial trade" and respect for China's territorial integrity.

Despite Hay's notes, China remained a tempting arena for imperial schemes. But the Open Door became a cardinal doctrine of American foreign policy in the twentieth century, a means by which the United States sought to dominate foreign markets. The United States promoted an informal or economic empire, as opposed to the traditional territorial colonial empire that Americans preferred to identify with European powers. Henceforth, American economic interests expected the U.S. government to oppose any developments that threatened to close other nations' economies to American penetration and to advance "private enterprise" abroad.

RIVALRY WITH JAPAN AND RUSSIA

At the turn of the twentieth century, both the Japanese and the Russians were more deeply involved in East Asia than was the United States. They expressed little support for the Open Door, which they correctly saw as favoring American interests over their own. But in pursuing their ambitions in China, the two came into conflict with each other. Alarmed at the threat of Russian expansion in Manchuria and Korea, Japan in 1904 attacked the Russian fleet at Port Arthur and defeated the Russians in Manchuria.

In this Russo-Japanese war, American sympathies lay with Japan, for the Russians were attempting to close Manchuria to foreign trade. President Theodore Roosevelt privately complained that a reluctant American public opinion meant that "we cannot fight to keep Manchuria open." He thus welcomed the Japanese attack in the belief that "Japan is playing our game." But he soon feared that an overwhelming Japanese victory could threaten American interests as much as Russian expansionism did, so he skillfully mediated an end to the war. In the Treaty of Portsmouth in 1905, Japan won control of Russia's sphere of influence in Manchuria, half the Russian island of Sakhalin, and recognition of its domination of Korea.

This treaty marked Japan's emergence as a great power, but, ironically, it worsened relations with the United States. Anti-American riots broke out in Tokyo. The Japanese people blamed Roosevelt for obstructing further Japanese gains and blocking a Russian indemnity that would have helped Japan pay for the war. Tensions were further aggravated by San Francisco's decision in 1906 to segregate Asian schoolchildren to avoid affecting the "youthful impressions" of white children. Japan regarded this as a racist insult, and Roosevelt worried that "the infernal fools in California" would provoke war. Finally he had the school order rescinded in exchange for his

limiting Japanese immigration, which lay at the heart of California's hostility. Under the **Gentlemen's Agreement**, worked out through a series of diplomatic notes in 1907 and 1908, Japan agreed to deny passports to workers trying to come to the United States, and the United States promised not to prohibit Japanese immigration overtly or completely.

To calm their mutual suspicions in East Asia, the United States and Japan adopted other agreements but failed to halt the deteriorating relationship. The Taft-Katsura Agreement (1905), the Root-Takahira Agreement (1908), and the Lansing-Ishii Agreement (1917) seemed to trade grudging American acceptance of Japan's special interests in Manchuria and control of Korea for Japanese promises to respect American rule in the Philippines and maintain the Open Door in China. But these agreements were vague, if not contradictory, and produced discord rather than harmony between the two countries.

Increasingly, Japan began to exclude American trade from its territories in East Asia and to press for further control over China. Elihu Root, Roosevelt's secretary of state, insisted that the Open Door and American access be maintained but asserted also that the United States did not want to be "a protagonist in a controversy in China with Russia and Japan or with either of them." The problem was that the United States could not sustain the Open Door without becoming a protagonist in China. This paradox, and the unwillingness to commit military force, would plague American foreign policy in Asia for decades.

IMPERIAL POWER: THE UNITED STATES AND LATIN AMERICA, 1899–1917

In Latin America, where no major powers directly challenged American objectives as Japan and Russia did in Asia, the United States was more successful in exercising imperial power (see Map 22-3). In the two decades after the Spanish-American War, the United States intervened militarily in Latin America no fewer than twenty times to promote its own strategic and economic interests (see the Overview table, "U.S. Interventions in Latin America, 1891–1933"). Policymakers believed that these goals required restricting the influence of European nations in the region, building an isthmian canal under American control, and establishing the order thought necessary for American trade and investments to expand. Intervention, at times, achieved these goals, but it often ignored the wishes and interests of Latin Americans, provoked resistance and disorder, and created lasting ill will.

Overview

U.S. Interventions in Latin America, 1891–1933

Country	Type of Intervention	Year
Chile	Ultimatum	1891–1892
Colombia	Military intervention	1903
Cuba	Occupation	1898–1902, 1906–1909, 1912, 1917–1922
Dominican Republic	Military and administrative intervention Occupation	1905–1907 1916–1924
Haiti	Occupation	1915–1934
Mexico	Military intervention	1914, 1916–1917
Nicaragua	Occupation	1912–1925, 1927–1933
Panama	Acquisition of Canal Zone	1904
Puerto Rico	Military invasion and territorial acquisition	1898

U.S. RULE IN PUERTO RICO

Well before 1898, expansionists such as James G. Blaine had advocated acquiring Puerto Rico because of its strategic location in the Caribbean. During the Spanish-American War, Roosevelt urged Washington, "Do not make peace until we get" Puerto Rico. Military invasion and the Treaty of Paris soon brought the island under American control, with mixed consequences. A military government improved transportation and sanitation and developed public health and education. But to the dismay of Puerto Ricans, who had been promised that American rule would bestow "the advantages and blessings of enlightened civilization," their political freedoms were curtailed. "We have suffered everything. No liberty, no rights," said José Henna, a physician who had led resistance to Spanish colonialism. "We are Mr. Nobody from Nowhere."

In 1900, the United States established a civil government, but it was under U.S. control, and popular participation was even less than under Spain. In the so-called *Insular Cases* (1901), the Supreme Court upheld Congress's authority to establish an inferior status for Puerto Rico, as an "unincorporated territory" without promise of statehood. Disappointed Puerto Ricans pressed to end this colonial status, some advocating independence, others statehood or merely greater autonomy. This division would continue throughout the twentieth century. In 1917, the United States granted citizenship and greater political rights to

Puerto Ricans, but their island remained an unincorporated territory under an American governor appointed by the president.

Economic development also disappointed most islanders, for American investors quickly gained control of the best land and pursued large-scale sugar production for the U.S. market. The landless peasants struggled to survive as workers on large plantations. By 1929, the new governor—ironically, Theodore Roosevelt, Jr.—found that under the domination of American capital, "poverty was widespread and hunger, almost to the verge of starvation, common." A subsequent investigation concluded that while "the influx of capital has increased the efficiency of production and promoted general economic development," the benefits had gone largely to Americans, not to ordinary Puerto Ricans, whose conditions were "deplorable." Increasingly, they left their homes to seek work in the United States.

CUBA AS A U.S. PROTECTORATE

Despite the Teller Amendment, the Spanish-American War did not leave Cuba independent. McKinley opposed independence and distrusted the Cuban revolutionaries. Many Americans considered the Cubans racial inferiors, and one U.S. general in Cuba snorted, "Why those people are no more fit for self-government than gun-powder is for hell." Accordingly, a U.S. military government was established in the island. Only in 1900, when the Democrats made an issue of imperialism, did the McKinley administration move

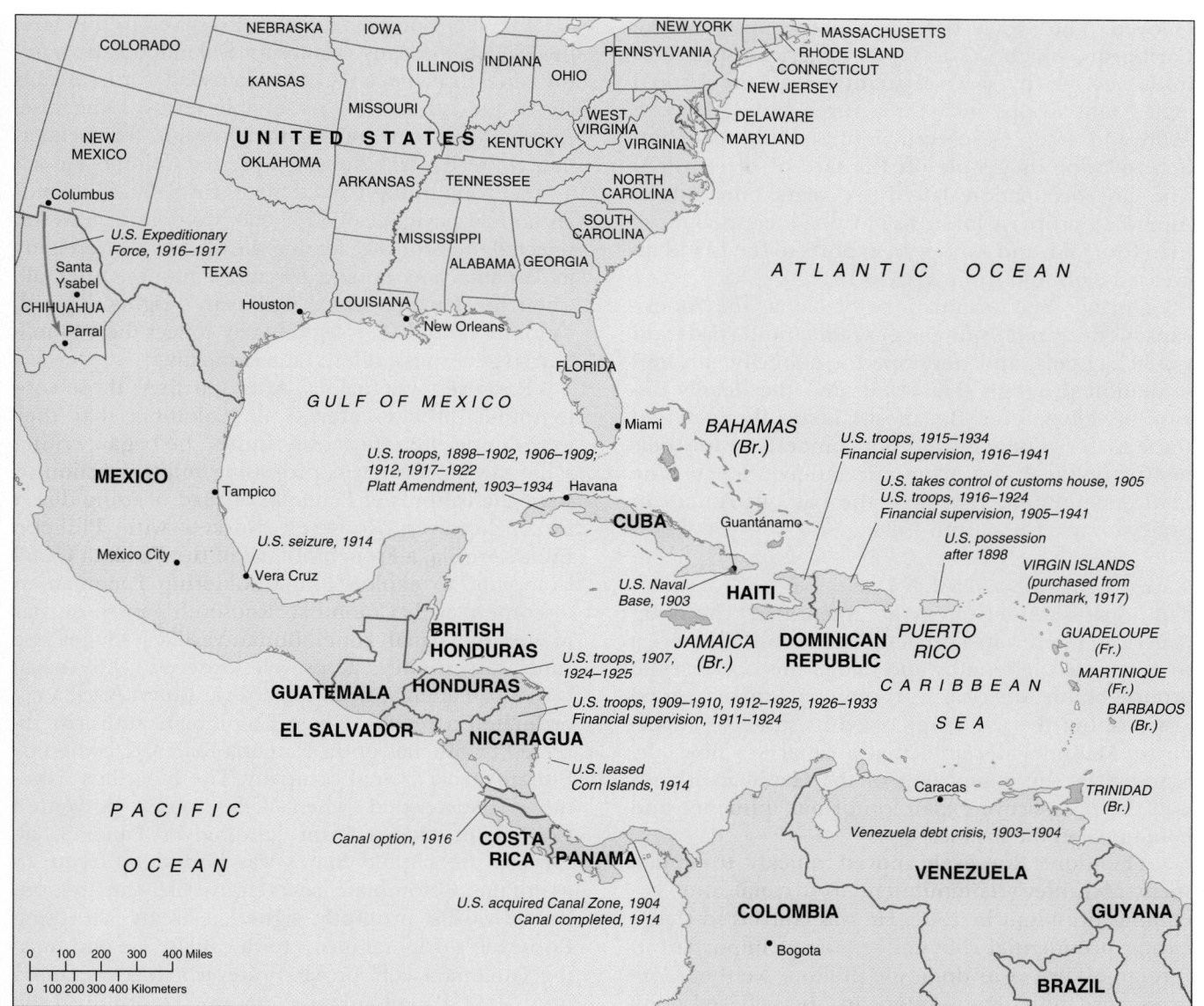

MAP 22-3   The United States in the Caribbean
For strategic and economic reasons, the United States repeatedly intervened in the Caribbean in the first three decades of the twentieth century. Such interventions protected the U.S. claim to dominance but often provoked great hostility among Latin Americans.

toward permitting a Cuban government and withdrawing American troops. McKinley summoned a Cuban convention to draft a constitution under the direction of the American military governor, General Leonard Wood. Reflecting the continuing U.S. fear of Cuban autonomy, this constitution restricted suffrage on the basis of property and education, leaving few Cubans with the right to vote.

Even so, before removing its troops, the United States wanted to insure its control over Cuba. It therefore made U.S. withdrawal contingent on Cuba's adding to its constitution the provisions of the **Platt Amendment**, drawn up in 1901 by the U.S.

secretary of war. The Platt Amendment restricted Cuba's autonomy in diplomatic relations with other countries and in internal financial policies, required Cuba to lease naval bases to the United States, and most important, authorized U.S. intervention to maintain order and preserve Cuban independence. Cubans resented this restriction on their sovereignty. As General Wood correctly observed, "There is, of course, little or no independence left Cuba under the Platt Amendment."

Cubans quickly learned that when the United States prevented Cuba from extending the same trade privileges to the British that U.S. merchants enjoyed. The Open Door would not apply in the Caribbean, which was to be an American sphere of influence. To preserve that influence, the United States sent troops into Cuba three times between 1906 and 1917 (Roosevelt admitted his recurrent itch to "wipe its people off the face of the earth"). The last occupation lasted six years. Meanwhile, American property interests in Cuba increased more than fourfold, and American exports to the island increased eightfold from 1898 to 1917.

During their occupations of Cuba, the Americans modernized its financial system, built roads and public schools, and developed a public-health and sanitation program that eradicated the deadly disease of yellow fever. But most Cubans thought that these material benefits did not compensate for their loss of political and economic independence. The Platt Amendment remained the basis of American policy toward Cuba until 1934.

THE PANAMA CANAL

The Spanish-American War intensified the long American interest in a canal through Central America to eliminate the lengthy and dangerous ocean route around South America. Its commercial value seemed obvious, but the war emphasized its strategic importance. McKinley declared that a canal was now "demanded by the annexation of the Hawaiian Islands and the prospective expansion of our influence and commerce in the Pacific."

Theodore Roosevelt moved quickly to implement McKinley's commitment to a canal after becoming president in 1901. He was convinced that a strong presidential role was at least as important in foreign affairs as in domestic politics. Neither Congress nor "the average American," he believed, took "the trouble to think carefully or deeply" about international affairs. Roosevelt's canal diplomacy helped establish the assertive presidency that has characterized U.S. foreign policy in the twentieth and early twenty-first centuries.

First, Roosevelt persuaded Britain to renounce its treaty right to a joint role with the United States in any canal venture. Britain's willingness reflected a growing friendship between the two nations, both wary of Germany's increasing aggressiveness. Where to build the canal was a problem. One possibility was Nicaragua, where a sea-level canal could be built. Another was Panama, then part of Colombia. A canal through Panama would require an elaborate system of locks. But the French-owned Panama Canal Company had been unsuccessfully trying to build a canal in Panama and was now eager to sell its rights to the project before they expired in 1904.

In 1902, Congress directed Roosevelt to purchase the French company's claims for $40 million and build the canal in Panama if Colombia ceded a strip of land across the isthmus on reasonable terms. Otherwise, Roosevelt was to negotiate with Nicaragua for the alternate route. In 1903, Roosevelt pressed Colombia to sell a canal zone to the United States for $10 million and an annual payment of $250,000. Colombia, however, rejected the proposal, fearing the loss of its sovereignty in Panama and hoping for more money. After all, when the Panama Canal Company's rights expired, Colombia could then legitimately collect the $40 million so generously offered the company.

Roosevelt was furious. After warning "those contemptible little creatures" in Colombia that they were "imperiling their own future," he began writing a message to Congress proposing military action to seize the isthmus of Panama. Instead of using direct force, however, Roosevelt worked with Philippe Bunau-Varilla, a French official of the Panama Canal Company, to exploit long-smoldering Panamanian discontent with Colombia. Roosevelt's purpose was to get the canal zone, Bunau-Varilla's to get the American money. Roosevelt ordered U.S. naval forces to Panama; from New York, Bunau-Varilla coordinated a revolt against Colombian authority directed by officials of the Panama Railroad, owned by Bunau-Varilla's canal company. The bloodless "revolution" succeeded when U.S. forces prevented Colombian troops from landing in Panama, although the United States was bound by treaty to maintain Colombian sovereignty in the region. Bunau-Varilla promptly signed a treaty accepting Roosevelt's original terms for a canal zone and making Panama a U.S. protectorate, which it remained until 1939. Panamanians themselves denounced the treaty for surrendering sovereignty in the zone to the United States, but they had to acquiesce because their independence depended on American forces. The United States took formal control of the canal zone in 1904 and completed construction of the Panama Canal in 1914.

Many Americans were appalled by what the *Chicago American* called Roosevelt's "rough-riding assault upon another republic over the shattered wreckage of international law and diplomatic usage." But others, as *Public Opinion* reported, wanted a "canal above all things" and were willing to overlook moral questions and approve the acquisition of the canal zone as simply "a business question." Roosevelt himself boasted, "I took the Canal Zone and let Congress debate," but his unnecessary and arrogant actions generated resentment among Latin Americans that rankled for decades.

Theodore Roosevelt at the controls of a giant steam shovel during the construction of the Panama Canal in 1906. Roosevelt's aggressive acquisition of the Canal Zone and its subsequent control by the United States angered Panamanians for nearly a century.

THE ROOSEVELT COROLLARY

To protect the security of the canal, the United States increased its authority in the Caribbean. The objective was to establish conditions there that would both eliminate any pretext for European intervention and promote American control over trade and investment. The inability of Latin American nations to pay their debts to foreign lenders raised the possibility of European intervention, as evidenced by a German and British blockade of Venezuela in 1903 to secure repayment of debts to European bankers. "If we intend to say hands off to the powers of Europe," Roosevelt concluded, "then sooner or later we must keep order ourselves."

In his 1904 annual message to Congress, Roosevelt announced a new policy, the so-called **Roosevelt Corollary** to the Monroe Doctrine. "Chronic wrongdoing," he declared, would cause the United States to exercise "an international police power" in Latin America. The Monroe Doctrine had expressed American hostility to European intervention in Latin America; the Roosevelt Corollary at-

tempted to justify U.S. intervention and authority in the region. Roosevelt invoked his corollary immediately, imposing American management of the debts and customs duties of the Dominican Republic in 1905. Commercial rivalries and political intrigue in that poor nation had created disorder, which Roosevelt suppressed for both economic and strategic reasons. Financial insolvency was averted, popular revolution prevented, and possible European intervention forestalled.

Latin Americans vigorously resented the United States' unilateral claims to authority. By 1907, the so-called Drago Doctrine (named after Argentina's foreign minister) was incorporated into international law, prohibiting armed intervention to collect debts. Still, the United States would continue to invoke the Roosevelt Corollary to advance its interests in the hemisphere. As Secretary of State Elihu Root asserted, "The inevitable effect of our building the Canal must be to require us to police the surrounding premises." He then added, "In the nature of things, trade and control, and the obligation to keep order which go with them, must come our way."

DOLLAR DIPLOMACY

Roosevelt's successor as president, William Howard Taft, hoped to promote U.S. interests without such combative rhetoric and naked force. He proposed "substituting dollars for bullets"—using government action to encourage private American investments in Latin America to supplant European interests, promote development and stability, and gain profits for American bankers. Under this **dollar diplomacy**, American investments in the Caribbean increased dramatically during Taft's presidency from 1909 to 1913, and the State Department helped arrange for American bankers to establish financial control over Haiti and Honduras.

But Taft did not shrink from employing military force to protect American property or to establish the conditions he thought necessary for American investments. In fact, Taft intervened more frequently than Roosevelt had, with Nicaragua a major target. In 1909, Taft sent U.S. troops there to aid a revolution fomented by an American mining corporation and to seize the Nicaraguan customs houses. Under the new government, American bankers then gained control of Nicaragua's national bank, railroad, and customs service. To protect these arrangements, U.S. troops were again dispatched in 1912. To control popular opposition to the American client government, the marines remained in Nicaragua for two decades. Military power, not the social and economic improvement promised by dollar diplomacy, kept Nicaragua's

THE BIG STICK IN THE CARIBBEAN SEA

The Roosevelt Corollary proclaimed the intention of the United States to police Latin America. Enforcement came, as this cartoon shows, with Roosevelt and subsequent presidents sending the U.S. Navy to one Caribbean nation after another.

repudiated the interventionist policies of his Republican predecessors. He promised that the United States would "never again seek one additional foot of territory by conquest" but would instead work to promote "human rights, national integrity, and opportunity" in Latin America. Wilson also named as his secretary of state the Democratic symbol of anti-imperialism, William Jennings Bryan. Their generous intentions were apparent when Bryan signed a treaty with Colombia apologizing for Roosevelt's seizure of the Panama Canal Zone in 1903.

Nonetheless, Wilson soon became the most interventionist president in American history, for a number of reasons. He agreed that the United States had to expand its exports and investments abroad and that U.S. dominance of the Caribbean was strategically necessary. He also shared the racist belief that Latin Americans were inferior and needed paternalistic guidance from the United States. In providing that guidance, through military force if necessary, Wilson came close to assuming that American principles and objectives were absolutes, that different cultural traditions and national aspirations were simply wrong. His self-righteousness and determination to transform other peoples' behavior led his policies to be dubbed "missionary diplomacy," but they also contained elements of Roosevelt's commitment to military force and Taft's reliance on economic power.

minority government stable and subordinate to the United States.

Dollar diplomacy increased American power and influence in the Caribbean and tied underdeveloped countries to the United States economically and strategically. By 1913, American investments in the region reached $1.5 billion, and Americans had captured more than 50 percent of the foreign trade of Costa Rica, Cuba, the Dominican Republic, Guatemala, Haiti, Honduras, Nicaragua, and Panama. But this policy failed to improve conditions for most Latin Americans. U.S. officials remained primarily concerned with promoting American control and extracting American profits from the region, not with the well-being of its population. One American diplomat, for instance, casually described a Guatemalan president in whose government San Francisco bankers had invested heavily under the premises of dollar diplomacy as a cruel despot who had "the good sense to be civil to our country and its citizens and to keep his cruelties . . . for home consumption." Not surprisingly, dollar diplomacy proved unpopular in Latin America.

WILSONIAN INTERVENTIONS

Taking office in 1913, the Democrat Woodrow Wilson

Caribbean interventions. In 1915, Wilson ordered U.S. Marines to Haiti. They went, explained Bryan, to restore order and preserve "American interests" that were "gravely menaced." The United States saved and even enhanced those interests by establishing a protectorate over Haiti and drawing up a constitution that increased U.S. property rights and commercial privileges. The U.S. Navy selected a new Haitian president, granting him nominal authority over a client government. Real authority, however, rested with the American military, which controlled Haiti until 1934, protecting the small elite who cooperated with foreign interests and exploited their own people. As usual, American military rule improved the country's transportation, sanitation, and educational systems, but the forced-labor program that the U.S. adopted to build such public works provoked widespread resentment. In 1919, marines suppressed a revolt against American domination, killing more than three thousand Haitians.

Wilson also intervened elsewhere in the Caribbean. In 1916, when the Dominican Republic refused to cede control of its finances to U.S. bankers, Wilson ordered the marines to occupy the country. The marines ousted Dominican officials, installed a military government to rule "on behalf of the Dominican government," and ran the nation until 1924. In 1917, the United States intervened in Cuba, which remained under American control until 1922.

Interfering with Mexico.

Wilson also involved himself in the internal affairs of Mexico. The lengthy dictatorship of Porfirio Díaz had collapsed in 1911 in revolutionary disorder. The popular leader Francisco Madero took power and promised democratic and economic reforms that alarmed both wealthy Mexicans and foreign investors, particularly Americans. In 1913, General Victoriano Huerta seized control in a brutal counterrevolution backed by the landed aristocracy and foreign interests. Most nations recognized the Huerta government, but Wilson, despite strong pressure from American investors, refused to do so. He was appalled by the violence of Huerta's power grab and was aware that opponents had organized to reestablish constitutional government.

Wilson hoped to bring the Constitutionalists to power and "to secure Mexico a better government under which all contracts and business and concessions will be safer than they have been." He authorized arms sales to their forces, led by Venustiano Carranza; pressured Britain and other nations to deprive Huerta of foreign support; and blockaded the Mexican port of Vera Cruz. In April 1914 Wilson exploited a minor incident to have the marines attack and occupy Vera Cruz. This assault damaged his image as a promoter of peace and justice, and even Carranza and the Constitutionalists denounced the American occupation as unwarranted aggression. By August, Carranza had toppled Huerta, and Wilson shifted his support to Francisco ("Pancho") Villa, who seemed more susceptible to American guidance. But Carranza's growing popular support in Mexico and Wilson's preoccupation with World War I in Europe finally led the United States to grant de facto recognition to the Carranza government in October 1915.

Villa then began terrorizing New Mexico and Texas, hoping to provoke an American intervention that would undermine Carranza. In 1916, Wilson ordered troops under General John J. Pershing to pursue Villa into Mexico, leading Carranza to fear a permanent U.S. occupation of northern Mexico. Soon the American soldiers were fighting the Mexican army rather than Villa's bandits. On the brink of full-fledged war, Wilson finally ordered U.S. troops to withdraw in January 1917 and extended full recognition to the Carranza government. Wilson lamely defended these steps as showing that the United States had no intention of imposing on Mexico "an order and government of our own choosing." That had been Wilson's original objective, however. His aggressive tactics had not merely failed but also embittered relations with Mexico.

CONCLUSION

By the time of Woodrow Wilson's presidency, the United States had been expanding its involvement in world affairs for half a century. Several themes had emerged from this activity: increasing American domination of the Caribbean, continuing interest in East Asia, the creation of an overseas empire, and the evolution of the United States into a major world power. Underlying these developments were an uneasy mixture of ideas and objectives. The American involvement in the world reflected a traditional, if often misguided, sense of national rectitude and mission. Generous humanitarian impulses vied with ugly racist prejudices as Americans sought both to help other peoples and to direct them toward U.S. concepts of religion, sanitation, capitalist development, and public institutions. American motives ranged from ensuring national security and competing with European colonial powers to the conviction that the United States had to expand its economic interests abroad. But if imperialism, both informal and at times colonial, brought Americans greater wealth and power, it also increased tensions in Asia and contributed to anti-American hostility and revolutionary ferment in Latin America. It also entangled the United States in the Great Power rivalries that would ultimately result in two world wars.

REVIEW QUESTIONS

1. After the Spanish-American War, General Leonard Wood asserted that Cubans believed that their American "liberators" were "still their faithful friends." Why might Cubans not agree with Wood?

2. What factors, old and new, shaped American foreign policy in the late nineteenth century? How were they interrelated?

3. How were individual politicians and diplomats able to affect America's foreign policy? How were they constrained by government institutions, private groups, and public opinion?

4. To what extent was the United States' emergence as an imperial power a break from, as opposed to a culmination of, its earlier policies and national development?

5. How effective were U.S. interventions in Latin America? What were the objectives and consequences?

KEY TERMS

Dollar diplomacy (p. 717)

Gentlemen's Agreement (p. 713)

Imperialism (p. 697)

Mahanism (p. 699)

Monroe Doctrine (p. 704)

Open Door (p. 712)

Pan American Union (p. 702)

Platt Amendment (p. 715)

Roosevelt Corollary (p. 717)

Spheres of Influence (p. 712)

Teller Amendment (p. 706)

Yellow press (p. 705)

RECOMMENDED READING

Beisner, Robert L. *From the Old Diplomacy to the New, 1865–1900,* 2d ed. (1986). An excellent analysis of historiographical issues.

Campbell, Charles S. *The Transformation of American Foreign Relations, 1865–1900* (1976). A comprehensive and cautious survey that provides many insights in U.S. foreign policy.

Hoganson, Kristin L. *Fighting for American Manhood: How Gender Politics Provoked the Spanish-American and Philippine-American Wars* (1998). An innovative and provocative book showing how gender concerns influenced U.S. foreign policy.

LaFeber, Walter. *The American Search for Opportunity, 1865–1913* (1993). A fascinating study documenting the disruptive international consequences of America's rise to world power.

LaFeber, Walter. *The New Empire: An Interpretation of American Expansion, 1860–1898* (1963). An influential study that emphasizes economic factors on American foreign policy.

Offner, John L. *An Unwanted War: The Diplomacy of the United States and Spain over Cuba, 1895–1898* (1992). A revisionist account maintaining that conflict over Cuba was inevitable.

Perez, Louis A, Jr. *The War of 1898: The United States and Cuba in History and Historiography* (1998). A brief book that emphasizes how relations between Cuba and the United States shaped the war and its meaning.

Pletcher, David. *The Diplomacy of Trade and Investment: American Economic Expansion in the Hemisphere, 1865–1900* (1998). Stresses the complex but inconsistent and unsystematic nature of American economic expansion.

ADDITIONAL SOURCES

Roots of Imperialism

Anderson, David L. *Imperialism and Idealism: American Diplomats in China, 1861–1898* (1985).

Anderson, Stuart. *Race and Rapprochement: Anglo-Saxonism and Anglo-American Relations, 1895–1904* (1981).

Hearden, Patrick J. *Independence and Empire: The New South's Cotton Mill Campaign, 1865–1901* (1982).

Hill, Patricia R. *The World Their Household: The American Woman's Foreign Mission Movement and Cultural Transformation, 1870–1920* (1985).

Hunt, Michael H. *Ideology and U.S. Foreign Policy* (1987).

Jacobson, Matthew Frye. *Barbarian Virtues: The United States Encounters Foreign Peoples at Home and Abroad* (2000).

Morris, Edmund. *The Rise of Theodore Roosevelt* (1979).

Paolino, Ernest. *The Foundations of the American Empire: William Henry Seward and U.S. Foreign Policy* (1973).

Plesur, Milton. *America's Outward Thrust: Approaches to Foreign Affairs, 1865–1890* (1971).

Pletcher, David M. *The Awkward Years: American Foreign Relations under Garfield and Arthur* (1962).

Rosenberg, Emily S. *Spreading the American Dream: American Economic and Cultural Expansion, 1890–1945* (1982).

Spector, Ronald. *Admiral of the New Empire* (1974).

Widenor, William. *Henry Cabot Lodge and the Search for an American Foreign Policy* (1980).

Williams, William A. *The Roots of the Modern American Empire* (1969).

The Spanish-American War

Challener, Richard. *Admirals, Generals, and American Foreign Policy, 1889–1914* (1973).

Cosmas, Graham A. *An Army for Empire: The United States Army and the Spanish-American War* (1971).

Dobson, John. *Reticent Expansionism: The Foreign Policy of William McKinley* (1988).

Gatewood, Willard B. Jr. *Black Americans and the White Man's Burden, 1898–1903* (1975).

Gould, Lewis L. *The Spanish-American War and President McKinley* (1982).

Healy, David F. *U.S. Expansionism: The Imperialist Urge in the 1890s* (1970).

Linderman, Gerald. *The Mirror of War: American Society and the Spanish-American War* (1974).

Milton, Joyce. *The Yellow Journalists* (1989).

Morgan, H. Wayne. *America's Road to Empire: The War with Spain and Overseas Expansion* (1965).

Pratt, Julius W. *Expansionists of 1898* (1936).

Trask, David R. *The War with Spain in 1898* (1981).

Anti-Imperialism

Beisner, Robert L. *Twelve against Empire: The Anti-Imperialists, 1898–1900* (1968).

Osborne, Thomas J. *"Empire Can Wait": American Opposition to Hawaiian Annexation, 1893–1898* (1981).

Schirmer, Daniel B. *Republic or Empire: American Resistance to the Philippine War* (1972).

Tompkins, E. Berkeley. *Anti-Imperialism in the United States: The Great Debate, 1890–1920* (1970).

Imperial Ambitions: The United States and East Asia, 1899–1917

Campbell, Charles S. *Special Business Interests and the Open Door Policy* (1951).

Cohen, Warren I. *America's Response to China* (1989).

Gates, John M. *Schoolbooks and Krags: The United States Army in the Philippines* (1973).

Hunt, Michael H. *The Making of a Special Relationship: The U.S. and China to 1914* (1983).

Iriye, Akira. *Pacific Estrangement: Japanese and American Expansion, 1897–1911* (1972).

McCormick, Thomas. *China Market: America's Quest for Informal Empire* (1967).

Miller, Stuart. *"Benevolent Assimilation": The American Conquest of the Philippines, 1899–1903* (1982).

Varg, Paul. *The Making of a Myth: The United States and China, 1897–1912* (1968).

Welch, Richard E. *Response to Imperialism: The United States and the Philippine-American War* (1979).

Imperial Power: The United States and Latin America, 1899–1917

Beale, Howard K. *Theodore Roosevelt and the Rise of America to World Power* (1956).

Benjamin, Jules. *Hegemony and Development: The United States and Cuba, 1890–1934* (1977).

Calder, Bruce. *The Impact of Intervention: The Dominican Republic during the U.S. Occupation of 1916 to 1924* (1984).

Carr, Raymond. *Puerto Rico: A Colonial Experiment* (1984).

Carrion, Arturo Morales. *Puerto Rico* (1983).

Cooper, John M. Jr. *The Warrior and the Priest: Woodrow Wilson and Theodore Roosevelt* (1983).

Eisenhower, John. *The United States and the Mexican Revolution, 1913–1917* (1993).

Healy, David F. *Drive to Hegemony: The United States in the Caribbean, 1898–1917* (1988).

Hitchman, James. *Leonard Wood and Cuban Independence, 1898–1902* (1971).

LaFeber, Walter. *Inevitable Revolutions: The United States in Central America* (1993).

LaFeber, Walter. *The Panama Canal* (1990).

Lane, Jack C. *Armed Progressive: General Leonard Wood* (1978).

Langley, Lester. *The Banana Wars: An Inner History of the American Empire, 1900–1934* (1983).

McCullough, David. *The Path between the Seas: The Creation of the Panama Canal* (1977).

Millett, Allan R. *The Politics of Intervention: The Military Occupation of Cuba, 1906–1909* (1968).

Perez, Louis A. Jr. *Cuba under the Platt Amendment, 1902–1934* (1986).

WHERE TO LEARN MORE

- **Mission Houses, Honolulu, Hawaii.** Built between 1821 and 1841, these buildings were homes and shops of missionaries sent to Hawaii by the American Board of Commissioners for Foreign Missions. Their exhibits include furnishings and memorabilia of a group important in developing American ties with Hawaii. www. missionhouses.org/.

- **Funston Memorial Home, Iola, Kansas.** Operated as a museum by the Kansas State Historical Society, this is the boyhood home of General Frederick Funston, prominent in the Spanish-American War and the Filipino-American War. For a virtual tour, together with military information, political cartoons, Roosevelt correspondence, and Funston links, see http://skyways. lib.ks.us/museums/funston/.

- **James G. Blaine House, Augusta, Maine.** The Executive Mansion of Maine's governor since 1919, this house was formerly Blaine's home and still contains his study and furnishings from the time he served as secretary of state and U.S. senator.

- **Rough Riders Memorial and City Museum, Las Vegas, New Mexico.** Together with the nearby Castaneda Hotel, this site provides intriguing information on Roosevelt's volunteer cavalry, recruited primarily from the Southwest. www. arco-iris.com/teddy/index.htm.

- **Seward House, Auburn, New York.** The home of William H. Seward contains furniture and mementos from his career as secretary of state.

 Please refer to the document CD-ROM for primary sources related to this chapter.

SEND THE EAGLE'S ANSWER
MORE SHIPS
UNITED STATES SHIPPING BOARD · EMERGENCY FLEET CORPORATION

➔ *In World War I, mobilization of the home front was basic to military success. Government posters exhorted Americans to increase industrial and agricultural production, buy war bonds, and suppress dissent.*

AMERICA AND THE GREAT WAR 23
1914–1920

CHAPTER OUTLINE

Waging Neutrality
The Origins of Conflict
American Attitudes
The Economy of War
The Diplomacy of Neutrality
The Battle over Preparedness
The Election of 1916
Descent into War

Waging War in America
Managing the War Economy
Women and Minorities:
    New Opportunities, Old Inequities
Financing the War
Conquering Minds
Suppressing Dissent

Waging War and Peace Abroad
The War to End All Wars
The Fourteen Points
The Paris Peace Conference

Waging Peace at Home
Battle over the League
*Economic Readjustment and Social
    Conflict*
Red Scare
The Election of 1920

Conclusion

I have been traveling for nearly three weeks through six Middle Western States, talking about the war, with all classes of people: farmers, labor leaders, newspaper editors, college professors, business men, and state officials. I have been trying to get at the bedrock sentiment of the people regarding it, and to set it down exactly as I find it.

Almost without exception, even among those who favor the war most vigorously, the people I have talked with have commented upon the lack of popular enthusiasm for the war. The more closely these people were connected with the farmers or the workingmen, the more sweeping and positive were their statements.

The attitude of the people is wholly different from what it was at the opening of our Spanish War in 1898. There are no heroic slogans, no boastfulness, no excitement, no glamour of war. There is still a great deal of haziness about the real issues and a great deal of doubt about how far America should go beyond mere defensive measures. One of the foremost political leaders of the West, himself an ardent supporter of the war, told me that if a secret ballot were taken as to whether American armies should be sent to France, the vote would be overwhelmingly against it. It is noteworthy, also, that the newspapers are full of a-b-c explanations of the reasons why we are at war and why we should go forward with it. . . . And finally, there are nowhere as yet any evidences of the passions and the hatred which war engenders. People do not hate Germans or Austrians or Turks; nor do they love the British.

On the other hand, if there is little enthusiasm, the people everywhere are taking the war as a grim necessity, feeling that they have been forced into it by events beyond their control, and they are going forward, more or less reluctantly, with the preparations; but they are really going forward. The draft was not popular; people wished it might have been done in some other way; and in some groups of population it was hated and feared, and yet, through all this country, there has been a wonderful and complete compliance with the law. In the same way the liberty loan is not popular. There is no popular rush to subscribe, and it has required an enormous amount of organization, advertising, and pressure to sell the bonds, and yet they are being sold and will be sold. . . . And there have been no signs of any popular rush to enlist, and men have been obtained only by dint of the most vigorous advertising and pressure. It is significant also that more than half of those registered in Chicago are demanding exemption.

The only real enthusiasm that I could find was in such campaigns as that of the Red Cross, the Y.M.C.A., and here and there in work for the American Ambulance in France. The work of women everywhere for the Red Cross is remarkably organized and well supported. . . . Of the value of these activities, no matter what happens, the people are convinced.

This is as nearly a true statement of the general situation as I can make. I have met a good many men who think that this state of the popular mind, this deliberate and passionless method of doing what is regarded as a disagreeable duty, is the best possible method of getting into the great war. . . .

On the other hand, I met a good many people, especially among the leaders of war organizations of various sorts, to whom the popular attitude is not only irritating but dangerous. They feel that the people are not fully awakened to the emergency, that they do not realize that the country is really at this moment at war, and that unless America meets with more enthusiasm and more speed the problems of raising money, producing food, and hurrying the training of men for armies in France the war may result in disaster.

Ray Stannard Baker, "West in Grim Business of War Without Passion," *St. Louis Post–Dispatch*, June 17, 1917.

Ray Stannard Baker, the famous journalist, thus described his journey across the Midwest in 1917, three years after World War I began in Europe and two months after the United States had joined the conflict by declaring war on Germany. Despite the official decision for war, the American people were reluctant participants, unconvinced that national interests were really involved. Instead, as Baker observed, they "seem to think that there was a fight between England and Germany with which Uncle Sam was not concerned in any way—but that he was simply an innocent bystander who happened to be in range and got hurt—quite as much by the fault of England as of Germany."

But as the perceptive Baker also discovered, the nation's leaders were determined to whip up popular support for the war effort through "organization, advertising, and pressure." The goal would be not only to train soldiers to fight in Europe but to demonize Germany, mobilize the economy, and transform social attitudes within America itself.

This determination profoundly shaped the American wartime experience. Not only was the

Great War the United States' first major military conflict on foreign soil, but it also changed American life. With economic management and social control considered essential to the war effort, government authority increased sharply. Business organizations, labor unions, farmers, ministers were all incorporated into the war effort. Women's organizational activities expanded dramatically beyond those noted by Baker and, in being focused broadly on the war effort, often developed in new and unexpected ways. Journalists, too, had their skills put to new and sometimes unfortunate uses; Baker himself, who had initially opposed the war as a threat to all progress, eventually went to Europe to file confidential reports for the State Department and then to organize the Press Department and control news at the Versailles Peace Conference.

Many of the changes in American life, from increased efficiency to Americanization, often reflected prewar progressivism, and the war years did promote some reforms. But the war also diverted reform energies into new channels, subordinated generous impulses to those that were more coercive ("the passions and the hatred" which Baker found lacking in mid-1917 were soon widespread), and strengthened the conservative opposition to reform. The results were often reactionary and contributed to a postwar mood that not only curtailed further reform but also helped defeat the peace treaty upon which so much had been gambled.

KEY TOPICS

- How sympathy for the Allies and outrage over German submarine warfare undermined U.S. neutrality during World War I

- Wilson's decision to join the conflict on the side of the Allies

- The reorganization of the U.S. economy and the challenge to civil liberties that resulted from the war effort

- Wilson's influence on the Versailles Treaty and his failure to gain its ratification in the U.S. Senate

- The postwar backlash

WAGING NEUTRALITY

Few Americans were prepared for the Great War that erupted in Europe in August 1914, but fewer still foresaw that their own nation might become involved in it. With near unanimity, they supported neutrality. But American attitudes, decisions, and actions, both public and private, undercut neutrality, and the policies of governments in Berlin, London, and Washington drew the United States into the war.

THE ORIGINS OF CONFLICT

There had been plenty of warning. Since the 1870s, the competing imperial ambitions of the European powers had led to economic rivalries, military expansion, diplomatic maneuvering, and international tensions. A complex system of alliances divided the continent into two opposing blocs. In central Europe, the expansionist Germany of Kaiser Wilhelm II allied itself with the multinational Austro-Hungarian Empire. Confronting them, Great Britain and France formed alliances with Tsarist Russia. A succession of crises threatened this precarious balance of power, and in May 1914, an American diplomat reported anxiously, "There is too much hatred, too many jealousies." He predicted "an awful cataclysm."

The cataclysm began a month later. On June 28, a Serbian terrorist assassinated Archduke Franz Ferdinand, the heir to the Austro-Hungarian throne, in Sarajevo. With Germany's support, Austria declared war on Serbia on July 28. Russia then mobilized its army against Austria to aid Serbia, its Slavic client state. To assist Austria, Germany declared war on Russia and then on Russia's ally, France. Hoping for a quick victory, Germany struck at France through neutral Belgium; in response, Britain declared war on Germany on August 4. Soon Turkey and Bulgaria joined Germany and Austria to form the **Central Powers**. The **Allies**—Britain, France, and Russia—were joined by Italy and Japan. Britain drew on its empire for resources, using troops from India, Canada,

Chronology

1914 World War I begins in Europe.

President Woodrow Wilson declares U.S. neutrality.

1915 Germany begins submarine warfare.

Lusitania is sunk.

Woman's Peace Party is organized.

1916 Gore-McLemore resolutions are defeated.

Sussex Pledge is issued.

Preparedness legislation is enacted.

Woodrow Wilson is reelected president.

1917 Germany resumes unrestricted submarine warfare.

The United States declares war on Germany.

Selective Service Act establishes the military draft.

Espionage Act is passed.

Committee on Public Information, War Industries Board, Food Administration, and other mobilization agencies are established.

American Expeditionary Force arrives in France.

East St. Louis race riot erupts.

Bolshevik Revolution occurs in Russia.

1918 Wilson announces his Fourteen Points.

Sedition Act is passed.

Eugene Debs is imprisoned.

The United States intervenes militarily in Russia.

Armistice ends World War I.

1919 Paris Peace Conference is held.

Steel, coal, and other strikes occur.

Red Scare breaks out.

Prohibition amendment is adopted.

Wilson suffers a massive stroke.

1920 Palmer Raids round up radicals.

League of Nations is defeated in the U.S. Senate.

Woman suffrage amendment is ratified.

U.S. troops are withdrawn from Russia.

Warren Harding is elected president.

1921 United States signs a separate peace treaty with Germany.

Australia, New Zealand, and South Africa. The war had become a global conflict, waged not only in Europe but also in Africa, the Middle East, and East Asia.

Mass slaughter enveloped Europe as huge armies battled to a stalemate. The British and French faced the Germans along a line of trenches stretching across France and Belgium from the English Channel to Switzerland. Little movement occurred despite great efforts and terrible casualties from artillery, machine guns, and poison gas. The British once suffered 300,000 casualties in an offensive that gained only a few square miles before being pushed back. Machine gunners went into shock at the carnage they inflicted. In the trenches, soldiers suffered in the cold and mud, surrounded by decaying bodies and human waste, enduring lice, rats, and nightmares and dying from disease and exhaustion. The belligerents subordinated their economies, politics, and cultures to military demands. The Great War, said one German soldier, had become "the grave of nations."

AMERICAN ATTITUDES

Although the United States had also competed for markets, colonies, and influence, few Americans had expected this calamity. As one North Carolina congressman said, "This dreadful conflict of the nations came to most of us as lightning out of a clear sky." Most people believed that the United States had no vital interest in the war and would not become involved. "Our isolated position and freedom from entangling alliances," noted the *Literary Digest*, "inspire our press with the cheering assurance that we are in no peril of being drawn into the European quarrel." President Wilson issued a proclamation of neutrality and urged Americans to be "neutral in fact as well as in name . . . impartial in thought as well as in action."

However, neither the American people nor their president stayed strictly neutral. German Americans often sympathized with Germany, and many Irish Americans hoped for a British defeat that would free Ireland from British rule. But most Americans sympathized with the Allies. Ethnic, cultural, and economic ties bound most Americans to the British and French. Politically, too, most Americans felt a greater affinity for the democratic Western Allies—Tsarist Russia repelled them—than for Germany's more authoritarian government and society. And whereas Britain and the United States had enjoyed a rapprochement since 1895, Germany had repeatedly appeared as a potential rival. Many Americans considered it a militaristic nation, particularly after it violated Belgium's neutrality.

Wilson himself admired Britain's culture and government and distrusted Germany's imperial ambitions. Like other influential Americans, Wilson believed that a German victory would threaten America's economic, political, and perhaps even strategic interests. "England is fighting our fight," he said privately. Secretary of State William Jennings Bryan was genuinely neutral, but most officials favored the Allies. Robert Lansing, counselor of the State Department; Walter Hines Page, the ambassador to England; and Colonel Edward House, Wilson's closest adviser on foreign affairs—all assisted British diplomats, undercut official U.S. protests against British violations of American neutrality, and encouraged Wilson's suspicions of Germany. Early in the war, House wrote to Page, "I cannot see how there can be any serious trouble between England and America, with all of us feeling as we do." House and Lansing assured the Allies privately that "we considered their cause our cause."

British propaganda bolstered American sympathies. British writers, artists, and lecturers depicted the Allies as fighting for civilization against a brutal Germany that mutilated nuns and babies. Although German troops, like most other soldiers, did commit outrages, they were not guilty of the systematic barbarity claimed by Allied propagandists. Britain, however, shaped America's view of the conflict. It cut the only German cable to the United States and censored war news to suit itself. German propaganda directed at American opinion proved so ineffectual that the German ambassador concluded it might as well be abandoned.

Sympathy for the Allies, however, did not mean that Americans favored intervention. The British ambassador complained that it was "useless" to expect any "practical" advantage from the Americans' sympathy, for they had no intention of joining the conflict. Indeed, few Americans doubted that neutrality was the appropriate course and peace the proper goal. The carnage in France solidified their convictions. Wilson was determined to pursue peace as long as his view of national interests allowed.

THE ECONOMY OF WAR

Economic issues soon threatened American neutrality. International law permitted neutral nations to sell or ship war material to all belligerents, and, with the economy mired in a recession when the war began, many Americans looked to war orders to spur economic recovery. But the British navy prevented trade with the Central Powers. Only the Allies could buy American goods. Their orders for steel, explosives, uniforms, wheat, and other products, however, pulled the country out of the recession. One journalist rejoiced that "war, for Europe, is meaning devastation and death; for America a bumper crop of new millionaires and a hectic hastening of prosperity revival."

Other Americans worried that this one-sided war trade undermined genuine neutrality. Congress even considered an embargo on munitions. But few Americans supported that idea. One financial journal declared of the Allied war trade: "We need it for the profits which it yields." Whatever its justification, however, the war trade strengthened U.S. ties with the Allies and embittered Germans. As the German ambassador noted, American industry was "actually delivering goods only to the enemies of Germany."

A second economic issue complicated matters. To finance their war purchases, the Allies borrowed from American bankers. Initially, Secretary of State Bryan persuaded Wilson to prohibit loans to the belligerents as "inconsistent with the true spirit of neutrality." But as the importance of the war orders to both the Allies and the American economy became clear, Wilson ended the ban. Secretary of the Treasury William McAdoo argued that it would be "disastrous" not to finance the Allies' purchases, on which "our prosperity is dependent." By April 1917, American loans to the Allies exceeded $2 billion, nearly one hundred times the amount lent to Germany. These financial ties, like the war trade they underwrote, linked the United States to the Allies and convinced Germany that American neutrality was only a formality.

THE DIPLOMACY OF NEUTRALITY

This same imbalance characterized American diplomacy. Wilson insisted on American neutral rights but acquiesced in British violations of those rights, while sternly refusing to yield on German actions. Wilson argued that while British violations of international law cost Americans property, markets, and time, German violations cost lives. As the *Boston Globe* noted, the British were "a gang of thieves" and the Germans "a gang of murderers. On the whole, we prefer the thieves, but only as the lesser of two evils."

When the war began, the United States asked belligerents to respect the 1909 **Declaration of London** on neutral rights. Germany agreed to do so; the British refused. Instead, skirting or violating established procedures, Britain instituted a blockade of Germany, mined the North Sea, and forced neutral ships into British ports to search their cargoes and confiscate material deemed useful to the German war effort. These British actions infringed U.S. trading rights. Wilson branded Britain's blockade illegal and unwarranted, but by October he had conceded many of America's neutral rights in order to avoid conflict with Britain. This concession reflected both Wilson's

English sympathies, for he thought it unfair and unrealistic to demand that Britain abandon its most effective weapon, and the profitable war trade with the Allies. He was also convinced that the Allied cause was vital to America's interests.

The British then prohibited food and other products that Germany had imported during peacetime, thereby interfering further with neutral shipping. Even the British admitted that these steps had no legal justification, and one American official complained privately, "England is playing a . . . high game, violating international law every day." But when the Wilson administration finally protested, it undermined its own position by noting that "imperative necessity" might justify a violation of international law. This statement virtually authorized the British to violate American rights. In January 1915, Wilson yielded further by observing that "no very important questions of principle" were involved in the Anglo-American quarrels over ship seizures and that they could be resolved after the war.

Submarine warfare.

This policy tied the United States to the British war effort and provoked a German response. With its army stalemated on land and its navy no match for Britain's, Germany decided in February 1915 to use its submarines against Allied shipping in a war zone around the British Isles. Neutral ships risked being sunk by mistake, partly because British ships illegally flew neutral flags. Germany maintained that Britain's blockade and the acquiescence of neutral countries in British violations of international law made submarine warfare necessary.

Submarines could not readily follow traditional rules of naval warfare. These rules had been drawn up for surface ships and required them to identify enemy merchant ships and insure the safety of passengers before attacking. But small and fragile submarines depended on surprise attacks. They could not surface without risking disaster from the deck guns of Britain's armed merchant ships, and they were too small to rescue victims of their sinkings. Yet Wilson refused to see the same "imperative necessity" in German tactics that he found in British tactics, and he warned that he would hold Germany responsible for any loss of American lives or property.

In May 1915, a German submarine sank a British passenger liner, the *Lusitania*. It had been carrying arms, and the German embassy had warned Americans against traveling on the ship, but the loss of life—1,198 people, including 128 Americans—caused Americans to condemn Germany. "To speak of technicalities and the rules of war, in the face of such wholesale murder on the high seas, is a waste of time," trumpeted one magazine. Yet only six of a thousand

editors surveyed called for war, and even the combative Theodore Roosevelt estimated that 98 percent of Americans still opposed war. Wilson saw that he had to "carry out the double wish of our people, to maintain a firm front in respect of what we demand of Germany and yet do nothing that might by any possibility involve us in the war."

That stance was difficult. Wilson demanded that Germany abandon its submarine campaign. His language was so harsh that Bryan resigned, warning that by requiring more of Germany than of Britain, the President violated neutrality and threatened to draw the nation into war. Bryan argued that "Germany has a right to prevent contraband from going to the Allies," and he protested Britain's use of American passengers as shields to protect contraband cargo. "This country cannot be neutral and unneutral at the same time," he declared. "If it is to be neutral it cannot undertake to help one side against the other." Bryan proposed prohibiting Americans from traveling on belligerent ships. His proposal gained support in the South and West, and Senator Thomas Gore of Oklahoma and Representative Jeff McLemore of Texas introduced it in congressional resolutions in February 1916.

Wilson moved to defeat the Gore-McLemore resolutions, insisting that they impinged on presidential control of foreign policy and on America's neutral rights. In truth, the resolutions abandoned no vital national interest while offering to prevent another provocative incident. Moreover, neither law nor tradition gave Americans the right to travel safely on belligerent ships. Wilson's assertion of such a right committed him to a policy that could only lead to conflict. Of the nation's "double wish," then, Wilson placed more priority on confronting what he saw as the German threat than on meeting the popular desire for peace.

Arguments over submarine warfare climaxed in April 1916. A German submarine torpedoed the French ship *Sussex*, injuring four Americans. Wilson threatened to break diplomatic relations if Germany did not abandon unrestricted submarine warfare against all merchant vessels, enemy as well as neutral. This threat implied war. Germany promised not to sink merchant ships without warning but made its **Sussex Pledge** contingent on the United States' requiring Britain also to adhere to "the rules of international law universally recognized before the war." Wilson's diplomatic victory, then, was hollow. Peace for America would depend on the British adopting a course they had already rejected. As Wilson saw it, however, "any little German lieutenant can put us into the war at any time by some calculated outrage." Wilson's diplomacy had left the nation's future at the mercy of others.

THE BATTLE OVER PREPAREDNESS

The threat of war sparked a debate over military policy. Theodore Roosevelt and a handful of other politicians, mostly northeastern Republicans convinced that Allied victory was in the national interest, advocated what they called **preparedness**, a program to expand the armed forces and establish universal military training. Conservative business groups also joined the agitation. The National Security League, consisting of eastern bankers and industrialists, combined demands for preparedness with attacks on progressive reforms.

But most Americans, certain that their nation would not join the bloody madness, opposed expensive military preparations. Many supported a large peace movement. Leading feminists, such as Jane Addams, Charlotte Perkins Gilman, and Carrie Chapman Catt, formed the Woman's Peace Party in 1915, and other organizations, such as the American League to Limit Armaments, also campaigned against preparedness. William Jennings Bryan denounced the militarism of Roosevelt as a "philosophy [that] can rot a soul" and condemned preparedness as a program for turning the nation into "a vast armory with skull and crossbones above the door." Most opponents agreed that military spending would undermine domestic reform and raise taxes while enriching arms merchants and financiers.

Wilson also opposed preparedness initially, but he reversed his position when the submarine crisis with Germany intensified. He also began to champion military expansion, lest Republicans accuse him in the 1916 election of neglecting national defense. In early 1916, he made a speaking tour to generate public support for expanding the armed forces. Continuing opposition to preparedness, especially in the South and West, forced Wilson to drop his proposal for a national reserve force. Nevertheless, the National Defense Act and the Naval Construction Act increased the strength of the army and authorized a naval construction plan. Draped in the flag, Wilson marched at

A preparedness parade winds its way through Mobile, Alabama, on July 4, 1916. By 1916, President Wilson, invoking the spirit of patriotism, had given his support to the preparedness program of military expansion.

the head of a huge preparedness parade in Washington to celebrate the military program.

THE ELECTION OF 1916

Wilson's preparedness plans stripped the Republicans of one issue in 1916, and his renewed support of progressive reforms (see Chapter 21) helped to hold Bryan Democrats in line. Wilson continued his balancing act in the campaign itself, at first stressing "Americanism" and preparedness but then emphasizing peace. The slogan "He Kept Us Out of War" appealed to the popular desire for peace, and the Democratic campaign became one long peace rally. Wilson disliked the peace emphasis but exploited its political appeal. He warned, "The certain prospect of the success of the Republican party is that we shall be drawn, in one form or another, into the embroilments of the European war."

The Republicans were divided. They had hoped to regain their progressive members after Roosevelt urged the Progressive Party to follow him back into the GOP. But many joined the Democratic camp instead, including several Progressive Party leaders, who endorsed Wilson for having enacted the party's demands of 1912. Roosevelt's frenzied interventionism had also alienated many midwestern Republicans opposed to preparedness and cost him any chance of gaining the nomination for himself. Instead, the GOP nominated Charles Evans Hughes, a Supreme Court justice and former New York governor. The platform denounced Wilson's "shifty expedients" in foreign policy and promised "strict and honest neutrality." Unfortunately for Hughes, Roosevelt's attacks on Wilson for not pursuing a war policy persuaded many voters that the GOP was a war party. The link with Roosevelt also kept Hughes from exploiting qualms about Wilson's own lack of neutrality. "If Hughes is defeated," wrote one observer, "he has Roosevelt to thank for it."

The election was the closest in decades (see Map 23-1). When California narrowly went for Wilson, it decided the contest. The results reflected sectional differences, with the South and West voting for Wilson and most of the Northeast and Midwest for Hughes. The desire for peace, all observers concluded, had determined the election.

DESCENT INTO WAR

Still, Wilson knew that war loomed, and he made a last effort to avert it. In 1915 and 1916, he had tried to mediate the European conflict, using Colonel House as a secret intermediary. Now he again appealed for an end to hostilities. In January 1917, he sketched out the

MAP 23-1 The Election of 1916
Woodrow Wilson won reelection in 1916—despite a reunified Republican party—by sweeping the South and West on campaign appeals to peace and progressive reform.

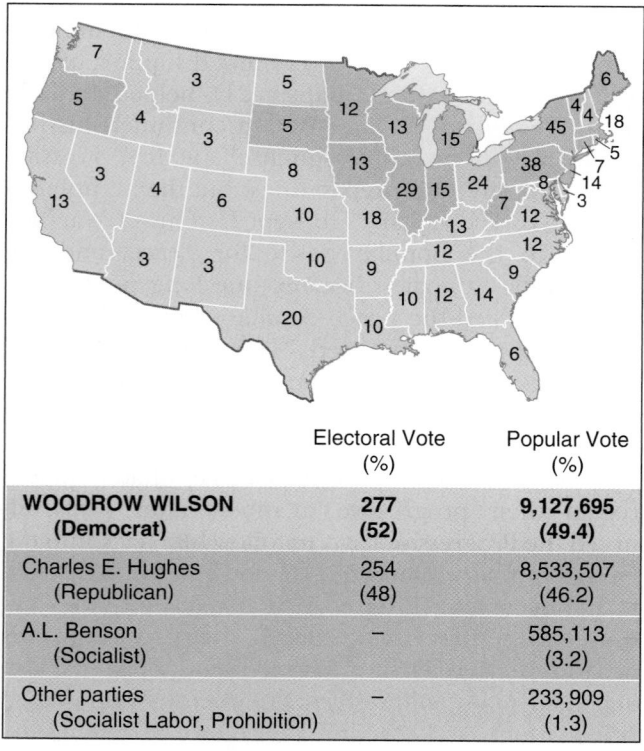

	Electoral Vote (%)	Popular Vote (%)
WOODROW WILSON (Democrat)	**277** (52)	**9,127,695** (49.4)
Charles E. Hughes (Republican)	254 (48)	8,533,507 (46.2)
A.L. Benson (Socialist)	–	585,113 (3.2)
Other parties (Socialist Labor, Prohibition)	–	233,909 (1.3)

terms of what he called a "peace without victory." Anything else, he warned, would only lead to another war. The new world order should be based on national equality and **self-determination**, arms reductions, freedom of the seas, and an international organization to insure peace. It was a distinctly American vision.

Neither the Allies nor the Central Powers were interested. Each side had sacrificed too much to settle for anything short of outright victory. Germany wanted to annex territory in eastern Europe, Belgium, and France and to take over Belgian and French colonies in Africa; Austria sought Balkan territory. The Allies wanted to destroy German military and commercial power, weaken the Austro-Hungarian empire, take Germany's colonies in Africa, and supplant Turkish influence in the Middle East. One British leader denounced Wilson as "the quintessence of a prig" for suggesting that, after three years of "this terrible effort," the two sides should accept American principles rather than their own national objectives. Wilson's initiative failed.

To break the deadlock, Germany decided to resume unrestricted submarine warfare. Such action seemed necessary: By 1917, nearly 700 German civilians died each day because of the British blockade, far more than the daily toll of British soldiers in the trenches. German generals believed that even if the United States declared war, it could do little more in the short run to injure Germany than it was already doing. German submarines, they hoped, would end the war by cutting the Allies off from U.S. supplies before the United States could send an army to Europe. On January 31, Germany announced its decision to unleash its submarines in a broad war zone.

Wilson commits to war. Wilson was now virtually committed to a war many Americans opposed. He broke diplomatic relations with Germany and asked Congress to arm American merchant vessels. When the Senate refused, Wilson invoked an antipiracy law of 1819 and armed the ships anyway. Although no American ships had yet been sunk, he also ordered the naval gun crews to shoot submarines on sight. Wilson's own secretary of the navy warned that these actions violated international law and were a step toward war; Wilson called his policy "armed neutrality." Huge rallies across America demanded peace.

Yet, several developments soon shifted public opinion. On March 1, Wilson released an intercepted message from the German foreign minister, Arthur Zimmermann, to the German minister in Mexico. It proposed that in the event of war between the United States and Germany, Mexico should ally itself with Germany; in exchange, Mexico would recover its "lost territory in Texas, New Mexico, and Arizona." The Zimmermann note produced a wave of hostility toward Germany and increased support for intervention in the war, especially in the Southwest, which had opposed involvement. A revolution in Russia overthrew the tsarist regime and established a provisional government. Russia was now "a fit partner" for the United States, said Wilson. When submarines sank four American freighters in mid-March, anti-German feeling broadened.

On April 2, 1917, Wilson delivered his war message, declaring that neutrality was no longer possible, given Germany's submarine "warfare against mankind." To build support for joining a war that most people had long regarded with revulsion and as alien to American interests, Wilson set forth the nation's war goals as simple and noble. The United States would not fight for conquest or domination but for "the ultimate peace of the world and for the liberation of its peoples. . . . The world must be made safe for democracy." Interventionists were delighted with the decision for war but often distanced themselves from any goal other than promoting national interests. Some progressives who had opposed involvement were won over by Wilson's appeal to idealism.

But others in Congress attacked war. Senator Robert La Follette assailed Wilson's policies as unneutral. Senator George Norris of Nebraska condemned the economic motives for American belligerency, crying out, "We are going to war upon the command of gold." Ridiculing Wilson's advocacy of war as a means to promote democracy, House Democratic leader Claude Kitchin of North Carolina insisted that the American people opposed war and unsuccessfully urged holding a popular referendum on the question. After vigorous debate, the Senate passed the war reso-

lution 82 to 6 and the House 373 to 50. On April 6, 1917, the United States officially entered the Great War, what Kitchin predicted would be "one vast drama of horrors and blood, one boundless stage upon which will play all the evil spirits of earth and hell."

WAGING WAR IN AMERICA

Mobilizing for military intervention was a massive undertaking. "It is not an army that we must shape and train for war," announced President Wilson; "it is a Nation." The government reorganized the economy to emphasize centralized management, developed policies to control public opinion and suppress dissent, and transformed the role of government itself. Mobilization often built on progressives' moralism and sense of mission and their work to resolve social and economic problems by government intervention. In other respects, however, the war experience undercut progressive achievements and withered the spirits of reformers. In many different ways, people on the home front—like soldiers in Europe—would participate in the Great War; all would find their lives changed.

MANAGING THE WAR ECONOMY

Surveying the nation's economy in May 1917, Secretary of War Newton Baker echoed Wilson. War no longer involved merely soldiers and weapons, he said. "It is the conflict of smokestacks now, the combat of the driving wheel and the engine." To harness those factories and machines for the war, federal and state governments developed a complex structure of agencies and controls for every sector of the economy, from industry and agriculture to transportation and labor (see the Overview table, "Major Government Wartime Agencies"). Supervised by the

Overview

Major Government Wartime Agencies

Agency	Purpose
War Industries Board	Reorganized industry to maximize wartime production
Railroad Administration	Modernized and operated the nation's railroads
Food Administration	Increased agricultural production, supervised food distribution and farm labor
National War Labor Board	Resolved labor-management disputes, improved labor conditions, and recognized union rights as means to promote production and efficiency
Committee on Public Information	Managed propaganda to build public support for the war effort

Council of National Defense, these agencies shifted resources to war-related enterprise, increased production of goods and services, and improved transportation and distribution.

Organizing industry.   The most important agency was the **War Industries Board (WIB)**, established in July 1917 to set industrial priorities, coordinate military purchasing, and supervise business. Led by financier Bernard Baruch, the WIB exercised unprecedented powers over industry by setting prices, allocating scarce materials, and standardizing products and procedures to boost efficiency. The number of sizes and styles of plows was reduced by 80 percent; the number of colors of typewriter ribbon dropped from 150 to 5. The WIB even specified how many trunks traveling salesmen could carry and how many stops elevators could make. Yet Baruch was not an industrial dictator; he aimed at business-government integration. The WIB promoted major business interests, helped suspend antitrust laws, and guaranteed huge corporate profits. So many business leaders became involved in the WIB that there was a popular outcry against business infiltration of the govern-

ment, and one corporate executive admitted, "We are all making more money out of this war than the average human being ought to." Some progressives began to see the dangers, and business leaders the advantages, of government economic intervention.

The Railroad Administration also linked business ambitions to the war economy. Under William McAdoo, it operated the nation's railroads as a unified system to move supplies and troops efficiently. Centralized management eliminated competition, permitted improvements in equipment, and brought great profits to the owners but higher prices to the general public. The Progressive Republican Senator Hiram Johnson of California protested that the Railroad Administration was "outrageously generous to the railroads and shamefully unjust to the people."

Assuring food supplies.   Equally effective and far more popular was the Food Administration, headed by Herbert Hoover. Hoover had organized relief supplies for war-torn Belgium and now controlled the production and distribution of food for the United States and its allies. He persuaded millions of Americans to accept meatless and wheatless days, so that

"Eat the potatoes, save the wheat; drive the Kaiser to defeat." Children in Wahoo, Nebraska, tend their victory garden. Government agencies tried to enlist everyone in the war effort.

the Food Administration could feed military and foreign consumers. Half a million women went door to door to secure food-conservation pledges from housewives. City residents planted victory gardens in parks and vacant lots, and President Wilson even pastured sheep on the White House lawn.

Hoover also worked closely with agricultural processors and distributors, assuring profits in exchange for cooperation. Farmers profited from the war, too. To encourage production, Hoover established high prices for commodities, and agricultural income rose by 30 percent. State and federal governments also provided commercial farmers with sufficient farm labor despite the military draft and competition from high-wage war industries. The Food Administration organized the Woman's Land Army to work in the fields. Most states formed units of the Boys' Working Reserve for agricultural labor. Many southern and western states required "loafers" or "slackers" to work in agriculture. Agribusinesses in the Southwest persuaded the federal government to permit them to import Mexicans to work under government supervision and be housed in special camps.

Overseeing labor relations. The National War Labor Board supervised labor relations. In exchange for labor's cooperation, this agency guaranteed the rights of unions to organize and bargain collectively. With such support, unions sharply increased their membership. The labor board also encouraged improved working conditions, higher wages, and shorter hours. War contracts stipulated an eight-hour day, and by the end of the war, nearly half the nation's workers had achieved the forty-eight-hour week. Wages rose, too, but often only as fast as inflation. These improvements limited labor disputes during the war, and Secretary of War Baker praised labor as "more willing to keep in step than capital." But when such unions as the Industrial Workers of the World did not keep in step, the government suppressed them.

Although these and other government regulatory agencies were dismantled when the war ended, their activities reinforced many long-standing trends in the American economy, from the consolidation of business to the commercialization of agriculture and the organization of labor. They also set a precedent for governmental activism that would prove valuable during the crises of the 1930s and 1940s.

WOMEN AND MINORITIES: NEW OPPORTUNITIES, OLD INEQUITIES.

The reorganization of the economy also had significant social consequences, especially for women and African Americans. In response to labor shortages, public officials and private employers exhorted women to join the work force—"For Every Fighter a Woman Worker," urged one poster. Women now took jobs previously closed to them. Besides farm work, they built airplanes, produced guns and ammunition, and manufactured tents and cartridge belts. More than 100,000 women worked in munitions plants and 40,000 in the steel industry. Women constituted 20 percent or more of all workers making electrical machinery, leather and rubber goods, and food. They operated drills and lathes, controlled cranes in steel mills, and repaired equipment in machine shops. "One of the lessons from the war," said one manufacturer, "has been to show that women can do exacting work." Harriot Stanton Blatch, a suffragist active in the Food Administration, estimated that a million women had replaced men in industry, where "their drudgery is for the first time paid for."

Many working women simply shifted to other jobs, where their existing skills earned better wages and benefits. The reshuffling of jobs among white women opened new vacancies for black women in domestic, clerical, and industrial employment. As black women

With women's labor crucial for the war effort, both government agencies and private industry recruited women for factory work. Here, four women, wearing "womanall" worksuits, pause at their jobs at the Westinghouse Electric Company in 1918.

replaced white women in the garment and textile industries, social reformers spoke of "a new day for the colored woman worker." But such optimism was unwarranted. Racial as well as gender segregation continued to mark employment, and wartime improvements were temporary. Federal efforts to prevent pay inequities and sexual harassment in the workplace were halfhearted and subordinated to the goals of efficiency and productivity. And, as one woman said of employers, "As usual, they did not want women to interfere in any way."

The war did help middle-class women reformers achieve two long-sought objectives: woman suffrage and prohibition. Women's support for the war effort prompted more Americans to support woman suffrage. Emphasizing the national cooperation needed to wage the war, one magazine noted that "arbitrarily to draw the line at voting, at a time when every man and woman must share in this effort, becomes an absurd anomaly." Even Woodrow Wilson finally endorsed the reform, terming it "vital to the winning of the war." Congress approved the suffrage amendment, which was ratified in 1920. Convinced that abstaining from alcohol would save grain and make workers and soldiers more efficient, Congress also passed the prohibition amendment, which was ratified in 1919.

The war also changed the lives of African Americans. The demand for industrial labor caused a huge migration of black people from the rural South, where they had had little opportunity, few rights, and no hope. In northern cities, they worked in shipyards, steel mills, and packing houses. Half a million African Americans moved north during the war, doubling and tripling the black populations of Chicago, Detroit, and other industrial cities.

Unfortunately, black people often encountered the kind of racial discrimination and violence in the North that they had hoped to leave behind in the South. Fearful and resentful white people started race riots in northern cities. In East St. Louis, Illinois, where thousands of black Southerners sought defense work, a white mob, in July 1917, murdered at least thirty-nine black people, sparing, as an investigating committee reported, "neither age nor sex in their blind lust for blood." Others

Black women work in a brick yard for wartime construction. Mobilization opened new jobs for women, but racial subordination and segregation persisted. Black women often performed the hardest and least desirable work.

placed the tragedy in a larger context. The *Literary Digest* noted, "Race-riots in East St. Louis afford a lurid background to our efforts to carry justice and idealism to Europe." And Wilson was told privately that the riot was "worse than anything the Germans did in Belgium."

FINANCING THE WAR

To finance the war, the government borrowed money and raised taxes. Business interests favored the first course, but southern and western progressives argued that taxation was more efficient and equitable and would minimize war profiteering. Conservative and business opposition to progressive taxation prompted California Senator Johnson to note, "Our endeavours to impose heavy war profit taxes . . . have brought into sharp relief the skin-deep dollar patriotism of some of those who have been loudest in declamations on war and in their demands for blood." Nevertheless, the tax laws of 1917 and 1918 established a graduated tax structure with increased taxes on large incomes, corporate profits, and wealthy estates. Conservative opposition, however, would frustrate progressives' hopes for permanent tax reforms.

The government raised two-thirds of the war costs by borrowing. Most of the loans came from banks and wealthy investors, but the government also campaigned to sell **Liberty Bonds** to the general public. Celebrities went to schools, churches, and rallies to persuade Americans to buy bonds as their patriotic duty. "Every person who refuses to subscribe," Secretary of the Treasury McAdoo told a California audience, "is a friend of Germany." Using techniques of persuasion and control from advertising and mass entertainment, the Wilson administration thus enlisted the emotions of loyalty, fear, patriotism, and obedience for the war effort.

CONQUERING MINDS

The government also tried to promote a war spirit among the American people by establishing propaganda agencies and enacting legislation to control social attitudes and behavior. This program drew from the restrictive side of progressivism: its impulses toward social control, behavior regulation, and nativism. It also reflected the interests of more conservative forces. The Wilson administration adopted this program of social mobilization because many Americans opposed the war: German Americans with ethnic ties to the Central Powers, Irish Catholics and Russian Jews who condemned the Allies for persecution and repression, Scandinavian immigrants averse to military service, pacifists who recoiled from what Wilson himself called "the most terrible and disastrous of all wars," radicals who denounced the war as capitalist and imperialist, and many others, especially among the rural classes of the South and Midwest, who saw no reason to participate in the distant war.

Government propaganda. To rally Americans behind the war effort, Wilson established the **Committee on Public Information (CPI)**, under the journalist George Creel. Despite its title, the CPI sought to manipulate, not inform, public opinion. Creel described his goal as winning "the fight for the minds of men, for the 'conquest of their convictions.'" The CPI flooded the country with press releases, advertisements, cartoons, and canned editorials. An average of six pounds of government publicity went each day to every newspaper in California, for example. The CPI made newsreels and war movies to capture public attention. It scheduled 75,000 speakers, who delivered a million speeches to 400 million listeners. Its women's division targeted American women in stereotyped emotional terms. It hired artists to draw posters, professors to write pamphlets in twenty-three languages, and poets to compose war poems for children.

Other government agencies launched similar campaigns. The Woman's Committee of the Council of National Defense established the Department of Educational Propaganda and Patriotic Education. Carrie Chapman Catt dropped her peace activism to head this bureau, in the hope that the war effort would increase support for woman suffrage.

"Beat Back the Hun," a poster to induce Americans to buy Liberty Bonds, demonizes the enemy in a raw, emotional appeal. Liberty bond drives raised the immense sum of $23 billion.

The agency worked to win over women who opposed the war, particularly in the rural Midwest, West, and South. It formed women's speakers' bureaus, developed programs for community meetings at country schools, and distributed millions of pamphlets.

Government propaganda had three themes: national unity, the loathsome character of the enemy, and the war as a grand crusade for liberty and democracy. Obsessed with national unity and conformity, Creel promoted fear, hatred, and prejudice in the name of a triumphant Americanism. Germans were depicted as brutal, even subhuman, rapists and murderers. The campaign suggested that any dissent was unpatriotic, if not treasonous, and dangerous to national survival. This emphasis on unreasoning conformity helped prompt hysterical attacks on German Americans, radicals, and pacifists.

SUPPRESSING DISSENT

The Wilson administration also suppressed dissent, now officially branded disloyalty. For reasons of their own, private interests helped shape a reactionary repression that tarnished the nation's professed idealistic war goals. The campaign also established unfortunate precedents for the future.

Congress rushed to stifle antiwar sentiment. The **Espionage Act** provided heavy fines and up to twenty years in prison for obstructing the war effort, a vague phrase but one "omnipotently comprehensive," warned one Idaho senator who opposed the law. "No man can foresee what it might be in its consequences." In fact, the Espionage Act became a weapon to crush dissent and criticism. Eventually, Congress passed the still more sweeping **Sedition Act of 1918**. Based on state laws in the West designed to suppress labor radicals, the Sedition Act provided severe penalties for speaking or writing against the draft, bond sales, and war production and for criticizing government personnel or policies. Congress emphasized the law's inclusive nature by rejecting a proposed amendment stipulating that "nothing in this act shall be construed as limiting the liberty or impairing the right of any individual to publish or speak what is true, with good motives, and for justifiable ends." Senator Hiram Johnson lamented, "It is war. But, good God, . . . when did it become war upon the American people?"

Postmaster General Albert Burleson banned antiwar or radical newspapers and magazines from the mail, suppressing literature so indiscriminately that one observer said he "didn't know socialism from rheumatism." Even more zealous in attacking radicals and presumed subversives was the reactionary attorney general, Thomas Gregory, who made little distinction between traitors and pacifists, war critics, and radicals. Eugene Debs was sentenced to ten years in prison for a "treasonous" speech in which he declared it "extremely dangerous to exercise the right of free speech in a country fighting to make democracy safe in the world." By war's end, a third of the Socialist party's national leadership was in prison, leaving the party in shambles. Other notable radicals imprisoned included Ricardo Flores Magon, a Mexican-American labor organizer who was sentenced to twenty years for publishing antiwar material in his Los Angeles Spanish-language newspaper, *Regeneración*.

Gregory also enlisted the help of private vigilantes, including several hundred thousand members of the reactionary American Protective League, which sought to purge radicals and reformers from the nation's economic and political life. They wiretapped telephones, intercepted private mail, burglarized

Police forcibly break up an antidraft protest by 5,000 women at New York City Hall on June 16, 1917. Insisting upon what President Wilson called "patriotic devotion," authorities at all levels vigorously suppressed dissent during the Great War.

union offices, broke up German-language newspapers, harassed immigrants, and staged mass raids, seizing thousands of people they claimed were not doing enough for the war effort. Even George Creel conceded that "at all times their patriotism was a thing of screams, violence, and extremes, and their savage intolerances had the burn of acid."

State and local authorities also suppressed what they saw as antiwar, radical, or pro-German activities. They established 184,000 investigating and enforcement agencies, known as councils of defense or public-safety committees. They encouraged Americans to spy on one another, required people to buy Liberty Bonds, and prohibited teaching German in schools or using the language in religious services and telephone conversations (see American Views: "Mobilizing America for Liberty"). Indeed, suppression of all things German reached extremes. Germanic names of towns, streets, and people were changed; sauerkraut became liberty cabbage, and the hamburger the liberty sandwich. In Tulsa, a member of the council of defense killed someone for making allegedly pro-German remarks. The council declared its approval, and community leaders applauded the killer's patriotism. A midwestern official of the Council of National Defense noted, "All over this part of the country men are being tarred and feathered and some are being lynched. . . . These cases do not get into the newspapers nor is an effort ever made to punish the individuals concerned."

Members of the business community exploited the hysteria to promote their own interests at the expense of farmers, workers, and reformers. As one Wisconsin farmer complained, businessmen "now under the guise of patriotism are trying to ram down the farmers' throats things they hardly dared before." On the Great Plains from Texas to North Dakota, the business target was the Nonpartisan League, a radical farm group demanding state control or ownership of banks, grain elevators, and flour mills. Although the League supported the war, oversubscribed bond drives, and had George Creel affirm its loyalty, conservatives depicted it as seditious to block its advocacy of political and economic reforms, including the confiscation of large fortunes to pay for the war. Minnesota's public-safety commission condemned members of the Nonpartisan League as traitors and proposed a "firing squad working overtime" to deal with them. Nebraska's council of defense barred League meetings. Public officials and self-styled patriots broke up the League's meetings and whipped and jailed its leaders.

In the West, business interests targeted labor organizations, especially the Industrial Workers of the World. In Arizona, for example, the Phelps-Dodge Company broke a miners' strike in 1917 by depicting the Wobblies as bent on war-related sabotage. A vigilante mob, armed and paid by the mining company, seized twelve hundred strikers, many of them Wobblies and one-third of them Mexican Americans, and herded them into the desert without food or water. Federal investigators found no evidence of sedition among the miners and reported that the company and its thugs had been inspired, not by "patriotism," but by "ordinary strike-breaking motives." Corporate management was merely "raising the false cry of 'disloyalty'" to suppress workers' complaints.

Nonetheless, the government itself assisted the business campaign. It used the army to break loggers' support for the IWW in the Pacific Northwest, and it raided IWW halls across the country in September 1917. The conviction of nearly two hundred Wobblies on charges of sedition in three mass trials in Illinois, California, and Kansas crippled the nation's largest industrial union.

In the end, the government was primarily responsible for the war hysteria, regardless of how such fears were used. It encouraged suspicion and conflict by its own inflammatory propaganda, repressive laws, and violation of basic civil rights, by supporting extremists who used the war for their own purposes, and by not opposing mob violence against German Americans. This ugly mood would infect the postwar world.

WAGING WAR AND PEACE ABROAD

While mobilizing the home front, the Wilson administration undertook an impressive military effort to help the Allies defeat the Central Powers. Wilson also struggled to secure international acceptance for his plans for a just and permanent peace.

THE WAR TO END ALL WARS

When the United States entered the war, the Allied military position was dire. The losses from three years of trench warfare had sapped military strength and civilian morale. French soldiers mutinied and refused to continue an assault that had cost 120,000 casualties in five days; the German submarine campaign was devastating the British. On the eastern front, the Russian army collapsed, and the Russian government gradually disintegrated after the overthrow of the tsarist regime.

What the Allies needed, said French Marshal Joseph Joffre in April 1917, was simple: "We want men, men, men." In May, Congress passed the **Selective Service Act of 1917**, establishing conscription. More than 24 million men eventually registered for the draft, and nearly 3 million entered the army when their numbers were drawn in a national lottery. Almost 2 million more men volunteered, as did more than ten thousand women, who served in the navy. Nearly one-fifth of America's soldiers were foreign-born (Europeans spoke of the "American Foreign Legion"); 367,000 were black. Many American Indians served with distinction as well; in response, Indian veterans were made citizens in 1919, a status extended to all Indians five years later.

Civilians were transformed into soldiers in hastily organized training camps, operated according to progressive principles. Prohibition prevailed in the camps; the poorly educated and largely working-class recruits were taught personal hygiene; worries about sin and inefficiency produced massive campaigns against venereal disease; and immigrants were taught English and American history. Some units were ethnically segregated: At Camp Gordon, Georgia, Italians and Slavs had separate units, with their own officers. Racial segregation was more rigid, not only in training camps and military units but in assignments as well. The navy assigned black sailors to menial positions, and the army similarly used black soldiers primarily as gravediggers and laborers. But one black combat division was created, and four black regiments fought under French command. France decorated three of these units with its highest citations for valor. (White American officers urged the French not to praise black troops, treat black officers as equals, or permit fraternization.)

AMERICAN VIEWS

Mobilizing America for Liberty

The war years witnessed official and popular efforts to repress dissent and diversity. Much of this repression was aimed at America's immigrant groups and sought to create national unity through coercive Americanization that trampled on the rights and values that the nation claimed to be defending. The following is an official proclamation of Governor W.L. Harding of Iowa, issued May 23, 1918.

- What is the rationale for the governor's proclamation? What do you think of his interpretation of the constitutional guarantees of individual rights?
- What other "inconvenience or sacrifice" might the proclamation impose on minorities?
- How might the proclamation incite vigilantism?

The official language of the United States and the State of Iowa is the English language. Freedom of speech is guaranteed by federal and State Constitutions, but this is not a guaranty of the right to use a language other than the language of this country—the English language. Both federal and State Constitutions also provide that "no laws shall be made respecting an establishment of religion or prohibiting the free exercise thereof." Each person is guaranteed freedom to worship God according to the dictates of his own conscience, but this guaranty does not protect him in the use of a foreign language when he can as well express his thought in English, nor entitle the person who cannot speak or understand the English language to employ a foreign language, when to do so tends in time of national peril, to create discord among neighbors and citizens, or to disturb the peace and quiet of the community.

Every person should appreciate and observe his duty to refrain from all acts or conversation which may excite suspicion or produce strife among the people, but in his relation to the public should so demean himself that every word and act will manifest his loyalty to his country and his solemn purpose to aid in achieving victory for our army and navy and the permanent peace of the world. . . .

The great aim and object of all should be unity of purpose and a solidarity of all the people under the flag for victory. This much we owe to ourselves, to posterity, to our country, and to the world.

Therefore, the following rules should obtain in Iowa during the war:

First. English should and must be the only medium of instruction in public, private, denominational, or other similar schools.

Second. Conversation in public places, on trains, and over the telephone should be in the English language.

Third. All public addresses should be in the English language.

Fourth. Let those who cannot speak or understand the English language conduct their religious worship in their homes.

This course carried out in the spirit of patriotism, though inconvenient to some, will not interfere with their guaranteed constitutional rights and will result in peace and tranquility at home and greatly strengthen the country in battle. The blessings of the United States are so great that any inconvenience or sacrifice should willingly be made for their perpetuity.

Therefore, by virtue of authority in me vested, I, W.L. Harding, Governor of the State of Iowa, commend the spirit of tolerance and urge that henceforth the within outlined rules be adhered to by all, that petty differences be avoided and forgotten, and that, united as one people with one purpose and one language, we fight shoulder to shoulder for the good of mankind.

Source: B.F. Shambaugh, ed., *Iowa and War* (Iowa City: State Historical Society of Iowa, 1919).

More than 40,000 women were recruited as non-combatant personnel, such as clerks, translators, and switchboard operators, thereby enabling more men to be assigned to combat duty. The navy awarded them equal rank with males performing the same tasks, and they were eligible after the war for veterans benefits. The army was a different story. Although serving in uniform and under military discipline, women had no formal military status, were ineligible for benefits, and often had their skills and contributions devalued. On the eve of a major battle in France, Merle Egan in the U.S. Army Signal Corps, working feverishly training soldiers to operate switchboards to help coordinate the massive military buildup, found that some of the men resented taking instructions from a woman. But "when I reminded them that any soldier could carry a gun but the safety of a whole division might depend on the switchboard one of them was operating, I had no more trouble."

The first American troops landed in France in June 1917. This American Expeditionary Force (AEF) was commanded by General John J. Pershing, a career officer who had chased Pancho Villa across northern Mexico (see Chapter 22). A gruff stickler for discipline (Secretary of War Baker worried that a man who had his mind so much on buttons would not have time to think about how to win a war), Pershing wanted to train his soldiers for a full two years before committing them to battle in 1919. But the AEF was rushed across the Atlantic in order to revive the collapsing morale among the French. Private Leo Bailey recalled that few of his company had ever discharged a firearm of any kind. "To have sent us to the front at that time would have been murder," he said. "We were woefully ignorant of the basic principles of the soldier." Months of training, under French direction, then followed as the Americans learned about trench warfare: using bayonets, grenades, and machine guns and surviving poison-gas attacks. Finally in October, the 1st Division, the Big Red One, moved into the trenches.

Full-scale American intervention began in the late spring of 1918 (see Map 23-2). General Tasker Bliss asked the French chief of staff, "Well, we have come over here to get killed. Where do you want to use us?" In June, the fresh American troops helped the French repulse a German thrust toward Paris at Château-Thierry. One soldier later recalled: "We saw the long lines of Marines leap from somewhere and start across the wheatfields. . . . As the first wave disappeared over the crest we heard the opening clatter of dozens of machine guns that sprayed our advancing lines. Then we heard some shrieks that made our blood run cold. High above the roar of the artillery and the clatter of machine guns we heard the war cries of the Marines. . . .

It seemed less than half an hour before all the machine guns had stopped firing." Further savage fighting at Belleau Wood blocked the Germans again, prompting a French officer to declare, "You Americans are our hope, our strength, our life." In July, the AEF helped defeat another German advance, at Rheims. The influx of American troops had tipped the balance toward Allied victory. By July 18, the German chancellor later acknowledged, "even the most optimistic among us knew that all was lost. The history of the world was played out in three days."

In July, Wilson also agreed to commit fifteen thousand American troops to intervene in Russia. Russia's provisional government had collapsed when the radical **Bolshevik** faction of the communist movement had seized power in November 1917. Under V.I. Lenin, the Bolsheviks had then signed an armistice with Germany in early 1918, which freed German troops for the summer offensive in France. The Allies' interventions were designed to reopen the eastern front and help overthrow the Bolshevik government. Lenin's call for the destruction of capitalism and imperialism alarmed the Allied leaders. One Wilson adviser urged the "eradication" of the Russian government. Soon, American and British troops were fighting Russians in an effort to influence Russia's internal affairs. U.S. forces remained in Russia until 1920, even after Germany had surrendered in 1918. These military interventions failed, but they did promote lasting Russian distrust of the West.

The Allies were more successful on the western front. Having stopped the German offensive in July, they launched their own advance. The decisive battle began in late September when an American army over 1 million strong attacked German trenches in the Argonne Forest. Many Americans were still inexperienced; some had been drafted only in July and had spent more time traveling than training. One officer worried, "With their unfamiliarity with weapons, a gun was about as much use as a broom in their hands." Nevertheless, the Americans advanced steadily, despite attacks with poison gas and heavy artillery. Lieutenant Maury Maverick (later a Texas congressman) described the shelling: "We were simply in a big black spot with streaks of screaming red and yellow, with roaring giants in the sky tearing and whirling and roaring." An exploding shell terrified him: "There is a great swishing scream, a smash-bang, and it seems to tear everything loose from you. The intensity of it simply enters your heart and brain, and tears every nerve to pieces."

The battle for the Argonne raged for weeks. One German general reported that his exhausted soldiers faced Americans who "were fresh, eager for fighting,

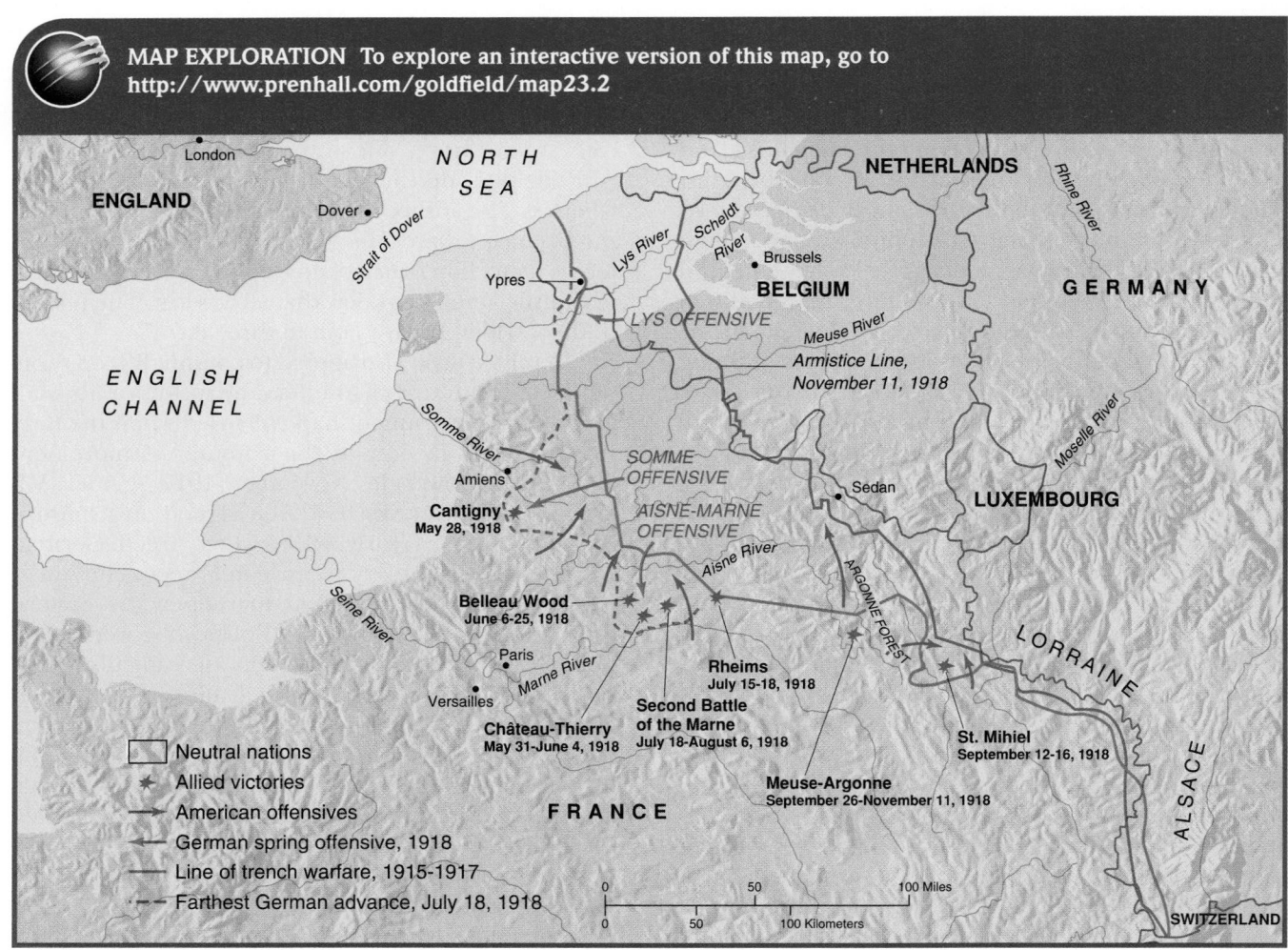

MAP EXPLORATION To explore an interactive version of this map, go to
http://www.prenhall.com/goldfield/map23.2

MAP 23-2   The Western Front, 1918
*After three years of trench warfare, the arrival of large numbers of American troops in 1918
enabled the Allies to launch an offensive that drove back the Germans and forced an armistice.*

and brave." But he found their sheer numbers most impressive. Eventually, this massive assault overwhelmed the Germans. Despite severe casualties, the AEF had helped the British and French to defeat the enemy. With its allies surrendering, its own army in retreat, and revolution breaking out among war-weary residents in its major cities, Germany asked for peace. On November 11, 1918, an armistice ended the Great War. More than 115,000 Americans were among the 8 million soldiers and 7 million civilians dead.

THE FOURTEEN POINTS

The armistice was only a step toward final peace. President Wilson had already enunciated American war objectives on January 8, 1918, in a speech outlining what became known as the Fourteen Points. In his 1917 war message, Wilson had advocated a more democratic world system, and this new speech spelled out

how to achieve it. But Wilson also had a political purpose. The Bolsheviks had published the Allies' secret treaties dividing up the expected economic and territorial spoils of war. Lenin called for an immediate peace based on the liberation of all colonies, self-determination for all peoples, and the rejection of annexations and punitive indemnities. Wilson's Fourteen Points reassured the American and Allied peoples that they were fighting for more than imperialist gains and offered an alternative to what he called Lenin's "crude formula" for peace.

Eight of Wilson's points proposed creating new nations, shifting old borders, or assuring self-determination for peoples previously subject to the Austrian, German, or Russian empires. The point about Russia would haunt Wilson after the Allied interventions there began, for it called on all nations to evacuate Russian territory and permit Russia "an unhampered

American soldiers advancing through smoke and shattered trees of the Argonne Forest in October 1918. Few participants found the Great War glorious or heroic. It was a conflict of relentless attrition, marked by the horrors of poison gas, artillery bombardment, pandemic disease, and what one American called the "unburied dead."

and unembarrassed opportunity for the independent determination of her own political development" under "institutions of her own choosing." Another five points invoked principles to guide international relations: freedom of the seas, open diplomacy instead of secret treaties, reduction of armaments, free trade, and the fair settlement of colonial claims. Wilson's fourteenth and most important point proposed a league of nations to carry out these ideals and ensure international stability.

Wilson and the German government had these principles in mind when negotiating the armistice. The Allies, however, had never explicitly accepted the Fourteen Points, and framing a final peace treaty would be difficult. While Wilson favored a settlement that would promote international stability and economic expansion, he recognized that the Allies sought "to get everything out of Germany that they can." Indeed, after their human and economic sacrifices, Britain and France wanted tangible compensation, not pious principles.

Convinced of the righteousness of his cause, Wilson decided to attend the peace conference in Paris himself, though no president had ever gone to Europe while in office. But Wilson weakened his position before he even set sail. First, he urged voters to support Democratic candidates in the November 1918 elections to indicate approval of his peace plans. But the electorate, responding primarily to domestic problems like inflation, gave the Republicans control of both houses of Congress. This meant that any treaty would have to be approved by Senate Republicans angry that Wilson had tried to use war and peace for partisan purposes. Second, Wilson refused to consult with Senate Republicans on plans for the peace conference and failed to name important Republicans to the Paris delegation. It would be Wilson's treaty, but Republicans would feel no responsibility to approve it.

THE PARIS PEACE CONFERENCE

The peace conference opened on January 18, 1919. Meeting at the Palace of Versailles, the delegations were dominated by the principal Allied leaders themselves: Wilson of the United States, David Lloyd George of Britain, Georges Clemenceau of France, and Vittorio Orlando of Italy. The Central Powers and Bolshevik Russia were excluded. The treaty would be one-sided except to the extent that Wilson could insist on the liberal terms of the Fourteen Points against French and British intransigence. As Clemenceau remarked, "God gave us the Ten Commandments and we broke them. Mr. Wilson has given us the Fourteen Points. We shall see."

Wilson himself had broken two of the Fourteen Points before the conference began. He had acquiesced in Britain's rejection of freedom of the seas. And he had sent U.S. troops to intervene in Russia in violation of its right to self-determination.

For months, the conference debated Wilson's other goals and the Allies' demands for compensation and security. Lloyd George later commented, with reference to the self-righteous Wilson and the assertive Clemenceau, "I think I did as well as might be expected, seated as I was between Jesus Christ and Napoleon Bonaparte." Under protest, Germany signed the **Treaty of Versailles** on June 28, 1919. Its terms were far more severe than Wilson had proposed or Germany had anticipated. Germany had to accept sole responsibility for starting the war, a stipulation that all Germans bitterly resented. It was required to pay huge reparations to the Allies; to give up land to France, Poland, Belgium, and Denmark; to cede its colonies; to limit its army and navy to small self-defense forces; to destroy military bases; and to promise not to manufacture or purchase armaments.

Wilson gained some acceptance of self-determination. As the German, Austro-Hungarian, Turkish, and Russian empires had collapsed at the end of the war, nationalist groups had proclaimed their independence. On one hand, the peace settlement formally recognized these new nation-states: Poland, Finland, Estonia, Latvia, and Lithuania in eastern Europe and Austria, Hungary, Czechoslovakia, and Yugoslavia in central Europe (see Map 23-3). On the other hand, France, Italy, Romania, and Japan all annexed territory regardless of the wishes of the inhabitants. Germans were placed under Polish control in Silesia and Czech control in Bohemia. Austrians were not allowed to merge with Germany. And the conference sanctioned colonialism by establishing a trusteeship system that enabled France, Britain, and Japan to take over German colonies and Turkish territory.

Moreover, Allied leaders endorsed the changes in eastern Europe in part because the new states there were anticommunist and would constitute a barrier against Bolshevism. Indeed, the Allies at Versailles were preoccupied with Bolshevik Russia, which one of Wilson's aides called the "black cloud of the east, threatening to overwhelm and swallow up the world." Communist movements in early 1919 in Germany, Austria, and Hungary caused the Allies to fear that "the Russian idea was still rising in power," and they hoped to isolate and weaken Bolshevik Russia. Allied armies were in Russia during the peace conference, and Wilson and the other leaders agreed to provide further aid to fight the

An exuberant President Wilson greeting an enthusiastic Paris crowd with French President Poincaré in December 1918. Within a few months, the Paris Peace Conference would produce disillusionment, bickering, and a flawed treaty that did little to insure international peace and stability.

Bolsheviks. This hostility to Russia, like the punitive terms for Germany and the concessions to imperial interests, boded ill for a stable and just postwar order.

But Wilson hoped that the final section of the Versailles treaty would resolve the flaws of the agreement by establishing his great international organization to preserve peace: the **League of Nations**. The Covenant, or constitution, of the League was built into the treaty. Its crucial feature, Article Ten, bound the member nations to guarantee each other's independence—a provision that was Wilson's concept of collective security. "At least," he told an aide, "we are saving the Covenant, and that instrument will work wonders, bring the blessing of peace, and then when the war psychosis has abated, it will not be difficult to settle all disputes that baffle us now." Sailing home, he mused, "Well, it is finished, and, as no one is satisfied, it makes me hope we have made a just peace; but it is all on the lap of the gods."

WAGING PEACE AT HOME

Wilson was determined to defeat opposition to the peace treaty. But many Americans were engaged in their own struggles with the new conditions of a nation suddenly at peace but riven by economic,

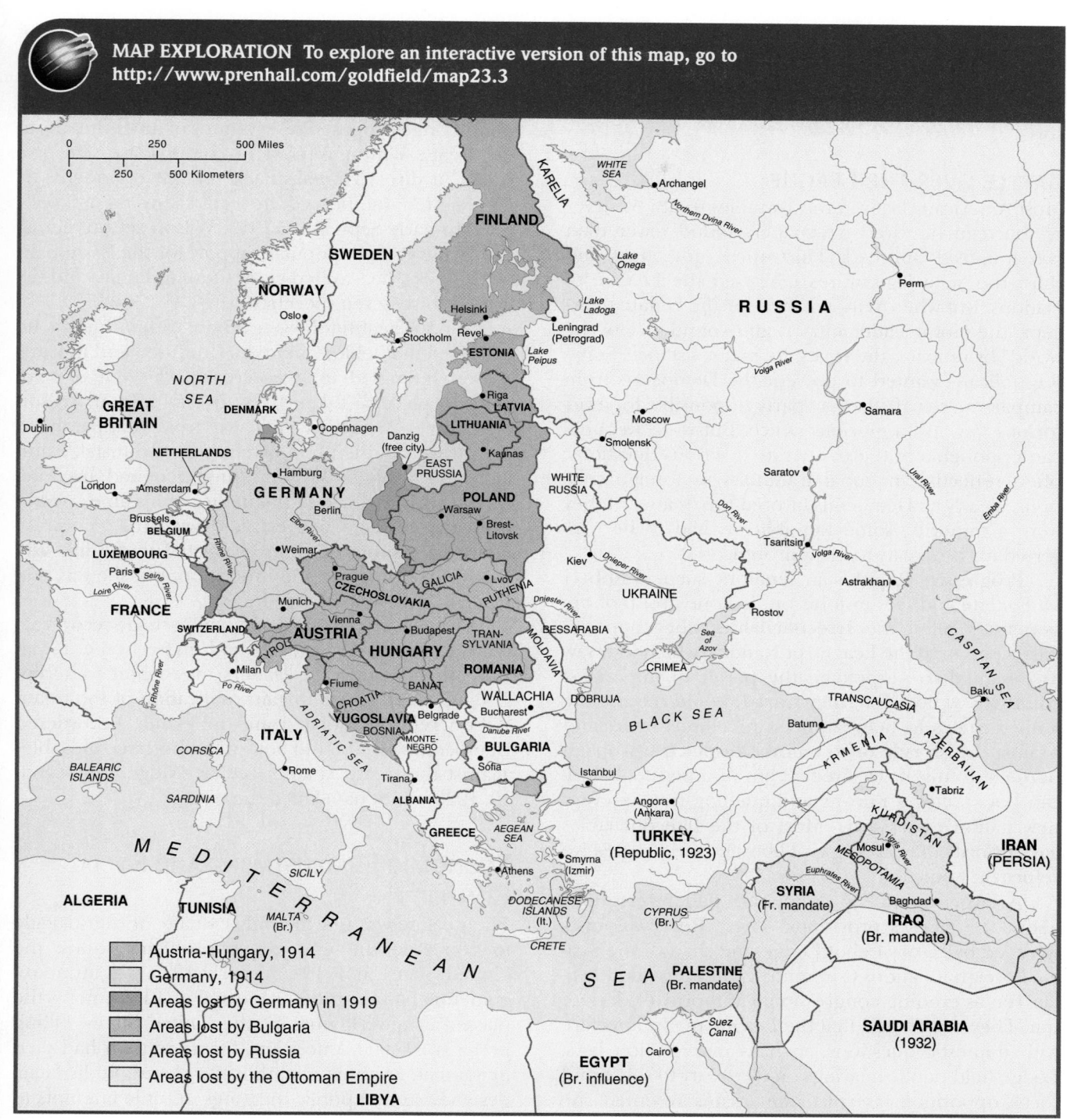

MAP EXPLORATION To explore an interactive version of this map, go to
http://www.prenhall.com/goldfield/map23.3

0   250   500 Miles
0   250   500 Kilometers

Austria-Hungary, 1914
Germany, 1914
Areas lost by Germany in 1919
Areas lost by Bulgaria
Areas lost by Russia
Areas lost by the Ottoman Empire

MAP 23-3   Europe and the Middle East after the Treaty of Versailles
*World War I and the Treaty of Versailles rearranged the borders of Europe and the Middle East.
Germany, Russia, and the Austrian and Turkish empires all lost land, and new nations were
recognized, but the principle of self-determination was only imperfectly observed.*

social, and political conflict shaped by the war experience. Wilson's battle for the League of Nations would fail tragically. The other conflicts would rage until the election of 1920 restored a normalcy of sorts.

BATTLE OVER THE LEAGUE

Most Americans favored the Versailles treaty. A survey of fourteen hundred newspapers found fewer than two hundred opposed. Thirty-three governors and thirty-two state legislatures endorsed the League of Nations. But when Wilson called for the Senate to accept "the moral leadership . . . and confidence of the world" by ratifying the treaty, he met resistance. Some Republicans wanted to prevent the Democrats from campaigning in 1920 as the party responsible for a victorious war and a glorious peace. But most Republican opponents of the treaty raised serious questions, often reflecting national traditions in foreign relations. Nearly all Democrats favored the treaty, but they were a minority; some Republicans had to be converted for the treaty to be approved.

Progressive Republican senators, such as Robert La Follette and Hiram Johnson, led one group of opponents. Called the **Irreconcilables**, they opposed participation in the League of Nations, which they saw as designed to perpetuate the power of imperialist countries. Article Ten, they feared, would require the United States to help suppress rebellions in Ireland against British rule or to enforce disputed European borders. Johnson declared, "I am opposed to American boys policing Europe and quelling riots in every new nation's backyard." Most of the Irreconcilables gave priority to restoring civil liberties and progressive reform at home.

A larger group of opponents had reservations about the treaty's provisions. These **Reservationists** were led by Henry Cabot Lodge, the chair of the Senate Foreign Relations Committee. They regarded Article Ten as eroding congressional authority to declare war. They also fretted that the League might interfere with domestic questions, such as immigration laws. Lodge held public hearings on the treaty to rouse and focus opposition. German Americans resented the war guilt clause; Italian and Polish Americans complained that the treaty did not satisfy the territorial ambitions of Italy and Poland; Irish Americans condemned the treaty's failure to give self-determination to Ireland. Many progressives also criticized the treaty's compromises on self-determination, reparations, and colonies. Linking these failures with Wilson's domestic policies, one former supporter concluded; "The administration has become reactionary, and deserves no support from any of us."

Lodge's own opposition was shaped by both partisanship and deep personal hostility. "I never expected to hate anyone in politics with the hatred I feel toward Wilson," Lodge confessed. Wilson reciprocated, and when Lodge proposed reservations or amendments to the treaty, Wilson refused to compromise. He proposed "a direct frontal attack" on his opponents. If they wanted war, he said, he would "give them a belly full." In early September 1919, Wilson set out across the country to win popular support for the League. In three weeks, he traveled eight thousand miles and delivered thirty-seven speeches.

In poor health following a bout with influenza, he collapsed in Pueblo, Colorado. Confused and in tears, Wilson mumbled to his secretary, "I seem to have gone to pieces." Taken back to Washington, Wilson on October 2 suffered a massive stroke that paralyzed his left side and left him psychologically unstable and temporarily blind. Wilson's physician and his wife, Edith Galt Wilson, kept the nature of his illness secret from the public, Congress, and even the vice president and cabinet. Rumors circulated that Edith Wilson was running the administration, but she was not. Instead, it was immobilized.

By February 1920, Wilson had partially recovered, but he remained suspicious and quarrelsome. Bryan and other Democratic leaders urged him to accept Lodge's reservations to gain ratification of the treaty. Wilson refused. Isolated and inflexible, he ordered Democratic senators to vote with the Irreconcilables against the treaty as amended by Lodge. On March 19, 1920, the Senate killed the treaty.

ECONOMIC READJUSTMENT AND SOCIAL CONFLICT

The League was not the only casualty of the struggle to conclude the war. Grave problems shook the United States in 1919 and early 1920. An influenza epidemic had erupted in Europe in 1918 among the massed armies. It now hit the United States, killing perhaps 700,000 Americans, far more than had died in combat. Frightened authorities closed public facilities and banned public meetings in futile attempts to stop the contagion.

Meanwhile, the Wilson administration had no plans for an orderly reconversion of the wartime economy, and chaos ensued. The secretary of the Council of National Defense later reported with but slight exaggeration, "The magnificent war formation of American industry was dissipated in a day; the mobilization that had taken many months was succeeded by an instantaneous demobilization." The government canceled war contracts and dissolved the regulatory agencies. Noting that "the war spirit of cooperation and sacrifice" had disappeared with the Armistice, Bernard Baruch decided to "turn industry absolutely free" and abolished the War Industries Board as of January 1, 1919. Other agencies followed in such haste that turmoil engulfed the economy.

The government also demobilized the armed forces. The army discharged 600,000 soldiers still in training camps; the navy brought AEF soldiers home from France so fast that it had to expand the troop fleet to four times its peak size during the war. With no planning or assistance, troops were hustled back into civilian life. There they competed for scarce jobs with workers recently discharged from the war industries.

As unemployment mounted, the removal of wartime price controls brought runaway inflation. The cost of food, clothing, and other necessities more than doubled over prewar rates. The return of the soldiers caused a serious housing shortage, and rents skyrocketed. Democratic leaders urged Wilson to devote less time to the League of Nations and more to the cost of living and the tensions it unleashed. Farmers also suffered from economic readjustments. Net farm income declined by 65 percent between 1919 and 1921. Farmers who had borrowed money for machinery and land to expand production for the war effort were left impoverished and embittered.

Postwar battles: gender and race.
Women also lost their wartime economic advances. Returning soldiers took away their jobs. Male trade unionists insisted that women go back to being housewives. One New York union maintained that "the same patriotism which induced women to enter industry during the war should induce them to vacate their positions after the war." At times, male workers struck to force employers to fire women and barred women from unions in jobs where union membership was required for employment. Most women were willing to relinquish their jobs to veterans who had previously held them but objected to being displaced by men without experience. "During the war they called us heroines," one woman complained, "but they throw us on the scrapheap now." Indeed, state legislatures actually passed new laws prohibiting women from working in many of the occupations they had successfully filled during the war. By 1919, half of the women newly employed in heavy industry during the war were gone; by 1920, women constituted a smaller proportion of the work force than they had in 1910.

The postwar readjustments also left African Americans disappointed. During the war, they had agreed with W.E.B. Du Bois to "forget our special grievances and close our ranks shoulder to shoulder with our own white fellow citizens." Participation in the war effort, they had hoped, might be rewarded by better treatment thereafter. African Americans had contributed to the fighting and home fronts. Now, the meagerness of their reward became clear.

Housing shortages and job competition interacted with racism in 1919 to produce race riots in twenty-six towns and cities, resulting in at least 120 deaths. In Chicago, thirty-eight people were killed and more than five hundred injured in a five-day riot that began when white thugs stoned to death a black youth swimming too near "their" beach. White rioters then fired a machine gun from a truck hurtling through black neighborhoods. But black residents fought back, no longer willing, the *Chicago Defender* reported, "to move along the line of least resistance as did their sires." The new militancy reflected both their experiences in the military and in industry and their exposure to propaganda about freedom and democracy. Racial conflict was part of a postwar battle between Americans hoping to preserve the new social relations fostered by the war effort and those wanting to restore prewar patterns of power and control.

Fighting for industrial democracy.
Even more pervasive discontents roiled as America adjusted to the postwar world. More than 4 million angry workers launched a wave of 3,600 strikes in 1919. They were reacting not only to the soaring cost of living, which undermined the value of their wages, but also to employers' efforts to reassert their authority and destroy the legitimacy labor had won by its participation in the war effort. The abolition of government controls on industry enabled employers not only to raise prices but also to rescind their recognition of unions and reimpose objectionable working conditions. Employers also protected their rising profits by insisting that workers' wages remain fixed. In response, strikers demanded higher wages, better conditions, and recognition of unions and the right of collective bargaining.

The greatest strike involved the American Federation of Labor's attempt to organize steelworkers, who endured dangerous conditions and twelve-hour shifts. When the steel companies refused to recognize the union or even discuss issues, 365,000 workers went out on strike in September 1919. Strikers in Pennsylvania pointed out that they had worked "cheerfully, without strikes or trouble of any kind" during the war to "make the world safe for democracy" and that they now sought "industrial democracy." Employers hired thugs to beat the strikers, used strikebreakers to take their jobs, and exploited ethnic and racial divisions

Postwar labor unrest met determined suppression. Here, mounted police attack striking steelworkers in Pittsburgh in 1919. The strikers were seeking union recognition and an end to twelve-hour days.

among them. To undercut support for the workers, management portrayed the strikers as disruptive radicals influenced by Bolshevism. After four months, the strike failed.

Employers used the same tactic to defeat striking coal miners, whose wages had fallen behind the cost of living. Refusing to negotiate with the United Mine Workers, coal operators claimed that Russian Bolsheviks financed the strike to destroy the American economy. Attorney General Mitchell Palmer secured an injunction against the strike under the authority of wartime legislation. Because the government no longer controlled coal prices or enforced protective labor rules, miners complained bitterly that the war had ended for corporations but not for workers.

Two municipal strikes in 1919 also alarmed the public when their opponents depicted them as revolutionary attacks on the social order. In Seattle, the Central Labor Council called a general strike to support 35,000 shipyard workers striking for higher wages and shorter hours. When 60,000 more workers from 110 local unions also walked out, the city ground to a halt. Workers behaved peacefully and protected public health and safety by operating garbage and fire trucks and providing food, water, and electricity. Nevertheless, Seattle's mayor, business leaders, and newspapers attacked the strikers as Bolsheviks and anarchists. Threatened with military intervention, the labor council called off the strike, but not before it had caused a public backlash against unions across the nation.

In Boston, the police commissioner fired police officers for trying to organize a union to improve their inadequate pay. In response, the police went on strike. As in Seattle, Boston newspapers, politicians, and business leaders attributed the strike to Bolshevism, although nothing indicated that the police wanted anything more than improved wages, conditions, and respect. Wilson denounced the Boston police strike as "a crime against civilization." Massachusetts Governor Calvin Coolidge mobilized the National Guard and gained nationwide acclaim when he stated, "There is no right to strike against the public safety by anybody, anywhere, anytime." The entire police force was fired; many of their replacements were war veterans.

THE RED SCARE

The strikes contributed to an anti-Bolshevik hysteria that swept the country in 1919. This **Red Scare** reflected fears that the Bolshevik revolution in Russia might spread to the United States. Steeped in the antiradical propaganda of the war years, many Americans were appalled by Russian Bolshevism, described by the *Saturday Evening Post* as a "compound of slaughter, confiscation, anarchy, and universal disorder." Their alarm grew in 1919 when Russia established the Third International to foster revolution abroad, and a few American socialists formed the American Communist Party. But the Red Scare also reflected the willingness of antiunion employers, ambitious politicians, sensational journalists, zealous veterans, and racists to exploit the panic to advance their own purposes.

Fed by misleading reports about Russian Bolshevism and its influence in the United States, the Red Scare reached panic levels by mid-1919. Bombs mailed anonymously to several prominent people on May Day seemed proof enough that a Bolshevik conspiracy threatened America. The Justice Department, Congress, and patriotic organizations like the American Legion joined with business groups to suppress radicalism, real and imagined. The government continued to enforce the repressive laws against Wobblies, socialists, and other dissenters; a Minnesota senator warned that the nation was more imperiled than during the war itself. Indeed, Wilson and Attorney General Mitchell Palmer called for more stringent laws and refused to release political prisoners jailed during the war. State governments harassed and arrested hundreds.

Palmer created a new agency, headed by J. Edgar Hoover, to suppress radicals and impose conformity. Its war on radicalism became the chief focus of the Justice Department. As an ambitious and ruthless bureaucrat, Hoover had participated in the government's assault on aliens and radicals during the war. Now he collected files on labor leaders and other "radical agitators" from Senator Robert La Follette to Jane Addams, issued misleading reports on communist influence in labor strikes and race riots, and contacted all major newspapers "to acquaint people like you with the real menace of evil-thinking, which is the foundation of the Red Movement." Indeed, the Justice Department itself promoted the Red Scare hysteria, which Palmer hoped would lead to his presidential nomination and Hoover hoped would enhance his own power and that of his bureau.

In November 1919, Palmer and Hoover began raiding groups suspected of subversion. A month later, they deported 249 alien radicals, including the anarchist Emma Goldman, to Russia. Rabid patriots endorsed such actions. One minister favored deporting radicals "in ships of stone with sails of lead, with the wrath of God for a breeze and with hell for their first port." In January 1920, Palmer and Hoover rounded up more than four thousand suspected radicals in thirty-three cities. Without warrants, they broke into union halls, club rooms, and private homes, assaulting and arresting everyone in sight. People were jailed without access to lawyers; some were beaten into signing false confessions. In Lynn, Massachusetts, thirty-nine people meeting to organize a bakery were arrested for holding a revolutionary caucus. Other arrests were just as outrageous, but the *Washington Post* clamored, "There is no time to waste on hairsplitting over infringement of liberty."

Other Americans began to recoil from the excesses and illegal acts. Assistant Secretary of Labor Louis Post stopped further deportations by demonstrating that most of the arrested were "working men of good character, who are not anarchists or revolutionists, nor politically or otherwise dangerous in any sense." They had been arrested, he said, "for nothing more dangerous than affiliating with friends of their own race, country, and language." Support for the Red Scare withered. Palmer's attempt to inflame public emotions to advance his own candidacy for the presidency backfired. When his predictions of a vio-

lent attempt to overthrow the government on May 1, 1920, came to naught, most Americans could see that no menace had ever existed. They agreed with the *Rocky Mountain News*: "We can never get to work if we keep jumping sideways in fear of the bewhiskered Bolshevik." Even one conservative Republican concluded that "too much has been said about Bolshevism in America." But if the Red Scare faded in mid-1920, the hostility to immigrants, organized labor, and dissent it reflected would endure for a decade. During the 1920s, the most acceptable forms of social change would be derived from technological and commercial innovations.

THE ELECTION OF 1920

Palmer failed to win the Democratic nomination, but it would have been an empty prize anyway. The Democratic coalition that Wilson had cobbled together on the issues of progressivism and peace came apart after the war. Workers resented the administration's hostility to the postwar strikes. Ethnic groups brutalized by the Americanization of the war years blamed Wilson for the war or condemned his peace settlement. Farmers grumbled about wartime price controls and postwar falling prices. Wartime taxes and the social and economic turmoil of 1919–1920 alienated the middle class. Americans were weary of great crusades and social sacrifices; in the words of Kansas journalist William Allen White, they were "tired of issues, sick at heart of ideals, and weary of being noble." They yearned for what Republican presidential candidate Warren Harding of Ohio called "normalcy."

The Republican ticket in 1920 symbolized the reassurance of simpler times. Harding was a genial politician who in a lengthy career had devoted more time to golf and poker than to public policy. An Old Guard conservative, he had stayed with the GOP when Theodore Roosevelt led the progressives out in 1912. His running mate, Calvin Coolidge, governor of Massachusetts, owed his nomination to his handling of the Boston police strike.

Wilson called the election of 1920 "a great and solemn referendum" on the League of Nations, but such lofty appeals fell flat. Harding was ambiguous about the League, and the Democratic national platform endorsed it but expressed a willingness to accept amendments or reservations. The Democratic nominees, James Cox, former governor of Ohio, and the young Franklin D. Roosevelt, Wilson's assistant secretary of the navy, favored the League, but it was not a decisive issue in the campaign.

Harding won in a landslide reflecting the nation's dissatisfaction with Wilson and the Democratic party. "The Democrats are inconceivably unpopular,"

In a 1920 cartoon, "A. Mitchell Palmer Out for a Stroll," the Chicago Tribune lampooned the Attorney General for his repeated but unfounded warnings about Bolshevik threats in America. The postwar Red Scare weakened civil liberties, promoted nativist hostilities, and undermined reform.

wrote Walter Lippmann, a prominent journalist. Harding received 16 million popular votes to Cox's 9 million. Running for president from his prison cell, Socialist Eugene Debs polled nearly a million votes. Not even his closest backers considered Harding qualified for the White House, but, as Lippmann said, the nation's "public spirit was exhausted" after the war years. The election of 1920 was "the final twitch" of America's "war mind."

CONCLUSION

The Great War disrupted the United States and much of the rest of the world. The initial American policy of neutrality yielded to sentimental and substantive links with the Allies and the pressure of German submarine warfare. Despite popular opposition, America joined the conflict when its leaders concluded that national interests demanded it. Using both military and diplomatic power, Woodrow Wilson sought to secure a more stable and prosperous world order, with an expanded role for the United States. But the Treaty of Versailles only partly fulfilled his hopes, and the Senate refused to ratify the treaty and its League of Nations. The postwar world order would be unstable and dangerous.

Participation in the war, moreover, had changed the American government, economy, and society. Some of these changes, including the centralization of the economy and an expansion of the regulatory role of the federal government, were already under way; some offered opportunities to implement progressive principles or reforms. Woman suffrage and prohibition gained decisive support because of the war spirit. But other consequences of the war betrayed both progressive impulses and the democratic principles the war was allegedly fought to promote. The suppression of civil liberties, manipulation of human emotions, repression of radicals and minorities, and exploitation of national crises by narrow interests helped disillusion the public. The repercussions of the Great War would linger for years, at home and abroad.

REVIEW QUESTIONS

1. What might have been the consequences, positive and negative, if the "deliberate and passionless method of doing what is regarded as a disagreeable duty" that Ray Stannard Baker found in 1917 had continued to characterize the U.S. war effort?

2. What were the major arguments for and against U.S. entry into the Great War? What position do you find most persuasive? Why?

3. How and why did the United States shape public opinion in World War I? What were the consequences, positive and negative, of the propaganda of the Committee on Public Information, Food Administration, and other government agencies?

4. How did other groups exploit the war crisis and the government's propaganda and repression?

5. Evaluate the role of Woodrow Wilson at the Paris Peace Conference. What obstacles did he face? How successful was he in shaping the settlement?

6. Discuss the arguments for and against American ratification of the Treaty of Versailles.

KEY TERMS

Allies (p. 725)

Bolshevik (p. 739)

Central Powers (p. 725)

Committee on Public Information (CPI) (p. 735)

Declaration of London (p. 727)

Espionage Act (p. 736)

Irreconcilables (p. 744)

League of Nations (p. 742)

Liberty Bonds (p. 734)

Preparedness (p. 729)

Red Scare (p. 746)

Reservationists (p. 744)

Sedition Act (p. 736)

Selective Service Act of 1917 (p. 737)

Self-determination (p. 730)

Sussex Pledge (p. 728)

Treaty of Versailles (p. 742)

War Industries Board (WIB) (p. 732)

RECOMMENDED READING

Clements, Kendrick A. *The Presidency of Woodrow Wilson* (1992). The best single volume on the Wilson presidency.

Coffman, Edward M. *The War to End All Wars* (1968). A valuable study of the U.S. military role in World War I.

Ferrell, Robert H. *Woodrow Wilson and World War I, 1917–1921* (1985). A useful synthesis that emphasizes diplomatic issues.

James, D. Clayton, and Anne Sharp Wells. *America and the Great War, 1914–1920* (1998). A fine, succinct synthesis of recent scholarship.

Kennedy, David M. *Over Here: The First World War and American Society* (1980). Thorough and illuminating discussion of the impact of World War I on American society.

Murray, Robert K. *The Red Scare: A Study in National Hysteria, 1919–1920* (1955). An important early study that retains much value.

Schaffer, Ronald. *America in the Great War: The Rise of the War Welfare State* (1991). An effective and provocative summary that illuminates the expanding role of government.

Zieger, Robert H. *America's Great War: World War I and the American Experience* (2000). A masterful account of the diplomatic, military, and domestic aspects of the war.

ADDITIONAL SOURCES

General Studies

Chambers, John Whiteclay II. *The Tyranny of Change* (1992).

Cooper, John M. Jr. *Pivotal Decades: The United States, 1900–1920* (1990).

Graham, Otis L. Jr. *The Great Campaigns: Reform and War in America* (1971).

Hawley, Ellis W. *The Great War and the Search for a Modern Order* (1992).

Lyons, Michael J. *World War I: A Short History* (1994).

Wynn, Neil. *From Progressivism to Prosperity: World War I and American Society* (1986).

Diplomacy of Neutrality, War, and Peace

Ambrosius, Lloyd. *Woodrow Wilson and the American Diplomatic Tradition* (1987).

Bailey, Thomas A. and Paul B. Ryan. *The Lusitania Disaster* (1975).

Burk, Kathleen. *Britain, America, and the Sinews of War* (1985).

Coogan, John. *The End of Neutrality* (1981).

Cooper, John M. Jr. *The Vanity of Power: American Isolationism and the First World War* (1969).

Cooper, John M. Jr. *Breaking the Heart of the World: Woodrow Wilson and the Fight for the League of Nations* (2001).

Foglesong, David S. *America's Secret War against Bolshevism: United States Intervention in the Russian Civil War, 1917–1920* (1995).

Gregory, Ross. *The Origins of American Intervention in the First World War* (1971).

Kaufman, Burton I. *Efficiency and Expansion: Foreign Trade Organization in the Wilson Administration* (1974).

Knock, Thomas J. *To End All Wars: Woodrow Wilson and the Creation of the League of Nations* (1992).

Levin, N. Gordon Jr. *Woodrow Wilson and World Politics: America's Response to War and Revolution* (1968).

Levine, Lawrence W. *Defender of the Faith: William Jennings Bryan, the Last Decade* (1965).

Link, Arthur S. *Woodrow Wilson and the Progressive Era, 1910–1917* (1954).

May, Ernest R. *The World War and American Isolation, 1914–1917* (1966).

McFadden, David W. *Alternative Paths: Soviets and Americans, 1917–1920* (1993).

Smith, Daniel M. *The Great Departure: The United States and World War I* (1965).

Stone, Ralph A. *The Irreconcilables* (1970).

Thompson, John A. *Woodrow Wilson* (2002).

Walworth, Arthur. *Wilson and the Peacemakers* (1986).

The Military

Barbeau, A. E. and Florette Henri. *The Unknown Soldiers: Black American Troops in World War I* (1974).

Bristow, Nancy. *Making Men Moral: Social Engineering During the Great War* (1996).

Chambers, John Whiteclay, II. *To Raise an Army* (1987).

Clifford, John Garry. *Citizen Soldiers: The Plattsburgh Training Camp Movement* (1972).

Coffman, Edward M. *The Hilt of the Sword: The Career of Peyton C. March* (1966).

Freidel, Frank. *Over There: The Story of America's First Great Overseas Crusade* (1964).

Patton, Gerald W. *War and Race: The Black Officer in the American Military* (1981).

Stallings, Laurence. *The Doughboys: The Story of the AEF, 1917–1918* (1963).

Trask, David. *The AEF and Coalition Warmaking, 1917–1918* (1993).

Vandiver, Frank E. *Black Jack: The Life and Times of John J. Pershing* (1977).

Wartime Economy and Society

Breen, William J. *Uncle Sam at Home: Civilian Mobilization, Wartime Federalism, and the Council of National Defense, 1917–1919* (1984).

Britten, Thomas. *American Indians in World War I: At Home and at War* (1997).

Connor, Valerie. *The National War Labor Board* (1983).

Cuff, Robert D. *The War Industries Board: Business-Government Relations during World War I* (1973).

Danbom, David. *The Resisted Revolution: Urban America and the Industrialization of Agriculture* (1979).

Greenwald, Maurine Weiner. *Women, War, and Work: The Impact of World War I on Women Workers in the United States* (1980).

Henri, Florette. *Black Migration: The Movement North, 1900–1920* (1975).

Koistinen, Paul. *Mobilizing for Modern War: The Political Economy of American Warfare, 1865–1919* (1997).

Luebke, Frederick C. *Bonds of Loyalty: German-Americans and World War I* (1974).

McCartin, Joseph A. *Labor's Great War: The Struggle for Industrial Democracy and the Origins of Modern American Labor Relations, 1912-1921* (1997).

Rudwick, Elliot M. *Race Riot at East St. Louis, July 2, 1917* (1964).

Thompson, John A. *Reformers and War: American Progressive Publicists and the First World War* (1987).

Vaughn, Stephen L. *Holding Fast the Inner Lines: Democracy, Nationalism, and the Committee on Public Information* (1980).

Wartime Dissent and Repression

Gibbs, Christopher. *The Great Silent Majority: Missouri's Resistance to World War I* (1989).

Kennedy, Kathleen. *Disloyal Mothers and Scurrilous Citizens: Women and Subversion During World War I* (1999).

Morlan, Robert. *Political Prairie Fire: The Nonpartisan League, 1915–1922* (1955).

Peterson, H. C. and Gilbert Fite. *Opponents of War, 1917–1918* (1957).

Preston, William. Jr. *Aliens and Dissenters: Federal Suppression of Radicals, 1903–1933* (1963).

Scheiber, Harry N. *The Wilson Administration and Civil Liberties* (1960).

Weinstein, James. *The Decline of Socialism in America* (1967).

Postwar Conflict

Brody, David. *Labor in Crisis: The Steel Strike of 1919* (1965).

Coben, Stanley A. *A. Mitchell Palmer, Politician* (1963).

Noggle, Burl. *Into the Twenties: The United States from Armistice to Normalcy* (1974).

Theoharis, Athan and John Stuart Cox. *The Boss: J. Edgar Hoover and the Great American Inquisition* (1988).

Tuttle, William M. Jr. *Race Riot: Chicago in the Red Summer of 1919* (1970).

WHERE TO LEARN MORE

- **National Infantry Museum, Fort Benning, Georgia.** This sprawling collection of weapons, uniforms, and equipment includes exhibits on World War I. www.benningmwr.com/index.cfm.

- **Fort George G. Meade Museum, Fort Meade, Maryland.** This museum contains unparalleled exhibits depicting U.S. military life during World War I, including artifacts, photographs, and French and American tanks designed for trench warfare.

- **General John J. Pershing Boyhood Home, Laclede, Missouri.** Maintained by the Missouri State Park Board, Pershing's restored nineteenth-century home exhibits some of his personal belongings and papers. www.mostateparks.com/pershingsite.htm.

- **Sgt. Alvin C. York Homeplace and State Historic Site, Pall Mall, Tennessee.** The home of America's greatest military hero of World War I contains fascinating artifacts, including York's letters written in the trenches. www.alvincyork.org.

- **Wisconsin Veterans Museum, Madison, Wisconsin.** The most stunning museum of its size in the United States, this large building combines impressive collections of artifacts ranging from uniforms to tanks, with substantive exhibits and video programs based on remarkable historical research. It both documents and explains the participation of Wisconsin soldiers in the nation's wars, including the Spanish-American War and World War I.

 Please refer to the document CD-ROM for primary sources related to this chapter.

More than a Car

Ford

A National Institution

→ *This image celebrates not only the centrality of the automobile but the mammoth size of the Ford enterprise and Henry Ford's vision of mass production in modern American society.*

TOWARD A MODERN AMERICA 24
THE 1920s

Happy times were here again. American industry, adopting Henry Ford's policy of mass production and low prices, was making it possible for everybody to have his share of everything. The newspapers, the statesmen, the economists, all agreed that American ingenuity had solved the age-old problem of poverty. There could never be another depression. . . .

The war had done something to Henry, it had taught him a new way to deal with his fellow men. . . . He became more abrupt in his manner, more harsh in his speech. "Gratitude?" he would say. "There's no gratitude in business. Men work for money." . . . From now on he was a business man, and held a tight rein on everything. This industry was his, he had made it himself, and what he wanted of the men he hired was that they should do exactly as he told them. . . .

Every worker had to be strained to the uttermost limit, every one had to be giving the last ounce of energy he had in his carcass. . . . They were tired when they started in the morning, and when they quit they were grey and staggering with fatigue, they were empty shells out of which the last drop of juice had been squeezed. . . .

Henry Ford was now getting close to his two million cars a year goal. . . . From the moment the ore was taken out of the ship at the River Rouge plant [in Detroit], through all the processes turning it into steel and shaping

CHAPTER OUTLINE

The Economy That Roared
Boom Industries
Corporate Consolidation
Open Shops and Welfare Capitalism
Sick Industries

The Business of Government
Republican Ascendancy
Government Corruption
Coolidge Prosperity
The Fate of Reform

Cities and Suburbs
Expanding Cities
The Great Black Migration
Barrios
The Road to Suburbia

Mass Culture in the Jazz Age
Advertising the Consumer Society
Leisure and Entertainment
The New Morality
The Searching Twenties

Culture Wars
Nativism and Immigration Restriction
The Ku Klux Klan
Prohibition and Crime
Old-Time Religion and the Scopes Trial

A New Era in the World?
War Debts and Economic Expansion
Rejecting War
Managing the Hemisphere

Herbert Hoover and the Triumph of the New Era

Conclusion

it into automobile parts with a hundred-ton press, and putting five thousand parts together into a car which rolled off the assembly line under its own power—all those processes were completed in less than a day and a half!

Some forty-five thousand different machines were now used in the making of Ford cars, in sixty establishments scattered over the United States. . . . Henry Ford was remaking the roads of America, and in the end he would remake the roads of the world—and line them all with filling stations and hot-dog stands of the American pattern.

Upton Sinclair, *The Flivver King: A Story of Ford–America.* (Chicago: Charles H. Kerr Publishing Company, 1999).

Upton Sinclair, one of America's most famous "muckraking" journalists, won his greatest recognition with the 1906 publication of his historical novel, *The Jungle,* which graphically depicted the wretched conditions endured by Chicago's immigrant meatpacking workers. In *The Flivver King,* Sinclair again points up his extraordinary ability to weave together a dramatic and historical account of industrial America, particularly the rise of the automobile industry and the revolutionizing vision of Henry Ford—the entrepreneur who captured the American mind and symbolized modern America to the world.

"Machinery," proclaimed Henry Ford, "is the new Messiah." Others in the 1920s thought that Ford, too, deserved homage. "Just as in Rome one goes to the Vatican and endeavours to get audience of the Pope," noted one British observer, "so in Detroit one goes to the Ford Works and endeavours to see Henry Ford." Ford had introduced the moving assembly line at his automobile factory on the eve of World War I, and, by 1925, it was turning out a Model T car every ten seconds. Mass production was becoming a reality; in fact, the term originated in Henry Ford's 1926 description of the system of flow production techniques popularly called "Fordism." The system symbolized the nation's booming economy: In the 1920s, Europeans used the word Fordize as a synonym for Americanize. Ford coupled machines and technology with managerial innovations. He established the "five-dollar day," twice the prevailing wage in Detroit's auto industry, and slashed the workweek from forty-eight to forty hours. These changes, Ford argued, would reduce the costs of labor turnover and boost consumer purchasing power, leading to further profits from mass production.

The assembly line, however, alienated workers, and even Ford himself conceded that the repetitive operations of the assembly line were "so monotonous that it scarcely seems possible that any man would care to continue long at the same job." Ford first tried to adapt his mostly immigrant workers to these conditions through an Americanization program. His "Education Department" taught classes in English, sobriety, obedience, and industrial efficiency to the unskilled laborers entering the factory. After the course, they participated in a symbolic pageant: They climbed into a huge "melting pot," fifteen feet across and seven feet deep. After Ford managers stirred the pot with ten-foot ladles, the workers emerged wearing new clothes and waving American flags—new Americans made for the factory. As one Ford leader said, "As we adapt the machinery in the shop to turning out the kind of automobile we have in mind, so we have constructed our educational system with a view to producing the human product in mind."

When the labor market became more favorable to management in the early 1920s, Ford abolished the Education Department and relied on discipline to control workers. As Sinclair observed, after the Great War, Ford dismissed the role of "gratitude" in business and determined to keep "a tight rein on everything." To maximize profits and increase efficiency, Ford even prohibited talking, whistling, sitting, or smoking on the job. Wearing fixed expressions—"Fordization of the face"—workers could communicate only without moving their lips in the "Ford whisper." In keeping with the actions of other employers, Ford also joined the assault on labor organization, banning unions altogether and enlisting the aid of spies and informants to guard against their formation.

But even greater control and higher profits did not satisfy Henry Ford, for, like the 1920s itself, he remained conflicted about the progress he championed—the changes he saw and had helped facilitate. The automobile not only represented the new consumer culture, but it also transformed forever America and Americans themselves—highways, filling stations, and hamburger stands sprang up across the nation, and the car even altered the dating practices of young Americans, alarming some parents and community leaders about what they feared as "bedrooms on wheels." Cars and cigarettes were among the most intensively advertised goods in the 1920s, and for some they signaled rebellion and freedom. Women in short skirts and the rise of the Jazz Age—all contributed to

Chronology

1915 Ku Klux Klan is founded anew.	**1922** Fordney-McCumber Act raises tariff rates.
1919 Volstead Act is passed.	Sinclair Lewis publishes *Babbitt.*
1920 Urban population exceeds rural population for the first time.	Country Club Plaza in Kansas City opens.
Warren Harding is elected president.	**1923** Harding dies; Calvin Coolidge becomes president.
Prohibition takes effect.	**1924** National Origins Act sharply curtails immigration.
First commercial radio show is broadcast.	Coolidge is elected president.
Sinclair Lewis publishes *Main Street.*	**1925** Scopes trial is held in Dayton, Tennessee.
1921 Sheppard-Towner Maternity and Infancy Act is passed.	F. Scott Fitzgerald publishes *The Great Gatsby.*
Washington Naval Conference limits naval armaments.	**1927** Charles A. Lindbergh flies solo across the Atlantic.
	1928 Kellogg-Briand Pact is signed.
	Herbert Hoover is elected president.
	1929 Ernest Hemingway publishes *A Farewell to Arms.*

what Ford saw as the evils of the "new America." Launching a "crusade" against this new direction America was headed, Ford decided, according to Sinclair, that "what America needed was to be led back to its past." Embracing nativism and protestantism, Ford, an ardent anti-Semite, targeted Jewish Americans in his diatribes, blaming them for radicalism and labor organization, and he singled out the "International Jew" for allegedly controlling the international financial community.

Henry Ford—and Fordism itself— thus reflected the complexity of the 1920s. Economic growth and technological innovation were paired with social conflict as traditions were destroyed, values were displaced, and new people were incorporated into a society increasingly industrialized, urbanized, and dominated by big business. Industrial production and national wealth soared, buoyed by new techniques and markets for consumer goods. Business values pervaded society and dominated government, which promoted business interests.

But not all Americans prospered. Many workers were unemployed, and the wages of still more were stagnant or falling. Farmers endured grim conditions and worse prospects. Social change brought pleasure to some and deep concern to others. City factories like the Ford Works attracted workers from the countryside, increasing urbanization; rapid suburbanization opened other horizons. Leisure activities flourished, and new mass media promoted modern ideas and stylish products. Workers would have to achieve personal satisfaction through consumption—and not production. But such experiences often proved unsettling, and some Americans sought reassurance by imposing their cultural or religious values on everyone around them. The tumultuous decade thus had many unresolved issues, much like the complex personality of Henry Ford himself. And Ford so dominated the age that when college students were asked to rank the greatest people of all time, Ford came in third—behind Christ and Napoleon.

KEY TOPICS

- The American economy in the 1920s
- The cult of business
- Change and social dislocation
- Materialism and mass culture
- The groups excluded from the prosperity of the 1920s

THE ECONOMY THAT ROARED

Following a severe postwar depression in 1920 and 1921, the American economy boomed through the remainder of the decade. Gross domestic product soared nearly 40 percent; output per worker-hour, or productivity, rose 72 percent in manufacturing; average per capita income increased by a third. Although the prosperity was not evenly distributed and some sectors of the economy were deeply troubled, most Americans welcomed the industrial expansion and business principles of the "New Era."

BOOM INDUSTRIES

Many factors spurred the economic expansion of the 1920s. The huge wartime and postwar profits provided investment capital that enabled business to mechanize. Mass production spread quickly in American industry; machine-made standardized parts and the moving assembly line increased efficiency and production. Businesses steadily adopted the scientific management principles of Frederick W. Taylor (see Chapter 21). These highly touted systems, though often involving little more than an assembly-line "speed-up," also boosted efficiency. The nation more than doubled its capacity to generate electricity during the decade, further bolstering the economy. In factories, electric motors cut costs and improved manufacturing; in homes, electricity spurred demand for new products. Henry Ford was right: Mass production and consumption went hand in hand. Although not one in ten farm families had access to electric power, most other families did by 1929, and many bought electric sewing machines, vacuum cleaners, washing machines, and other labor-saving appliances.

The automobile industry drove the economy. Its productivity increased constantly, and sales rose from about 1.9 million vehicles in 1920 to nearly 5 million by 1929, when 26 million vehicles were on the road (see Figure 24-1). The automobile industry also employed one of every fourteen manufacturing workers and stimulated other industries from steel to rubber and glass. It created a huge new market for the petroleum industry and fostered oil drilling in Oklahoma, Texas, and Louisiana. It launched new businesses,

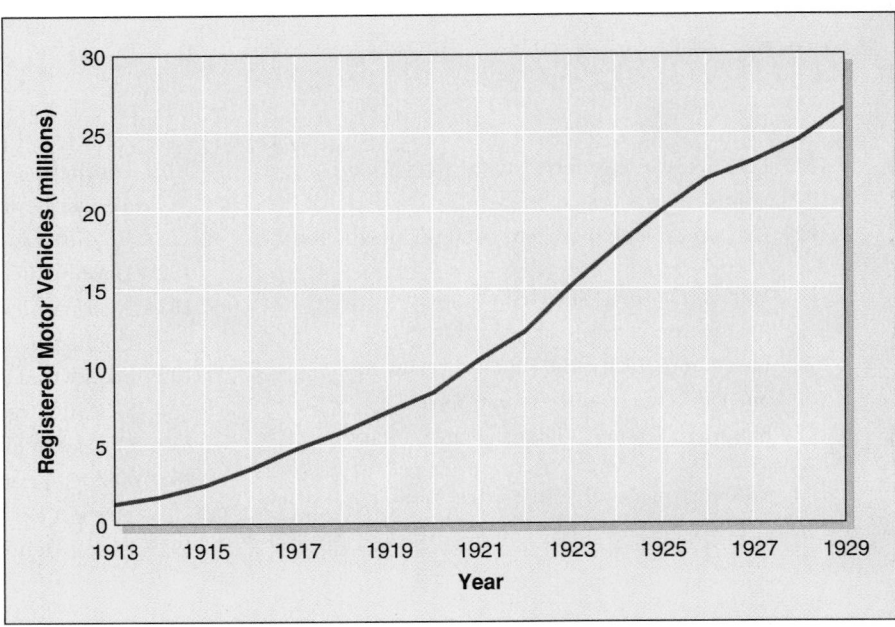

FIGURE 24-1   Registered Motor Vehicles, 1913–1929
The rapid adoption of automobiles shaped the 1920s, stimulating demand for steel and gasoline, encouraging the use of credit, facilitating suburbanization, promoting tourism, and suggesting new cultural horizons.

Data Source: U.S. Bureau of Public Roads.

from service stations (over 120,000 by 1929) to garages. It also encouraged the construction industry, a mainstay of the 1920s economy. Large increases in road building and residential housing, prompted by growing automobile ownership and migration to cities and suburbs, provided construction jobs, markets for lumber and other building materials, and profits.

New industries also sprang up. The aviation industry grew rapidly during the 1920s, with government support. The U.S. Post Office subsidized commercial air service by providing air-mail contracts to private carriers. Congress then authorized commercial passenger service over the mail routes, with regular traffic opening in 1927 between Boston and New York. By 1930, more than one hundred airlines crisscrossed America.

The Great War also stimulated the chemicals industry. The government confiscated chemical patents from German firms that had dominated the field and transferred them to such U.S. companies as DuPont. With this advantage, DuPont in the 1920s became one of the nation's largest industrial firms, a chemical empire producing plastics, finishes, dyes, and organic chemicals. It developed products for the commercial market: enamel for household appliances and automobile finishes, gasoline additives to eliminate engine knocks (many workers died from producing what the *New York World* called "loony gas"), rayon for women's clothing, cellophane to package consumer goods. Led

An Assembly Line
of the
Ford Motor Company

State Historical Society of Wisconsin

Ford Motor Company's assembly line at its River Rouge plant in Detroit. The increasing mechanization of work, linked to managerial and marketing innovations, boosted productivity in the 1920s and brought consumer goods within the reach of far more Americans than before.

still greater profits and power to the major studios, which alone could afford the increased engineering and production costs.

CORPORATE CONSOLIDATION

A wave of corporate mergers, rivaling that at the turn of the century, swept over the 1920s economy. Great corporations swallowed up thousands of small firms. Particularly significant was the spread of oligopoly—the control of an entire industry by a few giant firms. The number of automobile manufacturers dropped from 108 to 44, while only three companies—Ford, General Motors, and Chrysler—produced 83 percent of the nation's cars. Their large-scale, integrated operations eliminated competition from small firms. In the electric light and power industry, nearly four thousand local utility companies were merged into a dozen holding companies. Mergers also expanded oligopoly control over other industries. By 1929, the nation's two hundred largest corporations controlled nearly half of all nonbanking corporate wealth.

Oligopolies also dominated finance and marketing. Big banks extended their control through mergers and by opening branches. By 1929, a mere 1 percent of the nation's banks controlled half its banking resources. In marketing, national chain stores, such as A&P and Woolworth's, displaced local retailers. With fifteen thousand grocery stores and an elaborate distribution system, A&P could buy and sell goods for less than many corner grocers.

The corporate consolidation of the 1920s provoked little public fear or opposition. Independent retailers campaigned for local zoning regulations and laws to restrict chain stores, but for the most part, Americans accepted the idea that size brought efficiency and productivity.

OPEN SHOPS AND WELFARE CAPITALISM

Business also launched a vigorous assault on labor. In 1921, the National Association of Manufacturers organized an **open shop** campaign to break union-shop contracts, which required all employees to be union members. Denouncing collective bargaining as un-American, businesses described the open shop, in which union membership was not required and usually prohibited, as the "American plan." They forced workers to sign so-called **yellow-dog contracts** that bound

by such successes, the chemicals industry became a $4 billion giant employing 300,000 workers by 1929.

The new radio and motion picture industries also flourished. Commercial broadcasting began with a single station in 1920. By 1927, there were 732 stations, and Congress created the Federal Radio Commission to prevent wave-band interference. The rationale for this agency, which was reorganized as the Federal Communications Commission (FCC) in 1934, was that the airwaves belong to the American people and not to private interests. Nevertheless, corporations quickly dominated the new industry. Westinghouse, RCA, and General Electric began opening strings of stations in the early 1920s. Large corporations also came to control radio manufacturing. Factory-made crystal radio sets became available in 1920, and some 5 million sets were sold by mid-decade. But corporate pressure and patent control eliminated more than 90 percent of the 750 manufacturers by 1927.

The motion-picture industry became one of the nation's five largest businesses, with twenty thousand movie theaters selling 100 million tickets a week. Hollywood studios were huge factories, hiring directors, writers, camera crews, and actors to produce films on an assembly-line basis. While Americans watched Charlie Chaplin showcase his comedic genius in such films as *The Gold Rush* (1925), such corporations as Paramount were integrating production with distribution and exhibition to maximize control and profit and eliminate independent producers and theaters. The advent of talking movies later in the decade brought them to reject unions to keep their jobs. Business also used boycotts to force employers into a uniform antiunion front. Bethlehem Steel, for example, refused to sell steel to companies employing union labor. Where unions existed, corporations tried to crush them, using spies or hiring strikebreakers.

Some companies advocated a paternalistic system called **welfare capitalism** as an alternative to unions. Eastman Kodak, General Motors, U.S. Steel, and other firms provided medical services, insurance programs, pension plans, and vacations for their workers and established employee social clubs and sports teams. These policies were designed to undercut labor unions and to persuade workers to rely on the corporation. Home-financing plans, for instance, increased workers' dependence on the company, and stock ownership plans inculcated business values among employees. Welfare capitalism, however, covered scarcely 5 percent of the workforce and often benefited only skilled workers already tied to the company through seniority. Moreover, it was directed primarily at men. General Electric, for example, dismissed women workers when they married. Women rarely built up enough seniority to obtain vacations and pensions.

Corporations in the 1920s also promoted company unions, management-sponsored substitutes for labor unions. But company unions were usually forbidden to handle wage and hour issues. Their function was to implement company policies and undermine real unionism. General Electric's management reported that through its company union, "we have been able to educate and secure sympathy and support from a large body of employees who, under the old arrangement of bargaining with [AFL] craft unions, could not have been reached."

Partly because of these pressures, membership in labor unions fell from 5.1 million in 1920 to 3.6 million in 1929. But unions also contributed to their

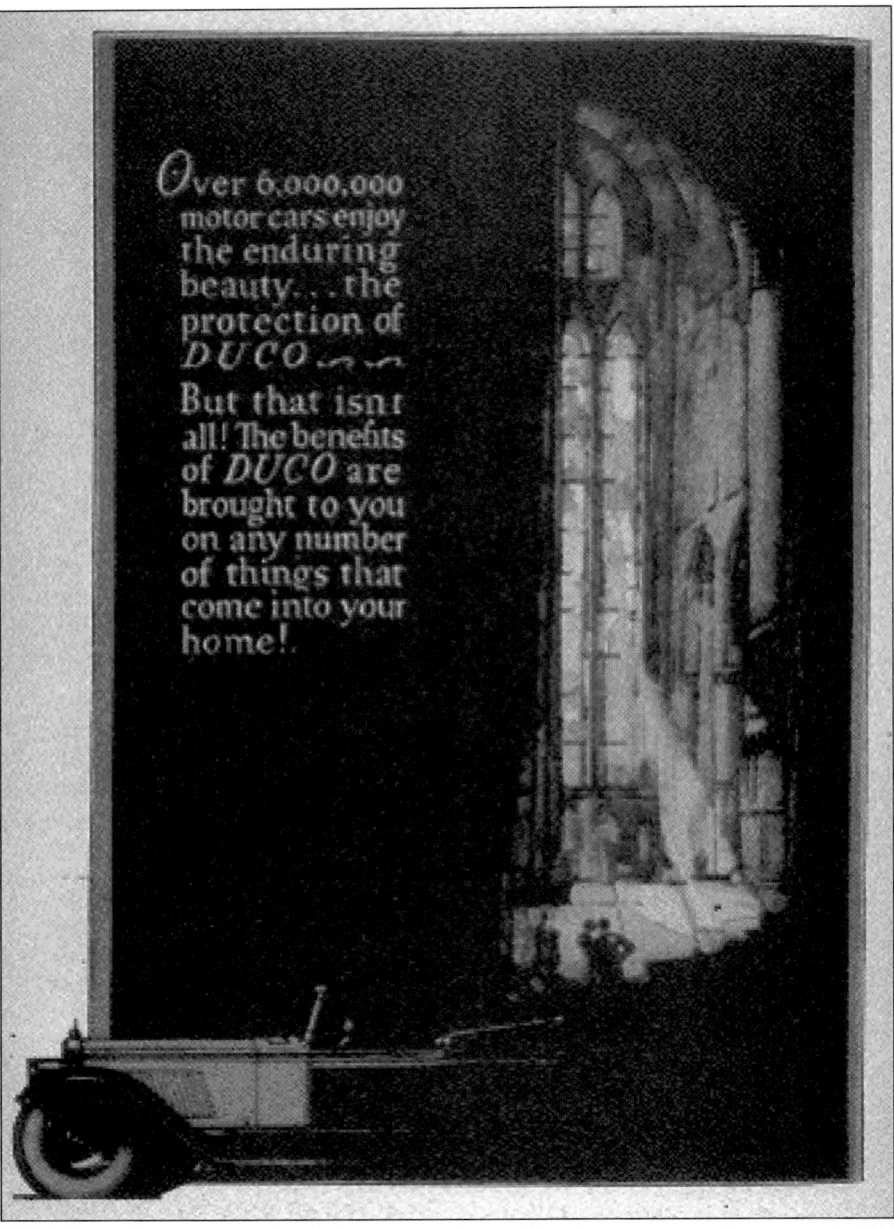

DuPont became one of the nation's largest industrial corporations in the 1920s by developing new consumer products and marketing them aggressively. This advertisement for Duco automobile finishes blends images of a cathedral and an auto showroom, placing consumerism in a favorable light.

own decline. Conservative union leaders neglected ethnic and black workers in mass-production industries. Nor did they try to organize women, by 1930 nearly one-fourth of all workers. And they failed to respond effectively to other changes in the labor market. The growing numbers of white-collar workers regarded themselves as middle class and beyond the scope of union action.

With increasing mechanization and weak labor unions, workers suffered from job insecurity and stagnant wages. Mechanization, *Fortune* concluded, meant that "from the purely productive point of view, a part of the human race is already obsolete." Unemployment reached 12 percent in 1921 and remained a persistent concern of many working-class Americans during the decade. And despite claims to the contrary, hours were long: The average workweek in manufacturing remained over fifty hours.

The promise of business to pay high wages proved hollow. Real wages (purchasing power) did improve, but most of the improvement came before 1923 and reflected falling prices more than it did rising wages. After 1923, American wages stabilized. Henry Ford made no general wage hike after 1919, although his workers would have needed an increase of 65 percent to recover the buying power they had enjoyed in 1914. Indeed, in 1928, Ford lowered wage rates.

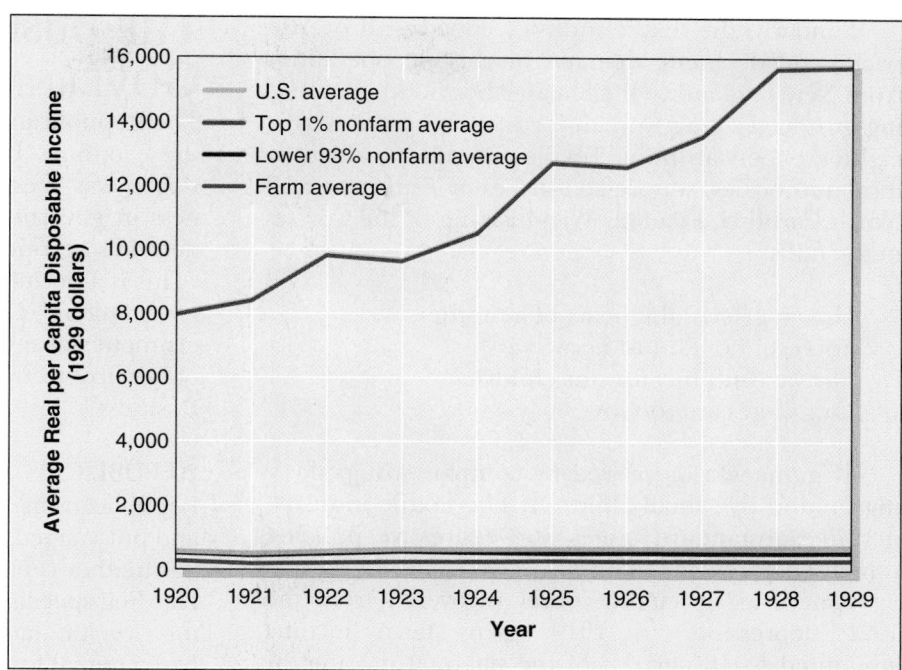

FIGURE 24-2   Growing Income Inequality in the 1920s
Despite the aura of prosperity in the 1920s, the vast majority of Americans received little or no increase in their real income. Farm families dragged the average down further while the wealthiest Americans doubled their own incomes.

Data Source: Charles Holt, "Who Benefited from the Prosperity of the Twenties?" *Explorations in Economic History,* 14 (1977).

U.S. Steel also reduced weekly wages, even while its profits almost doubled between 1923 and 1929. The failure to raise wages when productivity was increasing threatened the nation's long-term prosperity. In short, rising national income largely reflected salaries and dividends, not wages.

Some workers fared particularly badly. Unskilled workers—especially southern and eastern Europeans, black migrants from the rural South, and Mexican immigrants—saw their already low wages decline relative to those of skilled workers. Southern workers earned much less than Northerners, even in the same industry, and women were paid much less than men, even for the same jobs. Male furniture assemblers, for example, earned 56 cents an hour; females, only 32 cents. Overall, the gap between rich and poor widened during the decade (see Figure 24-2). By 1929, fully 71 percent of American families earned less than what the U.S. Bureau of Labor Statistics regarded as necessary for a decent living standard. The maldistribution of income meant that eventually Americans would be unable to purchase the products they made.

The expansion of consumer credit, rare before the 1920s, offered temporary relief by permitting consumers to buy goods over time. General Motors intro-

duced consumer credit on a national basis to create a mass market for expensive automobiles. By 1927, two-thirds of automobiles were purchased on the installment plan. By 1929, providing consumer credit had become the nation's tenth-largest business. Nevertheless, installment loans did not in the long run raise the purchasing power of an income; they simply added interest charges to the price of products.

SICK INDUSTRIES

Despite the general appearance of prosperity, several "sick" industries dragged on the economy. Coal mining, textile and garment manufacturing, and railroads suffered from excess capacity (too many mines and factories), shrinking demand, low returns, and management–labor conflicts. For example, U.S. coal mines had a capacity of a billion tons, but scarcely half of that amount was needed because of increasing use of oil, natural gas, and hydroelectricity. Using company police, strikebreakers, and injunctions, mine operators broke the United Mine Workers and slashed wages by up to one third. Unemployment in the industry approached 30 percent; by 1928, a reporter found "thousands of women and children literally starving to death" in Appalachia and the remaining miners held in "industrial slavery."

Similarly, the textile industry coped with overcapacity and declining demand by shifting operations from New England to the cheap-labor South, employing girls and young women for fifty-six-hour weeks at eighteen cents an hour. Textile companies, aided by local authorities, suppressed strikes in Tennessee and North Carolina. Ella May Wiggins sang of the worries in the mills:

> How it grieves the heart of a mother,
> You every one must know.
> For we can't buy for our children,
> Our wages are too low.

Wiggins was murdered by company thugs, leaving behind five small children. The textile industry, despite substandard wages and repressive policies, remained barely profitable.

American agriculture never recovered from the 1921 depression. In 1919, gross farm income amounted to 16 percent of the national income; by 1929, it had dropped to half that. Agricultural problems did not derive from inefficiency or low productivity. Mechanization (especially more tractors) and improved fertilizers and pesticides helped to produce crop surpluses. But surpluses and shrinking demand forced down prices. After the war, foreign markets dried up, and domestic demand for cotton slackened. Moreover, farmers' wartime expansion left them heavily mortgaged in the 1920s. Small farmers, unable to compete with larger, better-capitalized farmers, suffered most. Many lost their land and became tenants or farm hands. By 1930, only 57 percent of American farmers owned the land they worked, the lowest percentage ever.

Racial discrimination worsened conditions for black and Hispanic tenants, sharecroppers, and farm workers. In the South, black sharecroppers trapped in grinding poverty endured segregation, disfranchisement, and violence. Mexican immigrants and Hispanic Americans labored as migrant farm workers in the Southwest and California. Exploited by a contract labor system pervasive in large-scale agriculture, they suffered from poor wages, miserable living conditions, and racism that created, in the words of one investigation, "a vicious circle" from which "few can escape through their own efforts."

By the end of the 1920s, the average per capita income for people on the nation's farms was only one-fourth that of Americans off the farm. "Widespread agricultural disaster," warned one Iowa newspaper, was producing "a highly dangerous situation." Like textile workers in New England and the Piedmont and coal miners in Appalachia, rural Americans suffered in the 1920s.

THE BUSINESS OF GOVERNMENT

The Republican surge in national politics also shaped the economy. In the 1920 election, the Republican slogan was "Less government in business, more business in government." By 1924, Calvin Coolidge, the decade's second Republican president, proclaimed, "This is a business country . . . and it wants a business government." Under such direction, the federal government advanced business interests at the expense of other objectives (see "American Views: The Cult of Business").

REPUBLICAN ASCENDANCY

Republicans in 1920 had retained control of Congress and put Warren Harding in the White House. Harding was neither capable nor bright. One critic described a Harding speech as "an army of pompous phrases moving over the landscape in search of an idea." But he had a genial touch that contrasted favorably with Wilson. He pardoned Eugene Debs, whom Wilson had refused to release from prison, and he spoke out against racial violence. He also helped shape the modern presidency by supporting the Budget and Accounting Act of 1921, which gave the president authority over the budget and created the Budget Bureau and the General Accounting Office. Moreover, Harding recognized his own limitations and promised to appoint "the best minds" to his cabinet. Some of his appointees were highly accomplished, and two of them, Secretary of Commerce Herbert Hoover and Secretary of the Treasury Andrew Mellon, shaped economic policy throughout the 1920s.

A self-described progressive, dedicated to efficiency, Hoover made the Commerce Department the government's most dynamic office. He cemented its ties with the leading sectors of the economy, expanded its collection and distribution of industrial information, pushed to exploit foreign resources and markets, and encouraged innovation. His spreading influence led him to be called the secretary of commerce and "assistant secretary of everything else." Hoover's goal was to expand prosperity by making business efficient, responsive, and profitable.

Andrew Mellon had a narrower goal. A wealthy banker and industrialist, he pressed Congress to reduce taxes on businesses and the rich. He argued that lower taxes would enable wealthy individuals and corporations to increase their capital investments, thereby creating new jobs and general prosperity. But Mellon's hope that favoring the rich would cause prosperity to trickle down to the working and middle classes proved ill-founded. Nevertheless, despite the opposition of progressives in Congress, Mellon succeeded in lowering maximum tax rates and eliminating wartime excess-profits taxes in 1921.

The Harding administration promoted business interests in other ways, too. The tariff of 1922 raised import rates to protect industry from foreign competition. High new duties on foreign aluminum, for instance, permitted manufacturers—including Mellon's own Alcoa Aluminum—to raise prices by 40 percent. But by excluding imports, high tariffs made it difficult for European nations to earn the dollars to repay their war debts to the United States. High rates also impeded American farm exports and raised consumer prices.

The Harding administration aided the business campaign against unions. Attorney General Harry Daugherty secured an injunction against a railroad strike in 1922 and promised to "use the power of the government to prevent the labor unions of the country from destroying the open shop."

The Republicans also curtailed government regulation. By appointing advocates of big business to the Federal Trade Commission, the Federal Reserve Board, and other regulatory agencies established earlier by the progressives, Harding made government the collaborator rather than the regulator of business. Progressive Republican Senator George Norris of Nebraska angrily asked, "If trusts, combinations, and big business are to run the government, why not permit them to do it directly rather than through this expensive machinery which was originally honestly established for the protection of the people of the country against monopoly?" Norris condemned the new appointments as nullifying "federal law by a process of boring from within" and as setting "the country back more than twenty-five years."

Finally, Harding reshaped the Supreme Court into a still more aggressive champion of business. He named the conservative William Howard Taft as chief justice and matched him with three other justices. All were, as one of them proclaimed, sympathetic to business leaders "beset and bedeviled with vexatious statutes, prying commissions, and government intermeddling of all sorts." The Court struck down much of the government economic regulation adopted during the Progressive Era, invalidated restraints on child labor and a minimum wage law for women, and approved restrictions on labor unions.

GOVERNMENT CORRUPTION

The green light that Harding Republicans extended to private interests led to corruption and scandals. Harding appointed many friends and cronies, who saw public service as an opportunity for graft. Attorney General Daugherty's associates in the Justice Department took bribes in exchange for pardons and government jobs. The head of the Veterans Bureau went to prison for cheating disabled veterans of $200 million. Albert Fall, the secretary of the interior, leased petroleum reserves set aside by progressive conservationists to oil companies in exchange for cash, bonds, and cattle for his New Mexico ranch. Exposed for his role in the Teapot Dome scandal, named after a Wyoming oil reserve, Fall became the first cabinet officer in history to go to jail. Daugherty escaped a similar fate by destroying records and invoking the Fifth Amendment.

Harding was appalled by the scandals. "My God, this is a hell of a job!" he told William Allen White. "I have no trouble with my enemies. . . . But my damned friends, . . . they're the ones that keep me walking the floor nights!" Harding died shortly thereafter, probably of a heart attack.

COOLIDGE PROSPERITY

On August 3, 1923, Vice President Calvin Coolidge was sworn in as president by his father while visiting his birthplace in rural Vermont, thereby reaffirming his association with traditional values. This image reassured Americans troubled by the Harding scandals. Coolidge's calm appearance hid a furious temper and a mean spirit.

Coolidge supported business with ideological conviction. He opposed the activist presidency of the Progressive Era, cultivating instead a deliberate inactivity calculated to lower expectations of government. He endorsed Secretary of the Treasury Mellon's ongoing efforts to reverse the progressive tax policies of the Wilson years and backed Secretary of Commerce Hoover's persistent efforts on behalf of the business community (although he privately sneered at Hoover as the "Wonder Boy").

Like Harding, Coolidge installed business supporters in the regulatory agencies. To chair the Federal Trade Commission he appointed an attorney who had condemned the agency as "an instrument of oppression and disturbance and injury instead of help to business." Under this leadership, the FTC described its new goal as "helping business to help itself"—which meant approving trade associations and agreements to suppress competition. This attitude, endorsed by the Supreme Court, aided the mergers that occurred after 1925. The *Wall Street Journal* crowed, "Never before, here or anywhere else, has a government been so completely fused with business."

And Coolidge confined the government's role to helping business. When Congress tried to raise farm prices through government intervention, Coolidge vetoed the measure as "preposterous" special-interest legislation. One economist said Coolidge's vetoes revealed "a stubborn determination to do nothing," but

AMERICAN VIEWS

The Cult of Business

During the 1920s, publicists and politicians joined manufacturers and merchants in proclaiming that business promoted not only material but also social and even spiritual well-being. In his best-seller, *The Man Nobody Knows* (1924), advertising executive Bruce Barton portrayed Jesus Christ as the founder of modern business. The following excerpt from an article by Edward E. Purinton, a popular lecturer on business values and efficiency, makes even more extensive claims for business.

- How accurate are Purinton's claims of great opportunity in the corporate world of the 1920s? Of occupational mobility in the factory economy?

- What does this view of business imply about the role of government in American life?

- How do you think Protestant fundamentalists might have viewed the cult of business?

Among the nations of the earth today America stands for one idea: Business. National opprobrium? National opportunity. For in this fact lies, potentially, the salvation of the world.

Through business, properly conceived, managed, and conducted, the human race is finally to be redeemed. How and why a man works foretells what he will do, think, have, give, and be. And real salvation is in doing, thinking, having, giving, and being—not in sermonizing and theorizing. . . .

What is the finest game? Business. The soundest science? Business. The truest art? Business. The fullest education? Business. The fairest opportunity? Business. The cleanest philanthropy? Business. The sanest religion? Business.

You may not agree. That is because you judge business by the crude, mean, stupid, false imitation of business that happens to be located near you.

The finest game is business. The rewards are for everybody, and all can win. There are no fa-

they revealed more. For on the same day that Coolidge vetoed assistance to farmers, he raised by 50 percent the tariff on pig iron, thereby increasing manufacturers' profits and farmers' costs for tools. Government action was acceptable for business but not for nonbusiness interests.

"Coolidge prosperity" determined the 1924 election. The Democrats, hopelessly divided, took 103 ballots to nominate the colorless, conservative Wall Street lawyer John W. Davis. His election prospects, Davis conceded, were less "than a snowball in hell." A more interesting opponent for Coolidge was Robert La Follette, nominated by discontented farm and labor organizations that formed a new Progressive Party. La Follette campaigned against "the power of private monopoly over the political and economic life of the American people." The Progressive platform demanded government ownership of railroads and utilities, farm assis-

tance, and collective bargaining. The Republicans, backed by immense contributions from business, denounced La Follette as an agent of Bolshevism. The choice, Republicans insisted, was "Coolidge or Chaos." Thus instructed, Americans chose Coolidge, though barely half the electorate bothered to vote.

THE FATE OF REFORM

But progressive reform was not completely dead. Even Harding proposed social welfare measures, and, in the 1921 depression, he convened a conference on unemployment and helped spark voluntary relief. A small group in Congress, led by La Follette and George Norris, attacked Mellon's regressive tax policies and supported measures regulating agricultural processors, protecting workers' rights, and maintaining public ownership of a hydroelectric dam at Muscle Shoals, Alabama, that conservative Republicans vorites—Providence always crowns the career of the man who is worthy. And in this game there is no "luck"—you have the fun of taking chances but the sobriety of guaranteeing certainties. The speed and size of your winnings are for you alone to determine. . . .

The soundest science is business. All investigation is reduced to action, and by action proved or disproved. The idealistic motive animates the materialistic method. . . . Capital is furnished for the researches of "pure science"; yet pure science is not regarded pure until practical. Competent scientists are suitably rewarded—as they are not in the scientific schools. . . .

The fullest education is business. A proper blend of study, work and life is essential to advancement. The whole man is educated. Human nature itself is the open book that all business men study; and the mastery of a page of this educates you more than the memorizing of a dusty tome from a library shelf. In the school of business, moreover, you teach yourself and learn most from your own mistakes. What you learn here you live out, the only real test.

The fairest opportunity is business. You can find more, better, quicker chances to get ahead in a large business house than anywhere else on earth. . . . Recognition of better work, of keener

and quicker thought, of deeper and finer feeling, is gladly offered by the men higher up, with early promotion the rule for the man who justifies it. There is, and can be, no such thing as buried talent in a modern business organization. . . .

The sanest religion is business. Any relationship that forces a man to follow the Golden Rule rightfully belongs amid the ceremonials of the church. A great business enterprise includes and presupposes this relationship. I have seen more Christianity to the square inch as a regular part of the office equipment of famous corporation presidents than may ordinarily be found on Sunday in a verbalized but not vitalized church congregation. . . . You can fool your preacher with a sickly sprout or a wormy semblance of character, but you can't fool your employer. I would make every business house a consultation bureau for the guidance of the church whose members were employees of the house. . . .

The future work of the businessman is to teach the teacher, preach to the preacher, admonish the parent, advise the doctor, justify the lawyer, superintend the statesman, fructify the farmer, stabilize the banker, harness the dreamer, and reform the reformer.

Source: Edward E. Purinton, "Big Ideas from Big Business," *Independent*, April 16, 1921. National Weekly Corp., New York.

---

wanted to privatize. Yet reformers' successes were few and often temporary.

The fate of women's groups illustrated the difficulties reformers faced in the 1920s. At first, the adoption of woman suffrage prompted politicians to champion women's reform issues. In 1920, both major parties endorsed many of the goals of the new **League of Women Voters**. Within a year, many states had granted women the right to serve on juries, several enacted equal pay laws, and Wisconsin adopted an equal-rights law. Congress passed the **Sheppard-Towner Maternity and Infancy Act**, the first federal social-welfare law, in 1921. It provided federal funds for infant and maternity care, precisely the type of protective legislation that the suffragists had described as women's special interest.

But thereafter women reformers gained little. As it became clear that women did not vote as a bloc but

according to their varying social and economic backgrounds, Congress lost interest in "women's issues." In 1929, Congress killed the Sheppard-Towner Act. Nor could reformers gain ratification of a child-labor amendment after the Supreme Court invalidated laws regulating child labor. Conservatives attacked women reformers as "Bolsheviks."

Disagreements among women reformers and shifting interests also limited their success. Led by the National Woman's Party, some feminists campaigned for an Equal Rights Amendment. But other reformers feared that such an amendment would nullify the progressive laws that protected working women. Such reform organizations as the Consumers' League lost their energy and focus. The General Federation of Women's Clubs, always relatively conservative, promoted home economics and the use of electric appliances. Indeed, many younger women rejected the

One 1920s cartoon depicting a "View of Washington," showed Herbert Hoover everywhere at once. In fact, the talented and ambitious secretary of commerce was not a politician but a successful engineer, businessman, and administrator, who symbolized to many Americans the best of the New Era.

public reform focus of progressive feminists. The *Magazine of Business* even maintained that women valued the vacuum cleaner more than they did the vote. By 1927, the president of the Women's Trade Union League called the decade "hideous in the public life of our people and in the noisy flaunting of cheap hopes and cheaper materialism."

CITIES AND SUBURBS

The 1920 census reported that, for the first time, more Americans lived in urban than in rural areas. The trend toward urbanization accelerated in the 1920s as millions of Americans fled the depressed countryside for the booming cities. This massive population movement interacted with technological innovations to reshape cities, build suburbs, and transform urban life (see Map 24-1).

EXPANDING CITIES

Urbanization affected all regions of the country. In absolute terms, the older industrial cities of the Northeast and upper Midwest grew the most, attract-ing migrants from the rural South and distressed Appalachia. New York remained the nation's foremost metropolis. All other major cities expanded—none more spectacularly than Detroit, which grew to 1.6 million people. The "Motor City" thrived on the booming automobile industry and related industries like glass manufacturing. Old trees and wide lawns gave way to multilane highways as apartment houses and parking lots obliterated old Detroit.

Rural Southerners also headed for southern cities. In fact, the South was the nation's most rapidly urbanizing region. Migrants from the countryside poured into Atlanta, Birmingham, Memphis, and Houston. Little more than jungle before 1914, Miami became the fastest-growing city in the United States during the 1920s—"the Magic City." Not all Southerners welcomed urban growth and the values it represented. The novelist Thomas Wolfe cautioned against boosters in Asheville, North Carolina, "who shout 'Progress Progress Progress'—when what they mean is more Ford automobiles, more Rotary Clubs, more Baptist Ladies Social unions. . . . We are not necessarily four times as civilized as our grandfathers because we go four times as fast in automobiles, because our buildings are four times as tall."

In the West, Denver, Portland, and Seattle (each a regional economic hub) and several California cities grew rapidly. Los Angeles grew by 115 percent and by 1930 was the nation's fifth-largest city, with over 1.2 million people. Although it was the center of California's agricultural wealth and the motion-picture industry and one of the world's busiest ports, Los Angeles was also linked to the automobile industry. The southern California oil fields and the demand for gasoline made it the nation's leading refining center.

The population surge transformed the urban landscape. As land values soared, developers built skyscrapers, giving Cleveland, Kansas City, San Francisco, and many other cities modern skylines. By the end of the decade, American cities had nearly four hundred skyscrapers taller than twenty stories. The tallest, New York's 102-story Empire State Building, symbolized the urban boom.

THE GREAT BLACK MIGRATION

A significant feature of the rural-to-urban movement was the **Great Migration** of African Americans from the South. Like other migrants, they responded chiefly to economic factors. Southern segregation and violence made migration attractive, but job opportunities made it possible. Prosperity created jobs, and with the decline in European immigration, black workers filled the positions previously given to new immigrants. Though generally the lowest-paid and least secure jobs, they were better than sharecropping

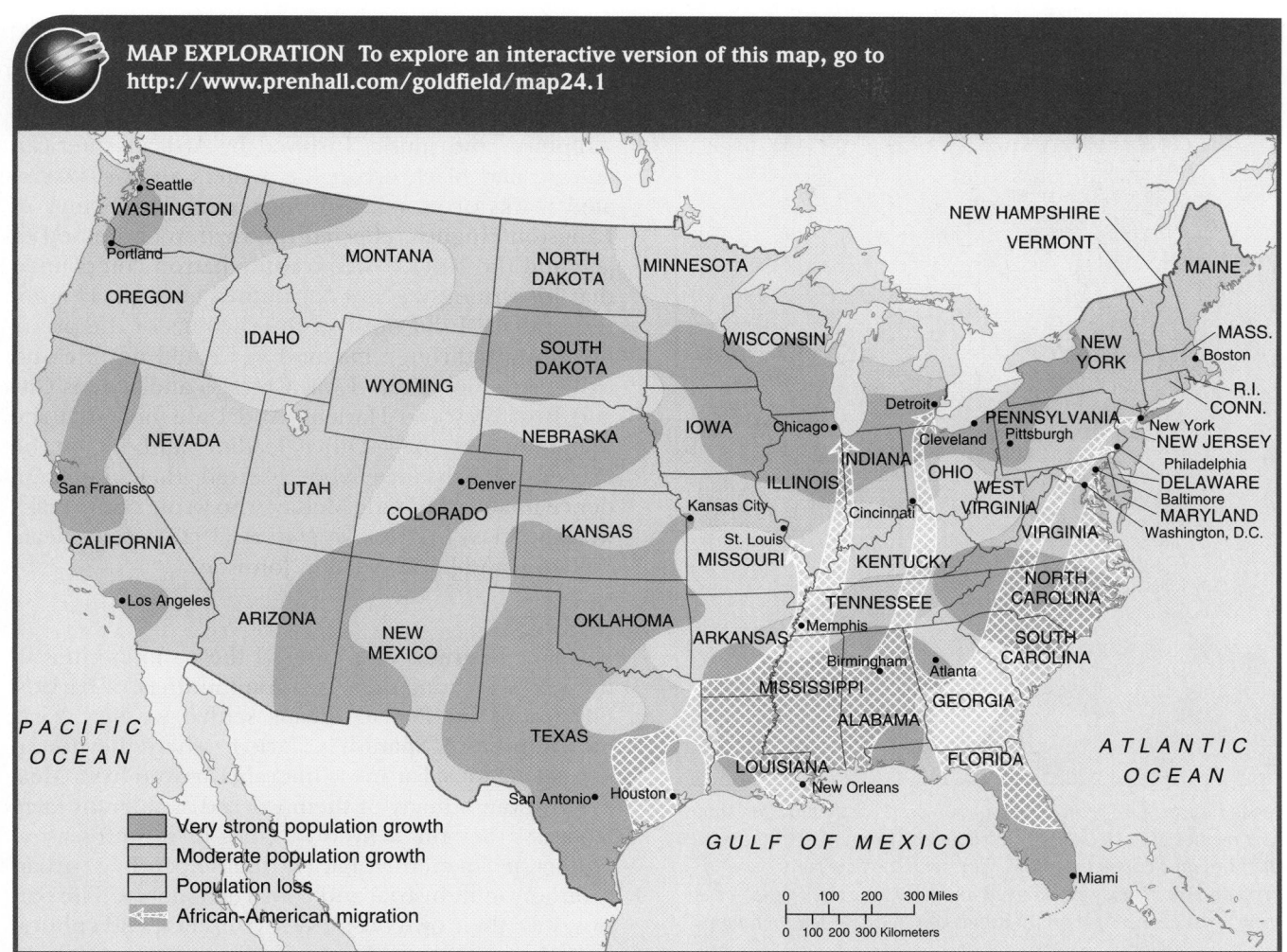

MAP EXPLORATION To explore an interactive version of this map, go to http://www.prenhall.com/goldfield/map24.1

Very strong population growth
Moderate population growth
Population loss
African-American migration

MAP 24-1 Population Shifts, 1920–1930
Rural Americans fled to the cities during the 1920s, escaping a declining agricultural economy to search for new opportunities. African Americans in particular left the rural South for eastern and midwestern cities, but the urban population also jumped in the West and in the South itself.

in the rural South. Black men worked as unskilled or semiskilled laborers; black women became domestics in white homes. The migrants often found adjustment to their new environment difficult. Southern rural black culture clashed with industrial work rhythms and discipline and with urban living. Still, more than a million and a half African Americans moved to northern cities in the 1920s.

There black ghettos usually developed, more because of prejudice than the wishes of the migrants. Although African Americans, like European immigrants, often wanted to live together to sustain their culture, racist restrictions meant that segregation, not congregation, most shaped their urban community. With thousands of newcomers limited to certain neighborhoods, housing shortages developed. Rapacious landlords charged ever-increasing rents for ever-declining housing. Rents doubled in New York's Harlem during the decade. In an example of the way racism exacer-

bated urban poverty, black workers earned less than working-class white workers but had to spend 50 percent more for housing. High rents and low wages forced black families to share inferior and unsanitary housing that threatened their health and safety. In Pittsburgh, only 20 percent of black houses had bathtubs, and only 50 percent had indoor toilets; in another city, an observer wrote that "the State would not allow cows to live in some of these apartments used by colored people." Continual migration disrupted efforts to develop a stable community; Harlem, said one social worker, was a "perpetual frontier."

However, the Great Migration also increased African Americans' racial consciousness, autonomy, and power. In 1928, for instance, black Chicagoans, using the ballot denied to African Americans in the South, elected the first black man to Congress since the turn of the century. Mutual-aid societies and fraternal orders proliferated. Churches were particularly

Jessie Fauset, Langston Hughes, and Zora Neale Hurston stand at a memorial to Booker T. Washington. Prominent authors in the Harlem Renaissance, they represented a new generation of African Americans seizing what another black intellectual called their "first chances for group expression and self-determination."

influential. A reporter in 1926 counted 140 black churches in a 150-block area of Harlem. Most of these were "storefront churches" where "cotton-field preachers" provided an emotional and fundamentalist religion familiar to migrants from the rural South.

Another organization also appealed to poor black ghetto dwellers. The Universal Negro Improvement Association (UNIA), organized by Marcus Garvey, a Jamaican immigrant to New York, rejected the NAACP's goal of integration. A black nationalist espousing racial pride, Garvey exhorted black people to migrate to Africa to build a "free, redeemed, and mighty nation." In the meantime, he urged them to support black businesses. UNIA organized many enterprises, including groceries, restaurants, laundries, a printing plant, and the Black Star Steamship Line, intended as a commercial link between the United States, the West Indies, and Africa. UNIA attracted half a million members, the first black mass movement in American history. When Garvey was con-

victed of mail fraud and deported, however, the movement collapsed.

Racial pride also found expression in the **Harlem Renaissance**, an outpouring of literature, painting, sculpture, and music. Inspired by African-American culture and black urban life, writers and artists created works of power and poignancy. The poetry of Langston Hughes reflected the rhythm and mood of jazz and the blues. When a white patron complained that his writing was not "primitive" enough, Hughes responded, "I did not feel the rhythms of the primitive surging through me, and so I could not live and write as though I did. I was Chicago and Kansas City and Broadway and Harlem. And I was not what she wanted me to be." Other leading authors of the Harlem Renaissance who asserted their independence included Claude McKay, who wrote of the black working class in *Home to Harlem* (1928), Zora Neale Hurston, and James Weldon Johnson.

BARRIOS

Hispanic migrants also entered the nation's cities in the 1920s, creating their own communities, or barrios. Fifty thousand Puerto Ricans settled in New York, mostly in East ("Spanish") Harlem, where they found low-paying jobs. Far more migrants arrived from Mexico. Although many of them worked as migrant farm laborers, they often lived in cities in the off-season. Others permanently joined the expanding urban economy in industrial and construction jobs. The barrios, with their own businesses, churches, and cultural organizations, created a sense of permanency.

These communities enabled the newcomers to preserve their cultural values and build social institutions, such as *mutualistas* (mutual aid societies), that helped them obtain credit, housing, and health care. But the barrios also reflected the hostility that Hispanics encountered in American cities, for racism often restricted them to such districts. The number of Mexicans in Los Angeles tripled during the 1920s to nearly 100,000, but segregation confined them to East Los Angeles. Other areas of the city, such as El Segundo and Lynwood, boasted of being "restricted to the white race" and having "no Negroes or Mexicans." Los Angeles maintained separate schools for Mexicans, and a social worker reported that "America has repulsed the Mexican immigrant in every step he has taken" toward integration. As new migrants streamed in, conditions in the barrios deteriorated, for few cities provided adequate public services for them. Denver's barrio was described in 1924 as an area "both God and Denver had forgotten" with "no paving, no sidewalks, no sewers."

Some Hispanics fought discrimination. *La Orden de Hijos de America* (The Order of the Sons of America), organized in San Antonio in 1921, campaigned against inequities in schools and the jury system. In 1929, it helped launch the larger League of United Latin American Citizens (LULAC), which would help advance civil rights for all Americans.

THE ROAD TO SUBURBIA

As fast as the cities mushroomed in the 1920s, the suburbs grew twice as fast. Park Ridge outside Chicago, Inglewood outside Los Angeles, Shaker Heights outside Cleveland, and many others expanded by 400 percent. New suburbs arose across the country. Fourteen hundred new subdivisions appeared in Los Angeles County during the 1920s; two-thirds of the new municipal incorporations in Illinois and Michigan were suburbs of Chicago, St. Louis, or Detroit. Some suburbs, such as Highland Park, where Henry Ford built his factory near Detroit, and Fairfield, Alabama,

Mexican Americans, like these farmworkers pitting apricots in Los Angeles County in 1924, often found jobs in the agribusiness enterprises of the Southwest but lived in barrios in the expanding cities of the region. More Mexicans than any other immigrants entered the United States in the 1920s.

were industrial, but most were havens for the middle and upper classes.

Automobiles created the modern suburb. Nineteenth-century suburbs were small and linear, stretching along the street railway system. The new developments were sprawling and dispersed, for the automobile enabled people to live in formerly remote areas. A single-family house surrounded by a lawn became the social ideal, a pastoral escape from the overcrowded and dangerous city. Many suburbs excluded African Americans, Hispanics, Jews, and working-class people. Shaker Heights, for instance, limited land sales to white buyers and required expensive building materials and professional architects. Suburbanites of more modest means found homes in such places as Westwood, outside Chicago, the "World's Largest Bungalow Development."

Suburbanization and the automobile brought other changes. The government provided federal money to states to build highways, and by the end of the decade, road construction was the largest single item in the national budget. Autos and suburbs also stimulated the growth of new industries. In 1922, J.C. Nichols opened the Country Club Plaza, the first suburban shopping center, in Kansas City; it provided free off-street parking. Department stores and other large retailers began leaving the urban cores for the suburbs, where both parking and more affluent customers were waiting. Drive-in restaurants began with Royce Hailey's Pig Stand in Dallas in 1921. Two years later, the first fast-food franchise chain, White Tower, appeared, with its standardized menu and building, serving hamburgers "by the sack" to Americans in record numbers. Enjoying remarkable success, owners Walt Anderson and Billy Ingram described their volume of sales in one year: "Picture a line of buns, laid side by side, one hundred and sixty-three miles long, forty-one truckloads of hamburger, weighing two tons each, two carloads of onions, three carloads of pickles, ninety-six-hundred five gallon urns of coffee and you have an idea of the output of the White Castle System for the year 1925."

MASS CULTURE IN THE JAZZ AGE

The White Tower chain symbolized a new society and culture. Urbanization and the automobile joined with new systems of distributing, marketing, and communications to mold a mass culture of standardized experiences and interests. Not all Americans participated equally in the new culture, however, and some attacked it.

ADVERTISING THE CONSUMER SOCIETY

Advertising and its focus on increasing consumption shaped the new society. President Coolidge considered advertising "the most potent influence in adopting and changing the habits and modes of life, affecting what we eat, what we wear, and the work and play of the whole nation." A less complacent observer calculated that in 1925, nearly 50 percent more was spent "to educate consumers in what they may or may not want to buy" than on education from grade school through university.

Advertisers exhorted consumers via newspapers, billboards, streetcar signs, junk mail, radio, movies, and even skywriting. They sought to create a single market where everyone, regardless of region and ethnicity, consumed brand-name products. Advertisers attempted to stimulate new wants by ridiculing previous models or tastes as obsolete, acclaiming the convenience of a new brand, or linking the latest

Advertisements for brand-name products, like this 1929 ad for Campbell's tomato soup, often tried to link simple consumption with larger issues of personal success and achievement.

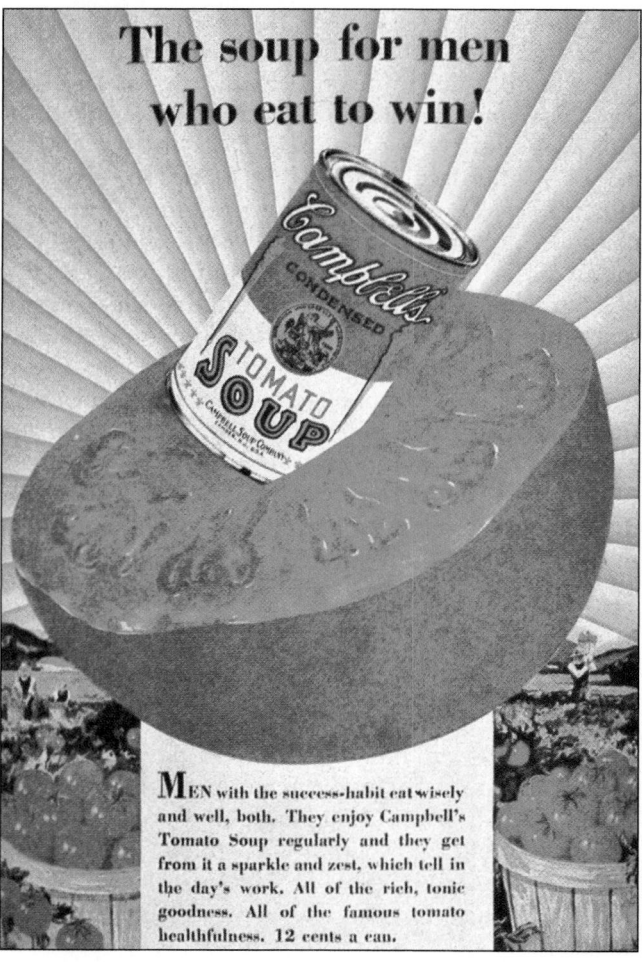

The soup for men who eat to win!

MEN with the success-habit eat wisely and well, both. They enjoy Campbell's Tomato Soup regularly and they get from it a sparkle and zest, which tell in the day's work. All of the rich, tonic goodness. All of the famous tomato healthfulness. 12 cents a can.

fashion with status or sex appeal. "If I wear a certain brand of underwear," observed one critic, "I have the satisfaction of knowing that my fellow-men not so fortunately clad are undoubtedly fouled swine."

The home became a focus of consumerism. Middle- and upper-class women purchased mass-produced household appliances, such as electric irons, toasters, vacuum cleaners, washing machines, and refrigerators. Working-class women bought packaged food, ready-made clothing, and other consumer goods to lighten their workload. Advertisers attempted to redefine the housewife's role as primarily that of a consumer, purchasing goods for her family. To promote sales of clothing and cosmetics, advertising depicted women as concerned with fashion, beauty, and sex appeal. It thus contributed to the declining interest in the larger social issues that the earlier women's movement had raised.

A shifting labor market also promoted mass consumption. The increasing number of white-collar workers had more time and money for leisure and consumption. Factory workers, whose jobs often provided little challenge, less satisfaction, and no prospect for advancement, found in consumption not only material rewards but, thanks to advertisers' claims, some self-respect and fulfillment as stylish and attractive people worthy of attention. Women clerical workers, the fastest-growing occupational group, found in the purchase of clothes and cosmetics a sign of social status and an antidote to workplace monotony. "People are seeking to escape from themselves," insisted a writer in *Advertising and Selling* in 1926. "They want to live in a more exciting world." Advertisers tried to portray popular fantasies rather than social realities.

Under the stimulus of advertising, consumption increasingly displaced the traditional virtues of thrift, prudence, and avoidance of debt. Installment buying became common. By 1928, fully 85 percent of furniture, 80 percent of radios, and 75 percent of washing machines were bought on credit. But with personal debt rising more than twice as fast as incomes, even aggressive advertising and the extension of credit could not indefinitely prolong the illusion of a healthy economy.

LEISURE AND ENTERTAINMENT

During the 1920s, Americans also spent more on recreation and leisure, important features of the new mass society. Millions of people packed into movie theaters, whose ornate style symbolized their social importance. In Chicago, the Uptown boasted a four-thousand–seat theater, an infirmary, a nursery, and a restaurant; its turreted façade soared eight stories. Inside was a four-story lobby with twin marble staircases, crystal chandeliers, and an orchestra to entertain people waiting to enter. "It is beyond human dreams of loveliness," exclaimed one ad, "achieving that overpowering sense of tremendous size and exquisite beauty."

Movies helped to spread common values and to set national trends in dress, language, and behavior. Studios made films to attract the largest audiences and fit prevailing stereotypes. Cecil B. De Mille titillated audiences while reinforcing conventional standards with such religious epics as *The Ten Commandments* (1923) and *The King of Kings* (1927). Set in ancient times, such movies depicted both sinful pleasures and the eventual triumph of moral order. One Hollywood executive called for "passionate but pure" films that would give "the public all the sex it wants with compensating values for all those church and women groups."

Violinist Carroll Dickerson, at the Sunset Café in 1922, led one of the jazz bands that flourished in Chicago's many clubs, pointing up the central role of African Americans in the Jazz Age. Variety *magazine dubbed Chicago the "hottest café town" in the U.S. but the Illinois Vigilance Association despaired that "in Chicago alone" it had "traced the fall of 1,000 girls…to jazz music" in just two years.*

Radio also helped to mold national popular culture. The first radio network, the National Broadcasting Company (NBC), was formed in 1926. Soon it was charging $10,000 to broadcast commercials to a national market. Networks provided standardized entertainment, personalities, and news to Americans across the nation. Radio incorporated listeners into a national society. Rural residents, in particular, welcomed the "talking furniture" for giving them access to the speeches, sermons, and business information available to city dwellers.

The phonograph, another popular source of entertainment, allowed families to listen to music of their choice in their own homes. The phonograph business boomed. Manufacturers turned out more than 2 million phonographs and 100 million records annually. Record companies promoted dance crazes, such as the Charleston, and developed regional markets for country, or "hillbilly," music in the South and West, as well as a "race market" for blues and jazz among the growing urban population, black and white. The popularity of the trumpet player Louis Armstrong and other jazz greats gave the decade its nickname, the **Jazz Age**.

Jazz derived from African American musical traditions. The Great Migration spread it from New Orleans and Kansas City to cities throughout the nation. Its improvisational and rhythmic characteristics differed sharply from older and more formal music and were often condemned by people who feared that jazz would undermine conventional restraints on behavior. One group in Cincinnati, arguing that the music would implant "jazz emotions" in babies, won an injunction against its performance near hospitals. Middle-class black Chicagoans frowned on jazz and favored "the better class of music." But conductor Leopold Stokowski defended jazz as the music of modern America: "Jazz has come to stay because it is an expression of the times, of the breathless, energetic, superactive times in which we are living; it is useless to fight against it."

Professional sports also flourished and became more commercialized. Millions of Americans, attracted by the popularity of such celebrities as Babe Ruth of the New York Yankees, crowded into baseball parks to follow major league teams. Ruth treated himself as a commercial commodity, hiring an agent, endorsing Cadillacs and alligator shoes, and defending a salary in 1932 that dwarfed that of President Hoover by declaring, "I had a better year than he did."

Large crowds turned out to watch such boxers as Jack Dempsey and Gene Tunney pummel each other; those who could not get tickets listened to radio announcers describe each blow. College football attracted frenzied followers among people with no interest in higher education. Universities built huge stadiums—Ohio State's had 64,000 seats. By 1929, the Carnegie Commission noted that the commercialization of college sports "overshadowed the intellectual life for which the university is assumed to exist."

Other crazes, from flagpole sitting to miniature golf, also indicated the spread of popular culture and its emphasis on leisure. Another celebrity who captured popular fascination was the aviator Charles Lindbergh, who flew alone across the Atlantic in 1927. In the *Spirit of St. Louis*, a tiny airplane built on a shoestring budget and nearly outweighed by the massive amount of fuel it had to carry, Lindbergh fought bad weather and fatigue for thirty-four hours before landing to a hero's welcome in Paris. Named its first "Man of the Year" by *Time*, one of the new mass-circulation magazines, Lindbergh won adulation and awards from Americans who still valued the image of individualism.

THE NEW MORALITY

The promotion of consumption and immediate gratification weakened traditional self-restraint and fed a desire for personal fulfillment. The failure of wartime sacrifices to achieve promised glories deepened Americans' growing disenchantment with traditional values. The social dislocations of the war years and growing urbanization accelerated moral and social change. Sexual pleasure became an increasingly open objective. Popularization of Sigmund Freud's ideas weakened prescriptions for sexual restraint; the growing availability of birth-control information enabled women to enjoy sex with less fear of pregnancy; and movie stars, such as Clara Bow, known as "the It Girl," and Rudolph Valentino, flaunted sexuality to mass audiences. Traditionalists worried as divorce rates, cigarette consumption, and hemlines went up while respect for parents, elders, and clergy went down. A sociological study of Muncie, Indiana—the nation's "Middletown"—found that "religious life as represented by the churches is less pervasive than a generation ago."

Young people seemed to embody the new morality. Rejecting conventional standards, they embraced the era's frenzied dances, bootleg liquor, smoking, more revealing clothing, and sexual experimentation. They welcomed the freedom from parental control that the automobile afforded—although the car was hardly the "house of prostitution on wheels" that one critic called it. The "flapper"—a frivolous young woman with short hair and a skimpy skirt who danced, smoked, and drank in oblivious self-absorption—was a major obses-sion in countless articles, bearing such titles as "These Wild Young People" and "The Uprising of the Young." Few people were more alarmed than the president of the University of Florida. "The low-cut gowns, the rolled hose and short skirts are born of the Devil," he cried, "and are carrying the present and future generations to chaos and destruction." But feminists also condemned this symbol of changing standards. "It is sickening," Charlotte Perkins Gilman wrote in 1923, "to see so many of the newly freed abusing that freedom in mere imitation of masculine vice and weakness."

But the new morality was neither as new nor as widespread as its advocates and critics believed. Signs of change had appeared before the war in the popularity of new clothing fashions, social values, and public amusements among working-class and ethnic groups. And if it now became fashionable for the middle class to adopt such attitudes and practices, most Americans still adhered to traditional beliefs and values. Legislators in Utah and Virginia, for example, proposed laws requiring hemlines within three inches of the ankle and necklines within three inches of the throat. Moreover, as Gilman's comment suggests, the new morality offered only a limited freedom. It certainly did not promote social equality for women, who remained subject to traditional double standards, with marriage and divorce laws, property rights, and employment opportunities biased against them.

THE SEARCHING TWENTIES

Many writers rejected what they considered the materialism, conformity, and provincialism of the emerging mass culture. Their criticism made the postwar decade one of the most creative periods in American literature. The brutality and hypocrisy of the war stimulated their disillusionment and alienation. What Gertrude Stein called the Lost Generation considered, in the words of F. Scott Fitzgerald, "all Gods dead, all wars fought, all faiths in man shaken." Ernest Hemingway, wounded as a Red Cross volunteer during the war, rejected idealism in his novel *A Farewell to Arms* (1929), declaring that he no longer saw any meaning in "the words sacred, glorious, and sacrifice."

Novelists also turned their attention to American society. In *The Great Gatsby* (1925), Fitzgerald traced the self-deceptions of the wealthy. Sinclair Lewis ridiculed middle-class society and its narrow business culture in *Babbitt* (1922), whose title character provided a new word applied to the smug and shallow. In 1930, Lewis became the first American to win the Nobel Prize in literature.

Other writers condemned the mediocrity and intolerance of mass society. The critic Harold Stearns

One of the famous American writers in Paris, Ernest Hemingway wrote in the preface to his first novel, The Sun Also Rises (1926), "You are all a lost generation," using the phrase earlier coined by Gertrude Stein to describe the alienation of the expatriates. Here, Hemingway poses in front of American expatriate Sylvia Beach's Paris bookstore, Shakespeare and Company in March, 1928. (Beach is to his left.) The bookstore was a favorite meeting place for English-speaking writers living in Paris.

edited *Civilization in the United States* (1922), a book of essays. Its depiction of a repressive society sunk in hypocrisy, conformity, and materialism prompted his departure for Paris, where he lived, like Hemingway and Fitzgerald, as an expatriate, alienated from America. H.L. Mencken made his *American Mercury* the leading magazine of cultural dissenters. Conventional and conservative himself, Mencken heaped vitriol on the "puritans," "peasants," and "prehensile morons" he saw everywhere in American life.

When President Coolidge declined a request to exhibit American paintings in Paris by declaring that there were none, he seemed to confirm for the critics the boorishness of American society. But many of the critics were as self-absorbed as their targets. When the old progressive muckraker Upton Sinclair complained that he found nothing "constructive" in Mencken's voluminous writings, Mencken was delighted. "Uplift," he retorted, "has damn nigh ruined the country." Fitzgerald claimed to have "no interest in politics at all." Such attitudes dovetailed with the society they condemned.

CULTURE WARS

Despite the blossoming of mass culture and society in the 1920s, conflicts divided social groups. Some of these struggles involved reactions against the new currents in American life, including technological and scientific innovations, urban growth, and materialism. But movements to restrict immigration, enforce prohibition, prohibit the teaching of evolution, and even sustain the Ku Klux Klan did not have simple origins, motives, or consequences. The forces underlying the culture wars of the 1920s would surface repeatedly in the future (see the Overview table, "Issues in the Culture Wars of the 1920s").

NATIVISM AND IMMIGRATION RESTRICTION

For years, many Americans, from racists to reformers, had campaigned to restrict immigration. In 1917, Congress required immigrants to pass a literacy test. But renewed immigration after the war revived the anti-immigration movement, and the propaganda of the war and the Red Scare years generated public support for more restriction. Depicting immigrants as radicals, racial inferiors, religious subversives, or criminals, nativists clamored for congressional action. The Emergency Quota Act of 1921 reduced immigration by about two-thirds and established quotas for nationalities on the basis of their numbers in the United States in 1910. Restrictionists, however, demanded more stringent action, especially against the largely Catholic and Jewish immigrants from southern and eastern Europe. Coolidge himself urged that America "be kept American," by which he meant white, Anglo-Saxon, and Protestant.

Congress adopted this racist rationale in the **National Origins Act of 1924**, which proclaimed its objective to be the maintenance of the "racial preponderance" of "the basic strain of our population." This law restricted immigration quotas to 2 percent of the foreign-born population of each nationality as recorded in the 1890 census, which was taken before the mass immigration from southern and eastern Europe. Another provision, effective in 1929, restricted total annual immigration to 150,000, with quotas that nearly eliminated southern and eastern Europeans. The law also completely excluded Japanese immigrants.

Other actions targeted Japanese residents in America. California, Oregon, Washington, Arizona, and other western states prohibited them from owning or leasing land, and in 1922, the Supreme Court ruled that, as nonwhites, they could never become naturalized citizens. A Japanese newspaper in Los Angeles criticized such actions as betraying America's own ideals. Dispirited by the prejudice of the decade, Japanese residents hoped for fulfillment through their children, the *Nisei*, who were American citizens by birth.

Ironically, as a U.S. territory, the Philippines was not subject to the National Origins Act, and Filipino

OVERVIEW

Issues in the Culture Wars of the 1920s

Issue	Proponent view	Opponent view
The new morality	Promotes greater personal freedom and opportunities for fulfillment	Promotes moral collapse
Evolutionism	A scientific advance linked to notions of progress	A threat to religious belief
Jazz	Modern and vital	Unsettling, irregular, vulgar, and primitive
Immigration	A source of national strength from ethnic and racial diversity	A threat to the status and authority of old-stock white Protestants
Great Migration	A chance for African Americans to find new economic opportunities and gain autonomy and pride	A threat to traditional white privilege, control, and status
Prohibition	Promotes social and family stability and reduces crime	Restricts personal liberty and increases crime
Fundamentalism	An admirable adherence to traditional religious faith and biblical injunctions	A superstitious creed given to intolerant interference in social and political affairs
Ku Klux Klan	An organization promoting community responsibility, patriotism, and traditional social, moral, and religious values	A group of religious and racial bigots given to violent vigilantism and fostering moral and public corruption
Mass culture	Increases popular participation in national culture; provides entertainment and relaxation	Promotes conformity, materialism, mediocrity, and spectacle
Consumerism	Promotes material progress and higher living standards	Promotes waste, sterility, and self-indulgence

immigration increased ninefold during the 1920s. Most Filipino newcomers became farm laborers, especially in California, or worked in Alaskan fisheries. Similarly, because the law did not apply to immigrants from the Western Hemisphere, Mexican immigration also grew. Nativists lobbied to exclude Mexicans, but agribusiness interests in the Southwest blocked any restrictions on low-cost migrant labor.

THE KU KLUX KLAN

Nativism was also reflected in the popularity of the revived Ku Klux Klan, the goal of which, according to its leader, was to protect "the interest of those whose forefathers established the nation." Although founded in Georgia in 1915 and modeled on its Reconstruction predecessor, the new Klan was a national, not only a southern, movement and claimed several mil-

lion members by the mid-1920s. Admitting only native-born white Protestants, the Klan embodied the fears of a traditional culture threatened by social change. Ironically, its rapid spread owed much to modern business and promotional techniques as hundreds of professional recruiters raked in hefty commissions selling Klan memberships to those hoping to defend their way of life.

In part, the Klan was a fraternal order, providing entertainment, assistance, and community for its members. Its picnics, parades, charity drives, and other social and family-oriented activities—perhaps a half-million women joined the Women of the Ku Klux Klan—sharply distinguished the organization from both the small, secretive Klan of the nineteenth century and the still smaller, extremist Klan of the later twentieth century. Regarding themselves as reformers, Klan members supported immigration restriction and prohibition.

But the Klan also exploited racial, ethnic, and religious prejudices and campaigned against many social groups and what it called "alien creeds." It attacked African Americans in the South, Mexicans in Texas, Japanese in California, and Catholics and Jews everywhere. A twisted religious impulse ran through much of the Klan's organization and activities. It hired itinerant Protestant ministers to spread its message, erected altars and flaming crosses at its meetings, and sang Klan lyrics to the tunes of well-known hymns. One Klan leader maintained that "the Klan stood for the same things as the Church, but we did the things the Church wouldn't do." This included publishing anti-Catholic newspapers, boycotting Catholic and Jewish businesses, and lobbying for laws against parochial schools and for compulsory Bible reading in the public schools. The Klan also resorted to violence. In 1921, for example, a Methodist minister who belonged to the Klan murdered a Catholic priest on his own doorstep, and other Klansmen burned down Catholic churches. The leader of the Oregon Klan insisted that "the only way to cure a Catholic is to kill him."

To the Klan, Catholics and Jews symbolized, not merely subversive religions, but also the ethnic diversity and swelling urban population that challenged traditional Protestant culture. To protect that culture, the Klan attempted to censor or disrupt "indecent" entertainment, assaulted those whom it accused of adultery, and terrorized doctors who performed abortions.

While the Klan's appeal seemed rooted in the declining countryside, it also attracted urban residents. Chicago had the largest Klan organization in the nation, with fifty thousand members, and Houston, Dallas, Portland, Indianapolis, Denver, and the satellite communities ringing Los Angeles were also Klan strongholds. Urban Klansmen were largely lower or lower middle class, many recently arrived from the country and retaining its attitudes; others were long-term urban residents who feared being marginalized by social changes, especially by competition from immigrants and new ideas.

The Klan also ventured into politics, with some success. But eventually it encountered resistance. In the North, Catholic workers disrupted Klan parades. In the South, too, Klan excesses provoked a backlash. After the Klan in Dallas flogged sixty-eight people in a "whipping meadow" along the Trinity River in 1922, respect turned to outrage. Newspapers demanded that the Klan disband, district attorneys began to prosecute Klan thugs, and in 1924 Klan candidates were defeated by a ticket headed by Miriam "Ma" Ferguson, whose gu-

Indiana Klanswomen pose in their regalia in 1924. The Klan combined appeals to traditional family and religious values with violent attacks upon these who were not white native-born Protestants.

bernatorial campaign called for anti-Klan laws and for the loss of tax exemptions for churches used for Klan meetings. Elsewhere the Klan was stung by revelations of criminal behavior and corruption by Klan leaders, who had been making fortunes pocketing membership fees and selling regalia to followers. The Klan crusade to purify society had bred corruption and conflict everywhere. By 1930, the Klan had nearly collapsed.

PROHIBITION AND CRIME

Like the Klan, prohibition both reflected and provoked social tensions in the 1920s. Reformers had long believed that prohibition would improve social conditions, reduce crime and family instability, increase economic efficiency, and purify politics. They rejoiced in 1920, when the Eighteenth Amendment, prohibiting the manufacture, sale, or transportation of alcoholic beverages, took effect. Congress then passed the **Volstead Act**, which defined the forbidden liquors and established the Prohibition Bureau to enforce the law. But many social groups, especially among urban ethnic communities, opposed prohibition, and the government could not enforce the law where public opinion did not endorse it.

Evasion was easy. By permitting alcohol for medicinal, sacramental, and industrial purposes, the Volstead Act gave doctors, priests, and druggists a huge loophole through which to satisfy their friends' needs. Hearing that the use of sacramental wines increased by 800,000 gallons under Prohibition, one Protestant leader complained that "not more than one-quarter of this is sacramental—the rest is sacrilegious." City-dwellers made "bathtub gin," and rural people distilled "moonshine." Scofflaws frequented the "speakeasies" that replaced saloons or bought liquor from bootleggers and rumrunners, who imported it from Canada, Cuba, or Mexico. The limited resources of the Prohibition Bureau often allowed bootleggers to operate openly. Dozens met publicly in a Seattle hotel in 1922 and adopted "fair prices" for liquor and a code of ethics "to keep liquor runners within the limits of approved business methods."

The ethics and business methods of bootleggers soon shocked Americans, however. The huge profits encouraged organized crime—which had previously concentrated on gambling and prostitution—to develop elaborate liquor distribution networks. Operating outside the law, crime "families" used violence to enforce contracts, suppress competition, and attack rivals. In Chicago, Al Capone's army of nearly a thousand gangsters killed hundreds. Using the profits from bootlegging and such new tools as the automobile and the submachine gun, organized crime corrupted city governments and police forces.

Gradually, even many "drys"—people who had initially favored prohibition—dropped their support, horrified by the boost the amendment gave organized crime and worried about a general disrespect for law that it promoted. A 1926 poll found that four-fifths of Americans wanted to repeal or modify prohibition. Yet it remained in force because it was entangled in party politics and social conflict. Many rural, Protestant Americans saw prohibition as a symbolic cultural issue. As the comedian Will Rogers said, "Mississippi will vote dry and drink wet as long as it can stagger to the polls." Prohibition represented the ability of rural Protestants to control the newcomers in the expanding cities. Democrats called for repeal in their 1928 and 1932 platforms, and in 1933, thirty-six states ratified an amendment repealing what Herbert Hoover had called a "noble experiment."

OLD-TIME RELIGION AND THE SCOPES TRIAL

Religion provided another fulcrum for traditionalists attempting to stem cultural change. Protestant fundamentalism, which emphasized the infallibility of the Bible, including the Genesis story of Adam and Eve, emerged at the turn of the century as a conserva-tive reaction to religious modernism and the social changes brought by the mass immigration of Catholics and Jews, the growing influence of science and technology, and the secularization of public education. But the fundamentalist crusade to reshape America became formidable only in the 1920s.

Fundamentalist groups, colleges, and publications sprang up throughout the nation, especially in the South. The anti-Catholic sentiment exploited by the Klan was but one consequence of fundamentalism's insistence on strict biblical Christianity. A second was the assault on Darwin's theory of evolution, which contradicted literal interpretations of biblical Creation. The Southern Baptist Convention condemned "every theory, evolutionary or other, which teaches that man originated or came by way of lower animal ancestry." Fundamentalist legislators tried to prevent teaching evolution in public schools in at least twenty states. In 1923, Oklahoma banned textbooks based on Darwinian theory, and Florida's legislature denounced teaching evolution as "subversive." In 1925, Tennessee forbade teaching any idea contrary to the biblical account of human origins. The governor signed the law, saying that "there is a widespread belief that something is shaking the fundamentals of the country, both in religion and in morals. It is the opinion of many that an abandonment of the old-fashioned faith and belief in the Bible is our trouble."

Through the historical figures of William Jennings Bryan and Clarence Darrow, the Scopes Trial symbolized the cultural battles of the twenties. And when Darrow (standing) interrogated Bryan on the accuracy of the Bible, the New York Times *called the exchange the "most amazing courtroom scene in Anglo-American history."*

Social or political conservatism, however, was not an inherent part of old-time religion. The most prominent antievolution politician, William Jennings Bryan, continued to campaign for political, social, and economic reforms. Never endorsing the Klan, he served on the American Committee on the Rights of Religious Minorities and condemned anti-Semitism and anti-Catholicism. Bryan feared that Darwinism promoted political and economic conservatism. The survival of the fittest, he complained, elevated force and brutality, ignored spiritual values and democracy, and discouraged altruism and reform. How could a person fight for social justice "unless he believes in the triumph of right?"

The controversy over evolution came to a head when the American Civil Liberties Union (ACLU) responded to Tennessee's violation of the constitutional separation of church and state by offering to defend any teacher who tested the antievolution law. John Scopes, a high-school biology teacher in Dayton, Tennessee, did so and was arrested. Scopes's trial attracted national attention after Bryan agreed to assist the prosecution and Clarence Darrow, a famous Chicago lawyer and prominent atheist, volunteered to defend Scopes.

Millions of Americans tuned their radios to hear the first trial ever broadcast. The judge, a fundamentalist, sat under a sign urging people to "Read Your Bible Daily." He ruled that scientists could not testify in support of evolution: Because they were not present at the Creation, their testimony would be "hearsay." But he did allow Darrow to put Bryan on the stand as an expert on the Bible. Bryan insisted on the literal truth of every story in the Bible, allowing Darrow to ridicule his ideas and force him to concede that some biblical passages had to be construed symbolically. Though the local jury took only eight minutes to convict Scopes, fundamentalists suffered public ridicule from reporters, including H.L. Mencken, who sneered at the "hillbillies" and "yokels" of Dayton.

But fundamentalism was hardly destroyed, and antievolutionists continued their campaign. New organizations, such as the Bryan Bible League, lobbied for state laws and an antievolution amendment to the constitution. Three more states forbade teaching evolution, but by 1929 the movement had faltered. Even so, fundamentalism retained religious influence and would again challenge science and modernism in American life (see From Then to Now, "The Culture Wars").

A NEW ERA IN THE WORLD?

Abroad, as at home, Americans in the 1920s sought peace and economic order. Rejection of the Treaty of Versailles and the League of Nations did not foreshadow isolationism. Indeed, in the 1920s, the United States became more deeply involved in international matters than ever before in peacetime. That involvement both produced important successes and sowed the seeds for serious future problems.

WAR DEBTS AND ECONOMIC EXPANSION

The United States was the world's dominant economic power in the 1920s, changed by the Great War from a debtor to a creditor nation. The loans that the United States had made to its allies during the war troubled the nation's relations with Europe throughout the decade. American insistence on repayment angered Europeans, who saw the money as a U.S. contribution to the joint war effort against Germany. Moreover, high American tariffs blocked Europeans from exporting goods to the United States and earning dollars to repay their debts. Eventually, the United States readjusted the terms for repayment, and American bankers extended large loans to Germany, which used the money to pay reparations to Britain and France, whose governments then used the same money to repay the United States. This unstable system depended on a constant flow of money from the United States.

America's global economic role expanded in other ways as well. Exports, especially of manufactured goods, soared; by 1929, the United States was the world's largest exporter, responsible for one-sixth of all exports. American investment abroad more than doubled between 1919 and 1930. To expand their markets and avoid foreign tariffs, many U.S. companies became **multinational corporations**, establishing branches or subsidiaries abroad. Ford built assembly plants in England, Japan, Turkey, and Canada. International Telephone and Telegraph owned two dozen factories in Europe and employed more overseas workers than any other U.S. corporation.

Other companies gained control of foreign supply sources. American oil companies invested in foreign oil fields, especially in Latin America, where they controlled more than half of Venezuelan production. The United Fruit Company developed such huge operations in Central America that it often dominated national economies. In Costa Rica, the company had a larger budget than the national government.

Europeans and Latin Americans alike worried about this economic invasion; even Secretary of Commerce Herbert Hoover expressed concerns. Multinationals, he warned, might eventually take markets from American manufacturers and jobs from American workers. Business leaders, however, dismissed such reservations.

Hoover's concerns, moreover, did not prevent him from promoting economic expansion abroad.

FROM THEN TO NOW

The Culture Wars

Cultural conflict raged through American society in the 1920s as people reacted to great social changes, including new roles for women, increasing ethnic and racial diversity, rapid urbanization, and the "new morality." Nativists demanded immigration restriction; the Ku Klux Klan played on fears of racial, ethnic, and religious minorities; prohibitionists grappled with the minions of Demon Rum; and Protestant fundamentalists campaigned to prohibit the teaching of evolution in public schools.

Such conflicts are rooted in the moral systems that give people identity and purpose. As a result, the challenges of the Great Depression and World War II dampened but did not extinguish them. Beginning in the 1960s, fueled as before by challenges to traditional values and beliefs—African American demands for civil rights, opposition to the Vietnam War, the women's rights movement and women's growing presence in the workplace, a new wave of immigration (dominated this time by Asians and Latin Americans), the gay rights movement—cultural conflict flared again and continues to burn.

In the 1920s, nativists succeeded in curtailing immigration with the passage of the National Origins Act of 1924. In 1994, the people of California approved Proposition 187, which barred undocumented aliens from public schools and social services. Again, as in the 1920s, fundamentalists are mounting an attack against the teaching of evolution in public schools, sometimes seeking to persuade local school boards to give equal time to the pseudoscience of creationism. And today rap and rock 'n' roll provoke the same kind of worried condemnation that jazz provoked in the 1920s.

The central battleground of today's culture wars, however, is women's rights, and especially abortion rights. Ever since the Supreme Court ruled in *Roe v. Wade* in 1973 that women had a right to an abortion, opponents, primarily religious conservatives, have sought to curtail or abolish that right in the name of "family values." Antiabortion protests became increasingly violent in the 1980s and 1990s. Demonstrators have harassed women trying to enter abortion clinics, clinics have been bombed, and several abortion providers have been murdered. Although the Supreme Court has upheld *Roe v. Wade* and laws restraining demonstrations at abortion clinics, it has also upheld state laws imposing limits on abortion rights. Abortions have become harder to obtain in many parts of the country.

Further complicating the issue of abortion rights is the recent challenge to fetal-tissue

---

The government worked to open doors for American businesses in foreign countries, helping them to secure access to trade, investment opportunities, and raw materials. Hoover's Bureau of Foreign Commerce opened fifty offices around the world to boost American business. Hoover also pressed the British to give U.S. corporations access to rubber production in the British colony of Malaya. Secretary of State Charles Evans Hughes negotiated access to Iraqi oil fields for U.S. oil companies. The government also authorized bankers and manufacturers to form combinations, exempt from antitrust laws, to exploit foreign markets.

REJECTING WAR

Although government officials cooperated with business leaders to promote American strategic and economic interests, they had little desire to use force in the process. Popular reaction against the Great War, strengthened by a strong peace movement, constrained policymakers. Having repudiated collective security as embodied in the League of Nations, the United States nonetheless sought to minimize international conflict and promote its national security. In particular, the State Department sought to restrict the buildup of armaments among nations.

research. Scientists have been engaged in fetal tissue research since the 1930s and point to such important discoveries as the polio vaccine—developed with the use of human kidney cells—as evidence for the continuing need for fetal tissue in biomedical research. Even as they and other advocates, including former First Lady Nancy Reagan, argue that fetal tissue research promises possible cures for such diseases as Alzheimer's and Parkinson's, their opponents passionately object to what they fear as biomedical engineering and continue to seek legislation prohibiting all fetal tissue research.

Gay rights is another battleground in the culture wars. Religious conservatives, again in the name of "family values," have sought to counter efforts to extend civil rights protections to gays and lesbians. In 1992, for example, Colorado approved a measure (overturned by the Supreme Court in 1996) that prohibited local governments from passing ordinances protecting gays and lesbians from discrimination. But Vermont recently passed legislation recognizing "civil unions" between same sex couples, and newspapers, including the *New York Times*, now carry announcements of same-sex unions in their engagement and wedding sections.

The hostility to the Catholic Church and Catholic immigrants that had long been characteristic of American nativism has been largely absent from the current culture wars. On the contrary, conservative Catholics have joined forces with evangelical Protestants on many fronts, particularly on abortion, gay rights, school prayer, and publicly funded vouchers for parochial schools. The last issue has ignited the opposition of organized public teachers whereas school prayer has divided communities, as in Pontotoc, Mississippi, where it produced a searing controversy now chronicled in an Emmy-award winning film titled *School Prayer: A Community At War.* For a fuller discussion of the battles continuing to rage over school prayer and vouchers, see Chapter 30.

According to one popular analysis, the antagonists in today's culture wars are, on one side, those who find authority in transcendent universal sources like those that religious traditions lay claim to, and, on the other, those who find authority in society and human reason. Republican leader Tom DeLay of Texas, for example, declared in 1999 that the impeachment debate over former President Clinton was "about relativism versus absolute truth," and with the failure to convict Clinton, another Republican lamented, "we probably have lost the culture war." But the election of President George W. Bush, who declared his opposition to fetal-tissue research and rallied those in support of "family values," suggests that the war is not over and that cultural conflict, motivated by deeply rooted convictions, is likely to remain a persistent undercurrent in American life.

At the invitation of President Harding, delegations from nine nations met in Washington at the Washington Naval Conference in 1921 to discuss disarmament. The conference drafted a treaty to reduce battleship tonnage and suspend the building of new ships for a decade. The terms virtually froze the existing balance of naval power, with the first rank assigned to Britain and the United States, followed by Japan and then France and Italy. Japan and the United States also agreed not to fortify their possessions in the Pacific any further and to respect the Open Door in East Asia. Public opinion welcomed the treaty; the U.S. Senate ratified it with only one dissenting vote, and the 1924 Republican platform hailed it as "the greatest peace document ever drawn."

The United States made a more dramatic gesture in 1928, when it helped to draft the Kellogg-Briand Pact. Signed by sixty-four nations, the treaty renounced aggression and outlawed war. Without provisions for enforcement, however, it was little more than symbolic. The Senate reserved the right of self-defense, repudiated any responsibility for enforcing the treaty, and maintained U.S. claims under the Monroe Doctrine. These limitations on the treaty, Senator Hiram Johnson noted, "have made its nothingness complete."

MANAGING THE HEMISPHERE

Senate insistence on the authority of the Monroe Doctrine reflected the U.S. claim to a predominant role in Latin America. The United States continued to dominate the hemisphere to promote its own interests. It exerted its influence through investments, control of the Panama Canal, invocation of the Monroe Doctrine, and, when necessary, military intervention.

In response to American public opinion, the peace movement, and Latin American nationalism, the United States did retreat from the extreme gunboat diplomacy of the Progressive Era, withdrawing troops from the Dominican Republic and Nicaragua. Secretary of State Hughes assured Latin Americans that "we covet no territory; we seek no conquest; the liberty we cherish for ourselves we desire for others; and we accept no rights for ourselves that we do not accord to others." But Haiti remained under U.S. occupation throughout the decade, American troops stayed in Cuba and Panama, and the United States directed the financial policies of other Latin American countries. Moreover, it sent the Marines into Honduras in 1924 and back to Nicaragua in 1926. Such interventions could establish only temporary stability while provoking further Latin American hostility. "We are hated and despised," said one American businessman in Nicaragua. "This feeling has been created by employing American marines to hunt down and kill Nicaraguans in their own country."

Latin American resentment led to a resolution at the 1928 Inter-America Conference denying the right of any nation "to intervene in the internal affairs of another." The U.S. delegation rejected the measure, but the anger of Latin Americans prompted the Hoover Administration to decline support for the Roosevelt Corollary, and J. Reuben Clark, chief legal officer of the State Department, drafted the Clark Memorandum. Not published until 1930, this document stated that the Roosevelt Corollary was not a legitimate extension of the Monroe Doctrine and, thereby, helped prepare the way for the so-called Good Neighbor Policy toward Latin America. Still, the United States did not pledge nonintervention and retained the means, both military and economic, to dominate the hemisphere.

HERBERT HOOVER AND THE FINAL TRIUMPH OF THE NEW ERA

As the national economy steamed ahead in 1928, the Republicans chose as their presidential candidate Herbert Hoover, a man who symbolized the policies of prosperity and the New Era. Hoover was not a politician—he had never been elected to office—but a successful administrator who championed rational and efficient economic development. A cooperative government, he believed, should promote business interests and encourage corporations to form trade associations to assure stability and profitability. It should not regulate economic activities. Hoover's stiff managerial image was softened by his humanitarian record and his roots in rural Iowa.

The Democrats, by contrast, chose a candidate who evoked the cultural conflicts of the 1920s. Alfred E. Smith, a four-term governor of New York, was a Catholic, an opponent of prohibition, and a Tammany politician tied to the immigrant constituency of New York City. He had failed to gain the presidential nomination in 1924, when the party split over prohibition and the Klan, but in 1928 he won the dubious honor of running against Hoover. His nomination plunged the nation into the cultural strife that had divided the Democrats in 1924. Rural fundamentalism, anti-Catholicism, prohibition, and nativism were crucial factors in the campaign. The fundamentalist assault was unrelenting. Billy Sunday attacked Smith and the Democrats as "the forces of hell," and a Baptist minister in Oklahoma City warned his congregation, "If you vote for Al Smith, you're voting against Christ and you'll all be damned."

But Hoover was, in fact, the more progressive candidate. Sympathetic to labor, sensitive to women's issues, hostile to racial segregation, and favorable to the League of Nations, Hoover had always distanced himself from what he called "the reactionary group in the Republican party." By contrast, despite supporting state welfare legislation to benefit his urban working-class constituents, Smith was essentially conservative and opposed an active government. Moreover, he was as parochial as his most rural adversaries and never attempted to reach out to them. H.L. Mencken, who voted for Smith, nevertheless said of him, "Not only is he uninterested in the great problems facing the nation, but he has never heard of them." Smith himself responded to a question about the needs of the states west of the Mississippi by asking, "What states *are* west of the Mississippi?"

Although many Americans voted against Smith because of his social background, those same characteristics attracted others. Millions of urban and ethnic voters, previously Republican or politically uninvolved, voted for Smith and laid the basis for a new Democratic coalition that would emerge in the 1930s. In 1928, however, with the nation still enjoying the economic prosperity so closely associated with Hoover and the Republicans, the Democrats were routed (see Map 24-2).

In his campaign, Hoover boasted that Republican policies could bring America to "the final triumph

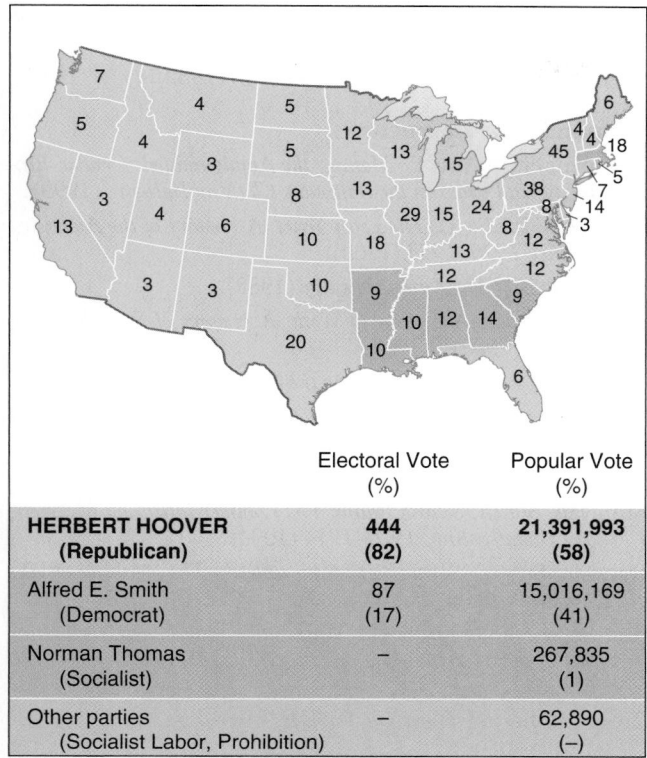

	Electoral Vote (%)	Popular Vote (%)
HERBERT HOOVER **(Republican)**	**444** **(82)**	**21,391,993** **(58)**
Alfred E. Smith (Democrat)	87 (17)	15,016,169 (41)
Norman Thomas (Socialist)	–	267,835 (1)
Other parties (Socialist Labor, Prohibition)	–	62,890 (–)

MAP 24-2 The Election of 1928
The cultural conflicts of the 1920s shaped the 1928 election. Al Smith carried the largest cities, but Herbert Hoover swept most of the rest of the nation, even attracting much of the usually Democratic South.

over poverty." But 1928 would be the Republicans' final triumph for a long time. The vaunted prosperity of the 1920s was ending, and the country faced a future dark with poverty.

CONCLUSION

The New Era of the 1920s changed America. Technological and managerial innovations produced giant leaps in productivity, new patterns of labor, a growing concentration of corporate power, and high corporate profits. Government policies from protective tariffs and regressive taxation to a relaxation of regulatory laws reflected and reinforced the triumphs of a business elite over traditional cautions and concerns.

The decade's economic developments, in turn, stimulated social change, drawing millions of Americans from the countryside to the cities, creating an urban nation, and fostering a new ethic of materialism, consumerism, and leisure and a new mass culture based on the automobile, radio, the movies, and advertising. This social transformation swept up many Americans but left others unsettled by the erosion of traditional practices and values. The concerns of traditionalists found expression in campaigns for prohibition and against immigration, the revival of the Ku Klux Klan, and the rise of religious fundamentalism. Intellectuals denounced the materialism and conformity they saw in the new social order and fashioned new artistic and literary trends.

But the impact of the decade's trends was uneven. Mechanization increased the productivity of some workers but cost others their jobs; people poured into the cities while others left for the suburbs; prohibition, intended to stabilize society, instead produced conflict, crime, and corruption; government policies advanced some economic interests but injured others. Even the notion of a "mass" culture obscured the degree to which millions of Americans were left out of the New Era. With no disposable income and little access to electricity, rural Americans scarcely participated in the joys of consumerism; racial and ethnic minorities were often isolated in ghettos and barrios; and many workers faced declining opportunities. Most ominous was the uneven prosperity undergirding the New Era. Although living standards rose for many Americans and the rich expanded their share of national wealth, more than 40 percent of the population earned less than $1,500 a year and fell below the established poverty level. The unequal distribution of wealth and income made the economy unstable and vulnerable to a disastrous collapse.

REVIEW QUESTIONS

1. How did the automobile industry affect the nation's economy and society in the 1920s? In the excerpt from *The Flivver King*, how does Upton Sinclair illustrate the tension between workers and technology even as they both served Henry Ford's vision of mass production and mass consumerism?

2. What factors characterized the "boom industries" of the 1920s? The "sick industries"? How accurate is it to label the 1920s the "decade of prosperity"?

3. What were the underlying issues in the election of 1924? Of 1928? What role did politics play in the public life of the 1920s?

4. What were the chief points of conflict in the "culture wars" of the 1920s? What were the underlying issues in these clashes? Why were they so hard to compromise?

5. In what ways did the World War I experience shape developments in the 1920s?

6. What were the chief features of American involvement in world affairs in the 1920s? To what extent did that involvement constitute a new role for the United States?

KEY TERMS

Great Migration (p. 764)

Harlem Renaissance (p. 766)

Jazz Age (p. 769)

League of Women Voters (p. 763)

Multinational corporations (p. 775)

National Origins Act of 1924 (p. 771)

Nisei (p. 771)

Open shop (p. 757)

Sheppard-Towner Maternity and Infancy Act (p. 763)

Volstead Act (p. 773)

Welfare capitalism (p. 758)

Yellow-dog contracts (p. 757)

RECOMMENDED READING

Braeman, John, Robert Bremner, and David Brody, eds. *Change and Continuity in Twentieth Century America: The 1920s* (1968). Stimulating essays that cover important features of economic, social, and political history.

Cohen, Warren I. *Empire without Tears: America's Foreign Relations, 1921–1933* (1987). A splendid brief analysis of diplomatic and economic policy.

Flink, James J. *The Car Culture* (1975). The fascinating history of the automobile and its social impact.

Hawley, Ellis W. *The Great War and the Search for a Modern Order* (1979). A valuable survey emphasizing economic and organizational changes.

Lewis, Sinclair, *Babbitt* (1922). An important novel of the 1920s that ridicules the empty business values of the booster society.

ADDITIONAL SOURCES

General Studies

Hicks, John D. *Republican Ascendancy, 1921–1933* (1960).

Leuchtenberg, William. *The Perils of Prosperity* (1958).

Parrish, Michael E. *Anxious Decades: America in Prosperity and Depression, 1920–1941* (1992).

Perrett, Geoffrey. *America in the Twenties* (1982).

Economic Developments

Argersinger, Jo Ann E. *Making the Amalgamated: Gender, Ethnicity, and Class in the Baltimore Clothing Industry* (1999).

Bernstein, Irving L. *The Lean Years: A History of the American Worker, 1920–1933* (1960).

Flink, James J. *The Automobile Age* (1988).

Kessler-Harris, Alice. *Out to Work: A History of Wage-Earning Women* (1982).

Marchand, Roland. *Advertising the American Dream* (1985).

Meyer, Stephen III. *The Five Dollar Day: Labor Management and Social Control in the Ford Motor Company* (1981).

Schatz, Ronald W. *The Electrical Workers* (1983).

Smulyan, Susan. *Selling Radio: The Commercialization of American Broadcasting, 1920–1934* (1994).

Strasser, Susan. *Satisfaction Guaranteed: The Making of the American Mass Market* (1989).

Tentler, Leslie Woodcock. *Wage-Earning Women: Industrial Work and Family Life in the United States, 1900–1930* (1979).

Zieger, Robert H. *American Workers, American Unions* (1994).

Politics and Government

Burner, David. *Herbert Hoover: A Public Life* (1979).

Burner, David. *The Politics of Provincialism* (1967).

Craig, Douglas B. *After Wilson: The Struggle for the Democratic Party* (1992).

Hawley, Ellis W. ed. *Herbert Hoover as Secretary of Commerce* (1981).

LaFeber, Walter. *Inevitable Revolutions: The United States in Central America* (1984).

Lichtman, Allan J. *Prejudice and the Old Politics: The Presidential Election of 1928* (1979).

Lowitt, Richard. *George W. Norris: The Persistence of a Progressive* (1971).

McCoy, Donald R. *Calvin Coolidge* (1967).

Murray, Robert. *The Politics of Normalcy* (1973).

Schulzinger, Robert D. *The Making of the Diplomatic Mind* (1975).

Trani, Eugene P., and David L. Wilson. *The Presidency of Warren G. Harding* (1977).

Wilson, Joan Hoff. *American Business and Foreign Policy, 1920–1933* (1968).

Wilson, Joan Hoff. *Herbert Hoover: Forgotten Progressive* (1975).

Cities and Suburbs

Deutsch, Sarah. *No Separate Refuge: Culture, Class, and Gender on an Anglo-Hispanic Frontier in the American Southwest* (1987).

Garcia, Juan. *Mexicans in the Midwest, 1900-1932* (1996).

Goldfield, David. *Cotton Fields and Skyscrapers* (1982).

Gottlieb, Peter. *Making Their Own Way: Southern Blacks' Migration to Pittsburgh, 1916–30* (1987).

Hogan, David Gerard. *Selling 'em by the Sack: White Castle and the Creation of American Food* (1997).

Jackson, Kenneth T. *Crabgrass Frontier: The Suburbanization of the United States* (1985).

Lewis, Earl. *In Their Own Interests: Race, Class, and Power in Twentieth-Century Norfolk, Virginia* (1991).

Osofsky, Gilbert. *Harlem: The Making of a Ghetto* (1968).

Romo, Ricardo. *East Los Angeles: History of a Barrio* (1983).

Teaford, John C. *Cities of the Heartland* (1993).

Worley, William. *J. C. Nichols and the Shaping of Kansas City* (1990).

Society and Culture

Alexander, Charles C. *The Ku Klux Klan in the Southwest* (1965).

Blee, Kathleen M. *Women and the Klan: Racism and Gender in the 1920s* (1991).

Carter, Paul. *Another Part of the Twenties* (1977).

Chafe, William H. *The American Woman: Her Changing Social, Economic, and Political Roles* (1972).

Clark, Norman. *Deliver Us from Evil: An Interpretation of American Prohibition* (1976).

Coben, Stanley. *Rebellion against Victorianism* (1991).

Cott, Nancy F. *The Grounding of American Feminism* (1987).

Dumenil, Lynn. *The Modern Temper: American Culture and Society in the 1920s* (1995).

Evans, Sara M. *Born for Liberty: A History of Women in America* (1989).

Ewen, Stuart. *Captains of Consciousness: Advertising and the Social Roots of the Consumer Culture* (1976).

Fass, Paula. *The Damned and the Beautiful: American Youth in the 1920s* (1977).

Hobson, Fred. *Mencken: A Life* (1994).

Huggins, Nathan. *Harlem Renaissance* (1971).

Jackson, Kenneth T. *The Ku Klux Klan in the City* (1967).

Lawrence, Bruce B. *Defenders of God: The Fundamentalist Revolt against the Modern Age* (1989).

Levine, Lawrence W. *Defender of the Faith: William Jennings Bryan, the Last Decade, 1915–1925* (1965).

Lewis, David L. *When Harlem Was in Vogue* (1981).

Maclean, Nancy. *Behind the Mask of Chivalry: The Making of the Second Ku Klux Klan* (1994).

May, Lary. *Screening Out the Past: The Birth of Mass Culture and the Motion Picture Industry* (1980).

Moore, Leonard. *Citizen Klansmen: The Ku Klux Klan in Indiana* (1991).

Muncy, Robyn. *Creating a Female Dominion in American Reform* (1991).

Ogren, Kathy H. *The Jazz Revolution* (1989).

Payne, Elizabeth A. *Reform, Labor, and Feminism: Margaret Dreier Robins and the Women's Trade Union League* (1988).

Peiss, Kathy. *Hope in a Jar: The Making of America's Beauty Culture* (1998).

Rader, Benjamin G. *American Sports: From the Age of Folk Games to the Age of Spectators* (1983).

Sklar, Robert. *Movie-Made America: A Cultural History of American Movies* (1994).

Stein, Judith. *The World of Marcus Garvey* (1986).

Wiggins, David. *Sport in America* (1995).

WHERE TO LEARN MORE

- **F. Scott and Zelda Fitzgerald Museum, Montgomery, Alabama.** The novelist and his wife lived a short while in this house in her hometown. www.alabamatravel.org/central/szfm.html.

- **Smithsonian Institution, Washington, D.C.** "From Farm to Factory," a permanent exhibition at the National Museum of American History, splendidly portrays the human side of the Great Migration.

- **Herbert Hoover National Historic Site, West Branch, Iowa.** Visitors may tour Hoover's birthplace cottage, presidential library, and museum.

- **Henry Ford Museum and Greenfield Village, Dearborn, Michigan.** Among many fascinating exhibits, "The Automobile in American Life" particularly and superbly demonstrates the importance of the automobile in American social history. www.hfmgv.org.

- **George Norris Home, McCook, Nebraska.** This museum, operated by the Nebraska State Historical Society, is dedicated to a leading progressive Republican of the 1920s. www.nebraskahistory.org/sites/norris/index.htm.

- **Warren G. Harding House, Marion, Ohio.** Harding's home from 1891 to 1921 is now a museum with period furnishings. www.ohiohistory.org/places/harding.

- **Rhea County Courthouse and Museum, Dayton, Tennessee.** The site of the Scopes Trial, the courtroom appears as it did in 1925; the museum contains memorabilia related to the trial.

- **Calvin Coolidge Homestead, Plymouth, Vermont.** Operated by the Vermont Division of Historic Sites, the homestead preserves the exact interiors and furnishings from when Coolidge took the presidential oath of office there in 1923. www.calvin-coolidge.org/pages/homestead and www.dhca.state.vt.us/HistoricSites/sites.htm.

 Please refer to the document CD-ROM for primary sources related to this chapter.

➔ Anguished faces tell a story of hard work and hard times. Farm families, such as the Barnetts of Woodward, Oklahoma, struggled throughout the Great Depression to survive on the land.

THE GREAT DEPRESSION AND THE NEW DEAL

25

1929–1939

My mother had two small babies on her hands. When I became sickly, Grandmother Josefa took me home with her, and I never returned to my parents. . . . My grandmother's house was located on the 'American' side of town, but there was nothing they could do about it because she was there before anybody else. . . . My grandmother worked very hard; I grew up in the Depression.

When it was time for me to go to school I was assigned to [the] Mexican side of town. We were segregated; [the] Anglo children were sent to Roosevelt and the Mexican children who lived closer to Roosevelt [still] had to go down to Harding. I'll admit, there was a lot of discrimination in those years.

During the Depression my grandmother sewed piecework for the WPA. My dad helped out when he could [and] Uncle Ernesto also worked. He used to dig graves.

The Depression years were very, very hard. I remember seeing the people passing on their way to California. . . . It hurt me to see the people in their rickety old cars, their clothes in tatters, escaping from the drought and the dust bowls.

Oral Testimony,
Carlotta Silvas Martin

On April 27 [1933], according to the *New York Times*, Paul Schneider, aged forty-four, a sick and crip-

CHAPTER OUTLINE

Hard Times in Hooverville
Crash!
The Depression Spreads
"Women's Jobs" and "Men's Jobs"
Families in the Depression
"Last Hired, First Fired"
Protest

Herbert Hoover and the Depression
The Limits of Voluntarism
Repudiating Hoover: The Election of 1932

Launching the New Deal
Action Now!
Creating Jobs
Helping Some Farmers
The Flight of the Blue Eagle
Critics Right and Left

Consolidating the New Deal
Lifting Up and Weeding Out
Expanding Relief
The Roosevelt Coalition and the Election of 1936

The New Deal and American Life
Labor on the March
Women and the New Deal
Minorities and the New Deal
The New Deal: North, South, East, and West
The New Deal and Public Activism

Ebbing of the New Deal
Challenging the Court
More Hard Times
Political Stalemate

Good Neighbors and Hostile Forces
Neutrality and Fascism
Edging Toward Involvement

Conclusion

pled Chicago school teacher, shot himself to death. His widow, left with three children, stated that he had not been paid for eight months. . . . Less than a month after Paul Schneider's discouragement drove him to suicide, the militant action of Chicago teachers— patient no more . . . resulted in the payment of $12,000,000 due them for the last months of 1932. Their pay for the five months of 1933 is still owed them. Five hundred of them are reported to be in asylums and sanitariums as a result of the strain. . . .

These are the conditions facing teachers fortunate enough to be employed. What of the unemployed? . . . "We are always hungry," wrote [one unemployed teacher]. "We owe six months' rent . . . . We live every hour in fear of eviction. . . . My sister, a typist, and I . . . have been out of work for two years. . . . We feel discouraged . . . and embittered. We are drifting, with no help from anyone."

> Eunice Langdon,
> *The Nation*, August 16, 1933

I am sitting in the city free employment bureau. It's the women's section. We have been sitting here now for hours. We sit here every day, waiting for a job. There are no jobs. . . .

. . . [W]e don't talk much. . . . There is a kind of humiliation . . . . We look away from each other. We look at the floor.

> Meridel LeSeur, "Women on the Breadlines,"
> 1932

Dear Mrs. Roosevelt,

I am now 15 years old and in the 10th grade. I have always been smart but I never had a chance as all of us is so poor. I hope to complete my education, but I will have to quit school I guess if there is no clothes can be bought. (Don't think that we are on the relief.) Mother has been a faithful servant for us to keep us together. I don't see how she has made it.

Mrs. Roosevelt, don't think I am just begging, but that is all you can call it I guess . . . . Do you have any old clothes you have throwed back. You don't realize how honored I would feel to be wearing your clothes.

> Your friend,
> M.I.
>
> Star Route One
> Albertville, Ala.
> January 1, 1936

"Carlotta Silvas Martin: A Mexican American Childhood during the Depression" and "Meridel LeSeur: The Despair of Unemployed Women," both from Susan Ware, *Modern American Women: A Documentary History* (New York: McGraw–Hill Higher Education, 2002), pp. 162–165, 145–146, respectively; Eunice Langdon, "The Teacher Faces the Depression," *The Nation* 137 (August 16, 1933): 182–187; Letter to Eleanor Roosevelt, January 1, 1936, http://www.newdeal.feri.org/eleanor/mi0136.htm.

Carlotta Silvas Martin, Eunice Langdon, and Meridel LeSeur convey some of the trauma of the Great Depression, but no one voice can capture its devastating effect on Americans. The American economy utterly collapsed, leaving millions of people jobless, homeless, or in constant fear of foreclosure, eviction, and even starvation. The decade of hard times constituted a journey into desperation and despair, and men, women, children everywhere saw their families and dreams shattered and felt the sting of humiliation as they stood in bread lines or begged for clothes or food scraps. The winter of 1932-1933 was particularly cruel: unemployment soared and stories of malnutrition and outright starvation made headlines in newspapers throughout the nation. Hunger was so widespread in Kentucky and West Virginia that one relief committee limited its handouts to those who were at least 10 percent below their normal weight for their height. The school teacher who committed suicide lived in the city of Chicago where, that winter, half the people were without jobs, where one-half the city's property tax bills were left unpaid, and, most striking, where one newspaper declared "Starvation Hits 14,000."

Natural disaster accompanied the economic crisis in the drought-stricken states of the Great Plains and forced families to leave their farms. They packed up their meager belongings and took to the road to escape the darkened skies of the "Dust Bowl"—in search of anything better. Their story, best chronicled in John Steinbeck's novel, *The Grapes of Wrath,* powerfully portrayed the westward movement of these homeless migrants—a book reviewed in 1939 by First Lady Eleanor Roosevelt, who described it as an "unforgettable experience." The poignant image of "the path of people in flight," as Steinbeck himself called it, also stayed with Carlotta Silvas, who as a young girl saw hungry and half-clothed families pass through her hometown of Superior, Arizona.

The election of Franklin D. Roosevelt, however, lifted spirits and hopes of jobless Americans throughout the nation. They enthusiastically responded to his **New Deal**, taking jobs, as did Carlotta's grandmother, with such programs as the Works Progress Administration (WPA). In unprecedented numbers, they also wrote to both FDR and Eleanor Roosevelt, asking for advice and for assistance for everything from a month's rent money to tide them over to old clothes to wear to school, as did the fifteen-old girl from Alabama. And they also wrote to thank the President and the First Lady for their compassionate support and leadership.

Throughout all such letters ran the common theme: the belief among poor and unemployed Americans that for the first time there were people in the White House who were interested in their welfare, who wanted to eliminate their hardships, and who would listen to their ideas.

Their stories about their experiences in the Great Depression further underscored that the decade of hard times affected people differently. The collapse hit hardest those industries dominated by male workers, leaving mothers and wives with new roles as the family breadwinners, sometimes straining family relationships and men's sense of purpose and respect. Some families drifted apart while others coped simply by making do. As Carlotta Silvas noted, her "dad helped out when he could." But the pressure for women to take on new economic responsibilities—especially married women—did not escape the wrath of the public. They were roundly condemned as "thieving parasites" and placed in the impossible position of being forced to work and told they should not hold jobs.

Race and ethnicity further complicated the problems of both joblessness and relief. Southern states routinely denied African Americans relief assistance as did southwestern states for Hispanic Americans. Although First Lady Eleanor Roosevelt pressed the president to challenge racism and discrimination and FDR did make some progress in assisting African Americans, the New Deal failed to overcome traditional attitudes and practices that targeted women and minorities and reinforced local prejudice and segregation. For Carlotta Silvas, that meant walking farther to school—a daily journey that she remembered throughout her life.

Hard times, then, both united and divided the American people. Franklin and Eleanor Roosevelt and the programs of the New Deal brought fresh hope and connected Americans to the White House as never before. And although the federal activism of the 1930s achieved neither full recovery nor systematic reform, it restored confidence to many Americans and permanently transformed the nation's responsibilities for the welfare of its citizens. By the end of the decade, President Roosevelt was proud of those changes and also frustrated by the persistence of hard times. But he was no longer worried that the economy—indeed the whole of society—teetered on the edge of catastrophe; his gaze now fixed abroad where even more ominous developments, he believed, threatened the nation's future and security.

KEY TOPICS

- The Great Depression
- Hoover's voluntary remedies
- FDR's New Deal
- The New Deal and organized labor, minorities, women, and farmers
- FDR's Democratic coalition of reformers, labor, urban ethnic groups, white Southerners, Westerners, and African Americans
- The faltering of the New Deal
- Diplomacy in the Great Depression

HARD TIMES IN HOOVERVILLE

The prosperity of the 1920s ended in a stock-market crash that revealed the flaws honeycombing the economy. As the nation slid into a catastrophic depression, factories closed, employment and incomes tumbled, and millions lost their homes, hopes, and dignity. Some protested and took direct action; others looked to the government for relief.

CRASH!

The buoyant prosperity of the New Era, more apparent than real by the summer of 1929, collapsed in October, when the stock market crashed. During the previous two years, the market had hit record highs, stimulated by optimism, easy credit, and speculators' manipulations. After peaking in September, it suffered several sharp checks, and on October 29, "Black Tuesday," panicked investors dumped their stocks at any price, wiping out the previous year's gains in one day. Confidence in the economy disappeared, and the slide continued for months, and then years. It hit bottom in July 1932. By then, the stock of U.S. Steel had plunged from 262 to 22, Montgomery Ward from 138 to 4. Much of the paper wealth of America had evaporated, and the nation sank into the **Great Depression**.

The Wall Street crash marked the beginning of the depression, but it did not cause it. The depression stemmed from weaknesses in the New Era economy. Most damaging was the unequal distribution of wealth and income. Workers' wages and farmers' incomes had fallen far behind industrial productivity and corporate profits; by 1929, the richest 0.1 percent of American families had as much total income as the bottom 42 percent (see Figure 25-1). With more than half the nation's people living at or below the subsistence level, there was not enough purchasing power to maintain the economy.

A second factor was that oligopolies dominated American industries. By 1929, the 200 largest corporations (out of 400,000) controlled half the corporate wealth. Their power led to "administered prices," prices kept artificially high and rigid rather than

FIGURE 25-1 Distribution of Income in the United States, 1929–1946
An unequal distribution of income contributed to the Great Depression by limiting purchasing power. Only slight changes occurred until after World War II, but other factors gradually stabilized the national economy.
Data Source: U.S. Bureau of the Census.

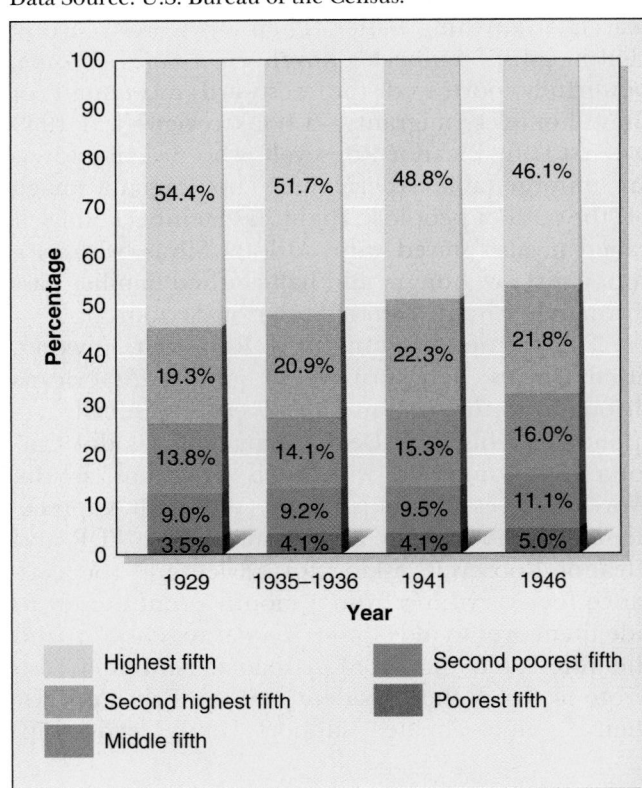

Chronology

1929 Stock market crashes.

1932 Farmers' Holiday Association organizes rural protests in the Midwest.

Reconstruction Finance Corporation is created to assist financial institutions.

Bonus Army is routed in Washington, D.C.

Franklin D. Roosevelt is elected president.

1933 Emergency Banking Act is passed.

Agricultural Adjustment Administration (AAA) is created to regulate farm production.

National Recovery Administration (NRA) is created to promote industrial cooperation and recovery.

Federal Emergency Relief Act provides federal assistance to the unemployed.

Civilian Conservation Corps (CCC) is established to provide work relief in conservation projects.

Public Works Administration (PWA) is created to provide work relief on large public construction projects.

Civil Works Administration (CWA) provides emergency winter relief jobs.

Tennessee Valley Authority (TVA) is created to coordinate regional development.

1934 Securities and Exchange Commission (SEC) is established.

Indian Reorganization Act reforms Indian policy.

Huey Long organizes the Share-Our-Wealth Society.

Democrats win midterm elections.

1935 Supreme Court declares NRA unconstitutional.

National Labor Relations Act (Wagner Act) guarantees workers' rights to organize and bargain collectively.

Social Security Act establishes a federal social insurance system.

Banking Act strengthens the Federal Reserve.

Revenue Act establishes a more progressive tax system.

Resettlement Administration is created to aid dispossessed farmers.

Rural Electrification Administration (REA) is created to help provide electric power to rural areas.

Soil Conservation Service is established.

Emergency Relief Appropriation Act authorizes public relief projects for the unemployed.

Works Progress Administration (WPA) is created.

Huey Long is assassinated.

1936 Supreme Court declares AAA unconstitutional.

Roosevelt is reelected president.

Sit-down strikes begin.

1937 Chicago police kill workers in Memorial Day Massacre.

FDR tries but fails to expand the Supreme Court.

Farm Security Administration (FSA) is created to lend money to small farmers to buy and rehabilitate farms.

National Housing Act is passed to promote public housing projects.

"Roosevelt Recession" begins.

1938 Congress of Industrial Organizations (CIO) is founded.

Fair Labor Standards Act establishes minimum wage and maximum hours rules for labor.

Roosevelt fails to "purge" the Democratic party.

Republicans make gains in midterm elections

---

determined by supply and demand. By not responding to purchasing power, this system not only helped bring on economic collapse but also dimmed prospects for recovery.

Weaknesses in specific industries had further unbalanced the economy. Agriculture suffered from overproduction, declining prices, and heavy debt; so did the coal and textile industries. These difficulties left the economy dependent on a few industries for expansion and employment; they could not carry the burden. Banking presented other problems. Poorly managed and regulated, banks had contributed to the instability of prosperity; they now threatened to spread the panic and depression.

International economic difficulties spurred the depression as well. Shut out from U.S. markets by high tariffs, Europeans had depended on American investments to manage their debts and reparation payments from the Great War. The stock market crash dried up the flow of American dollars to Europe, causing financial panics and industrial collapse and making the Great Depression global. In turn, European nations curtailed their imports of American goods and defaulted on their debts, further debilitating the U.S. economy. American exports fell by 70 percent from 1929 to 1932. As foreign markets shrank, so did hopes for economic recovery.

Government policies also bore some responsibility for the crash and depression. Failure to enforce antitrust laws had encouraged oligopolies and high prices; failure to regulate banking or the stock market had permitted financial recklessness and irresponsible speculation. Reducing tax rates on the wealthy had also encouraged speculation and contributed to the maldistribution of income. Opposition to labor unions and collective bargaining helped keep workers' wages and purchasing power low. The absence of an effective agricultural policy and the high tariffs that inhibited foreign trade and reduced markets for agricultural products hurt farmers in the same way. In short, the same government policies that shaped the booming 1920s economy also pointed to economic disaster.

But the crash did more than expose the weaknesses of the economy. Business lost confidence and refused to make investments that might have brought recovery. Instead, banks called in loans and restricted credit, and depositors tried to withdraw their savings, which were uninsured. The demand for cash caused banks to fail, dragging the economy down further. And the Federal Reserve Board prolonged the depression by restricting the money supply.

THE DEPRESSION SPREADS

By early 1930, the effects of financial contraction were painfully evident. Factories shut down or cut back, and industrial production plummeted; by 1932, it was scarcely 50 percent of its 1929 level. Steel mills operated at 12 percent of capacity, auto factories at 20 percent. Unemployment skyrocketed, as an average of 100,000 workers a week were fired in the first three years after the crash. By 1932, one-fourth of the labor

force was out of work (see Figure 25-2). In St. Louis, 75 percent of the workers in the building trades, a key sector of the 1920s economy, were jobless. Overall unemployment in Toledo reached 80 percent. The wages of those Americans lucky enough to work fell sharply. Personal income dropped by more than half between 1929 and 1932; by 1933, industrial workers had average weekly wages of only $16.73. Moreover, the depression began to feed on itself in a vicious circle: Shrinking wages and employment cut into purchasing power, causing business to slash production again and lay off workers, thereby further reducing purchasing power.

The depression particularly battered farmers. Commodity prices fell by 55 percent between 1929 and 1932, stifling farm income. Cotton farmers earned only 31 percent of the pittance they had received in 1929. Unable to pay their mortgages, many farm families lost their homes and fields. "We have no security left," cried one South Dakota farm woman. "Foreclosures and evictions at the point of sheriff's guns are increasing daily." The dispossessed roamed the byways, highways, and railways of a troubled country.

Urban families were also evicted when they could not pay their rent. Some moved in with relatives; others lived in **Hoovervilles**—the name reflects the bitterness directed at the President—shacks where people shivered, suffered, and starved. Oklahoma City's vast Hooverville covered one-hundred square miles; one witness described its hapless residents as squatting in "old, rusted-out car bodies," orange crates, and holes in the ground.

Soup kitchens became standard features of the urban landscape, with lines of the hungry stretching

FIGURE 25-2   Unemployment, 1925–1945

Unemployment soared in the early 1930s, spreading distress and overwhelming charities and local relief agencies. Federal programs improved conditions, but only American entry into World War II really ended the problem.

Data Source: U.S. Bureau of the Census.

Homeless Americans gathered in squalid "Hoovervilles," like this one in Seattle, and struggled to survive.

for blocks. But charities and local communities could not meet the massive needs, and neither state nor federal governments had welfare or unemployment compensation programs. To survive, people planted gardens in vacant lots and back alleys and tore apart empty houses or tapped gas lines for fuel. In immigrant neighborhoods, social workers found a "primitive communism" in which people shared food, clothing, and fuel in the belief that "what goes around comes around." Few Americans escaped hard times, but their experiences varied with their circumstances and expectations.

"WOMEN'S JOBS" AND "MEN'S JOBS"

The depression affected wage-earning women in complex ways. Although suffering 20 percent unemployment by 1932, women were less likely than men to be fired. Gender segregation had concentrated women in low-paid service, sales, and clerical jobs that shrank less than the heavy industries where men predominated. But while traditional attitudes somewhat insulated working women, they also reinforced opposition to female employment itself, especially that of married women. As one Chicago civic organization complained, "They are holding jobs that rightfully belong to the God-intended providers of the household." Nearly every state considered re-

stricting the employment of married women, and the city council of Akron, Ohio, resolved that public agencies and private employers should stop employing wives. Three-fourths of the nation's school systems refused to hire married women as teachers, and two-thirds dismissed female teachers who married. Many private employers, especially banks and insurance companies, also fired married women.

Firing women, however, rarely produced jobs for men because few men sought positions in the fields associated with women. Men did displace women as teachers, social workers, and librarians, but firing women simply aggravated the suffering of families already reeling from the depression. Disapproval of female employment implied that women did not deserve equal opportunities and probably stiffened the opposition to opening "men's jobs" to women when women were desperate for work. Despite such hostility, the proportion of married women in the work force increased in the 1930s as women took jobs to help their families survive.

FAMILIES IN THE DEPRESSION

"I have watched fear grip the people in our neighborhood around Hull House," wrote Jane Addams as the depression deepened in 1931 and family survival itself seemed threatened. Divorce declined because it was expensive, but desertion increased, and marriages were postponed. Birthrates fell. Husbands and fathers, the traditional breadwinners, were often humiliated and despondent when laid off from work. One social worker observed in 1931, "Like searing irons, the degradation, the sheer terror and panic which loss of job brings, the deprivation and the bitterness have eaten into men's souls." Unemployed men, sociologists reported, "lost much of their sense of time and dawdled helplessly and dully about the streets," dreading to return home.

Women's responsibilities, by contrast, often grew. The number of female-headed households increased sharply. Not only did some women become wage earners, but their traditional role as homemakers also gained new significance. To make ends meet, many women sewed their own clothing and raised and canned vegetables, reversing the trend toward consumerism. Some also took on extra work at home. In San Antonio, one in every ten families had boarders, and in Alabama, housewives took in laundry at 10 cents for a week's washload.

The depression also affected children. Some parents sacrificed their own well-being to protect their children. One witness described "the uncontrolled trembling of parents who have starved themselves for weeks so that their children might not go hungry." But children felt the tension and fear, and many went without food. In New York City, 139 people, most of them children, died of starvation and malnutrition in 1933. Boys and girls stayed home from school and church because they lacked shoes or clothing; others gave up their plans for college. As hope faded, family conflicts increased. Some parents nagged their children, even considering them burdens. Many teenagers left home, either to escape parental authority or so that younger children would have more to eat. These "juvenile transients" suffered from starvation, exposure, illness, and accidents. The California Unemployment Commission concluded that the depression had left the American family "morally shattered. There is no security, no foothold, no future."

"LAST HIRED, FIRST FIRED"

The depression particularly harmed racial minorities. With fewer resources and opportunities, they were less able than other groups to absorb the economic pain. African Americans were caught in a double bind, reported a sociologist at Howard University in 1932: They were "the last to be hired and the first to be fired." Black unemployment rates were more than twice the white rate, reflecting increased job competition and persistent racism. Jobless white workers now sought the menial jobs traditionally reserved for black workers, such as street cleaning and domestic service. In Atlanta, white citizens paraded with banners denouncing the hiring of black workers "Until Every White Man Has a Job."

Racism also limited the assistance African Americans received. Religious and charitable organizations often refused to care for black people. Local and state governments set higher requirements for black people than for white people to receive relief and provided them with less aid. One Memphis resident saw the result of such policies: "Colored men and women with rakes, hoes, and other digging tools, with buckets and baskets, digging around in the garbage and refuse for food." By 1932, most African Americans were suffering acute privation. "At no time in the history of the Negro since slavery," reported the Urban League, "has his economic and social outlook seemed so discouraging." African Americans were "hanging on by the barest thread."

Hispanic Americans also suffered. As mostly unskilled workers, they faced increasing competition for decreasing jobs paying declining wages. They were displaced even in the California agricultural labor force, which they had dominated. By the mid-1930s, they made up only a tenth of the state's migratory labor force, which increasingly consisted of white people who had fled the South and the Great Plains. Other jobs were lost when Arizona, California, and Texas barred Mexicans from public works and highway construction jobs. Vigilantes threatened employers who hired Mexicans rather than white Americans.

Economic woes and racism drove nearly half a million Mexican immigrants and their American-born children from the United States in the 1930s. Local authorities in the Southwest urged the federal government to deport Mexicans, offered free transportation to Mexico, and adopted discriminatory policies in providing relief. By 1931, a Los Angeles official announced that tens of thousands of Mexicans "have been literally scared out of southern California." Fear of deportation kept many Mexican-American families from seeking relief or even health care in Texas.

PROTEST

Bewildered and discouraged, most Americans reacted to the crisis without protest. Influenced by tra-

The Great Depression made more desperate the plight of Hispanic Americans. This family of pecan shellers in San Antonio, Texas, labored by day for 5 cents an hour and rented this hovel for 50 cents per week.

ditional individualism, many blamed themselves for their plight. But others did act, especially to protect their families. Protests ranged from small desperate gestures like stealing food and coal to more dramatic deeds. In Louisiana, women seized a train to call attention to the needs of their families; in New Jersey, in the "bloodless battle of Pleasantville," one hundred women held the city council hostage to demand assistance.

Communists, socialists, and other radicals organized more formal protests. Communists led the jobless into "unemployment councils" that staged hunger marches, demonstrated for relief, and blocked evictions. Mothers facing eviction in Chicago told their children: "Run quick and find the Reds." Socialists built similar organizations, including Baltimore's People's Unemployment League, which had twelve thousand members. Such groups provided protection and assistance. However, local authorities often suppressed their protests. In 1932, police fired on the Detroit Unemployment Council as it marched to demand food and jobs, killing four marchers and wounding many more.

Rural protests also broke out. Again, communists organized some of them, as in Alabama, where the Croppers' and Farm Workers' Union mobilized black agricultural laborers in 1931 to demand better treatment. In the Midwest, the Farmers' Holiday Association, formed among family farmers in 1932, stopped the shipment of produce to urban markets, hoping to drive up prices. A guerrilla war broke out as farmers blocked roads and halted freight trains, dumped milk in ditches, and fought bloody battles with deputy sheriffs. Midwestern farmers also tried to prevent foreclosure of their farms. In Iowa, farmers beat sheriffs and mortgage agents and nearly lynched a judge conducting foreclosure proceedings; in Nebraska, a Farmers' Holiday leader warned that if the state did not halt foreclosures, "200,000 of us are coming to Lincoln and we'll tear that new State Capitol Building to pieces."

HERBERT HOOVER AND THE DEPRESSION

The Great Depression challenged the optimism, policies, and philosophy that Herbert Hoover carried into the White House in 1929. The president took unprecedented steps to resolve the crisis but shrank back from the interventionist policies activists urged. His failures, personal as well as political and economic, led to his repudiation and to a major shift in government policies.

THE FAILURE OF VOLUNTARISM

Hoover fought economic depression more vigorously than had any previous president, but he believed that voluntary private relief was preferable to federal intervention. The role of the national government, he thought, was to advise and encourage the voluntary efforts of private organizations, individual industries, or local communities. As secretary of commerce, Hoover had championed trade associations as organizations to achieve economic order and social progress. As president, he persuaded Congress in 1929 to create the Federal Farm Board to promote voluntary agricultural cooperatives to raise farm income without government regulations. After the crash, he tried to apply this voluntarism to the depression.

Hoover first secured business leaders' pledges to maintain employment and wage levels. But most corporations soon repudiated these pledges, slashed wages, and laid off workers. An official of the Bureau of Labor Statistics complained that business leaders "are hell-bent to get wages back to the 1913 level." Hoover himself said, "You know, the only trouble with capitalism is capitalists; they're too damn greedy." Still, he rejected government action.

Hoover also depended on voluntary efforts to relieve the misery caused by massive unemployment. He created the President's Organization for Unemployment Relief to help raise private funds for voluntary relief agencies. Charities and local authorities, he believed, should help the unemployed; direct federal relief would expand government power and undermine the recipients' character. He vetoed congressional attempts to aid the unemployed. "The American way of relieving distress," said Hoover, was through "the voluntary agencies of self help in the community."

The depression rendered Hoover's beliefs meaningless. Private programs to aid the unemployed scarcely existed. Only a few unions, such as the Amalgamated Clothing Workers, had unemployment funds, and these were soon spent. Company plans for unemployment compensation covered less than 1 percent of workers, revealing the charade of the welfare capitalism of the 1920s. Some business leaders rejected any responsibility. "Even God Almighty never promised anybody that he should not suffer from hunger," snorted the president of the Southern States Industrial Council. Private charitable groups like the Salvation Army, church associations, and ethnic societies quickly exhausted their resources. By 1931, the director of Philadelphia's Federation of Jewish Charities conceded, "Private philanthropy is no longer capable of coping with the situation." Tens of thousands of Philadelphians, he noted, had been reduced to "the status of a stray cat prowling for food. . . . What this does to the innate dignity of the human soul is not hard to guess."

Nor could local governments cope, and their efforts declined as the depression deepened. New York City provided relief payments of $2.39 a week for an entire family, and other cities much less. By 1932, more than one hundred cities made no relief appropriations at all, and the commissioner of charity in Salt Lake City reported that people were sliding toward starvation. Only eight state governments provided even token assistance. Constitutional restrictions on taxes and indebtedness stopped some from responding to the relief crisis. Others lacked the will. Texas refused to issue bonds to fund relief. (See "American Views: An Ohio Mayor on Unemployment and Relief.")

Hoover blundered not in first relying on charities and local governments for relief but in refusing to admit that they were inadequate. Even his advisers warned that voluntarism and "individual initiative" had become obsolete. Both his vision and his efforts fell short.

As the depression worsened, Hoover adopted more activist policies. He persuaded Congress to cut taxes to boost consumers' buying power, and he increased the public works budget. The Federal Farm Board lent money to cooperatives and spent millions trying to stabilize crop prices. Unable to control production, however, the Board conceded failure by late 1931. More successful was the Reconstruction Finance Corporation (RFC). Established in January 1932, the RFC lent federal funds to banks, insurance companies, and railroads so that their recovery could "trickle down" to ordinary Americans. Hoover still opposed direct aid to the general public, although he finally allowed the RFC to lend small amounts to state and local governments for unemployment relief.

But these programs satisfied few Americans. "While children starve," cried Pennsylvania's gover-

Hands in their pockets, hungry men stand numbly in one of New York City's 82 breadlines.
Said one observer: "The wretched men, many without overcoats or decent shoes, usually began
to line up soon after six o'clock—in good weather or bad, rain or snow."

nor, Hoover "intends to let us have just as little relief as possible after the longest delay possible." Far more action was necessary, but Hoover remained committed to voluntarism and a balanced budget. The *New Republic* remarked in wonder: "Strangely enough, though he praises our government as representative and democratic, Mr. Hoover seems to regard most of the positive activities it might undertake as the intrusion of an alien sovereignty rather than the cooperative action of a people." Hoover's ideological limitations infuriated Americans who saw him as indifferent to their suffering and a reactionary protector of privileged business interests—an image his political opponents encouraged.

Bonus Marchers battling police in Washington, D.C., in 1932. Police and military assaults on these homeless veterans infuriated Americans and prompted Democratic Presidential nominee Franklin D. Roosevelt to declare, "Well, this will elect me."

REPUDIATING HOOVER: THE 1932 ELECTION

Hoover's treatment of the **Bonus Army** symbolized his unpopularity and set the stage for the 1932 election. In 1932, unemployed veterans of World War I gathered in Washington, demanding payment of service bonuses not due until 1945. Hoover refused to meet with them, and Congress rejected their plan. But ten thousand veterans erected a shantytown at the edge of Washington and camped in vacant public buildings. Hoover determined to evict the veterans, but General Douglas MacArthur disobeyed his cautious orders and on July 28 led cavalry, infantry, and tanks against the ragged Bonus Marchers. The troops cleared the buildings and assaulted the shantytown, dispersing the veterans and their families and setting their camp on fire.

This assault provoked widespread outrage. "What a pitiful spectacle is that of the great American Government, mightiest in the world, chasing unarmed men, women, and children with army tanks," commented the *Washington News*. The administration tried to brand the Bonus Marchers as communists and criminals, but official investigations refuted such claims. The marchers were anxious and discouraged Americans, not revolutionaries, and if any criminals were among them, noted one critic, they were proportionately fewer than in President Harding's cabinet. The incident confirmed Hoover's public image as harsh and insensitive.

In the summer of 1932, with no prospects for victory, Republicans renominated Hoover. Confident Democrats selected Governor Franklin D. Roosevelt of New York, who pledged "a new deal for the American people." A distant cousin of Theodore Roosevelt, FDR had prepared for the presidency. Born into a wealthy family in 1882, he had been educated at Harvard, trained in the law, and schooled in politics, as a state legislator, assistant secretary of the navy under Wilson, and the Democratic vice presidential nominee in 1920. In 1921, Roosevelt contracted polio, which paralyzed him from the waist down, leaving him dependent on braces or crutches. His struggle with this ordeal gave him greater maturity, compassion, and determination. His continued involvement in politics, meanwhile, owed much to his wife, Eleanor. A social reformer, she became a Democratic activist, organizing women's groups and campaigning across New York. In a remarkable political comeback, FDR was elected governor in 1928 and reelected in 1930.

The 1932 campaign gave scant indication of what Roosevelt's New Deal might involve. The Democratic platform differed little from that of the Republicans, and Roosevelt spoke in vague or general terms. He knew that the election would be a repudiation of Hoover more than an endorsement of himself. Still, observers gained clues from Roosevelt's record in New York, where he had created the first state system of unemployment relief and supported social welfare and conservation. More important was his outgoing personality, which radiated warmth and hope in contrast to Hoover's gloom. "If you put a rose in Hoover's hand," said one observer, "it would wilt."

FDR carried every state south and west of Pennsylvania (see Map 25-1). It was the worst rout of a Republican candidate ever (except in 1912, when the party had split). Yet Hoover would remain president for four more months, as the Constitution then required. And in those four months, the depression worsened, with rising unemployment, collapsing farm prices, and spreading misery. When teachers in Chicago, unpaid for months, fainted in their classrooms from hunger, it symbolized the imminent collapse of the nation itself. The final blow came in February 1933, when panic struck the banking system. Nearly six thousand banks had already failed, robbing 9 million depositors of their savings. Desperate Americans rushed to withdraw their funds from the remaining banks, pushing them to the brink as well. With the federal government under Hoover immobilized, state governments shut the banks to prevent their failure. By March, an eerie silence had descended on the nation. Hoover concluded, "We are at the end of our string."

LAUNCHING THE NEW DEAL

In the midst of national anxiety, Franklin D. Roosevelt pushed forward an unprecedented program to resolve the crises of a collapsing financial system, crippling unemployment, and agricultural and industrial breakdown and to promote reform. The early New Deal achieved successes and attracted support, but it also had limitations and generated criticism that suggested the need for still greater innovations.

"ACTION NOW!"

On March 4, 1933, Franklin Delano Roosevelt became president and immediately reassured the American people. He insisted that "the only thing we have to fear is fear itself—nameless, unreasoning, unjustified terror, which paralyzes needed efforts to convert retreat into advance." And he promised "action, and action now!" Summoning Congress, Roosevelt pressed forward on a broad front. In the first three months of his administration, the famous Hundred Days of the New Deal, the Democratic Congress passed many important laws (see the Overview table, "Major Laws of the Hundred Days").

Roosevelt's program reflected a mix of ideas, some from FDR himself, some from a diverse group of advisers, including academic experts dubbed the "brain trust," politicians, and social workers. It also incorporated principles from the progressive movement, precedents from the Great War mobilization,

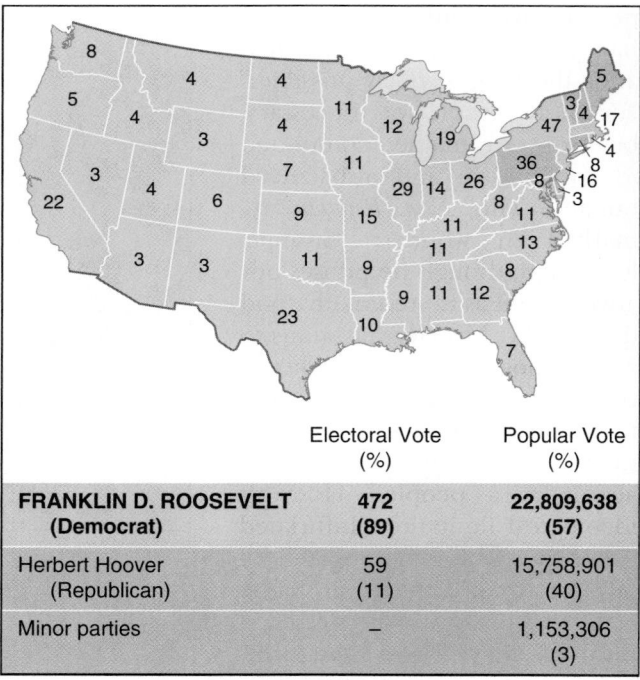

	Electoral Vote (%)	Popular Vote (%)
FRANKLIN D. ROOSEVELT (Democrat)	**472** **(89)**	**22,809,638** **(57)**
Herbert Hoover (Republican)	59 (11)	15,758,901 (40)
Minor parties	–	1,153,306 (3)

MAP 25-1   **The Election of 1932**
In the midst of the Great Depression, only the most rock-ribbed Republican states failed to turn to Franklin D. Roosevelt and the Democrats for relief. The election of 1932 was a landslide.

and even plans from the Hoover administration. Above all, the New Deal was a practical response to the depression. FDR had set its tone in his campaign when he declared, "The country needs, and, unless I mistake its temper, the country demands bold, persistent experimentation. . . . Above all, try something."

FDR first addressed the banking crisis. On March 5, he proclaimed a national bank holiday, closing all remaining banks. Congress then passed his Emergency Banking Act, a conservative measure that extended government assistance to sound banks and reorganized the weak ones. Prompt government action, coupled with a reassuring **fireside chat** over the radio by the president, restored popular confidence in the banks. When they reopened on March 13, deposits exceeded withdrawals. "Capitalism," said Raymond Moley of the brain trust, "was saved in eight days." In June, Congress created the **Federal Deposit Insurance Corporation (FDIC)** to guarantee bank deposits up to $2,500.

The financial industry was also reformed. The Glass-Steagall Act separated investment and commercial banking to curtail risky speculation. The Securities Act reformed the sale of stocks to prevent the insider abuses that had characterized Wall Street, and in 1934 the **Securities and Exchange Commission (SEC)** was created to regulate the stock market. Two

Overview

Major Laws of the Hundred Days

Law	Objective
Emergency Banking Act	Stabilized the private banking system
Agricultural Adjustment Act	Established a farm recovery program based on production controls and price supports
Emergency Farm Mortgage Act	Provided for the refinancing of farm mortgages
National Industrial Recovery Act	Established a national recovery program and authorized a public works program
Federal Emergency Relief Act	Established a national system of relief
Home Owners Loan Act	Protected homeowners from mortgage foreclosure by refinancing home loans
Glass-Steagall Act	Separated commercial and investment banking and guaranteed bank deposits
Tennessee Valley Authority Act	Established the TVA and provided for the planned development of the Tennessee River Valley
Civilian Conservation Corps Act	Established the CCC to provide work relief on reforestation and conservation projects
Farm Credit Act	Expanded agricultural credits and established the Farm Credit Administration
Securities Act	Required full disclosure from stock exchanges
Wagner-Peyser Act	Created a U.S. Employment Service and encouraged states to create local public employment offices

other financial measures in 1933 created the Home Owners Loan Corporation and the Farm Credit Administration, which enabled millions to refinance their mortgages.

CREATING JOBS

Roosevelt also provided relief for the unemployed. The Federal Emergency Relief Administration (FERA) furnished funds to state and local agencies. Harry Hopkins, who had headed Roosevelt's relief program in New York, became its director and one of the New Deal's most important members. FERA spent over $3 billion before it ended in 1935, and by then Hopkins and FDR had developed new programs that provided work rather than just cash. Work relief, they believed, preserved both the skills and the morale of recipients. In the winter of 1933–1934, Hopkins spent nearly $1 billion to create jobs for 4 million men and women through the Civil Works Ad-

ministration (CWA). The CWA hired laborers to build roads and airports, teachers to staff rural schools, and singers and artists to give public performances. The Public Works Administration (PWA) provided work relief on useful projects to stimulate the economy through public expenditures. Directed by Harold Ickes, the PWA spent billions from 1933 to 1939 to build schools, hospitals, courthouses, dams, and bridges.

One of FDR's personal ideas, the Civilian Conservation Corps (CCC), combined work relief with conservation. Launched in 1933, the CCC employed 2.5 million young men to work on reforestation and flood control projects, build roads and bridges in national forests and parks, restore Civil War battlefields, and fight forest fires. The men lived in isolated CCC camps and earned $30 a month, $25 of which had to be sent home. "I'd go anywhere," said one Baltimore applicant. "I'd go to hell if I could get work there."

A coal miner greeting Franklin D. Roosevelt in West Virginia in 1932. Roosevelt's promise of a New Deal revived hope among millions of Americans trapped in hard times.

One of the most popular New Deal agencies, the CCC lasted until 1942.

HELPING SOME FARMERS

Besides providing relief, the New Deal promoted economic recovery. In May 1933, Congress established the Agricultural Adjustment Administration (AAA) to combat the depression in agriculture caused by crop surpluses and low prices. The AAA subsidized farmers who agreed to restrict production. The objective was to boost farm prices to parity, a level that would restore farmers' purchasing power to what it had been in 1914. In the summer of 1933, the AAA paid southern farmers to plow up 10 million acres of cotton and midwestern farmers to bury 9 million pounds of pork. Restricting production in hard times caused public outrage. "Farmers are not producing too much," said one critic. "What we have overproduction of is empty stomachs and bare backs." Secretary of Agriculture Henry Wallace defended production controls as analogous to corporations maximizing profits: "Agriculture cannot survive in a capitalistic society as a philanthropic enterprise."

Agricultural conditions improved. Farm prices rose from 52 percent of parity in 1932 to 88 percent in 1935, and gross farm income rose by 50 percent. Not until 1941, however, would income exceed the level of 1929, a poor year for farmers. Moreover, some of the decreased production and increased prices stemmed from devastating droughts and dust storms on the Great Plains. The AAA itself harmed poor farmers while aiding larger commercial growers. As southern planters restricted their acreage, they dismissed tenants and sharecroppers, and with AAA payments, they bought new farm machinery, reducing their need for farm labor. A reporter in 1935 found thousands of sharecroppers "along the highways and byways of Dixie, . . . lonely figures without money, without homes, and without hope." Thus, while big producers moved toward prosperity, many small farmers were forced into a pool of rural labor for which there was decreasing need or into the cities, where there were no jobs.

The Supreme Court declared the AAA unconstitutional in 1936, but new laws established the farm subsidy program for decades to come. Increasing mechanization and scientific agriculture kept production high and farmers dependent on government intervention.

THE FLIGHT OF THE BLUE EAGLE

The New Deal attempted to revive American industry with the National Industrial Recovery Act (NIRA), which created the National Recovery Administration (NRA). The NRA sought to halt the slide in prices, wages, and employment by suspending antitrust laws and authorizing industrial and trade associations to draft codes setting production

New Deal agricultural programs stabilized the farm economy, but not all farmers benefited. Landowners who received AAA payments evicted these black sharecroppers huddled in a makeshift roadside camp in Missouri in 1935.

quotas, price policies, wages and working conditions, and other business practices. The codes promoted the interests of business generally and big business in particular, but Section 7a of the NIRA guaranteed workers the rights to organize unions and bargain collectively—a provision that John L. Lewis of the United Mine Workers called an Emancipation Proclamation for labor.

Hugh Johnson became director of the NRA. He persuaded business leaders to cooperate in drafting codes and the public to patronize participating companies. The NRA Blue Eagle insignia and its slogan "We Do Our Part" covered workplaces, storefronts, and billboards. Blue Eagle parades marched down the nation's main streets and climaxed in a massive demonstration in New York City.

Support for the NRA waned, however. Corporate leaders used it to advance their own goals and to discriminate against small producers, consumers, and labor. Minnesota's Governor Floyd Olson condemned the dominance within the NRA of the same selfish business interests he saw as responsible for the depression: "I am not satisfied with hanging a laurel wreath on burglars, thieves, and pirates and calling them code authorities."

Businesses also violated the labor rights specified in Section 7a. Defiant employers viewed collective bargaining as infringing their authority. Employers even used violence to smother unions. The NRA did little to enforce Section 7a, and Johnson—strongly probusiness—denounced all strikes. Workers felt betrayed.

Roosevelt tried to reorganize the NRA, but the act remained controversial until the Supreme Court declared it unconstitutional in 1935.

CRITICS RIGHT AND LEFT

The early New Deal had not ended the depression. Recovery was fitful and uneven; millions of Americans remained unemployed. Nevertheless, the New Deal's efforts to grapple with problems, its successes in reducing suffering and fear, and Roosevelt's own skills carried the Democratic party to victory in the 1934 elections. But New Deal policies also provoked criticism, from both those convinced that too little had been achieved and those alarmed that too much had been attempted.

Despite the early New Deal's probusiness character, conservatives complained that the expansion of government activity and its regulatory role weakened the autonomy of American business. They also condemned the efforts to aid nonbusiness groups as socialistic, particularly the "excessive" spending on unemployment relief and the "instigation" of labor organizing. By 1934, as *Time* magazine reported, "Private fulminations and public carpings against the New Deal have become almost a routine of the business day." Industrialists and bankers organized the American Liberty League to direct attacks on the New Deal.

AMERICAN VIEWS

An Ohio Mayor on Unemployment and Relief

Joesph Heffernan was the mayor of Youngstown, Ohio, when the nation sank into the Great Depression. Like other industrial cities, Youngstown soon confronted widespread unemployment and distress. In this document, written in 1932, Heffernan describes the obstacles he faced in responding to the suffering in Youngstown.

- What would Heffernan think of President Hoover's belief that private charities and local authorities would provide unemployment relief?
- What did Heffernan see as obstacles to a public response to the depression?
- What did he fear would be the consequences of the failure to devise a rational and humane system of relief?

[In 1930] I asked for a bond issue of $1,000,000 for unemployment relief. Many leading business men went out of their way to show their disapproval. One of them . . . said to me: "You make a bad mistake in talking about the unemployed. Don't emphasize hard times and everything will be all right." An influential newspaper chastised me for "borrowing trouble"; the depression would be over, the editor maintained, before relief would be needed. . . . The gravity of the situation was so deliberately misrepresented by the entire business community that when the bond issue finally came to a ballot, in November 1930, it was voted down.

Thus we passed into the early days of 1931—fourteen months after the first collapse—with no relief in sight except that which was provided by the orthodox charities. Not a single move had been made looking toward action by a united community.

Strange as it may seem, there was no way in which the city government could embark upon a program of its own. We had no funds available for emergency relief, and without specific authorization from the people we could not issue bonds. . . .

As time went on, business conditions showed no improvement. Every night hundreds of homeless men crowded into the municipal incinerator, where they found warmth even

---

The league distributed over 5 million copies of two hundred different pamphlets; it also furnished editorials and news stories to newspapers. These critics attracted little popular support, however, and their selfishness antagonized Roosevelt.

More realistic criticism came from the left. In 1932, FDR had campaigned for "the forgotten man at the bottom of the economic pyramid," and some radicals argued that the early New Deal had forgotten the forgotten man. Communists and socialists focused public attention on the poor, especially in the countryside. In California, Communists organized Mexican, Filipino,

and Japanese farm workers into their Cannery and Agricultural Workers Union; in Arkansas and Tennessee, socialists in 1934 helped organize sharecroppers into the Southern Tenant Farmers Union, protesting the "Raw Deal" they had received from the AAA. Both unions encountered violent reprisals. Growers killed three picketers in California's San Joaquin Valley; in Arkansas, landlords shot union organizers and led vigilante raids on sharecroppers' shacks. This terrorism, however, created sympathy for farmworkers.

Even without the involvement of socialists or communists, however, labor militancy in 1934 pressed Roothough they had to sleep on heaps of garbage. In January 1931, I obtained the cooperation of the City Council to convert an abandoned police station into a "flop house." The first night it was filled, and it has remained filled ever since. I made a point of paying frequent visits to this establishment so that I could see for myself what kind of men these down-and-outers were, and I heartily wish that those folk who have made themselves comfortable by ignoring and denying the suffering of their less fortunate neighbors could see some of the sights I saw. There were old men gnarled by heavy labor, young mechanics tasting the first bitterness of defeat, clerks and white-collar workers learning the equality of misery, derelicts who fared no worse in bad times than in good, Negroes who only a short time before had come from Southern cotton fields, now glad to find any shelter from the cold, immigrants who had been lured to Van Dyke's "land of youth and freedom"—each one a personal tragedy, and all together an overwhelming catastrophe for the nation. . . .

This descent from respectability, frequent enough in the best of times, has been hastened immeasurably by two years of business paralysis, and the people who have been affected in this manner must be numbered in millions. This is what we have accomplished with our bread lines and soup kitchens. I know, because I have seen thousands of these defeated, discouraged, hopeless men and women, cringing and fawn-

ing as they come to ask for public aid. It is a spectacle of national degeneration. That is the fundamental tragedy for America. If every mill and factory in the land should begin to hum with prosperity to-morrow morning, the destructive effect of our haphazard relief measures would not work itself out of the nation's blood until the sons of our sons had expiated the sins of our neglect.

Even now there are signs of rebellion against a system so out of joint that it can only offer charity to honest men who want to work. Sometimes it takes the form of social agitation, but again it may show itself in a revolt that is absolute and final. Such an instance was reported in a Youngstown newspaper on the day I wrote these lines:—

Father Of Ten Drowns Self

. . . Out of work two years, Charles Wayne, aged 57, father of ten children, stood on the Spring Common bridge this morning. . . . He took off his coat, folded it carefully, and jumped into the swirling Mahoning River. Wayne was born in Youngstown and was employed by the Republic Iron and Steel Company for twenty-seven years as a hot mill worker. "We were about to lose our home," sobbed Mrs. Wayne. "And the gas and electric companies had threatened to shut off the service."

Source: Joseph L. Heffernan, "The Hungry City: A Mayor's Experience with Unemployment," *Atlantic Monthly*, May 1932, pp. 538–540, 546.

sevelt. Workers acted as much against the failure of the NRA to enforce Section 7a as against recalcitrant corporations. The number of workers participating in strikes leaped from 325,000 in 1932 (about the annual average since 1925) to 1.5 million in 1934. From dockworkers in Seattle and copper miners in Butte to streetcar drivers in Milwaukee and shoemakers in Boston, workers demanded their rights. Textile workers launched the largest single strike in the nation's history, shutting down the industry in twenty states.

Rebuffing FDR's pleas for fair treatment, employers moved to crush the strikes, often using com-

plaisant police and private strikebreakers. In Minneapolis, police shot sixty-seven teamsters, almost all in the back, as they fled an ambush arranged by employers; in Toledo, company police and National Guardsmen attacked autoworkers with tear gas, bayonets, and rifle fire; in the textile strike, police killed six picketers in South Carolina, and soldiers wounded another fifty in Rhode Island. At times, the workers held their ground, and they often attracted popular support, even in general strikes that paralyzed such major cities as San Francisco. But against such powerful opponents, workers needed help to achieve their rights.

Harry Hopkins and other New Dealers realized that labor's demands could not be ignored.

Popular discontent was also mobilized by four prominent individuals who demanded government action to assist groups neglected by the New Deal. Representative William Lemke of North Dakota, an agrarian radical leader of the Nonpartisan League, called attention to rural distress. Lemke objected to the New Deal's limited response to farmers crushed by the depression. In his own state, nearly two-thirds of the farmers had lost their land through foreclosures. The AAA's strategy of simply restricting production, he thundered, was an "insane policy in the midst of hunger, misery, want, and rags."

Francis Townsend, a California physician, proposed to aid the nation's elderly, many of whom were destitute. The Townsend Plan called for a government pension to all Americans over the age of 60, provided they retire from work and spend their entire pension. This scheme promised to extend relief to the elderly, open jobs for the unemployed, and stimulate economic recovery. Townsend attracted people who, in his words, "believe in the Bible, believe in God, cheer when the flag passes by, the Bible Belt solid Americans." Over five thousand Townsend Clubs lobbied for government action to help the elderly poor.

Father Charles Coughlin, a Catholic priest in the Detroit suburb of Royal Oak, threatened to mobilize another large constituency against the limitations of the early New Deal. Thirty million Americans listened eagerly to his weekly radio broadcasts that mixed religion with anti-Semitism and demands for social justice and financial reform. Coughlin had condemned Hoover for assisting banks but ignoring the unemployed, and initially he welcomed the New Deal as "Christ's Deal." But after concluding that FDR's policies favored "the virile viciousness of business and finance," Coughlin organized the National Union for Social Justice to lobby for his goals. With support among lower-middle-class, heavily Catholic, urban ethnic groups, Coughlin posed a real challenge to Roosevelt's Democratic party.

Roosevelt found Senator Huey P. Long of Louisiana still more worrisome. Alternately charming and autocratic, Long had modernized his state with taxation and educational reforms and an extensive public-works program after his election as governor in 1928. Moving to the Senate and eyeing the White House, Long proposed more comprehensive social-welfare policies than the New Deal had envisaged. In 1934, he organized the Share-Our-Wealth Society. His plan to end poverty and unemployment called for confiscatory taxes on the rich to provide every family with a decent income, health coverage, education, and old-age pensions. Long's appeal was enormous. Within months, his organization claimed more than 27,000 clubs and 7 million members.

These dissident movements raised complex issues and simple fears. They built on concerns about the New Deal, both demanding government assistance and fretting about government intrusion; their programs were often ill-defined or impractical—Townsend's plan would cost more than half the national income; and some of the leaders, like Coughlin and Long, approached demagoguery. Nevertheless, their popularity warned Roosevelt that government action was needed to satisfy reform demands and assure his reelection in 1936.

CONSOLIDATING THE NEW DEAL

Responding to the persistence of the depression and political pressures, Roosevelt in 1935 undertook economic and social reforms that some observers have called the Second New Deal. The new measures shifted the relative weights accorded to the constant objectives of recovery, relief, and reform. Nor did FDR's interest in reform simply reflect cynical politics. He had frequently championed progressive measures in the past, and many of his advisers had deep roots in reform movements. After the 1934 elections gave the president an even more Democratic Congress, Harry Hopkins exulted: "Boys—this is our hour. We've got to get everything we want—a works program, social security, wages and hours, everything—now or never."

WEEDING OUT AND LIFTING UP

"In spite of our efforts and in spite of our talk," Roosevelt told the new Congress in 1935, "we have not weeded out the overprivileged and we have not effectively lifted up the underprivileged." To do so, he developed "must" legislation, to which his allies in Congress added. One of the new laws protected labor's rights to organize and bargain collectively. Drafted by Senator Robert Wagner of New York to replace Section 7a, it received Roosevelt's endorsement only after it was clear that both Congress and the public favored it. The Wagner National Labor Relations Act, dubbed "Labor's Magna Carta," guaranteed workers' rights to organize unions and forbade employers to adopt unfair labor practices, such as firing union activists and forming company unions. The law also set up the National Labor Relations Board (NLRB) to enforce these provisions, protect workers from coercion, and supervise union elections.

A symbol of progress and prosperity in the 1920s, automobility became something very different in the Great Depression. People fleeing the Dust Bowl, such as this family in Oklahoma, packed up their few tattered possessions and headed for California in hopes of getting a "little bit of this good dirt" for their own.

Social security.

Of greater long-range importance was the Social Security Act. Other industrial nations had established national social-insurance systems much earlier, but only the Great Depression moved the United States to accept the idea that the federal government should protect the poor and unemployed. Even so, the law was a compromise, framed by a nonpartisan committee of business, labor, and public representatives and then weakened by congressional conservatives. It provided unemployment compensation, old-age pensions, and aid for dependent mothers and children and the blind.

The conservative nature of the law appeared in its stingy benefit payments, its lack of health insurance, and its exclusion of more than one-fourth of all workers, including many in desperate need of protection, such as farm laborers and domestic servants. Moreover, unlike in other nations, the old-age pensions were financed through a regressive payroll tax on both employees and employers rather than through general tax revenues. Thus the new system was more like a compulsory insurance program. Roosevelt conceded as much but defended the taxes on workers as a tactic to protect the reform itself: "We put those payroll contributions there so as to give the contributors a legal, moral, and political right to collect their pensions and their unemployment benefits. With those taxes in there, no damn politician can ever scrap my social security program."

Roosevelt was justifiably proud. Despite its weaknesses, the Social Security Act was one of the most im-

portant laws in American history. It provided, he pointed out, "at least some measure of protection to the average citizen and to his family against the loss of a job and against poverty-ridden old age." Moreover, by establishing federal responsibility for social welfare, it inaugurated a welfare system that subsequent generations would expand.

Money, tax, and land reform.

Another reform measure, the Banking Act of 1935, increased the authority of the Federal Reserve Board over the nation's currency and credit system and decreased the power of the private bankers whose irresponsible behavior had contributed to the depression and the appeal of Father Coughlin. The Revenue Act of 1935, passed after Roosevelt assailed the "unjust concentration of wealth and economic power," provided for graduated income taxes and increased estate and corporate taxes. Opponents called it the Soak the Rich Tax, but with its many loopholes, it was scarcely that and was certainly not a redistributive measure such as Huey Long had proposed.

The New Deal enabled photographers and artists to take to the road to capture images of the nation's dispossessed. This famous photograph by Dorothea Lange of a mother and her children in a migrant labor camp in 1936 came to symbolize for all Americans the haunting stare of hunger and hardship.

Nevertheless, it set a precedent for progressive taxation and attracted popular support.

The Second New Deal also responded belatedly to the environmental catastrophe that had turned much of the Great Plains from Texas to the Dakotas into a "Dust Bowl" (see Map 25-2). Since World War I, farmers had stripped marginal land of its native grasses to plant wheat. When drought and high winds hit the plains in 1932, crops failed, and nothing held the soil. Dust storms blew away millions of tons of topsoil, despoiling the land and darkening the sky a thousand miles away. Families abandoned their farms in droves. Many of these poor "Okies" headed for California, their plight captured in John Steinbeck's novel, *The Grapes of Wrath* (1939).

In 1935, Roosevelt established the Resettlement Administration to focus on land reform and help poor farmers. Under Rexford Tugwell, this agency initiated soil erosion projects and attempted to resettle impoverished farmers on better land, but the problem exceeded its resources. Congress moved to save the land, if not its people, by creating the Soil Conservation Service in 1935.

EXPANDING RELIEF

If reform gained priority in the Second New Deal, relief remained critical. With millions still unemployed, Roosevelt pushed through Congress in 1935 the Emergency Relief Appropriation Act, authorizing $5 billion—at the time the largest single appropriation in history—for emergency public employment. Roosevelt created the Works Progress Administration (WPA) under Hopkins, who set up work relief programs to assist the unemployed and boost the economy. Before its end in 1943, the WPA gave jobs to 9 million people (more than a fifth of the labor force) and spent nearly $12 billion. Three-fourths of its expenditures went on construction projects that could employ manual labor: the WPA built 125,000 schools, post offices, and hospitals; 8,000 parks; nearly 100,000 bridges; and enough roads and sewer systems to circle the earth thirty times. From New York City's La Guardia Airport to Atlanta's sewer system to irrigation ditches in the Far West, the WPA laid much of the basic infrastructure on which the nation still relies.

The WPA also developed work projects for unemployed writers, artists, musicians, and actors. "Why not?" said FDR. "They are human beings. They have to live." The Federal Writers' Project put authors to work preparing state guidebooks, writing historical pamphlets, and recording the memories of ex-slaves. The Federal Art Project hired artists to teach art in night schools, prepare exhibits at museums, and paint murals on post office walls. The Federal Theatre Project

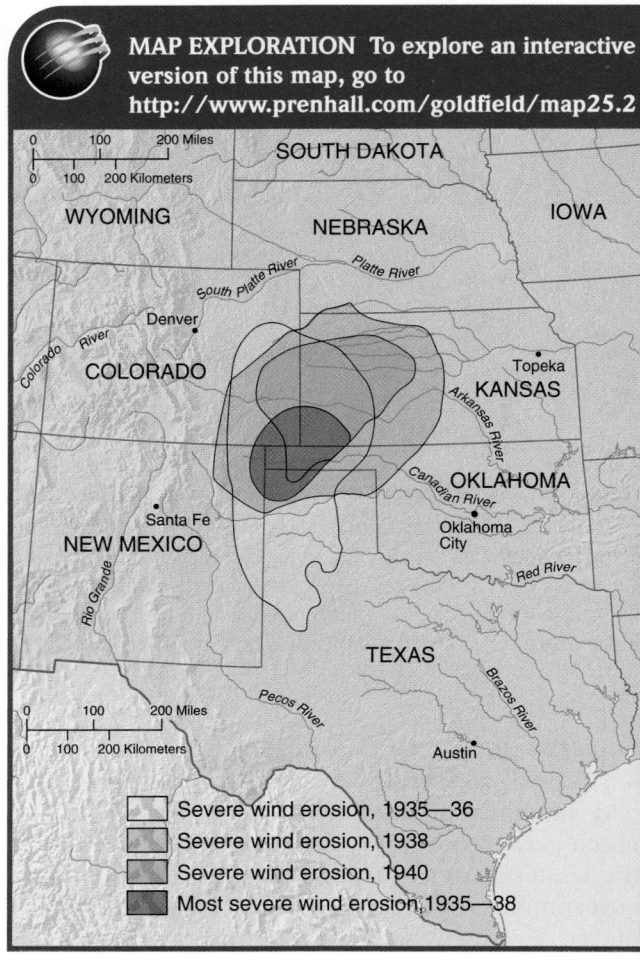

MAP 25-2   **The Dust Bowl**
Years of overcultivation, drought, and high winds created the Dust Bowl, which most severely affected the southern Great Plains. Federal relief and conservation programs provided assistance, but many residents fled the area, often migrating to California.

organized theatrical productions and drama companies that in four years played to 30 million Americans. The Federal Music Project hired musicians to collect and perform folk songs. These WPA programs allowed people to use their talents while surviving the depression, increased popular access to cultural performances, and established a precedent for federal support of the arts. "What has happened and in such a short time is almost incredible," said one reviewer. "From a government completely apathetic to art, we suddenly have a government very art conscious."

The National Youth Administration (NYA), another WPA agency, gave part-time jobs to students, enabling 2 million high school and college students to stay in school, learn skills, and do productive work. At the University of Nebraska, NYA students built an observatory; at Duke University, law student Richard M. Nixon earned 35 cents an hour doing research in the library. Lyndon Johnson, a Texas NYA official, believed that "if the Roosevelt administration had never done another thing, it would have been justified by the work of this great institution for salvaging youth."

THE ROOSEVELT COALITION AND THE ELECTION OF 1936

The 1936 election gave Americans an opportunity to judge FDR and the New Deal. Conservatives alarmed at the expansion of government, business people angered by regulation and labor legislation, and wealthy Americans furious with tax reform decried the New Deal. But they were a minority. Even the presidential candidate they supported, Republican Governor Alf Landon of Kansas, endorsed much of the New Deal, criticizing merely the inefficiency and cost of some of its programs. (Roosevelt remarked whimsically that he thought he could defeat himself with such a campaign.) The New Deal's earlier critics on the left had also lost most of their following. The reforms of 1935 had undercut their arguments, and the assassination of Huey Long in the same year had removed their ablest politician. They formed the Union party and nominated William Lemke for the presidency, but they were no longer a threat.

The programs and politicians of the New Deal had created an invincible coalition behind Roosevelt. Despite ambivalence about large-scale government intervention, the New Deal's agricultural programs reinforced the traditional Democratic allegiance of white Southerners while attracting many western farmers. Labor legislation clinched the active support of the nation's workers; Sidney Hillman of the Amalgamated Clothing Workers promised that his union would campaign for FDR "to see to it that we hold onto the gains labor has won." Middle-class voters, whose homes had been saved and whose hopes had been raised, also joined the Roosevelt coalition.

So did urban ethnic groups, who had benefited from welfare programs and appreciated the unprecedented recognition Roosevelt's administration gave them. FDR named the first Italian American to the federal judiciary, for example, and appointed five times as many Catholics and Jews to government positions as the three Republican presidents had during the 1920s. African Americans voted overwhelmingly Democratic for the first time. Women, too, were an important part of the Roosevelt coalition, and Eleanor often attracted their support as much as Franklin did. As one campaigner said to a roaring crowd in 1936, "Many women in this country when they vote for Franklin D. Roosevelt will also be thinking with a choke in the throat of Eleanor Roosevelt!"

This political realignment produced a landslide. Roosevelt polled 61 percent of the popular vote and the largest electoral vote margin ever recorded, 523 to 8. Landon even lost Kansas, his own state, and Lemke received fewer than 900,000 votes. Democrats also won huge majorities in Congress. Roosevelt's political coalition reflected a mandate for himself and the New Deal; it would enable the Democrats to dominate national elections for three decades.

Eleanor Roosevelt campaigns with FDR in Fremont, Nebraska in 1935. A visible activist for social and economic reform, she was also politically important in building the powerful Roosevelt coalition. "Previously," said the journalist Ruby Black, "a President's wife acted as if she didn't know that a political party existed."

THE NEW DEAL AND AMERICAN LIFE

The landslide of 1936 revealed the impact the New Deal had on Americans. Industrial workers mobilized to secure their rights, women and minorities gained increased, if still limited, opportunities to participate in American society, and Southerners and Westerners benefited from government programs they turned to their own advantage. Government programs changed daily life, and ordinary people often helped shape the new policies.

LABOR ON THE MARCH

The labor revival in the 1930s reflected both workers' determination and government support. Workers wanted not merely to improve their wages and benefits but also to gain union recognition and union contracts to limit arbitrary managerial authority and achieve some control over the workplace. This larger goal provoked opposition from employers and their allies and required workers to organize, strike, and become politically active. Their achievement was remarkable.

The Second New Deal helped. By guaranteeing labor's rights to organize and bargain collectively, the Wagner Act sparked a wave of labor activism. But if the government ultimately protected union rights, the unions themselves had to form locals, recruit members, and demonstrate influence in the workplace.

At first, those tasks overwhelmed the American Federation of Labor (AFL). Its reliance on craft-based unions and reluctance to organize immigrant, black, and women workers left it unprepared for the rush of industrial workers seeking unionization. More progressive labor leaders saw that industry-wide unions were more appropriate for unskilled workers in mass-production industries. Forming the Committee for Industrial Organization (CIO) within the AFL, they campaigned to unionize workers in the steel, auto, and rubber industries, all notoriously hostile to unions. AFL leaders insisted that the CIO disband and then in 1937 expelled its unions. The militants reorganized as the separate **Congress of Industrial Organizations**. (In 1955, the two groups merged as the AFL-CIO.)

The split roused the AFL to increase its own organizing activities, but it was primarily the new CIO that put labor on the march. It inspired workers previously neglected. The CIO's interracial union campaign in the Birmingham steel mills, said one organizer, was "like a second coming of Christ" for black workers, who welcomed the union as a chance for social recognition as well as economic opportunity. The CIO also employed new and aggressive tactics, particularly the sit-down strike, in which workers, rather than picketing outside the factory, simply sat inside the plant, thereby blocking both production and the use of strikebreakers. Conservatives were outraged, but Upton Sinclair said, "For seventy-five years big business has been sitting down on the American people, and now I am delighted to see the process reversed."

The CIO won major victories, despite bitter opposition from industry and its allies. The issue was not wages but labor's right to organize and bargain with management. Sit-down strikes paralyzed General Motors in 1937 after it refused to recognize the United Auto Workers. GM tried to force the strikers out of its Flint, Michigan, plants by turning off the heat, using police and tear gas, threatening strikers' families, and securing court orders to clear the plant by military force. But the governor refused to order National Guardsmen to attack, and the strikers held out, aided by the Women's Emergency Brigade, working-class women who picketed the building, heckled the police, and smuggled food to the strikers. After six weeks, GM signed a contract with the UAW. Chrysler soon followed suit. Ford refused to recognize the union until 1941, often violently disrupting organizing efforts.

Steel companies also used violence against unionization. In the Memorial Day Massacre in Chicago in 1937, police guarding a plant of the Republic Steel Company fired on strikers and their families, killing ten people as they tried to flee. Scores more were wounded and beaten in a police frenzy so violent that theaters refused to show a newsreel of the event. A Senate investigation found that Republic and other companies had hired private police to attack workers seeking to unionize, stockpiled weapons and tear gas, and corrupted authorities. The investigators concluded that "private corporations dominate their employees, deny them their constitutional rights, promote disorder and disharmony, and even set at naught the powers of the government itself." Federal court orders finally forced the companies to bargain collectively.

New Deal labor legislation, government investigations and court orders, and the federal refusal to use force against strikes helped the labor movement secure basic rights for American workers. Union membership leaped from under 3 million in 1932 to 9 million by 1939, and workers won higher wages, better working conditions, and more economic democracy.

WOMEN AND THE NEW DEAL

As federal programs proliferated in 1933, a Baltimore women's group urged the administration to "come out for a square and new deal for women." Although women did gain increased attention and influence, government and society remained largely bound by traditional values.

New Deal relief programs had a mixed impact on working women. Formal government policy required "equal consideration" for women and men, but local officials so flouted this requirement that Eleanor Roosevelt urged Harry Hopkins to "impress on state administrators that the women's programs are as important as the men's. They are so apt to forget us!" Women on relief were restricted to "women's work"— more than half worked on sewing projects, regardless of their skills—and were paid scarcely half what men received. WPA training programs also reinforced traditional ideas about women's work; black women, for example, were trained to be maids, dishwashers, and cooks. Although women constituted nearly one-fourth of the labor force, they obtained only 19 percent of the jobs created by the WPA, 12 percent of those created by the FERA, and 7 percent of those created by the CWA. The CCC excluded women altogether. Still, relief agencies provided crucial assistance to women in the depression.

Other New Deal programs also had mixed benefits for women. Despite demands by the League of Women Voters and the Women's Trade Union League for "equal pay for equal work and equal opportunity for equal ability regardless of sex," many NRA codes mandated lower wage scales for women than for men, which officials justified as reflecting "long-established customs." But by raising minimum wages, the NRA brought relatively greater improvements to women, who were concentrated in the lowest-paid occupations, than to male workers. The Social Security Act did not cover domestic servants, waitresses, and women who worked in the home, but it did help mothers with dependent children.

Still more significant, the Social Security Act reflected and reinforced prevailing notions about proper roles for men and women. The system was based on the idea that men should be wage earners and women should stay at home as wives and mothers. Accordingly, if women worked outside the home and their husbands were eligible for benefits, those working women would not receive their own retirement pensions. And if women were without husbands but had children, welfare authorities removed them from work-relief jobs, regardless of whether they wanted to continue to work, and gave them assistance from the Aid to Dependent Children (ADC) program, which was also created under the Social Security Act. These new programs, then, while providing much needed assistance, also institutionalized a modern welfare system that segregated men and women in separate spheres and reaffirmed the then popular belief that the success of the family depended on that separation.

Women also gained political influence under the New Deal, although Molly Dewson, the director of the Women's Division of the Democratic party, exaggerated when she exclaimed, "The change from women's status in government before Roosevelt is unbelievable." Dewson herself exercised considerable political power and helped to shape the party's campaigns. Around Dewson revolved a network of women, linked by friendships and experiences in the National Consumers' League, Women's Trade Union League, and other progressive reform organizations. Appointed to many positions in the Roosevelt administration, they helped develop and implement New Deal social legislation. Secretary of Labor Frances Perkins was the first woman cabinet member and a key member of the network; other women were in the Treasury Department, the Children's Bureau, and relief and cultural programs.

Eleanor Roosevelt was their leader. Described by a Washington reporter as "a cabinet member without portfolio," she roared across the social and political landscape of the 1930s, pushing for women's rights, demanding reforms, traveling across the country, writing newspaper columns and speaking over the radio, developing plans to help unemployed miners in West Virginia and abolish slums in Washington, and lobbying both Congress and her husband. FDR used her as his eyes and ears and sometimes his conscience. He rebuffed her critics with a jaunty, "Well, that is my wife; I can't do anything about her." Indeed, Eleanor Roosevelt had become not merely the most prominent first lady in history but a force in her own right and a symbol of the growing importance of women in public life.

MINORITIES AND THE NEW DEAL

Despite the move of African Americans into the Democratic party, the New Deal's record on racial issues was limited. Although Roosevelt deplored racial abuses, he never pushed for civil rights legislation, fearing to antagonize the influential Southern Democrats in Congress whose support he needed. For similar reasons, many New Deal programs discriminated against African Americans. The CCC segregated black workers; NRA codes so often specified lower wages and benefits for black workers relative to white workers or even excluded black workers from jobs that the black press claimed NRA stood for "Negro Run Around" or "Negroes Ruined Again." And racist officials discriminated in allocating federal relief. Atlanta, for instance, provided average monthly relief checks of $32.66 to white people but only $19.29 to black people.

However, disproportionately poor and unemployed, African Americans did benefit from the New Deal's welfare and economic programs. W.E.B. Du Bois asserted that "large numbers of colored people in the United States would have starved to death if it had not been for the Roosevelt policies," adding that the New Deal served to sharpen their sense of the value of citizenship by making clear the "direct connection between politics and industry, between government and work, [and] between voting and wages." And key New Dealers campaigned against racial discrimination. Eleanor Roosevelt prodded FDR to appoint black officials, wrote articles supporting racial equality, and flouted segregationist laws. Attacked by white racists, she was popular in the black community. Harry Hopkins and Harold Ickes also promoted equal rights. Ickes, a former president of Chicago's NAACP chapter, insisted that African Americans receive PWA relief jobs in proportion to their share of the population and ended segregation in the Department of the Interior, prompting other cabinet secretaries to follow suit. As black votes in northern cities became important, more pragmatic New Dealers also began to pay more attention to black needs.

African Americans themselves pressed for reforms. Civil rights groups protested discriminatory policies, including the unequal wage scales in the NRA codes and the CCC's limited enrollment of black youth. African Americans demonstrated against racial discrimination in hiring and their exclusion from federally financed construction projects.

In response, FDR took more interest in black economic and social problems. He prohibited discrimination in the WPA in 1935, and the NYA adopted enlightened racial policies. Roosevelt also appointed black people to important positions, including the first black federal judge. Many of these officials began meeting regularly at the home of Mary McLeod Bethune of the National Council of Negro Women. Dubbed the Black Cabinet, they worked with civil rights organizations, fought discrimination in government, influenced patronage, and stimulated black interest in politics.

The New Deal improved economic and social conditions for many African Americans. Black illiteracy dropped because of federal education projects, and the number of black college students and graduates more than doubled, in part because the NYA provided student aid to black colleges. New Deal relief and public health programs reduced black infant mortality rates and raised life expectancy rates. Conditions for black people continued to lag behind those

With an appointment in the National Youth Administration, the educator Mary McLeod Bethune served as the highest-ranking African American woman in the Roosevelt administration. She advised FDR on all racial matters and envisioned "dozens of Negro women coming after me, filling positions of trust and strategic importance."

for white people, and discrimination persisted, but the black switch to the Roosevelt coalition reflected the New Deal's benefits.

Native Americans also benefited from the New Deal. The depression had imposed further misery on a group already suffering from poverty, wretched health conditions, and the nation's lowest educational level. Many New Deal programs had limited applicability to Indians, but the CCC appealed to their interests and skills. More than eighty thousand Indians received training in agriculture, forestry, and animal husbandry, along with basic academic subjects. CCC projects, together with those undertaken by the PWA and the WPA, built schools, hospitals, roads, and irrigation systems on reservations.

New Deal officials also refocused government Indian policy, which had undermined tribal authority and promoted assimilation by reducing Indian landholding and attacking Indian culture. Protests had been ignored. Appointed commissioner of Indian affairs in 1933, John Collier prohibited interference with Indian religious or cultural life, directed the Bureau of Indian Affairs to employ more Indians, and prevented Indian schools from suppressing native languages and traditions.

Collier also persuaded Congress to pass the Indian Reorganization Act of 1934, often called the Indians' New Deal. The act guaranteed religious freedom, reestablished tribal self-government, and halted the sale of tribal lands. It also provided funds to expand Indian landholdings, support Indian students, and establish tribal businesses. But social and economic problems persisted on the isolated reservations, and white missionaries and business interests attacked Collier's reforms as atheistic and communistic.

Hispanic Americans received less assistance from the New Deal. Its relief programs aided many Hispanics in California and the Southwest but ignored those who were not citizens. Moreover, local administrators often discriminated against Hispanics, especially by providing higher relief payments to Anglos. Finally, by excluding agricultural workers, neither the Social Security Act nor the Wagner Act gave Mexican Americans much protection or hope. Farm workers remained largely unorganized, exploited, and at the mercy of agribusinesses.

THE NEW DEAL: NORTH, SOUTH, EAST, AND WEST

"We are going to make a country," President Roosevelt declared, "in which no one is left out." And with that statement along with his belief that the federal government must take the lead in building a new "economic constitutional order," FDR ensured that his New Deal programs and policies fanned out throughout the nation, bolstering the stock market and banking in New York, constructing public housing for poor immigrant families and African-Americans in most major cities, and building schools, roads, and bridges in all regions of the United States. Ironically, the New Deal also offered special benefits to the South, traditionally averse to government activism, and to the West, which considered itself the land of rugged individualism.

The New Deal's agricultural program boosted farm prices and income more in the South than any other region. By controlling cotton production, it also promoted diversification; its subsidies financed mechanization. The resulting modernization helped replace an archaic sharecropping system with an emergent agribusiness. The rural poor were displaced, but the South's agricultural economy advanced.

The New Deal also improved southern cities. FERA and WPA built urban sewer systems, airports,

bridges, roads, and harbor facilities. Whereas northern cities had already constructed such facilities themselves—and were still paying off their debts—the federal government largely paid for such modernization in the South, giving its cities an economic advantage.

Federal grants were supposed to be awarded to states in proportion to their own expenditures, but while southern politicians welcomed New Deal funds—"I'm gonna grab all I can for the state of Texas," said Governor Lee O'Daniel—they refused to contribute their share of the costs. Nationally, the federal proportion of FERA expenditures was 62 percent; in the South, it was usually 90 percent and never lower than 73 percent. Virginia officials refused to provide even 10 percent, declaring, "It takes people a long time to starve." Some southern cities and counties refused to contribute anything to relief, and Memphis spent less on relief—only 0.1 percent of its budget—than on maintaining public golf courses.

Federal money enabled southern communities to balance their own budgets, preach fiscal orthodoxy, and maintain traditional claims of limited government. Federal officials complained of the South's "parasitic" behavior in accepting aid but not responsibility, and even Southerners acknowledged the hypocrisy of the region's invocation of state's rights. "We recognize state boundaries when called on to give," noted the *Houston Press,* "but forget them when Uncle Sam is doing the giving."

The federal government had a particularly powerful impact on the South with the **Tennessee Valley Authority (TVA),** launched in 1933 (see Map 25-3). Coordinating activities across seven states, the TVA built dams to control floods and generate hydroelectric power, produced fertilizer, fostered agricultural and forestry development, encouraged conservation, improved navigation, and modernized school and health systems. Private utility companies denounced the TVA as socialistic, but most Southerners supported it. Its major drawback was environmental damage that only became apparent later. Over a vast area of the South, it provided electricity for the first time.

The New Deal further expanded access to electricity by establishing the Rural Electrification Administration (REA) in 1935. Private companies had refused to extend power lines into the countryside because it was not profitable, consigning 90 percent of the nation's farms to drudgery and darkness. The REA revolutionized farm life by sponsoring rural nonprofit electric cooperatives. By 1941, 35 percent of American farms had electricity; by 1950, 78 percent. By providing electric power to light and heat homes

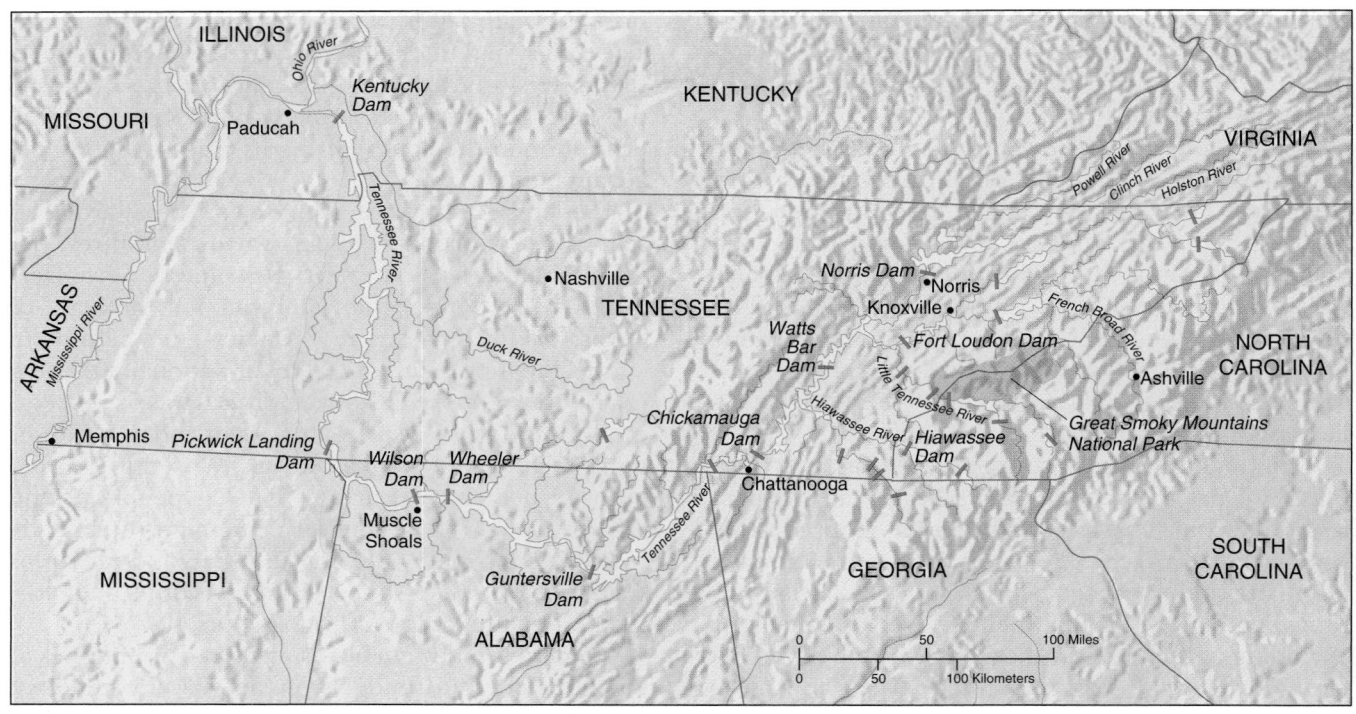

MAP 25-3   The Tennessee Valley Authority
*By building dams and hydroelectric power plants, the TVA controlled flooding and soil erosion
and generated electricity that did much to modernize a large region of the Upper South.*

and barns, pump water, and run refrigerators, washing machines, and radios, one Arkansas newspaper concluded, the REA had made "a reality" of what had been only a "utopian dream."

The New Deal also changed the West. Westerners received the most federal money per capita in welfare, relief projects, and loans. Like Southerners, they accepted federal aid and clamored for more. Utah, which received the most federal relief funds per capita, was the nation's "prize 'gimme state,'" said one FERA official. Western farmers and cattle raisers were saved by federal payments, and even refugees from the Dust Bowl depended on relief assistance and medical care in federal camps.

The Bureau of Reclamation, established in 1902, emerged as one of the most important government agencies in the West. It built huge dams to control the western river systems and promote large-scale development. The Hoover Dam on the Colorado River between Nevada and Arizona, completed in 1935; the Grand Coulee Dam on the Columbia River in Washington, finished in 1941; and other giant projects prevented flooding, produced cheap hydroelectric power, and created reservoirs and canal systems to bring water to farms and cities. By furnishing capital and expertise, the government subsidized and stimulated western economic development, particularly the growth of agribusiness.

Westerners welcomed such assistance but rarely shared the federal goals of rational resource management. Instead, they often wanted to continue to exploit the land and resented federal supervision as colonial control. In practice, however, the government worked in partnership with the West's agribusinesses and timber and petroleum industries.

THE NEW DEAL AND PUBLIC ACTIVISM

Despite Hoover's fear that government responsibility would discourage local initiative, the 1930s witnessed an upsurge in such activism. New Deal programs, in fact, often encouraged or empowered groups to shape public policy and social and economic behavior. Moreover, because the administration worried about centralization, some federal agencies fostered what New Dealers called "grassroots democracy." The AAA set up committees totaling more than 100,000 people to implement agricultural policy and held referendums on crop controls; local advisory committees guided the various federal arts projects; federal management of the West's public grasslands mandated cooperation with associations of livestock raisers.

At times, local administration of national programs enabled groups to exploit federal policy for their own advantage. Wealthy planters shaped AAA practices at the expense of poor tenant farmers; local control of TVA projects excluded black people. But federal programs often allowed previously unrepresented groups to contest traditionally dominant interests. By requiring that public housing projects be initiated locally, for example, New Deal programs prompted labor unions, religious and civic groups, neighborhood associations, and civil rights groups to form associations to overcome the hostility of realty agents and bankers to public housing. Often seeing greater opportunities for participation and influence in federal programs than in city and state governments, such community groups campaigned to expand federal authority. In short, depression conditions and New Deal programs actually increased citizen involvement in public affairs.

EBBING OF THE NEW DEAL

After his victory in 1936, Roosevelt committed himself to further reforms. "I see one-third of a nation ill-housed, ill-clad, ill-nourished," he declared in his second inaugural address. "The test of our progress is not whether we add more to the abundance of those who have much; it is whether we provide enough for those who have too little." But determined opponents, continuing economic problems, and the President's own misjudgments blocked his reforms and deadlocked the New Deal.

CHALLENGING THE COURT

Roosevelt regarded the Supreme Court as his most dangerous opponent. During his first term, the Court had declared unconstitutional several important measures. FDR complained that the justices held "horse-and-buggy" ideas about government that prevented the President and Congress from responding to changes. Indeed, most of the justices were elderly conservatives, appointed by Republicans and unsympathetic to an activist federal government. It seemed that the court would also strike down the Second New Deal.

Emboldened by the 1936 landslide, Roosevelt decided to restructure the federal judiciary. In early 1937, he proposed legislation authorizing the president to name a new judge for each one serving past the age of 70. Additional judges, he said, would increase judicial efficiency. But his real goal was to appoint new judges more sympathetic to the New Deal.

His court plan led to a divisive struggle. The proposal was perfectly legal: Congress had the authority, which it had used repeatedly, to change the number of judges on the Court. But Republicans and conservative Democrats attacked the plan as a scheme to "pack" the Court and subvert the separation of powers among the three branches of government. Some conservatives called the President a "dictator," but even many liberals expressed reservations about the plan or FDR's lack of candor in proposing it.

The Court itself undercut support for FDR's proposal by upholding the Social Security and Wagner Acts and minimum-wage legislation. Moreover, the retirement of a conservative justice allowed Roosevelt to name a sympathetic successor. Congress rejected Roosevelt's plan.

Roosevelt's challenge to the Court hurt the New Deal. It worried the public, split the Democratic party, and revived conservatives. Opponents promptly attacked other New Deal policies, from support for unions to progressive taxation. Henceforth, a conservative coalition of Republicans and Southern Democrats in Congress blocked FDR's reforms.

MORE HARD TIMES

A sharp recession, beginning in August 1937, added to Roosevelt's problems. The New Deal's deficit spending had reflected his desire to alleviate suffering, not a conviction that it would stimulate economic recovery. As the economy improved in 1936, Roosevelt decided to cut federal expenditures and balance the budget. But private investment and employment remained stagnant, and the economy plunged. A record decline in industrial production canceled the gains of the previous two years, and unemployment leaped from 7 million to 11 million within a few months. Republicans delighted in attacking the "Roosevelt recession," although it stemmed from retrenchment policies they themselves had advocated.

In 1938, Roosevelt reluctantly increased spending. His decision was based on the principles of British economist John Maynard Keynes. As Marriner Eccles of the Federal Reserve Board explained, the federal government had to serve as the "compensatory agent" in the economy: It should use deficit spending to increase demand and production when private investment declined and raise taxes to pay its debt and cool the economy when business activity became excessive. New appropriations for the PWA and other government programs revived the faltering economy, but neither FDR nor Congress would spend what was necessary to end the depression. Only the vast expenditures for World War II would bring full recovery.

POLITICAL STALEMATE

The recession interrupted the momentum of the New Deal and strengthened its opponents. In late 1937, their leaders in Congress issued a "conservative manifesto" decrying New Deal fiscal, labor, and regulatory policies. Holding seniority in a Congress malapportioned in their favor, they blocked most of Roosevelt's reforms. None of his "must" legislation passed a special session of Congress in December. In 1938, Congress rejected tax reforms and reduced corporate taxes.

The few measures that passed were heavily amended. The Fair Labor Standards Act established maximum hours and minimum wages for workers but authorized so many exemptions that one New Dealer asked "whether anyone is subject to this bill." The Farm Tenancy Act established the Farm Security Administration to lend money to tenant farmers and agricultural laborers to acquire their own land, but appropriations were so limited that centuries would have been required to meet the need. The National Housing Act created the United States Housing Authority to finance slum clearance and public housing projects, but its total funds were less than what was needed to demolish tenements in New York City alone.

To protect the New Deal, Roosevelt turned again to the public, with whom he remained immensely popular. In the 1938 Democratic primaries, he campaigned against the New Deal's conservative opponents. But FDR could not transfer his personal popularity to the political newcomers he supported. What his foes attacked as a "purge" failed. Roosevelt lost further political leverage when the Republicans gained seventy-five seats in the House and seven in the Senate and thirteen governorships.

The 1938 elections did not repudiate the New Deal, for the Democrats retained majorities in both houses of Congress. But the Republican revival and the survival of the conservative Southern Democrats guaranteed that the New Deal had gone as far as it ever would. With Roosevelt in the White House and his opponents controlling Congress, the New Deal ended in political stalemate.

GOOD NEIGHBORS AND HOSTILE FORCES

Even before FDR's conservative opposition derailed the New Deal, the President felt the impact of congressional limitations in the area of foreign policy as well. Isolationists in Congress counseled against any U.S. involvement in world affairs and appealed to the growing national disillusionment with America's participation in the Great War to support their position.

Responding to the spreading popular belief that World War I had been fought to protect the fortunes of financiers and munitions makers, Republican Senator Gerald Nye established a committee in 1934 to investigate the origins of U.S. involvement in what many Americans termed the European War. For two years, the Nye Committee sensationally exposed the greed of big business and intimated that President Woodrow Wilson had gone to war to save profits for capitalists—and not democracy for the world. Jobless and homeless Americans reacted with anger to the committee's findings and public sentiment against fighting another "foreign" war hardened. Moreover, Roosevelt himself, although not an isolationist, believed that the gravity of the nation's economic depression warranted a primary focus on domestic recovery, and in the early years of his presidency, he took few international initiatives.

Those actions he did take related directly to salvaging America's desperate economy. As the depression worsened in 1933, American businesses searched for new markets throughout the world, and key business leaders informed FDR that they would welcome the opportunity to expand trade to the Soviet Union. Moscow was also eager to renew ties to the U.S., and President Roosevelt extended formal recognition of the Soviet Union in November 1933. His decision was not without controversy; even his own mother denounced him for it. Still worse, the anticipated trade did not occur, although FDR believed that establishing diplomatic ties with the Soviets also served as a warning signal to Japan and its expansionist appetite.

Enhancing trade opportunities and rescuing the economy from the damage wrought by high tariffs figured prominently in Roosevelt's policies in the Western hemisphere. In large measure, Roosevelt merely extended the Good Neighbor policy begun by President Herbert Hoover. Hoover had altered the U.S. policy of interventionism so that by the time he left office in March 1933, all U.S. troops had been removed from Latin America. Still, the Great Depression strained U.S.-Latin American relations, sending economic shock waves throughout Central and South America and, in several instances, helping propel to power ruthless dictators who ruled with iron fists and U.S. support. Moreover, although FDR continued the policy of military nonintervention, displeased with the 1933 election of a radical in Cuba as president, he supported a coup there, which resulted in the coming to power of the infamous dictator Fulgencio Batista, and the Batista era lasted until it was overthrown by Fidel Castro in 1959.

Symbolic of "good neighbors," FDR visited the Caribbean in 1934, receiving an enthusiastic reception, and in 1936, he broke new ground by becoming the first U.S. president to sail to South America. He also worked to encourage trade by reducing tariffs.

On November 9, 1938, Nazi Germany launched an assault on Jews, destroying their businesses and burning their synagogues. This street scene in Berlin shows the shattered windows of Jewish businesses. Nazi leader Joseph Goebbels recorded the event, known as Kristallnacht, in his diary: "Yesterday: Berlin. There, all proceeded fantastically. One fire after another. It is good that way.... 100 dead. But no German property damaged."

Between 1929 and 1933, the volume of trade worldwide had collapsed by 40 percent and American exports had plummeted by 60 percent. Eager to increase American exports, FDR's Secretary of State, Cordell Hull, who, like Roosevelt himself, believed in the need for lower tariffs, finalized trade agreements with numerous Latin American nations that allowed "most favored nation" status and resulted in sharply increasing U.S. exports to its southern neighbors. Good neighbors were also good trading partners.

NEUTRALITY AND FASCISM

Outside the hemisphere, during his first term as president, Roosevelt generally followed the policy of avoiding involvement in Europe's political, economic, and social problems. But the aggressive actions of Adolf Hitler in Germany ultimately led Roosevelt to a differ-

ent position, and in the latter part of the decade, he faced the task of educating the American public, still resentful of U.S. participation in World War I, about the fascist danger that was spreading in Europe. Hitler came to power in 1933, shortly before FDR entered the White House, and he pledged to restore German pride and nationalism in the aftermath of the Versailles Treaty. As the leader of the National Socialist Workers Party—the Nazis—Hitler established a **fascist government**—a one-party dictatorship—closely aligned with corporate interests, committed to a "biological world evolution," and determined to establish a new empire, the Third Reich. He vowed to eliminate Bolshevik radicalism and purify the German "race" through the elimination of those he deemed undesirable, especially targeting the Jewish population—a group Hitler blamed for most, if not all, Germany's ills.

FROM THEN TO NOW

Social Security

No politician will "ever scrap my social security program." So predicted FDR when he signed the Social Security Act in 1935. He based his confidence on the provisions in the act that linked benefits to payroll deductions. Because workers contributed to the program, they would feel a "right to collect their pensions and unemployment benefits." But Roosevelt could not have imagined just how successful the Social Security program would become. Expanded over the years since the 1930s, it now assists more than 44 million Americans, including the elderly, the disabled, and the survivors of contributors to the program. Certain poverty would confront half the nation's elderly without their monthly checks.

But the successful expansion of the program has also called its future into question. By 2030, the number of eligible recipients will double, but the number of employees paying Social Security taxes will increase by only 17 percent. Annual funding deficits of more than $100 billion loom ahead.

Still, as FDR predicted, no political leader dares to propose "scrapping" Social Security. Rather, proposals to solve this problem reflect conflicting views about the expansion of the federal government—and especially its efforts to promote social welfare—that began with the New Deal. No longer does the public overwhelmingly endorse federal responsibility for solving social problems as it did during the economic crisis of the 1930s. On the contrary, an increasingly intense backlash against "big government" emerged in the 1960s, ultimately finding its champion in the 1980s in Republican President Ronald Reagan, who declared, "Government is not the solution to our problems; government is the problem." Reagan's administration sought to reduce the size of government and curtail its regulatory oversight of American business. This "Reagan Revolution" appealed to those who never supported government responsibility for social welfare and to those who had lost trust in the government's ability to fulfill that role. By the 1990s, even the Democratic

---

Others aided the spread of fascism. Italian leader Benito Mussolini, who had assumed power in 1922 and envisaged emulating the power and prestige of the Roman empire, brutally attacked Ethiopia in 1935. The following year, a young fascist military officer, Francisco Franco, led an uprising in Spain, and with the assistance of Italy and Germany, successfully ousted the Spanish Republicans by 1939 to create an authoritarian government. Meanwhile, Hitler implemented his plan of conquest: he remilitarized the Rhineland in 1936 and in 1938 he annexed Austria.

But the aggressive actions of Germany and Italy failed to eclipse American fears of being led into another European war. And Congress, too, made known its strong disinclination to get involved in international conflict by passing four Neutrality Acts designed to continue America's trade with its world partners but prohibit the president from taking sides

in the mounting European crisis. The first act, passed in 1935, prohibited Americans from traveling to a war zone, banned loans to belligerent nations, and instituted an embargo on armaments to belligerents. The following year Congress extended the legislation for another year and then in 1937 made the neutrality prohibitions permanent, with the addition of a "cash-and-carry" provision that required belligerent nations to pay for American goods in advance of their shipment. President Roosevelt reluctantly signed the bill into law, but continued to work to heighten public awareness of the dangers of Nazism.

Appeasement and more neutrality. After annexing Austria, Hitler pushed again in 1938 when he demanded the Sudetenland from Czechoslovakia. The French and the British refused to stand up to Hitler's insatiable reach, following instead a policy of appeasement. Meeting in Munich in September 1938, the

President Bill Clinton declared an end to the era of "big government."

Support has grown for private initiatives to replace government programs, and now critics, led by Republican President George W. Bush, are pressing to "privatize" the Social Security system itself. They have proposed such sweeping changes as limiting benefits to contributors only and requiring contributors to invest their Social Security accounts themselves, including in the stock market. The predicted payoff would be larger earnings.

Opponents of these critics argue for reforming, not overturning, the current Social Security system. Privatization, they argue, would undermine Social Security's fundamental principle: to guarantee retirees a dependable income base. Investing retirement savings in the stock market subjects them to market volatility, which might benefit some people but could leave others with serious losses just when they were ready to retire. The stock market decline beginning in 2000 powerfully reinforced that warning. Privatization would also eliminate the special assistance that Social Security provides to large families, cou-

ples with one partner who has had no or limited earnings, and low-income earners.

Rather than scrap the current system, reformers propose other changes. They suggest taxing all workers for Social Security; many, especially in state and local governments, are now outside the system. Extending the age of eligibility to receive benefits, justified by the increasing life expectancy of Americans, would also bolster the Social Security funds. Another proposal would abandon the current investment strategy but have a quasi-private government entity manage the system's portfolio. Such changes would enable Social Security to continue meeting the needs of all citizens.

The current argument over Social Security echoes the disputes of the 1930s about the role and function of our government and reflects continuing differences over the degree to which the government should attempt to make American society more equitable. Finding a solution to funding Social Security in the new century will require addressing the issue of America's core values.

leaders of England and France met with Hitler and Mussolini and abandoned their security obligations to the Czechs, yielding the Sudetenland to Hitler in exchange for a weak promise of no more annexations.

In America, too, the sentiment was for peace at all costs, and isolationism permeated the halls of Congress. Indeed, Hitler himself did not regard the United States as a threat to his expansionist plan: "America," he said in 1939, "is not dangerous to us." Hitler held FDR in low esteem and denounced America as a racially mixed nation of intellectual inferiors. "Transport a German to Kiev," Hitler declared, "and he remains a perfect German. But transplant him to Miami, and you make a degenerate out of him—in other words, an American." Isolationism also combined with anti-Semitism and with division among America's Jewish leadership to insure that the U.S. would not become a haven for Jews suffering under Nazi brutality. News of Nazi atrocities against Aus-

trian Jews in 1938 shocked the American press, and Hitler's violent pogrom, known as *Kristallnacht* (the Night of the Broken Glass), conducted against Jews throughout Germany in November 1938 added fresh proof of Nazi cruelty. Although the U.S. recalled its ambassador from Berlin to protest the pogrom (in response, Germany recalled its ambassador from Washington), the U.S. failed to alter its restrictive immigration quota system, the 1924 National Origins Act, to provide refuge for German Jews. Unchallenged, Hitler pressed on with his campaign of persecution and terror against what he termed "inferior races" and "anti-socials," herding Jews, Slavs, homosexuals, and handicapped citizens into concentration camps. As early as 1933, Hitler had established the first concentration camp at Dachau and by 1939, camps in Germany held over 25,000 people.

As Europe edged closer to war, the relationship between the U.S. and Japan, periodically tense in the twentieth century, became more strained. Japan resented U.S. economic interests in East Asia and was offended by American immigration policy which excluded Japanese immigrants. The U.S. regarded Japan's desires for empire as threatening but also needed Japan as a trading partner, especially in the economically depressed 1930s. Consequently, in September 1931, when Japan seized Manchuria, the U.S. did little more than denounce the action. Again in 1937, when Japanese troops attacked Chinese forces north of Beijing in an effort to extend Japanese economic influence, and outright war began between Japan and China, the U.S. merely condemned the action. And although, that same year, President Roosevelt denounced "the epidemic of world lawlessness," indicting the aggressiveness of Italy, Germany, and Japan and calling for a "quarantine" of aggressors, he continued his policy of refusing to risk war with Japan.

EDGING TOWARD INVOLVEMENT

After the Munich agreement, President Roosevelt moved away from domestic reform toward preparedness for war, fearful that conflict in Europe was unavoidable and determined to revise the neutrality laws. In his State of the Union address in January 1939, FDR explained that "our neutrality laws" might "actually give aid to an aggressor and deny it to the victim." By the fall of that year, he had won support for eliminating the prohibition of arms and adding armaments to the list of cash-and-carry items—a revision that would enable the U.S. to provide important assistance to Britain and France in the winter of 1939-1940. Hitler's defiance of the Munich agreement and his conquest of all of Czechoslovakia by March 1939 merely anticipated his next move toward Poland later that summer and also convinced the British and the French that war was imminent.

CONCLUSION

The Great Depression and the New Deal mark a major divide in American history. The depression cast doubt on the traditional practices, policies, and attitudes that underlay not only the nation's economy but its social and political institutions and relationships as well. The New Deal failed to restore prosperity, but it did bring partial economic recovery. Moreover, its economic policies, from banking and securities regulation to unemployment compensation, farm price supports, and minimum wages, created barriers against another depression. The gradual adoption of compensatory spending policies also expanded the government's role in the economy. Responding to the failures of both private organizations and state and local governments, the federal government also assumed the obligation to provide social welfare. The New Deal established pensions for the elderly, aid for dependent mothers and children and the blind, public housing for the poor, and public health services. Although such programs were limited in scope and access, they helped establish a responsible government. "Better the occasional faults of a Government that lives in a spirit of charity," Roosevelt warned, "than the constant omission of a Government frozen in the ice of its own indifference."

Roosevelt also expanded the role of the presidency. As his White House took the initiative for defining public policy, drafting legislation, lobbying Congress, and communicating with the nation, it became the model for all subsequent presidents. Not only was the president's power increased, but Roosevelt made the federal government, rather than state or local governments, the focus of public interest and expectations. Under Hoover, one secretary had handled all the White House mail; under FDR, a staff of fifty was overwhelmed.

Roosevelt and the New Deal also revitalized the Democratic party, drawing minorities, industrial workers, and previously uninvolved citizens into a coalition with white Southerners. The tensions in such a coalition sometimes prevented effective public policies, but the coalition made the Democrats the dominant national party.

Political constraints explained some of the New Deal's failures. Conservative southern Democrats and northern Republicans limited its efforts to curtail racial discrimination or protect the rural and urban poor. But Roosevelt and other New Dealers were often constrained by their own vision, refusing to consider the massive deficit spending necessary to end the depression or not recognizing the need to end gender discrimination. But if the New Deal did not bring the revolution its conservative critics claimed—it did not redistribute wealth or income—it did change American life.

By the end of the 1930s, as international relations deteriorated, FDR was already considering a shift, as he later said, from Dr. New Deal to Dr. Win-the-War. Reluctant to move beyond public opinion that did not want war and neutrality legislation that limited America's support of its allies, FDR cautiously led the nation toward war—this time against an enemy, he believed, far more threatening than even the Great Depression. Ironically, only then would President Roosevelt end the depression that had ravaged a nation for nearly a decade.

REVIEW QUESTIONS

1. In the series of quotes that introduce the chapter, what do these voices from the Great Depression suggest about the changed role of the family and the value placed on work and school?

2. Why did President Hoover's emphasis on voluntarism fail to resolve the problems of the Great Depression?

3. Describe the relief programs of the New Deal. What were they designed to accomplish? What were their achievements and their limitations?

4. What were the major criticisms of the early New Deal? How accurate were those charges?

5. How did the policies of the New Deal shape the constituency and the prospects of the Democratic party in the 1930s?

6. Describe the conflict between management and labor in the 1930s. What were the major issues and motivations involved? How did the two sides differ in resources and tactics, and how and why did these factors change over time?

7. How did the role of the federal government change in the 1930s? What factors were responsible for those changes?

KEY TERMS

Bonus Army (p. 793)

Congress of Industrial Organizations (p. 804)

Fascist government (p. 811)

Federal Deposit Insurance Corporation (FDIC) (p. 794)

Fireside chat (p. 794)

Great Depression (p. 786)

Hoovervilles (p. 788)

New Deal (p. 785)

Securities and Exchange Commission (SEC) (p. 794)

Tennessee Valley Authority (TVA) (p. 807)

RECOMMENDED READING

Conkin, Paul. *The New Deal*, 3rd ed. (1992). A brief and insightful critique of FDR's programs.

Fraser, Steve, and Gary Gerstle, eds. *The Rise and Fall of the New Deal Order, 1930–1980* (1989). A valu-able collection of essays that surveys the New Deal and explores its legacy.

Freidel, Frank. *Franklin D. Roosevelt: A Rendezvous with Destiny* (1990). The best one-volume biography of FDR.

Kennedy, David. *Freedom from Fear: The American People in Depression and War* (1999). The most recent and comprehensive survey of the period.

Leuchtenburg, William. *Franklin D. Roosevelt and the New Deal, 1932–1940* (1963). The best single-volume study of FDR's policies during his first two terms as president.

Sitkoff, Harvard, ed. *Fifty Years Later: The New Deal Evaluated* (1985). The New Deal analyzed in an excellent selection of essays.

Steinbeck, John. *The Grapes of Wrath* (1939). The classic novel of Dust Bowl migrants; still makes gripping reading.

ADDITIONAL SOURCES

Hard Times in Hooverville

Bernstein, Michael. *The Great Depression* (1987).

Blackwelder, Julia Kirk. *Women of the Depression: Caste and Culture in San Antonio* (1984).

Chafe, William H. *The American Woman, 1920–1970* (1972).

Galbraith, John Kenneth. *The Great Crash: 1929* (1989).

Garraty, John. *The Great Depression* (1986).

Kelley, Robin D. G. *Hammer and Hoe: Alabama Communists during the Great Depression* (1990)

Klein, Maury. *Rainbow's End: The Crash of 1929* (2001).

McElvaine, Robert. *The Great Depression: America, 1929–1941* (1984).

Mullins, William. *The Depression and the Urban West Coast, 1929–1933* (1991).

Reisler, Mark. *By the Sweat of Their Brow: Mexican Immigrant Labor in the United States* (1976).

Scharf, Lois. *To Work and to Wed: Female Employment, Feminism, and the Great Depression* (1980).

Shover, John. *Cornbelt Rebellion: The Farmers' Holiday Association* (1965).

Herbert Hoover and the Depression

Burner, David. *Herbert Hoover: A Public Life* (1979).

Daniels, Roger. *The Bonus March* (1971).

Fausold, Martin L. *The Presidency of Herbert C. Hoover* (1985).

Hamilton, David E. *From New Day to New Deal: American Farm Policy from Hoover to Roosevelt* (1991).

Lisio, Donald. *The President and Protest* (1974).

Romasco, Albert. *The Poverty of Abundance: Hoover, the Nation, the Depression* (1965).

Schwartz, Jordan A. *Interregnum of Despair* (1970).

Watkins, T. H. *The Hungry Years: A Narrative History of the Great Depression in America* (1999).

Wilson, Joan Hoff. *Herbert Hoover: Forgotten Progressive* (1975).

Launching the New Deal

Badger, Anthony J. *The New Deal: The Depression Years, 1933–1940* (1989).

Bernstein, Irving. *Turbulent Years: A History of the American Worker, 1933–1941* (1970).

Blackorby, Edward C. *Prairie Rebel: William Lemke* (1963).

Brinkley, Alan. *Voices of Protest: Huey Long, Father Coughlin, and the Great Depression* (1982).

Conrad, David. *The Forgotten Farmers: The Story of the Share-croppers in the New Deal* (1965).

Grubbs, Donald H. *Cry from the Cotton: The Southern Tenant Farmers Union and the New Deal* (1971).

Hawley, Ellis. *The New Deal and the Problem of Monopoly* (1966).

Leuchtenburg, William. *The FDR Years* (1995).

Ribuffo, Leo P. *The Old Christian Right: The Protestant Far Right from the Great Depression to the Cold War* (1983).

Romasco, Albert. *The Politics of Recovery: Roosevelt's New Deal* (1983).

Saloutos, Theodore. *The American Farmer and the New Deal* (1982).

Schlesinger, Arthur M. Jr. *The Coming of the New Deal* (1958).

Williams, T. Harry. *Huey Long* (1969).

Consolidating the New Deal

Allswang, John. *The New Deal and American Politics* (1978).

Andersen, Kristi. *The Creation of a Democratic Majority* (1979).

Berkowitz, Edward D. *America's Welfare State* (1991).

Biles, Roger. *A New Deal for the American People* (1991).

Gamm, Gerald. *The Making of New Deal Democrats* (1989).

Gordon, Colin. *New Deals: Business, Labor, and Politics in America* (1994).

McCoy, Donald R. *Landon of Kansas* (1966).

McJimsey, George. *Harry Hopkins* (1987).

The New Deal and American Life

Argersinger, Jo Ann E. *Toward a New Deal in Baltimore: People and Government in the Great Depression* (1988).

Arnold, Joseph L. *The New Deal in the Suburbs* (1971).

Barnard, John. *Walter Reuther and the Rise of the Auto Workers* (1983).

Biles, Roger. *The South and the New Deal* (1994).

Cohen, Lisabeth. *Making a New Deal: Industrial Workers in Chicago* (1990).

Faue, Elizabeth. *Community of Suffering and Struggle: Women, Men, and the Labor Movement in Minneapolis* (1991).

Fine, Sidney. *Sitdown: The General Motors Strike of 1936–1937* (1969).

Fraser, Steven. *Labor Will Rule: Sidney Hillman and the Rise of American Labor* (1991).

Gregory, James. *American Exodus: The Dust Bowl Migration and Okie Culture in California* (1989).

Gutierrez, David G. *Walls and Mirrors: Mexican Americans, Mexican Immigrants, and the Politics of Ethnicity* (1995).

Kelly, Laurence C. *The Assault on Assimilation: John Collier and the Origins of Indian Policy Reform* (1983).

Lichtenstein, Nelson. *The Most Dangerous Man in Detroit: Walter Reuther and the Fate of American Labor* (1995).

Lowitt, Richard. *The New Deal and the West* (1984).

Mink, Gwendolyn. *The Wages of Motherhood: Inequality in the Welfare State, 1917–1942* (1995).

Nelson, Bruce. *Workers on the Waterfront* (1988).

Sitkoff, Harvard. *A New Deal for Blacks* (1978).

Smith, Douglas L. *The New Deal in the Urban South* (1988).

Stock, Catherine. *Main Street in Crisis: The Great Depression and the Old Middle Class on the Northern Plains* (1992).

Taylor, Graham. *The New Deal and American Indian Tribalism* (1980).

Ware, Susan. *Beyond Suffrage: Women in the New Deal* (1981).

Ware, Susan. *Holding Their Own: American Women in the 1930s* (1982).

Worster, Donald. *Dust Bowl* (1979).

Worster, Donald. *Rivers of Empire* (1985).

Zieger, Robert. *The CIO, 1935–1955* (1995).

Zieger, Robert. *John L. Lewis* (1988).

Ebbing of the New Deal

Brinkley, Alan. *The End of Reform: New Deal Liberalism in Recession and War* (1995).

Cole, Wayne. *Roosevelt and the Isolationists, 1932–1945* (1983).

Dallek, Robert. *Franklin Delano Roosevelt and American Foreign Policy, 1932–1945* (1979).

Davis, Kenneth S. *FDR: Into the Storm, 1937–1940* (1993).

Dubofsky, Melvyn. *The State and Labor in Modern America* (1994).

Heinrichs, Waldo. *Threshold of War: Franklin D. Roosevelt and American Entry into World War II* (1988).

Leff, Mark. *The Limits of Symbolic Reform: The New Deal and Taxation* (1984).

Lipstadt, Deborah E. *Beyond Belief: The American Press and the Coming of the Holocaust, 1933–1945* (1986).

Patterson, James T. *Congressional Conservatism and the New Deal* (1967).

Patterson, James T. *The New Deal and the States* (1969).

Trout, Charles H. *Boston, the Great Depression, and the New Deal* (1977).

WHERE TO LEARN MORE

- **Center for New Deal Studies, Roosevelt University, Chicago, Illinois.** The center contains political memorabilia, photographs, papers, and taped interviews dealing with Franklin D. Roosevelt and the New Deal; it also sponsors an annual lecture series about the Roosevelt legacy.

- **Herbert Hoover National Historic Site, West Branch, Iowa.** This 186-acre site contains the birthplace cottage and grave of Herbert Hoover as well as his presidential library and museum, which contains a reconstruction of Hoover's White House office. www.nps.gov/heho; www.hoover.archives.gov.

- **Labor Museum and Learning Center of Michigan, Flint, Michigan.** Exhibits trace the history of the labor movement, including the dramatic "Sit-Down Strike" of 1936–1937.

- **Franklin D. Roosevelt Home and Presidential Library, Hyde Park, New York.** The Roosevelt home, furnished with family heirlooms, and the spacious grounds, where FDR is buried, personalize the president and provide insights into his career. The nearby library has displays and exhibitions about Roosevelt's presidency, and the Eleanor Roosevelt Wing is dedicated to the career of ER. www.fdrlibrary.marist.edu.

- **Eleanor Roosevelt National Historic Site, Hyde Park, New York.** These two cottages, where Eleanor Roosevelt worked and, after 1945, lived, contain her furniture and memorabilia. Visitors can also watch a film biography of ER and tour the grounds of this retreat where she entertained personal friends and world leaders. www.nps.gov/elro.

- **Civilian Conservation Corps Interpretive Center, Whidbey Island, Washington.** This stone and wood structure, built as a CCC project, now houses exhibits and artifacts illustrating the history of the CCC.

- **Bethune Museum and Archives National Historic Site, Washington, D.C.** This four-story townhouse was the home of Mary McLeod Bethune, a friend of Eleanor Roosevelt and the director of the New Deal's Division of Negro Affairs, and the headquarters of the National Council of Negro Women, which Bethune founded in 1935. Exhibits feature the contributions of black activist women and activities of the civil rights movement.

 Please refer to the document CD-ROM for primary sources related to this chapter.

✧ On June 6, 1944, American, British, and Canadian forces seized a beachhead in German-occupied France. The landings began the final phase of World War II in Europe, which ended eleven months later with German surrender to the U.S., Britain, the Soviet Union, and their allies.

WORLD WAR II 26
1939–1945

CHAPTER OUTLINE

The Dilemmas of Neutrality
The Roots of War
Hitler's War in Europe
Trying to Keep Out
Edging Toward Intervention
The Brink of War
December 7, 1941

Holding the Line
Stopping Germany
The Survival of Britain
Retreat and Stabilization in the Pacific

Mobilizing for Victory
Organizing the Economy
The Enlistment of Science
Men and Women in the Military
The Home Front
New Workers
Clashing Cultures
Internment of Japanese Americans
The End of the New Deal

War and Peace
Turning the Tide in Europe
Operation OVERLORD
Victory and Tragedy in Europe
The Pacific War
Searching for Peace
How the Allies Won

Conclusion

December, 1942

The scene [under the stadium] at The University of Chicago would have been confusing to an outsider, if he could have eluded the security guards and gained admittance. He would have seen only what appeared to be a crude pile of black bricks and wooden timbers. . . .

Finally, the day came when we were ready to run the experiment. We gathered on a balcony about 10 feet above the floor of the large room in which the structure had been erected. Beneath us was a young scientist, George Weil, whose duty it was to handle the last control rod that was holding the reaction in check. . . .

Finally, it was time to remove the control rods. Slowly, Weil started to withdraw the main control rod. On the balcony, we watched the indicators which measured the neutron count and told us how rapidly the disintegration of the uranium atoms under their neutron bombardment was proceeding.

At 11:35 A.M., the counters were clicking rapidly. Then, with a loud clap, the automatic control rods slammed home. The safety point had been set too low.

It seemed a good time to eat lunch. During lunch everyone was thinking about the experiment but nobody talked much about it.

> At 2:30, Weil pulled out the control rod in a series of measured adjustments. Shortly after, the intensity shown by the indicators began to rise at a slow but ever-increasing rate. At this moment we knew that the self-sustaining [nuclear] reaction was under way.
>
> The event was not spectacular, no fuses burned, no lights flashed. But to us it meant that release of atomic energy on a large scale would be only a matter of time.[1]

Enrico Fermi, in *The First Reactor* (Washington: U.S. Department of Energy, 1982), accessed at http://hep.uchicago.edu/cp; Laura Fermi, *Atoms in the Family* (Chicago: University of Chicago Press, 1954); Laura Fermi, "The Fermis' Path to Los Alamos," in Lawrence Badash, Joseph O. Hirschfelder, and Herbert P. Broida, eds. *Reminiscences of Los Alamos, 1943–45* (Boston and Dordrecht: D. Reidel Publishing Co.).

Enrico Fermi was describing the first controlled nuclear chain reaction—the critical experiment from which atomic weapons and atomic power would soon develop. Fermi himself had emigrated to escape the growing political repression of Fascist Italy. In 1938, he had received a Nobel Prize in physics. When he accepted the prize in Stockholm, Sweden, the family put secret plans into action and immigrated to the United States rather than returning to Italy. As the United States joined the ongoing global conflict of World War II, Fermi was placed in charge of nuclear fission research at the University of Chicago in 1942 and played a leading role in efforts to develop an atomic bomb. The following year found Fermi, other atomic scientists, and their families at Los Alamos, a science city that the government built hurriedly on a high plateau in northern New Mexico, where isolation was supposed to ensure secrecy and help the U.S. win the race with Nazi Germany to develop atomic weapons.

The instant city was a cross between a cheap subdivision and an army camp for deeply engaged but eccentric scientists. "I always pitied our Army doctors for their thankless job," Enrico's wife Laura Fermi later wrote: "They had prepared for the emergencies of the battlefields, and they were faced instead with a high-strung bunch of men, women, and children. . . . high-strung because we were too many of a kind, too close to one another, and we were all crackpots."* Scientists spent their days designing a bomb that would change world politics and returned to dinners cooked on wood-burning stoves.

The Fermis were not the only family to give Los Alamos a multinational flavor. Laura remembered that it was "all one big family and all one big ac-

cent. . . . Everybody in science was there, both from the United States and from almost all European countries." British and Canadians worked alongside U.S. scientists. So did refugees from Europe who made Los Alamos the most distinguished collection of physicists in the world and contributed greatly to American victory (Laura Fermi later wrote about them in the book *Illustrious Immigrants*). Niels Bohr had fled Denmark to escape Nazi invasion. Edward Teller was a Hungarian who had studied in Germany. Hans Bethe had left Germany, and Stanislaus Ulam was the only member of his family to survive the Nazi conquest of Poland. Absent were scientists from the Soviet Union, which was bearing the worst of the fighting against Germany but was carefully excluded from the secret of the atomic bomb.

The internationalism of Los Alamos mirrored the larger war effort. Japan's attack on Pearl Harbor in December 1941 thrust the United States into a war that spanned the globe. U.S. allies against Japan in the Pacific and East Asia included Great Britain, Australia, and China. In Europe, its allies against Nazi Germany and Fascist Italy included Great Britain, the Soviet Union, and more than twenty other nations. The men and women racing to perfect the atomic bomb knew that victory was far from certain. Germany and Japan had piled one conquest on another since the late 1930s, and they continued to seize new territories in 1942. Allied defeat in a few key battles could have resulted in standoff or Axis victory. Not until 1944 did American economic power allow the United States and its allies to feel confident of victory. A new weapon might end the war more quickly or make the difference between victory and defeat.

The war's domestic impacts were as profound as its international consequences. The race to build an atomic bomb was only one part of a vast effort to harness the resources of the United States to the war effort. The war highlighted racial inequalities, gave women new opportunities, and fostered growth in

---

* Quotations from Laura Fermi, *Atoms in the Family* (Chicago: University of Chicago Press, 1954), 226, 230, 232; Laura Fermi, "The Fermis' Path to Los Alamos," in Lawrence Badash, Joseph O. Hirschfelder, and Herbert P. Broida, eds. *Reminiscences of Los Alamos, 1943-45* (Boston and Dordrecht: D. Reidel Publishing Co.), 94, 102.

the South and West. By devastating the nation's commercial rivals, compelling workers to retrain and factories to modernize, World War II left the United States dominant in the world economy. It also increased the size and scope of the federal government and built an alliance among the armed forces, big business, and science that helped shape postwar America.

KEY TOPICS

- The reluctance of most Americans to get involved in World War II
- FDR's effort to support Britain and pressure Japan despite isolationism
- The nation's strategy for a two-front war against Germany and Japan
- The roles of the different allied nations in defeating Germany
- The social and economic transformation of the United States by the war
- The beginning of the Cold War and the emergence of the United States as a superpower.

THE DILEMMAS OF NEUTRALITY

Americans in the 1930s wanted no part of another overseas war. According to a Gallup Poll in 1937, 70 percent thought that the United States had made a mistake to fight in 1917. Despite two years of German victories and a decade of Japanese aggression against China, opinion polls in the fall of 1941 showed that a majority of voters still hoped to avoid war. President Roosevelt's challenge was to lead the United States toward rearmament and support for Great Britain and China without alarming a reluctant public.

THE ROOTS OF WAR

The roots of World War II can be found in the aftereffects of World War I. The peace settlement after that war created a set of small new nations in Eastern Europe that were vulnerable to aggression from large neighbors such as Germany and the Soviet Union (officially the Union of Soviet Socialist Republics, or USSR). Italy and Japan thought that the Treaty of Versailles failed to recognize their stature as world powers. Many Germans were convinced that Germany had been betrayed rather than defeated in 1918. In the 1930s, economic crisis undermined an already shaky political order. Unemployment rose in every country and the level of international trade worldwide dropped by two thirds. Economic hardship and political instability fueled the rise of right-wing dictatorships that offered territorial expansion by military conquest as the way redress old rivalries, dominate trade, and gain access to raw materials.

Japanese internal propaganda in the 1930s stressed the need to rebuild Japan's greatness. Japanese nationalists believed that the United States, Britain, and France after World War I had treated Japan unfairly, despite its participation against Germany. They believed that Japan should expel the French, British, Dutch, and Americans from Asia and create a **Greater East Asia Co-Prosperity Sphere**, in which Japan gave the orders and other Asian peoples complied. Adding Manchuria to an East Asian empire that included Korea and Taiwan emboldened Japan's military in 1931. A full-scale invasion of China followed in 1937. Japan took many of the key cities and killed tens of thousands of civilians in the "rape of Nanking," but failed to dislodge the government of Jiang Jieshi (Chiang Kai-shek) and settled into a war of attrition.

Italian aggression embroiled Africa and the Mediterranean. The Fascist dictator Benito Mussolini had sent arms and troups to aid General Francisco Franco's right-wing rebels in Spain. The three-year civil war, which ended with Franco's victory in 1939, became a bloody testing ground for new German military tactics and German and Italian ambitions against democratic Europe.

In Germany, Adolf Hitler mixed the desire to reassert national pride and power after the defeat of World War I with an ideology of racial hatred. Coming to power by constitutional means in 1933, Hitler quickly consolidated his grip by destroying opposition parties and made himself the German Führer, or absolute leader. Proclaiming the start of a thousand-year Reich (empire), he combined the historic German interest in eastward expansion with a long tradition of

The raspy-voiced Adolf Hitler had a remarkable ability to stir the German people. He and his inner circle made skillful use of propaganda, exploiting German resentment over the country's defeat in World War I and, with carefully staged mass rallies, such as this event in 1938, inspiring an emotional conviction of national greatness.

racialist thought about German superiority. In the Nazi scheme, Germany and other northern European nations ranked above the Slavs of eastern Europe, who were to be pushed aside in order to provide more territory for a growing German population.

Special targets of Nazi hatred were Jews, who were prominent in German business and professional life but who soon faced persecution aimed at driving them from the country. In 1935, the "Nuremberg laws" denied civil rights to Jews and the campaign against them intensified. On November 9, 1938 in vicious attacks that became known as *Kristallnacht* (Night of the Broken Glass), Nazi thugs rounded up, beat, and murdered Jews, smashed property, and burned synagogues. The Nazi government began expropriating Jewish property and excluded Jews from most employment.

Germany and Italy formed the Rome-Berlin Axis in October 1936 and the Tripartite Pact with Japan in 1940, leading to the term **Axis Powers** to describe the aggressor nations. Political dissidents in all three nations had already been suppressed. Mussolini boasted of burying the "putrid corpse of liberty." Politicians in Japan feared assassination if they spoke against the army, and the Thought Police intimidated the public. Hitler's Germany, however, was the most repressive. The Nazi concentration camp began as a device for political terrorism, where socialists and other dissidents and "antisocials"—homosexuals and beggars—could be separated from "pure" Germans. In the camps, the inmates were overworked and abused.

Hitler decreed that opponents should disappear into "night and fog." After conquering Poland, Nazi officials began to force Jews to wear yellow six-pointed stars. Homosexuals had to wear a pink triangle. Soon the systematic discrimination and concentration camps would evolve into massive forced labor camps and then into hellish extermination camps.

HITLER'S WAR IN EUROPE

After annexing Austria and Czechoslovakia through diplomatic bullying and uncontested coups, Germany demonstrated the worthlessness of the Munich agreement by invading Poland on September 1, 1939. Britain and France, Poland's allies, declared war on Germany but did nothing to stop the German war machine. Western journalists covering the three-week conquest of Poland coined the term ***Blitzkrieg***, or "lightning war," to describe the German tactics. Armored divisions with tanks and motorized infantry punched quick holes in defensive positions and raced forward thirty or forty miles per day. Dive bombers blasted defenses. Portable radios coordinated the tanks, trucks, and motorcycles. Ground forces with horse-drawn artillery and supply wagons encircled the stunned defenders.

Hitler's greatest advantage was the ability to attack when and where he chose. From September 1939 to October 1941, Germany marched from victory to victory (see Map 26-1). Striking from a central position against scattered enemies, Hitler chose the targets and timing of each new front: eastward to smash Poland in September 1939; northward to capture Denmark and Norway in April and May 1940; westward to defeat the Netherlands, Belgium, and France in May and June 1940, an attack that Italy also joined; southward into the Balkans, enlisting Hungary, Romania, and Bulgaria as allies and conquering Yugoslavia and Greece in April and May 1941. Hitler also launched the Battle of Britain in the second half of 1940. German planes bombarded Britain mercilessly, in an unsuccessful effort to pound Britain into submission.

Hitler gambled once too often in June 1941. Having failed to knock Britain out of the war, he invaded the Soviet Union. The attack caught the Red Army off guard. The Nazis and Soviets had signed a nonaggression pact in 1939, and the USSR had helped to dis-

Chronology

1931 Japan invades Manchuria.

1933 Hitler takes power in Germany.

1935 Congress passes first of three Neutrality acts.

Italy invades Ethiopia.

1936 Germany and Italy form the Rome Berlin Axis.

Civil war erupts in Spain.

1937 Japan invades China.

1938 Germany absorbs Austria.

Munich agreement between Germany, Britain and France.

1939 Germany and the Soviet Union sign a nonagression pact.

Germany absorbs Czechoslovakia.

Germany invades Poland; Great Britain and France declare war on Germany.

1940 Germany conquers Denmark, Norway, Belgium, the Netherlands, and France.

Japan, Germany, and Italy sign the Tripartite Pact.

Germany bombs England in the Battle of Britain.

The United States begins to draft men into the armed forces.

Franklin Roosevelt wins an unprecedented third term.

1941 The United States begins a lend-lease program to make military equipment available to Great Britain and later the USSR.

The Fair Employment Practices Committee is established.

Germany invades the Soviet Union.

Roosevelt and Churchill issue the Atlantic Charter.

Japan attacks U.S. military bases in Hawaii.

1942 American forces in the Philippines surrender to Japan.

President Roosevelt authorizes the removal and internment of Japanese Americans living in four western states.

Naval battles in the Coral Sea and off the island of Midway blunt Japanese expansion. U.S. forces land in North Africa.

Soviet forces encircle a German army at Stalingrad.

The first sustained and controlled nuclear chain reaction takes place at the University of Chicago.

1943 U.S. and British forces invade Italy, which makes terms with the Allies.

Race conflict erupts in riots in Detroit, New York, and Los Angeles.

The landing of Marines on Tarawa initiates the island-hopping strategy.

U.S. war production peaks.

Roosevelt, Churchill, and Stalin confer at Tehran.

1944 Allied forces land in Normandy.

The U.S. Navy destroys Japanese sea power in the battles of the Philippine Sea and Leyte Gulf.

The Battle of the Bulge is the last tactical setback for the Allies.

1945 Roosevelt, Stalin, and Churchill meet at Yalta to plan the postwar world.

The United States takes the Pacific islands of Iwo Jima and Okinawa.

Franklin Roosevelt dies; Harry S Truman becomes president.

Germany surrenders to the United States, Great Britain, and the USSR.

The United Nations is organized at an international meeting in San Francisco.

Potsdam Conference

Japan surrenders after the detonation of atomic bombs over Hiroshima and Nagasaki.

---

member Poland. The Soviet dictator Joseph Stalin had disregarded warnings of a German buildup as a British attempt to goad him into war with Germany. Hitler hoped that smashing the USSR and seizing its vast resources would make Germany invincible. From June until December 1941, more than 4 million Germans, Italians, Hungarians, and Romanians pushed through Belarus, Ukraine, and western Russia. They encircled and captured entire Soviet armies. Before desperate Soviet counterattacks and a bitter winter stopped the German columns, they had reached the outskirts of Moscow and expected to finish the job in the spring.

TRYING TO KEEP OUT

"We Must Keep Out!" shouted the September 7, 1939, *Chicago Daily News*. As war erupted in Europe, most Americans wanted to avoid foreign quarrels. People who opposed intervention in the European conflict were sometimes called isolationists, but they considered themselves realists. Drawing their lessons from 1914–1918, they assumed that the same situation applied in 1939. For more than two years after the invasion of Poland, strong isolationist sentiment shaped public debate and limited President Roosevelt's ability to help Britain and its allies.

MAP 26-1   Axis Europe, 1941, on the Eve of Hitler's Invasion of the Soviet Union
After almost two years of war, the Axis powers controlled most of Europe, from the Atlantic Ocean to the Soviet border through annexation, military conquest, and alliances. Failure to force Britain to make peace caused Hitler to look eastward in 1941 to attempt the conquest of the Soviet Union.

Much of the emotional appeal of neutrality came from disillusionment with the American crusade in World War I, which had failed to make the world safe for democracy. Many opponents of intervention wanted the United States to protect its traditional spheres of interest in Latin America and the Pacific. The aviator Charles A. Lindbergh spoke for many when he argued that the best way to assure the safety of the United States was to conserve resources to defend the Western Hemisphere. Like George Washing-

ton, whose Farewell Address they quoted, they wanted to avoid becoming entangled in the perpetual quarrels of the European nations.

Congressional hearings by the Nye committee on munitions manufacturers and financiers had strengthened antiwar leanings. Between 1935 and 1937, Congress had passed five neutrality acts, which forbade arms sales and limited economic relations with nations at war. Other legislation prohibited loans to nations that had not paid their debts from World War I (including France and Great Britain). Noninterventionists spanned the political spectrum from left-leaning labor unions to such ultra-conservative business tycoons as Henry Ford, from radicals who wanted the European nations to fight themselves into exhaustion to admirers of Hitler and Mussolini. Any move to intervene in Europe had to take these different views into account, meaning that Roosevelt had to move the U.S. slowly and carefully to the side of Britain.

EDGING TOWARD INTERVENTION

Despite the Nazi triumphs, nonintervention had direct emotional appeal. The case for supporting beleaguered Britain and China, by contrast, rested on such abstract values as the worth of free societies and free markets. Still, Roosevelt's appeals to democratic values gained support in 1939 and 1940. Radio broadcasts from England describing London under German bombing heightened the sense of imperiled freedom. The importance of open markets also bolstered interventionism. As Roosevelt pointed out, "Freedom to trade is essential to our economic life. We do not eat all the food we produce; we do not burn all the oil we can pump; we do not use all the goods we can manufacture." U.S. business leaders had little doubt that Axis victories would bring economic instability and require crushing defense budgets to protect Fortress America.

Because 85 percent of the American people agreed that the nation should fight only if it was directly attacked, Roosevelt had to chip away at neutrality. The first step came in October 1939. A month-long congressional debate inspired millions of letters and telegrams in favor of keeping the arms embargo against warring nations. Nevertheless, the lawmakers reluctantly allowed arms sales to belligerent nations on a "cash-and-carry" basis, to avoid expanding European debts. In control of the Atlantic, France and Britain were the only expected customers.

Isolationism and anti-Semitism help to explain why the United States accepted only a few thousand Jewish refugees. American law strictly limited the numbers of Europeans who could enter the United States, and Congress in 1939 declined to authorize the entry outside the quotas of 20,000 Jewish children. Bureaucrats at the State Department blocked entry to "undesirables," such as left-wing opponents of Hitler, and were unsympathetic to Jewish refugees. In 1939, officials turned the passenger ship *St. Louis* away from Miami and forced its 950 German Jewish refugees back to Europe. FDR made small gestures, such as allowing fifteen thousand German and Austrian refugees, including many scientists and artists, to remain in the United States on visitor permits, but polls showed that the public supported restrictions on immigration. The

consequences of these restrictions would prove tragic later in the war, as the Nazis began systematic genocide of European Jews.

The collapse of France and U.S. rearmament.
Despite the efforts of isolationists, in 1940 the U.S. edged closed to involvement in the war. In May, the Roosevelt administration established the National Defense Advisory Commission and the Council of National Defense to deal with the strategic planning necessary to get the economy and the government prepared for war. The collapse of France in June 1940 scared Americans into rearming. The United States had a very powerful navy, but its land forces ranked only eighteenth in the world in size. However, the sudden defeat of France, which had survived four years of German attacks in World War I, made the new war seem far more serious. In the summer of 1940, Congress voted to expand the army to 2 million men, build 19,000 new war planes, and add 150 ships to the navy. Lawmakers approved the nation's first peacetime draft in September, requiring 16.5 million men between the ages of twenty-one and thirty-five to register for military service on October 16.

In the same month, the United States concluded a "destroyer deal" with Britain. The British were desperate for small, maneuverable warships to guard imports of food and war materials against German submarines. The Americans had long wanted additional air and naval bases to guard the approaches to North America. Roosevelt met both needs by trading fifty old destroyers for the use of bases on British territories in the Caribbean, Bermuda, and Newfoundland.

The election of 1940.
In the presidential election of 1940, however, foreign policy was secondary. Wendell Willkie, the Republican nominee, was a successful lawyer and utility executive who had fought the New Deal. Combining a homespun manner and a sharp mind, he differed from many in his party by sharing Roosevelt's belief in the importance of aid to Britain. The big campaign issue was therefore whether FDR's unprecedented try for a third term represented arrogance or a legitimate concern for continuity in a time of peril. The election was tighter than in 1932 or 1936, but Roosevelt received 55 percent of the vote. The president pledged that no Americans would fight in a foreign war. But if the United States were attacked, he said privately, the war would no longer be "foreign."

THE BRINK OF WAR

After the election, FDR and his advisers edged the United States toward stronger support of Britain and put pressure on Japan. In January 1941, Roosevelt proposed the "lend-lease" program, which allowed Britain to "borrow" military equipment for the duration of the war. Roosevelt compared the program to lending a garden hose to a neighbor whose house had caught fire. Senator Robert Taft of Ohio countered that it was more like lending chewing gum, since you wouldn't want it back after it was used. Behind the scheme was Britain's inability to pay for American goods. "Well, boys," their ambassador explained to a group of reporters, "Britain's broke."

The **Lend-Lease Act** triggered intense political debate. The Committee to Defend America by Aiding the Allies argued the administration's position. In opposition, the strongly isolationist America First Committee claimed that lend-lease would allow the president to declare anything a "defense article." Their spokesperson, Charles Lindbergh, protested that the United States should not surrender weapons that it might need to defend itself. Congress finally passed the measure in March 1941, authorizing the president to lease, lend, or otherwise dispose of arms and other equipment to any country whose defense was considered vital to the security of the United States. The program proved invaluable in aiding Great Britain, to which the United States extended unlimited credit, and later in assisting the Soviet Union.

FDR soon began an undeclared war in the North Atlantic, instructing the navy to report sightings of German submarines to the British. In September, the U.S. destroyer *Greer* clashed with a German submarine. The encounter allowed Roosevelt to proclaim a "shoot on sight" policy for German subs and to escort British convoys to within 400 miles of Britain. In reply, German submarines torpedoed and damaged the destroyer *Kearny* on October 17 and sank the destroyer *Reuben James,* with the loss of more than one-hundred lives, on October 30. After the attack on the *Reuben James,* Congress repealed parts of the Neutrality Act of 1939 to allow U.S. merchant ships to be armed and to carry munitions to Great Britain. The United States was now approaching outright naval war with Germany in the storm-churned waters of the Atlantic.

The Atlantic Charter.

With U.S. ships on a war footing in the North Atlantic, Roosevelt and the British prime minister, Winston Churchill, met secretly off Newfoundland in August 1941 to map out military strategy and goals for a postwar world. They agreed that the defeat of Germany was their first priority, and Japan was secondary. Their joint proclamation, known as the **Atlantic Charter**, provided a political umbrella for American involvement in the war. Echoing Woodrow Wilson, Roosevelt insisted on a commitment to op-

pose territorial change by conquest, to support self-government, to promote freedom of the seas, and to create a system of economic collaboration. Churchill signed to keep Roosevelt happy, but the document papered over sharp differences in U.S. and British expectations about the future of world trade and European colonial possessions.

Roosevelt's intent in the North Atlantic remains uncertain. Some historians think that he hoped the United States could support Britain short of war. Others believe that he accepted the inevitability of war but hesitated to outpace public opinion (the House of Representatives renewed the military draft in August 1941 by just one vote). In this second interpretation, FDR wanted to eliminate Hitler without going to war if possible, with war if necessary. "I am waiting to be pushed into the situation," he told his secretary of the treasury.

Events in the Pacific.

That final shove came in the Pacific rather than the Atlantic. In 1940, as part of its rearmament program, the United States decided to build a "two-ocean navy." This decision antagonized Japan, prodding it toward a war that most U.S. leaders hoped to postpone or avoid. Through massive investment and national sacrifice, Japan had achieved roughly 70 percent of U.S. naval strength by late 1941. However, America's buildup promised to reduce that ratio to only 30 percent by 1944. Furthermore, the United States was restricting Japan's vital imports of steel, iron ore, and aluminum in an effort to curb its military aggression. In July 1941, after Japan occupied French Indochina, Roosevelt froze Japanese assets in the United States, blocked shipments of petroleum products, and began to build up U.S. forces in the Philippines. The actions caused Japan's rulers to consider war against the United States while Japan still had a petroleum reserve. Both militarily and economically, it looked in Tokyo as if 1942 was Japan's last chance for victory.

The Japanese military made its choice in September. Unless the United States and Britain ended aid to China and acquiesced in Japanese dominance of southeast Asia—impossible conditions—war preparations would be complete in October. The Japanese General Staff defined its aims as "expelling American, Dutch, and British influences from East Asia, consolidating Japan's sphere of autonomy and security, and constructing a new order in greater East Asia." War planners never seriously considered an invasion of the United States or expected a decisive victory. They hoped that attacks on American Pacific bases would shock the United States into letting Japan have its way in Asia or at least win time to create impenetrable defenses in the central Pacific.

DECEMBER 7, 1941

Since 1941, Americans have questioned Roosevelt's foreign policy. If he wanted an excuse for war, was the torpedoing of the *Reuben James* not enough? If he wanted to preserve armed neutrality, why threaten Japan by moving the Pacific fleet from California to Hawaii in 1940 and sending B-17 bombers to the Philippines in 1941? It now seems that Roosevelt wanted to restrain the Japanese with bluff and intimidation, so that the United States could focus on Germany, since the president and his advisers were nearly certain that defeating Hitler would require the United States' entry into the war. American moves were intended to be aggressive but measured in the Atlantic, firm but defensive in the Pacific. After July, however, Washington expected a confrontation with Japan over the oil fields and rubber plantations of Southeast Asia. Because the United States cracked Japanese codes, it knew by November that Japanese military action was imminent but expected the blow to come in Southeast Asia.

Instead, the Japanese navy launched a surprise attack on American bases in Hawaii. The Japanese fleet sailed a four-thousand-mile loop through the empty North Pacific, avoiding merchant shipping and American patrols. Before dawn on December 7, 1941, six Japanese aircraft carriers launched 351 planes in two bombing strikes on Pearl Harbor.

The Japanese attack on Pearl Harbor shocked the American people. Images of burning battleships confirmed the popular image of Japan as sneaky and treacherous and stirred a desire for revenge. The attack rendered the United States incapable of resisting Japanese aggression in Southeast Asia in early 1942, but it failed to achieve its goal of destroying U.S. naval power in the Pacific.

When the smoke cleared, Americans counted their losses: eight battleships, eleven other warships, and nearly all military aircraft damaged or destroyed, and 2,403 people killed. They could also count their good fortune. Dockyards, drydocks, and oil storage tanks remained intact because the Japanese admiral had refused to order a third attack. And the American aircraft carriers, at sea on patrol, were unharmed. They proved far more important than battleships as the war developed. Within hours, the Japanese attacked U.S. bases at Guam, Wake Island, and in the Philippines.

Speaking to Congress the following day, Roosevelt proclaimed December 7, 1941, "a date which will live in infamy." He asked for and got a declaration of war against Japan. Hitler and Mussolini declared war on the United States on December 11, following their obligation under the Tripartite Pact. On January 1, 1942, the United States, Britain, the Soviet Union, and twenty-three other nations subscribed to the principles of the Atlantic Charter and pledged not to negotiate a separate peace.

HOLDING THE LINE

When Japan was considering war with the United States and Great Britain in 1940, Admiral Isoroku Yamamoto, the chief of Japan's Combined Fleet, weighed the chances of victory: "If I am told to fight regardless of the consequences, I shall run wild for the first six months or a year, but I have utterly no confidence for the second or third year." The admiral was right. Japan's armies quickly conquered most of Southeast Asia; its navy forced the United States on the defensive in the central Pacific. As it turned out, Japan's conquests reached their limit after six months, but, in early 1942, it was far from clear that such would be the case. At the same time, in Europe, Allied fortunes went from bad to worse. Again, no one knew that German and Italian gains would peak at midyear. Decisive turning points did not come until November 1942, a year after the United States had entered the war, and not until the middle of 1943 could the **Allies**–the United States, Britain, the Soviet Union, China, and other nations at war with Germany, Japan and Italy–begin with confidence to plan for victory.

STOPPING GERMANY

In December 1941, the United States plunged into a truly global war that was being fought on six distinct fronts (see Map 26–2). In North Africa, the British battled Italian and German armies that were trying to seize the Suez Canal, a critical transportation link to Asia. Along the 1,000 miles of the vast **Eastern Front**, Soviet armies held defensive positions as German forces, pushing deeply into Soviet territory, reached the outskirts of Moscow and Leningrad (St. Petersburg). In the North Atlantic, German submarines stalked merchant ships carrying supplies to Britain. In China, Japan controlled the most productive provinces but could not crush Chinese resistance, which was supported by supplies airlifted from British India over the high mountains of Burma ("the hump" to the aviators). In Southeast Asia, Japanese troops attacked the Philippines, the Dutch East Indies (now Indonesia), New Guinea, Malaya, and Burma. In the central Pacific, the Japanese fleet faced the U.S. Navy.

Despite the popular desire for revenge against Japan, the Allies had already decided to defeat Germany first. The reasoning was simple: Germany, with its huge armies, massive industrial capacity, and technological expertise, was far stronger than Japan. Defeat of Japan would not assure the defeat of Germany, especially if it crushed the Soviet Union or starved Britain into submission. By contrast, a strategy that helped the Soviets and British survive and then destroyed German military power would doom Japan.

The Eastern Front and the Battle of Stalingrad.
The strategy recognized that the Eastern Front held the key to Allied hopes. In 1941, Germany had seized control of 45 percent of the Soviet population, 47 percent of its grain production, and more than 60 percent of its coal, steel, and aluminum industries. Hitler next sought to destroy the Soviet capacity to wage war. "Our aim," said the Führer Directive No. 41, "is to wipe out the entire defense potential remaining to the Soviets, and to cut them off. . . . from their most important centers of war industry." Hitler targeted southern Russia, an area rich in grain and oil. The German thrust in 1942 was also designed to eliminate the British from the Middle East.

The scheme was easier to plot on a map than to carry out in the fields of Russia. The German offensive opened with stunning success. Every day's advance, however, stretched supply lines. Tanks ran out of fuel and spare parts. The horses that pulled German supply wagons died for lack of food.

The turning point of the war in Europe came at Stalingrad (present-day Volgograd), an industrial center on the western bank of the Volga River. After initially aiming at the city, German armies had turned south toward Russian oil fields, leaving a dangerous strongpoint on their flank that the German command decided to capture. In September and October, 1942, German, Italian, and Romanian soldiers fought their way house by house into the city. At night, the Soviets ferried their wounded across the Volga and brought in new ammunition. For both Hitler and Stalin, the

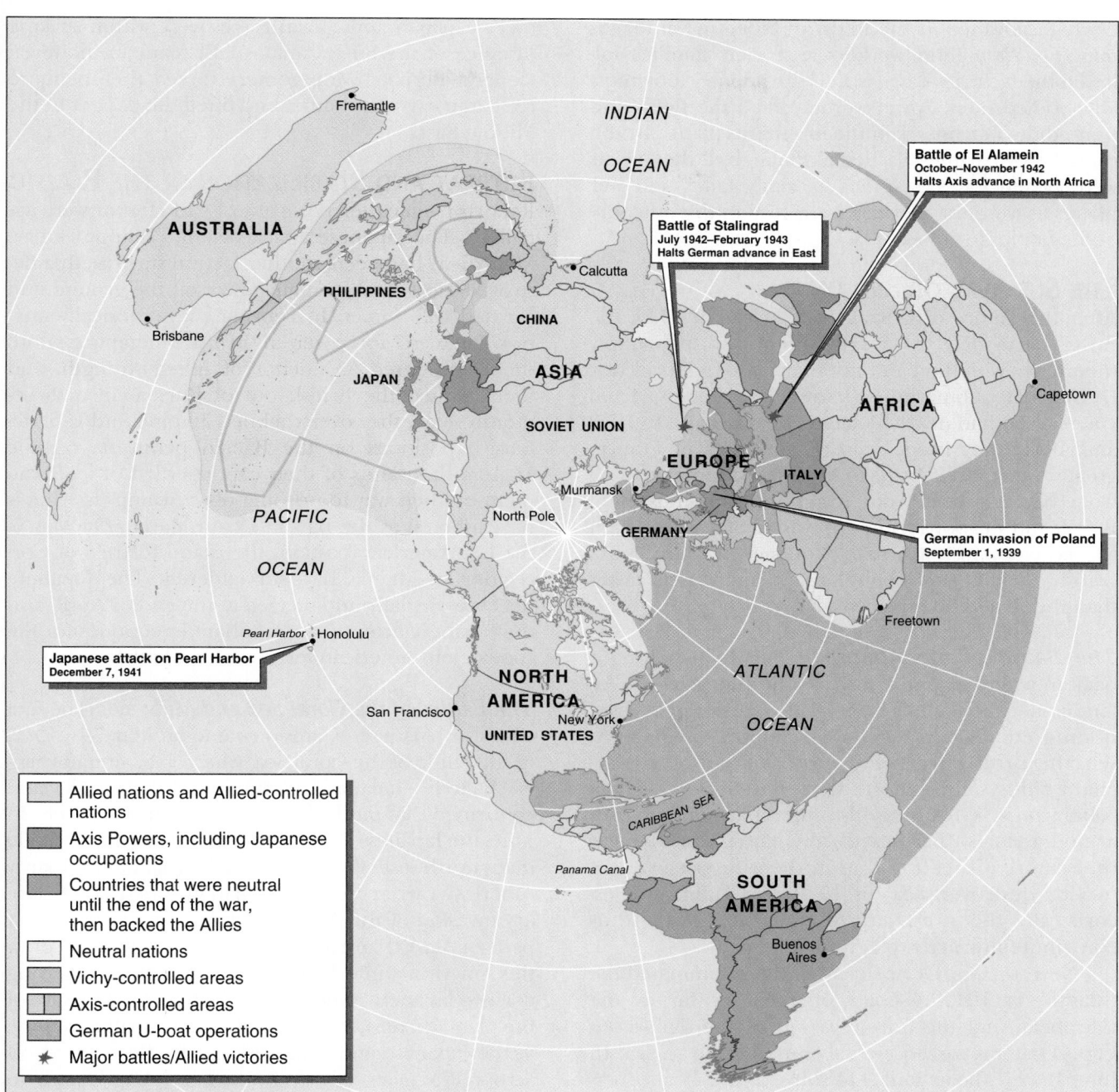

MAP 26-2   A Global War
World War II was truly a global war. As this map indicates, fighting engulfed both sides of the Eurasian continent and spread deep into the Atlantic, Pacific, and Indian oceans. The United States was the only major belligerent nation that was insulated from the battle fronts by two oceans.

city became a test of wills that outweighed even its substantial military importance.

The Red Army delivered a counterstroke on November 18 that cut off 290,000 Axis soldiers. Airlifts kept the Germans fighting for more than two additional months, but they surrendered in February 1943. This was the first German mass capitulation, and it came at immense human cost to both sides. The Soviet army suffered more deaths in this battle than the United States did in the entire war. Russians call the hills around Stalingrad "white fields" because human bones still turn up after spring thaws.

Behind the victory was an extraordinary revival of the Soviet capacity to make war. In the desperate months of 1941, the Soviets dismantled nearly 3,000 factories and rebuilt them far to the east of the

German advance in the midst of Siberian winter. As many as 25 million workers and their families followed the factories eastward. As the military took most able-bodied men, Soviet women tilled the fields and worked the machinery in the munitions plants. By the time the two armies clashed at Stalingrad, the Soviets were producing four times as many tanks and war planes as were the Germans, suggesting the outcome of the battles to come.

THE SURVIVAL OF BRITAIN

After the failure of German air attacks in 1940, the British struggled to save their empire and supply themselves with food and raw materials. In World War I, German submarines (known as U-boats, from *Unterseeboot*) had nearly isolated Great Britain. In 1940 and 1941, they tried again. From bases in France, greatly improved U-boats intercepted shipments of oil from Nigeria, beef from Argentina, minerals from Brazil, and weapons from the United States. Through the end of 1941, German "tonnage warfare" sank British, Allied, and neutral merchant vessels faster than they could be replaced.

The Battle of the Atlantic. The British fought back in what became known as the **Battle of the Atlantic**. Between 1939 and 1944, planning and rationing cut Britain's need for imports in half. At sea, the British organized protected convoys. Merchant ships sailing alone were defenseless against submarines. Grouping the merchant ships with armed escorts "hardened" the targets and made them more difficult to find in the wide ocean. Roosevelt's destroyer deal of 1940 and U.S. naval escorts in the western Atlantic in 1941 thus contributed directly to Britain's survival.

Nevertheless, German submarines dominated the Atlantic in 1942. U-boats operated as far as the Caribbean and the Carolinas, where the dangerous Cape Hatteras forced coastal shipping out to sea. In June 1942, U-boats sank 144 ships, and U-boats operating in "wolfpacks" continued to decimate convoys into 1943. The balance shifted only when Allied aircraft began to track submarines with radar, spot them with searchlights as they maneuvered to the surface, and attack them with depth charges. New sonar systems allowed escort ships to measure submarines' direction, speed, and depth. By the spring of 1943, American shipyards were also launching ships faster than the Germans could sink them

British ground fighting in 1942 centered in North Africa, where the British operated out of Egypt and the Italians and Germans from the Italian colony of Libya. By October 1942, Field Marshal Erwin Rom-

mel's German and Italian forces were within striking distance of the Suez Canal. At El Alamein, however, General Bernard Montgomery forced the enemy to retreat in early November and lifted the danger to the Middle East.

RETREAT AND STABILIZATION IN THE PACIFIC

Reports from eastern Asia after Pearl Harbor were appalling. The Japanese attack on the Philippines (see Map 26–3) had been another tactical surprise that destroyed most American air power on the ground and isolated U.S. forces. In February, a numerically inferior Japanese force seized British Singapore, until then considered an anchor of Allied strength, and then pushed the British out of Burma. In a three-month siege, they overwhelmed Filipino and U.S. defensive positions on the Bataan peninsula outside Manila; thousands of their captives died of maltreatment on their way to prisoner-of-war camps in what is remembered as the Bataan Death March. On May 6, the last American bastion, the island fortress of Corregidor in Manila Bay, surrendered. The Japanese fleet was virtually undamaged at the end of April, and the Japanese army was triumphant in conquest of European and American territories in Southeast Asia.

The Battles of the Coral Sea and Midway. The first check to Japanese expansion came on May 7–8, 1942, in the Battle of the Coral Sea, where U.S. aircraft carriers halted a Japanese advance toward Australia and confirmed that the U.S. navy could fight effectively. In June, the Japanese struck at the island of Midway, 1,500 miles northwest of Honolulu. Their goal was to destroy American carrier forces. The plan included a diversionary invasion of the Aleutian Islands (the westernmost parts of Alaska) and a main assault on Midway, to draw the Americans into battle on Japanese terms. Having cracked Japanese radio codes, U.S. forces were aware of the plan and refused the bait. On the morning of June 4, the Japanese and American carrier fleets faced off across 175 miles of ocean, each sending planes to search the other out. U.S. Navy dive bombers found the Japanese fleet and sank or crippled three aircraft carriers in five minutes; another Japanese carrier sank later in the day. The Battle of Midway ended Japanese efforts to expand in the Pacific.

MOBILIZING FOR VICTORY

News of the Japanese attack on Pearl Harbor shattered a bright Sunday afternoon. Twelve-year-old Jean Bartlett's family was headed to the movies when news of the attack came over the car radio. Elliott Johnson was eating in a Chinese restaurant in Portland, Ore-

MAP 26-3   World War II in the Pacific, from Pearl Harbor to Midway
The first six months after the Japanese attack on Pearl Harbor brought a string of Japanese victories and conquests in the Pacific, the islands southeast of Asia, and the British colonies of Malaya and Burma. Japan's advance was halted by a standoff battle in the Coral Sea, a decisive U.S. naval victory at Midway, and the length and vulnerability of Japanese supply lines to the most distant conquests.

gon, when the proprietor burst from the kitchen with a portable radio; the line was two blocks long by the time he got to the marine recruiting office. In Cincinnati, the enormously popular Andrews Sisters found that no one had shown up for their Sunday matinee concert. "Where is Pearl Harbor?" Maxine Andrews asked the theater's doorman.

War changed the lives of most Americans for the next four years and for some forever. Millions of men and women served in the armed forces and millions more worked in defense factories. In order to keep track of this staggering level of activity, the number of civilian employees of the federal government quadrupled to 3.8 million, a much greater increase than during the New Deal. Meanwhile, youngsters saved tin foil, collected scrap metal, and followed the freedom-fighting stories of Wonder Woman in the comics. College science students might be recruited to work at scientific espionage against the Nazis. The breadth of involvement in the war effort gave Americans a common purpose that softened the divisions of region, class, and national origin while calling attention to continuing inequalities of race.

ORGANIZING THE ECONOMY

The need to fight a global war brought a huge expansion of the federal government. Congress authorized the President to reorganize existing government departments and to create new agencies. The War Manpower Commission allocated workers among vital industries and the military. The War Production Board invested $17 billion for new factories and managed $181 billion in war-supply contracts, favoring large existing corporations because they had experience in large-scale production.

The Office of Price Administration (OPA) fought inflation with price controls and rationing that began with tires, sugar, and coffee and eventually included meat, butter, gasoline, and shoes. "Use it up, wear it out, make it do or do without" was the OPA's slogan. Consumers used ration cards and ration stamps to obtain scarce products. By slowing price increases, the OPA helped to convince Americans to buy the war bonds that financed half the war spending. Americans also felt the bite of the first payroll deductions for income taxes as the government secured a steady of flow of revenues and soaked up some of the high wages that would have pushed inflation. In total, the federal budget in 1945 was $98 billion, eleven times as large as in 1939, and the national debt had increased more than sixfold.

Industry had reluctantly begun to convert from consumer goods to defense production in 1940 and 1941. By the time of the attack on Pearl Harbor, 25 percent of the national economy was devoted to military needs. Although corporations hated to give up the market for toasters and automobiles just as Americans had more money, the last passenger car for the duration of the war rolled off the assembly line in February 1942. Existing factories retooled to make war equipment, and huge new facilities turned out thousands of planes and ships. Baltimore, Atlanta, Fort Worth, Los Angeles, and Seattle became centers for aircraft production. New Orleans, Portland, and the San Francisco Bay area were shipbuilding centers. Henry J. Kaiser, who had helped to build vast projects such as the Grand Coulee Dam, turned out cargo ships by the thousands. One of the Kaiser shipyards built a Liberty ship (a standard-model cargo carrier) in ten and one-half days.

The United States applied mass production technology to aircraft production at a time when Japan was still building warplanes one at a time and Germany in small batches. The most spectacular example was the new Ford plant at Willow Run, Michigan, designed to adapt assembly-line approaches to manufacturing B-24 bombers. Where the typical automobile had 15,000 parts, a B-24 had 1,550,000. The assembly line itself

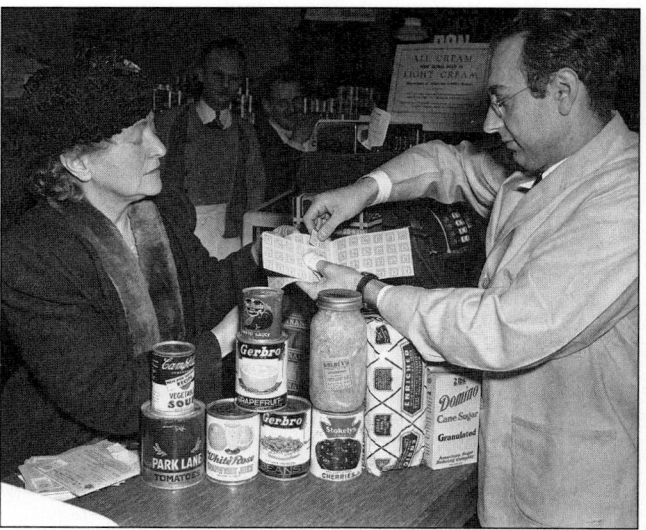

During the course of World War II, the government limited the consumption of a number of products to reserve supplies of products for the war effort and to prevent demand from pushing up the prices of scarce consumer goods. Shoppers, such as this woman at a grocery store counter, used ration stamps to obtain their share of controlled products.

was more than a mile long, starting with four separate tracks that gradually merged into one. By 1943, the plant was delivering ten planes a day. In factories all across the country, American aircraft workers were twice as productive as their German counterparts and four times more productive than Japanese.

Most defense contracts went to such established industrial states as Michigan, New York, and Ohio, but the relative impact was greatest in the South and West, where the war marked the takeoff of what Americans would later call the Sunbelt (see Map 26–4). Washington, D.C., teemed with staff officers, stenographers, and other office workers who helped to coordinate the war effort. Albuquerque, New Mexico, more than doubled in population during the 1940s. War-boom cities, such as San Diego (up 92 percent in population in the 1940s) and Mobile (up 68 percent), bustled with activity and hummed with tension. Factories operated three shifts, movies ran around the clock, and workers filled the streets after midnight.

The hordes of war workers found housing scarce. Workers in Seattle's shipyards and Boeing plants scrounged for living space in offices, tents, chicken coops, and rooming houses where "hot beds" rented in shifts. The situation was similar in small towns, such as Seneca, Illinois, home to a company that normally made river barges. Between June 1942 and June 1945, it also built 157 specialized ships to land tanks in amphibious assaults. Thousands of new workers flocked to Seneca. They lined up three deep at the bars with their Friday paychecks. Residents would sometimes find a stranger rolled up in a blanket on their front porch.

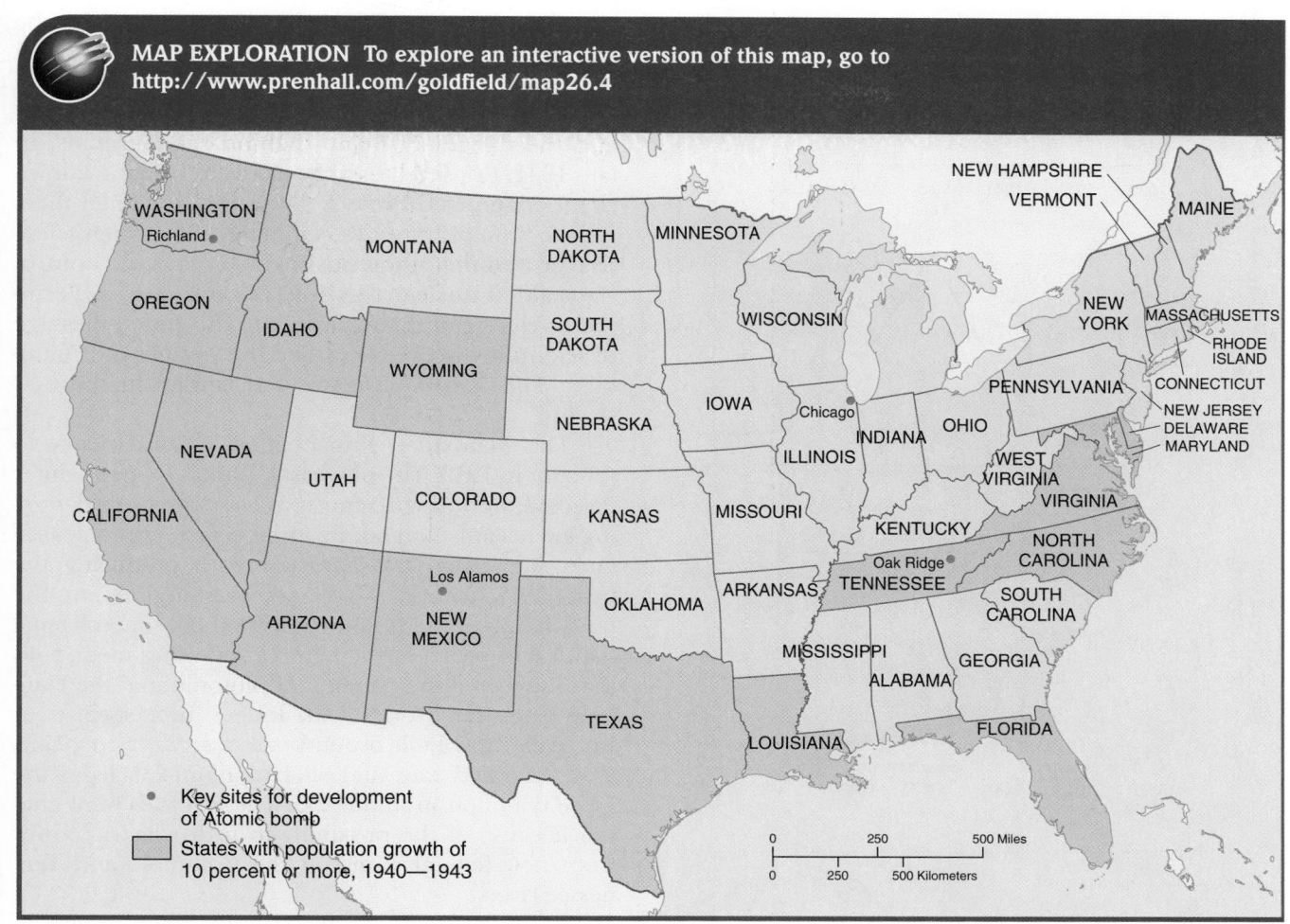

MAP EXPLORATION To explore an interactive version of this map, go to
http://www.prenhall.com/goldfield/map26.4

Key sites for development
of Atomic bomb

States with population growth of
10 percent or more, 1940—1943

MAP 26-4   **States with Population Growth of 10 Percent or More 1940–1943**
*The conversion of U.S. industry to defense production and the headlong expansion of the armed
forces pulled Americans to coastal states and cities and to the South, where the mild climate allowed year-round military training.*

The results of war production were staggering (see
Figure 26–1). One historian estimates that 40 percent
of the world's military production was coming from
the United States by 1944. Equally impressive is the 30
percent increase in the productivity of U.S. workers between 1939 and 1945. Surging farm income pulled
agriculture out of its long slump. The rich certainly got
richer, but overall per capita income doubled, and the
poorest quarter of Americans made up some of the
ground lost during the Great Depression.

THE ENLISTMENT OF SCIENCE

The war reached into scientific laboratories as well as
shops and factories. "There wasn't a physicist able to
breathe who wasn't doing war work," remembered
Professor Philip Morrison. At the center of the scientific enterprise was Vannevar Bush, former dean at the
Massachusetts Institute of Technology. As head of the
newly established Office of Scientific Research and De-

velopment, Bush guided spending to develop new
drugs, blood transfusion procedures, weapons systems,
radar, sonar, and dozens of other military technologies. The scale of research and development dwarfed
previous scientific work and set the pattern of massive
federal support for science that continued after the
war.

The most costly scientific effort was the development of radar, or radio detection and ranging devices.
Building on British research on microwaves, the
United States put $3 billion into the Radiation Labo-
ratory at MIT. Increasingly compact and sophisticated
radar systems helped to defeat the German and Japanese navies and to give the Allies control of the air over
Europe. Radar research and engineering laid the
basis for microwave technology, transistors, and integrated circuits developed after the war.

In the summer of 1945, *Time* magazine planned
a cover story on radar as the weapon that won the

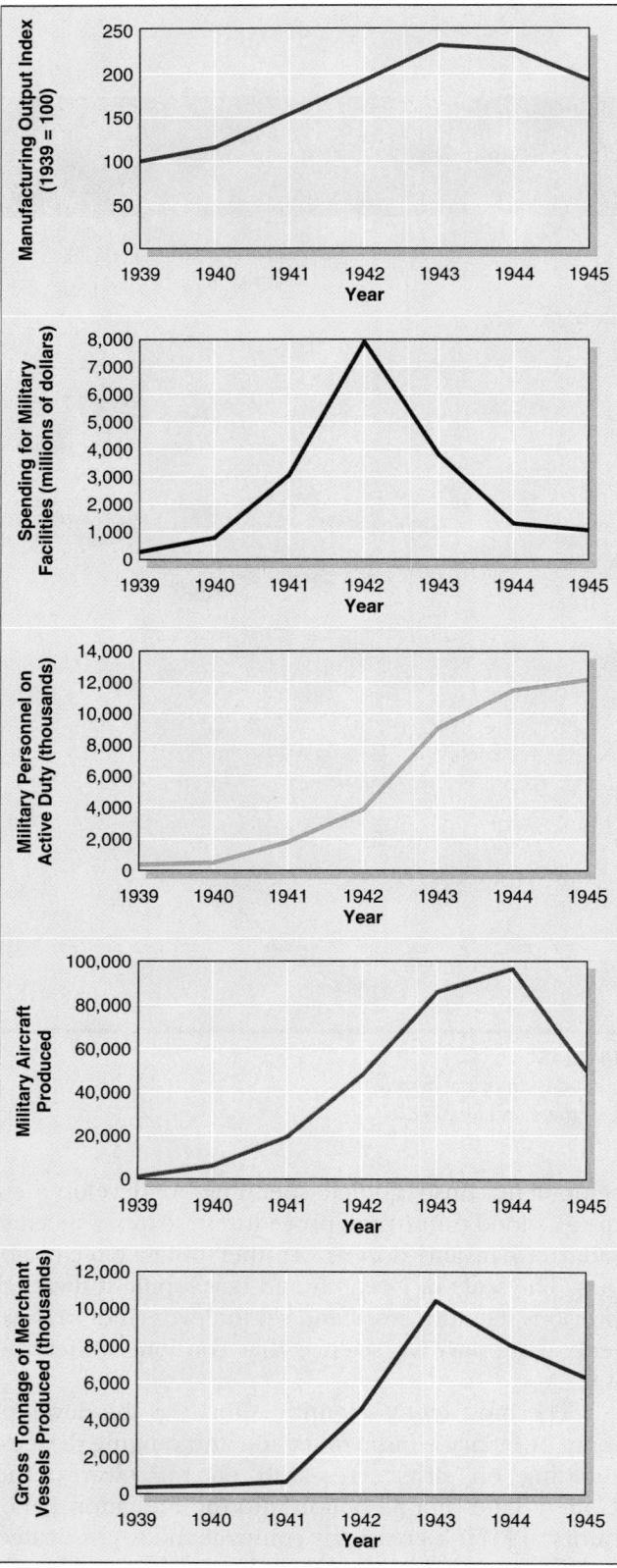

FIGURE 26-1   Making War: The United States Mobilizes, 1939-1945

The U.S. economic mobilization for World War II reached its peak in 1943, the year in which the Allies prepared for the offensives against Germany and Japan that they hoped would end the war. The number of men and women in uniform continued to grow until 1945.

war. However, the *Time* story was upstaged by the atomic bomb, the product of the war's other great scientific effort. As early as 1939, Albert Einstein had written to FDR about the possibility of such a weapon and the danger of falling behind the Germans. In late 1941, Roosevelt established what became known as the **Manhattan Project**. The work remained theoretical, however, until December 2, 1942, when scientists proved that it was possible to create and control a sustained nuclear reaction. Because Enrico Fermi was in charge of the experiment, the coded message of scientific discovery recalled the voyages of Columbus: "The Italian navigator has landed in the new world."

The Manhattan Project moved from theory to practice in 1943. The physicist J. Robert Oppenheimer directed the young scientists at Los Alamos in designing a nuclear-fission bomb. Engineers in other new science cities tried two approaches to producing the fissionable material. Richland, Washington, on the dusty banks of the Columbia River, burgeoned from a handful of peach farmers into a sprawling metropolis that supported the creation of plutonium at the Hanford Engineer Works. Oak Ridge, Tennessee, near Knoxville, was built around gaseous diffusion plants that separated rare and vital uranium-235 from the more common uranium-238. The two sites were chosen because of the proximity to hydroelectric power from new federal dams on the Columbia and Tennessee rivers.

The Manhattan Project ushered in the age of atomic energy. Plutonium from Hanford fueled the first bomb tested at the Trinity site in New Mexico on July 16, 1945. The explosion astonished even the physicists; Oppenheimer quoted from Hindu scriptures as he tried to comprehend the results: "Now I am become Death, destroyer of worlds."

MEN AND WOMEN IN THE MILITARY

World War II required a more than thirtyfold expansion of the U.S. armed forces from their 1939 level of 334,000 soldiers, sailors, and marines. By 1945, 8.3 million men and women were on active duty in the army and army air forces and 3.4 million in the navy and Marine Corps, totals exceeded only by the Soviet Union. The military establishment was four times larger than that of World War I. Once in the military, sailors and GIs served an average of thirty-three months. In total, some 350,000 women and more than 16 million men served in the armed forces; 292,000 died in battle, 100,000 survived prisoner-of-war camps, and 671,000 returned wounded.

Most of the Americans in uniform served in support jobs that kept the war machine going. They repaired airplanes and built runways, tracked supplies, and counted coffins. The poet John Ciardi wrote out commendations for valor. Bill Mauldin drew cartoons for the Army newspaper *Stars and Stripes.* But for many readers, Mauldin's cartoon GIs, Willie and Joe, came to represent the experience of the front lines. As was true in wars through history, it was loyalty to the men in their own unit that kept fighting men steady. "The only thing that kept you going was your faith in your buddies," recalled a Marine from the Pacific theater. "You couldn't let 'em down. It was stronger than flag and country."

Twenty-five thousand American Indians served in the armed forces. Most were in racially integrated units, and Harvey Natcheez, of the Ute tribe, was the first American to reach the center of conquered Berlin. Because the Navajo were one of the few tribes that had not been studied by German anthropologists, the Army Signal Corps decided that their language would be unknown to the Axis armies. More than three hundred members of the tribe were "code-talkers" who served in radio combat-communication teams in the Pacific theater, transmitting vital information in Navajo.

Approximately 1 million African Americans served in the armed forces during World War II. African American leaders had pressed for a provision in the Selective Service Act to bar discrimination "against any person on account of race or color." But as it had since the Civil War, the army organized black soldiers in segregated units and often assigned them to the more menial jobs, such as construction work, and excluded them from combat until manpower shortages forced changes in policy.

The average black soldier encountered discrimination on and off the base. Towns adjacent to army posts were sometimes open to white soldiers but off limits to blacks. At some southern bases, German prisoners of war watched movies from the first rows along with white GIs while African American soldiers watched from the back. Private Charles Wilson wrote President Roosevelt that Davis-Monthan Army Air Force Base in Tucson was color-coded: Barracks for African Americans were coated with black tar paper, and those for white soldiers sported white paint. Military courts were quick to judge and harsh to punish when black GIs were the accused. Despite the obstacles, all-black units, such as the 761st Tank Battalion and the 99th Pursuit Squadron, earned distinguished records. More broadly, the war experience helped to invigorate postwar efforts to achieve equal rights, as had also been true after World War I.

The nation had a different—but also mixed–reaction to the women who joined the armed forces as

"above and beyond the call of duty"

DORIE MILLER
Received the Navy Cross at Pearl Harbor, May 27, 1942

Dorie Miller, a mess attendant on the battleship West Virginia, *received the Navy Cross for "extraordinary courage" during the Japanese attack on Pearl Harbor. Miller helped to pull the* Arizona's *captain to safety and then manned a machine gun and shot down several Japanese planes. The War Department used Miller on recruiting posters such as this one but neglected to point out that it continued to restrict black recruits mostly to kitchen and other service jobs.*

army and navy nurses and as members of the WACS (Women's Army Corps), WAVES (Navy), SPARS (Coast Guard), and Marine Corps Women's Reserve. The armed services tried not to change established gender roles. Military officials told Congress that women in uniform could free men for combat. Many of the women hammered at typewriters, worked switchboards, inventoried supplies. Others, however, worked close to combat zones as photographers, code analysts, and nurses who tended the ill and injured. WAC officers battled the tendency of the popular press to call females in the service "girls" rather than "women" or "soldiers" yet emphasized that military service promoted "poise and charm."

The greatest departure from expected roles was the work of the 1,074 members of the Women's Air-force Service Pilots (WASPS), a civilian auxiliary of the

U.S. Army Air Forces. Many of the WASPS were women who had learned to fly as civilians. From 1942 to 1944, they ferried military aircraft across the United States, towed targets for antiaircraft practices, and tested new planes. Caro Bayley from Springfield, Ohio, lied about her height so that she could pilot B-25s and later flew high-hazard runs to test new radar systems. Nevertheless, WASPS were not allowed to carry male passengers, and the unit was dissolved when the supply of male pilots caught up with the demand.

THE HOME FRONT

The war inexorably penetrated everyday life. Residents in war-production cities had to cope with throngs of new workers. Especially in 1941 and 1942, many were unattached males—young men waiting for their draft call and older men without their families. They elbowed long-term residents in stores, snatched seats on the streetcars, and filled restaurants and theaters. Military and defense officials worried about sexually transmitted diseases and pressured cities to shut down their vice districts. At the same time, college officials scrambled to fill their classrooms, especially after the draft age dropped to 18 in 1942. Many colleges and universities responded to federal requests with special training programs for future officers and engineering and technical training for military personnel. Patricia Cain of Portland, Oregon, put off college to sign on as an electrician's helper in the shipyards. She remembered cartoons that asked; "What are you doing to help the war?" They showed women sipping tea, playing cards, and relaxing. "THIS?" And then a smiling woman worker with a lunch box, her hair tied up in a scarf, a large ship in the background, "Or THIS?"

Families in wartime. Americans put their lives on fast forward, as Judy Garland and Robert Walker did in the movie *The Clock* (1944). They played young people who meet in New York, fall in love, and are separated by the war in a matter of days. In real life, men and women often decided to beat the clock with instant matrimony. Couples who had postponed marriage because of the depression could afford to marry as the economy picked up. War intensified casual romances and heightened the appeal of marriage as an anchor in troubled times. Jewelers worried about running out of wedding rings. Altogether, the war years brought 1.2 million "extra" marriages, compared to the rate for the period 1920–1939.

The war's impact on families was gradual. The draft started with single men, then called up married men without children, and finally tapped fathers in 1943. Left at home were millions of "service wives," whose compensation from the government was $50 per month. Women who followed their husbands to stateside military posts and war factories often met cold welcomes from local residents. Harriet Arnow crafted a sensitive exploration of isolation from friends and family in her novel *The Dollmaker*, about a Kentucky farm woman who accompanied her husband to a Detroit war plant.

The war had mixed effects on children. "Latchkey children" of working mothers often had to fend for themselves, but middle-class kids whose mothers stayed home could treat the war as an interminable scout project, with salvage drives and campaigns to sell war bonds. Children in the rural Midwest picked milkweed pods to stuff life jackets; in coastal communities, they participated in blackout drills. Seattle high schools set aside one class period a day for the High School Victory Corps, training boys as messengers for air-raid wardens, while girls knitted sweaters and learned first aid. Between the end of the school day and suppertime, children listened as Captain Midnight, Jack Armstrong, and Hop Harrigan ("America's ace of the airways") fought the Nazis and Japanese on the radio.

War propaganda and censorship. The federal government tried to keep civilians of all ages committed to the war. It encouraged scrap drives and backyard victory gardens. The government also managed news about the fighting. Censors screened soldiers' letters. Early in the war, they blocked publication of most photographs of war casualties, although magazines such as *Life* were full of strong and haunting images. Worried about flagging commitment, censors later authorized photographs of enemy atrocities to motivate the public.

Government officials had a harder time controlling Hollywood. The Office of War Information wanted propaganda in feature films, but not so heavy-handed that it drove viewers from theaters. Officials told movie directors to tone down car chases because screeching tires implied wasted rubber. War films revealed the nation's racial attitudes, often drawing distinctions between "good" and "bad" Germans but uniformly portraying Japanese as subhuman and repulsive. The most successful films dramatized the courage of the Allies. *Mrs. Miniver* (1942) showed the British transcending class differences in their battle with the Nazis. *So Proudly We Hail* (1943) celebrated the heroism of navy nurses in the Pacific theater.

NEW WORKERS

As draft calls took men off the assembly line, women changed the composition of the industrial work force. The war gave them new job opportunities that were embodied in the image of Rosie the Riveter. Women made up one-quarter of West Coast shipyard workers at the peak of employment and nearly half of Dallas and Seattle aircraft workers. Most women in the shipyards were clerks and general helpers. The acute shortage of welders and other skilled workers, however, opened thousands of journeyman positions to them as well, work that was far more lucrative than waiting tables or sewing in a clothing factory. Aircraft companies, which compounded labor shortages by stubborn "whites only" hiring, developed new power tools and production techniques to accommodate the smaller average size of women workers, increasing efficiency for everyone along the production line.

Members of Women Fliers of America examine an aircraft engine. The organization had been asked by the U.S. Army to identify women with more than 200 flying hours who might ferry planes, freeing military aviators for other duties.

By July 1944, fully 19 million women held paid jobs, up 6 million in four years. Women's share of government jobs increased from 19 to 38 percent and their share of manufacturing jobs from 22 to 33 percent. Mirroring the sequence in which the military draft took men, employers recruited single women before turning to married women in 1943 and 1944. Some women worked out of patriotism. Many others, however, needed to support their families and already had years of experience in the work force. As one of the workers recalled of herself and a friend, "We both had to work, we both had children, so we became welders, and if I might say so, damn good ones."

Americans did not know how to respond to the growing numbers of working women. The country needed their labor, but many worried that their employment would undermine families. The federal government assisted female entry into the labor force by funding day-care programs that served 600,000 children. Employment recruitment posters showed strong, handsome women with rolled-up sleeves and wrenches in hand, but *Life* magazine reassured readers that women in factories could retain their sex appeal. Men and women commonly assumed that women would want to return to the home after victory; they were to work when the nation needed them and quit when the need was past.

Mexican American workers made special contributions to the war effort. As defense factories and the military absorbed workers, western farms and railroads faced an acute shortage of workers. In the 1930s, western states had tried to deport Mexican nationals who were competing for scarce jobs. In 1942, however, the U.S. and Mexico negotiated the *bracero* program, under which the Mexican government recruited workers to come to the United States on six-to-twelve month contracts. More than 200,000 Mexicans worked on U.S. farms under the program, and more than 100,000 worked for western railroads. Although *bracero* workers still faced discrimination, the U.S. government tried to improve working conditions because it wanted to keep public opinion in Latin America favorable to the Allied cause.

The war was a powerful force for the assimilation of Native Americans. Forty thousand moved to off-reservation jobs; they were a key labor force for military supply depots throughout the West. The average cash income of Indian households tripled during the war. Many stayed in cities at its end. The stress of balancing tribal life and urban America is depicted in M. Scott Momaday's 1968 novel, *House Made of Dawn*, which follows a World War II veteran as he moves between his home village in New Mexico and Los Angeles. The experience of the war accelerated the fight for full civil rights. Congress had made Indians citizens in 1924, in part to recognize their contributions in World War I, but several states continued to deny them the vote. Activists organized the National Congress of American Indians in 1944 and began the efforts that led the U.S. Supreme Court in 1948 to require states to grant voting rights.

African Americans, too, found economic advancement through war jobs. Early in the mobilization, labor leader A. Philip Randolph of the Brotherhood of Sleeping Car Porters worked with Walter White of the NAACP to plan a "Negro March on Washington" to protest racial discrimination by the federal government. To head off a major embarrassment, Roosevelt issued Executive Order 8802 in June 1941, barring racial discrimination in defense contracts and creating the **Fair Employment Practices Committee** (FEPC); the order coined a phrase that reverberated powerfully through the coming decades: "No discrimination on grounds of race, color, creed, or national origin."

The FEPC's small staff resolved fewer than half of the employment discrimination complaints, and white resistance to black coworkers remained strong. In Mobile, New Orleans, and Jacksonville, agreements between shipyards and segregated unions blocked skilled black workers from high-wage jobs. Attempts to overturn discrimination could lead to violence. When the Alabama Dry Dock Company integrated its work force in May 1943, white workers rioted. Transportation workers in Philadelphia struck the following year to protest upgrading of jobs held by black workers. Nevertheless, African American membership in labor unions doubled, and wartime prosperity raised the average black income from 41 percent of the white average in 1939 to 61 percent by 1950.

CLASHING CULTURES

As men and women migrated in search of work, they also crossed or collided with traditional boundaries of race and region. African American migration out of the South accelerated in the early 1940s. Many of the migrants headed for well-established black neighborhoods in northern cities. Others created new African American neighborhoods in western cities. White Southerners and black Northerners with different ideas of racial etiquette found themselves side by side in West Coast shipyards. In the Midwest, black migrants from the South and white migrants from Appalachia crowded into cities such as Cincinnati and Chicago, competing for the same high-wage jobs and scarce apartments.

Tensions between black and white residents exploded in at least fifty cities in 1943 alone. New York's Harlem neighborhood erupted in a riot after rumors of attacks on black servicemen. In Detroit, the issue was the boundary between white and black territories. In June 1943, an argument over the use of Detroit's Belle Isle Park set off three days of violence: Twenty-five black people and nine white people died in the most serious racial riot of the war.

Tensions were simultaneously rising between Mexican Americans and Anglos. As the Mexican community in Los Angeles swelled to an estimated 400,000, newspapers published anti-Mexican articles. On June 6, 1943, off-duty sailors and soldiers attacked Latinos on downtown streets and invaded Mexican-American neighborhoods. The main targets were so-called *pachucos*—young Chicanos who wore flamboyant "zoot suits" with long, wide-shouldered jackets and pleated, narrow-cuffed trousers, whom the rioters considered delinquents or draft dodgers. The attacks dragged on for a week of sporadic violence against black people and Filipinos as well as Latinos.

INTERNMENT OF JAPANESE AMERICANS

On February 19, 1942, President Roosevelt issued Executive Order 9066, which authorized the secretary of war to define restricted areas and remove civilian residents who were threats to national security. The primary targets were 112,000 Japanese Americans in California and parts of Washington, Oregon, and Arizona. Japanese immigrants and their children in the western states had experienced forty years of hostility because of racial prejudice, fear of the growing power of Japan, and jealousy of their economic success as farmers and business owners. The outbreak of war triggered anti-Japanese hysteria and gave officials an excuse to take action against both enemy aliens (immigrants who retained Japanese citizenship) and their American-born children. As the U.S. general commanding on the West Coast put it, "A Jap is a Jap. It makes no difference whether he is an American citizen or not."

In the months after Pearl Harbor, some West Coast Japanese managed to move to other parts of the country, but most of them were unable to leave because of ties to families and businesses. At the end of April, Japanese in the coastal states were given a week to organize their affairs and report to assembly centers at fairgrounds and armories, where they were housed for several weeks before being moved again to ten internment camps in isolated locations in the western interior (see American Views: "Internment of Japanese Americans: Life in Camp Harmony"). Here, they were housed in tar-paper barracks, hemmed in by barbed wire fences, and guarded by military police. The victims reacted to the hardship and stress in different ways. Several thousand second-generation Japanese-Americans renounced their citizenship in disgust. But many others demonstrated their loyalty by cooperating with the authorities, finding sponsors who would help

THE END OF THE NEW DEAL

Roosevelt's New Deal ran out of steam in 1938. The war had reinvigorated his political fortunes by focusing national energies on foreign policy, over which presidents have the greatest power. Especially after the 1942 election left Congress in the hands of Republicans and conservative southern Democrats, lawmakers followed the new tack. Conservative lawmakers ignored proposals that war emergency housing be used to improve the nation's permanent housing stock, abolished the National Resources Planning Board, curtailed rural electrification, and crippled the Farm Security Administration. Roosevelt himself declared that "Dr.-Win-the-War" had replaced "Dr. New Deal" at a 1943 press conference.

In 1942, the federal government removed Japanese Americans from parts of four western states and interned them in isolated camps scattered through the West.

them move to other parts of the country, or joining the 442nd Regimental Combat Team, the most decorated American unit in the European war.

Although the U.S. Supreme Court sanctioned the removals in *Korematsu v. United States* (1944), the nation officially recognized its liability with the Japanese Claims Act of 1948, for many internees had lost property that they had been powerless to protect. The nation acknowledged its broader moral responsibility in 1988, when Congress approved redress payments to each of the sixty thousand surviving evacuees.

The internment of West Coast Japanese contrasted with the treatment of Japanese Americans by the military government of Hawaii. Despite the greater threat that Japan posed to Hawaii than to California, local residents and officials avoided panic. Hawaii's long history as a multiethnic society made residents disinclined to look for a racial scapegoat. Less than 1 percent of Hawaii's Japanese American population of 160,000 was interned. The treatment of mainland Japanese Americans also contrasted with the situation of German Americans and Italian Americans. The government interned approximately 11,000 German nationals and German Americans who were explicitly seen as individual threats. Until November 1942, it imposed curfews and travel restrictions on Italians and Italian Americans on the West Coast, but it interned fewer than 2,000. Both numbers were tiny fractions of the total populations.

The presidential election of 1944 raised few new issues of substance. The Republicans nominated Governor Thomas Dewey of New York, who had made his reputation as a crime-fighting district attorney. The Democrats renominated Roosevelt for a fourth term. Missouri Senator Harry S Truman, a tough investigator of American military preparedness, replaced liberal New Dealer Henry Wallace as Roosevelt's running mate. The move appeased southern Democrats and moved the ticket toward the political center.

The most important issue was a fourth term for Roosevelt. Supporters argued that the nation could not afford to switch leaders in the middle of a war, but Dewey's vigor and relative youth (he was twenty years younger than FDR) pointed up the president's failing health and energy. Voters gave Roosevelt 432 electoral votes to 99, but the narrowing gap in the popular vote—54 percent for Roosevelt and 46 percent for Dewey—made the Republicans eager for 1948.

WAR AND PEACE

In January 1943, the U.S. War Department completed the world's largest office building, the Pentagon. The building housed 23,000 workers along 17.5 miles of corridors. It took three hundred telephone operators to direct the calls that came into the single Pentagon phone number for Secretary of War Henry Stimson, General George C. Marshall, and their thousands of

AMERICAN VIEWS

The Internment of Japanese Americans in 1942

In the spring of 1942, the U.S. army ordered that Japanese Americans in four western states be relocated to internment camps distant from the Pacific Coast. Monica Itoe Stone describes the experience of her Seattle family as they were transferred to temporary quarters—at the state fairgrounds renamed "Camp Harmony" by the military—before they were moved again to Idaho.

- How do the expectations of *issei* (immigrants who had been born in Japan) differ from those of *nisei* (their American-born children, including the author of this memoir)?
- Why did the U.S. army wait five months after Pearl Harbor before beginning the internment?
- Does the management of the assembly and internment suggest anything about stereotypes of Japanese Americans?

General DeWitt kept reminding us that E day, evacuation day, was drawing near. "E day will be announced in the very near future. If you have not wound up your affairs by now, it will soon be too late."

. . . On the twenty-first of April, a Tuesday, the general gave us the shattering news. "All the Seattle Japanese will be moved to Puyallup by May 1. Everyone must be registered Saturday and Sunday between 8 A.M. and 5 P.M.

Up to that moment, we had hoped against hope that something or someone would intervene for us. Now there was no time for moaning. A thousand and one details must be attended to in this one week of grace. Those seven days sputtered out like matches struck in the wind, as we rushed wildly about. Mother distributed sheets, pillowcases and blankets, which we stuffed into seabags. Into the two suitcases, we packed heavy winter overcoats, plenty of sweaters, woolen slacks and skirts, flannel pajamas and scarves. Personal toilet articles, one tin plate, tin cup and silverware completed our luggage. The one seabag and two suitcases apiece were going to be the backbone of our future home, and we planned it carefully.

Henry went to the Control Station to register the family. He came home with twenty tags, all numbered "10710," tags to be attached to each piece of baggage, and one to hang from our coat lapels. From then on, we were known as Family #10710.

[On the day set for relocation] we climbed into the truck. . . . As we coasted down Beacon Hill bridge for the last time, we fell silent, and stared out at the delicately flushed, morning

---

subordinates. The building provided the space in which military planners could coordinate the tasks of raising and equipping the armed forces that would strike directly at Germany and Japan. Indeed, while Congress was chipping away at federal programs, the war effort was massively expanding the government presence in American life. The gray walls of the Pentagon symbolized an American government that was outgrowing its prewar roots.

TURNING THE TIDE IN EUROPE

The unanswered military question of 1942 and 1943 was when the United States and Britain would open a second front against Germany by attacking across the English Channel. U.S. leaders wanted to justify massive mobilization with a war-winning campaign and to strike across Europe to occupy the heart of Germany. Stalin needed a full-scale invasion of western Europe to divert German forces from the Eastern Front,

THE AMERICAN JOURNEY
THIRD EDITION

GET THE BOOK THAT **GETS YOUR STUDENTS.**

AMERICAN VIEWS

The Internment of Japanese Americans in 1942

In the spring of 1942, the U.S. army ordered that Japanese Americans in four western states be relocated to internment camps distant from the Pacific Coast. Monica Itoe Stone describes the experience of her Seattle family as they were transferred to temporary quarters—at the state fairgrounds renamed "Camp Harmony" by the military—before they were moved again to Idaho.

- How do the expectations of *issei* (immigrants who had been born in Japan) differ from those of *nisei* (their American-born children, including the author of this memoir)?
- Why did the U.S. army wait five months after Pearl Harbor before beginning the internment?
- Does the management of the assembly and internment suggest anything about stereotypes of Japanese Americans?

General DeWitt kept reminding us that E day, evacuation day, was drawing near. "E day will be announced in the very near future. If [not we]... your affairs...

which we stuffed into seabags. Into the two suitcases, we packed heavy winter overcoats, plenty of sweaters, woolen slacks and skirts, flannel pa[jamas and scarves]...

GET THE BEST DOCUMENTS:
American Views

Understanding history means interpreting it from the perspectives of many people. What better way to offer students an interesting perspective than by integrating primary source documents throughout the text?

Each chapter of **THE AMERICAN JOURNEY, THIRD EDITION** contains an *American Views* box spotlighting a primary source document that is relevant to the chapter's content. These accounts of the American journey provide a valuable record of the American story designed to serve as a springboard for your students, connecting them to the rich heritage that is our nation's past.

Taken from letters, diaries, newspapers, government papers, and various written sources, these features bring the people of the past and their concerns vividly alive. An introduction and critical thinking questions relate the documents to the text and direct students' attention to important issues. In this example we learn from Monica Itoi Stone, in an excerpt from NISEI DAUGHTER, what it was like when her family was relocated from their home in Seattle, Washington to Idaho during the Japanese-American Internment that began in 1942 during World War II. *Other examples may be found on pages 306, 446, 672, 798, 872, and 944.*

Take a moment to look at *American Views*, and see how integrating primary source material into the text will help to impart authenticity and real, balanced perspective into your students' study of American history. Get Goldfield—and get your students the best documents.

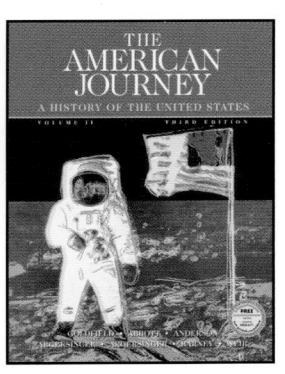

GET THE BOOK THAT GETS YOUR STUDENTS.

The authors of THE AMERICAN JOURNEY, THIRD EDITION **take educating students very seriously.** Every aspect of this new edition is geared towards providing the most important scholarship, as well as the best tools to ensure your students have a positive experience with our textbook, regardless of their individual learning style.

In addition, Prentice Hall believes in providing you with the most flexibility and your students with the most value for their investment. Therefore, we are offering THE AMERICAN JOURNEY, THIRD EDITION in a variety of options to serve your teaching needs, plus a selection of value packages designed to satisfy your students' budget concerns. In every way, THE AMERICAN JOURNEY is the book that gets your students.

GET THE BEST TEXT

- **The Best Pedagogy: Student Tool Kit** *(refer to tab 1 in this text)*
- **The Best Drama:** *Voices from the American Journey (refer to tab 2 in this text)*
- **The Best Maps:** *Map Explorations (refer to tab 3 in this text)*
- **The Best Presentation: Overviews and 3-Level Heads** *(refer to tab 4 in this text)*
- **The Best Relevance:** *From Then To Now (refer to tab 5 in this text)*
- **The Best Documents:** *American Views (refer to tab 6 in this text)*

GET THE BEST OPTIONS

THE AMERICAN JOURNEY: A HISTORY OF THE UNITED STATES, THIRD EDITION is available in the following formats, all of which include the FREE, exclusive **U.S. History Documents CD-ROM** from Prentice Hall:

- *Combined Edition—includes Chapters 1-31:* 0-13-182553-4
- *Volume 1—includes Chapters 1-15:* 0-13-182552-6
- *Volume 2—includes Chapters 16-31:* 0-13-182550-X

THE AMERICAN JOURNEY is also available in a convenient Brief Edition.

GET THE BEST PACKAGES

Take advantage of these SPECIAL VALUE PACKAGES available with new copies of THE AMERICAN JOURNEY, THIRD EDITION by Goldfield, et al. Get your students these great savings when your bookstore uses the corresponding package ISBNs below:

- **Combined Edition:**
  —*with FREE Study Guide/Practice Test:* 0-13-130271-X
  —*with FREE Common Sense by Thomas Paine AND The Jungle by Upton Sinclair: 0-13-130272-8*

- **Volume I:**
  —*with FREE Study Guide/Practice Test:* 0-13-130273-6
  —*with FREE Common Sense by Thomas Paine: 0-13-130274-4*

- **Volume II:**
  —*with FREE Study Guide/Practice Test:* 0-13-130275-2
  —*with FREE The Jungle by Upton Sinclair: 0-13-130276-0*

Additional FREE Value Packages are available. For details, please contact your local Prentice Hall sales representative.

PRENTICE HALL HISTORY
Connecting the past with the future
www.prenhall.com/history

sky of Puget Sound. We drove through bustling Chinatown, and in a few minutes arrived on the corner of Eighth and Lane. This area was ordinarily lonely and deserted but now it was gradually filling up with silent, labeled Japanese. . . .

Finally at ten o'clock, a vanguard of Greyhound busses purred in and parked themselves neatly along the curb. The crowd stirred and murmured. The bus doors opened and from each, a soldier with rifle in hand stepped out and stood stiffly at attention by the door. The murmuring died. It was the first time I had seen a rifle at such close range and I felt uncomfortable. . . .

Newspaper photographers with flash-bulb cameras pushed busily through the crowd. One of them rushed up to our bus, and asked a young couple and their little boy to step out and stand by the door for a shot. They were reluctant, but the photographers were persistent and at length they got out of the bus and posed, grinning widely to cover their embarrassment. We saw the picture in the newspaper shortly after and the caption underneath it read, "japs good-natured about evacuation."

Our bus quickly filled to capacity. . . . The door closed with a low hiss. We were now the Wartime Civil Control Administration's babies.

About noon we crept into a small town. . . . and we noticed at the left of us an entire block filled with neat rows of low shacks, resembling chicken houses. Someone commented on it with awe, "Just look at those chicken houses. They sure go in for poultry in a big way here." Slowly the bus made a left turn, drove through a wire-fenced gate, and to our dismay, we were inside the oversized chicken farm. . . .

The apartments resembled elongated, low stables about two blocks long. Our home was one room, about 18 by 20 feet, the size of a living room. There was one small window in the wall opposite the one door. It was bare except for a small, tinny wood-burning stove crouching in the center. The flooring consisted of two by fours laid directly on the earth, and dandelions were already pushing their way up through the cracks. . . .

I stared at our little window, unable to sleep. I was glad Mother had put up a makeshift curtain on the window for I noticed a powerful beam of light sweeping across it every few seconds. The lights came from high towers placed around the camp where guards with Tommy guns kept a twenty-four hour vigil. I remembered the wire fence encircling us, and a knot of anger tightened in my breast. What was I doing behind a fence like a criminal? If there were accusations to be made, why hadn't I been given a fair trial? Maybe I wasn't considered an American anymore. My citizenship wasn't real, after all. Then what was I? I was certainly not a citizen of Japan as my parents were. On second thought, even Father and Mother. . . . had little tie with their mother country. In their twenty-five years in America, they had worked and paid their taxes to their adopted government as any other citizen.

Of one thing I was sure. The wire fence was real. I no longer had the right to walk out of it. It was because I had Japanese ancestors. It was also because some people had little faith in the ideas and ideals of democracy.

Source: Monica Itoi Sone, *Nisei Daughter* (Seattle: University of Washington Press, 1979).

where Soviet troops were inflicting 90 percent of German battle casualties.

The Allies spent 1943 hammering out war aims and strategies. Meeting in Casablanca in January 1943, Roosevelt and Churchill demanded the "unconditional surrender" of Italy, Germany, and Japan. The phrase meant that there would be no deals that kept the enemy governments or leaders in power and was an effort to avoid the mistake of ending World War I

with Germany itself intact. Ten months later, the Allied leaders huddled again. Roosevelt and Churchill met with China's Jiang in Cairo and then flew on to meet Stalin in Tehran. Jiang and Stalin could not meet directly because the Soviet Union was neutral in the East Asian war. At Tehran, the United States and Britain promised to invade France within six months. "We leave here," said the three leaders, "friends in fact, in spirit, in purpose."

The superficial harmony barely survived the end of the war. The Soviets had shouldered the brunt of the war for nearly two-and-a-half years, suffering millions of casualties and seeing their nation devastated. Stalin and his generals scoffed at the small scale of early U.S. efforts. Roosevelt's ideal of self-determination for all peoples, embodied in the Atlantic Charter, seemed naive to Churchill, who wanted the major powers to carve out realistic spheres of influence in Europe. It was irrelevant to Stalin, who wanted control of eastern Europe.

The campaign in North Africa.
The United States entered the ground war in Europe with Operation TORCH. Soon after the British victory at El Alamein, British and American troops under General Dwight Eisenhower landed in French Morocco and Algeria on November 8, 1942, against little opposition. (see Map 26–5). These were territories that the Germans had left under a puppet French government after the French military collapsed in 1940. Despite the easy landings (French officials in Africa quickly switched sides), German troops that remained in North Africa taught U.S. forces hard lessons in tactics and leadership, but their stubborn resistance ended in May 1943, leaving all of Africa in Allied hands.

Eisenhower had already demonstrated his ability to handle the politics of military leadership, skills he perfected commanding a multinational army for the next two and one-half years. He also chose the right subordinates, giving operational command to Generals Omar Bradley and George Patton. Bradley was low-keyed and rock solid; to relax he worked algebra and calculus problems. Patton was a much flashier figure (he wore a pearl-handled revolver), with a mighty ego and a fierce commitment to victory.

The invasion of Italy.
The central Mediterranean remained the focus of U.S. and British action for the next year. The British feared military disaster from a premature landing in western Europe and proposed strikes in southern Europe, which Churchill inaccurately called the "soft underbelly" of Hitler's empire. U.S. Army Chief of Staff George Marshall and President Roosevelt agreed to invade Italy in 1943, in part so that U.S. troops could participate in the ground fighting in Europe. Allied forces overran Sicily in July and August, but the Italian mainland proved more difficult. When Sicily fell, the Italian king and army forced Mussolini from power and began to negotiate peace with Britain and America (but not the Soviet Union). In September, the Allies announced an armistice with Italy, and Eisenhower's troops landed south of Naples. Germany responded by occupying the rest of Italy.

Just as American military planners had feared, the Italian campaign soaked up Allied resources. The mountainous Italian peninsula was one long series of defensive positions, and the Allies repeatedly bogged down. Week after week, the experience of GIs on the line was the same: "You wake up in the mud and your cigarettes are all wet and you have an ache in your joints and a rattle in your chest." Despite months of bitter fighting, the Allies controlled only two-thirds of Italy when the war there ended on May 1, 1945.

Soviet advances and the Battle of Kursk.
Meanwhile, the Soviets recruited, rearmed, and upgraded new armies, despite enormous losses. They learned to outfight the Germans in tank warfare and rebuilt munitions factories beyond German reach. They also made good use of 17.5 million tons of U.S. lend-lease assistance. As Soviet soldiers recaptured western Russia and the Ukraine, they marched in 13 million pairs of American-made boots and ate U.S. rations (they called cans of Spam "second fronts"). They traveled in 78,000 jeeps and 350,000 Studebaker, Ford, and Dodge trucks. "Just imagine how we could have advanced from Stalingrad to Berlin without [lend-lease vehicles]," future Soviet Premier Nikita Khrushchev later commented.

The climactic battle of the German-Soviet war erupted on July 5, 1943. The Germans sent three thousand tanks against the Kursk Salient, a huge wedge that the Red Army had pushed into their lines. In 1941 and 1942, such a massive attack would have forced the Soviets to retreat, but now Soviet generals had prepared a defense in depth with three thousand tanks of their own. With 1 million men actively engaged on each side for more than two weeks, Kursk was the largest pitched battle of the war. It was a huge failure for Germany and marked the end of the last great German offensive, leaving Germany capable of a fighting retreat but too weak to have any hope of winning the war and expecting an American and British attack across the English Channel.

OPERATION OVERLORD
On **D-Day**—June 6, 1944—the western Allies landed on the coast of Normandy in northwestern France. Six divisions went ashore from hundreds of attack transports carrying four thousand landing craft, as vividly dramatized in the film *Saving Private Ryan*. Dozens of warships and twelve thousand aircraft provided support. One British and two American airborne divisions dropped behind German positions. When the sun set on the "longest day," the Allies had a tenuous toehold in France.

MAP EXPLORATION To explore an interactive version of this map, go to
http://www.prenhall.com/goldfield/map26.5

MAP 26-5   **World War II in Europe, 1942-1945**

*Nazi Germany had to defend its conquests on three fronts. Around the Mediterranean,
American and British forces pushed the Germans out of Africa and southern Italy, while
guerrillas in Yugoslavia pinned down many German troops. On the Eastern Front, Soviet
armies advanced hundreds of miles to drive the German Army out of the Soviet Union and
eastern Europe. In June 1944, U.S. and British landings opened the Western Front in northern
France for a decisive strike at the heart of Germany.*

Americans had been waiting for the news. In Montgomery, Alabama, word of the invasion spread quickly by radio and then by extra editions of the newspaper. Flags appeared along the streets and traffic halted at 5:00 P.M. for buglers from nearby bases and the high school to sound the "call to the colors." At 6:00 P.M. all movie projectors were stopped to allow time for prayer.

The next few weeks brought limited success. The Allies secured their beachheads and poured more than a million men and hundreds of thousands of vehicles ashore in the first six weeks. However, the German defenders kept them pinned along a narrow coastal strip. **Operation OVERLORD**, the code name for the entire campaign across northern France, met renewed success in late July and August. U.S. troops improved their fighting skills through "experience, sheer bloody experience." They finally broke through German lines around the town of St.-Lô and then drew a ring around the Germans that slowly closed on the town of Falaise. The Germans lost a quarter of a million troops.

The German command chose to regroup closer to Germany rather than fight in France. The Allies liberated Paris on August 25; Free French forces (units that had never surrendered to the Nazis) led the entry. The drive toward Germany was the largest U.S. operation of the war. The only impediments appeared to be winter weather and getting enough supplies to the rapidly advancing armies.

The story was similar on the Eastern Front, where the Soviets relentlessly battered one section of the German lines after another. By the end of 1944, the Red Army had entered the Balkans and reached central Poland. With the end in sight, the Soviets had suffered as many as 27 million military and civilian deaths and sustained by far the heaviest burden in turning back Nazi tyranny (see Table 26-1).

VICTORY AND TRAGEDY IN EUROPE

In the last months of 1944, massive air strikes finally reduced German war production, which had actually increased during 1943 and much of 1944. The Americans flew daylight raids from air bases in Britain with heavily armed B-17s ("Flying Fortresses") and B-24s, ("Libera-

American, British, and Canadian forces opened the long-awaited "second front" against Germany on June 6, 1944—D-Day—when tens of thousands of troops landed on the coast of Normandy in France. The landings were the largest amphibious operation ever staged. Although the Germans had expected the landings further north, their defenses pinned the Allies to a narrow beachhead for several weeks.

tors") to destroy factories with precision bombing. On August 17, 1943, however, Germans shot down or damaged 19 percent of the bombers that attacked the aircraft factories of Regensburg and the ball-bearing factories of Schweinfurt. Air crews who were expected to fly dozens of missions could count the odds, and the Americans had to seek easier targets.

Gradually, however, the balance shifted. The new American P-51 escort fighter helped B-17s overfly Germany in relative safety after mid-1944. Thousand-bomber raids on railroads and oil facilities began to cripple the German economy. The raids forced Germany to devote 2.5 million workers to air defense and damage repair and to divert fighter planes from the front lines. The air raids cut German military production by one-third through 1944, destroyed the transportation system, and left Germany a set of isolated regions living off stockpiles of food and raw materials. Politics, rather than military need, governed the final great action of the European air war. British and U.S. bombers in February 1945 staged a terror raid on the nonindustrial city of Dresden, packed with refugees, filled with great art, and undefended by the Germans; a firestorm fueled by incendiary bombs and rubble from blasted buildings killed tens of thousands of civilians.

Out of the bombing raids that pitted pilots and crews against unseen enemies would come some of the most vivid efforts to relive and comprehend the

TABLE 26.1	
Military and Civilian Deaths in World War II	
Nation	**Victims (millions)**
USSR	27
China	10-20
Germany and Austria	6
Poland	6
Japan	2.7
Yugoslavia	1.7
Romania	0.7
France	0.6
Great Britain	0.5
Hungary	0.5
Italy	0.4
Czechoslovakia	0.4
United States	0.3

experience of war. The movie *Twelve O'Clock High* (1949) focused on successive commanders of a U.S. bomber unit in Britain who became too involved with their men to function effectively. The literature of the bomber campaigns included anti-war novels like Joseph Heller's *Catch-22* (1961).

The Battle of the Bulge and the collapse of Germany.

Even as the air bombardment intensified, Hitler struck a last blow. Stripping the Eastern Front of armored units, he launched twenty-five divisions against thinly held U.S. positions in the Ardennes Forest of Belgium on December 16, 1944. He hoped to split U.S. and British forces by capturing the Belgian port of Antwerp. The attack surprised the Americans, who had treated the Ardennes as a "ghost front," where nothing was going on. Taking advantage of snow and fog that grounded Allied aircraft, the Germans drove a 50-mile bulge into U.S. lines. Although

Americans took substantial casualties, the German thrust literally ran out of gas beyond the town of Bastogne. The Battle of the Bulge never seriously threatened the outcome of the war, but pushing the Germans back through the snow-filled forest gave GIs a taste of the conditions that had marked the war in the Soviet Union.

The Nazi empire collapsed in the spring of 1945. American and British divisions crossed the Rhine in March and enveloped Germany's industrial core. The Soviets drove through eastern Germany toward Berlin. On April 25, American and Soviet Army troops met on the Elbe River. Hitler committed suicide on April 30 in his concrete bunker deep under devastated Berlin, which surrendered to the Soviets on May 2. The Nazi state formally capitulated on May 8.

The Holocaust.

The defeat of Germany revealed appalling evidence of the evil at the heart of the Nazi ideology of racial superiority. After occupying Poland in 1939, the Nazis also expanded concentration camps into forced-labor camps, where overwork, starvation, and disease killed hundreds of thousands of Jews, Gypsies, Poles, Russians, and others the Nazis classed as subhuman. As many as 7 million labor conscripts from both eastern and western Europe provided forced labor in fields, factories, mines, and repair crews, often dying on the job from overwork and starvation.

The "final solution" to what Hitler thought of as the "Jewish problem" went far beyond slave labor. The

Jewish residents of Cracow, Poland, boarding cattle cars under the eye of the German SS; their destination would be one of the extermination camps where Germans systematically killed millions of people.

The Nazi regime sent slave laborers who were too weak to continue working on its V-2 rocket projects to the Nordhausen concentration camp to die of starvation. When U.S. troops liberated the camp in April 1945, they found more than three thousand corpses.

German army in 1941 had gained practice with death by slaughtering hundred of thousands of Jews and other civilians as it swept across Russia. In the fall of that year, Hitler decided on the total elimination of Europe's Jews. The elite SS, Hitler's personal army within the Nazi party, in 1942 set out to do his bidding. At Auschwitz, Treblinka, and several other death camps, the SS organized the efficient extermination of up to 6 million Jews and 1 million Poles, Gypsies, and others who failed to fit the Nazi vision of the German master race. Prisoners arrived by forced marches and cattle trains. Those who were not worked or starved to death were herded into gas chambers and then incinerated in huge crematoriums.

The evidence of genocide—systematic racial murder—is irrefutable. Allied officials had begun to hear reports of mass murder midway through the war, but inaccurate propaganda about German atrocities in World War I made many skeptical. Moreover, the camps were located in the heart of German controlled territory that Allied armies did not reach until 1945. At Dachau in southwestern Germany, American forces found 10,000 bodies and 32,000 prisoners near death through starvation. Soviet troops that overran the camps in Poland found even more appalling sights–gas chambers as big as barns, huge ovens, the dead stacked like firewood. For more than half a century, the genocide that we now call the **Holocaust** has

given the world its most vivid images of inhumanity.

THE PACIFIC WAR

In the Pacific, as in Europe, the United States used 1943 to probe enemy conquests and to build better submarines, bigger aircraft carriers, and superior planes. Washington divided responsibilities in the Pacific theater. General Douglas MacArthur operated in the islands that stretched between Australia and the Philippines. Admiral Chester Nimitz commanded in the central Pacific. The Allies planned to isolate Japan from its southern conquests. The British moved from India to retake Burma. The Americans advanced along the islands of the southern Pacific to retake the Philippines. With Japan's army still tied down in China, the Americans then planned to bomb Japan into submission.

Racial hatred animated both sides in the Pacific war and fueled a "war without mercy." Americans often characterized Japanese soldiers as vermin. Political cartoons showed Japanese as monkeys or rats, and some Marines had "Rodent Exterminator" stenciled on their helmets. In turn, the Japanese depicted themselves as the "leading race" with the duty to direct the rest of Asia. Japan treated Chinese, Filipinos, and other conquered peoples with contempt and brutality, and the record of Japanese atrocities is substantial. Japanese viewed Americans as racial mongrels and called them demons. Each side expected the worst of the other and frequently lived up to expectations.

The Pacific campaigns of 1944 are often called **island hopping**. Planes from American carriers controlled the air, allowing the navy and land forces to isolate and capture the most strategically located Japanese-held islands while bypassing the rest. The process started in November 1943, when Marines took Tarawa (see Map 26–6). It worked to perfection with the assault on Saipan in June 1944. When the Japanese fleet challenged the attack, U.S. Navy flyers destroyed three aircraft carriers and hundreds of planes.

MacArthur used a version of the bypass strategy in the Solomon Islands and New Guinea, leapfrogging over Japanese strong points. The invasion of the Philippines repeated the approach by landing on

MAP 26-6   World War II in the Pacific, 1942-1945
The Allied strategy against Japan was to cut off Japan's southern conquests by retaking the central Pacific islands, the Philippines, and Burma and then to strike at the Japanese home islands. Submarine warfare and massive air attacks from November 1944 to August 1945 crippled Japan's capacity to wage war. The detonation of atomic bombs over Hiroshima and Nagasaki then forced surrender on August 15, 1945.

Leyte, in the middle of the island chain. The Philippine campaign also destroyed the last offensive capacity of the Japanese fleet. In the Battle of Leyte Gulf, the U.S. military sank four Japanese battleships, four carriers, and ten cruisers. The Japanese home islands were left with no defensive screen against an expected invasion.

During 1943 and 1944, the United States also savaged the Japanese economy. Submarines choked off food, oil, and raw materials bound for Japan and island bases. By 1945, imports to Japan were one-eighth of the 1940 level. Heavy bombing of Japan began in

early 1944, using the new long-range B-29. Japan's dense wooden cities were more vulnerable than their German counterparts, and Japanese air defenses were much weaker. A fire-bomb raid on Tokyo on the night of March 9, 1945, killed 124,000 people and left 1 million homeless; it was perhaps the single biggest mass killing of all time. Overall, conventional bombing destroyed 42 percent of Japan's industrial capacity. By the time the United States captured the islands of Iwo Jima and Okinawa in fierce fighting (April-June 1945) and neared the Japanese home islands, Japan's position was hopeless.

SEARCHING FOR PEACE

At the beginning of 1945, the Allies sensed victory. Conferring from February 4 to 11 in the Ukrainian town of Yalta, Roosevelt, Stalin, and Churchill planned for the postwar world. The most important American goal was to enlist the Soviet Union in finishing off the Pacific war. Americans hoped that a Soviet attack on Manchuria would tie down enough Japanese troops to reduce U.S. casualties in invading Japan. Stalin repeated his intent to declare war on Japan within three months of victory in Europe, in return for a free hand in Manchuria.

In Europe, the Allies had decided in 1944 to divide Germany and Austria into French, British, American, and Soviet occupation zones and to share control of Berlin. The Red Army already controlled Bulgaria, Romania, and Hungary, countries that had helped the Germans; Soviet officials were installing sympathetic regimes there. Soviet armies also controlled Poland. The most that Roosevelt could coax from Stalin were vague pledges to allow participation of non-communists in coalition governments in eastern Europe. Stalin also agreed to join a new international organization, the United Nations (UN), whose foundations were laid at a conference in San Francisco in the spring of 1945. The new organization was intended to correct the mistakes of World War I, when the United States had stayed aloof from the League of Nations and had relied on the "parchment peace" of international treaties without mechanisms of enforcement. American leaders wanted the UN to provide a framework through which the United States could coordinate collective security against potential aggressors while retaining its own military strength as the primary means to preserve the peace.

Conservative critics later charged that the western powers "gave away" eastern Europe at the **Yalta Conference**. In fact, the Soviet Union gained little that it did not already control. In East Asia as well, the Soviets could seize the territories that the agreements granted them. Roosevelt overestimated his ability to charm Stalin, but the Yalta talks could not undo the results of four years of fighting by the Soviet Army.

Truman and Potsdam.
On April 12, two months after Yalta, Roosevelt died of a cerebral hemorrhage. Harry Truman, the new president, was a shrewd politician, but his experience was limited; Roosevelt had not even told him about the Manhattan Project. Deeply distrustful of the Soviets, Truman first ventured into personal international diplomacy in July 1945 at a British-Soviet-American conference at Potsdam, near Berlin. Most of the sessions debated the future of Germany. The leaders endorsed the expulsion of ethnic Germans from eastern Europe and moved the borders of Poland 100 miles west into historically German territory. Truman also made it clear that the United States expected to dominate the occupation of Japan. Its goal was to democratize the Japanese political system and reintroduce Japan into the international community, a policy that succeeded. The **Potsdam Declaration** on July 26 summarized U.S. policy and gave Japan an opening for surrender. However, the declaration failed to guarantee that Emperor Hirohito would not be tried as a war criminal. The Japanese response was so cautious that Americans read it as rejection.

The atomic bomb.
Secretary of State James Byrnes now urged Truman to use the new atomic bomb, tested just weeks earlier. Japan's ferocious defense of Okinawa had confirmed American fears that the Japanese would fight to the death. Thousands of suicide missions by kamikaze pilots who tried to crash their planes into U.S. warships seemed additional proof of Japanese fanaticism. Prominent Americans

The ruins of Hiroshima in the aftermath of the atomic bomb. Atomic bombs, dropped first on Hiroshima and then on Nagasaki in August 1945, instantly destroyed most of each city. Now one airplane could wreak the kind of devastation that massive fire-bombing raids had inflicted on cities such as Hamburg and Tokyo, adding new terror to the idea of total war.

Getty/Liaison Agency, Inc.

Overview

The Decision to Use the Atomic Bomb

Americans have long argued whether the use of atomic bombs on the Japanese cities of Hiroshima and Nagasaki was necessary to end the war. Several factors probably influenced President Truman's decision to use the new weapon.

Military necessity	After the war, Truman argued that the use of atomic bombs was necessary to avoid an invasion of Japan that would have cost hundreds of thousand of lives. Military planners expected Japanese soldiers to put up the same kind of suicidal resistance in defense of the home islands as they had to American landings at the Philippines, Iwo Jima, and Okinawa. More recently, historians have argued that the Japanese military was near collapse and that an invasion would have met far less resistance than feared.
Atomic diplomacy	Some historians believe that Truman used atomic weapons to overawe the Soviet Union and induce it to move cautiously in expanding its influence in Europe and east Asia. Truman and his advisers were certainly aware of how the bomb might influence the Soviet leadership.
Domestic politics	President Roosevelt and his chief military advisers had spent billions on the secret atomic bomb project without the knowledge of Congress or the American public. The managers of the Manhattan Project may have believed that only proof of its military value would quiet critics and justify the huge cost.
Momentum of war	The United States and Britain had already adopted wholesale destruction of German and Japanese cities as a military tactic. Use of the atomic bomb looked like a variation on fire bombing, not the start of a new era of potential mass destruction. In this context, some historians argue, President Truman's choice was natural and expected.

were wondering if unconditional surrender was worth another six or nine months of bitter fighting. In contrast, using the bomb to end the conflict quickly would insure that the United States could occupy Japan without Soviet participation, and the bomb might intimidate Stalin (see the Overview table, "The Decision to Use the Atomic Bomb"). In short, a decision not to use atomic weapons was never a serious alternative in the summer of 1945.

In early August, the United States dropped two of three available nuclear bombs on Japan. On August 6, at Hiroshima, the first bomb killed at least eighty thousand people and poisoned thousands more with radiation. A second bomb, three days later, at Nagasaki, took another forty thousand lives. Japan ceased hostilities on August 14 and surrendered formally on September 2. The world has wondered ever since whether the United States might have defeated Japan without resorting to atomic bombs, but recent research shows that the bombs were the shock that allowed the Emperor and peace advocates to overcome military leaders who wanted to fight to the death.

HOW THE ALLIES WON

The Allies won with economic capacity, technology, and military skill. The ability to out-produce the enemy made victory certain in 1944 and 1945, but it was the ability to outthink and outmaneuver the Axis powers that staved off defeat in 1942 and 1943.

In the spring of 1942, an unbroken series of conquests had given the Axis powers control of roughly one third of the world's production of industrial raw materials, up from only 5 percent in 1939. But while Germany and Japan struggled to turn these resources into military strength, the Soviet Union accomplished wonders in relocating and rebuilding its manufacturing capacity after the disasters of 1941. The United States, meanwhile, rearmed with astonishing swiftness, accomplishing in one year what Germany had thought would take three. By 1944, the United States was outproducing all of its enemies combined; over the course of the war, it manufactured two-thirds of all the war materials used by the Allies.

The United States and Soviet Union not only built more planes and tanks than the Axis nations, but they

FROM THEN TO NOW

Nuclear Weapons

On May 11–12, 1998, India tested five nuclear weapons in its western desert. Two weeks later, Pakistan tested its own nuclear weapons. Neighbors and bitter rivals, the two became the six and seventh nations to publicly acknowledge the possession of nuclear weapons. Now the tensions between them, which have long fueled border clashes and twice erupted into open warfare, had become another factor in the delicate calculus of nuclear terror that has confronted the world since Hiroshima. As recently as 2002, the two nations came close to nuclear war.

It has been a central goal of U.S. policy since 1945 to limit the number of nations with atomic weapons and to place ceilings on the size of nuclear arsenals. The goal became more urgent when the Soviet Union deployed its own nuclear weapons after 1949, establishing the "balance of terror" that haunted the decades-long Cold War between the United States and the Soviet Union.

Two key steps toward reducing the nuclear threat were the Limited Test Ban Treaty of 1963—in which the United States, Britain, and the USSR outlawed atmospheric nuclear testing—and the Nuclear Non-Proliferation Treaty, signed in 1968 and extended indefinitely in 1995. As many as 180 nations have agreed not to acquire nuclear weapons, and the five acknowledged nuclear powers—the United States, Russia, Britain, France, China—have agreed to eventual elimination of their own weapons.

The power of international opinion was obviously not enough to stop the Indian and Pakistani weapons programs, and it may have failed elsewhere. One justification of the Gulf War in 1991 was to prevent Iraq from developing nuclear arms, and Iraqi interference with United Nations inspection teams triggered bombing raids on Iraq in 1998–1999, a new Security Council resolution in 2002, and the serious threat of new American military action. The United States also orchestrated international pressure on North Korea to cancel an admitted nuclear weapons program.

The 1990s saw advances in efforts to reduce the huge nuclear stockpiles of the superpowers. The first Strategic Arms Reduction Treaty (START I) went into effect in 1994. The United States and Russia each agreed to retain a maximum of 8,000 warheads each. START II, if implemented, would cut the total to 3,000 each. The breakup of the Soviet Union and the economic challenges that have confronted its constituent republics have created fears about the diversion of warheads into the hands of terrorists. The United States, however, has helped to pay for dismantling of Russian warheads and their removal from Ukraine and Kazakhstan, both formerly parts of the Soviet Union.

The frightening proliferation and growth of nuclear arsenals that began with the Manhattan Project and the atomic bombing of Japan to the 1980s remains a danger to the world. The 1990s may have initiated a new era of shrinking nuclear capacity, despite reversals such as those in India and Pakistan, fears that terrorists may access nuclear materials from nations such as Pakistan, and North Korea's threat in 2003 to restart a nuclear weapons program. South Africa, for example, announced in 1993 that it had destroyed six warheads that it had manufactured secretly. And planned reductions in the largest nuclear arsenals offer hope that the trend will continue in the new century. And the United States and Russia in 2002 announced plans for additional deep cuts in their stockpiles of atomic warheads.

---

also built better ones. The Soviets developed and mass-produced the T-34, the world's most effective tank. American aircraft designers soon jumped ahead of the Germans, who were unable to update the designs that had given them the edge in the 1930s. The United States and Britain gained the lead in communication systems, radar, code-breaking capacity, and, of course, atomic weapons. Even behind the lines the Allies had the technical advantage. The U.S. and British forces that invaded France were fully motorized, and Soviet forces increasingly so, while the German army still depended on more than a million horses to draw supply wagons and artillery.

Superior technology had its great impact because the Allies learned hard lessons from defeat and figured out how to outfight the Axis. Hitler's generals outsmarted the Soviet military in 1941, Japan outmaneuvered the British and Americans in the first months of the Pacific war, and the German navy came close to squeezing the life from Great Britain in 1942. In 1943 and 1944, the tables were turned. The Russians reexamined every detail of their military procedures and devised new tactics that kept the vast German armies off guard and on the defensive. New ways to fight U-boats in the Atlantic devastated the German submarine service and staved off defeat. Americans in the Pacific utilized the full capacity of aircraft carriers, while Japanese admirals still dreamed of confrontations between lines of battleships.

Finally, the Allies had the appeal of democracy and freedom. The Axis nations were the clear aggressors. Germany and Japan made deep enemies by exploiting and abusing the people of the countries that they conquered, from Yugoslavia and France to Malaya and the Philippines, and incited local resistance movements. The Allies were certainly not perfect, but they fought for the ideals of political independence and were welcomed as liberators as they pushed back the Axis armies.

CONCLUSION

World War II changed the lives of tens of millions of Americans. It made and unmade families. It gave millions of women new responsibilities and then sent them back to the kitchen. It put money in pockets that had been emptied by the Great Depression and turned struggling business owners into tycoons. In war zones and behind the lines, it introduced millions of men and women in the armed forces to people and places outside the United States.

Whether on the home front or the fighting front, Americans knew that victory was uncertain. World War II adventure movies in which Americans always win leave the impression that triumph was necessary and inevitable. In fact, victory was the hard-fought result of public leadership and military effort. Under other leadership, the United States might have stood aside until it was too late to reverse the Axis conquest of Europe and east Asia. The collapse of the Soviet Union or failure of the North Atlantic convoy system might have made Germany unbeatable. In 1941 and 1942 in particular, Americans faced each day with fear and uncertainty

The war unified the nation in new ways, while confirming old divisions. People of all backgrounds shared a common cause. Farm boys mixed with city slickers, Northerners with Southerners. "When I woke up the first morning on the troop train in Fulton, Kentucky," recalled one Midwesterner, "I thought I was in Timbuktu." The war narrowed the distance between native-born, small-town Americans and recent European immigrants from the big cities. The chasms between Protestant, Catholic, and Jewish Americans were far narrower in 1945 than they had been in 1940.

But nothing broke the barriers that separated white and black Americans. Unequal treatment in a war for democracy outraged black soldiers, who returned to fight for civil rights. The uprooting of Japanese Americans was another reminder of racial prejudice. After the war, however, memories of the contrast between the nation's fight against Axis tyranny and the unequal treatment of American citizens fueled a gradual shift of public attitudes that climaxed in the civil rights movements of the 1950s and 1960s.

The United States ended the war as the world's overwhelming economic power. It had put only 12 percent of its population in uniform, less than any other major combatant. For every American who died, twenty Germans and dozens of Russians perished. Having suffered almost no direct destruction, the United States was able to dictate a postwar economic trading system that favored its interests

Nevertheless, the insecurities of the war years influenced the United States for decades. A nation's current leaders are often shaped by its last war. Churchill had directed strategy, and Hitler, Mussolini, and Truman had all fought in World War I and carried its memories into World War II. The lessons of World War II would similarly influence the thinking of presidents from Dwight Eisenhower in the 1950s to George Bush in the 1990s. Even though the United States ended 1945 with the world's mightiest navy, biggest air force, and only atomic bomb, the instability that had followed World War I made Western leaders nervous about the shape of world politics.

One result in the postwar era was conflict between the United States and the Soviet Union, whose only common ground had been a shared enemy. After Germany's defeat, their wartime alliance gave way to hostility and confrontation in the Cold War. At home, international tensions fed pressure for social and political conformity. The desire to enjoy the fruits of victory after fifteen years of economic depression and sacrifice made the postwar generation sensitive to perceived threats to steady jobs and stable families. For the next generation, the unresolved business of World War II would haunt American life.

REVIEW QUESTIONS

1. What motivated German, Italian, and Japanese aggression in the 1930s? How did Great Britain, the USSR, and other nations respond to the growing conflict?

2. What arguments did Americans make against involvement in the war in Europe? Why did President Roosevelt and many others believe it necessary to block German and Japanese expansion? What steps did Roosevelt take to increase U.S. involvement short of war?

3. What was the military balance in early 1942? What were the chief threats to the United States and its allies? Why did the fortunes of war turn in late 1942?

4. Assess how mobilization for World War II altered life in the United States. How did the war affect families? How did it shift the regional balance of the economy? What opportunities did it open for women?

5. Did World War II help or hinder progress toward racial equality in the United States? How did the experiences of Japanese Americans, African Americans, and Mexican Americans challenge American ideals?

6. What factors were decisive in the defeat of Germany? How important were Soviet efforts on the Eastern Front, the bomber war, and the British-American landings in France?

7. What was the U.S. strategy against Japan, and how well did it work? What lay behind President Truman's decision to use atomic bombs against Japanese cities?

8. What role did advanced science and technology play in World War II? How did the scientific lead of the U.S. affect the war's outcome?

KEY TERMS

Allies (p. 828)

Atlantic Charter (p. 826)

Axis Powers (p. 822)

Battle of the Atlantic (p. 830)

Blitzkrieg (p. 822)

D-Day (p. 842)

Eastern Front (p. 828)

Fair Employment Practices Committee (p. 838)

Greater East Asia Co-Prosperity Sphere (p. 821)

Holocaust (p. 846)

Island hopping (p. 846)

Lend-Lease Act (p. 826)

Manhattan Project (p. 834)

Operation OVERLORD (p. 844)

Potsdam Declaration (p. 848)

Yalta Conference (p. 848)

RECOMMENDED READING

Bailey, Beth, and David Farber. *The First Strange Place: The Alchemy of Race and Sex in World War II Hawaii* (1992). Explores the effects of the war on American ideas about the proper roles of men and women, black people, white people, and Asian Americans.

Goodwin, Doris Kearns. *No Ordinary Time: Franklin and Eleanor Roosevelt, the Home Front in World War II* (1994). Presents the tensions and crises of World War II through the daily lives of President Roosevelt and his wife Eleanor.

Hersey, John. *Hiroshima* (1946). Recounts the atomic bombing through the eyes of victims and survivors.

Keegan, John. *The Second World War* (1990). A comprehensive and readable account giving a strong sense of the relative importance of the various fronts.

O'Neill, William L. *A Democracy at War: America's Fight at Home and Abroad in World War II* (1993). Explores the choices that the United States made in mobilizing and conducting the war.

Sherwin Martin J. *A World Destroyed: The Atomic Bomb and the Grand Alliance* (1975). Explains why American leaders never seriously considered alternatives to the atomic bomb.

Terkel, Studs. *The Good War: An Oral History of World War II* (1984). Eloquent testimony about the effects of the war on both ordinary and extraordinary Americans.

ADDITIONAL SOURCES

The Politics of War

Cole, Wayne S. *Roosevelt and the Isolationists* (1983).

Dallek, Robert. *Franklin D. Roosevelt and American Foreign Policy, 1932-1945* (1979).

Doenecke, Justus D. *Storm on the Horizon: The Challenge to American Intervention, 1939-1941* (2000)

Iriye, Akira. *Power and Culture: The Japanese-American War, 1941-1945* (1981).

Kimball, Warren. *The Juggler: Franklin Roosevelt as Wartime Statesman* (1991).

Schneider, James. *Should America Go to War? The Debate over Foreign Policy in Chicago, 1939-1941* (1989).

Military Operations

Beevor, Anthony. *Stalingrad* (1998).

Chappell, John D. *Before the Bomb: How Americans Approached the Pacific War* (1997).

Keegan, John. *Six Armies in Normandy; From D-Day to the Liberation of Paris* (1982).

Morrison, Samuel Eliot. *The Two-Ocean War: A Short History of the United States Navy in the Second World War* (1963).

Prange, Gordon. *At Dawn We Slept: The Untold Story of Pearl Harbor* (1981).

Spector, Ronald H. *Eagle against the Sun: The American War with Japan* (1985).

Syrett, David. *The Defeat of the German U-Boats: The Battle of the Atlantic* (1994).

Tuchman, Barbara W. *Stillwell and the American Experience in China, 1911-1945* (1970).

Weinberg, Gerhard. *A World at Arms: A Global History of World War II* (1994).

The Experience of War

Ambrose, Stephen. *Citizen Soldiers: The U.S. Army from the Normandy Beaches to the Bulge to the Surrender of Germany, June 7, 1944 - May 7, 1945* (1997).

Cameron, Craig M. *American Samurai: Myth, Imagination, and the Conduct of Battle in the First Marine Division, 1941-1951* (1994).

Doubler, Michael. *Closing with the Enemy: How GIs Fought the War in Europe, 1944-1945* (1994).

Fussell, Paul. *Wartime: Understanding and Behavior in the Second World War* (1989).

Leinbaugh, Harold P. and John D. Campbell *The Men of Company K: The Autobiography of a World War II Rifle Company* (1985).

Manchester, William. *Goodbye Darkness: A Memoir of the Pacific War* (1980).

Salisbury, Harrison. *The 900 Days: The Siege of Leningrad* (1969).

Schrijvers, Peter. *The Crash of Ruin: American Combat Soldiers in Europe during World War II* (1996).

Sledge, E. B. *With the Old Breed at Peleliu and Okinawa* (1981).

Mobilizing the Home Front

Blum, John M. *V Was for Victory: Politics and American Culture during World War II* (1976).

Doherty, Thomas. *Projections of War: Hollywood, American Culture, and World War II* (1994).

Johnson, Marilynn. *The Second Gold Rush* (1993).

Koppes, Clayton, and Gregory Black, *Hollywood Goes to War* (1987).

Lichtenstein, Nelson. *Labor's War at Home: The CIO in World War II* (1983).

Nash, Gerald. *The American West Transformed: The Impact of the Second World War* (1985).

Newton, Wesley P. *Montgomery in the Good War: Portrait of a Southern City, 1939-1946* (2000).

Polenberg, Richard. *War and Society: The United States, 1941-1945* (1972).

Rhodes, Richard *. The Making of the Atomic Bomb* (1986).

Tuttle, William M. *Daddy's Gone to War: The Second World War in the Lives of America's Children* (1993).

Vatter, Harold. *The U.S. Economy in World War II* (1985).

Women and the War Effort

Anderson, Karen. *Wartime Women: Sex Roles, Family Relations, and the Status of Women during World War II* (1981).

Campbell, D'Ann. *Women at War with America: Private Lives in a Patriotic Era* (1984).

Hartmann, Susan. *The Home Front and Beyond: American Women in the 1940s* (1982).

Kesselman, Amy. *Fleeting Opportunities: Women in Portland and Vancouver Shipyards during World War II and Reconversion* (1990).

Litoff, Judy Barrett. *We're in This War Too: World War II Letters of American Women in Uniform* (1994).

Racial Attitudes and U.S. Policy

Daniels, Roger. *Concentration Camps U.S.A.: Japanese Americans and World War II* (1971).

Dower, John. *War without Mercy: Race and Power in the Pacific War* (1986).

Capeci, Jr. Dominic J. *Race Relations in Wartime Detroit: The Sojourner Truth Controversy of 1942* (1984).

Wyman, David S. *The Abandonment of the Jews: America and the Holocaust, 1941-1945* (1984).

WHERE TO LEARN MORE

- **Air Force Museum, Dayton, Ohio.** Visitors can walk among World War II fighter planes and bombers, including the B-29 that dropped the atomic bomb in Nagasaki, and learn about the role of aviation in the war.

- **Museum of the Pacific War, Fredericksburg, Texas.** In the birthplace of Admiral Chester Nimitz, this new museum is an excellent introduction to the war with Japan.

- **Los Alamos County Historical Museum and Bradbury Science Museum, Los Alamos, New Mexico.** The museum traces the origins of atomic energy for military and civilian uses. Nearby is the Los Alamos County Historical Museum, which gives the feel of everyday life in the atomic town.

- **United States Holocaust Memorial Museum, Washington, D.C.** The Holocaust Museum gives visitors a deeply moving depiction of the deadly impacts of Nazi ideas in the 1930s and 1940s. The museum's website at .http://www.ushmm.urlorg also explores virtually every facet of the Holocaust experience for Jews during World War II.

 Please refer to the document CD-ROM for primary sources related to this chapter.

→ As international tensions rose with the onset of the Cold War, Americans wondered how to prepare for a possible nuclear war. Many families stocked extra food and water and bought a battery-powered radio, but few actually installed backyard bomb shelters like the one being tested by this family in a Long Island suburb not far from Levittown.

THE COLD WAR AT HOME AND ABROAD 1946–1952

27

My eyes popped when I got to town hall because the lobby and the stairs leading up to the hearing room were loaded with people. The upstairs hallway was jammed and the room was packed. People were standing along the walls. I remember there were a lot of children, toddlers—some in strollers—and many babies held by men and women. We expected there would be quite a turnout. But the extent of the crowd was a big surprise to me. . . . The meeting itself was rather brief. There were some speeches. No screaming and yelling the way people do at town meetings today. Everyone was quiet, anxious. I remember one guy in uniform, holding a baby, made a strong statement. These people were desperate. It was very moving. When the decision was announced, the crowd broke into applause.

Levittown was the last place on the planet I thought I would be living. But, as it turned out, we moved there because the house was such a good buy. . . . We loved living there. I came into work and told [Newsday managing editor Alan] Hathway that I would be eating crow for the rest of my days.*

Bernadette Rischer Wheeler, in "Levittown at Fifty: Long Island Voices," at www.lihistory.com/specsec/hsvoices.htm; originally published in *Newsday*.

CHAPTER OUTLINE

Launching the Great Boom
Reconversion Chaos
Economic Policy
The GI Bill
Assembly-Line Neighborhoods
Steps Toward Civil Rights
Consumer Boom and Baby Boom

Truman, Republicans, and the Fair Deal
Truman's Opposition
Whistle-Stopping across America
Truman's Fair Deal

Confronting the Soviet Union
The End of the Grand Alliance
The Truman Doctrine and the Marshall Plan
Soviet Reactions
American Rearmament

Cold War and Hot War
The Nuclear Shadow
The Cold War in Asia
NSC-68 and Aggressive Containment
War in Korea, 1950–1953
The Politics of War

The Second Red Scare
The Communist Party and the Loyalty Program
Naming Names to Congress
Subversion Trials
Senator McCarthy on Stage
Understanding McCarthyism

Conclusion

Bernadette Wheeler was a reporter for *Newsday*, the daily newspaper for the Long Island suburbs of New York, who covered the birth of the new community of Levittown. She remembers the meeting on May 21, 1947, when the local governing board approved construction of the new subdivision. The size of the crowd indicates the severity of the housing shortage after World War II and the intense desire of Americans to return to normal life. After years of hardship, they defined American ideals in terms of economic opportunity and the chance to enjoy national prosperity. Even President Truman replaced the model gun on his White House desk with a model plow. Over the next decade, the residents who moved to Levittown and thousands of other new subdivisions would start the baby boom and rekindle the economy with their purchases of automobiles, appliances, and televisions.

This compelling desire to enjoy the promise of American life after years of sacrifice helps to explain why Americans reacted so fiercely to new challenges and threats. They watched as congressional conservatives and President Truman fought over the fate of New Deal programs. More worrisome was the con-frontation with the Soviet Union that was soon being called the **Cold War**. Triggered by the Soviet Union's imposition of communist regimes throughout eastern Europe, the Cold War grew into a global contest in which the United States tried to counter Soviet influence around the world. By the time real war broke out in Korea in 1950, many Americans were venting their frustration by blaming international setbacks on internal subversion and by trying to root out suspected "reds."

The Cold War began in the late 1940s, but it would shape the United States and the world for another generation. Massive rearmament allowed U.S. presidents to act as international policemen in the name of democratic values—a vast change from earlier American goals to remain disengaged from the problems of other nations. Defense spending also reshaped American industry and helped stimulate twenty-five years of economic growth. The Cold War narrowed the range of political discussion, making many of the left-wing ideas of the 1930s taboo by the 1950s. It also made racial segregation and limits on immigration into international embarrassments and thus nudged the nation to live up to its ideals.

KEY TOPICS

- Post-war shortages and the massive exit of women from the workforce

- The beginning of a twenty-five-year economic boom

- The beginning of the postwar civil rights movement

- The origins of the Cold War

- The reelection of Harry Truman

- The Korean War and the nuclear arms race

- McCarthy and the Second Red Scare

LAUNCHING THE GREAT BOOM

In 1947, *The Best Years of Our Lives* swept seven Oscars at the Academy Awards. The immensely popular movie dealt with the problems of returning veterans as squarely as Hollywood could. It follows three veterans as they try to readjust to civilian life. The plot cuts between the personal problems of reconnecting with wives and sweethearts and the social challenge of finding meaningful work.

Behind the story line was nagging concern about the future. "Hard times are coming," one character predicts. When World War II ended, Americans feared that demobilization would bring a return of the inflation and unemployment that had followed World War I. Indeed, in the first eighteen months of peace, rising prices, strife between labor and management, and shortages of everything from meat to automobiles confirmed their anxiety. But in fact, 1947 and 1948 ushered in an economic expansion that lasted for a quarter-century. The resulting prosperity would finance a military buildup and an activist foreign policy.

Chronology

1944 Servicemen's Readjustment Act (GI Bill) is passed.

1945 United Nations is established.

1946 Employment Act creates Council of Economic Advisers.

George Kennan sends his "long telegram."

Winston Churchill delivers his "iron curtain" speech.

1947 Truman Doctrine is announced.

Truman establishes a federal employee loyalty program.

Kennan explains containment policy in an anonymous article in *Foreign Affairs*. Marshall Plan begins providing economic aid to Europe.

HUAC holds hearings on Hollywood.

Taft-Hartley Act rolls back gains of organized labor.

National Security Act creates National Security Council and Central Intelligence Agency.

1948 Communists stage coup in Czechoslovakia.

Berlin airlift overcomes Soviet blockade.

Truman orders desegregation of the armed forces.

Selective Service is reestablished.

Truman wins reelection.

1949 North Atlantic Treaty Organization is formed.

Communist Chinese defeat Nationalists.

Soviet Union tests an atomic bomb.

Department of Defense is established.

1950 Senator McCarthy begins his Red hunt.

Alger Hiss is convicted of perjury.

NSC-68 is drafted and accepted as U.S. policy.

Korean War begins.

1951 Senate Internal Security Subcommittee begins hearings.

Truman relieves MacArthur of his command.

Julius and Ethel Rosenberg are convicted of conspiring to commit espionage.

Truce talks begin in Korea.

1952 United States tests the hydrogen bomb.

Eisenhower is elected president

It also supported continuity in domestic politics from the late 1940s to the mid-1960s.

RECONVERSION CHAOS

Japan's sudden surrender took the United States by surprise. Plans called for a two-year phase-out of military spending, while gradually reintroducing veterans to the domestic economy. Now these plans were obsolete. The Pentagon, already scaling back defense spending, canceled $15 billion in war contracts in the first two days after Japanese surrender. Public pressure demanded that the military release the nation's 12 million servicemen and servicewomen as rapidly as possible. GIs in Europe and the South Pacific waited impatiently for their turn on slow, crowded troop ships and calculated their order of discharge according to length of time in uniform, service overseas, combat decorations, and number of children. Even at the rate of 25,000 discharges a day, it took a year to get veterans back to the States and civilian life.

Veterans came home to shortages of food in the grocery stores and consumer goods in the department stores. High demand and short supply meant inflationary pressure, checked temporarily by continuing the Office of Price Administration until October

1946. Meanwhile, producers, consumers, and retailers scrambled to evade price restrictions and scarcities. Farmers sold meat on the black market, bypassing the big packing companies for one-on-one deals at higher prices. Automobiles were especially scarce; the number of vehicles registered in the United States had declined by 4 million during the war. For the privilege of spending a few hundred dollars on a junker, consumers sometimes had to pay used-car dealers for such so-called accessories as $150 batteries and $100 lap robes.

A wave of strikes made it hard to retool factories for civilian products. Inflation squeezed factory workers, who had accepted wage controls during the war effort. Since 1941, prices had risen twice as fast as base wages. In the fall of 1945, more and more workers went on strike to redress the balance; the strikes interrupted the output of products from canned soup to copper wire. By January 1946, some 1.3 million auto, steel, electrical, and packinghouse workers were off the job. Strikes in these basic industries shut other factories down for lack of supplies. Presidential committees finally crafted settlements that allowed steel and auto workers to make up ground lost during the war, but they also allowed corporations to pass on higher costs to consumers. One Republican senator

The Best Years of Our Lives *dealt realistically with the problems facing veterans trying to readjust to civilian life. Director William Wyler strove for a feeling of accuracy, shooting on location in Cincinnati and costuming the actors in clothing bought in local stores.*

complained of "unionists who fatten themselves at the expense of the rest of us." Bill Nation, who inspected window moldings at a GM plant in Detroit, wondered who the senator was talking about. The strike gave him an hourly raise of 18 cents, pushing his weekly income to $59. After paying for food, housing, and utilities, Bill was left with $13.44 for himself, his wife, and five children to spend on clothes, comic books, and doctor bills.

ECONOMIC POLICY

The economic turmoil of 1946 set the stage for two major and contradictory efforts to deal more systematically with peacetime economic readjustment. The Employment Act of 1946 and the Taft-Hartley Act of 1947 represented liberal and conservative approaches to the peacetime economy.

The Employment Act was an effort by congressional liberals to ward off economic crisis by fine-tuning government taxation and spending. It started as a proposal for a full-employment bill that would have committed the federal government to insure everyone's "right to a useful and remunerative job." Watered down in the face of business opposition, it still defined economic growth and high employment as national goals. It also established the **Council of Economic Advisers** to assist the president. Even this weak legislation, putting the federal government at the center of economic planning, would have been unthinkable a generation earlier.

In the short term, the Employment Act aimed at a problem that did not materialize. Economists had predicted that the combination of returning veterans and workers idled by canceled defense work would bring depression-level unemployment of 8 to 10 million. In fact, more than 2 million women provided some slack by leaving the labor force outright. Federal agencies hastened their departure by publishing pamphlets asking men the pointed question, "Do you want your wife to work after the war?" In addition, consumer spending from a savings pool of $140 billion in bank accounts and war bonds created a huge demand for workers to fill. Total employment rose rather than fell with the end of the war, and unemployment in 1946–1948 stayed below 4 percent.

From the other end of the political spectrum, the **Taft-Hartley Act** climaxed a ten-year effort by conservatives to reverse the gains made by organized labor in the 1930s. The act passed in 1947 because of anger about continuing strikes. For many Americans, the chief culprit was John L. Lewis, head of the United Mine Workers, who had won good wages for coal miners with a militant policy that included wartime walkouts. In a country that still burned coal for most of its energy, the burly, bushy-browed, and combative Lewis was instantly recognizable, loved by his workers and hated by nearly everyone else. In April 1946, a forty-day coal strike hampered industrial production. The coal settlement was only days old when the nation faced an even more crippling walkout by railroad workers. Truman asked for the unprecedented power to draft strikers into the army; the threat undercut the union and led to a quick and dramatic settlement. Many middle-class Americans were convinced that organized labor needed to be curbed.

In November 1946, Republicans capitalized on the problems of reconversion chaos, labor unrest, and dissatisfaction with Truman. Their election slogan was simple: "Had enough?" The GOP won control of Congress for the first time since the election of 1928, continuing the political trend toward the right that had been apparent since 1938.

Adopted by the now firmly conservative Congress, the Taft-Hartley Act was a serious counterattack by big business against large unions. It outlawed several union tools as "unfair labor practices." It barred the closed shop (the requirement that all workers hired in a particular company or plant be union members) and blocked secondary boycotts (strikes against suppliers or customers of a targeted business). The federal government could postpone a strike by imposing a "cooling-off period," which gave companies time to stockpile their output. Officers of national unions had to swear that they were not Communists or Communist sympathizers, even though corporate executives had no similar obligation. The bill passed over Truman's veto.

THE GI BILL

Another landmark law for the postwar era passed Congress without controversy. The Servicemen's Readjustment Act of 1944 was designed to ease veterans back into the civilian mainstream. Popularly known as the **GI Bill of Rights**, it was one of the federal government's most successful public assistance programs. Rather than pay cash bonuses to veterans, as after previous wars, Congress tied benefits to specific public goals. The GI Bill guaranteed loans of up to $2,000 for buying a house or farm or starting a business, a substantial sum at a time when a new house cost $6,000. The program encouraged veterans to attend college with money for tuition and books plus monthly stipends.

The GI Bill democratized American higher education by making college degrees accessible to men with working-class backgrounds. It brought far more students into higher education than could otherwise have enrolled. In the peak year of 1947, veterans made up half of all college students. "We're all trying to get where we would have been if there hadn't been a war," one veteran attending Indiana University told *Time* magazine. Veterans helped convert the college degree, once available primarily to the socially privileged, into a basic business and professional credential. However, an unfortunate side effect of the GI tide was to crowd women out of classrooms, although sixty thousand servicewomen did take advantage of educational benefits. Cornell University made room for veterans by limiting women to 20 percent of its entering class; the University of Wisconsin closed its doors to women from out of state. Women's share of bachelor's degrees dropped from 40 percent in 1940 to 25 percent in 1950.

College life in 1946 and 1947 meant close quarters. Universities were unequipped to deal with older or married students. Prefabricated apartments from the wartime atomic-energy project at Richland, Washington, were trucked to college campuses around the West to house newly enrolled veterans. Recycled Quonset huts became as much a part of campus architecture as gothic towers and ivy-covered halls. States rented surplus defense facilities for big-city extension campuses that would be easier for veterans to attend than traditional small-town universities. Many of these campuses evolved into major public universities, such as the University of Illinois at Chicago and Portland State University in Oregon.

ASSEMBLY-LINE NEIGHBORHOODS

Americans faced a housing shortage after the war. In 1947, fully 3 million married couples were unable to set up their own households. Most doubled up with relatives while they waited for the construction industry to respond. Hunger for housing was fierce. Eager buyers lined up for hours and paid admission fees to tour model homes or to put their names in drawings for the opportunity to buy. When in 1946 the *Des Moines Register and Tribune* ran a fake apartment ad to check real-estate industry claims that the housing crisis was over, 351 people answered it. Fifty-six of them said that they lived in a hotel or rented room; sixty-eight lived with parents.

The solution started with the federal government and its Veterans Administration (VA) mortgage program. By guaranteeing repayment, the VA allowed veterans to get home purchase loans from private lenders without a down payment. Neither the VA program nor the New Deal-era Federal Housing Administration (FHA) mortgage insurance program, however, could do any good unless there were houses to buy. Eyeing the mass market created by the federal programs, innovative private builders devised their own solution. In 1947, William Levitt, a New York builder who had developed defense housing projects, built two thousand rental houses for veterans on suburban Long Island. His basic house had 800 square feet of living space in two bedrooms, living room, kitchen, and bath, a 60-by-100-foot lot, and an unfinished attic waiting for the weekend handyman. It was only one-third the size of the typical new house fifty years later, but it gave new families a place to start. There were six thousand **Levittown** houses by the end of 1948 and more than seventeen thousand by 1951.

Other successful builders worked on the same scale. They bought hundreds of acres of land, put in utilities for the entire tract, purchased materials by the carload, and kept specialized workers busy on scores of identical houses. Floor plans were square, simple, and easy for semiskilled workers to construct. For the first time, kitchens across America were designed for preassembled cabinets and appliances in standard sizes. "On-site fabrication" was mass production without an assembly line. Work crews at the Los Angeles suburb of Lakewood started a hundred houses a day as they moved down one side of the street and back up the other, digging foundation trenches, pouring concrete, and working through the dozens of other stages of home building.

From 1946 through 1950, the federal government backed $20 billion in VA and FHA loans, approximately 40 percent of all home-mortgage debt. Housing starts neared 2 million in the peak year of 1950. New subdivisions were starting places for couples in their late twenties or early thirties making up for lost time on a tight budget. By the end of the 1940s, 55 percent of American households owned their homes. The figure continued to climb until the 1980s, broadening access to the dream of financial security for many families. All during this time, the suburban population grew much faster than the population of central cities, and the population outside the growing reach of metropolitan areas actually declined (see Figure 27–1).

Isolation and discrimination.

Unfortunately, the suburban solution to housing shortages also had costs. Vast new housing tracts tended to isolate women and children from traditional community life. They also did little to help African Americans. As the migration of black workers and their families to northern and western cities continued after the war, discrimination excluded them from new housing. As late as 1960, the 82,000 residents of Levittown had no African American neighbors; not until 1957 did a black family move into a second Levittown near Philadelphia. Federal housing agencies and private industry worsened the problem by **redlining** older neighborhoods, which involved withholding home-purchase loans and insurance coverage from inner-city areas.

Public and private actions kept African Americans in deteriorating inner-city ghettos. When severe flooding in 1948 drove thousands of African Americans from leftover wartime housing in Portland, Oregon,

for example, their only choice was to crowd into the city's small black neighborhood. Chicago landlords squeezed an estimated 27,000 black migrants per year into run-down buildings, subdividing larger apartments into one-room "kitchenette" units, with sinks and hot plates but no private bathrooms. One tenant commented that rats came "in teams." Families who tried to find new homes in white neighborhoods on the edge of black ghettos often met violence in the form of rocks thrown through their windows, fire-bombs, and angry white mobs.

STEPS TOWARD CIVIL RIGHTS

The problem of securing decent housing helped to motivate African Americans to demand full rights as citizens. The wartime experience of fighting for freedom abroad while suffering discrimination at home steeled a new generation of black leaders to reduce the gap between America's ideal of equality and its performance. As had also been true after World War I, some white Americans held the opposite view, hoping to reaffirm racial segregation. A wave of racist violence surged across the South after the war; special targets were black veterans who tried to register to vote. However, many white Americans felt uneasy about the contradiction between a crusade for freedom abroad and racial discrimination at home.

In this era of rapid change and racial tension, the Truman administration recognized the importance of securing civil rights for all Americans. Caught between pressure from black leaders and the fear of alienating southern Democrats, the president in 1946 appointed the Committee on Civil Rights, whose report developed an agenda for racial justice that would take two decades to put into effect. The NAACP had already begun a campaign of antisegregation lawsuits, which the Justice Department now began to support. The administration ordered federal housing agencies to modify their racially restrictive policies and prohibited racial discrimination in federal employment. Federal committees began to push for desegregation of private facilities in the symbolically important city of Washington, D.C.

The president also ordered "equality of treatment and opportunity" in the armed services in July 1948. The army in particular dragged its feet, hoping to limit black enlistees to 10 percent of the total. Manpower needs and the record of integrated units in Korea from 1950 to 1953 persuaded the reluctant generals. Over the next generation, African Americans would find the military an important avenue for career opportunities.

Changes in national policy were important for ending racial discrimination, but far more Americans

FIGURE 27-1 The Suburbanizing Nation
In the decades after World War II, Americans moved in unprecedented numbers to new communities surrounding established cities. In the early 1960s, the combined population of suburban areas passed the populations of large central cities and of smaller towns and rural areas.

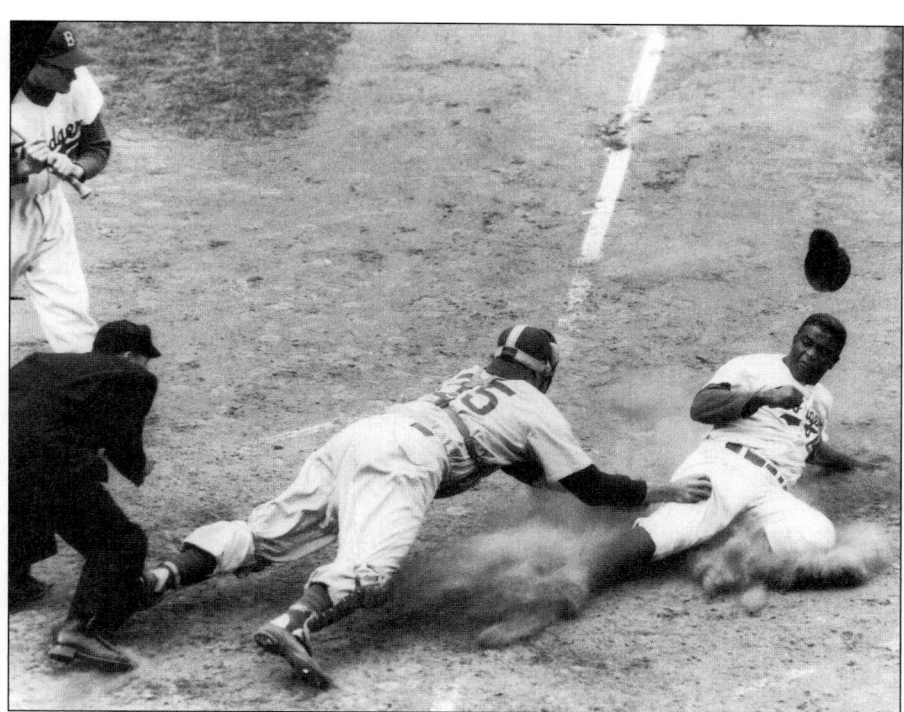

CORBIS

Jackie Robinson, the first black player in modern major league baseball, joined the Brooklyn Dodgers in 1947. He was both personally courageous and an outstanding player. Here he steals home against the Chicago Cubs in 1952.

were interested in the lowering of racial barriers in professional team sports. Americans had applauded individual black champions, such as heavyweight boxer Joe Louis and sprinter Jesse Owens, but team sports required their members to travel, practice, and play together. The center of attention was Jack Roosevelt (Jackie) Robinson, a gifted African American athlete, who opened the 1947 baseball season as a member of the Brooklyn Dodgers. Black baseball players had previously displayed their talents in the Negro leagues, but Robinson broke the color line that had reserved the modern major leagues for white players. His ability to endure taunting and hostility and still excel on the ball field opened the door for other African Americans and Latinos. In the segregated society of the 1940s, Robinson also found himself a powerful symbol of racial change.

CONSUMER BOOM AND BABY BOOM

The housing boom was a product of both pent-up demand and a postwar "family boom." Americans celebrated the end of the war with weddings; the marriage rate in 1946 surpassed even its wartime high. Many women who left the labor force opted for marriage, and at increasingly younger ages. By 1950, the median age at which women married would be just over 20 years—lower than at any previous time in the twentieth century. Movies in the 1930s had abounded with independent career women. By the late 1940s, Holly-

wood reflected new attitudes and social patterns by portraying women as helpless victims or supportive wives and publicizing hard-edged stars, such as Joan Crawford, as homebodies at heart. The United States ended the 1940s with 7 million more married couples than at the decade's start.

New marriages jump-started the "baby boom," as did already married couples who decided to catch up after postponing childbearing during the war. In the early 1940s, an average of 2.9 million children per year were born in the United States; in 1946–1950, the average was 3.6 million. Those 3.5 million "extra" babies needed diapers, swing sets, lunch boxes, bicycles, and schoolrooms (see Figure 27–2).

Fast-growing families also needed to stock up on household goods. Out of an average household income of roughly $4,000 in 1946 and 1947, a family of four had $300 to $400 a year for furnishings

FIGURE 27-2   The Postwar Baby Boom: The U.S. Birthrate. 1930-1995
The baby boom after World War II was a product of high marriage rates and closely spaced children. The generation of Americans born between 1945 and 1960 has strongly affected American society and politics as its members have gone to school and college, entered the workforce, started their own families, and begun to plan for retirement in the twenty-first century.

Americans were eager to enjoy the most modern appliances and houses. Manufacturers promoted streamlined kitchens to make life easier for housewives and their families.

and appliances. A couple who studied *Consumer Reports* might equip its new Levittown kitchen with a Dripolator coffee maker for $2.45 and or Mirro-Matic pressure cooker for $12.95. The thrifty family could get along with a Motorola table radio in brown plastic for under $30; for $100, it could have a massive radio-phonograph combination in a four-foot console as the centerpiece of a well-equipped living room before the arrival of television.

TRUMAN, REPUBLICANS, AND THE FAIR DEAL

From new radios to new homes to new jobs, the economic gains of the postwar years propelled Americans toward the political center. After fifteen years of economic crisis and world war, they wanted to enjoy prosperity. They wanted to keep the gains of the New Deal, but without risking new experiments. William Levitt tried to humorously capture the American satisfaction with the fruits of free enter-

prise when he said in 1948 that "no man who owns his house and lot can be a Communist; he has too much to do."

Recognizing this attitude, Harry Truman and his political advisers tried to define policies acceptable to moderate Republicans as well as to Democrats. This project meant creating a bipartisan coalition to block Soviet influence in western Europe and defending the core of the New Deal's social and economic agenda at home.

This political package is known as the strategy of the "vital center," after the title of a 1949 book by Arthur Schlesinger, Jr. The book linked anti-communism in foreign policy with efforts to enact inclusive social and economic policies to extend freedom abroad and at home at the same time. The vital center reflected the political reality of the Cold War years, when Democrats had to prove that they were tough on Communism before they could enact domestic reforms. The approach defined the heart of the Democratic Party for twenty years and found full expression in the administrations of John Kennedy (1961–1963) and Lyndon Johnson (1963–1969).

TRUMAN'S OPPOSITION

Truman had unexpected luck in his campaign for a full term as president in 1948. Besides the Republicans, he faced new fringe parties on the far right and far left that allowed him to position himself in the moderate center. The blunt, no-nonsense Missourian entered the campaign an underdog, but, compared to his rivals, he soon looked like the country's best option for steering a steady course.

Truman's opponents represented the left-leaning American Progressive party, the **Dixiecrats** (officially the States' Rights Democrats), and the Republicans. The Progressive candidate was Henry Wallace, who had been FDR's vice president from 1941 to 1945, before being dumped in favor of Truman himself; more recently, he had been Truman's secretary of commerce. The Dixiecrat, Governor Strom Thurmond of South Carolina, had bolted the Democratic party over civil rights. The most serious challenger was the Republican, Thomas Dewey, who had run against Roosevelt in 1944.

Wallace cast himself as the prophet for "the century of the common man." His background as a plant geneticist and farm journalist prepared him to deal with domestic policy but not with world affairs. After Truman fired him from the cabinet in 1946 for advocating a conciliatory stance toward the Soviet Union, Wallace went to Europe to praise the Soviet Union and to denounce U.S. foreign policy. On his return, enthusiastic college crowds raised his sights from "scaring the Democratic Party leftward" to running for president. Most liberal Democrats ran the other way when Wallace organized the Progressive Party, leaving the Communist Party to supply many of his campaign workers.

Wallace argued that the United States was forcing the Cold War on the Soviet Union and undermining American ideals by diverting attention from poverty and racism at home. He wanted to repeal the draft and destroy atomic weapons. His arguments had merit, for the United States was becoming a militarized society, but Wallace was the wrong person to change American minds. With his shy personality, disheveled appearance, and fanaticism about health food, he struck most voters as a kook rather than a statesman, and he made skepticism about the Cold War increasingly vulnerable to right-wing attack.

At the other political extreme were the Southerners who walked out when the 1948 Democratic National Convention called for full civil rights for African Americans. The raucous convention debate previewed the politics of the 1960s. Mayor Hubert Humphrey of Minneapolis challenged the Democratic Party "to get out of the shadow of states' rights and walk forthrightly into the bright sunshine of human rights." His speech foreshadowed Humphrey's twenty years of liberal influence in the Democratic Party, culminating in his presidential nomination in 1968.

When the angry Southerners met to nominate their own candidate, however, the South's important politicians stayed away. They had worked too long to throw away seniority and influence in Congress and the Democratic Party. Major southern newspapers called the revolt futile and narrow-minded. Strom Thurmond claimed that the Dixiecrats were really trying to defend Americans against government bureaucracy, not fighting to preserve racial segregation, but few listened outside the deep South.

Tom Dewey, Truman's real opponent, had a high opinion of himself. He had been an effective governor of New York and represented the moderate eastern establishment within the Republican Party. Fortunately for Truman, Dewey lacked the common touch. Smooth on the outside, he alienated people who should have been his closest supporters; as one political acquaintance put it, "You have to know Dewey really well to dislike him." He was an arrogant campaigner, refusing to interrupt his morning schedule to talk to voters. He acted like a snob and dressed like the groom on a wedding cake.

Harry Truman greets supporters and railroad workers in Pittsburgh at the start of an eighteen-state campaign tour in June 1948. Truman's grassroots campaign and down-home style helped him pull out an unexpected victory in November 1948.

Dewey was also saddled with the results of the Republican-controlled "do-nothing" 80th Congress (1947–1948). Truman used confrontation with Congress to rally voters who had supported the New Deal. He introduced legislation that he knew would be ignored, and he used his veto even when he knew Congress would override it. All the while he was building a list of campaign issues by demonstrating that the Republicans were obstructionists. Vote for me, Truman argued, to protect the New Deal, or vote Republican to bring back the days of Herbert Hoover. After his nomination in July 1948, Truman called Congress back into session and dared Republicans to enact all the measures for which their party claimed to stand. Congress did nothing, and Truman had more proof that the Republicans were all talk and no show.

WHISTLE-STOPPING ACROSS AMERICA

The 1948 presidential campaign mixed old and new. For the last time, a major candidate crisscrossed the nation by rail and made hundreds of speeches from the rear platforms of trains. For the first time, national television broadcast the two party conventions, although the primitive cameras showed the handful of viewers little more than talking heads. The Republican campaign issued a printed T-shirt that read "Dew-It With Dewey," the earliest advertising T-shirt in the collections of the Smithsonian Institution.

Truman ran on both character and issues. He was a widely read and intelligent man who cultivated the image of a backslapper. "I'll mow 'em down. . . . and I'll give 'em hell," he told his vice presidential running mate. Crowds across the country greeted him with "Give 'em hell, Harry!" He covered 31,700 miles in his campaign train and gave ten speeches a day. Republicans belittled the small towns and cities he visited, calling them "whistle stops." Democrats made the term a badge of pride for places like Laramie, Wyoming, and Pocatello, Idaho.

Truman brought the campaign home to average Americans. He tied Dewey to inflation, housing shortages, and fears about the future of Social Security (an issue that Democrats would continue to use into the next century). In industrial cities, he hammered at the Taft-Hartley Act. In the West, he pointed out that Democratic administrations had built dams and helped to turn natural resources into jobs. He called the Republicans the party of privilege and arrogance. The Democrats, he said, offered opportunity for farmers, factory workers, and small business owners.

Truman got a huge boost from Dewey's unwillingness to fight. Going into the fall with a huge lead in the public opinion polls, Dewey sought to avoid mistakes. He failed to counter Truman's attacks and packed his speeches with platitudes: "Our streams abound with fish." "You know that your future is still ahead of you." The results astounded the poll takers, who had stopped sampling opinion in mid-October just as a swing to Truman gathered strength. Wallace and Thurmond each took just under 1.2 million votes. Dewey received nearly 22 million popular votes and 189 electoral votes, but Truman won more than 24 million popular votes and 303 electoral votes (see Map 27–1).

TRUMAN'S FAIR DEAL

Truman hoped to build on the gains of the New Deal. In his State of the Union address in January 1949, he called for a Fair Deal for all Americans. He promised to extend the New Deal and insure "greater economic opportunity for the mass of the people." Over the next four years, however, conservative Republicans and southern Democrats forced Congress to choose carefully among Truman's proposals, accepting those

MAP 27-1   The Election of 1948
Harry Truman won a narrow victory in the presidential election of 1948 by holding many of the traditionally Democratic states of the South and West and winning key industrial states in the Middle West. His success depended on the coalition of rural and urban interests that Franklin Roosevelt had pulled together in the 1930s.

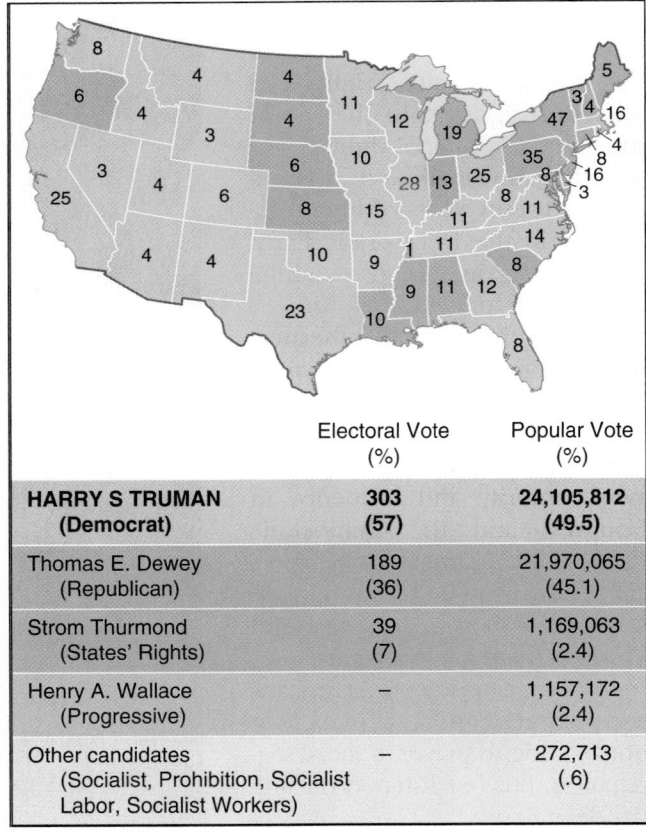

	Electoral Vote (%)	Popular Vote (%)
HARRY S TRUMAN (Democrat)	**303** **(57)**	**24,105,812** **(49.5)**
Thomas E. Dewey (Republican)	189 (36)	21,970,065 (45.1)
Strom Thurmond (States' Rights)	39 (7)	1,169,063 (2.4)
Henry A. Wallace (Progressive)	–	1,157,172 (2.4)
Other candidates (Socialist, Prohibition, Socialist Labor, Socialist Workers)	–	272,713 (.6)

that expanded existing programs but rejecting new departures. The result was a set of disconnected measures rather than the consistent program that Truman had advocated.

In the Housing Act of 1949, the federal government reaffirmed its concern about families who had been priced out of the private market. Passed with the backing of conservative Senator Robert Taft, "Mr. Republican" to his admirers, the act provided money for local housing agencies to buy, clear, and resell land for housing. The intent was to clear "substandard and blighted areas" and replace them with affordable modern apartments. The program never worked as intended because of scanty appropriations and poor design of the replacement housing, but it established the goal of decent housing for all Americans.

In 1950, Congress revitalized the weak Social Security program. Benefits went up by an average of 80 percent, and 10.5 million additional people received old-age and survivors' insurance. Most of the new coverage went to rural and small-town people, thus consolidating the broad support that has made it politically difficult to change Social Security ever since, even in the face of projected shortages in the twenty-first century.

Congress rejected other Fair Deal proposals that would remain on the national agenda for decades. A plan to alter the farm subsidy system to favor small farmers rather than agribusiness went nowhere. A Senate filibuster killed a permanent Fair Employment Practices Commission to fight racial discrimination in hiring, halting progress toward civil rights. The medical establishment blocked a proposal for national health insurance as "socialistic," leaving the issue to be revisited in the 1960s (with the passage of Medicare and Medicaid) and 1990s (with Bill Clinton's proposals for health-care reform). The overall message from Truman's second term was clear: Americans liked what the New Deal had given them but were hesitant about new initiatives.

CONFRONTING THE SOVIET UNION

In 1945, the United States and the Soviet Union were allies, victorious against Germany and planning the defeat of Japan. By 1947, they were engaged in a diplomatic and economic confrontation and soon came close to war over the city of Berlin. The business tycoon and presidential adviser Bernard Baruch characterized the conflict in April 1947 as a "cold war," and the newspaper columnist Walter Lippmann quickly popularized the term.

Over the next forty years, the United States and the Soviet Union contested for economic, political, and military influence around the globe. The heart of Soviet policy was control of eastern Europe as a buffer zone against Germany. The centerpiece of American policy was to link the United States, western Europe, and Japan into an alliance of overwhelming economic power. Both sides spent vast sums on conventional military forces and atomic weapons that held the world in a "balance of terror." They also competed for political advantage in Asia and Africa as newly independent nations replaced European colonial empires. For the United States, the Cold War was simultaneously an effort to promote democracy in Europe, maintain a strategically favorable military position in relation to the Soviet Union, and preserve its leadership of the world economy.

Each side in the Cold War thought the worst of the other. Behind the conflicts were Soviet insecurity about an aggressive West and American fear of Communist expansionism. Americans and Soviets frequently interpreted each other's actions in the most threatening terms, turning miscalculations and misunderstandings into crises. A U.S. public that had suffered through nearly two decades of economic depression and war reacted to international problems with frustration and anger. The emotional burdens of the Cold War warped and narrowed a generation of American political life around the requirements of anticommunism.

THE END OF THE GRAND ALLIANCE

The Yalta Conference of February 1945 had recognized military realities by marking out rough spheres of influence. The Soviet defeat of Germany on the Eastern Front had made the Soviet Union the only military power in eastern Europe. The American and British attacks through Italy and France had made the Western allies dominant in western Europe and the Mediterranean. The Soviets, Americans, British, and French shared control of defeated Germany, each with its own occupation zone and its own sector of Berlin. The Western allies had the better of the bargain. Defeated Italy and Japan, whose reconstruction was firmly in Western hands, had far greater economic potential than had Soviet-controlled Bulgaria, Romania, or Hungary. In addition, the British, French, and American occupation zones in western Germany held more people and industrial potential than did the Russian zone in eastern Germany.

As the victorious powers tried to put their broad agreements into operation, they argued bitterly about Germany and eastern Europe. Was the Soviet Union to dominate eastern Europe, or was the region to be open to Western economic and political influence? For Poland, Truman and his advisers claimed that Yalta had assumed open elections on the American model. The Soviet Union saw Poland as the historic invasion route from the west; it claimed that Yalta had insured that any Polish government would be friendly to Soviet interests and acted to guarantee that this would be so.

Facing Soviet intransigence over eastern Europe, Truman decided that the United States should "take the lead in running the world in the way the world ought to be run." One technique was economic pressure. The State Department "mislaid" a Soviet request for redevelopment loans. The United States and Britain objected to Soviet plans to take industrial equipment and raw materials from the western occupation zones in Germany, compensation that the Soviets thought they had been promised.

The United States also tried to involve the Soviet Union and eastern Europe in new international organizations. The Senate approved American membership in the newly organized United Nations (UN) with only two opposing votes, a sharp contrast to its rejection of the League of Nations in 1920. The Washington-based **International Monetary Fund** (IMF) and the **World Bank** were designed to revive international trade. The IMF stabilized national currencies against the short-term pressures of international trade. The World Bank drew on the resources of member nations to make economic development loans to governments for such projects as new dams or agricultural modernization. These organizations insured that a reviving world economy would revolve around the industrial and technological power of the United States, and they continue to dictate economic policy of many developing nations into the twenty-first century.

In 1946, the United States also presented a plan in the United Nations to control atomic energy. Bernard Baruch suggested that an international agency should oversee all uranium production and research on atomic explosives. The Baruch plan emphasized enforcement and inspections that would have opened the Soviet nuclear effort to American interference, an unacceptable prospect for a nation trying to catch up with the United States by building its own atomic bombs. On-site inspection would remain a problem in arms control negotiations for the next half-century.

While UN delegates debated the future of atomic energy, American leaders were becoming convinced of Soviet aggressiveness. In February 1946, George Kennan, a senior American diplomat in Moscow, sent a "long telegram" to the State Department. He depicted a Soviet Union driven by expansionist Communist ideology. The Soviets, he argued, would con-

stantly probe for weaknesses in the capitalist world. The best response was firm resistance to protect the western heartlands.

The British encouraged the same tough stand. Lacking the strength to shape Europe on its own, Great Britain repeatedly nudged the United States to block Soviet influence. Speaking at Westminster College in Missouri in March 1946, Winston Churchill warned that the Soviet Union had dropped an "iron curtain" across the middle of Europe and urged a firm Western response.

Churchill's speech matched the mood in official Washington. Truman's foreign-policy advisers shared the belief in an aggressive Soviet Union, and the president himself saw the world as a series of either-or choices. Administration leaders did not fear an immediate Soviet military threat to the United States itself, for they knew that World War II had exhausted the Soviet Union. But they also knew that the Soviets were strong enough to brush aside the U.S. occupation forces in Germany. Added to military apprehension were worries about political and economic competition. Communist parties in war-ravaged Europe and Japan were exploiting discontent. In Asia and Africa, the allegiance of nationalists who were fighting for independence from France, Great Britain, and the Netherlands remained in doubt. America's leaders worried that much of the Eastern Hemisphere might fall under Soviet control and turn its back on North America.

Were Truman and his advisers right about Soviet intentions? The evidence is mixed. In their determination to avoid another Munich, Truman and the "wise men" who made up his foreign-policy circle ignored examples of Soviet caution and conciliation. The Soviets withdrew troops from Manchuria in northern China and acquiesced in America's control of defeated Japan. They allowed a neutral but democratic government in Finland and technically free elections in Hungary and Czechoslovakia (although it was clear that Communists would do well there). They demobilized much of their huge army and reduced their forces in eastern Europe while expecting a falling out between capitalist Britain and the United States.

However, the Soviet regime also did more than enough to justify American fears. The Soviet Union could not resist exerting influence in the Middle East. It pressured Turkey to give it partial control of the exit from the Black Sea. It retained troops in northern Iran until warned out by the United States. The Soviets were ruthless in support of Communist control in Eastern Europe in 1946 and 1947; they aided a Communist takeover in Bulgaria, backed a coup in Romania, and undermined the last non-Communist political opposition in Poland. U.S. policymakers read these Soviet actions as a rerun of Nazi aggression and determined not to let a new totalitarian threat undermine Western power.

THE TRUMAN DOCTRINE AND THE MARSHALL PLAN

Whatever restraint the Soviet Union showed was too late or too little. Early in 1947, Truman and his advisers acted decisively. The British could no longer afford to back the Greek government that was fighting Communist rebels, and U.S. officials feared that a Communist takeover in Greece would threaten the stability of Italy, France, and the Middle East. Truman coupled his case for intervention in Greece with an appeal for aid to neighboring Turkey, which lived under the shadow of the Soviet Union. On March 12, he told Congress that the United States faced a "fateful hour." Taking the advice of Senator Arthur Vandenberg to "scare the hell out of the country," he said that only the appropriation of $400 million to fight Communism in Greece and Turkey could secure the free world. Congress agreed, and the United States became the dominant power in the eastern Mediterranean.

Framing the specific request was a sweeping declaration that became known as the **Truman Doctrine**. The president pledged to use U.S. economic power to help free nations everywhere resist internal subversion or aggression. "It must be the policy of the United States," he said, "to support free peoples who are resisting attempted subjugation by armed minorities or by outside pressures. . . . I believe that our help should be primarily through economic and financial aid, which is essential to economic stability and orderly political processes."

Meanwhile, Europe was sliding toward chaos. Germany was close to famine after the bitter winter of 1946–1947. Western European nations were bankrupt and unable to import raw materials for their factories. Overstressed medical systems could no longer control diseases such as tuberculosis. Communist parties had gained in Italy, France, and Germany. Winston Churchill, again sounding the alarm, described Europe as "a rubble-heap, a charnel house, a breeding ground of pestilence and hate."

The U.S. government responded with unprecedented economic aid. Secretary of State George C. Marshall announced the European Recovery Plan on June 5, 1947. What the press quickly dubbed the **Marshall Plan** committed the United States to help rebuild Europe. The United States invited Soviet and eastern European participation, but under terms that

would have reduced Moscow's control over its satellite economies. The Soviets refused, fearing that the United States wanted to undermine its influence, instead organizing their eastern European satellites in their own association for Mutual Economic Assistance, or Comecon, in 1949. In western Europe, the Marshall Plan was a success. Aid totaled $13.5 billion over four years. It met many of Europe's economic needs and quieted class conflict. Unlike the heavy-handed Soviet role in eastern Europe, the Marshall Plan expanded American influence through cooperative efforts. Because Europeans spent much of the aid on U.S. goods and machinery, and because economic recovery promised markets for U.S. products, business and labor both supported it. In effect, the Marshall Plan created an "empire by invitation," in which Americans and Europeans jointly planned European recovery.

U.S. policy in Japan followed the pattern set in Europe. As supreme commander of the Allied Powers, General Douglas MacArthur acted as Japan's postwar dictator. He tried to change the values of the old war-prone Japan through social reform, democratization, and demilitarization. At the end of 1947, however, the United States decided that democracy and pacifism could go too far. Policymakers were fearful of economic collapse and political chaos, just as in Europe. The "reverse course" in occupation policy aimed to make Japan an economic magnet for other nations in East Asia, pulling them toward the American orbit and away from the Soviet Union. MacArthur reluctantly accepted the new policy of "economic crank-up" by preserving Japan's corporate giants and encouraging American investment. At American insistence, the new Japan accepted American bases and created its own "self-defense force" (with no capacity for overseas aggression).

George Kennan summed up the new American policies in the magazine *Foreign Affairs* in July 1947. Writing anonymously as "X," Kennan argued that the Soviet leaders were committed to a long-term strategy of expanding Communism. The proper posture of the United States, he said, should be an equally patient commitment to "firm and vigilant **containment** of Russian expansive tendencies." Kennan warned that the emerging Cold War would be a long conflict, with no quick fixes.

SOVIET REACTIONS

The bold American moves in the first half of 1947 put the Soviet Union on the defensive. In response, Soviet leaders orchestrated strenuous opposition to the Marshall Plan by French and Italian Communists. East of the Iron Curtain, Hungarian Communists expelled other political parties from a coalition government. Bulgarian Communists shot opposition leaders. Romania, Bulgaria, and Hungary signed defense pacts with the Soviet Union.

In early 1948, the Soviets targeted Czechoslovakia. For three years, a neutral coalition government there on the model of Finland had balanced trade with the West with a foreign policy friendly to the Soviet Union. In February 1948, while Russian forces assembled on the Czech borders, local Communists took advantage of political bumbling by other members of the governing coalition. Taking control of the government through a technically legal process, they pushed aside Czechoslovakia's democratic leadership and turned the nation into a dictatorship and Soviet satellite within a week.

The climax of the Soviet reaction came in divided Berlin, located 110 miles inside the Soviet Union's East German occupation zone. The city was divided into one sector controlled by the Soviets and the other by the U.S. Britain, and France. On June 4, 1948, Soviet troops blockaded surface traffic into Berlin, cutting off the United States, British, and French sectors. The immediate Soviet aim was to block Western plans to merge their three occupation zones into an independent federal republic (West Germany). Rather than abandon 2.5 million Berliners or shoot their way through, the Western nations responded to the **Berlin blockade** by airlifting supplies to the city. Planes landed every two minutes at Berlin's Tempelhof Airport. Stalin decided not to intercept the flights. After eleven months, the Soviets abandoned the blockade, making the Berlin airlift a triumph of American resolve.

AMERICAN REARMAMENT

The coup in Czechoslovakia and the Berlin blockade shocked American leaders and backfired on the Soviets. The economic assistance strategy of 1947 now looked inadequate. Congress responded in 1948 by reinstating the military draft and increasing defense spending. Much of the money bought new war planes, as thrifty congressmen decided that air power was the easiest way for the United States to project its military power abroad.

The United States had already begun to modernize and centralize its national security apparatus, creating the institutions that would run foreign policy in the second half of the century. The National Security Act of July 1947 created the **Central Intelligence Agency** (CIA) and the **National Security Council** (NSC). The CIA handled intelligence gathering and covert operations. The NSC assembled top diplomatic and military advisers in one committee. In

1949, legislation also created the Department of Defense to oversee the army, navy, and air force (independent from the army since 1947). The civilian secretary of defense soon emerged as a position with influence on foreign policy equal to that of the secretary of state. The new post of chairman of the joint chiefs of staff was supposed to coordinate the rival branches of the military.

In April 1949, ten European nations, the United States, and Canada signed the North Atlantic Treaty as a mutual defense pact. American commitments to the **North Atlantic Treaty Organization (NATO)** included military aid and the deployment of U.S. troops in western Europe. As Republican Senator Robert Taft warned in the ratification debate, NATO was the sort of "entangling alliance" that the United States had avoided for 160 years. It was also the insurance policy that western Europeans required if they were to accept the dangers as well as the benefits of a revived Germany, which was economically and militarily necessary for a strong Europe. In short, NATO was a sort of marriage contract between Europe and the previously standoffish United States. After 1955, its counterpart would be the **Warsaw Pact** for mutual defense among the Soviet Union and its European satellites (see Map 27–2).

Two years later, the United States signed similar but less comprehensive agreements in the western Pacific: the ANZUS Pact with Australia and New Zealand and a new treaty with the Philippines. The alliances reassured Pacific allies who were nervously watching the United States negotiate a unilateral peace treaty with Japan (ignoring the Soviet Union). The United States overcame opposition from nations that Japan had attacked in World War II by promising to assist their defense and maintaining military bases in Japan. Taken together, peacetime rearmament and mutual defense pacts amounted to a revolution in American foreign policy.

COLD WAR AND HOT WAR

The first phase of the Cold War reached a crisis in the autumn of 1949. The two previous years had seen an uneasy equilibrium in which American success in southern and western Europe and the standoff over Berlin (the blockade ended in May 1949) balanced the consolidation of Soviet power in eastern Europe. Now, suddenly, two key events seemed to tilt the world balance against the United States and its allies. In September, Truman announced that the Soviet Union had tested its own atomic bomb. A month later, the Chinese Communists under Mao Zedong (Mao Tsetung) took power in China. The following summer,

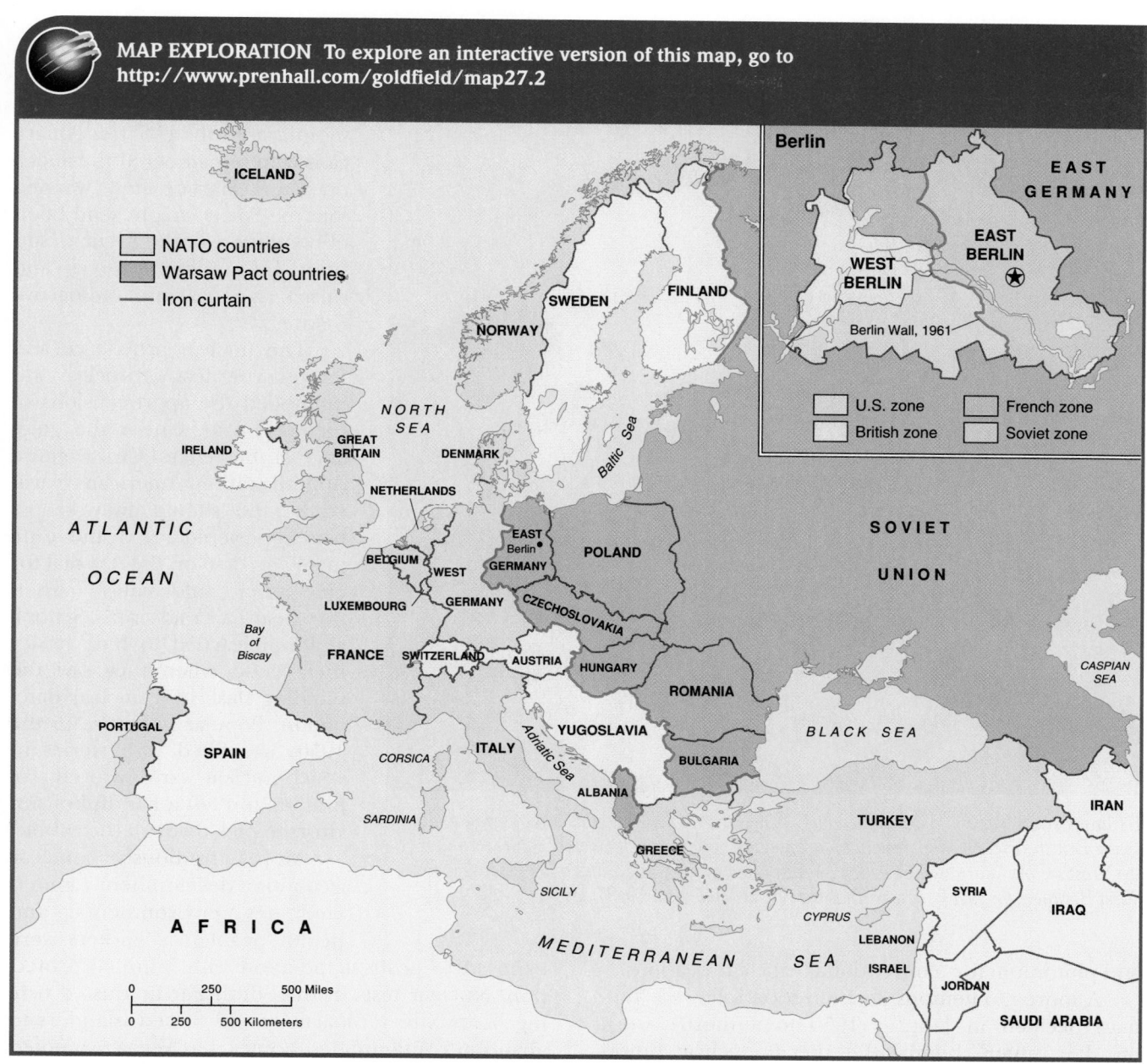

MAP EXPLORATION To explore an interactive version of this map, go to http://www.prenhall.com/goldfield/map27.2

MAP 27-2   **Cold War in Europe**
In the late 1940s and 1950s, the Cold War split Europe into rigidly divided western and eastern blocs. Members of NATO allied with the United States to oppose Soviet expansion. The Soviet Union directed the military and foreign policies of members of the Warsaw Pact.

civil war in Korea sucked the United States into a fierce war with Communist North Korea and China. While Americans studied maps that showed communism spreading across Europe and Asia, their government accelerated a forty-year arms race with the Soviet Union.

THE NUCLEAR SHADOW

Experts in Washington had known that the Soviets were working on an A-bomb, but the news dismayed the average citizen. As newspapers and magazines scared their readers with artists' renditions of the effects of an atomic bomb on New York or Chicago, the shock tilted U.S. nuclear policy toward military uses. In 1946, advocates of civilian control had won a small victory when Congress gave control of atomic energy to the new Atomic Energy Commission (AEC). The AEC tried to balance research on atomic power with continued testing of new weapons. Now Truman told the AEC to double the output of fissionable uranium

TimePix

Berlin in 1948 was still a devastated city. When the Soviet Union closed off ground access to the British, French, and American occupation zones, the city also became a symbol of the West's Cold War resolve. Allied aircraft lifted in food, fuel, and other essentials for West Berliners for nearly a year until the Soviets ended the blockade.

floor. Great Britain became the third nuclear power in the same year. The Soviet Union tested its own hydrogen bomb only nine months after the U.S. test. Americans who remembered the attack on Pearl Harbor now worried that the Soviets might send fleets of bombers over the Arctic to surprise U.S. military forces and smash its cities into radioactive powder.

The nuclear arms race and the gnawing fear of nuclear war multiplied the apprehensions of the Cold War. Under the guidance of the Federal Civil Defense Administration, Americans learned that they should always keep a battery-powered radio and tune to 640 or 1240 on the AM dial for emergency information when they heard air raid sirens. Schoolchildren learned to hide under their desks when they saw the blinding flash of a nuclear detonation. Popular literature in the 1950s was filled with stories in which nuclear war destroyed civilization and left a handful of survivors to pick through the rubble.

More insidiously, nuclear weapons development generated new environmental and health problems. Soldiers were

and plutonium for "conventional" nuclear weapons.

A more momentous decision soon followed. Truman decided in January 1950 to authorize work on the "super" bomb—the thermonuclear fusion weapon that would become the hydrogen bomb (H-bomb). The debate over the "super" pitted a cautious scientific advisory committee and J. Robert Oppenheimer against powerful political figures and a handful of scientists who believed, correctly, that the Soviets were already at work on a similar weapon. As would be true in future nuclear-defense debates, the underlying question was how much capacity for nuclear destruction was enough (see American Views: "Deciding on a Nuclear Arms Race").

Nuclear weapons proliferated in the early 1950s. The United States exploded the first hydrogen bomb in the South Pacific in November 1952. Releasing one hundred times the energy of the Hiroshima bomb, the detonation tore a mile-long chasm in the ocean

exposed to posttest radiation with minimal protection. Nuclear tests in the South Pacific dusted fishing boats with radioactivity and forced islanders to abandon contaminated homes. Las Vegas promoted tests in southern Nevada as tourist attractions, but radioactive fallout contaminated large sections of the West and increased cancer rates among "downwinders" in Utah. Weapons production and atomic experiments contaminated vast tracts in Nevada, Washington, and Colorado and left huge environmental costs for later generations (see Map 27–3).

THE COLD WAR IN ASIA

Communist victory in China's civil war was as predictable as the Soviet nuclear bomb but no less controversial. American military and diplomatic missions in the late 1940s pointed out that the collapse of Jiang Jieshi's Nationalist regime was nearly inevitable, given its corruption and narrow support. Nevertheless,

AMERICAN VIEWS

Deciding on a Nuclear Arms Race

In 1950, the United States began work on a hydrogen (thermonuclear) bomb. The decision locked the United States and the Soviet Union into a nuclear arms race that lasted another forty years. In the first document reprinted here, an excerpt from a letter to President Truman written on November 25, 1949, Lewis Strauss, chairman of the Atomic Energy Commission, urged work on the H-bomb. In the second, scientist Edward Teller agreed. A refugee from Nazi-dominated Europe who had worked at Los Alamos, Teller remained an advocate of massive defense spending through the 1980s.

- How did memories of World War II affect this Cold War decision?
- How did U.S. policymakers evaluate the intentions of the Soviet Union?

Lewis Strauss, November 1949:

Dear Mr. President:

As you know, the thermonuclear (super) bomb was suggested by scientists working at Los Alamos during the war. . . . I believe that the United States must be as completely armed as any possible enemy. From this, it follows that I believe it unwise to renounce, unilaterally, any weapon which an enemy can reasonably be expected to possess. I recommend that the President direct the Atomic Energy Commission to proceed with the development of the thermonuclear bomb, at highest priority. . . . Obviously the current atomic bomb as well as the proposed thermonuclear weapon are horrible to contemplate. All war is horrible. Until, however, some means is found of eliminating war, I cannot agree with those of my colleagues who feel that an announcement should be made by the President to the effect that the development of the thermonuclear weapon will not be undertaken by the United States at this time. This is because I do not think the statement will be credited in the Kremlin . . . and because primarily until

disarmament is universal, our arsenal must be not less well equipped than with the most potent weapons that our technology can devise.

Edward Teller, March 1950:

President Truman has announced that we are going to make a hydrogen bomb. . . . The scientist is not responsible for the law of nature. It is his job to find out how these laws operate. . . . However, it is not the scientist's job to determine whether a hydrogen bomb should be constructed, whether it should be used, or how it should be used. This responsibility rests with the American people and their chosen representatives. Personally, as a citizen, I do not know in what other way President Truman could have acted. . . . To my mind we are in a situation no less dangerous than the one we were facing in 1939, and it is of the greatest importance that we realize it. We must realize. . . . that democracy will not be saved by ideals alone.

Source: Lewis L. Strauss, *Men and Decisions* (1962).

Americans looked for a scapegoat when Jiang's anti-Communist government and fragments of the Nationalist army fled to the island of Taiwan off China's southern coast.

Advocates for Jiang, mostly conservative Republicans from the Midwest and West, were certain that

Truman's administration had done too little. "China asked for a sword," complained one senator, "and we gave her a dull paring knife." Critics looked for scapegoats. Foreign service officers who had honestly analyzed the weakness of the Nationalists were accused of communist sympathies and hounded from their jobs.

MAP 27-3 The Landscape of Nuclear Weapons

The development and production of nuclear weapons was concentrated in the West and South. The World War II sites of Hanford, Los Alamos, and Oak Ridge remained active after the war. Workers at Savannah River, Rocky Flats, and Pantex produced nuclear materials. Scientists and engineers at Lawrence-Livermore and Sandia laboratories designed and assembled weapons that were tested at the Nevada Proving Grounds. Prospectors with Geiger counters swarmed over the canyons of southwestern Colorado and southeastern Utah in a uranium mining rush in the early 1950s.

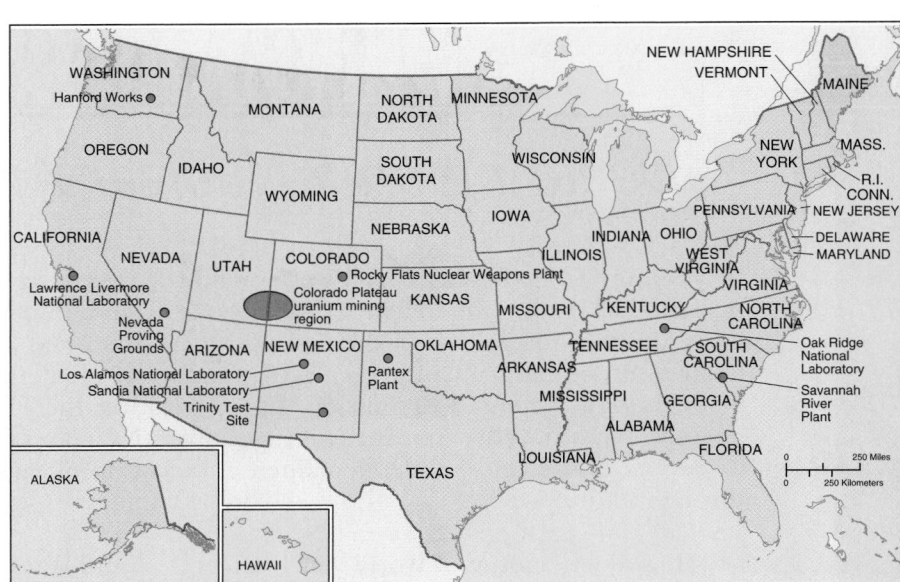

The results were tragedy for those unfairly branded as traitors and damage to the State Department, a weakness that would haunt the United States as it became entangled in southeast Asia in the 1950s and 1960s.

Mao's victory expanded a deep fissure between "Europe first" and "Asia first" approaches to American foreign policy. Both during and after World War II, the United States had made Europe its first priority. Strong voices, however, had persistently argued that America's future lay with China, Japan, and the Pacific nations. Influential senators claimed that the "loss of China" was the disastrous result of putting the needs of England and France above the long-term interests of the United States.

NSC-68 AND AGGRESSIVE CONTAINMENT

The turmoil of 1949 led to a comprehensive statement of American strategic goals. In April 1950, the State Department prepared a sweeping report known as **National Security Council Paper 68 (NSC-68)**. The document described a world divided between the forces of "slavery" and "freedom" and assumed that the Soviet Union was actively aggressive, motivated by greed for territory and a "fanatic faith" in Communism. To defend civilization itself, said the experts, the United States should use as much force as needed to resist communist expansion anywhere and everywhere.

The authors of NSC-68 thought in terms of military solutions. Truman and his advisers in 1947 and 1948 had hoped to contain the Soviets by diplomacy and by integrating the economies of Europe and Japan with that of the United States. Now that the Soviets had the atomic bomb, however, the American

atomic shield might be neutralized. Instead, NSC-68 argued that the United States needed to press friendly nations to rearm and to make its former enemies into military allies. It also argued that the nation needed expensive conventional forces to defend Europe on the ground and to react to crises as a "world policeman." NSC-68 thus advocated nearly open-ended increases in the defense budget (which, in fact, tripled between 1950 and 1954).

NSC-68 summed up what many people already believed. Although it was not a public document, its portrait of implacable Communist expansion would have made sense to most Americans; it certainly did to Harry Truman. The outbreak of war in Korea at the end of June 1950 seemed to confirm that Communism was a military threat. The thinking behind the report led the United States to approach the Cold War as a military competition and to view political changes in Africa and Asia as parts of a Soviet plan. The need for a flexible military response became the centerpiece of an American policy of active intervention that led eventually to the jungles of Vietnam in the 1960s. And the report's implied strategy of bankrupting the communists through competitive defense spending helped destroy the Soviet Union at the end of the 1980s.

WAR IN KOREA, 1950–1953

The success of Mao and the Chinese Communists forced the Truman administration to define national interests in eastern Asia and the western Pacific. The most important U.S. interest was Japan, still an industrial power despite its devastating defeat. The United States had denied the Soviet Union any part in the occupation of Japan in 1945 and had shaped a more de-mocratic nation that would be a strong and friendly trading partner. Protected by American armed forces, Japan would be part of a crescent of offshore strong points that included Alaska, the Philippines, Australia, and New Zealand.

Two questions remained at the start of 1950 (and were still troublesome at the turn of the century). One was the future of Taiwan and the remnants of Jiang's regime. Some American policymakers wanted to defend Jiang against the Communists. Others as-sumed that his tattered forces would collapse and allow Mao to complete the Communist takeover of Chinese territory. The other question was Korea, whose own civil war would soon bring the world to the brink of World War III.

The Korean peninsula is the closest point on the Asian mainland to Japan. With three powerful neigh-bors—China, Russia, and Japan—Korea had always had to fight for its independence. From 1910 to 1945, it had been an oppressed colony of the Japanese em-pire. As World War II ended, Soviet troops moved down the peninsula from the north and American forces landed in the south, creating a situation similar to that in Germany. The 38th parallel, which Russians and Americans set as the dividing line between their zones of occupation, became a *de facto* border. The United States in 1948 recognized an independent South Korea, with its capital at Seoul, under a conser-vative government led by Syngman Rhee. Rhee's sup-port came from large landowners and from a police force trained by the Japanese before 1945. The Soviets recognized a separate North Korea, whose leader, Kim Il Sung, advocated radical social and political change. Both leaders saw the 38th parallel as a tempo-rary barrier and hoped to unify all Koreans under their own rule. Each crushed political dissent and tried to undermine the other with economic pressure and commando raids.

As early as 1947, the United States had decided that Korea itself was not essential to American military strategy. Planners assumed that U.S. air power in Japan could neutralize unfriendly forces on the Ko-rean peninsula. But Korea remained politically impor-tant as the only point of direct confrontation with the Soviet Union in Asia. In January 1950, Secretary of State Dean Acheson carefully excluded Korea from the primary "defensive perimeter" of the United States but kept open the possibility of international guarantees for Korean security.

On June 25, 1950, North Korea, helped by Soviet equipment and Chinese training, attacked South Korea, an act that started the **Korean War**, which lasted until 1953 (see Map 27–4). Truman and Ache-

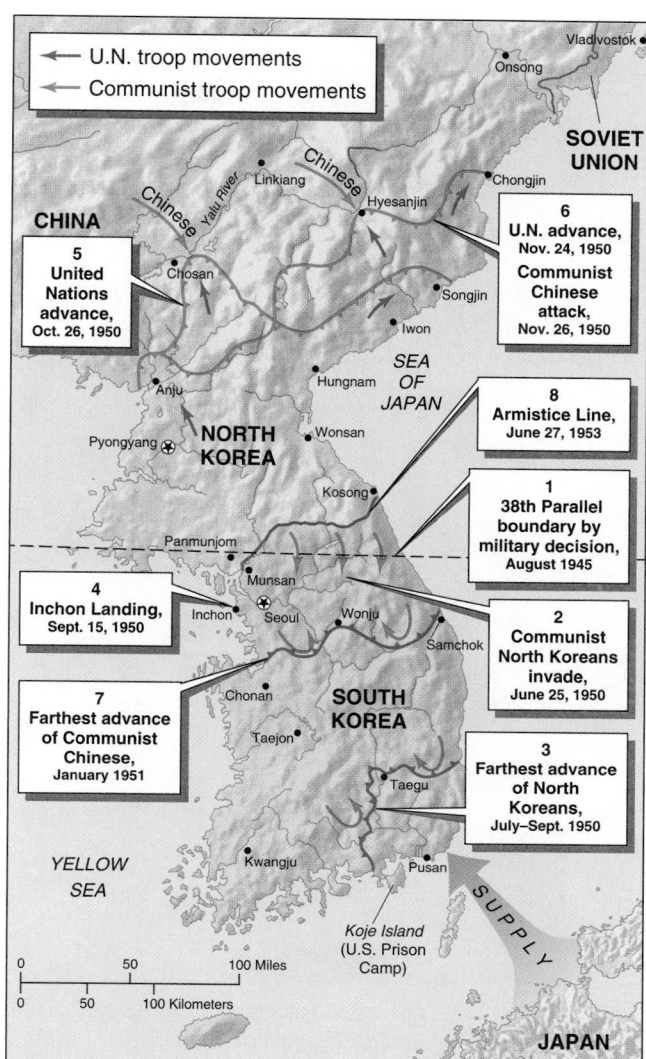

MAP 27-4   The Korean War
After rapid reversals of fortune in 1950 and early 1951, the war in Korea settled into stalemate. Most Americans agreed with the need to contain Communist expansion but found it deeply frustrating to fight for limited objectives rather than total victory.

son believed that Moscow lay behind the invasion. They worried that the attack was a ploy to suck Amer-ica's limited military resources into Asia before a bigger war came in Europe or the Middle East. Re-publicans blamed Acheson's speech for inviting an in-vasion, but the war was really an intensification of an ongoing civil war that Stalin was willing to exploit. In fact, Kim originated the invasion plan and spent a year persuading Stalin to agree to it. Stalin hoped that the conquest of South Korea would force Japan to sign a favorable treaty with the USSR.

The explosion of a hot war after five years of world tension seemed to American leaders to demand

United Nation forces in Korea fought the weather as well as Communist North Korean and Chinese. Baking summer heat alternated with fierce winters. Snow and cold were a major help to the Chinese when they surprised United States forces in November 1950 and drove American troops such as these southward.

a military response. As the South Korean army collapsed, Truman committed American ground troops from Japan on June 30. The United States also had the good fortune of securing an endorsement from the United Nations. Because the Soviet Union was boycotting the UN (hoping to force the seating of Mao's People's Republic of China in place of Jiang's government), it could not use its veto when the Security Council asked UN members to help South Korea. The Korean conflict remained officially a United Nations action, although U.S. Generals Douglas MacArthur, Matthew Ridgway, and Mark Clark ran the show as the successive heads of the UN command.

THE POLITICS OF WAR

Fortunes in the first year of the Korean conflict seesawed three times. The first U.S. combat troops were outnumbered, outgunned, and poorly trained. They

could not stop the North Koreans. By early August, the Americans clung to a narrow toehold around the port of Pusan on the tip of the Korean peninsula. As reinforcements arrived from the United States, however, MacArthur transformed the war with a daring amphibious counterattack at Inchon, 150 miles behind North Korean lines. The North Korean army was already overextended and exhausted. It collapsed and fled north.

The temptation to push across the 38th parallel and unify the peninsula under Syngman Rhee was irresistible. MacArthur and Washington officials disregarded warnings by China that it would enter the war if the United States tried to reunite Korea by force. U.S. and South Korean troops rolled north, drawing closer and closer to the boundary between North Korea and China.

Chinese forces attacked MacArthur's command in late October but then disappeared. MacArthur dismissed the attacks as a token gesture. In fact, they were a final warning. On November 26, the Chinese struck the overextended American columns. They had massed 300,000 troops without detection by American aviation. Their assault drove the UN forces into a two-month retreat that again abandoned Seoul.

Despite his glaring mistake, MacArthur remained in command until he publicly contradicted national policy. In March 1951, with the UN forces again pushing north, Truman prepared to offer a cease-fire that would have preserved the separate nations of South and North Korea. MacArthur tried to preempt the president by demanding that China admit defeat or suffer the consequences. He then published a direct attack on the administration's policy of limiting the Asian war to insure the security of Europe.

President Truman had no choice. To protect civilian control of the armed forces, he relieved MacArthur of his commands on April 11, 1951. The general returned to parades and a hero's welcome when he addressed a joint session of Congress. He quoted a line from an old barracks song: "Old soldiers never die; they just fade away." The song was soon heard on the radio, but Truman remained in charge of the war.

In Korea itself, U.S. and South Korean forces stabilized a strong defensive line that cut diagonally across the 38th parallel. Here the conflict settled into trench warfare. UN and Communist armies faced each other across steep bare hills that choked in clouds of summer dust and froze in winter. For two years, boredom alternated with fierce inch-by-inch battles for territory with such names as Heartbreak Ridge and Pork Chop Hill. The war's only glamour was in the air, where the arrival of new F-86 Saberjets in 1952 allowed American pilots to clear the skies of Chinese aviators in Russian-made MIG 15s.

Stabilization of the Korean front ushered in two years of truce negotiations beginning in July 1951, for none of the key actors wanted a wider war. The Chinese were careful to keep their war planes north of the ground combat zone. The Russians had stayed out of the war. The United States learned a painful lesson in 1950 and was willing to accept a divided Korea.

Negotiations stalled over thousands of Chinese prisoners of war who might not want to return to China. The political decision to turn free choice for POWs into a symbol of resistance to Communism left Truman's administration bogged down in a grinding war. Nearly half of the 140,000 U.S. casualties came after the truce talks started. The war was a decisive factor behind the Republican victory in the November 1952 elections and dragged on until June 1953, when an armistice returned the peninsula roughly to its prewar political division, a situation that endured into the twenty-first century.

The blindly ambitious attack into North Korea was one of the great failures of intelligence and strategic leadership in American military history. Nearly everyone in Washington shared the blame for letting the excitement of battlefield victories obscure limited war aims. Civilian leaders could not resist the desire to roll back communism. Truman hoped for a striking victory before the 1950 congressional elections. The Joint Chiefs of Staff failed to question a general with MacArthur's heroic reputation. MacArthur himself allowed ambition and wishful thinking to jeopardize his army.

Consequences of the Korean War. The war in Korea was a preview of Vietnam fifteen years later. American leaders propped up an undemocratic regime to defend democracy. Both North Koreans and South Koreans engaged in savage political reprisals as the battlefront shifted back and forth.

American soldiers found it hard distinguish between allied and enemy Koreans. American emphasis on the massive application of firepower led U.S. forces to demolish entire villages to kill single snipers. The air force tried to break North Korean resistance by pouring bombs on cities, power stations, factories, and dams; General Curtis Le May estimated that the bombings killed a million Koreans.

The Korean War had global consequences. It helped to legitimize the United Nations. In Washington, it confirmed the ideas underlying NSC-68, with its call for the United States to expand its military and to lead an anti-Communist alliance. Two days after the North Korean invasion, President Truman ordered the Seventh Fleet to protect the Nationalist Chinese on Taiwan, a decision that guaranteed twenty years of hostility between the United States and the People's Republic of China. In the same month, the United States began to aid France's struggle to retain control over its Southeast Asian colony of Indochina, which included Laos, Cambodia, and Vietnam.

In Europe, the United States now pushed to rearm West Germany as part of a militarized NATO and sent troops to Europe as a permanent defense force. It increased military aid to European governments and secured a unified command for the national forces allocated for NATO. The unified command made West German rearmament acceptable to France and the smaller nations of western Europe. Rearmament also stimulated German economic recovery and bound West Germany to the political and economic institutions of the North Atlantic nations. In 1952, the European Coal and Steel Community marked an important step toward economic cooperation that would evolve into the European Union by the end of the century. Dwight Eisenhower, who had led the Western allies in the invasion of France and Germany, became the new NATO commander in April 1951; his appointment symbolized the American commitment to western Europe.

THE SECOND RED SCARE

The Korean War reinforced the second Red Scare, an assault on civil liberties that stretched from the mid-1940s to the mid-1950s and dwarfed the Red Scare of 1919–1920. The Cold War fanned fears of communist subversion on American soil. Legitimate concerns about espionage mixed with suspicions that communist sympathizers in high places were helping Stalin and Mao. The scare was also a weapon that the conservative wing of the Republican party used against men and women who had built Roosevelt's New Deal (see the Overview table, "The Second Red Scare").

Efforts to root out suspected subversives operated on three tracks. National and state governments established loyalty programs to identify and fire suspect employees. The courts punished members of suspect organizations. Congressional and state legislative investigations followed the whims of committee chairs. Anti-Communist crusaders often relied on dubious evidence and eagerly believed the worst. They also threatened basic civil liberties.

THE COMMUNIST PARTY AND THE LOYALTY PROGRAM

The Communist Party in the United States was in rapid decline after World War II. Many intellectuals had left the party over the Nazi Soviet Pact in 1939. The wartime glow of military alliance with the Soviet Union helped the party recover to perhaps eighty thousand members—still fewer than one in every fifteen hundred Americans—but the postwar years brought a series of failures. In 1946, Walter Reuther defeated a Communist for the presidency of the huge United Auto Workers union, and other CIO unions froze Communists out of leadership positions. Communist support for Henry Wallace reduced the party's influence and separated it from the increasingly conservative mainstream of American politics.

Nevertheless, Republicans used Red-baiting as a campaign technique in 1944 and 1946, setting the stage for a national loyalty program. In 1944 they tried to frighten voters about "commydemocrats" by linking FDR, CIO labor unions, and Communism. Democrats slung their own mud by trying to convince voters that Hitler preferred the Republicans. Two years later, Republican campaigners told the public that the basic choice was "between Communism and Republicanism." Starting a thirty-year political career, a young Navy veteran named Richard Nixon won a southern California congressional seat by hammering on his opponent's connections to supposedly "Communist-dominated" organizations.

President Truman responded to the Republican landslide with Executive Order 9835 in March 1947, initiating a loyalty program for federal employees. Truman may have been trying to head off more drastic action by Congress. Nevertheless, Order 9835 was a blunt instrument. It authorized the attorney general to prepare a list of "totalitarian, Fascist, Communist, or subversive" organizations and made membership or even "sympathetic association" with such groups grounds for dismissal. The loyalty program applied to approximately 8 million Americans working for the federal government or defense contractors; similar state laws affected another 5 million.

Loyalty was a moving target. The attorney general's list grew by fits and starts, with often arbitrary additions. Many accusations were just malicious gossip, but allegations stayed in a worker's file even if refuted. Appointment to a new job in the federal government triggered a new investigation, in which officials might paw through the same old material. Many New Dealers and people associated with presumably liberal East Coast institutions were targets. An Interior Department official boasted that he had been especially effective in squeezing out graduates of Harvard and Columbia.

Federal employees worked under a cloud of fear. Would the cooperative store they had once patron-

Overview

The Second Red Scare

Type of Anticommunist Effort	Key Tools	Results
Employee loyalty programs	U.S. attorney general's list of subversive organizations	Thousands of federal and state workers fired, careers damaged
Congressional investigations	HUAC McCarren Committee Army-McCarthy hearings	Employee blacklists, harassment of writers and intellectuals, Hollywood Ten
Criminal prosecutions	Trials for espionage and conspiracy to advocate violent overthrow of the U.S. government	Convictions of Communist Party leaders (1949), Alger Hiss (1950), and Rosenbergs (1951)

ized or the protest group they had joined in college suddenly appear on the attorney general's list? Would someone complain that they had disloyal books on their shelves? Loyalty boards asked about religion, racial equality, and a taste for foreign films; they also tried to identify homosexuals, who were thought to be targets for blackmail by foreign agents. The loyalty program resulted in 1,210 firings and 6,000 resignations under Truman and comparable numbers during Dwight Eisenhower's first term from 1953 to 1956.

NAMING NAMES TO CONGRESS

Congress was even busier than the executive branch. The congressional hunt for subversives had its roots in 1938, when Congressman Martin Dies, a Texas Democrat, created the Special Committee on Un-American Activities. Originally intended to ferret out pro-Fascists, the Dies Committee evolved into the permanent **House Un-American Activities Committee (HUAC)** in 1945. It investigated "un-American propaganda" that attacked constitutional government.

One of HUAC's juiciest targets was Hollywood. In the last years before television, the movie industry stood at the height of its capacity to influence public opinion. In 1946, Americans bought an average of 90 million tickets every week. But Hollywood's reputation for loose morals, foreign-born directors, Jewish producers, and left-leaning writers aroused the suspicions of many congressmen. HUAC sought to make

sure that no un-American messages were being peddled through America's most popular entertainment.

When the hearings opened in October 1947, studio executives, such as Jack Warner of Warner Brothers and Louis B. Mayer of MGM, assured HUAC of their anti-Communism. So did the popular actors Gary Cooper and Ronald Reagan. By contrast, eight screenwriters and two directors—the so called Hollywood Ten—refused to discuss their past political associations, citing the free-speech protections of the First Amendment to the Constitution. HUAC countered with citations for contempt of Congress. The First Amendment defense failed when it reached the Supreme Court, and the Ten went to jail in 1950.

HUAC changed the politics of Hollywood. Before 1947, it had been fashionable to lean toward the left; even *The Best Years of Our Lives* contained criticism of American society. After the hearings, it was imperative to tilt the other way. Humphrey Bogart apologized for being a "dope" about politics. The government refused to let British-born Charlie Chaplin reenter the United States in 1952 because of his left-wing views. Other actors, writers, and directors found themselves on the Hollywood blacklist, banned from jobs where they might insert Communist propaganda into American movies.

At the start of 1951, the new Senate Internal Security Subcommittee joined the sometimes bumbling HUAC. The McCarran Committee, named for the

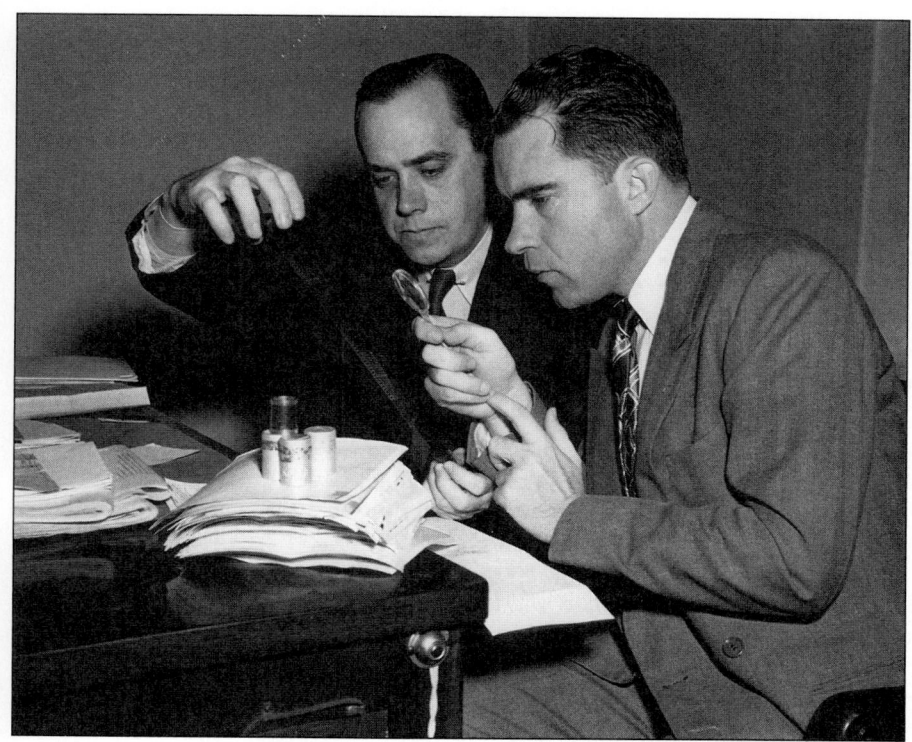

Richard Nixon (right) and the chief investigator for the House Committee on Un-American Activities inspect microfilm of the "pumpkin papers." Hidden inside a pumpkin on the Maryland farm of committee informant Whittaker Chambers, the papers helped convict Alger Hiss of perjury. Nixon's role in pursuing Hiss launched a political career that took him to the White House.

Nevada senator who chaired it, targeted diplomats, labor union leaders, professors, and schoolteachers. Both committees turned their investigations into rituals. The real point was not to force personal confessions from witnesses but to badger them into identifying friends and associates who might have been involved in suspect activities.

The only sure way to avoid "naming names" was to respond to every question by citing the Fifth Amendment to the Constitution, which protects Americans from testifying against themselves. When the states adopted the Fifth Amendment in 1791, they wanted to protect citizens against false confessions coerced by intimidation and torture. The ordeal triggered by a congressional subpoena was certainly intimidating. Many Americans assumed that citing the amendment was a sure sign of guilt, not a matter of principle, and talked about Fifth Amendment Communists. "Taking the Fifth" could not protect jobs and reputations.

State legislatures imitated Congress by searching for "Reducators" among college faculty in such states as Oklahoma, Washington, and California. College presidents frequently fired faculty who took the Fifth Amendment. Harvard apparently used its influence to stay out of the newspapers, cutting a deal in which the FBI fed it information about suspect faculty, whom the university quietly fired. More common was the experience of the economics professor fired from the University of Kansas City after testimony before the McCarran Committee. He found it hard to keep any job once his name had been in the papers. A local dairy fired him because it thought its customers might be uneasy having a radical handle their milk bottles.

The moral dilemma posed by the investigations was revisited in 1954's Oscar-winning movie *On the Waterfront*. The director, Elia Kazan, and the scriptwriter, Budd Schulberg, had both "named names." They used the movie as a parable to justify their actions. The film's hero, played by Marlon Brando, agonizes about informing against corrupt officials in a dockworkers union. He finally speaks out at the urging of an activist priest. Most Americans called before HUAC and the McCarran Committee thought that Kazan and Schulberg had missed the point, for witnesses were usually being asked about previous political affiliations and beliefs, not current criminal activity.

SUBVERSION TRIALS

In 1948, the Justice Department indicted the leaders of the American Communist Party under the Alien Registration Act of 1940. Eleven men and women were convicted in 1949 of conspiring to advocate the violent overthrow of the United States government through their speech and publications. Some of the testimony came from Herbert Philbrick, an advertising manager and FBI informer who had posed as a party member. Philbrick parlayed his appearance into a bestseller titled *I Led Three Lives* and then into a popular television series on which the FBI foiled Communist spies every Friday night.

The case of Alger Hiss soon followed. In 1948, a former Communist, Whittaker Chambers, named Hiss as a Communist, with whom he had associated in the 1930s. Hiss, who had held important posts in the State Department, first denied knowing Chambers but then admitted to having known him under another name. He continued to deny any involvement with Communists and sued Chambers for slander. As proof, Chambers gave Congressman Richard Nixon microfilms that he had hidden inside a pumpkin on his Maryland farm. Tests seemed to show that the "pumpkin papers" were State Department documents that had been copied on a typewriter that Hiss had once owned. With the new evidence, the Justice Department indicted Hiss for perjury—lying under oath. A first perjury trial ended in deadlock, but a second jury convicted Hiss in January 1950.

Hiss was more important as a symbol than as a possible spy. For more than forty years, the essence of his case was a matter of faith, not facts. Even his enemies agreed that any documents he might have stolen were of limited importance. What was important, they said, was the sort of disloyalty and "weak thinking" that Hiss represented. Moreover, his smugness as a member of the East Coast establishment enraged them. To his opponents, Hiss stood for every wrong turn that the nation had taken since 1932. In contrast, his supporters found a virtue in every trait that his enemies hated, from his refined taste to his education at The Johns Hopkins University and Harvard Law School. Many supporters believed that he had been framed. Both sides claimed support from Soviet records that became public in the 1990s, but the weight of evidence seems to confirm that he did pass information to the Soviets from the mid-1930s through 1945.

The case of Julius and Ethel Rosenberg represented a similar test of belief. In 1950, the British arrested nuclear physicist Klaus Fuchs, who confessed to passing atomic secrets to the Soviets when he worked at Los Alamos in 1944 and 1945. The "Fuchs spy ring" soon implicated the Rosenbergs, New York radicals of strong beliefs but limited sophistication. Convicted in 1951 of the vague charge of conspiring to commit espionage, they were sent to the electric chair in 1953 after refusing to buy a reprieve by naming other spies.

As with Alger Hiss, the government had a plausible but not an airtight case. After their trial, the Rosenbergs became a cause for international protest. Their small children became pawns and trophies in political demonstrations, an experience recaptured in E.L. Doctorow's novel *The Book of Daniel* (1971). There is no doubt that Julius Rosenberg was a convinced Communist, and it is likely that he was a minor participant in an atomic spy net, but Ethel Rosenberg was charged, in the words of FBI director J. Edgar Hoover, "as a lever" to pressure her husband into naming his confederates.

SENATOR MCCARTHY ON STAGE

The best-remembered participant in the second Red Scare was Senator Joseph McCarthy of Wisconsin. Crude, sly, and ambitious, McCarthy had ridden to victory in the Republican landslide of 1946. His campaign slogan, "Congress needs a tail gunner," claimed a far braver war record than he had earned. He burst into national prominence on February 9, 1950. In a rambling speech in Wheeling, West Virginia, he latched on to the issue of Communist subversion. Although no transcript of the speech survives, he supposedly stated; "I have here in my hand a list of 205 that were known to the Secretary of State as being members of the Communist Party and who, nevertheless, are still working and shaping the policy of the State Department." In the following days, the 205 Communists changed quickly to 57, to 81, to 10, to 116. McCarthy's rise to fame climaxed with an incoherent six-hour speech to the Senate. He tried to document the charges by mixing previously exposed spies with people who no longer worked for the government or who had never worked for it. Over the next several years, his speeches were aimed at moving targets, full of multiple untruths. He threw out so many accusations, true or false, that the facts could never catch up.

Senator Joe McCarthy used press releases and carefully managed congressional committee hearings to attack suspected communists, although he had almost no hard information. At the Army-McCarthy hearings in June, 1954 he clashed with attorney Joseph Welch. Here Welch listens as McCarthy points to Oregon on a map that supposedly showed Communist party organization in the United States.

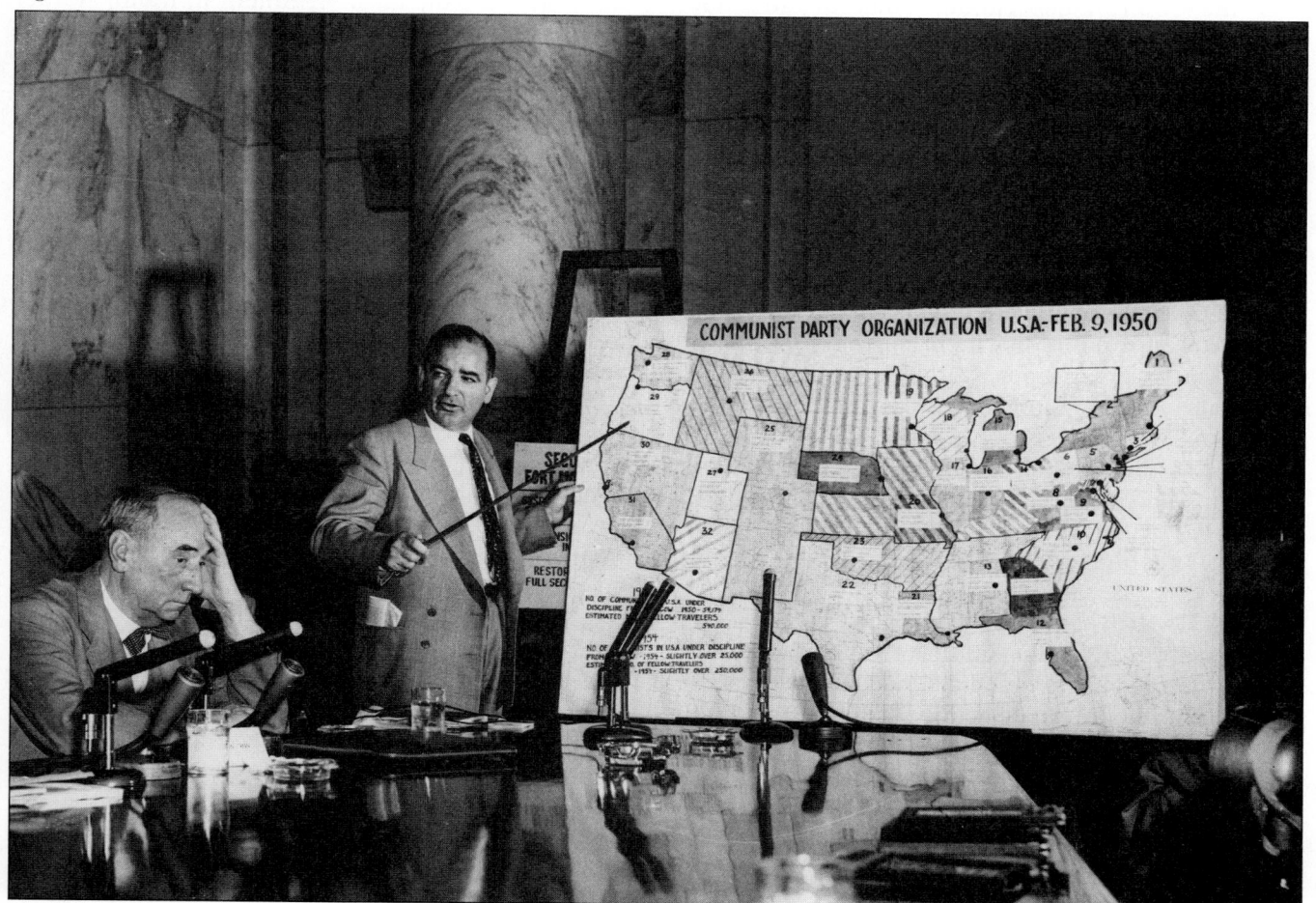

The Senate disregarded McCarthy, but the public heard only the accusations, not the lack of evidence. Senators treated McCarthy as a crude outsider in their exclusive club, but voters in 1950 turned against his most prominent opponents. Liberal politicians ran for cover; conservatives were happy for McCarthy to attract media attention away from HUAC and the McCarran Committee. In 1951, McCarthy even called George Marshall, then serving as secretary of defense, an agent of Communism. The idea was ludicrous. Marshall was one of the most upright Americans of his generation, the architect of victory in World War II, and a key contributor to the stabilization of Europe. Nevertheless, McCarthy was so popular that the Republicans featured him at their 1952 convention. That fall, the Republicans' presidential candidate, Dwight Eisenhower, appeared on the same campaign platform with McCarthy and conspicuously failed to defend George Marshall, who had been chiefly responsible for Eisenhower's fast-track career.

McCarthy's personal crudeness made him a media star but eventually undermined him. Given control of the Senate Committee on Government Operations in 1953, he investigated dozens of agencies from the Government Printing Office to the Army Signal Corps. Early in 1954, he began to harass the U.S. Army about the promotion of an army dentist with a supposedly subversive background. The confrontation turned into two months of televised hearings that revealed the emptiness of the charges. The cameras also put McCarthy's style on trial. "Have you no decency?" asked the army's lawyer, Joseph Welch, at one point.

The end came quickly. McCarthy's "favorable" rating in the polls plummeted. The comic strip *Pogo* began to feature a foolishly menacing figure with McCarthy's face named Simple J. Malarkey. The U.S. Senate finally voted 67 to 22 in December 1954 to condemn McCarthy for conduct "unbecoming a Member of the Senate." Until his death from alcoholism in 1957, he was an increasingly isolated figure, repudiated by the Senate and ignored by the media who had built him up.

UNDERSTANDING MCCARTHYISM

The antisubversive campaign that everyone now calls **McCarthyism**, however, died a slower death. Legislation, such as the Internal Security Act (1950) and the Immigration and Nationality Act (1952), remained as tools of political repression. HUAC continued to mount investigations as late as the 1960s.

Fear of Communist subversion reached deep into American society. In the early 1950s, Cincinnati's National League baseball team was phasing in a new double-play duo of second baseman Johnny Temple and shortstop Roy McMillan. The team was also trying out a new name, for it was important not to let the national game be tainted by Communism. Harking back to its origins as the Red Stockings, the team was now the "Redlegs," not the "Reds." The brief revision of baseball history was one example of how the fear of Communists spread from Washington through the grassroots. Cities and states required loyalty oaths from their employees; Ohio even required oaths from recipients of unemployment compensation.

In retrospect, at least four factors made Americans afraid of Communist subversion. One was a legitimate but exaggerated concern about atomic spies. A second was an undercurrent of anti-Semitism and nativism, for many labor organizers and Communist Party members (like the Rosenbergs) had Jewish and eastern European backgrounds. Third was southern and western resentment of the nation's Ivy League elite. Most general, finally, was a widespread fear that the world was spinning out of control. Many people sought easy explanations for global tensions. It was basically reassuring if Soviet and Chinese Communist successes were the result of American traitors rather than of Communist strengths.

Partisan politics mobilized the fears and resentments into a political force. From 1946 through 1952, the conservative wing of the Republican party used the Red Scare to attack New Dealers and liberal Democrats. HUAC, the McCarran Committee, and McCarthy were all tools for bringing down the men and women who had been moving the United States toward a more active government at home and abroad. The Republican elite used McCarthy until this group won control of the presidency and Congress in 1952, and then it abandoned him.

The broader goal of the second Red Scare was conformity of thought. Many of the professors and bureaucrats targeted for investigation had indeed been Communists or interested in Communism, usually in the 1930s and early 1940s. Most saw it as a way to increase social justice, and they sometimes excused the failures of Communism in the Soviet Union. Unlike the handful of real spies, however, they were targeted not for actions but for ideas. The investigations and loyalty programs were efforts to insure that Americans kept any left-wing ideas to themselves.

CONCLUSION

In the face of confrontation over Berlin, fighting in Korea, and growing numbers of nuclear weapons,

THE CONFIDENT YEARS
1953–1964

28

The first day I was able to enter Central High School [in Little Rock, Arkansas, September 23, 1957], what I felt inside was terrible, wrenching, awful fear. On the car radio I could hear that there was a mob. I knew what a mob meant and I knew that the sounds that came from the crowd were very angry. So we entered the side of the building, very, very fast. Even as we entered there were people running after us, people tripping other people. . . . There has never been in my life any stark terror or any fear akin to that.

I'd only been in the school a couple of hours and by that time it was apparent that the mob was just overrunning the school. Policemen were throwing down their badges and the mob was getting past the wooden sawhorses because the police would no longer fight their own in order to protect us. So we were all called into the principal's office, and there was great fear that we would not get out of this building. We were trapped. And I thought, Okay, so I'm going to die here, in school. . . . Even the adults, the school officials, were panicked, feeling like there was no protection. . . . [A] gentleman, who I believed to be the police chief, said . . . "I'll get them out." And we were taken to the basement of this place. And we were put into two cars, grayish blue Fords. And the man instructed the drivers, he said, "Once you start driving, do not stop." And he told us to put our heads down. This guy revved up his engine and he came up out of the bowels of this building, and as he came up, I could just see hands reaching across this car, I could hear the yelling, I could see guns, and he was told not to stop. "If you hit somebody, you keep rolling, 'cause the kids are dead." And he did just that, and he didn't hit anybody, but he certainly was forceful and aggressive in the way he exited this driveway, because people tried to stop him and he didn't stop. He dropped me off at home. And I remember saying, "Thank you for the ride," and I should've said, "Thank you for my life."*

Melba Patillo Beals in Henry Hampton and Steve Frayer, eds., *Voices of Freedom: An Oral History of the Civil Rights Movement from the 1950s through the 1980s* (New York: Bantam, 1990).

CHAPTER OUTLINE

A Decade of Affluence
What's Good for General Motors
Reshaping Urban America
Comfort on Credit
The New Fifties Family
Inventing Teenagers
Turning to Religion
The Gospel of Prosperity
The Underside of Affluence

Facing Off with the Soviet Union
Why We Liked Ike
A Balance of Terror
Containment in Action
Global Standoff

John F. Kennedy and the Cold War
The Kennedy Mystique
Kennedy's Mistakes
Getting into Vietnam
Missile Crisis: A Line Drawn in the Waves
Science and Foreign Affairs

Righteousness Like a Mighty Stream: The Struggle for Civil Rights
Getting to the Supreme Court
Deliberate Speed
Public Accommodations
The March on Washington, 1963

"Let Us Continue"
Dallas, 1963
War on Poverty
Civil Rights, 1964-1965
War, Peace, and the Landslide of 1964

Conclusion

Melba Pattillo was one of the nine African American students who entered previously all-white Central High in the fall of 1957. Her enrollment in the high school, where she managed to last through a year of harassment and hostility, was a symbolic step in the journey toward greater racial equality in American society. School integration in Little Rock implemented the U.S. Supreme Court decision in the case of *Brown v. Board of Education* in 1954, which declared that racially segregated schools violated the mandate that all citizens receive equal protection of the law. The violence with which some white residents of Little Rock responded, and the courage of the students, marked one of the key episodes in the civil rights revolution that spanned roughly a decade from the *Brown* decision to the Voting Rights Act of 1965.

The struggle for full civil rights for all Americans was rooted in national ideals, but it was also shaped by the continuing tensions of the Cold War. President Dwight Eisenhower acted against his own inclinations and sent federal troops to keep the peace in Little Rock in part because he worried about public opinion in other nations. As the United States and the Soviet Union maneuvered for influence in Africa and Asia, domestic events sometimes loomed large in foreign relations. Few Americans questioned the rightness or necessity of contesting the Cold War—or of America's ultimate triumph. This consensus gave U.S. policy an overarching goal of containment but also narrowed American options by casting issues at home and abroad in terms of the U.S.-Soviet rivalry.

Melba Pattillo's life after Little Rock also reveals something about the increasing economic opportunities available to most Americans. She eventually graduated from San Francisco State University, earned a master's degree from Columbia University, and went on to a career as a television reporter and writer. San Francisco State, which was rapidly expanding on a new campus, was itself part of the great expansion of higher education that helped millions of Americans move into middle-class jobs and neighborhoods. The prosperous years from 1953 to 1964 spread the economic promise of the 1940s across American society. Young couples could afford large families and new houses. Labor unions grew conservative because cooperation with big business offered immediate gains for their members.

Despite challenges at home and abroad, Americans were fundamentally confident during the decade after the Korean War. They expected corporations to use scientific research to craft new products for eager customers and medical researchers to conquer diseases such as polio, as Dr. Jonas Salk's vaccine had. When the USSR challenged U.S. preeminence and launched the first artificial space satellite in 1957, Americans responded with shock followed by redoubled efforts to regain what they considered their rightful world leadership in science and technology.

KEY TOPICS

- Affluence and conformity in the middle class during the 1950s
- The Cold War confrontation with the USSR during the Eisenhower and Kennedy administrations
- The struggle for African American civil rights
- Lyndon Johnson and the Great Society

A DECADE OF AFFLUENCE

Americans in the 1950s believed in the basic strength of the United States. Television's General Electric Theater was third in the ratings in 1956-1957. Every week, its host, Ronald Reagan, a popular Hollywood lead from the late 1930s, stated, "At General Electric, progress is our most important product." It made sense to his viewers. Large, technologically sophisticated corporations were introducing new marvels: Orlon sweaters and Saran Wrap, long-playing records and Polaroid cameras. As long as the United States defended free enterprise, Reagan told audiences on national speaking tours, the sky was the limit.

Many Americans valued free enterprise and family life as part of the anti-Communist crusade. Social and intellectual conformity assured a united front. Congress established Loyalty Day in 1955. National leaders argued that strong families were bulwarks

Chronology

1953 CIA backed coup returns the Shah, Reza Pahlevi, to power in Iran.

Soviet Union detonates hydrogen bomb.

1954 Vietnamese defeat the French; Geneva conference divides Vietnam.

United States and allies form SEATO.

Supreme Court decides *Brown v. Board of Education of Topeka*.

CIA overthrows the government of Guatemala.

China provokes a crisis over Quemoy and Matsu.

1955 Salk polio vaccine is announced.

Black citizens boycott Montgomery, Alabama, bus system.

Soviet Union forms the Warsaw Pact.

AFL and CIO merge.

1956 Interstate Highway Act is passed.

Soviets repress Hungarian revolt.

Israel, France, and Britain invade Egypt.

1957 U.S. Army maintains law and order in Little Rock after violent resistence to integration of Central High School.

Soviet Union launches *Sputnik*, world's first artificial satellite.

1958 U.S. and Soviet Union voluntarily suspend nuclear tests.

1959 Fidel Castro takes power in Cuba.

Nikita Khrushchev visits the United States.

1960 U-2 spy plane shot down over Russia

Sit-in movement begins in Greensboro, North Carolina.

1961 Bay of Pigs invasion fails.

Kennedy establishes the Peace Corps.

Vienna summit fails.

Freedom rides are held in the Deep South.

Berlin crisis leads to construction of the Berlin Wall.

1962 John Glenn orbits the earth.

Cuban missile crisis brings the world to the brink of nuclear war.

Michael Harrington publishes *The Other America*.

1963 Civil rights demonstrations rend Birmingham.

Civil rights activists march in Washington.

Betty Friedan publishes *The Feminine Mystique*.

Limited Test Ban Treaty is signed.

Ngo Dinh Diem is assassinated in South Vietnam.

President Kennedy is assassinated.

1964 Civil Rights Act is passed.

Freedom Summer is organized in Mississippi.

Office of Economic Opportunity is created.

Gulf of Tonkin Resolution is passed.

Wilderness Act marks new direction in environmental policy.

1965 Medical Care Act establishes Medicare and Medicaid.

Elementary and Secondary Education Act extends direct federal aid to local schools.

Selma-Montgomery march climaxes era of nonviolent civil rights demonstrations.

Voting Rights Act suspends literacy tests for voting

---

against Communism and that churchgoing inoculated people against subversive ideas. Under the lingering cloud of McCarthyism, the range of political ideas that influenced government policy was narrower than in the 1930s and 1940s. Nevertheless, critics began to voice the discontents that exploded in the 1960s and 1970s.

WHAT'S GOOD FOR GENERAL MOTORS

Dwight Eisenhower presided over the prosperity of the 1950s. Both Democrats and Republicans had courted him as a presidential candidate in 1948. Four years later, he picked the Republicans because he wanted to make sure that the party remained committed to NATO and collective security in Europe rather than retreating into isolationism. He easily defeated the De-

mocrat, Adlai Stevenson, the moderately liberal governor of Illinois. Stevenson was a thoughtful politician, a witty campaigner, and a favorite in academic circles. He also carried Truman's negative legacy of domestic policy confrontation, the hated war in Korea, and the "loss" of China, and he had no chance of winning.

Eisenhower and the politics of the middle. Over the next eight years, Eisenhower claimed the political middle for Republicans. Publicists tried a variety of labels for his domestic views: "progressive moderation," "New Republicanism," "dynamic conservatism." Satisfied with postwar America, Eisenhower accepted much of the New Deal but saw little need for further reform. In a 1959 poll, liberals considered him a fellow liberal and conservatives thought him a conservative.

Eisenhower's first secretary of defense, "Engine Charlie" Wilson, had headed General Motors. At his Senate confirmation hearing, he proclaimed, "For years, I thought what was good for the country was good for General Motors and vice versa." Wilson's statement captured a central theme of the 1950s. Not since the 1920s had Americans been so excited about the benefits of big business. When *Fortune* magazine began in 1957 to publish an annual list of the 500 largest American corporations, it tapped a national fascination with America's productive capacity.

The new prosperity. The economy in the 1950s gave Americans much to like. Between 1950 and 1964, output grew by a solid 3.2 percent per year. Automobile production, on which dozens of other industries depended, neared 8 million vehicles per year in the mid-1950s; less than 1 percent of new car sales were imports.

American workers in the 1950s had more disposable income than ever before. Their productivity, or output per worker, increased steadily. Average compensation per hour of work rose faster than consumer prices in nine of eleven years from 1953 to 1964. Rising productivity made it easy for corporations to share gains with large labor unions. The steel and auto industries set the pace with contracts that gave their workers a middle-class way of life. In turn, labor leaders lost interest in radical changes in American society. In 1955, the older and politically more conservative American Federation of Labor absorbed the younger Congress of Industrial Organizations. The new AFL-CIO positioned itself as a partner in prosperity and foe of communism at home and abroad.

For members of minority groups with regular industrial and government jobs, the 1950s were also economically rewarding. Industrial cities, such as Detroit, Dayton, and Oakland, offered them factory jobs at wages that could support a family. Black people worked through the Urban League, the National Association of Colored Women, and other race-oriented groups to secure fair employment laws and jobs with large corporations. Many Puerto Rican migrants to New York found steady work in the Brooklyn Navy Yard. Mexican American families in San Antonio benefited from maintenance jobs at the city's military bases. Steady employment allowed black people and Latinos to build strong community institutions and vibrant neighborhood business districts.

However, there were never enough family-wage jobs for all of the African American and Latino workers who continued to move to northern and western cities. Many Mexican Americans were still migrant

farm laborers and workers in nonunionized sweatshops. Minority workers were usually the first to suffer from the erosion of industrial jobs that began in the 1960s and black unemployment crept upward to twice the white rate.

Native Americans faced equally daunting prospects. To cut costs and accelerate assimilation, Congress pushed the policy of termination between 1954 and 1962. The government sold tribal land and assets, distributed the proceeds among tribal members, and terminated its treaty relationship with the tribe. Applied to such tribes as the Klamaths in Oregon and the Menominees in Wisconsin, termination gave thousands of Indians onetime cash payments but cut them adrift from the security of tribal organizations. The Bureau of Indian Affairs also encouraged Indians to move to large cities, but jobs were often unavailable. The new urban populations would nourish growing militancy among Native Americans in the 1960s and 1970s.

RESHAPING URBAN AMERICA

If Eisenhower's administration opted for the status quo on many issues, it nevertheless reshaped American cities around an agenda of economic development. In 1954, Congress transformed the public housing program into urban renewal. Cities used federal funds to replace low-rent businesses and run-down housing on the fringes of their downtowns with new hospitals, civic centers, sports arenas, office towers, and luxury apartments. Urban renewal temporarily revitalized older cities in the Northeast and Midwest that were already feeling the competition of the fast-growing South and West. *Fortune* in 1956 concluded that some of the largest cities were the best run—Cincinnati, New York, Philadelphia, Detroit, Milwaukee.

Only a decade later, the same cities would top the list of urban crisis spots, in part because of accumulating social costs from urban renewal. The bulldozers often leveled minority neighborhoods in the name of downtown expansion. Urban renewal displaced Puerto Ricans in New York, African Americans in Atlanta and Norfolk, Mexican Americans in Denver. Los Angeles demolished the seedy Victorian mansions of Bunker Hill, just northwest of downtown, for a music center and bank towers. A mile to the north was Chavez Ravine, whose Mexican American population lived in substandard housing but maintained a lively community. When conservative opposition blocked plans for public housing, the residents were evicted, and Dodger Stadium was built. Here as elsewhere, urban showplaces rose at the expense of minority groups.

The Eisenhower administration also revolutionized American transportation. Americans had long dreamed of something better than two-lane highways that routed motorists through the stop-and-go traffic of cities and trapped them behind creeping trucks. By the early 1950s, they were fed up with roads designed for Model A Fords: They wanted to enjoy their new V-8 engines. The solution was the **Federal Highway Act of 1956**, creating a national system of interstate and defense highways. The legislation wrapped a program to build 41,000 miles of freeways in the language of the Cold War. The roads would be wide and strong enough for trucks hauling military hardware; they were also supposed to make it easy to evacuate cities in case of a Soviet attack.

Although the first interstate opened in Kansas in 1956, most of the mileage came in use in the 1960s and 1970s. Interstates halved the time of city-to-city travel. They were good for General Motors, the steel industry, and the concrete industry, requiring the construction equivalent of sixty Panama Canals. The highways promoted long-distance trucking at the expense of railroads. They also wiped out hundreds of homes per mile when they plunged through large cities. As with urban renewal, the bulldozers most often plowed through African American or Latino neighborhoods, where land was cheap and white politicians could ignore protests. Some cities, such as Miami, used the highways as barricades between white and black neighborhoods.

Interstates accelerated suburbanization. The beltways or perimeter highways that began to ring most large cities made it easier and more profitable to develop new subdivisions and factory sites than to reinvest in city centers. Federal grants for sewers and other basic facilities further cut suburban costs. Continuing the pattern of the late 1940s, suburban growth added a million new single-family houses per year.

COMFORT ON CREDIT

Prosperity transformed spending habits. The 1930s had taught Americans to avoid debt. The 1950s taught them to buy on credit. Families financed their new houses with 90 percent Federal Housing Administration (FHA) mortgages and 100 percent Veterans Administration (VA) mortgages. They filled the rooms by signing installment contracts at furniture and appliance stores and charging the drapes and carpeting on department-store credit cards. The value of consumer debt, excluding home mortgages, tripled from 1952 to 1964.

New forms of marketing facilitated credit-based consumerism. The first large-scale suburban shopping center was Northgate in Seattle, which assembled all the pieces of the full-grown mall—small stores facing an interior corridor between anchor department stores and surrounded by parking. By the end of the

decade, developers were building malls with 1 million square feet of shopping floor. At the start of the 1970s, the universal credit card (Visa, MasterCard) made shopping even easier.

Surrounding the new malls were the servants and symbols of America's car culture. Where cities of the early twentieth century had been built around the public transportation of streetcars and subways, the 1950s depended on private automobiles. Interstate highways sucked retail business from small-town main streets to interchanges on the edge of town. Nationally franchised motels and fast-food restaurants sprang up along suburban shopping strips, pioneered by Holiday Inn (1952) and McDonald's (nationally franchised in 1955). By shopping along highways rather than downtown, suburban whites also opted to use places that minimized contact with people of other races.

More extreme than the mall were entirely new environments for high-intensity consumption and entertainment that appeared in the Southwest. Mobster Bugsy Siegel transformed Las Vegas with the Flamingo Hotel in 1947. Other hotel-casinos soon turned Vegas into a middle-class adult fantasy land. Disneyland was Las Vegas for the whole family, a walk-through fantasy designed to outperform wide-screen movies as a "real" experience. Opening in Orange County, California, in 1955, Disneyland offered a carefully tended environment that was as safe as a shopping mall and as artificial as Las Vegas—a never-ending state fair without the smells and dust.

THE NEW 1950S FAMILY

Family life in the Eisenhower years departed from historic patterns. Prosperity allowed children to finish

Levittown, Pennsylvania, was the second suburban community built by William Levitt, following Levittown, New York. As Bernadette Wheeler described at the beginning of Chapter 27 for the first Levittown, residents quickly settled in to enjoy their new home and began to put their individual stamp on the houses, yards, and community.

school and young adults to marry right after high school. Young women faced strong social pressure to pursue husbands rather than careers; women went to college, people said, to get the "Mrs." degree rather than the B.A. In a decade when the popular press worried about "latent homosexuality," single men were also suspect. The proportion of single adults reached its twentieth-century low in 1960. At all social levels, young people married quickly and had an average of three children spaced closely together, adding to the number of baby boomers whose needs would influence American society for the rest of the century. Family activities replaced the street corner for kids and the neighborhood tavern for men. Strong families, said experts, defended against communism by teaching American values.

The impact of television.

Television was made to order for the family-centered fifties. By 1960, fully 87 percent of households had sets (see Figure 28–1). Popular entertainment earlier had been a community activity; people saw movies as part of a group, cheered baseball teams as part of a crowd. TV was watched in the privacy of the home.

Television programming was up for grabs. Experts hoped that 90-minute dramas would elevate popular taste, but morning talk shows, quiz shows, and such puppet shows as *Howdy Doody* were common in the early days because they were cheap to produce. Variety hours recycled old vaudeville formats. Soap operas, fifteen-minute newscasts, and Saturday morning adventure shows were adapted straight from radio.

Situation comedies were the most successful programs. Viewers liked continuing characters who resolved everyday problems in half an hour. A few shows dealt with characters outside the middle-class mainstream, such as the bus driver and sewer worker played by Jackie Gleason and Art Carney on *The Jackie Gleason Show* and *The Honeymooners* (1952-1957). Most successful shows depicted the ideal of family togetherness. Lucille Ball and Desi Arnaz in *I Love Lucy* (1951-1955) started a family and left New York for suburbia. The families on *The Adventures of Ozzie and Harriet* (1952-1966), *Father Knows Best* (1954-1962), and *Leave It to Beaver* (1957-1962) were white, polite, and happy. The Nelsons, Andersons, and Cleavers bore northern European names and lived in single-family houses with friendly neighbors. Thousands of school-aged baby boomers wondered why their families didn't have good times like the families on the picture tube.

Stay-at-home moms and working women.

The 1950s extended the stay-at-home trend of the postwar years. Women in the fifties gave up some of their earlier educational gains. Their share of new college degrees and professional jobs fell. Despite millions of new electric appliances, the time spent on housework increased. Magazines proclaimed that proper families maintained distinct roles for dad and mom, who was urged to find fulfillment in a well-scrubbed house and children. While television programming helped limit women's roles by power of example, TV actresses assured readers that they were housewives first and career women second.

In fact, far from allowing women to stay home as housewives, family prosperity in the 1950s often depended on their earnings. The number of employed women reached new highs. By 1960, nearly 35 percent of all women held jobs, including 7.5 million mothers with children under 17 (see Figure 28–2). The pressures of young marriages, large families, and economic needs interacted to erode some of the assumptions behind the idealized family and laid the groundwork for dramatic social changes in the 1960s and 1970s.

INVENTING TEENAGERS

Teenagers in the 1950s joined adults as consumers of movies, clothes, and automobiles. Advertisers tapped

FIGURE 28-1   Households with Telephones, Televisions, and VCRs

American life in the twentieth century was transformed by a sequence of electronic consumer goods, from telephones to laptop computers. Entertainment items (televisions and videocassette recorders) spread even more rapidly among consumers than did the home telephone.

Data Source: *Statistical Abstract of the United States.*

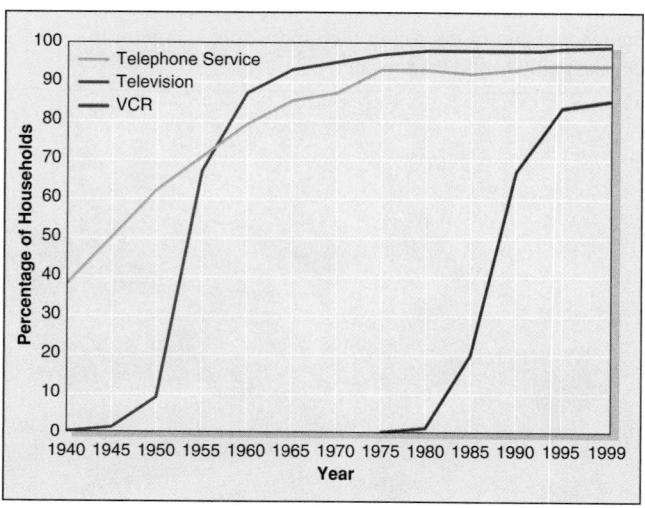

and expanded the growing youth market by promoting a distinct "youth culture," an idea that became omnipresent in the 1960s and 1970s. While psychologists pontificated on the special problems of adolescence, many cities matched their high schools to the social status of their students: college-prep curricula for middle-class neighborhoods, vocational and technical schools for future factory workers, and separate schools or tracks for African Americans and Latinos. "Maturity" in middle-class high schools meant self-confidence and leadership; at vocational schools, it meant neatness and respect for authority. In effect, the schools trained some children to be doctors and officers and others to be mechanics and enlisted men.

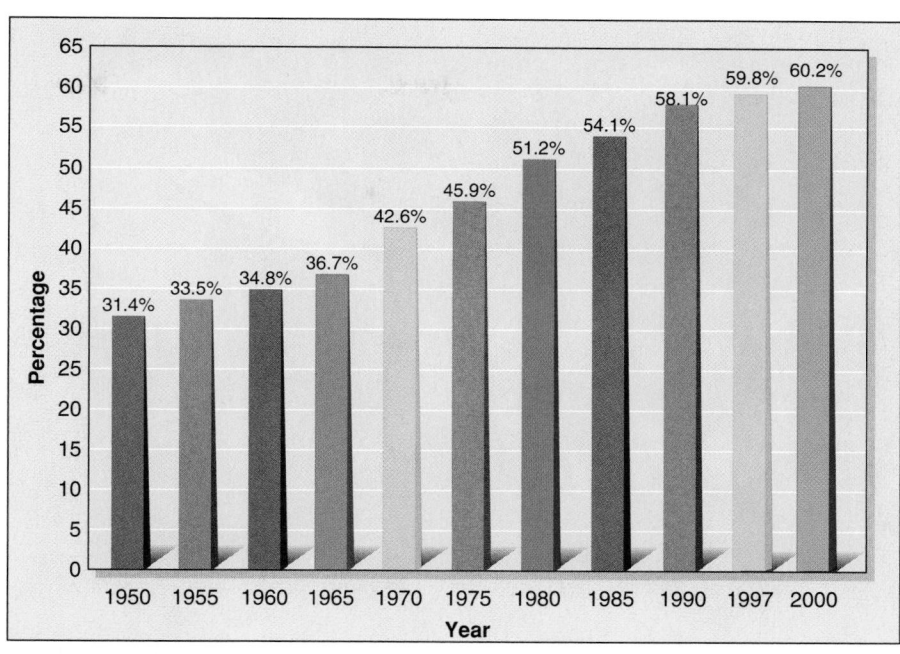

FIGURE 28-2   Working Women as a Percentage of All Women, 1950-2000
The proportion of American women who are part of the labor force (working or looking for work) has increased steadily since 1950, with the fastest increase between 1965 and 1985.

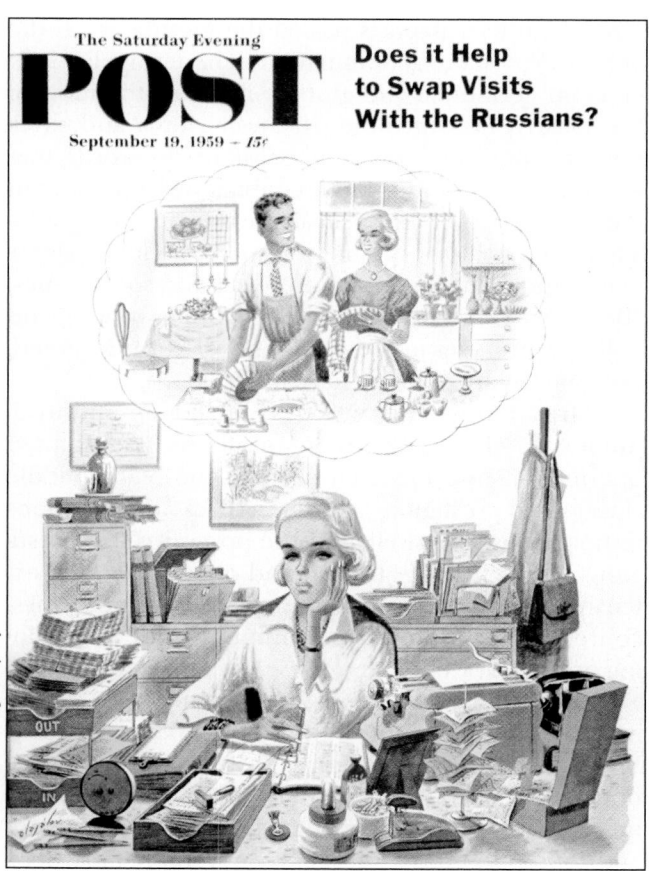

All teenagers shared rock-and-roll, a new music of the mid-1950s that adapted black urban rhythm-and-blues for a white mass market. Rhythm-and-blues was the hard-edged and electrified offspring of traditional blues and gospel music. In turn, rock music augmented its black roots by drawing vitality from poor white Southerners (Buddy Holly, Elvis Presley), Hispanics (Richie Valens), and, in the 1960s, the British working class (the Beatles). Record producers played up the association between rock music and youthful rebellion. The 1955 movie *Blackboard Jungle* depicted juvenile delinquency to the music of Bill Haley's "Rock Around the Clock." Elvis Presley's meteoric career, launched in 1956 with "Heartbreak Hotel," depended both on his skill at blending country music with rhythm-and-blues and the sexual suggestiveness of his stage act.

Technological changes helped rock split off from adult pop music. Portable phonographs and 45-rpm records let kids listen to rock-and-roll in their own rooms. Car radios and transistor radios (first marketed

Middle class women in the 1950s faced conflicting pressures and messages. The popular media idealized the woman whose life revolved around her house and family. As this magazine cover suggests, however, that image was as much a myth as a reality. Despite real limitations on available careers, increasing numbers of women entered the labor force and made necessary contributions to their families' incomes—while daydreaming about getting help with never-ending household tasks.

In his first years as a star, Elvis Presley brought new energy to the world of popular music.

Frank Driggs/Archive Photos

around 1956) let disc jockeys reach teenagers outside the home. The result was separate music for young listeners and separate advertising for teenage consumers, the roots of the teenage mall culture of the next generation.

The raucous sounds and rebellious lyrics of early rock and roll gave adult authorities even more reason to emphasize social conformity. Schools, churches, and elected officials responded with dress codes, campaigns against sinful comic books, and worry about juvenile delinquency. Young people responded by crowding movie theaters for *Rebel Without a Cause* (1955), in which James Dean played an anguished teenager in stifling suburbia.

TURNING TO RELIGION

Leaders from Dwight Eisenhower to FBI Director J. Edgar Hoover advocated churchgoing as an antidote for Communism. Regular church attendance grew from 48 percent of the population in 1940 to 63 percent in 1960. Moviegoers flocked to biblical epics: *The Robe* (1953), *The Ten Commandments* (1956), and *Ben-Hur* (1959). Newsweek talked about the "vast resurgence of Protestantism," and Time claimed that "everybody knows that church life is booming in the U.S."

The situation was more complex. Growing church membership looked impressive at first, but the total barely kept pace with population. In some ways, the so-called return to religion was new. Congress created new connections between religion and government when it added "under God" to the Pledge of Allegiance in 1954 and required currency to bear the phrase "In God We Trust" in 1955.

Radio and television preachers added a new dimension to religious life. Bishop Fulton J. Sheen brought vigorous anticommunism and Catholic doctrine to millions of TV viewers who would never have entered a Catholic church. Norman Vincent Peale blended popular psychology with Protestantism, presenting Jesus Christ as "the greatest expert on human nature who ever lived." His book *The Power of Positive Thinking* (1952) told readers to "stop worrying and start living" and sold millions of copies.

Another strand in the religious revival was found among revitalized evangelical and fundamentalist churches. During the 1950s, the theologically and socially conservative Southern Baptists passed the Methodists as the largest Protestant denomination. The evangelist Billy Graham continued the grand American tradition of the mass revival meeting. In auditoriums and stadiums, he preached personal salvation in words that everyone could understand. Graham was a pioneer in the resurgence of evangelical Christianity that gradually shifted the tone of American religious life by stressing an individual approach to belief and social issues. "Before we can solve the economic, philosophical, and political problems in the world," he said, "pride, greed, lust, and sin are going to have to be erased."

African American churches were community institutions as well as religious organizations. With limited options for enjoying their success, the black middle class joined prestigious churches. Black congregations in northern cities swelled in the postwar years. Prestigious black churches thrived and often supported extensive social service programs. In southern cities, churches were centers for community pride and training grounds for the emerging civil rights movement.

Other important changes to come in American religion had their roots in the 1950s and early 1960s. Boundaries between many Protestant denominations blurred as church leaders emphasized national unity, paving the way for the ecumenical movement and denominational mergers. Supreme Court deci-

JAMES DEAN

The overnight sensation of 'East of Eden'

Warner Bros. put all the force of the screen into a challenging drama of today's juvenile violence!

"REBEL WITHOUT A CAUSE"

CINEMASCOPE AND WARNERCOLOR

and they both come from 'good' families!

Movie actor James Dean died in an automobile accident shortly after completing Rebel Without a Cause. *His tragic death and his depiction of alienated youth made him a symbol of dissatisfaction with the middle-class 1950s.*

sions sowed the seeds for later political activism among evangelical Christians. In *Engel v. Vitale* (1962), the Court ruled that public schools could not require children to start the school day with group prayer. *Abington Township v. Schempp* (1963) prohibited devotional Bible reading in the schools. Such decisions alarmed many evangelicals; within two decades, school prayer would be a central issue in national politics.

THE GOSPEL OF PROSPERITY

Writers and intellectuals often marveled at the prosperity of Eisenhower's America. For scholars and journalists who had grown up during the Great Depression, the lack of economic hardship was the big story. William H. Whyte, Jr., searched American corporations for the changing character of the United States in *The Organization Man* (1956). The historian David Potter brilliantly analyzed Americans in *People of Plenty* (1954), contending that their national character had been shaped by the abundance of natural resources. In *The Affluent Society* (1958), economist John Kenneth Galbraith predicted that the challenge of the future would be to insure the fair distribution of national wealth.

At times in these years, production and consumption even outweighed democracy in the American message to the world. Officially, the argument was that abundance was a natural by-product of a free society. In fact, it was easy to present prosperity as a goal in itself, as Vice President Richard Nixon did when he represented the United States at a technology exposition in Moscow in 1959. The American exhibit included twenty-one models of automobiles and a complete six-room ranch house. In its "miracle kitchen," Nixon engaged Soviet Communist Party chairman Nikita Khrushchev in a carefully planned "kitchen debate." The vice president claimed that the "most important thing" for Americans was "the right to choose": "We have so many different manufacturers and many different kinds of washing machines so that the housewives have a choice."

Khrushchev heard a similar message when he visited the United States in September 1959. His itinerary started with a helicopter ride over rush-hour Washington to show the ubiquity of individually owned automobiles. He went to a farm in Coon Rapids, Iowa, a machine shop in Pittsburgh, and Hollywood movie studios. Although Khrushchev never believed that ordinary workers had miracle kitchens, he returned to Moscow knowing that America meant "business."

THE UNDERSIDE OF AFFLUENCE

The most basic criticism of the ideology of prosperity was the simplest—that affluence concealed vast inequalities. Michael Harrington had worked among the poor before writing *The Other America* (1962). He reminded Americans about the "underdeveloped nation" of 40 to 50 million poor people who had missed the last two decades of prosperity. The poor were walled off in urban and rural backwaters. They were old people living on stale bread in bug-infested hotels. They were white families in the valleys of Appalachia, African Americans in city ghettos who could not find decent jobs, and Hispanic migrant workers whose children went for months without a glass of milk.

If Harrington found problems at the bottom of U.S. society, C. Wright Mills found dangers in the way that the Cold War distorted American society at the top. *The Power Elite* (1956) described an interlocking alliance of big government, big business, and the

The United States exhibit at a technology exposition in Moscow in 1959 displayed a wide range of American consumer goods, from soft-drink dispensers to sewing machines. It included a complete six-room ranch house with an up-to-date kitchen where, in a famous encounter dubbed the "kitchen debate," Vice President Richard Nixon and Soviet Communist Party chairman Nikita Khrushchev disputed the merits of capitalism and Communism.

military. The losers in a permanent war economy, said Mills, were economic and political democracy. His ideas would reverberate in the 1960s during the Vietnam War.

Other critics targeted the alienating effects of consumerism and the conformity of homogeneous suburbs. Journalists indicted suburban society with coined terms like "slurb" and books like *The Crack in the Picture Window* (1957) and *The Split Level Trap* (1961). Sociologist David Riesman saw suburbia as the home of "other-directed" individuals who lacked inner convictions. Although much of the antisuburban rhetoric was based on intellectual snobbery rather than research, it represented significant dissent from the praise of affluence.

There was far greater substance to increasing dissatisfaction among women, who faced conflicting images of the perfect woman in the media. On one side was the comforting icon of Betty Crocker, the fictional spokeswoman for General Mills who made housework and cooking look easy. On the other side were sultry sexpots, such as Marilyn Monroe and the centerfold women of *Playboy* magazine, which first appeared in 1953. Women wondered how to be both Betty and Marilyn.

In 1963, Betty Friedan's book *The Feminine Mystique* recognized that thousands of middle-class housewives were seething behind their picture windows. It followed numerous articles in *McCall's*, *Redbook*, and the *Ladies' Home Journal* about the unhappiness of college-educated women who were expected to find total satisfaction in kids and cooking. Friedan repackaged the message of the women's magazines along with re-

sults of a survey of her Smith College classmates who were then entering their forties. What Friedan called "the problem that has no name" was a sense of personal emptiness. "I got up one morning," remembered Geraldine Bean, "and I got my kids off to school. I went in to comb my hair and wash my face, and I stood in front of the bathroom mirror crying . . . because at eight-thirty in the morning I had my children off to school. I had my housework done. There was absolutely nothing for me to do the rest of the day." She went on to earn a Ph.D. and win election to the board of regents of the University of Colorado.

Eventually, the critical analyses of Harrington, Mills, and Friedan would fuel radical political change; in the short run, they inspired radical art. New York and San Francisco had long sheltered cultural rebels who liked to confront the assumptions of mainstream Americans. The artsy bohemians of New York's Greenwich Village began to use Pop Art to satirize consumer culture. Meanwhile, the Beats came together in San Francisco, where poets, artists, and musicians drifted in and out of the City Lights bookstore. They attracted national attention in 1955 when Allen Ginsberg first chanted his poem "Howl," with its blistering attack on stifling materialism.

FACING OFF WITH THE SOVIET UNION

Americans got a reassuring new face in the White House in 1953, but not new policies toward the world. As had been true since 1946, the nation's leaders weighed every foreign policy decision for its effect on the Cold War. The United States pushed ahead in an arms race with the Soviet Union, stood guard on the borders of China and the Soviet empire, and judged political changes in Latin America, Africa, and Asia for their effect on the global balance of power.

U.S. and Soviet actions created a bipolar world that mimicked the effects of a magnet on a scattering of iron filings. The two poles of a magnet draw some filings into tightly packed clusters, pull others into looser alignments pointing toward one pole or the other, and leave a few in the middle unaffected. In the later 1950s and early 1960s, the United States and the USSR were the magnetic poles. Members of NATO, the Warsaw Pact, and other formal alliances made up the tight clusters. The third world of officially uncommitted nations felt the influence of both blocs, sometimes aligning with one or the other and sometimes struggling to remain neutral.

WHY WE LIKED IKE

In the late twentieth century, few leaders were able to master both domestic policy and foreign affairs. Some presidents, such as Lyndon Johnson, have been more adept at social problems than diplomacy. By contrast, Richard Nixon and George Bush were more interested in the world outside the United States.

Dwight Eisenhower was one of these "foreign-policy presidents." As a general, he had understood that military power should serve political ends. He had helped to hold together the alliance that defeated Nazi Germany and built NATO into an effective force in 1951–1952. He then sought the Republican nomination, he said, to insure that the United States kept its international commitments. He sealed his victory in 1952 by emphasizing his foreign-policy expertise, telling a campaign audience that "to bring the Korean war to an early and honorable end . . . requires a personal trip to Korea. I shall make that trip . . . I shall go to Korea."

What makes Eisenhower's administration hard to appreciate is that many of its accomplishments were things that did not happen. Eisenhower refused to dismantle the social programs of the New Deal. He exerted American political and military power around the globe but avoided war. Preferring to work behind the scenes, he knew how to delegate authority and keep disagreements private.

In his "hidden-hand" presidency, Eisenhower sometimes masked his intelligence. It helped his political agenda if Americans thought of him as a smiling grandfather. The "Ike" whose face smiled from "I Like Ike" campaign buttons and who gave rambling, incoherent answers at White House press conferences

knew exactly what he was doing—controlling information and keeping the opposition guessing. When his press secretary advised him to duck questions at one press conference, Ike replied, "Don't worry, I'll just confuse them." He was easily reelected in 1956, when Americans saw no reason to abandon competent leadership.

A BALANCE OF TERROR

The backdrop for U.S. foreign policy was the growing capacity for mutual nuclear annihilation. The rivalry between the United States and the USSR was therefore carried out within a framework of deterrence, the knowledge that each side could launch a devastating nuclear attack. The old balance of power had become a balance of terror.

The Eisenhower administration's doctrine of **massive retaliation** took advantage of America's superior technology while economizing on military spending. Eisenhower and his advisers worried that matching the land armies of China and the Soviet Union would inflate the role of the federal government in American society (see Figure 28-3). Eisenhower compared uncontrolled military spending to crucifying humankind on a "cross of iron." "Every gun that is fired," he warned, "every warship launched, every rocket fired signifies . . . a theft from those who hunger and are not fed, those who are cold and not clothed." The administration concentrated military spending where the nation already had the greatest advantage—on atomic weapons. In response to any serious attack, the United States would direct maximum force against the homeland of the aggressor. Secretary of State Dulles called for "a maximum deterrent at a bearable cost." Reporters translated the policy as "more bang for the buck."

The massive-retaliation doctrine treated nuclear weapons as ordinary or even respectable. It put European and American cities on the frontline in the defense of Germany, for it meant that the United States would react to a Soviet conventional attack on NATO by dropping nuclear bombs on the Soviet Union, which would presumably retaliate in kind. The National Security Council in 1953 made reliance on "massive retaliatory damage" by nuclear weapons official policy.

The doctrine grew even more fearful as the Soviet Union developed its own hydrogen bombs. The chairman of the Atomic Energy Commission terrified the American people by mentioning casually that the Soviets could now obliterate New York City. Dozens of nuclear weapons tests in the late 1950s made the atomic threat immediate. So did signs for

FIGURE 28-3 **Defense Spending as a Percentage of Gross Domestic Product, 1950–2000**

Defense spending has been an important force for economic development and innovation. The impact of the defense budget on the domestic economy was greatest in the mid-1950s, at the height of the Cold War. Lesser peaks came during the Vietnam War in the late 1960s and the Reagan administration defense buildup in the early 1980s.

Data Source: *Statistical Abstract of the United States*

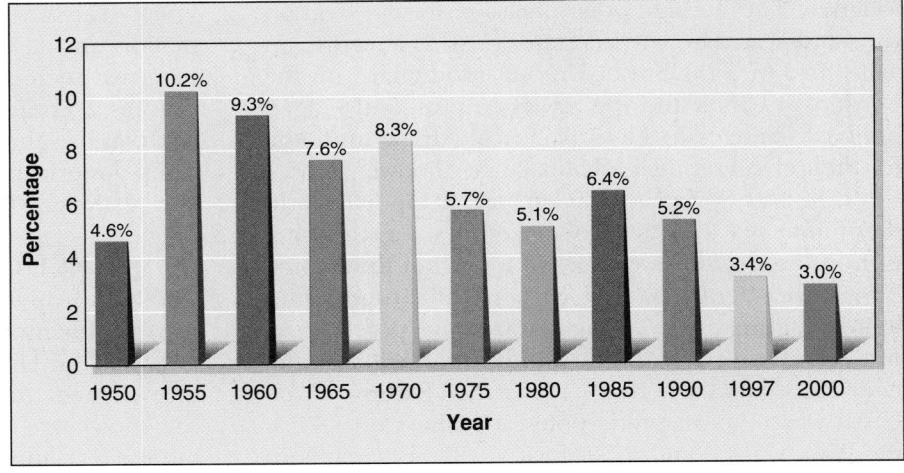

air-raid shelters posted on downtown buildings and air-raid drills that taught schoolchildren to duck under their desks if they saw the flash of an atomic bomb. Radioactivity carried by fallout from the tests appeared in milk supplies in the form of the isotope strontium 90. Stories about handfuls of survivors groping through the ruins of atomic war filled popular literature.

The Soviet Union added to worries about atomic war by launching the world's first artificial satellite. On the first Sunday of October 1957, Americans discovered that Sputnik—Russian for "satellite"—was orbiting the earth. The Soviets soon lifted a dog into orbit while U.S. rockets fizzled on the pad. Soviet propagandists claimed that their technological "first" showed the superiority of communism, and Americans wondered if the United States had lost its edge. Schools beefed up science courses and began to introduce the "new math," Congress passed the National Defense Education Act to expand college and postgraduate education, and the new **National Aeronautics and Space Administration (NASA)** took over the satellite program in 1958.

The crisis was more apparent than real. Eisenhower had rejected the use of available military rockets for the U.S. space program in favor of developing new launch vehicles, and he overlooked the symbolic impact of Sputnik. He thus built himself into a political box, for the combination of Soviet rocketry and nuclear capacity created alarm about a missile gap. The Soviet Union was said to be building hundreds of intercontinental ballistic missiles (ICBMs) to overwhelm American air defenses designed to intercept piloted bombers. By the early 1960s, critics charged, a do-nothing administration would have put the United States in peril. Although there was no such gap, Eisenhower was unwilling to reveal secret information that might have allayed public anxiety.

CONTAINMENT IN ACTION

Someone who heard only the campaign speeches in 1952 might have expected sharp foreign-policy changes under Eisenhower, but there was more continuity than change. John Foster Dulles, Eisenhower's secretary of state, had attacked the Democrats as defeatists and appeasers. He demanded that the United States liberate eastern Europe from Soviet control and encourage Jiang Jieshi to attack Communist China. Warlike language continued after the election. In 1956, Dulles proudly claimed that tough-minded diplomacy had repeatedly brought the United States to the verge of war: "We walked to the brink and looked it in the face. We took strong action." Critics protested that such "brinkmanship" endangered the entire world.

In fact, Eisenhower viewed the Cold War in the same terms as Truman. He worried about the "sullen weight of Russia" pushing against smaller nations and saw a world caught between incompatible values of freedom and communism, but caution replaced campaign rhetoric about "rolling back" Communism. Around the periphery of the communist nations, from eastern Asia to the Middle East to Europe, the United States accepted the existing sphere of communist influence but attempted to block its growth, a policy most Americans accepted.

The American worldview assumed both the right and the need to intervene in the affairs of other nations, especially countries in Latin America, Asia, and Africa. Policymakers saw these nations as markets for U.S. products and sources of vital raw materials. When political disturbances arose in these states, the United States blamed Soviet meddling to justify U.S. intervention. If Communism could not be rolled back in eastern Europe, the CIA could still undermine anti-American governments in the third world. The Soviets themselves took advantage of local revolutions,

Schoolchildren in the 1950s regularly practiced taking cover in case of atomic attack. If there was warning, they were to file into interior hallways, crouch against the walls, and cover their heads with their jackets as protection from flying glass. If they saw the blinding flash of an atomic explosion without warning, they were to "duck and cover" under their school desks.

brought the Chinese to a truce that left Korea divided into two nations.

The following year, China began to shell the small islands of Quemoy and Matsu, from which the Nationalist Chinese on Taiwan were launching commando raids on the mainland. Again, Secretary Dulles rattled the atomic saber, and China stopped the attacks. Evidence now suggests that Washington misread the situation. Mao's "theatrical" shelling was a political statement, not a prelude to military assault. Stepping to the "brink of war" did not deter Chinese aggression, because China never planned to attack.

Halfway around the world, there was a new crisis when three American friends—France, Britain, and Israel—ganged up on Egypt. France was angry at Egyptian support for revolutionaries in French Algeria. Britain was even angrier at Egypt's nationalization of the British-dominated Suez Canal. And Israel wanted to weaken its most powerful Arab enemy. On October 29, 1956, Israel attacked Egypt. A week later, British and French forces attempted to seize the canal. The United States forced a quick cease-fire, partly to maintain its standing with oil-producing Arab nations. Because Egypt blocked the canal with sunken ships, the war left Britain and France dependent on American oil that Eisenhower would not provide until they left Egypt. Resolution of the crisis involved one of the first uses of peace-keeping troops under the United Nations flag.

In Europe, Eisenhower accepted the status quo because conflicts there could result in nuclear war. In 1956, challenges to Communist rule arose in East Germany, Poland, and Hungary and threatened to break up the Soviet empire. The Soviets replaced liberal Communists in East Germany and Poland with hard-liners. In Hungary, however, reformers took the fatal step of proposing to quit the Warsaw Pact. Open warfare broke out when the Soviet army rolled across the border to preserve the Soviet empire. Hungarian freedom fighters in Budapest used rocks and firebombs against Soviet tanks for several days, while pleading in vain for Western aid. NATO would not risk war with the USSR. Tens of thousands

even when they did not instigate them; they thus confirmed Washington's belief that the developing world was a game board on which the superpowers carried on their rivalry by proxy.

Twice during Eisenhower's first term, the CIA subverted democratically elected governments that seemed to threaten U.S. interests. In Iran, which had nationalized British and U.S. oil companies in an effort to break the hold of western corporations, the CIA in 1953 backed a coup that toppled the government and helped the young Shah, or monarch, gain control. The Shah then cooperated with the United States until his overthrow in 1979. In Guatemala, the leftist government was upsetting the United Fruit Company. When the Guatemalans accepted weapons from the Communist bloc in 1954, the CIA imposed a regime friendly to U.S. business (see Map 28–1).

For most Americans in 1953, democracy in Iran was far less important than ending the war in Korea and stabilizing relations with China. Eisenhower declined to escalate the Korean War by blockading China and sending more U.S. ground forces. Instead he shifted atomic bombs to Okinawa, only four hundred miles from China. The nuclear threat, along with the continued cost of the war on both sides,

MAP EXPLORATION To explore an interactive version of this map, go to
http://www.prenhall.com/goldfield/map28.1

MAP 28-1   **U.S. Intervention around the Caribbean since 1954**
*The United States has long kept a careful eye on the politics of neighboring nations to the south.
In the second half of the twentieth century, the United States frequently used military assistance
or force to influence or intervene in Caribbean and Central American nations. The most common purpose has been to counter or undermine left-leaning governments; some interventions, as
in Haiti, have been intended to stabilize democratic regimes.*

of Hungarians died, and 200,000 fled when the Soviets crushed the resistance.

GLOBAL STANDOFF

The Soviet Union, China, and the United States and
its allies were all groping in the dark as they maneuvered for influence in the 1950s and 1960s. In one
international crisis after another, each player misinter-

preted the other's motivations and diplomatic signals.
As documents from both sides of the Cold War become available, historians have realized what dangerously different meanings the two sides gave to
confrontations between 1953 and 1964.

A good example was the U-2 affair of 1960, which
derailed progress toward nuclear disarmament. The
Kremlin was deeply worried that West Germany and

China might acquire nuclear bombs. Washington wanted to reduce military budgets and nuclear fallout. Both countries voluntarily suspended nuclear tests in 1958 and prepared for a June 1960 summit meeting in Paris, where Eisenhower intended to negotiate a test ban treaty.

But on May 1, 1960, Soviet air defenses shot down an American U-2 spy plane over the heart of Russia and captured the pilot, Francis Gary Powers. The cover story for the U-2 was weather research, but the frail-looking black plane was a CIA operation. Designed to soar above the range of Soviet antiaircraft missiles, U-2s had assured American officials that there was no missile gap.

When Moscow trumpeted the news of the downing, Eisenhower took personal responsibility in hopes that Khrushchev would accept the U-2 as an unpleasant reality of international espionage. Unfortunately, the planes meant something very different to the Soviets, touching their festering sense of inferiority. They had stopped protesting the flights in 1957, because complaints were demeaning. The Americans thought that silence signaled acceptance. Khrushchev had staked his future on good relations with the United States; when Eisenhower refused to apologize in Paris, Khrushchev stalked out. Disarmament was set back for years because the two sides had such different understandings of the same events.

The most important aspect of Eisenhower's foreign policy was continuity. Despite militant rhetoric, the administration pursued containment as defined under Truman. The Cold War consensus, however, prevented the United States from seeing the nations of the developing world on their own terms. By viewing every independence movement and social revolution as part of the competition with communism, American leaders created unnecessary problems. In the end, Eisenhower left troublesome and unresolved issues—upheaval in Latin America, civil war in Vietnam, tension in Germany, a nuclear arms race—for his successor, John Kennedy, who wanted to confront international Communism even more vigorously. (see American Views: Two Presidents Assess the Implications of the Cold War).

JOHN F. KENNEDY AND THE COLD WAR

John Kennedy was a man of contradictions. Many Americans recall his presidency (1961-1963) as a golden age, but we are more taken by his memory than we were by Kennedy himself. A Democrat who promised to get the country moving again, he presided over policies whose direction was set under Eisenhower. Despite stirring rhetoric about leading the nation toward a **New Frontier** of scientific and social progress, he recorded his greatest failures and successes in the continuing Cold War.

THE KENNEDY MYSTIQUE

Kennedy won the presidency over Richard Nixon in a cliff-hanging election that was more about personality and style than about substance (see Map 28-2). Both candidates were determined not to yield another inch to Communism. The charming and eloquent Kennedy narrowly skirted scandal in his personal life. Well publicized as a hero from World War II, he tempered ruthless ambition with respect for public service. His forthright campaigning allayed voter concern about his Roman Catholicism. Nixon had wider experience and was a shrewd tactician, but he was also self-righteous and awkward. Eisenhower had wanted to drop Nixon as vice president in 1956 and gave him only lukewarm support in 1960—when a reporter asked Eisenhower to cite important decisions to which Nixon had contributed, Ike replied, "Give me a week and I might think of one."

Television was crucial to the outcome. The campaign featured the first televised presidential debates. In the first session, Nixon actually gave better replies, but his nervousness and a bad makeup job turned off millions of viewers, who admired Kennedy's energy. Nixon never overcame the setback, but the race was tight with tiny margins in crucial states giving Kennedy the victory. His televised inauguration was the perfect setting for an impassioned plea for national unity: "My fellow Americans," he challenged, "ask not what your country can do for you—ask what you can do for your country."

Kennedy brought dash to the White House. His beautiful and refined wife, Jackie, made sure to seat artists and writers next to diplomats and businessmen at White House dinners. Kennedy's staff and large family played touch football, not golf. No president had shown such verve since Teddy Roosevelt. People began to talk about Kennedy's "charisma," his ability to lead by sheer force of personality. In fact, the image of a fit, vigorous man concealed the reality that he was battling severe physical ailments that demanded constant medical attention.

Behind the glamorous façade, Kennedy remained a puzzle. One day, Kennedy could propose the Peace Corps, which gave thousands of idealistic young Americans a chance to help developing nations; another day, he could approve plots to assassinate Fidel

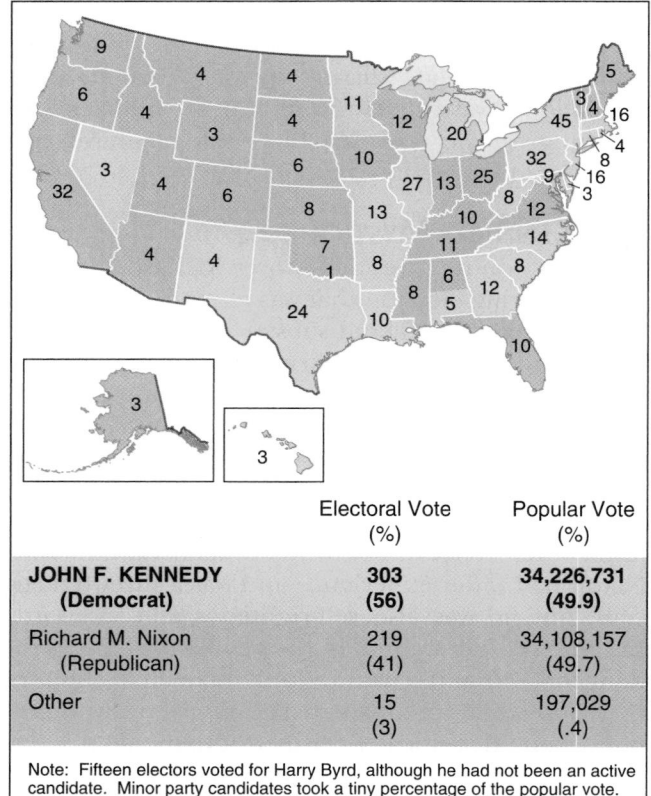

	Electoral Vote (%)	Popular Vote (%)
JOHN F. KENNEDY (Democrat)	**303 (56)**	**34,226,731 (49.9)**
Richard M. Nixon (Republican)	219 (41)	34,108,157 (49.7)
Other	15 (3)	197,029 (.4)

Note: Fifteen electors voted for Harry Byrd, although he had not been an active candidate. Minor party candidates took a tiny percentage of the popular vote.

MAP 28-2 **The Election of 1960**
The presidential election of 1960 was one of the closest in American history. John Kennedy's victory depended on his appeal in northern industrial states with large Roman Catholic populations and his ability to hold much of the traditionally Democratic South. Texas, the home state of his vice-presidential running mate, Lyndon Johnson, was vital to the success of the ticket.

Castro. Visitors who expected a shallow glad-hander were astonished to meet a sharp, hard-working man who was eager to learn about the world. One savvy diplomat commented, "I have never heard of a president who wanted to know so much."

KENNEDY'S MISTAKES

Kennedy and Khrushchev perpetuated similar problems. Talking tough to satisfy their more militant countrymen, they pushed each other into corners, continuing the problems of mutual misunderstanding that had marked the 1950s. When Khrushchev promised, in January 1961, to support "wars of national liberation," he was really fending off Chinese criticism. But Kennedy overreacted in his first State of the Union address by asking for more military spending.

Three months later, Kennedy fed Soviet fears of American aggressiveness by sponsoring an invasion of Cuba. At the start of 1959, Fidel Castro had toppled corrupt dictator Fulgencio Batista, who had made Havana infamous for Mafia-run gambling and prostitution. Castro then nationalized American investments, and thousands of Cubans fled to the United States.

When fourteen hundred anti-Castro Cubans landed at Cuba's **Bay of Pigs** on April 17, 1961, they were following a plan from the Eisenhower administration. The CIA had trained and armed the invaders and convinced Kennedy that the landing would trigger spontaneous uprisings. But when Kennedy refused to commit American armed forces to support them, Cuban forces captured the attackers.

Kennedy followed the Bay of Pigs debacle with a hasty and ill-thought-out summit meeting with Khrushchev in Vienna in June. Poorly prepared and nearly incapacitated by agonizing back pain, Kennedy made little headway. Khrushchev saw no need to bargain and subjected him to intimidating tirades. "He just beat the hell out of me," Kennedy told a reporter. Coming after Kennedy's refusal to salvage the Bay of Pigs by military intervention, the meeting left the Soviets with the impression that the president was weak and dangerously erratic.

To exploit Kennedy's perceived vulnerability, the Soviet Union renewed tension over Berlin, deep within East Germany. The divided city served as an escape route from Communism for hundreds of thousands of East Germans. Khrushchev now threatened to transfer the Soviet sector in Berlin to East Germany, which had no treaty obligations to France, Britain, or the United States. If the West had to deal directly with East Germany for access to Berlin, it would have to recognize a permanently divided Germany. Kennedy sounded the alarm; He doubled draft calls, called up reservists, and warned families to build fallout shelters. Boise, Idaho, families paid $100 for a share in a community shelter with its own power plant and hospital. Outside New York, Art Carlson and his son Claude put up a prefabricated steel shelter in four hours; Sears planned to sell the same model for $700.

Rather than confront the United States directly, however, the Soviets and East Germans on August 13, 1961, built a wall around the western sectors of Berlin while leaving the access route to West Germany open. The **Berlin Wall** thus isolated East Germany without challenging the Western allies in West Berlin itself. In private, Kennedy accepted the wall as a clever way to stabilize a dangerous situation: "A wall," he said, "is a hell of a lot better than a war." Tensions remained high for months as the two sides tested each other's resolve. Berlin remained a point of East-West tension until East German communism collapsed in 1989 and Berliners tore down the hated wall.

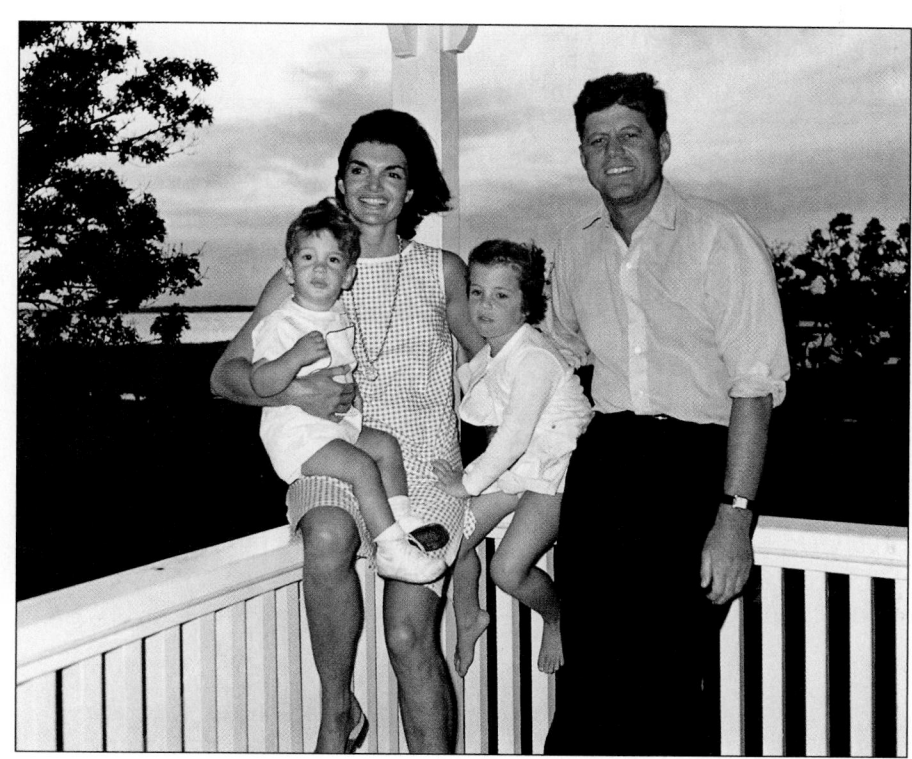

For many Americans in the early 1960s, John and Jacqueline Kennedy and their two children represented the ideal family, although the carefully posed pictures with happy smiles concealed the president's severe health problems and deep rifts in the marriage.

GETTING INTO VIETNAM

American involvement in Vietnam, located in Southeast Asia on the southern border of China, dated to the mid-1950s. Since the end of World War II, France had fought to maintain its colonial rule there against rebels who combined communist ideology with fervor for national independence under the leadership of Ho Chi Minh. The United States picked up three-quarters of the costs, but the French military position collapsed in 1954 after Vietnamese forces overran the French stronghold at Dien Bien Phu. The French had enough, and President Eisenhower was unwilling to join another Asian war. A Geneva peace conference "temporarily" divided Vietnam into a Communist north and a non-Communist south and scheduled elections for a single Vietnamese government.

The United States then replaced France as the supporter of pro-Western Vietnamese in the south. Washington's client was Ngo Dinh Diem, an anticommunist from South Vietnam's Roman Catholic elite. U.S. officials encouraged Diem to put off the elections and backed his efforts to construct an independent South Vietnam. Ho meanwhile consolidated the northern half as a communist state that claimed to be the legitimate government for all Vietnam. The United States further reinforced containment in Asia

by bringing Thailand, the Philippines, Pakistan, Australia, New Zealand, Britain, and France together in the **Southeast Asia Treaty Organization (SEATO)** in 1954 (see Map 28–3).

Another indirect consequence of the Vienna summit was growing American entanglement in South Vietnam, where Kennedy saw a chance to take a firm stand and reassert America's commitment to containment. In the countryside, Communist insurgents known as the **Viet Cong** were gaining strength. The anti-Communist leader, Diem, controlled the cities with the help of a large army and a Vietnamese elite that had worked with the French. The United States stepped up its supply of weapons and sent advisers, including members of one of Kennedy's military innovations, the Army Special Forces Group (Green Berets).

U.S. aid did not work. Despite overoptimistic reports and the help of sixteen thousand American troops, Diem's government by 1963 was losing the loyalty—the "hearts and minds"—of many South Vietnamese. North Vietnamese support for the Viet Cong canceled the effect of U.S. assistance. Diem courted a second civil war by violently crushing opposition from Vietnamese Buddhists. Kennedy's administration tacitly approved a coup on November 1 that killed Diem and his brother and installed an ineffective military junta.

MISSILE CRISIS: A LINE DRAWN IN THE WAVES

The escalating tensions of 1961 in Southeast Asia, the Caribbean, and Germany were a prelude to the crisis that came closest to triggering a nuclear war. In the summer of 1962, congressional Republicans had hounded Kennedy about the Soviet military presence in Cuba. On October 15, reconnaissance photos revealed Soviets at work on launching sites from which nuclear missiles could hit the United States. Top officials spent five exhausting and increasingly desperate days sorting through the options. Doing nothing was never considered: The missiles would be political disaster and a threat to national security. A full-scale invasion of Cuba was not feasible on short notice, and

AMERICAN VIEWS

Two Presidents Assess the Implications of the Cold War

In speeches two days apart in January 1961, outgoing President Dwight Eisenhower and incoming President John Kennedy offered contrasting interpretations of America's Cold War crusade. Eisenhower spoke with concern about the effects of defense spending on American society. Kennedy promised an unlimited commitment of resources to achieve national goals.

- Why did Kennedy define the American mission to the world so broadly?
- What changes in the 1950s led Eisenhower to warn about the dangers of pursuing that mission?
- Do the selections show basic agreement or disagreement about the goals of national policy?

Dwight D. Eisenhower
Farewell Address, January 18, 1961

Our military organization today bears little relation to that known by any of my predecessors in peacetime. . . .

This conjunction of an immense military establishment and a large arms industry is new in the American experience. The total influence—economic, political, even spiritual—is felt in every city, every State house, every office of the federal government. We recognize the imperative need for this development. Yet we must not fail to comprehend its grave implications. . . .

In the councils of government, we must guard against the acquisition of unwarranted influence, whether sought or unsought, by the military-industrial complex. The potential for the disastrous rise of misplaced power exists and will persist.

We must never let the weight of this combination endanger our liberties or democratic processes. We should take nothing for granted.

Only an alert and knowledgeable citizenry can compel the proper meshing of the huge industrial and military machinery of defense with our peaceful methods and goals.

John F. Kennedy
Inaugural Address, January 20, 1961

Let the word go forth from this time and place, to friend and foe alike, that the torch has been passed to a new generation of Americans—born in this century, tempered by war, disciplined by a hard and bitter peace, proud of our ancient heritage—and unwilling to witness or permit the slow undoing of those human rights to which this nation has always been committed, and to which we are committed today at home and around the world.

Let every nation know, whether it wishes us well or ill, that we shall pay any price, bear any burden, meet any hardship, support any friends, oppose any foe to assure the survival and the success of liberty.

"surgical" air strikes were technically impossible. Either sort of military operation would kill hundreds of Soviet personnel and force Moscow to react. Secretary of Defense Robert McNamara suggested demanding removal of the missiles and declaring a naval "quarantine" against the arrival of further offensive weapons. A blockade would buy time for diplomacy.

Kennedy imposed the blockade in a terrifying speech on Monday, October 22. He emphasized the "deceptive" deployment of the Russian missiles and raised the specter of nuclear war. Americans would have been even more afraid had they known that some of the missiles were operational and that Soviets in Cuba were authorized to use them in self-defense.

MAP 28-3　SEATO and Other East Asian Countries with Ties to the United States
In East Asia and the western Pacific, the United States in the 1950s constructed a series of alliances to resist Soviet and Chinese Communist influence.

viet commitment to anti-Western regimes in the developing world. Americans hated the Castro government out of proportion to its geopolitical importance, but they rightly feared that Cuba would try to export revolution throughout Latin America. Kennedy had tried to preempt Castroism in 1961 by launching the **Alliance for Progress**, an economic development program for Latin America that tied aid to social reform. However, the United States had also orchestrated the Bay of Pigs invasion and funded a CIA campaign to sabotage Cuba. High American officials were not contemplating a full-scale invasion, but Castro and Khrushchev had reason to fear the worst.

Khrushchev also hoped to redress the strategic balance. As Kennedy discovered on taking office, the United States actually led the world in the deployment of strategic missiles. Intermediate-range rockets gave the USSR a nuclear club over western Europe, but in October 1962, the Soviet Union had fewer than fifty ICBMs to aim at the United States and China. The United States was creating a defensive triad of a thousand land-based Minuteman missiles, five hundred long-range bombers, and six hundred Polaris missiles on nuclear submarines targeted on the USSR. The strategic imbalance had sustained NATO during the Berlin confrontation, but forty launchers in Cuba with two warheads each would have doubled the Soviet capacity to strike at the United States.

Soviet missiles in Cuba thus flouted the Monroe Doctrine and posed a real military threat. Kennedy and Khrushchev had also backed each other into untenable positions. In September, Kennedy had warned that the United States could not tolerate Soviet offensive weapons in Cuba, never dreaming that they were already there. Had Khrushchev acted openly (as the United States had done when it placed missiles in Turkey), the United States would have been hard pressed to object under international law. By acting in secret

While Khrushchev hesitated, Soviet ships circled outside the quarantine line. On Friday, Khrushchev offered to withdraw the missiles in return for an American pledge not to invade Cuba. On Saturday, a second communication nearly dashed this hopeful opening by raising a new complaint about American missiles on the territory of NATO allies. The letter was the result of pressure by Kremlin hard-liners and Khrushchev's own wavering. Kennedy decided to accept the first letter and ignore the second. The United States pledged not to invade Cuba and secretly promised to remove obsolete Jupiter missiles from Turkey. Khrushchev accepted these terms on Sunday, October 28.

Why did Khrushchev risk the Cuban gamble? One reason was to protect Castro as a symbol of So-

and breaking previous promises, the Soviets outsmarted themselves. When the missiles were discovered, Kennedy had to act.

In the end, both sides were cautious. Khrushchev backed down rather than fight. Kennedy fended off hawkish advisers who wanted to destroy Castro. The world had trembled, but neither nation wanted war over "the missiles of October."

SCIENCE AND FOREIGN AFFAIRS

The two superpowers competed through science as well as diplomacy. When Kennedy took office, the United States was still playing catch-up in space technology. A Russian, Yuri Gagarin, was the first human to orbit the earth, on April 12, 1961. American John Glenn did not match Gagarin's feat until February 1962. Kennedy committed the United States to placing an American astronaut on the moon by 1970. The decision narrowed a multifaceted scientific and military program to a massive engineering project that favored the economic capacity of the United States.

The Soviet Union and U.S. were also fencing about nuclear weapons testing. After the three-year moratorium, both resumed tests in 1961–1962. The U.S. started with underground tests to minimize fallout, but then followed with atmospheric detonations. Renewed testing let the Russians show off huge hydrogen bombs with yields of 20 and 30 megatons—roughly one thousand times the power of the bombs dropped on Japan. Both nations worked on multiple targetable warheads, anti-ballistic missiles, and other innovations that might destabilize the balance of terror.

After the missile crisis showed his toughness, however, Kennedy had enough political maneuvering room to respond to pressure from liberal Democrats and groups like Women Strike for Peace and the Committee for a Sane Nuclear Policy by giving priority to disarmament. In July 1963, the United States, Britain, and the USSR signed the **Limited Test Ban Treaty**, which outlawed nuclear testing in the atmosphere, in outer space, and under water, and invited other nations to join in. A more comprehensive treaty was impossible because the Soviet Union refused the on-site inspections the United States deemed necessary to distinguish underground tests from earthquakes. France and China, the other nuclear powers, refused to sign, and the treaty did not halt weapons development, but it was the most positive achievement of Kennedy's foreign policy and a step toward later disarmament treaties.

RIGHTEOUSNESS LIKE A MIGHTY STREAM: THE STRUGGLE FOR CIVIL RIGHTS

Supreme Court decisions are based on abstract principles, but they involve real people. One was Linda Brown of Topeka, Kansas, a third-grader whose parents were fed up with sending her past an all-white public school to attend an all-black school a mile away. The Browns volunteered to help the NAACP challenge Topeka's school segregation by trying to enroll Linda in their neighborhood school, beginning a legal case that reached the Supreme Court. Three years later, on May 17, 1954, the Court decided **Brown v. Board of Education of Topeka,** opening a new civil rights era. The justices reversed the 1896 case of *Plessy v. Ferguson* by ruling that sending black children to "separate but equal" schools denied them equal treatment under the Constitution. Linda's mother heard about the decision on the radio while she was ironing and told her daughter when she got home from school; when Linda's father heard the news, his eyes filled with tears, and he said, "Thanks be to God."

The *Brown* decision made the growing effort to secure equal legal treatment for African Americans an inescapable challenge to American society. The first phase of the civil rights struggle built from the Supreme Court's decision in 1954 to a vast gathering at the Lincoln Memorial in 1963. In between, African Americans chipped away at the racial segregation of schools, universities, and public facilities with marches, boycotts, sit-ins, and lawsuits, forcing segregated communities to choose between integration and violent defiance. In the two years following the 1963 March on Washington, the federal government passed landmark legislation.

GETTING TO THE SUPREME COURT

The *Brown* decision climaxed a twenty-five-year campaign to reenlist the federal courts on the side of equal rights (see the Overview table, "Civil Rights: The Struggle for Racial Equality"). The work began in the 1930s when Charles Hamilton Houston, dean of Howard University's law school, trained a corps of civil-rights lawyers. Working on behalf of the NAACP, he hoped to erode *Plessy* by suits focused on interstate travel and professional graduate schools (the least defensible segregated institutions, because states seldom provided alternatives). In 1938, Houston's student Thurgood Marshall, a future Supreme Court justice, took over the NAACP job. He and other NAACP lawyers such as Constance Baker Motley risked personal danger crisscrossing the South to file civil rights lawsuits wherever a local case emerged. In 1949, Motley was the first black lawyer to argue a case in a Mississippi courtroom since Reconstruction.

The *Brown* case combined lawsuits from Delaware, Virginia, South Carolina, the District of Columbia, and Kansas. In each instance, students and families braved community pressure to demand equal access to a basic public service. Chief Justice Earl Warren brought a divided Court to unanimous agreement. Viewing public education as central for the equal opportunity that lay at the heart of American values, the Court weighed the consequences of segregated school systems and concluded that separate meant unequal. The reasoning fit the temper of a nation that was proud of making prosperity accessible to all.

Brown also built on efforts by Mexican Americans in the Southwest to assert their rights of citizenship. After World War II, Latino organizations such as the League of United Latin American Citizens battled job discrimination and ethnic segregation. In 1946, the federal courts had prohibited segregation of Mexican American children in California schools. Eight years later, the Supreme Court forbade Texas from excluding Mexican Americans from juries. These cases provided precedents for the Court's decision in *Brown* and subsequent civil-rights cases.

DELIBERATE SPEED

Racial segregation by law was largely a southern problem, the legacy of Jim Crow laws from early in the century. The civil rights movement therefore focused first on the South and allowed Americans elsewhere to think of racial injustice as a regional issue.

Southern responses to *Brown* emphasized regional differences. Few southern communities desegregated schools voluntarily, for to do so undermined the entrenched principle of a dual society. Their reluctance was bolstered in 1955 when the Supreme Court allowed segregated states to carry out the 1954 decision "with all deliberate speed" rather than immediately. The following year, 101 southern congressmen and senators issued the **Southern Manifesto**, which asserted that the Court decision was unconstitutional. President Eisenhower privately deplored the desegregation decision, which violated his sense of states' rights and upset Republican attempts to gain southern votes; he called both those who resisted the decision and those who wanted to enforce it "extremists."

Eisenhower's distaste for racial integration left the Justice Department on the sidelines. Courageous parents and students had to knock on schoolhouse doors, often carrying court orders. Responses varied: School districts in border states, such as Maryland,

Overview

Civil Rights: The Struggle for Racial Equality

Area of Concern	Key Actions	Results
Public school integration	Federal court cases	*Brown v. Board of Education of Topeka* (1954) Enforcement by presidential action, Little Rock (1957) Follow-up court decisions, including mandatory busing programs
Equal access to public facilities	Montgomery bus boycott (1955) Lunch counter sit-ins (1960) Freedom rides (1961) Birmingham demonstrations (1963) March on Washington (1963)	Civil Rights Act of 1964
Equitable voter registration	Voter registration drives, including Mississippi Summer Project (1964) Demonstrations and marches including Selma to Montgomery march (1965)	Voting Rights Act of 1965

Elizabeth Eckford, one of the first black students to attend Central High in Little Rock, Arkansas, in 1957, enters the school amid taunts from white students and bystanders.

Kentucky, and Oklahoma, desegregated relatively peacefully. Further south, African American children often met taunts and violence.

The first crisis came in Little Rock, Arkansas, in September 1957. The city school board admitted nine African Americans, including Melba Pattillo, to Central High, while segregrationist groups, such as the White Citizens Council, stirred up white fears. Claiming to fear violence, Governor Orval Faubus surrounded Central High with the National Guard and turned the new students away. Under intense national pressure, Faubus withdrew the Guard. When the black students entered the school, a howling mob forced the police to sneak the students out after two hours. Fuming at the governor's defiance of federal authority, which bordered on insurrection, Eisenhower reluctantly nationalized the National Guard and sent in the 101st Airborne Division to keep order. Eight of the students endured a year of harassment in the hallways of Central.

Virginians in 1958–1959 tried avoidance rather than confrontation. Massive resistance was a state policy that required local school districts to close rather than accept black students. When court orders to admit nineteen black students triggered the shut-down of four high schools and three junior highs in Norfolk, white parents tried to compensate with private academies and tutoring, but it was soon apparent that a modern community could not dismantle public education without becoming a laughing-stock. Norfolk's leaders realized that no large business was going to locate in a city whose claim to fame was the "lost class of '59," and Virginia's elite privately welcomed federal court decisions that got them off the hook by striking down their own law.

Change came slowly to state universities. Border states desegregated colleges and professional schools with few incidents. Again, the story was different in the lower South. In 1956, the University of Alabama admitted Autherine Lucy under court order but then expelled her before she could attend classes. In September 1962, James Meredith tried to enter the University of Mississippi, igniting a riot that the state refused to control. Because the governor directly defied the federal courts and broke promises to the administration, President Kennedy sent in the army. A year later, Governor George Wallace of Alabama grabbed headlines by "standing in the schoolhouse door" to prevent integration of the University of Alabama, gaining a national prominence that culminated in a third-party candidacy for president in 1968.

The breakthrough in school integration did not come until the end of the 1960s, when the courts rejected further delays, and federal authorities threatened to cut off education funds. As late as 1968, only 6 percent of African American children in the South attended integrated schools. By 1973, the figure was 90 percent. Attention thereafter shifted to northern communities, whose schools were segregated, not by law, but by the divisions between white and black neighborhoods and between white suburbs and multiracial central cities, a situation known as *de facto* segregation.

PUBLIC ACCOMMODATIONS

The civil-rights movement also sought to integrate public accommodations. Most southern states separated the races in bus terminals and movie theaters.

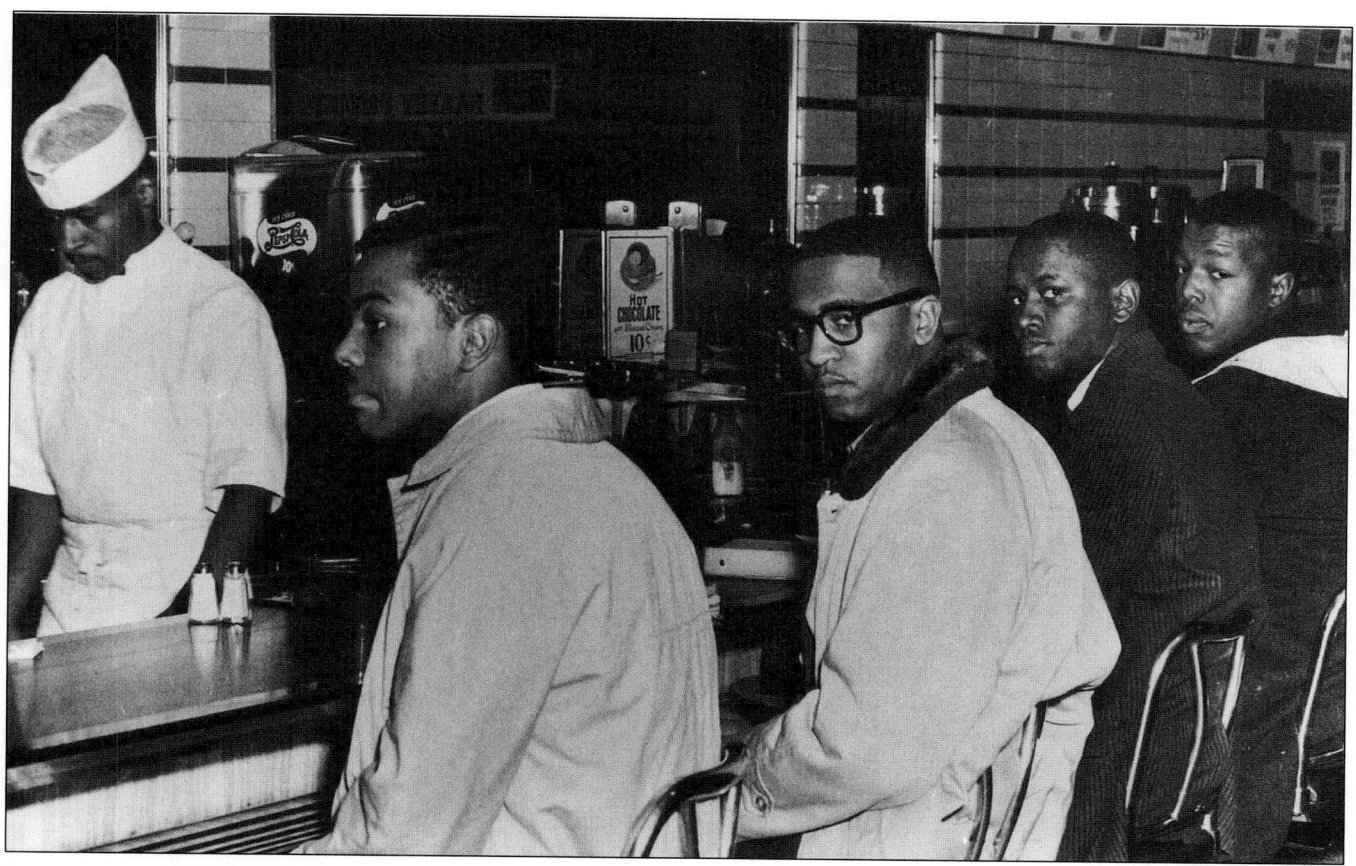

Students from North Carolina A&T, an all-black college, began the lunch-counter sit-in movement in February 1960. Here four students sit patiently in the Greensboro Woolworth's without being served. Participants wore their best clothes and suffered politely through days of verbal and sometimes physical abuse.

They required black riders to take rear seats on buses. They labeled separate restrooms and drinking fountains for "colored" users. Hotels denied rooms to black people, and restaurants refused them service.

The struggle to end segregated facilities started in Montgomery, Alabama. On December 1, 1955, Rosa Parks, a seamstress who worked at a downtown department store, refused to give up her bus seat to a white passenger and was arrested. Parks acted spontaneously, but she was part of a network of civil-rights activists who wanted to challenge segregated buses and was the secretary of the Montgomery NAACP. As news of her action spread, the community institutions that enriched southern black life went into action. The Women's Political Council, a group of college-trained black women, initiated a mass boycott of the privately owned bus company. Alabama State College professor Jo Ann Robinson worked through the night to mimeograph 52,500 flyers and enlisted students to spread them through the city. Martin Luther King, Jr., a 26-year-old pastor, led the boycott. He galvanized a mass meeting with a speech

that quoted the biblical prophet Amos: "We are determined here in Montgomery to work and fight until justice runs down like water, and righteousness like a mighty stream."

Montgomery's African Americans organized their boycott in the face of white outrage. A car pool substituted for the buses despite police harassment. As the boycott survived months of pressure, the national media began to pay attention. After nearly a year, the Supreme Court agreed that the bus segregation law was unconstitutional.

Victory in Montgomery depended on the steadfastness of African American involvement. Leaders included Ralph Abernathy, other black preachers, and faculty members from Alabama State College. Participants cut across the class lines that had divided black Southerners. Success also revealed the discrepancy between white attitudes in the Deep South and national opinion. For white Southerners, segregation was a local concern best defined as a legal or constitutional matter. For other Americans, it was increasingly an issue of the South's deviation from national moral norms.

The Montgomery boycott won a local victory and made King famous, but it did not propel a wave of immediate change. King formed the **Southern Christian Leadership Conference (SCLC)** and sparred with the NAACP about community-based versus court-based civil rights tactics, but four African American college students in Greensboro, North Carolina, started the next phase of the struggle. On February 1, 1960, they put on jackets and ties and sat down at the segregated lunch counter in Woolworth's, waiting through the day without being served. Their patient courage brought more demonstrators; within two days, eighty-five students packed the store. Nonviolent sit-ins spread throughout the South.

The sit-ins had both immediate and long-range effects. In such comparatively sophisticated border cities as Nashville, Tennessee, sit-ins integrated lunch counters. Elsewhere, they precipitated white violence and mass arrests. Like soldiers on a battlefield, nervous participants in sit-ins and demonstrations drew strength from one another. "If you don't have courage," said one young woman in Albany, Georgia, "you can borrow it." King welcomed nonviolent confrontation. SCLC leader Ella Baker helped the students form a new organization, the **Student Nonviolent Coordinating Committee (SNCC)**.

The year 1961 brought "freedom rides" to test the segregation of interstate bus terminals. The idea came from James Farmer of the **Congress of Racial Equality (CORE)**, who copied a little-remembered 1947 Journey of Reconciliation that had tested the integration of interstate trains. Two buses carrying black and white passengers met only minor problems in Virginia, the Carolinas, and Georgia, but Alabamians burned one of the buses and attacked the riders in Birmingham, where they beat demonstrators senseless and clubbed a Justice Department observer. The governor and police refused to protect the freedom riders. The riders traveled into Mississippi under National Guard protection but were arrested at the Jackson bus terminal. Despite Attorney General Robert Kennedy's call for a cooling-off period, freedom rides continued through the summer. The rides proved that African Americans were in charge of their own civil rights revolution.

THE MARCH ON WASHINGTON, 1963

John Kennedy was a tepid supporter of the civil-rights movement and entered office with no civil-rights agenda. He appointed segregationist judges to mollify southern congressmen and would have preferred that African Americans stop disturbing the fragile Democratic Party coalition. As Eisenhower did at Little Rock, Kennedy intervened at the University of Mississippi in

Martin Luther King, Jr.'s speech on August 28, 1963, was an emotional high point of the civil rights revolution.

1962 because of a state challenge to federal authority, not to further racial justice.

In the face of slow federal response, the SCLC concentrated for 1963 on rigidly segregated Birmingham. April began with sit-ins and marches that aimed to integrate lunch counters, restrooms, and stores and secure open hiring for some clerical jobs. Birmingham's commissioner of public safety, Bull Connor, used fire hoses to blast demonstrators against buildings and roll children down the streets. When demonstrators fought back, his men chased them with dogs. Continued marches brought the arrest of hundreds of children. King's own "Letter from Birmingham City Jail" stated the case for protest: "We have not made a single gain in civil rights without determined legal and nonviolent pressure. . . . Freedom is never voluntarily given by the oppressor; it must be demanded by the oppressed."

The Birmingham demonstrations were inconclusive. White leaders accepted minimal demands on May 10 but delayed enforcing them. Antiblack violence continued, including a bomb that killed four children in a Birmingham church. Meanwhile, the events in Alabama had forced President Kennedy to board the freedom train with an eloquent June 11 speech and to send a civil-rights bill to Congress. "Are we to say . . . that this is the land of the free, except for Negroes, that we have no second-class citizens, except Negroes . . . ? Now the time has come for the nation to fulfill its promise."

On August 28, 1963, a rally in Washington transformed African-American civil rights into a national cause. A quarter of a million people, black and white, marched to the Lincoln Memorial. The day gave Martin Luther King, Jr., a national pulpit. His call for progress toward Christian and American goals had immense appeal. Television cut away from afternoon programs for his "I Have a Dream" speech.

The March on Washington demonstrated the mass appeal of civil rights and its identification with national values. It also papered over growing tensions within the civil rights movement. John Lewis of SNCC wanted to challenge Kennedy for doing "too little, too late" but dropped the criticism under intense pressure. He was the only speaker at the march to talk about "black people" rather than "Negroes," an indication of growing militancy that split the civil-rights effort in the mid-1960s and moved younger African Americans, as well as Latinos and Native Americans, to emphasize their own distinct identities within American society.

"LET US CONTINUE"

The two years that followed King's speech mingled despair and accomplishment. The optimism of the March on Washington shattered with the assassination of John Kennedy in November 1963. In 1964 and 1965, however, President Lyndon Johnson pushed through Kennedy's legislative agenda and much more in a burst of government activism unmatched since the l930s. Federal legislation brought victory to the first phase of the civil-rights revolution, launched the **War on Poverty**, expanded health insurance and aid to education, and opened an era of environmental protection.

DALLAS, 1963

In November 1963, President Kennedy visited Texas to patch up feuds among Texas Democrats. On November 22, the president's motorcade took him near the Texas School Book Depository building in Dallas, where Lee Harvey Oswald had stationed himself at a window on the sixth floor. When Kennedy's open car swung into the sights of his rifle, Oswald fired three shots that wounded Texas Governor John Connally and killed the president. As doctors vainly treated the president in a hospital emergency room, Dallas police arrested Oswald. Vice President Lyndon Johnson took the oath of office as president on Air Force One while the blood-spattered Jacqueline Kennedy looked on. Two days later, as Oswald was being led to a courtroom, the Texas nightclub owner Jack Ruby killed Oswald with a handgun, in full view of TV cameras.

Lee Oswald was a 24-year old misfit. He had served in the Marines and worked maintaining U-2 spy planes before defecting to the Soviet Union, which he found to be less than a workers' paradise. He returned to the United States after three years with a Russian wife and a fervent commitment to Fidel Castro's Cuban revolution. It was later learned that he had tried to shoot a right-wing general in 1963. He visited the Soviet and Cuban embassies in Mexico City in September trying to drum up a job, but neither country thought him worth hiring.

Some Americans believe there is more to the story. Why? One possibility is the expectation that important events should have great causes. Oswald seems too insignificant to be responsible on his own for the murder of a charismatic president. The sketchy job done by the Warren Commission, appointed to investigate the assassination, also bred doubts in some minds. The commission hurried to complete its work before the 1964 election. It also sought to assure Americans that Kennedy had not been killed as part of a communist plot. The Warren Commission calmed fears in the short run but left loose ends that have fueled conspiracy theories.

All of the theories remain unproved. Until they are, logic holds that the simplest explanation for cutting through a mass of information is usually the best. Oswald was a social misfit with a grievance against American society. Ruby was an impulsive man who told his brother on his deathbed that he thought he was doing the country a favor. Like presidents Garfield and McKinley before him, Kennedy died at the hands of one unbalanced man acting alone.

WAR ON POVERTY

Five days after the assassination, Lyndon Johnson claimed Kennedy's progressive aura for his new administration. "Let us continue," he told the nation, promising to implement Kennedy's policies. In fact, Johnson was vastly different from Kennedy. He was a professional politician who had reached the top through Texas politics and congressional infighting. As Senate majority leader during the 1950s, he had

After the assassination of John Kennedy in Dallas, Lyndon Johnson, with Jackie Kennedy looking on, took the oath of office as president aboard Air Force One at Love Field in Dallas.

built a web of political obligations and friendships. Johnson's presence on the ticket in 1960 had helped to elect Kennedy by attracting southern voters, but the Kennedy entourage loathed him. He lacked Kennedy's polish and easy relations with the eastern elite. He knew little about foreign affairs but was a master of domestic politics. Johnson's upbringing in rural Texas shaped a man who was endlessly ambitious, ruthless, and often personally crude, but also deeply committed to social equity. He had entered public life with the New Deal in the 1930s and believed in its principles. Johnson, not Kennedy, was the true heir of Franklin Roosevelt.

Johnson inherited a domestic agenda that the Kennedy administration had defined but not enacted. Kennedy's New Frontier had met the same fate as Truman's Fair Deal. Initiatives in education, medical insurance, tax reform, and urban affairs had stalled or been gutted by conservatives in Congress.

Kennedy's farthest-reaching initiative was rooted in the acknowledgment that poverty was a persistent American problem. Michael Harrington's study *The Other America* became an unexpected bestseller. As poverty captured public attention, Kennedy's economic advisers devised a community action program that emphasized education and job training, a national service corps, and a youth conservation corps. They prepared a package of proposals to submit to Congress in 1964 that downplayed the option of large-scale income transfers as politically unpopular. Instead, they focused on social programs to alter behaviors that were thought to be passed from generation to generation, thus following the American tendency to attribute poverty to the failings of the poor themselves.

Johnson made Kennedy's antipoverty package his own. Adopting Cold War rhetoric, he declared "unconditional war on poverty." The core of Johnson's program was the **Office of Economic Opportunity (OEO)**. Established under the direction of Kennedy's brother-in-law R. Sargent Shriver in 1964, the OEO operated the Job Corps for school dropouts, the Neighborhood Youth Corps for unemployed teenagers, the Head Start program to prepare poor children for school, and VISTA (Volunteers in Service to America), a domestic Peace Corps. OEO's biggest effort went to Community Action Agencies. By 1968, more than five hundred such agencies provided health and educational services. Despite flaws, the War on Poverty improved life for millions of Americans.

CIVIL RIGHTS, 1964–1965

Johnson's passionate commitment to economic betterment accompanied a commitment to civil rights. In Johnson's view, segregation not only deprived African Americans of access to opportunity but also distracted white Southerners from their own poverty and underdevelopment. As he complained in a speech in New Orleans, southern leaders ignored the region's economic needs in favor of racial rabble-rousing.

One solution was the **Civil Rights Act of 1964**, which Kennedy had introduced but which Johnson got enacted. The law prohibited segregation in public accommodations, such as hotels, restaurants, gas stations, theaters, and parks, and outlawed employment discrimination on federally assisted projects. It also created the Equal Employment Opportunity Commission (EEOC) and included gender in list of categories protected against discrimination, a provision whose consequences were scarcely suspected in 1964.

Even as Congress was debating the 1964 law, **Freedom Summer** moved political power to the top of the civil-rights agenda. Organized by SNCC, the Mississippi Summer Freedom Project was a voter registration drive that sent white and black volunteers to the small towns and back roads of Mississippi. The target was a political system that used rigged literacy tests and intimidation to keep black Southerners from voting. In Mississippi in 1964, only 7 percent of eligible black citizens were registered voters. Local black activists had laid the groundwork for a registration effort with years of courageous effort through the NAACP and voter leagues. Now an increasingly militant SNCC took the lead. The explicit goal was to increase the number of African American voters. The tacit intention was to attract national attention by putting middle-class white college students in the line of fire. Freedom Summer gained sixteen hundred new voters and taught two thousand children in SNCC-run Freedom Schools at the cost of beatings, bombings, church arson, and the murder of three project workers.

Another outgrowth of the SNCC effort was the Mississippi Freedom Democratic Party (MFDP), a biracial coalition that bypassed Mississippi's all-white Democratic Party, followed state party rules, and sent its own delegates to the 1964 Democratic convention. To preserve party harmony, President Johnson refused to expel the "regular" Mississippi Democrats and offered instead to seat two MFDP delegates and enforce party rules for 1968. The MFDP walked out, seething with anger. Fannie Lou Hamer, a MFDP delegate who had already suffered in the struggle for voting rights, remembered, "We learned the hard way that even though we had all the law and all the righteousness on our side—that white man is not going to give up his power to us. We have to build our own power."

Freedom Summer and political realities both focused national attention on voter registration. Lyndon Johnson and Martin Luther King, Jr., agreed on the need for federal voting legislation when King visited the president in December 1964 after winning the Nobel Peace Prize. For King, power at the ballot box would help black Southerners to take control of their own communities. For Johnson, voting reform would fulfill the promise of American democracy. It would also benefit the Democratic party by replacing with black voters the white Southerners who were drifting toward anti-integration Republicans.

The target for King and the SCLC was Dallas County, Alabama, where only 2 percent of eligible black residents were registered, compared with 70 percent of white residents. Peaceful demonstrations started in January 1965. By early February, jails in the county seat of Selma held 2,600 black people whose offense was marching to the courthouse to demand the vote. The campaign climaxed with a march from Selma to the state capital of Montgomery. SNCC leader John Lewis remembered, "I don't know what we expected. I think maybe we thought we'd be arrested and jailed, or maybe they wouldn't do anything to us. I had a little knapsack on my shoulder with an apple, a toothbrush, toothpaste, and two books in it: a history of America and a book by [Christian theologian] Thomas Merton."

On Sunday, March 7, five hundred marchers crossed the bridge over the Alabama River, to meet a sea of state troopers. The troopers gave them two minutes to disperse and then attacked on foot and horseback "as if they were mowing a big field." The attack drove the demonstrators back in bloody confusion while television cameras rolled.

As violence continued, Johnson addressed a joint session of Congress to demand a voting-rights law: "Our mission is at once the oldest and the most basic of this country: to right wrong, to do justice, to serve man." He ended with the refrain of the civil rights movement: "We shall overcome." By opening the political process to previously excluded citizens, the Voting Rights Act was as revolutionary and far reaching as the Nineteenth Amendment, guaranteeing women the right to vote, and the Labor Relations Act of 1935, which recognized labor unions as the equals of corporations.

Johnson signed the **Voting Rights Act** on August 6, 1965. The law outlawed literacy tests and provided for federal voting registrars in states where registration or turnout in 1964 was less than 50 percent of eligible population. It applied initially in seven southern states. Black registration in these states jumped from 27 percent to 55 percent within the first year. In 1975, Congress extended coverage to Hispanic voters in the Southwest. By the end of 1992, Virginia had elected a black governor, and nearly every southern state had elected black representatives to Congress. Less obvious but just as revolutionary were the thousands of black and Latino candidates, who won local offices, and the new moderation of white leaders, who had to satisfy black voters. In the long run, the Voting Rights Act climaxed the battle for civil rights and shifted attention to the continuing problems of economic opportunity and inequality.

WAR, PEACE, AND THE LANDSLIDE OF 1964

Lyndon Johnson was the peace candidate in 1964. Johnson had maintained Kennedy's commitment to

FROM THEN TO NOW

Medical Research on Polio and AIDS

When Dr. Jonas Salk announced an effective vaccine for polio on April 12, 1955, the United States gained a new hero. In the confident mid-1950s, the polio vaccine seemed another proof of American ability to improve the world.

Poliomyelitis, or infantile paralysis, attacks the nervous system; it can paralyze the legs or kill by short-circuiting muscles in the throat and chest. Before 1900, infants had often encountered the polio virus in their first months and developed lifelong immunity. In the twentieth century, cleaner houses and streets delayed contact with polio until the preschool years or later, when the disease could be devastating. The virus sometimes struck adults; it cost Franklin Roosevelt the use of his legs when he was in his thirties, but most victims were children.

Fear of polio haunted American families after World War II. The disease killed fewer people than heart disease or cancer, but it seemed grossly unfair. Most Americans knew at least one child who hobbled through life on crutches and metal leg braces. Hospitals filled with new cases every summer—58,000 in 1952 alone. Many children clung to life inside iron lungs, metal cylinders that pumped air in and out of a hole in the throat.

Polio season peaked in July and August. Worried parents kept their children out of movie theaters and swimming pools, but the disease struck even the most careful families. One woman who grew up in the 1950s remembered: "Polio? That was the big fear when I was young. . . . I remember going to Dallas and seeing television for the first time. . . . Every day they would report 'another so many polio cases today.'"

Salk's announcement was welcome news. A generation later, President Ronald Reagan would list the polio vaccine with the steam engine and silicon chip as one of the great modern discoveries. By 2002, the number of new polio cases around the world had fallen to fewer than 1,000 in only ten countries—not including the United States.

However, medical research in the new century was vastly different than in the 1950s. Salk's work was financed largely by private contributions—many made by individuals and families to the March of Dimes. Fifty years later, the federal government is by far the largest supporter of medical research, spending to the

---

South Vietnam. On the advice of such Kennedy hold-overs as Defense Secretary Robert McNamara, he stepped up commando raids and naval shelling of North Vietnam, on the assumption that North Vietnam controlled the Viet Cong. On August 2, North Vietnamese torpedo boats attacked the U.S. destroyer *Maddox* in the Gulf of Tonkin while it was eavesdropping on North Vietnamese military signals. Two days later, the *Maddox* and the *C. Turner Joy* reported another torpedo attack (probably false sonar readings). Johnson ordered a bombing raid in reprisal and asked Congress to authorize "all necessary measures" to protect American forces and stop further aggression. Congress passed the **Gulf of Tonkin Resolution** with only two nay votes, effectively authorizing the president to wage undeclared war.

Johnson's militancy paled beside that of his Republican opponent. Senator Barry Goldwater of Arizona represented the new right wing of the Republican party, which was drawing strength from the South and West. A department store heir, Goldwater wanted minimal government interference in free enterprise. As a former Air Force pilot, he also wanted aggressive confrontation with communism. Campaign literature accurately described him as "a choice, not an echo." He declared that "extremism in the defense of liberty is no vice," raising visions of vigilantes and mobs. Goldwater's campaign made Johnson look moderate. Johnson pledged not "to send American boys nine or ten thousand miles from home to do what Asian boys ought to be doing for themselves" while Goldwater proposed an all-out war.

amount of nearly $20 billion annually (30 times the level of 1955 in constant dollars). The money finances researchers in hundreds of universities and medical schools as well as a huge complex of federal laboratories and programs grouped as the National Institutes of Health, located in Bethesda, Maryland.

Federal medical research touches on nearly every disease and health condition—from cancer to Alzheimer's disease, from mental health to heart disease—but much of the public's attention focused on HIV/AIDS research after the mid-1980s. Scientists first identified a new disease pattern, acquired immune deficiency syndrome (AIDS), in 1981. The name described the symptoms resulting from the human immunodeficiency virus (HIV), which destroys the body's ability to resist disease. HIV is transferred through blood and semen. In the 1980s, the most frequent American victims were gay men or intravenous drug users, with transmissions to heterosexual women increasing in the 1990s. By the beginning of the twenty-first century, HIV infection had been responsible for approximately 500,000 deaths in the United States. Worldwide the HIV death toll is in the millions and climbing fast.

HIV/AIDS triggers many of the same intense emotions as polio. It strikes people in their prime and gradually wastes their strength. Because it first seemed narrowly targeted at specific groups, the spread of the epidemic inspired intense anger among gays who believed that straight society and government agencies were indifferent to their plight. The Aids Coalition to Unleash Power, or ACT UP, used aggressive and sometimes outrageous tactics to pressure the government to increase funding and speed the approval process for new drugs. According to AIDS researcher Anthony Fauci, AIDS activists changed the practice of medicine in the U.S. for the better by giving patients greater control of their own treatment.

At the same time, HIV/AIDS remains as daunting scientifically as it has been politically volatile. Even as new drugs extended survival rates and made the disease relatively manageable for hundred of thousands of U.S. victims, a preventive vaccine has been much more elusive than the polio vaccine. In 2002, the federal budget allocated $2.8 billion for HIV/AIDS research and another $10 billion for prevention and treatment programs in the U.S. and other nations, amounts vastly greater than the funds spent fighting polio. If Salk's success confirmed American confidence in the 1950s, the global struggle against HIV and AIDS mirrors the complexity of the twenty-first century.

The election was a landslide. Johnson's 61 percent of the popular vote was the greatest margin ever recorded in a presidential election. Democrats racked up two-to-one majorities in Congress. For the first time in decades, liberal Democrats could enact their domestic program without begging votes from conservative Southerners or Republicans, and Johnson could achieve his goal of a **Great Society** based on freedom and opportunity for all.

The results were a series of measures that Johnson pushed through Congress before the Vietnam War eroded his political standing and distracted national attention. The National Endowment for the Arts and the National Endowment for the Humanities seemed noncontroversial at the time but would later become the focus of liberal and conservative struggles over the character of American life. The Wilderness Act (1964), which preserved 9.1 million acres from all development, would prove another political battlefield in the face of economic pressures in the next century.

The goal of increasing opportunity for all Americans stirred the president most deeply. As he told a July 1965 news conference, "When I was young, poverty was so common that we didn't know it had a name. An education was something that you had to fight for. . . . It is now my opportunity to help every child get an education, to help every Negro and every American citizen have an equal opportunity, to have every family get a decent home, and to help bring healing to the sick and dignity to the old." The Elementary and Secondary Education Act was the first general federal aid program for public schools, allocating $1.3 billion for textbooks and special education. The Higher Education Act funded low-interest student loans and university research facilities. The Medical Care Act created **Medicare**, federally funded health insurance for the elderly and **Medicaid**, which helped states offer medical care to the poor. The Appalachian Regional Development Act funded economic development in the depressed mountain counties of twelve states from Georgia to New York and proved a long-run success.

It is sometimes said that the United States declared war on poverty and lost. In fact, the nation came closer in to winning the war on poverty than it did the war in Vietnam. New or expanded social insurance and income support programs, such as Medicare, Medicaid, Social Security, and food stamps, cut the proportion of poor people from 22 percent of the American population in 1960 to 13 percent in 1970 (see Fig. 28–4). Infant mortality dropped by a third because of improved nutrition and better access to health care for mothers and children. Taken together, the political results of the 1964 landslide moved the United States far toward the vision of an end to poverty and racial injustice

CONCLUSION

The era commonly remembered as "the 1950s" stretched from 1953 to 1964. Consistent goals guided American foreign policy through the entire period, including vigilant anticommunism and the confidence to intervene in trouble spots around the globe. At home, the Supreme Court's *Brown* decision introduced a decade-long civil rights revolution that reached its emotional peak with the March on Washington and its political climax with the Civil Rights Act (1964) and Voting Rights Act (1965). However, many patterns of personal behavior and social relations remained unchanged. Women faced similar expectations from the early fifties to the early sixties. Churches showed more continuity than change.

In retrospect, it is remarkable how widely and deeply the Cold War shaped U.S. society. Fundamental social institutions, such as marriage and religion, got extra credit for their contributions to anticommunism. The nation's long tradition of home-grown radicalism was virtually silent in the face of the Cold War consensus. Even economically meritorious programs like more money for science and better roads went down more easily if linked to national defense.

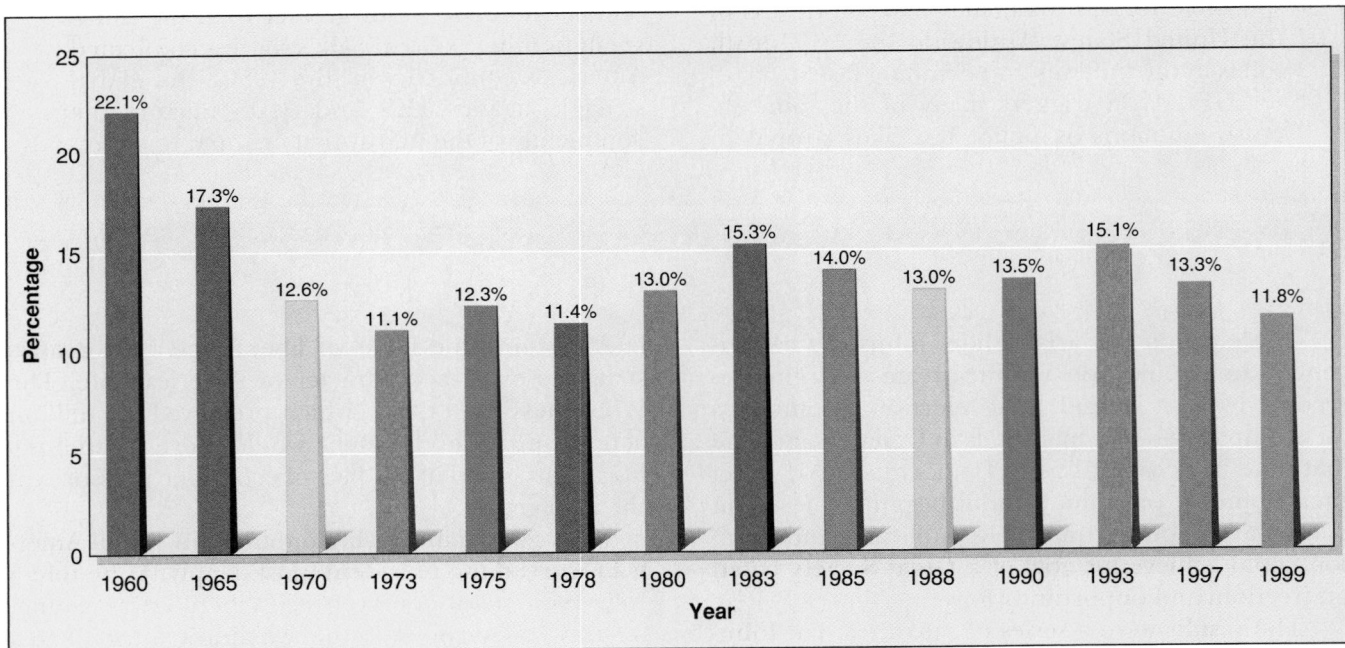

FIGURE 28-4   Poverty Rate, 1960-1999
With the improvement of federal health insurance, assistance for the elderly, and antipoverty programs, the proportion of Americans living in poverty dropped dramatically in the later 1960s. It began to inch upward again in the 1980s, when the priorities of the federal government shifted.
Data Source: *Statistical Abstract of the United States*

But the consistency and stability of the 1950s were fragile. The larger world was too complex to fit forever within the narrow framework of bipolar conflict. American society was too disparate and dynamic for Cold War conformity. In the later 1960s and the 1970s, contradictions burst through the surface of the American consensus. Foreign competitors, resource scarcities, and environmental damage diminished economic abundance and sapped national confidence. Nations from Vietnam to Iran refused to cooperate with American plans for the world. Corrupt politicians threatened the constitutional order.

Under these pressures, the national consensus splintered after 1964. Some members of minority groups turned their back on integration. Some younger Americans dropped out of mainstream society to join the aptly named counterculture. Others sought the security of religious commitment and community. Perhaps most divisively, "hawks" battled "doves" over Vietnam. If civil rights and Cold War had been the defining issues for "the fifties," Vietnam would define "the sixties," which stretched from 1965 to 1974.

REVIEW QUESTIONS

1. What were the sources of prosperity in the 1950s and 1960s? How did prosperity shape cities, family life, and religion? What opportunities did it create for women and for young people? How did it affect the American role in the world? Why did an affluent nation still need a war on poverty in the 1960s?

2. What assumptions about the Soviet Union shaped U.S. foreign policy? What assumptions about the United States shaped Soviet policy? What did American leaders think was at stake in Vietnam, Berlin, and Cuba?

3. Who initiated and led the African American struggle for civil rights? What role did the federal government play? What were the goals of the civil rights movement? Where did it succeed, and in what ways did it fall short?

4. How did the growth of nuclear arsenals affect international relations? How did the nuclear shadow affect American politics and society?

5. In what new directions did Lyndon Johnson take the United States? Were there differences in the goals of the New Frontier and the Great Society?

6. Why was school integration the focus of such strong conflict? How did the work of Mexican Americans and African Americans support the same goal of equal access to education.

KEY TERMS

Alliance for Progress (p. 903)

Bay of Pigs (p. 900)

Berlin Wall (p. 900)

Brown v. Board of Education of Topeka (p. 904)

Civil Rights Act of 1964 (p. 910)

Congress of Racial Equality (CORE) (p. 908)

Federal Highway Act of 1956 (p. 889)

Freedom Summer (p. 911)

Great Society (p. 913)

Gulf of Tonkin Resolution (p. 912)

Limited Test Ban Treaty (p. 904)

Massive retaliation (p. 895)

Medicaid (p. 914)

Medicare (p. 914)

National Aeronautics and Space Administration (NASA) (p. 896)

New Frontier (p. 899)

Office of Economic Opportunity (OEO) (p. 910)

Southeast Asia Treaty Organization (SEATO) (p. 901)

Southern Christian Leadership Conference (SCLC) (p. 908)

Southern Manifesto (p. 905)

Student Nonviolent Coordinating Committee (SNCC) (p. 908)

Viet Cong (p. 901)

Voting Rights Act (p. 911)

War on Poverty (p. 909)

RECOMMENDED READING

Beschloss, Michael. *May-Day: Eisenhower, Khrushchev, and the U-2 Affair* (1986). The drama and confusion of the U-2 affair are used to interpret the meaning of the Cold War for the United States and the Soviet Union.

Graebner, William. *Coming of Age in Buffalo* (1990). In words and pictures, places the complexity of teenage life in the 1950s within the American patterns of class and race.

Halberstam, David. *The Fifties* (1993). Provides a readable and detailed account of political and social change.

Harrington, Michael. *The Other America* (1962). Published early in the Kennedy years, an impassioned study that reminded Americans of continuing economic inequality and helped launch the War on Poverty.

McWhurter, Diane. *Carry Me Home: Birmingham, Alabama: The Climactic Battle of the Civil Rights Revolutaion* (2000). A sweeping depiction of race relations in one of the nation's most divided cities.

Posner, Gerald. *Case Closed* (1993). A detailed analysis of John Kennedy's death that refutes the most popular conspiracy theories.

White, Theodore. *The Making of the President, 1960* (1961). A vivid account of the issues and personalities of the 1960 campaign.

Williams, Juan. *Eyes on the Prize: America's Civil Rights Years, 1954-1965* (1988). A graphic and fast-moving account of the civil rights movement, written in conjunction with a PBS television series.

Wolfe, Tom. *The Right Stuff* (1979). An irreverent account of the early years of the U.S. space program that captures the atmosphere of the 1950s and early 1960s.

ADDITIONAL SOURCES

The Eisenhower Presidency

Ambrose, Stephen E. *Ike's Spies: Eisenhower and the Espionage Establishment* (1981).

Bowie, Robert, and Richard Immerman. *Waging Peace: How Eisenhower Shaped an Enduring Cold War Strategy* (1998).

Brands, H. W. *Cold Warriors: Eisenhower's Generation and American Foreign Policy* (1988).

Divine, Robert. *Eisenhower and the Cold War* (1981).

Dudziak, Mary. *Cold War Civil Rights: Race and the Image of American Democracy* (2000).

Greenstein, Fred. *The Hidden-Hand Presidency: Eisenhower as Leader* (1982).

Hixson, Walter. *Parting the Curtain: Propaganda, Culture and the Cold War* (1997).

Immerman, Richard. *The CIA in Guatemala: The Foreign Policy of Intervention* (1982).

Pach, Chester. *The Presidency of Dwight David Eisenhower* (1991).

Pickett, William B. *Eisenhower Decides to Run: Presidential Politics and Cold War Strategy* (2001).

Science, Politics, and Society

Clowse, Barbara. *Brainpower for the Cold War: The Sputnik Crisis and the National Defense Education Act* (1981).

Divine, Robert. *The Sputnik Challenge* (1993).

Grossman, Andrew. *Neither Dead nor Red: Civil Defense and American Political Development during the Early Cold War* (2001).

Kleidman, Robert. *Organizing for Peace: Neutrality, the Test Ban, and the Freeze* (1993).

McEnaney, Laura. *Civil Defense Begins at Home: Militarization Meets Everyday Life in the Fifties* (2000).

McDougall, Walter. *The Heavens and the Earth: A Political History of the Space Age* (1985).

Smith, Jane. *Patenting the Sun* (1990).

Titus, M. Costandina. *Bombs in the Backyard: Atomic Testing and American Politics* (1986).

Winkler, Allan. *Life under a Cloud: American Anxiety about the Atom* (1993).

The Politics of Growth

Abbott, Carl. *The New Urban America: Growth and Politics in Sunbelt Cities* (1986).

Fones-Wolf, Elizabeth. *Selling Free Enterprise: The Business Assault in Labor and Liberalism, 1945-1960* (1994).

Jackson, Kenneth. *The Crabgrass Frontier* (1985).

McQuaid, Kim. *Uneasy Partners: Big Business in American Politics, 1945-1990* (1993).

O'Neill, William L. *American High: The Years of Confidence, 1945-1960* (1986).

Rose, Mark. *Interstate: Express Highway Politics* (1990).

Teaford, Jon. *The Rough Road to Renaissance: Urban Revitalization in America* (1990).

Family Life and Culture

Altschuler, Glenn, and David Grossvogel. *Changing Channels: America in TV Guide* (1992).

Breines, Wini. *Young, White and Miserable: Growing Up Female in the 1950s* (1992).

Doherty, Thomas. *Teenagers and Teenpics: The Juvenilization of American Movies in the 1950s* (rev. ed.: 2002).

Horowitz, Daniel. *Vance Packard and American Social Criticism* (1994).

Jamison, Andrew, and Ron Eyerman. *Seeds of the Sixties* (1994).

Kaledin, Eugenia. *Mothers and More: American Women in the 1950s* (1984).

May, Elaine Tyler. *Homeward Bound: American Families in the Cold War Era* (1988).

Rupp, Leila, and Verta Taylor. *Survival in the Doldrums: The American Women's Rights Movement, 1945 to the 1960s* (1987).

Weiss, Jessica. *To Have and To Hold: Marriage, the Baby Boom, and Social Change* (2000).

Whyte, William. *The Organization Man* (1956).

The Early 1960s

Beschloss, Michael. *The Crisis Years: Kennedy and Khrushchev, 1960-1963* (1991).

Burner, David. *John F. Kennedy and a New Generation* (1988).

Freedman, Lawrence. *Kennedy's Wars: Berlin, Cuba, Laos, and Vietnam* (2001)

Giglio, James. *The Presidency of John F. Kennedy* (1991).

Goldberg, Robert Alan. *Barry Goldwater* (1995).

Hoffman, Elizabeth Cobbs. *All You Need Is Love: The Peace Corps and the Spirit of the 1960s* (1998).

Kearns, Doris. *Lyndon Johnson and the American Dream* (1976).

Moise, Edward. *Tonkin Gulf and the Escalation of the Vietnam War* (1996).

Patterson, James T. *America's Struggle against Poverty, 1900-1985* (1986).

Perlstein, Rick. *Before the Storm: Barry Goldwater and the Unmaking of American Consensus* (2001)

Stern, Mark. *Calculating Visions: Kennedy, Johnson, and Civil Rights* (1992).

Wyden, Peter. *Bay of Pigs: The Untold Story* (1979).

Struggles for Equal Rights

Acuña, Rudolfo. *Occupied America: A History of Chicanos* (1988).

Branch, Taylor. *Parting the Waters: America in the King Years, 1954-1963* (1988).

Burner, Eric. *And Gently He Shall Lead Them: Robert Parris Moses and Civil Rights in Mississippi* (1994).

Carson, Claybourne. *In Struggle: SNCC and the Black Awakening of the 1960s* (1981).

Chafe, William. *Civilities and Civil Rights: Greensboro, North Carolina, and the Black Struggle* (1980).

Dittmer, John. *Local People: A History of the Mississippi Movement* (1994).

Egerton, John. *Speak Now Against the Day: The Generation before the Civil Rights Movement in the South* (1994).

Garrow, David. *Bearing the Cross: Martin Luther King Jr. and the Southern Christian Leadership Conference* (1986).

Goldman, Roger, and David Gallen. *Thurgood Marshall: Justice for All* (1993).

Halberstam, David. *The Children* (1998).

Huckaby, Elizabeth. *Crisis at Central High: Little Rock, 1957-1958* (1980).

Kluger, Richard. *Simple Justice: The History of Brown v. Board of Education* (1976).

Marsh, Charles. *God's Long Summer: Stories of Faith and Civil Rights* (1998).

Mills, Kay. *This Little Light of Mine: The Life of Fannie Lou Hamer* (1993).

Payne, Charles. *I've Got the Light of Freedom: The Organizing Tradition and the Mississippi Freedom Struggle* (1995).

Sitkoff, Harvard. *The Struggle for Black Equality; 1954-1992* (1992).

WHERE TO LEARN MORE

- **National Air and Space Museum, Washington, D.C.** Part of the Smithsonian Institution's complex of museums in Washington, the Air and Space Museum is the richest source for artifacts and discussion of the American space program. www.nasm.edu.

- **Kansas Cosmosphere, Hutchinson, Kansas.** A rich collection of artifacts and equipment from the U.S. space program. www.cosmo.org.

- **Sixth Floor Museum, Dallas, Texas.** Occupying the sixth floor of the former Texas School Book Depository building, exhibits examine the life, death, and legacy of John F. Kennedy. www.jfk.org.

- **Birmingham Civil Rights Institute Museum, Birmingham, Alabama.** This museum and archive deal with the background of southern racial segregation, civil rights activism, and the 1963 demonstrations in Birmingham. www.bcri.bham.al.us.

- **Martin Luther King, Jr., National Historical Site, Atlanta, Georgia.** The birthplace and grave of Reverend King are the nucleus of a park set in the historic black neighborhood of Auburn. http://www.nps.gov/malu/.

- **National Civil Rights Museum, Memphis, Tennessee.** Located in the Lorraine Motel, where Martin Luther King, Jr., was killed, the museum traces the participants, background, and effects of key events in the civil rights movement. http://www.civilrightsmuseum.org.

- **National Afro-American Museum and Cultural Center, Wilberforce, Ohio.** The exhibit "From Victory to Freedom: Afro-American Life in the Fifties" looks at home, family, music, and religion. www.ohiohistory.org/places/afroam/.

- **John F. Kennedy Library and Museum, Boston, Massachusetts.** Exhibits offer a sympathetic view of Kennedy's life and achievements. www.cs.umb.edu/jfklibrary/.

 Please refer to the document CD-ROM for primary sources related to this chapter.

➔ *1968 was a year of escalating violence and disorder, from the Tet Offensive in Vietnam to political assassinations and riots in American cities. Many of the tensions converged and exploded during the Democratic Party convention in Chicago on August, where 20,000 law enforcement officials and National Guard were mobilized to face thousands of antiwar demonstrators. Public order collapsed on the night of August 28, when police attacked demonstrators trying to march to the convention center.*

SHAKEN TO THE ROOTS 29
1965–1980

Contact light! O.K., engine stop. . . . Houston, Tranquility Base here. The Eagle has landed! . . .

We opened the hatch and Neil, with me as navigator, began backing out of the tiny opening [in the Lunar Module *Eagle*]. It seemed like a small eternity before I heard Neil say, "That's one small step for man. . . . one giant leap for mankind." In less than fifteen minutes I was backing awkwardly out of the hatch on onto the surface to join Neil, who, in the tradition of all tourists, had his camera ready to photograph my arrival.

I took off jogging to test my maneuverability. The exercise gave me an odd sensation and looked even more odd when I later saw the films of it. With bulky suits on, we seemed to be moving in slow motion. . . . At one point, I remarked that the surface was "Beautiful, beautiful. Magnificent desolation." I was struck by the contrast between the starkness of the shadows and the desert-like barrenness of the rest of the surface. It ranged from dusty gray to light tan and was unchanging except for one startling sight: our LM sitting there with its black, silver and bright yellow-orange thermal coating shining brightly in the otherwise colorless landscape.

During a pause in experiments, Neil suggested we proceed with the flag. . . . To our dismay the staff of the pole wouldn't go far enough into the lunar surface. . . . I dreaded the possibility of the American flag collapsing into the lunar dust in front of the television camera.[1]

Edgar Cortright, ed., *Apollo Expeditions to the Moon* (Washington: NASA SP 350, 1975).

CHAPTER OUTLINE

The End of Consensus
Deeper into Vietnam
Voices of Dissent
New Left and Community Activism
The Feminist Critique
Youth Culture and Counterculture
Sounds of Change
Communes and Cults

Cities Under Stress
Diagnosing an Urban Crisis
Racial Rioting
Minority Separatism
Suburban Independence: The Outer City

The Year of the Gun, 1968
The Tet Offensive
LBJ's Exit
Red Spring
Violence and Politics: Kennedy, King, and Chicago

Nixon and Watergate
Getting Out of Vietnam, 1969–1975
Nixon and the Wider World
Courting Middle America
Oil, OPEC, and Stagflation
Americans as Environmentalists
From Dirty Tricks to Watergate
The Ford Footnote

Jimmy Carter: Idealism and Frustration in the White House
Carter, Energy, and the Economy
Closed Factories and Failed Farms
Building a Cooperative World
New Crises Abroad

Conclusion

Buzz Aldrin and Neil Armstrong, on July 20, 1969, completed the longest journey that any person had yet taken. Landing the Apollo 11 lunar module on the surface of the moon climaxed a five-day trip across the quarter million miles separating the earth from the moon. Six and a half hours after the landing, Armstrong and Aldrin were the first humans to walk on the moon's surface.

The Apollo 11 expedition combined science and Cold War politics. The American flag waving on the lunar surface was a symbol of victory in one phase of the space race between the U.S. and Soviet Union. NASA had been working since 1961 to meet John F. Kennedy's goal of a manned trip to the moon before the end of the decade. The trial runs were Apollo 8, which sent American astronauts in orbit around the moon on Christmas Eve of 1968, and Apollo 10 in May 1969. After the Apollo ll expedition, American Astronauts made five more trips to the moon between 1969 and 1972, which helped to restore the nation's standing as the world's scientific and technological leader.

Even with the excitement of Apollo's success, however, the United States was increasingly shaken and divided in the later 1960s and 1970s. The failure to win an easy victory in Vietnam eroded the nation's confidence and fueled bitter divisions about the nation's goals. Most Americans had agreed about the goals of the Cold War, the benefits of economic growth, and the value of equal opportunity. Stalemate in Southeast Asia, political changes in third world countries, and an oil supply crisis in the 1970s challenged U.S. influence in the world. Frustrated with slow progress toward racial equality, many minority Americans advocated separation rather than integration, helping to plunge the nation's cities into crisis, while other Americans began to draw back from some of the objectives of racial integration

Political scandals, summarized in three syllables as "Watergate," undercut faith in government. Fifteen years of turmoil forced a grudging recognition of limits to American military power, economic capacity, governmental prerogatives, and even the ideal of a single American dream.

KEY TOPICS

- Vietnam, civil rights, and the unraveling of the national consensus

- The prolonged military struggle that resulted from Lyndon Johnson's decision to commit American forces to direct combat in Vietnam

- Growing opposition to the Vietnam War from 1965 to 1972

- The unraveling of the New Deal coalition beginning with the election of 1968

- Nixon's presidency and the Watergate scandal

- The growing militance of the struggle for civil rights among African Americans, Hispanic Americans, and Native Americans

THE END OF CONSENSUS

Pleiku is a town in Vietnam 240 miles north of Saigon (now Ho Chi Minh City). In 1965, Pleiku was the site of a South Vietnamese army headquarters and American military base. At 2 A.M. on February 7, Viet Cong attacked the U.S. base, killing eight Americans and wounding a hundred. The national security adviser, McGeorge Bundy, in Saigon on a fact-finding visit; Ambassador Maxwell Taylor; and General William Westmoreland, the commander of U.S. forces South Vietnam, all quickly recommended a retaliatory air strike against North Vietnam. President Johnson con-

curred, and navy bombers roared off aircraft carriers in Operation FLAMING DART. A month later, Johnson ordered a full-scale air offensive code-named ROLLING THUNDER.

The attack at Pleiku triggered plans that were waiting to be put into effect since the Gulf of Tonkin resolution the previous summer. The official reason for the bombing was to pressure North Vietnam to negotiate an end to the war. As the South Vietnamese government lost control of the countryside, air strikes on North Vietnam looked like an easy way to redress the balance. In the back of President Johnson's mind

Chronology

1962 Rachel Carson publishes *Silent Spring*.

Port Huron Statement launches Students for a Democratic Society.

1965 Congress approves Wilderness Act.

Malcolm X is assassinated.

Residents of Watts neighborhood in Los Angeles riot.

1967 African Americans riot in Detroit and Newark.

1968 Viet Cong launches Tet Offensive.

James Earl Ray kills Martin Luther King, Jr.

Lyndon Johnson declines to run for reelection.

SDS disrupts Columbia University.

Sirhan Sirhan kills Robert Kennedy.

Peace talks start between the United States and North Vietnam.

Police riot against antiwar protesters during the Democratic National Convention in Chicago.

Richard Nixon is elected president.

1969 Neil Armstrong and Buzz Aldrin walk on the moon.

1970 United States invades Cambodia.

National Guard units kill students at Kent State and Jackson State Universities.

Earth Day is celebrated.

Environmental Protection Agency is created.

1971 New York Times publishes the secret "Pentagon Papers."

President Nixon freezes wages and prices.

"Plumbers" unit is established in the White House.

1972 Nixon visits China.

United States and Soviet Union adopt SALT I.

Operatives for Nixon's reelection campaign break into Democratic headquarters in the Watergate complex in Washington, D.C.

1973 Paris accords end direct U.S. involvement in South Vietnamese war.

United States moves to all-volunteer armed forces.

Watergate burglars are convicted.

Senate Watergate hearings reveal the existence of taped White House conversations.

Spiro Agnew resigns as vice president, is replaced by Gerald Ford.

Arab states impose an oil embargo after the third Arab-Israeli War.

1974 Nixon resigns as president, is succeeded by Gerald Ford.

1975 Communists triumph in South Vietnam.

United States, USSR, and European nations sign the Helsinki Accords.

1976 Jimmy Carter defeats Gerald Ford for the presidency.

1978 Carter brings the leaders of Egypt and Israel to Camp David for peace talks.

1979 SALT II agreement is signed but not ratified.

OPEC raises oil prices.

Three Mile Island nuclear plant comes close to disaster.

Iranian militants take U.S. embassy hostages.

1980 Iranian hostage rescue fails.

Soviet troops enter Afghanistan.

Ronald Reagan defeats Jimmy Carter for the presidency.

---

were the need to prove his toughness and the mistaken assumption that China was aggressively backing North Vietnam.

The air strikes pushed the United States over the line from propping up the South Vietnamese government to leading the war effort. A president who desperately wanted a way out of Southeast Asia kept adding American forces. Eventually, the war in Vietnam would distract the United States from the goals of the Great Society and drive Johnson from office. It hovered like a shadow over the next two presidents, set back progress toward global stability, and divided the American people.

DEEPER INTO VIETNAM

Lyndon Johnson faced limited options in Vietnam (see Map 29–1). The pervasive American determination to contain Communism and Kennedy's previous commitments there hemmed Johnson in. Advisers persuaded him that controlled military escalation—a middle course between withdrawal and all-out war—could secure Vietnam. They failed to understand the extent of popular opposition to the official government in Saigon and the willingness of North Vietnam to sacrifice to achieve national unity.

ROLLING THUNDER put the United States on the up escalator to war. Because an air campaign required ground troops to protect bases in South Vietnam, U.S. Marines landed on March 8. Over the next four months, General Westmoreland wore away Johnson's desire to contain American involvement. More bombs, a pause, an offer of massive U.S. aid—nothing brought North Vietnam to the negotiating table. Meanwhile, defeat loomed. Johnson dribbled in new forces and expanded their mission from base security to combat. On July 28, he finally gave Westmoreland doubled draft calls and an increase in U.S. combat troops from 75,000 to 275,000 by 1966 (see Figure 29–1).

Johnson's decision turned a South Vietnamese war into an American war. Secretary of Defense McNamara was clear about the change: "We have relied on South Vietnam to carry the brunt. Now we would be responsible for a satisfactory military outcome." At the end of 1967, American forces in South Vietnam totaled 485,000; they reached their maximum of 543,000 in August 1969.

The U.S. strategy on the ground was **search and destroy**. As conceived by Westmoreland, it used sophisticated surveillance and heavily armed patrols to locate enemy detachments, which could then be destroyed by air strikes, artillery, and reinforcements carried in by helicopter. The approach made sense when the opposition consisted of North Vietnamese troops and large Viet Cong units. It worked well in the sparsely populated Ia Drang Valley, where the First Air Cavalry chewed up North Vietnamese regulars in November 1965.

However, most opponents were not North Vietnamese divisions but South Vietnamese guerrillas. The Viet Cong avoided

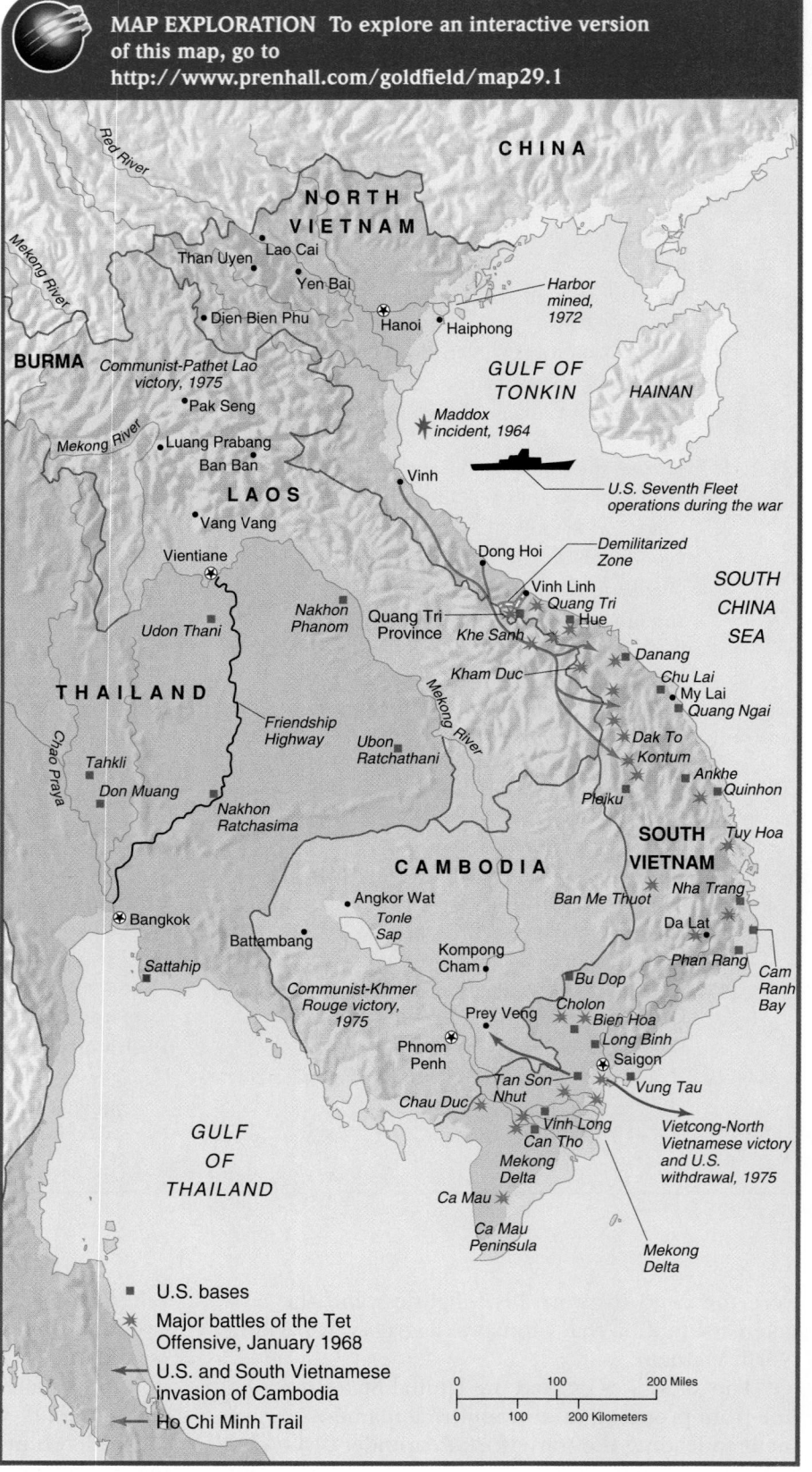

MAP 29-1 The War in Vietnam
The United States attacked North Vietnam with air strikes but confined large-scale ground operations to South Vietnam and Cambodia. In South Vietnam, U.S. forces faced both North Vietnamese army units and Viet Cong rebels, all of whom received supplies by way of the so-called Ho Chi Minh Trail, named for the leader of North Vietnam. The coordinated attacks on cities and towns throughout South Vietnam during the Tet Offensive in 1968 surprised the United States.

FIGURE 29-1   The United States in Vietnam

American involvement in Vietnam grew slowly in the Kennedy administration from 1961 to 1963, expanded rapidly under Lyndon Johnson from 1964 to 1968, and fell just as rapidly under Richard Nixon from 1969 to 1973. The "Nixon Doctrine" tried to substitute American weapons and equipment for American military personnel but failed to prevent a North Vietnamese victory in 1975 after United States withdrawal.

Statistical Abstract of the United States

"set-piece" battles. Instead, they forced the United States to make repeated sweeps through farms and villages. The enemy were difficult for Americans to recognize among farmers and workers, making South Vietnamese society itself the target. The American penchant for massive firepower killed thousands of Vietnamese and made millions refugees. Because the South Vietnamese government was unable to secure areas after American sweeps, the Viet Cong often reappeared after the Americans had crashed through a district.

The American air war also had limited results. Pilots dropped a vast tonnage of bombs on the "Ho Chi Minh Trail," a network of supply routes from North Vietnam to South Vietnam through the mountains of neighboring Laos. Despite the bombing, thousands of workers converted rough paths into roads that were repaired as soon as they were damaged. Air assault on North Vietnam itself remained "diplomatic," intended to force North Vietnam to stop intervening in the South Vietnamese civil war. Since North Vietnam's leadership considered North and South to be one country, the American goal was unacceptable. Attacking North Vietnam's poorly developed economy, the United States soon ran out of targets. The CIA estimated that it cost nearly $10 to inflict every $1 of damage.

VOICES OF DISSENT

At home, protest against the war quickly followed the commitment of American combat forces. In the 1950s, dissenters on the left had been too intimidated by McCarthyism to protest overcommitment to the Cold War. Now a coalition of experienced antiwar workers and new college activists openly challenged the Cold Warriors. The first national antiwar march took place in Washington on April 17, 1965. Twenty-five thousand people picketed the White House, assembled at the Washington Monument for speeches by Senator Ernest Gruening of Alaska (one of the two dissenting votes on the Gulf of Tonkin Resolution) and African American leaders, and walked up the Mall to the Capitol.

One group of opponents were "realists" who argued that the war was a mistake. Foreign policy expert Hans Morgenthau, for example, fully supported anti-Soviet containment in Europe but maintained that the U.S. had no vital interests in South Vietnam. Policy-makers in Washington, he said, were misreading

*The city of Hue suffered severe damage in the Tet Offensive and its aftermath. Here refugees
return to the rubble of bombed-out houses.*

the situation, wasting American lives and resources, and weakening the American presence in regions such as Europe that were truly important to national security. Respected figures such as the Cold War strategist George Kennan joined in the dissent. Senator J. William Fulbright held well publicized hearings in 1966 and 1967, at which respectable critics of the war could state their case to a national audience, and published *The Arrogance of Power* (1967), a book that argued that even the U.S. needed to recognize limits on its vast political and military power.

If the realists thought that the U.S. was simply being stupid, more radical critics found the roots of the war in basic flaws in the American character and system. Novelist Norman Mailer compared the American military to big-game trophy hunters in Alaska in *Why Are We in Vietnam?* (1967). Others called the war an example of economic imperialism that showed the power of multinational corporations to control American foreign policy. A generation later, some of the same analysis would reappear in arguments against the North American Free Trade Agreement and the World Trade Organization.

From protest to confrontation.

In 1966 and 1967, antiwar activity changed from respectful protest to direct confrontations with what protesters called the war machine. Protesters lay down in front of trains carrying munitions. Representatives of Women Strike for Peace journeyed to North Vietnam to explore possible solutions. Religious groups such as the American Friends Service Committee, tried to dispense medical and humanitarian aid even-handedly in both North Vietnam and South Vietnam.

The tone of the debate became nastier. Johnson and his associates ridiculed dissenters (for example, Fulbright became "Halfbright" among the administration's inner circle). In turn, protesters chanted "Hey, hey, LBJ! How many kids did you kill today?" Much of the anger was directed at the military draft administered by the **Selective Service System**. In theory, the Selective Service picked the young men who could best serve the nation as soldiers and deferred induction of those with vital skills. As the war expanded, the administration tried to hold the allegiance of the middle class by finding ways to exempt their sons from service in Vietnam. Full-time college enrollment was good for a deferment; so was the right medical diagnosis from the right doctor. As a result, draftees and enlistees tended to be small-town and working-class youth. They were also young. The average GI in World War II had been in his mid-twenties; the typical soldier in Vietnam was 19 or 20. Women who served as military nurses tended to come from the same small-town

Overview

Why Were We in South Vietnam?

American leaders offered a number of justifications for American military involvement in Vietnam. Here are some of the key arguments, with points that supported or questioned the explanation.

To Prop Up a Domino:	Communist success in South Vietnam would undermine pro-American regimes in adjacent nations, which would topple like a row of dominoes,	
	Pro	The firm U.S. stand contributed to an anti-Communist coup in Indonesia in 1965 and encouraged pro-American interests in Thailand and the Philippines.
	Con	Detailed knowledge of each nation in Southeast Asia shows that their own histories and internal issues that were far more important in determining their futures than was American action in Vietnam.
To Contain China:	China's Communist regime wanted to expand its control throughout Asia.	
	Pro	The People's Republic of China was hostile to the United States, as shown in the Korean War, and had a long history of trying to control Vietnam.
	Con	North Vietnam had closer ties to the Soviet Union than to China and played the two communist nations against each other to preserve its own independence from China.
To Defeat Aggression:	South Vietnam was an independent nation threatened by invasion.	
	Pro	The major military threat to South Vietnam after 1965 came from the growing presence of the North Vietnamese army, and U.S. military intervention was necessary to counter that invasion.
	Con	The conflict in South Vietnam originated as a civil war within South Vietnam. Moreover, South and North Vietnam were a single nation, artificially divided in 1954, so that North Vietnam was trying to reunify rather than invade South Vietnam.
To Protect Democracy:	South Vietnam was a democratic nation that deserved American support.	
	Pro	South Vietnam had an emerging middle class and an opportunity to develop democratic institutions.
	Con	South Vietnam was never a true democracy, ruled first by civilian dictator Ngo Dinh Diem and them a series of military strongmen.

and working-class backgrounds where patriotism was unquestioned. The resentment created by the draft was an important wedge that began to erode the long-standing alliance between working-class Americans and the Democratic Party.

Military service also deepened the gap between blacks and white. The black community supplied more than its share of combat soldiers. In 1965, when African Americans made up 11 percent of the nation's population, 24 percent of the soldiers who died in Vietnam were black. This disparity forced the Defense Department to revise its combat assignments. Martin Luther King, Jr., joined the protest in 1967. King

called the war a moral disaster whose costs weighed most heavily on the poor and a new form of colonialism that was destroying Vietnamese society.

Draft resistance provided a direct avenue for protest against the war. Some young men burned the small paper cards that indicated their selective service classification, causing Congress to enact steep penalties for the act. Several thousand moved to Canada, to spend a decade or more in exile. Because of the well-publicized impact of the war on civilians and noncombatants, thousands of others described their religious and ethical opposition to war in applications for conscientious-objector classification. Much smaller

Antiwar protests were simultaneously symbolic and disruptive. Some activists dumped jars of animal blood over draft-board records. Others tried to block munitions trains. In October 1967, a hundred thousand people marched on the Pentagon and surrounded it with the light of burning draft cards. Some in front stuck flowers in the rifle barrels of the soldiers ringing the building; others kicked and spat. The troops and police cleared the grounds with tear gas and clubs.

numbers went to jail for refusing to cooperate in any way with the Selective Service System. And a handful of activists, including the Catholic priests Daniel Berrigan and Philip Berrigan, directly disrupted the operations of the draft by invading draft-board offices and trying to burn files or douse them with animal blood. Resistance mounted through the entire decade. By the end of 1969, over half the men drafted in California were refusing to show up, and prosecutions for draft evasion would peak in 1972 at nearly 5,000.

The popular media portrayed the conflicting visions of the Vietnam war. Barry McGuire's "Eve of Destruction" climbed the charts. Folksinger Phil Ochs sang "I Ain't Marching Anymore." "And it's one, two, three, what are we fighting for?" sang Country Joe and the Fish. Supporters countered with an aging John Wayne as a heroic American soldier saving South Vietnam in the movie *The Green Berets*. Country signer Merle Travis spoke for many small-town Americans who supported the war in "Okie from Muskogee" (where they didn't burn draft cards).

NEW LEFT AND COMMUNITY ACTIVISM

The antiwar movement was part of a growing grassroots activism that took much of its tone from the university-based **Students for a Democratic Society (SDS)**. The group was important for its ideas, not its size. Its Port Huron Statement, adopted in 1962, called for grassroots action and "participatory democracy." Building on ideas of such 1950s dissenters as C. Wright Mills, SDS tried to harness youthful disillusionment about consumerism, racism, and imperialism. It

wanted to counter the trends that seemed to be turning Americans into tiny cogs in the machinery of big government, corporations, and universities. SDS thought of itself as a "New Left" that was free from the doctrinal squabbles that hampered the old left of the 1930s and 1940s.

Many of the original SDS leaders were also participants in the civil-rights movement. The same was true of Mario Savio, founder of the **Free Speech Movement (FSM)** at the University of California at Berkeley in 1964. Savio hoped to build a multi-issue "community of protest" around the idea of "a free university in a free society." FSM protests climaxed with a December sit-in that led to 773 arrests and stirred protest on other campuses.

What SDS wanted to do with its grassroots organizing resembled the federal community-action programs associated with the war on poverty. The **Model Cities Program** (1966) invited residents of poor neighborhoods to write their own plans for using federal funds to improve local housing, education, health services, and job opportunities. Model Cities assemblies challenged the racial bias in programs like urban renewal and helped train community leaders.

In the 1970s and 1980s, when SDS was long gone and the Model Cities Program was fading, the lessons of grassroots reform would still be visible in alternative organizations and political movements that strengthened democracy from the bottom up. Activists staffed food cooperatives, free clinics, women's health groups, and drug counseling centers across the country. Community-based organization was a key element in self-help efforts by African Americans, Asian Americans, and Latinos. Neighborhood associations and community-development corporations that provided affordable housing and jobs extended the "backyard revolution" into the 1980s and beyond. Social conservatives, such as antiabortionists, used the same techniques on behalf of their own agendas.

THE FEMINIST CRITIQUE

The growing dissatisfaction of many women with their domestic roles helped set the stage for a revived feminism that was another result of the ferment of the 1960s. Important steps in this revival included the Presidential Commission on the Status of Women in 1961; the addition of gender as one of the categories protected by the Civil Rights Act of 1964 (see Chapter 28); and creation of the National Organization for Women (NOW) in 1966.

Mainstream feminism targeted unequal opportunity in the job market. Newspapers in the early 1960s segregated help-wanted ads by sex, listing "Girl Friday" jobs in one column and professional work in another. College-educated baby boomers encountered "glass ceilings" and job discrimination, in which companies hired less qualified men who "needed the job" rather than more qualified women who supposedly did not. Throughout the mid-1960s and 1970s, activists battled to open job categories to women, who proved that they could indeed use tools, run computers, or pick stocks on Wall Street. They also battled for equal pay for everyone with equal qualifications and responsibilities.

Changes in sexual behavior paralleled efforts to equalize treatment in the workplace. More reliable methods of contraception, especially birth-control pills introduced in the early 1960s, gave women greater control over childbearing. In some ways a replay of ideas from the 1920s, a new sexual revolution eroded the double standard that expected chastity of women but tolerated promiscuity among men. Starting in the 1960s, women began to catch up to men by acting as if marriage was not necessary to sanction sexual relations. One consequence was a singles culture that accepted sexual activity between unmarried men and women.

More radical versions of the feminist message came from women who had joined the civil-rights and antiwar movements only to find themselves working the copy machine and the coffeemaker while men plotted strategy. Radicals caught the attention of the national media with a demonstration against the 1968 Miss America pageant. Protesters crowned a sheep as Miss America and encouraged women to make a statement by tossing their bras and makeup in the trash.

Women's liberation took off as a social and political movement in 1970 and 1971 as influential books probed the roots of inequality between men's and women's opportunities. Women shared their stories and ideas in small "consciousness-raising" sessions. *Ms.* magazine gave the movement a national voice in 1972. Within a few years, millions of women had recognized events and patterns in their lives as discrimination based on gender. The feminist movement, and specific policy measures related to it, put equal rights and the fight against sexism (a word no one knew before 1965) on the national agenda and gradually changed how Americans thought about the relationships between men and women. Feminists focused attention on rape as a crime of violence and called attention to the burdens the legal system placed on rape victims. In the 1980s and 1990s, they also challenged sexual harassment in the workplace, gradually refining the boundaries between acceptable and unacceptable behavior.

Ms. magazine published its first issue in 1972. Edited by Gloria Steinem, the magazine attempted to bring a radical feminist message to a wide audience. Ms. emphasized the need for women to have equal access with men to education, health care, and employment and tried to help Americans rethink traditional gender roles.

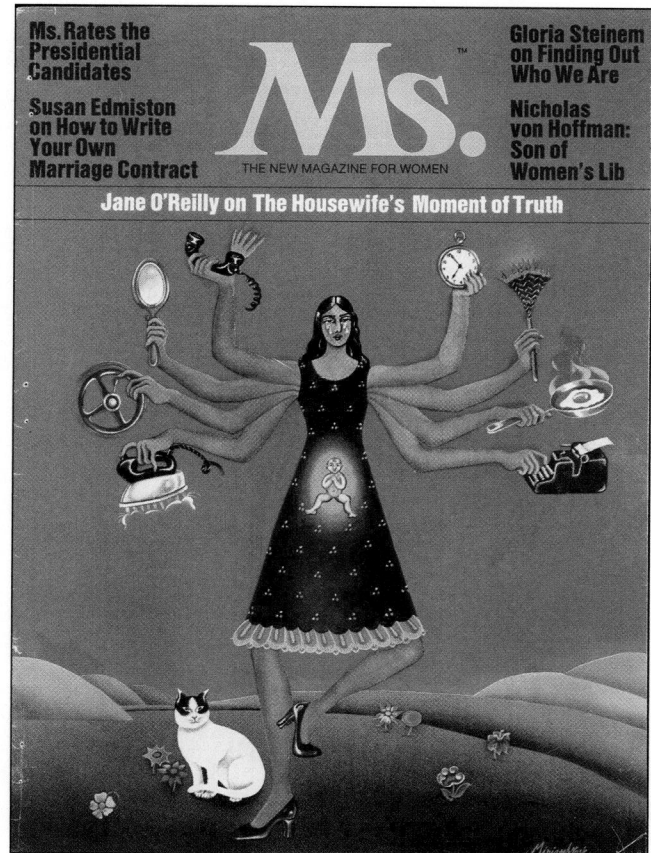

YOUTH CULTURE AND COUNTERCULTURE

The popular context for the serious work of the New Left was the growing youth culture and **counterculture**. Millions of young people in the second half of the 1960s expressed their alienation from American society by sampling drugs or chasing the rainbow of a youth culture. Some just smoked marijuana, grew long hair, and listened to psychedelic rock. Others plunged into ways of life that scorned their middle-class backgrounds. The middle-aged and middle-class ignored the differences and dubbed the rebellious young "hippies."

The youth culture took advantage of the nation's prosperity. It was consumerism in a tie-dyed T-shirt. A high point was the 1969 Woodstock rock festival in New York State, a weekend of "sex, drugs, and rock-and-roll" for 400,000 young people. But Woodstock was an excursion, not a life-altering commitment. Members of the Woodstock Generation were consumers in a distinct market niche, dressing but not living like social reformers or revolutionaries. The musical *Hair* (1968) and

During the late 1960s, the peace sign became a common gesture with a wide range of meanings—from advocacy of the hippie lifestyle to opposition to the war in Vietnam.

Getty Images, Inc. – Taxi

the film *Easy Rider* (1969) harnessed their social ferment to the box office as mass culture absorbed the youth culture.

Within the youth culture was a smaller and more intense counterculture that added Eastern religion, social radicalism, and evangelistic belief in the drug LSD. The Harvard professor Timothy Leary and the writer Aldous Huxley claimed that hallucinogenic or psychedelic drugs, such as mescaline and LSD, would swing open the "doors of perception." Rock lyrics began to reflect the drug culture in 1966 and 1967, and young people talked about Leary's advice to "tune in, turn on, and drop out."

The mecca of the dropouts was San Francisco's Haight-Ashbury district. In the early 1960s, its cheap apartments had housed African Americans, beatniks, and homosexuals. Its radical atmosphere attracted a sudden influx of students and college dropouts in 1966. In 1967's "Summer of Love," the Haight was home to perhaps seven thousand permanent hippies and seventy thousand short-time visitors. "If you're going to San Francisco," said one song, "be sure to wear some flowers in your hair." Drugs and violence soon took over the streets, psychedelic businesses closed, and a respectable middle class bought the cheap real estate. Meanwhile, hippie districts sprang up around university campuses across the country.

The cultural rebels of the late 1950s and early 1960s had been trying to combine personal freedom with new social arrangements. Many hippies were more interested in altering their minds with drugs than with politics or poetry. Serious exploration of societal alternatives was left for the minority who devoted themselves to the political work of the New Left, communal living, women's liberation, and other movements.

SOUNDS OF CHANGE

The youth culture was shaped by films and philosophers, by pot and poets, but above all by music. Many changes in American society are mirrored in the abrupt shift from the complacent rock-and-roll of the early 1960s to the more provocative albums of mid-decade: Bob Dylan's *Highway 61 Revisited* (1965), the Beatles *Rubber Soul* (1965) and *Sergeant Pepper's Lonely Hearts Club Band* (1967), the Jefferson Airplane's *Surrealistic Pillow* (1967). The songs were still aimed at popular success, but the musicians were increasingly self-conscious of themselves as artists and social critics.

At the start of the decade, the African American roots of rock-and-roll were unmistakable, but there was no social agenda. Elvis Presley and the Everly Brothers kept the messages personal, and there was no reason to anticipate any departure from popular music's normal concerns about love and loss. Music that criticized American society initially found a much smaller audience through the folk-music revival in a few big cities and university campuses. Folk singers, such as the long-established Pete Seeger and the younger Joan Baez, drew on black music, white country music, and old labor-organizing songs to keep alive dissenting voices.

Then, in an artistic revolution, the doors opened to a new kind of rock music. The Beatles capitalized on their immense popularity to begin a career of artistic experimentation. They also opened the way for such hard-edged British bands as the Rolling Stones and The Who to introduce social criticism and class consciousness into rock lyrics. San Francisco's new psychedelic-rock scene took its name from drugs, such as LSD, and centered on shows at the Fillmore Auditorium, where performers in 1966 included the Jefferson Airplane, the Grateful Dead, and Buffalo Springfield. The Texan Janis Joplin came to San Francisco to draw on black musical styles after reading the Beat writers who had celebrated the city's jazz and racial openness.

Bob Dylan, a folksinger with an acoustic guitar, "went electric" at the Newport, Rhode Island, folk festival in 1965 and further transformed the music scene. Songs like "Blowin' in the Wind" and "Like a Rolling Stone" were personal and political at the same time; Dylan's music was musically exciting and socially critical in a way that expressed much of the discontent of American young people. Dylan paved the way for later singers like Bruce Springsteen and Kurt Cobain.

The transformation of rock in the mid-1960s invited far more explicit treatment of sex and illegal drugs than was previously accepted in pop music. Jim Morrison and The Doors, Lou Reed and the Velvet Underground, and Jimi Hendrix exploded onto the scene in 1967. Their driving rhythms and sexually aggressive stage personalities blended the tensions of big cities with influences from white rock and roll and black rhythm and blues. Hendrix spanned the greatest distance from ghetto blues clubs of the 1950s to the mass market of the late 1960s, with albums such as *Are Your Experienced* (1967). By 1972, both Morrison and Hendrix were dead of hard living and drug abuse. Meanwhile, *Rolling Stone* magazine had published its first issue in November 1967, giving the new sounds a forum for serious analysis.

COMMUNES AND CULTS

Out of the half-secular, half-spiritual vision of the counterculture came people who not only dropped

At the Newport (Rhode Island) Jazz Festival in 1963, Joan Baez and Bob Dylan performed as folksingers who worked in the tradition of protest songs. Two years later in Newport, Dylan shocked the popular music world by replacing his acoustic instrument with an amplified guitar and backup and jump-starting a fruitful blending of folk, country, and rock music into radical new sounds.

out of mainstream institutions but also tried to drop into miniature societies built on new principles. Thousands of Americans in the late 1960s and 1970s formed "intentional communities" or "communes," many as a response to the collapse of the Haight-Ashbury neighborhood into crime and drug abuse after 1967. Their members usually tried to combine individual freedom and spontaneity with cooperative living. Upper New England and the Southwest were commune country. The northern California coast and the Pacific Northwest were also attractive because of their fine climate for growing marijuana. Rural communes usually located on marginal land too poor to support commercial farming; members pored over *The Whole Earth Catalog* (1968) to figure out how to live on the land. There were also thousands of smaller and less conspicuous urban communes whose members occupied large old houses and tried to pursue experiments in socialism, environmentalism, or feminism.

A few communes followed coherent social theories, but many were free-form. It is easy to make fun of them in retrospect, with their tepees, log cabins, and eccentric architecture. Children ended up with off-the-tent names like Catnip, Psyche Joy, and Hummingbird. Adults practiced odd combinations of vegetarianism, Asian religion, and campfire sing-alongs. Communes were artificial families, financed by inheritances, food stamps, and handicraft sales, and they suffered from the same inequality between men and women that was fueling the feminist revolt. Like natural families, they were emotional hothouses; most collapsed because their members had incompatible goals.

Similar to communes but far more organized were exotic religious communities. Following an American tradition, they have offered tightly knit group membership and absolute answers to basic questions of human life. One of the most successful has been the Holy Spirit Association for the Unification of World Christianity (Unification Church), which Sun Myung Moon brought from Korea to the United States in 1973. Converts ("Moonies") have never numbered more than a few tens of thousands, but Moon amassed a huge fortune and dabbled in conservative politics.

Americans usually hear about cults only if they clash with authorities or end in disaster. Most tragic was the case of Jim Jones, who founded the People's Temple in California on a program of social justice but became increasingly dictatorial and abusive. He moved nearly a thousand followers to Guyana in South America and violently resisted authorities' efforts to penetrate his walls of secrecy. A congressional investigation of abuses within the colony led to the murder of Congressman Leo Ryan and mass suicide by nine hundred of Jones's followers, who drank cyanide-laced punch on November 18, 1978.

CITIES UNDER STRESS

In the confident years after World War II, big cities had an upbeat image. The typical movie with a New York setting opened with a shot of the towering Manhattan skyline and plunged into the bustling business or theater districts. By the 1970s, however, slums and squalid back streets dominated popular imagery. *The French Connection* (1971) followed a drug dealer from Fifth Avenue to empty and menacing warehouses. *Klute* (1971) and *Taxi Driver* (1976) took moviegoers through the twilight world of prostitution. *Blade Runner* (1982) showed a Los Angeles driven mad by corporate violence and social isolation. Such television cop shows as *Hill Street Blues* (1981–1987) and *Miami Vice* (1984–1990) repeated the message that cities had become places of random and frequent violence.

DIAGNOSING AN URBAN CRISIS

Popular entertainment reflected Americans' growing discomfort with their cities. The nation entered the 1960s with the assumption that urban problems were growing pains. Exploding metropolitan areas needed money for streets, schools, and sewers. Politicians viewed the difficulties of central cities as by-products of exuberant suburban growth, which left outmoded downtowns in need of physical redevelopment. In mid-decade, however, TV networks and news magazines began to run stories about "Battlefield, USA" and "Crisis in the Cities" that described cities as sinking under racial violence, crime, and unemployment.

Central cities had a special burden in caring for the domestic poor. Baltimore had 27 percent of the Maryland population in 1970 but 66 percent of the state's welfare recipients. Boston had 14 percent of the Massachusetts population but 32 percent of the welfare clients. Impoverished, and often fragmented, families needed schools to serve as social-work agencies as well as educational institutions. Poor people with no other access to health care treated city hospital emergency rooms as the family doctor.

Many urban problems were associated with the "second ghettos" created by the migration of 2.5 million African Americans from southern farms to northern and western cities in the 1950s and 1960s. At the start of World War II, black Americans had been much more rural than white Americans. By 1970, they were more urban. Fully one-third of all African Americans lived in the twelve largest cities, crowding into ghetto neighborhoods dating from World War II.

Postwar black migrants found systems of race relations that limited their access to decent housing, to the best schools, and to many unionized jobs. Many families also arrived just in time to face the consequences of industrial layoffs and plant closures in the 1970s and 1980s. Already unneeded in the South because of the mechanization of agriculture, the migrants found themselves equally unwanted in the industrial North, caught in decaying neighborhoods and victimized by crime.

The residential ghetto trapped African American families who tried to follow the expectations of mainstream society. Because ghettos grew block by block, middle-class black families had to pioneer as intruders into white neighborhoods and then see ghetto problems crowd in behind them. Their children faced the seductions of the street, which became increasingly violent with the spread of handguns and trade in illegal drugs.

Central cities faced additional financial problems unrelated to poverty and race. Many of their roads, bridges, fire stations, and water mains were 50 to 100 years old by the 1960s and 1970s, and they were wearing out. Closure of the elevated West Side Highway along the Hudson River in Manhattan after huge chunks fell out of the roadway symbolized a spreading urban problem. Decay of urban utility and transportation systems was a by-product of market forces and public policy. Private developers often borrowed money saved through northeastern bank accounts, insurance policies, and pension funds to finance new construction in the suburbs. The defense budget pumped tax dollars from the old industrial cities into the South and West.

High local taxes in older cities was one result, for the American system of local government demands that cities and the poor help themselves. By the early 1970s, the average resident of a central city paid roughly twice the state and local taxes per $1,000 of income as the average suburbanite. As Mayor Moon Laundreau of New Orleans commented, "We've taxed everything that moves and everything that stands still; and if anything moves again, we tax that, too."

RACIAL RIOTING

African Americans and Hispanics who rioted in city streets in the mid-1960s were fed up with lack of job opportunities, and with substandard housing and crime in their neighborhoods. Prominent black writers, such as James Baldwin in *The Fire Next Time* (1963), had warned of mounting anger. Suddenly the fires were real. Riots in Rochester, Harlem, and Brooklyn in July 1964 opened four years of racial violence. Before they subsided, the riots scarred most big cities and killed two hundred people, most of them African Americans.

The explosion of the Watts neighborhood in Los Angeles fixed the danger of racial unrest in the public mind. Trouble started on August 11, 1965, when a white highway-patrol officer arrested a young African American for drunken driving. Loud complaints drew a crowd, and the arrival of Los Angeles police turned the bystanders into an angry mob that attacked passing cars. Rioting, looting, and arson spread through Watts for two days until the National Guard cordoned off the trouble spots and occupied the neighborhood on August 14 and 15.

The outburst frightened white Americans. In most previous race riots, whites had used violence to keep blacks "in their place." In Watts, blacks were the instigators. The primary targets were the police and ghetto businesses that had reputations for exploiting their customers. The National Advisory Commission on Civil Disorders concluded in 1968 that most property damage was the "result of deliberate attacks on white-owned businesses characterized in the Negro community as unfair or disrespectful." In short, the riots were protests about the problems of ghetto life.

After Watts, Americans expected "long hot summers" and got them. Scores of cities suffered riots in 1966, including a riot by Puerto Ricans in Chicago that protested the same problems blacks faced. The following year, the worst violence was in Newark, New Jersey, and in Detroit, where forty-three deaths and blocks of blazing buildings stunned television viewers.

Few politicians wanted to admit that African Americans and Hispanics had serious grievances. Their impulse was to blame riffraff and outside agitators—"lawbreakers and mad dogs," to quote California Governor Ronald Reagan. This theory was wrong. Almost all participants were neighborhood residents. Except that they were younger, they were representative of the African American population, and their violence came from the frustration of rising expectations. Despite the political gains of the civil rights movement, unemployment remained high, and the police still treated all blacks as potential criminals. The urban riots were political actions to force the problems of African Americans onto the national agenda. "What are these people rioting about?" asked one resident. "They want recognition, and the only way they're going to get it is to riot."

MINORITY SEPARATISM

Minority separatism tapped the same anger that fueled the urban riots. Separatists challenged the central goal of the civil rights movement, which sought full participation in American life. The phrase "**Black Power**" summed up the new alternative. The term came from frustrated SNCC leader Stokely Carmichael in 1966: "We've been saying freedom for six years—and we ain't got nothing. What we're going to start saying now is 'Black Power'!"

Black power translated many ways—control of one's own community through the voting machine, celebration of the African American heritage, creation of a parallel society that shunned white institutions. At the personal level, it was a synonym for black pride. It propelled the successful political campaigns of Richard Hatcher in Gary, Indiana, and Carl Stokes in Cleveland, the first African Americans elected mayors of large northern cities.

Black Power also meant increased interest in the **Nation of Islam**, or Black Muslims, who combined a version of Islam with radical separatism. They called for self-discipline, support of black institutions and businesses, and total rejection of whites. The Nation of Islam appealed to blacks who saw no future in integration. It was strongest in northern cities, such as Chicago, where it offered an alternative to the life of the ghetto streets.

In the early 1960s, Malcolm X emerged as a leading Black Muslim. Growing up as Malcolm Little, he was a streetwise criminal until he converted to the Nation of Islam in prison. After his release, Malcolm preached that blacks should stop letting whites set the terms by which they judged their appearance, communities, and accomplishments. He emphasized the African cultural heritage and economic self-help and proclaimed himself an extremist for black rights. In the last year of his life, however, he returned from a pilgrimage to Mecca willing to consider limited acceptance of whites. Rivals within the movement assassinated him in February 1965, but his ideas lived on in *The Autobiography of Malcolm X*.

The **Black Panthers** pursued similar goals. Bobby Seale and Huey Newton grew up in the Oakland, California, area and met as college students. They saw African American ghettos as internal colonies in need of self-determination. They created the Panthers in 1966, began to carry firearms, and recruited Eldridge Cleaver as the group's chief publicist.

The Panthers asserted their equality. They shadowed police patrols to prevent mistreatment of African Americans and carried weapons into the California State Legislature in May 1967 to protest gun control. As Seale recalled, the goal was "to read a message to the world" and use the press to "blast it across the country." The Panthers also promoted community-based self-help efforts, such as a free breakfast program for school children and medical clinics, and ran political candidates. In contrast to the rioters in Watts, the Panthers had a political program, if not the ability to carry it through. The movement was shaken when Newton was convicted of manslaughter for killing a police officer, Cleaver fled to Algeria, and an unjustified police raid killed Chicago Panther leader Fred Hampton. Panther chapters imploded when they attracted thugs and shakedown artists as well as visionaries. Nevertheless, the Panthers survived as a political party into

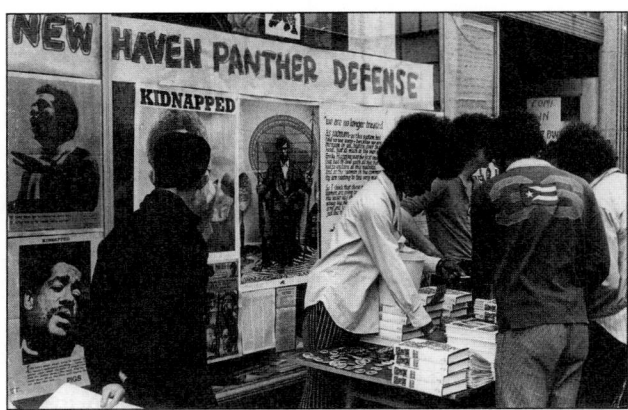

Some members of the Black Panther party raised funds to pay for the legal fees of those arrested and charged with various offenses, such as Bobby Seale and Ericka Huggins. The Panthers advocated a radical economic, social, and educational agenda that made the group the target of a determined campaign of suppression by the police and the FBI.

the 1970s. Former Panther Bobby Rush entered Congress in 1992.

Hispanic activism in the Southwest. Latinos in the Southwest developed a their own "Brown Power" movement in the late 1960s. Led by Reies López Tijerina, Hispanics in rural New Mexico demanded the return of lands that had been lost to Anglo Americans despite the guarantees of the Treaty of Guadalupe Hidalgo in 1848. Tijerina's "Letter from the Santa Fe Jail" denounced the "rich people from outside the state with their summer homes and ranches" and "all those who have robbed the people of their land and culture for 120 years." Mexican Americans in the 1970s organized for political power in southern Texas communities where they were a majority. In Denver, Rodolfo Gonzales established the Crusade for Justice. His "Plan for the Barrio" emphasized Hispanic cultural traditions, community control of schools, and economic development.

The best-known Hispanic activism combined social protest with the crusading spirit of earlier labor union organizing campaigns. César Chávez organized the multiracial United Farm Workers (UFW) among Mexican American agricultural workers in California in 1965. Chavez was committed both to nonviolent action for social justice and to the labor movement. UFW demands included better wages and safer working conditions, such as less exposure to pesticides. UFW Vice President Dolores Huerta spoke for the special needs of women who labored in the fields. Because farm workers were not covered by the National

Labor Relations Act of 1935, the issue was whether farm owners would recognize the union as a bargaining agent and sign a contract. Chávez supplemented work stoppages with national boycotts against table grapes, lettuce, and certain brands of wine, making *la huelga* ("the strike") into *la causa* for urban liberals. Rival organizing by the Teamsters Union and the short attention span of the national public gradually undermined the UFW's initial success. Nevertheless, Chávez's dogged toughness and self-sacrifice gave both Chicanos and the country a new hero.

Latino political activism had strong appeal for young people. Ten thousand young Chicanos stormed out of Los Angeles high schools in March 1968 to protest poor education and racist teachers. Some students organized as Brown Berets to demand more

Dolores Huerta and César Chávez confer at the 1973 convention of the United Farm Workers. Chávez and Huerta tried to build a union that welcomed workers of all ethnic backgrounds, but the UFW leaders were largely Hispanic, and the union took much of its symbolism from the Mexican heritage shared by most of its members.

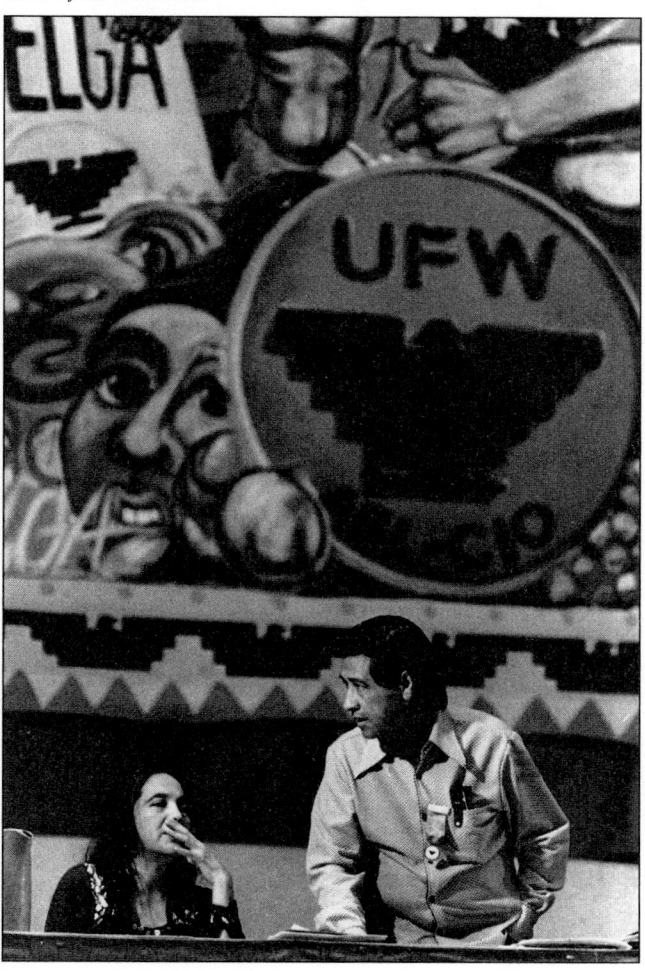

relevant education and fairer police treatment. Many rejected assimilation in favor of community self-determination and began to talk about *la raza* ("the people"), whose language and heritage descended from centuries of Mexican history. "Chicano" itself was a slang term with insulting overtones that was now adopted as a badge of pride and cultural identity.

Native Americans assert their identity. Native Americans also fought both for equal access to American society and to preserve cultural traditions through tribal institutions. Congress in 1968 restored the authority of tribal laws on reservations. A few years later, it granted native Alaskans 40 million acres to settle claims for their ancestral lands. Legally sophisticated tribes sued for compensation and enforcement of treaty provisions, such as fishing rights in the Pacific Northwest. Larger tribes established their own colleges, such as Navajo Community College (1969) and Oglala Lakota College (1971). Navajo Community College, said its catalog, "exists to fulfill many needs of the Navajo people. . . . It provides a place where Navajo history and culture can be studied and learned; it provides training in the skills necessary for many jobs on the reservation which today are held by non-Navajos."

A second development was newly media-oriented protest that assented "Red Power." Native American students gained national attention by seizing the abandoned Alcatraz Island for a cultural and educational center (1969–1971). Indians in Minneapolis created the **American Indian Movement (AIM)** in 1968 to increase economic opportunity and stop police mistreatment. AIM participated in the cross-country Broken Treaties Caravan, which climaxed by occupying the Bureau of Indian Affairs in Washington in 1972. AIM also allied with Sioux traditionalists on the Pine Ridge Reservation in South Dakota against the tribe's elected government. In 1973, they took over the village of Wounded Knee, where the U.S. Army in 1890 had massacred three hundred Indians. They held out for seventy days before leaving peacefully. Since these events of the early 1970s, Indians have continued to assert their distinctiveness within American society.

The slogans of Black Power, Brown Power, and Red Power spanned goals that ran from civil rights to cultural pride to revolutionary separatism. They were all efforts by minorities to define themselves through their own heritage and backgrounds, not simply by looking in the mirror of white society. They thus questioned the American assumption that everyone wanted to be part of the same homogeneous society.

The American Indian Movement (AIM) drew its strength from young Indians in the cities. In 1972, AIM joined a march of Native Americans along the "Trail of Broken Treaties" to Washington, D.C., where members occupied the offices of the Bureau of Indian Affairs. The occupation ended after a week but succeeded in publicizing Native American grievances.

SUBURBAN INDEPENDENCE: THE OUTER CITY

In the mid-1960s, the United States became a suburban nation. The 1970 census found more people living in the suburban counties of metropolitan areas (37 percent) than in central cities (31 percent) or in small towns and rural areas (31 percent). Just after World War II, most new suburbs had been bedroom communities that depended on the jobs, services, and shopping of central cities. By the late 1960s, suburbs were evolving into "outer cities," whose inhabitants had little need for the old central city. The *New York Times* in 1978 found that 40 percent of the residents of New York's Long Island and New Jersey suburbs visited the city fewer than three times a year, and most denied that they were part of the New York area. New residents in a suburban community had typically moved from other suburbs and felt no personal connection to or responsibility for old city neighborhoods. For them, suburban malls and shopping strips were the new American Main Street and suburban communities the new Middle America.

Suburban economic growth and political influence. Suburbs captured most new jobs, leaving the urban poor with few opportunities for employment. In the fifteen largest metropolitan areas, the number of central city jobs fell by 800,000 in the 1960s, while the number of suburban jobs rose by 3.2 million. The shift from rail to air for business travel accentuated suburban job growth. Sales representatives and executives could arrive at airports on the edge of town rather than at railroad stations at the center and transact business without ever going downtown. The trend was first obvious at Chicago's O'Hare Airport in the 1960s; by the 1970s, every major airport had a fringe of hotels, office parks, and corporate offices. Around many cities, suburban retailing, employment, and services fused into so-called "edge cities." Examples are the Galleria Post Oak district in Houston and the Tysons Corner area in northern Virginia. Huge complexes of shopping malls, high-rise hotels, and glass-sided office buildings have far more space than old business districts in such cities as Fort Wayne and Wichita.

Suburban rings gained a growing share of public facilities intended to serve the entire metropolitan area. As pioneered in California, community colleges served the suburban children of the baby boom. Many of the new four-year schools that state university systems added in the 1960s and early 1970s were also built for suburbanites, from George Mason University and the University of Maryland Baltimore County in the Washington-Baltimore area to California State University campuses at Northridge and Fullerton. The California Angels in baseball and New York Islanders in hockey gave suburban regions exclusive claims to their own major league sports franchises.

Suburban political power grew along with economic clout. In 1962, the Supreme Court handed down a landmark decision in the case of ***Baker v. Carr***. Overturning laws that treated counties or other political subdivisions as the units to be represented in state legislatures, *Baker* required that legislative seats be apportioned on the basis of population. This principle of "one person, one vote" broke the stranglehold of rural counties on state governments, but the big beneficiaries were not older cities, but fast-growing suburbs. By 1975, suburbanites held the largest block of seats in the House of Representatives—131 suburban districts, 130 rural, 102 central city, and 72 mixed. Reapportionment in 1982, based on the 1980 census, produced a House that was even more heavily suburban.

School busing controversies. School integration controversies in the 1970s reinforced a tendency for suburbanites to separate themselves from city problems. In ***Swann v. Charlotte-Mecklenburg Board of Education*** (1971), the U.S. Supreme Court held that crosstown busing was an acceptable solution to the *de facto* segregation that resulted from residential patterns within a single school district. When school officials around the country failed to achieve racial balance, federal judges ordered their own busing plans. Although integration through busing occurred peacefully in dozens of cities, many white people resented the practice. Working-class students who depended on public schools found themselves on the front lines of integration, while many middle-class families switched to private education. For many Americans, the image of busing for racial integration was fixed in 1975, when white citizens in Boston reacted with violence against black students who were bused to largely white high schools in the South Boston and Charlestown neighborhoods. The goal of equal opportunity clashed with equally strong values of neighborhood, community, and ethnic solidarity.

Because the Supreme Court also ruled that busing programs normally stopped at school-district boundaries, suburbs with independent districts escaped school integration. One result was to make busing self-defeating, for it caused white families to move out of the integrating school district. Others placed their children in private academies, as happened frequently in the South. Busing also caused suburbanites to defend their political independence fiercely. In Denver, for example, a bitter debate lasted from 1969 until court-ordered busing in 1974. By-products included incorporation or expansion of several large suburbs and a state constitutional amendment that blocked further expansion of the city boundaries (and thus of the Denver school district).

THE YEAR OF THE GUN, 1968

Some years are turning points that force society to reconsider its basic assumptions. In 1914, the violence of World War I undermined Europe's belief in progress. In 1933, Americans had to rethink the role of government. In 1968, mainstream Americans turned against the war in Vietnam, student protest and youth counterculture turned ugly, and political consensus shattered.

THE TET OFFENSIVE

The longer the Vietnam War continued and the less interest that China or the Soviet Union showed in it, the less valid the conflict seemed to the American people. It looked more and more like a war for pride, not national security.

The Viet Cong's Tet Offensive on January 30, 1968, undermined that pride. At the end of 1967, U.S. officials were overconfidently predicting victory. They also fell for a North Vietnamese feint by committing U.S. forces to the defense of Khe Sanh, a strongpoint near the North-South border. The defense was a tactical success for the United States but thinned its forces elsewhere in South Vietnam. Then, at the beginning of Tet, the Vietnamese New Year, the Viet Cong attacked thirty-six of forty-four provincial capitals and the national capital, Saigon. They hit the U.S. embassy and reached the runways of Tan Son Nhut air base. If the United States was winning, the Tet offensive should not have been possible.

As a military effort, the attacks failed. U.S. and South Vietnamese troops repulsed the attacks and cleared the cities. But the offensive was a psychological blow that convinced the American public that the war was quicksand.

Television coverage of the Tet battles made the bad publicity worse. During World War II, officials had censored pictures from the front. Images from Vietnam went directly to the evening news; it was a "living room war." At least until Tet, the commentary from network news anchors had supported the American effort, but the pictures undermined civilian morale. Viewers could hear cigarette lighters clicking open to set villages in flames. A handful of images stayed in people's memories—a Buddhist monk burning himself to death in protest; a child with flesh peeled off by napalm; a South Vietnamese official executing a captive on the streets of Saigon.

In the wake of the Tet crisis, General Westmoreland's request for 200,000 more troops forced a political and military reevaluation. Clark Clifford, a dedicated Cold Warrior, was the new secretary of defense. Now he had second thoughts. Twenty "wise men"—the big names of the Cold War—told the president that the war was unwinnable on terms acceptable to America's allies and to many Americans. By devouring resources and souring relations with other nations, it endangered rather than enhanced American security. Most scholars have agreed with this assessment. The best option, the wise men told LBJ, was disengagement. "He could hardly believe his ears," Clifford remembered.

LBJ's EXIT

The president was already in political trouble. After other prominent Democrats held back, Minnesota's liberal Senator Eugene McCarthy had decided to challenge Johnson in the presidential primaries.

Because he controlled the party organizations in two-thirds of the states, Johnson did not need the primary states for renomination and ignored the first primary in New Hampshire. Enthusiastic college students staffed McCarthy's campaign. McCarthy won a startling 42 percent of the popular vote and twenty of twenty-four delegates in the New Hampshire primary. The vote was a protest against Johnson's Vietnam policy rather than a clear mandate for peace. As an unknown, McCarthy attracted voters who wanted the United States out of Vietnam and those who wanted all-out victory. Nevertheless, the vote proved that the political middle ground would no longer hold.

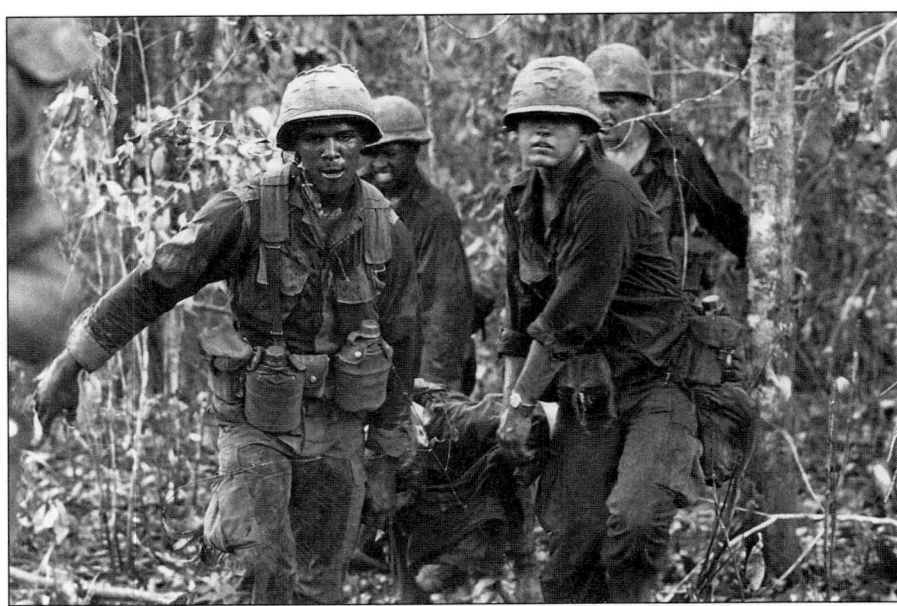

GIs evacuate a wounded comrade from fighting near the border between Vietnam and Cambodia.

By showing Johnson's vulnerability, New Hampshire also drew Robert Kennedy into the race. The younger brother of the former president, Kennedy inspired both fervent loyalty and strong distaste. In the 1950s, he had worked for Senator Joe McCarthy and had been initially a reluctant supporter of civil rights during his brother's administration. He was arrogant and abrasive, but also bright and flexible. More than other mainstream politicians of the 1960s, he touched the hearts of Hispanic and African American voters as well as the white working class. He had left his position as attorney general to win election to the Senate from New York in 1964. Now he put the Kennedy mystique on the line against a man whom he despised.

Facing political challenges and an unraveling war, on March 31, 1968, Johnson announced a halt to most bombing of North Vietnam, opening the door for peace negotiations that formally began in May 1969. He then astounded the country by withdrawing from the presidential race. It was a statesmanlike act by a man who had been consumed by a war he did not want, had never understood, and could not end. As he told an aide, the war made him feel like a hitchhiker in a hailstorm: "I can't run, I can't hide, and I can't make it stop." Hoping to save his domestic program, he served out his term with few friends and little credit for his accomplishments.

RED SPRING

In the months that followed the Tet crisis, much of the industrial world was in ferment. Grassroots rebellion shook the Soviet grip on eastern Europe. University students in Poland protested the stifling of political discussion. Alexander Dubček, the new leader of the Czech Communist Party, brought together students and the middle class around reforms that caused people to talk about "Prague Spring"—a blossoming of democracy inside the iron curtain. In August, the Soviets sent in their tanks to crush the reforms and bring Czechoslovakia back into line.

Western Europe was also in turmoil. Students rioted in Italy and Berlin. Workers and students protested against the Franco regime in Spain. In Paris, student demonstrations against the Vietnam War turned into attacks on the university system and the French government. Students fought police in the Paris streets in the first days of May. Radical industrial workers called a general strike. The government nearly toppled.

Students at Columbia University in New York echoed Europe with their own rebellion. Columbia's African American students and its SDS chapter had several grievances. One was the university's cooperation with the Pentagon-funded Institute for Defense Analysis. Another was its plan to build a gymnasium on park land that might better serve the residents of Harlem. Some students wanted changes in university policy, others a confrontation that would recruit new radicals. They occupied five university buildings, including the library and the president's office, for a week in April until police evicted them. A student strike and additional violence lasted until June. The "battle of Morningside Heights" (the location of Columbia) was tame when compared to the events in Warsaw or Paris, but it gave Americans a glimpse of the gap that divided radicalized students from national institutions.

VIOLENCE AND POLITICS: KING, KENNEDY, AND CHICAGO

Red Spring in France, Prague Spring in Czechoslovakia, and turmoil in New York were the background for the violent disruption of American politics through assassination and riot. On April 4, 1968, an ex-convict, James Earl Ray, shot and killed Martin Luther King, Jr. as he stood on the balcony of a Memphis motel. King's death was the product of pure racial hatred, and it triggered a climactic round of violence in black ghettos. Fires devastated the West Side of Chicago and downtown Washington, D.C. The army guarded the steps of the Capitol, ready to protect Congress from its fellow citizens.

The shock of King's death was still fresh when another political assassination stunned the nation. On June 5, Robert Kennedy won California's primary election. He was still behind Vice President Hubert Humphrey in the delegate count but coming on strong. As Kennedy walked out of the ballroom at his headquarters in the Ambassador Hotel in Los Angeles, a Jordanian immigrant named Sirhan Sirhan put a bullet in his brain. Sirhan may have wanted revenge for America's tilt toward Israel in that country's victorious Six-Day War with Egypt and Jordan in 1967.

Kennedy's death insured the Democratic nomination for Humphrey, a liberal who had loyally supported Johnson's war policy. After his nomination, Humphrey faced the Republican Richard Nixon and the Independent George Wallace. Nixon positioned himself as the candidate of the political middle. Wallace appealed to southern whites and working-class Northerners who feared black militancy and hated "the ivory-tower folks with pointy heads."

Both got great help from the Democratic Convention, held in Chicago on August 26–29. While Democrats feuded among themselves, Chicago Mayor Richard Daley and his police department monitored antiwar protesters. The National Mobilization Committee to End the War in Vietnam drew from the New Left and from older peace activists—sober and committed people who had fought against nuclear weapons in the 1950s and the Vietnam War throughout the 1960s. They wanted to embarrass the Johnson-Humphrey administration by marching to the convention hall on nomination night. Mixed in were the Yippies. (The term supposedly stood for Youth International Party, but the idea of hippies making yip-

pie! came first and the word later.) The Yippies planned to attract young people to Chicago with a promise of street theater, media events, and confrontation that would puncture the pretensions of the power structure. To the extent they had a program, it was to use youth culture to attract converts to radical politics.

The volatile mix was ready for a spark. On August 28, the same night that Democratic delegates were nominating Humphrey, tensions exploded in a police riot. Protesters and Yippies had congregated in Grant Park, across Michigan Avenue from downtown hotels. Undisciplined police waded into the crowds with clubs and tear gas. Young people fought back with rocks and bottles. Television caught the hours of violence that ended when the National Guard separated police from demonstrators. On the convention floor, Senator Abraham Ribicoff of Connecticut decried "Gestapo tactics" on the streets of Chicago. Mayor Daley shouted back obscenities. For Humphrey, the convention was a catastrophe, alienating liberal Democrats and associating Democrats with disorder in the public mind.

The election was closer than Humphrey had any right to hope (see Map 29–2). Many Americans who liked Wallace's message were unwilling to vote for a radical third party. Nixon appealed to the white middle class and claimed that he had a secret plan to end the war. Humphrey picked up strength in October after he separated himself from Johnson's war policy. Election day gave Wallace 13.5 percent of the popular vote, Humphrey 42.7 percent of the popular vote and 191 electoral votes, and Nixon 43.4 percent of the popular vote and 301 electoral votes.

The Wallace candidacy was a glimpse of the future. The national media saw Wallace in terms of bigotry and a backlash against civil rights, getting only part of the story. Many of Wallace's northern backers were unhappy with both parties. Liberal on economic issues but conservative on family and social issues, many of these working-class voters evolved into "Reagan Democrats" by the 1980s. In the South, Wallace was a transitional choice for conservative voters who would eventually transfer their allegiance from the Democratic to the Republican party.

NIXON AND WATERGATE

The new president was an unlikely politician, ill-at-ease in public and consumed by a sense of inferiority. A product of small-town California, he felt rejected by the eastern elite. After losing a 1962 race for governor of California, he announced that he was quitting politics and that the press would no

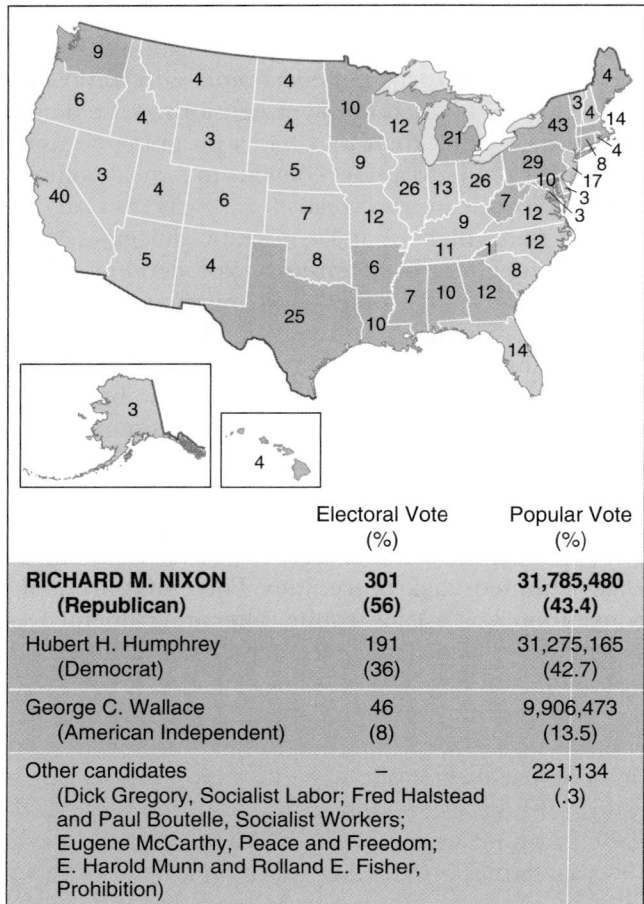

	Electoral Vote (%)	Popular Vote (%)
RICHARD M. NIXON (Republican)	**301** **(56)**	**31,785,480** **(43.4)**
Hubert H. Humphrey (Democrat)	191 (36)	31,275,165 (42.7)
George C. Wallace (American Independent)	46 (8)	9,906,473 (13.5)
Other candidates (Dick Gregory, Socialist Labor; Fred Halstead and Paul Boutelle, Socialist Workers; Eugene McCarthy, Peace and Freedom; E. Harold Munn and Rolland E. Fisher, Prohibition)	–	221,134 (.3)

MAP 29-2 **The Election of 1968**
Richard Nixon won the presidency with the help of the American Independent Party candidate, George Wallace. Wallace won several southern states, offering an alternative to white Southerners unhappy with the Democratic Party but not yet prepared to vote Republican. He also drew northern working-class votes away from Hubert Humphrey and helped Nixon to take several midwestern states.

longer have Dick Nixon "to kick around." In 1968, he skillfully sold a "new Nixon" to the media. Seven years later, the press was his undoing as it uncovered the Watergate scandal.

Nixon's painful public presence and dishonesty have tended to obscure his administration's accomplishments. He reduced tensions in the Cold War. He reluctantly upgraded civil-rights enforcement, set goals for minority hiring by federal contractors, and presided over impressive environmental legislation.

GETTING OUT OF VIETNAM, 1969–1975

After 1968, things got worse in Southeast Asia before they got better. Nixon had no secret plan to end the war. Protests culminated in 1969 with the Vietnam

Moratorium on October 15, when 2 million protesters joined rallies across the country. Disaffection also mounted in Vietnam. Racial tensions sapped morale on the front lines. Troops lost discipline, took drugs, and hunkered down waiting for their tours of duty to end. Soldiers "fragged" (killed) their own gung-ho or racist officers, and the high command had to adapt its code of justice to keep an army on the job.

Nixon and Vice President Spiro Agnew responded by trying to isolate the antiwar opposition, but Nixon also reduced the role of U.S. ground forces. He claimed that his policies represented "the great silent majority of my fellow Americans." Agnew blamed bad morale on journalists and intellectuals—on "nattering nabobs of negativism" and "an effete corps of impudent snobs." The administration arranged for a "spontaneous" attack by construction workers on antiwar protesters in New York. The hard-hat counterattack was a cynically manipulated symbol, but Nixon and Agnew tapped genuine anger about failure in Asia and rapid change in American society.

The New Left had already split into factions. Many activists continued to focus on peace work, draft resistance, and other efforts to link radical and liberal agendas. About a hundred angry SDS members, however, declared themselves the Weather Underground in 1969, taking their name from a Bob Dylan lyric ("You don't need a weatherman to know which way the wind blows"). They tried to disrupt Chicago and Washington with window-smashing "days of rage." Three Weatherpeople accidentally blew themselves up with a homemade bomb in New York in 1970. Others robbed a Boston bank to get money for the revolution. Still others bombed a University of Wisconsin building and killed a student.

"Vietnamization" and the secret war against Cambodia. Nixon's secretary of defense, Melvin Laird, responded to the antiwar sentiment with "Vietnamization," withdrawing U.S. troops as fast as possible without undermining the South Vietnamese government. In July 1969, the president announced the **Nixon Doctrine**. The United States would help other countries fight their wars with weapons and money but not with soldiers. The policy substituted machines for men. Americans rearmed and expanded the South Vietnamese army and surreptitiously bombed Communist bases in neutral Cambodia.

The secret war against Cambodia culminated on April 30, 1970, with an invasion. Americans who had hoped that the war was fading away were outraged. Students shut down hundreds of colleges. At Kent State University in Ohio, the National Guard was called in to maintain order. Taunts, tossed bottles, and the recent record of violence put them on edge. On May 4, one unit unexpectedly fired on a group of nonthreatening students and killed four of them. At Jackson State University in Mississippi, two unsuspecting students were killed when troops fired on their dormitory.

Stalemate and cease-fire.
The Cambodian "incursion" extended the military stalemate in Vietnam to U.S. policy. Beginning in December 1969, a new lottery system for determining the order of draft calls by birthdate let two-thirds of young men know they would not be drafted. In December 1970, Congress repealed the Gulf of Tonkin Resolution and prohibited the use of U.S. ground troops outside South Vietnam. Cambodia, however, was already devastated. The U.S. invasion had destabilized its government and opened the way for

The shootings at Kent State University in May 1970 reflected the deep divisions in American society created by the Vietnam War, including those between antiwar college students and young people serving in the armed forces.

the bloodthirsty Khmer Rouge, who killed millions of Cambodians in the name of a working-class revolution. Vietnamization continued; only ninety thousand U.S. ground troops were still in Vietman by early 1972. A final air offensive in December smashed Hanoi into rubble and helped to force four and a half years of peace talks to a conclusion.

The cease-fire began on January 27, 1973. It confirmed American withdrawal from Vietnam. North Vietnamese and Viet Cong forces would remain in control of the territory they occupied in South Vietnam, but they were not to be reinforced or substantially reequipped. The United States promised not to increase its military aid to South Vietnam. There were no solid guarantees for the South Vietnamese government. Immediately after coming to terms with North Vietnam, Nixon suspended the draft in favor of an all-volunteer military.

In 1975, South Vietnam collapsed. Only the American presence had kept its political, ethnic, and religious factions together. For the first two years after the Paris agreement, North Vietnam quietly rebuilt its military capacity. In the spring of 1975, it opened an offensive, and South Vietnamese morale evaporated. Resistance crumbled so rapidly that the United States

had to evacuate its embassy in Saigon by helicopter while frantic Vietnamese tried to join the flight.

NIXON AND THE WIDER WORLD
To his credit, Richard Nixon took American foreign policy in new directions even while he was struggling to escape from Vietnam and Cambodia. Like Dwight Eisenhower before him, Nixon's reputation as an anti-Communist allowed him to improve relations with China and the Soviet Union. Indeed, he hoped to distract the American people from frustration in Southeast Asia with accomplishments elsewhere.

Nixon and Henry Kissinger, his national security adviser (and, later, secretary of state), shared what they considered a realistic view of foreign affairs. For both men, foreign policy was not about crusades or moral stands. It was about the balance of world economic and military power and securing the most advantageous agreements, alliances, and military positions. In particular, they hoped to trade improved relations with China and the Soviet Union for help in settling the Vietnam War.

Since 1950, the United States had acted as if China did not exist, refusing economic relations and insisting that the Nationalist regime on Taiwan was the legitimate Chinese government. But the Republic of China was increasingly isolated within the Communist world. In 1969, it almost went to war with the Soviet Union. Nixon was eager to take advantage of Chinese-Soviet tension. Secret talks led to an easing of the American trade embargo in April 1971 and a tour of China by a U.S. table-tennis team. Kissinger then arranged for Nixon's startling visit to Mao Zedong in Beijing in February 1972.

Playing the "China card" helped to improve relations with the Soviet Union. The Soviets needed increased trade with the United States and a counterweight to China, the United States was looking for help in getting out of Vietnam, and both countries wanted to limit nuclear armaments. In 1969, the Senate came within one vote of stopping the development of defensive antiballistic missiles (ABMs). Opponents feared that strong antimissile defenses would encourage the idea that a nation could launch a first strike and survive the retaliation. Nixon treated the ABM program as a bargaining chip. Protracted negotiations led to arms agreements known as **SALT** (Strategic Arms Limitation Treaty) that Nixon signed in Moscow in May 1972. The agreements blocked creation of extensive ABM systems but failed to limit bombers, cruise missiles, or multiple independently targeted warheads on single missiles.

Diplomats used the French word **détente** to describe the new U.S. relations with China and the Soviet Union. *Détente* means an easing of tensions, not friendship or alliance. It facilitated travel between the United States and China. It allowed U.S. farmers to sell wheat to the Soviets. More broadly, *détente* implied that the United States and China recognized mutual interests in Asia and that the United States acknowledged the Soviet Union as an equal in world affairs. *Détente* made the world safer.

COURTING MIDDLE AMERICA

Nixon designed domestic policy to help him win reelection. His goal was to solidify his "Middle American" support. The strategy targeted the growing populations of the South and the suburbs, as well as blue-collar voters who were ready to abandon the Democrats for law-and-order Republicans.

The Nixon White House preferred to ignore troubled big cities. Spokesmen announced that the "urban crisis" was over and dismantled the urban initiatives of Johnson's Great Society, even though such programs as Model Cities had never been given enough money to work. Instead, Nixon tilted federal assistance to the suburbs. The centerpiece of his **New Federalism** was General Revenue Sharing (1972) which passed federal funds directly to local govern-

ments with no limits on use. By 1980, it had transferred more than $18 billion from the federal treasury to the states and more than $36 billion to local governments. Revenue sharing was a suburban-aid program. Its "no-strings" grants supplemented the general funds of every full-service government, whether a city of 2 million or a suburban town of five hundred.

Nixon pursued the southern strategy through the symbolism of Supreme Court nominations. His first nominees were Clement Haynsworth of Florida and G. Harrold Carswell of Alabama. Although the Senate rejected both as unqualified, the nominations nonetheless gave Nixon a reputation as a champion of the white South. He hoped to move cautiously in enforcing school desegregation, but a task force led by Secretary of Labor George Shultz crafted an approach that allowed substantial desegregation. In this instance, as elsewhere with his domestic policies, Nixon was inflammatory in speeches but moderate in action, increasing the funding of federal civil rights agencies.

OIL, OPEC, AND STAGFLATION

One of the most troublesome domestic issues was inflation. The cost of living began to outpace wages in the late 1960s. Economists saw the situation as a classic example of "demand-pull" inflation, in which too many dollars from government and consumer spending were chasing too few goods and services. One of the causes was LBJ's decision to fight in Vietnam without tax increases until 1968. An income tax cut in 1969, supported by both parties, made the situation worse. Inflation eroded the value of savings and pensions. It also made U.S. goods too expensive for foreign buyers and generated a trade deficit that placed pressures on the international value of the dollar.

In August 1971, Nixon detached the dollar from the gold standard. The Treasury would no longer sell gold at $35 an ounce, a practice that had made the dollar the anchor around which other currencies fluctuated. The dollar could now float in value relative to other currencies, making U.S. exports more competitive but undercutting the nation's ability to lead global economic policy. Nixon took the action without consulting America's allies, even though it triggered drastic readjustments of international markets. It was an example of the political expediency with which he sometimes operated.

The U.S. economy took another hit from inflation in 1973–74. This time it was "cost-push" inflation, in which a price increase for one key product raises the cost of producing other items. The main cause was sharp increases in the price of energy, an input to every product and service. Angry at American support for Israel in the Arab-Israeli War of October 1973, Arab nations imposed an embargo on oil exports that lasted from October 1973 to March 1974. Gasoline and heating oil became scarce and expensive. Long lines at gas pumps and hurried rationing systems (such as allowing half the nation to buy gas on odd-numbered days and the other half in even-numbered days) panicked auto-dependent Americans. The shortages eased when the embargo ended, but the **Organization of Petroleum Exporting Countries (OPEC)** had challenged the ability of the industrial nations to dictate world economic policy.

Rising energy prices forced Americans to switch off unused lights, turn down thermostats, and put on sweaters. Consumers compared the efficiency ratings of appliances and the gas mileage of cars. Congress required states to enforce a fuel-saving highway speed limit of 55 miles per hour to get federal highway funds. Congress also enacted the first fuel economy standards for automobiles. The fuel efficiency of the average new car doubled from 14 miles per gallon in 1973 to 28 miles per gallon by the late 1980s, and more efficient imports captured a third of the U.S. car market by 1980.

While Nixon searched for short-term political advantage, underlying problems of the American economy went untreated. After thirty years at the top, the United States could no longer dominate the world economy by itself. The newly found power of OPEC was obvious. Just as important was the surging industrial capacity of Germany and Japan, which now had economies as modern as that of the United States. Declining rates of saving and investment in industrial capacity seemed to put the United States in danger of following the British road to economic obsolescence and second-level status. Indeed, a new term entered the popular vocabulary in 1971: *Stagflation* was the painful combination of stagnant economic growth, high unemployment, and inflation that matched no one's economic theory but everyone's daily experience (see Figure 29-2).

AMERICANS AS ENVIRONMENTALISTS

In the turbulent 1970s, Americans found one issue they could agree on. In the 1970s, resource conservation grew into a multifaceted environmental movement. Environmentalism dealt with serious problems. It was broad enough for both scientific experts and activists, for both Republican Richard Nixon and Democrat Jimmy Carter.

After the booming 1950s, Americans had started to pay attention to "pollution," a catchall for the damage that advanced technologies and industrial production did to natural systems. Rachel Carson's *Silent*

Spring in 1962 pushed pollution onto the national agenda. Carson, a well-regarded science writer, described the side effects of DDT and other pesticides on animal life. In her imagined future, spring was silent because all the birds had died of pesticide poisoning. Other side effects of the industrial economy made headlines. An offshore oil well polluted the beaches of Santa Barbara, California, in 1969. Fire danced across the Cuyahoga River in Cleveland when industrial discharges ignited.

Environmentalism gained strength among Americans in 1970. On April 22, ten thousand schools and 20 million other people took part in Earth Day, an occasion first conceived by Wisconsin Senator Gaylord Nelson. Earth Day gained a grassroots following in towns and cities across the country. New York closed Fifth Avenue to automobiles for the day. Companies touted their environmental credentials.

The first Earth Day in 1970 tapped growing concern about the environment. It helped turn the technical field of pollution control into the broad-based environmental movement.

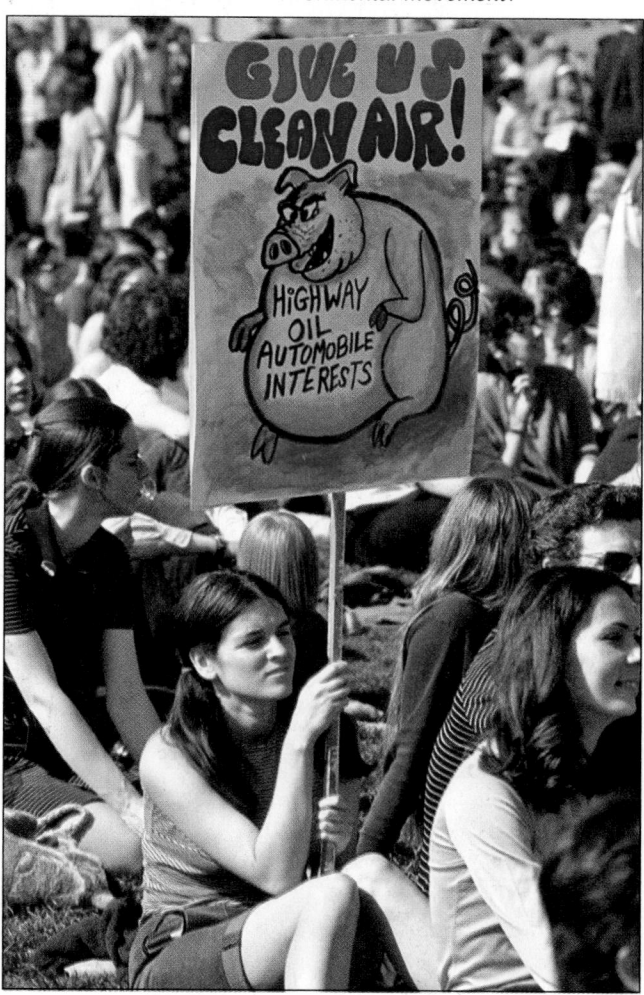

The American establishment had been looking for a safe and respectable crusade to divert the idealism and discontent of the 1960s. Now the mainstream media discovered the ravaged planet. So did a politically savvy president. An expedient proenvironmental stance might attract some of the antiwar constituency. Nixon had already signed the National Environmental Policy Act on January 1, 1970, and later in the year created the **Environmental Protection Agency (EPA)** to enforce environmental laws. The rest of the Nixon years brought legislation on clean air, clear water, pesticides, hazardous chemicals, and endangered species (see the Overview table, "The Environmental Decades") that made environmental management and protection part of governmental routine.

As Americans became more aware of human-caused environmental hazards, they realized that minority and low-income and communities had more than their share of problems. In the Louisiana petrochemical belt along the Mississippi River, African Americans often lived downstream and downwind. Landfills and waste disposal sites were frequently located near minority neighborhoods. In Buffalo, white working-class residents near the Love Canal industrial site discovered in 1978 that an entire neighborhood was built on land contaminated by decades of chemical dumping. Activists sought to understand the health effects and force compensation, paving the way for the Superfund cleanup legislation (see American Views: Grassroots Community Action).

FROM DIRTY TRICKS TO WATERGATE

The **Watergate** crisis pivoted on Richard Nixon's character. Despite his solid political standing, Nixon saw enemies everywhere and overestimated their strength. Subordinates learned during his first administration that the president would condone dishonest actions—"dirty tricks"—if they stood to improve his political position. In 1972 and 1973, dirty tricks grew from a scandal into a constitutional crisis when Nixon abused the power of his office to cover up wrongdoing and hinder criminal investigations.

The chain of events that undermined Nixon's presidency started with the **Pentagon Papers**. In his last year as secretary of defense, Robert McNamara had commissioned a report on America's road to Vietnam. The documents showed that the country's leaders had planned to expand the war even while they claimed to be looking for a way out. In June 1971, one of the contributors to the report, Daniel Ellsberg, leaked it to the *New York Times*. Its publication infuriated Nixon.

In response, the White House compiled a list of journalists and politicians who opposed Nixon. As

Overview

The Environmental Decades

Administration	Focus of Concern	Legislation
Johnson	Wilderness and wildlife	Wilderness Act (1964) National Wildlife Refuge System (1966) Wild and Scenic Rivers Act (1968)
Nixon	Pollution control and endangered environments	National Environmental Policy Act (1969) Environmental Protection Agency (1970) Clean Air Act (1970) Occupational Safety and Health Act (1970) Water Pollution Control Act (1972) Pesticide Control Act (1972) Coastal Zone Management Act (1972) Endangered Species Act (1973)
Ford	Energy and hazardous materials	Toxic Substances Control Act (1976) Resource Conservation and Recovery Act (1976)
Carter	Energy and hazardous materials	Energy Policy and Conservation Act (1978) Comprehensive Emergency Response, Compensation, and Liability Act (Superfund) (1980)

one White House staffer, John Dean, put it, the president's men could then "use the available federal machinery [Internal Revenue Service, FBI] to screw our political enemies." Nixon set up a special investigations unit in the White House. Two former CIA employees, E. Howard Hunt and G. Gordon Liddy, became the chief "plumbers," as the group was known because its job was to prevent leaks of information. The plumbers contributed to an atmosphere of lawlessness in the White House. They cooked up schemes to embarrass political opponents and ransacked the office of Ellsberg's psychiatrist.

Early in 1972, Hunt went to work for CREEP—the Committee to Re-Elect the President—while Liddy took another position on the presidential staff. CREEP had already raised millions from corporations and was hatching plans to undermine Democrats with rumors and pranks. Then, on June 17, 1972, five inept burglars hired with CREEP funds were caught breaking into the Democratic National Committee office in Washington's Watergate apartment building. The people involved knew that an investigation would lead directly to CREEP and then to the White House. Nixon felt too insecure to ride out what would probably have been a small scandal. Instead, he initiated a coverup. On June 23, he ordered his assistant H. R. Haldeman to warn the FBI off the case with the excuse that national security was involved. Nixon compounded this obstruction of justice by arranging a $400,000 bribe to keep the burglars quiet.

The coverup worked in the short run. As midlevel officials from the Justice Department pursued their investigation, the public lost interest in what looked more like slapstick than a serious crime. Nixon's opponent in the 1972 election was South Dakota Senator George McGovern, an impassioned opponent of the Vietnam War. McGovern was honest, intelligent, and well to the left on such issues as the defense budget and legalization of marijuana. He did not appeal to the white Southerners and blue-collar Northerners whom Nixon and Agnew were luring from the Democrats. An assassination attempt that took George Wallace out of national politics also helped Nixon win in a landslide.

The coverup began to come apart with the trial of the Watergate burglars in January 1973. Federal Judge John Sirica used the threat of heavy sentences to pressure one burglar into a statement that implied that higher-ups had been involved. Meanwhile, the *Washington Post* was linking Nixon's people to dirty tricks and illegal campaign contributions. The White House scrambled to find a defensible story. White House Counsel John Dean, who coordinated much of the effort, reported to Nixon in March that the scandal and coverup had become a "cancer on the presidency." Nixon was aware of many of the actions that his subordinates had undertaken. He now began to coach people on what they should tell investigators, claimed his staff had lied to him, and tried to set up Dean to take the fall.

In the late spring and early summer, attention shifted to the televised hearings of the Senate's Select Committee on Presidential Campaign Activities. Its chair was Sam Ervin of North Carolina, whose down-home style masked a clever mind. A parade of White House and party officials described their parts in the affair, often accusing each other and revealing the plumbers and the enemies list. The real questions, it became obvious, were what the president knew and when he knew it. It seemed to be John Dean's word against Richard Nixon's.

A bombshell turned the scandal into a constitutional crisis. A mid-level staffer told the committee that Nixon made tape recordings of his White House conversations. Both the Senate and the Watergate special prosecutor, Archibald Cox, subpoenaed the tapes. Nixon refused to give them up, citing executive privilege and the separation of powers. In late October, after he failed to cut a satisfactory deal, he fired his attorney general and the special prosecutor. This "Saturday-night massacre" caused a storm of protest, and many Americans thought that it proved that Nixon had something to hide. In April 1974, he finally issued edited transcripts of the tapes, with foul language deleted and key passages missing; he claimed that his secretary had accidentally erased crucial material. Finally, on July 24, 1974, the U.S. Supreme Court ruled unanimously that Nixon had to deliver sixty-four tapes to the new special prosecutor.

Congress was now moving to impeach the president. On July 27, the House Judiciary Committee took up the specific charges. Republicans joined Democrats in voting three articles of impeachment: for hindering the criminal investigation of the Watergate break-in, for abusing the power of the presidency by using federal agencies to deprive citizens of their rights, and for ignoring the committee's subpoena for the tapes. Before the full House could vote on the articles of impeachment and send them to the Senate for trial, Nixon delivered the tapes. One of them contained the "smoking gun," direct evidence that Nixon had participated in the coverup on June 23, 1972, and had been lying ever since. On August 8 he announced his resignation, effective the following day.

Watergate was two separate but related stories. On one level, it was about individuals who deceived or manipulated the American people. Nixon and his cronies wanted to win too badly to play by the rules

AMERICAN VIEWS

Grassroots Community Action

In the 1950s, a major chemical company closed a waste dump in Niagara Falls, New York. The site, known as Love Canal, was soon surrounded by a park, school, and hundreds of modest homes. Residents put up with noxious odors and seepage of chemical wastes until 1978, when they learned that the State Health Department was concerned about the health effects on small children and pregnant women. Over the next two years, residents battled state and federal bureaucracies and reluctant politicians for accurate information about the risks they faced and then for financial assistance to move from the area (often their homes represented their only savings). In October, 1980, President Carter signed a bill to move all families permanently from the Love Canal area.

One of the leaders of the grassroots movement was housewife Lois Gibbs. The following excepts from her story show her increasing sophistication as a community activist, starting by ringing doorbells in 1978 and ending with national television exposure in 1980. Although the Love Canal case itself was unusual, community based organizations in all parts of the country learned the tactics of effective action in the 1960s and 1970s.

- What public programs in the 1960s and 1970s gave citizens experience in grassroots action?

- How might the Internet change the tactics of community organizing?

Knocking on Doors

I decided to go door-to-door with a petition. It seemed like a good idea to start near the school, to talk to the mothers nearest it. I had already heard that a lot of the residents near the school had been upset about the chemicals for the past couple of years. I thought they might help me. I had never done anything like this. . . . I was afraid a lot of doors would be slammed in my face, that people would think I was some crazy fanatic. But I decided to do it anyway. . . . and knocked on my first door. There was no answer. I just stood there, not knowing what to do. It was an usually warm June day and I was perspiring. I thought: What am I doing here? I must be crazy. People are going to think I am. Go home, you fool! And that's just what I did.

---

and repeatedly broke the law. Nixon paid for his over-reaching ambition with the end of his political career; more than twenty others paid with jail terms.

On another level, the crisis was a lesson about the Constitution. The separation of powers allowed Congress and the courts to rein in a president who had spun out of control. The Ervin Committee hearings in 1973 and the House Judiciary Committee proceedings in 1974 were rituals to assure Americans that the system still worked. Nevertheless, the sequence of political events from 1968 to 1974 disillusioned many citizens.

THE FORD FOOTNOTE

Gerald Ford was the first president who had not been elected as either president or vice president. Ford was Nixon's appointee to replace Spiro Agnew, who had resigned and pleaded no contest to charges of bribery and income tax evasion in 1973 as Watergate was gathering steam. Ford was competent but unimaginative. His first major act was his most controversial—the pardon of Nixon for "any and all crimes" committed while president. Since Nixon had not yet been indicted, the pardon saved him from future prosecution. To many Americans, the act looked

It was one of those times when I had to sit down and face myself. I was afraid of making a fool of myself, I had scared myself, and I had gone home. When I got there, I sat at the kitchen table with my petition in my hand, thinking. Wait. What if people do slam doors in your face? People may think you're crazy. But what's more important—what people think or your child's health? Either you're going to do something or you're going to have to admit you're a coward and not do it. . . .

The next day, I went out on my own street to talk to people, I knew. It was a little easier to be brave with them. If I could convince people I knew—friends—maybe it would be less difficult to convince others. . . . I went to the back door, as I always did when I visited a neighbor. Each house took about twenty or twenty-five minutes. . . .

Phil Donahue and Political Action

The *Phil Donahue Show* called. They wanted us to appear on their June 18 show. The reaction in the office was different this time, compared to the show in October 1978. In October, everyone was excited. "Phil Donahue—wow!" Now, residents reacted differently. "Donahue. That's great press. Now we'll get the politicians to move!" . . . Now our people looked at the show as a tool to use in pushing the government to relocate us permanently. By this time we understood how politicians react to public pressure, how to play the political game. We eagerly

agreed to go, and found forty other residents to go with us. . . .

[After arriving in Chicago] We then planned how we would handle the *Phil Donahue Show*. . . . We had to get the real issues across. Each resident was assigned an issue. One told of the chromosome tests. Another was to concentrate on her multiple miscarriages. Another was to ask for telegrams from across the country to the White House in support of permanent relocation. I coached them to get their point in, no matter the question asked. For example, if Donahue asked what you thought of the mayor, and your assignment was to discuss miscarriages, you should answer: "I don't like the mayor because I have had three miscarriages and other health problems, and he won't help us." Or; "My family is sick, and the mayor won't help us. That's why we need people to send telegrams to the White House for permanent relocation." . . . The residents were great! Each and every one followed through with our plan.

In July, I went on a speaking tour of California arranged by Jane Fonda and Tom Hayden. I visited many sites with problems similar to ours. I was able to give advice, based on our experiences. I told the leaders of each community that it wasn't hopeless that they could win. "Stick with it. We are!"

Source: Lois Marie Gibbs, as told to Murray Levine, *Love Canal: My Story* (Albany: State University of New York Press, 1982), pp. 12–13, 161–64.

---

like a payoff. Ford insisted that the purpose was to clear the decks so that the nation could think about the future rather than the past. He also offered clemency to thousands of draft resisters.

Ford's administration presided over the collapse of South Vietnam in 1975, but elsewhere in the world, *détente* continued. American diplomats joined the Soviet Union and thirty other European nations in the capital of Finland to sign the **Helsinki Accords**. The agreements called for increased commerce between the Eastern and Western blocs and for human-rights guarantees. They also legitimized

the national boundaries that had been set in eastern Europe in 1945.

At home, the federal government did little new during Ford's two and a half years in office. The economy slid into recession; unemployment climbed above 10 percent; inflation diminished the value of savings and wages. Ford beat back Ronald Reagan for the Republican presidential nomination, but he was clearly vulnerable.

His Democratic opponent was a political enigma. James Earl Carter, Jr., had been a navy officer, a farmer, and the governor of Georgia. He was one of several new-style politicians who transformed southern politics in the 1970s. Carter and the others left race-baiting behind to talk like modern New Dealers, emphasizing that whites and blacks both needed better schools and economic growth. He appealed to Democrats as someone who could reassemble LBJ's political coalition and return the South to the Democratic party. In his successful campaign, Carter presented himself as an alternative to party hacks and Washington insiders (see Map 29–3).

JIMMY CARTER: IDEALISM AND FRUSTRATION IN THE WHITE HOUSE

Johnson and Nixon had both thought of themselves as outsiders even after nearly thirty years in national politics. Carter was the real thing, a stranger to the national policy establishment that revolves around Washington think tanks and New York law firms. As an outsider, Carter had one great advantage: freedom from the narrow mind-set of experts who talk only to each other. However, he lacked both the knowledge of key political players and the experience to resolve legislative gridlock.

The new president's personal background compounded his problems. Intellectuals found this devout Baptist hard to fathom. Labor leaders and political bosses did not know what to make of a deep Southerner. The national press was baffled. It was only after his presidency, when Americans took a clear look at Carter's moral character, that they decided they liked what they saw.

Even had he been the most skilled of politicians, however, Carter took office with little room to maneuver. Watergate bequeathed him a powerful and self-satisfied Congress and a combative press. OPEC oil producers, Islamic fundamentalists, and Soviet generals followed their own agendas. The American people themselves were fractionalized and quarrelsome, uneasy with the new advocacy of equality for women, uncertain as a nation whether they shared the same values and goals. Carter's attempt to govern like a preacher, with appeals to moral principles, did more to reveal divisions than establish common ground.

CARTER, ENERGY, AND THE ECONOMY

Carter was refreshingly low-key. After his inauguration, he walked from the Capitol to the White House, as Jefferson had. He preferred sweaters to tuxedos and signed official documents "Jimmy." He tended to tell the public what he thought rather than what pollsters said the people wanted to hear.

Carter's approach to politics reflected his training as an engineer. He was analytical, logical, and given to breaking a problem into its component parts. He was better at working with details than at defining broad goals. He filled his cabinet with experts rather than with political operators. He failed to understand the importance of personalities and was uncomfortable with compromise. He did not seem to understand the basic rules of Washington politics. For example, he and his cabinet officers developed policies and made appointments without consulting key congressional committee chairs.

The biggest domestic problem remained the economy, which slid into another recession in 1978. Another jump in oil prices helped make 1979 and 1980 the worst years for inflation in the postwar era. Interest rates surged past 20 percent as the Federal Reserve tried to reduce inflation by squeezing business and consumer credit. Carter himself was a fiscal conservative whose impulse was to cut federal spending. This course worsened unemployment and alien-

MAP 29-3   The Election of 1976
Georgian Jimmy Carter ran in 1976 as an outsider to Washington politics. He capitalized on a reputation as a progressive governor and on the Watergate scandal, which had damaged the Republican Party.

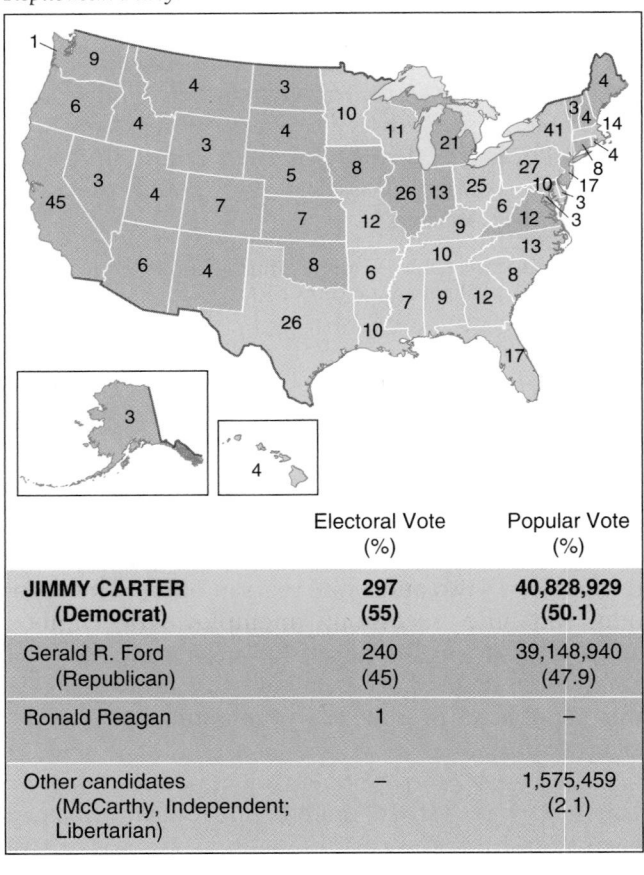

	Electoral Vote (%)	Popular Vote (%)
JIMMY CARTER (Democrat)	**297 (55)**	**40,828,929 (50.1)**
Gerald R. Ford (Republican)	240 (45)	39,148,940 (47.9)
Ronald Reagan	1	–
Other candidates (McCarthy, Independent; Libertarian)	–	1,575,459 (2.1)

ated liberal Democrats, who wanted to revive the Great Society.

Carter simultaneously proposed a comprehensive energy policy. He asked Americans to make energy conservation the moral equivalent of war—to accept individual sacrifices for the common good. Congress created the Department of Energy but refused to raise taxes on oil and natural gas to reduce consumption. However, the Energy Policy and Conservation Act (1978) did encourage alternative energy sources to replace foreign petroleum. Big oil companies poured billions of dollars into western Colorado to squeeze a petroleum substitute from shale. Solar energy research prospered. Breezy western hillsides sprouted "wind farms" to wring electricity out of the air.

However, antinuclear activism blocked one obvious alternative to fossil fuels. The antinuclear movement had started with concern about the ability of the Atomic Energy Commission to monitor the safety of nuclear-power plants and about the disposal of spent fuel rods. In the late 1970s, activists staged sit-ins at the construction sites of nuclear plants. A near-meltdown at the Three Mile Island nuclear plant in Pennsylvania in March 1979 stalemated efforts to expand nuclear-power capacity. Utilities were soon worrying about the costs of shutting down and dismantling their old nuclear plants rather than trying to build new ones.

When the OPEC price hikes undermined the inflation-fighting effort in the summer of 1979, Carter told the nation that a "moral and spiritual crisis" demanded a rebirth of the American spirit. He also proposed new steps to solve the energy crisis. The public did not know whether he had preached a sermon or given them marching orders. A cabinet reshuffle a few days later was supposed to show that he was firmly in charge. Instead, the media painted the president as inconsistent and incompetent.

Carter's problems were both personal and structural. In effect, opinion leaders by 1979 had decided that he was not capable of leading the nation and then interpreted every action as confirming that belief. There was also the practical problem of trying to hold the loyalty of Democratic liberals while attracting middle-of-the-road voters.

CLOSED FACTORIES AND FAILING FARMS

Ford and Carter both faced massive problems of economic transition that undercut their efforts to devise effective government programs. Here is how novelist John Updike described the fictional city of Brewer, Pennsylvania, at the start of the 1970s:

> Railroads and coal made Brewer. Everywhere in this city. . . . structures speak of expended energy. Great shapely stacks that have not issued smoke for half a century. . . . The old textile plants given over to discount clothing outlets teeming with a gimcrack cheer of banners FACTORY FAIR and slogans Where a Dollar Is Still a Dollar. . . . All this had been cast up in the last century by what now seem giants, in an explosion of iron and brick still preserved intact in this city where the sole new buildings are funeral parlors and government offices.

Updike's Brewer was like dozens of specialized industrial cities that fell behind a changing economic world in the 1970s and 1980s. Industrial decay stalked such "gritty cities" as Allentown, Pennsylvania; Trenton, New Jersey; and Gary, Indiana. Communities whose workers had made products in high volume for mass markets found that technological revolutions made them obsolete. When radial tires replaced bias-ply tires, Akron rubber workers paid the price. Merchants who replaced mechanical cash registers with electronic models left Dayton with block after block of outmoded factories. Asian steelmakers undercut the aging mills of Pittsburgh and Birmingham. Critics renamed the old manufacturing region of the Northeast and Middle West the Rustbelt in honor of its abandoned factories.

Stories of **deindustrialization** were similar in small cities such as Springfield, Ohio, and large cities such as Cleveland. Springfield lost ten thousand manufacturing jobs and four thousand people during the 1970s, suffered unemployment of 17 percent, and needed $30 million in public subsidies to keep its largest factory going in 1982. Cleveland had built a century of prosperity on oil refining, steel, and metalworking; the metropolitan area had grown from 1.3 million in 1940 to 2.1 million in 1970. In the 1970s, however, it lost 165,000 people. As high-paying jobs in unionized industries disappeared, sagging income undermined small businesses and neighborhoods. Falling tax revenue brought the city to the verge of bankruptcy in 1978; bankers forced public service cuts and tax increases, which meant further job losses.

Plant closures were only one facet of business efforts to increase productivity by substituting machinery for employees. Between 1947 and 1977, American steelmakers doubled output while cutting their work force from 600,000 to 400,000. Lumber companies used economic recession in the early 1980s to automate mills and rehired only a fraction of their workers when the economy picked up. High interest rates in the early 1980s, the result of a ballooning federal deficit (see Chapter 30), attracted foreign investors and strengthened the dollar in relation to other currencies. A strong dollar made U.S. exports too expensive and foreign imports cheap, forcing American manufacturers to cut costs or perish.

Despite the despairing headlines, some older industries and their workers did find new roles in the sink-or-swim environment of technological and international competition. Buffalo, New York, lost much of its steel industry but retained smaller and more flexible factories making diverse products. The auto industry went through a similar cycle of crisis and response. Prosperity in the 1950s had led automobile executives to believe that they knew how to manipulate U.S. consumers. Booming imports of well-made Toyotas and Hondas and customer demand for smaller cars destroyed that complacency in the fuel-short 1970s. In response, Ford, Chrysler, and finally General Motors remade themselves on the Japanese model as lean and flexible manufacturers. They cast off old plants, workers, and executives, started over, often in new locations, and forced Japanese companies to shift production to U.S. localities and workers.

Parallel to the decline of heavy industry was the continuing transformation of American agriculture from small, family enterprises to corporate agribusinesses. Agriculture was a national success story in the aggregate, but one accompanied by many human and environmental costs. The early 1970s brought an unexpected boom in farming. Crop failures and food shortages around the world in 1972 and 1973 expanded markets and pushed up prices for U.S. farm products. For a few years, agriculture looked like the best way for the United States to offset the high cost of imported oil. But the boom was over by the 1980s, when global commodity prices slumped. Farmers found themselves with debts they could not cover. Farm bankruptcies in Iowa reached levels unseen since the 1930s, and rock stars staged "Farm Aid" concerts to raise money to fend off foreclosures.

The boom of the 1970s was thus a brief interruption in the long-term transformation of U.S. agriculture. The number of farms slid from 4 million in 1960 to 2.4 million in 1980 and 1.9 million in 2000. Many farmers sold out willingly, glad to escape from drudgery and financial insecurity. Others could not compete in an agricultural system that favored large-scale production by demanding large amounts of capital for equipment and fertilizer.

Corporate farming substituted capital investment for labor in the time-tested manner of industrial maturity. By the 1990s, the 600,000 largest farms and ranches were responsible for 94 percent of total production of U.S. farm products. Many of them were owned by large corporations that measured success by the bottom line rather than the stability of rural communities. Fewer than 2 percent of all American workers now make their living from farming, down from 8 percent in 1960.

BUILDING A COOPERATIVE WORLD

Despite troubles on the home front, Carter's first two years brought foreign-policy successes that reflected a new vision of a multilateral world. As a relative newcomer to international politics, Carter was willing to work with African, Asian, and Latin American nations on a basis of mutual respect. He appointed Andrew Young—an African American from Georgia with long experience in the civil-rights movement—as ambassador to the United Nations, where he worked effectively to build bridges to third-world nations.

Carter's moral convictions were responsible for a new concern with human rights around the globe. He criticized the Soviet Union for preventing free speech and denying its citizens the right to emigrate, angering Soviet leaders, who didn't expect the human rights clauses of the Helsinki Accords to be taken seriously. Carter was also willing to criticize some (but not all) American allies. He withheld economic aid from South Africa, Guatemala, Chile, and Nicaragua, which had long records of human rights abuses. In Nicaragua, the change in policy helped left-wing Sandinista rebels topple the Somoza dictatorship.

The triumph of the new foreign policy was the **Camp David Agreement** between Egypt and Israel. Carter risked his reputation and credibility in September 1978 to bring Egyptian President Anwar al-Sadat and Israeli Prime Minister Menachem Begin together at Camp David, the presidential retreat. He refused to admit failure and dissuaded the two leaders from walking out. A formal treaty was signed in Washington on March 26, 1979. The pact normalized relations between Israel and its most powerful neighbor and led to Israel's withdrawal from the Sinai Peninsula. It was a vital prelude to further progress toward Arab-Israeli peace in the mid 1990s.

NEW CRISES ABROAD

The Cold War was a noxious weed that *détente* trimmed but did not uproot. In the last two years of Carter's administration, it sprang back to life around the globe and smothered the promise of a new foreign policy. The Soviets ignored the human-rights provisions of the Helsinki Accords. Soviet advisers or Cuban troops intervened in African civil wars. At home, Cold Warriors who had never accepted *détente* found it easier to attack Carter than Nixon.

CORBIS

Egyptian President Anwar al-Sadat, U.S. President Jimmy Carter, and Israeli Prime Minister Menachem Begin share a symbolic handshake after the signing of a peace treaty between Egypt and Israel on August 26, 1979. The treaty codified the historic agreement that the leaders had hammered out at Camp David, Maryland, in September 1978.

The failure of SALT II.

Carter inherited negotiations for SALT II—a strategic arms-limitation treaty that would have reduced both the American and Soviet nuclear arsenals—from the Ford administration. SALT II met stiff resistance in the Senate. Opponents claimed it would create a "window of vulnerability" in the 1980s that would invite the Soviets to launch a nuclear first strike. Carter tried to counter criticism by stepping up defense spending, starting a buildup that would accelerate under Ronald Reagan.

Hopes for SALT II vanished on January 3, 1980, when Soviet troops entered Afghanistan, a neutral Muslim nation on the southern border of the Soviet Union. Muslim tribespeople unhappy with modernization had attacked Afghanistan's pro-Communist government, which invited Soviet intervention. The situation resembled the American involvement in South Vietnam. Similar, too, was the inability of Soviet forces to suppress the Afghan guerrillas, with their American weapons and control of the mountains. In the end, it took the Soviets a decade to find a way out.

The Iranian hostage crisis.

The final blow to Carter's foreign policy came in Iran. Since 1953, the United States had strongly backed Iran's monarch, Shah Reza Pahlevi. The Shah modernized Iran's economy but his feared secret police jailed and tortured political opponents. U.S. aid and oil revenues helped him build a large army, but the Iranian middle class despised his authoritarianism, and Muslim fundamentalists opposed the Westernizing influence of modernization. A revolution toppled the Shah at the start of 1979.

The upheaval installed a nominally democratic government, but the Ayatollah Ruhollah Khomeini, a Muslim cleric who hated the United States, exercised real power. Throughout 1979, Iran grew increasingly anti-American. After the United States allowed the exiled Shah to seek medical treatment in New York, a mob stormed the U.S. embassy in Tehran on November 4, 1979, and took more than sixty Americans hostage. They demanded that Carter surrender the Shah.

Television brought pictures of blindfolded hostages and anti-American mobs burning effigies of Uncle Sam and wrapping American flags around garbage. The administration tried economic pressure and diplomacy, but Khomeini had no desire for accommodation. When Iran announced in April 1980 that the hostages would remain in the hands of the militants rather than be transferred to the government, Carter ordered an airborne rescue. Even a perfectly managed effort would have been difficult. The hostages were held in the heart of a city of 4 million hostile Iranians, hundreds of miles from the nearest aircraft carrier and thousands of miles from U.S. bases. Hampered by lack of coordination among the military services, the attempt misfired when three of eight helicopters malfunctioned and one crashed in the Iranian desert. The fiasco added to the national embarrassment. The United States and Iran finally reached agreement on the eve of the 1980 election. The hostages gained their freedom after 444 days, at the moment Ronald Reagan took office as the new president.

The hostage crisis consumed Jimmy Carter the way that Vietnam had consumed Lyndon Johnson. It gripped the public and stalemated other issues. For weeks, Carter limited public appearances to statements in the White House Rose Garden. The public blamed him for problems literally beyond his control, for failing to use military force, and then for using it and failing. Carter's tragedy was that "his" Iranian crisis was the fruit of policies hatched by the Eisenhower administration and pursued by every president since then, all of whom overlooked the

The Iran hostage crisis reflected intense anti-American feelings in Iran and provoked an equally bitter anti-Iranian reaction in the United States. Fifty-two of the more than sixty U.S. embassy employees first seized were held for 444 days, giving the United States a painful lesson about the limits on its ability to influence events around the world.

Shah's despotic government because of his firm anti-Communism.

After thirty years in which the United States had viewed the entire world as a Cold War battlefield, Carter was willing to accept the developing world on its own terms. His human-rights efforts showed that evangelical religious convictions could be tied to progressive aims. He wanted to avoid supporting oppressive regimes, but the past was too burdensome. Iranian rage at past policies of the sort Carter hoped to change destroyed his ability to direct a new course. After he left office, his continuing work for peace and humanitarian efforts would earn him the Nobel Peace Prize in 2002.

CONCLUSION

In the mid-1970s, Americans encountered real limits to national capacity. From 1945 to 1973, they had enjoyed remarkable prosperity. That ended in 1974.

Long lines at gas stations showed that prosperity was fragile. Cities and regions felt the costs of obsolete industries. Environmental damage caused many Americans to reconsider the goal of economic expansion.

The nation also had to recognize that it could not run the world. American withdrawal from Vietnam in 1973 and the collapse of the South Vietnamese government in 1975 were defeats; the United States ended up with little to show for a long and painful war. SALT I stabilized the arms race, but it also recognized that the Soviet Union was an equal. The American nuclear arsenal might help deter a third world war, but it could not prevent the seizure of hostages in Iran.

These challenges came amid deep economic changes in the United States. The ways that Americans made their livings and the range of opportunities that they faced were in flux. The nation finished the 1970s more egalitarian than it had been in the early

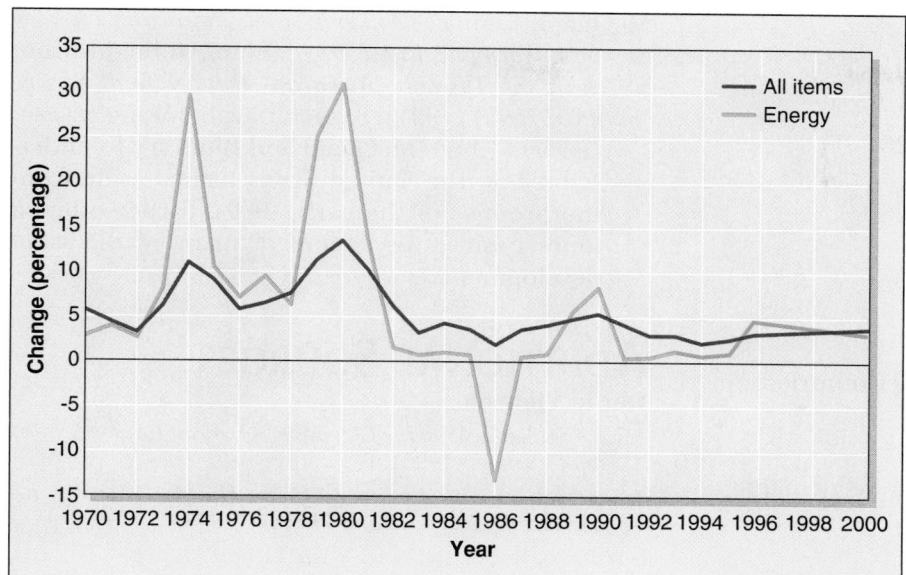

FIGURE 29-2   Year-to-Year Percentage Changes in the Consumer Price Index and Energy Prices
From 1974 to 1982, price inflation was one of the nation's most serious problems. Rapid increases in energy prices were one cause. Another was the effort to fight a war in southeast Asia without raising taxes to offset federal defense spending. Inflation eroded the value of savings and hurt people on fixed incomes, such as the elderly.

Data Source: *Statistical Abstract of the United States*

1960s but also more divided. More citizens had the opportunity to advance economically and to seek political power, but there were deepening fissures between social liberals and cultural conservatives, old and new views about roles for women, rich and poor,

whites and blacks. In 1961, John Kennedy had called on his fellow citizens to "bear any burden, pay any price" to defend freedom. By 1980, the nation had neither the economic capacity to pay any price nor the unity to agree on what burdens it should bear.

REVIEW QUESTIONS

1. Why did the United States fail to achieve its objectives in Vietnam? What factors limited President Johnson's freedom of action there? How did the Tet Offensive affect U.S. policy? How did antiwar protests in the United States influence national policy?

2. How did racial relations change between 1965 and 1970? What were the relationships between the civil rights movement and minority separatism? What were the similarities and differences among African American, Latino, and Native American activism?

3. In what ways was 1968 a pivotal year for American politics and society?

4. What were the implications of *détente?* Why did the Cold War reappear in the late 1970s? How and why did U.S. influence over the rest of the world change during the 1970s?

5. How did Richard Nixon's political strategy respond to the growth of the South and West? How

did it respond to the shift of population from central cities to suburbs?

6. How did the backgrounds of Presidents Johnson, Nixon, and Carter shape their successes and failures as national leaders?

7. What political and constitutional issues were at stake in the Watergate scandal? How did it change American politics?

8. Why was the "space race" important for the United States? How did it strengthen the alliance among American science, government and industry?

KEY WORDS

American Indian Movement (AIM) (p. 933)

Baker v. Carr (p. 934)

Black Panthers (p. 932)

Black Power (p. 931)

Camp David Agreement (p. 948)

Counterculture (p. 928)

Deindustrialization (p. 947)

Détente (p. 940)

Environmental Protection Agency (p. 942)

Free Speech Movement (FSM) (p. 926)

Helsinki Accords (p. 945)

Model Cities Program (p. 926)

Nation of Islam (p. 932)

New Federalism (p. 940)

Nixon Doctrine (p. 938)

Organization of Petroleum Exporting Countries (OPEC) (p. 941)

Pentagon Papers (p. 942)

SALT (Strategic Arms Limitation Treaty) (p. 940)

Search and destroy (p. 922)

Selective Service System (p. 924)

Students for a Democratic Society (SDS) (p. 926)

Swann v. Charlotte-Mecklenburg Board of Education (p. 935)

Watergate (p. 942)

RECOMMENDED READING

Bates, Tom. *Rads: The 1970 Bombing of the Army Math Research Center at the University of Wisconsin and Its Aftermath* (1992). Bates attempts to use a specific episode to understand the collapse of the New Left.

Caute, David. *Year of the Barricades* (1988). Tour the events of 1968 on both sides of the Atlantic.

Emerson, Gloria. *Winners and Losers* (1976). The impact of the war in Vietnam on American society is told through the stories of individuals changed by the war.

Farber, David. *Chicago '68* (1988); *Medium Cool* (1969), directed by Haskell Wexler. Farber's book contrasts the perspectives and language of city officials and protesters. Wexler's film captures the tension of Chicago in the hot summer through the eyes of a reporter.

Halberstam, David. *October 1964* (1994). Halberstam uses the baseball season of 1964 and the World Series between the St. Louis Cardinals and New York Yankees to encapsulate the impacts of changing racial relations on American society.

Karnow, Stanley. *Vietnam: A History* (1983). This comprehensive history of American involvement in Vietnam details the collapse of French rule and early U.S. relations with Vietnam.

McQuaid, Kim. *The Anxious Years: America in the Vietnam-Watergate Era (1989)*; Blum, John Morton. *Years of Discord: American Politics and Society, 1961–1974* (1991); Farber, David, *The Age of Great Dreams* (1994). McQuaid and Blum try to understand how the United States turned aside from the promise of the early 1960s. Farber offers a more positive assessment of many of the same developments.

ADDITIONAL SOURCES

War in Vietnam

Appy, Christian. *Working-Class War: American Combat Soldiers and Vietnam* (1993).

Auster Albert. and Leonard Quart. *How the War Was Remembered: Hollywood and Vietnam* (1988).

Buzzanco, Robert. *Masters of War* (1996).

Fitzgerald, Frances. *Fire on the Lake* (1972).

Herring, George. *America's Longest War* (1986).

Levy, David W. *The Debate over Vietnam* (1991).

Shawcross, William. *Sideshow: Kissinger, Nixon, and the Destruction of Cambodia* (1979).

Schulzinger, Robert. *A Time for War. The United States and Vietnam, 1941–1975 (1997)*.

Sheehan, Neil. *A Bright Shining Lie: John Paul Vann and America in Vietnam* (1988).

Van De Mark, Brian. *Into the Quagmire: Johnson and the Escalation of the Vietnam War* (1991).

Van Devanter, Lynda. *Home before Morning* (1984).

Wells, Tom. *The War Within: America's Battle over Vietnam* (1994).

Young, Marilyn. *The Vietnam Wars, 1945–1990* (1991).

The Revolt of the Young

Anderson, Terry. *The Movement and the Sixties* (1995).

Breines, Wini. *Community and Organization in the New Left, 1962–1968* (1982).

Evans, Sara. *Personal Politics: The Roots of Women's Liberation in the Civil Rights Movement and the New Left* (1979).

Gitlin, Todd. *The Sixties: Years of Hope, Days of Rage* (1987).

Jezer, Marty. *Abbie Hoffman: American Rebel* (1992).

Miller, James. *"Democracy Is in the Streets": From Port Huron to the Siege of Chicago* (1987).

Perry, Charles. *The Haight-Ashbury* (1985).

Rorabaugh, William. *Berkeley at War* (1989).

Sale, Kirkpatrick. *SDS* (1973).

Minority Rights and Minority Separatism

Giddings Paula, and Cornel West, *Regarding Malcolm X* (1994).

Mathiesson, Peter. *In the Spirit of Crazy Horse* (1983).

Means, Russell. *Where White Men Fear to Tread* (1995).

Padilla, Felix. *Puerto Rican Chicago* (1987).

Parman, Donald. *Indians and the American West in the Twentieth Century* (1994).

Thomas, Piri. *Down These Mean Streets* (1967).

Van Deburg, William L. *New Day in Babylon: The Black Power Movement and American Culture, 1965–1975* (1993).

Foreign Policy in the 1970s

Bill, James A. *The Eagle and the Lion: The Tragedy of American-Iranian Relations* (1988).

Garthoff, Raymond. *Détente and Confrontation* (1985).

Isaacson, Walter. *Kissinger: A Biography* (1992).

Le Feber, Walter. *The Panama Canal: The Crisis in Historical Perspective* (1978).

Litwak, Robert. *Détente and the Nixon Doctrine* (1984).

Nelson, Keith. *The Making of Détente* (1995).

Quando, William B. *Camp David: Peacemaking and Politics* (1986).

Schulzinger, Robert. *Henry Kissinger: Doctor of Diplomacy* (1989).

Smith, Gaddis. *Morality, Reason, and Power* (1986).

Talbot, Strobe. *Endgame: The Inside Story of SALT II* (1979).

Watergate and Politics in the Nixon Years

Ambrose, Stephen E. *Nixon: Ruin and Recovery, 1973–1990* (1991).

Carter, Dan T. *The Politics of Rage: George Wallace, the Origins of the New Conservatism, and the Transformation of American Politics* (1996).

Greene, John Robert. *The Limits of Power: The Nixon and Ford Administrations* (1992).

Kutler, Stanley. *The Wars of Watergate* (1990).

Schudson, Michael. *Watergate in American Memory: How We Remember, Forget, and Reconstruct the Past* (1992).

Jimmy Carter and His Presidency

Carter, Jimmy. *Keeping Faith: Memoirs of a President* (1982).

Glad, Betty. *Jimmy Carter, In Search of the Great White House* (1980).

Hargrove, Erwin C. *Jimmy Carter as President: Leadership and the Politics of the Public Good* (1988).

Jones, Charles O. *The Trusteeship Presidency: Jimmy Carter and the United States Congress* (1988).

Kaufman, Burton I. *The Presidency of James Earl Carter, Jr.* (1993).

Miller, William Lee. *Yankee from Georgia: The Emergence of Jimmy Carter* (1978).

Environmental Politics

Gottlieb, Robert. *Forcing the Spring: The Transformation of the American Environmental Movement* (1993).

Hays, Samuel. *Beauty, Health, and Permanence: Environmental Politics in the United States, 1955–1985* (1987).

Sale, Kirkpatrick *The Green Revolution: The American Environmental Movement, 1962–1992* (1993).

WHERE TO LEARN MORE

- *Lyndon B. Johnson National Historical Park, Johnson City, Texas.* Johnson's ranch, southwest of Austin, gives visitors a feeling for the open landscape in which Johnson spent his early years. www.nps.gov/lypo/

- *Vietnam Veterans Memorial, Washington, D.C.* A simple wall engraved with the names of the nation's Vietnam War dead is testimony to one of the nation's most divisive wars. www.nps.gov/vive/

- *Richard Nixon Library and Birthplace, Yorba Linda, California.* Exhibits trace Nixon's political career and related world events with a sympathetic interpretation. www.nixonfoundation.org/index.shtml

- *Titan Missile Museum, Green Valley, Arizona.* The Green Valley complex near Tucson held eighteen Titan missiles. They were deactivated after SALT I, and the complex is now open to visitors. www.pimaair.org/titan_01.htm.

 Please refer to the document CD-ROM for primary sources related to this chapter.

➤ *Americans in the 1980s struggled to understand the nation's place in a rapidly changing world. President Ronald Reagan appealed to traditional patriotism and vigorously asserted American power abroad at the same time that Americans were increasingly focused on the benefits of prosperity and the good life.*

THE REAGAN REVOLUTION AND A CHANGING WORLD

30

1981–1992

The Khmer Rouge marched into the city [Phnom Penh, the capital of Cambodia], dressed in black. . . . Young Khmer Rouge [Marxist revolutionary] soldiers, eight or ten years old, were dragging their rifles, which were taller than them. . . . The whole city, more than two million people was forced out of their homes into the streets. My family walked until we reached Mao Tse-Tung Boulevard, the main boulevard in Phnom Penh. All the population of the city was gathered there. The Khmer Rouge were telling everyone to leave the city.

Although my two middle children were safe in France, my oldest and youngest daughters were close beside me. Parika was only seven. Mealy, who was nineteen, carried her infant son. I kept my children huddled together. As soon as a parent let go, a child would be lost in the huge crowd. . . . And the Khmer Rouge kept ordering everybody, "You must go forward." They shot their guns in the air. Even during the middle of the night the procession was endless. The Khmer Rouge kept shooting and we kept moving forward. . . .

Recently I saw the movie *Doctor Zhivago*, about the Russian Revolution. If you compare that to what happened in Phnom Penh, the movie is only on a very small scale. Even *Killing Fields* only gives you part of the idea of what happened in Cambodia. The reality was much more incredible. . . .

CHAPTER OUTLINE

Reagan's Domestic Revolution
Reagan's Majority
The New Conservatism
Reaganomics: Deficits and Deregulation
Crisis for Organized Labor
An Acquisitive Society
Poverty amid Prosperity
Consolidating the Revolution: George Bush

The Second (Short) Cold War
Confronting the Soviet Union
Risky Business: Foreign Policy Adventures
Embracing Perestroika
Crisis and Democracy in Eastern Europe
The Persian Gulf War

Growth in the Sunbelt
The Defense Economy
New Americans
Old Gateways and New
The Graying of America

Values in Collision
Women's Rights and Public Policy
Coming Out
Churches in Change
Culture Wars

Conclusion

Each night, when we came back to the village from working in the fields, Mom would say, "Children, let's all go to sleep." She would quietly warn me that the wood had eyes and ears. She'd say, "It's nine o'clock now. Go to sleep. . . . There is nothing else to do but work. All the men are gone in our family." Mom was actually saying for the Khmer Rouge spies to hear, "They are only girls. Don't kill them. We are the only members left of the family." . . . We were lying to them about our identity. It was a horrible game.

If you hid your identity, that meant you wanted your past forgotten. We had changed from people who were intellectual, who used to think independently. . . . You became humiliated, allowed to live only as a slave. . . . We were accepted into the United States thanks to my husband's military service. . . . My daughters and I flew to the United States on July 4, 1979. . . . As we landed, I thought, "This is real freedom." . . .

I've found that America is a country where people have come from all over the world. You do your job, you get paid like anybody else, and you're accepted. But Cambodians I know in France, like my sister, feel differently. People are not accepted if they are not French. But in America you're part of the melting pot. . . . In 1983, I came to Los Angeles for my daughter Monie's wedding. I decided to stay. . . . Long Beach has the largest concentration of Cambodians in the country. I called the community center in Long Beach. They said they had no job openings. So I decided to get involved in running a store. . . . Donut shops are very American. . . .

All that refugees have is our work, our dreams. Do I still hurt from what happened in the past? When I opened my mouth to tell you my story, I don't know where my tears came from. . . .My daughters don't like to talk about the past in Cambodia. They want to forget and think about their future. They ask me why I would talk about the past with anybody. I said, "The past cannot be erased from my memory."

Celia Noup in Al Santoli, *New Americans: An Oral History* (New York, 1988).

Celia Noup taught school for twenty years in Cambodia, which borders on South Vietnam. In 1975, after a long civil war, the Communist Khmer Rouge insurgents took over Cambodia's capital, Phnom Penh, and forced its inhabitants into the countryside to work in the fields. Four years later, Noup managed to make her way to a refugee camp in neighboring Thailand and then to the United States. Here she joined hundreds of thousands of other refugees who arrived in the later 1970s and 1980s from war-devastated nations such as Cambodia, Vietnam, Laos, Ethiopia, and Afghanistan. Within a decade, she was working from 5:00 a.m. to 7:00 p.m. in her own donut shop near Los Angeles airport and worrying about helping her children buy houses.

Celia Noup's life shows some of the ways that new waves of immigration from Asia, Latin America, and Africa have changed the United States over the last generation. Immigrants fueled economic growth in the 1980s and 1990s with their labor and their drive to succeed in business. They revitalized older neighborhoods in cities from coast to coast and changed the ethnic mix of major cities. And they created new racial tensions that found their way into national political debates about immigration and into open conflict in places such as Miami and Los Angeles.

Noup's story is also a reminder of the drawn-out consequences of the U.S. involvement in Vietnam and the long shadow of the Cold War. The Cambodian civil war was fueled by reactions to the Vietnamese war and the American invasion of Cambodia in 1969. American refugee policy was humanitarian but also political, opening the door to people fleeing Communist regimes but holding it shut against refugees from right-wing dictatorships. In Washington, foreign policy decisions in the 1980s started with the desire of a new administration to reaffirm American toughness after failures in Vietnam and ended with the astonishing evaporation of the Cold War.

By the end of Ronald Reagan's presidency (1981-89), new rules governed domestic affairs as well as international relations. Since World War II, politics had followed a well-thumbed script. Lessons about full employment and social services that were accepted in 1948 still applied in 1968 or 1972. In the 1980s, however, Americans decided to reverse the growth of federal government responsibilities that had marked both Republican and Democratic administrations since the 1930s. By the 1990s, the center of U.S. politics had shifted substantially to the right, and even a "liberal" Democrat like Bill Clinton

would sound like an Eisenhower Republican. The backdrop to the political changes were massive readjustments in the American economy that began in the 1970s with the decline of heavy industry and then continued to shift employment from factory jobs to service jobs in the 1980s (Celia's Noup's small shop was part of the service economy). The ideology of unregulated markets celebrated economic success and made "yuppies" or young urban professionals the center of media attention; some of the yuppies probably grabbed a donut on their way to catch a flight from Los Angeles to New York to help close a deal. But behind the lifestyle stories was a troubling reality: a widening gap between the rich and poor. The result by 1992 was a nation that was much more secure in the world than it had been in 1980, but also more divided against itself.

KEY TOPICS

- Economic and social change during the Reagan administration
- The changing balance of American regions
- The rise of conservative thought
- The collapse of the Soviet Union and the end of the Cold War
- Instability and war in the Middle East
- Changes in the legal standing of women
- Conflict over family values and religious beliefs

REAGAN'S DOMESTIC REVOLUTION

Political change began in 1980, when Ronald Reagan and running his mate, George Bush, rode American discontent to a decisive victory in the presidential election (see Map 30–1). Building on a conservative critique of American policies and developing issues that Jimmy Carter had placed on the national agenda, Reagan presided over revolutionary changes in American government and policies. He was a "Teflon president" who managed to take credit for successes but avoid blame for problems, and he rolled to a landslide reelection in 1984 and set the stage for George Bush's victory in 1988. The consequences of his two terms included an altered role for government, powerful but selective economic growth, and a shift of domestic politics away from bread-and-butter issues toward moral or lifestyle concerns.

An unresolved question is whether Ronald Reagan planned an economic revolution, or simply presided over changes initiated by others. Most memoirs by White House insiders suggest the latter; so do journalists who titled books about the Reagan administration *Sleepwalking through History, The Acting President,* and *The Role of a Lifetime.* Even if Reagan was acting out a role that was scripted by others, however, he was a hit at the polling place. Americans, worried about inflation at home and declining power abroad, elected Reagan by voting *against* Jimmy Carter in 1980, but they enthusiastically voted *for* Reagan in 1984.

REAGAN'S MAJORITY

Ronald Reagan reinvented himself several times on his unusual journey to the White House. A product of small-town Illinois, he succeeded in Hollywood in the late 1930s as a romantic lead actor while adopting the

Chronology

1973 *Roe v. Wade:* Supreme Court struck down state laws banning abortion in the first trimester of pregnancy.

1980 Ronald Reagan is elected president.

1981 Economic Recovery and Tax Act, reducing personal income tax rates, is passed.

Reagan breaks strike by air traffic controllers.

AIDS is recognized as a new disease

1982 Nuclear freeze movement peaks.

United States begins to finance Contra rebels against the Sandinista government in Nicaragua.

Equal Rights Amendment fails to achieve ratification.

1983 241 Marines are killed by a terrorist bomb in Beirut, Lebanon.

Strategic Defense Initiative introduced.

U.S. invades Grenada.

1984 Reagan wins reelection.

1985 Mikhail Gorbachev initiates economic and political reforms in the Soviet Union.

1986 Tax Reform Act is adopted.

1987 Congress holds hearings on the Iran-Contra scandal.

Reagan and Gorbachev sign the Intermediate Nuclear Force treaty.

1988 George Bush is elected president.

1989 Communist regimes in eastern Europe collapse; Germans tear down Berlin Wall.

Financial crisis forces federal bailout of many savings and loans.

United States invades Panama to capture General Manuel Noriega.

1990 Iraq invades Kuwait; and United States sends forces to the Persian Gulf.

West Germany and East Germany reunite.

Americans with Disabilities Act is adopted.

1991 Persian Gulf War: Operation Desert Storm drives the Iraqis from Kuwait.

Soviet Union dissolves into independent nations.

Strategic Arms Reduction Treaty (START) is signed.

1992 Acquittal of officers accused of beating Rodney King triggers Los Angeles riots.

---

liberal politics common at the time. After World War II, he moved rapidly to the political right as a spokesman for big business. For several years, he traveled the country under the sponsorship of the General Electric Company, giving a standard speed that extolled the virtues of free enterprise. He entered politics with a rousing conservative speech at the 1964 Republican convention and then accepted the invitation of wealthy California Republicans to run for governor in 1966. In two terms in that office, he offered little formal leadership but spoke for a state and then a nation that were drifting toward more conservative values and expectations.

With a common touch that made him a favorite for a sizable segment of the public, Reagan tapped into the nostalgia for a simpler America. Although he was 69 when elected, his status as a movie and television personality made him seem up-to-date. His Hollywood background made it easy for him to use popular films to make his points. He once threatened to veto legislation by challenging Congress with Clint Eastwood's "Make my day." Many blockbuster movies reinforced two of Reagan's messages. One was the importance of direct confrontation with bad guys ranging from terrorists (*Die Hard*) to drug dealers (*Lethal Weapon*). The second was the incompetence of

government bureaucracies, whose elitist mistakes could only be set right by tough individuals, like the movie heroes Dirty Harry Callahan and John Rambo.

Some of Reagan's most articulate support came from anti-Communist stalwarts of both parties, who feared that the United States was losing influence in the world. Despite Jimmy Carter's tough actions in 1979 and 1980 and increased defense spending, such conservatives had not trusted him to do enough. The inability to free the hostages in Iran grated. The Panama Canal and SALT II treaties seemed to give away American power. Soviet military buildup, charged the critics, was creating a "window of vulnerability," a dangerous period when the Soviet Union might threaten the United States with a first strike by nuclear weapons.

Other Reagan voters directed their anger at government bureaucracies. Christian conservatives worried that social activists were using the federal courts to alter traditional values. Wealthy entrepreneurs from the fast-growing South and West believed that Nixon-era federal offices such as the Environmental Protection Agency and the Occupational Safety and Health Administration, were chok-

Ronald Reagan and his wife Nancy celebrate Reagan's inauguration as president.

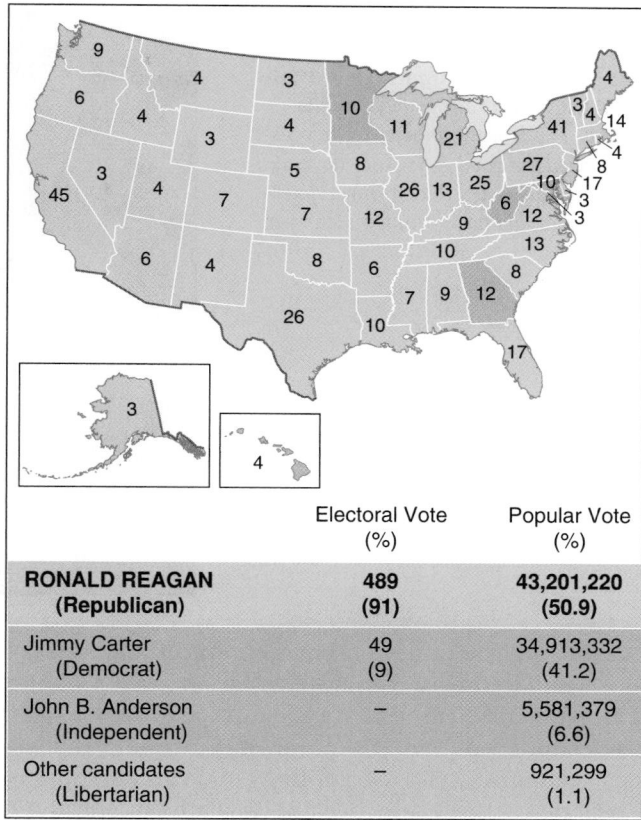

	Electoral Vote (%)	Popular Vote (%)
RONALD REAGAN (Republican)	**489 (91)**	**43,201,220 (50.9)**
Jimmy Carter (Democrat)	49 (9)	34,913,332 (41.2)
John B. Anderson (Independent)	–	5,581,379 (6.6)
Other candidates (Libertarian)	–	921,299 (1.1)

MAP 30-1   The Election of 1980
Ronald Reagan won in a landslide in 1980. Independent candidate John Anderson took more votes from Jimmy Carter than from Reagan, but Reagan's personal magnetism was a powerful political force. His victory confirmed the shift of the South to the Republican Party.

ing their businesses in red tape. Many of these critics had amassed new fortunes in oil, real estate, and retailing and hated the taxes that funded social programs. In many ways, the two groups were mismatched. Christian moralists had little in common with the high-rolling hedonists and Hollywood tycoons with whom Reagan rubbed shoulders. But they shared a deep distrust of the federal establishment.

Foreign policy activists and opponents of big government would have been unable to elect Reagan without disaffected blue-collar and middle-class voters who deserted the Democrats. Reagan's campaign hammered on the question; "Are you better off than you were four years ago?" Democrats faced a special dilemma with the deepening tension between working-class white voters and black voters. They needed both groups to win but found white blue-collar voters deeply alienated by affirmative action and busing for school integration. When pollsters read white Detroiters a statement from Robert Kennedy that called on Americans to recognize special obligations to black citizens who had endured racial discrimination, responses were vehement: "I can't go along with that!" "That's bull!" The same sorts of voters worried about inflation and blamed their difficulties on runaway government spending.

A further Democratic challenge was Ronald Reagan's personal appeal. The new president won over many Americans by surviving a 1981 assassination attempt in fine spirits. Reagan's popularity compounded the Democrats' inability to excite younger voters. The mid-1980s consistently showed that roughly two-thirds of people in their twenties and early thirties were choosing the Republicans as the party of energy and new ideas, leaving the Democrats to the middle-aged and elderly.

In the election of 1984, Democrats sealed their fate by nominating Walter Mondale, who had been vice president under Carter. Mondale was earnest, honest, and dull. Reagan ran on the theme, "It's Morning in America," with the message that a new age of pride and prosperity had begun. Mondale assumed that Americans cared enough about the exploding federal deficit that Reagan's defense spending had produced to accept an across-the-board tax increase. With the economy growing and inflation now in check, most voters did not want Mondale to remind them of long-range financial realities, and Reagan won reelection with 98 percent of the electoral votes. His election confirmed that the American public found conservative ideas increasingly attractive.

THE NEW CONSERVATISM

Reagan's approach to public policy drew on conservative intellectuals who offered a coherent critique of the New Deal–New Frontier approach to American government. Some of the leading figures were jour-

As the movie character John Rambo, actor Sylvester Stallone in the early 1980s gave voice to American frustrations with the country's place in the world. The Rambo movies clearly distinguished the good guys from the bad guys and suggested that stronger determination could have brought victory in Vietnam.

nalists and academics who had embraced the ideas of the Vital Center a generation earlier (see Chapter 27). Now they feared that the antiwar movement had undermined the anti-Communist stance and that social changes were corrupting mainstream values. *Commentary* magazine became a platform for these combative neoconservative arguments. *The Public Interest* was a new magazine for conservative or skeptical academic writers.

Downsizing the Great Society.
Worries about big government permeated the critique of domestic policy. Edward Banfield's radical ideas about the failures of the Great Society set the tone of the neoconservative analysis. In *The Unheavenly City* (1968), he questioned the basic idea of public solutions for social problems. He argued that inequality is based on human character and rooted in the basic structure of society; government action can solve only the problems that require better engineering, such as pollution control, better highways, or the delivery of explosives to military targets. Government's job, said Banfield, was to preserve public order, not to right wrongs or encourage unrealistic expectations.

Other conservative writers elaborated Banfield's ideas. The most influential was Charles Murray, whose 1984 book, *Losing Ground*, tried to do for neoconservative domestic policy what Michael Harrington's *The Other America* had done for liberal policy. Murray's basic argument was simple: Welfare assistance hurt more than it helped, by encouraging dependency and discouraging individual efforts at self-improvement. Despite massive antipoverty and welfare efforts since 1965, he contended, poverty, minority unemployment, and deviant behavior had increased rather than decreased. The blame, he said, must lie in welfare programs themselves. Scholars have shown that Murray's book distorts the evidence and makes flawed arguments, but it had a major impact on political debates.

Free market utopians.
Another strand of conservative argument came from free market utopians. After years of stagflation, Americans were eager to hear that unleashing free markets would trigger renewed prosperity. The *Wall Street Journal* evolved from a narrow business newspaper into a national conservative forum by devoting its editorial page to outspoken versions of neoconservatism. Politicians such as Congressman Jack Kemp built support for specific steps to cut economic regulation and encourage business enterprise.

The common themes of the conservative critique were simple: Free markets work better than government programs; government intervention does more harm than good; government assistance may be acceptable for property owners, but it saps the initiative of the poor. In 1964, three-quarters of Americans had trusted Washington "to do what is right." By 1980, three-quarters were convinced that the federal government wasted tax money. The neoconservatives offered the details to support Reagan's own summary: "Government is not the solution to our problems; government is the problem." The cumulative effect of the neoconservative arguments was to trash the word "liberal" and convince many Americans that labor unions and minorities were "special interests" but that oil tycoons, defense contractors, and other members of Reagan's coalition were not.

The conservative cause found support in new "think tanks" and political lobbying organizations. Many conservatives were convinced that university faculty members were hopelessly liberal. In response, wealthy businesspeople funded alternative organizations, such as the Manhattan Institute, the Heritage Foundation, and the American Enterprise Institute, where conservative analysts could take the time to develop their own policy proposals and opinion pieces for newspapers. The cumulative effect was to shift the terms of political discussion substantially in a conservative direction between 1975 and 1990.

Conservative political tactics.   Conservatives promoted their ideology with new political tactics. Targeted mailings raised funds and mobilized voters with emotional appeals while bypassing the mass media, with their supposed preference for mainstream or liberal policies. Conservative organizers also knew how to use radio call-in shows to spread their message. Such appeals contrasted with the Democrats's reliance on more traditional ways to get out the vote through personal contacts and labor unions. Through the 1980s, Democrats repeatedly found themselves blindsided by creative Republican campaign tactics.

REAGANOMICS: DEFICITS AND DEREGULATION

The heart of the 1980s revolution was the **Economic Recovery and Tax Act of 1981 (ERTA)**, which reduced personal income tax rates by 25 percent over three years. The explicit goal was to stimulate business activity by lowering taxes overall and slashing rates for the rich. Cutting the government's total income by $747 billion over five years, ERTA meant less money for federal programs and more money in the hands of consumers and investors to stimulate economic growth.

Reagan's first budget director, David Stockman, later revealed a second goal. ERTA would lock in deficits by "pulling the revenue plug." Because defense spending and Social Security were untouchable, Congress would find it impossible to create and fund new programs without cutting old ones. Compared with spending patterns in effect in 1980, the Reagan administration also shifted $70 billion per year from domestic to military programs. The first year's tax reductions were accompanied by cuts of $40 billion in federal aid to mass transit, school lunches, and similar programs. If Americans still wanted social programs, they could enact them at the local or state level, but Washington would no longer pay.

The second part of the economic agenda was to free capitalists from government regulations, in the hope of increasing business innovation and efficiency. The **deregulation** revolution built on a head start from the 1970s. A federal antitrust case had split the unified Bell System of AT&T and its subsidiaries into seven regional telephone companies and opened long-distance service to competition. Congress also deregulated air travel in 1978. During the first forty years of commercial air service, the Federal Aviation Administration had matched airlines and routes (treating air service like a public utility); deregulation now allowed air carriers to start and stop service at will, resulting in cheaper and more frequent air service for major hubs and poorer and more expensive service for small cities. Economists tend to be satisfied that the net gains have outweighed the costs.

Environmental regulation and federal lands.   Corporate America used the Reagan administration to attack environmental legislation as "strangulation by regulation." Reagan's new budgets sliced funding for the Environmental Protection Agency. Vice President Bush headed the White House Task Force on Regulatory Relief, which delayed or blocked regulations on hazardous wastes, automobile emissions, and exposure of workers to chemicals on the job.

Most attention, however, went to the controversial appointment of a Colorado lawyer, James Watt, as secretary of the interior. Watt had long worked to open up federal lands in the West to more intensive development. He was sympathetic to a western movement known as the **Sagebrush Rebellion**, which wanted the vast federal land holdings in the West transferred to the states for less environmental protection and more rapid economic use. He once blamed air pollution on natural emissions from trees and compared environmentalists to Nazis and Bolsheviks. Federal resource agencies sold trees to timber companies at a loss to the Treasury, expanded offshore oil drilling, and expedited exploration for minerals.

Deregulation of the banking industry.   The early 1980s also transformed American financial markets. Savings and loans had traditionally been conservative financial institutions that funneled individual savings into safe home mortgages. Under new rules, they began to compete for deposits by offering high interest rates and reinvested the money in much riskier commercial real estate. By 1990, the result was a financial crisis in which bad loans destroyed hundreds of S&Ls, especially in the Southwest. American taxpayers were left to bail out depositors to the tune of hundreds of billions of dollars to prevent a collapse of the nation's financial and credit system.

With the deregulation of financial markets, corporate consolidations and mergers flourished. Corporate raiders raised money with "junk bonds" —high-interest, high-risk securities—and snapped up profitable and cash-rich companies that could be milked of profits and assets. The merger mania channeled capital into paper transactions rather than investments in new equipment and products. Another effect was to damage the economies of small and middle-sized communities by transferring control of local companies to outside managers.

In the short term, the national economy boomed in the mid-1980s. Deregulated credit, tax cuts, and massive deficit spending on defense fueled exuberant growth. The decade as a whole brought nearly 20 million new jobs, especially for professional and managerial workers, office support staff, sales people, and workers providing personal services. Inflation dipped to 3 percent per year. The stock market mirrored the overall prosperity; the Dow Jones average of blue-chip industrial stock prices more than tripled from August 1982 to August 1987.

CRISIS FOR ORGANIZED LABOR

The flip side of the economic boom was another round in the Republican offensive against labor unions. Reagan set the tone when he fired more than eleven thousand members of the Professional Air Traffic Controllers Organization for violating a no-strike clause in their hiring agreements. He claimed to be enforcing the letter of the law, but the message to organized labor was clear. For many years, corporations had hesitated to hire permanent replacements for striking workers. With Reagan's example, large companies, such as Hormel and Phelps-Dodge, chose that option, undercutting the strike as an effective union strategy. During the Reagan administration, the National Labor Relations Board and other federal agencies also weakened collective bargaining by their interpretation of labor-management regulations.

Decline of union membership and blue-collar jobs.
Organized labor counted a million fewer members at the end of Reagan's administration in 1989 than in 1964, even though the number of employed Americans had nearly doubled. Many unions that had been the mainstays of the labor movement in the Roosevelt and Truman years found themselves in trouble, saddled with leaders who were unable to cope with restructuring of the economy. As union membership declined and unions struggled to cope with the changing economy, corporations seized the

opportunity to demand wage rollbacks and concessions on working conditions as trade-offs for continued employment, squeezing workers in one plant and then using the settlement to pressure another. Workers in the 1970s and 1980s faced the threat that employers might move a factory to a new site elsewhere in the United States or overseas. Or a company might sell out to a new owner, who could close a plant, and reopen without a union contract. One 16-year-old described the changes in the grocery chain where her father worked for twenty-six years: "They're letting people go with no feelings for how long they've worked there, just lay 'em off. It's sad. He should be getting benefits after all these years and all the sacrifices he's made. Now they're almost ready to lay him off without a word."

Another cause for shrinking union membership was the overall decline of blue-collar jobs, from 36 percent of the American work force in 1960 to roughly 25 percent at the end of the 1990s. Unionization of white-collar workers made up only part of the loss from manufacturing. Unions were most successful in recruiting government workers, such as police officers, teachers, and bus drivers. By the late 1980s, the American Federation of State, County, and Municipal Employees had twice the membership of the United Steel Workers. In the private sector, however, many white-collar jobs were in small firms and offices that were difficult to organize.

Impact of economic restructuring. Popular culture's best take on the problems of blue collar America was the television situation comedy *Roseanne* (1988–97). Living in an industrial satellite of Chicago, Roseanne and Dan Conner struggle to raise a family on the income from a series of jobs as small business owner, assembly-line worker, waitress, skilled laborer. The lifelong unionized factory job is a thing of the past as the shifting economy makes it hard to accumulate savings and stay ahead of the financial crises of normal life, let alone keep kids in college. A telling statistic about the problems of the real equivalents of the "Conners" was the increase in personal bankruptcy filings from roughly 300,000 per year in the early 1980s to 1,200,000 per year by the later 1990s.

The community depicted in *Roseanne* represented the impacts of economic restructuring on the blue-collar success story of the 1950s and 1960s when increasing productivity, expanding markets for U.S. goods, and strong labor unions had made it possible for factory workers to enter the middle class. In an era of deindustrialization, however, companies replaced machine operators, assemblers, inspectors, and other

The working class family depicted on the television show Roseanne *offered viewers a glimpse of the problems facing many Americans in an era of economic change marked by deindustrialization and the rise of service jobs.*

production workers with more sophisticated machinery or shifted production to nonunion plants. The corporate merger mania of the 1980s added to instability when takeover specialists loaded old companies with new debt, triggering efforts to cut labor costs, sell off plants, or raid pension funds for cash to pay the interest. Manufacturing employment in the 1980s declined by nearly 2 million jobs, with the expansion of high tech manufacturing concealing much higher losses in traditional industries. In sum, while corporate merger specialists steered their BMWs along the fast lane to success, displaced mill hands drove battered pickups along potholed roads to nowhere.

AN ACQUISITIVE SOCIETY

The new prosperity fueled lavish living by the wealthy and a fascination with the "lifestyles of the rich and famous." The television show of the same name, which premiered in 1984, offered its viewers glimpses of "champagne wishes" and "caviar dreams" as lived by entertainment stars and business tycoons. Prime time soap operas flourished, bringing to the small screen stories of intrigue among the rich folks of fast-growing Texas in *Dallas* (1978–91), Colorado in *Dynasty* (1981–89), and California in *Knots Landing* (1979–93). With a few exceptions, even the "middle class" in television sitcoms enjoyed lives available only to the top 20 percent of Americans.

The national media in the early 1980s discovered "yuppies," or young urban professionals, who were both a marketing category and a symbol of social change. These upwardly mobile professionals supposedly defined themselves by elitist consumerism. Such middle-line retailers as Sears had clothed Americans for decades and furnished their homes. With the help of catalog shopping, status-seeking consumers now flocked to such upscale retailers as Neiman-Marcus and Bloomingdale's. Yuppie as a marketing category meanwhile spawned variations, such as "buppie" for black urban professional. It was difficult for most Americans to feel much sympathy for the family in a *New York Times* profile in 1987 who had difficulty making ends meet on $600,000 a year.

Far richer than even such atypical yuppies were wheeler-dealers who made themselves into media stars of finance capitalism. The autobiography of Lee Iacocca, who had helped revive the fortunes of the Chrysler Corporation, was a bestseller in 1984, portraying the corporate executive as hero. *Forbes* magazine began to publish an annual list of the nation's 400 richest people. The real-estate developer Donald Trump made himself a celebrity with a well-publicized personal life and a stream of projects crowned with his name: office tower, hotel, casino. Before he admitted to violating the law against profiting from insider information, the corporate-merger expert Ivan Boesky had told a business-school audience; "Greed is all right. . . . You shouldn't feel guilty," epitomizing an era of big business takeovers driven by paper profits rather than underlying economic fundamentals. Hollywood portrayed this era of corporate takeovers in the 1987 film *Wall Street*. The actor Michael Douglas

"They're museum quality!"

This 1993 cartoon contrasting a yuppie couple and a family dressed as hippies makes two points. While highlighting the rapid changes in American styles and tastes from the 1970s to the 1990s, it also satirizes the supposed yuppie tendency to value everything as a commodity or "collectible."

plays Gordon Gekko, a Boesky-like character who mesmerizes an audience of shareholders when he intones, "Greed is good."

The superficial glamour of this era of acquisitiveness and corporate greed had its underside of loneliness and despair. Young novelists in the 1980s explored the emptiness of life among the privileged, repeating some of the themes of the 1920s in the process. Bret Easton Ellis in *Less Than Zero* (1985) dissected the despair and drug habits of college students from the affluent west side of Los Angeles. *In Bright Lights, Big City* (1986), Jay McInerney took on the same problems of glamour and depression among young professionals in New York, where the real incomes of people on the lower third of the economic ladder declined during the 1980s, while those of the top 10 percent rose by 40 percent. Novelist Tom Wolfe fictionalized the cold statistics in his bestselling novel *The Bonfire of the Vanities* (1987), depicting a New York where the art dealers and stockbrokers of glitzy Manhattan meet the poor of the devastated South Bronx only through an automobile accident to their mutual incomprehension and ruin.

New movements in popular music reacted to the acquisitive 1980s. Punk rock pared rock-and-roll to its basics, lashing out at the emptiness of 1970s disco sounds and the commercialization of youth culture. Punk music influenced grunge bands such as Nirvana, which expressed alienation from consumerism. Hip-Hop originated among African Americans and

Latinos in New York, soon adding the angry and often violent lyrics of rap. Rap during the 1980s was about personal power and sex, but it also dealt with social inequities and deprivation and tapped some of the same anger and frustration that had motivated black power advocates in the 1960s. It crossed into the mainstream culture with the help of MTV, which had begun broadcasting in 1981, but it retained a hard-edged "attitude" that undercut any sense of complacency about an inclusive American society.

POVERTY AMID PROSPERITY

Federal tax and budget changes had different effects on the rich and poor. (see Figure 30–1) Popular attention to the lifestyles of upscale Manhattan and Beverly Hills obscured the economic realities for many Americans. Those in the top fifth increased their share of after-tax income relative to everyone else during the 1980s, and the richest 1 percent saw their share of all privately held wealth grow from 31 percent to 37 percent. The 1981 tax cuts also came with sharp increases in the Social Security tax, which hit lower-income workers the hardest. The tax changes meant that the average annual income of households in the bottom 20 percent *declined* and that many actually paid higher taxes.

The budget changes that fueled conspicuous consumption put pressure on American cities. Cities and their residents absorbed approximately two-thirds of the cuts in the 1981-1982 federal budget.

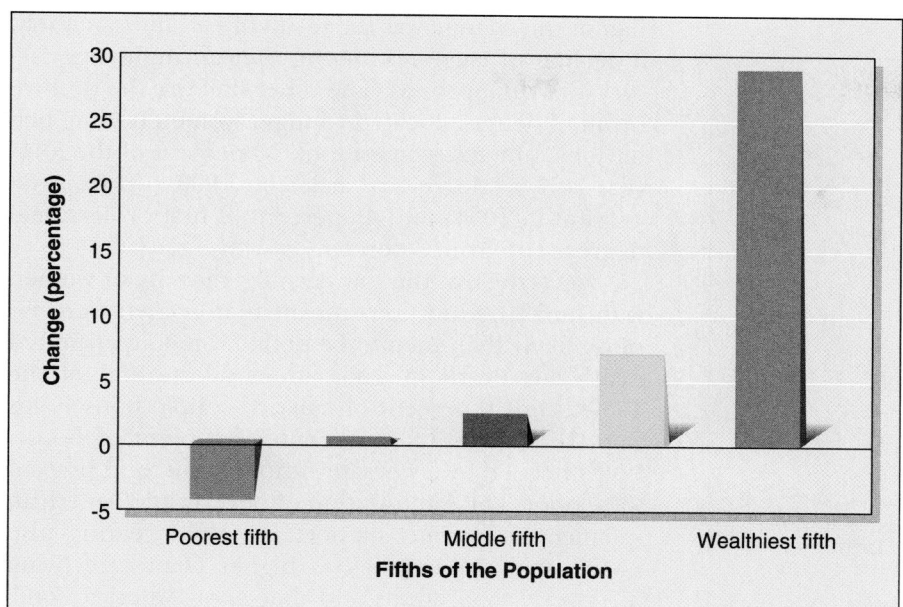

FIGURE 30-1 Changes in Real Family Income, 1980-1990
In the 1980s, the poor got poorer, the middle class made slight gains, and the most affluent 20 percent of the American people did very well. Tax changes that helped well-off households were one factor. Another factor was the erosion of "family-wage jobs" in manufacturing.

Provisions for accelerated depreciation (tax write-offs) of factories and equipment in the 1981 tax act encouraged the abandonment of center-city factories in favor of new facilities in the suburbs. One result was a growing jobs-housing mismatch. There were often plenty of jobs in the suburbs, but the poorer people who most needed the jobs were marooned in city slums and dependent on public transit that seldom served suburban employers.

Federal tax and spending policies in the 1980s decreased the security of middle-class families. As the economy continued to struggle through deindustrialization, average wage rates fell in the 1980s when measured in real purchasing. The squeeze put pressure on traditional family patterns and pushed into the workforce women who might otherwise have stayed home. Even with two incomes, many families found it hard to buy a house because of skyrocketing prices in urban markets and sky-high interest rates. The national home ownership rate actually fell for the first time in almost fifty years, from 66 to 64 percent of American households. Many Americans no longer expected to surpass their parents' standard of living.

Corporate downsizing and white-collar jobs.
Lower-paying office jobs fell under the same sorts of pressure as factory jobs. Banks substituted ATMs for tellers, telephone companies replaced operators with automated information lines, and credit card companies computerized their operations to eliminate hand sorting of charge slips. Increasing numbers of clerical and office workers were "temps" who shifted from job to job. Organizations of all sorts, from corporations to universities, realized that a shift toward temporary

and part-time workers not only kept wages low but also allowed less spending on health insurance and other benefits.

The chill of corporate "downsizing" hit white-collar families most heavily toward the end of the 1980s. Big business consolidations delivered improved profits by squeezing the ranks of middle managers as well as assembly-line workers. With fewer workers to supervise and with new technologies to collect and distribute information, companies could complete their cost cutting by trimming administrators. Takeovers sometimes meant the elimination of the entire management and support staff of target companies. In the 1950s, a college graduate could sign on with a large corporation like IBM or General Motors, advance through the ranks, and expect to retire from the same company. Now the expectation of a "job for life" looked dubious; AT&T, for one example, eliminated 76,000 jobs—one-fifth of its total—between 1985 and 1989. Those white-collar workers whose jobs survived clung to them more firmly than ever. The combined result was to clog the ladder of economic opportunity for college graduates, making the cab-driving Ph.D. and the *barrista* with the B.A. popular clichés.

Increase in the poverty rate.
At the lower end of the economic ladder, the proportion of Americans living in poverty increased. After declining steadily from 1960 to a low of 11 percent in 1973, the poverty rate climbed back to the 13 to 15 percent range. Although the economy in the 1980s created lots of new jobs, half of them paid less than poverty-level wages. Conservative critics began to talk about an underclass of

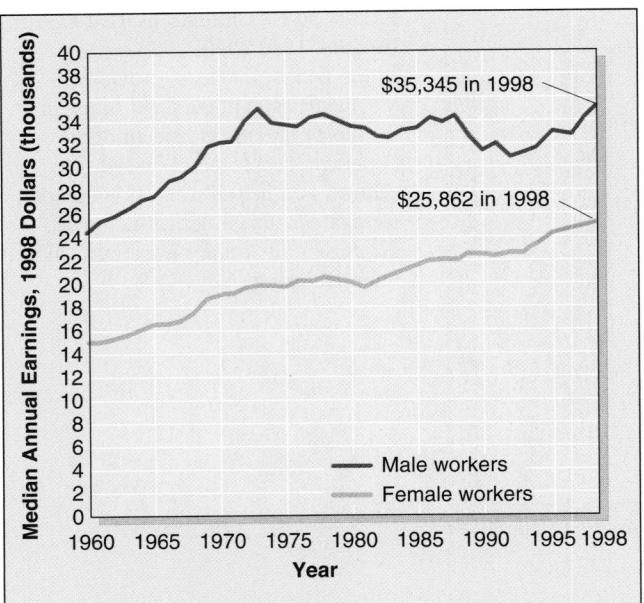

FIGURE 30-2 **Median Salary of Women and Men, 1960-1998**
Since the 1960s, the gap between the earnings of women and men working full time and year-round has narrowed. One reason is better pay for jobs traditionally considered "women's work," but another has been the declining earning power of men without college educations. Nevertheless, the gender gap in earning power remain an important economic problem.

Americans permanently outside the mainstream economy because of poor education, drug abuse, or sheer laziness. In fact, talk of an underclass was a way to avoid confronting the realities of limited economic opportunity. Most of the nation's millions of poor people lived in households with employed adults. In 1992, fully 18 percent of all full-time jobs did not pay enough to lift a family of four out of poverty, a jump of 50 percent over the proportion of underpaid jobs in. One of the biggest barriers to better employment was not a disinterest in work, but rather the isolation of many job seekers in poverty neighborhoods without access to suburban jobs or the informal social networks that are the best way to find good employment.

The wage gap and the feminization of poverty.

Nor could most women, even those working full time, expect to earn as much as men. In the 1960s and 1970s, the average working woman earned just 60 percent of the earnings of the average man (see Figure 30-2). Only part of the wage gap could be explained by measurable factors, such as education or experience. The gap narrowed in the 1980s, with women's earnings rising to 74 percent of men's by 1996 but falling back to 72 percent in 2000. About half of the change was the result of bad news, namely, a decline of earnings among men as high-wage factory jobs disappeared. The other half was the positive result of better-educated younger women finding better jobs. Indeed, women took 56 percent of the four-year college degrees awarded in 1998 (up from 38 percent in 1960) and 43 percent of first professional degrees (up from 3 percent).

Nevertheless, the low earning capacity of women with limited educations meant that women were far more likely than men to be poor. Women constituted nearly two-thirds of poor adults at the end of the 1980s. Only 6 percent of married-couple households were below poverty level, but 32 percent of households headed by a woman without a husband present were poor. The feminization of poverty and American reliance on private support for child rearing also meant that children had a higher chance of living in poverty than adults and that poor American children were worse off than their peers in other advanced nations.

Homelessness in America.

Falling below even the working poor were growing numbers of homeless Americans. Large cities have always had transient laborers, derelict alcoholics. and voluntarily homeless hobos. In the 1980s, several factors made homelessness more visible and pressing. A new approach to the treatment of the mentally ill reduced the population of mental hospitals from 540,000 in 1960 to only 140,000 in 1980. Deinstitutionalized patients were supposed to receive community-based treatment, but many ended up on the streets and in overnight shelters. New forms of self-destructive drug abuse, such as crack addiction, joined alcoholism. A boom in downtown real estate destroyed old skid-row districts with their bars, missions, and dollar-a-night hotels.

These factors tripled the number of permanently homeless people during the early and middle 1980s, from 200,000 to somewhere between 500,000 to 700,000. Twice or three times that many may have been homeless for part of a given year. For every person in a shelter on a given night, two people were sleeping on sidewalks, in parks, in cars, and in abandoned buildings. Because homeless people made middle-class Americans uncomfortable, it was reassuring to assume they were outsiders attracted by local conditions, such as tolerant attitudes (as some claimed in Seattle) or mild climate (as some claimed in Phoenix). In fact, few among the down-and-out have the resources to move from town to town. Bag ladies, panhandlers, working people, and yuppies were all parts of the same communities, neighbors in the broadest sense.

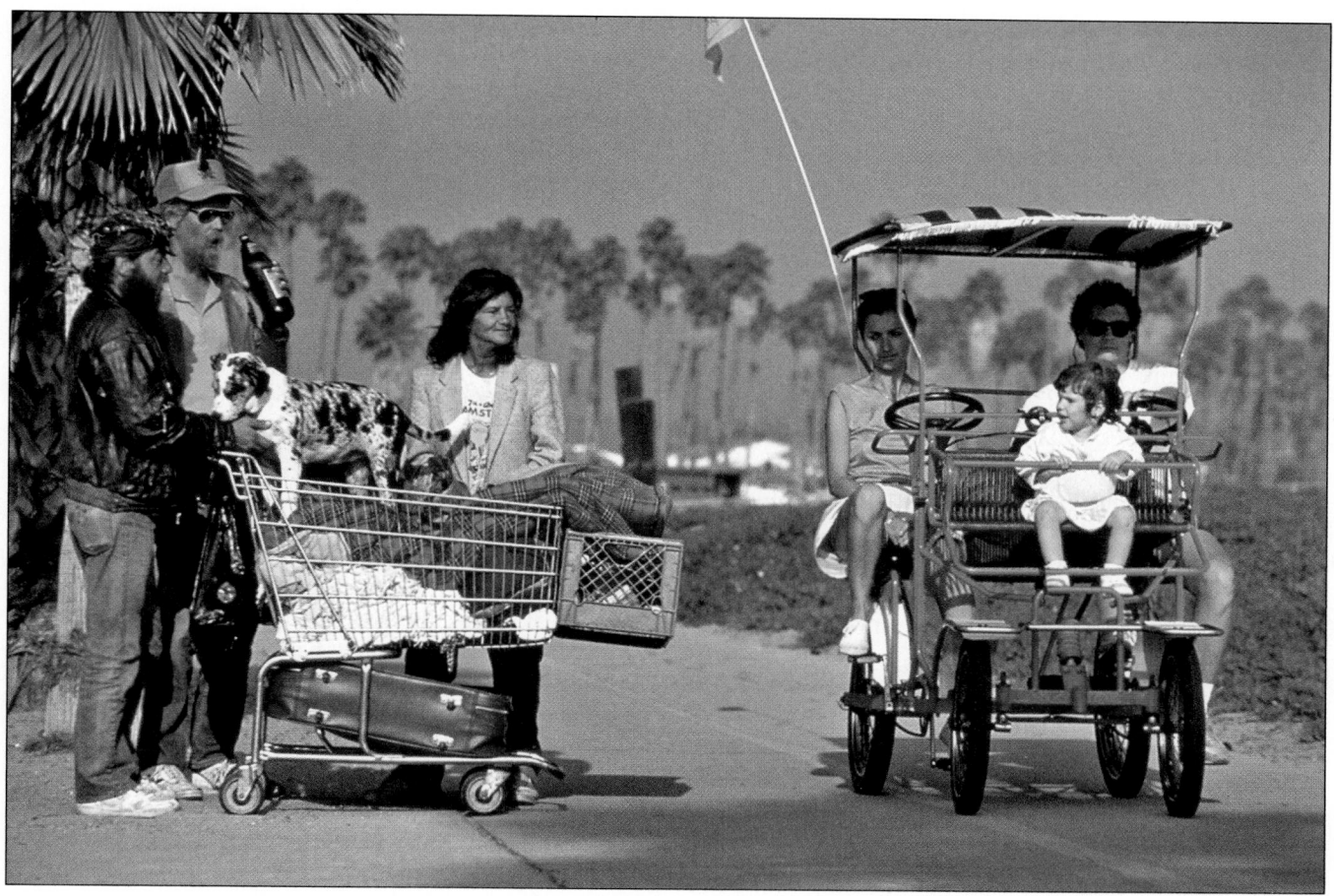

An affluent family pedals by a group of homeless people in Santa Barbara, California. In the 1980s a combination of rising housing prices and the closure of most mental hospitals pushed increasing numbers of Americans onto the streets. Estimates of the number of homeless Americans in the late 1980s ranged from 300,000 to 3 million, depending on the definition of homelessness and the political goals of the estimator.

CONSOLIDATING THE REVOLUTION: GEORGE BUSH

In 1988 George Bush, Reagan's vice-president for 8 years, won the presidential election with 56 percent of the popular vote and 40 out of 50 states. Bush's view of national and world politics reflected a background in which personal connections counted. He was raised as part of the New England elite, built an oil business in Texas, and then held a series of high-level federal appointments. As someone who had survived twenty years of bureaucratic infighting, his watchword was prudence. Using a comparison from baseball, Bush described himself as the sort of guy who would play the averages and "bunt 'em over" rather than go for the big inning.

Michael Dukakis, the Democratic nominee in 1988, was a dry-as-dust, by-the-numbers manager who offered the American people "competence." The Bush campaign director, Lee Atwater, looked for "hot-but-ton" issues that could fit onto a three-by-five card. He found that Dukakis as governor of Massachusetts had delayed cleanup of Boston Harbor, favored gun control, and had vetoed a bill requiring schoolchildren to recite the Pledge of Allegiance (arguing correctly that it would be overturned in the courts). Even more damaging was that Massachusetts officials had allowed a murderer named Willie Horton a weekend furlough from prison, during which he had committed a brutal rape. Pro-Bush advertisements tapped into real worries among the voters—fear of crime, racial tension (Horton was black), worry about eroding social values. George Bush, despite his background in prep schools and country clubs, came out looking tough as nails, while the Democrats looked inept.

The ads locked Bush into a rhetorical war on crime and drugs that was his major domestic policy. Americans had good cause to be worried about public safety, but most were generally unaware that the likelihood of becoming the target of a violent crime had leveled off and would continue to fall in the 1990s or that crime was far worse in minority communities than elsewhere, in part due to gang- and drug-related activities.

The Bush administration stepped up the fight against illegal drugs and the federal drug-control budget tripled. In the early 1980s, a quarter of federal prison inmates were in jail for drug offenses. Longer sentences, mandatory jail time, and tougher parole terms for drug crimes pushed the proportion over 50 percent by 1990. The United States tried to stop the flow of cocaine by blockading its borders with airplanes, sea patrols, and specially trained dogs at airport customs lines. Casual and middle-class use of cocaine and marijuana began to decline in the mid-1980s. Drug use and drug sales were increasingly a problem of poor and minority neighborhoods.

George Bush believed that Americans wanted government to leave them alone. He ignored a flood of new ideas from entrepreneurial conservatives, such as HUD Secretary Jack Kemp. The major legislation from the Bush administration were a transportation bill that shifted federal priorities from highway building toward mass transit and the **Americans with Disabilities Act** (1990) to prevent discrimination against people with physical handicaps. In the areas of crime and health care, however, Bush's lack of leadership left continuing problems.

The same attitude produced weak economic policies. The national debt had amounted to 50 percent of personal savings in 1980 but swelled to 125 percent by 1990. The massive budget deficits of the 1980s combined with growing trade deficits to turn the United States from an international creditor to a debtor nation. When Reagan took office, foreigners owed the United States and its citizens the equivalent of $2,500 for every American family. When Bush took office, the United States had used up its foreign assets and become the world's biggest debtor, with liabilities that averaged $7,000 per family. After pledging "no new taxes" in his campaign, Bush backed into a tax increase in 1990. A strong leader might have justified the taxes to the nation, but voters found it hard to forget the president's waffling and attempts to downplay the importance of his decision.

The most conspicuous domestic event of the Bush administration—the "Rodney King riot" of April 1992 in Los Angeles—was a reminder of the nation's inattention to the problems of race and poverty. Rodney King was a black motorist who had been savagely clubbed and kicked by police officers while being arrested after a car chase on March 3, 1991. A nearby resident captured the beating on videotape from his apartment. Within two days, the tape was playing and replaying on national television. The grainy pictures shocked the nation and confirmed the worst black fears about biased police behavior. Early the next year, the four officers stood trial for unjustified use of force before a suburban jury. The televised trial and the unexpected verdict of not guilty on April 29 stirred deep anger that escalated into four days of rioting.

The disorder revealed multiple tensions among ethnic groups and was far more complex than the Watts outbreak of 1965. African Americans from south central Los Angeles participated, but so did Central American and Mexican immigrants in adjacent districts, who accounted for about one third of the 12,000 arrests. The disorder spread south to Long Beach and north to the edge of upscale neighborhoods in Westwood and Beverly Hills. Rioters assaulted the downtown police headquarters, city hall, and the *Los Angeles Times* building. As in 1965, some targets were white passers-by and symbols of white authority. But members of competing minority groups were also victims as angry black people targeted hundreds of Korean-owned and Vietnamese-owned shops as symbols of economic discrimination. Four days of disorder left fifty-eight people dead, mostly African Americans and Latinos.

THE SECOND (SHORT) COLD WAR

Ronald Reagan entered office determined to reassert U.S. leadership in world affairs and not to lose the Cold War. He considered the Soviet Union not a co-equal nation with legitimate world interests but an "evil empire," like something from the *Star Wars* movies. After the era of *détente*, global tensions had started to mount in the late 1970s. They were soon higher than they had been since the 1960s. But by the end of Reagan's two terms, unexpected changes were rapidly bringing the Cold War to an end, and George Bush faced a radically new set of foreign-policy issues.

CONFRONTING THE SOVIET UNION

Who renewed the Cold War after Nixon's diplomacy of *détente* and Carter's early efforts at negotiation? The Soviets had pursued military expansion in the 1970s, triggering the fear that they might stage a nuclear Pearl Harbor. The Soviet Union in 1980 was supporting Marxist regimes in civil wars in Angola, Ethiopia, Nicaragua, and especially Afghanistan, where its 1980 intervention led to a decade of costly and futile military occupation. Were these actions parts of a careful plan? Or did they result from the Cold War inertia of a rudderless nation that reacted to situations one at a time? Given the aging Soviet leadership and the economic weaknesses revealed in the late 1980s, it makes more sense to see the Soviets as muddling along rather than executing a well-planned global strategy.

On the American side, Reagan's readiness to confront "the focus of evil in the modern world" reflected the views of many conservative supporters that the Soviet Union was a monolithic and ideologically motivated foe bent on world conquest. In hindsight, some Reaganites claim that the administration's foreign policy and massive increases in defense spending were part of a deliberate and coordinated scheme to check a Soviet offensive and bankrupt the Soviet Union by pushing it into a new arms race. It is just as likely, however, that the administration's defense and foreign policy initiatives were a set of discrete but effective decisions.

The Reagan administration reemphasized central Europe as the focus of superpower rivalry, just as it had been in the 1950s and early 1960s. To counter improved Soviet armaments, the United States began to place cruise missiles and midrange Pershing II missiles in Europe in 1983. NATO governments approved the action, but it frightened millions of their citizens. By the mid-1980s, many Europeans saw the United States as the dangerous and aggressive force in world affairs and the Soviet Union as the voice of moderation—international attitudes that continue to this day.

The controversy over new missiles was part of new thinking about nuclear strategy. Multiple warheads on U.S. missiles already allowed Washington to target 25,000 separate places in the Soviet Union. National Security Directive D-13 (1981) set forth a new doctrine that it might be possible to fight and win a nuclear war, despite its enormous costs. A reactivated civil-defense program also suggested that the United States was serious about nuclear war. All Americans needed for survival, said one administration official, were "enough shovels" to dig fallout shelters.

Escalation of the nuclear arms race reinvigorated the antiwar and antinuclear movement in the United States as well as Europe. Drawing on the experience of the antiwar movement, the nuclear-freeze campaign caught the imagination of many Americans in 1981 and 1982. It sought to halt the manufacture and deployment of new atomic weapons by the great powers. The movement gained urgency when distinguished scientists argued that the smoke and dust thrown up by an atomic war would devastate the ecology of the entire globe by triggering "nuclear winter." Nearly a million people turned out for a nuclear-freeze rally in New York in 1982. Hundreds of local communities endorsed the freeze or took the symbolic step of declaring themselves "nuclear-free zones."

In response, Reagan announced the **Strategic Defense Initiative (SDI)** or "Star Wars" program in 1983. SDI was to deploy new defenses that could intercept and destroy ballistic missiles as they rose from the ground and arced through space. Ideas included superlasers, killer satellites, and clouds of projectiles to rip missiles to shreds before they neared their targets. All of the technologies were untested; some existed only in the imagination. Few scientists thought that SDI could work. Many arms control experts thought that defensive systems were dangerous and destabilizing, because strong defenses suggested that a nation might be willing to risk a nuclear exchange. Nevertheless, President Reagan found SDI appealing, for it offered a way around the balance of terror.

RISKY BUSINESS: FOREIGN-POLICY ADVENTURES

The same administration that sometimes seemed reckless in its grand strategy also took risks to assert U.S. influence in global trouble spots to block or roll back Soviet influence. Reagan asserted America's right to intervene anywhere in the world to support local groups who were fighting against Marxist governments. The assumption underlying this assertion, which later became known as the **Reagan Doctrine**, was that Soviet-influenced governments in Asia, Africa, and Latin America needed to be eliminated if the United States was to win the Cold War.

Nevertheless, Reagan kept the United States out of a major war and backed off in the face of serious trouble. Foreign interventions were designed to achieve symbolic victories rather than change the global balance of power. The exception was the Caribbean and Central America, the "backyard" where the United States had always claimed an overriding interest and where left-wing action infuriated Reagan's conservative supporters.

On October 25, 1983, for example, U.S. troops invaded the small independent Caribbean island of Grenada. A left-leaning government had invited Cuban help in building an airfield, which the United States feared would turn into a Cuban military base. Two thousand American troops overcame Cuban soldiers who were thinly disguised as construction workers, "rescued" American medical students, and put a more sympathetic and locally popular government in power.

Intervention and covert activities in Central America. The Reagan administration attributed political turmoil in Central America to Soviet influence and to arms and agitators from Soviet-backed Cuba. Between

1980 and 1983, the United States sent more military aid to conservative governments and groups in Central America than it had during the previous thirty years. Indeed, Central America became the focus of a secret foreign policy operated by the CIA and then by National Security Council (NSC) staff, since a Democratic Congress was not convinced of the danger. The CIA and the NSC engaged not just in espionage but in direct covert operations. The chief target was Nicaragua, the Central American country where leftist Sandinista rebels had overthrown the Somoza dictatorship in 1979. Reagan and his people were determined to prevent Nicaragua from becoming "another Cuba," especially when Sandinistas helped left-wing insurgents in neighboring El Salvador. In the early 1980s, Reagan approved CIA plans to arm and organize approximately 10,500 so-called Contras, from the remnants of Somoza's national guard. From bases in Honduras, the Contras harassed the Sandinistas with sabotage and raids. Reagan called the Contras "freedom fighters," listened to stories of their exploits, and hunched over maps to follow their operations in detail. Meanwhile, Americans with different views aided refugees from the war zones of Central America through the church-based sanctuary movement ("sanctuary" could imply both legal economic assistance and direct defiance of efforts to deport refugees).

The Reagan administration bent the law to support this covert effort to overthrow the Sandinista regime. An unsympathetic Congress blocked U.S. funding for the Contras. In response, CIA director William Casey directed Lieutenant Colonel Oliver North of the National Security Council staff to illegally organize aid from private donors. The arms pipeline operated until a supply plane was shot down in 1986. The Contras failed as a military effort, but the civil war and international pressure persuaded the Sandinistas to allow free elections that led to a democratic, centrist government.

The war against drugs.

The American war against drugs was simultaneously shaping U.S. policy in the Caribbean and straining relations with Latin America. The United States pressured South American nations such as Colombia and Peru, to uproot coca plants grown by poor farmers. As president, George Bush also parlayed the war on drugs into war on Panama during his first year in office. General Manuel Noriega, the Panamanian strongman, had once been on the CIA payroll. He had since turned to international drug sales in defiance of United States antismuggling efforts. On December 20, 1989, American troops invaded Panama, hunted down Noriega, and brought him back to stand trial in the United States on drug-trafficking charges. A handful

of Americans and thousands of Panamanians died, many of them civilians caught in crossfire.

Intervention in the Middle East.

If the results of intervention in Nicaragua and Panama were mixed, intervention in the Middle East was a failure. In 1982 Israel invaded Lebanon, a small nation to its north, to clear Palestinian guerrillas from its borders and to set up a friendly Lebanese government. The Israeli army bogged down in a civil war between Christian Arabs and Muslims. Reagan sent U.S. Marines to preserve the semblance of a Lebanese state and to provide a face-saving exit for Israel. Although the Marines arrived in Beirut to interpose themselves between Israeli tanks and the Lebanese, they remained on an ill-defined "presence mission" that angered Arabs and motivated terrorist actions against Israel and the U.S. among Islamic radicals. In October 1983, a terrorist car bomb killed 241 Marines in their barracks. The remainder were soon gone, confirming the Syrian observation that Americans were "short of breath" when it came to Middle East politics. The debacle in Lebanon undermined United States-backed peace initiatives in the Middle East. Continuing terrorist acts such as taking Americans hostage, bombing cruise ships, and sabotaging airliners were aiming at inhibiting U.S. support of Israel.

The Iran-Contra Affair.

Even less effective were the Reagan administration's secret efforts to sell weapons to Iran in return for Iranian help in securing the release of Americans held hostage by pro-Iranian Islamic radicals in Lebanon. The United States in 1985 joined Israel in selling five hundred antitank missiles to Iran, then embroiled in a long, bitter war with Iraq. The deal followed stern public pronouncements that the United States would never negotiate with terrorists—and considered Iran's religious leaders to be backers of international terrorism. It also violated this nation's official trade embargo against Iran that had been in place since the U.S. embassy seizure in 1980. In May 1986, National Security adviser Robert McFarlane flew to Iran for more arms-for-hostages talks, carrying a chocolate cake and a Bible autographed by Reagan to present to the Iranian leader Ayatollah Khomeini. The pro-Iranian radicals released several hostages, but others were soon taken. When the deals came to light in 1986 and Congressional hearings were held in the summer of 1987, Americans were especially startled to learn that Colonel North had funneled millions of dollars from the arms sales to the Nicaraguan Contras, in a double evasion of the law.

As had been true with Watergate, the Iran-Contra affair was a two-sided scandal. First was the blatant misjudgment of operating a secret, bumbling, and unlawful foreign policy that depended on international arms dealers and ousted Nicaraguan military officers. Second was a concerted effort to cover up the illegal and unconstitutional actions. North shredded relevant documents and lied to Congress. In his final report in 1994, Special Prosecutor Lawrence Walsh found that President Reagan and Vice President Bush were aware of much that went on and participated in efforts to withhold information and mislead Congress.

U.S. policy in Asia. American policy in Asia was a refreshing contrast with practices in Central America and the Middle East. In the Philippines, American diplomats helped push corrupt President Ferdinand Marcos out and opened the way for a popular uprising to put Corazon Aquino in office. Secretary of State George Shultz made sure that the United States supported popular democracy while reassuring the Philippine military. In South Korea, the United States similarly helped ease out an unpopular dictator by firmly supporting democratic elections that brought in a more popular but still pro-United States government.

EMBRACING *PERESTROIKA*

Thaw in the Cold War started in Moscow. Mikhail Gorbachev became general secretary of the Communist Party in 1985, when the Soviet Union was trapped in the sixth year of its failed attempt to control Afghanistan. Gorbachev was the picture of vigor compared to his three elderly predecessors. A master of public relations who charmed western Europe's leaders and public, he was also a modernizer in a long Russian tradition that stretched back to Tsar Peter the Great in the eighteenth century. Gorbachev startled Soviet citizens by urging *glasnost,* or political openness with free discussion of issues and relaxation of controls on the press. He followed by setting the goal of *perestroika,* or restructuring of the painfully bureaucratic Soviet economy that was falling behind capitalist nations. His hope was that market-oriented reforms would help the Soviet Union keep up with the United States.

Gorbachev decided that he needed to reduce the crushing burden of Soviet defense spending if the Soviet Union was to have any chance of modernizing. During Reagan's second term, the Soviets offered one concession after another in a drive for arms control. They agreed to cut the number of land-based strategic weapons in half. They gave up their demand for an end to SDI research. In negotiations on conventional forces in Europe, they accepted bigger cuts for the Warsaw Pact nations than for NATO. They even agreed to on-site inspections to control chemical weapons.

Mikhail Gorbachev and Ronald Reagan sign the Intermediate Nuclear Forces treaty at the White House in 1987. The treaty marked a radical transformation in Reagan's approach to relations with the Soviet Union and lessened the military tension between NATO and the Soviet bloc in Europe.

Reagan had the vision (or audacity) to embrace the new Soviet position. He cast off decades of belief in the dangers of Soviet Communism and took Gorbachev seriously. One of his reasons for SDI had been his personal belief that the abolition of nuclear weapons was better than fine-tuning the balance of terror. Now he was willing to forget his own rhetoric. He frightened his own staff when he met with Gorbachev in the summer of 1986 and accepted the principle of deep cuts in strategic forces. Reagan explained that when he railed against the "evil empire," he had been talking about Brezhnev and the bad old days; Gorbachev and *glasnost* were different.

In the end, Reagan negotiated the **Intermediate Nuclear Force Agreement (INF)** over the strong objections of the CIA and the Defense Department. INF was the first true nuclear disarmament treaty (see the Overview table, "Controlling Nuclear Weapons: Four Decades of Progress"). Previous agreements had only slowed the growth of nuclear weapons; they were "speed limits" for the arms race. The new pact matched Soviet SS-20s with American cruise missiles as an entire class of weapons that would be destroyed, with on-site inspections for verification.

CRISIS AND DEMOCRACY IN EASTERN EUROPE

President Bush loved to run the world by Rolodex. When someone's name came up at a formal dinner, he was likely to grab a phone and call the person up. When Congress was heading in the wrong direction, he started dialing senators and representatives. When a crisis threatened world peace, he would start chatting with presidents and prime ministers. He viewed diplomacy as a series of conversations and friendships

Overview

Controlling Nuclear Weapons: Four Decades of Progress

Limiting the Testing of Nuclear Weapons	Limited Test Ban Treaty (1963)	Banned nuclear testing in the atmosphere, ocean, and outer space.
	Comprehensive Test Ban Treaty (1996)	Bans all nuclear tests, including underground tests. Rejected by U.S. Senate in 1999.
Halting the Spread of Nuclear Weapons	Nuclear Non-Proliferation Treaty (1968)	Pledged five recognized nuclear nations (United States, Soviet Union, Britain, France, China) to pursue disarmament in good faith, and 140 other nations not to acquire nuclear weapons.
	Strategic Arms Limitation Treaty (SALT I, 1972)	Limited the number of nuclear-armed missiles and bombers maintained by the United States and Soviet Union. Closely associated with United States-Soviet Union agreement to limit deployment of antiballistic missile systems to one site each.
	Strategic Arms Limitation Treaty (SALT II, 1979)	Further limited the number of nuclear-armed missiles and bombers. Not ratified but followed by Carter and Reagan administrations.
Reducing the Number of Nuclear Weapons	Intermediate Nuclear Force Agreement (1987)	Required the United States to eliminate 846 nuclear armed cruise missiles, and the Soviet Union to eliminate 1,846 SS-20 missiles.
	Strategic Arms Reduction Treaty (START I, 1991)	By July 1999, led to reductions of approximately 2,750 nuclear warheads by the United States and 3,725 warheads by the nations of the former USSR.
	Strategic Arms Reduction Treaty (START II, 1993)	Set further cuts in nuclear arsenals. Ratified by Russia in April 2000.

Data Source: Warhead data from Arms Control Association.

among leaders, not the reconciliation of differing national interests.

As a believer in personal diplomacy, George Bush based much of his foreign policy on his changing attitudes toward Mikhail Gorbachev. He started lukewarm, talking tough to please the Republican right wing. Bush feared that Gorbachev, by instituting reforms that challenged the entrenched Communist Party leaders, was being imprudent: one of the worst things he could say about another leader. Before 1989 was over, however, the president had decided that Gorbachev was OK. For the next two years, the United States pushed the prodemocratic transformation of Eastern Europe while being careful not to gloat in public or damage Gorbachev's position at home. He tried not to push the Soviet Union too hard and infuriate Russian hard-liners. "I don't want to do something that would inadvertently set back the progress," Bush said. Later asked whether the United States had a new foe after the end of the Cold War, Bush answered without hesitation; "The enemy is unpredictability. The enemy is instability."

The end of Communist regimes in eastern Europe.

The people of eastern Europe overcame both American and Soviet caution. Gorbachev had urged his eastern European allies to emulate perestroika to free their economies from stifling controls and proclaimed what his foreign ministry called the "Sinatra doctrine," alluding to the ballad, "My Way," popularized by Frank Sinatra. Each Communist nation could "do it its way" without fearing the Soviet tanks that had crushed change in Hungary in 1956 and Czechoslovakia in 1968. Instead of careful economic liberalization, the Warsaw Pact system collapsed. Poland held free elections in June l989, Hungary adopted a democratic constitution in October, and prodemocracy demonstrations then forced out Communist leaders in other Eastern European countries. When East Germans began to flee westward through Hungary, the East German regime bowed to mounting pressure and opened the Berlin Wall on November 9. By the end of 1989, there were new democratic or non-Communist governments in Czechoslovakia, Romania, Bulgaria, and East Germany. These largely peaceful revolutions destroyed the military and economic agreements that had harnessed the satellites to the Soviet economy (the Warsaw Pact and Comecon). The Soviet Union swallowed hard, accepted the loss of its satellites, and slowly withdrew its army from eastern Europe.

German reunification and the dissolution of the Soviet Union.

Events in Europe left German reunification as a point of possible conflict. Soviet policy since 1945 had sought to prevent the reemergence of a strong, united Germany that might again threaten its neighbors. West German Chancellor Helmut Kohl removed one obstacle when he reassured Poland and Russia that Germany would seek no changes in the boundaries drawn after World War II. By July 1990, the United States and Soviet Union had agreed that a reunited Germany would belong to NATO. The decision satisfied France and Britain that a stronger Germany would still be under the influence of the Western allies. In October, the two Germanies completed their political unification, although it would be years before their mismatched economies functioned as one. Reunification was the last step in the diplomatic legacy of World War II.

The wall that divided East from West Berlin from 1962 to 1989 was a hated symbol of the Cold War. When the Communist government of East Germany collapsed in November 1989, jubilant Berliners celebrated the opening of the wall and the reuniting of the divided city.

The final act in the transformation of the Soviet Union began with a failed coup against Mikhail Gorbachev in August, 1991. The Soviet Union had held free elections in 1989. Now Gorbachev scheduled a vote on a new constitution that would decrease the power of the central Soviet government. Old-line Communist bureaucrats who feared the change arrested Gorbachev in his vacation house and tried to take over the government apparatus in Moscow. They turned out to be bumblers and drunks who had not secured military support and even failed to take over radio and television stations. Boris Yeltsin, president of the Russian Republic, organized the resistance. Muscovites flocked to support Yeltsin and defied tank crews in front of the Russian parliament building. Within three days, the plotters themselves were under arrest.

The coup hastened the fragmentation of the Soviet Union. Before the month was out, the Soviet parliament banned the Communist Party. Gorbachev soon resigned. Previously suppressed nationalist feelings caused all of the fifteen component republics of the Soviet Union to declare their independence. The superpower Union of Soviet Socialist Republics ceased to exist. Russia remained the largest and strongest of the new states, followed by Ukraine and Kazakhstan.

The end of the Cold War leaves the historical assessment of the last half-century of U.S. foreign policy open to debate. Analysts agree that the relentless pressure of American defense spending helped bankrupt and undermine the Soviet Union. It is an open question whether this same American defense spending also weakened the United States' economy and its ability to compete in the world marketplace. Some scholars see the demise of the Soviet empire as ultimate justification for forty years of Cold War. Dissenters argue the opposite— that the collapse of European Communism shows that American leaders had magnified its threat. Before we can choose among differing views, we need to wait for scholars to explore Russian archives and develop a fuller history of Soviet Cold War policy to

place alongside our understanding of U.S. policy (see the Overview table, "Why Did the Cold War End?").

THE PERSIAN GULF WAR

On August 2, 1990, President Saddam Hussein of Iraq seized the small neighboring oil-rich country of Kuwait. The quick conquest gave Iraq control of 20 percent of the world's oil production and reserves. President Bush demanded unconditional withdrawal, enlisted European and Arab allies in an anti-Iraq coalition, and persuaded Saudi Arabia to accept substantial U.S. forces for its protection against Iraqi invasion. Within weeks, the Saudis were host to tens of thousands of U.S. soldiers and hundreds of aircraft.

The background for Iraq's invasion was a simmering dispute over border oil fields and islands in the Persian Gulf. Iraq was a dictatorship that had just emerged from an immensely costly eight-year war with Iran. Saddam Hussein had depended on help from the United States and Arab nations in this war, but Iraq was now economically exhausted. Kuwait itself was a small, rich nation whose ruling dynasty enjoyed few friends but plenty of oil royalties. The U.S. State Department had signaled earlier in 1990 that it might support some concessions by Kuwait in the disputes. Saddam Hussein read the signal as an open invitation to do what he wanted; having been favored in the past by the United States, he probably expected denunciations but no military response.

The Iraqis gave George Bush a golden opportunity to assert America's world influence. The Bush administration was concerned that Iraq might target

George Bush visits American troops in Saudi Arabia on Thanksgiving Day, 1990. The United States had countered Iraq's seizure of Kuwait in August by rushing forces to protect Saudi Arabia's vital oil fields. The buildup lasted until January, when U.S. planes began a systematic air assault on Iraq.

Overview	
Why Did the Cold War End?	
Commentators have offered a number of explanations for the rapid failure of the USSR and the collapse of Soviet power at the end of the 1980s. All of these factors made contributions to the complex unraveling of the Cold War.	
Economic exhaustion:	The United States in the late 1970s embarked on a great modernization and expansion of its military forces. The USSR exhausted its economy and revealed its technical backwardness by trying to keep pace. Gorbachev's policy of *perestroika* was an attempt to reduce the bureaucratic inertia of the economy.
Failure of leadership:	The Soviet Union in the 1970s and early 1980s was governed by unimaginative bureaucrats. A closed elite that thought only of preserving their privileges and authority could not adapt to a changing world. The policy of *glasnost* was an effort to encourage new ideas.
Intervention in Afghanistan:	The disastrous intervention in Afghanistan revealed the limits of Soviet military power. It alienated the large Muslim population of the USSR and brought disillusionment with the incompetence of its leaders.
Triumph of democratic ideas:	As political discussion became more free, the appeal of democratic ideas took on its own momentum, especially in eastern European satellite nations such as East Germany, Czechoslovakia, and Poland.
Power of nationalism:	The collapse of the Soviet empire was triggered by the resurgence of national sentiments throughout the Soviet empire. National sentiments fueled the breakaway of the eastern European satellite nations such as Hungary, Rumania, and Poland. Nationalism also broke up the USSR itself as fourteen smaller "socialist republics" declared independence of the Russian-dominated Union

oil-rich Saudi Arabia. The importance of Middle Eastern oil helped enlist France and Britain as military allies and secure billions of dollars from Germany and Japan. Iraq itself had antagonized nearly all its neighbors. The collapse of Soviet power and Gorbachev's interest in cooperating with the United States meant that the Soviets would not interfere with U.S. plans.

Bush and his advisers offered a series of justifications for American actions. First, and most basic, were the desire to punish armed aggression and the presumed need to protect Iraq's other neighbors. In fact, there was scant evidence of Iraqi preparations against Saudi Arabia. The buildup of American air power plus the effective economic sanctions would have accomplished both protection and punishment. Sanctions and diplomatic pressure might also have brought withdrawal from most or all of Kuwait. However, additional American objectives—to destroy Iraq's capacity to create nuclear weapons and to topple Saddam's regime—would require direct military action.

The Persian Gulf itself offered an equally golden opportunity to the American and allied armed forces. Here were no tangled jungles, invisible guerrillas, or civilians caught in a civil war. The terrain was open and nearly uninhabited. The enemy had committed regular forces to traditional battle, where the superiority of American equipment and training would be telling. Indeed, the United States could try out the tactics of armored maneuver and close land-air cooperation that the Pentagon had devised to protect Germany against Soviet invasion.

Bush probably decided on war in October, eventually increasing the number of American troops in Saudi Arabia to 580,000. The United States stepped up diplomatic pressure by securing a series of increasingly tough United Nations resolutions that culminated in November 1990 with Security Council Resolution 678, authorizing "all necessary means" to liberate Kuwait. The president convinced Congress to agree to military action under the umbrella of the UN. The United States also ignored compromise plans floated by France and last-minute concessions from Iraq.

War began one day after the UN's January 15 deadline for Iraqi withdrawal from Kuwait. **Operation Desert Storm** opened with massive air attacks on command centers, transportation facilities, and Iraqi forward positions. The air war destroyed 40 to 50 percent of Iraqi tanks and artillery by late February. The attacks also seriously hurt Iraqi civilians by disrupting utilities and food supplies.

Americans found the **Persian Gulf War** fascinating. They bought millions of Middle East maps to follow the conflict. They watched CNN's live transmission of Baghdad under bombardment and stared at pictures of Patriot missiles presumably intercepting Iraqi Scud missiles. They read about Stealth fighter bombers that were invisible to radar and about precision-guided missiles (although most of the damage came from traditional bombing and low-tech A-10 antitank aircraft).

The forty-day rain of bombs was the prelude to a ground attack. (see Map 30–2). Despite Saddam Hussein's threats that the coalition faced the "mother of all

MAP 30-2 The Persian Gulf War

Ground operations against Iraq in the Persian Gulf War followed six weeks of aerial bombardment. The ground attack, which met quick success, was a multinational effort by the United States, Britain, France, Saudi Arabia, and other Arab nations threatened by an aggressive Iraq. The war freed Kuwait from Iraqi occupation but stopped before forcing a change in Iraq's government.

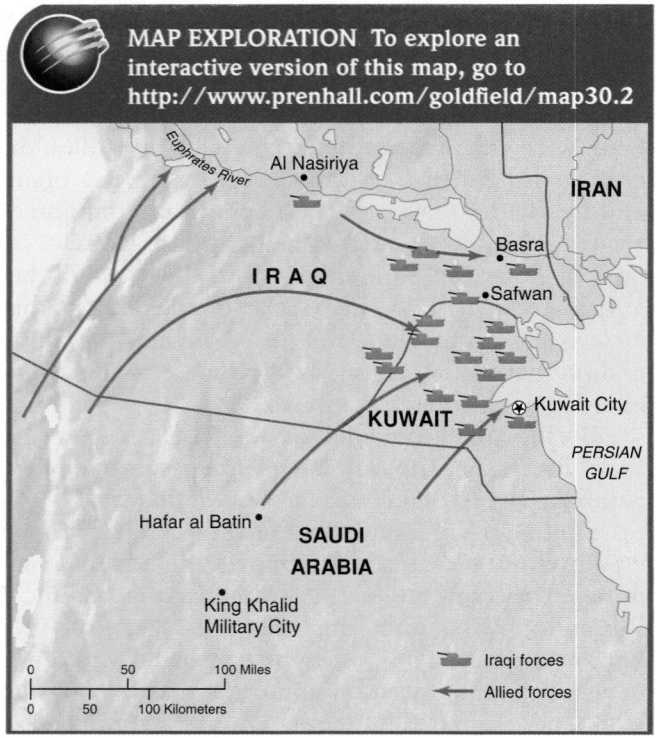

MAP EXPLORATION To explore an interactive version of this map, go to http://www.prenhall.com/goldfield/map30.2

battles," the Iraqi military made the land war easy. They concentrated their forces near the Persian Gulf in Kuwait itself because they expected an amphibious landing near Kuwait City and a direct strike north along the coast. Instead, the allies moved 235,000 U.S., French, and British soldiers far into the interior. On February 24, 1991, these forces swept into Iraq in a great arc. Americans, Saudis, Syrians, and Egyptians advanced directly to liberate Kuwait. A cease-fire came one hundred hours after the start of the ground war. The Iraqis had been driven out of Kuwait, but the relatively slow advance of the left wing failed to prevent many of the Iraqi troops from escaping. Allied forces suffered only 240 deaths in action, compared to perhaps 100,000 for the Iraqis.

Bush directed Desert Storm with the "Vietnam syndrome" in mind, believing that Americans were willing to accept war only if it involved overwhelming U.S. force and ended quickly. The desire for a quick war, however, posed a problem. The United States hoped to replace Saddam Hussein without disrupting Iraqi society. Instead, the hundred-hour war incited armed rebellions against Saddam by Shi'ite Muslims in southern Iraq, a branch of Muslims who are a minority in that nation, and by ethnically distinct Kurds in the north. Because Bush and his advisers were unwilling to get embroiled in a civil war, they stood by while Saddam crushed the uprisings. In one sense, the United States won the war but not the peace. Saddam Hussein became a hero to many in the Islamic world simply by remaining in power. In another sense, Bush had accomplished exactly what he wanted: the restoration of the status quo. In 2002, however, President George W. Bush (the president's son, elected in 2000), made a change in the Iraqi regime a centerpiece of U.S. foreign policy.

GROWTH IN THE SUNBELT

The rise in the military and defense spending from the late 1970s through the early 1990s and the Persian Gulf War, was one of the most powerful sources of growth in the **Sunbelt**, the southern and western regions of the United States. Americans had discovered this "new" region in the 1970s. Kevin Phillips's book *The Emerging Republican Majority* (1969) first popularized the term "Sunbelt." Phillips pointed out that people and economic activity had been flowing southward and westward since World War II, shifting the balance of power away from the Northeast. Sections of the South and West, historically controlled from the northeastern industrial core, have developed as independent centers of economic change.

The Sunbelt was a region of conservative voting habits where Republicans solidified their status as a

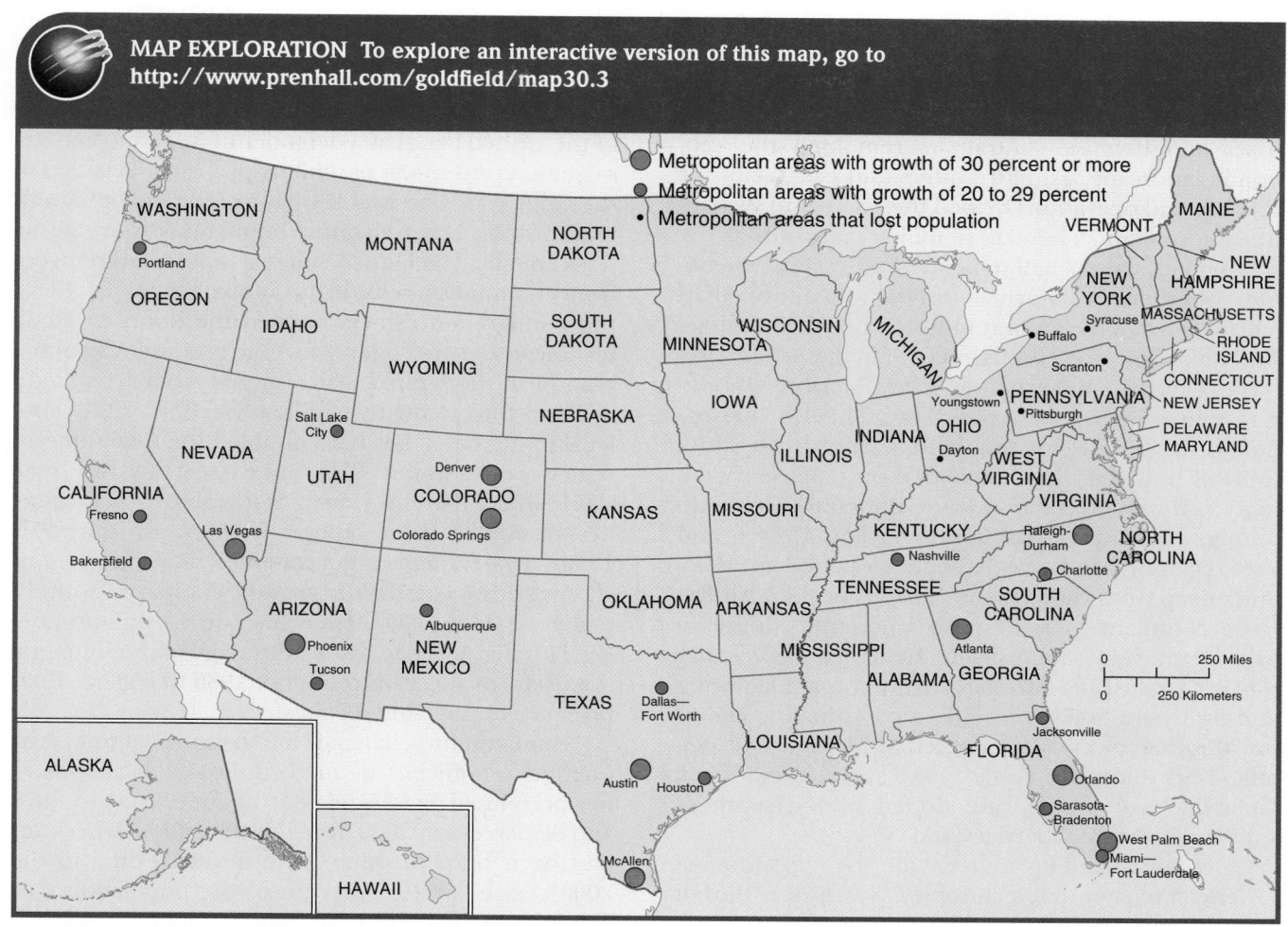

MAP EXPLORATION To explore an interactive version of this map, go to
http://www.prenhall.com/goldfield/map30.3

MAP 30-3   **Fast-Growing and Shrinking Metropolitan Areas, 1900-2000**
In the 1990s, boom cities were found in the Southeast, Southwest, and on the West Coast. In contrast, all of the large metropolitan areas that lost population were in Ohio, New York, or Pennsylvania, the area hardest hit by the decline of jobs in established manufacturing industries.

majority party, a process continuing to the present. In the 1990s, the region's economic power was reflected in a conservative tone in both the Republican and Democratic parties and in the prominence of southern political leaders. Indeed, the career of George Bush, who got his start in New England but gained his greatest success as a new Texan, epitomized the political trend toward the Sunbelt. (See Map 30-3).

The rise of the Sunbelt, which is anchored by Florida, Texas, and California, reflected the leading economic trends of the 1970s and 1980s, including military spending, immigration from Asia and Latin America, and recreation and retirement spending. Corporations liked the business climate of the South, which had weak labor laws, low taxes, and generally lower costs of living and doing business.

New factories dotted the southern landscape, often in smaller towns rather than cities. General Motors closed factories in Flint, Michigan, but invested in a new Saturn plant in Spring Hill, Tennessee. In contrast to troubled industrial cities in the Northeast and Midwest, journalists and scholars found headlong prosperity in cities like Orlando, Charlotte, Atlanta, Dallas, and Phoenix. Houston, with sprawling growth, business spinoffs from NASA, and purring air conditioners epitomized the booming metropolitan areas of the South and West. It was, said one reporter, "the place that scholars flock to for the purpose of seeing what modern civilization has wrought."

THE DEFENSE ECONOMY

The Vietnam buildup and reinvestment in the military during the Carter (1977–1981) and Reagan

(1981–1989) administrations fueled the growth of the Sunbelt. Over the forty years from the Korean conflict to the Persian Gulf War, the United States made itself the mightiest military power ever known. Military bases and defense contractors remolded the economic landscape, as mild winters and clear skies for training and operations helped the South and West attract more than 75 percent of military payrolls.

Big cities and small depended on defense spending. Southern California thrived on more than 500,000 jobs in the aircraft industry. Lockheed's huge Burbank plant drew thousands of families to the new suburbs of the San Fernando Valley; McDonnell-Douglas shaped the area around Los Angeles International Airport. Twelve thousand smaller firms and a third of the area's jobs depended on defense spending. A thousand miles away, visitors to Colorado Springs could drive past sprawling Fort Carson and visit the new Air Force Academy, opened in 1958. Sunk deep from view was the North American Air Defense command post beneath Cheyenne Mountain west of the city. Malmstrom Air Force Base transformed Great Falls, Montana, from a manufacturing and transportation center into a coordinating center for Minuteman missiles targeted at Moscow and Beijing. Dark blue Air Force vans carried crews from Great Falls to missile sites dotted over a swath of rolling plains as vast as Maryland.

Defense spending underwrote the expansion of American science and technology. Nearly one-third of all engineers worked on military projects. Large universities, such as MIT, the University of Michigan, California Institute of Technology, and Stanford, were leading defense contractors. The modern electronics business started in New York, Boston and the San Francisco Bay Area with research and development for military uses, such as guided-missile controls. California's Silicon Valley grew with military sales long before it turned to consumer markets. The space component of the aerospace industry was equally reliant on the defense economy, with NASA spending justified by competition with the USSR. NASA's centers were scattered across the South: launch facilities at the Kennedy Space Center in Cape Canaveral, Florida; research labs at Huntsville, Alabama; and Houston's Manned Spacecraft Center as the control center for the space exploration.

NEW AMERICANS

Few Americans anticipated the effects of the **Immigration and Nationality Act of 1965**, which transformed the ethnic mix of the United States and helped to stimulate the sunbelt boom. The new law initiated a change in the composition of the American people by abolishing the national quota system in effect since 1924. Quotas had favored immigrants from western Europe and limited those from other parts of the world. The old law's racial bias contradicted the self-proclaimed role of the United States as a defender of freedom, and immigration reform was part of the propaganda battles of the Cold War. The new law gave preference to family reunification and welcomed immigrants from all nations equally. The United States also accepted refugees from communism outside the annual limits.

Immigration reform opened the doors to Mediterranean Europe, Latin America, and Asia. Legal migration to the United States surged from 1.1 million in 1960–1964 to nearly 4 million for 1990–1994. Nonlegal immigrants may have doubled the total number of newcomers in the 1970s and early 1980s. Not since World War I had the United States absorbed so many new residents from other countries. By the early 1990s, legal immigration accounted for 37 percent of all American population growth, compared with 10 percent before 1965. Meanwhile, over 2 million nonlegal immigrants had taken advantage of the Immigration Reform and Control Act of 1986 to legalize their presence in the United States.

Immigration changed the nation's ethnic mix. Members of officially defined ethnic and racial minorities accounted for 25 percent of Americans in 1990 and 30 percent in 2000. Roughly 28 million Americans had been born in other countries according to the 2000 census, or 10.4 percent of the population (see Table 30–1). This was lower than the high of 14.7 percent in 1910 but a great increase from the low of 4.7 percent in 1970. One-third of the foreign born were from Latin America and one-fourth were from Asia.

The largest single group of new Americans came from Mexico. The long shared border has facilitated easy movement from south to north. Especially in the border states of Texas, New Mexico, Arizona, and California, permanent immigrants have mingled with tourists, family members on visits, temporary workers, and other workers without legal permission to enter the U.S. Mexican Americans in the later twentieth century were the largest minority group in many southwestern and western states. They were also transforming neighborhoods in Chicago and other midwestern cities and changing everything from politics to the Catholic church.

The East Coast has especially welcomed migrants from the West Indies and Central America. Many Puerto Ricans, who hold U.S. citizenship, came to Philadelphia and New York in the 1950s and 1960s. The 110th Street subway station in East Harlem marked the center of *El Barrio de Nueva York* for that city's 600,000 Puerto Ricans. Other countries sending

TABLE 30.1

Major Racial and Ethnic Minorities in the United States

	1960 Population (in millions)	Percentage of total	2000 Population (in millions)	Percentage of total
American Indians	.5	0.3	2.5	0.9
Asians and Pacific Islanders	1.1	0.6	10.6	3.7
African Americans	18.9	10.5	34.7	12.3
Hispanics	not available		35.3	12.5

large numbers of immigrants include Haiti, the Dominican Republic, Guatemala, Honduras, Nicaragua, El Salvador, and Jamaica. Cuban refugees from Castro's regime concentrated in Miami and in major cities such as Chicago and New York.

Another great immigration has occurred eastward across the Pacific. Chinese, Filipinos, Koreans, Samoans, and other Asians and Pacific Islanders constituted only 6 percent of newcomers to the United States in 1965 but nearly half of all arrivals in 1990. The numbers of ethnic Chinese in the United States jumped from a quarter of a million in 1965 to 1,645,000 in 1990. Immigrants from Taiwan, Hong Kong, and the People's Republic created new Chinatowns in Houston and San Diego and crowded into the historic Chinatowns of New York and San Francisco.

The most publicized Asian immigrants were refugees from Indochina after Communist victories in 1975. The first arrivals tended to be highly educated professionals who had worked with the Americans. Another 750,000 Vietnamese, Laotians, and Cambodians arrived after 1976 by way of refugee camps in Thailand, as did Celia Noup. Most settled on the West Coast. The San Francisco Bay area, for example, had more than a dozen Vietnamese-language newspapers, magazines, and cable television programs. People in Silicon Valley knew Hewlett-Packard as "Little Vietnam" in the mid-1980s and Advanced Micro Devices as "Little Manila."

In addition to southeast Asians, political conflicts and upheavals sent other waves of immigrants to the United States. Many Iranians fled the religious regime that took power in their country in the late 1970s, at the same time that Ethiopians were fleeing a nation shattered by drought, civil war, and doctrinaire Marxism. To escape repression in the Soviet Union, Jews and conservative Christians came to the U.S. in the

George P. Bush, son of Jeb Bush and his Mexican American wife Columba, and nephew of President George W. Bush, marches in New York's Puerto Rican Day Parade in June 2002. Both George W. Bush in Texas and Jeb Bush in Florida were more successful than many Republicans in winning the approval of Hispanic voters. George P. Bush appeared in television ads during the 2000 campaign saying "I am a young Latino and very proud of my bloodline."

1980s, and the collapse of Communism in the Soviet Union opened the door for Russians, Ukrainians, Rumanians, and other eastern Europeans in the 1990s to emigrate to the United States.

Recent immigrants have found both economic possibilities and problems. On the negative side, legal and illegal immigration has added to the numbers of nonunion workers. By one estimate, two-thirds of the workers in the Los Angeles garment trade were undocumented immigrants. Most worked for small, nonunion firms in basements and storefronts, without health insurance or pensions. But a positive contrast was the abundance of opportunities for talent and ambition in the expanding economy of the mid-1980s and 1990s. The 130,000 Vietnamese immigrants of 1975 now have an average adjusted income above the national average. Asians and Pacific islanders by 2000 constituted 22 percent of students in California's public universities. Like earlier European immigrants, many newcomers have opened groceries, restaurants, and other businesses that serve their own group before expanding into larger markets. Juan Fernandez found it easier to set up a successful car repair shop in Gary, Indiana, than in Guadalajara, Mexico, because his fellow immigrants prefer a Spanish-speaking mechanic. Asian-born business owners have filled retail vacuums in central city neighborhoods abandoned by chain stores. One Korean told a typical story: "A friend of mine came over with his family. He invested a few dollars in a vegetable stand in downtown Manhattan. He and his sons got up early, went to the market early. . . . He took some of his earnings and invested in a candy store. Then he bought two more vegetable and fruit stands. . . . Their kids work hard too and they make a lot of money."

OLD GATEWAYS AND NEW

The new immigration from the Asia, Latin America, and the Caribbean had its most striking effects in coastal and border cities. New York again became a great mixing bowl of the American population. By 1990, some 28 percent of the population of New York City was foreign-born, compared to 42 percent at the height of European immigration in 1910. Journalist Andy Logan described the new immigrants' impact by the 1970s: "A third of the children now in the city's public schools are said to be the children of parents who were born in other countries. . . . Whole areas of the city, such as Washington Heights, in Manhattan, and Elmhurst, in Queens, would be half empty without the new arrivals." ZIP code 11373 in North Queens was reportedly the most diverse neighborhood in the world.

Just as important was the transformation of southern and western cities into gateways for immigrants from Latin America and Asia. Los Angeles emerged as "the new Ellis Island" that rivaled New York's historic role in receiving immigrants. As *Time* magazine put it in 1983, the arrival of more than 2 million immigrants in greater Los Angeles altered "the collective beat and bop of L.A." In 1960, a mere 1 percent of the Los Angeles County population was Asian and 11 percent was Hispanic. By 2000, the figures for a population of 9.5 million were 12 percent Asian and 45 percent Hispanic. The sprawling neighborhoods of East Los Angeles make up the second-largest Mexican city in the world. New ethnic communities appeared in Los Angeles suburbs Iranians in Beverly Hills, Chinese in Monterey Park, Japanese in Gardena, Thais in Hollywood, Samoans in Carson, Cambodians in Lakewood. One hundred languages are spoken among students entering Los Angeles schools.

New York and Los Angeles are world cities as well as immigrant destinations. Like London and Tokyo, they are capitals of world trade and finance, with international banks and headquarters of multinational corporations. They have the country's greatest concentrations of international lawyers, accounting firms, and business consultants. The deregulation of international finance and the explosive spread of instant electronic communication in the 1980s confirmed their importance as global decision centers.

Similar factors turned Miami into the economic capital of the Caribbean. A quarter-million Cuban businessmen, white-collar workers, and their families had moved to the United States between 1959 and 1962 to escape Castro's new socialist government. New "freedom flights" carried 150,000 additional Cubans to the U.S. from 1966 to 1973 and a third round added 125,000 in 1980. Most of the newcomers stayed in South Florida. Cubans by the late 1970s owned about one-third of the area's retail stores and many of its other businesses. Their success in business made Miami a major Latino market and helped to attract two million Latin American tourists and shoppers to its stores and hotels during the 1980s. Access to the Caribbean and South America also make Miami an international banking and commercial center with hundreds of offices for corporations engaged in U.S. Latin American trade.

Cross-border communities in the Southwest, such as El Paso, Texas, and Juarez, Mexico, or San Diego, California, and Tijuana, Mexico, are "Siamese twins joined at the cash register." Employees with work permits commute from Mexico to the United States. American popular culture flows southward. Bargain hunters and tourists pass in both directions. A shopping center near San Diego made 60 percent of its sales to Mexicans.

Both nations have promoted the cross-border economy. The Mexican government in the mid-1960s began to encourage a "platform economy" by allowing companies on the Mexican side of the border to import components and inputs duty-free as long as 80 percent of the items were reexported and 90 percent of the workers were Mexicans. The intent is to encourage American corporations to locate assembly plants south of the border. Such *maquila* industries can employ lower-wage workers and avoid strict antipollution laws (leading to serious threats to public health on both sides of the border). From the Gulf of Mexico to the Pacific Ocean, eighteen hundred *maquiladora* plants employed half a million workers. North of the border, U.S. factories supplied components under laws that meshed with the Mexican regulations.

THE GRAYING OF AMERICA

Retirees were another factor contributing to the growth of the Sunbelt. Between 1965 and 2000, the number of Americans aged 65 and over jumped from 18.2 million to 35 million, or 12.4 percent of the population. For the first time, most Americans could expect to survive into old age. The "young old" are people in their sixties and seventies who remain sharp, vigorous, and financially secure because of better private pensions, Social Security, and Medicare. The "old old" are the 9 million people in their eighties and nineties who often require daily assistance, although data show that improved medical services have made such Americans healthier and more self-sufficient than they were ten or twenty years ago.

Older Americans have become a powerful voice in public affairs. They tend to vote against local taxes but fight efforts to slow the growth of Social Security, even though growing numbers of the elderly are being supported by a relatively smaller proportion of working men and women. By the 1990s, observers noted increasing resentment among younger Americans, who fear that public policy is biased against the needs of men and women in their productive years. In turn, the elderly fiercely defend the programs of the 1960s and 1970s that have kept many of them from poverty. Protecting Medicare and Social Security was one of the Democrats' best campaign issues in 1996 and 2000, after Republicans suggested cuts in spending growth.

Retired Americans changed the social geography of the United States. Much growth in the South and Southwest has been financed by money earned in the Northeast and Midwest and transferred by retirees. Florida in the 1980s absorbed nearly 1 million new residents aged sixty or older. California, Arizona, Texas, the Carolinas, and the Ozark Mountains of Missouri and Arkansas have all attracted retirees, many of them in age-segregated communities such as Sun City near Phoenix.

VALUES IN COLLISION

In 1988, two very different religious leaders sought a presidential nomination. Pat Robertson's campaign for the Republican nomination tapped deep discontent with the changes in American society since the 1960s. A television evangelist, Robertson used the mailing list from his 700 Club program to mobilize conservative Christians and pushed the Republican Party further to the right on family and social issues. Jesse Jackson, a civil-rights leader and minister from Chicago, mounted a grassroots campaign with the opposite goal of moving the Democratic Party to the left on social and economic policy. Drawing on his experience in the black civil-rights movement, he assembled a "Rainbow Coalition" that included labor unionists, feminists, and others whom Robertson's followers feared. Both Jackson and Robertson used their powerful personalities and religious convictions to inspire support from local churches and churchgoers.

In diagnosing social ills, Robertson pointed to the problems of individual indulgence, while Jackson pointed to racism and economic inequality. Their sharp divergence expressed differences in basic values that divided Americans in the 1980s and beyond. In substantial measure, the conflicts were rooted in the social and cultural changes of the 1960s and 1970s that had altered traditional institutions, especially the 1950s ideal of a "Ward and June Cleaver" family. Changes in roles and expectations among women and new openness about gay and lesbian sexuality were particularly powerful in dividing American churches and politics.

WOMEN'S RIGHTS AND PUBLIC POLICY

The women's liberation movement of the 1960s achieved important gains when Congress wrote many of its goals into law in the early 1970s. Title IX of the Educational Amendments (1972) to the Civil Rights Act prohibited discrimination by sex in any educational program receiving federal aid. The legislation expanded athletic opportunities for women and slowly equalized the balance of women and men in faculty positions. In the same year, Congress sent the Equal Rights Amendment (ERA) to the states for ratification. The amendment read, "Equal rights under the law shall not be denied or abridged by the United States or by any state on account of sex." More than twenty states ratified in the first few months. As conservatives who wanted to preserve traditional family patterns rallied strong opposition, however, the next dozen states ratified only after increasingly tough battles in state legislatures. The ERA then stalled, three states short, until the time limit for ratification expired in 1982.

Abortion rights and the conservative backlash.

In January 1973, the U.S. Supreme Court expanded the debate about women's rights with the case of **Roe v. Wade.** Voting 7 to 2, the Court struck down state laws forbidding abortion in the first three months of pregnancy and set guidelines for abortion during the remaining months. Drawing on the earlier decision of *Griswold v. Connecticut,* which dealt with birth control, the Court held that the Fourteenth Amendment includes a right to privacy that blocks states from interfering with a woman's right to terminate a pregnancy. The Supreme Court later upheld congressional limitations on the use of federal funds for abortion in *Webster v. Reproductive Health Services* (1989) and allowed some state restrictions in *Planned Parenthood v. Casey* (1992). Nevertheless, the *Roe* decision remained in place.

These changes came in the context of increasingly sharp conflict over the feminist agenda. Both the ERA and *Roe* stirred impassioned support and equally passionate opposition. Behind the rhetoric were male fears of increased job competition during a time of economic contraction and concern about changing families. Also fueling the debate was a deep split between the mainstream feminist view of women as fully equal individuals and the contrary conservative belief that women had a special role as anchors of families, an updating of the nineteenth-century idea of separate spheres. For conservative politicians, the ERA was a good "wedge issue" that could help split religious conservatives from the Democratic Party. The debate about abortion drew on the same issue of women's relationship to families but added strong religious voices, particularly the formal opposition of the Roman Catholic church to abortion. The arguments also tapped such deep emotion that the two sides could not even agree on a common language, juxtaposing a right to life against rights to privacy and freedom of choice.

Women in the work force.

The most sweeping change in the lives of American women did not come from federal legislation or court cases, but from the growing likelihood that a woman would work outside the home. In 1960, some 32 percent of married women were in the labor force; forty years later, 61 percent were working or looking for work (along with 69 percent of single women). Federal and state governments slowly responded to the changing demands of work and family with new policies such as a federal child care tax credit.

More women entered the work force as inflation in the 1970s and declining wages in the 1980s eroded the ability of families to live comfortable lives on one income. Between 1979 and 1986, fully 80 percent of married households saw the husband's income fall in constant dollars. The result, headlined the Wall Street Journal in 1994: "More Women Take Low-Wage Jobs Just So Their Families Can Get By."

A second reason for the increase in working women from 29 million in 1970 to 66 million in 2000 was the broad shift from manufacturing to service jobs, reducing demand for factory workers and manual laborers and increasing the need for such "women's jobs" as data entry clerks, reservation agents, and nurses. Indeed, the American economy still divides job categories by sex. There was some movement toward gender-neutral hiring in the 1970s because of legal changes and the pressures of the women's movement. Women's share of lawyers more than quadrupled, of economists more than tripled, and of police detectives more than doubled. Nevertheless, job types were more segregated by sex than by race in the 1990s.

COMING OUT

New militancy among gay men and lesbians drew on several of the social changes of the late 1960s and 1970s. Willingness to acknowledge and talk about nonstandard sexual behavior was part of a change in public values. Tactics of political pressure came from the antiwar and civil rights movements. The timing, with a series of key events from 1969 to 1974, coincided with that of women's liberation.

Gay activism spread from the biggest cities to smaller communities, from the coasts to Middle America. New York police had long harassed gay bars and their customers. When police raided Manhattan's Stonewall Inn in June 1969, however, patrons fought back in a weekend of disorder. The **"Stonewall Rebellion"** was a catalyst for homosexuals to assert themselves as a political force. San Francisco also became a center of gay life. Its large homosexual community dated to World War II, when gays discharged from the armed forces in the Pacific theater were processed out through San Francisco. Openly gay poets and artists were prominent in the city's avant-garde circles. By the late 1970s, the city had more than three hundred business and social gathering places identified as gay and lesbian.

With New Yorkers and San Franciscans as examples, more and more gay men and lesbians "came out," or went public about their sexual orientation. They published newspapers, organized churches, and lobbied politicians for protection of basic civil rights such as equal access to employment, housing, and public accommodations. They staged "gay pride" days and marches. In 1974, the American Psychiatric Association eliminated homosexuality from its official list of mental disorders.

The character of life in gay communities took an abrupt turn in the 1980s when a new worldwide epidemic began to have an impact on the United States. Scientists first identified a new disease pattern, **acquired immune deficiency syndrome (AIDS)**, in 1981. The name described the symptoms resulting from the human immunodeficiency virus (HIV), which destroys the body's ability to resist disease. HIV is transferred through blood and semen. In the 1980s, the most frequent American victims were gay men and intravenous drug users.

A decade later, it was clear that HIV/AIDS was a national and even global problem. By the end of 1998, AIDS had been responsible for 411,000 deaths in the United States, and transmission to heterosexual women was increasing. The U.S. Centers for Disease Control and Prevention estimated roughly forty thousand new cases of HIV infection per year in the late 1990s, bringing the total close to 800,000. Once a problem of big cities, HIV infection had spread to every American community and had helped to change American attitudes about the process of dying through the spread of hospices for the care of the terminally ill. Meanwhile, the toll of AIDS deaths in other parts of the world, particularly eastern Africa, dwarfed that in the United States and made it a world health crisis.

By the 1990s, Americans were accustomed to open discussion of gay sexuality, if not always accepting of its reality. Television stars and other entertainers could "come out" and retain their popularity. So could politicians in selected districts. Tony Kushner's drama *Angels in America* (1993) won national prizes for its intense exploration of the impact of AIDS on an ordinary American community. On the issue of gays in the military, however, Congress and the Pentagon were more cautious, accepting a policy that made engaging in homosexual acts, though not sexual orientation itself, grounds for discharge.

CHURCHES IN CHANGE

Americans picture mining frontiers as rip-roaring places, where a handful of women hold the fort while the men work hard, drink deep, and carry on. Modern Grand Junction, Colorado, however, is far less exciting. Between 1980 and 1984, efforts to develop the oil-shale resources of western Colorado pushed the population of Grand Junction from sixty thousand to eighty thousand. Hopes were high and money was easy, but there was also a boom in religion. Newcomers to Grand Junction, a fast-changing city within a rapidly evolving society, searched for family stability and a sense of community by joining established congregations and organizing new churches. The telephone book in 1985 listed twenty-eight mainstream Protestant and Catholic churches, twenty-four Baptist

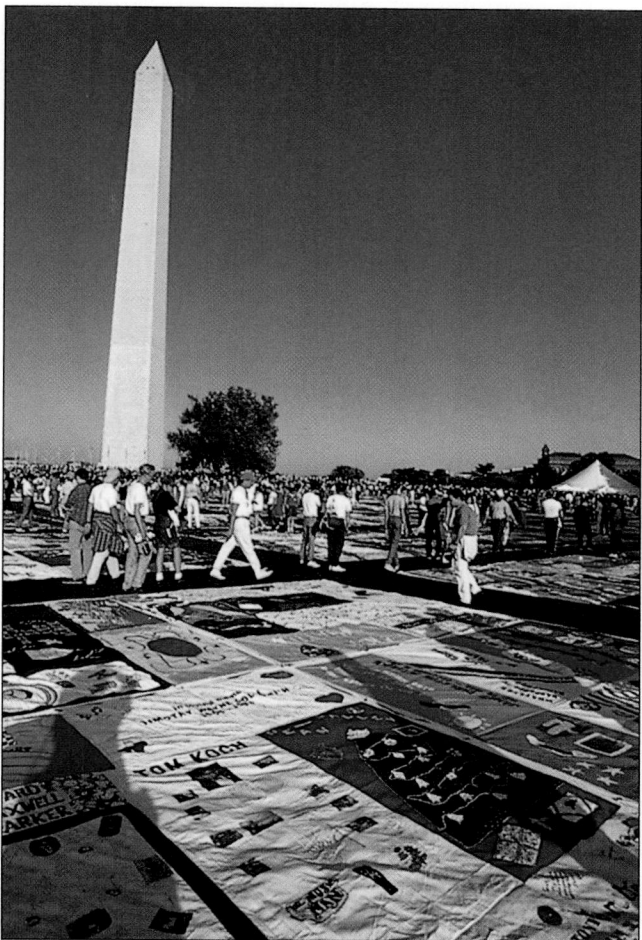

The AIDS Quilt, displayed in Washington in October 1992, combined individual memorials to AIDS victims into a powerful community statement. The quilt project reminded Americans that AIDS had penetrated every American community.

churches (reflecting the Oklahoma and Texas roots of many oil workers), five more liberal churches (such as Unitarians), and more than fifty Pentecostal, Bible, and Evangelical churches. Nearly a dozen Christian schools supplemented the public schools.

Grand Junction's religious bent is typical of the contemporary United States, where religion is prominent in daily lives, institutions, and public policy debates. Americans take their search for spiritual grounding much more seriously than do citizens of other industrial nations. Roughly half of privately organized social activity (such as charity work) is church related. In the mid-1970s, 56 percent of Americans said that religion was "very important" to them, compared to only 27 percent of Europeans.

As the Grand Junction statistics also suggest, mainline Protestant denominations that traditionally defined the center of American belief struggled after 1970. The United Methodist Church, the Presbyterian Church U.S.A., the United Church of Christ, and the

AMERICAN VIEWS

The Religious Imperative in Politics

The strong religious faith of many Americans frequently drives them to different stands on political issues. The first of these two documents, a letter by Jerry Falwell to potential supporters of the Moral Majority, reflects the politically conservative outlook of many evangelical Christians. Falwell is pastor of the Thomas Road Baptist Church in Lynchburg, Virginia. He founded the Moral Majority, a conservative religious lobbying and educational organization, in 1979 and served as its president until 1987, the year he wrote the letter reprinted here. The second document, from an open letter issued by the Southside United Presbyterian Church in Tucson in 1982, expresses the conviction of other believers that God may sometimes require civil disobedience to oppose oppressive government actions. The letter explains the church's reasons for violating immigration law to offer sanctuary to refugees from repressive Central American regimes supported by the United States.

- How do Falwell and the Southside Presbyterian Church define the problems that demand a religious response?
- Are there any points of agreement?
- How does each statement balance the claims of God and government?

From the Reverend Jerry Falwell:

I believe that the overwhelming majority of Americans are sick and tired of the way that amoral liberals are trying to corrupt our nation from its commitment to freedom, democracy, traditional morality, and the free enterprise system.

And I believe that the majority of Americans agree on the basic moral values which this nation was founded upon over 200 years ago.

Today we face four burning crises as we continue in this Decade of Destiny the 1980s loss of our freedom by giving in to the Commu-

---

Episcopal Church battled internally over the morality of U.S. foreign policy, the role of women in the ministry, and the reception of gay and lesbian members. They were strengthened by the ecumenical impulse, which united denominational branches that had been divided by ethnicity or regionalism. However, they gradually lost their position among American churches, perhaps because ecumenism diluted the certainty of their message. Liberal Protestantism has also historically been strongest in the slow-growing Northeast and Midwest.

By contrast, evangelical Protestant churches have benefited from the direct appeal of their message and from strong roots in the booming Sunbelt. Members of evangelical churches (25 percent of white Americans) now outnumber the members of mainline Protestant churches (20 percent). Major evangelical denomina-

tions include Baptists, the Church of the Nazarene, and the Assemblies of God. Fundamentalists, defined by a belief in the literal truth of the Bible, are a subset of evangelicals. So are 8 to 10 million Pentecostals and charismatics, who accept "gifts of the spirit," such as healing by faith and speaking in tongues.

Outsiders know evangelical Christianity through "televangelists." Spending on religious television programming rose from $50 to $600 million by 1980. The "electronic church" built on the radio preaching and professional revivalism of the 1950s. By the 1970s, it reached 20 percent of American households. Americans everywhere recognized the Big Four. Oral Roberts had a television show and Oral Roberts University in Oklahoma. Pat Robertson had the Christian Broadcasting Network in Virginia. Jerry Falwell claimed leadership of the Moral Majority (See "American nists; the destruction of the family unit; the deterioration of the free enterprise system; and the crumbling of basic moral principles which has resulted in the legalizing of abortion, widespread pornography, and a drug problem of epidemic proportions.

That is why I went to Washington, D.C., in June of 1979, and started a new organization The Moral Majority.

Right now you may be wondering: "But I thought Jerry Falwell was the preacher on the Old-Time Gospel Hour television program?"

You are right. For over twenty-four years I have been calling the nation back to God from the pulpit on radio and television.

But in recent months I have been led to do more than just preach. I have been compelled to take action.

I have made the commitment to go right into the halls of Congress and fight for laws that will save America. . . .

I will still be preaching every Sunday on the Old-Time Gospel Hour and I still must be a husband and father to my precious family in Lynchburg, Virginia.

But as God gives me the strength, I must do more. I must go into the halls of Congress and fight for laws that will protect the grand old flag . . . for the sake of our children and grandchildren.

From Southside United Presbyterian Church.

We are writing to inform you that Southside Presbyterian Church will publicly violate the Immigration and Nationality Act, Section 274 (A). . . .

We take this action because we believe the current policy and practice of the United States Government with regard to Central American refugees is illegal and immoral. We believe our government is in violation of the 1980 Refugee Act and international law by continuing to arrest, detain, and forcibly return refugees to the terror, persecution, and murder in El Salvador and Guatemala.

We believe that justice and mercy require the people of conscience actively assert our God-given right to aid anyone fleeing from persecution and murder. . . .

We beg of you, in the name of God, to do justice and love mercy in the administration of your office. We ask that "extended voluntary departure" be granted to refugees from Central America and that current deportation proceedings against these victims be stopped.

Until such time, we will not cease to extend the sanctuary of the church. . . . Obedience to God requires this of us all.

Sources: Gary E. McCuen, ed., *The Religious Right* (G. E. McCuen Publishers, 1989); Ann Crittenden, *Sanctuary* (Weidenfeld and Nicolson, 1988).

Views: The Religious Imperative in Politics"). Jim and Tammy Faye Bakker had grand plans for real-estate developments before their schemes collapsed in fraud.

Behind the glitz and hype of the television pulpit, evangelical churches emphasized religion as an individual experience focused on personal salvation. Unlike many of the secular and psychological avenues to fulfillment, however, they also offered communities of faith that might stabilize fragmented lives. The conservative nature of their theology and social teaching in a changing society offered certainty that was especially attractive to many younger families.

Another important change in national religious life has been the continuing "Americanization" of the Roman Catholic church following the Second Vatican Council in 1965, in which church leaders sought to respond to postwar industrial society. In the United States, Roman Catholicism moved toward the center of American life, helped by the popularity of John Kennedy and by worldly success that made Catholics the economic peers of Protestants. Even as the tight connection between Catholicism and membership in European immigrant communities gradually faded, Asian and Latino immigrants brought new vigor to many parishes and many inner city churches have been centers for social action. Church practice lost some of its distinctiveness; celebrating Mass in English rather than Latin was an important move toward modernization, but it also sparked a conservative counter-effort to preserve the traditional liturgy. Traditional and nontraditional Catholics also disagree about whether priests should be allowed to marry and other adaptations to American culture

CULTURE WARS

In the 1950s and 1960s, Americans argued most often over foreign policy, racial justice, and the economy. Since the 1980s, they have also quarreled over beliefs and values, especially as the patterns of family life have become more varied. In the course of these quarrels, religious belief has heavily influenced politics as individuals and groups try to shape America around their particular, and often conflicting, ideas of the godly society. One expert talks about a division between cultural liberals and conservatives, another about "culture wars" between progressivism and orthodoxy. Americans who are undogmatic in religion are often liberal in politics as well, hoping to lessen economic inequities and strengthen individual social freedom. Religious and political conservatism also tend to go together. To some degree, this cultural division runs all the way through American society, dividing liberal North from conservative South, cities from small towns, and college professors from Kiwanis Club members .

The division on social issues is related to theological differences within Protestantism. The "conservative" emphasis on personal salvation and the literal truth of the Bible also expresses itself in a desire to restore "traditional" social patterns. Conservatives worry that social disorder occurs when people follow personal impulses and pleasures. In contrast, the "liberal" or "modern" emphasis on the universality of the Christian message restates the Social Gospel with its call to build the Kingdom of God through social justice and may recognize divergent pathways toward truth. Liberals worry that greed in the unregulated marketplace creates disorder and injustice.

The cultural conflict also transcends the historic three-way division of Americans among Protestants, Catholics, and Jews. Instead, the conservative-liberal division now cuts through each group. For example, Catholic reformers, liberal Protestants, and Reform Jews may find agreement on issues of cultural values despite theologies that are worlds apart. The same may be true of conservative Catholics, fundamentalist Protestants, and Orthodox Jews.

Conservatives have initiated the culture wars, trying to stabilize what they fear is an American society spinning out of control because of sexual indulgence. In fact, the evidence on the sexual revolution is mixed. Growing numbers of teenagers reported being sexually active in the 1970s, but the rate of increase tapered off in the 1980s. The divorce rate began to drop after 1980. Births to teenagers dropped after 1990, and the number of two-parent families increased. Sexual advice and self-help books proliferated, with such titles as *Open Marriage* (1972) and *The Joy of Sex* (1972), but most adults remained staid and monogamous, according to data from 1994. Perhaps the logical extension of

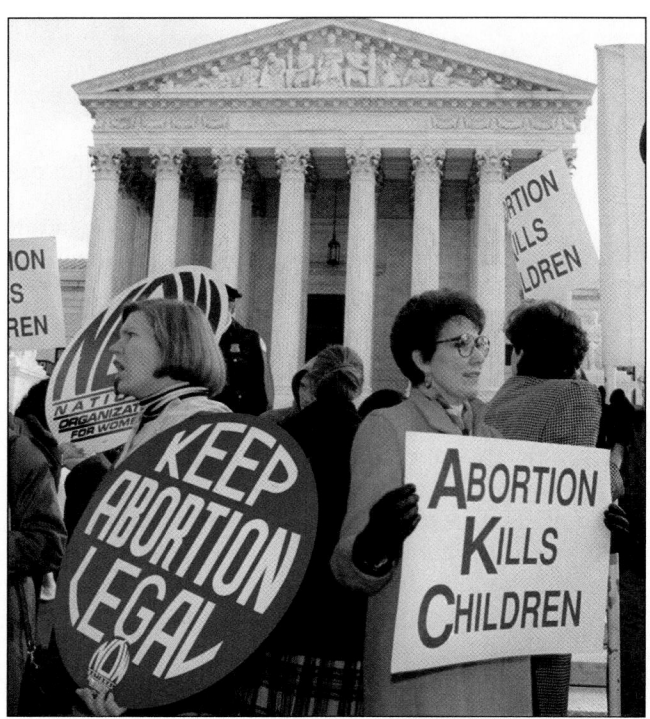

In December 1993, the U.S. Supreme Court heard arguments on whether states could require protesters to remain a certain distance from abortion clinics. These anti-abortion and pro-abortion protesters revealed the deep divisions over this and other issues in the culture wars.

reading about sex in the 1970s was an astonishing eagerness to talk about sex in the 1990s, a decade when soap opera story lines and talk shows covered everything from family violence to exotic sexual tastes.

The explosion of explicit attention to sexual behavior set the stage for religiously rooted battles over two sets of issues. One cluster revolves around so-called family values, questioning the morality of access to abortion, the acceptability of homosexuality, and the roles and rights of women. A second set of concerns has focused on the supposed role of public schools in undermining morality through sex education, unrestricted reading matter, nonbiblical science, and the absence of prayer. Opinion polls show clear differences among religious denominations on issues such as censorship of library books, acceptability of racially segregated neighborhoods, freedom of choice in terminating pregnancy, and homosexuality.

Not all issues of the culture wars carry the same weight. Censorship of art exhibits and library collections has mostly been an issue for political grandstanding. U.S. senators grabbed headlines in 1989 by attacking the National Endowment for the Arts for funding "obscene" art, but a local jury in Cincinnati later proved tolerant of sexually explicit images in a photographic exhibition. Efforts to restrict legal access to abortion mobilized thousands of "right to life" advocates in the late 1980s and early 1990s, but illegal acts remained the work of a radical fringe.

A culturally conservative issue with great popular appeal in the early 1990s was an effort to prevent states and localities from protecting homosexuals against discrimination. Under the slogan "No special rights," antigay measures passed in Cincinnati, Colorado, and communities in Oregon in 1993 and 1994, only to have the Supreme Court overturn the Colorado law in *Romer v. Evans* (1996). It is important to note that public support for lesbian and gay civil rights varies with different issues (strong support for equal employment opportunity, much less for granting marriage rights to same-sex couples) and whether the issues are framed in terms of specified rights for gays or in terms of the right of everyone, including gays, to be free from government interference with personal decisions, such as living arrangements and sexual choices.

CONCLUSION

Americans entered the 1980s searching for stability. The 1970s had brought unexpected and uncomfortable change. Soviet actions in Asia and Africa seemed to be destabilizing the world. The memory of defeat in Vietnam left a bitter taste, and hostages in Tehran seemed to signal the end to America's global postwar dominance. Energy crises, inflation, and boarded-up factories eroded purchasing power and undermined confidence in the future. Traditional values seemed under siege. Ronald Reagan's presidential campaign played to these insecurities by promising to revitalize the older ways of life and restore the United States to its former influence.

Taken as a whole, the years from 1981 through 1992 brought transformations that redirected the course of American life. Because many changes were associated with national policy choices, it is fair to call this the era of the Reagan revolution. The astonishing

collapse of the Soviet Union ended forty years of Cold War. New political leadership in Washington reversed the fifty-year expansion of federal government programs to deal with economic and social inequities. Prosperity alternated with recessions that shifted the balance between regions. The stock market rode a roller coaster, familiar corporate names vanished, and the national media made temporary heroes of business tycoons. Economic inequality increased after narrowing for a generation at the same time that more and more leaders proclaimed that unregulated markets could best meet social needs. Middle-class Latinos and African Americans made substantial gains while many other minority Americans sank deeper into poverty.

At the same time, it is important to recognize that every revolution has its precursors. Intellectuals had been clarifying the justifications for Reagan administration actions since the 1960s. The Reagan-Bush years extended changes that had begun in the 1970s, particularly the conservative economic policies and military buildup of the troubled Carter administration. In retrospect, the growing weakness of the USSR should also have been apparent in the same decade, had not the United States been blinded by its fear of communist power. Intervention in the Persian Gulf amplified American policies that had been in place since the CIA intervened in Iran in 1953. The outbreak of violence in Los Angeles after the Rodney King verdict showed that race relations were as tense as they had been in the 1960s.

In 1992, the United States stood as the undisputed world power. Its economy was poised for a surge of growth at the same time that rivals such as Japan were mired in economic crisis. It was the leader in scientific research and the development of new technologies. Its military capacities far surpassed those of any rival and seemed to offer a free hand in shaping the world–capacities that would be tested and utilized in the new century.

REVIEW QUESTIONS

1. Is it accurate to talk about a Reagan Revolution in American politics? Did Reagan's presidency change the economic environment for workers and business corporations? How did economic changes in the 1980s affect the prospects of the richest and poorest Americans?

2. How did American ideas about the proper role of government change during the 1980s? What were the basis of these changes?

3. What caused the breakup of the Soviet Union and the end of the Cold War? Did U.S. foreign policy under Reagan and Bush contribute significantly to the withdrawal of Soviet power from eastern Europe? Did the collapse of the USSR show the strength of the United States and its allies or the weakness of Soviet communism?

4. How did the United States use military force during the Reagan and Bush administrations? Did military actions achieve the expected goals?

5. What were some of the important economic trends that shifted American growth toward the Sunbelt (South and West)? How has immigration from other nations affected the different American regions?

6. What changes in family roles and sexual behavior became divisive political issues? How have churches responded to cultural changes? What are some of the ways in which churches and religious leaders have tried to influence political decisions?

7. How did U.S. military involvement in southeast Asia in the 1960s continue to affect American society for decades to come?

KEY TERMS

Acquired immune deficiency syndrome (AIDS) (p. 983)

Americans with Disabilities Act (p. 968)

Deregulation (p. 961)

Economic Recovery and Tax Act of 1981 (ERTA) (p. 961)

Glasnost (p. 971)

Immigration and Nationality Act of 1965 (p. 978)

Intermediate Nuclear Force Agreement (p. 971)

Operation Desert Storm (p. 976)

Persian Gulf War (p. 976)

Perestroika (p. 971)

Reagan Doctrine (p. 969)

Roe v. Wade (p. 982)

Sagebrush Rebellion (p. 961)

Stonewall Rebellion (p. 982)

Strategic Defense Initiative (SDI) (p. 969)

Sunbelt (p. 976)

RECOMMENDED READING

Anderson, Elijah. *Streetwise: Race, Class, and Change in an Urban Community* (1990). This is a deeply troubling portrait of the culture of the streets in the Philadelphia ghetto during the Reagan years.

Beschloss, Michael, and Strobe Talbott. *At the Highest Levels* (1993). A dramatic narrative of the last years of the Cold War, based on detailed interviews with American and Soviet participants.

Coutin, Susan Bibler. *The Culture of Protest: Religious Activism and the U.S. Sanctuary Movement* (1993). Examining foreign policy from the grassroots, sympathetically portrays the meanings that participants in the sanctuary movement gave their actions.

Edsall, Thomas Byrne, and Mary D. Edsall. *Chain Reaction: The Impact of Race, Rights, and Taxes on American Politics* (1991). Argues that the Democratic party has systematically alienated its working-class supporters.

Fitzgerald, Frances. *Way Out There in the Blue: Reagan, Star Wars, and the End of the Cold War* (2000). A detailed analysis of the technical weaknesses and political appeal of strategic missile defense.

Liebow, Elliot. *Tell Them Who I Am: The Lives of Homeless Women* (1993). A sensitive depiction of "street people" and "bag ladies" as complex individuals coping with personal problems and economic crisis.

Phillips, Kevin. *Boiling Point: Democrats, Republicans, and the Decline of Middle-Class Prosperity* (1992). Expresses the belief that the economic policies of the Reagan and Bush administrations systematically damaged working- and middle-class families.

Rubin, Lillian. *Families on the Fault Line: America's Working Class Speaks about the Family, the Economy, Race, and Ethnicity* (1994). Interviews with American families about their efforts to cope with economic and social change.

Wills, Garry. *Reagan's America: Innocents at Home* (1987). A biography critical of Reagan's ideas but insightful about his personality.

ADDITIONAL SOURCES

Economic Change: Opportunity and Inequality

Beam, Frank, and Gillian Stevens, *American's Newcomers and the Dynamics of Diversity* (2003).

Ehrenreich, Barbara. *Fear of Falling: The Inner Life of the Middle Class* (1989).

Levy, Frank. *The New Dollars and Dreams: American Incomes and Economic Change* (1998).

Markusen, Ann. et al. *The Rise of the Gunbelt: The Military Remapping of Industrial America* (1991).

Spain, Daphne, and Suzanne Bianchi. *Balancing Act: Motherhood, Marriage and Employment among American Women* (1996).

Stewart, James B. *Den of Thieves* (1991).

Susser, Ida. *Norman Street: Poverty and Politics in an Urban Neighborhood* (1982).

Zukin, Sharon. *Loft Living: Culture and Capital in Urban Change* (1982).

African American Experiences

Clavel, Pierre and Wim Wiewel. eds. *Harold Washington and the Neighborhoods* (1991).

Coyle, Daniel. *Hardball: A Season in the Projects* (1993).

Duneier, Mitchell. *Slim's Table: Race, Respectability and Masculinity* (1992).

Hacker, Andrew. *Two Nations: Black and White, Separate, Hostile, Unequal* (1992).

Lawson, Steven F. *In Pursuit of Power: Southern Blacks and Electoral Politics* (1985).

Wilson, William Julius. *The Truly Disadvantaged* (1987).

The New Conservatism

Bennett, William. *The De-Valuing of America: The Fight for Our Culture and Our Children* (1992).

Edwards, Lee. *The Conservative Revolution: The Movement That Remade America* (1999).

Ehrman, John. *The Rise of Neo-Conservative Intellectuals and Foreign Affairs, 1945-1994* (1995).

Hoeveler, Jr., J. David. *Watch on the Right: Conservative Intellectuals in the Reagan Era* (1991).

Katz, Michael. *The Undeserving Poor: From the War on Poverty to the War on Welfare* (1989).

Kintz, Linda. *Between Jesus and the Market: The Emotions That Matter in Right-Wing America* (1997).

Kristol, Irving. *Neoconservatism: The Autobiography of an Idea* (1995).

Lowi, Theodore J. *The End of the Republican Era* (1995).

Murray, Charles. *Losing Ground: American Social Policy, 1950-1980* (1984).

Politics, Society, and the Mass Media

Denisoff, R. Serge. *Inside MTV* (1988).

Flournoy, Don. *CNN World Report: Ted Turner s International News Coup* (1992).

Gitlin, Todd. *Watching Television* (1987).

Goodwin, Andrew. *Dancing in the Distraction Factory: Music Television and Popular Culture* (1992).

Mills, Nicolaus. *Culture in an Age of Money* (1990).

Military and Foreign Policy

Allin, Dana H. *Cold War Illusions: America, Europe, and Soviet Power, 1969-1989* (1998).

Cortright, David. *Peace Works: The Citizen's Role in Ending the Cold War* (1993).

Draper, Theodore. *A Very Thin Line* (1991).

Freedman, Lawrence, and Efraim Karsh. *The Gulf Conflict, 1990 1991: Diplomacy and the New World Order* (1993).

Friedberg, Aaron L. *In the Shadow of the Garrison State: America's Anti-Statism and the Cold War* (2000).

Gaddis, John L. *Now We Know; Rethinking Cold War History* (1997).

Graubard, Stephen. *Mr. Bush's War* (1992).

Hogan, Michael J. ed. *The End of the Cold War: Its Meaning and Implications* (1992).

Smith, Christian. *Resisting Reagan: The U.S. Central American Peace Movement* (1997).

Tucker, Robert W., and David C. Hendrickson. *The Imperial Temptation: The New World Order and America's Purposes* (1992).

Daniel Wirls, *Buildup: The Politics of Defense in the Reagan Era* (1992).

Politics and Politicians in the 1980s

Anderson, Martin. *Revolution* (1989).

Berman, William. *America's Right Turn: From Nixon to Bush* (1994).

Duffy, Michael, and Dan Goodgame. *Marching in Place: The Status Quo Presidency of George Bush* (1992).

Greene, John Robert. *The Presidency of George Bush* (2000).

Gallon, Steven M. *The Democrats Dilemma: Walter F. Mondale and the Liberal Legacy* (1992).

Johnson, Haynes. *Sleepwalking through History: America in the Reagan Years* (1991).

Pemberton, William. *Exit with Honor: The Life and Presidency of Ronald Reagan* (1997).

Noonan, Peggy. *What I Saw at the Revolution: A Political Life in the Reagan Era* (1990).

Schaller, Michael. *Reckoning with Reagan: American and Its President in the 1980s* (1992).

Sloan, John W. *The Reagan Effect: Economics and Presidential Leadership* (1999).

Stockman, David. *The Triumph of Politics: How the Reagan Revolution Failed* (1986).

WHERE TO LEARN MORE

- **Ronald Reagan Boyhood Home, Dixon, Illinois.** The home where Reagan lived from 1920 to 1923 tells relatively little about Reagan himself but a great deal about the small-town context that shaped his ideas.

- **The Causes of Homelessness in America** Social and political policies since the 1980s that have contributed to the gap bewteen rich and poor and the rise of homelessness. http://www. stanford.edu/class/e297c/poverty_prejudice/soc _sec/hcauses.htm.

- **The Intermediate Nuclear Force Agreement (INF).** The full text document of the INF agreement between the United States and the Soviet Union, the first true nuclear disarmament treaty. http://www.state.gov/www/global/arms/treaties /inf1.html.

- **The Gulf War** Read about the Persian Gulf war commanders, see testimony of American combat soldiers, and learn about the events leading up to the invasion. http://www.pbs.org/wgbh/pages/ frontline/gulf/.

- **A Concrete Curtain: The Life and Death of the Berlin Wall** Traces the wall from creation in the 1960s to its destruction after the collapse of communist East Germany. Http:www.wall-berlin.org/ gb/berlin.htm.

 Please refer to the document CD-ROM for primary sources related to this chapter.

➔ *The terrorist attack on the World Trade Center on September 11, 2001, brought a spontaneous outpouring of efforts to assist the victims. The collapse of the World Trade Center towers also killed hundreds of emergency workers. This New York City firefighter looks toward the collapsing buildings where many of his co-workers perished.*

COMPLACENCY AND CRISIS
1993–2003

31

I'm a firefighter for the FDNY [Fire Department New York]. I had gotten off the night before. . . . My friend woke me up early that morning to borrow my car to take his sick cat to the vet. . . . I was up so I went to my local bagel store for my coffee and paper. . . . when I heard a lady scream a plane had hit the Trade Center. . . . I thought since it was a beautiful day that perhaps a Cessna with the pilot having a heart attack had accidentally done this. . . . I ran home to put the TV on. . . . as soon as I saw what damage was done I knew this wasn't any Cessna. . . . my god people were jumping . . . phone rang it was a fellow from my station and he hadn't turned his TV on yet. . . . I screamed to him to turn his #*#* TV on. . . .

When the second plane hit. . . . I said goodbye and told him I was going in. . . . I jumped in my car and was off to the races. . . . the highway was closed. . . . but open for us. . . . I had the gas pedal to the floor as I headed toward the city looking out my window I see both towers burning. . . . when I hear a rumble and see the south tower #2 fall. . . . I have to get my gear so I pull off the highway going down the on ramp. . . . arriving at the firehouse everyone's in shock and we know we gotta get there now to help. . . . as we're getting ready to leave the 2nd tower fell. . . . we commandeer a bus and we're off. . . .

We arrived at a staging area and then finally got the ok to go in. . . . who's in charge? . . . Shoes, papers, and dust are

CHAPTER OUTLINE

Politics of the Center
The Election of 1992: A New Generation
Policing the World
Clinton's Neoliberalism
Contract with America and the Election of 1996
The Dangers of Everyday Life
Morality and Partisanship

A New Economy?
The Prosperous 1990s
A Service Economy
The High Tech Sector
An Instant Society
In the World Market

Broadening Democracy
Americans in 2000
Women from the Grassroots to Congress
Minorities at the Ballot Box
Rights and Opportunities

Edging into a New Century
The 2000 Election
Reaganomics Revisited
Downsized Diplomacy

Paradoxes of Power
9-11-01
Security and Conflict
Iraq and Conflicts in the Middle East

Conclusion

everywhere. . . . we wait til [building] 7 collapses. . . . chief gets us into the site by going thru the financial center and bam there we are. . . . pieces of the outside wall sticking out of the highway. . . . cars on fire . . . buses gutted. . . . I saw numerous acts of courage that day both civilian and uniformed. . . . the looks on the faces of the people coming out of the city that day will haunt me forever . . . everyone was the same color. . . . dust white. . . . women crying. . . . men crying. . . .we must never forget the men and women that died that day. . . . their sacrifice will live on for generations to come. . . .

John McNamara Story #400, The September 11 Digital Archive, 13 April, 2002, http://911digitalarchive.org/stories/details/400

John McNamara was one of the many off-duty New York City fire fighters who rushed to the World Trade Center after the terrorist attack on September 11, 2001. Hijacking four commercial jetliners, the terrorists crashed one plane into the Pentagon and one into each of the twin towers of the World Trade Center, high 110-story buildings that housed 50,000 workers at the peak of the workday. Like John McNamara, tens of millions of Americans were jolted out of morning routines by riveting television coverage of the burning towers and watched in horror as first one tower and then the other disintegrated into itself. September 11 was the occasion for terror and courage. Passengers on the fourth plane fought the hijackers and made sure that it crashed in the Pennsylvania mountains rather than hitting a fourth target. Altogether, 479 police officers, fire fighters, and other emergency workers died in the collapse of the towers. Thousands of volunteers rushed to assist rescue efforts or contribute to relief efforts. The total confirmed death toll was 2,795 in New York, 184 at the Pentagon, and 40 in Pennsylvania.

The attacks, masterminded by the Al-Qaeda network of Muslim extremists, ended a decade of prosperity at home and complacency about the place of the United States in the world. In their aftermath, as Americans noticed millions of Muslim neighbors and tried to balance civil liberties against national security, they realized how diverse the nation had become. For most of the 1990s, prosperity allowed politics to focus on social issues, such as health care and education, as well as on bitterly partisan but often superficial battles over personalities and presidential behavior. However, the terrorists attacked buildings that were the symbols of the nation's economic and military power. The aftermath of the attacks deepened a business recession that had followed a decade of growth spurred by new technologies. At the same time, the vulnerability of the targets undermined Americans' sense of security and isolation from world problems, underscored the global reach of terrorism, and made understanding its sources more necessary than ever.

KEY TOPICS

- Moderate policies and conservative reactions during the Clinton administration.
- Broadening participation in American politics.
- Information technologies and economic prosperity.
- New policies under President George W. Bush.
- Terrorist attacks and a dangerous world.

THE POLITICS OF THE CENTER

In Bill Clinton's race for president in 1992, the "war room" was the decision center where Clinton and his staff planned tactics and countered Republican attacks. On the wall was a sign with a simple message:

"It's the economy, stupid." The short sentence was a reminder that victory lay in emphasizing everyday problems that George Bush had neglected.

Clinton promised economic leadership and stressed the need for private investment to create

Chronology

1969 First version of Internet (ARAPnet) launched.

1980 CNN begins broadcasting.

1991 World Wide Web launched.

1992 Bill Clinton elected president.

1993 Congress approves the North American Free Trade Agreement (NAFTA).

Congress adopts Family Leave Act.

1994 Independent Counsel Kenneth Starr begins investigation of Bill and Hilary Clinton. Paula Jones files sexual harassment lawsuit against Bill Clinton.

Republicans sweep to control of Congress.

Federal government temporarily shuts down for lack of money.

1995 United States sends troops to Bosnia.

1996 Clinton wins a second term as president.

1998 Paula Jones lawsuit dismissed.

House of Representatives impeaches Clinton.

1999 Senate acquits Clinton of impeachment charges.

United States leads NATO intervention in Kosovo.

2000 George Bush defeats Al Gore, Jr. in nation's closest presidential election.

2001 Congress passes massive ten-year tax reduction.

U.S. refuses to agree to Kyoto Treaty to limit global warning.

Terrorists crash airliners into World Trade Center and Pentagon.

U.S. military operations eliminate Taliban regime in Afghanistan.

Congress passes U.S. Patriot Act to combat domestic terror.

2002 U.S. and Russia agree to cut number of deployed nuclear warheads.

Congress creates Department of Homeland Security.

United Nations Security Council passes resolution requiring Iraq to allow open inspections of weapons systems.

---

jobs. He promised to reduce government bureaucracy and the deficit, touted the value of stable families, and talked about health care and welfare reform. His message revealed an insight into the character of the United States in the 1990s. What mattered most were down-to-earth issues, not the distant problems of foreign policy, which seemed to have little urgency with the end of the Cold War. As voters worried about the changing economy and its social consequences, they were eager for leaders who promised practical responses. The mid-1990s brought erratic swings between the two major parties, but the most reliable position was the center. As had happened time and again, the nation's two-party system punished extremes and rewarded practical leaders who claimed the middle of the road with such issues as economic growth.

Bill Clinton's election, first term, and reelection in 1996 showed the attraction of the political center. The later 1990s and the beginning of the new century also suggest that national politics may be stabilizing around a relatively even balance between political parties and partisan agendas, somewhat like the years from 1876 to 1896. In his first inaugural address in January 1993, Clinton pledged "an end to the era of deadlock and drift and a new season of American renewal." What he found in his first four years in office

was an equilibrium that resulted in narrow, bipartisan victories and defeats. In 1996, voters showed that they liked the nation's break from an activist government by keeping the balance of a Democratic White House and Republican Congress, and the presidential election of 2000 proved the closest in history.

THE ELECTION OF 1992: A NEW GENERATION

Every fifteen to twenty years, a new group of voters and leaders comes to power, driven by the desire to fix the mess that the previous generation left behind. The men and women who came of age during the crusade of World War II learned to accept the need to struggle and the expectation of success. Their attitudes shaped the Cold War, dynamic conservatism, the New Frontier, and foreign policy under Johnson and Nixon. The conservative agenda for Ronald Reagan's and George Bush's administrations arose from the disillusion and crises of the late 1960s and 1970s, shaping leaders who believed that the answer was to turn the nation's social and economic problems over to the market while asserting America's influence and power around the world.

The mid-1990s brought another generation into the political arena. The members of "Generation X" came of voting age with deep worries about the foreclosing of opportunities. They worried that previous administrations had ignored growing economic divisions and let the competitive position of the United States deteriorate. The range of suggested solutions differed widely—individual moral reform, a stronger labor movement, leaner competition in world markets—but the generational concern was clear.

This generational change made 1992 one of the most volatile national elections in decades. A baby boomer and successful governor of Arkansas who was not widely known nationally, Democrat Bill Clinton, decided that George Bush was vulnerable when more senior Democrats opted to pass on the contest. His campaign for the nomination overcame minimal name recognition, accusations of womanizing, and his use of a student deferment to avoid military service in Vietnam. Clinton made sure that the Democrats fielded a full baby boomer (and Southern) ticket by choosing the equally youthful Tennessean Albert Gore, Jr., who had served in the Senate for two terms and was widely known for his book on the environment, *Earth in the Balance*, as his running mate.

Bush, the last politician of the World War II generation to gain the White House, won renomination by beating back the archconservative Patrick Buchanan, who claimed that the last twelve years had been a long betrayal of true conservatism. The Republican National Convention in Houston showed how important cultural issues had become to the Republican Party. The party platform conformed to the beliefs of the Christian right. Buchanan delivered a startling speech that called for right-thinking Americans to crusade against unbelievers. Buchanan's divisive comments were a reminder of the multiple ways that religious belief was reshaping American politics.

The wild card was the Texas billionaire Ross Perot, whose independent campaign started with an appearance on a television talk show. Perot loved flip charts, distanced himself from professional politicians, and claimed to talk sense to the American people. He also tried to occupy the political center, appealing to the middle of the middle-class to small business owners, middle managers, and professionals who had approved of Reagan's antigovernment rhetoric but distrusted his corporate cronies. In May, Perot outscored both Bush and Clinton in opinion polls, but his behavior became increasingly erratic. He withdrew from the race and then reentered after floating stories that he was the target of dark conspiracies.

Bush campaigned as a foreign-policy expert. He expected voters to reward him for the end of the Cold War, but he ignored anxieties about the nation's direction at home. His popularity had surged immediately after the victory of the Persian Gulf war, only to fall rapidly as the country became mired in a recession. In fact, voters in November 1992 ranked the economy first as an issue, the federal budget deficit second, health care third, and foreign policy eighth. Clinton hammered away at economic concerns, appealing to swing voters, such as suburban independents and blue-collar Reagan Democrats. He presented himself as the leader of new, pragmatic, and livelier Democrats. He put on sunglasses and played the saxophone on a late-night talk show. His campaign theme song came from Fleetwood Mac, a favorite rock group of thirty-something Americans: "Don't stop thinking about tomorrow. . . . Yesterday's gone. Yesterday's gone."

Election day gave the Clinton-Gore ticket 43 percent of the popular vote, Bush 38 percent, and Perot 19 percent. Clinton held the Democratic core of northern and midwestern industrial states and loosened the Republican hold on the South and West. (see Map 31–1). Millions who voted for Perot were casting a protest vote for "none of the above" and against "politics as usual" rather than hoping for an actual Perot victory. Clinton ran best among voters over 65, who remembered FDR and Harry Truman, and voters under 30.

Despite personal flaws, Bill Clinton was enormously effective as a political campaigner.

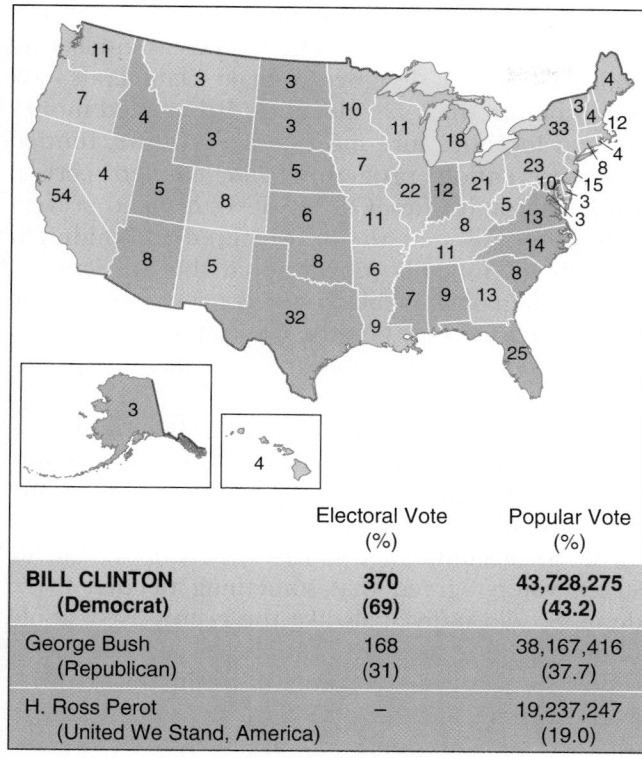

	Electoral Vote (%)	Popular Vote (%)
BILL CLINTON (Democrat)	**370** **(69)**	**43,728,275** **(43.2)**
George Bush (Republican)	168 (31)	38,167,416 (37.7)
H. Ross Perot (United We Stand, America)	–	19,237,247 (19.0)

MAP 31-1   The Election of 1992
Bill Clinton defeated George Bush in 1992 by reviving the Democratic Party in the industrial Northeast and enlisting new Democratic voters in the western states, where he appealed both to Hispanic immigrants and to people associated with fast-growing high-tech industries. He won reelection in 1996 with the same pattern of support. However, the coalition was an unstable combination of "Old Democrats," associated with older industries and labor unions, and "New Democrats," favoring economic change, free trade, and globalization.

POLICING THE WORLD

Although Clinton was much more interested in domestic policies, and the election had hinged on the economy, he inherited an expectation that the United States could keep the world on an even keel and counter ethnic hatred. During the administration's first years, U.S. diplomats helped broker an Israel-PLO accord that gave Palestinians self-government in Gaza and the West Bank, only to watch extremists on both sides undermine the accords and plunge Israel into a near-civil war by 2002. The United States in 1994 used diplomatic pressure to persuade North Korea to suspend building nuclear weapons, calming a potentially explosive trouble spot. The world also benefited from a gradual reduction of nuclear arsenals and from a 1996 treaty to ban the testing of nuclear weapons.

Elsewhere in the world, Clinton used military power with caution. Given the national distaste for overseas entanglements, he responded far more effec-

tively than critics expected. He inherited a U.S. military presence in Somalia (in northeastern Africa) because of a postelection decision by George Bush; he withdrew American forces when their humanitarian mission of guarding food relief to starving Somalis was overshadowed by the need to take sides in a civil war. Clinton intervened decisively in Haiti to restore an elected president.

Bosnia and Kosovo.   Clinton reluctantly committed the United States to a multinational effort to end bloody civil war in ethnically and religiously divided **Bosnia** in 1995. In the early 1990s, the former Communist nation of Yugoslavia, in southeastern Europe, fragmented into five independent nations: Slovenia, Montenegro, Croatia, Bosnia, and Yugoslavia (the name retained by the predominantly Serbian nation with its capital at Belgrade). Bosnia, divided both ethnically and religiously between Christians and Muslims, erupted in bitter civil war. Christian Serbs, who were supported by Belgrade, engaged in massacres and deportations of Muslim Bosnians with the goal of creating "ethnically clean" Serbian districts. Too late to stop most bloodshed, NATO eventually intervened in 1995. U.S. and European troops enforced a brittle peace accord and a division of territory into Bosnian and Serb sectors under a shaky federated government.

The American military revisited the same part of Europe in 1999, when the United States and Britain led NATO's intervention in **Kosovo**. The overwhelming majority of people in this Yugoslav province were ethnic Albanians who have chafed under the control of the Serb-controlled Yugoslav government. When a Kosovar independence movement began a rebellion, Yugoslav president Slobodan Milosevic responded with brutal repression that threatened to drive over 1 million ethnic Albanians out of the province. To protect the Kosovars, NATO in March 1999 began a bombing campaign that targeted Yugoslav military bases and forces in Kosovo. In June, Yugoslavia agreed to withdraw its troops and make way for a multinational NATO peacekeeping force with 50,000 troops from Britain, France, Germany, Italy, the Netherlands and the United States, marking a measured success for U.S. policy.

The reinvention of NATO.   In order to satisfy Russia, the peacekeeping force that entered Kosovo in June was technically a U.S. operation, but it was a reinvented NATO that negotiated with Yugoslavia. Fifty years earlier, the North Atlantic Treaty Organization had been created for three purposes. The first was to unite non-Communist nations of western Europe in an alliance against the Soviet Union. The second was to formally commit the United States and Canada to the defense of western Europe by placing substantial U.S. military forces in Europe. The third was to establish a framework that would make the rearmament of West Germany acceptable to other European nations. For the next forty years—until the collapse of eastern European Communism—NATO coordinated western European defense planning and remained a foundation stone of United States foreign policy.

The new NATO is a product of the new Europe of the 1990s. A key step was expansion into the former Soviet sphere in eastern Europe. At the anniversary summit in 1999, NATO formally admitted Poland, Hungary, and the Czech Republic. Over the objections of Russia, the action erased the last vestige of the buffer of satellite nations that the Soviet Union, had created after World War II. Three years later, NATO agreed to give Russia a formal role in discussions about a number of its policy decisions, further eroding the barriers of the Cold War.

CLINTON'S NEOLIBERALISM

Domestic policy attracted Clinton's greatest interest, and his first term can be divided into two parts. In 1993–1994, he worked with a slim Democratic majority in Congress to modernize the American economy, taking advantage of an economic upturn that lasted for most of the decade. In 1995 and 1996, however, he faced solid Republican majorities, the result of an unanticipated Republican tide in the November 1994 elections.

The heart of Clinton's agenda was efforts to make the United States economy more equitable domestically and more competitive internationally; these goals marked Clinton as a **neoliberal** who envisioned a partnership between a leaner government and a dynamic private sector. Steps to "reinvent" government cut federal employment below Reagan administration levels. A new tax bill reversed some of the inequities of the 1980s by increasing taxes on the well-off (the top 1.2 percent of households). At the other end of the income scale was expansion of the Earned Income Tax Credit, a Nixon-era program that helped lift working Americans out of poverty. An improved college student-aid program spread benefits to more students by allowing direct federal loans. The National and Community Service Trust Act created a pilot program for a domestic Peace Corps. In early 1993, Clinton pushed through the Family and Medical Leave Act, which provided up to twelve weeks of unpaid leave for workers with newborns or family emergencies and had been vetoed twice by George Bush.

The 1994 crime bill demonstrated the nation's delicate political balance. The bill was as much symbolic as practical, designed to make Democrats look tough before the 1994 elections. It included money to help localities hire more police officers, funded crime-prevention programs, and banned certain kinds of assault rifles. Conservatives disliked prevention programs that they caricatured as "midnight basketball." Liberals thought that the bill ignored the problem of racial bias in the court system. A compromise passed only because Clinton managed to recruit moderate Republicans to make up for defecting Democrats.

Clinton's biggest setback was the failure of comprehensive health-care legislation. The goals seemed simple at first: containment of health care costs and extension of basic medical insurance from 83 percent of Americans under age 65 to 100 percent. In the abstract, voters agreed that something needed to be done. So did individuals like the twenty-five-year-old photographer's assistant who found herself facing cancer surgery without savings or health insurance: "I work full-time, and because it's a very small business, we don't get any benefits. . . . It just devastated everybody financially. And that shouldn't happen. That's the American dream that's lost."

Clinton appointed his wife, Hillary Rodham Clinton, to head the health-care task force. Many found this an inappropriate role for a first lady, while others distrusted her preference for a substantial government role. The plan that emerged from the White House ran to 1,342 pages of complex regulations, with something for everyone to dislike. Senior citizens worried about limits on Medicare spending. Insurance companies did not want more regulations. Businesses did not want the costs of insuring their workers. Taxpayers liked the idea of wider medical insurance coverage but not the idea of paying for it through higher taxes or rationing of medical services. Thus the reform effort went nowhere.

If Reagan avoided blame for mistakes, Clinton in his first two years in office seemed to avoid credit for successes. Despite his legislative accomplishments, the press emphasized his difficulty in reaching decisions. Perhaps because he sometimes started with absolute statements and positions, what might look in another leader like a willingness to compromise looked like waffling in Clinton. Both the president and his wife attracted extreme and bitter hatred from the far right, of a sort previously reserved for Franklin and Eleanor Roosevelt and the Kennedy family. Indeed, Hillary Rodham Clinton became a symbol of discomfiting changes in American families.

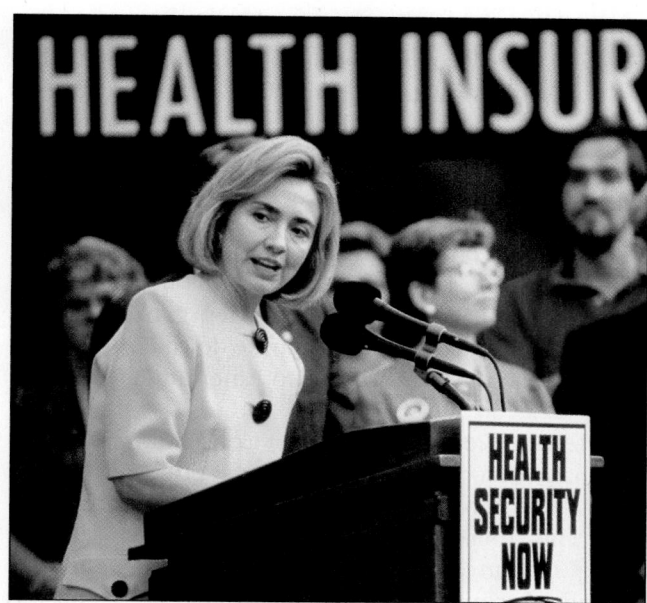

Hillary Rodham Clinton's mastery of policy details seemed to some critics to be inappropriate for a first lady, but it helped her be an effective senator from New York beginning in 2001.

CONTRACT WITH AMERICA AND THE ELECTION OF 1996

Conservative political ideology and personal animosity against the Clintons were both parts of the background for an extraordinary off-year election in 1994, in which voters defeated dozens of incumbents and gave Republicans control of Congress. For most of 1995, the new Speaker of the House, Newt Gingrich of Georgia, dominated political headlines as he pushed the **Contract with America**, the official Republican campaign platform for the 1994 elections, which called for a revolutionary reduction in federal responsibilities.

Clinton laid low and let the new Congress attack environmental protections, propose cuts in federal benefits for the elderly, and try to slice the capital-gains tax to help the rich. As Congress and president battled over the budget, congressional Republicans refused to authorize interim spending and forced the federal government to shut down for more than three weeks between November 1995 and January 1996. Gingrich was the clear loser in public opinion, both for the shutdowns and for his ideas. Democrats painted Gingrich and his congressional allies as a radical fringe who wanted to gut Medicare and Medicaid, undermine education, punish legal immigrants, and sell off national parks—core values and programs that most Americans wanted to protect. Democrats, of course, proclaimed themselves the defenders of national values.

After the budget confrontations, 1996 brought a series of measures to reward work—a centrist position acceptable to most Americans. The minimum wage increased. Congress made pension programs easier for employers to create and made health insurance portable when workers changed jobs. After tough negotiations, Clinton signed bi-partisan legislation to "end welfare as we know it." The new program of **Temporary Assistance to Needy Families (TANF)** replaced Aid to Families with Dependent Children (AFDC). TANF had strict requirements that aid recipients be seeking work or be enrolled in schooling, and it set a time limit on assistance. By 2001, the number of public-assistance recipients had declined 58 percent from its 1994 high, but there are doubts that many of the former recipients have found jobs adequate to support their families.

Clinton's reelection in 1996 was a virtual replay of 1992. His opponent, Robert Dole, represented the World War II generation of politicians. The Republican Party was uncertain whether to stress free markets or morality. The party tried to paper over its uneasy mix of traditional probusiness and socially moderate country-club Republicans, radical proponents of unregulated markets, and religious conservatives increasingly active in politics. Evangelicals dominated many state parties, but they made many traditional party regulars uncomfortable and carried few statewide elections. The Republicans thus displayed many of the internal fractures that characterized American society as a whole.

Because the nation was prosperous and at peace, and because Clinton had claimed the political center, which allowed him to sound like Dwight Eisenhower, the results were never in doubt. Clinton became the first Democratic president to be elected to a second term since Franklin Roosevelt. The Clinton-Gore ticket took 70 percent of the electoral votes and 49 percent of the popular vote (versus 41 percent for Dole and 9 percent for a recycled Ross Perot). Clinton easily won the Northeast, the industrial Midwest, and the Far West; Hispanic voters alienated by anti-immigrant rhetoric from the Republicans helped Clinton also take usually Republican states, such as Florida and Arizona.

The election confirmed that voters liked the pragmatic center. They were cautious about the radical free-market advocates on the extreme right, showing little interest in having Republicans actually put the Contract with America into practice. They were equally unimpressed by liberal advocates of extensive entitlements on the European model. What voters wanted was to continue the reduction of the federal role in domestic affairs that began in the 1980s without damaging social insurance programs.

THE DANGERS OF EVERYDAY LIFE

Part of the background for the sometimes vicious politics of mid-decade was a sense of individual insecurity and fear of violence that coexisted with an economy that was booming in some sectors but still leaving many Americans behind. The solutions, however, seemed inadequate. The liberal response of tighter limitations on the acquisition of firearms could not stop every irrational individual. The conservative response of harsher and mandatory prison terms was equally futile to prevent irrational actions.

Random violence and domestic terrorism.

One after another, headlines and news flashes proclaimed terrifying random acts of violence. In April 1999, two high-school students in Littleton, Colorado took rifles and pipe bombs into Columbine High School to kill twelve classmates, a teacher, and themselves; schools in Arkansas and Oregon experienced similar terror from gun-wielding students. A national manhunt in 1997 captured Ted Kaczynski, the so-called Unabomber, who since 1978 had mailed more than a dozen bombs to college professors and airlines as protest against an industrialized economy.

The greatest losses of life came in Waco, Texas, and in Oklahoma City. On April 19, 1993, federal agents raided the fortified compound of the Branch Davidian cult outside Waco after a fifty-one day siege. The raid triggered a fire, probably set from inside, that killed more than eighty people. On the second anniversary of the Waco raid, Timothy McVeigh packed a rented truck with explosive materials and detonated it in front of the federal office building in downtown Oklahoma City. The blast collapsed the entire front of the nine-story building and killed 169 people, presumably as revenge against what McVeigh considered an oppressive government.

Gun control.

Office-place assassins, schoolroom murders, and domestic terrorism invigorated efforts to monitor access to firearms. The Brady Handgun Violence Prevention Act, passed in 1994, took its name from James Brady, President Reagan's first press secretary, who was seriously injured in the 1981 attempt to kill the president. The act set up a waiting period and background checks for purchases of firearms from retailers, pawnshops, and licensed firearm dealers. Congress also debated detailed restrictions on certain types of weapons, such as assault rifles, and particularly lethal types of ammunition and discovered that police forces and urban residents tended to line up in favor, and rural representatives in opposition.

Gun control was political dynamite, for Americans have drastically differing understandings of the Second Amendment, which states: "A well regulated militia, being necessary to the security of a free State, the right of the people to keep and bear arms, shall not be infringed." The powerful National Rifle Association, the major lobby for gun owners and manufacturers, now argued that the amendment establishes an absolute individual right. Until the 1980s, in contrast, federal courts consistently interpreted the amendment to apply to the possession of weapons in connection with citizen service in a government-organized militia, and federal courts have yet to strike down any gun control law for violating the Second Amendment.

Crime and the war on drugs.

Conservatives, including many gun-ownership absolutists, put their faith in strict law enforcement as the best route to pubic security. The 1990s saw numerous states adopt "three strike" measures that drastically increased penalties for individuals convicted of a third crime. One result was an explosive growth of the prison industry. Mandatory minimum sentencing caused Louisiana's prison population to grow by 50 percent between 1994 and 2001. Mississippi legislation that severely restricted the possibility of parole caused an even greater jump in the state's prison population from 10,700 in 1994 to 37,700 in 2001. States diverted funds from education and health care to build and staff more prisons. The number of people serving sentences of a year or longer in state and federal prisons grew from 316,000 in 1980 to 740,000 in 1990 and 1,305,000 in 1999, with another 606,000 being held for shorter periods in local jails.

The war on drugs, begun in the 1980s, was the biggest contributor to the prison boom. As the drug war dragged on through the 1990s, the federal government poured billions of dollars into efforts to stop illegal drugs from crossing the Mexican border or from landing by boat or airplane in the Southeast. The United States intervened in South American nations that produced cocaine, particularly Peru and Colombia, aiding local military efforts to uproot crops and battle drug lords. By 2002, the United States was edging perilously close to full involvement in a Colombian civil war. Meanwhile, aggressive enforcement of domestic laws against drug possession or sales filled American prison cells. The antidrug campaign fell most heavily on minorities. Connecticut, for example, required mandatory sentences for selling or possessing drugs within two-thirds of a mile of a school, daycare center, or public housing project. Because these criteria encompassed nearly all the neighborhoods in Hartford and New Haven with large minority populations, minority offenders arrested on drug charges were nine times more likely than white offenders to end up in jail.

The strict enforcement of laws against the possession and sale of drugs, and "three-strikes" laws in many states, rapidly expanded the nation's prison population in the 1990s. These laws have tended to most heavily impact black, Hispanic, and low-income offenders with limited access to legal resources, as reflected in the population of this Texas prison.

In fact, crime fell steadily for a decade after reaching a peak in 1991. The rate of violent crime (murder, rape, robbery, aggravated assault) fell by 31 percent from 1991 to 1999, including a 37 percent drop in number of murders. The rate of major property crimes (burglary, larceny-theft, and motor vehicle theft) fell by 27 percent over the same period. Easing fears combined with escalating costs to cause some states to rethink the reliance on prison terms. California voters adopted a measure that provides for treatment rather than prison for many drug offenders. A handful of states adopted measures legalizing marijuana for medical use. Other states, ranging from Mississippi to Connecticut to North Dakota, softened some of their sentencing laws.

MORALITY AND PARTISANSHIP

If the economy was the fundamental news of the later 1990s, Bill Clinton's personal life was the hot news. In 1998 and 1999, the United States was riveted by revelations about the president's sex life, doubts about his integrity, and debates about his fitness for high office. Years of rumors, innuendoes, and law suits culminated in 1999 in the nation's second presidential impeachment trial. To his enemies, Clinton's behavior seemed one more example of disregard for law and morality, while his supporters found the questions they raised to be nothing but partisan politics.

The attacks on the President Clinton were accompanied by unprecedented assaults on the reputation of Hillary Clinton, attacks which showed that tension over social values remained an important dimension of American life. Both her active role in shaping policy and her stands on social issues made her a symbol of changes in American families and values that distressed many conservatives. Talk-show hosts and ultra-conservative activists tried repeatedly to link her to scandals and wrong-doing.

Clinton's problems began in 1994 with the appointment of a special prosecutor to investigate possible fraud in the **Whitewater** development, an Arkansas land promotion in which Bill and Hillary Clinton had invested in the 1980s. The probe by Kenneth Starr, the independent counsel, however, expanded beyond Whitewater into a wide-ranging investigation that encompassed the firing of the White House travel-office staff early in 1993, the suicide of White House aide Vincent Foster, and the sexual behavior of the president. Meanwhile, Paula Jones had brought a lawsuit claiming sexual harassment by then-governor Clinton while she was a state worker in Arkansas. The investigation of Whitewater brought convictions of several friends and former associates of the Clintons, but no evidence pointing directly at either Bill or Hillary Clinton themselves.

The legal landscape changed in January 1998, when allegations surfaced about an affair between the president and Monica Lewinsky, a former White House intern. Lewinsky admitted to the relationship privately and then to Starr's staff after the president had denied it in a sworn deposition for the Paula Jones case. This opened Clinton to charges of perjury and obstruction of justice. Although a federal judge dismissed Jones's suit in April, the continued unfolding of the Lewinsky affair treated the nation to a barrage of personal details about Bill Clinton and to semantic debates over what exactly constituted a "sexual relationship." The affair certainly revealed deep flaws in Clinton's character and showed his willingness to shade the truth. Newspaper editorials, radio talk shows, and politicians debated whether such flaws were relevant to his ability to perform his Constitutional duties.

In the fall of 1998, the Republican leaders who controlled Congress decided that Clinton's statements and misstatements justified the Constitutional process of impeachment. In December, the Republican majority on the House Judiciary Committee recommended four articles of impeachment, or specific charges against the president, to the House of Representatives. By a partisan vote, the full House approved two of the charges and forwarded them to the Senate. The formal trial of the charges by the Senate began in January 1999 and ended on February 12. Moderate

Republicans joined Democrats to assure that the Senate would fall far short of the two-thirds majority required for conviction and removal from office. Article 1, charging that the president had perjured himself, failed by a vote of 45 to 55. Article 2, charging that he had obstructed justice, failed by a vote of 50 to 50.

Why did Congressional Republicans pursue impeachment to the bitter end? It was clear by the end of 1998 that a majority of Americans strongly disapproved of Clinton's conduct but did not think that his personal behavior merited removal from office (see Overview table, "Presidential Impeachment"). The 1998 election, which reduced the Republican majority in the House and resulted in the resignation of Newt Gingrich, confirmed the opinion polls. At the same time, 25 to 30 percent of Americans remained convinced that Clinton was a disgrace whose presence in the White House demeaned the nation. It was not so much that they disliked his policies, which were often quite conservative, but that they felt that his personal flaws and sins made him unfit to lead and represent the nation and deprived him of the moral authority necessary to inspire its people. In other words, although anti-Clinton people are a powerful force within the Republican Party and impeachment was certainly motivated by politics, it was also another battle in America's continuing culture wars.

A NEW ECONOMY?

Within months of the impeachment trial, Americans had a new worry. In the closing months of 1999, many Americans stocked up on canned food and kerosene, powdered milk, ammunition, and cash. They were preparing to survive, not foreign invasion or natural disaster, but rather the possible collapse of the global computer network. Europeans called the problem the "millennium bug," Americans the "Y2K" problem (for

Overview

Presidential Impeachment

Andrew Johnson, 1868	Charges:	Failure to comply with Tenure of Office Act, requiring Congressional approval to fire cabinet members.
	Political Lineup:	Radical Republicans against Johnson; Democrats and moderate Republicans for him.
	Actions:	Tried and acquitted by Senate.
	Underlying Issues:	Johnson's opposition to Republican plans for reconstruction of southern states after the Civil War.
Richard Nixon, 1974	Charges:	Obstruction of justice in Watergate investigation; abuse of power of federal agencies for political purposes; refusal to recognize Congressional subpoena.
	Political Lineup:	Democrats and many Republicans against Nixon.
	Actions:	Charges approved by House committee; Nixon resigned before action by the full House of Representatives.
	Underlying Issues:	Nixon's construction of a secret government and his efforts to undermine integrity of national elections.
Bill Clinton, 1999	Charges:	Perjury and obstruction of justice in the investigation of sexual misconduct allegations by Paula Jones.
	Political Lineup:	Conservative Republicans against Clinton; Democrats and some moderate Republicans for him.
	Actions:	Tried and acquitted by Senate.
	Underlying Issues:	Republican frustration with Clinton's ability to block their agenda; deep concern about Clinton's character and moral fitness for presidency.

Year 2000). In the early years of computers, memory space was precious, causing programmers to designate dates with only the last two digits of the year (thus, "82" for 1982). In the mid-1990s, many realized that such programs might treat the year 2000 as 1900, or might choke in electronic confusion, throwing information systems into chaos. Paychecks might be miscalculated, automatic-teller machines might crash, electric power grids might fall apart. While a small army of programmers worked to rewrite and repair the software, the media offered a steady diet of dire stories that urged preparations. . . . just in case.

In fact, almost nothing happened. The software patches worked. Americans on the evening of December 31, 1999, could watch the progression of millennium celebrations and fireworks from Singapore to Rome and then to London as midnight swept westward across the globe. Since civilization did not collapse in Asia and Europe, North Americans could let midnight arrive with a sigh of relief.

In larger perspective, the Y2K worries illustrate how much the American economy had changed in even the previous decade, and how mysterious the changes seemed. More than ever, it was a global economy. And, unlike any time in the past, it was an economy that depended on electronic computing to manage and transmit vast quantities of data. The impacts of the electronic revolution were still being absorbed into the structures and routines of everyday life as Americans put Y2K behind them and looked to a new century.

THE PROSPEROUS 1990s

From 1992 through 2000, Americans enjoyed nine years of continuous economic expansion. Unemployment dropped from 7.2 percent in 1992 to 4.0 percent at the start of 2000 as American businesses created more than 12 million new jobs. Key states like California rebounded from economic recession with new growth driven by high-tech industries, entertainment, and foreign trade. The stock market soared during the nineties; rising demand for shares in established blue-chip companies and new **Internet** firms swelled the value of individual portfolios, IRA accounts, and pension funds. The rate of homeownership rose after declining for fifteen years. Prosperity also trickled down to Americans at the bottom of the economic ladder. The proportion of Americans in poverty dropped to 12 percent in 1999, and the gap between rich and poor began to narrow (slightly) for the first time in two decades.

The economic boom was great news for the federal budget. Tight spending and rising personal income turned perennial deficits into surpluses for

1998, 1999, and 2000. Reduced borrowing by the U.S. Treasury resulted in low interest rates, which further fueled corporate expansion and consumer spending. Both political parties anticipated a growing surplus for the next decade and debated whether to offer massive tax cuts, to buy down the national debt, or to shore up Social Security and Medicare. In 1997, Clinton signed a deficit-reduction bill that seemed to promise fiscal stability.

Behind the statistics were substantial gains in the efficiency of the American economy. International rivals, especially Japan, experienced severe economic slumps in the mid-1990s. In the United States, in contrast, by the end of the decade the productivity of manufacturing workers was increasing more than 4 percent per year, the highest rate in a generation. Part of the gain was the payoff from the painful business restructuring and downsizing of the 1970s and 1980s. Another cause was improvements in efficiency from the full incorporation of personal computers and electronic communication into everyday life and business practice.

It remains to be seen whether the growth of the 1990s marked the beginning of a new wave of sustained economic expansion like earlier waves triggered by technological innovation. In the past, such waves have followed fifty-year cycles that begin with a thirty-year period of rapid expansion followed by two decades of consolidation and slow growth. From 1945 to 1974, for example, the automobile and aerospace industries helped Europe, Japan, and the United States enjoy an era of sustained growth that was followed by two decades of painful economic readjustment and problems. In the later 1990s, fast-growing information-based industries such as electronic communications, software, biotechnology, and medicine may have jump-started another era of prosperity, although many individual technology companies failed in 2001 and 2002, dragging down the stock market.

THE SERVICE ECONOMY

At the beginning of the twenty-first century, the United States was an economy of services. As fewer Americans drove tractors and toiled on assembly lines, more became service workers. The service sector includes everyone not directly involved in producing and processing physical products. Service workers range from lawyers to hairstylists, from police officers who write traffic tickets to theater employees who sell movie tickets. In 1965, services already accounted for more than half of American jobs. By the 1990s, their share rose to more than 70 percent.

Service jobs vary greatly. At the bottom of the scale are minimum-wage jobs held mostly by women, immigrants, and the young such as cleaning people, child care workers, hospital orderlies, and fast-food workers. These positions offer little in terms of advancement, job security, or benefits. In contrast, many of the best new jobs are in information industries. Teaching, research, government, advertising, mass communications, and professional consulting depend on producing and manipulating information. All of these fields have grown. They add to national wealth by creating and applying new ideas rather than by supplying standardized products and services.

The information economy flourishes in large cities with libraries, universities, research hospitals, advertising agencies, and corporate headquarters. New York's bankers and stockbrokers made Manhattan an island of prosperity in the 1980s. Pittsburgh, with major universities and corporate headquarters, made the transition to the information economy even while its steel industry failed. A good benchmark of a brain-powered economy is whether more than a quarter of the adults (people aged 25 or over) have finished college. The District of Columbia, with its high-priced lawyers and lobbyists, ranked first in 1999, with 42 percent. Next was Colorado (39 percent), followed closely by Maryland, Connecticut, Minnesota, Virginia, and Massachusetts.

The rise of the service economy had political consequences. Rapid expansion of jobs in state and local government triggered popular revolts against state taxes that started in 1978 with passage of California's Proposition 13, which limited property taxes, and continued into the 1990s. Another growth industry was health care. Spending on medical and health services amounted to 12 percent of the gross domestic product in 1990, up from 5 percent in 1960. The need to share this huge expense fairly was the motivation for Medicare and Medicaid in the 1960s and the search for a national health insurance program in the 1990s.

THE HIGH TECH SECTOR

The epitome of the "sunrise" economy was electronics, which grew hand-in-glove with the defense budget. The first computers in the 1940s were derived in part from wartime code-breaking efforts. In the 1950s, IBM got half its revenues from air defense computers and guidance systems for B-52 bombers. "It was the Cold War that helped IBM make itself the king of the computer business," commented the company president, Thomas J. Watson. Employment in computer manufacturing rose in the mid-1960s with the expansion of mainframe computing. Large machines from IBM, Honeywell, NCR and other established corporations required substantial support facilities and staff and were used largely by universities, government

agencies, and corporations. In the 1970s, new companies began to compete with smaller, specialized machines for purposes such as word processing. One cluster of firms sprang up outside Boston around Route 128, benefiting from proximity to MIT and other Boston-area universities. California's **Silicon Valley**, north of San Jose, took off with corporate spin-offs and civilian applications of military technologies and benefited equally from proximity to Stanford University.

Invention of the microprocessor in 1971 kicked the industry into high gear. The farmlands of Santa Clara County, California, became a "silicon landscape" of neat one-story factories and research campuses. In 1950, the county had 800 factory workers. In 1980, it had 264,000 manufacturing workers and 3,000 electronics firms. Related hardware and microchip factories spread the industry throughout the West, to such cities as Austin, Phoenix, Portland, Boise, and Salt Lake City, creating "silicon prairies," "silicon forests," and "silicon deserts" to complement California's original Silicon Valley.

The electronics boom was driven by extraordinary improvements in computing capacity. At the start of the microcomputer era, Intel co-founder Gordon Moore predicted that the number of transistors on a microchip would double every eighteen months, with consequent increases in performance and drops in price. "Moore's Law" worked at least to the opening of a new century as producers moved from chips with 5,000 transistors to ones with 50,000,000. The practical result was vastly increased capacities and portability of computers. The "portable" Osborne and Apple of the early 1980s were suitcase-sized packages with limited hard drives and tiny random access memories for running programs. Twenty years later, when students and business travelers pulled out their laptops at every opportunity, the first generation of personal computers were as outmoded as a Spanish galleon in an age of supertankers.

The computer industry generated an accompanying software industry as a major component of information technology employment (see American Views: "Creating and Working in the New Economy"). Every computer needed a complexly coded operating system, word-processing programs, spreadsheet programs, file-reading programs, Internet browsers, and, of course, games. Seattle-based Microsoft parlayed an alliance with IBM into a dominant position that eventually triggered federal anti-trust action. Other software firms rose and fell with innovative and then outmoded programs. Software writing skills also spawned a new world of multimedia entertainment A

The spread of the information economy meant new jobs at all levels, from writing multi-media software to repairing computer equipment, as these young people are learning.

sequence of new films, such as *The Matrix* (1999), repeatedly pushed the possibilities of combining computer simulation and live action.

Personal computers and consumer electronics became part of everyday life in the 1990s. Automakers built computers into their cars to diagnose engine problems; high-end models added global positioning systems for drivers too hurried to unfold a map. New buildings came with "smart" climate control systems that were touted as self-regulating. Busy people replaced their appointment books with hand-held personal organizers. In 2000, 45 percent of adults reported that they had Internet access at home or work, up from around 14 percent in 1996, and nearly all of them had used it in the previous month. It took radio thirty-eight years and television thirteen years before 50 million Americans tuned in; the Internet reached the same level of use in four years. Children aged 10–14 used computers more frequently than any other age group, and nine out of ten could access the Internet at home or at school. The most networked state was Alaska, where computers helped to make up for vast distances and isolating winters. Close behind were New Hampshire, Washington, Utah, and Oregon.

The electronics boom was part of a larger growth of "high technology" industries. If "high tech" is applied to industries that devote a substantial portion of their income to research and development, it also covers chemicals, synthetic materials, cosmetics, aircraft and space satellites, drugs, measuring instruments, and many other products. Pharmaceuticals, medical imaging and diagnosis, bioengineering, and genetic engineering were all areas of rapid advance in the 1990s with momentum for the future. In fundamental ways, they were all examples of activities based on the acquisition and processing of information.

AN INSTANT SOCIETY

On June 1, 1980, CNN Cable News Network gave television viewers their first chance to watch news coverage twenty-four hours a day. Newscasters Bernard Shaw and Mary Alice Williams brought instant information to an initial audience of 1.7 million subscribers; a decade later, CNN had hundreds of millions of viewers in more than seventy-five countries. Business executives in Zurich, college students in Nairobi, and farmers in Omaha, all tuned in to the version of world events pulled together in CNN's Atlanta headquarters. CNN made a global reputation with live reporting on the pro-democracy protests of Chinese students in Beijing in 1989. When American bombs began to fall on Baghdad in January 1991, White House officials watched CNN to find out how their war was going.

Fourteen months after CNN went on the air, another new cable channel, MTV: Music Television, started broadcasting and had an immediate impact. By the time it reached the key New York and Los Angeles markets in January 1983, MTV's round-the-clock programming of music videos had created a new form of popular art and advertising. With its own programming aimed at viewers aged 18 to 34, MTV inspired Nickelodeon for kids and VH-1 for baby boomers.

CNN, MTV, and the rest of cable television reflected both the fragmentation of American society in the 1980s and 1990s and the increasing dependence on instant communication. As late as 1980, ordinary Americans had few shared choices for learning about their nation and world: virtually identical newscasts on NBC, CBS, and ABC and similar stories in *Time* and *Newsweek*. Fifteen years later, they had learned to surf through dozens of cable channels in search of specialized programs and were beginning to explore the Internet. Hundreds of magazines for niche markets had replaced the general-circulation periodicals of the postwar generation. Vast quantities of information were more easily available, but much of it was packaged for a subdivided marketplace of specialized consumers.

The electronic society in the 1990s also learned to communicate by e-mail and to look up information on the **World Wide Web**. No longer did messages need the delays of the postal system or the costs of long-distance telephone calls. Students could avoid inconvenient trips to the library to look up information in books because it was so much quicker to search the Web. (Many of the data for this section on the new economy were compiled in just that way.) The United States was increasingly a society that depended on instant information and expected instant results.

AMERICAN VIEWS

Creating and Working in the New Economy

Like many American industries, the booming information technology sector that employed millions of workers by the 1990s started with a few key ideas and innovators. Bill Gates and Paul Allen, the founders of software giant Microsoft Corporation, talk about their early encounters with computers as high school students and the origins of Allen's idea of a "wired world" in the early 1970s. Following their interview are the reflections of a worker in the huge high tech industry at the end of the 1990s.

- What do the experiences suggest about the pace of change in the high technology economy?
- What do they suggest about the process of technological innovation and industrial change?
- How do high tech workers cope with the pace of change in their industry, and what are the implications for their jobs?

Bill Gates, Paul Allen, and the Seeds of the Personal Computer Revolution

GATES: Our friendship started [in high school] after the mothers' club paid to put a computer terminal in the school in 1968. The notion was that, of course, the teachers would figure out this computer thing and then teach it to the students. But that didn't happen. It was the other way around. There was a group of students who kind of went nuts.

ALLEN: The teletype room was full of rolled-up paper-tape programs and manuals and everything else. Between classes, or whenever any of us hard-core computer types had a spare period, we would congregate there.

GATES: We were always scrounging free computer time. One year a student's mother arranged for us to go downtown to a new commercial center. We didn't have to pay for the time as long as we could find bugs in their system and report them. . . .

ALLEN: At the end of every school day, a bunch of us would take our little leather satchel briefcases and ride the bus downtown to the computer center. Bill and I were the guys that stayed the latest, and afterward we'd eat pizza at this hippie place across the street. . . .

GATES: The event that started everything for us business-wise was when Paul found an article in 1971 in an electronics magazine. . . . about Intel's 4004 chip, which was the world's first microprocessor. Paul comes up and says "Whoa" and explains that this microprocessor thing's only going to get better and better. . . .

ALLEN: I remember having pizza at Shakey's in Vancouver, Washington, in 1973, and talking

The Internet grew out of concerns about defense and national security. Its first form in 1969 was ARPANet (for Advanced Research Projects Administration part of the Defense Department), intended to be a communication system to survive nuclear attack. As the Internet evolved into a system that connected universities and national weapons laboratories, the Pentagon gave up control in 1984. Through the 1980s, it was used mainly by scientists and academics to share data and communicate by e-mail. The World Wide Web, created in 1991, expanded the Internet's uses by allowing organizations and companies to create websites that placed political and commercial information only a few clicks away from wired consumers. Addresses with the .com suffix (pronounced "dotcom") soon outnumbered those with .edu, .gov, and .org. The equally rapid expansion of bandwidth and modem capacities allowed web pages filled with about the fact that eventually everyone is going to be online and have access to newspapers and stuff and wouldn't people be willing to pay for information on a computer terminal.

Source: "Bill Gates and Paul Allen Talk," *Fortune*, 132, October 2, 1995, pp 69–72. Copyright (c) 1995 *Fortune*, reprinted by permission.

Susie Johnson, Computer Chip Layout Designer

I design the layout of computer chips for Cirrus Logic in Austin, Texas. We're what they call a "chip solutions company." . . . [Laughs] Right now, we're laying out audio chips that go into computers and improve the sound of the speakers. I saw a demo of them recently. They had a regular PC with those regular little speakers and it sounded very weak. Then they put our chip in there, and the speakers sounded like this huge stereo. It was pretty wild.

My job is I'm given a schematic of the chip by the engineers, and it's basically just a bunch of symbols-triangles and rectangles with lines going in and out of them. Each symbol represents a device on the chip that hooks up to something else, and each of these little devices is designed to perform some function electronically. . . . I translate this technical information into the way the chip will actually look—how all this information will be contained in this tiny space. I draw it out using a computer program. It's mostly an automated process. In the past, I'd draw the devices by hand, but the chips I'm working on now are too complicated for that. . . .

I did lots of different jobs before—I was a waitress and I worked in a bunch of stores. . . .

So I was wanting to change. . . . I certainly didn't think that I could do this, but one night I came into work with my ex-husband and he let me do some simple layout, and I thought, this is really cool, I want to try it. So I took a couple of classes at Austin Community College—an electrical design class and an integrated circuit layout class—so I'd understand a little more of the theory angle. . . . I've been doing this for three years. I have no plans to stop. I love it. . . .

There is some art to it. You could take one of these audio chips and give it to five different layout people and it would probably come back five different ways, you know? It's not all automated. Different people will put different things next to each other.

The way I think of it is I'm making little tiny highways for electrons. Some people say it's like New York City on a postage stamp. And it is! I mean, there are so many devices that I have to put into a tiny space. The one I was working on last week had over a hundred thousand. . . .

Sometimes there's problems that the computer catches and can't fix. I'm not sure why that happens, but it's the toughest part of the job. The computer will tell you what area of the chip the problem's in, but you have to go within that area yourself and find the problem and correct it. Like if something is too close to something else, then it needs to be moved over. . . . I think it's kind of fun. You have to figure it out, you have to be a detective. . . .

Source: From *GIG* by John Bowe, Marisa Bowe and Sabin Streeter, copyright © 2000, 2001 by John Bowe, Marisa Bowe, and Sabin Streeter. Used by permission of Crown Publishers, a division of Random House, Inc.

pictures and graphics to replace the text-only sites of the 1980s. By the start of the new century, Web surfers could find vast quantities of material, from Paris hotel rates to pornography, from song lyrics to stock prices.

Instant satisfaction was one of the principles behind the boom of dotcom businesses in 1998, 1999, and 2000. Many were services that repackaged information for quick access. Others were essentially online versions of mail order catalogs, but capable of listing hundreds of thousands of items. Still others were instant delivery services designed to save consumers a trip to the video store or minimart. Although many of the dotcom companies crashed in 2001, they can be viewed as extensions of ongoing trends in retailing and services. Americans in 2000 spent 48 cents on meals out for every 52 cents spent on food to eat at home, paying for the convenience of quick meals without preparation and clean up time. Automatic-teller machines had been a convenience when introduced in the early 1980s, but they were a necessity twenty years later, when Americans expected to be able to pull cash from their bank accounts 168 hours a week rather than finding a bank open perhaps 30 hours a week.

Mobile telephones or "cell phones" were part of the same instant society. They exploited underutilized radio bands and communication satellites to allow wireless conversations among "cells" or geographic areas linked by special microwave broadcasting towers. Technological changes again drove demand. The chunky car phone built into a vehicle gave way to sleek handheld devices the size of *Star Trek* communicators. Wireless phone companies originally sold their phones as emergency backups and business necessities, just as wired telephones had been sold in the first years of the twentieth century. The 5 million cell phone subscribers of 1990 had exploded to 86 million before the end of the decade. The phone had become ubiquitous, beeping in concerts and classrooms, in buses and on street corners. In the disaster of September 11, 2001, portable phones utilizing satellite links offered some final communications from passengers on hijacked airlines.

IN THE WORLD MARKET

Instant access to business and financial information accelerated the globalizing of the American economy. Expanding foreign commerce had become a deliberate goal of national policy with the General Agreement on Tariffs and Trade (GATT) in 1947. GATT regularized international commerce after World War II and helped to secure one of the goals of World War II by insuring that world markets remained open to American industry. The Trade Expansion Act in 1962 had authorized President Kennedy to make reciprocal trade agreements to cut tariffs by up to 50 percent, to keep American companies competitive in the new European Common Market. Although both measures were aimed at trade with Europe, they also helped to expand American commerce across the Pacific.

With the help of national policy and booming economies overseas, the value of American imports and exports more than doubled, from 7 percent of the gross domestic product in 1965 to 16 percent in 1990—the largest percentage since World War I. Americans in the 1970s began to worry about a "colonial" status, in which the United States exported food, lumber, and minerals and imported automobiles and television sets. By the 1980s, foreign economic competitiveness and trade deficits, especially with Japan, became issues of national concern.

The effects of international competition were more complex than "Japan-bashers" acknowledged. Mass-production industries, such as textiles and aluminum, suffered from cheaper and sometimes higher-quality imports, but many specialized industries and services such as Houston's oil equipment and exploration firms thrived. Globalization also created new regional winners and losers. In 1982, the United States began to do more business with Pacific nations than with Europe.

More recent steps to expand the global reach of the American economy were the **North American Free Trade Agreement (NAFTA)** in 1993 and a new worldwide GATT approved in 1994. Negotiated by Republican George Bush and pushed through Congress in 1993 by Democratic Bill Clinton, NAFTA combined 25 million Canadians, 90 million Mexicans, and 250 million U.S. consumers in a single "common market" similar to that of western Europe. GATT cut tariffs among 100 nations. A larger free-trade zone was intended to open new markets and position the United States to compete more effectively against the European Community and Japan. The agreement may have been a holdover from the Bush years, but it matched Clinton's ideas about reforming the American economy.

NAFTA was a hard pill for many Democrats, and it revived the old debate between free traders and protectionists. Support was strongest from professional businesses and industries that sought foreign customers, including agriculture and electronics. Opponents included organized labor, communities already hit by industrial shutdowns, and environmentalists worried about lax controls on industrial pollution in Mexico. In contrast to the nineteenth-century arguments for protecting infant industries, new industries now looked to foreign markets, while older and uncompetitive firms hoped for protected domestic markets. The readjustments from NAFTA have tended to produce obvious pain in the form of closed factories or farms made unprofitable by cheaper imports, while its gains are less visible—a new job here, larger sales there. Evidence from the early years favored NAFTA supporters, indicating that few manufacturing jobs relocated to Mexico.

The **World Trade Organization (WTO)** which replaced GATT in 1996, became the unexpected target of a global protest movement. Seattle officials, committed to promoting Seattle as a "world class" city, lobbied hard to get the 1999 WTO meeting. With finance and foreign affairs ministers and heads of government expected to attend, it would give Seattle world attention. Instead, it gave the city a headache. Fifty thousand protesters converged on the meeting, held from November 30 to December 4, 1999. Most demonstrators were peaceful, but several hundred started a rampage through downtown that triggered massive overreaction by unprepared police.

The battle of Seattle was part of an international movement. It was preceded by similar disturbances around an earlier WTO meeting Geneva, Switzerland, and was followed by large demonstrations against the International Monetary Fund in Washington in 2000 and against a WTO meeting in Genoa, Italy, in 2001. Protesters were convinced that the WTO is a tool of huge transnational corporations that tramples on local labor and environmental protections in the name of "free trade" that benefits only the wealthy nations and their businesses. WTO defenders pointed to the long-term effects of open trade in raising net production in the world economy and thereby making more wealth available for developing nations. Opponents asserted, in turn, that such wealth never reaches the workers and farmers in those nations. American opponents demanded that U.S. firms, such as sportswear companies, that make their products overseas make sure that those overseas workers have decent living conditions and wages.

Protests against the WTO have united environmentalists and labor unions, interests that are often in opposition over domestic issues.

BROADENING DEMOCRACY

Closely related to the changes in the American economy were the changing composition of the American people and the continued emergence of new participants in American government. Bill Clinton's first cabinet, in which three women and four minority men balanced seven white men, recognized the make-up of the American population and marked the maturing of minorities and women as distinct political constituencies. The first cabinet appointed by George W. Bush in 2001 included four minority men and four women, one of whom was Asian American. In both administrations, the new prominence of women and minorities in the national government followed years of growing success in cities and states.

AMERICANS IN 2000

The federal census for the year 2000 found 281,400,000 Americans in the 50 states, District of Columbia, and Puerto Rico (and probably 2–3 million more residents were not counted). The increase from 1990 was 13.2 percent, or 32,700,000. It was the largest ten-year population increase in U.S. history, evidence of the nation's prosperity and its attractiveness for immigrants. One third of all Americans lived in four states: California, Texas, New York, and Florida. These were the key prizes in presidential elections. Their regulations and consumer preferences conditioned national markets for products ranging from automobiles to textbooks.

The West grew the fastest. The super boom states were Nevada (66 percent growth), Arizona (40 percent), Colorado (31 percent), Utah (30 percent), and Idaho (29 percent). Fast growth implies young populations, and the states with the lowest average ages were also western: Utah, Alaska, Idaho, and Texas. The Southwest and South also had the fastest growing metropolitan areas. Las Vegas topped them all with an increase of 83 percent. Among large metro areas with over 500,000 people in 2000, all twenty of the fastest growing of were in the West and Southeast.

In contrast, parts of the American midlands grew slowly. Rural counties continued to empty out in Appalachia and across the Great Plains as fewer and fewer Americans were needed for mining and farming or for the small towns associated with those industries. No state lost population, but North Dakota and West Virginia had ten year gains of only 1 percent.

Another important trend was increasing ethnic and racial diversity (Table 31–1). Hispanics were the fastest-growing group in the American population. Indeed, the number of Hispanics in 2000 (35.2 million) surprised many officials and matched the number of African Americans. Although immigrants concentrated in the coastal and border states, Hispanics and Asian Americans were also spreading into interior states. Both Asians and Hispanics who had been in the U.S. for some time showed substantial economic success. Non-Hispanic whites are now a minority in California at 47 percent, in the District of Columbia, in Hawaii, and in New Mexico.

The changing ethnicity of the American people promised to be increasingly apparent in coming decades. Immigrants tend to be younger adults who are likely to form families, and birth rates have been particularly high among Hispanics and Asian Americans. The result is a sort of multi-ethnic baby boom. In 1972, at the peak of the post World War II baby boom, 80 percent of elementary and high school students were non-Hispanic whites. By 1999 the figure was 63 percent and falling. Over the coming decades, the effects of ethnic change will be apparent not only in schools but also in the workplace, popular culture, and politics.

WOMEN FROM THE GRASSROOTS TO CONGRESS

The increasing prominence of women and family issues in national politics was a steady, quiet revolution that bore fruit in the 1990s, when the number of women in Congress more than doubled. In 1981, President Reagan had appointed Arizona judge Sandra Day O'Connor to be the first woman on the United States Supreme Court. In 1984, Walter Mondale chose New York Congresswoman Geraldine Ferraro as his vice presidential candidate. In 1993 Clinton appointed the second woman to the Supreme Court, U.S. Appeals Court judge Ruth Bader Ginsburg. Clinton appointee Janet Reno was the first woman to serve as Attorney General and Madeleine K. Albright the first to serve as Secretary of State. In 2001, George W. Bush continued to break new ground by naming Condoleezza Rice as his National Security Advisor.

Political gains for women at the national level reflected their growing importance in grassroots politics. The spreading suburbs of postwar America were "frontiers" that required concerted action to solve immediate needs like adequate schools and decent parks. Because pursuit of such community services was often viewed as "woman's work" (in contrast to the "man's work" of economic development), postwar metropolitan areas offered numerous opportunities for women to engage in volunteer civic work, learn political skills, and run for local office. Moreover, new

TABLE 31.1

States with Highest Proportions of Minority Residents in 2000 (percent of total population)

Hispanic	
New Mexico	42%
California	32%
Texas	32%
Arizona	35%
Nevada	20%
Asian and Pacific Islander	
Hawaii	51%
California	11%
Washington	6%
New Jersey	6%
New York	6%
Black	
Mississippi	36%
Louisiana	33%
South Carolina	30%
Georgia	29%
Maryland	28%
American Indian	
Alaska	16%
New Mexico	10%
South Dakota	8%
Oklahoma	8%
Montana	6%

As leadership opportunities for African Americans have increased in recent decades, they have gained positions of influence in a growing range of activities. In the field of foreign policy, for example, President George W. Bush chose Colin Powell as Secretary of State and Condoleezza Rice as National Security Advisor. Here Powell (2nd from left) and Rice (right) observe a White House meeting between Bush and United Nations Secretary General Kofi Annan.

cities and suburbs had fewer established political institutions, such as political machines and strong parties; their politics were open to energetic women.

The entry of more women into politics is a bipartisan affair. Important support and training grounds are the League of Women Voters, which does nonpartisan studies of basic issues, and the National Women's Political Caucus, designed to support women candidates of both parties. Most women in contemporary politics have been more liberal than men—a difference that political scientists attribute to women's interest in the practical problems of schools, neighborhoods, and two-earner families. But women's grassroots mobilization, especially through evangelical churches, has also strengthened groups committed to conservative social values.

Regional differences have affected women's political gains. The West has long been the part of the country most open to women in state and local government and in business. Many of the same skills learned from politics were also useful as women played a growing role as independent business proprietors (see Map 31-2). Several western states granted voting rights to women before the adoption of the Nineteenth Amendment. Westerners have been more willing than voters in the East or South to choose

women as mayors of major cities and as members of state legislatures.

In 1991, the nomination of Judge Clarence Thomas, an African American, to the U.S. Supreme Court insured that everyone knew that the terms of American politics were changing. Because of his conservative positions on social and civil-rights issues, Thomas was a controversial nominee. Controversy deepened when law professor Anita Hill accused Thomas of harassing her sexually while she had served on his staff at the U.S. Civil Rights Commission. The accusations led to riveting hearings before a U.S. Senate committee. Critics tried to discredit Hill with vicious attacks on her character, and the committee failed to call witnesses who could have supported her position. The public was left with Hill's plausible but unproved allegations and Thomas's equally vigorous but unproved denials. The Senate confirmed Thomas to the Supreme Court. Partisans on each side continued to believe the version that best suited their preconceptions and agendas.

Whatever the merits of her charges, Hill's badgering by skeptical senators angered millions of women. In the shadow of the hearings, women made impressive gains in the 1992 election, which pushed women's share of seats in the fifty state legislatures above 20 percent (it was 22 percent in 1999). The number of women in the U.S. Senate jumped from two to six (and grew further to six Democrats and three Republicans after November 1996). In 2000, Hillary Rodham Clinton won a Senate seat from New York. Her husband had appointed women to 37 percent of the five hundred or so high-level jobs in the White House and federal departments. That is far higher than Jimmy Carter's 15 percent or Lyndon Johnson's 4 percent, and also above George W. Bush's 26 percent (see figure 31-1).

Women have influenced national politics as voters as well as candidates and cabinet members. Since the 1980s, voting patterns have shown a widening gender gap. Women in the 1990s identified with the Democratic party and voted for its candidates at a higher rate than men. The reasons include concerns

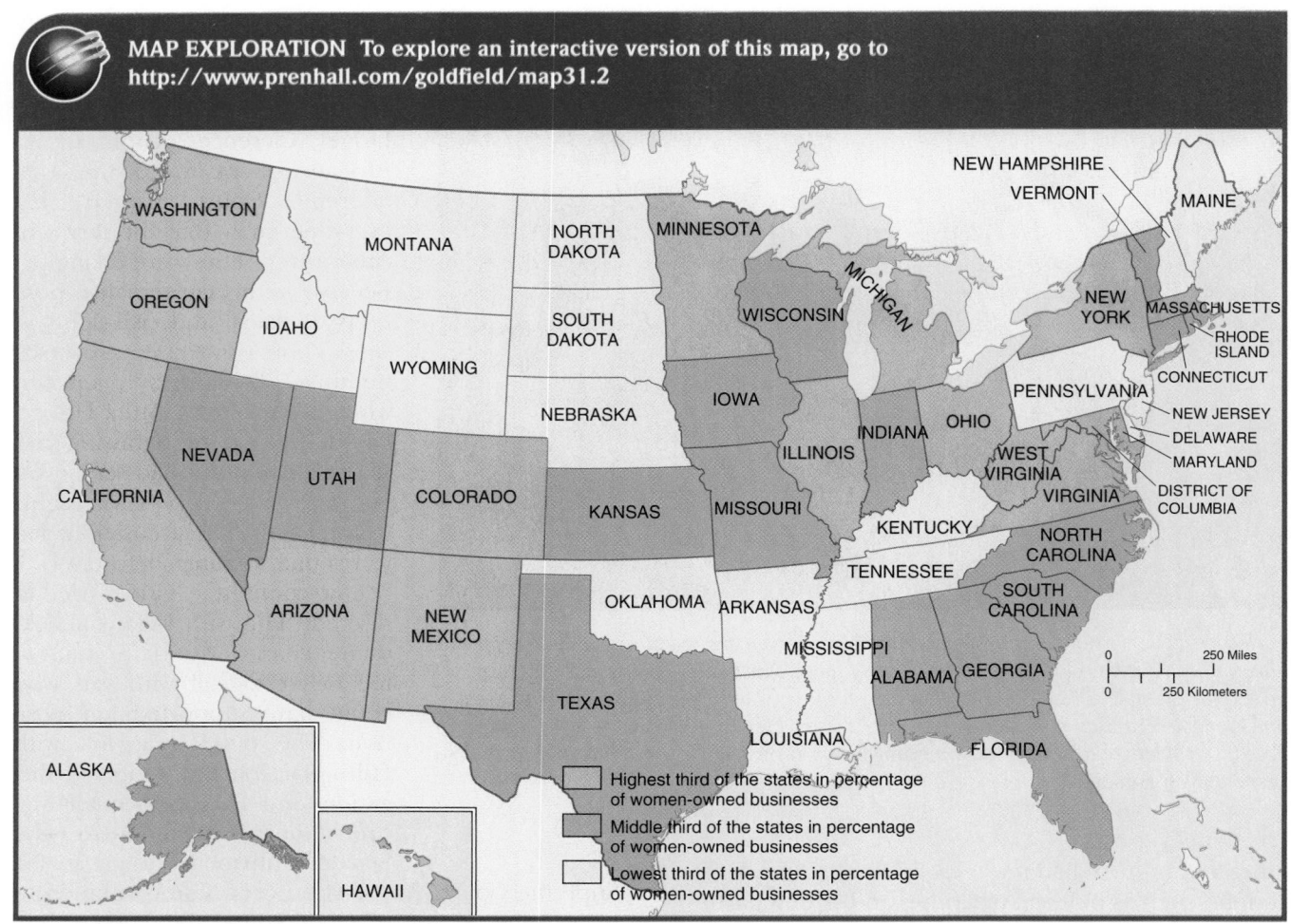

MAP EXPLORATION To explore an interactive version of this map, go to
http://www.prenhall.com/goldfield/map31.2

MAP 31-2   Women as Business Owners, 1997
Some parts of the nation are more inviting to women-owned businesses than are others. The western and Great Lakes states, with histories of innovative politics, stand out as supportive of business opportunities for women.
U.S. Census Bureau, *1997 Economic Census*

about the effects of government spending cuts and interest in measures to support families rather than conservative rhetoric. This gender gap has helped keep Democrats competitive and dampened the nation's conservative swing.

MINORITIES AT THE BALLOT BOX

The changing makeup of the American populace also helped black and Latino candidates for public office to increased success. After the racial violence of the 1960s, many black people had turned to local politics to gain control of their own communities. The first black mayor of a major twentieth-century city was Carl Stokes in Cleveland in 1967. The 1973 election brought victories for Tom Bradley in Los Angeles, Maynard Jackson in Atlanta, and Coleman Young in Detroit. By 1983, three of the nation's four largest cities had black mayors. In 1989, Virginia made Dou-

glas Wilder the first black governor in any of the United States since Reconstruction.

The election of a minority mayor was sometimes more important for its symbolism than for the transfer of real power. Efforts to restructure the basis of city council elections, however, struck directly at the balance of power. Most mid-sized cities had stopped electing city councils by wards or districts during the first half of the twentieth century. Voting at large shifted power away from geographically concentrated ethnic groups. It favored business interests who claimed to speak for the city as a whole but who could assign most of the costs of economic growth to older and poorer neighborhoods.

In the 1970s, minority leaders and community activists realized that a return to district voting could convert neighborhood segregation from a liability to a political resource. As amended in 1975, the federal

Voting Rights Act allowed minorities to use the federal courts to challenge at-large voting systems that diluted the impact of their votes. Blacks and Mexican Americans used the act to reestablish city council districts in the late 1970s and early 1980s in city after city across the South and Southwest.

The political rebalancing meant that local leaders faced strong pressures to assure equitable distribution of the benefits and burdens of growth. Newly empowered minorities began to press for a fair share of an expanding economic pie. In San Antonio and Denver, for example, young Hispanic politicians brought new ideas into city government in the 1980s. Henry Cisneros of San Antonio defeated a representative of the downtown establishment in 1981, and in Denver, Federico Peña ousted a sixteen-year incumbent with the help of an army of volunteers. Both men ran on platforms of planned growth and later served in Clinton's cabinet. Progressive African American mayors in the 1990s included Dennis Archer in Detroit and Andrew Young in Atlanta, leaders who won on positive platforms of growth and equity and who mended fences with business leaders. Meanwhile, Washington state elected a Chinese American as governor, and Hawaii elected Japanese American, native Hawaiian, and Filipino American governors.

At the national level, minorities gradually increased their representation in Congress. Ben Nighthorse Campbell of Colorado, a Cheyenne, brought a Native American voice to the U.S. Senate in 1992. The number of African Americans in the House of Representatives topped forty after 1992, with the help of districts drawn to concentrate black voters. Even after a series of Supreme Court cases invalidated districts drawn with race as the "predominant factor," however, African Americans held most of their gains, while the number of Latino members rose to 22 by 2003 (see figure 31-2).

In struggling for political influence, recent immigrants have added new panethnic identities to their national identities. In the nineteenth century, English-speaking Americans looked at European immigrants from widely separated regions and backgrounds and saw "Italians" or "Jews." In turn, newcomers found economic and political strength by making common cause across their differences, molding identities as ethnic groups within the U.S. context. Newer immigrants have gone through a parallel process. Hispanic activists revived the term "Chicano" to bridge the gap between recent Mexican immigrants and Latinos whose families had settled in the Southwest before the American conquest in 1848. Great gaps of experience and culture separated Chinese, Koreans, Filipinos, and Vietnamese, but they gained political recognition and influence if they dealt with other Americans as "Asians." Native Americans have similarly downplayed tribal differences in efforts to secure better opportunities for Indians as a group.

RIGHTS AND OPPORTUNITIES

The increasing presence of Latinos and African Americans in public life highlighted a set of troublesome questions about the proper balance between equal rights and equal opportunities. Was government justified in seeking to equalize outcomes as well as starting points? More broadly, was the United States to be a unitary society in which everyone assimilated to a single culture and adhered to a single set of formal and informal rules, or might it be a plural society in which different groups accepted different goals and behaviors? The debates at the end of the twentieth century replayed many of the questions that European immigration had raised at the century's beginning.

Illegal immigration and bilingual education. One issue has been the economic impact of illegal

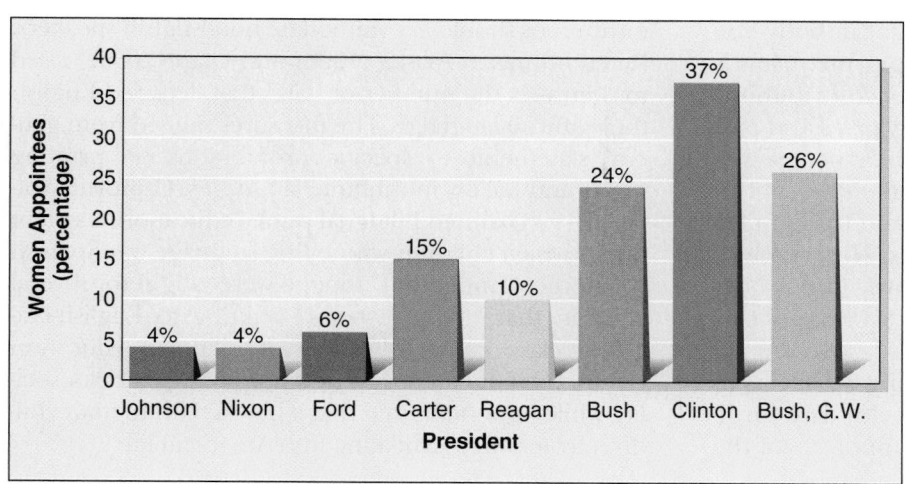

FIGURE 31-1   **Women as a Percentage of Initial High-Level Presidential Appointments: Lyndon Johnson to George W. Bush**
By the 1990s, Americans were willing to accept women in positions that would have been reserved "for men only" in earlier decades, such as attorney general, secretary of state, and national security advisor.

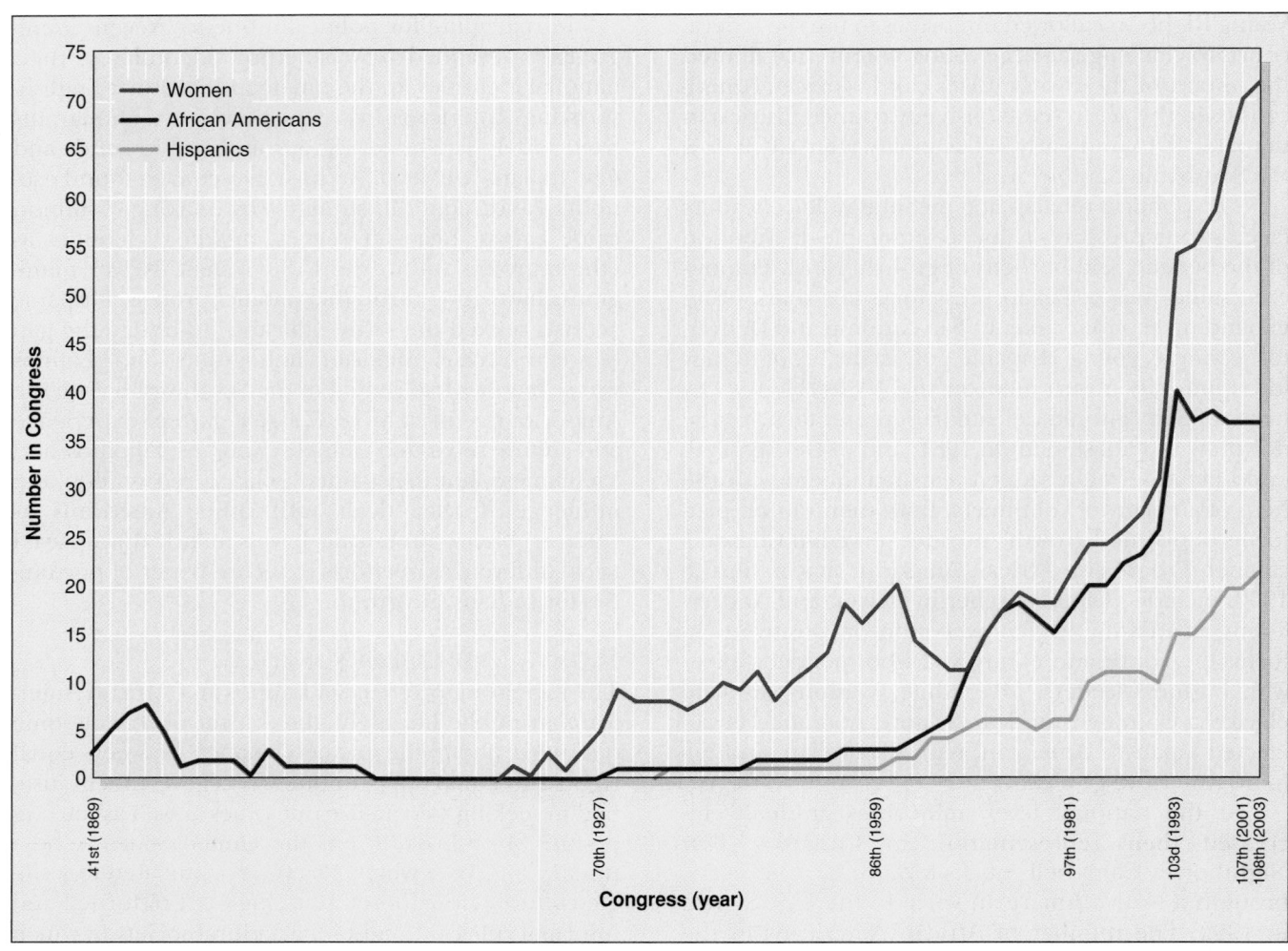

FIGURE 31-2 Minorities and Women in Congress, 1869-2001
The number of African Americans, Hispanics, and women serving in the House of Representatives and Senate increased rapidly in the 1980s and early 1990s and more slowly in the middle 1990s. The increases reflected changing attitudes, the impact of the Voting Rights Act, and decades of political activism at the grassroots.

immigration. Advocates of tight borders assert that illegal immigrants take jobs away from legal residents and eat up public assistance. Many studies, however, find that illegal immigrants fill jobs that nobody else wants. Over the long run, high employment levels among immigrants mean that their tax contributions through sales taxes and Social Security taxes and payroll deductions more than pay for their use of welfare, food stamps, and unemployment benefits, which illegal immigrants are often afraid to claim for fear of calling attention to themselves. Nevertheless, high immigration can strain local government budgets even if it benefits the nation as a whole. Partly for this reason, 60 percent of California voters approved **Proposition 187** in 1994, cutting off access to state-funded public education and health care for illegal immigrants. The mostly white supporters of the

measure said that it was about following the rules; Hispanic opponents saw it as racism.

A symbolic issue was the degree to which American institutions should accommodate non-English speakers. Referendums in Alaska (1996) and Utah (2000) raised to twenty-six the number of states that declared English their official language. The measures ranged from general statements to specific prohibitions on printing forms and ballots in multiple languages. California voters in 1998 banned bilingual public education, a system under which children whose first language was Spanish or another "immigrant" tongue were taught for several years in that language before shifting to English-language classrooms. Advocates of bilingual education claimed that it eased the transition into American society, while opponents said that it blocked immigrant children from fully assimilating into American life.

Affirmative action. A more encompassing issue was a set of policies that originated in the 1960s as **affirmative action**, a phrase that first appeared in executive orders issued by presidents Kennedy and Johnson. The initial goal was to require businesses that received federal contracts to "take affirmative action to ensure that applicants are employed, and that employees are treated during employment without regard for their race, creed, color, or national origin." By the 1970s, many states and cities had adopted similar policies for hiring their own employees and choosing contractors and extended affirmative action to women as well as minorities. Colleges and universities used affirmative action policies in recruiting faculty and admitting students.

As these efforts spread, the initial goal of nondiscrimination evolved into expectations and requirements for active ("affirmative") efforts to achieve greater diversity among employees, students, or contractors. Government agencies began to set aside a small percentages of contracts for woman-owned or minority-owned firms. Cities actively worked to hire more minority police officers and fire fighters. Colleges made special efforts to attract minority students. The landmark court case about affirmative action was ***University of California v. Bakke*** (1978). Allan Bakke was an unsuccessful applicant to the medical school at the University of California at Davis. He argued that the university had improperly set aside 16 of 100 places in its entering class for minority students, thereby engaging in reverse discrimination against white applicants. In a narrow decision, the U.S. Supreme Court ordered Bakke admitted because the only basis for his rejection had been race. At the same time, the Court stated that race or ethnicity could legally be one of several factors considered in college and university admissions as long as a specific number of places were not reserved for minorities.

In 1996, California voters took grassroots action, approving a ballot measure to eliminate state-sponsored affirmative action. One effect was to prohibit state-funded colleges and universities from using race or ethnicity as a factor in deciding which applicants to admit. In the same year, the Supreme Court let stand a lower-court ruling in *Hopwood v. Texas,* which had forbidden the University of Texas to consider race in admission decisions. The number of black freshmen in the University Texas dropped by half in 1997 and the number of blacks and Hispanics among first-year law students by two-thirds. The results were similar at the University of California at Berkeley, where the number of blacks among entering law students dropped from twenty to one.

Affirmative action has come under such close scrutiny and attack because it is a lightning rod for disagreements about the character of American society. The problem is that the goal of diversity seems to conflict with the fundamental American value of individual opportunity. In opinion polls, a majority of Americans reject the idea that past injustice and unequal opportunity can justify special consideration for all members of a group. Instead, they believe that individual merit and qualifications should be the sole basis for getting into school or getting a job, and that such factors as SAT scores and civil-service exams can measure those qualifications. Others argue that the merit system is severely flawed, that students from poor families lack the advantages at home and at school that give upper middle class and wealthy students a head start for success. Affirmative action, they argue, helps to level the field. Nevertheless, many minorities worry that affirmative action undermines their own success by suggesting that they received jobs or contracts by racial preference rather than merit.

The nation surely benefits when members of minority groups are able to build successful businesses. Both cities with large minority populations and suburbs with few minorities benefit when members of all groups are serving on their police forces and working in their classrooms. Students benefit when they interact with people of diverse backgrounds and opinions in the course of their studies. Despite opposition, court cases and legislation through the late 1990s suggested that affirmative action programs would survive in substantially limited form "mended but not ended," to paraphrase President Clinton, although the Supreme Court in 2003 considered important new cases.

EDGING INTO A NEW CENTURY

On the evening of November 7, 2000, CBS-TV made a mistake that journalists dread. Relying on questions put to a sample of voters after they cast their ballots in the presidential contest between Albert Gore, Jr. and George W. Bush, the CBS newsroom first projected that Gore would win Florida and likely the election, then reversed itself and called the election for Bush, only to find that it would be days or even weeks before the votes in several pivotal states, including Florida, could be certified.

The miscue was reminiscent of the premature *Chicago Tribune* headline in November, 1948, which proclaimed "Dewey Beats Truman" when the actual results were the reverse. The inability to predict the outcome in 2000 was also an indication of the degree to which Americans were split down the middle in their political preferences and their visions for the future. The United States entered the twenty-first century both divided and balanced, with extremes of opinion revolving around a center of basic goals and values.

THE 2000 ELECTION

On November 8, 2000, the day after their national election, Americans woke up to the news that neither Republican George W. Bush nor Democrat Albert Gore, Jr., had secured a majority of votes in the electoral college. For the next five weeks, they woke to the same news. Although Gore held a lead in the popular vote (about 340,000 votes out of more than 100 million cast), both candidates needed a majority in Florida to secure its electoral votes and the White House. After protracted protests of voting irregularities and malfunctioning voting equipment, politically divided Floridians engaged in an on-again off-again recount in key counties. The U.S. Supreme Court finally preempted the state process and ordered a halt to recounting on December 12 by the politically charged margin of 5 to 4. The result was to

make Bush the winner in Florida by a few hundred votes and the winner nationwide by 271 electoral votes to 267 (see map 31-3).

The heart of the controversy involved how to read Florida's punch-card ballots. Americans learned a new word, "chad," for the little paper ovals that get punched out. How should election officials count dangling chads that were partially detached? What should they do with ballots where the chad was dimpled but not punched through? Until the Supreme Court put an end to the discussion, teams of officials struggled through recounts. Both parties put their own spin on the process. Republicans framed the issue as "following the rules," while Democrats framed it as "making every vote count."

It is difficult to know who "really" won Florida. There is good evidence that African American voters, who strongly favored Gore, were turned away in disproportionate numbers because of technical challenges to their registration. In one county, a ballot with a particularly poor design probably caused several thousand mistaken votes for a minor candidate rather than Gore. Overseas absentee ballots, likely to favor Bush, were counted despite their frequent failure to meet the criteria for legitimate votes. But recounts by teams of newspaper reporters came to different conclusions about who might have won, depending on what criteria were used to accept or reject disputed punch card ballots. In the aftermath,

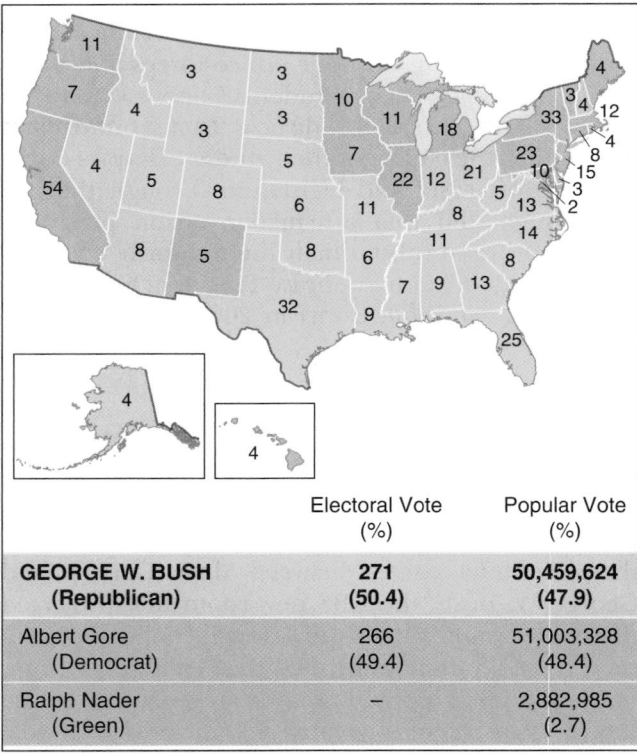

	Electoral Vote (%)	Popular Vote (%)
GEORGE W. BUSH (Republican)	**271** **(50.4)**	**50,459,624** **(47.9)**
Albert Gore (Democrat)	266 (49.4)	51,003,328 (48.4)
Ralph Nader (Green)	–	2,882,985 (2.7)

MAP 31-3 The Election of 2000
In the nation's closest presidential election, Democrat Al Gore was most successful in the Northeast and Far West, while George W. Bush swept the South and won most of the Great Plains states. Green Party candidate Ralph Nader took most of his votes from Gore, and, in a twist of irony, helped to swing the election to Bush.

Despite sophisticated exit polls and computer-based voting models, the 2000 presidential election was too close to call in the hours—and then the weeks—after the voting ended. The Chicago Sun-Times reflected the suspense and confusion in the news media, trying four different headlines as the lead see-sawed between George W. Bush and Albert Gore, Jr.

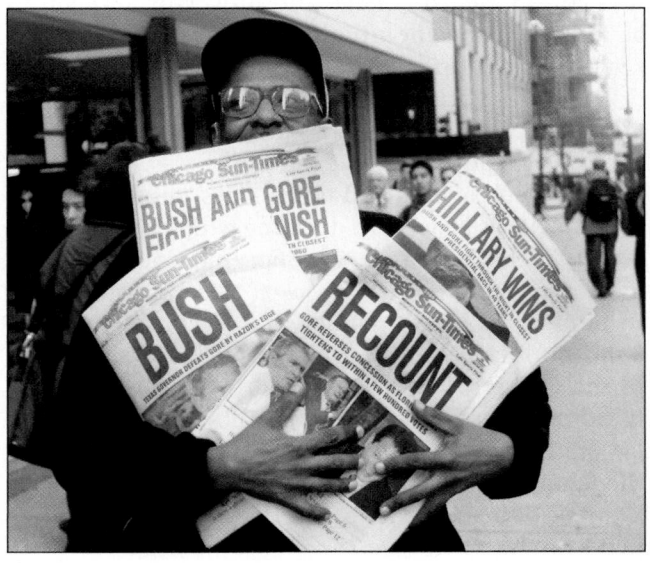

each side could claim to have won, but the Supreme Court ruling and Bush's inauguration made the point irrelevant.

The outcome of the election showed a nation that was paradoxically divided around a strong center. The votes showed basic differences between the parties. Gore appealed especially to residents of large cities, to women, to African Americans, and to families struggling to make it economically. Bush appealed to people from small towns, to men, and to members of households that had benefited the most from the prosperity of the Clinton era. These were divisions that had marked the two parties since the 1930s, and their persistence was a reminder of the nation's diversity of opinions and values. The nation also divided regionally, with Gore strong in the Northeast, upper Middle West, and Pacific Coast, Bush in the South, Ohio Valley, Great Plains, and Rocky Mountain states.

At the same time, both Bush, governor of Texas and son of President George Bush (1989–93), and Gore, vice-president for the previous eight years, targeted their campaigns at middle Americans. Each offered to cut taxes, reduce the federal government, and protect Social Security, differing in the details rather than the broad goals. In trying to claim the political middle, they reflected the successful political message of the Clinton administration. Voters also shaved the Republican control of Congress to razor-thin margins, further undermining any chance of radical change in either a conservative or a liberal direction. To those on the political left and right who had hoped for new directions for the nation, it looked like a formula for paralysis; for the majority of Americans, it looked like stability.

REAGANOMICS REVISITED

Despite the message of stability, the Bush administration took the return to executive power as opportunity to tilt domestic policy abruptly to the right. In effect, the new administration decided it had a mandate for change and acted boldly to implement its goals. Following the example of Ronald Reagan, Bush made massive tax cuts the centerpiece of his first months in office. By starting with proposals for ten-year cuts so large that two generations of federal programs were threatened, Bush and congressional Republicans forced the Democrats to "compromise" on reductions far higher than the economy could probably support. The resulting cuts to income taxes and estate taxes were projected to total $1,350 billion over the decade, with one-third of the benefits going to families earning more than $200,000. By 2003, officials were forecasting a budget deficit of $300 billion for the coming year, undoing the careful political balancing and fiscal discipline of the Clinton administration. Nevertheless, the administration seemed likely to achieve its goal of making the tax cuts permanent after the 2002 elections confirmed a Republican majority in Congress.

The Bush team also moved quickly to deregulate the economy. It opened many of the environmental and business regulations of last two decades to reconsideration—from arsenic standards in drinking water to protections for wetlands to the pollution controls required of electric utilities. In many cases, the administration proposed to rely on the market through voluntary compliance and incentives to replace regulations. Vice President Dick Cheney developed a new production-oriented energy policy in consultation with energy companies but not with environmental or consumer groups. The administration failed to secure congressional approval for oil drilling in the Arctic National Wildlife Refuge in the far north of Alaska but crafted development-friendly policies for other federal lands. Collapse of the energy-trading company Enron in a hailstorm of criticism over

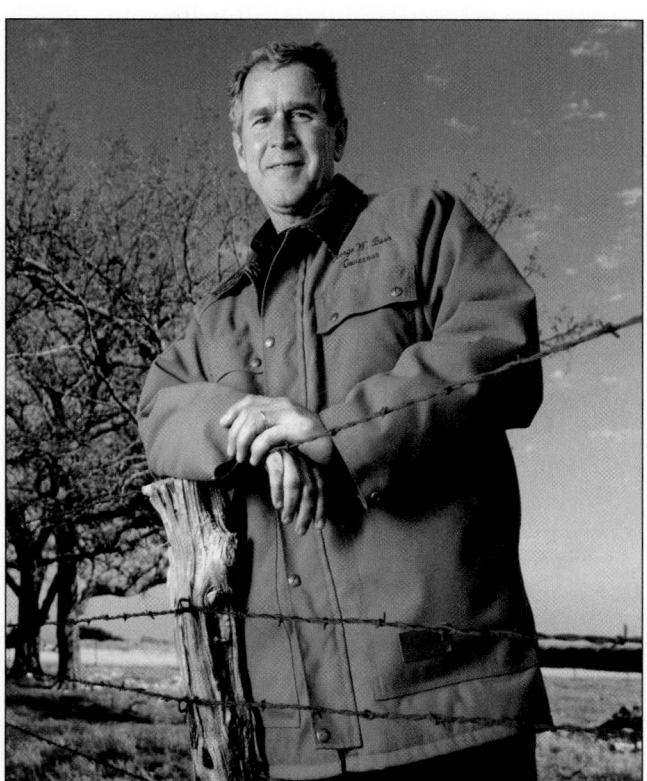

Awaiting the final results of the 2002 election on his Texas ranch, George W. Bush presented himself as a westerner. His environmental policies, emphasizing the easing of environmental constraints on the development of natural resources, were particularly popular in rural sections of the West.

deceptive accounting and shady market manipulations to create an energy crisis in California in early 2000 slowed the push to deregulate. In turn, Enron proved to the first of many companies that had to restate earnings in 2002, depressing the stock market and raising questions about the ethics of big business and business accounting practices. Stock market declines and the evaporation of retirement savings for many workers raised doubts about the solidity of the 1990s boom and helped to hold down economic growth for the third year.

Education policy, a centerpiece of Bush's image as an innovator from his service as governor of Texas, was another legislative front. Tough battles with Congress resulted in compromise legislation, reminiscent of the 1990s, that included national testing standards, as Bush wanted, balanced by more federal funding. More important for both education and religion was the narrow decision by the Supreme Court in *Zelman v. Simmons-Harris* (2002) to uphold the use of taxpayer-funded assistance, or vouchers, to help students attend religious schools. By declaring that both religious and secular institutions can compete for government money as long as it is channeled through individuals who decided how to spend it, the court continued a two-decade trend to narrow the constitutional prohibition on the "establishment of religion."

DOWNSIZED DIPLOMACY

Strong conservatives had long criticized subordinating U.S. authority and freedom of action to international agreements. The new Bush administration heeded this criticism and brought a revolutionary approach to foreign affairs. The administration repeatedly adopted unilateral or bilateral policies in preference to the complexities of negotiations with an entire range of nations.

In his first eighteen months, Bush opted out of a series of treaties and negotiations on

global issues, sometimes after years of careful bargaining. In each case he pointed to specific flaws or problems, but the goal was to reduce restrictions on U.S. business and its military. The administration undercut efforts to implement the Convention on Biological Warfare because of possible adverse effects on drug companies. It refused to sign on to efforts to reduce the international trade in armaments, declined to acknowledge a new International Criminal Court that is designed to try war criminals, and ignored an international compact on the rights of women in def-

Fire fighters work in the rubble of one of the World Trade Center towers soon after its destruction on September 11, 2001.

New Yorkers assembled an informal memorial to victims in the September 11 attacks, with photos and posters of the missing.

erence to cultural conservatives. Most prominently, it refused to accept the Kyoto Agreement, aimed at combating the threat of massive environmental change through global warming resulting from the carbon dioxide released by fossil fuels, dismissing a growing scientific consensus on the problem.

In the field of arms control, Bush entered office with the intention of ending the 1972 treaty that had limited the deployment of anti-missile defenses by the U.S. and Russia in order to stabilize the arms race. The treaty had been a cornerstone of national security policy. Despite the objection of Russia, however, he formally withdrew from the treaty in December 2001. In its place he revived Ronald Reagan's idea of a Strategic Defense Initiative with proposals for new but unproven technologies to protect the U.S. against nuclear attacks by "rogue states." This argument was supported in 2002 by North Korea's revelation that it was pursuing a nuclear weapons program, even though it had agreed not to do so in 1994.

Bush also decided not to implement the START II treaty, which had been one of the major accomplishments of his father's term as president. In its place, he worked directly to improve relations with Russia and negotiated a bilateral agreement to reduce substantially the number of nuclear warheads that Russia and the United States actively deploy for potential use. A new U.S. policy that explicitly claimed the right to act militarily to preempt potential threats confirmed the go-it-alone approach.

PARADOXES OF POWER

The United States in the twenty-first century faced the paradox of power: The enormous economic, military, and technological capacity that allowed it to impose its will on other nations did not extend to an ability to prevent anti-American actions by deeply enraged individuals.

In the 1990s, the U.S. economy had surged while Japan stagnated, Europe marked time, and Russia verged on economic collapse. The American economy in the early twenty-first century was twice the size of Japan's; California alone had economy capacity equal to France or Britain. Its lead was nurtured by research and development spending equal to that of the next six countries combined. The American military budget exceeded the total military spending of the next dozen nations. The U.S. had the world's only global navy and a huge edge in military technology.

But the U.S. remained vulnerable. Terrorist attacks by Islamic radicals killed nineteen American soldiers at military housing in Saudi Arabia in 1996 and seventeen sailors on the destroyer *Cole* while in port in the Arab nation of Yemen in 2000. Bombs at the U.S. embassies in Kenya and Tanzania in 1998 killed more than 200 people. These bombings followed the detonation of explosives in basement garage of the World Trade Center in New York in February 1993, killing six people. New acts of terror remained a constant threat—realized in an appalling manner on September 11, 2001.

FROM THEN TO NOW

Loyalty in 2001 and 1917

In mid-October of 2001, Congress completed work on anti-terrorism legislation that President George W. Bush and Attorney General John Ashcroft had demanded in the aftermath of the September 11 tragedy. The Patriot Act gave federal authorities substantial new capacity to conduct criminal investigations, in most provisions for the next three to five years. These included the power to request "roving" wiretaps of individuals rather than single telephones; to obtain nationwide search warrants; to tap information in computerized records; and to detain foreigners without filing charges for up to a week.

These measures raised a number of concerns about the protection of civil liberties, as noted by the several dozen members of Congress who voted against the act. In historical perspective, however, it is comparatively restrained. Congress deliberated for several weeks rather than instantly ratifying the administration's request. And it seemed as if some history lessons had sunk in, for numerous lawmakers and commentators raised the painful memory of the unnecessary internment of Japanese Americans during World War II.

Perhaps the most useful historical comparison—and contrast—is not World War II but World War I. (see Chapter 23). When Americans plunged into war in April 1917, the nation's political and economic leaders took the occasion to muffle dissent in the name of unity. Congress rushed through an Espionage Act that set prison terms for obstructing the war effort and quickly became a tool for squashing dissenting voices. The Sedition Act of 1918 was even broader, establishing penalties for speaking or writing against the draft, bond sales, or war production.

Federal authorities in the Justice Department cooperated with the private, reactionary American Protective League and with tens of thousands of local councils of defense. Neighbors spied on each other and reported suspicious conversations. The "loyalty" efforts targeted African Americans and Asian Americans as well as German Americans. The Post Office censored mail. Schools stopped teaching German, and immigrants spoke the language at their peril. Workers who failed to buy war bonds were fired. Loyalty became an excuse for crushing working class organizing. Socialist Party leader Eugene Debs was put in jail for noting, accurately, that it

9-11-01

The men who hijacked four commercial jetliners on the morning of September 11 were part of the Al-Qaeda network of terrorists coordinated by Osama Bin-Laden. A Saudi Arabian businessman who had turned against the U.S. because of its role in the Gulf War and its support for Israeli, Bin-Laden was probably the brains behind the attacks on the U.S. military and on diplomats overseas and the earlier blast at the World Trade Center. Operating from exile in Afghanistan, he now masterminded the new and spectacular assault. The first hijacked plane hit the North Tower of the World Trade Center at 8:46 AM eastern time, and the second plane hit the South Tower at

9:30. As flames billowed upward, the South Tower disintegrated at 10:05 and the North Tower at 10:28. Each building took only ten seconds to fall in on itself, but television replays burned the image into the national memory.

The events of September 11 were an enormous shock to the American people, but worries about escalating terrorism were not new. Security specialists such as Defense Secretary William Cohen had been sounding the alarm through the 1990s. The U.S. Commission on National Security/21st Century, appointed by President Clinton, had included detailed warnings in its February 2001 report, although the new administration had ignored its recommendations to reorganize federal homeland security. The was now hard to exercise free speech. Authorities and their allies raided labor union offices and used the war emergency as an excuse for violent strike breaking.

The anti-radical vigilantism of 1917–18 segued into the Red Scare of 1919–20, when federal and local authorities targeted immigrants and labor organizers as potential revolutionaries. The Wilson administration kept wartime political prisoners in jail and arrested thousands more before the nation got tired of fighting off a revolution that never came.

In contrast to the 1910s, Americans in 2001 and 2002 were careful on the homefront. The leaders and supporters of the War on Terrorism have reacted to dissenting voices, particularly those from a pacifist tradition, with caustic remarks rather than repression. Censorship to date consists of careful management of the news and stonewalling of requests under the Freedom of Information Act rather than direct censorship of speech and the press. Violations of civil liberties have affected individuals rather than entire groups. Ethnic profiling has resulted in heightened suspicion and surveillance of Muslims, selective enforcement of immigration laws on visitors from twenty Muslim nations, and detention of several hundred U.S. residents of middle eastern origin, rather than incarceration of entire ethnic groups. Because a number of the detainees have been held without formal charges for periods of many months, a close analogy is the suspension of the writ of habeas corpus by President Lincoln during the Civil War rather than the wholesale constriction of freedom during World War I.

The different reactions can be linked to the far greater sense of national identity at the start of the twenty-first century than early in the twentieth century. Americans in the twenty-first century worry about the challenges of racial and ethnic variety and the stresses of immigration, but mass media and easy travel have helped to promote a shared sense of "being American." There are small fringe groups that advocate or practice violent preservation of a "white nation," but the middle and upper classes do not fear immigration or working class revolution in the way that was common a hundred years ago. Despite a number of individual hate crimes, the formal effort to recognize the Americanness of most of the nation's six million Muslims and Arab Americans stands in contrast to the demonizing of Japanese-Americans in the 1940s and discrimination against German-Americans in 1917–1918. Through the second half of the twentieth century, Americans seem to have learned at least something about tolerance, diversity, and the value of civil liberties.

problem, however, has been to connect broad concerns to specific threats. After September 11, there were reports of information-gathering failures by the FBI and CIA, to be investigated by a commission appointed by President Bush at the end of 2002. However, it is always enormously difficult to separate and correlate key points in the vast flood of information that flows through law-enforcement and intelligence agencies. Experts call this the problem of discerning real "signals" in the "noise" of information. It is much easier to read the warnings after an event has occurred than to pick out the essential data before the unexpected happens—something as true about the attack on Pearl Harbor, for example, as about the attack of 9-11.

SECURITY AND CONFLICT

On September 12, President George W. Bush called the Pentagon and World Trade Center attacks "acts of war." Three days later, Congress passed a Joint Resolution that gave the president sweeping powers "to use all necessary and appropriate force against those nations, organizations, or persons he determines planned, authorized, committed, or aided the terrorist attacks that occurred on September 11, 2001." Only one member voted against the resolution—the same level of agreement that the nation showed after December 7, 1941.

The government response in the U.S. was a hodge-podge of security measures and arrests. Air

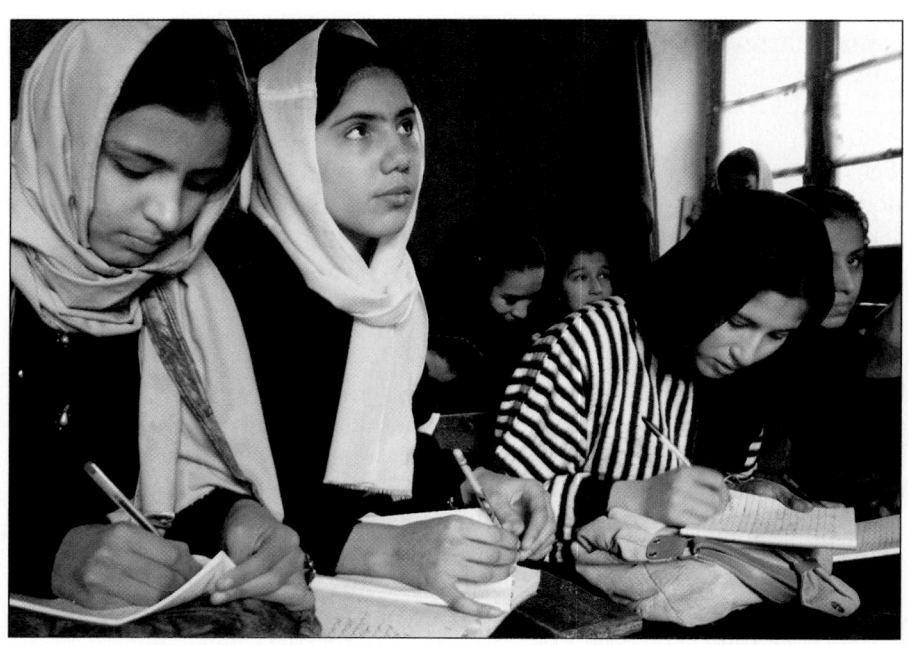

The overthrow of the Taliban regime in Afghanistan reopened many opportunities for women, including access to education as called for in Muslim scriptures. These young women are among 600 who were studying at the Cheva school for girls in Kabul by December 2002.

travelers found endless lines and stringent new screening procedures, watched over by army reservists called to duty by the president. Members of Congress and journalists received letters containing potentially deadly anthrax spores, heightening fears of biological warfare (the source of the letters remained a mystery a year later). Federal agents detained more than one thousand terrorist suspects, mostly men from the Middle East, releasing some but holding hundreds without charges, evidence, or legal counsel. President Bush also declared that "enemy combatants" could be tried by special military tribunals, although domestic and international protest caused the administration to agree to more legal safeguards than originally planned. Congress passed the **Patriot Act** (Providing Appropriate Tools Required to Intercept and Obstruct Terrorists) in late October. The legislation tries to bring surveillance and information gathering into the electronic age (See From Then to Now: "Loyalty in 2001 and 1917").

In November 2002, Congress approved a massive reorganization of the federal government to improve security at home. The new Department of Homeland Security includes the Immigration and Naturalization Service, Customs Service, Coast Guard, Secret Service, federal airport security workers, bioterrorism experts, and many others. With 170,000 employees, it is the second-largest federal agency, after the Defense Department, but will leave unsolved the problem of an ineffective FBI and CIA.

In the months after 9-11, the military response overseas focused on Afghanistan, where the ruling Taliban regime was harboring Bin-Laden. Afghanistan had been wracked by civil war since it had been invaded by the Soviet Union in 1979. The Taliban, who came to power after Soviet withdrawal and civil war, were politically and socially repressive rulers with few international friends. American bombing attacks on Taliban forces began in early October 2001, and internal opposition groups within Afghanistan threw the Taliban out of power by December. Bin-Laden, however, apparently escaped with the aid of mountainous terrain and the confusion of war, leaving the U.S. with an uncertain commitment to rebuild a stable Afghanistan. The Al-Qaeda network and sympathetic groups remained active around the world with bombings in places as distant as Indonesia and Kenya.

IRAQ AND CONFLICTS IN THE MIDDLE EAST

Even while the U.S. was intervening in Afghanistan, the administration was expanding its attention to other nations that supported or condoned anti-American terrorists or had the capability to produce chemical, biological, or nuclear weapons of mass destruction. George Bush named North Korea, Iran, and Iraq as an "axis of evil" for these reasons, and then focused on Iraq. After the Gulf War, Iraq had grudgingly accepted a United Nations requirement that it eliminate such weapons, but had gradually made UN inspections impossible. Such resistance caused Bush to reject the previous policy of containing and isolating Iraq and to make the overthrow of Iraq's ruthless dictator, Saddam Hussein, the center of foreign policy. In effect, he declared one small, and possibly dangerous nation to be the greatest menace that the United States faced. In the meantime, North Korea created a further crisis by actively pursuing its atomic weapons program with the threat of additional war.

In addition to the direct fallout from the Persian Gulf War, background to deep-seated tensions in the

In the early years of the twenty-first century the United States took on long term military commitments in southern Asia.

Middle East included U.S. support of Israel amidst deterioration of relations between Israel and the Arab Palestinians in territories occupied by Israel since 1967. The U.S. has consistently backed Israel since the 1960s. The cornerstones of American policy have been the full endorsement of Israel's right to exist with secure borders and agreement on the right of Palestinians to a national state—in effect, a policy of coexistence. The U.S. had helped to broker an Israel-Egypt peace agreement in 1977 and agreements pointing toward an independent Palestinian state in the 1990s. But it has repeatedly found that hardline Israeli governments have taken advantage of U.S. support from the 1980s in Lebanon (see Chapter 30) to the present.

In 2001–2002, the U.S. watched from the sidelines as the Israeli-Palestinian agreements for transition to a Palestinian state fell apart. Palestinian extremists and suicide bombers and an Israeli government that favored military responses locked each other into a downward spiral that turned anti-Israel demonstrations into civil war. The result for many

Arabs has been to identify the U.S. as an enemy of Arab nations and peoples, despite formal U.S. policy. The deep and seemingly unsolvable Israel-Palestinian conflict helps to explain anti-American terrorism among Arabs, and sometimes other Muslims.

In the spring and summer of 2002, the administration escalated threats of unilateral intervention to change the Iraqi regime and began preparations for a second war in the Persian Gulf region. On October 10, Congress authorized preemptive military action against Iraq. However, international pressure from unenthusiastic allies and from other Arab nations persuaded Bush to place diplomacy ahead of war and devote two months making his case at the United Nations. On November 8, the UN Security Council unanimously adopted a compromise resolution whose effect was to give Iraq three and a half months to allow full and open inspections before military action might be considered. In the following months, UN inspectors searched Iraqi military sites while the U.S. built up forces in the Middle East in preparation for possible war. On March 17, 2003, Bush suspended further diplomatic efforts and on March 19 began a full scale U.S.-British invasion of Iraq.

CONCLUSION

If there was a dominant theme that ran through the changes and challenges of the 1990s and early 2000s, it was interconnection. The Internet, e-mail, and cell phones brought instant communication. The national economy was more and more deeply engaged with the rest of the world through trade, investment, travel, and immigration. Corporate mismanagement affected far more people than before because of pensions and savings invested in the stock market.

The nation's growing diversity—closely connected to its internationalized economy—was reflected in the political gains of African Americans and Hispanics, as well as women. The same diversity fueled battles over affirmative action and language politics. It underlay the effort to increase security against terrorism without endangering the civil liberties of Muslim Americans.

Despite what some might have wished, Americans also found that they could not always isolate the nation from the problems and conflicts that wracked much of the rest of the world. The Clinton administration joined international peacekeeping efforts in Bosnia and Kosovo. The Bush administration chose to ignore several international agreements, but still sought United Nations approval for action against Iraq.

The events of September 11 sparked a renewed sense of national unity, at least in the short run. Stories of heroism were inspiring, whether by emergency workers, by ordinary men and women who helped each other escape from the WTC, or by passengers who kept the fourth airplane from its target. So was the outpouring of volunteers and contributions for rescue and relief efforts. As the nation slowly settled back into routines, however, the question that remained was whether Americans could sustain a new sense of unity and inclusiveness under the pressures of economic uncertainty, threats of terrorism, and war.

REVIEW QUESTIONS

1. Was the American political system more polarized and divided in 1992 than in 1980? How did religiously conservative Americans understand issues of foreign relations and economic policy? How did religiously liberal Americans understand these same issues? What was the gender gap in national politics in the 1990s? Why were Republicans unable to appeal to most black and Hispanic voters in 1992?

2. What were Bill Clinton's major policy accomplishments? Do these represent "liberal," "moderate," or "conservative" positions?

3. What was the Contract with America? What are other examples of a conservative political trend in the 1990s?

4. What issues were involved in Clinton's impeachment? How does the impeachment compare with the challenges to presidents Andrew Johnson and Richard Nixon?

5. Did the American economy undergo fundamental changes in the 1990s? What has been the impact of the computer revolution? Of the growing importance of world markets?

6. What new directions did George W. Bush establish for U.S. domestic and foreign policy?

7. How did the terrorist attacks of September 11, 2001 change life inside the United States? How did ordinary Americans respond at the time and since the attacks?

KEY TERMS

Affirmative action (p. 1013)

Bosnia (p. 995)

Contract with America (p. 997)

Internet (p. 1001)

Kosovo (p. 995)

Neoliberal (p. 996)

North American Free Trade Agreement (NAFTA) (p. 1006)

Patriot Act (p. 1020)

Proposition 187 (p. 1012)

Silicon Valley (p. 1002)

Temporary Assistance for Needy Families (TANF) (p. 997)

University of California vs. Bakke (p. 1013)

Whitewater (p. 999)

World Trade Organization (WTO) (p. 1006)

World Wide Web (p. 1003)

RECOMMENDED READING

Berman, William C. *From the Center to the Edge: A History of the Clinton Presidency* (2001). An assessment of the Clinton administration in historical perspective.

Friedman, Thomas *The Lexus and the Olive Tree* (1999). A positive assessment of the increasing integration of the world economy.

Langewiesche, William. *American Ground: Unbuilding the World Trade Center* (2002). The story of the clearance and rehabilitation efforts at the World Trade Center after September 11.

Mitchell, William. *E-Topia: Urban Life, Jim, But Not As We Know It* (2000). An evaluation of the impacts of new electronic communications on the American economy and society.

Posner, Richard A. *An Affair of State: The Investigation, Trial and Impeachment of President Clinton* (1999). An evenhanded account of the Clinton-Lewinsky scandal that finds few heros.

ADDITIONAL SOURCES

The New Economy

Castells, Manuel. *The Internet Galaxy: Reflections on the Internet, Business, and Society* (2001).

Gilpin, Robert. *Global Political Economy* (2001).

Kidder, Tracy. *The Soul of a New Machine* (1981).

Micklethwait, John and Adrian Wooldridge. *A Future Perfect: The Challenge and Hidden Promise of Globalization* (2000).

Rogers, Everett. *Silicon Valley Fever* (1984).

Markusen, Ann, Peter Hall, and Amy Glasmeier. *High Tech America: The What, How, Why and When of the Sunrise Industries* (1986).

Sassen, Saskia. *The Global City* (1991).

Wallace, James, and Jim Erickson. *Hard Drive: Bill Gates and the Making of the Microsoft Empire* (1993).

Wresch, William. *Disconnected: Haves and Have-Nots in the Information Age* (1996).

Politics

Balz Dan, and Ronald Brownstein. *Storming the Gates: Protest Politics and the Republican Revival* (1996).

Barber, Benjamin. *The Truth of Power: Intellectual Affairs in the Clinton White House* (2001).

Colburn, David, and Jeffrey Adler, eds. *African-American Mayors: Race, Politics and the American City* (2001).

Dionne, Jr., E. J. *Why Americans Hate Politics* (1991).

Gillman, Howard. *The Votes That Counted: How the Courts Decided the 2000 Presidential Election* (2001).

Maraniss, David. *First in His Class: The Biography of Bill Clinton* (1996).

Renshon, Stanley. *High Hopes: The Clinton Presidency and the Politics of Ambition* (1998).

Rozell, Mark, and Clyde Wilcox. *Second Coming: The New Christian Right in Virginia Politics* (1996).

Sunstein, Cass, and Richard Epstein. *The Vote: Bush, Gore, and the Supreme Court* (2001).

Social Issues

Bowen, William, and Derek Bok. *The Shape of the River: The Long-Term Consequences of Considering Race in College and University Admissions* (1998).

Cohen, Michael Lee. *The Twenty-Something American Dream* (1993).

Linenthal, Edward. *The Unfinished Bombing: Oklahoma City in American Memory* (2001).

Weiss, Michael J. *The Clustered World: How We Live, What We Buy, and What It Means about Who We Are* (2000).

The New American Landscape

Blackford, Mansel. *Fragile Paradise: The Impact of Tourism on Maui* (2001).

Calthorpe, Peter, and William Fulton. *The Regional City* (2001).

Riebsame, William. et al. *Atlas of the New West* (1997).

Rothman, Hal. *Neon Metropolis: How Las Vegas Started the Twenty-First Century* (2002).

WHERE TO LEARN MORE

● **Oklahoma City National Memorial Center Museum, Oklahoma City, OK** Exhibits about the federal building bombing and its impacts on the community. **www.oklahomacitynationalmemorial.org**.

 Please refer to the document CD-ROM for primary sources related to this chapter.

THE DECLARATION OF INDEPENDENCE

When in the course of human events it becomes necessary for one people to dissolve the political bands which have connected them with another and to assume, among the powers of the earth, the separate and equal station to which the laws of nature and of nature's God entitle them, a decent respect to the opinions of mankind requires that they should declare the causes which impel them to the separation.

We hold these truths to be self-evident, that all men are created equal; that they are endowed by their Creator with certain unalienable rights; that among these are life, liberty, and the pursuit of happiness. That, to secure these rights, governments are instituted among men, deriving their just powers from the consent of the governed; that, whenever any form of government becomes destructive of these ends, it is the right of the people to alter or to abolish it, and to institute a new government, laying its foundation on such principles, and organizing its powers in such form, as to them shall seem most likely to effect their safety and happiness. Prudence, indeed, will dictate that governments long established should not be changed for light and transient causes; and, accordingly, all experience hath shown that mankind are more disposed to suffer, while evils are sufferable, than to right themselves by abolishing the forms to which they are accustomed. But when a long train of abuses and usurpations, pursuing invariably the same object, evinces a design to reduce them under absolute despotism, it is their right, it is their duty, to throw off such government and to provide new guards for their future security. Such has been the patient sufferance of these colonies, and such is now the necessity which constrains them to alter their former systems of government. The history of the present King of Great Britain is a history of repeated injuries and usurpations, all having, in direct object, the establishment of an absolute tyranny over these States. To prove this, let facts be submitted to a candid world:

He has refused his assent to laws the most wholesome and necessary for the public good.

He has forbidden his governors to pass laws of immediate and pressing importance, unless suspended in their operation till his assent should be obtained; and, when so suspended, he has utterly neglected to attend to them.

He has refused to pass other laws for the accommodation of large districts of people, unless those people would relinquish the right of representation in the legislature, a right inestimable to them and formidable to tyrants only.

He has called together legislative bodies at places unusual, uncomfortable, and distant from the depository of their public records, for the sole purpose of fatiguing them into compliance with his measures.

He has dissolved representative houses, repeatedly for opposing, with manly firmness, his invasions on the rights of the people.

He has refused, for a long time after such dissolutions, to cause others to be elected; whereby the legislative powers, incapable of annihilation, have returned to the people at large for their exercise; the state remaining, in the meantime, exposed to all the danger of invasion from without and convulsions within.

He has endeavored to prevent the population of these States; for that purpose, obstructing the laws for naturalization of foreigners, refusing to pass others to encourage their migration hither, and raising the conditions of new appropriations of lands.

He has obstructed the administration of justice by refusing his assent to laws for establishing judiciary powers.

He has made judges dependent on his will alone for the tenure of their offices and the amount and payment of their salaries.

He has erected a multitude of new offices and sent hither swarms of officers to harass our people and eat out their substance.

He has kept among us, in time of peace, standing armies, without the consent of our legislatures.

He has affected to render the military independent of, and superior to, the civil power.

He has combined with others to subject us to a jurisdiction foreign to our Constitution and unacknowledged by our laws, giving his assent to their acts of pretended legislation—

For quartering large bodies of armed troops among us;

For protecting them by mock trial, from punishment for any murders which they should commit on the inhabitants of these States;

For cutting off our trade with all parts of the world;

For imposing taxes on us without our consent;

For depriving us, in many cases, of the benefit of trial by jury;

For transporting us beyond seas to be tried for pretended offences;

For abolishing the free system of English laws in a neighboring province, establishing therein an arbitrary government, and enlarging its boundaries, so as to render it at once an example and fit instrument for introducing the same absolute rule into these colonies;

For taking away our charters, abolishing our most valuable laws, and altering, fundamentally, the powers of our governments.

For suspending our own legislatures and declaring themselves invested with power to legislate for us in all cases whatsoever.

He has abdicated government here by declaring us out of his protection and waging war against us.

He has plundered our seas, ravaged our coasts, burnt our towns, and destroyed the lives of our people.

He is, at this time, transporting large armies of foreign mercenaries to complete the works of death, desolation, and tyranny already begun with circumstances of cruelty and perfidy scarcely paralleled in the most barbarous ages, and totally unworthy the head of a civilized nation.

He has constrained our fellow citizens, taken captive on the high seas, to bear arms against their country, to become the executioners of their friends and brethren, or to fall themselves by their hands.

He has excited domestic insurrections amongst us and has endeavored to bring on the inhabitants of our frontiers, the merciless Indian savages, whose known rule of warfare is an undistinguished destruction of all ages, sexes, and conditions.

In every stage of these oppressions, we have petitioned for redress in the most humble terms; our repeated petitions have been answered only by repeated injury. A prince whose character is thus marked by every act which may define a tyrant is unfit to be the ruler of a free people.

Nor have we been wanting in attention to our British brethren. We have warned them, from time to time, of attempts made by their legislature to extend an unwarrantable jurisdiction over us. We have reminded them of the circumstances of our emigration and settlement here. We have appealed to their native justice and magnanimity, and we have conjured them, by the ties of our common kindred, to disavow these usurpations, which would inevitably interrupt our connections and correspondence. They, too, have been deaf to the voice of justice and consanguinity. We must, therefore, acquiesce in the necessity which denounces our separation, and hold them, as we hold the rest of mankind, enemies in war, in peace, friends.

We, therefore, the representatives of the United States of America, in general Congress assembled, appealing to the Supreme Judge of the world for the rectitude of our intentions, do, in the name and by the authority of the good people of these colonies, solemnly publish and declare, that these united colonies are, and of right ought to be, free and independent states: that they are absolved from all allegiance to the British Crown, and that all political connection between them and the state of Great Britain is, and ought to be, totally dissolved; and that, as free and independent states, they have full power to levy war, conclude peace, contract alliances, establish commerce, and to do all other acts and things which independent states may of right do. And, for the support of this declaration, with a firm reliance on the protection of Divine Providence, we mutually pledge to each other our lives, our fortunes, and our sacred honor.

THE ARTICLES OF CONFEDERATION AND PERPETUAL UNION*

Between the states of New Hampshire, Massachusetts-bay Rhode Island and Providence Plantations, Connecticut, New York, New Jersey, Pennsylvania, Delaware, Maryland, Virginia, North Carolina, South Carolina, and Georgia.

ARTICLE 1
The Stile of this Confederacy shall be "The United States of America."

ARTICLE 2
Each state retains its sovereignty, freedom, and independence, and every power, jurisdiction, and right, which is not by this Confederation expressly delegated to the United States, in Congress assembled.

ARTICLE 3
The said States hereby severally enter into a firm league of friendship with each other, for their common defense, the security of their liberties, and their mutual and general welfare, binding themselves to assist each other, against all force offered to, or attacks made upon them, or any of them, on account of religion, sovereignty, trade, or any other pretense whatever.

ARTICLE 4
The better to secure and perpetuate mutual friendship and intercourse among the people of the different States in this Union, the free inhabitants of each of these States, paupers, vagabonds, and fugitives from justice excepted, shall be entitled to all privileges and immunities of free citizens in the several States; and the people of each State shall have free ingress and regress to and from any other State, and shall enjoy therein all the privileges of trade and commerce, subject to the same duties, impositions, and restrictions as the inhabitants thereof respectively, provided that such restrictions shall not extend so far as to prevent the removal of property imported into any State, to any other State of which the owner is an inhabitant; provided also that no imposition, duties or restriction shall be laid

---

*Agreed to in Congress November 15, 1777; ratified March 1781.

by any State, on the property of the United States, or either of them.

If any person guilty of, or charged with, treason, felony, or other high misdemeanor in any State, shall flee from justice, and be found in any of the United States, he shall, upon demand of the Governor or executive power of the State from which he fled, be delivered up and removed to the State having jurisdiction of his offense.

Full faith and credit shall be given in each of these States to the records, acts, and judicial proceedings of the courts and magistrates of every other State.

ARTICLE 5

For the most convenient management of the general interests of the United States, delegates shall be annually appointed in such manner as the legislatures of each State shall direct, to meet in Congress on the first Monday in November, in every year, with a power reserved to each State to recall its delegates, or any of them, at any time within the year, and to send others in their stead for the remainder of the year.

No State shall be represented in Congress by less than two, nor by more than seven members; and no person shall be capable of being a delegate for more than three years in any term of six years; nor shall any person, being a delegate, be capable of holding any office under the United States, for which he, or another for his benefit, receives any salary, fees or emolument of any kind.

Each State shall maintain its own delegates in a meeting of the States, and while they act as members of the committee of the States.

In determining questions in the United States in Congress assembled, each State shall have one vote.

Freedom of speech and debate in Congress shall not be impeached or questioned in any court or place out of Congress, and the members of Congress shall be protected in their persons from arrests or imprisonments, during the time of their going to and from, and attendence on Congress, except for treason, felony, or breach of the peace.

ARTICLE 6

No State, without the consent of the United States in Congress assembled, shall send any embassy to, or receive any embassy from, or enter into any conference, agreement, alliance or treaty with any King, Prince or State; nor shall any person holding any office of profit or trust under the United States, or any of them, accept any present, emolument, office or title of any kind whatever from any King, Prince or foreign State; nor shall the United States in Congress assembled, or any of them, grant any title of nobility.

No two or more States shall enter into any treaty, confederation or alliance whatever between them, without the consent of the United States in Congress assembled, specifying accurately the purposes for which the same is to be entered into, and how long it shall continue.

No State shall lay any imposts or duties, which may interfere with any stipulations in treaties, entered into by the United States in Congress assembled, with any King, Prince or State, in pursuance of any treaties already proposed by Congress, to the courts of France and Spain.

No vessel of war shall be kept up in time of peace by any State, except such number only, as shall be deemed necessary by the United States in Congress assembled, for the defense of such State, or its trade; nor shall any body of forces be kept up by any State in time of peace, except such number only, as in the judgement of the United States in Congress assembled, shall be deemed requisite to garrison the forts necessary for the defense of such State; but every State shall always keep up a well-regulated and disciplined militia, sufficiently armed and accoutered, and shall provide and constantly have ready for use, in public stores, a due number of filed pieces and tents, and a proper quantity of arms, ammunition and camp equipage.

No State shall engage in any war without the consent of the United States in Congress assembled, unless such State be actually invaded by enemies, or shall have received certain advice of a resolution being formed by some nation of Indians to invade such State, and the danger is so imminent as not to admit of a delay, till the United States in Congress assembled can be consulted; nor shall any State grant commissions to any ships or vessels of war, nor letters of marque or reprisal, except it be after a declaration of war by the United States in Congress assembled, and then only against the Kingdom or State and the subjects thereof, against which war has been so declared, and under such regulations as shall be established by the United States in Congress assembled, unless such State be infested by pirates, in which case vessels of war may be fitted out for that occasion, and kept so long as the danger shall continue, or until the United States in Congress assembled shall determine otherwise.

ARTICLE 7

When land forces are raised by any State for the common defense, all officers of or under the rank of colonel, shall be appointed by the legislature of each State respectively, by whom such forces shall be raised, or in such manner as such State shall direct, and all vacancies shall be filled up by the State which first made the appointment.

ARTICLE 8

All charges of war, and all other expenses that shall be incurred for the common defense or general welfare, and allowed by the United States in Congress assembled, shall be defrayed out of a common treasury, which shall be supplied by the several States in proportion to the value of all land within each State, granted to or surveyed for any person, as such land and the buildings and improvements thereon shall be estimated according to such mode as the United States in Congress assembled, shall from time to time direct and appoint.

The taxes for paying that proportion shall be laid and levied by the authority and direction of the legislatures of the several States within the time agreed upon by the United States in Congress assembled.

ARTICLE 9

The United States in Congress assembled, shall have the sole and exclusive right and power of determining on peace and war, except in the cases mentioned in the sixth article; of sending and receiving ambassadors; entering into treaties and alliances, provided that no treaty of commerce shall be made whereby the legislative power of the respective States shall be restrained from imposing such imposts and duties on foreigners, as their own people are subjected to, or from prohibiting the exportation or importation of any species of goods or commodities whatsoever; of establishing rules for deciding in all cases, what captures on land or water shall be legal, and in what manner prizes taken by land or naval forces in the service of the United States shall be divided or appropriated; of granting letters of marque and reprisal in times of peace; appointing courts for the trial of piracies and felonies committed on the high seas and establishing courts for receiving and determining finally appeals in all cases of captures, provided that no member of Congress shall be appointed a judge of any of the said courts.

The United States in Congress assembled shall also be the last resort on appeal in all disputes and differences now subsisting or that hereafter may arise between two or more States concerning boundary, jurisdiction or any other causes whatever; which authority shall always be exercised in the manner following. Whenever the legislative or executive authority or lawful agent of any State in controversy with another shall present a petition to Congress stating the matter in question and praying for a hearing, notice thereof shall be given by order of Congress to the legislative or executive authority of the other State in controversy, and a day assigned for the appearance of the parties by their lawful agents, who shall then be directed to appoint by joint consent, commissioners or judges to constitute a court for hearing and determining the matter in question: but if they cannot agree, Congress shall name three persons out of each of the United States, and from the list of such persons each party shall alternately strike out one, the petitioners beginning, until the number shall be reduced to thirteen; and from that number not less than seven, nor more than nine names as Congress shall direct, shall in the presence of Congress be drawn out by lot, and the persons whose names shall be so drawn or any five of them, shall be commissioners or judges, to hear and finally determine the controversy, so always as a major part of the judges who shall hear the cause shall agree in the determination: and if either party shall neglect to attend at the day appointed, without showing reasons, which Congress shall judge sufficient, or being present shall refuse to strike, the Congress shall proceed to nominate three persons out of each State, and the secretary of Congress shall strike in behalf of such party absent or refusing; and the judgement and sentence of the court to be appointed, in the manner before prescribed, shall be final and conclusive; and if any of the parties shall refuse to submit to the authority of such court, or to appear or defend their claim or cause, the court shall nevertheless proceed to pronounce sentence, or judgement, which shall in like manner be final and decisive, the judgement or sentence and other proceedings being in either case transmitted to Congress, and lodged among the acts of Congress for the security of the parties concerned: provided that every commissioner, before he sits in judgement, shall take an oath to be administered by one of the judges of the supreme or superior court of the State, where the cause shall be tried, "well and truly to hear and determine the matter in question, according to the best of his judgement, without favor, affection or hope of reward:" provided also, that no State shall be deprived of territory for the benefit of the United States.

All controversies concerning the private right of soil claimed under different grants of two or more States, whose jurisdictions as they may respect such lands, and the States which passed such grants are adjusted, the said grants or either of them being at the same time claimed to have originated antecedent to such settlement of jurisdiction, shall on the petition of either party to the Congress of the United States, be finally determined as near as may be in the same manner as is before prescribed for deciding disputes respecting territorial jurisdiction between different States.

The United States in Congress assembled shall also have the sole and exclusive right and power of regulating the alloy and value of coin struck by their own authority, or by that of the respective States; fixing the standards of weights and measures throughout the United States; regulating the trade and managing all affairs with the Indians not members of any of the States; provided that the legislative right of any State within its own limits be not infringed or violated; establishing or regulating post offices from one State to another, throughout all the United States, and exacting such postage on the papers passing through the same as may be requisite to defray the expenses of the said office; appointing all officers of the land forces in the service of the United States, excepting regimental officers; appointing all the officers of the naval forces, and commissioning all officers whatever in the service of the United States; making rules for the government and regulation of the said land and naval forces, and directing their operations.

The United States in Congress assembled shall have authority to appoint a committee, to sit in the recess of Congress, to be denominated "A Committee of the States," and to consist of one delegate from each State; and to appoint such other committees and civil officers as may be necessary for managing the general affairs of the United States under their direction; to appoint one of their members to preside, provided that no person be allowed to serve in the office of president more than one year in any term of three years; to ascertain the necessary sums of money to be raised for the service of the United States, and to appropriate and apply the same for defraying the public expenses; to borrow money, or emit bills on the credit of the United States, transmitting every half year to the respective States an account of the sums of money so borrowed or emitted; to build and equip a navy; to agree upon the number of land forces, and to make requisitions from each State for its quota, in proportion to the number of white inhabitants in such State; which requisition shall be binding, and thereupon the legislature of each State shall appoint the regimental officers, raise the men and cloath, arm and equip them in a soldierlike manner, at the expense of the United States; and the officers and men so cloathed, armed and equipped shall march to the place appointed, and within the time agreed on by the United States in Congress assembled; but if the United States in Congress assembled shall, on consideration of circumstances judge proper that any State should not raise men, or should raise a smaller number of men than the quota thereof, such extra number shall be raised, officered, cloathed, armed and equipped in the same manner as the quota of each State, unless the legislature of such State shall judge that such extra number cannot be safely spared out in the same, in which case they shall raise, officer, cloath, arm and equip as many of such extra number as they judge can be safely spared. And the officers and men so cloathed, armed, and equipped, shall march to the place appointed, and within the time agreed on by the United States in Congress assembled.

The United States in Congress assembled shall never engage in a war, nor grant letters of marque or reprisal in time of peace, nor enter into any treaties or alliances, nor coin money, nor regulate the value thereof, nor ascertain the sums and expenses necessary for the defense and welfare of the United States, or any of them, nor emit bills, nor borrow money on the credit of the United States, nor appropriate money, nor agree upon the number of vessels of war, to be built or purchased, or the number of land or sea forces to be raised, nor appoint a commander in chief of the army or navy, unless nine States assent to the same: nor shall a question on any other point, except for adjourning from day to day be determined, unless by the votes of the majority of the United States in Congress assembled.

The Congress of the United States shall have power to adjourn to any time within the year, and to any place within the United States, so that no period of adjournment be for a longer duration than the space of six months, and shall publish the journal of their proceedings monthly, except such parts thereof relating to treaties, al-

liances or military operations, as in their judgement require secrecy; and the yeas and nays of the delegates of each State on any question shall be entered on the journal, when it is desired by any delegates of a State, or any of them, at his or their request shall be furnished with a transcript of the said journal, except such parts as are above excepted, to lay before the legislatures of the several States.

ARTICLE 10

The Committee of the States, or any nine of them, shall be authorized to execute, in the recess of Congress, such of the powers of Congress as the United States in Congress assembled, by the consent of the nine States, shall from time to time think expedient to vest them with; provided that no power be delegated to the said Committee, for the exercise of which, by the Articles of Confederation, the voice of nine States in the Congress of the United States assembled is requisite.

ARTICLE 11

Canada acceding to this confederation, and adjoining in the measures of the United States, shall be admitted into, and entitled to all the advantages of this Union; but no other colony shall be admitted into the same, unless such admission be agreed to by nine States.

ARTICLE 12

All bills of credit emitted, monies borrowed, and debts contracted by, or under the authority of Congress, before the assembling of the United States, in pursuance of the present confederation, shall be deemed and considered as a charge against the United States, for payment and satisfaction whereof the said United States, and the public faith are hereby solemnly pledged.

ARTICLE 13

Every State shall abide by the determination of the United States in Congress assembled, on all questions which by this confederation are submitted to them. And the Articles of this Confederation shall be inviolably observed by every State, and the Union shall be perpetual; nor shall any alteration at any time hereafter be made in any of them; unless such alteration be agreed to in a Congress of the United States, and be afterwards confirmed by the legislatures of every State.

These articles shall be proposed to the legislatures of all the United States, to be considered, and if approved of by them, they are advised to authorize their delegates to ratify the same in the Congress of the United States; which being done, the same shall become conclusive.

THE CONSTITUTION OF THE UNITED STATES OF AMERICA

We the people of the United States, in order to form a more perfect union, establish justice, insure domestic tranquillity, provide for the common defense, promote the general welfare, and secure the blessings of liberty to ourselves and our posterity, do ordain and establish this Constitution for the United States of America.

ARTICLE I

SECTION 1. All legislative powers herein granted shall be vested in a Congress of the United States, which shall consist of a Senate and House of Representatives.

SECTION 2. 1. The House of Representatives shall be composed of members chosen every second year by the people of the several States, and the electors in each State shall have the qualifications requisite for electors of the most numerous branch of the State legislature.

2. No person shall be a representative who shall not have attained to the age of twenty-five years, and been seven years a citizen of the United States, and who shall not, when elected, be an inhabitant of that State in which he shall be chosen.

3. Representatives and direct taxes[1] shall be apportioned among the several States which may be included within this Union, according to their respective numbers, which shall be determined by adding to the whole number of free persons, including those bound to service for a term of years, and excluding Indians not taxed, three fifths of all other persons.[2] The actual enumeration shall be made within three years after the first meeting of the Congress of the United States, and within every subsequent term of ten years, in such manner as they shall by law direct. The number of representatives shall not exceed one for every thirty thousand, but each State shall have at least one representative; and until such enumeration shall be made, the State of New Hampshire shall be entitled to choose three, Massachusetts eight, Rhode Island and Providence Plantations one, Connecticut five, New York six, New Jersey four, Pennsylvania eight, Delaware one, Maryland six, Virginia ten, North Carolina five, South Carolina five, and Georgia three.

4. When vacancies happen in the representation from any State, the executive authority thereof shall issue writs of election to fill such vacancies.

5. The House of Representatives shall choose their speaker and other officers; and shall have the sole power of impeachment.

SECTION 3. 1. The Senate of the United States shall be composed of two senators from each State, chosen by the legislature thereof,[3] for six years; and each senator shall have one vote.

2. Immediately after they shall be assembled in consequence of the first election, they shall be divided as equally as may be into three classes. The seats of the senators of the first class shall be vacated at the expiration of the second year, of the second class at the expiration of the fourth year, and of the third class at the expiration of the sixth year, so that one third may be chosen every second year; and if vacancies happen by resignation, or otherwise, during the recess of the legislature of any State, the executive thereof may make temporary appointments until the next meeting of the legislature, which shall then fill such vacancies.[4]

3. No person shall be a senator who shall not have attained to the age of thirty years, and been nine years a citizen of the United States, and who shall not, when elected, be an inhabitant of that State for which he shall be chosen.

4. The Vice President of the United States shall be President of the Senate, but shall have no vote, unless they be equally divided.

5. The Senate shall choose their other officers, and also a president pro tempore, in the absence of the Vice President, or when he shall exercise the office of the President of the United States.

6. The Senate shall have the sole power to try all impeachments. When sitting for that purpose, they shall be on oath or affirmation. When the President of the United States is tried, the chief justice shall preside: and no person shall be convicted without the concurrence of two thirds of the members present.

7. Judgment in cases of impeachment shall not extend further than to removal from office, and disqualification to hold and enjoy any office of honor, trust or profit under the United States: but the party convicted shall nevertheless be liable and subject to indictment, trial, judgment and punishment, according to law.

SECTION 4. 1. The times, places, and manner of holding elections for senators and representatives, shall be prescribed in each State by the legislature thereof; but the Congress may at any time by law make or alter such regulations, except as to the places of choosing senators.

2. The Congress shall assemble at least once in every year, and such meeting shall be on the first Monday in December, unless they shall by law appoint a different day.

SECTION 5. 1. Each House shall be the judge of the elections, returns and qualifications of its own members, and a majority of each shall constitute a quorum to do business; but a smaller number may adjourn from day to day, and

---

[1]See the Sixteenth Amendment.
[2]See the Fourteenth Amendment.

[3]See the Seventeenth Amendment.
[4]See the Seventeenth Amendment.

may be authorized to compel the attendance of absent members, in such manner, and under such penalties as each House may provide.

2. Each House may determine the rules of its proceedings, punish its members for disorderly behavior, and, with the concurrence of two thirds, expel a member.

3. Each House shall keep a journal of its proceedings, and from time to time publish the same, excepting such parts as may in their judgment require secrecy; and the yeas and nays of the members of either House on any question shall, at the desire of one fifth of those present, be entered on the journal.

4. Neither House, during the session of Congress, shall, without the consent of the other, adjourn for more than three days, nor to any other place than that in which the two Houses shall be sitting.

SECTION 6. 1. The senators and representatives shall receive a compensation for their services, to be ascertained by law, and paid out of the Treasury of the United States. They shall in all cases, except treason, felony, and breach of the peace, be privileged from arrest during their attendance at the session of their respective Houses, and in going to and returning from the same; and for any speech or debate in either House, they shall not be questioned in any other place.

2. No senator or representative shall, during the time for which he was elected, be appointed to any civil office under the authority of the United States, which shall have been created, or the emoluments whereof shall have been increased, during such time; and no person holding any office under the United States shall be a member of either House during his continuance in office.

SECTION 7. 1. All bills for raising revenue shall originate in the House of Representatives; but the Senate may propose or concur with amendments as on other bills.

2. Every bill which shall have passed the House of Representatives and the Senate, shall, before it become a law, be presented to the President of the United States; If he approves he shall sign it, but if not he shall return it, with his objections, to that House in which it shall have originated, who shall enter the objections at large on their journal, and proceed to reconsider it. If after such reconsideration two thirds of that House shall agree to pass the bill, it shall be sent, together with the objections, to the other House, by which it shall likewise be reconsidered, and if approved by two thirds of that House, it shall become a law. But in all such cases the votes of both Houses shall be determined by yeas and nays, and the names of the persons voting for and against the bill shall be entered on the journal of each House respectively. If any bill shall not be returned by the President within ten days (Sundays excepted) after it shall have been presented to him, the same shall be a law, in like manner as if he had signed it, unless the Congress by their adjournment prevent its return, in which case it shall not be a law.

3. Every order, resolution, or vote to which the concurrence of the Senate and the House of Representatives may be necessary (except on a question of adjournment) shall be presented to the President of the United States; and before the same shall take effect, shall be approved by him, or being disapproved by him, shall be repassed by two thirds of the Senate and House of Representatives, according to the rules and limitations prescribed in the case of a bill.

SECTION 8. 1. The Congress shall have the power

1. To lay and collect taxes, duties, imposts, and excises, to pay the debts and provide for the common defense and general welfare of the United States; but all duties, imposts, and excises shall be uniform throughout the United States.

2. To borrow money on the credit of the United States;

3. To regulate commerce with foreign nations, and among the several States, and with the Indian tribes;

4. To establish a uniform rule of naturalization, and uniform laws on the subject of bankruptcies throughout the United States;

5. To coin money, regulate the value thereof, and of foreign coin, and fix the standard of weights and measures;

6. To provide for the punishment of counterfeiting the securities and current coin of the United States;

7. To establish post offices and post roads;

8. To promote the progress of science and useful arts, by securing for limited times to authors and inventors the exclusive right to their respective writings and discoveries;

9. To constitute tribunals inferior to the Supreme Court;

10. To define and punish piracies and felonies committed on the high seas, and offenses against the law of nations;

11. To declare war, grant letters of marque and reprisal, and make rules concerning captures on land and water;

12. To raise and support armies, but no appropriation of money to that use shall be for a longer term than two years;

13. To provide and maintain a navy;

14. To make rules for the government and regulation of the land and naval forces;

15. To provide for calling forth the militia to execute the laws of the Union, suppress insurrections and repel invasions;

16. To provide for organizing, arming, and disciplining the militia, and for governing such part of them as may be employed in the service of the United States, reserving to the States respectively, the appointment of the officers, and the authority of training the militia according to the discipline prescribed by Congress;

17. To exercise exclusive legislation in all cases whatsoever, over such district (not exceeding ten miles square) as may, by cession of particular States, and the acceptance of Congress, become the seat of the government of the United States, and to exercise like authority over all places purchased by the consent of the legislature of the State in which the same shall be, for the erection of forts, magazines, arsenals, dockyards, and other needful buildings; and

18. To make all laws which shall be necessary and proper for carrying into execution the foregoing powers, and all other powers vested by this Constitution in the government of the United States, or any department or officer thereof.

SECTION 9. 1. The migration or importation of such persons as any of the States now existing shall think proper to admit, shall not be prohibited by the Congress prior to the year one thousand eight hundred and eight, but a tax or duty may be imposed on such importation, not exceeding ten dollars for each person.

2. The privilege of the writ of habeas corpus shall not be suspended, unless when in cases of rebellion or invasion the public safety may require it.

3. No bill of attainder or ex post facto law shall be passed.

4. No capitation, or other direct, tax shall be laid, unless in proportion to the census or enumeration hereinbefore directed to be taken.[5]

5. No tax or duty shall be laid on articles exported from any State.

6. No preference shall be given by any regulation of commerce or revenue to the ports of one State over those of another: nor shall vessels bound to, or from, one State be obliged to enter, clear, or pay duties in another.

7. No money shall be drawn from the treasury, but in consequence of appropriations made by law; and a regular statement and account of the receipts and expenditures of all public money shall be published from time to time.

8. No title of nobility shall be granted by the United States: and no person holding any office of profit or trust under them, shall, without the consent of the Congress, accept of any present, emolument, office, or title, of any kind whatever, from any king, prince, or foreign State.

SECTION 10. 1. No State shall enter into any treaty, alliance, or confederation; grant letters of marque and reprisal; coin money; emit bills of credit; make any thing but gold and silver coin a tender in payment of debts; pass any bill of attainder, ex post facto law, or law impairing the obligation of contracts, or grant, any title of nobility.

2. No State shall, without the consent of the Congress, lay any imposts or duties on imports or exports, except what may be absolutely necessary for executing its inspection laws: and the net produce of all duties and imposts laid by any State on imports or exports, shall be for the use of the treasury of the United States; and all such laws shall be subject to the revision and control of the Congress.

3. No State shall, without the consent of the Congress, lay any duty of tonnage, keep troops, or ships of war in time of peace, enter into any agreement or compact with another State, or with a foreign power, or engage in war, unless actually invaded, or in such imminent danger as will not admit of delay.

ARTICLE II

SECTION 1. 1. The executive power shall be vested in a President of the United States of America. He shall hold his office during the term of four years, and, together with the Vice President, chosen for the same term, be elected, as follows:

2. Each State shall appoint, in such manner as the legislature thereof may direct, a number of electors, equal to the whole number of senators and representatives to which the State may be entitled in the Congress: but no senator or representative, or person holding any office of trust or profit under the United States, shall be appointed an elector.

The electors shall meet in their respective States, and vote by ballot for two persons, of whom one at least shall not be an inhabitant of the same State with themselves. And they shall make a list of all the persons voted for, and of the number of votes for each; which list they shall sign and certify, and transmit sealed to the seat of the government of the United States, directed to the president of the Senate. The president of the Senate shall, in the presence of the Senate and House of Representatives, open all the certificates, and the votes shall then be counted. The person having the greatest number of votes shall be the President, if such number be a majority of the whole number of electors appointed; and if there be more than one who have such majority, and have an equal number of votes, then the House of Representatives shall immediately choose by ballot one of them for President; and if no person have a majority, then from the five highest on the list the said House shall in like manner choose the President. But in choosing the President, the votes shall be taken by States, the representation from each State having one vote; a quorum for this purpose shall consist of a member or members from two thirds of the States, and a majority of all the States shall be necessary to a choice. In every case after the choice of the President, the person having the greatest number of votes of the electors shall be the Vice President. But if there should remain two or more who have equal votes, the Senate shall choose from them by ballot the Vice President.[6]

3. The Congress may determine the time of choosing the electors, and the day on which they shall give their votes; which day shall be the same throughout the United States.

4. No person except a natural born citizen, or a citizen of the United States, at the time of the adoption of this Constitution, shall be eligible to the office of President; neither shall any person be eligible to the office who shall not have attained to the age of thirty-five years, and been fourteen years a resident within the United States.

5. In case of the removal of the President from office, or of his death, resignation, or inability to discharge the powers and duties of the said office, the same shall devolve on the Vice President, and the congress may by law pro-

---

[5]See the Sixteenth Amendment.

[6]Superseded by the Twelfth Amendment.

vide for the case of removal, death, resignation or inability, both of the President and Vice President, declaring what officer shall then act as President, and such officer shall act accordingly until the disability be removed, or a President shall be elected.

6. The President shall, at stated times, receive for his services a compensation which shall neither be increased nor diminished during the period for which he shall have been elected, and he shall not receive within that period any other emolument from the United States, or any of them.

7. Before he enter on the execution of his office, he shall take the following oath or affirmation:—"I do solemnly swear (or affirm) that I will faithfully execute the office of President of the United States, and will to the best of my ability, preserve, protect and defend the Constitution of the United States."

SECTION 2. 1. The President shall be commander in chief of the army and navy of the United States, and of the militia of the several States, when called into the actual service of the United States; he may require the opinion in writing, of the principal officer in each of the executive departments, upon any subject relating to the duties of their respective offices, and he shall have power to grant reprieves and pardons for offenses against the United States, except in cases of impeachment.

2. He shall have power, by and with the advice and consent of the Senate, to make treaties, provided two thirds of the senators present concur; and he shall nominate, and by and with the advice and consent of the Senate, shall appoint ambassadors, other public ministers and consuls, judges of the Supreme Court, and all other officers of the United States, whose appointments are not herein otherwise provided for, and which shall be established by law; but the Congress may by law vest the appointment of such inferior officers, as they think proper, in the President alone, in the courts of laws, or in the heads of departments.

3. The President shall have power to fill up all vacancies that may happen during the recess of the Senate, by granting commissions which shall expire at the end of their next session.

SECTION 3. He shall from time to time give to the Congress information of the state of the Union, and recommend to their consideration such measures as he shall judge necessary and expedient; he may, on extraordinary occasions, convene both Houses, or either of them, and in case of disagreement between them with respect to the time of adjournment, he may adjourn them to such time as he shall think proper; he shall receive ambassadors and other public ministers; he shall take care that the laws be faithfully executed, and shall commission all the officers of the United States.

SECTION 4. The President, Vice President, and all civil officers of the United States, shall be removed from office on impeachment for, and conviction of, treason, bribery, or other high crimes and misdemeanors.

ARTICLE III

SECTION 1. The judicial power of the United States shall be vested in one Supreme Court, and in such inferior courts as the Congress may from time to time ordain and establish. The judges, both of the Supreme and inferior courts, shall hold their offices during good behavior, and shall, at stated times, receive for their services, a compensation, which shall not be diminished during their continuance in office.

SECTION 2. 1. The judicial power shall extend to all cases, in law and equity, arising under this Constitution, the laws of the United States, and treaties made, or which shall be made, under their authority;—to all cases of admiralty and maritime jurisdiction;—to controversies to which the United States shall be a party;[7]—to controversies between two or more States;—between a State and citizens of another State;—between citizens of different States;—between citizens of the same State claiming lands under grants of different States, and between a State, or the citizens thereof, and foreign States, citizens or subjects.

2. In all cases affecting ambassadors, other public ministers and consuls, and those in which a State shall be party, the Supreme Court shall have original jurisdiction. In all the other cases before mentioned, the Supreme Court shall have appellate jurisdiction, both as to law and fact, with such exceptions, and under such regulations as the Congress shall make.

3. The trial of all crimes, except in cases of impeachment, shall be by jury; and such trial shall be held in the State where the said crimes shall have been committed; but when not committed within any State, the trial shall be such place or places as the congress may by law have directed.

SECTION 3. 1. Treason against the United States shall consist only in levying war against them, or in adhering to their enemies, giving them aid and comfort. No person shall be convicted of treason unless on the testimony of two witnesses to the same overt act, or on confession in open court.

2. The Congress shall have power to declare the punishment of treason, but no attainder of treason shall work corruption of blood, or forfeiture except during the life of the person attained.

ARTICLE IV

SECTION 1. Full faith and credit shall be given in each State to the public acts, records, and judicial proceedings of every other State. And the Congress may by general laws prescribe the manner in which such acts, records and proceedings shall be proved, and the effect thereof.

SECTION 2. 1. The citizens of each State shall be entitled to all privileges and immunities of citizens in the several States.[8]

---

[7]See the Eleventh Amendment.
[8]See the Fourteenth Amendment, Sec. 1.

2. A person charged in any State with treason, felony, or other crime, who shall flee from justice, and be found in another State, shall on demand of the executive authority of the State from which he fled, be delivered up to be removed to the State having jurisdiction of the crime.

3. No person held to service or labor in one State under the laws thereof, escaping into another, shall, in consequence of any law or regulation therein, be discharged from such service or labor, but shall be delivered up on claim of the party to whom such service or labor may be due.[9]

SECTION 3. 1. New States may be admitted by the Congress into this Union; but no new State shall be formed or erected within the jurisdiction of any other State, nor any State be formed by the junction of two or more States, or parts of States, without the consent of the legislatures of the States concerned as well as of the Congress.

2. The Congress shall have power to dispose of and make all needful rules and regulations respecting the territory or other property belonging to the United States; and nothing in this Constitution shall be so construed as to prejudice any claims of the United States, or of any particular State.

SECTION 4. The United States shall guarantee to every State in this Union a republican form of government, and shall protect each of them against invasion; and on application of the legislature, or of the executive (when the legislature cannot be convened) against domestic violence.

ARTICLE V

The Congress, whenever two thirds of both Houses shall deem it necessary, shall propose amendments to this Constitution, or, on the application of the legislatures of two thirds of the several States, shall call a convention for proposing amendments, which in either case shall be valid to all intents and purposes, as part of this Constitution, when ratified by the legislatures of three fourths of the several States, or by conventions in three fourths thereof, as the one or the other mode of ratification may be proposed by the Congress; Provided that no amendment which may be made prior to the year one thousand eight hundred and eight shall in any manner affect the first and fourth clauses in the ninth section of the first article; and that no State, without its consent, shall be deprived of its equal suffrage in the Senate.

ARTICLE VI

1. All debts contracted and engagements entered into, before the adoption of this Constitution, shall be as valid against the United States under this Constitution, as under the Confederation.[10]

2. This Constitution, and the laws of the United States which shall be made in pursuance thereof; and all treaties made, or which shall be made, under the authority of the United States, shall be the supreme law of the land; and the judges in every State shall be bound thereby, any thing in the Constitution or laws of any State to the contrary notwithstanding.

3. The senators and representatives before mentioned, and the members of the several State legislatures, and all executive and judicial officers, both of the United States and of the several States, shall be bound by oath or affirmation to support this Constitution; but no religious test shall ever be required as a qualification to any office or public trust under the United States.

ARTICLE VII

The ratification of the conventions of nine States shall be sufficient for the establishment of this Constitution between the States so ratifying the same.

Done in Convention by the unanimous consent of the States present the seventeenth day of September in the year of our Lord one thousand seven hundred and eighty-seven, and of the independence of the United States of America the twelfth. In witness whereof we have hereunto subscribed our names.

[Signatories' names omitted]

Articles in addition to, and amendment of, the Constitution of the United States of America, proposed by Congress, and ratified by the legislatures of the several States, pursuant to the fifth article of the original Constitution.

Amendment I

[First ten amendments ratified December 15, 1791]

Congress shall make no law respecting an establishment of religion, or prohibiting the free exercise thereof; or abridging the freedom of speech, or of the press; or the right of the people peaceably to assemble, and to petition the government for a redress of grievances.

Amendment II

A well regulated militia, being necessary to the security of a free State, the right of the people to keep and bear arms, shall not be infringed.

Amendment III

No soldier shall, in time of peace be quartered in any house, without the consent of the owner, nor in time of war, but in a manner to be prescribed by law.

Amendment IV

The right of the people to be secure in their persons, houses, papers, and effects, against unreasonable searches and seizures, shall not be violated, and no warrants shall issue, but upon probable cause, supported by oath or affirmation, and particularly describing the place to be searched, and the persons or things to be seized.

---

[9]See the Thirteenth Amendment.
[10]See the Fourteenth Amendment, Sec. 4.

Amendment V

No person shall be held to answer for a capital or otherwise infamous crime, unless on a presentment or indictment of a grand jury, except in cases arising in the land or naval forces, or in the militia, when in actual service in time of war or public danger; nor shall any person be subject for the same offense to be twice put in jeopardy of life or limb; nor shall be compelled in any criminal case to be a witness against himself, nor be deprived of life, liberty, or property, without due process of law; nor shall private property be taken for public use, without just compensation.

Amendment VI

In all criminal prosecutions, the accused shall enjoy the right to a speedy and public trial, by an impartial jury of the State and district wherein the crime shall have been committed, which district shall have been previously ascertained by law, and to be informed of the nature and cause of the accusation; to be confronted with the witnesses against him; to have compulsory process for obtaining witnesses in his favor, and to have the assistance of counsel for his defense.

Amendment VII

In suits at common law, where the value in controversy shall exceed twenty dollars, the right of trial by jury shall be preserved, and no fact tried by a jury shall be otherwise reexamined in any court of the United States, than according to the rules of the common law.

Amendment VIII

Excessive bail shall not be required, nor excessive fines imposed, nor cruel and unusual punishments inflicted.

Amendment IX

The enumeration in the Constitution of certain rights shall not be construed to deny or disparage others retained by the people.

Amendment X

The powers not delegated to the United States by the Constitution, nor prohibited by it to the States, are reserved to the States respectively, or to the people.

Amendment XI [January 8, 1798]

The judicial power of the United States shall not be construed to extend to any suit in law or equity, commended or prosecuted against one of the United States by citizens of another State, or by citizens or subjects of any foreign State.

Amendment XII [September 25, 1804]

The electors shall meet in their respective States, and vote by ballot for President and Vice President, one of whom, at least, shall not be an inhabitant of the same State with themselves; they shall name in their ballots the person voted for as President, and in distinct ballots, the person voted for as Vice President, and they shall make distinct lists of all persons voted for as President and of all persons voted for as Vice President, and of the number of votes for each, which lists they shall sign and certify, and transmit sealed to the seat of the government of the United States, directed to the President of the Senate;—The President of the Senate shall, in the presence of the Senate and House of Representatives, open all the certificates and the votes shall then be counted;—The person having the greatest number of votes for President, shall be the President, if such number be a majority of the whole number of electors appointed; and if no person have such majority, then from the persons having the highest numbers not exceeding three on the list of those voted for as President, the House of Representatives shall choose immediately, by ballot, the President. But in choosing the President, the votes shall be taken by States, the representation from each State having one vote; a quorum for this purpose shall consist of a member or members from two thirds of the States, and a majority of all the States shall be necessary to a choice. And if the House of Representatives shall not choose a President whenever the right of choice shall devolve upon them, before the fourth day of March next following, then the Vice President shall act as President, as in the case of the death or other constitutional disability of the President. The person having the greatest number of votes as Vice President shall be the Vice President, if such number be a majority of the whole number of electors appointed, and if no person have a majority, then from the two highest numbers on the list, the Senate shall choose the Vice President; a quorum for the purpose shall consist of two thirds of the whole number of Senators, and a majority of the whole number shall be necessary to a choice. But no person constitutionally ineligible to the office of President shall be eligible to that of Vice President of the United States.

Amendment XIII [December 18, 1865]

SECTION 1. Neither slavery nor involuntary servitude, except as a punishment for crime whereof the party shall have been duly convicted, shall exist within the United States, or any place subject to their jurisdiction.

SECTION 2. Congress shall have power to enforce this article by appropriate legislation.

Amendment XIV [July 28, 1868]

SECTION 1. All persons born or naturalized in the United States, and subject to the jurisdiction thereof, are citizens of the United States and of the State wherein they reside. No State shall make or enforce any law which shall abridge the privileges or immunities of citizens of the United States; nor shall any State deprive any person of life, liberty, or property, without due process of law; nor deny to any person within its jurisdiction the equal protection of the laws.

SECTION 2. Representatives shall be apportioned among the several States according to their respective numbers, counting the whole number of persons in each State, excluding Indians not taxed. But when the right to vote at any election for the choice of electors for President and Vice President of the United States, representatives in Congress, the executive and judicial officers of a State, or the members of the legislature thereof, is denied to any of the male inhabitants of such State, being twenty-one years of age, and citizens of the United States, or in any way abridged, except for participating in rebellion, or other crime, the basis of representation there shall be reduced in the proportion which the number of such male citizens shall bear to the whole number of male citizens twenty-one years of age in such State.

SECTION 3. No person shall be a senator or representative in Congress, or elector of President and Vice President, or hold any office, civil or military, under the United States, or under any State, who having previously taken an oath, as a member of Congress, or as an officer of the United States, or as a member of any State legislature, or as an executive or judicial officer of any State, to support the Constitution of the United States, shall have engaged in insurrection or rebellion against the same, or given aid or comfort to the enemies thereof. But Congress may by a vote of two thirds of each House, remove such disability.

SECTION 4. The validity of the public debt of the United States, authorized by law, including debts incurred for payment of pensions and bounties for services in suppressing insurrection or rebellion; shall not be questioned. But neither the United States nor any State shall assume or pay any debt or obligation incurred in aid of insurrection or rebellion against the United States, or any claim for the loss or emancipation of any slave; but all such debts, obligations, and claims shall be held illegal and void.

SECTION 5. The Congress shall have the power to enforce, by appropriate legislation, the provisions of this article.

Amendment XV [March 30, 1870]
SECTION 1. The right of citizens of the United States to vote shall not be denied or abridged by the United States or by any State on account of race, color, or previous condition of servitude.

SECTION 2. The Congress shall have power to enforce this article by appropriate legislation.

Amendment XVI [February 25, 1913]
The Congress shall have power to lay and collect taxes on incomes, from whatever source derived, without apportionment among the several States, and without regard to any census or enumeration.

Amendment XVII [May 31, 1913]
The Senate of the United States shall be composed of two senators from each State, elected by the people thereof, for six years; and each senator shall have one vote. The electors in each State shall have the qualifications requisite for electors of the most numerous branch of the State legislature.

When vacancies happen in the representation of any State in the Senate, the executive authority of such State shall issue writs of election to fill such vacancies: Provided, That the legislature of any State may empower the executive thereof to make temporary appointments until the people fill the vacancies by election as the legislature may direct.

This amendment shall not be so construed as to affect the election or term of any senator chosen before it becomes valid as part of the Constitution.

Amendment XVIII[11] [January 29, 1919]
After one year from the ratification of this article, the manufacture, sale, or transportation of intoxicating liquors within, the importation thereof into, or the exportation thereof from the United States and all territory subject to the jurisdiction thereof for beverage purposes is thereby prohibited.

The Congress and the several States shall have concurrent power to enforce this article by appropriate legislation.

This article shall be inoperative unless it shall have been ratified as an amendment to the Constitution by the legislatures of the several States, as provided in the constitution, within seven years from the date of the submission hereof to the States by Congress.

Amendment XIX [August 26, 1920]
The right of citizens of the United States to vote shall not be denied or abridged by the United States or by any State on account of sex.

Congress shall have the power to enforce this article by appropriate legislation.

Amendment XX [January 23, 1933]
SECTION 1. The terms of the President and Vice President shall end at noon on the 20th day of January and the terms of Senators and Representatives at noon on the 3d day of January, of the years in which such terms would have ended if this article had not been ratified; and the terms of their successors shall then begin.

SECTION 2. The Congress shall assemble at least once in every year, and such meeting shall begin at noon on the 3d day of January, unless they shall by law appoint a different day.

SECTION 3. If, at the time fixed for the beginning of the term of President, the President-elect shall have died, the Vice President-elect shall become President. If a President shall not have been chosen before the time fixed for the beginning of his term, or if the President-elect shall have failed to qualify, then the Vice President-elect shall act as President until a President shall have qualified; and the Congress may by law provide for the case wherein neither a President-elect nor a Vice President-elect shall have qualified, declaring who shall then act as President, or the manner in which one who is to act shall be selected, and such person shall act accordingly until a President or Vice President shall have qualified.

---

[11]Repealed by the Twenty-first Amendment.

SECTION 4. The Congress may by law provide for the case of the death of any of the persons from whom, the House of Representatives may choose a President whenever the right of choice shall have devolved upon them, and for the case of the death of any of the persons from whom the Senate may choose a Vice President whenever the right of choice shall have devolved upon them.

SECTION 5. Sections 1 and 2 shall take effect on the 15th day of October following the ratification of this article.

SECTION 6. This article shall be inoperative unless it shall have been ratified as an amendment to the Constitution by the legislatures of three-fourths of the several States within seven years from the date of its submission.

Amendment XXI [December 5, 1933]

SECTION 1. The Eighteenth Article of amendment to the Constitution of the United States is hereby repealed.

SECTION 2. The transportation or importation into any State, Territory, or possession of the United States for delivery or use therein of intoxicating liquors in violation of the laws thereof, is hereby prohibited.

SECTION 3. This article shall be inoperative unless it shall have been ratified as an amendment to the Constitution by conventions in the several States, as provided in the Constitution, within seven years from the date of the submission thereof to the States by the Congress.

Amendment XXII [March 1, 1951]

No person shall be elected to the office of the President more than twice, and no person who has held the office of President, or acted as President, for more than two years of a term to which some other person was elected President shall be elected to the office of the President more than once.

But this article shall not apply to any person holding the office of President when this article was proposed by the Congress, and shall not prevent any person who may be holding the office of President, or acting as President, during the term within which this article becomes operative from holding the office of President or acting as President during the remainder of such term.

This article shall be inoperative unless it shall have been ratified as an amendment to the Constitution by the legislatures of three-fourths of the several States within seven years from the date of its submission to the States by the Congress.

Amendment XXIII [March 29, 1961]

SECTION 1. The District constituting the seat of Government of the United States shall appoint in such manner as the Congress may direct.

A number of electors of President and Vice President equal to the whole number of Senators and Representatives in Congress to which the District would be entitled if it were a State, but in no event more than the least populous State; they shall be in addition to those appointed by the States, but they shall be considered, for the purposes of the elec-tion of President and Vice President, to be electors appointed by a State; and they shall meet in the District and perform such duties as provided by the twelfth article of amendment.

SECTION 2. The Congress shall have power to enforce this article by appropriate legislation.

Amendment XXIV [January 23, 1964]

SECTION 1. The right of citizens of the United States to vote in any primary or other election for President or Vice President, for electors for President or Vice President, or for Senator or Representative in Congress, shall not be denied or abridged by the United States or any State by reason of failure to pay any poll tax or other tax.

SECTION 2. The Congress shall have power to enforce this article by appropriate legislation.

Amendment XXV [February 10, 1967]

SECTION 1. In case of the removal of the President from office or of his death or resignation, the Vice President shall become President.

SECTION 2. Whenever there is a vacancy in the office of the Vice President, the President shall nominate a Vice President who shall take office upon confirmation by a majority of both Houses of Congress.

SECTION 3. Whenever the President transmits to the President pro tempore of the Senate and the Speaker of the House of Representatives his written declaration that he is unable to discharge the powers and duties of his office, and until he transmits to them a written declaration to the contrary, such powers and duties shall be discharged by the Vice President as Acting President.

SECTION 4. Whenever the Vice President and a majority of either the principal officers of the executive departments or of such other body as Congress may by law provide, transmit to the President pro tempore of the Senate and the Speaker of the House of Representatives their written declaration that the President is unable to discharge the powers and duties of his office, the Vice President shall immediately assume the powers and duties of the office as Acting President.

Thereafter, when the President transmits to the President pro tempore of the Senate and the Speaker of the House of Representatives his written declaration that no inability exists, he shall resume the powers and duties of his office unless the Vice President and a majority of either the principal officers of the executive departments or of such other body as Congress may by law provide, transmit within four days to the President pro tempore of the Senate and the Speaker of the House of Representatives their written declaration that the President is unable to discharge the powers and duties of his office. Thereupon Congress shall decide the issue, assembling within forty-eight hours for that purpose if not in session. If the Congress, within twenty-one days after receipt of the latter written declaration, or, if Congress is not in session, within twenty-one days after Congress is required to assemble, determines by two-thirds vote of both Houses that the President is unable to discharge the powers and duties of his office, the Vice President shall continue to discharge the same as Acting President; otherwise, the President shall resume the powers and duties of his office.

Amendment XXVI [June 30, 1971]

SECTION 1. The right of citizens of the United States who are eighteen years of age or older to vote shall not be denied or abridged by the United States or by any State on account of age.

SECTION 2. The Congress shall have power to enforce this article by appropriate legislation.

Amendment XXVII[12] [May 7, 1992]

No law, varying the compensation for services of the Senators and Representatives, shall take effect until an election of Representatives shall have intervened.

---

[12]James Madison proposed this amendment in 1789 together with the ten amendments that were adopted as the Bill of Rights, but it failed to win ratification at the time. Congress, however, had set no deadline for its ratification, and over the years—particularly in the 1980s and 1990s—many states voted to add it to the Constitution. With the ratification of Michigan in 1992 it passed the threshold of 3/4ths of the states required for adoption, but because the process took more than 200 years, its validity remains in doubt.

PRESIDENTIAL ELECTIONS

Year	Number of States	Candidates	Party	Popular Vote*	Electoral Vote†	Percentage of Popular Vote
1789	11	GEORGE WASHINGTON	No party designations		69	
		John Adams			34	
		Other Candidates			35	
1792	15	GEORGE WASHINGTON	No party designations		132	
		John Adams			77	
		George Clinton			50	
		Other Candidates			5	
1796	16	JOHN ADAMS	Federalist		71	
		Thomas Jefferson	Democratic-Republican		68	
		Thomas Pinckney	Federalist		59	
		Aaron Burr	Democratic-Republican		30	
		Other Candidates			48	
1800	16	THOMAS JEFFERSON	Democratic-Republican		73	
		Aaron Burr	Democratic-Republican		73	
		John Adams	Federalist		65	
		Charles C. Pinckney	Federalist		64	
		John Jay	Federalist		1	
1804	17	THOMAS JEFFERSON	Democratic-Republican		162	
		Charles C. Pinckney	Federalist		14	
1808	17	JAMES MADISON	Democratic-Republican		122	
		Charles C. Pinckney	Federalist		47	
		George Clinton	Democratic-Republican		6	
1812	18	JAMES MADISON	Democratic-Republican		128	
		DeWitt Clinton	Federalist		89	
1816	19	JAMES MONROE	Democratic-Republican		183	
		Rufus King	Federalist		34	
1820	24	JAMES MONROE	Democratic-Republican		231	
		John Quincy Adams	Independent-Republican		1	
1824	24	JOHN QUINCY ADAMS	Democratic-Republican	108,740	84	30.5
		Andrew Jackson	Democratic-Republican	153,544	99	43.1
		William H. Crawford	Democratic-Republican	46,618	41	13.1
		Henry Clay	Democratic-Republican	47,136	37	13.2
1828	24	ANDREW JACKSON	Democrat	647,286	178	56.0
		John Quincy Adams	National Republican	508,064	83	44.0
1832	24	ANDREW JACKSON	Democrat	687,502	219	55.0
		Henry Clay	National Republican	530,189	49	42.4
		William Wirt	Anti-Masonic	} 33,108	7	2.6
		John Floyd	National Republican		11	

* *Percentage of popular vote given for any election year may not total 100 percent because candidates receiving less than 1 percent of the popular vote have been omitted.*

† *Prior to the passage of the Twelfth Amendment in 1904, the electoral college voted for two presidential candidates; the runner-up became Vice-President. Data from Historical Statistics of the United States, Colonial Times to 1957 (1961), pp. 682–683, and The World Almanac.*

PRESIDENTIAL ELECTIONS (continued)

Year	Number of States	Candidates	Party	Popular Vote	Electoral Vote	Percentage of Popular Vote
1836	26	MARTIN VAN BUREN	Democrat	765,483	170	50.9
		William H. Harrison	Whig		73	
		Hugh L. White	Whig	739,795	26	49.1
		Daniel Webster	Whig		14	
		W. P. Mangum	Whig		11	
1840	26	WILLIAM H. HARRISON	Whig	1,274,624	234	53.1
		Martin Van Buren	Democrat	1,127,781	60	46.9
1844	26	JAMES K. POLK	Democrat	1,338,464	170	49.6
		Henry Clay	Whig	1,300,097	105	48.1
		James G. Birney	Liberty	62,300		2.3
1848	30	ZACHARY TAYLOR	Whig	1,360,967	163	47.4
		Lewis Cass	Democrat	1,222,342	127	42.5
		Martin Van Buren	Free Soil	291,263		10.1
1852	31	FRANKLIN PIERCE	Democrat	1,601,117	254	50.9
		Winfield Scott	Whig	1,385,453	42	44.1
		John P. Hale	Free Soil	155,825		5.0
1856	31	JAMES BUCHANAN	Democrat	1,832,955	174	45.3
		John C. Frémont	Republican	1,339,932	114	33.1
		Millard Fillmore	American ("Know Nothing")	871,731	8	21.6
1860	33	ABRAHAM LINCOLN	Republican	1,865,593	180	39.8
		Stephen A. Douglas	Democrat	1,382,713	12	29.5
		John C. Breckinridge	Democrat	848,356	72	18.1
		John Bell	Constitutional Union	592,906	39	12.6
1864	36	ABRAHAM LINCOLN	Republican	2,206,938	212	55.0
		George B. McClellan	Democrat	1,803,787	21	45.0
1868	37	ULYSSES S. GRANT	Republican	3,013,421	214	52.7
		Horatio Seymour	Democrat	2,706,829	80	47.3
1872	37	ULYSSES S. GRANT	Republican	3,596,745	286	55.6
		Horace Greeley	Democrat	2,843,446	*	43.9
1876	38	RUTHERFORD B. HAYES	Republican	4,036,572	185	48.0
		Samuel J. Tilden	Democrat	4,284,020	184	51.0
1880	38	JAMES A. GARFIELD	Republican	4,453,295	214	48.5
		Winfield S. Hancock	Democrat	4,414,082	155	48.1
		James B. Weaver	Greenback-Labor	308,578		3.4
1884	38	GROVER CLEVELAND	Democrat	4,879,507	219	48.5
		James G. Blaine	Republican	4,850,293	182	48.2
		Benjamin F. Butler	Greenback-Labor	175,370		1.8
		John P. St. John	Prohibition	150,369		1.5
1888	38	BENJAMIN HARRISON	Republican	5,447,129	233	47.9
		Grover Cleveland	Democrat	5,537,857	168	48.6
		Clinton B. Fisk	Prohibition	249,506		2.2
		Anson J. Streeter	Union Labor	146,935		1.3

* *Because of the death of Greeley, Democratic electors scattered their votes.*

PRESIDENTIAL ELECTIONS (continued)

Year	Number of States	Candidates	Party	Popular Vote	Electoral Vote	Percentage of Popular Vote
1892	44	GROVER CLEVELAND	Democrat	5,555,426	277	46.1
		Benjamin Harrison	Republican	5,182,690	145	43.0
		James B. Weaver	People's	1,029,846	22	8.5
		John Bidwell	Prohibition	264,133		2.2
1896	45	WILLIAM MCKINLEY	Republican	7,102,246	271	51.1
		William J. Bryan	Democrat	6,492,559	176	47.7
1900	45	WILLIAM MCKINLEY	Republican	7,218,491	292	51.7
		William J. Bryan	Democrat; Populist	6,356,734	155	45.5
		John C. Woolley	Prohibition	208,914		1.5
1904	45	THEODORE ROOSEVELT	Republican	7,628,461	336	57.4
		Alton B. Parker	Democrat	5,084,223	140	37.6
		Eugene V. Debs	Socialist	402,283		3.0
		Silas C. Swallow	Prohibition	258,536		1.9
1908	46	WILLIAM H. TAFT	Republican	7,675,320	321	51.6
		William J. Bryan	Democrat	6,412,294	162	43.1
		Eugene V. Debs	Socialist	420,793		2.8
		Eugene W. Chafin	Prohibition	253,840		1.7
1912	48	WOODROW WILSON	Democrat	6,296,547	435	41.9
		Theodore Roosevelt	Progressive	4,118,571	88	27.4
		William H. Taft	Republican	3,486,720	8	23.2
		Eugene V. Debs	Socialist	900,672		6.0
		Eugene W. Chafin	Prohibition	206,275		1.4
1916	48	WOODROW WILSON	Democrat	9,127,695	277	49.4
		Charles E. Hughes	Republican	8,533,507	254	46.2
		A. L. Benson	Socialist	585,113		3.2
		J. Frank Hanly	Prohibition	220,506		1.2
1920	48	WARREN G. HARDING	Republican	16,143,407	404	60.4
		James M. Cox	Democrat	9,130,328	127	34.2
		Eugene V. Debs	Socialist	919,799		3.4
		P. P. Christensen	Farmer-Labor	265,411		1.0
1924	48	CALVIN COOLIDGE	Republican	15,718,211	382	54.0
		John W. Davis	Democrat	8,385,283	136	28.8
		Robert M. La Follette	Progressive	4,831,289	13	16.6
1928	48	HERBERT C. HOOVER	Republican	21,391,993	444	58.2
		Alfred E. Smith	Democrat	15,016,169	87	40.9
1932	48	FRANKLIN D. ROOSEVELT	Democrat	22,809,638	472	57.4
		Herbert C. Hoover	Republican	15,758,901	59	39.7
		Norman Thomas	Socialist	881,951		2.2
1936	48	FRANKLIN D. ROOSEVELT	Democrat	27,752,869	523	60.8
		Alfred M. Landon	Republican	16,674,665	8	36.5
		William Lemke	Union	882,479		1.9
1940	48	FRANKLIN D. ROOSEVELT	Democrat	27,307,819	449	54.8
		Wendell L. Willkie	Republican	22,321,018	82	44.8

PRESIDENTIAL ELECTIONS (continued)

Year	Number of States	Candidates	Party	Popular Vote	Electoral Vote	Percentage of Popular Vote
1944	48	FRANKLIN D. ROOSEVELT	Democrat	25,606,585	432	53.5
		Thomas E. Dewey	Republican	22,014,745	99	46.0
1948	48	HARRY S. TRUMAN	Democrat	24,105,812	303	49.5
		Thomas E. Dewey	Republican	21,970,065	189	45.1
		J. Strom Thurmond	States' Rights	1,169,063	39	2.4
		Henry A. Wallace	Progressive	1,157,172		2.4
1952	48	DWIGHT D. EISENHOWER	Republican	33,936,234	442	55.1
		Adlai E. Stevenson	Democrat	27,314,992	89	44.4
1956	48	DWIGHT D. EISENHOWER	Republican	35,590,472	457*	57.6
		Adlai E. Stevenson	Democrat	26,022,752	73	42.1
1960	50	JOHN F. KENNEDY	Democrat	34,227,096	303†	49.9
		Richard M. Nixon	Republican	34,108,546	219	49.6
1964	50	LYNDON B. JOHNSON	Democrat	42,676,220	486	61.3
		Barry M. Goldwater	Republican	26,860,314	52	38.5
1968	50	RICHARD M. NIXON	Republican	31,785,480	301	43.4
		Hubert H. Humphrey	Democrat	31,275,165	191	42.7
		George C. Wallace	American Independent	9,906,473	46	13.5
1972	50	RICHARD M. NIXON‡	Republican	47,165,234	520	60.6
		George S. McGovern	Democrat	29,168,110	17	37.5
1976	50	JIMMY CARTER	Democrat	40,828,929	297	50.1
		Gerald R. Ford	Republican	39,148,940	240	47.9
		Eugene McCarthy	Independent	739,256		
1980	50	RONALD REAGAN	Republican	43,201,220	489	50.9
		Jimmy Carter	Democrat	34,913,332	49	41.2
		John B. Anderson	Independent	5,581,379		
1984	50	RONALD REAGAN	Republican	53,428,357	525	59.0
		Walter F. Mondale	Democrat	36,930,923	13	41.0
1988	50	GEORGE BUSH	Republican	48,901,046	426	53.4
		Michael Dukakis	Democrat	41,809,030	111	45.6
1992	50	BILL CLINTON	Democrat	43,728,275	370	43.2
		George Bush	Republican	38,167,416	168	37.7
		H. Ross Perot	United We Stand, America	19,237,247		19.0
1996	50	BILL CLINTON	Democrat	45,590,703	379	49.0
		Robert Dole	Republican	37,816,307	159	41.0
		H. Ross Perot	Reform	7,866,284		8.0
2000	50	GEORGE W. BUSH	Republican	50,459,624	271	47.9
		Albert Gore, Jr.	Democrat	51,003,328	266	49.4
		Ralph Nader	Green	2,882,985		2.7

Walter B. Jones received 1 electoral vote.

†Harry F. Byrd received 15 electoral votes.

‡Resigned August 9, 1974: Vice President Gerald R. Ford became President.

SUPREME COURT JUSTICES

Name*	Years on Court	Appointing President
JOHN JAY	1789–1795	Washington
James Wilson	1789–1798	Washington
John Rutledge	1790–1791	Washington
William Cushing	1790–1810	Washington
John Blair	1790–1796	Washington
James Iredell	1790–1799	Washington
Thomas Jefferson	1792–1793	Washington
William Paterson	1793–1806	Washington
JOHN RUTLEDGE†	1795	Washington
Samuel Chase	1796–1811	Washington
OLIVER ELLSWORTH	1796–1800	Washington
Bushrod Washington	1799–1829	J. Adams
Alfred Moore	1800–1804	J. Adams
JOHN MARSHALL	1801–1835	J. Adams
William Johnson	1804–1834	Jefferson
Brockholst Livingston	1807–1823	Jefferson
Thomas Todd	1807–1826	Jefferson
Gabriel Duvall	1811–1835	Madison
Joseph Story	1812–1845	Madison
Smith Thompson	1823–1843	Monroe
Robert Trimble	1826–1828	J. Q. Adams
John McLean	1830–1861	Jackson
Henry Baldwin	1830–1844	Jackson
James M. Wayne	1835–1867	Jackson
ROGER B. TANEY	1836–1864	Jackson
Philip P. Barbour	1836–1841	Jackson
John Cartron	1837–1865	Van Buren
John McKinley	1838–1852	Van Buren
Peter V. Daniel	1842–1860	Van Buren
Samuel Nelson	1845–1872	Tyler
Levi Woodbury	1845–1851	Polk
Robert C. Grier	1846–1870	Polk
Benjamin R. Curtis	1851–1857	Fillmore
John A. Campbell	1853–1861	Pierce
Nathan Clifford	1858–1881	Buchanan
Noah H. Swayne	1862–1881	Lincoln
Samuel F. Miller	1862–1890	Lincoln
David Davis	1862–1877	Lincoln
Stephen J. Field	1863–1897	Lincoln
SALMON P. CHASE	1864–1873	Lincoln
William Strong	1870–1880	Grant
Joseph P. Bradley	1870–1892	Grant
Ward Hunt	1873–1882	Grant
MORRISON R. WAITE	1874–1888	Grant
John M. Harlan	1877–1911	Hayes
William B. Woods	1881–1887	Hayes
Stanley Matthews	1881–1889	Garfield
Horace Gray	1882–1902	Arthur
Samuel Blatchford	1882–1893	Arthur

SUPREME COURT JUSTICES (continued)

Name*	Years on Court	Appointing President
Lucious Q. C. Lamar	1888–1893	Cleveland
MELVILLE W. FULLER	1888–1910	Cleveland
David J. Brewer	1890–1910	B. Harrison
Henry B. Brown	1891–1906	B. Harrison
George Shiras, Jr.	1892–1903	B. Harrison
Howell E. Jackson	1893–1895	B. Harrison
Edward D. White	1894–1910	Cleveland
Rufus W. Peckham	1896–1909	Cleveland
Joseph McKenna	1898–1925	McKinley
Oliver W. Holmes	1902–1932	T. Roosevelt
William R. Day	1903–1922	T. Roosevelt
William H. Moody	1906–1910	T. Roosevelt
Horace H. Lurton	1910–1914	Taft
Charles E. Hughes	1910–1916	Taft
EDWARD D. WHITE	1910–1921	Taft
Willis Van Devanter	1911–1937	Taft
Joseph R. Lamar	1911–1916	Taft
Mahlon Pitney	1912–1922	Taft
James C. McReynolds	1914–1941	Wilson
Louis D. Brandeis	1916–1939	Wilson
John H. Clarke	1916–1922	Wilson
WILLIAM H. TAFT	1921–1930	Harding
George Sutherland	1922–1938	Harding
Pierce Butler	1923–1939	Harding
Edward T. Sanford	1923–1930	Harding
Harlan F. Stone	1925–1941	Coolidge
CHARLES E. HUGHES	1930–1941	Hoover
Owen J. Roberts	1930–1945	Hoover
Benjamin N. Cardozo	1932–1938	Hoover
Hugo L. Black	1937–1971	F. Roosevelt
Stanley F. Reed	1938–1957	F. Roosevelt
Felix Frankfurter	1939–1962	F. Roosevelt
William O. Douglas	1939–1975	F. Roosevelt
Frank Murphy	1940–1949	F. Roosevelt
HARLAN F. STONE	1941–1946	F. Roosevelt
James F. Brynes	1941–1942	F. Roosevelt
Robert H. Jackson	1941–1954	F. Roosevelt
Wiley B. Rutledge	1943–1949	F. Roosevelt
Harold H. Burton	1945–1958	Truman
FREDERICK M. VINSON	1946–1953	Truman
Tom C. Clark	1949–1967	Truman
Sherman Minton	1949–1956	Truman
EARL WARREN	1953–1969	Eisenhower
John Marshall Harlan	1955–1971	Eisenhower
William J. Brennan, Jr.	1956–1990	Eisenhower
Charles E. Whittaker	1957–1962	Eisenhower
Potter Stewart	1958–1981	Eisenhower
Byron R. White	1962–1993	Kennedy
Arthur J. Goldberg	1962–1965	Kennedy

SUPREME COURT JUSTICES (continued)

Name*	Years on Court	Appointing President
Abe Fortas	1965–1970	L. Johnson
Thurgood Marshall	1967–1991	L. Johnson
WARREN E. BURGER	1969–1986	Nixon
Harry A. Blackmun	1970–1994	Nixon
Lewis F. Powell, Jr.	1971–1987	Nixon
William H. Rehnquist	1971–1986	Nixon
John Paul Stevens	1975–	Ford
Sandra Day O'Connor	1981–	Reagan
WILLIAM H. REHNQUIJST	1986–	Reagan
Antonin Scalia	1986–	Reagan
Anthony Kennedy	1988–	Reagan
David Souter	1990–	Bush
Clarence Thomas	1991–	Bush
Ruth Bader Ginsburg	1993–	Clinton
Stephen Breyer	1994–	Clinton

* Capital letters designate Chief Justices
† Never confirmed by the Senate as Chief Justice

ADMISSION OF STATES INTO THE UNION

State	Date of Admission	State	Date of Admission
1. Delaware	December 7, 1787	26. Michigan	January 26, 1837
2. Pennsylvania	December 12, 1787	27. Florida	March 3, 1845
3. New Jersey	December 18, 1787	28. Texas	December 29, 1845
4. Georgia	January 2, 1788	29. Iowa	December 28, 1846
5. Connecticut	January 9, 1788	30. Wisconsin	May 29, 1848
6. Massachusetts	February 6, 1788	31. California	September 9, 1850
7. Maryland	April 28, 1788	32. Minnesota	May 11, 1858
8. South Carolina	May 23, 1788	33. Oregon	February 14, 1859
9. New Hampshire	June 21, 1788	34. Kansas	January 29, 1861
10. Virginia	June 25, 1788	35. West Virginia	June 20, 1863
11. New York	July 26, 1788	36. Nevada	October 31, 1864
12. North Carolina	November 21, 1789	37. Nebraska	March 1, 1867
13. Rhode Island	May 29, 1790	38. Colorado	August 1, 1876
14. Vermont	March 4, 1791	39. North Dakota	November 2, 1889
15. Kentucky	June 1, 1792	40. South Dakota	November 2, 1889
16. Tennessee	June 1, 1796	41. Montana	November 8, 1889
17. Ohio	March 1, 1803	42. Washington	November 11, 1889
18. Louisiana	April 30, 1812	43. Idaho	July 3, 1890
19. Indiana	December 11, 1816	44. Wyoming	July 10, 1890
20. Mississippi	December 10, 1817	45. Utah	January 4, 1896
21. Illinois	December 3, 1818	46. Oklahoma	November 16, 1907
22. Alabama	December 14, 1819	47. New Mexico	January 6, 1912
23. Maine	March 15, 1820	48. Arizona	February 14, 1912
24. Missouri	August 10, 1821	49. Alaska	January 3, 1959
25. Arkansas	June 15, 1836	50. Hawaii	August 21, 1959

DEMOGRAPHICS OF THE UNITED STATES

POPULATION GROWTH

Year	Population	Percent Increase
1630	4,600	
1640	26,600	478.3
1650	50,400	90.8
1660	75,100	49.0
1670	111,900	49.0
1680	151,500	35.4
1690	210,400	38.9
1700	250,900	19.2
1710	331,700	32.2
1720	466,200	40.5
1730	629,400	35.0
1740	905,600	43.9
1750	1,170,800	29.3
1760	1,593,600	36.1
1770	2,148,100	34.8
1780	2,780,400	29.4
1790	3,929,214	41.3
1800	5,308,483	35.1
1810	7,239,881	36.4
1820	9,638,453	33.1
1830	12,866,020	33.5
1840	17,069,453	32.7
1850	23,191,876	35.9
1860	31,443,321	35.6
1870	39,818,449	26.6
1880	50,155,783	26.0
1890	62,947,714	25.5
1900	75,994,575	20.7
1910	91,972,266	21.0
1920	105,710,620	14.9
1930	122,775,046	16.1
1940	131,669,275	7.2
1950	151,325,798	14.5
1960	179,323,175	18.5
1970	203,302,031	13.4
1980	226,542,199	11.4
1990	248,718,301	9.8
2000	281,421,906	13.1

Source: *Historical Statistics of the United States* (1975); *Statistical Abstract by the United States* (2001).
Note: Figures for 1630–1780 include British colonies within limits of present United States only; Native American population included only in 1930 and thereafter.

WORK FORCE

Year	Total Number Workers (1000s)	Farmers as % of Total	Women as % of Total	% Workers in Unions
1810	2,330	84	(NA)	(NA)
1840	5,660	75	(NA)	(NA)
1860	11,110	53	(NA)	(NA)
1870	12,506	53	15	(NA)
1880	17,392	52	15	(NA)
1890	23,318	43	17	(NA)
1900	29,073	40	18	3
1910	38,167	31	21	6
1920	41,614	26	21	12
1930	48,830	22	22	7
1940	53,011	17	24	27
1950	59,643	12	28	25
1960	69,877	8	32	26
1970	82,049	4	37	25
1980	106,940	3	43	23
1990	125,840	3	45	16
2000	140,863	2	47	12

Source: *Historical Statistics of the United States* (1975); *Statistical Abstract of the United States* (2001).

VITAL STATISTICS
(in thousands)

Year	Births	Deaths	Marriages	Divorces
1800	55	(NA)	(NA)	(NA)
1810	54.3	(NA)	(NA)	(NA)
1820	55.2	(NA)	(NA)	(NA)
1830	51.4	(NA)	(NA)	(NA)
1840	51.8	(NA)	(NA)	(NA)
1850	43.3	(NA)	(NA)	(NA)
1860	44.3	(NA)	(NA)	(NA)
1870	38.3	(NA)	9.6 (1867)	0.3 (1867)
1880	39.8	(NA)	9.1 (1875)	0.3 (1875)
1890	31.5	(NA)	9.0	0.5
1900	32.3	17.2	9.3	0.7
1910	30.1	14.7	10.3	0.9
1920	27.7	13.0	12.0	1.6
1930	21.3	11.3	9.2	1.6
1940	19.4	10.8	12.1	2.0
1950	24.1	9.6	11.1	2.6
1960	23.7	9.5	8.5	2.2
1970	18.4	9.5	10.6	3.5
1980	15.9	8.8	10.6	5.2
1990	16.7	8.6	9.8	4.7
1997	14.6	8.6	8.9	4.3

Source: *Historical Statistics of the United States* (1975); *Statistical Abstract of the United States* (1999).

RACIAL COMPOSITION OF THE POPULATION
(in thousands)

Year	White	Black	Indian	Hispanic	Asian/Pacific Islander
1790	3,172	757	(NA)	(NA)	(NA)
1800	4,306	1,002	(NA)	(NA)	(NA)
1820	7,867	1,772	(NA)	(NA)	(NA)
1840	14,196	2,874	(NA)	(NA)	(NA)
1860	26,923	4,442	(NA)	(NA)	(NA)
1880	43,403	6,581	(NA)	(NA)	(NA)
1900	66,809	8,834	(NA)	(NA)	(NA)
1910	81,732	9,828	(NA)	(NA)	(NA)
1920	94,821	10,463	(NA)	(NA)	(NA)
1930	110,287	11,891	(NA)	(NA)	(NA)
1940	118,215	12,866	(NA)	(NA)	(NA)
1950	134,942	15,042	(NA)	(NA)	(NA)
1960	158,832	18,872	(NA)	(NA)	(NA)
1970	178,098	22,581	(NA)	(NA)	(NA)
1980	194,713	26,683	1,420	14,609	3,729
1990	208,727	30,511	2,065	22,372	2,462
2000	211,461	34,658	2,476	35,306	10,642

Source: U.S. Bureau of the Census, U.S. *Census of Population: 1940,* vol. II, part 1, and vol. IV, part 1; *1950,* vol. II, part 1; *1960,* vol. I, part 1; *1970,* vol. I, part B; and *Current Population Reports,* P25-1095 and P25-1104; *Statistical Abstract of the United States* (2001).

THE ECONOMY AND FEDERAL SPENDING

Year	Gross National Product (GNP) (in billions)	Foreign Trade (in millions)			Federal Budget (in billions)	Federal Surplus/Deficit (in billions)	Federal Debt (in billions)
		Exports	Imports	Balance of Trade			
1790	(NA)	$ 20	$ 23	$ −3	$ 0.004	$ +0.00015	$ 0.076
1800	(NA)	71	91	−20	0.011	+0.0006	0.083
1810	(NA)	67	85	−18	0.008	+0.0012	0.053
1820	(NA)	70	74	−4	0.018	−0.0004	0.091
1830	(NA)	74	71	+3	0.015	+0.100	0.049
1840	(NA)	132	107	+25	0.024	−0.005	0.004
1850	(NA)	152	178	−26	0.040	+0.004	0.064
1860	(NA)	400	362	−38	0.063	−0.01	0.065
1870	$ 7.4	451	462	−11	0.310	+0.10	2.4
1880	11.2	853	761	+92	0.268	+0.07	2.1
1890	13.1	910	823	+87	0.318	+0.09	1.2
1900	18.7	1,499	930	+569	0.521	+0.05	1.2
1910	35.3	1,919	1,646	+273	0.694	−0.02	1.1
1920	91.5	8,664	5,784	+2,880	6.357	+0.3	24.3
1930	90.7	4,013	3,500	+513	3.320	+0.7	16.3
1940	100.0	4,030	7,433	−3,403	9.6	−2.7	43.0
1950	286.5	10,816	9,125	+1,691	43.1	−2.2	257.4
1960	506.5	19,600	15,046	+4,556	92.2	+0.3	286.3
1970	992.7	42,700	40,189	+2,511	195.6	−2.8	371.0
1980	2,631.7	220,783	244,871	+24,088	590.9	−73.8	907.7
1990	5,524.5	394,030	494,042	−101,012	1,251.8	−220.5	3,233.3
2000	9,958.7	1,068,397	1,438,086	−369,689	1,788.8	+236.4	5,629.0

Source: *U.S. Office of Management and Budget, Budget of the United States Government, annual; Statistical Abstract of the United States,* 2001.

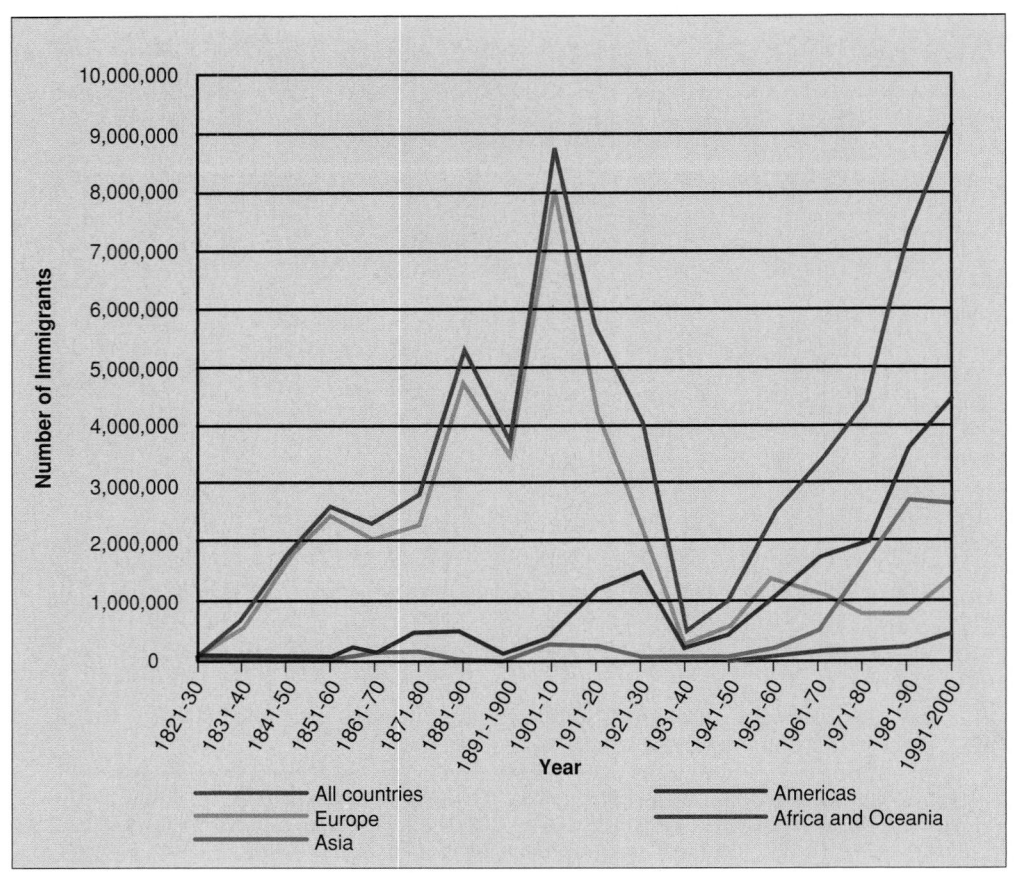

Immigration to the United States since 1820, by decade
Source: *Statistical Yearbook of the Immigration and Naturalization Service,* 2001.

GLOSSARY

Act for Religious Toleration The first law in America to call for freedom of worship for all Christians. It was enacted in Maryland in 1649 to quell disputes between Catholics and Protestants, but it failed to bring peace.

Actual representation The practice whereby elected representatives normally reside in their districts and are directly responsive to local interests.

Affirmative Action A set of policies to open opportunities in business and education for members of minority groups and women by allowing race and sex to be factors included in decisions to hire, award contracts, or admit students to higher education programs.

Age of Enlightenment Major intellectual movement occurring in western Europe in the late seventeenth and early eighteenth centuries. Inspired by recent scientific advances, thinkers emphasized the role of human reason in understanding the world and directing its events. Their ideas placed less emphasis on God's role in ordering worldly affairs.

Agricultural Wheel One of several farmer organizations that emerged in the South during the 1880s. It sought federal legislation to deal with credit and currency issues.

AIDS (Acquired immune deficiency syndrome) A complex of deadly pathologies resulting from infection with the human immunodeficiency virus (HIV).

Alamo Franciscan mission at San Antonio, Texas, that was the site in 1836 of a siege and massacre of Texans by Mexican troops.

Albany Plan of Union Plan put forward in 1754 by Massachusetts Governor William Shirley, Benjamin Franklin, and other colonial leaders, calling for an intercolonial union to manage defense and Indian affairs. The plan was rejected by participants at the Albany Congress.

Alien and Sedition Acts Collective name given to four acts passed by Congress in 1798 that curtailed freedom of speech and the liberty of foreigners resident in the United States.

Alien Friends Act Law passed by Congress in 1798 authorizing the president during peacetime to expel aliens suspected of subversive activities; one of the **Alien and Sedition Acts**.

Alliance for Progress Program of economic aid to Latin America during the Kennedy administration.

Allies In World War I, Britain, France, Russia, and other belligerent nations fighting against the **Central Powers** but not including the United States, which insisted upon being merely an associated nation. In World War II, the Allies fighting the **Axis Powers** included the United States as well as the Soviet Union, Great Britain, France, China, and other nations.

American Anti-Slavery Society The first national organization of abolitionists, founded in 1833.

American Colonization Society Organization, founded in 1817 by antislavery reformers, that called for gradual emancipation and the removal of freed blacks to Africa.

American Federation of Labor (AFL) Union formed in 1886 that organized skilled workers along craft lines and emphasized a few workplace issues rather than a broad social program.

American Female Moral Reform Society Organization founded in 1839 by female reformers that established homes of refuge for prostitutes and petitioned for state laws that would criminalize adultery and the seduction of women.

American Indian Movement (AIM) Group of Native American political activists who used confrontations with the federal government to publicize their case for Indian rights.

American Liberty League Business group organized to sway popular opinion against the **New Deal**.

American Revenue Act See **Sugar Act**.

Americans with Disabilities Act Legislation in 1992 that banned discrimination against physically handicapped persons in employment, transportation, and public accommodations.

American System The program of government subsidies favored by Henry Clay and his followers to promote American economic growth and protect domestic manufacturers from foreign competition.

American system of manufacturing A technique of production pioneered in the United States in the first half of the nineteenth century that relied on precision manufacturing with the use of interchangeable parts.

American Temperance Society National organization established in 1826 by evangelical Protestants that campaigned for total abstinence from alcohol and was successful in sharply lowering per capita consumption of alcohol.

Anarchist A person who believes that all government interferes with individual liberty and should be abolished by whatever means.

Anglican Of or belonging to the Church of England, a Protestant denomination.

Anglo–American Accords Series of agreements reached in the British–American Convention of 1818 that fixed the western boundary between the United States and Canada at the 49th parallel, allowed for the joint occupation of the Oregon Country, and restored to Americans fishing rights off Newfoundland.

Anglo-Saxon Broadly, a person of English descent.

Annapolis Convention Conference of state delegates at Annapolis, Maryland, that issued a call in September 1786 for a convention to meet at Philadelphia in May 1787 to consider fundamental changes to the **Articles of Confederation**.

Antifederalist An opponent of the **Constitution** in the debate over its ratification.

Anti-Masons Third party formed in 1827 in opposition to the presumed power and influence of the Masonic order.

Articles of Confederation Written document setting up the loose confederation of states that comprised the first national government of the United States from 1781 to 1788.

Atlanta Compromise Booker T. Washington's policy accepting segregation and **disfranchisement** for African Americans in exchange for white assistance in education and job training.

Atlantic Charter Statement of common principles and war aims developed by President Franklin Roosevelt and British Prime Minister Winston Churchill at a meeting in August 1941.

Australian ballot Secret voting and the use of official ballots rather than party tickets.

Axis Powers The opponents of the United States and its allies in World War II. The Rome–Berlin Axis was formed between Germany and Italy in 1936 and included Japan after 1940.

Aztecs   A warrior people who dominated the Valley of Mexico from about 1100 until their conquest in 1519–21 by Spanish soldiers led by Hernán Cortés.

Bacon's Rebellion   Violent conflict in Virginia (1675–1676), beginning with settler attacks on Indians but culminating in a rebellion led by Nathaniel Bacon against Virginia's government.

Baker v. Carr   U.S. Supreme Court decision in 1962 that allowed federal courts to review the apportionment of state legislative districts and established the principle that such districts should have roughly equal populations ("one person, one vote").

Bank War   The political struggle between President Andrew Jackson and the supporters of the **Second Bank of the United States**.

Battle of the Atlantic   The long struggle between German submarines and the British and U.S. navies in the North Atlantic from 1940 to 1943.

Bay of Pigs   Site in Cuba of an unsuccessful landing by fourteen hundred anti-Castro Cuban refugees in April 1961.

Beaver Wars   Series of bloody conflicts, occurring between 1640s and 1680s, during which the Iroquois fought the French and their Indian allies for control of the fur trade in eastern North America and the Great Lakes region.

Benevolent empire   Network of reform associations affiliated with Protestant churches in the early nineteenth century dedicated to the restoration of moral order.

Berlin blockade   Three-hundred-day Soviet blockade of land access to United States, British, and French occupation zones in Berlin, 1948–1949.

Berlin Wall   Wall erected by East Germany in 1961 and torn down in 1989 that isolated West Berlin from the surrounding areas in Communist-controlled East Berlin and East Germany.

Bill of rights   A written summary of inalienable rights and liberties.

Black codes   Laws passed by states and municipalities denying many rights of citizenship to free blacks before the Civil War. Also, during the **Reconstruction era**, laws passed by newly elected southern state legislatures to control black labor, mobility, and employment.

Black Hawk's War   Short 1832 war in which federal troops and Illinois militia units defeated the Sauk and Fox Indians led by Black Hawk.

Black Panthers   Political and social movement among black Americans, founded in Oakland, California, in 1966 and emphasizing black economic and political power.

Black Power   Philosophy emerging after 1965 that real economic and political gains for African-Americans could come only through self-help, **self-determination**, and organizing for direct political influence. Latinos and Native Americans developed their own versions as Brown Power and Red Power, respectively.

"Bleeding Kansas"   Violence between pro- and antislavery forces in Kansas Territory after the passage of the **Kansas-Nebraska Act** in 1854.

Blitzkrieg   German war tactic in World War II ("lightning war") involving the concentration of air and armored firepower to punch and exploit holes in opposing defensive lines.

Bolshevik   Member of the communist movement in Russia that established the Soviet government after the 1917 Russian Revolution; hence, by extension, any radical or disruptive person or movement seeking to transform economic and political relationships.

Bosnia   A nation in southeast Europe that split off from Yugoslavia and became the site of bitter civil war and religious war, requiring NATO and U.S. intervention in the 1990s.

Boston Tea Party   Incident that occurred on December 16, 1773, in which Bostonians, disguised as Indians, destroyed £9,000 worth of tea belonging to the British East India Company in order to prevent payment of the duty on it.

British Constitution   The principles, procedures, and precedents that governed the operation of the British government. These could be found in no single written document; Parliament and the king made the Constitution by their actions.

Brook Farm   A utopian community and experimental farm established in 1841 near Boston.

Brown v. Board of Education of Topeka   Supreme Court decision in 1954 that declared that "separate but equal" schools for children of different races violated the **Constitution**.

Bureau of Reclamation   Federal agency established in 1902 providing public funds for irrigation projects in arid regions; played a major role in the development of the West by constructing dams, reservoirs, and irrigation systems, especially beginning in the 1930s.

Cahokia   Located near modern St. Louis, this was one of the largest urban centers created by Mississippian peoples, containing perhaps 30,000 residents in 1250.

Camp David Agreement   Agreement to reduce points of conflict between Israel and Egypt, hammered out in 1977 with the help of U.S. President Jimmy Carter.

Central Intelligence Agency (CIA)   Agency that coordinates the gathering and evaluation of military and economic information on other nations, established in 1947.

Central Powers   Germany and its World War I allies Austria, Turkey, and Bulgaria.

Chain migration   Process common to many immigrant groups whereby one family member brings over other family members, who in turn bring other relatives and friends and occasionally entire villages.

Charles River Bridge v. Warren Bridge   Supreme Court decision of 1837 that promoted economic competition by ruling that the broader rights of the community took precedence over any presumed right of monopoly granted in a corporate charter.

Cherokee War   Conflict (1759–1761) on the southern frontier between the Cherokee Indians and colonists from Virginia southward. It caused South Carolina to request the aid of British troops and resulted in the surrender of more Indian land to white colonists.

Chesapeake **Incident**   Attack in 1807 by the British ship *Leopard* on the American ship *Chesapeake* in American territorial waters that nearly provoked an Anglo-American war.

Chisholm Trail   The route followed by Texas cattle raisers driving their herds north to markets at Kansas railheads.

Church of Jesus Christ of Latter-day Saints   *See* **Mormon Church.**

Civil Rights Act of 1866   Law that defined national citizenship and specified the civil rights to which all national citizens were entitled.

Civil Rights Act of 1875   Law that prohibited racial discrimination in jury selection, public transportation, and public accommodations; declared unconstitutional by the U.S. Supreme Court in 1883.

Civil Rights Act of 1964   Federal legislation that outlawed discrimination in public accommodations and employment on the basis of race, skin color, sex, religion, or national origin.

Claims club   A group of local settlers on the nineteenth-century frontier who banded together to prevent the price of their land claims from being bid up by outsiders at public land auctions.

Coercive Acts   Legislation passed by Parliament in 1774; included the Boston Port Act, the Massachusetts Government Act, the Administration of Justice Act, and the **Quartering Act** of 1774.

Cold War The political and economic confrontation between the Soviet Union and the United States that dominated world affairs from 1946 to 1989.

Collective bargaining Representatives of a union negotiating with management on behalf of all members.

Colored Farmers' Alliance An organization of southern black farmers formed in Texas in 1886 in response to the **Southern Farmers' Alliance**, which did not accept black people as members.

Columbian exchange The transatlantic exchange of plants, animals, and diseases that occurred after the first European contact with the Americas.

Committees of correspondence Committees formed in Massachusetts and other colonies in the pre-Revolutionary period to keep Americans informed about British measures that would affect the colonies.

Committee of Safety Any of the extralegal committees that directed the Revolutionary movement and carried on the functions of government at the local level in the period between the breakdown of royal authority and the establishment of regular governments under the new state constitutions. Some Committees of Safety continued to function throughout the Revolutionary War.

Committee on Public Information (CPI) Government agency during World War I that sought to shape public opinion in support of the war effort through newspapers, pamphlets, speeches, films, and other media.

Communism A social structure based on the common ownership of property.

Conciliatory Proposition Plan proposed by Lord North and adopted by the House of Commons in February 1775 whereby Parliament would "forbear" taxation of Americans in colonies whose assemblies imposed taxes considered satisfactory by the British government. The Continental Congress rejected this plan on July 31, 1775.

Confederate States of America Nation proclaimed in Montgomery, Alabama, in February 1861 after the seven states of the Lower South seceded from the United States.

Confiscation Act of 1862 Second confiscation law passed by Congress, ordering the seizure of land from disloyal Southerners and the emancipation of their slaves.

Congressional Reconstruction Name given to the period 1867–1870 when the Republican-dominated Congress controlled **Reconstruction Era** policy. It is sometimes known as Radical Reconstruction, after the radical faction in the **Republican party**.

Congress of Industrial Organizations An alliance of industrial unions that spurred the 1930s organizational drive among the mass-production industries.

Congress of Racial Equality (CORE) Civil rights group formed in 1942 and committed to nonviolent civil disobedience, such as the 1961 "freedom rides."

Conservation The efficient management and use of natural resources, such as forests, grasslands, and rivers, as opposed to **preservation** or uncontrolled exploitation.

Constitutional Convention Convention that met in Philadelphia in 1787 and drafted the **Constitution of the United States**.

Constitutional Union party National party formed in 1860, mainly by former **Whigs**, that emphasized allegiance to the Union and strict enforcement of all national legislation.

Constitution of the United States The written document providing for a new central government of the United States, drawn up at the **Constitutional Convention** in 1787 and ratified by the states in 1788.

Containment The policy of resisting further expansion of the Soviet bloc through diplomacy and, if necessary, military action, developed in 1947–48.

Continental Army The regular or professional army authorized by the Second Continental Congress and commanded by General George Washington during the Revolutionary War. Better training and longer service distinguished its soldiers from the state militiamen.

Continental Association Agreement, adopted by the **First Continental Congress** in 1774 in response to the **Coercive Acts**, to cut off trade with Britain until the objectionable measures were repealed. Local committees were established to enforce the provisions of the association.

Contract theory of government The belief that government is established by human beings to protect certain rights—such as life, liberty, and property—that are theirs by natural, divinely sanctioned law and that when government protects these rights, people are obligated to obey it. But when government violates its part of the bargain (or contract) between the rulers and the ruled, the people are no longer required to obey it and may establish a new government that will do a better job of protecting them. Elements of this theory date back to the ancient Greeks; John Locke used it in his *Second Treatise on Government* (1682), and Thomas Jefferson gave it memorable expression in the Declaration of Independence, where it provides the rationale for renouncing allegiance to King George III.

Contract with America Platform on which many Republican candidates ran for Congress in 1994. Associated with House Speaker Newt Gingrich, it proposed a sweeping reduction in the role and activities of the federal government.

Copperheads A term Republicans applied to Northern war dissenters and those suspected of aiding the Confederate cause during the Civil War.

Council of Economic Advisers Board of three professional economists established in 1946 to advise the president on economic policy.

Counterculture Various alternatives to mainstream values and behaviors that became popular in the 1960s, including experimentation with psychedelic drugs, communal living, a return to the land, Asian religions, and experimental art.

Country (Real Whig) ideology Strain of thought first appearing in England in the late seventeenth century in response to the growth of governmental power and a national debt. Main ideas stressed the threat to personal liberty posed by a standing army and high taxes and emphasized the need for property holders to retain the right to consent to taxation.

Coureur de bois French for "woods runner," an independent fur trader in New France.

Coxey's Army A protest march of unemployed workers, led by Populist businessman Jacob Coxey, demanding inflation and a public works program during the depression of the 1890s.

Cult of domesticity The belief that women, by virtue of their sex, should stay home as the moral guardians of family life.

Currency Act Law passed by Parliament in 1764 to prevent the colonies from issuing **legal tender** paper money, which often depreciated.

Dartmouth College v. Woodward Supreme Court decision of 1819 that prohibited states from interfering with the privileges granted to a private corporation.

Dawes Act An 1887 law terminating tribal ownership of land and allotting some parcels of land to individual Indians with the remainder opened for white settlement.

D-Day June 6, 1944, the day of the first paratroop drops and amphibious landings on the coast of Normandy, France, in the first stage of **Operation OVERLORD** during World War II.

Declaration of Independence The document by which the Second Continental Congress announced and justified its decision (reached July 2, 1776) to renounce the colonies' allegiance to the British government. Drafted mainly by Thomas Jefferson and adopted by Congress on July 4, the declaration's indictment of the king provides a remarkably full catalog of the colonists' grievances, and Jefferson's eloquent and inspiring statement of the **contract theory of government** makes the document one of the world's great state papers.

Declaration of London Statement drafted by an international conference in 1909 to clarify international law and specify the rights of neutral nations.

Declaration of Rights and Grievances Resolves, adopted by the **Stamp Act Congress** at New York in 1765, asserting that the **Stamp Act** and other taxes imposed on the colonists without their consent, given through their colonial legislatures, were unconstitutional.

Declaration of Sentiments The resolutions passed at the **Seneca Falls Convention** in 1848 calling for full female equality, including the right to vote.

Declaration of the Causes and Necessity of Taking Up Arms Document, written mainly by John Dickinson of Pennsylvania and adopted on July 6, 1775, by which the Second Continental Congress justified its armed resistance against British measures.

Declaratory Act Law passed in 1766 to accompany repeal of the **Stamp Act** that stated that Parliament had the authority to legislate for the colonies "in all cases whatsoever." Whether "legislate" meant tax was not clear to Americans.

Deindustrialization The process of economic change involving the disappearance of outmoded industries and the transfer of factories to new low-wage locations, with devastating effects in the Northeast and Middle West, especially in the 1970s and 1980s.

Deism Religious orientation that rejects divine revelation and holds that the workings of nature alone reveal God's design for the universe.

Democratic Party Political party formed in the 1820s under the leadership of Andrew Jackson; favored states' rights and a limited role for the federal government, especially in economic affairs.

Denmark Vesey's Conspiracy The most carefully devised slave revolt, named after its leader, a free black in Charleston. The rebels planned to seize control of Charleston in 1822 and escape to freedom in Haiti, a free black republic, but they were betrayed by other slaves, and seventy-five conspirators were executed.

Deregulation Reduction or removal of government regulations and encouragement of direct competition in many important industries and economic sectors.

Disfranchisement The use of legal means to bar individuals or groups from voting.

Dollar diplomacy The U.S. policy of using private investment in other nations to promote American diplomatic goals and business interests.

Dominion of New England James II's failed plan of 1686 to combine eight northern colonies into a single large province, to be governed by a royal appointee (Sir Edmund Andros) with an appointed council but no elective assembly. The plan ended with James's ouster from the English throne and rebellion in Massachusetts against Andros's rule.

Dred Scott **decision** Supreme Court ruling, in a lawsuit brought by Dred Scott, a slave demanding his freedom based on his residence in a free state and a free territory with his master, that slaves could not be U.S. citizens and that Congress had no jurisdiction over slavery in the territories.

Eastern Front The area of military operations in World War II located east of Germany in eastern Europe and the Soviet Union.

Economic Recovery and Tax Act of 1981 (ERTA) A major revision of the federal income tax system.

Emancipation Proclamation Decree announced by President Abraham Lincoln in September 1862 and formally issued on January 1, 1863, freeing slaves in all Confederate states still in rebellion.

Embargo Act of 1807 Act passed by Congress in 1807 prohibiting American ships from leaving for any foreign port.

Empresario An agent who received a land grant from the Spanish or Mexican government in return for organizing settlements.

Encomienda In the Spanish colonies, the grant to a Spanish settler of a certain number of Indian subjects, who would pay him tribute in goods and labor.

Enumerated products Items produced in the colonies and enumerated in acts of Parliament that could be legally shipped from the colony of origin only to specified locations, usually England and other destinations within the British empire.

Environmental Protection Agency (EPA) Federal agency created in 1970 to oversee environmental monitoring and cleanup programs.

Era of Good Feelings The period from 1817 to 1823 in which the disappearance of the **Federalists** enabled the **Republicans** to govern in a spirit of seemingly nonpartisan harmony.

Espionage Act of 1917 Law whose vague prohibition against obstructing the nation's war effort was used to crush dissent and criticism during World War I.

Fair Employment Practice Committee (FEPC) Federal agency established in 1941 to curb racial discrimination in war production jobs and government employment.

Farmers' Alliance A broad mass movement in the rural South and West during the late nineteenth century, encompassing several organizations and demanding economic and political reforms; helped create the **Populist party**.

Fascist Subscribing to a philosophy of governmental dictatorship that merges the interests of the state, armed forces, and big business; associated with the dictatorship of Italian leader Benito Mussolini between 1922 and 1943 and also often applied to Nazi Germany.

Federal Deposit Insurance Corporation (FDIC) Government agency that guarantees bank deposits, thereby protecting both depositors and banks.

Federal Highway Act of 1956 Measure that provided federal funding to build a nationwide system of interstate and defense highways.

Federalism The sharing of powers between the national government and the states.

Federalist A supporter of the **Constitution** who favored its ratification.

Federal Reserve Act The 1913 law that revised banking and currency by extending limited government regulation through the creation of the Federal Reserve System.

Federal Trade Commission (FTC) Government agency established in 1914 to provide regulatory oversight of business activity.

Field Order No. 15 Order by General William T. Sherman in January 1865 to set aside abandoned land along the southern Atlantic coast for forty-acre grants to freedmen; rescinded by President Andrew Johnson later that year.

Fireside chats Speeches broadcast nationally over the radio in which President Franklin Roosevelt explained complex issues and programs in plain language, as though his listeners were gathered around the fireside with him.

First Continental Congress   Meeting of delegates from most of the colonies held in 1774 in response to the **Coercive Acts**. The Congress endorsed the **Suffolk Resolves**, adopted the **Declaration of Rights and Grievances**, and agreed to establish the **Continental Association** to put economic pressure on Britain to repeal its objectionable measures. The Congress also wrote addresses to the king, the people of Britain, and the American people.

Fletcher v. Peck   Supreme Court decision of 1810 that overturned a state law by ruling that it violated a legal contract.

Fort Sumter   Begun in the late 1820s to protect Charleston, South Carolina, it became the center of national attention in April 1861 when President Lincoln attempted to provision federal troops at the fort, triggering a hostile response from on-shore Confederate forces, opening the Civil War.

Fourierist communities   Short-live utopian communities in the 1840s based on the ideas of economic cooperation and self-sufficiency popularized by the Frenchman Charles Fourier.

Fourteenth Amendment   Constitutional amendment passed by Congress in April 1866 incorporating some of the features of the **Civil Rights Act of 1866**. It prohibited states from violating the civil rights of its citizens and offered states the choice of allowing black people to vote or losing representation in Congress.

Franco-American Accord of 1800   Settlement reached with France that brought an end to the **Quasi-War** and released the United States from its 1778 alliance with France.

Freedmen's Bureau   Agency established by Congress in March 1865 to provide social, educational, and economic services, advice, and protection to former slaves and destitute whites; lasted seven years.

Freedom Summer   Voter registration effort in rural Mississippi organized by black and white civil rights workers in 1964.

Free silver   Philosophy that the government should expand the money supply by purchasing and coining all the silver offered to it.

Free Speech Movement (FSM)   Student movement at the University of California, Berkeley, formed in 1964 to protest limitations on political activities on campus.

French and Indian War   The last of the Anglo-French colonial wars (1754–1763) and the first in which fighting began in North America. The war (which merged with the European conflict known as the Seven Years' War) ended with France's defeat and loss of its North American empire.

Fugitive Slave Act   Law, part of the Compromise of 1850, that required that authorities in the North to assist southern slave catchers and return runaway slaves to their owners.

Fundamental Constitutions of Carolina   A complex plan for organizing the colony of Carolina, drafted in 1669 by Anthony Ashley Cooper and John Locke. Its provisions included a scheme for creating a hierarchy of nobles who would own vast amounts of land and wield political power; below them would be a class of freedmen and slaves. The provisions were never implemented by the Carolina colonists.

Fundamentalists   Religious conservatives who believe in the literal accuracy and divine inspiration of the Bible; the name derives from an influential series of pamphlets, *The Fundamentals* (1909–1914).

Gabriel Prosser's Rebellion   Slave revolt that failed when Gabriel Prosser, a slave preacher and blacksmith, organized a thousand slaves for an attack on Richmond, Virginia, in 1800. A thunderstorm upset the timing of the attack, and a slave informer alerted the whites. Prosser and twenty-five of his followers were executed.

Gang system   The organization and supervision of slave field hands into working teams on southern plantations.

General Union for Promoting the Observance of the Christian Sabbath   See **Sabbatarian movement**.

Gentlemen's Agreement   A diplomatic agreement in 1907 between Japan and the United States curtailing but not abolishing Japanese immigration.

Ghent, Treaty of   Treaty signed in December 1814 between the United States and Britain that ended the **War of 1812**.

GI Bill of Rights   Legislation in June 1944 that eased the return of veterans into American society by providing educational and employment benefits.

Gibbons v. Ogden   Supreme Court decision of 1824 involving coastal commerce that overturned a steamboat monopoly granted by the state of New York on the grounds that only Congress had the authority to regulate interstate commerce.

Gilded Age   Term applied to late-nineteenth-century America that refers to the shallow display and worship of wealth characteristic of the period.

Glasnost   Russian for "openness," applied to Mikhail Gorbachev's encouragement of new ideas and easing of political repression in the Soviet Union.

Glorious Revolution   Bloodless revolt that occurred in England in 1688 when parliamentary leaders invited William of Orange, a Protestant, to assume the English throne and James II fled to France. James's ouster was prompted by fears that the birth of his son would establish a Catholic dynasty in England.

Gospel of Wealth   Thesis that hard work and perseverance lead to wealth, implying that poverty is a character flaw.

Grandfather clause   Rule that required potential voters to demonstrate that their grandfathers had been eligible to vote; used in some southern states after 1890 to limit the black electorate, as most black men's grandfathers had been slaves.

Grand Settlement of 1701   Separate peace treaties negotiated by Iroquois diplomats at Montreal and Albany that marked the beginning of Iroquois neutrality in conflicts between the French and the British in North America.

Grange   The National Grange of the Patrons of Husbandry, a national organization of farm owners formed after the Civil War.

Granger laws   State laws enacted in the Midwest in the 1870s that regulated rates charged by railroads, grain elevator operators, and other middlemen.

Great Awakening   Tremendous religious revival in colonial America. Sparked by the tour of the English evangelical minister George Whitefield, the Awakening struck first in the Middle Colonies and New England in the 1740s and eventually spread to the southern colonies by the 1760s.

Great Compromise   Plan proposed by Roger Sherman of Connecticut at the 1787 **Constitutional Convention** for creating a national bicameral legislature in which all states would be equally represented in the Senate and proportionally represented in the House.

Great Depression   The nation's worst economic crisis, extending throughout the 1930s, producing unprecedented bank failures, unemployment, and industrial and agricultural collapse and prompting an expanded role for the federal government.

Great Migration   The mass movement of African Americans from the rural South to the urban North, spurred especially by new job opportunities during World War I and the 1920s.

Great Society   Theme of Lyndon Johnson's administration, focusing on poverty, education, and civil rights.

Great Uprising Unsuccessful railroad strike of 1877 to protest wage cuts and the use of federal troops against strikers; the first nationwide work stoppage in American history.

Greenback party A third party of the 1870s and 1880s that garnered temporary support by advocating currency inflation to expand the economy and assist debtors.

Greenville, Treaty of Treaty of 1795 in which Native Americans in the Old Northwest were forced to cede most of the present state of Ohio to the United States.

Halfway Covenant Plan adopted in 1662 by New England clergy to deal with the problem of declining church membership. It allowed adults who had been baptized because their parents were church members but who had not yet experienced conversion to have their own children baptized. Without the Halfway Covenant, these third-generation children would remain unbaptized until their parents experienced conversion.

Harlem Renaissance A new African-American cultural awareness that flourished in literature, art, and music in the 1920s.

Helsinki Accords Agreement in 1975 among NATO and Warsaw Pact members that recognized European national boundaries as set after World War II and included guarantees of human rights.

Holocaust The systematic murder of millions of European Jews and others deemed undesirable by Nazi Germany.

Homestead Act Law passed by Congress in May 1862 providing homesteaders (mainly in the West) with 160 acres of free land in exchange for improving the land (as by cultivating it and erecting a house) within five years of the grant.

Hooverville Shantytown, sarcastically named after President Hoover, in which unemployed and homeless people lived in makeshift shacks, tents, and boxes. Hoovervilles cropped up in many cities in 1930 and 1931.

House of Burgesses The legislature of colonial Virginia. First organized in 1619, it was the first institution of representative government in the English colonies.

Hull House Chicago **settlement house** that became part of a broader neighborhood revitalization project led by Jane Addams.

Immigration and Nationality Act of 1965 Federal legislation that replaced the national quota system for immigration with overall limits of 170,000 immigrants per year from the Eastern Hemisphere and 120,000 per year from the Western Hemisphere.

Imperialism The policy and practice of exploiting nations and peoples for the benefit of an imperial power either directly through military occupation and colonial rule or indirectly through economic domination of resources and markets.

Indentured servant An individual—usually male but occasionally female—who contracted to serve a master for a period of four to seven years in return for payment of the servant's passage to America. Indentured servitude was the primary labor system in the Chesapeake colonies for most of the seventeenth century.

Independent Treasury System Fiscal arrangement first instituted by President Martin Van Buren in which the federal government kept its money in regional vaults ("pet banks") and transacted its business entirely in hard money.

Initiative Procedure by which citizens can introduce a subject for legislation, usually through a petition signed by a specific number of voters.

Intermediate Nuclear Force Agreement (INF) Disarmament agreement between the United States and the Soviet Union under which an entire class of missiles would be removed and destroyed and on-site inspections would be permitted for verification.

International Monetary Fund (IMF) International organization established in 1945 to assist nations in maintaining stable currencies.

Internet The system of interconnected computers and servers that allows the exchange of e-mail, posting of web sites, and other means of instant communication.

Interstate and Defense Highways Federal legislation in 1956 committed the federal government to finance more than 40,000 miles of new limited access freeways to criss-cross the United States.

Interstate Commerce Act The 1887 law that expanded federal power over business by prohibiting pooling and discriminatory rates by railroads and establishing the first federal regulatory agency, the **Interstate Commerce Commission**.

Interstate Commerce Commission (ICC) The first federal regulatory agency, established in 1887 to oversee railroad practices.

Intolerable Acts American term for the **Coercive Acts** and the **Quebec Act**.

Iroquois League The union of five Indian nations (Mohawks, Oneidas, Onondagas, Cayugas, and Senecas) formed around 1450, also known as the League of Five Nations. Essentially a religious organization, its purpose was to maintain peace among the five nations and unite them to fight against other enemies. After the Tuscarora War (1713–1715), the Tuscaroras joined the league, thereafter known as the League of Six Nations.

Irreconcilables Group of U.S. senators adamantly opposed to ratification of the **Treaty of Versailles** after World War I.

Jacksonian Democrats See **Democratic Party**.

Jay's Treaty Treaty with Britain negotiated in 1794 in which the United States made major concessions to avert a war over the British seizure of American ships.

Jazz Age The 1920s, so called for the popular music of the day as a symbol of the many changes taking place in the mass culture.

Jeffersonian Republicans See **Republican Party (Jeffersonian)**.

Jim Crow laws Segregation laws that became widespread in the South during the 1890s, named for a minstrel show character portrayed satirically by white actors in blackface.

John Brown's Raid New England abolitionist John Brown's ill-fated attempt to free Virginia's slaves with a raid on the federal arsenal at Harpers Ferry, Virginia, in 1859.

Joint-stock company Business enterprise in which a group of stockholders pooled their money to engage in trade or to fund colonizing expeditions. Joint-stock companies participated in the founding of the Virginia, Plymouth, and Massachusetts Bay colonies.

Judicial review A power implied in the **Constitution** that gives federal courts the right to review and determine the constitutionality of acts passed by Congress and state legislatures.

Judiciary Act of 1789 Act of Congress that implemented the judiciary clause of the **Constitution** by establishing the Supreme Court and a system of lower federal courts.

Kansas-Nebraska Act Law passed in 1854 creating the Kansas and Nebraska Territories but leaving the question of slavery open to residents, thereby repealing the **Missouri Compromise**.

King George's War The third Anglo-French war in North America (1744–1748), part of the European conflict known as the War of the Austrian Succession. During the North American fighting, New Englanders captured the French fortress of Louisbourg, only to have it returned to France after the peace negotiations.

King Philip's War Conflict in New England (1675–1676) between Wampanoags, Narragansetts, and other Indian peoples against English settlers; sparked by English encroachments on native lands.

King William's War The first Anglo-French conflict in North America (1689–1697), the American phase of Europe's War of the League of Augsburg. Ended in negotiated peace that reestablished the balance of power.

Knights of Labor Labor union that included skilled and unskilled workers irrespective of race or gender; founded in 1869, peaked in the 1880s, and declined when its advocacy of the eight-hour workday led to violent strikes in 1886.

Know-Nothing Party Anti-immigrant party formed from the wreckage of the **Whig Party** and some disaffected northern Democrats in 1854.

Kosovo Province of Yugoslavia, in southeast Europe, where the U.S. and NATO intervened militarily in 1999 to protect ethnic Albanians from expulsion by Yugoslavia.

Ku Klux Klan Perhaps the most prominent of the vigilante groups that terrorized black people in the South during **Reconstruction Era**, founded by Confederate veterans in 1866.

Laissez-faire The doctrine that government should not intervene in the economy, especially through regulation.

Lancaster, Treaty of Negotiation in 1744 whereby Iroquois chiefs sold Virginia land speculators the right to trade at the Forks of the Ohio. Although the Iroquois had not intended this to include the right to settle in the Ohio Country, the Virginians assumed that it did. Ohio Valley Indians considered this treaty a great grievance against both the English and the Iroquois.

Land Grant College Act Law passed by Congress in July 1862 awarding proceeds from the sale of public lands to the states for the establishment of agricultural and mechanical (later engineering) colleges. Also known as the Morrill Act, after its sponsor, Congressman Justin Morrill of Vermont.

Land Ordinance of 1785 Act passed by Congress under the **Articles of Confederation** that created the grid system of surveys by which all subsequent public land was made available for sale.

League of Nations International organization created by the **Versailles Treaty** after World War I to ensure world stability.

Lecompton Constitution Proslavery draft written in 1857 by Kansas territorial delegates elected under questionable circumstances; it was rejected by two governors, supported by President Buchanan, and decisively defeated by Congress.

Legal tender An attribute of money that results from legislation declaring it to be, as in the case of modern United States currency, "legal tender for all debts public and private." Creditors must therefore accept it at face value.

Lend-Lease Program begun in 1941 through which the U.S. transferred military equipment to Britain and other World War II allies.

Liberal Republicans Members of a reform movement within the **Republican Party** in 1872 that promoted measures to reduce government influence in the economy and restore control of southern governments to local white elites.

Liberty Bonds Interest-bearing certificates sold by the U.S. government to finance the American World War I effort.

Liberty Party The first antislavery political party, formed in 1840.

Lincoln-Douglas debates Series of debates in the 1858 Illinois senatorial campaign during which Democrat Stephen A. Douglas and Republican Abraham Lincoln staked out their differing opinions on the issue of slavery in the territories.

Little Bighorn, Battle of the Battle in which Colonel George A. Custer and the Seventh Cavalry were defeated by the Sioux and Cheyennes under Sitting Bull and Crazy Horse in Montana in 1876.

Lost Cause The phrase many white Southerners applied to their Civil War defeat. They viewed the war as a noble cause but only a temporary setback in the South's ultimate vindication.

Lynching Execution, usually by a mob, without trial.

Mahanism The ideas advanced by Alfred Thayer Mahan, stressing U.S. naval, economic, and territorial expansion.

Manhattan Project The effort, using the code name Manhattan Engineer District, to develop an atomic bomb under the management of the U.S. Army Corps of Engineers during World War II.

Manifest Destiny Doctrine, first expressed in 1845, that the expansion of white Americans across the continent was inevitable and ordained by God.

Marbury v. Madison Supreme Court decision of 1803 that created the precedent of judicial review by ruling as unconstitutional part of the **Judiciary Act of 1789**.

Massive retaliation Popular name for the military doctrine adopted in the 1950s, whereby the U.S. promised to respond to any attack on itself or its allies with massive force, including nuclear weapons.

McCarthyism Anticommunist attitudes and actions associated with Senator Joe McCarthy in the early 1950s, including smear tactics and innuendo.

McCulloch v. Maryland Supreme Court decision of 1819 that established the supremacy of federal over state authority by declaring that states could not tax federal institutions.

Medicaid Supplementary medical insurance for the poor, financed through the federal government; program created in 1965.

Medicare Basic medical insurance for the elderly, financed through the federal government; program created in 1965.

Mercantilism Economic system whereby the government intervenes in the economy for the purpose of increasing national wealth. Mercantilists advocated possession of colonies as places where the mother country could acquire raw materials not available at home.

Middle Passage The voyage between West Africa and the New World slave colonies.

Minute Men Special companies of militia formed in Massachusetts and elsewhere beginning in late 1744. These units were composed of men who were to be ready to assemble with their arms at a minute's notice.

Missouri Compromise Sectional compromise in Congress in 1820 that admitted Missouri to the Union as a slave state and Maine as a free state and prohibited slavery in the **Louisiana Purchase** territory above 36°30′ north latitude.

Model Cities Program Effort to target federal funds to upgrade public services and economic opportunity in specifically defined urban neighborhoods between 1966 and 1974.

Monroe Doctrine Declaration by President James Monroe in 1823 that the Western Hemisphere was to be closed off to further European colonization and that the United States would not interfere in the internal affairs of European nations.

Mormon Church (Church of Jesus Christ of Latter-day Saints) Church founded in 1830 by Joseph Smith and based on the revelations in a sacred book he called the Book of Mormon.

Muckraking Journalism exposing economic, social, and political evils, so named by Theodore Roosevelt for its "raking the muck" of American society.

Mugwumps Elitist and conservative reformers who favored **sound money** and limited government and opposed tariffs and the **spoils system**.

Multinational corporation Firm with direct investments, branches, factories, and offices in a number of countries.

National Aeronautics and Space Administration (NASA) Federal agency created in 1958 to manage American space flights and exploration.

National American Woman Suffrage Association The organization, formed in 1890, that coordinated the ultimately successful campaign to achieve women's right to vote.

Nationalists Group of leaders in the 1780s who spearheaded the drive to replace the **Articles of Confederation** with a stronger central government.

National Origins Act A 1924 law sharply restricting immigration on the basis of immigrants' national origins and discriminating against southern and eastern Europeans and Asians.

National Security Council (NSC) The formal policymaking body for national defense and foreign relations, created in 1947 and consisting of the president, the secretary of defense, the secretary of state, and others appointed by the president.

National Security Council Paper 68 (NSC-68) Policy statement that committed the United States to a military approach to the **Cold War**.

National War Labor Board Government agency that supervised labor relations during World War I, guaranteeing union rights in exchange for industrial stability.

Nation of Islam Religious movement among black Americans that emphasizes self-sufficiency, self-help, and separation from white society.

Nativist/Nativism Favoring the interests and culture of native-born inhabitants over those of immigrants.

Nat Turner's Rebellion Uprising of slaves in Southampton County, Virginia, in the summer of 1831 led by Nat Turner that resulted in the death of fifty-five whites.

Natural rights Political philosophy that maintains that individuals have an inherent right, found in nature and preceding any government or written law, to life and liberty.

Neoconservative Advocate of or participant in the revitalized conservative politics of the 1980s and 1990s, calling for a strong government role in defense and foreign policy and a limited role in social and economic policy.

Neoliberal Advocate of or participant in the effort to reshape the **Democratic party** for the 1990s around a policy emphasizing economic growth and competitiveness in the world economy.

New Deal The economic and political policies of the Roosevelt administration in the 1930s.

New Federalism President Richard Nixon's policy to shift responsibilities for government programs from the federal level to the states.

New Freedom Woodrow Wilson's 1912 program for limited government intervention in the economy to restore competition by curtailing the restrictive influences of trusts and protective tariffs, thereby providing opportunities for individual achievement.

New Frontier John F. Kennedy's domestic and foreign policy initiatives, designed to reinvigorate a sense of national purpose and energy.

New Harmony Short-lived utopian community established in Indiana in 1825, based on the socialist ideas of Robert Owen, a wealthy Scottish manufacturer.

New Jersey Plan Proposal of the New Jersey delegation at the 1787 **Constitutional Convention** for a strengthened national government in which all states would have equal representation in a **unicameral legislature**.

New Lights People who experienced conversion during the revivals of the **Great Awakening**.

New Nationalism Theodore Roosevelt's 1912 program calling for a strong national government to foster, regulate, and protect business, industry, workers, and consumers.

New Orleans, Battle of Decisive American **War of 1812** victory over British troops in January 1815 that ended any British hopes of gaining control of the lower Mississippi River Valley.

New York Draft Riot A mostly Irish-immigrant protest against conscription in New York City in July 1863 that escalated into class and racial warfare that had to be quelled by federal troops.

Niagara Movement African-American group organized in 1905 to promote racial integration, civil and political rights, and equal access to economic opportunity.

Nineteenth Amendment Constitutional revision that in 1920 established women citizens' right to vote.

Nisei U.S. citizens born of immigrant Japanese parents.

Nixon Doctrine In July, 1969, President Nixon described a new American policy toward Asia, in which the U.S. would honor treaty commitments but would gradually disengage and expect Asian nations to handle military defense on their own.

Nonimportation Movement A tactical means of putting economic pressure on Britain by refusing to buy its exports to the colonies. Initiated in response to the taxes imposed by the **Sugar** and **Stamp Acts**, it was used again against the **Townshend duties** and the **Coercive Acts**. The nonimportation movement popularized resistance to British measures and deepened the commitment of many ordinary people to a larger American community.

Nonintercourse Act Law passed by Congress in 1809 that prohibited American trade with Britain and France.

North American Free Trade Agreement (NAFTA) Agreement reached in 1993 by Canada, Mexico, and the United States to substantially reduce barriers to trade.

Northwest Ordinance of 1787 Legislation passed by Congress under the **Articles of Confederation** that prohibited slavery in the Northwest Territories and provided the model for the incorporation of future territories into the Union as coequal states.

Nullification A constitutional doctrine holding that a state has a legal right to declare a national law null and void within its borders.

Nullification crisis Sectional crisis in the early 1830s in which a **states' rights** party in South Carolina attempted to nullify federal law.

Office of Economic Opportunity (OEO) Federal agency that coordinated many programs of the **War on Poverty** between 1964 and 1975.

Olive Branch Petition Petition, written largely by John Dickinson and adopted by the Second Continental Congress on July 5, 1775, as a last effort of peace that avowed America's loyalty to George III and requested that he protect them from further aggressions. Congress continued military preparations, and the king never responded to the petition.

Omaha Platform The 1892 platform of the **Populist party** repudiating laissez-faire and demanding economic and political reforms to aid distressed farmers and workers.

Oneida Community Utopian community established in upstate New York in 1848 by John Humphrey Noyes and his followers.

Open Door American policy of seeking equal trade and investment opportunities in foreign nations or regions.

Open shop Factory or business employing workers whether or not they are union members; in practice, such a business usually refuses to hire union members and follows antiunion policies.

Operation Desert Storm Code name for the successful offensive against Iraq by the United States and its allies in the Persian Gulf War (1991).

Operation OVERLORD   U.S. and British invasion of France in June 1944 during World War II.

Oregon Trail   Overland trail of more than two thousand miles that carried American settlers from the Midwest to new settlements in Oregon, California, and Utah.

Organization of Petroleum Exporting Countries (OPEC)   Cartel of oil-producing nations in Asia, Africa, and Latin America that gained substantial power over the world economy in the mid- to late 1970s by controlling the production and price of oil.

Pan American Union   International organization originally established as the Commercial Bureau of American Republics by Secretary of State James Blaine's first Pan-American Conference in 1889 to promote cooperation among nations of the Western Hemisphere through commercial and diplomatic negotiations.

Panic of 1857   Banking crisis that caused a credit crunch in the North; it was less severe in the South, where high cotton prices spurred a quick recovery.

Pan-Indian resistance movement   Movement calling for the political and cultural unification of Indian tribes in the late eighteenth and early nineteenth centuries.

Patriot Act   Federal legislation adopted in 2001, in response to the terrorist attacks of September 11, intended to facilitate anti-terror actions by federal law enforcement and intelligence agencies.

Peace of Paris   Treaties signed in 1783 by Great Britain, the United States, France, Spain, and the Netherlands that ended the Revolutionary War. First in a preliminary agreement and then in the final treaty with the United States, Britain recognized the independence of the United States, agreed that the Mississippi River would be its western boundary, and permitted it to fish in some Canadian waters. Prewar debts owed by the inhabitants of one country to those of the other were to remain collectible, and Congress was to urge the states to return property confiscated from Loyalists. British troops were to evacuate United States territory without removing slaves or other property. In a separate agreement, Britain relinquished its claim to East and West Florida to Spain.

Pendleton Civil Service Act   A law of 1883 that reformed the **spoils system** by prohibiting government workers from making political contributions and creating the Civil Service Commission to oversee their appointment on the basis of merit rather than politics.

Pentagon Papers   Classified Defense Department documents on the history of the United States' involvement in Vietnam, prepared in 1968 and leaked to the press in 1971.

People's Party   *See* **Populist Party**.

Pequot War   Conflict between English settlers (who had Narragansett and Mohegan allies) and Pequot Indians over control of land and trade in eastern Connecticut. The Pequots were nearly destroyed in a set of bloody confrontations, including a deadly English attack on a Mystic River village in May 1637.

Perestroika   Russian for "restructuring," applied to Mikhail Gorbachev's efforts to make the Soviet economic and political systems more modern, flexible, and innovative.

Persian Gulf War   War (1991) between Iraq and a U. S. led coalition that followed Iraq's invasion of Kuwait and resulted in the expulsion of Iraqi forces from that country.

Pietists   Protestants who stress a religion of the heart and the spirit of Christian living.

Pilgrims   Settlers of Plymouth Colony, who viewed themselves as spiritual wanderers.

Pinckney's Treaty   Treaty with Spain in 1795 in which Spain recognized the 31st parallel as the boundary between the United States and Spanish Florida and opened the Mississippi River through the port of New Orleans to American shipping.

Platt Amendment   A stipulation the United States had inserted into the Cuban constitution in 1901 restricting Cuban autonomy and authorizing U.S. intervention and naval bases.

Plattsburg, Battle of   American naval victory on Lake Champlain in September 1814 in the **War of 1812** that thwarted a British invasion from Canada.

Pogroms   Government-directed attacks against Jewish citizens, property, and villages in tsarist Russia beginning in the 1880s; a primary reason for Russian Jewish migration to the United States.

Poll tax   A tax imposed on voters as a requirement for voting. Most southern states imposed poll taxes after 1900 as a way to disfranchise black people; the measures also restricted the white vote.

Pontiac's Rebellion   Indian uprising (1763–1766) led by Pontiac of the Ottawas and Neolin of the Delawares. Fearful of their fate at the hands of the British after the French had been driven out of North America, the Indian nations of the Ohio River Valley and the Great Lakes area united to oust the British from the Ohio-Mississippi Valley. They failed and were forced to make peace in 1766.

Populist Party   A major third party of the 1890s, also known as the **People's Party**. Formed on the basis of the **Southern Farmers' Alliance** and other reform organizations, it mounted electoral challenges against the Democrats in the South and the Republicans in the West.

Potsdam Declaration   Statement issued by the United States during a meeting of U.S. President Harry Truman, British Prime Minister Winston Churchill, and Soviet Premier Joseph Stalin held at Potsdam, near Berlin, in July 1945 to plan the defeat of Japan and the future of eastern Europe and Germany. In it, the United States declared its intention to democratize the Japanese political system and reintroduce Japan into the international community and gave Japan an opening for surrender.

Predestination   The belief that God decided at the moment of Creation which humans would achieve salvation.

Preparedness   Military buildup in preparation for possible U.S. participation in World War I.

Preservation   Protecting forests, land, and other features of the natural environment from development or destruction, often for aesthetic appreciation.

Proclamation Line   Boundary, decreed as part of the **Proclamation of 1763**, that limited British settlements to the eastern side of the Appalachian Mountains, thereby threatening colonial expansionists and causing resentment. It proved unenforceable.

Proclamation of 1763   Royal proclamation setting the boundary known as the **Proclamation Line**.

Prohibition   A ban on the production, sale, and consumption of liquor, achieved temporarily through state laws and the Eighteenth Amendment.

Prohibition Party   A venerable third party still in existence that has persistently campaigned for the abolition of alcohol but has also introduced many important reform ideas into American politics.

Proposition 187   California legislation adopted by popular vote in California in 1994, which cuts off state-funded health and education benefits to undocumented or illegal immigrants.

Proprietary colony   A colony created when the English monarch granted a huge tract of land to an individual or group of individuals, who became "lords proprietor." Many lords proprietor had distinct social visions for their colonies, but these plans were hardly ever implemented. Examples of proprietary colonies are Maryland, Carolina, New York (after it was seized from the Dutch), and Pennsylvania.

Pueblo Revolt   Rebellion in 1680 of Pueblo Indians in New Mexico against their Spanish overlords, sparked by religious conflict and excessive Spanish demands for tribute.

Puritan   An individual who believed that Queen Elizabeth's reforms of the Church of England had not gone far enough in improving the church, particularly in ensuring that church members were among the saved. Puritans led the settlement of Massachusetts Bay Colony.

Put-in-Bay, Battle of   American naval victory on Lake Erie in September 1813 in the **War of 1812** that denied the British strategic control over the Great Lakes.

Putting-out system   System of manufacturing in which merchants furnished households with raw materials for processing by family members.

Quakers   Members of the Society of Friends, a radical religious group that arose in the mid-seventeenth century. Quakers rejected formal theology and an educated ministry, focusing instead on the importance of the "Inner Light," or Holy Spirit that dwelt within them. Quakers were important in the founding of Pennsylvania.

Quartering Acts   Acts of Parliament requiring colonial legislatures to provide supplies and quarters for the troops stationed in America. Americans considered this taxation in disguise and objected. None of these acts passed during the pre-Revolutionary controversy required that soldiers be quartered in an occupied house without the owner's consent.

Quasi-War   Undeclared naval war of 1797 to 1800 between the United States and France.

Quebec Act   Law passed by Parliament in 1774 that provided an appointed government for Canada, enlarged the boundaries of Quebec southward to the Ohio River, and confirmed the privileges of the Catholic Church. Alarmed Americans termed this act and the **Coercive Acts** the **Intolerable Acts.**

Queen Anne's War   American phase (1702–1713) of Europe's War of the Spanish Succession. At its conclusion, England gained Nova Scotia.

Radical Republicans   A shifting group of Republican congressmen, usually a substantial minority, who favored the abolition of slavery from the beginning of the Civil War and later advocated harsh treatment of the defeated South.

Reagan Doctrine   The policy assumption that Soviet-influenced governments in Asia, Africa, and Latin America needed to be eliminated if the United States was to win the Cold War.

Recall   The process of removing an official from office by popular vote, usually after using petitions to call for such a vote.

Reconquista   The long struggle (ending in 1492) during which Spanish Christians reconquered the Iberian peninsula from Muslim occupiers, who first invaded in the eighth century.

Reconstruction Era   The era (1865–1877) when the resolution of two major issues—the status of the former slaves and the terms of the Confederate states' readmission into the Union—dominated political debate.

Redeemers   Southern Democrats who wrested control of governments in the former Confederacy, often through electoral fraud and violence, from Republicans beginning in 1870.

Redemptioners   Similar to **indentured servants**, except that redemptioners signed labor contracts in America rather than in Europe, as indentured servants did. Shipmasters sold redemptioners into servitude to recoup the cost of their passage if they could not pay the fare upon their arrival.

Red Scare   Post–World War I public hysteria over **Bolshevik** influence in the United States directed against labor activism, radical dissenters, and some ethnic groups.

Referendum   Submission of a law, proposed or already in effect, to a direct popular vote for approval or rejection.

Regulators   Vigilante groups active in the 1760s and 1770s in the western parts of North and South Carolina. The South Carolina Regulators attempted to rid the area of outlaws; the North Carolina Regulators sought to protect themselves against excessively high taxes and court costs. In both cases, westerners lacked sufficient representation in the legislature to obtain immediate redress of their grievances. The South Carolina government eventually made concessions; the North Carolina government suppressed its Regulator movement by force.

Repartimiento   In the Spanish colonies, the assignment of Indian workers to labor on public works projects.

Republicanism   A complex, changing body of ideas, values, and assumptions, closely related to **country ideology**, that influenced American political behavior during the eighteenth and nineteenth centuries. Derived from the political ideas of classical antiquity, Renaissance Europe, and early modern England, republicanism held that self-government by the citizens of a country, or their representatives, provided a more reliable foundation for the good society and individual freedom than rule by kings. The benefits of monarchy depended on the variable abilities of monarchs; the character of republican government depended on the virtue of the people. Republicanism therefore helped give the American Revolution a moral dimension. But the nature of republican virtue and the conditions favorable to it became sources of debate that influenced the writing of the state and federal constitutions as well as the development of political parties.

Republican Party   Party that emerged in the 1850s in the aftermath of the bitter controversy over the **Kansas-Nebraska Act**, consisting of former **Whigs**, some northern Democrats, and many **Know-Nothings**.

Republican Party (Jeffersonian)   Party headed by Thomas Jefferson that formed in opposition to the financial and diplomatic policies of the **Federalist Party**; favored limiting the powers of the national government and placing the interests of farmers and planters over those of financial and commercial groups; supported the cause of the French Revolution.

Rescate   Procedure by which Spanish colonists would pay ransom to free Indians captured by rival natives. The rescued Indians then became workers in Spanish households.

Reservationists   Group of U.S. senators favoring approval of the **Treaty of Versailles**, the peace agreement after World War I, after amending it to incorporate their reservations.

Rhode Island system   During the industrialization of the early nineteenth century, the recruitment of entire families for employment in a factory.

Roe v. Wade   U.S. Supreme Court decision in 1973 that disallowed state laws prohibiting abortion during the first three months (trimester) of pregnancy and established guidelines for abortion in the second and third trimesters.

Roosevelt Corollary   President Theodore Roosevelt's policy asserting U.S. authority to intervene in the affairs of Latin American nations; an expansion of the **Monroe Doctrine**.

Rush–Bagot Agreement   Treaty of 1817 between the United States and Britain that effectively demilitarized the Great Lakes by sharply limiting the number of ships each power could station on them.

Sabbatarian movement   Reform organization founded in 1828 by Congregationalist and Presbyterian ministers that lobbied for an end to the delivery of mail on Sundays and other Sabbath violations.

"Sack of Lawrence"   Vandalism and arson committed by a group of proslavery men in Lawrence, the free-state capital of Kansas Territory.

Sagebrush Rebellion   Political movement in the western states in the early 1980s that called for easing of regulations on the economic use of federal lands and the transfer of some or all of those lands to state ownership.

SALT   Strategic Arms Limitation Treaty signed in 1972 by the United States and the Soviet Union to slow the nuclear arms race.

Sand Creek Massacre   The near annihilation in 1864 of Black Kettle's Cheyenne band by Colorado troops under Colonel John Chivington's orders to "kill and scalp all, big and little."

San Jacinto, Battle of   Battle fought in eastern Texas on April 21, 1836, in which Texas troops under General Sam Houston overwhelmed a Mexican army and forced its commander, General Antonio López de Santa Anna, to recognize the independence of Texas.

San Lorenzo, Treaty of   *See* **Pinckney's Treaty**.

Scalawags   Southern whites, mainly small landowning farmers and well-off merchants and planters, who supported the southern **Republican Party** during **Reconstruction** for diverse reasons; a disparaging term.

Search and destroy   U.S. military tactic in South Vietnam, using small detachments to locate enemy units and then massive air, artillery, and ground forces to destroy them.

Second Bank of the United States   A national bank chartered by Congress in 1816 with extensive regulatory powers over currency and credit.

Second Continental Congress   An assemblage of delegates from all the colonies that convened in May 1775 after the outbreak of fighting in Massachusetts between British and American forces. It became the national government that eventually declared independence and conducted the Revolutionary War.

Second Great Awakening   Series of religious revivals in the first half of the nineteenth century characterized by great emotionalism in large public meetings.

Second party system   The national two-party competition between **Democrats** and **Whigs** from the 1830s through the early 1850s.

Second Treaty of Fort Laramie   The treaty acknowledging U.S. defeat in the Great Sioux War in 1868 and supposedly guaranteeing the Sioux perpetual land and hunting rights in South Dakota, Wyoming, and Montana.

Securities and Exchange Commission (SEC)   Federal agency with authority to regulate trading practices in stocks and bonds.

Sedition Act of 1918   Broad law restricting criticism of America's involvement in World War I or its government, flag, military, taxes, or officials.

Segregation   A system of racial control that separated the races, initially by custom but increasingly by law during and after **Reconstruction**.

Selective Service Act of 1917   The law establishing the military draft for World War I.

Selective Service System   Federal agency that coordinated military conscription before and during the Vietnam War.

Self-determination   The right of a people or nation to decide on its own political allegiance or form of government without external influence.

Seneca Falls Convention   The first convention for women's equality in legal rights, held in upstate New York in 1848. *See also* **Declaration of Sentiments**.

Separatist   Member of an offshoot branch of Puritanism. Separatists believed that the Church of England was too corrupt to be reformed and hence were convinced that they must "separate" from it to save their souls. Separatists helped found Plymouth Colony.

Settlement house   A multipurpose structure in a poor neighborhood that offered social welfare, educational, and homemaking services to the poor or immigrants; usually under private auspices and directed by middle-class women.

Seventeenth Amendment   Constitutional change that in 1913 established the direct popular election of U.S. senators.

Shakers   The followers of Mother Ann Lee, who preached a religion of strict celibacy and communal living.

Sharecropping   Labor system that evolved during and after **Reconstruction** whereby landowners furnished laborers with a house, farm animals, and tools and advanced credit in exchange for a share of the laborers' crop.

Shays's Rebellion   An armed movement of debt-ridden farmers in western Massachusetts in the winter of 1786–1787. The rebellion shut down courts and created a crisis atmosphere, strengthening the case of **nationalists** that a stronger central government was needed to maintain civil order in the states.

Sherman Antitrust Act   The first federal antitrust measure, passed in 1890; sought to promote economic competition by prohibiting business combinations in restraint of trade or commerce.

Silicon Valley   The region of California between San Jose and San Francisco that holds the nation's greatest concentration of electronics firms.

Sixteenth Amendment   Constitutional revision that in 1913 authorized a federal income tax.

***Slaughterhouse* cases**   Group of cases resulting in one sweeping decision by the U.S. Supreme Court in 1873 that contradicted the intent of the **Fourteenth Amendment** by decreeing that most citizenship rights remained under state, not federal, control.

Slave codes   Sometimes known as "black codes." A series of laws passed mainly in the southern colonies in the late seventeenth and early eighteenth centuries to define the status of slaves and codify the denial of basic civil rights to them. Also, after American independence and before the Civil War, state laws in the South defining slaves as property and specifying the legal powers of masters over slaves.

Slave Power   A key concept in abolitionist and northern antislavery propaganda that depicted southern slaveholders as the driving force in a political conspiracy to promote slavery at the expense of white liberties.

Social Darwinism   The application of Charles Darwin's theory of biological evolution to society, holding that the fittest and the wealthiest survive, the weak and the poor perish, and government action is unable to alter this "natural" and beneficial process.

Socialism   A social order based on government ownership of industry and worker control over corporations as a way to prevent worker exploitation.

Solid South   The one-party (Democratic) political system that dominated the South from the 1890s to the 1950s.

Sons of Liberty   Secret organizations in the colonies formed to oppose the **Stamp Act**. From 1765 until independence, they spoke, wrote, and demonstrated against British measures. Their actions often intimidated stamp distributors and British supporters in the colonies.

Sound money   Misleading slogan that referred to a conservative policy of restricting the money supply and adhering to the gold standard.

Southeast Asia Treaty Organization (SEATO)   Mutual defense alliance signed in 1954 by the United States, Britain, France, Thailand, Pakistan, the Philippines, Australia, and New Zealand.

Southern Christian Leadership Conference (SCLC)   Black civil rights organization founded in 1957 by Martin Luther King, Jr., and other clergy.

Southern Farmers' Alliance The largest of several organizations that formed in the post-Reconstruction South to advance the interests of beleaguered small farmers.

Southern Homestead Act Largely unsuccessful law passed in 1866 that gave black people preferential access to public lands in five southern states.

Southern Manifesto A document signed by 101 members of Congress from southern states in 1956 that argued that the Supreme Court's decision in **Brown v. Board of Education of Topeka** itself contradicted the **Constitution**.

Southwest Ordinance of 1790 Legislation passed by Congress that set up a government with no prohibition on slavery in U.S. territory south of the Ohio River.

Specie Circular Proclamation issued by President Andrew Jackson in 1836 stipulating that only gold or silver could be used as payment for public land.

Sphere of influence A region dominated and controlled by an outside power.

Spoils system The awarding of government jobs to party loyalists.

Stamp Act Law passed by Parliament in 1765 to raise revenue in America by requiring taxed, stamped paper for legal documents, publications, and playing cards. Americans opposed it as "taxation without representation" and prevented its enforcement. Parliament repealed it a year after its enactment.

Stamp Act Congress October 1765 meeting of delegates sent by nine colonies, held in New York City, that adopted the **Declaration of Rights and Grievances** and petitioned against the **Stamp Act**.

States' rights Favoring the rights of individual states over rights claimed by the national government.

Stonewall Rebellion On June 27, 1969, patrons fought back when police raided the gay Stonewall Inn in New York; the name refers to that event and to the increase in militancy by gay Americans that it symbolizes.

Stono Rebellion Uprising in 1739 of South Carolina slaves against whites; inspired in part by Spanish officials' promise of freedom for American slaves who escaped to Florida.

Strategic Defense Initiative (SDI) President Reagan's program, announced in 1983, to defend the United States against nuclear missile attack with untested weapons systems and sophisticated technologies; also known as "Star Wars."

Student Nonviolent Coordinating Committee (SNCC) Black civil rights organization founded in 1960 and drawing heavily on younger activists and college students.

Students for a Democratic Society (SDS) The leading student organization of the New Left of the early and mid-1960s.

Subtreasury plan A program promoted by the **Southern Farmers' Alliance** in response to low cotton prices and tight credit. Farmers would store their crop in a warehouse (or "subtreasury") until prices rose, in the meantime borrowing up to 80 percent of the value of the stored crops from the government at a low interest rate.

Suffolk Resolves Militant resolves adopted in September 1774 in response to the **Coercive Acts** by representatives from the towns in Suffolk County, Massachusetts, including Boston. They termed the **Coercive Acts** unconstitutional, advised the people to arm, and called for economic sanctions against Britain. The **First Continental Congress** endorsed these resolves.

Suffrage The right to vote in a political election.

Sugar Act Law passed in 1764 to raise revenue in the American colonies. It lowered the duty from 6 pence to 3 pence per gallon on

foreign molasses imported into the colonies and increased the restrictions on colonial commerce.

Sunbelt The states of the American South and Southwest.

Sussex Pledge Germany's pledge during World War I not to sink merchant ships without warning, on the condition that Britain also observe recognized rules of international law.

Swann v. Charlotte-Mecklenburg Board of Education U.S. Supreme Court decision in 1971 that upheld cross-city busing to achieve the racial integration of public schools.

Sweatshops Small, poorly ventilated shops or apartments crammed with workers, often family members, who pieced together garments.

Taft-Hartley Act Federal legislation of 1947 that substantially limited the tools available to labor unions in labor–management disputes.

Tammany Hall New York City's **Democratic party** organization, dating from well before the Civil War, that evolved into a powerful political machine after 1860, using patronage and bribes to maintain control of the city administration.

Taos Revolt Uprising of Pueblo Indians in New Mexico that broke out in January 1847 over the imposition of American rule during the Mexican War; the revolt was crushed within a few weeks.

Tariff Act of 1789 Apart from a few selected industries, this first tariff passed by Congress was intended primarily to raise revenue and not protect American manufacturers from foreign competition.

Tariff Act of 1798 Law placing a duty of 5 percent on most imported goods, designed primarily to generate revenue and not to protect American goods from foreign competition.

Tea Act of 1773 Act of Parliament that permitted the East India Company to sell tea through agents in America without paying the duty customarily collected in Britain, thus reducing the retail price. Americans, who saw the act as an attempt to induce them to pay the Townshend duty still imposed in the colonies, resisted this act through the **Boston Tea Party** and other measures.

Tejano A person of Spanish or Mexican descent born in Texas.

Teller Amendment A congressional resolution adopted in 1898 renouncing any American intention to annex Cuba.

Temperance Reform movement originating in the 1820s that sought to eliminate the consumption of alcohol.

Temporary Assistance for Needy Families (TANF) Federal program created in 1996 to replace earlier welfare programs to aid families and children; it involves explicit work requirements for receiving aid and places a time limit on benefits.

Tenement Four- to six-story residential dwelling, once common in New York and certain other cities, built on a tiny lot without regard to providing ventilation or light.

Tennessee Valley Authority (TVA) Federal regional planning agency established to promote **conservation**, produce electric power, and encourage economic development in seven southern states.

Thirteenth Amendment Constitutional amendment ratified in 1865 that freed all slaves throughout the United States.

Tonnage Act of 1789 Duty levied on the tonnage of incoming ships to U.S. ports; tax was higher on foreign-owned ships to favor American shippers.

Tordesillas, Treaty of Treaty negotiated by the pope in 1494 to resolve the territorial claims of Spain and Portugal. It drew a north–south line approximately 1,100 miles west of the Cape Verde Islands, granting all lands west of the line to Spain and all lands east of the line to Portugal. This limited Portugal's New World empire to Brazil but confirmed its claims in Africa and Asia.

Tories A derisive term applied to **Loyalists** in America who supported the king and Parliament just before and during the American Revolution. The term derived from late-seventeenth-century English politics when the Tory party supported the Duke of York's succession to the throne as James II. Later the Tory party favored the Church of England and the crown over dissenting denominations and Parliament.

Townshend Duty Act Act of Parliament, passed in 1767, imposing duties on colonial tea, lead, paint, paper, and glass. Designed to take advantage of the supposed American distinction between internal and external taxes, the Townshend duties were to help support government in America. The act prompted a successful colonial nonimportation movement.

Trail of Tears The forced march in 1838 of the Cherokee Indians from their homelands in Georgia to the Indian Territory in the West; thousands of Cherokees died along the way.

Transcendentalism A philosophical and literary movement centered on an idealistic belief in the divinity of individuals and nature.

Trans-Continental Treaty of 1819 Treaty between the United States and Spain in which Spain ceded Florida to the United States, surrendered all claims to the Pacific Northwest, and agreed to a boundary between the Louisiana Purchase territory and the Spanish Southwest.

Transportation revolution Dramatic improvements in transportation that stimulated economic growth after 1815 by expanding the range of travel and reducing the time and cost of moving goods and people.

Truman Doctrine President Harry Truman's statement in 1947 that the United States should assist other nations that were facing external pressure or internal revolution; an important step in the escalation of the **Cold War**.

Underground Railroad Support system set up by antislavery groups in the Upper South and the North to assist fugitive slaves in escaping the South.

Underwood-Simmons Tariff Act The 1913 reform law that lowered tariff rates and levied the first regular federal income tax.

Unicameral legislature A legislative body composed of a single house.

Union League A **Republican party** organization in northern cities that became an important organizing device among freedmen in southern cities after 1865.

University of California v. Bakke U.S. Supreme Court case in 1978 that allowed race to be used as one of several factors in college and university admission decisions but made rigid quotas unacceptable.

Valley Forge Area of Pennsylvania approximately 20 miles northwest of Philadelphia where General George Washington's continental troops were quartered from December 1777 to June 1778 while British forces occupied Philadelphia during the Revolutionary War. Approximately 2,500 men, about a quarter of those encamped there, died of hardship and disease.

Versailles, Treaty of The treaty ending World War I and creating the **League of Nations**.

Vertical integration The consolidation of numerous production functions, from the extraction of the raw materials to the distribution and marketing of the finished products, under the direction of one firm.

Viet Cong Communist rebels in South Vietnam who fought the pro-American government established in South Vietnam in 1954.

Virginia Plan Proposal of the Virginia delegation at the 1787 **Constitution Convention** calling for a national legislature in which the states would be represented according to population. The national legislature would have the explicit power to veto or overrule laws passed by state legislatures.

Virtual representation The notion, current in eighteenth-century England, that parliamentary members represented the interests of the nation as a whole, not those of the particular district that elected them.

Volstead Act The 1920 law defining the liquor forbidden under the Eighteenth Amendment and giving enforcement responsibilities to the Prohibition Bureau of the Department of the Treasury.

Voting Rights Act Legislation in 1965 that overturned a variety of practices by which states systematically denied voter registration to minorities.

Waltham system During the industrialization of the early nineteenth century, the recruitment of unmarried young women for employment in factories.

War Hawks Members of Congress, predominantly from the South and West, who aggressively pushed for a war against Britain after their election in 1810.

War Industries Board (WIB) The federal agency that reorganized industry for maximum efficiency and productivity during World War I.

War of 1812 War fought between the United States and Britain from June 1812 to January 1815 largely over British restrictions on American shipping.

War on Poverty Set of programs introduced by Lyndon Johnson between 1963 and 1966 designed to break the cycle of poverty by providing funds for job training, community development, nutrition, and supplementary education.

Watergate A complex scandal involving attempts to cover up illegal actions taken by administration officials and leading to the resignation of President Richard Nixon in 1974.

Webster–Ashburton Treaty Treaty signed by the United States and Britain in 1842 that settled a boundary dispute between Maine and Canada and provided for closer cooperation in suppressing the African slave trade.

Welfare capitalism A paternalistic system of labor relations emphasizing management responsibility for employee well-being. While providing some limited benefits, its function was primarily to forestall the formation of unions or public intervention.

Whig party Political party, formed in the mid-1830s in opposition to the **Jacksonian Democrats**, that favored a strong role for the national government in promoting economic growth.

Whigs The name used by advocates of colonial resistance to British measures during the 1760s and 1770s. The Whig party in England unsuccessfully attempted to exclude the Catholic Duke of York from succession to the throne as James II; victorious in the **Glorious Revolution**, the Whigs later stood for religious toleration and the supremacy of Parliament over the crown.

Whiskey Rebellion Armed uprising in 1794 by farmers in western Pennsylvania who attempted to prevent the collection of the excise tax on whiskey.

Whitewater Arkansas real estate development in which Bill and Hillary Clinton were investors; several fraud convictions resulted from investigations into Whitewater, but evidence was not found that the Clintons were involved in wrong-doing.

Wide Awakes Group of red-shirted, black-caped young men who paraded through city streets in the North extolling the virtues of the **Republican party** during the 1860 presidential election campaign.

Wobblies Popular name for the members of the Industrial Workers of the World (IWW).

Women's Christian Temperance Union (WCTU) National organization formed after the Civil War dedicated to prohibiting the sale and distribution of alcohol.

World Trade Organization International organization that sets standards and practices for global trade, and the focus of international protests over world economic policy in the late 1990s.

World Wide Web Since 1991, the Web has expanded the use of the Internet by allowing organizations and companies to create websites that place political and commercial information only a few clicks away from wired consumers.

Wounded Knee Massacre The U.S. Army's brutal winter massacre in 1890 of at least two hundred Sioux men, women, and children as part of the government's assault on the tribe's Ghost Dance religion.

Writs of assistance Documents issued by a court of law that gave British officials in America the power to search for smuggled goods wherever they wished. The legality of these writs became an important cause of controversy in Massachusetts in 1761 and 1762.

XYZ Affair Diplomatic incident in 1798 in which Americans were outraged by the demand of the French for a bribe as a condition for negotiating with American diplomats.

Yalta Conference Meeting of U.S. President Franklin Roosevelt, British Prime Minister Winston Churchill, and Soviet Premier Joseph Stalin held in February 1945 to plan the final stages of World War II and postwar arrangements.

Yellow-dog contracts Employment agreements binding workers not to join a union.

Yellow press A deliberately sensational journalism of scandal and exposure designed to attract an urban mass audience and increase advertising revenues.

COVER AND TITLE PAGE "The Prairie is my Garden," Sodbusters/Homesteaders (1866–1900). Pugsly Union, South Dakota State University, Brooking. S.D.

CHAPTER 1 The Granger Collection, 1; The Granger Collection, 4; David Muench Photography, Inc., 7; Cahokia Mounds State Historic Site, 9; By permission of the Houghton Library, Harvard University, 15; The Granger Collection, 16; Courtesy of the Library of Congress, 19; From the collections of the James Ford Bell Library, University of Minnesota, Minneapolis, Minnesota, 19; The Art Archive/Biblioteca Nacional Madrid/Dagli Orti, 21; Courtesy of the Library of Congress, 26.

CHAPTER 2 Mrs. Elizabeth Freake and Baby Mary (American), oil on canvas, 1963.134. Worcester Art Museum, Worcester Massachusetts, Gift of Mr. and Mrs. Albert W. Rice, 34; Samuel de Champlain, "Les Voyages . . .," Paris, 1613. Illustration opp. pg. 322. Early battle with the Iroquois. Rare Books Division, The New York Public Library, Astor Lenox and Tilden Foundations, 39; Rijksmuseum, 41 (top); CORBIS, 41; Courtesy of the Library of Congress, 44; Arents Collection, The New York Public Library, Astor, Lenox and Tilden Foundations, 45; The Granger Collection, 56; AP/Wide World Photos, 61.

CHAPTER 3 Archives Charmet, Musee des Arts d'Afrique et d'Oceanie, Paris, France, 66; Courtesy of the Library of Congress, 71; Courtesy of the Library of Congress, 75; TLM Photo, 80; Courtesy of the American Antiquarian Society, 86; Courtesy of the Library of Congress, 87.

CHAPTER 4 Samuel Scott (c. 1702–1772) "Old East India Wharf at London Bridge" (CT2825). ©Victoria & Albert Museum, London/Art Resource, NY, 103; Courtesy of the Museum of Fine Arts, Boston. Reproduced with permission, 109; The Maryland Historical Society, Baltimore, Maryland, 110; Henry Glassie, Pattern in the Material Folk Culture of the Eastern United States, 123; Art Resource, N.Y., 124; North Wind Picture Archives, 127.

CHAPTER 5 Courtesy of the Library of Congress, 136; North Wind Picture Archives, 142; Museum of the Cherokee Indian, Cherokee, NC, 143; The New York Public Library, 145; The Granger Collection, 149; Courtesy of the Library of Congress, 153; Christie's Images Inc., 154.

CHAPTER 6 National Museum of American History/Smithsonian Institution, Photographic Collection, 164; Peale, Charles Willson (1741–1827). (after): George Washington after the battle of Princeton, January 3, 1777. 1779. Oil on canvas, 234.5 x 155 cm. Inv.:MV 4560. Photo: Gerard Blot. Chateaux de Versailles et de Trianon, Versailles, France, 170; The Granger Collection, 172; Courtesy of the Library of Congress, 173; The Granger Collection, 174; Independence National Historical Park, 180; Anne S.K. Brown Military Collection, John Hay Library, Brown University, 194.

CHAPTER 7 The Granger Collection, 200; CORBIS, 204; ©Bettmann/CORBIS, 205; The Granger Collection, 212; The Granger Collection, New York, 215; Charles Allen Munn Collection, Fordham University Library, Bronx, NY, 221; Print and Picture Collection, The Free Library of Philadelphia, 223; The Granger Collection, 228.

CHAPTER 8 The Granger Collection, 232; The New York Public Library, 239; Tontine Coffee House, Francis Guy, New York Historical Society, New York, USA/ The Bridgeman Art Library International, Ltd., London/New York, 243; The Granger Collection, 252; White House Collection, Courtesy White House Historical Association, 254; The New-York Historical Society, negative #35609, 255.

CHAPTER 9 The Granger Collection, 260; The Granger Collection, 266; William Clark Papers, Clark Family Collection, Missouri Historical Society, St. Louis, 267; North Wind Picture Archives, 269; Courtesy of the Library of Congress, 272; McCord Museum of Canadian History, 275; National Archives and Records Administration, 279; © CORBIS, 280.

CHAPTER 10 The Granger Collection, 303; The Granger Collection, 304; Courtesy of the Library of Congress, 311; Smithsonian Institution/Office of Imaging, Printing, and Photographic Services, 315.

CHAPTER 11 The Granger Collection, New York, 322; Courtesy of The New-York Historical Society, New York City, 329; Courtesy of the Library of Congress, 332; Abby Aldrich Rockefeller Folk Art Museum, Williamsburg, VA, 335; Courtesy of the Library of Congress, 336; Courtesy of the Library of Congress, 347.

CHAPTER 12 North Wind Picture Archives, 350; I.N. Phelps Stokes Collection, Miriam and Ira D. Wallach Division of Art, Prints and Photographs, The New York Library, Astor, Lenox and Tilden Foundations, 357; American Textile History Museum, Lowell, MA, 360; CORBIS, 363; Courtesy of the Library of Congress, 369; Getty Images Inc. - Hulton Archive Photos, 370; Richard Nowitz Photography, 373; Courtesy of the Library of Congress, 374; CORBIS, 382.

CHAPTER 13 Mary Evans Picture Library Ltd, 388; The Old Print Shop, 395; Courtesy of the Library of Congress (top), 402; Courtesy of the Lane County Historical Museum, 402; Art Resource, N.Y., 404; © Christie's Images Inc., 410.

CHAPTER 14 Courtesy of the Library of Congress, 425; CORBIS, 426; The Newberry Library, 430; Courtesy of the Library of Congress, 433; Robert Marshall Root, "Lincoln-Douglas Debate at Charleston, Illinois." Henry Horner Lincoln Collection. Courtesy of the Illinois State Historical Library, 435; The Granger Collection, 439.

CHAPTER 15 National Archives and Records Administration, 452; Boston Public Library / Rare Books Department - Courtesy of the Trustees, 464; CORBIS, 465; CORBIS, 475; Culver Pictures, Inc., 479; Center of Military History, U.S. Army, 480; CORBIS, 482; National Archives and Records Administration, 484; Courtesy of the Library of Congress, 487; Harper's Weekly, March 18, 1865. Courtesy of William C. Hine, 488; Courtesy of the Library of Congress, 490.

CHAPTER 16 The Granger Collection, New York, 496; The Granger Collection, 501; The Granger Collection, 502; Courtesy of Hampton University Archives, 503; The Granger Collection, 505; The Granger Collection, 511; The Granger Collection, 513; The Granger Collection, New York, 517; Courtesy of the Library of Congress, 520.

CHAPTER 17 Courtesy of the Library of Congress, 528; Shivery Family Photograph Collection, Photographs and Prints Division, Schomburg Center for Research in Black Culture, The New York Public Library, Astor, Lenox and Tilden Foundations, 531; T. E. Armitstead Collection, University of South Alabama Archives, 537; Courtesy of The North Carolina Division of Archives and History, 541; Courtesy of the Library of Congress, 545; Courtesy of the Library of Congress, 546; The Granger Collection, 547; The Ohio Historical Society, 549; North Carolina Mutual Life Insurance Company, 554; (Booker T. Washington) The Granger Collection, 558; (W.E.B. DuBois) The Granger Collection, 558.

CHAPTER 18 Courtesy of the Library of Congress, 562; Ford Motor Company, 569; Rhode Island Economic Development Corporation, 570; George Eastman House, 572; Culver Pictures, Inc., 573; Getty Images Inc. - Hulton Archive Photos, 575; The Granger Collection, 579; Southern Pacific, 582; Courtesy of the Library of Congress, 583; Brown Brothers, 587; Culver Pictures, Inc., 593.

CHAPTER 19 The Granger Collection, New York, 598; Union Pacific Historical Collection, 600; The Granger Collection, New York, 605; A Pictographic History of the Oglala Sioux, The University of Nebraska Press, 606; Western History Collections, University of Oklahoma Libraries, 607; Courtesy of the Library of Congress, 612; The Denver Public Library, Western History Department, 616; Kansas State Historical Society, 619; Wyoming State Archives, 620; CORBIS, 621.

CHAPTER 20 The Granger Collection, New York, 628; Reproduced from the collections of the Ohio Historical Society Archives/Library, 633; The Granger Collection, 635; The Granger Collection, 636; Stock Montage, Inc./Historical Pictures Collection, 639; Courtesy of the Library of Congress, 642; Kansas State Historical Society, 645; Courtesy of the Library of Congress, 650; Culver Pictures, Inc., 651; The Granger Collection, New York, 652.

CHAPTER 21 The Granger Collection, New York, 658; Kheel Center, Cornell University, Ithaca, NY 14853-3901, 664; Cornell University School of Industrial & Labor Relations, 667; Kheel Center, Cornell University, Ithaca, NY 14853-3901, 670; Courtesy National Archives, photo no. 102-LH-1986, 671; AP/Wide World Photos, 674; Indiana Historical Society, 677; CORBIS, 678; Portrait #65, The Bancroft Library, University of California at Berkeley, 684; The Granger Collection, 685; The Granger Collection, 687.

CHAPTER 22 The Granger Collection, New York, 694; By permission of the Houghton Library, Harvard University, 699; CORBIS, 704; National Archives and Records Administration, 708; Wisconsin Historical Society/WHi-3916, 709; Theodore Roosevelt Collection, Harvard College Library, 710; Kansas State Historical Society Topeka, Kansas, 711; Stock Montage, Inc./Historical Pictures Collection, 712; Theodore Roosevelt Collection, Harvard College Library, 717; The Granger Collection, 718.

Italic page references refer to illustrations.

A

A&P, 757
Abbott, Robert, 588
Abenakis, 48
Abernathy, Ralph, 907
Abington Township v. Schempp, 893
Abolitionist movement, 309, 352
  Brown's raid and, 436, 438–440,
    439
  development of, 379–381
  Garrison and, 312, 378, 379–381
  political, 382–383
  violence against, 380–381, *381*
  women and, 376–377, 380–381
Abortion, 776–777, 982
Acheson, Dean, 873
Acoma Pueblo, *7,* 24, 404
Act for Religious Toleration (1649),
  47
Actual representation, 120
Adams, Abigail, 193
Adams, Charles Francis, Jr., 551
Adams, Henry, 566
Adams, John, 146, *173, 254*
  as American minister to London,
    219
  American Revolution and, 170,
    190, 191, *192*
  Declaration of Independence
    and, 173
  election of 1796 and, 251–252
  First Continental Congress and,
    157
  presidency of, 252–257
  republicanism and, 174
  as vice president, 241
Adams, John Quincy
  election of 1824 and, 287–288
  election of 1828 and, 301
  gag rule and, 382
  as secretary of state, 282–283
Adams, Samuel, 148, *148,* 152, 154,
  157, 168, 228
Adamson Act (1916), 689
Addams, Jane, 574–575, 669, 670, 677,
  687, 709, 729, 747, 789
Adena-Hopewell culture, 8
Administration of Justice Act (1774),
  154, 155
Adventures of Ozzie and Harriet, 890
Advertising
  in the early 1900s, 591
  in the 1920s, 768
Aetna Insurance Co., 94
Affirmative action programs, 1013
Affluent Society, The (Galbraith), 893
Afghanistan, 949, 1020
AFL-CIO, 804, 888
Africa
  See also West African societies
  slaves from West, 12–13, 81–82
African Americans
  See also Civil rights movement;
    Race riots; Racism
  as cowhands, 616
  Depression of 1929 and, 790

disfranchisement, 547, 548–550,
  552–553
employment, 586–587, 888
Exodus to the West, 619
ghettos, 587
in government, 1008–1011, *1012*
Great Migration, 586–588,
  764–766
Jim Crow laws, 548
lynching, 546–547, *546*
New Deal and, 808–806
redlining, 860
religion, 892
response of black community,
  551–557
segregation by law, 547–548
in Spanish-American War,
  707–708, *708*
treatment of, following
  Reconstruction, 545–557
Vietnam War and, 925
voting rights, 548–550, 632
white backlash, 546
women, 554, 587
World War I and, 734, *734,* 737,
  745
World War II and, 835, 838
African Americans, free
  American Revolution and, 180,
    205
  before the American Revolution,
    87, 109
  in Civil War, 458, 469–471, *471,*
    488–490
  culture, 342–344
  Dred Scott v. Sandford,, 432–433,
    445, 510
  employment, 343
  growth of communities following
    American Revolution, 205–206
  in nineteenth-century cities, 343
  religion, 343, 345
  voting and, 296–297
African Americans, free (after
  Reconstruction)
  black codes, 342, 508–509
  education, 501–502
  employment, 502–504
  land ownership, 502–504
  migration to cities, 504–505
  in politics, 514
  Progressive Era racism, 674,
    677–678
  religion, 505–506
  sharecropping, 523
  voting rights, 510–513, 524
African Methodist Episcopal (AME)
  Church, *206,* 336, 502, 506
Afro-American Council, 551
Age of Enlightenment, 112–113
Age of Reason (Paine), 255–256
Aging of America, 981
Agnew, Spiro T., 938, 944
Agricultural Adjustment
  Administration (AAA), 795, 796
Agricultural Wheel, 540
Agriculture
  See also under type of crop
  agrarian revolt in the South,

538–543
Archaic period, 4–5
Colored Farmers' Alliance, 541
cooperatives, 540
crowded conditions in the East
  and affects on, 391, 393
Depression of 1929 and, *782,* 785,
  788, 791
dry farming, 623
Dust Bowl, 785, 802, *802*
exchange between Old and New
  Worlds, 25–26
Farmers' Alliances, 644–645
Grange, 540
impact of transportation on, 353
mound-building societies, 8
Native Americans and, 4–5, *4,*
  403–404
New Deal and, 795, 796
in New England, 55
in the 1920s, 760
in the 1960s and 1970s, 948
in Old Northwest, 393–395
in Old Southwest, 395–397
protests in the 1890s, 644–645
reforms in the 1840s, 329–330
sharecropping, 523
Southern Farmers' Alliance,
  540–541
technological improvements, 364,
  394–395, 623–624
in West African societies, 11, 12
westward expansion and exploitation, 617–624
yeoman, 341–342
Agriculture, Department of, 675
Aguinaldo, Emilio, 710
AIDS (acquired immune deficiency
  syndrome), 913, 983, *983*
Aid to Dependent Children (ADC),
  805
Aid to Families with Dependent
  Children (AFDC), 997
Akans, 12
Alabama
  admitted to Union, 295, 395
  Birmingham campaign, 908–909
  Civil War, 482
  Montgomery bus boycott,
    907–908
  secession, 442, *443*
  Selma campaign, 911
  as a slave state, 284
Alamo, 124, 406
Alaska, purchase of, 701
Albany Congress (1754), *127,* 129, 144
Albany Plan of Union, 129
Albany Regency, 300
Albright, Madeleine K., 1008
Alcatraz Island, 933
Alcoa Aluminum, 761
Alcoholism, 592–593
  in the mining camps, 612
  Prohibition, 676, 773–774
  temperance movement, 543–544,
    636
Aldrich, Nelson, 642, 686
Aldrin, Buzz, 920
Aleuts, 5

Alexander II, 467
Algonquians, 41–42, 72
Ali, Sunni, 11
Alien and Sedition Acts (1789),
  253–254
Alien Enemies Act (1789), 253
Alien Friends Act (1789), 253
Alien Registration Act (1940), 878
Allen, Ethan, 170, 219
Allen, Paul, 1004
Alliance for Progress, 903
Allies
  in World War I, 725
  in World War II, 828
Al-Qaeda, 1018, 1020
Amalgamated Clothing Workers, 666,
  791, 803
America First Committee, 826
American and Foreign Anti-Slavery
  Society, 381
American Anti-Slavery Society, 379,
  380, 381
American Association (AA), 592
American Association for Labor
  Legislation, 667
American Bankers' Association, 668
American Bible Society, 368
American Board of Commissioners
  for Foreign Missions, 368
American Civil Liberties Union
  (ACLU), 775
American Colonization Society, 378
American Committee on the Rights of
  Religious Minorities, 775
American Communist party, 746, 878
American Equal Rights Association,
  511
American Expeditionary Force (AEF),
  739
American Federation of Labor (AFL),
  578, 666, 745–746, 804, 888
  See also AFL-CIO
American Federation of State, County,
  and Municipal Employees, 962
American Federation of Teachers, 680
American Female Moral Reform
  Society, 370
American Friends Service Committee,
  924
American Fur Company, 399
American Home Missionary Society,
  368
American Indian Movement (AIM),
  933, *934*
American Iron and Steel Association,
  636
Americanization
  of immigrants, 675–676
  of Native Americans, 607–610,
    622–623
American League to Limit
  Armaments, 729
American Legion, 746
American Liberty League, 797–798
American Missionary Association, 502
American Mercury, 771
American Missionary Association, 502
American Protective Association
  (APA), 585

American Protective League, 736, 1018
American Protective Tariff League, 636
American Railway Union (ARU), 579
American Revenue Act. *See* Sugar Act
American Revolution
 African Americans in, 180–181, 193–194, 205
 battles, list of, 178
 battles (1775–1776), 168–170, *169*
 battles (1776–1777), 181–184
 battles (1778–1781), 184–190
 British policies and events leading to, 139–160
 casualties, 169, 171, 183, 184, 193, 196
 chronology of, 168
 Declaration of Independence and, 172–174
 early fighting (Massachusetts, Virginia, the Carolinas, and Canada), 171–172
 economic consequences, 191, 194, 196
 financing of, 211–212
 foreign support for, 175, 177, 183, 184–185
 Lexington and Concord, battles of (1775), 168–170, *169*, 178
 Native Americans in, 181, 185, 194
 naval battles, 185–186
 Olive Branch Petition, 170, 172
 outbreak of, 167–168
 Peace of Paris, (1783), 190–192, *191*
 professional soldiers, 175–177, 179, *179*
 republicanism, 174–175, 203–210
 Second Continental Congress, 170
 societal impact of, 193–194
 women and, 180, 193, 203–205
"American Scholar, The" (Emerson), 376–377
American Slavery As It Is: Testimony of a Thousand Witnesses (Weld), 352, 379
American Sugar Refining Co., 648–649
American Sunday School Union, 368
Americans with Disabilities Act (1990), 968
American System
 of federal subsidies, 288
 of manufacturing, 364
American Temperance Society, 369
American Tobacco Co., 533, 536
American Tract Society, 368
American Woman's Home, 590
Amusement parks, 566, 593, *593*
Anarchists, 380
Anasazis, 7–8, *7*
Anderson, John B., *959*
Anderson, Robert, 445–446
Anderson, Walt, 767
Andover South Parish Society for the Reformation of Morals, 368
André, John, *179*
Andrew, John, 469
Andros, Edmund, 117
Angels in America, 983
Anglican Church (Church of England), 48, 49–50, 113–114, 117, 155, 207, 208
Anglo-American Accords (1818), 282
Annapolis Convention (1786), 221

Anthony, Susan B., 382, 510–511, 513, 633, 636, *636*
Antietam, battle of (1862), 467–468, 489
Antifederalists, 226–228
Antigua, 59
Anti-Imperialist League, 709, 711
Anti-Masons, 313–314
Anti-Monopoly party, 635
Antin, Mary, 563–564, 592
Anti-Saloon League, 676
Antislavery reform, types of, 380
ANZUS Pact, 868
Apaches, 77, 404, 602, 607
Apalachees, 23
Appalachian Mountains, 240
Appalachian Regional Development Act, 914
Appeal to Reason, 668
Appeal to the Colored Citizens of the World (Walker), 378
Applied Sociology (Ward), 665
Appomattox Courthouse, surrender at, 490
Apprentices, 361, 362
Apthorp, Charles, *107*
Aquino, Corazon, 971
Arapahos, 397, 399, 602, 603, 606
Archaic period
 agriculture, 4–5
 burial practices, 4
 division of labor in, 3
 hunting and gathering, 3
 trade, 3–4
Archer, Dennis, 1011
Argonne, battle for, 739–740
Arikaras, 397
Arkansas
 admitted to Union, 395
 Civil War, 477
 secession, 448, 455, 460
Arkansas Federation of Women's Clubs, 544
Arkansas Territory, 285
Armstrong, Louis, 769
Armstrong, Neil, 919–920
Arnaz, Desi, 890
Arnold, Benedict, 170, 172, 179
Arnow, Harriet, 836
Arrogance of Power, The (Fulbright), 924
Art/artisans
 apprentices, 361, 362
 Archaic period, 5
 colonial, 107–108
 free blacks as, 343
 journeymen, 361–362
 Mesoamerican, 7
 in nineteenth century, 361–362, 367
 putting-out system, 361
 slaves as, 328, 333
 unions and, 367
 in West African societies, 11, *11*
Arthur, Chester A., 637, 640, 644
Articles of Confederation, 210
 Constitution compared to, 224
Asante, 11
Ashcroft, John, 1018
Ashley, Henry, 399
Asia
 See also specific country
 Cold War in, 870–872
 immigration from, 979
Asylum reform, 373–374
AT&T, 961, 965
Atahualpa, 22

Atlanta, Georgia
 Civil War, 485–486, *486*, 489
 growth of, 588
 population of freed blacks in, 504
Atlanta Compromise, 555–556
Atlantic, battle of the, 830
Atlantic Charter, 826
Atomic bomb, 820, 834, 848–849
Atomic diplomacy, 868–870, 871
Atomic Energy Commission (AEC), 869, 947
Attucks, Crispus, 152, *153*
Atwater, Lee, 967
Austin, Moses, 405
Austin, Stephen F., 405
Australian ballot, 679
Austria, 725, 822
Autobiography of Malcolm X, The, 932
Automobile industry
 following World War II, 857
 in the 1920s, *752*, 754, 756, *756*, 757, *757*, 767
 in the 1950s, 889
Axis Powers, 822
Ayer, Frederick, 504
Aztecs, 5, 6, 20–22, *26*

B

Babbitt (Lewis), 770
Backus, Isaac, 207
Bacon, Nathaniel, 77
Bacon's Rebellion, 76, 77
Baker, Ella, 908
Baker, Newton, 731, 733, 739
Baker, Ray Stannard, 667, 723–724
Baker v. Carr, 934
Bakke, Allan, 1013
Bakker, Jim, 984–985
Bakker, Tammy Faye, 985
Balboa, Vasco Núñez de, 20
Baldwin, James, 931
Ball, Lucille, 890
Ballard, Allan B., 491
Ballinger, Richard, 686
Ballou, Sullivan, 453–454
Baltimore
 growth of colonial, 107
 in the nineteenth century, 357
Baltimore & Ohio Railroad, 356, 577
Banfield, Edward, 960
Banking Act (1935), 801
Banking/financial industry
 Bank of North America (first commercial bank), 211–212
 Bank of the United States, 243, 264, 278
 deregulation in the 1980s, 961–962
 National Banking Act (1863), 478
 New Deal and, 794–795
 reform, 688
 Second Bank of the United States, 280–281, 283, 284, 302, 308–309
Bank of America, 584
Bank of Italy, 584
Bank War, 301, 308–309
Bannocks, 407
Baptists, 113, 114, 115, 274, 297–299, 335, 345
Barbados, 56, 57, 59
Barber, Susan, 615
Barré, Isaac, 145
Barrett, W. H., 546–547
Barrios, 766–767
Barrows, J. H., 698
Barton, Bruce, 762–763

Barton, Clara, 480
Baruch, Bernard, 732, 745, 865, 866
Batista, Fulgencio, 810, 900
Battle of One Hundred Slain, 605
Bay of Pigs, 900
Beasley, David, 557
Beatles, 891, 928, 929
Beauregard, P. G. T., 447, 462
Beaver Wars, 71–72, 76, 78–80
Beecher, Catherine, 352, 418, 590
Beecher, Lyman, 352, 368, 369, 418
Begin, Menachem, 948, *949*
Belgium, 725
Belk, William Henry, 538
Belknap, Jeremy, 208
Bell, Ann, *480*
Bell, John, 441, *442*
Benevolent empire, 368–369
Ben-Hur, 892
Benin, 11, *11*
Benton, Jessie, 432
Benton, Thomas Hart, 410, 427, 432
Berkeley, William, 77, *110*
Berlin blockade, 868
Berlin Wall, 900, 973, *973*
Berrigan, Daniel, 926
Berrigan, Philip, 926
Best Years of Our Lives, 856, *858*, 877
Bethlehem Steel, 758
Bethune, Mary McLeod, 806, *806*
Biddle, Nicholas, 308
Biddle Institute, 502
Bill of rights, in state constitutions, 207
Bill of Rights (England) (1689), 119
Bill of Rights (U.S.) (1791), 241
Bini, 11
Bin-Laden, Osama, 1018, 1020
Birmingham, Alabama
 campaign, 908–909
 following Reconstruction, 532, 536
Birney, James G., 382, 383
Birth control, 674, 770, 927
Birth of a Nation, 550
Birth rates (1930–1995), 861, *861*
Bitter Cry of the Children, The (Spargo), 670
Blackboard Jungle, 891
Black Cabinet, 806
Black codes, 342, 508–509
Black Death, 13
Black Hawk's War (1832), 304–305, 398
Black Kettle, 603
Black Legend, 24
Black Man's Burden Association, 709
Black Muslims, 932
Black Panthers, 932, *932*
Black Power, 931–932
Black Reconstruction (Du Bois), 522
Blade Runner, 930
Blaine, James G., 641, 701–702, 714
Bland-Allison Act (1878), 644
Blatch, Harriot Stanton, 733
Bleeding Kansas, 429–430, 445
Blitzkrieg, 822
Board of Trade, 119
Boesky, Ivan, 963
Bogart, Humphrey, 877
Bolsheviks, 739, 746–747
Bondwoman's Narrative, The (Crafts), 324
Bonfire of the Vanities, The (Wolfe), 964
Bon Homme Richard, 186, *186*

Bonus Army, 793
Book of Common Prayer, 48
Book of Daniel, The (Doctorow), 879
Book of Mormon, The (Smith), 371
Booth, John Wilkes, 490–491
Bosnia, 995
Boston
    American Revolution in, 168–170, 171
    growth of colonial, 107
    Massacre, 152, *153*
    in the nineteenth century, 357
    Port Act (1774), 154, 155
    slave population of, 107
    Tea Party, 153–154, *154*
Boston and Worcester railroad, 356, 357–358
Boston Associates, 362, 364
Boston Children's Friend Society, 373
Boston News-Letter, 111, 118
Boston Seamen's Aid Society, 370–371
Bow, Clara, 770
Bowery, Charity, 334, 336
Bowery, Richard, 334, 336
Boxer Rebellion, 712
Boyd, Belle, 483
Bozeman Trail, 605
Braddock, Edward, 130
Bradford, William, 49, *145*
Bradley, Omar, 842
Bradley, Tom, 1010
Brady, James, 998
Brady Handgun Violence Prevention Act (1994), 998
Bragg, Braxton, 475, 485, 499
Branch Davidians, 998
Brandeis, Louis, 689
Brandywine Creek, battle of, 178, 184
Brannan, Sam, 421
Brant, Joseph (Thayendanegea), 181, 183
Breckinridge, John C., 441–443, *442*
Breeds Hill, battle of, 171, *172,* 178
Brennan, William, 524
Brent's Old Fort, 407
Britain
    battle of, 822, 830
    in World War I, 725, 726–727
    in World War II, 822, 826, 830, 840–842
British Constitution, 146
Brocas, William, 48
Brook Farm, 375–376
Brooklyn Heights, battle of, 178, 182
Brooks, Preston, 430
Brown, Henry, 337
Brown, John
    Kansas civil war and, 430
    raid on Harpers Ferry, 436, 438–440, *439,* 445
Brown, John (Revolutionary era merchant), 153
Brown, Linda, 904
Brown, Mather, *173*
Brown v. Board of Education, 904–905
Bryan, William Jennings
    election of 1896 and, 651–653, *651*
    election of 1908 and, 685
    evolution and 775
    imperialist views and, 709–710, 718
    World War I and, 727, 728, 729
Bryan Bible League, 775
Buchanan, James, 478
    Dred Scott v. Sandford and, 432–433

election of 1856 and, 432
    Lecompton Constitution, 433–434
    secession and, 443
Buchanan, Patrick, 994
Budget and Accounting Act (1921), 760
Budget Bureau, 760
Buffalo, slaughter of, *605,* 606
Bulgaria, 725
Bulge, battle of the, 845
Bull, Amos Bad Heart, *606*
Bull Run
    first battle of (1861), 462, *462,* 489
    second battle of (1862), 466, 489
Bunau-Varilla, Philippe, 716
Bundy, McGeorge, 920
Bunker Hill, battle of, 171, *172,* 178
Bureau of Foreign Commerce, 776
Bureau of Indian Affairs, 607–608, 609, 807, 933
Bureau of Reclamation, 684, 808
Bureau of Refugees, Freedmen, and Abandoned Lands, 501
Burgess, John W., 698
Burgoyne, John, 183–184
Burleson, Albert, 736
Burnside, Ambrose E., 471–472
Burr, Aaron, 255, 257, 269
Burroughs, Nannie H., 554
Bush, George, 256, 412
    election of 1980 and, 957, *959*
    election of 1988 and, 967–968
    election of 1992 and, 993–994, *995*
    environmental issues, 690
    Persian Gulf War, 974–976, *976*
Bush, George P., *979*
Bush, George W., 195, 256, 287, 412, 777
    domestic issues, 1015–1016
    election of 2000 and, 1013–1015, *1014*
    environmental issues, 690
    9-11-01 attacks, *990,* 991–992, *1016, 1017,* 1018–1020
    Social Security and, 813
    war with Iraq, 1020–1021
Bush, Vannevar, 833
Business
    deregulation, 961
    following World War I, 756–760
    multinational corporations, 775
    New Deal and, 796–797
    T. Roosevelt and regulation of, 684–685
    welfare capitalism, 757–759
    women as owners of, *1010*
Butler, Andrew, 430
Butler, Benjamin F., 469, 484
Butler, Nicholas Murray, 576
Byrd, William II, 112, 122
Byrnes, James, 848

C

Cabeza de Vaca, Álvar Núñez, 22–23
Cabinet, formation of presidential, 241
Cabot, John, 28, 30
Caddos, 124
Cahokia, 8, *9*
Cahokia, battle of, 178, 185
Cahuillas, 601
Calhoun, Floride, 307
Calhoun, John C., 287, 295, 313
    Compromise of 1850 and, 422–423

economic policy of, 280, 281
    nullification crisis, 306–308
    states' rights and, 306
    Texas and, 317–318
    as vice president, 306
    as a War Hawk, 272
California
    gold rush, 421–422, *421*
    Native Americans in, 403–404
    rancho era, 406–407
    settlement of, 406–407, 422
    Spanish in, 123–125, 139, 140
Californios, 406
Calvert, Cecilius, 46, 47
Calvert, George, 46, 117
Calvert, Rosalie, 261–262
Calvin, John, 15, 48
Calvinists, 15
Cambodia, 938–939
Camden (South Carolina), battle of, 178, 188–189
Campbell, Ben Nighthorse, 1011
Campbell Soup, 591, *768*
Camp David Agreement, 948
Canada
    See also New France
    American Revolution in, 172
    War of 1812, 273–280, *274*
Canals, 353 355, *356*
Canary Islands, 17
Cannery and Agricultural Workers Unions, 798
Canning, George, 283
Cannon, "Uncle Joe," 686
Capone, Al, 774
Caribbean islands
    English in, 55–57
    history of, 9
    principal European possessions in, *54*
    slave colonies in, 19
    Spanish conquest of, 2, 17, 19–20, 55
Caribbean, U.S. interventions
    since 1954, *894,* 985
    Wilson and, 718–719
Caribs, 9, 19, 20
Carleton, Guy, 192
Carmichael, Stokely, 931
Carnegie, Andrew, 570, 575, 578, 709
Carnegie Steel Co., 570
Carney, Art, 890
Carolina
    See also North Carolina; South Carolina
    colony, overview of, 59
    settlement of, 57–60
    slavery in, 58–59, 81, 83
Carpetbaggers, 514
Carranza, Venustiano, 719
Carson, Rachel, 941
Carswell, G. Harrold, 940
Carter, Jimmy
    economy, 946–948
    election of 1976 and, 945–946, *946*
    election of 1980 and, 958, *959*
    environmental issues, 942, 947
    foreign policy, 948–950
    Iran hostage crisis, 949–950
Carter, Landon, 89
Carter, Robert, 111
Cartier, Jacques, 27
Casey, William, 970
Cass, Lewis, 420
Castro, Fidel, 810, 900, 903

Catawbas, 73, 181
Catch-22 (Heller), 845
Catherine of Aragon, 28
Catherine the Great, 185
Catholic Church, 14–15
Catholics, in Maryland, 46–47
Catlin, George, 389–390, *404*
Cato's Letters, 147
Catt, Carrie Chapman, 678, 729, 735
Cattle ranching, exploitation of
    cattle drives and cow towns, 614–615
    cowhands, 616–617
    rise and fall of open-range ranching, 615–616
Cayugas, 71
Cayuses, 401
Central America, Reagan administration and, 969–970
Central Intelligence Agency. *See* CIA
Central Pacific Railroad, *582,* 600, *600*
Central Powers, 725
Chain migration, 582
Chamberlain, Daniel H., 519
Chambers, Whittaker, *877,* 878
Champlain, Samuel de, 37, *39*
Chandler, Asa, 533
Chaplin, Charlie, 757, 877
Charles I, king of England, 46–47, 50
Charles II, king of England, 57, 60, 62, 116
Charles V, king of Spain, 15
Charles River Bridge v. Warren Bridge, 356–357
Charleston, South Carolina
    American Revolution in, 178, 187, *188*
    Fort Sumter, 444–448
    growth of colonial, 107
    slavery in, 90
Charleston Mercury, 440
Chase, Samuel, 266
Chattanooga, battle of (1863), 475, *476,* 477, 489
Chancellorsville, battle of (1863), 472, *472,* 489
Chávez, César, 932–933, *933*
Cheek, Joel, 591
Chemical industry, 756–757
Cheney, Dick, 1015
Cherokee, 71, 73, 181, 194, 220, 247, 477
    Indian Removal Act (1830), 303–305, *304, 305,* 306–307
    Trail of Tears, 304, *304,* 306–307
Cherokee Nation v. Georgia, 305
Cherokee War (1759–1761), 142–143, *143*
Cherry Valley, battle of, 178, 185
Chesapeake
    community life in, 47–48
    economy, 44–46, *46*
    indentured servants, 45–46
    Jamestown, 42–43
    laborers in, source of, 91
    Maryland, 46–47
    population of, *37,* 77, *84*
    slavery in, 83, 239
    tobacco in, 44–46, *46*
    Virginia, 42–44
    warfare in, 43–44, 48
Chesapeake incident, 270
Chesnut, Mary, 482, 488
Cheyenne, 397, 399, 602, 603–604, 606
Chiang Kai-shek (Jiang Jieshi), 821, 841, 870–871

Chicago, 359, 590
Chicago Defender, 586, 588, 745
Chickasaws, 181, 220
    Indian Removal Act (1830),
        303–305, *304, 305*
Chief executive, office of, 223–224,
    241
Child, Lydia Maria, 376–377, 379, 440
Child labor, 92, 362, 367, 571, 663,
    670, *670, 671,* 672–673, 763
Children
    colonial, 53, *53*
    Depression of 1929 and, 790
    slave, 327, 334
    in textile mills, 362
    West African, 12
    World War II and, 836
Children's Bureau, 670
Chile, 704–705
    U.S. intervention in, 714
China
    Boxer Rebellion, 712
    Eisenhower administration and,
        896
    Korean War, 872–875, *873, 874*
    Nixon administration and,
        939–940
    Open Door policy, 712–713
Chinese Consolidated Benevolent
    Association, 583
Chinese Exclusion Act (1882), 585
Chinese immigrants, 582, 583
    in the mining camps, 581,
        612–613, *613*
    racism, 584, 585–586
    on the railroads, 581, *582,* 600
Chinooks, 5, 601
Chippewas, 216, 398
Chisholm Trail, 614–615
Chivington, John, 603–605
Choctaws, 125, 181, 220
    Indian Removal Act (1830),
        303–305, *304, 305*
Cholera, 333, 402
Christian Coalition, 448
Christian History, The, 115
Christianity and the Social Crisis
    (Rauschenbusch), 664
Chrysler Corp., 757, 804, 963
Chumashes, 403
Churchill, Winston, 826, 841, 842,
    848, 866
Church of England. *See* Anglican
    Church
Church of God, 541
Church of Jesus Christ of Latter-day
    Saints, 371, 407–408
CIA (Central Intelligence Agency)
    formation of, 868
    intervention by, 897, *898,* 970
    Nicaraguan Contras and, 970
Cincinnati, Ohio, 359
Cisneros, Henry, 1011
Cities and towns
    See also Communities
    edge, 934
    growth of (1820–1860), 357–361,
        358, 359
    growth of (1880–1900), 588–589,
        589
    growth of (1920s), 764, *765*
    growth of, following
        Reconstruction, 531
    growth of colonial, 107–109
    impact of globalization on,
        980–981

impact of immigration on,
    360–361
industrial, 359–360
industrial (1877–1900), 533–534,
    536–537
inland, 358–359
living conditions and sanitation,
    358
metropolitan areas (1900–2000),
    comparison of, *977*
migration to, after the Civil War,
    504–505
Model Cities Program, 926
in the 1950s, 859, 888
port, 357–358
reform in, 668–670, 680
suburbs, development of, 589–590
suburbs in the 1920s, 767
suburbs in the 1960s–1990s, 934
urban crisis in the 1970s, 930–931
Civilian Conservation Corps (CCC),
    795–796
Civilization in the United States, 771
Civil rights
    for Hispanic Americans, 932–933,
        933
    for Native Americans, 933, *934*
    minority separatism, 931–933
Civil Rights Act (1866), 510–511, 521
Civil Rights Act (1875), 510, 519–520,
    521
Civil Rights Act (1964), 905, 910, 927
Civil rights movement
    Birmingham campaign, 908–909
    Brown v. Board of Education,
        904–905
    Eisenhower administration and,
        904–908
    freedom rides, 908
    Freedom Summer project, 911
    Johnson administration and,
        910–911
    Kennedy administration and,
        906–909
    Little Rock crisis, 906, *906*
    March on Washington (1963), 908
    Montgomery bus boycott,
        907–908
    origins of, 904–906
    overview of, 905
    Plessy v. Ferguson, 548, *549,* 904
    public accommodations, 906–908
    Selma campaign, 911
    sit-ins, *907,* 908
    Southern Christian Leadership
        Conference (SCLC), 908
    Student Nonviolent Coordinating
        Committee (SNCC), 908
    Truman administration and steps
        toward, 860–861
Civil Service Commission, 640
Civil service reform, 639–640
Civil War, *452*
    African Americans in, 458,
        469–471, *471,* 488–490
    Appomattox Courthouse, surren-
        der at, 490
    arming the Confederacy's slaves,
        488–490
    border states, Lincoln's fight for,
        460–461
    casualties, 463–465, 466, 468, 472,
        474, 484–485
    chronology, 456
    comparison of North and South
        (1860), 436–438, 458–459

conscription/draft riots, 457, 458,
    478
desertions/dissenters, 477–478,
    483
diseases in, 464
East, fighting in the, 465–466
economy of the North, 479–480
economy of the South, 482
financing of, 456, 459
leadership, 459–460
life of a common soldier, *461,*
    464–465
migration for, 455–461
Native Americans in, 477
naval fighting, 466–467
outbreak of, 444–448
peace movements, 481
politics, in the South, 481
politics/legislation, in the North,
    477–478
strategies and tactics, 461
in trans-Mississippi West, 477
West, fighting in the, 462–463,
    463
women in, 458, 464, *464,* 465, 480,
    480, 482, 482, 483
Civil War, battles
    Antietam, 467–468, 489
    Atlanta, 485–486, *486,* 489
    Bull Run, first battle of, 462, *462,*
        489
    Bull Run, second battle of, 466,
        489
    Chancellorsville, 472, *472,* 489
    Chattanooga, 475, *476,* 477, 489
    Franklin and Nashville, 488, 489
    Fredericksburg, 471–472, *472,* 489
    Gettysburg, 472–474, *474, 475,*
        489, 491
    major battles 1861–1865, 489
    Sherman's March, 488, *488,* 489
    Vicksburg, 463, 475, *476,* 489
    Wilderness and Cold Harbor,
        484–485, *485,* 489
Civil Works Administration (CWA),
    795
Claims clubs, 394
Clalin, Frances, *464*
Clansman, The, 550
Clark, George Rogers, 185, 206
Clark, Mark, 874
Clark, J. Reuben, 778
Clark, William, 267, *267,* 286–287, 399
Clark Memorandum, 778
Clay, Henry, 308, 313, 316–317, 378
    Compromise of 1850 and,
        422–423
    economic policy of, 280
    election of 1824 and, 287–288
    election of 1844 and, 318
    Missouri Compromise and,
        284–285
    as a War Hawk, 272
Clayton, Powell, 517
Clayton Anti-Trust Act (1914), 688
Cleaver, Eldridge, 932
Clemenceau, Georges, 741
Clermont, 353
Cleveland, Grover, 412, 579, 637, 641,
    644, 647, 648–650, 703–704
Cleveland, Ohio, 359
Clifford, Clark, 935
Clinton, Bill, 94, 412
    domestic policy, 996–997
    election of 1992 and, 993–994,
        994, 995

election of 1996 and, 997
foreign policy, 995–996
impeachment of, 999–1000
morality and Whitewater, 999
Social Security and, 813
Clinton, DeWitt, 276
Clinton, Henry, 180, 185, 186–188
Clinton, Hillary Rodham, 996, *997,*
    999, 1009
Clock, The, 836
CNN (Cable News Network), 1003
Coahuila, 405
Cobb, Howell, 488
Cobb, Thomas R. R., 332
Coca-Cola, 533
Coercive Acts, 154
Cohen, William, 1018
Colbert, Jean-Baptiste, 38
Cold Harbor, battle of (1864),
    484–485, *485, 487,* 489
Cold War, 856
    in Asia, 870–872
    atomic diplomacy, 868–870, 871
    Bay of Pigs, 900
    Berlin blockade and formation of
        NATO, 868
    Berlin Wall, 900, 973, *973*
    containment policy, 867, 872,
        896–898
    Cuban missile crisis, 901–904
    division of Europe, 865–868, *869*
    Eisenhower administration and,
        894–899
    end of, 974, 975
    glasnost and perestroika, 971
    Kennedy administration and,
        899–904
    Korean War, 872–875
    Marshall Plan, 867
    massive retaliation doctrine,
        895–896
    McCarthyism, 879–880
    origin of term, 865
    policies of, summary of, 972
    Reagan administration and,
        968–969
    satellites, launching of, 896
    Truman Doctrine, 867
    U-2 incident, 898–899
Cole, 1017
Colfax Massacre (1873), 516–517
Collective bargaining, 578
Colleges
    black, 502
    colonial, 115
Collier, John, 806–807
Colombia, U.S. intervention in, 714
Colonial period
    See also under name of colony
    art/artisans, 107–108
    backcountry expansion, 121–125
    diverging politics between
        England and, 119–121
    ethnic distribution of immigrants
        in, 93, 95, *93, 95*
    Glorious Revolution, 117, 118–119
    growth of cities, 107–109
    houses, 48, 110–111, *110*
    importation of goods, 110
    population in, 53, *84, 121, 122*
    religion, 113–116
Colonial wars
    See also American Revolution
    French and Indian War
        (1756–1763), 126, 129–132
    King George's War (1739–1748),

126, 127–129
King Philip's War, 76–77
King William's War (1689–1697), 126–127
Queen Anne's War (1702–1713), 126–127
Colonization, rejection of, 378–379
Colorado Fuel and Iron Co., 668
Colored Farmers' Alliance, 541, 644, 645
Colored Masons, 553
Colored Methodist Episcopal Church, 506
Colored Monitor Union club, 514
Colored Odd Fellows, 553
Columbian exchange, 25–26
Columbia University, student demonstrations at, 936
Columbine High School, 998
Columbus, Christopher, 2, 9, 13, 17, 19, 25, 26, 27, 55
Comanches, 388, 404, 404, 405, 406, 477, 602, 603, 607
Comecon, 867
Commerce, regulation of interstate, 641–643
Committee for Industrial Organization (CIO), 804
    See also AFL-CIO
Committee of Safety, 167
Committee on American Interests in China, 712
Committee on Civil Rights, 860
Committee on Public Information (CPI), 731, 735
Committees of Correspondence, 153
Committee to Defend America by Aiding the Allies, 826
Committee to Re-Elect the President (CREEP), 943
Common Sense (Paine), 172, 412
Commonwealth v. Hunt, 367
Communes and cults in the 1970s, 929–930
Communism/communists, 375
    See also Cold War
    collapse of, 974, 975
    containment policy, 867, 872, 896–898
    Red Scare, 746–747, 748
    Red Scare, following World War II, 875–880
Communist party, 876–877
Communities
    growth of free black communities following American Revolution, 205–206
    Native American, 29
    slave, 89
    utopian, 375–378
Community Action Agencies, 910
Company of New France, 37, 38
Comprehensive Test Ban Treaty, 972
Compromise of 1850, 422–423, 424, 445
Compromise of 1877, 520
Compromise Tariff of 1833, 308
Computers, 1002–1003
Comstock Lode, 610
Concentration camps, 813, 822, 845–846, 846
Conciliatory Proposition, 168
Concord, battle of (1775), 168–170, 169, 178
Cone, Spencer Houghton, 274
Conestogas, 143

Coney Island, 593, 593
Confederate battle flag, 556–557
Confederate States of America
    See also Civil War
    Davis as president, 442
    disintegration of, 481–483
    financing of, 457, 459
    formation of, 442–443, 443
Confederation Congress
    Articles of Confederation, 210, 224
    economic problems, 211–214
    England, relations with, 218–219
    France, relations with, 218
    Land Ordinance (1785), 216
    Native American lands and, 206
    Northwest Ordinance (1787), 218
    Spain, relations with, 219–221
    western lands and, 216–218
Confiscation Act (1862), 468, 469
Congregationalists, 113, 207, 235
Congress
    See also Confederation Congress;
        Continental Congress
    Articles of Confederation, 210, 224
    Bill of Rights and, 241
    Constitutional Convention, 221–224
    in 1871–1901, 637–638, 638
    minorities and women in, 1008–1011, 1012
    Red Scare investigations, 877–878
Congressional Reconstruction, 512–513
Congress of Industrial Organizations, 804, 888
Congress of Racial Equality (CORE), 908
Connally, John, 909
Connecticut
    colony, overview of, 59
    labor system in, 91, 92
    ratification of Constitution, 227
    religion in, 235
    settlement of, 50–51, 59
Connor, Bull, 908
Conquistadores, 19–20
Conscience Whigs, 421
Conservation, 663, 682–684
Constantinople, 16
Constitutional Amendments
    Bill of Rights, 241
    Eighteenth, 669, 676, 773
    Fifteenth, 513, 517, 520, 521, 524, 525, 549
    Fifth, 878
    Fourteenth, 510–511, 521, 520, 524, 525
    Ninth, 241
    Nineteenth, 669, 679
    role of, 241
    Second, 241
    Seventeenth, 669, 681
    Sixteenth, 669, 685
    Tenth, 241, 245
    Thirteenth, 501, 509, 521
Constitutional Convention, 221–224
Constitutional Union party, 441
Constitution of the United States, 221
    compared with the Articles of Confederation, 224
    overview of, 224–225
    ratification of, 225–228
Consumer credit
    introduction of, 759

in the 1950s, 889
Consumerism
    in early 1900s, 591–592
    in the 1920s, 768
    in the 1950s, 861–862, 889
    in the 1980s, 963–964
Consumers' League, 763
Containment policy, 867, 872, 896–898
Continental Army, 166, 170, 175–177, 179, 192
Continental Association, 157
Continental Congress
    See also Confederation Congress
    First, 154, 155, 157
    Second, 170
Continental dollar, 170, 194, 211
Contract theory of government, 173
Contract with America, 997
Coolidge, Calvin, 746, 747, 760, 761–762, 768
Cooper, Anna J., 529–530
Cooper, Anthony Ashley, 57
Cooper, Gary, 877
Cooperatives, 540
Copley, John Singleton, 109, 148, 151
Copperheads, 478
Coral Sea, battle of the, 830
Coram, Thomas, 60
Cornwallis, Charles, 188, 189–190, 190
Coronado, Francisco Vásquez de, 24
Corporations
    consolidation in the 1920s, 757
    deregulation, 961
    downsizing, 965
    multinational, 775
    role of, 567–570
Cortés, Hernán, 1, 20–21, 26
Cosmopolitan, 665
Cotton
    between 1877–1900, 538–539, 539, 541–542
    gin, 363–364, 396
    mills, 362
    prices 1825–1845, 310
    production 1800–1860, 327, 330
    slavery and, 325–326
    southern expansion with, 396–397
Coughlin, Charles, 800, 801
Council of Economic Advisers, 858
Council of National Defense, 732, 825
Council of the Indies, 23
Counterculture, 928
Counter-Reconstruction, 516–519
Counter-Reformation, 15
Country clubs, 592
Country ideology, 127, 146–147, 174
Country Life movement, 663, 675
Coureurs de bois, 38, 39, 125
Court system, formation of, 241–242
Covenant, 50
Cowhands, 616–617
Cowpens, battle of, 178, 189
Cox, Archibald, 943
Cox, George, 635
Cox, James M., 747
Coxey, Jacob, 647–648, 650
Coxey's Army, 647, 650
Craft, Ellen, 337
Crafts, Hannah, 323–324
Crawford, William H., 287
Crazy Horse, 606, 606
Creeks, 181, 220, 240, 247, 278–279, 280
    Indian Removal Act (1830),

303–305, 304, 305
Creel, George, 735, 736, 737
CREEP (Committee to Re-Elect the President), 943
Crees, 5
Creoles, 88
Crèvecoeur, J. Hector St. John, 208–209
Crime, Prohibition and, 773–774
Criollos, 403
Crisis, The, 678
Crittenden, John J., 444
Crittenden Plan, 444
Croatoan Indians, 29
Croker, Richard, 635
Cromwell, Oliver, 47
Croppers' and Farm Workers' Union, 791
Crow, 397, 608
CSX Corp., 94
Cuba
    Bay of Pigs, 900
    missile crisis, 901–904
    Ostend Manifesto, 427
    Revolution (1959), 900
    Spanish-American War, 705–710, 707, 708
    Spanish exploration of, 19, 55
    Ten Years' War, 705
    as a U.S. protectorate, 714–716
Cult of domesticity, 365–366
Culture wars, 986–987
Cumming, Kate, 464
Currency
    continental dollar, 170, 194, 211
    establishment of national, 478
    greenbacks, 459, 643
    paper money pre-American Revolution, 144
    silver coinage, 643–644
    sound money, 643, 651–652
    Specie Circular, 311
Currency Act (1764), 144, 156
Currency Act (1897), 653
Custer, George A., 606
Custis, Mary, 466
Czechoslovakia
    following World War I, 742
    new government, 973
    Prague Spring, 936
    World War II, 822, 868

D

Dahomey, 11
Dakotas, 477
Daley, Richard, 937
Dance, of slaves, 335
Dare, Virginia, 29
Darrow, Clarence, 775
Dartmouth, 154
Dartmouth College v. Woodward, 282
Darwin, Charles, 575
Darwinism, 697, 699, 775
Daugherty, Harry M., 761
Daughters of the American Revolution, 675
Davenport, James, 115
Davenport, John, 52
Davis, Edmund J., 517
Davis, Jefferson, 440, 442, 447, 459–460, 469, 475, 477, 481, 486, 488–490
Davis, John W., 762
Dawes Act (1887), 609, 618
Day, Thomas, 343
D-Day, 842, 844

Dean, James, 892, *893*
Dean, John, 943
Dearborn, Henry, 275
Debs, Eugene V., 579, 668, 687, 736, 748, 760, 1018–1019
Declaration of Independence and, 172–174
Declaration of London, 727
Declaration of Rights and Grievances, 148
Declaration of Sentiments, 381
Declaration of the Causes and Necessity of Taking Up Arms, 170
Declaratory Act, 149
Deere, John, 394
Deindustrialization, 947–948
Deism, 255, 256
Delany, Martin, 424
Delavan, Edward, 369
Delaware
    labor system in, 92
    ratification of Constitution, 227
    secession, 460
Delawares, 61, 73, 127, 128, 129, 131, 181, 216
DeLay, Tom, 777
De Mille, Cecil B., 769
Democratic party
    Civil War and, 478
    compared with the Whigs, 313
    during 1870–1900, 531, 633–635
    election of 1848 and, 420
    election of 1852 and, 426–427
    election of 1860 and, 440–442, *442*, 445
    election of 1864 and, 486–487
    election of 1896 and, 650–653, *653*
    Jacksonian Democrats, 295, 299–301
    Reconstruction, 508, 519
    Redeemer, 540
Democratic-Republican societies, 246–247
Dempsey, Jack, 769
Denmark Vesey's Conspiracy (1822), 336
Denver, Colorado, 588
Department stores, 573, 590, 591–592, 767
Depression, following American Revolution, 212–214
Depression of 1893, 646–650
Depression of 1929
    See also New Deal
    agriculture in, 785, 788, 791
    chronology, 787
    the crash, 786–788
    families in, 789–790
    Hoover and, 791–794
    minorities in, 790
    protests during, 790–791
    spread of, 788–789
    underlying weaknesses, 786–788
    unemployment in, 788, 789, 798–799
    voluntarism, limits of, 791–793
    women and, 789–790
Deregulation, 961
Desert Storm, 976
De Soto, Hernán, 23–24
Détente, 940
Detroit, Michigan, 185, 359
    growth of in the 1920s, 764
Dew, Thomas R., 347
Dewey, George, 706

Dewey, John, 672
Dewey, Thomas E., 839, 862, 863, 864
Dewson, Molly, 805
Días, Bartholomew, 17
Díaz, Porfirio, 719
Dickens, Charles, 358, 374
Dickerson, Carroll, *769*
Dickinson, Anna, 633
Dickinson, John, 151, 173, 210
Die Hard, 958
Diem, Ngo Dinh, 901
Dies, Martin, 877
Diggs, Annie, 645
Direct Tax of 1798, 253, 254
Discourse on Western Planting (Hakluyt), 30–31
Diseases
    AIDS, 913, 983, *983*
    in American Revolution, 177
    among slaves, 333
    Black Death, 13
    cholera, 333, 402, 603
    in the Civil War, 464
    in colonies, 47
    influenza epidemic of 1919, 744
    introduced in the Americas, 21
    Native Americans and, 21–22, 25–26, 70–71, 399, 401, 603
    polio, 912–913
    smallpox, 21, 25, 26, *26*, 399
    typhoid, 574
Disfranchisement, 547, 548–550, 552–553
Disneyland, 889
Divorce, 770, 789, 986
Dix, Dorothea, 374, *374*
Dixiecrats, 862, 863
Dixon, Thomas, 550
Djenné, 12
Doctorow, E. L., 879
Dole, Robert, 997
Dollar diplomacy, 717–718
Dollmaker, The (Arrow), 836
Dominican Republic, 701, 714, 717, 719
Dominion of New England, 117
Dominy family, 363
Doolittle, Amos, *169*
Douglas, Stephen A.
    Civil War and, 456
    Compromise of 1850 and, 423
    debates with Lincoln, 434–435, *435*
    election of 1856 and, 432
    election of 1860 and, 440–442, *442*
    Kansas-Nebraska Act, 428–429, *429*
    Lecompton Constitution, 434
Douglass, Frederick, 382–383, *383*, 424, 439, 471, 501, 522
Douglass, Lewis, 471
Dragging Canoe, 181
Drago Doctrine, 717
Drake, Francis, 28
Drayton, William Henry, 158–159
Dream songs, 404
Dred Scott v. Sandford, 432–433, 445, 510
Dreiser, Theodore, 588
Drugs, fight against, 928, 968, 970, 998
Dubek, Alexander, 936
Du Bois, W. E. B., 522, 531, 551, 555–556, *558*, 677–678, 745, 806
Dudley, Thomas, 36, 49, 50

Dukakis, Michael, 967
Duke, James B., 533, 536–537, 570
Duke Power Co., 537
Duke University, 537
Dulles, John Foster, 895, 896
Dunmore, Lord (John Murray), 171–172, 180
Dunning, William A., 551
DuPont Co., 567, 756, *758*
Dust Bowl, 785, 802, *802*
Dutch, *236*, 237
    Anglo-Dutch wars, 62
    in the Caribbean, 55, 56
    colonies, 40–41
    exploration/colonization by, 39–42
    map of colonies in North America, *42*
Dutch East India Company, 40
Dutch Reformed Church, 207, 237
Dylan, Bob, 928, 929, 938

E

Earl, Ralph, *169*
Early, Jubal, 484
Earned Income Tax Credit, 996
Earth Day, 941
Earth in the Balance (Gore), 994
East India Company, 153, 154
Eastwood, Clint, 958
Easy Rider, 928
Eaton, Margaret "Peggy," 307
Eaton Affair, 306–307
Eccles, Marriner, 809
Eckford, Elizabeth, *906*
Economic Recovery Tax Act (ERTA) (1981), 961
Economy
    American Revolution impact on, 191, 194, 196
    Bush (George) administration, 968
    Bush (George W.) administration, 1015
    Carter administration, 946–948
    Chesapeake tobacco, 44–46, *46*
    Civil War economy of the North, 479–480
    Civil War economy of the South, 482
    Clinton administration, 996
    colonial, 101–107
    defense, 977–978
    Depression of 1893, 646–650
    Depression of 1929, 785–791
    development of the West and, *611*
    following Reconstruction, 531, 534–536
    following World War I, 756–760, 775
    following World War II, 858
    Ford administration, 945
    Hamilton's economic programs, 242–244, 245
    legacy of slavery, 346
    mercantilism, 101
    national debt issues, 243–244, 245
    nationalism, 280–281
    New England, 53–55, 101–107
    in the 1950s, 861–862, 886–894
    in the 1990s, 1001
    in the nineteenth century, 364
    Nixon administration, 940–941
    Panic of 1819, 283–284
    Panic of 1837, 309–311
    Panic of 1857, 434

problems following the American Revolution, 211–214
    Reaganomics, 961–962
    F. Roosevelt recession, 809
    service, 1001–1002
    slave, 326–328
    World War I, 727, 731–733, 744–746
    World War I debts and expansion of, 775–776
    World War II, 832–833
Edison, Thomas Alva, 566–567
Education
    affirmative action programs, 1013
    for African Americans, in Reconstruction period, 501–502, 535–536, 554, *555*
    bilingual, 1011–1012
    Brown v. Board of Education, 904–905
    Bush (George W.) administration, 1016
    busing of children, 935
    of colonial women, 111, 204–205, 235, 237, *237*
    Elementary and Secondary Education Act (1965), 914
    GI Bill of Rights, 859
    Head Start, 910
    Higher Education Act (1963), 914
    integration of public schools, 904–906
    of Native Americans, *607, 608,* 674
    prayer in schools, 893
    public, 372
    public school system, growth and reform of, 671–674
    reform, 372–373
    women as teachers, 373, 501–502
    of women following the Civil War, 480
    of women in the early 1900s, 573–574
Educational Amendments, Title IX of, 981
Edwards, Jonathan, 115
Egypt, 830, 842, 897, 948
Eighteenth Amendment, 669, 676, 773
Einstein, Albert, 834
Eisenhower, Dwight D., 875
    civil rights and, 904–908
    foreign policy, 894–899
    as president, 887–899
    World War II and, 842
El Alamein, 830, 842
Elections, presidential
    of 1796, 251–252
    of 1800, 255–257
    of 1804, 263
    of 1808, 270
    of 1812, 276
    of 1816, 280
    of 1820, 287
    of 1824, 287–288, *288,* 299
    of 1828, 300–301, *301*
    of 1832, 309
    of 1836, 309
    of 1840, 315–316, *315*
    of 1844, 318
    of 1848, 420–421
    of 1852, 426–427, 445
    of 1856, 432, 445
    of 1860, 440–442, *442*, 445
    of 1864, 478, 486–488
    of 1868, 512

of 1872, 518–519
of 1876, 520, *522*
of 1880, 640
of 1884, 641
of 1892, 646
of 1896, 650–653, *653, 705–706*
of 1900, 710
of 1904, 684
of 1908, 685
of 1912, 686–687, *688*
of 1916, 729–730, *730*
of 1920, 747–748
of 1924, 762
of 1928, 778–779, *779*
of 1932, 793–794, *794*
of 1936, 803
of 1940, 825
of 1944, 839
of 1948, 862–864, *864*
of 1952, 887
of 1956, 895
of 1960, 899, *900*
of 1964, 911–914
of 1968, 937, *938*
of 1972, 943
of 1976, 945–946, *946*
of 1980, 957, *959*
of 1984, 959
of 1988, 967–968
of 1992, 993–994, *995*
of 1996, 997
of 2000, 1013–1015, *1014*
Electoral reform, 679–680
Electricity, 566–567, *568,* 756
Elementary and Secondary Education
    Act (1965), 914
Eliot, John, 76
Elizabeth I, queen of England, 28, 46,
    48, 49
Elliott, Robert B., *514*
Ellis, Bret Easton, 964
Ellsberg, Daniel, 942
Ely, Richard T., 665, 667
Emancipation Proclamation (1829),
    405
Emancipation Proclamation (1863),
    468–469
Embargo Act (1807), 269–270
Emergency Banking Act (1933), 794,
    795
Emergency Quota Act (1921), 771
Emergency Relief Appropriations Act
    (1935), 802
Emerging Republican Majority, The
    (Phillips), 976
Emerson, Ralph Waldo, 170, 376–377,
    438, 440
Employment
    See also Industrialization and man-
        ufacturing; Labor
    affirmative action programs, 1013
    for African Americans, 586–587
    of children, 92, 362, 367
    corporate downsizing, 965
    in defense economy, 977–978
    deindustrialization, 947–948
    Equal Employment Opportunity
        Commission (EEOC), 910
    for free blacks, 343
    of immigrants during 1870–1900,
        570–574, 581–584
    for Irish immigrants, 363
    Job Corps, 910
    in the 1950s, 888
    for women, 362–363, *363,*
        365–366

for women from 1970–2000, 981,
    982
working classes, 366–367
Employment Act (1946), 858
Empresario, 405
Encomienda, 69, 77, 78
Energy, Department of, 947
Energy crisis of the 1970s, 940–941
Energy Policy and Conservation Act
    (1978), 947
Enforcement Act (1870), 517
Engel v. Vitale, 893
England
    See also American Revolution
    Anglo-Dutch wars, 62
    in the Caribbean, 55–57
    Chesapeake colonies, 42–48
    Civil War (U.S.) and, 467
    Confederation Congress and,
        218–219
    diverging politics between
        colonies and, 119–121
    exploration/colonization by,
        28–31, 42–55, 121–123
    French and Indian War
        (1756–1763), 126, 129–132
    Glorious Revolution, 118–119
    impressment of American sailors
        by, 250, 268–270
    Jay's Treaty (1794), 250–251
    King George's War (1739–1748),
        126, 127–129
    King William's War (1689–1697),
        126–127
    map of colonies in North
        America, *42, 58*
    mercantilism, 101
    New England, 48–55
    North American territories
        1750–1763, *121*
    overview of seventeenth-century
        colonies, 59
    proprietary colonies, 46, 57–62
    Queen Anne's War (1702–1713),
        126–127
    slave trade and, 82–83
    U.S. relations with, 250–251
    War of 1812, *260,* 261–262,
        273–280, *274, 279*
Enlightenment, 112–113
Enrollment Act (1862), 458
Enron Corp., 1015–1016
Entertainment
    See also Sports; *under type of*
    amusement parks, 566, 593, *593*
    colonial, 111
    in cow towns, 615
    in the early 1900s, 572–573, 590,
        592–594
    in mining camps, 610–612
    in nineteenth century, 364–365,
        365
    in the 1920s, 757, 768–770
    in the 1950s, 890, 891–892
    vaudeville, 588
Enumerated products, 101
Environmental issues
    Bush (George) administration, 690
    Bush (George W.) administration,
        690
    Carter administration, 942, 947
    Ford administration, 942
    Johnson administration, 942
    Nixon administration, 690,
        941–942
    Reagan administration, 690, 961

Roosevelt (Theodore) administra-
    tion, 663, 682–684
Environmental Protection Agency
    (EPA), 690, 942, 961
Episcopalians, 207
Equal Employment Opportunity
    Commission (EEOC), 910
Equal Rights Amendment (ERA), 763,
    981
Equiano, Olaudah, 68, 82, *83*
Era of Good Feelings, 280–283
Erie Canal, 313, 353, 355, *356,* 357,
    359
Erskine, David, 271
Ervin, Sam, 943
Eskimos, 5
Espionage Act (1917), 736
Essex Junto, 269
Established churches, 207–208
Estonia, 742
Ethnic groups
    in 1770s British North America,
        93, 95, *93, 95*
    in 1790s, *236,* 237
Europe
    See also Exploration and coloniza-
        tion; *specific countries*
    Middle Ages, 13
    patriarchal, 13
    Renaissance, 13
European Coal and Steel Community,
    875
European Recovery Plan, 867
Evangelicalism, 298–299, 345,
    365–366, 369
Evangelists/televangelists, 892
Everybody's, 665, 667
Executive Order 8802, 838
Executive Order 9066, 838
Executive Order 9835, 876
Exodusters, 619
Exploration and colonization
    by Dutch, 39–42
    by England, 28–31, 42–55,
        121–123
    expansion in 1750s, *121*
    by France, 27–28, 37–39, 125
    maps of, *18, 20*
    by Portugal, 12–13, 16–17, 27
    by Spain, 2, 9, 12, 13–14, 16, 17,
        19–25, 123–125

F

Factories. *See* Industrialization and
    manufacturing
Facts of Reconstruction (Lynch), 522
Fair Deal, 864–865
Fair Employment Practices
    Committee (FEPC), 838, 865
Fair Labor Standards Act (1938), 810
Fall, Albert, 761
Fallen Timbers, battle of, 247, 248
Falwell, Jerry, 448, 984–985
Family and Medical Leave Act (1993),
    996
Family life
    in Chesapeake colonies, 47–48
    cultural perceptions and misper-
        ceptions, 26–27
    Depression of 1929 and, *782,*
        783–785, 789–790
    in the 1880s, 571
    middle class, 365, *366*
    New England, 52–55
    in the 1950s, 889–890
    slave, 57, 88–89, 334–336

West African, 12
westward expansion and, 401–402
World War II and, 836
Farewell to Arms, A (Hemingway), 770
Fargo, William, 421
Farmar, Eliza, 137–139
Farm Credit Administration, 795
Farmer, James, 908
Farmer-Paellmann, Deandria, 94
Farmers' Alliances, 644–645
Farmers' Holiday Association, 791
Farming. *See* Agriculture
Farm Tenancy Act, 810
Farragut, David G., 463
Fascism, 811–812
Fast-food franchise chains, 767, 889
Father Knows Best, 890
Faubus, Orval, 906
Faulkner, William, 491
Fauset, Jessie, *766*
Federal Art Project, 802
Federal Aviation Administration
    (FAA), 961
Federal bureaucracy and the spoils
    system, 638
Federal Civil Defense Administration,
    870
Federal Communications Commission
    (FCC), 757
Federal Council of Churches of Christ
    in America, 664
Federal Deposit Insurance Corp
    (FDIC), 794
Federal Emergency Relief
    Administration (FERA), 795
Federal Farm Board, 791
Federal Farm Loan Act (1916), 689
Federal Highway Act (1956), 889
Federal Housing Administration
    (FHA), 859, 889
Federalism, 225, 226
Federalist, The, 228
Federalist Gazette, 246
Federalist party
    differences between Republican
        party and, 244
    formation of, 245
    policies of, 244, 245
Federalists, 225, 226–228
    High, 253–257
Federal Music Project, 802
Federal Radio Commission, 757
Federal Reserve Act (1913), 669, 688
Federal Reserve Board, 688, 801
Federal Theatre Project, 802
Federal Trade Commission Act
    (1914), 669, 688, 761
Felton, Rebecca Latimer, 543–544
Feminine Mystique, The (Friedan), 894
Feminism, 381–382, *382*
Feminist Alliance, 666
Feminist movement, 927, 981–982
Ferdinand, Franz, 725
Ferdinand, king of Spain, 13, 14
Ferguson, Clementia, 108
Ferguson, Miriam, 773
Fermi, Enrico, 819–820, 834
Fermi, Laura, 820
Ferraro, Geraldine, 1008
Ferris, George Washington, 593
Ferris, Warren A., 399, 400
Field Order No. 15, 503
Fifteenth Amendment, 513, 517, 520,
    521, 524, 525, 549
Fifth Amendment, 878

Filipino-American War, 710–712, *711*
Fillmore Millard, 423, 426, 432
Finland, 742
Finney, Charles G., 365
Fire Next Time, The (Baldwin), 931
First African Baptist Church, 505, *505*
First Colored Baptist Church, 505
First Continental Congress, 154, 155, 157
First International American Conference, 702
Fishermen, 92
Fishing, 30–31
Fiske, John, 697
Fisk University, 502
Fitzgerald, F. Scott, 770, 771
Five Points slum area, 358
Flapper, 770
FleetBoston Financial Corp., 94
Fletcher v. Peck, 282
Flivver King, The (Sinclair), 754
Florida
    admitted to Union, 395
    annexation of West, to the U.S., 268–269, 272
    British control of, following French and Indian War, 133, 140
    French exploration/colonization of, 28
    Jackson's invasion of, 283
    missionaries in, 73–74, *74*
    secession, 442, *443*
    Spanish exploration/colonization of, 20, 23, 24
Folwell, John, 108
Food Administration (FA), 731, 732–733
Foote, Andrew H., 462
Force Bill (1833), 308
Ford, Gerald R., 942, 944–946
Ford, Henry, 753–755, 759, 825
Fordism, 755
Ford Motor Co., *569, 752, 757,* 757, 775, 804, 832
Foreign policy
    Bush (George) administration, 974–976, *976*
    Carter administration, 948–950
    Clinton administration, 995–996
    Eisenhower administration, 894–899
    Kennedy administration, 899–904
    McKinley administration, 706–710
    Nixon administration, 938–940
    Reagan administration, 968–971
    Roosevelt (Theodore) administration, 700, 702–703
    Truman administration, 865–867, 872–875
    Wilson administration, 718–719
Forest Management Act (1897), 682
Forest Reserve Act (1891), 682
Forrest, Nathan Bedford, 516
Fort Dearborn, 275
Fort Donelson, 462, 463, 489
Fort Duquesne, 129, 130, 131
Fort Henry, 462, 463, 489
Fort Laramie, *403*
Fort Laramie, treaty of (1851), 403
Fort Laramie, treaty of (1868), 605
Fort Loudoun, 143
Fort McIntosh, treaty of (1785), 216
Fort Michilimackinac, 275
Fort Necessity, 129
Fort Orange, 40

Fort Oswego, 130
Fort Stanwix, treaty of (1784), 216
Fort Sumter, 444–448
Fort Ticonderoga, 170, 178, 183
Fortune, T. Thomas, 497–498
Fort Wagner, 471
Fort Wayne, treaty of (1809), 272
Fort William Henry, 130
Forty-Niners, *421*
Foster, J. Ellen, 633
Foster, Vincent, 999
Fourier, Charles, 375
Fourierist communities, 375
Fourteen Points, 740–741
Fourteenth Amendment, 510–511, 521, 520, 524, 525
Fox (Indians), 304, 398
Frame of Government, 61
France
    See also New France
    American Revolution and, 184–185
    in the Caribbean, 55
    Civil War (U.S.) and, 467
    Confederation Congress and, 218
    control of Native Americans, 71
    exploration/colonization by, 27–28, 37–39, 125
    French and Indian War (1756–1763), 126, 129–132
    in Louisiana, 125
    in the Mississippi Valley, 125
    North American territories 1750–1763, *121*
    Red Spring, 936, 937
    Vietnam and, 901
    War of the Austrian Succession (1739–1748), 126, 127–129
    War of the League of Augsburg (1689–1697), 126–127
    World War I, 725
    World War II, 821, 825, 842, 844
    XYZ Affair, 252–253
Francis I, king of France, 27
Franciscans, 73–75, 78, 124, 403
Franco, Francisco, 812, 821
Franco-American Accord (1800), 255
Franco-American Alliance (1778), 246
Franklin, battle of (1864), 488, 489
Franklin, Benjamin, 110, *112,* 115, 122, 143, 584
    Albany Plan of Union, 129
    American Revolution and, 172, 184, 186, 190, *192*
    inventions, 112–113
    taxation and, 149
Franklin, Deborah, 110
Franklin, John Hope, 94, 525
Freake, Elizabeth, *34*
Fredericksburg, battle of (1862), 471–472, *472,* 489
Free blacks. *See* African Americans, free
Freedmen's Bureau, 501–502, 503, 504, 510, 521
Freedom rides, 908
Freedom's Journal, 378
Freedom Speech Movement (FSM), 926
Freedom Summer, 911
Freemen, New England, 50
Freeport Doctrine, 435
Free silver policy, 643, 705
Free-Soil party, formation of, 383, 421
Frémont, John C., 432, 441
French, Benjamin B., 293–294

French and Indian War (1756–1763), 126, 129–132
French Connection, 930
French Revolution (1789), 245–247
Freud, Sigmund, 593, 770
Frick, Henry Clay, 578
Friedan, Betty, 894
Fries, John, 254
Fries's Rebellion, 254
Frobisher, Martin, 28
Fry, Lewis, 647
Fuchs, Klaus, 878
Fugitive Slave Act (1850), 423–425
Fulbright, J. William, 924
Fulton, Robert, 353
Fundamental Constitutions of Carolina, 57–58
Fundamentalists, 668, 774, 775
Fundamental Orders, 51
Fur trade
    Dutch, 41
    French in, 37–38, 70, 125
    westward expansion and, 399–400, *399, 400*

G

Gabriel Prosser's Rebellion (1800), 336
Gadsden, Christopher, 148, 157
Gagarin, Yuri, 904
Gage, Thomas, 154, 167, 168, 171, 181
Gag rule, 312, 380, 383
Galbraith, John Kenneth, 893
Gallatin, Albert, 264, 265, 278
Galloway, Joseph, 157
Gálvez, José de, 124
Gama, Vasco da, 17
Gang system, 326
Gardoqui, Don Diego de, 220
Garfield, James A., 501, 634, 637, 640, 643, 701
Garland, Judy, 836
Garrison, William Lloyd, 378, 379–381, 440
    Liberator, 312, 379, *379*
Garvey, Marcus, 766
Gaspee, 153
Gates, Bill, 1004
Gates, Horatio, 184
General Accounting Office, 760
General Agreement on Tariffs and Trades (GATT), 1006
General Electric Co., 567, 757, 758, 958
General Electric Theater, 886
General Federation of Women's Clubs, 666, 763
General Motors, 757, 758, 759, 804
General Union for Promoting the Observance of the Christian Sabbath, 368–369
Genêt, Edmond, 246
Gentlemen's Agreement, 713
George, Henry, 578
George II, king of England, 118, 119
George III, king of England, 139, 146, 152, 170, 172, 173, 190
Georgia
    American Revolution in, 187, *188*
    Civil War, 469, 485–486, *486,* 488, 489
    Indian removal, 303–305, *304, 305*
    ratification of Constitution, 227
    secession, 442, *443*
    settlement of, 85
    slavery in, 85, 239

Germans
    in colonial settlements, *236,* 237
    immigration of, in the nineteenth century, 360, 361, 430, 580
Germany
    Berlin blockade, 868
    Berlin Wall, 900, 973, *973*
    reunification of, 973, *973*
    in World War I, 725, 726–727
    in World War II, 821–823, *822,* 828–830, 844–846
Geronimo, 607
Gerry, Elbridge, 226
Gettysburg, battle of (1863), 472–474, *474, 475,* 489, 491
Ghana, 11
Ghent, treaty of (1814), 278
Ghettos, 587, 765, 930
Ghost Dance, 608
Giannini, Amadeo Pietro, 584
Gibbons, Thomas, 356
Gibbons v. Ogden 356
GI Bill of Rights (Servicemen's Readjustment Act) (1944), 859
Giddings, Joshua R., 383
Gilbert, Humphrey, 28–29
Gilded Age, 565
Gilman, Charlotte Perkins, 729, 770
Gilmore, Quincy Adams, 469
Gingrich, Newt, 997
Ginsberg, Allen, 894
Ginsburg, Ruth Bader, 1008
Gladden, Washington, 664
Gladstone, William, 467
Glasnost, 971
Glass-Steagall Act, 794, 795
Gleason, Jackie, 890
Glenn, John, 904
Glorieta Pass, battle of (1862), 477
Glorious Revolution, 117, 118–119
Goldman, Emma, 747
Gold rush, 421–422, *421,* 610
Gold Rush, The, 757
Gold standard, 653, 940
Goldwater, Barry, 912
Goliad, 406
Gompers, Samuel, 578, 709
Gonzales, Rodolfo, 932
Good Neighbor Policy, 778
Gorbachev, Mikhail, 971, *971,* 972–974
Gordon, John B., 516
Gordon, Thomas, 147
Gore, Al, 994
    election of 2000 and, 1013–1015, *1014*
Gore, Thomas, 728
Gorsuch, Edward, 425
Gospel of Wealth, 575–576
Government
    contract theory of, 173
    growth of, 1877–1900, 637–639
    minorities and women in, 1008–1011, *1012*
    in the 1920s, 760–764
    progressive reforms of state, 68–681
    representation, colonial, 120
Graham, Billy, 892
Grand Banks, 30–31
Grand Coulee Dam, 808, 832
Grandfather clauses, 549
Grand Settlement of 1701, 127
Grange, 540, 635–636
Granger, A. O., 544
Granger laws, 635, 642

Grant, Ulysses S., *487, 637*
  Civil War and, 462–463, 475, 484–486, 490
  election of 1868 and, 512
  election of 1872 and, 518–519
Grapes of Wrath (Steinbeck), 785, 802
Great Awakening, 114–116
Great Bridge, battle at, 172, 178
Great Compromise, 222–223
Great Depression. *See* Depression of 1929
Greater East Asia Co-Prosperity Sphere, 821
Great Gatsby, The (Fitzgerald), 770
Great League of Peace and Power, 71–72
Great Migration, 586–588, 764–766
Great Northern Railroad, 579
Great Plains, 397–400
Great Society, 913–914, 960
Great Uprising, 576–577, *579*
Great War. *See* World War I
Greeley, Horace, 441, 468, 518–519
Green, Anne Catherine, 108
Greenback party, 635, 643
Greenbacks, 459, 643
Greene, Nathaniel, 189
Greenhow, Rose O'Neal, 483
Greenpeace, 690
Green Spring Mansion, *110*
Greenville, treaty of (1795), 247, *247, 271*
Greer, 826
Gregg, William, 328
Gregory, Thomas, 736
Grenville, George, 144, 145
Griffith, D. W., 550
Grimké, Angelina, 351–352, 381
Grimké, Sarah, 352, 381
Griswold, Roger, *253*
Griswold v. Connecticut, 982
Guadalupe Hidalgo, treaty of (1848), 413
Guam, 708
Guanahaní, *19*
Guanahatabeys, 9
Guatemala, Eisenhower administration and, 897
Guilford Court House, 178, 189
Gulf of Tonkin Resolution, 912, 939
Gulf Oil, 569
Gun control, 998

H

Habeas Corpus Act (1863), 477–478
Hakluyt, Richard, 30–31
Hailey, Royce, 767
Hair, 928
Haiti, 701, 714, 718–719, 778
Haldeman, H. R., 943
Hale, Sarah Josepha, 371
Haley, Bill, 891
Halfway Covenant (1662), 113
Hamburg-American Line (HAPAG), 580
Hamer, Fannie Lou, 911
Hamilton, Alexander, 269
  Annapolis Convention (1786), 221
  Constitutional Convention and, 222
  dispute with Jefferson and Madison, 245
  economic programs, 242–244, 245
  election of 1796 and, 253
  Federalist and, 228

French Revolution and, 246
national debt and, 256
as secretary of the Treasury and fiscal program of, 242
Whiskey Rebellion and, 250
Hammond, James Henry, 328, 440, 467
Hammond, Lily, 543
Hampton, Fred, 932
Hampton Institute, 502, *503,* 555
Hancock, John, *148,* 151, 167, 168, 228
Hanna, Mark A., 651, 652, 712
Harding, Warren G., 747–748, 760–761
Harding, W. L., 738
Hariot, Thomas, 29
Harlan, John Marshall, 548
Harlem Renaissance, 766, *766*
Harpers Ferry, Virginia
  federal arsenal at, 364
  John Brown's raid on, 436, 438–440, *439,* 445
Harrington, Michael, 893, 910
Harrison, Benjamin, 637, 641, 647, 699, 701, 703, 704
Harrison, William Henry, 313, 314, 315–317
  pan-Indian resistance movement and, 271–272
  War of 1812 and, 277
Harrison Act (1914), 669, 676
Harvard College, 112, 113
Hat Act (1732), 102
Hatcher, Richard, 932
Havana, Cuba, 132
Hawaii, annexation of, 702–704, 707
Hawkins, John, 28
Hawthorne, Nathaniel, 376, 377–378
Hay, John, 700, 712–713
Hayes, Rutherford B., 520, 577, 637, 639–640
Haygood, Atticus G., 547
Haygood, Laura, 543
Haymarket Square demonstrations, 578
Haynes, March, 469
Haynesworth, Clement, 940
Hays, Mary Ludwig, 180
Headright system, 43
Head Start, 910
Health care, Clinton administration and, 996
Hearst, William Randolph, 591, 705
Hebrew Emigrant Aid Society, 618
Hefferman, Joseph, 798–799
Heller, Joseph, 845
Helsinki Accords, 945, 948
Hemingway, Ernest, 770, 771, *771*
Henderson, Julia, 640
Henna, José, 714
Henry, Andrew, 399
Henry, Patrick, 144, 147, 157, 222
Henry IV, king of France, 37
Henry VII, king of England, 13, 28
Henry VIII, king of England, 14, 28
Henry the Navigator, 16
Hepburn Act (1906), 669, 684–685
Hidatsas, 397
Higher Education Act (1963), 914
High Federalists, 253–257
Highway Act (1916), 689
Hill, Anita, 1009
Hill, John, *356*
Hillman, Sidney, 803
Hillsborough, Lord, 150

Hill Street Blues, 930
Hine, Lewis, *562, 572, 671*
Hippies, 928
Hirohito, emperor, 848
Hiroshima, *848,* 849
Hispanic Americans
  See also Mexican Americans
  barrios, 766–767
  civil rights and, 932–933
  Depression of 1929 and, 790
  immigration of, 978
Hispaniola, 19, 24, 55
Hiss, Alger, *877,* 878
Hitler, Adolf, 811–814, 821–822, *822,* 828, 845
Ho Chi Minh, 901
Ho Chi Minh Trail, 923
Hohokams, 7
Holiday Inn, 889
Holiness movement, 541
Holly, Buddy, 891
Holmes, James Henry, 505
Holocaust, 845–846
Holy Roman Empire, 15
Homeless in the 1980s, 966, *967*
Home mission societies, 543
Home Owners Loan Corp., 795
Homer, Winslow, *461*
Homestead Act (1862), 478, 617, 618
Homestead strike (1892), 578
Home to Harlem (McKay), 766
Homosexuals, 777, 982–983
Honduras, 778
Honeymooners, The, 890
Hood, John Bell, 486, 488
Hooker, Joseph, 472
Hooker, Thomas, 51
Hooper, William, 209
Hoover, Herbert, 732
  crash of 1929 and, 791–793
  election of 1928 and, 778–779, *779*
  election of 1932 and, 793–794, *794*
  as secretary of commerce, 760, 761, *764, 775*–776
Hoover, J. Edgar, 747, 879
Hoover Dam, 808
Hoovervilles, 788, *789*
Hope, Lugenia Burns, 554
Hopi, 8, 75, 404, 407, 601
Hopkins, Harry, 795, 800, 802, 806
Hopwood v. Texas, 1013
Horizontal integration, 569
Horses
  introduced to the Americas, 398
  Plains Indians and, 25, 398, 602
Horseshoe Bend, battle of (1814), 278–279, *280*
Horton, Willie, 967
House, Edward, 727, 730
House Made of Dawn (Momaday), 837
House of Burgesses, 43, 44, 77, 87
House of Commons, 119, 146
House of Lords, 119
House of the Seven Gables (Hawthorne), 377
House Un-American Activities Committee (HUAC), 877–878
Housing
  Archaic period, 5
  backcountry log, *123*
  barrios, 766–767
  Chesapeake, 48
  colonial, 48, 110–111, *110, 123*
  fallout shelters, *854,* 900

ghettos, 587, 765, 860, 930
Hoovervilles, 788, *789*
kivas, 8, 404
log cabins, *123, 239*
Model Cities Program, 926
settlement houses, 543, 574–575, 663, 668–670
shortages following World War I, 745
shortages following World War II, 859–860
slave, *60,* 89, 333
slums, 358
sod, *621*
subdivisions/row housing, 591
suburbs of the 1950s, 859–860, 861
tenements, 574, *575,* 576–577
Housing Act (1949), 865
Houston, Charles Hamilton, 904
Houston, Sam, 406
Howard University, 502
Howdy Doody, 890
Howe, Richard, 181–183
Howe, Samuel Gridley, 373
Howe, William, 181–183, 184
Howell, Varina, 459
Howell, William Dean, 522
Howl (Ginsberg), 894
How the Other Half Lives (Riis), 574, 576
Hudson, Henry, 40
Hudson's Bay Company, 399, 401
Huerta, Dolores, 932, *933*
Huerta, Victoriano, 719
Hughes, Charles Evans, 681, 730, *730, 776, 778*
Hughes, John, 468
Hughes, Langston, 766, *766*
Hull, Cordell, 811
Hull, William, 275
Hull House, 574–575, 669
Human sacrifice, 7
Humphrey, Hubert H., 863, 937, *938*
Hundred Years' War, 13
Hungary, 742, 973
Hunt, E. Howard, 943
Hunter, Addie W., 587
Hunter-gatherers, 3–5
Hurons, 26, 38, *39,* 70–72
Hurston, Zora Neale, 766, *766*
Hussein, Saddam, 974–976, 1020
Hutchinson, Anne, 51–52
Hutchinson, Thomas, 148, 153, 167
Huxley, Aldous, 928

I

Iacocca, Lee, 963
IBM, 1002
Ickes, Harold, 795, 806
If Christ Came to Chicago (Stead), 667
Igbos, 11, 12, 68
I Led Three Lives, 878
Illinois
  admitted to Union, 295, 393
  settlement of, 125
I Love Lucy, 890
Illinois Woman's Alliance, 636
Immigration/immigrants, *562*
  changes in from 1960–2000, 978–981
  during 1870–1900, 579–588
  employment of, 570–574, 581–584
  German, 360, 361
  illegal, 1011–1012
  Irish, 360–361

in the mining camps, 612–613
National Origins Act (1924), 771, 776
nativism, 584–586, 675–676, 771–772, 776
neighborhoods, 582–583
in the nineteenth century, 360–361, *361*, 384
old-world backgrounds, 579–582
patterns of (1820–1914), *580, 581*
Progressive Era and, 663–664, 675–676
reactions to, 384
roots of the Great, 586–588
westward expansion and, 618–621
Immigration and Nationality Act (1952), 880
Immigration and Nationality Act (1965), 978
Immigration Reform and Control Act (1986), 978
Immigration Restriction League (IRL), 585, 675
Impeachment, 207
of Clinton, 999–1000
of Andrew Johnson, 512, 637, 1000
Nixon resignation to avoid, 943, 1000
Imperialism
Chile and Venezuela, 704–705
East Asia, 710–713
expansion in the Pacific 1867–1899, *701*
Hawaii, 702–704
Latin America, 713–719
rationales for, 697–700
Seward and Blaine, 701–702
Spanish-American War, 705–710
Impressment of American sailors by Britain, 250, 269–270
In Bright Lights, Big City (McInerney), 964
Incas, 22–23
In Defense of the Indians (Las Casas), 24
Indentured servants, 38, 45–46, 56, 83, 91
Independent Treasury System, 311–312
Independent Whig, 147
Indian
See also Native Americans; *under name of tribe*
origin of the term, 2
Indiana, admitted to Union, 295, 393
Indian Removal Act (1830), 303–305, *304, 305*, 397
Indian Reorganization Act (1934), 807
Indian Rights Association, 607
Indian Territory of Oklahoma, 285, 304, *304*, 397–398, 477
Industrialization and manufacturing
by artisans, 361–362
assembly line, 754
between 1870–1900, 565–579
children as workers, 362
conditions in the early 1900s, 662–663, 665–666
corporations, role of, 567–570
cotton mills, 362
deindustrialization, 947–948
factory system, 362
following World War I, 756–760
Gospel of Wealth, 575–576
horizontal integration, 569

in Jefferson's America, 361
household manufacturing, 361
interchangeable machine-made parts/ American system of, 364
mass production, 756
New Deal and, 796–797
in the New South, 532–537
pollution from, 364
Progressive Era, 662–664
putting-out system, 361
reconversion following World War II, 857–858
role of technology, 362, 363–364
sources of workers for, 362–363
technology, role of, 565–567
textile mills, 359–360, *360, 361*
use of British technology, 362
vertical integration, 569
women as workers, 362–363, *363*
World War II, effects of, 832
Industrial Workers of the World (IWW), 666, 737
Infant mortality, in the early 1900s, 574
Inflation
in the 1970s, 940
Reagan administration and, 961–962
Influence of Sea Power Upon History, The (Mahan), 699
Ingram, Billy, 767
In His Steps (Sheldon), 664, 667
Initiative, 680–681
Insular Cases, 714
Intendants, 38, 139
Inter-America Conference, 778
Intermediate Nuclear Force (INF), 971, 972
Internal Security Act (1950), 880
International Association for Labor Legislation, 667
International Ladies Garment Workers Union (ILGWU), 666
International Monetary Fund (IMF), 866
International Telephone and Telegraph, 775
Internet, 1001, 1002, 1003–1006
Interstate Commerce Act (1887), 641, 642
Interstate Commerce Commission (ICC), 642, 684
Intolerable Acts (1774), 154–155
Iowa
admitted to Union, 395
settlement of, 398
Iran
-Contra scandal, 970–971
Eisenhower administration and, 897
hostage crisis, 949–950, *950*
Iraq
Coalition war against, 1020–1021
Persian Gulf War, 974–976, *976*
Ireland, 28
Irish immigrants, 360–361, 363, 384, 430–431, 584
Iroquois, 9, 26, 27, *39*, 41
American Revolution and, 181, 185, 194
Beaver Wars, 71–72, 76, 78–80
Confederacy, 181, 206, 216
French and Indian War (1756–1763), 126, 129–132
Grand Settlement of 1701, 127
King George's War (1739–1748),

126, 128–129
King William's War (1689–1697), 126–127
Lancaster, treaty of (1744), 129
League, 71–72, 126, 127
Irreconcilables, 744
Isabella, queen of Spain, 13, 14, 19
Islam, 12
Island hopping campaign, 846–847
Israel, 897, 948, 1021
Italian immigrants, 580, 582, 584, 586
Italy
in World War I, 725
in World War II, 821, 822, 842
Iwo Jima, 847

J

Jackie Gleason Show, The, 890
Jackson, Andrew, *301*
Bank War, 301, 308–309
Battle of New Orleans and, 278–280
Creeks and, 278–279, *280*
Eaton Affair, 306–307
election of 1824 and, 287–288
election of 1828 and, 300–301
inauguration of, 302, *302*
Indian Removal Act (1830), 303–305, *304, 305*
invasion of Florida, 283
nullification crisis, 301, 305–308
presidency of, 301–309
Texas and, 317
Jackson, Jesse, 981
Jackson, Maynard, 1010
Jackson, Stonewall, 462, 465, 472
Jacksonian Democrats, 295, 299–301
Jamaica, 19, 55, 59
James I, king of England, 42, 44, 49
James II, king of England (duke of York), 62, 116–117, 119
Jamestown, 42–43
Japan
invasion of China and Manchuria, 821
occupation of, 867
Russo-Japanese War, 713
in World War I, 725
in World War II, 821, 826–828, 830, 846–847
Japanese Association of America, 583
Japanese Claims Act (1948), 839
Japanese immigrants, 581, 584, 586, 771
internment of, during World War II, 838–839, *839*, 840–841
Jay, John, 190, *192*, 219, 220–221, 228, 250
Jay's Treaty (1794), 250–251
Jazz, 769
Jefferson, Thomas, 112, *173*, 208, 239
Alien and Sedition Acts (1789) and, 253–254
Declaration of Independence and, *173*–174
dispute with Hamilton, 245
election of 1796 and, 252
election of 1800 and, 257
election of 1804 and, 263
Embargo Act (1807), 269–270
Florida and western schemes, 268–269
French Revolution and, 246
Louisiana Purchase and, 266–268, *268*
Ordinance of 1784 and, 216

presidency of, 263–270
reforms, 263–266
slaves/slavery and, 174, 216
states' rights and, 254
Jell-O, 591
Jesuits, 38, 75, *75*, 139
Jews
anti-Semitism, 773, 775, 822, 825
concentration camps, 813, 822, 845–846, *846*
Holocaust, 845–846
immigrants, 580, 581, 584, 586
Kristallnacht, *811*, 813, 822
Jiang Jieshi (Chiang Kai-shek), 821, 841, 870–871
Jim Crow laws, 548, *549*
Job Corps, 910
Joffre, Joseph, 737
Johnson, Andrew, 701
impeachment of, 512, 637, 1000
Reconstruction plan, 507–512
Southern Homestead Act and, 503
Johnson, Anthony, 86–87
Johnson, Hiram, 681, 732, 734, 736, 744, 777
Johnson, Hugh, 797
Johnson, James Weldon, 766
Johnson, Lyndon B., 803
civil rights and, 910–911
election of 1964 and, 911–914
environmental issues, 942
Great Society, 913–914
oath of office as President, 909, *910*
Vietnam War, 912, 920–926, 935–936
War on Poverty, 909–910
Johnson, Richard M., 295
Johnston, Joseph E., 462, 465, 484, 485–486, 488, 490, 492
Joint-stock companies, 42, 50
Jones, Charles Colcock, 345
Jones, Jim, 930
Jones, John Paul, 186, *186*
Jones, Mother (Mary Harris), 672–673
Jones, Paula, 999
Jones, Sam, 538
Jones, Samuel "Golden Rule," 680
Journeymen, 361–362, 367
Juárez, Benito, 467
Judicial nationalism, 281–282
Judicial review, 225
Judiciary Act (1789), 242, 266
Judiciary Act (1801), 265–266
Julian, George W., 508, 509–510
Jungle, The (Sinclair), 571, 665, 754

K

Kaczynski, Ted, 998
Kaiser, Henry J., 832
Kalb, Johann, 177
Kansas
Bleeding, 429–430, 445
cattle ranching in, 614–615
homesteading, 617
Kansas Farmer, 617, 645
Kansas Indians, 397
Kansas-Nebraska Act, 428–429, *429*, 445
Kaskaskia, battle of, 178, 185
Kazan, Elia, 878
Kearney, 826
Kearny, Stephen W., 413
Keating-Owen Act (1916), 669, 670–671, 689
Kelley, Abby, 381

Kelley, Florence, 666
Kellogg-Briand Pact (1928), 777
Kellor, Frances, 676
Kemp, Jack, 960, 968
Kennan, George, 866, 867, 924
Kennedy, Jacqueline, 899, *901, 910*
Kennedy, John F., *901*
  assassination of, 909
  civil rights and, 906–909
  Cuban missile crisis, 901–904
  election of 1960 and, 899, *900*
  mistakes, 900–901
  mystique, 899–900
Kennedy, Robert, 908, 936, 937
Kent State University, 938–939, *939*
Kentucky
  Civil War, 462
  secession, 460–461
  settlement of, 240
  as a slave state, 284
  statehood for, 240
Kern-McGillicuddy Act, 689
Kettle Creek, battle of, 178, 187
Key, Francis Scott, 278
Keynes, John Maynard, 809
Khomeini, Ayatollah Ruholla, 949
Khrushchev, Nikita, 893, *894*, 899, 900, 903
Kieft, Willem, 41–42
Kim Il Sung, 873
King, Martin Luther, Jr.
  assassination of, 937
  Birmingham campaign, 908–909, *908*
  March on Washington (1963), 908–909
  Montgomery bus boycott, 907, 982
  Selma campaign, 911
  Southern Christian Leadership Conference (SCLC), 908
  Vietnam War and, 925
King, Rodney, 968
King George's War (1739–1748), 126, 127–129
King of Kings, The, 769
King Philip's War, 76–77
Kingsley, Bathsheba, 116
Kings Mountain, battle of, 178, 189
King William's War (1689–1697), 126–127
Kiowas, 404, 603, 606, 609
Kissinger, Henry A., 939, 940
Kitchin, Claude, 731
Kivas, 8, 404
Klamaths, 888
Klute, 930
Knights of Labor, 554, 577–578, 636
Know-Nothings, 431, 432, 584
Eastman Kodak, 567, 758
Kohl, Helmut, 973
Korean War, 872–875, *873, 874*
Korematsu v. U.S., 839
Kosciuszko, Tadeusz, 175, 177
Kosovo, 995
Kristallnacht, 811, 813, 822
Ku Klux Klan, 516–517, *517,* 550, 772–773, *773*
Ku Klux Klan Act (1871), 517
Kursk Salient, 842
Kushner, Tony, 983
Kuwait, Persian Gulf War, 974–976, *976*
Kwakiutls, 5

L

Labor
  See also Employment;

Industrialization and manufacturing; Slavery; Slaves; Strikes; Unions
  apprentices, 108
  changing nature of, 570–571
  child, 92, 362, 367, 571, 663, 670, *670, 671,* 672–673, 763
  conditions in the early 1900s, 662–663, 665–666
  in 1870–1910, *567,* 570–574
  eight-hour workday, 685
  in English colonies, 91–93
  Fordism, 755
  immigrant, 93, 95
  indentured servants, 38, 45–46, 56, 83, 91
  in the mining camps, 614
  Progressive Era and, 662–663, 665–666
  redemptioner system, 91
  T. Roosevelt and, 682
  sweatshops, 571
  tenancy, 91
  unions, 367
  uprisings, 576–579
  women in, 571–574
Ladies' Association of Philadelphia, 193
Ladies' Memorial Associations, 544
Lafayette, Marquis de, 175
La Follette, Robert M., 681, 685, 686, 731, 744, 747, 762
Laird, Melvin, 938
Laissez-faire politics, 637
Lake Erie, 276–277
Lakotas, 477, 602, 605
Lancaster, treaty of (1744), 129
Land Grant College Act (1862), 478
Landon, Alfred M., 803
Land Ordinance (1785), 216–217, *217*
Land ownership
  See also Westward expansion
  for African Americans, in Reconstruction period, 502–504
  claims clubs, 394
  contractual property rights, 282
  differences between England and colonies, 120
  European seizure of Native American land, 72–73, 123, 142
  government land policy in 1865–1890, 618
  headright system, 43
  Homestead Act (1862), 478
  Land Grant College Act (1862), 478
  problems of overcrowding (1790–1850), 391–393
  republicanism and, 203
  sharecropping, 523
  squatters, 240, 394
  women and, 204
Langdon (Landon), Eunice, 784, 785
Lange, Dorothea, *801*
Lansing, Robert, 727
Lansing-Ishii Agreement (1917), 713
Larkin, Thomas, 410
La Salle, Sieur de (Robert), 39
Las Casas, Bartolomé de, 24
Las Gorras Blancas (White Caps), 620
Lathrop, Julia, 670
Latin America (1899–1917)
  Cuba as U.S. protectorate, 714–716
  dollar diplomacy, 717–718

overview of U.S. interventions in, 714
  Panama Canal, 716
  Roosevelt Corollary, 717
  U.S. rule in Puerto Rico, 714
  Wilsonian interventions, 718–719
Latvia, 742
Laurens, Henry, 151, 166, *192*
Laurens, John, 165–167, 180, *180*
Lawes Divine, Morall and Martiall, 43
League of Armed Neutrality, 185
League of Freedom, 424
League of Nations, 742, 744
League of United Latin American Citizens (LULAC), 767
League of Women Voters, 763, 805, 1009
Leary, Timothy, 928
Lease, Mary E., 645, 646
Leave It to Beaver, 890
Leaves of Grass (Whitman), 377
Lebanon, 970, 1021
Lecompton Constitution, 433–434, 445
Lee, Ann (Mother Ann), 375
Lee, Jason, 401
Lee, Richard Henry, 173
Lee, Robert E., 439, 465–466, *465,* 467–468, 472–474, 484, 484–486, 487, 490, 499, 499, 557
Legislative action, overview of colonial, 156
Leisler, Jacob, 117
Lemke, William, 800, 803
Lend-lease program (1941), 826
Lenin, V. I., 739, 740
Leopard, 270
Le Seur, Meridel (Merideth), 784, 785
Less Than Zero (Ellis), 964
Lethal Weapon, 958
Letters from an American Farmer (Crèvecoeur), 208–209
Levitt, William, 859, *889*
Levittown, 856, 859, 860, *889*
Lewelling, Lorenzo D., 648–649
Lewinsky, Monica, 999
Lewis, John, 909, 911
Lewis, John L., 797, 858
Lewis, Sinclair, 770
Lewis and Clark expedition, 267, *268,* 286–287, 399
Lexington, battle of (1775), 168–170, *169,* 178
Leyte Gulf, battle of, 847
Liberal Republicans, 516, 518
Liberator, 312, 379, 379
*Liberty, 151
Liberty Association, 424
Liberty Bonds, 734–735, *735*
Liberty party, 382, 383
Liddy, G. Gordon, 943
Life, 836
Liliuokalani, Queen, 703
Limited Test Ban Treaty (1963), 850, 904, 972
Lincoln, Abraham, 384, 439, *490,* 506–507, 701
  assassination of, 490–492
  Civil War, 455–456, 459, 460–461, 462, 465, 471, 474, 477, 484, 490
  debates with Douglas, 434–435, *435*
  election of 1860 and, 441–442, *442*
  election of 1864 and, 478,

487–488
  Emancipation Proclamation (1863), 468–469
  Fort Sumter, 446–447
  habeas corpus and, 477–478
  inauguration, 444
  Reconstruction plan of, 506–507
  secession and, 443, 444
  on slavery, 446–447
Lincoln, Benjamin, *190*
Lincoln, Mary Todd, 434
Lindbergh, Charles, 770, 824, 826
Linn, William, 255
Lippmann, Walter, 748, 865
Literacy rates, colonial, 111
Literature
  Age of Enlightenment, 112–113
  colonial, 111–112
  Harlem Renaissance, 766, *766*
  Lost Generation, 770–771
  muckraking journalism, 663, 665
  in the 1980s, 964
Lithuania, 742
Little, Malcolm, 932
Little Bighorn, battle of (1876), 606
Little Crow, 398
Little Mountain, 609
Little Rock, Arkansas, 906, *906*
Little Turtle (Mishikinakwa), 247, *247,* 248
Lloyd George, David, 741–742
Lochner v. New York, 668
Locke, John, 57, 59–60, 112, 146, 173
Lodge, Henry Cabot, 697, 700, 702, 705, 706, 744
Logan, James, 73
London Company, 42
Lone Star Federation, 544
Long, Huey P., 800, 801, 803
Long, Stephen, 397
Long Island, slavery on, 62
Longstreet, James, 475, 519
Lords of Trade, 117, 119
Los Alamos, 820, 834
Los Angeles
  growth of, 588, 764
  Mexican Americans in, 766
Losing Ground (Murray), 960
Lost Cause, 499–500, 544, *545,* 556
Lost Generation, 770–771
Loudoun, Lord, 130
Louis, Joe, 861
Louis XI, king of France, 13, 14
Louis XIV, king of France, 38, 126, 246
Louisbourg, 128, 131
Louisiana
  French settlement of, 125
  naming of, 39
  secession, 442, *443*
  as a slave state, 284
Louisiana Purchase, 266–268, *268*
Love Canal, 942, 944–945
Lovejoy, Elijah P., 380
L'Ouverture, Touissant, 267
Lowell, Massachusetts, 359–360, *360*
Lower South, defined, 325
Loyalists/Tories, 160, 167–168
Loyalty programs, 876–877, 1018–1019
Lucas, John Gray, 545–546
Lucy, Autherine, 906
Lusitania, 728
Luther, Martin, 14–15
Luther, Seth, 296
Lutheranism, 114, 207, 237

Lynch, John R., 522
Lynching, 546–547, *546*
Lyon, Matthew, 253, *253*
Lyon, Pat, *362*

M

MacArthur, Douglas
    Bonus Army and, 793
    Korean War and, 874–875
    occupation of Japan and, 867
    World War II and, 846–847
Macdonough, Thomas, 278
MacIntosh, Ebenezer, 147–148
Maclay, William, 233–234
Macon, Nathaniel, 271
Macon's Bill No. 2 (1810), 271
Macune, Charles W., 540, 541, 542
Maddox, 912
Madero, Francisco, 719
Madison, Dolley, *266*
Madison, James, 214, 221, *228*, 268,
    378
    Alien and Sedition Acts (1789)
      and, 253–254
    Annapolis Convention (1786)
      and, 221
    Bill of Rights and, 241
    Constitutional Convention and,
      222, 223, 225
    dispute with Hamilton, 245
    election of 1808, 270
    election of 1812, 276
    Federalist and, 228
    Marbury v. Madison, 266
    presidency of, 270–280
    ratification of Constitution and,
      228
    states' rights and, 254
    Tonnage Act of 1789 and, 242
    Virginia Plan, 222
    War of 1812, 272–280, *274, 279*
Maentel, Jacob, *237*
Magon, Ricardo Flores, 736
Mahan, Alfred Thayer, 699–700, 702,
    705
Mahanism, 699–700
Mailer, Norman, 924
Maine, 706
Maine, admitted to Union, 284, 295
Malcolm X, 932
Mali, 11
Mallory, Stephen R., 427
Manassas. *See* Bull Run
Mandans, 8, 397
Mandingo, 82
Manhattan Project, 834
Manifest Destiny, 390, 408–410, 412,
    697, 700
Manila, Philippines, 132, 710, 829
Mann, Horace, 372
Mann-Elkins Act (1910), 676, 685
Man Nobody Knows, The (Barton),
    762–763
Manufacturing. *See* Industrialization
    and manufacturing
Mao Zedong (Mao Tse-tung), 868,
    872, 940
Marbury, William, 266
Marbury v. Madison, 266
March on Washington (1963), 908
Marcos, Ferdinand, 971
Marcy, Moses, *98*
Marion, Francis, 189
Marriage
    changing views of in the 1970s,
      927, 928

English-Indian, 43, 47
interracial, 87, *124*
in New England, 53, 237
in the 1950s, 861
of slaves, 88, 334
World War II and, 836
Married Women's Property Act
    (1860), 382
Marshall, George C., 842, 867, 880
Marshall, James, 421
Marshall, John, 266, 269, 281–282,
    281, 305, 356
Marshall, Thurgood, 904
Marshall Plan, 867
Martí, José, 705
Martine, Carlotta Silvas, 783, 785
Mary I, queen of England, 28, 117
Maryland
    Civil War, 467–468, 489
    colony, overview of, 59
    labor system in, 92
    ratification of Constitution, 228
    secession, 460
    settlement of, 46–47, 59
    slavery in, 83
Maryland Gazette, 108
Mason, David, *53*
Mason, George, 207, 226
Mason, James M., 423, 440
Mason, Margaretta, 440
Masons, 313–314
Massachusetts
    American Revolution in, 168–170,
      171
    Conciliatory Proposition, 168
    Government Act (1774), 154, 155
    Lexington and Concord, battles of
      (1775), 168–170, *169,* 178
    labor system in, 92
    ratification of Constitution, 228
    religion in, 235
Massachusetts Bay Colony, 49–52, 59
Massachusetts Bay Company, 50
Massasoit, 49
Massive retaliation doctrine, 895–896
Mather, Cotton, 112
Mauldin, Bill, 835
Maverick, Maury, 739
Maximilian, 467
Maxwell House coffee, 591
Mayans, 5
Mayer, Louis B., 877
Mayflower, 49
Mayflower Compact, 49
Mayhew, Thomas, Jr., 76
Maysville Road Bill, 302–303
McAdoo, William, 727, 732, 735
McCarran Committee, 877–878
McCarthy, Eugene, 935–936
McCarthy, Joseph R., 879–880, *879*
McCarthyism, 879–880
McClellan, George B., 465, 466, 468,
    471, 478, 484, 486
McClure, Samuel S., 665
McClure's Magazine, 665, 667, 676
McCormick, Cyrus, 394, *395*
McCormick reaper, 394–395
McCoy, Joseph, 614
McCrea, Jane, 181
McCulloch v. Maryland, 282
McDonald's, 889
McDowell, Calvin, 546–547
McDowell, Irvin, 462
McFarlane, Robert, 970
McGillivray, Alexander, 220, *221*
McGovern, George, 943

McInerney, Jay, 964
McKay, Claude, 766
McKelway, Alexander, 676
McKinley, William, 640
    assassination of, 681
    election of 1896 and, 651–653,
      652
    foreign policy, 706–710
McKinley Tariff Act (1890), 641, 651,
    703
McLemore, Jeff, 728
McNamara, John, 991–992
McNamara, Robert S., 902, 912, 922,
    942
McVeigh, Timothy, 998
Meade, George Gordon, 472–474,
    484, 485
Meadows, William R., 516
Meat Inspection Act (1906), 669, 684
Meatpacking industry, 569, 571, 665
Medicaid, 914
Medical Care Act, 914
Medicare, 914
Mellon, Andrew, 760–761
Melville, Herman, 377, 378, 593
Memorial Day Massacre, 804
Memphis Appeal, 441
Mencken, H. L., 771, 775, 778
Mendes, 11
Mennonites, 114, 237
Menominees, 888
Mercantilism, 101
Meredith, James, 906
Merrick, John, *554*
Mesoamerica, 5–7
Mestizos, 75, *124,* 403
Metacom, 76–77
Methodist Episcopal Church, 345
Methodists, 205, 274, 297–299
Mexican Americans
    See also Hispanic Americans
    civil rights for, 905
    as cowhands, 616
    Depression of 1929 and, 790
    employment in the 1950s, 888
    New Deal and, 807
    westward expansion and, 620–621
    World War II and, 837
Mexican borderlands, 403–405
Mexican Cession of 1848, 408
Mexican immigrants, 583–584, 675, 978
Mexican War, 408, 410–413, *411*
Mexico
    Spanish conquest of, 24
    U.S. intervention in, 714, 719
    Wilson administration and, 719
Miamis, 181, 240, 247, *247,* 248
Miami Vice, 930
Miantonomo, 52
Michigan, admitted to Union, 395
Microsoft Corp., 1004–1005
Middle class, 365, *366*
    black, in the 1880s, 552–554
    new, 590–591
Middle Passage, description of cross-
    ing the Atlantic, 82, *85*
Midway, battle of, 830
Mifflin, Thomas and Sara Morris, *151*
Migration, Great, 586–588, 764–766
Milholland, Inez, 659–661
Military Reconstruction Acts (1867),
    512, 521
Miller, Alfred James, *403*
Miller, Dorrie, *835*
Mills, C. Wright, 893, 926
Milwaukee, 359

Miners' Union Library, 614
Mining industry
    exploitation of, 610–613
    strikes, 614, 737, 746, 759
Minorities
    Depression of 1929 and, 790
    in government, 1008–1011, *1012*
Minor v. Happersett, 632
Minuit, Peter, 40
Minutemen, 167, 169
Miranda, Francisco de, 203
Mishikinakwa (Little Turtle), 247,
    247, 248
Missionaries
    imperialism and, 698–699
    Native Americans and, 73–76, 123,
      401, 403
Mississippi
    admitted to Union, 295, 395
    Civil War, 463, 475, 477
    Freedom Summer project, 911
    secession, 442, *443*
    as a slave state, 284
Mississippians, 8
Mississippi Freedom Democratic Party
    (MFDP), 911
Mississippi River, Spain and, 219–221
Mississippi Valley, French in, 125
Missouri
    admitted to Union, 295, 395
    Civil War, 477
    secession, 460
Missouri Compromise, 284–285, 428,
    444
Mitchell, John, 682, 711
Moby Dick (Melville), 378
Moctezuma, *1,* 20, *21,* 22
Model Cities Program, 926
Modocs, 606
Mohawks, 71, 181
Mohegans, 51
Molasses Act (1733), 102, 104
Momaday, M. Scott, 837
Mondale, Walter, 959, 1008
Monmouth Court House, battle of,
    180, 178, 185
Monopolies, 356–357
Monroe, James, 218, 378
    presidency of, 280–283
Monroe Doctrine, 283, 704, 717, 778
Montagnais, 38
Montauks, 116
Montcalm, Marquis de, 130, 131
Montgomery, Bernard, 830
Montgomery bus boycott, 907–908
Montgomery Ward, 622, 786
Monticello, *265*
Montreal, 37, 38
Montserrat, 59
Moody, Dwight, *554*
Moon, Sun Myung, 930
Moore, A. M., *554*
Moore, John Bassett, 710
Moore's Creek Bridge, battle of, 172,
    178
Morality
    in the 1920s, 770
    in the 1970s, 986
Moral Majority, 448, 984–985
Moral reform movement
    backlash against, 371
    benevolent empire, 368–369
    Sabbatarian movement, 368–369
    Sunday schools, 368
    temperance movement, 369–370
    women, role of, 370–371

Morals Efficiency League, 676–677
Moravians, 76, 237
Morgan, Daniel, 189
Morgan, John, 700
Morgan, J. P., 569, 650, 684
Morgan, William, 313
Mormons, 371, 407–408, 603, 618
Morrill Act (1862), 617, 618
Morris, Robert, 173, 211–212
Morrison, Philip, 833
Morse, Omar H., 391
Mortality rates, trappers and, 400
Moss, Tom, 546–547
Mother Bethel Church, 206
Motley, Constance Baker, 904–905
Mott, Lucretia, 381, 382
Mound-building societies, 8–9
Mount Vernon, 111
Movies
    Hollywood and 1920s, 757, 769
    in the 1950s, 891, 892
    urban crisis depicted in, 930
    World War II, 836
Mrs. Miniver, 836
Ms., 927, 927
MTV (Music Television), 1003
Muckrakers, 663, 665
Mugwumps, 636, 639, 641
Muir, John, 684, 690
Mulattoes, 344
Mulberry Plantation, 60
Muller v. Oregon, 671
Multinational corporations, 775
Munn v. Illinois, 642
Murray, Charles, 960
Murray, Judith Sargeant, 235
Music
    jazz, 769
    in the 1980s, 964
    protest, 926, 928–929
    rock 'n' roll, 891–892, 892
    Woodstock, 928
Mussolini, Benito, 812, 821, 828

N

NAACP (National Association for the
    Advancement of Colored People)
    Confederate battle flag and, 557
    formation of, 556, 678
Nagasaki, 848, 849
Napier, J. C., 553
Napoleon Bonaparte, 267–268, 270,
    271, 277
Napoleon III, 467
Narragansetts, 49, 51, 70, 73, 76
Narrative of the Life of Frederick Douglass,
    an American Slave (Douglass), 382
NASA (National Aeronautics and
    Space Administration)
    formation of, 896
    space exploration, 896
Nash, Gary, 195
Nashville, battle of (1864), 488, 489
Nast, Thomas, 520
Nation, 518
National Advisory Commission on
    Civil Disorders, 931
National Americanization Committee,
    676
National American Woman Suffrage
    Association (NAWSA), 636, 663,
    678
National and Community Service
    Trust Act, 996
National Association for the
    Advancement of Colored People.

See NAACP
National Association of Colored
    Women, 554, 888
National Association of
    Manufacturers, 668, 680, 757
National Banking Act (1863), 478
National Birth Control League,
    674–675
National Black Convention, 424, 426
National Child Labor Committee,
    663, 670, 676
National Civil Service Reform League,
    636
National Congress of American
    Indians, 837–838
National Congress of Mothers, 666
National Consumers' League, 663,
    666, 667, 805
National Council of Negro Women,
    806
National debt issues, 242, 256, 264
National Defense Act (1916), 729
National Defense Advisory
    Commission, 825
National Defense Education Act
    (NDEA) (1958), 896
National Endowment for the Arts, 913
National Endowment for the
    Humanities, 913
National Environmental Policy Act
    (1970), 942
National Farmers Union, 680
National Gazette, 251
National History Standards, 195
National Housing Act, 810
National Housing Association, 670
National Industrial Recovery Act
    (NIRA) (1933), 795, 796–797
Nationalists, 211
National Labor Relations Act (1935),
    800
National Labor Relations Board
    (NLRB), 800, 962
National League, 592
National Mobilization Committee to
    End the War in Vietnam, 937
National Organization for Women
    (NOW), 927
National Origins Act (1924), 771, 776
National parks, creation of, 683, 683
National Progressive League, 686
National Reclamation Act (1902), 684
National Recovery Administration
    (NRA), 796–797
National Republicans, 300, 312
National Rifle Association, 998
National Security Act (1947), 868
National Security Council (NSC)
    formation of, 868
    Iran-Contra scandal and, 970–971
    Nicaraguan Contras and, 970
    Paper 68, 872
National Security League, 729
National Trades Union (NTU), 367
National Union for Social Justice, 800
National War Labor Board (NWLB),
    731, 733
National Woman's Party (NWP), 763
National Women's Political Caucus,
    1009
National Youth Administration
    (NYA), 802–803
Nation of Islam (NOI), 932
Native American Graves Protections
    and Repatriation Act (1990), 623
Native American Religious Freedom

Act (1978), 623
Native Americans
    See also Archaic period; under name
        of tribe
    after the American Revolution,
        206–207, 240
    agriculture, 4–5, 4, 403–404
    Americanization, 607–610,
        622–623
    American Revolution and, 181,
        185, 194
    Bacon's Rebellion, 76, 77
    Beaver Wars, 71–72
    before 1492, 2–9
    Black Hawk's War, 304–305, 398
    Cherokee War (1759–1761),
        142–143, 143
    civil rights for, 933, 934
    Civil War and, 477
    contacts with Europeans, 68–80
    cultural perceptions and misper-
        ceptions, 26–27
    Dawes Act (1887), 609
    destruction of buffalo, 605, 606
    diseases introduced to, 21–22,
        25–26, 70–71, 399, 401, 603
    education of, 607, 608, 674
    European seizure of land, 72–73,
        123, 142
    federal government policy toward,
        603
    fighting between, 71–72
    French and Indian War
        (1756–1763), 126, 129–132
    Ghost Dance, 608
    Indian Removal Act (1830),
        303–304, 304, 305
    King George's War (1739–1748),
        126, 127–129
    King Philip's War, 76–77, 78–79
    King William's War (1689–1697),
        126–127
    as laborers, 69–70
    land cessions (1784–1800), 247,
        249
    land cessions (1860–1894), 604
    life on the reservation, 607–610
    missionaries and, 73–76, 123, 401,
        403
    New Deal and, 806–807
    in the 1950s, 888
    in the 1990s, 622–623
    origin of the term Indian, 2
    pan-Indian resistance movement,
        271–272
    Pontiac's Rebellion (1763–1766),
        143
    population of, from 1600–1730,
        70
    Pueblo Revolt, 76, 77–78
    religion, 602–603, 607–608
    as slaves, 77, 81
    Sun Dance, 607
    trade between Europeans and,
        70–72
    Trail of Tears, 304, 304, 306–307
    tribes and cultures, 601–603
    warfare and dispossession,
        603–607
    westward expansion and affects
        on, 240, 397–403
    women, 609
    World War I and, 737
    World War II and, 835, 837–838
Native Sons of the Golden State, 586
Nativism, 584–586, 675–676, 771–772,

776
Nativists, 367, 384
NATO (North Atlantic Treaty
    Organization)
    formation of, 868
    massive retaliation doctrine,
        895–896
    reinvention of, 995–996
Nat Turner's Rebellion (1831), 306,
    336, 336, 378–379
Naturalization Act (1798), 253
Naturalization Act (1870), 585
Natural rights, 206
Navajo Community College, 933
Navajos, 404, 407, 477, 602, 607, 835
Naval Advisory Board, 700
Naval Construction Act, 729
Navigation Acts (1651, 1660, 1696),
    101, 102, 117, 119
Navy
    American Revolution and,
        185–186, 186
    Civil War and, 466–467
    formation of, 170
    Quasi-War and, 253
    War of 1812 and, 275, 276–277
NBC (National Broadcasting Co.),
    769
Nebraska
    Kansas-Nebraska Act, 428–429,
        429
    settlement of, 428
Negro Seamen's Act, 336
Neighborhood Guild, 574
Neighborhood Union, 554, 677
Nelson, Gaylord, 941
Neoconservative, 960
Neoliberal, 996
Neolin, 143
Neutrality acts (1935, 1936, 1937),
    812, 824
Nevis, 59
New Amsterdam, 40–41
New Deal, 785
    African Americans and, 805–806
    agricultural policy, 796
    banking industry and, 794–795
    chronology, 787
    coalition, 803
    criticism of, 797–800
    Dust Bowl, 802, 802
    end of, 809–810
    Hispanic Americans and, 807
    Hundred Days, 794, 795
    industry and, 796–797
    jobs, creating, 795–796
    legislation, summary of, 795
    Native Americans and, 806–807
    relief programs, 801–802
    second, 800–803
    in the South, 807–808
    unions and, 800, 804
    water policies, 807, 808
    in the West, 808
    women and, 804–805
New Echota, treaty of (1835), 306
New England
    agriculture, 55
    economy, 53–55
    founding of, 48–55
    government in, 50, 54
    growth of, 53
    King Philip's War, 76–77
    laborers in, 91–93
    Massachusetts Bay Colony, 49–52
    missionaries in, 75–76

Plymouth Colony, 48–49
population of, 53, *84*
Puritanism in, 48–50
in the 1790s, 235, 237
slavery in, 235
social classes in, 54
towns, 53–54
women in, 53, 235, 237, *237*
New England Anti-Slavery Society, 379
New England Non-Resistant Society, 380
New England Woman Suffrage Association, 513
New Federalism, 940
Newfoundland, 29
New France
See also Canada
Beaver Wars, 71–72, 76, 78–80
establishment of, 27, 37, 38–39
French in, 37
fur trade, 37
map of, *38*
missionaries in, *74,* 75
population of, *40*
New Freedom, 687–689
New Frontier programs, 899
New Hampshire
colony, overview of, 59
labor system in, 92
ratification of Constitution, 228
settlement of, 52, 59
New Harmony, 375
New Haven, Connecticut, 52, 59
New Jersey
American Revolution in, 181–183, *182*
ethnic diversity in, 237
labor system in, 91, 92
overview of, 59
ratification of Constitution, 227
settlement of, 59, 62
slavery in, 206, 238
voting rights for women, 204, *204,* 296–297
New Jersey Plan, 222
Newlands Act (1902), 669
New Lights, 115
New Mexico
ceded to U.S., 413
Civil War, 477
missionaries in, 73–75, *74*
Pueblo Revolt, 76, 77–78
settlement of, 405–406, 422
Spanish colonists in, 24, 69
New Nationalism, 686–687
New Netherland, 41, 62
New Orleans
battle of (1815), 278–280
Civil War, 463
founding of, 125
New South
African Americans in 545–557
agriculture in, 538–543
cities, growth of, 533–534
impact on Southerners, 537–538
industry in, 532–537
newness of, 531–532
racial issues, 545–557
railroads in, 533, *534*
Southern Populists, 542–543
women in, 543–545
New Spain, 23
Newspapers
abolitionist, 379, *379,* 383
colonial, 108, 111–112, 118, 251
in the early 1900s, 591

immigrant, 583
yellow press, 705
Newton, Huey P., 932
Newton, Isaac, 112
New York City
Bowery, *568*
conditions in the early 1900s, 574, *583*
draft riots, 478, *479*
Five Points slum area, 358
growth of, 588
Mulberry, 574, *583*
in the nineteenth century, 357, *357*
New York colony
American Revolution in, 181–184, *182*
ethnic diversity in, 237
growth of, 107
labor system in, 92
overview of, 59
ratification of Constitution, 228
settlement of, 59, 62
slave revolts in, 90
slavery in, 86, 107, 205–206, 238
New York Female Moral Reform Society, 370
New York Journal, 591, 705, 706
New York State Factory Commission, 666
New York Stock Exchange, *243,* 357
New York Tenement House Law (1901), 669, 670
New York Times, 551
New York World, 591, 705
Nez Percé, 606–607
Niagara Movement, 677–678
Nicaragua, 714, 717–718, 778, 948, 970
Nicols, J. C., 767
Nimitz, Chester, 846
9-11-01, *990,* 991–992, *1016, 1017, 1018–1020*
Nineteenth Amendment, 669, 679
Ninth Amendment, 241
Nisei, 771
Nixon, Richard M., 803
civil rights and, 938, 940
Doctrine, 938
domestic policy, 940–941
election of 1960 and, 899, *900*
election of 1968 and, 937, *938*
election of 1972 and, 943
energy crisis and, 940–941
environmental issues, 690, 941–942
foreign policy, 938–940
Hiss case and, *877,* 878
kitchen debate, 893, *894*
pardon of, 944–945
resignation, 943, 1000
Vietnam War and, 938–939
Watergate, 942–944
Nonimportation movement, 147, 151–152, 155, 157, 158–159
Nonintercourse Act (1809), 270, 271
Nonpartisan League, 737, 800
Noriega, Manuel, 970
Norris, Frank, 642, 665
Norris, George, 731, 761
North, Lord, 152, 153, 168, 190
North, Oliver, 970, 971
North Africa, World War II in, 842
North American Free Trade Agreement (NAFTA), 1006
North Atlantic Treaty Organization.

See NATO
North Carolina
American Revolution in, 172, 178, 188, 189
Civil War, 481, 488
formation of, 59
labor system in, 92
ratification of Constitution, 228
secession, 447, 455
settlement of, 59
slavery in, 83
North Carolina Mutual Life Insurance Co., 553, *554*
Northern New Mexico Cowboys Union, 617
Northern Pacific Railroad, 606, 618
Northern Securities Co., 684
North Korea, 873
North Star, 383
Northwest Ordinance (1787), 218, 284, 394, 425
Northwest Passage, 27, 28
Noup, Celia, 955–956
Nova Scotia, 126
Noyes, John Humphrey, 375
Nuclear arms race
beginnings of, 868–870, *871*
Cuban missile crisis, 901–904
first hydrogen bomb testing, 870, *871*
Limited Test Ban Treaty (1963), 850, 904
massive retaliation doctrine, 895–896
overview of, 972
proliferation of, 850
Reagan administration, 969, 971
SALT I, 940
SALT II, 949
Strategic Defense Initiative (SDI) (Star Wars), 969
U-2 incident, 898–899
Nuclear Non-Proliferation Treaty (1968), 850, 972
Nullification, doctrine of, 254
Nullification crisis, 301, 305–308
Nye, Gerald, 810

O

Occom, Samson, 116
O'Connor, Sandra Day, 1008
Octopus, The (Norris), 642, 665
Office of Economic Opportunity (OEO), 910
Office of Price Administration (OPA), 832, 857
Office of Scientific Research and Development, 833
Office of War Information (OWI), 836
Ogden, Aaron, 356
Oglala Lakota College, 933
Oglethorpe, James Edward, 85
Ohio, admitted to Union, 393
Ohio Company, 217
Ohio Indians, 240, 248
Oil, crisis of 1973, 941
Okinawa, 847
Oklahoma City, violence in, 998
Old Northwest territories, settlement of, 393–395
Old Republicans, 284
Old Southwest territories
peoples of, 403–405
settlement of, 395–397
Olive Branch Petition, 170, 172

Olmecs, 5
Olney, Richard, 704
Olson, Floyd, 797
Omaha Platform, 646
Omahas, 397
On the Waterfront, 878
Opechancanough, 43–44, *44,* 48
Open Door policy, 712–713
Open shops, 757
Operation Desert Storm, 976
Operation OVERLOAD, 842, 844
Operation Rescue, 449
Operation ROLLING THUNDER, 920, 921–922
Operation TORCH, 842, *843*
Oppenheimer, J. Robert, 834, 870
Order of the Heroes of America, 481
Order of the Sons of America, 767
Orders in Council, 271
Ordinance of 1784, 216
Oregon, settlement of, 318, 401
Oregon Trail, 390, 397, 400–403, *402*
Organization Man, The (Whyte), 893
Organization of Petroleum Exporting Countries (OPEC), 941, 947
Orlando, Vittorio, 741
Orwell, George, 501
Osages, 397
Osceola, 305
Ostend Manifesto, 427
O'Sullivan, John L., 408–409
Oswald, Lee Harvey, 909
Oswald, Richard, *192*
Other America, The (Harrington), 893, 910
Otis, James, Jr., 146
Ottawas, 79, 143, 216
Outlook, 551
Overland trails/overlanders, 390, 400–403, *401, 402*
Owen, Robert, 375
Owens, Jesse, 861
Oyo, 11

P

Paddock, Adino, 108
Page, Walter Hines, 727
Pahlavi, Muhammad Reza, 897, 949
Paine, Thomas, 172, 183, 255–256, 412
Paiutes, 403, 404, 601
Pakenham, Edward, 278
Pakenham, Richard, 317
Paleo-Indians, 3
Palestinians, 1021
Palmer, Mitchell, 746, 747, *748*
Panama, 970
Panama Canal, 702, 714, 716, *717*
Pan American Union, 702
Panhandle Stock Association, 617
Panic of 1819, 283–284
Panic of 1837, 309–311
Panic of 1857, 434
Pan-Indian resistance movement, 271–272
Paris, treaty of (1763), 132–133
Paris, treaty of (1783), 190–192, *192,* 218–219
Paris, treaty of (1899), 708–710
Paris Peace conference, 741–742
Parker, Alton B., 684
Parker, William, 425

Parks
amusement, 566, 593, *593*
national, creation of, 683, *683*
Parks, Rosa, 907
Parsons, Theophilus, 204
Parson's Cause, 144
PATCO (Professional Air Traffic Controllers Organization), 962
Paterson, William, 222
Patriot Act (2001), 1018, 1020
Patroonships, 41
Pattillo, Melba, 885–886, 906
Patton, George, 842
Patuxets, 49
Pawnees, 8, 81, 398, 603
Paxton Boys, 143
Peace of Paris (1783), 190–192, *192*
Peale, Charles Willson, *129, 170, 180*
Peale, Norman Vincent, 892
Pea Ridge, battle of (1862), 460, 477
Pearl Harbor, attack on, 827–828, *827*
Peffer, William A., 645
Pemberton, John, 475, 533
Peña, Federico, 1011
Pendleton Civil Service Act (1883), 640
Peninsula Campaign, 465–466
Penn, William, 60, 61–62, *61,* 73
Pennsylvania
American Revolution in, *182,* 183, 185
Civil War, 472–474
colony, overview of, 59
ethnic diversity in, 237
labor system in, 91, 92
ratification of Constitution, 227
settlement of, 59, 60–62
slavery in, 86, 238
Whiskey Rebellion, 250
Pennsylvania Gazette, 127
Pennsylvania Journal, 145
Pentagon, 839–840
attack on, *990,* 991–992, *1016, 1017,* 1018–1020
Pentagon Papers, 942–943
People of Plenty (Pope), 893
People's Grocery, 546–547
People's party. *See* Populist party
People's Temple, 930
People's Unemployment League, 791
Pequots, 50–51, 73
Pequot War (1637), 51, 73
Perdue, Sonny, 557
Perestroika, 971
Perkins, Frances, 805
Perot, H. Ross, 994, *995*
Perpetual Emigrating Fund Co., 618
Perry, Matthew, 700
Perry, Oliver Hazard, 277
Pershing, John J., 719, 738
Persian Gulf War, 974–976, *974, 976*
Petersburg, Virginia, 471, 489, 485
Phelps-Dodge Co., 737
Philadelphia
American Revolution in, 181, *182*
growth of colonial, 107, *108*
in the nineteenth century, 357
settlement of, 61–62
slave population of, 86, 107
Philadelphia Centennial Exposition, 564–565, 591
Philbrick, Herbert, 878
Philip, King (Metacom), 76–77
Philippines, 771–772, 971
U.S. conquest of, 706–707, 710–712

World War II and, 830, 846–847
Phillips, Kevin, 976
Phillips, Wendell, 510
Phonograph, 769, 891
Pickens, Francis, 312
Pickering, John, 266
Pickett, George, 474
Pierce, Franklin, 426–427, 428
Pietists, 237
Pig Stand, 767
Pike, Zebulon, 397
Pilgrims, 48–49
Pinchot, Gifford, 682, 683, 686
Pinckney, Charles Cotesworth, 255, 270
Pinckney's Treaty (San Lorenzo Treaty) (1795), 251
Pitcher, Molly, 180
Pitt, William, 130–131
Pittsburgh, Pennsylvania, 358–359
Pizarro, Francisco, 22
Place, Francis, *61*
Plains Indians, 8, 25–26
See also under name of
Planned Parenthood v. Casey, 982
Plantation Duty Act (1673), 102
Plantations
Mulberry, *60*
rice, 58
social classes, 337–342
sugar, 55–56
wives, role of, 340
Platt Amendment, 715
Plattsburgh, battle of (1814), 278
Plessy, Homer, 548
Plessy v. Ferguson, 548, *549,* 904
Plymouth colony, 48–49, 59, 117
Plymouth Company, 42, 48
Pocahontas, 43, 47
Pogroms, 580
Poland, 742, 822, 866, 973
Political parties
See also under name of
comparison of, in the 1890s, 634
development of second (two)-party system, 312, 313
emergence of, 245
growth of, 1877–1900, 631–637
Politics
diverging, between colonies and England, 119–121
dominion of New England and limits of British control, 116–118
Politics, growth of, 1877–1900
associational, 635–637
campaigns and elections, 631–633
partisan, 633–635
Polk, James K.
election of 1844 and, 318
Mexican War, 408, 410–413, *411*
westward expansion and, 318
Poll taxes, 549
Pomeiooc, *29*
Pomos, 403
Ponce de León, Juan, 20
Pontiac, 143
Pontiac's Rebellion (1763–1766), 143
Poor Richard's Almanac (Franklin), 186
Popé, 77–78, *80*
Pope, Alexander, 147
Pope, John, 466
Popular sovereignty, 420
Population
in cities (1820–1860), 357, *358, 359*

colonial, 53, *84, 121, 122*
growth of free blacks (1750–1800), 205, *205*
Native American (1600–1730), *70*
shift of (1790–1850), 391, *392, 393*
slave, 80, *84*
in Southern states in 1850, *343*
Population shifts
and agricultural land uses in late 1800s, *619*
in the 1920s, *765*
in 2000, 1007–1008
Populist party, 542–543, 635, 645–646, 648–649
Port Huron Statement, 926
Portugal
exploration/colonization by, 12–13, 16–17, 27
slave trade and, 55, 82
Post, Louis, 747
Potawatomis, 398
Potomac Company, 221
Potsdam Declaration, 848
Potter, David, 893
Poverty
colonial, 109
feminization of, 966
in the 1980s, 965–966
rate for 1870–1900 and responses to, 574–576
rate for 1960–1999, *914*
War on Poverty, 909–910
Powderly, Terence V., 577
Power Elite, The (Mills), 893–894
Power of Positive Thinking, The (Peale), 892
Powers, Francis Gary, 899
Powhatan, 43
Powhatans, 26, 30, 43–44, 48, 77
Prague Spring, 936
Prairie Cattle Co., *616*
Predestination, 15, 48
Preemption Act (1841), 393
Preparedness program, 729
Presbyterians, 114, 207, 237, 345
Preservation, 683
Presidency
Constitutional Convention and determining duties and election methods for, 223–224
how to address, 241
Presidential Commission on the Status of Women, 927
Presidential electors, methods of electing, 295
President's Organization for Unemployment Relief, 791
Presley, Elvis, 891, *892,* 928
Prevost, George, 278
Price, Charles, 546
Princeton, battle of, *170,* 178, 183
Printing press, 15, *15*
Prison reform, 373–374
Proclamation Line, 141, *141*
Proclamation of 1763, 141, 144
Progressive Era, 661
chronology of, 662
church and campus, 664–665
country life, 675
education, reshaping of public, 671–674
electoral reform, 679–680
gender restrictions, 674–675
gospel of efficiency, 665
industrial and urban tensions,

662–664
labor's demand for rights, 665–666
major laws of, 669
major organizations/groups of, 663
moral crusades, 675–677
muckrakers, 665
opponents of reform, 668
political and government reform, 678–681
protective legislation for women and children, 670–671
racism, 677–678
Roosevelt presidency and, 681–686
settlement houses and urban reform, 668–670
socialism, 667–668
Wilson presidency and, 686–689
women in, 666–667, 674–675, 678–679
Progressive party, 687
Prohibition, 676, 773–774
Prohibition party, 635
Prophet's Town, 272
Prophet Tenkswatawa, 271–272, *272*
Proposition 187, 776, 1012
Proprietary colonies, 46, 57–62
Prosser, Gabriel, 336
Prostitution, 370, 465
in the mining camps, 610–612
social reform and, 676–677
Protective tariffs, 242, 243
Protestantism, 14–16, 76–77, 114
Provident Hospital, 588
Public Works Administration (PWA), 795
Pueblo Bonito, 8
Pueblo Revolt, 76, 77–78, *80,* 404
Pueblos, 7–8, 24, 25, 26, 75, 77–78, 123, 404, 413, 601
Puerto Rico, 708
immigrants from, 978
Spanish exploration of, 19, 55
U.S. rule in, 714
Pulaski, Kazimierz, 177
Pulitzer, Joseph, 591, 705
Pullman, George, 568, 578
Pullman Palace Sleeping Car Co., 578
Pullman strike (1894), 578–579, 648
Pure Food and Drug Act (1906), 669, 684
Puritans/Puritanism
in England, 46–47
in New England, 48–50, 113
relations with Indians, 76
Put-in-Bay, battle of (1813), 277
Putting-out system, 361

Q

Quakers, 60–61, 114, 207, 237
Quartering Act (1765), 141–142, 149–150
Quartering Act (1774), 154
Quasi-War, 253
Quebec, 37, 38
Act (1774), 154–155, *155*
battle of (1759), 131, *131*
Siege of (1775), 172, 178
Queen Anne's War (1702–1713), 126–127
Queenston Heights, battle of (1812), 275
Quiberon, battle of (1759), 131

R

Race riots
    in the 1900s, 677–678
    in the 1920s, 745
    in the 1960s, 931
    in the 1990s, 968
    World War II and, 838
Racism
    Chinese immigrants, 584, 585–586
    Depression of 1929 and, 790
    1877–1890, 545–556
    imperialism and, 697–698, 699
    nativism, 584–586
    in the 1920s, 760
    Progressive Era, 674, 677–678
    scientific, 585
    World War II and, 835–836
Radical Republicans, 478, 507, 510
Radio broadcasting
    fireside chats of F. Roosevelt, 794
    in the 1920s, 757, 769
    preachers in the 1950s, 892
Railroad Administration, 731, 732
Railroads
    in the 1830s, 355–356, 357–358
    in 1860, *437*
    land grants, 600, 617, 618
    plans for a transcontinental, 428
    regulation of, 642
    segregation laws, 548
    in the South (1859–1899), 533,
        534
    strike of 1877, 576–577
    strike of 1894, 578–579, 648
    transcontinental, 600–601, *600*
    westward expansion and role of,
        600–601, *600*
Rainbow Coalition, 981
Raleigh, Walter, 29, 30
Rambo, 960
Rancheros, 406–407
Randolph, A. Philip, 838
Randolph, Edmund, 226
Ranger, 186
Rauschenberg, Robert, *884*
Rauschenbusch, Walter, 664, 668
Ray, James Earl, 937
Rayner, John B., 542
RCA, 757
Reagan, Nancy, 777
Reagan, Ronald
    as an actor, 886, 957
    deficits and deregulation, 961–962
    Doctrine, 969
    domestic policy, 959–963
    election of 1980 and, 957, *959*
    election of 1984 and, 959
    environmental issues, 690, 961
    foreign policy, 968–971
    Iran-Contra scandal, 970–971
    Red Scare and, 877
    Social Security and, 812
Real Whig ideology, 127
Rebel Without a Cause, 892, *893*
Recall, 681
Reconquista, 14, 16, 17, 19, 24
Reconstruction, 521
    African-American aspirations,
        500–506
    agriculture in, 502–504, 523
    amendments/legislation, list of,
        521
    congressional, 512–513
    counter, 516–519
    education, 501–502

failure of, 522–525
government in the South,
    513–516
Ku Klux Klan, 516
land redistribution programs,
    502–504
Lincoln's Ten Percent Plan,
    506–507
migration to cities, 504–505
presidential, 507–512
redemption period, 519–522
religion, 505–506
voting rights, 510–513, 524
Reconstruction Finance Corp. (RFC),
    792
Red-baiting, 876
Red Cloud, 607
Red Eagle, *280*
Redeemer Democrats, 540
Redeemers, 519
Redemption period, 519–522
Redemptioner system, 91
Red Light Saloon, 610
Redlining, 860
Red Scare, 746–747, *748,* 875–880
Referendum, 680, 681
Reformation, 15–16
Regulators, 150
Reid, Whitelaw, 504, 700
Religion
    See also under type of
    for African Americans following
        the Civil War, 505–506, *505*
    colonial, 113–116
    communes and cults in the 1970s,
        929–930
    cultural perceptions and misper-
        ceptions, 26
    decline in devotion in colonial
        period, 255
    in the 1820s, 338–369
    evangelists/televangelists,
        984–985
    free blacks, 343, 345, 505–506
    Ghost Dance, 608
    Great Awakening, 114–116
    human sacrifice, 7
    missionaries and Native
        Americans, 73–76, 123, 401, 403
    Native American, 38, 404,
        602–603, 607–608
    in the 1950s, 892–893
    in the 1960s–1990s, 928, 983–985
    old-time, and Scopes trial,
        774–775
    politics and, 448–449, 984–985
    Second Great Awakening,
        297–299, *298*
    of slaves, 89, 335–336
    Social Gospel movement, 663,
        664–665, 667–668
    state constitutions and pluralism
        in, 207–208
    Sun Dance, 607
    West African, 12
    women and, 116, 298–299
Renaissance, 13
Reno, Janet, 1008
Repartimiento, 69
Republicanism, 174–175
    Articles of Confederation, 210
    defining the people, 203–207
    state constitutions, 207–209
Republican party
    Civil War and, 478
    differences between Federalist

party and, 244
during 1870–1900, 633–635
in 1854, 431–432
election of 1856 and, 432
election of 1860 and, 440–442,
    442, 445
election of 1864 and, 487–488
election of 1896 and, 650–653,
    653
formation of, 245, 431
Liberal, 516, 518
moderate, 507
National, 300, 312
in the 1920s, 760–761
Old Republicans, 284
policies of, 244, 245
Radical, 478, 507, 510
Reconstruction and, 507
slavery issues and, 345
in the South after Reconstruction,
    513–516
Republic Steel Co., 804
Rescate, 69
Reservationists, 744
Resettlement Administration (RA),
    802
Retroactive I, 884
Reuben James, 826, 827
Reuther, Walter, 876
Revenue Act (1935), 801
Revere, Paul, 108, *109, 153,* 168
*Review of the Debates in the Virginia
    Legislature of 1831 and 1832* (Dew),
    347
Rhee, Syngman, 873
Rhett, Robert Barnwell, 429, 440
Rhode Island
    colony, overview of, 59
    labor system in, 92
    ratification of Constitution, 228
    Rogue's Island, 215–216
    settlement of, 51, 59
    slavery in, 86
Rhode Island system, 362
Ribicoff, Abraham, 937
Rice
    exports, 105
    plantations, 58
Rice, Condoleezza, 1008, *1009*
Rice, Thomas, 548
Richmond Whig, 440
Ridgway, Matthew, 874
Riesman, David, 894
Riis, Jacob, 574, *575,* 576–577, 673
Ring shout, 335
Roach, Isaac, 276
Roads, development of, 353
Roanoke Island, 29–31, 42
Robe, The, 892
Roberts, Oral, 984
Robertson, Pat, 448, 981, 984
Roberval, Jean-François de la, 27
Robinson, Jackie, 861, *861*
Rochester, New York, 358
Rockefeller, John D., 569, 576, 665,
    668
Rockingham, Lord, 190
Rocky Mountain Fur Co., 399
Roe v. Wade, 776, 982
Rogers, Will, 774
Rolfe, John, 43, 44, 47
Rome-Berlin Axis, 822
Rommel, Edwin, 830
Roosevelt, Eleanor, 785, 793, 803, *803,*
    805, 806
Roosevelt, Franklin D., 412

See also New Deal
death of, 848
discrimination and, 805, 838
election of 1932 and, 793–794,
    794
election of 1936 and, 803
election of 1940 and, 825
election of 1944 and, 839
fireside chats, 794
packing of Supreme Court, 809
World War II and, 823, 825–826,
    839, 841–842, 848
Roosevelt, Theodore, 591, 665, 675
    Corollary, 717, *718*
    corporate regulation, 684–685
    election of 1904 and, 684
    election of 1912 and, 686
    imperialist views, 700, 702–703
    labor and, 682
    natural resources, 682–684, *683,
        684*
    New Nationalism, 686–687
    Panama Canal, 716, *717*
    as president, 681–685
    Russo-Japanese War and, 713
    Spanish-American War and, 681,
        705, 706, 707–709, *710*
    World War I and preparedness
        program, 729
Roosevelt, Theodore, Jr., 714
Root, Elihu, 700, 713, 717
Root-Takahira Agreement (1908), 713
Roseanne, 962–963, *963*
Rosebud, battle of (1876), 606
Rosecrans, Willaim S., 475
Rosenberg, Ethel, 878–879
Rosenberg, Julius, 878–879
Ross, John, 306
Roughing It (Twain), 612
Rough Riders, 707–708
Rowlandson, Mary, 78–79
Royal African Company, 83
Royal Society of London, 112
Ruby, Jack, 909
Ruffin, Edmund, 329, 330–331
Rural Electrification Administration
    (REA), 807–808
Rural Free Delivery, 622
Rush, Benjamin, 204–205
Rush, Bobby, 932
Rush–Bagot Agreement (1817), 282
Russell, Andrew J., 613–614
Russell, Charles E., 667
Russia
    See also Soviet Union
    Bolsheviks, 739, 746–747
    Russo-Japanese War, 713
    U.S. Civil War and, 467
    in World War I, 725
Russian Republic, 974
Russo-Japanese War, 713
Ruth, Babe, 769
Rutledge, Edward, 210
Ryan, Leo, 930

S

Sabbatarian movement, 368–369
Sack of Lawrence, 430
Sadat, Anwar al-, 948, *949*
Sagadahoc, 49
Sagebrush Rebellion, 690, 961
St. Augustine, 24
St. Christopher, 59
St. Clair, Arthur, 247
St. Domingue (Haiti), 250, 267
St. Lawrence River, 27, 37, 39

St. Leger, Barry, 183
St. Louis, 825
St. Louis, Missouri, 359
Salary Act (1816), 295
Salish Indians, 400
Salk, Jonas, 912
Saloons, 592–593, 612
SALT. *See* Strategic Arms Limitation Treaty
Samoset, 49
San Antonio, Texas
    Alamo, 124, 406
    founding of, 124
Sánchez, José María, 408–409
Sand Creek massacre, 603–605
Sandinista rebels, 948, 970
San Francisco, 421–422, 588
Sanger, Margaret, 674, *674*
San Jacinto, battle of (1836), 406
San Juan Hill, 708
San Lorenzo (Pinckney's Treaty), treaty of (1795), 251
Santa Anna, Antonio López de, 405–406
Santa Fe Trail, 404, 407
Santee Sioux, 398
São Tomé, 17
Saratoga, battle of (1777), 178, 184
Sargent, Henry, *365*
Sauks, 304, 398
Savannah, battles of (1778, 1779), 177, 178
Savio, Mario, 926
Scalawags, 513–514
Scandinavian Immigration Society, 618
Scarlet Letter, The (Hawthorne), 377
Schaw, Janet, 176
Schaw, Robert, 176
Schenck, David, 546
Schlesinger, Arthur, Jr., 862
Schofield, Martha, 501–502
School and Society, The (Dewey), 672
School Prayer: A Community At War, 777
Schulberg, Budd, 878
Schumacker, General, *237*
Schurz, Carl, 518, 709
Scientific management, 665
Scopes, John, 775
Scopes trial, 775
Scots-Irish, 93, *236,* 237
Scott, Dred, 432–433, *433*
Scott, Evelyn, 538
Scott, Harriet, 432–433, *433*
Scott, Winfield, 413, 426, 446, 466
Scrooby separatists, 49
SEATO (Southeast Asia Treaty Organization), 901, *903*
Secession, 442–444, *443*
Second Amendment, 241
Second Bank of the United States, 280–281, 283, 284, 302, 308–309
Second Continental Congress, 170
Second Great Awakening, 297–299, *298*
Second (two)-party system, 313
Securities and Exchange Commission (SEC), formation of, 794
Sedition Act (1798), 253
Sedition Act (1918), 736, 1018
Segregation by law, 547–548
Selective Service Act (1917), 737
Selective Service System, 924
Selma, Alabama, 911
Seminoles, 283

Indian Removal Act (1830), 303–305, *304, 305*
Seneca Falls Convention (1848), 381–382
Senecas, 71, 79, 128, 185
Separatists, 49
September 11, 2001. *See* 9-11-01
Sequoyah, *303*
Serapis, 186, *186*
Serbia, 725
Serra, Junípero, 124
Servicemen's Readjustment Act. *See* GI Bill of Rights
Settlement houses, 543, 574–575, 663, 668–670
Seven Cities of Cíbola, 24
Seven Days' Battles (1862), 465–466, 489
Seventeenth Amendment, 669, 681
Seven Years' War (1756–1763), 126, 129–132
Seward, William, 314, 422, 429, 432, 441, 446, 491
Seward, William Henry, 701–702
Seymour, Horatio, 512
Shakers, 375
Sharecropping, 523
Share-Our-Wealth Society, 800
Shastas, 403
Shaw, Albert, 700
Shaw, Bernard, 1003
Shaw v. Reno, 524
Shawnees, 128, 129, 131, 181, 194
Shays, Daniel, 201
Shays' Rebellion, 201–203, 215, *215*
Shepard, William, 201–203
Sheen, Fulton J., 892
Shelburne, Lord, 190
Sheldon, Charles, 664, 667
Shepard, William, 201–203
Sheppard-Towner Maternity and Infancy Act (1921), 763
Sheridan, Philip H., 487, 490, 603, 605
Sherman, Roger, 222, 223
Sherman, William Tecumseh, 456, 484, 485, 486, 488, *488,* 503, 605, 606
Sherman Antitrust Act (1890), 641, 642–643, 648–649
Sherman Silver Purchase Act (1890), 644, 649–650
Shiloh Church, battle of, (1862), 463, 489
Shima, George, 584
Shipping/ship building
    flatboats, 394
    late Middle Ages, 16–17, *16*
    New England, 106
    steamboats, 353, 355
    World War II and, 832
Shirley, William, 129
Shopping centers, 767, 889
Shoshone, 5, 601
Shriver, R. Sargent, 910
Shultz, George, 940, 971
Siegel, Bugsy, 889
Sierra Club, 690
Silent Spring (Carson), 941
Silicon Valley, 1002
Silver currency, 643–644
Simpson, "Sockless Jerry," 645
Sinclair, Upton, 571, 665, 667, 754, 771, 804
Singleton, Benjamin, 551
Sioux, 389–390, 397–399, 403, 602–603, 605–606, 608
Sirhan, Sirhan, 937

Sirica, John, 943
Sit-ins, *907,* 908
Sitting Bull, 602–603, 606
Sixteenth Amendment, 669, 685
Slater, Samuel, 362
Slaughterhouse cases, 525
Slave codes, 57, 87–88, 332
Slave Power, 383, 434, 446
Slaves/slavery
    See also Civil War
    in the American Revolution, 180–181
    arguments for, 344–347
    as artisans and skilled workers, 328, 333
    auction, *322*
    changing patterns in, 331–332, *331*
    changing race relations in the colonies, 86–87
    chartered generation of, 87
    communities, 88–89
    Constitutional Convention and issues of, 223
    cotton and, 325–326
    creole, 88
    daily life/culture, description of, 323–324, 332–337
    decline of, 331–332
    destination of, *81*
    economic legacy of, 346
    families, 88–89, 334–336
    field work of, 333
    as house servants, 333
    labor needs and the turn to, 80–81, 91
    legacy of, 94
    in the lower South, 325–326
    Middle Passage, description of, 82, *85*
    Missouri Compromise, 284–285
    Native Americans as, 77, 81
    in New Amsterdam, *41*
    in the northern colonies, 85–86
    origins of, 81, *82*
    personal accounts, 67–68
    population estimations, 80, *84*
    profits of, 326–328
    religion, 89, 335–336
    resistance/rebellions, 89–91, 336–337, 378–379, 425
    runaways, 337, 338–339
    shock of enslavement, 81–82
    social classes, 337–344
    in the southern colonies, 83, 85
    spread, *326*
    three-fifths rule, 222, 279
    in the upper South, 328–332
    urban, 328
    women, 334
Slave ship, *66*
Slave trade
    Africans as slavers, 81–82
    Atlantic islands and, 17
    in the Caribbean islands, 19, 55–57
    evolution of, 80–81
    New Spain, 23
    West African, 12–13, 81–82
    in the West Indies, 17, 55–57
Slidell, John, 411
Smallpox, 21, 25, 26, *26,* 143, 399
Smalls, Robert, 552–553
Smith, Alfred E., 778, *779*
Smith, Anna, 647
Smith, Gerrit, 383

Smith, Hoke, 677
Smith, John, 43, *44*
Smith, Joseph, 371, 407
Smith, Kirby, 490
Smith-Lever Act (1914), 669, 675
Social classes
    black middle class in the 1880s, 552–554
    Caribbean islanders, 9
    colonial, 54, 57–58, 108–109
    free blacks, 342–344
    indentured servants, 38, 45–46, 56, 83, 91
    Middle Ages, 13, *14*
    middle class, 365, *366*
    middle class, new, 590–591
    mulattoes, 344
    in the nineteenth century, 364–367
    the old rich, 364–365
    plantation, 337–342
    working classes, 366–367
    yeomen, 341–342
Social Darwinism, 575–576, 585
Social Gospel movement, 663, 664–665, 667–668
Socialism, 579, 667–668
Socialism, utopian, 375
Socialist Party of America, 668
Social reform
    See also Progressive Era
    educational reform, 372–373
    prisons, workhouses, and asylums, 373–374
    utopian alternatives, 375–378
    women and, 543–544, 666–667
Social Security Act (1935), 801, 811, 865
    controversy over, 812–813
Society for the Propagation of the Gospel in Foreign Parts, 113
Society for the Relief of Poor Widows with Small Children, 370
Society of Friends. *See* Quakers
Soil Conservation Service, 802
Solid South, 531
Solomon, Job ben, 82
Songhai empire, 11
Sons of Liberty, 145, *145,* 147–148, 153–154
Sons of the Confederate Veterans, 556
So Proudly We Hail, 836
Soulé, Pierre, 427
Souls of Black Folk, The (Du Bois), 556
Sound money policy, 643
South Carolina
    American Revolution in, 172, 178, 187–189, *188*
    Civil War, 444–448, 488
    formation of, 59
    labor system in, 92
    ratification of Constitution, 228
    secession, 442, *443*
    settlement of, 59
    slave revolts in, 89–91
    slavery in, 83, 87, *90,* 239
    Stono Rebellion, 90
    tariff of 1828 and nullification, 305–308
South Carolina Exposition and Protest, 306
South Carolina Gazette, 108
Southeast Asia Treaty Organization (SEATO), 901, *903*
Southern Baptist Convention, 774
Southern Christian Leadership

Conference (SCLC), 908
Southern Farmers' Alliance, 540–541
Southern Homestead Act (1866), 503, 521
Southern Manifesto, 905
Southern Methodist Church, 506
Southern Pacific Railroad, 665
Southern Power Co., 536
Southern Tenant Farmers Union, 798
South Korea, 873
Southwest Ordinance (1790), 218, 284, 397
Soviet Union (USSR)
   See also Cold War; Russia
   Carter administration and, 948–949
   collapse of, 973–974
   glasnost and perestroika, 971
   Nixon administration and, 939, 940
   Reagan administration and, 968–969
   World War II, 821, 822–823, 828–830, 842, 848
Space exploration, 896, 904, 919–920
Spain
   American Revolution and, 185
   in California, 123–125, 139, 140
   Caribbean islands, conquest by, 2, 17, 19–20, 55
   Confederation Congress and, 219–221
   control of Native Americans, 69–70
   exploration/colonization by, 2, 9, 12, 13–14, 16, 17, 19–25, 123–125
   in Florida, 20, 23, 24, 139
   in Mexico, 24
   North American territories 1750–1763, *121*
   slave trade and, 23, 82
   in Texas, 123–125
   U.S. relations with, 250, 251
   War of the Austrian Succession (1739–1748), 126, 127–129
   War of the Spanish Succession (1702–1713), 126–127
Spanish-American War, 681, *694*, 695–696, 705–710, *707, 708, 709, 710*
Spargo, John, 670
Spaulding, C. C., *554*
Specie Circular, 311
Spectator, The, 111, 112
Spice Islands, 40
Spirit of St. Louis, 770
Spoils system, 302, 638
Sports
   baseball, 592, 769, 861
   boxing, 769, 861
   football, 592, 769–770
   in the 1920s, 769–770
   professional leagues, formation of, 592
   racism in, 861
Spotsylvania, battle of, 485
Sputnik, 896
Squanto, 49
Squatters, 240, 394
Stagflation, 941
Stalin, Joseph, 823, 841, 848
Stalingrad, 828–830
Stallone, Sylvester, *960*
Stamp Act (1765), 145, 147, 148, 149, *149*

Stamp Act Congress, 148
Standard Oil Co., 567, 569, 642, 652, 665, 668
Stanton, Edwin M., 512
Stanton, Elizabeth Cady, 381, 513
Staple Act (1663), 102
Starr, Kenneth, 999
"Star-Spangled Banner, The" (Key), 278
START. *See* Strategic Arms Reduction Treaty
State, constitutions, 207–209
State Department, formation of, 241
States' rights, 254
Stead, William T., 667
Steamboats, 353, 355
Steam engines, 565
Stearns, Harold, 770–771
Steel industry, 532, 536, 566, 745–746, 804
Steffens, Lincoln, 665, 667
Stein, Gertrude, 770
Steinbeck, John, 785, 802
Stephens, Alexander H., 442
Steuben, Baron von, 177, 184
Stevens, John, 703
Stevens, Thaddeus, 510
Stevenson, Adlai E., Jr., 887
Stewart, T. McCants, 545
Stewart, William, 546–547
Stockman, David, 961
Stockton and Darlington, 356
Stono Rebellion, 90
Stowe, Harriet Beecher, 417–418, 425–426, 502, 590
Strategic Arms Limitation Treaty
   SALT I, 940, 972
   SALT II, 949, 972
Strategic Arms Reduction Treaty
   START I, 850, 972
   START II, 850, 972, 1017
Strategic Defense Initiative (SDI) (Star Wars), 969, 1017
Strauss, Levi, 421
Strauss, Lewis L., 871
Strikes
   by cowhands, 616–617
   in 1894, 578–579
   following World War I, 745–746
   following World War II, 857–858
   Great Uprising (1877), 576–577, *579*
   Homestead strike (1892), 578
   mining, 614, 737, 746, 759
   New Deal and, 804
   PATCO, 962
   Pullman strike (1894), 578–579, 648
Student demonstrations, 936, 938, *939*
Student Nonviolent Coordinating Committee (SNCC), 908, 911
Students for a Democratic Society (SDS), 926
Stuyvesant, Peter, 42, 62
Submarine warfare
   in World War I, 728–729
   in World War II, 826, 830
Subtreasury plan, 541–542
Suburbs
   development of, 589–590
   in the 1920s, 767
   in the 1950s, 859, 888
   in the 1960s–1990s, 934
   politics and, 934
Suez Canal crisis, 897

Suffolk Resolves, 157
Suffrage. *See* Voting
Sugar
   trade, 17, 104, 105
   in the West Indies, 55–56
Sugar Act (1764), 144–145, 147, 148
Sumner, Charles, 430, 510, *514*, 519
Sumter, Thomas, 189
Sun Also Rises, The (Hemingway), *771*
Sunbelt states, 976–977
Sun Dance, 607
Sunday, Billy, 668, 778
Supreme Court
   abortion and, 776, 982
   affirmative action and, 1013
   busing and, 935
   civil rights and, 548, 904–905
   Constitution on, and the formation of, 225, 242
   contractual property rights and, 282
   Judiciary Act (1789), 242, 266
   Judiciary Act (1801), 265–266
   monopolies and, 356–357
   national power over states, 281–282
   in the 1920s, 761
   Nixon administration and, 940
   F. Roosevelt's packing of, 809
Supreme Court cases
   Abington Township v. Schempp, 893
   Baker v. Carr, 934
   Brown v. Board of Education, 904–905
   Cherokee Nation v. Georgia, 305
   Dred Scott v. Sandford, 432–433, 510
   Engel v. Vitale, 893
   Griswold v. Connecticut, 982
   Hopwood v. Texas, 1013
   Insular Cases, 714
   Korematsu v. U. S., 839
   Lochner v. New York, 668
   Minor v. Happersett, 632
   Muller v. Oregon, 671
   Munn v. Illinois, 642
   Planned Parenthood v. Casey, 982
   Plessy v. Ferguson, 548, *549*, 904
   Roe v. Wade, 776, 982
   Swann v. Charlotte-Mecklenburg Board of Education, 935
   U.S. v. E.C. Knight Co., 648–649
   University of California v. Bakke, 1013
   Wabash, St. Louis, and Pacific Railway Co. v. Illinois, 642
   Webster v. Reproductive Health Services, 982
   Zelman v. Simmons-Harris, 1016
Susquehannocks, 42, 77, 127
Sussex, 728
Sutter, John, 421
Swan Land and Cattle Co., 615
Swann v. Charlotte-Mecklenburg Board of Education, 935
Sweatshops, 571
Swift, Gustavus, 569

T

Taft, Horace, 629–630
Taft, Robert, 826, 865, 868
Taft, Will, 630
Taft, William Howard, 685–686, 712, 717–718, 761
Taft-Hartley Act (1947), 858
Taft-Katsura Agreement (1905), 713
Tainos, 9, 19, *19*, 20, 26, 27

Tallmadge, James, 284
Tallmadge Amendment, 284
Tammany Hall, 517
Taney, Roger B., 309, 356–357, 432–433
Taos Revolt (1847), 413
Tappan, Arthur, 379
Tappan, Lewis, 379
Tarbell, Ida, 665
Tariff Act of 1789, 242
Tariffs, 640–641
   Compromise Tariff of 1833, 308
   of 1816, 281
   of 1824 and 1828 (Abominations), 305–306
   nullification crisis, 301, 305–308
   protective, 242, 243
Tarleton, Banastre, 188, 189
Tatler, The, 111
Taxation, colonial
   British versus American views on, 145–147
   overview of, 156
   protests against, 147–148
   Stamp Act (1765), 145, 147, 148, 149, *149*
   Sugar Act (1764), 144–145, 147, 148
   Tea Act (1773), 153–154
   Townshend Duty Act (1767), 150–151
   whiskey, 243
Taxes
   Clinton administration, 996
   Economic Recovery Tax Act (ERTA) (1981), 961
   introduction of income, 688
Taxi Driver, 930
Taylor, Frederick W., 665, 756
Taylor, John, 284
Taylor, Maxwell, 920
Taylor, Zachary
   Compromise of 1850 and, 422, 423
   death of, 423
   election of 1848 and, 420–421
   Mexican War, 410–411
Tea Act (1773), 153–154
Teapot Dome scandal, 761
Tea Room, The (Sargent), *365*
Technology
   agricultural, 623–624
   high tech sector, 1002–1003
   impact on industrialization, 565–567
   industrialization and role of, 362, 363–364, 394
   Internet, 1001, 1002, 1003–1006
   mining camps, and, 613–614
Tecumseh, 271–272, 275, 277
Teenagers, in the 1950s and, 890–892
Tejanos, 405, 406
Tekakwitha, Kateri, 38
Telephone, 591
Television
   first presidential debates, 899
   in the 1950s, 864, 886, 890, 892
   in the 1980s, 962–963
   urban crisis depicted in, 930
Teller Amendment, 706, 714
Temperance movement, 365, 369–370, 543–544, 636
Temporary Assistance to Needy Families (TANF), 997
Tenancy, 91
Ten Commandments, The, 769, 892
Tenements, 574, *575*, 576–577

Tenkswatawa (Prophet), 271–272, *272*
Tennent, Gilbert, 115
Tennent, William, 114, 115
Tennessee
 Civil War, 462, 463, 475–477, 485, 488
 secession, 447, 455
 settlement of, 240
 as a slave state, 284
Tennessee Valley Authority (TVA), 795, 807, *808*
Tenochtitlán, 1, 2, 7
Ten Percent Plan, 506–507
Tenth Amendment, 241, 245
Tenure of Office Act (1867), 512, 521
Teotihuacán, 5
Territorial expansion, overview of, 156
Terrorism
 domestic, 998
 9-11-01 attacks, *990,* 991–992, *1016, 1017,* 1018–1020
Terry, Randall, 449
Tet offensive, 935
Tetons, 398
Texas
 admitted to Union, 395
 Alamo, 124, 406
 Americanization of, 405–406
 annexation of, 316, 317–318
 cattle ranching in, 614
 Civil War, 477
 independence from Mexico, 406
 secession, 442, *443*
 slavery in, 405
 Spanish in, 123–125
 Tejanos in, 405, 406
Texas and Pacific Railway, 533
Texas Oil Co. (Texaco), 569
Textile industry
 in the New South, 533, 536, 537, *537*
 in the 1920s, 760
Textile mills, 359–360, *360,* 361
Thames, battle of (1814), 277
Thayendanegea (Joseph Brant), 181, 183
Thirteenth Amendment, 487–488, 501, 509, 521
Thomas, Clarence, 1009
Thomas, Gertrude, 544
Thompson, Cyrus, 541
Thomson, Elihu, 567
Thoreau, Henry David, 377, 438, 440
Thoughts upon Female Education (Rush), 204–205
Three-fifths rule, 222, 279
Three Mile Island, Pennsylvania, 947
Three Rivers Land and Cattle Co., 615
Thurmond, Strom, 862, 863, 864
Tijerina, Reies López, 932
Tilden, Samuel J., 520
Tillamooks, 601
Tilyou, George C., 593
Timbuktu, 11, 12
Timothy, Elizabeth, 108
Tippecanoe, battle of (1811), 272
Tobacco
 economics and, 104–105
 following Reconstruction, 533, 536–537
 in Virginia, 44–46, *46*
Toltecs, 5
Tomasito, 413
Tonkin Gulf resolution, 912, 939
Tonnage Act of 1789, 242

Tontine Coffee House, *243*
Toombs, Robert, 419, 432
Tordesillas, treaty of (1494), 27
Tories/Loyalists, 160, 167–168
Townsend, Charles, 150–151
Townsend, Francis, 800
Townshend Duty Act (1767), 150–151
Trade
 See also Fur trade; Slave trade
 acts, 102
 Anglo-American transatlantic, 103–106, *104*
 Archaic period, 3–4
 between Europeans and Native Americans, 70–72
 British regulation and taxation of colonial, 101–109
 colonial exports, 103–106
 colonial exports, value of, *105*
 colonial imports, 106–107
 Constitutional Convention and issues of, 223
 Embargo Act (1807), 269–270
 globalization of, 1006–1007
 imperialism and, 700
 Macon's Bill No. 2 (1810), 271
 Mesoamerican, 7
 nullification crisis, 301, 305–308
 overview of colonial, 102, 156
 spice, 16
 sugar, 17
 Tariff Act of 1789, 242
 Tariff of 1816, 281
 West African, 11–13
Trade Expansion Act (1962), 1006
Trail of Tears, 304, *304,* 306–307
Transcendentalism, 376–378
Trans-Continental Treaty (1819), 283, 397
Transportation
 See also under type of
 canals, 353 355, *356*
 effects of, 353
 flatboats, 394
 funding and role of government, 356–357
 impact on agriculture, 353
 impact on traveling time, 309
 map of 1830–1850 network, *354*
 in the 1950s, 888–889
 omnibuses, 357
 railroads, 355–356, 357–358
 roads, 353
 steamboats, 353, 355
 wagon trains, 402
 westward expansion and role of, 600–601, *600*
Travis, Joseph, 336
Treasury Department
 formation of, 241
 Independent Treasury System, 311–312
Treaties
 Fort Laramie (1851), 403
 Fort Laramie (1868), 605
 Fort McIntosh (1785), 216
 Fort Stanwix (1784), 216
 Fort Wayne (1809), 272
 Ghent (1814), 278
 Greenville (1795), 247, *247,* 271
 Guadalupe Hidalgo (1848), 413
 Jay's Treaty (1794), 250–251
 Lancaster (1744), 121
 New Echota (1835), 306
 Paris (1763), 132–133
 Paris (1783), 190–192, *192,*

218–219
 Paris (1899), 708–710
 San Lorenzo (Pinckney's Treaty) (1795), 251
 Tordesillas (1494), 27
 Trans-Continental (1819), 283, 397
 Versailles (1919), 741–742, *743*
 Vincennes (1804), 271
 Webster-Ashburton (1843), 317
Tredegar Iron Works, 334, 458, 459
Trenchard, John, 147
Trenton, battle of, 178, 183
Triangle Shirtwaist Co., 663, *664,* 666
Tripartite Pact, 822, 828
Trois-Rivières, 37, 38
Trujillo, Jesús, 413
Truman, Harry S
 atomic bomb and, 849
 atomic diplomacy, 868–870, 871
 civil rights and, 860–861
 Doctrine, 867
 election of 1944 and, 839
 election of 1948 and, 862–864, *864*
 Fair Deal, 864–865
 Korean War, 872–875
 Potsdam Declaration, 848
 as president, 862–865
 relations with Soviet Union, 866–867
Trumbull, John, *172, 190, 221*
Trump, Donald, 963
Truth, Sojourner, 334, 471
Tryon, William, 150
Tubman, Harriet, *337*
Tugwell, Rexford, 802
Tunney, Gene, 769
Turkey, in World War I, 725
Turner, Henry McNeal, 506, 551–552
Turner, Nat, 306, 336, *336,* 378–379
Tuscaroras, 73, 181
Tuskegee Institute, 502, 555
Twain, Mark, 500, 593, 612, 681, 709
Tweed, William M., 517
Twelve O'Clock High, 845
Twitchell, Marshall Harvey, 519
Two Penny Act, 144
Tyler, John, 315, 316–317, 383, 444

U

Uncle Tom's Cabin (Stowe), 414–418, *416,* 425–426, *426*
Underground Railroad, 337
Underwood-Simmons Tariff Act (1913), 669, 688
Unemployment
 Depression of 1929 and, 788, 789, 798–799
 following World War I, 745
Unheavenly City, The (Banfield), 960
Unification Church, 930
Union Labor party, 635
Union Leagues, 514
Union Pacific Railroad, 600, *600*
Union party, 803
Unions
 African Americans excluded from, 548
 Amalgamated Clothing Workers, 666, 791, 803
 American Federation of Labor (AFL), 578, 666, 745–746
 beginnings of trade, 367
 business unionism, 578
 in the cattle industry, 616–617

 Civil War and, 479
 craft, 577, 578
 following World War I, 757–759
 Industrial Workers of the World (IWW), 666, 737
 International Ladies Garment Workers Union (ILGWU), 666
 Knights of Labor, 577–578
 in the mining industry, 614
 New Deal and, 800, 804
 in the 1980s, 962
 open shops, 757
 women in, 367
 workers organize (1870–1900), 576–579
United Automobile Workers (UAW), 804
United Daughters of the Confederacy (UDC), 544, 556
United Farm Workers, 932–933
United Fruit Co., 775, 897
United Mine Workers (UMW), 682, 746, 759, 797
United Nations, 848, 866
U.S. Chamber of Commerce, 680
U.S. Commission on National Security/21st Century, 1018
U.S. Department of Homeland Security, 1020
U.S. Geological Survey, establishment of, 638
U.S. Housing Authority, 810
U.S. Post Office, 756
U.S. Rubber, 567
United States Sanitary Commission, 464
U.S. Steel Corp., 570, 571, 662, 758, 759, 786
United States v. Cruikshank, 524, 525
U.S. v. E.C. Knight Co., 648–649
United Steel Workers, 962
Universal Negro Improvement Association (UNIA), 766
University of California v. Bakke, 1013
Updike, John, 947
Upper South, defined, 328–329
Upshur, Abel P., 317
Urban League, 790, 888
Urban slavery, 328
Utah, settlement of, 407–408
Utes, 5, 404, 407, 606
Utopianism, 375–378
U-2 incident, 898–899

V

Valens, Richie, 891
Valentino, Rudolph, 770
Valley Forge, 184
Van Buren, Martin
 Albany Regency and, 300
 election of 1836 and, 309
 election of 1840 and, 315–316
 election of 1848 and, 421
 gag rule, 312
 Independent Treasury System, 311–312
 presidency of, 309–312
Vandenburgh, Arthur H., 867
Vanderbilt, William K., *570*
Van Rensselaer, Stephen, 275, 369
Vardaman, James, 677
Veiller, Lawrence, 669–670
Venezuela, 704–705
Verger, Jean-Baptiste-Antoine de, *194*
Vermont, statehood for, 240
Verrazano, Giovanni da, 27

Versailles, treaty of (1919), 741–742, *743*
Vertical integration, 569
Vesey, Denmark, 336
Vest, George, 704
Vice-admiralty courts, 145
Vicksburg, battle of (1863), 463, 475, *476*, 489
Viet Cong, 901
Vietnam
 division of, 901
 Eisenhower administration and, 901
Vietnam War
 antiwar protests, 923–926, 938–939
 cease-fire, 939
 Ho Chi Minh Trail, 923
 Johnson administration and, 912, 920–926
 Kennedy administration and, 901
 map of, *922*
 Nixon administration and, 938–939
 Operation ROLLING THUNDER, 920–923
 overview of, 925
 search and destroy, 922–923
 Tet offensive, 935
 Tonkin Gulf resolution, 912, 939
Villa, Francisco Pancho, 719
Vincennes, battle of, 178, 185
Vincennes, treaty of (1804), 271
Virginia
 American Revolution in, 171–172, 188, 189–190
 Bacon's Rebellion, 76, 77
 Civil War, 462, 465–466, 471–472, 484–485, 490
 colony, overview of, 59
 founding of, 42, 59
 Jamestown, 42–43
 labor system in, 92
 life in early, 47–48
 Parson's Cause, 144
 ratification of Constitution, 228
 Roanoke Island, 29–31, 42
 secession, 447, 455, 461, 481
 slavery in, 83, 87, 239
 as a tobacco colony, 44–46, *46*, 59
Virginia Company, 42, 44
Virginia Declaration of Rights, 207
Virginia Plan, 222
Virtual representation, 120
VISTA (Volunteers in Service to America), 910
Voice from the South, A (Cooper), 530
Volstead Act (1919), 773
Voting
 African Americans following Civil War and, 510–513, 524
 after the American Revolution, 204
 disfranchisement movement, 547, 548–549, 552–553
 Fifteenth Amendment, 513, 521, 517, 524, 549
 free black males and, 296–297
 property requirements for, 295, 296
 universal white male, 295–297
 women and, 204, *204*, 296–297, 381–382, 513, 632, 636, *658*, 678–679, *678, 679*, 763
 written ballots, use of, 295
Voting Rights Act (1965), 905, 911

Voting Rights Act (1975), 1010–1011

W

Wabash, St. Louis, and Pacific Railway Co. v. Illinois, 642
Waco, Texas, 998
Wade, Benjamin F., 510
Wade-Davis Bill, 506
Wages
 changes in, 1980–1990, 964–965, *964*, 966
 growing income inequality in the 1920s, 759, *759*
Wagner, Robert F., 800
Wagner Act. *See* National Labor Relations Act
Wagon trains, 402
Waite, Morrison, 632
Walden, or Life in the Woods (Thoreau), 377
Walker, David, 378
Walker, Robert (actor), 836
Walker, Robert (friend of Buchanan), 433–434
Walker, William, 427–428
Wallace, George C., 906, 937, *937*, 943
Wallace, Henry A., 796, 839, 862–863, 864, 876
Wallace, Mary, 108
Wall Street Journal, The, 960
Walsh, Lawrence, 971
Waltham, Massachusetts, 362–363
Wampanoags, 26, 49, 76–77
Ward, Lester, 595
Ward, Samuel, 382
War Department, formation of, 241
Warehouse Act (1916), 689
War for Independence. *See* American Revolution
War Hawks, 272
War Industries Board (WIB), 731, 732, 745
War Manpower Commission, 832
Warmoth, Henry C., 515
Warner, Jack, 877
War of 1812, *260*, 261–262, 273–280, *274, 279*
War of the Austrian Succession (1739–1748), 126, 127–129
War of the League of Augsburg (1689–1697), 126–127
War of the Spanish Succession (1702–1713), 126–127
War on Poverty, 909–910
War Production Board, 832
Warren, Earl, 905
Warren, Joseph, *172*
Warren Bridge Co., 356–357
Warren Commission, 909
Warri, 13
Warsaw Pact, 868, *869*
Washington, Booker T., 554–555, *558*, 674, 677
Washington, D.C., British burning of, *260*, 261, 278, *279*
Washington, George, *164, 170, 190*
 American Revolution and, 171, 175, 181–182, 183, 184, 185, 192
 Annapolis Convention (1786) and, 221
 background of, 99–100
 as commander of Continental Army, 170–171, 179
 Constitutional Convention and, 222, *223*
 farewell address, 251

 foreign policy, 250–251
 French and Indian War and, 129, *129*, 131
 French Revolution and, 246
 importation of goods by, 110
 Mount Vernon, 111
 presidency of, *232*, 241
 Whiskey Rebellion and, 250
Washington, Martha, 184
Washington Naval Conference, 777
Washington Post, 943
Washington Temperance Societies, 370
Watergate, 942–944
Watie, Stand, 477
Watling Island, 17
Watson, Thomas J., 1002
Watson, Tom, 542, 646, 651
Watt, James, 961
Watts riots, 931
Wayne, Anthony, 247, *247*
Weather Bureau, establishment of, 638
Weather Underground, 938
Weaver, James B., 646, 650
Webster, Daniel, 313, 314, 317
 Compromise of 1850 and, 423
Webster-Ashburton Treaty (1843), 317
Webster v. Reproductive Health Services, 982
Weed, Thurlow, 314
Welch, Joseph, *879*, 880
Welch, Mary Josephine, 610
Weld, Theodore Dwight, 352, 379, 380, 438–439
Welfare capitalism, 758
Wells, Henry, 421
Wells, Ida B. (Wells-Barnett), 547, *547*, 554, 677
Wesley, John, 543
Wesley Houses, 543
West, Benjamin, *131*, 192
West African societies, 9–13
 agriculture, 12
 artisans and merchants, 11–12
 division of labor in, 12
 family structure, 12
 map of, *10*
 religion, 12
 slavery, 12–13, 81–82
 trade, 11–13
Western Federation of Miners, 614
West India Company, 40
West Indies, 17, 55–57, *84*
Westinghouse Electric Co., *733*, 757
Westmoreland, William, 920, 922, 935
West Point, 179, 265
West Virginia, admitted to Union, 461
Westward expansion
 after the American Revolution, 210, *211*, 216–217, *217*, 218, 240
 agricultural frontier, 391–397
 agriculture, exploitation of, 617–624
 cattle ranching, exploitation of, 614–617
 fur traders and, 399–400, *399, 400*
 Land Ordinance (1785), 216–217, *217*
 Lewis and Clark expedition, 267, *268*, 286–287, 399
 Louisiana Purchase, 266–268, *268*
 Mexican borderlands, 403–405
 mines, exploitation of, 610–614
 Native Americans and, 397–403,

 598, 601–610
 Northwest Ordinance (1787), 218, 394
 Old Northwest, 393–395
 Old Southwest, 395–397
 overview of (1815–1850), 396
 railroads, role of, 600–601, *600*
 shift of population (1790–1850), *392*
 Southwest Ordinance (1790), 218, 397
Wheat, 106, 394
Wheatley, Phillis, *205*
Wheeler, Bernadette, 855–856
Wheeler, John Hill, 324
Whig party
 compared with the Democrats, 313
 Conscience, 421
 election of 1840 and, 313, 315–316
 election of 1844 and, 318
 election of 1848 and, 420–421
 election of 1852 and, 426–427
 formation of, 311
 rise of, 312–318
 Texas issue, 317–318
Whigs, 160, 167–168
Whipper, W. J., 550
Whiskey Rebellion, 247, 250
Whiskey tax, 243
White, Hugh Lawson, 314
White, John, 29–30
White, Walter, 838
White, William Allen, 747
Whitefield, George, 114–115, *114*
White League, 519
White Plains, battle of, 178, 183
Whiteside, James A., *341*
White Tower, 767
Whitewater, 999
Whitman, Marcus, 401
Whitman, Narcissa, 401
Whitman, Walt, 357, 377
Whitmer, John, 371
Whitney, Eli, 363–364, 396
Whitney, Jackson, 338–339
Why Are We in Vietnam? (Mailer), 924
Whyte, William H., Jr., 893
Wide Awakes, 441
Wiggins, Ella May, 760
Wilder, Douglas, 1010
Wilderness, battle of (1864), 484–485, *485*, 489
Wilderness Act (1964), 913
Wilhelm II, 725
Wilkie, Wendell L., 825
Wilkinson, Eliza, 204
Wilkinson, James, 220, 269
Willard, Frances, 636–637
William of Orange, 117, 119, 126
Williams, Daniel Hale, 588
Williams, Fannie Barrier, 587
Williams, Mary Alice, 1003
Williams, Roger, 51, 52, 73
Wilmot, David, 419
Wilmot Proviso, 419–420, 445
Wilson, Charles, 888
Wilson, Edith Galt, 744
Wilson, James, 158–160
Wilson, Woodrow, 412, 637, 663, 675, 687, 742
 See also World War I
 Caribbean interventions, 718–719
 election of 1912 and, 686–687, *688*

election of 1916 and, 729–730, *730*
Fourteen Points, 740–741
interventionist policies of, 718–719
League of Nations, 742
Mexico and, 719
New Freedom, 687–689
reform expansion under, 689
Wingina, 29
Winslow, John, 132
Winthrop, John, 50, *50*, 51, 56
Wirt, William, 314
Wisconsin, admitted to Union, 395
Wise, Henry A., 432
Witchcraft, 117
Wobblies, 666, 737
Wolfe, James, 131, *131*
Wolfe, Thomas, 764, 964
Woman Rebel, 674
Woman's Land Army, 733
Woman's Municipal League, 636
Women
    abolitionists, 376–377, 380–381
    African American, 554, 587
    American Revolution and, 180, 193, 203–205
    in Archaic period, 3, 4
    in associational politics, 636–637
    as business owners, *1010*
    Civil War and, 458, 464, *464,* 465, 480, *480,* 482, *482,* 483
    in clubs, 544–545, 554, 666, 672
    colonial, 47, 53, 108, 111
    cult of domesticity, 365–366
    Depression of 1929 and, 789–790
    during 1877–1900, 531–532
    education of, in the early 1900s, 573–574
    education of, following the Civil War, 480, 501–502
    education of colonial, 111, 204–205, 235, 237, *237*
    employment of (1870–1900), 571–574, 671
    employment of (1970–2000), 981, 982
    evangelicalism and, 298–299, 366
    as federal clerks in 1890s, 640
    in government, 1008–1010
    in industry, 362–363, *363,* 365–366
    in the Ku Klux Klan, 772, *773*
    land ownership and, 204
    in mining camps, 610–612
    moral reform and role of, 370–371
    Native American, 26, 609
    New Deal and, 804–805
    in New England, 53, 235, 237, *237*
    in the New South, 543–545
    in the 1950s and 1960s, 890, 894
    plantation mistresses, 340
    political activism and, 251
    Progressive era and, 666–667, 674–675, 678–679
    religion and, 116, 298–299
    republicanism and, 203–205
    rights movement, 381–382, *382,* 927, 981–982
    as slaves, 334
    social reform and, 374, 543–544, 666–667
    as teachers, 373, 501–502
    temperance movement and, 369
    unions and, 367, 666
    voting and, 204, *204,* 296–297,

381–382, 513, 632, 636, *658,* 678–679, *678, 679,* 763
    wage gap and poverty for, 966
    West African, 12
    westward expansion and life for, 402, 621–622
    World War I and, 733–734, *733, 734,* 739, 745
    World War II and, 834, 835–837
Women's Christian Temperance Union (WCTU), 543–544, 554, 636–637
Women's Emergency Brigade, 804
Women's National Indian Association, 607
Women's National Republican Association, 633
Women's Peace Party, 729
Women's Political Council (WPC), 907
Women's Trade Union League (WTUL), 663, 666, 671, 764, 805
Wood, Jethro, 394
Wood, Leonard, 695–696, 707, 715
Woodlands Indians, 8–9
Woodmason, Charles, 122–123
Woodstock Generation, 928
Woolens Act (1699), 102
Woolworth's, 757, *907,* 908
Worcester v. Georgia, 305
Workhouses, 373–374
Working classes, 366–367
Workingmen's movement, 372
Works Progress Administration (WPA), 802
World Bank, 866
World Trade Center, *990,* 991–992, *1016, 1017,* 1018–1020
World Trade Organization (WTO), 1006–1007
World War I
    African Americans in, 734, *734,* 737
    American attitudes, 726–727
    chronology, 726
    diplomacy of neutrality, 727–729
    economic readjustment and social conflict following, 744–746
    economy and, 727, 731–733
    financing, 734–735
    Fourteen Points, 740–741
    Native Americans in, 737
    origins of conflict, 725–726
    overview of government wartime agencies, 731
    Paris Peace conference, 741–742
    preparedness for, 729
    propaganda in, 735
    start of, 730–731
    submarine warfare, 728–729
    suppressing dissent, 736–737
    U.S. declaration of war, 737–740
    women and, 733–734, *733, 734,* 739, 745
World War II
    African Americans in, 835, 838
    Atlantic Charter, 826
    atomic bomb, 820, 834, 848–849
    in the Atlantic, 830
    bombing raids, 844–845
    casualties, 828, 845
    chronology, 823
    D-Day, 842, 844
    Eastern Front, 828–830, 845–846
    events leading to, 821–822
    Hitler's war in Europe, 822–823

    internment of Japanese Americans, 838–839, *839,* 840–841
    in Italy, 842
    mobilizing the home front, 830–839
    Native Americans in, 835, 837–838
    in North Africa, 842
    in the Pacific, 826–828, *827,* 830, 846–847
    Pearl Harbor, attack on, 827–828, *827*
    Potsdam Declaration, 848
    submarine warfare, 826, 830
    U.S. declares war, 828
    U.S. neutrality, 823–826
    women and, 834, 835–837
    Yalta conference, 848
Worth, Jonathan, 481
Wounded Knee, South Dakota, 608, 622–623, 933
Writs of assistance, 146
Wyandots, 79, 181, 216
Wyoming Valley, battle of, 178, 185

X

XYZ Affair, 252–253

Y

Yale University, 113
Yalta conference, 848, 865
Yamamoto, Isoroku, 828
Yamasees, 73
Yankees, use of term, 62
Yanktonais, 398
Yanktons, 398
Yaquis, 25
Yellow-dog contracts, 757–758
Yellow press, 705
Yelstin, Boris, 974
Yeoman, 341–342, 396
Yippies, 937
Yorktown, battle of, *170,* 178, 189–190, *190*
Yorubas, 12
Young, Andrew, 1011
Young, Brigham, 407
Young, Coleman, 1010
Young America movement, 426, 427–428
Young Citizens' Club, 575
Young Men's Christian Association (YMCA), 588
Young Women's Christian Association (YWCA), 545, 554, 588
Youth culture and counterculture, 928
Y2K problem, 1000–1001
Yugoslavia, 742
Yumans, 404, 406
Yuppies, 963

Z

Zeeuw, Cornelius de, *41*
Zelman v. Simmons-Harris, 1016
Zimmermann, Arthur, 730
Zimmerman note, 731
Zitkala-Sa (Red Bird), 608–609
Zuni, 8, 75, 601

SINGLE PC LICENSE AGREEMENT AND LIMITED WARRANTY

READ THIS LICENSE CAREFULLY BEFORE OPENING THIS PACKAGE. BY OPENING THIS PACKAGE, YOU ARE AGREEING TO THE TERMS AND CONDITIONS OF THIS LICENSE. IF YOU DO NOT AGREE, DO NOT OPEN THE PACKAGE. PROMPTLY RETURN THE UNOPENED PACKAGE AND ALL ACCOMPANYING ITEMS TO THE PLACE YOU OBTAINED THEM. THESE TERMS APPLY TO ALL LICENSED SOFTWARE ON THE DISK EXCEPT THAT THE TERMS FOR USE OF ANY SHAREWARE OR FREEWARE ON THE DISKETTES ARE AS SET FORTH IN THE ELECTRONIC LICENSE LOCATED ON THE DISK:

1. GRANT OF LICENSE and OWNERSHIP: The enclosed computer programs <<and data>> ("Software") are licensed, not sold, to you by Prentice-Hall, Inc. ("We" or the "Company") and in consideration of your purchase of the accompanying Company textbooks and/or other materials, and your agreement to these terms. We reserve any rights not granted to you. You own only the disk(s) but we and/or our licensors own the Software itself. This license allows you to use and display your copy of the Software on a single computer (i.e., with a single CPU) at a single location for academic use only, so long as you comply with the terms of this Agreement. You may make one copy for back up, or transfer your copy to another CPU, provided that the Software is usable on only one computer.

2. RESTRICTIONS: You may not transfer or distribute the Software or documentation to anyone else. Except for backup, you may not copy the documentation or the Software. You may not network the Software or otherwise use it on more than one computer or computer terminal at the same time. You may not reverse engineer, disassemble, decompile, modify, adapt, translate, or create derivative works based on the Software or the Documentation. You may be held legally responsible for any copying or copyright infringement which is caused by your failure to abide by the terms of these restrictions.

3. TERMINATION: This license is effective until terminated. This license will terminate automatically without notice from the Company if you fail to comply with any provisions or limitations of this license. Upon termination, you shall destroy the Documentation and all copies of the Software. All provisions of this Agreement as to limitation and disclaimer of warranties, limitation of liability, remedies or damages, and our ownership rights shall survive termination.

4. LIMITED WARRANTY AND DISCLAIMER OF WARRANTY: Company warrants that for a period of 60 days from the date you purchase this SOFTWARE (or purchase or adopt the accompanying textbook), the Software, when properly installed and used in accordance with the Documentation, will operate in substantial conformity with the description of the Software set forth in the Documentation, and that for a period of 30 days the disk(s) on which the Software is delivered shall be free from defects in materials and workmanship under normal use. The Company does not warrant that the Software will meet your requirements or that the operation of the Software will be uninterrupted or error-free. Your only remedy and the Company's only obligation under these limited warranties is, at the Company's option, return of the disk for a refund of any amounts paid for it by you or replacement of the disk. THIS LIMITED WARRANTY IS THE ONLY WARRANTY PROVIDED BY THE COMPANY AND ITS LICENSORS, AND THE COMPANY AND ITS LICENSORS DISCLAIM ALL OTHER WARRANTIES, EXPRESS OR IMPLIED, INCLUDING WITHOUT LIMITATION, THE IMPLIED WARRANTIES OF MERCHANTABILITY AND FITNESS FOR A PARTICULAR PURPOSE. THE COMPANY DOES NOT WARRANT, GUARANTEE OR MAKE ANY REPRESENTATION REGARDING THE ACCURACY, RELIABILITY, CURRENTNESS, USE, OR RESULTS OF USE, OF THE SOFTWARE.

5. LIMITATION OF REMEDIES AND DAMAGES: IN NO EVENT, SHALL THE COMPANY OR ITS EMPLOYEES, AGENTS, LICENSORS, OR CONTRACTORS BE LIABLE FOR ANY INCIDENTAL, INDIRECT, SPECIAL, OR CONSEQUENTIAL DAMAGES ARISING OUT OF OR IN CONNECTION WITH THIS LICENSE OR THE SOFTWARE, INCLUDING FOR LOSS OF USE, LOSS OF DATA, LOSS OF INCOME OR PROFIT, OR OTHER LOSSES, SUSTAINED AS A RESULT OF INJURY TO ANY PERSON, OR LOSS OF OR DAMAGE TO PROPERTY, OR CLAIMS OF THIRD PARTIES, EVEN IF THE COMPANY OR AN AUTHORIZED REPRESENTATIVE OF THE COMPANY HAS BEEN ADVISED OF THE POSSIBILITY OF SUCH DAMAGES. IN NO EVENT SHALL THE LIABILITY OF THE COMPANY FOR DAMAGES WITH RESPECT TO THE SOFTWARE EXCEED THE AMOUNTS ACTUALLY PAID BY YOU, IF ANY, FOR THE SOFTWARE OR THE ACCOMPANYING TEXTBOOK. BECAUSE SOME JURISDICTIONS DO NOT ALLOW THE LIMITATION OF LIABILITY IN CERTAIN CIRCUMSTANCES, THE ABOVE LIMITATIONS MAY NOT ALWAYS APPLY TO YOU.

6. GENERAL: THIS AGREEMENT SHALL BE CONSTRUED IN ACCORDANCE WITH THE LAWS OF THE UNITED STATES OF AMERICA AND THE STATE OF NEW YORK, APPLICABLE TO CONTRACTS MADE IN NEW YORK, AND SHALL BENEFIT THE COMPANY, ITS AFFILIATES AND ASSIGNEES. HIS AGREEMENT IS THE COMPLETE AND EXCLUSIVE STATEMENT OF THE AGREEMENT BETWEEN YOU AND THE COMPANY AND SUPERSEDES ALL PROPOSALS OR PRIOR AGREEMENTS, ORAL, OR WRITTEN, AND ANY OTHER COMMUNICATIONS BETWEEN YOU AND THE COMPANY OR ANY REPRESENTATIVE OF THE COMPANY RELATING TO THE SUBJECT MATTER OF THIS AGREEMENT. If you are a U.S. Government user, this Software is licensed with "restricted rights" as set forth in subparagraphs (a)-(d) of the Commercial Computer-Restricted Rights clause at FAR 52.227-19 or in subparagraphs (c)(1)(ii) of the Rights in Technical Data and Computer Software clause at DFARS 252.227-7013, and similar clauses, as applicable.

Should you have any questions concerning this agreement or if you wish to contact the Company for any reason, please contact in writing: Prentice Hall, One Lake Street, Upper Saddle River, NJ 07458.